Advanced Guide to

Programming with Microsoft® Visual Basic® .NET

Michael V. Ekedahl
University of Nevada, Reno

THOMSON

COURSE TECHNOLOGY

Australia • Canada • Mexico • Singapore • Spain • United Kingdom • United States

Advanced Guide to Programming with Microsoft® Visual Basic® .NET

by Michael V. Ekedahl

Managing Editor:
Jennifer Muroff

Product Manager:
Alyssa Pratt

Associate Product Manager:
Janet Aras

Associate Production Manager:
Christine Freitas

Developmental Editor:
Jill Batistick

Cover Designer:
Abby Scholz

Manufacturing Coordinator:
Laura Burns

Compositor:
GEX Publishing Services

BRIEF
Contents

TABLE OF

Contents

Preface

Advanced Guide to Programming with Microsoft Visual Basic .NET was written to provide the Visual Basic .NET programmer with the tools to create programs that conform to well-adopted Windows standards. The intent is to provide the reader with a rich set of tools to create programs that satisfy the demands of today's business environment.

Organization and Approach

This book presumes a familiarity with Visual Basic .NET syntax and the use of intrinsic controls. If you are new to Visual Basic or Visual Basic .NET, then an introductory text that discusses VB .NET syntax, and event driven programming, will be necessary.

The book is relatively modular in design. Some readers may be interested in database-related topics, while others may want specific information about class modules and object-oriented programming. As such, some chapters are functionally related and others are not.

Chapter 1 supplies a conceptual introduction to Visual Studio .NET, including the Common Language Runtime, the .NET Framework class library, intermediate language, and the Just-In-Time compiler. In addition, the supported Visual Studio .NET languages are compared. Calling the VB .NET compiler without the aid of the Visual Studio .NET integrated development environment is discussed.

Chapter 2 explores the core concepts necessary to implement a desktop Windows application. Creating form and control instances both at design time and dynamically at run-time are discussed. The essential skills required to set properties and create dynamic event handlers is also presented.

Chapter 3 supplies an in depth presentation of the types that comprise a VB .NET application and how those types are used and organized. Namespaces, enumerations, structures, classes, and module blocks are discussed. Understanding the material in this chapter is essential to creating complex .NET applications.

Chapter 4 expands on the material presented in Chapter 3. In this chapter, significant object-oriented concepts are introduced, including inheritance and overloading. The inheritance rules of constructors are also discussed. Finally, the topic of handling program errors is presented. Note that understanding the material presented in Chapters 3 and 4 is essential understanding the material presented in subsequent chapters.

Chapter 5 discusses how to work with the Windows file system by navigating between directories and has creating, moving, and deleting directories. In addition, reading sequential and random files is presented. Finally, the chapter contains a discussion of the ArrayList, SortedList, Queue, and Stack classes. Together, these classes implement some of the more commonly used data structures.

Chapter 6 presents the concept of an interface, how to implement predefined .NET interfaces, and how to create custom interfaces. By implementing interfaces, the reader will be able to call predefined methods to sort lists, and enumerate lists with For Each loops. Understanding interface-based programming is also an important part of developing .NET applications.

Chapter 7 introduces ADO.NET and the essential ADO.NET classes. These classes include the OleDbConnection class used to establish a database connection, the OleDbDataAdapter class used to retrieve and save database data, and the DataSet and DataTable classes used to store an in-memory representation of database information. In this chapter, programmatic use of these classes is introduced.

Chapter 8 expands on the material presented in Chapter 7. In this chapter, the reader uses Toolbox controls and tools supplied by the Visual Studio .NET IDE to create OleDbConnections and OleDbDataAdapters. In addition, typed DataSets are introduced along with how to work with DataSets containing multiple tables and one-to-many relationships between those tables. In addition, the DataReader is introduced, which provides an efficient, forward-only tool to read records from a database table. The DataGrid control and scalar queries are also introduced.

Chapter 9 presents the topic of Crystal Reports. The essentials of creating control break reports with formulas, subtotals, and totals is presented in this chapter. Exporting reports to other formats, including HTML, Excel workbooks, and Word documents, is discussed. Finally, the reader is shown how to select report information dynamically.

Chapter 10 discusses how to use the Windows common controls including the ToolBar, StatusBar, TreeView, and ListView controls. This chapter is applicable to anyone who is creating a user interface that uses common Windows metaphors.

Chapter 11 discusses the supported techniques to create custom .NET controls, and how to use them. Control licensing and custom property editors are discussed.

Chapter 12 introduces drawing and the Graphical Device Interface and how to create two-dimensional bar and pie charts. The essential drawing shapes are presented in this chapter. In addition, drawing to a printer and the .NET printing objects are discussed.

Chapter 13 discusses MDI programming concepts and how to implement MDI programs. Menu integration and context menus are also presented in this chapter.

Appendix A is intended to demonstrate how to use the Visual Studio .NET IDE to locate program errors and how to correct them.

Features

Chapter Organization Each chapter begins with a programming-related problem that the reader could expect to encounter in business, followed by a demonstration of an application that could be used to solve the problem. By allowing the user to see the application he or she will be able to create after completing the chapter, the reader will see how the programming concepts can be used and, therefore, why the concepts are important. The completed application contains numerous comments that will also help the reader to understand the application's implementation.

Each chapter contains review questions and programming questions. Following these questions, four to five Hands-on Projects are provided. By completing these Hands-on Projects, the reader can apply the skills presented in the chapter. Each Hands-on Project is successively more difficult. Some Hands-on Projects require that the reader apply skills from multiple chapters.

- **Read This Before You Begin Page** This page is consistent with Course Technology's unequaled commitment to helping instructors introduce technology into the classroom. Technical considerations and assumptions about hardware, software, and default settings are listed in one place to help instructors save time and eliminate unnecessary aggravation.

- **Chapter Case and Previewing the Application** Each chapter begins with a programming-related problem that the reader could expect to encounter in business, followed by a demonstration of an application that could be used to solve the problem.

- **Step-by-Step Methodology** The unique Course Technology methodology keeps students on track. The text reinforces where students are in the development process and emphasizes how each phase relates to the others. Students also learn development concepts and techniques in the context of creating a contemporary application.

- **Objectives** The Objectives call out the main concepts that will be presented in the chapter.

- **Syntax Windows** Syntax Windows for statements, methods, and so on, is presented in a manner similar to its appearance in the online Help system. Syntax is then "dissected," with a complete definition of each keyword and arguments. Syntax Windows for class members lists the properties, methods, and events. Together, these Syntax Windows gather important information about programming constructs and objects in an easy-to-reference format.

- **Code Examples** In addition to code examples included with the syntax, actual code is used within the text of the chapter to provide additional examples of a concept or illustrate further peculiarities. The completed application that accompanies each chapter is fully commented and will often contain additional code beyond the code entered in the step-by-step instructions included in the chapters. The intent is to demonstrate a reasonably robust example.

- **Tips** Tips supply additional information, such as references to materials to enhance the learning experience.

- **Summary** Following each chapter is a section highlighting the programming concepts, commands, and controls covered in the chapter.

- **Review Questions** Each chapter concludes with meaningful, conceptual review questions that test the reader's understanding of the material presented in the chapter.

- **Programming Questions** Short programming questions appear at the end of each chapter. These short programming questions test comprehension of the syntactical elements presented in the chapter.

- **Hands-on Projects** The programming questions are followed by Hands-on Projects that test the readers understanding of how to complete business-related programs pertaining to the chapter. The Hands-on Projects provide additional practice of skills and concepts presented in the chapter. Finally, some of the Hands-on Projects test skills from preceding chapters so the reader develops increasingly complex business applications.

- **Software** Visual Basic .NET 2002 or Visual Basic .NET 2003 Standard Edition software.

The Visual Basic Environment

This book was written using Microsoft Visual Studio .NET – Professional Edition installed on a Windows XP personal computer. The Enterprise Architect Edition of Visual Basic .NET will produce the same results. Screen shots were captured using the Windows XP theme. This book has also been tested using the Professional Edition of Windows 2000. Specific instructions for installing Visual Studio .NET are provided in the Instructor's Manual. If you are using Visual Studio .NET 2003, you will receive messages to update the solution files to the Visual Studio .NET 2003 format.

Teaching Tools

All of the teaching tools for this text are found in the Instructor's Resource Kit, which is available from the Course Technology Web site (*www.course.com*) and on the CD-ROM.

- **Instructor's Manual** The Instructor's Manual has been written by the author and has been quality assurance tested. It is available on CD-ROM and online at *www.course.com*. The Instructor's Manual contains the following items:

  - Additional coverage of Visual Basic concepts.

  - Answers to all of the questions and solutions to all of the exercises.

  - Chapter Notes, which contain background information from the author about the Chapter Case and the instructional progression of the chapter.

  - Technical Notes, which include troubleshooting tips as well as information on how to customize the readers' screens to closely emulate the screen shots in the book.

- **ExamView Engine and Test Bank** ExamView is a Windows-based testing software program that helps instructors design and administer examinations and practice tests. This full-featured program allows instructors to randomly generate practice tests that provide immediate on-screen feedback and detailed study guides for incorrectly answered questions. Instructors can also use ExamView to create printed and online tests over the network. Tests on any or all chapters of this textbook can be created, previewed, and administered entirely over a local area network. ExamView can grade the tests automatically at the computer and can generate statistical information on individual as well as group performance. An ExamView test bank has been written to accompany this text and is included on the CD-ROM. The test bank includes multiple-choice, true/false, short answer, programming, and essay questions.

- **Solution Files** Solution files contain possible solutions to all the problems students are asked to create or modify in the chapters and cases. (Due to the nature of software development, student solutions can differ from these solutions and still be correct.)

- **Data Files** Data files, containing all data that readers will use for the chapters and exercises in this textbook, are provided through Course Technology's Online Companion on the Instructor's Resources CD-ROM and online at *www.course.com*. A Help file includes technical tips for lab management. See the inside front cover of this textbook and the "Read This Before You Begin" page preceding Chapter 1 for more information on data files.

Acknowledgements

First, I would like to thank Terri for standing by me throughout this long project and to my dog Rio for sitting at my feet.

Thanks to Sergiu Pascutiu for his efforts on the test bank and his help with the problem sets. Thanks also to Mukesh Motwani for his endless hours of research. Thanks also to my colleagues and students at the University of Nevada, Reno. To Bill Newman: thanks for all of your help along the way. To Jill Batistick: my developmental editor, thanks for all of the great ideas and being so enjoyable to work with. Finally, thanks to Alyssa Pratt, and the staff at Course Technology for turning an idea into reality. Thanks also to the following reviewers for their comments and support:

Ann Rovetto: Horry-Georgetown Technical College
Stan Kurkovsky: Columbus State University
Louis Fuxan: Delgado Community College
Robert Marcus: Clayton College and State University
Larry Langellier: Moraine Valley Community College
Anthony Basilico: Community College of Rhode Island
Chris Panell: Heald College
Melinda White: Seminole Community College
Peter Van Der Goes: Rose State College

Read This Before You Begin

TO THE USER OF THE DATA FILES

To complete the steps and projects in this book, you will need data files that have been created specifically for this book. Your instructor will provide the data files to you. You also can obtain the files electronically from the Course Technology Web site by connecting to *www.course.com*, and then searching for this book title.

You can use a computer in your school lab or your own computer to complete the Hands-on Projects in this book.

The data files for this book are organized such that the examples and exercises are divided into folders named Chapter.*xx*, where *xx* is the chapter number. Each chapter contains a completed program and a partially completed program that you finish by performing the hands-on steps appearing throughout each chapter. The completed program appears in the folder Complete*xx* and the startup program appears in the folder Startup*xx* within the Chapter.*xx* folder. Compiled solutions to the Hands-on Projects appear in the Solutions*xx* folder. Use these precompiled solutions to help you visualize the end result of the Hands-on Projects. You can save the student files anywhere on your system unless specifically indicated in the chapter.

Using Your Own Computer

To use your own computer to complete the Hands-on Projects, you will need the following:

- **Software** Microsoft Visual Studio .NET Professional Edition including the Microsoft .NET Framework. Windows NT (Service pack 6 or greater), Windows 2000, or Windows XP.

- **Hardware** A Pentium II-class processor, 450 MHz or higher personal computer. We suggest a minimum of 256MB of memory.

- **Data files** You will not be able to complete the chapters and projects in this book using your own computer unless you have the data files. You can get the data files from your instructor, or you can obtain the data files electronically from the Course Technology Web site by connecting to *www.course.com*, and then searching for this book title.

Visit Our World Wide Web Site

Additional materials designed especially for this book might be available for your course on the World Wide Web. Go to **www.course.com**. Periodically search *www.course.com* for more details.

1

THE PHILOSOPHY OF VISUAL STUDIO .NET

In this chapter, you will:

♦ Be introduced to Visual Basic .NET and Visual Studio .NET
♦ Learn about the features of Visual Studio .NET
♦ Learn how to choose a development language
♦ Learn about the design and implementation of the .NET Framework
♦ Understand the purpose of the Common Language Runtime
♦ Receive an introduction to assemblies
♦ Understand the organization of namespaces
♦ Understand the .NET Framework class library
♦ Create a first VB .NET application
♦ Understand the syntax of Intermediate Language

This chapter is largely theoretical and describes several design philosophies behind .NET and how the elements of Visual Studio .NET are related. In this chapter you will not use the Visual Studio .NET Integrated Development Environment (IDE) to create an application. Instead, so that you can better understand the underlying Visual Studio .NET compiler and the elements of a Visual Studio .NET application, you will create a very simple application using a text editor such as Notepad, although any other text editor will work. You will then compile and execute that application from a Command Prompt window.

The structure of this chapter differs slightly from the other chapters in this book, as well. With the exception of this chapter, each chapter begins by previewing a completed application that you can examine and run inside of the Visual Studio .NET IDE. A completed version of the application for this chapter does appear in the folder named Chapter.01\Complete01. The completed application file is named Complete01.vb. However, you will not be asked to open the file as part of the hands-on steps.

INTRODUCTION TO VISUAL BASIC .NET AND VISUAL STUDIO .NET

Prior to the introduction of Visual Basic, writing applications for the Windows operating system required that developers use Visual C++. However, Visual C++ was difficult to learn, and creating Windows applications in C++ was both complex and time consuming. Microsoft developed Visual Basic in 1991 to simplify the development of Windows applications.

Early versions of Visual Basic revolutionized software development for personal computers because of its ease of use compared to Visual C++. Furthermore, each successive version of Visual Basic provided additional features and functionality making it suitable for the development of real-world business applications. However, these versions of Visual Basic lacked some of the sophisticated features provided by C++. With the release of Visual Studio .NET and Visual Basic .NET, these limitations no longer exist.

Visual Studio .NET revolutionizes Windows software development for the following reasons:

- Microsoft supplies four Visual Studio .NET languages: C++, C#, Visual J#, and Visual Basic .NET (VB .NET). No matter which Visual Studio .NET language you choose, the integrated development environment used to create, test, and deploy applications is the same. In fact, Visual Studio .NET allows you to create part of an application in one language, and other parts of an application in another language.

- Each Visual Studio .NET language supplies nearly identical functionality so the decision of which Visual Studio .NET language to use is no longer based on the features provided by a particular language. Rather, a developer can choose the programming language with which they are most familiar.

- The performance of all .NET languages is nearly identical, so again, the language that you choose does not matter.

Although you will likely use the Visual Studio .NET IDE to create most .NET applications, you need not do so. You could create any and all .NET applications with a text editor such as Notepad, and compile those applications by calling the appropriate compiler from a Command Prompt window. In fact, Visual Studio .NET need not even be installed on your computer to create VB .NET applications. The reason for this is simple. Another underlying software component, called the .NET Framework, is responsible for compiling and executing applications. The only software component required to develop and test an application is the .NET Framework itself. In this chapter you will begin by creating a simple application using Notepad so that you can visualize the elements of a VB .NET application and how to call the VB .NET compiler directly.

SUMMARIZING THE NEW VISUAL STUDIO .NET FEATURES

The Visual Studio .NET IDE has evolved considerably from previous versions and provides several new features. Furthermore, the syntax and implementation of the supported languages have evolved considerably too. The following list describes selected improvements to the Visual Studio .NET IDE:

- All Visual Studio .NET languages share the same integrated development environment. When Visual Studio .NET is installed on a computer, three languages (C++, C#, and VB .NET) are installed by default along with the .NET Framework itself. Depending on the Visual Studio .NET version you are using, Visual J# is also installed by default. You can, however, select which languages to install. You can also select specific tools to install.

- The Help system has been significantly reorganized. Most index topics are now organized by namespaces and the types defined within those namespaces. Namespaces and their contents are discussed in detail later in this chapter.

- Visual Studio .NET introduces several new controls. One group of controls provides access to Windows services such as writing data to the system message logs. Other controls supply access to databases via ADO .NET.

- Visual Studio .NET allows you to create several different types of applications. For example, you can create ASP.NET and ASP.NET Web Service applications. ASP.NET is the successor to ASP. ASP.NET Web Services are new to Visual Studio .NET and provide a general model for building distributed applications on the Internet. Visual Studio .NET also allows you to create Console applications and applications that operate as a desktop service. A desktop service is an application that starts automatically when Windows itself starts and responds to requests without user intervention.

- Visual Studio .NET relies on the Extensible Markup Language (XML) to save, send, and receive data across the Web and to communicate information between applications.

- Microsoft added several new debugging windows and debugging tools, making it easier to fix errors. Appendix A discusses these debugging tools in detail.

- The Visual Studio .NET deployment tools were overhauled, providing a developer the means to customize the setup application run by users on their target computer. Users can now optionally install parts of an application and customize how an application is installed on their computers.

In addition to improvements in the IDE, the Visual Studio .NET languages have improved too. The following list describes selected language enhancements:

- All of the Visual Studio .NET languages are formally considered object-oriented languages. Whether you choose to develop applications in VB .NET, C#, or Visual J#, you have access to the same object-oriented features. Furthermore, all .NET languages support true inheritance and polymorphism. These features are a requirement of any object-oriented programming language.

- Although the syntax differs from one .NET language to another, all applications have a similar structure no matter the language you choose. In other words, all of the .NET languages support classes having the same types of members. (For example, the syntax of the statements to declare a class differs to match the syntax of the underlying language.)

- Microsoft has introduced several new keywords to the VB .NET language to handle all of the new object-oriented features. C# is an entirely new language with syntax similar to C++. Visual J# is also a new language with syntax similar to Java.

- The file structure for modules is the same for all .NET languages. Module files are grouped into projects. One or more projects can be grouped into a solution. The structure of a project and solution is the same no matter the Visual Studio .NET development language that you choose.

- No matter which .NET language you choose for development, all applications are compiled into the same format, called Intermediate Language (IL). The purpose and format of IL is discussed in detail in this chapter.

 Microsoft had to make significant changes to the Visual Basic language itself to migrate it from an object-aware programming language to an object-oriented programming language. The reason that the Visual Basic language has changed so much is simple. Microsoft has reengineered VB .NET to work with Visual Studio .NET and the .NET Framework, making all of the Visual Studio .NET languages compatible with each other. Thus, several new keywords and statements were added to VB .NET.

Having said that all .NET languages are roughly equivalent, subtle differences between languages do exist which may influence the decision to use one language over another. We discuss these subtleties next.

CHOOSING A DEVELOPMENT LANGUAGE

VB .NET, C#, and Visual J# are the three primary languages supported by Microsoft for use with the .NET Framework. Again, other languages have been developed by third-party vendors that target the .NET Framework, but these third-party languages are not compared in this chapter. The following list illustrates some of the differences between VB .NET, C#, and Visual J#:

- Syntactically, the C# language closely resembles the C++ language and both use the same terse syntax. Thus, many developers consider Visual Basic an easier language to learn than C#. Furthermore, if a developer is already familiar with VB 6 then he or she should continue using VB .NET since the language syntax is already familiar. For C++ developers, C# will likely be the language of choice.

- C# supports functionality that is similar to C++. Specifically, C# supports a form of pointers, which VB .NET does not. Also, C# supports unsigned numeric variables, while VB .NET supports only signed numeric variables. With a signed numeric variable, one bit is reserved to denote whether a number is positive or negative. With an unsigned numeric variable, this bit represents part of the number. Thus, for a 16 bit signed Short Integer, the maximum value is 32,727. For an unsigned Short Integer, the maximum value is 65,535. Of course, unsigned Integers cannot store negative numbers. This limitation poses no real problem as the Common Language Specification, discussed later in the chapter, specifies support only for signed Integers. To maintain compatibility with the largest number of .NET Framework components, use of non-standard types such as unsigned Integers is discouraged.

- Strict type checking is optional in VB .NET but is required in C#. That is, VB .NET will allow data to be converted from one type to another implicitly at runtime through a process called type coercion. Through type coercion, VB .NET attempts to convert one type to another without the developer explicitly calling a type conversion method.

- C# will not use type coercion to implicitly convert less restrictive types to more restrictive types. Rather, C# requires that the developer explicitly call a type conversion method to convert data from a less restrictive type to a more restrictive type. For example, VB .NET will, by default, implicitly convert less restrictive types, such as a Long, to a more restrictive type, such as an Integer, even though an error may occur or data may be lost in the type conversion process. The new VB .NET Option Strict statement prohibits implicit type conversion from less restrictive types to more restrictive types, making the type conversion rules the same for both VB .NET and C#. All of the applications in this book will include the Option Strict statement, and will perform explicit type conversion where necessary. Use of Option Strict also eliminates type conversion errors resulting from implicit type conversion between incompatible types.

- VB .NET does continue to support optional procedure arguments while C# does not. Because both VB .NET and C# support overloading of methods, however, this limitation does not pose a problem. Overloading is simply the ability to call different versions of a procedure based on the number and data types of the arguments passed to that procedure. The number and data types of the arguments expected by a procedure are referred to as a procedure's **signature**. Overloading is discussed in detail in Chapter 4.

- C# and Visual J# have a similar syntax. Visual J# was designed to leverage the skills of Java developers wanting to target applications for the .NET Framework. Note that applications developed with Visual J# will not execute on the Java Virtual Machine (JVM) defined by Sun Microsystems. Rather, J# applications rely on the same .NET Framework services as any other .NET language.

In summary, each .NET language has its subtle advantages and disadvantages. However, the tradeoffs between the different languages are minimal. Most importantly, VB .NET, C#, and Visual J# all have access to all of the services supplied by the .NET Framework. Thus, choosing one language over another is a matter of personal preference and language familiarity. Finally, although we compare the Microsoft-supplied development languages, development in other languages such as COBOL is certainly possible. This complete language independence is one of the most significant benefits of the programming with Visual Studio .NET and the .NET Framework.

Before starting to develop VB .NET applications, this chapter begins by describing some of the significant design philosophies behind Visual Studio .NET and by explaining characteristics shared by all of the Visual Studio .NET languages.

THE DESIGN AND IMPLEMENTATION OF THE .NET FRAMEWORK

At the heart of the Visual Studio .NET application development environment is a software component known as the .NET Framework. In general, the .NET Framework defines the rules for language interoperability and how an application is compiled into executable code. The .NET Framework is also responsible for managing the execution of an application created in any Visual Studio .NET language. The design and implementation of the .NET Framework is the focus of the following sections in this chapter.

Relationship Between Visual Studio .NET and the .NET Framework

The .NET Framework must be installed on a computer to develop and run any .NET application. The .NET Framework contains all of the compilers required to translate a .NET application into an executable file. Thus, a developer could build applications using any text editor, such as Notepad, without using the Visual Studio .NET IDE.

The purpose of the Visual Studio .NET IDE is to provide a robust integrated development environment used to develop, test, and deploy a .NET application written in VB .NET, C#, Visual J#, or Visual C++. Visual Studio .NET contains the visual designers to create forms and manage XML documents. It also contains the tools to manage large multi-file projects, and compile those projects into an executable file. Visual Studio .NET also contains tools to deploy applications and to deploy the .NET Framework itself to another computer. Thus, although complex applications could be developed without the Visual Studio .NET IDE, doing so would be neither practical nor efficient. Figure 1-1 illustrates the relationship between the .NET Framework and Visual Studio .NET.

Figure 1-1   Relationship between the .NET Framework and Visual Studio .NET

As shown in Figure 1-1, the Visual Studio .NET IDE relies on the services provided by the .NET Framework. These services include the language compilers supplied by Microsoft and, optionally, third-party vendors. The language compilers are part of the .NET Framework itself, rather than Visual Studio .NET. Visual Studio .NET, in turn, provides sophisticated tools to call each installed compiler.

The **Common Language Runtime (CLR)** is part of the .NET Framework. It supplies four roles. First, the Common Language Runtime defines the rules for standard data types and language interoperability through the Common Type System and Common Language Specification, respectively. The Just-In-Time compiler translates Intermediate Language code (IL) to executable code before running the application. The Common Language Runtime also manages the application, allocating and deallocating memory as the application runs. The Common Language Runtime and the services it provides are discussed in detail in the following sections.

The final part of the .NET Framework is the .NET Framework class library. The developers of the .NET Framework created reusable components to perform nearly every conceivable task. Collectively, these components are referred to as the .NET Framework class library. With these reusable components you can read and write files, manipulate database data, perform drawing operations, send and receive data over the Internet, and so on.

Requirements of the .NET Framework

For a user to execute an application developed with any .NET Framework language, the user's computer must have the .NET Framework itself installed. The .NET Framework is installed automatically when Visual Studio .NET is installed. The .NET Framework can also be freely downloaded from Microsoft and installed for older versions of Windows that were not distributed with the .NET Framework. The latest releases of Windows, including Windows XP service pack 1, are shipped with the .NET Framework installed.

 At the time of this printing, the .NET Framework can be downloaded from *http://msdn.microsoft.com/netframework/downloads*. Follow the instructions on the Web site to download and install the .NET Framework. As the .NET Framework is relatively new software, additional service packs will likely be released frequently by Microsoft.

The .NET Framework will run on all Windows versions except for Windows 95. Thus, the .NET Framework will run on Windows 98, Windows 98 Second Edition, Windows ME, Windows NT 4 (Service Pack 6 is required), Windows 2000, and Windows XP. Note, however, that some features of the .NET Framework are not available under Windows 98 and Windows ME because of limitations of the operating system itself.

.NET Framework Versions

Microsoft distributes the .NET Framework in two versions. The desktop version of the .NET Framework is used by all the preceding Windows versions. The compact version is designed for use by small devices such as PDAs, and other mobile devices such as Internet-enabled cellular telephones. Currently, the compact version runs only on Windows CE. However, Microsoft is working with third-party manufacturers so that the .NET Framework will run on other proprietary operating systems.

Installation of the .NET Framework

Installation of the .NET Framework is required regardless of the .NET programming language that you choose for development. That is, whether you develop applications in VB .NET, C#, or Visual J#, all .NET languages rely on the .NET Framework to compile and execute those applications. In addition, third-party languages such as COBOL and Eiffel have also been developed that take advantage of the .NET Framework. Again, you must have the .NET Framework installed on your computer to run applications developed in these third-party languages.

THE COMMON LANGUAGE RUNTIME

An integral part of the .NET Framework is the Common Language Runtime. You should know the following facts about the services supplied by the Common Language Runtime (CLR):

- The Common Type System (CTS) defines the standard data types and their format, for all .NET languages. For example, the CTS defines that an Integer is 32 bits in size, and it also specifies the internal format for an Integer number.

- The Common Language Specification (CLS) defines rules for language interoperability. Because of the rules defined by the CLS, a class created in one .NET language can be used by any other .NET language.

- When a .NET application is first compiled, it is compiled into an intermediate language that is shared by all .NET languages. Just before an application is executed, the Just-In-Time (JIT) compiler translates the intermediate language file into an executable file that can execute on the target computer.

- The CLR manages the execution of a running application. That is, the CLR is responsible for allocating and deallocating memory as objects are created and destroyed.

- The Garbage Collector (GC) deallocates memory.

We discuss each of these services in turn.

The Common Type System

The **Common Type System (CTS)** is part of the CLR. The CTS defines standards for how types are declared and used so that the CLR can manage those standardized types between applications developed in different languages, and communicate data in a standardized format from one computer to another. The following list describes the functions of the CTS:

- The CTS defines the primary .NET data types used by all applications and the internal format of those types. For example, the CTS specifies the size and format of primitive numeric data types such as Integer and Single.

- The CTS specifies how the memory for structures and classes is allocated.

- The CTS allows components developed in different languages to operate seamlessly with each other.

- Type safety is enforced by the CTS. Type safety prohibits one application from interfering with the memory allocated to another application.

Closely related to the CTS is the Common Language Specification.

The Common Language Specification

The **Common Language Specification (CLS)** is a subset of the Common Type System and works in conjunction with the CTS to define a set of standards allowing different programming languages, and the applications written in those programming languages, to operate seamlessly with each other.

The CLS and the .NET Framework itself rely on low-level services provided by the Windows Application Programmer Interface. The **Windows Application Programmer Interface (API)** provides classes for elementary controls such as text boxes, buttons, scroll bars, list boxes, and combo boxes, among others. The Windows API also supplies the elementary Windows services to manage files, processes, and memory.

The CLS defines a minimum set of features, which all languages based on the .NET Framework must support. In general, the rules defined by the CLS can be categorized as follows:

- The CLS defines standard rules for naming variables. For example, all CLS-compliant variable names must begin with a letter and must not contain intervening spaces. Variable names must also differ by something other than the variable's case.

- The CLS defines primitive data types such as Int32, Int64, Single, Double, and Boolean.

- The CLS prohibits unsigned numeric data types. A signed numeric data type is a data type with one bit reserved to indicate whether the value is positive or negative. In an unsigned numeric data type, no bit is reserved to store the sign of the number.

- The CLS defines support for 0-based arrays.

- The CLS specifies rules for function argument lists, and how arguments are passed to functions. For example, the CLS prohibits the use of optional arguments.

- Event names and the rules for passing arguments to events are defined by the CLS.

- The CLS disallows memory pointers, and pointers to functions. Note that type-safe pointers are supplied through delegates. Delegates are discussed in detail in subsequent chapters.

The CLS defines additional standards beyond those described in the preceding list. However, as this book is not intended to describe the entire CLS, only a few of the standards are discussed in this chapter.

Any language may extend the base CLS requirements. For example, some languages, such as C#, provide support for unsigned Integers. Use of non-standard features is discouraged though, because the benefits of language interoperability are diminished. Any language that fully adheres to the rules of the CLS is called a **CLS-compliant language**.

Intermediate Language and the Just-In-Time Compiler

Any application developed in a .NET language, such as VB .NET, C#, or Visual J#, must be compiled into an executable file before that application can be executed. A traditional executable file contains native instructions allowing that file to be executed on the architecture of a particular CPU. The CPUs built by different manufacturers each have a unique architecture. That is, they each have different registers and execute a unique set of instructions. For example, the CPU instruction set for a Macintosh differs from the instruction set for an Intel Pentium processor. To overcome this problem, Apple's Virtual PC application allows Mac users to run Windows software by translating Pentium CPU instructions into Macintosh CPU instructions. This type of application is commonly referred to as an **emulator**.

Other computer vendors manufacture emulators too. Although the software emulation solution works, software emulators tend to execute applications more slowly than executing a native executable. Furthermore, software emulators are not always able to take advantage of the subtle enhancements made to CPUs, such as the evolution from the Pentium III to the Pentium IV.

The .NET Framework solves this problem of differing hardware architectures by compiling an application into a hardware independent format called **Microsoft Intermediate Language (MSIL)**. The term **Intermediate Language (IL)** is often used for brevity and will be used in this book.

IL has a format similar to assembly language. Assembly language statements are directly related to the instructions supported by the underlying CPU architecture. The format of IL is generic, however, and is not bound to the architecture of a particular CPU. That is, IL does not reference CPU registers or execute any CPU instruction directly. Rather, when the user executes an application stored in IL format, another utility called the **Just–In–Time (JIT)** compiler further translates the IL into a native executable that the target CPU can execute. The JIT compiler is discussed in further detail later in this section. The process of translating an IL file into a native executable file using the JIT compiler is often called **JITting**.

In addition to CPU manufacturers building different incompatible hardware, a single manufacturer, such as Intel, regularly builds new CPUs with additional features that support specialized instructions. By compiling an application to a machine independent IL, that IL can be optimized for a particular CPU when the user executes it. Thus, Microsoft will supply different versions of the JIT compiler for each target CPU version to take advantage of the unique capabilities of that CPU, thereby improving performance.

Execution Management

Code that is executed by the CLR is called **managed code**. One purpose of managed code is to prohibit one application from interfering with another application. This process is called **type safety**. Using type-safe managed code, it is impossible for one application to overwrite any memory allocated to another application. Applications developed in VB .NET execute under the control of the CLR and are therefore considered managed executables. Creating a managed executable involves four steps:

1. First, you must choose an appropriate compiler that produces code suitable for execution by the CLR and that utilizes the resources supplied by the .NET Framework. As mentioned, Microsoft supplies four .NET Framework-compatible languages at this time: VB .NET, C#, Visual J#, and C++. Third-party vendors also supply .NET Framework-compatible languages.

2. The application is then compiled into a machine independent intermediate language called IL. IL is discussed in a moment.

3. When executed, the IL code must be translated into a native executable file. It is the native executable file that will execute on the hardware of the target CPU. This process is referred to as Just-In-Time (JIT) compilation.

4. As an application executes, it calls upon the resources supplied by the .NET Framework class library, and the CLR itself.

Figure 1-2 illustrates this process.

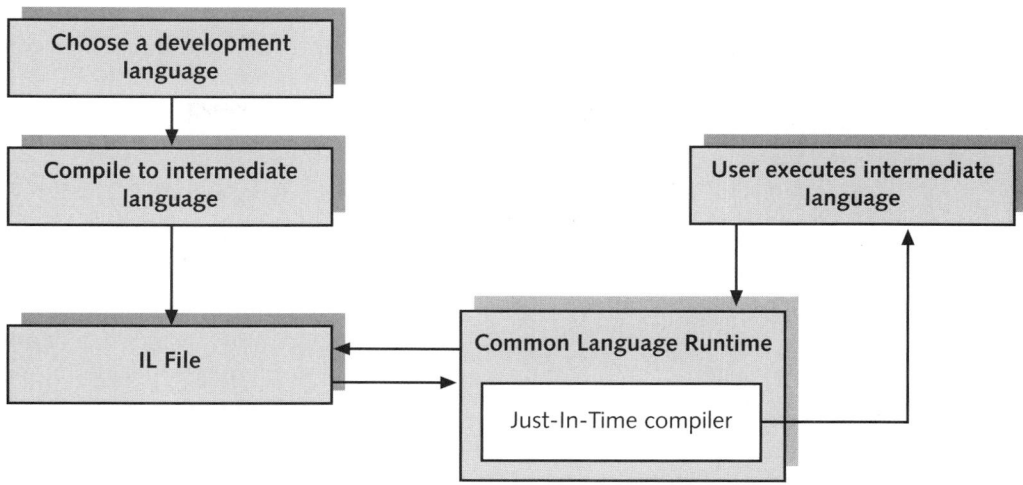

Figure 1-2   Creating and executing a managed executable

Some executables produced by Visual Studio .NET do not rely on the services provided by the CLR. This type of executable is referred to as an **unmanaged executable** or unmanaged code. C++ applications, for example, can produce either managed executables or unmanaged executables. A C++ application that uses pointers directly will produce an unmanaged executable, because pointers are not type safe.

Introduction to the Garbage Collector

One of the functions provided by the CLR is memory management. When an application (process) starts, the CLR allocates a contiguous area of memory to that process. This contiguous region of memory is called the **managed heap**. As the CLR creates objects from classes, it allocates memory for those objects from the managed heap. Remember that in VB .NET, objects are created from classes with the New keyword. If the CLR allocated memory forever, the available memory would become exhausted. Thus, the CLR periodically reclaims memory from the managed heap using another component called the **Garbage Collector (GC)**. The GC runs periodically to reclaim memory that is no longer needed by a running application (process).

Every running application has a set of **roots**. This set of roots includes global and static object pointers. Simply put, roots are global or static variables that store references to objects. Roots also include local variables and CPU registers. When memory needs to be reclaimed, the GC examines these roots (variables) and creates a list of all of the objects reachable from these roots. Any object that is not reachable from a process' roots is considered garbage. In other words, the memory allocated to a particular object is no longer needed. The GC will release this memory and return it to the managed heap. For example, suppose that you have declared a local variable in a procedure and that procedure has finished executing. Because the variable (root) no longer exists, the memory allocated to the variable is no longer reachable, so the GC will reclaim that memory.

To optimize the performance of the GC, the objects stored in the managed heap are divided into three generations identified by the values 0, 1, and 2 (a generation refers to how long an object has existed):

- A newly created object is stored as a generation 0 object. For performance reasons, generation 0 objects are typically allocated from L2 Cache rather than being stored in memory. When the managed heap space for generation 0 objects is full, the GC performs a collection operation on the generation 0 objects. Objects that are considered garbage are released back to the managed heap. Objects that are not garbage are migrated to generation 1. The logic for storing newly created objects and first reclaiming them from generation 0 is simple. Empirically, many objects exist for a very short time period. Frequently, the GC can reclaim enough memory from generation 0 without examining the objects allocated to generations 1 and 2, which significantly improves performance.

- Generation 0 objects that survive the first round of garbage collection are promoted to generation 1. If the GC cannot reclaim memory from generation 0, it then examines the objects allocated from generation 1, and attempts to reclaim memory from the generation 1 objects. Those objects that survive generation 1 garbage collection are then promoted to generation 2.

- Generation 2 objects have the longest lifetime. Objects will continue to appear in the generation 2 heap until they can be reclaimed.

Much more can be said about the internals of the GC. However, our purpose here is just to introduce how garbage collection works within the .NET Framework. Note also that you, as the developer, typically do not need to run the GC directly. The CLR automatically calls the GC in the background when necessary. However, Visual Studio .NET does provide the means to call the GC directly in special circumstances.

At this point, we have described the logical structure of the .NET Framework, and the relationships between the components that comprise the .NET Framework. In the next section of this chapter, we begin to apply these theoretical fundamentals to create a .NET application.

INTRODUCTION TO ASSEMBLIES

As mentioned, Visual Studio .NET compiles an application into an IL file. This IL file has a well-defined format. The contents of this file are commonly referred to as an assembly. An **assembly** is the primary physical building block of any .NET application. Every application that you create is considered an assembly. The .NET Framework class library itself also supplies several assemblies. Remember that the .NET Framework class library is part of the .NET Framework itself. All of the classes that comprise the .NET

Framework class library are stored in physical assemblies. Assemblies have common characteristics as described in the following list:

- The name of an assembly must be globally unique. When an assembly is deployed as a shared assembly, a developer can be assured that the assembly name will not conflict with another assembly name.

- The identity of an assembly's publisher is stored in the assembly. Thus, you, as a developer, can be assured that an assembly came from the actual publisher of the assembly. Thus, spoofing is not possible.

Every assembly contains an assembly manifest. The **assembly manifest** describes the assembly and the modules that make up the assembly. The assembly manifest is often referred to as **assembly metadata**. The following list describes the basic elements of an assembly manifest:

- An assembly contains a descriptive name, and optional localization information used when an assembly is designed to support different languages. This descriptive name and localization information is referred to as the **assembly's identity**.

- The manifest describes an assembly's contents. The **assembly contents** describe the types (classes, for example) exposed by the assembly.

- An assembly may rely on one or more other assemblies to operate. Thus, the assembly manifest contains a list of **dependencies**.

- The manifest also contains permissions. **Assembly permissions** dictate who can use the contents of the assembly.

In addition to assembly metadata, an assembly typically contains another kind of metadata called **type metadata**. Type metadata describes the types, and members of those types, contained in an assembly. For example, if an assembly contained a class named StreamReader, with methods named Read and ReadLine, that information would be stored in the assembly's type metadata. In addition to assembly and type metadata, an assembly contains the actual IL code itself. Finally, an assembly may contain optional resources. Resources include such elements as bitmap and icon files, along with other support files required by the application.

The .NET Framework class library is comprised of numerous assemblies that read and write files, store and retrieve information from databases, and provide the functionality for a form. In addition, third-party vendors supply additional assemblies that extend the functionality of the .NET Framework class library. Selected third-party vendors and their Web sites appear in the following list:

- ComponentOne (*www.componentone.com*) sells grid controls to display and manage database data.

- Data Dynamics (*www.datadynamics.com*) sells sophisticated reporting tools.

- Dundas Software (*www.dundas.com*) develops products to create charts and graphs.

- Infragistics (*www.infragistics.com*) sells numerous controls that extend the controls supplied by the .NET Framework class library.

- Northwoods Software (*www.nwoods.com*) has a product called Go.Net used to create interactive graphics.

The preceding list mentions only a few of the vendors supplying third-party .NET tools.

If you have worked with the Windows API or used and developed ActiveX components, you have incorporated various DLLs into your applications by means of the Declare statement or by including a reference to a COM library in an existing project. Assemblies in .NET serve the same purpose. By referencing an assembly in an application, you gain access to a group of components defined by that assembly. Although assemblies have a file suffix of .dll, they are not DLLs in the same way that the Windows API functions are DLLs. That is, .NET assemblies have a unique internal format.

The following list describes but a few of the assemblies that make up the .NET Framework class library and their purpose. These assemblies are used by nearly every desktop form-based application that you create.

- The assembly named **System.dll** defines the primary data types such as Integer and Long, along with the most elemental types such as System.Object.

- The assembly named **System.Data.dll** defines the components that make up ADO.NET. ADO.NET supplies the database processing services used by Visual Studio .NET.

- The assembly named **System.Drawing.dll** contains the components used to draw various shapes to an output device, such as the screen or a printer. These shapes include rectangles and lines, among others.

- The assembly named **System.Windows.Forms.dll** contains the components used to implement the forms used in a desktop application, along with the controls that you create on those forms.

- **System.XML.dll** contains the necessary components to process Extensible Markup Language (XML) documents. XML is the primary transport protocol for ADO.NET and other Internet-related services.

Each of the preceding assemblies (library files) contains a part of the .NET Framework class library. Note that the preceding list describes only a few of the assemblies that comprise the .NET Framework class library. In total, there are nearly 100 different assemblies. This group of assemblies defines the components that make up the .NET Framework class library.

THE ORGANIZATION OF NAMESPACES

Physical assemblies are organized into logical components called namespaces. Through **namespaces**, the physical file(s) that comprise an assembly are translated into logical components that comprise the hierarchy that forms the .NET Framework class library. To begin, Microsoft has divided VB .NET into two primary namespaces as follows:

- Namespaces created by the .NET team begin with the name **System**. All .NET languages use the members of the System namespace.

- Namespaces created by Microsoft but by groups other than the .NET team begin with the name **Microsoft**. For example, the Microsoft.VisualBasic namespace contains those components that are unique to VB .NET.

VB .NET is not formally considered part of the .NET Framework. Rather, VB .NET is a language that relies on the services provided by the .NET Framework, so it appears under the Microsoft namespace rather than under the System namespace. Thus, the Microsoft.VisualBasic namespace defines the components unique to the Visual Basic language. Namespaces are organized into a hierarchy and are syntactically connected together with a period (.). Thus, the VisualBasic namespace belongs to the Microsoft namespace.

An assembly may contain one or more namespaces. For example, the System and System.IO namespaces are stored in the System.dll assembly. In addition, it is possible for one namespace to be stored into two assemblies.

The following list describes selected namespaces used by nearly every .NET desktop application:

- The **System** namespace contains the fundamental classes that define data types, events, and event handlers.

- The **System.Data** namespace contains the namespaces and classes that provide data access capabilities. Collectively these namespaces and classes form ADO.NET.

- The **System.Drawing** namespace contains the classes that provide the interface to the Windows Graphical Device Interface (GDI). These classes define various drawing shapes such as lines and rectangles.

- The **System.IO** namespace contains classes to read and write sequential files and data from other sources.

- The **System.Windows.Forms** namespace defines the classes containing the controls appearing in the Toolbox, along with the capabilities of the form itself.

We have said that assemblies are the building blocks of the .NET Framework, and that a physical assembly contains one or more namespaces. Namespaces, in turn, contain one or more **types**. In the .NET Framework, an Integer or String is considered a type. Every class is also considered a type. To illustrate, the System namespace contains a type named

Int32, which represents an Integer. In VB .NET, types are divided into two primary categories: value types and reference types.

- **Value types** store data directly in the variable. Many built-in data types such as Short (Int16), Integer (Int32), Long (Int64), Single, and Double are all value types. Structures and enumerations are also value types. The .NET Framework allocates memory for value types from the program stack.

- **Reference types** store a memory address in the variable. That memory address, in turn, points to the memory address that stores the actual data or object. Classes defined by the .NET Framework class library and classes that you create are reference types. Arrays and strings are also reference types. The .NET Framework allocates the memory for reference types from the managed heap.

Namespaces contain classes, delegates, structures, enumerations, and interfaces, each of which is considered a type. Each of these preceding types is either a value type or a reference type. We briefly identify each of these types in the following list. These types will be discussed in significant detail in subsequent chapters.

- **Classes** are reference types, meaning that a variable having a data type of a particular class stores a memory address. That memory address, in turn, points to the memory allocated to the actual object. Classes support events, fields, methods, and properties. Controls appearing in the Toolbox are all classes. A form is also a class.

- **Delegates** are also reference types. However, they have a much more specific purpose than classes. Delegates provide the mechanism through which your program registers events to the Windows operating system, so that Windows can raise those events at runtime, thereby calling the appropriate event handler. Delegates (event handlers) can also be created dynamically at runtime.

- **Structures** are value types rather than reference types, meaning that the data is stored directly in the variable itself. Structures can have both properties and methods. The primary data types such as Integer (Int32) or Single are considered structures by the .NET Framework.

- **Enumerations** are a limited form of a value type. Enumerations do not have methods or properties. Rather, they have only fields. Enumerations provide the mechanism to associate a mnemonic name with a constant value. Thus, enumerations are conceptually similar to constants. Many control properties are enumerations. For example, the TextAlign property of a TextBox has an enumerated data type of HorizontalAlignment. This enumeration has possible values of Center, Left, and Right.

- **Interfaces** define the members (methods, properties, etc.) that other classes that implement the interface must support. Simply put, an interface defines the task that a class must perform, but not how the class performs that task. For example, an array can be sorted by calling the Sort method of the Array class. The Sort method uses an implementation of an interface named IComparable or IComparer to determine how the elements in the array will be sorted. As the developer, you create a class that implements one or both of these interfaces. The interface does not define specifically what type of object will be sorted, nor does it define how the object will be sorted. It is the implementation of the interface you create that specifies how a list will be sorted.

Every type created by the developers of .NET, and any type that you create in a .NET application, falls into one of the preceding type categories. For example, every form in a desktop application is considered a class, forming its own type. Formally, an Integer is also a type. That is, an Integer is a structure with members to convert an Integer to a string, and to determine the largest value that an Integer can store. Figure 1-3 illustrates the relationship between an assembly, namespaces, and types.

Figure 1-3   Relationship between types

Figure 1-3 illustrates the relationship between a small subset of the types contained in the System.dll assembly. The System and System.IO namespaces are contained in the System assembly. Remember that an assembly may contain multiple namespaces. The System namespace contains the primary types that comprise the .NET Framework, including the Integer and String types. An Integer is a structure, so it is a value type. A String is a class, so it is a reference type. The System.IO namespace in the System assembly contains the classes to perform file input and output. The File class has methods to create, remove, and manage files. FileMode is an enumeration used to determine how the operating system should open a file.

To illustrate a namespace and how the classes in a namespace relate to each other, examine the following statement to print a string to a Command Prompt window:

```
System.Console.WriteLine("Course Technology")
```

All components in the .NET Framework, along with any developer-created components, are organized into namespaces containing types. In the preceding statement, System is the namespace. Namespaces may contain other namespaces or other types such as a class. In the preceding statement, the Console class applies to the System namespace. Classes, in turn, contain members. These members include properties, methods, and fields. The WriteLine method applies to the Console class and prints a string to the Console (Command Prompt) window. Thus, the preceding statement prints the string "Course Technology" to a Console window by calling the WriteLine method of the Console class of the System namespace. The WriteLine method accepts one argument: the value to write.

The Console class of the System namespace supports the following members:

Syntax

System.Console class

Definition

The methods of the **Console** class read and write characters or lines from a system console. If a Console window is not available, then the data is discarded and no error is produced.

Public Methods

- The **Read** method reads a character from the input stream. The method returns the character read in the form of an Integer, or returns –1 if no character exists in the input stream.

- The **ReadLine** method reads a line from the input stream. The method returns the line read or returns –1 if no data exists in the input stream. The carriage return appearing at the end of the line is discarded.

- The **Write** method writes a character or string to the output stream.

- The **WriteLine** method writes a line to the output stream. The line is terminated by a carriage return character.

The following examples illustrate the use of the preceding members of the Console class:

```
Dim pintCharacter As Integer
Dim pstrLine As String
pintCharacter = System.Console.Read()
pstrLine = System.Console.ReadLine()
System.Console.Write("Course Technology")
System.Console.WriteLine("Course Technology")
```

The first two of the preceding statements declare local variables to store the input read from the console. The first call to the Read method reads a single character and stores the character read in the Integer variable pintCharacter. The call to the ReadLine method reads an entire line—discarding the carriage return character appearing at the end of the line—and stores the line in the variable pstrLine. The last two statements write the string "Course Technology" to the Console window. The WriteLine method writes a carriage return at the end of the line, but the call to the Write method does not.

As we have said, the .NET Framework organizes namespaces and classes into a hierarchy, and that part of the .NET Framework is called the .NET Framework class library.

THE .NET FRAMEWORK CLASS LIBRARY

The .NET Framework class library contains all of the types defined by the .NET Framework. Remember that classes, delegates, enumerators, interfaces, and structures are all considered types by .NET. Figure 1-4 illustrates how the .NET Framework class library fits into the .NET Framework itself, and presents selected members of the .NET Framework class library.

Figure 1-4   The .NET Framework class library

Types are built from other types using inheritance. Through **inheritance,** one type gains access to the methods and properties defined by another type. Inheritance is discussed fully in Chapter 4. In addition to inheriting the properties and methods of a type, it is also possible to alter the actions of existing methods or the behavior of properties. This process is called **overriding.** Overriding is discussed fully in Chapter 5.

All of the types belonging to the .NET Framework, along with any types that you create, are organized into a hierarchy. The type at the base of the .NET Framework hierarchy is System.Object. In other words, System.Object exists at the root of the hierarchical tree and is called the **superclass.** The System.Object superclass supplies the most elemental features of all types that make up the .NET Framework.

The following list describes the services provided by System.Object:

- System.Object supplies a constructor. A **constructor** provides the means to create an object from its underlying type. Syntactically, a constructor is a procedure named New appearing in a class that VB .NET executes when creating an instance of that class. Note that structures and modules can also have constructors.

- The **Equals** method tests whether two objects contain the same data. The definition of equality varies from one type to another. Thus, the Equals method tests for value equality rather than reference equality.

- The **GetHashCode** method defines the hashing function for the type. Hashing and the purpose of the GetHashCode method are discussed in more detail in subsequent chapters.

- The **GetType** method returns the data type of the object. GetType returns another object having the data type of Type. The Type object itself supports numerous properties that describe the data type.

- The **ReferenceEquals** method tests for reference equality. That is, it tests whether two object variables reference the same instance of the class. In other words, ReferenceEquals tests that two object variables reference the same memory address, rather than testing whether two different object variables contain the same data. Note that in VB .NET you can use the equals (=) operator to test for reference equality.

- The **ToString** method converts the value of the object to a string. Again, most classes override this method. If the method is not overridden, the ToString method returns the fully qualified name of the class.

Because System.Object is the superclass, and all other types are derived from System.Object, all types must, by definition, support the preceding methods. Next, we discuss the primary .NET Framework data types.

Primary .NET Framework Data Types

Table 1-1 lists and describes the primary .NET Framework data types, the memory needed to store each data type, and the possible values.

Table 1-1 Primary data types

Data type	Memory needed	Possible values
Boolean (System.Boolean)	2 bytes	True or False
Byte (System.Byte)	1 byte	0 to 255
Short (System.Int16)	2 bytes	–32,768 to 32,767
Integer (System.Int32)	4 bytes	–2,147,483,648 to 2,147,483,647
Long (System.Int64)	8 bytes	–9,223,372,036,854,775,808 to 9,223,372,036,854,775,807
Single (System.Single)	4 bytes	Floating point numbers with 6 digits of precision
Double (System.Double)	8 bytes	Floating point numbers with 16 digits of precision
Char (System.Char)	2 bytes	0 to 65,535
String (System.String)	Depends on string length	0 to approximately 2 billion characters
Date (System.DateTime)	8 bytes	January 1, 0001 to December 31, 9999

Note that the memory allocation listed in the preceding table may be misleading. Depending on the CPU architecture, and whether the system is a 32-bit or 64-bit system, the actual required memory allocation will differ.

Declaring a Variable

Declaring a variable requires that you use an access modifier, such as Dim, followed by the variable name, and followed by the data type. Access modifiers and variable scope are discussed in detail in subsequent chapters. Examine the following equivalent statements to declare a local Integer variable:

```
Dim pintCurrent As System.Int32
Dim pintCurrent As Integer
```

The two preceding statements are equivalent. The first statement uses the formal .NET Framework syntax to declare the variable named pintCurrent, as the actual data type is System.Int32. The second statement uses convenience syntax to declare an Integer variable. VB .NET permits both syntax variations to provide backward compatibility with previous versions of Visual Basic.

Type Inheritance

Given the inheritance model that the .NET Framework uses, every type is inherited from the base class System.Object. For example, System.ValueType inherits from System.Object. System.ValueType overrides the methods of System.Object to provide functionality appropriate to value types. Data types such as Int32 (Integer) and Single are value types and therefore derive from System.ValueType.

Note that additional types inherit from System.ValueType. For example, System.Enum derives from System.ValueType to provide the functionality of an enumeration. System.Enum overrides methods supplied by System.ValueType and expands the implementation, providing several methods that apply to enumerations. Figure 1-5 illustrates the relationship between selected types defined by the .NET Framework class library.

Figure 1-5   The .NET Framework type hierarchy

As shown in Figure 1-5, the Int16, Int32, Int64, Single, and Double structures all derive from System.ValueType, which, in turn, derives from the System.Object class. The System.Enum class also derives from System.ValueType. The String and Array classes derive directly from System.Object. The key point to remember is that no matter the type, every type fits into the .NET Framework class hierarchy somewhere. In addition, no matter the type, every type ultimately derives from the base type (superclass) System.Object. Understanding this concept is the key to understanding the .NET Framework class library.

The Implementation of Structures

Structures, such as Int32, have methods and fields. For example, the Int32 structure has fields named MinValue and MaxValue that retrieve the minimum and maximum possible values for an Int32 structure, respectively. In addition, the Int32 structure has a method named ToString used to convert the Int32 value to a String data type. Every type, by definition, has a method named ToString because System.Object defines ToString.

Examine the following statements to get the minimum and maximum possible values that can be stored in an Integer (Int32):

```
Dim pintMin As Integer
Dim pintMax As Integer
Dim pstrMin As String
Dim pstrMax As String
pintMin = System.Int32.MinValue
pintMax = System.Int32.MaxValue
pstrMin = pintMin.ToString()
pstrMax = pintMax.ToString()
```

The preceding statements use the MinValue and MaxValue fields of the Int32 structure to get and store into variables the minimum and maximum allowable values for an Integer. The final two statements convert those numeric values into a string and store the results in the corresponding String variables. Again, note that the syntax is consistent. The MinValue field of the Int32 structure of the System namespace is connected using a period. This same syntax is used to reference all .NET Framework types. The ToString method for primitive numeric data types support arguments that control how a string is formatted.

Examine the following statements:

```
pstrMin = pintMin.ToString("c")
pstrMax = pintMax.ToString("f")
```

The preceding statements format the Integer as a currency value and a fixed decimal value, respectively. The "c" argument denotes currency, and the "f" argument denotes fixed.

Type Conversion

Type conversion is the process of converting the data stored in a variable from one type to another. Suppose that a value was stored in a variable having a data type of Single and that data needed to be converted to an Integer value. VB .NET can accomplish this task using one of two forms of type conversion: implicit type conversion or explicit type conversion.

Using **implicit type conversion**, VB .NET will attempt to convert data from one type to another without calling a type conversion method. Implicit type conversion poses no problem when data are converted from a more restrictive type to a less restrictive type, because no risk of data loss exists. For example, when converting data from an Integer to a Long, or converting a Single to a Double, VB .NET will use implicit type conversion correctly to convert the data. However, the reverse is not true. For example, data stored in a Long variable may be lost when an attempt is made to store the data in an Integer. A loss of precision may also occur when converting data from the Double data type to a Single. Examine the following statements that rely on implicit type conversion:

```
Dim psngCurrent As Single = 123456.789
Dim pintCurrent As Integer
Dim pshoCurrent As Short
pintCurrent = psngCurrent
pshocurrent = pintCurrent
```

The first of the preceding statements declares a variable of type Single and initializes the value to 123456.789. The assignment statement that stores the Single value stored in psngCurrent in the Integer value pintCurrent will work, but the value will be rounded to 123457. The final statement will cause a numeric overflow error because the largest value that can be stored in a variable having a data type of Short is 32767.

With strict type checking enabled, assignment statements that attempt implicit type conversion will succeed only when converting from a more restrictive type to a less restrictive type. For example, implicit type conversion from an Integer to a Long will succeed, but implicit type conversion from a Long to an Integer will fail because an Integer is a more restrictive type than a Long. The purpose of strict type conversion is to eliminate those errors that cause data loss when a variable having a Single data type is stored in a variable having a Long or other more restrictive data type. Furthermore, VB .NET will not implicitly convert strings to numeric data types when strict type checking is enabled.

The following statements enable and disable strict type checking, respectively:

```
Option Strict On
Option Strict Off
```

The Option Strict statement must appear at the beginning of a module. VB .NET continues to support the Option Explicit statement, although the syntax has changed slightly. When Option Explicit is enabled, all variables must be explicitly declared before those variables are used. The following statements enable and disable Option Explicit:

```
Option Explicit On
Option Explicit Off
```

Both the Option Strict and Option Explicit statements apply to the file containing the statements. Thus, if a project contains multiple module files, then the Option Strict and Option Explicit statements should appear in every module file.

Even though the Option Strict statement prohibits certain types of implicit type conversion, data can still be converted from one type to another explicitly by calling methods of the System.Convert class. The Convert class of the System namespace supplies the **explicit type conversion** methods to convert data from one data type to another, as follows:

Syntax

System.Convert Class

Public Methods

- The **ToBoolean** method converts its argument to a Boolean value.
- The **ToDateTime** method converts its argument to a DateTime structure.
- The **ToInt16** method converts its argument to a Short Integer.
- The **ToInt32** method converts its argument to an Integer.
- The **ToInt64** method converts its argument to a Long Integer.
- The **ToSingle** method converts its argument to a single precision number (Single).
- The **ToDouble** method converts its argument to a double precision number (Double).
- The **ToString** method converts its argument to a string representation (String).

These are but a few of the methods supplied by the System.Convert class. Figure 1-6 illustrates how the System.Convert class and its methods fit into the .NET Framework class hierarchy.

The following example illustrates how to read an input value from the console and convert that value to an Integer using the ToInt32 method. The syntax to call the other methods is the same.

```
Dim pstrCurrent As String
Dim pintCurrent As Integer
pstrCurrent = System.Console.Readline()
pintCurrent = System.Convert.ToInt32(pstrCurrent)
```

Figure 1-6   The System.Convert class

The preceding statements declare String and Integer variables named pstrCurrent and pintCurrent, respectively. The third statement reads a string from the console into the variable pstrCurrent. The final statement converts that value to an Integer and stores the result in the variable pintCurrent. Note that if the variable named pstrCurrent does not contain a valid number, the ToInt32 method will fail and an error will occur.

The Math Class of the System Namespace

Another class supplied by the System namespace is the Math class. Its methods perform common mathematical and trigonometric functions as follows:

Syntax

System.Math Class

Public Fields

- The Field **E** represents the natural logarithmic base specified by the constant *e*.
- The Field **PI** stores the constant value of Pi.

Public Methods

- The **Abs** method accepts one numeric argument and returns the absolute value of that argument.
- The **Cos** method accepts one numeric argument and returns the cosine of an angle.

- The **Sign** method returns a value indicating whether a number is positive or negative.
- The **Sin** method accepts one numeric argument and returns the sine of an angle.
- The **Sqrt** method accepts one numeric argument and returns the square root of a number.
- The **Tan** method accepts one numeric argument and returns the tangent of an angle.

Figure 1-7 illustrates how the System.Convert class and the System.Math class fit into the .NET Framework class hierarchy.

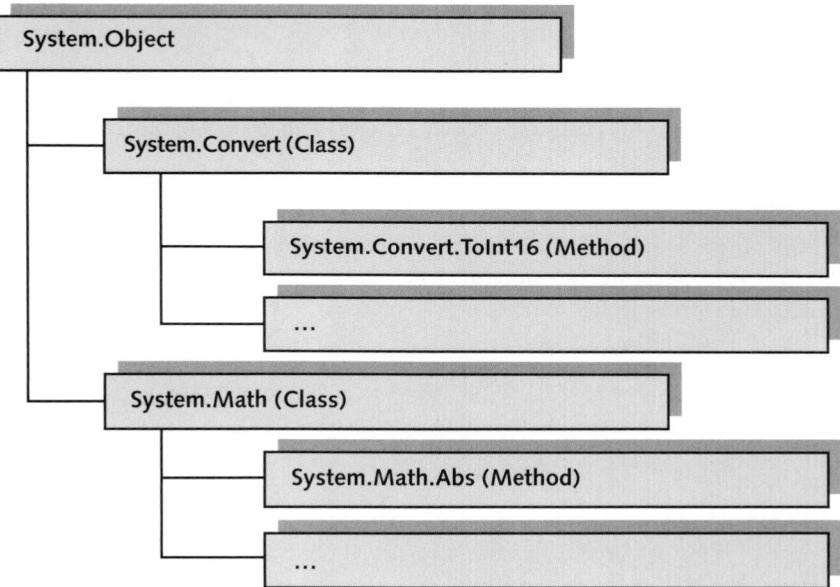

Figure 1-7   The System.Convert and System.Math classes

The following example illustrates how to call the Abs method to determine the absolute value of a number. The syntax to call the other methods of the System.Math class is the same.

```
Dim pintPositive As Integer
pintPositive = System.Math.Abs(-334)
```

 Refer to the Help topic for the System.Math class for a complete list of the supported mathematical methods.

CREATING A FIRST VISUAL BASIC .NET APPLICATION

To demonstrate the use of the VB .NET compiler, and IL, you will create the simplest of Console applications that will print a string to a Command Prompt window.

 Many developers refer to a Command Prompt window as a DOS window. The term Command Prompt window will be used in this book for technical accuracy.

In addition, so that you can see how to call the VB .NET compiler directly, you will create the application in Notepad without the aid of Visual Studio .NET. Chapter 2 explains more fully the structure of a complete VB .NET application and how to use the Visual Studio .NET IDE to create an application. However, as the purpose of this chapter is to introduce the fundamental concepts surrounding the .NET Framework, only the most elemental structure of a VB .NET application is introduced.

The Structure of a Visual Basic .NET Application

In the .NET Framework, all files containing VB .NET form, module, and classes have a file suffix of .vb, which should not be changed. Furthermore, VB .NET introduces new keywords to denote whether a file contains a form, or whether a file is a module file. A module has the following syntax:

Syntax

Module *name*
   Statements
End Module

Syntax Description

Just as classes are reference types, standard modules declared with the Module statement are also reference types. Thus, the CLR allocates the memory for a module from the managed heap instead of the program stack. An application may have zero or more module files. Multiple module blocks (Module and End Module statements) may appear in the same file. Module blocks may not be nested. That is, one module block cannot contain another module block. A module may contain variable declarations and procedures. A module is marked with the Module and End Module statements.

Dissection

- The **Module** statement marks the beginning of the module.
- The **End Module** statement marks the end of the module.

- *name* defines the name of the module. The name must comply with the standard .NET Framework naming rules for identifiers. Note that VB .NET is a case insensitive language.

- The *statements* that comprise the module appear between the Module and End Module keywords.

Code Example

```
Module Startup01
    ' statements
End Module
```

Code Dissection

The preceding statements define a module named Startup01.

A module may contain variable declarations and procedures. VB .NET must know which procedure to execute when an application begins executing. One possibility is to create a sub procedure named Main in a module. VB .NET considers a Public procedure named Main in a module as a startup procedure. VB .NET executes the statements in this startup procedure when the application begins to execute. The following code segment illustrates a Sub Main procedure in a Module block:

```
Module Startup01
    Public Sub Main()
        ' statements
    End Sub
End Module
```

The preceding code segment declares a Public Sub procedure named Main in the module named Startup01. The italicized text is a placeholder for the statements in the module.

Writing the Application

You now have the skills to create a first Console application. In this first Console application, you will write an application that will get input from the user, convert that string input to a number, calculate the square root of that value, and display the result to the user. The application will continue to calculate output until the user enters an input value of negative one (-1).

Again, in this chapter you will create the application using a text editor instead of using the Visual Studio .NET IDE. The purpose of using Notepad, as you will see in a moment, is to understand how to call the VB .NET compiler directly, and understand the output produced by the compiler.

To create a Console application:

1. Start Notepad and enter the following statements in the empty file:

```
Option Strict On
Option Explicit On

Module Startup01

    Sub Main()
        Dim pstrLine As String
        Dim pdblValue As Double
        Do While True
            System.Console.Write("Enter a number: ")
            pstrLine = System.Console.ReadLine()
            pdblValue = System.Convert.ToDouble(pstrLine)
            If pdblValue = -1 Then
                Exit Do
            Else
                pdblValue = System.Math.Sqrt(pdblValue)
                System.Console.Write("The result is ")
                System.Console.WriteLine(pdblValue.ToString())
            End If
        Loop
    End Sub
End Module
```

2. Save the file using the name **Startup01.vb** in the folder named **Chapter.01\ Startup01**.

Examining the statements that you just wrote, the Do loop executes until the user enters an input value of -1 causing the Exit Do statement to execute. The following statement in the Do loop displays a prompt to the user by calling the Write method of the System.Console class:

```
System.Console.Write("Enter a number: ")
```

The subsequent statements read an input value and then convert that value to a Double (note that if the user enters a value that is not a number, an error will occur):

```
pstrLine = System.Console.ReadLine()
pdblValue = System.Convert.ToDouble(pstrLine)
```

The If statement tests whether or not the input value was -1. If it was, the loop exits and then the program itself will exit. If the value was not -1, the following statements execute:

```
pdblValue = System.Math.Sqrt(pdblValue)
System.Console.Write("The result is ")
System.Console.WriteLine(pdblValue.ToString())
```

The first of the preceding statements calculates the square root of the input value. The final two statements display the output with a descriptive prompt.

Locating the Visual Basic .NET Compiler

Having written a first application, that application must be compiled into an executable file before the user can run it. Unfortunately, the VB .NET compiler is not stored in a folder that is automatically searched by Windows. One way to call the compiler is to specify the full path name of the compiler executable file on the command line. Alternatively, Visual Studio .NET supplies a batch file that you can run from the command line (Command Prompt window) so that Windows will know where to locate the VB .NET compiler. By default, this batch file is stored in the file named C:\Program Files\ Microsoft Visual Studio .NET\FrameworkSDK\Bin\corvars.bat. So that you can easily run this batch file, you will copy it to a searchable Windows folder such as C:\Windows for Windows XP or C:\WINNT for Windows 2000.

 If you are running Visual Studio .NET 2003, then the batch file name is vsvars32.bat. This file is stored in the folder named C:\Program Files\ Microsoft Visual Studio .NET 2003\Common7\Tools\vsvars32.bat.

To change the Windows search path to locate the VB .NET compiler:

1. Using Windows Explorer, copy the file **C:\Program Files\Microsoft Visual Studio .NET\FrameworkSDK\Bin\corvars.bat** to the folder named **C:\Windows**.

   Note that this folder name may vary if Visual Studio .NET is not installed in the default location.

2. To open a Command Prompt window, click **Start**, point to **All Programs**, point to **Accessories**, and then click **Command Prompt**. Note that this step will vary if you are running Windows 2000 or are running Windows XP in Classic view.

3. In the Command Prompt window, run the batch file by typing **corvars.bat**. Running this batch file will modify the necessary environment variables so that Windows will search the folder containing the VB .NET compiler. Note that Windows will be able to locate the corvars.bat file because the default search path should contain the directory C:\Windows. Figure 1-8 shows how to run the file corvars.bat and the output produced.

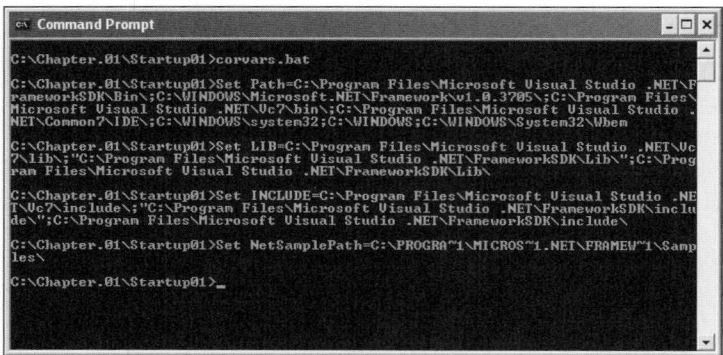

Figure 1-8   Command Prompt window running corvars.bat

Do not close the Command Prompt window.

Note the following about the preceding steps. First, if your computer is in a lab you may not have permission to change the environment. In this situation, you will need to call the VB .NET compiler by supplying the full path name. Second, you may not have permission to open a Command Prompt window. Finally, each time you open a new instance of a Command Prompt window, you will need to run the corvars.bat file again, as the changes to the environment are not consistent from one Command Prompt window to another.

Compiling a Visual Basic .NET Application

Having created the application and set up the Visual Studio .NET environment such that it can locate the VB .NET compiler, you must compile the VB .NET source statements into IL. Although the Visual Studio .NET IDE can accomplish this task, the purpose of this simple illustration is to call the compiler directly from the command line (Command Prompt window).

The VB .NET compiler uses a command line interface to translate source files into an IL file. Compiling applications from a Command Prompt window can be useful when memory is limited on the development computer, or when an application is so simple that it does not require the rich features supplied by the IDE. In addition, using a Command Prompt window may be necessary if Visual Studio .NET is not available on the target computer.

The VB .NET compiler is named vbc.exe (Visual Basic Compiler), and by default is stored in the folder named C:\Windows\Microsoft.Net\Framework\v1.0.3705. Note that the final directory named v1.0.3705 represents the version and build number of the .NET Framework. This build number will vary based on the version of the .NET Framework you are running.

 If you are using Windows 2000 instead of Windows XP, the default path name is C:\WINNT\Microsoft.Net\Framework\v1.0.3705.

To compile an application from a Command Prompt window, you call the compiler directly, with the source file name as an argument. In this example the source file is named Startup01.vb. In addition to supplying the file name to compile, you supply the command line directives that describe how the application should be compiled, any external references that are necessary to compile the application, and the name of the output file that will be produced.

The syntax of the VB .NET compiler is simple. Each command line directive is preceded by a forward slash. The following optional argument is separated from the directive by a full colon. Either a space or a comma separates each compiler directive and argument pair. The following list describes but a few of the command line directives defined by the VB .NET compiler:

- The **/debug** directive causes the compiler to produce debugging information.

- The **/libpath** directive works with the /reference directive and is used to specify a directory to search for assemblies. The compiler first searches for references in the current working directory. Then the CLR system directory is searched. Next, any directories specified by /libpath are searched, and finally, any directories specified by the LIB environment variable are searched.

- The **/main** directive specifies the class or module that contains the Sub Main procedure. The /main directive can also specify the name of the form designated as the startup form.

- The **/nowarn** directive suppresses warning messages.

- The **/optionexplicit** directive enforces explicit variable declaration. When enabled, variables must be declared before they are referenced. Using this directive has the same effect as including the Option Explicit statement in a module.

- The **/optionstrict** directive enforces strict type checking. When enabled, less restrictive types will not be implicitly converted to more restrictive types. Furthermore, strings will not be implicitly converted into numeric data types. Using this directive has the same effect as including the Option Strict statement in a module.

- The **/out** directive defines the file name of the executable file produced. If omitted, the output file has the same name as the module name containing the Sub Main procedure.

- The **/reference** directive makes an assembly or multiple assemblies available.

- The **/verbose** directive causes the compiler to display additional descriptive information about the compile.

 For a full list of compiler options, refer to the Help topic regarding Visual Basic compiler options.

The following statement illustrates how to call the compiler to produce an executable file. Even though the statement appears on two lines, it is a single statement.

```
vbc /verbose /reference:System.dll /out:Startup01.exe
Startup01.vb
```

The preceding statement illustrates that the VB .NET compiler is named vbc.exe. The file named Startup01.vb will be compiled into an IL file. The /reference directive specifies that the application uses the resources supplied by the assembly named System.dll. The optional /out directive specifies that the IL file will be stored in the file named Startup01.exe.

You will now enter the command line statement to compile the Visual Studio .NET source file into an IL file that can be executed by the .NET Framework.

To compile and test an application from a Command Prompt window:

1. In the Command Prompt window, make sure that the current working directory is Chapter.01\Startup01. This is the directory where you created the Startup01.vb file. Note that you can use the CD command to change directories.

2. Enter the following statement and then press **Enter** to compile the application. Even though the following statement appears on two lines, it is a single statement.

```
vbc.exe /verbose /reference:System.dll /out:Startup01.exe
Startup01.vb
```

As VB .NET compiles the application, log messages appear describing the status of the compilation process. Also, any syntax errors are reported as they are found. If any syntax errors are detected, Visual Studio .NET will not produce the executable file.

Figure 1-9 shows the results of the compile.

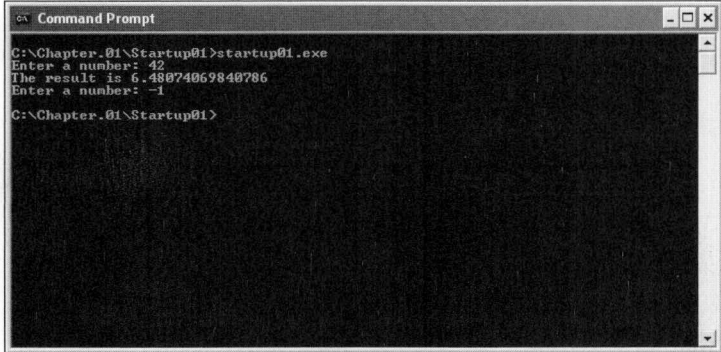

Figure 1-9   Compiling the application

As shown in Figure 1-9, the compiler first displays the version information and a copyright notice. Next, the compiler indicates that a reference to the System.dll assembly is added, and that the file Starutp01.vb is added to the compile. Next, the necessary dll's are loaded, and finally the compiler indicates that the application is being built.

Next, you can test the application that you just created.

To test the application:

1. Test the executable file by typing **Startup01.exe** in the Command Prompt window, and then pressing **Enter**. Type the value **42** in response to the prompt, and then press **Enter**. The application calculates the square root of the number.

2. Type the value **–1** to end the application. Figure 1-10 shows the results.

Figure 1-10   Executing the application

Having created, compiled, and tested the application, you will now explore the output produced by the compiler.

THE SYNTAX OF INTERMEDIATE LANGUAGE

As mentioned, when you compile a VB .NET application, that application appears in IL format and is not a true executable file. Visual Studio .NET provides a tool that will convert the IL file into a text form allowing you to view and optionally modify the IL. In this chapter, we introduce the concepts of IL. However, understanding the complete syntax of IL is beyond the scope of this chapter and this book.

 The ability to disassemble programs to examine the underlying source code has been a criticism of the .NET Framework for security and copyright reasons. Although disassembling IL will not produce the original VB .NET or C# code written by a developer, any developer familiar with assembly language and IL itself would be able to understand the essential operation of an application. In reality, most production applications will have sufficient complexity that the disassembled code will be difficult to interpret. In addition, Microsoft is working on a product called the Obfuscator that will scramble the .NET IL, making it difficult, if not impossible, for other developers to reverse engineer.

Visual Studio .NET provides a tool to translate the machine-readable IL code into a human-readable form. This tool is called the IL disassembler and is named ILDasm.exe. ILDasm.exe can be run in one of the following two ways:

- ILDasm.exe can be run from a Command Prompt window and will produce a disassembled output file.

- In addition, ILDasm.exe also provides a graphical forms-based interface. Note that this interface is fairly simple. Its purpose is to allow you to navigate through the structure of an assembly.

First, we illustrate how to run ILDasm.exe from a Command Prompt window producing an output file.

To disassemble an IL file using the command line:

1. Type the following statement in the Command Prompt window to disassemble the Startup01.exe file and produce the file named Startup01.il. Note that the file suffix of a disassembled IL file is .il. Then, press **Enter**.

   ```
   ILDasm Startup01.exe /Out=Startup01.il
   ```

   As shown in the preceding statement, the disassembler named ILDasm is called. The first argument contains the name of the executable file to be disassembled. The second argument specifies the name of the output file produced. This output file is a text file containing the machine independent IL instructions.

2. Open the file named **Startup01.il** in a text editor such as Notepad. We then can discuss selected elements of this file next.

The following are selected IL statements generated by the IL disassembler:

```
.assembly extern mscorlib
{
  .publickeytoken = (B7 7A 5C 56 19 34 E0 89 )
// .z\V.4..
  .ver 1:0:3300:0
}
```

The first line of the preceding code segment specifies that this application will reference the assembly named mscorlib. This assembly is considered the System assembly and contains the definitions for the .NET base types such as Integer. Each shared assembly has a public key that uniquely identifies the assembly. This public key is stored in .publickeytoken. The .ver statement defines the version number of the assembly. The lines beginning with two forward slashes are comments. IL uses a block structured syntax that is similar to C# or C++. That is, blocks are enclosed in braces ({}).

The following statements reference the Microsoft.VisualBasic assembly:

```
.assembly extern Microsoft.VisualBasic
{
  .publickeytoken = (B0 3F 5F 7F 11 D5 0A 3A )
// .?_....:
  .ver 7:0:3300:0
}
```

The preceding code segment is similar to the first and specifies that this application will use the Microsoft.VisualBasic assembly. It also includes the public key token and version number of the assembly.

The following statements define the name of the assembly (Startup01) that represents the application you created:

```
.assembly Startup01
{
  .hash algorithm 0x00008004
  .ver 0:0:0:0
}
```

The preceding statements define the name of this assembly. In this case, the assembly is named Startup01. Every application that you create belongs to an assembly, and this application is no exception. Note that the extern keyword is absent because we are defining this assembly rather than a reference to an external assembly. The .hash statement defines the hashing algorithm for the assembly. Again, the assembly has a version number.

Remember that a module is class (reference type); the following statements define the module named Startup01:

```
.class private auto ansi sealed Startup01
       extends [mscorlib]System.Object
```

The preceding statement contains a type definition. That is, the preceding statement defines the class named Startup01. The keyword private defines the visibility of the class, and means that the class is for internal use only. The keyword auto defines how the loader will layout the class. The keyword ansi defines how strings will be converted when working with unmanaged code. The ansi keyword indicates that strings will be converted to and from C-style strings. C-style strings are simply a consecutive sequence of bytes terminated by a null byte. The keyword sealed indicates that no other class can derive from this class. The keyword extends defines the base class for this class. In this example, we say that this class extends the base System.Object class. By default, all classes are derived from System.Object.

The following statements represent the constructor for the class:

```
{
  .custom instance void
[Microsoft.VisualBasic]Microsoft.VisualBasic.CompilerServic
es.StandardModuleAttribute::.ctor() = ( 01 00 00 00 )
```

The preceding code segment illustrates the IL for the constructor. The constructor executes when VB .NET creates the instance of the class.

The following statements represent the code for the Main procedure itself:

```
.method public static void  Main() cil managed
{
  .entrypoint
  .custom instance void
[mscorlib]System.STAThreadAttribute::.ctor() = ( 01 00 00
00 )
  // Code size        74 (0x4a)
  .maxstack 2
  .locals init (float64 V_0,
          string V_1)
  IL_0000:  br.s       IL_0046

  IL_0002:  ldstr      "Enter a number: "
  IL_0007:  call       void
[mscorlib]System.Console::Write(string)
  IL_000c:  call       string
[mscorlib]System.Console::ReadLine()
  IL_0011:  stloc.1
  IL_0012:  ldloc.1
  IL_0013:  call       float64
[mscorlib]System.Convert::ToDouble(string)
  IL_0018:  stloc.0
  IL_0019:  ldloc.0
```

```
     IL_001a:   ldc.r8      -1.
     IL_0023:   bne.un.s    IL_0029

     IL_0025:   br.s        IL_0049

     IL_0027:   br.s        IL_0046

     IL_0029:   ldloc.0
     IL_002a:   call        float64
[mscorlib]System.Math::Sqrt(float64)
     IL_002f:   stloc.0
     IL_0030:   ldstr       "The result is "
     IL_0035:   call        void
[mscorlib]System.Console::Write(string)
     IL_003a:   ldloca.s    V_0
     IL_003c:   call        instance string
[mscorlib]System.Double::ToString()
     IL_0041:   call        void
[mscorlib]System.Console::WriteLine(string)
     IL_0046:   ldc.i4.1
     IL_0047:   brtrue.s    IL_0002

     IL_0049:   ret
   } // end of method Startup01::Main

 } // end of class Startup01
```

In addition to reverse engineering a compiled program from an IL executable back to the underlying IL code, it is also possible to compile IL into an executable by calling the IL assembler named ILasm.exe The following command line statement will translate the IL file generated previously back to an IL executable file:

```
ILasm.exe Startup01.il
```

In addition to using ILDasm from the command line and producing a text file, ILDasm also has a traditional Windows interface that can be used to examine the elements of the executable file.

To use ILDasm in a Windows environment:

1. From the Command Prompt window, type the following statement to run the IL disassembler, and then press **Enter**.

```
ILDasm Startup01.exe
```

Figure 1–11 shows the IL disassembler running in a window.

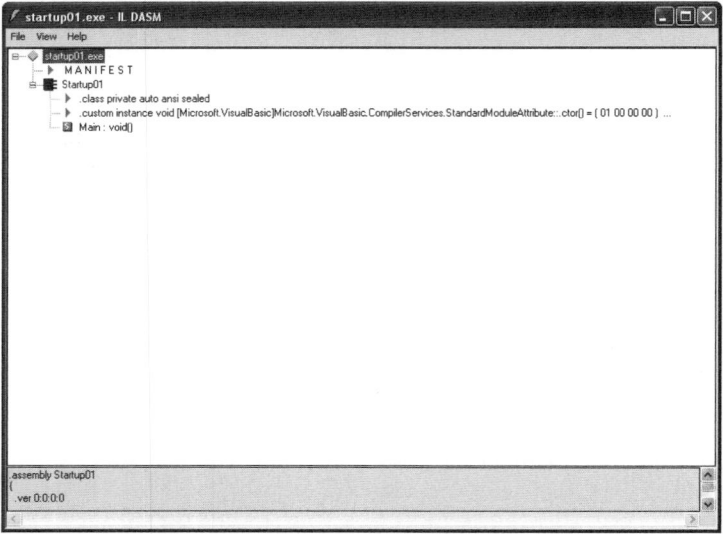

Figure 1-11   ILDasm running in a window

As shown in Figure 1–11, the assembly named Startup01.exe contains a manifest. The manifest contains the information that describes the assembly.

To view the assembly manifest:

    1. Double-click **MANIFEST**. The assembly manifest appears in another window as shown in Figure 1–12.

Figure 1-12   Assembly manifest

As shown in Figure 1-12, the information in the assembly manifest is the same as the manifest information discussed in the preceding section.

2. Close the MANIFEST window and the ILDASM window.

Because the IL program generated by Visual Studio .NET appears as a pseudo-assembly language executable, it cannot run on any processor until the IL code is translated into a native executable file for the target CPU. Performing this task is the responsibility of the **Just–In–Time (JIT)** compiler. In some ways, the JIT compiler operates similarly to the Java Virtual Machine. That is, JIT translates intermediate machine independent code into native executable instructions. The user does not need to call the JIT compiler directly. In fact, the user does not even need to be aware that the JIT compiler exists. When the user runs the IL application, the .NET Framework automatically calls the JIT compiler.

The JIT compiler does not compile an entire application into native executable code when an application is run. Rather, the JIT compiler translates IL into a native executable file such that the code for each individual method is translated when the method is called. Once a method has been compiled it need not be compiled again.

Compiling an application on demand using the JIT compiler does have performance implications. Applications that tend to call many methods during startup will force the JIT compiler to compile those methods, resulting in increased load time. However, applications that do not call many methods at startup will begin to execute more quickly.

In spite of possible increased load time at startup, JIT compiled applications will run just as fast as any native executable file. One significant benefit of the JIT technology is the ability to compile machine independent code into native code such that the native code takes advantage of any specialized hardware built into the CPU. Thus, the JIT compiler can generate code for specialized CPUs including the Itanium and Athlon processors. Furthermore, JIT compilers could be developed for any software and hardware configuration. Thus, it is possible that a third-party developer will create a JIT compiler (and port the .NET Framework) for Sun's Solaris operating system or other open development environments such as Linux.

The CLR supplies another means of compilation called **install-time code generation**. Using this mode of code generation, the compiler translates the IL code to a native executable in the same way as the JIT compiler. However, the entire application is converted into a native executable. A native executable file will start running faster than an executable that has not been JITted. Compiling an application to a native executable happens when the application is installed. This topic will be discussed more fully in the Deployment chapter.

Another point needs to be made about the translation from an IL file into a native executable file. When the JIT compiler translates an IL file, security checks are made on that IL file to make sure that the executable file is type safe. Remember that type safety is required by the CLR and prohibits an application from accessing memory outside of the application domain. Note that an administrator may configure a security policy that will bypass the normal security checks. By default, however, the CLR performs the following checks to make sure that an application is type safe:

- Memory will not be overrun.
- The MSIL code has been properly generated.
- Identities are what they claim to be.

CHAPTER SUMMARY

- ❏ This chapter introduced the concept of Visual Studio .NET and the implementation of the .NET Framework. In addition, you have seen how to compile a .NET application, as well as disassemble and assemble that application using ILDasm.exe and ILAsm.exe, respectively. The chapter also summarized some of the features that make Visual Studio .NET a revolutionary programming environment.

- ❏ Microsoft supplies four languages with Visual Studio .NET: C++, C#, Visual J#, and Visual Basic .NET (VB .NET). Each language supplies the same features. The performance of an application written in any .NET language will be roughly the same.

- ❏ To run any .NET application, a software component known as the .NET Framework must be installed on the target computer. The .NET Framework will run on any Windows version except for Windows 95. Because of differences in operating system versions, some features may not be available under Windows 98 or Windows ME.

- ❏ At the heart of Visual Studio .NET is the .NET Framework. The .NET Framework defines the rules for language interoperability, and how applications are compiled into executable code.

- ❏ The Common Language Specification defines the rules to which all .NET languages must adhere. These rules include how arguments are passed to procedures, and the naming conventions for variables.

- ❏ The Common Language Runtime (CLR) manages the execution of a running application. Code that is executed by the CLR is called managed code. The CLR is responsible for allocating memory to an application and releasing that memory using another utility called the Garbage Collector (GC).

- ❏ When a .NET application is compiled, that application is compiled to Microsoft Intermediate Language (MSIL). When the user executes the IL, another utility called the Just-In-Time (JIT) compiler converts the machine independent IL code into a native code executable.

- ❏ One role of the CLR is garbage collection. The GC runs periodically to reclaim memory that is no longer needed by a running application.

- ❏ The .NET Framework class library contains all of the types defined by .NET. Types are built from other types using inheritance. Through inheritance, one type gains access to the methods and properties defined by a base type. The behavior of methods and properties can be overridden. All types are derived from a superclass named System.Object.

- All types fall into one of the following categories: classes, delegates, structures, enumerations, and interfaces. All of these types are either value types or reference types. Value types store their data directly in the variable. The memory for value types is allocated from the program stack. Reference types store a memory address. That memory address, in turn, points to the actual object allocated from the managed heap.

- Types are stored in assemblies. All assemblies contain a manifest that describes the assembly and the modules that make up the assembly. The manifest is often referred to as metadata. The manifest contains a descriptive name, the contents of the assembly, and any dependencies. Assemblies also contain permissions that dictate who can use the contents of the assembly.

- Assemblies contain one or more logical components called namespaces. Namespaces that were developed by the .NET team begin with the name System. Other namespaces developed by Microsoft begin with the name Microsoft.

- Namespaces contain one or more types. For example, the System namespace defines the primary data types such as Int32 and Single. The System.Convert class contains type conversion methods. The System.Math class contains methods to perform mathematical operations. The System.Console class contains methods to read and write data from and to the console.

- To compile a .NET application, call the compiler as shown in the following statement:

  ```
  vbc.exe /reference:System.dll /out:Startup01.exe
  Startup01.vb
  ```

- To examine the IL produced by the compiler, call ILDasm as shown in the following statement:

  ```
  ILDasm Startup01.exe /Out=Startup01.il
  ```

REVIEW QUESTIONS

1. Which of the following statements describes the languages that comprise Visual Studio .NET?

   a. Microsoft distributes four Visual Studio .NET languages: C++, C#, Visual J#, and Visual Basic .NET (VB .NET).

   b. The performance of all Visual Studio .NET languages is roughly equivalent.

   c. The capabilities of all Visual Studio .NET languages are nearly equivalent.

   d. Visual Studio .NET compiles an application written in any language to Intermediate Language (IL).

   e. all of the above

2. Which of the following statements is true of the relationship between Visual Studio .NET and the .NET Framework?

   a. Visual Studio .NET and the .NET Framework have nothing to do with each other.

   b. You could create applications using the Visual Studio .NET IDE or using a simple text editor such as Notepad.

   c. The .NET Framework is required to develop applications, but is not necessary to run the applications created with Visual Studio .NET.

   d. all of the above

   e. none of the above

3. Which of the following statements describes the differences between VB 6 and VB .NET?

   a. VB 6 was considered an object-aware language, while VB .NET is truly an object-oriented programming language.

   b. VB .NET supports limited capabilities compared to the other Visual Studio .NET languages.

   c. The VB .NET language is identical to the VB 6 language.

   d. all of the above

   e. none of the above

4. Which of the following statements correctly describes the .NET Framework?

   a. The .NET Framework represents the part of Visual Studio .NET that provides the graphical developer interface.

   b. The .NET Framework replaces older versions of the Windows operating system and is required to run all versions of Windows.

   c. It defines the rules for language interoperability, how applications are compiled into executable code, and how those applications execute.

   d. The .NET Framework and Visual Studio .NET are synonymous terms used to describe the .NET environment.

   e. all of the above

5. Which of the following are parts of the .NET Framework?

   a. The Application Development Service and the Application Execution Service.

   b. The Design Time Specification and the Runtime Specification.

   c. The Common Language Specification and the .NET Framework class library.

   d. The Shared Compiler Service and the Shared Runtime Service.

   e. none of the above

6. Which of the following statements applies to CLS languages?

   a. All CLS languages must support 1-based arrays.

   b. A language should not extend the features beyond those formally defined by the CLS. Otherwise, the language will not be "CLS compliant."

   c. The CLS is divided into two parts: the Common Data Specification, and the Common Execution Specification.

   d. Primary data types, such as an Integer, can be represented differently in different CLS languages. For example, in one language an Integer may be 32 bits although in another language, an Integer may be 16 bits.

   e. none of the above

7. What is the difference between managed code and unmanaged code?

   a. Unmanaged code relies on the services provided by the CLR, while managed code does not.

   b. Managed code relies on the services provided by the CLR, while unmanaged code does not.

   c. Managed code allows the use of C++ pointers.

   d. There exists no difference between managed code and unmanaged code.

   e. none of the above

8. Which of the following statements correctly describes the Microsoft Intermediate Language?

   a. IL represents the native executable produced by all Visual Studio .NET languages that executes on a target CPU.

   b. Visual Studio .NET does not produce IL.

   c. IL is similar to assembly language. However, its format is generic and not bound to a particular CPU architecture.

   d. The IL produced by the Visual Studio .NET compilers will vary depending on the target CPU.

   e. none of the above

9. What kind of data is allocated from the managed heap?

   a. reference types

   b. value types

   c. both reference types and value types

   d. Integers

   e. none of the above

10. Which of the following statements applies to Visual Studio .NET inheritance?

    a. Inheritance allows one type to gain access to the methods and properties defined by another type.

    b. All types ultimately inherit from the superclass named System.Object.

    c. Visual Studio .NET supports a type of inheritance called single inheritance.

    d. all of the above

    e. none of the above

11. Which of the following are type categories in Visual Studio .NET?

    a. properties and methods

    b. managed types and unmanaged types

    c. classes, delegates, structures, enumerations, and interfaces

    d. assemblies and namespaces

    e. both c and d

12. What is the difference between a reference type and a value type?

    a. Reference types store a memory address in the variable, while value types store their data directly in the variable.

    b. Reference types store their data directly in the variable, while value types store a memory address in the variable.

    c. Reference types and value types store their data in exactly the same way.

    d. The .NET Framework does not support value types as all types are now reference types.

    e. none of the above

13. What is contained in an assembly manifest?

    a. The assembly manifest allows older applications that use COM to interact with .NET applications.

    b. The assembly manifest contains a descriptive name, localization information, and the classes exposed by the assembly.

    c. The assembly manifest contains the actual code that the CLR calls as a program executes.

    d. Assemblies do not have a manifest.

    e. Both a and b

14. Which of the following are valid methods of the System.Convert class?

    a. ToInteger, ToNumber, ToData

    b. ToInt32, ToInt64, ToSingle, ToDouble

    c. IsNumeric, IsDate

     d. ConvertString, ConvertNumber

     e. none of the above

15. Which of the following statements applies to the System.Math class?

     a. It is part of the .NET Framework class library.

     b. It derives from System.Object.

     c. It contains methods to perform mathematical operations.

     d. all of the above

     e. none of the above

16. List and describe the differences and similarities between C# and VB .NET.

17. List and describe the command line options used to compile a VB .NET application.

18. What is the purpose of the ILDasm.exe and ILAsm.exe programs?

19. What is the relationship between an assembly and a namespace?

20. Describe the purpose of the Just-In-Time compiler.

PROGRAMMING QUESTIONS

1. Write the statements to declare a module named Demo1.

2. Write the statements to declare a module named Chapter01. Enable strict type checking and explicit variable declaration.

3. Assume that a String variable named pstrQuestion has been declared. Write the statement to convert the variable to an Integer, storing the value in the variable pintQuestion.

4. Write the statement to read a line from the console and store the string read into the variable named pstrInput.

5. Write the statement to write the string "Chapter01" to the Console window. Do not write a trailing carriage return to the end of the line.

6. Write the statement to write the string "Chapter01" to the Console window. Write a trailing carriage return to the end of the line.

7. Write the statements to create a module named Echo having a Sub Main procedure. The code in the Sub Main procedure should read a line from the Console window into a string variable named pstrLine. Write the line read back out to the Console window. Write a carriage return at the end of the line.

8. Write the statements to create a module named EchoRepeat having a Sub Main procedure. The code in the Sub Main procedure should repeatedly read a line from the Console window into a String variable named pstrLine. Write the line read back out to the Console window. Write a carriage return at the end of the line. The module should stop reading lines when the user enters the text "End" in the line.

9. Write the statements to declare a module named PrintOut having a Sub Main procedure. The code in the Sub Main procedure should print the text "Hello" to the Console window. Do not write a trailing carriage return at the end of the line.

10. Write the statements to declare a module named PrintName having a Sub Main procedure. The code in the Sub Main procedure should print your name to the Console window, followed by a carriage return.

11. Write the statements to declare a module named Absolute, having a Sub Main procedure. The code in the Sub Main procedure should read a string value into the variable pstrValue1. Write the statement to convert the input value into a double precision number storing the value in the variable pdblCurrent. Display the absolute value of the number entered to the Console window. Declare the variables as necessary.

12. Write the statements to declare a module named Add, having a Sub Main procedure. The code in the Sub Main procedure should read two string input values. Store the data in the String variables pstrValue1 and pstrValue2. Convert the input to Integers storing the values in the variables pintValue1 and pintValue2. Write the statement to add the two numbers together and display the result to the Console window. Use the variable pintResult to store the output value.

13. Write the statements to declare a module named Trig, having a Sub Main procedure. The code in the Sub Main procedure should read a string input value. Store the data in the String variable pstrInput. Convert the input value to a number and store it in a variable named psngInput having a data type of Single. Call the appropriate math methods to calculate the Sine, Cosine, and Tangent of the number, storing the result in the variable named psngOutput. Write the calculated output to the Console window. Write the strings "Sine," "Cosine," and "Tangent" to the left of the output value. Write each output value on a separate line.

14. Write the statement to call the Visual Basic compiler. Assume that the source file is named Question.vb and that the program references the library named System.dll.

15. Write the statement to call the Visual Basic compiler. Assume that the source file is named Demo.vb and that that the program references the library named System.dll. Enable the verbose option.

HANDS-ON PROJECTS

1. In this project you will create an application that calculates the volume of a cube. The user will be prompted to enter the length, height, and width of the cube. Then the application will calculate the result and display it to the user. The project will use a sentinel value of –1 for any value to indicate the end of the input.

   a. Using Notepad or another text editor, create a new file named **Ch01Ex1.vb** in a folder named **Ch01Ex1**.

   b. Create a module named **Cube** and a Sub Main procedure in that module.

1

   c. Enable strict type checking and explicit variable declaration.

   d. Write the statements to prompt the user to enter the three input values. Each input value should be entered on a separate line. Store the input values entered by the user into String variables. For each input value that the user enters, display a prompt indicating the meaning of the input value.

   e. Convert the input values to the appropriate numeric data types as necessary.

   f. Write the statements to calculate the volume of the cube (multiply the length, height, and width to calculate the result).

   g. Display the output to the user. Again, display a prompt to the left of the calculated output value.

   h. Create a Do loop so that the user will continue to enter input until a value of −1 is specified for the height, length, or width.

   i. Compile and test the application.

2. In this project, you will create an application that uses the System.Math class to perform calculations in an input value.

   a. Using Notepad or another text editor, create a new module file named **Ch01Ex2.vb** in a folder named **Ch01Ex2**.

   b. Create a module named **MathCalc** and a Sub Main procedure in that module.

   c. Enable strict type checking and explicit variable declaration.

   d. Write a loop to get an input value from the user, and then perform mathematical calculations on that input value. Write the loop such that the application will continue to process input until the user enters an input value of −1.

   e. For each input value entered, calculate the sine, cosine, and tangent angle of the input value. In addition, calculate the Log of the input value by calling the Log method.

   f. Display descriptive prompts to the user for the input value and display prompts to describe the output values.

   g. Compile and test the application.

3. In this project you will create an application that uses the Pythagorean Theorem to calculate a side of a right triangle based on the data given for the other two sides. Remember that the formula of the Pythagorean Theorem is $a^2 + b^2 = c^2$, where a and b represent the sides of the right triangle, and c represents the hypotenuse.

   a. Using Notepad or another text editor, create a new module file named **Ch01Ex3.vb** in a folder named **Ch01Ex3**.

   b. Create a module named **PythagoreanTheorem** and a Sub Main procedure in that module.

   c. Enable strict type checking and explicit variable declaration.

d. Write a loop to get an input value from the user. If the user enters the value −1, then the program should exit. If the user enters the value 2, assume the user is calculating the value for one of the sides. If the user enters the value 1, assume that the user is calculating the value for the hypotenuse.

e. Declare the necessary variables to store the input values.

f. Write the necessary statements to get the input from the user. Display a prompt to the user for all of the input values.

g. Write the statements to determine the length of a side or the hypotenuse depending on which calculation the user has requested. Display a prompt for the output.

h. Compile and test the application.

4. In this project you will create an application that allows a user to input a list of numbers. Once the user has entered the list of numbers, the application will display the minimum, maximum, and average value from the list.

a. Using Notepad or another text editor, create a new module file named **Ch01Ex4.vb** in a folder named **Ch01Ex4**.

b. Create a module with a Sub Main procedure. Name the module **List**.

c. Enable strict type checking and explicit variable declaration.

d. In the Sub Main procedure, write a loop to read input lines. Create the loop such that the user signifies that they are finished entering input when the value −1 is entered.

e. When the user has completed entering the input values, calculate the minimum, maximum, and average value of the numbers entered. *Hint*: As the user enters each value, determine whether or not the value entered represents a new minimum or maximum value. Store the current minimum or maximum value in a variable. In addition, you will also need a counter variable to store the number of values entered by the user.

f. Write the statements to display prompts for user input and display prompts indicating the meaning of any output.

g. Display the minimum and maximum list values. Display the average list value. Finally, display the number of list items.

h. Compile and test the application.

5. In this project you will create an application that calculates the surface area of a round tank. The user will be able to enter input options to specify whether the tank has a top, and a base, and whether the surface area includes the inside and outside surfaces.

a. Using Notepad or another text editor, create a new program file named **Ch01Ex5.vb** in a folder named **Ch01Ex5**.

b. Create a module with a Sub Main procedure. Name the module **SurfaceArea**.

c. Enable strict type checking and explicit variable declaration.

d. In the Sub Main procedure, write a loop to read the input data. The input data should include the following values: the radius of the tank, the height of the tank, whether the tank has a top, whether the tank has a base, and whether the inside surface area should be calculated.

e. Create the loop such that the user signifies that they are finished entering input when the value −1 is entered.

f. Write the statements to display prompts for user input and display prompts indicating the meaning of any user output.

g. Write the statements to calculate the output. The output should determine the surface area of the tank. You will need to apply the following formulas: the circumference of a circle is $2\pi r$, where π is the value of Pi, and r is the radius of the circle; the formula for a circle's area is πr^2.

h. Write the statements to display the output values.

i. Compile and test the application.

2

DESKTOP APPLICATIONS: CORE CONCEPTS

In this chapter you will:

- Explore the types of VB .NET applications
- Understand the organization of a VB .NET application
- Examine the windows that comprise the Visual Studio .NET integrated development environment (IDE)
- Work with a Form module
- Understand the basic operation of Windows forms
- Learn how to manage forms
- Understand the purpose of VB .NET controls, create control instances, and set properties for those control instances
- Set the tab order for controls
- Understand the operation of VB .NET event handlers
- Dynamically create event handlers and control instances at runtime
- Understand the collections of controls

In this chapter, and in most subsequent chapters of this book, a completed solution has already been created that corresponds to the material presented in the chapter. This completed solution is the same solution that you create when opening the startup solution and then performing all the hands-on steps described in the chapter. The completed solution also contains numerous comments that describe specific application statements and their purpose. You may want to print the completed solution and use it as a reference as you work through the chapter and the hands-on steps.

For brevity, you will not enter comments in the hands-on steps. The startup solution does not contain any comments other than a header comment appearing at the beginning of each module.

PREVIEWING THE COMPLETED SOLUTION

Assume that an airline needs to keep track of passengers as they board an airplane, and that different types of airplanes have different seating configurations. The purpose of the application developed in this chapter is to create a seating chart for two different airplane configurations.

In the application's main form, the user selects the type of airplane and specifies other information such as the flight number, the origin of the flight, and the flight's destination. From the information specified by the user, the application displays another form containing the seating chart. On the seating chart form, the user clicks a check box to indicate that a seat is occupied. As the user checks each check box, the form is updated to indicate the number of seats filled and the number of empty seats.

To preview the completed solution:

1. Start Visual Studio .NET and open the solution file named **Chapter.02\Complete02\Complete02.sln**.

2. Run the solution by pressing **F5**.

   The splash screen appears for five seconds to identify the solution to the user. Splash screens are common to most applications. Figure 2-1 shows the splash screen.

Figure 2-1   Completed solution – splash screen

After the splash screen appears for five seconds, the main form appears. Figure 2-2 shows the main form after the input has been entered.

Figure 2-2   Completed solution – main form

As shown in Figure 2-2, the main form contains a menu, radio buttons to select the airplane type, list boxes to select the origin and destination of the flight, and a text box used to enter the flight number.

3. Using the radio buttons, click an airplane type, and then click the origin and destination cities as shown in Figure 2-2. On the menu bar, click **Display**, and then click **Airplane**.

The form containing the airplane seating chart appears as shown in Figure 2-3. The control instances at the top of the form contain the flight information. The two buttons allow the user to clear the check boxes and to close the form. Note that the application can display multiple seating forms at the same time. Also, the CheckBox control instances are created dynamically when the form loads. Thus, if you examine the form at design time, you will not see these check boxes.

4. Click several of the check boxes to indicate that the seats are occupied. The counters at the top of the form are updated. Click the scroll bar to the right of the form to scroll through the seat rows. This feature to create a scrollable control and form is new to VB .NET. Figure 2-3 shows the seating form with some occupied seats.

5. Click the **Clear** button. The check boxes are cleared and the counters are reset.

6. End the solution by clicking the **Close** button on the seating form, then clicking **File** on the menu bar, and then clicking **Exit**.

Figure 2-3   Completed solution – seating form

A NOTE ABOUT THIS CHAPTER

This chapter and Chapter 3 briefly summarize the new or changed Visual Studio .NET developer interface windows. This chapter focuses on the changes and enhancements to forms, controls, and event handlers, while Chapter 3 focuses on the changes and enhancements to the VB .NET language itself. Thus, the materials in Chapters 2 and 3 are intertwined.

We do not attempt in these two chapters to teach you about the elemental syntax of VB .NET. We assume that you are familiar with creating control instances and setting their properties. Thus, in this chapter we address controls that are new to VB .NET and selected new control features. If you have not created control instances on a form, or created event handlers for those control instances, you will again need to refer to an introductory VB .NET text.

Note that the Visual Studio .NET developer interface is the same no matter the language chosen for development. That is, the same windows appear and operate the same way whether you are creating an application in C++, C#, Visual J#, or VB .NET. As this book is based on VB .NET, the other .NET Framework languages will not be discussed further.

TYPES OF VISUAL BASIC .NET APPLICATIONS

Chapter 1 illustrated how to create a Console application using Notepad, and how to compile that application without the aid of the Visual Studio .NET integrated developer environment (IDE). This approach would seldom be used in practice. The purpose of Chapter 1 was to introduce the purpose of the .NET Framework, the parts of the .NET Framework, and how those parts fit together. In this chapter, you will use the Visual Studio .NET IDE to create a Windows Application.

A Windows Application has a user interface made up of one or more forms. VB .NET allows you to create many different types of applications, each designed for a particular purpose. For example, some types of applications are designed to run on a desktop computer, while other types of applications are designed to run on the Internet or an intranet. These different types of applications are called **projects**. The following list describes the project types supported by VB .NET and gives a brief description of their purpose:

- **Windows Application**: This project type is a desktop application run directly by the end user via forms appearing on the desktop. In this chapter, and in most of the chapters in this book, you will create Windows Application projects.

- **Class Library**: Class Library projects contain components designed for use by other developers. The components built from Class Library projects are not run directly by a user. Rather, you, as another developer, typically import a Class Library project into a Windows Application project, and then use its components. Think of the components provided by a namespace, such as the System namespace, as a Class Library project.

- **Windows Control Library**: VB .NET allows a developer to create controls that extend the intrinsic controls appearing in the VB .NET Toolbox. These controls are typically used by Windows Application projects, much in the same way a developer would use a Class Library project.

- **ASP.NET Web Application**: ASP.NET Web Applications run on the Internet or an intranet. A Web server executes an ASP.NET Web Application by sending Web pages to a Web browser and receiving requests for information from that Web browser. ASP.NET is not discussed in detail in this book.

- **ASP.NET Web Service**: An ASP.NET Web Service is similar to an ASP.NET Web Application. However, the client using an ASP.NET Web Service need not be a Web browser. Rather, the client can be any type of application, including a Windows Application. This book will introduce the topic of creating an ASP.NET Web Service.

- **Web Control Library**: Similar to a Windows Control Library, a Web Control Library project allows you to create controls designed for use in an ASP.NET Web Application project. Web Control Libraries will not be discussed in this book.

- **Console Application**: Console applications do not run from a Form window as Windows Applications do. Rather, their input and output appears in a Command Prompt window. Chapter 1 described the basics of a Console application.
- **Windows Service**: Windows Services are applications that start as Windows boots. They have no user interface. Windows Services perform such tasks as monitoring system performance or dealing with system errors.

No matter the type of application you create, you use the same Visual Studio .NET IDE windows to create and manage the parts of that application. However, the IDE windows work differently for different types of applications. For example, the Properties window operates differently for Windows Applications and ASP.NET Web Applications because the objects they manage differ significantly. In addition, the visual designer that you use to create the forms in a Windows Application and an ASP.NET Web Application differ as well.

To create a new solution, you use the New Project dialog box shown in Figure 2-4.

Figure 2-4   New Project dialog box

As shown in Figure 2-4, the Project Types pane lists the projects for the various .NET languages installed. In the Templates pane, the application templates corresponding to the selected project type appear. In the Name text box, you specify the name of the solution to create, and in the Location list box, you define the folder where Visual Studio .NET will create the solution. Note that Visual Studio .NET creates a new folder with the same name as the solution.

The following list describes the steps to create a new solution:

1. On the menu bar, click File, point to New, and then click Project.

2

2. In the New Project dialog box, change the location, if necessary, to the folder where the solution will be created.

3. In the Project Types pane, click Visual Basic Projects.

4. Assign a name to the project.

5. In the Templates pane, select the application type.

ORGANIZATION OF A VISUAL BASIC .NET APPLICATION

As you saw in Chapter 1, you can create the files that comprise an application with any text editor, and then compile that application into an IL executable file from a Command Prompt window. However, the Visual Studio .NET IDE supplies a rich set of tools to manage and compile the files that comprise an application.

When you create an application via Visual Studio .NET, that application is organized into a solution. The contents of a solution are stored in a solution file with a file suffix of .sln. The solution file is a text file. Another file called the solution user options file has a file suffix of .suo. This file contains configuration information about the solution, and specifies which windows are currently open in the Visual Studio .NET IDE. Note that the solution user options file is a binary file and can only be edited by Visual Studio .NET itself.

All the files that comprise a solution are typically stored in a unique directory called the solution directory. Visual Studio .NET automatically creates the solution directory when it creates the solution. Using the Visual Studio .NET IDE, you manage the files that comprise a solution using the Solution Explorer. As the Solution Explorer is the key to managing the files that comprise a solution, it is discussed first in this section of the chapter.

The Solution Explorer

The Solution Explorer is a tool window used to manage the solution, the project(s) that comprise the solution, and the files that comprise each project.

To view the Solution Explorer:

1. Start Visual Studio .NET and open the solution file named **Startup02.sln** from the **Chapter.02\Startup02** folder.

   If the Solution Explorer is not visible, display it by clicking **View**, and then clicking **Solution Explorer** on the menu bar.

2. Just below the title bar in the Solution Explorer, click the **Show All Files** button to display all the files that comprise the solution, if necessary.

3. The Solution Explorer displays the solution contents hierarchically. Click the plus signs to the left of the folders until the Solution Explorer displays the folders shown in Figure 2-5.

Figure 2-5   Solution Explorer

Figure 2-5 shows the Solution Explorer for a solution containing a single project having multiple modules. The following list describes the elements appearing in Figure 2-5:

- The solution named **Startup02** organizes all the files and references that make up the application. Thus, the solution appears at the top of the hierarchy. The physical file Startup02.sln corresponds to the solution file.

- The project named **Startup02** appears at the second level of the hierarchy. Project files have a file suffix of .vbproj. Thus, the project file is named Startup02.vbproj. When you compile a project, that project gets compiled into an executable file. Visual Studio .NET creates a different type of executable file based on the type of project. For example, Visual Studio .NET will compile a Windows Application project into an executable (.exe) file, while it will compile a Class Library project into a dynamic link library (.dll) file.

- The **References** folder lists the namespaces currently used by the project. By default, Visual Studio .NET references the five namespaces shown in Figure 2-5. Note that the references are not stored as physical disk files. Rather, this information is stored in the project file itself.

- The folder named **bin** contains the executable file produced when Visual Studio .NET compiles the project.

- The folder named **obj** and its subdirectories contain another copy of the executable file and other support files necessary to debug and test the application from within the IDE.

- The file **AssemblyInfo.vb** contains attributes that describe the assembly.

- The project named Startup02 contains four forms, named **frmAbout.vb**, **frmMain.vb**, **frmSeating.vb,** and **frmSplash.vb**. Each of these forms corresponds to a physical disk file. A project may contain any number of forms.

- The completed project also contains a module file named **modMain**. This module also has a file suffix of .vb. The purpose of the module file is the same as its purpose in Chapter 1. It contains a Sub Main procedure that the CLR calls when the application starts. This module does not appear in the startup project. You will add it as you complete the chapter's hands-on steps.

- Each form file has an associated resource file having a file suffix of .resx. Resource files contain information about the form and support elements such as bitmaps or icon files. This file is an XML document.

The Solution Explorer manages its elements in one of two ways. Some solution elements are managed as files, such that these files are stored within the solution folder itself. Other solution elements are stored in the solution file as links. Solution items that are not part of a project are stored as links.

The Solution Explorer and Solution File

The Solution Explorer and the corresponding solution file fulfill three roles in the management of a VB .NET application, as described in the following list:

- The Solution Explorer contains references to the project(s) that comprise the application.

- For each project, the solution file defines the configuration files available to each project, and which configuration file will be used to compile the project. Configuration files are discussed in detail in Chapter 21. However, for now, understand that a configuration file defines specific statements to be included or excluded from a particular software release. VB .NET supplies two generic configurations to build executable files for debugging purposes and executable files to be released for distribution to other computers. When a project is compiled for distribution, debugging information is typically removed for performance and security reasons.

- The solution file may also contain references to files that are relevant to developing the solution, but need not be deployed with the compiled application. These files are stored as links.

You can rename files using the Solution Explorer by right-clicking a file and selecting Rename from the context menu. If you need to rename files, rename them using the Solution Explorer instead of Windows Explorer. If you rename files using Windows Explorer, Visual Studio .NET will not be able to locate the renamed file.

To understand the contents of a solution file, you will open the Complete02.sln file in Notepad and examine its contents.

To examine the contents of a solution file:

1. Start Notepad, and then open the file **Chapter.02\Complete02\ Complete02.sln**.

As you can see, the solution file is a text file. The statement defines the version of the solution file and the project(s) managed by the solution, as shown in the following code segment. For formatting reasons, the following statement appears on multiple lines. However, it appears on a single line in Notepad.

```
Microsoft Visual Studio Solution File, Format Version 7.00
Project("{F184B08F-C81C-45F6-A57F-5ABD9991F28F}") =
"Complete02", "Complete02.vbproj", "{1013CFD2-0C8D-4666-
B63A-2BAC54FBE6BB}"
EndProject
```

As illustrated in the preceding code segment, the solution contains one project named Complete02. The file name for this project is Complete02.vbproj.

The solution file is a block structured file, which means that the solution file is divided into sections. Each section is surrounded by statements that mark the beginning and end of the section. For example, the previous section was marked by the Project and EndProject keywords.

Examine the following code segment that defines a GlobalSection named SolutionConfiguration. VB .NET, by default, supplies two solution configurations appearing in the GlobalSection named SolutionConfiguration. These two solution configurations are named Debug and Release. As mentioned, these configurations control how the project(s) in the solution are compiled into an executable file.

```
GlobalSection(SolutionConfiguration) = preSolution
    ConfigName.0 = Debug
    ConfigName.1 = Release
EndGlobalSection
```

The remaining contents of the solution file are omitted here. These remaining elements are discussed in Chapter 21, which discusses deployment.

As mentioned, a solution file contains one or more project files. Visual Studio .NET compiles each project in a solution into its own executable file. To illustrate the relationship between a project and a solution, consider a scenario involving a Windows Application project with multiple forms. At some point, a project must be deployed to another computer. Given this scenario, you create two projects within the same solution: a Windows Application project and a Deployment project. The solution file groups these two projects so that you can easily build and deploy an application from the same instance of Visual Studio .NET.

Project Files

A project file defines the type of executable file that Visual Studio .NET will produce, along with the various component files necessary to build the project. The following list describes the information contained in a project file:

- **The type of project**: In this chapter, you will complete a Windows Application project.

- **References to assemblies and namespaces**: These are the same assemblies and namespaces discussed in Chapter 1. Visual Studio .NET uses this information to call the compiler (vbc.exe), just as you called the compiler in Chapter 1.

- **Compilation information specific to a project**: Note that the solution file contains global information describing how the solution gets compiled and the project(s) that make up the solution. On the other hand, each project file contains configuration information that is unique to the project, such as the files that comprise the project, rather than global to the solution.

- **Module files**: They make up the files representing the forms and classes in the project.

Figure 2-6 summarizes the relationships among the solution, project, and module files.

Figure 2-6   Relationships among the solution, project, and module files

To illustrate the purpose and contents of a project file, we examine selected elements. While Visual Studio .NET will modify the contents of the project file automatically, the purpose of the following steps is to illustrate the relationship between the Solution Explorer and the project(s) it manages.

To examine the contents of a project file:

1. Start Notepad, if necessary, and open the project file named **Chapter.02\ Complete02\Complete02.vbproj**.

In the file, the first line indicates that the project is a Visual Studio .NET project. The second line indicates that the project is a VB .NET project. The ProjectType directive indicates that this is a local Windows Application project. The ProductVersion directive defines the version of Visual Studio .NET as 7.0.9466. This version number will vary based on the version of Visual Studio .NET that you are using. The SchemaVersion directive indicates the version of the XML schema used by the project, and the final directive named ProjectGuid is called a globally unique identifier. This number is guaranteed to be unique and uniquely defines the project among all other projects.

The Build section defines how the project will be compiled. The following code segment illustrates selected parts of the Build section:

```
<Build>
    <Settings
    . . .
        AssemblyName = "Complete02"
        . . .
        OptionExplicit = "On"
        OptionStrict = "Off"
        RootNamespace = "Complete02"
        . . .
    />
</Settings>
```

The AssemblyName setting defines the name of the executable file produced. In this case, the file name will be Complete02.exe. Explicit variable declaration is enabled and strict type checking is disabled. These values may vary depending on the settings on your computer. The root namespace is named Complete02.

Next, the References section identifies the namespaces and assemblies used in the project. This project uses five namespaces. The following code segment shows the statements to reference the System namespace. The syntax for the other namespace references is the same.

```
<References>
    <Reference
        Name = "System"
        AssemblyName = "System"
    />
    Statements to reference the other namespaces
</References>
```

2

 Note that the preceding code segments resemble the syntax of an HTML or XML document. The preceding code segment defines a References block, which creates a reference to the System assembly, hence the System namespace.

Finally, the Files block defines all the files that comprise the project. Again, for brevity, the following code segment shows only a portion of the Files block:

```
<Files>
    <Include>
        <File
            RelPath = "AssemblyInfo.vb"
            SubType = "Code"
            BuildAction = "Compile"
        />
        File directives for other forms
        <File
            RelPath = "frmSeating.vb"
            SubType = "Form"
            BuildAction = "Compile"
        />
        <File
            RelPath = "frmSeating.resx"
            DependentUpon = "frmSeating.vb"
            BuildAction = "EmbeddedResource"
        />
        File directives for other modules
    </Include>
</Files>
```

The project contains five files. The RelPath directive defines the relative path for the files and the file names. The SubType directive defines the type of the file (form or code), and the BuildAction directive tells the VB .NET compiler what to do with the file. Some files should be compiled, and other files are dependency files that are used by another file. For example, the resource file named frmSeating.resx is a dependency file for the form named frmSeating.vb.

SUMMARY OF THE IDE WINDOWS

Having examined the files that comprise a VB .NET solution, you can now examine the windows that comprise the Visual Studio .NET IDE, and how those windows are used to create applications.

First, Visual Studio .NET supports two developer interface modes. In MDI mode, the Visual Studio .NET interface closely resembles the one found in previous versions. Tabbed documents mode is new to Visual Studio .NET, although it is similar to the one supplied by Visual Studio 6. This book will use Tabbed documents mode. In Tabbed documents mode, Visual Studio .NET displays windows differently based on their type. Windows are categorized into two types as described in the following list:

- **Document windows** appear on one or more tab groups. The Win Forms Designer and Code Editor are both document windows. In the Win Forms Designer, you define the visual interface for a form. In the Code Editor, you write the statements that execute at runtime as the user interacts with the control instances created on the form.

- **Tool windows** appear differently depending on how they are configured. Tool windows can be configured to float on the desktop, or be docked along any edge of the IDE. In addition, tool windows can be auto hidden. The Solution Explorer, Toolbox, Properties window, and debugging windows are all tool windows. Refer to Appendix A Debugging for a list of the debugging windows and how to use them.

Document Windows

Again, in this section, we only point out the significant changes to the IDE. Figure 2-7 shows the Visual Studio .NET IDE.

Document windows appear on a tab group

Solution Explorer appears as a tool window

Figure 2-7   The Visual Studio .NET IDE

As shown in Figure 2-7, three document windows appear on a tab group below the toolbar. Only one document window can be active at a time in a tab group. However, additional tab groups can be created by right-clicking a tab group, and then clicking New Horizontal Tab Group or New Vertical Tab Group. To activate a document window, click the tab on the tab group. To close a document window, activate it, and then click the Close button to the right of the tab group. If the number of open windows will not fit on a tab group, click the left or right arrows to the right of the tab group to scroll through the windows.

Tool Windows

In addition to document windows, Visual Studio .NET supplies tool windows that are common to all the solutions that you create. You activate a tool window by clicking View on the menu bar, and then clicking the desired tool window from the menu.

The following list describes the primary tool windows and their purposes:

- The **Solution Explorer** manages all the projects that comprise the solution and the modules in those projects.

- The **Properties window** allows you to set design-time properties for the current form, and the control instances created on the current form.

- The **Toolbox** contains the controls that you create on a form and controls intended for use by the developer. By default, VB .NET divides the controls in the Toolbox into four tabs, based on their functions. The Components tab contains controls used to interact with Windows itself. For example, you can write messages to the system message logs, or monitor changes to the file system. The controls appearing on the Data tab are used with ADO.NET. By default, the General tab contains only the Pointer tool. The controls that you create on a form appear on the Windows Forms tab. It is possible to create custom tabs or modify the controls appearing on the default tabs.

Tool windows operate differently from document windows. Tool windows can appear in one of four display modes. To change the display mode of a tool window, right-click on the title bar of the tool window, and then select one of the following options:

- The **Auto Hide** option causes the tool window to be hidden along an edge of the IDE when the mouse passes off of the window. For a tool window to be auto hidden, the window must be docked along an edge of the IDE.

- The **Dockable** option causes a tool window to be docked along an edge of the IDE. After selecting Dockable, drag the tool window to the edge of the IDE where the window should be docked.

- The **Floating** option causes a tool window to appear unconstrained by the parent IDE window. Thus, a floating window can appear anywhere on the desktop.

- Some tool windows can appear as document windows by dragging the tool window to a tab group.

The Properties Window and its Property Editors

The Properties window has two columns. The left column lists the property names, and the right column allows you to edit the value for the selected property. If a property stores an object or structure, then the property can be expanded or collapsed so that you can assign values to the members of that object or structure. Depending on the data type of the property, the Properties window displays a dialog box called a **property editor**, allowing you to set certain properties more easily. To illustrate selected property editors, you will activate the splash screen and set a few of its properties.

To examine the Properties window:

1. Activate the Win Forms Designer for the form named **frmSplash.vb**, if necessary, by double-clicking the form in the Solution Explorer. Activate the Properties window for the form by pressing **F4**.

2. Click the **value column** for the BackColor property, and then click the **list arrow** to activate the Color property editor. Click the **Web** tab, and then select the color **SteelBlue**, as shown in Figure 2-8.

Figure 2-8 Properties window – Color property editor

3. In the Object list box of the Properties window, select the control instance named **lblName**. Set the Back Color property to **Steel Blue**. Click the **value** column for the TextAlign property and then click the **list box**. Right-justify the text by clicking the middle-right box, as shown in Figure 2-9.

Middle-right justification

Figure 2-9   Properties window – Alignment property editor

WORKING WITH A FORM MODULE

As mentioned, VB .NET stores every form in a project in a text file having a file suffix of .vb. As the developer, you use the Win Forms Designer to create the form's visual interface and the Code Editor to create the statements that execute as the user interacts with the control instances created on the form. These two windows are discussed in turn. We then touch on the structure of the class module when the Win Forms Designer generates it.

The Win Forms Designer

The **Win Forms Designer** always appears as a document window on a tab group. The Win Forms Designer contains two regions. One region contains a visual representation of the form that the user will see at runtime. Control instances seen by the user at runtime appear on the visible region of the form. Optionally, below the visible form region appears a resizable tray. This resizable tray displays any control instances that are not visible to the user as the application runs. If no invisible control instances exist, the resizable tray does not appear.

Control instances are created on a form by clicking the desired control in the Toolbox, and then drawing the control instance at the desired position on the form. If a control instance is not visible at runtime, it will automatically appear in the resizable tray below the form, no matter where you position the control instance. After a control instance has been created, it can be moved or resized by selecting the control instance and then dragging it to the new position on the form, or by dragging the sizing handles to resize it.

When you create a control instance on a form using the Win Forms Designer, Visual Studio .NET writes statements in the corresponding module file to actually create the control instance as the application runs. We examine this automatically generated code in the following section.

The Code Editor

The **Code Editor** is a text editor specifically designed to edit VB .NET module files. Again, any text editor can be used to edit these files, but the features supplied by the Code Editor make it far superior to any other text editor. The following list describes some of the new features that Microsoft has added to the Code Editor:

- The Code Editor will automatically indent statement blocks. If and Select Case statements are automatically indented, as are statements in Do loops and For loops.

- The Code Editor automatically completes statement blocks. For example, when writing an If statement, pressing Enter after completing the If part of the statement causes the Code Editor to automatically add the corresponding End If statement. Statement completion for Select Case statements, Do loops, and For loops is also performed automatically.

- Copy and paste operations are added to a clipboard ring in a manner similar to Microsoft Office. Thus, Visual Studio .NET supports multiple clipboards.

- Procedures and groups of procedures can be collapsed or expanded.

- The Code Editor allows you to use the clipboard to copy and paste rectangular blocks of code by holding down the Alt key while dragging the mouse to mark the rectangular region. After marking the rectangular region, you can copy it to the clipboard.

To understand how to navigate through the Code Editor and how it interacts with the Win Forms Designer, you will examine selected statements automatically generated by the Win Forms Designer. These statements are generated as the developer creates the control instances on the form.

To examine the features of the Code Editor:

1. Activate the Code Editor for the form named **frmSplash.vb** by right-clicking the form in the Solution Explorer, and then clicking **View Code**. Figure 2-10 illustrates the Code Editor. Note that line numbers may or may not appear depending on the configuration of your computer.

Class Name list box
Method Name list box

Expand or collapse region

Windows Form Designer
generated code is collapsed

Figure 2-10 Code Editor

 Tip

As shown in Figure 2-10, the Class Name list box allows you to select the form or a control instance. The Method Name list box allows you to select an event supported by the form or control instance. Plus and minus signs appear in the left margin of the Code Editor. Clicking a minus sign collapses a procedure or a region. Clicking a plus sign expands that region. In addition, line numbers appear in the left margin. To enable line numbers, click Tools, and then click Options on the menu bar. In the Options dialog box, click the Text Editor tab, and then click Basic. Check the Line numbers check box.

2. Click the plus sign to the left of the text "Windows Form Designer generated code." Note that the statements in the Region directive are expanded.

Examine the following code that should be on your screen:

```
#Region " Windows Form Designer generated code "
    ' Statements
#End Region
```

The #Region and #End Region directives mark a block of statements that can be expanded or collapsed. The Win Forms Designer automatically encloses the statements it generates between the #Region and #End Region directives. You can also create your own regions to mark large blocks of code.

Reexamine the statements shown in Figure 2-10. The module begins with a comment block. Remember that the lines beginning with an apostrophe character (') are considered comments and are ignored by VB .NET. Next, the Option Strict and Option

Explicit statements appear to indicate that strict type checking and explicit variable declaration are enabled for all the statements in this module. Option Strict and Option Explicit will be enabled for all of the applications created in this book.

> Depending on the configuration of your computer, strict type checking (Option Strict), and explicit variable declaration (Option Explicit) may be enabled from within the IDE. We will, however, explicitly enable these options programmatically both for clarity and consistency.

The Structure of a Win Forms Designer Generated Class Module

When you create a form, and control instances on the form, the Win Forms Designer creates a class. That class contains all of the necessary statements to define the characteristics of the form, and the control instances drawn on the form. In addition, it contains procedures to create an instance of the form and to destroy the form instance. In this section, we discuss selected statements automatically generated by the Win Forms Designer.

The following code segment illustrates the structure of the class corresponding to the form named frmSplash:

```
Public Class frmSplash
    Inherits System.Windows.Forms.Form
    #Region " Windows Form Designer generated code "
    ' Statements
    #End Region
End Class
```

The preceding code segment illustrates the structure of a class module. A class is just one of the types supported by the .NET Framework. Chapter 1 presented a module block marked by the Module and End Module statements. A class block has a similar syntax. The Class and End Class statements mark the beginning and end of the class. In the preceding code segment, the class is named frmSplash. Remember that classes are derived from other classes. The Inherits statement defines the class from which this class is derived. In this case, the class name frmSplash derives from the class named System.Windows.Forms.Form. All forms are derived from the System.Windows.Forms.Form class. Classes and the Inherits statement are discussed fully in Chapters 3 and 4.

Inside the class named frmSplash, the Win Forms Designer creates a procedure named New. This procedure executes when VB .NET creates an instance of the class. The following statements show the New procedure for the form class named frmSplash:

```
Public Sub New()
    MyBase.New()
    'This call is required by the Windows Form Designer.
    InitializeComponent()
    'Add any initialization after the InitializeComponent() call
End Sub
```

VB .NET executes a procedure named New (as shown in the preceding code) each time it creates an instance of a class. Thus, when VB .NET creates the form instance, it executes the New procedure automatically. This procedure is called a **constructor** because it is used to construct an instance of a class. The first statement in the constructor reads MyBase.New(). The MyBase keyword allows you to reference the members of the base class. The base class for the frmSplash class is System.Windows.Forms.Form. Thus, the statement MyBase.New() calls the constructor in the base Form class. Constructors, and the MyBase keyword, are discussed fully in Chapter 4.

The statement InitializeComponent() is just a call to the procedure named InitializeComponent appearing in this class. The Win Forms Designer automatically generates the InitializeComponent procedure and its code. The purpose of the statements in this procedure is to create the form's control instances and set their properties. These are the same properties defined using the Properties window.

Just as any procedure can accept arguments, so too can a constructor. In this chapter's solution, the constructor for the form named frmSeating accepts arguments to define the airplane type, and other information as shown in the following code segment:

```
Public Sub New(ByVal AircraftType As String, _
    ByVal pstrOrigin As String, _
    ByVal pstrDestination As String)
    ' Statements
End Sub
```

As shown in the preceding constructor, the New procedure takes three arguments, each having a data type of String. The syntax to pass arguments to a constructor is the same as the syntax to pass arguments to any procedure.

 Do not modify the code generated by the Win Forms Designer. If you make an error, the Win Forms Designer will not be able to display the control instances or the form itself. Furthermore, do not create a procedure named New for anything else but a constructor.

In addition to creating a constructor, the Win Forms Designer created a procedure named Dispose, which is called when the instance of the class is destroyed. The Dispose procedure is called the **destructor**. The following code segment shows the Dispose procedure generated by the Win Forms Designer:

```
Protected Overloads Overrides Sub Dispose(ByVal
disposing As Boolean)
    If disposing Then
        If Not (components Is Nothing) Then
            components.Dispose()
        End If
    End If
    MyBase.Dispose(disposing)
End Sub
```

When VB .NET destroys a class instance, the Dispose procedure runs. The purpose of the Dispose procedure is to release the memory allocated to the class instance, which in this case is the form itself.

In addition to generating the constructor and destructor, the Win Forms Designer generates statements to create and configure the control instances that you created on the form. First, the Win Forms Designer declares variables to store the control instances as shown in the following statements:

```
Friend WithEvents lblCompany As System.Windows.Forms.Label
Friend WithEvents lblName As System.Windows.Forms.Label
```

The preceding statements declare two variables in the class. The Friend access modifier defines the scope of the variable. Variable scope is discussed fully in Chapter 3. The keyword WithEvents declares the variable such that VB .NET will raise events for the control instances. In this case, VB .NET is declaring two variables to store the two Label control instances created on the form.

The following code segment generated by the Win Forms Designer customizes the debugging environment:

```
<System.Diagnostics.DebuggerStepThrough()>
```

The preceding statement fragment may be unfamiliar as the syntax is new to VB .NET. The less-than and greater-than signs define what is called a **metadata attribute**. VB .NET uses metadata attributes for several tasks including debugging. For example, the DebuggerStepThrough attribute tells the debugger that when stepping through the statements in the module, this procedure will be ignored. Ignoring this procedure is logical as it was automatically generated by the Win Forms Designer, and does not contain any errors. Ignoring the procedure saves time when debugging because you need not ever step through its contents.

As mentioned above, the Win Forms Designer generates a procedure named InitializeComponent. This procedure contains the necessary statements to initialize the control instances and the form itself. It has the following syntax:

```
Private Sub InitializeComponent()
    ' Statements
End Sub
```

The preceding statements contain the declaration for the Sub procedure named InitializeComponent. The syntax of this sub procedure declaration is no different from any other procedure declaration. The procedure begins with the Private Sub keywords and ends with the End Sub keywords.

The following statements appear inside the InitializeComponent procedure.

```
Me.lblCompany = New System.Windows.Forms.Label()
Me.lblName = New System.Windows.Forms.Label()
```

The purpose of these statements is to create the control instances and set their properties. The Me keyword references the current class instance. In this case, Me references the instance of the class named frmSplash (the form). The preceding statements create two instances of the Label control and store those control instances in the variables named lblCompany and lblName, respectively. The New keyword creates an instance of a class.

> The preceding statements assign an object reference. In VB 6, the Set statement was required when assigning object references. The Set statement is obsolete in VB .NET.

The following statements set the properties of the Label control instance named lblCompany. Specifically, they assign values to the Font, ForeColor, Location, Name, Size, TabIndex, and Text properties. In VB .NET, all the statements necessary to create the control instances on the form appear in the statements automatically generated by the Win Forms Designer. Because these statements are new to VB .NET, we discuss them briefly. Chapter 13 discusses the Font, Point, and Size classes and structures in detail.

```
Me.lblCompany.Font = New System.Drawing.Font( _
    "Microsoft Sans Serif", 24.0!, _
    System.Drawing.FontStyle.Regular, _
    System.Drawing.GraphicsUnit.Point, CType(0, Byte))
Me.lblCompany.ForeColor = System.Drawing.Color.Azure
Me.lblCompany.Location = New System.Drawing.Point(40, 64)
Me.lblCompany.Name = "lblCompany"
Me.lblCompany.Size = New System.Drawing.Size(328, 56)
Me.lblCompany.TabIndex = 0
Me.lblCompany.Text = "Course Technology"
```

The Font property defines the font of the text appearing in the label, and the ForeColor property defines the color used for the text font. The Location property defines the position of the label on the form. The Location property has a data type of Point. Thus, to define the position of a control instance on the form, you create an instance of the Point structure. The first argument contains the x coordinate, and the second argument contains the y coordinate. These values are, by default, measured in pixels. The Size property defines the size of the label as it will appear on the form. Like the Location property, you create an instance of the Size structure and assign it to the Size property.

The Name, TabIndex, and Text properties define the name of the control instance, the position of the label in the tab order, and the text that appears in the visible region of the Label control instance. Note that we have omitted the settings for the Label control instance named lblName for brevity.

The following statements set up the visual characteristics of the form:

```
Me.BackColor = System.Drawing.Color.SteelBlue
Me.ClientSize = New System.Drawing.Size(488, 349)
Me.FormBorderStyle = _
    System.Windows.Forms.FormBorderStyle.None
Me.Name = "frmSplash"
Me.ShowInTaskbar = False
Me.StartPosition = _
    System.Windows.Form.FormStartPosition.CenterScreen
Me.ResumeLayout(False)
```

The first statement sets the background color of the form, and the second statement defines the size of the form's client area. The client area of a form is the visible region of the form appearing inside the form's border, and does not include the region of the title bar. The statement that sets the FormBorderStyle property indicates that the form has no border. The next statement defines the Name property of the form as frmSplash. The ShowInTaskbar property is set to False. Thus, the splash screen will not appear in the taskbar. Finally, the StartPosition property is set such that the splash screen will appear in the center of the desktop. Note that all these properties were set using the Properties window. As the developer set these properties, the Win Forms Designer automatically generated the preceding statements.

THE BASICS OF WINDOWS FORMS

A Windows Application project contains one or more forms, and each form is derived from the System.Windows.Forms.Form class. The following list describes selected properties, methods, and events of the Form class:

Syntax

System.Windows.Forms.Form class

Public Properties

- The **AcceptButton** property defines the Button control instance designated as the Accept button. When the user presses the Enter key, Windows fires the Click event handler for this button.

- If the **AutoScroll** property is set to True, scroll bars will automatically appear if the control instances are placed outside of the form's client area. If set to False, scroll bars will not appear.

- The **CancelButton** property defines the Button control instance designated as the Cancel button. Windows fires the Click event handler for this button when the user presses the Escape key.

2

- The **FormBorderStyle** property defines if a border surrounds the form, and, if so, the appearance of the border, and if the user can resize the form. If set to None, then no border surrounds the form, and the form has no title bar. If set to FixedSingle or Fixed3D, then the form is not resizable but a border does appear. The setting Sizable allows the user to resize the form at runtime. The settings FixedToolWindow and SizableToolWindow create tool windows. Tool windows have a slightly smaller title bar.

- The **Opacity** property defines the transparency of the form. Valid values are between 0 and 1. The value 0 indicates that the form is transparent, and the value 1 indicates that the form is solid. Note that the Properties window displays the value as a percentage. Note also that Windows 98 does not support opacity.

- The **StartPosition** property controls where on the desktop the form appears when it is displayed.

Public Events

- The **Enter** event fires when the form gets input focus.

- The **Leave** event fires when the form loses input focus.

Public Methods

- The **Hide** method hides a form. Calling the Hide method is equivalent to setting the Visible property to False.

- The **Show** method displays a form as a modeless form.

- The **ShowDialog** method displays a form as a modal form. The user cannot interact with the calling form in the application until the modal form has been hidden or unloaded.

This chapter contains four forms, each having different characteristics as described in the following list:

- An introductory form called a splash screen will appear when the solution starts running. This form will have no border. The user will not interact with this form in any way. This form will not appear in the taskbar.

- The main form will have a border and not be resizable.

- The seating form will be resizable, and will display the seating configuration for different types of airplanes.

- The about form will display a dialog box containing information about the application.

You will now configure the forms that comprise this application.

To configure forms:

1. Click **View** on the menu bar, and then click **Designer**. Activate the Properties window for the form named **frmSplash**.

2. Set the FormBorderStyle property to **None**, if necessary. Set the Opacity property to **95%**.

3. Activate the Properties window for the form named **frmMain**. Set the FormBorderStyle property to **FixedSingle**.

4. Activate the Properties window for the form named **frmSeating**. Note that the FormBorderStyle property is set to Sizable.

5. Activate the Properties window for the form named **frmAbout**. Set the FormBorderStyle property to **FixedSingle**.

MANAGING FORMS

In Chapter 1, the default startup object was set to a sub procedure named Main in the single module that comprised the application. Any form in the application can also be designated as the startup object. This is accomplished using the Project Properties Pages dialog box shown in Figure 2-11.

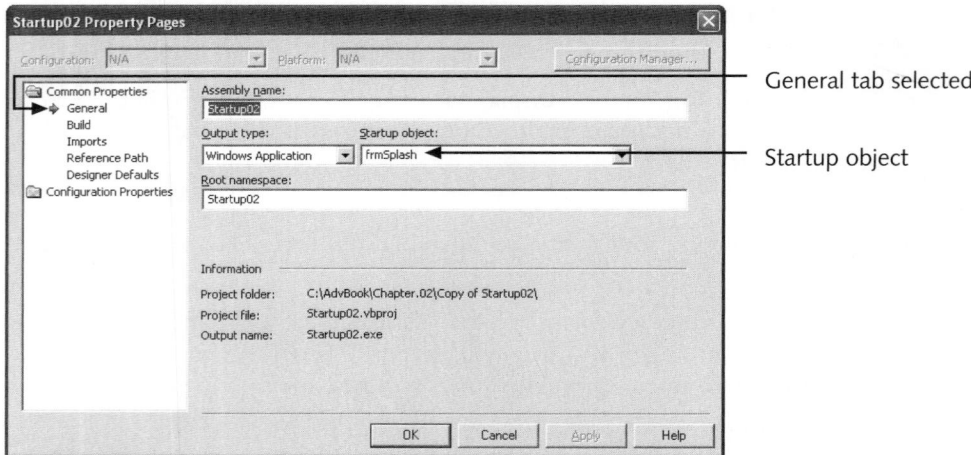

Figure 2-11   Project Properties Pages dialog box

As shown in Figure 2-11, the Project Properties Pages dialog box uses a drill-down interface to set the properties for a project. Figure 2-11 shows the General tab selected. The startup object is currently set to the splash screen named frmSplash.

2

Technically, you could designate the splash screen as the startup object in this project. However, when the splash screen has appeared for five seconds it will be unloaded and closed. This situation poses a problem because once the startup form (or any startup object) has been unloaded, the application ends. Thus, if the splash screen was designated as the startup object, the main form in the application would never appear. The solution to this problem is to create a Sub Main procedure in a module, and designate that procedure as the startup procedure. The startup procedure will, in turn, create an instance of the splash screen and display it as a modal dialog box. When the splash screen is closed, the statements in the Sub Main procedure will display the main form as a modal dialog box. When the user closes the main form, the Sub Main procedure ends causing the application itself to end.

To display a form, you must explicitly create an instance of the form from its class, store a reference to that form instance in a variable, and then display the form, as shown in the following statements:

```
Dim frmSplashNew As New frmSplash()
frmSplashNew.ShowDialog()
```

The New keyword creates an object from its class. In the preceding code segment, the first statement creates an instance of the form named frmSplash and stores a reference to that form instance in the variable named frmSplashNew. The second statement displays that form as a modal dialog box by calling the ShowDialog method.

The preceding statements can also be written such that one statement declares a variable, and a second statement creates an instance of the class, as shown in the following code segment:

```
Dim frmSplashNew As frmSplash
frmSplashNew = New frmSplash()
frmSplashNew.ShowDialog()
```

Next, examine the statements that will appear in the Sub Main procedure to display the splash screen, and then the main form:

```
Public Sub Main
    Dim frmSplashNew As New frmSplash()
    Dim frmMainNew As New frmMain()
    frmSplashNew.ShowDialog()
    frmMainNew.ShowDialog()
End Sub
```

The execution flow of the preceding statements is significant. First, the splash screen is displayed as a modal dialog box. Execution of the statements in this procedure is suspended until the modal dialog box is either hidden or closed. When the splash screen is closed, the main form is then displayed as a modal dialog box, and execution of the statements in the Main procedure are suspended again. When the main form is closed, execution of the Main procedure continues. When VB .NET has executed all of the statements in the Main procedure, the application itself ends. Figure 2-12 illustrates the execution flow of the preceding statements:

Figure 2-12   Execution flow of displaying modal dialog boxes

Thus, in any solution having multiple forms you have two choices to define the startup object. A form can be designated as the startup object if that form will exist for the life of the running application. If, however, the first form displayed to the user will be closed, then you must use the preceding technique designating Sub Main as the startup object and displaying the forms as modal dialog boxes.

You will now create a module and a Sub Main procedure to display the splash screen and main form.

To create a module and a Sub Main procedure:

1. Add a new module to the project by clicking **Project**, then click **Add Module** on the menu bar. The Add New Item dialog box appears as shown in Figure 2-13.

2. Make sure that the **Module** template is selected.

3. In the Name text box, set the name to **Startup.vb**. Click **Open** to close the dialog box and add the module to the project. Note that there is no difference between this module file and the module file you created in Chapter 1. In this chapter, however, you are using the Code Editor instead of Notepad to edit the file.

2

Select Module to add a
module, if necessary

Specify the module name

Figure 2-13   Add New Item dialog box

4. Activate the Code Editor, if necessary, for the Startup.vb module, and then
enter the following statements (shown in bold) in the Code Editor. Again, to
activate the Code Editor select the desired module in the Solution Explorer.
Then, either click **View**, **Code** on the menu bar or click the **View Code**
button appearing at the top of the Solution Explorer.

```
Option Strict On
Option Explicit On
Module Startup
    Public Sub Main()
        Dim frmSplashNew As New frmSplash()
        Dim frmMainNew As New frmMain()
        frmSplashNew.ShowDialog()
        frmMainNew.ShowDialog()
    End Sub
End Module
```

5. Set the startup object by right-clicking the project name (**Startup02**) in the
Solution Explorer, and then clicking **Properties**. Be careful to select the project rather than the solution.

6. Set the Startup object to **Sub Main** and then click **OK** to save the changes.

7. Test the solution. The splash screen appears. The main form does not appear
next because you have not yet written the statements to hide the splash screen.
End the solution by clicking the **Stop Debugging** button on the Toolbar.

THE BASICS OF CONTROLS

The controls appearing in the Toolbox are part of the .NET Framework class library and are shared by all Visual Studio .NET languages. Again, remember that the inherited types making up the .NET Framework are organized hierarchically, one type being derived from another type. Controls are derived from the System.Windows.Forms.Control class. The Control base class supplies the keyboard input and mouse input functionality, along with updating the display for those control instances appearing to the user. Controls can be categorized by their purpose as described in the following list:

- The Button, CheckBox, and RadioButton controls form a group of clickable buttons. Each of these controls derives from the System.Windows.Forms.ButtonBase class.

- The ComboBox and ListBox controls are considered list controls, as the user selects an item from a list. Both of these controls derive from the System.Windows.Forms.ListControl class.

- The horizontal scroll bar (HScrollBar) and vertical scroll bar (VScrollBar) derive from the System.Windows.Forms.ScrollBar class.

- The TextBoxBase class provides the implementation for editable controls. These controls include the TextBox and RichTextBox.

- The Label class derives directly from System.Windows.Forms.Control.

- The Panel control contains other controls and acts as a container for those controls. The Panel control derives from System.Windows.Forms.Control.ScrollableControl.

Figure 2-14 illustrates the organization of selected controls within the .NET Framework class hierarchy.

Again, this chapter assumes that you are familiar with controls and their operation. Thus, we provide only a summary discussion of selected controls. Microsoft has made several enhancements to controls in VB .NET. The following list summarizes these enhancements:

- VB .NET no longer supports control arrays. This change poses no problem because VB .NET supplies a new way to create control instances dynamically at runtime. Additionally, because of the changes to the operation of event handlers, one event handler can handle the same event for multiple control instances. The changes to event handlers and dynamic control creation are discussed later in this chapter.

- Controls no longer have a Caption property. The Text property replaces the Caption property for the Button, Label, and other controls.

- The ToolTip property is no longer supported. Instead, a new control called the ToolTip control provides the support for ToolTips.

Figure 2-14   Control Hierarchy

- The Image control is no longer supported. Its features have been merged into the PictureBox control.

- The GroupBox control replaces the Frame control.

- Controls no longer support a default property. For example, to reference the Text property of a TextBox, you must now explicitly specify the Text property. This change was required because of the removal of the Set statement.

The steps to create a control instance are simple. First, activate the Win Forms Designer. Second, click the desired control in the Toolbox to select it, then draw the control instance on the form. Using the Properties window, set the Name and other properties as necessary.

The Timer Control

The purpose of the Timer control is simple. It fires an event named Tick at regular intervals as defined by the Interval property. The Tick event only fires when the Enabled property is set to True. The Interval property stores a 32-bit Integer. Intervals are measured in milliseconds, so an interval of 1000 is equal to 1 second. In this chapter, the Timer control will be used to display the splash screen for five seconds. When the Tick event for the Timer control fires, the splash screen will close.

To create an instance of the Timer control and configure it:

1. Activate the Win Forms Designer for the form named **frmSplash**, if necessary.

2. Using the Toolbox, create an instance of the Timer control on the form. Because the Timer control is not visible at runtime, it appears in the resizable tray below the form. Using the Properties window, set the Name property to **tmrClose**, the Enabled property to **True**, if necessary, and the Interval property to **5000**.

3. Create the Tick event handler for the Timer control instance by double-clicking the control instance.

4. Enter the following statement into the Tick event handler to unload the form:

```
Me.Close()
```

The preceding statement to close the form uses the Me keyword. VB .NET uses the Me keyword to reference the current instance of a class. In this case the class is the form. The Close method unloads the form, thereby removing the form and its objects from memory.

5. Test the solution. The splash screen appears for five seconds, and then the main form appears.

Menus and Menu Items

A menu system gives the user a way to perform tasks as an alternative to clicking buttons on a form. A menu system consists of a menu bar that displays drop-down menus. A drop-down menu may contain menu items or menus that display sub-menus. Although the user could click buttons on a form to perform the same tasks, the number of buttons on a form can become excessive, causing the form to appear cluttered and disorganized. This chapter only introduces the most basic elements of how to create a menu. Refer to Chapter 14 for a full discussion of menus and how to integrate menus between forms. Because a menu system is bound to a form, each form in a solution can have a unique menu system associated with it. In addition, a form may contain more than one instance of the MainMenu control.

To create the menu system for a form, you first create an instance of the MainMenu control. When you create an instance of the MainMenu control on a form, the Win Forms Designer writes the necessary statements in the Code Editor to create an instance of the control and configure it. Each individual menu appearing on the form is a member of the MenuItem class. The MenuItem class derives from the System.Windows.Forms class and supports the following properties and events:

Syntax

System.Windows.Forms.MenuItem class

2

Public Properties

- The Boolean **Checked** property is used to define a checked menu item, which is a menu item that displays a check mark to the left of the menu text. The check box can either be checked or unchecked.

- The Boolean **Enabled** property defines whether or not the menu item is enabled or disabled. An enabled menu item responds to a Click event, while a disabled menu item does not. Disabled menu items appear shaded.

- The **Name** property defines the name of the menu item.

- The **Shortcut** and Boolean **ShowShortcut** properties work together. The Shortcut property defines a shortcut key used to execute the Click event handler for a menu item. The Shortcut key only appears on the menu item if the ShowShortcut property is set to True.

- The **Text** property defines the text that appears in the visible region of the menu item. To create a hot key for a menu item, preface the character designated as the hot key with an ampersand (&).

- The **Visible** property defines whether or not the menu item is visible to the user. If a menu title or menu is invisible, any subordinate menus are invisible too.

Public Events

- Windows fires the **Click** event for a menu item when the user clicks it.

This book will use the standard prefix "mmu" followed by a descriptive name for the Name property of a menu. The descriptive name will be the same as the menu's caption with all the spaces removed.

To create the menu system for a form, you first create an instance of the MainMenu control on the form, and then you configure the menu by editing it in place in the Win Forms Designer.

To create a menu:

1. Activate the Win Forms Designer for the form named **frmMain.vb**, if necessary.

2. Create an instance of the MainMenu control on the form. Because the control instance is not visible at runtime, it appears in the resizable tray at the bottom of the Win Forms Designer.

3. Using the Properties window, set the Name property of the control instance to **mmuMain**.

Notice that the Win Forms Designer displays the text "Type Here" immediately below the form's title bar, as shown in Figure 2-15.

Figure 2-15   Creating a menu

4. To create the menu titles, click the text that reads **Type Here** and then enter the text **&File**.

5. To enter other menu titles, click the text to the right of the File menu that you just created, and then enter the text **&Display**. To the right of the text that reads Display, enter the text **&Help**.

   To create menu items, you enter text below a menu title in the same way that you entered the text for the menu title.

6. Click the **File** menu. The text Type Here appears below the File menu. Enter the text **&Exit** below the File menu.

7. Continue to create a menu item with the text **&Airplane** below the Display menu, and a menu item with the text **&About** below the Help menu.

Having created the menu title and menu items, you can now define the names for the menu titles and menu items. To define the names for menu items, you activate the MainMenu control to display the menu on the form. Next, right-click on the menu appearing on the form, and then select Edit Names from the context menu. Finally, type in the names.

To define the menu names:

1. Right-click the menu appearing in the Win Forms Designer, and then click **Edit Names** to edit the Name property for the menu titles and menu items.

2. Define the menu names as follows: File — **mmuFile**, Exit — **mmuFileExit**, Display — **mmuDisplay**, Airplane — **mmuDisplayAirplane**, Help — **mmuHelp**, About — **mmuHelpAbout**. Figure 2-16 illustrates the menu while the names are being edited.

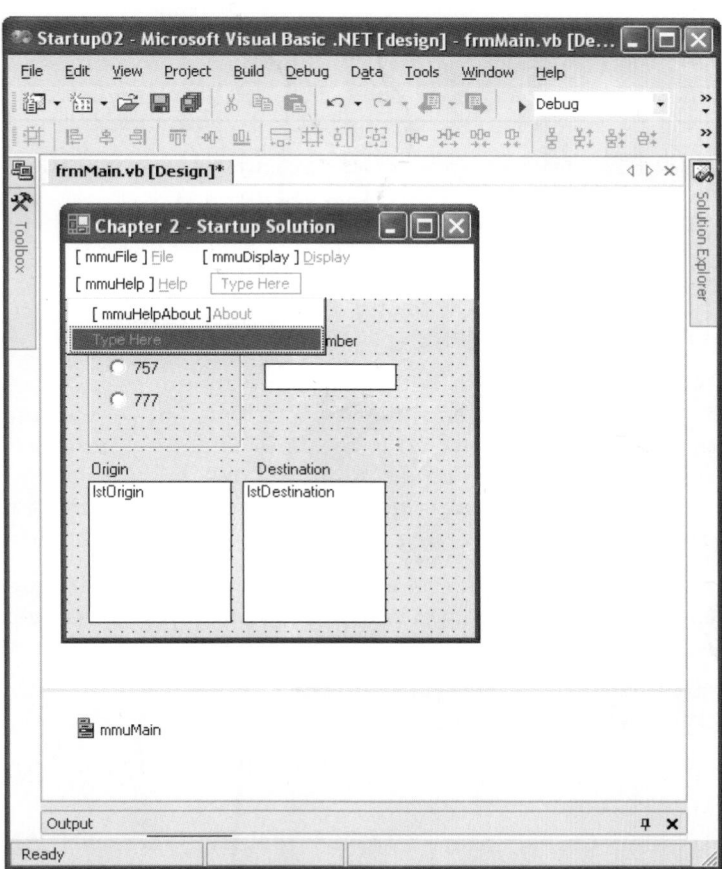

Figure 2-16   Editing menu names

3. Right-click again on the menu. Click **Edit Names** again from the context menu. The names that you entered are recorded.

In addition to a main menu, a form can have context menus, also called pop-up menus.

Having created the menu on the main form, you can now create the event handlers for those menu items. These event handlers will exit the application and display the other forms in the application.

To create an event handler for a menu item:

1. Activate the Win Forms Designer for the form named **frmMain.vb**, if necessary. Click the **File** menu on the form, and then double-click the **Exit** menu item. VB .NET activates the Code Editor and creates the Click event handler for the menu item. Enter the following statement into the event handler to close the form:

```
Me.Close()
```

2. Activate the Win Forms Designer for the form named **frmMain.vb**. Click the **Display** menu on the form, then double-click the **Airplane** menu item. Enter the following statements into the event handler to display the seating form:

```
Dim frmSeatingNew As New frmSeating(mstrAirplaneType, _
    lstOrigin.SelectedItem.ToString, _
    lstDestination.SelectedItem.ToString)

frmSeatingNew.Show()
frmSeatingNew.Text = "Flight Number " & _
    txtFlightNumber.Text
```

The Dim statement creates an instance of the seating form. The constructor takes three arguments. The first is the airplane type. The second and third are the origin and destination selected in the ListBox control instance. The Show method displays the form as a modeless dialog box. The final statement updates the text appearing on the form's title bar. At this point in the solution's development, though, you have not yet populated the contents of the list boxes.

3. Activate the Win Forms Designer for the form named **frmMain.vb**. Click the **Help** menu on the form and then double-click the **About** menu item. Enter the following statements into the Click event handler to display the About form:

```
Dim frmAboutNew As New frmAbout()
frmAboutNew.ShowDialog()
```

The preceding statements create an instance of the form named frmAbout and then display the form as a modal dialog box.

4. Test the solution. On the main form, click **Help** and then click **About**. The About dialog box appears. Close the dialog box.

5. End the application.

The CheckBox Control

The CheckBox control contains a check box that the user can check, along with text that describes the purpose of the check box. The developer can specify both the placement of the check box and the text within the visible region of the control instance.

The CheckBox control operates either as a two-state or a three-state control. Operating as a two-state control, the check box can either be checked or unchecked. Operating as a three-state control, the check box can be checked, unchecked, or indeterminate. The indeterminate setting indicates that the check box is neither checked nor unchecked. The ThreeState property, if set to False, causes the check box to operate in two-state mode. If the ThreeState property is set to True, then the check box operates in three-state mode.

In two-state mode, the Checked property defines whether the check box is checked or not. Use the CheckedChanged event to determine when the value of the Checked property changes. In three-state mode, use the CheckState property to determine if the check box is checked, unchecked, or indeterminate. Use the CheckStateChanged event in three-state mode to determine when the value of the CheckState property changes.

Regardless of whether the check box is operating in two-state or three-state mode, the Boolean AutoCheck property controls whether the check box becomes checked or unchecked when the user clicks on any part of the visible region of the control instance instead of just the check box.

Label and TextBox Controls

The Label control displays a textual prompt or an image to the user. The Text property contains the textual prompt and the Image property defines the image. The TextBox control supplies the user with an editable control used for both input and output. The following list summarizes selected properties and events of the TextBox control:

Syntax

System.Windows.Forms.TextBox class

Public Properties

- If the Boolean **AcceptsReturn** property is set to True, pressing the Enter key will cause the carriage return character to be embedded into the text string. If the property is set to False, pressing the Enter key will cause the Click event handler to execute for the button designated as the default button.

- If the Boolean **AcceptsTab** property is set to False, pressing the Tab key will cause the next control instance in the tab order to get input focus. If set to True, the tab character will be embedded into the contents of the text box.

- The **Lines** property contains an array of strings. Each string in the array represents one line in the text box. A carriage return character separates each line.

- The **MaxLength** property defines the maximum number of characters that the user can enter into the text box.

- The Boolean **ReadOnly** property controls if the user can change the contents of the text box at runtime.

Public Methods

- The **Clear** method clears the contents from the control instance.

- The **Cut**, **Copy**, and **Paste** methods perform cut, copy, and paste operations to and from the clipboard.

- The **Focus** method sets the focus to the control instance.

Public Events

- The **Enter** event fires when the control instance gets input focus.

- The **Leave** event fires just before the control instance loses input focus.

- When the user changes the text in the control instance, the **TextChanged** event fires.

- The **Validating** event fires just before the control instance loses input focus as the input is being validated. The **Validated** event fires after the Validating event.

In the startup solution, the text box has already been created on the main form and its properties have been set.

Button Control

The Button control provides the user with a clickable button. Most commonly, you, as the developer, create a Click event handler that executes in response to the user clicking the button. Some new features have been added to the Button control. The new FlatStyle property defines the 3-D appearance of the Button control instance. Possible values are Flat, Popup, Standard, and System. The Image property contains the image that appears within the visible region of the control instance, and the ImageAlign property defines how the image will be aligned within the visible region of the button. The Appearance property replaces the Style property. The new Focus method sets input focus to the button, and the new PerformClick method fires a Click event for the button.

Scroll Bar Controls

VB .NET supports horizontal and vertical scroll bars. Both operate the same way. The Minimum and Maximum properties define the valid lower bound and upper bound of the Value property, respectively. The Value property contains the current value of the control instance. The Value property is an Integer. The SmallChange and LargeChange properties define the amount of change to the Value property when the user clicks the scroll arrows at the ends of the scroll bar or the scroll region, respectively. The ValueChanged event fires when the user changes the Value property or the Value property is changed programmatically. VB .NET does not allow the Maximum property to have a value less than the Minimum property.

GroupBox and Panel Controls

Both the GroupBox and Panel controls are container controls, meaning, both contain other control instances created on the form. Moving a GroupBox or Panel control instance causes the contained control instances to be moved too. That is, if radio buttons are created in a group box or panel, those radio buttons must appear inside the region of the group box or panel, and will be repositioned on the form when the developer repositions the group box or panel.

The Text property of the GroupBox control contains a descriptive prompt. However, the Panel control does not have a caption. The most notable feature of the Panel control is its ability to act as a scrollable control. That is, you can create control instances that are contained by the panel that will scroll within the region of the Panel control instance. If the control instances created in the region of the Panel control will not fit within the visible region of the Panel, and the AutoScroll property is set to True, then scroll bars will appear in the panel. You will see how to make a Panel control a scrollable control later in the chapter when you dynamically create control instances at runtime.

Radio Buttons

Radio buttons—formerly called option buttons—allow the user to select one button from a group of buttons. The group of buttons is called a **button group**. If only one button group exists on a form, then the radio buttons can be created directly on the form and will be considered a button group. If, however, a form requires multiple button groups, then the radio buttons of each button group must be enclosed in a GroupBox or Panel control instance.

When creating radio buttons in a GroupBox or Panel control instance, create the radio buttons directly in the GroupBox or Panel. If you attempt to drag an existing radio button control instance into a GroupBox or Panel, it will not be part of the button group. To make an existing radio button control instance a member of a button group, cut the control instance, select the desired control instance, and then paste the radio button from the clipboard into the GroupBox or Panel.

In this chapter's solution, the radio buttons have already been created on the main form and are contained by an instance of the GroupBox control. Additionally, an instance of the Panel control has been created on the seating form. Later in the chapter, you will dynamically add CheckBox control instances into the Panel control instance.

List and Combo Boxes

List boxes and combo boxes are similar. The user typically selects one or more items from a list of items in a List or ComboBox control instance. The primary difference between a list box and a combo box is that a combo box can display list items in a drop-down list, while the region of the ListBox control is fixed.

 Use the ComboBox control instead of the ListBox control to conserve space on a form.

Syntax

System.Windows.Forms.ListBox class
System.Windows.Forms.ComboBox class

Public Properties

- The **Items** property contains a reference to the Items collection. Each item in the Items collection represents a list item in the control instance. The data type of an item is System.Object. Thus, any type of object can be stored as a list item.

- The **SelectedIndex** property stores the 0-based index of the selected item. If no item is selected, then the SelectedIndex property has a value of –1.

- The **SelectedItem** property stores the currently selected item in the list or combo box. Again, the SelectedItem property has a data type of System.Object.

- The **Sorted** property, if set to True, causes the items in the list or combo box to appear in sorted order.

- The **TopIndex** property defines the first visible item appearing in the list or combo box control instance.

Public Methods

- The **ClearSelected** method deselects all the items in the control instance.

Public Events

- The **SelectedIndexChanged** event fires when the user selects a different item in the list or combo box.

In this chapter's solution, list boxes on the main form will be used to display the origin and destination airports. Technically, the list boxes could be configured at design time or runtime. However, to illustrate both techniques, you will now configure one list box at design time and configure the other list box at runtime.

To configure a list box:

1. Activate the Win Forms Designer for the form named **frmMain.vb**, if necessary.

2. Click the **lstOrigin** control instance on the form to select it.

3. Activate the Properties window, and then click the **value** column for the Items property to display the build button. Click the **build** button to display the String Collection Editor.

4. Enter the values shown in Figure 2-17:

Figure 2-17   String Collection Editor

5. Click **OK** to close the String Collection Editor. The items you entered appear in the list box.

In addition to adding items to a list box at design time, the Add method of the Items collection allows list box or combo box items to be added at runtime, as shown in the following code segment:

```
lstDestination.Items.Add("Atlanta")
```

The preceding code segment adds an item to the list box by calling the Add method of the Items collection. Of course, the Add method would need to be called for the remaining three cities as well. In addition to adding a single item to a ListBox control instance,

VB .NET supplies a new technique that adds multiple items to a ListBox control instance at the same time, as shown in the following code segment:

```
Dim pstrCities() As String = {"Atlanta", "Chicago", _
    "Los Angeles", "New York"}
lstDestination.Items.AddRange(pstrCities)
```

The first statement declares a dynamic array of strings. However, the array is initialized at design time. The list of items in the array is enclosed in braces ({ }). The items in the list appear separated by commas. VB .NET allows all arrays to be initialized in this manner. The second statement calls the AddRange method instead of the Add method. The AddRange method adds an array of items instead of a single item.

To illustrate how to call the AddRange method, you will initialize the list box named lstDestination when the main form loads. Thus, you will perform the initialization tasks in the frmMain_Load event handler.

To initialize a ListBox control instance at runtime:

1. Activate the Win Forms Designer for the form named **frmMain.vb**, if necessary.

2. Double-click the mouse on the form but not on a control instance to create the frmMain_Load event handler, and then enter the following statements:

```
Dim pstrCities() As String = {"Atlanta", "Chicago", _
    "Los Angeles", "New York"}
lstDestination.Items.AddRange(pstrCities)
```

3. Test the solution. When the main form appears, both list boxes are initialized.

ToolTip Control

The ToolTip control is new to VB .NET. This category of control is called a provider control. A **provider control** is one that works in conjunction with another control instance, having the effect of expanding that other control's features. The ToolTip control is invisible at runtime, so it appears in the resizable tray below the form. When you create a ToolTip control instance, a property named ToolTip on *xxxx* appears in the Properties window for the form and the control instances created on the form. (*xxxx* is a placeholder for the name of the ToolTip control instance.)

The ToolTip control has the following properties allowing you to define when to display a ToolTip and how long the ToolTip should be displayed (these properties are measured in milliseconds):

- The **AutoPopupDelay** property controls how long the ToolTip is displayed.

- The **InitialDelay** property controls how long the mouse must hover over a control instance before the ToolTip is displayed.

- The **AutomaticDelay** property is used to configure the preceding properties automatically.

2

Next, you will create a ToolTip control instance on the main form to display ToolTips for other control instances.

To create and configure a ToolTip:

1. Activate the Win Forms Designer for the form named **frmMain**.

2. Create a ToolTip control instance on the form. It appears in the resizable tray below the form.

3. Using the Properties window, set the Name property to **tipGeneral**.

4. Activate the Properties window for the ListBox control instance named **lstOrigin**, and then set the ToolTip on tipGeneral property to **Click to select the origin of the flight**.

5. Activate the Properties window for the ListBox control instance named **lstDestination**, then set the ToolTip on tipGeneral property to **Click to select the destination of the flight**.

6. Test the solution. When the main form appears, move the mouse over the two list boxes and let it hover for a few seconds. The ToolTip that you created appears.

UNDERSTANDING TAB ORDER

Every form has exactly one active control instance at runtime. For example, when the user enters text in a text box, that text box has input focus and is considered the active control instance. The **tab order** represents the order in which the control instances on a form get input focus as the user presses the Tab key.

Each control instance that can get input focus supports the TabIndex property. You define the tab order by setting a unique value to the TabIndex property for each visible control instance, such that the first control to get focus will have a TabIndex value of 0, the second control instance a TabIndex value of 1, and so on.

To set the tab order:

1. Activate the Win Forms Designer for the form named **frmMain.vb**, if necessary.

2. On the Menu bar, click **View**, and then click **Tab Order**.

   The control instances appear on the form with small boxes in the upper-left corner of each control instance. The number in the box indicates the relative tab order.

3. Click each of the control instances in turn so that the tab order is the same as the tab order shown in Figure 2-18.

Figure 2-18   Setting the tab order

4. On the Menu bar, click **View**, and then click **Tab Order** again to save your changes.

INTRODUCTION TO VISUAL BASIC .NET EVENT HANDLERS

Event handling has evolved considerably in VB .NET. In VB .NET, event handlers are still implemented as sub procedures. However, the arguments to event handlers have changed, and the procedure name is no longer significant. A procedure is designated as an event handler by adding the Handles clause to the end of the procedure declaration, as shown in the following code segment:

```
Private Sub btnDemo_Click(ByVal sender As System.Object, _
    ByVal e As System.EventArgs) Handles btnDemo.Click
End Sub
```

The preceding code segment illustrates three significant changes to VB .NET event handlers. First, all VB .NET handlers have two arguments. The first argument—named sender—contains a reference to the object that generated the event. For example, if the user clicked the button named btnDemo, then the sender argument would contain a reference to the Button control instance named btnDemo. The second argument—named e—supplies the means to pass any necessary information to the event handler. Notice that the data type of the second argument is System.EventArgs. Remember that System.Object is the superclass and that all types derive from System.Object. System.EventArgs is no different and derives directly from System.Object. The System.EventArgs class itself does very little. It is merely the base class for events that pass data. To illustrate the purpose of the second argument, examine the following MouseMove event for the form named frmMain:

```
Private Sub frmMain_MouseMove(ByVal sender As Object, _
    ByVal e As System.Windows.Forms.MouseEventArgs) _
    Handles MyBase.MouseMove
End Sub
```

Note that the data type for the MouseMove event is System.Windows.Forms.MouseEventArgs. The MouseEventArgs class supplies properties that allow you to determine which mouse button was clicked, and the state of any modifier keys (Shift, Ctrl, Alt). The important concept to remember is that all data is passed to an event via the second event argument, and the data type of this argument varies based on the type of the event. The following list describes some of the more significant event classes:

- The KeyUp and KeyDown event handlers use the **KeyEventArgs** class. Its properties allow you to determine the scan code for the keyboard character that was pressed or released.

- The KeyPress event handler uses the **KeyPressEventArgs** class to retrieve the ASCII character that was pressed.

- The second argument to the MouseDown and MouseUp events handlers has a data type of **MouseEventArgs**. The properties of this class allow you to determine which mouse button was pressed or released and the state of any modifier keys.

- The **CancelEventArgs** class is often used with the Validating event. It allows the developer to cancel the event in situations where input is not valid. If the Validating event is cancelled then the subsequent Validated event does not fire. Input validation is discussed in Chapter 3.

The other significant change to the syntax of an event handler is the Handles clause. Examine the following statement fragment:

```
Handles btnDemo.Click
```

The Handles clause defines the control instance and the event to be handled. The control instance and the event name are separated by a period. Thus, the preceding code segment denotes that the Click event for the button named btnDemo will be handled.

VB .NET supports two ways to create the Click event handler for the Button control instance. Double-clicking the Button control instance in the Win Forms Designer will create the Click event handler for the button and activate the Code Editor. Selecting the Button control instance in the Code Editor's Class Name list box, and then selecting the Click event in the Method Name list box will also work. In the following steps you will use the second technique.

To select an event handler in the Code Editor:

1. Activate the Code Editor for the form named **frmSeating.vb**.

2. Click the **list arrow** in the Class Name list box, and then select the Button control instance named **btnClose**.

3. Click the list arrow in the Method Name list box and then select the **Click** event.

4. Enter the following statement in the event handler to close the form:

   ```
   Me.Close()
   ```

Another important point needs to be made about VB .NET event handling: control arrays are no longer supported. Control arrays were commonly used with such controls as radio buttons. The event handler for the control array of radio buttons would handle the event for a button group. This change may seem to pose a problem, but it does not. The reason is simple. The Handles clause can be modified so that one event handler will handle events for multiple control instances. VB .NET calls an event handler that handles events for multiple control instances a **multicast event handler**.

Examine the following multicast event handler for a group of radio buttons:

```
Private Sub radAirplaneType_CheckedChanged( _
    ByVal sender As System.Object, _
    ByVal e As System.EventArgs) _
    Handles rad757.CheckedChanged, rad777.CheckedChanged
    ' Statements in event handler
End Sub
```

As shown in the preceding code segment, the procedure named radAirplaneType_CheckedChanged handles the CheckedChanged event for two radio buttons. Note that a comma separates each control instance in the Handles clause. In this chapter's solution, you will handle the CheckedChanged event to store the current airplane type in a string variable. The contents of this variable will be used later in the solution.

To create a multicast event handler:

1. Activate the Code Editor for the form named **frmMain.vb**, if necessary, and then enter the following statements (shown in bold) to create the multicast event handler for the button group:

```
Private Sub radAirplaneType_CheckedChanged(ByVal sender As _
    System.Object, ByVal e As System.EventArgs) _
    Handles rad737.CheckedChanged, rad777.CheckedChanged

    Dim radCurrent As System.Windows.Forms.RadioButton
    radCurrent = CType(sender, System.Windows.Forms.RadioButton)
    mstrAirplaneType = radCurrent.Text
End Sub
```

Analyzing the preceding code segment, the procedure named radAirplaneType_CheckedChanged will handle the CheckedChanged event for the two radio buttons. The statements in this event handler require explanation. Examine the following statement:

```
Dim radCurrent As System.Windows.Forms.RadioButton
```

The preceding statement declares a local variable named radCurrent having a data of RadioButton.

The following statement stores a reference to the RadioButton control instance clicked by the user:

```
radCurrent = CType(sender, System.Windows.Forms.RadioButton)
```

The variable sender contains a reference to the object that fired the event—in this case, the RadioButton control instance clicked by the user. However, note that the data type of the variable sender is System.Object while the data type of radCurrent is RadioButton. Because Option Strict is enabled, VB .NET will not implicitly convert a variable from a less restrictive type to a more restrictive type. The CType function explicitly converts a variable from one data type to another.

The CType function accepts two arguments. The first argument contains the object to convert, and the second argument defines the data type to which the data should be converted. Thus, the preceding statement explicitly converts the generic System.Object type to the RadioButton type. This book will use the CType function to explicitly convert data types from a generic type (System.Object) to a specific type.

Examine the following statement:

```
mstrAirplaneType = radCurrent.Text
```

The final statement stores the Text property of the clicked RadioButton control instance in the string variable named mstrAirplaneType. This variable will be used later in the chapter to configure and display the seating form for a particular type of airplane.

Dynamic Event Handlers

In addition to creating event handlers using the Handles clause, VB .NET supplies another means to create event handlers dynamically at runtime using the AddHandler and RemoveHandler statements, which have the following syntax:

Syntax

AddHandler *event,* **AddressOf** *eventhandler*
RemoveHandler *event,* **AddressOf** *eventhandler*

Definition

The **AddHandler** statement dynamically creates an event handler at runtime, while the **RemoveHandler** statement removes a dynamically created event handler.

Dissection

- The *event* argument contains the name of the control instance and event for which you want to designate an event handler. For example, you may create a CheckedChanged event for several instances of a CheckBox control.

- The *eventhandler* argument contains the procedure name of the procedure designated as the event handler.

- The **AddressOf** operator is called a function delegate. Note that the *eventhandler* argument follows the AddressOf operator. Thus, this part of the statement gets the memory address of a procedure. The AddHandler statement registers the memory address of this procedure, allowing VB .NET to call the event handler at runtime.

Code Example

```
AddHandler chkSeats.CheckedChanged, AddressOf _
    chkSeats_CheckedChanged
```

Code Dissection

- The preceding statement creates an event handler dynamically at runtime. The procedure named chkSeats_CheckedChanged is designated as the event handler for the CheckedChanged event of the check box named chkSeats.

In addition to creating event handlers at runtime, VB .NET allows you to create control instances at runtime too. The two processes are intertwined, because after a control instance gets created at runtime, the corresponding event handlers need to get created. Examine the following statements to create a CheckBox control instance dynamically at runtime and then set its properties. Note that the following statements are similar to those automatically generated by the Win Forms Designer.

```
Private chkSeats As System.Windows.Forms.CheckBox
chkSeats = New System.Windows.Forms.CheckBox()
chkSeats.Visible = True
chkSeats.Location = New System.Drawing.Point(50, 50)
chkSeats.Size = New System.Drawing.Size(80, 20)
```

The preceding statements first declare a variable to store a reference to a CheckBox control. The second statement creates the control instance. Again, remember that the New keyword is used to create any object from its underlying class. The third statement makes the check box visible. The final two statements define the position and size of the check box by creating instances of the Point and Size structures, respectively.

In this chapter, you will dynamically create instances of the CheckBox control on the seating form. Instead of creating a single CheckBox control instance, you will create several of them; one for each seat on the airplane. Before doing so, however, the structure of the code in the seating form needs some explanation. The seating form contains two arrays to store references to the dynamically created CheckBox and Label control instances as shown in the following statements:

```
Private chkSeats(,) As System.Windows.Forms.CheckBox
Private lblRow() As System.Windows.Forms.Label
```

The first of the preceding statements declares a dynamic two-dimensional array of check boxes. This two-dimensional array will store references to check boxes in rows and columns. The second statement declares a dynamic array of labels that will be used to identify the row number. Note that a dynamic array has no initial size and is declared without subscripts. When the seating form gets loaded the constructor calls the procedure named ConfigureSeating. This procedure accepts one argument: the type of airplane to configure.

A Select Case statement is used to configure the two airplane types. The preceding dynamic arrays must be given a size before they can be used. Changing the size of an array is accomplished with the ReDim statement, as shown in the following statements:

```
Private Sub ConfigureSeating(ByVal AircraftType As String)
    Dim pintSeatCurrent, pintRowCurrent As Integer
    Select Case AircraftType
        Case "757"
            ReDim chkSeats(cint757Seats, cint757Rows)
            ReDim lblRow(cint757Rows)
            mintEmpty = cint757Seats * cint757Rows
            ' statements to initialize the check boxes
            ' and labels
```

```
        Case "777"
            ReDim chkSeats(cint777Seats, cint777Rows)
            ReDim lblRow(cint777Rows)
            mintEmpty = cint777Seats * cint777Rows
            ' statements to initialize the check boxes
            ' and labels
    End Select
End Sub
```

The selected statements from the ConfigureSeating procedure redimension the arrays that store the check boxes and labels based on the type of airplane. The ReDim statement redimensions an array, giving the array a size. In the statements cint757Seats, cint757Rows, cint777Seats and cint777Rows are constants. Constants have already been declared in the startup solution for each airplane type. Initially, the airplane will be empty. The final statements in each Case defines the number of empty seats by multiplying the number of seats per row by the number of rows.

The following nested For loops create the CheckBox control instances and configure them for the 757 airplane type:

```
For pintSeatCurrent = 0 To cint757Seats - 1
    For pintRowCurrent = 0 To cint757Rows - 1
        pntCurrent = New Point((pintSeatCurrent + 1) * _
            cintCheckBoxWidth, (pintRowCurrent + 1) * _
            cintCheckBoxHeight)
        Call CreateCheckBox(pintSeatCurrent, _
            pintRowCurrent, pntCurrent)
    Next
Next
```

The outer For loop iterates through the seats, while the inner For loop iterates through the rows. Constants that have already been declared are used as the loop counters. The constant cint757Seats defines the seats per row on the 757 airplane type and the constant cint757Rows defines the number of rows. The variable pntCurrent stores a Point structure used to position the check box on the form. The constants cintCheckBoxWidth and cintCheckBoxHeight store the size of the check box. These values are multiplied by the current seat number and current row number to calculate the position. For each seat, a new check box is dynamically created at runtime using the following CreateCheckBox procedure:

```
Private Sub CreateCheckBox(ByVal pintSeatCurrent As _
    Integer, ByVal pintRowCurrent As Integer, _
    ByVal pnt As Point)
    chkSeats(pintSeatCurrent, pintRowCurrent) = _
        New CheckBox()
```

```
      chkSeats(pintSeatCurrent, pintRowCurrent).Visible = _
         True
      chkSeats(pintSeatCurrent, pintRowCurrent).Size = _
         New System.Drawing.Size(cintCheckBoxWidth, _
         cintCheckBoxHeight)
      chkSeats(pintSeatCurrent, pintRowCurrent).Location = _
         pnt
      AddHandler chkSeats(pintSeatCurrent, _
         pintRowCurrent).CheckedChanged, _
         AddressOf chkseats_CheckedChanged
      Me.pnlSeats.Controls.Add(chkSeats(pintSeatCurrent, _
         pintRowCurrent))
   End Sub
```

The current seat and current row are passed as arguments to the CreateCheckBox procedure, along with the Point structure that defines the position where the CheckBox control instance will get created. The statements create the instance of the CheckBox control, make it visible, and set its size and location. Finally, the AddHandler statement creates the dynamic event handler for the check box.

Label control instances are also dynamically created to the right of the check boxes as shown in the following code segment:

```
   For pintRowCurrent = 0 To cint757Rows - 1
      Call CreateLabel(pintRowCurrent)
      lblRow(pintRowCurrent).Left = 120
      lblRow(pintRowCurrent).Top = (pintRowCurrent + 1) * _
         cintCheckBoxHeight
      lblRow(pintRowCurrent).Height = 15
      lblRow(pintRowCurrent).Width = 25
   Next
```

In the preceding code segment, the For loop creates one Label control instance for each airplane row. The CreateLabel procedure does the work of actually creating each control instance. Instead of creating Point and Size structures, the Left, Top, Height, and Width properties are used to position and size the control instance. Note that both techniques will work. Figure 2-19 illustrates the logic to create the control instances dynamically on the seating form.

Figure 2-19 Creating the seating form

COLLECTIONS OF CONTROLS

Each form supports a collection named Controls. The Controls collection contains a reference to each control instance created directly on the form. You can enumerate the Controls collection—or any collection for that matter—by writing a For Each loop. The following illustrates how to create a For Each loop to enumerate the Controls collection of a form:

```
Dim ctlCurrent As Control
For Each ctlCurrent In Me.Controls
    ' Statements to process the current control instance
Next
```

In VB .NET, multiple Controls collections may exist for a form. These collections are organized hierarchically such that all container controls have their own Controls collection.

To illustrate the hierarchical Controls collections, suppose that a GroupBox control instance appears on the form named frmMain, and that GroupBox control instance, in turn, contains four radio buttons. In this situation the form itself has a Controls collection that stores references to the control instances created directly on the form.

Note that the GroupBox control instance has another Controls collection. The Controls collection of the GroupBox control contains the radio buttons created in the GroupBox. This nesting can continue for multiple levels. That is, if a GroupBox control instance contains another GroupBox control instance, then each GroupBox control instance would have its own Controls collection.

The Panel control instance already created on the seating form is also a container control. In this chapter's solution you will configure check boxes that you dynamically created in the preceding steps so that they are contained by the Panel rather than the form itself.

For those control instances created using the Win Forms Designer, VB .NET automatically generates the statements to add the control instances to the correct Controls collection. However, in this chapter you have dynamically created several CheckBox control instances. VB .NET will not automatically add these control instances to the proper Controls collection. Instead, you must write the necessary statements to perform this task. Examine the following statement:

```
Me.pnlSeats.Controls.Add(chkSeats(pintSeatCurrent, _
    pintRowCurrent))
```

The preceding statement will add a check box from the array of check boxes to the Controls collection of the panel named pnlSeats.

To create control instances and event handlers dynamically at runtime:

1. Activate the Code Editor for the form named **frmSeating.vb**. Enter the following statements in the **CreateCheckBox** procedure:

```
chkSeats(pintSeatCurrent, pintRowCurrent) = New CheckBox()
chkSeats(pintSeatCurrent, pintRowCurrent).Visible = True
chkSeats(pintSeatCurrent, pintRowCurrent).Size = _
    New System.Drawing.Size(cintCheckBoxWidth, _
    cintCheckBoxHeight)
chkSeats(pintSeatCurrent, pintRowCurrent).Location = pnt
AddHandler chkSeats(pintSeatCurrent, _
    pintRowCurrent).CheckedChanged, _
    AddressOf chkseats_CheckedChanged
Me.pnlSeats.Controls.Add(chkSeats(pintSeatCurrent, _
    pintRowCurrent))
```

2. Enter the following statements in the **CreateLabel** procedure:

```
lblRow(pintRowCurrent) = New Label()
lblRow(pintRowCurrent).Visible = True
lblRow(pintRowCurrent).Text = _
    (pintRowCurrent + 1).ToString()
Me.pnlSeats.Controls.Add(lblRow(pintRowCurrent))
```

3. Locate the **ConfigureSeating** procedure, and then enter the following statements:

```
Dim pintSeatCurrent, pintRowCurrent As Integer
Select Case AircraftType
    Case "757"
        ReDim chkSeats(cint757Seats, cint757Rows)
        ReDim lblRow(cint757Rows)
        mintEmpty = cint757Seats * cint757Rows
        For pintSeatCurrent = 0 To cint757Seats - 1
            For pintRowCurrent = 0 To cint757Rows - 1
                pntCurrent = New Point(( _
                    pintSeatCurrent + 1) * _
                    cintCheckBoxWidth, _
```

```
                            (pintRowCurrent + 1) * _
                            cintCheckBoxHeight)
                        Call CreateCheckBox(pintSeatCurrent, _
                            pintRowCurrent, pntCurrent)
                    Next
                Next
                For pintRowCurrent = 0 To cint757Rows - 1
                    Call CreateLabel(pintRowCurrent)
                    lblRow(pintRowCurrent).Left = 120
                    lblRow(pintRowCurrent).Top = _
                        (pintRowCurrent + 1) * cintCheckBoxHeight
                    lblRow(pintRowCurrent).Height = 15
                    lblRow(pintRowCurrent).Width = 25
                Next

            Case "777"
                ReDim chkSeats(cint777Seats, cint777Rows)
                ReDim lblRow(cint777Rows)
                mintEmpty = cint777Seats * cint777Rows
                For pintSeatCurrent = 0 To cint777Seats - 1
                    For pintRowCurrent = 0 To cint777Rows - 1
                        pntCurrent = New Point(( _
                            pintSeatCurrent + 1) * _
                            cintCheckBoxWidth, _
                            (pintRowCurrent + 1) * _
                            cintCheckBoxHeight)
                        Call CreateCheckBox(pintSeatCurrent, _
                            pintRowCurrent, pntCurrent)
                    Next
                Next

                For pintRowCurrent = 0 To cint777Rows - 1
                    Call CreateLabel(pintRowCurrent)
                    lblRow(pintRowCurrent).Left = 220
                    lblRow(pintRowCurrent).Top = _
                        (pintRowCurrent + 1) * _
                        cintCheckBoxHeight
                    lblRow(pintRowCurrent).Height = 15
                    lblRow(pintRowCurrent).Width = 25
                Next
        End Select
```

4. Enter the following statements in the **chkSeats_CheckedChanged** procedure:

```
Dim chkCurrent As System.Windows.Forms.CheckBox
chkCurrent = CType(sender, System.Windows.Forms.CheckBox)
Select Case chkCurrent.Checked
    Case True
        mintFull += 1
        mintEmpty -= 1
```

2

```
        Case False
            mintFull -= 1
            mintEmpty += 1
    End Select
    lblFull.Text = mintFull.ToString()
    lblEmpty.Text = mintEmpty.ToString()
```

The preceding statements execute whenever the user checks or unchecks one of the dynamically created check boxes, because this is the procedure you designated as the CheckedChanged event handler with the AddHandler statement. The procedure is simple. The first argument to the procedure is named sender. This argument is converted from the generic System.Object type to a check box. The number of occupied and empty seats are updated as necessary, depending on whether the check box is checked or unchecked, and the results displayed in the corresponding label control instances.

5. Test the solution. Select an airplane type of **777**. Select **Atlanta** as the origin city and **Los Angeles** as the destination city, and enter a flight number of **1422**.

6. On the menu, click **Display**, and then click **Airplane** to display the seating form.

Having dynamically created the CheckBox and Label control instances and added them to the Controls collection for the Panel control instance, you can write a For Each loop to enumerate the Controls collection for the Panel.

Examine the following code segment:

```
Dim ctlCurrent As Control
Dim chkCurrent As System.Windows.Forms.CheckBox
For Each ctlCurrent In pnlSeats.Controls
    If TypeOf (ctlCurrent) Is _
        System.Windows.Forms.CheckBox Then
        chkCurrent = CType(ctlCurrent, _
            System.Windows.Forms.CheckBox)
        chkCurrent.Checked = False
    End If
Next
lblFull.Text = ""
lblEmpty.Text = ""
```

The preceding code segment declares two variables. The first has a data type of Control and the second has a data type of CheckBox. The For Each loop examines the Controls collection for the Panel control instance named pnlSeats. The TypeOf statement checks whether the type of the current control instance is CheckBox. If it is, the control instance is converted to a check box and the Checked property is then set to False. Remember that explicit type conversion is required because the type Control is a less restrictive type than CheckBox.

To enumerate a Controls collection:

1. Activate the Code Editor for the form named **frmSeating.vb**. Enter the following statements in the **Click** event handler for the button named **btnClear**:

```
Dim ctlCurrent As Control
Dim chkCurrent As System.Windows.Forms.CheckBox
For Each ctlCurrent In pnlSeats.Controls
    If TypeOf (ctlCurrent) Is _
        System.Windows.Forms.CheckBox Then
        chkCurrent = CType(ctlCurrent, _
            System.Windows.Forms.CheckBox)
        chkCurrent.Checked = False
    End If
Next
lblFull.Text = ""
lblEmpty.Text = ""
```

2. Test the solution. Select an airplane type, an origin and destination city, and a flight number. Click **Display**, **Airplane** on the main form's menu bar.

3. When the seating form appears, click several of the check boxes. As you do, the number of full and empty seats is updated. Finally, click the **Clear** button on the form. The statements that you just wrote iterate through the Controls collection for the Panel control instance. All the check boxes are unchecked.

You have completed the programming for this chapter. You learned about the windows that make up the IDE and how to create control instances and set their properties. You have also learned how to create control instances and event handlers dynamically.

Chapter Summary

❏ VB .NET supports different types of applications, each designed for a particular purpose. For example, VB .NET supports Windows Applications, Class Libraries, Windows Control Libraries, ASP.NET Web Applications, ASP.NET Web Services, Web Control Libraries, and Console Applications. When you create a solution you define the type of application (project) to create.

❏ A solution file is the heart of every VB .NET application. The solution file contains global configuration options. Additionally, it manages the projects that make up the solution. A solution contains one or more projects. Projects, in turn, contain references to the files that make up the project. The solution file also contains the references to the namespaces used by the project. All these files are text files.

❏ Visual Studio .NET divides windows into two types. Document windows appear on tab groups in the IDE. The Win Forms Designer and Code Editor are document windows. Tool windows work the same way for all Visual Studio .NET applications. Tool windows can be configured to float on the desktop, be docked along an edge

2

of the IDE, or auto hidden. Some tool windows can appear as document windows. The Toolbox, Properties window, and Solution Explorer are all tool windows.

❑ Every form is a class that inherits from System.Windows.Forms.Form. Every form contains code automatically generated by the Win Forms Designer. This code includes a constructor, a destructor, and a procedure named InitializeComponent. This code is automatically generated by the Win Forms Designer as the developer creates the control instances on the form. Note that the code to create the control instances on the form is exposed to the developer and appears in the InitializeComponent procedure. Do not modify the statements generated by the Win Forms Designer.

❑ The process to create and display an instance of a form has changed considerably in VB .NET. Instead of simply calling the Show method for the form name, an instance of the form must first be created by declaring a variable and creating the instance with the New keyword. Then the form can be displayed using the Show or ShowDialog methods. In a multi-form application, if the initial form is unloaded, then the application ends. Thus, a Sub Main procedure in a standard module can be used to display the main form as a modal dialog box to prevent the application from ending.

❑ Controls have been enhanced in VB .NET. All controls are derived from the System.Windows.Forms.Control class. Some properties have changed. For example, the Text property replaces the Caption property for all controls. Additionally, most controls have improved text alignment capabilities. The GroupBox control replaces the Frame control. The ToolTip control is considered a provider control and is new to VB .NET.

❑ The implementation of menus has changed considerably in Visual Studio .NET. The MainMenu control provides the means to create a menu on a form, and replaces the Menu Editor. Menus are edited in place by entering menu titles and menu items directly on the form itself.

❑ Tab order can now be edited in place instead of having to set the TabOrder property using the Properties window.

❑ The syntax of event handlers have changed significantly in VB .NET. Every event has two arguments. The first argument—named sender—contains a reference to the object that generated the event. The second argument—named e—supplies the means by which VB .NET passes information to the event. The data type of this argument varies based on the event. Finally, the name of the procedure for an event handler is no longer significant. In VB .NET, the Handles keyword designates a procedure as an event handler. Furthermore, VB .NET supports multicast event handlers.

❑ VB .NET also supports dynamic event handlers. The AddHandler statement creates an event handler at runtime, while the RemoveHandler statement deletes an event handler created by the AddHandler statement.

❐ Control instances can be created dynamically too. To create a control instance dynamically, declare a variable and then create an instance of the desired control. Finally, configure the control instance by setting the necessary properties, and then add it to the Controls collection of the form or a container control such as a Panel.

❐ The VB .NET Controls collection applies to the form and contains a reference to the control instances created directly on the form. The VB .NET Controls collection is hierarchical, meaning that container controls have their own Controls collection.

REVIEW QUESTIONS

1. Which of the following are valid types of VB .NET applications?

    a. Data application, Desktop application, Library application

    b. Form application, Internet application, Library application

    c. Windows Application, Class Library, Windows Control Library, ASP.NET Web Application, ASP.NET Web Service

    d. Display application, Object library

    e. none of the above

2. Which of the following statements is true of a solution file?

    a. A solution file organizes the elements of an application and can contain one or more projects.

    b. A project file contains at least one solution file. The purpose of this solution file is to deploy an application to another computer.

    c. To compile any and all applications a solution file must be created.

    d. The Solution Editor manages a solution file. The Solution Editor uses key and value pairs and appears to the developer similar to the Properties window.

    e. none of the above

3. Which of the following statements is correct in relation to a project?

    a. VB .NET supports different types of projects.

    b. A Windows Application project typically contains one or more forms.

    c. Project files carry a file suffix of .vbproj.

    d. all of the above

    e. none of the above

4. Which of the following statements is true of the Win Forms Designer?

    a. Invisible control instances appear directly on the form as icons.

    b. As you create control instances on the form the Win Forms Designer automatically generates code to create those control instances at runtime. These statements should not be modified directly.

    c. The Win Forms Designer is considered a tool window.

    d. all of the above

    e. none of the above

5. What is a constructor?

    a. The VB .NET New keyword is considered a constructor.

    b. A constructor is a procedure named New that VB .NET executes to create an instance of a class.

    c. A constructor is a special procedure named Construct that is automatically generated by VB .NET and hidden from the developer. The contents of this procedure cannot be modified by the developer.

    d. VB .NET does not support constructors.

    e. none of the above

6. Which of the following statements is true of the Point and Size structures?

    a. To define the location and position of a control instance on the form, create an instance of the Point and Size structures and assign the instance to the Location and Position properties of the control instance.

    b. The Point and Size structures are commonly used to define the location and position of a control instance on a form.

    c. The Point and Size structures belong to the System.Drawing namespace.

    d. all of the above

    e. VB .NET does not support the Point and Size structures.

7. Which of the following properties apply to the Form class?

    a. Accept, Scroll, Cancel, BorderStyle

    b. EnterButton, EscapeButton, Transparency

    c. AcceptButton, AutoScroll, CancelButton, FormBorderStyle, Opacity

    d. FixedBorder, SizableBorder, ToolBorder

    e. none of the above

8. Which of the following general statements applies to controls?

    a. All controls are ultimately derived from the System.Windows.Forms.Control class.

    b. Buttons, check boxes, and radio buttons derive from the System.Windows.Forms.Buttons class.

    c. The ComboBox and ListBox controls derive from the List class.

    d. The RichTextBox and TextBox controls are editable controls and are derived from the Text class.

    e. none of the above

9. Which of the following statements apply to the CheckBox control?

   a. It can be configured as a two-state or three-state control.

   b. The position of the check box relative to the text is fixed and cannot be changed.

   c. A check box cannot display a graphical icon.

   d. all of the above

   e. none of the above

10. Which of the following statements correctly describes how to create a ToolTip?

   a. Every control instance supports a ToolTip property. The text stored in the ToolTip property will be displayed automatically when the mouse hovers over the control instance for a few seconds.

   b. Create an instance of the ToolTip control on the form. Then, set the ToolTip on *xxxx* property to the text that you want to appear in the ToolTip.

   c. Add a ToolTip file to the project. Then, for each control instance that you want to display a ToolTip, add an entry to the ToolTip file.

   d. Edit the ToolTip property using the Win Forms Designer.

   e. none of the above

11. What a multicast event handler?

   a. It is a special type of event handler used only for the Panel control.

   b. Multicast event handlers are used to change the normal order that Windows fires events.

   c. It is used for buttons, when an instance of the Button control should be designated as either the accept button or the cancel button.

   d. It is an event handler that is designed to handle events for multiple control instances instead of a single control instance.

   e. VB .NET does not support multicast event handlers.

12. Which of the following statements would you use to create and destroy event handlers at runtime?

   a. AddEvent, RemoveEvent

   b. AddHandler, RemoveHandler

   c. CreateEvent, DeleteEvent

   d. Event, RaiseEvent

   e. VB .NET does not allow you to create and destroy event handlers at runtime.

13. Which of the following statements is true of the Controls collection in VB .NET?

   a. A form always has exactly one Controls collection.

   b. A form can have one or more Controls collections. Each control instance that operates as a container control has its own Controls collection.

c. VB .NET no longer supports the Controls collection.

d. all of the above

e. none of the above

14. Describe the difference between document windows and tool windows. Describe the different ways a tool window can appear.

15. Describe the difference between a modal form and a modeless form.

16. Describe the purpose of the Timer control and how to create and configure the Timer control.

17. Describe how to create a menu system for a form and the controls used to create a menu system.

18. List and describe the common arguments to event handlers.

19. What is a multicast event handler?

20. What is the purpose of the TabOrder property? How do you set the TabOrder for control instances?

PROGRAMMING QUESTIONS

1. Write the statement to unload the current form using the Me keyword.

2. Write the statements to declare a local variable named frmNewQuestion having a data type of frmQuestion. The variable declaration should create an instance of the class. Display the form as a modeless form. Assume that the constructor accepts no arguments.

3. Write the statements to declare a local variable named frmNewQuestion having a data type of frmQuestion. The variable declaration should create an instance of the class. Display the form as a modal dialog box. Assume that the constructor accepts an Integer argument. Pass the literal value 1 as the argument to the constructor.

4. Write the statements to add the counting numbers 1 to 100 to the list box named lstNumbers by calling the Add method of the Items collection. Use an Integer variable named pintCount as the loop's counter.

5. Write the statement to remove all the items from the list box named lstNumbers.

6. Declare and initialize an array of strings named pstrStates having values of Arizona, California, and Nevada. Add the contents of this array to the ListBox control instance named lstQuestion.

7. Write the statements to create an instance of the CheckBox control dynamically at runtime. Name the CheckBox control chkQuestion. In addition, write the statement to make the control instance visible, and make its size 80 by 20. Position the control instance so that it appears one inch from the top and left of the form. Store the text "Check Me" in the check box. Add the check box to the Controls collection of the form.

8. Write the statements to create an instance of the Button control dynamically at runtime. Name the Button control instance btnDemo. Make the control instance visible. Make the size of the control instance 50 by 50. Position the control instance so that it appears two inches from the upper-left corner of the form. Add the button to the form's Controls collection. Store the text "Click Me" in the Button.

9. Create a multicast CheckedChanged event handler for a group of radio buttons named rad1, rad2, and rad3. In the event handler, store the name of the selected radio button in the String variable named pstrCurrent.

10. Write the statement to add an event handler dynamically at runtime. Add the Click event for the button named btnQuestion. Assume that the procedure is named ClickDemo.

11. Write the statement to dynamically remove the event handler you created in the preceding question.

12. Write the statement to add the CheckBox control instance named chkCurrent to the Controls collection for the panel named pnlQuestion.

13. Write the statement to add the Button control instance named btnQuestion to the Controls collection of-or-in the form.

14. Write the statements to enumerate the Controls collection for the panel named pnlQuestion. If the type of the control instance is a text box, then remove the text from the Text property.

15. Write the statements to enumerate the Controls collection for the form. If the type of the control instance is a button, then enable the button by setting the Enabled property to True.

HANDS-ON PROJECTS

1. In this project you will create a solution that creates control instances on a form dynamically. The form will resemble a calendar when complete. The file named Chapter.02\Exercises02\Ch02Ex1.exe contains the compiled executable application. Figure 2-20 shows the completed main form for the solution.

   a. Start Visual Studio .NET and create a solution named **Ch02Ex1.sln**.

   b. Add a splash screen to the solution. Create the necessary control instances and write the necessary statements so that the splash screen appears for five seconds, then closes. On the splash screen, display the text Chapter 2 — Project 1 in a Label control instance. The splash screen should have no border and should appear in the center of the desktop. The background color should be light blue.

   c. Add a module named **Startup.vb** to the solution and create a Sub Main procedure in the module. Write the necessary statements in the Sub Main procedure to display the splash screen, and then display the main form as modal dialog boxes.

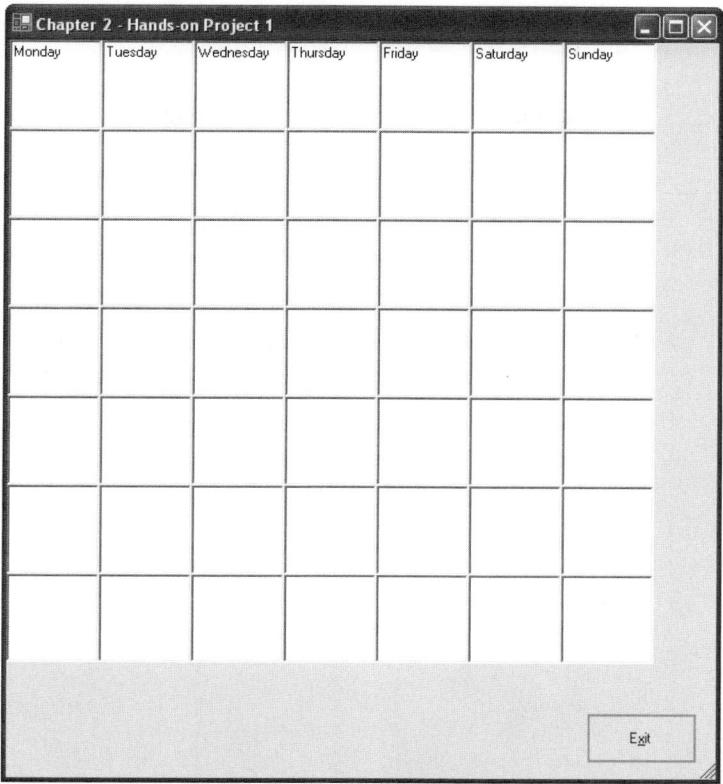

Figure 2-20   Chapter 2 – Hands-on Project 1

    d. Configure the main form so that it is not resizable. The main form should appear in the center of the desktop. Set the text in the title bar as shown in Figure 2-20. Create a Button on the form and designate that button as the AcceptButton. Set the caption to Exit. Write the statements to exit the application.

    e. Write the statements so that when the main form loads, it will dynamically create text boxes on the form to resemble a calendar. Each text box should be 75 by 75 pixels. Store the day of the week in the text boxes appearing on the first row as shown in Figure 2-20. Set the MultiLine property for the text boxes to True. You should create 7 rows and 7 columns of text boxes.

2. In this project you will create a form that displays a seating chart for a small theater. Assume that the theatre has 25 rows, and each row has 10 seats. The file named Chapter.02\Exercises02\Ch02Ex2.exe contains the compiled executable application. Figure 2-21 shows the completed main form for the solution.

Figure 2-21   Chapter 2 – Hands-on Project 2

a. Start Visual Studio .NET and create a solution named **Ch02Ex2.sln**.

b. Add a splash screen to the solution. On the splash screen, display the text Chapter 2 — Project 2. Create a Timer control instance on the splash screen and configure it so that the form will close after it has appeared for seven seconds. Configure the splash screen so that it does not have a border and appears in the center of the desktop when displayed. The background color should be light blue.

c. Add a module named **Startup.vb** to the solution and create a Sub Main procedure. Write the necessary statements to display the splash screen, then display the main form as modal dialog boxes.

2

d. Write the statements so that when the main form loads it will dynamically create the check boxes on the form. The check boxes should be created inside a scrollable Panel control instance. Above the scrollable Panel control instance, display the column number (1 to 10). The seating chart should resemble the seating chart shown in Figure 2-21.

e. Additionally, dynamically create the event handlers for the check boxes so that you can calculate the number of occupied seats and the number of empty seats. Display this information in Label control instances on the form.

f. Create a menu for the form. Create a File menu with an Exit menu item. Create a menu having a caption of Seats. Create a menu item named Clear within the Seats menu that will reset all of the form's dynamically created check boxes so that none of the check boxes are checked.

g. Write the statement for the Exit menu item to close the main form.

3. In this project you will dynamically create a form that a dispatcher may use to schedule deliveries. The main form contains list boxes allowing the dispatcher to specify the number of trucks and the number of deliveries per truck. Using this information, the dispatch form will display a matrix of text boxes. The file named Chapter.02\Exercises02\Ch02Ex3.exe contains the compiled executable application. Figure 2-22 shows the completed main form for the solution.

Figure 2-22   Chapter 2 – Hands-on Project 3

a. Start Visual Studio .NET and create a solution named **Ch02Ex3.sln**.

b. Add a splash screen to the solution. On the splash screen, display the text Chapter 2 — Project 3. Create a Timer control instance on the splash screen and configure it so that the form will close after it has appeared for seven seconds. Configure the splash screen so that it does not have a border and appears in the center of the desktop when displayed. The background color should be light blue.

c. Add a module named **Startup.vb** to the solution and create a Sub Main procedure. Write the necessary statements to display the splash screen, then display the main form as modal dialog boxes.

d. On the main form, create the control instances shown in Figure 2-22. In the Load event handler for the main form, populate the list boxes so that the user can select from between 1 and 10 trucks and between 1 and 20 deliveries per truck.

e. Create a Display Dispatch button on the main form. When the user clicks this button, it will create an instance of the Dispatch form shown in Figure 2-23 passing the number of trucks and the number of deliveries per truck to the form's constructor.

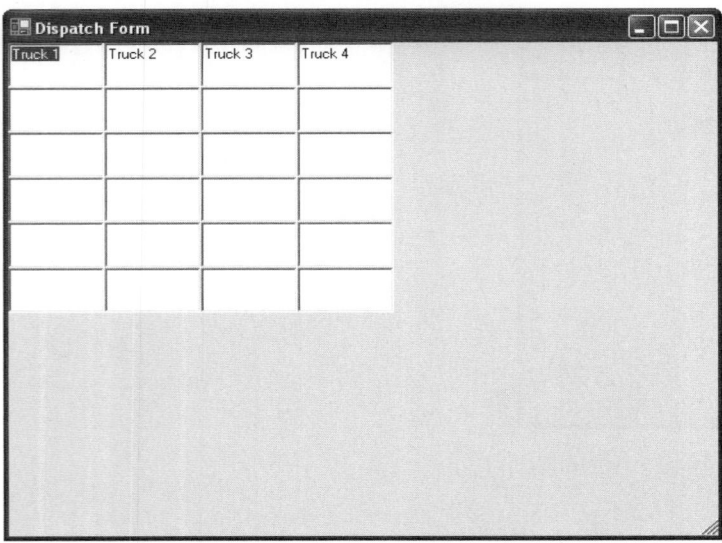

Figure 2-23 Dispatch form

f. Write the necessary statements to create the control instances shown in Figure 2-23 dynamically based on the number of trucks and the number of deliveries selected. Make the size of the control instances 75 by 400.

4. In this project you will create a solution that allows the user to create an electronic invoice. The user will be able to add to the invoice, calculate the invoice totals, and clear the invoice in preparation for another invoice. The file named Chapter.02\Exercises02\Ch02Ex4.exe contains the compiled executable application. Figure 2-24 shows the completed main form for the solution.

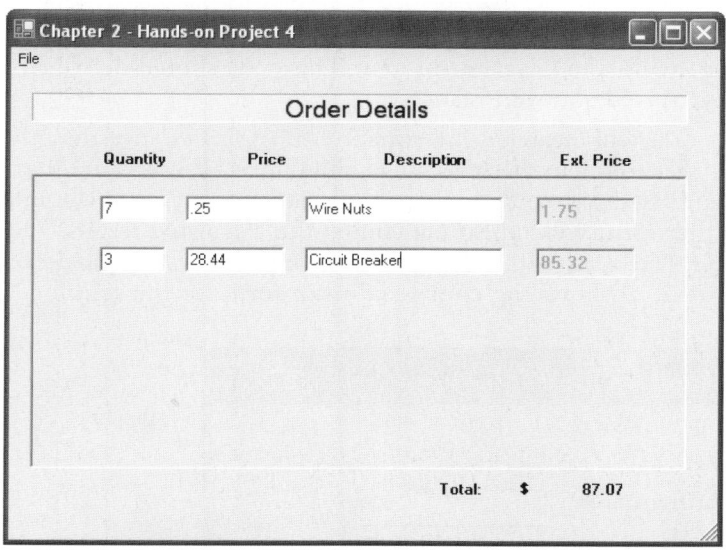

Figure 2-24   Chapter 2 – Hands-on Project 4

a. Start Visual Studio .NET and create a solution named **Ch02Ex4.sln**.

b. Add a splash screen to the solution. Write the necessary statements so that the splash screen appears for five seconds, and then displays the main form. On the splash screen, display the text Chapter 2 — Project 4. Display the text "Invoice Generator" on the splash screen.

c. Add a module to the solution and create a Sub Main procedure. Write the necessary statements to display the splash screen, and then display the main form.

d. On the main form, create a menu. Create a menu title named File, with menu items named Add, Calculate, Clear, and Exit. The Exit menu item should exit the solution. The Add menu item should add a new line to the invoice. The Calculate menu item should calculate the invoice total. The Clear menu item should remove all of the dynamically created control instances.

e. Create the static control instances on the main form as shown in Figure 2-24. These control instances include the Panel and the Label control instances appearing above the Panel. Configure the Panel control instance so that it will display scroll bars when the dynamically allocated control instances will not fit within the region of the Panel.

f. Write the code for the Add menu item to add a new row to the end of the invoice. You will need to create the necessary control instances at runtime and display those control instances at the proper location on the form. If you are storing these control instances in arrays, then you will need to redimension the arrays.

g. Write the code for the Calculate menu item. This code should use the quantity and price to calculate the extended price for each row. The solution should calculate the invoice total.

h. Write the code for the Clear menu item. This code should delete all of the dynamically created control instances.

5. In this project, you will create an investment estimator. The investment estimator will allow the user to select the investment time horizon, compounding period, interest rate, and fixed payments applied to the investment. From the information provided, another form will appear containing the calculated results. The file named Chapter.02\Exercises02\Ch02Ex5.exe contains the compiled executable program. Figure 2-25 shows the completed main form for the solution.

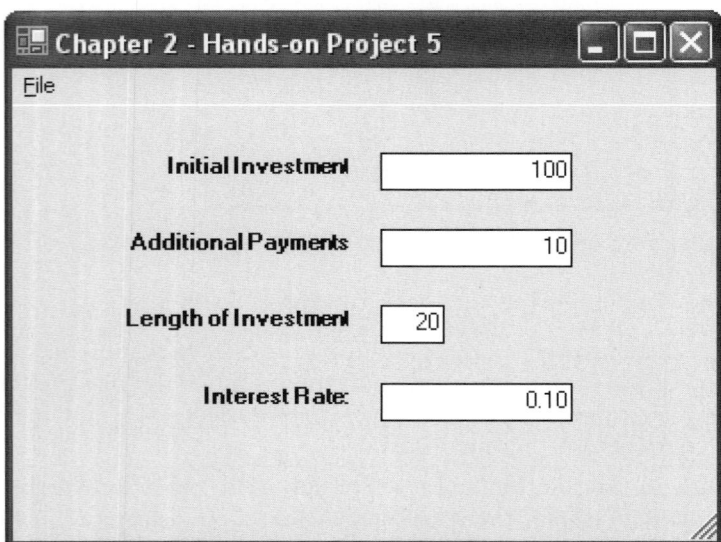

Figure 2-25   Chapter 2 – Hands-on Project 5

a. Start Visual Studio .NET and create a solution named **Ch02Ex5.sln**.

b. Add a splash screen to the solution. Write the necessary statements so that the splash screen appears for five seconds, and then displays the main form. On the splash screen, display the text Chapter 2 — Project 5. Additionally, display the text "Investment Estimator" on the splash screen.

c. Add a module to the solution and create a Sub Main procedure. Write the necessary statements to display the splash screen, and then display the main form.

2

   d. Create the control instances on the main form as shown in Figure 2–25.

   e. Create a File menu on the main form with menu items named Calculate and Exit.

   f. When the user clicks the Calculate menu item your application should display another form containing an amortization schedule, as shown in Figure 2–26.

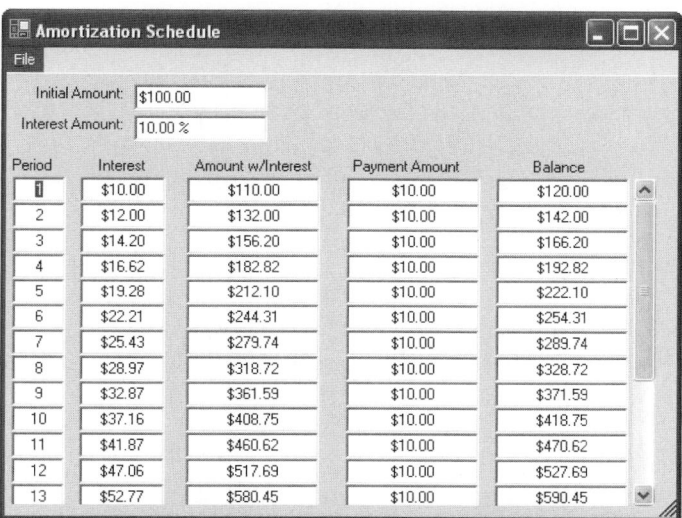

Figure 2-26   Amortization schedule

   g. Use the following guidelines to create the amortization schedule. You will need to calculate the interest for each period and display those calculations. Multiply the interest rate by the current balance to determine the interest for the period. Add the amount of the regular payment to that value, and then add that total to the current balance to determine the balance at the end of the period. This value becomes the starting balance for the next period.

CHAPTER

3

DESKTOP APPLICATIONS: CORE SYNTAX CONCEPTS

In this chapter, you will:

♦ Learn the basics of component programming
♦ Control visibility with access modifiers
♦ Organize components into namespaces
♦ Use enumerations to improve code readability
♦ Organize data using structures
♦ Work with module blocks
♦ Work with classes
♦ Create constructors for classes
♦ Work with shared data and shared methods

In Chapters 1 and 2, you saw how to create a Console application and a Windows application. In addition, you learned about the basic concepts of an assembly and how an assembly contains one or more namespaces. This chapter explains more fully how to create namespaces and how to organize namespaces. It also explains the contents of a namespace, including enumerations, structures, classes, and modules. It also more fully explains the scope and lifetime of variables. Shared and instance methods are also discussed.

The classes created in this chapter are simplified and do not exploit all of the OOP features supplied by VB .NET. Chapter 4 further expands upon the concepts presented in this chapter.

Previewing the Completed Solution

The completed solution presented in this chapter illustrates many of the new object-oriented syntax elements that Microsoft has added to make VB .NET a full featured object-oriented programming language. The completed solution contains two namespaces. One namespace, named Shipping, contains a class named ShippingCost used to calculate the cost to ship a package. The Shipping namespace also contains a structure named CostDetail containing all of the cost information applicable to a particular shipment. Another namespace named Validate contains a subordinate class named ValidatePostalInfo. In addition, it contains subordinate namespaces named ValidateStrings and ValidateNumbers. These two namespaces, in turn, contain modules used to perform general input validation. These namespaces and their classes are used by the forms to validate user input and calculate the cost of a shipment. Figure 3-1 illustrates the design and organization of the solution.

To preview the completed solution:

1. Start Visual Studio .NET and open the solution file named **Chapter03\ Complete03\Complete03.sln**.

   Examine the Solution Explorer. In addition to containing forms and a module (Startup.vb), the solution contains two additional modules named Shipping.vb and Validate.vb. These two modules contain the additional namespaces and classes used by the forms. As with all projects, the module named AssemblyInfo.vb contains information about the assembly itself.

2. Run the solution. A splash screen appears, and then the login form appears.

3. Enter your first and last name in the login form, as shown in Figure 3-2, and then click **OK** to display the main form. Note that you must enter data in both text boxes to proceed to the main form.

3

Main form	Shipping (namespace)
Calls members of ShippingCost to create and calculate the cost of a shipment	**CostDetail (structure)** Stores members related to the cost of a shipment
Calls members of Validate namespace to validate string and numeric input	**ShippingCost (class)** Contains properties and methods to calculate the cost of a shipment

Login form	Validate (namespace)
Calls members of Validate namespace to validate string input	**ValidatePostalCode (class)** Validates postal codes for correctness
	ValidateStrings (namespace) Contains methods to validate string data for correctness
	ValidateNumbers (namespace) Contains methods to validate numeric data for correctness

Figure 3-1   Solution design

Figure 3-2   Completed solution – login form

4. Enter the information shown in Figure 3-3.

Figure 3-3   Completed solution – main form

5. Click the **Ship To Australia** button.

Figure 3-4 shows the main form with the calculated output.

Figure 3-4   Completed solution – main form output

6. End the solution and exit Visual Studio .NET.

AN INTRODUCTION TO COMPONENT PROGRAMMING

In Chapter 2, you used predefined .NET Framework components, including controls, to create an application. In VB .NET, you can create your own classes, called components, designed for use by other developers. Defined simply, building a **component** involves nothing more than building a black box. The developer using the black box does not need to know how the black box works to use it. Think of a garage door remote control as a simple black box. You click the button and the garage door goes up. Click it again, and the garage door goes down. You don't need to know exactly how the garage door opener works to use it.

Defined formally, a component is a .NET type, such as a class, that exposes one or more members (properties, methods, etc.) so as to hide the details necessary to perform a complex or repetitive task. For example, consider the task of validating common input formats for telephone numbers and Social Security numbers. You could create a component (class) with members (methods) named IsValidTelephoneNumber, and IsValidSocialSecurityNumber. Each method would accept one argument, the input value to be tested, and return True or False depending on whether the input was valid. After the component has been created, many developers can use that component to validate these common input fields. Thus, the developer views the component as a black box.

When creating and using components, you must keep in mind the following two terms:

- The person creating a reusable component is called the **author**.

- The person who writes an application that uses a component created by the author is called the **developer**.

In this chapter, you will assume the roles of both author and developer. When you create the components to perform input validation and calculate the cost of a shipment, you will assume the role of the author. When you write the code in the forms that call upon the services supplied by the components, you will assume the role of the developer.

The Implementation and Interface of a Component

A component has a well-defined interface by which it communicates with other applications. The data and processes acting on that data that are accessible to other components constitute a component's **interface**. The coupling of data with the processes acting on that data is referred to as **encapsulation**. In .NET terms, the properties (data) and methods (processes) are encapsulated together, thereby forming the component's interface. The interface of a component is commonly called the **exposed part** or the **public part** of the component.

In addition to a public or exposed part, every component has a **private part**, known as the hidden part. The **hidden part** of a component is not visible to the applications that use the component. The term **implementation** refers to the hidden part of the component. It does not matter how the hidden part of a component performs its tasks, as long as the exposed part (interface) does not change. The reason is simple. To illustrate, consider a text box. So long as the properties, events, and methods of a text box do not change, it does not matter how the text box is implemented. Any application using that text box will continue to work correctly, regardless of the changes made to the implementation.

The Design and Organization of Components

The rules for organizing and designing components are not absolute. Subjective decisions are often made about which members to expose in the interface and which members to hide in the implementation. Additionally, components often interact with each other so you must decide which members to place in which component. For example, in this chapter we have separated the Shipping component from the Validate component. Although the Shipping and Validate components could have been combined together, other components could utilize the interface of the Validate component for purposes other than calculating the cost of a shipment. In general, a component should be designed to perform one or more related tasks.

Benefits of Component-Based Programming

Component-based programming has many benefits as described in the following list:

- Programmer productivity improves because complex tasks can be performed without the developer having to worry about how the component performs a particular task. For example, consider the intrinsic TextBox control as a component. You, as a developer, can create text boxes, set their properties, and handle text box events without knowing anything about the internal workings of a text box.

- Because a component performs a standard and well-defined set of tasks, multiple applications can use the same component. For example, every Windows application that you create can utilize the services supplied by the TextBox control, thereby improving productivity.

- The internal workings of a component (implementation) can be changed as long as the interface (the component's properties, methods, and events) remains constant. Thus, the developer responsible for maintaining a component can modify its implementation to improve performance without disturbing the component's interface as viewed by other developers.

CONTROLLING VISIBILITY WITH ACCESS MODIFIERS

The **visibility** of a variable or procedure determines which classes and modules, and possibly other assemblies, can reference the variable or procedure. The visibility of a variable or procedure is controlled by keywords called **access modifiers**. Which access modifier you use to declare a variable or procedure determines if that variable or procedure will be part of a component's interface or implementation, as described in the following list:

- Any class or module in a project (assembly) can reference variables or procedures declared with the **Public** keyword. In addition, Public members are accessible to other assemblies. Thus, members declared with the Public keyword have no access restrictions. Public members are part of a component's interface rather than part of the component's implementation.

- Only the class containing the declaration can access members declared with the **Private** keyword. Thus, Private members are part of a component's implementation rather than part of the component's interface.

- **Friend** variables and procedures are something of a hybrid between Public and Private variables. All of the modules in a project (assembly) can access Friend variables and procedures, but classes outside the assembly containing the declaration cannot access them. Friend variables are commonly used when two components are coupled together.

- **Static** variables must be declared at the procedure level (within a procedure). Only the procedure containing the declaration can access a Static variable, so it is part of a component's implementation. The value of a Static variable persists from one procedure call to the next.

- **Protected** variables can be declared only at the class level. They cannot be declared at the namespace or module level. Protected variables are accessible from the class containing the declaration and any derived classes. Chapter 4 explains Protected variables further.

- **Protected Friend** variables can be used throughout the assembly containing the declaration. In addition, derived classes can also access Protected Friend variables. Chapter 4 explains Protected Friend variables, derived classes, and inheritance further.

- Declaring a variable with the **Dim** keyword inside of a procedure creates a local variable. Local variables are part of a component's implementation.

- The **Shared** keyword indicates that a variable's data is shared between all instances of the class or structure.

- Shadowing occurs when a variable in a derived class hides a variable in a base class. The **Shadows** keyword shadows a variable.

As you work through this chapter, you will use these access modifiers to declare variables and define the accessibility of procedures. The naming convention used for variables will vary based on the access modifier. Hidden variables declared with the Private keyword will appear in **Hungarian notation**, that is, the variable name will carry a prefix denoting the variable's data type and the accessibility of the variable. For example, the following code segment illustrates two variables declared using Hungarian notation:

```
Private mintIDCurrent As Integer
Private mstrPostalCode As String
```

The first character in the preceding declaration denotes module-level access. The following three characters denote the data type of the variable. The prefix "int" denotes Integer and the prefix "str" denotes String. This book will also use prefixes of "bln" to denote Boolean, "sng" to denote Single, "dbl" to denote Double, and "lng" to denote Long.

Exposed variables and all procedure names will appear in **camel case**, meaning, exposed variables and procedure names will consist of whole words, and the first character of each word will be capitalized. Microsoft recommends using camel case for all exposed properties and methods. The following variable names appear in camel case:

```
Public VatCost As Double
Public TariffCost As Double
```

Not everyone agrees on the naming conventions for variables. Even though Microsoft pioneered Hungarian notation, Microsoft is now discouraging its use. Whatever naming convention you choose for variables, be consistent.

ORGANIZING COMPONENTS INTO NAMESPACES

In Chapters 1 and 2, you used a few of the namespaces defined by the .NET Framework class library. The System namespace is considered the root namespace for the .NET Framework class library, and the Microsoft.VisualBasic namespace contains those types unique to VB .NET. Remember that the namespaces comprising the .NET Framework class library are organized hierarchically based on their purpose. Namespaces that you create should be organized hierarchically based on their purpose too.

Microsoft recommends that namespaces be named in the format *companyname.technologyname*.

Every project that you create forms an assembly and contains a root namespace. That root namespace may, in turn, contain other namespaces. Using the Project Property Pages dialog box shown in Figure 3-5, you specify the assembly name and the name of the root namespace.

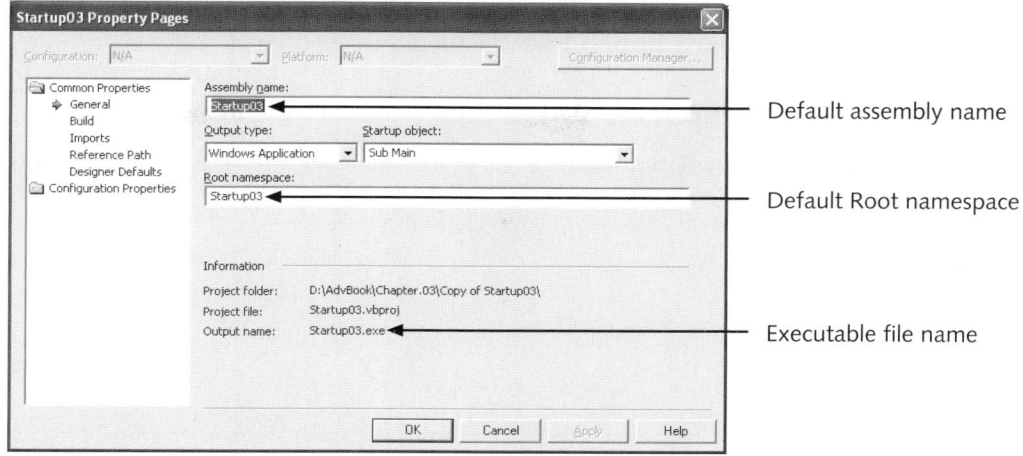

Figure 3-5   Project Property Pages dialog box

By default, the name of the assembly is the same as the project name having a suffix of .exe or .dll, depending on the type of project. (Recall that Windows Application projects are compiled to .exe files and Class Library projects are compiled to .dll files.) By default, the name of the root namespace is the same as the project name.

VB .NET will not allow you to change the name of the root namespace for a project while any of the forms are open.

To define the assembly name and the name of the root namespace:

1. Start Visual Studio .NET, and then open the solution file named **Chapter.03\ Startup03\Startup03.sln**.

2. Make sure that the Win Forms Designer and Code Editor are closed for all of the forms in the solution. Remember, to close a document window, select the document window and then click the **Close** button on the **Group** tab.

3. Activate the Solution Explorer, if necessary, and then right-click the **Startup03** project. Make sure to click the project rather than the solution. Click **Properties** to activate the Property Pages.

   Note that the default name for the assembly and root namespace is the same as the project name.

4. Set the Assembly name to **ShippingManager**.

5. Set the Root namespace to **Course**, and then click **OK**.

As you have seen, namespaces of the .NET Framework class library are organized hierarchically based on their purpose. For example, the System namespace contains another namespace named Drawing, thus, we say the System.Drawing namespace. The namespaces that you create should be organized hierarchically too, based on their purpose.

Declaring Namespaces

The Namespace statement appears in a module file and defines a namespace that will become part of the root namespace. A namespace is marked by the Namespace and End Namespace statements having the following syntax:

Syntax

Namespace { *name* | *name.name* }
   [*componenttypes*]
End Namespace

Definition

The **Namespace** and **End Namespace** statements define a namespace block. A module file can contain multiple namespace blocks, and one namespace block can contain another namespace block, meaning, namespaces can be nested.

Dissection

- The Namespace statement marks the beginning of the namespace block. The End Namespace statement marks the end of the namespace block.

- The *name* argument defines the unique namespace name. The name must be a valid identifier. Use camel case for namespace names.

- Between the Namespace and End Namespace statements appear the types that comprise the namespace. These types include enumerations, structures, classes, and modules, among others.

Code Example

```
Namespace Validate
    ' componenttypes
End Namespace
```

Code Discussion

The preceding statement block declares a namespace named Validate.

Namespaces are open ended. In other words, one namespace can be divided into different module files. For example, you may create multiple classes that belong to the same namespace. To keep the project organized, you may want to create each class such that it appears in its own physical file. Figure 3-6 shows how one namespace can be split into multiple files.

Figure 3-6   Splitting a namespace into multiple files

As shown in Figure 3-6, the Shipping namespace contains a class and a structure stored in two physical files. The first file contains the structure named CostDetail, and the second file contains the class named ShippingCost.

 Note that a class or module block cannot be divided into multiple physical files.

Within a namespace you can create nested namespaces. For example, you may want to divide a namespace named Validate into two namespaces, one to validate numbers and another to validate strings. The following code segment illustrates how namespaces can be organized hierarchically based on their purpose. The Validate namespace contains a class named ValidatePostalInfo. In addition, it contains two namespaces named ValidateStrings and ValidateNumbers. These namespaces, in turn, can contain classes, modules, and structures, which, in turn, will validate user input.

```
Namespace Validate
    Public Class ValidatePostalInfo

    End Class
    Namespace ValidateStrings
        ' Classes, modules, and structures
    End Namespace
```

```
      Namespace ValidateNumbers
          ' Classes, modules, and structures
      End Namespace
End Namespace
```

In this chapter's project, you will define a namespace named Validate containing classes and methods to validate user input.

To create a namespace:

1. Create a new module in the project by clicking **Project**, and then clicking **Add Module** on the Visual Studio .NET menu bar. In the Add New Item dialog box, enter the name **Validate.vb**, and then click **Open** to create the module.

2. Remove all of the existing statements in the module and then enter the following statements:

```
Option Explicit On
Option Strict On
Namespace Validate
    Namespace ValidateStrings

    End Namespace
    Namespace ValidateNumbers

    End Namespace
End Namespace
```

3. Create a second new module in the project by clicking **Project**, and then clicking **Add Module** on the Visual Studio .NET menu bar. In the Add New Item dialog box, enter the name **Shipping.vb**, and then click **Open** to create the module.

4. Remove all of the existing statements in the module and then enter the following statements:

```
Option Explicit On
Option Strict On
Namespace Shipping

End Namespace
```

As you can see, a single assembly can contain any number of namespaces, and these namespaces may or may not be organized hierarchically. Figure 3-7 illustrates the organization of the namespaces in the ShippingManager project.

As shown in Figure 3-7, ShippingManager is the root namespace. The root namespace, in turn, contains the Validate and Shipping namespaces. The Validate namespace, in turn, contains namespaces named ValidateNumbers and ValidateStrings. There is no limit to the depth of the namespace hierarchy.

Figure 3-7   Namespace organization

Namespace references can get quite long, so the statements to reference a particular namespace, its classes, and the methods in those classes can become quite long too. For example, you will find yourself frequently calling the methods of the System.Convert class to convert variables from one data type to another, or using the members of the System.Windows.Forms.Form class. Fortunately, VB .NET provides a shorthand notation for referencing the members of a namespace, class, or other types. We discuss that topic next.

Importing Namespaces

The **Imports** statement allows you to reference the members of a particular namespace or class without fully qualifying the namespace or class name. The Imports statement does not, however, make an assembly and its namespace(s) available for use in a project. You use the Add Reference dialog box for that purpose. The Imports statement has the following syntax:

Syntax

Imports [*aliasname* =] *namespace* [*.element*]

Definition

When using the Imports statement, you can call a method or reference a class without including the namespace name. The Imports statement must appear in a module file before any declaration statements and after the Option Explicit and Option Strict statements. That is, it must appear in a module file before any Namespace, Class, or Module blocks. A module file may contain any number of Imports statements. In addition to importing namespaces, you can import other types such as classes.

Dissection

- The optional *aliasname* argument defines an alias for the namespace being imported. The *aliasname* argument is useful when two classes in different namespaces have the same member names. When the *aliasname* argument is specified, it must be used to reference the components belonging to the imported namespace. The *aliasname* can be any valid identifier.

- The *namespace* argument contains the name of the namespace, or other type, to be imported. The name must be fully qualified. That is, you must specify the namespace name beginning with the root namespace.

- The optional *element* argument contains a class, structure, or other member name to be imported.

Code Example

```
Imports System.Windows.Forms
Imports System.Convert
```

Code Dissection

The first of the preceding statements imports the System.Windows.Forms namespace, while the second statement imports the System.Convert class.

After a namespace or class has been imported, you can reference its components without qualification. For example, the following statements will call the ToInt32 method of the System.Convert class. The first statement uses the fully qualified name of the System.Convert class, and the second does not.

```
Dim pstrDemo As String = "123.45"
Dim pintDemo As Integer

' The following two statements are equivalent.
pintDemo = System.Convert.ToInt32(pstrDemo)
pintDemo = ToInt32(pstrDemo)

' The following two statements are also equivalent.
Dim txtCurrent As New System.Windows.Forms.TextBox()
Dim txtCurrent As New TextBox()
```

To illustrate how to apply an alias with the Imports statement, examine the following statement to import the System.Convert class:

```
Imports Conv = System.Convert
```

The preceding statement uses an alias named Conv for the System.Convert class. Thus, to call the ToInt32 method of the System.Convert class using the Conv alias, you would write the following statements:

```
Dim pstrDemo As String = "123.45"
Dim pintDemo As Integer
pintDemo = Conv.ToInt32(pstrDemo)
```

> The decision to import a namespace is subjective. You should import a namespace when several statements reference the members of that namespace. Defining an alias with the Imports statement can be helpful when two imported classes share members having the same name.

A final point needs to be made about importing namespaces. The Imports statement requires fully qualified namespace references. The following statements will import the System.Drawing and System.Drawing.Drawing2D namespaces:

```
Imports System.Drawing
Imports System.Drawing.Drawing2D
```

However, the following statement to import the System.Drawing.Drawing2D namespace will not work. That is, the second statement will cause an error because the Drawing2D namespace must be fully qualified.

```
Imports System.Drawing
Imports Drawing2D
```

In this chapter's solution, you will import the .NET Framework namespaces used most commonly. In addition, you will import the Shipping and Validate namespaces that you created. There is no difference between the steps to import a .NET Framework namespace and the steps to import a namespace that you create.

To import a namespace:

1. Activate the Code Editor for the module file named **Validate.vb**, and then enter the following Imports statement (shown in bold) immediately after the Option Strict On statement:

```
Option Strict On
Imports System.Convert
Namespace Validate
```

2. Activate the Code Editor for the form named **frmMain.vb**, and then enter the following Imports statements (shown in bold) to import the Shipping and Validate namespaces:

```
Option Strict On
Imports Course.Shipping
Imports Course.Validate
Public Class frmMain
```

3. Activate the Code Editor for the form named **frmLogin.vb**, and then enter the following Imports statement (shown in bold) to import the Validate namespace:

```
Option Strict On
Imports Course.Validate
Public Class frmLogin
```

4. Activate the Code Editor for the module named **Shipping.vb**, and then enter the following Imports statement (shown in bold) to import the ControlChars class:

```
Option Strict On
Imports Microsoft.VisualBasic.ControlChars
Namespace Shipping
```

Namespaces contain types, such as classes, structures, enumerations, and module blocks. Note that you cannot create a procedure directly in a namespace, nor can you declare a variable directly in a namespace. Procedure and variable declarations must appear in a module, class, or structure declaration.

IMPROVING CODE READABILITY USING ENUMERATIONS

Enumerations are value types that inherit from the System.Enum class. Their purpose is to supply mnemonic (descriptive) names to a group of constant values. Enumerations are more restrictive than classes and structures as they cannot have properties or methods and cannot handle events. An enumeration can appear within a namespace block, a class or structure block, or a module. An enumeration cannot be declared inside of a procedure, however. Enumerations have the following syntax:

Syntax

[**Public** | **Private** | **Friend**] **Enum** *name* [**As** *type*]
   membername [= *initexpr*]
    . . .
End Enum

Definition

The **Enum** and **End Enum** statements mark the beginning and end of an enumeration block.

Dissection

- The **Public**, **Private**, and **Friend** keywords are used as access modifiers to define the accessibility of the enumeration.

- The *name* argument defines the name of the enumeration and must be a valid identifier.

- The **As** *type* clause for an enumeration is new to VB .NET. By default, an enumeration has a data type of Integer if the As *type* clause is omitted. Other possible types are Byte, Short, or Long.

- The *membername* lines define the members that comprise the enumeration. An enumeration must have at least one member name although most enumerations have several members. A constant is more suitable than declaring an enumeration with only one member.

- By default, member numbering begins at 0, and subsequent members are numbered sequentially. The *initexpr* argument changes the default numbering of member names.

Code Example

```
Public Enum ShipType
    Ground
    TwoDay
    NextDay
End Enum
```

Code Dissection

The preceding code segment declares a Public enumeration named ShipType having members named Ground, TwoDay, and NextDay. Ground has a value of 0, TwoDay has a value of 1, and NextDay has a value of 2.

You can change the starting enumeration value and the data type, as shown in the following enumeration block:

```
Public Enum MonthsOfYear As Byte
    January = 1
    February = 2
    . . .
    December = 12
End Enum
```

The preceding enumeration named MonthsOfYear begins member numbering at 1 instead of 0. Each member is numbered sequentially. In addition, the data type is Byte because the range of values is less than 255. Using a one-based enumeration is logical in this case, as the month of January is typically associated with a value of 1 instead of 0.

 Microsoft recommends that you create enumerations with a starting value of 0. This way, an enumeration variable that has not been initialized will have a valid value.

Enumeration values need not be consecutive or unique. For example, the following example, albeit abbreviated, shows how to declare an enumeration for the number of days in each month of the year:

```
Public Enum DaysInMonth
    January = 31
    February = 28
```

```
      March = 31
      April = 30
      . . .
      December = 31
End Enum
```

After declaring an enumeration type, you typically declare variables of that enumeration type, just as you declare any other variable, as shown in the following statements:

```
Public CurrentType As ShipType
Public CurrentType As ShipType = ShipType.Ground
```

The first of the preceding statements declares a variable named CurrentType having a data type of ShipType (an enumeration). The second statement illustrates how to use an initializer when declaring an enumerated variable. The syntax is the same as the syntax to initialize any other variable. After declaring a variable having an enumerated type, you can then store values in that enumerated variable. The following statements store a shipment type in the variable CurrentType:

```
CurrentType = ShipType.Ground
CurrentType = ShipType.TwoDay
```

VB .NET applies different rules for the data that you can store in an enumeration variable, depending on whether strict type checking is enabled (Option Strict). If strict type checking is enabled, then the data type of the enumeration and the data type of the value stored in the enumeration must be the same. If strict type checking is disabled, Integer values can be stored in the enumeration. Thus, the following statement will produce a syntax error if strict type checking is enabled. If strict type checking is disabled, the following statement is legal:

```
CurrentType = 2
```

The **CType** function will explicitly convert one data type to another when strict type checking is enabled. The following statement will convert the Integer value 2 to a data type of ShipType:

```
CurrentType = CType(2, ShipType)
```

In this chapter, you will declare an enumeration to define the valid shipping types. The valid enumeration values are Ground, TwoDay, and NextDay. As the enumeration is declared with the Public access modifier, any assembly will be able to use the enumeration.

To declare an enumeration:

1. Activate the Code Editor for the module named **Shipping.vb**, if necessary, and then enter the following statements (shown in bold), immediately after the Namespace statement:

```
Namespace Shipping
    Public Enum ShipType
        Ground = 1
        TwoDay = 2
```

```
        NextDay = 3
    End Enum
End Namespace
```

Later in the chapter you will declare variables and use this enumeration to define a shipment type.

In addition to creating enumerations in a namespace, a namespace can also contain any number of structure blocks. We discuss structures next.

STRUCTURES

Structures provide the means to group related data together. Structures support Public, Private, and Friend members. A structure can also have exposed and hidden methods. That is, you can create function and sub procedures in a structure with an access modifier. Syntactically, a structure declaration can appear in a namespace, in a class, or in a module. Structure declarations cannot appear inside of a procedure, however. Structures can also be nested. That is, one structure block can contain another structure block. In addition, a structure can have members that are themselves structures. Structures are value types. When you declare a variable having a structure data type, VB .NET automatically creates an instance of the structure even if the New keyword does not appear in the declaration.

A structure has the following syntax:

Syntax

[**Public** | **Private** | **Friend**] **Structure** *name*
   variabledeclarations
   proceduredeclarations
End Structure

Definition

- The **Structure** and **End Structure** keywords mark the beginning and end of the structure block, respectively.

Dissection

- The **Public**, **Private**, and **Friend** access modifiers define the accessibility of the structure to classes, modules, and other types. For example, a Public structure is accessible to any class or other assembly, just as a Public variable is globally accessible. If an access modifier is not specified, then the default accessibility for the structure is Friend.

- The *name* argument defines the name of the structure, and must be a valid identifier name. Use camel case for structure names.

- *variabledeclarations* allow you to declare the members that are part of the structure. The Public, Private, and Friend access modifiers allow you to control the accessibility of each structure member. For example, only the other members of the structure can reference a member declared with Private access, even though the structure itself may be declared with Public access. Note that an access modifier must precede each member declaration. Structure members can also contain initializers, but those initializers must contain constant values. A structure must also contain at least one member with Public accessibility.

- *proceduredeclarations* are function or sub procedures that are part of a structure. A structure can contain any number of procedures, and procedures can be declared with different access modifiers.

Code Example

```
Public Structure DataEntry
    Public FirstName As String
    Public LastName As String
    Public DataEntryTime As DateTime

    Public Function FullName() As String
        Return FirstName & " " & LastName
    End Function
End Structure
```

Code Discussion

The preceding structure contains three members named FirstName, LastName, and DataEntryTime, each having Public access. The Public method FullName returns the first and last names concatenated together. A space separates the first and last names.

The following code segment illustrates a nested structure declaration. The Employee structure contains another structure named Dates having members named DateHired and DateTerminated.

```
Public Structure Employee
    Public ID As Integer
    Public Name As String
    Public Structure Dates
        Public DateHired As DateTime
        Public DateTerminated As DateTime
    End Structure
End Structure
```

In addition to nested structures, structures can have members that are themselves structures, as shown in the following statements:

```
Public Structure Person
    Public FirstName As String
    Public LastName As String
End Structure
```

```
Public Structure Employee
    Public EmployeeName As Person
    Public Wage As Single
End Structure

Public Structure Customer
    Public CustomerName As Person
    Public BalanceDue As Single
End Structure
```

The preceding statements declared a structure named Person. The Employee and Customer structures, in turn, have members named EmployeeName and CustomerName, respectively. The data type of these members is Person.

After you have declared a structure, you can declare variables that have the structure as their data type, as shown in the following statement:

```
Dim CurrentUser As Course.DataEntry
```

The preceding statement declares a variable named CurrentUser having a data type of DataEntry. However, because VB .NET automatically creates an instance of the structure, the following statements are equivalent to the preceding statement:

```
Dim CurrentUser As New DataEntry()
Dim CurrentUser As DataEntry = New DataEntry()
```

After you have declared a structure variable, you store and retrieve values from its members using *object.property* syntax, as shown in the following statements:

```
CurrentUser.FirstName = "Mary"
CurrentUser.LastName = "Jones"
```

Some final notes should be made about structures. Structures cannot be inherited. Thus, the Inherits statement cannot appear inside of a structure block. Structures can contain arrays, however, those arrays must be declared with no initial size.

You will now declare the structure used to store the information about the clerk who performed the data entry for a shipment.

To declare a structure:

1. Activate the Code Editor for the module named **Startup.vb**.

2. Enter the following statements (shown in bold), immediately after the Option Strict statement:

```
Option Strict On

Public Structure DataEntry

    Public FirstName As String
    Public LastName As String
    Public DataEntryTime As DateTime
```

```
    Public Function FullName() As String
        Return FirstName & " " & LastName
    End Function

End Structure
Module Startup
```

Next, you need to declare a variable to store the clerk's information. The clerk will specify this information in the login form. However, other forms in the application will use the information. Therefore, you will declare the variable in a Public module that is shared by all of the other modules in the application.

3. Enter the following statement (shown in bold) in the Startup module:

```
Module Startup
    Public CurrentUser As Course.DataEntry
    Public Sub Main()
        'Statements
    End Sub
End Module
```

Having declared the CurrentUser variable, you can now store the user information into the variable when the user closes the login form.

4. Activate the Code Editor for the form named **frmLogin.vb**, and then enter the following statements in the **Click** event handler for the button named **btnOK**. These statements will copy the data out of the text boxes into the structure variable, and then close the form.

```
CurrentUser.FirstName = txtFirstName.Text
CurrentUser.LastName = txtLastName.Text
CurrentUser.DataEntryTime = System.DateTime.Now
Me.Close()
```

The current user will appear on the title bar of the main form. Thus, you will set the Text property of the main form as it loads so that the current user will appear.

5. Activate the Code Editor for **frmMain.vb**, and then enter the following statement in the **frmMain_Load** event handler for the form:

```
Me.Text = Me.Text & " - " & CurrentUser.FullName
```

6. Test the solution. Enter your name in the login form. When the main form appears, your name appears in the title bar of the main form.

The Shipping namespace will also contain a structure named CostDetail to store all of the costs related to a shipment. These costs include the value added cost, the tariff cost, the actual shipping cost, and the total cost.

To create a structure in a namespace:

1. Activate the Code Editor for the module named **Shipping.vb**.

2. Enter the following statements (shown in bold) immediately after the enumeration that you declared previously:

```
End Enum
Public Structure CostDetail
    Public VatCost As Double
    Public TariffCost As Double
    Public ShippingCost As Double
    Public TotalCost As Double
End Structure
```

Again, you will use the CostDetail structure later in the chapter, when you calculate the cost of a shipment.

In addition to enumerations and structures, a namespace can also contain one or more module blocks. We discuss them next.

MODULE BLOCKS

In Chapter 2, you defined a module and a sub procedure in that module named Main that executed when the application started. Note that the application in this chapter works the same way. The module named Startup.vb already contains a procedure named Main to display the forms in the application. First the splash screen is displayed, then the login form, and then the main form.

In addition to a Sub Main procedure, modules can contain additional procedures and variable declarations. Modules are similar to classes in that both are reference types. However, you do not create an instance of a module as you create an instance of a class. Rather, the data for a module exists while a project runs. All of the variables declared in a module are shared. That is, one copy of the data exists for all of the variables declared in a module. In addition, you do not create an instance of a module so as to call its methods.

You define a new module by declaring a block with the Module and End Module statements, having the following syntax:

Syntax

[Public | Friend] Module *name*
    [*statements*]
End Module

Definition

The **Module** and **End Module** statements form a block. A physical file can contain any number of module blocks. One or more module blocks can appear inside of a namespace block. If a module block does not appear inside of a namespace block, then that module will belong to the project's root namespace. Module blocks cannot be nested. That is, one module block cannot contain another module block. Module blocks cannot appear inside of a class declaration either. However, a class can appear nested inside of a module block.

Dissection

- The Public and Friend access modifiers define the visibility of the module. Other assemblies reference the members appearing in **Public** modules. The members of **Friend** modules can be referenced only from the assembly containing the module declaration. If you omit the access modifier, modules are declared as Friend by default.

- *name* defines the name of the module. It must be a valid identifier.

Code Example

```
Public Module Strings
    ' statements
End Module
```

Code Discussion

The preceding code segment creates a Public module named Strings.

Creating Procedures within Modules

A module block can contain variable declarations, classes, structures, and procedures. Next, you will create a module named Strings and a function procedure in the Strings module that will determine whether the length of a string argument is within a specified range.

To create a module and a function procedure within a module:

1. Activate the Code Editor for the module named **Validate.vb**, and then enter the following statements (shown in bold) in the ValidateStrings namespace to declare the Strings module and the IsStringInRange method:

```
Namespace ValidateStrings
    Public Module Strings
        Public Function IsStringInRange(ByVal pstrArg As _
            String, ByVal pintMin As Integer, _
            ByVal pintMax As Integer) As Boolean
            If pstrArg.Length >= pintMin And _
                pstrArg.Length <= pintMax Then
                Return True
            Else
                Return False
            End If
        End Function
    End Module
End Namespace
```

The preceding Boolean function procedure named IsStringInRange will determine whether a string is within a specified length range. The string to be tested is passed as the first argument to the function along with the minimum and maximum valid lengths. The If statement tests to verify that the length of the string is within the valid length range. If it is, the function returns True, and returns False otherwise. Again, referring back to the component design principles discussed at the beginning of the chapter, this method could be used by any application that needs to validate the length of a string.

Next, you will create another module named Numeric in the ValidateNumbers namespace. This module will contain two functions that will validate that a string argument can be converted to an Integer number, and that a string argument contains a number within a range of numbers.

To create a module to validate numeric data:

1. Activate the Code Editor for the module named **Validate.vb**, if necessary, and then enter the following statements (shown in bold) in the ValidateNumbers namespace:

```
Namespace ValidateNumbers

    Public Module Numeric

        Public Function IsInteger( _
            ByVal pstrArg As String) As Boolean
            Dim psngArg As Integer
            Dim pintArg As Single
            If IsNumeric(pstrArg) Then
                pintArg = ToInt32(pstrArg)
                psngArg = ToSingle(pstrArg)
                If pintArg = psngArg Then
                    Return True
                End If
            End If
            Return False
        End Function

        Public Overloads Function IsIntegerInRange( _
            ByVal pstrArg As String, _
            ByVal pintMin As Integer, _
            ByVal pintMax As Integer) As Boolean
            Dim pintArg As Integer
            If IsInteger(pstrArg) Then
                pintArg = ToInt32(pstrArg)
                If pintArg >= pintMin _
                    And pintArg <= pintMax Then
                    Return True
                End If
            End If
        End Function
    End Module
End Namespace
```

The IsInteger function tests that the string argument contains an Integer. The outer If statement first tests that the argument is numeric. If it is, then the argument is converted to an Integer and a Single. If the converted values are the same, then the argument is an Integer so the function returns True. If the values are not the same, then the value is a floating point number, so the function returns False.

The second procedure, named IsIntegerInRange, tests that the first argument is an Integer by calling the IsInteger function. If the value is an Integer, then it is further tested to determine whether the value is within the valid range. The valid range is specified by the second and third arguments named pintMin and pintMax.

Again, reviewing the component-based programming principles, you are creating a generalized component that will validate different types of input. The members of this component could likely be used by many applications.

Working with a Validating Event

To illustrate how to call the function procedures you just created, you will program the Validating event for the text boxes appearing on the login form and the main form so as to validate the input specified by the user.

VB .NET supplies two validation events named Validating and Validated. Windows fires the Validating event just before a control instance loses input focus. If the event is not cancelled, then the Validated event fires, and then the control instance loses input focus. If the Validating event is cancelled, Windows does not fire the subsequent Validated event or the subsequent Leave event, so the control instance does not lose focus. Figure 3-8 illustrates the sequence of events that fire as a control instance gets focus and loses focus.

Remember that all VB .NET event handlers have two arguments. The first argument, named sender, identifies the object that fired the event. The second argument supplies the means by which VB .NET sends information to the event. For the Validating event, the data type of the argument is System.ComponentModel.CancelEventArgs. The System.ComponentModel namespace provides classes that implement the runtime and design-time behavior of controls. The CancelEventArgs class, in turn, allows an event to be cancelled. By canceling an event, subsequent events do not fire. An event gets canceled by setting the Cancel argument to True.

To create a Validating event handler:

1. Activate the Code Editor for the form named **frmLogin.vb**.

2. Enter the following statements in the **Validating** event handler for the text box named **txtFirstName**:

```
If Not ValidateStrings.IsStringInRange( _
    txtFirstName.Text, 1, 30) Then
    e.Cancel = True
End If
```

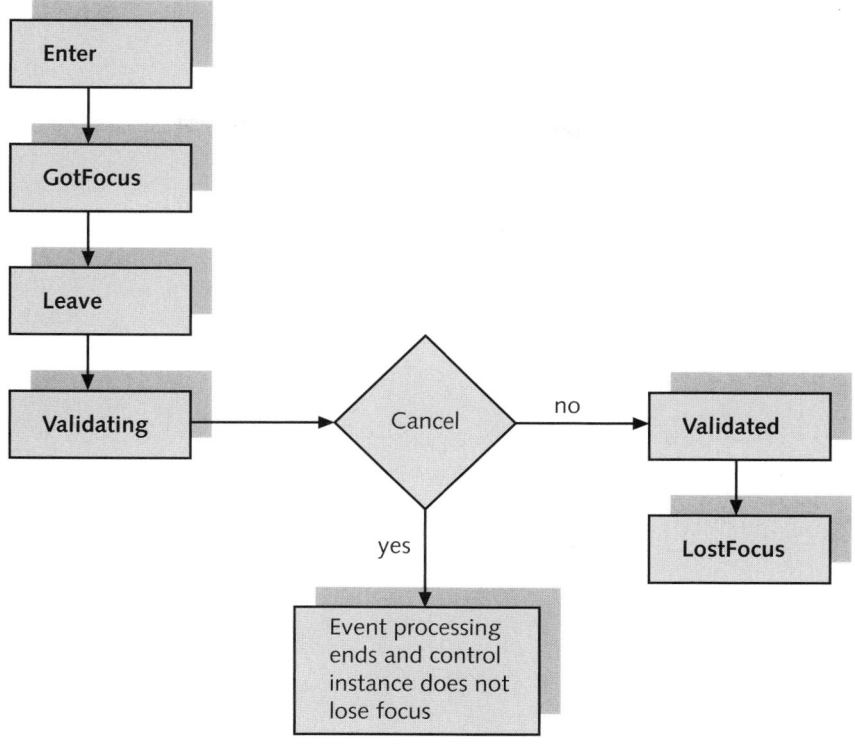

Figure 3-8   Sequence of focus events

3. Enter the following statements in the **Validating** event handler for the text box named **txtLastName**:

```
If Not ValidateStrings.IsStringInRange(txtLastName.Text, _
    1, 30) Then
    e.Cancel = True
End If
```

The preceding statements call the IsStringInRange method that you just created. If the string stored in the respective text box is not between 1 and 30 characters in length, then the event is cancelled. In such a case, the subsequent Validated and Leave events do not fire, so the text box does not lose input focus.

4. Test the solution. The splash screen appears for about 5 seconds, and then the login form appears. Press the **Tab** key. Because the text box is empty, the Validating event gets cancelled so the text box will not lose input focus. Enter your first and last name in the text boxes, and then click **OK** to display the main form. End the solution.

In addition to validating string input, you can also validate numeric input by calling the IsIntegerInRange method that you just created. For example, you can validate the weight of a package and its value to verify that they both contain Integer values within some range.

To validate numeric input:

1. Activate the Code Editor for the form named **frmMain.vb**.

2. Enter the following statements in the **Validating** event handler for the text box named **txtWeight**:

```
If Not ValidateNumbers. _
    IsIntegerInRange(txtWeight.Text, 1, 100) Then
        e.Cancel = True
End If
```

3. Enter the following statements in the **Validating** event handler for the text box named **txtValue**:

```
If Not ValidateNumbers. _
    IsIntegerInRange(txtValue.Text, 1, 10000) Then
        e.Cancel = True
End If
```

In addition to enumerations, structures, and modules, a project may also contain one or more classes. You used classes in Chapter 2 implicitly, as all forms are really classes that inherit from System.Windows.Forms.Form. In addition to using the classes defined by the .NET Framework class library, you can create your own.

INTRODUCTION TO CLASSES

Classes are reference types and implicitly inherit from the System.Object superclass. Remember that all classes ultimately derive from the System.Object superclass. Examine the following simple class declaration:

```
Public Class ShippingCost
End Class
```

The preceding class does not explicitly inherit from System.Object. However, the inheritance is implicit, because, class declaration that explicitly inherits System.Object is the same as the preceding declaration:

```
Public Class ShippingCost
    Inherits System.Object
End Class
```

Many classes inherit from classes other than System.Object. For example, when you create a form, that class inherits from System.Windows.Forms.Form as shown in the following code segment:

```
Public Class frmLogin
    Inherits System.Windows.Forms.Form
        'Statements
End Class
```

A physical file may contain any number of modules and classes. You define a new class by declaring a block with the Class and End Class statements, having the following syntax:

Syntax

[**Public** | **Private** | **Friend**] **Class** *classname*
    [*statements*]
End Class

Definition

The **Class** and **End Class** statements form a block. Classes can be nested, meaning, one class block can contain another class block. A module block may contain any number of class blocks. Classes may also be declared inside or outside of a namespace block.

Dissection

- The **Public**, **Private**, and **Friend** access modifiers define the visibility of the class with respect to other classes and modules. A class declared with Public access can be referenced by other projects (assemblies). Classes declared with Friend access can be referenced by other classes and modules, so long as those modules appear in the same project (assembly). Only the classes within the declaration context of the current class can reference Private classes. If an access modifier is not supplied, the default access for a class is Friend.

- The *classname* argument forms the name of the class and must be a valid identifier.

Code Example

```
Public Class ShippingCost
    Public User As String
End Class
```

Code Discussion

The preceding statements declare a class named ShippingCosts. The class is declared with the Public access modifier so any assembly can reference the class. The class contains one field named User. Fields are discussed in a moment.

Having declared a class, you can declare variables to store a reference to a class instance or create an instance of the class, as shown in the following statements (remember that the New keyword creates an instance of a class):

```
Dim Ship As Shipping.ShippingCost
Dim Ship As New Shipping.ShippingCost()
```

The first declaration declares a variable named Ship but does not create an instance of the ShippingCost class. Thus, the variable references Nothing. The second statement declares a variable named Ship and creates an instance of the ShippingCost class.

VB .NET allows you to create arrays to store references to classes, as shown in the following statement:

```
Dim Shipments() As Shipping.ShippingCost
```

The preceding declaration defines a dynamic array named Shipments of type Shipping.ShippingCost. The array has no initial size.

Classes and Shared Methods

Classes can contain two types of members: instance members and shared members. You are already familiar with instance members. When you work with an instance member you must first create an instance of the class to call the instance member. Put in simple terms, you must first create an instance of a control, such as a Label, before setting its Text property. Shared members work differently. You can reference a shared member (procedure or property) without first creating an instance of the underlying class.

If a method is declared as a shared method, then it can only use shared variables. That is, referencing an instance variable from a shared method will cause an error. Conceptually, this is logical because if a shared method were to reference instance data, the question then arises as to which instance variable should be used.

To create a shared method, you include the Shared keyword in the method declaration as shown in the following statements:

```
Public Class ValidatePostalInfo
    Public Shared Function IsValidPostalCode( _
        ByVal pstrCode As String) As Boolean
    ' Statements
    End Function
End Class
```

The preceding code segment declares a shared method named IsValidPostalCode. Unlike instance methods, you do not create an instance of the class (ValidatePostalInfo) before calling the method, as shown in the following statements:

```
If ValidatePostalInfo.IsValidPostalCode("1234") Then
    ' Statements
End If
```

In addition to creating shared methods, you can also define shared data by including the Shared keyword in the variable declaration, as shown in the following statement:

```
Public Class ShippingCost
    Private Shared mintShipmentCount As Integer
End Class
```

The only difference between the preceding variable declaration and any other variable declaration is the inclusion of the Shared keyword. No matter how many instances of the ShippingCost class that you create, only one copy of the variable named mintShipmentCount exists. That is, all instances of the ShippingCost class share the data stored in the variable mintShipmentCount.

In the following steps, you will create a class named ValidatePostalInfo with a shared method named IsValidPostalCode to validate a postal code. Note that you could have just as easily declared this class as a module. There is no difference between either a class and a shared method, or a module with a method.

To create a shared method:

1. Activate the Code Editor for the module named **Validate.vb**. Create the ValidatePostalInfo class and shared IsValidPostalCode function by entering the following statements (shown in bold) after the Validate namespace declaration:

```
Namespace Validate

    Public Class ValidatePostalInfo

        Public Shared Function IsValidPostalCode( _
            ByVal pstrCode As String) As Boolean
            If pstrCode.Length = 4 Then
                If Validate.ValidateNumbers. _
                    IsIntegerInRange( _
                        pstrCode, 1, 9999) Then
                    Return True
                Else
                    Return False
                End If
            End If
        End Function
    End Class
```

2. Activate the Code Editor for the form named **frmMain.vb**. Enter the following statements in the Validating event for the text box named txtPostalCode:

```
If Not Course.Validate.ValidatePostalInfo. _
    IsValidPostalCode(txtPostalCode.Text) Then
    e.Cancel = True
End If
```

3. Test the solution. Enter your name in the login form, and then click **OK**. On the main form, enter a postal code of "12345". Press the **Tab** key. The postal code is not valid so the text box will not lose input focus. End the solution.

3

Using Instance Members in Classes

In this section, you will create a class named ShippingCost that will calculate the cost of a shipment based on the value of the shipment, its weight, and the type of shipment. To do so, you will define an interface consisting of the members shown in Figure 3-9.

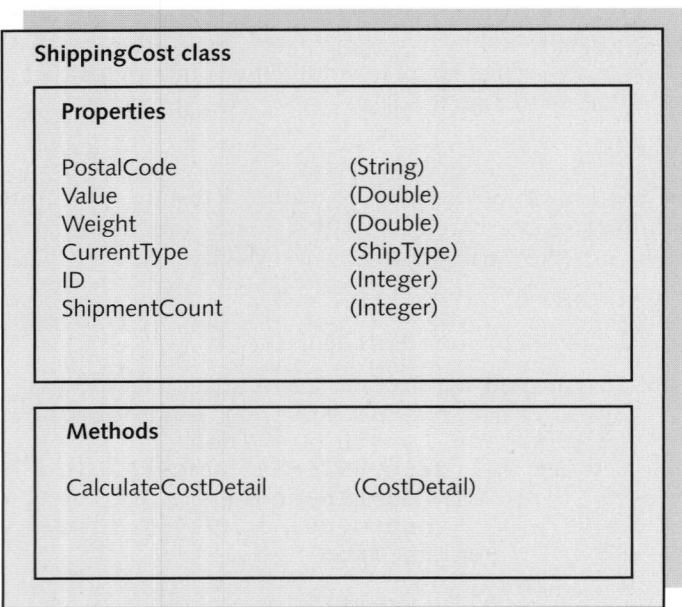

Figure 3-9   Members of the ShippingCost class

The properties and methods shown in Figure 3-9 define the interface of the ShippingCost class.

You can now, as the author, create the ShippingCost class of the Shipping namespace.

To create a class:

1. Activate the Code Editor for the module named **Shipping.vb**, and then enter the following statements (shown in bold) after the End Structure statement marking the end of the CostDetail structure:

```
Public Structure CostDetail
    ' Statements
End Structure
Public Class ShippingCost
End Class
```

The preceding statements declare the ShippingCost class that will calculate the cost of a shipment.

Having declared the ShippingCost class, you need to provide the interface and the implementation for this class.

Hiding Data in a Component

Remember that one purpose of creating a component is to build a black box whose inner-workings are hidden from the developer using the component. As the author of a component, you hide data and functions in the class (component) so that it is hidden from the developer. That is, you want to create data that is part of the implementation rather than part of the interface. Creating hidden data and hidden procedures is simple. Just declare variables and procedures with an access modifier of Private. Local variables declared with the Dim statement are also hidden. Data and procedures declared with the Friend keyword will become part of the implementation too, because Friend variables are not visible outside the project (assembly) containing the declaration.

To declare hidden data:

1. Activate the Code Editor for the module named **Shipping.vb**, if necessary, and then enter the following statements (shown in bold) in the **ShippingCost** class:

```
Public Class ShippingCost
    Private Shared mintShipmentCount As Integer
    Private Const cdblVatRateAustralia _
        As Double = 0.06
    Private Const cdblTariffRateAustralia _
        As Double = 0.05
    Private Const cdblShippingRateAustralia _
        As Double = 5.66

    Private mintIDCurrent As Integer

    Private mstrPostalCode As String
    Private mdblVatRate As Double
    Private mdblTariffRate As Double
    Private mdblValue As Double
    Private mdblWeight As Double
    Private mShipType As ShipType

    Private mblnValidPostalCode As Boolean
    Private mblnValidValue As Boolean
    Private mblnValidWeight As Boolean
End Class
```

The preceding statements declare the data hidden in the ShippingCost class. The shared variable mintShipmentCount will store the number of shipments made. The constants store the rate of the value added tax, the tariff rate, and the base shipping rate. The variable mintIDCurrent will store the current shipment ID. The variable named mstrPostalCode will store the postal code of the shipment. The variables named mdblVatRate and mdblTariffRate will store the rate of the value added tax and the rate of the tariff. The variables mdblValue and mdblWeight will store the value of the shipment and the weight of the shipment. The variable mShipType will store the shipment type. The final three Boolean variables will indicate whether the postal code, shipment value, and shipment weight are valid.

In addition to hidden data, data should be exposed to the developer through fields and properties.

Creating Exposed Class Data

VB .NET supplies two ways to define properties for a class: Public variables and property procedures. The simplest way to create a property for a class is to declare a Public variable in a class module. A Public variable has no access restrictions and can be used by all of the modules in an assembly, and by other assemblies. VB .NET refers to a Public variable declared in a class as a **field**. To illustrate how to declare a field, examine the following statements:

```
Public Class ShippingCost
    Public User As String
End Class
```

The preceding statements declare a field named User in the class named ShippingCost. The statements to create an instance of the class and to reference the field are the same as the statements to create any other class instance and reference its properties, as shown in the following code segment:

```
Dim Ship As Shipping.ShippingCost
Ship = New Shipping.ShippingCost()
Ship.User = CurrentUser.FullName
```

In this chapter's solution you will create a field in the ShippingCost class to store the full name of the user creating the shipment.

To create a field:

1. Activate the Code Editor for the module named **Shipping.vb**, if necessary.

2. Enter the following statement (shown in bold) in the **ShippingCost** class, just after the class declaration.

```
Public Class ShippingCost
    Public User As String
```

Overcoming the Limitations of Fields

Although fields work as a means to create properties, they have limitations. First, as the author, you cannot write code in a class to validate a field's value when the developer sets it. In fact, you cannot execute any code at all when the developer reads or writes a field's value. Property procedures solve these problems. You can create properties by declaring and writing code for property procedures in a class module. Structures can also contain property procedures.

VB .NET supports three types of properties:

- A developer can get a value from a **read-only** property but cannot store a value in the property.

- A developer can store a value in a **write-only** property but cannot read that stored value.

- **Read–write** properties can be both read and written by a developer.

Property procedures have the following syntax:

Syntax

[**Public** | **Private** | **Friend**] [**ReadOnly** | **WriteOnly**] [**Shared**] **Property**
varname(**ByVal** *parameterlist*) [**As** *typename*]
   Get
     [*block*]
   End Get
   Set(**ByVal** *value* **As** *typename*)
     [*block*]
   End Set
End Property

Definition

The **Property** statement declares the name of a property, and defines whether the property is read-only, read-write, or write-only.

Dissection

- The **Public**, **Private**, and **Friend** keywords are access modifiers used to define which classes or assemblies can reference the property. Their meaning is the same for property procedures as it is for variables and procedure declarations. By default, property procedures have Public access. The **Shared** keyword marks the property as shared.

- The optional **ReadOnly** and **WriteOnly** keywords define whether the property is a read-only property or a write-only property, respectively. If omitted, the property is read-write, and the property procedure must include both a Get and a Set block. When creating a read-only property, include the Get block but omit the Set block and include the ReadOnly keyword in the property declaration. When creating a write-only property, include the Set block but omit the Get block, and include the WriteOnly keyword in the declaration.

- Arguments are passed to the property procedure via *parameterlist*.

- The optional **As** *typename* clause defines the data type of the property. If omitted, the default data type is System.Object. As this book uses Option Strict for all applications, the As *typename* clause is required.

- *varname* contains the name of the property and must be a valid identifier name.

- The **Get** block contains the statements that execute when the developer reads the value of the property. Local variables can be declared in the Get block.

- The **Set** block contains the statements that execute when the developer writes the value of the property. Note that the Set block contains an argument. This argument is used to set the property's value. Local variables can be declared in the Set block.

Code Example

```
Private mdblValue As Double
Public Property Value() As Double
    Get
        Return mdblValue
    End Get
    Set(ByVal Value As Double)
        Value = mdblValue
        mblnValidValue = True
    End Set
End Property
```

Code Dissection

The preceding statements illustrate how to create a read-write property procedure named Value. The value of the property is stored in the hidden variable named mdblValue.

Implementing Property Procedures

When you implement property procedures, you typically store the value of the property in a hidden variable. This hidden (Private or Friend) variable, although global to the class, is not visible to the developer using the class. When the developer writes a statement to set the property, the statement in the Set block of the property procedure executes and saves the value to the hidden variable. When the developer writes a statement to read the property's value, then the Get block executes, which returns the value from a hidden variable. Figure 3-10 illustrates the Value property implemented as a pair of property procedures.

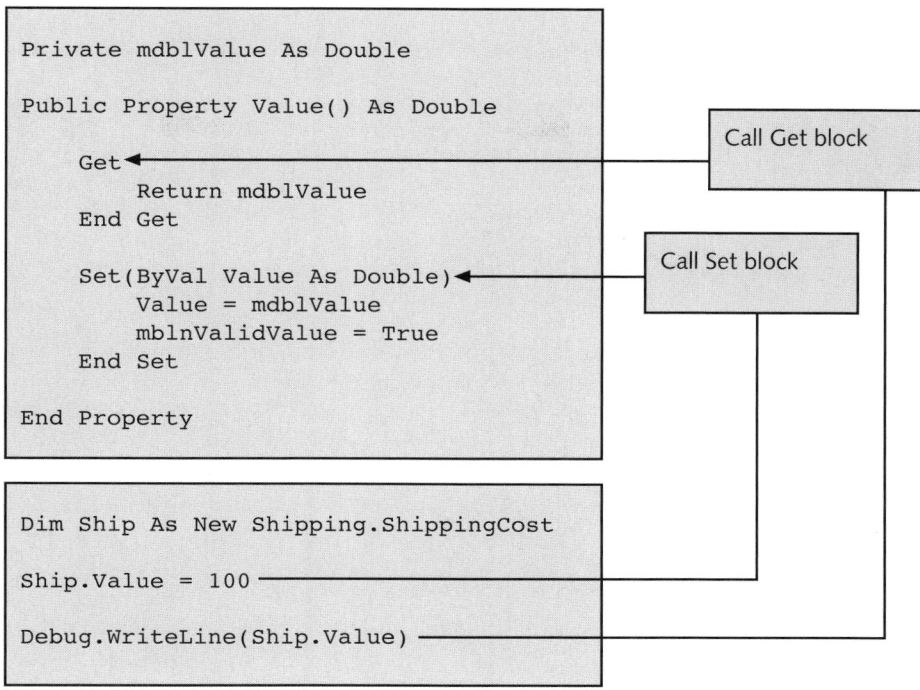

Figure 3-10   Implementation of a property procedure

In addition to creating a read-write property, you can create a read-only property by adding the ReadOnly keyword to the property declaration and omitting the Set block from the property procedure. The following code segment illustrates a read-only property procedure:

```
Public ReadOnly Property ShipmentCount() As Integer
    Get
        Return mintShipmentCount
    End Get
End Property
```

You previously declared a hidden variable named mintShipmentCount to store the number of shipments created. The preceding read-only property procedure returns the value of this hidden variable.

Sometimes, you must create a write-once property, but VB .NET does not explicitly support write-once properties. However, you can create a write-once property by declaring a Static hidden variable in the property procedure. Examine the following statements:

```
Private mintID As Integer
Public Property ID() As Integer
    Get
        Return mintID
```

```
        End Get
        Set(ByVal Value As Integer)
            Static pblnSet As Boolean
            If pblnSet Then
                ' Error
            Else
                pblnSet = True
                mintID = Value
            End If
        End Set
    End Property
```

As shown in the preceding code segment, the Static Boolean hidden variable named pblnSet will be True or False depending on whether the developer has previously set the property or not. The first time the property is set, the variable's value is False. The If statement sets the variable's value to True. If the developer attempts to set the property's value a second time, an error should occur. Chapter 4 discusses in detail how to handle and generate errors.

Creating Properties

In the ShippingCost class of the Shipping namespace, you will create several read–write properties. The PostalCode property will store the destination postal code of the shipment, the Value property will store the value of the shipment, and the Weight property will store the weight of the shipment. The CurrentType property will contain the current type of the shipment (ground, two day, next day). The ShippingCost class will contain a read-only property named ShipmentCount that will return the number of shipments.

To create property procedures:

1. Activate the **Shipping.vb** module, if necessary, and then enter the following statements (shown in bold) at the end of the **ShippingCost** class to create the read–write property procedures:

```
Private mblnValidWeight As Boolean
Public Property PostalCode() As String
    Get
        Return mstrPostalCode
    End Get
    Set(ByVal Value As String)
        mblnValidPostalCode = True
        mstrPostalCode = Value
    End Set
End Property
Public Property Value() As Double
    Get
        Return mdblValue
    End Get
```

```
        Set(ByVal Value As Double)
            mdblValue = Value
            mblnValidValue = True
        End Set
    End Property

    Public Property Weight() As Double
        Get
            Return mdblWeight
        End Get
        Set(ByVal Value As Double)
            mblnValidWeight = True
            mdblWeight = Value
        End Set
    End Property
    Public Property CurrentType() As ShipType
        Get
            Return mShiptype
        End Get
            Set(ByVal Value As ShipType)
            mShipType = Value
        End Set
    End Property
```

2. Enter the following statements at the end of the **ShippingCost** class to create the read-only properties:

```
Public ReadOnly Property ID() As Integer
    Get
        ID = mintIDCurrent
    End Get
End Property

Public ReadOnly Property ShipmentCount() As Integer
    Get
        Return mintShipmentCount
    End Get
End Property
```

Having defined the hidden and exposed data for the ShippingCost class, you can now create its constructor and define the methods.

CONSTRUCTORS

Remember that a constructor is a procedure named New that VB .NET executes when it creates an instance of a class. All constructors can accept 0 or more arguments, as can any procedure. Just as a form can have a constructor, so too can a class. When the developer creates an instance of a class, the statements in the constructor execute. There is no difference between the constructor in a form and the constructor in any other class. Examine the following constructor for the ShippingCost class:

```
Public Sub New()
    mintShipmentCount += 1
    mintIDCurrent = mintShipmentCount
End Sub
```

The preceding constructor accepts no arguments. The sub procedure is a constructor by virtue of the fact that the procedure appears in a class block and has the name New. The statements increment the shipment counter (mintShipmentCount), and set the hidden variable mintIDCurrent to the shipment counter.

To create a constructor:

1. Activate the Code Editor for the **Shipping.vb** module, if necessary.

2. Enter the following constructor (shown in bold) in the **Shipping** class just after the variable declarations:

```
Private mblnValidWeight As Boolean
Public Sub New()
    mintShipmentCount += 1
    mintIDCurrent = mintShipmentCount
End Sub
```

CREATING METHODS

As the author of a class, you implement methods in a class by creating function and sub procedures just as you create them in any other module. Function methods return a value, but sub methods do not. The purpose of the Public, Private, and Friend access modifiers is the same as it is for variables and procedures. Thus, Public methods are part of the class's interface while Private methods are part of the class's implementation. Methods may accept any number of arguments, including none.

To illustrate how to create a method, you will create a procedure named CalculateCostDetail in the ShippingCost class that will calculate the cost of a shipment.

To create a method:

1. Enter the following statements at the end of the **ShippingCost** class just before the End Class statement to create the CalculateCostDetail method:

```
Public Function CalculateCostDetail() As CostDetail
    Dim pCostDetail As CostDetail
    If mblnValidPostalCode AndAlso mblnValidValue _
        AndAlso mblnValidWeight Then
        pCostDetail.VatCost = mdblValue * _
            cdblVatRateAustralia
        pCostDetail.TariffCost = mdblValue * _
```

```
                cdblTariffRateAustralia
            pCostDetail.ShippingCost = mdblWeight * _
                (cdblShippingRateAustralia * mShipType)
            pCostDetail.TotalCost = pCostDetail.VatCost + _
                pCostDetail.TariffCost + _
                pCostDetail.ShippingCost
            Return pCostDetail
        End If
    End Function
```

The CalculateCostDetail method first tests that the postal code, value, and weight are valid. If they are, the elements of the CostDetail structure are completed.

You have completed the programming for the classes. Now, as the developer, you can create the code that will use the classes that you have created. The button named btnShipToAustralia will create an instance of the ShippingCost class, set its properties, and then calculate the cost of a shipment.

To create a shipment:

1. Activate the Code Editor for the form named **frmMain.vb**, and then enter the following statement in the module immediately after the statement generated by the Win Forms Designer. This statement declares a variable to reference the ShippingCost class.

```
Private Ship As Shipping.ShippingCost
```

2. On the form named **frmMain.vb**, enter the following statements in the **Click** event handler for the button named **btnShipToAustralia**:

```
Dim pcostDetail As Shipping.CostDetail
Ship = New Shipping.ShippingCost()
Ship.User = CurrentUser.FullName
Ship.PostalCode = txtPostalCode.Text
Ship.Value = System.Convert.ToDouble(txtValue.Text)
Ship.Weight = System.Convert.ToDouble(txtWeight.Text)
If radGround.Checked = True Then
    Ship.CurrentType = ShipType.Ground
ElseIf radTwoDay.Checked = True Then
    Ship.CurrentType = ShipType.TwoDay
Else
    Ship.CurrentType = ShipType.NextDay
End If
pcostDetail = Ship.CalculateCostDetail
txtID.Text = Ship.ID.ToString
CopyToTextBoxes(pcostDetail)
```

The preceding statements create an instance of the ShippingCost class. The values from the text boxes are copied into the properties of the class instance named Ship. The If statement checks which of the three radio buttons are selected and sets the CurrentType property accordingly. Then the CalculateCostDetail method is called. This method returns the detailed costs in the form of a CostDetail structure. This structure is passed to the CopyToTextBoxes procedure.

3. On the main form, create the **CopyToTextBoxes** procedure by entering the following statements:

```
Private Sub CopyToTextBoxes( _
    ByVal scd As Shipping.CostDetail)
    txtVatCost.Text = scd.VatCost.ToString("c")
    txtTariffCost.Text = scd.TariffCost.ToString("c")
    txtShippingCost.Text = scd.ShippingCost.ToString("c")
    txtTotalCost.Text = scd.TotalCost.ToString("c")
End Sub
```

The CopyToTextBoxes procedure is simple. It copies the members out of the structure, converts the values to strings, and stores each value in the appropriate text box.

4. Test the solution. Enter your first and last name in the login dialog box. When the main form appears, enter the information shown in Figure 3-11. Click the **Ship To Australia** button. The output values appear.

Figure 3-11   Completed form

You have completed the programming for this chapter. You have seen how to divide an application into components that can be shared by one or more applications.

CHAPTER SUMMARY

In this chapter you have learned about the organization of a VB .NET application. That is, you have seen how enumerations, structures, classes, and modules fit together to create an application.

❐ Component-based programming can save development time and reduce development costs because a component can be reused by several applications. When working with components, the author creates the component and the developer uses components created by authors. A component has a private part, which is hidden from the developer, and a public part that is exposed to the developer.

❐ This chapter discussed three access modifiers. Variables and procedures declared with Public access have no access restrictions. That is, they can be used by any assembly. Variables declared with Friend access can be used only by the project containing the declaration. Private variables can be referenced only by the class containing the declaration.

❐ Namespaces are at the heart of every VB .NET application. In addition to the namespaces defined by the .NET Framework class library, every project that you create belongs to a namespace. Namespaces are hierarchical. The Namespace and End Namespace statements define a namespace block. Namespaces are open-ended, meaning that a namespace can be split into multiple files.

❐ The Imports statement allows a namespace or class to be referenced without fully qualifying the namespace or class name. The optional alias clause allows you to specify a shorthand alias to reference the namespace or class. The Imports statement must use fully qualified namespaces or class names. The Imports statement appears after the Option Strict and Option Explicit statements but before the Namespace statement. A module may import any number of namespaces.

❐ Enumerations allow you to attach a mnemonic name to a constant whole number value. An enumeration block begins with the Enum statement and ends with the End Enum statement. By default, enumeration numbering begins at zero and enumeration members are numbered sequentially. However, an enumeration can begin numbering with some other value, and enumeration values need not be sequential or unique.

❐ Structures organize related data. A structure block begins with the Structure statement and ends with the End Structure statement. Structures can contain Public, Friend, and Private variables and methods. Structures can be nested. In addition, a structure member can itself be another structure. Structure declarations cannot appear inside of a procedure. Structures cannot be inherited.

❐ Namespaces can contain any number of module blocks. Modules are similar to classes, as they are both reference types. Modules, however, are shared, meaning that only one copy of a module's data exists for the running project.

❐ Namespaces can contain any number of classes. By default, classes inherit from System.Object, but may inherit from any other class. A class block is marked by the Class and End Class statements. Classes can contain hidden data that is part of the implementation, and exposed data that is part of the interface. The Private and Friend access modifiers create hidden data; the Public access modifier creates exposed data. Classes can also contain structures and enumerations.

❐ Classes can also contain properties. The easiest way to create a property is to declare a Public variable in a module. This type of property is called a field. Properties are also declared with property procedures. VB .NET supports read-only, write-only, and read-write properties. Read-only properties have a Get block but no corresponding Set block. Write-only properties have a Set block but no corresponding Get block. Read-write properties have both a Get block and a Set block.

❐ Classes can have constructors. A constructor is a Public sub procedure named New that VB .NET calls when it creates a class instance at runtime. Constructors can accept 0 or more arguments.

❐ Methods are created by developing Public function or sub procedures in a class. The syntax of a function or sub procedure in a class module is the same as the syntax in any other module.

❐ Methods and data can be shared. To declare a shared variable or shared method, include the Shared keyword in the variable or method declaration. Note that a shared method will only work with shared data. Trying to reference instance data from a shared method will cause an error.

Review Questions

1. Which of the following statements correctly describes the difference between a component's interface and implementation?

   a. A component's interface is exposed to other developers, while a component's implementation is hidden inside of the component and is not available to other developers.

   b. A component's implementation is exposed to other developers, while a component's interface is hidden inside of the component and is not available to other developers.

   c. The terms "interface" and "implementation" have nothing to do with component-based programming.

   d. none of the above

2. What is the difference between members declared with the Public and Private access modifiers?

   a. Only the assembly containing the declaration can reference variables and procedures declared with Public access. Any assembly can reference variables declared with Private access.

   b. Any assembly can reference a variable or procedure declared with Public access. Variables declared with Private access can only be referenced by the class containing the declaration.

   c. A variable declared with Private access can be referenced by the assembly containing the declaration but not outside the assembly. Variables can be declared with Public access inside of a module block.

   d. If a class contains variables declared with Public access, is cannot contain variables declared with Private access.

   e. none of the above

3. Which of the following statements is true of namespaces?

   a. A namespace can contain another namespace.

   b. While assemblies created by Microsoft contain one or more namespaces, the assemblies that you create do not.

   c. You cannot define a root namespace. Only Microsoft can create root namespaces.

   d. all of the above

   e. none of the above

4. What is the purpose of the Imports statement?

   a. It retrieves the code appearing in a module file into another module file.

   b. It establishes a reference to the namespaces in an assembly, thereby making those namespaces available to an application.

   c. It allows you to reference the members of a namespace or type without fully qualifying the names of those members.

   d. It imports a project into a solution.

   e. none of the above

5. Which of the following statements is true of the Imports statement?

   a. It can be used to import classes and structures but it cannot be used to import namespaces.

   b. It can be used to import namespaces but it cannot be used to import other types, such as classes.

   c. You can import a class using a relative reference. For example, if you have imported the System namespace, you can import the System.Convert class without specifying the System namespace.

   d. It can be used to import namespaces, classes, and other types.

   e. none of the above

6. Which of the following statements applies to enumerations?

    a. An enumeration is declared in a block with the Enum and End Enum statements.

    b. By default, the first member of an enumeration has a value of 1.

    c. The members of an enumeration must have sequential values.

    d. Use of enumerations should be avoided as they make the statement in an application harder to understand.

    e. none of the above

7. Which of the following statements applies to structures?

    a. Structures cannot be nested.

    b. You declare a structure with the Type statement.

    c. Structures cannot be declared inside of a Namespace block.

    d. Structures are reference types.

    e. none of the above

8. What items can appear in a module block?

    a. Public and Private variables

    b. function and sub procedures

    c. structures

    d. enumerations

    e. all of the above

9. Which of the following statements is correct related to the Validating and Validated events?

    a. The Validating event is supported by the TextBox control, but is not supported by any other types of controls because the user does not enter text.

    b. The Validating event fires before the Validated event. If the Validating event is cancelled, then the Validated event does not fire.

    c. The Validated event always fires after the Validating event, whether or not the Validating event was cancelled.

    d. The data type of the second argument to the Validating and Validated event is System.ValidateEventArgs.

    e. none of the above

10. How do you hide data in a class?

    a. Declare a variable with the Public keyword.

    b. Declare a variable with the Private keyword.

    c. Declare a variable with the Hidden keyword.

    d. Declare a variable in a hidden Namespace block.

    e. none of the above

11. What is meant by the term "field" with regard to a class module?

    a. Class modules cannot contain fields.

    b. Fields are always hidden.

    c. A field is merely a Public variable declared in a class module.

    d. If you create fields in a class module, then you cannot create property procedures in a class module.

    e. none of the above

12. How do you create an exposed method in a class?

    a. Create a procedure with the Method keyword having Public access.

    b. Create a procedure with either the Sub or Function keywords having Public access.

    c. Create a property procedure with Public access.

    d. Create a procedure with either the Sub or Function keywords having Exposed access.

    e. none of the above

13. Which of the following statements is true of property procedures?

    a. VB .NET supports read-only, read-write, and write-only property procedures.

    b. A read-only property procedure has a Get block, but the Set block is omitted.

    c. A write-only property has a Set block, but the Get block is omitted.

    d. A read-write property has both a Get block and a Set block.

    e. all of the above

14. Which of the following statements is true of constructors?

    a. Every class can have a constructor.

    b. A constructor is a sub procedure named New, appearing in a class module.

    c. A constructor can accept 0 or more arguments.

    d. all of the above

    e. none of the above

15. Which of the following statements is true of shared methods and shared data?

    a. You declare a shared method with the Shared keyword.

    b. A shared method can use instance data.

    c. If one method in a class module is shared, then all of the methods in that class module must be shared.

    d. all of the above

    e. none of the above

16. Describe the similarities and differences between a module block and a class block.

17. Referring to component-based programming, describe the role of the author and developer.
18. List and describe the benefits of component-based programming.
19. Describe how to create read-only, write-only, and write-once properties.
20. Describe the purpose of a shared method.

PROGRAMMING QUESTIONS

1. Write the statements to declare a namespace named Automobiles, having two subordinate namespaces named Cars and Trucks.
2. Write the statements to declare a namespace named Course, having two Public modules named Sales and Marketing.
3. Write the statements to import the System.Windows.Forms namespace and the System.Windows.Forms.Form class. Do not use an alias.
4. Write the statement to import the System.Drawing namespace using an alias of Draw.
5. Write the statement to declare a shared Public variable named InstanceCount, having a data type of Integer.
6. Write the statements to declare a Public enumeration named VisualAppearance, having named values of Strong, Normal, and Soft. Use the default values for the three members.
7. Write the statements to declare a Public enumeration named Magnitude, having named values of Ten, Hundred, and Thousand with values of 10, 100, and 1000, respectively.
8. Write the statements to declare a Public class named Employee containing fields named FirstName and LastName. Both fields should have a data type of String. Create a method named FullName that will concatenate the FirstName and LastName fields such that a space appears between the two names.
9. Write the statements to declare a Public structure named Payroll, having the following Public members and data types: ID (Integer), Name (String), HourlyWage (Single).
10. Write the statements to declare a Public structure named Coordinates, having Public members named X, Y, and Z, each with a data type of Double. Declare a Private member named ID, having a data type of String.
11. Write the statements to declare a read-write property named EmployeeName, having a data type of String. Store the value of the property in the hidden variable mstrEmployeeName.
12. Write the statements to declare a read-write property named Format, having an enumerated data type of FormatType. Store the value of the property in the hidden variable mFormatType.

13. Write the statements to declare a read–only String property named ID. Write the statements in the property procedure to return the value stored in the hidden variable named pstrID.

14. Write the statements to create a write-once property named IDLocked. Store the value of the property in the hidden variable named mintIDLocked. Assume that the property has a data type of Integer.

15. Write the statements to declare a class named IsValid, having a shared method named IsCharacter. The method should accept one argument having a data type of String. The method should return True if the string has a length of one and contains an upper case character (A–Z).

HANDS-ON PROJECTS

1. In this project you will create a solution similar to the one presented in the chapter. However, instead of calculating the cost of a shipment, the solution will create a quotation for an insurance policy based on a person's age, gender, and whether or not they smoke. The file named Chapter.03\Exercises03\Ch03Ex1.exe contains the compiled executable application. Figure 3-12 shows the completed main form for the solution with the calculated output.

Figure 3-12   Chapter 3 – Hands-on Project 1

a. Create a solution named **Ch03Ex1.sln**.

b. Create a splash screen for the form. Create a Sub Main procedure that will display the splash screen for five seconds and then display the main form.

c. Define the root namespace as **Course** and the assembly name as **Ch03Ex1**. Add a module named **Validate** to validate the input provided by the user.

d. In the Validate module, declare a namespace named **Validate** with two subordinate namespaces named **ValidateStrings** and **ValidateNumbers**.

e. In the ValidateStrings namespace, create an exposed method named **IsStringInRange**. The method should accept three arguments: the string to check, the minimum length, and the maximum length. The method should return True if the string has a valid length and False otherwise.

f. In the ValidateNumbers namespace, create an exposed method named **IsInteger** that accepts one string argument. The method should return True if the argument can be converted to an Integer and False otherwise. Create a second exposed method in the ValidateNumbers namespace named **IsIntegerInRange** that accepts three arguments. The first argument should contain the string to be checked. The second and third arguments should contain integers denoting the minimum and maximum valid values, respectively.

g. Add a module file named **Insurance** to calculate the cost of an insurance policy. Declare a namespace named **Insurance** in the file. The Insurance namespace should expose a structure named **InsuranceQuote**, an enumeration named **GenderType**, and a class named **InsuranceCost**.

h. Declare the **InsuranceQuote** structure, having public members named **BaseRate**, **AgeSurcharge**, **SmokerSurcharge**, **GenderDiscount**, and **TotalQuote**. Each member should have a data type of Single.

i. Declare an enumeration named **GenderType** having names of **Male** and **Female**. Use the default enumeration values.

j. Next, in the Insurance namespace, declare a class named **InsuranceCost**. Expose the following read-write properties, having the following data types: **Age** (Integer), **Gender** (GenderType), and **Smoker** (Boolean). Declare the necessary hidden variables to store the property values. Also write the necessary statements for each property that you declared to read and write the property value.

k. Create a method named **Calculate** in the InsuranceCost class that will calculate the cost of the quotation. The base rate for an insurance policy is $100.00. The age surcharge is $2.50 for each year of age over 20. The gender discount is a flat $25.00 for females regardless of age. The smoking surcharge is $50.00 regardless of the person's gender or age.

l. On the main form, create the user interface as shown in Figure 3-12.

m. Import any namespaces as necessary.

n. Create the necessary Validating event handlers to check if the name is between 1 and 30 characters long, and if the age is an Integer number between 20 and 100.

o. Write the statements for the **Calculate Quote** button that will create an instance of the InsuranceCost class and store the valid data in its properties. Call the necessary method to calculate the cost of the quotation.

p. Display the quote in the output text boxes as necessary.

2. In this project, you will create a class that will calculate volume discounts based on the amount of a product purchased. Assume that a gravel company sells three products: sand, gravel, and mixed concrete. The charge for each product is based on the amount of each product ordered and the type of customer. The file named Chapter.03\Exercises03\Ch03Ex2.exe contains the compiled executable application. Figure 3-13 shows the completed form for the solution.

3

Figure 3-13   Chapter 3 – Hands-on Project 2

a. Create a solution named **Ch03Ex2.sln**.

b. Create a splash screen for the form. Create a Sub Main procedure that will display the splash screen for five seconds and then display the main form.

c. Define the root namespace as **Course**, and the assembly name as **Ch03Ex2**.

d. Add a module named **Validate** to validate the input provided by the user.

e. In the Validate module, declare a namespace named **Validate** with two subordinate namespaces named **ValidateFields** and **ValidateNumbers**.

f. In the ValidateFields namespace, create a module named **Fields** and an exposed method named **IsValidTelephone**. The method should accept one string argument, the telephone number to validate, and return True if the telephone number is valid and False otherwise. A valid telephone number has a format of *xxx-xxx-xxxx* where *x* is a digit.

g. In the ValidateNumbers namespace, create a module named **Numbers** and exposed methods named **IsInteger** and **IsIntegerInRange**.

h. Create a new module file named **Products.vb**. Declare a namespace named **Products** in the Products.vb file having a structure named **ProductQuote** and a class named **ProductCost**.

i. Declare an enumeration named CustomerType having members named Retail, Government, and Commerical.

j. Assume that the company sells the following three products: sand, gravel, and mixed cement. Declare a structure to store the total cost of the three products along with the total cost of all three products combined.

k. In the **ProductCost** class, declare read-write properties to store the quantity of sand, gravel, and concrete, and the CustomerType.

l. Create a method named **Calculate** that will return a ProductQuote structure. Calculate the cost based on the following rules. The base price for sand is $23.00 per cubic yard, the base price for gravel is $21.00 per cubic yard, and the base price for mixed concrete is $41.00 per yard. If a customer orders between 11 and 20 yards, they receive a 10% discount on that product. Between 21 and 30 yards they receive a 15% discount. Between 31 and 40 yards, a 20% discount is given. For order quantities above 41 yards, a 25% discount is awarded. An additional discount is awarded based on the customer type. Retail customers receive no discount. Government customers receive a 5% discount, and commercial customers receive a 7% discount. The customer discount is calculated off of the discounted volume price rather than the base price.

m. Create the control instances on the main form as shown in Figure 3–13.

n. Write the statements to create an instance of the ProductCost class, set the necessary properties, and display the output.

3. In this project, you will create a utility class. The utility class will provide information about the control instances appearing on a form. That is, it will calculate the number of Button, CheckBox, Label, and TextBox control instances on a form. Figure 3–14 shows the completed main form for the solution. The file named Chapter.03\Exercises03\Ch03Ex3.exe contains the compiled executable application. Note that the control instances on the main form serve no purpose other than to test the class that examines a collection of controls.

a. Create a solution named **Ch03Ex3.sln**.

b. Create a splash screen for the form. Create a Sub Main procedure that will display the splash screen for five seconds and then display the main form.

c. Define the root namespace as **Course**, and the assembly name as **Ch03Ex3**. Add a module named **ListControls** to the project.

d. In the module, declare a class named **ListControls**. Do not declare an additional namespace.

Figure 3-14 Chapter 3 – Hands-on Project 3

e. In the ListControls class, create a constructor so that it accepts one argument having a data type of **System.Windows.Forms.Form.ControlCollection**. You will pass a Controls collection to the constructor.

f. The constructor should accept one argument. The statements in the constructor should examine the ControlCollection, searching for the following four types of controls: Button, CheckBox, Label, and TextBox. Using a hidden accumulator, count the number of each type of control.

g. Declare four read-only properties named **ButtonCount**, **CheckBoxCount**, **LabelCount**, and **TextBoxCount**. Write the statements to return the number of Buttons, CheckBoxes, Labels, and TextBoxes appearing in the Controls collection passed as a constructor.

h. Create methods named **GetButtonNames**, **GetCheckBoxNames**, **GetLabelNames**, and **GetTextBoxNames**. These methods should return a string containing the names of the respective control instances. That is, GetButtonNames should return the value of the Name property for the Button control instances. Return the string such that each control instance name is separated by a carriage return. Use the Microsoft.VisualBasic.ControlChars.CrLf enumeration to accomplish this task.

i. Create a method named **GetAllNames** that will return the names of all the control instances created on the form.

j. Create the control instances on the main form as shown in Figure 3-14. Write the necessary statements in the Click event handler for the ListControls button to test the members of the class that you just created.

4. In this project, you will create a credit scoring system. Points are awarded or removed based on various criteria. A person's credit score is based on the following guidelines:

- ❏ 100 points are awarded for each $10,000.00 of income. That is, 110 points would be awarded for $11,000.00 in annual income.

- ❏ 25 points are deducted for each $10,000.00 of annual revolving debt.

- ❏ 15 points are deducted for each $10,000.00 in annual house payments.

- ❏ 25 points are deducted for each late payment.

- ❏ 15 points are deducted for each dependant.

- ❏ 15 points are awarded for each $10,000.00 in the bank.

- ❏ 50 points are awarded if a person owns their house outright.
  The file named Chapter.03\Exercises03\Ch03Ex4.exe contains the compiled executable application. Figure 3-15 shows the completed main form for the solution.

Figure 3-15   Chapter 3 – Hands-on Project 4

a. Create a solution file named **Ch03Ex4.sln**.

b. Create a splash screen for the form. Create a Sub Main procedure that will display the splash screen for five seconds and then display the main form.

c. Create a namespace named **Validate**, having modules to validate a person's Social Security number and telephone number. Create other modules to validate the above input values.

d. Create a second namespace and the necessary classes and structures to calculate the credit score.

e. Using Figure 3-15 as a template, create the control instances on the form, and then call the members of the classes to validate the input and calculate the credit score.

3

4

.NET PROGRAMMING PILLARS

In Chapter 3, you learned about several core concepts related to component-based programming. Specifically, you learned how to create components using namespaces containing modules and classes. In addition, you saw that by using different access modifiers you can hide members, making those members part of a component's implementation, or expose members, making them part of a component's interface. This chapter expands upon the component-based programming concepts presented in Chapter 3.

In this chapter, you will learn how to create more complex components that contain overloaded members and how to create classes that are inherited from other classes. In addition, you will modify classes so that they support events and handle exceptions.

PREVIEWING THE COMPLETED SOLUTION

The completed solution in this chapter expands on the material presented in Chapter 3 by explaining additional features of classes and the interrelationships that can exist between classes. This solution calculates the cost to ship a parcel to one of three countries, based on the cost and weight of the parcel. This chapter's solution illustrates how to create a class that defines the general shipping characteristics common to all countries. Specific classes are derived from the general class so as to calculate the shipping cost for each particular country supported. Different classes exist to calculate the shipment cost to Australia, Canada, and Mexico. Each of these classes calculates the cost of a shipment based on the value added tax, tariffs, shipment weight, and value of the shipment. Table 4-1 shows the costs applicable to a shipment for each country. Of course, these values are simulated.

Table 4-1   Shipping costs

	Value added tax	Tariff	Cost per pound
Australia	6%	5%	$5.66
Canada	7%	0	$3.01
Mexico	0	0	$2.82

To preview the completed solution:

1. Start Visual Studio .NET and open the solution file named **Chapter.04\ Complete04\Complete04.sln**.

2. Open the Solution Explorer, if necessary, and examine its contents. The solution contains two projects: a Windows Application project and a Class Library project. The component named Shipping is a Class Library project and contains the classes to calculate the shipping costs.

3. Run the solution. The splash screen appears, and then the main form appears. Enter the input values shown in Figure 4-1 (complete with the capitalization shown).

4. Click **Ship To Canada** to determine the cost to ship the package to Canada. Note that if you supply invalid input, the solution will display a message box indicating that the input is incorrect and request that you provide correct input values. Figure 4-2 shows the results of the shipment information entered in Figure 4-1.

5. Enter a postal code of **1234**, a weight of **25**, and a declared value of **200**. Click the **Ship To Australia** button to calculate the cost of a shipment to Australia.

6. Enter a postal code of **12345**, a weight of **10**, and a declared value of **100**. Click the **Ship To Mexico** button to calculate the cost of a shipment to Mexico.

7. Enter a postal code of **22**, a declared value of **–3**, and a weight of **–3**. Click the **Ship To Mexico** button. A message box appears indicating that the input is not valid. Click **OK** to close the message box.

8. End the solution, and then exit Visual Studio .NET.

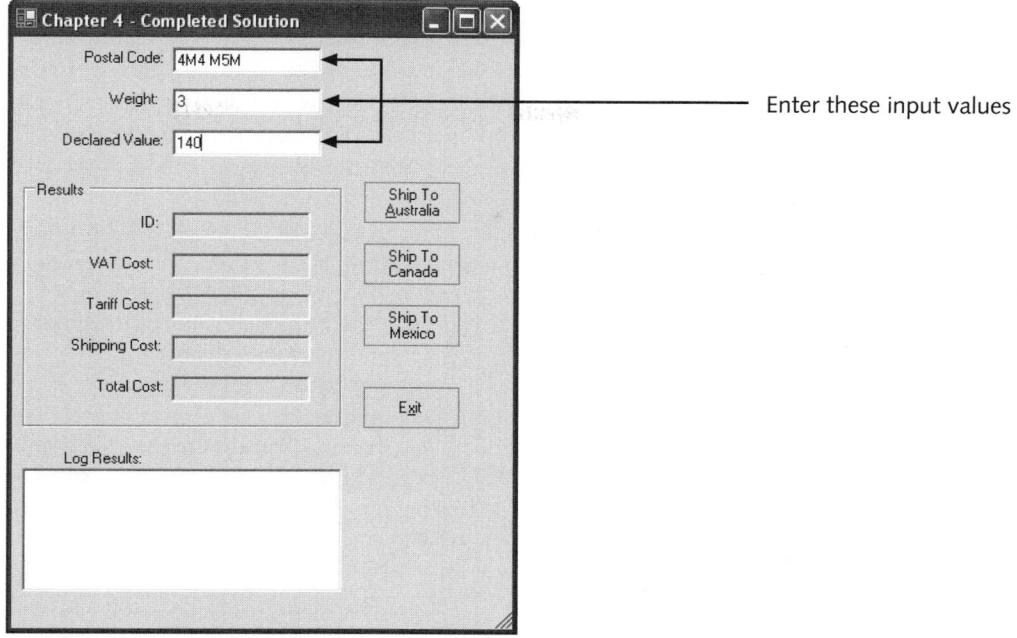

Enter these input values

Figure 4-1   Completed solution – main form

Details of shipping costs

Total shipping costs

Text box contains shipment log

Figure 4-2   Completed solution – shipment output

The design of this solution is similar to the design of the solution from Chapter 3. First, the component named Shipping performs the tasks necessary to calculate the cost of a shipment to one of three countries. The members of the Validate class perform all of the necessary input validation. The main form calls on the services provided by the Shipping component. The Shipping component, in turn, calls upon the services of the Validate component. Figure 4-3 illustrates the design of the Shipping and Validate components.

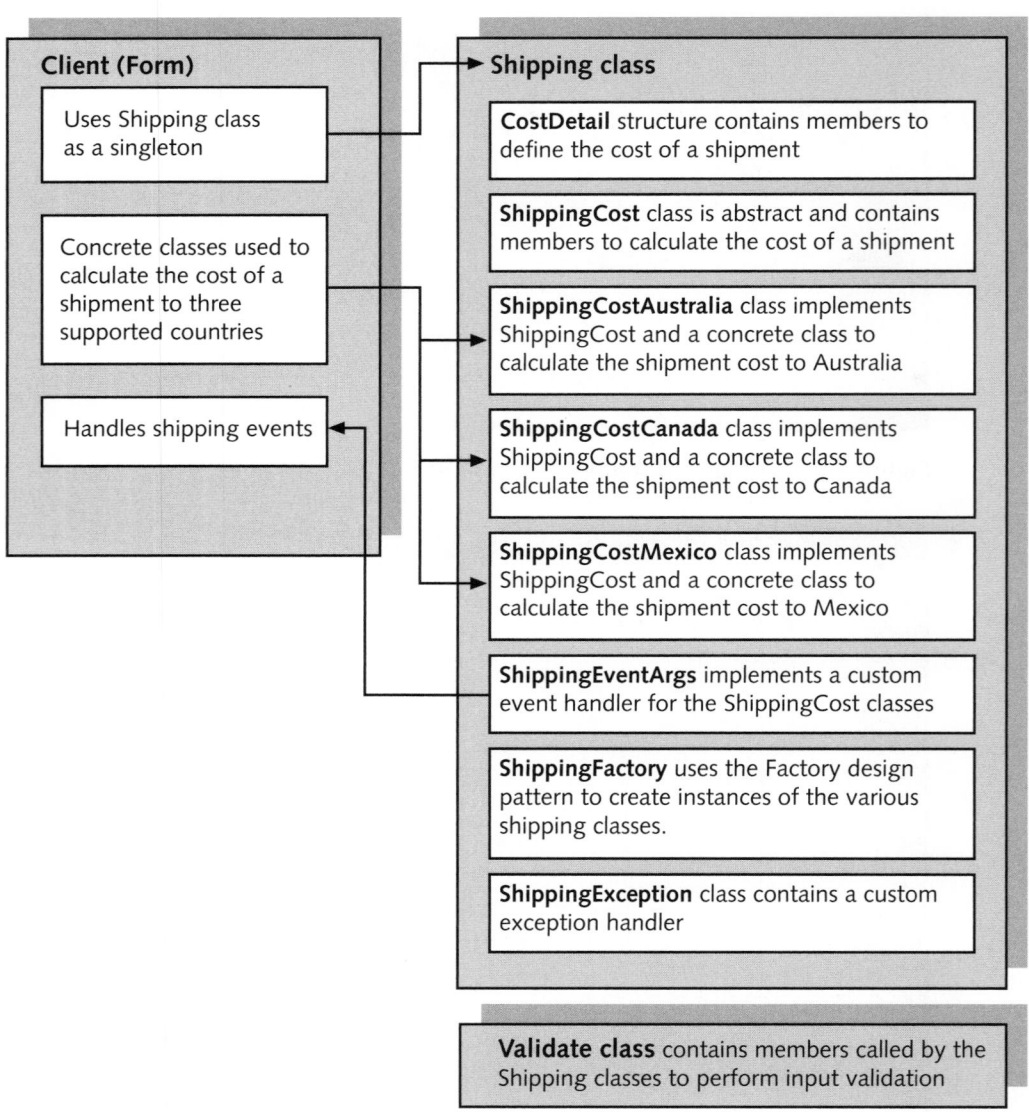

Client (Form)

Uses Shipping class as a singleton

Concrete classes used to calculate the cost of a shipment to three supported countries

Handles shipping events

Shipping class

CostDetail structure contains members to define the cost of a shipment

ShippingCost class is abstract and contains members to calculate the cost of a shipment

ShippingCostAustralia class implements ShippingCost and a concrete class to calculate the shipment cost to Australia

ShippingCostCanada class implements ShippingCost and a concrete class to calculate the shipment cost to Canada

ShippingCostMexico class implements ShippingCost and a concrete class to calculate the shipment cost to Mexico

ShippingEventArgs implements a custom event handler for the ShippingCost classes

ShippingFactory uses the Factory design pattern to create instances of the various shipping classes.

ShippingException class contains a custom exception handler

Validate class contains members called by the Shipping classes to perform input validation

Figure 4-3 Solution design

As shown in Figure 4–3, the Shipping class contains nested classes and structures. The CostDetail structure stores the costs applicable to a shipment. Three classes named ShippingCostAustralia, ShippingCostCanada, and ShippingCostMexico inherit from the base ShippingCost class. The class named ShippingException is used to manage errors (exceptions) that may arise from supplying invalid input to the application. As a result, the developer using the Shipping component does not need to perform any input validation. That responsibility is hidden inside of the implementation of the Shipping component. The Validate component is similar to the one used in Chapter 3.

WORKING WITH MULTI-PROJECT SOLUTIONS

Until now, you have created solutions having a single project. However, Visual Studio .NET will allow you to create solutions containing multiple projects. As the author of a component, you typically create a Class Library project containing a reusable component that is designed for use by other developers. However, acting as the developer, you need to test the Class Library project to make sure that it works correctly. This is the purpose of a multi-project solution.

This chapter's solution contains two projects: a Windows Application project and a Class Library project. The purpose of the Windows Application project is to test the component contained within the Class Library project. When the Class Library project gets compiled, it will be compiled to a .dll file as a separate assembly. This assembly can be distributed to developers independently of the Windows Application project.

Figure 4–4 shows the Solution Explorer with two projects.

Figure 4-4   Solution Explorer with two projects

As shown in Figure 4-4, the Windows Application project is named Complete04 and the Class Library project is named Shipping. The Windows Application project contains forms but the Class Library project does not. By definition, Class Library projects have no visible interface. Rather, other developers use the components they expose programmatically. Note also that the Complete04 project appears in a bold typeface. The project appearing in bold is always the startup project.

To add an existing project to a solution:

1. Start Visual Studio .NET and open the solution named **Chapter.04\ Startup04\Startup04.sln**.

2. On the menu bar, click **File**, point to **Add Project**, and then click **Existing Project**.

3. The Add Existing Project dialog box appears. Select the project named **Chapter.04\Startup04\Shipping\Shipping.vbproj**, and then click **Open** to add the Class Library project to the solution.

    The newly added project will appear in the Solution Explorer. Note that if you were adding a new project you would have selected New Project instead of Existing Project, and then selected the project type and name.

If you tried to create an instance of the class contained in the Class Library project from the Windows Application project, you would find that it will not work. The reason is simple: just as you must add references to the assemblies that comprise the .NET Framework class library, you must also add a reference to the assembly that comprises the Class Library project.

To add a reference to an assembly:

1. In the Solution Explorer, right-click on the project named **Startup04**, and then click **Add Reference**. Make sure to right-click on the project rather than the solution. The Add Reference dialog box appears.

2. Three tabs appear on the Add Reference dialog box. Click the **Projects** tab.

    The Projects tab allows multiple projects within the same solution to communicate with each other.

3. Click **Shipping**, if necessary, and then click the **Select** button. The project appears in the Selected Components pane. Your screen should resemble Figure 4-5.

4. Click **OK** to add the reference. Expand the folders appearing in the Solution Explorer to display the references, if necessary. Note that the reference to the Shipping assembly appears.

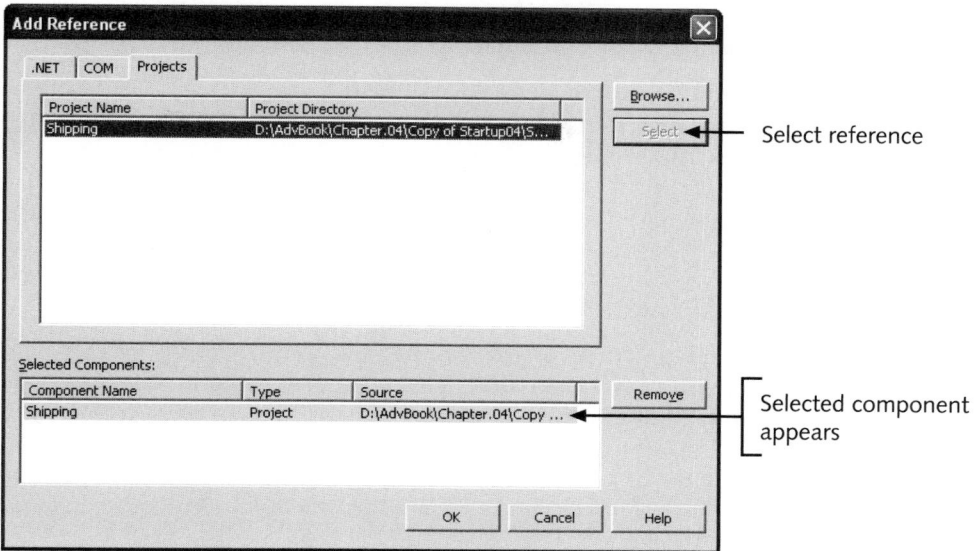

Figure 4-5 Add Reference dialog box

THE BASICS OF OOP DESIGN

One of the primary goals of object-oriented programming is to create components that can be used again and again by different developers. Those components should be designed in such a way that they are easily modifiable, upgradeable, and expandable. This level of sharing and reusability ultimately reduces the cost to develop and maintain a particular component.

Consider the task of input validation. As you have seen, it is logical to create a reusable component to validate input. For example, a Validate component could contain methods to validate the format of fields such as a person's Social Security number, a United States telephone number, or a postal code, because all of these data items have well-known formats. Once the component has been created to validate this input, developers across the enterprise can use and reuse that same component. Thus, each developer does not need to "reinvent the wheel" for each application created, because that component can be viewed as a black box.

Many theories have been expressed about the best way to design software components so as to promote reusability and expandability. One such theory identifies common abstract repeating patterns, called problems, and describes common solutions to those problems. These repeating patterns are referred to as design patterns. **Design patterns** are abstract patterns that describe common problems appearing in object-oriented programs, and well-known solutions to those common problems. Generally, design patterns can be categorized by their purpose, as described in the following list:

- **Creational patterns** define a systematic process that describes how objects get created. For example, given a print spooler, you may want to apply a creation rule that only one instance of the class (print spooler) exists. This one instance of a print spooler is shared by all applications. This type of pattern is called a singleton. Other creational patterns include the factory pattern. Think of a factory as an assembly line creating the same product, or similar products, over and over again. The singleton and factory patterns are discussed in more detail in the next section of this chapter.

- **Structural patterns** define the organization (structure) of classes. The adapter pattern is a structural pattern used to make incompatible interfaces compatible. For example, imagine that you have an electrical device, such as a clock, that is designed to plug into a standard 3-prong U.S. electrical outlet, but you want to use the clock in Germany. An adapter allows you plug the clock into a receptacle in Germany thereby making incompatible devices compatible.

- **Behavioral patterns** define the interaction between classes and the division of responsibility between two or more classes. The chain of responsibility pattern is a behavioral pattern. Given a single request, there may be several different classes specifically designed to handle that request. For example, consider a component designed to display images such that each class is designed to display an image having a different file format. The request to display the image is passed from class to class until one of the classes recognizes the image format and can display it.

 Entire books have been written on the topic of design patterns; we only introduce the concepts in this chapter. Furthermore, many more design patterns exist than the singleton and factory patterns discussed in this chapter. As you progress through the chapters in this book, we will revisit the topic of design patterns and introduce new design patterns as the applications produced fall into one or more of the various design pattern categories.

The Singleton Design Pattern

A **singleton** is a component (class) configured such that a developer can only create one instance of that component. As a singleton describes how a class instance gets created, it falls into the category of a creational pattern. That is, one instance of the singleton should be universally available to all of the applications using the component.

The singleton pattern applies to several types of tasks. For example, consider a shared message log or a print spooler. Given the scenario of a shared message log, no matter the number of applications (processes) running on the system, they should all write entries to the same shared message log. Thus, only one instance of the class responsible for writing to the message log should exist and should be shared by all processes.

A print spooler works the same way, meaning, all of the applications on a single computer share the same print spooler. In this chapter you will define the Shipping class as a singleton. That is, the developer will only be able to create one instance of the Shipping class.

The .NET Framework makes the process of creating a singleton surprisingly easy. First, make the constructor for a class Private instead of Public. This change has the effect of preventing a developer from creating an instance of the class. Then, create a Shared method or declare a Shared field to create an instance of the class. By convention, this method or field is named Instance although any legal identifier name will work. The following statements create a singleton:

```
Public NotInheritable Class Shipping
    Private Sub New()
    End Sub
    Public Shared ReadOnly Instance As Shipping = _
        New Shipping()
End Class
```

The preceding code segment declares the Shipping class. Note that the constructor for the class is declared with the Private access modifier instead of the Public access modifier. By making the constructor Private, the developer cannot use the New keyword to create an instance of the class. The key to implementing the singleton is the Instance variable. By declaring the Instance variable as Shared and initializing the variable upon declaration, the .NET Framework will initialize the variable (create an instance of the Shipping class) only the first time that the variable is referenced. If the variable is never referenced, no instance of the Shipping class will ever be created. If the variable is referenced repeatedly, additional instances of the Shipping class will not be created. Note that the class is declared with the NotInheritable keyword. This keyword, discussed in detail in the next section, prevents another class from inheriting this class.

The developer creates an instance of the Shipping class by referencing the Instance field of the Shipping class, as shown in the following statement:

```
Dim shpCurrent = Course.Shipping.Instance
```

Again, because the constructor is hidden (declared with the Private access modifier), the following statement will not work to create an instance of the Shipping class:

```
Dim shpCurrent = New Course.Shipping()
```

To create a singleton:

    1. Insert a new module named Shipping into the Shipping project. Select the **Shipping** project in the Solution Explorer. On the menu bar, click **Project**, and then click **Add Class**. In the Add New Item - Shipping dialog box, set the class name to **Shipping.vb**. Click **Open**.

2. Activate the Code Editor for the Shipping class, if necessary and then enter the following statements (shown in bold) into the module:

```
Option Explicit On
Option Strict On
Imports Microsoft.VisualBasic.ControlChars
Public NotInheritable Class Shipping
    Private Sub New()
    End Sub
    Public Shared ReadOnly Instance As Shipping = _
        New Shipping()
    Public Enum ShippingCountryEnum
        Australia
        Canada
        Mexico
    End Enum
    Public Structure CostDetail
        Public VatCost As Double
        Public TariffCost As Double
        Public ShippingCost As Double
        Public TotalCost As Double
    End Structure
End Class
```

The preceding statements create the singleton. The enumeration named ShippingCountryEnum will be used by the component to define the valid countries. The structure named CostDetail will be used by the component to store the detailed costs of a shipment.

3. Activate the Code Editor for the main form named **frmMain.vb**, and then enter the following statement immediately after the Win Forms Designer generated code declare a variable to store the singleton:

```
Private Ship As Course.Shipping
```

4. Enter the following statement in the **frmMain_Load** event handler to create an instance of the singleton:

```
Ship = Course.Shipping.Instance
```

The Factory Design Pattern

Another creational pattern is the factory design pattern. In the **factory** design pattern, one class is responsible for creating instances of the various classes derived from an abstract class. An abstract class is one that declares an interface but no implementation. In other words, an abstract class contains function and sub procedure declarations but does not contain any code to define the implementation of those members.

In the Shipping component, you will create an abstract class that defines the common elements to ship a package to any country. Derived classes will subsequently be created to ship packages to specific countries. The factory design pattern involves the following:

- Logically, you implement a factory design pattern such that the **client** uses the factory. In this solution the client is the Windows Application project.

- The **factory**, in turn, is responsible for creating products. By using an abstract class to create the products, additional products can be added without affecting existing clients.

- The **products** represent the elements created by the factory. In this chapter's solution, each shipment to a different country is considered a product.

In this solution, consider the factory to be the Shipping class. The Shipping class contains a nested class named ShippingFactory with one method named CreateShippingCost. The CreateShippingCost method is responsible for creating a shipment to each of the three supported countries. Thus, the shipments become the products. The component author can add classes to create shipments to additional countries without affecting existing clients. The methods already created to ship a package to an existing country need not be changed. Figure 4-6 illustrates the factory design pattern used in this chapter to create the shipments.

Figure 4-6 Factory design pattern

As shown in Figure 4-6, the Windows Application project represents the client. The client creates an instance of the factory (Shipping class), which itself is a singleton, meaning, there exists only one instance of the Shipping class. The factory, in turn, is responsible for creating instances of the various products (shipments), and returning those shipments to the client.

As you work through the chapter, you will learn about abstract classes, inheritance, and how to inherit one class from another. Using inheritance, you will implement the factory design pattern.

 In this section we have introduced only two of the 23 defined design patterns. As you progress through the chapters in this book, the topic of design patterns will be revisited where appropriate.

Having introduced design patterns and how those patterns can be used to create reusable components, we now explore the VB .NET syntax to implement those components. First, we discuss the concept of overloading.

OVERLOADING MEMBERS

Overloading provides the means by which VB .NET allows multiple function, sub, or property procedures in a class, or other module, to share the same name. We refer generically to an overloaded function procedure, sub procedure, property procedure, or constructor as an **overloaded member**.

Signatures in Overloaded Members

When creating an overloaded member, each overloaded member may have a different argument count. Two overloaded members may also have the same argument count. In the second case, at least one of the corresponding argument data types must differ. For example, two overloaded members may have one argument. If they do, then the data type of that argument must differ for each of the members. The unique combination of arguments for a member, and the data types of those arguments, form a member's **signature**.

Any member (function procedure, sub procedure, property procedure, or constructor) can be overloaded. Furthermore, both shared and instance members may be overloaded. The CLR calls the correct overloaded member based on that member's unique signature. If you try to create a member without a unique signature, VB .NET will identify a syntax error.

The following list describes the syntactical rules for creating overloaded members:

- Include the optional Overloads keyword in all of the declarations for an overloaded member. If the Overloads keyword appears in one member declaration, then it must appear in all of the declarations for that overloaded member. The examples in this book will include the optional Overloads keyword to improve readability and clarity. (Thus, you can include the Overloads keyword for clarity, but its use is not required.)

- By creating multiple members having the same name, VB .NET will automatically consider that member as an overloaded member.

- Even though constructors (the New procedure) can be overloaded, the Overloads keyword must not appear in a constructor. The reason for this is simple. Even though the New procedure looks like any other sub procedure, it is not. Rather, constructors have unique inheritance rules and other unique attributes. Overloading and inheriting constructors is discussed in further detail in the section titled Inheritance and Constructors of this chapter.

- The return data type for overloaded methods must be the same, meaning, overloaded functions or properties must return a value having the same data type for all members.

The following code segment illustrates how to create an overloaded Shared method named IsIntegerInRange:

```
Private Overloads Shared Function IsIntegerInRange( _
    ByVal pintArg As Integer, ByVal pintMin As Integer, _
    ByVal pintMax As Integer) As Boolean
    If pintArg >= pintMin And pintArg <= pintMax Then
        Return True
    End If
End Function

Private Overloads Shared Function IsIntegerInRange( _
    ByVal pstrArg As String, ByVal pintMin As Integer, _
    ByVal pintMax As Integer) As Boolean
    Dim pintArg As Integer
    If IsInteger(pstrArg) Then
        pintArg = ToInt32(pstrArg)
        If pintArg >= pintMin And pintArg <= pintMax Then
            Return True
        End If
    End If
End Function

Private Shared Function IsInteger( _
    ByVal pstrArg As String) As Boolean
    Dim pintArg As Integer, pdblArg As Double
    If IsNumeric(pstrArg) Then
        pintArg = ToInt32(pstrArg)
        pdblArg = ToDouble(pstrArg)
        If pintArg = pdblArg Then
            Return True
        End If
    End If
End Function
```

The preceding code segment defines a method named IsIntegerInRange having two unique signatures. The CLR will call the appropriate method based on the data type and number of arguments passed to the method. The first method determines whether an Integer argument is within the valid range of values defined in the second and third arguments. The second method accepts three arguments too, but as the first argument is a string, the string is first validated to determine whether it contains a valid Integer number. The IsInteger function performs the validation for the string value.

The following statements illustrate how to call the preceding overloaded method:

```
Dim pblnValid As Boolean
pblnValid = IsIntegerInRange(7, 1, 10)      ' True
pblnValid = IsIntegerInRange("17", 1, 10) ' False
```

Figure 4-7 illustrates the logic that VB .NET uses to call the preceding overloaded methods.

```
Overloaded method

    Private Overloads Shared Function IsIntegerInRange( _
        ByVal pintArg As Integer, _
        ByVal pintMin As Integer, _
        ByVal pintMax As Integer) As Boolean
        . . .
    End Function

    Private Overloads Shared Function IsIntegerInRange( _
        ByVal pstrArg As String, _
        ByVal pintMin As Integer, _
        ByVal pintMax As Integer) As Boolean
        . . .
    End Function
```

Signatures vary by argument type

Call correct method based on the data type of the first argument

```
    Dim pstrCurrent As String = "17"
    pblnValid = IsIntegerInRange(pstrCurrent, 1, 10)
```

```
    Dim pintCurrent As Integer = 7
    pblnValid = IsIntegerInRange(pintCurrent, 1, 10)
```

Figure 4-7   Calling an overloaded method

The statements in Figure 4-7 call the overloaded IsIntegerInRange method discussed already. In the first call to the method, pstrCurrent has a value of 17, which is not between 1 and 10, so the method returns False. The Integer value 7 in the second call to IsIntegerInRange is between 1 and 10 so the method returns True.

In this solution you will create an overloaded Shared method named IsValidPostalCode that will validate the postal codes for the supported countries. This Shared method will call the overloaded IsIntegerInRange methods just shown. You will validate the postal code based on the rules described in the following list:

- Australian postal codes consist of a four-digit number.
- Canadian postal codes have the form *LDL DLD* where *L* represents a letter and *D* represents a digit. Note that a space appears in the postal code.
- Mexican postal codes consist of a five-digit number similar to U.S. postal codes.

In this solution you will create an overloaded method to validate the postal codes for the countries supported. The first method will accept one argument having a data type of String. Canada will be used as the default country. The second overloaded method will allow the developer to specify the country name.

To create an overloaded method:

1. Activate the Code Editor for the module named **Validate.vb**, and then enter the following statements (shown in bold) in the PostalInfo class to implement the overloaded **IsValidPostalCode** method:

```
Public Class PostalInfo
    Public Overloads Shared Function IsValidPostalCode( _
        ByVal pstrCode As String) As Boolean
        Return IsValidCanadianPostalCode(pstrCode)
    End Function

    Public Overloads Shared Function IsValidPostalCode( _
        ByVal pstrCode As String, _
        ByVal Country As Shipping.ShippingCountryEnum) _
            As Boolean

        Select Case Country
            Case Shipping.ShippingCountryEnum.Australia
                Return _
                    IsValidAustralianPostalCode(pstrCode)
            Case Shipping.ShippingCountryEnum.Canada
                Return IsValidCanadianPostalCode(pstrCode)
            Case Shipping.ShippingCountryEnum.Mexico
                Return IsValidMexicanPostalCode(pstrCode)
        End Select
    End Function

    Private Shared Function IsValidAustralianPostalCode( _
        ByVal pstrCode As String) As Boolean
        If pstrCode.Length = 4 Then
            If IsIntegerInRange(pstrCode, 1, 9999) Then
                Return True
            End If
        End If
    End Function

    Private Shared Function IsValidCanadianPostalCode( _
        ByVal pstrCode As String) As Boolean
        If pstrCode.Length = 7 Then
            If IsDigit(pstrCode.Substring(0, 1)) And _
                IsCharacter(pstrCode.Substring(1, 1)) And _
                IsDigit(pstrCode.Substring(2, 1)) And _
                pstrCode.Substring(3, 1) = " " And _
                IsCharacter(pstrCode.Substring(4, 1)) And _
```

4

```
                        IsDigit(pstrCode.Substring(5, 1)) And _
                        IsCharacter(pstrCode.Substring(6, 1)) Then
                        Return True
                End If
            End If
        End Function

        Private Shared Function IsValidMexicanPostalCode( _
            ByVal pstrCode As String) As Boolean
            If pstrCode.Length = 5 Then
                If IsIntegerInRange(pstrCode, 1, 99999) Then
                    Return True
                End If
            End If
        End Function
        ' Statements
    End Class
```

You just created two methods named IsValidPostalCode having unique signatures. The Public
overloaded methods call Private function procedures named IsValidAustralianPostalCode,
IsValidCanadianPostalCode, and IsValidMexicanPostalCode respectively, to perform the
actual validation of the various postal codes. These procedures, in turn, call additional procedures named IsCharacter and IsDigit to determine whether a character is a letter or digit.
This code is fully commented on in the completed solution.

Implicit Type Conversion and Overloaded Members

Remember that VB .NET performs implicit type conversion from more restrictive types
to less restrictive types. These type conversion rules have implications for overloaded
members. The following code segment illustrates an important point about type conversion and overloaded methods:

```
Public Overloads Function IsMajorityAge( _
    pstrArg As String) As Boolean
    ' Statements
End Function

Public Overloads Function IsMajorityAge( _
    pdblArg As Double) As Boolean
    ' Statements
End Function
```

The preceding overloaded IsMajorityAge method has two signatures. Each method
accepts one argument; the argument of the first method has a data type of String and
the argument of the second method has a data type of Double. You may wonder what
would happen if a developer called this overloaded method with an argument having a
data type of Integer or Single, that is, which method would be called, or would an error

occur? The answer lies in the way that VB .NET performs type coercion. Remember that when strict type checking is enabled (Option Strict = On), VB .NET will automatically convert more restrictive types to less restrictive types. Thus, if you called the IsMajorityAge method with an Integer, Long, or Single argument, VB .NET would call the version of the method that accepts a Double data type as an argument because it has the closet matching less restrictive type. Figure 4-8 illustrates how VB .NET performs type coercion with overloaded members.

4

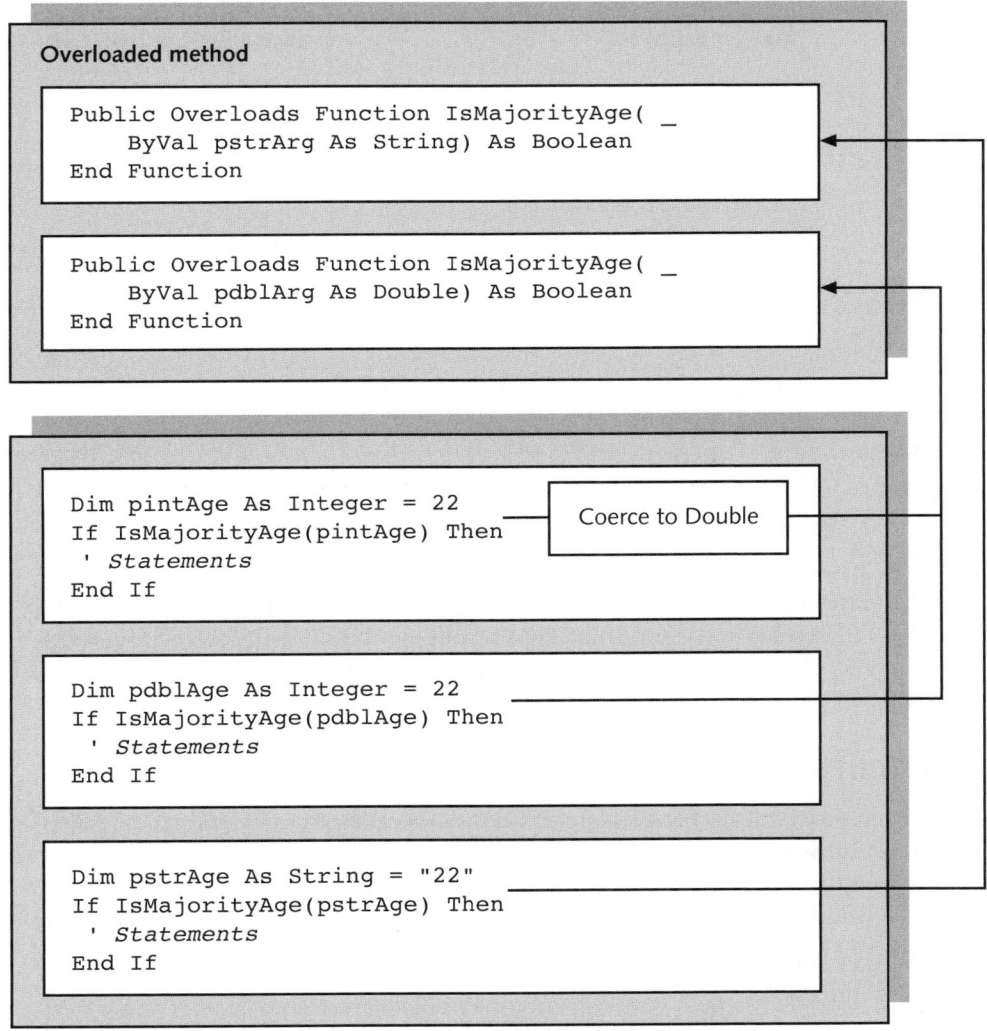

Figure 4-8   Type coercion with overloaded methods

When you create an overloaded member, each member must have a unique signature. Each member must also return a value having the same data type. To illustrate, examine the following invalid function prototypes for an overloaded IsValid method:

```
Public Overloads Function IsValid(pstrArg As String) _
    As Boolean
    . . .
End Function

Public Overloads Function IsValid(pstrArg As String) _
    As Integer
    . . .
End Function
```

The preceding attempt to overload the IsValid method will cause an error because both methods have identical signatures, meaning, both versions accept one argument having a data type of String. In addition, the preceding methods will not compile because the two methods return different data types: Boolean and Integer.

 When you call an overloaded method, Intellisense technology takes over and displays the appropriate ToolTip for the correct version of that overloaded member. It also displays the member number within the list of members. Numbering in the ToolTip begins at 1 rather than 0.

Another object-oriented feature new to VB .NET is true inheritance. We discuss it next.

INHERITANCE

Inheritance is the ability of one class to obtain, or inherit, all of the members of another class. The inherited class is called the **base class**, and the inheriting class is called the **derived class**. When you, as the developer, create an instance of the derived class, VB .NET implicitly makes the exposed members in the base class available.

Inheritance Rules of Different Languages

Different languages have different inheritance rules. For example, C++ supports **multiple inheritance**, meaning that a derived class can inherit from multiple base classes. By definition, all .NET Framework classes support **single inheritance**, however, a derived class can inherit from one and only one base class.

To introduce the concept of inheritance, examine the following statements common to all Windows forms:

```
Public Class frmMain
    Inherits System.Windows.Forms.Form
End Class
```

The Class and End Class statements define the block forming the class for a particular form (frmMain), and the Public access modifier indicates that any other assembly can use the class. The Inherits statement must immediately follow the Class statement and specifies the base class to be inherited. In this case, the form named frmMain (the derived class) is inheriting from System.Windows.Forms.Form (the base class). By inheriting from a base class, you can immediately call all of the methods contained in the base class and reference any of the properties defined in the base class. That is, you can call methods of the System.Windows.Forms.Form class such as Show, ShowDialog, and Focus, along with handling the events defined in the base class such as Enter and Leave.

Because the .NET Framework utilizes single inheritance, the following inheritance model is illegal because one derived class cannot inherit from two or more base classes:

```
Public Class frmMain
    Inherits System.Windows.Forms.Form
    Inherits System.Windows.Forms.Control
End Class
```

Inheritance Keywords

Understanding inheritance involves more than just inheriting one class from another class. For example, some classes can be inherited while others cannot. The following VB .NET keywords define the inheritance rules for a class and the inheritance rules for the members of that class:

- The **Inherits** keyword indicates that a class (the derived class) inherits the members of a base class. The Inherits keyword must appear inside of a Class block and appear as the first statement in the Class block. The Inherits keyword cannot appear in a module or structure, as these types cannot be inherited.

- The **MustInherit** keyword is used to create an abstract class and appears in the statement that declares the class. An abstract class defines the class's interface but not its implementation, meaning, an abstract class defines the members of the class but not what those members will do. It is not possible to create an instance of an abstract class. Rather, abstract classes provide a base class from which derived classes inherit. A class that is declared with the MustInherit keyword cannot be declared as NotInheritable.

- The optional **Overridable** keyword appears in a member declaration (function, sub, or property procedure) and indicates that the member may be overridden in a derived class. If the member is not overridden in the derived class, the member of the same name appearing in the base class will be called. Constructors cannot be declared with the Overridable keyword. Members are, by default, overridable so the Overridable keyword is optional.

- The **Overrides** keyword appears in the declaration for a member and indicates that a member in a derived class overrides a member having the same name and signature appearing in a base class. The member in the base class must be declared with the MustOverride or Overridable keywords. As an example, all classes support a method named ToString because the ToString method is defined by the System.Object superclass, and all types derive from System.Object. Thus, any class that you create can override the ToString method of the base class.

- The **MustOverride** keyword appears in the declaration for a member in a base class. It indicates that a derived class must override a particular member in a base class. The MustOverride keyword is typically used to define the interface of abstract classes.

- The **NotInheritable** keyword indicates that a class cannot be inherited. This type of class is often referred to as a sealed class. Because another class cannot inherit a class declared with the NotInheritable keyword, members in a NotInheritable class cannot be declared with the MustOverride or Overridable keywords.

Scope and Inheritance

Chapter 3 discussed the Public, Friend, and Private access modifiers. The Protected access modifier is used with nested classes and inherited classes. If a Protected member (variable, method, property) is declared in a base class, then it is visible to the members of the base class and any derived classes. In this chapter's solution, several Protected variables are declared in the ShippingCost class to store the data used to calculate the shipping costs. As Protected members, these variables (members) are exposed to the three derived classes. Examine the following statements that illustrate the scope of a Protected member:

```
Public MustInherit Class ShippingCost
    Protected mblnValidValue As Boolean = False
End Class

Public NotInheritable Class ShippingCostAustralia
    Inherits ShippingCost
    Public Function CalculateCostDetail() _
        As CostDetail
        Dim pCostDetail As CostDetail
        If mblnValidValue = True Then
            pCostDetail.TotalCost = 100.0
            Return pCostDetail
        End If
    End Function
End Class

Public Class OtherCost
    Public Function CalculateCostDetail() _
        As CostDetail
        Dim pCostDetail As CostDetail
        If mblnValidValue = True Then ' Error
```

```
            pCostDetail.TotalCost = 100.0
            Return pCostDetail
        End If
    End Function
End Class
```

The Protected variable named mblnValidValue will indicate whether the shipment value is valid. Any class derived from the ShippingCost class can reference this variable. In this case, the ShippingCostAustralia class inherits from the ShippingCost class, so the CalculateCostDetail method has access to the Protected member. The class named OtherCost does not derive from the ShippingCost class, so it does not have access to the Protected member named mblnValidValue and will cause an error. Protected members are part of a component's implementation. Thus, the following statements that try to reference the Protected member will cause an error:

```
Dim Ship As New ShippingCostAustralia()
Ship.mblnValidValue = True
```

Next, you will declare Protected variables to indicate whether a valid postal code, shipment value, and shipment weight have been specified. By declaring a Protected variable in a base class, it can be used in the derived classes.

To declare Protected variables:

1. Activate the Code Editor for the module named **Shipping.vb**, and then enter the following statements (shown in bold) to declare the ShippingCost class and its Protected members:

```
Public Structure CostDetail
    ' Statements
End Structure
Public MustInherit Class ShippingCost
    Protected mintIDCurrent As Integer
    Protected mstrPostalCode As String
    Protected mdblVatRate As Double
    Protected mdblTariffRate As Double
    Protected mdblValue As Double
    Protected mdblWeight As Double

    Protected mblnValidPostalCode As Boolean
    Protected mblnValidValue As Boolean
    Protected mblnValidWeight As Boolean
    Private SharedmintIDCount As Integer
End Class
```

The Protected variables named mintIDCurrent and mstrPostalCode store the identification number of the shipment and the postal code. The next four variables store the value added tax rate, tariff rate, value, and weight of the shipment, respectively. The final variables named mblnValidPostalCode, mblnValidValue, and mblnValidWeight indicate whether input values are correct or incorrect. The variable named mintIDCount will be used to store a counter for the current shipment ID.

4

Nested Classes

A nested class is simply a class that contains another class. That is, one Class block appears nested inside of another Class block, as shown in the following statements:

```
Public Class Shipping
    Public MustInherit Class ShippingCost
    End Class
    Public Class ShippingCostAustralia
        Inherits ShippingCost
    End Class
End Class
```

The preceding statements illustrate a nested class. The Shipping class contains classes named ShippingCost and ShippingCostAustralia. Again, this is logical as there exists a hierarchical relationship between the Shipping class and the destination countries. Note that an outer class can reference the inner classes without expressly specifying the class name.

Abstract Classes and Inheritance

To illustrate the inheritance model used in this Shipping component, we begin by examining the logic presented in Figure 4-9.

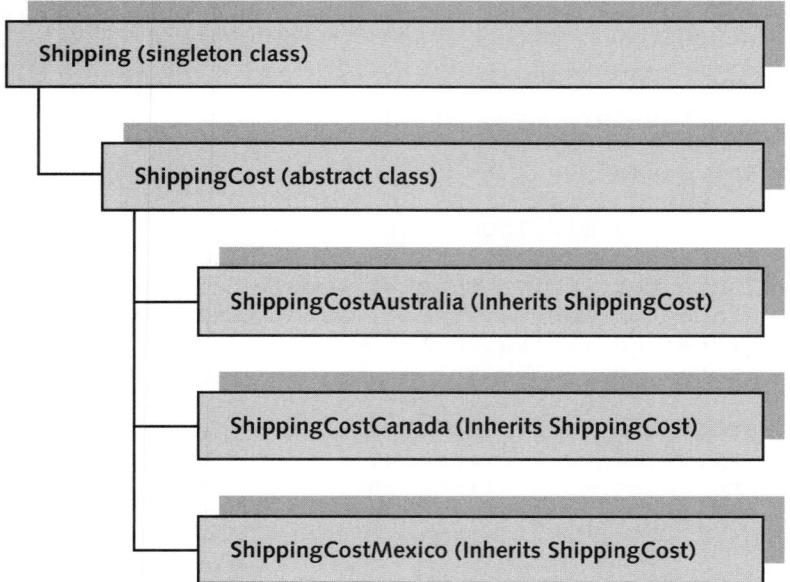

Figure 4-9   Inheritance in the Shipping component

As shown in Figure 4-9, the Shipping component (class) contains another class named ShippingCost. The developer does not create an instance of the ShippingCost class directly. Thus, the ShippingCost class is considered an **abstract class** and is declared with the MustInherit keyword, as shown in the following code:

```
Public MustInherit Class ShippingCost
End Class
```

By including the MustInherit keyword in the preceding class declaration, you are saying that neither the author nor another developer can create an instance of the ShippingCost class. Rather, a derived class must inherit the base class (ShippingCost). Thus, the following statement will cause an error:

```
Private CostNew As New ShippingCost()
```

In an abstract class, you typically define members (properties and methods) that will be implemented by a derived class. Thus, in the abstract class, you are defining the interface for the class. In the derived class, you define the implementation. In other words, you implement the interface. To declare an abstract member, you create a member prototype, as shown in the following code segment for the abstract ShippingCost class:

```
Public MustInherit Class ShippingCost
    Public MustOverride Function CalculateCostDetail() _
        As CostDetail
End Class
```

The preceding statements declare an abstract method named CalculateCostDetail, having a data type of CostDetail. Note that no implementation is provided for the abstract method. An abstract class may, however, contain one or more members having an implementation. In such a case, the derived class will inherit that member.

To create abstract members:

1. Activate the Code Editor for the module named **Shipping.vb**, if necessary, and then enter the following statements (shown in bold) to create the abstract members of the **ShippingCost** class:

```
Public MustInherit Class ShippingCost
    ' Statements
    Protected mblnValidWeight As Boolean
    Private Shared mintIDCount As Integer
    Public MustOverride Function CalculateCostSummary() _
        As String
    Public MustOverride Function CalculateCostDetail() _
        As CostDetail
End Class
```

The preceding code segment declares two abstract methods named CalculateCostSummary and CalculateCostDetail. Any class derived from the ShippingCost class must implement these methods, as they are declared with the MustOverride keyword. Note that the preceding members are only prototypes. The prototypes define the argument lists and the return data types for the members. However, the implementation of these members is left up to the derived classes.

The Overridable keyword declares a member that can be overridden in a derived class. If the member is not overridden in a derived class, VB .NET calls the member appearing in the base class. To illustrate, the ShippingCost class will contain two overridable methods named SetValue and SetWeight, and an overridable property named ID. The following code segment illustrates the SetValue method:

```
Public Overridable Function SetValue( _
    ByVal pstrArg As String) As Boolean
    If Validate.PostalInfo.IsIntegerInRange( _
        pstrArg, 1, 10000) Then
        mblnValidValue = True
        mdblValue = System.Convert.ToInt32(pstrArg)
    End If
End Function
```

The preceding overridable function procedure appears in the abstract ShippingCost class. Its purpose is to set a flag indicating whether the developer using the component has assigned a valid value for the value of the shipment. When the developer sets a value for this property, a hidden Boolean flag (mblnValidValue) is set to True indicating that the value has been set. In addition, the argument is copied to a hidden variable which is used later to calculate the cost of the shipment.

To create overridable members:

1. Activate the Code Editor for the module named **Shipping.vb**, if necessary, and then enter the following statements (shown in bold) in the **ShippingCost** class:

```
Public MustOverride Function CalculateCostDetail() _
    As CostDetail
Public Overridable Function SetValue( _
    ByVal pstrArg As String) As Boolean
    If Validate.PostalInfo.IsIntegerInRange( _
        pstrArg, 1, 10000) Then
        mblnValidValue = True
        mdblValue = System.Convert.ToInt32(pstrArg)
    End If
End Function

Public Overridable Function SetWeight( _
    ByVal pstrArg As String) As Boolean
    If Validate.PostalInfo.IsIntegerInRange( _
        pstrArg, 1, 100) Then
        mblnValidWeight = True
        mdblWeight = System.Convert.ToInt32(pstrArg)
    End If
End Function
```

```
Public Overridable ReadOnly Property ID() As Integer
    Get
        ID = mintIDCurrent
    End Get
End Property
```

Having created the abstract class, you can create the classes that will inherit from that abstract class.

Inheriting a Class

In this solution, three classes named ShippingCostAustralia, ShippingCostCanada, and ShippingCostMexico will be derived from the ShippingCost class. Each of these derived classes will calculate the shipping costs to the supported countries. Classes derived from an abstract class to provide an implementation are commonly called **concrete classes**.

The solution will calculate the cost of a shipment to three countries: Australia, Canada, and Mexico. Thus, three different classes will derive from the ShippingCost class (ShippingCostAustralia, ShippingCostCanada, and ShippingCostMexico). Examine the following class declarations:

```
Public MustInherit Class ShippingCost
    ' Statement
End Class
Public Class ShippingCostAustralia
    Inherits ShippingCost
    ' Statement
End Class
```

The preceding code segment illustrates the abstract class named ShippingCost. The concrete class named ShippingCostAustralia inherits from the base ShippingCost class. Presently, the application is designed to support three countries. However, as additional countries are added, you, as the author, merely need to create a new derived class for the new country you want to support.

Given the preceding declarations, other classes could inherit from the ShippingCostAustralia class, so, the following statements would be legal:

```
Public Class NewCountry
    Inherits ShippingCostAustralia
End Class
```

In some situations, this inheritance model may make sense. For example, suppose that an abstract class named ShippingCost was defined, and another class named ShippingCostEU provided an implementation for the ShippingCost class for the

European Union. Thus, you may want to derive specific classes from the ShippingCostEU class for particular countries within the European Union as shown in the following code segment:

```
Public MustInherit Class ShippingCost
End Class
Public Class ShippingCostEU
    Inherits ShippingCost
End Class
Public Class ShippingCostGermany
    Inherits ShippingCostEU
End Class
```

Prohibiting Inheritance

Just as you can force a class to be inherited, you can also prohibit a class from being inherited. A class that cannot be inherited is referred to as a **sealed class**. Many of the .NET Framework classes are sealed classes. If you examine the Help page for the String class, you will see the following declaration indicating that the String class cannot be inherited by another class:

```
NotInheritable Public Class String
    Implements IComparable, ICloneable, IConvertible, _
    IEnumerable
```

As you can see from the preceding declaration, the String class is declared as a sealed class because class declaration contains the NotInheritable keyword. (For now, don't worry about the Implements keyword. The Implements keyword indicates that a class implements one or more interfaces, and interfaces are discussed in Chapter 6.) Because the String class is not inheritable, the following declaration will cause an error:

```
Public Class Demo
    Inherits System.String
End Class
```

If you think about the ShippingCostAustralia, ShippingCostCanada, and ShippingCostMexico classes presented in this chapter, each provides a full implementation to calculate the cost of a shipment to a particular country. It is therefore logical that the classes should not be inherited.

To create sealed classes:

1. Activate the Code Editor, and then enter the following statements (shown in bold) for the **Shipping** class:

```
Public MustInherit Class ShippingCost
    ' Statements
End Class
Public NotInheritable Class ShippingCostAustralia
    Inherits ShippingCost
End Class
```

```
Public NotInheritable Class ShippingCostCanada
    Inherits ShippingCost
End Class
Public NotInheritable Class ShippingCostMexico
    Inherits ShippingCost
End Class
```

Note that at this point in the solution's development, the statements that you just wrote will cause errors. The reason is simple. You declared abstract methods in the base class that must be implemented in the derived classes. You will perform that task next.

OVERRIDING MEMBERS

There may be occasions when a member in a base class should perform a different action from a member of the same name in a derived class. Furthermore, members in a derived class must provide an implementation for the corresponding abstract members declared in a base class. This process is called **overriding**.

To see how overriding works, we begin with a simple example. Remember that every type you create is ultimately derived from the base class named System.Object, and that this base class defines the method named ToString, among others. Thus, any class derived from System.Object will have a default implementation for this method.

In this chapter's solution, you already declared a structure named CostDetail in the Shipping class to store the shipping cost of a parcel. If you called the ToString method on a variable of type CostDetail, the following string would be returned:

```
Course.Shipping.CostDetail
```

By default, calling the ToString method on a structure will return the fully qualified class name of the structure (in this case, the CostDetail structure of the Shipping class of the Course namespace). To change the default behavior of the ToString method, you can override it in a structure as shown in the following statements:

```
Public Overrides Function ToString() As String
    ' Statements
End Function
```

The rules to create an overridable method in a base class and optionally override that method in a derived class are simple. In the base class, include the Overridable or MustOverride keywords in the method or property declaration. In the derived class, include the Overrides keyword in the method or property declaration. Note that if you override a method, the method in the derived class must have the same signature as the method in the base class. Note also that it is possible to override overloaded members. Next, you will override the ToString method in the CostDetail structure.

To override a method:

1. Activate the Code Editor for the module named **Shipping.vb**, if necessary, and then enter the following statements (shown in bold) to override the ToString method in the **CostDetail** structure:

```
Public Structure CostDetail
    Public VatCost As Double
    Public TariffCost As Double
    Public ShippingCost As Double
    Public TotalCost As Double
    Public Overrides Function ToString() As String
        Return "Vat Cost = " & VatCost.ToString("c") _
        & CrLf & _
        "Tariff Cost = " & TariffCost.ToString("c") _
        & CrLf & _
        "Shipping Cost = " & _
        ShippingCost.ToString("c") & CrLf & _
        "Total Cost = " & TotalCost.ToString("c")
    End Function
End Structure
```

There exist some variations on the concept of overriding. There may be times when a method in a base class should not be overridden in a derived class. The NotOverridable keyword prevents a derived class from overriding a particular method in a base class. Overriding overloaded members has implications too. An overloaded member can be overridden. However, you need not override all of the overloaded members (members with different signatures). Furthermore, you can add methods with new signatures in a derived class.

At this point, you have all the necessary tools to create the concrete classes named ShippingCostAustralia, ShippingCostCanada, and ShippingCostMexico that will inherit the abstract ShippingCost class. Consider the following points about these classes:

- Private constants are declared in each concrete class to store the value added tax rate, the tariff rate, and the shipping rate per pound.

- Each concrete class will contain an overloaded constructor, which you will create later in the chapter.

- Each class overrides the abstract CalculateCostSummary and CalculateCostDetail methods declared with the MustOverride keyword in the base ShippingCost class.

To create a concrete class:

1. Activate the Code Editor for the module named **Shipping.vb**, if necessary, and then enter the following statements (shown in bold) in the **ShippingCostAustralia** class:

```
Public NotInheritable Class ShippingCostAustralia
    Inherits ShippingCost
```

4

```
        Private Const cdblVatRate As Double = 0.06
        Private Const cdblTariffRate As Double = 0.05
        Private Const cdblShippingRate As Double = 5.66
        Public Overrides Function CalculateCostSummary() _
            As String
            If mblnValidPostalCode AndAlso mblnValidValue _
                AndAlso mblnValidWeight Then
                Return CalculateCostDetail.ToString
            End If
        End Function

        Public Overrides Function CalculateCostDetail() _
            As CostDetail
            Dim pCostDetail As CostDetail
            If mblnValidPostalCode AndAlso mblnValidValue _
                AndAlso mblnValidWeight Then
                pCostDetail.VatCost = mdblValue * cdblVatRate
                pCostDetail.TariffCost = mdblValue * _
                    cdblTariffRate
                pCostDetail.ShippingCost = mdblWeight * _
                    cdblShippingRate
                pCostDetail.TotalCost = pCostDetail.VatCost + _
                    pCostDetail.TariffCost + _
                    pCostDetail.ShippingCost
                Return pCostDetail
            End If
        End Function
End Class
```

The constants named cdblVatRate, cdblTariffRate, and cdblShippingRate define the value added tax rate, tariff rate, and shipping rate per pound to ship a package. The CalculateCostSummary procedure first tests whether the input fields are valid. If they are, the CalculateCostDetail method is called. The CalculateCostDetail method calculates the cost of the value added tax, tariff cost, shipping cost, and total cost. This structure is returned by the method.

2. Activate the Code Editor for the module named **Shipping.vb**, if necessary, and then enter the following statements (shown in bold) in the **ShippingCostCanada** class:

```
Public NotInheritable Class ShippingCostCanada
    Inherits ShippingCost
    Private Const cdblVatRate As Double = 0.07
    Private Const cdblTariffRate As Double = 0
    Private Const cdblShippingRate As Double = 3.01
    Public Overrides Function CalculateCostSummary() _
        As String
        If mblnValidPostalCode AndAlso mblnValidValue _
            AndAlso mblnValidWeight Then
```

```
                    Return CalculateCostDetail.ToString
              End If
          End Function

          Public Overrides Function CalculateCostDetail() _
          As CostDetail
              Dim pCostDetail As CostDetail
              If mblnValidPostalCode AndAlso mblnValidValue _
                  AndAlso mblnValidWeight Then
                  pCostDetail.VatCost = mdblValue * cdblVatRate
                  pCostDetail.TariffCost = mdblValue * _
                      cdblTariffRate
                  pCostDetail.ShippingCost = mdblWeight * _
                      cdblShippingRate
                  pCostDetail.TotalCost = pCostDetail.VatCost + _
                      pCostDetail.TariffCost + _
                      pCostDetail.ShippingCost
                  Return pCostDetail
              End If
          End Function
      End Class
```

3. Activate the Code Editor for the module named **Shipping.vb**, if necessary, and then enter the following statements (shown in bold) in the **ShippingCostMexico** class:

```
Public NotInheritable Class ShippingCostMexico
    Inherits ShippingCost
    Private Const cdblVatRate As Double = 0
    Private Const cdblTariffRate As Double = 0
    Private Const cdblShippingRate As Double = 4.88
    Public Overrides Function CalculateCostSummary() _
        As String
        If mblnValidPostalCode AndAlso mblnValidValue _
            AndAlso mblnValidWeight Then
            Return CalculateCostDetail.ToString
        End If
    End Function

    Public Overrides Function CalculateCostDetail() _
        As CostDetail
        Dim pCostDetail As CostDetail
        If mblnValidPostalCode AndAlso mblnValidValue _
            AndAlso mblnValidWeight Then
            pCostDetail.VatCost = mdblValue * cdblVatRate
            pCostDetail.TariffCost = mdblValue * _
                cdblTariffRate
            pCostDetail.ShippingCost = mdblWeight * _
                cdblShippingRate
            pCostDetail.TotalCost = pCostDetail.VatCost + _
```

```
                    pCostDetail.TariffCost + _
                    pCostDetail.ShippingCost
            Return pCostDetail
        End If
    End Function
End Class
```

4

INHERITANCE AND CONSTRUCTORS

Remember that a constructor is a procedure named New that VB .NET calls to create an instance of a class. You may think that a constructor is an ordinary sub procedure having the special name New, but it is not. If you declare a constructor in a base class and then create derived classes from that base class, you would expect the derived class to inherit the constructor from the base class, just as other members would be inherited. This is not the case, however. The following list describes the inheritance rules for constructors:

- If a constructor appears in a base class and accepts no arguments, that constructor will be implicitly called from any derived classes. Thus, the derived class need not have a constructor at all. It is also possible for both base classes and derived classes to have no constructors at all.

- If a constructor in a base class has parameters, then the constructor must be implemented in any derived classes. Furthermore, the first statement in the constructor must call the corresponding constructor in the base class using the MyBase keyword.

First we examine the scenario of constructors without arguments, as shown in the following code segment:

```
Public MustInherit Class ShippingCost
    Public Sub New()
        ' Initialization statements
    End Sub
End Class

Public NotInheritable Class ShippingCostAustralia
    Inherits ShippingCost
End Class
Public NotInheritable Class ShippingCostCanada
    Inherits ShippingCost
    Public Sub New()
        ' Initialization statements
    End Sub
End Class
```

If a base class has a Public constructor that accepts no arguments, then the derived class implicitly calls the constructor of the base class. Including the MyBase keyword in the constructor for the derived class is optional. To illustrate, consider what happens when the following statement executes:

```
Dim shpAustralia As New ShippingCostAustralia()
```

The preceding statement creates an instance of the ShippingCostAustralia class. Because the ShippingCostAustralia class has no constructor, the parameterless constructor in the base Shipping class is called. However, consider the following statement, which creates an instance of the ShippingCostCanada class:

```
Dim shpCanada As New ShippingCostCanada()
```

The execution of the constructors for the preceding statement is much different because the ShippingCostCanada class has a constructor too. Figure 4-10 illustrates the execution flow of the constructors.

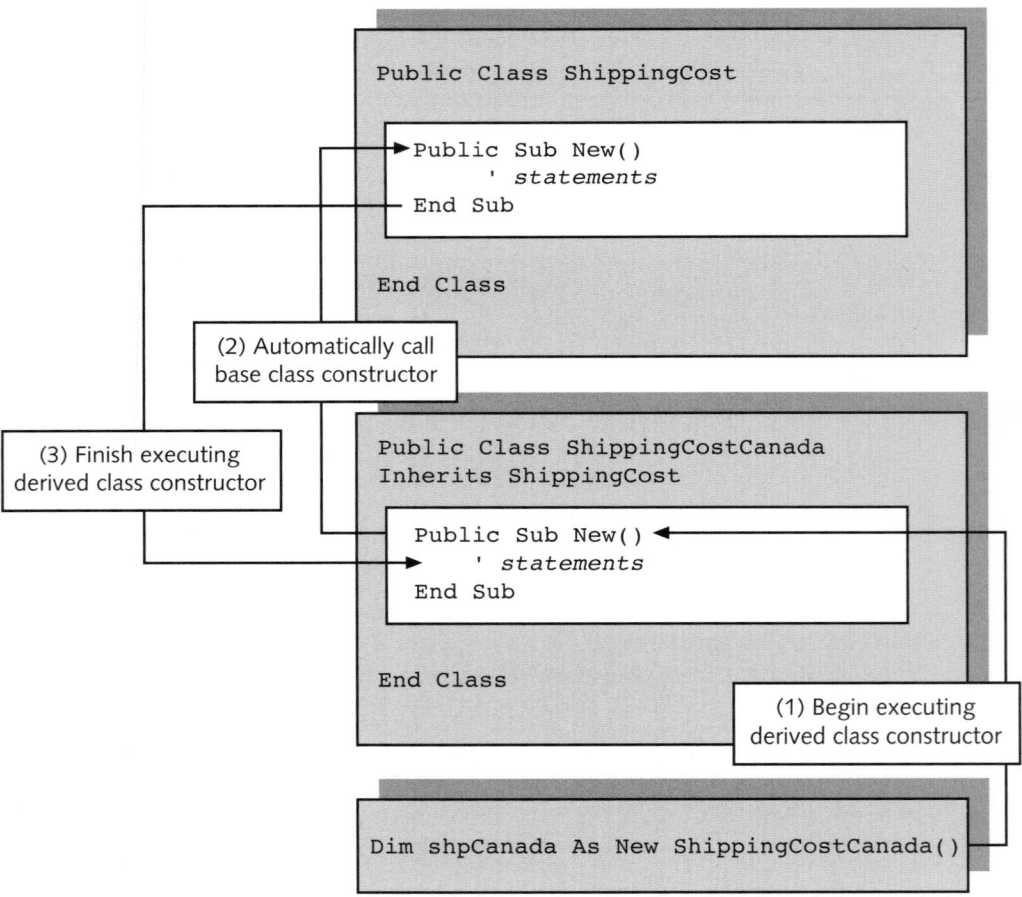

Figure 4-10   Inheriting constructors without parameters

When an instance of the ShippingCostCanada class gets created, the parameterless constructor in the derived class is implicitly called. Before executing the statements in the derived class's constructor, the statements in the base class's constructor execute. Then the statements in the constructor for the derived class execute.

If a base class has a constructor that accepts arguments, then the derived class must explicitly implement a constructor having the same signature. That is, the parameterized constructor is not implicitly inherited. To illustrate, the following constructors will not work because the derived class does not implement a constructor having the same signature as the constructor in the base class:

```
Public MustInherit Class ShippingCost
    Public Sub New(ByVal pstrPostalCode As String)
        ' Initialization statements
    End Sub
End Class

Public Class ShippingCostAustralia
    Inherits ShippingCost
End Class
```

A derived class will not implicitly inherit a constructor with arguments. Thus, assuming the above class declaration, the following statement to create an instance of the ShippingCostAustralia class will cause an error:

```
Dim shpAustralia As New ShippingCostAustralia("1234")
```

VB .NET will display an error message for the ShippingCostAustralia class indicating that there are too many arguments for Public Sub New. The reason is simple. Constructors with arguments are not implicitly inherited. Thus, you must explicitly create a constructor in the derived class. Thus, you may expect that the following change would remedy the error:

```
Public MustInherit Class ShippingCost
    Public Sub New()
        ' Initialization statements
    End Sub
    Public Sub New(ByVal pstrPostalCode As String)
        ' Initialization statements
    End Sub
End Class
Public NotInheritable Class ShippingCostAustralia
    Inherits ShippingCost
    Public Sub New(ByVal pstrPostalCode As String)
        ' Initialization statements
    End Sub
End Class
```

Even though the classes in the preceding code segment implement a constructor having one String argument (the same signature), the execution of that constructor may not be what you would expect. Remember, only constructors without parameters are inherited. Given this rule, examine Figure 4-11, which illustrates the execution flow of the constructors in the base and derived classes.

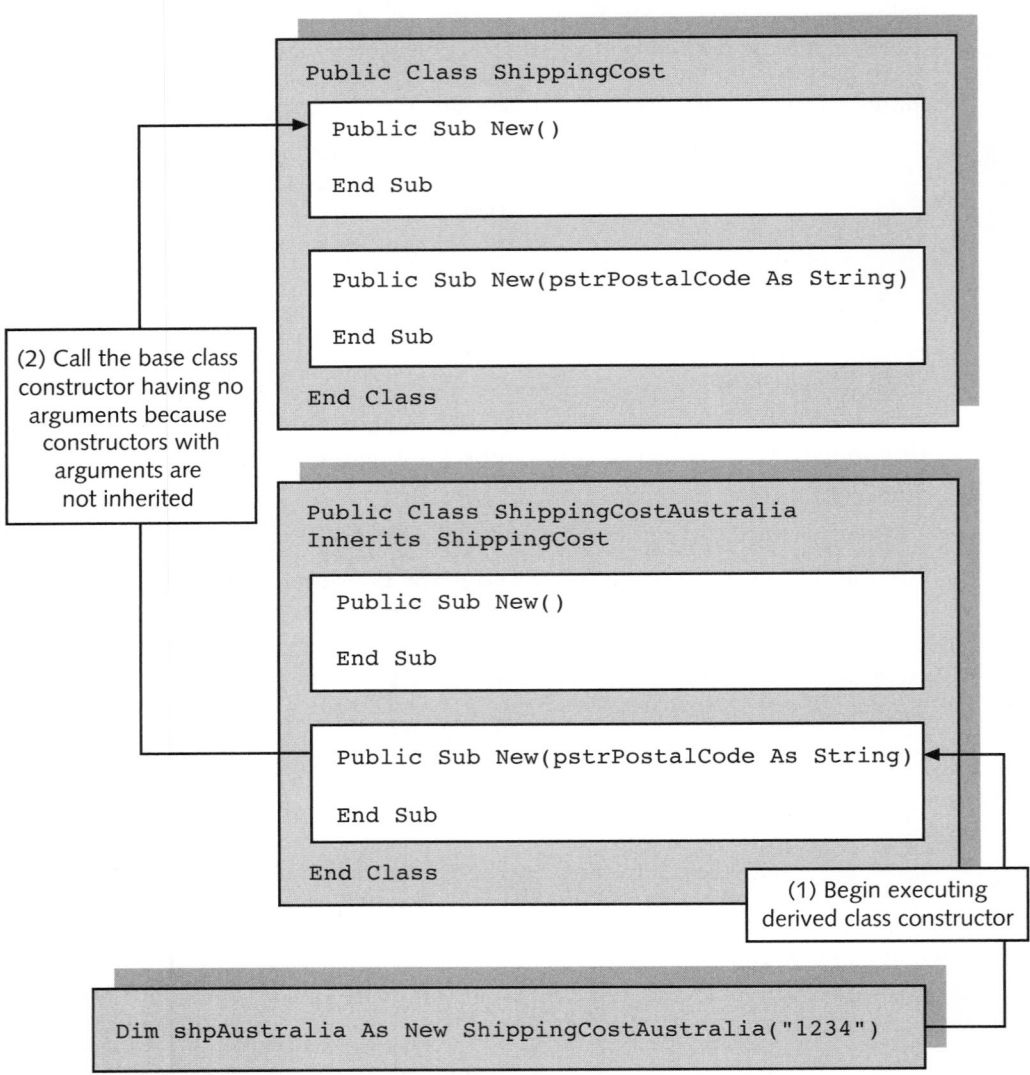

Figure 4-11   Inheriting constructors with parameters

While the code in Figure 4-11 works, it may not work as you expect. Because constructors with parameters are not inherited, but parameterless constructors are, the constructor having no arguments in the base class is called from the constructor in the derived class. The constructor in the base class with arguments is hidden from the derived class. Getting to this constructor is one purpose of the MyBase keyword. The **MyBase** keyword provides a reference to the base class.

The MyBase keyword works like an object variable and is used in a derived class to call the member in a base class. You can use MyBase to call a constructor in a base class although MyBase can call other methods too. Several rules surround the use of the MyBase keyword, as described in the following list:

- MyBase cannot be assigned to a variable or passed to a procedure because it is not a real object.
- MyBase cannot be used in modules because modules cannot be inherited.
- MyBase cannot be used to call members declared in a base class with the MustOverride keyword.

The following modification to the ShippingCostAustralia class calls the correct constructor for the base ShippingCost class:

```
Public NotInheritable Class ShippingCostAustralia
    Inherits ShippingCost
    Public Sub New(ByVal pstrPostalCode As String)
        MyBase.New(pstrPostalCode)
        ' Initialization statements
    End Sub
End Class
```

MyBase.New calls the constructor for the base class. That is, the New procedure in the base ShippingCost class is called. Because the constructor in the base class is declared with one argument, the call to MyBase.New also has one argument. Note that when calling MyBase, it *must* be the first statement appearing in the constructor. Figure 4-12 illustrates how calling MyBase works.

Considering inheritance and class visibility, you must examine the unique behavior of constructors with different access modifiers. Most of the constructors that you have created were Public. This means that a developer can create an instance of the class, and the code in the constructor will execute. However, suppose that you declared a constructor with an access modifier of Friend or Private.

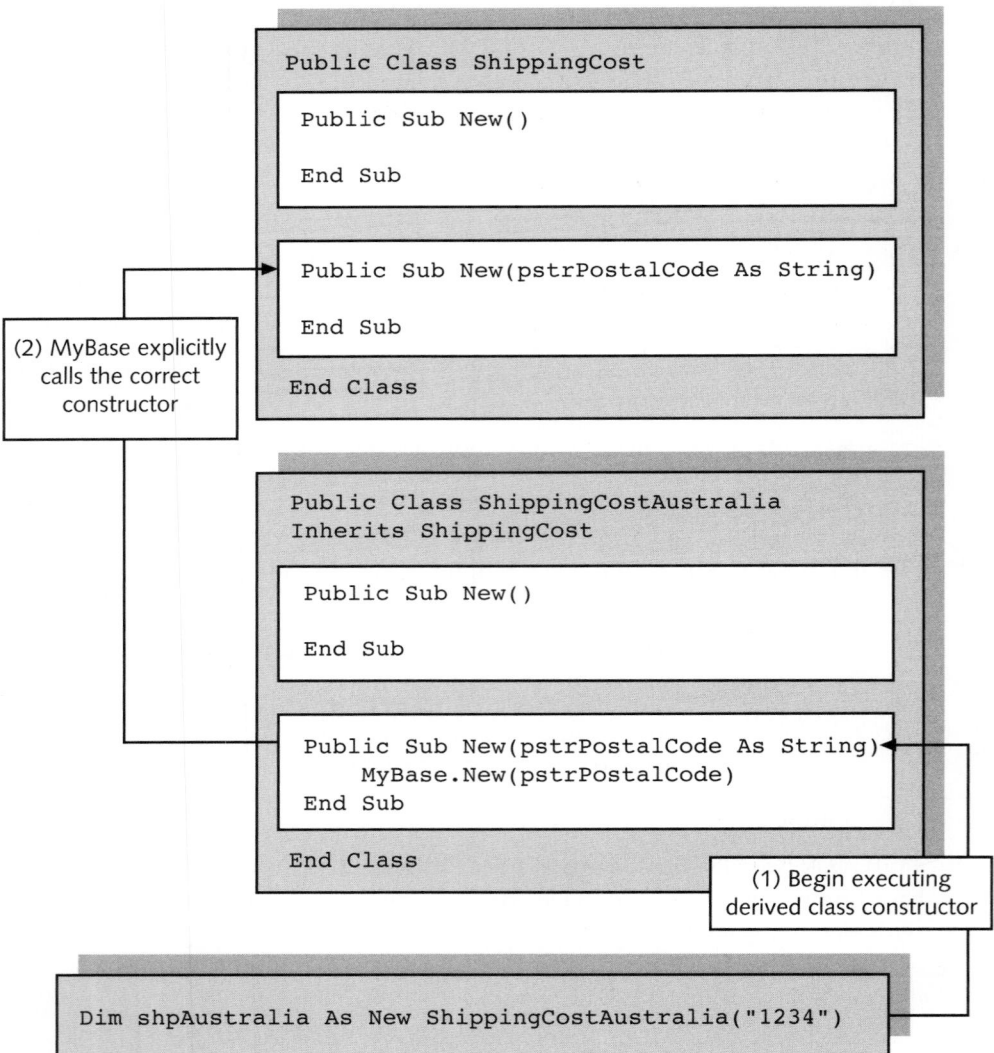

Figure 4-12   Understanding the MyBase keyword

If you declare a constructor with an access modifier of Friend, an instance of the class can be created from within the assembly. However, the class cannot be instantiated from outside of the assembly. The behavior is consistent with the meaning of the Friend access modifier to declare other members. Declaring a constructor with the Private access modifier works similarly. If a constructor is declared with Private access, then the class cannot be instantiated either from inside of the assembly or from outside of the assembly. Creating a Private constructor is useful when a class contains only shared members. In such a case, there never exists a need to create an instance of the class. Next, you will create the constructors for the classes:

To create and inherit constructors:

1. Activate the Code Editor for the module named **Shipping.vb**, if necessary. Enter the following statements (shown in bold) in the base **ShippingCost** class:

```
Public MustInherit Class ShippingCost
    Public Sub New()
        mblnValidValue = False
        mblnValidWeight = False
        mblnValidPostalCode = False
        mintIDCount +=1
        mintIDCurrent = mintIDCount
    End Sub
```

The preceding statements set the initial status of the shipment to indicate that the shipment value, shipment weight, and postal code are False (invalid). The shared variable mintIDCount is incremented. Thus, this variable is used as the shipment counter. The variable mintIDCurrent stores the current shipment ID number.

2. Enter the following statements (shown in bold) in the **ShippingCostAustralia** class:

```
Private Const cdblShippingRate As Double = 5.66
Public Sub New(ByVal pstrPostalCode As String)
    MyBase.New()
    If Validate.PostalInfo.IsValidPostalCode( _
        pstrPostalCode, ShippingCountryEnum.Australia) Then
        Me.mstrPostalCode = pstrPostalCode
        Me.mblnValidPostalCode = True
    End If
End Sub
```

3. Enter the following statements (shown in bold) in the **ShippingCostCanada** class:

```
Private Const cdblShippingRate As Double = 3.01
Public Sub New(ByVal pstrPostalCode As String)
    MyBase.New()
```

```
        If Validate.PostalInfo.IsValidPostalCode( _
            pstrPostalCode, ShippingCountryEnum.Canada) Then
            Me.mstrPostalCode = pstrPostalCode
            Me.mblnValidPostalCode = True
        End If
    End Sub
```

4. Enter the following statements (shown in bold) in the
ShippingCostMexico class:

```
Private Const cdblShippingRate As Double = 4.88
Public Sub New(ByVal pstrPostalCode As String)
    MyBase.New()
    If Validate.PostalInfo.IsValidPostalCode( _
        pstrPostalCode, ShippingCountryEnum.Mexico) Then
        Me.mstrPostalCode = pstrPostalCode
        Me.mblnValidPostalCode = True
    End If
End Sub
```

All of the preceding constructors that you created work roughly the same
way. They first call the constructor in the base ShippingCost class. Then they
validate that the postal code, passed as an argument, is correct. If it is, then
the postal code is set, and the flag mblnValidPostalCode is set to indicate that
the postal code is valid.

Closely related to the MyBase keyword is the MyClass keyword. The **MyClass** keyword
works similarly to the Me keyword. In fact, the difference between Me and MyClass
only appears when called in a derived class. The MyClass keyword calls a member in the
base class, even if it has been overridden in a derived class. Figure 4-13 illustrates the
operation of the MyClass keyword.

Note that the MyClass keyword has similar restrictions as the MyBase keyword. That is,
it cannot be assigned to a variable or passed as an argument to a procedure.

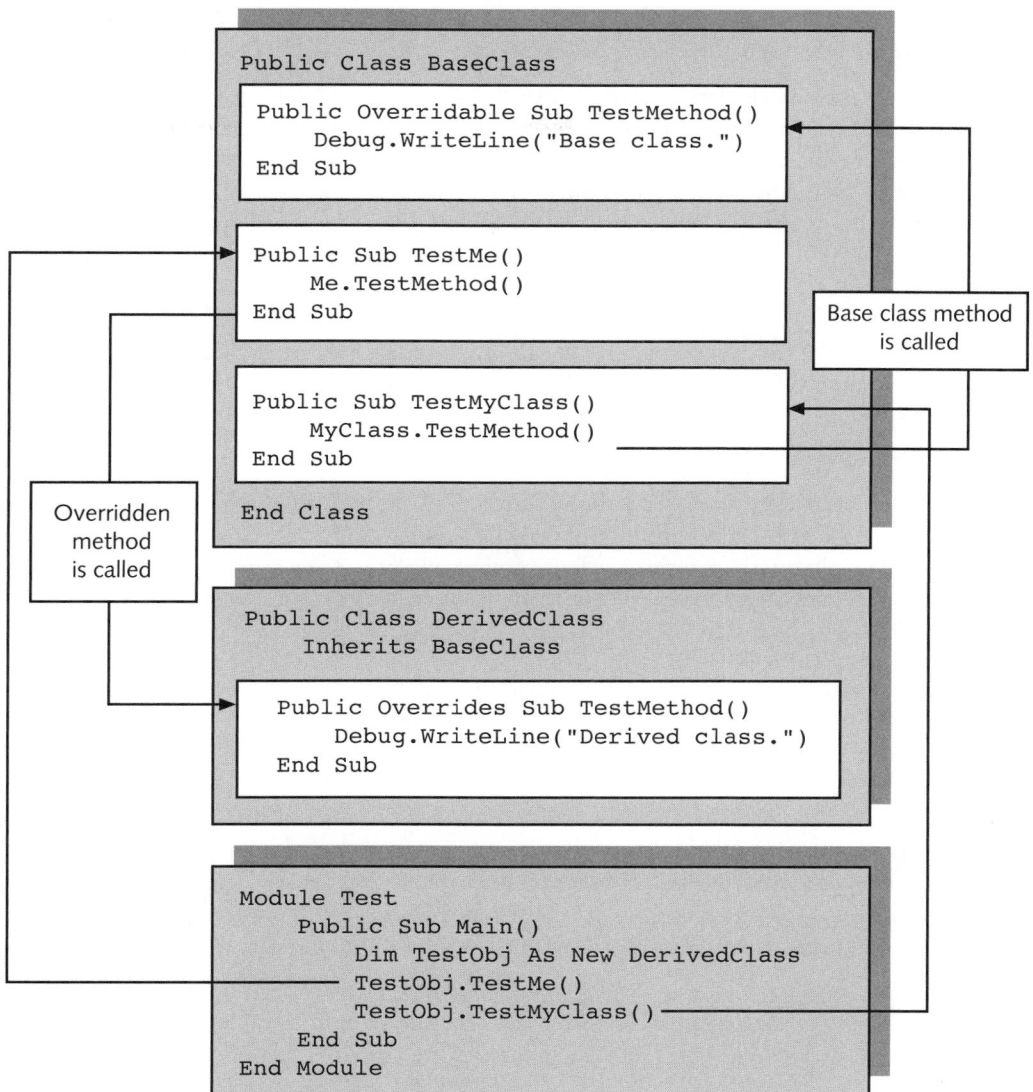

```
Public Class BaseClass

    Public Overridable Sub TestMethod()
        Debug.WriteLine("Base class.")
    End Sub

    Public Sub TestMe()
        Me.TestMethod()
    End Sub

    Public Sub TestMyClass()
        MyClass.TestMethod()
    End Sub

End Class


Public Class DerivedClass
    Inherits BaseClass

    Public Overrides Sub TestMethod()
        Debug.WriteLine("Derived class.")
    End Sub



Module Test
    Public Sub Main()
        Dim TestObj As New DerivedClass
        TestObj.TestMe()
        TestObj.TestMyClass()
    End Sub
End Module
```

Base class method
is called

Overridden
method
is called

4

Figure 4-13   Understanding the MyClass keyword

CLASS EVENTS

You have seen that control instances raise events as the user interacts with them. In addition, you have also seen how to create and destroy event handlers dynamically with the AddHandler and RemoveHandler statements. The classes you create can support events too. For example, the base Shipping class and derived classes can both define and raise events intended for use by a developer.

The steps to declare and raise events are simple. The Event keyword declares an event and its arguments, and the RaiseEvent keyword fires the event. Note that for the developer to handle the event, the class instance must be declared with the WithEvents keyword. Syntactically, this is consistent with declaring control instances so that they will handle events. For example, the following statement declares the variable ShipCurrent so that it will handle the events fired by the ShippingCost class:

```
Private WithEvents ShipCurrent As _
    Course.Shipping.ShippingCost
```

Examine the following statement to declare an event named Action that accepts no arguments:

```
Public Event Action()
```

To declare an event, you specify an access modifier, followed by the Event keyword, followed by the event name (Action). The event name can be any valid identifier. The preceding event declaration is legal but it violates the standard argument list for events. Remember that VB .NET events typically accept two arguments. The first argument has a data type of System.Object and the second argument has a data type of System.EventArgs, or a type that derives from System.EventArgs. Events that you create should work the same way. Examine the following event declaration:

```
Public Event Action(ByVal sender As System.Object, _
    ByVal e As System.EventArgs)
```

The preceding event declaration conforms to the standard argument list for events. However, suppose that you wanted to pass data back to the event handler. The System.EventArgs class does not allow you to pass custom information to an event. The solution to the problem is simple. You create a class that derives from System.EventArgs, and pass an instance of that class back to the event handler. Examine the following class:

```
Public Class ShippingEventArgs
    Inherits System.EventArgs

    Public ReadOnly ID As Integer
    Public ReadOnly Description As String

    Public Sub New(ByVal pintID As Integer, _
        ByVal pstrDescription As String)
        Me.ID = pintID
        Me.Description = pstrDescription
    End Sub
End Class
```

The preceding code segment declares a class named ShippingEventArgs that inherits from System.EventArgs. Ultimately, an instance of this class will be passed to the Action event. The class has two read-only properties to store information about the event: an Integer ID and a text description. The parameterized constructor stores the event data. Note that the event inherits from System.EventArgs, as all events should.

 When declaring event classes, Microsoft recommends that the class name end with EventArgs so that it is easily recognizable as an event.

Having declared the event, you now need to create an instance of the event class and raise the event using the RaiseEvent statement, as shown in the following code segment:

```
Dim e As New ShippingEventArgs(1, _
    "Added Shipment to Canada")
RaiseEvent Action(Me, e)
```

The preceding statement creates an instance of the ShippingEventArgs class, and then raises the event.

Once you, as the author, have declared an event, written the statements to create an instance of the event argument class, and then raised the event, the developer can create an event handler just as he or she would create any other event handler.

Implications when Declaring Events

There are implications when declaring events in base classes and derived classes. First, you cannot use the Overrides keyword to override an event. That is, you cannot declare an event in a base class and then override that event in a derived class. Although on the surface this may seem to be a limitation, it is not. To manage events in base and derived classes, you declare a procedure in the base class. The procedure in the base class is responsible for raising the event. Then, in any derived class, you call the procedure in the base class to raise the event to the developer. Examine the following statements appearing in the abstract ShippingCost class to raise the Action event:

```
Protected Sub EventSink(ByVal sender As System.Object, _
    ByVal e as ShippingEventArgs)
    RaiseEvent Action(sender, e)
End Sub
```

The procedure named EventSink serves no purpose other than to raise the Action event for any classes that derive from the ShippingCost class. Note that the procedure is declared with the Protected keyword so it is available to any classes that derive from the ShippingCost class.

Examine the following code:

```
Dim e As New ShippingEventArgs(1, "Shipment to Australia")
MyBase.EventSink(Me, e)
```

Statements in the ShippingCostAustralia class call the EventSink procedure.

Defining Events for a Class

In this solution, you will write the statement to raise an event whenever the developer calculates the cost of a shipment.

To declare and raise events:

1. In the module named **Shipping.vb**, create a nested class named **ShippingEventArgs** inside of the Shipping class:

```
Public Class ShippingEventArgs
    Inherits System.EventArgs

    Public ReadOnly ID As Integer
    Public ReadOnly Description As String

    Public Sub New(ByVal pintID As Integer, _
        ByVal pstrDescription As String)
        Me.ID = pintID
        Me.Description = pstrDescription
    End Sub
End Class
```

2. In the **ShippingCost** class, write the following statement immediately after the Class declaration to declare the **Action** event:

```
Public MustInherit Class ShippingCost
    Public Event Action( _
    ByVal sender As System.Object, _
    ByVal e As ShippingEventArgs)
```

3. Create the **EventSink** procedure immediately after the Action event that you just declared by entering the following statements:

```
Public Sub EventSink(ByVal sender As System.Object, _
    ByVal e As ShippingEventArgs)
    RaiseEvent Action(sender, e)
End Sub
```

4. Having declared the event, you now need to write the statements to raise the event. Enter the following statements (shown in bold) in the **CalculateCostDetail** method for the **ShippingCostAustralia** class:

```
Public NotInheritable Class ShippingCostAustralia
    ' Statements
    Public Overrides Function CalculateCostDetail() _
        As CostDetail
        ' Statements
        Dim e As New ShippingEventArgs(1, _
            "Shipment to Australia")
        MyBase.EventSink(Me, e)
        Return pCostDetail
    End Sub
End Class
```

5. Enter the following statements (shown in bold) in the **CalculateCostDetail** method for the **ShippingCostCanada** class:

```
Public NotInheritable Class ShippingCostCanada
    ' Statements
    Public Overrides Function CalculateCostDetail() _
        As CostDetail
        ' Statements
        Dim e As New ShippingEventArgs(1, _
            "Shipment to Canada")
        MyBase.EventSink(Me, e)
        Return pCostDetail
    End Sub
End Class
```

6. Enter the following statements (shown in bold) in the **CalculateCostDetail** method for the **ShippingCostMexico** class:

```
Public NotInheritable Class ShippingCostMexico
    ' Statements
    Public Overrides Function CalculateCostDetail() _
        As CostDetail
        ' Statements
        Dim e As New ShippingEventArgs(1, _
            "Shipment to Mexico")
        MyBase.EventSink(Me, e)
        Return pCostDetail
    End Sub
End Class
```

Having, as the component's author, written the statements to declare and raise the event, you can now, as the developer, write the statements to handle the event.

To handle an event:

1. Activate the Code Editor for the module named **frmMain.vb**. Enter the following statement (shown in bold) that declares the ShipCurrent variable so that it will handle events:

```
Private Ship As Course.Shipping
Private WithEvents ShipCurrent As _
    Course.Shipping.ShippingCost
```

2. As the developer, you can select and create the event handler for the ShippingCost class in the same way that you would create any other event handler. In the Class Name list box, select the object named **ShipCurrent**. In the Method Name list box, select the **Action** event. Note that the data type of the second argument is ShippingEventArgs. Enter the following statement in the event handler:

```
txtLog.Text = txtLog.Text & crlf & e.Description
```

The preceding statement appends the event description to the text box appearing at the bottom of the main form.

Figure 4-14 illustrates the execution flow of the event handler.

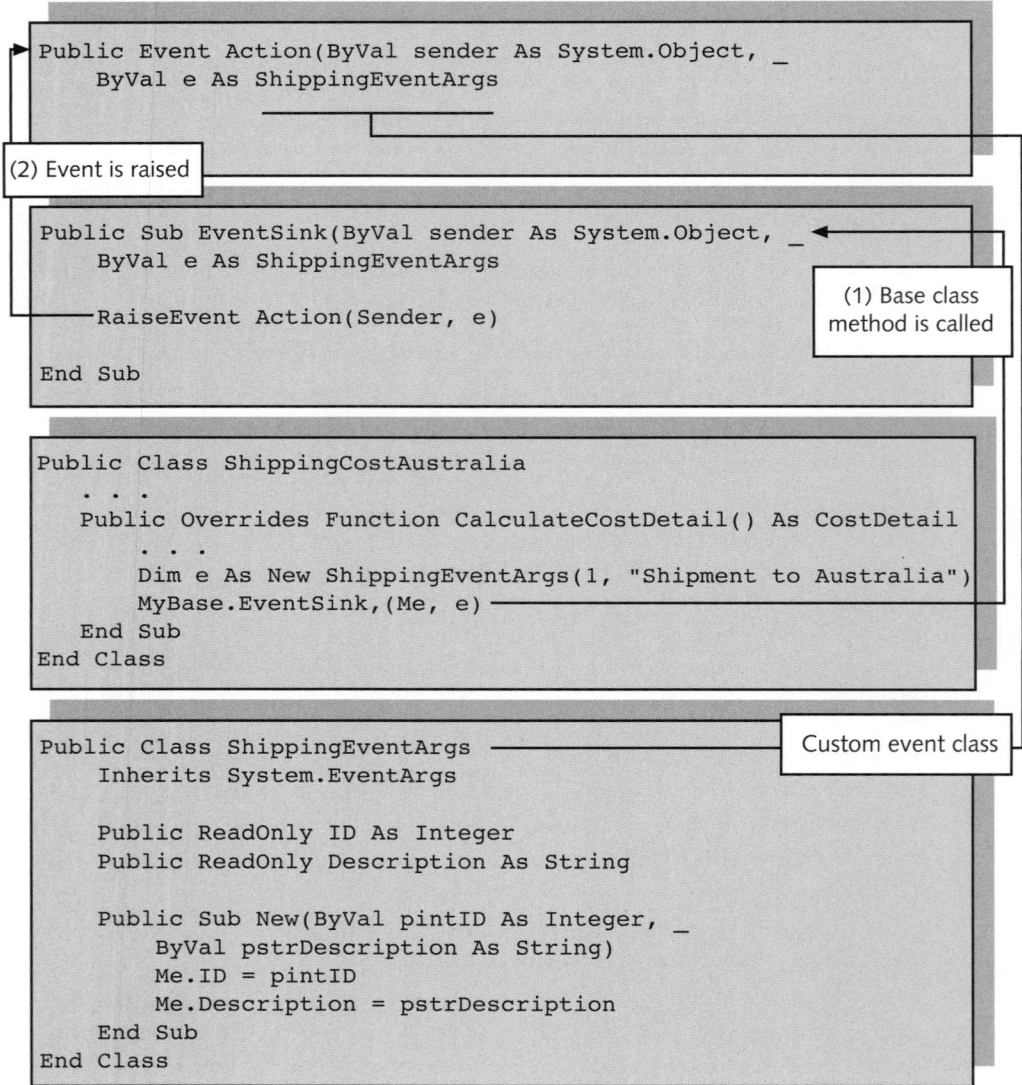

Figure 4-14   Execution flow of an event handler

As shown in Figure 4-14, the concrete ShippingCostAustralia class creates an instance of the ShippingEventArgs class, and then calls the EventSink procedure in the base class using the MyBase keyword. The EventSink procedure, in turn, raises the event. The event handler in the form module then handles the event.

EXCEPTION HANDLING

As a solution runs, runtime errors will often occur as a result of some abnormal condition. For example, trying to read a file from a floppy disk when no disk is in the drive will cause a runtime error. Invalid type conversion will also cause a runtime error. VB .NET refers to errors as **exceptions**.

One of the services provided by the Common Language Runtime is to notify an application that an exception has occurred. Note here that we use the term exception rather than the term error. While many exceptions indicate an error, some exceptions may occur in the normal course of an application's execution.

The exception model of the Common Language Runtime operates the same way regardless of the programming language being used. The following list describes the key concepts of exceptions and the .NET Framework:

- When an exception occurs, statements execute to process the exception in some way. This process is referred to as **catching an exception** or **handling an exception**.

- A component may generate an exception that will be caught by another component. This process is called **throwing an exception**.

Each .NET language can, and often does, have a unique syntax to process exceptions. VB .NET uses the Try, Catch, Finally, and End Try statements to build structured exception handlers to catch exceptions. The concept of a **structured exception handler** is new to VB .NET. Structured exception handlers are just a specialized form of a decision-making statement that executes to detect and handle exceptions.

VB 6 used the On Error and Resume keywords to define error handlers. These statements remain supported by VB .NET but only for backward compatibility. The On Error syntax may also degrade the performance of an application. Thus, the obsolete On Error syntax will not be discussed further in this book.

You create a structured exception handler by enclosing statements in a Try, Catch, Finally, End Try block having the following syntax:

Syntax

Try
> *Statements that could cause an exception*

Catch *name* **As** *exception*
    Code that executes when an exception occurs in the Try block
[**Catch** *name* **As** *exception*]
    Code that executes when an exception occurs in the Try block
 [**Finally** *name* **As** *exception*]
    Statements that always execute regardless of whether an exception occurs
End Try
    Statements following exception handler

Definition

The **Try**, **Catch**, **Finally**, and **End Try** statements declare a structured exception handler.

Dissection

- The statements in the **Try** block contain the executable statements that could cause an exception to occur. The statements in this block are commonly referred to as guarded code.

- If an exception occurs, the statements in a **Catch** block execute. An exception handler may have multiple Catch blocks to handle different types of exceptions.

- The statements in the optional **Finally** block always execute, regardless of whether an exception occurred. The optional Finally block typically contains statements to perform housekeeping chores such as closing files or closing database connections.

- The *name* argument defines a variable to store the exception.

- The **As** *exception* clause contains the name of the exception that the Catch block should handle. We discuss exception types in a moment.

Code Example

```
Dim pintCurrent As Integer
Try
    pintCurrent = System.Int32.MaxValue + 1
Catch ex As System.Exception
    MessageBox.Show("Numeric overflow")
End Try
```

Code Dissection

The preceding statements illustrate the most simple of exception handlers. The statement in the Try block will cause a numeric overflow error because the value stored in the variable pintCurrent is greater than the largest possible Integer value. Thus, the statement in the Catch block will execute and then display the message box to the user. Thus, the overflow error was caught and the application will continue to run.

Figure 4-15 illustrates the logic to detect and handle an exception.

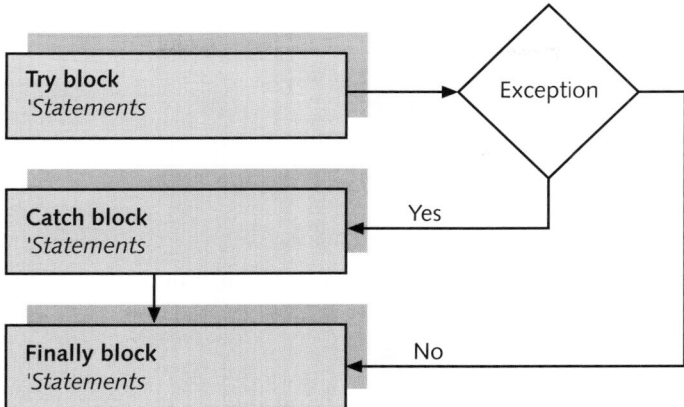

Figure 4-15   Handling an exception

As shown in Figure 4-15, if an exception occurs, then the statements in the Catch block execute, and then the statements in the Finally block execute. If an exception does not occur, the statements in the Try block finish, and then the statements in the Finally block execute.

Internally, the .NET Framework sends an exception to an application when an error occurs. The method can handle the exception with a Try, Catch, Finally block. If the exception is not caught, it will propagate to the caller. That is, if the calling method has an exception handler, then the process begins again. If a method handles an exception, then, you, as the developer, write statements to determine whether the procedure can recover from the exception. If a method can successfully recover from the exception, the process ends and the exception is said to be caught. Otherwise, the called method can optionally add information about the exception, and then propagate it to the caller. Exception propagation continues until the calling procedure is the Main procedure. Figure 4-16 illustrates how an exception is propagated to calling procedures.

Figure 4-16   Propagating exceptions

Understanding the Exception Hierarchy

Like most classes that comprise the .NET Framework, the Exception class is hierarchical and all exceptions ultimately derive from the System.Exception class. Two classes derive from System.Exception. The System.SystemException class contains the exceptions defined by the .NET Framework itself. The System.ApplicationException class is designed for exceptions that pertain to a particular application. Figure 4-17 illustrates a part of the exception hierarchy.

As shown in Figure 4-17, the System.Exception class contains two classes. All of the exceptions defined by the .NET Framework belong to the System.SystemException class. Exceptions that occur because of an application error should derive from the System.ApplicationException class. Arithmetic exceptions derive from the System.SystemException class. Specific types of arithmetic exceptions such as System.DivideByZeroException and System.OverflowException derive from the System.ArithmeticException class. The CLR throws these exceptions when an attempt is made to divide an Integer by 0 or when a numeric overflow error occurs, respectively.

Figure 4-17   Exception hierarchy

The System.IO namespace defines additional exceptions related to file handling. These include exceptions such as the DirectoryNotFoundException and the FileNotFoundException. Note that exceptions are organized into a hierarchy. This organization is significant. When handling different exceptions, the Catch blocks must be organized from the most specific exception to the most general exception.

Examine the following exception handler having multiple Catch blocks to handle three different exceptions:

```
Dim pintCurrent As Integer
Try
    pintCurrent = System.Int32.MaxValue + 1
Catch ex As System.OverflowException
    MessageBox.Show("Overflow")
Catch ex As System.ArithmeticException
    MessageBox.Show("Arithmetic Exception")
Catch ex As System.Exception
    MessageBox.Show("General Exception")
End Try
```

The order of the Catch blocks in the preceding statements is significant. Note that the Catch blocks are ordered from the most specific exception to the least specific exception. Thus, if the exception is a numeric overflow exception, then the statement in the first Catch block will execute. If an arithmetic exception other than an overflow exception occurs, then the statement in the second Catch block will execute. If, however, an exception other than an arithmetic exception occurs, then the statement in the final Catch block will execute.

Examine the following incorrect exception handler:

```
Dim pintCurrent As Integer
Try
    pintCurrent = System.Int32.MaxValue + 1
Catch ex As System.Exception
    MessageBox.Show("General Exception")
Catch ex As System.OverflowException
    MessageBox.Show("Overflow Exception")
End Try
```

In the preceding exception handler, the statements in the System.OverflowException block will never execute because catching System.Exception catches all exceptions. Thus, always order the exceptions in a Catch block from the most specific exception to the least specific exception.

Optionally, a Catch block can contain a When clause. The When clause allows you to add an additional condition to the Catch block. The condition in the When clause has the same syntax as the condition in an If statement. Examine the following statements:

```
Public Sub ValidateInput()
    Dim pintStep As Integer
    Try
        pintStep = 1
        pintStep = 2
        pintStep = 3
    Catch ex As System.Exception When pintStep = 1
    Catch ex As System.Exception When pintStep = 2
    Catch ex As System.Exception When pintStep = 3
    End Try
End Sub
```

The preceding code segment illustrates a common use of the When clause in a Catch block. The first Catch block will handle all exceptions only when the variable pintStep is equal to 1. The second Catch block will handle all exceptions only when the variable pintStep is equal to 2, and so on.

Use the When clause in multiple Catch blocks when a process has sequential states such as an initialization state, a processing state, and a shutdown state. By knowing the current state when an error occurred, it may be possible to correct the error and restart from the current state.

In addition to catching exceptions, it is also possible to raise them. The process of creating an exception is called throwing an exception. To throw an exception, you create an instance of an exception class, and then call the Throw statement with the exception variable as an argument, as shown in the following statements:

```
Dim exp As New System.IO.FileNotFoundException( _
    "Input file not found.")
Throw exp
```

The preceding statements throw a FileNotFoundException. The Throw statement accepts one optional argument: a string message describing the exception.

All exceptions share similar properties, as described in the following list:

- One exception may generate another exception. The **InnerException** property allows the application to store the exception that led up to the current exception.

- The **Message** property contains a textual message describing the exception.

- The **Source** property gets the name of the application or object that caused the exception to occur.

Avoid using exceptions for errors that an application should expect. For example, a method designed to validate a Social Security number should return False if the input is not valid, rather than raising an exception to the caller. The reason to minimize exception handlers is simple. Exception handlers consume more resources than returning a value to the called method.

Defining an Exception Handling Strategy for an Application

When an exception occurs you must decide how best to handle the exception. Compare how exceptions may be handled differently in a Windows Application project and a Class Library project (component). In a form, you would likely display a message box describing the error and allowing the user to correct it. However, a Class Library project should not have a visible interface. The reason is simple. A Class Library project is not aware of the application using the component. For example, the Shipping component could easily be used by an application other than a Windows Application. That application may not have a visible interface. In this solution, the exceptions that occur in the Shipping component will attempt to handle errors and, if necessary, throw an exception so that it can be handled by the Windows Forms application.

Users require more simplified information than developers. Furthermore, developers are typically more interested in detail information explaining why the exception occurred. Thus, create data for exception handlers that are suitable for the target audience.

Conceptually, there exist four strategies for defining the exception handlers in an application:

- Ignore the exception, allowing it to propagate automatically up through the call stack. That is, the error will propagate to each called procedure from the most recently called procedure to the least recently called procedure.

- Catch the exception and handle it.

- Catch the exception and rethrow it.

- Divide the exception into two parts. One part is called the inner exception, and the other is called the outer exception.

Ignoring Exceptions

A procedure may simply ignore an exception. That is, say a statement causes the .NET Framework to raise an exception. However, there exists no Catch block to handle the exception. In this situation, the exception propagates to the procedure that called the method. Propagation continues up the call stack until a Catch block is found. If no Catch block is found, then the program will end abnormally.

Catching and Handling Exceptions

Many times, an exception handler can handle an exception and there is no need to propagate the exception to the calling procedure. For example, a Button control may have code to open a disk file. If the file cannot be opened, the CLR will raise an exception. An exception handler in the Button's Click event handler can handle the exception and display a message box to the user describing the error and possibly how to fix it. For example, you could display a message that the file was not found.

Catching and Rethrowing Exceptions

When the .NET Framework raises an exception, the procedure in which the exception occurs has the opportunity to catch the exception. The statements in the procedure may be able to handle the problem. However, there may be occasions when the exception is of a nature that it cannot be handled. In such a situation, the same exception is rethrown to the caller.

Custom Exceptions

The .NET Framework already supplies a rich hierarchy of exceptions. There may be times, however, when a component needs to define an exception that is not part of the existing .NET Framework exception hierarchy. Creating a new exception class is mechanical. You define a new class that inherits from the System.ApplicationException class. In that class, override any desired methods and properties, as shown in the following code segment:

```
Public Class ShippingException
    Inherits System.ApplicationException

    Private mstrAppSource As String
    Public Sub New(ByVal pstrMessage As String)
        MyBase.New(pstrMessage)
        Me.mstrAppSource = "General shipping error"
    End Sub
End Class
```

The preceding code segment illustrates an exception class named ShippingException. The class inherits from the base class named System.ApplicationException. Note that exception classes you create should derive from System.ApplicationException, or from another class that, in turn, derives from System.ApplicationException. In the preceding code segment, the constructor calls the constructor in the base class, passing an error message as an argument. Exception classes can derive from one another. Suppose that in the Shipping class you wanted to create more detailed exceptions based on the type of shipping exception that occurred. In this situation, you can create classes that derive from the ShippingException class, as shown in the following code segment:

```
Public Class ShippingPostalException
    Inherits ShippingException

    Public Sub New(ByVal pstrMessage As String)
        MyBase.New("Invalid postal code")
    End Sub
End Class
```

Next, you will implement the code in the component to declare custom exceptions, catch exceptions, and rethrow them as necessary.

To catch and throw exceptions:

1. Enter the following statements at the end of the **Shipping.vb** module, making sure to declare them after the end of the Shipping class:

```
Public Class ShippingException
    Inherits System.ApplicationException

    Private mstrAppSource As String
    Public Sub New(ByVal pstrMessage As String)
        MyBase.New(pstrMessage)
        Me.mstrAppSource = "General shipping error"
    End Sub
End Class
```

```
Public Class ShippingPostalException
    Inherits ShippingException

    Public Sub New(ByVal pstrMessage As String)
        MyBase.New("Invalid postal code")
    End Sub
End Class

Public Class ShippingNumericException
    Inherits ShippingException
    Public Sub New(ByVal pstrMessage As String)
        MyBase.New("Invalid numeric argument")
    End Sub
End Class
```

2. Modify the statements in the **SetValue** function appearing in the ShippingCost class as follows:

```
If Validate.PostalInfo.IsIntegerInRange( _
    pstrArg, 1, 10000) Then
    mblnValidValue = True
    mdblValue = System.Convert.ToInt32(pstrArg)
Else
    Dim exp As New ShippingNumericException( _
        "Invalid numeric argument")
    Throw exp
End If
```

3. Modify the statements in the **SetWeight** function appearing in the **ShippingCost** class as follows:

```
If Validate.PostalInfo.IsIntegerInRange( _
    pstrArg, 1, 100) Then
    mblnValidWeight = True
    mdblWeight = System.Convert.ToInt32(pstrArg)
Else
    Dim exp As New ShippingNumericException( _
        "Invalid numeric argument")
    Throw exp
End If
```

4. Modify the statements in the constructor (New procedure) in the class named **ShippingCostAustralia** by entering the following statements (shown in bold):

```
Public Sub New(ByVal pstrPostalCode As String)
    MyBase.New()
    If Validate.PostalInfo.IsValidPostalCode( _
        pstrPostalCode, ShippingCountryEnum.Australia) Then
        Me.mstrPostalCode = pstrPostalCode
        Me.mblnValidPostalCode = True
```

```
        Else
            Dim exp As New ShippingPostalException( _
                "Invalid PostalCode - Australia")
            Throw exp
        End If
    End Sub
```

5. Modify the statements in the constructor (New procedure) in the class named **ShippingCostCanada** by entering the following statements (shown in bold):

```
Public Sub New(ByVal pstrPostalCode As String)
    MyBase.New()
    If Validate.PostalInfo.IsValidPostalCode( _
        pstrPostalCode, ShippingCountryEnum.Canada) Then
        Me.mstrPostalCode = pstrPostalCode
        Me.mblnValidPostalCode = True
    Else
        Dim exp As New ShippingPostalException( _
            "Invalid PostalCode - Canada")
        Throw exp
    End If
End Sub
```

6. Modify the statements in the constructor (New procedure) in the class named **ShippingCostMexico** by entering the following statements (shown in bold):

```
Public Sub New(ByVal pstrPostalCode As String)
    MyBase.New()
    If Validate.PostalInfo.IsValidPostalCode( _
        pstrPostalCode, ShippingCountryEnum.Mexico) Then
        Me.mstrPostalCode = pstrPostalCode
        Me.mblnValidPostalCode = True
    Else
        Dim exp As New ShippingPostalException( _
            "Invalid PostalCode - Mexico")
        Throw exp
    End If
End Sub
```

At this point in the solution's development, you have one final task to perform. While you, as the developer, could create instances of the sealed ShippingCostAustralia, ShippingCostCanada, and ShippingCostMexico classes, you will instead create another class used as a factory to create these class instances.

To create the ShippingFactory class:

1. Activate the Code Editor for the **Shipping.vb** module, if necessary, and then enter the following statements (shown in bold) in the **Shipping** class after the **ShippingEventArgs** class:

```
Public Class ShippingEventArgs
  ' Statements
```

```
End Class
Public Class ShippingFactory

    Public Shared Function CreateShippingCost( _
        ByVal pstrType As ShippingCountryEnum, _
        ByVal pstrPostalCode As String) As ShippingCost

        Select Case pstrType
            Case ShippingCountryEnum.Australia
                Dim scCurrent As New _
                    ShippingCostAustralia(pstrPostalCode)
                Return scCurrent
            Case ShippingCountryEnum.Canada
                Dim scCurrent As New _
                    ShippingCostCanada(pstrPostalCode)
                Return scCurrent
            Case ShippingCountryEnum.Mexico
                Dim scCurrent As New _
                    ShippingCostMexico(pstrPostalCode)
                Return scCurrent
        End Select
    End Function
End Class
```

At this point, you have completed the programming for the Shipping component. The only remaining task is to create the code on the main form to test the component. The following statements illustrate the code to calculate the cost of a shipment to Australia:

```
Try
    Dim pcostDetail As Course.Shipping.CostDetail
    ShipCurrent = Course.Shipping.ShippingFactory. _
        CreateShippingCost( _
        Course.Shipping.ShippingCountryEnum.Australia, _
        txtPostalCode.Text)
    ShipCurrent.SetValue(txtValue.Text)
    ShipCurrent.SetWeight(txtWeight.Text)
    pcostDetail = ShipCurrent.CalculateCostDetail
    txtID.Text = ShipCurrent.ID.ToString
    CopyToTextBoxes(pcostDetail)
Catch ex As Course.ShippingException
    MessageBox.Show(ex.Message, "Error", _
        MessageBoxButtons.OK)
End Try
```

The preceding statements use the ShippingFactory class to create an instance of the shipment cost. The value and weight are set from the text box and the cost of the shipment is calculated. The results are then copied to the text boxes on the form.

To test the Shipping component:

1. Open **frmMain.vb**. Enter the following statements at the end of the form to create the CopyToTextBoxes procedure:

```
Private Sub CopyToTextBoxes( _
    ByVal scd As Course.Shipping.CostDetail)
    txtVatCost.Text = scd.VatCost.ToString("c")
    txtTariffCost.Text = scd.TariffCost.ToString("c")
    txtShippingCost.Text = scd.ShippingCost.ToString("c")
    txtTotalCost.Text = scd.TotalCost.ToString("c")
End Sub
```

2. Position the cursor inside the Click event handler for the button named **btnShipToAustralia**. Instead of typing in all of the statements to calculate the cost of a shipment, you will insert a preexisting file into the module.

3. On the menu bar, click **Edit**, and then click **Insert File As Text**. In the Insert File dialog box, insert the file named **Chapter.04\Data\ Australia.txt**. The code in the file appears in the event handler.

4. Position the cursor inside the Click event handler for the button named **btnShipToCanada**. On the menu bar, click **Edit**, and then click **Insert File As Text**. In the Insert File dialog box, insert the file named **Chapter.04\Data\Canada.txt**.

5. Position the cursor inside the Click event handler for the button named **btnShipToMexico**. On the menu bar, click **Edit**, and then click **Insert File As Text**. In the Insert File dialog box, insert the file named **Chapter.04\ Data\Mexico.txt**.

6. Test the solution.

CHAPTER SUMMARY

This chapter discussed several key features of object-oriented programming including inheritance, creating abstract classes and sealed classes, overloading, and overriding.

◻ Repeating patterns, called design patterns, tend to appear in applications. These design patterns are divided into creational patterns, structural patterns, and behavioral patterns. Different design patterns can be used to define how objects get created and the relationship between objects. The singleton pattern is used to create a class that can have only one instance. The factory pattern is used to abstract the process of object creation.

◻ Overloading is the process whereby multiple procedures have the same name but different signatures. VB .NET calls the correct overloaded member based on the member's signature. Function procedures, sub procedures, property procedures, and constructors can be overloaded. To overload a procedure, include the Overloads keyword in the member declaration. Note that the Overloads keyword does not appear when overloading a constructor.

❑ Inheritance is the ability of one class to inherit the members of a base class. The inherited class is called the base class and the inheriting class is called the derived class. VB .NET supports single inheritance, meaning that a derived class can only inherit from one base class. To inherit a class, include the Inherits keyword followed by the base class as the first statement after the class declaration.

❑ VB .NET allows you to create abstract classes. An abstract class has an interface but no implementation. To create an abstract class, declare the class with the MustInherit keyword. In addition, declare the members without any implementation.

❑ Sealed classes are those classes that cannot be inherited. To create a sealed class, declare the class with the NotInheritable keyword.

❑ Overriding is the process of replacing a member in a base class with a member in a derived class. To override a member, include the Overrides keyword in the member declaration in the derived class. Declare members in the base class with the Overridable keyword.

❑ Constructors have special inheritance rules. Constructors having arguments are not implicitly inherited. To inherit a constructor, create the constructor in the derived class, and then use the MyBase keyword to call the constructor in the base class.

❑ Classes that you create can support events. To declare an event, use the Event statement. To raise an event, use the RaiseEvent statement. Events that you create should have two arguments just as predefined VB .NET events have two arguments. The second argument to the event should be derived from the System.EventArgs class. Note that events cannot be inherited. However, this situation does not pose a problem. Declare the event in the base class, and create a procedure to raise that event in the base class. In any derived class, call the procedure in the base class to raise the event.

❑ Occasionally, exceptions will occur in an application. You can handle an exception by creating an exception handler. An exception handler consists of a Try, Catch, Finally, End Try block. Enclose the statements in the Try block that may cause an exception. Create one or more Catch blocks to handle the exception. The statements in the Finally block execute whether or not an exception occurred.

REVIEW QUESTIONS

1. Which of the following are categories of design patterns?

   a. abstract, concrete

   b. simple, complex

   c. conditional, logical, functional

   d. representational, automation

   e. creational, structural, behavioral

2. Which of the following statements is true of design patterns?

a. Design patterns represent common patterns that repeat themselves in object-oriented programming.

b. Singleton and factory are examples of design patterns.

c. When applying the singleton design pattern, the developer typically only creates a single instance of a class.

d. all of the above

e. none of the above

3. Which of the following statements is true of overloading?

a. Function and sub procedures may be overloaded but properties may not.

b. Overloaded procedures share the same name but have different signatures.

c. When creating an overloaded procedure, the Overloads keyword must always appear in the procedure declaration.

d. An overloaded procedure must always have a different number of arguments.

e. You can overload a class by including the Overloads keyword in the class declaration.

4. What is meant by the term "signature"?

a. A signature represents the unique combination of argument type and argument count. VB .NET uses an overloaded method's signature to call the correct method at runtime.

b. The name of a procedure alone define that procedure's signature.

c. The term signature refers to multiple inheritance. A signature specifies the base classes to be inherited.

d. A signature is used to implement a singleton.

e. none of the above

5. What is the purpose of the Inherits keyword?

a. The Inherits keyword specifies that a class can be inherited by another class.

b. The Inherits keyword specifies that a derived class inherits, or can call the members of, the base class.

c. The Inherits keyword specifies that a procedure in one class can be inherited by another class.

d. The Inherits keyword is used in a derived class to call the methods appearing in the base class.

e. none of the above

6. Which of the following statements is true of inheritance in VB .NET?

   a. VB .NET supports multiple inheritance while other languages, such as C++, support single inheritance.

   b. The inherited class is called the base class and the inheriting class is called the derived class.

   c. The Sealed keyword is used to create a sealed class, which is a class that cannot be inherited by another class.

   d. The Inheritable keyword indicates that a class can be inherited by another class.

   e. none of the above

7. What is the purpose of the Overrides keyword?

   a. The Overrides keyword appears in a class declaration. Its purpose there is to tell VB .NET that the methods in the class containing the Overrides keyword will override all of the methods in the base class.

   b. The Overrides keyword is used in a derived class to inherit a method appearing in the base class.

   c. The Overrides keyword appears in a procedure declaration. It is used to override a member in a base class.

   d. If you override a member, you can call the member of the same name using the MyBaseMethod keyword.

   e. VB .NET does not support the Overrides keyword.

8. Which of the following statements is correct about an abstract class?

   a. An abstract class is declared with the Abstract keyword in the Class block.

   b. An abstract class is a class containing an interface but no implementation.

   c. An abstract class contains variables and properties but does not contain methods.

   d. all of the above

   e. none of the above

9. Which of the following statements is true of a variable declared with the Protected keyword?

   a. A Protected variable can only be referenced by those methods in a class that are declared with the Protected keyword.

   b. The Protected keyword is used to declare a hidden namespace.

   c. Protected variables are typically declared inside of a procedure.

   d. A Protected variable can be referenced by the class containing the declaration and any derived class.

   e. none of the above

10. How to you create a nested class in VB .NET?

  a. Declare a class with the Nested keyword followed by the name of the parent class.

  b. Declare a Class block inside of another Class block.

  c. Create two classes in different modules. Use the Property Pages for the module to specify that a class is a nested class.

  d. VB .NET does not support nested classes.

  e. none of the above

11. Which of the following statements is true of constructors in inherited classes?

  a. If a constructor appears in a base class, then the constructor is inherited by the derived class just as any other procedure is inherited by the derived class.

  b. Constructors are not inherited in the same way as procedures. If a base class has a constructor that accepts arguments, it must be explicitly called in the derived class using the MyBase keyword.

  c. To inherit a constructor, you declare the constructor in the derived class. Then, in the derived class, you call the constructor in the base class with the CallBase keyword.

  d. Declare the constructor with the Inherits keyword appearing in the procedure declaration.

  e. none of the above

12. What is the name of the class from which all event arguments should derive?

  a. System.Object

  b. System.Event

  c. System.RaiseEvent

  d. System.SuperClass

  e. System.EventArgs

13. Which of the following statements describes how to declare and raise an event?

  a. Declare the event by calling the CreateEvent method of the Event class. Raise the event by calling the Raise method of the Event class.

  b. Declare a class named Event. Register the event by calling the RegisterEvent method using the event name as an argument.

  c. Create a class that inherits from System.Event. Create methods in the class named Event and RaiseEvent.

  d. You cannot declare and raise events in a class module.

  e. First, declare an event with the Event statement having two arguments. Raise the event with the RaiseEvent statement.

4

14. Which of the following statements accurately describes how to create a structured exception handler?

    a. Create a Try block containing the statements that may cause an exception. Create one or more Catch blocks to handle the exception. Create an optional Finally block to execute statements that will execute whether or not an exception occurs.

    b. Create an Error block containing the statements that may cause an exception. Create one or more HandleError blocks to handle the exception.

    c. Create a procedure named Error that Windows will execute when and if an error occurs.

    d. Use the On Error Goto statement to create the error handler.

    e. VB .NET does not support structured exception handlers.

15. How do you create a custom exception handler?

    a. Create a Module block named CustomException. In that module block, create a procedure named Exception.

    b. Create a class named CustomException. Include a Try, Catch, Finally, End Try block in that class.

    c. Create a class that derives from the System.Object superclass. Create a method in that class named Exception to implement the custom exception.

    d. Create a class that derives from the System.ApplicationException class.

    e. You cannot create exceptions beyond those provided by the .NET Framework itself.

16. What is a signature?

17. What is a sealed class?

18. Describe the relationship of constructors between a base class and a derived class. In your answer, be sure to discuss constructors with and without arguments, and the purpose of the MyBase and MyClass keywords.

19. Describe the process to create nested classes and the purpose of the Protected keyword in a nested class.

20. Describe how to create a structured exception handler. In your answer, be sure to describe the purpose of the Try, Catch, Finally, and End Try statements.

PROGRAMMING QUESTIONS

1. Write the statements to create a Public overloaded function method named IsPositiveNumber. One of the methods should accept a String argument and the other should accept an argument having a data type of Double. Both of the function methods should return a Boolean data type. Write the statements in the methods to determine if the argument is an Integer number whose value is greater than 0.

2. Write the statements to create an overloaded Public sub procedure named CreateList. Both procedures should accept a reference to a ListBox control. For the first overloaded method, add the items to display the years 2000 to 2005 in the list box. The second overloaded method should accept two additional Integer arguments named pintMin and pintMax containing the minimum and maximum years to display. Write a loop to add the specified years to the list box. Assume that the list box argument for both methods is named plstDemo.

3. Write the statements to create an overloaded Public sub procedure named FormatControl. Both procedures should accept a reference to a TextBox control. In the first overloaded method, set the foreground and background colors to Black and White, respectively. The second overloaded method should accept an enumeration named FormatType having members named Bold, Normal, and Light. Write the statements in the second overloaded method so that the Bold format has foreground and background colors of DarkBlue and LightBlue, the Light format has colors of Gray and White, and the Normal format has colors of Black and White as in the first overloaded method.

4. Write the statements to declare a Public class named Employee that is derived from the Class named Course.Person.

5. Write the statements to declare an abstract Public class named GenericCustomer having a field named Name with a data type of String. Create prototypes for two methods that must be overridden by any derived class. The first method should be named GetID, accept no arguments, and return an Integer. The second, named GetInfo, should accept no arguments and return a String.

6. Write the statements to declare a Public abstract class named BankCustomer having a String field named Name. Create a class named CreditCardCustomer that derives from the BankCustomer class having an additional String field named CreditCardNumber. Create a second derived class named CheckingCustomer having an additional String field named CheckingAccountNumber. Make these two derived classes sealed classes.

7. Write the statements to declare a Public structure named FullName having three Public String members named FirstName, MiddleInitial, and LastName. Override the default ToString method of the structure so that it returns the three name parts concatenated together. Embed a space between each part.

8. Write the statements to create a nested class. Create the outer class named HouseSize, and three inner classes named Bedroom, Bathroom, and Kitchen. All of the classes should be publicly accessible.

9. Create a Public class named CannotCreate such that the developer cannot create an instance of the class. Use the constructor to perform this task.

10. Assume that a class named Customer is derived from the class named Person. Write the statements to create the Customer class. Create the constructor for the derived class so that it accepts one String argument. In the constructor for the derived class, call the constructor for the base class having the same number of arguments.

11. Write the statements to declare a class named CustomerEventArgs designed to be used as the second argument to an event handler. The class should inherit from the System.EventArgs class. The class should have two read-only properties: CustomerID having a data type of Integer, and CustomerAction having a data type of String. Create the constructor for the class as necessary.

12. Write the statement to declare an event named CustomerAction having two arguments. The first argument named sender should have a data type of System.Object, and the second argument, named e, should have a data type of CustomerEventArgs.

13. Write the statement to raise the event that you declared in the preceding question.

14. Write the statements to create a function procedure named Cube that accepts one Integer argument. The function procedure should calculate the cube of the argument. Create an exception handler such that an overflow exception will be trapped. If overflow occurs, display a message box.

15. Write the statements to create a class named CustomException that inherits from the System.ApplicationException class. Create the exception such that it has one additional argument named pstrMessage. Store the string "Invalid Format" in the message.

HANDS-ON PROJECTS

1. In this project, you will use the completed solution from the chapter as a template, and extend the example to handle an additional country. The file named Chapter.04\Exercises04\Ch04Ex1.exe contains the compiled executable application. Figure 4-18 shows the completed main form for the solution.

   a. Create a solution named **Ch04Ex1.sln** made up of a Windows Application project. Add a new Class Library project to the solution.

   b. For the Class Library project, define the root namespace as **Course** and the assembly name as **Shipping**. Add a module named **Validate** to validate the input provided by the user.

   c. Using the completed solution as a template, expand the Validate class to validate German postal codes. Assume that a German postal code has 6 digits.

   d. Expand the Shipping component to create a class named **ShippingCostGermany**. Override the methods of the abstract Shipping class as necessary. Assume that the value added tax rate is 5%, the tariff rate is 2% and the cost per pound to ship a package is $3.95.

   e. Expand the ShippingFactory class as necessary to handle the additional country.

   f. On the form, create a button to ship a package to Germany. Call the components of the Shipping class as necessary to calculate the cost of a shipment.

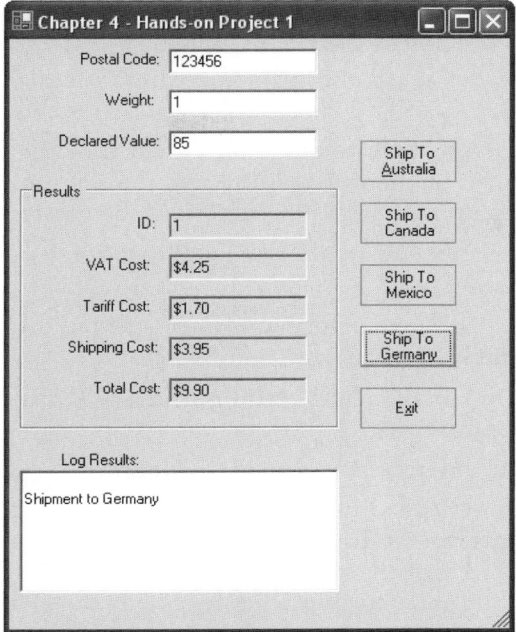

Figure 4-18   Chapter 4 – Hands-on Project 1

2. In this project, you create a solution that will convert units of measure between the U.S. and metric measures. The project will allow the user to convert values from among the U.S. measures of inches, feet, and yards, and metric measures of millimeters, centimeters, and meters. The file named Chapter.04\ Exercises04\Ch04Ex2.exe contains the compiled executable application. Figure 4-19 shows the completed main form for the solution.

Figure 4-19   Chapter 4 – Hands-on Project 2

a. Create a solution named **Ch04Ex2.sln** made up of a Windows Application project. Add a new Class Library project to the solution.

b. For the Class Library project, define the root namespace as **Course** and the assembly as **Convert**.

c. Add a module named **Validate** to validate the input provided by the user. Create the necessary overloaded methods to validate that the user input is correct. All input values can contain a decimal point and must be greater than 0.

d. Create a class named **Conversion**. Create the class such that the developer cannot create an instance of the class.

e. In the Conversion class, create a Public enumeration named **MetricUnit** having members named **Millimeter**, **Centimeter**, and **Meter**.

f. In the Conversion class, create a Public enumeration named **USUnit** having members named **Inch**, **Feet**, and **Yard**.

g. In the Conversion class create a nested class named **ToMetric**.

h. In the ToMetric class, create overloaded Function methods named **ToMillimeters**, **ToCentimeters**, and **ToMeters**. Each overloaded method should have four signatures. The first should accept one argument having a data type of Double. The method should convert inches to millimeters. The second method should accept a Double data type as the first argument. The second argument should have a data type of USUnit to denote the measurement unit of the first argument. The third and fourth methods should have the same number of arguments as the first and second methods. However, the data type of the first argument, instead of having a data type of Double, should have a data type of String. Each of the methods should return a Double.

i. Create the code for each of the preceding methods to convert the data. Note that there are 2.54 centimeters per inch.

j. In the Conversion class, create a nested class named **ToUS**.

k. In the ToUS class, create overloaded Function methods named **ToInches**, **ToFeet**, and **ToYards**. Each overloaded method should have four signatures. Instead of the USUnit enumeration, use the MetricUnit enumeration to denote the measurement unit. Create the code to convert the data.

l. Handle overflow exceptions as necessary.

m. Create the control instances on the form as shown in Figure 4-19 and the necessary code to test the Class Library project.

3. In this project, you will create a solution designed to play Blackjack. The rules of the game are simple. Assume that there exists a player and a dealer. The winner of the game is the player who gets closest to 21 without exceeding 21 or "going bust." If both players have the same points, then neither player wins the hand. An ace has a value of 1 or 11. Face cards have a value of 10. The dealer must take a card if the dealer's hand is worth 16 or less. The dealer may not take a card if the

hand is worth 17 or more. As the player, you can take another card at any time. The file named Chapter.04\Exercises04\Ch04Ex3.exe contains the compiled executable application. Figure 4-20 shows the completed main form for the solution.

Figure 4-20   Chapter 4 – Hands-on Project 3

a. Create a solution named **Ch04Ex3.sln** made up of a Windows Application project. Add a new Class Library project to the solution.

b. For the Class Library project, define the root namespace as **Course** and the assembly name as **Cards**.

c. Create a class named **Cards**. Implement this class as a singleton.

d. Store the deck of cards in an array of structures.

e. In the Cards class, create an overloaded method named **Shuffle**. One method should accept no arguments and shuffle one deck of cards. The second method should accept one argument, the number of decks to shuffle.

f. Write the statements to shuffle the deck of cards. There exist several ways to shuffle the deck. One way is to generate random numbers used to exchange array elements. Refer to the Help system for the Randomize and Rnd functions.

g. Create another class that inherits from the Cards class, named **Game21**. The Game21 class should also be implemented as a singleton.

h. Create a method named **Deal** that will deal two cards to the player and two cards to the dealer. Create the constructor such that each time an instance of the Game21 class is created, the deck of cards is shuffled. Use an overloaded parameterized constructor so as to shuffle either one deck of cards or several decks of cards.

i. Create read-only properties named **PlayerValue** and **DealerValue** that will return the current value of the player's hand and the dealer's hand.

j. Create a method named **Hit** that will deal another card to the player. The method should recalculate the value of the player's hand.

k. Create a method named **Stand** that will deal cards to the dealer until the dealer's hand has a value of 17 or greater.

l. Create a form and objects on the form to test the class modules. Validate the input and provide the error handling routines as necessary. Dynamically create the text box control instances on the form as each card is dealt.

4. In this project, you will create a group of classes that will calculate the cost of a car insurance policy based on several factors. The file named Chapter.04\Exercises04\Ch04Ex4.exe contains the compiled executable application. Figure 4-21 shows the completed main form for the solution.

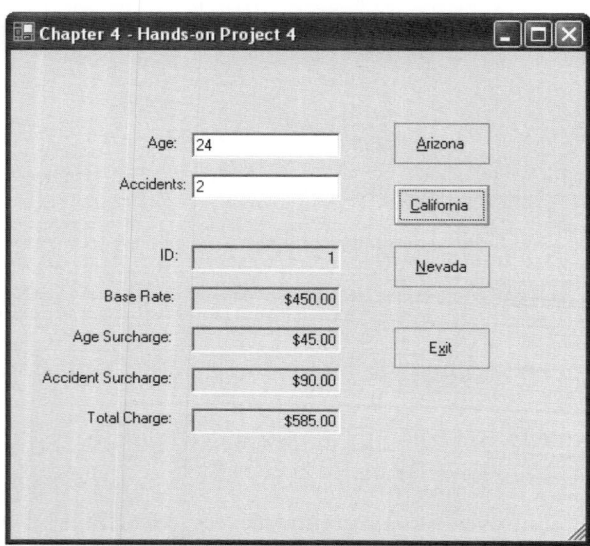

Figure 4-21   Chapter 4 – Hands-on Project 4

a. Create a solution named **Ch04Ex4.sln** made up of a Windows Application project. Add a new Class Library project to the solution.

b. For the Class Library project, define the root namespace as **Course**, and the assembly name as **Insurance**. Implement the Insurance class as a singleton.

c. In the Insurance class, create an enumeration named **StateEnum** having members named **Arizona**, **California**, and **Nevada**.

d. Create a structure named **CostDetail** having the following members: **BaseRate**, **AgeSurcharge**, **AccidentSurcharge**, and **TotalCharge**, each having a data type of Double.

e. Create an abstract class named **InsuranceCost**. Write the statements to declare and raise an event named **Action**. The data type of the event's second argument should be **InsuranceEventArgs**. The Description property should display a message indicating to which state the insurance policy was quoted.

f. Using the techniques presented in the chapter, declare the Protected variables to indicate whether all of the input values have been supplied, and store the hidden data. Create overridable methods to store values for the person's age, and number of accidents.

g. Create abstract methods to calculate the costs of the insurance.

h. Create derived classes named **InsuranceArizona**, **InsuranceCalifornia**, and **InsuranceNevada**. In these classes, calculate the insurance costs based on the following information. The base cost for insurance is $400.00 in Arizona, $450.00 in California, and $500.00 in Nevada. A 10% surcharge is added for each accident. If a person is between the ages of 18 and 25, a 10% surcharge is added to the base rate.

i. Implement the methods in the derived class as necessary.

j. Create a customized exception handler as necessary.

k. Create a class named **Validate** to perform any input validation.

l. Create the control instances on the form as shown in Figure 4–21. Create the necessary procedures to test the Class Library project.

4

5

WORKING WITH THE WINDOWS FILE SYSTEM AND ESSENTIAL DATA STRUCTURES

In this chapter, you will:

- ♦ Understand the members of the System.IO namespace
- ♦ Understand the organization of the Windows file system and how to manage directories and files
- ♦ Configure the OpenFileDialog and SaveFileDialog controls as a means for the user to select files to open and save
- ♦ Read and write sequential files using the StreamReader and StreamWriter classes
- ♦ Understand the basics of collections and work with enumerators
- ♦ Create and manage lists of data with the ArrayList class
- ♦ Create and manage sorted lists of data with the SortedList class
- ♦ Create first-in first-out lists, called queues
- ♦ Understand last-in first-out lists, called stacks
- ♦ Read and write random files

This chapter contains two primary topics. The first topic shows you how to work with the Windows file system so as to navigate from directory to directory, and how to open and save different types of files. The second topic shows you how to work with collections of data in different ways. For example, you will learn how to work with records in the form of sorted and unsorted lists, and how to work with queues and stacks.

PREVIEWING THE COMPLETED SOLUTION

The completed solution in this chapter contains multiple forms. Each form stores and manages similar data in a different way. For example, one form displays data as an unsorted list, and another as a sorted list. Another form manages a queue, while yet another form allows you to examine file attributes. The following list describes the forms that comprise the solution and their purpose:

- The form named frmFiles illustrates how to determine the attributes of a particular file.

- The form named frmArrayList manages a list of data in an unsorted order. This data represents calls made to a call center.

- The form named frmSortedList manages a list of data so that the data remains sorted at all times. This data contains records representing the calls made to the call center and the responses to those calls.

- The form named frmQueue implements a data structure called a queue. A queue operates such that the first element added to the queue is the first element removed from the queue. The queue implemented in this chapter mimics the pending calls made to the call center that have not been completed.

- The form named frmRandomFiles manages a random file. A random file is one in which any record in the file can be accessed directly. This file contains one record for each employee working at the call center.

To preview the completed solution:

1. Start Visual Studio .NET and open the solution file named **Chapter.05\ Complete05\Complete05.sln**.

2. Run the solution. On the menu, click **Windows**, and then click **Display Calls** to display the form that stores data in an ArrayList.

3. On the form's menu bar, click **File**, and then click **Open** to display the Open dialog box. Select the file named **Chapter.05\Data\DemoCalls.txt**. The data appears in the form's text boxes. Figure 5-1 shows the ArrayList form after the data has been loaded.

4. Navigate to different records by clicking the **Next**, **First**, **Previous**, and **Last** menu items on the Navigate menu. Close the form.

5. On the main form menu, click **Windows**, and then click **Display Responses** to display the form that sorts the records based on the ID number. The form looks the same as the ArrayList form and displays the same data, but in sorted order by ID number.

Figure 5-1   Completed solution – ArrayList form

6. Click **File**, and then click **Open** to display the Open dialog box. Select the file named **Chapter.05\Data\DemoResponses.txt**. The data appears in the form's text boxes.

7. Click **Navigate**, **Find By ID** on the menu bar. In the input box, enter an ID number of **99**. Click **OK** to display the corresponding record. Close the form.

8. On the menu, click **Windows**, and then click **Edit Employees**. The form that processes a random file appears. Click **File**, and then click **Open** to display the Open dialog box. Select the file named **Chapter.05\Data\EmployeeList.rnd**. Figure 5-2 shows the form.

Figure 5-2   Completed solution – Random File form

9. To locate a record, click **Records**, and then click **Find Record**. Enter the value **2** in the input box, and then click **OK** to display the selected record. Note that if you select a record that does not exist, a message box will appear. Close the form.

10. On the menu, click **Windows**, and then click **Display Customer Queue**. The Queue form appears.

11. Enter a new customer into the text boxes with the following information: ID = **1**, First Name = **Jeff**, Last Name = **Hough**. Click the **Add Call Enqueue** button to add the customer to the queue.

12. Add a second customer using the information shown in Figure 5-3, and then click the **Add Call Enqueue** button again.

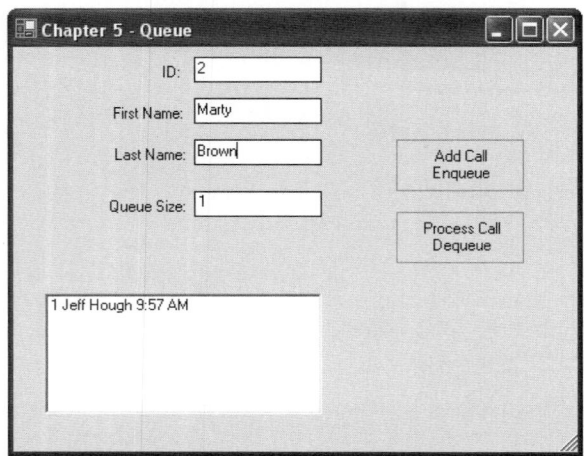

Figure 5-3   Completed solution – Queue form

As you add each customer, the information for the added customer appears in the list box to show the status of the queue.

13. Click the **Process Call Dequeue** button to remove the first customer from the front of the queue. Click the **Process Call Dequeue** button again to delete the only remaining customer from the queue. Close the form.

14. End the solution, and then exit Visual Studio .NET.

The completed solution is organized into components. For example, a class named RequestList manages the file containing the calls made to the call center. The class named ResponseList manages the file containing the calls made to the call center and the responses to those calls. Note that the forms themselves contain the code to manage the random file and the queue. Figure 5-4 illustrates the organization of the solution.

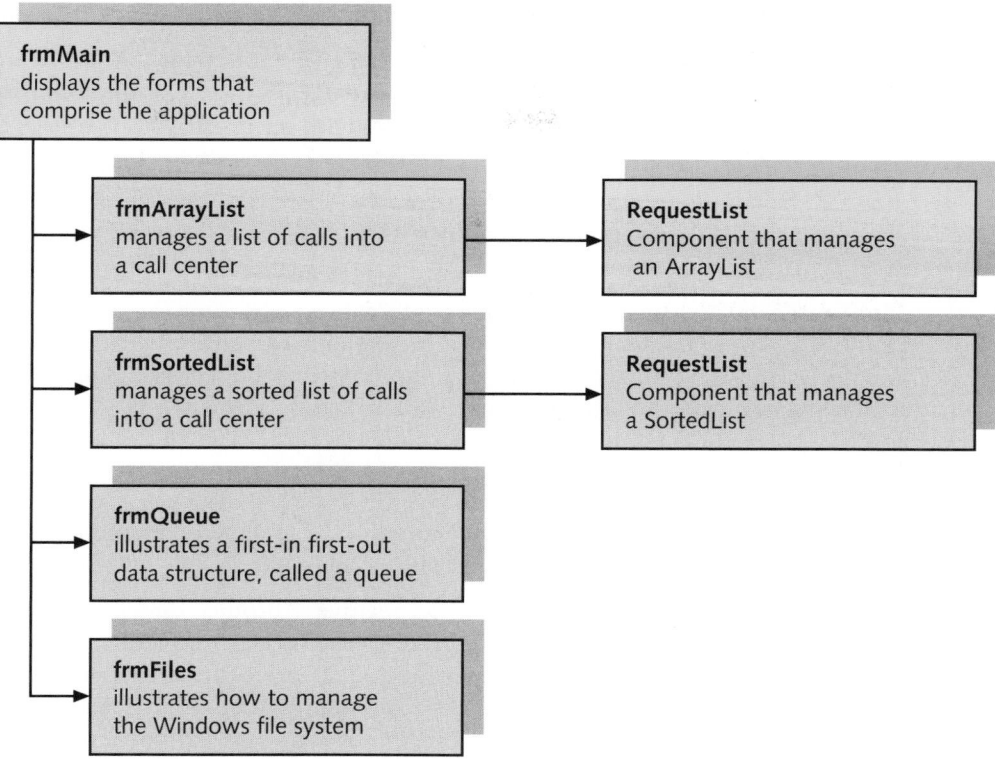

Figure 5-4   Solution organization

INTRODUCTION TO THE SYSTEM.IO NAMESPACE

The System.IO namespace, as its name implies, supplies the classes used to manage folders and files, and to read and write files in various ways.

> The terms "folder" and "directory" have the same meaning. As you work with Windows Explorer you will have likely used the former term. However, the System.IO namespace uses the latter term. For consistency with Visual Studio .NET, we will use the term "directory" in this chapter, rather than the term "folder."

The following list describes the classes discussed in this chapter that relate to file management and the purpose of those classes:

- The **System.IO.Directory** class contains methods to create, move, rename, and delete directories.

- The **System.IO.File** class works similarly to the System.IO.Directory class but manages files instead of directories and subdirectories.

- The members of the **System.IO.StreamReader** and **System.IO.StreamWriter** classes are used to read and write sequential files, respectively.

For those of you who have not worked with a Command Prompt window to navigate through the Windows file system, the organization of files may be unclear. Thus, before discussing how to use the classes of the System.IO namespace, we briefly describe the organization of the Windows file system.

The Windows file system is organized into a hierarchy. Physical or logical disk drives (A:, B:, C:, D:, etc.) appear at the base of the hierarchy. Logical disk drives, in turn, contain directories and files. Directories, in turn, can contain subdirectories and files. A backward slash separates each directory, subdirectory, or file, as shown in the following directory and file reference:

```
C:\Windows\Temp\Temp.doc
```

The preceding statement fragment references the file named Temp.doc in the directory named \Windows\Temp on the C: drive.

Directory references may be absolute or relative. Absolute directory references begin with a drive designator followed by a leading backslash (e.g., "C:\"). (If the drive designator is omitted, then the current drive is used.) Relative directory references begin with a directory name, but the leading backslash is omitted. Searching begins at the current working directory. Directory names can contain the special pattern ".." (two periods appearing together without an intervening space). Windows interprets this pattern to mean the parent directory of the current working directory. Examine the following relative directory reference:

```
..\Chapter.05\Complete\Temp.doc
```

The preceding code segment illustrates a relative directory reference to the file named Temp.doc. The two periods reference the parent directory of the current working directory. From the parent directory, the directory Chapter.05\Complete is referenced. Examine the following relative directory references:

```
.\Complete\Temp.doc
Complete\Temp.doc
```

Both of the preceding statements illustrate a relative directory reference. The file Temp.doc is assumed to appear in the Complete subdirectory of the current working directory. To create a relative directory reference, you either precede the reference with a leading period and a backslash, as shown in the first statement, or just begin with the directory name, as shown in the second statement.

Having seen how to specify the path names for directories and subdirectories, you will now learn how to use those path names to create directories and files.

WORKING WITH THE WINDOWS FILE SYSTEM

The System.IO.Directory class contains shared methods to manage the Windows file system. Thus, you do not create an instance of the Directory class before calling its methods. When working with the System.IO.Directory class, you must understand the concept of the current working directory. At any given time, as an application runs, one directory is designated as the **current working directory**. If you use relative references for directories or files, VB .NET will use the current working directory as the basis for the relative reference. If you use an absolute reference, the current working directory is ignored.

5

Methods of the Directory Class

The following list describes the methods of the Directory class:

- The **CreateDirectory** method creates a new directory or subdirectory. The method accepts one argument—the directory to create. The method returns an instance of the DirectoryInfo class. The DirectoryInfo class will be discussed later in the chapter. Note that if the directory already exists, the method will return a DirectoryInfo class instance representing the specified directory but will not create the directory. An exception will not occur.

- The overloaded **Delete** method accepts either one or two arguments. In both overloaded methods, the first argument contains the directory to delete. If the single argument version is used, VB .NET will throw a System.IO.IOException if the directory is not empty. The second overloaded method requires one additional Boolean argument. If True, all subdirectories and files are removed from the directory. If False, the directory must be empty for the directory to be removed. Otherwise, VB .NET will again throw a System.IO.IOException. Note that a directory cannot be deleted if it is the current working directory or a subdirectory of the current working directory. Furthermore, a directory cannot be deleted if another program is referencing that directory or a file in that directory.

- The **Exists** method accepts one argument—a String containing a directory name, and returns a Boolean value indicating whether the directory exists. If the directory exists, then the method returns True, and False otherwise.

- The **GetCurrentDirectory** method accepts no arguments and returns a String containing the current working directory. Initially, the current working directory is the directory from which the application is started. The SetCurrentDirectory method changes the current working directory and thus changes the value returned by the GetCurrentDirectory method.

- The **GetLogicalDrives** method accepts no arguments. It returns an array of strings listing the logical drives installed on the system. These drives include floppy disks, hard disks, CD-ROM devices, and other disks such as Zip disks.

- The **Move** method accepts two arguments and moves an existing directory to another directory. The source directory appears as the first argument and the destination directory appears as the second argument. The Move method can also be used as a mechanism to rename directories. Relative or absolute directory references may be used.

- The **SetCurrentDirectory** method accepts one argument—an existing directory. Calling this method resets the current working directory. Thus, subsequent calls to the GetCurrentDirectory method will return this new directory. If the directory cannot be found, VB .NET throws a System.IO.FileNotFoundException.

Using the Methods of the Directory Class

The following simple examples illustrate the use of the preceding methods of the Directory class. For example, the following code segment illustrates how to create a directory:

```
Dim dinfoCurrent As DirectoryInfo
dinfoCurrent = Directory.CreateDirectory("C:\Demo")
dinfoCurrent = Directory.CreateDirectory("Demo")
```

The preceding statements create an absolute directory named "C:\Demo" and a relative directory named "Demo" in the current working directory. The CreateDirectory method returns an instance of the DirectoryInfo class. The DirectoryInfo class, discussed in a moment, contains detailed information about the directory, such as the creation time and the last modification time. Because the methods of the Directory class are shared, you do not create an instance of the Directory class before calling its methods.

The following statements delete a directory:

```
Directory.Delete("C:\Demo")
Directory.Delete("C:\Demo", True)
```

The preceding statements delete the absolute directory named "C:\Demo". The first statement will delete the directory only if it is empty. The second statement will delete the directory and any subdirectories and files contained in the directory.

 Be careful when deleting directories. If you delete a directory having subdirectories, those subdirectories will be deleted without getting any confirmation from the user. For example, the following statement will remove everything from the C: drive, which is an unlikely request: `Directory.Delete("C:\", True)`.

The following statements determine if the directory named "C:\Demo" exists. The method returns True if the directory exists and False otherwise.

```
Dim pblnExists As Boolean
pblnExists = Directory.Exists("C:\Demo")
```

Examine the following statements to change the current working directory:

```
Dim pstrDirectory As String
pstrDirectory = Directory.GetCurrentDirectory()
```

```
If pstrDirectory <> "C:\" Then
    Call Directory.SetCurrentDirectory("C:\")
End If
```

The preceding statements get the current working directory and store the directory name in the String variable pstrDirectory. If the current working directory is not the root directory on the C drive, then the current working directory is set to "C:\". This directory must already exist or VB .NET will throw an exception.

The Move method of the directory class will move one directory to another directory on the same logical drive. It can also be used to rename a directory. Directories cannot be moved from one logical drive to another. For example, you cannot move a directory from the "C:" drive to the "D:" drive. The Move method accepts two arguments—the source file and the destination file, as shown in the following statements:

```
Directory.Move("C:\Demo", "C:\Backup\Demo")
Directory.Move("C:\Demo", "C:\Demo1")
```

The first of the preceding statements moves the directory named "C:\Demo", its subdirectories, and files, to the directory named "C:\Backup" without changing the directory name. The second of the preceding statements renames the directory from "C:\Demo" to "C:\Demo1". Note that the Directory class was explicitly specified in the preceding method calls. This is required because Move is an event of the form and will take precedence over the Move method of the Directory class.

Applying the Methods of the Directory Class

In this solution, you will create a directory structure to store the files containing the logs that are generated each day at the call center. You will create directories for each day of the year. Figure 5-5 illustrates the organization of these files.

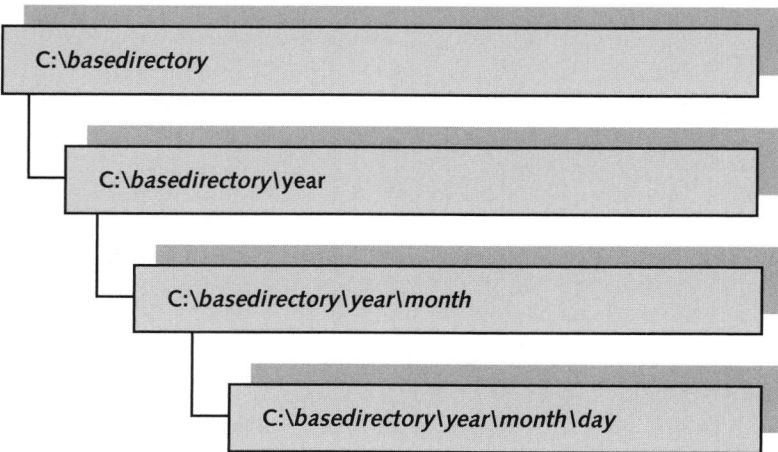

Figure 5-5   Logical file structure

As shown in Figure 5-5, the base directory contains a directory (*year*) to store the log files for the year. Subdirectories appear for each month of the year. Further subdirectories appear for each day of the month. Thus, the log files for a particular day will be stored in a separate directory. Even though you will create the directories to store each day's log files, you will not create each of the log files.

To accomplish this task, you will create a small component that will create directories based on the arguments passed to the overloaded method named CreateDirectoryTree. The first overloaded method will accept two arguments: the base directory where the tree should be created, and the year. The second overloaded method accepts an additional Boolean argument. If True, the component will create directories for each day of the month. If False, only the directories for the month names will be created. Figure 5-6 illustrates the organization and operation of this component.

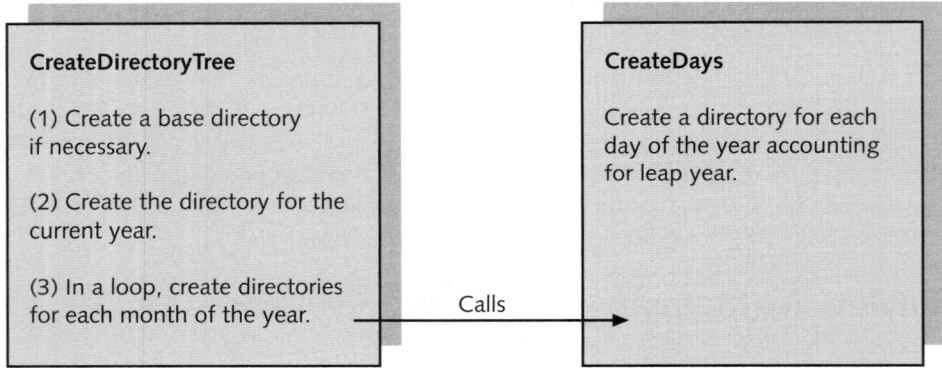

Figure 5-6   Operation of the DirectoryManager component

Three arrays have been declared in the component already to store the month names and the number of days in a month. The String array named pstrMonths stores the month names. The arrays to store the number of days in the month, shown below, have also been created but need to be examined as they account for a leap year.

```
Private Shared mintDaysInMonth() As Integer = { _
    0, 31, 28, 31, 30, 31, 30, _
    31, 31, 30, 31, 30, 31}

Private Shared mintDaysInMonthLeap() As Integer = { _
    0, 31, 29, 31, 30, 31, 30, _
    31, 31, 30, 31, 30, 31}
```

As you can see, the preceding two arrays are almost identical. Notice that the first element has a value of 0. This element is not used, so that the first month, January, has a subscript of 1, rather than 0. This way, we can write For loops that iterate from 1 to 12 rather than from 0 to 11. The purpose is simply to make the code more intuitive. Second, notice that the third element (February) has 28 days in one array and 29 days in another.

The following statements illustrate how these two different arrays are used to account for leap year:

```
Dim pintArrayToUse() As Integer
If System.DateTime.IsLeapYear(pintYear) Then
    pintArrayToUse = mintDaysInMonthLeap
Else
    pintArrayToUse = mintDaysInMonth
End If
```

As shown in the preceding statements, the IsLeapYear method of the System.DateTime class is called to determine if the current year is a leap year. If it is, then the array named mintDaysInMonthLeap will be used instead of the array named mintDaysInMonth. Note that because arrays are classes (reference types), the preceding assignment statements do not copy the array data, but just store a reference to the appropriate array in the variable named pintArrayToUse.

Next, you will write the statements to build the directory tree.

To create directories:

1. Start Visual Studio .NET, and open the solution file named **Chapter05\Startup05\Startup05.sln**.

2. In the module named **DirectoryManager.vb**, enter the following statement (shown in bold) in the first **CreateDirectoryTree** procedure, which accepts two arguments:

```
Public Overloads Shared Sub CreateDirectoryTree( _
    ByVal pstrBase As String, _
    ByVal pintYear As Integer)
    Call CreateDirectoryTree(pstrBase, pintYear, True)
End Sub
```

All that the preceding statement does is to call the CreateDirectoryTree procedure having three arguments. The final argument (True) indicates that the directories for the days in a month should be created.

3. Enter the following statements (shown in bold) in the second **CreateDirectoryTree** procedure, which accepts three arguments:

```
Public Overloads Shared Sub CreateDirectoryTree( _
    ByVal pstrBase As String, _
    ByVal pintYear As Integer, _
    ByVal pblnDays As Boolean)
    Dim pintMonth As Integer
    If Not Directory.Exists(pstrBase) Then
        Directory.CreateDirectory(pstrBase)
    End If
    Directory.SetCurrentDirectory(pstrBase)
    Directory.CreateDirectory(pintYear.ToString)
```

5

```
Directory.SetCurrentDirectory(pstrBase & "\" & _
    pintYear.ToString)
For pintMonth = 1 To 12
    Directory.CreateDirectory(pstrMonths(pintMonth))
    If pblnDays Then
        Call CreateDays(pintYear, pintMonth)
    End If
Next
Directory.SetCurrentDirectory("C:\")
End Sub
```

4. Enter the following statements in the **CreateDays** procedure:

```
Dim pintDay As Integer
Dim pstrTempDir As String
Dim pintArrayToUse() As Integer

If System.DateTime.IsLeapYear(pintYear) Then
    pintArrayToUse = mintDaysInMonthLeap
Else
    pintArrayToUse = mintDaysInMonth
End If

For pintDay = 1 To pintArrayToUse(pintMonth)
    pstrTempDir = pstrMonths(pintMonth) & "/" & _
        pintDay.ToString
    Directory.CreateDirectory(pstrTempDir)
Next
```

5. On the form named **frmMain.vb**, enter the following statements (shown in bold) in the **Click** event handler for the menu item named **mmuCreateDirectories**:

```
Dim pstrBaseDir As String = InputBox("Enter Directory", _
    "Directory", "C:\Test")
DirectoryManager.CreateDirectoryTree(pstrBaseDir, _
System.DateTime.Today.Year, False)
```

6. In the **Click** event handler for the menu item named **mmuDeleteDirectories**, write the following statements to delete the preceding directories:

```
Dim pstrRoot As String = InputBox( _
    "Enter Directory", "Directory", "C:\Test")
Directory.Delete(pstrRoot, True)
```

7. Test the solution. On the main form, click **File, Create Directories** on the main menu.

8. An input box appears with a default directory name. In the input box, click **OK** to create the directories and files in those directories. Using Windows Explorer, verify that the directories were built correctly.

9. Close Windows Explorer. As mentioned, if Windows Explorer is displaying a directory that you are trying to delete, then an exception will occur.

10. Remove the directories that you just created by clicking **File, Delete Directories**. Click **OK** to close the dialog box. Verify that the directories were deleted.

The File Class

The File class operates similarly to the Directory class and has static methods to create, delete, move, and open files, as described in the following list:

- The **Copy** method copies a source file to a destination file. Absolute or relative directory references may be used. If the destination file already exists, or the destination file is a directory, then an exception will occur. The exception raised by the CLR will vary.

- The **Create** method creates a new file. The Create method returns an instance of the FileStream class. Note that if the file already exists, it will be overwritten and VB .NET will not raise an exception. Thus, to prevent accidentally overwriting a file, call the Exists method first to make sure that the file does not already exist.

- The **Delete** method deletes a file. Again, absolute or relative directory references may be used. If the directory or file cannot be found, or the argument to the Delete method contains an empty string, the CLR will again raise an exception.

- The **Exists** method accepts one argument: a file name. It returns a Boolean value if the file exists.

- The **Move** method moves a source file to a destination file. You can use the Move method to rename files by using a different file name but the same directory for the source and destination files. The Move method allows you to move files from one logical drive to another.

- Every file has attributes. Attributes define a file's general characteristics, such as whether or not the file is a hidden file, a read-only file, and so on. The **GetAttributes** and **SetAttributes** methods get and set file attributes, respectively.

- The **GetCreationTime**, **GetLastAccessTime**, and **GetLastWriteTime** methods get the date and time the file was created, the time the file was last accessed, and the time the file was last written, respectively.

The following statements illustrate how to create, copy, move, and delete files:

```
File.Create("C:\Demo\DemoFile.txt")
File.Copy("C:\Demo\DemoFile.txt", "C:\Demo\DemoFile1.txt")
File.Move("C:\Demo\DemoFile.txt", "C:\Demo\DemoFile2.txt")
File.Delete("DemoFile1.txt")
```

The first of the preceding statements creates the file named "DemoFile.txt" in the folder named "C:\Demo" using an absolute directory reference. The second and third statements copy and rename the file respectively using absolute directory references. The final statement removes the file named "DemoFile1.txt" from the current working directory because no absolute directory name appears.

Next, you will modify the procedure that you created in the preceding steps to copy template files into the folders.

To create and copy files:

1. In the component named **DirectoryManager.vb**, enter the following statements (shown in bold) in the **CreateDirectoryTree** procedure having a signature accepting three arguments:

```
For pintMonth = 1 To 12
    Directory.CreateDirectory(pstrMonths(pintMonth))
    File.Create(pstrMonths(pintMonth.ToString) & _
        "\" & "Readme.doc")
    ' Statements
Next
```

2. Enter the following statement (shown in bold) in the **CreateDays** procedure:

```
Directory.CreateDirectory(pstrTempDir)
File.Create(pstrTempDir & "\" & "Readme.doc")
```

3. Test the solution. On the main form, click **File, Create Directories**. In the input box, click **OK** to create the directories and files in those directories. Using Windows Explorer, examine that the directories were built correctly and that an empty file named Readme.doc appears in each directory.

4. Close Windows Explorer.

5. Remove the directories that you just created by clicking **File, Delete Directories**. Click **OK**. Verify that the directories were deleted.

As mentioned, every file has attributes, and the static GetAttributes and SetAttributes methods of the File class allow you to work with the attributes of files. Both of these methods store file attributes in a FileAttributes enumeration. This enumeration contains bitwise flags that allow you to define each attribute. The following list describes selected file attributes, and their purpose:

- The **Archive** flag is used to mark files for backup or removal.
- If a file is compressed, the **Compressed** flag is set.
- The **Directory** flag indicates that the file is a directory.
- The **Hidden** flag indicates that a file should not be viewed by ordinary users. Hidden files are typically files used only by the system.
- If a file should be read-only, set the **ReadOnly** attribute.
- System files are typically marked by the **System** attribute.

The preceding list describes only a few of the supported attributes. Attributes are bit flags. That is, each bit in an Integer value indicates whether the attribute is enabled or disabled.

As an Integer is 32 bits in size, the value can store up to 32 attributes, one for each bit. To determine whether a particular attribute is enabled or disabled, you call the GetAttributes method of the File class, storing the result in a variable of type FileAttributes. Then, by performing an And operation, you can determine whether the bit is on or off, as shown in the following statements:

```
Dim faCurrent As FileAttributes
Dim pblnAttribute As Boolean
faCurrent = File.GetAttributes(ofdMain.FileName)
pblnAttribute = System.Convert.ToBoolean( _
    faCurrent And FileAttributes.System)
chkSystem.Checked = pblnAttribute
```

The preceding code segment illustrates how to determine whether or not the System attribute is set. First, the GetAttributes method is called on a file and stored in the variable faCurrent having a data type of FileAttributes. The And operator is applied to the variable faCurrent and the FileAttributes.System attribute, and the result is stored in the variable pblnAttribute. Thus, if the bit representing the System attribute is set, then the result will be True. Figure 5-7 illustrates how the process works.

Figure 5-7 Bitwise And operation

As shown in Figure 5-7, the bit patterns of two variables are compared. If both bits are on then the corresponding result bit is turned on. If one of the bits in the result variable is on then the result is True.

THE OPENFILEDIALOG AND SAVEFILEDIALOG CONTROLS

In any application involving file management, you must provide the user with a means to select a file to open or a file to save. Obviously, you could have the user enter a directory and file name in a text box or input box. However, this technique does not supply a user-friendly means to select a file. So VB .NET supplies the OpenFileDialog and SaveFileDialog controls, which allow the user to select a file to open and save, respectively, using standard dialog boxes. These two dialog boxes allow the user to select a directory by navigating through the file system, and then select the file to open or save. These two controls do not actually open or save files. They merely supply the means for the user to select a file to open or save. It is up to the code in your application to actually open or save the selected file.

The OpenFileDialog and SaveFileDialog controls are both derived from the FileDialog control. Thus, the two controls share nearly identical members, as described in the following syntax diagram:

Syntax

System.Windows.Forms.OpenFileDialog control
System.Windows.Forms.SaveFileDialog control

Public Properties

- The Boolean **AddExtension** property defines whether or not the system adds the current file extension if the file extension is omitted by the user.

- The Boolean **CheckFileExists** and **CheckPathExists** properties, if set to True, require that the user select a file and directory that already exist. These properties are typically set to True when opening a file, because it is illogical to open a file that does not already exist.

- The **FileName** property contains the file name selected by the user.

- The **FileNames** property contains an array of strings. Each element in the array contains the full path and file name selected by the user. The FileNames property works in conjunction with the MultiSelect property.

- The **FilterIndex** and **Filter** properties work in unison. Together, they define the possible file extensions selectable by the user, and the current file extension. If the Filter property is set to an invalid string, the CLR will throw a System.ArgumentException. The FilterIndex property is 1-based, meaning, the first filter has a value of 1, the second filter a value of 2, and so on.

- The **InitialDirectory** property contains a string that defines the directory that VB .NET will initially search for files. By default, the current working directory is searched.

- The Boolean **MultiSelect** property defines if the user can select multiple files from the dialog boxes. If set to True, the list of files is stored in the FileNames property. If set to False, the user cannot select multiple files.

- By default, the current working directory is reset to the directory selected by the user after the user closes the dialog box. If the **RestoreDirectory** property is set to True, the current working directory is restored to its original state after the dialog box closes.

- The contents of the **Title** property appear on the title bar of the dialog boxes.

Public Methods

- The **ShowDialog** method displays the OpenFileDialog or SaveFileDialog box.

- The **Reset** method sets all the properties to their default values.

Public Events

- The **FileOK** event fires when the user clicks the Open or Save button in the OpenFileDialog or SaveFileDialog box, respectively.

Figure 5-8 shows the OpenFileDialog control and how the various property settings affect the display of the control instance.

Figure 5-8   OpenFileDialog control

The Filter Property

Most common file types have standard file extensions. For example, Word documents have a file extension of ".doc" and an Excel Workbook has a file extension of ".xls." These common file extensions serve two purposes. By associating a file extension with a particular application, the user can double-click a file in Windows Explorer to start the application and open the file. In addition, when using the OpenFileDialog or SaveFileDialog controls to open or save a file, the list of files displayed is typically restricted to those having a particular file extension. The Filter property restricts the files displayed based on a particular file extension. The Filter property stores a String containing description value pairs separated by a vertical bar.

The following statement illustrates a filter having two description value pairs:

```
ofdDemo.Filter = "Text Files (*.txt)|*.txt" & _
    "|All Files (*.*)|*.*"
```

As shown in the preceding statement, the Filter property contains a text string. The first description contains the text "Text Files (*.txt)" and the first filter is "*.txt". To define a filter, you specify the file extension preceded by the "*." characters. The second filter description is "All Files (*.*)" and the second filter is "*.*". Thus, the first filter displays only those files having a suffix of ".txt" and the second filter will display all files. While the preceding statement defined two filters, you can create as many filters as needed. Note that no embedded spaces appear before or after the vertical bar character. If you include extra spaces, the filter will not work properly.

 When defining filters, always define an "All Files" filter. In the event the user changed the file extension, they will be able to find the desired file using this filter. The All Files filter should appear as the last filter. Set the FilterIndex property to the most commonly used filter if one exists.

The dialog boxes return a value having a data type of DialogResult, allowing you to determine which button the user clicked. If the user clicks the Open or Save buttons, the value DialogResult.OK is returned. If the user clicks the Cancel button, the value DialogResult.Cancel is returned.

Using the OpenFileDialog Control

As a first example of using the OpenFileDialog control, you will configure an instance of the OpenFileDialog control to determine file attributes. An instance of the OpenFileDialog control already appears on the form named frmFiles. Because the control instance is invisible at runtime, it appears in the resizable tray below the form.

To create and configure an instance of the OpenFileDialog control:

1. Activate the Code Editor for the form named **frmFiles.vb**.

2. Enter the following statements (shown in bold) in the **Click** event handler for the menu item named **mmuDisplayAttributes** to display the OpenFileDialog control instance:

```
Dim pblnAttribute As Boolean
Dim dlgResult As DialogResult
dlgResult = ofdFiles.ShowDialog()
If dlgResult <> DialogResult.OK Then
    Exit Sub
End If
faCurrent.File.GetAttributes(ofdFiles.FileName)
```

The preceding statements display an instance of the OpenFileDialog control. The ShowDialog method returns a DialogResult data type. The variable dlgResult is checked to determine whether the user clicked the Open button or the Cancel button. If the user clicked the Open button, then the value of dlgResult is DialogResult.OK, so the procedure continues to execute. The statements to get the file attributes have already been completed. Refer to the commented code in the solution for an explanation of these statements.

3. Test the solution. On the main form, click **Windows**, and then click **File Attributes**. On the File Attributes form, click **File**, and then click **Display Attributes** to display the Open dialog box. Select a file of your choosing. One outcome of this step sequence is shown in Figure 5-9.

Figure 5-9   File attributes

While the preceding statements illustrated how to open a single file, you can also allow the user to select multiple files to open by setting the MultiSelect property to True. The FileNames property contains an array of strings. Each String in the array contains the path name and file name selected by the user. Examine the following statements:

```
Dim pstrCurrentFile As String
For Each pstrCurrentFile In ofdFiles.FileNames
```

```
        Debug.WriteLine(pstrCurrentFile)
    Next
```

The preceding statements assume that ofdFiles is an instance of the OpenFileDialog control. The For Each loop enumerates the list of files stored in the FileNames property. Each time through the loop, the variable pstrCurrentFile contains one of the files from the list of files. Again, it is up to the code in your program to process the files as necessary.

Now that you know how to allow the user to select files, you can write the statements to work with those files. To manage directories and files, you use the classes of the System.IO namespace.

READING AND WRITING FILES

VB .NET supplies considerable flexibility in reading and writing files. You can call the methods of several different classes to achieve the same result. The techniques presented in this section represent but one way to read and write files from and to the disk.

Files can roughly be categorized into the following two types:

- **Sequential files** contain records of varying lengths. Typically, a carriage return separates each record. Each record contains one or more fields. A special character, called a delimiter, separates fields. The delimiter character is typically a comma but other characters can be used as a delimiter. Sequential files are typically text files, editable by any text editor such as Notepad. Sequential files must be read and written from beginning to end. Thus, you cannot read a record without reading all of the records that precede it. Sequential files are useful for several reasons. Many applications can exchange data using sequential files and many applications generate log files that appear as sequential files.

- **Random files**, also known as direct access files, are typically binary files. Records in a random file have a fixed size. Thus, it is possible to locate a specific record directly without reading the preceding records first. Random files have the benefit of performance, as it is possible to read any record directly with having first read the records preceding it. Random files are discussed in the last section of this chapter.

Reading Sequential Files with the StreamReader Class

To open a sequential file for reading, you create an instance of the StreamReader class. The overloaded constructor for the StreamReader class allows you to specify a file name as an argument, and optionally specify the character encoding system to use. Subsequently, calling the methods of the StreamReader class allows you to read the file character by character, or record by record, or to read the entire file at once. The following syntax dissection describes the methods of the StreamReader class:

Syntax

System.IO.StreamReader class

Public Methods

- The **Close** method closes the file associated with the StreamReader instance. A file should be explicitly closed after it has been read.

- The overloaded **Read** method reads one or more characters into a buffer as Integer values. With no arguments, the Read method reads a single character. The Read method can also be called to read an array of characters. When no more characters remain to be read in the file, the Read method returns the value –1.

- The **ReadLine** method reads a line (record) into a string. The line is read up to and including the carriage return character appearing at the end of the line. The carriage return character is discarded and does not appear in the returned string. When the records in the file have been read completely, the ReadLine method returns Nothing.

- The **ReadToEnd** method reads from the current position in the file to the end of the file. If the current file position is the beginning of the file, then the ReadToEnd method reads the entire file.

The following statements illustrate how to open a file by creating an instance of the StreamReader class:

```
Dim pstrFileName As String = "C:\Demo.txt"
Dim psrdCurrent As New System.IO.StreamReader(pstrFileName)
```

Assuming that pstrFileName is a String containing a valid file name, the preceding statements create an instance of the StreamReader class, thereby making the file available for reading. The variable psrdCurrent stores the instance of the StreamReader class. If the file does not exist, then the variable psrdCurrent references Nothing.

Calling the methods of the StreamReader class allows you to read the file. To illustrate the simplest possible case, the following statement reads an entire text file and stores the file's contents in a multi-line text box named txtFile:

```
txtFile.Text = psrdCurrent.ReadToEnd()
```

Suppose that you wanted to read a file and replace any tab characters with a space. The following code segment does this:

```
ofdFiles.ShowDialog()

Dim psrdCurrent As New _
    System.IO.StreamReader(ofdFiles.FileName)
Dim pintCurrent As Integer, pchrCurrent As Char
Dim pstrCurrent As String
pintCurrent = psrdCurrent.Read()
Do Until pintCurrent = -1
    pchrCurrent = ToChar(pintCurrent)
    If pchrCurrent = ControlChars.Tab Then
        pchrCurrent = Chr(32)
```

```
        End If
        pstrCurrent &= pchrCurrent
        pintCurrent = psrdCurrent.Read()
    Loop
    psrdCurrent.Close()
```

The preceding statements first create an instance of the StreamReader class, then the first character is read. If the file is empty, the statements in the Do loop will never execute. (Remember that the Read method returns –1 when no more characters remain in the file to be read.) The first statement in the Do loop converts the Integer representation of the character read to the actual character. The If statement tests if the character is a tab. If it is, the Chr function replaces the character with a space ("Chr(32)"). The current character is concatenated to the String variable pstrCurrent and then the next character is read. After all of the characters have been read, the file is closed. Figure 5-10 illustrates the logic to read a sequential file.

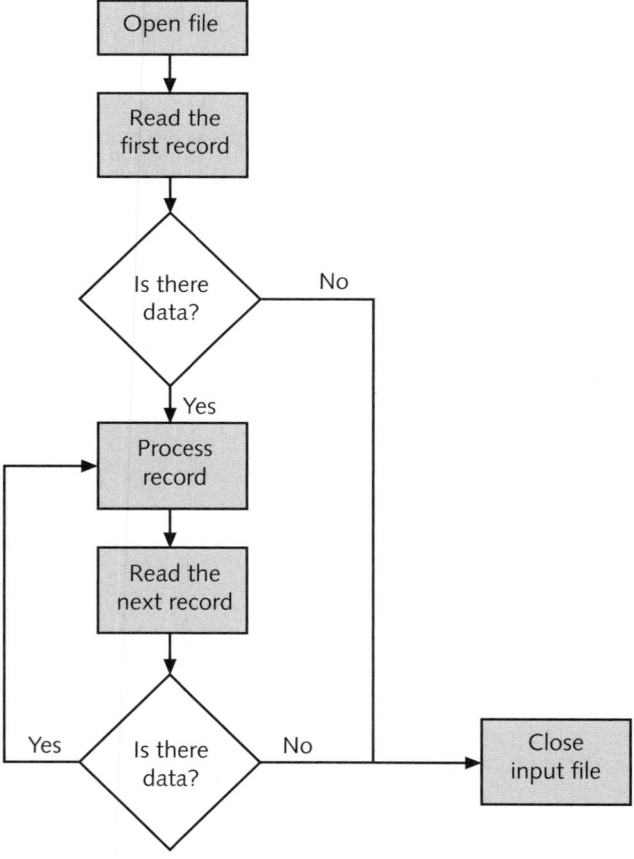

Figure 5-10   Logic to read a sequential file

Reading a file one line at a time is a bit more complex than reading one character at a time or reading the entire file at once. As mentioned, sequential files are typically organized such that each line contains one record. Each record, in turn, contains fields separated by a delimiter character. Typically, a comma is used as the delimiter character. Thus, to read and process the file, you read each record one at a time from the beginning of the file to the end of the file. For each line read, you split the line into its individual fields and store the data. The groups of code segments below illustrate the steps to read a sequential file.

```
Dim pstrCurrent As String
Dim pstrFields() As String
Dim pchrDelimiter() As Char = {ToChar(",")}
```

The preceding statements declare the variables to store the current line read (pstrCurrent) and the array of strings that will store the fields in the current record (pstrFields). The final statement declares a variable to store the delimiter. To split the input line into its individual fields, you call the Split method of the String class. The Split method accepts two arguments: the String to split and an array of type Char that stores the delimiter character(s). Thus, the last of the preceding statements declares an array of type Char named pchrDelimiter. The array is initialized to store a single character which is a comma. The ToChar method of the System.Convert class explicitly converts the String to a Char data type.

```
Dim psrdCurrent As New System.IO.StreamReader(pstrFileName)
pstrCurrent = psrdCurrent.ReadLine()
```

The first of the preceding statements opens the file stored in the String variable pstrFileName. The second statement calls the ReadLine method to read the first record into the String variable pstrCurrent. This step is important. By attempting to read the first record of the file before entering the following Do loop, we account for the possibility that the file may be empty. That is, if the file is empty, then the ReadLine method returns Nothing and the following statements that process the records in the file will never execute. The remaining steps to read and process the sequential file involve a Do loop. A Do loop is used instead of a For loop because you cannot determine in advance the number of records appearing in the file. The statements in the Do loop process the current line and then attempt to read another line. When all of the lines have been read, the loop exits and the file is closed.

Examine the following loop to read a sequential file:

```
Do Until pstrCurrent = Nothing
    pstrFields = pstrCurrent.Split(pchrDelimiter)
    custNew.ID = System.Convert.ToInt32(pstrFields(0))
    recNew.ID = pstrFields(0)
    recNew.Employee = pstrFields(1)
    recNew.CallReceived = ToDateTime(pstrFields(2))
    recNew.Request = CType(pstrFields(3), TypeOfRequest)
    pstrCurrent = psrdCurrent.ReadLine()
Loop
psrdCurrent.Close()
```

In the preceding loop, the Split method is called to break up the current line into its component fields. Figure 5-11 illustrates how the Split method operates.

```
pstrFields = pstrCurrent.Split(pchrDelimiter)
```

Figure 5-11   Operation of the Split method

After the Split method is called, the dynamic String array named pstrFields contains one element for each field read. You will read a sequential file later in the chapter into an ArrayList and complete the hands-on steps when the ArrayList class is discussed.

The Join method can be thought of as the inverse of the Split method. It joins an array of strings into a single String and separates each string in the array with a delimiter character, as shown in the following statements:

```
Dim pstrList() As String = {"January", "February", "March"}
Dim pstrJoined As String
pstrJoined = String.Join(",", pstrList)
```

The preceding statements join the String array named pstrList into a single String using the comma character as the delimiter. When complete, the String pstrJoined contains the following text:

```
January,February,March
```

Writing Files with the StreamWriter Class

The steps to write a file with the StreamWriter class are similar to those steps used to read a file, meaning, you create an instance of the StreamWriter class using the file name as an argument, and then call its methods to write the file character by character, or record by record. The StreamWriter class supports the following members:

Syntax

System.IO.StreamWriter class

Public Properties

- The **NewLine** property defines the character, a carriage return by default, that marks the end of a line. The NewLine property works in conjunction with the WriteLine method.

Public Methods

- The **Close** method closes the open file. Again, a file should be explicitly closed after it has been written to prevent loss of data.
- The **Write** method writes a character or characters to the file.
- The **WriteLine** method writes a character or characters to the file. The line terminator stored in the NewLine property is written after the characters are written.

Expanding on one of the preceding examples, suppose that you wanted to read a file, replace the tab characters with space characters, and then create a new file. The following code segment illustrates the steps to read and write a file, replacing tab characters with space characters:

```
ofdFiles.ShowDialog()
sfdFiles.ShowDialog()
Dim psrdCurrent As New _
    System.IO.StreamReader(ofdFiles.FileName)
Dim pswriCurrent As New _
    System.IO.StreamWriter(sfdFiles.FileName)
Dim pintCurrent As Integer, pchrCurrent As Char
pintCurrent = psrdCurrent.Read()

Do Until pintCurrent = -1
    pchrCurrent = ToChar(pintCurrent)
    If pchrCurrent = ControlChars.Tab Then
        pchrCurrent = Chr(32)
    End If
    pswriCurrent.Write(pchrCurrent)
    pintCurrent = psrdCurrent.Read()
Loop
psrdCurrent.Close()
pswriCurrent.Close()
```

The preceding code segment is simplified in that it has no error handling. However, it does illustrate how to read and write a file, replacing the tab characters with spaces. Instances of the StreamReader and StreamWriter classes are created based on the file names obtained from instances of the OpenFileDialog and SaveFileDialog controls, and the first character is read from the input stream. Thus, if the input file is empty, the statements in the Do loop will not execute. The statements in the Do loop test the value of the input character. If it is a tab, the character is replaced with a space and then the character is written to the output file. After all of the characters have been read, both the input file and the output file are closed. Note that this procedure has already been created in the startup and completed solution. The procedure appears in the form named frmFiles.

Having seen how to read and write sequential files, you will now learn about different ways to store that data in memory, and how to process that data.

WORKING WITH COLLECTIONS

A **collection** is nothing more than multiple objects, typically of the same type, organized in some way. In this solution, you will read a sequential file representing the calls made to the call center and summarize its contents. No matter the type of object managed by a collection, all collections supply a means to enumerate the objects contained in the collection using a For Each loop. Collections mimic common data structures including lists, sorted lists, stacks, and queues. You can also override the features of existing collections and create your own collections.

All of the predefined .NET collection classes belong to the System.Collections namespace. The following classes of the System.Collections namespace allow you to implement collections in different ways. Note that all of the following classes can work with any type of object. Thus, they all work with lists containing items of type System.Object. If strict type checking is enabled, you must call the CType function to convert the generic System.Object type to a specific type.

The following list describes the collections discussed in this chapter:

- The **ArrayList** class works similarly to an array. It contains additional methods beyond those provided by the Array class to add and remove elements, along with methods to sort the list and locate elements in the list.

- The **SortedList** class is similar to the ArrayList class, but it maintains elements in a sorted order automatically.

- The **Queue** class implements a first-in first-out list. That is, the first element added to the list is the first element removed from the list.

- The **Stack** class works the opposite of a queue. That is, it is a last-in first-out list. The element most recently added to the stack is the first element removed from the stack.

VB .NET supplies other classes that belong to the System.Collections namespace beyond those mentioned in the preceding list.

In the sections that follow, we discuss each of the preceding collections in turn. However, each of the preceding collections supports a group of common members. We discuss them in the following list rather than repeating these same properties and methods in each syntax dissection.

- The **Count** property returns the number of elements in the collection. The Count property is 1–based, so if there were 10 objects in the collection, then the Count property would have a value of 10.

- The **Clear** method removes all of the elements from the collection.

- The **ToArray** method converts the elements in a collection into an array.

- The **ToString** method returns a String representing the collection.

THE ARRAYLIST CLASS

The ArrayList class is used to maintain a list of objects, similar to a 1-dimensional array storing a list of numbers, structures, or other objects. However, the ArrayList class has additional properties and methods, making the ArrayList more robust than the Array class. The ArrayList class has the following members:

Syntax

System.Collections.ArrayList class

Public Properties

- The **Capacity** property defines the number of elements that the ArrayList can contain. As objects are added to the ArrayList, VB .NET will increase the capacity as necessary. As elements are added to an ArrayList, the Capacity property is not incremented by 1. Rather, VB .NET allocates increasingly larger blocks of elements in anticipation of more elements being added.

- The **Count** property contains the number of elements actually stored in the ArrayList. Thus, the value of the Count property is always less than or equal to the value of the Capacity property.

Public Methods

- The **Add** method adds an element to the end of the ArrayList.

- The **AddRange** method adds multiple elements to the end of the ArrayList.

- The **BinarySearch** method uses a type of search algorithm called a binary search to locate an element quickly within a sorted ArrayList.

- The **Remove** method removes the first occurrence of a specific element from the ArrayList.

- The **RemoveAt** method removes an element from the ArrayList. The method accepts one argument: the 0-based index of the element to remove. Note that an ArrayList uses an index in much the same way an array uses an index.

- The **Reverse** method reverses the order of the elements stored in the ArrayList. The Reverse method may also be called to reverse the elements stored in a portion of the ArrayList.

- The **Sort** method sorts the elements in all or part of the ArrayList.

In this chapter's solution, you will read the records contained in a sequential file and store them in an ArrayList. Then you will provide the functionality for the user to locate a given record, and to add, change, and delete those records. Finally, you will write the statements to save the contents of the ArrayList back to the disk as a sequential file. Thus, you will use the methods of the StreamReader and StreamWriter classes discussed previously in the chapter.

Managing the Call Records

While you could certainly create all of the statements to accomplish the task of managing the call records in the form itself, you will instead create a component named RequestList to handle this task, multiple applications could use this component to process the sequential file containing call records. Figure 5-12 illustrates the organization of the component and the form using the component.

frmMain form

Calls upon the services of the RequestList class to add, change, and delete records

RequestList class

Navigate method performs record navigation from record to record

AddRequest method adds a new record to the call list

SaveRequest method makes changes to an existing request

DeleteRequest method deletes an existing request

OpenFile method reads and processes the sequential file

SaveFile method saves the list to a sequential file

Figure 5-12   Organization of the RequestList component

The members of the RequestList class abstract the processing to create the ArrayList and read records from a sequential file into the ArrayList. Additional methods provide support for record navigation and adding, changing, and deleting records.

First, you will write the statements to open a sequential file and read its contents into an ArrayList. The following class has already been declared in the module named Global.vb to store the objects in the ArrayList. The data type named TypeOfRequest is an enumeration. This enumeration has also been declared and stores the type of the request that was made.

```
Public Class CallRecord
    Public ID As String
    Public Employee As String
    Public CallReceived As DateTime
    Public Request As TypeOfRequest
End Class
```

In addition, the following variable has been declared to store the ArrayList:

```
Private alRecords As New ArrayList()
```

Using the techniques already presented, you will write the statements to open the sequential file and read its contents into the ArrayList.

To open a file and read it into an ArrayList:

1. Activate the Code Editor for the module named **RequestList.vb**, and then enter the following statements in the **OpenFile** procedure:

```
Dim pstrCurrent As String
Dim pstrFields() As String
Dim pstrDelimiter() As Char = {ToChar(",")}
Try
    Dim psrdCurrent As New _
    System.IO.StreamReader(pstrFileName)
    pstrCurrent = psrdCurrent.ReadLine()
    Do Until pstrCurrent = Nothing
        Dim recNew As New CallRecord()
        pstrFields = pstrCurrent.Split(pstrDelimiter)
        recNew.ID = pstrFields(0)
        recNew.Employee = pstrFields(1)
        recNew.CallReceived = ToDateTime(pstrFields(2))
        recNew.Request = CType(pstrFields(3), _
            TypeOfRequest)
        alRecords.Add(recNew)
        pstrCurrent = psrdCurrent.ReadLine()
    Loop
    psrdCurrent.Close()
    mintCurrent = 0
    Return True
```

5

```
Catch ex As System.Exception
    Return False
End Try
```

The preceding statements open and read a sequential file as previously discussed in the chapter. First, an instance of the StreamReader class is created, thereby opening the file. The first call to the ReadLine method reads the first line of the file. If the first line contains data, the statements in the Do loop execute. A new instance of the CallRecord class is created to store the record. The next statements split the line into fields by calling the Split method, and store those fields in the class instance. Calling the Add method adds the call record to the end of the ArrayList. The final statements close the file and set the hidden variable named mintCurrent to 0. The variable mintCurrent is used to mark which record in the ArrayList is the current record. Note that an exception handler surrounds the statements to open and read the file. If the file is read correctly then the method returns True. If, for any reason the file cannot be read, the method will return False.

2. Activate the Code Editor for the form named **frmArrayList.vb**, and then enter the following statements in the **Click** event handler for the menu item named **mmuFileOpen**:

```
Dim dlgResult As DialogResult
Dim pstrCurrentFile As String
ofdArrayList.Filter = "Text Files (*.txt)|*.txt" & _
    "|All Files (*.*)|*.*"
ofdArrayList.FilterIndex = 1
ofdArrayList.CheckPathExists = True
ofdArrayList.CheckFileExists = True
dlgResult = ofdArrayList.ShowDialog()
If dlgResult = DialogResult.OK Then
    If Not ( _
        mCurrentList.OpenFile(ofdArrayList.FileName)) Then
        MessageBox.Show("Cannot read file", "Error", _
            MessageBoxButtons.OK)
    Else
        SetEditState(EditState.Browsing)
        Dim recCurrent As CallRecord
        recCurrent = _
        mCurrentList.Navigate( _
            RequestList.NavigateWhere.NavigateFirst)
        Call DisplayCurrentRecord(recCurrent)
    End If
End If
```

The preceding statements display the OpenFileDialog control instance, set the filter, and then display the dialog box. If the user clicks OK, then the file is opened. Note that the variable mCurrentList has already been declared and creates an instance of the RequestList class. If the OpenFile method returns False, then the file was invalid and a message box appears to the user. The call to the procedure DisplayCurrentRecord copies the data out of the current record into the form's text boxes. This procedure has already been created. The call to the SetEditState procedure enables and disables appropriate menu items along with enabling and disabling the form's text boxes. This procedure is fully commented on in the completed solution. Enabling and disabling the various control instances prevents the user from attempting to perform an impossible action.

Having seen how to read a sequential file into an ArrayList, the next statements that you will write in the RequestList component will allow the developer to navigate through the records stored in the list. The Navigate method accepts one argument: an enumeration indicating whether to navigate to the first, previous, next, or last record. This enumeration, named NavigateWhere, has already been declared in the RequestList component.

To navigate through the records in an ArrayList:

1. Activate the Code Editor for the class named **RequestList.vb**, and then enter the following statements (shown in bold) in the **Navigate** procedure:

```
Public Function Navigate(ByVal eWhere As NavigateWhere) _
    As CallRecord
    Select Case eWhere
        Case NavigateWhere.NavigateFirst
            mintCurrent = 0

        Case NavigateWhere.NavigatePrevious
            If mintCurrent > 0 Then
                mintCurrent -= 1
            Else
                Return Nothing
            End If
        Case NavigateWhere.NavigateNext
            If mintCurrent < alRecords.Count - 1 Then
                mintCurrent += 1
            Else
                Return Nothing
            End If
        Case NavigateWhere.NavigateLast
            mintCurrent = alRecords.Count - 1
    End Select
    Return CType(alRecords(mintCurrent), CallRecord)
End Function
```

The Select Case statement uses the enumeration to determine where to navigate. Each Case sets the current record by setting the value of the hidden variable named mintCurrent. The NavigatePrevious and NavigateNext cases have an additional statement to test whether the first record or the last record is the current record, respectively. In such a case, record navigation is not possible so the value Nothing is returned. Otherwise, the desired record from the ArrayList is returned.

2. Activate the Code Editor for the form named **frmArrayList.vb**, and then enter the following statements in the **Click** event handler for the menu item named **mmuNavigateNext**:

```
Dim recCurrent As CallRecord
recCurrent = mCurrentList.Navigate( _
    RequestList.NavigateWhere.NavigateNext)
If Not (recCurrent Is Nothing) Then
    Call DisplayCurrentRecord(recCurrent)
Else
    MessageBox.Show("Last record is already current", _
    "Error", MessageBoxButtons.OK)
End If
```

The preceding statements call the Navigate method that you just wrote to locate the next record in the list and display it. If there is no next record, a message box is displayed.

3. Enter the following statements in the **Click** event handler for the menu item named **mmuNavigatePrevious**:

```
Dim recCurrent As CallRecord
recCurrent = mCurrentList.Navigate( _
    RequestList.NavigateWhere.NavigatePrevious)
If Not (recCurrent Is Nothing) Then
    Call DisplayCurrentRecord(recCurrent)
Else
    MessageBox.Show("First record is already current", _
    "Error", MessageBoxButtons.OK)
End If
```

The process to locate the previous record is nearly the same as the process to locate the next record. The If statement tests if there is a previous record, and either displays the record, or displays a message box indicating that the first record is the current record.

4. Enter the following statements in the **Click** event handler for the menu item named **mmuNavigateFirst**:

```
Dim recCurrent As CallRecord
    recCurrent = mCurrentList.Navigate( _
    RequestList.NavigateWhere.NavigateFirst)
Call DisplayCurrentRecord(recCurrent)
```

5. Enter the following statements in the **Click** event handler for the menu item named **mmuNavigateLast**:

```
Dim recCurrent As CallRecord
recCurrent = mCurrentList.Navigate( _
    RequestList.NavigateWhere.NavigateLast)
Call DisplayCurrentRecord(recCurrent)
```

6. Test the solution. On the main form, click **Windows** and then click **Display Calls**. On the form, click **File**, and then click **Open** to display the OpenFileDialog control instance. Select the file named **Chapter05\Data\ DemoCalls.txt**, and then click **Open**. In the ArrayList form, click the **First**, **Next**, **Previous**, and **Last** menu items on the Navigate menu to locate and display records.

Next, you will see how to add new records to an ArrayList, make changes to existing records, and delete records. To add a new record to an ArrayList, you call the Add method. To change a record, you merely replace its contents. To delete a record, you call the Remove or RemoveAt methods. Again, you will first create methods in the RequestList component to add, change, and delete records, and then you will write the statements in the form to test the component.

To add, change, and delete records in an ArrayList:

1. Activate the Code Editor for the class named **RequestList.vb**, and then enter the following statement (shown in bold) in the procedure named **AddRequest**:

```
Public Function AddRequest(ByVal cr As CallRecord) _
    As Boolean
    alRecords.Add(cr)
End Function
```

As shown in the preceding statement, an instance of the CallRecord class is passed as an argument to the procedure. This CallRecord is added to the hidden ArrayList named alRecords by calling the Add method.

2. Enter the following statement in the procedure named **SaveRequest**:

```
alRecords.Item(mintCurrent) = cr
```

Again, an instance of the CallRecord class is passed as an argument to the procedure. Remember that the hidden variable named mintCurrent indicates which object in the ArrayList is the current object. Thus, the preceding statement replaces the current CallRecord with the CallRecord passed as an argument to the procedure.

3. Enter the following statements in the procedure named **DeleteRequest**:

```
alRecords.RemoveAt(mintCurrent)
mintCurrent = 0
```

Again, the variable mintCurrent identifies the current list element. Calling the RemoveAt method removes that element. The final statement sets the current record indicator to 0 because the existing current record was deleted.

4. In the form named **frmArrayList.vb**, enter the following statements in the **Click** event handler for the menu item named **mmuRecordsAdd**:

```
Call SetEditState(EditState.Adding)
txtID.Clear()
```

```
txtEmployee.Clear()
txtTime.Clear()
```

These statements merely clear the contents of the text boxes, allowing the user to complete the information for the record that will be added. Additionally, they set the edit state to enable the text boxes and the appropriate menu items.

5. Enter the following statements in the **Click** event handler for the menu item named **mmuRecordsSaveAdd**:

```
Dim recCurrent As New CallRecord()
Try
    With recCurrent
        .ID = txtID.Text
        .Employee = txtEmployee.Text
        .CallReceived = ToDateTime(txtTime.Text)
        .Request = CType(lstType.SelectedIndex, _
            TypeOfRequest)
    End With
    mCurrentList.AddRequest(recCurrent)
Catch ex As System.Exception
    MessageBox.Show("Invalid Data")
    Call DisplayCurrentRecord(recCurrent)
Finally
    Call SetEditState(EditState.Browsing)
End Try
```

The preceding statements create an instance of the CallRecord class, and then copy the contents of the text boxes into that class instance. The final statement in the With block uses the SelectedIndex property of the list box named lstType to determine which of the enumerated values is selected. Finally, the AddRequest method is called to add the new CallRecord to the list. The exception handler deals with any type conversion errors that may arise as a result of the user entering invalid data.

6. Enter the following statement in the **Click** event handler for the menu item named **mmuRecordsChange**:

```
Call SetEditState(EditState.Editing)
```

The preceding statement enables the text boxes on the form and updates the menu items so that the user can save the changed record.

7. Enter the following statements in the **Click** event handler for the menu item named **mmuRecordsSaveChange**:

```
Dim recCurrent As CallRecord
Try
    With recCurrent
        .ID = txtID.Text
        .Employee = txtEmployee.Text
        .CallReceived = ToDateTime(txtTime.Text)
```

```
        .Request = CType(lstType.SelectedIndex, _
            TypeOfRequest)
    End With
    mCurrentList.SaveRequest(recCurrent)
Catch ex As System.Exception
    MessageBox.Show(ex.Message, "Error", _
        MessageBoxButtons.OK)
Finally
    Call SetEditState(EditState.Browsing)
End Try
```

The preceding statements again create a new CallRecord. The data stored in the text boxes is copied to the CallRecord class instance. Next, the SaveRequest method is called to save the current record. If the data is invalid, then the exception handler catches the error and displays a message box.

8. Enter the following statements in the **Click** event handler for the menu item named **mmuRecordsDelete**:

```
Dim recCurrent As CallRecord
mCurrentList.DeleteRequest()
recCurrent = mCurrentList.Navigate( _
    RequestList.NavigateWhere.NavigateFirst)
```

The preceding statements call the DeleteRequest method of the RequestList component to remove the current record. Because the current record is removed, the current record is set to the first record, and then displayed. The choice of which record to display, however, is arbitrary.

9. Test the solution. On the main form, click **Windows** and then click **Display Calls**. Click **File** and then click **Open** to open the file named **Chapter.05\Data\DemoCalls.txt**. Click **Records**, and then click **Add** to begin adding a new record. Enter the information shown in Figure 5-13. Click **Records**, **Save Add** to save the record back to ArrayList.

Figure 5-13   Call list

10. Using the items on the Navigate menu, locate other records and then the record that you just added. Click **Records**, **Delete** to delete the record.

Having shown how to add, change, and delete records, those changes need to be saved back to the sequential file. To save a sequential file, you call the methods of the StreamWriter class as previously discussed.

To save an ArrayList:

1. Activate the Code Editor for the class named **RequestList.vb**, and then enter the following statements in the procedure named **SaveFile**:

```
Dim pswriCurrent As New _
    System.IO.StreamWriter(pstrFileName)
Dim recCurrent As CallRecord
For Each recCurrent In alRecords
    pswriCurrent.Write(recCurrent.ID)
    pswriCurrent.Write(",")
    pswriCurrent.Write(recCurrent.Employee)
    pswriCurrent.Write(",")
    pswriCurrent.Write(recCurrent.CallReceived.ToString)
    pswriCurrent.Write(",")
    pswriCurrent.WriteLine(recCurrent.Request)
Next
pswriCurrent.Close()
```

2. Activate the Code Editor for the form named **frmArrayList.vb**, and then enter the following statements in the **Click** event handler for the menu item named **mmuFileSave**:

```
Dim dlgResult As DialogResult
sfdArrayList.Filter = "Text Files (*.txt)|*.txt"
sfdArrayList.FilterIndex = 1
dlgResult = sfdArrayList.ShowDialog
If dlgResult = DialogResult.OK Then
    Call mCurrentList.SaveFile(sfdArrayList.FileName)
End If
```

The preceding statements display the SaveFileDialog control instance already created on the form. If the user clicks the OK button, then the file is saved.

3. Test the solution. On the menu bar, click **Windows**, and then click **Display Calls**. Open the file named **DemoCalls.txt**. Save the file by clicking **File**, **Save** to display the Save File Dialog. Use the name **Chapter.05\Data\ DemoCallsBak.txt** to make an exact copy of the file.

The final task that you will perform with the ArrayList is to enumerate its contents with a For Each loop to tally the different categories of calls. The function that you create will return a string containing a description of the call type followed by the number of calls.

To enumerate an ArrayList:

1. Activate the Code Editor for the class named **RequestList.vb**, and then enter the following statements in the procedure named **RequestSummary**:

```
Dim recCurrent As CallRecord
Dim objCurrent As Object
Dim pintMakeReservation As Integer
Dim pintOtherInfo As Integer
Dim pintPriceTicket As Integer
For Each objCurrent In alRecords
    recCurrent = CType(objCurrent, CallRecord)
    Select Case recCurrent.Request
        Case TypeOfRequest.MakeReservation
            pintMakeReservation += 1
        Case TypeOfRequest.OtherInfo
            pintOtherInfo += 1
        Case TypeOfRequest.PriceTicket
            pintPriceTicket += 1
    End Select
Next
Return "Reservations = " & pintMakeReservation.ToString & _
    CrLf & "Other info = " & pintOtherInfo.ToString & _
    CrLf & "Price of ticket = " & pintPriceTicket
```

The preceding statements use a For Each loop to examine the ArrayList. Because strict type checking is enabled, the generic object type must be converted to the CallRecord type. The type of call for each record is examined and the totals calculated. After all of the records have been examined, a String is built containing the summarized information.

2. Activate the Code Editor for the form named **frmArrayList.vb**, and then enter the following statements in the **Click** event handler for the menu item named **mmuRecordsSummary**:

```
Dim pstrSummary As String
pstrSummary = mCurrentList.RequestSummary()
    MessageBox.Show(pstrSummary, "Summary", _
        MessageBoxButtons.OK)
```

3. Test the solution. Activate the Call List form that you have been working with, and then open the file named **DemoCalls.txt**. On the menu bar, click **Records** and then click **Summary**. A message box appears containing the summarized data.

At this point, you have seen how to manage an ArrayList. The SortedList class, discussed next, works similarly.

THE SORTEDLIST CLASS

The SortedList class is similar to an array or an ArrayList in that it stores a list of objects. However, the SortedList class internally maintains two arrays. One array stores the keys used to locate the values associated with those keys. The SortedList class allows you to retrieve a value directly from the list given a specific key, and allows you to add and remove items easily from the list. Figure 5-14 illustrates the key / value relationships.

Figure 5-14   Key / value relationships in a SortedList

As shown in Figure 5-14, you use a key to look up the associated value. The SortedList keeps the keys sorted at all times so it is able to look up the value associated with a particular key directly. Note that the key values must be unique.

As a developer, you typically add, change, and remove items from a SortedList. As you add, change, and delete items from a SortedList, those items are kept in sorted order automatically. The SortedList class supports the following members:

- The **Add** method adds an element to the SortedList. When adding an element to the SortedList, you call the Add method with two arguments: the key and the value associated with that key.

- Just as each element in an ArrayList has a 0-based index, so too does each element in a SortedList. As items are added and removed from a SortedList, the index value will be updated automatically. The **GetByIndex** method gets the value associated with the associated index. The **SetByIndex** method works similarly to the GetByIndex method but stores a value based on a specific index.

- The **Item** method allows you to retrieve a value from the list given a specific key. Having retrieved that value, you can modify and change its contents. Note that the Item method does not produce the same result as the GetByIndex method. For example, a key may have a value of 99, but the index value may be 0.

- The **Remove** method removes an item from the SortedList. The Remove method accepts one argument: the key to remove.

- The **RemoveAt** method removes an item from the SortedList and accepts one argument: the index of the key to remove.

- The **Values** property contains a collection. Each element in the collection represents an object in the collection.

In this solution, you will add records to a SortedList in much the same way you added records to an ArrayList, but the records will be sorted by ID number. In addition to containing a record indicating the time that a call was placed, another record appears in the sequential file indicating the time that the call was completed. Most of the code to read the sequential file and populate the SortedList has already been created, as it is similar to the code you wrote to manage the ArrayList. Thus, in the following section you will only write the statements that materially differ from the statements to process the ArrayList. You will begin by supplying the navigation capabilities.

Locating an Item in a SortedList

The Item method of the SortedList class accepts one argument, which is the key of the item to retrieve. The method returns the value associated with the corresponding key. Examine the following code segment:

```
Public Function FindRequest(ByVal ID As String) _
    As CallRecord
    Return CType(slRecords.Item(ID), CallRecord)
End Function
```

The Item method of the SortedList class returns a value from the SortedList based on the corresponding key. Thus, in the preceding statements, the key that is stored in the variable named ID causes the corresponding call record (value) to be returned by the function. As the SortedList returns values in the generic form of System.Object, we call the CType function explicitly to convert the value to the CallRecord data type. Note that if a corresponding value is not found, the Item method will return Nothing.

In addition to locating a record directly using its key, you can call the GetByIndex method to get a record using its ordinal index value. Conceptually, this process is similar to the one that you used to navigate through the records in the ArrayList. Examine the following statements:

```
Dim cr As CallRecord
cr = CType(slRecords.GetByIndex(mintCurrent), CallRecord)
```

The preceding statements assume that slRecords represents an instance of the SortedList class, and that mintCurrent is a hidden variable used as a counter to store the position of the current record within the SortedList. Thus, the preceding statements retrieve the current record and store a reference to that record in the variable cr.

To locate items in a SortedList:

1. Activate the Code Editor for the module named **ResponseList.vb**, and then enter the following statement (shown in bold) at the end of the **Navigate** procedure:

```
Select Case eWhere
    ' Statements
End Select
Return CType(slRecords.GetByIndex(mintCurrent), CallRecord)
```

2. Enter the following statement in the **FindRequest** procedure:

```
Return CType(slRecords.Item(ID), CallRecord)
```

3. Test the solution. On the menu bar, click **Windows, Display Responses** to display the form that manages the SortedList. Open the file named **Chapter.05\Data\DemoResponses.txt**.

   Note that the OpenFile procedure appearing in the component has been completed already and is nearly identical to the one used to process the ArrayList.

4. Navigate from record to record. Note that the records appear in sorted order by ID number.

Adding a SortedList Item

To add an item to a SortedList, you call the Add method, having the following syntax:

Syntax

System.Collections.SortedList.Add(*key* **As Object,** *value* **As Object)**

Definition

The **Add** method of the SortedList class adds a key / value pair to the SortedList.

Dissection

- The first argument to the Add method contains the *key*. As the key argument has a type of System.Object, the key can be of any type.

- The second argument, *value*, can also be of any type. Thus, the data associated with the key can be any class instance or structure. As this book uses strict type checking, you must explicitly convert the generic object variable to another data type.

Code Example

```
Dim slRecords As New SortedList
Dim cr As New CallRecord()
    ' Statements to store data in the CallRecord
slRecords.Add(cr.ID, cr)
```

Code Dissection

Adding a new item (key / value pair) to a sorted list requires that you call the Add method with two arguments. The first argument contains the key and the second argument contains the object (value) that is associated with the key. In the preceding code segment, the key is stored in the member named cr.ID, and the value added is the class instance named CallRecord. The items in the list will be automatically reordered to keep the list sorted.

Modifying a SortedList Item

The SetByIndex method replaces a value in the SortedList. The SetByIndex method requires two arguments: the numeric index to set and the value associated with that index. Examine the following statements to save a record to the sorted list:

```
Public Function SaveRequest(ByVal cr As CallRecord) _
    As Boolean
    slRecords.SetByIndex(slRecords.IndexOfKey(cr.ID), cr)
End Function
```

The preceding statements get the index value associated with the key by calling the IndexOfKey method. The SetByIndex method replaces the CallRecord.

Removing a SortedList Item

The steps to remove an item from a SortedList are similar to the steps to add an item. The RemoveAt method of the SortedList class accepts one argument: the index of the item to remove. The following statement illustrates how to remove an item from a SortedList:

```
Public Function DeleteRequest(ByVal cr As CallRecord) _
    As Boolean
    slRecords.RemoveAt(slRecords.IndexOfKey(cr.ID))
    mintCurrent = 0
End Function
```

Again, the preceding statement uses the value of a particular key to remove the key / value pair from the sorted list, meaning, the Remove method accepts one argument: the index for the key / value pair to remove.

To add, change, and delete records from a SortedList:

1. Activate the Code Editor for the module named **ResponseList.vb,** if necessary, and then enter the following statement in the **AddRequest** procedure:

   ```
   slRecords.Add(cr.ID, cr)
   ```

2. Enter the following statement in the **SaveRequest** procedure:

   ```
   slRecords.SetByIndex(slRecords.IndexOfKey(cr.ID), cr)
   ```

3. Enter the following statements in the **DeleteRequest** procedure:

   ```
   slRecords.RemoveAt(slRecords.IndexOfKey(cr.ID))
   mintCurrent = 0
   ```

   Note that the statements have already been created on the form named frmSortedList to call the preceding methods. Again, they are nearly identical to the statements that manage the ArrayList.

4. Test the solution. On the main form, click **Windows**, and then click **Display Responses** to display the SortedList form. Open the file named **DemoResponses.txt**. Click **Records**, and then click **Add** to add a new record. Add the record using the information shown in Figure 5-15.

Figure 5-15   Adding a record to a SortedList

5. Click **Records**, and then click **Save Add**. Delete the record that you just created.

QUEUES

A queue stores a list of objects much like an ArrayList stores a list of objects, however, queues are first-in first-out data structures. The first item added to a queue is the first item removed from the queue. In other words, elements are added to the back of the queue and removed from the front of the queue. Imagine that calls enter the call center at a rate that is greater than the rate that the calls can be processed. Those waiting calls are stored in a queue. Figure 5-16 illustrates the operation of a queue.

Figure 5-16   Operation of a queue

As shown in Figure 5-16, an enqueue operation adds an element to the back of the queue, and a dequeue operation removes an element from the front of the queue. VB .NET supplies the Queue class to implement a queue, having the following members:

Syntax

System.Collections.Queue class

Public Properties

- The **Count** property gets the number of elements stored in the queue. If the value of the Count property is 0, then the queue is empty.

Public Methods

- The **Dequeue** method returns the element at the front of the queue and removes that element from the queue.

- The **Enqueue** method adds an element to the back of the queue.

- The **Peek** method returns the element at the front of the queue but does not remove the element from the queue.

In this chapter, you will implement a queue for customers telephoning the call center. The form named frmQueue contains a structure named CallWaiting to store a waiting call.

To create a queue:

1. Activate the Code Editor for the form named **frmQueue.vb**. Enter the following statements in the **Click** event handler for the button named **btnEnqueue**:

```
Dim cwCurrent As New CallWaiting()
With cwCurrent
    .ID = txtID.Text
    .LastName = txtLastName.Text
    .FirstName = txtFirstName.Text
    .CallTime = System.DateTime.Now
End With

queCurrent.Enqueue(cwCurrent)
lstqueue.Items.Add(cwCurrent.ToString)
lblCount.Text = queCurrent.Count.ToString
txtID.Clear()
txtFirstName.Clear()
txtLastName.Clear()
```

The variable queCurrent stores a reference to the queue instance, which has already been declared. Calling the Enqueue method adds a customer to the end of the queue. Referencing the Count property returns the number of elements in the queue.

2. Enter the following statements in the **Click** event handler for the button named **btnDequeue**:

```
Dim cwCurrent As CallWaiting
If queCurrent.Count > 0 Then
    cwCurrent = CType(queCurrent.Dequeue(), CallWaiting)
    lstqueue.Items.RemoveAt(0)
    lblCount.Text = queCurrent.Count.ToString
End If
```

The If statement first determines whether or not an element exists in the queue. Calling the Dequeue method removes the customer from the front of the queue and returns that customer. Again, because strict type checking is used in this book, the generic System.Object type returned by the Dequeue method must be explicitly converted to a CallWaiting type. The corresponding element is removed from the list box, and the text box storing the number of elements in the queue is updated.

3. Test the solution. On menu of the main form, click **Windows**, and then click **Display Customer Queue**. Enter an ID of **1**, a first name of **Joe**, and a last name of **Smith**. Click the **Add Call Enqueue** button to add the customer to the queue. Using an ID of **2**, and your name, add a second customer to the queue. Click the **Process Call Dequeue** button to remove the first customer (Smith) from the queue.

Queues and stacks are similar. A queue is a first-in, first-out list, a stack is a last-in, first-out list.

STACKS

A stack is a last-in, first-out list, meaning, the item most recently added to the stack is the first item removed from the stack. To understand a stack, think of a person's inbox in which requests pile up from bottom to top. Those requests are satisfied by removing the latest request from the top of the pile (stack). Figure 5-17 illustrates the order in which items are added to and removed from the stack, respectively.

Figure 5-17   Operation of a stack

The Stack class supports the following members:

Syntax

System.Collections.Stack class

Public Properties

- The **Count** property contains the number of elements in the stack.

Public Methods

- The **Push** method adds an item to the stack.

- The **Pop** method returns the most recently added item from stack. The item returned is also removed from the stack.

- The **Peek** method returns the object at the top of the stack without removing it.

So far, you have worked with sequential files and stored the contents of those sequential files in various types of collections. Next, you will learn about another kind of file: a random file.

OPENING, READING, AND WRITING RANDOM FILES

The steps to read and write random files are very different from the steps to read and write sequential files. The following list summarizes the characteristics of opening, reading, and writing records in random files:

- To open a random file for reading and writing, you call the FileOpen function.

- The records in a random file have a fixed length. Thus, the records in a random file typically consist of structures. The String data in those structures also has a fixed length.

- While a random file is open, any record can be read or written at any time, depending on how the file is opened. That is, you do not need to open a file for reading only or for writing only.

- The FileGet function reads a record and the FilePut function writes a record. These functions can read or write any record from a random file without first reading or writing the preceding records.

- The Seek method locates a record.

First, we discuss how to open a file for random access, and then we discuss how to read and write the records that comprise that random file. You will notice a significant difference in the statements to open, read, and write random files compared to the statements to manage sequential files. Instead of calling methods of a particular class, you call intrinsic functions to manage random files.

 When reading and writing random files, we break our usual rule of enabling strict type checking, because of the complexities of performing explicit type conversion.

Opening a Random File

Before reading or writing the records contained in a random file, you must open it. To open a random file, you call the FileOpen function having the following syntax:

Syntax

FileOpen function

Public Sub FileOpen(ByVal *filenumber* **As Integer, ByVal** *filename* **As String, ByVal** *mode* **As OpenMode,**
Optional ByVal *access* **As OpenAccess = OpenAccess.Default,**
Optional ByVal *share* **As OpenShare = OpenShare.Default,**
Optional ByVal *recordlength* **As Integer = -1)**

Dissection

- The *filenumber* argument contains a unique Integer value to reference the open file. Typically, the first open file has a value of 1, the second a value of 2, and so on.

- The *filename* argument contains a String that defines the name of the file to open. The file name may contain an absolute or relative directory reference.

- The *mode* argument defines the type of file. For random files, use the enumeration value OpenMode.Random.

- The optional *access* argument defines the operations that can be performed on the file. The OpenAccess enumeration defines the possible values. OpenAccess.Default allows the file to be read or written. OpenAccess.Read allows the file to be read but not written, and OpenAccess.Write allows the file to be written only.

- The optional *share* argument defines whether or not other processes can access the open file, and the actions that those processes can perform on that open file. The value OpenShare.Default allows the file to be read and written by other processes.

- The *recordlength* argument defines the length of each record.

In this section you will open a random file for reading and writing. The random file will contain employee records having an ID, first name, last name, accrued vacation days, and accrued sick days. Random access files differ from sequential files in that each record must be exactly the same size. This poses no problem if the records contain fixed size data such as Integers. But suppose that a record contains Strings that typically have a variable size. What do you do then?

VB .NET provides a unique solution to the fixed-length String problem. This solution involves attributes. To understand the syntax of an attribute, examine the following structure declaration used to store each record:

```
Private Structure Employeef
    Public EmployeeID As Integer
```

```
<VBFixedString(20)> Public FirstName As String
<VBFixedString(20)> Public LastName As String
Public AccruedVacation As Integer
Public AccruedSick As Integer
End Structure
```

The preceding structure declaration resembles any other structure declaration. It contains a Structure block and Public members. However, each String member declaration contains an attribute defining the length of the structure as follows:

```
<VBFixedString(20)>
```

The preceding attribute tells the CLR that the String member is 20 characters in length. Thus, the Employeef structure is 56 bytes in size. Each String is 20 bytes, and an Integer is 4 bytes. Note that the preceding structure has already been declared in the startup solution. Attributes will be discussed further in subsequent chapters. For now, however, realize that attributes are surrounded between less than (<) and greater than (>) signs, and can have zero or more arguments. The VBFixedString attribute accepts one argument: the length of the fixed length string.

To open a random file:

1. Activate the Code Editor for the form named **frmRandomFile.vb**, and then enter the following statements in the **Click** event handler for the menu item named **mmuFileOpen**:

```
Dim dlgResult As DialogResult
Dim fiCurrent As FileInfo
ofdRandom.CheckFileExists = False
ofdRandom.CheckPathExists = True
dlgResult = ofdRandom.ShowDialog()

If dlgResult = DialogResult.OK Then
    Try
        FileOpen(1, ofdRandom.FileName, OpenMode.Random, _
            OpenAccess.Default, , Len(EmpCurrent))
            mblnFileIsOpen = True

        fiCurrent = New FileInfo(ofdRandom.FileName)

        If fiCurrent.Length = 0 Then
            mintRecordCount = 0
        Else
            mintRecordCount = ToInt32(fiCurrent.Length _
                / Len(EmpCurrent))
            FileGet(1, EmpCurrent, 1)
            mintRecordCurrent = 1
            Call CopyToTextBoxes()
        End If
```

```
        Catch ex As System.Exception
            MessageBox.Show("Can't Open file", "Error", _
                MessageBoxButtons.OK)
        End Try
    End If
    Call SetEditState(EditState.Browsing)
```

The preceding statements display the OpenFileDialog box. If the user clicks the Open button, the statements in the outer If block execute. The statements in the Try block first attempt to open the file as a random file. The final argument, Len(EmpCurrent), defines the length of each record. Note that in addition to its use in determining the length of a String, the Len function can also be used to determine the length of members that comprise the structure.

In the code, note that the flag mblnFileIsOpen is set to True. This flag is used elsewhere in the form. The next statement creates an instance of the FileInfo class. The inner If statement uses the length of the file to determine the number of records in the file. If the length of the file is 0, then the file is empty. Otherwise, the file length is divided by the record size to calculate the number of records and the result stored in the variable mintRecordCount. Then the FileGet function is called to retrieve the first record and store that record in the form's text boxes by calling the CopyToTextBoxes procedure. This sub procedure has already been created and merely copies the EmpCurrent structure to the text boxes on the form. Note that the FileGet function is discussed in detail in a moment.

Reading and Writing Records

Having defined the structure of each record in the random access file, you will now see how to read and write records. To write a record to a random file, you call the FilePut function having the following syntax:

Syntax

FilePut function

Public Overloads Sub FilePut(*filenumber* **As Integer**, *value* **As Object**, **Optional** *recordnumber* **As Integer = −1)**

Definition

The **FilePut** function writes a record to a random file.

Dissection

- The *filenumber* argument contains a valid file number. This is the file number obtained when the file was opened with the FileOpen function.

- The *value* argument contains the data to be written. This argument can be of any type.

- The optional *recordnumber* argument contains the record number to write. The argument is one-based, so to write the first record, the record number would have a value of 1. To add a new record to a random file, write a record having a record number one greater than the current largest record number.

Code example

```
FilePut(1, EmpCurrent, 2)
```

Code dissection

Assuming that a structure variable named EmpCurrent has been declared, and file number 1 represents an active file handle created with the FileOpen function, the preceding statement writes the second record to the random file. If that record already exists, the record will be overwritten.

Now it's time to write the statements that will allow the user to add and change records.

To add and change records in a random file:

1. Activate the Code Editor for the form named **frmRandomFile.vb**, if necessary, and then enter the following statements in the **Click** event handler for the menu item named **mmuRecordsSaveAdd**:

```
Call CopyToStructure()
FilePut(1, EmpCurrent, EmpCurrent.EmployeeID)
Call SetEditState(EditState.Browsing)
```

2. Enter the following statements in the **Click** event handler for the menu item named **mmuRecordsSaveRecord**:

```
Call CopyToStructure()
FilePut(1, EmpCurrent, EmpCurrent.EmployeeID)
Call SetEditState(EditState.Browsing)
```

The preceding statements first call a procedure named CopyToStructure. This procedure already exists in the startup solution. The procedure merely copies the contents of the form's text boxes to the variable EmpCurrent. Then the FilePut method is called to write the record to the random file. Again, the first argument to the FilePut function is the reference to the open file. The second argument contains the data to write and the last argument contains the record number.

The steps to read a record from a random file are similar to the steps to write a record. Instead of calling the FilePut function, however, you call the FileGet function. The arguments for both functions are the same. Examine the following statement:

```
FileGet(1, EmpCurrent, 2)
```

The preceding statement to get a record from a random file has the same syntax as to put a record. It retrieves the second record from the open random file and stores the data in the variable named EmpCurrent.

To read a record from a random file:

1. In the form named **frmRandomFile.vb**, enter the following statements in the **Click** event handler for the menu item named **mmuRecordsFindRecord**:

```
Dim pintRecordCurrent As Integer
Try
    pintRecordCurrent = ToInt32(InputBox( _
        "Enter Record Number", _
        "Random Files", 1))
    FileGet(1, EmpCurrent, pintRecordCurrent)
    mintRecordCurrent = pintRecordCurrent
    Call CopyToTextBoxes()
Catch ex As System.Exception
    MessageBox.Show("Cannot find record", "Error", _
        MessageBoxButtons.OK)
End Try
```

The preceding statements use an input box to get the record number from the user. That value is converted to an Integer. Then the FileGet function is called to get the record, and then that record is displayed in the form's text boxes. If the record cannot be found, then the statement in the Catch block executes and displays the message box to the user indicating that the record cannot be found.

In the final steps, you will write the statements to close the file when the user closes the form. Again, all files should be explicitly closed to prevent loss of data.

To close a random file:

1. Enter the following statement in the **Click** event handler for the menu item named **mmuFileCloseForm**:

```
FileClose(1)
Me.Close()
```

The syntax of the FileClose function is simple. The function accepts one argument: the number of the file handle to close.

2. Test the solution. On the main menu, click **Windows**, and then click **Edit Employees**. Click **File** and then click **Open**. Open the file named **EmployeeList.rnd**. Click **Records**, and then click **Find Records**. In the input box, enter **2** to locate that employee. Add and change a record of your choosing.

In this section, we have generally discussed the steps to read and write sequential and random files, using various types of lists. You can apply these techniques to several different scenarios.

CHAPTER SUMMARY

❑ The OpenFileDialog and SaveFileDialog controls allow the user to select a file to open or save, respectively. These controls do not actually open or save files. They merely allow the user to select a file. The Filter and FilterIndex properties define the possible file filters and the current filter, respectively. Calling the ShowDialog method displays the dialog box to the user. The FileName property contains the file selected by the user.

❑ The System.IO.Directory class contains static methods to manage the file system. The CreateDirectory method creates a new directory and the Delete method removes an existing directory. The Exists method determines whether or not a directory exists. The GetCurrentDirectory method gets the current working directory and the SetCurrentDirectory method sets the current working directory. The GetLogicalDrives method returns an array of strings containing the logical drives installed on the system. The File class works similarly to the Directory class and has methods to create, copy, move, and delete files. The GetAttributes and SetAttributes methods get and set the attributes for a particular file. Attributes define whether or not a file is a directory, a hidden file, a compressed file, a read-only file, and so on.

❑ Reading a sequential file involves first creating an instance of the StreamReader class. The constructor for the StreamReader class accepts one argument: the name of the file to read. To read a file all at once, call the ReadToEnd method, which reads a file into a String. The ReadLine method reads a record up to and including the carriage return. The carriage return character is discarded. Typically, each line is read and processed in a loop. The Read method reads one or more characters. After reading a file, explicitly close it by calling the Close method of the StreamReader class.

❑ To write a sequential file, create an instance of the StreamWriter class. The Write method writes a String. The WriteLine method writes a String terminated by a special character, typically a carriage return. This special character is defined by the NewLine property. Again, after writing a file it should be explicitly closed by calling the Close method of the StreamWriter class.

❑ The ArrayList class is similar to an array but supports additional methods to add and remove elements from the list. The Add method adds a new element to the list. The Remove method removes the first occurrence of a specific element from the list. The RemoveAt method removes an element from the list based on an index value. The ArrayList can be sorted by calling the Sort method.

❑ The SortedList class is similar to the ArrayList class but maintains list elements in sorted order based on a key. The key must be unique. Each key corresponds to a value. The value can be any object. Like an ArrayList, the Add method adds an element to the list. The Remove and RemoveAt methods remove an element from the List. To iterate through the objects in an ArrayList, use the Values property, which references the collection of values.

❑ A queue is a first-in, first-out data structure. The Enqueue method of the Queue class adds an element to the back of the queue and the Dequeue method removes an element from the front of the queue.

❒ A stack is a last-in, first-out data structure. The Push method adds an element to the top of the stack and the Pop method removes the element that exists at the top of the stack.

❒ The steps to read and write random files are very different from the steps to read and write a sequential file. First, call the FileOpen function to open a file for random input and output. Call the FileGet function to read a record from the random file and call the FilePut function to write a record to the random file. Note that records in a random file have a fixed length. To determine the length of a record, call the Len function on the structure containing the record. When finished reading and writing the file, call the FileClose function explicitly to close the random file.

5

REVIEW QUESTIONS

1. Which of the following statements is true of the Directory class?

    a. The methods of the Directory class are static, thus, to call the methods you need not create an instance of the Directory class.

    b. To remove a directory, you call the RemoveDirectory method of the Directory class.

    c. The Directory class applies to the System.FileSystem namespace.

    d. To remove a directory, that directory must always be empty.

    e. none of the above

2. What is the difference between an absolute and a relative directory reference?

    a. An absolute directory reference can begin with the characters "..", indicating the parent directory.

    b. A relative directory reference must begin with a leading backslash. An absolute directory reference must not begin with a leading backslash.

    c. If a directory reference begins with a drive designator such as C:, then that reference is considered a relative directory reference.

    d. An absolute directory reference contains a full path name while a relative directory reference does not.

    e. none of the above

3. Which of the following statements is true of the File class?

    a. The methods of the File class allow you to create files, move files, copy files, and delete files.

    b. The methods of the File class are shared, meaning that you need not create an instance of the File class before calling its methods.

    c. File names can be absolute or relative.

    d. The file class applies to the System.IO namespace.

    e. all of the above

4. What is the purpose of the DirectoryInfo and FileInfo classes?

   a. The methods of the DirectoryInfo and FileInfo classes allow you to move directories and files from one disk to another.

   b. Both classes allow you to get attributes related to a directory or file, such as the time of creation.

   c. To reference a DirectoryInfo or FileInfo class, you call the constructor with one argument: the name of the directory or file.

   d. Both a DirectoryInfo and FileInfo class must be explicitly closed after they are opened.

   e. VB .NET does not support classes named DirectoryInfo and FileInfo.

5. Referring to the OpenFileDialog and SaveFileDialog controls, which property controls the type of files displayed?

   a. Selection

   b. Filter

   c. Index

   d. Files

   e. FileType

6. Which of the following statements applies to the StreamReader and StreamWriter classes?

   a. To read or write a file, you first create an instance of the StreamReader or StreamWriter classes, respectively.

   b. Using an instance of the StreamReader class, a file can be read one character at a time, one line at a time, or the entire file can be read all at once.

   c. Methods of the StreamWriter class allow you to write text or write a line such that it is terminated with a carriage return.

   d. After opening a file with the StreamReader or StreamWriter class, the StreamReader or StreamWriter class instance must be explicitly closed.

   e. all of the above

7. What is the name of the method typically used to read a record from a sequential file?

   a. Read

   b. ReadLine

   c. ReadRecord

   d. ReadToEnd

   e. none of the above

8. Which of the following general statements applies to collections?

   a. You enumerate the items in a collection with a For Item InCollection loop.

   b. Most collections are one-based, meaning that the first item in the collection has an index value of 1.

c. The CollectionCount property always returns the number of items in a collection.

d. The ArrayList and SortedList classes are considered collections.

e. Collections are always shared. Thus, you never create an instance of a collection class.

9. Which of the following statements correctly describes the characteristics of an ArrayList?

a. The size of an ArrayList is fixed. That is, you cannot add objects to an ArrayList once is has been created.

b. The Capacity property defines the number of objects that an ArrayList can contain, while the Count property stores the number of elements actually stored in the ArrayList.

c. To add an item to an ArrayList, you call the AddItem method, and to remove an item, you call the RemoveItem method.

d. To retrieve an item from an ArrayList, you call the GetItem method.

e. Once an item has been added to an ArrayList, it cannot be removed.

10. Which of the following statements is true of a SortedList?

a. When adding items to a SortedList, those items are added in a random order. After adding an item you must explicitly call the Sort method to sort the items.

b. A Sorted list always contains structures. The first element of the structure is always considered the key. Thus, the items in a SortedList will be sorted by the first structure member.

c. For the items in a SortedList to appear in sorted order, those items must be added in sorted order.

d. When adding an item to a SortedList, you use two arguments: the key of the item that is being added, and the value corresponding to that item.

e. none of the above

11. Which of the following statements correctly describes a queue?

a. A queue represents a sorted list. Items can be added anywhere to the list. Locate an item in a queue by calling the Find method of the Queue class.

b. Objects can be added to a queue in any order. The Remove method of the Queue class can be used to remove any object from the queue. To get the first object in the queue, call the GetFirst method. To get the last object in the queue, call the GetLast method.

c. A queue is a first-in first-out data structure. Using the Queue class, you add items to the queue by calling the Enqueue method and remove items from the queue by calling the Dequeue method.

d. A queue is a last-in first-out data structure. You add items to the queue by calling the AddItem method and remove items by calling the RemoveItem method.

e. none of the above

12. Which of the following statements correctly describes a stack?

   a. A stack is a first-in first-out data structure. Objects are added and removed from the stack by calling the AddItem and RemoveItem methods.

   b. Objects can be added to the stack in any order by calling the AddItem method. In addition, objects can be added to the top of the stack by calling the AddTop method and removed from the bottom of the stack by calling the RemoveBottom method.

   c. A stack is a last-in first-out data structure. The Stack class has methods named Push and Pop used to add an object to the stack and remove an object from the stack, respectively.

   d. VB .NET supports the List structure to implement both queues and stacks. You pass an argument to the constructor for the List class to specify whether the List will operate as a Queue or a stack.

   e. none of the above

13. Which of the following statements correctly describes how to open a file for random access?

   a. Create an instance of the RandomReader class.

   b. Call the FileOpen function.

   c. Create an instance of the StreamReader class. As an argument to the constructor, specify that the file should be opened for random access.

   d. Call the OpenBinary method of the RandomReader class.

   e. VB .NET does not support random file access.

14. Which of the following statements is true of random access files?

   a. Random access files work exactly the same way as sequential files. That is, you call the same methods to read and write records in a random file as you call for sequential files.

   b. Each record in a random access file has the same length, thereby making it possible to search for a particular record based on an index.

   c. Each record in a random access file has a prefix that denotes the length of that record, allowing the length of each record in the file to vary.

   d. When reading a random access file you must read the first record, which defines the size of subsequent records.

   e. none of the above

15. Describe the purpose of the Filter property pertaining to the OpenFileDialog and the SaveFileDialog controls. In your answer, describe the syntax of the Filter property.

16. Describe the general logic to read and process the records in a sequential file.

17. Describe the differences between an ArrayList and a SortedList.

18. List and describe the steps to add, locate, update, and remove items from a SortedList.

19. Describe the differences between a Stack and a Queue.

20. Describe the steps to open a file for random access, and how to read and write records from a random file. Finally, describe the characteristics of a random file.

PROGRAMMING QUESTIONS

1. Write the statements to create 20 directories named Question1 through Question20. Assume that the directory named C:\Book is the parent directory.

2. Write the statements to test if the file named C:\Question exists. If it does, display a message box containing the text "File Exists". Otherwise, do nothing.

3. Write the statements to create a filter for an instance of the OpenFileDialog control named ofdQuestion. Create the filter such that it specifies the following three file types: Word Documents (*.doc), Rich Text Files (*.rtf), and Text Files (*.txt).

4. Write the statements to open the text file named "C:\Question.txt" so that you can read it. Use the variable named msrdCurrent to store the instance of the StreamReader class. Assume that the file contains records having a single field: an Integer number. Write the statements to read the file into the Integer array named mintList. Redimension the array as necessary. Close the file after you have read it.

5. Write the statements to create an instance of the StreamWriter class. Use a variable named mswriCurrent. Write the file named "C:\Count.txt". Write the counting numbers 1 through 100 to the file such that each number appears on its own line. Close the file after you have written it.

6. Write the statements to add the counting numbers 1 through 100 to the ArrayList named alCurrent. Also, write the statements to declare and create an instance of the ArrayList class.

7. Write the statement to determine the number of items in the ArrayList named alCurrent, and store the result in the Integer variable named pintCount.

8. Assume that an ArrayList exists named alData containing structures of type Coordinate, having members named X and Y of the data type Double. Write the statements to enumerate all of the ArrayList members, calculating the total for the X and Y members. Store the total in the Double variables named pdblXTotal and pdblYTotal. Assume that strict type checking is enabled.

9. Assume that a variable named InventoryCurrent exists, having a data type of Inventory. Write a statement to add the item to the back of the queue named queInventory. Write another statement that will return the item from the front of the queue and store the returned item in the variable InventoryCurrent. Perform explicit type conversion as necessary.

10. Write the statements to push the counting numbers 1 through 10 to the stack named stkNumber.

11. Write the statements to test that the stack named stkQuestion is empty. If it is, display a message box with the text "Stack Empty".

12. Assume that a SortedList exists named slQuestion that stores structures having a data type of QuestionInfo. Assume that the key field is named QuestionNumber, having a data type of Integer. Write the statements to find the record having a key value of 3. Declare the variable to store the structure, as necessary. Assume that strict type checking is enabled.

13. Assume that a SortedList named slRecords stores structures named slData, having members named X and Y, each of the data type Double. Write the statements to enumerate the sorted list, writing the contents to the file named C:\data.txt as a comma delimited file.

14. Write the statements to open the random file named "C:\Demo.rnd". Use a file handle of 1. After opening the file, read the first record of the file into the variable named QuestionDemo. Finally, close the file.

15. Write the statements to determine whether the random file named "C:\Demo.rnd" is empty. If it is, display a message box having the text "Empty File".

HANDS-ON PROJECTS

1. In this project, you will read and write text files from an ArrayList. The file named Chapter.05\Exercises05\Ch05Ex1.exe contains the compiled executable application. Figure 5-18 shows the completed main form for the solution. The file named Chapter.05\Data\Ch05Ex1Data.txt contains the data file for the application. Assume that employees can borrow against their upcoming checks up to a certain amount, and that the Employee structure has the following members and data types: ID (Integer), FirstName (String), LastName (String), BalanceDue (Double), CreditLimit(Double).

Figure 5-18   Chapter 5 – Hands-on Project 1

a. Start Visual Studio .NET and create a new solution named **Ch05Ex1.sln**.

b. Create a Sub Main procedure in a module that will display the splash screen, and then the main form.

c. Create a component named **Employee**. In that component, create a class named **Employee** to store the above Employee structure. Create another class named **EmployeeList** to manage an ArrayList.

d. In the EmployeeList class, create a **Navigate** method using the same technique presented in the chapter. Create methods named **AddEmployee**, **SaveEmployee**, and **DeleteEmployee** (the latter will delete underlying employees from the hidden ArrayList).

e. In the EmployeeList class, create methods to open and save the sequential file containing the employees. Each of these methods should accept one argument: the file to open and save, respectively.

f. Create the control instances on the main form as shown in Figure 5-18.

g. Create a **File** menu on the form with menu items to open and save the sequential file, and to exit the solution.

h. Create instances of the OpenFileDialog and SaveFileDialog controls on the form. Write the statements to configure these control instances as necessary, allowing the user to select a file to open and save. Write the code for the **Open** and **Save** menu items that will call upon the component you previously created to open and save the file, respectively.

i. Create a **Navigate** menu with menu items to locate the first, previous, next, and last records. Write the statements to display the correct record using the methods of the component that you already created.

j. Create menu items and write the statements so that the user can add, change, and delete records. Enable and disable the menu items and text boxes as necessary so as to prevent errors.

k. Add exception handlers to the solution as necessary.

2. In this project, you will read and write text files using a SortedList. The file named Chapter.05\Exercises05\Ch05Ex2.exe contains the compiled executable application. Figure 5-19 shows the completed main form for the solution. The file named Ch05Ex2Data.txt contains the data file for the application. Assume that an Employee structure has the following members and data types: FirstName (String), LastName (String), Address (String), City (String), State (String), GrossPay (Double), NetPay (Double). Use the FirstName and LastName fields as the unique key for the records.

Figure 5-19   Chapter 5 – Hands-on Project 2

a. Start Visual Studio .NET and create a new solution named **Ch05Ex2.sln**.

b. Create a Sub Main procedure in a module that will display the splash screen and then the main form.

c. Create a component named **Employee**. In that component, create a class named **Employee** to store the above Employee structure. Create another class named **EmployeeList** to manage a SortedList.

d. In the EmployeeList class, create a **Navigate** method using the same technique presented in the chapter. Create methods named **AddEmployee**, **SaveEmployee**, and **DeleteEmployee** (the latter will delete underlying Employees from the hidden SortedList).

e. In the EmployeeList class, create methods to open and save the sequential file containing the employees. Each of these methods should accept one argument: the file to open and save, respectively.

f. Create the control instances on the main form as shown in Figure 5-19.

g. Create a File menu on the form with menu items to open and save the sequential file, and to exit the solution.

h. Create instances of the OpenFileDialog and SaveFileDialog controls on the form. Write the statements to configure these control instances as necessary, allowing the user to select a file to open and save. Write the code for the **Open** and **Save** menu items that will call upon the component you previously created to open and save the file, respectively.

i. Create a **Navigate** menu with menu items to locate the first, previous, next, and last records. Write the statements to display the correct record using the methods of the component that you already created.

j. Create menu items and write the statements so that the user can add, change, and delete records. Enable and disable the menu items and text boxes as necessary so as to prevent errors.

k. Add exception handlers to the solution as necessary.

3. In this project, you will read and write random files. The file named Chapter.05\ Exercises05\Ch05Ex3.exe contains the compiled executable application. The file named Ch05Ex3Data.rnd contains the data file for the application. Figure 5-20 shows the completed main form for the solution. The random file you will manage operates with inventory records having the following fields: PartNumber (Integer), Description (String – 20 characters), Quantity (Double), Price (Double). The part number is the key field.

Figure 5-20   Chapter 5 – Hands-on Project 3

a. Start Visual Studio .NET and create a new solution named **Ch05Ex3.sln**.

b. Create a Sub Main procedure in a module that will display the splash screen and then the main form.

c. Create a menu with an **Open** menu item. Write the statements to display an OpenFileDialog control instance. Open the file if the user clicks the Open button. Display the first record in the file if one exists.

d. Create menu items to add a new record. Write the statements to save the newly added record to the random file. Do not let the user enter ID numbers. The program should automatically generate them.

e. Write the statements that will allow the user to edit the current record and save that record to the file.

f. Create exception handlers for the program as necessary.

4. In this project, you will work with multiple sequential files in the same application. Assume that a bank has account numbers stored in one sequential file, and transactions corresponding to those account numbers in a second file. Assume that the account file contains an account number, the customer's name, and address. The transaction file contains a unique transaction ID number, a transaction type, a transaction date, and a transaction amount. Sample data files for this application have been created, named Ch05Ex4Master.txt and Ch05Ex4Trans.txt. The file named Chapter.05\Exercises05\Ch05Ex4.exe contains the compiled executable application.

   a. Start Visual Studio .NET and create a new solution named **Ch05Ex4.sln**.

   b. Create a Sub Main procedure in a module that will display the splash screen and then the main form.

   c. On the main form, create the necessary control instances to display the records in the master file.

   d. Create menu items and write the statements that will allow the user to navigate through the records in the master file.

   e. Create menu items and write the necessary code that will allow the user to edit the records appearing in the master file. The records in the master file should be sorted by the account number. Make sure that the user cannot delete a record in the master file if corresponding records exist in the transaction file. Do not let the user change the account number once the account number has been assigned.

   f. Provide a means for the user to select a record from the master file and display the records in the corresponding transaction file. For any given account, there may be several transaction records. The number of transaction records will vary. You program should also handle the possibility that no transactions exist for a given account.

   g. Display the transaction records on a second form as a modal dialog box such that each transaction record appears on a separate row. Use dynamically created control instances, such as text boxes, to accomplish this task. Account for the possibility that there will be more transactions than will fit on the form. Use a scrollable control such as a panel to hold the dynamically created control instances. Notify the user if there are no transactions for a particular account.

   h. Create totals for the transactions. Transactions are of two types: checks and deposits. Total the value of checks and deposits. Display the total number of transactions also.

   i. Create error handlers for the application as necessary.

5. In this project, you will read a sequential file and create multiple sequential files based on a date range. The sequential file used for input contains log records for Internet requests. Each log record has the following fields: SourceAddress, DestinationAddress, Date, and Bytes. The file named Ch05Ex5Logs.txt contains

the sample data for the application. The file named Chapter.05\Exercises05\ Ch05Ex5.exe contains the compiled executable application.

a. Start Visual Studio .NET and create a new solution named **Ch5Ex5.sln**.

b. Create a Sub Main procedure in a module that will display the splash screen, and then the main form.

c. On the main form, allow the user to navigate and edit the records contained in the file.

d. Determine the oldest and newest date in the file. Using the same directory structure as in the chapter, create directories for each date between the two dates. You can assume that the dates will all be in the same year.

e. Create an output file containing the records for a single date. Store each output file in the appropriate directory.

f. Next, create a summary file for each output file. The summary file should contain the number of records in the detail file, and a total of the number of bytes identified in each record.

5

6

INTERFACE-BASED PROGRAMMING

In this chapter you will:

- ◆ Understand the concept of an interface
- ◆ Understand how to implement and declare interfaces
- ◆ Implement the IComparable interface
- ◆ Sort a list with the IComparable interface
- ◆ Implement the IComparer interface
- ◆ Add For Each support to a list by implementing the IEnumerator and IEnumerable interfaces
- ◆ Understand the details of the IEnumerable interface
- ◆ Create a custom interface that inherits from the ICollection interface
- ◆ Understand cloning and how to implement the ICloneable interface

The completed solution in this chapter further expands on the array and list processing concepts introduced in Chapter 5. In Chapter 5, you examined the Array, ArrayList, SortedList, Queue, and Stack classes. Each of these different classes implement what is referred to as an interface.

Some classes implement a single interface while other classes implement multiple interfaces. Consider an array: the System.Array class implements four interfaces, one of them named IEnumerable. By implementing the IEnumerable interface, the System.Array class allows you to enumerate the items in any array using a For Each loop. Any other classes that implement the IEnumerable interface can be enumerated with a For Each loop. This is one of the benefits of programming with interfaces.

In this chapter, you will find out that by defining and implementing interfaces, any developer can apply a consistent syntax to perform common tasks such as enumerating through the items in a list.

PREVIEWING THE COMPLETED SOLUTION

The completed solution for this chapter works with a common Employee structure stored in the file Employee.vb. In addition, the ToString method has been overridden. That is, we have changed the behavior of ToString from the default behavior provided by System.Object. The ToString method now concatenates the structure members, embedding a space between each member.

The following statements illustrate the Employee structure used in the chapter:

```
Public Structure Employee
    Public ID As String
    Public LastName As String
    Public FirstName As String
    Public Address As String
    Public Telephone As String

    Public Overrides Function ToString() As String
        Return Me.ID & " " & Me.LastName & " " & _
        Me.FirstName & " " & Me.Address & " " & _
        Me.Telephone
    End Function

    End Structure
```

The Employee structure declared above is simplified. A real Employee structure would have additional fields to define the hourly wage and deduction information. However, the purpose of this chapter is not to discuss the structure itself. The Employee structure merely provides the data from which you will implement various interfaces.

Each form in the solution manages a list of Employee structures in different ways. Furthermore, each form—and the classes used by each form—implement various interfaces. Figure 6-1 illustrates the relationships between the forms and the classes used in this solution. Each of the classes implements one or more of the interfaces. Note that, by convention, all interface names begin with a capital "I" to denote Interface.

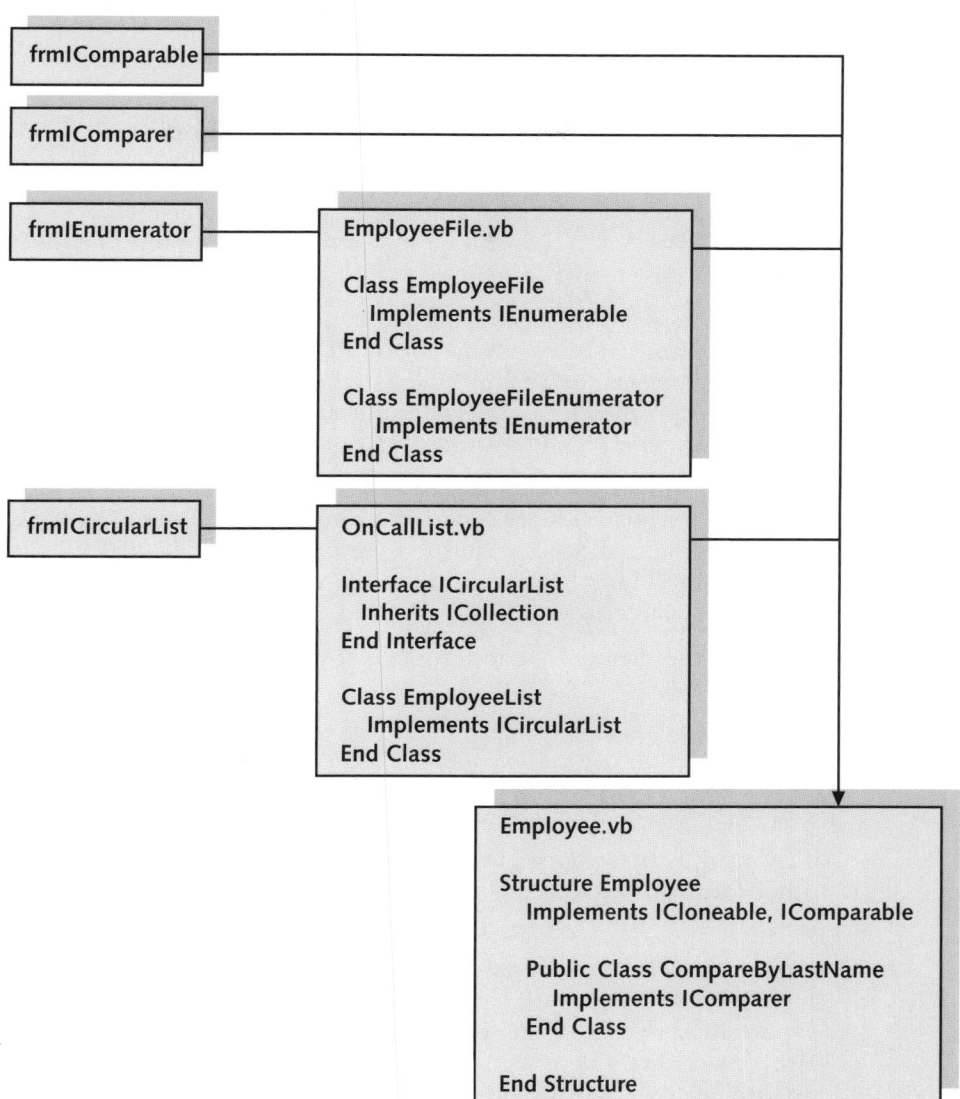

Figure 6-1   Form and class relationships

The following list describes the purpose of the forms listed in Figure 6-1:

- The form named frmIComparable reads a sequential file into a list of
  Employee structures. The statements in the form call the Sort method of
  the System.Array class to sort the list. The Employee structure implements
  the IComparable interface, which defines how the Sort method will sort the
  items in the list.

- The purpose of the form named frmIComparer is similar to that of the frmIComparable form. However, it calls the Sort method with two arguments. The first argument contains the list to sort. The second argument contains a reference to a class that implements the IComparer interface. Two nested classes named CompareByLastName and CompareByFirstName appear in the Employee structure. Both of these classes implement the IComparer interface. By implementing the IComparer interface, the Sort method of the Array class can be used to sort the employees either by first name or by last name.

- The form named frmIEnumerator illustrates how to enumerate a list with a For Each loop. The statements in the form call on the class named EmployeeFile, which implements the IEnumerable interface. The EmployeeFile class contains another class named EmployeeFileEnumerator that implements the IEnumerator interface. These classes, in turn, also reference the Employee structure.

- The form named frmICircularList calls upon the class named OnCallList. This class, in turn, also references the Employee structure. The OnCallList module contains a declaration for a custom interface named ICircularList. The EmployeeList class appearing in the same module implements the ICircularList interface.

Having discussed the elements that comprise the completed solution, you will now preview it.

To preview the completed solution:

1. Start Visual Studio .NET and run the solution file named **Chapter.06\Complete06\Complete06.sln**.

   The main form appears. The sole purpose of the main form is to display the other forms in the solution. Each of these different forms illustrates the purpose of various interfaces.

2. On the main form, click the **IComparable** button to display the IComparable Interface form. On the IComparable Interface form, click **File**, and then click **Open**. In the Open dialog box, open the file named **Chapter.06\Data\ Employees.txt**. The statements to open and read the sequential file have already been created in both the completed and startup solution. These statements use the same logic to create an instance of the StreamReader class and to read the sequential file as discussed in Chapter 5.

3. Click the **Navigate**, **Next** menu items to navigate through the records in the list. The order of the records is the same as the order that they appear in the sequential file. Click the **Sort By ID** button. Navigate through the records again, and note that they are sorted in ascending order by ID number. Figure 6-2 shows the IComparable Interface form.

Figure 6-2   Completed solution – IComparable Interface form

The Employee structure contains a procedure named CompareTo that implements the CompareTo method of the IComparable interface. When the System.Array.Sort method is called on an array of Employee structures, VB .NET automatically calls the comparison procedure (CompareTo), as necessary, to sort the records by ID number. The System.Array.Sort method was called when you clicked the Sort By ID button.

4. Close the IComparable Interface form.

5. On the main form, click the **IComparer** button to display the IComparer Interface form. On the form's menu, click **File**, and then click **Open**. In the Open dialog box, open the file named **Chapter.06\Data\Employees.txt** again. The file is read and the data is stored in an array. Click the **Sort By First Name** button. Again, navigate through the records and note that they are sorted in ascending order by the employee's first name.

6. Click the **Sort By Last Name** button. Using the items on the **Navigate** menu, note that the items are sorted by last name instead of by first name.

7. Close the IComparer Interface form.

The buttons to sort the employee list also call the System.Array.Sort method. An additional argument is supplied to the Sort method containing an instance of a class that implements the IComparer interface. This class appears as a nested class in the Employee structure. Implementing the IComparer interface allows items to be based on multiple key values rather than just a single key value.

8. On the main form, click the **IEnumerator** button to display the IEnumerator Interface form. The classes that implement the IEnumerator and IEnumerable interfaces appear in the file named EmployeeFile.vb.

9. Click the **Enumerate List** button. In the Open dialog box, select and open the file named **Chapter.06\Data\Employees.txt**. The file is read and displayed in the form's multiline text box. Note that the file is read simply by enumerating a list. Figure 6–3 shows the IEnumerator Interface form with the contents of the Employee file loaded.

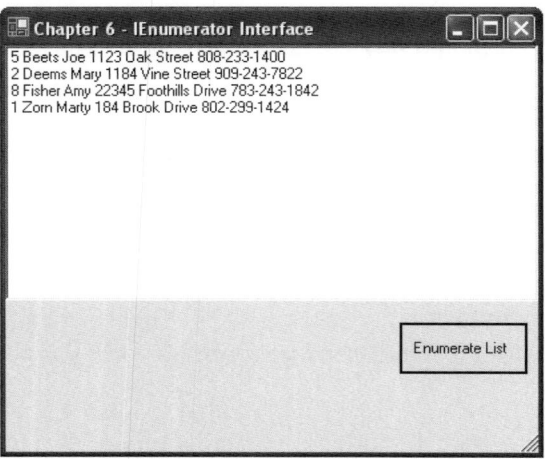

Figure 6-3   Completed solution – IEnumerator Interface form

10. Close the IEnumerator Interface form.

11. On the main form, click the **ICircularList** button.

The ICircularList Interface form is more complicated than the other two forms. This form calls upon the methods of the OnCallList class, which implements multiple interfaces instead of just a single interface. That is, the OnCallList class implements the IEnumerator and IEnumerable interfaces, allowing the items in the list to be enumerated using a For Each loop. The class also implements the ICollection interface. In addition, the OnCallList class implements a custom interface named ICircularList. Figure 6-4 shows the ICircularList Interface form with data.

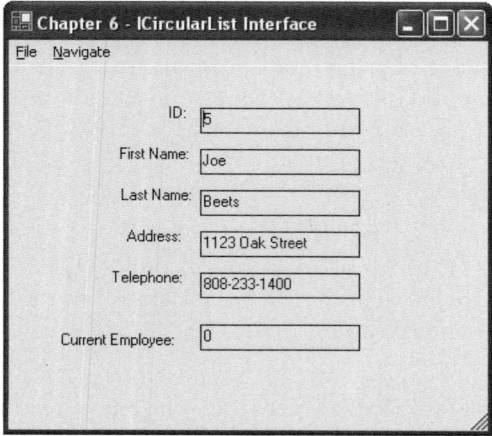

Figure 6-4   Completed solution – ICircularList form

12. On the form's menu bar, Click **File**, and then click **Open**. In the Open dialog box, select and open the file named **Chapter.06\Data\Employees.txt**.

13. On the menu bar, click **Navigate**, **Next** 5 times. Note that when the last record is the current record, clicking the Navigate Next menu item will cause the first record to become the current record. Thus, the list is circular.

14. End the solution, and then exit Visual Studio .NET.

UNDERSTANDING THE CONCEPT OF AN INTERFACE

To understand the concept of an interface, think about the mouse attached to your computer. Windows expects all mice to provide the same functionality. Combined, those functions make up the interface of a mouse.

- The user must be able to use the mouse to position the cursor on the desktop.

- The user must be able to click the left and right mouse buttons.

- Mice support some form of a mouse wheel used for scrolling.

Different vendors may implement the mouse interface differently. For example, consider three different ways to implement mouse movement:

- Some mice detect movement via a rolling ball beneath the mouse.

- Some mice detect movement via an optical sensor beneath the mouse.

- Other mice detect movement through a rolling ball placed on top of a stationary mouse.

In addition to providing different ways to move the mouse cursor, different vendors may position the left and right mouse buttons differently. For example, some vendors position mouse buttons on the side of the mouse, rather than on top of the mouse. Thus, an interface defines what an object, such as a mouse, will do, but not how to do it. That task is left up to the implementation of the interface.

VB .NET interfaces work similarly. As mentioned, VB .NET defines an interface named IEnumerator. All the IEnumerator interface does is to define the signature of properties and methods that allow the items in a list to be examined using a For Each loop. The IEnumerator interface does not define the type of object returned when the list is enumerated or the order in which the items in a list will be returned. That is the job of any class or structure that implements the IEnumerator interface. The ArrayList, SortedList, Queue, and Stack classes all implement the IEnumerator interface, so any instance of these classes can be enumerated with a For Each loop.

Interface-based applications work somewhat differently from the applications that you have created in previous chapters. In all the applications you have created so far, you have written statements in a procedure to call the methods of a particular class explicitly. When you implement an interface, however, VB .NET automatically calls the methods that you create. These methods supply the implementation for a particular interface. For example, suppose that you create a class that implements the IEnumerator interface. In that class, you must implement a property named Current and two methods named MoveNext and Reset. However, you do not write statements to call these members directly. Rather, VB .NET calls them automatically when it enumerates a list with a For Each loop. VB .NET first calls the Reset method when it begins executing the For Each loop. VB .NET then calls the move Next method to locate the next item in the list, and it then reads the Current property to get the current item from the list.

This chapter discusses the following predefined VB .NET interfaces:

- The IComparable and IComparer interfaces define how two objects will be compared for equality or inequality. The purpose of these two interfaces is simple. By telling VB .NET how to compare two objects for equality, you can call the Sort method of the Array class to sort a list of objects. The Sort method, in turn, calls the methods that implement the IComparable and IComparer interfaces to actually compare two objects and ultimately sort the list. By implementing the IComparable or IComparer interfaces, you, as the developer, can define the order in which VB .NET will sort the items in a list.

- Together, the IEnumerator and IEnumerable interfaces allow the items in a list to be examined using a For Each loop. When you write a For Each loop, VB .NET calls the members of the IEnumerator and IEnumerable interfaces to iterate through each item in the list. Each time through the For Each loop, the next item in the list is returned until all of the list items have been examined. Again, the System.Array, System.Collections.ArrayList, and System.Collections.SortedList classes all implement the IEnumerator and IEnumerable interfaces, so you can enumerate these lists with a For Each loop.

- The ICollection interface allows you to implement a simple collection.

- Implementing the ICloneable interface allows you to make a copy of an object's data. Again, the Array, ArrayList, and SortedList classes implement the ICloneable interface. By implementing the ICloneable interface, you can make an exact copy of an object's data instead of simply copying an object reference.

Note that the preceding list only describes the interfaces implemented in this chapter. VB .NET supports many other interfaces too.

IMPLEMENTING AND DECLARING INTERFACES

In previous chapters, we have used the term interface to describe the members (methods, properties, events, and fields) exposed by the author of a class to the developer using the class. In addition, you have likely used to the term interface to refer to a graphical user interface (GUI). The term interface in VB .NET has a much more specific meaning though.

Classes and interfaces are both reference types. Like abstract classes, interfaces define member signatures but do not contain any executable code. The implementation of an abstract class is left up to the concrete class(es) that inherit the abstract class. The purpose of an interface is similar to that of an abstract class. An **interface** defines a contract, which, in turn, can be implemented by other classes and structures. That contract defines the signatures of the members that comprise the interface, but supplies no implementation for those members.

Any class or structure that implements an interface must adhere to the contract defined by that interface exactly. In other words, an interface defines a set of members and the signatures of those members. Any class or structure that implements an interface must implement all of the members defined by that interface. That is, a class cannot implement selected members and omit the implementation for other members.

An interface contains no executable statements. That is, an interface contains declarations for property procedures, function procedures, and sub procedures, but must not contain the implementation for those members. Thus, the interface defines the members and the signatures of those members, but the interface does not define the actions that those members will perform. That task is left up to the classes or structures that implement the interface. As an interface contains no data, it is illegal to declare variables in an interface.

Implementing an Interface

Any class or structure may implement any number of interfaces. That is, a class may implement one, two, three, or more interfaces. Also, as you have seen before, a class might not implement any interfaces at all. To implement an interface, you use the Implements statement, which has the following syntax:

Syntax

Implements *interfacename* [, ...]

Definition

The **Implements** statement tells VB .NET that a class or structure implements one or more interfaces.

Dissection

- The *interfacename* argument contains the name of the interface being implemented. If the class or structure is implementing multiple interfaces, then those interface names can appear as a comma-separated list following the Implements statement. In addition, multiple Implements statements may appear.

Code Example

```
Public Class Demo
    Implements ICloneable, IEnumerable
End Class
```

Code Dissection

The preceding Implements statement indicates that the Demo class implements the interfaces named ICloneable, and IEnumerable.

The preceding comma-separated list can also be written with individual Implements statements, as shown in the following code segment:

```
Public Class Demo
    Implements ICloneable
    Implements IEnumerable
End Class
```

As another example, consider the SortedList class that you used in Chapter 5. If you examine the Help page for the SortedList class, you will see that it implements four interfaces, as shown in the following code segment:

```
Public Class SortedList
    Implements IDictionary, ICollection, _
        IEnumerable, ICloneable
End Class
```

In the preceding code segment, the class named SortedList implements four interfaces named IDictionary, ICollection, IEnumerable, and ICloneable. The Implements keyword appears after the Class declaration and contains a comma-separated list of the interfaces that are implemented by the class. The Implements keyword must appear after the Inherits statement, if one exists, and before any other declaration statements or methods.

Declaring an Interface

In addition to implementing an interface, you can create your own interfaces with the Interface statement, which has the following syntax:

Syntax

[**Public** | **Private** | **Protected** | **Friend** | **Protected Friend**] _
[**Shadows**] **Interface** *name*
  [**Inherits** *interfacename*[, *interfacename*]]
  [**Property** *propertyname*]
  [**Function** *membername*]
  [**Sub** *membername*]
  [**Event** *membername*]
End Interface

Definition

The **Interface** statement declares an interface. An interface may be inherited by other interfaces. In addition, an interface may inherit from a base interface.

Dissection

- The optional access modifiers define the scope of the interface. Their meaning is the same as their meaning when used to declare a class or variable or other member.

- The **Interface** statement marks the beginning of the Interface block. An interface declaration may appear in a namespace, structure, class, or module block.

- The **name** keyword defines the name of the interface. The interface name can be any valid identifier name.

- The optional **Inherits** keyword defines any interfaces inherited by this interface. The inherited interfaces appear as a comma-separated list. An interface may inherit any number of other interfaces.

- The **Property** keyword defines the signatures for any properties defined by the interface.

- The **Function** keyword defines the signatures for any function methods defined by the interface. An interface may define any number of function methods.

- The **Sub** keyword defines the signatures for any sub methods defined by the interface.

- The **Event** keyword defines the signatures for any events defined by the interface.

- The **End Interface** statement marks the end of the interface declaration.

Code Example

```
Public Interface IEnumerator
    ReadOnly Property Current As Object
    Function MoveNext() As Boolean
    Sub Reset()
End Interface
```

Code Dissection

The preceding statements declare an interface named IEnumerator. This is the actual IEnumerator interface defined by VB .NET. The interface defines a read-only property named Current, a function method named MoveNext that returns a Boolean value, and a sub method named Reset. Any class that implements the IEnumerator interface must implement these three members with exactly the same member signatures. Note that the member prototypes declared in an interface do not contain an access modifier.

Inheriting Interfaces

Interfaces can be inherited, but the inheritance rules differ between interfaces and classes. Remember that VB .NET uses single inheritance for classes. That is, a derived class can inherit from only one base class. However, an interface may inherit from any number of other interfaces. For example, the IList interface defines the contract to manage a list of items.

In the Help system for the IList interface, you will see the following prototype:

```
Public Interface IList
    Inherits ICollection, IEnumerable
    ' Statements
End Interface
```

The preceding code segment shows the declaration for the IList interface. The Interface and End Interface statements mark the beginning and end of the interface block. The IList interface inherits the ICollection and IEnumerable interfaces. This means any class that implements the IList interface must implement all of the members of both the ICollection interface and the IEnumerable interface. Note that while an interface can inherit other interfaces, an interface cannot inherit other types such as a class or a structure.

UNDERSTANDING THE ICOMPARABLE INTERFACE

Frequently, an application may need to sort data. That is, you may need to sort an array of structures or an array of other objects. Of course, you could write the code to sort the array elements by hand, exchanging the list elements as necessary, but implementing a predefined interface makes the process surprisingly easy.

To get started with implementing an interface, we examine one of the predefined interfaces supplied by VB .NET. Each interface defines prototypes for a fixed set of properties, methods, and events, which may be overloaded. To illustrate the declaration of an interface using the simplest of examples, consider the IComparable interface, which defines how VB .NET will compare two objects for equality or inequality. The designers of the IComparable interface declared the interface as follows:

```
Public Interface IComparable
    Function CompareTo(ByVal obj As Object) As Integer
End Interface
```

The preceding code segment declares an interface named IComparable. The IComparable interface supports a single function method named CompareTo. The method accepts one argument, an object (System.Object), and returns an Integer. This function prototype has the same syntax as the function prototype for an abstract class. Note that the function prototype contains no access modifier. In addition, note that interface member prototypes always have Public access, but that the interface declaration itself may contain an access modifier. The reason that an interface member is declared with Public access is simple. Interfaces are designed for use by other applications and assemblies. Thus, if an interface member was declared with an access modifier other than Public, that interface member could not be referenced by other assemblies, and would be useless.

By designing this generic interface into VB .NET, any class or structure that you create can implement the IComparable interface to define how the records in a list will be sorted.

 The benefit of implementing an interface will become clear in a moment, when you see how VB .NET calls the CompareTo method of a class or structure that implements the IComparable interface.

To implement an interface, you include the Implements keyword in a class or structure declaration, as shown in the following code segment:

```
Public Structure Employee
    Implements IComparable
    ' Structure members

    Function CompareTo(ByVal obj As Object) As Integer
        Implements IComparable.CompareTo
        ' Statements to perform comparison
    End Function
End Structure
```

The preceding statements declare a structure named Employee. The Implements IComparable statement denotes that the structure will implement the IComparable interface. Remember that the IComparable interface defines a single member named CompareTo, and that the CompareTo method will compare two objects for equality or inequality. Thus, the preceding Employee structure must implement the CompareTo method before VB .NET can compile the application. The CompareTo method must have a signature that matches the one defined by the interface itself.

Examine the following code segment that implements the CompareTo method of the IComparable interface:

```
Public Structure Employee
    Implements IComparable
    Public ID As String
    ' Other members

    Public Function CompareTo(ByVal obj As Object) _
        As Integer Implements IComparable.CompareTo

        If Me.ID < CType(obj, Employee).ID Then
            Return -1
        ElseIf Me.ID > CType(obj, Employee).ID Then
            Return 1
        Else
            Return 0
        End If

    End Function

End Structure
```

6

First, examine carefully the declaration of the CompareTo method. Note that the data type of the argument is System.Object and that the function procedure returns an Integer. As an interface defines a contract, any class that implements the interface must adhere to that contract exactly. Thus, the CompareTo procedure must be a function procedure and must accept one argument having a data type of System.Object. Finally, the function procedure must return an Integer. If the signatures do not match exactly, then a syntax error will occur. Examine the following statement that performs the comparison between two instances of the Employee structure:

```
If Me.ID < CType(obj, Employee).ID Then
    Return -1
```

Remember that the Me keyword references the current instance of the class or structure, so Me.ID references the ID property of the current structure instance. The argument passed to the CompareTo method has a data type of System.Object. Because strict type checking is enabled, the CType function must be called to convert the generic System.Object type to the type Employee. Thus, the preceding If statement compares the value of the ID property for the current structure instance with an instance passed as an argument.

The CompareTo method returns an Integer indicating whether the current class or structure instance is equal to, less than, or greater than the instance passed as an argument. If the value of the current instance is greater than the value of the object passed as an argument, then a positive value is returned. If the value of the current instance is less than the value of the object passed as an argument, then a negative value is returned. If the values of the two objects are equal, then the CompareTo method returns 0. While the CompareTo procedure returns a negative or positive 1, returning any negative or positive number will have the same result.

Consider the values returned by the CompareTo method. When VB .NET sorts a list, it calls the CompareTo method as necessary to compare two objects for equality or inequality. The Sort method interprets positive values to mean greater than, negative values to mean less than, and a value of 0 to mean equal to. If your implementation of the CompareTo method did not return the correct values, then the Sort method would sort the list incorrectly. Thus, when you implement an interface you must adhere to the contract, so that any data returned by a member has a value consistent with the value expected by the VB .NET utility that is calling the member.

The other significant part of the function declaration is the Implements keyword. A class or structure implements a member defined by an interface by way of the Implements keyword appearing at the end of the procedure declaration. The actual procedure name "CompareTo" has no significance at all.

Examine the following statement fragment:

```
Implements IComparable.CompareTo
```

It is the preceding statement fragment that causes the CompareTo method to implement the CompareTo method of the IComparable interface. Note that the interface name and the member name are separated by a period. This syntax is consistent with the syntax to implement any interface member. Figure 6-5 illustrates the relationship between an interface declaration and a class that implements an interface.

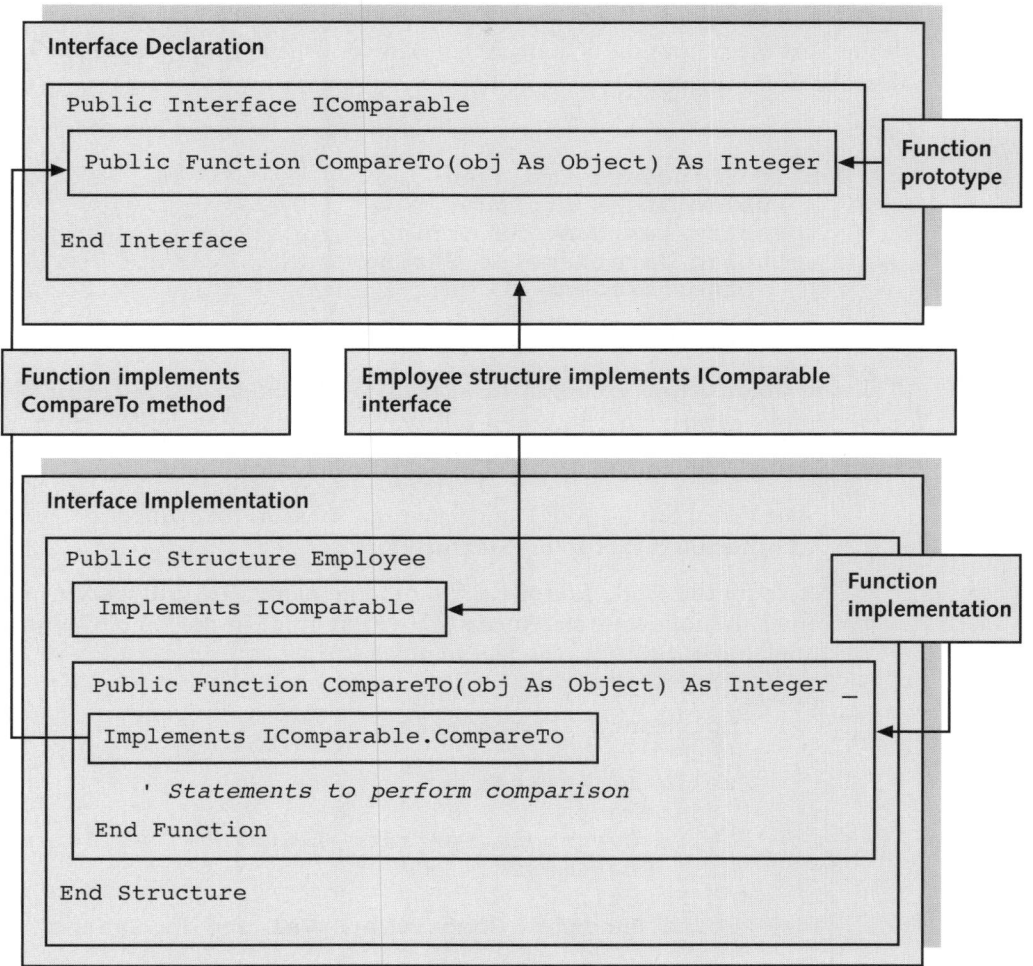

Figure 6-5   Interface relationships

As shown in Figure 6-5, the Employee structure implements the IComparable interface by way of the Implements keyword appearing in the Structure declaration. The CompareTo function implements the CompareTo function defined by the interface. This is the only function prototype defined by the IComparable interface.

SORTING A LIST WITH THE ICOMPARABLE INTERFACE

In this chapter's solution, the form named frmIComparable contains the statements to open a sequential file, and read that file into an array of Employee structures named EmployeeList using the same techniques presented in Chapter 5. The statements to navigate from record to record have already been written. In the hands-on steps that follow, you will implement the IComparable interface for the Employee structure, and then call the Sort method of the System.Array class to sort the list of employees based on the value of the ID member.

Suppose that an array of the following structure needs to be sorted by a unique ID number:

```
Public Structure Employee
    Public ID As String
    Public LastName As String
    Public FirstName As String
    ' Other members
End Structure
Public EmployeeList() As Employee
```

All that is required to accomplish this task is to implement the IComparable interface for the Employee structure, and then call the Sort method of the System.Array class.

To sort a list by implementing the IComparable interface:

1. Start Visual Studio .NET and open the solution file named **Chapter.06\Startup06\Startup06.sln**.

2. Activate the Code Editor for the module named **Employee.vb**, and then enter the following statements (shown in bold) in the Employee structure to implement the IComparable interface:

```
Public Structure Employee
    Implements IComparable

    Public ID As String
    ' Statements
    Public Overrides Function ToString() As String
        ' Statements
    End Function
    Public Function CompareTo(ByVal obj As System.Object) _
```

```
        As Integer Implements IComparable.CompareTo
        If Me.ID < CType(obj, Employee).ID Then
            Return -1
        ElseIf Me.ID > CType(obj, Employee).ID Then
            Return 1
        Else
            Return 0
        End If
    End Function
End Structure
```

The preceding code segment illustrates the mechanics to implement the IComparable interface. The first statement in the structure—Implements IComparable—indicates that the structure implements the interface named IComparable. The IComparable interface defines one method named CompareTo, which the structure implements. Note that the preceding implementation of the CompareTo function compared the ID member. However, the CompareTo function could have been implemented to compare any other member, such as the LastName or FirstName members.

3. Activate the Code Editor for the form named **frmIComparable.vb**.

4. Enter the following statement in the **Click** event handler for the button named **btnSort**:

```
System.Array.Sort(EmployeeList)
mintCurrent = 0
Call DisplayCurrentRecord(mintCurrent)
```

The first of the preceding statements calls the Sort method of the System.Array class. The argument passed to the Sort method tells the method which list to sort. The Sort method will sort the array named EmployeeList by calling the CompareTo method of the IComparable interface automatically. The remaining statements display the current record.

5. Test the solution. On the main form, click the **IComparable** button to display the IComparable Interface form. On the IComparable Interface form, click **File**, and then click **Open** to display the Open dialog box. Open the file named **Chapter.06\Data\Employees.txt**. Note that the records appear in an unsorted order.

6. Click the **Sort By ID** button on the form. Using the items on the **Navigate** menu, scroll through the records to observe that the records are sorted in ascending order by the ID number.

When the Sort method is called, the Sort method itself calls the CompareTo method as necessary to sort the items in the list. Figure 6-6 illustrates how the Sort method calls the CompareTo method.

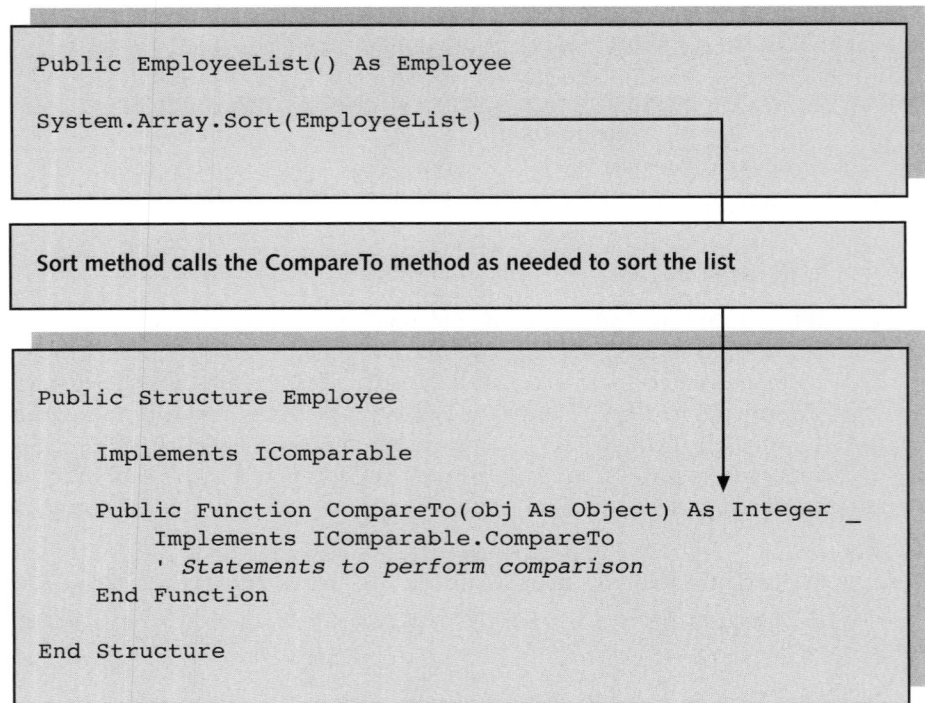

```
Public EmployeeList() As Employee

System.Array.Sort(EmployeeList)
```

Sort method calls the CompareTo method as needed to sort the list

```
Public Structure Employee

    Implements IComparable

    Public Function CompareTo(obj As Object) As Integer _
        Implements IComparable.CompareTo
        ' Statements to perform comparison
    End Function

End Structure
```

Figure 6-6   Calling an implemented interface

As shown in Figure 6-6, the Sort method calls the CompareTo method to determine equality. If two items in the list need to be exchanged, then the Sort method takes care of this task automatically.

The purpose of the IComparer interface is the same as that of the IComparable interface. However, the IComparer interface allows you to sort a list based on different key fields or multiple key fields. We discuss the IComparer interface next.

IMPLEMENTING THE ICOMPARER INTERFACE

As mentioned, VB .NET defines two interfaces to sort lists: IComparable and IComparer. The purpose of the two interfaces is the same; they both compare two objects for equality or inequality. Implementing the IComparer or IComparable interfaces allows you to sort an array by calling the overloaded Sort method of the System.Array class.

The two interfaces differ though in the following way:

- Implementing the IComparable interface allows data to be sorted by a single key.

- Implementing the IComparer interface allows data to be sorted either by a single key or by different keys.

By implementing the IComparer interface, you could sort the EmployeeList array (as shown in the code in the previous section of this chapter) by the ID member, the LastName member, or any other combination of members. To implement the IComparer interface to sort a list, you create one or more nested classes. Each of these nested classes, in turn, must implement the IComparer interface. When you want to sort the list, you call the Sort method of the System.Array class as before. However, you supply the list to sort as the first argument, and an instance of the desired nested class that implements the IComparer interface as the second argument.

The IComparer interface defines one function method named Compare. This method has the same purpose as the CompareTo method defined by the IComparable interface. However, the signature of the Compare method requires two arguments instead of one, as shown in the following interface declaration:

```
Interface IComparer
    Function Compare(ByVal x As System.Object, _
        ByVal y As System.Object) As Integer
End Interface
```

As shown in the preceding interface declaration, the Compare method accepts two arguments instead of just one. Both arguments are of type System.Object and contain the two objects that will be used in the comparison. If the value of x is less than the value of y, then the Compare function should return a negative number. If the values of x and y are equal, then the Compare function should return 0. If the value of x is greater than the value of y, then the Compare function should return a positive number.

Examine the following code segment, which shows the Employee structure with multiple implementations of the IComparer interface:

```
Public Structure Employee
    Public ID As String
    Public FirstName As String
    Public LastName As String

    ' Other members

    Public Class CompareByFirstName
        Implements IComparer
        Public Function Compare(ByVal x As System.Object, _
            ByVal y As System.Object) As Integer _
            Implements IComparer.Compare
            ' Statements to compare x and y
        End Function
    End Class

    Public Class CompareByLastName
        Implements IComparer
```

6

```
      Public Function Compare(ByVal x As System.Object, _
          ByVal y As System.Object) As Integer _
          Implements IComparer.Compare
          ' Statements to compare x and y
      End Function
    End Class
End Structure
```

As shown in the preceding statements, the Employee structure contains two classes named CompareByFirstName and CompareByLastName. Each class implements the IComparer interface. However, the CompareByFirstName class will perform the comparison based on the contents of the FirstName member, and the CompareByLastName class will perform the comparison based on the contents of the LastName member.

Additional classes could be created that implement the IComparer interface to supply comparison methods based on different members or based on multiple members. For example, you could create a class that would perform the comparison based on the contents of both the LastName and FirstName members combined.

Given the preceding declarations, the Sort method can be called as before. However, the syntax differs slightly, as shown in the following code segment:

```
Dim SortByFirstName As New Employee.CompareByFirstName()
System.Array.Sort(EmployeeList, SortByFirstName)

Dim SortByLastName As New Employee.CompareByLastName()
System.Array.Sort(EmployeeList, SortByLastName)
```

As shown in the preceding statements, the first statement creates an instance of the CompareByFirstName class that implements the IComparer interface. This class instance, in turn, is used as the second argument to the array's Sort method. The last two statements also sort the list. However, instead of sorting the list based on the contents of the FirstName member, the records are sorted based on the contents of the LastName member. Figure 6-7 illustrates how the IComparer interface works.

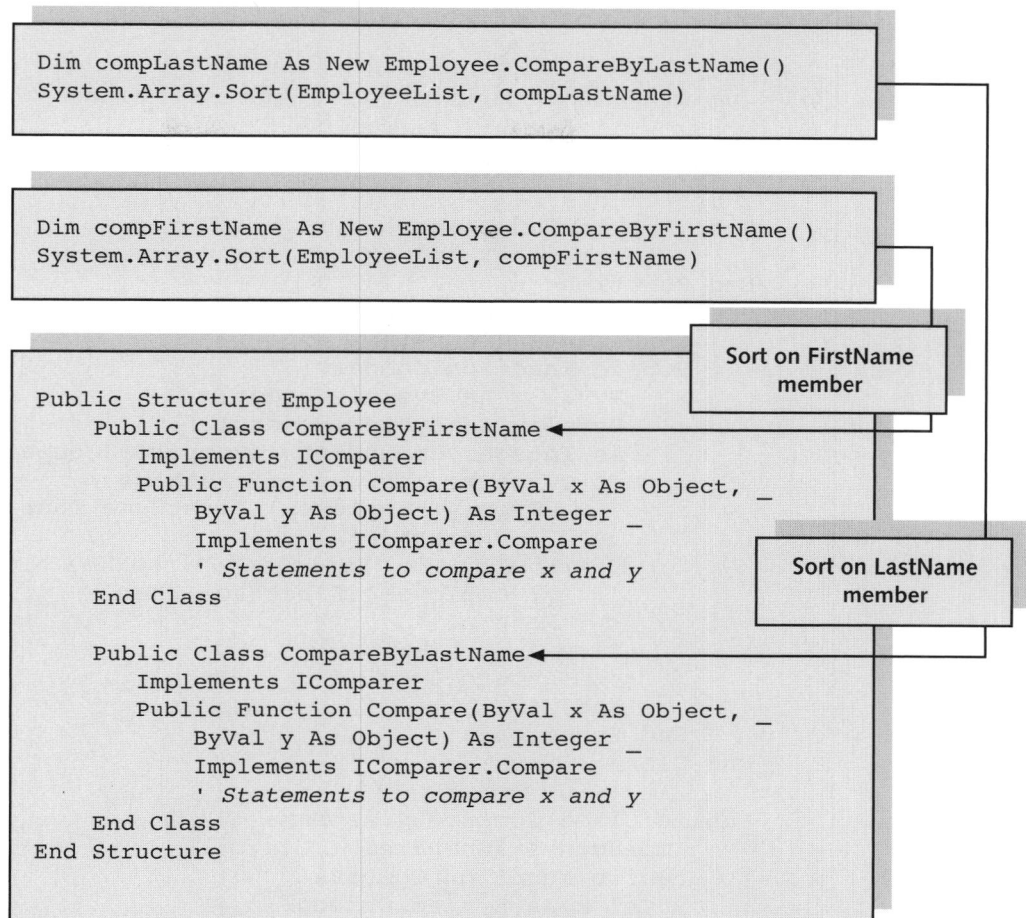

Figure 6-7   The IComparer interface

As shown in Figure 6-7, two nested classes are declared in the Employee structure. Each nested class supplies its own implementation for the IComparer interface. Which implementation gets called depends on which class instance is passed to the Sort method of the System.Array class.

Next, you will implement the IComparer interface to sort the EmployeeList array either by the LastName or FirstName members.

To implement the IComparer interface:

1. Activate the Code Editor for the module named **Employee.vb**. Enter the following statements (shown in bold) in the Employee structure to provide two implementations for the IComparer interface:

```
Public Structure Employee
    ' Statements
    Public Function CompareTo(. . .)
        ' Statements
    End Function
    Public Class CompareByFirstName
        Implements IComparer
        Public Function Compare( _
            ByVal x As System.Object, _
            ByVal y As System.Object) _
            As Integer Implements IComparer.Compare
            If CType(x, Employee).FirstName < _
                CType(y, Employee).FirstName Then
                    Return -1
            ElseIf CType(x, Employee).FirstName > CType( _
                y, Employee).FirstName Then
                Return 1
            Else
                Return 0
            End If
        End Function
    End Class

    Public Class CompareByLastName
        Implements IComparer
        Public Function Compare( _
        ByVal x As System.Object, _
        ByVal y As System.Object) _
        As Integer Implements IComparer.Compare
            If CType(x, Employee).LastName < _
                CType(y, Employee).LastName Then
                Return -1
            ElseIf CType(x, Employee).LastName > _
                CType(y, Employee).LastName Then
                Return 1
            Else
                Return 0
            End If
        End Function
    End Class
End Structure
```

Both the CompareByFirstName and CompareByLastName classes implement the IComparer interface. As the IComparer interface defines the contract for the Compare method, both of the classes must implement that method. However, the CompareByFirstName class compares two objects using the FirstName member of the Employee structure, and the CompareByLastName method compares two objects using the LastName member of the Employee structure.

2. Activate the Code Editor for the form named **frmIComparer.vb**. Enter the following statements in the **Click** event handler for the button named **btnSortByFirstName**:

```
Dim SortByFirstName As New Employee.CompareByFirstName
System.Array.Sort(EmployeeList, SortByFirstName)
mintCurrent = 0
Call DisplayCurrentRecord(mintCurrent)
```

The preceding statements first create a new instance of the nested class that implements the IComparer interface. That class instance is then used as the second argument to the overloaded Sort method of the Array class. The final statements display the current record.

3. Enter the following statements in the **Click** event handler for the button named **btnSortByLastName**:

```
Dim SortByLastName As New Employee.CompareByLastName
System.Array.Sort(EmployeeList, SortByLastName)
mintCurrent = 0
Call DisplayCurrentRecord(mintCurrent)
```

These statements are nearly identical to the statements you just wrote to sort the list by the FirstName field. However, these statements create an instance of the CompareByLastName class and pass that class instance as an argument to the Sort method of the Array class.

4. Test the solution. On the main form, click the button named **IComparer** to display the IComparer Interface form. On the form's menu, click **File**, and then click **Open** to display the Open dialog box. Open the file named **Chapter.06\Data\Employees.txt**. Click the button named **Sort By Last Name**. Using the menu items on the **Navigate** menu, verify that the records in the list are sorted by last name. Click the button named **Sort By First Name**. Verify that the records in the list are sorted by the employee's first name.

Most interfaces are more complex than the IComparable interface, thereby supporting additional members. For example, the IEnumerator interface has three members named Current, MoveNext, and Reset, instead of just a single member. When implementing the IEnumerator interface, you must again implement all of the defined members per the interface contract.

THE RELATIONSHIP BETWEEN THE IENUMERATOR AND IENUMERABLE INTERFACES

You have used For Each loops before to enumerate through the objects contained in different collections. The For Each loop is able to enumerate through the objects in any collection because the collection implements two interfaces: the IEnumerator and IEnumerable interfaces.

The IEnumerator and IEnumerable interfaces are tightly coupled. That is, you always implement both of these interfaces together. Combined, these two interfaces allow the objects in a list to be examined, or enumerated, using a For Each loop. For example, the elements in the Array, ArrayList, and SortedList classes can be enumerated using a For Each loop because all of these classes implement the IEnumerator and IEnumerable interfaces.

As a first simple example, consider an array. The System.Array class allows you to examine its elements using a For Each loop, as shown in the following code segment:

```
Private pstrList() As String = {"One", "Two", "Three"}
Dim objCurrent As Object
For Each objCurrent In pstrList
    txtOutput.Text &= objCurrent.ToString & CrLF
Next
```

The preceding For Each loop enumerates the elements of the String array named pstrList. Each time through the For Each loop, the object variable "objCurrent" stores a reference to the next array element. The array elements are concatenated to the multi-line text box named txtOutput. Thus, the multi-line text box would contain the following output:

```
One
Two
Three
```

You could write similar statements to enumerate an array of Integer, Single, or Double values, or an array of any other data type. A String can be enumerated in the same way, because the String class also implements the IEnumerable interface. By definition, when you enumerate a String, the enumerator returns one character from the String at a time, as shown in the following statements:

```
Dim pstrCurrent As String = "abc"
Dim pchrCurrent As Char
For Each pchrCurrent In pstrCurrent
    Debug.WriteLine(pchrCurrent.ToString)
Next
```

The preceding statements enumerate a String much in the same way the statements that enumerated an array. Each time through the For Each loop, the Debug.WriteLine statement prints the current character in the String. Thus, the letters "a", "b", and "c" will each be written to the Output window.

In addition to using the enumerators supplied by other classes, the classes that you create can support an enumerator by implementing the IEnumerable and IEnumerator interfaces.

UNDERSTANDING THE DETAILS OF THE IENUMERABLE INTERFACE

The IEnumerable interface supports a single method named GetEnumerator. The GetEnumerator method, in turn, returns an instance of a second class that implements the IEnumerator interface. Examine the following simple class that implements the IEnumerable interface:

```
Public Class EmployeeFile
    Implements IEnumerable
    Public SourceFile As String

    Public Sub New(ByVal SourceFile As String)
        Me.SourceFile = SourceFile
    End Sub

    Public Overloads Function GetEnumerator() _
        As IEnumerator Implements IEnumerable.GetEnumerator
        Return New EmployeeFileEnumerator(SourceFile)
    End Function
End Class
```

The preceding class named EmployeeFile implements one interface: the IEnumerable interface. The statement appearing in the GetEnumerator method is quite simple. The function procedure creates an instance of a second class that implements the IEnumerator interface and returns that instance. All GetEnumerator methods work in exactly the same way. That is, they all return an instance of the enumerator.

The IEnumerator interface defines a property named Current and two methods named MoveNext and Reset, as discussed in the following syntax diagram:

Syntax

System.Collections.IEnumerator interface

Public Properties

- The **Current** property returns the current item in the list. If the last call to the MoveLast method returned False, then referencing the Current property will cause VB .NET to throw an exception.

Public Methods

- The **MoveNext** method advances the enumerator to the next item in the list. The method should return True if there are more items in the list and False otherwise.

- The **Reset** method resets the enumerator to its initial position in preparation for enumerating the items in the list. The initial position should be one element before the first element in the list.

Figure 6-8 illustrates the relationship between the IEnumerable and the IEnumerator interfaces.

EmployeeFile class implements the IEnumerable interface

```
Public Class EmployeeFile
    Implements IEnumerable
    Public Overloads Function GetEnumerator() As IEnumerator _
        Implements IEnumerable.GetEnumerator
        Return New EmployeeFileEnumerator(SourceFile)
    End Function
End Class
```

Create an instance of the enumerator

EmployeeFileEnumerator class implements the IEnumerator interface

```
Public Class EmployeeFileEnumerator
    Implements IEnumerator
End Class
```

Figure 6-8   Relationship between the IEnumerable and IEnumerator interfaces

As with most interfaces, you do not explicitly call the members of the IEnumerable and the IEnumerator interfaces. Rather, VB .NET calls the following members as it executes a For Each loop. Figure 6-9 illustrates the order in which VB .NET calls the members of an enumerator.

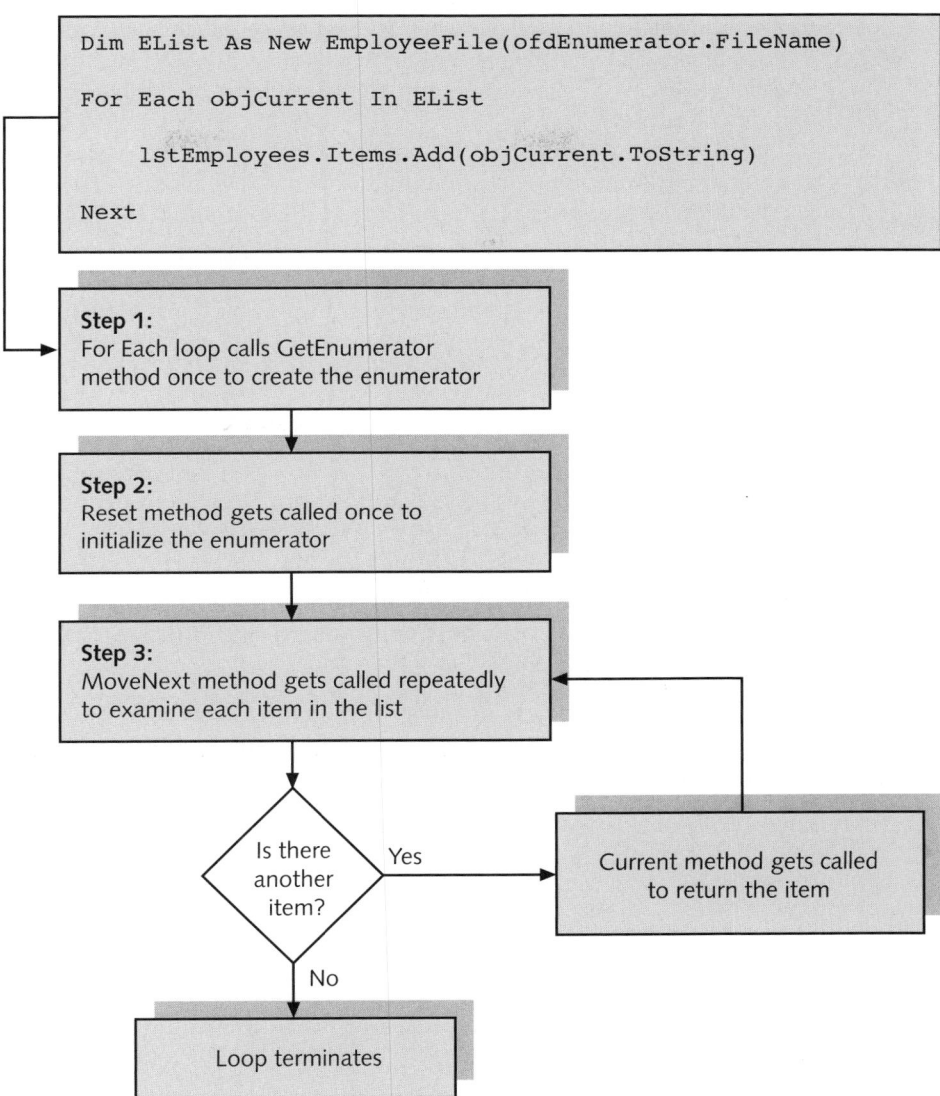

```
Dim EList As New EmployeeFile(ofdEnumerator.FileName)

For Each objCurrent In EList

    lstEmployees.Items.Add(objCurrent.ToString)

Next
```

Step 1:
For Each loop calls GetEnumerator
method once to create the enumerator

Step 2:
Reset method gets called once to
initialize the enumerator

Step 3:
MoveNext method gets called repeatedly
to examine each item in the list

Is there
another
item?

Yes

Current method gets called
to return the item

No

Loop terminates

Figure 6-9   Calling an enumerator

As shown in Figure 6-9, when the For Each loop begins execution, the GetEnumerator method gets called to return the actual enumerator. Then, the Reset method is called to initialize the enumerator. Each time through the For Each loop, the MoveNext method gets called to increment the enumerator and then the Current method gets called. These two methods are called repeatedly until no more items remain in the list, that is, until MoveNext returns False.

Collections are not inherently thread safe. That is, if another process modifies a collection while it is being enumerated, then VB .NET will throw an InvalidOperationException when any of the methods of the IEnumerator interface are called.

In this solution, you will implement an enumerator that will allow the developer to read a sequential file. However, instead of having to read the sequential file directly, the developer will be able to read the sequential file using a For Each loop. The constructor for the EmployeeFileEnumerator class calls a procedure named ReadFile. This procedure is documented in both the completed and startup solution. It is not discussed here because the procedure uses the exact same technique to read a sequential file into an array as the technique used in Chapter 5.

The following variables are already declared in the EmployeeFile.vb module in the startup solution:

```
Private EmployeeList() As Employee
Private mintCount As Integer
Private mintCurrent As Integer
```

The EmployeeList array stores the records read from the sequential file. The variable mintCount contains the number of elements in the array, and the variable mintCurrent contains the current array element.

The statements to implement the Current property and Reset and MoveNext methods deserve careful analysis. The following procedure implements the Reset method of the IEnumerator interface:

```
Public Sub Reset() Implements IEnumerator.Reset
    mintCurrent = -1
End Sub
```

By definition, the Reset method should position the enumerator one item before the first item in the list. As the underlying data structure is a 0-based array named EmployeeList, the Reset method sets the variable mintCurrent to -1. The Current property returns the current item from the list, as shown in the following statements:

```
Public ReadOnly Property Current() _
    As Object Implements IEnumerator.Current
    Get
        Return EmployeeList(mintCurrent)
    End Get
End Property
```

The read-only Current property returns the current employee from the array named EmployeeList. Again, the variable mintCurrent is used as the index into the array. This is the same variable that was set in the Reset method.

The purpose of the MoveNext method is to advance the current record pointer to the next item in the list, as shown in the following statements:

```
Public Function MoveNext() As Boolean _
    Implements IEnumerator.MoveNext
    If mintCurrent >= mintCount Then
        Return False
    Else
        mintCurrent += 1
        Return True
    End If
End Function
```

The If statement in the MoveNext method checks to see if more items remain in the list. That is, the current item is compared against the total number of items. If the list contains no more items, the MoveNext method returns False. If more items remain to be enumerated, then the method increments the variable mintCurrent and the method returns True.

To implement an enumerator:

1. Activate the Code Editor for the class named **EmployeeFile** appearing in the module named **EmployeeFile.vb**. Enter the following statements (shown in bold) in the class module named **EmployeeFile**:

```
Public Class EmployeeFile
    Implements IEnumerable
    Public SourceFile As String

    Public Sub New(ByVal SourceFile As String)
        Me.SourceFile = SourceFile
    End Sub

    Public Overloads Function GetEnumerator() _
        As IEnumerator _
        Implements IEnumerable.GetEnumerator
        Return New EmployeeFileEnumerator(SourceFile)
    End Function
End Class
```

Note that the Return statement will have an error at this point because you have not yet created the appropriate constructor for the EmployeeFileEnumerator class.

The preceding EmployeeFile class implements the IEnumerable interface. The constructor accepts one argument: the name of the file to read. The GetEnumerator method, in turn, creates an instance of the EmployeeFileEnumerator class. The constructor in the EmployeeFileEnumerator class calls another procedure to read the sequential file.

6

2. Next, you must create the EmployeeFileEnumerator class, which implements the IEnumerable interface. Enter the following statements (shown in bold) into the **EmployeeFileEnumerator** class:

```
Public Class EmployeeFileEnumerator
    Implements IEnumerator

    Private EmployeeList() As Employee
    Private mintCount As Integer
    Private mintCurrent As Integer

    Public Sub New(ByVal pstrFile As String)
        Call ReadFile(pstrFile)
        Reset()
    End Sub

    Public ReadOnly Property Current() As Object _
        Implements IEnumerator.Current
        Get
            Return EmployeeList(mintCurrent)
        End Get
    End Property

    Public Sub Reset() Implements IEnumerator.Reset
        mintCurrent = -1
    End Sub

    Public Function MoveNext() As Boolean _
        Implements IEnumerator.MoveNext
        If mintCurrent >= mintCount Then
            Return False
        Else
            mintCurrent += 1
            Return True
        End If
    End Function

    Private Sub ReadFile(ByVal pstrFile As String)
        ' Statements
    End Sub
End Class
```

3. Activate the Code Editor for the form named **frmIEnumerator.vb**. Enter the following statements in the **Click** event handler for the button named **btnEnumerateList**:

```
Dim dlgResult As DialogResult
Dim objCurrent As Object

Try
```

```
        ofdEnumerator.ShowDialog()
        Dim EList As New EmployeeFile(ofdEnumerator.FileName)

        For Each objCurrent In EList
            lstEmployees.Items.Add(objCurrent.ToString)
        Next

    Catch ex As System.Exception
        MessageBox.Show(ex.Message, "Error", _
            MessageBoxButtons.OK)
    End Try
```

4. Test the solution. On the main form, click the **IEnumerator** button to activate the IEnumerator Interface form. Click the **Enumerate List** button to display the Open dialog box. Select the file named **Chapter.06\Data\ Employees.txt**. The enumerator reads the sequential file and the contents are added to the list box.

So far you have seen how to implement the IComparable and IComparer interfaces. While the IEnumerable and IEnumerator interfaces required that you implement more than a single method, the interface remained fairly simple. Now we proceed to implement a custom interface.

THE ICOLLECTION INTERFACE

The ICollection interface inherits the IEnumerable interface. The purposes of the ICollection and IEnumerable interfaces are related. By implementing the ICollection interface, you provide the means to group objects of a similar type in a list. The ICollection interface defines a member named Count that returns the number of items in a collection.

When you implement the ICollection interface, you must also implement the members of the IEnumerable interface because the ICollection interface inherits IEnumerable. The following code segment shows the declaration for the ICollection interface:

```
    Public Interface ICollection
        Inherits IEnumerable
    End Interface
```

In addition to the members of the IEnumerable interface, the ICollection interface defines the following additional members related to managing the items in a list:

Syntax

System.Collections.ICollection interface

6

Public Properties

- The read-only **Count** property returns the number of items in the collection.
- The purpose of the **IsSynchronized** and **SyncRoot** properties relates to multi-threaded applications, and whether or not the collection is thread-safe.

Public Methods

- The **CopyTo** method copies the contents of the list to an array.

In this chapter's solution, you will create your own interface named ICircularList that inherits the ICollection and IEnumerable interfaces. The interface that you will define is similar to a queue. However, unlike a queue, the interface that you will implement has no beginning or end. Thus, we will call this interface ICircularList to denote a circular list.

To understand the concept of a circular list, suppose that one employee is "on call" at a time, and the employee currently on call rotates through a list of employees. Once all of the employees have been on call, the first employee that was on call becomes on call again. Thus, you will create a list that is circular. Figure 6-10 illustrates the operation of the circular list.

First, you must define the interface for the circular list. To declare an interface, you use the Interface statement. Inside the interface that you declare, you declare the members that will be supported by that interface. Again, the members that you declare are only prototypes. The class that ultimately implements the interface will contain the code for these members.

To define an interface:

1. Activate the Code Editor for the module named **OnCallList.vb**. Enter the following statements (shown in bold) immediately after the Option Strict statement:

```
Option Strict On
Public Interface ICircularList
    Inherits ICollection
    Function Add(ByVal value As Object) As Integer
    Function Current() As Object
    Function GetIndex() As Integer
    Function MoveNext() As Object
End Interface
Public Class OnCallList
```

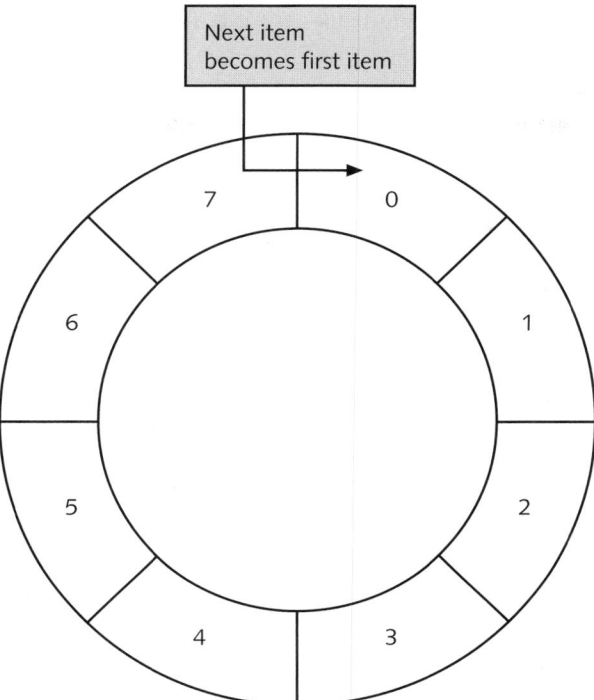

Next item
becomes first item

Figure 6-10   Operation of the circular employee list

The preceding statements declare an interface named ICircularList. The ICircularList interface inherits the ICollection interface, so any class that inherits from ICircularList must implement the methods of the ICollection interface. Furthermore, the ICircularList interface extends the behavior of the ICollection interface by exposing methods to add and locate items. The following list describes the purpose of each method:

- The Add method adds a new item to the end of the list. The item to be added to the list is passed as an argument.

- The Current method returns the current item in the list.

- The GetIndex method gets the index of the current item in the list.

- The MoveNext method is defined as a function method, and returns an object. As you will see later in this section, the MoveNext method will be used to locate the next item in the circular list. If the last item is the current item, then the MoveNext method will locate the first item in the list.

While you are implementing a circular list made up of on-call employees, other applications could make use of a circular list as well. For example, a stoplight or traffic intersection is a circular list in that a pattern repeats itself indefinitely.

Next, you will begin to implement the OnCallList class so that it implements the ICircularList interface.

To implement the ICircularList interface:

1. Activate the Code Editor for the module named **OnCallList.vb**, if necessary. Enter the following statements (shown in bold) in the **OnCallList** class to indicate that this class implements the ICircularList interface:

```
Public Class OnCallList
    Implements ICircularList
    Private EmployeeArray() As Employee
    Private mintCount As Integer
    Private mintCurrent As Integer
    ' Statements
End Class
```

The first of the preceding statements indicates that the OnCallList class implements the ICircularList interface. The remaining statements declare hidden variables that will store the list of employees, the number of employees in the list, and the index of the current employee.

 At this point in the development of the class, the Implements statement that you just wrote contains an error. The reason is simple: You have not yet implemented the members of the ICollection or ICircularList interfaces.

Having stated that the OnCallList class implements the ICircularList interface, you must now write the statements to actually implement the interface. That is, you must implement the properties and methods defined by the ICollection and IEnumerable interfaces, along with implementing the methods required by the ICircularList interface. First, you will implement the Add method.

To implement the Add method of the ICircularList interface:

1. Enter the following statements (shown in bold) in the **OnCallList** class:

```
Private mintCurrent As Integer
Public Function Add(ByVal value As Object) _
    As Integer Implements ICircularList.Add
    Dim empCurrent As Employee
    Static pblnFirst As Boolean = True
    Dim pintCount, pintCurrent As Integer
    If TypeOf value Is Employee Then
        empCurrent = CType(value, Employee)

        If pblnFirst Then
            ReDim Preserve EmployeeArray(mintCount)
            EmployeeArray(mintCount) = empCurrent
            pblnFirst = False
        Else
```

```
            mintCount += 1
            ReDim Preserve EmployeeArray(mintCount)
            EmployeeArray(mintCount) = empCurrent
        End If
        mintCurrent += 1
        Return mintCount
    Else
        Return -1
    End If
End Function
```

The Add method accepts one argument of type System.Object and returns an Integer. The value returned contains the index of the newly added item. The item is added such that the new employee added appears at the end of the list. The Add method adds the item to the list by redimensioning the EmployeeList array, increasing its size by one. The object passed as an argument is added to the list.

2. Activate the Code Editor for the form named **frmICircularList.vb**, and then enter the following statements in the **Click** event handler for the menu item named **mmuFileOpen**:

```
Dim dlgResult As DialogResult
Dim empCurrent As Employee
Dim objCurrent As Object
Try

    ofdICollection.ShowDialog()
    Dim EList As New EmployeeFile(ofdICollection.FileName)

    For Each objCurrent In EList
        OnCallListCurrent.Add(objCurrent)
    Next
    empCurrent = CType(OnCallListCurrent.Current(), _
        Employee)
    Call CopyToTextBoxes(empCurrent)

Catch ex As System.Exception
    MessageBox.Show(ex.Message, "Error", _
        MessageBoxButtons.OK)
End Try
```

The preceding statements create an instance of the EmployeeFile class you created previously in the chapter. The For Each loop enumerates the list using the enumerator you previously created. The statement in the For Each loop adds each employee to the OnCallList array.

The CopyTo member of the ICollection interface copies the list elements to an array and returns that array. You will implement that method next.

To implement the CopyTo method of the ICollection interface:

1. Activate the Code Editor for the module named **OnCallList.vb**. Enter the following statements (shown in bold) in the **CopyTo** method:

```
Public Overloads Sub CopyTo(ByVal array As Array, _
    ByVal index As Integer) Implements ICollection.CopyTo
    Dim pintElements As Integer
    Dim pintCount As Integer
    pintElements = EmployeeArray.GetUpperBound(0) - index
    Dim NewEmployeeArray(pintElements) As Employee
    For pintCount = 0 To pintElements
        NewEmployeeArray(pintCount) = _
        EmployeeArray(pintCount + index)
    Next
    array = NewEmployeeArray
End Sub
```

The procedure creates a new EmployeeArray array and copies the data from the original EmployeeArray to NewEmployeeArray. The newly created NewEmployeeArray is stored in the array argument.

The Count property is defined by the ICollection interface, and simply returns the number of items in the list.

To implement the Count property:

1. Activate the Code Editor for the module named **OnCallList.vb**, if necessary. Enter the following statements (shown in bold) for the **Count** property:

```
Public ReadOnly Property Count() _
    As Integer Implements ICollection.Count
    Get
        Return mintCount
    End Get
End Property
```

The implementation for the Count property is simple. The read-only Count property returns the number of items in the list. The number of list items is stored in the hidden variable mintCount.

As defined in the ICircularList interface, the Current method will accept no arguments and return a value having a data type of System.Object. The method returns the current item in the list.

To implement the Current method of the ICircularList interface:

1. Activate the Code Editor for the module named **OnCallList.vb**, if necessary. Enter the following statements (shown in bold) in the **Current** method:

```
Public Function Current() _
    As Object Implements ICircularList.Current
    If mintCurrent > mintCount Then
        mintCurrent = 0
    End If
    Return EmployeeArray(mintCurrent)
End Function
```

The statements in the Current procedure return the current employee in the EmployeeList array. Thus, the If statement sets the current item to 0 if the current item has a greater value than the number of items. Next, you will implement the GetIndex method, which will return the numeric index of the current item.

2. Enter the following statements (shown in bold) in the **GetIndex** procedure:

```
Public Function GetIndex() _
    As Integer Implements ICircularList.GetIndex
    If mintCurrent > mintCount Then
        mintCurrent = 0
    End If
    Return mintCurrent
End Function
```

The GetIndex method returns the index of the current item. When the list is first created, the variable mintCurrent will have a value one greater than the end of the list. Thus, the If statement sets the current item to 0.

3. The MoveNext method will return the next employee in the list. Enter the following statements (shown in bold) in the **MoveNext** method:

```
Public Function MoveNext() _
    As Object Implements ICircularList.MoveNext
    If mintCurrent < mintCount Then
        mintCurrent += 1
    Else
        mintCurrent = 0
    End If
    Return EmployeeArray(mintCurrent)
End Function
```

The MoveNext method will iterate through the employees in the list. If the last employee is the current employee, then the MoveNext method will set the current employee to the first employee. The current employee is returned by the MoveNext method.

6

In addition to the preceding methods, you must implement the IsSynchronized and SyncRoot methods required by the ICollection interface. While the purpose of these properties may seem mysterious at this point, their purpose is to synchronize the collection with other processes. Even though the CircularList class does not provide thread safety, you must implement the properties because you must implement all of the properties and methods defined by an interface. Thus, you will just return the value False for the IsSynchronized property and Nothing for the SyncRoot property, causing the properties to return no synchronization object.

To implement the IsSynchronized and SyncRoot properties of the ICollection interface:

1. Enter the following statements (shown in bold) in the **IsSynchronized** property:

```
Public ReadOnly Property IsSynchronized() _
    As Boolean Implements ICollection.IsSynchronized
    Get
        Return False
    End Get
End Property
```

2. Enter the following statements (shown in bold) in the **SyncRoot** property:

```
Public ReadOnly Property SyncRoot() _
    As Object Implements ICollection.SyncRoot
    Get
        Return Nothing
    End Get
End Property
```

Next, you must implement the enumerator for the IList interface because the IList interface inherits the IEnumerable interface. However, for this enumerator, we illustrate how to make an interface operate without fully implementing all of its members. The ICollection interface requires that you implement the GetEnumerator method. However, you can just return Nothing so that the GetEnumerator method does nothing.

To implement an enumerator:

1. Enter the following statements (shown in bold) in the **GetEnumerator** method:

```
Public Function GetEnumerator() _
    As IEnumerator Implements ICollection.GetEnumerator
    Return Nothing
End Function
```

Next, you can write the statements in the ICircularList form to call the methods of the OnCallList class.

To implement the circular list:

1. Activate the Code Editor for the form named **frmICircularList.vb**, and then enter the following statements in the **Click** event handler for the menu item named **mmuNavigateNext**:

```
Dim empCurrent As Employee
empCurrent = CType(OnCallListCurrent.MoveNext, Employee)
Call CopyToTextBoxes(empCurrent)
```

2. Test the solution. On the main form, click the ICircularList button to display the ICircularList Interface form. On the menu bar, click **File**, and then click **Open**. Open the file named **Chapter.06\Data\Employees.txt**.

3. Click the **Navigate, Next** menu item several times. Note that when the last employee is the current employee, the first employee becomes the next employee.

Another important interface implemented by most classes is the ICloneable interface. Unlike other interfaces, such as IComparable and IComparer, the system never calls the method of the ICloneable interface. Rather, the one method of the ICloneable interface is designed for use solely by the developer. Its purpose is to make an exact copy of a particular object.

CLONING

Cloning is the process of making copies of objects. To understand the concept of cloning, consider first what happens when you assign two object variables, as shown in the following statements:

```
Dim txtX As New TextBox
Dim txtY As TextBox
txtY = txtX
```

The preceding statements assign an object reference. That is, the variables txtX and txtY both reference the same text box, as shown in Figure 6-11.

There may be times, however, when instead of assigning an object reference, you may want to create a copy of the object and its data. This process is called cloning because an exact copy of the original object is made. To illustrate the scenario further, examine the following assignment statements:

```
Dim pstrList() As String = {"First", "Second"}
Dim pstrListCopy() As String
pstrListCopy = pstrList
pstrList(0) = "Last"
```

```
Dim txtX As New TextBox
```

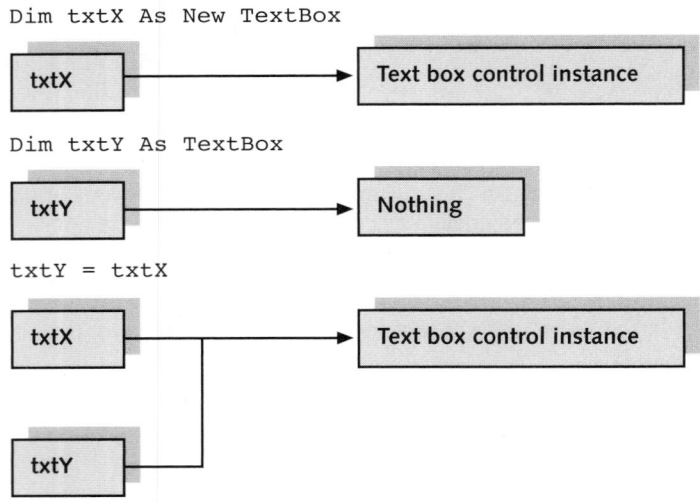

```
Dim txtY As TextBox
```

```
txtY = txtX
```

Figure 6-11   Assigning object references

You may think that a copy of the array pstrList is made and stored in the variable named pstrListCopy, so changing the contents of pstrList would not affect the contents of the array pstrListCopy. This is not the case, however. Remember that VB .NET arrays are reference types. When you assign reference type variables, only the object reference is assigned. The data is not copied. Thus, in the preceding statements, both pstrList and pstrListCopy reference the same array.

To allow the user to clone an object, you implement the ICloneable interface and its one method named Clone as shown in the following statements:

```
Public Structure Employee
    Implements ICloneable
    Public Function Clone() Implements ICloneable.Clone
        Dim objCurrent As Object
        objCurrent = Me.MemberwiseClone
        Return objCurrent
    End Function
End Class
```

As shown in the preceding statements, the structure Employee implements the ICloneable interface. The syntax is the same as the syntax used to implement any other interface.

The preceding code segment is fairly simple. The statements in the Clone method create a new variable to store a copy of the Employee structure. The following statement requires careful examination:

```
objCurrent = Me.MemberwiseClone
```

The MemberwiseClone method creates a new instance of the object, which in this case is the Employee structure, and then performs what is called a **shallow copy** on that object. The shallow copy performs a bit-by-bit copy of the data stored in the original object to the new object.

In many cases a shallow copy works fine. However, consider a situation where a class or structure contains other classes. In this situation, a shallow copy may not have the desired results. To illustrate the problem, examine the following class declarations:

```
Public Class PayrollInfo
    Public YTDGrossPay As Double
    Public YTDNetPay As Double
End Class

Public Class Employee
    Implements ICloneable

    Public Name As String
    Public Info As PayrollInfo

    Public Function Clone() _
        As Object Implements ICloneable.Clone
        Dim objCurrent As Object
        objCurrent = Me.MemberwiseClone
        Return objCurrent
    End Function

End Class
```

As you can see from the preceding statements, the Employee class contains a member named Info, having a data type of PayrollInfo. As this type is a reference type, the shallow copy will not have the desired effect because of the way the MemberwiseClone method performs copies with reference types. While the Name member is copied properly, only a reference to the PayrollInfo object is copied. Thus, the variables named empCurrent and empCopy reference the same instance of the PayrollInfo class. Figure 6-12 illustrates the process.

To solve the preceding problem, you must explicitly create an instance of the PayrollInfo class in the Clone method to make a deep copy. A **deep copy** is one where all of the data is copied instead of just the data corresponding to the value types. The following code segment illustrates the same Employee class with a deep copy implemented for the Clone method:

```
Public Function Clone() _
    As Object Implements ICloneable.Clone
    Dim objCopy As New Employee()
    Dim pr As New PayrollInfo()
    pr.YTDGrossPay = Me.Info.YTDGrossPay
```

```
            pr.YTDNetPay = Me.Info.YTDNetPay
            objCopy.Name = Me.Name
            objCopy.Info = pr
            Return objCopy
    End Function
```

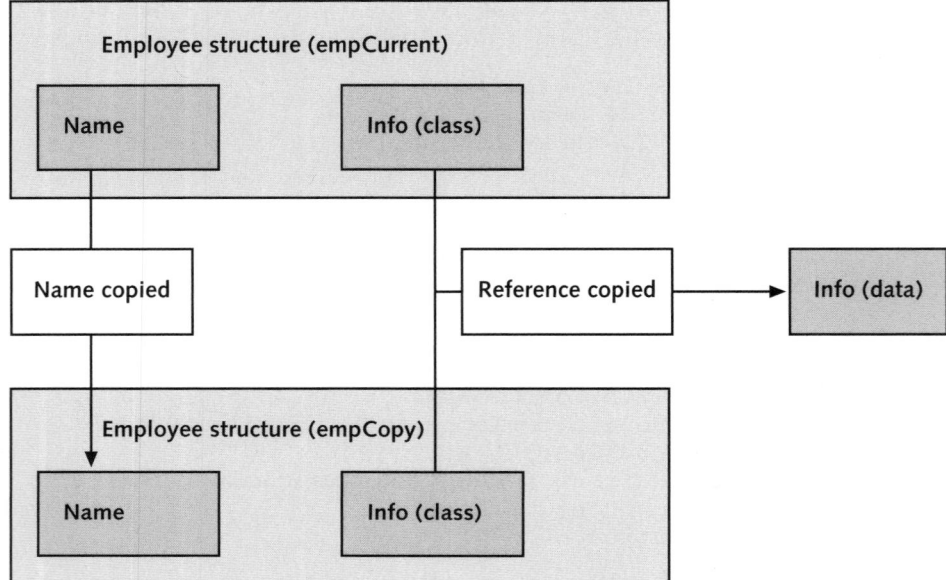

Figure 6-12   Cloning – Shallow copies

In the preceding code segment, new instances of the Employee and PayrollInfo classes are explicitly created, and the data copied from the original objects into the new objects. Thus, two entirely separate copies of the data exist.

You have completed the programming for this chapter. You have seen how to implement several of the interfaces defined by VB .NET, and how to create your own interface that inherits from other interfaces.

CHAPTER SUMMARY

❐ An interface defines a contract. That contract defines the properties and methods that any class or structure must implement. The signatures of the methods in the implementation must exactly match the signatures of the members defined by the interface. One unique characteristic of interfaces is that you do not usually call the members of a class that implements a particular interface. Rather, VB .NET calls these members automatically. For example, VB .NET automatically calls the members of an enumerator as it executes a For Each loop, or the members of the IComparable and IComparer interfaces as it sorts a list.

❐ To implement an interface, include the Implements keyword inside the class or structure declaration. Then, create an implementation for all of the members of that interface. Note that a class or structure may implement multiple interfaces.

❐ To declare an interface, declare a block with the Interface statement. An interface may inherit any number of other interfaces. In the interface block, declare the prototypes for the members that will make up the interface.

❐ One of the simplest interfaces to implement is the IComparable interface. The IComparable interface defines one member named CompareTo. This member accepts one argument of type System.Object. The method should return a negative Integer if the current instance of the class or structure is less than the instance passed as an argument to the CompareTo method. If the current instance is greater than the argument, the method should return a positive Integer. Finally, if the values are equal, the method should return 0.

❐ The purpose of the IComparer interface is similar to the purpose of the IComparable interface. To implement the IComparer interface, you create a nested class. That nested class contains one method named Compare that compares two objects, passed as arguments, for equality or inequality. The value returned by the Compare method is the same as the value returned by the CompareTo method.

❐ To create an enumerator, you implement the IEnumerator and IEnumerable interfaces. The IEnumerable interface defines one member named GetEnumerator. In the GetEnumerator member, you typically return an instance of a second class that implements the IEnumerator interface. The IEnumerator interface defines three members named Current, Reset, and MoveNext. The Current property returns the current object from the list being enumerated. The Reset method, as its name implies, resets the enumerator. By definition, the Reset method should reset the enumerator so that the current index value is one item before the first item. The MoveNext method returns a Boolean value indicating whether or not more items remain in the list to be examined.

❐ Cloning is the process whereby a copy of an object and its data is made from an existing object. A class supports cloning by implementing the Clone method of the ICloneable interface. There exist two types of clones. A shallow copy performs a bit-by-bit copy of a structure or class instance. Thus, the data for value types are copied. However, the data for reference types are not copied. A deep copy copies all of the data for both value types and reference types. Note that the MemberwiseClone method only performs shallow copies. To perform a deep copy, you must write the statements to create an instance of all the necessary objects, and then copy the data for each member.

REVIEW QUESTIONS

1. Which of the following general statements is true about interfaces?

    a. A class can only implement one interface.

    b. When you implement an interface, you can implement a subset of the methods defined by the interface itself. If you omit the code to implement a method, the base method of the interface will be called.

    c. An interface is a contract. When you implement an interface, you must implement all of the members defined by the interface.

    d. An interface cannot have overloaded members.

    e. none of the above

2. Which of the following statements correctly indicates that a class implements the ICloneable and IList interfaces?

    a. Interface ICloneable, IList

    b. Implements Interface ICloneable, IList

    c. Implements ICloneable, IList

    d. Interface.ICloneable, Interface.IList

    e. none of the above

3. Which of the following statements correctly describes the rules for inheriting an interface?

    a. The inheritance rules for interfaces differ from the rules for inheriting classes. While a class can only inherit from one base class, an interface can inherit any number of base interfaces.

    b. Because VB .NET uses a single inheritance model, an interface can only inherit from one base interface.

    c. To inherit an interface, you add the InheritsInterface statement as the first statement in an Interface block.

    d. Interfaces cannot be inherited.

    e. none of the above

4. Which of the following are valid interfaces defined by VB .NET?

    a. IComparable, IComparer, ICollection

    b. Comparable, Compare, Collection

    c. IForm, IControl, IStream

    d. all of the above

    e. none of the above

5. Which of the following statements related to comparing two objects for equality is correct?

   a. You can implement the IComparer or IComparable interfaces, and then call the Sort method of the Array class.

   b. The IComparer and IComparable interfaces are used to compare two objects for equality.

   c. If you implement the IComparable interface, you must provide an implementation for the CompareTo method.

   d. If you implement the IComparer interface, you create a nested class or classes that actually implement IComparer. Each class that implements the IComparer interface must implement the Compare method.

   e. all of the above

6. Which of the following statements is true of the IComparable interface?

   a. It defines one method named CompareLessThan. The CompareLessThan method takes two arguments having a data type of System.Object. It returns the object with the smallest value.

   b. It defines three methods named GreaterThan, LessThan, and EqualTo. Each method returns a Boolean value.

   c. It defines one method named Compare, which returns an Integer.

   d. You can either implement the Compare or CompareTo methods but not both.

   e. none of the above

7. Which of the following statements is true of the IComparer interface?

   a. It defines one method named CompareTo that accepts one argument—the value to compare—and returns a Boolean value True if the objects are equal.

   b. It defines one method named Compare. The Compare method accepts two arguments. The method returns an Integer.

   c. It defines one method named Equal, which returns True if two objects are equal and False otherwise.

   d. It defines two methods named CompareEquality and CompareInequality.

   e. none of the above

8. Which of the following statements is true of an enumerator?

   a. When implementing an enumerator, both the IEnumerable and IEnumerator methods must be implemented.

   b. The IEnumerable interface defines one method named ReturnEnumerator. This method returns the current object in the collection.

   c. The IEnumerator interface inherits the IList interface as a means to return the items in the collection in a sorted order.

   d. all of the above

   e. none of the above

6

9. Which of the following properties and methods must be implemented when implementing the IEnumerable and IEnumerator interfaces?

   a. GetEnumerator

   b. Current, MoveNext, Reset

   c. For, Each

   d. both a and b

   e. all of the above

10. Which of the following statements correctly describes the rules for implementing the IEnumerator interface?

    a. The Current property is a read-only property and should return the current item in the list.

    b. The Reset method should be configured so that it positions the current list item to a value that is one before the first list item.

    c. The MoveNext method returns a Boolean value indicating whether or not there are more items in the list.

    d. all of the above

    e. none of the above

11. What is the name of the statement to declare an interface?

    a. Inherits

    b. Declare Interface

    c. Interface

    d. ImplementInterface

    e. none of the above

12. Which of the following statements is true of the ICloneable interface?

    a. VB .NET automatically calls the Clone method when you assign an object reference.

    b. Unlike most other interfaces, the developer calls the Clone method directly to make a copy of an object.

    c. The ICloneable interface supports two methods named DeepCopy and ShallowCopy.

    d. There exists no interface named ICloneable.

    e. none of the above

13. What is the name of the method that you must implement when you implement the ICloneable interface?

    a. Copy

    b. Create

    c. Clone

    d. IClone

    e. none of the above

14. What is the name of the method that you call to make a shallow copy of an object?

    a. Copy

    b. Clone

    c. MemberwiseClone

    d. ShallowCopy

    e. Duplicate

15. Describe the difference between the IComparer interface and the IComparable interface.

16. Describe the steps to implement a VB .NET interface. In your answer, discuss the inheritance rules surrounding interfaces.

17. Describe the steps to create your own interface.

18. Describe the purpose of an enumerator, and the interfaces required to implement an enumerator. In your answer, be sure to describe the methods of each interface and their purpose.

19. What is the purpose of the MemberwiseClone method?

20. Describe the difference between a deep copy and a shallow copy in relation to cloning.

PROGRAMMING QUESTIONS

1. Write the statements to declare a structure named Inventory, having String members named ID and PartNumber. Write the statements to declare the structure and implement the IComparable interface using PartNumber as the key. Assume that strict type checking is enabled.

2. Write the statements to declare a class named Inventory, having String members named ID, PartNumber, and PartDescription. Write the statements to declare the structure and implement the IComparer interface by creating two nested classes named CompareByID and CompareByPartNumber. The CompareByID class should compare two class instances based on the contents of the ID member, and the CompareByPartNumber class should compare the two class instances based on the PartNumber member. Assume that strict type checking is enabled.

3. Write the statements to declare a class named Question having the following fields: ID (Integer), Name (String), Type (String), Answer (Integer). Write the statements to implement the IComparable interface using ID as the key. Write the statements to implement the IComparer interfaces using methods named CompareByName and CompareByType, choosing the Name and Type fields as key fields, respectively.

4. Write the statements to declare a class named Employee, having String members named EmployeeID, EmployeeName, and EmployeeZipCode. Write the statements to declare nested classes named CompareByID, CompareByName, and CompareByZipCode. Each of these classes should implement the IComparer interface, comparing two objects based on the contents of the respective field.

5. Write the statements to declare an array named Questions, having a data type of Question. Write the statement to create an instance of the CompareByType class (assume that it is a nested class of the Question class that implements the IComparer interface). Write the statements to sort the question list named Questions.

6. Write the statements to declare a class named MyList that implements the ICollection interface.

7. Write the statements to declare an interface named QuestionList that inherits the IList interface.

8. Write the statements to declare a class named QuestionList. The QuestionList class should implement the IEnumerable interface. Create the necessary method in the QuestionList class to implement the method defined by the IEnumerable interface. The method that you create should return an instance of the enumerator named QuestionEnumerator. Assume that the constructor for the QuestionEnumerator class accepts no arguments.

9. Write the statements to declare a class named QuestionEnumerator that implements the IEnumerator interface. Assume that the class contains an array of structures named QuestionList. Enumerate this list.

10. Assume that a class implements the ICollection interface. Write the statement to implement the Count method so that it returns the value of the hidden variable named mintCount.

11. Write the statements to declare a class named MakeList. Write the statement in the class to indicate that the class inherits the ICollection interface.

12. Write the statements to declare an interface named IGetChunk. The interface should inherit the ICollection interface. The interface should define function methods named GetTenth and GetHundredth. The methods should accept no arguments, and return an Integer.

13. Write the statements to declare a class named Demo. Write the statement to call the MemberwiseClone method on the current class instance, storing the result in the variable objCurrent.

14. Write the statements to declare a class named QuestionExists, having members named Name, Description, and Answer, each with a data type of String. Write the statements to implement the Clone method of this class to copy the member data. Do not call the MemberwiseClone method.

HANDS-ON PROJECTS

1. In this project you will create a solution that implements the IComparer and IComparable interfaces. The file named Chapter.06\Exercises06\Ch06Ex1.exe contains the compiled executable application. The corresponding sequential data file is named Chapter.06\Data\Inventory.txt. The solution will read a sequential file into an array of structures. The sequential file contains inventory records. The user will be able to sort the inventory records based on either the part number or the part description. Figure 6-13 shows the completed main form for the solution.

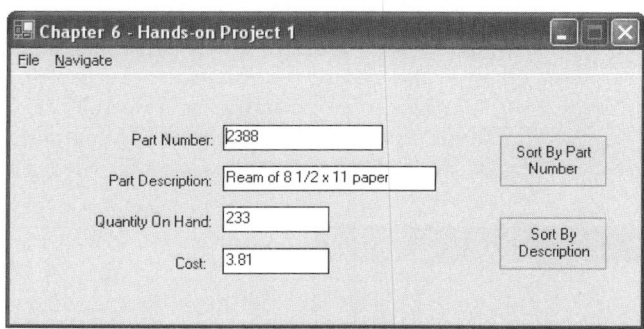

Figure 6-13   Chapter 6 – Hands–on Project 1

a. Start Visual Studio .NET and create a new solution named **Ch06Ex1.sln**.

b. Create a splash screen for the solution.

c. Create the control instances shown in Figure 6-13.

d. Declare a structure named **Inventory**, having the following members and data types: **PartNumber** — Integer, **PartDescription** — String, **OnHand** — Integer, **Cost** — Single.

e. Implement the IComparable interface so that the comparison is performed on the PartNumber field. Enable strict type checking.

f. In the same structure, create a class named **CompareByPartDescription** that will implement the IComparer interface. The method in this class should compare inventory items based on the contents of the PartDescription member.

g. In the form, declare a dynamic array to store the Inventory structures.

h. Create a menu on the form. The **File** menu should have **Open** and **Exit** menu items. The Open menu item should open a sequential file using an OpenFileDialog control instance. Write the necessary statements to open the file, and then read the file into the array that you declared. Write the code for the Exit menu item.

i. Create a menu named **Navigate** with menu items named **First**, **Previous**, **Next**, and **Last**. Write the necessary statements for these menu items to locate the first, previous, next, and last records, respectively.

j. Create a **Sort By Part Number** button on the form. Write the statements to sort the array based on the contents of the PartNumber member. After sorting the array, display the first record in the list.

k. Create a **Sort By Description** button on the form. Write the statements to sort the array based on the contents of the PartDescription member. After sorting the array, display the first record in the list.

2. In this project, you will again create a solution that implements the IComparable and IComparer interfaces. However, the user will be able to perform sorts based on different key fields and sort data in ascending or descending order. In addition, the user will be able to add, change, and delete records from the list. The file named Chapter.06\Exercises06\Ch06Ex2.exe contains the compiled executable application. The corresponding sequential data file is named Chapter.06\Data\Customers.txt. Figure 6-14 shows the completed main form for the solution.

Figure 6-14   Chapter 6 – Hands–on Project 2

a. Start Visual Studio .NET and create a new solution named **Ch06Ex2.sln**.

b. Create a splash screen for the solution.

c. Create the control instances on the main form as shown in Figure 6-14.

d. Declare a structure named **Customer** having the following members and data types: **ID** — Integer, **LastName** — String, **FirstName** — String, **CreditLimit** — Single, **BalanceDue** — Single, **DueDate** — Date, **PastDue** — Boolean.

e. Declare a dynamic array to store the Customer structures.

f. Implement the IComparable interface so that the comparison is performed on the ID member. Enable strict type checking.

g. In the same structure, create a class named **CompareByName** that will perform a comparison on the LastName and FirstName fields concatenated together. This class should implement the IComparer interface.

h. Create two more classes to implement the IComparer interface named **CompareByBalanceDueAsc** and **CompareByBalanceDueDesc**. The first should sort on the BalanceDue field in ascending order. The second should sort on the BalanceDue field in descending order. *Hint:* Reverse the return values for the less than and greater than conditions.

i. Create a menu on the form. The **File** menu should have **Open**, **Save**, and **Exit** menu items. The Open menu item should open a sequential file using an OpenFileDialog control instance. Write the necessary statements to open the file, and then read the file into the array that you declared. Write the necessary statements to save the file. Use an instance of the SaveFileDialog control.

j. Create a menu named **Navigate** with menu items named **First**, **Previous**, **Next**, and **Last**. Write the necessary statements for these menu items to locate the first, previous, next, and last records, respectively. Display the minimum payment. The calculated minimum payment is 5% of the balance due.

k. Create a **Records** menu on the form having menu items named **Add**, **Save Add**, **Change**, **Save Change**, and **Delete**. Write the necessary statements for these menu items to add, change, and delete records. Perform exception handling as necessary. Enable and disable menu items as necessary to prevent the user from attempting to perform an impossible action.

l. Create a **Sort** menu, having menu items named **By ID**, **By Name**, **Ascending Balance Due**, and **Descending Balance Due**.

m. Write the necessary statements to sort the list by ID, by Name, by the BalanceDue field in ascending order, and by the BalanceDue field in descending order.

3. In this project, you will create a solution that implements an enumerator. The file named Chapter.06\Exercises06\Ch06Ex3.exe contains the compiled executable application. The corresponding sequential data file is named Chapter.06\Data\Customers.txt. Figure 6-15 shows the completed main form for the solution.

a. Start Visual Studio .NET and create a new solution named **Ch06Ex3.sln**.

b. Create a splash screen for the solution.

c. Write the statements to declare the **Customer** structure so that it has the same members as the Customer structure in project 2. Override the ToString method as necessary to return all of the members as a comma-separated list.

6

d. Create a class named **CustomerFile** that will implement the IEnumerable interface. The constructor for the CustomerFile class should accept one argument: the name of the file to read.

e. Implement the necessary function in the CustomerFile class that will return the enumerator.

f. Next, create the actual enumerator. Name the class that implements the IEnumerator interface **CustomerFileEnumerator**.

g. Create the methods in the CustomerFileEnumerator class so as to provide the implementation for the interface named IEnumerator.

h. On the main form, write the statements to create an instance of the CustomerFile class, thereby reading the file. Enumerate the instance of the CustomerFile class, displaying the contents in a list box.

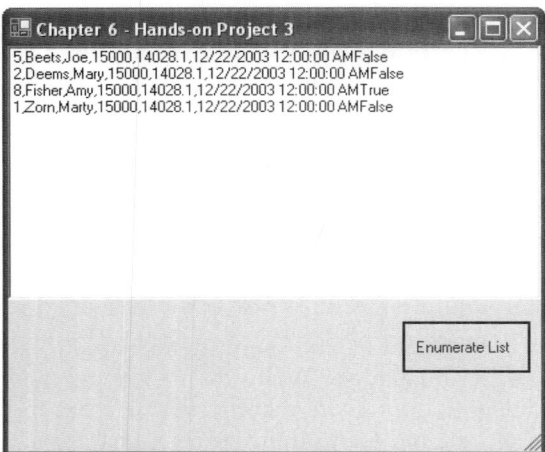

Figure 6-15   Chapter 6 – Hands–on Project 3

4. In this project you will implement the IList interface. Even though the IList interface was not fully discussed in the chapter, the steps to implement IList are the same as the steps to implement any other interface. The file named Chapter.06\Exercises06\Ch06Ex4.exe contains the compiled executable application. The corresponding sequential data file is named Chapter.06\Data\ Customers.txt. This is the same file used in projects two and three.

a. Start Visual Studio .NET and create a new solution named **Ch06Ex4.sln**.

b. Create a splash screen for the solution.

c. Write the statements to declare a **Customer** class such that it has the same members as the Customer structure in Project 2. Override the ToString method as necessary to return all of the members as a comma-separated list.

d. Create an interface named **ICustomerList** that implements the IList interface. Define members named **MoveFirst**, **MovePrevious**, **MoveNext**, and **MoveLast** in the ICustomerList interface. Each of these methods should return an instance of the Customer class.

e. Create a class named **CustomerList** that implements the members of the IList interface along with the members that you just defined. The CustomerList class should implement the ICustomerList interface. The CustomerList class should manage a hidden array of Customer class instances.

f. Create the constructor for the CustomerList class such that it accepts one argument; a file name. When the instance of the CustomerList class gets created, read the sequential file and populate the array.

g. Implement the members required by the IList interface. Refer to the Help system to determine the members defined by IList and the signatures of those members. For example, the Add method required by the IList interface must accept one argument; and object, and returns an Integer. Thus, you must implement this method such that it adds an Employee object to the hidden array. Methods, such as remove, work similarly.

h. Create a form and the necessary control instances to test the CustomerList class that you just created. Make sure that you provide features to add, change, and delete records, and to navigate through the records in the list. The statements that you write on the form should not deal with the sequential file or its data directly. That is, the form should only use the members of the CustomerList class to locate, add, change, and delete records.

6

CHAPTER

7

INTRODUCTION TO ADO.NET

In this chapter, you will:

- Learn about fundamental database concepts
- Understand the OleDbConnection class
- Work with the OleDbDataAdapter class
- Learn about the DataSet class
- Modify data in a DataTable
- Use input validation
- Learn about SQL query parameters
- Record DataSet changes to the database

In preceding chapters, you used sequential files to read and write data. In this chapter, you will use a database to accomplish the task of navigating through data, and adding, changing, and deleting data.

PREVIEWING THE COMPLETED SOLUTION

The completed solution in this chapter uses a single database table to implement an electronic Rolodex. The data for the Rolodex is stored in a database that was created using Microsoft Access.

> The database used in this chapter was created with an Access 2000 file format. The database can be read and processed by both Access 2000 and Access XP. It will not work, however, with previous versions of Access.

Although you will not use Microsoft Access in this chapter, you can open the database in Access to examine the database, its table, and its fields. The database is named Rolodex.mdb, and appears in the Chapter.07\Data folder. It contains a single table named tblNames, having the fields shown in Table 7-1.

Table 7-1   Fields in the table named tblNames

Field Name	VB .NET Data Type	Field Description
fldID	Integer	Identification number
fldFirstName	String	First name
fldLastName	String	Last name
fldDateAdded	DateTime	Date the record was added
fldEstimatedSales	Single	Estimated sales amount
fldActive	Boolean	Active/inactive flag

> This chapter will use the Hungarian notation of "tbl" to denote a database table and "fld" to denote a database field. Using Hungarian names for tables and fields prevents hard-to-find errors resulting from using field names such as Transaction and Sum. Although these are legal variable names, some databases consider these names reserved words thereby causing SQL statements to be evaluated incorrectly.

The completed solution in this chapter contains a single main form. The purpose of the main form is to allow the user to navigate through the records in the table and to add, change, and delete records.

To preview the completed solution:

1. Start Visual Studio .NET. Open and run the solution file named **Chapter.07\Complete07\Complete07.sln**.

2. When the form loads, statements execute to establish a connection between your solution and the database. In addition, the first record is displayed in the form's control instances. Figure 7-1 shows the completed form with the records loaded.

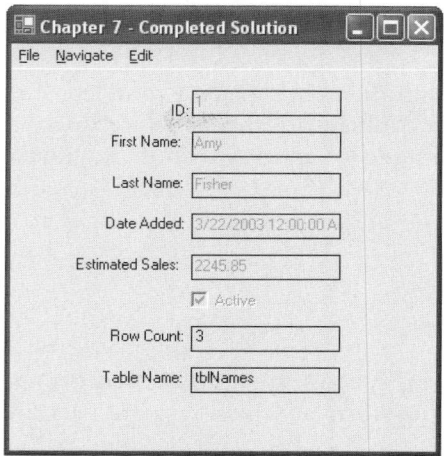

Figure 7-1   Completed solution – main form

3. Using the items on the Navigate menu, click the **Last**, **First**, **Next**, and **Previous** menu items to navigate through the database records.

4. On the main menu, click **Edit**, and then click **Add**. The control instances on the form are enabled and the contents are cleared, allowing you to add a new record. Enter the information shown in Figure 7-2.

Figure 7-2   Adding a record

5. Click **Edit**, and then click **Save Add** to record the change. The control instances are disabled, and the appropriate menu items are enabled and disabled as necessary to prevent the user from trying to perform an invalid action.

6. On the main menu, click **Navigate**, and then click **Last** to locate the record you just added.

7. On the main menu, click **Edit**, and then click **Delete** to delete the record that you just added. Click **Yes** to confirm the change. Note that the menu also allows you to change the contents of existing records and save changes back to the underlying database.

8. Exit the solution, and then exit Visual Studio .NET.

FUNDAMENTAL DATABASE CONCEPTS

Prior to the advent of database management systems, applications that manipulated data did so via a **traditional file-processing system** in which separate data files typically existed for each application. For example, the data for a sales system and an accounts receivable system would be stored in separate files. This approach often resulted in inconsistent data being stored in those different files. For example, a customer's name in one file would often differ from the customer name found in another file. In addition, redundant data were stored in these different files. For example, a customer's address might exist in an accounts receivable file as well as a sales file. To solve the limitations of traditional file-processing systems, most organizations now use database management systems to process their data.

In a database management system, a **database** contains a set of information related to a particular topic or purpose. A database may also store all of the data for a particular organization. In a database, the data are stored inside a table. Most databases contain several tables. Each **table** consists of rows and columns. The column defines the name and the characteristics of the stored information. The columns in a table are called **fields**, and the rows in a table are called **records**.

A variety of software companies such as Microsoft, IBM, and Oracle, manufacture database management systems. VB .NET can operate with any of these database management systems. In this chapter, you will work with the **Microsoft Jet database engine** (also known as Jet or the Jet engine). This is the same database manager used by Microsoft Access.

Properly designing the structure of a database requires an understanding of several key concepts:

- The tables in a database should be organized to eliminate data redundancy. For example, a customer's address should be stored in a database once and only once. This process of eliminating data redundancy is commonly called **normalization**.

- Each row (record) in a table should have a unique index, enabling the code you write to locate a record directly without examining other rows in the table first. This unique index may consist of one or more fields. The unique index for a table is referred to as the **primary key**.

- The data stored in one table are often related to another table in some way. For example, consider a situation where customer information is stored in one table and a unique customer ID (primary key) identifies a customer. Assume that orders pertaining to customers are stored in a different table. In this scenario, the customer ID is stored in both tables and a relationship is defined between the two fields in the two different tables. The customer ID in the second table is known as the **foreign key**. While in this chapter you will work only with a single table, you will work with multiple related tables in Chapter 8.

Fundamentally, ADO.NET operates in two modes: disconnected mode and connected mode.

- In **connected mode**, the developer establishes a connection to a database. Commands are then sent over that connection. Data is returned from the database into another object called a DataReader. Using ADO.NET in connected mode with the DataReader is discussed in Chapter 8.

- In **disconnected mode**, ADO.NET operates much differently. The disconnected DataSet object allows a developer to retrieve data from a database, work with it offline, and then establish a new connection over which changes are sent back to the database. In this chapter, you will explore how to work with ADO.NET in disconnected mode.

Like all other .NET classes, the ADO.NET classes are organized into namespaces. The following list describes selected namespaces and classes that comprise ADO.NET:

- At the heart of ADO.NET is the **System.Data** namespace. This namespace contains all the other namespaces and classes used to manage data for several types of databases, including Jet (Microsoft Access) and SQL Server.

- The **System.Data.Common** namespace contains additional classes that are shared by both Jet and SQL Server databases. That is, different providers share the classes in the System.Data.Common namespace.

- The **System.Data.OleDb** namespace contains the classes to send and receive data between your application and the database using a software component known as a generic provider. Generic providers operate with many databases, including Microsoft Access, SQL Server, and Oracle. It is the responsibility of the provider to accept requests to retrieve or update database data, process those requests, and return any data back to your application.

- The classes of the **System.Data.SqlClient** namespace work only with SQL Server databases. While the classes of the System.Data.OleDb namespace can also be used with SQL Server databases, the performance of the classes in the SqlClient namespace is significantly better.

- The **System.Data.SqlTypes** namespace contains classes that map native SQL Server data types to .NET Framework data types. Using OleDb, this type conversion is performed using the **System.Data.OleDbType** enumeration.

- The **System.XML** class, while not explicitly part of ADO.NET, contains the classes used to read, write, and parse XML data. ADO.NET uses XML to transport other objects, such as DataSets, between client and server.

As you progress through this chapter and Chapter 8, you will examine the preceding namespaces and classes.

Visual Studio .NET and ADO.NET supply several ways to create applications that work with a database, as described in the following list:

- The Data Form Wizard will create a form with all of the necessary code to establish a database connection, display that data in control instances appearing on the form, and update that data.

- You can also use controls appearing on the Data tab of the Toolbox to establish that same database connection and to update database data.

- Alternatively, you can create all of the necessary ADO.NET objects programmatically.

In this chapter, so that you can best understand how ADO.NET works, you will create the entire application programmatically without the aid of the Data Form Wizard or the Toolbox controls. In Chapter 8, you will learn how to use the Toolbox controls.

In this chapter, you will use the following .NET Framework classes to create an ADO.NET application:

- The **OleDbConnection** class of the System.Data.OleDb namespace allows you to establish a database connection over which commands are sent to retrieve and update data.

- The **OleDbDataAdapter** class of the System.Data.OleDb namespace is responsible for sending SQL statements over an OleDbConnection and loading any data returned into another object called a DataSet. The OleDbDataAdapter also sends commands over an OleDbConnection to add, change, and delete records.

- The **DataSet** class of the System.Data namespace stores an in-memory representation of the data returned through the OleDbDataAdapter.

- The **DataTable** class of the System.Data namespace is tightly coupled with a DataSet. A DataTable corresponds to a database table appearing in a DataSet.

As creating and opening a connection is the first step in retrieving data from a database, we discuss the OleDbConnection class first.

THE OLEDBCONNECTION CLASS

To send and receive data from a database using ADO.NET, you first establish a connection to that database. A **connection** is nothing more than a pipeline between your client application and ADO.NET, and is used in both connected and disconnected mode. Another software component, known as a provider, processes the commands sent over a connection. A **provider** receives requests to retrieve or update database data, processes those requests, and optionally returns data to the client solution. Figure 7-3 illustrates the relationship between a client solution, a connection and provider, and the database.

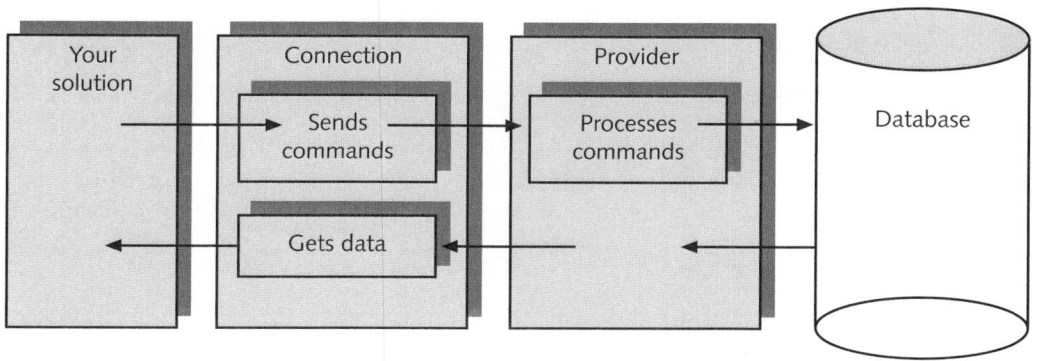

Figure 7-3   Connection relationships

The Connection Classes in ADO.NET

ADO.NET supplies two classes to create a connection. The first is the generic OleDbConnection class, which creates connections that operate with different types of databases including Microsoft Access (Jet), SQL Server, and Oracle. The second class, SqlConnection, operates only with SQL Server and is optimized for performance. In this chapter, we discuss the OleDbConnection class.

VB .NET allows you to create an instance of the OleDbConnection class using the OleDbConnection control appearing on the Data tab of the Toolbox, or to create a connection programmatically. In this chapter, you will create the connection programmatically. The OleDbConnection class supports the following members:

Syntax

System.Data.OleDb.OleDbConnection class

Definition

The OleDbConnection class is used to establish a database connection over which data is sent and received.

Public Properties

- The **ConnectionString** property, as the name implies, contains a String that the OleDbConnection class uses to establish the database connection. The contents of the ConnectionString will vary based on the type of database you are using. For example, the ConnectionString will differ depending on whether you are using Jet or SQL Server. The syntax of the ConnectionString will be discussed in a moment.

- The **ConnectionTimeout** property contains an Integer that defines how long the provider will wait to establish a connection. If the value is set to 0, the connection will wait indefinitely. The default value is 15 (15 seconds). If you try to set the ConnectionTimeout property to a value less than 0, then a System.ArgumentException will occur.

- The **State** property gets the current state of the connection. Specifically, you use the State property to determine whether the connection is open or closed. The data type of the State property is ConnectionState. With the first release of ADO.NET, the only possible values for the ConnectionState property are Open and Closed. Future releases of ADO.NET will support additional connection states.

Public Methods

- The **Close** method closes an open connection.

- The **Open** method reads the contents of the ConnectionString property, sends a request to a provider, and then opens a connection. Some classes, such as OleDbDataAdapter, will open a connection automatically.

- The **BeginTransaction** method starts a database transaction.

- The **ChangeDatabase** method operates on an open connection and changes the database for that connection.

Public Events

- Windows fires the **StateChanged** event when the state of the connection changes. That is, when the connection opens or closes, the StateChanged event fires. The second argument of the StateChanged event is of type StateChangedEventArgs. Its properties contain the current and previous state of the connection.

Creating a Connection Programmatically

To create a connection, you first create an instance of the OleDbConnection class, and then configure the ConnectionString property. The ConnectionString property contains a list of key/value pairs. An equals sign separates each key from its corresponding value, and a semicolon separates each key/value pair.

Examine the following statements that create an instance of the OleDbConnection class and set the ConnectionString property:

```
Private mconCurrent As New OleDbConnection()
mconCurrent.ConnectionString = _
    "Provider=Microsoft.Jet.OLEDB.4.0;" _ &
    "Password="""";User ID=Admin;" _ &
    "Data Source=C:\Rolodex.mdb"
```

The first of the preceding statements creates an instance of the OleDbConnection class named mconCurrent. The second statement configures the ConnectionString property by defining the necessary key/value pairs. As shown in the preceding code segment, the first key is named Provider, and the corresponding value is Microsoft.Jet.OLEDB.4.0. This key/value pair defines the provider that the connection will use to interact with the database. The second and third keys are Password and User ID, respectively. These keys and values supply security information for the connection. The fourth key is Data Source, and the value for that key is C:\Rolodex.mdb. The Data Source key defines the database to which the connection will be established. Thus, in the preceding ConnectionString, the database named Rolodex.mdb is assumed to exist in the root directory on the C: drive. Note the semicolon separating each key/value pair.

 For simplicity, the database that you are using in this chapter has no password. By default, all Access databases have a user name of Admin. Furthermore, the preceding ConnectionString is simplified. There exist several additional key/value pairs that control how the database and connection will be shared by other users, and other key/value pairs that define security information.

You will now create a connection programmatically by declaring a variable of type OleDbConnection, and then configuring the ConnectionString property.

To create a connection programmatically:

1. Start Visual Studio .NET, and then open the solution named **Chapter.07\Startup07\Startup07.sln**.

2. Activate the Code Editor for the form named **frmMain.vb**, if necessary, and then enter the following statement (shown in bold) immediately after the Windows Forms Designer generated code to create an instance of the OleDbConnection class. For brevity, the System.Data, System.DataCommon, and System.Data.OleDb namespaces have already been imported into the startup solution.

```
Windows Form Designer generated code
Private mconCurrent As New OleDbConnection()
```

3. Enter the following statements in the **InitializeDatabase** procedure. Note that the statement to call this procedure has already been created in the form's Load event handler.

```
mconCurrent.ConnectionString = _
    "Provider=Microsoft.Jet.OLEDB.4.0;" & _
    "Data Source=..\..\Data\Rolodex.mdb"
```

The statements that you just entered define a connection. The ConnectionString property sets the Provider key to connect to a Jet database, and the Data Source key to connect to the database named Rolodex.mdb. Note that the directory name is '..\..\Data'. (Remember that '..' means the parent directory of the current directory.) Thus, for the application to locate the database, the database must appear in the Chapter.07\Data directory, because the working directory for your solution is Chapter.07\Startup07\bin. Depending on how you have organized the files on your computer, change this directory name as necessary.

 The syntax of connection strings varies from one provider to another. The ConnectionString for an Oracle database will differ from the ConnectionString for a Jet database. Furthermore, the ConnectionString will also vary for a SQL Server database. Refer to the supplier of the database that you are using to configure the ConnectionString properly.

Sending Requests over a Connection

Having created the database connection, the next step is to send requests over that connection to select data. In general, ADO.NET supplies two means to retrieve data over a connection:

- Using the DataReader class, data is read through an input stream much in the same way that data is read using the StreamReader class discussed in Chapter 5. The DataReader is discussed in Chapter 8.

- The OleDbDataAdapter class retrieves data from one or more database tables into another object called a DataSet, which contains an in-memory representation of the data contained in those tables. To retrieve the data into the DataSet, the OleDbDataAdapter automatically opens the connection as necessary, and then reads database data into the DataSet on the client computer. When the data has been read, the OleDbDataAdapter automatically closes the connection. The user then makes additions, changes, and deletions to the disconnected DataSet on the client computer. When the modifications are complete, the OleDbDataAdapter reopens the connection, sends the changes back to the database, and then closes the connection again.

In this chapter, we discuss how to create an OleDbDataAdapter and how to use the OleDbDataAdapter to select data from the database into a DataSet. First we discuss the OleDbDataAdapter class, and then we discuss the DataSet class.

THE OLEDBDATAADAPTER CLASS

The OleDbDataAdapter class sends SQL statements over a connection to a provider for processing. That provider then returns the records retrieved from a query to the OleDbDataAdapter. The OleDbDataAdapter, in turn, populates a DataSet, or in the case of a query that does not return records, a provider returns whether the request succeeded or failed. Figure 7-4 illustrates the role of the OleDbDataAdapter.

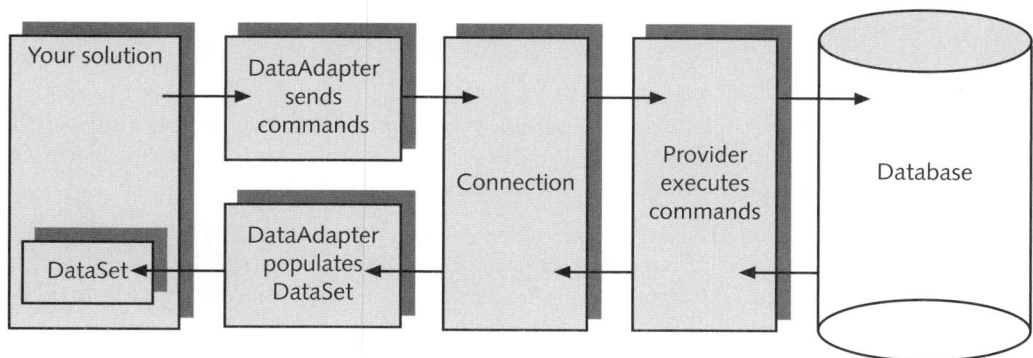

Figure 7-4   Role of the OleDbDataAdapter

As shown in Figure 7-4, the OleDbDataAdapter sends commands over a connection for processing, and then retrieves that returned data and populates another object called a DataSet. As you will see later in the chapter, the OleDbDataAdapter also supplies the means to add new rows, change the contents of existing rows, and delete rows from the database. The OleDbDataAdapter works in conjunction with the DataSet class to accomplish all of these tasks.

The OleDbDataAdapter supports the following members:

Syntax

System.Data.OleDb.OleDbDataAdapter class

Public Properties

- The OleDbDataAdapter retrieves data by sending a SQL SELECT statement over a connection. The syntax of the SQL SELECT statement will be discussed in a moment. This SELECT statement is stored in the **SelectCommand** property. The OleDbDataAdapter automatically opens the connection as necessary, and then calls upon the provider to execute the SELECT statement. The records returned by the SELECT statement are then stored into a DataSet.

- The **InsertCommand** property stores a SQL INSERT statement that will insert a row into a database table. Again, the OleDbDataAdapter automatically opens the connection and sends the INSERT statement to the provider for processing. Unlike the SELECT statement, the INSERT statement does not return any records.

- The **UpdateCommand** property stores a SQL UPDATE statement to update the contents of an existing row in a database table.

- The **DeleteCommand** property stores a SQL DELETE statement that will remove a row from a database table.

- The **TableMappings** property maps names between the underlying database table and the DataTable object contained by a DataSet.

Public Methods

- The **Fill** method uses an OleDbConnection to retrieve database records, and then store them in a DataSet. The database records retrieved are based on the SQL SELECT statement stored in the SelectCommand property.

- The **Update** method examines the DataSet for any added, changed, or deleted records. The SQL statements stored in the InsertCommand, UpdateCommand, and DeleteCommand properties are then used to make the modifications to the underlying database table.

Public Events

- The **FillError** event fires if an error occurs while populating the DataSet.

- The **RowUpdating** event fires just before an attempt is made to update a row in the data source (database).

- The **RowUpdated** event fires just after a row in the data source is updated.

The OleDbCommand Class

Before creating an OleDbDataAdapter and DataSet, the SelectCommand, InsertCommand, UpdateCommand, and DeleteCommand properties warrant a detailed discussion. Each of the preceding four properties has a data type of OleDbCommand, which supports the following members:

Syntax

System.Data.OleDb.OleDbCommand class

Public Properties

- The **CommandText** property stores a SQL statement that will be executed against a provider. This SQL statement can be an INSERT, UPDATE, DELETE, or SELECT statement.

- The **Connection** property stores a reference to an existing OleDbConnection object. Note that the connection need not be open, as the OleDbDataAdapter will open and close the connection as necessary.

- The **Parameters** property stores a reference to a Parameters collection. For each parameter in the Parameters collection, the OleDbDataAdapter dynamically fills in the data that is used to add, change, or delete a database record. The Parameters collection is discussed in detail later in the chapter.

Public Methods

- The **ExecuteNonQuery** method executes a SQL statement that does not return database rows.

- The **ExecuteReader** method creates a DataReader. Chapter 8 discusses the DataReader class.

- The **ExecuteScalar** method executes a SELECT statement. It returns the first column of the first row retrieved by the SELECT statement.

Examine the following statements to create an instance of the OleDbCommand class and configure it:

```
Private modbcmdSelect As New OleDbCommand()
modbcmdSelect.CommandText = "SELECT * FROM tblNames"
modbcmdSelect.Connection = modbconCurrent
```

The preceding statements first create an instance of the OleDbCommand class. The System.Data.OleDb namespace has been imported for brevity. Next, the CommandText property stores the SQL SELECT statement. Finally, the Connection property is set to modbconCurrent. This variable is assumed to store an instance of the OleDbConnection class.

When changes made to a DataSet need to be recorded to the database, the OleDbDataAdapter sends the necessary INSERT, UPDATE, and DELETE statements over the connection. The provider then executes those statements to update the data as necessary. The topic of updating data is discussed in detail later in the chapter.

Creating an OleDbDataAdapter Programmatically

Just as you can create an OleDbConnection with a control or programmatically, you can also create an OleDbDataAdapter with a control or programmatically. In this chapter, you will learn how to create and configure the OleDbDataAdapter programmatically.

You configure the OleDbDataAdapter by writing SQL statements and storing those statements in the respective SelectCommand, InsertCommand, UpdateCommand, and DeleteCommand properties. The overloaded constructor for the OleDbDataAdapter class allows you to supply an optional SQL statement, an existing connection, or a ConnectionString causing the OleDbDataAdapter to create the connection dynamically.

First you will learn how to select data using the OleDbDataAdapter. Before creating the statements to select data, however, we first explore the syntax of the SQL SELECT statement:

Syntax

SELECT * | *fieldlist* **FROM** *tablename* **WHERE** *conditionlist* **ORDER BY** *fieldlist*

Definition

The SQL **SELECT** statement selects one or more rows (records) from a database table or query.

Dissection

- The *fieldlist* argument specifies the field(s) to select from the database table and contains a comma-separated list of field names. To select all of the fields, use an asterisk in place of the field names.

- The *tablename* argument contains the name of the database table or query from which data will be selected.

- The **WHERE** *conditionlist* argument contains a condition used to restrict the rows selected and resembles the condition in an If statement. Creating conditions is discussed in more detail later in the chapter.

- The **ORDER BY** *fieldlist* argument contains a comma-separated list. This list contains the field names that the SELECT statement will use to sort the data.

Code Example

```
SELECT * FROM tblNames ORDER BY fldLastName
SELECT * FROM tblNames ORDER BY fldLastName, fldFirstName
SELECT fldFirstName, fldLastName FROM tblNames
```

Code Dissection

The first of the preceding SQL SELECT statements selects all of the fields from the table named tblNames. The records are sorted by the contents of the field fldLastName. Note that all of the rows are selected because the WHERE clause is omitted. The second SELECT statement retrieves all of the rows from the same table and sorts them by the field named fldLastName. If two records have the same value for the last name, then those records are further sorted by the field named fldFirstName. The final statement selects only the fields named fldFirstName and fldLastName from the table.

In the preceding syntax diagram, the SQL keywords appeared in all upper case characters. Although SQL keywords typically appear in upper case characters, this capitalization scheme is not required. The SQL language itself, like VB .NET, is a case insensitive language.

The WHERE clause appears in a SQL statement to restrict the rows that are selected, updated, or deleted. The condition in a WHERE clause has roughly the same syntax as the condition in an If statement, as shown in the following code segment:

```
SELECT * FROM tblNames WHERE fldID = 3
```

The preceding statement illustrates the use of a WHERE clause. The statement returns only those records where the contents of the field named fldID are equal to 3. Because the field named fldID is the primary key in the table named tblNames, the SELECT statement will return at most one record. A WHERE clause can be more complex, containing comparison and logical operators, as shown in the following statement:

```
SELECT * FROM tblNames WHERE fldID > 1 AND fldID < 10
```

The preceding statement selects only those records where the contents of the field named fldID are greater than 1 and less than 10. The ORDER BY clause can also appear in a SELECT statement containing a WHERE clause, as follows:

```
SELECT * FROM tblNames WHERE fldID > 1 AND fldID < 10 ORDER
BY fldLastName
```

The preceding statement selects the same records but sorts those records by the field named fldLastName.

In the preceding statements the field in the WHERE clause was numeric. However, if a field has a data type of String, then the string is enclosed in single quotation marks. Date values are enclosed in pound signs. See the following statements:

```
SELECT * FROM tblNames WHERE fldLastName = 'Smith'
SELECT * FROM tblNames WHERE fldDate = #12/22/2003#
```

As this book is not designed to be a tutorial on the SQL language, we will explore only the most elemental SQL syntax and features.

Configuring the OleDbDataAdapter Programmatically

Just as you created and configured an instance of the OleDbConnection class programmatically, you will also configure the OleDbDataAdapter programmatically. First, you will declare the OleDbDataAdapter and the necessary OleDbCommand objects that will store the SELECT, INSERT, UPDATE, and DELETE statements.

To configure an OleDbDataAdapter programmatically:

1. Activate the Code Editor for the form named **frmMain.vb**, and then enter the following statements (shown in bold) after the code generated by the Win Forms Designer:

```
Private mconCurrent As New OleDbConnection()
Private modbdaCurrent As New OleDbDataAdapter()
Private modbcmdSelect As New OleDbCommand()
Private modbcmdInsert As New OleDbCommand()
Private modbcmdUpdate As New OleDbCommand()
Private modbcmdDelete As New OleDbCommand()
Private dsCurrent As New DataSet()
Private WithEvents dtNames As DataTable
```

The first of the preceding statements creates an instance of the OleDbDataAdapter class. The next four statements create the four instances of the OleDbCommand class that will store the SELECT, INSERT, UPDATE, and DELETE statements. The final two statements declare variables named dsCurrent and dtNames to store the DataSet and DataTable, respectively.

2. Enter the following statements (shown in bold) at the end of the **InitializeDatabase** procedure to configure the OleDbDataAdapter and the OleDbCommand objects for the SELECT statement:

```
mconCurrent.ConnectionString = . . .
modbcmdSelect.CommandText = "SELECT * FROM tblNames " & _
    "ORDER BY fldLastName"
modbcmdSelect.Connection = mconCurrent
modbdaCurrent.SelectCommand = modbcmdSelect
```

The preceding statements store the SELECT statement in the OleDbCommand object named modbcmdSelect, and associate that OleDbCommand object with the connection named mconCurrent. The final statement stores the OleDbCommand object in the SelectCommand property of the OleDbDataAdapter.

At this point, you have configured the OleDbDataAdapter to retrieve all of the records from the database table named tblNames. The records will be returned in ascending order by the field named fldLastName. Again, these statements do not actually retrieve the records from the database into the DataSet. Rather, they merely configure the OleDbDataAdapter to select the records.

Table Mappings

By default, when you populate the DataSet, the OleDbDataAdapter names the first table in the DataSet "Table," the second table in the DataSet "Table1," and so on. However, you will likely want to reference the table using a more intuitive name. Naming tables is one purpose of the DataTableMapping class. The DataTableMapping class supports the following properties:

- The **ColumnMappings** property contains a reference to a DataColumnMappingCollection. This collection maps column names in much the same way that the DataTableMapping class maps table names. When a DataTable is mapped, the columns in the table are mapped automatically.

- The **DataSetTable** property contains a String. This String defines the table name, as it will be known in the DataSet.

- The **SourceTable** property contains the source table that will be mapped, for example Table or Table1.

As the developer, you have considerable flexibility in how you create a DataTableMapping. You can either supply arguments to the constructor or you can set the properties one at a time. Examine the following code segment to create a DataTableMapping:

```
Dim dtmtblNames As DataTableMapping
dtmtblNames = modbdaCurrent.TableMappings.Add( _
    "Table", "tblNames")
```

The preceding statements call the Add method of the TableMappings collection to create a DataTableMapping object. The DataTableMapping object maps the default table named "Table" to the name "tblNames." Thus, when the OleDbDataAdapter fills the DataSet, the table will be named tblNames instead of Table. The following statements illustrate a second technique to accomplish the same task:

```
Dim dtmtblNames As New DataTableMapping("Table", _
    "tblNames")
modbdaCurrent.TableMappings.Add(dtmtblNames)
```

The first of the preceding statements creates a DataTableMapping instance, and the second statement adds that DataTableMapping object to the OleDbDataAdapter's TableMappings collection.

Having seen how to create a SQL SELECT statement and an OleDbDataAdapter, you will now write the code to map the table.

To create a DataTableMapping object in the TableMappings collection:

1. In the form named **frmMain.vb**, enter the following statements (shown in bold) at the end of the **InitializeDatabase** procedure:

```
modbdaCurrent.SelectCommand = modbcmdSelect
Dim dtmtblNames As DataTableMapping
dtmtblNames = modbdaCurrent.TableMappings.Add("Table", _
    "tblNames")
```

At this point, you have created and configured an OleDbDataAdapter so that it will retrieve all of the records from the table named tblNames. Next, you will see how to use the OleDbDataAdapter to load data into the DataSet.

Filling the OleDbDataAdapter

After the OleDbDataAdapter has been configured, calling the overloaded Fill method populates the DataSet. The OleDbDataAdapter fills the DataSet by opening the connection and sending the SQL SELECT statement stored in the SelectCommand property to the provider for execution. The provider then compiles and executes that SELECT statement and optionally returns records to the OleDbDataAdapter in the form of a DataSet. Figure 7-5 illustrates the process.

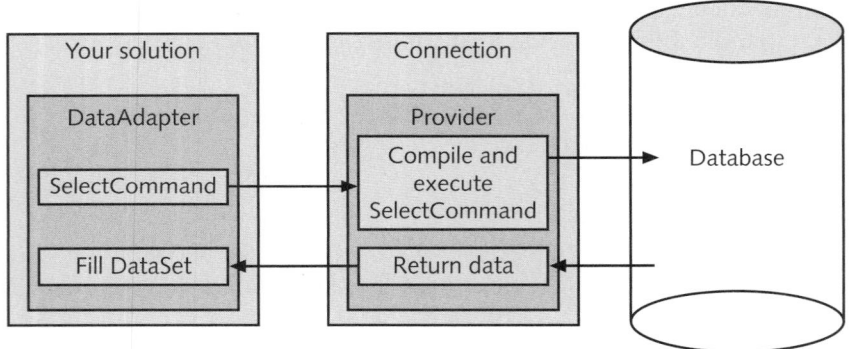

Figure 7-5   Relationship between a DataSet, DataTables, and DataColumns

The overloaded Fill method has the following syntax:

Syntax

System.Data.OleDb.OleDbDataAdapter.Fill method

Overrides Overloads Public Function Fill(ByVal *DataSet* **As DataSet) As Integer**
Overloads Public Function Fill(ByVal DataSet As *DataSet***, ByVal** *SrcTable* **As String) As Integer**

Dissection

- The first overloaded method accepts one argument: the *DataSet* to fill.

- The second overloaded method is similar to the first. It accepts a second argument containing the name of a particular table to fill. Note that additional overloaded methods exist beyond those presented here.

Code Example

```
Dim modbdaCurrent As New OleDbDataAdapter()
Dim dsCurrent As New DataSet()
' Statements to configure the DataAdapter
modbdaCurrent.Fill(dsCurrent)
modbdaCurrent.Fill(dsCurrent, "tblNames")
```

Code Dissection

The preceding statements create an instance of the OleDbDataAdapter and DataSet classes. The statements to configure the OleDbDataAdapter and SelectCommand property have been omitted for brevity. The final two statements call the Fill method of the OleDbDataAdapter. The first statement uses one argument: the name of the DataSet to populate. The second statement specifies that the DataTable in the DataSet will be named tblNames. Note that this second technique allows you to omit creating the DataTableMapping object for the OleDbDataAdapter, because the table name is explicitly defined when the DataSet gets filled.

7

Having configured the OleDbDataAdapter to select database records, and having mapped the database table, you can now populate the DataSet by calling the Fill method of the OleDbDataAdapter.

To populate a DataSet using the OleDbDataAdapter:

1. Enter the following statement (shown in bold) at the end of the **InitializeDatabase** procedure:

```
dtmtblNames = modbdaCurrent.TableMappings.Add( _
    "Table", "tblNames")
modbdaCurrent.Fill(dsCurrent)
```

If you were to test the solution at this point, the DataSet would be populated. However, you have yet to write the statements to display the data on the form's control instances, or process the data in the DataSet in any way.

By calling the Fill method of the OleDbDataAdapter, you have populated the DataSet named dsCurrent. This DataSet contains an in-memory representation of the data in the underlying database table. Next, you will see how to reference the data contained in the DataSet.

INTRODUCING THE DATASET CLASS

As mentioned, ADO.NET works in either a connected or disconnected mode. The DataSet object represents a disconnected view of the data stored in one or more database tables. The DataSet provides a rich set of features, as described in the following list:

- You can sort the data appearing in a DataSet based on the contents of one or more columns.

- You can search through the rows in a DataSet searching for a particular row based on specific criteria.

- The DataSet is designed to store and manage hierarchical data. For example, the DataSet can be configured to perform operations on multiple tables used in one-to-many relationships.

DataSets can be roughly categorized into untyped and typed DataSets. In order to reference the tables and fields in an untyped DataSet, you must reference the tables and fields through their corresponding collections. For example, a DataSet supplies a collection named Tables. The Tables collection contains a reference to each DataTable in the DataSet. Untyped DataSets are discussed in the following section. A typed DataSet is derived from the System.Data.DataSet class. This class contains additional properties and methods, allowing you to reference tables and fields directly, by name, without having to reference the underlying collection. Typed DataSets are discussed in Chapter 8.

The following list describes the members of the DataSet class:

Syntax

System.Data.DataSet class

Public Properties

- The Boolean **CaseSensitive** property controls whether String comparisons are made in a case sensitive or case insensitive way. For example, if the CaseSensitive property were set to True, then the values "Course" and "course" would be different values. By default, the CaseSensitive property is set to False.

- The **DataSetName** property defines the name of the DataSet. The default name for a DataSet is "NewDataSet."

- A DataSet may contain constraints. A constraint is simply a rule defined for a particular piece of data that may not be violated. For example, a constraint may be defined that prohibits two rows from having the same value for a particular field. The **EnforceConstraints** property defines whether ADO.NET checks these rules when adding, changing, or deleting data.

- The **Tables** property returns the collection of DataTable objects in the DataSet. Each item in the Tables collection has a data type of DataTable. A DataSet contains one or more tables.

Public Methods

- As you make changes to a DataSet's data, records are marked as new, changed, or deleted. Calling the **AcceptChanges** method causes any changed records to be marked as unchanged records. The AcceptChanges method is typically called just after the changed data is recorded to the database to synchronize the DataSet with the database.

- The **Clear** method removes all rows from all tables in the DataSet.

- The **Clone** method makes a copy of the DataSet schema (structure). The data, however, is not copied. Cloning was discussed in Chapter 6.

- The **Copy** method copies both the schema and the data from a DataSet, thereby creating an exact copy of the original DataSet.

- The overloaded **GetChanges** method examines an existing DataSet and returns a new DataSet containing the changed records. Depending on the arguments specified, you can get all modified records, added records, changed records, or deleted records.

- The **HasChanges** method returns a Boolean value indicating whether the DataSet has pending changes. Thus, the HasChanges method will return False immediately after the AcceptChanges method has been called.

- The **RejectChanges** method causes any pending changes to be cancelled, restoring any data to their original values.

When the DataAdapter executes a SQL SELECT statement and retrieves rows into the DataSet, those rows are stored in another object called a DataTable. The Tables collection of the DataSet class contains a reference to each DataTable object contained in the DataSet. Each DataTable can be referenced through the Tables collection via a numeric index or string key, as shown in the following statements:

```
Private dtNames As DataTable
dtNames = dsCurrent.Tables(0)
dtNames = dsCurrent.Tables("tblNames")
```

Previously in the chapter, you set the TableMapping object so that the table named Table would be known as tblNames in the DataSet named dsCurrent. Thus, the preceding statements will both store a reference to the same DataTable in the variable dtNames. The first statement uses a numeric index and the second statement uses the string key tblNames.

The DataTable Class

A DataSet object typically contains one or more DataTable objects. Each DataTable, in turn, contains one or more DataColumn objects representing the columns in the under-lying table. A DataColumn does not contain the data, but rather contains information about the column such as its data type. Figure 7-6 illustrates the relationship between a DataSet, its DataTables, and its DataColumns.

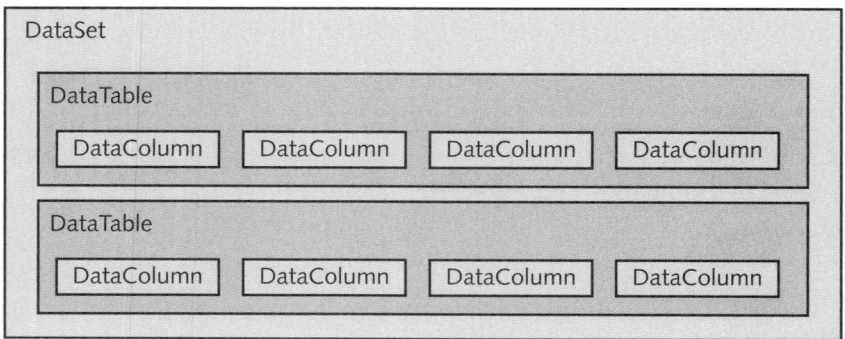

Figure 7-6   Relationship between a DataSet, DataTables, and DataColumns

The following syntax diagram lists the members of the DataTable class. Note that many of these members are shared by both the DataSet and DataTable classes:

Syntax

System.Data.DataTable class

Public Properties

- By default, the **CaseSensitive** property of the DataTable has the same value as the CaseSensitive property of the parent DataSet. Setting the CaseSensitive property for a specific DataTable does not affect the other DataTable objects in the DataSet, however, or the CaseSensitive property for the DataSet itself.

- The **Columns** property contains a reference to a DataColumnCollection. This col-lection, in turn, provides the reference to the DataColumn objects in the DataTable.

- Errors may occur as records are added, changed, or deleted from a DataTable. Those changes may result in errors when attempting to update the database. The Boolean **HasErrors** property is set to True if any of the rows contain errors.

- The **PrimaryKey** property contains Nothing if no primary key is defined. If a pri-mary key is defined, it contains an array of DataColumn objects. Each DataColumn object, in turn, corresponds to a column in the DataTable. The purpose of the PrimaryKey property is to define the field or fields that uniquely identify a row. No two rows may have the same value for the PrimaryKey. The PrimaryKey property is used primarily when calling the Find method of the Rows collection to locate a particular DataRow based on the value of its key.

- The **Rows** property is a collection having a data type of DataRowCollection. Each object in the collection corresponds to a DataRow in the underlying DataTable. Through the Rows property, you reference the individual rows containing the table's data.

Public Method

- The **NewRow** method creates a new DataRow object using the schema information obtained from the DataTable itself. Calling the NewRow method creates a new DataRow object with the same number of DataColumn objects as exist in the DataTable.

Public Events

- The **ColumnChanging** event fires just before a new value is stored in a particular column. The second argument to the ColumnChanging event has a data type of System.ColumnChangeEventArgs.

- The **ColumnChanged** event fires after a value is stored in a column, meaning, the ColumnChanged event fires after the ColumnChanging event.

- The **RowChanging** event fires before a new value is stored in a row. When the event fires depends on whether the BeginEdit method was called or not. If the BeginEdit method was not called, the event fires as each column is edited and after the ColumnChanging event fires. Thus, as you attempt to change the values of multiple columns in the same row, the RowChanging event will fire as a change is made to each column. When using the BeginEdit and EndEdit methods, the RowChanging event fires only when the EndEdit method is called.

- The **RowChanged** event fires after a new value has been stored in a row.

Each DataTable object contains a Rows collection. This Rows collection represents the rows in the DataTable and has a data type of DataRowCollection. The following statements illustrate how to reference the first row in the DataTable named tblNames:

```
Private dtNames As DataTable
Private drCurrent As DataRow
dtNames = dsCurrent.Tables("tblNames")
drCurrent = dtNames.Rows(0)
```

The first and second statements declare variables of type DataTable and DataRow. The third statement uses the Tables collection of the DataSet named dsCurrent to obtain a reference to the DataTable. The final statement stores the first row in the DataTable into the variable drCurrent. Note that like most collections, the Rows collection is 0-based. Figure 7-7 illustrates the relationship between a DataTable and the Rows collection.

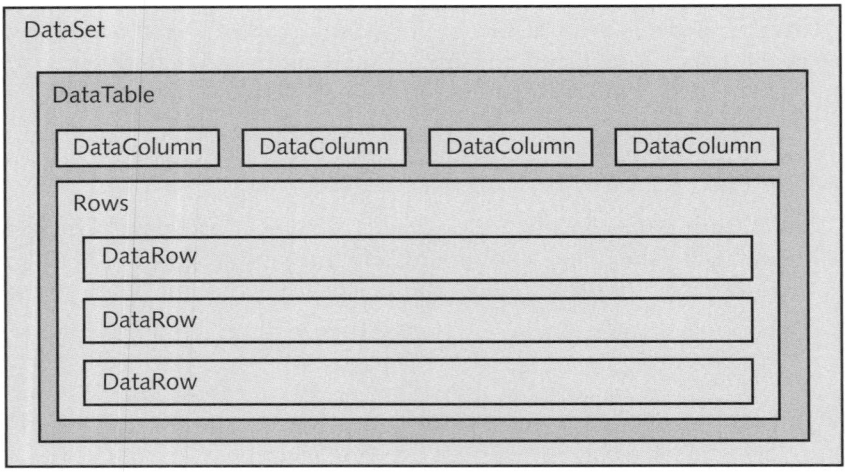

Figure 7-7   Relationship between a DataTable and its Rows collection

As shown in Figure 7-7, a DataTable contains one Rows collection. The Rows collection contains one DataRow for each record in the DataTable. The DataRowCollection, like most collections, supports methods to add, remove, and locate items (rows) in the collection, as described in the following syntax diagram:

Syntax

System.Data.DataRowCollection class

Public Properties

- The **Count** property gets the number of rows in the collection (records in the DataTable).

- The **Item** property returns a row having the specified index. Remember that the collection is 0-based, so the first row has an index of 0.

Public Methods

- The **Add** method adds a new DataRow to the end of the Rows collection.

- The **Clear** method removes all of the DataRow objects from the Rows collection, thereby removing all of the rows from the underlying DataTable itself.

- The **Find** method locates a single DataRow in the Rows collection. The Find method uses the primary key to search for the requested DataRow.

- The **Remove** method accepts one argument, a DataRow object. The DataRow in the Rows collection corresponding to the DataRow object is removed from the DataTable, and all of the data for that row is lost.

- The **RemoveAt** method has the same purpose as the Remove method but accepts the numeric index of the row to remove as its one argument.

As you progress through the chapter, you will use the preceding members to locate, add, change, and delete DataRow objects from a DataTable.

Each row in the Rows collection has a data type of DataRow, having the following members:

Syntax

System.Data.DataRow class

Public Properties

- The **Item** property is used to get or set the value for a particular column in a DataRow and accepts one argument. An item can be referenced using either the 0-based numeric index or a string key. The string key typically corresponds to a field name.

- The **RowState** property indicates whether the DataRow is a new row, a deleted row, or a row whose contents have been modified.

Public Method

- The **Delete** method of the DataRow class marks the row for deletion. The row is not actually deleted until the AcceptChanges method of the DataSet or DataTable is called.

Navigating through the Rows in a DataTable

At this point in the solution's development, you have created the OleDbConnection and OleDbDataAdapter objects, and populated the DataSet, causing VB .NET to create the corresponding DataTable object. In this section, you will see how to navigate through the rows in that DataTable.

The variable named mintCurrent has already been declared in the startup solution and will designate the current row in the DataTable. To display a row from a DataSet, you retrieve a DataRow from the DataTable, and then use the Item method to reference a particular column in the DataRow, as shown in the following statements:

```
Dim drCurrent As DataRow = dtNames.Rows(mintCurrent)
txtID.Text = drCurrent.Item("fldID").ToString
```

The first of the preceding statements stores a DataRow in the variable drCurrent. If mintCurrent has a value of 0, then the first row is stored in drCurrent. The second statement retrieves the field named fldID from the current row, converts that value to a String, and stores the value in the text box named txtID. Figure 7-8 illustrates how to reference a field in a DataRow.

Figure 7-8   Referencing a field in a DataRow

To get the number of rows in a DataTable, you reference the Count property of the Rows collection as shown in the following statement:

```
lblCount.Text = dtNames.Rows.Count.ToString
```

You can now write the statements to display a row from a DataTable in the control instances appearing on the form.

To display a row from a DataTable:

1. Activate the Code Editor for the form named **frmMain.vb**, if necessary. Enter the following statements (shown in bold) in the procedure shown:

```
Private Overloads Sub ShowCurrentRecord( _
    ByVal drCurrent As DataRow)
    txtID.Text = drCurrent.Item("fldID").ToString
    txtFirstName.Text = _
        drCurrent.Item("fldFirstName").ToString
    txtLastName.Text = _
        drCurrent.Item("fldLastName").ToString
    txtDateAdded.Text = _
        drCurrent.Item("fldDateAdded").ToString
    txtEstimatedSales.Text = _
        drCurrent.Item("fldEstimatedSales").ToString
```

```
    chkActive.Checked = _
        ToBoolean(drCurrent.Item("fldActive"))
    lblCount.Text = dtNames.Rows.Count.ToString
End Sub
```

The preceding overloaded ShowCurrentRecord procedure accepts one argument having a data type of DataRow. The Item method of the DataRow class retrieves the field from the row. The field name and the string key in the collection have the same value. Thus, the field name appears as the string key to get a DataRow from the Rows collection.

2. Enter the following statements (shown in bold) in the ShowCurrentRecord procedure:

```
Private Overloads Sub ShowCurrentRecord( _
    ByVal pintCurrent As Integer)
    Dim drCurrent As DataRow = dtNames.Rows(pintCurrent)
    Call ShowCurrentRecord(drCurrent)
End Sub
```

The preceding version of the overloaded ShowCurrentRecord procedure calls the first version. The first of the preceding statements gets the current row (DataRow) based on the numeric index of the row in the collection.

Having created the ShowCurrentRecord procedure, you can now write the statements for the various navigational menu items that will display a record.

To navigate through the rows in a DataTable:

1. Activate the Code Editor for the form named **frmMain.vb**, if necessary, and then enter the following statements in the **Click** event handler for the menu item named **mmuNavigateFirst**:

```
mintCurrent = 0
Call ShowCurrentRecord(mintCurrent)
```

The preceding statements set the current record indicator mintCurrent to 0 (the first record), and then call the ShowCurrentRecord procedure.

2. Enter the following statements in the **Click** event handler for the menu item named **mmuNavigatePrevious**:

```
If mintCurrent > 0 Then
    mintCurrent -= 1
    Call ShowCurrentRecord(mintCurrent)
End If
```

The preceding statements locate the previous record. The If statement tests whether the first record is the current record, thereby preventing an exception from occurring because of trying to locate a record that does not exist.

3. Enter the following statements in the **Click** event handler for the menu item named **mmuNavigateNext**:

```
If mintCurrent < dtNames.Rows.Count - 1 Then
    mintCurrent += 1
    Call ShowCurrentRecord(mintCurrent)
End If
```

The preceding statements locate the next record in the DataTable. The If statement tests whether the last record is the current record using the Count property of the Rows collection. The value 1 is subtracted from the Count property because the variable mintCurrent is 0-based while the Count property is 1-based.

4. Enter the following statements in the **Click** event handler for the menu item named **mmuNavigateLast**:

```
mintCurrent = dtNames.Rows.Count - 1
Call ShowCurrentRecord(mintCurrent)
```

The preceding statements locate the last record in the DataTable. As before, the value 1 is subtracted from the row count because the Count property is 1-based and the variable mintCurrent is 0-based.

5. Enter the following statements (shown in bold) at the end of the **InitializeDatabase** procedure to define the DataTable and display the first database record:

```
modbdaCurrent.Fill(dsCurrent)
dtNames = dsCurrent.Tables("tblNames")
Call ShowCurrentRecord(0)
Call SetEditState(EditState.Browsing)
```

The purpose of the already created SetEditState procedure is the same as the procedure of the same name used in Chapters 5 and 6. It enables and disables the menu items and control instances so as to prevent the user from attempting to perform an impossible action.

6. Test the solution. Click the menu items on the **Navigate** menu to locate various records in the database table.

In addition to navigating through the rows in a DataTable, it is possible to locate a row directly using a primary key.

Creating a Primary Key

Using a primary key to navigate through the records in a DataTable is a two-step process. First, you must define the column(s) that will comprise the primary key, and then you search for a record based on that key. The following statements define a primary key for the fldID column in the DataTable named dtNames:

```
Dim dcKeyfldID() As DataColumn = _
    {dtNames.Columns("fldID")}
dtNames.PrimaryKey = dcKeyfldID
```

The preceding statements first declare an array of DataColumn objects named dcKeyfldID. The array has one element, the DataColumn object corresponding to the column (field) named fldID. The second statement defines this DataColumn as the primary key for the DataTable. Even though this table contains a primary key comprised of a single field, the primary key could be made up of multiple fields. To create a primary key using multiple fields, create an array of DataColumn objects with multiple elements instead of just one. Each element in the array corresponds to a field of the primary key.

The following statements show how to create a primary key made up of two columns (fldID and fldLastName) instead of just a single column:

```
Dim dcKeyfldIDLastName() As DataColumn = _
    {dtNames.Columns("fldID"), _
    dtNames.Columns("fldLastName")}
dtNames.PrimaryKey = dcKeyfldIDLastName
```

The second part of the process involves searching for a row based on the value of the primary key, as shown in the following statements:

```
Dim drCurrent As DataRow
drCurrent = dtNames.Rows.Find(txtID.Text)
Call ShowCurrentRecord(drCurrent)
```

The preceding statements illustrate how to locate a specific DataRow from a DataTable by searching for a record with a corresponding primary key. The first statement declares a variable named drCurrent to store the retrieved row. The second statement searches for the row based on the primary key. The final statement calls the ShowCurrentRecord procedure with the DataRow as an argument to display the record in the form's text boxes.

To locate a record using a primary key:

1. Activate the Code Editor for the form named **frmMain.vb**, and then enter the following statements (shown in bold) in the **InitializeDatabase** procedure:

```
dtNames = dsCurrent.Tables("tblNames")
Dim dcKeyfldID() As DataColumn = _
    {dtNames.Columns("fldID")}
dtNames.PrimaryKey = dcKeyfldID
Call ShowCurrentRecord(0)
```

7

2. Enter the following statements in the **Click** event handler for the menu item named **mmuNavigateFind**:

```
Dim drCurrent As DataRow
Dim pstrID As String
pstrID = InputBox("Enter an ID:", "Find")
If pstrID.Length > 0 Then
    drCurrent = dtNames.Rows.Find(pstrID)
    If drCurrent Is Nothing Then
        MessageBox.Show("Record not found", "Error", _
        MessageBoxButtons.OK, MessageBoxIcon.Information)
    Else
        Call ShowCurrentRecord(drCurrent)
    End If
End If
```

The preceding statements first declare a DataRow object to store the row returned by the Find method, and a String variable to store the search string. The InputBox function gets a string specified by the user. If the user entered a value, the Find method is called to search for the row. If a row is not found, then the DataRow contains Nothing and a message box is displayed. Otherwise, the found record is displayed.

3. Test the solution. On the menu bar, click **Navigate**, and then click **Find**. In the input box, enter **2** to search for the person with an ID of 2. Click **OK**. The respective record is displayed. Click **Navigate**, and then click **Find** again. Enter a value of **99**. Click **OK**. The record is not found, so the message box appears indicating that the record could not be located.

Having seen how to create and fill a DataSet and its corresponding DataTable, and how to navigate through the records in a DataTable, you will now learn how to make changes to the contents of that DataTable, and then save those changes back to the underlying database.

MODIFYING DATA IN A DATATABLE

Modifying the records in a DataSet and its DataTable(s) and recording those changes back to the database is a two-step process. Remember that the DataSet and its DataTables operate in a disconnected mode. Changes that you make to the records in a DataTable are not automatically recorded to the database. In this section, we first explain how to add, change, and delete records in the DataTable. In the next section, we discuss how to record those changes back to the database.

Adding a Row to a DataTable

To add a row to a DataTable, you first create a new DataRow object by calling the NewRow method of the DataTable class. The NewRow method creates a new

DataRow object with the same schema as the underlying DataTable, meaning, the DataRow created by the NewRow method will have the same number of columns as the columns in the underlying DataTable. In addition, each column will have the same data type as the corresponding column in the DataTable. Once the new DataRow has been created, you store data in the fields. Because the new row has the same schema as the rows in the underlying DataTable, the field names are the same as those appearing in the DataTable itself. Finally, you add the newly created row to the Rows collection of the DataTable, as shown in the following code segment:

```
Dim drCurrent As DataRow
drCurrent = dtNames.NewRow
drCurrent.Item("fldID") = txtID.Text
' Statements to copy other fields
dtNames.Rows.Add(drCurrent)
```

The first of the preceding statements declares a variable of type DataRow to store the new row, and the second statement creates that row by calling the NewRow method of the DataTable named dtNames. The first statement copies the data from the text box named txtID into the field named fldID using a string key. The statements to copy the other fields have been omitted for brevity. The final statement adds the newly created row to the Rows collection of the DataTable. Again, while the row has been added to the DataTable, the newly added row has not been recorded to the database. This topic is addressed later in the chapter. In the following steps, you will write the statements to add a record to the DataTable.

To add a row to an untyped DataTable:

1. Activate the Code Editor for the form named **frmMain.vb**, and then enter the following statements in the **Click** event handler for the menu item named **mmuEditAdd**:

```
Call SetEditState(EditState.Adding)
txtID.Clear()
txtFirstName.Clear()
txtLastName.Clear()
txtDateAdded.Clear()
txtEstimatedSales.Clear()
chkActive.Checked = False
```

2. The SetEditState procedure contains the necessary statements to enable the appropriate menu items so that the user must either save the new record or cancel the addition before continuing. The remaining statements clear the contents of the text boxes so that the user can enter new information into those text boxes.

7

3. Enter the following statements (shown in bold) in the **Click** event handler for the menu item named **mmuEditSaveAdd**:

```
Call SetEditState(EditState.Browsing)
Dim drCurrent As DataRow
Try
    drCurrent = dtNames.NewRow
    drCurrent("fldID") = txtID.Text
    drCurrent("fldFirstName") = txtFirstName.Text
    drCurrent("fldLastName") = txtLastName.Text
    drCurrent("fldDateAdded") = txtDateAdded.Text
    drCurrent("fldEstimatedSales") = txtEstimatedSales.Text
    drCurrent("fldActive") = chkActive.Checked
    dtNames.Rows.Add(drCurrent)
    mintCurrent += 1
    Call SaveChanges()
Catch ex As System.ArgumentException
    dtNames.Rows(mintCurrent).CancelEdit()

Catch ex As System.Data.ConstraintException
    MessageBox.Show( _
        "ID must be unique. Addition cancelled", _
        "Error", MessageBoxButtons.OK)
    dtNames.Rows(mintCurrent).CancelEdit()

Finally
    Call ShowCurrentRecord(mintCurrent)
End Try
```

The preceding statements first call the SetEditState procedure, thereby enabling and disabling the appropriate menu items. The statements in the Try block first create a new DataRow and then copy the data from the text boxes to the newly created DataRow. Next, calling the Add method adds the DataRow to the DataTable, and then the record counter (mintCurrent) is incremented to accurately reflect the number of records. If an exception occurs, the edit is canceled.

4. Test the solution. Click **Edit**, and then click **Add** to begin adding a new record. The text boxes are enabled. Enter an ID of **123**. Use your name as the first name and last name. Enter the current date as the date added, and an estimated sales amount of **1000.25**. On the menu bar, click **Edit**, and then click **Save Add**. Note that the data is added to the DataTable. However, you have not yet written the statements to record the changes back to the database. Thus, when you end the solution, the newly added record will be lost.

Two exceptions were possible in the code segment that you just entered. A System.ArgumentException will be raised if the user enters a value in a TextBox having a data type that is not compatible with the underlying database field. A

System.Data.ConstraintException will occur if the user attempts to add a record with an ID that already exists in the DataTable. This exception occurs because you defined a primary key for the field named fldID. A DataTable cannot contain two records having the same value for the primary key.

Having seen how to add a new row to a DataTable, you will now learn how to modify the data of an existing row.

Modifying a DataRow

The steps to modify an existing row in a DataTable are simple. Using an index to the Rows collection, you reference a field within that row as shown in the following statement:

```
dtNames.Rows(0).Item("fldID") = txtID.Text
```

The preceding statement references the first row in the DataTable named dtNames. The Item property and its corresponding string key reference the field named fldID in the current row. The contents of the text box named txtID are then stored in that row. Although the preceding statement stores the data for a single field, the steps to save the other fields are the same. Again, the preceding statement saves the changes to the DataTable. Those changes are not automatically recorded back to the database. You can now proceed to write the statements that will modify the contents of the current row.

To modify a row in a DataTable:

1. Activate the Code Editor for the form named **frmMain.vb**, if necessary, and then enter the following statement in the **Click** event handler for the menu item named **mmuEditEdit**:

```
Call SetEditState(EditState.Editing)
```

2. Enter the following statements in the **Click** event handler for the menu item named **mmuEditSaveChanges**:

```
Call SetEditState(EditState.Browsing)
Try
    dtNames.Rows(mintCurrent).BeginEdit()
    dtNames.Rows(mintCurrent).Item("fldID") = txtID.Text
    dtNames.Rows(mintCurrent).Item("fldFirstName") = _
        txtFirstName.Text
    dtNames.Rows(mintCurrent).Item("fldLastName") = _
        txtLastName.Text
    dtNames.Rows(mintCurrent).Item("fldDateAdded") = _
        txtDateAdded.Text
    dtNames.Rows(mintCurrent).Item("fldEstimatedSales") = _
        txtEstimatedSales.Text
    dtNames.Rows(mintCurrent).Item("fldActive") = _
        chkActive.Checked
```

7

```
        dtNames.Rows(mintCurrent).EndEdit()
        Call SaveChanges()

    Catch ex As System.ArgumentException
        dtNames.Rows(mintCurrent).CancelEdit()

    Catch ex As System.Data.ConstraintException
        MessageBox.Show( _
            "ID must be unique. Change cancelled", _
            "Error", MessageBoxButtons.OK)
        dtNames.Rows(mintCurrent).CancelEdit()

    Finally
        Call ShowCurrentRecord(mintCurrent)
    End Try
```

The preceding statements use the variable mintCurrent to reference the current row in the DataTable. Again, the statements in the Try block begin editing on the current row, and then store the contents of the corresponding text boxes in the fields of the current row. If an exception occurs, the edit is canceled by calling the CancelEdit method on the DataRow.

3. Enter the following statements in the **Click** event handler for the menu item named **mmuEditCancel**:

```
Call SetEditState(EditState.Browsing)
Call ShowCurrentRecord(mintCurrent)
```

4. Test the solution. On the menu bar, click **Edit**, and then click **Change** to enable editing on the first record. Change the first name and the last name to your name. Click **Edit**, and then click **Save Change** to record the edit to the DataTable. Again, while the change is saved to the DataTable, it is not recorded to the underlying database. You will see how to record changes back to the database later in the chapter.

Having learned how to add and modify a row in a DataTable, you will now learn how to delete a row.

Deleting a Row from a DataTable

To delete a row from a DataTable, you call the Delete method of the DataRow class. There are different ways to accomplish this task. One is shown in the following code segment:

```
dtNames.Rows(0).Delete
```

The preceding statement deletes the first row from the DataTable named dtNames. The following statements produce the same result:

```
Dim drCurrent As DataRow
drCurrent = dtNames.Rows(0)
drCurrent.Delete()
```

In the preceding statements, a variable named drCurrent is declared and a reference to the first DataRow is stored in the variable. The Delete method is then called on the DataRow object to delete the row. Again, the preceding statements only delete the row from the DataTable. The row is not removed from the underlying DataSet.

To delete a row from a DataTable:

1. Activate the Code Editor for the form named **frmMain.vb**, and then enter the following statements in the **Click** event handler for the menu item named **mmuEditDelete**:

```
Dim drCurrent As DataRow
Dim dlgResult As DialogResult
dlgResult = MessageBox.Show("Delete Record?", "Confirm", _
    MessageBoxButtons.YesNo)
If dlgResult = DialogResult.Yes Then
    drCurrent = dtNames.Rows(mintCurrent)
    drCurrent.Delete()
    Call SaveChanges()
    mintCurrent = 0
    Call ShowCurrentRecord(mintCurrent)
End If
```

2. Test the solution. Navigate to the last record. On the menu bar, click **Edit**, and then click **Delete**. A message box appears. Click **Yes** to delete the row. The current row is deleted and the record counter is updated.

INPUT VALIDATION

Just as you should validate other user input before processing that input, you should validate proposed record additions and changes before attempting to save those changes to the DataTable. The DataTable class supports events that allow you to perform input validation before recording new or changed records to the DataTable itself, as described in the following list:

- The **RowChanging** event fires just before recording a changed or newly added row to the DataTable. After the row has been changed, the **RowChanged** event fires.

- The **ColumnChanging** event fires just before changes are made to a particular column. The ColumnChanging event fires for each column in the row that is being changed. After the column has been changed, the **ColumnChanged** event fires.

- Windows fires the **RowDeleting** event just before a row is deleted. After the row has been deleted, the **RowDeleted** event fires.

When working with the RowChanging and ColumnChanging events, you can create event handlers for one event or the other, or create event handlers for both the RowChanging and ColumnChanging events. However, you need not typically handle both events in the same application because if you do, you are validating the same input twice. Thus, you typically handle changes on a column-by-column basis with the ColumnChanging event, or for the entire row with the RowChanging event.

Exactly when the RowChanging event fires depends on whether the BeginEdit method has been called on the DataRow. If you call the BeginEdit method before changing the data in the DataRow, the RowChanging event fires once when the EndEdit method is called. If the BeginEdit method is not called when editing the columns in a DataRow, then the RowChanging event fires each time the data in a column changes. Figure 7-9 illustrates when the RowChanging event fires.

Figure 7-9 The order of RowChanging events

As shown in Figure 7-9, three fields are changed in the first data row. If the BeginEdit method is called, the RowChanging event fires once when the EndEdit method is called. If the BeginEdit method is not called, then the RowChanging event fires once for each field.

Examine the following event handler for the RowChanging event:

```
Private Sub dtNames_RowChanging( _
    ByVal sender As Object, _
    ByVal e As System.Data.DataRowChangeEventArgs) _
    Handles dtNames.RowChanging

    Dim pblnError As Boolean
    Dim pstrMessage As String
    If e.Row.Item("fldFirstName").ToString.Length = 0 Then
        pstrMessage = "First name must exist."
        pblnError = True
    End If

    If e.Row.Item("fldLastName").ToString.Length = 0 Then
        pstrMessage &= "Last name must exist."
        pblnError = True
    End If
    If pblnError Then
        MessageBox.Show(pstrMessage, "Error", _
        MessageBoxButtons.OK)
        Throw New System.Exception(pstrMessage)
    End If
End Sub
```

As shown in the preceding code segment, the data type of the second argument is DataRowChangeEventArgs. This class has two properties. The Action property is of type DataRowAction and contains an enumerated value indicating the action that caused the event to fire. The second property, named Row, is of type DataRow. Thus, you can reference the fields in the Row argument in the same way that you can reference the fields in any other DataRow. The preceding statements check that the fields named fldFirstName and fldLastName contain a value. Otherwise, a message box is displayed and an exception thrown.

The purpose of the ColumnChanging event is similar to the RowChanging event. However, the ColumnChanging event always fires for each column just before the column's value is changed. The data type of the ColumnChanging event's second argument is DataColumnChangeEventArgs. This event supports the following properties allowing you to validate the proposed value for the column:

- The **Column** property is of type DataColumn. It contains the data type of the column, and the original value of the column.

- The **ProposedValue** property contains the new value that will be stored in the column.

- The **Row** property contains the underlying DataRow object containing the column.

In this section, you will program the ColumnChanging event to handle the validation task. However, you could easily create similar statements for the RowChanging event. The choice of which to use is arbitrary.

To validate record additions or record changes:

1. Activate the Code Editor for the form named **frmMain.vb**, if necessary. Create the **ColumnChanging** event handler for the DataTable named **dtNames**, and then enter the following statements:

```
Select Case e.Column.ColumnName
    Case "fldEstimatedSales"
        If Not IsNumeric(e.ProposedValue) Then
            MessageBox.Show("Sales must be numeric", _
                "Error", MessageBoxButtons.OK)

        End If
    Case "fldDateAdded"
        If Not IsDate(e.ProposedValue) Then
            MessageBox.Show("Date added is not a date", _
                "Error", MessageBoxButtons.OK)
        End If
End Select
```

2. Test the solution. Click **Edit**, and then click **Change** to begin modifying the first record. Enter an invalid date, and then click **Edit**, **Save Change**. A message box appears indicating that the date is not valid. Click **OK** in the message box. The record is restored to its original value.

At this point, you have completed the portion of the solution that allows the user to add, change, and delete records in a DataTable. In addition, you have seen how to validate that data. The next section describes how to record changes in a DataSet and DataTable back to the underlying database using parameterized SQL statements.

INTRODUCING SQL QUERY PARAMETERS

You have seen how to execute a SQL SELECT statement that returns all of the records from a database table. Suppose, however, that you only wanted to retrieve a particular record or select records that matched some criteria, and you wanted to retrieve those different records based on user input. To solve this problem, you dynamically build a SQL WHERE clause that will select specific records from the records in a DataTable.

To select records dynamically, you build a parameterized query. Conceptually, a **parameterized query** is similar to a function or sub procedure that accepts one or more arguments. Just as you pass different values to the arguments of a procedure, you can supply different values for the parameters of a SQL statement.

To create a parameterized query, you create a SQL SELECT statement as you did before. However, the values for the criteria in a WHERE clause are defined dynamically at run-time. To begin, examine the following statement to specify the CommandText property for the OleDbCommand object named odbcmdSelect:

```
odbcmdSelect.CommandText = "SELECT * FROM tblNames " _
    "WHERE fldID = ? ORDER BY fldLastName"
```

In the preceding SELECT statement, the WHERE clause defines a condition in which the field named fldID will be compared for equality against some value. A question mark (?) defines the placeholder for that dynamic value. Having defined a dynamic placeholder in a SELECT statement, you must supply the means to store data in that placeholder so that data can be selected based on the user-specified input.

 The syntax of a parameterized query varies from provider to provider. For example, Jet uses a question mark to denote each parameter in the query.

The OleDbCommand class contains a collection named Parameters that works with these placeholder characters. This collection contains one OleDbParameter object for each positional value appearing in the CommandText property. The OleDbParameter class has the following members:

Syntax

System.Data.OleDb.OleDbParameter class

Public Properties

■ Data types may vary from database to database. For example, different database vendors may use a different number of bytes to store an Integer. To provide compatibility between the .NET Framework and the data types used by various databases, the **OleDbType** property maps a database type to its corresponding .NET Framework type.

■ The **Size** property defines the number of bytes required to store the data. For numeric and Boolean data types, the size is inferred from the data type itself. For example, the Size property for an Integer will automatically be set to 32 (32 bits). For Strings, however, the maximum String length cannot be determined. Thus, you explicitly set the Size property to define the maximum length of a String.

■ At runtime, the **Value** property stores the current value of the parameter. This value is used to build the SQL statement to retrieve the desired record(s).

For each parameter in a SQL statement, you create an instance of the preceding OleDbParameter class, and then add it to the Parameters collection of the OleDbCommand object. The OleDbParameter constructor has the following syntax:

Syntax

Public Sub New (*name* **As String**, *datatype* **As OleDbType**, *size* **As Integer**, *srccolumn* **As String)**

Definition

The constructor for the **OleDbParameter** class creates a parameter that will be used in a SQL statement.

Dissection

- The *name* argument contains the name of the parameter.

- The *datatype* argument contains a value that defines the data type of the argument. Note that the data type is OleDbType. The data type used corresponds to the data type of the column in the database, which may differ from the corresponding VB .NET data type.

- The *size* argument contains the maximum size of the data. For a String argument, you explicitly specify the maximum size of the string. However, for numeric data types use the value 0 for the *size* argument, as the size is inferred from the corresponding OleDbType.

- The *srccolumn* argument contains the name of the column in the underlying DataTable.

Code Example

```
odbcmdSelect.CommandText = "SELECT * FROM tblNames" _ &
    " WHERE fldID = ? "
Dim odbParam As New OleDbParameter("fldID", _
    OleDbType.Integer, 0, "fldID")
odbcmdSelect.Parameters.Add(odbParam)

odbcmdSelect.Parameters("fldID").Value = 2
odbcmdSelect.Connection = mconCurrent
odbdaCurrent.SelectCommand = odbcmdSelect
dsCurrent.Clear()
odbdaCurrent.Fill(dsCurrent)
```

Code Dissection

The preceding statements define a parameterized SELECT statement. The variable odbcmdSelect is assumed to be an OleDbCommand object. The second statement creates the new parameter having a data type of Integer. The size argument is 0, so the size will be inferred from the OleDbType.Integer type. The field name in the DataTable is fldID. After the parameter has been created, calling the Add method of the Parameters collection adds the parameter. At this point, the parameter has been created. The subsequent statements use the parameter. The Value property of the parameter is set to 2. Thus, the record having the value 2 for the field named fldID will be retrieved. The remaining statements actually select the desired record into the DataSet named dsCurrent.

At runtime, the OleDbDataAdapter uses the OleDbSelectCommand and its parameters to create a SELECT statement dynamically, as shown in Figure 7-10.

Figure 7-10   SQL parameters

As shown in Figure 7-10, the CommandText property contains a SELECT statement with a single parameter. The OleDbParameter constructor creates the actual parameter. These statements configure the parameter. At runtime, VB .NET uses this information to perform the parameter substitution and send the completed SELECT statement to the provider for execution.

Having seen how to create a parameter for a SQL SELECT statement, you will now create parameters for INSERT, UPDATE, and DELETE statements. The process to create parameters is the same no matter the type of SQL statement.

RECORDING DATASET CHANGES TO THE DATABASE

At this point in the solution's development, you have seen how to make changes to the DataTable contained in a DataSet. However, because the DataSet and the DataTable(s) in that DataSet are disconnected from the database, you must explicitly record any changes back to the database using the OleDbDataAdapter.

The following members are used to record changes back to the database:

- The Update method of the OleDbDataAdapter records the changes made to the DataTable(s) in a DataSet.

- The RowState property marks whether a particular DataRow was added, changed, or deleted. This information is used by the OleDbDataAdapter to update the rows in a database table, as necessary.

- The InsertCommand, UpdateCommand, and DeleteCommand properties of the OleDbDataAdapter contain SQL statements used to add, change, and delete records, respectively.

- The OleDbDataAdapter sends the appropriate parameterized SQL statements, over the OleDbConnection, as necessary, to record additions, changes, and deletions.

Before discussing how to create the INSERT, UPDATE, and DELETE statements, examine the following statements to retrieve any changed records from the DataSet and record those changes to the database:

```
Dim dsUpdates As DataSet
Try
    dsUpdates = dsCurrent.GetChanges()
    If Not (dsUpdates Is Nothing) Then
        odbdaCurrent.Update(dsUpdates)
    End If
Catch ex As System.Exception
    Debug.WriteLine(ex.Message)
End Try
```

The first of the preceding statements declares a variable named dsUpdates, having a data type of DataSet. This DataSet will store only those records that have been added, changed, or deleted. The first statement in the Try block gets the changed rows from the original DataSet named dsCurrent, and returns those changed rows in the DataSet named dsUpdates. The If statement tests whether or not dsUpdates is Nothing. The purpose of this If statement is to determine whether the new DataSet is empty. If the DataSet references Nothing, then there were no added, changed, or deleted rows in the original DataSet. If the new DataSet is not empty, then the Update method of the DataSet class is called to record the changes to the underlying database.

 The OleDbDataAdapter will automatically open the connection, make the changes, and then close the connection after those changes have been recorded.

After the preceding statements have executed, any changes made in the DataSet have been recorded to the database. However, now the RowState property for each row in the DataSet needs to be updated to synchronize the DataSet with the database. The changed records in the DataSet must be marked as unchanged. Examine the following statement to accomplish this task:

```
dsCurrent.AcceptChanges()
```

After the DataSet changes have been recorded to the underlying database, the AcceptChanges method is called to synchronize the database with the DataSet. To discard the changes, you call the RejectChanges method. Figure 7-11 illustrates the process of recording database changes:

Figure 7-11   Recording DataSet changes

Next, you will create the procedure to record additions, changes, and deletions. Consider the topic of when to update the database data. One strategy would be to save the changes each time a record is added, changed, or deleted. A second strategy would be to cache the updates until the user explicitly requests the database be updated. In this chapter you will use the first strategy.

If several users are simultaneously making changes to a database, then you should record the changes as they are made so that those changes will be visible to other users. If, however, a database is used by a single user, cache the changes to improve performance.

To record changes to the database:

1. Activate the Code Editor for the form named **frmMain.vb**, if necessary, and then enter the following statements in the **SaveChanges** procedure to record any changed records to the database:

```
Dim dsUpdates As DataSet
Try
    dsUpdates = dsCurrent.GetChanges()
    If Not (dsUpdates Is Nothing) Then
        modbdaCurrent.Update(dsUpdates)
        dsCurrent.AcceptChanges()
    End If

Catch ex As System.Exception
    MessageBox.Show(ex.Message, "Error", _
        MessageBoxButtons.OK)
End Try
```

Having created the statements to record the changes made to the DataSet, you must now finish configuring the OleDbDataAdapter so that it can create the necessary parameterized INSERT, UPDATE, and DELETE statements that will be sent to the provider when the Update method is called.

Configuring the OleDbDataAdapter to Record Additions

As discussed, when you add a record to a DataTable, that new record is not automatically recorded to the underlying database table. So that the newly added DataTable records can be recorded to the underlying database, you define the properties for the InsertCommand property of the OleDbDataAdapter. When you ultimately save the DataSet changes, ADO.NET will execute the appropriate SQL INSERT statement after having substituted values for the corresponding positional parameters. The SQL INSERT statement adds a record to a database table and has the following syntax:

Syntax

INSERT INTO *tablename* (*field1*[, *field2* [, …]]) **VALUES** (*value1*[, *value2* [,…]])

Definition

The **Insert** statement inserts one record into a database table.

Dissection

- The *tablename* argument contains the name of the table or query where the record will be inserted.

- For each *field* in *tablename*, the INSERT statement will store the corresponding *value* in the field. Parentheses enclose the list of fields and a comma separates each field.

- The values stored in the fields are specified via the **VALUES** clause, which is followed by the values *value1, value2,* and so on. Each value is inserted such that *value1* corresponds to *field1*, *value2* corresponds to *field2*, and so on. If the number of fields and values do not match, an exception will occur.

Code Example

```
INSERT INTO tblNames (fldID, fldFirstName, fldLastName, fldDate
Added, fldEstimatedSales, fldActive) VALUES _
(?, ?, ?, ?, ?, ?)
```

7

Code Dissection

Although the preceding statement appears on multiple lines, it is a single statement. The inserted record has six fields. The VALUES clause defines the values to be inserted. Although these could be literal values, the above INSERT statement is parameterized so the question mark character marks each positional parameter. Just as a parameterized SELECT statement uses the question mark character to denote a parameter, so too does a parameterized INSERT statement. The number of fields and values (parameters) in the INSERT statement must match and the values must be enclosed in parentheses.

The INSERT statement can contain parameters just as any other SQL statement can contain parameters. As a simple example, examine the following statements to configure the parameters for the INSERT statement that will add records to the table named tblNames:

```
modbcmdInsert.CommandText = "INSERT INTO tblNames " & _
    "(fldID, fldFirstName, fldLastName, fldDateAdded, " & _
    "fldEstimatedSales, fldActive) VALUES " & _
    "(?, ?, ?, ?, ?, ?)"

Dim odbInsertParamID As New OleDbParameter( _
    "fldID", OleDbType.Integer, 0, "fldID")
Dim odbInsertParamFirstName As New OleDbParameter( _
    "fldFirstName", OleDbType.VarWChar, 20, "fldFirstName")
' Statements to configure the parameters for the
' remaining fields
```

```
modbcmdInsert.Parameters.Add(odbInsertParamID)
modbcmdInsert.Parameters.Add(odbInsertParamFirstName)
' Statements to add the remaining parameters
```

In the preceding statements, the INSERT statement stored in the CommandText property contains positional parameters corresponding to the fields in the DataTable. The second statement calls the constructor for the OleDbParameter class to associate the database field and data type with the positional parameter. The third statement configures the parameter for the field named fldFirstName. The statements to create the parameters for the remaining fields have been omitted for brevity. The final two statements add the parameters to the Parameters collection of the OleDbCommand object named modbcmdInsert.

Figure 7-12 illustrates how the OleDbDataAdapter builds the INSERT statement for a new row.

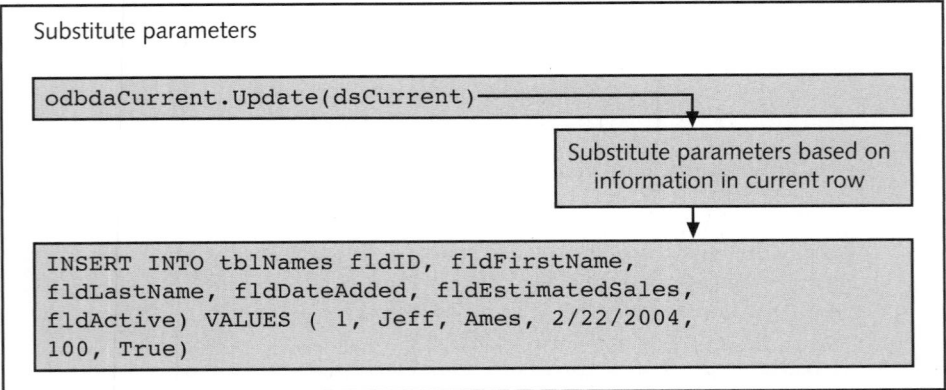

Figure 7-12   Building a parameterized INSERT statement

When the Update method of the OleDbDataAdapter gets called, the OleDbDataAdapter will locate any inserted rows. For each inserted row, the OleDbDataAdapter will configure the INSERT statement using the specified parameters, and send the INSERT statement to the provider for processing.

In the solution for this chapter, you must insert multiple columns corresponding to the columns of the underlying DataTable. In addition, different columns have different data types. Thus, instead of a single parameter, the INSERT statement used to insert a record into the list of names will require multiple parameters of varying data types.

To record the inserted rows from a DataTable to the database:

1. Activate the Code Editor for the form named **frmMain.vb**, and then enter the following statements (shown in bold) in the **InitializeDatabase** procedure:

```
dtNames.PrimaryKey = dcKeyfldID
modbcmdInsert.CommandText = "INSERT INTO tblNames " & _
    "(fldID, fldFirstName, fldLastName, fldDateAdded, " & _
    "fldEstimatedSales, fldActive) " & _
    "VALUES (?, ?, ?, ?, ?, ?)"

Dim odbInsertParamID As New OleDbParameter("fldID", _
    OleDbType.Integer, 0, "fldID")
Dim odbInsertParamFirstName As New _
    OleDbParameter("fldFirstName", OleDbType.VarWChar, _
    20, "fldFirstName")
Dim odbInsertParamLastName As New _
    OleDbParameter("fldLastName", OleDbType.VarWChar, _
    20, "fldLastName")
Dim odbInsertParamDateAdded As New _
    OleDbParameter("fldDateAdded", OleDbType.DBDate, 0, _
    "fldDateAdded")
Dim odbInsertParamEstimatedSales As New _
    OleDbParameter("fldEstimatedSales", OleDbType.Single, _
    0, "fldEstimatedSales")
Dim odbInsertParamActive As New OleDbParameter( _
    "fldActive", OleDbType.Boolean, 0, "fldActive")

modbcmdInsert.Parameters.Add(odbInsertParamID)
modbcmdInsert.Parameters.Add(odbInsertParamFirstName)
modbcmdInsert.Parameters.Add(odbInsertParamLastName)
modbcmdInsert.Parameters.Add(odbInsertParamDateAdded)
modbcmdInsert.Parameters.Add(odbInsertParamEstimatedSales)
modbcmdInsert.Parameters.Add(odbInsertParamActive)
```

7

```
modbcmdInsert.Connection = mconCurrent
modbdaCurrent.InsertCommand = modbcmdInsert
Call ShowCurrentRecord(0)
```

2. Test the solution. Add a new record containing the information shown in Figure 7-13.

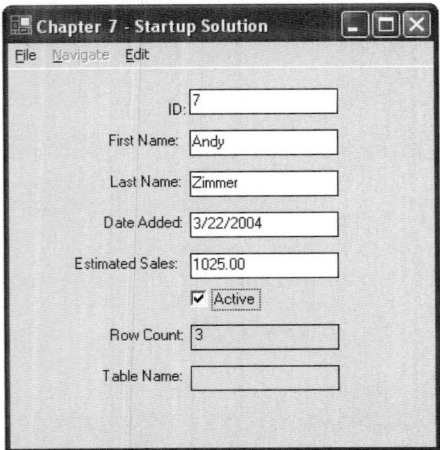

Figure 7-13   Adding a record

The preceding statements configure the OleDbCommand object named odbcmdInsert. First, the CommandText property is set to the parameterized INSERT statement. The next group of statements creates each parameter corresponding to each field in the DataTable. For the numeric fields the size is set to zero. For the string fields (fldFirstName and fldLastName) the size is set to 20. The final parameter stores a Boolean value. The next block of statements adds each parameter to the Parameters collection. The final two statements set the Connection and InsertCommand property of the DataAdapter.

Recording Updates

The SQL UPDATE statement records changes to a record or records. The number of records updated depends on the contents of the WHERE clause. The syntax of a WHERE clause in an UPDATE statement is the same as the syntax of a WHERE clause in a SELECT statement. The UPDATE statement has the following syntax:

Syntax

UPDATE *tablename* **SET** *fieldname = newvalue* [, *fieldname = newvalue*] [, *fieldname = newvalue*] **WHERE** *criteria*

Definition

The **UPDATE** statement updates the contents of one or more fields in one or more rows in a table. The rows updated are defined by the condition in the WHERE clause.

Dissection

- The *fieldname* argument is a field from the DataTable specified by *tablename*.

- The *newvalue* argument can contain a literal value or expression. The *fieldname* argument is set to the literal value or expression contained in *newvalue*.

- The WHERE clause follows the SET clause. The WHERE clause contains an expression having the same syntax as the WHERE clause used in a SELECT statement.

Code Example

```
UPDATE tblNames SET fldFirstName = ?, fldLastName = ?
WHERE fldID = ?
```

Code Dissection

Even though the preceding statement appears on multiple lines, it is a single statement. The above parameterized SQL UPDATE statement updates the values for the fields named fldFirstName and fldLastName where the field named fldID has a specific value. Again, the preceding statement assumes that the parameters will be filled in at runtime.

In this solution, you will update a database record based on the contents of the field named fldID. Note that in this solution, the field named fldID cannot be updated.

To record database updates:

1. Activate the Code Editor for the module named **frmMain.vb**, if necessary, and then enter the following statements (shown in bold) in the **InitializeDatabase** procedure:

```
modbdaCurrent.InsertCommand = modbcmdInsert
modbcmdUpdate.CommandText = "UPDATE tblNames SET " & _
    "fldFirstName = ?, " & _
    "fldLastName = ?, fldDateAdded = ?, " & _
    "fldEstimatedSales = ?, " & _
    "fldActive = ? WHERE fldID = ?"

Dim odbUpdateParamFirstName As New _
    OleDbParameter("fldFirstName", OleDbType.VarWChar, _
    20, "fldFirstName")
Dim odbUpdateParamLastName As New _
```

```
                 OleDbParameter("fldLastName", OleDbType.VarWChar, _
                 20, "fldLastName")
        Dim odbUpdateParamDateAdded As New _
                 OleDbParameter("fldDateAdded", OleDbType.DBDate, _
                 0, "fldDateAdded")
        Dim odbUpdateParamEstimatedSales As New _
                 OleDbParameter("fldEstimatedSales", OleDbType.Single, _
                 0, "fldEstimatedSales")
        Dim odbUpdateParamActive As New _
                 OleDbParameter("fldActive", OleDbType.Boolean, _
                 0, "fldActive")
        Dim odbUpdateParamID As New _
                 OleDbParameter("fldID", OleDbType.Integer, 0, "fldID")

        modbcmdUpdate.Parameters.Add(odbUpdateParamFirstName)
        modbcmdUpdate.Parameters.Add(odbUpdateParamLastName)
        modbcmdUpdate.Parameters.Add(odbUpdateParamDateAdded)
        modbcmdUpdate.Parameters.Add(odbUpdateParamEstimatedSales)
        modbcmdUpdate.Parameters.Add(odbUpdateParamActive)
        modbcmdUpdate.Parameters.Add(odbUpdateParamID)

        modbcmdUpdate.Connection = mconCurrent
        modbdaCurrent.UpdateCommand = modbcmdUpdate
```

2. Test the solution. On the menu bar, click **Edit**, and then click **Change** to begin editing the first record. Enter your name as the first and last names. Click **Edit**, and then click **Save Change** to record the changes to the database.

Having written the statements to perform additions and changes, you can now write the statements to delete records.

Recording Deletions

The SQL DELETE statement removes one or more rows from a database table. The WHERE clause selects the rows that will be deleted. The DELETE statement has the following syntax:

Syntax

DELETE * FROM *table* **WHERE** *conditionlist*

Definition

The **DELETE** statement removes one or more rows from a table based on the condition appearing in the WHERE clause.

Dissection

- The *table* argument is the name of the database table from which records are deleted.

- The *conditionlist* argument contains an expression that determines which records to delete. The syntax of *conditionlist* is the same as its syntax when used in a SELECT or UPDATE statement.

Code Example

```
DELETE * FROM tblNames
DELETE * FROM tblNames WHERE fldID = 32
DELETE * FROM tblNames WHERE fldID = ?
```

Code Dissection

The first of the preceding statements will delete all of the rows from the table named tblNames. The second statement will delete the row where the value of the field named fldID is 32. The final statement implements a parameterized DELETE statement.

To record the deletion of records from a DataSet back to the database, you must configure the DeleteCommand property of the OleDbDataAdapter. Again, you create an instance of the OleDbCommand class and configure it to contain a parameterized SQL DELETE statement. The OleDbDataAdapter will send the necessary DELETE statements to the provider when the Update method of the OleDbDataAdapter is called.

To delete database records:

1. Activate the Code Editor for the form named **frmMain.vb**, if necessary, and then enter the following statements (shown in bold) in the **InitializeDatabase** procedure:

```
modbcmdUpdate.Connection = mconCurrent
modbdaCurrent.UpdateCommand = modbcmdUpdate
modbcmdDelete.CommandText = "DELETE * FROM tblNames " & _
    "WHERE fldID = ?"
Dim odbDeleteParam As New OleDbParameter("fldID", _
    OleDbType.Integer, 0, "fldID")
modbcmdDelete.Parameters.Add(odbDeleteParam)
modbcmdDelete.Connection = mconCurrent
modbdaCurrent.DeleteCommand = modbcmdDelete
```

The preceding statements configure the OleDbCommand object named modbcmdDelete to delete records from the table named tblNames. The CommandText property contains the parameterized DELETE statement. The DELETE statement has one parameter: the field named fldID. The variable named odbDeleteParam stores the Integer parameter. Again, the Connection property is set to the active connection, and the DeleteCommand property of the OleDbDataAdapter itself is set to the OleDbCommand object. When the OleDbDataAdapter needs to record a deletion, the statement will configure the parameters as necessary and send the statement to the provider for processing.

2. Test the solution. Delete the first record by clicking **Edit**, **Delete**.

You have completed the programming for this chapter. You have seen how to establish a connection with a database, send commands over that connection, and display data. You have also learned how to add, update, and delete data, and save those changes from the disconnected DataSet back to the underlying database.

CHAPTER SUMMARY

❑ A database contains a set of information related to a particular topic or purpose. Data are stored in one or more tables. Each table contains one or more columns, also known as fields. The rows in a table are called records. Through the process of normalization, redundant data is eliminated.

❑ A connection forms the pipeline between a client application and the database. The OleDbConnection class allows you to establish a connection to an Access (Jet) database, while the SQLConnection class provides the means to establish a connection to a SQL Server database. To create a connection, create an instance of the OleDbConnection class and set the ConnectionString property to configure the connection. When using the OleDbDataAdapter, it is not necessary to open a connection explicitly as the OleDbDataAdapter class will open and close the connection automatically.

❑ The OleDbDataAdapter class sends SQL statements to a provider for processing. The Fill method causes VB .NET to execute the SELECT statement stored in the SelectCommand property, thereby populating the DataSet. The InsertCommand, UpdateCommand, and DeleteCommand properties contain the respective INSERT, UPDATE, and DELETE statements. These statements execute when the UPDATE method of the DataAdapter is called.

❑ The InsertCommand, UpdateCommand, and DeleteCommand properties of the DataAdapter have a data type of OleDbCommand. The CommandText property contains the parameterized SQL statement, and the Parameters collection contains the OleDbParameter objects that correspond to the respective command parameters.

❑ The DataSet object contains an in-memory representation of the data retrieved from the database table(s). Each table in the DataSet is contained in a DataTable. Each DataTable, in turn, has a Rows collection containing each row. Each row has a data type of DataRow.

❏ A DataTable may have a primary key made up of one or more fields in the DataTable. Each record must have a unique value for the primary key. To create a primary key, create an array of DataColumn objects. Each element in the array contains a column in the DataTable. Assign the array to the PrimaryKey property of the DataTable.

❏ To add a row to a DataTable, call the NewRow method of the DataTable storing the result in a variable of type DataRow. Update the fields in the DataRow as necessary. Finally, call the Add method of the Rows collection of the DataTable with one argument: the DataRow object to add.

❏ To modify a DataRow, update the fields as necessary. To suspend events from firing while the row is being edited, call the BeginEdit method. Call the EndEdit method when editing is complete.

❏ To delete a DataRow, call the Delete method of the DataRow object.

❏ To save DataSet changes, call the GetChanges method on the original DataSet to return a DataSet containing only the changed record(s). Then call the Update method of the DataAdapter with one argument: the DataSet containing the changes. Finally, call the AcceptChanges method on the original DataSet to synchronize the DataSet with the database.

❏ To insert rows added to the DataSet to the underlying database table, configure the InsertCommand property of the OleDbDataAdapter.

❏ To update rows that have been changed in the DataSet, configure the UpdateCommand property of the OleDbDataAdapter.

❏ To delete database rows, configure the DeleteCommand property of the OleDbDataAdapter.

REVIEW QUESTIONS

1. Which of the following statements is correct related to database processing?

   a. Data in a database are stored in one or more tables.

   b. A database table consists of rows and columns.

   c. The columns in a database table are referred to as fields.

   d. The rows in a database table are called records.

   e. all of the above

2. Which of the following statements is true of establishing a connection with the OleDbConnection class?

   a. The Connect method causes the OleDbConnection to be opened, allowing requests to be sent over that connection.

   b. A connection must be explicitly opened by calling the Connect method before any data can be retrieved over that connection.

   c. A program can have only one connection open at a time. Thus, having two connections open to two different databases is not possible.

   d. You determine whether or not a connection is open by checking the value of the Connection property.

   e. none of the above

3. Referring to the OleDbConnection class, what is the purpose of the ConnectionString property?

   a. The ConnectionString property has an enumerated type of ConnectionType. The various enumerated values are used to define the type of database.

   b. The ConnectionString property has a data type of Connection. The Database property contains the name of the database, and the Provider property defines the type of the database.

   c. The ConnectionString property is a string made up of key/value pairs. A semi-colon separates each key/value pair.

   d. No matter which type of database you use (Jet, SQL Server, etc.), the ConnectionString property will have the same value.

   e. none of the above

4. Which of the following statements is true of the OleDbDataAdapter class?

   a. The OleDbDataAdapter sends requests over a connection to select, add, update, or delete data.

   b. When you call the SelectCommand method, the database data is retrieved into the DataSet.

   c. To update changes in the DataSet, you call the SaveChanges method of the OleDbDataAdapter.

   d. all of the above

   e. none of the above

5. What is the purpose of the TableMappings collection of the OleDbDataAdapter class?

   a. It is used to rename default table names to more meaningful table names.

   b. It associates the table or tables in a DataSet with the underlying OleDbDataAdapter.

   c. It is used to populate a DataSet.

d. The TableMappings collection has nothing to do with the OleDbDataAdapter class.

e. none of the above

6. How do you populate a DataSet with data?

   a. After creating an instance of the DataSet class, call the Load method supplying an instance of the OleDbDataAdapter as an argument.

   b. Create an instance of the DataSet class. The constructor populates the DataSet automatically.

   c. Call the overloaded Fill method of the OleDbDataAdapter using the DataSet to fill as the argument to the method.

   d. Create an instance of the DataSet class. Then, for each table in the DataSet that you want to populate, create an instance of the DataTable class.

   e. none of the above

7. Which of the following statements is correct related to a DataSet?

   a. A DataSet typically contains one or more DataTable objects.

   b. To remove all of the rows from a DataSet, you call the Clear method.

   c. The Copy method makes a copy of a DataSet's schema and data.

   d. If a DataSet contains records whose data has been changed, the HasChanges property will be True.

   e. all of the above

8. Which of the following statements correctly describes the relationship between a DataSet and a DataTable?

   a. A DataSet contains one or more DataTable objects.

   b. A DataSet can contain one and only one DataTable.

   c. A DataTable contains one or more DataSet objects.

   d. There exists no relationship between a DataSet and a DataTable, as the two objects are independent.

   e. none of the above

9. Referring to a DataTable, which of the following statements is correct related to defining a primary key?

   a. To define the primary key for a DataTable, you set the Key property of the DataTable to a string. That string contains the name of the field designated as the key.

   b. A primary key can be made up of a single column or multiple columns.

   c. A primary key is always made up of a single column.

   d. all of the above

   e. none of the above

10. Which of the following statements correctly describes the steps to add a new DataRow to a DataTable?

    a. First, call the Add method of the DataTable. Second, store the data in the fields.

    b. Create a new instance of the Row class. Specify the number of fields to the over-loaded constructor. Finally, add the new row to the DataTable's Rows collection.

    c. First, call the NewRow method of the underlying DataTable to create the row. Second, store data in the fields of the new row. Finally, add the new row to the Rows collection of the DataTable.

    d. Any of the above will work.

    e. none of the above

11. Which of the following statements accurately describes the ColumnChanging event of the DataTable?

    a. The DataTable does not support an event named ColumnChanging.

    b. The ColumnChanging event fires as an attempt is made to change a value in a DataTable column. However, the event does not fire as a new row is being added. If a column is being added, then the ColumnAdding event fires.

    c. The ColumnChanging event fires for each column as a row in a DataTable is being added or changed.

    d. The ColumnChanging event fires once as the contents of a row in a DataTable are being changed. The second argument to the event contains a reference to all of the columns in the current row.

    e. none of the above

12. What is the name of the method of the DataAdapter used to record any changes made to a DataSet back to the database?

    a. Save

    b. GetChanges

    c. Update

    d. AcceptChanges

    e. none of the above

13. What is the purpose of the OleDbParameter class?

    a. It is used to configure the columns that will be retrieved into a DataSet.

    b. It can be used to configure the ConnectionString property of the OleDbConnection class dynamically.

    c. It allows you to supply dynamic parameters that are used by OleDbCommand objects to build SELECT, INSERT, UPDATE, and DELETE statements.

    d. all of the above

    e. none of the above

14. When creating a parameterized query using the Jet engine, what special character do you use to indicate a positional parameter?

    a. @

    b. *

    c. $

    d. ?

    e. #

15. What method do you call to record changes made to a DataSet back to the underlying Database?

    a. Record

    b. Save

    c. Update

    d. Change

    e. none of the above

16. Referring to the OleDbDataAdapter, what is the purpose of the SelectCommand, InsertCommand, UpdateCommand, and DeleteCommand properties?

17. Describe the purpose of the DataSet and DataTable objects. In your answer, be sure to describe the relationship between the two objects.

18. Describe the steps to add, change, and delete records in a DataTable.

19. Describe the difference between the RowChanging event and the ColumnChanging event.

20. Describe the steps necessary to record any changes made to a DataSet back to the underlying database.

PROGRAMMING QUESTIONS

1. Write the statements to create an instance of the OleDbConnection class, storing the instance in the variable named odbconList. Configure the connection to use the Jet provider. Assume that the database is stored in the file "C:\List.mdb". Finally, assume that you need not supply any security information.

2. Write the statements to create an instance of the OleDbCommand class, storing the instance in the variable named odbcmdSelect. Configure the OleDbCommand to retrieve all of the records from the table named tblQuestion, sorting the records by the field fldQuestionNumber. Assume that an existing connection exists named odbconCurrent. Associate the OleDbCommand class with this connection.

3. Assume that an instance of the OleDbDataAdapter exists named odbdaQuestion. Write the statement to add a table mapping such that the default table named "Table" is mapped to the table named tblQuestions.

4. Assume that an instance of the OleDbDataAdapter named odbdaQuestion exists. Write the statement to fill the OleDbDataAdapter to populate the DataSet named dsCurrent.

5. Assume that a DataSet exists named dsQuestion. Write the statement to get the first table from the DataSet and store a reference to the table in the variable named dtQuestion, having a data type of DataTable.

6. Write the statements to create a primary key by declaring an array of DataColumn objects named dcQuestions. Assume that a DataTable named dtQuestions exists having a column named fldQuestionNumber. Use this column for the primary key.

7. Write the statements to create a primary key by declaring an array of DataColumn objects named dcPerson. Assume that a DataTable exists, named tblEmployees. Create the primary key using the fields named fldLastName and fldFirstName.

8. Assume that a PrimaryKey exists for the DataTable named dtQuestion and that the primary key contains a single field. Write the statement to find the record based on the primary key. Assume that the value is stored in the string variable pstrVal. Store the returned DataRow in the variable drQuestion.

9. Write the statement to create a new row in the DataTable named dtQuestion, storing the newly created row in the variable drQuestion.

10. Assume that a DataTable named dtQuestion exists having a field named fldQuestionName. Write the statements to begin editing on the first row, and then store the string "Question 1" in the field. Finally, write the statement to end editing on that row.

11. Assume that a DataTable exists named dtQuestion. Write the statement(s) to remove the last row from the DataTable.

12. Assume that an instance of the OleDbDataAdapter named odbQuestion exists, and that an instance of the DataSet also exists. Write the statement to get the changed records from the DataSet named dsQuestion and store those records in another DataSet named dsTemp. Write an If statement that will test whether any changes exist, and update the database as necessary. Accept the changes to the primary DataSet.

13. Write the statements to declare an instance of the OleDbCommand object named odbcmdInsert. Configure the object to insert the fields named fldOne, fldTwo, and fldThree into the table. Assume that each of the fields is a string field 20 characters in length. Create the parameters as necessary and add them to the Parameters collection of the OleDbCommand object. Finally, associate the OleDbCommand object with an instance of the OleDbDataAdapter named odbdaCurrent.

14. Write the statements to declare an instance of the OleDbCommand object named odbcmdDelete. Configure the object to delete a record from the table named tblQuestion using the field named fldID as an argument. Create the parameters as necessary to perform the deletion. Associate the OleDbCommand object with the OleDbDataAdapter named odbdaCurrent.

15. Write the statement to create the ColumnChanging event handler for the DataTable named dtDemo. Test that the field named fldNumber is numeric and that the field named fldDate is a date. Display a message box if invalid data is encountered.

HANDS-ON PROJECTS

All of the hands-on projects use the same database named Factory.mdb located in the Chapter.07\Data folder. The following list describes the fields in the table named tblFactory:

- ❑ fldFactoryName (String)—Unique factory name
- ❑ fldAddress (String)
- ❑ fldCity (String)
- ❑ fldState (String)
- ❑ fldZipCode (String)
- ❑ fldEmployeeCount (Integer)

The following list describes the fields in the table named tblEmployees:

- ❑ fldEmployeeID (Integer)—Unique employee identification number
- ❑ fldFirstName (String)
- ❑ fldLastName (String)
- ❑ fldType (String)—Hourly or salaried employee
- ❑ fldHireDate (DateTime)
- ❑ fldWage (Single)

The following list describes the fields in the table named tblInventory:

- ❑ fldPartNumber (Integer)—Unique part number
- ❑ fldPartDescription (String)
- ❑ fldCost (Single)
- ❑ fldSalesPrice (Single)
- ❑ fldQtyOnHand (Integer)

The following list describes the fields in the table named tblSales:

□ fldSalesID (Integer)—Unique sales record number

□ fldPartNumber (Integer)

□ fldQtySold (Integer)

□ fldSalesPrice (Single)

□ fldSalesDate (DateTime)

1. In this project, you will create a solution that will allow the user to navigate through the records in a database table, and allow the user to add, change, and delete those records. The file named Chapter.07\Exercises07\Ch07Ex1.exe contains the compiled executable application. Figure 7-14 shows the completed main form for the solution.

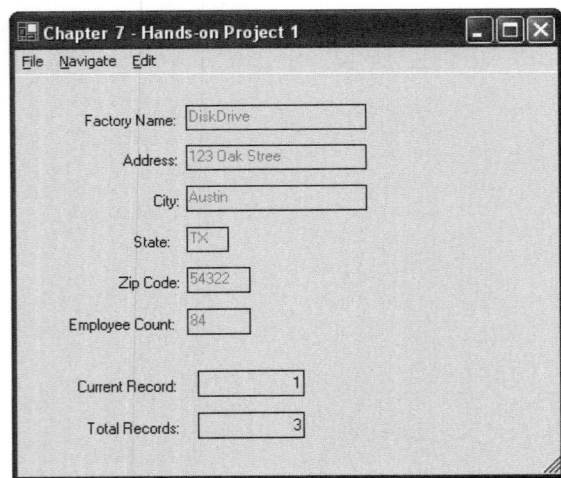

Figure 7-14   Chapter 7 – Hands-on Project 1

   a. Create a new solution named **Ch07Ex1.sln**.

   b. Create the control instances on the form as shown in Figure 7-14.

   c. Create a procedure to initialize the database connection. Configure the database connection as necessary to connect to the database named **Factory.mdb**. Configure an instance of the OleDbDataAdapter so that it will select all of the records from the table named tblFactory. In addition, configure the data adapter so that it will use OleDbCommand objects that will insert, update, and delete records from the database table.

   d. Create a menu for the form.

   e. Create a **File** menu with one menu item to exit the solution.

f. Create a **Navigate** menu with menu items to locate the first, previous, next, and last record in the database table. Write the necessary statements for each of the menu items to locate and display the correct records.

g. Next, create an **Edit** menu with menu items to add a new record and save the newly added record. In addition, create menu items to edit an existing record and save that record. Create a menu item to delete the current record. Write the necessary statements for these menu items to add, change, and delete records. Allow the user to cancel a record addition or modification. Get confirmation from the user before deleting a record.

h. Write the necessary statements that will save the changes made to the disconnected DataTable back to the database.

i. Write the necessary statement to perform error handling. If the user enters invalid data while adding or editing a record, display message boxes as necessary indicating that there is an error.

j. Write the statements to display the current record number and the total number of records. Display this information in the control instances appearing on the form.

2. In this project, you will create a solution that will allow the user to navigate through the records in the table named tblEmployees. The file named Chapter.07\ Exercises07\Ch07Ex2.exe contains the compiled executable application. Figure 7-15 shows the completed main form for the solution.

Figure 7-15   Chapter 7 – Hands-on Project 2

a. Create a new solution named **Ch07Ex2.sln**.

b. Create the control instances on the form as shown in Figure 7-15.

7

c. Create a procedure to initialize the database connection. Configure the database connection as necessary to connect to the database named **Factory.mdb**. The records that you display should be sorted by last name.

d. Create a menu with the necessary menu items so that the user can navigate from record to record, and can add, change, and delete records.

e. Create the necessary validate code to require that the employee ID be unique, and that the first name and last name both exist. The employee type must contain the value "Salary" or "Hourly", the wage must be a number greater than 0, and the hire date must be a date in the past.

f. Write the statements to display the current record and the total number of records. Update the values as necessary as the user navigates from record to record, or adds and deletes records.

g. Write the statements to examine all of the rows in the DataTable. Calculate the total number of salaried and hourly employees by examining the field named fldType for each data row. Display this information in a message box.

3. In this project, you will create a solution that will allow the user to navigate through the records in the table named tblInventory. The file named Chapter.07\Exercises07\Ch07Ex3.exe contains the compiled executable application. Figure 7-16 shows the completed main form for the solution.

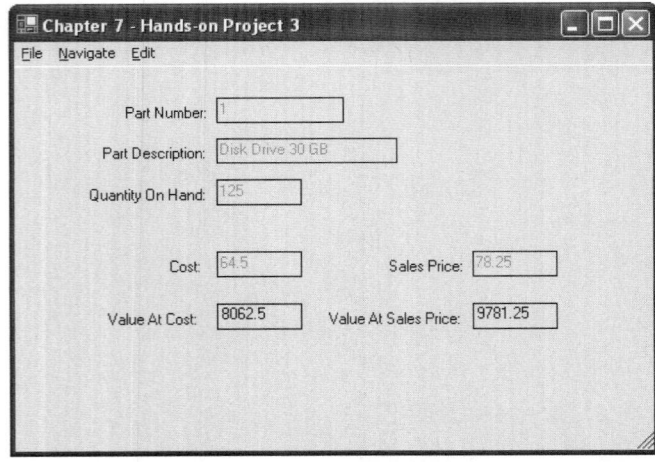

Figure 7-16   Chapter 7 – Hands-on Project 3

a. Create a new solution named **Ch07Ex3.sln.**

b. Create the control instances on the form as shown in Figure 7-16.

c. Create a procedure to initialize the database connection. Configure the database connection as necessary to connect to the database named **Factory.mdb**. The records that you display should be sorted by part number.

d. Create a menu with the necessary menu items so that the user can navigate from record to record, and can add, change, and delete records.

e. Validate that the part number is an integer, that the part description exists, and that the cost and sales price are positive numbers. Validate that the sales price is greater than the cost. The quantity on hand must be a positive integer number.

f. Each time the current record position changes or a record is added or changed, display the value at cost and the value at sales price. To calculate these values, multiple the quantity on hand by the cost and sales price, respectively. Display these values in the output labels on the form.

g. Create a **Summary** menu item on the File menu. Calculate the total value of the inventory at cost and at the sales price. Display these totals in a message box. You will need to write a For loop to examine all of the rows in the DataTable.

4. In this project, you will create a solution that will allow the user to navigate through the records in a database table, and to add, change, and delete those records. Finally, the user will be able to read data from a sequential file into the database table, and write data from the database to a sequential file. Figure 7-17 shows the completed main form for the solution.

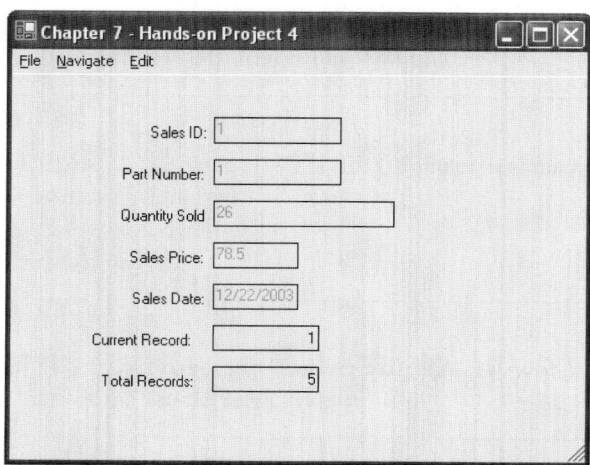

Figure 7-17   Chapter 7 – Hands-on Project 4

a. Create a new solution named **Ch07Ex4.sln**.

b. Create a splash screen for the application and create the control instances on the main form as shown in Figure 7-17.

c. Create menu items that will allow the user to locate the first, next, previous, and last record in the table.

d. Configure the OleDbDataAdapter so that it will send parameterized INSERT, UPDATE, and DELETE statements to the provider. Create a menu item and the necessary statements that will save the changes made to the disconnected DataTable back to the database.

e. Create the necessary statements that will allow the user to copy the contents of the database table to a comma-delimited sequential file. Allow the user to select the name of the sequential file using a SaveFileDialog dialog box. Use the StreamWriter class discussed in Chapter 6 to accomplish this task.

f. Display the current record number and the total number of records in the control instances appearing on the form.

g. Create a menu item named **Summarize By Part**. Display an input box allowing the user to select a part number. Calculate the total sales for the selected part number and display the results in a message box.

h. Create another menu item named **Summarize By Date**. Display a modal dialog box allowing the user to select two dates. In a message box, display the total sales amounts for records between those two dates. Validate the input by prohibiting the user from entering values beyond the minimum and maximum date range stored in the database table.

WORKING WITH DATA FROM MULTIPLE TABLES

In this chapter, you will:

♦ Create an OleDbConnection and OleDbDataAdapter using Toolbox controls

♦ Create and manage strongly typed DataSets

♦ Design one-to-many relationships between data

♦ Create DataRelations to relate data from two tables programmatically

♦ Bind control instances to a DataSet using simple binding and complex binding

♦ Work with the DataGrid control

♦ Work with the DataReader class

♦ Execute scalar queries

In Chapter 7, you performed database operations on a single table and created instances of the OleDbConnection, OleDbDataAdapter, and DataSet classes programmatically. Instead of a single table, most database applications work with multiple tables related in different ways. Using ADO.NET to manage and relate data stored in multiple tables is one topic discussed in this chapter. In addition, you will learn how to create an OleDbConnection, OleDbDataAdapter, and DataSet using VB .NET controls. Chapter 7 also introduced an untyped DataSet. In this chapter, you will use a strongly typed DataSet. Finally, in Chapter 7 you used the disconnected DataSet. In this chapter you will use the disconnected DataSet too, however, you will also use the DataReader to work with ADO.NET in connected mode.

PREVIEWING THE COMPLETED SOLUTION

The completed solution in this chapter illustrates an accounts receivable system. The accounts receivable system contains two tables. The first table, named tblCustomers, contains general information about a customer, such as name and address information. The second table, named tblTransactions, contains one record for each charge or payment made on the customer's account.

The customers and transactions tables are linked together by a common field named fldID that appears in the table tblCustomers and represents the table's primary key. Records having the same value for the field named fldID appearing in the table named tblTransactions represent transactions for the corresponding customer. Figure 8-1 illustrates the relationships between the two tables.

Figure 8-1   Table relationships

Table 8-1 lists the fields and VB .NET data types in the table named tblCustomers.

Table 8-1   Fields in tblCustomers

Field name	.NET data type	Description
fldID	Integer	Identification number (primary key)
fldFirstName	String	First name
fldLastName	String	Last name
fldAddress	String	Address
fldCity	String	City
fldState	String	State
fldZipCode	String	Zip code
fldActive	Boolean	Active/inactive flag

Table 8-2 lists the fields and VB .NET data types in the table named tblTransactions.

Table 8-2   Fields in tblTransactions

Field name	.NET data type	Description
fldID	Integer	Customer identification number (foreign key)
fldTransactionID	Integer	Transaction identification number (primary key)
fldDate	Date/Time	Transaction date
fldAmount	Single	Transaction amount
fldType	Integer	Transaction type (1 = Charge, 2 = Payment)

Note

This chapter uses a control called the OleDbConnection control to establish the database connection. By default, the OleDbConnection control embeds an absolute path name into the ConnectionString property. Thus, depending on where you installed the files associated with this book, that absolute path name may be incorrect. To solve this problem, we overwrite the ConnectionString property in the constructor (New procedure) for each form to use relative path names.

Examine the commented code in the constructors for the forms in the completed solution. In that commented code, you will see that the statements to set the ConnectionString property use a constant named pstrDatabase. This constant is declared in the module named Global.vb. Change the value of this constant, as necessary, depending on where you installed the data files associated with this book.

Furthermore, if you attempt to change the configuration of the DataSets in the completed solution, you may need to change the ConnectionString properties for the OleDbConnection controls in each of the forms.

To preview the completed solution:

1. Start Visual Studio .NET. Open and run the solution file named **Chapter.08\ Complete08\Complete08.sln**. Note that for the solution to run correctly, the folder named Complete08 and the folder named Data must appear as child folders of the Chapter.08 folder, because relative folder names are used to reference the database from the solution. The main form appears as shown in Figure 8-2.

Figure 8-2   Completed solution – main form

As shown in Figure 8-2, the main form contains a menu allowing the user to navigate from record to record, and to edit records. The logic for this form is similar to the logic for the form you created in Chapter 7. However, this form uses a typed DataSet instead of an untyped DataSet. In addition, OleDbConnection, OleDbCommand, and DataSet objects were created using controls instead of being created programmatically.

2. Using the items on the **Navigate** menu, locate different database records. Note that the Edit menu contains menu items to add, change, and delete records.

3. On the main form, click **Windows**, **Transactions** on the menu to display the transactions form shown in Figure 8-3.

As shown in Figure 8-3, the transactions form displays the data for a single customer in text boxes. The transactions for the selected customer appear in a DataGrid control instance that appears below the text boxes. As you click the menu items on the Navigate menu, the transaction records for the selected customer appear in the DataGrid. In addition, the solution allows you to add, change, and delete transaction records using the DataGrid control instance.

Figure 8-3   Completed solution – transactions form

4. Click the menu items on the **Navigate** menu to locate different customer records. As you do, note that the corresponding transaction records appear for the selected customer.

5. Close the transactions form.

6. End the solution and exit Visual Studio .NET.

In this chapter, the following namespaces have been imported in all of the forms to simplify the references to the ADO.NET classes:

```
Imports System.Data
Imports System.Data.Common
Imports System.Data.OleDb
```

CREATING A CONNECTION WITH THE OLEDBCONNECTION CONTROL

To create a connection with the OleDbConnection control, you first create an instance of the OleDbConnection control on the form. Then you set the ConnectionString property by defining the provider and the database using the tabs appearing on the Data Link Properties dialog box. In the following steps, you will establish a connection to the database named Customer.mdb.

To create a connection with the OleDbConnection control:

1. Start Visual Studio .NET, and open the solution file named **Chapter.08\ Startup08\Startup08.sln.**

2. Activate the Win Forms Designer for the form named **frmUtility.vb**. Activate the **Data tab** on the Toolbox. On the form named **frmUtility**, create an instance of the **OleDbConnection** control. Because the control instance is invisible to the user at runtime, it appears in the resizable tray below the form. Activate the Properties window, and then set the Name property to **odbconUtility**.

3. In the Properties window, click the **value** column for the **ConnectionString** property. A list arrow appears.

4. Click the **list arrow**. If existing connections have been created on the computer you are using, those connections will appear in the drop-down list. The New Connection list item allows you to create a new connection.

5. Click **<New Connection...>** to activate the Data Link Properties dialog box and begin configuring the connection. In the Data Link Properties dialog box, click the **Provider** tab.

6. On the Provider tab, click the provider named **Microsoft Jet 4.0 OLE DB Provider**. Again, this is the same OLE DB provider that you used in Chapter 7. Figure 8-4 shows the Provider tab.

Figure 8-4   Data Link Properties dialog box – Provider tab

7. Click **Next** to activate the Connection tab.

8. On the Connection tab, click the **Build** button. In the Select Access Database dialog box, select the database named **Chapter.08\Data\Customer.mdb**. Click **Open** to select the database. The Select Access Database dialog box closes and the database and its directory path appear in the text box. Figure 8-5 shows the Connection tab with the database selected. The absolute path name will vary.

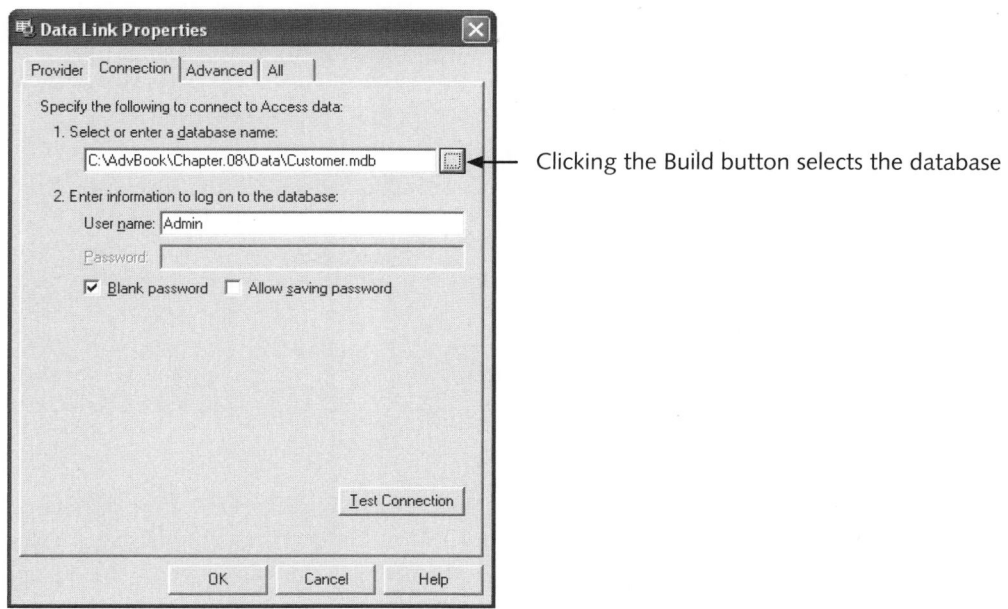

Clicking the Build button selects the database

8

Figure 8-5   Data Link Properties dialog box – Connection tab

9. Click the **Test Connection** button. A dialog box should appear with the message "Test connection succeeded." Click **OK** to close the dialog box.

10. In the Data Link Properties dialog box, click **OK** to close it and configure the connection.

The ConnectionString property appearing in the Properties window is the same ConnectionString property that you created programmatically in Chapter 7.

By setting the ConnectionString to a fully qualified path name, the solution you are creating will only run if the location of the database does not change. If you change the database location, you must modify the value of the ConnectionString property. The completed solution will work from any directory because it has been modified to use relative directory names.

The OleDbConnection control instances have already been created on the forms named frmMain and frmCustomersTransactions. However, the ConnectionString property for those control instances is likely incorrect because of different database directories. In the following steps, you will update the ConnectionString property to coincide with the location of the database file.

To revise the ConnectionString property:

1. Activate the Win Forms Designer for the form named **frmMain.vb**. Click the OleDbConnection control instance named **odbconCustomers** to select it. In the Properties window, select the **ConnectionString** property. In the drop-down list box, select the connection that reflects the location of the database file on your computer, if it does not already exist.

2. Activate the Win Forms Designer for the form named **frmCustomersTransactions.vb**. Click the OleDbConnection control instance named **odbconCurrent** to select it. In the Properties window, select the **ConnectionString** property. In the drop-down list box, select the connection that reflects the location of the database file on your computer, if necessary.

If you move this application from computer to computer, you will need to repeat the preceding steps so that Visual Studio .NET can locate the associated database file.

When you closed the Data Link Properties dialog box, VB .NET wrote the necessary statements to configure the connection (ConnectionString property). These are nearly the same statements that you wrote in Chapter 7 to create a connection.

The following code segment illustrates the statements automatically generated by the Win Forms Designer. Note that the following ConnectionString property setting has been reformatted to make it more readable. However, the resulting connection string is the same as the one generated by the Win Forms Designer.

```
Friend WithEvents odbconCustomers As _
    System.Data.OleDb.OleDbConnection
Me.odbconCustomers = New _
    System.Data.OleDb.OleDbConnection()
Me.odbconCustomers.ConnectionString = _
    "Provider=Microsoft.Jet.OLEDB.4.0;" & _
    "Password="""";User ID=Admin;" & _
    "Data Source=D:\Chapter.08\Data\Customer.mdb;" . . .
```

The preceding statements set the same ConnectionString property of the OleDbConnection class that you used in Chapter 7. However, the preceding ConnectionString contains additional key/value pairs to configure the connection. Note that the preceding code segment displays only part of the ConnectionString property, for brevity.

THE OLEDBDATAADAPTER CONTROL

Having created and configured the OleDbConnection control, you can proceed to create and configure the OleDbDataAdapter control instances. Again, in Chapter 7, you created the OleDbDataAdapter programmatically. In this chapter, you will use the OleDbDataAdapter control and its associated Wizard to accomplish the same task. The dialog boxes that comprise the Wizard allow you to select the connection over which commands will be sent, and then define the SQL statements that will retrieve and update data. After you complete the dialog boxes that comprise the Wizard, the Wizard automatically generates the statements to configure the OleDbDataAdapter.

To create an OleDbDataAdapter with the OleDbDataAdapter control:

1. Activate the Win Forms Designer for the form named **frmUtility.vb**.

2. Using the Data tab on the Toolbox, create an instance of the **OleDbDataAdapter** control on the form. Because the control instance is invisible at runtime, it appears in the resizable tray at the bottom of the Win Forms Designer.

   When you create the OleDbDataAdapter control instance on the form, VB .NET automatically activates the Data Adapter Configuration Wizard and displays an introductory dialog box.

3. In the Welcome dialog box, click **Next** to activate the Choose Your Data Connection dialog box shown in Figure 8-6.

Figure 8-6   Choose Your Data Connection dialog box

4. In the Choose Your Data Connection dialog box, select the connection named **ACCESS.C:\AdvBook\Chapter.08\Data\Customer.mdb.Admin**, if necessary. The database path name will vary based on where you installed the files on your computer. In addition, the list of available connections may also vary.

5. Click **Next** to activate the Choose a Query Type dialog box shown in Figure 8-7.

Figure 8-7   Choose a Query Type dialog box

The Choose a Query Type dialog box contains three radio buttons allowing you to define how the OleDbDataAdapter will generate the SQL statements. Which radio buttons are enabled depends on the provider that you selected in the preceding steps. The Use SQL statements radio button is the only enabled option because the OleDbConnection class does not support stored procedures.

6. Click **Next** to activate the Generate the SQL statements dialog box.

In the Generate the SQL statements dialog box, you can either manually enter the SQL SELECT statement or use the Query Builder to assist you with the task.

7. Click the **Query Builder** button to activate the Query Builder and the Add Table dialog boxes. The Add Table dialog box displays the two tables appearing in the database. In the Add Table dialog box, click the table named **tblCustomers** if necessary, and then click the **Add** button to add the table to the Query Builder.

8. In the Add Table dialog box, click the **Close** button to close the dialog box and enable the Query Builder.

9. In the Query Builder, click the check boxes for each of the columns in the following order: **fldID**, **fldFirstName**, **fldLastName**, **fldAddress**, **fldCity**, **fldState**, **fldZipCode**, **fldActive**. When you check each box, VB .NET adds the field to the SQL statement that the Query Builder will generate. Note that the field named fldID appears in a boldface font because this field is designated as the primary key. Figure 8-8 shows the Query Builder dialog box.

Figure 8-8   Query Builder dialog box

10. Click **OK** to close the Query Builder, and return to the Generate the SQL statements dialog box. Note that the SQL SELECT statement generated by the Query Builder appears in the dialog box as shown in Figure 8-9.

11. In the Generate the SQL statements dialog box, click **Advanced Options** to display the Advanced SQL Generation Options dialog box shown in Figure 8-10.

If the Generate Insert, Update and Delete statements box is checked, VB .NET will configure the OleDbDataAdapter so as to create the OleDbCommand objects containing SQL INSERT, UPDATE, and DELETE statements similar to those that you wrote in Chapter 7. We discuss the automatically generated statements following these steps. The Use optimistic concurrency check box causes VB .NET to generate the UPDATE and DELETE statements differently so as to prevent errors that may arise when two users try to update the same record at the same time. This topic is also discussed following these steps.

12. Click **OK** to close the Advanced SQL Generation dialog box.

Figure 8-9   Generate the SQL statements dialog box

Figure 8-10   Advanced SQL Generation Options dialog box

13. Click **Next** to configure the OleDbDataAdapter. The View Wizard Results dialog box displays a summary report. If any errors occurred while generating the SQL statements, those errors will appear in the View Wizard Results dialog box.

14. **Finish** to close the View Wizard Results dialog box.

15. Activate the Properties window for the OleDbDataAdapter and set the Name property to **odbdaCustomers**.

When you configured the OleDbDataAdapter, VB .NET generated SQL statements similar to those that you wrote in Chapter 7, writing the parameterized SELECT, INSERT, UPDATE, and DELETE statements for you automatically.

In addition to an OleDbDataAdapter to retrieve records from the table named tblCustomers, this form will also use data from the table named tblTransactions. Thus, you need to create a second OleDbDataAdapter to read and write the records from that table.

To create a second OleDbDataAdapter:

1. Using the Data tab on the Toolbox, create a second instance of the **OleDbDataAdapter** control on the form.

2. In the Welcome dialog box, click **Next** to activate the Choose Your Data Connection dialog box. Select the connection named **ACCESS:C:\AdvBook\ Chapter.08\Data\Customer.mdb.Admin** if necessary. Again, the path name may vary.

3. Click **Next** to activate the Choose a Query Type dialog box.

4. Click **Next** to activate the Generate the SQL statements dialog box.

5. Click the **Query Builder** button to activate the Query Builder and the Add Table dialog box. Click the table named **tblTransactions**. Click **Add** to add the table, and then click **Close**.

6. In the Query Builder, click each of the column choices in the order that they appear. Click **OK** to close the Query Builder.

7. Click **Next** to configure the OleDbDataAdapter. Click **Finish** to close the View Wizard Results dialog box. Activate the Properties window for the OleDbDataAdapter, and set the Name property to **odbdaTransactions**.

If you examine the Properties window for the OleDbDataAdapter control instance, you will see hierarchical properties named InsertCommand, UpdateCommand, and DeleteCommand. If you expand these properties, you will see the SQL statements generated by the Wizard.

 If you modify the structure of the database table(s) used by the OleDb-DataAdapter, then you will need to regenerate the statements that were built by the Wizard, otherwise the statements automatically generated by the OleDbDataAdapter will be incorrect. To regenerate the statements created by the OleDbDataAdapter, right-click on the control instance appearing in the tray below the Win Forms Designer, and then click Configure Data Adapter from the context menu. Then complete the dialog boxes that comprise the Wizard to generate the new SQL statements.

At this point, you have configured the OleDbDataAdapter control instances. The Wizard wrote the necessary statements to configure the OleDbDataAdapters.

Understanding the InsertCommand Property

Examine the following statements to configure the OleDbCommand object that will insert a row into the table named tblCustomers. Note that these statements appear in the code automatically generated by the Win Forms Designer. Again, the following statements have been reformatted for readability.

```
Friend WithEvents OleDbInsertCommand1 As _
    System.Data.OleDb.OleDbCommand
Me.OleDbInsertCommand1 = New _
    System.Data.OleDb.OleDbCommand()
Me.odbdaCustomers.InsertCommand = Me.OleDbInsertCommand1
Me.OleDbInsertCommand1.CommandText = "INSERT INTO " & _
    "tblCustomers(fldID, fldFirstName, fldLastName, " & _
    "fldAddress, fldCity, fldState, fldZipCode, " & _
    "fldActive) VALUES (?, ?, ?, ?, ?, ?, ?, ?)"
Me.OleDbInsertCommand1.Connection = Me.odbconCustomers
```

The first of the preceding statements declares a variable named OleDbInsertCommand1 to store the parameterized INSERT statement, and the next two statements configure InsertCommand using the same technique presented in Chapter 7.

The following statement defines the first parameter to the INSERT statement:

```
Me.OleDbInsertCommand1.Parameters.Add( _
    New System.Data.OleDb.OleDbParameter("fldID", _
    System.Data.OleDb.OleDbType.Integer, 0, _
    System.Data.ParameterDirection.Input, False, _
    CType(10, Byte), CType(0, Byte), "fldID", _
    System.Data.DataRowVersion.Current, Nothing))
```

The preceding statement adds an OleDbParameter to the Parameters collection. However, the preceding statement uses a more complex version of the overloaded constructor than the one that you used in Chapter 7.

The following list describes the arguments to the constructor:

- The first argument contains the parameter name that uniquely identifies the parameter in the Parameters collection.

- The second argument specifies the OleDb data type of the parameter (Integer).

- The third argument specifies the size of the parameter. As you have seen before, by specifying a parameter size of 0, the size of the parameter is inferred from the underlying data type (Integer).

- The fourth argument specifies the direction of the parameter. Parameters can be used for input, output, or both. When you store a value in a parameter, as you are doing here, the parameter is used for input. When a parameter returns a value, then the parameter is used for output. The value has a data type of ParameterDirection.

- The fifth argument specifies whether or not the value of the parameter can be null. As the first parameter is the primary key, it cannot be null so the value is False.

- The next two arguments define the precision and scale of the parameter. The precision defines the number of digits to the right of the decimal point and the scale defines the number of digits.

- The eighth argument contains the name of the column in the DataSet (fldID).

- Each row in a DataSet may have an original version, a current version, or a proposed version. The HasVersion property of the DataRow stores the version of the row. The ninth argument stores the version of the row used to get the values for the parameterized query.

- The final argument contains the default value of the parameter. No default parameter is supplied so the value is Nothing.

The OleDbDataAdapter Wizard generated additional parameters for the remaining parameterized fields. Those parameters are omitted here for brevity. In addition, the OleDbDataAdapter Wizard generated the INSERT statement for the table named tblTransactions.

Understanding the UpdateCommand Property

The statements to update a row are more complex than the UPDATE statements that you wrote in Chapter 7. The following UPDATE statement will update a row in the table named tblCustomers:

```
Me.OleDbUpdateCommand1.CommandText = _
    "UPDATE tblCustomers SET fldID = ?, " & _
    "fldFirstName = ?, fldLastName = ?, fldAddress " & _
    "= ?, fldCity = ?, fldState = ?, fldZipCode = ?, " & _
    "fldActive = ? WHERE (fldID = ?) " & _
    "AND (fldActive = ?) " & _
    "AND (fldAddress = ? OR ? IS NULL " & _
    "AND fldAddress IS NULL) AND" & _
    " (fldCity = ? OR ? IS NULL AND fldCity IS NULL) " & _
    "AND (fldFirstName = ? OR ? IS NULL " & _
    " AND fldFirstName IS NULL) AND " & _
    "(fldLastName = ? OR ? IS NULL AND fldLastName IS " & _
    "NULL) AND (fldState = ? OR ? IS NULL AND fldState " & _
    "IS NULL) AND (fldZipCode = ?" & _
    " OR ? IS NULL AND fldZipCode IS NULL)"
```

The preceding UPDATE statement created by the OleDbDataAdapter Wizard updates the fields in the table named tblCustomers, however, the WHERE clause is expanded. Instead of just comparing the record to update against the primary key field, the WHERE clause is modified to compare the contents of each field value. The original value of the field is compared against the field contents appearing in the database table.

The purpose of this WHERE clause is to prevent one user from accidentally overwriting changes made by another user to the same record. To explain, two or more users create their own DataSets based on the same database data. Furthermore, each user can make modifications to the data in those DataSets. Because a DataSet is disconnected from the database, changes made by one user to one DataSet do not appear in another DataSet. Figure 8-11 illustrates the problem.

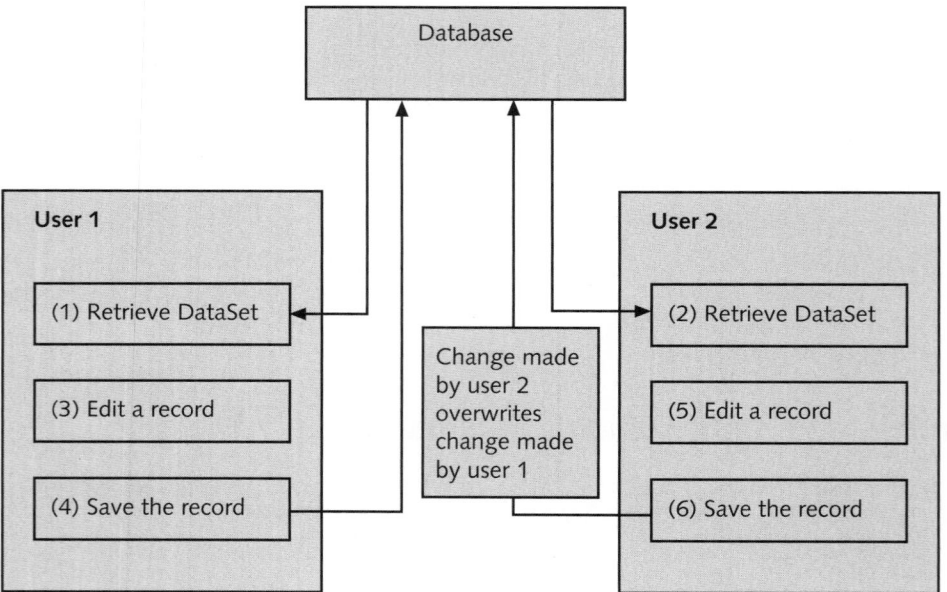

Figure 8-11   Overwriting database changes

As shown in Figure 8-11, user 1 creates a DataSet, and then user 2 creates a DataSet containing the same records. User 1 then edits and updates a record. Then user 2 edits and updates the same record. Given this scenario, user 1 is not aware that the change was overwritten, nor is user 2 aware that the record was changed since the time is was read into the DataSet.

To solve the problem, VB .NET builds the INSERT, UPDATE, and DELETE statements so that changes made to one DataSet will not accidentally be overwritten by changes made to another DataSet by another user. In the preceding UPDATE statement, the WHERE clause compares the contents of every field against the original value stored in the corresponding parameter. The effect of this WHERE clause is significant. If another user has modified any field in the selected record, then no record will match the criteria defined in the WHERE clause, so no record will be updated. This is one way that ADO.NET provides concurrency control between multiple database users.

The preceding UPDATE statement has additional parameters to specify the current version of a field and the new original version of the field. The following statements illustrate the parameters for the field named fldID:

```
Me.OleDbUpdateCommand1.Parameters.Add( _
    New System.Data.OleDb.OleDbParameter("fldID", _
    System.Data.OleDb.OleDbType.Integer, 0, _
    System.Data.ParameterDirection.Input, False, _
    CType(10, Byte), CType(0, Byte), "fldID", _
    System.Data.DataRowVersion.Current, Nothing))
' Statements for other parameters
Me.OleDbUpdateCommand1.Parameters.Add(New _
    System.Data.OleDb.OleDbParameter("Original_fldID", _
    System.Data.OleDb.OleDbType.Integer, 0, _
    System.Data.ParameterDirection.Input, False, _
    CType(10, Byte), CType(0, Byte), "fldID", _
    System.Data.DataRowVersion.Original, Nothing))
```

The preceding statements define the parameters for the UPDATE statement. However, the Wizard has generated statements to better handle any concurrency problems arising from multiple users trying to update the same record. Notice that the first parameter used in the WHERE clause stores the current version of the field (System.Data.DataRowVersion.Current). The second argument contains the new changed version.

When the update is performed, if another user has made changes to any fields in the record, then no records will match in the WHERE clause and the UPDATE statement will not succeed.

Figure 8-12 illustrates the operation of the parameterized UPDATE statement automatically generated by the OleDbDataAdapter.

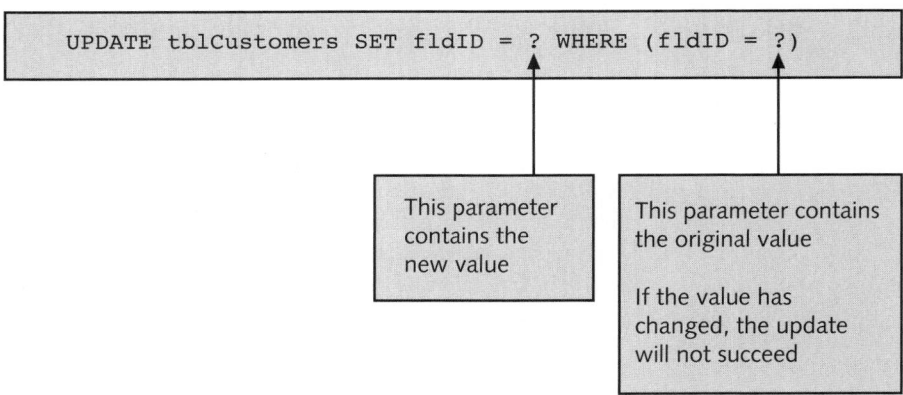

Figure 8-12   UPDATE statement with concurrency parameters

Note that the DELETE statement generated by the Wizard is nearly the same as the one that you previously created and is not discussed in detail here.

At this point in the solution's development, you have created and configured the OleDbConnection and OleDbDataAdapter control instances. Next, you need to generate and fill the DataSet.

STRONGLY TYPED DATASETS

In Chapter 7, you worked with an untyped DataSet. In this part of the chapter, you will learn how to work with strongly typed DataSets. For brevity, we will use the term typed DataSet to mean strongly typed DataSet.

Typed DataSets versus Untyped DataSets

A **typed DataSet** is a DataSet that derives from the System.Data.DataSet class and defines additional properties and methods to reference the tables and fields in that DataSet, based on the names of the underlying tables and fields appearing in the database itself. To get started, examine the following statements that reference a field using both an untyped DataSet and a typed DataSet:

```
Dim pstrID As String
pstrID = DsCustomers1.Tables("tblCustomers"). _
    Rows(0).Item(0).ToString
pstrID = DsCustomers1.tblCustomers(0).fldID.ToString
```

The preceding statements both reference the field named fldID in the DataTable named tblCustomers. The first statement uses the Tables and Rows collections to reference the field as you have seen before. This first reference uses an untyped DataSet. The final statement illustrates how to reference the same field using a typed DataSet. The table named tblCustomers can be referenced directly without referencing the Tables collection. Note also that the Rows collection need not be explicitly referenced either.

The following list describes selected differences between typed and untyped DataSets:

- A typed DataSet reduces the amount of code you must write to reference the tables and fields in the DataSet.

- A typed DataSet tends to perform faster than an equivalent untyped DataSet.

- When you call the Item method of the DataRow class to reference a field and its data, that data is returned as a generic Object type. This can cause run-time type conversion errors because the data type of the field is not known at compile time. In a typed DataSet, a property is exposed for each field. That property has the same data type as the data type of the underlying field. Thus, possible type conversion errors can be detected at compile time.

- Intellisense technology displays the names of the tables and fields in a strongly typed DataSet.

Creating a Typed DataSet

You create a typed DataSet using an existing OleDbDataAdapter and a dialog box called the Generate Dataset dialog box. A typed DataSet can contain data from a single table or data from multiple tables.

To generate a typed DataSet:

1. Activate the Win Forms Designer for the form named **frmUtility.vb**, if necessary. On the menu bar, click **Data**, **Generate Dataset** to activate the Generate Dataset dialog box shown in Figure 8-13.

Figure 8-13   Generate Dataset dialog box

2. Click the **New** radio button, and then enter the name **dsUtility** as the name of the DataSet. Make sure that the **Add this dataset to the designer.** check box is checked.

   If you do not add the DataSet to the designer, VB .NET writes the statements to create a typed DataSet but does not declare a variable in the form to store an instance of the typed DataSet class. By adding the DataSet to the designer, VB .NET declares a variable in the form to reference the typed DataSet class, and then creates an instance of that class. We show this variable declaration in a moment.

3. Click **OK** to close the dialog box and generate the DataSet.

VB .NET performed several tasks when you generated the typed DataSet. Because you elected to add the DataSet to the designer, VB .NET wrote the following statements to declare a variable named DsUtility1 to store an instance of the typed DataSet class named dsUtility:

```
Friend WithEvents DsUtility1 As Startup08.dsUtility
Me.DsUtility1 = New Startup08.dsUtility()
```

Through the variable named DsUtility1, you reference the typed DataSet. Note that the class is named Startup08.dsUtility. This custom class was created by VB .NET when you generated the DataSet. VB .NET uses the class name followed by the number 1 as the name of the instance variable.

 If you make changes to the OleDbDataAdapter, you should regenerate the DataSet. Unless you regenerate the DataSet, the OleDbDataAdapter will likely be using a SELECT statement that is inconsistent with schema defined in the DataSet's .xsd file.

The Schema Definition File

To represent the structure of the typed DataSet, VB .NET created a file called a schema definition file when you generated the DataSet. A **schema definition file** is an XML document that describes the structure of the DataSet, the structure of the DataTable(s) that comprise the DataSet, and the fields in those tables. The schema definition file may also contain elements to define the primary key and to define any relations between the tables in the DataSet. This file has a suffix of .xsd and appears in the Solution Explorer. The .xsd file generated by VB .NET can be modified and edited using the XML Designer. This visual designer, like all document windows, appears on a group tab.

The XML Designer operates in two modes. When the DataSet tab is active, you edit the XML document using a visual interface and various dialog boxes. When the XML tab is active, you edit the XML document directly. In this chapter, you will edit the XML document using the visual designer.

To view the schema definition file visually:

1. Activate the **Solution Explorer**, if necessary.

2. In the Solution Explorer, double-click the icon for the file named **dsUtility.xsd** to activate the XML Designer shown in Figure 8-14. Click the **DataSet** tab if necessary.

As shown in Figure 8-14, the XML Designer has two tabs. The DataSet tab displays the visual designer used to manage the schema definition file. The XML tab allows you to edit the XML statements directly. Through the XML Designer, you may add fields to a DataSet table, modify field data types, and change the XML in other ways too. These capabilities will be discussed as you use them.

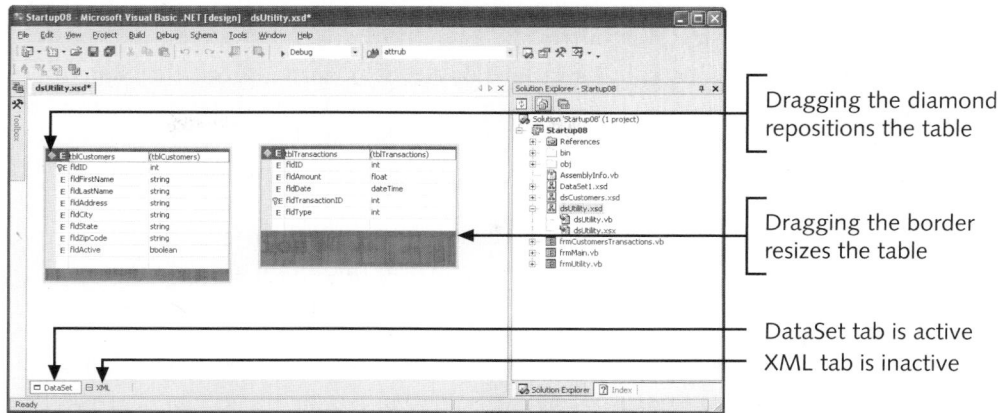

Figure 8-14   XML Designer – DataSet tab

Entire books have been written on the topic of XML. We will introduce the XML language only to the extent that it describes the XML document created by the XML Designer.

From the XML document stored in the schema definition file, VB .NET created another file named dsUtility.vb that defines a class derived from System.Data.DataSet. (Note that the names of the .xsd file and the .vb file are the same. Only the file extension differs.) This class corresponds to the DataSet configuration contained in the .xsd file. If the contents of the .xsd file are changed, the corresponding .vb file should be regenerated. You regenerate the derived class from the .xsd file by right-clicking the XML document in the XML Designer, and then clicking Generate Dataset from the context menu. Do not ever modify the contents of the .vb file directly, as regenerating the DataSet will cause VB .NET to overwrite the .vb file.

So that you can best understand how a typed DataSet works, we suggest that you print the corresponding module file and use it for reference as you work through this section of the chapter.

To print a typed DataSet class:

1. Activate the **Solution Explorer**, and then click the **Show All Files** button, if necessary. Expand the **dsUtility.xsd** folder to display the module named dsUtility.vb.

2. Activate the Code Editor for the module named **dsUtility.vb**, and then print the module.

To help explain how a strongly typed DataSet works, we discuss selected classes exposed by the dsUtility.vb module.

Elements of a Typed DataSet

A typed DataSet is merely a custom DataSet that derives from the System.Data.DataSet class using the same inheritance rules you have worked with before. In the next group of statements, you will explore the organization of this class to see how it works. Note that we do not examine all of the statements in the typed DataSet class. As the purpose of a typed DataSet is to simplify DataSet programming, we examine only those members that are exposed to you and omit the discussion of most hidden members. The typed dsUtility class appears in the dsUtility.vb file as shown in the following statements:

```
Imports System.Data
  ' Statements
Public Class dsUtility
    Inherits DataSet
    ' Statements
End Class
```

What is significant about the dsUtility class is that it exposes properties and methods allowing you to access each DataTable, its rows, and the fields in those rows by name instead of having to use the Tables and Rows collections of the underlying DataSet class itself. In addition, these properties and methods have data types corresponding to the data type of the underlying table, row, and field.

For each DataTable in the DataSet, the class contains a Public nested class named *xxx*DataTable where *xxx* is the name of the underlying database table. Thus, this DataSet contains a class named tblCustomersDataTable for the table named tblCustomers in the DataSet. An additional class named tblTransactionsDataTable also appears, which corresponds to the table named tblTransactions. Remember that the DataSet contains two tables. Examine the following statements:

```
Imports System.Data
Public Class dsUtility
    Inherits DataSet
    ' Statements
    Public ReadOnly Property tblCustomers As _
        tblCustomersDataTable
    Get
        Return Me.tabletblCustomers
    End Get
    End Property
    ' Statements
    Public Class tblCustomersDataTable
        Inherits System.Data.DataTable
        ' Statements
    End Class
  ' Statements
End Class
```

The preceding DataSet defines a read-only property named tblCustomers to reference the typed DataTable named tblCustomersDataTable. The class tblCustomersDataTable inherits from the class named System.Data.DataTable and supplies strongly typed methods and properties to reference each row in the DataTable. Assuming that DsUtility1 is an instance of the dsUtility class, the following statements will reference the typed DataTable:

```
Dim dtCustomers As tblCustomersDataTable
dtCustomers = DsUtility1.tblCustomers
```

Each derived DataTable class, in turn, contains another nested class named *xxx*Row, where *xxx* again contains the name of the underlying database table. Thus, this DataSet class contains a class named tblCustomersRow. The *xxx*Row class is just a strongly typed version of the DataRow class. This typed class derives from the DataRow class, as shown in the following statements:

```
Public Class tblCustomersDataTable
    Inherits System.Data.DataTable
    ' Statements
    Public Class tblCustomersRow
        Inherits DataRow
        ' Statements
    End Class
    ' Statements
    Public Default ReadOnly Property Item( _
        ByVal index As Integer) As tblCustomersRow
        Get
            Return CType(Me.Rows(index),tblCustomersRow)
        End Get
    End Property
End Class
```

As shown in the preceding statements, the class tblCustomersDataTable contains a nested class named tblCustomersRow. The Item property, like the Item property of any DataTable class, returns a DataRow from the DataTable using a 0-based numeric index. However, the Item property of the derived DataTable is also strongly typed (tblCustomersRow). The following statements reference the first row in the table:

```
Dim drCurrent As tblCustomersRow
tblCustomersRow = DsUtility1.tblCustomers(0)
```

Each DataRow in a DataTable, in turn, contains properties having the same name as the underlying fields. These properties are strongly typed too. That is, each property has a data type that corresponds to the data type of the underlying table field. This is one of the advantages to using strongly typed DataSets. They eliminate the need to explicitly perform much of the type conversion required when implementing an untyped DataSet. The following statements illustrate the property procedure named fldID in the typed DataRow class tblCustomersRow:

```
Public Class tblCustomersRow
    Inherits DataRow
```

```
' Statements
Public Property fldID As Integer
    Get
        Return CType(Me( _
            Me.tabletblCustomers.fldIDColumn),Integer)
    End Get
    Set
        Me(Me.tabletblCustomers.fldIDColumn) = _
            value
    End Set
End Property
' Property procedures for other fields
End Class
```

As shown in the preceding code segment, the DataRow (tblCustomersRow) contains a property named fldID corresponding to the field in the DataTable having the same name. Note that this property is strongly typed. That is, the value returned is explicitly converted to an Integer data type. Thus, the following statements will reference the field named fldID from the first row in the DataTable:

```
Dim pintID As Integer
pintID = DsUtility1.tblCustomers(0).fldID
```

A typed method named FindByfldID appears in the tblCustomersDataTable class. This method will locate a DataRow based on the field named fldID, as shown in the following statements:

```
Public Class tblCustomersDataTable
    Inherits DataTable
    Implements System.Collections.IEnumerable
    ' Statements
    Public Function FindByfldID(ByVal fldID As Integer) _
        As tblCustomersRow
        Return CType(Me.Rows.Find(New Object() _
            {fldID}), tblCustomersRow)
    End Function
    ' Statements
End Class
```

The preceding statements call the same Find method of the Rows collection that you saw in Chapter 7. However, instead of returning a generic DataRow object, the returned row has an explicit data type of tblCustomersRow.

Having explored selected classes and methods exposed by a typed DataSet, you will now learn how they are used.

Referencing Fields in a Typed DataSet

The form named frmMain.vb contains all of the statements to locate records, and to add, change, and delete records using a strongly typed DataSet. All of the code for this form has already been created. In this section, we review selected code segments in this form so as to describe the differences between a typed DataSet and an untyped DataSet.

As mentioned, when you generate a typed DataSet, VB .NET creates properties for the typed DataRow corresponding to each field name. Examine the following statements to reference selected fields corresponding to the table named tblCustomers:

```
Dim pintID As Integer
Dim pstrFirstName, pstrLastName As String

Dim drCurrent As dsCustomers.tblCustomersRow
drCurrent = DsCustomers1.tblCustomers(0)
pintID = drCurrent.fldID
pstrFirstName = drCurrent.fldFirstName
pstrLastName = drCurrent.fldLastName
```

The variable drCurrent is declared as a strongly typed DataRow (tblCustomersRow). dsCustomers is the name of the typed DataSet class that you already generated. The next statement stores the first row in the table into the variable drCurrent. The variable DsCustomers1 is assumed to store an instance of the dsCustomers DataSet class. Again, note that the typed DataSet table named tblCustomers defines the table. The last three statements retrieve the contents of the three fields into variables to illustrate how to reference the fields in the typed DataRow. The following equivalent statement illustrates how to reference a field in a typed DataRow without declaring an intermediate variable to store the DataRow itself:

```
pintID = DsCustomers1.tblCustomers(0).fldID
```

Remember that the DataTable class supports a method named Find, which will return a DataRow corresponding to a primary key. A typed DataSet supplies a typed version of the same Find method.

Locating a Record in a Typed DataSet

The field named fldID was designated as the primary key in the database table. Thus, the typed DataSet exposes a method named FindByfldID that will return an object of type tblCustomersRow, which is just a strongly typed version of the DataRow class. Examine the following statements to locate a row in the DataTable:

```
Dim drCurrent As dsCustomers.tblCustomersRow
drCurrent = _
    DsCustomers1.tblCustomers.FindByfldID(1)
```

The form named frmMain.vb already contains a typed DataSet to reference the fields in the table. This typed DataSet is similar to the one that you just created and is named dsCustomers. The form already contains all of the statements to locate records and to add, change, and delete records from the typed DataSet. The following statements appear in the ShowCurrentRecord procedure. Its purpose is to display one of the records in a DataSet. The following selected statements show how to use the typed DataSet to reference fields named fldID and fldFirstName. The statements to reference the other fields have been omitted for brevity.

```
Private Sub ShowCurrentRecord( _
    ByVal drCurrent As dsCustomers.tblCustomersRow)

    txtID.Text = drCurrent.fldID.ToString
    txtFirstName.Text = drCurrent.fldFirstName
    ' Statements to store the remaining fields
End Sub
```

Using a typed DataSet, you reference a field's contents through a property of a typed DataRow. Thus, the ShowCurrentRecord method accepts one argument of type tblCustomersRow. The field name is appended to the DataRow. This is possible because the typed DataSet exposes properties of the DataRow having the same name as the field names themselves. In both the completed and startup solutions, the statements to navigate from record to record have also been completed for brevity.

Adding a Record to a Typed DataSet

Conceptually, the steps to add a new record to a typed DataSet are the same as the steps to add a new record to an untyped DataSet. You create a new row based on the schema of a DataTable, modify the contents of that new row, and then add the newly created row to the underlying DataTable. As both a typed and untyped DataSet are disconnected from the database, you again use the OleDbDataAdapter to record the DataSet changes back to the database.

Two modifications exist for the steps necessary to add a record from those shown in Chapter 7. First, the typed table named tblCustomers contains a method named NewtblCustomersRow to create the new typed DataRow object, and the method named AddtblCustomersRow adds the new DataRow to the underlying DataTable. The following statements appear on the form named frmMain.vb, in the Click event handler for the menu item named mmuEditSaveAdd:

```
Call SetEditState(EditState.Browsing)
Dim drCurrent As dsCustomers.tblCustomersRow

Try
    drCurrent = _
        DsCustomers1.tblCustomers.NewtblCustomersRow
    With drCurrent
        .fldID = System.Convert.ToInt32(txtID.Text)
        .fldFirstName = txtFirstName.Text
        .fldLastName = txtLastName.Text
        .fldAddress = txtAddress.Text
        .fldCity = txtCity.Text
        .fldState = txtState.Text
        .fldZipCode = txtZipCode.Text
        .fldActive = chkActive.Checked
```

```
        End With
        DsCustomers1.tblCustomers.AddtblCustomersRow(drCurrent)
        mintCurrent += 1
        Call SaveChanges()

    Catch ex As System.ArgumentException
        DsCustomers1.tblCustomers(mintCurrent).CancelEdit()

    Catch ex As System.Data.ConstraintException
        MessageBox.Show( _
            "ID must be unique. Addition cancelled", _
            "Error", MessageBoxButtons.OK)
            DsCustomers1.tblCustomers(mintCurrent).CancelEdit()

    Finally
        Call ShowCurrentRecord(mintCurrent)
    End Try
```

Modifying a Record

The steps to modify a row with a typed DataSet are not that much different from the steps to modify a row with an untyped DataSet. However, instead of referencing individual fields through the Tables and other collections, you reference the tables and fields through the properties and methods exposed by the typed DataSet itself, just as you did when adding a record. The following statements appear in the Click event handler for the menu item named mmuEditSaveChange on the form named frmMain.vb:

```
Dim drCurrent As dsCustomers.tblCustomersRow
drCurrent = DsCustomers1.tblCustomers(mintCurrent)
drCurrent.BeginEdit()
drCurrent.fldID = System.Convert.ToInt32(txtID.Text)
drCurrent.fldFirstName = txtFirstName.Text()
' Statements to store values in other fields
drCurrent.EndEdit()
```

The preceding statements create a typed DataRow object named drCurrent. Then data are stored into each field as you have seen before. The BeginEdit and EndEdit methods have the same purpose as you have also seen before. The BeginEdit method temporarily suspends the RowChanging event on the row as it is being edited.

Deleting a Record

Again, deleting a row from a typed DataSet is similar to adding and changing a row. The Delete method is called on a DataRow as you have seen before. The following statements illustrate how to delete a record from a typed DataSet:

```
Dim drCurrent As dsCustomers.tblCustomersRow
drCurrent = DsCustomers1.tblCustomers(mintCurrent)
drCurrent.Delete()
```

```
Call SaveChanges()
mintCurrent = 0
Call ShowCurrentRecord(mintCurrent)
```

Again, for brevity, the statements appearing in the form named frmMain.vb to delete a record have already been completed in both the startup and completed solutions.

UNDERSTANDING ONE-TO-MANY RELATIONSHIPS

As mentioned, a database seldom contains a single table, rather, most databases contain multiple tables. The information in these multiple tables is typically related in some way. For example, the table named tblCustomers in this database has one row for each customer. The table named tblTransactions contains the transactions for all customers. The field named fldID in the table named tblCustomers is that table's primary key, and the field named fldID in the table named tblTransactions is that table's foreign key. A DataSet can be created that links the customers with their associated transactions using the primary and foreign keys from the two tables.

The form named frmCustomersTransactions.vb contains a user interface that links the customer information with the associated transaction information for each customer. The form named frmUtility.vb also uses the same two tables.

Examining the form named frmCustomersTransactions.vb, you can see that it already contains an instance of the OleDbConnection control over which commands will be sent. Two OleDbDataAdapter control instances have already been configured on the form. The first, named odbdaCustomers, retrieves all of the records from the table named tblCustomers. The second, named odbdaTransactions, retrieves all of the records from the table named tblTransactions. The steps to create and configure these OleDbDataAdapters are the same as you have seen before. A typed DataSet named dsCustomersTransactions has also been created that stores data from both tables.

Having created the DataSet objects for the form named frmUtility.vb and the form named frmCustomersTransactions.vb, you can now proceed to define how the data contained in the two tables are related together. To relate two or more tables in a DataSet you use another class called a DataRelation.

 Even though a database may contain defined relationships, these relationships are not propagated to the disconnected DataSet. You must define these relationships manually.

THE DATARELATION CLASS

ADO.NET supplies two ways to define the relations between multiple tables in a DataSet. You can create a relation programmatically or use a tool supplied by VB .NET. At the heart of the process is the DataRelation object. Its purpose is to define a one-to-many relationship between two DataTable objects in a DataSet. In such a relationship, one table is considered the parent (one) table, and another is considered the child (many) table.

In this section, you will create a DataRelation programmatically, and then create that same DataRelation using a VB .NET tool so as best to understand the process.

Defining a DataRelation Programmatically

Every DataSet has a collection named Relations. The Relations collection, in turn, contains one DataRelation object for each relation defined in the DataSet. As a DataSet can have several tables, you can define multiple DataRelation objects to describe complex relationships between those tables. The DataRelation class has the following members:

Syntax

System.Data.DataRelation class

Public Properties

- The **ChildTable** property references the DataTable configured as the child table.

- The **ChildColumns** property returns an array of DataColumn objects that define the column(s) in the child table.

- The **ParentTable** property references the DataTable configured as the parent table.

- The **ParentColumns** property returns an array of DataColumn objects that define the column(s) that comprise the primary key in the parent table.

The process to create a DataRelation involves three steps. First, you retrieve the column(s) representing the primary key and the foreign key from the two tables involved in the relation. These columns have a data type of DataColumn. Second, you create the DataRelation using its constructor. Third, you add the new DataRelation to the Relations collection of the underlying DataSet. The overloaded DataRelation constructor has the following syntax:

Syntax

Overloads Public Sub New(*relationname* **As String**, *parentcolumn* **As DataColumn**, *childcolumn* **As DataColumn**)
Overloads Public Sub New(*relationname* **As String**, *parentcolumns*() **As DataColumn**, *childcolumns*() **As DataColumn**)

Definition

The overloaded **DataRelation** constructor creates a DataRelation using the primary key from the parent table, and the foreign key from the child table.

Dissection

- The *relationname* argument specifies a unique name for the DataRelation.

- The *parentcolumns()* and *parentcolumn* arguments define the primary key field(s) from the parent table.

- The *childcolumns()* and *childcolumn* arguments define the foreign key field(s) from the child table.

The groups of statements below illustrate the three steps to create a DataRelation.

```
Dim dcParent As DataColumn
Dim dcChild As DataColumn
Dim drUtility As DataRelation
```

The preceding statements declare the necessary variables to store the two columns that will be used in the DataRelation and a variable to store the DataRelation itself. The following statements store the column representing the primary and foreign keys into the DataColumn variables just declared:

```
dcParent = _
    DsUtility1.tblCustomers.fldIDColumn
dcChild = _
    DsUtility1.tblTransactions.fldIDColumn
```

The preceding statements use the typed DataSet named DsUtility1 to get the fldID columns from both of the DataTable objects. Note that you can accomplish the same task using an untyped DataSet, but the syntax is more cumbersome. The following statements create the DataRelation using the two columns you just defined as the primary and foreign keys:

```
drUtility = New DataRelation( _
    "drUtility", dcParent, dcChild)
DsUtility1.Relations.Add(drUtility)
```

The first of the preceding statements creates the DataRelation itself. The first argument defines the unique name for the DataRelation (drUtility). The second and third arguments to the constructor contain the DataColumn objects from the parent and child tables. The final statement adds the DataRelation to the Relations collection of the DataSet.

In this section, you will create a DataRelation between the customers and transactions tables. You will then use this DataRelation to get the transaction records for the active customers.

To create a DataRelation programmatically:

1. Activate the Code Editor for the form named **frmUtility.vb**. Enter the following statements in the **Load** event handler for the form:

```
Dim dcParent As DataColumn
Dim dcChild As DataColumn
Dim drUtility As DataRelation
```

```
dcParent = _
    DsUtility1.tblCustomers.fldIDColumn
dcChild = _
    DsUtility1.tblTransactions.fldIDColumn
drUtility = New DataRelation("drUtility", _
    dcParent, dcChild)
DsUtility1.Relations.Add(drUtility)

odbdaCustomers.Fill(DsUtility1)
odbdaTransactions.Fill(DsUtility1)
```

The preceding statements declare the necessary variables to store the fields used in the DataRelation, and then create that DataRelation. The final two statements populate the DataSet.

The GetChildRows Method

The primary purpose of the DataRelation is to get all of the rows from the detail table corresponding to a single row appearing in the parent table. The GetChildRows method of the DataRow class uses the DataRelation to retrieve all of the child rows corresponding to a parent row, and has the following syntax:

Syntax

System.Data.DataRow.GetChildRows method

Overloads Public Function GetChildRows(*relation* **As DataRelation) As DataRow()**
Overloads Public Function GetChildRows(*relationname* **As String) As DataRow()**
Overloads Public Function GetChildRows(*relation* **As DataRelation,** *version* **As DataRowVersion) As DataRow()**
Overloads Public Function GetChildRows(*relationname* **As String,** *version* **As DataRowVersion) As DataRow()**

Definition

For a given DataRow, the overloaded *GetChildRows* method returns an array of DataRow objects corresponding to the records in a child table. Note that an array of DataRow objects is different from a DataTable.

Dissection

■ The *relation* argument contains an existing DataRelation object.

■ Instead of specifying the DataRelation as the argument, you can also use the *relationname* you assigned to the DataRelation when you created it.

■ The *version* argument allows you to get the current or proposed values from the child rows.

The following statements illustrate how to get the child rows corresponding to the first parent row in the dsUtility DataSet. Again, as the focus of this chapter involves working with typed DataSets, the following statements use the typed DataRow named tblTransactionsRow. An untyped DataSet would also work, however.

```
Dim drTransactions() As _
    dsUtility.tblTransactionsRow
drTransactions = DsUtility1. _
    tblCustomers(0).GetChildRows("drUtility")
```

The first statement uses the typed DataSet to declare an array named drTransactions that will store the DataRow objects returned by the GetChildRows method. The second statement gets the child rows corresponding to the first record in the parent DataSet table named tblCustomers. The statement fragment DsUtility1.tblCustomers(0) references the first row in the parent customers table. By calling the GetChildRows method on this DataRow, the corresponding child rows are returned and stored in the array drTransactions. The name of the DataRelation (drUtility) is passed as the argument to the GetChildRows method. Figure 8-15 illustrates how this process works.

```
drTransactions = DsUtility1.tblCustomers(0).GetChildRows("drUtility")
```

Figure 8-15   Getting the child rows from a DataRelation

As shown in Figure 8-15, the GetChildRows method is called on a particular DataRow, and returns an array of DataRow objects. The array contains one DataRow object for each child row. Note that an array of DataRow objects is different from a DataTable. That is, the GetChildRows method returns an array, so you use array processing techniques to examine the DataRow objects in the array as shown in the following code segment:

```
drTransactions = drCustomer.GetChildRows("drUtility")
For pintCount = 0 To drTransactions.GetUpperBound(0)
    ' Statements to process each DataRow
Next
```

In this chapter's solution, you will use a DataRelation to examine each active customer. For each active customer you will write the statements to tally the total amount of charges and payments for that customer.

To get the child rows in a DataRelation:

1. Activate the Code Editor for the form named **frmUtility.vb**, and then enter the following statements in the **Click** event handler for the button named **btnCalculateTotal**:

```
Dim drTransactions() As _
    dsUtility.tblTransactionsRow
Dim drCustomer As dsUtility.tblCustomersRow
Dim pintCount As Integer
Dim psngCharges, psngPayments As Single
Dim pstrOutput As String

For Each drCustomer In _
    DsUtility1.tblCustomers.Rows
    drTransactions = drCustomer.GetChildRows("drUtility")

For pintCount = 0 To drTransactions.GetUpperBound(0)
    If drTransactions(pintCount).fldType = 1 Then
        psngCharges += _
            drTransactions(pintCount).fldAmount
    Else
        psngPayments += _
            drTransactions(pintCount).fldAmount
    End If
Next
pstrOutput &= vbCrLf & drCustomer.fldLastName & _
    "," & drCustomer.fldFirstName & vbTab & _
    psngCharges.ToString("f") & vbTab & _
    psngPayments.ToString("f")
psngCharges = 0
psngPayments = 0
Next
txtOutput.Text = pstrOutput
```

8

The preceding statements declare a variable named drTransactions to store the array of tblTransactionsRow objects. The For Each loop examines each DataRow in the table named tblCustomers. For each row in the parent table (tblCustomers), the GetChildRows method is called to get the child rows (transactions) corresponding to the current customer. The inner For loop examines each row in the array of DataRows. The statement in the For loop checks to determine whether the transaction is a charge (fldType = 1), or a payment (fldType = 2). The respective accumulator is updated accordingly. Then, for each parent record, a string is built containing the customer name, charges, and payments. After all of the parent records have been processed, the contents of the string are stored in the text box.

2. Test the solution. On the main form, click **Windows**, **Utilities** to display the utilities form. Click the **Calculate** button to calculate the total charges and payments for each customer and display the results in the form's multiline text box.

In addition to creating a DataRelation programmatically, you can also use the XML Designer to accomplish the same task.

Using the XML Designer to Create a DataRelation

The XML Designer provides a graphical means to create the same DataRelation that you just created programmatically. In this section, you will define the DataRelation for the DataSet on the form named frmCustomersTransactions.vb. The DataRelation that you are defining on this form has the same characteristics as the one you just created. The only difference is that you will use the XML Designer to accomplish the same task.

You saw previously in the chapter that the XML Designer can be used to configure and edit a typed DataSet. You can also use the XML Designer to define the relations between the DataTable objects in a DataSet. To create a DataRelation with the XML Designer, you right-click the parent table in the XML Designer to select it, and then click Add, New Relation from the context menu to display the Edit Relation dialog box shown in Figure 8-16. Finally, you fill in the fields in the XML Designer to create and configure the DataRelation.

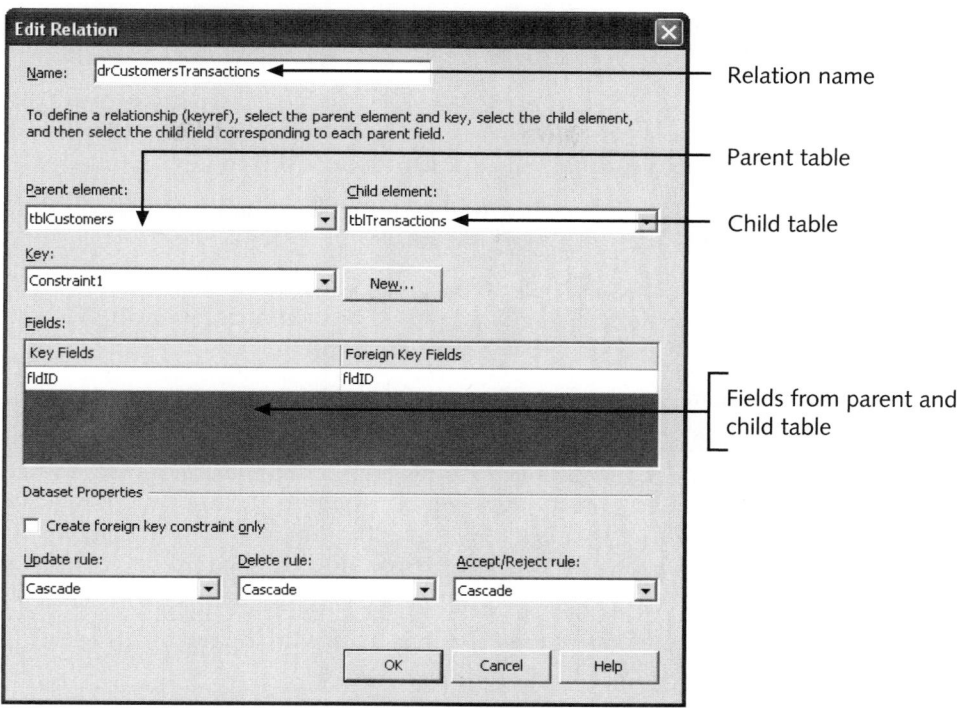

Figure 8-16   Edit Relation dialog box

Figure 8–16 shows the completed DataRelation between the tables named tblCustomers and tblTransactions. The following list describes the meaning of the various fields:

- In the Parent element list box, you select the master table, in this case tblCustomers.

- In the Child element list box, you select the detail table, in this case tblTransactions.

- The XML Designer automatically defines the key fields based on the primary key in the master (parent) table and the foreign key in the child table. In this case, the primary and foreign keys are fldID. You can change these key fields if necessary.

- The Update, Delete, and Accept/Reject rule list boxes define how changes to the primary key in the parent table will affect the corresponding records and foreign key in the child table. If set to Cascade, changing the primary key value in the parent table will cause values of the foreign keys to be changed to that same value in the child table. The setting SetNull will cause the corresponding foreign key values in the child table to be set to null values. The setting SetDefault will cause the foreign key values in the child table to be set to a default value, if one exists.

Next, you will use the XML Designer to visually define the DataRelation between the table named tblCustomers, and the table named tblTransactions.

1. Activate the XML Designer for the DataSet named **dsCustomersTransactions**. Remember, to activate the XML Designer, right-click the .xsd file in the Solution Explorer, and then click **Open** from the context menu.

2. In the XML Designer, click the master table named **tblCustomers** to select it. A hatched border surrounds the table.

3. On the menu bar, click **Schema**, select **Add**, and then click **New Relation**. The Edit Relation dialog box appears as shown in Figure 8-16. Note that the relation appears after it has been fully configured.

4. Set the name of the DataRelation to **drCustomersTransactions**.

   The DataRelation you created programmatically used this same DataSet and was named dsUtility. Indeed, this is redundant, but the purpose is to illustrate how to create a DataRelation both programmatically and visually. Note that the names of the two DataRelations are different. If you tried to create two DataRelations having the same name, an error would occur because two elements in a collection cannot have the same value for a string key.

5. Set the name of the Parent element to **tblCustomers**, if necessary. This is the name of the master table in the DataSet.

6. Set the name of the Child element to **tblTransactions**.

7. Set the Update rule, Delete rule, and Accept/Reject rule to **Cascade**.

8. Click **OK** to create the relation and close the Edit Relation dialog box.

   Note that a line connects the master and detail tables in the DataRelation. If you later want to change the characteristics of the DataRelation, right-click on the diamond of the DataRelation, and then click Edit Relation from the context menu.

9. On the menu bar, click **File**, and then click **Save All** to save the changes that you just made to the DataSet.

When you created the DataRelation, VB .NET regenerated the typed class named dsCustomersTransactions.vb and generated the DataRelation as shown in the following code segment:

```
Private relationtblCustomerstblTransactions As DataRelation
Me.relationtblCustomerstblTransactions = New _
    DataRelation("drCustomerstblTransactions", _
    New DataColumn() {Me.tabletblCustomers.fldIDColumn}, _
    New DataColumn() _
    {Me.tabletblTransactions.fldIDColumn}, False)
```

The preceding statements to create the DataRelation are very similar to those you wrote for the utilities form. However, the columns are created in the constructor without intermediate variables. In addition, the DataColumn objects are arrays, which allow the keys to contain multiple fields.

DATA BINDING

Data binding associates a control instance with data from a data source. In this chapter, you will bind control instances to a DataSet. However, data binding works with other objects too. For example, you could bind control instances to the elements in an ArrayList. VB .NET supplies two types of data binding, as described in the following list:

- Using **simple binding**, you bind a control instance to a row in a DataTable. A control instance, such as a text box, stores the data from one field appearing in a single row.
- Using **complex binding**, you bind a control instance to multiple rows in a DataTable. Controls such as combo boxes and list boxes are complex bound and can be configured to display all of the rows from a field in a DataTable. The DataGrid control, which you will explore in a moment, is also complex bound.

In the following three sections you will first explore simple binding, and then see how to work with complex bound controls.

Simple Binding

You can bind a control instance using tools supplied by VB .NET or write the statements yourself. When you bind a control instance to a data source, you bind a single property, such as the Text property of a text box to a field in a DataTable. When the solution is run, VB .NET automatically stores the contents of the field in the bound property for the control instance. You accomplish this task programmatically by first creating a Binding object using the Binding constructor, and then adding that Binding object to the DataBindings collection of the control instance.

The Binding constructor has the following syntax:

Syntax

System.Windows.Forms.Binding constructor

Public Sub New (ByVal *propertyname* **As String, ByVal** *datasource* **As Object, ByVal** *datamember* **As String) As String**

Definition

The **Binding** constructor creates a Binding. This Binding is then used to bind a control instance to a data source.

Dissection

- The *propertyname* argument contains the name of a property supported by the control instance. For example, if you were binding a data source to a text box you would typically bind the Text property. If, however, you were binding a scroll bar, you would typically bind the Value property. Creating a Binding does not bind a control instance to a field in a DataTable. It merely defines which property will be bound to a field in the DataTable.

- The *datasource* argument contains the source of the data: typically a DataSet or DataTable object.

- The *datamember* argument provides a navigation path to the field in the DataSet.

Code Example

```
Dim pbndTemp As Binding
pbndTemp = New Binding("Text", DsCustomersTransactions1, _
    "tblCustomers.fldID")
```

Code Dissection

The preceding statement first declares a variable of type Binding. The second statement actually creates the Binding by calling the Binding constructor. The first argument contains the property to be bound, the second argument defines the DataSet, and the final argument defines the navigation path to the table and field in the DataSet.

Having defined the Binding, the next step is to associate that binding with a control instance. You do this by adding the Binding to the DataBindings collection supported by each control. Examine the following statements to associate a Binding with a control instance:

```
Dim pbndTemp As Binding
pbndTemp = New Binding("Text", DsCustomersTransactions1, _
    "tblCustomers.fldID")
txtID.DataBindings.Add(pbndTemp)
```

The preceding statements first create the Binding as you just saw. The final statement actually associates the Binding with the TextBox named txtID by adding the Binding to the DataBindings collection of the TextBox. The effect of this statement requires additional explanation.

When you bind a control instance to a data source, VB .NET transparently creates another object called the CurrencyManager. The purpose of the CurrencyManager object is to synchronize a group of bound control instances with a data source. You may have noticed that a data source, such as a DataTable, has no notion of position. That is, when using unbound control instances, you kept track of the current record via an Integer variable because the DataTable itself has no property to denote the current record. One role of the CurrencyManager is to keep track of the current record.

In this chapter, you will bind all of the control instances to the same data source, thereby implicitly creating one CurrencyManager object. However, this is not a requirement. On a single form you can create multiple DataBindings (bind control instances to different data sources). For each different DataBinding you create, VB .NET will implicitly create a separate CurrencyManager object. Next, you will see how to reference the CurrencyManager through the BindingContext.

Binding and Record Navigation

To navigate from record to record using simple bound controls, you reference the BindingContext of the form itself. VB .NET manages the elements in this collection when you add a Binding to the DataBindings collection of a control instance. The BindingContext object is a collection. However, unlike other collections, you reference an element in the collection with two arguments instead of just a single argument. The first argument contains a data source, and the second argument contains the navigation path to a table in that data source.

The BindingContext supports a property named Position used to define the current record in the data source. For example, the following statement positions the bound text boxes to the first item in the underlying bound list:

```
Me.BindingContext(DsCustomersTransactions1, _
    "tblCustomers").Position = 0
```

The preceding statement locates the first record in a BindingContext using the data source (DataSet) named DsCustomersTransactions1. The second argument specifies the navigation path to the table named tblCustomers.

In the following steps, you will bind the text boxes appearing on the form named frmCustomersTransactions.vb. In addition, you will write the statements that will allow the user to navigate through the bound control instances.

To navigate through records using a BindingContext:

1. Activate the Code Editor for the form named **frmCustomersTransactions.vb,** and then enter the following statements in the **Load** event handler for the form:

```
Dim pbndTemp As Binding
pbndTemp = New Binding("Text", DsCustomersTransactions1, _
    "tblCustomers.fldID")
txtID.DataBindings.Add(pbndTemp)

pbndTemp = New Binding("Text", DsCustomersTransactions1, _
    "tblCustomers.fldFirstName")
txtFirstName.DataBindings.Add(pbndTemp)

pbndTemp = New Binding("Text", DsCustomersTransactions1, _
    "tblCustomers.fldLastName")
txtLastName.DataBindings.Add(pbndTemp)
```

8

2. Enter the following statement in the **Click** event handler for the menu item named **mmuNavigateFirst**:

```
Me.BindingContext(DsCustomersTransactions1, _
    "tblCustomers").Position = 0
```

3. Enter the following statement in the **Click** event handler for the menu item named **mmuNavigatePrevious**:

```
Me.BindingContext(DsCustomersTransactions1, _
    "tblCustomers").Position -= 1
```

4. Enter the following statement in the **Click** event handler for the menu item named **mmuNavigateNext**:

```
Me.BindingContext(DsCustomersTransactions1, _
    "tblCustomers").Position += 1
```

5. Enter the following statement in the **Click** event handler for the menu item named **mmuNavigateLast**:

```
Me.BindingContext(DsCustomersTransactions1, _
    "tblCustomers").Position = _
    DsCustomersTransactions1.tblCustomers.Count - 1
```

6. Test the solution. On the main form, click **Windows**, **Transactions** to display the transactions form. Click the items on the **Navigate** menu to locate different records in the customers table.

Modifying Records in Complex Bound Controls

When control instances are bound to a DataSet, changes made to the bound control instances are automatically recorded to the DataSet itself. You save those changes just as you have done before. That is, you call the Update method of the OleDbDataAdapter, using the DataSet or DataTable as an argument. Then, you call the AcceptChanges method of the DataSet to synchronize the DataSet with the database itself.

THE DATAGRID CONTROL

The DataGrid control displays data from one or more tables as a series of rows and columns, in much the same way that Microsoft Access displays a table. Because the DataGrid control displays data from multiple rows, the DataGrid control is considered a complex bound control. The DataGrid control has the following members:

Syntax

System.Windows.Forms.DataGrid control

Public Properties

- The Boolean **AllowSorting** property defines whether or not the grid can be sorted by clicking a column header.

- The **CaptionVisible** and **CaptionText** properties define whether or not the caption (title bar) is visible and the contents of the caption, respectively.

- The **DataMember** property defines the navigation path to a table in the DataSource.

- The **DataSource** property defines the DataSet or DataTable bound to the DataGrid.

- The **Item** method gets or sets the value of a particular cell.

Public Methods

- The **BeginEdit** and **EndEdit** methods enable and disable editing in the DataGrid.

- The **CurrentCellChanged** event occurs when the user selects a different cell in the DataGrid.

Binding a DataGrid

The process of binding a DataGrid to a DataSet or DataTable is quite simple. You need only set the DataSource property to the DataSet, and then set the DataMember property to either the name of the DataTable or the name of a DataRelation.

To bind a DataGrid to a DataTable:

1. Activate the Win Forms Designer for the form named **frmCustomersTransactions.vb**, if necessary.

2. Create an instance of the DataGrid control on the form, as shown in Figure 8-17.

3. Activate the Properties window for the DataGrid control instance that you just created.

4. Set the Name property to **dgTransactions**.

5. Using the Properties window, set the DataSource property to **DsCustomersTransactions1** and set the DataMember property to **tblTransactions**.

   Note that when you define the DataMember, the field names are retrieved from the DataSet and are displayed as column headers in the DataGrid.

6. Test the solution. Click **Windows**, **Transactions** to display the transactions form. The transaction records appear in the DataGrid.

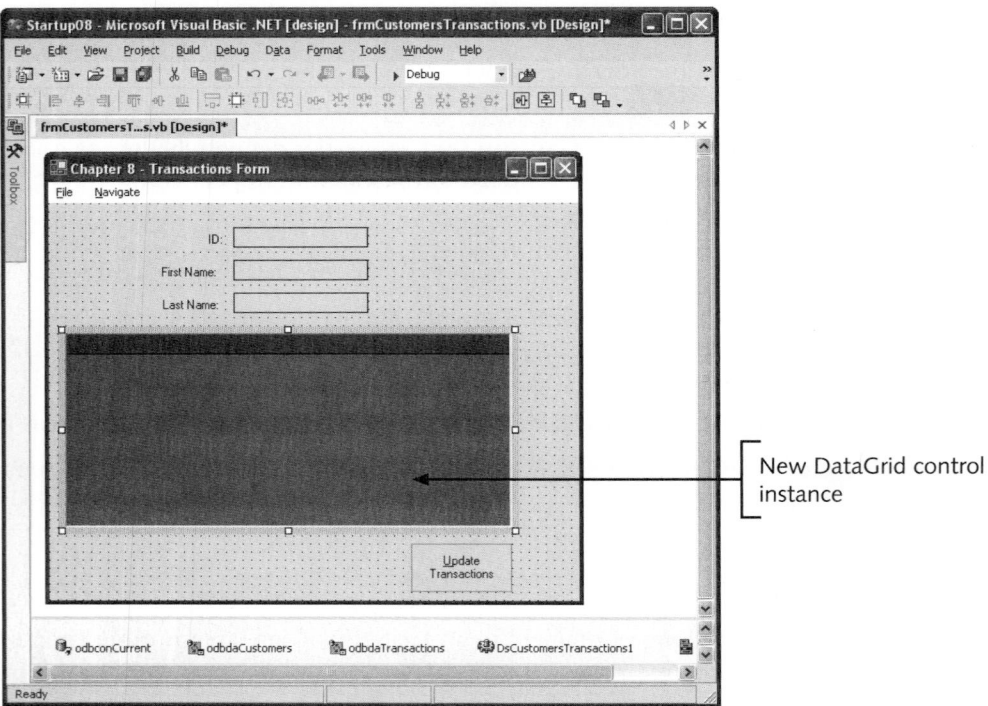

Figure 8-17   Creating a DataGrid control instance

Displaying Selected Transaction Records

Although the DataGrid displays transaction records, it is currently configured to display all of the transaction records, rather than just those transaction records corresponding to the current customer. To solve this problem, you again use a DataRelation. Remember that you used the XML Designer to create a DataRelation to link the records between the customers and transactions tables. To display only the child rows in the DataGrid, you bind the DataGrid to the DataRelation instead of the child table.

To bind a DataGrid to a DataRelation:

1. Activate the Properties window for the DataGrid on the form named **frmCustomersTransactions.vb**.

2. Activate the **DataMember** property. Expand the table named **tblCustomers**. The DataRelation appears as a member of tblCustomers.

3. Set the DataMember property to **tblCustomers.drCustomersTransactions**.

4. Test the solution. Click **Windows, Transactions** to display the transactions form. The transaction records appear in the DataGrid. Using the **Navigate** menu items, navigate from customer record to customer record. As you do, the corresponding transaction records appear in the DataGrid control instance.

The user can make changes to the records in a bound DataGrid. Those changes are automatically propagated back to the underlying DataSet. As the DataSet is disconnected from the database, you must explicitly save those changes using the same technique that you have seen before. That is, you call the GetChanges method on the DataSet to get the changed records, and then call the Update method on the underlying OleDbDataAdapter so as to record those changes back to the database. Finally, you call the AcceptChanges method on the DataSet so as to synchronize the DataSet with the underlying database.

To save changes made to a DataGrid:

1. Activate the **Code Editor** for the form named **frmCustomersTransactions.vb**, if necessary, and then enter the following statements in the **Click** event handler for the button named **btnUpdate**:

```
Dim dsCurrent As dsCustomersTransactions
dsCurrent = DsCustomersTransactions1.GetChanges
If Not (dsCurrent Is Nothing) Then
    odbdaTransactions.Update(dsCurrent)
    DsCustomersTransactions1.AcceptChanges()
End If
```

2. Test the solution. Click **Windows**, **Transactions** to display the transaction form. Add a new record to the transactions table by entering a new row in the DataGrid control instance. Save those changes by clicking the **Update Transactions** button.

So far, the database processing that you have performed involved using a DataSet containing one or more DataTables. ADO.NET supplies another means to process database data that does not involve the DataSet or DataTable.

THE DATAREADER CLASS

In Chapter 7, and in this chapter, you configured the OleDbDataAdapter manually, and used the OleDbDataAdapter control to configure SQL statements using a Wizard. The OleDbCommand class has other purposes too. First, it allows you to create another object called a DataReader. There are two forms of the DataReader class:

- The **SqlDataReader** class is optimized for performance and works only with SQL Server.

- The **OleDbDataReader** class is generic and used by several providers.

 Like a DataSet, a **DataReader** reads data from one or more database tables. However, the logic to read data with a DataReader is similar to reading data from a sequential file.

The following list describes the differences between the DataReader and the DataSet:

- Unlike the DataSet, the DataReader works in a connected mode rather than a disconnected mode. That is, the underlying connection must remain open while reading data into a DataReader. While the connection is open, the connection cannot process other requests. Thus, you must explicitly close the connection used by the DataReader immediately after reading all of the data.

- Together, the DataAdapter and DataSet classes allow you to save changes to the database. As the DataReader is a read-only object, you cannot make changes to the data you read with the DataReader.

- Because the contents of the DataReader cannot be changed, it follows that the DataReader cannot be used to save changes to the database.

- The DataSet class provides methods to locate records directly and navigate from record to record. The DataReader, like a StreamReader, is a forward-only object. That is, using the DataReader, you can read records and fields but you must read them from beginning to end. You cannot navigate backward through records using the DataReader.

Understanding the DataReader

While the DataReader supplies more limited functionality than the DataSet, it is very efficient. Thus, if your application does not need to record any changes back to the database, then the DataReader may be a better alternative to creating and populating a DataSet. The OleDbDataReader class supports the following members:

Syntax

System.Data.OleDb.OleDbDataReader class

Public Properties

- The **FieldCount** property gets the number of fields in the current row. This property is useful if you don't know the schema of the underlying table. Note that unlike a DataSet, a DataReader does not contain schema information.

- The Boolean **IsClosed** method indicates whether the DataReader is open (False) or closed (True).

Public Methods

- The **Close** method closes the DataReader. Once the records have been read from the DataReader, the DataReader must be explicitly closed. The underlying connection must be explicitly closed too.

- The DataReader reads a record into columns, each having an ordinal value (index). The first column in the DataReader has an index of 0, the second column 1, and so on. The **GetInt16**, **GetInt32**, and **GetInt64** methods all accept one argument, the ordinal value of the column to retrieve. The data is converted to a 16 bit, 32 bit, or 64 bit Integer, respectively.

- The **GetFloat** and **GetDouble** methods get data as a single-precision and double-precision number, respectively.

- The **GetBoolean** method works the same way as the preceding methods but converts the column data to a Boolean data type.

- The **GetDateTime** method gets a column value in DateTime format.

- The **GetChar** and **GetString** methods retrieve a Char or a String, respectively.

- The **GetValue** method gets the value of a column. However, the value is returned in its native format.

- The Boolean **Read** method advances the current record indicator to the next record. When you first create an instance of the DataReader, the current record indicator is positioned just before the first record. Thus, the Read method must be called once before attempting to process the first record. Each successive call to the Read method positions the current record indicator at the next record. If there are more records, then the method returns True; it returns False when there are no more records.

8

To read a table's data with an OleDbDataReader, you first create the OleDbDataReader itself, read the data sequentially, and then close the reader, as shown in Figure 8-18.

As shown in Figure 8-18, you first create the OleDbDataReader, then you call the Read method to position the current record indicator at the first record. The next statements are part of a loop in which you get the data out of the current record and process it, and then you read the next record. When all of the records have been read and processed, you close both the OleDbDataReader and the connection. The groups of statements below illustrate how to create an OleDbDataReader, and process its data.

```
Dim drCurrent As OleDbDataReader
Dim pblnActive As Boolean, pintActiveCount As Integer
Dim pblnMoreData As Boolean
```

The preceding statements declare an OleDbDataReader. The System.Data.OleDb namespace has been imported for brevity. The other two variables will store the data as it is read.

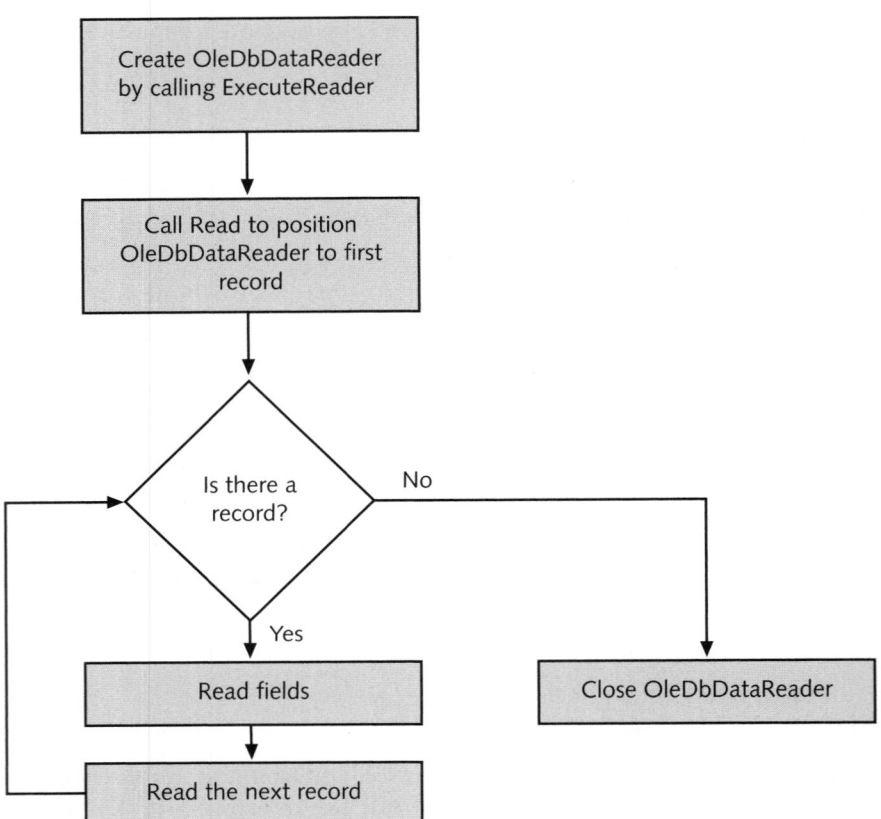

Figure 8-18 Operation of an OleDbDataReader

```
Dim odbcmdCurrent As New OleDbCommand( _
    "SELECT fldActive FROM tblCustomers", odbconUtility)
```

Next, the OleDbCommand object gets created. The first argument to the overloaded constructor contains the SELECT statement. The SELECT statement retrieves only the field named fldActive from the table named tblCustomers. The second argument assumes that odbconUtility represents the instance of the OleDbConnection control created on the form named frmUtility.

```
odbconUtility.Open()
drCurrent = odbcmdCurrent.ExecuteReader
```

When you read data using an OleDbDataReader, you must explicitly open the connection. Remember that the OleDbDataAdapter opens and closes the connection automatically. You do not create the OleDbDataReader using a constructor. Rather, the OleDbDataReader gets created when the ExecuteReader method gets called. Thus, the second of the preceding statements creates the OleDbDataReader.

The following statement initializes the OleDbDataReader:

```
pblnMoreData = drCurrent.Read()
```

When the ExecuteReader method creates the OleDbDataReader, the position of the reader is one record before the first record. Thus, before attempting to process the first record, you must first call the Read method. Once the Read method has been called the first time, the OleDbDataReader is positioned at the first row.

The statements to process and read each record are part of a loop as the following code segment illustrates:

```
While pblnMoreData
    pblnActive = drCurrent.GetBoolean(0)
    If pblnActive Then
        pintActiveCount += 1
    End If
    pblnMoreData = drCurrent.Read()
End While
```

Remember that the SQL statement selected one field (fldActive), so the DataReader itself contains a single field, having an ordinal value of 0. Thus, the preceding statements get the first field's contents as a Boolean value and store the result in the variable pblnActive. The If statement tests whether or not the customer is active, and increments the accumulator accordingly. After the current record has been processed, the next record is read. The statements in the loop continue to execute while more records remain to be processed (pblnMoreData = True).

```
drCurrent.Close()
odbconUtility.Close()
```

Once the records have been read from the OleDbDataReader, the underlying connection must be explicitly closed. While the OleDbDataReader is open, the underlying connection cannot accept or process other commands.

Using the OleDbDataReader

To illustrate the use of the OleDbDataReader, you will see how to read the contents of the table named tblCustomers using an OleDbDataReader, and create a sequential file from the records in the underlying DataTable. The capability to create a sequential file is useful, as some applications can only import and export data using a sequential file.

To create a sequential file with an OleDbDataReader:

1. Activate the Code Editor for the form named **frmUtility.vb**, and then enter the following statements in the **Click** event handler for button named **btnCreateFile**:

```
Dim pswriCurrent As StreamWriter
Dim drCurrent As OleDbDataReader
Dim dlgResult As DialogResult
Dim pblnMoreData As Boolean

Dim odbcmdCurrent As New OleDbCommand( _
    "SELECT * FROM tblCustomers", odbconUtility)
odbconUtility.Open()
dlgResult = sfdUtility.ShowDialog()
If dlgResult = DialogResult.Cancel Then
    Exit Sub
End If

pswriCurrent = New StreamWriter(sfdUtility.FileName)
drCurrent = odbcmdCurrent.ExecuteReader
pblnMoreData = drCurrent.Read()
While pblnMoreData
    With pswriCurrent
        .Write(drCurrent.GetInt32(0))
        .Write(",")
        .Write(drCurrent.GetString(1))
        .Write(",")
        .Write(drCurrent.GetString(2))
        .Write(",")
        .Write(drCurrent.GetString(3))
        .Write(",")
        .Write(drCurrent.GetString(4))
        .Write(",")
        .Write(drCurrent.GetString(5))
        .Write(",")
        .Write(drCurrent.GetString(6))
        .Write(",")
        .WriteLine(drCurrent.GetBoolean(7))
    End With
    pblnMoreData = drCurrent.Read
End While
pswriCurrent.Close()
drCurrent.Close()
odbconUtility.Close()
```

The preceding statements create the StreamWriter as you have seen before and declare a variable to store the OleDbDataReader. All of the fields from the table named tblCustomers use the existing connection named odbconUtility. Next, the connection is opened and the ExecuteReader method is called to create the OleDbDataReader. The While loop reads each record, and the statements in the loop write each field to the sequential file. After all of the records have been written, the StreamWriter, OleDbDataReader, and connection are closed.

2. Test the solution. On the main form, click **Windows**, **Utilities** to activate the Utilities form. On the Utilities form, click **Create File** to create the sequential file.

Another useful feature supplied by ADO.NET is the ability to execute scalar queries, which return only a single data item.

EXECUTING SCALAR QUERIES

The **ExecuteScalar** method of the OleDbCommand class executes a SELECT statement. It returns the first column of the first row returned. Any additional rows or columns are discarded. Note that if additional rows or columns are returned, an exception will not be thrown. The additional data is merely discarded. One use of the ExecuteScalar method is to determine whether or not a specific primary key exists in a database table, or to find the maximum primary key on file.

Examine the following statements:

```
Dim odbcmdCurrent As New OleDbCommand( _
    "SELECT Max(fldID) FROM tblCustomers", odbconCustomers)
Dim pstrMax As String
odbconCustomers.Open()
pstrMax = odbcmdCurrent.ExecuteScalar.ToString
odbconCustomers.Close()
```

The preceding statements first create an instance of the OleDbCommand object. The SELECT statement selects the largest value for the field named fldID from the table named tblCustomers. The variable odbconCustomers is assumed to be an instance of the OleDbConnection control. As with the OleDbDataReader, you must explicitly open the connection before calling the ExecuteScalar method, and then close the connection when complete. The ExecuteScalar method returns a data type of System.Object, which in the preceding statements is explicitly converted to a string.

To execute a scalar query:

1. Activate the Code Editor for the form named **frmUtility.vb**. Enter the following statements in the **Click** event handler for the button named **btnScalarQuery**:

```
Dim pstrMax, pstrCount As String
Dim odbcmdCurrent As New OleDbCommand( _
    "SELECT Max(fldID) FROM tblCustomers", odbconUtility)
odbconUtility.Open()
pstrMax = odbcmdCurrent.ExecuteScalar.ToString
odbcmdCurrent = New OleDbCommand( _
    "SELECT Count(fldID) FROM tblCustomers", odbconUtility)
pstrCount = odbcmdCurrent.ExecuteScalar.ToString
```

8

```
odbconUtility.Close()
txtOutput.Text = "There are " & pstrCount.ToString & _
    " records. The maximum ID number is " & _
    pstrMax.ToString
```

2. Test the solution. On the menu bar, click **Windows**, **Utilities**. Click the **Scalar Demo** button. The largest ID number and the number of records from the customers table appears in the multiline text box.

You have completed the programming for this chapter. This chapter has shown how to use the various controls supplied by VB .NET to create a Connection, DataAdapter, and strongly typed DataSet. In addition, you have seen how to use a DataRelation to relate records from master and detail tables. You have also explored how to bind control instances to a DataSet table, thereby simplifying the process of record navigation. Finally, you have seen how to use the OleDbDataReader to read the records from a database table efficiently and use the ExecuteScalar method to read a single database field.

Chapter Summary

❒ The OleDbConnection control allows you to create a connection by completing dialog boxes rather than creating the connection programmatically. To create a connection with the OleDbConnection control, you create an instance of the control on the form, and then configure the ConnectionString property by selecting the provider and the database in the Data Link Properties dialog box.

❒ The OleDbDataAdapter control allows you to create an OleDbDataAdapter and build the necessary statements to add, change, and delete records using a Wizard. Using the dialog boxes that comprise the Wizard, you select the connection that you want to use and define the SQL statements to be executed. When you complete the Wizard's dialog boxes, VB .NET generates the SQL SELECT, UPDATE, and DELETE statements automatically.

❒ A typed DataSet is nothing more than a class that derives from System.Data.DataSet. This class exposes properties and methods that correspond to the underlying table names and fields. Thus, when using a typed DataSet you can reference individual tables and fields by name without having to navigate through the underlying Tables and Rows collections. A .xsd file forms the basis for a typed DataSet. The .xsd file is an XML file that defines the schema for the DataSet, its DataTables, fields, keys, and so on. From the .xsd file, VB .NET generates a class module containing nested classes for each DataTable and properties to represent the fields in each DataTable. In addition, it creates a strongly typed version of the DataRow class.

❒ Most database applications work with multiple tables instead of just a single table. Multiple DataAdapters can be created on a form to fill a DataSet with the data from multiple tables. Data from each table is stored in a unique DataTable object.

❐ Multiple tables are typically related to each other in some way. One such relationship is a one-to-many relationship. The DataRelation class defines how two or more tables are related. You create a DataRelation by defining the key field from the two tables, and assigning a name to that DataRelation. Once you have defined the DataRelation, you add it to the Relations collection of the underlying DataSet.

❐ By itself, the DataRelation is of little use. Its primary purpose is to allow you to get the child rows corresponding to a parent DataRow. The GetChildRows method applies to a DataRow. It uses the DataRelation supplied as an argument to get an array of DataRow objects from the child table that corresponds to the current DataRow. You can create a DataRelation programmatically or create it using the XML Designer.

❐ The GetChildRows method of the DataRow class accepts one argument: the name of an existing DataRelation. The method returns an array of DataRow objects from the child table corresponding to the current row in the parent table.

❐ DataBinding is the process of binding a control instance to the data in a DataSet or DataTable. Simple binding is used to bind controls such as text boxes, while complex binding is used for controls that display data from multiple rows. Complex bound controls include list boxes, combo boxes, and the DataGrid control. To simple bind a control, create an instance of the Binding class, and then add that object to the BindingCollection of a form.

❐ When control instances are bound to a DataSet table, you use the BindingContext collection of the form to navigate through the records in the DataSet by setting the 0-based Position property.

❐ The complex bound DataGrid control displays records from one or more tables. The DataSource property defines the DataSet or DataTable to be bound, and the DataMember property defines the navigation path to a table in the DataSource. To display the child rows corresponding to a parent row, bind the DataMember to a DataRelation.

❐ The OleDbDataReader class operates independently of the DataSet class and reads records from a database table in a manner similar to that of reading a sequential file. To read a file with the OleDbDataReader, you first create an instance of the OleDbCommand class, and then define the SELECT statement to be used and the OleDbConnection over which the command will be sent. Then you explicitly open the connection and call the ExecuteReader method of the OleDbCommand object to create the actual OleDbDataReader. Next, call the Read method to initialize the OleDbDataReader. Then, in a While loop, process each record and attempt to read the next record if one exists. When reading is complete, explicitly close both the DataReader and the OleDbConnection itself.

❐ The ExecuteScalar method works similarly to the ExecuteReader method of the OleDbCommand class. It returns a single field from a single row in a database table. Again, before calling the ExecuteScalar method, a connection must be explicitly opened and the connection must be closed after the ExecuteScalar method has been called.

REVIEW QUESTIONS

1. Which of the following statements is true of the OleDbConnection control?

    a. The OleDbConnection control differs from a connection created programmatically in that the OleDbConnection control does not use a connection string.

    b. If you want to work with multiple tables on a form, you must create one OleDbConnection control for each table in the database that you are using.

    c. The OleDbConnection control configures the same properties that you would use if you created a connection programmatically.

    d. To configure the OleDbConnection control, you activate the Connection String dialog box. This dialog box contains various list boxes corresponding to each key/value pair supported by the ConnectionString property.

    e. none of the above

2. Which of the following statements is true of the OleDbDataAdapter control?

    a. The OleDbDataAdapter control can be used to configure a parameterized SELECT statement, but it cannot be used to configure the INSERT, UPDATE, and DELETE statements.

    b. Unlike the OleDbDataAdapter that you created programmatically, the OleDbDataAdapter control does not use SQL statements.

    c. The OleDbDataAdapter control can create a complex SQL UPDATE statement to reduce the errors that can arise when multiple users attempt to update the same record.

    d. Unlike the OleDbDataAdapter that you created programmatically, when you use the OleDbDataAdapter control, you do not create a new connection or use an existing connection.

    e. none of the above

3. How do you create a DataSet having multiple DataTables?

    a. Instead of using the OleDbDataAdapter, create an instance of the OleDbMultiTableAdapter control, and then fill it as you would with an ordinary OleDbDataAdapter.

    b. Using multiple OleDbDataAdapters, call the Fill method with the same DataSet as the argument to the OleDbDataAdapter's Fill method.

    c. Instead of calling the Fill method of the DataSet class, call the FillMultiple method.

    d. A DataSet cannot have multiple DataTables.

    e. none of the above

4. Which of the following statements correctly identifies the files accompanying a typed DataSet?

   a. The .xsd file contains an XML document. Embedded in that document are the VB .NET statements to create the DataSet and manage its contents. The corresponding .vb file contains additional methods that are called by the statements embedded in the .xsd file.

   b. The .xsd file, called a schema definition file, contains an XML document that describes the members of the DataSet. A file of the same name having a suffix of .vb contains a strongly typed class that derives from System.Data.DataSet.

   c. The .xsd file contains the SQL statements that make up a schema document. The corresponding .vb file contains the necessary OleDbConnection and OleDbCommand objects to populate the DataSet and record changes to the database.

   d. A typed DataSet contains a type file having a suffix of .typ. The type file defines the data types of the various DataTables and the fields contained in those DataTables.

   e. none of the above

5. Which of the following statements is true of a DataRelation?

   a. It defines a parent/child relationship between two tables.

   b. A DataRelation typically provides a link between two parent tables in a DataSet.

   c. The columns that relate two tables cannot be primary keys.

   d. all of the above

   e. none of the above

6. How do you create a DataRelation programmatically?

   a. Call the CreateRelation method of the table designated as the parent table with three arguments: the key field in the parent table, the key field in the child table, and the name of the child table.

   b. Create an instance of the DataRelation class, specifying the key fields from the parent and child tables as arguments to the constructor. Then add the DataRelation to the Relations collection of the DataSet.

   c. For the table designated as the parent table in the DataSet, set the ParentField property to the key field in the parent table and the ChildField property to the key field in the child table.

   d. It is not possible to create a DataRelation programmatically.

   e. none of the above

8

7. Which of the following statements is correct related to the GetChildRows method of the DataRow class?

   a. The method requires that you specify the DataRelation that will be used to determine the child table from which rows will be returned.

   b. If you do not specify the DataRelation to use, the GetChildRows method will use the DataRelation designated as the default DataRelation.

   c. The GetChildRows method returns a new DataTable containing the rows in the child table that match the row in the parent table.

   d. all of the above

   e. none of the above

8. Which of the following steps correctly describes how to create a DataRelation visually using the XML Designer?

   a. Using the XML Designer, drag the common field in the parent table to the same field in the child table.

   b. Select the master (parent) table in the XML Designer, and then activate the Edit Relation dialog box. Specify the parent and child tables, and the common fields between those two tables.

   c. In the child table, right-click on the common field, and then click Create Relation from the context menu.

   d. Create an instance of the DataRelation control. Then bind that control to the DataSet by setting the DataSet property. Next, using the Properties window, define the tables designated as the parent and child tables, and the key fields from those two tables.

   e. none of the above

9. Which of the following statements is correct pertaining to data binding?

   a. The Binding constructor creates a Binding. By creating a Binding, a control instance is associated with a particular field in a DataSet table.

   b. When you create a Binding from the Binding class, you specify an array as an argument. That array contains a reference to each control instance that should be bound.

   c. The Binding constructor creates a Binding. However, for the Binding to be associated with a particular control instance it must be added to the DataBindings collection of a particular control instance.

   d. You can bind control instances to a DataTable in a DataSet. However, a Binding cannot be associated with other objects such as an ArrayList.

   e. none of the above

10. Which of the following controls would be simple bound?

   a. TextBox

   b. Label

c. CheckBox

d. all of the above

e. none of the above

11. Which of the following statements is correct related to data binding and record navigation?

    a. The Position property of the BindingContext defines which record is considered the current record.

    b. The MoveFirst, MoveNext, MovePrevious, and MoveLast methods update the current record, thereby updating the Position property.

    c. Using a Binding, you can navigate forward through the bound records but it is not possible to navigate backward.

    d. A Binding has no notion of the current record.

    e. none of the above

12. Which of the following statements is true of the DataGrid control?

    a. The DataGrid control is a read-only control. That is, the records in the DataGrid cannot be edited.

    b. The DataGrid control is considered a simple bound control.

    c. The DataMember and DataSource properties define the navigation path to the data source, and the data source itself.

    d. all of the above

    e. none of the above

13. Which of the following statements applies to the DataReader?

    a. It is a forward-only object, meaning that you must read records in a table from beginning to end.

    b. When the DataReader is first opened, the current record indicator is positioned just before the first record.

    c. The fields in each record are retrieved using the ordinal value of the field.

    d. all of the above

    e. none of the above

8

14. Which of the following statements correctly describes the ExecuteScalar method of the OleDbCommand class?

   a. The ExecuteScalar method returns all of the fields from a specific row in a DataTable. The row returned is specified by the Row argument to the method.

   b. The ExecuteScalar method returns a single field from a single row. If multiple rows or fields are selected, then only the first field from the first row is actually returned.

   c. If you call the ExecuteScalar method such that it returns more than one field from one row, then an InvalidDataException will occur.

   d. The ExecuteScalar method applies to the DataSet class.

   e. none of the above

15. Describe the differences between an untyped DataSet and a typed DataSet.

16. Describe the purpose of a DataRelation and how to create a DataRelation, both programmatically and using the XML Designer.

17. What is the purpose of the GetChildRows method of the DataRow?

18. Describe the difference between complex binding and simple binding. In your answer, describe the steps necessary to simple bind and to complex bind a control instance.

19. Compare and contrast the DataSet and DataReader classes.

20. Describe the syntax and purpose of the ExecuteScalar method of the OleDbCommand class.

PROGRAMMING QUESTIONS

1. Assume that a DataSet class instance named DsCurrent1 should contain two tables. Write the statements to fill the DataSet using OleDbDataAdapter control instances named odbdaMaster and odbdaChild.

2. Using a typed DataSet reference, write the statement to reference the field named fldNumber in the DataTable named tblQuestion in the DataSet named DsList1. Reference the field in the first row of the DataTable and store the result in the String variable named pstrNumber.

3. Assume that a strongly typed DataSet class instance named DsSamples1 exists, having a DataTable named tblWaterSamples. Write the statements to iterate through the rows in the DataTable. Assume that a field exists named fldWaterLevel. Using an accumulator, calculate the total water level for all samples. Divide the total water level by the number of records to calculate the average water level. Store the results in the variables named psngTotalWaterLevel and psngAverageWaterLevel.

4. Write the statement to declare a DataRow object named drCurrent, having a data type of tblSamplesRow (tblSamplesRow is a typed DataRow from the DataSet class DsSamples). Store in the DataRow the first row from the strongly typed DataSet class instance named DsSamples1, having a table named tblSamples.

5. Assume that a typed DataSet class named DsQuestion has been declared. Write the statements to create a DataRelation named drQuestion and add that DataRelation to the Relations collection of the DataSet class instance named DsQuestion1. Assume that the key field is named fldQuestionID. Assume that the parent and child tables are named tblQuestions and tblResponses, respectively.

6. Write the statements to store an array of DataRow objects in the variable drPayroll. Declare the variable named drPayroll to store typed DataRow objects named DsPr1.tblPayrollRow. Assume that the typed DataSet class instance is named DsPr1 and that the typed parent data table is named tblEmployees. Write the statements to get the child rows for the first row in the table named tblEmployees.

7. Assume that the GetChildRows method has been called and returned an array of DataRow objects named drQuestions. Write the statements to accumulate the total for the field named fldResponse. Store the total in the single precision variable named psngResponseTotal.

8. Assume that the DataSet class named DsDemo has a master table named tblMaster and has a DataRelation defined, named drIDs. Write the statements to get the child rows for each parent row using the instance variable DsDemo1. Assume that the data type of the child row is DsDemo.tblChildRow. For each group of child rows, calculate the average value for the field named fldAmount in the child table, and write that value to the Output window.

9. Write the statements to declare a binding such that the Text property of the TextBox control instance named txtDemo will be bound to the DataSet class instance named DsDemo1. Assume that the DataTable is named tblDemo and that the field is named fldDemo.

10. Assume that a BindingContext exists having a DataSet class instance named DsCurrent1 and a table named tblTransactions. Write the statements to locate the first, next, previous and last records using the BindingContext.

11. Assume that an instance of the OleDbCommand class named odbcmdCurrent exists and has been configured with a SQL SELECT statement. Write the statements to create a DataReader named drDemo. Assume that the SELECT statement selects one field having a data type of Integer. Assume that the connection has already been opened. Write a loop to read all of the records. Calculate the average of the field contents, storing the result in the variable named pintAverage. When complete, close the OleDbDataReader.

12. Assume that an instance of the OleDbConnection class exists named odbconCurrent. Write the statements to declare an instance of the OleDbCommand class to select the fields named fldActive (Boolean) and fldAmount (Single) from the table named tblTransactions. Write the statements to open the connection and create an instance of the OleDbDataReader class. Read the data. If the field named fldActive is True, then add the value of the second field named fldAmount to an accumulator named psngTotal. Close the OleDbDataReader and OleDbConnection after you read the data.

13. Assume that an existing connection has been declared named odbconQuestion. Create the necessary SELECT statement to select the field named fldTotal from the table named tblData. Write the statements to create the OleDbDataReader, and then read each record. For each record that you read, accumulate the total in the variable named psngTotal. Assume that the field fldTotal has a data type of Single. Open and close the connection and DataAdapter as necessary.

14. Write the statements to declare an instance of the OleDbCommand class named odbcmdSelect. Configure the variable to select the maximum value from the field named fldID from the table named tblEmployees. Assume that an instance of the OleDbConnection class exists named odbconCurrent. Write the statements to open the connection, execute the query, and then close the connection. Store the result of the query in the Integer variable named pintID.

15. Write the statements to declare an instance of the OleDbCommand class named odbcmdSelect. Configure the variable to select the total of the values from the field named fldAmount from the table named tblTransactions. Assume that an instance of the OleDbConnection class exists, named odbconCurrent. Write the statements to open the connection, execute the query, and then close the connection. Store the result of the query in the Single variable named psngTotal.

HANDS-ON PROJECTS

All of the Hands-on projects use the same database, named Ledger.mdb, in the Chapter.08\ Data folder. Note that to run any of the previously compiled hands-on projects, the database named Ledger.mdb must appear in the same folder as the compiled hands-on project.

The following list describes the fields in the table named tblUsers:

❑ fldUserID (Integer) — Unique user identification number

❑ fldUserLogin (String) — Unique user login

❑ fldUserPassword (String) — User password

The following list describes the fields in the table named tblAccounts:

❑ fldAccountNumber (Integer) — Unique ledger account number

❑ fldCategory (String) — Account category (Asset, Liability, Capital)

❑ fldDescription (String) — Account description

❑ fldBeginningBalance (Single) — Beginning balance

The following list describes the fields in the table named tblTransactions:

❑ fldTransactionID (Integer) — Unique Transaction ID

❑ fldAccountNumber (Integer) — Account number

❑ fldTransactionDate (Date) — Date of transaction

❐ fldTransactionAmount (Single) — Transaction amount

❐ fldTransactionDescription (String) — Transaction description

❐ fldDebitCredit (Integer) — a value of 1 indicates a debit and a value of 2 indicates a credit.

1. In this project, you will create an application that allows an administrator to manage a password file using a strongly typed DataSet. The file named Chapter.08\Exercises08\ Ch08Ex1.exe contains the compiled executable application. Figure 8-19 shows the completed main form for the solution.

Figure 8-19   Chapter 8 – Hands-on Project 1

    a. Create a new project named **Ch08Ex1.sln**.

    b. Create and display a splash screen for the solution.

    c. Create a login form for the administrator. The login form should appear after the splash screen. For simplicity, you can assume that the administrator login is Admin and the password for the administrator is Password. Assume that the login and password are case sensitive. If the administrator logs in correctly, display the application's main form as shown in Figure 8-19. Configure the login form so that the administrator can only make three login attempts. After three failed attempts, exit the program.

    d. On the main form, create the control instances as shown in Figure 8-19.

    e. Using the OleDbConnection control, create a connection to the database stored in **Chapter.08\Data\Ledger.mdb**.

    f. Using the OleDbDataAdapter control, create and configure the DataAdapter to retrieve all of the records in the table named tblUsers. Order the records in ascending order based on the contents of the field named fldUserLogin.

    g. Generate the DataSet for the OleDbDataAdapter.

h. In the form's Load event handler, write the necessary statements to fill the DataSet. Create a procedure to display the current record using the techniques presented in the chapter. Do not use a Binding.

i. Create the menu for the form. Create a **Navigate** menu having menu items named **First**, **Previous**, **Next**, and **Last**. Again, do not use data binding.

j. Create an **Edit** menu with menu items to add, change, and delete records. Write the statement to add, change, and delete the current record. Enable and disable the menu items on the form as necessary to prevent errors from occurring.

k. Write the statements to update changes made to the DataSet back to the database.

2. In this project, you will display the totals for various ledger accounts based on the account number requested by the user. The file named Chapter.08\Exercises08\ Ch08Ex2.exe contains the compiled executable application. Figure 8-20 shows the completed main form for the solution.

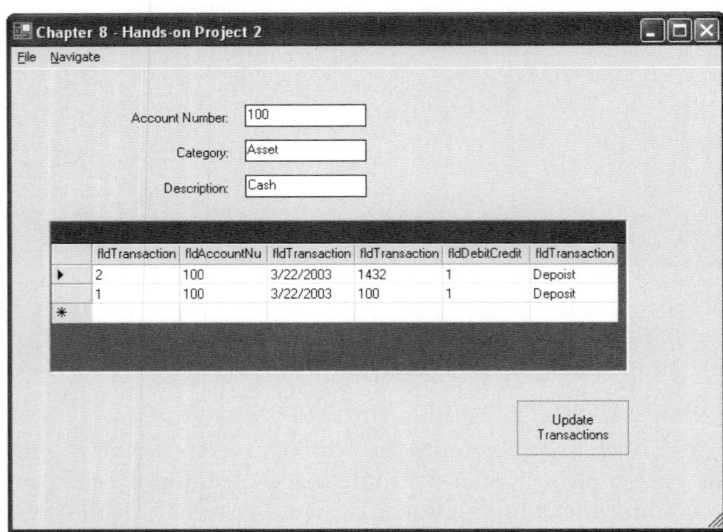

Figure 8-20   Chapter 8 – Hands-on Project 2

a. Create a new project named **Ch08Ex2.sln**.

b. Create a splash screen for the solution.

c. Create the control instances on the main form as shown in Figure 8-20.

d. Create the necessary OleDbConnection control to establish the connection to the database named **Chapter.08\Data\Ledger.mdb**.

e. Create two instances of the OleDbDataAdapter control. One of the control instances should select all of the records from the table named tblAccounts sorted by account number, and the other OleDbDataAdapter should select all of the records from the table named tblTransactions sorted by transaction date.

f. Generate a typed DataSet from the two OleDbDataAdapters that you just created.

g. Using the XML Designer, create a data relation between the two tables using the key field named fldAccountNumber. Set the update, delete, and accept/reject rules to Cascade.

h. Write the statements in the form's Load event handler to populate the DataSet.

i. Write the necessary statement to bind the fields from the table named tblAccounts to the form's text boxes. Perform this task in the form's Load event handler.

j. Create a **Navigate** menu on the form with menu items to locate the first, previous, next, and last records. Write the statements for the Navigate menu to display the current record using the BindingContext.

k. Create an instance of the DataGrid control on the form. Configure the DataGrid control instance so that it will display the transactions for the currently selected account number.

l. Create a button on the form to display the total debit and credit transactions for the selected master record. Display the results in a message box.

m. Create a button on the form to save any changes made in the DataGrid control instance back to the database.

3. In this project, you will work with a typed DataSet and programmatically create DataRelation objects. The file named Chapter.08\Exercises08\Ch08Ex3.exe contains the compiled executable application.

a. Create a new project named **Ch08Ex3.sln**.

b. Create a splash screen for the solution.

c. Create a login form for the solution. Using the techniques presented in the chapter, validate that the user's login exists and that the password is correct. To do this, create the necessary OleDbConnection, OleDbCommand, and typed DataSet on the login form. Look up the login and password in the DataSet as necessary. If the user entered correct information, then continue to display the main form. If the user incorrectly enters his or her login information three times, then exit the solution.

d. On the main form, create the control instances to display the records from the master table named tblAccounts. Use data binding to display the data in the control instances.

e. Create a **Navigate** menu on the form with menu items to locate the first, previous, next, and last records. Write the statements for the Navigate menu to display the correct record.

f. Create the necessary menu items and code such that the following information is displayed on the form's text boxes: the total debits and total credits for the selected account. Also display the number of debit transactions and the number of credit transactions. Use a DataRelation to accomplish this task.

8

4. In this project, you will work with a DataRelation and manipulate data using one-to-many relationships. The file named Chapter.08\Exercises08\Ch08Ex4.exe contains the compiled executable application.

   a. Create a new project named **Ch08Ex4.sln**.

   b. Create a splash screen and a login form for the solution. The splash screen should appear for five seconds, and then display the login form.

   c. Configure the login form so that it contains text boxes allowing the user to enter their login and password. Use a DataReader to read the data from the table named tblUsers. Do not use a DataSet. Create a login button on the form. When the user clicks the Login button, determine whether or not the login and password are valid. If user information is valid, display the main form. Exit the solution if the user enters an incorrect login more than three times.

   d. On the main form, create the control instances to display the records from the master table named tblAccounts. Provide the means for the user to navigate from record to record using DataBinding.

   e. Allow the user to add, change, and delete records from the table named tblAccounts. When adding a record, first verify that the account does not already exist.

   f. On the main form, create a button to display the transaction record corresponding to the selected account number. Display the transaction records on a second form. Display each transaction record in a dynamically created text box.

   g. On the transactions form, create a button that will allow the user to write the currently selected transaction records to a sequential file. Allow the user to select the output file via a SaveFileDialog box.

CHAPTER

9

CRYSTAL REPORTS

In this chapter, you will:

♦ Create a blank Crystal Report
♦ Preview a report with the CrystalReportViewer control
♦ Create fields on a Crystal Report
♦ Create reports based on the data from multiple database tables
♦ Create a tabular report with a control break
♦ Export reports
♦ Configure a report to display information dynamically

Crystal Reports is a reporting tool that allows you to define the contents and layout of a report in a visual way, similar to the way that you define a form's visual interface. That is, you create control instances on a report and set their properties. After defining the report's layout, you preview the report using the CrystalReportViewer control or send the report directly to a printer.

In this chapter, you will learn how to create and print reports using Crystal Reports. Note that this chapter does not describe all of the capabilities supplied by Crystal Reports. Rather, this chapter is intended to be an introduction to Crystal Reports.

PREVIEWING THE COMPLETED SOLUTION

The completed solution in this chapter reads data from an Access 2000 database file using ADO.NET. The solution uses the OleDbConnection, OleDbDataAdapter, DataSet, and DataTable objects to retrieve data from the database. Of course, a SQL Server database could also be used with Crystal Reports. The reports read data directly from the DataSet and DataTable objects at runtime, and then they display that data.

The database used in this chapter contains employee records and payroll records. There exists a one-to-many relationship between the employees table (tblEmployees) and the payroll table (tblPayroll). The two tables are linked by the field named fldID. The table named tblEmployees contains general information about each employee. Table 9-1 lists the fields in tblEmployees.

Table 9-1   tblEmployees table

Field Name	.NET Data type	Description
fldID	Integer	Unique identification number (primary key)
fldFirstName	String	Employee first name
fldLastName	String	Employee last name
fldDepartment	String	Employee department
fldEmployeeType	String	Salaried or hourly employee
fldDeductions	Integer	Deductions
fldWage	Single	Hourly wage or monthly salary depending on employee type
fldPension	Boolean	True if the employee belongs to the pension plan

The table named tblPayroll contains one record per employee for each pay period. The payroll example used in the chapter is simplified, as the only payroll deductions are federal income tax and Social Security tax. Table 9-2 lists the fields in tblPayroll.

Table 9-2   tblPayroll table

Field Name	.NET Data type	Description
fldID	Integer	Employee identification number (foreign key)
fldDate	Date/Time	Payroll date
fldHoursWorked	Single	Number of hours worked during the period (value is 0 for salaried employees)
fldGrossPay	Single	Gross pay or monthly salary
fldFIT	Single	Federal income tax withholding
fldFICA	Single	Social Security deduction
fldNetPay	Single	Net payroll amount

You must have a printer installed on the system to run this solution or develop reports with Crystal Reports. In addition, Crystal Reports is licensed software. Thus, before using Crystal Reports for the first time, you may need to register it.

To preview the completed solution:

1. Start Visual Studio .NET. Open the solution file named **Chapter.09\ Complete09\Complete09.sln**.

2. Activate the Solution Explorer. Click the **Show All Files** button in the Solution Explorer. Note that the solution file contains two report files, named EmployeeReport.rpt and PayrollReport.rpt. A Crystal Report file consists of a binary file having a suffix of .rpt, and a class having the same name with a file suffix of .vb. These files correspond to the reports in the solution. Figure 9–1 shows the Solution Explorer with multiple report files.

Report files

Figure 9-1 Solution Explorer containing report files

3. Run the solution. The main form appears as shown in Figure 9–2.

The main form displays data in two DataGrid control instances. The first DataGrid control instance displays employee records. The second DataGrid control instance displays multiple payroll records corresponding to the selected employee in the first DataGrid control instance. The only purpose of the DataGrid control instances is to allow you to visualize the data contained in the reports. The reports in the chapter perform calculations on this data, summarize it, and format it. That formatted data can be viewed by the user in a form, or sent to a printer.

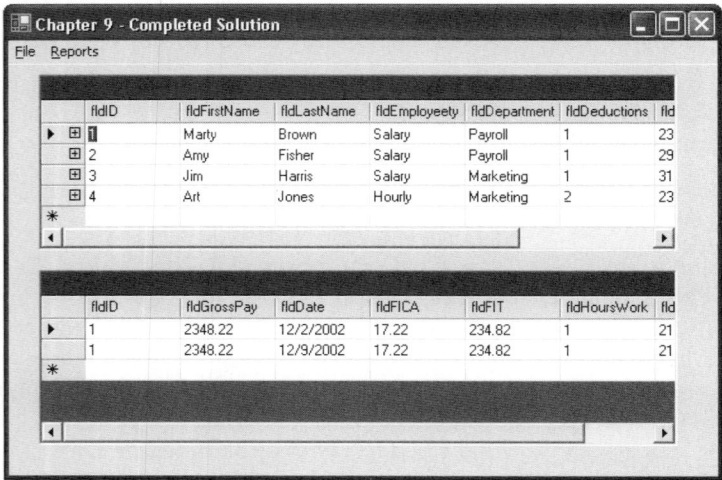

Figure 9-2 Completed solution – main form

4. On the main form, click **Reports**, and then click **Employee Report**. A second form appears containing the report.

Crystal Reports displays a report on a form via the CrystalReportViewer control. This control contains a visible region displaying the report itself and an optional toolbar allowing the user to zoom in and out of the current page, select pages, and print the report to the printer. Figure 9-3 shows the Employee Report displayed in an instance of the CrystalReportViewer control.

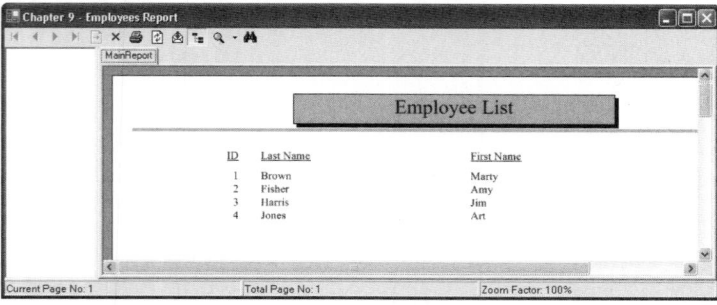

Figure 9-3 Completed solution – employee report

As shown in Figure 9-3, the CrystalReportViewer control instance is docked so as to fill the visible region of the form. The buttons on the toolbar allow the user to select different pages and to send the report to the printer.

5. Click the **Print Report** button to display the Print dialog box. Click **OK** to print the report. The printed report copy will be useful as you work through the chapter. Close the employee report form.

6. On the main form, click **Reports**, and then click **Payroll Report**. A dialog box appears allowing you to select report data dynamically. Check all of the check boxes appearing in the list box. Click **OK** to display the Payroll Report. Another form appears and the report fills the region of the displayed CrystalReportViewer control instance. Again, print the report for reference. Figure 9-4 shows the completed Payroll Report.

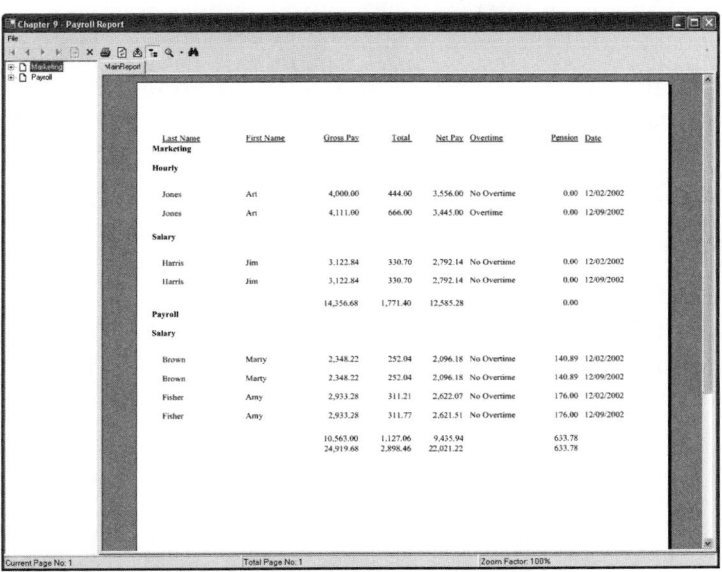

Figure 9-4   Completed solution – payroll report

7. End the solution and exit Visual Studio .NET.

 As you have experienced before, the OleDbConnection control stores an absolute path name in the ConnectionString property. Modify the ConnectionString property as necessary depending on where you installed the files associated with this book.

INTRODUCTION TO CRYSTAL REPORTS

Crystal Reports is a reporting tool that allows you, the developer, to design and implement presentation quality reports using a visual designer called the **Crystal Reports Designer**. You design a report with the Crystal Reports Designer in much the same way that you design a form. You create control instances on the report and set properties for those control instances. With Crystal Reports, you can create reports designed for both the desktop and the Web. Crystal Reports can create several types of reports, including tabular reports, form letters, and graphs. In this chapter, you will learn how to create tabular reports designed to be displayed and printed by desktop applications.

The steps to create a report with Crystal Reports differ from the steps to a create form and the code behind the form, as Crystal Reports hides most of the programming logic from the developer. That is, you, as the developer, do not write statements to navigate from record to record, or to advance the printer to the next page when a page is full. Instead, you define what will appear on the report header, page header, page footer, detail lines, totals, and subtotals all by creating fields on the report itself.

When the user prints the report, Crystal Reports displays and formats the report automatically based on the data contained in one or more database tables. All of this programming logic is built into Crystal Reports and cannot be altered. At runtime, Crystal Reports builds and prints a report in three stages.

Processing Stage 1

In Stage 1, the values of any constant formulas are evaluated. This step is performed once for the entire report. Crystal Reports then reads each record, and calculates the formulas defined for each record. In addition, records are sorted and grouped, and most of the subtotals are calculated in this processing stage. The following list details the processing that takes place in Stage 1:

1. Just before Stage 1 processing begins, Crystal Reports evaluates the values for constant formulas. A constant formula is similar to a VB .NET constant. The value of a constant formula does not change as the report is printed.

2. Each record is retrieved from the DataSet or DataTable.

3. Detail formulas that rely on Database fields or constant values are evaluated for each record. For example, you may have a detail formula that calculates an extended price for each record based on the quantity ordered and a unit price.

4. Records are then sorted and grouped, as necessary. If the report contains groups, then the records are sorted according to the hierarchical organization of each group. Group totals are calculated based on the sorted data. The records in the Payroll Report, for example, are grouped by department, and subtotals printed for the employees working in each department.

5. The sorted data and calculated totals are saved both to memory and to a temporary file for later use. Thus, the data need not be read from the database again in Stage 2.

6. Once all of the records have been read, Stage 2 processing begins as the records are formatted and printed.

Processing Stage 2

In Stage 2, totals that were not calculated in Stage 1 are evaluated, and report totals are evaluated. In addition, each page is formatted. Crystal Reports formats each page "on demand." That is, Crystal Reports does not format a page until the user previews or prints that page. The following list describes the processing that occurs during Stage 2:

1. Running totals are calculated.

2. Formulas that reference subtotals are evaluated. For example, a formula may reference the subtotals for all departments to calculate a grand total.

3. Charts and maps are formatted.

4. Finally, the page images are rendered as requested. (By page image, we mean the image of the printed page.) Note that Crystal Reports only renders a page when it is previewed or printed, thus, if you print a subset of the pages in a report, the pages that are not printed will not be rendered, for efficiency.

In the optional third processing stage, the page count is determined. This stage only executes if you have selected a Page Total field or an *n* of *m* field. Figure 9-5 gives a general overview of the processing stages for a Crystal Report.

9

```
Stage 1

1. Evaluate constant formulas
2. Retrieve database records
3. Sort records


Stage 2

1. Calculate running totals
2. Calculate subtotals
3. Render pages


Stage 3

1. Calculate page count if necessary
```

Figure 9-5   Processing stages of a Crystal Report

CREATING A REPORT

You add a Crystal Report to a project just as you add any other module file to a project, using the Add New Item dialog box. After adding the report with the Add New Item dialog box, another dialog box appears allowing you to define the type of report to create.

Defining the Report Type

When you add a Crystal Report to a project, you define the type of the report using the Crystal Report Gallery dialog box. Crystal Reports provides three ways to create a report:

- When you create a report using a Report Expert, you select from one of seven Report Experts to guide you through the process of creating a particular type of report. Each Report Expert is similar to a Wizard in that you complete a sequence of dialog boxes to define the data associated with the report, the detail information contained on the report, and how the subtotals and totals will be calculated. The contents of these dialog boxes vary from one Report Expert to another, based on the type of report being generated. If you create a report with the Report Expert, you can later modify the report using Crystal Reports. However, a Report Expert cannot be used to modify an existing report.

- You can create a blank report. A blank report contains five default sections. These default sections contain regions that describe the report header, the header and footer that appear at the top and bottom of each page, and a footer that appears at the end of the report itself. A section also appears for each detail line that will print on the report. However, the report is not automatically connected to a database nor does Crystal Reports create any fields on the report.

- You can create a new report based on an existing report. In this case, Crystal Reports just makes a copy of a previously defined report, and adds it to the project.

So that you can best understand the elements of a report, you will first create a blank report and define its characteristics without using a Report Expert. (The other two options in the preceding list will not help you understand the elements of a report because Crystal Reports will automatically generate the report elements for you.)

The first report you create will contain a list of employees based on the data from the table named tblEmployees. This first report will have a simplified visual appearance so that you can focus on only the most essential report elements. Later, you will create a second report with data from multiple tables and explore the more complex display and formatting capabilities supplied by Crystal Reports.

To add a blank Crystal Report to a project:

1. Start Visual Studio .NET, and then open the solution file named **Chapter.09\Startup09\Startup09.sln**.

   The main form contains two DataGrid control instances so that you can view the data that is being reported. This is the same DataGrid control that you have used in previous chapters. At this point, you will create a new blank report.

2. On the menu bar, click **Project**, and then click **Add New Item**. In the Add New Item dialog box, select **Crystal Report**. You will need to scroll down in the Templates pane to locate the Crystal Report icon. In the Name text box,

enter the name **EmployeeReport.rpt**. Make sure that you type the suffix. Do not change the file suffix of the report file or VB .NET will not be able to locate or recognize the file as a Crystal Report file.

3. Click the **Open** button to create the report and add it to the solution. In the Crystal Report Gallery dialog box, click the **As a Blank Report** radio button. The Crystal Report Gallery dialog box is shown in Figure 9-6.

If Crystal Reports has not yet been registered, a dialog box will appear requesting you to register the software. You may either register the software now or click the Register Later button to begin using Crystal Reports without registering it.

Figure 9-6   Crystal Report Gallery dialog box

4. Click **OK** to close the dialog box and create a blank report. The new report appears in a document window, as shown in Figure 9-7.

As shown in Figure 9-7, a new tool window appears called the Field Explorer. The Field Explorer allows you to define the visual interface for the report. Note that the Field Explorer may be hidden initially.

Figure 9-7   Blank Crystal Report

The Five Sections of the Crystal Reports Designer

The Crystal Reports Designer displays a visual representation of the report divided into five sections. The ruler across the top of the report defines the width of the page. As a page is typically measured in inches, the ruler uses inches as the unit of measure. Horizontal title bars mark each section. Note that each section is given a unique number. For example, the Report Header is designated as Section1. The height of each section defines the height of the section as it will appear on the printed page. Rulers along the left side of the Crystal Reports Designer mark the height of each section. Again, the unit of measure is inches. To decrease or increase the height of a section, drag the section title bar up or down, respectively.

The following list describes the purpose of the five default sections shown in Figure 9-7:

- The Report Header section appears once at the top of the first report page. The Report Header may also be configured to appear on its own page.

- The contents of the Page Header section appear at the top of each page. In a columnar report, you typically place column headers in this section to describe the rows of data appearing in the Details section.

- The Details section contains the report data. In this section, you typically select the Database fields that will appear. When the report is printed, the fields appearing in the Details section are printed for each record processed. When the page is full, Crystal Reports automatically advances the printer to the next page allowing enough space on the page to print the contents of the Page Footer section, if necessary.

- The contents of the Page Footer section appear at the bottom of each page. Page footers often contain a page number, the date the report was printed, and so on.

- The contents of the Report Footer section appear at the end of the report. In this section, you typically print report totals or other summary information. Note that the Report Footer section appears before the Page Footer section in the Crystal Reports Designer.

The preceding list describes only the default report sections created by Crystal Reports. As you progress through the chapter, you will create additional sections to display summarized payroll totals by department and display grand totals.

Crystal Reports Namespaces

When you added the Crystal Report to the project, VB .NET added references to the following three namespaces. The modules in this chapter will import these following namespaces:

- The classes of the **CrystalDecisions.CrystalReports.Engine** namespace allow you to access the elements of a report, and to define how the report will be printed. Its runtime classes also allow you to specify parameters dynamically to select specific records as the solution runs. You define parameters in a manner similar to the way you define parameters for an OleDbCommand object.

- You typically need not work with the **CrystalDecisions.ReportSource** namespace directly. Its classes provide an interface layer between the Crystal Reports Engine and a Windows form.

- The **CrystalDecisions.Shared** namespace contains generic classes to define parameters, page margins, and how the page is aligned about the report.

The Crystal Reports Files

When you create a blank report, Crystal Reports generates the following two files:

- One file has a suffix of .rpt. The .rpt file contains the report itself. Unlike most VB .NET files, the .rpt file is a binary file and can only be edited by the Crystal Reports Designer.

- Crystal Reports also generates a corresponding .vb file. Note that the .vb file only appears in the Solution Explorer if the Show All Files button is selected. Conceptually, this .vb file is similar to a strongly typed DataSet in that it contains a class that derives from the generic Crystal Reports ReportClass. This class has the same name as the report itself. Thus, when you created the blank report above, Crystal Reports created a class named EmployeeReport in the file named EmployeeReport.vb.

As mentioned, a Crystal Report contains five default sections. The EmployeeReport class contains read-only properties named Section1, Section2, and so on that correspond to these default sections. Just as you can call the typed methods of the DataSet class, you can use these properties and methods to create the report, and reference the data in the report programmatically. You will reference the report programmatically later in the chapter.

COMMON REPORT ELEMENTS

Crystal Reports supports controls and fields, which you use to create the report's visual interface, as described in the following list:

- **Crystal Reports controls** contain constant information such as a report title or a column header. These controls appear on the Crystal Reports tab of the Toolbox. You cannot use Win Forms controls on a Crystal Report.

- **Crystal Reports fields** typically store dynamic and calculated data. For example, you use fields to store the data for each record as the record is displayed. Fields are also used to store such information as page numbers or the date that the report was printed. Fields appear in the Field Explorer.

Crystal Reports Controls

Crystal Reports controls work the same way as the controls you have created on a form. That is, you create a control instance on a report, and then set its properties.

 Do not let the words "control" and "object" in Crystal Reports confuse you. Just because the word "Object" appears in a control name does not mean that the control itself is an object; it is still a control. For example, Crystal Reports uses the name "Text Object" as the name of a control.

Crystal Reports supports three controls, as described in the following list:

- The **Text Object** control is used to create a box containing literal text that does not change as the report is printed. Note that when you create Database fields in the Details section of the report, Crystal Reports automatically creates a corresponding Text Object control instance in the report's Page Header section to describe the column. The default text appearing in the Text Object control instance is the same as the field name. Fields will be discussed in a moment.

- The **Line Object** control is used to draw a horizontal or vertical line. Crystal Reports cannot draw diagonal lines.

- The **Box Object** control draws a flat or three-dimensional rectangle on the report.

When the Crystal Reports Designer is active, the Toolbox displays the Crystal Reports tab listing the preceding three controls. You create an instance of a Crystal Reports control in almost the same way as you create an instance of a Win Forms control on a form. That is, you create the control instance on the report, and then set its properties. Subtle differences, however, appear in the specific keystrokes required to create, move, and format the data appearing in a control instance. The following list describes selected differences:

- To reposition a control instance, click the control instance to select it. The control instance appears with a hatched border and sizing handles. Drag the control instance to move it, or drag the sizing handles to resize it. Note that if you increase the font size of the text appearing in a control instance, you must manually resize that control instance so that the text will fit within its visible region.

- Delete a control instance by selecting it, and then pressing the Delete key.

- The steps to enter text in a Text Object differ from the steps used to define the text for a TextBox or Label control instance. You edit the text in-place in the control instance. By default, the Text Object is activated when you create it so that the text can be entered directly into the Text Object. To activate the Text Object manually, right-click on the Text Object to select it, and then click Edit Text Object from the context menu.

- You do not always define the height of a Crystal Reports control instance. Crystal Reports uses the height of the current font to determine the height of the control instance. If you change the font or font size, you will subsequently need to resize the control instance.

To create a Text Object control instance on the report:

1. Make sure that the **Crystal Reports Designer** is active for the report named **EmployeeReport.rpt**. To activate the Crystal Reports Designer, double-click the report in the Solution Explorer.

2. In the Toolbox, click the **Crystal Reports** tab, if necessary, to activate it.

3. Click the Crystal Reports **Text Object** control, and then drag the control instance to the center of the **Report Header** section. The control instance appears with a hatched border. Again, note that Crystal Reports defines the default size of the control instance. Thus, you do not draw the control instance to define its size.

4. Enter the text **Employee List** in the Text Object control instance. Remember that you edit the text in-place.

 If the text you type does not appear in the visible region of the control instance, right-click the control instance, and then select Edit Text Object from the context menu.

Formatting the Contents of a Crystal Reports Control Instance

Having created a Text Object on the report, you can format its contents. Crystal Reports supplies two ways to format a Text Object. You can select the Text Object and then set many of its properties using the Properties window, or you can use the Format Editor. To activate the Format Editor, you right-click the desired Text Object in the Crystal Reports Designer, and then click Format from the context menu. Note that other control instances and fields are formatted using the same Format Editor.

As you create any Crystal Report, you use numerous dialog boxes, including the Format Editor. Because Crystal Reports has so many dialog boxes, the term dialog box will be omitted during subsequent discussions in this chapter.

The Format Editor displays different tabs depending on the type of object you are formatting. The following list describes the purpose of the context-sensitive tabs appearing on the Format Editor. All of the tabs appear in the following list. Note that some of these tabs do not apply to the text box. For example, the Box and Rounding tabs do not appear.

- The Box and Rounding tabs are used to format a Box control instance. The Box tab defines the thickness and color of the border surrounding the box. The Rounding tab allows you to round the corners of the box.

- On the Common tab, you define when, and if, a field should be hidden. You can create a hidden field and use that hidden field in calculations while not displaying the field's data to the user. You can also hide a field to prevent duplicate values from being printed on multiple rows. The Common tab also contains items that allow you to rotate text.

- On the Border tab, you define the border surrounding the control instance or field. You can also create formulas that Crystal Reports will evaluate at run-time to configure a particular border.

- From the Font tab, you define the font and any font attributes. You can define fonts for Text Objects and most types of fields.

- From the Line tab, you define the length, thickness, and color of a line.

- The Paragraph tab is used when a Text Object or field contains or displays multiple lines. Crystal Reports can interpret and format rich text files and HTML documents on multiple lines.

Next, you will see how to format the Text Object that you just created.

To format a Text Object:

1. Make sure that the Crystal Reports Designer is active for the report named **EmployeeReport.rpt**.

2. In the Crystal Reports Designer, right-click the **Text Object** that you just created to select it, and then click **Format** from the context menu to display the Format Editor.

3. Click the **Border** tab.

   If the Border tab does not appear on the Format Editor, close the Format Editor, deselect the Text Object, and then repeat Step 2. If text is currently being edited in the Format Editor, the Border tab will not appear.

4. Select a single line border for all of the borders by selecting **Single** from each of the four list boxes in the Line Style section of the Format Editor. Click the

Background check box. Set the background color to **Silver** if necessary. Click the **Drop Shadow** check box. Note that as you change each formatting element, a preview appears at the bottom of the Format Editor. Figure 9-8 shows the Border tab after the border, font, and alignment have been configured.

Figure 9-8 Format Editor – Border tab

5. Click the **Font** tab to activate it. Select an **18 point** font. Click **OK** to close the Format Editor and apply the changes.

   Even though you selected a larger font, Crystal Reports does not automatically resize the control instance.

6. In the Crystal Reports Designer, resize the Text Object so that the control instance is centered in the report. Increase the height and width of the control instance so that the text will fit within the visible region. To do so, click the control instance to select it, and then drag the sizing handles as necessary.

Other Formatting Properties

In addition to using the Format Editor to format the contents of a Text Object, you can also set several of the same properties using the Properties window. Which technique you choose is up to you. Many of these property names are unique to Crystal Reports, however.

Note that just as a VB .NET control instance has a name, so too does a Crystal Reports control instance. You use the value of the Name property to reference the control instance or field programmatically.

The following properties are shared by most types of controls and fields:

- You can individually define the borders surrounding a control instance or field by setting the **BottomLineStyle**, **LeftLineStyle**, **RightLineStyle**, and **TopLineStyle** properties. By setting these properties individually, you can hide or display a specific border line, draw single lines or double lines, or create dashed lines. For example, to underline a total field, draw the field with only a bottom border and hide the remaining borders.

- Crystal Reports works with color and color printers. The **BackColor**, **BorderColor**, and **TextColor** properties define the background color, border color, and text color, respectively.

- The **HorAlignment** property allows you to specify the horizontal alignment of the text within the visible region of the control instance or field. Again, this property name is unique to Crystal Reports.

Numerous properties are designed to format currency values, as described in the following list:

- The **CurrencyPositionType** property defines whether the currency symbol appears before or after the value. It also defines the position of the currency symbol relative to the negative number symbol when the number is negative.

- The **CurrencySymbol** property defines the character that marks a currency value. Typically, the character is a dollar sign ($), however, for international applications, this character will differ.

- The **CurrencySymbolType** property is used to suppress the currency symbol, cause the currency symbol to appear at a fixed position, or cause it to float with the data appearing in the field.

- The **DecimalPlaces** property defines the number of digits printed to the right of the decimal place.

In addition to currency values, Crystal Reports provides considerable flexibility with regard to formatting date values. The following properties apply to formatting date values:

- The **DateCalendarType** property defines which international calendar is used to calculate date values, because different cultures use different calendars.

- The **DateOrder** property defines the order of the year, month, and day parts of a date. Typically, U.S. dates appear in month/day/year format. European dates often appear in year/month/day format.

- The **TimeBase** property causes times to be displayed using a 12 or 24 hour clock.

- The **YearType** property can be configured to display four digit years or two digit years, or to omit displaying the year.

Next, you will see how to use the Properties window to format the Text Object control instance that you previously created.

To set Text Object properties using the Properties window:

1. Click the **Text Object** you created to select it, if necessary, and then activate the Properties window. Note that you can also use the Object list box in the Properties window to select the Text Object.

2. Set the HorAlignment property to **crHorCenterAlign** to center the text in the visible region of the control instance.

3. Set the Name property to **txtReportName**.

Having seen how to create a Text Object on the report, you will now create and format a horizontal line on the report.

To create a horizontal line:

1. In the Toolbox, click the **Line Object** to select it. In the Crystal Reports Designer, the cursor changes to a pencil.

2. Draw the line in the **Report Header** section such that it occupies the entire width of the report and appears below the Text Object that you just created.

3. Right-click on the line to select it, if necessary, and then click **Format** on the context menu to display the Format Editor.

4. The Format Editor appears with a single tab allowing you to configure the format of the line, its color, and its thickness, as shown in Figure 9-9.

5. Format the line as shown in Figure 9-9, and then click **OK** to close the Format Editor.

Before proceeding to create the rest of the report, you will learn how to preview the report using the CrystalReportViewer control. The reason for this organization is simple. By learning how to preview the report, you can interactively examine the report as you design and develop it.

9

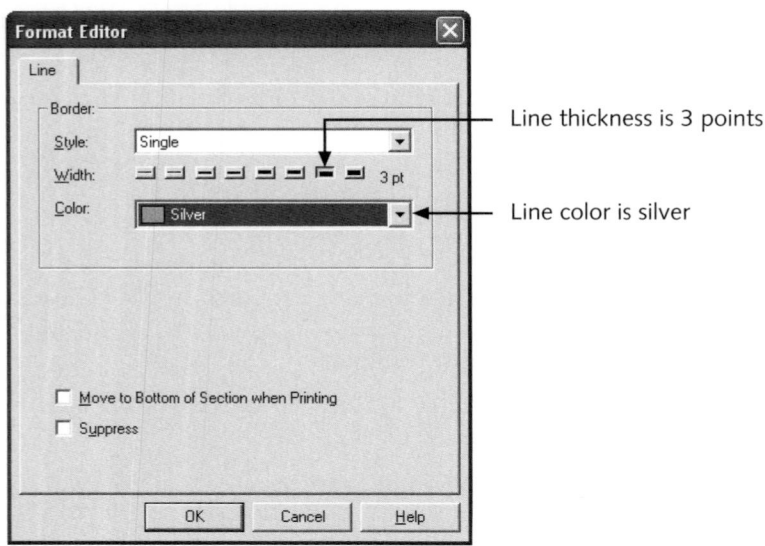

Figure 9-9   Format Editor – Line tab

PREVIEWING A REPORT

Having created the report, you can preview it on a form or send it directly to the printer. Most applications, such as Microsoft Word, provide such capabilities. Many users may want to preview a report, checking it for correctness, before sending it to a printer.

To display a report, you create an instance of the CrystalReportViewer control on a form. Crystal Reports displays the report in the visible region of the control instance. The CrystalReportViewer control supports the following members:

Syntax

System.Windows.Forms.UserControl.CrystalReportViewer control

Public Properties

- The **Dock** property has the same meaning as the Dock property of other controls. It defines how the control instance will be docked on the form.

- The Boolean **DisplayToolbar** property defines whether or not a toolbar appears along the top of the control instance. By default, a toolbar appears.

- If the Boolean **EnableDrillDown** property is True, then a drill–down interface appears along the left side of the control instance. This drill–down interface allows the user to navigate to specific sections of the report, or to locate specific records. It also allows the user to expand or collapse specific report sections. This property is True by default.

- The **ReportSource** property defines the name of the Crystal Reports file. This file has the suffix of ".rpt". This is the same file that Crystal Reports created when you created the report itself. The ReportSource property can be set at design time using the Properties window, or programmatically at runtime.

- The **ShowPageNavigationButtons** property defines whether or not the user can navigate to different report pages. These buttons appear on the toolbar.

- The **ShowPrintButton** property defines whether or not the Print button appears at the top of the control instance. This button appears on the toolbar.

- The **ShowZoomButton** property defines whether or not zooming is enabled. This button appears on the toolbar.

Public Methods

- Calling the **PrintReport** method prints the report displayed in the CrystalReportViewer control instance.

- The current page displayed can be set by calling the **ShowFirstPage**, **ShowNextPage**, **ShowPreviousPage**, and **ShowLastPage** methods.

- The **ShowNthPage** method displays a particular report page.

- Calling the **Zoom** method changes the magnification level.

Public Events

- The **Navigate** event fires as the user navigates from one report page to another.

- If an exception fires in the CrystalReportViewer, you can create an event handler for the **HandleException** event.

Next, you will display the Employee Report by creating and configuring an instance of the CrystalReportViewer control. The solution already contains a form named frmEmployees.vb to display the report. In addition, the main form contains the statements to display the Employee Report form.

To display a report created with Crystal Reports:

1. Using the Windows Forms tab on the Toolbox, create an instance of the **CrystalReportViewer** control on the form named **frmEmployees.vb**.

2. Activate the Properties window for the CrystalReportViewer control instance, if necessary. Set the Dock property to **Fill**.

3. Set the Name property to **crvEmployees**.

4. Set the ReportSource property by clicking the **value** column in the Properties window to display the list arrow. Click the list arrow, and then click **Browse** to activate the Open an Existing Crystal Report dialog box. Select the report named **Chapter.09\Startup09\EmployeeReport.rpt**, and then click **Open**.

Note that by setting the ReportSource at design time, the path name is hard coded into the application. Thus, if the application is moved to another directory, it will not run correctly. We solve this problem later in the chapter.

5. Test the solution. On the main form, click **Reports** and then click **Employee Report** to display the report shown in Figure 9-10. As mentioned, your report may differ slightly.

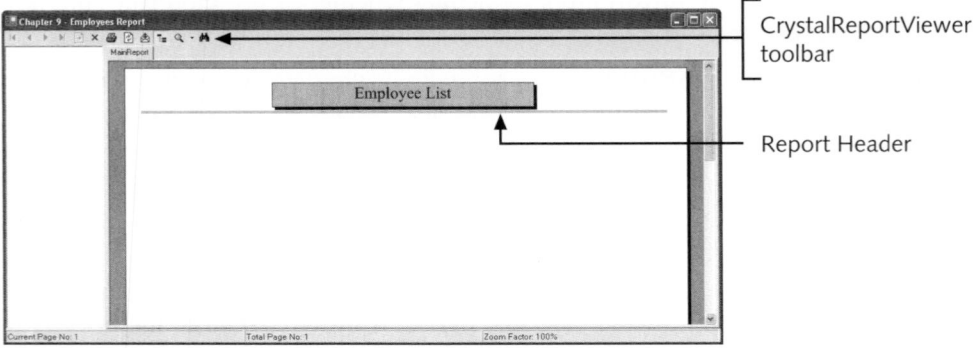

Figure 9-10   Displaying a Crystal Report

While the report appears in the CrystalReportViewer, it displays only the report header. The reason is simple: you have yet to define the data that will appear on the report, or any other fields that will appear on the report.

In this section, you used controls to define the constant information appearing on a report. That is, you defined lines and text that will not change as Crystal Reports displays the report in the CrystalReportViewer control instance. Other report elements are created using fields.

CRYSTAL REPORTS FIELDS

You create fields on a report in much the same way that you create control instances on a form. However, instead of creating control instances with the Toolbox, you create fields with the Field Explorer. The Field Explorer categorizes fields into the following seven types using a drill-down interface:

- A **Database field** corresponds to a field in a database table(s). Database fields are commonly used to print detail records from one or more database tables. Database fields may appear in any report section, however.

- **Formula fields** allow you to perform calculations using the contents of Database fields, other Formula fields, or Unbound fields.

- **Parameter fields** allow you to select or specify data dynamically at runtime either from a Crystal Reports-supplied dialog box or programmatically.

- **Group Name fields** allow similar data to be grouped together to form a control break report. A control break report is one containing subtotals based on a categorical grouping of records. Control break reports are discussed later in the chapter.

- **Running Total fields** allow you to tally the values for multiple rows and to perform calculations on those rows. For example, you can calculate the total gross pay for several employees or calculate the minimum or maximum gross pay.

- **Special fields** provide the means to display information common to most reports, such as the current date or page number.

- **Unbound fields** store numeric, string, or Boolean data that is not associated with a Database field.

Before you can create the report fields that will display data from the database, you must first connect the report with a database.

CONNECTING THE REPORT TO A DATABASE

9

Crystal Reports can create reports from the data contained in an ADO.NET DataSet. This is the same ADO.NET DataSet that you have used in previous chapters. Thus, you create the DataSet using the same OleDbConnection and OleDbDataAdapter objects that you have used before. Again, these objects can be created using the VB .NET tools, or programmatically.

Crystal Reports and ADO.NET

Crystal Reports works with ADO.NET through a .xsd file and a typed DataSet. You can create the necessary .xsd file by saving a DataSet to a file. Or you can use the same typed DataSet object that you have created before both programmatically and using the same OleDbConnection and OleDbDataAdapters that you have used in previous chapters.

 When you use a DataSet with Crystal Reports, it is imperative that the .xsd file and the DataSet itself have exactly the same schema (structure), as Crystal Reports uses both objects concurrently. Thus, if you change the structure of the in-memory DataSet such that it differs from the one defined in the .xsd file, Crystal Reports will raise an exception.

By using a DataSet with a Crystal Report, both the Crystal Report and the application itself can share the same data. For example, you can display a DataSet and its tables in a DataGrid control instance, and then use that same DataSet to print a report. Again, because the DataSet is disconnected from the database, Crystal Reports does not need to access the database either. Finally, you can sort, filter, and manipulate the data in the DataSet before sending it to Crystal Reports.

The first step in associating a Crystal Report with a DataSet is to create the typed DataSet. You create a typed DataSet for a report using the same OleDbConnection and OleDbDataAdapter controls that were discussed in Chapter 7.

To create a typed DataSet for use with Crystal Reports:

1. Activate the Win Forms Designer for the form named **frmEmployees.vb**.
2. Create an instance of the **OleDbConnection** control on the form using the Data tab of the Toolbox. Set its Name property to **odbconEmployees**.
3. Set the **ConnectionString** property to establish a connection with the database named **Chapter.09\Data\Payroll.mdb**. Use the Microsoft **Jet 4.0 OLE DB Provider**. Remember that you set the properties using the Data Link Properties dialog box. Activate the dialog box by clicking the list arrow for the **ConnectionString** property and clicking **<New Connection>**.
4. Create an instance of the OleDbDataAdapter object on the form. Using the DataAdapter's Configuration Wizard, configure the control instance to select all of the fields from the table named **tblEmployees**. Sort the data in ascending order using the field named **fldID**. Set the Name property of the control instance to **odbdaEmployees**. Refer to Chapter 7 for further information on configuring the OleDbDataAdapter.
5. Generate a **DataSet** by activating the form and clicking **Data**, **Generate Dataset** from the menu. In the Generate Dataset dialog box, make sure to add the DataSet to the designer. Name the DataSet **dsEmployees**.

   If a dialog box appears indicating that the project must be rebuilt, rebuild the project as requested. Regenerate and replace the DataSet as necessary.

Even though you have generated the DataSet, there exists no association with the DataSet and the Crystal Report yet. Before you can create the Database fields on the report itself, you must associate the .xsd file with the Crystal Report. Another dialog box called the Database Expert is used to accomplish this task.

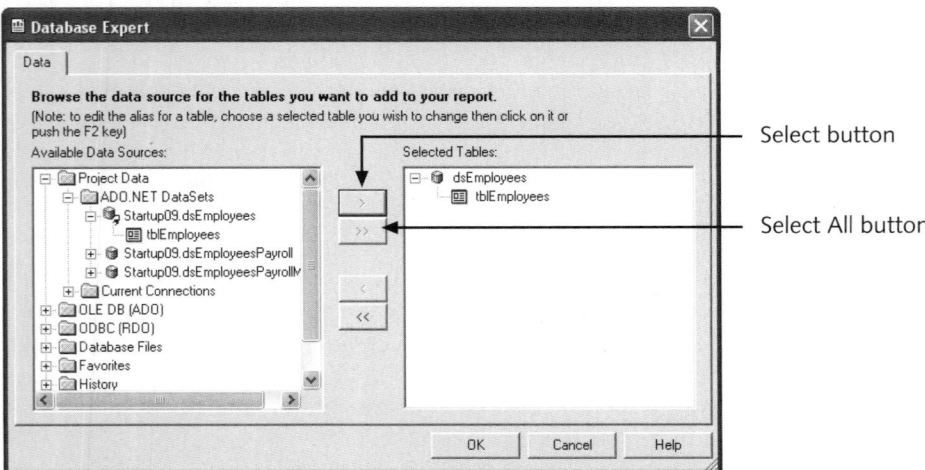

Figure 9-11 Database Expert

As shown in Figure 9-11, the Database Expert has a drill-down interface with which you select data from different data sources. The Project Data folder associates a Crystal Report with data from the project itself. ADO.NET DataSets are considered Project Data. The option OLE DB (ADO) allows you to use classic ADO. Classic ADO is not discussed in this book.

To associate an .xsd file with a Crystal Report:

1. Activate the Crystal Reports Designer for the report by double-clicking the report named **EmployeeReport.rpt** in the Solution Explorer, if necessary.

2. In the Field Explorer, right-click **Database Fields**. Click **Add/Remove Database** from the context menu to display the Database Expert shown in Figure 9-11. Note that Figure 9-11 shows the Database Expert after the DataSet table has been selected.

   If the Field Explorer is not visible, click View, select Other Windows, and then click Document Outline.

3. In the Available Data Sources pane, click the **plus** (+) sign to the left of the **Project Data** folder. Expand the **ADO.NET DataSets** folder to display the DataSet (Startup09.DsEmployees). Expand this folder to display the DataTable in the DataSet (tblEmployees).

4. In the Available Data Sources pane, click the table named **tblEmployees** to select it, and then click the **Select** (>) button to select the table. The DataSet and DataTable appear in the **Selected Tables** pane. Click **OK** to select the table and close the Database Expert.

5. In the Field Explorer, expand the **Database Fields** folder. Expand the folder named **tblEmployees**. The table's fields appear.

By generating a DataSet and a corresponding .xsd file, Crystal Reports is able to read that file at design time and select the DataTable(s) and fields into the Field Explorer. Note that these steps do not associate the runtime DataSet with the report, however. That topic will be discussed in a moment.

Next you will create instances of the Database fields so that they will appear on the printed report. To create the Database fields that will appear on the report, you use the Field Explorer. Conceptually, the purpose of the Field Explorer is similar to that of the Toolbox. You create Database fields on a report just as you create control instances on a form. Furthermore, you drag and drop fields onto a report in almost the same way as you create control instances on a form.

Database Fields

By creating Database fields on a report, you cause Crystal Reports to display the data contained in the underlying database table(s) at runtime. If you create a Database field in the details section of the report, Crystal Reports will print one line for each record appearing in the table. That is, Crystal Reports will generate one record during Stage 1 of report processing and print one record during Stage 2. Next, you will create Database fields for the DataSet fields named fldID, fldFirstName, and fldLastName.

To create Database fields:

1. Make sure that the Crystal Reports Designer is active for the report named **EmployeeReport.rpt**.

2. Expand the **Field Explorer** for the table named **tblEmployees**, if necessary.

3. Create the first Database field by dragging the field named **fldID** to the Details section of the report, as shown in Figure 9-12. Figure 9-12 shows the Crystal Reports Designer after all of the Database fields have been created and formatted.

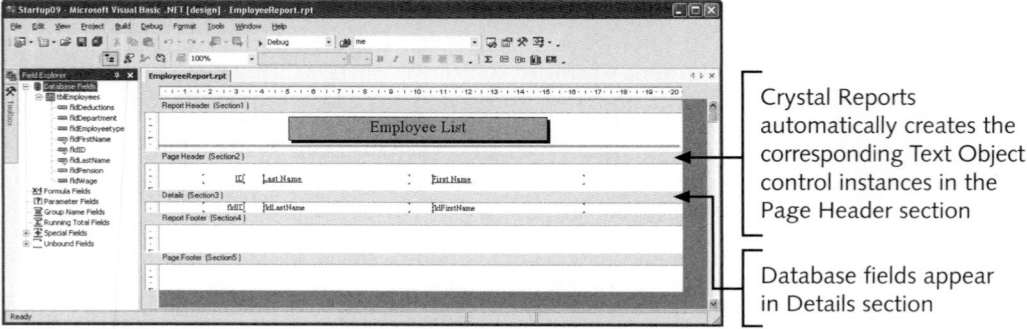

Crystal Reports automatically creates the corresponding Text Object control instances in the Page Header section

Database fields appear in Details section

Figure 9-12   Creating Database fields

Note that when you created the Database field, Crystal Reports automatically created a Text Object control instance in the Page Header section to identify the column.

4. Create the remaining Database fields for the fields named **fldFirstName** and **fldLastName** as shown in Figure 9-12.

5. Resize and position the fields and change the Text property so that the column headers match those shown in Figure 9-12. Remember, to change the text appearing in a Text Object, right-click the Text Object to select it, and then click Edit Text Object.

To move multiple Database fields (or other fields) at the same time, drag a rectangle around the desired fields to select them. The fields are selected and appear highlighted. Drag the fields to their new position. It is also possible to drag and drop fields from one report section to another.

If you were to run the application to preview the report with the data, it would not work. While Crystal Reports has read the .xsd file so that you could specify the report fields, you have not configured the report so that it will read data from a runtime instance of the DataSet. Remember that a DataSet does not get populated until you call the Fill method of the OleDbDataAdapter. Thus, to display DataSet data in a Crystal Report, you must create the DataSet, fill it, and then configure the Crystal Report to read the data from that populated DataSet. To accomplish this task, you must work with the Crystal Report programmatically.

Managing a Crystal Report Programmatically

Every Crystal Report is exposed to your application through a class having the same name as the report itself. When you created the report named EmployeeReport.rpt, Crystal Reports defined a class named EmployeeReport in the file named EmployeeReport.vb. The following statements declare a variable and create an instance of the EmployeeReport class:

```
Dim crReportDocument As EmployeeReport
crReportDocument = New EmployeeReport()
```

The preceding statements declare a variable of type EmployeeReport, and then create an instance of that class. Think of the EmployeeReport class as a strongly typed DataSet. That is, the EmployeeReport class is derived from the ReportDocument class. It contains typed members that allow you to manage the fields in the various report sections. This report derives from the ReportDocument class, having the following members:

9

Syntax

System.Component.ReportDocument class

Public Properties

- The **DataBase** property references a DataBase object. This object is unique to Crystal Reports and does not represent a physical database. The DataBase object, in turn, contains a Tables collection through which Crystal Reports retrieves data from a database table. Again, this collection is unique to Crystal Reports and differs from the Tables collection of the DataSet class.

- The various field categories, such as Database fields, Formula fields, and Parameter fields, correspond to collections contained within the **DataDefinition** property. The objects in these subordinate collections allow you to access the Database fields, Formula fields, and Parameter fields of the report itself at runtime.

- The **ExportOptions** property allows a report to be exported to another format. Crystal Reports supports document formats for HTML, Microsoft Word, Microsoft Excel, and others.

- The **PrintOptions** property stores a reference to a PrintOptions object, which has properties to specify the page margins and the paper size, and to select a printer.

- The **SummaryInfo** property defines general information about the report, including the report author, report title, and comments.

Public Methods

- The **Close** method destroys the ReportDocument, thereby destroying the elements of the report, such as the DataDefinition.

- The **Export** method uses the contents of the ExportOptions property to export a report to a file or other destination.

- The **FilePath** property returns the path and file name of the report.

- The **Load** method explicitly loads a report. Once a report is loaded you can access the properties of the report, such as the DataDefinition.

- The **PrintToPrinter** method sends the report to a printer on the system. The arguments allow you to specify minimum and maximum page numbers to print, the number of copies to print, and, when printing multiple copies, how to collate those copies.

- The **SetDataSource** method associates a populated DataSet with the Crystal Reports engine.

Public Events

- The **InitReport** event fires for the report just after the report loads.

To associate a DataSet with a report you must populate the DataSet, create an instance of the report itself, and then associate that DataSet with the report. Examine the following statements to accomplish this task:

```
Dim crReportDocument As New EmployeeReport()
odbdaEmployees.Fill(DsEmployees1)
crReportDocument.SetDataSource(DsEmployees1)
crvEmployees.ReportSource = crReportDocument
```

The first statement creates an instance of the EmployeeReport class, and the second statement populates the DataSet named DsEmployees1 using the Fill method of the OleDbDataAdapter that you created previously. Remember that the typed DataSet class is named dsEmployees and the instance variable is named DsEmployees1. The third statement associates the DataSet with the Crystal Reports engine by calling the SetDataSource method. The SetDataSource method accepts one argument having a data type of System.Object. If the actual data type of the argument is a DataSet, then Crystal Reports will obtain its data from that DataSet. The final statement associates the CrystalReportViewer control instance named crvEmployees with the report itself. As you have seen, the ReportSource property can also be set at design time, however, when set at design time, the report's path and file name are hard coded into the application.

Next, you will associate the report with the DataSet and then view its data.

To associate a Crystal Report with a DataSet:

1. Activate the Properties window for the CrystalReportViewer control instance appearing on the form named **frmEmployees.vb**. Set the ReportSource property to **None**, as you will be defining the ReportSource programmatically in the following step.

2. Activate the Code Editor for the form named **frmEmployees.vb**. Enter the following statements in the form's **Load** event handler:

```
Dim crReportDocument As New EmployeeReport()
odbdaEmployees.Fill(DsEmployees1)
crReportDocument.SetDataSource(DsEmployees1)
crvEmployees.ReportSource = crReportDocument
```

3. Test the solution. On the main form, click **Reports**, and then click **Employee Report** to display the Employee Report as shown in Figure 9-13.

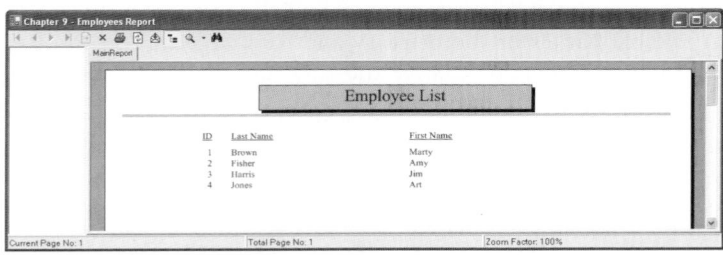

Figure 9-13   Report containing data

As shown in Figure 9-13, the report contains a page header with three columns. Four detail records are printed beneath the page headers.

Now that you have seen how to use Crystal Reports with a single database table, you will create a more complex report that displays data from multiple tables, and create formulas, subtotals, and grand totals.

WORKING WITH MULTIPLE TABLES IN CRYSTAL REPORTS

Working with multiple tables in Crystal Reports is not that much different from working with a single table. You define a DataSet containing multiple tables, fill that DataSet, and then associate the DataSet with a Crystal Report.

The form named frmPayroll has already been created. This form has instances of the OleDbConnection, OleDbDataAdpater, and DataSet classes. The DataSet has been configured with a DataRelation to relate the field named fldID from the master table named tblEmployees and the detail table named tblPayroll. In addition, a report named PayrollReport.rpt has already been created. You use the same Database Expert to associate multiple DataSet tables with a report.

The multi-table report that you will create in the following steps will not exactly match the report in the completed solution. For brevity, you will not be changing the text in the automatically generated column headers.

To create a multi-table report:

1. Activate the Crystal Reports Designer for the report named **PayrollReport.rpt**.

2. In the Field Explorer, right-click **Database Fields**. Click **Add/Remove Database** from the context menu to display the Database Expert.

3. Click the **plus** (+) sign to the left of the **Project Data** folder, if necessary. Expand the **ADO.NET DataSets** folder to display the DataSet (Startup09.dsEmployeesPayroll).

4. Select the tables named **tblEmployees** and **tblPayroll** by clicking the database name, and then clicking the **Select All** (>>) button.

   Crystal Reports automatically attempts to link the underlying DataSet tables based on the table names or the primary and foreign keys. You can use the Links tab of the Database Expert to change the way the two tables are linked together.

5. Activate the **Links tab** of the Database Expert. The two tables appear with an arrow drawn between them to indicate the relationship. Note that the tables are linked by the field named fldID.

6. Click **OK** to establish the link and close the Database Expert.

7. Activate the Code Editor for the form named **frmPayroll.vb**. Enter the following statement immediately after the code generated by the Win Forms Designer:

   Private crReportDocument As New PayrollReport()

8. On the same form, enter the following statements in the **Load** event handler to populate the DataSet and associate it with the report:

   ```
   odbdaEmployees.Fill(DsEmployeesPayroll1)
   odbdaPayroll.Fill(DsEmployeesPayroll1)
   crReportDocument.SetDataSource(DsEmployeesPayroll1)
   crvPayroll.ReportSource = crReportDocument
   ```

9. Activate the Crystal Reports Designer for the report named **PayrollReport.rpt**.

10. Create Database fields for the fields named **fldLastName**, **fldFirstName**, and **fldGrossPay** in the Details section of the report. Change the text for the Text Objects to match Figure 9-14. Resize the control instances and fields, as necessary.

11. Test the solution. On the main menu, click **Reports**, and then click **Payroll Report** to display the Payroll Report. The employee records should appear in the Details section of the report.

In addition to creating Database fields, you can also perform calculations using Formula fields.

Figure 9-14   Creating fields from multiple tables

CREATING FORMULA FIELDS

Formulas are an integral part of most reports. Formulas allow you to perform calculations on Database fields, Unbound fields, or other Formula fields. For example, suppose that you wanted to calculate the total federal and Social Security taxes for an employee. Assuming that this value is not stored in a database table, you can perform the calculation using a Formula field. To create a Formula field, you use the Formula Editor shown in Figure 9-15.

Figure 9-15   Formula Editor

As shown in Figure 9-15, the Formula Editor contains a toolbar. The toolbar buttons allow you to configure the Formula Editor, save formulas, and select formulas for editing.

The Formula Editor is divided into three panes, called trees. Each tree has a drill-down interface. The following list describes the purpose of each tree:

- The **Field Tree** appears in the left pane and lists the fields that have been created on the report in the Report Fields section. In addition, the Field Tree shows the DataSet associated with the report, allowing you to use fields in a calculation that do not appear on the report itself.

- The **Function Tree** appears in the middle pane and lists the mathematical and statistical functions that you can apply to the fields appearing in the Field Tree.

- The right column contains the **Operator Tree**. The Operator Tree contains the mathematical, string, relational, and conditional operators supported by Crystal Reports.

 The panes in the Formula Editor are configurable. You can resize the Formula Editor itself, or you can drag the border of each tree, allowing you to increase or decrease the width of a particular tree.

As you build a formula by clicking on fields, functions, and operators, Crystal Reports displays the formula in the multi-line text box appearing at the bottom of the Formula Editor. In addition to clicking the various entries in the Field, Function, and Operator Trees, you can also type the formula directly into the Formula Editor or modify an existing formula. To modify an existing formula, right-click the formula in the Field Explorer, and then select Edit from the context menu. The same context menu contains options to delete and rename formulas.

To explore how to create a simple formula, you will create a Formula field that will add the federal tax and Social Security tax together and display that value for each detail record.

To create a Formula field:

1. Activate the Crystal Reports Designer for the report named **PayrollReport.rpt**, if necessary.

2. In the Field Explorer, right-click **Formula Fields**, and then click **New** from the context menu.

3. The Formula Name dialog box appears, requesting that you give the formula a unique name. Every Crystal Reports field must have a unique name. Enter the name **TotalTaxes** in the Formula Name dialog box, and then click **OK** to close the Formula Name dialog box and display the Formula Editor.

   When you activate the Formula Editor, the Report Fields section appears expanded and contains the Database fields that you just created on the report. In the following formula, you will use fields from the database not yet used on the report. Another section contains all of the fields defined in the DataSet itself. This folder appears collapsed, by default.

4. Expand the DataSet named **dsEmployeesPayroll** to display the DataSet tables. Expand the table named **tblPayroll**.

5. Double-click the field named **fldFIT**. The field appears in the formula section at the bottom of the Formula Editor. In the Operators pane, expand the **Arithmetic** folder and double-click the **Add (x + y)** operator to add the operator to the formula. Note that the formula "(x + y)" is just part of the prompt. It does not describe the formula that you are creating.

6. In the Field Tree, double-click the field named **fldFICA**. This field is added to the formula.

7. Click the **Save** button to save the Formula field. Close the Formula Editor.

   Note that the toolbar contains a "Check" button allowing you to check the syntax of the current formula. In addition, the "Save and close" button will save the formula and then close the Formula Editor.

8. Having created the Formula field, you can now create an instance of the Formula field on the report itself. You create a Formula field on a report in the same way that you create a Database field on a report. You drag the field from the Field Explorer to the report itself.

9. In the Field Explorer, expand the **Formula Fields** folder. The Formula field named TotalTaxes appears. Create the field on the PayrollReport, positioning the field to the right of the GrossPay field.

   Note that Crystal Reports puts an @ at the begining of every formula field.

10. Create a second Formula field named **NetPay**. Subtract the formula named **@TotalTaxes** from the field named **fldGrossPay** to create the following Formula field:

    ```
    {tblPayroll.fldGrossPay} - {@TotalTaxes}
    ```

    From the preceding Formula field, you can see that a Formula field itself can contain another Formula field.

11. Create an instance of the @**NetPay** Formula field on the report to the right of the @TotalTaxes field that you just created.

12. Save the report.

13. Test the solution. On the menu, click **Reports**, and then click **Payroll Report** to display the report. The total taxes and net pay appear for each detail record.

Note that the syntax of a Crystal Reports Formula field differs from the syntax of a VB .NET expression. Examine the syntax of the @TotalTaxes formula that you just created:

```
{tblPayroll.fldFIT} + {tblPayroll.fldFICA}
```

The preceding formula uses two Database fields. The field names appear surrounded by braces. Furthermore, unlike an assignment statement, a Formula field has no left side.

Once you have created a Formula field, you can edit it by right-clicking the Formula field in the Field Editor, and then clicking Edit from the context menu. Delete a Formula field by clicking Delete from the context menu. In addition, you can format the contents of a Formula field in the same way that you formatted the contents of a Text Object.

Crystal Reports allows you to create much more complex Formula fields than the one you just created. The following list describes just a few of the functions supplied by Crystal Reports:

- Supported financial functions include present value (PV), future value (FV), and internal rate of return (IRR).

- Numerous string functions are supported to convert a string to uppercase or lowercase characters, perform string concatenation, and manipulate the data contained in a string. These string functions appear in the Strings folder of the Operator Tree. Additional string functions appear in the Strings folder of the Function Tree.

- Formulas can also contain loops and If statements. Conditional operators appear in the Control Structures folder of the Operator Tree.

- Logical operators such as And, Or, and Not are supported. Logical operators appear in the Boolean folder of the Operator Tree.

Next, you will create a more complex Formula field using a condition. The condition will determine whether an employee worked more than 40 hours during the pay period. If so, the text "Overtime" will appear on the report. Otherwise, the text "No Overtime" should be displayed. Note that the Crystal Reports syntax for an If statement differs from the VB .NET syntax as shown in the following code segment:

```
If {tblPayroll.fldHoursWorked} > 40 then
    "Overtime"
else
    "No Overtime"
```

The syntax of the condition in the If statement is similar to the VB .NET syntax with the exception that the field name(s) appears in braces. The syntax for the assignment part of the statement differs considerably, though. The string "Overtime" or "No Overtime" is stored in the formula, based on the outcome of the If statement. However, the left side of the assignment statement along with the equals sign is omitted. Finally, notice that the End If is missing.

To create a Formula field having a condition:

1. Create a new Formula field named **Overtime** by right-clicking **Formula Fields** in the Field Explorer, and then clicking New from the context menu. Enter the following formula in the Formula Editor:

```
If {tblPayroll.fldHoursWorked} > 40 then
    "Overtime"
else
    "No Overtime"
```

2. Save the Formula field and close the Formula Editor.

   Note that if you make an error entering the formula, Crystal Reports will display a dialog box describing the cause of the error. Examine the message in the dialog box, fix the error, and attempt to save the formula again.

3. Create an instance of the @**Overtime** Formula field on the report to the right of the @NetPay field in the Details section of the report. Resize the field as necessary.

   Next, you will see how to create a conditional Formula field using numeric data. If an employee is signed up for the company pension plan, the pension amount is 6% of the gross pay.

4. Create another Formula field named **Pension**, having the following formula:

```
If {tblEmployees.fldPension} then
    {tblPayroll.fldGrossPay} * 0.06
else
    0
```

5. Create an instance of the @**Pension** Formula field on the report to the right of the @Overtime field.

6. Create a Database field using the field named **fldDate** to the right of the @Pension field that you just created.

7. Save the report.

8. Test the solution. On the menu, click **Reports**, **Payroll Report**. The overtime value appears on the report along with the pension deduction.

The next type of Crystal Reports field discussed is the Special field.

SPECIAL FIELDS

Special fields are nothing more than ordinary field objects that Crystal Reports automatically configures for you to form specific tasks, such as displaying a page number, the current date, a record number, or a title. The following list describes selected Special fields:

- The **Print Date** field prints the current date and the **Print Time** field prints the current time.
- The **Record Number** field prints the 1-based record number.
- The **Page Number** field prints the 1-based page number.
- The **Page N of M** field prints the current page number and the total number of pages.
- The **Total Page Count** field prints the total number of pages.

In the Payroll Report, you will print the date and the page number in the report's page footer using Special fields.

To create Special fields:

1. Using the Field Explorer, expand the **Special Fields** section to display the supported Special fields.

2. Create a **Print Date** field in the Page Footer section as shown in Figure 9-16. You create a Special field the same way you create any other Crystal Reports field. In the Field Explorer, click the Special field to select it, and then drag the field to its position in the Page Footer section of the report.

3. Create a **Page N of M** field in the Page Footer section as shown in Figure 9-16. Right-align the field.

4. Save the report.

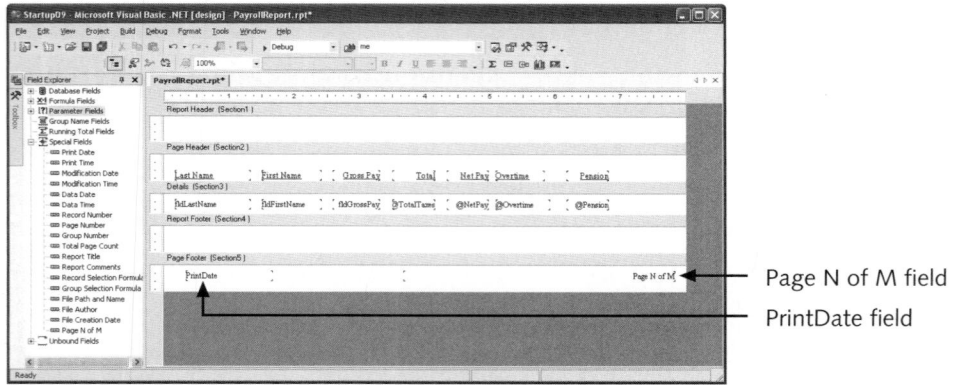

Page N of M field
PrintDate field

Figure 9-16   Creating Special fields

5. Test the solution. Display the Payroll Report. The date printed and the page number appears in the page footer.

At this point, your report prints one line for each detail record appearing in the payroll table.

CONTROL BREAK REPORTS

Crystal Reports allows you to create control break reports. A **control break report** is a report where some special processing occurs when the value of a particular field changes. When the value of some defined field changes, a control break occurs, normal processing is suspended, special processing occurs, and then normal processing resumes until that field's value changes again. This special processing may include printing a subtotal, or resetting the value of an accumulator.

An employee works for a particular department in the organization. In the control break report you create, payroll records will be sorted and grouped by department. When the department changes, subtotals will be printed for that department. Finally, a grand total will be printed for all departments.

Creating a Control Break with the Group Name Field

To create a report with a control break, you create a Group Name field with the Insert Group dialog box shown in Figure 9-17.

Figure 9-17   Insert Group dialog box

The following list describes the fields in the Insert Group dialog box:

- In the top list box, you select the field that marks the control break. That is, the control break will occur when the contents of the selected field change.

- In the second list box, you select whether the records will be sorted in ascending order, descending order, a custom order, or not sorted at all.

- The Group Options section allows you to customize the behavior of the group.

- If the Keep Group Together check box is checked, then Crystal Reports will try to print the records in the group on the same page. However, this is not possible if the members of a group will not fit on a single page.

- If the records in a group span multiple pages and the Repeat Group Header On Each Page check box is checked, then the Group header will be printed on the continuation pages for the group.

Next you will create a Group Name field that will group the employee payroll records by employee department. For each employee department, you will print subtotals for the employees working in that department.

To create a Group Name field:

1. Activate the Crystal Reports Designer for the report named **PayrollReport.rpt**, if necessary.

2. In the Field Explorer, right-click **Group Name Fields**, and then click **Insert Group** on the context menu.

3. In the top list box, select **fldDeparment** from the table named **tblEmployees**. Note that the default sort order is ascending. You can sort records in descending order or select the records in their default order. The default order is the order of the records as they appear in the DataSet itself. It is also possible to define a custom sort order.

4. Click the **Keep Group Together** check box. Click the **Repeat Group Header On Each Page** check box.

5. Click **OK** to close the Insert Group dialog box and create the group.

6. Test the solution. Click **Reports**, **Payroll Reports** to display the Payroll Report.

When you created the group, Crystal Reports added two additional sections to the Crystal Reports Designer, as shown in Figure 9-18.

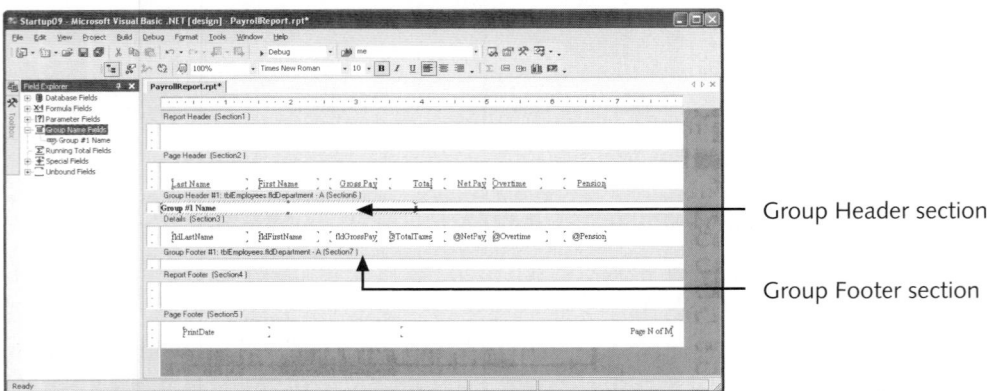

Figure 9-18   Report with Group headers

The Group Header #1 section will print when the value for the field named fldDepartment changes. Then the detail records for that department will print. When the department changes, subtotals appearing in the Group Footer #1 section will print. You will create the subtotals in a moment.

Nested Control Breaks

Control breaks can be nested. That is, you can create a control break within a control break. For example, in this report, you will create a control break to further categorize the hourly and salaried employees in a department.

To create a nested Group Name field:

1. In the Field Explorer, right-click **Group Name Fields**, and then click **Insert Group** on the context menu.

2. In the top list box, select **tblEmployees.fldEmployeeType**.

3. Click **OK** to close the dialog box and create the group.

   Crystal Reports creates a second Group Header and Group Footer on the report.

4. Save the report.

5. Test the solution. Display the Payroll Report.

The order in which the Group Name fields appear is significant. Group Header #1 (Department) is the primary group header and Group Header #2 is the secondary group header (Employee Type). If you wanted the grouping to be reversed, you would reorder the Group headers. To do this, right-click Group Name Fields in the Field Explorer, and then click Change Group Expert from the context menu. The Change Group dialog box appears as shown in Figure 9-19.

Figure 9-19   Change Group dialog box

As shown in Figure 9-19, the Change Group dialog box lists the groups in the order that they will be categorized. Click the up and down arrows to change order of the categories.

Creating Running Totals

Running totals summarize the value of a particular column. Running totals can be created to tally the values for a particular control break (subtotal) or to create a grand total. Crystal Reports supplies numerous mathematical functions to create subtotals and grand totals. For example, you can accumulate a total for a column of numbers, determine the average, maximum, or minimum value, or perform more complex statistics such as calculating the standard deviation of a list of numbers.

The steps to create a Running Total field are similar to the steps used to create a Formula field. First you create a Running Total field and configure it using a dialog box. Figure 9-20 shows the Create Running Total Field dialog box.

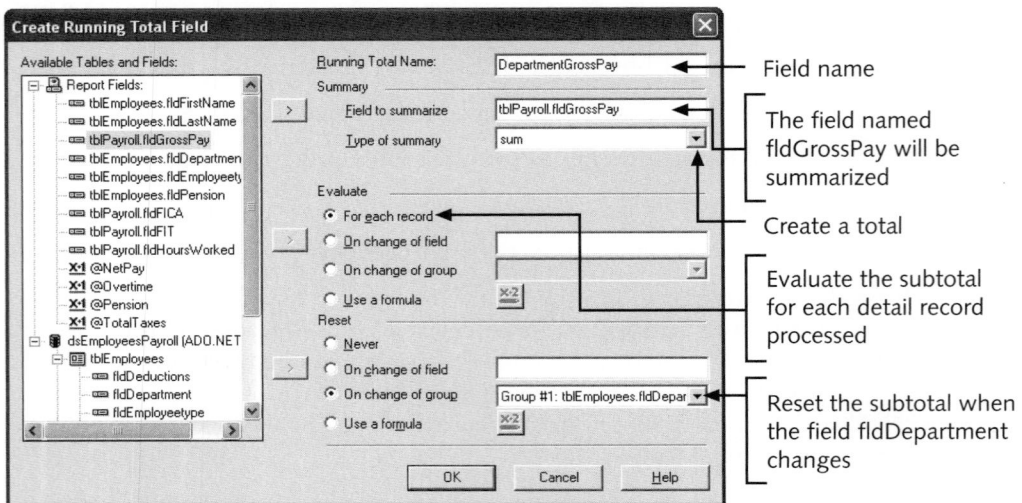

Figure 9-20   Create Running Total Field dialog box

The following list describes the general options applicable to all Running Total fields:

- Like all other fields, a Running Total field must have a unique name. This name appears in the Running Total Name text box.

- In the Summary section, you define the field that you want to summarize. This field can be a Database field or a Formula field. You select the field either by entering the table and field name separated by a period, or by selecting the field in the Available Tables and Fields pane, and then clicking the Select button.

- Once a field has been selected, the Type of Summary list box is enabled allowing you to specify how the data should be summarized. You can calculate the sum, average, maximum, minimum, mode, or various percentiles.

In the Evaluate section, you define when the running total will be calculated as described in the following list:

- If the For each record option is selected, then the running total will be calculated for each detail record processed. Thus, if you selected the sum function, the subtotal or total would be accumulated for each detail record.

- The On change of field option is typically used with control break reports. The field value is only recalculated when the value of the corresponding Group Name field changes.

- The On change of group option is also used with control break reports. The value is only recalculated when the group value changes.

- The Use a formula option is used to create a custom condition, which is then used to determine when the total should be recalculated. When this option is enabled, you again use the Formula Editor to define the condition.

In the Reset section, you define when and if the value of the Running Total field will be reset. The options correspond to the options appearing in the Evaluate section and are described in the following list:

- If the Never option is selected, the running total is never reset. That is, if you sum the records, you will sum all of the detail records in a report.

- The On change of field option is used with control break reports. The value is reset when the value of the field changes.

- The On change of group option is used with control break reports. The value is reset when the group value changes. Thus, this option is commonly used to print a subtotal for a particular group.

- The Use a formula option is used to create a custom condition, which is then used to determine when the total should be reset.

After having created and configured the Running Total field, you create an instance of it on the Crystal Reports Designer. In this section, you will first create multiple Running Total fields to calculate the total gross pay, taxes, and pension deduction for the employees in each department.

To create a Running Total field:

1. Activate the Crystal Reports Designer for the report named **PayrollReport.rpt**, if necessary.

2. In the Field Explorer, right-click **Running Total Fields**. Click **New** from the context menu. The Create Running Total Field dialog box appears.

3. Set the Running Total Name field to **DepartmentGrossPay**.

4. In the Available Tables and Fields section, expand the **Report Fields** section, if necessary. Click the field named **tblPayroll.fldGrossPay**.

5. Click the **Select** button in the Summary section to select the field.

   When you select the field, Crystal Reports adds the field named tblPayroll.fldGrossPay to the Field to summarize text box and sets the Type of summary to "sum", indicating that the value of all the records will be tallied.

6. In the Evaluate section, click **For each record**, if necessary. This setting causes the value to be tallied for each detail record read.

7. In the Reset section, click **On change of group**. The running total will be reset whenever the value of the employee department field changes. Note that the list box is enabled, indicating the Group Name field that will be used for the control break. By default the field named Group #1: tblEmployees.fldDepartment is selected, which is the correct group.

8. Click **OK** to create the Running Total field, and close the dialog box.

9. In the Field Explorer, expand the **Running Total Fields** section to display the Running Total field that you just created. Drag the field named DepartmentGrossPay to the Group Footer #1 section so that it appears just below the Gross pay column in the details section.

   Note that if you place the field in the wrong section, the total will not be displayed correctly when the control break occurs.

10. Create a second Running Total field to summarize the Formula field named **@TotalTaxes**. Set the Running Total Name field to **DepartmentTotalTaxes**. Use the same options as you used in the previous steps. Create an instance of the Running Total field to the right of the Running Total field that you just created.

11. Create a third Running Total field to summarize the Formula field named **@NetPay**. Set the name to **DepartmentNetPay**. Use the same options in the Evaluate and Reset sections that you used in the previous steps. Create an instance of the Running Total field on the report.

12. Create a final Running Total field to summarize the Formula field named **@Pension**. Set the name to **DepartmentPension**. Use the same options you used in the previous steps. Create an instance of the Running Total field on the report.

13. Save the report, and then test the solution. Click **Reports**, **Payroll Report** on the menu to display the report. The running totals summarize the columns for each department.

If you want later to modify a Running Total field that you have created, right-click on the Running Total field in the Field Explorer, and then click Edit on the context menu.

In addition to creating running totals for subtotals, you can create running totals for grand totals too. The steps to do so are nearly identical.

To create a running total for a grand total:

1. In the **Field Explorer**, right-click **Running Total Fields**. Click **New** from the context menu. The Create Running Total Field dialog box appears.

2. In the Available Tables and Fields section, expand the **Report Fields** section, if necessary. Click the field named **tblPayroll.fldGrossPay**, and then click the **Select** button.

3. Set the Running Total Name field to **GrandTotalGrossPay**, and close the dialog box. Note that the Type of summary field is set to sum, however, the Reset option is set to Never so a grand total will be calculated. The total will never be reset.

4. Create an instance of the Running Total field in the Report Footer section below the GrossPay field.

5. Create Running Total fields to create grand totals for the fields named **fldTotalTaxes**, **fldNetPay**, and **fldPension**. Name the fields **GrandTotalTaxes**, **GrandTotalNetPay**, and **GrandTotalPension**, respectively. Again, the type of summary should be sum and the Reset option should be set to Never. Figure 9-21 shows the report with the group totals and the grand totals created.

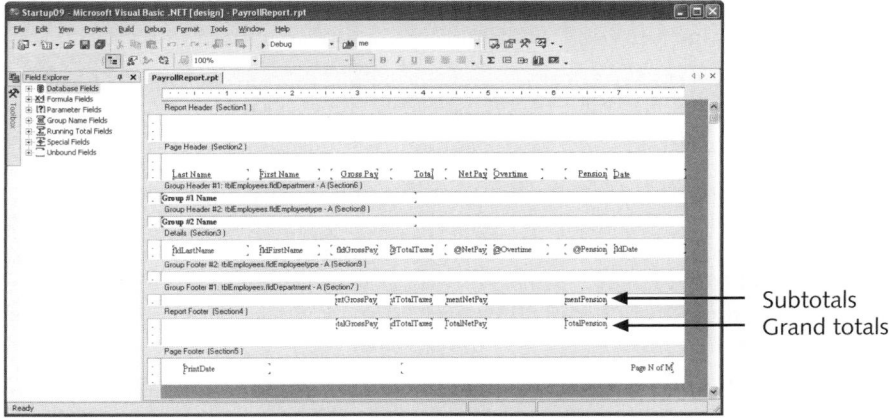

                    Subtotals
                    Grand totals

Figure 9-21   Report with subtotals and grand totals

6. Test the solution. Click **Reports**, **Payroll Report** on the menu to display the report. The grand totals appear in the Report Footer section.

At this point, the report itself is complete. Next you will see how to work with the report dynamically at runtime. First you will learn how to export a report for use in another application, then you will learn how to define report parameters to select data dynamically at runtime.

EXPORTING REPORTS

You have seen how to call the SetDataSource method of the ReportDocument class to associate a DataSet with a report. The ExportOptions object of the ReportDocument class allows you to export a report into a Word document, an Excel workbook, or an HTML document based on the options that you select.

The ExportOptions object supports four properties. Together, these properties define how and where a report will be exported, as described in the following list:

- The **DestinationOptions** property can store one of three different object types. The DiskFileDestinationOptions class has one property (FileName), used to specify the name of the disk file. The classes ExchangeFolderDestinationOptions and MicrosoftMailDestinationOptions allow a report to be exported to Microsoft Exchange Server or Microsoft Mail, respectively. These last two options are not discussed in this chapter.

- The **DestinationType** property works with the DestinationOptions property. The DestinationType property contains one of three enumeration values—DiskFile, ExchangeFolder, or MicrosoftMail—and is used to describe the type of the destination option. If the DestinationType and DestinationOptions do not correspond with each other, then an exception will occur. For example, if the DestinationType is set to DiskFile, then the FileName property of the DestinationOptions class should be set to the actual file name.

- The **ExportFormatType** property defines the type of output Crystal Reports will produce. The following formats are supported: Excel, HTML32, HTML40, NoFormat, PDF (Portable Document Format), RichText, and WordForWindows.

- The **FormatOptions** property stores one of three object types. The object type corresponds to the ExportFormatType. When exporting to Excel, the object is of type ExcelFormatOptions. When exporting a report as an HTML document, use HTMLFormatOptions. For other types, use PdfRtfWordFormatOptions. Again, the ExportFormatType and FormatOptions must correspond or an exception will occur.

By configuring the ExportOptions, you specify how Crystal Reports will export a report which can then be used by another application. Examine the following statements to declare the variables used to export a report as an Excel workbook:

```
Dim FileName As String = "C:\ExcelFile.xls"
Dim diskOpts As New DiskFileDestinationOptions()
Dim exportOpts As New ExportOptions()
```

The first of the preceding statements define the exported file name. The String variable is set to an arbitrary file name for brevity. The second and third statements declare two variables that will be used to configure the export. The first (diskOpts) stores the output disk file. The second (exportOpts) defines the export file type and how the file will be exported when it is saved. The following statements illustrate how to configure and export the report as an Excel workbook:

```
diskOpts.DiskFileName = FileName
crReportDocument.ExportOptions.DestinationOptions = _
    diskOpts
crReportDocument.ExportOptions.ExportFormatType = _
    CrystalDecisions.Shared.ExportFormatType.Excel
```

```
crReportDocument.ExportOptions.ExportDestinationType = _
    CrystalDecisions.Shared.ExportDestinationType.DiskFile
crReportDocument.Export()
```

The preceding statements configure the ExportOptions and assume that the variable crReportDocument references an instance of a Crystal Report. First, the DestinationOptions are configured to save a file name. The ExportFormatType is set to Excel, indicating that the file will be exported as an Excel workbook. The next statement indicates that the report will be exported to a disk file. Finally, the report is exported by calling the Export method.

In this chapter, you will create event handlers for menu items to export a report to an Excel workbook, a Word document, and an HTML document.

To export a report:

1. Activate the Code Editor for the form named **frmPayroll.vb**. Enter the following statements in the **Click** event handler for the menu item named **mmuFileExportToExcel**:

```
Dim dlgResult As DialogResult
dlgResult = sfdCommon.ShowDialog()
If dlgResult = DialogResult.OK Then
    Dim diskOpts As New DiskFileDestinationOptions()
    Dim exportOpts As New ExportOptions()
    diskOpts.DiskFileName = sfdCommon.FileName

    crReportDocument.ExportOptions.DestinationOptions = _
        diskOpts
    crReportDocument.ExportOptions.ExportFormatType = _
        CrystalDecisions.Shared.ExportFormatType.Excel
    crReportDocument.ExportOptions.ExportDestinationType = _
        CrystalDecisions.Shared.ExportDestinationType.DiskFile
    crReportDocument.Export()
End If
```

The preceding statements create instances of the DiskFileDestinationOptions and ExportOptions classes used to export the report. The DiskFileName property is set to the file name returned by the SaveFileDialog control instance. Finally, the ExportOptions are configured to export the report as an Excel workbook.

2. Enter the following statements in the **Click** event handler for the menu item named **mmuFileExportToHTML**:

```
Dim dlgResult As DialogResult
dlgResult = sfdCommon.ShowDialog()
If dlgResult = DialogResult.OK Then
    Dim diskOpts As New DiskFileDestinationOptions()
    Dim htmlOpts As New HTMLFormatOptions()
    diskOpts.DiskFileName = sfdCommon.FileName
    htmlOpts.HTMLFileName = sfdCommon.FileName
    crReportDocument.ExportOptions.FormatOptions = htmlOpts
```

9

```
    crReportDocument.ExportOptions.DestinationOptions = _
        diskOpts
    crReportDocument.ExportOptions.ExportFormatType = _
        CrystalDecisions.Shared.ExportFormatType.HTML40
    crReportDocument.ExportOptions.ExportDestinationType = _
        CrystalDecisions.Shared.ExportDestinationType.DiskFile
    crReportDocument.Export()
End If
```

The preceding statements save the report as an HTML document. The statements are similar to those used to save the report as an Excel workbook. However, the ExportFormatType is set to HTML40. In addition, the HTMLFormatOptions are used for the FormatOptions.

3. Enter the following statements in the **Click** event handler for the menu item named **mmuFileExportToWord**:

```
Dim dlgResult As DialogResult
dlgResult = sfdCommon.ShowDialog()
If dlgResult = DialogResult.OK Then
    Dim diskOpts As New DiskFileDestinationOptions()
    diskOpts.DiskFileName = sfdCommon.FileName
    crReportDocument.ExportOptions.DestinationOptions = _
        diskOpts
    crReportDocument.ExportOptions.ExportFormatType = _
        CrystalDecisions.Shared.ExportFormatType. _
        WordForWindows
    crReportDocument.ExportOptions.ExportDestinationType = _
        CrystalDecisions.Shared.ExportDestinationType.DiskFile
    crReportDocument.Export()
End If
```

The preceding statements export the report to a Word document. Again, the statements are similar. The ExportFormatType is set to WordForWindows, however.

4. Test the solution. Display the Payroll Report. On the form's menu, click **File**, and then click **Export to Excel** to export the report to an Excel workbook. In the Save As dialog box specify a file name of **C:\PayrollReport.xls**.

Note that pound signs appear in some cells because the column width is too narrow.

5. Start Excel and open the file named **C:\PayrollReport.xls** to view the exported report.

6. Export the file as a Word document using a file name of your choosing.

7. Export the file as an HTML document. Use the file name **C:\PayrollReport.htm**. Note that Crystal Reports creates a temporary directory from the directory you specify. This directory name will vary and will appear in the directory that you specify for the file name.

Having seen how to use the ReportDocument object to export a report, you will use that same object to configure the report dynamically as the solution runs.

PARAMETER FIELDS

Parameter fields allow you to define parameters that restrict the rows displayed in a report and supply other report information dynamically. Conceptually, a Parameter field works similarly to an OleDbParameter used in the WHERE clause of a SQL statement. However, the Crystal Reports implementation differs significantly.

Defining and using a Crystal Reports Parameter field is a two step process. First you define the Parameter field in the report itself. Second, you write the code to fill in the parameter value at runtime. We discuss each step in turn.

The Operation of Parameter Fields

To create a Parameter field, you activate the Field Explorer, and then create a new Parameter field using the Create Parameter Field dialog box shown in Figure 9-22.

Figure 9-22   Create Parameter Field dialog box

The Create Parameter Field dialog box defines how Crystal Reports will create the Parameter field, as described in the following list:

- In the Name text box, you specify the name of the Parameter field. This is the same name that you subsequently use to reference the parameter using VB .NET statements. Like other field names, Parameter field names must be unique.

- Crystal Reports can automatically prompt the user to fill in the values of a Parameter field. To display a descriptive prompt, define a caption in the Prompting text text box.

- In the Value type list box, you select the data type of the Parameter field.
- In the Options section, you define how the Parameter field will be configured. Crystal Reports supports two categories of Parameter fields:
  - Discrete values are used to select a single value.
  - Range values, as the name implies, are used to select a range of values.
- Checking the Allow multiple values check box allows you to define a Parameter field containing multiple discrete or range values.

To illustrate, you could create a discrete Parameter field for the Database field named fldDepartment, causing the report to display only that data applicable to the selected department. You could also define a Range parameter to select only those payroll records between a range of dates. Once you have created the Parameter field, you associate that Parameter field with a Database field using another dialog box called the Select Expert.

First, you will see how to create a Discrete Parameter field allowing the user to select specific departments from the available departments. The user will select these departments from a CheckedListBox control instance appearing on another dialog box. The list of departments will be obtained from the DataSet.

To create a Parameter field:

1. Activate the Field Explorer for the report named **PayrollReport.rpt**, if necessary.

2. In the Field Explorer, right-click **Parameter Fields**, and then click **New** from the context menu to display the Create Parameter Field dialog box.

3. Set the Name to **Department**. Through the value of the Name field, you will later reference the parameter with VB .NET code. Note that the value type is set to String. This data type corresponds to the data type for the underlying field. As the department is a string, the default value is correct.

4. Check the **Allow multiple values** check box. Note that the Discrete value(s) radio button is checked. By checking these options, you will be able to select multiple departments to print from a list of departments and supply that list as a list of discrete parameters.

5. Click **OK** to close the dialog box and create the Parameter field.

Once you have created the Parameter field, you can associate it with a Database field, as follows:

1. In the Field Explorer, expand the table named **tblEmployees**, if necessary. Right-click the field named **fldDepartment** from the Database Fields section, and then click **Select Expert** from the context menu.

2. The Choose Field dialog box allows you to select the field that you want to compare against a particular parameter. In the Report Fields section,

click **tblEmployees.fldDepartment,** and then click **OK** to display the Select Expert.

In the left list box, you select a comparison operator. In the right list box, you specify the name of the parameter using the same syntax that you use to create a formula.

3. In the left list box, select **is equal to**. In the right list box, select the named Parameter field **{?Department}**. Figure 9-23 shows the Select Expert.

Figure 9-23   Select Expert

Note that if a dialog box appears asking you to create a connection, close the dialog box and the Select Expert. Activate the Win Forms Designer for the form named frmPayroll.vb. Reset the ConnectionString property for the OleDbConnection control instance named odbconEmployees to the correct location of the database.

4. Click **OK** to close the Select Expert and associate the Parameter field with the Database field.

5. Save the report.

6. Test the solution. On the main form, click **Reports**, **Payroll Report**. Crystal Reports requires that you specify a discrete value or values for the parameter using the Enter Parameter Values dialog box shown in Figure 9-24.

7. Enter the parameter **Payroll** in the Discrete values list box. Click **Add** to add the parameter, causing it to appear in the Values section of the dialog box. Click **Finish** to display the report. The records printed are restricted to employees working in the Payroll department.

At this point, you have defined the Parameter field and defined a Select query to restrict the rows displayed based on the contents of the parameter's value. The next step in the process is to fill in the Parameter field at runtime with your own code instead of using the dialog box defined by Crystal Reports. When you used the Enter Parameter Values dialog box, Crystal Reports supplied the parameters you defined so as to restrict the rows printed in the report. You can also store information in those parameters programmatically at runtime.

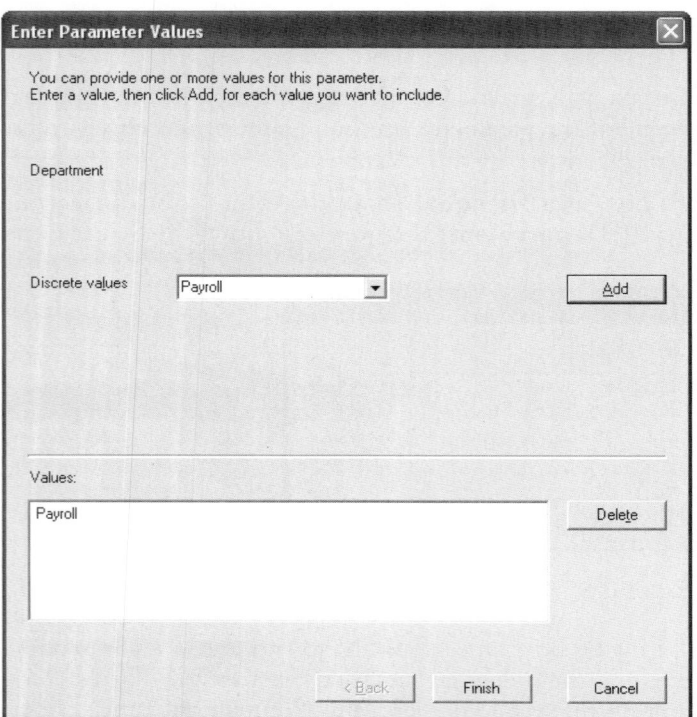

Figure 9-24   Enter Parameter Values dialog box

Communicating with Parameters Programmatically

As you have seen, you communicate with a report at runtime through an instance of the ReportDocument class. Additionally, you have seen that Crystal Reports contains various types of fields including Formula fields and Parameter fields. You can reference each of these fields programmatically through the DataDefinition class of the ReportDocument.

The DataDefinition class has properties that correspond to the field categories appearing in the Field Explorer. Each of these properties references a collection. The individual objects in each collection store the attributes of a specific field category. That is, each object in a collection references a report field.

The following list describes selected properties of the DataDefinition class and the types of fields they manage:

- The **FormulaFields** property has a data type of FormulaFieldDefinitions. Each element in the collection describes a particular Formula field.

- The **GroupNameFields** property has a data type of GroupNameFieldDefinitions. Each object in the collection corresponds to a Group Name field appearing on the report.

- The **ParameterFields** property has a data type of ParameterFieldDefinitions. Each object in the collection corresponds to a Parameter field defined in the report.

- The **RunningTotalsFields** property corresponds to the running totals appearing on the report.

The topic of this section is to fill in the data for the Parameter fields that you just defined for the Department Parameter field. When you created the Parameter field in the report, you assigned a value to the Name property and configured several attributes. Crystal Reports exposes a Parameter field as a ParameterFieldDefinition object in the ParameterFields collection. Examine the following statements:

```
Dim crParameterFieldDefinitions As _
    ParameterFieldDefinitions
Dim crParameterFieldDefinition As _
    ParameterFieldDefinition
```

The preceding statements declare variables to store a reference to the ParamaterFieldDefinitions collection and a single ParameterFieldDefinition object.

Examine the following code:

```
Dim crParameterValues As ParameterValues
Dim crParameterDiscreteValue As ParameterDiscreteValue
```

The first of the preceding statements declares a variable of type ParameterValues. This collection will store the list of discrete parameter values. The second of the preceding statements declares a variable to store an individual discrete parameter value from the collection.

The following statements reference a single Parameter field in the collection:

```
crParameterFieldDefinitions = _
    crReportDocument.DataDefinition.ParameterFields
crParameterFieldDefinition = _
    crParameterFieldDefinitions.Item("Department")
```

The preceding statements assume that the report contains a Parameter field named "Department." The name of the Parameter field allows you to look up the Parameter field in the collection using a String key. The value of the String key corresponds to the value of the Name property of the Parameter field. This is the same value that you defined for the Name property when you created the Parameter field.

The CurrentValues property of the ParameterFieldDefinition class returns a collection of Parameter fields. For example, in this chapter you will store a discrete list of departments as parameters. Examine the following statement to reference the CurrentValues collection for the Parameter field named Department:

```
crParameterValues = _
    crParameterFieldDefinition.CurrentValues
```

As you have seen, parameter values are of two types: range parameters and discrete parameters. Range parameters, as the name implies, define a range of values, while discrete parameters define a single value. The ParameterRangeValue object supplies the following properties to define the range of values:

- The **StartValue** property defines the minimum value of the range.
- The **EndValue** property defines the maximum value of the range.
- If the **LowerBoundType** property is set to Inclusive, then the StartValue is included in the range. If the property is set to Exclusive, then the StartValue is not included in the range.
- The **UpperBoundType** property works in the same way as the LowerBoundType property, but works with the EndValue instead of the StartValue.

The following statements illustrate how to define a range parameter value:

```
crParameterRangeValue = New ParameterRangeValue()

With crParameterRangeValue
    .EndValue = "92445"
    .LowerBoundType = RangeBoundType.BoundInclusive
    .StartValue = "92442"
    .UpperBoundType = RangeBoundType.BoundInclusive
End With
```

The preceding statements define a range parameter having values from 92442 to 92445. Once you have created the ParameterRangeValue, it needs to be added to the ParameterValues collection. Remember, you can define multiple ranges rather than just a single range, as shown in the following statements:

```
crParameterValues.Add(crParameterRangeValue)
crParameterFieldDefinition.ApplyCurrentValues( _
    crParameterValues)
```

The first of the preceding statements adds the ParameterRangeValue named crParameterRangeValue to the ParameterValues collection. The second statement applies the Parameter field to the report.

The purpose of the ParameterDiscreteValue class is to supply a parameter having a single value instead of a range of values. The ParameterDiscreteValue class supports a property named Value to store the discrete value, as shown in the following statements:

```
Dim crParameterDiscreteValue As ParameterDiscreteValue
crParameterDiscreteValue = New ParameterDiscreteValue()
crParameterDiscreteValue.Value = 3
```

The preceding statements create a discrete parameter value. The value stored in the parameter is 3.

Figure 9-25 illustrates the steps to configure parameters programmatically.

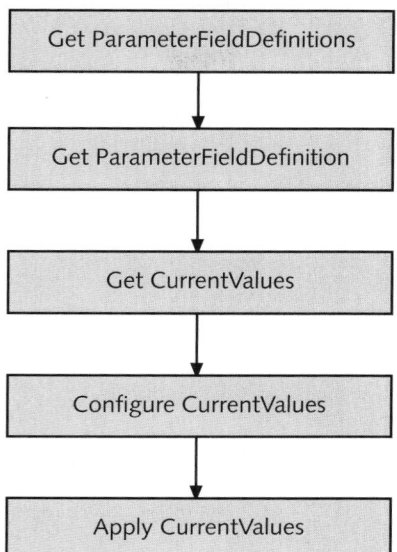

Figure 9-25   Configuring parameters programmatically

Next you will write the necessary statements to configure the values for the Parameter fields defined in the report.

To define runtime report parameters:

1. Enter the following statements (shown in bold) at the end of the **Load** event handler for the form named **frmPayroll.vb**:

```
crReportDocument.SetDataSource(DsEmployeesPayroll1)

Dim drCurrent As dsEmployeesPayroll.tblEmployeesRow
Dim pstrDepartment As String
Dim pintCount As Integer

Dim crParameterFieldDefinitions As _
    ParameterFieldDefinitions
Dim crParameterFieldDefinition As ParameterFieldDefinition
Dim crParameterValues As ParameterValues
Dim crParameterDiscreteValue As ParameterDiscreteValue

crParameterFieldDefinitions = _
    crReportDocument.DataDefinition.ParameterFields
crParameterFieldDefinition = _
    crParameterFieldDefinitions.Item("Department")
crParameterValues = _
    crParameterFieldDefinition.CurrentValues
```

```
Dim frmSelectNew As New frmSelect()

For Each drCurrent In DsEmployeesPayroll1.tblEmployees
    If pstrDepartment <> drCurrent.fldDepartment Then
        frmSelectNew.lstDepartments.Items.Add( _
            drCurrent.fldDepartment)
        pstrDepartment = drcurrent.fldDepartment
    End If
Next
frmSelectNew.ShowDialog()
For pintCount = 0 To _
    frmSelectNew.lstDepartments.CheckedItems.Count - 1
    crParameterDiscreteValue = New ParameterDiscreteValue()
    crParameterDiscreteValue.Value = _
        frmSelectNew.lstDepartments.CheckedItems( _
        pintCount).ToString
    crParameterValues.Add(crParameterDiscreteValue)
Next
crParameterFieldDefinition.ApplyCurrentValues( _
    crParameterValues)
crvPayroll.ReportSource = crReportDocument
```

Next, you need to delete the Select formula that you previously created. This formula is no longer needed because you are now performing the task programmatically.

2. Activate the Crystal Reports Designer for the report named PayrollReport.rpt. In the Field Explorer, right-click the Database field named **fldDepartment**. Click **Select Expert** on the context menu. In the Select Expert, click **Delete**. Close the Select Expert.

3. Save the report.

4. Test the solution. Click **Reports**, **Payroll Report** on the menu to display the Select Departments dialog box. Click the check boxes to select all of the departments, and then click **OK** to display the Payroll Report.

You have completed the programming for this chapter. You have seen the elements that make up a Crystal Report. Finally, you have used the CrystalReportViewer control to display the report on a form.

CHAPTER SUMMARY

❏ To add a Crystal Report to a solution, click Project, and then click Add New Item to activate the Add New Item dialog box. Click Local Project Items in the Categories pane, and then click Crystal Report in the Templates pane. Assign a name to the report.

❏ To connect a report to a database, create the necessary Connection, DataAdapter, and DataSet. Associate the DataSet with the report by calling the SetDataSource method of the Crystal Report.

❏ To create a control instance on a report, activate the Crystal Reports tab of the Toolbox. Create a control instance by dragging it to a particular report section. Set the properties for the control instance with either the Properties window or the Format Editor.

❏ To display a report, create an instance of the CrystalReportViewer control on the form. Using the Properties window or with code, set the ReportSource property to the name of the desired Crystal Report. Set the properties of the CrystalReportViewer control instance to define whether or not the toolbar appears in the control instance, and the buttons that appear on the toolbar.

❏ To create a Database field on a report, first activate the Field Explorer. Expand the Database Fields section to display the tables and fields appearing in the DataSet. Drag the desired field(s) to a report section.

❏ To create a Formula field, right-click Formula Fields in the Field Explorer. Click New from the context menu. In the Formula Name dialog box, assign the Formula field a unique name. In the Formula Editor, build the field by selecting Database fields or other Formula fields. Select the functions and operators as desired. As you add elements to the Formula field, they appear in the Formula pane at the bottom of the Formula Editor. Create an instance of the Formula field on the report.

❏ To create a Running Total field, right-click Running Total Fields in the Field Explorer, and then click New to activate the Running Total Field Editor. Select the field that you want to summarize and the type of summary (sum, average, minimum, maximum, etc.). Create an instance of the Running Total field in the desired summary section on the report.

❏ Crystal Reports can export reports to Microsoft Word or Excel, or as an HTML document. To export a report, configure an instance of the ExportOptions class. Set the DestinationOptions as necessary. Specify the ExportFormatType to define how the report will be exported. Finally, call the Export method of the ReportDocument to export the report.

❏ Parameter fields allow you to define parameters that restrict the rows displayed in a report and supply other report information dynamically. To create a Parameter field, you activate the Field Explorer, and then create a new Parameter field using the Create Parameter Field dialog box. Parameter fields can also be configured programmatically.

9

REVIEW QUESTIONS

1. Which of the following statements is true of configuring a Crystal Report?

   a. Crystal Reports hides the logic of printing each detail line, subtotals, and totals.

   b. Reports that print subtotals when the value of some field changes are called control break reports.

   c. Crystal Reports can establish a connection using ADO.NET.

   d. all of the above

   e. none of the above

2. Which of the following statements is true of the programming logic used by Crystal Reports?

   a. Crystal Reports reads records based on the different group names, if group names are defined. When a control break occurs, the group totals are calculated, and then the records in the group are printed.

   b. Crystal Reports reads a record from a DataSet, and then immediately prints that record on the report.

   c. Crystal Reports first reads all of the report records and then evaluates any constant formulas. Crystal Reports saves this data for later use. In processing Stage 2, data is formatted and printed on demand.

   d. Crystal Reports reads all of the report records, formats each record, and then prints the record, regardless of whether or not the user views a specific record or page of records.

   e. none of the above

3. Which of the following statements correctly describes the files that comprise a Crystal Report?

   a. A binary file with the suffix of .rpt contains the report. A file with the suffix of .vb contains a strongly typed class that derives from the ReportClass.

   b. A report is stored as a text file. The text file has a format similar to a form created by the Win Forms Designer. That is, Crystal Reports writes code to generate the control instances on the report.

   c. A report is stored as an XML document much like an ADO.NET DataSet. The corresponding .vb file contains a method to navigate through the records in the report.

   d. If a project contains multiple reports, then all of those reports are stored together in one report file.

   e. none of the above

4. Which of the following are considered default report sections?

   a. Header, Footer, Detail

   b. Group Header, Group Footer, Total

   c. Report Header, Page Header, Page Footer, Detail

   d. Report Title, Page Title, Detail Record

   e. none of the above

5. Which of the following controls are supported by Crystal Reports?

   a. TextBox, Label, Rectangle

   b. Text, Line, Box

   c. Special, Formula, Database

   d. all of the above

   e. none of the above

6. Which of the following statements is true of currency formatting in a Crystal Report?

   a. Currency values must always be formatted with two decimal places.

   b. The currency symbol always appears to the left of the numeric values.

   c. By setting the CurrencySymbolType property, you define the symbol that will appear in a field.

   d. all of the above

   e. none of the above

7. Which of the following statements is true of date formatting?

   a. Different types of calendars can be used.

   b. You can define the order of the month, day, and year parts of a date.

   c. Times can be specified using a 12 hour or 24 hour clock.

   d. Years can be displayed with two or four digits.

   e. all of the above

8. Which of the following statements applies to the CrystalReportViewer control?

   a. You define the DataSet for the CrystalReportViewer control by setting the DataSet property.

   b. You define the report to be viewed by setting the Report property.

   c. You can display or hide the toolbar, which allows the user to zoom in and out of a page, or to select pages.

   d. all of the above

   e. none of the above

9. Which of the following statements correctly describes how to associate an ADO.NET DataSet with a Crystal Report?

a. Call the SetDataSource method of the report with one argument, the name of the DataSet to associate.

b. Set the DataSet property of the report.

c. Call the SetDataSet method of the report with one argument, the name of the DataSet to associate.

d. In the Properties window, set the DataSet property of the report. This property cannot be set at runtime, however.

e. none of the above

10. Which of the following statements is true of Formula fields?

a. You create a Formula field with the Formula Editor.

b. Formula fields have exactly the same syntax as the right-side of a VB .NET assignment statement.

c. Formula fields cannot contain references to Database fields.

d. all of the above

e. none of the above

11. Which of the following statements correctly describes the capabilities of a Running Total field?

a. You can use a Running Total field to create a grand total for the data in a particular column.

b. Running Total fields can be used to calculate averages or to find the minimum and maximum values.

c. Running totals can be calculated for a particular control break.

d. all of the above

e. none of the above

12. Which of the following formats are valid Crystal Reports export formats?

a. PowerPoint, Binary

b. Word, Excel, HTML

c. DataSet

d. all of the above

e. none of the above

13. What is the purpose of a Parameter field?

    a. It allows you to specify information to a report at runtime to select specific data.

    b. Parameter fields are a form of a Special field used to obtain information directly from the system.

    c. To create a Parameter field, you add a Parameter to the Parameters collection of an OleDbDataAdapter.

    d. Parameter fields always have a String data type.

    e. none of the above

14. What is the purpose of the DataDefinition class?

    a. It allows you to store and retrieve information from the fields in the report.

    b. It allows you to change the contents of the DataSet's .xsd file.

    c. It stores and retrieves the data types for the fields in the underlying DataSet.

    d. Crystal Reports does not support the DataDefinition class.

    e. none of the above

15. Describe how to associate a Crystal Report with data using ADO.NET.

16. Describe the processing stages that Crystal Reports goes through when printing a report.

17. List and describe the purpose of the namespaces supported by Crystal Reports.

18. What is a Crystal Reports field? List and describe the different types of fields.

19. Describe how to create a control break report with Group Name fields.

20. Describe how to export a report to Microsoft Excel or Microsoft Word. In your answer, be sure to describe the required classes used to export the report.

PROGRAMMING QUESTIONS

1. Using the variable named crQuestion, write the statements to create an instance of the Crystal Report named QuestionReport. Set the data source of the report to the existing DataSet named dsQuestion.

2. Assume that a CrystalReportViewer control instance named crvQuestions exists. Write the statement to associate the CrystalReportViewer with the ReportDocument named crReportQuestions.

3. Assume that a CrystalReportViewer control instance named crvQuestions exists. Write the statements to display the first, previous, next, and last report page. Finally, write the statement to display the fifth page.

4. Assume that a ReportDocument exists named crQuestion. Write the statements to configure the ExportOptions to export the report to an Excel file named C:\Question.xls.

5. Assume that a ReportDocument exists named crQuestion. Write the statements to configure the ExportOptions to export the report as a Microsoft Word document. Export the report to the file named C:\Question.doc.

6. Assume that a ReportDocument exists named crQuestion. Write the statements to configure the ExportOptions to export the report as an HTML document. Export the report to the file named C:\Question.html.

HANDS-ON PROJECTS

All of the hands-on projects in this chapter use the same database named Warehouses.mdb in the Chapter.09\Data folder. The following list describes the fields in the table named tblWarehouse:

- fldWarehouseID (Integer)—Unique warehouse identification number
- fldWarehouseDescription (String)—Warehouse description
- fldWarehouseCity (String)—City
- fldWarehouseState (String)—State
- fldWarehouseZipCode (String)—Zip code

The following list describes the fields in the table named tblEmployees:

- fldWarehouseID (Integer)—Warehouse where employee works
- fldEmployeeID (Integer)—Unique employee identification number
- fldName (String)—Employee name
- fldCity (String)—Employee city
- fldState (String)—Employee state
- fldZipCode (String)—Employee Zip code
- fldWage (Single)—Employee wage

The following list describes the fields in the table named tblInventory:

- fldWarehouseID (Integer)—Location of part
- fldPartNumber (Integer)—Unique part number
- fldPartDescription (String)—Part description
- fldPartCategory (String)—Part category
- fldPartCost (Single)—Cost of part
- fldSalesPrice (Single)—Sales price of part
- fldPartQuantity (Integer)—Quantity of part in inventory

The following list describes the fields in the table named tblSales:

- ❏ fldWarehouseID (Integer)—Location of part
- ❏ fldSalesDate (DateTime)—Sales date
- ❏ fldPartNumber (Integer)—Part number
- ❏ fldSalesQuantity (Integer)—Sales quantity
- ❏ fldCost (Single)—Cost per part
- ❏ fldGrossSalesPrice (Single)—Sales amount
- ❏ fldDiscountPercentage (Single)—Discount percentage

1. In this project, you will create a Crystal Report that displays data from a single database table. Figure 9-26 shows the completed report for the solution. The file named Chapter.09\Exercises09\Ch09Ex1.exe contains the compiled executable application.

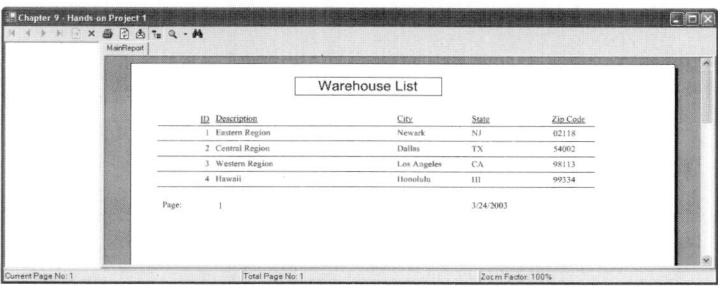

Figure 9-26   Chapter 9 – Hands-on Project 1

a. Create a new project named **Ch09Ex1.sln**.

b. Create a splash screen for the solution.

c. Create the necessary control instances to define a connection to the database named Warehouses.mdb. Create an instance of the OleDbDataAdapter to get all of the records from the table named tblWarehouse. Create a DataSet to store the records from the table.

d. Create a new Crystal Report named **Warehouse.rpt**. Associate the report with the .xsd file corresponding to the DataSet that you just created. Create the Database fields in the Details section of the report as shown in Figure 9-26.

e. Create the necessary fields to display the current date and page number in the report's page footer.

f. Create a Line Object to separate each record appearing in the Details section. Change the height of the Details section, as necessary.

g. Create a report header as shown in Figure 9-26. Use a 16 point bold Arial font for the text. Surround all of the text with a single line border.

h. Create an instance of the CrystalReportViewer control on the main form. Dock the control instance.

i. Write the statements in the form's Load event handler to fill the DataSet and associate the DataSet with the report.

2. In this project, you will create a Crystal Report that will display data from multiple tables. Figure 9-27 shows the completed report for the solution. The file named Chapter.09\Exercises09\Ch09Ex2.exe contains the compiled executable application.

Figure 9-27   Chapter 9 – Hands-on Project 2

a. Create a new solution named **Ch09Ex2.sln**.

b. Create a splash screen for the solution.

c. Create the necessary control instances to define a connection to the database named Warehouses.mdb. Create instances of the OleDbDataAdapter to get all of the records from the tables named tblWarehouse and tblEmployees. Create a DataSet to store the records from the two tables. Define the database link between the two tables, as necessary.

d. Create a Crystal Report named **WarehouseEmployees.rpt**. Create the report header, page header, and page footer fields as shown in Figure 9-27.

e. Create the detail lines for the report such that the report will print the employee ID, employee name, and hourly wage.

f. Create a control break report such that the records will be sorted and grouped by the warehouse description. Display the warehouse description in the group header.

g. Create a Running Total field to calculate the average wage for all workers in a particular warehouse. Display the average wage so that it appears with a single underline.

h. Create another Running Total field to calculate the average wage for all workers across all warehouses. Display this average wage so that it appears with a double underline.

i. Create Running Total fields to count the number of employees working in each warehouse, and the total number of employees working in all warehouses.

j. Display the page number and current date in the page footer.

k. Create a horizontal line in both the Page Header section and the Page Footer section.

l. Create an instance of the CrystalReportViewer control on the main form.

m. Write the statements in the form's Load event handler to fill the DataSet and associate the DataSet with the report.

3. In this project, you will create a report to display inventory information based on the warehouse. In addition, you will create a control break report and write Formula fields. Figure 9-28 shows the completed main form for the solution. The file named Chapter.09\Exercises09\Ch09Ex3.exe contains the compiled executable application.

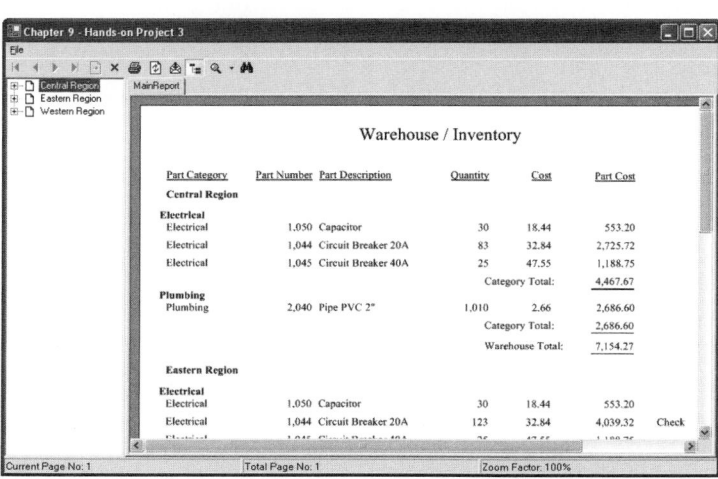

Figure 9-28 Chapter 9 – Hands-on Project 3

a. Create a new solution named **Ch09Ex3.sln**.

b. Create a splash screen for the solution.

c. Create the necessary control instances to define a connection to the database named Warehouses.mdb. Create a DataSet to store the records from the tables named tblWarehouse and tblInventory. Create the necessary DataRelation and links.

d. Create a Crystal Report named **WarehouseInventory.rpt**.

e. Create the report header, page header, and detail fields as shown in Figure 9-28.

f. Create a control break report such that the records will be grouped by warehouse, and then further grouped by part category.

g. Create a Formula field to calculate the dollar amount of each product in inventory. (Multiply the quantity on hand by the cost).

h. Create Running Total fields for the warehouse and category groups that will tally the extended inventory amounts for each category and warehouse. Create a grand total of extended inventory amounts for all warehouses. Underline the category and warehouse totals. Double underline the grand total.

i. If the dollar amount of a part is greater then $4,000.00, conditionally display the text **Check** in the Formula field.

j. Display the page number and current date in the page footer. Display the page number as a Page N of M field.

k. Create a **File** menu. On the File menu, create menu items that will allow the user to export the report as a Word document, an HTML document, or an Excel workbook. Use an instance of the SaveFileDialog control so that the user can specify the file name.

4. In this project, you will again create a report that works with multiple tables. In addition, you will export the report as a Word document, an Excel workbook, and an HTML document. You will also write the statements that will allow the user to select parameters dynamically at runtime. Figure 9-29 shows the completed main form for the solution. The file named Chapter.09\Exercises09\Ch09Ex4.exe contains the compiled executable application.

a. Create a new project named **Ch09Ex4.sln**.

b. Create a splash screen for the solution.

c. Create the necessary control instances to define a connection to the database named Warehouses.mdb. Create a DataSet to store the record from the tables named tblWarehouse and tblSales. Create the necessary DataRelation and links.

d. Create a Crystal Report named **WarehouseSales.rpt**.

e. Create the necessary fields to display the date and page number on the report. Display the page number as a Page N of M field.

f. Create Database fields in the Details section of the report as shown in Figure 9-29.

g. Create Formula fields to calculate the net price and extended price.

h. Create Running Total fields to tally the extended sales by warehouse, and the total extended sales.

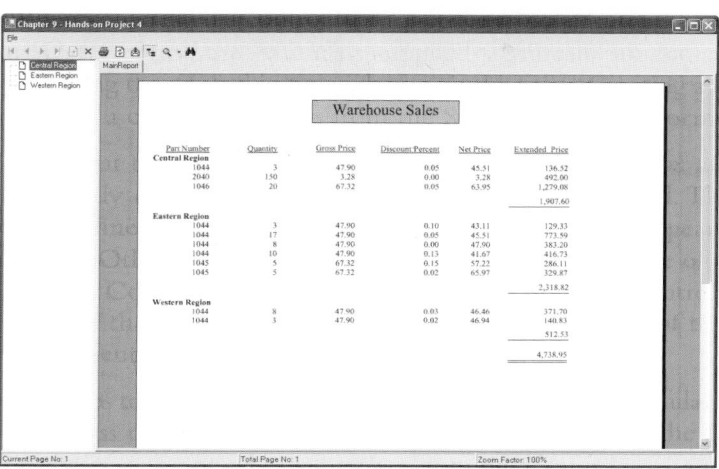

Figure 9-29   Chapter 9 – Hands-on Project 4

i. On the menu, create menu items that will allow the user to export the report as a Word document, an HTML document, or an Excel workbook. Use an instance of the SaveFileDialog control so that the user can specify the file name.

j. Using the technique presented in the chapter, allow the user to select specific warehouse data to be included in the report.

COMMON WINDOWS CONTROLS

In this chapter, you will:

♦ Learn about common Windows controls

♦ Load, display, and share images with other control instances using the ImageList control

♦ Create a ToolBar control instance on a form and configure it

♦ Create a status bar on a form to display application-specific information

♦ Create a drill-down interface using the TreeView and ListView controls

♦ Configure the ListView control to work with Details view

In this chapter, you will learn about controls common to most Windows applications. These controls include the ImageList, ToolBar, StatusBar, TreeView, and ListView controls.

PREVIEWING THE COMPLETED SOLUTION

The user interface for the completed solution resembles the user interface of Windows Explorer. A ToolBar control instance appears just below the form's menu. Its buttons supply the same functionality as equivalent menu items. A StatusBar control instance appears at the bottom of the form. The status bar displays context-sensitive information related to the current state of the application. Together, the TreeView and ListView controls display data from a typed DataSet. The TreeView control instance appears on the left side of the form, allowing the user to "drill down" through an organization's structure so as to locate an employee. The ListView control instance appears on the right side of the form. Its purpose is to display the information related to one or more selected employees.

 This solution obtains its data from a database and uses a typed ADO.NET DataSet to display the data in the ListView and TreeView control instances.

The database contains three tables, as shown in Tables 10-1 through 10-3.

Table 10-1   Fields in the table named tblOffices

Field name	VB .NET data type	Field description
fldOfficeID	Integer	Office identification number (Primary key)
fldOfficeDescription	String	Office description

Table 10-2   Fields in the table named tblDepartments

Field name	VB .NET data type	Field description
fldOfficeID	Integer	Office ID
fldDepartmentID	Integer	Department identification number (Primary key)
fldDepartmentDescription	String	Department description

Table 10-3   Fields in the table named tblEmployees

Field name	VB .NET data type	Field description
fldEmployeeID	Integer	Employee identification number (Primary key)
fldName	String	Employee name
fldPhone	String	Telephone number
fldExtension	String	Telephone extension
fldInOut	Boolean	Flag indicating whether the employee is in or out of the office

To preview the completed solution:

1. Start Visual Studio .NET. Open and run the solution file named **Chapter.10\
   Complete10\Complete10.sln**.

   For the completed solution to work correctly, the relative directory structure
   of the Chapter.10 folder must be preserved. That is, the Data directory must
   appear as a child directory of the Chapter.10 directory.

2. On the menu bar, click **File**, and then click **Open**. The solution loads data
   into an ADO.NET DataSet. This DataSet is then used to populate the
   TreeView control instance. Figure 10-1 shows the completed main form for
   the solution, with selected nodes expanded and data appearing in the
   ListView control instance.

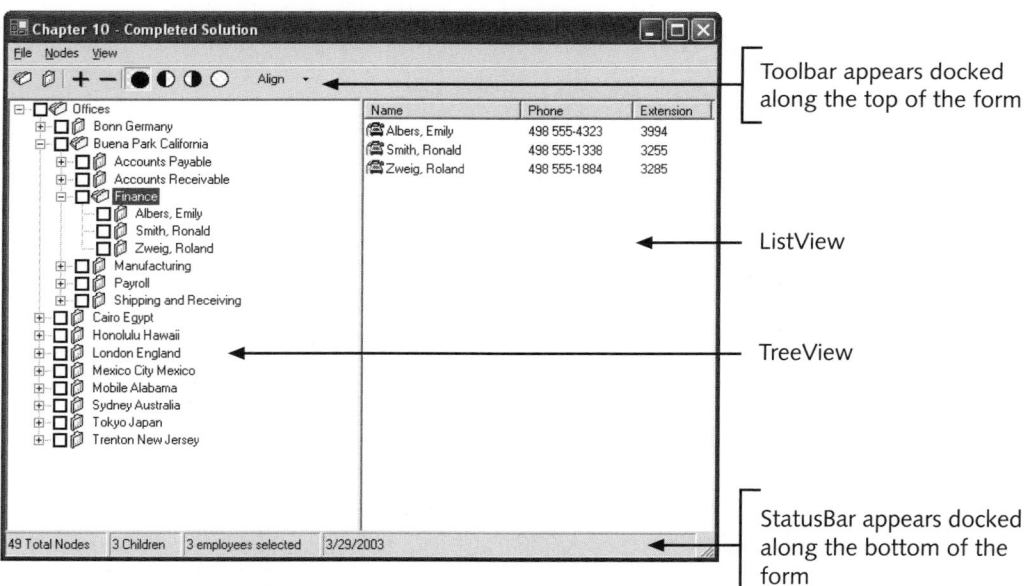

Figure 10-1   Completed solution – main form

As shown in Figure 10-1, a ToolBar control instance appears docked along
the top of the form and a StatusBar control instance appears docked along
the bottom of the form. The TreeView control instance appears on the left
side of the form, providing a drill-down interface to locate an employee or a
group of employees from within the organization. The ListView control
instance appears on the right side of the form and displays the selected
employee(s) that work for the organization, a particular office, or a particular
department within the organization.

3. Click the **plus** (+) sign to the left of the **Offices** node to expand it. Click
   the **plus** sign to the left of the **Buena Park California** node to expand it,
   and then click the **plus** sign next to the **Finance** node.

Note that as you click the plus sign for a node, it expands. Clicking the minus sign to the left of a node collapses it.

4. Click the **Finance** node. The employees working in the Finance department for the Buena Park, California office appear in the ListView control instance on the right side of the form. As you click other nodes in the TreeView control instance, the corresponding employees appear in the ListView control instance.

Note that as you click different nodes, the contents of the status bar are updated to reflect the number of child nodes. In addition, the number of items in the ListView control instance also appears in the status bar.

5. The ListView control displays data in one of four views. Click the four **View buttons** on the toolbar to change the current view. Note also that these functions are mimicked by the menu items on the View menu.

6. Click the **Expand** and **Collapse** buttons on the toolbar to expand and collapse all of the nodes, respectively. Note that these functions are mimicked by the Expand and Collapse menu items on the Nodes menu.

7. Check the **check box** next to the **Offices** node. Note that all of the children of the Offices node become checked. Finally, click **File**, and then click **Save Checked**. In the Save As dialog box, enter a file name of your choosing having a suffix of .txt. Click **Save** to save the file. The employee records corresponding to the checked nodes are saved as a comma–delimited sequential file.

8. Resize the form. The TreeView and ListView control instances are resized along with the form.

9. End the solution, and then exit Visual Studio .NET.

Both the completed and startup solutions utilize typed DataSets. If the program will not establish a connection to the database, recreate the ConnectionString property for the OleDbConnection control instance on the main form so that it can access the database named Chapter.10\Data\ETC.mdb. Regenerate the DataSet named dsEmployees, if necessary. Note that the DataSet contains references to all three tables and has DataRelations named drOfficesDepartments and drDepartmentsEmployees to link the three tables together. In addition, because of the extensive type conversion required in this chapter, we have disabled strict type checking for brevity.

INTRODUCING COMMON WINDOWS CONTROLS

The Windows operating system supplies much more than a user interface. It also supplies a rich set of software libraries available to the developer, which allows you to create familiar user interface elements. The controls supplied by these libraries are exposed to the .NET developer by means of various classes of the System.Windows.Forms namespace.

Many of these controls were historically referred to as the Windows Common Controls. In this chapter, we discuss the following common Windows controls:

- The **ImageList** control stores images typically used by other control instances, such as the ListView and TreeView controls.

- The **ToolBar** control displays buttons. Each button typically duplicates the functionality of some menu item. Although technically this design is not required, the goal is to supply an easy-to-use interface for both keyboard and mouse oriented users. The ToolBar control typically appears docked across the top of the form.

- The **StatusBar** control displays a horizontal bar that typically appears docked along the bottom of a form, although it can technically be docked along any edge of the form. The StatusBar control is made up of one or more panels used to store status information. This information typically contains the state of various keyboard keys, or information about the running state of the application itself.

- The **TreeView** control allows you to create a hierarchical interface called a drill-down interface. This interface works similarly to the left pane of Windows Explorer. That is, information is displayed hierarchically. The information displayed in this hierarchy can be expanded and collapsed by the user.

- The **ListView** control, as its name implies, displays data in the form of a list. The ListView control is commonly used in conjunction with the TreeView control. It displays data in one of four views. Again, these four views correspond to the four views of Windows Explorer. For example, the ListView control will display data as a large icon and description, as a small icon and description, as a columnar list, or as a tabular report, depending on the selected view.

First, we examine the ImageList control, as it is the image repository for the other types of controls used throughout the chapter.

THE IMAGELIST CONTROL

The **ImageList control** stores graphical files such as bitmap (.bmp), icon (.ico), and cursor (.cur) files. The ImageList control is not a visible control, so it appears in the resizable tray below the Win Forms Designer.

The ImageList control is not used by itself, rather, it is used in conjunction with other control instances that display graphical images. These controls include the TreeView, ListView, and ToolBar controls, among others. When a TreeView, ListView, or ToolBar control instance displays images, the control instance itself does not store those images. Rather, an instance of the ImageList control holds the images, which can then be shared by all of the control instances appearing on the form.

A good reason exists for separating images from the control instances that use them. Consider an application that contains instances of both the ListView and TreeView controls. Furthermore, assume that both of the control instances require many of the same graphic images. Rather than storing multiple copies of the same graphical image in the ListView and TreeView control instances, one ImageList control instance stores all of the graphical images, which can then be shared by other control instances. This design ultimately reduces the size of the executable program and improves performance.

An ImageList control has a property named Images. This property, in turn, contains a reference to an ImageCollection. This collection, in turn, contains one or more Image objects corresponding to the images in the collection. Just as with all collections, you reference an individual Image object in the collection at runtime by its 0-based numeric index.

When you load images into an instance of an ImageList control, those images are stored in the resource file corresponding to the form. This resource file has a file suffix of .resx and is an XML document.

You can add images to the ImageCollection at runtime, or use the Image Collection Editor at design time. First, you will begin by creating and configuring the ImageList control instance at design time using the Image Collection Editor.

To create the ImageList control instance and set the image size:

1. Start Visual Studio .NET, and then open the solution file named **Chapter.10\ Startup10\Startup10.sln**.

2. Create an instance of the **ImageList** control on the form named **frmMain.vb**. Again, because an ImageList control instance is not visible at runtime, it appears in the resizable tray below the Win Forms Designer.

3. Set the Name property to **ilsSmall** using the Properties window.

   Note that the image size is set to 16x16, the default. Thus, the ImageList control instance will scale the images to 16 by 16 pixels. All images stored in an instance of the ImageList control must have the same size. If an application needs images of varying sizes, create multiple instances of the ImageList control, such that each control instance stores images of a particular size.

4. Activate the Image Collection Editor by clicking the **value** column for the Images property, and then clicking the **Build** button.

   The Image Collection Editor appears.

VB .NET contains numerous graphic files in the folder "Program Files\ Microsoft Visual Studio .NET\Common7\Graphics". This folder contains sub folders for different types of graphic files. For example, the Graphics folder contains folders named "icons" and "bitmaps". These folders contain additional sub folders, which categorize images based on their purpose. For brevity, we have included the graphical files used in this chapter in the Chapter.10\Data folder.

Next you will add the images to the ImageList control instance that you just created. These images will be shared by the ToolBar, TreeView, and ListView control instances that you will create and configure later in the chapter.

1. In the Image Collection Editor, click **Add** to activate the Open dialog box. Select the file named **Chapter.10\Data\PhoneIn.ico**. Click **Open** to insert the image.

   As you add each image to the ImageList control instance, VB .NET assigns a unique numeric index to the image. To change the value of the numeric index, click the desired image to select it, and then click the up or down arrows to reorder the image.

2. Continue to add the icons named **PhoneOut.ico**, **Open.ico**, **Close.ico**, **Expand.ico**, **Collapse.ico**, **SmallIcon.ico**, **LargeIcon.ico**, **List.ico**, and **Details.ico** from the same **Chapter.10\Data** folder. Figure 10-2 shows the Image Collection Editor after the images have been added.

Figure 10-2   Image Collection Editor

   Make sure that you add the icons in the same order that they appear in this step. Otherwise, the numeric index of the images in the collection will be incorrect. This will result in the ToolBar and other control instances that rely on the ImageList control instance displaying incorrect images.

3. Click **OK** to close the Image Collection Editor.

Note that a second ImageList control instance named ilsLarge appears in the resizable tray below the form. This second control instance contains only the first two graphics from the ImageList control instance that you just created. The images in this second control instance are scaled to 32 by 32 pixels, and will be used later by the ListView control instance.

When loading images into an instance of the ImageList control, the control instance itself scales those images to the correct size by selecting bits from the larger picture. Thus, if scaling a large image, the selected bits may appear random and the scaled image will not resemble the original graphic. Therefore, use an image size that closely approximates the size of the image defined in the ImageList control instance.

In addition to adding images to the ImageList control at design time, you can add images programmatically at runtime. Examine the following statements:

```
Dim imgCurrent As Image
imgCurrent = Image.FromFile("C:\Balloon.bmp")
ilsSmall.Images.Add(imgCurrent)
```

The preceding statements add an image to the ImageList control instance named ilsSmall. However, the Add method cannot read the image from the file directly. Rather, the image must be first loaded by calling the FromFile method of the Image class, and then that loaded image is added to the Images collection of the ImageList control.

Now that you have created the ImageList control instance that will be used by the other control instances on the form, you can begin to create those other control instances. First you will begin by creating a toolbar. The buttons on the toolbar will mimic the functionality of equivalent menu items. Note that the menu has already been created on the form.

THE TOOLBAR CONTROL

A ToolBar control typically contains buttons that the user clicks to perform an action, in much the same way that the user clicks a menu item. As mentioned, comparable toolbar buttons and menu items both perform the same task as a way to supply keyboard-based and mouse-based users with the most flexible user interface.

To create menu items and toolbar buttons so that they have the same functionality, create a general procedure. Call that general procedure from the equivalent menu item and toolbar button.

Members of the ToolBar Control

Each toolbar button can contain text, a graphical image, or both. Buttons can be configured as drop-down buttons or as push buttons. Drop-down buttons display a menu, while push buttons typically execute a procedure that corresponds to a menu item. The ToolBar control supports the following members:

Syntax

System.Windows.Forms.ToolBar class

Public Properties

- The **Appearance** property defines whether the buttons on the toolbar appear raised off the surface of the toolbar or appear flat. Valid values are Normal and Flat for raised and flat buttons, respectively. Most current Windows applications use flat toolbars and buttons.

- One or more buttons appear on a toolbar. The **Buttons** property references a collection containing the ToolBarButton objects appearing on the toolbar. Each object in the collection references a button appearing on the toolbar itself.

- The **ImageList** property stores a reference to an instance of the ImageList control. The ToolBar control instance obtains the button images from this ImageList control instance.

- Toolbar buttons can be configured to display ToolTips. The Boolean **ShowToolTips** property defines whether or not the ToolTips will appear as the mouse hovers over a button. The text appearing in a particular ToolTip is a property of each individual button.

- The **TextAlign** property defines how the text will be aligned about the button when the button displays text.

Public Events

- When the user clicks a button on the toolbar, a **ButtonClick** event fires. The ButtonClick event fires for the toolbar itself, rather than for each individual button on the toolbar. As always, the first argument, named sender, has a data type of System.Object. The second argument has a data type of ToolBarButtonClickEventHandler. A reference to the clicked button is passed in the Button property of this class. Thus, you use this argument to determine which button the user clicked, and then execute the desired statements.

- The **ButtonDropDown** event fires when a ToolBarButton having a drop-down style is clicked.

In the next sections, you will create a toolbar with buttons to manage the TreeView and ListView control instances that you will create later in the chapter.

Creating the ToolBar Control Instance

First, you will begin by creating the ToolBar control instance itself, and then you will learn how to create and configure the buttons appearing on the toolbar.

To create a ToolBar control instance:

1. Create an instance of the **ToolBar** control on the form named **frmMain.vb**. By default, the toolbar is docked along the top of the form since the Dock property is set to Top.

2. Using the Properties window, set the Name property to **tbrMain**. Set the Appearance property to **Flat** and set the TextAlign property to **Right**.

3. Set the ImageList property to **ilsSmall**. By setting the ImageList property of the ToolBar control instance, the toolbar will obtain its graphical images from this ImageList control instance.

The ToolBar Control Buttons

Having created the toolbar, you can proceed to create its buttons. Buttons appearing on a toolbar have a data type of ToolBarButton. The properties of a ToolBarButton are similar to the properties of a Button control instance, as described in the following list:

- The **Enabled** and **Visible** properties have the same purpose as other control instances. They enable or disable the ToolBarButton or make it visible or invisible, respectively.

- The **ImageIndex** property contains the numeric index of the image defined in an instance of the ImageList control. This image will appear in the ToolBarButton.

- Each button has a **Name** property with which you can reference the button programmatically. You can also use the **Tag** property to accomplish the same task. The purpose of the Tag property is discussed in a moment.

- The **Style** property defines how the button operates. The details of the Style property are also discussed in a moment.

- In addition to containing an icon, a button may also contain text. The **Text** property defines the optional text appearing in the button.

- The **ToolTipText** property contains the text that will appear in the button's ToolTip. Again, ToolTips will only appear if the ShowToolTips property of the toolbar itself is set to True.

How a button operates and interacts with the other buttons appearing on the toolbar is controlled by the setting of the button's Style property. A button can have one of the four following styles:

- A button configured as a **DropDownButton** displays a context menu.

- A button configured as a **PushButton** works much like an ordinary Button control. That is, some code executes when the user clicks the button. The button appears recessed while the ButtonClick event handler is executing.

- A **Separator** button does nothing other than to visually separate one button from another. If the toolbar is flat, a Separator button appears as a vertical line between two buttons. If the buttons are raised off of the toolbar, then creating a Separator button causes a small vertical space to appear between the two buttons.

- A **ToggleButton** works similarly to a check box or checked menu item, in that it can be checked or unchecked. A checked button appears recessed while an unchecked button appears raised. ToggleButtons typically operate as a group, meaning, one ToggleButton appears pressed in a group of ToggleButtons. It is up to the statements in your application to update the state of the ToggleButtons appearing in a group.

In this chapter, you will create buttons that mimic the functionality of equivalent menu items. These buttons will allow the user to expand and collapse the nodes appearing in the TreeView control instance, define the current view in the ListView control instance, and open and close the database. You will program these buttons as you progress through the chapter.

To define the buttons appearing on the toolbar, you use the ToolBarButton Collection Editor. The interface of the ToolBarButton Collection Editor is similar to the Collection Editor of the ImageList control, in that the ToolBarButton Collection Editor contains two panes. The left pane displays the buttons and the right pane allows you to set the properties for each button.

To create toolbar buttons:

1. Activate the Properties window for the ToolBar control instance, if necessary. Click the **Build** button for the Buttons property to activate the ToolBarButton Collection Editor shown in Figure 10-3. Note that Figure 10-3 shows the buttons after they have already been created and configured.

Figure 10-3 ToolBarButton Collection Editor

2. Click **Add** to create a new ToolBarButton. The new button appears in the ToolBarButton Collection Editor. VB .NET assigns the button a default name of ToolBarButton1. Using the Properties pane, set the Name property to **tbbOpen**, and the ImageIndex property to **2**. Set the Tag property to **tbbOpen**. You will later use the Tag property to reference the button at runtime. Set the ToolTipText property to **Open the database**.

3. Create the remaining buttons listed in Table 10-4.

Table 10-4   Creating toolbar buttons

Member index	Name	Tag	Style	ImageIndex	ToolTipText
1	tbbClose	tbbClose	PushButton	3	Exit the application.
2	tbbSep1		Separator		
3	tbbExpand	tbbExpand	PushButton	4	Expand
4	tbbCollapse	tbbCollapse	PushButton	5	Collapse
5	tbbSep2		Separator		
6	tbbSmallIcon	tbbSmallIcon	ToggleButton	6	Small Icon view
7	tbbLargeIcon	tbbLargeIcon	ToggleButton	7	Large Icon view
8	tbbList	tbbList	ToggleButton	8	List view
9	tbbDetails	tbbDetails	ToggleButton	9	Details view

4. Click **OK** to close the dialog box.

When complete, the toolbar appears as shown in Figure 10-4.

DropDown Buttons

DropDown buttons operate differently from other buttons. A DropDown button displays a context menu. To create a context menu, you first create an instance of the ContextMenu control. Then you create the menu in-place as you have done before with the MainMenu control. That is, you select the instance of the ContextMenu control to activate it, and then you enter the menu items. Finally, you create a Click event handler for each menu item. To associate a ToolBarButton with a context menu, you set the DropDownMenu property of the button to the name of the ContextMenu control instance, set the Style of the button to DropDownButton, and then VB .NET does the rest. The ContextMenu control instance has already been created for you in this solution.

You used the ToolBarButton Collection Editor to create buttons thus far. While you could use it to create and configure the DropDown button, you will create the button programmatically to see how the process works.

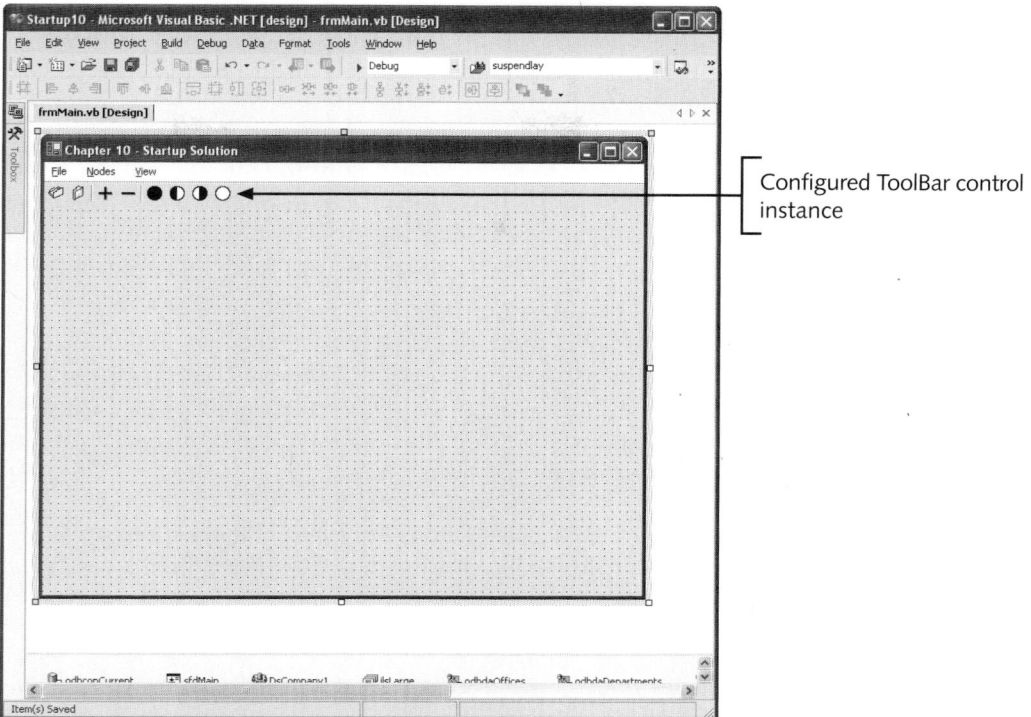

Figure 10-4   Configured ToolBar control instance

To create a ToolBarButton programmatically:

1. Activate the Code Editor for the form named **frmMain.vb**, if necessary, and then enter the following statements (shown in bold) at the end of the **Load** event handler for the form:

```
odbdaEmployees.Fill(DsCompany1)
Dim tbbTemp As New ToolBarButton("Align")
tbbTemp.DropDownMenu = Me.cmuAlign
tbbTemp.Style = ToolBarButtonStyle.DropDownButton
tbrMain.Buttons.Add(tbbTemp)
```

The preceding statements first create an instance of the ToolBarButton class. The argument contains the text that will appear in the button. By setting the Style property to DropDownButton, the button will display a drop-down menu. The ContextMenu control instance named cmuAlign appears as the DropDown menu. VB .NET will automatically display the context menu when the user clicks the drop-down button on the toolbar.

2. Test the solution. Notice that the Align button appears on the toolbar. Click the arrow to the right of the button to display the context menu. You will program these menu items later in the chapter after you learn about the ListView control.

Creating Event Handlers for Toolbar Buttons

Having created the ToolBar control instance and its buttons, you can now create the event handler for those buttons. When the user clicks a button on the toolbar, the ButtonClick event fires for the toolbar. Unlike a Button control instance, the ButtonClick event applies to the toolbar itself, rather than to an individual button. Thus, the statements in the event handler must first determine which button was clicked, and then execute the appropriate statements based on which button was clicked. The second argument to the ButtonClick event handler is of type ToolBarButtonClickEventArgs. A reference to the clicked button is passed in this argument.

Most controls and many classes support a property named Tag, which is used to supply additional descriptive information about a control instance. The Tag property has a data type of System.Object. VB .NET itself does not use the Tag property in any way. Rather, the Tag property exists solely for you, the developer, to store additional information about a class or control instance.

Using the Tag property supplies one way to augment the properties of a particular class. As an alternative, create a class that inherits from a base class, then add new properties or methods to supplement the interface supplied by the base class.

As you will see later in the chapter, you will use the Tag property to store information about a TreeNode appearing in an instance of the TreeView control. The Tag property will be used to describe whether the TreeNode applies to an office, a department, or an employee, or if the TreeNode is a root node.

Remember that a Tag is just a generic object that is ignored by VB .NET. As a first example, the following statements illustrate how to store a string in the Tag property:

```
Private ptnRoot As New TreeNode
ptnRoot.Tag = "Root"
```

For the toolbar that you created, you set the Tag property for each button when you created the button. You can use the event argument and the Tag property together to determine which button the user clicked, as shown in the following code segment:

```
Private Sub tbrMain_ButtonClick( _
    ByVal sender As System.Object, ByVal e As _
    System.Windows.Forms.ToolBarButtonClickEventArgs) _
    Handles tbrMain.ButtonClick
    Select Case e.Button.Tag
        Case "tbbOpen"
        ' Case statements for other buttons
    End Select
End Sub
```

The preceding code segment illustrates a prototype for the toolbar's ButtonClick event handler. A reference to the clicked button is passed in the second argument to the event handler. As always, the first argument, named sender, contains a reference to the object that fired the event. Thus, the statement fragment e.Button.Tag references the Tag property of the clicked button. Using the Tag property, you can determine which button was clicked and execute different code accordingly.

 In addition to using the Tag property to determine the button that was clicked, you could also use the button's Name property. Which strategy to apply is a matter of personal preference.

Next, you will create the structure of the ButtonClick event handler for the toolbar. As you complete the steps in the chapter, you will expand the following procedure to perform specific tasks.

To handle toolbar events:

1. Activate the Code Editor for the form named **frmMain.vb**, if necessary. Create the **ButtonClick** event hander for the ToolBar control instance named **tbrMain**, and then enter the following statements:

```
Select Case e.Button.Tag
    Case "tbbOpen"
    Case "tbbClose"
    Case "tbbExpand"
    Case "tbbCollapse"
    Case "tbbSmallIcon"
    Case "tbbLargeIcon"
    Case "tbbList"
    Case "tbbDetails"
End Select
```

The preceding Select Case statement defines the structure for the ButtonClick event handler by determining which button was clicked and creating a Case for each button. Again, you will write the statements later in the chapter to call various procedures as you create them.

THE STATUSBAR CONTROL

Most applications, including Microsoft Word and Excel, support a status bar as a user interface element. A status bar typically appears docked along the bottom of a form and displays information pertaining to the program state or the state of specific keyboard keys. For example, you can create a status bar that indicates the status of keyboard keys such as the Caps Lock or Insert keys. In the case of an application that works with a database, you can display the current record number or the total number of records in a status bar. To create a status bar on a form, you create an instance of the StatusBar control. The StatusBar control supports the following members:

Syntax

System. Windows. Forms. StatusBar control

Public Properties

- The **Panels** property contains a reference to the StatusBarPanelCollection. This collection contains a reference to each panel defined in the status bar.

- The Boolean **ShowPanels** property, if False, causes the value of the Text property to appear across the entire status bar. If True, the individual panels appear in the visible region of the status bar. By default, the ShowPanels property is set to False.

- The value of the **Text** property appears in the status bar only when the value of the ShowPanels property is False. When set to True, the value of the Text property is hidden and the individual panels are displayed.

Public Events

- The **PanelClick** event fires when the user clicks on the status bar. A reference to the panel that was clicked is passed in the second argument to the event handler. This argument has a data type of StatusBarPanelClickEventArgs.

The StatusBar control works in conjunction with another class called the StatusBarPanel class. The visible region of a status bar is divided into panels. Each panel can contain text, a picture, or both. A panel is implemented as a StatusBarPanel object in the StatusBarPanelCollection. The StatusBarPanel class supports the following properties:

Syntax

System. Windows. Forms. StatusBarPanel class

Public Properties

- The **Alignment** property can be set to Left, Right, or Center, to align the text within the visible region of the panel.

- Usually a status bar occupies the width of the form. Thus, as the user resizes the form, the panels appearing in the status bar are resized too. The **AutoSize** property allows you to specify how a panel is resized relative to the other panels in the status bar. If set to None, the size of the panel is fixed and will not be resized. If set to Contents, the size of the panel changes so that the contents (text and icon) will fit within the panel's visible region. If set to Spring, the size of the panel increases or decreases to fill the width of the status bar, based on the contents of the other panels.

- The **BorderStyle** property defines how the border appears around a status bar panel. Valid values are None, Sunken, and Raised. Typically, a status bar panel appears sunken. Creating a raised panel causes it to appear to the user as a clickable button. If set to None, the panel appears flat.

- The **Icon** property contains an image. This image will appear in the panel along with any text. Unlike the ToolBar control, the images are stored directly in the status bar itself, rather than in an associated instance of the ImageList control.

- The **MinWidth** and **Width** properties work together. The MinWidth property defines the minimum width of the panel. The Width property defines the actual or maximum panel width. The MinWidth property is typically used with panels that resize based on their contents, and to define the minimum panel width.

In this chapter, you will create a status bar that will display the number of nodes in the TreeView, the number of child nodes of the current node, and the number of items currently appearing in the ListView control instance. Each of these values will be updated at runtime as the user selects different items in the TreeView and ListView control instances. A final panel will display the current date. You will write the statements to store data in the panels later in the chapter when you work with the ListView and TreeView control instances.

To create and configure a status bar:

1. Create an instance of the StatusBar control on the form named **frmMain.vb**. Set the Name property to **sbrMain**. By default, the control instance is docked along the bottom of the form.

2. Activate the Properties window for the StatusBar control instance, if necessary.

3. Set the ShowPanels property to **True**, causing the status bar to display individual panels.

4. Click the **Build** button for the Panels property to activate the StatusBarPanel Collection Editor. The StatusBarPanel Collection Editor shown in Figure 10-5 shows the panels after they have been configured.

   The StatusBarPanel Collection Editor has the same interface as the other Collection Editors you have used. That is, each object appears in the left pane and the properties for the selected object appear in the right pane. The up and down arrows reorder the individual panels.

5. In the StatusBarPanel Collection Editor, click **Add** to create a new panel. A default name of StatusBarPanel1 is assigned to the panel. Set the Name property to **sbpAllNodes**. Set the AutoSize property to **Contents**. Remove the text from the Text property.

6. Create a second panel, setting the name to **sbpChildNodes**. Remove the text from the Text property. Set the AutoSize property to **Contents**.

7. Create a third panel, setting the name to **sbpListNodes**. Remove the text from the Text property. Set the AutoSize property to **Contents**.

10

Figure 10-5   StatusBarPanel Collection Editor

8. Create a final panel, setting the name to **sbpDate**. Remove the text from the Text property. Set the AutoSize property to **Spring**.

9. Click **OK** to close the StatusBarPanel Collection Editor.

You may have noticed that the StatusBarPanel class does not support a Visible property. To hide a panel, set the MinWidth and Width properties to 0.

Having created the status bar and defined the Name property for each panel, each panel can then be referenced at runtime so as to store and display status information. VB .NET supplies two ways to reference the panel. First, you can reference the panel using its ordinal value in the Panels collection as shown in the following statement:

```
sbrMain.Panels(3).Text = _
        System.DateTime.Today.ToShortDateString
```

The preceding statement stores the date in the fourth panel of the status bar, because the ordinal panel value is 0-based.

When you create a panel, VB .NET and the Win Forms Designer declare a variable having the same name as the panel itself. For example, you set the name of the panel that will display the current date to sbpDate. Thus, the following statement will also store the current date in the panel.

```
sbpDate.Text = System.DateTime.Today.ToShortDateString
```

As a first example, you will store the current date in one of the panels.

To store data in a StatusBarPanel at runtime:

1. Activate the Code Editor for the form named **frmMain.vb**, and then enter the following statements (shown in bold) in the form's **Load** event handler:

```
odbdaEmployees.Fill(DsCompany1)
sbrMain.Panels(3).Text = _
    System.DateTime.Today.ToShortDateString
sbrMain.ShowPanels = False
sbrMain.Text = "Database not open."
```

2. Test the solution. Because you set the ShowPanels property to False, the panels do not appear and the contents of the Text property appear across the entire status bar. When the ShowPanels property is set to True, the panels you created, along with the one to display the current date, will appear.

INTRODUCTION TO DRILL-DOWN INTERFACES

Many Windows programs utilize a drill-down user interface that operates with hierarchically organized data. A **drill-down** interface is one in which the user navigates through hierarchical data from the most general to the most specific. The Windows Explorer program shown in Figure 10-6 illustrates a well-known example of a drill down interface.

10

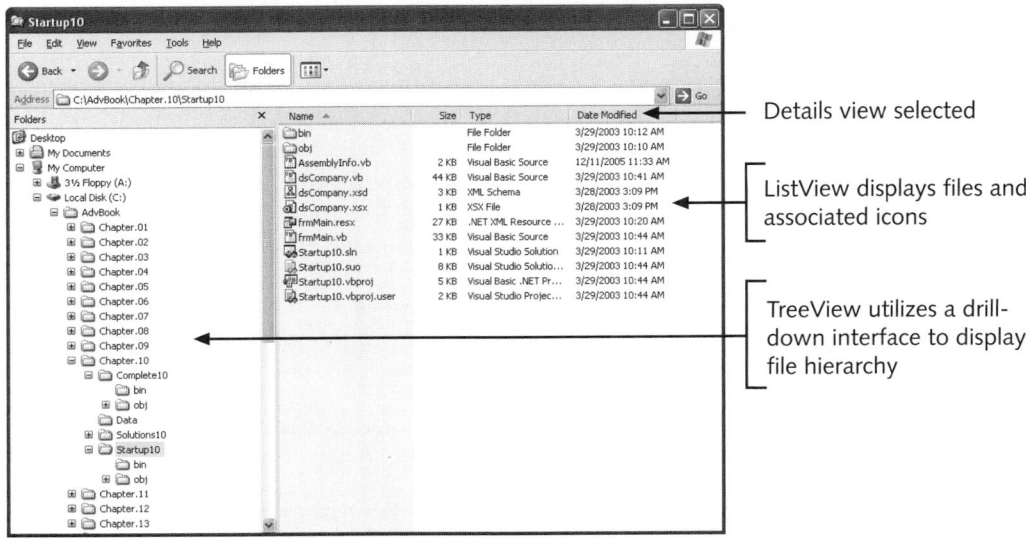

Details view selected

ListView displays files and associated icons

TreeView utilizes a drill-down interface to display file hierarchy

Figure 10-6   Drill-down interface used by Windows Explorer

As shown in Figure 10-6, Windows Explorer consists of two separate panes. The left pane displays the folders and files in a hierarchy. This left pane corresponds to a TreeView control instance. The interface allows individual folders to be expanded and collapsed. When a folder is expanded, the contents of the folder, including files and other folders, appear. The right pane displays the specific information pertaining to the folders and files in the selected folder. The right pane corresponds to a ListView control instance.

In Figure 10-6, the right pane displays several columns when Details view is selected. Each column typically displays the same type of information on each line. For Windows Explorer, the first column contains the file name, the second column contains the file size, and so on. Both panes can display an icon adjacent to each column.

In VB .NET, you use two different controls to create the two parts of a similar drill-down interface. You use the **TreeView control** to create the hierarchical part of the user interface, which appears in the left pane of Windows Explorer. The **ListView control** appears in the right pane of Windows Explorer and displays detailed information about the selected item(s) appearing in the TreeView.

The TreeView and ListView controls commonly work in tandem. For example, in Windows Explorer, the files and folders displayed in a ListView control instance are synchronized with the selected folder in the TreeView control instance. This synchronization process is not automatic. Rather, you, as the developer, must write the necessary statements to update the contents of the ListView control instance when the user selects a different element in the TreeView control instance. First we discuss how to create and populate an instance of the TreeView control. Then we discuss how to display information in an instance of the ListView control.

THE TREEVIEW CONTROL

The TreeView control displays information in a hierarchical manner much like Windows Explorer. It could therefore be used to display a hierarchy of files stored on a physical disk or to display hierarchically organized database data. In this chapter, you will use an instance of the TreeView control to provide the means for the user to navigate the hierarchical structure of the employees working for a company. That is, the company has offices, which have departments, which in turn have employees, as shown in Figure 10-7.

Figure 10-7 Relationships of employees in an organization

The Nodes property of the TreeView control provides the key to understanding how the TreeView works. This property references a collection which, in turn, stores references to TreeNode objects. Each TreeNode object in the Nodes collection represents an element in the TreeView hierarchy. Each TreeNode object has a visual component consisting of a textual label and an optional bitmap.

Relationships exist between individual nodes in any hierarchy. The hierarchy of relationships is expressed as an inverted tree structure. The terms used to describe these hierarchical relationships mimic those used to describe genealogical relationships. For instance, the **root node** appears at the top of the hierarchy (family tree) and can have zero or more **children**. All nodes, with the exception of the root node, have a single **parent** node. The root node has no parent node. All children having the same parent node are called **siblings**. Of the siblings sharing a common parent, one sibling is designated as the **first sibling**, and another is designated as the **last sibling**. A child node can have only one parent, but a parent can have multiple children. Child nodes can, in turn, have their own children, which in turn can have their own children. The terms **grandchildren** and **great grandchildren** describe these additional relationships.

Figure 10-8 illustrates hierarchical relationships. In Figure 10-8, the root TreeNode has two children (Node1 and Node2). These two TreeNodes are siblings. Node2 is the parent of three children: Node3, Node4, and Node5. These three TreeNodes are siblings. Node3 is the first sibling and Node5 is the last sibling.

10

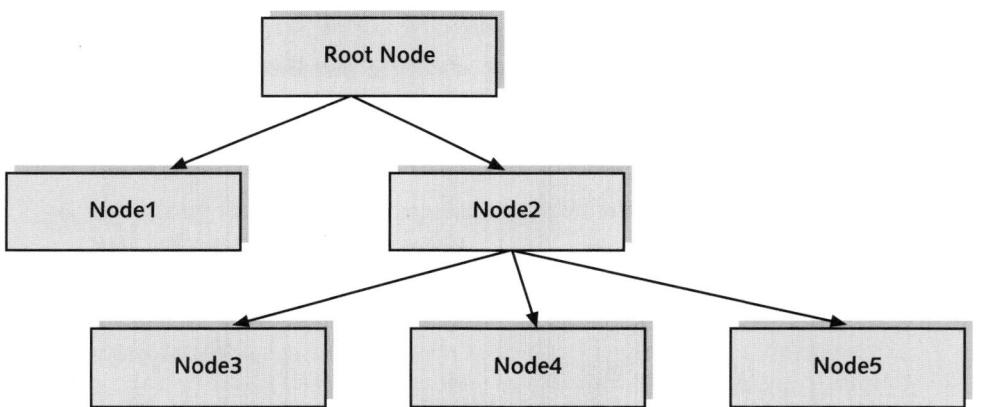

Figure 10-8   Hierarchical relationships between TreeNodes

Before working with the TreeNode objects, you must understand the properties and methods of the TreeView control itself.

Syntax

System.Windows.Forms.TreeView control

Public Properties

- The **CheckBoxes** property can be set to True or False. If set to True, check boxes appear to the left of each TreeNode. If set to False, they do not.

- The **ImageIndex** property contains the numeric index of the image from an associated ImageList control instance. This is the default image that appears for the TreeNode objects in the control instance.

- The **ImageList** property contains a reference to an instance of the ImageList control. Using the associated ImageList control instance, the TreeView control obtains the images that will appear in each TreeNode.

- The Boolean **LabelEdit** property defines whether or not the user can edit the textual contents of each TreeNode. The BeginEdit and EndEdit methods enable and complete editing on a node, respectively.

- The **Nodes** property references a collection of TreeNode objects. The data type for the Nodes property is TreeNodeCollection.

- The **PathSeparator** property is useful when a TreeView control instance operates with files. The PathSeparator property defines the character that separates the TreeNodes appearing in the hierarchy of a TreeView control instance.

- The Boolean **Scrollable** property defines whether or not scroll bars will appear when the expanded TreeNodes will not fit within the visible region of the control instance.

- The **SelectedImageIndex** property contains the numeric index of an image appearing in the associated ImageList control instance. This image appears when a TreeNode in the TreeView is selected.

- The **SelectedNode** property has a data type of TreeNode. It gets the selected TreeNode or selects a TreeNode.

- The Boolean **ShowLines** property defines whether or not lines connect the visible TreeNodes. If the **ShowRootLines** property is set to True, then child TreeNodes appear connected to the root TreeNode. If the **ShowPlusMinus** property is set to True, then a plus sign appears to the left of TreeNode's text if the TreeNode is collapsed, and a minus sign appears if the TreeNode is expanded. For the plus and minus signs to appear, the ShowRootLines property must also be set to True.

- The **Sorted** property, if set to True, causes the TreeNode objects to be sorted in alphabetical order.

Public Methods

- The **BeginUpdate** and **EndUpdate** methods suppress painting of the TreeView control instance while TreeNodes are being added or removed. To suppress painting of the TreeView control instance, call the BeginUpdate method, and then update the nodes as necessary. When updating is completed, call the EndUpdate method. Suppressing painting of the control instance while nodes are being added or removed eliminates possible flicker and improves performance.

- The **CollapseAll** method collapses all TreeNode objects in the hierarchy so that only the root-level node(s) are visible.

- The **ExpandAll** method expands all of the TreeNode objects in the hierarchy.

- The **GetNodeAt** method is typically used with a mouse event to get a TreeNode at a particular point or x,y coordinate pair.

- The **GetNodeCount** method accepts one Boolean argument. If the argument is False, then the GetNodeCount method gets the number of immediate children of the specified TreeNode. If the argument's value is True, then the method returns the count of all of the child TreeNodes in the TreeView control instance.

Public Events

- The **AfterCheck** event only fires when the CheckBoxes property is set to True. The event fires just after a TreeNode is checked or unchecked.

- The **BeforeExpand** and **AfterExpand** events fire just before and just after a TreeNode is being expanded, respectively. The TreeNode being expanded is passed as an argument to the event.

- The **BeforeCollapse** and **AfterCollapse** events fire just before and just after a TreeNode is collapsed, respectively.

- The **AfterSelect** event fires after a TreeNode is selected in the control instance. The data type of the second argument is TreeViewEventArgs. This class contains a reference to the TreeNode that was selected.

- The **BeforeSelect** event fires just before a TreeNode is selected. The data type of the second argument is TreeViewCancelEventArgs. The class contains a reference to the TreeNode that was selected. The event can also be cancelled, causing the subsequent AfterSelect event not to fire.

The TreeView control expands and collapses TreeNodes automatically as the user clicks the plus and minus signs to the left of each node. You can also write code to expand and collapse these nodes programmatically.

Creating a TreeView Control Instance

Next, you will create an instance of the TreeView control and configure its general properties.

To create the TreeView control instance:

1. Activate the Win Forms Designer for the form named **frmMain.vb**, if necessary.

2. Using the **TreeView** button on the Toolbox, create an instance of the TreeView control as shown in Figure 10-9.

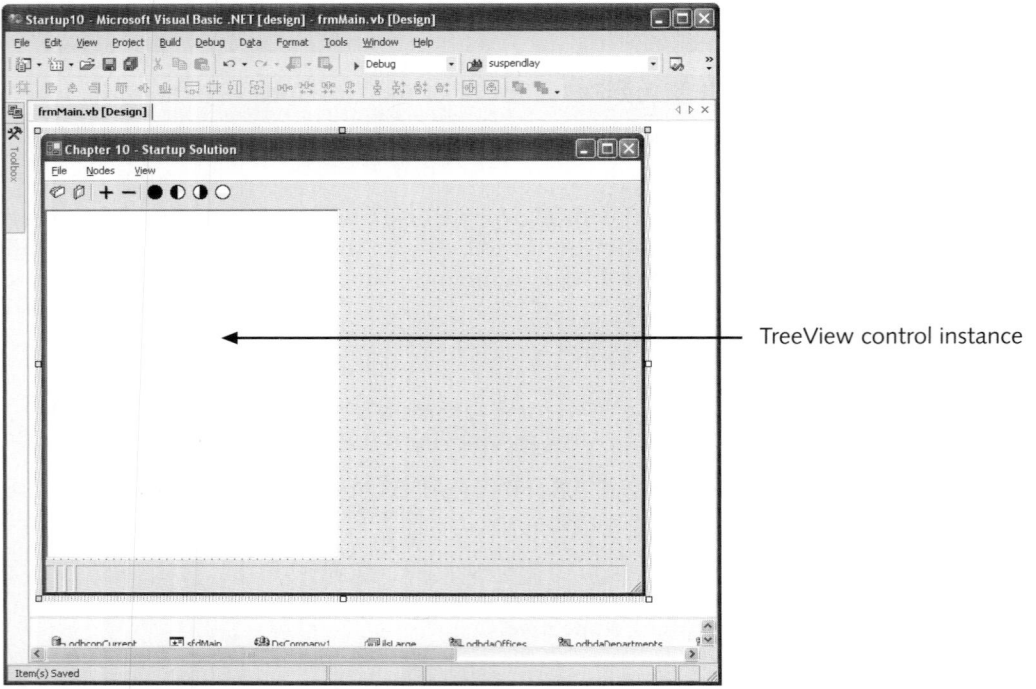

TreeView control instance

Figure 10-9   Creating an instance of the TreeView control

3. Using the Properties window, set the name to **tvwMain**.

4. Set the ImageList property to **ilsSmall**. This is the name of the ImageList control instance that you created earlier in the chapter. Thus, the TreeView control instance will obtain its images from this ImageList control instance.

5. Set the **Sorted** property to True. This property setting will cause sibling nodes to be sorted in alphabetical order.

6. Set the ImageIndex property to **3**. Setting this property defines the default image appearing to the left of each TreeNode. Set the SelectedImageIndex property to **2**.

   Note that the ShowLines, ShowPlusMinus, and ShowRootLines properties are set to True by default.

Adding Nodes to a TreeView Control Instance

Now that an instance of the TreeView control exists, you can write the code to add nodes to the TreeView control instance at runtime. Common sources for data include databases and text files.

The implementation designed in this chapter to create the TreeNodes uses four procedures. The first procedure named InitTreeRoot creates the root-level TreeNode and then calls a procedure named InitTreeOffices to create a TreeNode for each of the different offices. For each office, this second procedure calls a third procedure named InitTreeDepartments to create the TreeNodes for the departments pertaining to that office. The procedure to create the department TreeNodes calls a fourth procedure named InitTreeEmployees to create the TreeNodes representing the employees working in that particular department. Thus, a different procedure performs the processing for each level of the hierarchy. Figure 10-10 illustrates these procedures and their organization.

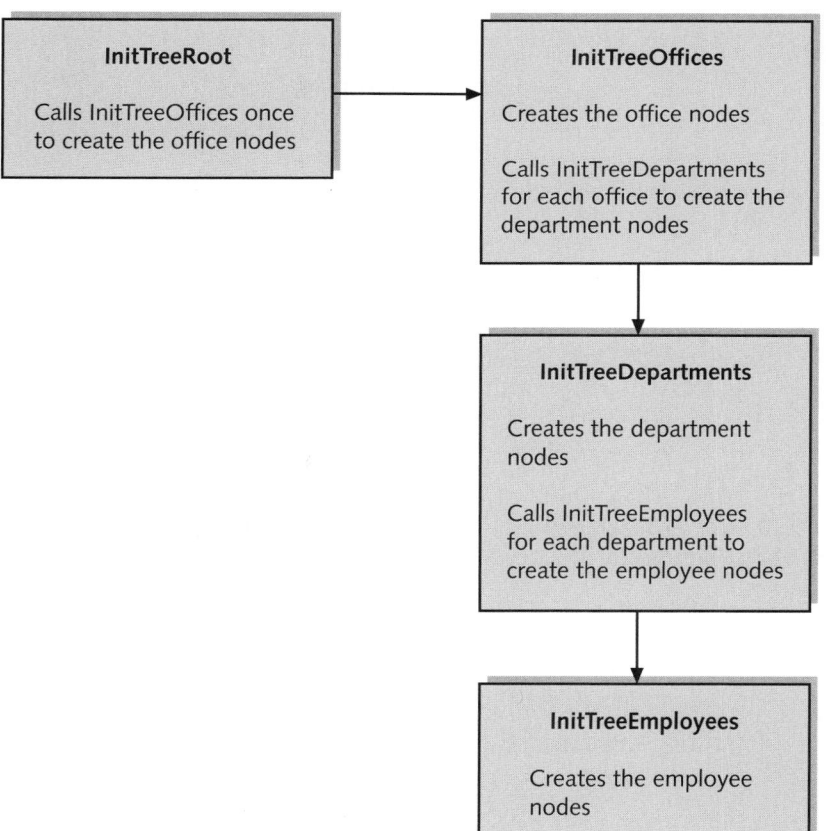

Figure 10-10   Populating the TreeNode hierarchy

The TreeView control groups TreeNode objects in a collection having a data type of TreeNodeCollection. Like any collection, the TreeNodeCollection class implements the ICollection, IEnumerable, and IList interfaces, so TreeNodes can be added and removed from the list and the list can be enumerated using a For Each loop.

The TreeNode Object

The TreeNode object supports the following members used to define the behavior of each TreeNode and its relationship to other TreeNodes in the hierarchy. As you review the properties and methods of the TreeView control and the TreeNode object, you will see that both support similar members.

Syntax

System.Windows.Forms.TreeNode class

Public Properties

■ The **Checked** property, if True, indicates that the TreeNode is checked. If the TreeNode is not checked, then the Checked property has a value of False. The Checked property is only useful if the CheckBoxes property of the TreeView control itself is set to True.

■ The **ImageIndex** property contains the numeric index of the image appearing in the corresponding ImageList control instance. This image appears to the left of the text appearing in the TreeNode.

■ Several properties are used to check the status of a particular TreeNode. The Boolean **IsVisible** property returns True if the TreeNode is visible, and False otherwise. The **IsSelected** property returns True if the TreeNode is selected, and False otherwise. The **IsExpanded** property returns True if the TreeNode is expanded, and False otherwise.

■ Several properties are used to locate sibling TreeNodes. The **FirstNode** property gets the first sibling TreeNode of the current TreeNode. The **PreviousNode** and **NextNode** properties get the previous and next sibling, respectively. The **LastNode** property gets the last sibling.

■ The **SelectedImageIndex** property contains the numeric index of an image appearing in the corresponding ImageList control instance. This image appears to the left of the text when the TreeNode is selected.

■ The **Tag** property has the same meaning as the Tag property of other control instances. It contains a generic object that is ignored by VB .NET.

■ The text appearing in the TreeNode is stored in the **Text** property.

Public Methods

■ The **Collapse** method collapses the child TreeNodes of the current TreeNode.

■ The **Expand** method expands the child TreeNodes of the current TreeNode.

■ The **Toggle** property collapses expanded nodes or expands collapsed nodes depending on the current state of the TreeNode.

■ The **BeginEdit** and **EndEdit** methods enable and disable editing of the current TreeNode, respectively.

- The **Remove** method removes the current TreeNode.

- The **EnsureVisible** method makes the TreeNode visible, expanding or collapsing other TreeNodes as necessary.

- The **GetNodeCount** method returns the number of child TreeNodes of the current TreeNode.

Having described the relationship of a TreeNode to the TreeView control itself, you can now begin to add TreeNodes to the TreeView. TreeNodes can be added either at design time using the TreeNode Editor or programmatically at runtime. Figure 10-11 shows the TreeNode Editor.

Figure 10-11   TreeNode Editor

The TreeNode Editor allows you to create the root TreeNode, child TreeNodes of that root TreeNode, and sibling TreeNodes using the following buttons:

- The Add Root button is the only enabled button when the TreeView control instance contains no TreeNodes. This is logical, as a TreeView must have a root TreeNode. Note that a TreeView control instance may have multiple root nodes.

- To add a child TreeNode, select an existing TreeNode, and then click the Add Child button. The new TreeNode will be created as a child of the selected TreeNode.

- To delete a TreeNode, select the TreeNode to be deleted, and then click the Delete button.

In the Label text box, you define the text that will appear in the TreeNode itself. The Image and Selected image list boxes allow you to select an image from the associated ImageList control instance. In this chapter, however, you will add each TreeNode programmatically using data read from a database. First you will learn how to add a root TreeNode.

Adding a TreeNode Programmatically

The code that you will write calls the Add method of the Nodes collection to add a TreeNode. The Nodes collection has a data type of TreeNodeCollection. This process of adding objects to a collection is consistent with the process for adding objects to other collections. The Add method has the following syntax:

Syntax

Overridable Overloads Public Function Add(ByVal *text* **As String) As TreeNode**
Overridable Overloads Public Function Add(ByVal *node* **As TreeNode) As Integer**

Definition

The overloaded **Add** method adds a new TreeNode object to the Nodes collection.

Dissection

- In the first overloaded method, the Add method creates a new instance of the TreeNode class. The method accepts one argument: the text string stored in the TreeNode. The method returns the instance of the TreeNode that was added.

- In the second overloaded method, the Add method accepts one argument: an existing TreeNode object. The method returns the index of the node in the Nodes collection.

Code Example

```
tvwMain.Nodes.Add("First Node")

Dim ptnCurrent As New TreeNode()
ptnCurrent.Text = "Second Node"
tvwMain.Nodes.Add(ptnCurrent)
```

Code Dissection

The first of the preceding statements adds a new TreeNode to the TreeView control instance named tvwMain. The text "First Node" appears in the TreeNode. The next three statements also add a TreeNode. However, these statements first create an instance of the TreeNode class, and then set its Text property. The final statement adds the newly created TreeNode to the Nodes collection.

Creating the Root-Level Node

The sub procedure to create the root TreeNode is relatively simple. It creates the TreeNode and defines its text and icons. Then the procedure calls another procedure to add the child TreeNodes that represent the offices. After the statements in this second procedure add the offices, it sorts the child nodes and expands the current node. The children are then displayed.

To create the root-level node:

1. Activate the Code Editor for the form named **frmMain.vb**, if necessary. Enter the following statements in the **InitTreeRoot** procedure:

```
Dim pintNodeCount As Integer
Dim ptnRoot As TreeNode
tvwMain.BeginUpdate()
tvwMain.Nodes.Clear()
ptnRoot = tvwMain.Nodes.Add("Offices")
ptnRoot.Tag = "Root"
Call InitTreeOffices(ptnRoot)
tvwMain.EndUpdate()
pintNodeCount = tvwMain.Nodes(0).GetNodeCount(True)
sbpAllNodes.Text = pintNodeCount.ToString & " Total Nodes"
sbpChildNodes.Text = "0 child nodes"
sbpListNodes.Text = "0 employees selected"
sbrMain.ShowPanels = True
```

The preceding statements create a new TreeNode by adding a TreeNode to the Nodes collection of the TreeView itself. The newly created TreeNode is returned by the Add method. The Tag property is set to "Root", identifying the TreeNode as a root-level node. Remember that the Tag property is only used by your code and not by VB .NET. The Tag property will be used later in the chapter. The next statement calls the InitTreeOffices procedure to initialize the Office nodes that will appear beneath the root TreeNode. By calling the BeginUpdate and EndUpdate methods on the TreeView control instance, the control instance will not be refreshed as the individual nodes are being added. The next statements get the total number of TreeNodes by calling the GetNodeCount method of the root node. This information is displayed in the StatusBar control instance. The final two statements display default information in the other two status bar panels and set the ShowPanels property to True.

2. Next you need to call this procedure from both the menu and the appropriate toolbar button. Enter the following statement in the **Click** event handler for the menu item named **mmuFileOpen**:

```
Call InitTreeRoot()
```

3. Enter the same statement (shown in bold) in the **ButtonClick** event handler for the toolbar named **tbrMain**:

```
Select Case e.Button.Tag
    Case "tbbOpen"
```

10

```
        Call InitTreeRoot()
Case "tbbClose"
' Statements
```

4. Test the solution. Click the **Open the database** button on the toolbar. The root TreeNode appears in the TreeView control instance. In addition, the contents of the status bar are updated.

Having created the root TreeNode, you will now proceed to create the remaining TreeNodes that will comprise the hierarchy.

Creating Child Nodes

Before you can add nodes that appear at different levels of the hierarchy, you need to understand how to create a TreeNode relative to other TreeNodes. Each TreeNode object contains its own Nodes collection. This Nodes collection, in turn, stores the immediate children of the current TreeNode. Thus, the TreeNode objects are organized into a hierarchy. Examine the following statements to add two child TreeNodes to the root TreeNode:

```
Dim ptnRoot As TreeNode
Dim ptnChild As TreeNode
ptnRoot = tvwMain.Nodes.Add("Root Node")
ptnChild = tvwMain.Nodes(0).Nodes.Add("First Child")
ptnChild = tvwMain.Nodes(0).Nodes.Add("Second Child")
```

The previous statements first create the root TreeNode. The final two statements add two TreeNodes that appear as children of the root TreeNode. The statement fragment tvwMain.Nodes(0) references the first TreeNode in the Nodes collection, which is the root TreeNode. Each TreeNode, in turn, has its own Nodes collection. Thus, these statements add two child TreeNodes to the Nodes collection of the root TreeNode.

The preceding statements can be written another way. The variable ptnRoot references the root TreeNode, thus, the next two statements also add two child TreeNodes to the root TreeNode.

```
ptnChild = ptnRoot.Nodes.Add("First Child")
ptnChild = ptnRoot.Nodes.Add("Second Child")
```

Figure 10-12 illustrates how the TreeNodes added in the preceding code segments are organized.

In the following steps, you will begin by initializing the nodes for the offices. As mentioned, an OleDbConnection, OleDbDataAdapter, and typed DataSet have already been created on the form. Using the data from the table named tblOffices in the DataSet, you will add Office nodes to the TreeView control.

```
Dim ptnRoot As TreeNode
Dim ptnChild As TreeNode
```

```
ptnRoot = tvwMain.Nodes.Add("Root Node")

ptnChild = ptnRoot.Nodes.Add("First Child")

ptnChild = ptnRoot.Nodes.Add("Second Child")
```

Figure 10-12   TreeNode hierarchy

To populate a TreeView control instance from a DataSet:

1. Enter the following statements (shown in bold) in the procedure named **InitTreeOffices**:

```
Private Sub InitTreeOffices(ByVal tnRoot As TreeNode)
    Dim drCurrent As dsCompany.tblOfficesRow
    Dim tnCurrent As TreeNode
    Dim pintCount As Integer

    For pintCount = 0 To _
        DsCompany1.tblOffices.Rows.Count - 1
        drCurrent = DsCompany1.tblOffices(pintCount)
        tnCurrent = _
            tnRoot.Nodes.Add( _
            drCurrent.fldOfficeDescription)
        tnCurrent.Tag = "Office," & drCurrent.fldOfficeID
        Call InitTreeDepartments(tnCurrent, drCurrent)
    Next
End Sub
```

The preceding statements use a typed DataSet named dsCompany. Again, VB .NET declares an object variable named DsCompany1 to reference the instance of the DataSet. The first statement in the For loop retrieves the current typed DataRow from the table named tblOffices. The For loop examines all of the rows in the DataSet table. For each row examined, a TreeNode is added to the TreeView control instance containing the contents of the field named fldOfficeDescription. The variable named tnRoot references the root TreeNode so the TreeNodes will appear as immediate children of the root TreeNode.

The setting of the Tag property is important and will become evident when you display items in the ListView control instance corresponding to the currently selected TreeNode. If the current office ID had a value of 1, then the Tag property would contain the following string:

```
Office,1
```

The Tag property stores the constant string "Office" to indicate that the TreeNode applies to an office rather than a department or employee. The second field stores the ID number of that office. The final statement calls the procedure named InitTreeDepartments with two arguments: the department node and the current DataRow. You will create the procedure in a moment to initialize the department level nodes.

To test the solution:

1. On the menu, click **File**, and then click **Open**. Expand the root TreeNode. The offices appear in the TreeView control instance as children of the root-level node.

At this point, you have initialized the TreeNodes for the offices. The next step is to initialize the TreeNodes for the departments within each office. The InitTreeDepartments procedure is called once for each office, thereby initializing the departments corresponding to a particular office. The InitTreeDepartments procedure accepts two arguments. The first argument stores a TreeNode representing a particular office. The department TreeNodes will be added as children of the tnOffice TreeNode.

1. Enter the following statements (shown in bold) in the **InitTreeDepartments** procedure:

```
Private Sub InitTreeDepartments( _
    ByVal tnOffice As TreeNode, _
    ByVal drOffice As dsCompany.tblOfficesRow)
    Dim tnCurrent As TreeNode
    Dim drCurrent() As dsCompany.tblDepartmentsRow
    Dim pintCount As Integer
    drCurrent = _
        drOffice.GetChildRows("drOfficesDepartments")
    For pintCount = 0 To drCurrent.GetUpperBound(0)
        tnCurrent = _
            tnOffice.Nodes.Add(drCurrent(pintCount). _
                fldDepartmentDescription)
        tnCurrent.Tag = "Department," & _
            drCurrent(pintCount).fldDepartmentID
        Call InitTreeEmployees(tnCurrent, _
            drCurrent(pintCount))
    Next
End Sub
```

The InitTreeDepartments procedure accepts two arguments: a TreeNode containing the office to which the departments will be added, and the corresponding DataRow for the office. The first of the preceding statements you entered declares a TreeNode named tnCurrent to store the newly created node. The second statement declares an array of DataRow objects to store the departments. The fourth statement uses the GetChildRows method of a DataRelation named drOfficesDepartments to get the departments corresponding to the particular office. The For loop examines each row in the array, and then adds a TreeNode to the applicable office node. Note that this procedure gets called once for each department. After adding the department node, the InitTreeEmployees procedure is called so as to initialize the employees working in a particular department. You will create that procedure next. Again, the Tag property is set so that it contains the string "Department", followed by the unique department ID. The Tag will be used later in the chapter when you display data in the ListView control instance.

To test the solution:

1. Test the solution. On the menu bar, click **File**, and then click **Open**. Expand the root Offices node. Expand the node for the Buena Park California office. The departments corresponding to the selected office appear.

Finally, you need to initialize the TreeNodes for the employees working in each department. The process to initialize the employees working in a department is similar to the process to initialize the departments applicable to a particular office.

To initialize the Employee nodes:

1. Enter the following statements (shown in bold) in the **InitTreeEmployees** procedure:

```
Private Sub InitTreeEmployees( _
    ByVal tnDepartment As TreeNode, _
    ByVal drDepartment As dsCompany.tblDepartmentsRow)
    Dim tnCurrent As TreeNode
    Dim drCurrent() As dsCompany.tblEmployeesRow
    Dim pintCount As Integer
    drCurrent = _
        drDepartment.GetChildRows("drDepartmentsEmployees")
    For pintCount = 0 To drCurrent.GetUpperBound(0)
        tnCurrent = _
            tnDepartment.Nodes.Add(drCurrent(pintCount). _
            fldName)
        tnCurrent.Tag = "Employee," & _
            drCurrent(pintCount).fldEmployeeID
    Next
End Sub
```

The InitTreeEmployees procedure accepts two arguments. The first argument contains the department level TreeNode. The employee TreeNodes will be added as children of the department TreeNode. The second argument contains a DataRow representing the department. The GetChildRows method is called on the department DataRow, thereby retrieving all of the employees working in that department. Each employee is then added as a child of the department TreeNode, and the Tag property set so that it will store the string "Employee", followed by the employee ID number.

2. Test the solution. On the menu bar, click **File**, and then click **Open**. Expand the root TreeNode. Expand the TreeNode for the Buena Park California office. Expand the TreeNode for the Finance department. The employees working in the selected department appear.

At this point in the solution's development, you have fully populated the TreeView control instance. Next, you will begin to write the statements to expand and collapse the nodes in the TreeView, and display status information in the various status bar panels. To expand and collapse all of the nodes in a TreeView control instance, you call the ExpandAll and CollapseAll methods, respectively.

To expand and collapse nodes programmatically:

1. Enter the following statements (shown in bold) in the **ButtonClick** event handler for the ToolBar control instance named **tbrMain** to expand and collapse the nodes:

```
Case "tbbExpand"
    tvwMain.ExpandAll()
Case "tbbCollapse"
    tvwMain.CollapseAll()
```

2. Enter the following statement in the **Click** event handler for the menu item named **mmuNodesExpand** to expand the nodes:

```
tvwMain.ExpandAll()
```

3. Enter the following statement in the **Click** event handler for the menu item named **mmuNodesCollapse** to collapse the nodes:

```
tvwMain.CollapseAll()
```

As mentioned, a toolbar button and equivalent menu items typically perform the same task. That is why you wrote the same statements for both the toolbar buttons and the menu items.

4. Create the **AfterExpand** event handler for the TreeView control instance and then enter the following statement:

```
e.Node.ImageIndex = 2
```

The preceding statement associates the image having an index of 2 in the associated ImageList control instance with the ImageIndex property of the node. This image will appear when the node is expanded.

5. Create the **AfterCollapse** event handler for the TreeView control instance and then enter the following statement:

```
e.Node.ImageIndex = 3
```

The preceding statement associates the image having an index of 3 in the associated ImageList control instance with the ImageIndex property of the node. This image will appear when the node is collapsed.

6. Test the solution. Open the database. Click the **Expand** and **Collapse** buttons on the toolbar. The TreeNodes are expanded and collapsed.

In addition to expanding and collapsing nodes, you can determine information about a particular node including the number of children, and the total number of nodes appearing in the TreeView itself.

To display status information in the StatusBar control instance:

1. Activate the Code Editor for the form named **frmMain.vb**, if necessary.

2. Create the **AfterSelect** event handler for the TreeView control instance named **tvwMain**, and then enter the following statements:

```
Dim pintChildCount As Integer
pintChildCount = e.Node.GetNodeCount(False)
sbpChildNodes.Text = pintChildCount.ToString & " Children"
```

The preceding statements get the number of immediate children of the current node. The final statement stores the number of children in the StatusBarPanel named sbpChildNodes.

3. Test the solution. On the menu bar, click **File**, and then click **Open**. Click on the text of various nodes. The number of children appears in the StatusBarPanel.

Iterating through TreeNodes

When working with a hierarchical structure such as the TreeNode objects in a TreeView control instance, it is often necessary to examine all of the TreeNodes in the hierarchy. One way to examine all of the TreeNodes in a TreeView is to create a **recursive procedure**. A recursive procedure is simply a procedure that calls itself. Examine the following statements to create a recursive procedure named CheckChildren:

```
Call CheckChildren(e.Node, True)

Private Sub CheckChildren( _
    ByVal tnCurrent As TreeNode,
    ByVal pblnChecked As Boolean)
    Dim tnLocal As TreeNode
    For Each tnLocal In tnCurrent.Nodes
        ' Statements
        Call CheckChildren(tnLocal, pblnChecked)
    Next
End Sub
```

The CheckChildren procedure accepts two arguments: a TreeNode and a value indicating whether the child nodes should be checked or unchecked. The procedure enumerates the child TreeNodes of the current TreeNode. For each child TreeNode, the procedure then calls itself thereby enumerating the grandchild TreeNodes. The process continues until a TreeNode has no child TreeNodes. Figure 10-13 illustrates the process of calling a recursive procedure.

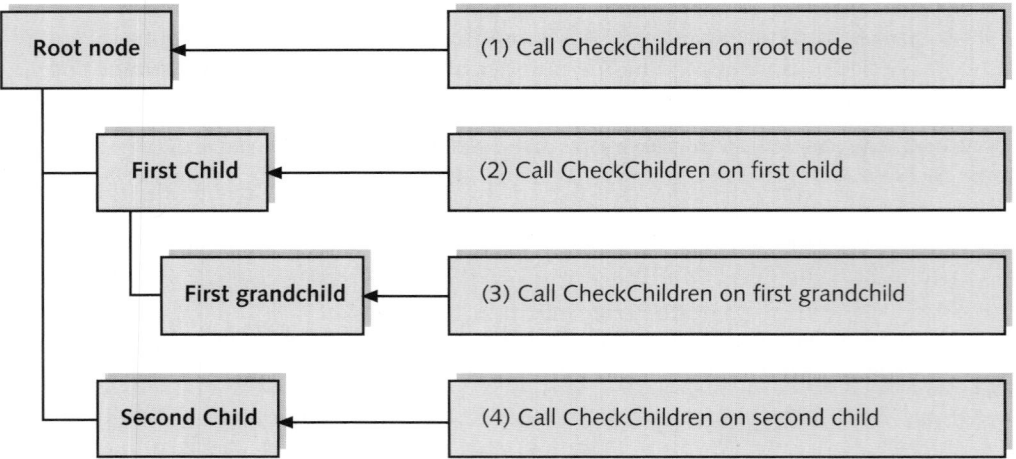

Figure 10-13   Calling a recursive procedure

In this chapter's solution, you will configure the TreeView to display check boxes next to each TreeNode. When the user clicks a particular TreeNode, thereby checking or unchecking it, the recursive procedure named CheckChildren will be called to check or uncheck all of the children of the selected TreeNode.

To create a recursive procedure:

1. Set the CheckBoxes property to **True** for the TreeView control instance named **tvwMain**.

2. Create the **AfterCheck** event handler for the TreeView control instance named **tvwMain**. The AfterCheck event fires just after the TreeNode is checked or unchecked. Enter the following statements in the event handler that you just created:

```
If e.Node.Checked Then
    Call CheckChildren(e.Node, True)
Else
    Call CheckChildren(e.Node, False)
End If
```

3. Enter the following statements (shown in bold) in the **CheckChildren** procedure:

```
Private Sub CheckChildren( _
    ByVal tnCurrent As TreeNode, _
    ByVal pblnChecked As Boolean)
```

```
        Dim tnLocal As TreeNode
        For Each tnLocal In tnCurrent.Nodes
            tnLocal.Checked = pblnChecked
            Call CheckChildren(tnLocal, pblnChecked)
        Next
    End Sub
```

4. Test the solution. On the menu bar, click **File**, and then click **Open**. As you check or uncheck individual TreeNodes, the child and grandchild TreeNodes are checked or unchecked.

Allowing the user to check or uncheck boxes has very little use in and of itself. Usually, when working with the TreeView with check boxes, you want to traverse all of the TreeNodes, and perform some action only for the TreeNodes that are checked. In this solution, you will traverse all of the TreeNodes, searching for those that are checked. If a TreeNode is checked and the TreeNode stores an employee, then that node will be written to a sequential file. This sequential file could likely be used by another application. Again, to accomplish this task, you will create a recursive procedure.

To traverse all of the TreeNodes in a TreeView:

1. Enter the following statements in the **Click** event handler for the menu item named **mmuFileSaveChecked**:

```
sfdMain.ShowDialog()
mswriCurrent = New StreamWriter(sfdMain.FileName)
Call SaveChecked(tvwMain.Nodes(0))
mswriCurrent.Close()
```

The preceding statements display a SaveFileDialog and create an instance of the StreamWriter class. The third statement calls the recursive SaveChecked procedure that you will create next. The root TreeNode is passed as an argument to the procedure. Finally, the StreamWriter is closed.

2. Enter the following statements (shown in bold) in the **SaveChecked** procedure:

```
Private Sub SaveChecked(ByVal tnCurrent As TreeNode)
    Dim tnLocal As TreeNode
    Dim pstrFields() As String
    Dim pchrDelimiter() As Char = {ToChar(",")}


    For Each tnLocal In tnCurrent.Nodes
        pstrFields = tnLocal.Tag.Split(pchrDelimiter)
        If pstrFields(0) = "Employee" Then
            If tnLocal.Checked Then
                Call SaveEmployee(pstrFields(1))
            End If
        End If
        Call SaveChecked(tnLocal)
    Next
```

10

The SaveChecked procedure recursively calls itself. The procedure examines each TreeNode to determine whether or not it is an Employee TreeNode. To do this, the Tag property is examined to determine whether or not the first field in the Tag contains the string "Employee". If it does, and the TreeNode is checked, then the SaveEmployee procedure is called to write the selected employee to the file.

3. Enter the following statements (shown in bold) in the **SaveEmployee** procedure:

```
Private Sub SaveEmployee(ByVal pintEmployee As Integer)
    Dim drEmployee As dsCompany.tblEmployeesRow
    drEmployee = _
        DsCompany1.tblEmployees. _
        FindByfldEmployeeID(pintEmployee)
    With mswriCurrent
        .Write(drEmployee.fldEmployeeID)
        .Write(",")
        .Write(drEmployee.fldName)
        .Write(",")
        .Write(drEmployee.fldPhone)
        .Write(",")
        .Write(drEmployee.fldExtension)
        .WriteLine()
    End With
End Sub
```

The preceding statements should be familiar. A unique employee ID number is passed as an argument to the procedure. The strongly typed FindByfldEmployeeID method is called to retrieve the DataRow corresponding to the employee ID number, which is passed as an argument to the procedure. The remaining statements write the contents of the DataRow using the instance of the StreamWriter class.

4. Test the solution. On the menu bar, click **File**, and then click **Open**. Check various TreeNodes in the TreeView control instance.

5. On the menu bar, click **File** and then click **Save Checked**. In the Save As dialog box, enter a file name having a file suffix of .txt and then click **Save**. Open the file you saved using a text editor such as Notepad. It contains a sequential file representing the selected TreeNode objects.

At this point, you have completed the programming for the TreeView control. Next, you will create an instance of the ListView control and write code for it to display information related to the currently selected TreeView node.

THE LISTVIEW CONTROL

The ListView control displays data in the form of lists or organized into columns. The view defines how the data are displayed within the control instance. In LargeIcon and SmallIcon view, data appear with an icon and a short description. In List and Details view, data appear organized into columns. Depending on specific property settings, data can appear sorted and columns of data can be rearranged. The ListView control also allows the user to select one or multiple items. The ListView control supports the following members:

Syntax

System.Windows.Forms.ListView control

Public Properties

- The **Alignment** property defines the alignment of the icons within the visible region of the control instance. The data type of the property is ListViewAlignment. Common settings are Top and Left, which are used to align the elements along the top or left border of the control instance, respectively.

- The Boolean **AllowColumnReorder** property defines whether or not the user can reorder the columns using drag-and-drop.

- The Boolean **CheckBoxes** property defines whether or not check boxes appear along with the list items. This property works in conjunction with the CheckedItems property.

- The **Columns** property references a collection of type ColumnHeaderCollection. Each element in the ColumnHeaderCollection represents a column header appearing in the control instance.

- The **FullRowSelect** property is only relevant while the ListView is in Details view. If an item is selected, then all of the sub items are selected.

- The Boolean **LabelEdit** property defines whether or not the user can edit the text of an item. The text of sub items cannot be modified, however.

- The Boolean **MultiSelect** property, if set to True, allows the user to select multiple items in the control instance. If the property is set to False, the user cannot select multiple items.

- The Boolean **Scrollable** property defines whether or not scroll bars appear in the control instance when the items will not fit within the visible region.

- The **Sorting** property allows you to specify whether or not and how the items in the ListView will be sorted. The enumeration value SortOrder.Ascending will cause the items to be sorted in ascending order, while the value SortOrder.Descending will cause the items to be sorted in descending order. The setting SortOrder.None will cause the items to appear in the order that they were added to the control instance.

- The **View** property defines which of the four supported views is the current view. Valid values are SmallIcon, LargeIcon, List, and Details.

10

Public Methods

- The **ArrangeIcons** method arranges the icons along the top or left border of the control instance.

- When adding or removing several items from the list, suspend repainting the control instance by calling the **BeginUpdate** method, performing the updates, and then calling the **EndUpdate** method, so as to improve performance and eliminate flicker.

- The **Clear** method removes all of the items from the control instance.

- The **Sort** method sorts the items in the control instance.

Public Events

- The **BeforeLabelEdit** event fires just before the user begins editing the text in a label.

- The **AfterLabelEdit** event fires just after the user finishes editing the text in a label.

- The **ItemCheck** event fires when the user checks or unchecks an item.

The ListView control displays information in one of four views, as determined by the setting of the View property. The value of the View property can be changed at runtime or at design time. The following list describes the four different views and how the data is displayed in those different views:

- In **LargeIcon** view, items are displayed with large (32 by 32) pixel icons. LargeIcon view is the default view.

- In **SmallIcon** view, items are displayed with small (16 by 16) pixel icons.

- In **List** view, items are displayed in a list. Data can be aligned in rows or columns.

- **Details** view displays the richest set of information. Items are displayed in multiple columns having column headers. The ListView control supports any number of columns.

In this chapter's solution, you will create and configure an instance of the ListView control to display the employee or employees working in a particular office or department.

To create and configure a ListView control instance:

1. Create an instance of the ListView control on the form named **frmMain.vb**, as shown in Figure 10-14.

2. Set the Name property to **lvwMain**.

3. Set the SmallImageList property to **ilsSmall**, and the LargeImageList property to **ilsLarge**. Setting these properties associates the ListView control instance with the ImageList control instances appearing on the form.

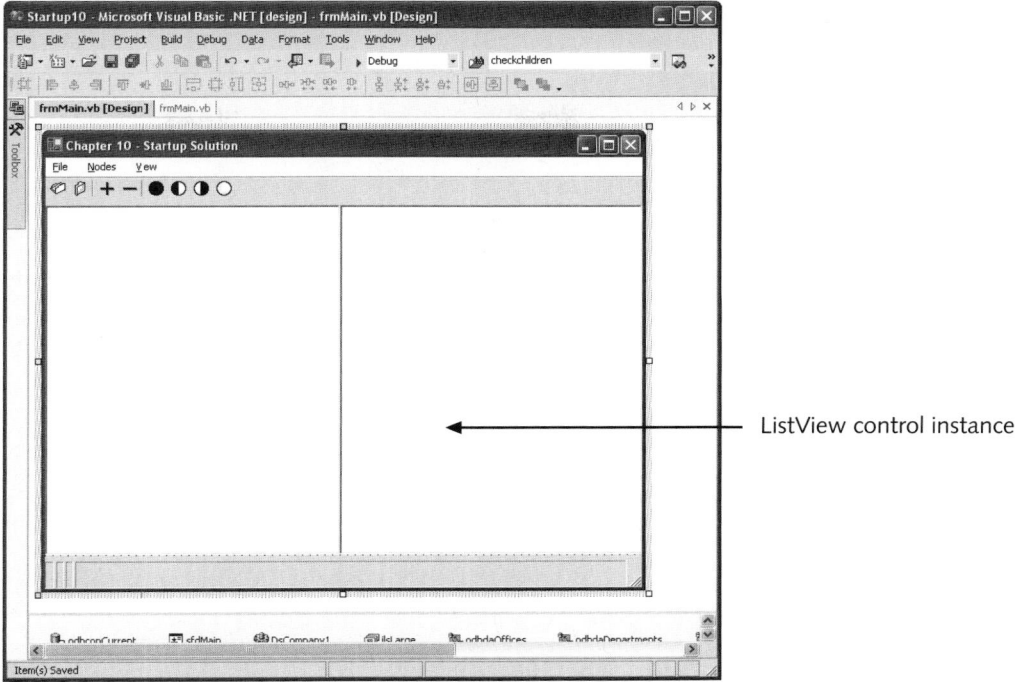

ListView control instance

Figure 10-14 Creating a ListView control instance

4. So that the TreeView and ListView control instances will resize with the form when the form is resized, enter the following statements in the **Resize** event handler for the form named **frmMain.vb**:

```
tvwMain.Width = Me.ClientSize.Width / 2
tvwMain.Height = Me.ClientSize.Height - _
    sbrMain.Height - tbrMain.Height
lvwMain.Width = Me.ClientSize.Width / 2
lvwMain.Left = Me.ClientSize.Width / 2
lvwMain.Height = Me.ClientSize.Height - _
    sbrMain.Height - tbrMain.Height
```

The preceding statements resize the TreeView and ListView control instances such that each fills ½ of the form. The height of the two control instances accounts for the toolbar and status bars.

5. Test the solution. Resize the form. The ListView and TreeView control instances are resized.

Once you have created an instance of the ListView control, you can populate it. The steps to populate an instance of the ListView control are similar to the steps to populate a TreeView control instance. Instead of adding TreeNodes to the Nodes collection, however, you add ListViewItem objects to the Items collection. Each item appearing the ListView control has a data type of ListViewItem. Figure 10-15 shows an instance of the ListView control with three ListViewItem objects while the ListView control instance appears in LargeIcon view.

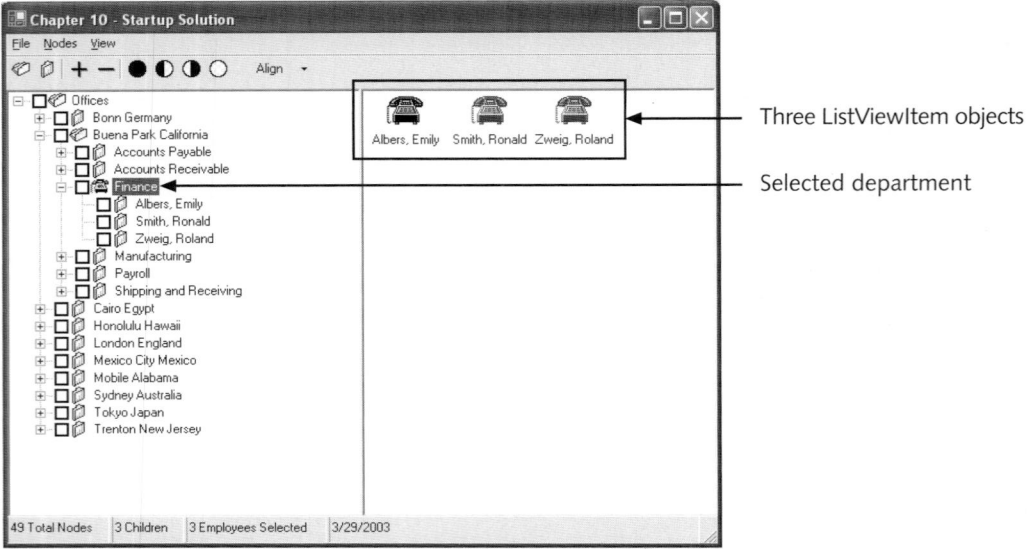

Figure 10-15   ListView control and ListViewItemCollection

In Figure 10-15 a different colored telephone icon appears next to each employee indicating whether the employee is in or out of the office. Each ListViewItem object contains a textual description and an associated icon. The ListView control is typically associated with two instances of the ImageList control, whereas the TreeView control is associated with only one. Remember that one ImageList control instance can contain only icons of the same size. When LargeIcon view is selected, the LargeImageList property determines which images appear in the control instance at runtime. When the other three views are active, the SmallImageList property specifies the images that appear. The text that accompanies the image is stored in the ListViewItem's Text property. The ListViewItem class supports the following members:

Syntax

System.Windows.Forms.ListViewItem class

Public Properties

■ The **ImageIndex** property contains the index of the image associated with the ListViewItem. This index corresponds to the image associated with a particular index in the ImageList control instance.

- The **ImageList** property returns the ImageList control instance associated with the ListViewItem.

- The **SubItems** property references a collection of type ListViewSubItemCollection. The items in this collection appear when the ListView control instance is in Details view. ListViewSubItems are discussed in a moment.

- The text appearing in the visible region of the ListViewItem is stored in the **Text** property.

Public Methods

- The **BeginEdit** method enables editing of the ListViewItem.

- The **EndEdit** method disables editing.

Loading the ListViewItem objects into the ListViewItemCollection is the first step in configuring the ListView control instance. You call the Add method to add ListViewItem objects to the collection. Many sources for the data exist. These sources can include ASCII files or the data contained in a DataSet. No matter the source of the data, the process to add ListViewItem objects is the same. You call the Add method of the ListViewItemCollection, having the following syntax:

Syntax

Overridable Overloads Public Function Add(ByVal *value* **As ListViewItem) As ListViewItem**
Overridable Overloads Public Function Add(ByVal *text* **As String) As ListViewItem**
Overridable Overloads Public Function Add(ByVal *text* **As String, ByVal** *imageIndex* **As Integer) As ListViewItem**

Definition

The overloaded **Add** method adds a new ListViewItem to the ListViewItemCollection, thereby adding an item to the ListView control instance. Each of the overloaded methods returns an instance of the ListViewItem created.

Dissection

- The first overloaded method accepts one argument: an existing instance of the ListViewItem class. The ListViewItem is added to the end of the list.

- The second overloaded method accepts one argument: a string. The string appears in the visible region of the control instance.

- The third overloaded method accepts two arguments. The first argument contains the string appearing in the visible region of the control instance. The second argument contains the index of an image from an instance of the ImageList control.

10

Code Example

```
lvwDemo.Items.Add("Item 1")

Dim lviDemo As New ListViewItem()
lviDemo.Text = "Item 2"
lvwDemo.ImageIndex = 1
lvwDemo.Items.Add(lviDemo)

lvwDemo.Items.Add("Item 3", 1)
```

Code Dissection

The first statement adds a new ListViewItem object having the text "Item 1". The second block of statements first creates an instance of the ListViewItem class, and then sets the value for the Text and ImageIndex properties. This ListViewItem object is then added to the Items collection of the ListView control instance. The final statement adds a new ListViewItem object having the text "Item 3". The second argument contains an Integer that references the index of an image in the corresponding ImageList control instance. Remember that the index is 0-based.

Next you will begin to configure the ListView control instance. In the ListView control instance, you will store the employees that work for the selected office or department. The selected office or department is defined by the currently selected TreeNode in the TreeView control instance.

To add items to a ListView control instance:

1. Enter the following statement (shown in bold) in the **AfterSelect** event handler for the TreeView control instance named **tvwMain**:

```
sbpChildNodes.Text = pintChildCount.ToString & " Children"
Call InitListView(e.Node)
```

2. Enter the following statements in the **InitListView** procedure:

```
Dim drEmployee As dsCompany.tblEmployeesRow
Dim drEmployees() As dsCompany.tblEmployeesRow
Dim lvwitmCurrent As ListViewItem
Dim pstrID, pstrLevel As String
Dim pintCount, pintCount1 As Integer


Dim pstrNodeType As String
Dim pstrFields() As String
Dim pchrDelimiter() As Char = {ToChar(",")}
pstrFields = tnCurrent.Tag.Split(pchrDelimiter)

lvwMain.Items.Clear()
lvwMain.Sorting = SortOrder.Ascending
```

```
        Select Case pstrFields(0)
            Case "Root"
                For Each drEmployee In DsCompany1.tblEmployees
                    Call AddEmployeeToListView(drEmployee)
                Next
            Case "Office"
                Dim pintOfficeID As Integer = pstrFields(1)
                Dim drDepartments() As dsCompany.tblDepartmentsRow
                Dim drOffice As dsCompany.tblOfficesRow
                drOffice = _
                    DsCompany1.tblOffices.FindByfldOfficeID( _
                    pintOfficeID)
                drDepartments = _
                    drOffice.GetChildRows("drOfficesDepartments")
                    For pintCount = 0 To _
                        drDepartments.GetUpperBound(0)
                        drEmployees = _
                            drDepartments(pintCount). _
                            GetChildRows("drDepartmentsEmployees")
                        For pintCount1 = 0 To _
                            drEmployees.GetUpperBound(0)
                            Call AddEmployeeToListView( _
                                drEmployees(pintCount1))
                        Next
                    Next
            Case "Department"
                Dim pintDepartmentID As Integer = pstrFields(1)
                Dim drDepartment As dsCompany.tblDepartmentsRow
                drDepartment = _
                    DsCompany1.tblDepartments. _
                        FindByfldDepartmentID(pintDepartmentID)
                    drEmployees = _
                        drDepartment.GetChildRows( _
                        "drDepartmentsEmployees")
                For pintCount1 = 0 To _
                    drEmployees.GetUpperBound(0)
                    Call AddEmployeeToListView( _
                        drEmployees(pintCount1))
                Next
            Case "Employee"
                drEmployee = _
                DsCompany1.tblEmployees. _
                    FindByfldEmployeeID(pstrFields(1))
                Call AddEmployeeToListView(drEmployee)
        End Select
        sbpListNodes.Text = lvwMain.Items.Count.ToString & _
            " Employees Selected"
```

The preceding statements require careful analysis. The Split method splits the contents of the Tag property and examines the first field to determine whether the node is a root node, an office node, or a department node. Remember that as you created each TreeNode, you stored the string "Root", "Office", "Department", or "Employee" in the Tag property, followed by a comma, then followed by the corresponding ID number.

Each type of node is treated similarly in the Select Case statement. If the node is a root node, the Select Case statement enumerates the table named tblEmployees in the DataSet and adds all of the rows to the ListView control instance by calling the AddEmployeeToListView procedure. You will create that procedure in a moment. If the node is an office node, however, the process is more complex. Nested For loops use two DataRelations to get the departments for the selected office, and the employees for the selected department, respectively. If the node is a department node, then the employees are retrieved only for the selected department using the DataRelation named drDepartmentsEmployees.

Next you will write the statements to add each employee to the ListView control instance.

To add items to a ListView control instance:

1. Enter the following statements (shown in bold) in the **AddEmployeeToListView** procedure:

```
Private Sub AddEmployeeToListView( _
    ByVal drEmployee As dsCompany.tblEmployeesRow)
    Dim lvwitmCurrent As ListViewItem
    lvwitmCurrent = lvwMain.Items.Add(drEmployee.fldName)

    If drEmployee.fldInOut = True Then
        lvwitmCurrent.ImageIndex = 0
    Else
        lvwitmCurrent.ImageIndex = 1
    End If
End Sub
```

The AddEmployeeToListView procedure adds the contents of a DataRow to the ListView control instance. The contents of the field named fldName are stored in the text of the ListViewItem. Based on the value of the field named fldInOut, a different icon is displayed so as to indicate whether the employee is in the office or out of the office.

2. Test the solution. On the menu bar, click **File**, and then click **Open**. Click the text of the **Offices** node. All of the employees appear in the ListView control instance. Expand the Offices node, and then click the text of the **Buena Park California** node. The employees working for that office appear in the ListView control instance. Finally, expand the **Buena Park California** node, and then click the **Finance** node. Only those employees working in the Finance department appear.

Having created the ListView control instance and added the ListItem objects, you will now see the effect of the four different views and the effect of the Alignment property.

To configure the alignment and view of the ListView:

1. Enter the following statements in the procedure named **ConfigureView**:

```
tbbSmallIcon.Pushed = False
tbbLargeIcon.Pushed = False
tbbList.Pushed = False
tbbDetails.Pushed = False
Select Case ViewCurrent
    Case View.SmallIcon
        lvwMain.View = View.SmallIcon
        tbbSmallIcon.Pushed = True
    Case View.LargeIcon
        lvwMain.View = View.LargeIcon
        tbbLargeIcon.Pushed = True
    Case View.List
        lvwMain.View = View.List
        tbbList.Pushed = True
    Case View.Details
        lvwMain.View = View.Details
        tbbDetails.Pushed = True
End Select
```

The preceding statements accomplish two tasks. First they set the current view for the ListView control instance, then they set the Pushed property of the appropriate toolbar button so that the buttons in the group are synchronized with the current view. Note that Details view will not work correctly yet because you have not yet defined the column headings.

2. Enter the following statements (shown in bold) in the **ButtonClick** event handler for the ToolBar control instance named **tbrMain**:

```
Case "tbbSmallIcon"
    Call ConfigureView(View.SmallIcon)
Case "tbbLargeIcon"
    Call ConfigureView(View.LargeIcon)
Case "tbbList"
    Call ConfigureView(View.List)
Case "tbbDetails"
    Call ConfigureView(View.Details)
```

The preceding statements call the ConfigureView procedure with the appropriate argument, depending on which toolbar button was clicked.

Because the toolbar buttons mimic equivalent menu items, you must call the ConfigureView procedure from the menu items too.

10

3. Enter the following statement in the **Click** event handler for the menu item named **mmuViewSmallIcon**:

```
Call ConfigureView(View.SmallIcon)
```

4. Enter the following statement in the **Click** event handler for the menu item named **mmuViewLargeIcon**:

```
Call ConfigureView(View.LargeIcon)
```

5. Enter the following statement in the **Click** event handler for the menu item named **mmuViewList**:

```
Call ConfigureView(View.List)
```

6. Enter the following statement in the **Click** event handler for the menu item named **mmuViewDetails**:

```
Call ConfigureView(View.Details)
```

7. Enter the following statement in the **Click** event handler for the menu item named **mmuViewAlignLeft** and the ContextMenu named **cmuLeft**:

```
lvwMain.Alignment = ListViewAlignment.Left
```

8. Enter the following statement in the **Click** event handler for the menu item named **mmuViewAlignTop** and the ContextMenu named **cmuTop**:

```
lvwMain.Alignment = ListViewAlignment.Top
```

You must enter the statements in the Click event handlers for the context menu too, because it is these click events handlers that execute when the context menu appears for the drop-down toolbar button.

9. Test the solution. On the menu bar, click **File**, and then click **Open**. Click the **Offices** node to display the employees. On the menu bar, click each of the four different views. Note that Details view does not work. You will see how to add the detail information next.

USING DETAILS VIEW

Using the ListView control in Details view adds considerable functionality beyond that available with the other three views. This additional functionality increases the programming complexity, however. Details view displays records from a database table, text file, or other information source, as a columnar grid.

To support this functionality, you need a mechanism to store the column headers and the information in the rows that appear beneath the column headers. The ColumnHeaderCollection and ListViewSubItemCollection collections perform this task. These two collections are only pertinent in Details view. Figure 10–16 depicts the relationship between the ListView control and the objects that apply to it.

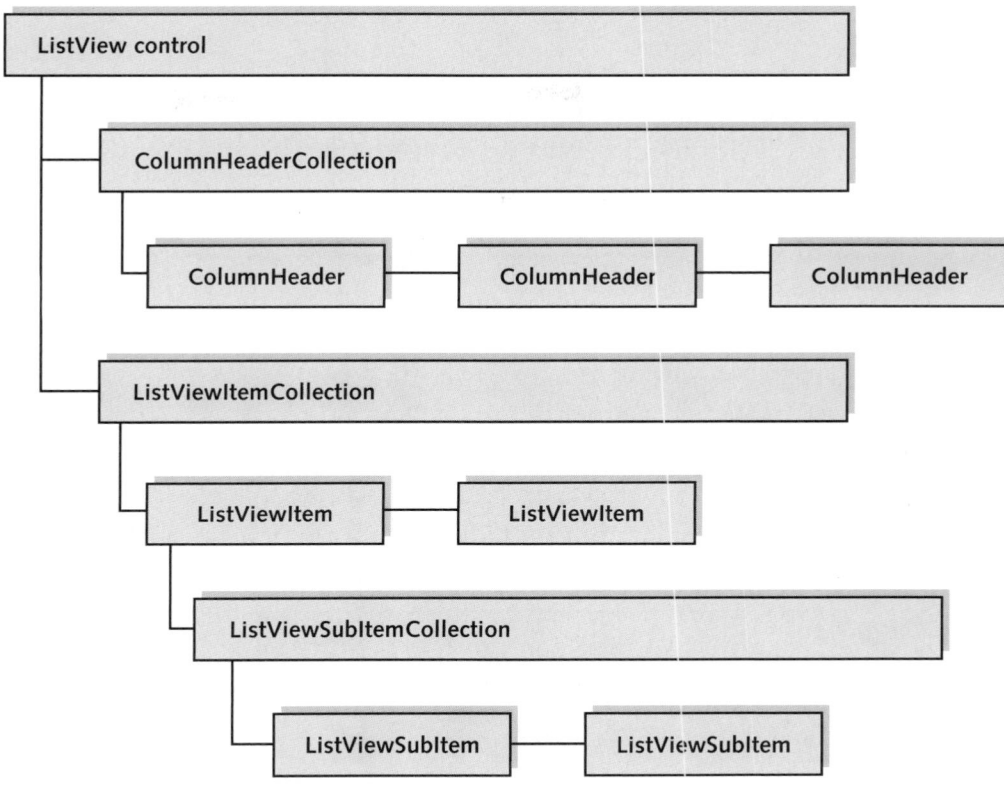

Figure 10-16 ListView collections and objects

As shown in Figure 10-16, The ListView control has one ColumnHeaderCollection storing each ColumnHeader object. The one ListViewItemCollection stores each of the ListViewItem objects. Each ListViewItem object, in turn, references a ListViewSubItemCollection having ListViewSubItem objects.

The ColumnHeaderCollection

The ListView control supports the Columns property, which in turn references a ColumnHeaderCollection. The ColumnHeaderCollection contains one or more ColumnHeader objects representing each column. The ColumnHeader class supports the following members:

Syntax

System.Windows.Forms.ColumnHeader class

Public Properties

- The **Text** property contains the text that appears in the column header.

- The **TextAlign** property defines horizontal alignment of the text within the column. Text may be left justified, right justified, or centered.

- The **Width** property defines the width of the column. This column width is measured in pixels.

Column headers can be added at design time using the ColumnHeader Collection Editor or at runtime by calling the Add method of the ColumnHeaderCollection, which has the following syntax:

Syntax

Overridable Overloads Public Function Add(ByVal *value* **As ColumnHeader) As Integer**
Overridable Overloads Public Function Add(ByVal *str* **As String, ByVal** *width* **As Integer, ByVal** *textalign* **As HorizontalAlignment) As ColumnHeader**

Definition

The **Add** method of the ColumnHeaderCollection creates a new ColumnHeader.

Dissection

- The first overloaded method requires one argument: an existing ColumnHeader object. The method returns the numeric index in the collection where the ColumnHeader object was added.

- The second overloaded method contains the arguments to configure the ColumnHeader fully. The first argument contains the text that will appear in the ColumnHeader. The second argument defines the width of the column, and the final argument defines the alignment of the column.

Code Example

```
Dim lvwchCurrent As New ColumnHeader()
lvwchCurrent.Text = "Column 1"
lvwchCurrent.Width = 72
lvwchCurrent.TextAlign = HorizontalAlignment.Center
lvwDemo.Columns.Add(lvwchCurrent)

lvwDemo.Columns.Add("Column 2", 72, _
    HorizontalAlignment.Center)
```

Code Dissection

- The first block of statements creates a new instance of the ColumnHeader class, configures the class instance by individually setting each property, and then adds the ColumnHeader to the Columns collection.

- The final statement adds a new ColumnHeader. However, instead of adding a pre-defined ColumnHeader object, the statement causes VB .NET to create a new ColumnHeader object based on the arguments provided. The first argument contains the text that will appear in the ColumnHeader. The second argument defines the width of the column, and the final argument defines the column's alignment.

Next you will create the column headers for the ListView control instance. The columns will store each employee's name, telephone number, and telephone extension.

To create column headers:

1. Enter the following statements (shown in bold) at the end of the **Load** event handler for the form to define the column headers for the ListView control instance:

```
sbrMain.Text = "Database not open."
lvwMain.Columns.Add("Name", 140, HorizontalAlignment.Left)
lvwMain.Columns.Add("Phone", 70, HorizontalAlignment.Left)
lvwMain.Columns.Add("Extension", 70, _
    HorizontalAlignment.Left)
```

2. Test the solution. On the menu bar, click **File**, and then click **Open**. Click the text for the **Offices** node to display data in the ListView control instance. Select **Details** view. The column headers appear. Note that the data does not appear for the ListSubItems. You will perform that task next.

Having defined the column headers, you will now write the statements to store data in those columns.

ListViewSubItems

Each ListViewItem object has another collection named SubItems having a data type of ListViewSubItemCollection. These sub items appear in additional columns while the ListView control instance is in Details view. SubItems do not respond to events and support only the BackColor and ForeColor properties that define the text color, and the Text property to define the text itself that appears in the sub item. Figure 10-17 shows an instance of the ListView control and the relationship between the ListViewSubItem objects and the other objects in the ListView.

As shown in Figure 10-17, each value in the Name column represents one ListViewItem. Each ListViewItem has its own ListViewSubItemCollection. That collection, in turn, contains two ListViewSubItem objects.

10

Figure 10-17   ListViewSubItems relationships

To create ListViewSubItems:

1. Enter the following statements (shown in bold) in the **AddEmployeeToListView** procedure:

```
lvwitmCurrent = lvwMain.Items.Add(drEmployee.fldName)
lvwitmCurrent.SubItems.Add(drEmployee.fldPhone)
lvwitmCurrent.SubItems.Add(drEmployee.fldExtension)
If drEmployee.fldInOut = True Then
' Statements
```

The variable lvwitmCurrent references a ListViewItem. By calling the Add method of the SubItems collection, ListViewSubItem objects are added to the respective ListViewItem object.

2. Test the solution. On the menu bar, click **File**, and then click **Open**. Set the current view for the ListView control instance to Details view. Select various nodes. The employees appear in the ListView control instance.

You have completed the programming for the ListView and TreeView control instances. In this chapter, you have seen how to improve an application's user interface by including the StatusBar and ToolBar controls. You have also seen how to implement a drill-down interface using the TreeView and ListView controls.

CHAPTER SUMMARY

❐ The ImageList control acts as a repository for images used by other control instances in the solution. Images can be added at design time using the Image Collection Editor or programmatically. Each image added to the ImageList is referenced by its 0-based numeric index in the ImageCollection. Note that all images in an instance of the ImageList control must be of the same size. Create multiple instances of the ImageList control to display images of varying sizes.

❐ The ToolBar control allows you to create a toolbar that typically appears docked along the top border of the form. A toolbar contains one or more buttons. To add or remove buttons, use the ToolBarButton Collection Editor at design time. Buttons can also be created programmatically. For each button, set the Name, Tag, and ImageIndex properties. At runtime, handle the ButtonClick event for the toolbar itself.

❐ The StatusBar control displays information about the state or status of an application. The region of the status bar is divided into panels. Each panel can contain text, an icon, or both. Each StatusBarPanel object can be configured with a fixed size, configured to resize based on its contents or configured to expand to fill the width of the form. At runtime, a StatusBarPanel can be referenced through the panel's ordinal value in the Panels collection. In addition, VB .NET declares a variable having the same name as the panel itself, which you can use to reference the panel.

❐ The TreeView control supplies a drill-down interface used to display information in a hierarchical manner. Each item in an instance of the TreeView control has a data type of TreeNode. You build the hierarchy of TreeNodes by adding new TreeNode objects to the Nodes collection of a particular TreeNode object, or the Nodes collection of the TreeView control instance itself.

❐ The ListView control typically works in conjunction with the TreeView control. Data in the ListView control appears in one of four views: LargeIcon, SmallIcon, List, and Details. The ListView control supports collections to store the ColumnHeader objects and the ListViewItem objects. Each ListViewItem object supports another collection named SubItems. This collection stores the ListViewSubItem objects corresponding to a particular ListViewItem.

10

REVIEW QUESTIONS

1. Which of the following statements pertaining to the ImageList control is true?

   a. Images are dynamically loaded at runtime, rather than being stored in an internal file such as a resource file.

   b. The images stored in an instance of the ImageList control must all be of the same size.

   c. Images can be bitmaps, but other image formats, such as icons, are not supported.

   d. all of the above

   e. none of the above

2. Where are images stored once they are added to an instance of the ImageList control?

   a. The files are stored as individual graphic files on the disk. The control instance itself stores the path name and file name of the graphic in the Images collection.

   b. The images are stored in the resource file corresponding to the form.

   c. Images are grouped in a special file called an Image Catalog File. This file contains a header block listing the images in the file. Following the header block, the images appear.

   d. Images are stored in the assembly information file.

   e. none of the above

3. Which of the following statements is correct pertaining to the ToolBar control?

   a. When the user clicks a button on the toolbar, a separate ButtonClick event fires for each individual button. Thus, if a toolbar had six buttons, you would create six ButtonClick event handlers.

   b. A toolbar button can contain text or an icon, but not both.

   c. A toolbar must be docked along the top of the form.

   d. all of the above

   e. none of the above

4. Which of the following are valid toolbar button styles?

   a. TextButton, IconButton

   b. PushButton, ToggleButton, Separator, DropDownButton

   c. ClickButton, CheckButton, Space

   d. PressButton, CheckedButton, MenuButton, PlaceholderButton

   e. none of the above

5. Which of the following statements is correct pertaining to a StatusBar control instance?

   a. A status bar can be configured to display individual panels or a single panel. The display mode is controlled by the ShowPanels property of the status bar itself.

   b. A status bar is typically docked along the bottom of the form.

   c. The Panels property of the StatusBar control references a StatusBarPanel collection. This collection, in turn, contains a reference to each panel appearing in the status bar.

   d. An individual panel can be configured to appear raised or recessed.

   e. all of the above

6. Which of the following statements correctly describes the sizing of panels in a status bar?

   a. All panels have a fixed size. The size of a panel cannot change as the program runs and the user resizes the form.

   b. A panel size can be configured to increase or decrease based on the panel's contents.

   c. A panel's width is determined by the PanelSize property.

   d. Only one panel can have its Style property set to Spring.

   e. none of the above

7. Which of the following statements pertaining to the TreeView control is true?

   a. The TreeView control supports the Nodes collection.

   b. A TreeNode must have at least one child.

   c. A TreeNode can have at most 10 children.

   d. Nodes that share a common parent node are called equivalent nodes.

   e. none of the above

8. How do you associate icons with the TreeNodes appearing in a TreeView control instance?

   a. Set the Image property of each TreeNode object in the TreeView.

   b. Set the ImageList property of the TreeView itself to an instance of the ImageList control appearing on the form.

   c. Set the IconType property based on the type of icons specified in the IconList property.

   d. Use the Icon Editor to select the icons that will appear in the TreeView. Then for each TreeNode, set the Icon property to the name of the graphical image you selected in the Icon Editor.

   e. none of the above

10

9. Which of the following properties define how lines are drawn between TreeNodes in a TreeView?

   a. ConnectLines, ConnectRootLines

   b. ShowLines, ShowRootLines

   c. Line, LineOrientation

   d. ShowNodeLines, ShowRootNodeLines

   e. none of the above

10. What is the purpose of the BeginUpdate and EndUpdate methods of the TreeView control?

    a. The TreeView control does not support the BeginUpdate and EndUpdate methods.

    b. These methods start and end editing on an instance of the TreeView control.

    c. You must call the BeginUpdate method before adding a TreeNode, and the EndUpdate method after adding the TreeNode, or an exception will occur.

    d. The BeginUpdate and EndUpdate methods are used to edit the Text property of a TreeNode.

    e. They are used to prevent the control instance from being refreshed while items are added to the control instance.

11. Which of the following statements is true pertaining to the ListView control?

    a. Data can be displayed in one of three different views.

    b. The ListView control is always associated with one and only one ImageList control instance.

    c. To define the items appearing in an instance of the ListView control, you set the List property.

    d. all of the above

    e. none of the above

12. Which of the following statements is correct related to the ListViewSubItem object of the ListView control?

    a. There exists a separate SubItems collection for each ListViewItem object.

    b. ListViewSubItem objects only appear when the ListView control instance is in Details view.

    c. A ListViewItem need not have any ListViewSubItem objects.

    d. all of the above

    e. none of the above

13. How do you create column headers in a ListView control?

    a. Add items to the ColumnHeaderCollection programmatically.

    b. Use the ColumnHeader Collection Editor at design time.

c. Create a menu bar in the ListView control.

d. Both a and b

e. all of the above

14. Which of the following views are supported by the ListView control?

    a. Icon, Columnar, Details

    b. LargeIcon, Icon, SmallIcon, Details

    c. SmallIcon, LargeIcon, List, Details

    d. RowView, ColumnView

    e. none of the above

15. Which of the following statements is correct pertaining to the icons appearing in an instance of the ListView control?

    a. Depending on the selected view, the ListView control will display large or small icons which are obtained from two different instances of the ImageList control.

    b. When the view is set to Details, the ListView control instance displays large icons.

    c. When the view is set to List, the ListView control instance displays large icons.

    d. When the view is set to List, no icons are displayed.

    e. none of the above

16. List and describe the types of buttons appearing on a toolbar.

17. Describe how panels in a StatusBar control instance can be resized.

18. Referring to the TreeView control, describe the hierarchical organization of the TreeNode objects. In your answer, discuss how to add and remove nodes.

19. Referring to the ListView control, what is the difference between the ListViewItem and ListViewSubItem classes?

20. List and describe the different views supported by the ListView control.

PROGRAMMING QUESTIONS

1. Assume that a toolbar named tbrQuestion exists, having a push button as the first button. Write the statement to mark the button as unpressed.

2. Assume that a toolbar named tbrQuestion exists, having buttons with the following values for the Tag property: "Open", "Close", "Exit". Create the ButtonClick event handler for the toolbar. In the event handler, determine which button was clicked. If the Open button was clicked, call the procedure named OpenFile. If the Close button was clicked, call the procedure named CloseFile. If the Exit button was clicked, end the program. Assume that the OpenFile and CloseFile procedures accept no arguments.

3. Assume that a StatusBar control instance exists named sbrQuestion. Write the statements to store the text "10 Records" in the panel named pnlRecordCount.

4. Assume that a StatusBar control instance named sbrList exists having some number of panels. Write the necessary statements to remove the text from all of the panels appearing in the status bar. *Hint*: Examine the Panels collection.

5. Write two statements to change the display of the status bar named sbrQuestion to display the individual panels and display the contents of the Text property.

6. Write the statements to add a TreeNode object to the TreeView control instance named tvwDemo. Set the text to NewNode. Add the object so that it appears as a root node.

7. Assume that an instance of the TreeView control exists named tvwQuestion. Write the statements to create 10 child nodes of the node named tnRoot, having captions of 1, 2, 3, 4, and so on.

8. Declare the necessary variables and write a loop to print the value to the Text property for all of the children of the TreeNode object named tnDemo. Print the values to the Output window.

9. Create a recursive procedure named PrintNodes that accepts one argument having a data type of TreeNode. Print the text of all the child nodes of the node passed as an argument to the Output window.

10. Write the statements to create four column headers for a ListView control instance named lvwQuestion. The column headers should have captions of First, Second, Third, and Fourth, respectively. Set the width of each column to 72 pixels.

11. Write the statement(s) to clear the contents of the ListView control instance named lvwQuestion.

12. Write the statements to set the view of the ListView control instance named lvwQuestion to SmallIcon, LargeIcon, List, and Details view, respectively.

13. Assume that a ListView control instance named lvwQuestion exists. Write the statements to add 10 items to the ListView, having captions of Question1, Question2, Question3, and so on. Use a For loop to accomplish this task.

14. Assume that a ListView control instance named lvwQuestion exists having a ListItem object named lviCurrent. Write the statements to add three ListSubItems having captions of One, Two, and Three, respectively.

15. Assume that a ListView control instance named lvwQuestion exists. Write the statements to add three ListItem objects having captions of 1, 2, and 3, respectively. For each ListItem object you add, add ListSubItem objects having captions of a, b, c, d, and e.

HANDS-ON PROJECTS

1. In this project, you will use the TreeView control to display the numbers 0-9 and the letters A-Z in a node hierarchy. This application does not require any data to run. Rather, the data are initialized using ASCII character codes. The file named Chapter.10\Exercises10\Ch10Ex1.exe contains the compiled executable application. Figure 10-18 shows the completed main form for the solution.

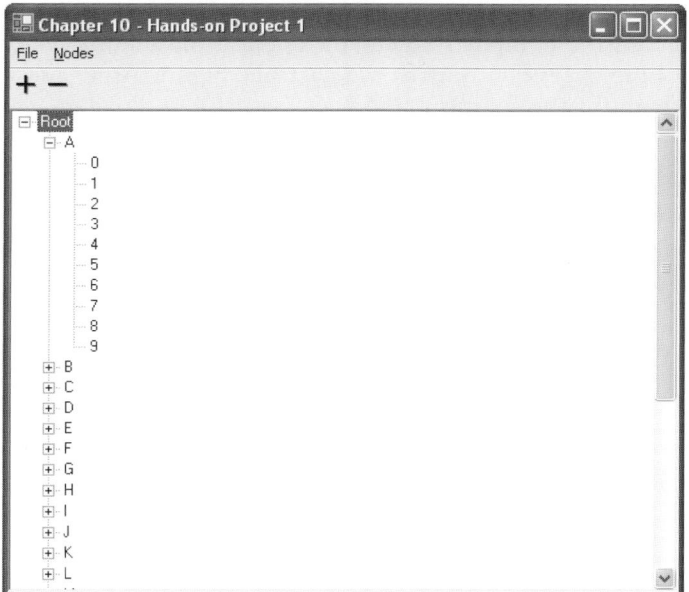

Figure 10-18   Chapter 10 – Hands-on Project 1

a. Create a new project named **Ch10Ex1.sln** and a splash screen for the solution.

b. Create the control instances in the form as shown in Figure 10-18.

c. Create a root-level node having a caption of **Root**.

d. Create a child node of the root node for each letter of the alphabet. There should be 26 TreeNode objects, each having as its caption a letter of the alphabet. (Use a For loop and the Chr function to accomplish this task.)

e. For each letter node, create 10 child nodes so that the nodes will display the values 0 through 9. (Again, use the Chr function to accomplish this task.)

f. Create menu items on the form to expand and collapse all of the nodes in the hierarchy. Suspend painting of the control while the nodes are being expanded or collapsed.

10

g. Create an instance of the ImageList control on the form. Add the images named **Expand.ico** and **Collapse.ico** from the Chapter.10\Data folder.

h. Create a toolbar on the form. Associate the toolbar with the ImageList that you just created. Create buttons to expand and collapse all of the nodes that will mimic the menu items that you already created.

i. Write the statements to resize the TreeView control instance so that it fills the form.

2. In this project, you will read the contents of a sequential file into instances of a TreeView and ListView control. The file named Chapter.10\Exercises10\ Ch10Ex2.exe contains the compiled executable application. The file named Chapter.10\Data\Employees.txt contains the data file. Figure 10-19 shows the completed main form for the solution.

Figure 10-19 Chapter 10 – Hands-on Project 2

a. Create a new project named **Ch10Ex2.sln**.

b. Create the instances of the ListView and TreeView controls on the form as shown in Figure 10-19.

c. Create an ImageList control on the form to display icons in the TreeView control instance.

d. Create a ToolBar control instance on the form. The toolbar should have buttons to open the file, exit the solution, expand and collapse all of the nodes, and allow the user to select the four different views. Use icons of your choice for the buttons.

e. Assume that the sequential file contains the following fields: ID – Integer, Department – String, Last Name – String, First Name – String, Address – String, Telephone – String.

f. Write the statements to read the sequential file into the TreeView control such that the unique employee departments appear as root-level nodes. *Hint:* You may want to store the sequential file into an ArrayList or other data structure to facilitate displaying the appropriate selected data in the ListView control instance.

g. Create root-level nodes to store the unique departments.

h. Write the statements to create the child nodes of the root-level nodes. The child nodes should store the employee's first name and last name concatenated together with a comma separating the two fields.

i. Write the statements that will execute when the user clicks a node in the TreeView control instance. If the user clicked a node for a department, display all of the employees that work in that department in the ListView control instance. If the user clicked a node for an employee, display only the selected employee in the ListView control instance. Again, you will want to store information in the Tag property to store the type of node and information about that node.

j. Provide support for the four different views. When in Details view, the ListView control instance should display the employee ID, last and first name, address, and telephone number.

k. Create a status bar control instance on the form. When the program starts, the status bar should display a single panel having the text **No file open**. When the user opens a file, display the total number of records, the number of selected records, and the current date. Also display the file name opened by the user.

l. Allow the user to collapse and expand all of the nodes in the TreeView control instance. Write the statements to display an appropriate icon in a TreeNode to indicate whether the node is expanded or collapsed.

m. Write the statements to resize the ListView and TreeView control instances when the user resizes the form.

3. In this project, you will use the TreeView and ListView control in much the same way that you used them in the chapter. In this exercise, however, you will create a drill-down interface that will look up a part number in inventory. The file named Chapter.10\Exercises10\Ch10Ex3.exe contains the compiled executable application. Figure 10-20 shows the completed main form for the solution.

a. Create a new project named **Ch10Ex3.sln**.

b. Create the control instances in the form as shown in Figure 10-20.

10

Figure 10-20   Chapter 10 – Hands-on Project 3

c. Create the necessary OleDbConnection, OleDbDataAdapters, and DataSet object to retrieve the data from the three database tables. Write the statements that will populate the DataSet. Create the DataRelations as necessary. The database named Inventory.mdb appears in the Chapter.10\Data folder. The table named tblCategory has the following fields: fldCategoryID – Integer, fldCategoryDescription – String. The table named tblSubCategory has the following fields: fldCategoryID – Integer, fldSubCategoryID – Integer, fldSubCategoryDescription – String. The table named tblParts has the following fields: fldCategoryID – Integer, fldSubCategoryID – Integer, fldPartNumber – Integer, fldPartDescription – String, fldQuantityOnHand – Integer, fldCost – Single.

d. Create a procedure that will initialize the root node of the tree. The root node should have a caption of **Inventory**.

e. Create a procedure that will create the category nodes as children of the root node.

f. For each category created, the corresponding subcategories must be added to the TreeView control instance. Create another procedure to accomplish this task.

g. For each subcategory created, the corresponding part numbers must be added to the TreeView control instance. Create another procedure to accomplish this task.

h. Write the statements to manage the ListView control instance. When the user clicks on a category in the TreeView control instance, the program should display all of the records in that category. Note that multiple subcategories may be selected simultaneously. When the user selects a subcategory, select and display only the matching category and subcategory records in the ListView control instance. When the user selects a part number in the TreeView control instance, display only that part number. Calculate the total cost (quantity on hand * price), and display that value in the ListView.

i. Create a StatusBar control instance on the form. Create panels on the status bar to display the total number of nodes appearing in the TreeView control instance, the number of child nodes of the current node, and the number of items currently displayed in the ListView control instance.

j. Create the toolbar on the form. Create buttons on the toolbar to expand and collapse all of the nodes in the TreeView control instance. Create buttons to display the ListView control instance in the four possible views. Create a button to exit the program.

4. In this project, you again will work with the ListView and TreeView controls, and create a status bar and toolbar. The file named Chapter.10\Exercises10\Ch10Ex4.exe contains the compiled executable application.

a. Create a new project named **Ch10Ex4.sln**.

b. Create the necessary OleDbConnection, OleDbDataAdapters, and DataSet object to retrieve the data from the two database tables. Write the statements that will populate the DataSet. Create the DataRelations as necessary. The database named Customer.mdb appears in the Chapter.10\Data folder. The table named tblCustomers has the following fields: fldID – Integer, fldFirstName – String, fldLastName – String, fldAddress – String, fldCity – String, fldState – String, fldZipCode – String, fldActive – Boolean. The table named tblTransactions has the following fields: fldID – Integer, fldTransactionID – Integer, fldDate – DateTime, fldAmount – Single, fldType – Integer. The field named fldType stores the value 1 to indicate a charge and 2 to indicate a payment.

c. Configure the TreeView control instance to display a root node named Customers. The root node should contain child nodes for each state. Each state node should display the customer's first name and last name.

d. Configure the ListView control instance such that it will display all of the transactions for the selected customer.

e. Configure the StatusBar control instance to display the total debits and total credits for the selected customer.

f. Create a menu on the form. Create menu items to expand and collapse all of the nodes in the TreeView control instance. Create menu items to set the ListView control instance to each of the four possible views.

g. Create an instance of the ToolBar control. Configure it to expand and collapse nodes, and display the ListView control instance in the four different views.

In this chapter, you will:

♦ Learn about the reasons to create a control

♦ Create a control by inheriting from an existing control

♦ Work with control attributes

♦ Create a control by inheriting from System.Windows.Forms. UserControl

♦ Aggregate and delegate properties

♦ Create a control by inheriting from System.Windows.Forms.Control

♦ Create a custom property editor

♦ Work with control licensing

Throughout this book, you have used existing Toolbox controls to create a form's visual interface. In this chapter, you will learn about the different ways to create a custom control designed for use by other developers. These custom controls can be inherited from other existing controls, such as the TextBox or Label controls, or created from scratch. In addition, you will learn how to implement licensing for controls to prevent their unauthorized use.

In this chapter, we refer to two roles when creating a custom control and using a custom control created by someone else. The person who creates the custom control is referred to as the author, and the person who uses that custom control is referred to as the developer. These are the same roles defined when creating and using a custom component.

PREVIEWING THE COMPLETED SOLUTION

The completed solution in this chapter is not an application in the sense of being a form with a user interface. Rather, the completed solution is made up of two projects: a Windows Application project and a Windows Control Library project. The Windows Control Library project contains several modules. Each module contains a class that defines a custom control. Note, however, that multiple control classes could be contained in a single module file. The only purpose of the Windows Application project in this solution is to test the custom controls contained in the Windows Control Library project. Thus, the completed Windows Application does almost nothing.

Before you test the completed solution, you will license those custom controls that require a license. The licensing scheme works by reading a file called a license file. This license file must appear in the Windows system directory.

To preview the completed solution:

1. Copy the file named **Chapter.11\Complete11\LocalControls\bin\ LocalControls.SuperText.lic** to the Windows system directory. This directory is named C:\WINDOWS\System if you are using Windows XP, and C:\WINNT\system if you are using Windows 2000.

2. Start Visual Studio .NET and open the solution file named **Chapter.11\ Complete11\Complete11.sln**.

3. Activate the Win Forms Designer for the form named **frmMain.vb**.

4. To use the custom controls created in this chapter, you must first add them to the Toolbox. Right-click the **Windows Forms** tab of the Toolbox, and then click **Customize Toolbox**. The Customize Toolbox dialog box appears.

5. Click the **.NET Framework Components** tab. Click the **Browse** button to activate the Open dialog box. Select the library named **Chapter.11\ Complete11\LocalControls\bin\LocalControls.dll**, and then click **Open**. Click **OK** in the Customize Toolbox dialog box to close it and add the custom controls to the Toolbox.

6. Activate the Win Forms Designer for the form named **frmMain.vb**, if necessary. Activate the Toolbox. Note that the Toolbox contains three additional controls named SuperText, FractionalScrollBar, and Box.

7. Create an instance of the FractionalScrollBar on the form. The FractionalScrollBar control works much like an intrinsic HScrollBar, however, instead of operating with Integer values, it operates with fractional values.

8. Activate the Properties window for the FractionalScrollBar. The Precision property is set to 2, which is the default. The FractionalScrollBar will have a numeric precision of two decimal places.

9. Create an instance of the SuperText control on the form. Note that the SuperText control is made up of two controls: a label used as a descriptive prompt and a text box in which the user can enter text.

10. Create an instance of the Box control on the form. Activate the Properties window for the Box control. Set the LineColor property to **Green**. Note that the Properties window displays a color editor, just as would be used with any other property involving color. Set the Thickness property to **3**. Note that the values for the Thickness property appear in a drop-down list box. This drop-down list box is considered a custom property editor. The border surrounding the Box control becomes green. Figure 11-1 shows the control instances created on the form.

Figure 11-1 Custom control instances created on a form

11. Exit the solution and Visual Studio .NET. Do not save any changes.

REASONS TO CREATE A CONTROL

There are three different reasons to create your own control. Knowing these reasons will help you navigate this chapter, put the information you are learning into context, and apply what you learn to other situations.

First you may want to enhance or change the behavior of an existing control. For example, you may want to create a control that expands upon the properties of the intrinsic TextBox control. That is, you may want to create a new property that applies specific formatting attributes. Or you may want to hide specific properties from the developer. For example, to enforce organizational standards, you may only want developers to have access to selected control properties. Second, you may want to create a control that combines the features of two or more intrinsic controls. For example, you may want to create a control made up of a label and a text box. The label would be used to display a prompt while the user enters text in the text box. Third, you may want to create an entirely new control that is not based on a control appearing in the Toolbox. VB .NET will allow you to create controls based on each of these different scenarios.

CREATING A CONTROL BY INHERITING FROM AN EXISTING CONTROL

You can create a class that inherits from another control class. By inheriting from an existing control class, the derived class inherits all of the members of the base class. After inheriting from the base class, you can define new members or modify the behavior of existing members.

The simplest way to create a control is to create a class that derives from another control class such as a TextBox, Label, HScrollBar, or any other control type. This approach to control creation is surprisingly easy. In this solution, you will create a control that is derived from a constituent horizontal scroll bar (HScrollBar). However, you will modify the control to work with fractional values instead of Integer values.

Inheriting a Control

To create a control that derives from an existing control class, you create a new class that derives from an existing control, such as an HScrollBar, using inheritance. That is, you write the same Inherits statement that you have used before. In this solution, you will create a control named FractionalScrollBar that inherits from the System.Windows.Forms.HScrollBar class, as shown in the following statements:

```
Public Class FractionalScrollBar
    Inherits System.Windows.Forms.HScrollBar
End Class
```

The preceding statements should look familiar. The class named FractionalScrollBar inherits from the base System.Windows.Forms.HScrollBar class. As always, when a class inherits from a base class, the Inherits keyword must appear as the first statement in the derived class. Also, as VB .NET supports single inheritance, the control that you create must inherit from a single control. By inheriting from a class such as HScrollBar, your control inherits all of the members of the base HScrollBar class. That is, all of the properties and methods of the base HScrollBar class are available to the derived FractionalScrollBar class.

Creating a Windows Control Library Project

Typically, when you create your own control(s) you will want to distribute that control to other computers in its own assembly. That way, many developers can use the control(s) as part of their Windows Application projects. To create a control as part of its own assembly, you create a Windows Control Library project in the same way that you create any other type of project. In addition, you can test that Windows Control Library project by creating a solution made up of two projects: the first project being a Windows Application project, and the second project being a Windows Control Library project.

As you have seen when working with multiple projects in the same solution, one project must be designated as the startup project. Only one project in a solution can be designated as the startup project. When working with a Windows Application project and a Windows Control Library project, you must also add a reference to the Windows Control Library project from the Windows Application project. Furthermore, you usually want to add the new control to the Toolbox itself. You will perform these tasks in the following steps.

To create a Windows Control Library project:

1. Start Visual Studio .NET, and then open the solution file named **Chapter.11\Startup11\Startup11.sln**. Note that the project named Startup11 is already designated as the startup project.

2. Click **File**, point to **Add Project**, and then click **New Project** to activate the Add New Project dialog box. In the Templates pane, click **Windows Control Library**. Set the location to **Chapter.11\Startup11** by clicking **Browse**, and then selecting the directory. Set the name to **LocalControls**, as shown in Figure 11-2.

   Note that the root path name may differ from the one shown in Figure 11-2, depending on where you installed the solution files corresponding to this book.

3. Click **OK** to close the Add New Project dialog box and create the project.

   VB .NET creates a new project with a single class having a default name of UserControl1. This is the name by which your class (control) will be known to the developer. You should change this name to a name that better reflects the purpose of the control.

11

Figure 11-2   Creating a Windows Control Library project

4. In the Solution Explorer, rename the module by right-clicking the module named **UserControl1.vb**, clicking **Rename** from the context menu, and then entering the name **FractionalScrollBar.vb**.

Figure 11-3 shows the Solution Explorer with two projects.

Figure 11-3   Solution Explorer with two projects

5. Activate the Code Editor for the module named **FractionalScrollBar.vb**. Modify the automatically generated statements so that the class appears as follows. Do not modify the Win Forms Designer generated code.

```
Option Explicit On
Option Strict On

Imports System.Convert
Imports System.ComponentModel

Public Class FractionalScrollBar
    Inherits System.Windows.Forms.HScrollBar
    Win Forms Designer generated code
End Class
```

The System.ComponentModel namespace contains numerous classes that supply the design time and run-time behavior of controls. In addition, data binding is also accomplished using the classes of the System. ComponentModel namespace. The class is named FractionalScrollBar, which inherits from the System.Windows.Forms.HScrollBar class.

At this point, you have created a fully functional control, although it does nothing more than the intrinsic HScrollBar control.

 When you create a control that derives from an intrinsic control such as the HScrollBar, there exists no visual designer corresponding to the class. That is, the only way to modify the characteristics of the FractionalScrollBar is to use the Code Editor.

Compiling and Referencing a Windows Control Library Project

Before the Windows Application project can use the FractionalScrollBar control appearing in the LocalControls project, two steps need to be performed. First the Windows Control Library project must be compiled. A Windows Control Library project is compiled to a Dynamic Link Library (DLL) rather than to an executable file run directly by the user. This DLL, in turn, can be used by a Windows Application project.

Because the Windows Application project and the FractionalScrollBar control appear in different projects, you must add a reference to the FractionalScrollBar project from the Windows Application project so that the form can use the new control. To accomplish this task, you add a reference to the Inherited control (FractionalScrollBar) to the Windows Application project. In addition, you need to add the control to the Toolbox. By adding the control to the Toolbox, you, as the developer, can create one or more instances of the FractionalScrollBar control on the form just as you would create instances of any other intrinsic control.

11

To compile and reference a Windows Control Library project:

1. Click the **LocalControls** project in the Solution Explorer to select it.

2. On the menu bar, click **Build**, and then click **Build LocalControls**. VB .NET produces a file named LocalControls.dll in the project's bin directory (Chapter.11\Startup11\LocalControls\bin\LocalControls.dll). It is this DLL that will be used by the Windows Application project.

3. Activate the Win Forms Designer for the form named **frmMain.vb**, and then activate the Toolbox.

4. Right-click the **Windows Forms** tab, and then click **Customize Toolbox** from the context menu to activate the dialog box shown in Figure 11-4. Note that Figure 11-4 shows the Customize Toolbox dialog box with the .NET Framework Components tabs active.

Figure 11-4 shows callouts: "Available controls appear in Name column", "Namespace of control", "Assembly name containing control", "Checked controls appear in Toolbox".

Figure 11-4 Customize Toolbox dialog box

The Customize Toolbox dialog box allows you to add references to two categories of components. COM components use older ActiveX technology used by previous versions of Visual Basic. .NET Framework Components are .NET assemblies and work just like any other component.

5. Click the **.NET Framework Components** tab to activate it.

The Browse button allows you to add a reference to a Windows Control Library not already appearing in the Toolbox. The Reset button at the bottom of the dialog box removes any custom controls that were added to the Toolbox, restoring the Toolbox to its default state.

6. Click **Reset** to reset the Toolbox to its default state. A dialog box appears. Click **Yes** to confirm the reset.

7. Click **Browse** to activate an Open dialog box. Select the file named **Chapter.11\Startup11\LocalControls\bin\LocalControls.dll**. Click **Open** to add the DLL.

   This .dll file contains the Windows Control Library that you just compiled. The FractionalScrollBar control is added to the dialog box and the control is checked indicating that it will be added to the Toolbox.

8. Click **OK** to close the Customize Toolbox dialog box and add the FractionalScrollBar to the Toolbox.

   By adding a reference to the LocalControls project and the FractionalScrollBar, VB .NET added the new control to the Toolbox.

9. In the Toolbox, scroll to the bottom of the Windows Forms or General tab, depending on where you added the FractionalScrollBar. Note that the FractionalScrollBar control appears.

When you add controls to the Toolbox, the controls are added to the selected tab. Because .NET selects the General tab when you reset the Toolbox, the FractionalScrollBar control is added to the General tab, by default.

To see how the control works, you can create an instance of it on the form.

To create and examine the FractionalScrollBar control instance:

1. Create an instance of the **FractionalScrollBar** on the form. Activate the Properties window for the control instance. Note that it supports exactly the same properties as an HScrollBar. This is logical as the custom control that you created derives from the HScrollBar control.

2. Activate the Code Editor for the form. Using the Class Name and Method Name list boxes, note that the FractionalScrollBar supports the same events as the HScrollBar.

3. Delete the FractionalScrollBar control instance that you just created.

Overriding Members of an Inherited Control

At this point, the FractionalScrollBar control that you created works exactly like an intrinsic HScrollBar. In the steps that follow, you will modify the behavior of the FractionalScrollBar so that instead of operating on Integer values, it will work with fractional single precision values. To do so, you will override various methods of the HScrollBar itself.

In the derived FractionalScrollBar class, you can override existing properties and methods of the base HScrollBar class and create new properties and methods. Overriding a member of the base class is accomplished by declaring a member having the same name as a member declared in the base class. This member should be declared with the Shadows keyword so as to hide the member of the same name appearing in the underlying base class. For the FractionalScrollBar control, we shadow members of the base HScrollBar class so as to provide a new implementation that operates with fractional values. Thus, we override the Value, Minimum, Maximum, LargeChange, and SmallChange properties of the base HScrollBar class.

Examine the following statements to override the Value property of the base HScrollBar class:

```
Private msngValue As Single

Public Shadows Property Value() As Single
    Get
        Return msngValue
    End Get
    Set(ByVal Value As Single)
        msngValue = Value
        MyBase.Value = ToInt32(msngValue * _
            (10 ^ (mintPrecision)))
    End Set
End Property
```

The read-write property procedure shown in the preceding code segment has the same syntax as any other property procedure. That is, the declaration defines the property name (Value). The statements in the Get and Set blocks execute when the developer reads and writes the property's value, respectively. Through shadowing, the preceding statements override the Value property of the base HScrollBar class. The fractional value is stored in the hidden variable msngValue. When the developer reads the Value property, the statement in the Get block executes and returns the fractional value stored in the hidden variable. When the developer stores a number in the Value property, the statements in the Set block execute.

Do not be misled by the argument name in the Set block of the Value property. The procedure has the name Value. When you enter the property procedure, Intellisense technology creates the Get and Set blocks for you and uses the name Value as the argument. While we could change the name of the Value argument to avoid confusion, we will not do so to remain consistent with the Intellisense technology chosen names.

The first statement stores the fractional value in the hidden variable named msngValue. The second statement requires careful examination:

```
MyBase.Value = ToInt32(msngValue * (10 ^ (mintPrecision)))
```

As the FractionalScrollBar control inherits from the base System.Windows.Forms. HScrollBar class, you need to set the properties of that base class for the control's display to be updated. That is, if you do not set the value of the base scroll bar, the visible scroll bar's thumbs will not be updated. As the HScrollBar can only store whole numbers in its Value property, the preceding statements convert the single precision number to a whole number by multiplying the number by 10, 100, 1,000, or 10,000 based on setting of the Precision property and the variable mintPrecision. (You will create the Precision property in a moment.) In addition to shadowing the Value property, you must also shadow the other properties that operate with the Value property. These properties include the Maximum, Minimum, SmallChange, and LargeChange properties. You will override all of these properties next.

To override the members of a base control:

1. Activate the Code Editor for the module named **FractionalScrollBar.vb**, and then enter the following statements (shown in bold) immediately after the statements generated by the Win Forms Designer:

```
Win Forms Designer generated code
    Private msngValue As Single
    Private msngMinimum As Single
    Private msngMaximum As Single
    Private msngLargeChange As Single
    Private msngSmallChange As Single
    Private mintPrecision As Integer = 2
End Class
```

The preceding statements declare module-level variables to store the current value of the Value property, the Minimum property, the Maximum property, and the SmallChange and LargeChange properties. The variable mintPrecision stores the current decimal precision setting. The default decimal precision is 2.

2. Enter the following statements (shown in bold) to override the Value property:

```
Private mintPrecision As Integer = 2
Public Shadows Property Value() As Single
    Get
        Return msngValue
    End Get
    Set(ByVal Value As Single)
        msngValue = Value
        MyBase.Value = ToInt32(msngValue * _
            (10 ^ (mintPrecision)))
    End Set
End Property
```

3. Enter the following statements (shown in bold) to override the Minimum, Maximum, LargeChange, and SmallChange properties:

```
End Property
Public Shadows Property Minimum() As Single
    Get
        Return msngMinimum
    End Get
    Set(ByVal Value As Single)
        msngMinimum = Value
        MyBase.Minimum = ToInt32(msngMinimum * _
            (10 ^ (mintPrecision)))
    End Set
End Property

Public Shadows Property Maximum() As Single
    Get
        Return msngMaximum
    End Get
    Set(ByVal Value As Single)
        msngMaximum = Value
        MyBase.Maximum = ToInt32(msngMaximum * _
            (10 ^ (mintPrecision)))
    End Set
End Property

Public Shadows Property LargeChange() As Single
    Get
        Return msngLargeChange
    End Get
    Set(ByVal Value As Single)
        msngLargeChange = Value
        MyBase.LargeChange = ToInt32(msngLargeChange * _
            (10 ^ (mintPrecision)))
    End Set
End Property

Public Shadows Property SmallChange() As Single
    Get
        Return msngSmallChange
    End Get
    Set(ByVal Value As Single)
        msngSmallChange = Value
        MyBase.SmallChange = ToInt32(msngSmallChange * _
            (10 ^ (mintPrecision)))
    End Set
End Property
```

The preceding property procedures shadow the Minimum, Maximum, SmallChange, and LargeChange properties. The statements for these properties are similar to the statements in the property procedure that you created to shadow the Value property, meaning, each property has a data type of Single. When the developer reads the value of the property, the value of the corresponding hidden variable is returned. When the developer sets the value of the property, the new value is stored in the corresponding hidden variable, then the value is converted to a whole number. That whole number is stored in the corresponding property of the base HScrollBar class.

Extending Members of an Inherited Control

In addition to shadowing properties, you can declare new properties that augment those properties of the base class. The rules for creating a new property are simple: you declare a new property procedure. However, since the new property is not shadowing a property of the base class, the Shadows keyword is omitted.

Next, you will create a property named Precision. This property will store an Integer value between 1 and 4. If the developer attempts to store a value outside of this range, an exception will be thrown advising the developer that the proposed value is not valid. This property will store the decimal precision used by the other properties such as the Value, Maximum, and Minimum properties.

To create a new property:

1. Enter the following property procedure named Precision (shown in bold) after the statements that you just created:

```
End Property
Public Property Precision() As Integer
    Get
        Return mintPrecision
    End Get
    Set(ByVal Value As Integer)
        If Value < 1 Or Value > 4 Then
            Throw New _
                System.ArgumentOutOfRangeException( _
                "Value must be between 1 and 4")
        Else
            mintPrecision = Value
        End If
    End Set
End Property
```

The statements to declare the Precision property are similar to the statements you wrote to shadow the properties of the base HScrollBar. The value of the Precision property is stored in the hidden variable named mintPrecision. Note that you do not call MyBase to set a property of the base HScrollBar class because the Precision property is a new property. If the developer attempts to store a value that is not between 1 and 4, then a System.ArgumentOutOfRangeException is thrown.

11

In addition to shadowing and overriding properties, you can also override events. For an HScrollBar, the OnValueChanged method raises the ValueChanged event. In the following code segment, you will override the OnValueChanged method so as to store the new fractional value in the hidden variable msngValue.

To override an event:

1. Enter the following statements (shown in bold) to create the OnValueChanged method immediately after the property procedures that you just created:

```
End Property
Protected Overrides Sub OnValueChanged( _
    ByVal e As System.EventArgs)
    msngValue = MyBase.Value
    msngValue = ToSingle(msngValue / _
        (10 ^ (mintPrecision)))
End Sub
End Class
```

The first of the preceding statements gets the Integer value out of the base HScrollBar class. The second statement converts that value to the single precision number used by the derived class.

Before testing the FractionalScrollBar you must recompile the project. Recompiling the project containing the FractionalScrollBar causes VB .NET to regenerate the DLL. If you do not recompile the LocalControls project before creating an instance of the FractionalScrollBar on the form, the Win Forms Designer will use the old version of the DLL.

To perform the recompile:

1. Select the **LocalControls** project in the Solution Explorer.

2. Click **Build**, and then click **Rebuild LocalControls**.

3. Test the solution. Activate the Win Forms Designer for the form named **frmMain.vb**. Create an instance of the FractionalScrollBar on the form. Note that the FractionalScrollBar control appears on the General tab of the Toolbox. Activate the Properties window for the control. Note that the Precision property is set to 2, which is the default value. Try to set the Precision property to **5**, which is an invalid value. A dialog box appears as shown in Figure 11-5.

Figure 11-5   Properties Window dialog box

4. Click **Details**. The detail information about the exception appears in the message. Close the dialog box.

5. Store values in the Minimum, Maximum, and Value properties having two decimal places.

6. Delete the instance of the FractionalScrollBar from the form.

You saw briefly how to use attributes and the System.ComponentModel namespace in Chapter 3. Attributes are commonly used with controls to alter the design-time behavior of the control. For example, attributes are used to define how and where a property appears in the Properties window. Attributes are also used to supply custom property editors for a property and to perform control licensing. We discuss control attributes next.

USING ATTRIBUTES WITH CONTROLS

Attributes are used to alter the design-time behavior of custom controls. Some attributes apply to the control class itself, while other attributes apply to a particular member.

The following list describes the purpose of the attributes used in this chapter:

- The Boolean **Browsable** attribute accepts one argument that defines whether or not a property should appear in the Properties window. If the value is True, then the property appears in the Properties window. If the value is False, then the property does not appear. Hiding properties in the Properties window is useful when a property only has meaning at runtime. By default, properties are browsable.

- The **Category** attribute is relevant when the Categorized tab of the Properties window is active. The attribute accepts one String argument: the name of the category where the property should appear in the Properties window.

- The **DefaultValue** attribute allows you to specify a default value for a particular property. The property accepts one argument: the default value of the property.

- The **DefaultProperty** attribute allows you to define the property that will be selected, by default, when the user activates the Properties window. The attribute accepts one argument: the property designated as the default property. The value appears as a quoted string containing the property name. Thus, if a developer activates the control instance and presses F4 to activate the Properties window, the property designated as the default property will be selected in the Properties window.

- The **Description** attribute contains a string. The value of this string appears in the Description section at the bottom of the Properties window.

- The **Editor** attribute is used to define a class that will operate as a custom property editor. Instead of displaying data in the form of a simple value, you can create a custom property editor to display a drop-down dialog box containing a single control instance or a modal dialog box containing multiple control instances. Custom property editors are discussed later in the chapter.

- The **Localizable** attribute defines whether or not a property can be localized. Localization is used to configure applications to work with different languages.

- As you know, only certain properties appear in the Properties window when multiple instances of a control are selected. The Boolean **MergableProperty** attribute defines whether or not the property will appear in the Properties window when multiple control instances are selected. By default, properties are Mergable (the MergableProperty attribute is set to True) so this property need only be set to False, when a property should not be Mergable.

- The **RefreshProperties** attribute defines how the visual designer should refresh other properties appearing in the Properties window when the value of a particular property is changed. If set to All, the visual designer requeries all of the properties and refreshes their values in the Properties window. This setting is useful when setting one property effects the value of other properties. If set to None, the other property values are not refreshed. If set to Repaint, the Properties window is refreshed.

- The **ToolboxBitmap** attribute defines the bitmap that appears in the Toolbox. If not specified, VB .NET adds a default bitmap based on the underlying project type.

The following code segment illustrates how to set the Category attribute for a property named Precision:

```
<Category("Behavior")> _
Public Property Precision() As Integer
    ' Statements
End Property
```

All attributes are enclosed in less-than and greater-than signs, similar to the way that HTML tags are enclosed in less-than and greater-than signs. As the attribute is part of the procedure declaration, a continuation character appears after the attribute.

Multiple attributes can be applied to a particular member. The following statements show four attributes applied to the Precision property:

```
<DefaultValue(2), _
    Description("The decimal precision."), _
    Category("Behavior"), _
    MergableProperty(False)> _
Public Property Precision() As Integer
    ' Statements
End Property
```

All of the attributes specified in the preceding code segment apply to the Precision property. A comma separates each attribute, and all of the attributes combined appear between one pair of less-than and greater-than symbols.

The DefaultValue attribute is set to 2. The description appearing in the Properties window will be "The decimal precision." The Category attribute is set to "Behavior" so the property will appear in the Behavior section of the Properties window. Because the MergableProperty attribute is set to False, the property will not appear in the Properties window when multiple control instances are selected.

 You cannot embed a blank line between each attribute, or between the attributes and the member declaration, because the attributes, and the member that they describe, must all be part of the same statement.

Next you will create the attributes for properties of the FractionalScrollBar. As mentioned, some attributes, such as the ToolboxBitmap and DefaultValue attributes, apply to the class itself and are therefore part of the class declaration. Other attributes apply to a particular member and thus appear as part of that member's declaration.

To create member attributes:

1. Activate the Code Editor for the module named **FractionalScrollBar.vb**.

2. Enter the following attributes (shown in bold) for the **LargeChange** property:

```
<Description("The change in the thumb position " & _
    "when the user clicks the scroll area."), _
    Category("Behavior")> _
    Public Shadows Property LargeChange() As Single
```

The preceding statement sets the Description and Category attributes for the LargeChange property. Note the continuation characters for the textual string description.

3. Enter the following attributes (shown in bold) for the **SmallChange** property:

```
<Description("The change in the thumb position " & _
    "when the user clicks the arrows."), _
    Category("Behavior")> _
    Public Shadows Property SmallChange() As Single
```

The preceding statement sets the Description and Category attributes for the SmallChange property.

4. Enter the following Description and Category attributes (shown in bold) for the **Minimum** property:

```
<Description("The minimum position of the thumb."), _
    Category("Behavior")> _
    Public Shadows Property Minimum() As Single
```

11

5. Enter the following Description and Category attributes (shown in bold) for the **Maximum** property:

```
<Description("The maximum position of the thumb."), _
    Category("Behavior")> _
    Public Shadows Property Maximum() As Single
```

6. Enter the following Description and Category attributes (shown in bold) for the **Value** property:

```
<Description("The value of the thumb."), _
    Category("Behavior")> _
    Public Shadows Property Value() As Single
```

7. Enter the following DefaultValue, Description, and Category attributes (shown in bold) for the **Precision** property:

```
<DefaultValue(2), _
    Description("The decimal precision."), _
    Category("Behavior")> _
    Public Property Precision() As Integer
```

The preceding statement assigns the Precision property a default value of 2. It also sets the Description and Category attributes.

8. Before testing these changes you must again recompile the DLL so that the Win Forms Designer will use the correct library containing the changes. In the Solution Explorer, select the **LocalControls** project. On the menu bar, click **Build** and then click **Rebuild LocalControls**.

9. Test the solution. Create an instance of the **FractionalScrollBar** on the form. In the Properties window, activate the Precision property. Note that it appears in the Behavior section and has a default value of 2. Note also that the description appears. Test the attributes for the Minimum, Maximum, LargeChange, and SmallChange properties.

10. Delete the FractionalScrollBar control instance that you just created.

In addition to creating attributes for individual members, other attributes apply to the entire class. For example, the ToolboxBitmap and DefaultProperty attributes apply to the class rather than to an individual member.

To define class level attributes:

1. Activate the Code Editor for the module named **FractionalScrollBar.vb**, if necessary, and then enter the following statement (shown in bold) just before the class module declaration:

```
<ToolboxBitmap(".\FractionalScrollBar.bmp"), _
    DefaultProperty("Value")> _
    Public Class FractionalScrollBar
```

2. Note that a relative file name is used to specify the bitmap. For VB .NET to locate and load the bitmap, it must reside in the same folder as the assembly itself. Copy the file named FractionalScrollBar.bmp from the **Chapter.11\ Data** folder to **Chapter.11\Startup11\LocalControls\bin**.

3. Recompile the project by clicking **Build**, and then clicking **Rebuild LocalControls**.

   Note that the Toolbox does not automatically refresh its icons. Thus, the new icon specified by the ToolboxBitmap attribute will not appear in the Toolbox. To refresh the display, you must remove the control and control library from the Toolbox, and then add the library again using the same steps that you used to add the Windows Control Library the first time.

4. Activate the Win Forms Designer for the form named **frmMain.vb**. On the Toolbox, right-click the **Windows Forms** tab, and then click **Customize Toolbox** from the context menu. Click the **.NET Framework Components** tab.

5. In the Customize Toolbox dialog box, click **Reset** to restore the Toolbox to its default configuration. Click **Yes** in the dialog box to confirm the reset. Add the Windows Control Library back to the project by clicking **Browse** to activate the Open dialog box. Select the file named **Chapter.11\Startup11\ LocalControls\bin\LocalControls.dll**. Click **Open** to select the control. Click **OK** to close the Customize Toolbox dialog box.

6. Activate the Win Forms Designer for the form named **frmMain.vb**, if necessary, and then activate the Toolbox. The new icon appears in the Toolbox. Create an instance of the FractionalScrollBar on the form. Press **F4** to activate the Properties window. Note that the Value property is selected because you set the Default attribute.

7. Delete the FractionalScrollBar control instance that you just created.

By default, a property is Mergable. That is, the property will appear in the Properties window when multiple control instances are selected. Because the MergableProperty attribute is True by default, you only need to set the attribute's value when a property should not be Mergable. For the FractionalScrollBar control, you will configure the Value property so that it is not Mergable.

To define a property as not Mergable:

1. Activate the Code Editor for the module named **FractionalScrollBar.vb**, and then enter the following statement (shown in bold) to set the MergableProperty attribute for the **Value** property:

```
<Description("The value of the thumb."), _
    MergableProperty(False), _
    Category("Behavior")> _
    Public Shadows Property Value() As Single
```

11

2. Recompile the LocalControls library.

3. Test the solution. Create multiple instances of the FractionalScrollBar control on the form. Activate the Properties window. Select multiple control instances. The Value property is hidden because the MergableProperty attribute for the Value property is False.

4. Delete the control instances that you just created.

At this point the FractionalScrollBar is complete. Another way to create a custom control is to derive a control from the System.Windows.Forms.UserControl class instead of a specific Toolbox control. We discuss this next.

INHERITING FROM SYSTEM.WINDOWS.FORMS.USERCONTROL

You can inherit a control from the base class named System.Windows.Forms. UserControl. When you inherit a control from the UserControl class, VB .NET supplies a visual designer similar to the Win Forms Designer. Using this visual designer, you create instances of other controls on the UserControl.

Basically, when you create a control that derives from the UserControl class, you use a visual designer that resembles the Win Forms Designer. You create other control instances, called constituent controls, on the UserControl Designer. A **constituent control** is nothing more than an existing intrinsic control, such as a TextBox or Label, used as a basis to create another control. The reason that you can create control instances in the UserControl Designer is that the UserControl class derives from the ContainerControl class. The ContainerControl class supplies the functionality to display other control instances.

The UserControl class has the following members:

Syntax

System.Windows.Forms.UserControl class

Public Properties

■ The Boolean **DesignMode** property of the base Component class, if True, signifies that the control is in design mode. If False, the control is running.

■ The **ForeColor** and **BackColor** properties define the foreground and background colors of the control, respectively.

■ The **ClientRectangle** property returns a Rectangle structure representing the client area of the control instance.

- The **ClientSize** property returns the height and width of the client area.

Public Methods

- The **BringToFront** and **SendToBack** methods reorder the control instance in the z-order.

Public Events

- The UserControl supports mouse events such as **MouseOver**, **MouseUp**, and **MouseDown**.

- The UserControl supports keyboard events such as **KeyUp**, **KeyDown**, and **KeyPress**.

- The **Resize** event fires when the developer resizes the UserControl.

Next you will create a control that is comprised of a constituent TextBox and a constituent Label. Thus, you will add another control to the LocalControls project. Note that a User Control Library project can contain any number of custom controls. It need not contain only one. Thus, each custom control you add to a User Control Library project will become part of the same assembly.

To add a UserControl to a project:

1. Make sure that the project named **LocalControls** is active. Activate the project by clicking it in the Solution Explorer.

2. Add a UserControl to the project by clicking **Project**, and then clicking **Add User Control**.

3. In the Add New Item–LocalControls dialog box, click **User Control** in the Templates pane, if necessary. Set the name to **SuperText.vb**, and then click **Open** to create the UserControl and add it to the project.

When you create the UserControl, VB .NET displays the control in a window resembling the Win Forms Designer. This window is called the UserControl Designer and is shown in Figure 11-6. Note that Figure 11-6 shows the UserControl Designer after the constituent TextBox and Label controls have been added.

Developing a control derived from the UserControl class is quite similar to creating control instances on a form, setting the properties for those control instances, and creating event handlers. In this project, you will create a UserControl that is made up of a constituent text box and a constituent label. You create these constituent control instances with the UserControl Designer in the same way that you create control instances on a form. That is, you activate the UserControl Designer and then, using the intrinsic Toolbox controls, create the visual interface for your control.

Figure 11-6   UserControl Designer

To create a UserControl based on constituent controls:

1. Activate the Code Editor for the module named **SuperText.vb**, and then enter the following statements (shown in bold) to enable strict type checking and to import the System.ComponentModel and System.IO namespaces:

```
Option Explicit On
Option Strict On
Imports System.ComponentModel
Imports System.IO
Public Class SuperText
```

2. Activate the UserControl Designer for the control named **SuperText.vb**.

3. Using the Toolbox, create instances of the **Label** and **TextBox** controls as shown in Figure 11-6.

4. Set the Multiline property of the constituent TextBox control to **True**.

   It does not matter exactly where the constituent control instances are positioned in the UserControl Designer, as you will write statements to position and resize them in a moment.

5. Rebuild the **LocalControls** project. Again, the DLL is not regenerated until the Windows Control Library project is built. Thus, the SuperText control will not appear in the Toolbox until the library is rebuilt.

While you create the constituent controls on the UserControl, consider what happens when the developer creates an instance of that control on the form and resizes the control instance. Even though the developer can create an instance of your control (SuperText) on the form and resize it, the constituent controls will not be resized automatically. The following steps illustrate the problem.

To create an instance of a UserControl on a form:

1. Activate the Win Forms Designer for the form named **frmMain.vb**. Create an instance of the SuperText control on the form as shown in Figure 11-7. Note that by default, the SuperText control appears on the Windows Forms tab of the Toolbox.

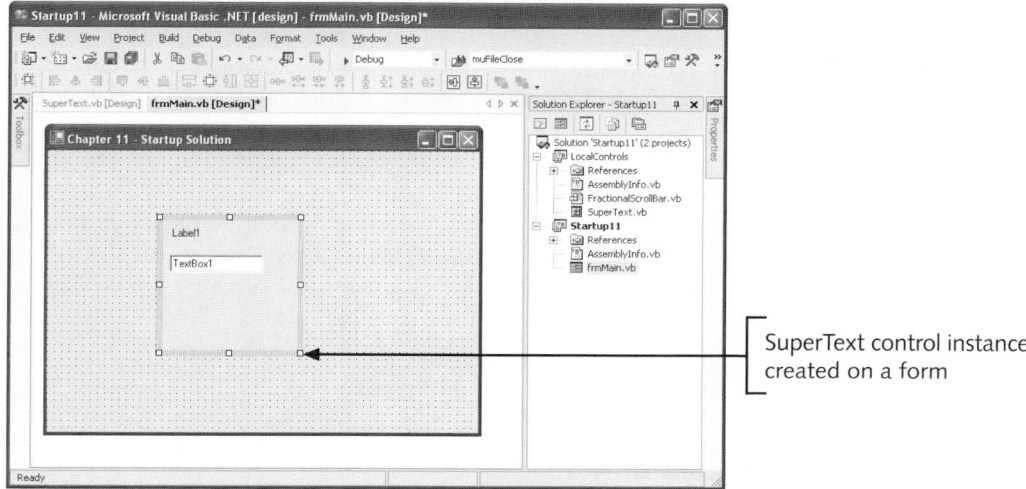

SuperText control instance created on a form

Figure 11-7   SuperText control instance created on a form

2. Resize the control instance.

In the previous step sequence, note that as you resized the control instance, the size of the constituent control instances did not change. To understand why, consider that the UserControl class has members just as a form or any other class has members. That is, just as a form supports properties and events, so too does the UserControl. Thus, you can set properties of the UserControl, and create event handlers just as you do for an ordinary form.

To view the properties exposed by the UserControl class:

1. Activate the Properties window for the SuperText control instance that you just created.

    Note that several common properties appear in the Properties window, including the BackColor, ForeColor, Dock, and Anchor properties. These are properties of the UserControl itself. These properties are commonly referred to as **ambient properties**, however, these properties do not represent the properties of the constituent TextBox or Label controls.

2. Delete the SuperText control instance that you just created.

11

In the following steps, you will handle the Resize event of the UserControl itself. This event handler will contain the necessary statements to resize the constituent Label and TextBox control instances when the developer resizes the UserControl. How you decide to resize the constituent control instances is somewhat subjective. That is, you need to decide, for example, whether or not to change the height of the text box or label when the user changes the height of the UserControl itself. You could change the height of one control instance or the other, or adjust the height of both control instances. For the SuperText control, the height of the label will remain fixed while the height of the text box will be adjusted. In addition, when the developer changes the width of the control instance, the width of the constituent control instances will be adjusted to fill the width of the UserControl itself.

To handle a UserControl event:

1. Activate the Code Editor for the module named **SuperText.vb**. Create the Resize event handler by clicking **(Base Class Events)** in the Class Name list box, and then clicking **Resize** in the Method Name list box. Enter the following statements in the Resize event handler:

```
Dim pintWidth As Integer
Dim pintTextHeight As Integer
pintWidth = Me.Width
pintTextHeight = Me.Height - Label1.Height
TextBox1.Top = 25
TextBox1.Height = pintTextHeight
TextBox1.Width = pintWidth
TextBox1.Left = 0

Label1.Top = 0
Label1.Width = pintWidth
Label1.Left = 0
Label1.Height = 24
```

The preceding statements are relatively simple. The variable Me.Width contains the current width of the UserControl itself. As always, the Me keyword references the current instance of the class. The width of the constituent label and text box are set to this value. The height of the label is fixed. The height of the text box is set to the height of the UserControl minus the height of the label.

2. Recompile the LocalControls project.

3. Create an instance of the SuperText control on the form. Resize the control instance. Note that as you resize the SuperText control instance the constituent controls are resized accordingly.

4. Delete the control instance that you just created.

An important point needs to be made at this time. When you, as the developer, create an instance of a control on the form and set its properties, VB .NET is in design mode. However, the control itself is actually running. That is, when you resize the control instance, the Resize event fires for the running control instance and the control itself is resized. Consider also what happens when you set a property for a control instance using the Properties window. Again, even though VB .NET is in design mode, the control is running. Thus, when you set a value for a property using the Properties window, the statements in the corresponding property procedure execute.

Having created the constituent controls, you then define the properties that you want to expose to the developer, along with any events that you want to expose through aggregation and delegation.

DELEGATING AND AGGREGATING PROPERTIES

The constituent TextBox and Label control instances that you created on the UserControl are hidden from the developer using your control. If you examine the code automatically generated by the UserControl Designer, you will see that it resembles the code generated by the Win Forms Designer. That is, the automatically generated statements to create the constituent control instances on the UserControl appear in a #Region #EndRegion block. The same statements appear to declare the variables and create the control instances.

Examine the following automatically generated statements:

```
Public Class SuperText
    Inherits System.Windows.Forms.UserControl

#Region " Windows Form Designer generated code "
    ' Statements
    Friend WithEvents Label1 As System.Windows.Forms.Label
    Friend WithEvents TextBox1 As _
        System.Windows.Forms.TextBox
    ' Statements
    Me.Label1 = New System.Windows.Forms.Label()
    Me.TextBox1 = New System.Windows.Forms.TextBox()
    ' Statements
#End Region
End Class
```

As you can see from the preceding statements, the constituent Label and TextBox control instances are hidden from the developer because they are declared with the Friend access modifier. Remember that the Friend access modifier declares variables that are not visible outside of the current assembly.

You expose selected properties to the developer using two techniques, delegation and aggregation, as described in the following list:

- **Delegation** exposes a property of a constituent control. For example, you may delegate the Text property of the constituent TextBox control to the developer so that the hidden Text property of the text box can be read and written.

- **Aggregation** is used to group properties when building a control from multiple constituent controls. For example, both the Label and TextBox controls support common properties such as ForeColor. Through aggregation, when the developer sets the value of a property such as ForeColor, the property's value is set for both the constituent label and text boxes.

Figure 11-8 illustrates the processes of delegation and aggregation.

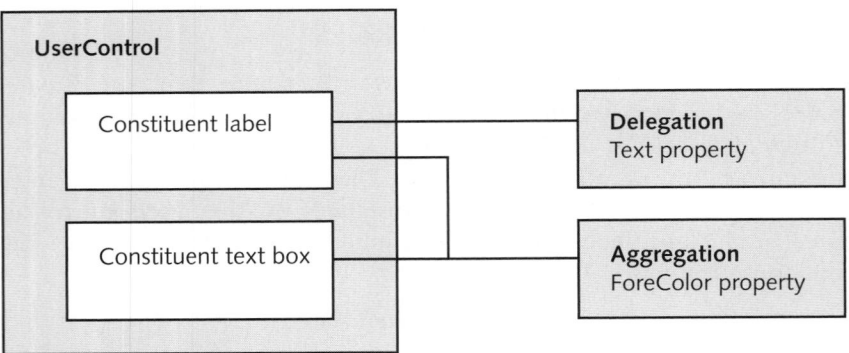

Figure 11-8   Delegation and aggregation

As shown in Figure 11-8, the Text property of the constituent text box is delegated. However, the ForeColor property of both the constituent text box and label are aggregated into a single property.

In the following steps, you will delegate and aggregate selected properties to see how the process works. First you will delegate the Text property of the text box.

To delegate a property:

1. Activate the Code Editor for the module named **SuperText.vb**, and then enter the following statements (shown in bold) in the class module:

```
Windows Form Designer generated code
<Browsable(True)> _
Public Shadows Property Text() As String
    Get
        Return TextBox1.Text
    End Get
```

```
    Set(ByVal Value As String)
        TextBox1.Text = Value
    End Set
End Property
```

The preceding statements delegate the Text property of the constituent TextBox control using a property procedure. The syntax of the property procedure is the same as you have seen before. However, instead of declaring a hidden variable to store the value of the property, the Text property of the constituent text box is used. Thus, when the developer reads the property's value, the statement in the Get block executes and the value of the Text property of the constituent text box is returned. When the developer stores a value in the Text property, the statement in the Set block executes and the value is stored in the Text property of the constituent text box. By setting the Browsable attribute to True, the property will appear in the Properties window.

2. Recompile the LocalControls project before testing it. Activate the Win Forms Designer for the form named **frmMain.vb**.

3. Create an instance of the SuperText control on the form. Activate the Properties window for the SuperText control instance. Note that the Text property you delegated appears in the Properties window. Store a new value in the Text property. That text appears in the control instance created on the form.

4. Delete the SuperText control instance that you just created.

At this point in the control's development, there exists a problem. Both the constituent Label and TextBox control instances have a Text property. To set the property of the constituent label, you must use a different name, such as TextPrompt, thereby creating a new property.

To create a new property:

1. Activate the Code Editor for the module named **SuperText.vb**, and then enter the following statements (shown in bold) in the class module:

```
Public Shadows Property Text() As String
    ' Statements
End Property
<Browsable(True)> _
Public Property TextPrompt() As String
    Get
        Return Label1.Text
    End Get
    Set(ByVal Value As String)
        Label1.Text = Value
    End Set
End Property
```

11

2. Recompile the LocalControls project before testing it. Create an instance of the SuperText control on the form. Activate the Properties window. Note that the TextPrompt property appears. Delete the SuperText control instance that you just created.

Aggregation works much like delegation. Using aggregation, the developer sets the value for a single property. Your code then sets the property's value for multiple control instances—in this case, the constituent label and text box. Next you will aggregate the TextAlign property for the constituent Label and TextBox controls.

To aggregate a property:

1. Activate the Code Editor for the module named **SuperText.vb**, and then enter the following statements (shown in bold) in the class module:

```
Public Shadows Property TextPrompt() As String
    ' Statements
End Property
<Browsable(True)> _
Public Property TextAlign() As HorizontalAlignment
    Get
        Return TextBox1.TextAlign
    End Get
    Set(ByVal Value As HorizontalAlignment)
        Select Case Value
            Case HorizontalAlignment.Center
                Label1.TextAlign = _
                    ContentAlignment.MiddleCenter
            Case HorizontalAlignment.Left
                Label1.TextAlign = _
                    ContentAlignment.MiddleLeft
            Case HorizontalAlignment.Right
                Label1.TextAlign = _
                    ContentAlignment.MiddleRight
        End Select
        TextBox1.TextAlign = Value
    End Set
End Property
```

One important point needs to be made about the preceding property procedure. While both the TextBox and Label controls support a property named TextAlign, the two properties have different data types. Thus, the data type of the TextAlign property was chosen as HorizontalAlignment, the data type for the TextBox control. The Select Case statement converts the value to the correct data type for the constituent label.

2. Recompile the solution before testing it. Activate the Win Forms Designer for the form named **frmMain.vb**. Create an instance of the SuperText control on the form. Activate the Properties window for the control instance that you just created.

Note that the TextAlign property that you aggregated appears. Note also that the possible values of the property appear in a list box. When the data type of a property is an enumeration such as HorizontalAlignment, the Properties window automatically displays the valid enumeration values.

3. Set the TextAlign property to **Center**. The alignment of the text is updated in both the constituent Label and constituent TextBox control instances.

4. Delete the SuperText control instance from the form.

As a further example of aggregating a property, you will aggregate the ForeColor and BackColor properties of the constituent TextBox and Label control instances.

To aggregate a property:

1. Activate the Code Editor for the module named **SuperText.vb**, and then enter the following statements (shown in bold) in the class module:

```
Public Property TextAlign() As HorizontalAlignment
    ' Statements
End Property
<Browsable(True)> _
Public Shadows Property ForeColor() As Color
    Get
        Return TextBox1.ForeColor
    End Get
    Set(ByVal Value As Color)
        TextBox1.ForeColor = Value
        Label1.ForeColor = Value
    End Set
End Property

<Browsable(True)> _
Public Shadows Property BackColor() As Color
    Get
        Return TextBox1.BackColor
    End Get
    Set(ByVal Value As Color)
        TextBox1.BackColor = Value
        Label1.BackColor = Value
    End Set
End Property
```

2. Test the solution by recompiling the LocalControls project, and then creating a SuperText control instance on the form. Set the **ForeColor** property to a color of your choosing. Note that because the property has a data type of Color, VB .NET displays the Color property editor.

3. Delete the control instance that you just created.

One final point needs to be discussed about the UserControl that you have created. Properties such as AutoScroll, AutoScrollMargin, and AutoScrollMinSize appear in the

11

Properties window. However, your control, as it exists, is not a scrollable container control. Thus, you should hide these properties from the developer. To hide a property, you create a property procedure that shadows a property of the base class, and set the Browsable attribute to False. In addition, you must prevent a developer from accessing this property at runtime.

Examine the following statements:

```
If Not Me.DesignMode Then
    Throw New System.NotImplementedException()
End If
```

The preceding statements check that the control is not in design mode by testing the DesignMode property of the UserControl. If the control is running, a NotImplementedException is thrown to the developer.

To hide a property from a developer:

1. Activate the Code Editor for the module named **SuperText.vb**, and then enter the following statements (shown in bold) in the class module:

```
Public Shadows Property BackColor() As Color
    ' Statements
End Property
<Browsable(False)> _
Public Shadows Property AutoScroll() As Boolean
    Get
        If Not Me.DesignMode Then
            Throw New System.NotImplementedException()
        End If
    End Get
    Set(ByVal Value As Boolean)
        If Not Me.DesignMode Then
            Throw New System.NotImplementedException()
        End If
    End Set
End Property
```

   The preceding statements hide the AutoScroll property by setting the Browsable attribute to False, thereby causing the property to be hidden from the Properties window. If the control is running, then an exception is thrown.

2. Test the solution by recompiling the LocalControls project, and then creating a SuperText control instance on the form. Note that the AutoScroll property does not appear in the Properties window.

3. Delete the control instance.

In reality, you would need to create nearly the same property procedures for all other properties that you wanted to hide, including AutoScrollMargin and AutoScrollMinSize. However, we have omitted those steps for brevity.

INHERITING FROM SYSTEM.WINDOWS.FORMS.CONTROL

You can create a control from scratch by inheriting a class from System.Windows.Forms. Control. When you create a control from scratch, you must write the statements to paint the control. Creating a control from scratch is the most difficult control creation technique.

When you created a control that inherited from an intrinsic control, such as an HScrollBar or UserControl, the base class supplied significant functionality related to drawing and refreshing the control instance drawn on the form. Creating a control from scratch involves creating a class that inherits from the System.Windows.Forms.Control class.

Note that the intrinsic controls appearing in the Toolbox and the UserControl class all ultimately derive from System.Windows.Forms.Control. The members of the Control class define the size of the control instance as it will appear on a visual surface such as a form. Other members define the color and appearance of the control. Note, however, that the Control class itself does not define how the control will be painted. The properties of the Control class are similar to the properties of the UserControl class and are not presented in detail here.

The steps to derive a control from the Control class are similar to the steps you used to create a class derived from an intrinsic Toolbox control or the UserControl class. You add a new class to the project that derives from the Control class, and then add it to the Toolbox.

To create a control from scratch:

1. Add a new class module named Box to the LocalControls project by selecting the **LocalControls** project in the Solution Explorer and then clicking **Project**, **Add Class**. In the Add New Item–LocalControls dialog box, name the class **Box.vb**, and then click **Open** to close the dialog box and create the class module.

2. In the Code Editor, enter the following statements (shown in bold):

```
Option Explicit On
Option Strict On
Imports System.ComponentModel
Imports System.Drawing.Design
Imports System.Windows.Forms.Design
Public Class Box
    Inherits System.Windows.Forms.Control
End Class
```

3. Test the solution by recompiling the LocalControls project. Reset the Toolbox as you have done in previous steps. Add the LocalControls assembly back to the project so as to add the Box control to the Toolbox.

4. Create an instance of the Box control on the form. While the Box control appears, it displays no visible contents. You will add content in the next step sequence. Delete the Box control instance.

11

Having created the Box control, you can define new properties and override those properties supplied by the Control class itself. The syntax to create a property procedure for a class derived from the Control class is the same as the syntax to create any other property procedure. For this control, you will create two properties. The Thickness property will define the thickness of the line surrounding the control, and the LineColor property will define the color of the line that will be drawn around the border of the control.

To create properties for a control:

1. In the module named Box.vb, enter the following statements (shown in bold) to declare the LineColor and Thickness properties:

```
Public Class Box
    Inherits System.Windows.Forms.Control
    Private mcolLine As System.Drawing.Color
    Private mintThickness As Integer = 1
    Public Property LineColor() As System.Drawing.Color
        Get
            Return mcolLine
        End Get
        Set(ByVal Value As System.Drawing.Color)
            mcolLine = Value
            Me.Invalidate()
        End Set
    End Property

    Public Property Thickness() As Integer
        Get
            Return mintThickness
        End Get
        Set(ByVal Value As Integer)
            mintThickness = Value
            Me.Invalidate()
        End Set
    End Property
End Class
```

The preceding statements declare the property procedures for the LineColor and Thickness properties. The current property values are stored in the corresponding hidden variables. Note that when the properties are set, the Invalidate method is called. Calling Invalidate forces VB .NET to fire the Paint event for the control, thereby causing the control instance to be redrawn. Conceptually, the process is the same as calling the Invalidate method for a form. You will develop the code for the Paint event next.

If you were to test the control at this point, you would not see the line drawn surrounding the control instance. You must write the statements to do this. Thus, you must override the OnPaint event of the Control class. You will create the code for the Protected OnPaint event to draw a rectangle around the region of the control instance.

To handle OnPaint events:

1. Enter the following statements in the **Box** class to override the OnPaint event:

```
Protected Overrides Sub OnPaint(ByVal e As _
    System.Windows.Forms.PaintEventArgs)
    MyBase.OnPaint(e)
    Dim penCurrent As New Pen(Me.LineColor, mintThickness)
    Dim pintX As Integer = Me.ClientRectangle.X
    Dim pintY As Integer = Me.ClientRectangle.Y
    Dim pintHeight As Integer = _
    Me.ClientRectangle.Height - 2
    Dim pintWidth As Integer = Me.ClientRectangle.Width - 2
    Dim recCurrent As New Rectangle(pintX, pintY, _
        pintWidth, pintHeight)
    e.Graphics.DrawRectangle(penCurrent, recCurrent)
End Sub
```

The preceding statements override the OnPaint event for the Box control and calculate the size of the control. This size is used to draw a bordered rectangle around the control by creating a new instance of the Rectangle class, and then calling the DrawRectangle method. Note that drawing is fully discussed in Chapter 12.

2. Test the solution by recompiling the LocalControls project. Create an instance of the Box control on the form. Using the Properties window, set the Line Color property to **Black**. The control appears with a black border, as shown in Figure 11-9.

11

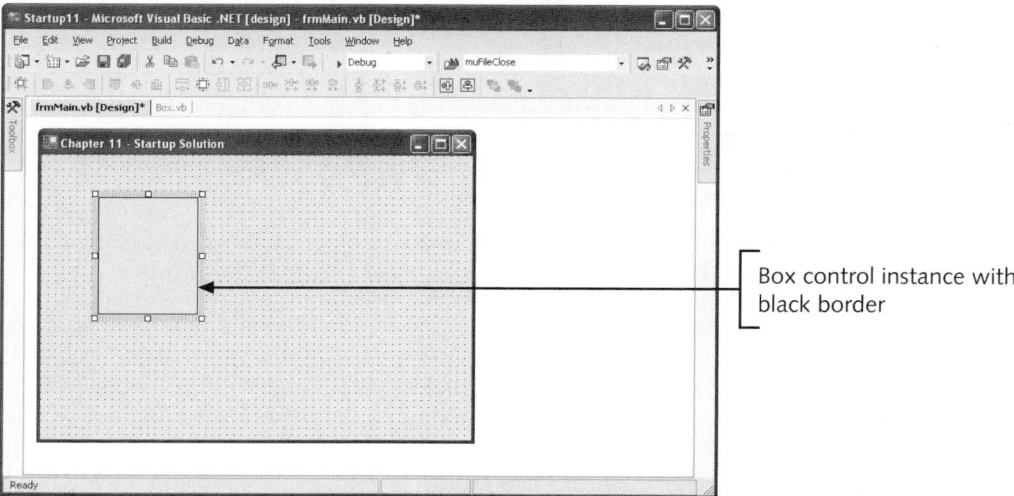

Figure 11-9　Creating the Box control instance on the form

3. Delete the Box control instance.

At this point, the control does not paint correctly as it is resized. To solve this problem, you must advise VB .NET that the control instance needs to be repainted when it is resized. You accomplish this task by invalidating the control when the developer resizes it.

To force a control to repaint when resized:

1. Activate the Code Editor for the module named **Box.vb**. Enter the following statements to handle the OnResize event for the Box control:

```
Protected Overrides Sub OnResize( _
    ByVal e As System.EventArgs)
    Me.Invalidate()
End Sub
```

2. Recompile the Local Controls project and test the solution. Activate the Win Forms Designer for the form named **frmMain.vb**. Create an instance of the Box control on the form. Resize the control instance. The border resizes as the control instance is resized.

3. Delete the control instance that you just created.

CREATING A CUSTOM PROPERTY EDITOR

You have seen that VB .NET displays custom property editors for properties having specific data types. If a property has a data type of Color, VB .NET will automatically display the Color property editor in the Properties window. In addition to using the various property editors supplied by VB .NET, you can also create your own custom property editor. Creating a custom property editor requires that you use two different namespaces, as described in the following list:

- The **System.Drawing.Design** namespace contains classes that define existing property editors. For example, there exist classes for Color, Font, and Image editors. In addition, the UITypeEditor class supplies the base class from which you create your own custom property editor.

- The classes of the **System.Windows.Forms.Design** namespace allow you to extend the design-time support for forms and controls.

When you create a custom property editor, you are essentially customizing the design-time environment supplied by VB .NET. To illustrate, consider what happens when you set a property such as ForeColor. Instead of making you enter a color manually, VB .NET displays a drop-down menu allowing you to select a color from a list of colors. Thus, VB .NET has created a custom property editor in which you set properties having a data type of Color. Custom property editors also exist for setting fonts and for docking. Figure 11-10 illustrates how the general process works.

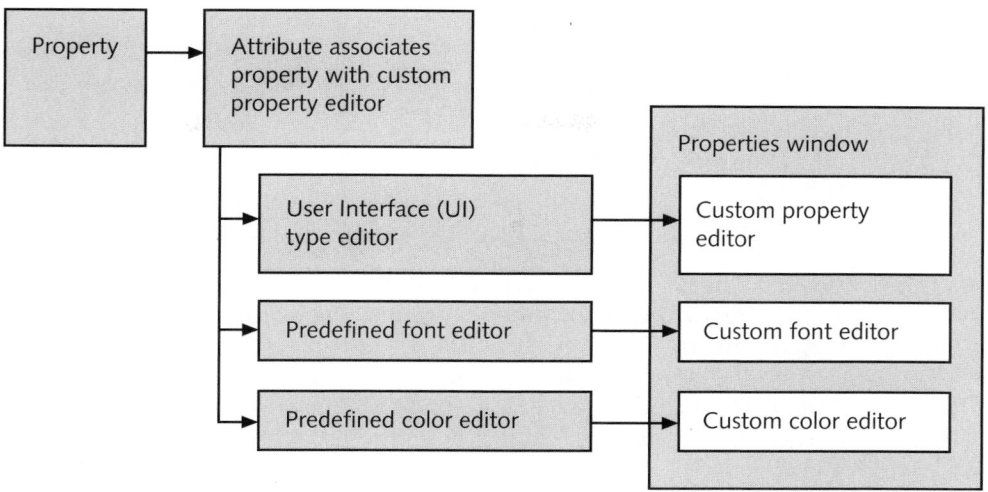

Figure 11-10   Organization of the VB .NET design time environment

As shown in Figure 11-10, the design-time environment uses attributes to determine whether or not a property editor is associated with a particular property. If so, then that editor is used to edit the property. You can create your own custom property editor or use property editors defined by .NET itself.

Creating and using a custom property editor and associating it with an existing property is a two-step process. First, you create a class that derives from the UITypeEditor class. Note that predefined property editors such as the Color and Font editors are derived from the UITypeEditor class. Second, you supply an attribute to a specific property so that the VB .NET design-time environment will be able to use the custom property editor.

Examine the following statements to associate the Thickness property with the custom property editor named ThicknessEditor:

```
<Editor(GetType(ThicknessEditor), GetType(UITypeEditor))> _
    Public Property Thickness() As Integer
```

The preceding attribute, named Editor, specifies that the Properties window should use the class named ThicknessEditor as the design-time editor for the Thickness property. The constructor accepts two arguments: the first contains the type (the class named ThicknessEditor) that will be used as the custom property editor, and the second contains the base type from which the custom property editor derives. Thus, the preceding attribute defines the ThicknessEditor class as the editor and UITypeEditor as the base class. The GetType method returns the type of a particular class.

11

Having defined the Editor attribute, the next step is to define the ThicknessEditor class itself, which must inherit from the base UITypeEditor class, as shown in the following statements:

```
Public Class ThicknessEditor
    Inherits UITypeEditor
End Class
```

The UITypeEditor class supplies two methods that are significant in creating a custom property editor, as described in the following list:

- The **GetEditStyle** method determines the editor style used to edit the specified property. Presently, VB .NET supports two editor styles. A DropDown style editor will display a drop-down menu within the region of the Properties window. The editors for the Color and TextAlign properties are DropDown style editors. A Modal style editor causes the Properties window to display a build button. Clicking the build button displays a modal dialog box. Collection editors, such as the ToolBarButton Collection editor that you have used to create the buttons on a ToolBar control instance, are Modal style editors.

- The **EditValue** method is responsible for creating the control instance that will be used to edit a value in the Properties window. For example, you may create a ListBox control instance that will appear as a DropDown style editor.

Figure 11-11 illustrates the operation of a custom property editor.

When the developer activates the Properties window for a control instance, VB .NET calls the GetEditStyle method for all of the registered custom property editors for the underlying control type. Remember, a custom property editor is registered by defining the Editor attribute for a particular property. When the developer begins to edit the property, VB .NET calls the EditValue method to edit the property. The EditValue method returns the new property setting, which VB .NET then displays in the Properties window.

First we examine the GetEditStyle method, and then we examine the EditValue method. The following statements override the GetEditStyle method of the base UITypeEditor class:

```
Public Overloads Overrides Function GetEditStyle( _
    ByVal context As _
    System.ComponentModel.ITypeDescriptorContext) _
    As System.Drawing.Design.UITypeEditorEditStyle

    If Not (context Is Nothing) _
        AndAlso Not (context.Instance Is Nothing) Then
        Return UITypeEditorEditStyle.DropDown
    Else
        Return MyBase.GetEditStyle(context)
    End If
End Function
```

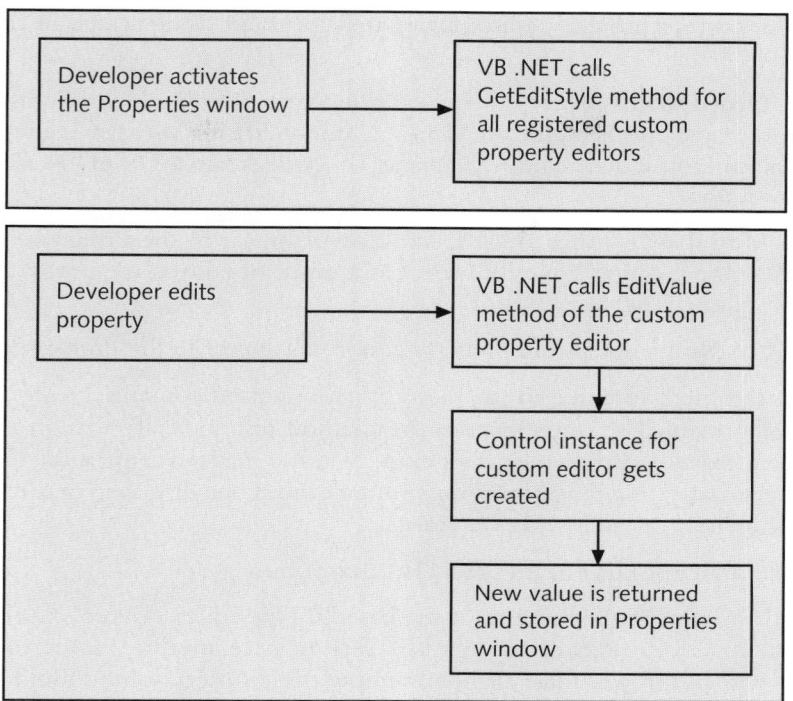

Figure 11-11   Operation of a custom property editor

VB .NET calls the GetEditStyle method to determine how the Properties window should display the custom property editor. Note that the data type of the argument to the GetEditStyle method is ITypeDescriptorContext. This argument provides information about the container, in this case the Win Forms Designer. If the context argument is Nothing, then the container cannot support this interface. In other words, the container cannot display the custom property editor. The reason for this test is simple. In this case, your control is being hosted in the Win Forms Designer, which does support custom property editors. However, suppose that your control was being hosted inside of Internet Explorer. In this situation, Internet Explorer does not support this interface so the context would have a value of Nothing.

The Instance property of the context argument supplies a reference to the control instance that invoked this method. The preceding code segment tests that the interface is available (context is Nothing), and then tests that the control instance is available (context.Instance is Nothing). If both are available, then the EditStyle is set to DropDown. Otherwise, the EditStyle is set to the EditStyle of the container itself. In other words, by calling MyBase. GetEditStyle, VB .NET will use the property editor defined by the base class.

11

Three types of custom property editor styles are supported, as described in the following list:

- If a **DropDown** style editor is used, the Properties window will display a list arrow at the right side of the Value column. Clicking that list arrow causes an in-place DropDown editor to appear. You will create a DropDown editor in this section.

- If a **Modal** style editor is used, ellipses will appear in the Properties window and a modal dialog box will appear as a result of editing the property. The Font editor is a Modal editor.

- If set to **None**, no custom property editor will appear in the Properties window.

The context argument supplied to the GetEditStyle method contains a reference to the associated component. The statements in the method test to verify that an instance of the component exists. If an instance does exist, then the method returns the DropDown editor style type indicating that a drop-down menu should be displayed in the Properties window, as shown in the following statement:

```
Return UITypeEditorEditStyle.DropDown
```

Overriding the GetEditStyle method of the base UITypeEditor class solves only part of the problem. In addition to creating the GetEditStyle method so as to return a DropDown style editor, you must also define how the property value should be edited. This task is the responsibility of the EditValue method of the base UITypeEditor class. Fundamentally, the purpose of the EditValue method is to create an instance of a subordinate control, such as a list box, that will appear in the Properties window. The EditValue method is also responsible for configuring that subordinate control instance. Note that a custom property editor having a DropDown style can only display a single control instance. Thus, you cannot create a drop-down property editor with two controls, such as a list box and a button.

In this solution, you will display a list box containing the possible values for the Thickness property. These values will be displayed in a subordinate list box. Examine the following declaration and arguments to the EditValue method:

```
Public Overloads Overrides Function EditValue( _
    ByVal context As _
    System.ComponentModel.ITypeDescriptorContext, _
    ByVal provider As System.IServiceProvider, _
    ByVal value As Object) _
    As Object
```

The first argument to the EditValue method has a data type of ITypeDescriptorContext. The Instance property of ITypeDescriptorContext returns the instance of the class that made this request—in this case, the instance of the Box control. The Container property returns a reference to the container—in this case, the Win Forms Designer itself.

The second argument is of type IServiceProvider. A service provider supplies support for other objects. It is through a service provider that the Win Forms Designer is able to display the drop-down control, as you will see in a moment.

Examine the following statements that appear in the EditValue method:

```
If (context Is Nothing) Or (context.Instance Is _
    Nothing) Or (provider Is Nothing) Then
        Return value
End If
```

The preceding If statement verifies that the component exists and has a container. In addition, the statement tests for a valid service provider. If there is a valid service provider, then the following statements execute (these statements also appear in the EditValue method):

```
Dim wfes As IWindowsFormsEditorService
wfes = CType(provider.GetService( _
    GetType(IWindowsFormsEditorService)), _
    IWindowsFormsEditorService)
If wfes Is Nothing Then
    Return value
End If
```

The provider argument is of type IServiceProvider. The second of the preceding statements returns the service provider by calling the GetService method of the provider. If the service provider can be found, then the variable wfes contains a reference to that service provider. All the preceding code does is to test that the container supports the service to display the custom property editor. If it does, then the following statements execute to actually create and configure the ListBox control instance that will appear in the Properties window:

```
lstThickness = New ListBox()
lstThickness.Size = New Size(100, 200)
lstThickness.Items.Add(1)
lstThickness.Items.Add(2)
lstThickness.Items.Add(3)
lstThickness.Items.Add(4)
wfes.DropDownControl(lstThickness)
```

The purpose of all but the last of the preceding statements should be obvious. They create a new instance of the ListBox control and add items to it. The final statement associates the ListBox control instance with the service provider. It is this final statement that displays the ListBox control instance in the region of the Properties window.

The preceding statements configure and display the ListBox control instance as a custom property editor. Next you must copy the selected item out of the list box and return that value as the property's value as shown in the following statements:

```
EditValue = _
    System.Convert.ToInt32( _
    lstThickness.SelectedItem.ToString)
lstThickness.Dispose()
lstThickness = Nothing
```

The value of the selected list box item is retrieved, and then returned to the calling procedure. Finally, the last two statements destroy the instance of the ListBox control.

The final step in the process is to close the drop-down menu, as the custom property editor does not perform this task automatically. In the following code segment, we close the drop-down menu when the user releases the mouse button. Thus, we handle the MouseUp event for the ListBox control instance as shown in the following statements:

```
Private Sub lstThickness_MouseUp( _
    ByVal sender As Object, _
    ByVal e As System.Windows.Forms.MouseEventArgs) _
    Handles lstThickness.MouseUp
    If Not (wfes Is Nothing) Then
        wfes.CloseDropDown()
    End If
End Sub
```

As shown in the preceding code segment, the If statement verifies that the service provider exists. If it does, then the CloseDropDown method is called to close the drop-down menu.

Next you will create the custom property editor for the Box control.

To create a custom property editor:

1. Activate the Code Editor for the module named **Box.vb**, and then enter the following statements (shown in bold) in the class declaration so as to specify the Editor attribute for the Thickness property:

```
<Editor(GetType(ThicknessEditor), GetType(UITypeEditor))> _
    Public Property Thickness() As Integer
```

2. Create the ThicknessEditor class by entering the following statements as a nested class within the Box class:

```
Public Class ThicknessEditor
    Inherits UITypeEditor

    Public Overloads Overrides Function GetEditStyle( _
        ByVal context As _
        System.ComponentModel.ITypeDescriptorContext) _
        As System.Drawing.Design.UITypeEditorEditStyle
```

```
            If Not (context Is Nothing) AndAlso Not _
                (context.Instance Is Nothing) Then
                Return UITypeEditorEditStyle.DropDown
            Else
                Return MyBase.GetEditStyle(context)
            End If
        End Function

        Private WithEvents lstThickness As ListBox
        Private wfes As IWindowsFormsEditorService

        Public Overloads Overrides Function EditValue( _
            ByVal context As _
            System.ComponentModel.ITypeDescriptorContext, _
            ByVal provider As System.IServiceProvider, _
            ByVal value As Object) _
            As Object
            If (context Is Nothing) Or _
                (context.Instance Is Nothing) _
                Or (provider Is Nothing) Then
                Return value
            End If
            wfes = CType(provider.GetService( _
                GetType(IWindowsFormsEditorService)), _
                IWindowsFormsEditorService)
            If wfes Is Nothing Then
                Return value
            End If
            lstThickness = New ListBox()
            lstThickness.Size = New Size(100, 200)
            lstThickness.Items.Add(1)
            lstThickness.Items.Add(2)
            lstThickness.Items.Add(3)
            lstThickness.Items.Add(4)
            wfes.DropDownControl(lstThickness)

            Return(System.Convert.ToInt32( _
                lstThickness.SelectedItem.ToString))
            lstThickness.Dispose()
            lstThickness = Nothing
        End Function

        Private Sub lstThickness_MouseUp( _
            ByVal sender As Object, _
            ByVal e As System.Windows.Forms.MouseEventArgs) _
            Handles lstThickness.MouseUp
```

11

```
        If Not (wfes Is Nothing) Then
            wfes.CloseDropDown()
        End If
    End Sub
End Class
```

3. Recompile the LocalControls project. Create an instance of the Box control on the form. Activate the Properties window for the control instance, and then set the Thickness property to a value of your choosing. The custom property editor that you created appears. Figure 11-12 shows the custom property editor.

Figure 11-12   Custom property editor

4. Delete the instance of the Box control that you created.

CONTROL LICENSING

When you create and distribute a control, you will likely want to prevent any unauthorized use of that control. You have two options to supply licensing for a control: you can use the built-in license provider supplied by VB .NET, or you can create your own custom license provider. This section of the chapter discusses the built-in license provider supplied by VB .NET, the Environment class, and how to create a custom license provider.

Using the Built-in LicFileLicenseProvider

The easiest way to license a control is to use the LicenseProvider attribute and the built-in LicFileLicenseProvider class. Examine the following attribute to use the built-in license provider for the SuperText class:

```
<LicenseProvider(GetType(LicFileLicenseProvider))> _
Public Class SuperText
```

As shown in the preceding statement, the LicenseProvider attribute creates an instance of the built-in LicFileLicenseProvider class. The LicenseProvider constructor accepts one argument: the class that manages the license itself. In the preceding statement, the predefined class named LicFileLicenseProvider is used. Having specified the built-in license provider, the next step in the process is to determine whether or not the developer has a valid license. This task is accomplished by calling the Validate method of the LicenseManager class. The shared LicenseManager class belongs to the System. ComponentModel namespace.

Examine the following code:

```
Private licCurrent As License
Public Sub New()
    MyBase.New()
    InitializeComponent()
    licCurrent = _
        LicenseManager.Validate(GetType(SuperText), Me)
End Sub
```

As shown in the preceding statements, the license is validated in the constructor for the class. The Validate method of the LicenseManager class checks to see whether or not a valid license exists. The Validate method accomplishes this task by reading the license file corresponding to the control. A control's license file has a well-defined file name and syntax. First, the name of the license file must be the same as the fully qualified name of the control. The file name has a suffix of .lic, thus the license file for the SuperText control must be LocalControls.SuperText.lic. LocalControls is the name of the root namespace and SuperText is the name of the control. The license file itself must begin with the fully qualified name of the control followed by a message of your choosing.

The following code segment illustrates the license file for the SuperText control:

```
LocalControls.SuperText is a licensed component.
```

When the control instance is destroyed you must destroy the license, as shown in the following code segment:

```
If Not (licCurrent Is Nothing) Then
    licCurrent.Dispose()
    licCurrent = Nothing
End If
```

The preceding statements will appear in the destructor for the control. If the license exists, it is explicitly destroyed by calling the Dispose method. Figure 11-13 summarizes the steps involved in creating and destroying a license manager.

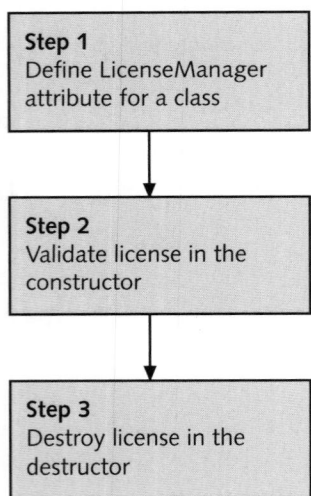

Figure 11-13   Creating and destroying a license manager

Next you will create the license file for the SuperText control using the built-in license manager.

To create a license for a control:

1. Activate the Code Editor for the module named **SuperText.vb**, and then enter the following statement (shown in bold) in the class declaration:

```
<LicenseProvider(GetType(LicFileLicenseProvider))> _
Public Class SuperText
```

2. Enter the following statement (shown in bold) immediately after the Win Forms Designer generated code to declare the variable named licCurrent to store the license:

```
Private licCurrent As License
```

3. Enter the following statement (shown in bold) in the constructor to validate the license. Remember that the constructor appears in the Win Forms Designer generated code. Expand this region block as necessary.

```
InitializeComponent()
licCurrent = _
    LicenseManager.Validate(GetType(SuperText), Me)
```

4. Enter the following statements (shown in bold) in the destructor to destroy the license. The destructor also appears in the Win Forms Designer generated code.

```
If disposing Then
    If Not (licCurrent Is Nothing) Then
        licCurrent.Dispose()
        licCurrent = Nothing
    End If
    If Not (components Is Nothing) Then
        components.Dispose()
    End If
End If
```

5. Recompile the LocalControls project, and then test the solution. Try to create an instance of the SuperText control on the form. The license file does not exist, so the dialog box shown in Figure 11-14 appears.

Figure 11-14   Dialog box indicating an invalid license

As you can see, the statements that you just wrote test for the existence of the license file. However, because the license file does not exist, the developer cannot create an instance of the SuperText control in the Win Forms Designer. Thus, you must create the license file and save it in the folder containing the control.

To create a license file:

1. Start Notepad or another text editor and create a file named **LocalControls. SuperText.lic**. It is imperative that the file name is correct or VB .NET will not be able to locate the license file.

2. Enter the following statement in the license file:

LocalControls.SuperText is a licensed component.

3. Save the file in the folder named **Chapter.11\Startup11\LocalControls\ obj\Debug**.

4. Test the solution again. Try to create an instance of the SuperText control on the form. Because the license file exists, VB .NET will let the developer create a design-time instance of the control. Delete the control instance.

Creating your own security management scheme or custom license provider is much more complex than using the built-in provider supplied by VB .NET. Before creating your own security manager, we discuss the Environment class as a means to locate the license file dynamically.

The Environment Class

The Environment class supplies the means to obtain information about the current computer's configuration. This information includes such items as the Windows system directory and command line arguments passed to the application, as follows:

Syntax

System.Environment class

Public Properties

- The **CurrentDirectory** property gets the directory from which the process (application) started.

- The **SystemDirectory** property gets the path name of the Windows system directory. The Windows system directory for Windows XP is typically C:\WINDOWS\system.

Public Methods

- The **GetEnvironmentVariable** method gets the value of a specific environment variable, such as the path.

- The **GetEnvironmentVariables** method gets all of the defined environment variables.

As mentioned, another way to license a control is to create a custom license provider. Using a custom license provider, you can add additional security beyond that supplied by the built-in file license provider.

Creating a Custom License Provider

The steps to create a custom license provider require that you create a class that inherits from the abstract LicenseProvider class. The LicenseProvider class supplies an abstract method named GetLicense that you must implement. It is the responsibility of this method to load and process the license file. That is, the class you implement must perform the same tasks as those supplied by the built-in license provider. Examine the following code segment that illustrates the structure of a custom license provider:

```
Public Class LicCustomFileLicenseProvider
    Inherits LicenseProvider

    Public Overrides Function GetLicense( _
        ByVal context As LicenseContext, _
        ByVal typ As System.Type, _
        ByVal instance As Object, _
        ByVal allowExceptions As Boolean) As License
    Public Class DesignTimeLicense
        Inherits License
    End Class
    Public Class RunTimeLicense
        Inherits License
    End Class
End Class
```

To create a custom license provider, you create a class that inherits from the LicenseProvider class. This class must implement a method named GetLicense having the following argument types:

- The LicenseContext argument specifies when the license can be used. The UsageMode property of the LicenseContext class has enumeration values of LicenseUsageMode.Runtime and LicenseUsageMode.Designtime for runtime and design-time licenses, respectively.

- The type of the component requesting the license appears in the second argument, having a data type of System.Type.

- The third argument has a data type of System.Object. This argument contains an instance of the component that is requesting the license.

- The final argument has a data type of Boolean. A value of True indicates that an exception should be thrown if the component cannot be granted a license and False otherwise.

Examine the following code segment for the GetLicense method:

```
Public Overrides Function GetLicense(
    ByVal context As LicenseContext,
    ByVal typ As System.Type, _
    ByVal instance As Object,
    ByVal allowExceptions As Boolean) As License
```

```
Dim ctlCurrent As String
Dim psrdCurrent As StreamReader
Dim pstrLicenseText As String

ctlCurrent = typ.FullName
If context.UsageMode = LicenseUsageMode.Designtime Then
    Try
        Dim fname As String = _
            Environment.SystemDirectory()
        fname = fname & "\" & ctlCurrent & ".lic"
        psrdCurrent = New StreamReader(fname)
        pstrLicenseText = psrdCurrent.ReadToEnd
        If pstrLicenseText = ctlCurrent & _
            " is a licensed component." Then
            Throw New System.ArgumentException()
        End If
    Catch ex As Exception
        If allowExceptions Then
            Throw New LicenseException(typ, instance, _
                "Can't find design-time license")
        Else
            Return Nothing
        End If
    Finally
        psrdCurrent.Close()
    End Try
    Return New DesignTimeLicense(Me, typ)
Else
    Return New RunTimeLicense(Me, typ)
End If
End Function
```

Examining the preceding statements, the UsageMode property of the context argument is checked to determine whether the component is in design time or runtime. If the component is in design time, then an attempt is made to validate the license. The statements attempt to open and read the license file from the Windows system directory. If the file contents are not valid, then an exception is thrown. If the license is valid, then an instance of the License class is returned. The preceding custom license provider always grants a run-time license, although this need not be the case.

To create a custom license provider:

1. Activate the Code Editor for the module named **SuperText.vb**. Modify the class declaration to use the custom license provider instead of the built-in license provider as follows:

```
<LicenseProvider(GetType(LicCustomFileLicenseProvider))> _
Public Class SuperText
```

2. Enter the following statements (shown in bold) to create the custom license provider:

```
Public Class SuperText
    ' Statements
End Class
Public Class LicCustomFileLicenseProvider
    Inherits LicenseProvider

    Public Overrides Function GetLicense( _
    ByVal context As LicenseContext, _
    ByVal typ As System.Type, _
    ByVal instance As Object, _
    ByVal allowExceptions As Boolean) As License

    Dim ctlCurrent As String
    Dim psrdCurrent As StreamReader
    Dim pstrLicenseText As String

    ctlCurrent = typ.FullName
    If context.UsageMode = LicenseUsageMode.Designtime Then
        Try
            Dim fname As String = _
                Environment.SystemDirectory()
            fname = fname & "\" & ctlCurrent & ".lic"
            psrdCurrent = New StreamReader(fname)
            pstrLicenseText = psrdCurrent.ReadToEnd
            If pstrLicenseText = ctlCurrent & _
                " is a licensed component." Then
                Throw New System.ArgumentException()
            End If
        Catch ex As Exception
            If allowExceptions Then
                Throw New LicenseException(typ, instance, _
                    "Can't find design-time license")
            Else
                Return Nothing
            End If
        Finally
            psrdCurrent.Close()
        End Try
        Return New DesignTimeLicense(Me, typ)
    Else
        Return New RunTimeLicense(Me, typ)
    End If
    End Function
End Class
```

11

```
Public Class DesignTimeLicense
    Inherits License

    Private owner As LicCustomFileLicenseProvider
    Private typ As Type

    Public Sub New( _
        ByVal owner As LicCustomFileLicenseProvider, _
        ByVal typ As Type)
        Me.owner = owner
        Me.typ = typ
    End Sub

    Public Overrides Sub Dispose()
    End Sub

    Public Overrides ReadOnly Property LicenseKey() _
        As String
        Get
            Return typ.FullName
        End Get
    End Property
End Class

Public Class RunTimeLicense
    Inherits License
    Private owner As LicCustomFileLicenseProvider
    Private typ As Type
    Public Sub New( _
        ByVal owner As LicCustomFileLicenseProvider, _
        ByVal typ As Type)
        Me.owner = owner
        Me.typ = typ
    End Sub

    Public Overrides Sub Dispose()
    End Sub

    Public Overrides ReadOnly Property LicenseKey() _
        As String
        Get
            Return typ.FullName
        End Get
    End Property
End Class
```

The preceding statements expect the license provider file to appear in the Windows system directory. When you tested the completed solution, you copied the license file to the appropriate system directory.

3. Recompile the LocalControls project, and then test the solution. Create an instance of the SuperText control on the form.

4. Delete the control instance.

You have completed the programming steps for this chapter. You have seen the three different ways that VB .NET will allow you to create a custom control, how to create custom property editors, and how to license a control.

CHAPTER SUMMARY

- VB .NET supplies three ways to create a control. First, you can create a control that inherits from an intrinsic control such as TextBox. Second, you can create a control that inherits from the UserControl class. Third, you can create a control from scratch by inheriting from System.Windows.Forms.Control.

- When you inherit from an existing intrinsic control, all of the members of the control in the base class are exposed to the developer. You can override these members or create additional members. Note that no visual designer exists when you create a control that derives from an existing intrinsic Toolbox control. When you override a member, call MyBase to call the member of the same name in the base class.

- When you create a control that derives from the UserControl class, VB .NET supplies a visual designer called the UserControl Designer. In the UserControl Designer, you create instances of intrinsic controls called constituent controls. By default, the members of constituent controls are hidden from the developer. You expose members through aggregation or delegation.

- The third way to create a control is to create one that derives from System.Windows. Forms.Control. When you create a control that derives from System.Windows.Forms. Control, you must override the OnPaint event so as to render an image of the control instance on the form. Call the Invalidate method on the control when it is resized to force the control to repaint. You may override members of the base Control class and create new members.

- Control attributes are used to configure the design-time behavior of custom controls. Attributes such as ToolboxBitmap and DefaultProperty apply to the class itself. Other attributes such as Browsable, Category, DefaultValue, Description, Editor, and Localizable apply to the individual members. Attributes are supplied by the System.ComponentModel namespace. Multiple attributes can be associated with a single member.

- VB .NET allows you to create a custom property editor for any property. To create a custom property editor for a property, you use the Editor attribute to specify the class that represents the custom property editor. This class must derive from the UITypeEditor class. In the class that derives from the UITypeEditor class, you override a method named GetEditStyle that returns the editor style to use. In addition,

11

you override a method named EditValue. Finally, you need to handle an event to hide the control instance displayed in the custom property editor.

❏ VB .NET allows you to license controls so as to prevent their unauthorized use. The easiest way to license a control is to use the built-in LicFileLicenseProvider. To use the built-in license provider, you create a class-level LicenseProvider attribute specifying the name of the LicenseProvider (LicFileLicenseProvider) as an argument to the constructor. In the constructor for the control, you call the Validate method of the LicenseManager class. In the destructor, explicitly dispose of the license by calling the Dispose method. You must manually create and install the license file for any licensed control.

❏ Creating a custom license provider is much more difficult than using the built-in LicFileLicenseProvider. To create a custom license provider, you create a class that derives from the LicenseProvider class. Then you override the GetLicense method of the class.

REVIEW QUESTIONS

1. Which of the following is a possible way to create a VB .NET control?

    a. Create a class that inherits from another control such as a TextBox.

    b. Create a class that inherits from System.Windows.Forms.Form.

    c. Use the classes of System.ComponentModel to create a new control.

    d. Create a class that inherits from System.Windows.CustomControl.

    e. none of the above

2. What type of project do you typically use to create a control?

    a. Win Forms application

    b. Dynamic Control project

    c. Windows Control Library project

    d. Custom Control Library project

    e. none of the above

3. Which of the following statements is correct referring to inheriting a control from another control such as a TextBox or ScrollBar?

    a. The properties of the base class are hidden from the developer and must be either aggregated or delegated so that the developer can use them.

    b. The properties of the base class are, by default, exposed to the developer. However, the properties of the base class can be overridden through shadowing.

   c. The properties of the base class are exposed to the developer and cannot be overridden.

   d. To override a property of the base class, you create a property having the same name as the property of the base class. Then, you override the property using the OverrideProperty attribute.

   e. none of the above

4. What is the purpose of control attributes?

   a. They can be used to configure the design-time behavior of custom controls.

   b. Through attributes, you define new properties for a custom control.

   c. Through attributes, you define new events for a custom control.

   d. You use attributes to define the base class of a particular control.

   e. none of the above

5. Which of the following are valid attributes for properties?

   a. Browsable, Category, DefaultValue, DefaultProperty

   b. Browser, Section, Default

   c. Enabled, Disabled, Visible

   d. Refresh, Bitmap, Viewable

   e. none of the above

6. What happens if you set the MergableProperty attribute for a property to False?

   a. The property will not appear in the Properties window when multiple instances of the control are selected.

   b. The property will appear in the Properties window when multiple instances of the control are selected.

   c. By setting the MergableProperty attribute of a property to False, the property will not appear in the tab order.

   d. The MergableProperty attribute defines where the property will appear in the Properties window. That is, it defines the section where the property will appear.

   e. none of the above

7. How do you prevent a property from appearing in the Properties window?

   a. Create a custom property editor.

   b. Set the Visible property of the UserControl class to False.

   c. Set the Browsable attribute to False.

   d. Set the Visible attribute to False.

   e. none of the above

11

8. What is meant by the term constituent control?

   a. The controls appearing on a UserControl are considered constituent controls.

   b. When you inherit from an intrinsic control such as a TextBox, the TextBox is considered a constituent control.

   c. When you create a control using the UserControl class, the UserControl class is considered a constituent control.

   d. When you inherit from the Control class, the Control class itself is considered a constituent control.

   e. none of the above

9. Which of the following statements is true of controls derived from the System.Windows.Forms.Control class?

   a. When you create a control that derives from the Control class, you can use the UserControl Designer to create constituent controls on the UserControl.

   b. You must write statements that define how the control instance is painted on the form.

   c. When you create a control that derives from the Control class, you must implement the IControl interface.

   d. all of the above

   e. none of the above

10. Which of the following is/are valid members of the UserControl class?

    a. TextBox, Label

    b. DesignMode, ClientRectangle, ClientSize

    c. Constituent control

    d. all of the above

    e. none of the above

11. If a property has a data type that is an enumeration, how is the data displayed in the Value column of the Properties window?

    a. The numeric values are displayed in a drop-down menu.

    b. The enumeration names are displayed in a drop-down menu.

    c. You specify the value by entering the numeric value associated with the enumeration. If the number is not valid, an exception will occur.

    d. You must implement a custom property editor whenever a property has a data type that is an enumeration.

    e. none of the above

12. Which of the following statements is valid related to creating a custom property editor?

   a. To create a custom property editor you create a class that derives from the CustomProperty class.

   b. In the property that should have a property editor, you create a nested class named CustomProperty. This class must implement the IProperty interface.

   c. To create a custom property editor, you use the Editor attribute for the property and specify, as an argument, a class that inherits from UITypeEditor.

   d. VB .NET does not allow you to create editors beyond those already defined by the Properties window itself.

   e. none of the above

13. How many subordinate controls can you display in a drop-down custom property editor?

   a. Only one

   b. No more than 3

   c. Any number that you want

   d. Custom property editors do not display subordinate controls.

   e. none of the above

14. Which of the following statements correctly describes how to license a control using the built-in LicFileLicenseProvider?

   a. You use the LicenseProvider attribute to indicate that the control is licensed. The argument to the constructor is the class named LicFileLicenseProvider.

   b. You check that the license is correct by calling the Validate method of the LicenseManager class.

   c. A license file having a well-defined name and content must reside on the target system.

   d. all of the above

   e. none of the above

15. What is the purpose of the Environment class?

   a. The Environment class returns information related to the hardware installed on the computer such as the type of graphics card installed and the amount of disk space available.

   b. The Environment class can be used to obtain the system directory or the current working directory.

   c. The Environment class obtains information about the assembly of the running application.

   d. all of the above

   e. none of the above

11

16. Which of the following statements is correct related to creating a custom license provider?

    a. You create a class that inherits from CustomLicenseProvider.

    b. The class that inherits from CustomLicenseProvider must implement the GetCustomLicense method.

    c. When you use a CustomLicenseProvider, you do not use an attribute.

    d. all of the above

    e. none of the above

17. List and describe the three ways to create a custom control.

18. What is the difference between delegating a property and aggregating a property?

19. Describe the differences between using the built-in license provider supplied by VB .NET, and creating a custom license provider.

20. Describe the difference between a drop-down custom property editor and a modal custom property editor.

PROGRAMMING QUESTIONS

1. Write the statements to declare a class named CustomLabel that inherits from the intrinsic Label class.

2. Write the statements to declare a class named BoxWithX that derives from the System.Windows.Forms.Control class. Override the OnPaint event as necessary so that the CustomLabel will draw a black X through the visible region of the control instance.

3. Write the statements to declare attributes for a property named Value. The description should be set to "Value of the control". The property should appear in the Behavior section of the Properties window. The property should not be mergable.

4. Write the statements to create class-level attributes for the class named SuperLabel. The bitmap appearing in the Toolbox should be obtained from the file named C:\BitFile.bmp. The default property should be the Text property.

5. Assume that a UserControl named SuperLabel exists, having a constituent Label control instance named Label1. Create the necessary procedure to hide the Dock property so that it will not appear in the Properties window. In addition, throw a System.NotImplementedException if the developer attempts to read or write the property's value.

6. Assume that a UserControl named SuperLabel exists, having a constituent Label control instance named Label1. Write the statements to delegate the Text property.

7. Assume that a UserControl named DoubleText exists, having constituent TextBox control instances named Text1 and Text2. Write the statements to aggregate the ForeColor property of the two constituent control instances.

8. Assume that a class named ToggleButton exists that is derived from the UserControl class. Assume that the ToggleButton class contains two constituent instances of the Button control named btnOn and btnOff. Create the Resize event handler such that each button will occupy the entire width of the control instance. Together, the two buttons should fill the vertical region of the control instance so that one button appears at the top of the control instance and the other button appears at the bottom of the control instance. Both buttons should have the same height.

9. Write the statements to create a class named BlackBox that derives from the System.Windows.Forms.Control class. Create the necessary OnPaint event handler so that the control region will be filled with a black rectangle.

10. Write the statements to create a property named VisualAppearance having an enumeration type of VisualOptions. Create the necessary attribute for the property so that it will use the custom property editor named VisualEditor that derives from the base class UITypeEditor.

11. Write the statements to create a class named VisualEditor that inherits the UITypeEditor class. Override the GetEditStyle and EditValue methods as necessary to populate a list box with the values Emphasis, Normal, and NoEmphasis, and to return the selected value.

12. Write the statements to retrieve the current working directory and the system directory. Store the results in the String variables named pstrDir and pstrSysDir.

13. Write the statement to declare an attribute for the class named VisualBox so that it will use the intrinsic LicFileLicenseProvider class.

14. Write the statement designed to appear for a licensed control to validate the license. Assume that the license variable is named licCurrent and that the type of the control is named VisualBox.

15. Write an If statement designed to appear in the GetLicense method for a licensed control. Using the context argument, write the If statement to test whether or not VB .NET is operating in design mode. If it is, throw a LicenseException. Otherwise, do nothing.

HANDS-ON PROJECTS

1. In this project, you will create a control that derives from the intrinsic ListBox class. Figure 11-15 shows the visual interface for the control. To test the control, create a new project. Add a reference to the control named Chapter.11\Exercises11\CustomListBox.dll.

Figure 11-15 Chapter 11 – Hands-on Project 1

 a. Create a new Windows Application project and solution named **Ch11Ex1.sln**.

 b. Add a Windows Control Library project to the solution named **CustomListBox**.

 c. Name the control **CustomListBox**.

 d. Modify the class so that the CustomListBox derives from the intrinsic ListBox control.

 e. Write the statements in the control's constructor to add the following descriptive state names to the Items collection: **Arizona**, **California**, **Nevada**, and **Utah**.

 f. Write the statements to override the SelectedItem property so that instead of returning the descriptive state name, the property will return the state abbreviation—AZ, CA, NV, and UT—based on which of the states is selected.

 g. Override the necessary procedure and create the necessary attribute so that the SelectionMode property will not appear in the Properties window.

2. In this project, you will create a control comprised of a constituent Timer control, a constituent Label control, and constituent buttons. The control that you create will work in much the same way as a stopwatch. Figure 11-16 shows the visual interface for the control. To test the control, create a new project. Add a reference to the control named Chapter.11\Exercises11\StopWatch.dll.

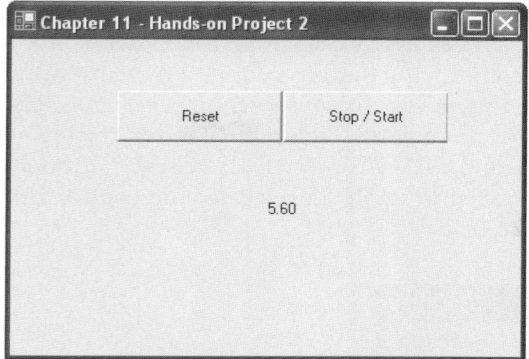

Figure 11-16   Chapter 11 – Hands-on Project 2

a. Create a new Windows Application project named **Ch11Ex2.sln**.

b. Add a Windows Control Library project to the solution named **StopWatch**. The class that you create should derive from the UserControl class.

c. Name the control **StopWatch**.

d. Create a constituent Label control on the form. The constituent Label control instance will display the elapsed stopwatch seconds.

e. Create two constituent buttons on the form. The first should reset the stopwatch. The second should operate as a toggle switch. When clicked, the stopwatch should start counting. When clicked again, the stopwatch should stop counting. The stopwatch should have a precision of 1/10 of a second.

f. Write the statements to handle the Resize event. The label should fill the width and height of the control instance. The two buttons should appear above the label. Each button should be resized so that both have equal widths. The buttons should have a fixed height

g. Write the statements to delegate the Text and TextAlign properties of the constituent Label control instance.

h. Delegate the Text property of the label so that it will store the current value (number of elapsed seconds) of the stopwatch. Make this property the default property.

i. Hide the Dock property from the developer.

j. Write the code for the Button's click event handlers to start, stop, and reset the stopwatch.

k. Create attributes so that each of the properties you just created has a description. Use description values of your choice.

l. Create attributes so that each of the properties you just created are not mergable.

11

3. In this project, you will create a FractionalScrollBar control similar to the one appearing in the chapter. However, this FractionalScrollBar will derive from the UserControl class and contain constituent controls to display the current value of the Value, Minimum, and Maximum properties in constituent labels. Figure 11-17 shows the completed visual interface for the control. To test the control, create a new project. Add a reference to the control named Chapter.11\Exercises11\TextScrollBar.dll. Note that even though you are asked to create a license for the control, it has been omitted from the sample for ease of use.

Figure 11-17   Chapter 11 – Hands-on Project 3

a. Create a new project named **Ch11Ex3.sln**.

b. Add a Windows Control Library project to the solution named **TextScrollBar**. The TextScrollBar class should derive from the UserControl class.

c. Create a constituent HScrollBar and three constituent labels on the control instance.

d. Write the statements to handle the Resize event. The HScrollBar should appear across the top of the control and occupy the width of the control. The constituent Label control instances should appear along the bottom of the control. Each Label control instance should have exactly the same width.

e. Delegate the following properties of the constituent HScrollBar: Maximum, Minimum, LargeChange, SmallChange, and Value. Write the necessary statements so that when the value of the Maximum, Minimum, or Value property gets updated, the value of the corresponding constituent label gets updated. The Value property should be the default property. The default value for the Minimum property should be 0 and the default value for the Maximum property should be 100.

f. Aggregate the following properties of the constituent Label control instances: ForeColor, BackColor, TextAlign.

g. Create descriptive attributes for each of the properties that you aggregate or delegate.

h. Implement licensing for the control using the built-in LicFileLicenseProvider. Create the license file as necessary.

i. Make all of the properties mergable except for the Value property.

j. Define an icon of your choosing for the control.

4. In this project, you will create a control from scratch. This control will operate similarly to the control that you created from scratch in the chapter. However, you will define additional properties that manage how the control instance is drawn on the form.

a. Create a new project named **Ch11Ex4.sln**.

b. Add a Windows Control Library project to the solution named **PatternBox**. The control should derive from the System.Windows.Forms.Control class.

c. Override the ForeColor and BackColor properties. The ForeColor property should define the color of the lines drawn on the control instance. The BackColor property should define the background color of the control instance.

d. Declare a property named **Pattern** having a data type of PatternType. The enumeration values for the PatternType property should be **Outline**, **X**, and **Fill**.

e. Write the necessary statements so that when the developer sets the Pattern property the control instance will be redrawn with an outline surrounding the control instance when the value of the property is Outline. Draw an X through the control instance when the property's value is set to X. Fill the region of the control instance with the foreground color when the value is set to Fill.

f. Implement licensing for the control using a custom license provider. Create the license file as necessary.

11

12

DRAWING AND THE GDI+

In this chapter, you will:

♦ Understand the GDI+

♦ Understand color and the Color structure

♦ Define lines, rectangles, text, and polygons

♦ Draw images to a graphical device

♦ Understand the different graphical transformations

♦ Send graphical output to a printer

♦ Create bar and pie charts

In this chapter, you will learn how to draw graphical shapes such as lines and rectangles to various output devices. These output devices include windows on the desktop and attached printers. You will begin by first learning how to create simple shapes on a splash screen. Then you will see how to combine those shapes together to create graphical charts including bar charts and pie charts.

PREVIEWING THE COMPLETED SOLUTION

The purpose of this solution is to illustrate how to draw graphical shapes, thus the completed solution in this chapter contains a splash screen similar to those appearing in other chapters. However, this splash screen does not contain control instances that display text. Instead, the code for this splash screen draws shapes and text on the form dynamically as VB .NET paints the form on the desktop. In addition to the splash screen, the application reads data from a sequential file and creates graphs on the main form based upon that data. Finally, the completed solution contains another form that allows the user to view graphical images.

To preview the completed solution:

1. Start Visual Studio .NET. Open, and then run the solution file named **Chapter.12\Complete12\Complete12.sln**. The splash screen appears as shown in Figure 12-1. Notice that the splash screen contains lines and geometric shapes.

Figure 12-1   Completed solution – splash screen

2. After the splash screen appears, the main form appears. On the main form, click **File** and then click **Open**. Open the file named **Chapter.12\Data\Sales.txt**. In the client area of the main form, the bar chart appears as shown in Figure 12-2.

3. On the main form, click **View**, and then click **Pie Chart**. Figure 12-3 shows the main form displaying the same data appearing as a pie chart.

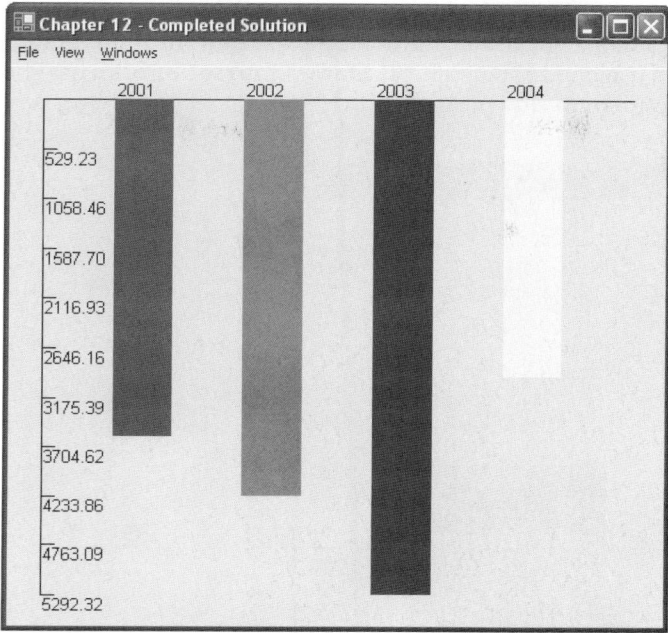

Figure 12-2   Completed solution – main form displaying bar chart

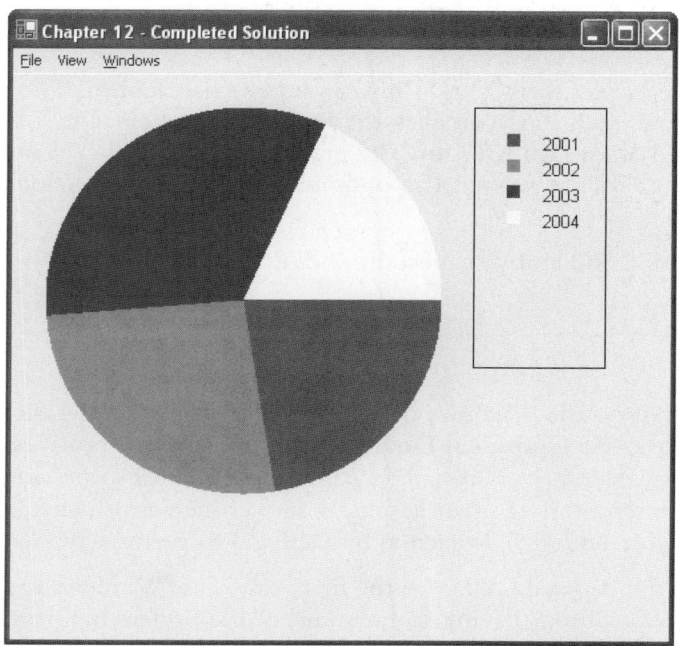

Figure 12-3   Completed solution – main form displaying pie chart

4. On the main form, click **Windows**, and then click **Image Viewer**. On the image viewer form, click **File**, and then click **Open**. In the Open dialog box, select the image named **Chapter.12\Data\CourseLogo.bmp**. The image appears in the form as shown in Figure 12-4.

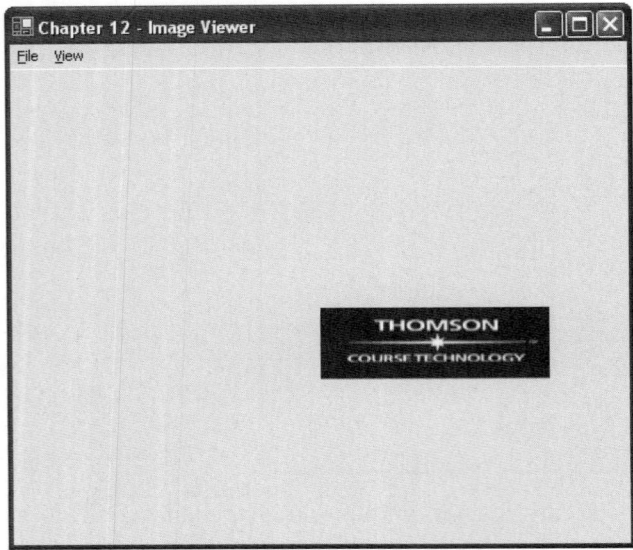

Figure 12-4   Completed solution – image viewer form

5. On the image viewer form, click **View**, and then click **Rotate**. The image is rotated 1 degree each time you click the Rotate menu item. Click **View**, **Zoom In** and **View**, **Zoom Out**. The image is zoomed. Click **View**, select **Pan**, and then click the various Pan options. The image is repositioned about the form.

6. End the solution and exit Visual Studio .NET.

INTRODUCING THE GDI+

Drawing text or graphics to the Windows desktop involves programming the Graphical Device Interface (GDI+). The **Graphical Device Interface (GDI+)** provides the means by which Windows displays text, lines, rectangles, and more complex shapes, such as polygons and curves, to the screen or to other graphical devices such as printers. In addition, the GDI+ allows you to render images such as bitmaps and to perform typography.

Microsoft introduced the original GDI with the first versions of Windows as a means to display graphical output without having to be aware of the underlying graphics hardware installed on a particular computer. For example, because of the GDI, a developer could write a single statement to display a white line, instead of having to write several statements to make a row of pixels white, one pixel at a time.

While the versions of the GDI supplied with Windows 95 and Windows 98 allowed a developer to draw lines and shapes, newer versions of Windows, such as Windows 2000 and Windows XP, supply additional features such as opacity, gradient brushes, and lines with custom endpoints. This new version of the GDI is called the GDI+.

The GDI+ allows a developer to define explicitly the appearance of a line's endpoints and the pattern of a line. Lines can be capped with arrows or custom shapes. Instead of filling a shape with a solid color or pattern, the GDI+ allows a developer to fill shapes with complex patterns and gradient colors too. The .NET Framework class library gives a developer full access to the Windows GDI+.

The services provided by the GDI+ can be roughly divided into the following four categories:

- The GDI+ supplies classes to draw simple shapes, such as lines and rectangles, or more complex shapes, such as polygons and curves. Note that all of the shapes defined by the GDI+ are two-dimensional. To create three-dimensional graphics, other products such as DirectX or OpenGL are appropriate. DirectX is a proprietary Microsoft technology providing graphics and multimedia services to Windows applications. OpenGL provides similar three-dimensional graphics services. However, OpenGL is a standard technology which can be used with Microsoft Windows, UNIX, and different software and hardware environments.

- The GDI+ allows a developer to display bitmaps and other types of images.

- The GDI+ allows a developer to display text of varying fonts. That text can be filled with a specific color, gradient colors, or an image. Collectively, these features are referred to as typography.

- The GDI+ performs transformations. Transformations include rotating graphics, zooming, and panning.

Each of the preceding GDI+ capabilities is discussed in this chapter.

 If you are developing .NET applications for older versions of Windows, such as Windows 98, some of the extended GDI+ features will not work properly. Most of these new features are contained in the classes of the System.Drawing.Drawing2D namespace.

Working with the GDI+ involves using the following namespaces and classes:

- The members of the **System.Drawing** namespace define the shapes that you can draw and how those shapes should be outlined or filled. For example, the Pen class defines the characteristics of a line. Lines are used to draw a straight line, a border around a rectangle or polygon, or an arc. The Brush class defines how a shape, such as a rectangle or polygon, will be filled.

- The members of the **System.Drawing.Drawing2D** namespace extend the features of the System.Drawing namespace. In general, the System.Drawing.Drawing2D namespace contains those classes that are new to the GDI+. The classes of the System.Drawing.Drawing2D namespace allow a shape to be filled with a gradient brush. That is, the filled region of a shape varies from one color to another. In addition, the members of the Drawing2D namespace allow you to create custom lines with custom endpoints.

- The **System.Graphics** class serves two purposes. First, it contains members used to draw shapes, such as lines and rectangles, draw images, and perform typography. The same members are used whether drawing to a form or other drawing surface, such as a printer. Second, an instance of the Graphics class provides a reference to the drawing surface itself.

UNDERSTANDING COLOR AND THE COLOR STRUCTURE

Combining varying intensities of red, green, and blue creates a color. The term **RGB** refers to the three colors (red, green, and blue) used to create a color. Each RGB value ranges from 0 to 255. If the value is 0, then the color is off. If the value is 255, then the color is applied at full intensity. Thus, if each RGB value is 0, then the color produced is black. If each RGB value is set to 255, then the color produced is white. VB .NET predefines several named colors for you. In addition, you can create custom colors from RGB values.

Programmatically, you work with color using the Color structure, which has the following members:

Syntax

System.Drawing.Color structure

Public Properties

- The **A** property returns the alpha component of the color. One purpose of the alpha component is to control opacity.

- The **R** property returns the red component of the color.

- The **G** property returns the green component of the color.

- The **B** property returns the blue component of the color.

- In addition to the preceding properties, the Color structure supplies several named colors. For example, Color.Red, Color.Blue and Color.Green are all named colors. The preceding three colors are but a few of the over 100 named colors.

Public Methods

- The overloaded shared **FromArgb** method creates a color based on R, G, B, and alpha values.

To illustrate the use of the Color structure, examine the following statement that references a named color:

```
Dim colCurrent As Color = Color.Red
```

The preceding statement declares a Color structure named colCurrent, and stores the named color Color.Red in the variable.

The FromArgb method creates custom colors from component RGB values. One version of the overloaded FromArgb method accepts three arguments: the red, green, and blue values, respectively. The following statements illustrate how to create a custom color using the FromArgb method:

```
Dim colCurrent As Color
colCurrent = Color.FromArgb(255, 255, 255)
colCurrent = Color.FromArgb(0, 0, 255)
```

The first of the preceding statements declares a variable to store a color. The second of the preceding statements creates a new custom color using RGB values. The color produced is white. The color produced by the third statement is blue, because the red and green colors are turned off and the color blue is applied at full intensity.

 Different computers have different color capabilities based on the installed graphics hardware, and how that hardware is configured. The graphics cards in nearly all newer computers support true 24-bit color, allowing more than 3 million possible colors. Older computers are limited to displaying 256 colors. If the solutions in this chapter do not work correctly, activate the Control Panel, select Display, and then select Settings. Make sure that the current color setting is 24-bit or greater.

Colors are used in conjunction with pens to draw lines.

DRAWING LINES

The most basic shape defined by the .NET Framework is a line. A straight line is drawn between two points using a pen. Pens are of two types: cosmetic pens and geometric pens. **Cosmetic pens** are used to draw solid lines. **Geometric pens** allow you to create custom lines with custom endpoints.

A line is drawn to a graphical device by calling the overloaded DrawLine method of the Graphics class. The overloaded DrawLine method can be called either with existing

Point structures, or by specifying the x and y coordinate values for the line's endpoints. A pen is used to define the color and thickness of the line. In the following sections, we first discuss how to define a Point structure, and then how to create an instance of the Pen class. Finally, we discuss how to draw a line using that point and pen.

Defining a Point

A straight line is drawn from a starting point to an ending point. A rectangle is defined by a point that marks the origin of the rectangle. In addition, a rectangle has a size, which is defined by the values of its height and width. To define a point, you create an instance of a Point structure using the following constructor:

Syntax

System.Drawing.Point constructor

Public Sub New(ByVal x As Integer, ByVal y As Integer)

Definition

The **Point** structure defines a position on a graphical output device having x and y coordinate values.

Dissection

- The x argument defines the horizontal distance from the left edge of the graphical device to the point.

- The y argument defines the vertical distance from the top of the graphical device to the point.

Code Example

```
Dim pntCurrent As New Point(0, 0)
```

Code Dissection

The preceding statement creates a new Point structure at the origin (upper-left corner) of the output device, such as a form or a PictureBox control instance.

Having seen how to define a point, you can now define a pen that will specify a line's color and thickness.

Defining a Pen

Pens are used to define the color and thickness of a line or the border surrounding other shapes, such as rectangles or polygons. The following properties define the style and color of a pen:

- The **Color** property defines the color of the pen.

- The **DashStyle** property contains the value of a DashStyle enumeration member. The enumeration members define standard dash styles. VB .NET also allows you to define custom dash styles and custom end caps.

- The **EndCap** property defines the shape of the cap appearing at the end of the line. Its data type is a LineCap enumeration.

- The **StartCap** property defines the shape of the cap appearing at the beginning of a line. Its data type is also a LineCap enumeration.

To create a pen, you call the overloaded Pen constructor, which has the following syntax:

Syntax

System.Drawing.Pen constructor

Public Sub New(*color* **As Color**)
Public Sub New(*color* **As Color**, *width* **As Width**)

Definition

The **Pen** constructor creates a new pen. The pen has a color and an optional width.

Dissection

- The *color* argument contains an existing color. This color may be a named color or a color created as a result of calling the FromArgb method.

- The optional *width* argument defines the width of the line. The default width of a line is 1 (one pixel).

Code Example

```
Dim penCurrent As New Pen(Color.Red)
Dim penCurrentWide As New Pen(Color.Red, 3)
' Statements to draw a line or outline a shape
penCurrent.Dispose()
penCurrentWide.Dispose()
```

Code Dissection

The first of the preceding statements creates a new red pen that is one pixel wide. The second statement also creates a red pen, but the pen is three pixels wide instead of being one pixel wide. The final two statements dispose of the custom pens by calling the Dispose method. Explicitly calling the Dispose method releases the resources used by the pen and the pen itself.

Whenever you create a custom pen, it must be explicitly disposed by calling the Dispose method. Even though the GC will ultimately release the memory allocated to the custom pen, other resources, such as device contexts, may not be released quickly enough causing errors to occur.

Once you have created a pen, you can customize the endpoints of the line that will be rendered, along with the format of the line itself, by setting the EndCap, StartCap and DashStyle properties. The EndCap and StartCap properties have an enumeration data type of System.Drawing.Drawing2D.LineCap.

VB .NET supports numerous LineCap styles to draw arrows, blocks, and other shapes on a line's endpoints. Examine the following statements to define the EndCap and StartCap for the pen named penCurrent:

```
penCurrent.EndCap = Drawing.Drawing2D.LineCap.Triangle
penCurrent.StartCap = Drawing.Drawing2D.LineCap.Triangle
```

The preceding statements set the style of the starting and ending points of the line. A triangle (arrow) will be drawn at the line's endpoints.

In addition to customizing a line's endpoints, you can customize the format of the line itself by setting the DashStyle property of the pen, as shown in the following statement:

```
penCurrent.DashStyle = Drawing.Drawing2D.DashStyle.Dash
```

The line drawn with the preceding pen will appear as a dashed line.

THE GRAPHICS CLASS

At the heart of all drawing operations is the Graphics class. It supplies the methods to clear a drawing surface and to draw all shapes to an output device (window or printer). It also contains members to scale drawings and images and to rotate drawings. The Graphics class supports the following members:

Syntax

System.Drawing.Graphics class

Public Properties

- The **DpiX** and **DpiY** properties return the horizontal and vertical resolution of the graphics device. Dpi is an acronym for "dots per inch."

Public Methods

- The **Clear** method clears the drawing surface and fills that surface with a background color. The background color is supplied as an argument to the Clear method.
- The **DrawArc** method draws an arc using a pen.
- The **DrawEllipse** method draws an ellipse bounded by a rectangle.
- The **DrawImage** and **DrawImageScaled** methods draw an image to the output device.
- The **DrawLine** method draws a line between two points using a pen.

- The **DrawLines** method draws a series of connected lines.

- The **DrawPie** method draws a pie shape. A pie is part of an ellipse. A pie is sliced from the ellipse using two radial lines.

- The **DrawPolygon** method draws an outline of a polygon using a pen. The vertices of the polygon are represented as an array of points.

- The **DrawRectangle** method draws a bordered rectangle using a pen. A point marks the origin of the rectangle. The height and width arguments to the DrawRectangle method define the rectangle's size.

- The **DrawString** method represents the GDI's typography capabilities. It allows you to draw filled and outlined text.

- The **FillPie** method fills a pie slice with a brush.

- The **FillPolygon** method fills a polygon with a brush.

- The **FillRectangle** method fills a rectangle with a brush.

- The **Flush** method forces all graphical requests to be processed. That is, all pending graphical requests will be drawn to the output device when the Flush method is called.

- The **RotateTransform** method rotates images using an angle between 1 and 360 degrees.

- By calling the **ScaleTransform** method, you effectively zoom in and zoom out of the graphics displayed on an output device.

- By default, the upper-left corner of the form is considered the form's origin. Thus, the x and y coordinates of the upper-left corner of the form are $(0, 0)$. The x coordinate value increases to the right, and the y coordinate value increases downward. By calling the **TranslateTransform** method you can change the point that VB .NET considers the origin.

12

Graphical shapes are drawn to a window by calling the methods of the Graphics class in the form's Paint event handler or the Paint event handler of a PictureBox. The Paint event fires as a form or PictureBox control instance is rendered on the screen. Just as all event handlers have two arguments, so too does the Paint event handler. As always, the first argument, named sender, has a data type of System.Object and contains a reference to the object that fired the event. The second argument to the Paint event handler is of type System.Windows.Forms.PaintEventArgs. The Graphics property of the PaintEventArgs class references an instance of the Graphics class. It is through this property and the corresponding Graphics object that you perform drawing operations. Figure 12-5 illustrates the arguments of the Paint event handler.

```
Private Sub frmMain_Paint( _
    ByVal sender As Object, _
    ByVal e As System.Windows.Forms.PaintEventArgs) _
    Handles MyBase.Paint

    e.Graphics.DrawLine(Pens.Red, 0, 0, 10, 10)

End Sub
```

Argument e contains a
reference to the Graphics class

Figure 12-5   The Paint event handler

To force Windows to fire a Paint event, you call the Invalidate method of the form or PictureBox as shown in the following statements:

```
Me.Invalidate()
picGraph.Invalidate()
```

The first of the preceding statements invalidates the form using the Me keyword. The second statement invalidates the PictureBox control instance named picGraph.

DRAWING LINES

Having learned how to define the endpoints and characteristics of a line, you call the DrawLine method of the Graphics class to draw a line to the graphical output device. The overloaded DrawLine method has the following syntax:

Syntax

System.Drawing.Graphics.DrawLine method

Overloads Public Sub DrawLine(ByVal *pen* As Pen, *pt1* As Point, *pt2* As Point)
Overloads Public Sub DrawLine(ByVal *pen* As Pen, *x1* As Integer, *y1* As Integer, *x2* As Integer, *y2* As Integer)

Definition

The overloaded **DrawLine** method draws a straight line to an output device using an existing instance of the Pen class. The position of the line is specified using two existing Point structures or by specifying the *x* and *y* coordinate values of the line's endpoints.

Dissection

- The *pen* argument contains a reference to an existing pen.

- The *pt1* and *pt2* arguments reference existing Point structures that define the endpoints of the line.

- The *x1* and *y1* arguments define the line's starting point and the *x2* and *y2* arguments define the line's endpoint.

Code Example

```
Dim penCurrent As New Pen(Color.Red)
Dim pntStart As New Point(0, 0)
Dim pntEnd As New Point(50, 50)
e.Graphics.DrawLine(penCurrent, pntStart, pntEnd)
e.Graphics.DrawLine(penCurrent, 0, 0, 50, 50)
penCurrent.Dispose()

e.Graphics.DrawLine(Pens.Red, 0, 0, 50, 50)
```

Code Dissection

The first call to the DrawLine method draws a line using a custom pen named penCurrent, and existing Point structures named pntStart and pntEnd. The second call draws the same line by using *x* and *y* coordinate values. The two statements are equivalent. The next statement disposes of the custom pen named penCurrent. The final statement illustrates how to draw a line using a predefined named pen (Pens.Red). The default unit of measure used to draw pens and other shapes is pixels. Unlike custom pens, you need not explicitly dispose of predefined named pens.

12

As a first example, you will draw a line on a splash screen. Later in the chapter, you will create a bar chart using lines and other shapes.

When using predefined named pens, you need not call the Dispose method to destroy the pen. However, you must explicitly dispose of all custom pens.

So that you can focus on the syntax of creating and drawing lines and other shapes, you will first create simple shapes on a splash screen. Later in the chapter you will combine different shapes together to create graphs. In reality, you could create the splash screen using controls such as a Label or TextBox. However, the purpose of this splash screen is to introduce how to draw simple graphical shapes.

To create a line:

1. Start Visual Studio .NET, and then open the file named **Chapter12\ Startup12\Startup12.sln**. Activate the Code Editor for the form named **frmSplash.vb**, and then enter the following statements in the form's **Paint** event handler:

```
Dim pntStart As New Point(10, Me.ClientSize.Height - 10)
Dim pntEnd As New Point(Me.ClientSize.Width - 10, _
   Me.ClientSize.Height - 10)
Dim penLine As New Pen(Color.SkyBlue, 3)
e.Graphics.DrawLine(penLine, pntStart, pntEnd)
penLine.Dispose()
```

The preceding statements draw a horizontal SkyBlue line 10 pixels from the bottom of the form. The line's endpoints are 10 pixels from the form's left and right border. After the line is drawn, the custom pen is explicitly disposed.

2. Test the solution. The SkyBlue line appears along the bottom of the splash screen.

The steps to draw a rectangle are similar to the steps to draw a line. In addition to using a pen to outline the rectangle and a point to mark the rectangle's origin, you can specify the rectangle's width and height.

DRAWING RECTANGLES

A rectangle consists of Point and Size structures. The Point structure defines the origin of the rectangle, and the Size structure defines the rectangle's height and width. The Size constructor has the following syntax:

Syntax

System.Drawing.Size constructor

Public Sub New(ByVal *width* **As Integer, ByVal** *height* **As Integer)**

Definition

The **Size** constructor is used to define the size of a bounding rectangle.

Dissection

- The *width* argument defines the width of the rectangle.

- The *height* argument defines the height of the rectangle.

Code Example

```
Dim sizCurrent As New Size(72, 72)
```

Code Dissection

The preceding statement creates a new instance of the Size structure that is roughly one inch square.

Creating a rectangle involves calling the overloaded Rectangle constructor having the following syntax:

Syntax

System.Drawing.Rectangle constructor

Overloads Public Sub New(ByVal *location* **as Point, ByVal** *size* **As Size)**
Overloads Public Sub New(ByVal *x* **As Integer, ByVal** *y* **As Integer, ByVal** *width* **As Integer, ByVal** *height* **As Integer)**

Definition

The overloaded **Rectangle** constructor creates a new instance of the Rectangle structure using existing Point and Size structures or using Integer coordinates.

Dissection

- The *location* argument contains an existing Point structure.
- The *size* argument contains an existing Size structure.
- The *x* and *y* arguments define the origin of the rectangle.
- The *width* and *height* arguments define the size of the rectangle.

Code Example

```
Dim pntCurrent As New Point(0, 0)
Dim sizCurrent As New Size(100, 100)
Dim recCurrent As New Rectangle(pntCurrent, sizCurrent)
Dim recCurrent1 As New Rectangle(0, 0, 100, 100)
```

Code Dissection

The first call to the Rectangle constructor creates a new rectangle using existing Point and Size structures. The second call creates a new rectangle using *x* and *y* coordinates along with the width and height. Both of the calls to the Rectangle's constructor create the same rectangle.

Once you have created a rectangle, you draw an outline of that rectangle by calling the DrawRectangle method of the Graphics class. One version of the overloaded

DrawRectangle method accepts two arguments: an existing Pen and an existing Rectangle structure. Another allows you to define the rectangle's shape by specifying the *x* and *y* coordinates along with the width and height.

Examine the following statements to draw a rectangle outline:

```
Dim recCurrent As New Rectangle(0, 0, 100, 100)
e.Graphics.DrawRectangle(Pens.Red, recCurrent)
e.Graphics.DrawRectangle(Pens.Red, 0, 0, 100, 100)
```

The preceding statements draw the same rectangle outline. In the preceding statements e.Graphics is assumed to appear in a Paint event handler and reference an instance of the Graphics class. The first call to the DrawRectangle method uses an existing Rectangle structure. The second call to the DrawRectangle method explicitly defines the origin of the rectangle, the width, and the height. The outline drawn will be red as a predefined named pen, Pens.Red, is used. Again, because a custom pen was not used, the pen need not be explicitly disposed.

Next, you will create a rectangle outline on the splash screen.

To create and draw a rectangle outline:

1. Activate the Code Editor for the form named **frmSplash.vb**, if necessary, and then enter the following statements (shown in bold) at the end of the **Paint** event handler:

```
e.Graphics.DrawLine(penLine, pntStart, pntEnd)
penLine.Dispose()
Dim pntOutline As New Point(10, 260)
Dim sizOutline As New Size(Me.ClientSize.Width -20, 80)
Dim penOutline As New Pen(Color.LightSkyBlue, 2)
Dim recOutline As New Rectangle(pntOutline, sizOutline)
e.Graphics.DrawRectangle(penOutline, recOutline)
penOutline.Dispose()
```

The preceding statements create instances of the Point, Size, Pen, and Rectangle classes and structures. Calling the DrawRectangle method draws an outline of the rectangle. The final statement disposes of the custom pen.

2. Test the solution. The outlined rectangle that you just created appears on the splash screen just above the line that you drew previously.

In addition to drawing a rectangle outline, you can also fill the region of a rectangle.

FILLING THE REGION OF A RECTANGLE

Although you draw a rectangle outline with a pen, you fill a rectangle's region with a brush. In addition to filling rectangles with brushes, you also fill the region of other shapes, such as polygons, with brushes. VB .NET supports four types of brushes:

- A **SolidBrush** fills a shape with a solid color.

- A **HatchBrush** has a foreground and background color. The foreground color specifies the color of the horizontal, vertical, or diagonal lines drawn on the background. A HatchBrush supports over 20 different styles. See the Help page for the HatchStyle enumeration for a list of the different styles.

- A **LinearGradientBrush** defines a brush with two colors. The colors painted in the shape are varied from the starting color to the ending color. The colors can be varied horizontally, vertically, or diagonally.

- A **TextureBrush** fills a shape with an image.

Filling a Shape with a SolidBrush

To create a SolidBrush, you create an instance of the SolidBrush class using its constructor. The constructor accepts one argument: a color. Once a SolidBrush has been created, you can use that SolidBrush to fill a shape such as a rectangle or polygon.

Examine the following statements to create a rectangle and a SolidBrush, and then fill that rectangle using the SolidBrush:

```
Dim sbCurrent As New SolidBrush(Color.Red)
Dim recCurrent As New Rectangle(1, 1, 100, 100)
e.Graphics.FillRectangle(sbCurrent, recCurrent)
sbCurrent.Dispose()
```

The preceding statements first create a red SolidBrush and then a rectangle. The FillRectangle method of the Graphics class fills a rectangle using a SolidBrush or other type of brush. The FillRectangle method accepts two arguments: the SolidBrush and the rectangle to fill. Just as you should explicitly dispose of a custom pen, so should you dispose of a custom brush by calling the Dispose method.

In addition to custom brushes, you can use named brushes just as you can use named pens, as shown in the following statements:

```
Dim recCurrent As New Rectangle(1, 1, 100, 100)
e.Graphics.FillRectangle(Brushes.Red, recCurrent)
```

The preceding statements fill a rectangle using a named brush instead of a custom SolidBrush. Named brushes, like named pens, need not be explicitly disposed.

12

Filling a Shape with a HatchBrush

A HatchBrush fills a region with a pattern instead of a solid color. To fill a rectangle or other region with a HatchBrush, you create an instance of the HatchBrush class, and then use that HatchBrush as an argument to the FillRectangle method. The HatchBrush constructor has the following syntax:

Syntax

System.Drawing.Drawing2D.HatchBrush constructor

Public Sub New HatchBrush(*hatchstyle* **As HatchStyle,** *forecolor* **As Color**)
Public Sub New HatchBrush(*hatchstyle* **As HatchStyle,** *forecolor* **As Color,** *backcolor* **As Color**)

Definition

The **HatchBrush** constructor creates a new HatchBrush having a particular style. The arguments define the foreground and optional background colors.

Dissection

- The *hatchstyle* argument specifies the type of HatchBrush to use. The HatchStyle enumeration defines the possible values.

- The *forecolor* and *backcolor* arguments specify the color of the hatch pattern and the background color, respectively. Notice that the first overloaded version of the constructor has no backcolor. In this case, the brush is drawn without a background.

Code Example

```
Dim hbCurrent As New HatchBrush(HatchStyle.Cross, _
    Color.Red)
Dim recCurrent As New Rectangle(5, 5, 100, 100)
e.Graphics.FillRectangle(hbCurrent, recCurrent)
hbCurrent.Dispose()
```

Code Dissection

The first of the preceding statements creates a HatchBrush using a Cross style. The foreground color of the HatchBrush is red. There is no background color. The second statement defines the rectangle. The final statements fill the region of the rectangle using the HatchBrush and then dispose of the HatchBrush.

To illustrate the use of a HatchBrush, you will fill a rectangle that is the same size as the splash screen:

To create filled rectangles with brushes:

1. Activate the Code Editor for the form named **frmSplash.vb**, if necessary, and then enter the following statements (shown in bold) at the beginning of the **Paint** event handler:

```
Dim recHatchFill As New Rectangle(0, 0, _
    Me.ClientSize.Width, Me.ClientSize.Height)
Dim hbCurrent As New HatchBrush( _
    HatchStyle.Percent90, Color.Gray)
e.Graphics.FillRectangle(hbCurrent, recHatchFill)
hbCurrent.Dispose()
Dim pntStart As New Point(10, Me.ClientSize.Height - 10)
```

The preceding statements create a filled rectangle using a HatchBrush. Again, note that the HatchBrush, being a custom brush, is explicitly disposed. Notice that the first argument to the HatchBrush constructor is HatchStyle.Percent90. This value specifies a 90 percent hatch. This is the ratio of the foreground color to the background color. Again, refer to the HatchStyle enumeration Help page for a complete list of possible values.

2. Test the solution. The filled rectangle appears on the splash screen.

Notice that you filled the rectangle that covers the splash screen before drawing the other shapes. The order in which you draw shapes is significant. Each successive shape that is drawn or filled is drawn or filled on top of the previous shape.

Filling Shapes with a LinearGradientBrush

The LinearGradientBrush class defines a brush used to fill a shape. A bounding rectangle defines the shape of the LinearGradientBrush. The colors of the rectangle are then gradated from one color to another. Examine the following statements to create a LinearGradientBrush and fill a rectangle:

```
Dim recLGB As New Rectangle(10, 10, _
    Me.ClientSize.Width - 20, 235)
Dim lgbRectangle As New LinearGradientBrush(recLGB, _
    Color.AliceBlue, Color.SteelBlue, _
    LinearGradientMode.Horizontal)
e.Graphics.FillRectangle(lgbRectangle, recLGB)
lgbRectangle.Dispose()
```

The first of the preceding statements declares a rectangle. Then a horizontal LinearGradientBrush is created that is the same size as the rectangle. The color will be gradated from left to right starting from AliceBlue and moving to SteelBlue. Note that the other gradient modes are BackwardDiagonal, ForwardDiagonal, and Vertical. The final statements fill the same rectangle using the LinearGradientBrush. Again, the preceding statements would appear in a Paint event handler and e.Graphics references an instance of the Graphics class. As with all custom brushes, you must explicitly dispose of a LinearGradientBrush.

To create and fill a rectangle with a LinearGradientBrush:

1. Activate the Code Editor for the form named **frmSplash.vb**, if necessary, and then enter the following statements (shown in bold) at the end of the **Paint** event handler:

```
penOutline.Dispose()
Dim recLGB As New Rectangle(10, 10, _
    Me.ClientSize.Width - 20, 235)
Dim lgbRectangle As New LinearGradientBrush(recLGB, _
    Color.AliceBlue, Color.SteelBlue, _
    LinearGradientMode.Horizontal)
e.Graphics.FillRectangle(lgbRectangle, recLGB)
lgbRectangle.Dispose()
```

2. Test the solution. The filled rectangle appears on the splash screen.

Painting an Image with a TextureBrush

A TextureBrush is used to fill a shape with an image. The overloaded TextureBrush constructor allows you to specify the image and the rectangle that will fill the region, as shown in the following statements:

```
Dim imgCurrent As Image
imgCurrent = Image.FromFile("..\..\Data\CourseLogo.bmp")
Dim tbCurrent As New TextureBrush(imgCurrent)
e.Graphics.FillRectangle(tbCurrent, 1, 1, 200, 200)
```

The preceding statements read an image from a file, and then create a TextureBrush from that image. The final statement fills a rectangle with the image. Again, the preceding statements assume that e.Graphics references an instance of the Graphics class.

DRAWING TEXT

Drawing text involves creating a font with the overloaded Font constructor, and then calling the DrawString method to paint a string having a particular font. The overloaded Font constructor has numerous syntax variations. Only one is discussed in the following syntax diagram:

Syntax

System.Drawing.Font constructor

Public Sub New(ByVal *familyName* **As String, ByVal** *emSize* **As Single, ByVal** *style* **As FontStyle)**

Definition

The **Font** constructor creates a new instance of the Font class having a particular typeface, font characteristic, and size.

Dissection

- The *familyName* argument defines the font family, such as "Arial" or "Tahoma," used to create the font.

- The *emSize* argument defines the font size.

- The *style* argument allows you to specify font attributes such as boldface or underlining.

Code Example

```
Dim fntCurrent As New Font("Arial", 14, FontStyle.Bold)
```

Code Dissection

The preceding statement creates a new 14-point bold Arial font.

Once you have created an instance of the Font class, you call the DrawString method of the Graphics class to display the text on the drawing surface. The overloaded DrawString method has the following syntax:

Syntax

System.Drawing.DrawString method

Overloads Public Sub DrawString(ByVal *s* **As String, ByVal** *font* **As Font, ByVal** *brush* **As Brush, ByVal** *point* **As PointF)**
Overloads Public Sub DrawString(ByVal *s* **As String, ByVal** *font* **As Font, ByVal** *brush* **As Brush,** *layoutrectangle* **As RectangleF)**
Overloads Public Sub DrawString(ByVal *s* **As String, ByVal** *font* **As Font, ByVal** *brush* **As Brush, ByVal** *point* **As PointF, ByVal** *format* **As StringFormat)**
Overloads Public Sub DrawString(ByVal *s* **As String, ByVal** *font* **As Font, ByVal** *brush* **As Brush,** *layoutrectangle* **As RectangleF,** *format* **As StringFormat)**

Definition

The overloaded **DrawString** method draws a string to a graphical output device using a brush.

Dissection

- The first argument *s* contains the string to be drawn.

12

- The *font* argument contains an instance of the Font class representing the font to be drawn.

- The *point* argument contains a Point structure defining the origin of the drawn string.

- The string is drawn using *brush* as the brush.

- The *layoutrectangle* argument contains a bounding rectangle in which the string will be drawn.

- The *format* argument is used to left-justify or right-justify the text within a bounded rectangle.

Code Example

```
e.Graphics.DrawString("This is a string.", _
    fntCurrent, Brushes.Red, 0, 0)
```

Code Dissection

The preceding statement draws a string at the upper-left corner of the output device using an instance of the Font class named fntCurrent. The string is drawn using a named red brush. Again, e.Graphics is assumed to reference an instance of the Graphics class.

Next you will draw a string on the splash screen by creating an instance of the Font class, and then calling the DrawString method. The string that you draw will appear inside of the outlined rectangle you have already created.

To draw text to a graphical output device:

1. Activate the Code Editor for the form named **frmSplash.vb**, if necessary, and then enter the following statements (shown in bold) at the end of the **Paint** event handler:

```
lgbRectangle.Dispose()
Dim recText As New Rectangle(1, 1, 390, 80)
Dim fntCurrent As New Font("Arial", 48, FontStyle.Bold)
Dim lgbCurrent As New LinearGradientBrush(recText, _
    Color.AliceBlue, Color.SteelBlue, _
    LinearGradientMode.Horizontal)
e.Graphics.DrawString( _
    "Chapter 12", fntCurrent, lgbCurrent, 10, 260)
fntCurrent.Dispose()
lgbCurrent.Dispose()
```

2. Test the solution. The text appears on the splash screen in a LinearGradientBrush.

As with custom pens and brushes, you should explicitly dispose of a Font instance when you are finished with it.

COMPLEX SHAPES

In addition to creating simple lines and rectangles, VB .NET allows you to draw much more complex shapes such as polygons, arcs, and lines. The following list summarizes the complex shapes that you will create in this section:

- Three or more points may be connected together to form a polygon. VB .NET allows you to draw outlined polygons or fill polygons.

- Ellipses are created by defining a bounding rectangle. The center of the ellipse is the center of the bounding rectangle. Ellipses may be outlined or filled.

- An arc represents a portion of an ellipse.

- Essentially, a pie is created using that part of an ellipse formed by an arc. The pie is drawn or filled from the center of the ellipse using the angle defined by the arc.

We discuss each of these preceding shapes in turn.

Drawing and Filling Polygons

The Graphics class supplies methods to draw a polygon outline using a pen (DrawPolygon), and to fill a polygon using a brush (FillPolygon). The DrawPolygon method accepts two arguments: a pen and an array of Point structures. The FillPolygon method also accepts two arguments: a brush and an array of Point structures. Examine the following statements to draw a polygon outline and fill a polygon:

```
Dim pnt1 As New Point(100, 100)
Dim pnt2 As New Point(150, 200)
Dim pnt3 As New Point(50, 200)
Dim pntList() As Point = {pnt1, pnt2, pnt3}
e.Graphics.DrawPolygon(Pens.Black, pntList)
e.Graphics.FillPolygon(Brushes.Plum, pntList)
```

The preceding statements create the polygon shown in Figure 12-6. As the polygon has three sides, the polygon drawn is a triangle.

You will now create a polygon on the splash screen with three sides, fill that polygon with a brush, and then draw an outline around the polygon. In other words, you will create a triangle. In addition, you will also fill a rectangle and then draw an outline around the rectangle.

12

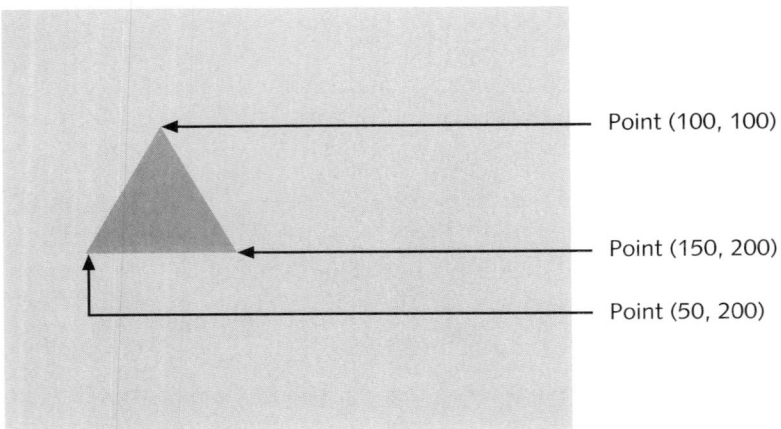

Point (100, 100)

Point (150, 200)

Point (50, 200)

Figure 12-6   Drawing a polygon

To create a polygon:

1. Activate the Code Editor for the form named **frmSplash.vb**, if necessary, and then enter the following statements (shown in bold) at the end of the **Paint** event handler:

```
lgbCurrent.Dispose()
Dim recSolidFill As New Rectangle(50, 50, 100, 100)
e.Graphics.FillRectangle(Brushes.Thistle, recSolidFill)
e.Graphics.DrawRectangle(Pens.Black, recSolidFill)

Dim pnt1 As New Point(100, 100)
Dim pnt2 As New Point(150, 200)
Dim pnt3 As New Point(50, 200)
Dim pntArray() As Point = {pnt1, pnt2, pnt3}
e.Graphics.FillPolygon(Brushes.Plum, pntArray)
e.Graphics.DrawPolygon(Pens.Black, pntArray)
```

2. Test the solution. The filled triangle appears on the splash screen with a black outline. A filled rectangle appears behind the triangle.

Next, you will learn how to draw and fill an ellipse.

Drawing and Filling Ellipses

Drawing an ellipse involves defining a bounding rectangle. The shape of the bounding rectangle defines the shape of the ellipse. Once you have defined the shape of the rectangle, you call the DrawEllipse method of the Graphics class to draw an outline of the ellipse using a pen, or call the FillEllipse method to fill the region of the ellipse with a brush. Figure 12-7 illustrates an ellipse drawn within a bounding rectangle.

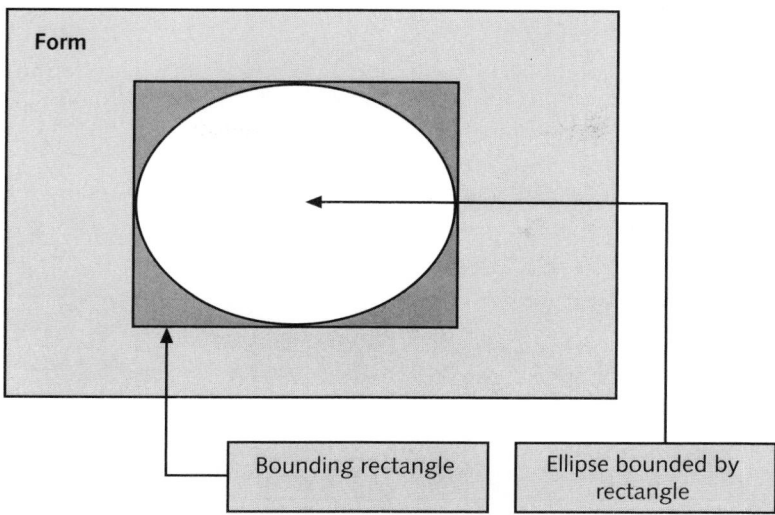

Figure 12-7   Drawing an ellipse

The following statements create a filled ellipse and draw a border around that ellipse:

```
Dim recCircle As New Rectangle(125, 125, 100, 100)
e.Graphics.FillEllipse(Brushes.DarkOrchid, recCircle)
e.Graphics.DrawEllipse(Pens.Black, recCircle)
```

The first of the preceding statements defines the bounding rectangle for the ellipse. The second statement fills the ellipse with a solid named brush, and then the final statement draws a black outline around that same ellipse.

Next, you will create an ellipse whose bounding rectangle is a square. Thus, the ellipse that you create will form a circle:

To create an ellipse:

1. Activate the Code Editor for the form named **frmSplash.vb**, if necessary, and then enter the following statements (shown in bold) at the end of the **Paint** event handler:

```
e.Graphics.DrawPolygon(Pens.Black, pntArray)
Dim recCircle As New Rectangle(125, 125, 100, 100)
e.Graphics.FillEllipse(Brushes.DarkOrchid, recCircle)
e.Graphics.DrawEllipse(Pens.Black, recCircle)
```

2. Test the solution. The filled and outlined ellipses appear on the splash screen.

Next, you will learn how to create an arc.

12

Drawing Arcs

The steps to create an arc require that you define an ellipse, along with defining an angle that encompasses a portion of the ellipse. The origin of the angle begins along the *x* axis. The radius of the defined arc increases clockwise from the origin. The radius is measured in degrees. Figure 12-8 illustrates how an arc is drawn.

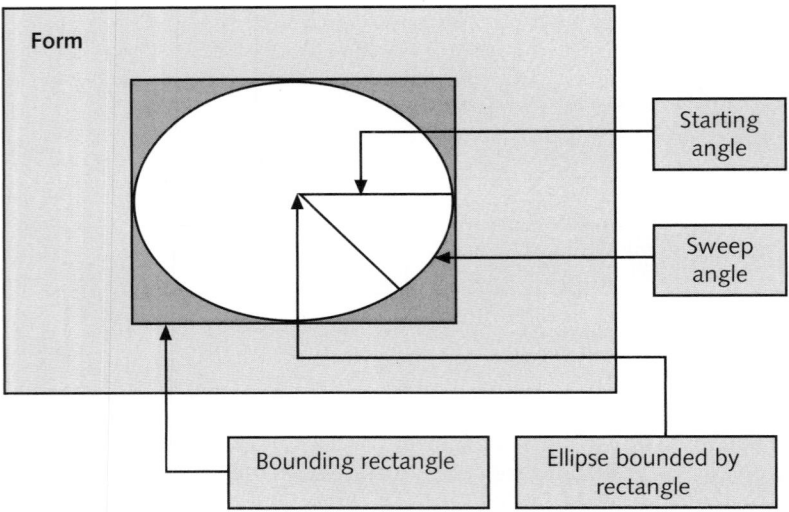

Figure 12-8   Drawing an arc

As shown in Figure 12-8, the bounding rectangle defines the shape of the ellipse. The starting angle identifies the staring point of the arc along the ellipse. The sweep angle defines the number of degrees of rotation along the ellipse.

To draw an arc, you call the overloaded DrawArc method. There exists no corresponding FillArc method because it makes no sense to fill an arc. An arc, by definition, has no filled region. Examine the following statements that define and draw an arc:

```
Dim recArc As New Rectangle(5, 5, 100, 100)
e.Graphics.DrawArc(Pens.Red, recArc, 0, 90)
```

The first of the preceding statements defines a bounding rectangle. The ellipse formed by the preceding rectangle is a circle. The DrawArc method draws an arc along that circle starting with an angle of 0. The sweep angle of the arc is 90 degrees in the clockwise direction.

Creating a Pie Shape

Having seen how to draw an ellipse and how to draw an arc from an ellipse, the steps to create a pie are relatively easy. First you create a rectangle that defines the bounds of the ellipse. Second, you call the DrawPie method, having the same arguments as the DrawArc method. These arguments specify the pen, bounding rectangle, starting angle, and sweep angle. Again, the DrawPie method draws an outline of a pie, and the FillPie method fills the pie.

The following statements illustrate how to fill a pie with a brush and draw an outline of the pie using a pen:

```
Dim recCircle As New Rectangle(155, 40, 200, 200)
e.Graphics.FillPie(Brushes.Purple, recCircle, 0, 45)
e.Graphics.DrawPie(Pens.Black, recCircle, 0, 45)
```

The first of the preceding statements declares the rectangle that will define the shape and size of the ellipse. The starting angle is 0 and the sweep angle is 45 degrees. The second and third statements fill the pie and draw an outline around the pie, respectively.

To create a pie:

1. Activate the Code Editor for the form named **frmSplash.vb**, if necessary, and then enter the following statements (shown in bold) at the end of the **Paint** event handler:

```
e.Graphics.DrawEllipse(Pens.Black, recCircle)
e.Graphics.FillPie(Brushes.Purple, recCircle, 0, 45)
e.Graphics.DrawPie(Pens.Black, recCircle, 0, 45)
```

2. Test the solution. The filled pie appears on the splash screen. A black border surrounds the filled pie.

In addition to drawing graphical shapes, you can also load images, such as bitmaps, and draw them to a graphics surface.

12

DRAWING IMAGES

Just as you use members of the Graphics class to draw shapes such as lines and rectangles, you also use members of the Graphics class to draw images to a graphical device. Drawing an image requires that you first load the image into memory. The FromFile method of the Image class loads an image into memory. The method accepts one argument: the file name containing the image. Valid file formats for images are bitmaps, icons, and Windows metafiles.

Examine the following statements to load an image:

```
Dim imgCurrent As Image
imgCurrent = Image.FromFile("C:\image.bmp")
```

Once an image has been loaded into memory, you draw it to a graphics surface by calling the DrawImage method of the Graphics class. The overloaded DrawImage method has the following syntax:

Syntax

System.Drawing.DrawImage method

Overloads Public Sub DrawImage(ByVal *image* **As Image, ByVal** *point* **As Point)**
Overloads Public Sub DrawImage(ByVal *image* **As Image, ByVal** *rect* **As Rectangle)**

Definition

The overloaded **DrawImage** method draws an image to a graphical device.

Dissection

- The first overloaded method accepts two arguments: the image to draw and a Point structure. The image is drawn using the point as the origin. The size of the drawn image is the same as the size of the underlying image.

- The second overloaded method also accepts two arguments: the image to draw and a bounding rectangle. The image will be stretched or scaled to fit within the bounds of the rectangle.

Code Example

```
Dim imgCurrent As Image
Dim pntImage As New Point(0, 0)
Dim recImage As New Rectangle(40, 40, 80, 160)
imgCurrent = Image.FromFile("C:\image.bmp")

e.Graphics.DrawImage(imgCurrent, pntImage)
e.Graphics.DrawImage(imgCurrent, recImage)
```

Code Dissection

The preceding statements create instances of the Point and Rectangle structures. The image is read into the variable named imgCurrent. The first call to the DrawImage method draws the unscaled image at the point specified by pntImage. The second call stretches the image so that it is drawn within the region of the rectangle defined by recImage.

Next, you will draw an image. You will use the Course Technology logo as the image.

To draw an image:

1. Activate the Code Editor for the form named **frmSplash.vb**, if necessary, and then enter the following statements (shown in bold) at the end of the **Paint** event handler:

```
e.Graphics.DrawPie(Pens.Black, recCircle, 0, 45)

Dim imgCurrent As Image
imgCurrent = Image.FromFile("..\..\Data\CourseLogo.bmp")
Dim recImage As New Rectangle(300, 175, _
    imgCurrent.Size.Width, imgCurrent.Size.Height)
e.Graphics.DrawImage(imgCurrent, recImage)
```

The preceding statements create a bounding rectangle to store the image such that the rectangle is the same size as the image, and then draw the image inside the region of the bounding rectangle.

2. Test the solution. The image appears in the splash screen.

At this point in the solution's development, you have completed programming the splash screen. Next you will learn how to scale and manipulate the graphics that appear on a form.

GRAPHICAL TRANSFORMATIONS

By default, when you draw to a graphical surface such as a form, the origin of the form is its upper-left corner and the unit of measure is pixels. Furthermore, x values increase to the right and y values increase in a downward direction. However, you can call various methods to change the form's origin or change the unit of measure. To understand how to perform these tasks, we first introduce how the GDI+ uses coordinate systems.

When you call a method of the Graphics class to draw a shape such as a line, the endpoints of that line are expressed in **world coordinates**. Examine the following statement:

```
e.Graphics.DrawLine(Pens.Black, 0, 0, 50, 50)
```

The preceding call to the DrawLine method draws a line from the origin (0, 0) to a point 50 pixels to the right on the x axis and 50 pixels down on the y axis. However, it is possible to perform graphical transformations that will alter the position of the objects drawn on the output device. The first graphical transformation that takes place is called the world transformation, which we discuss next.

World Transformation

When a line is drawn on a form, the GDI+ maps world coordinates to page coordinates. Page coordinates are discussed in a moment. Suppose that the form's origin is not the upper-left corner of the form's client area. Rather, assume that the origin of the form is shifted 50 pixels to the right on the x axis, and 50 pixels down on the y axis. In such a

12

case, the GDI+ translates world coordinates into page coordinates before drawing the line on the form. Figure 12-9 illustrates the process.

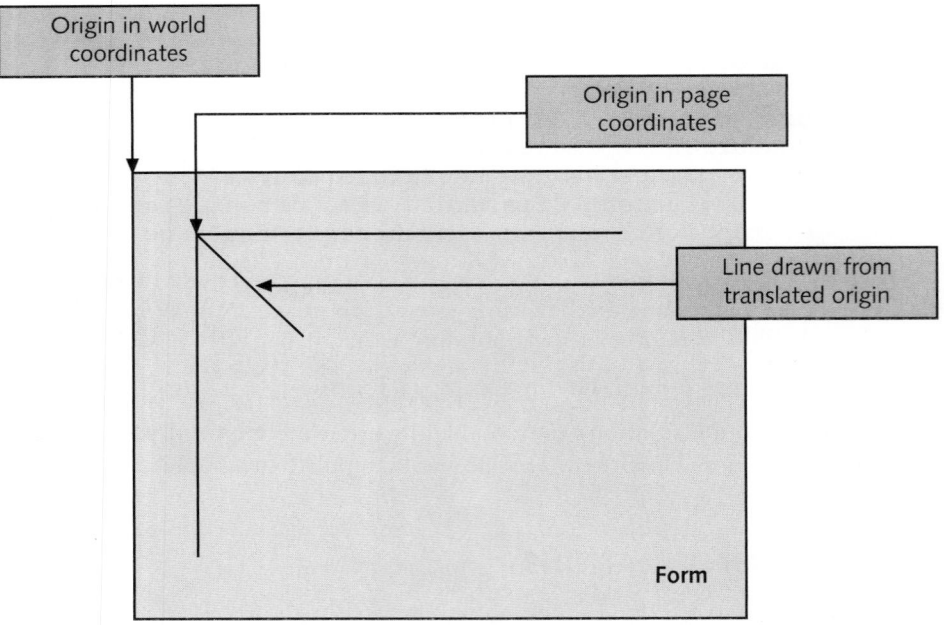

Figure 12-9   Mapping world coordinates to page coordinates

Instead of the line having points of (0, 0) and (50, 50), the line is shifted down and to the right so that the page coordinates are (50, 50) and (100, 100). This mapping of world coordinates to page coordinates is called **world transformation**.

Suppose that you wanted the origin of the drawing coordinates to be in the center of the form, rather than appearing in the upper-left corner of the form. To accomplish this task, you call the TranslateTransform method of the Graphics class to move the origin. The TranslateTransform method accepts two arguments. The first argument contains the number of units to shift the x axis, and the second argument contains the number of units to shift the y axis. Positive x values shift the x axis to the right and negative values shift the x axis to the left. Positive y values shift the y axis downward and negative values shift the y axis upward.

Examine the following statements to move the origin to the center of the form:

```
e.Graphics.TranslateTransform( _
    ToSingle(Me.ClientSize.Width / 2), _
    ToSingle(Me.ClientSize.Height / 2))
```

The preceding statements move the form's origin from its current position (0, 0) to the center of the form by setting *x* and *y* transformation values to ½ the width and ½ the height of the form's client area, respectively.

Page Transformation

Another transformation may also take place before the graphical shape is drawn on the output device. By default, the unit of measure applied by the GDI+ is expressed in pixels. However, suppose that you wanted to express values in a different unit of measure such as points or inches. In this case, the GDI+ performs a **page transformation**, converting page coordinates into device coordinates.

As mentioned, the GDI+ uses pixels as the default unit of measure for all distances. Thus, the page coordinates are the same as the device coordinates when the default unit of measure is used. However, suppose that you wanted to perform drawing operations using a different unit of measure, such as inches. To change the unit of measure, you set the PageUnit property of the Graphics class. Then, when you call drawing methods of the Graphics class, the unit of measure specified by the PageUnit property is applied. For example, examine the following statements:

```
e.Graphics.PageUnit = GraphicsUnit.Inch
e.Graphics.DrawLine(Pens.Black, 0, 0, 0, 1)
```

The preceding statements draw a line that is one inch long from the form's origin, because the unit of measure is changed to inches by setting the PageUnit property to GraphicsUnit.Inch.

If you were to draw the line using the preceding statements, you would find that a problem exists. Because the unit of measure is expressed in inches, the line would be drawn one inch wide. Remember that the default width of a pen is one unit. To solve this problem, you can use the following two properties exposed by the Graphics class:

- The **DpiX** property gets the horizontal resolution of the *x* axis.

- The **DpiY** property gets the vertical resolution of the *y* axis.

Thus, to create a pen that will draw a line one pixel wide, you can create a new pen and draw the line using the following statements:

```
e.Graphics.PageUnit = GraphicsUnit.Inch
Dim penCurrent As New Pen(Color.Black, 1 / e.Graphics.DpiX)
e.Graphics.DrawLine(penCurrent, 0, 0, 1, 1)
penCurrent.Dispose()
```

The preceding statements create a new pen and then draw a line. The width of the pen is 1 (one inch) divided by the horizontal resolution of the *x* axis. Thus, the pen drawn will be one pixel in width.

In addition to changing the origin of the form, you can also rotate graphics about the form.

12

Graphical Rotation

When you call the **RotateTransform** method of the Graphics class, graphics are rotated about the form's origin. Again, the origin is (0, 0) by default, but can be changed by calling the Translate Transform method first. To rotate graphics, you call the Rotate Transform method of the Graphics class with one argument. That argument defines the number of degrees of rotation to be applied. Rotating graphics by a positive number causes the graphics to be rotated in a clockwise direction. Rotating by a negative number causes the graphics to be rotated in a counterclockwise direction. Examine the following statements:

```
e.Graphics.RotateTransform(90)
e.Graphics.RotateTransform(180)
```

The preceding statements perform a rotate transformation rotating graphical objects 90 and 180 degrees, respectively.

In addition to rotating graphics, you can also change the scaling, thereby allowing the user to zoom in or zoom out of the drawing surface.

Scaling Graphics

Essentially, scaling allows you to change the magnification of the graphics drawn about the form. The normal scale factor is 1. Calling the Scale Transform method of the Graphics class changes the scaling. The Scale Transform method accepts two arguments. The first argument defines the scaling for the x axis, and the second argument defines the scaling for the y axis. Thus, if you apply different values for the x and y axes, the graphics will be stretched along one axis or the other.

Examine the following statements to change the scaling:

```
e.Graphics.ScaleTransform(2, 2)
e.Graphics.ScaleTransform(0.5, 0.5)
```

The first of the preceding statements effectively sets the zoom-factor to two. One transformation is based on the existing transformation. Thus, the second statement takes the existing scaling and scales it by 50%. Thus, after the second statement has executed, the scaling is the same as it was before the first ScaleTransform was performed.

To illustrate transformations, you will create a simple image viewer. The image viewer will use module-level variables to store the rotation angle, zooming, and panning units, as shown in the following variable declarations:

```
Private imgCurrent As Image
Private msngScale As Single = 1
Private msngSweepAngle As Single
Private msngPanX As Single
Private msngPanY As Single
```

The preceding variables have already been declared in the startup solution. As the user clicks the menu items, the code that you will write changes the value of these variables, and then invalidates the form, causing the form's Paint event to fire. In the Paint event handler, these variables will be used to perform the desired transformation.

To create an image viewer:

1. Activate the Code Editor for the form named **frmImageViewer.vb**, and then enter the following statements in the **Click** event handler for the menu item named **mmuFileOpen**:

```
Dim dlgResult As DialogResult
dlgResult = ofdImage.ShowDialog()
If dlgResult = DialogResult.OK Then
    imgCurrent = Image.FromFile(ofdImage.FileName)
    Me.Invalidate()
End If
```

The preceding statements allow the user to select an image using an instance of the OpenFileDialog control. If the user clicks the OK button, the image is read. Calling the Invalidate method of the form causes the Paint event to fire, thereby causing the image to be drawn on the form. For brevity, we have omitted an exception handler. Thus, if the user opens a file that is not a valid image file, then an exception will be thrown.

2. Enter the following statements in the **Click** event handler for the menu item named **mmuRotate**:

```
msngSweepAngle += 1
Me.Invalidate()
```

3. Enter the following statements in the **Click** event handler for the menu item named **mmuZoomIn**:

```
msngScale = ToSingle(msngScale * 1.1)
Me.Invalidate()
```

4. Enter the following statements in the **Click** event handler for the menu item named **mmuZoomOut**:

```
msngScale = ToSingle(msngScale * 0.9)
Me.Invalidate()
```

5. Enter the following statements in the **Click** event handler for the menu item named **mmuPanLeft**:

```
msngPanX -= 5
Me.Invalidate()
```

6. Enter the following statements in the **Click** event handler for the menu item named **mmuPanRight**:

```
msngPanX += 5
Me.Invalidate()
```

12

7. Enter the following statements in the **Click** event handler for the menu item named **mmuPanUp**:

```
msngPanY -= 5
Me.Invalidate()
```

8. Enter the following statements in the **Click** event handler for the menu item named **mmuPanDown**:

```
msngPanY += 5
Me.Invalidate()
```

9. Enter the following statements in the **Paint** event handler for the form:

```
Try
    e.Graphics.TranslateTransform( _
        ToSingle(Me.ClientSize.Width / 2 + msngPanX ), _
        ToSingle(Me.ClientSize.Height / 2 + msngPanY))
    e.Graphics.RotateTransform(msngSweepAngle)
    e.Graphics.ScaleTransform(msngScale, msngScale)
    e.Graphics.DrawImage(imgCurrent, 0, 0)
Catch ex As System.Exception
End Try
```

The preceding statements apply the various transformations. The call to the TranslateTransform method moves the image using the values stored in the variables msngPanX and msngPanY. The second statement performs the rotation. The third statement performs the scaling. The final statement draws the image.

10. Test the solution. Click **Windows**, and then click **Image Viewer**. Load the image named **Chapter.12\Data\CourseLogo.bmp**. Using the menu items, zoom in and out of the window, and rotate the image.

So far, you have performed all the drawing operations to a window. You use the same process to draw graphics to a printer.

DRAWING TO A PRINTER

Drawing graphics to a printer involves using the same GDI+ methods that you have used previously in the chapter. Instead of drawing to the screen using the form's Paint event handler, however, you draw shapes to a printer using the PrintDocument class. VB .NET supplies several related classes that support the printing process, as described in the following list:

- The **PageSettings** class has members to define the page orientation and page margins.

- The **PrinterSettings** class allows you to define settings for the printer itself and to select a printer.

■ The **PrintDialog** class works similarly to the OpenFileDialog or the SaveFileDialog classes. It allows the user to select print options, such as whether the document should be printed using portrait or landscape orientation, or to select the number of copies to print.

 To complete the following steps that relate to printing, you must have a printer installed on your computer.

Understanding the PrintDocument Class

You can create an instance of the PrintDocument class programmatically, or use the PrintDocument control to accomplish the same task. The PrintDocument class supports the following members:

Syntax

System.Drawing.Printing.PrintDocument class

Public Properties

■ The **DefaultPageSettings** property references an object of type PageSettings. The PageSettings class has members that describe the characteristics of a printed page, such as the page margins and whether the page will be printed in portrait mode or landscape mode.

■ The **DocumentName** property contains the name of the document. The name will appear in the dialog box that appears while the document is printing. The document name will also appear in the print queue.

■ The **PrinterSettings** property allows you to define which printer will be used to print the document.

Public Methods

■ Calling the **Print** method begins the printing process.

Public Events

■ The **BeginPrint** event fires just before printing begins, and the **EndPrint** event fires after printing completes.

■ The **PrintPage** event fires after the BeginPrint event. In this event handler, you typically write the necessary statements to send a document to the printer.

Printing with the PrintDocument class is a two-step process. First you call the Print method of the PrintDocument class to fire a PrintPage event. Conceptually, the process is similar to calling the Invalidate method of the form to fire the Paint event. Second, you write the statements in the PrintPage event handler to perform the actual task of printing. The following statement calls the Print method of the PrintDocument class instance named pdImage:

```
pdImage.Print()
```

When you call the Print method of the PrintDocument class, the PrintPage event of the PrintDocument class is raised. Again, the first argument of the PrintPage event, named sender, has a data type of System.Object. The second argument has a data type of PrintPageEventArgs. The Graphics property of this object references an instance of the Graphics class in the same way as the Graphics property of the PaintEventArgs class. Examine the following statements to print an image to the printer instead of displaying it on a form:

```
e.Graphics.DrawImage(imgCurrent, 0, 0)
e.HasMorePages = False
```

As you can see from the preceding statement, you call the DrawImage method as before. We assume that the variable imgCurrent stores the current image. Instead of painting the image to a form, however, the image is sent to the printer. As you can see, the steps to draw objects to a printer are the same as the steps to draw objects to the screen. The final statement sets the HasMorePages property to False, forcing the page to be printed. The page will not print until the HasMorePages property is set to False. Note that if you set the HasMorePages property to True, the page will be printed. Then, the PrintPage event is fired again so as to allow you to print the data for the next page.

In the steps that follow, you will load and print an image to the printer:

To load and print an image to the printer:

1. Create an instance of the PrintDocument control on the form named **frmImageViewer.vb**. Set its name to **pdImage**.

2. Enter the following statement in the **Click** event handler for the menu item named **mmuFilePrint**:

```
pdImage.Print()
```

3. Create the **PrintPage** event handler for the PrintDocument control named **pdImage**, and then enter the following statements:

```
e.Graphics.DrawImage(imgCurrent,0 , 0)
e.HasMorePages = False
```

4. Test the solution. Display the image viewer form. Open the image named **Chapter.12\Data\CourseLogo.bmp**. On the menu bar, click **File**, and then click **Print** to print the image to the printer.

At this point, you have provided the user with the most simple of printing capabilities. However, to improve the user interface you should allow the user to select a printer and describe how they want the document printed. To allow the user to select a printer and select print options, you use the PrintDialog control in conjunction with the PrinterSettings and PageSettings classes.

The PrintDialog Control

The PrintDialog control operates similarly to the OpenFileDialog and SaveFileDialog controls. That is, you display the PrintDialog control by calling the ShowDialog method. The ShowDialog method returns a value having a data type of DialogResult, which you can use to determine whether the user clicked the OK or Cancel button. Figure 12-10 shows an instance of the PrintDialog control.

Figure 12-10 PrintDialog control instance

As shown in Figure 12-10, the PrintDialog control allows the user to select which pages to print, the number of copies to print, and which printer to use. Clicking the Properties button allows the user to set more detailed properties including whether to print in portrait or landscape mode, and the order in which the pages should be printed. The PrintDialog control supports the following members:

Syntax

System.Windows.Forms.PrintDialog control

Public Properties

- The **AllowSomePages** property enables the radio buttons in the Print range section allowing the user to select which pages to print.
- The **AllowSelection** property enables the Selection radio button allowing the user to print the selection. Note that the All button is always enabled.

- The **PrinterSettings** property references a PrinterSettings object. When you set properties using the PrintDialog control, those settings are stored in an associated PrinterSettings object.

Public Methods

- The **ShowDialog** method displays the PrintDialog control. The method returns a value of DialogResult.OK if the user clicks the OK button and DialogResult.Cancel if the user clicks the Cancel button.

Before you call the ShowDialog method to display an instance of the PrintDialog control, you must associate the control instance with an instance of the PrinterSettings class. It is through this instance of the PrinterSettings class that you determine the selections made by the user.

Examine the following statements to configure an instance of the PrintDialog control named dlgImage and display it:

```
Dim psImage As New PrinterSettings()
Dim dlgResult As DialogResult
dlgImage.PrinterSettings = psImage
dlgResult = dlgImage.ShowDialog()
If dlgResult = DialogResult.OK Then
    ' Statements to print output
End If
```

The first of the preceding statements creates an instance of the PrinterSettings class. The third statement associates that PrinterSettings class instance with the PrinterSettings property of the PrintDialog control instance. If the PrinterSettings property of the PrintDialog control is not associated with an instance of the PrinterSettings class, then an exception will occur. The remaining statements display the PrintDialog control instance. If the user clicks the OK button, then the statements inside the If statement will execute.

Just as the OpenFileDialog control does not open a file, the PrintDialog control does not print a document. The PrintDialog control merely sets the properties of the associated PrinterSettings class. You then use the values of those properties to print the document. The PrinterSettings class supports the following members:

Syntax

System.Drawing.Printing.PrinterSettings class

Public Properties

- The **Copies** property contains the number of copies to print.

- The **FromPage** property contains the starting page to print and the **ToPage** property contains the ending page to print. Again, it is up to your program to use the information and print the selected pages.

- The **IsValid** property examines the value of the PrinterName property to determine whether or not the printer is a valid printer.

- The **PrinterName** property contains the name of the printer to use.

- The Boolean **PrintToFile** property, if True, causes the document to be printed to a file. If False (the default), then the document is printed to the selected printer.

Next, you will enhance the mmuFilePrint_Click event handler on the image viewer form to display an instance of the PrintDialog control. Using the options stored in the PrinterSettings object, you will configure the instance of the PrintDocument class.

To create and use the PrintDialog control:

1. Activate the Code Editor for the form named **frmImageViewer.vb**, if necessary, and then enter the following statements (shown in bold) in the Click event handler for the menu item named **mmuFilePrint**:

```
Dim dlgResult As DialogResult
Dim pintCount As Integer
Dim psImage As New PrinterSettings()
Dim psPage As New PageSettings()

dlgImage.PrinterSettings = psImage
dlgImage.AllowSomePages = True
dlgImage.AllowSelection = True
dlgResult = dlgImage.ShowDialog()

If dlgResult = DialogResult.OK Then
    If psImage.IsValid Then
        pdImage.DocumentName = ofdImage.FileName
        If dlgImage.PrinterSettings.LandscapeAngle > 0 Then
            psPage.Landscape = True
            pdImage.DefaultPageSettings = psPage
        End If

        pdImage.PrinterSettings = psImage
        For pintCount = 1 To _
            dlgImage.PrinterSettings.Copies
            pdImage.Print()
        Next
    End If
End If
```

12

The preceding statements first configure, and then display the PrintDialog control instance. If the user clicks the OK button, then the nested If statement tests whether or not the PageSettings are valid. If they are, the document is printed based on the information selected by the user.

2. Test the solution. On the main form, click **Windows**, and then click **Image Viewer**. Open the image named **Chapter.12\Data\CourseLogo.bmp**. On the menu bar, click **File**, and then click **Print** to display the Print dialog box. Click **OK** to print the document.

In addition to the PrintDialog control, you can preview a printout with the PrintPreviewDialog and PrintPreview controls.

The PrintPreviewDialog and PrintPreview Controls

The PrintPreviewDialog and PrintPreview controls have the same purpose. They allow you to preview a document before printing it. However, the PrintPreviewDialog control previews the document in a separate dialog box. This dialog box contains buttons to navigate from page to page, and to send the document to the printer. The PrintPreview control previews the document inside the visible region of the control instance appearing on the form.

Previewing a report with the PrintPreviewDialog control is surprisingly simple. First, you associate an instance of the PrintPreviewDialog control with an instance of the PrintDocument class. This is the same PrintDocument class that you have used before in the chapter. Second, you call the ShowDialog method of the PrintPreviewDialog control. Calling the ShowDialog method of the PrintPreviewDialog control causes the PrintPage event to fire for the associated instance of the PrintDocument class. The data is then printed in the instance of the PrintPreviewDialog control.

To use the PrintPreviewDialog control:

1. Create an instance of the PrintPreviewDialog control on the form named **frmImageViewer.vb**.

2. Using the Properties window, set the Name property to **ppdCurrent**, and then set the Document property to **pdImage**. This is the name of the PrintDocument control instance you have already created.

3. Enter the following statement in the **Click** event handler for the menu item named **mmuFilePrintPreview**:

```
ppdCurrent.ShowDialog()
```

4. Test the solution. On the main form, click **Windows**, and then click **Image Viewer**. On the image viewer form, load the image named **Chapter.12\Data\CourseLogo.bmp**. On the menu bar, click **File**, and then click **Print Preview**. The image appears in the region of the PrintPreviewDialog control instance.

The PrintPreviewDialog control instance displays a toolbar across the top of the form. The buttons on the toolbar allow the user to navigate from printed page to printed page, zoom in and out, and pan.

At this point, you have seen that the steps to print to a form and print to a printer are quite similar. Next, you will see how to build a more complex drawing application.

CONNECTING THE DOTS

So far, we have shown how to draw elementary shapes but have yet to use those shapes in a business context. In this section, we show how to use the drawing classes to create a bar chart and a pie chart. To do so, we read annual sales data from a sequential file. The sequential file contains two fields. The first field stores the sales year, and the second field stores the annual sales amount corresponding to that year. The sequential file is read into an ArrayList named alDataList. The menu item named mmuFileOpen appearing on the main form contains the statements to open the sequential file and read each record into an ArrayList storing DataList elements, having the following structure:

```
Public Structure DataList
    Public BrushColor As Brush
    Public Year As Integer
    Public SalesAmount As Single
    Public SalesPercent As Single
End Structure
```

Note that the member named SalesPercent is calculated at runtime. The value stores the percentage of sales for the current year, relative to the total sales amount. Values are also stored in the BrushColor member at runtime.

As the steps to open a sequential file and read the contents into an ArrayList have already been discussed, you will not enter those statements in these hands-on steps. Refer to the commented code in the solution for further details, if necessary.

As mentioned, you will print a bar chart and a pie chart using the data stored in the same ArrayList. The following enumeration and variable have been declared to store the current chart type:

```
Private Enum GraphType
    Bar
    Pie
End Enum
Private CurrentGraphType As GraphType
```

Two menu items exist from which the user selects the type of chart to render. The following statements appear in the Click event handler for the menu item named mmuViewBar to set the chart type:

```
CurrentGraphType = GraphType.Bar
picGraph.Invalidate()
```

12

The preceding statements set the current chart type and then invalidate the PictureBox control instance, thereby causing its Paint event to fire. The following statements appear in the Paint event handler for the PictureBox control instance:

```
Select Case CurrentGraphType
    Case GraphType.Bar
        Call DrawBarChart(e)
    Case GraphType.Pie
        Call DrawPieChart(e)
End Select
```

The procedures named DrawBarChart and DrawPieChart perform the task of drawing the charts. As these statements appear in the Paint event handler, the variable e is assumed to reference an instance of the Graphics class. You will complete the code in the hands-on steps that follow.

Creating a Bar Chart

You have likely created bar charts using a graphics program such as Microsoft Excel. Unlike Excel, in VB .NET you must write the code to create the graphical shapes that comprise the chart. Creating a bar chart using the VB .NET drawing tools involves performing the following general steps:

- The *x* and *y* axes must be drawn. In this solution, the graph will have a border. Thus, we apply a transformation to move the origin of the graph down and to the right 25 points.

- A legend needs to be drawn along the *y* axis containing the data values. In this solution, we arbitrarily display ten values from the range of values contained in the data file. Next to each value, a tick mark appears.

- The bars themselves need to be drawn. In this solution, we assume that the chart may have a variable number of data points or bars. One bar will be drawn on the bar chart for each sales year.

- A legend needs to be printed along the *x* axis to indicate the year corresponding to the bar.

The bar chart that you will create will be inside a PictureBox control instance instead of directly on the form. The decision for this implementation is somewhat arbitrary. However, the purpose of using the PictureBox control is to illustrate that the steps to draw graphical shapes to a PictureBox are no different from the steps to draw graphical shapes to a form. Finally, the bar chart that you will create will scale as the user resizes the form.

Drawing the *x* and *y* axes involves specifying the origin of the axis lines and the length of each line. The graph will be created with a 25 pixel border around all sides of the graph.

To draw the *x* and *y* axes around a graph:

1. Activate the Code Editor for the form named **frmMain.vb**, and then enter the following statements (shown in bold) at the end of the **DrawBarChart** procedure:

```
End If
e.Graphics.TranslateTransform(25, 25)
e.Graphics.DrawLine(Pens.Black, 0, 0, _
    picGraph.ClientSize.Width - 50, 0)
e.Graphics.DrawLine(Pens.Black, 0, 0, 0, _
    picGraph.ClientSize.Height - 50)
```

The first of the preceding statements calls the TranslateTransform method to move the origin of the PictureBox down and to the right 25 pixels. Note that the PictureBox is docked to fill the region of the form. The final two statements draw the lines that comprise the *x* and *y* axes. The lines are drawn from the translated origin to 25 pixels from the left and bottom border.

2. Test the solution. On the main form, click **File**, and then click **Open**. Open the file named **Chapter.12\Data\Sales.txt**. The *x* and *y* axes appear on the form.

Tick marks will appear along the *y* axis to display the values of the corresponding bars. In addition to the tick marks, the numeric value associated with the tick mark will appear just below the tick mark itself. To display this data, you need to declare variables that will store the distance between each tick mark and the values associated with each tick mark.

To create tick marks along the *y* axis:

1. Activate the Code Editor for the form named **frmMain.vb**, if necessary, and then enter the following statements (shown in bold) at the end of the **DrawBarChart** procedure:

```
e.Graphics.DrawLine(Pens.Black, 0, 0, 0, _
    picGraph.ClientSize.Height - 50)
Dim pintCount As Integer
Dim psngTickCurrent As Single
Dim psngTickValueCurrent As Single
```

The preceding statements declare a variable named pintCount, which will store the tick mark currently being printed. The variable psngTickCurrent will store the current position of the tick mark along the *y* axis, and the variable psngTickValueCurrent will store the value associated with the current tick mark.

2. Enter the following statements (shown in bold) at the end of the **DrawBarChart** procedure:

```
Dim psngTickValueCurrent As Single
Dim pintGraphHeight As Integer = _
    picGraph.ClientSize.Height - 50
```

```
Dim pintGraphWidth As Integer = _
    picGraph.ClientSize.Width - 50
Dim psngTickHeight As Single = _
    System.Convert.ToSingle(pintGraphHeight / 10)
Dim psngTickValue As Single = ToSingle(msngMax / 10)
```

The first two statements store the height and width of the graph. The third statement stores the distance between two tick marks. The height of the graph is divided by 10 to calculate the distance between two tick marks. (We assume that the graph will always display 10 tick marks.) The value corresponding to the distance between each tick mark is stored in the variable psngTickValue. The maximum data value stored in the variable msngMax is divided by the number of tick marks to perform this calculation. The statements that read the sequential file store the maximum sales amount in the accumulator named msngMax.

3. Enter the following statements (shown in bold) at the end of the **DrawBarChart** procedure to draw the 10 tick marks:

```
Dim psngTickValue As Single = ToSingle(msngMax / 10)
psngTickCurrent = psngTickHeight
psngTickValueCurrent = psngTickValue

For pintCount = 1 To 10
    e.Graphics.DrawLine(Pens.Black, 0, psngTickCurrent, _
        10, psngTickCurrent)
    e.Graphics.DrawString( _
        psngTickValueCurrent.ToString("f"), fntCurrent, _
        Brushes.Black, 0, psngTickCurrent)
    psngTickCurrent += psngTickHeight
    psngTickValueCurrent += psngTickValue
Next
```

The previous code segment generates 10 tick marks, evenly spaced, along the *y* axis. The variable psngTickHeight stores the distance between two tick marks. The variable psngTickCurrent stores the position along the *y* axis of the current tick mark. The variables psngTickValue and psngTickValueCurrent store the incremental value displayed next to the tick mark and the current value of the tick mark, respectively. Thus, each time through the For loop, the position of the tick mark and the associated value are incremented.

4. Test the solution. On the main form, click **File**, and then click **Open**. Open the file named **Chapter.12\Data\Sales.txt**. The tick marks and corresponding values appear on the form. Resize the form. Note that the graph is resized when the form is resized, because the code in the Resize event for the form calls the Invalidate method of the PictureBox control instance.

Having drawn the *x* and *y* axes and the tick marks, the next set of statements you write will draw the bar chart itself.

To create the bar chart:

1. Enter the following statements (shown in bold) at the end of the **DrawBarChart** procedure:

```
For pintCount = 1 To 10
    ' Statements
Next
Dim psngDataScale As Single = _
    ToSingle((picGraph.ClientSize.Height - 50) / msngMax)
Dim psngBarWidth As Single = _
    ToSingle(pintGraphWidth * 0.4) / alDataList.Count
Dim psngSpaceWidth As Single = _
    ToSingle(pintGraphWidth * 0.6) / (alDataList.Count + 1)
```

The first of the preceding statements calculates the scaling used to convert the data values to GDI+ world coordinates. That is, the variable psngDataScale stores a ratio between the data values and coordinate values. The second and third statements calculate the relative width of the bars and the space between the bars. We arbitrarily assume that the bar width will occupy 40% of the graph width, and the space between the bars will occupy 60% of the graph width. By dividing this intermediate value by the number of bars, the width of each bar and the space between each bar is calculated based on the size of the PictureBox control instance.

2. Enter the following statements (shown in bold) at the end of the **DrawBarChart** procedure:

```
Dim psngSpaceWidth As Single = _
    ToSingle(pintGraphWidth * 0.6) / (alDataList.Count + 1)
Dim psngX As Single = psngSpaceWidth
Dim pbrushColor As Brush
Dim psngAmount As Single
```

The first of the preceding statements stores the position of the bar along the *x* axis. This value will be incremented as each bar is printed. The second statement declares a variable that will store the color of the current brush used to fill the bar, and the final statement declares a variable that will store the sales amount for the current bar.

3. Enter the following statements (shown in bold) at the end of the **DrawBarChart** procedure to create the bars that comprise the chart:

```
Dim psngAmount As Single
For pintCount = 0 To alDataList.Count - 1
    psngAmount = CType(alDataList(pintCount), _
        DataList).SalesAmount
```

12

```
        pbrushColor = CType(alDataList(pintCount), _
            DataList).BrushColor
        Dim recCurrent As New RectangleF(psngX, 0, _
            psngBarWidth, psngAmount * psngDataScale)
        e.Graphics.FillRectangle(pbrushColor, recCurrent)
        e.Graphics.DrawString(CType(alDataList(pintCount), _
            DataList).Year.ToString, fntCurrent, _
            Brushes.Black, psngX, -15)
        psngX = psngX + psngBarWidth + psngSpaceWidth
Next
```

The preceding statements iterate through the values in the ArrayList, convert-ing the data types as necessary. For each element in the ArrayList, a new rec-tangle is created and filled. A string is drawn just above the bar to indicate the sales year. The variable named psngX keeps track of the current bar position.

4. Test the solution. On the main form, click **File**, and then click **Open**. Open the file named **Chapter.12\Data\Sales.txt**. The bar chart appears on the form. Resize the form. The bar chart resizes along with the form itself.

Creating a Pie Chart

The steps to create a pie chart are simpler than the steps to create the bar chart. Again we assume that the data contains annual sales values. The pie chart will display the rel-ative percentage of each annual sales amount.

The following steps describe the processing necessary to create the pie chart:

- Create the bounding rectangle for the ellipse and the pie shapes that will appear in the ellipse.

- Based on the percentage of sales for each year, calculate the number of degrees of angle for each slice of pie.

- Draw each pie slice.

Next, you will create the pie chart:

To create a pie chart:

1. Activate the Code Editor for the form named **frmMain.vb**, if necessary, and then enter the following statements at the end of the **DrawPieChart** procedure:

```
Dim psngStartAngle As Single
Dim psngDegreesPerSlice(alDataList.Count - 1) As Single
Dim pintCount As Integer
Dim pintY As Integer
e.Graphics.TranslateTransForm(25, 25)
```

The variable named psngStartAngle will store the starting angle. The starting angle will be 0. The array named psngDegreesPerSlice will store the number of degrees in the angle for each pie slice. There exists one element in the array for each sales year. The ArrayList named alDataList is used to determine the number of years. The final variable named pintCount is a counter that will be used in a For loop to print each pie slice. The final statement moves the origin of the form down and to the right 25 pixels.

2. Enter the following statements (shown in bold) at the end of the **DrawPieChart** procedure to create the bounding rectangle and calculate the number of degrees for each pie slice:

```
e.Graphics.TranslateTransForm(25, 25)
Dim recPie As New Rectangle(0, 0, _
      ToInt32(picGraph.ClientSize.Width * 0.6), _
      ToInt32(Me.ClientSize.Width * 0.6))

For pintCount = 0 To alDataList.Count - 1
      psngDegreesPerSlice(pintCount) = _
          CType(alDataList(pintCount), _
          DataList).SalesPercent * 360 / 100
Next
```

The ArrayList named alDataList contains one element for each sales year. The member named SalesPercent contains the percentage of sales for that year. This value has already been calculated. As the total percentage is 100 and the total number of degrees in a circle is 360, we multiply the percentage by 360 degrees and divide that value by 100 to calculate the number of degrees in the angle. The For loop performs the same calculation for each year, storing the number of degrees of each pie slice in the array named psngDegreesPerSlice.

3. Enter the following statements (shown in bold) at the end of the **DrawPieChart** procedure to draw the pie:

```
Next
For pintCount = 0 To alDataList.Count - 1
      e.Graphics.FillPie(sbList(pintCount), recPie, _
          psngStartAngle, psngDegreesPerSlice(pintCount))
      psngStartAngle = psngStartAngle + _
          psngDegreesPerSlice(pintCount)
Next
```

The preceding statements draw a slice of pie for each element in the ArrayList. Remember that the FillPie method requires four arguments: a brush, the bounding rectangle, the starting angle, and the number of degrees in the pie slice. The following list describes the data for each argument:

- The first argument uses the CurrentBrush member from the current ArrayList element to define the brush.

- The second argument defines the bounding rectangle.

12

- The third argument defines the starting angle. The first time through the loop the starting angle is 0. Each time through the loop the starting angle is incremented by the angle of the pie slice that was just drawn.

- The final argument contains the angle of the current pie slice. Again, this value is obtained from the current index of the ArrayList.

To test the solution:

1. Test the solution. On the main form, click **File**, and then click **Open**. Open the file named **Chapter.12\Data\Sales.txt**. Click **View**, and then click **Pie Chart** on the main form. The pie chart appears.

The final steps involve creating the legend. You will create the legend so that it appears in a rectangle along the right side of the form. Again, you will use ratios based on the width of the PictureBox so that the legend will be repositioned as the user resizes the form.

To create the legend:

1. Activate the Code Editor for the form named **frmMain.vb**, if necessary, and then enter the following statements (shown in bold) at the end of the **DrawPieChart** procedure:

```
Next
e.Graphics.DrawRectangle(Pens.Black, _
    ToInt32(Me.ClientSize.Width * 0.65), 0, _
    ToInt32(Me.ClientSize.Width * 0.2), 200)
For pintCount = 0 To alDataList.Count - 1
    pintY = pintY + 20
    Dim recCurrent As New _
        Rectangle(ToInt32(Me.ClientSize.Width * 0.7), _
        pintY, 10, 10)
    e.Graphics.FillRectangle(sbList(pintCount), recCurrent)
    e.Graphics.DrawString(( _
        CType(alDataList(pintCount), _
        DataList).Year).ToString, _
        fntCurrent, Brushes.Black, _
        ToInt32(Me.ClientSize.Width * 0.75), pintY)
Next
```

The first of the preceding statements creates a rectangle that will surround the legend. The For loop then executes, which prints the legend itself. Each time through the For loop, a small filled rectangle is displayed. The color of the rectangle corresponds to the color of the pie slice. To the right of the rectangle, a text string is printed containing the year.

2. Test the solution. On the main form, click **File**, and then click **Open**. Open the file named **Chapter.12\Data\Sales.txt**. Click **View**, and then click **Pie Chart** on the main form. The pie chart appears with the legend.

You have completed the programming for this chapter, having seen how to create elementary shapes, and then how to use those shapes to create graphs, including bar charts and pie charts.

CHAPTER SUMMARY

❐ The Graphical Device Interface (GDI+) supplies the means to paint graphics to an output device such as the screen or a printer. The System.Graphics class, System.Drawing namespace, and System.Drawing.Drawing2D namespace comprise the GDI+.

❐ At the heart of all drawing operations is the Graphics class. Its methods use various types of pens and brushes to draw and fill shapes to a graphics device. The Graphics class also contains methods to rotate graphics, scale graphics, and perform panning. The actual drawing operations are typically performed in the Paint event handler. The second argument to the Paint event handler supplies a reference to an instance of the Graphics class. To force a Paint event to occur, call the Invalidate method of the form or instance of the PictureBox control.

❐ To work with color, you use the Color structure. VB .NET supplies over 100 named colors. To create custom colors, call the FromArgb method to create a custom color from composite RGB values.

❐ Drawing a line involves defining the starting point and ending point of the line. The DrawLine method of the Graphics class draws a line using an existing color, the points marking the line's starting point and ending point, and an optional width.

❐ Drawing a rectangle involves creating Point and Size structures to define the origin and size of the rectangle. The DrawRectangle method draws a rectangle outline with a pen. The FillRectangle method fills a rectangle with a brush. VB .NET supports numerous types of brushes.

❐ The Graphics class also supports typography. Through typography, you can draw text using fonts and brushes. To draw text, first create an instance of the Font class. Then, call the DrawString method of the Graphics class to draw the text to the output device. Text can be drawn using any type of brush.

❐ Drawing a polygon involves creating an array of Point structures that mark the points that comprise the polygon. The DrawPolygon method draws an outline of a polygon using a pen. The FillPolygon method draws a filled polygon using a brush.

❐ Drawing an ellipse involves defining a bounding rectangle. The ellipse is drawn inside that bounding rectangle. The DrawEllipse method of the Graphics class draws a border around an ellipse. The FillEllipse method fills an ellipse with a brush.

❐ To create an arc, you start with an ellipse. An arc represents a segment of the ellipse. The segment is defined by specifying the starting angle of the arc and the number of degrees of the sweep angle. The DrawArc method draws an arc. There exists no corresponding FillArc method because it makes no sense to fill an arc.

❐ The steps to create a pie are roughly the same as the steps to create an arc. You define the bounding ellipse, the start angle, and the sweep angle. The FillPie method fills a pie while the DrawPie method draws the outline of a pie.

12

❑ By default, the form's origin is the upper-left corner of the form's client area. By calling the TranslateTransform method of the Graphics class, a world transformation is performed thereby changing the form's origin.

❑ Rotating graphics is accomplished by calling the RotateTransform method of the Graphics class. The RotateTransform method accepts one argument: the number of degrees of rotation. Positive values rotate graphics in a clockwise direction, and negative values rotate graphics in a counterclockwise direction.

❑ Scaling allows you to change the magnification of the graphics drawn about the form. Calling the ScaleTransform method of the Graphics class changes the scaling. The ScaleTransform method accepts two arguments. The first argument defines the scaling for the x axis, and the second argument defines the scaling for the y axis.

❑ The steps to print to a printer are nearly identical to the steps that you apply to print to a form. That is, you call the same methods of the Graphics class.

REVIEW QUESTIONS

1. Which of the following statements correctly describes the GDI+?
   a. The GDI+ supplies classes to draw two-dimensional shapes such as lines, rectangles, and polygons.
   b. All of the methods that comprise the GDI+ are contained within the System.GDI namespace.
   c. The GDI+ supports methods to draw and animate three-dimensional graphics.
   d. The methods of the GDI+ can be used to draw to the screen but not to a printer.
   e. all of the above

2. Which of the following methods are supported by the Graphics class?
   a. Ellipse, Arc, Polygon
   b. Point, Size, Rectangle, Line
   c. DrawLine, DrawRectangle, DrawPie
   d. DrawOutline, DrawFill
   e. none of the above

3. Which of the following statements about color is correct?
   a. You can create a color using named colors or by calling the FromArgb method.
   b. You create a custom color by calling the Color constructor.
   c. The Color structure belongs to the System.Graphics class.
   d. You can use existing predefined VB .NET colors but you cannot create new ones.
   e. none of the above

4. Which of the following statements describe the process used to draw a line?

   a. First create an instance of the Line class, then call the DrawLine method of the Graphics class using the instance of the Line class as an argument.

   b. First create a pen using the Pen constructor, then call the DrawLine method of the Graphics class using the pen and either existing Point structures or x and y coordinate values.

   c. First create an instance of the Shape class using a Line enumeration as an argument, then call the DrawLine method using the instance of the Shape class.

   d. Call the DrawLine method with three arguments. The first and second arguments define the endpoints of the line. The third argument has a data type of Color and defines the color of the line.

   e. none of the above

5. Which of the following statements related to drawing a rectangle is correct?

   a. A rectangle structure can be defined using x and y coordinates along with the height and width, or by using Point and Size structures.

   b. To draw a bordered rectangle, call the DrawRectangleBorder method of the Graphics class.

   c. To draw a filled rectangle, call the DrawRectangleFill method of the Graphics class.

   d. all of the above

   e. none of the above

6. Which of the following statements is true of brushes?

   a. To create a brush that fills a shape with an image, you use a type of brush called in ImageBrush.

   b. The MultiColor brush is a brush having two colors.

   c. A HatchBrush has a foreground color and a background color. Vertical or horizontal lines appear in the foreground color.

   d. Brushes are commonly used to fill the region of an arc.

   e. all of the above

7. Which of the following statements applies to creating and drawing polygons?

   a. A Polygon structure can have at most six points.

   b. The DrawPolygon method uses an array of Point structures to define the points that comprise the polygon.

   c. The DrawPolygon method accepts two arguments: the first contains a reference to a pen and the second contains a reference to a Polygon structure.

   d. It is possible to draw an outlined polygon, but VB .NET does not allow you to fill polygons.

   e. none of the above

8. How would you draw a circle?

    a. Call the DrawCircle method with two arguments: the Point structure that marks the center of the circle and the radius of the circle.

    b. Define a rectangle whose shape is a square. Then call the DrawEllipse method with the rectangle as an argument.

    c. Call the DrawCircle method with the rectangle as an argument.

    d. Call the overloaded DrawRectangle method, setting the RectangleType enumeration to Circle.

    e. none of the above

9. Which of the following statements describe how to draw an arc?

    a. First create an instance of the Arc class, and then call the DrawArc method using the already defined arc as an argument.

    b. Define a rectangle. Then call the DrawArc method with a pen and a rectangle as arguments. In addition, supply arguments to specify the starting angle and the sweep angle.

    c. Define a line. Then call the DrawArc method with the line and the arc angle of the line.

    d. Create an instance of the Arc class using the following arguments to the constructor: a point, the radius of the arc, and the angle of the arc.

    e. none of the above

10. How would you create and fill a pie?

    a. First create an instance of the Pie class, and then call the Fill method of the Graphics class. Define an arc. Then call the FillArc method with a brush.

    b. Define a polygon. Then call the FillPie method with a brush and polygon as arguments. In addition, supply arguments to specify the starting angle and the sweep angle.

    c. Define a rectangle. Then call the FillPie method with a brush and rectangle as arguments. In addition, supply arguments to specify the starting angle and the sweep angle.

    d. none of the above

11. Which of the following statements is correct related to the DrawString method?

    a. It draws a string using a font and a brush.

    b. You can optionally specify a point where drawing will begin.

    c. You can optionally specify a bounding rectangle.

    d. Strings can be justified within a bounding rectangle.

    e. all of the above

12. What is the name of the method you call to perform a scaling transformation?

   a. Scale

   b. ScaleTransform

   c. Transform

   d. Scaling

   e. none of the above

13. Which of the following statements correctly describe how to draw graphics to a printer?

   a. First create an instance of the Printer class. Then call the various Print methods of that class.

   b. You handle the PrintPage event of the PrintDocument class. The second argument of the PrintPage event contains a reference to a Graphics object.

   c. When you draw graphics to a printer, you call entirely different methods than you would call if you were drawing to the screen.

   d. Create an instance of the Printer object. Then call the graphical methods of the Printer object.

   e. none of the above

14. Which of the following statements is true of the PrintDialog control?

   a. It sends a document to the printer.

   b. It displays a dialog box containing a preview of the document that will eventually be printed.

   c. It allows the user to select print options such as the number of copies to print or which pages to print.

   d. all of the above

   e. none of the above

15. Which of the following statements are true of the PrintPreviewDialog control?

   a. To print using the PrintPreviewDialog control, you create an instance of the control on the form. The Graphics property of the PrintPreviewDialog control supplies the means to print the graphical shapes.

   b. The PrintPreviewDialog control works with the PrintDocument class and supplies the means to print graphics to a dialog box which can then be sent to the printer.

   c. The PrintPreviewDialog control appears on the form containing the control instance. The control instance is typically docked so as to fill the region of the form.

   d. all of the above

   e. none of the above

12

16. What is the purpose of the Invalidate method? Describe the relationship between the Invalidate method and the Paint event.

17. Describe the effect of drawing an image using a point and bounding rectangle.

18. Describe the relationship between world coordinates, page coordinates, and device coordinates.

19. Describe the significance of the order in which you apply graphical transformations.

20. What is the purpose of the PrintDocument class?

PROGRAMMING QUESTIONS

1. Write the statements to create a diagonal blue line that starts at the upper-left corner of the form's client area and ends at the lower-right corner for the form's client area. Use the named color Blue. The pen should be three pixels in width.

2. Write the statements to draw a green outlined rectangle. The rectangle should be three pixels in width. Use the named color Green for the rectangle. The rectangle should be roughly one inch square. The origin of the rectangle should be the upper-left corner of the form.

3. Write the statements to draw a rectangle using a HatchBrush. The HatchBrush should have a Cross style, a red foreground color, and a blue background color. Draw the rectangle such that it is positioned at the upper-left corner of the form. The rectangle should be roughly one inch square.

4. Write the statements to create a LinearGradientBrush named lgbCurrent. Assume that the starting and ending points of the brush are (0, 0) and (100, 100), respectively. Write the statements to declare a rectangle named recCurrent having the same coordinates as the LinearGradientBrush that you just created. Write the statements to fill the rectangle using the LinearGradientBrush. Assume that the variable e.Graphics references an instance of the Graphics class. Use Vertical gradient mode.

5. Write the statements to create a polygon named plyCurrent having the following points: (1, 1), (10, 10), (1, 10). Write the statements to draw the polygon using a black pen. Assume that the variable e.Graphics references an instance of the Graphics class.

6. Write the statements to create a polygon named plyCurrent having the following points: (1, 1), (10, 10), (20, 15), (1, 10). Write the statements to fill the polygon with a blue solid brush. Assume that the variable e.Graphics references an instance of the Graphics class.

7. Write the statements to create and draw an arc having the following characteristics: The bounding rectangle should have an origin of (10, 10) and be 250 pixels in both width and height. The starting angle should be 90 degrees, and the sweep angle should be 180 degrees. Assume that the variable e.Graphics references an instance of the Graphics class.

8. Write the statements to create and draw an ellipse having the following characteristics: The origin of the bounding rectangle should be at point (10, 10). The size of the rectangle should be 50 by 50. Assume that the variable e.Graphics references an instance of the Graphics class. Write the statements to fill the ellipse with a solid red brush, and outline the same ellipse with a black pen.

9. Write the statements to create and draw an arc having the following characteristics: The origin of the bounding rectangle should be at point (25, 25). The size of the rectangle should be 75 by 125. Assume that the starting angle is 90 degrees and the sweep angle is also 90 degrees. Write the statements to draw the arc with a blue pen.

10. Write the statements to create and draw a pie slice having the following characteristics: The origin of the bounding rectangle should be at point (15, 15). The size of the rectangle should be 50 by 50. Assume that the starting angle is 45 degrees and the sweep angle is 30 degrees. Write the statements to draw a border around the pie with a black pen and fill the pie with a yellow brush.

11. Write the statements to create four pie slices. The origin of the bounding rectangle should be at point (50, 50). Assume that the size of the rectangle is 100 by 100. Create four filled pie slices in each quadrant (the sweep angle for each slice will be 90 degrees). Fill each slice using the named colors Red, Blue, Green, and Yellow, respectively.

12. Write the statements to perform the following transformations: Move the origin of the form 50 units to the right and 50 units down. Set the scaling to 1.5 times the original size. Rotate 90 degrees.

13. Write the statements to make the origin of the form the center of the form. Draw two black lines along the x axis and y axis.

14. Assume that an instance of the PrintDocument class exists. Write the statement to begin printing.

15. Write the statement to associate a PrintDialog control instance named pdCurrent with an instance of the PrinterSettings object named psImage. Display the PrintDialog control instance.

12

HANDS-ON PROJECTS

Hands-on
Projects

1. In this project, you will draw a bar chart based on data obtained from a sequential file. On the x axis, the bar chart displays tick marks and values. On the y axis, the chart displays a legend. The file named Chapter.12\Exercises12\Ch12Ex1.exe contains the compiled executable application. The file named Ch12Ex1Data.txt contains the data file for the application. Figure 12-11 shows the completed main form for the solution.

   a. Start Visual Studio .NET and create a new project named **Ch12Ex1.sln**.

   b. Create a splash screen for the solution using the compiled application as a template.

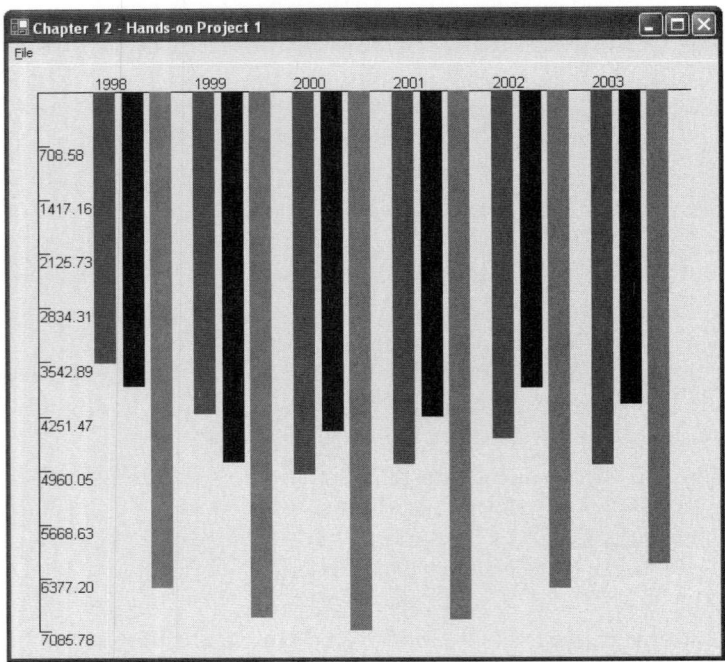

Figure 12-11   Chapter 12 – Hands-on Project 1

c. Create a **File** menu with menu items named **Open** and **Exit**. The Open menu item should contain the necessary statements to open the sequential file, read its contents into a list, and display the bar chart.

d. Write the statements to open and read the sequential file. Each record in the file contains annual sales records and has the following fields: Year (Integer), SalesWest (Single), SalesCentral (Single), and SalesEast (Single). Read the file into an ArrayList of structures corresponding to the sequential file.

e. Write the statements to create the x and y axes. The y axis should display 10 tick marks. Using the techniques presented in the chapter, display values corresponding to the tick marks. The maximum value should be obtained from the maximum sales amount found in the sequential file.

f. Write the statements to display the graph shown in Figure 12-11. Note that three bars appear for each year, representing the sales regions. The statements that you write to display the graph should operate such that the graph will resize when the form is resized. In addition, your program should be able to display the graph such that it will support a different number of years. Assume that the sales data file can contain sales data for between one and six years.

g. Devise a color scheme for the graph as you see fit.

2. In this project, you will draw a pie chart. The data for the pie chart will be obtained from a sequential file instead of being entered by the user. The file named Chapter.12\Exercises12\Ch12Ex2.exe contains the compiled executable application. The file named Ch12Ex2Data.txt contains the data file for the application. Figure 12-12 shows the completed main form for the solution.

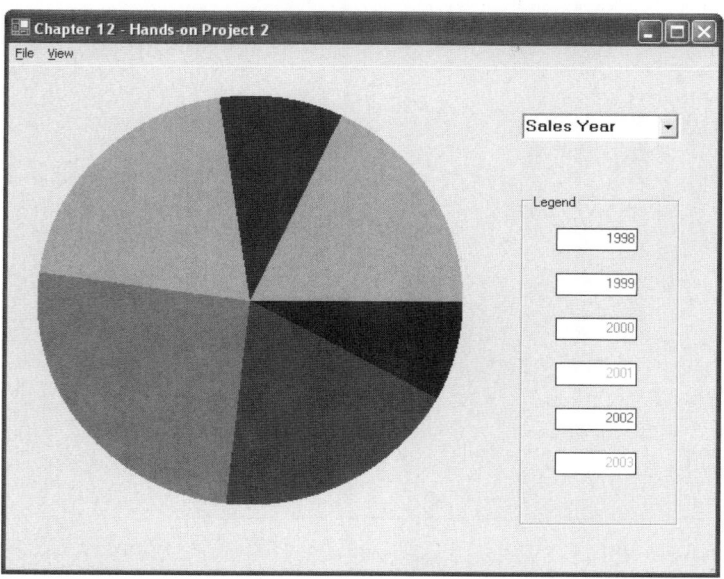

Figure 12-12   Chapter 12 – Hands-on Project 2

a. Start Visual Studio .NET and create a new project named **Ch12Ex2.sln**.

b. Create a splash screen for the solution using the compiled application as a template.

c. Create a **File** menu with menu items named **Open** and **Exit**. The Open menu item should contain the necessary statements to open the sequential file, read its contents into a list, and display the pie chart.

d. Create a list box on the form. Load the sales years into the list box. Obtain this data from the sequential file.

e. When the user selects a year, display the pie chart such that it contains slices for each sales region for the selected year. Display a legend for the pie chart.

f. Allow the user to display the pie chart such that it displays the cumulative data for all years instead of just one year.

g. Allow the user to display the pie chart such that it displays sales data by year instead of by sales region. Thus, there will be one slice of pie for each sales year (as shown in Figure 12-12). Each slice of pie will display the data for all regions instead of just the sales data for a single region.

3. In this project, you will create charts based on data obtained from a database. The database named Chapter.12\Data\Sales.mdb contains the sample database. The user will be able to select the range of data to be plotted. In addition, the user will be able to select whether a pie chart or a bar chart should be drawn. The file named Chapter.12\Exercises12\Ch12Ex3.exe contains the compiled executable application. Figure 12-13 shows the completed main form for the solution.

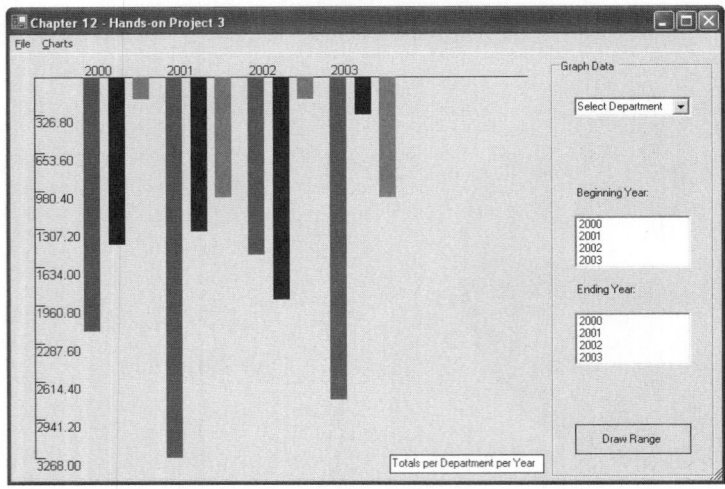

Figure 12-13   Chapter 12 – Hands-on Project 3

    a. Create a new project named **Ch12Ex3.sln**.

    b. Create a splash screen for the solution using the compiled application as a template.

    c. Establish a connection to the database. Create a typed DataSet based on the table named tblSales having the following fields and data types: fldID (Integer), fldDepartment (String) fldSalesDate (DateTime), fldSalesAmount (Single), fldSalesCost (Single). The field named fldDepartment contains one of the following values: "Services", "Parts", "Other".

    d. The data file contains multiple sales records for each year. Write the statements to tally the sales records so that you have one record for each department for each year.

    e. Display a bar chart such that each bar represents the total sales amount for a particular year. Use the field fldSalesAmount.

    f. Write the code so that the user can display pie charts based on the same data. Allow the user to display one pie chart having a slice of pie for each year. Display the relative sales percentage for the year. Also allow the user to display the pie chart based on the department.

g. Allow the user to select the range of years displayed using two list boxes: one storing the starting year and another storing the ending year.

h. Using instances of the PrintPreviewDialog control and the PrintDialog control, allow the user to send the current graph to the printer. In addition, allow the user to preview the graph before printing it. *Hint:* You can use the same drawing procedures for both the screen and printed images. Pass an argument containing a reference to the Graphics class to the drawing procedures. Call those procedures from the Paint or PrintPage event with the appropriate instance of the Graphics class.

4. In this project, you will create graphs that print both to the screen and to the printer. The database named Chapter.12\Data\Sales.mdb contains the sample database. The file named Chapter.12\Exercises12\Ch12Ex4.exe contains the compiled executable application. Figure 12-14 shows the completed main form for the solution.

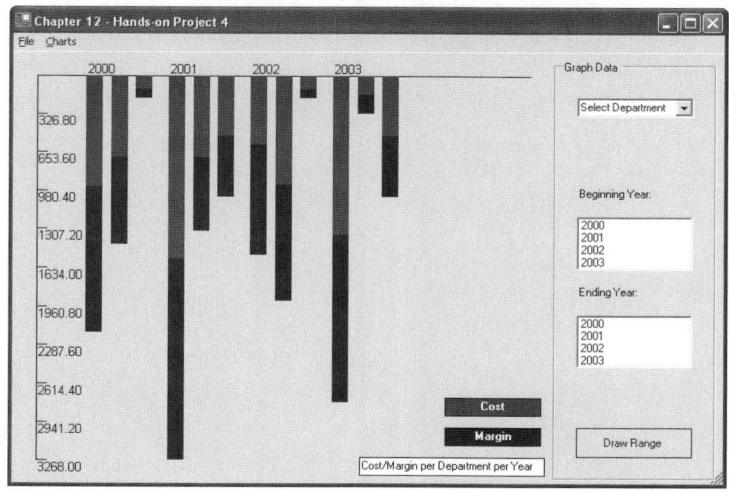

Figure 12-14   Chapter 12 – Hands-on Project 4

a. Create a new project named **Ch12Ex4.sln**.

b. Create a splash screen for the solution using the compiled application as a template.

c. Establish a connection to the database. Create a data reader to read the data from the table named tblSales having the following fields and data types: fldID (Integer), fldDepartment (String) fldSalesDate (DateTime), fldSalesAmount (Single), fldSalesCost (Single). The field named fldDepartment contains one of the following values: "Services", "Parts", "Other". Read the records into an ArrayList.

d. Based on the data you read, create a second ArrayList to store summarized data. The summarized data should have one record per department per year.

e. Create a stacked bar chart such that one bar appears for each year. Allow the user to select the data from all departments or from a particular department. Calculate the gross margin by subtracting the sales cost from the sales amount. The sales amount should encompass the entire region of each bar. The bar should have two segments: the cost and the margin.

f. Allow the user to select the range of years displayed using two list boxes: one storing the starting year and another storing the ending year.

g. Write the statements that will allow the user to display the bar chart such that the sales amounts are sorted in descending order from the largest sales amount to the smallest sales amount.

h. Using instances of the PrintPreviewDialog control and the PrintDialog control, allow the user to send the current graph to the printer. In addition, allow the user to preview the graph before printing it. *Hint:* Pass an argument containing a reference to the Graphics class to the drawing procedures. Call those procedures from the Paint or PrintPage event with the appropriate instance of the Graphics class.

In this chapter, you will:

♦ Understand the characteristics of MDI applications

♦ Organize the procedures between forms in MDI applications

♦ Understand the role of standard forms in an MDI application

♦ Integrate menus in an MDI application and create context menus

♦ Understand the relationships between events in an MDI application

♦ Manage and organize the forms that make up an MDI application

♦ Configure the RichTextBox control to display custom fonts and colors

♦ Read and write files with the RichTextBox control

♦ Format a RichTextBox control instance

♦ Use zooming

♦ Detect links to Web pages

In this chapter, you will learn how to create a multiple-document interface (MDI) application. That is, you will learn how to create a form called an MDI parent form. You will also learn how to create other forms called MDI child forms that appear inside of the visible region of the MDI parent form. In addition, you will learn how to integrate menus between the MDI parent form and MDI child forms, and create a context menu. Context menus typically appear when the user right-clicks on an MDI parent or MDI child form or a particular control instance on a form. You will also learn how to manage the loaded MDI child forms in an application. Finally, you will learn how to display text using the RichTextBox control and how to format the text appearing in an instance of that control.

PREVIEWING THE COMPLETED SOLUTION

Unlike the solutions you have created in previous chapters, you will implement this solution using a multiple-document interface (MDI). In an MDI application, each new window appears inside the region of another window, referred to as a parent form or parent window. MDI applications are not unique to VB .NET. In fact, applications such as Microsoft Excel and Microsoft Access are both MDI applications. The MDI application that you will create in this chapter will implement a simplified word processor.

To preview the completed solution:

1. Start Visual Studio .NET and open the solution file named **Chapter.13\ Complete13\Complete13.sln**. The project consists of three form modules: an MDI child form containing the interface for a text editor, an MDI parent form that acts as a container for the MDI child form, and a third form that operates as a standard form. A module file also appears in the application. This module file contains variables used to store data that must be shared by all the forms in the solution.

2. Run the solution. The MDI parent form appears on the screen. Because a new file has not yet been created, or an existing file opened, an instance of the MDI child form used to edit data does not yet appear.

3. On the MDI parent form's menu bar, click **File**, and then click **New** to create a new document. Another form, called an MDI child form, appears inside the region of the MDI parent form, as shown in Figure 13-1.

Figure 13-1   Completed solution with MDI parent and MDI child forms

Figure 13-1 shows the menu displayed on the MDI parent form. At this point, one instance of the MDI child form appears inside the region of the MDI parent form. This MDI child form contains an instance of the RichTextBox control, which is docked to fill the region of the form itself.

4. Move the MDI child form inside the region of the MDI parent form. Notice that the visible region of the MDI child form cannot extend beyond the region of the MDI parent form. This is one characteristic of all MDI applications.

5. Create a second instance of the MDI child form by clicking **File**, and then clicking **Open** on the menu bar. Open the file named **Chapter.13\Data\ Demo.rtf**. This file is a rich text file and has formatting directives embedded in the file. The RichTextBox control interprets these formatting directives and applies them to the text. Figure 13-2 shows the formatted text inside an instance of the RichTextBox control.

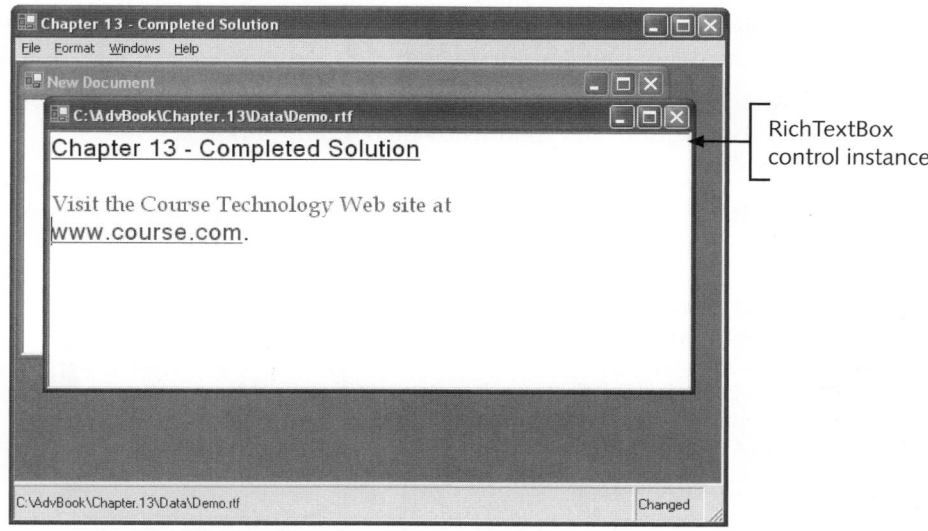

RichTextBox
control instance

Figure 13-2   RichTextBox control instance displaying formatted text

As you can see from Figure 13-2, the RichTextBox control instance can display text in different fonts and colors. Font attributes such as boldface, underlines, and italics can also be applied to the text. In addition, note that URLs appear underlined.

6. Select text in the rich text box having the same font and typeface. Click the various menu items on the **Format** menu to apply the selected formatting attribute to the selected text.

7. As shown in Figure 13-2, the text contains a hyperlink to the Course Technology Web site. Click the link (**www.course.com**). The Web page appears in Internet Explorer. Of course, you must be connected to the Internet.

8. On the menu bar, click **Windows**, and then click **Summary**. The solution examines all of the loaded MDI child forms and displays a summary dialog box as shown in Figure 13-3. The content of the dialog box may differ depending on the number and names of the MDI child forms you have open. The summary dialog box contains information about the loaded MDI child forms in the application.

Figure 13-3   Summary dialog box

9. On the menu bar, click **Help**, and then click **About**. The "About" form is configured as a standard form. Note that it appears as a modal dialog box and is not constrained by the MDI parent window.

10. End the solution, and then exit Visual Studio .NET.

The design of this solution requires that data be shared and that communication exist between the MDI parent and MDI child forms. Figure 13-4 illustrates the design of this solution.

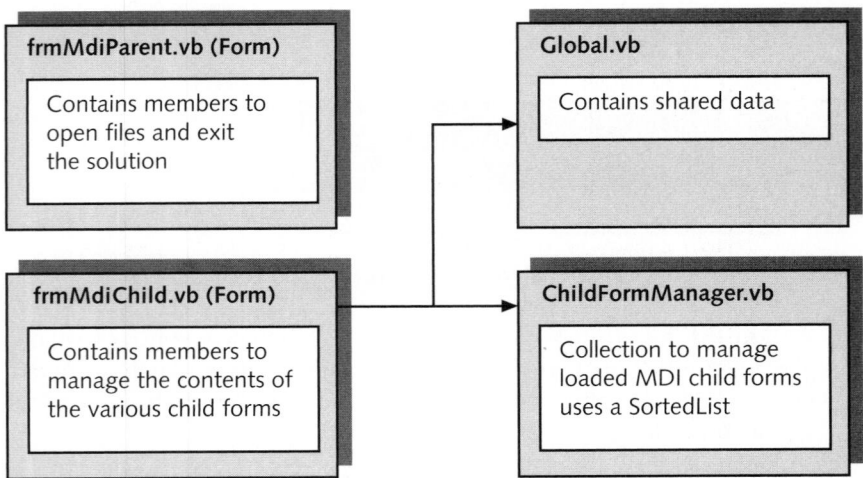

Figure 13-4   Solution design

As shown in Figure 13-4, the module named Global.vb contains references to the data that needs to be shared between the MDI parent and MDI child forms. The class named ChildFormManager implements an enumerated SortedList, which is used to keep track of the loaded MDI child forms. This is the same SortedList class discussed in Chapter 5. A reference to each MDI child form is added to this list when an instance of the MDI child form is created, and that reference is destroyed when the MDI child form instance is destroyed. The form named frmMdiParent.vb contains procedures to open MDI child forms containing new or existing documents, and to exit the solution. All of the procedures to manage the contents of an MDI child form appear in the MDI child form named frmMdiChild.vb.

CHARACTERISTICS OF MDI PROGRAMS

In the applications you have developed so far in this book, you have created forms that could appear anywhere on the desktop. This type of application is called a **single-document interface (SDI)** application. It is also common to create multiple instances of the same form, and then display those multiple form instances such that they appear inside the region of another form. These applications are called **multiple-document interface (MDI)** applications.

The decision of when to create an application as an MDI or SDI application is somewhat subjective. Suppose that you are creating an application that processes data contained in a sequential file. If only one file was open and being processed at a time, an SDI application with a single standard form to display the data would be sufficient. Suppose, however, that you wanted to be able to open multiple data files so that each form displayed the data from a different sequential file independently of the other forms. An MDI application is suitable in such a situation. Each MDI child form would display and process the data from a different sequential file. You could also create applications that operate with databases in the same way.

To illustrate an MDI application, consider Microsoft Excel. When working in Excel, you can open one or more workbooks. Each open workbook appears as a separate form, called an MDI child form, and contains the data from a different .xls file. Each MDI child form (workbook) appears inside the region of another form called an MDI parent form.

You can use three different types of forms in an MDI application, as described in the following list:

- An **MDI parent form** acts as the container for the MDI child forms in the solution. VB .NET allows an application to have multiple MDI parent forms although this is not common. In fact, the ability to have multiple MDI parent forms in an application is new to Visual Studio .NET.

- An **MDI child form** always appears inside the visible region of its MDI parent form. An MDI child form cannot be displayed as a modal form. Remember that a modal form is a form that must be closed before another form in the application can get input focus. A project may have several MDI child forms. Technically, it is possible to create an MDI application with no MDI child forms, but it is illogical to do so because creating MDI child forms is the whole reason for creating an MDI application in the first place.

13

- MDI applications can also contain zero or more standard forms. You have been using standard forms throughout this book. **Standard forms** can be displayed anywhere on the screen and are not contained by the MDI parent form. Standard forms in MDI applications are typically displayed as modal dialog boxes, and do not have menus associated with them. Again, however, this is not a technical requirement.

When you create an MDI application, the MDI parent form and its MDI child form(s) have unique characteristics that differ from those of standard forms. First, an MDI child form always appears inside the visible region of the MDI parent form. MDI child forms can be moved and resized. (Of course, you can resize the MDI parent form itself, maximize it, and minimize it.) Second, when the user minimizes an MDI child form, its icon appears, by default, at the bottom of the MDI parent form, rather than on the Taskbar. Iconified MDI child forms never appear on the Taskbar. Instead, the user positions the icon anywhere inside the visible region of the MDI parent form. Finally, when an MDI child form is maximized, the MDI child form's caption appears in brackets on the title bar of the MDI parent form. Maximized MDI child forms occupy the entire visible region of the MDI parent form, rather than the entire desktop. If the user minimizes the MDI parent form, the parent form does appear on the Taskbar, but the MDI child forms do not.

To configure a solution so that it will operate as an MDI application, you first designate a form as an MDI parent form by setting the form's IsMdiContainer property to True. A form configured as an MDI parent form supports the same properties as any other form. That is, you can set the FormBorderStyle and StartupPosition properties as you have done in the past. Note, however, that you cannot change the background color of an MDI parent form.

 MDI parent forms are typically displayed with a FormBorderStyle setting of FixedSingle. This way the user can resize the MDI parent form to view the MDI child forms.

Next, you will create the MDI parent form that will contain the MDI child forms in the application.

To configure a form as an MDI parent form:

1. Start Visual Studio .NET, and open the solution file named **Chapter.13\ Startup13\Startup13.sln**. Note that the solution already contains the two forms that will act as the MDI parent form and the MDI child form. (However, these forms have not yet been configured to operate as MDI parent or MDI child forms.) Furthermore, menus have already been created on both forms. You will configure these menus later in the chapter so that they operate properly when used with an MDI application. A Help "About" form has also been added to the solution already.

2. Activate the Win Forms Designer for the form named **frmMdiParent.vb**. Using the Properties window, set the IsMdiContainer property to **True**. Note that the background color of the MDI parent form changes to dark gray. As the developer, you cannot change the background color of an MDI parent form.

3. Designate the MDI parent form as the startup object by right-clicking the project in the Solution Explorer, and then clicking **Properties**. In the Startup13 Property Pages, designate the Startup object as the form named **frmMdiParent**, if necessary.

4. Test the solution. The startup form appears as an MDI parent form.

Having created the MDI parent form, you now need to write the statements to create instances of the MDI child form and to display those form instances. These steps to create an instance of an MDI child form are similar to the steps you have used in the past to create and display an instance of a standard form. That is, you create an instance of the form from its underlying class, and then display it, as shown in the following statements:

```
Dim frmCurrentChild As New frmMdiChild()
frmCurrentChild.MdiParent = Me
frmCurrentChild.Show()
```

The first of the preceding statements creates an instance of the MDI child form named frmMdiChild and stores the reference in the variable named frmCurrentChild. The final statement displays that form. The second statement is new, however, and it appears so that the Me keyword, in this context, will reference the MDI parent form. You designate a form as an MDI child form by setting the MdiParent property of the child form to an instance of the MDI parent form. If you do not set the MdiParent property to an instance of the MDI parent form, the form will operate as an ordinary standard form.

Consider why we placed the preceding statements in the MDI parent form. The MDI parent form is responsible for creating instances of the MDI child form. Imagine that the preceding statements appeared in a procedure appearing in the MDI child form. If there were no instances of the MDI child form open, then there would be no way to call the procedure.

13

 Be careful when setting the MdiParent property. The form reference stored in the MdiParent property must be an instance of an MDI parent form (the IsMdiContainer property of the form must be set to True). If the form is not an MDI parent form, a System.ArgumentException will occur.

Next you will see how to create instances of the form named frmMdiChild and configure those form instances so that they appear as MDI child forms.

To create instances of an MDI child form:

1. Activate the Code Editor for the MDI parent form named **frmMdiParent.vb**, and then enter the following statements in the **Click** event handler for the menu item named **mmuFileNew**:

```
Dim frmCurrentChild As New frmMdiChild()
frmCurrentChild.Text = "New Document"
frmCurrentChild.MdiParent = Me
frmCurrentChild.Show()
```

The preceding statements create an instance of the MDI child form named frmMdiChild and set that form's Text property to the literal string "New Document". By setting the MdiParent property to an instance of the MDI parent form, the form will operate as an MDI child form.

2. Test the solution. On the menu bar, click **File**, and then click **New**. An instance of the MDI child form appears. Click **File**, and then click **New** again. A second instance of the MDI child form appears. You could continue to create as many MDI child forms as you want.

ORGANIZING PROCEDURES IN MDI APPLICATIONS

Organizing the procedures in MDI applications poses unique challenges, because the MDI parent and MDI child forms in an application often need to communicate with each other. The following list describes the problems shared by nearly all MDI applications:

- Procedures and data must often be shared by both MDI parent forms and MDI child forms.

- An MDI parent form often needs to know which MDI child form instance is active. For example, if a toolbar appears on the MDI parent form containing buttons to format a RichTextBox control instance on the MDI child form, then the MDI parent form must know which MDI child form is active. The ActiveMdiChild property of the MDI parent form contains a reference to the MDI child form having focus.

- From the MDI child form, you must often reference members of the MDI parent form or the MDI parent form itself.

When organizing the procedures and variables in an MDI application, consider the following simple rules:

- In the MDI parent form, create the procedures that create instances of the MDI child forms. Furthermore, create the procedures to exit the application in the MDI parent form. Note that the procedure you just created in the preceding steps appeared in the MDI parent form because it created instances of the MDI child form.

- In the MDI child form(s), create the procedures responsible for managing each instance of the MDI child form. For example, in this chapter, all of the procedures to format the contents of the RichTextBox control instance appear in the MDI child form.

- To share a global reference to the MDI parent form, you can declare a Friend or global variable in a module file. Then, when the MDI parent form loads, store a reference to the MDI parent form in the Friend or global variable.

Next, you will create a global shared variable that can be referenced by both the MDI parent and MDI child forms.

To create a shared reference to the MDI parent form:

1. Enter the following statement (shown in bold) in the module named **Global.vb**.

```
Module Global
    Public gMdiParent As frmMdiParent
End Module
```

The preceding statement declares a global variable named gMdiParent. Because this variable is declared as Public it can be referenced throughout the application. Remember that because the variable is declared in a module, it is implicitly shared. That is, only one copy of the data exists.

2. Activate the Code Editor for the form named **frmMdiParent.vb**. Expand the region containing the Win Forms Designer generated code.

3. Enter the following statement (shown in bold) in the constructor (New procedure) for the form named **frmMdiParent.vb**:

```
InitializeComponent()
gMdiParent = Me
```

The preceding statement stores a reference to the MDI parent form in the variable named gMdiParent. Because this variable is declared as a Public variable in a module, the reference is globally available to the MDI parent form and all instances of the MDI child form. Note that you will use this global variable as you progress through the chapter's hands-on steps.

In addition to MDI parent and MDI child forms, an MDI application may contain any number of standard forms.

13

THE ROLE OF STANDARD FORMS IN AN MDI APPLICATION

Standard forms in an MDI application are typically displayed as modal dialog boxes and do not have menus. In this Application, you will display an "About" form as a standard form.

To display a standard form in an MDI application:

1. Activate the Code Editor for the form named **frmMdiParent.vb**, if necessary, and then enter the following statements in the **Click** event handler for the menu item named **mmuHelpAbout**:

```
Dim frmNewHelpAbout As New frmHelpAbout()
frmNewHelpAbout.ShowDialog()
```

2. Test the solution. On the menu, click **Help**, and then click **About** to display the About dialog box.

3. Move the dialog box. Note that it is not constrained by the MDI parent form. Click on the MDI parent form. Note that that MDI parent and child forms cannot get input focus until the modal dialog box is closed. Close the modal dialog box.

A point needs to be made about the placement of control instances in an MDI application. While VB .NET will allow you to create any control instance on an MDI parent form, you typically create control instances on the MDI parent form that apply to all of the MDI child forms. That is, you typically create a ToolBar control instance with buttons to open and save files, and you may create a StatusBar control instance to display status information applicable to the MDI child form having input focus. While it is technically possible to create other control instances such as buttons, text boxes, and labels on an MDI parent form, the process is not common.

MENUS AND MDI APPLICATIONS

Each MDI parent form and any MDI child form in a solution can have its own menu system. However, in an MDI application menus have unique characteristics as described in the following list:

- Only one menu bar appears below the title bar of the MDI parent form. The menu bar displays the menus for the MDI parent form and any MDI child forms. A menu bar never appears below the title bar of the MDI child form.

- The MDI parent form's menu appears when no MDI child forms are loaded.

- When an instance of an MDI child form is loaded or has focus, the menu of the MDI parent form is merged with the menu of the MDI child form. The merged menus appear just below the title bar of the MDI parent form. We discuss how those menus are merged together in a moment. The merged menus of the MDI parent and MDI child forms appear even when all of the MDI child forms in an application are iconified.

- Technically, standard forms in an MDI application can have an associated menu. However, standard forms typically appear as modal dialog boxes and do not have menus.

Next you will see how to merge the menus appearing on the MDI parent and MDI child forms.

Merging Menus

When an MDI child form is loaded or has focus, its menu is merged with the menu of the MDI parent form. The process of merging menus betweens MDI parent and MDI child forms involves working with the following two properties that work in tandem:

- The **MergeOrder** property applies to a MenuItem and contains an Integer value. That value is used with menus and menu items to indicate the relative order in which two menus or menu items will be merged.

- The **MergeType** property works in conjunction with the MergeOrder property and defines whether one menu will replace another menu, one menu will be added to another menu, or the menu items on two menus will be merged together.

The MergeType property has a data type of MenuMerge. The following list describes the possible enumeration values for this property and the purpose of each value:

- If set to **Add**, the menu on the MDI child form will be added to the menu of the MDI parent form. The position of the added menu is based on the relative setting of the MergeOrder property. For example, if a File menu on the MDI parent form had a MergeOrder value of 1, and an Edit menu on the MDI child form had a MergeOrder value of 2, then the Edit menu would appear after the File menu.

- If set to **MergeItems**, the menu items on the MDI child form menu will be merged with the menu items on the MDI parent form menu. The two menus that will be merged must have the same value for the MergeOrder property. How the menu items will be merged is based on the value of the MergeOrder property for each individual menu item.

- If set to **Remove**, the menu or menu item will not appear in the merged menu. This setting allows you to remove a menu from the MDI parent form when an instance of the MDI child form has focus. This setting is not logical for a menu on an MDI child form, because when the MDI child form becomes visible the menu will be removed. Thus, the menu would never appear to the user.

- The setting **Replace** causes the menu of the MDI child form to replace the menu appearing on the MDI parent form. The two menus on the MDI parent and MDI child forms must have the same relative value for the MergeOrder property. Both menu titles or menu items must also have their MergeOrder value set to Replace.

Figure 13-5 illustrates how two menus having unique values for the MergeOrder property will be merged together when the MergeType property is set to Add. In Figure 13-5, the value of the MergeOrder property appears in parentheses to the right of the menu caption.

As shown in Figure 13-5, the value of the MergeOrder property assigned to each menu title determines the relative order in which the two menus are merged. The menu title with the smallest value for the MergeOrder property appears first. This menu is the File menu from the MDI parent form, which has a MergeOrder value of 1. The Format menu on the MDI child form has a MergeOrder value of 2, so it appears next. The Windows menu from the MDI child form has a MergeOrder value of 3, so it appears after the Format menu. The Help menu from the MDI parent form appears last because it has a MergeOrder value of 4. The MergeType property is set to Add for all the menus.

In the preceding example, the values for the MergeOrder property were sequential. However, sequential numbering is not a requirement. If you anticipate adding additional menus or menu items at a later time, consider using non-sequential numbering so that you will not need to change the MergeOrder property value for existing menus or menu items.

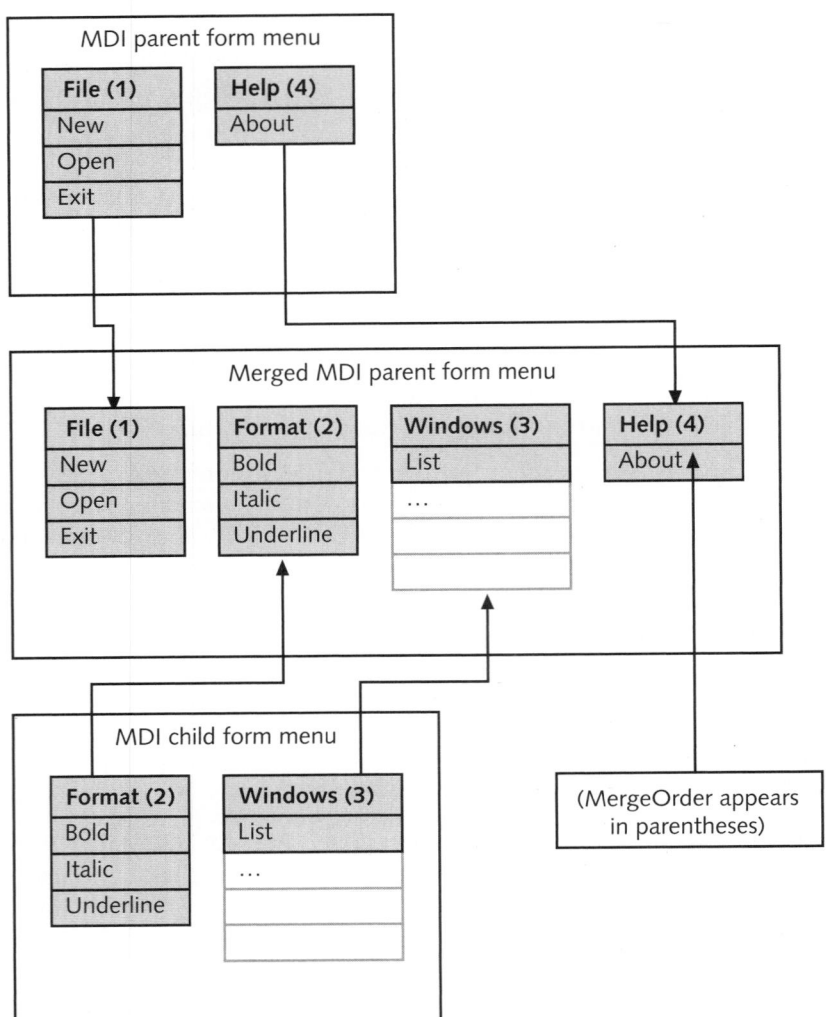

Figure 13-5   Merging menus

Replacing and Removing Menus and Menu Items

A menu can be configured to replace or remove another menu or menu item. To replace a menu title of an MDI parent form with a menu title of an MDI child form, you assign the same relative value to the MergeOrder property for both menu titles, and then set the MergeType property for both menu titles to Replace.

To remove a menu or menu item, you set the MergeType property to Remove for the menu or menu item appearing on the MDI parent form. Figure 13-6 illustrates how a menu title can be removed and another menu title replaced. Again, the value of the MergeOrder property appears in parentheses so that you can see how the menus will be merged.

As shown in Figure 13-6, the Help menu of the MDI parent form has a value of Remove for the MergeOrder property so it is removed when the MDI child menu is displayed. The File menu of the MDI child form replaces the File menu of the MDI parent form.

Figure 13-6   Removing and replacing menus

Merging Menu Items

In addition to merging menu titles, VB .NET allows you to merge the menu items on a menu. When two menus have the same value for the MergeOrder property and both menus have a MergeType setting of MergeItems, the menu items on the two menus will be merged. When merging the menu items on a menu, the relative order of the MergeOrder property for each menu item is again used to specify the order in which the menu items will be merged. Figure 13-7 illustrates the process.

 By default, when a menu or menu item is created, the value of the MergeOrder property is set to 0, and the value of the MergeType property is set to Add.

Figure 13-7 Merging menus and menu items

In this solution, you will merge menu items on the File menu so that the menu items applicable to opening and saving files will appear on the menu bar only when an instance of the MDI child form is active. This organization is logical as these menu items have no purpose when an instance of the MDI child form is not visible. In addition, you will add menus from the MDI child form applicable to formatting and window organization only when an instance of the MDI child form is loaded. Again, these menus only serve a purpose when an instance of the MDI child form is active.

To merge menu items:

1. Activate the Win Forms Designer for the form named **frmMdiParent.vb**.

2. Activate the Properties window for the menu named **mmuFile**. Set the MergeOrder property to **1**, and set the MergeType property to **MergeItems**.

3. Activate the Properties window for the menu item named **mmuFileNew**. Set the MergeOrder property to **1**, and set the MergeType property to **MergeItems**.

4. Activate the Properties window for the menu item named **mmuFileOpen**. Set the MergeOrder property to **2**, and set the MergeType property to **MergeItems**.

5. Activate the Properties window for the menu item named **mmuFileExit**. Set the MergeOrder property to **5**, and set the MergeType property to **MergeItems**.

6. Activate the Properties window for the menu item named **mmuHelp**. Set the MergeOrder property to **4**. Note that the MergeType property is already set to Add.

7. Activate the Win Forms Designer for the form named **frmMdiChild.vb**.

8. Activate the Properties window for the menu named **mmuFile**. Set the MergeOrder property to **1**, and set the MergeType property to **MergeItems**.

9. Activate the Properties window for the menu item named **mmuFileSave**. Set the MergeOrder property to **3**, and set the MergeType property to **MergeItems**.

10. Activate the Properties window for the menu item named **mmuFileClose**. Set the MergeOrder property to **4**, and set the MergeType property to **MergeItems**.

11. Activate the Properties window for the menu item named **mmuFormat**. Set the MergeOrder property to **2**. Note that the MergeType property is already set to Add.

12. Activate the Properties window for the menu item named **mmuWindows**. Set the MergeOrder property to **3**. Note that the MergeType property is already set to Add.

13. Test the solution. On the menu bar, click **File**, and then click **New**. Note that the Save menu item is merged with the menu items on the File menu. Note also that the Format and Windows menus appearing on the MDI child form are integrated with the menus appearing on the MDI parent form.

In addition to merging menus and menu items, you can customize a menu item so that it will allow the user to activate an MDI child form from a list of the loaded MDI child forms.

Using Menus to Select MDI Child Forms

Generally, the user of an MDI application will open multiple instances of the same MDI child form, much as you might have multiple Excel workbooks open at the same time. Well-written MDI applications should give the user an easy way to navigate between one MDI child form instance and another.

To select and display an MDI child form from a menu, you set the MdiList property pertaining to a menu item to True. This setting causes the menu item to display a list of all instances of the loaded MDI child forms. The caption appearing in the menu is the same as the caption appearing in the title bar of the MDI child form. The process is automatic. You need not write any statements to display the MDI child forms.

13

In this solution, the menu to select windows appears on the MDI child form. Again, the placement of this menu is logical. If no MDI child forms are loaded, then there are no MDI child forms to organize.

To configure a menu item as a WindowList menu:

1. Activate the Win Forms Designer for the form named **frmMdiChild.vb**. Activate the Properties window for the menu item named **mmuWindowsList**.

2. Set the MdiList property to **True**.

3. Test the solution. Open two instances of the MDI child form. On the menu bar, click **Windows**, and then select **List**. Note that the MDI child forms appear on the menu. Click one of the menu items that appear in the list. The MDI child form corresponding to that menu item is made the topmost form and gets input focus.

In addition to allowing the user to select a particular MDI child form, you can arrange the active MDI child forms within the region of the MDI parent form.

Arranging MDI Child Forms

A method named LayoutMdi applies to the MDI parent form. It accepts one argument having a data type of MdiLayout. The following list describes the four valid enumeration values:

- If set to **ArrangeIcons**, the iconified MDI child windows are arranged along the bottom of the MDI parent form.

- If set to **Cascade**, the visible MDI child windows are arranged such that each MDI child window appears below another MDI child window and is indented.

- The setting **TileHorizontal** divides the MDI child forms horizontally to fill the visible region of the MDI parent form.

- The setting **TileVertical** divides the MDI child forms vertically to fill the visible region of the MDI parent form.

In this solution, the menu items used to organize the MDI child forms appear on the menu for the MDI child form. However, the statements need to reference the MDI parent form instance so as to reference the LayoutMdi parent property of the MDI parent form itself. Thus, each MDI child form instance must be able to reference the MDI parent form. You can use the global variable named gMdiParent that you declared previously to accomplish this task, as shown in the following statement:

```
gMdiParent.LayoutMdi(MdiLayout.ArrangeIcons)
```

The preceding statement calls the LayoutMdi method of the MDI parent form. The argument MdiLayout.ArrangeIcons causes the icons of the MDI child forms to be arranged along the bottom of the MDI parent form.

To arrange MDI child windows:

1. Activate the Code Editor for the MDI child form named **frmMdiChild.vb**, and then enter the following statement in the **Click** event handler for the menu item named **mmuWindowsArrangeIcons**:

```
gMdiParent.LayoutMdi(MdiLayout.ArrangeIcons)
```

The preceding statement uses the global shared variable gMdiParent, which you declared previously, to reference the MDI parent form. Calling the LayoutMdi method, with the ArrangeIcons argument, causes VB .NET to arrange the iconified MDI child windows.

2. Enter the following statement in the **Click** event handler for the menu item named **mmuWindowsCascade**:

```
gMdiParent.LayoutMdi(MdiLayout.Cascade)
```

3. Enter the following statement in the **Click** event handler for the menu item named **mmuWindowsTileHorizontal**:

```
gMdiParent.LayoutMdi(MdiLayout.TileHorizontal)
```

4. Enter the following statement in the **Click** event handler for the menu item named **mmuWindowsTileVertical**:

```
gMdiParent.LayoutMdi(MdiLayout.TileVertical)
```

5. Test the solution. Create two instances of the MDI child form. On the menu bar, click **Windows**, and then click the appropriate menu items to cascade and tile the visible MDI child windows. Iconify the two windows, and then reposition those iconified windows within the region of the MDI parent form. On the menu bar, click **Windows** and then click **Arrange Icons**. The iconified windows are moved to the lower-left corner of the MDI parent form.

In chapter 11, you were introduced to context menus as a means to display menus for dropdown toolbar buttons. Context menus have other purposes too. We discuss them next.

Context Menus

Context menus typically appear when the user right-clicks on a control instance or the form itself. To create a context menu, you create an instance of the ContextMenu control just as you have created an instance of the MainMenu control: you create an instance of the appropriate control using the Toolbox. Then you create the menu items in place as you have done before. That is, you select the instance of the ContextMenu control instance to activate it, and then you enter the menu items in place in the Win Forms Designer. Then you associate the context menu with a form or a particular control instance by setting the ContextMenu property of the desired form or control instance to the context menu that you created. When the user right-clicks the associated form or control instance, VB .NET displays the corresponding context menu automatically.

13

A form may have several context menus, each associated with a different control instance. Furthermore, you can set the ContextMenu property at runtime to associate the context menu with a different control instance. This way, you can dynamically display specific context menus based on the current state of the application.

To illustrate how a context menu works, you will create a context menu on the MDI child form that will display three formatting menu items.

To create a context menu:

1. Create an instance of the ContextMenu control on the MDI child form named **frmMdiChild.vb**. Set the Name property to **cmuFormat**.

2. Enter the menu items as shown in Figure 13-8.

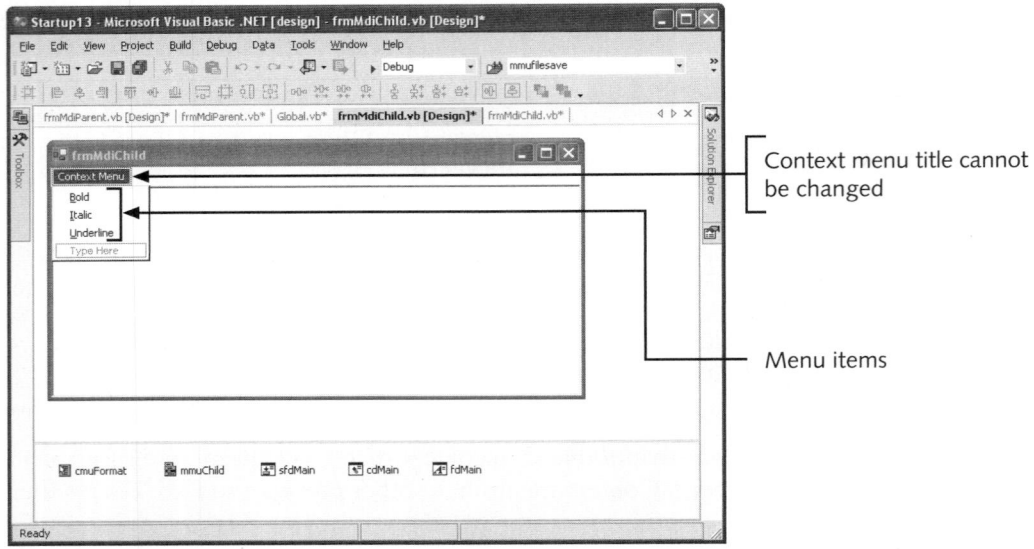

Figure 13-8   Creating a context menu

Unlike an ordinary menu, context menus do not have a menu title. Thus, you cannot change the "Context Menu" text appearing in the title bar. Context menus can, however, display submenus.

3. Set the Name property of the menu items as follows: Bold—**cmuFormatBold**, Italic—**cmuFormatItalic**, Underline—**cmuFormatUnderline**.

4. Activate the Properties window for the RichTextBox control instance named **rtfText**. Set the ContextMenu property to **cmuFormat** to associate the rich text box with the context menu.

5. Test the solution. Click **File**, and then click **New** to create an instance of the MDI child form. Right-click in the RichTextBox control instance appearing on the MDI child form. The context menu appears.

You will write the statements in a moment that will perform the formatting as the user clicks each context menu item. However, note that the process to create an event handler for a context menu item is the same as the process to create an event handler for an ordinary menu item. You can double-click the menu item in the Win Forms Designer, or you can select the Click event handler in the Code Editor using the Class Name and Method Name list boxes.

MDI EVENT RELATIONSHIPS

Windows fires various events as the user navigates from form to form in an MDI application. In addition, events fire as the user attempts to close either the MDI parent form or the MDI child form. The following list describes these events:

- The **Closing** event fires for both the MDI parent and MDI child forms. If the user is closing an instance of the MDI child form, then the Closing event fires for only that MDI child form. If the user is attempting to close the MDI parent form, then the Closing event fires first for each of the open MDI child forms. If any of the Closing events are cancelled, then Windows stops firing any subsequent Closing events. After the Closing event has fired for all of the MDI child forms, the Closing event fires for the MDI parent form itself. Conceptually, canceling a Closing event is the same as canceling a Validating event—subsequent events do not fire.

- When the user activates an MDI child form instance, the **Enter** event fires for the MDI child form getting focus. Typically, you handle this event to update status bar or toolbar information related to the selected MDI child form.

- Windows fires the **Leave** event just before an instance of the MDI child form loses focus.

Figure 13-9 illustrates the operation of the Closing event for MDI parent and MDI child forms.

To understand the reason for handling Closing events, consider what happens when you try to exit programs such as Microsoft Excel or Microsoft Word. First, if there are unsaved changes to a workbook or document file, the user is prompted to save the changes, abandon them, or cancel the close. Here, Excel and Word handle the Closing event.

13

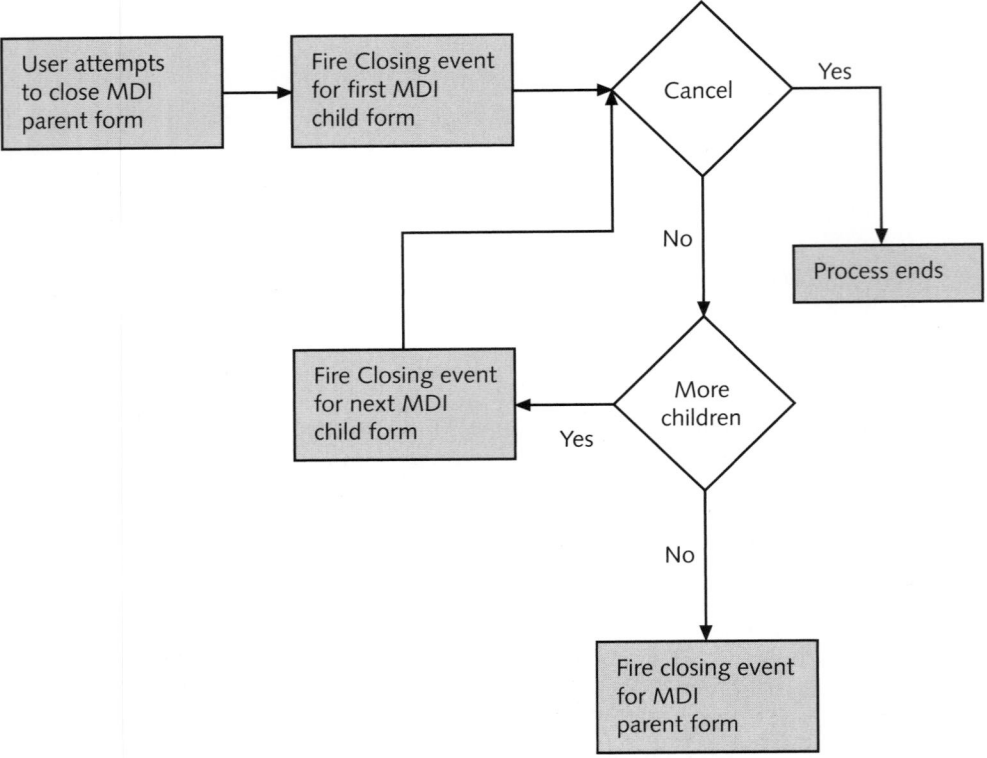

Figure 13-9   Order of Closing events

In the steps that follow, you will write the statements to handle the Closing events for the MDI parent and MDI child forms. The Closing event handler for the MDI parent form will get user confirmation to exit the solution. The Closing event handler for the MDI child form will check whether there exist any unsaved changes to the RichTextBox control instance. If there are unsaved changes, the user will be prompted to save those changes, abandon them, or cancel the Closing event and thus cancel all subsequent Closing events. To determine whether there are unsaved changes, a Boolean variable named mblnDirty has been declared in the MDI child form. The variable's value is True if there exist unsaved changes, and False otherwise. While we discuss the RichTextBox control fully later in the chapter, at this point, you should know that the TextChanged event fires whenever the contents of the control instance change. The following statement appears in the TextChanged event handler to indicate that unsaved changes exist:

```
mblnDirty = True
```

As you will also see later in the chapter, the variable's value is reset to False when the changes are saved.

To create the Closing event handlers for the MDI parent and MDI child forms:

1. Enter the following statements in the **Closing** event handler on the MDI child form named **frmMdiChild.vb**:

```
Dim dlgResult As DialogResult
If mblnDirty = True Then
    dlgResult = MessageBox.Show("Save changes?", _
        "Confirm", MessageBoxButtons.YesNoCancel, _
        MessageBoxIcon.Question)
    Select Case dlgResult
        Case DialogResult.Yes
            Call SaveFile()
        Case DialogResult.No
        Case DialogResult.Cancel
            e.Cancel = True
    End Select
End If
```

The preceding statements display a message box with Yes, No, and Cancel buttons. If the user clicks the Yes button, the file is saved. (You will write the statements for the SaveFile procedure later in the chapter). If the user clicks No, the changes are abandoned and the file is closed. If the user clicks Cancel, then the Closing event is cancelled so the form does not close.

2. Enter the following statements in the **Closing** event handler on the MDI parent form named **frmMdiParent.vb**:

```
Dim dlgResult As DialogResult
dlgResult = MessageBox.Show("Exit the program?", _
    "Confirm", MessageBoxButtons.YesNo, _
    MessageBoxIcon.Question)
If dlgResult = DialogResult.No Then
    e.Cancel = True
End If
```

The preceding statements display a message box to get user confirmation before exiting the application. If the user clicks Yes, then the application ends. If the user clicks No, then the Closing event is cancelled, and the application continues to run. Note that the Closing event fires for the MDI parent form only after it has fired for all of the MDI child forms.

3. On the MDI child form named **frmMdiChild.vb**, enter the following statement in the Click event handler for the menu item named **mmuFileClose**:

```
Me.Close()
```

The preceding statement fires the Closing event only for the MDI child form having focus.

4. On the MDI parent form named **frmMdiParent.vb**, enter the following statement in the Click event handler for the menu item named **mmuFileExit**:

```
Me.Close()
```

13

The preceding statement fires the Closing event for each of the MDI child forms. If none of the Closing events are cancelled, then the Closing event fires for the MDI parent form.

5. Test the solution. Create two new documents, and make changes to both documents. On the menu bar, click **File**, and then click **Close**.

6. In the message box that appears, click **Cancel** to cancel the Closing event for the current MDI child form. The form does not close and subsequent Closing events are cancelled.

7. Click **File** on the menu bar again, and then click **Exit**. The same message box appears as the first MDI child form attempts to close. Click **No** to abandon the changes.

8. The message box appears for the second MDI child form. Click **No** again to abandon the changes.

9. Finally, the Closing event fires for the MDI parent form itself. Click **Yes** to exit the solution.

So that you can see the Enter and Leave events, you will update the status bar appearing on the MDI parent form so that it will contain the name of the current form and display whether or not unsaved changes exist:

To program the Enter and Leave event handlers:

1. Activate the Code Editor for the MDI child form named **frmMdiChild.vb**, and then enter the following statements in the **Enter** event handler:

```
gMdiParent.sbpFileName.Text = Me.Text
If mblnDirty = True Then
    gMdiParent.sbpChanged.Text = "Changed"
Else
    gMdiParent.sbpChanged.Text = "Not changed"
End If
```

The preceding statements use the global variable gMdiParent to reference the MDI parent form. The status bar panels on the form are named sbpFileName and sbpChanged. The first statement stores the form's caption in the status bar panel. The If statement uses the variable mblnDirty to test whether or not unsaved changes exist. If they do, then the text "Changed" appears in the panel. Otherwise, the text "Not changed" appears in the same panel.

2. Enter the following statements in the **Leave** event handler:

```
gMdiParent.sbpFileName.Text = ""
gMdiParent.sbpChanged.Text = ""
```

The purpose of the preceding statements may not be obvious. When the Leave event fires for an MDI child form, another MDI child form may not be getting focus. For example, all of the MDI child forms may be iconified. Thus, the preceding statements clear the contents of both panels.

3. Test the solution. Open two instances of the MDI child form. Make changes to one of the forms. Navigate between the two child form instances to see that the panel indicating changes is updated. Iconify both MDI child form instances. The Leave event fires for an instance of the MDI child form but a subsequent Enter event does not fire. Thus, the panels are cleared.

At this point in the solution's development, you have configured the MDI parent form and the MDI child form. Next, you will learn how to keep track of the loaded MDI child forms.

MANAGING MDI CHILD FORMS

You have seen already that VB .NET supports a Controls collection for forms, and for those controls that act as container controls. You may therefore expect VB .NET to support a Forms collection that would manage all of the loaded MDI forms in an application, but it does not. Therefore, if you need to keep track of the loaded MDI child forms in an application, then you must perform that task yourself. One possible option would be to create an instance of the ArrayList or SortedList class on the MDI parent form, and then store references to the MDI child forms in either class instance. In this solution, you will create a small component that could be used by any MDI application to keep track of a collection of MDI child forms.

The class you create in this chapter will operate as a simple collection. The developer will be able to add and remove forms from the collection, and enumerate the collection with a For Each loop. Thus, the class you create will implement the IEnumerable and IEnumerator interfaces using the same techniques that you used in Chapter 6. The class named ChildFormManager will support the following members:

- The **Add** method will add a form to the list. It accepts one argument having a data type of Form.

- The **Remove** method will accept one argument, a form, and remove that form from the list.

- The **GetEnumerator** method will implement an enumerator.

While several implementation possibilities exist, we have chosen here to store form references in a hidden instance of the SortedList class.

As you enter the following hands-on steps, several statements will temporarily indicate syntax errors. Remember that as you implement an interface, you must implement all of the methods defined by that interface. Until the interface is fully implemented, certain statements will have syntax errors.

To create a collection to manage MDI child forms:

1. Activate the Code Editor for the module named **ChildFormManager.vb**. Enter the following statements (shown in bold) in the ChildFormManager

class. Note that as you enter the following statements, syntax errors will appear until you have fully implemented the IEnumerable interface.

```
Public Class ChildFormManager
    Implements IEnumerable

    Private Shared mintIDCount As Integer
    Private slCurrent As SortedList

    Public Sub New()
        slCurrent = New SortedList()
    End Sub

    Public Sub Add(ByVal frmCurrent As Form)
        mintIDCount += 1
        frmCurrent.Tag = mintIDCount
        slCurrent.Add(frmCurrent.Tag, frmCurrent)
    End Sub

    Public Sub Remove(ByVal frmCurrent As Form)
        slCurrent.Remove(frmCurrent.Tag)
    End Sub

    Public Function GetEnumerator() As IEnumerator _
        Implements IEnumerable.GetEnumerator
        Return New ChildFormEnumerator(slCurrent)
    End Function
End Class
```

The preceding statements declare a class named ChildFormManager that implements the IEnumerable interface. The variable mintIDCount stores a counter used to uniquely identify each form instance stored in the SortedList. The Add method adds a form to the SortedList, and the Remove method removes a form from the same SortedList. The Tag property is used to store the unique key value. The GetEnumerator function returns an instance of the enumerator as discussed in Chapter 6.

2. In the same module, enter the following statements (shown in bold) in the class named **ChildFormEnumerator** to implement the enumerator. Again, syntax errors will appear as you are entering the following statements until you implement all of the members of the enumerator.

```
Public Class ChildFormEnumerator
    Implements IEnumerator

    Private slEnum As SortedList
    Private mintIndex As Integer

    Public Sub New(ByVal sl As SortedList)
        slEnum = sl
```

```
            mintIndex = -1
    End Sub

    Public ReadOnly Property Current() As Object _
        Implements IEnumerator.Current
        Get
            Return slEnum.GetByIndex(mintIndex)
        End Get
    End Property

    Public Function MoveNext() As Boolean Implements _
        IEnumerator.MoveNext
        If mintIndex >= slEnum.Count - 1 Then
            Return False
        Else
            mintIndex += 1
            Return True
        End If
    End Function

    Public Sub Reset() Implements IEnumerator.Reset
        mintIndex = -1
    End Sub
End Class
```

The preceding statements implement the enumerator by implementing the Reset, MoveNext, and Current members. Refer to Chapter 6 for additional information related to implementing interfaces and the IEnumerator interface. In addition, the completed solution contains comments. Next, you must write the statements to add the forms to the collection.

3. Activate the Code Editor for the module named **Global.vb**, and then enter the following statement (shown in bold) to create an instance of the ChildFormManager class:

```
Public gMdiParent As frmMdiParent
Public gChildForms As New ChildFormManager()
```

4. Activate the Code Editor for the MDI parent form named **frmMdiParent.vb**, and then enter the following statement (shown in bold) in the **Click** event handler for the menu item named **mmuFileNew**:

```
frmCurrentChild.MdiParent = Me
gChildForms.Add(frmCurrentChild)
```

5. Activate the Code Editor for the MDI child form named **frmMdiChild.vb**, and then enter the following statements (shown in bold) so that the Closing event handler will remove the MDI child forms as they are closed:

```
If mblnDirty = True Then
    dlgResult = MessageBox.Show("Save changes?", _
        "Confirm", MessageBoxButtons.YesNoCancel, _
```

```
                    MessageBoxIcon.Question)
        Select Case dlgResult
            Case DialogResult.Yes
                Call SaveFile()
            Case DialogResult.No
                gChildForms.Remove(Me)
            Case DialogResult.Cancel
                e.Cancel = True
        End Select
    Else
        gChildForms.Remove(Me)
    End If
```

6. Enter the following statements in the **Click** event handler for the menu item named **mmuWindowsSummary**:

```
Dim pstrMessage As String
Dim frmCurrent As frmMdiChild
For Each frmCurrent In gChildForms
    pstrMessage &= CrLf & frmCurrent.Text
Next
MessageBox.Show(pstrMessage, "Children", _
    MessageBoxButtons.OK)
```

7. Test the solution. Open two instances of the MDI child form. On the menu bar click **Windows**, and then click **Summary**. A summary of the open MDI child windows appears in the dialog box. Close one of the MDI child forms and display the summary again. Note that the form no longer appears.

Next, you will program the RichTextBox control instance to format the text that it displays.

RICH TEXT FILES AND THE RICHTEXTBOX CONTROL

The RichTextBox control allows the user to edit files having a standardized file format called **Rich Text Format (RTF)**. Embedded inside RTF files are formatting directives. The rich text box does not display these directives. Rather, the control instance interprets the directives to perform a desired formatting task. Figure 13-10 shows a short RTF file with formatting directives.

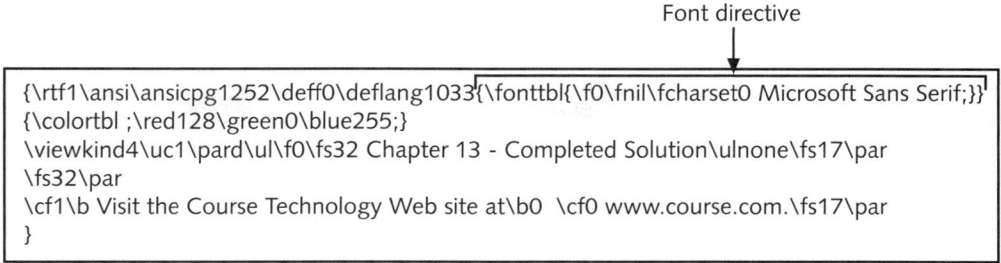

Figure 13-10   Rich text file

As shown in Figure 13–10, directives specify the font, font size, and font attributes. The text displayed in the RichTextBox control instance is embedded in the directives. Fortunately, you as the developer do not have to worry about these directives. Rather, the RichTextBox control interprets these directives automatically. In addition, when formatting is applied to specific text, the RichTextBox control stores the relevant directives in the file. The rich text box can read and write ordinary text files as well as process rich text files. The text shown in Figure 13–10 appears formatted as shown in Figure 13–11.

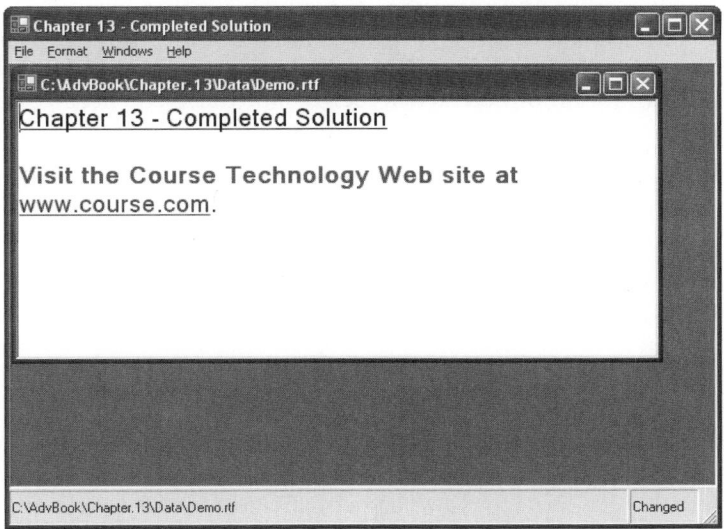

Figure 13-11   Formatted text in a RichTextBox control instance

If you are familiar with HTML, you will recognize that HTML tags resemble RTF directives. The RichTextBox control interprets RTF formatting directives in much the same way that a Web browser interprets HTML tags and displays the formatted output.

READING AND WRITING FILES WITH THE RICHTEXTBOX CONTROL

At the core of the text editor implemented in this chapter is the RichTextBox control. Both the RichTextBox control and the TextBox control are derived from the TextBoxBase class. The RichTextBox control supports additional properties and methods to apply formatting to text, including setting fonts and font attributes. The RichTextBox control supports the following members:

Syntax

System.Windows.Forms.RichTextBox class

Public Properties

- The Boolean **AcceptsTab** property defines what happens when the user presses the Tab key. If set to True, a tab character is inserted into the control instance. If set to False, pressing the Tab key causes the next control instance in the tab order to get focus.

- The **DetectUrls** property causes the RichTextBox control to recognize URLs. The text of a recognized URL appears as a link. When the user clicks the link, the LinkClicked event fires. The RichTextBox control detects that a string contains a URL when the text "www" or "http" is found. In addition, "ftp" (File Transfer Protocol) and "https" (HTTP secure) are also recognized as valid URLs. Note, however, that VB .NET cannot detect whether or not the URL itself references an actual address on the Web. An RTF file can contain multiple links.

- The **Lines** property returns an array of strings. The array of strings contains one element for each line appearing in the control instance. A line is marked by a carriage return character at the end of the line.

- The **MultiLine** property has the same purpose as the MultiLine property of the TextBox control. If set to True, the control instance will display text on multiple lines.

- The **RightMargin** property sets the rightmost limit for the text that appears on a line. This property is measured in points.

- The **ScrollBars** property defines whether or not scroll bars appear in the region of the control instance. The RichTextBox control can be configured to display either horizontal or vertical scroll bars, or both horizontal and vertical scroll bars. The control can also be configured to display scroll bars only when necessary, or all the time.

- The **SelectedRTF** property contains the selected text, including all rich text formatting directives. Thus, you can copy formatted text to the clipboard and then paste that text to other applications that can interpret RTF files.

- The **SelectedText** property contains the selected text. However, only the selected text is represented. The formatting directives are removed.

- The **SelectionColor** property defines the color of the selected text or insertion point.

- The **SelectionFont** property defines the font of the selected text or insertion point.

- The **SelectionStart** property contains an Integer and defines the position of the starting character of the selection.

- The **SelectionLength** property contains the number of characters in the selection.

Public Methods

- The **Clear** method removes all the text from the control instance.

- The **Copy** method copies the selected text to the Windows clipboard.

- The **Cut** method removes the selected text and places it in the Windows clipboard.

- The **Paste** method copies the contents of the Windows clipboard into an instance of the RichTextBox control. If no characters are selected, then the text is inserted at the insertion point. If text is selected, the text in the Windows clipboard replaces the selected text in the rich text box.

- The **LoadFile** method reads a file into the RichTextBox control instance. The control can read and write both plain text and rich text files. The LoadFile method is discussed in detail in a moment.

- The **SaveFile** method saves the contents of a RichTextBox control instance to a file.

Public Events

- The **LinkClicked** event only fires when the DetectUrls property is set to True. The event fires when the user clicks a link.

- The **TextChanged** event fires when the user modifies the contents of a RichTextBox control instance.

- The **SelectionChanged** event fires when the user selects different text or moves the insertion point.

One function supported by the RichTextBox control is the capability to read and write text and RTF files. Instead of writing the statements to open, read or write, and then close a file, all of the necessary functionality to read and write files is built into the RichTextBox control itself. Thus, you do not need to read a file by creating an instance of the StreamReader class, reading each line, and storing the lines read in an instance of the RichTextBox control. The LoadFile and SaveFile methods have the following syntax:

Syntax

Overloads Public Sub LoadFile(*path* **As String**, *filetype* **As RichTextBoxStreamType**)
Overloads Public Sub SaveFile(*path* **As String**, *filetype* **As RichTextBoxStreamType**)

Definition

The **LoadFile** and **SaveFile** methods read and write a text file or rich text file, respectively.

Dissection

- The *path* argument contains the folder and file name of the file to open or save.

- The optional *filetype* enumeration defines how the LoadFile or SaveFile methods will interpret the file contents. The enumeration value **PlainText** causes the RichTextBox control to read and display each text character. The value **RichText** causes the control to interpret the file as a rich text file, and apply any formatting directives before displaying the text in the region of the control instance.

Code Example

```
rtfText.LoadFile("C:\Demo.rtf", _
    RichTextBoxStreamType.RichText)
rtfText.SaveFile("C:\Demo.rtf", _
    RichTextBoxStreamType.RichText)
```

Code Dissection

The preceding statements read and write the text file named Demo.rtf as a rich text file.

If you attempt to open a file as a rich text file, and the file format is not valid, then a System.ArgumentException will occur.

Next you will write the statements to open and save the rich text files.

To open and save rich text files:

1. Activate the Code Editor for the form named **frmMdiParent.vb**. Enter the following statements in the **Click** event handler procedure named **mmuFileOpen**:

```
Dim dlgResult as DialogResult
dlgResult = ofdMain.ShowDialog()
Try
    If dlgResult = DialogResult.OK Then
        Dim frmCurrentChild As New frmMdiChild()
        frmCurrentChild.MdiParent = Me
        frmCurrentChild.rtfText.LoadFile( _
            ofdMain.FileName, _
            RichTextBoxStreamType.RichText)
        frmCurrentChild.Text = ofdMain.FileName
        gChildForms.Add(frmCurrentChild)
        frmCurrentChild.Show()
    End If
Catch ex As System.ArgumentException
    MessageBox.Show("Invalid file format", "Error", _
        MessageBoxButtons.OK)
End Try
```

The preceding statements display the OpenFileDialog already created on the MDI parent form. If the user clicks the Open button, then an instance of the MDI child form gets created and configured as an MDI child form using the same techniques you have already seen. Then the file specified by the user is loaded into the RichTextBox control instance appearing on the main form. If the file contents cannot be interpreted as an RTF file, then the statement in the exception handler displays a message box. Note also that the form is added to the instance of the ChildFormManager class just as the form was added when a new file was created by the user.

2. Activate the Code Editor for the form named **frmMdiChild.vb**. Enter the following statements in the procedure named **SaveFile**:

```
Dim dlgResult As DialogResult
dlgResult = sfdMain.ShowDialog()
If dlgResult = DialogResult.OK Then
    rtfText.SaveFile(sfdMain.FileName, _
    RichTextBoxStreamType.RichText)
    Me.Text = sfdMain.FileName
    gMdiParent.sbpFileName.Text = Me.Text
    gMdiParent.sbpChanged.Text = "Not changed"
    mblnDirty = False
End If
```

The preceding statements first display the SaveFileDialog. If the user clicks the Save button, then the SaveFile method of the RichTextBox control instance is called to save the file. Note that the file is saved in rich text format. The variable mblnDirty is set to False to indicate that no unsaved changes exist and the status bar panels are updated.

3. Test the solution. On the menu bar, click **File**, and then click **Open**. In the Open dialog box, open the file named **Chapter.13\Data\Demo.rtf**. Modify the file contents in some way. Click **File**, and then click **Save** to display the Save As dialog box.

4. Save the file using the name **Chapter.13\Data\Demo1.rtf**.

Now that you have seen how to open and save rich text files, you will learn how to format the contents of the rich text box itself.

FORMATTING A RICH TEXT BOX

In this solution, the user will format text appearing in the RichTextBox control instance by selecting the desired text, and then applying the desired font or color, or formatting attribute such as bold, italic, or underline. When formatting the contents of the rich text box, two concepts are important: the insertion point and the selection.

- When no text is selected in the control instance, the cursor position is referred to as the **insertion point**. If the user applies formatting attributes

13

such as boldface, or a font, the characters typed by the user at the insertion point will appear in boldface and have that selected font.

- When the user selects text, then the marked text is called the **selection**. Any formatting attributes chosen by the user will be applied to the selection.

The RichTextBox control supports several properties that work with the insertion point and the selection. The SelectionFont property returns the font of the insertion point or selection. The SelectionFont property, in turn, has properties named Bold, Italic, and Underline. These three properties can store the following values:

- If set to **Nothing**, then the selected text contains characters having different fonts. To prevent exceptions from firing, make sure the SelectionFont references a font before attempting to reference the members of the SelectionFont property.

- If set to **True**, the characters in the selection or the character following the insertion point have the selected font style applied.

- If set to **False** (the default), neither the characters in the selection nor the character following the insertion point have the selected font style applied.

In the sections that follow, you will see how to change the color of text, change the font, apply and remove font attributes, and add additional features to support zooming and linking.

Setting Colors

Just as VB .NET supports the OpenFileDialog and SaveFileDialog controls—which provide a means for the user to select files to open and save—the ColorDialog control allows the user to select a color from a standard dialog box. Just as the OpenFileDialog and SaveFileDialog controls do not open or save files, the ColorDialog control does not set the color of an object. It merely returns a color. The ColorDialog control contains two sections. The first section displays basic colors and the second section allows the user to define custom colors. Figure 13-12 shows the two parts of the ColorDialog control.

As shown in Figure 13-12, the left side of the Color dialog box displays basic colors, and the right side of the Color dialog box allows the user to define custom colors. Whether the user can only select colors from the basic set of colors, or define custom colors as well, depends on the setting of the FullOpen and AllowFullOpen properties. If the AllowFullOpen property is set to True, the user can expand the Color dialog box so as to display the section allowing custom color creation. If set to False, the user can only select colors from the basic set of colors. If the FullOpen property is set to True, then the custom colors section is displayed by default. Figure 13-12 shows the ColorDialog control while FullOpen is True.

Basic colors

Custom colors

Figure 13-12   Parts of the ColorDialog control

Note that the actual colors supported will depend on the graphics hardware installed on the user's computer.

The steps to apply a color to the selection in an instance of the RichTextBox control are simple. Display the ColorDialog control instance by calling its ShowDialog method, and then set the SelectionColor property to the color returned by the ColorDialog control instance.

To format colors:

1. Create an instance of the ColorDialog control on the form named **frmMdiChild.vb**. Set the name property to **cdMain**. Make sure that the FullOpen and AllowFullOpen properties are set to **True**.

2. Activate the Code Editor for the form named **frmMdiChild.vb**, and then enter the following statements in the **Click** event handler for the menu item named **mmuFormatColor**:

```
Dim dlgResult As DialogResult
dlgResult = cdMain.ShowDialog()
If dlgResult = DialogResult.OK Then
    rtfText.SelectionColor = cdMain.Color
End If
```

3. Test the solution. On the menu bar, click **File**, and then click **New** to create a new file. Enter a line of text, and then select that line of text. On the menu bar, click **Format**, and then click **Color**. Select a color, and then click **OK**. The text that you selected appears in the new color.

In addition to the ColorDialog control, VB .NET also supplies the FontDialog control with which the user can set fonts.

Setting Fonts

Just as the OpenFileDialog and SaveFileDialog controls allow the user to select a file to open or save, the FontDialog control allows the user to select fonts. To use the FontDialog control, you first set properties to define the options that will appear to the user on the dialog box, and then display the control instance. The Font property of the control instance stores the font and related font attributes selected by the user. As the developer, you read those attributes and apply them as necessary. The FontDialog control supports the following members:

Syntax

System.Windows.Forms.FontDialog control

Public Properties

- The **Color** property defines the font color. This property duplicates some of the capabilities of the ColorDialog control. Note, however, that the color selection is more limited.

- The **Font** property defines the selected font. The property contains a reference to an instance of the Font class.

- The **MinSize** and **MaxSize** properties allow you to specify the minimum and maximum user selectable font sizes. If the values are set to 0, then the size is ignored. Note that the value of the MinSize property must be less than the value of the MaxSize property.

- The **ShowApply** property, if set to True, causes the Font dialog box to display an Apply button.

- The Boolean **ShowColor** property, if set to True, allows the user to select colors in the Font dialog box. By default, the ShowColor property is set to False. The colors displayed represent a small subset of the colors displayed in the ColorDialog control.

- The Boolean **ShowEffects** property defines whether or not the user can select font effects, such as boldface and underlining.

Public Events

- The **Apply** event fires when the user clicks the Apply button. The Apply button only appears if the ShowApply property is set to True.

Public Methods

- The **ShowDialog** method displays the Font dialog box.

Figure 13-13 illustrates the parts of the FontDialog control.

Figure 13-13   Parts of the FontDialog control

As shown in Figure 13-13, the FontDialog control displays a list box allowing you to select specific fonts and to define the style of the selected font. The contents of these list boxes are determined by the fonts installed on the system. The minimum and maximum selectable font size is defined by the MinSize and MaxSize properties. The Effects section and the check boxes that it contains appear because the ShowEffects property is True.

To set fonts using the FontDialog control:

1. Create an instance of the **FontDialog** control on the form named **frmMdiChild.vb**. The control instance appears in the resizable tray below the Win Forms Designer.

2. Set the Name property of the control instance to **fdMain**. Set the ShowColor and ShowEffects properties to **True**, if necessary.

3. Activate the Code Editor for the form named **frmMdiChild.vb**. Enter the following statements in the **Click** event handler for the menu item named **mmuFormatFonts**:

```
Dim dlgResult As DialogResult
dlgResult = fdMain.ShowDialog
If dlgResult = DialogResult.OK Then
    rtfText.SelectionFont = fdMain.Font
    rtfText.SelectionColor = fdMain.Color
End If
```

The preceding statements display the FontDialog control named fdMain. If the user clicks the OK button, then the font and color selected by the user are stored in the SelectionFont and SelectionColor properties of the rich text

13

box, thereby setting the font and color of the selected text, or the insertion point if no text is selected.

4. Test the solution. On the menu bar, click **File**, and then click **New** to create a new file. Enter a line of text, and then select that line of text. On the menu bar, click **Format**, and then click **Fonts**. In the Font dialog box, select a font of your choosing. When you close the dialog box, the selected text appears in the new font.

In addition to setting fonts using the FontDialog control, you will now see how to set individual font attributes such as boldface, underlining, and italics, without the aid of the FontDialog control. Enabling or disabling a particular font attribute is more difficult, because rather than just overwriting existing font attributes such as boldface, you must first determine whether or not the current font attribute is applied. If the attribute is applied, then the attribute should be removed. If the attribute is not applied, then it should be. In addition, you must programmatically create an instance of the Font class.

Examine the following blocks of statements to apply or remove the boldface Font attribute.

```
Dim pfntCurrent As System.Drawing.Font
Dim pintStyle As Integer
```

The preceding statements declare a variable to store an instance of the Font class. The Integer variable named pintStyle will be used to store bit flags to indicate whether a particular font attribute is applied or not. The operation of these flags will be discussed in a moment.

```
pfntCurrent = rtfText.SelectionFont
If pfntCurrent Is Nothing Then
    MessageBox.Show("Cannot apply font attributes " & _
    "when multiple fonts are selected", "Error", _
    MessageBoxButtons.OK)
    Exit Sub
End If
```

The preceding statements first store the selected font in the variable named pfntCurrent. If the selection contains multiple fonts, then the RichTextBox control instance cannot determine the current font, so pfntCurrent will contain Nothing. The If statement tests for this condition. If multiple fonts are selected, then the message box is displayed and the sub procedure exits.

In the situation where multiple fonts are selected, it is technically possible to handle this problem by examining the font of each character in the selection using the SelectionStart and SelectionLength properties to get the selection. Then check and apply the selected font attribute character by character.

The following statements check whether the underline or italic attributes are applied for the currently selected text. If they are, the value of the FontStyle is added to the bit flag variable named pintStyle. Again, the operation of this flag will be discussed in a moment.

```
If rtfText.SelectionFont.Underline = True Then
    pintStyle += FontStyle.Underline
End If
If rtfText.SelectionFont.Italic = True Then
    pintStyle += FontStyle.Italic
End If
```

The preceding statements preserve the existing status of the underline and italic attributes. If the attributes are currently applied to the selected text, then the bit flag is set by adding the attribute value to the bit flag named pintStyle. If the attribute is not currently set, then the contents of the bit flag are not changed.

```
If rtfText.SelectionFont.Bold = False Then
    pintStyle += FontStyle.Bold
End If
```

The preceding statements enable the bold attribute if the existing selection is not bold. However, if the bold font attribute is already applied to the selection, then the statements do nothing, thereby removing the bold attribute. Figure 13-14 illustrates the operation of the bit flag in the preceding statements.

As shown in Figure 13-14, each attribute has an associated decimal value. Examining the binary value for each attribute, notice that a different bit is set for each attribute. Thus, if the bold and underline attributes were enabled, the numeric value of the bit flag would be 5 and the bit pattern would be "0101".

13

Attribute	Decimal value	Binary value
Bold	1	0001
Italic	2	0010
Underline	4	0100

Bold on	1	0001
	+	+
Italic off	0	0000
	+	+
Underline on	4	0100
	=	=
Result	5	0101

Figure 13-14   The operation of font attributes

The following statements apply a new font to the selection by creating a new instance of the Font class:

```
rtfText.SelectionFont = New System.Drawing.Font( _
    pfntCurrent.FontFamily, _
    pfntCurrent.Size, _
    CType(pintStyle, System.Drawing.FontStyle))
```

The preceding statement constructs a new font based on the current font family and current font size. Remember that the current selection font is stored in the variable pfntCurrent. The final argument sets the font attributes by converting the Integer variable named pintStyle to a FontStyle type. Again, explicit type conversion is required because strict type checking is enabled.

The preceding blocks of statements describe how to apply or remove the bold font attribute. The logic to apply and remove the underline or italic font attributes is nearly the same. Next you will write the statements to apply or remove the bold, italic, and underline font attributes. Because the user can format the selected text using items on the main menu and equivalent items on the context menu, you will create general procedures to apply or remove each formatting attribute, and then call those procedures from both the menu item and context menu item.

To set font attributes:

1. Activate the Code Editor for the MDI child form named **frmMdiChild.vb**, and then enter the following statements in the **FormatBold** procedure:

```
Dim pfntCurrent As System.Drawing.Font
Dim pintStyle As Integer

pfntCurrent = rtfText.SelectionFont
If pfntCurrent Is Nothing Then
    MessageBox.Show("Cannot apply font attributes " & _
    "when multiple fonts are selected", "Error", _
    MessageBoxButtons.OK)
    Exit Sub
End If
If rtfText.SelectionFont.Underline = True Then
    pintStyle += FontStyle.Underline
End If

If rtfText.SelectionFont.Italic = True Then
    pintStyle += FontStyle.Italic
End If

If rtfText.SelectionFont.Bold = False Then
    pintStyle += FontStyle.Bold
End If

rtfText.SelectionFont = New System.Drawing.Font( _
    pfntCurrent.FontFamily, _
```

```
        pfntCurrent.Size, _
        CType(pintStyle, System.Drawing.FontStyle))
    Call UpdateFormatMenu()
```

2. Enter the following statement in the **Click** event handler for the context menu item named **cmuFormatBold** and the main menu item named **mmuFormatBold**:

```
Call FormatBold()
```

3. Enter the following statements in the **FormatItalics** procedure:

```
Dim pfntCurrent As System.Drawing.Font
Dim pintStyle As Integer

pfntCurrent = rtfText.SelectionFont
If pfntCurrent Is Nothing Then
    MessageBox.Show("Cannot apply font attributes " & _
    "when multiple fonts are selected", "Error", _
    MessageBoxButtons.OK)
    Exit Sub
End If

If rtfText.SelectionFont.Underline = True Then
    pintStyle += FontStyle.Underline
End If

If rtfText.SelectionFont.Italic = False Then
    pintStyle += FontStyle.Italic
End If

If rtfText.SelectionFont.Bold = True Then
    pintStyle += FontStyle.Bold
End If

rtfText.SelectionFont = New System.Drawing.Font( _
    pfntCurrent.FontFamily, _
    pfntCurrent.Size, _
    CType(pintStyle, System.Drawing.FontStyle))
    Call UpdateFormatMenu()
```

4. Enter the following statement in the **Click** event handler for the context menu item named **cmuFormatItalic** and the main menu item named **mmuFormatItalic**:

```
Call FormatItalics()
```

5. Enter the following statements in the **FormatUnderline** procedure:

```
Dim pfntCurrent As System.Drawing.Font
Dim pintStyle As Integer
```

13

```
pfntCurrent = rtfText.SelectionFont
If pfntCurrent Is Nothing Then
    MessageBox.Show("Cannot apply font attributes " & _
        "when multiple fonts are selected", "Error", _
        MessageBoxButtons.OK)
    Exit Sub
End If

If rtfText.SelectionFont.Underline = False Then
    pintStyle += FontStyle.Underline
End If

If rtfText.SelectionFont.Italic = True Then
    pintStyle += FontStyle.Italic
End If

If rtfText.SelectionFont.Bold = True Then
    pintStyle += FontStyle.Bold
End If

rtfText.SelectionFont = New System.Drawing.Font( _
    pfntCurrent.FontFamily, _
    pfntCurrent.Size, _
    CType(pintStyle, System.Drawing.FontStyle))
Call UpdateFormatMenu()
```

6. Enter the following statement in the **Click** event handler for the context menu item named **cmuFormatUnderline** and the main menu item named **mmuFormatUnderline**:

```
Call FormatUnderline()
```

7. Enter the following statements in the procedure named **UpdateFormatMenu**:

```
With rtfText.SelectionFont
    mmuFormatBold.Checked = .Bold
    cmuFormatBold.Checked = .Bold
    mmuFormatItalic.Checked = .Italic
    cmuFormatItalic.Checked = .Italic
    mmuFormatUnderline.Checked = .Underline
    cmuFormatUnderline.Checked = .Underline
End With
```

The purpose of the preceding statements is to update the checked formatting menu items on both the main menu and the context menu so that they reflect the current format.

8. Test the solution. Enter a line of text in the RichTextBox control instance, select some text, and then right-click while the cursor is positioned over the rich text box. Click **Bold** to apply a bold typeface to the selected text.

9. Select different text. Test the **Italic** and **Underline** attributes using both the main menu and the context menu.

As a final improvement, you can update the checked formatting menu items to indicate the current formatting attributes applied to the selected text. Each time the selection or insertion point changes, the SelectionChanged event fires for the RichTextBox control instance. In this event handler, you can call the UpdateFormatMenu procedure you just created to update the checked menu items.

To synchronize the selection with the formatting menu items:

1. Activate the Code Editor for the form named **frmMdiChild.vb**, if necessary, and then enter the following statements in the **SelectionChanged** event handler for the RichTextBox control instance named **rtfText**:

```
Dim pfntCurrent As Font = rtfText.SelectionFont
If pfntCurrent Is Nothing Then
    Exit Sub
Else
    Call UpdateFormatMenu()
End If
```

The preceding statements get the font of the selection. Again, the If statement tests that multiple fonts are not selected. If multiple fonts are selected, the procedure exits. Otherwise, the procedure updates the checked menu items.

2. Test the solution. Create a new file. Enter text and apply font attributes. Note that as you select different text, the checked formatting menu items are updated.

Another feature supported by the RichTextBox control is zooming, which is discussed next.

13

ZOOMING

Using Microsoft Word, you can zoom in and out of a document's contents. The RichTextBox control supports the same capabilities. The ZoomFactor property allows you to change the magnification of the text displayed in a RichTextBox control instance. A ZoomFactor of 1 displays the text in normal magnification. A setting of 1.5 displays the text as 150% of normal, and so on.

To set the magnification of text in the rich text box:

1. Activate the Code Editor for the form named **frmMdiChild.vb**, if necessary. Enter the following statement in the **Click** event handler for the menu item named **mmuWindowsZoom75**.

```
rtfText.ZoomFactor = 0.75
```

2. Enter the following statement in the **Click** event handler for the menu item named **mmuWindowsZoom100**.

```
rtfText.ZoomFactor = 1
```

3. Enter the following statement in the **Click** event handler for the menu item named **mmuWindowsZoom150**.

```
rtfText.ZoomFactor = 1.5
```

4 Test the solution. Create a new document and enter text in that document. Click **Windows**, and then point to **Zoom**. Select each of the three magnification levels.

One new feature of the RichTextBox control is the ability to detect URLs. The user can then click on a URL to jump to a Web page.

DETECTING LINKS TO WEB PAGES

By setting the DetectUrls property to True, VB .NET will automatically detect when the user types a URL into the RichTextBox control instance. When VB .NET detects a URL, the text appears highlighted and underlined. In addition to detecting a URL, you must also create a LinkClicked event handler that will execute when the user clicks on the URL.

Typically, when the user clicks on a URL, the user wants to start a Web browser and navigate to that URL. To start another program such as Internet Explorer, you call the Start method of the Process class of the System.Diagnostics namespace, having the following syntax:

Syntax

System.Diagnostics.Process.Start method

Overloads Public Shared Function Start(*filename* **As String**) **As Process**
Overloads Public Shared Function Start(*filename* **As String**, *arguments* **As String**) **As Process**

Definition

The overloaded **Start** method starts a new process such as Internet Explorer.

Dissection

The *filename* argument contains the path and the file name of the program to start. The *arguments* argument contains any command-line arguments that should be passed to the program.

Code Example

```
System.Diagnostics.Process.Start("Iexplore", _
    "www.course.com")
```

Code Dissection

The preceding statement will start Internet Explorer and display the Web page *www.course.com*.

As mentioned, the LinkClicked event fires when the user clicks on text recognized as a link. As always, the first argument in the event is named sender and has a data type of System.Object. The second argument to the event handler has a data type of LinkClickedEventArgs. The argument variable e contains a reference to the link stored in the LinkText property. Thus, the following statement can be used to start Internet Explorer and navigate to the link:

```
System.Diagnostics.Process.Start("IExplore", e.LinkText)
```

In the preceding statement, the first argument contains the application to start (Internet Explorer), and the second argument contains the name of the link (e.LinkText).

To configure a RichTextBox to display URLs:

1. Activate the Properties window for the RichTextBox control instance appearing on the MDI child form. Set the DetectUrls property to **True**, if necessary.

2. Enter the following statement in the **LinkClicked** event handler for the RichTextBox control instance named **rtfText**:

```
System.Diagnostics.Process.Start(IExplore", e.LinkText)
```

3. Test the solution. Create a new document. Enter the URL **www.course.com**. As you type the URL, it appears as a link. Click the link. Internet Explorer starts, and if you are connected to the Internet, the home page for *www.course.com* will appear.

You have completed the programming for this chapter. You have seen how to work with MDI applications. Specifically, you have seen how to manage the interaction between MDI parent and MDI child forms. In addition, you have seen how to merge menus between MDI parent and MDI child forms, and how to create context menus. Finally, you saw how to use the RichTextBox control, and apply formatting to text.

CHAPTER SUMMARY

- An MDI application consists of one or more MDI parent forms, and one or more MDI child forms. The visible region of an MDI child form cannot extend beyond the visible region of the MDI parent form. In addition, when an MDI child form is iconified, it appears at the bottom of the MDI parent form rather than on the Taskbar. Standard forms typically appear in MDI applications as modal dialog boxes.

❏ To designate a form as an MDI parent form, set the form's IsMdiContainer property to True. To designate a form as an MDI child form, create an instance of the MDI child form and set the MdiParent property of the MDI child form to the instance of the MDI parent form.

❏ When working with menus in an MDI application, the menu bar for both the MDI parent and MDI child forms appears just below the title bar of the MDI parent form. When an instance of the MDI child form has input focus, the menu of the MDI parent form and the menu of the MDI child form are merged together based on the settings of the MergeType and MergeOrder properties for each menu. Standard forms in an MDI application do not typically have menus.

❏ Menus may be merged such that an MDI child menu is added to the MDI parent menu. The menu items of a parent and child menu may be merged together by setting the MergeType property to MergeItems. A parent menu may be deleted by setting the MergeType property to Remove. A child menu will replace a parent menu when the MergeType property is set to Replace.

❏ A menu item may be configured to list the active MDI child forms by setting the MdiList property of the menu item to True.

❏ MDI child forms may be arranged by calling the LayoutMdi method of the MDI parent form. Windows may be tiled, cascaded, or iconified, by specifying an argument to the LayoutMdi method.

❏ In addition to ordinary menus, an application can contain one or more context menus. To create a context menu, simply create an instance of the ContextMenu control on the form, and then create and edit the menu items in place as you have done before. To associate a context menu with a control instance, set the ContextMenu property of that control instance to the desired context menu. Note that a form can have several context menus and those context menus can be associated with different control instances.

❏ There exist relationships between the events in an MDI application. When the user activates an instance of an MDI child form, the Enter event fires for that MDI child form. When an MDI child form loses input focus, the Leave event fires. The Closing event fires for both MDI parent and MDI child forms when an attempt is made to close the MDI parent form or MDI child form, respectively. If a Closing event is cancelled, then subsequent Closing events do not fire. The Closing event first fires for all of the MDI child forms and then for the MDI parent form.

❏ The RichTextBox control allows the user to edit files having a standardized file format called Rich Text Format (RTF). The LoadFile method reads text or RTF files into the control instance, and the SaveFile method saves the contents to a text or RTF file.

❏ You format the contents of the RichTextBox control based on the selection or the insertion point. The SelectionFont property allows you to define the font of the selection or insertion point. The SelectionColor property allows you to define the color.

❑ The ColorDialog control supplies a standard dialog box that allows the user to select a color. The ShowDialog method displays the control instance. The color selected by the user is stored in the Color property.

❑ The FontDialog control supplies a standard dialog box that allows the user to select a font. Again, the ShowDialog method displays the control instance. The font selected and the font attributes are stored in the Font property.

❑ The RichTextBox control supports zooming in much the same way that Microsoft Word allows you to zoom in and zoom out of a document. A value of 1 indicates normal magnification, and a value of 2 indicates a magnification level of 200%.

❑ The RichTextBox control will search an RTF document for URLs. VB .NET recognizes URLs based on the strings "http", "www", "ftp", and "https". Set the DetectUrls property to True so that the rich text box will recognize URLs. In the LinkClicked event handler for the rich text box, call the Start method of the System.Diagnostics.Process class with two arguments. The first argument contains the name of the program to start and the second argument contains the text of the link.

REVIEW QUESTIONS

1. Which of the following statements correctly describes the relationships between forms in an MDI application?

   a. An MDI child form must appear inside the visible region of an MDI parent form.

   b. A standard from must appear inside the visible region of an MDI parent form.

   c. An MDI child form must always have a menu.

   d. Only one form in an MDI application can be designated as an MDI child form.

   e. all of the above

2. How do you configure a form as an MDI parent form?

   a. Call the Show method of the form designated as the MDI parent form with an argument having the enumeration value of ModeMdiParent.

   b. Instead of creating a Windows Form application project, create an MDI application project.

   c. Using the Project Properties dialog box, set the IsMdiApplication property to True, and then set the startup object to the form that will operate as the MDI parent form.

   d. Set the MdiParent property to True for the form that should be designated as the MDI parent form.

   e. none of the above

13

3. How to you designate a form as an MDI child form?

   a. Set the MdiChild property to True.

   b. Set the MdiChildForm property to True.

   c. Set the MdiParent property of the MDI child form to reference an instance of the MDI parent form.

   d. Call the GetParentForm method of the MdiChild class to get a reference to the MDI parent form. Store that reference in the Parent property of the MDI child form.

   e. none of the above

4. Which of the following types of controls can be created on an MDI parent form?

   a. TextBox, Button, Label

   b. ComboBox, ListBox

   c. StatusBar, ToolBar

   d. You can create any type of control on an MDI parent form.

   e. none of the above

5. Which of the following statements related to menu negotiation is correct?

   a. The MergeType and MergeOrder properties are used to configure how menus will be negotiated.

   b. A menu on an MDI child form can be configured to replace a menu on an MDI parent form.

   c. It is possible to remove a menu from the MDI parent form when the menus of the MDI parent and MDI child forms are merged.

   d. It is possible to insert a menu anywhere in a menu system.

   e. all of the above

6. Which of the following statements describes the relative order of menus and the MergeOrder property?

   a. The MergeOrder property contains an Integer value used to indicate the relative order of the menus and menu items that will be merged between MDI parent and MDI child forms.

   b. Two menu items on an MDI parent and MDI child form must always have unique values for the MergeOrder property. If two menus have the same value for the MergeOrder property, then an exception will occur.

   c. Two menu items on an MDI parent and MDI child form must have the same values for the MergeOrder property, or an exception will occur.

   d. If you want a menu on an instance of an MDI child form to replace a menu on the MDI parent form, then the two menus must have a value of 0 for the MergeOrder property.

   e. none of the above

7. How do you configure a menu to display a list of loaded MDI child forms?

a. Create an instance of the WindowList provider control, and then associate that control instance with a menu item.

b. Iterate through the ChildForms collection of the MDI parent form. For each MDI child form found, create a new instance of the MenuItem class to store a reference to the MDI child form.

c. Set the MenuType property of a menu item to WindowList.

d. Set the MdiList property of a menu item to True.

e. none of the above

8. What are the possible layout options to display MDI child forms?

a. Arrange, Overlay, Horizontal, Vertical

b. ArrangeIcons, Cascade, TileHorizontal, TileVertical

c. Icon, Minimize, Maximize

d. Icon, List, Report

e. none of the above

9. Which of the following statements correctly describes how to create a context menu?

a. Create an instance of the MainMenu control. Set its ContextMenu property to True so that the menu will appear as a context menu.

b. Create an instance of the ListBox control in a modal dialog box. Then display the modal dialog box.

c. You create a context menu by creating an instance of the ContextMenu control, and then editing the menu items in place.

d. You cannot create context menus in VB .NET.

e. none of the above

10. Which of the following statements correctly describes the relationship between focus events as the user navigates from MDI child form to MDI child form?

a. As the user navigates from one MDI child form to another, the Leave event fires for the form losing focus, and then the Enter event fires for the MDI child form that is getting focus.

b. The Enter and Leave events fire for the MDI parent form in addition to any MDI child forms.

c. You can update status bar information by creating an event handler for an MDI child form's Enter event.

d. all of the above

e. none of the above

13

11. Which of the following statements is true of the Closing event handlers for MDI parent and child forms?

   a. The Closing event cannot be canceled.

   b. If the MDI parent form is closing, the Closing event first fires for the MDI parent form, and then for each of the MDI child forms.

   c. If the MDI parent form is closing, the Closing event first fires for each of the MDI child forms, and then for the MDI parent form.

   d. The Closing event fires only for MDI child forms. The event does not apply to an MDI parent form.

   e. none of the above

12. Which of the following statements is correct regarding the RichTextBox control?

   a. As well as reading and writing RTF files, the RichTextBox control can read and write HTML files.

   b. The RichTextBox control can read and write text files and RTF files.

   c. A file read as an RTF file cannot be saved as a text file.

   d. While it is possible to set formatting attributes such as bold, underline, and italic, it is not possible to format fonts or select colors for text.

   e. none of the above

13. Which of the following statements is correct of the FontDialog control?

   a. The Font property contains the font selected by the user. The data type is Font.

   b. The user can set font colors using the FontDialog control.

   c. You can set properties to define the minimum and maximum allowable font sizes.

   d. The ShowDialog method displays the dialog box.

   e. all of the above

14. Which of the following statements is correct of the ColorDialog control?

   a. The color is returned in the Color property.

   b. The Color property has a data type of Double.

   c. You call the ShowColor method to display the dialog box.

   d. all of the above

   e. none of the above

15. How do you allow the RichTextBox control to recognize links to Web pages?

   a. Set the RecognizeUrls property to True, and handle the Click event.

   b. Set the DetectUrls property to True, and create an event handler for the LinkClicked event.

   c. Create an event handler for the URLClicked event.

   d. Create an event handler for the URLSelected event.

   e. none of the above

16. Describe how MDI parent, MDI child, and standard forms are typically used in an MDI application.

17. List and describe the events pertaining to input focus with regard to MDI parent and MDI child forms.

18. List and describe the valid settings for the MergeType property for menus and menu items, and the effect of each setting on how two menus and their menu items will be merged together.

19. Describe how to configure and use the FontDialog and ColorDialog controls.

20. Describe how to configure and display a context menu.

PROGRAMMING QUESTIONS

1. Write the statements to create an instance of the form class named frmChild, storing the instance in the variable named frmNewChild. Configure the form so that it will appear as an MDI child form of the MDI parent form instance named frmNewParent.

2. Write the statements to create and display 10 instances of the MDI child form named frmChild. Display the values "Document 1" to "Document 10" on the title bar of each MDI child form instance that you create.

3. Assume that a variable named frmMdiParentForm exists that references an instance of an MDI parent form. Write the statements to arrange the icons and set the layout to cascade, horizontal tiling, and vertical tiling.

4. Assume that an MDI child form instance exists named frmChild. Write the statements to create the Enter and Leave event handlers for the form such that when the form gets input focus, the text Active will appear in the title bar of the form and the text Inactive will appear in the title bar when the form loses input focus.

5. Write the statements to create the Closing event handler for the MDI child form named frmChild. Write the statements in the event handler that will display a message box that gets confirmation before closing the form. If the user does not want to close the form, then cancel the event.

6. Assume that an instance of an MDI parent form exists named frmParent. Write the statement to set the title bar text for the active MDI child form to "Active Form".

7. Assume that an instance of the RichTextBox control exists named rtfMain. Write the statement to select all of the characters appearing in the rich text box.

8. Assume that an instance of the RichTextBox control exists named rtfMain. Write the two statements to load and save the file named "C:\Question.rtf" as a rich text file.

9. Write the statements to display an instance of the ColorDialog control instance named cdCurrent such that the user can select custom colors. When the user closes the instance of the ColorDialog control, apply the formatting to the selected text appearing in the RichTextBox control instance named rtfMain.

13

10. Assume that an instance of the RichTextBox control exists named rtfMain. Write the statements to format the selection such that the text will appear in a bold, italicized, and underlined typeface.

11. Assume that an instance of the RichTextBox control exists named rtfMain. Write the statements to display an instance of the FontDialog control named fdCurrent. If the user clicks the OK button on the FontDialog control instance, apply the font to the selected text in the RichTextBox control instance.

12. Assume that an instance of a RichTextBox control exists named rtfMain. Write the statements to set the zoom factor to 25%, 50%, 75%, and 100%.

13. Assume that URL recognition is enabled for the RichTextBox control named rtfMain. Write the statements to create the necessary event hander and code that will display the contents of the URL in Internet Explorer.

14. Assume that an instance of the RichTextBox control named rtfMain exists. Write the statements to examine each line appearing in the control instance. If the line contains more than 80 characters, increment the value of the Integer counter variable named pintLongLines.

HANDS-ON PROJECTS

1. In this project, you will extend the word processing application discussed in the chapter by adding additional controls and features. The file named Chapter.13\Exercises13\Ch13Ex1.exe contains the compiled executable solution. Figure 13-15 shows the completed solution with multiple instances of the MDI child form loaded and visible.

   a. Create a new project named **Ch13Ex1.sln**. Create the same menu items and functionality as found in the completed chapter solution.

   b. Create a **SaveAll** menu item that will go through all of the open MDI child forms, determine which documents have unsaved changes, and then save those documents. If the document has never been saved before, display a Save File dialog box allowing the user to select a file name.

   c. Create a status bar control instance on the form. In the status bar, display the number of open documents. Display the number of characters, words, and lines in the current document in the status bar. A word is separated by space characters. A line ends with the carriage return character (CrLf). Update the current number of characters, words, and lines as the user modifies text in the RichTextBox control instance. In addition, update these values as the user navigates from MDI child form to MDI child form.

   d. Create a menu item that will allow the user to abandon all files. That is, all of the MDI child forms should be closed without displaying any prompts to save the changes.

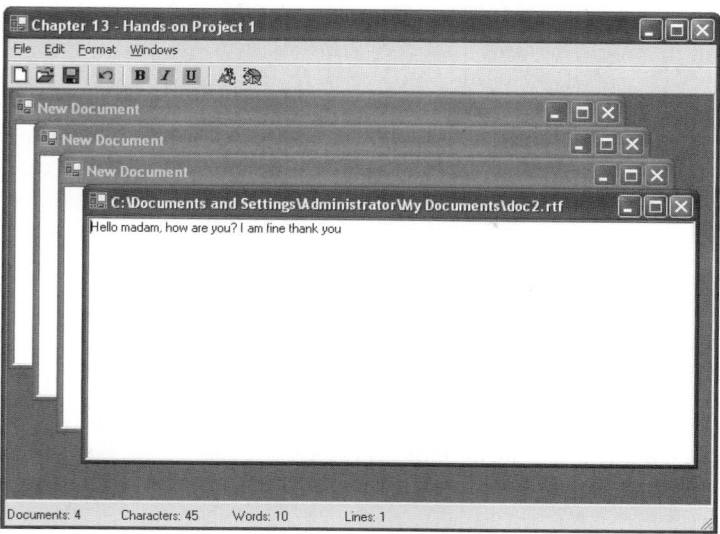

Figure 13-15   Chapter 13 – Hands-on Project 1

e. Create a menu item that will display a summary form instead of simply displaying summary information in a modal dialog box. Examine each loaded MDI child form. For each loaded MDI child form, display the file name appearing on the title bar and whether or not unsaved changes exist. In addition, display the number of characters in the file. Finally, display the total number of documents open and the total number of characters in all of the files. Use control instances of your choosing to display this information.

f. Create a toolbar on the MDI parent form. Create toolbar buttons that allow the user to open a file and display that file in an instance of the MDI child form. Create buttons that allow the user to apply a bold, italic, and underlined typeface to the selected text. These toolbar buttons should mimic equivalent menu items. In addition, write the statements such that when the user changes the selection or the insertion point, the bold, underline, and italic toggle buttons appearing on the toolbar will be updated accordingly. Use icons of your choosing for the toolbar buttons. Create appropriate ToolTips for each button.

g. Create buttons on the toolbar that display dialog boxes allowing the user to apply colors and fonts to the selected text.

h. Create a menu item that allows the user to clear the contents of the RichTextBox control instance for the active MDI child form, and another menu item that selects all of the text in the active MDI child form. Configure the menu integration as necessary. Also create an undo menu item.

13

2. In this project, you will work with a subordinate class to manage the MDI child forms in the application. Assume that a retail operation, such as a store or bank, has some number of clerks serving customers. In this solution, you will keep track of the number of customers waiting in each line, and the number of customers that have been served. The solution will also keep track of the total number of customers in line for all clerks and the total number of customers served by all clerks. The file named Chapter.13\Exercises13\Ch13Ex2.exe contains the compiled executable application. Figure 13-16 shows the completed solution.

a. Create a new solution named **Ch13Ex2.sln**.

b. Using the techniques presented in the chapter, create a class that will keep track of all the loaded MDI child forms.

c. On the MDI parent form, create a File menu with menu items named **Initialize**, **Add Clerk**, and **Remove Clerk**.

d. The Initialize menu item should allow the user to enter an Integer value into an input box. Based on the number entered, create that number of MDI child forms. Display captions on the title bar as shown in Figure 13-16. Add each MDI child form to the collection responsible for managing the MDI child form instances.

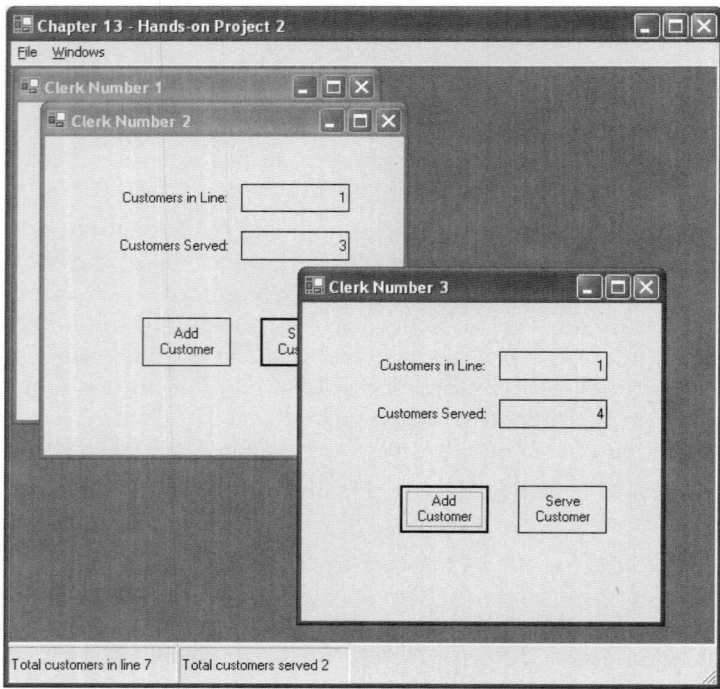

Figure 13-16   Chapter 13 – Hands-on Project 2

e. The Add Clerk menu item should add a single clerk, thereby creating one more instance of the MDI child form, and then add that MDI child form to the collection.

f. The Remove Clerk menu item should remove the active MDI child form.

g. On the MDI child form, create a **Windows** menu having menu items that will allow the user to navigate from MDI child form to MDI child form, and iconify and cascade the MDI child windows.

h. Create the control instances on the MDI child form as shown in Figure 13-16. Increment the number of customers in line when the user clicks the Add Customer button, and decrement the number of customers in line when the user clicks the Serve Customer button. When a customer is served, increment the number of customers served, and decrement the number of customers in line. Make sure that the number of customers in line cannot be negative.

i. Create a status bar on the MDI parent form. In the status bar, display the total number of customers in all lines and the number of customers served in all lines. Display this information for the current MDI child form. Be sure to update the data as different MDI child forms get input focus.

j. Create a menu item that will display the summary dialog box. Create the form for the custom dialog box. Add an instance of the ListBox control to the summary form, and display the total number of customers currently in line and the total number of customers served in the list box.

k. On the MDI parent form, create a menu item to exit the solution. Handle the closing event for the MDI parent form. Get confirmation before exiting the solution.

3. In this project, you will process sequential files and display their contents in multiple MDI child windows. A sequential file named Ch13Ex3.txt contains the data for this exercise. The file has the following fields and data types: TellerName (String), TransactionDate (Date/Time), TransactionType (String), AccountNumber (Integer), Amount (Single). The file named Chapter.13\Exercises13\Ch13Ex3.exe contains the compiled executable application. Figure 13-17 shows the completed solution with instances of the MDI child form appearing in the main form.

a. Create a new solution named **Ch13Ex3.sln**.

b. Create an MDI parent form for the application. On the MDI parent form, create a **File** menu with menu items to open the sequential file and to exit the application.

c. Create the MDI child form and its control instances as shown in Figure 13-17.

d. Allow the user to open the file with an instance of the OpenFileDialog control. The sequential file is sorted by teller name. When the user opens the file, read the file so that the records for each teller appear in a separate instance of the MDI child form. Only one record should appear at a time on each MDI child form. (*Hint*: you may want to create one instance of the ArrayList class for each MDI child form to manage the records for that form.

13

Figure 13-17   Chapter 13 – Hands-on Project 3

e. Create menu items that will allow the user to navigate from record to record.

f. Create a status bar on the form. In the status bar, display the teller name corresponding to the active MDI child form. In addition, display the total number of transactions for that teller and display the current record number. As the user navigates from MDI child form to MDI child form, make sure that you update the contents of the status bar accordingly.

g. Create a **Windows** menu with menu items that will allow the user to navigate from MDI child form to MDI child form. Create the necessary menu items that will allow the user to arrange the windows.

h. Create a **Context** menu that will allow the user to format the text appearing in the text boxes. From the Context menu, the user should also be able to specify the font and color for the text. Create menu items that will allow the user to individually set the bold, italic, and underline attributes.

i. Write the statements so that when text has been modified in the current MDI child form, two asterisks (**) will be added to the caption on the MDI child form to indicate that the text needs to be saved.

j. Allow the user to save the data back to the sequential file. You must iterate through all of the open forms, saving the records for each form. Create a menu item to accomplish this task. Allow the user to select the file name using an instance of the SaveFileDialog control.

4. In this project, you will work with a database so that database information is stored in instances of MDI child forms. Instead of a single type of MDI child form, you will work with multiple instances of an MDI child form. Each instance of the MDI

child form may display different database data. Note that this hands-on project extensively uses the ADO.NET material presented in Chapters 8 and 9. The file named Chapter.13\Exercises13\Ch13Ex4.exe contains the compiled executable application. The file named Chapter13.mdb contains the corresponding database file. Figure 13-18 shows the completed solution.

a. Create a new project named **Ch13Ex4.sln**.

b. On the MDI parent form, create a **File** menu with the menu items named **Open CAS Index**, **Open Borehole**, and **Open Lab Data**.

c. The Open CAS Index menu item should open an instance of an MDI child form that will display all of the data from the table named tblCASIndex. The table has the following fields and data types: fldCASIndexNumber – Integer, fldChemicalName – String, fldCASRegNo – String, fldCarcinogenic – Boolean. Display the records sorted by the chemical name field. You will need to create the necessary connection, OleDbDataAdapter, and DataSet, and bind that DataSet to the DataGrid control instance appearing on the form. Configure the application so that only one instance of this MDI child form can be open at a time.

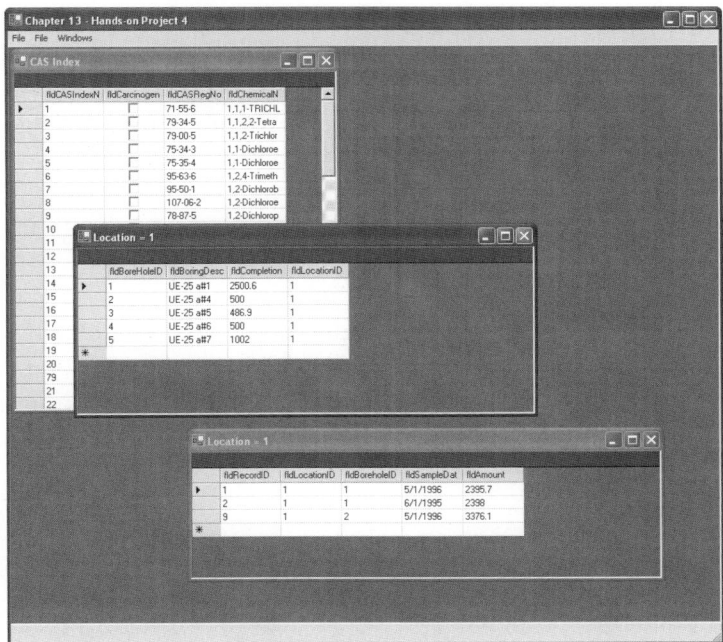

13

Figure 13-18   Chapter 13 – Hands-on Project 4

d. The task to open the data for the boreholes is more complicated than the Open CAS Index form. The borehole data represents wells drilled into the ground. Wells are grouped into locations, thus, there is a one-to-many relationship between the table named tblLocation and the table named tblBoreholeData. The field name fldLocationID is the key field that links the two tables. The table named tblLocation has the following members: fldLocationID – Integer, fldLocationName – String, fldLocationAddress – String. The table named tblBoreholeData has the following fields: fldRecordNumber – Integer, fldBoreholeIID – Integer, fldLocationID – Integer, fldBoringDescription – String, fldCompletionDepth – Single. When the user clicks the Open Borehole menu item, display a dialog box listing all of the valid locations. The dialog box should display the unique locations in the list box. When the user selects a location description in the list box, display an instance of the Borehole form containing only that data corresponding to the current location.

e. The Open Lab Data menu item should work similarly to the Open Borehole menu item. The user first must select a valid location. Then, in the MDI child form, display the records from the table named tblLabData having the following fields: fldRecordID – Integer, fldLocationID – Integer, fldBoreHoleID – Integer, fldSampleDate – Date/Time, fldDepth – Single, fldAmount – Single. Note that there are other fields in the table but you need not use them.

f. The MDI child form should have a menu allowing the user to update and save any of the records displayed in the various DataGrid control instances. Merge this menu with the menu on the MDI parent form.

g. Create a status bar on the MDI parent form. The status bar should be updated as the user navigates from MDI child form to MDI child form. In the status bar, display the number of records in the DataSet.

h. Create a **Windows** menu that will allow the user to navigate from MDI child form to MDI child form. Create this menu on the MDI child form.

i. Program the Closing events for both the MDI parent and MDI child forms. In the Closing event for the MDI parent form, confirm that the user wants to exit the application. In the Closing event for the MDI child form, confirm that there exist no unsaved changes.

APPENDIX
A
DEBUGGING

In this appendix, you will:

♦ Be introduced to the debugging environment

♦ Configure the debugging environment

♦ Understand Visual Studio .NET debugging tools

♦ Trace the execution of program statements

♦ Set breakpoints to suspend program execution temporarily

♦ Use the Command window to examine data values

♦ Use Watch windows and create watch expressions

♦ Examine the order in which procedures are called using the Call Stack window

♦ Examine the values of local variables using the Locals window

♦ Examine the values of variables and properties using the Autos window

---

In any program you write, you will likely make mistakes. Locating and correcting those mistakes is an important part of the development process, and is called **debugging**. The purpose of this appendix is to help you learn how to debug the programs that you write using the debugging windows supplied by Visual Studio .NET. Visual Studio .NET supplies multiple windows to help you debug an application.

You use the various debugging windows of the Visual Studio .NET IDE to help you locate and correct errors. The Visual Studio .NET debugging tools are useful to help you locate and correct both runtime errors and logic errors. However, the debugging tools can do nothing to help you resolve syntax errors appearing in a statement or statements. Thus, we do not discuss syntax errors in this appendix.

Syntax errors appear underlined in the Code Editor. In addition, the Task List window displays any syntax errors that you have made.

INTRODUCTION TO THE CONCEPT OF DEBUGGING

Compiling and executing a .NET application is a two-step process. First the source code for an application is compiled into IL by one of the Visual Studio .NET compilers. The compiler used depends upon the language chosen for development. Remember that a Visual Studio .NET solution is compiled into a machine-independent intermediate language called IL. That IL is then translated into an executable file by the Just-In-Time (JIT) compiler. When you debug an application, the process works in reverse. Visual Studio .NET reverse engineers the executable file back to IL. That IL is then mapped back to the original source code using a corresponding program database file (PDB file). Thus, to debug an application, an up-to-date program database file must exist.

Visual Studio .NET writes the program database file to the bin and obj\debug directories in the solution folder. This file is a binary file and is used internally by VB .NET. You cannot edit this file.

CONFIGURING THE DEBUGGING ENVIRONMENT

To debug any VB .NET application from within the Visual Studio .NET IDE, you must first configure that application for debugging. When you compile a VB .NET application to an executable file, you apply what is called a **configuration** so as to specify how that application will be compiled.

Visual Studio .NET supplies two default configurations: Debug and Release. In addition, you can also create custom configurations. Creating custom configurations is not discussed in this appendix. A list box appearing on the Standard toolbar allows you to select a configuration from the available configurations, as described in the following list:

- If **Debug** is the current configuration, then Visual Studio .NET builds a program database file having a suffix of ".pdb". This file stores debugging information and has the same name as the executable file corresponding to the project. When the Debug configuration is used, the program is not optimized. When a program is optimized, the compiler often reorders statements to improve performance. If statements are reordered, then Visual Studio .NET cannot reverse engineer the executable file using the program database file.

■ If the current configuration is set to **Release**, then the debugging information is stripped from the application. Thus, no corresponding .pdb file is
built. This means that you cannot use the Visual Studio .NET debugging
windows to debug the application. In addition, statements are reordered and
optimized for performance. Thus, when you are going to debug an application, you must select the Debug configuration.

If you have selected the Release configuration and attempt to debug an application, Visual Studio .NET will only be able to display the IL for the application.

First, you will verify that Visual Studio .NET and the application are properly configured for debugging.

To verify the debugging environment:

1. Start Visual Studio .NET, and then open the solution named
AppendixA\AppendixA.sln.

   The purpose of the completed solution appearing in this appendix is merely
   to demonstrate selected programming errors and how to correct them. It is
   not a complete solution in the sense of the solutions appearing in other
   chapters.

2. Make sure that the Standard and Debug toolbars are visible. Right-click anywhere on the toolbar. In the context menu that appears, make sure that
   Standard is checked. Make sure that the **Debug** toolbar is also active.

3. Verify that the configuration is set to Debug, as shown in Figure A-1.

Figure A-1 shows the completed main form for the solution.

Figure A-1 Completed form

THE VISUAL STUDIO .NET DEBUGGING TOOLS

Visual Studio .NET's debugging tools consist of commands that allow you to suspend the execution of a program temporarily by entering break mode, and then trace the execution of statements and procedures as they are called. You can execute each statement in a program line by line while suspending execution as each line executes, suspend execution when the value of a particular variable changes, or suspend execution when some condition becomes true.

The Visual Studio .NET debugging tools are just that. They are tools. How and when you use them is up to you. That is, some developers prefer to set watch variables and other developers may prefer to examine the values of variables in the Command window. Furthermore, some developers prefer to set breakpoints while others prefer to single-step through the statements in the application. In addition, depending on the error that you are experiencing, you may choose to use one window over another.

Learning how to use these debugging tools, and how to use them effectively, will help you program more efficiently. The time you spend working with these tools, and thoroughly understanding them, will help you in the long run to program more efficiently, and to locate and correct the errors that you make much more quickly.

The Visual Studio .NET debugging tools consist of windows that you use together to locate and correct errors in a program, as described in the following list:

- The **Breakpoints** window lets you define statements in a program where Visual Studio .NET will suspend execution. Once execution is suspended, you typically examine the values of variables and object properties so as to determine the cause of a particular error. In addition, you can use the Code Editor, along with buttons on the Debug toolbar, to execute statements one at a time.

- The **Command** window serves two purposes by operating in two different modes, called views. In Command view, you execute commands appearing on the Visual Studio .NET menu bar. For example, you can use Command view to open a solution and save it. Visual Studio .NET also allows you to combine multiple commands together into macros. Command view will not be discussed further in this appendix. In Immediate view, you enter expressions that display the values of variables and object properties. As you enter each expression, Visual Studio .NET evaluates the expression and displays the result.

- Four separate **Watch** windows display lists of variables or properties and their corresponding values. Each Watch window works the same way. Four windows are provided so that you can logically organize the variables and object properties that you want to watch.

- The **Call Stack** window allows you to examine the procedures that have been called and the order in which those procedures were called.

- The **Locals** window allows you to examine the values of local variables, the properties of a form, and its control instances.

- The **Autos** window operates similarly to the Locals window. The Autos window displays variables and their corresponding values for the currently executing statement and the statements surrounding the statement that just executed.

- The **Me** window allows you to use the Me keyword to debug the elements corresponding to the current class instance.

- The **Memory**, **Disassembly**, and **Registers** windows are typically used to debug assembly language IL. The Memory window allows you to examine the contents of memory directly. The Disassembly window displays statements in the form of IL. The Registers window allows you to view and change the contents of the underlying CPU registers. As you will not debug the underlying IL or assembly language for the program, these windows are not discussed in this appendix.

In this appendix, we discuss how to use most of the debugging windows presented in the preceding list.

TRACING THE EXECUTION OF PROGRAM STATEMENTS

The simplest way to examine the statements in your program as they execute is to trace their execution. The following list describes the buttons appearing on the Debug toolbar that you use to step through statements as Visual Studio .NET executes them:

- Visual Studio .NET executes one statement and then enters break mode when you click the **Step Into** button. The Step Into button traces execution as procedures are called and as they complete. The order of statement execution is exactly the same as it would be if the user were running the application. Thus, if you click the Step Into button on a statement containing a procedure call, then you can trace the execution of the statements in that procedure, and any procedures called by that procedure.

- The **Step Over** button works similarly to the Step Into button. If the statement is a procedure call, however, Visual Studio .NET executes all of the statements in the procedure, and then enters break mode just before executing the statement following the procedure call. Stepping over a procedure is useful when you know that the procedure does not contain errors.

- The **Step Out** button works similarly to the Step Over button. When clicked, Visual Studio .NET executes all of the remaining statements in the current procedure, and then enters break mode at the statement following the statement that called the procedure.

In addition to using the buttons on the Debug toolbar, equivalent menu items appear on the Debug menu. You can also use the following equivalent function keys: Step Over (F10), Step Into (F11), Step Out (Shift+F11). If the preceding keys do not appear to work correctly, then Visual Studio .NET is likely configured such that the keyboard keys are mapped to be compatible with an older version of Visual Studio. On the menu bar, click Tools, and then click Options. In the Options dialog box, click Environment, and then click Keyboard. Make sure that the Keyboard mapping scheme is set to Default Settings.

To step through program statements:

1. Compile the solution by clicking **Build**, **Rebuild AppendixA** to compile the solution. Again, compiling the solution updates the corresponding .pdb file.

2. Click the **Step Into** button on the Debug toolbar to begin program execution. The New procedure (constructor) executes first.

The New procedure is highlighted in the Code Editor, indicating that the constructor (New procedure) is about to execute. Figure A-2 shows the Code Editor in break mode.

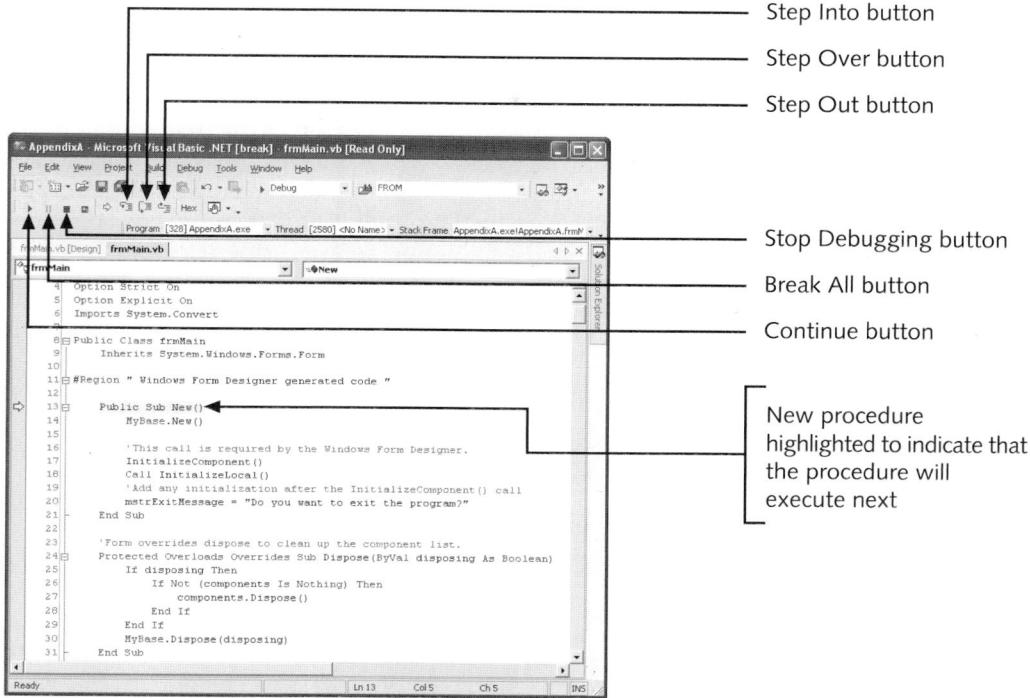

Figure A-2 Code Editor in break mode

Examining Figure A-2, you will see that the Continue and Stop Debugging buttons are enabled. Clicking the Continue button will cause Visual Studio .NET to continue program execution. Clicking the Stop Debugging button will end execution, causing Visual Studio .NET to return to design mode. The Break All button is disabled because Visual Studio .NET is already in break mode. Note that the Step Into, Step Over, and Step Out buttons are also enabled.

3. Click the **Step Into** button again. The call to the statement MyBase.New() is highlighted, indicating that this statement will execute next.

The statement highlighted in the Code Editor is the statement that Visual Studio .NET will execute next, not the statement that has just executed. Furthermore, notice that the MyBase.New() call and the call to the InitializeComponent procedure appear in the form's constructor. Thus, you can see that the constructor for a class executes first.

4. Click the **Step Into** button again. The InitializeComponent procedure is highlighted, indicating that it will execute next.

5. Click the **Step Into** button again. The InitializeComponent procedure executes. Note that Visual Studio .NET does not suspend execution for the statements in the InitializeComponent procedure because the following attribute appears in the procedure declaration:

```
<System.Diagnostics.DebuggerStepThrough()> _
    Private Sub InitializeComponent()
```

By setting the DebuggerStepThrough attribute, the Visual Studio .NET debugging environment will not step through the statements in the InitializeComponent procedure. Applying this attribute is logical because the statements in the InitializeComponent procedures were automatically generated by the Win Forms Designer. Thus, they do not contain errors. Note that the Win Forms Designer declared this attribute automatically.

6. Click the **Step Into** button again. The InitializeLocal procedure gets called. Visual Studio .NET traces the execution of each procedure that is called and the statements in those procedures as they execute.

7. Click the **Step Out** button. Execution of the InitializeLocal procedure completes and then control returns to the form's constructor.

8. End the solution by clicking the Stop Debugging button.

How you write the statements in an application can affect your ability to debug those statements. To illustrate, examine the following code segment:

```
Dim pstrVal1 As String = "23.4"
Dim pstrVal2 As String = "24.4"
Dim psngVal1, psngVal2 As Single
Dim psngResult As Single
Dim pblnValid1, pblnValid2 As Boolean

pblnValid1 = IsNumeric(pstrVal1)
pblnValid2 = IsNumeric(pstrVal2)

If pblnValid1 And pblnValid2 Then
    psngVal1 = ToSingle(pstrVal1)
    psngVal2 = ToSingle(pstrVal2)
    psngResult = psngVal1 + psngVal2
Else
    Exit Sub
End If
```

In the preceding statements, local variables are declared to store intermediate results. However, the preceding If statement could have been written as follows without using intermediate local variables:

```
If IsNumeric(pstrVal1) And IsNumeric(pstrVal2) Then
    psngResult = ToSingle(pstrVal1) + ToSingle(pstrVal2)
Else
    Exit Sub
End If
```

Writing the If statement in the preceding manner may make it more difficult to debug the statements because you cannot examine the values of the intermediate variables to determine whether they are correct. That is, you can single-step only on a statement-by-statement basis. You cannot step through the execution of part of a statement. Again, how you write equivalent statements is up to you. However, if you nest complex statements, they become more difficult to debug.

 While in break mode, you cannot modify any program statements and then continue execution. Instead, you must end the program, make the necessary changes, and then recompile the solution thereby generating a new executable file and .pdb file.

SETTING BREAKPOINTS

When you suspect that a problem is occurring in a particular procedure or that a particular statement is incorrect, you can suspend execution of the solution at any executable statement by setting a breakpoint. A **breakpoint** is an executable statement where Visual Studio .NET will suspend execution and enter break mode just before executing the marked statement. Once Visual Studio .NET has entered break mode, you can step through the statements following the breakpoint or examine the values of variables and object properties. Visual Studio .NET supports four types of breakpoints, as described in the following list:

- A **function breakpoint** is a breakpoint set on an executable statement in a procedure. Breakpoints cannot be set on declaration statements.

- **Data breakpoints** suspend execution when the value of a variable changes. Note that VB .NET does not support data breakpoints, but certain other Visual Studio .NET languages do.

- Two other types of breakpoints called file breakpoints and address breakpoints are not discussed in this appendix. **File breakpoints** allow you to set a breakpoint at a particular line in a module file. You can more easily set the same breakpoint by setting a function breakpoint, so we do not discuss file breakpoints. **Address breakpoints** are used to set a breakpoint at a particular memory address, and are typically used when debugging IL.

Statements containing breakpoints appear to the developer with filled circles in the left margin of the Code Editor. In addition, breakpoints are listed in the Breakpoints window. Figure A-3 shows the Visual Studio .NET IDE with two enabled breakpoints set in the Code Editor, and the same two enabled breakpoints in the Breakpoints window.

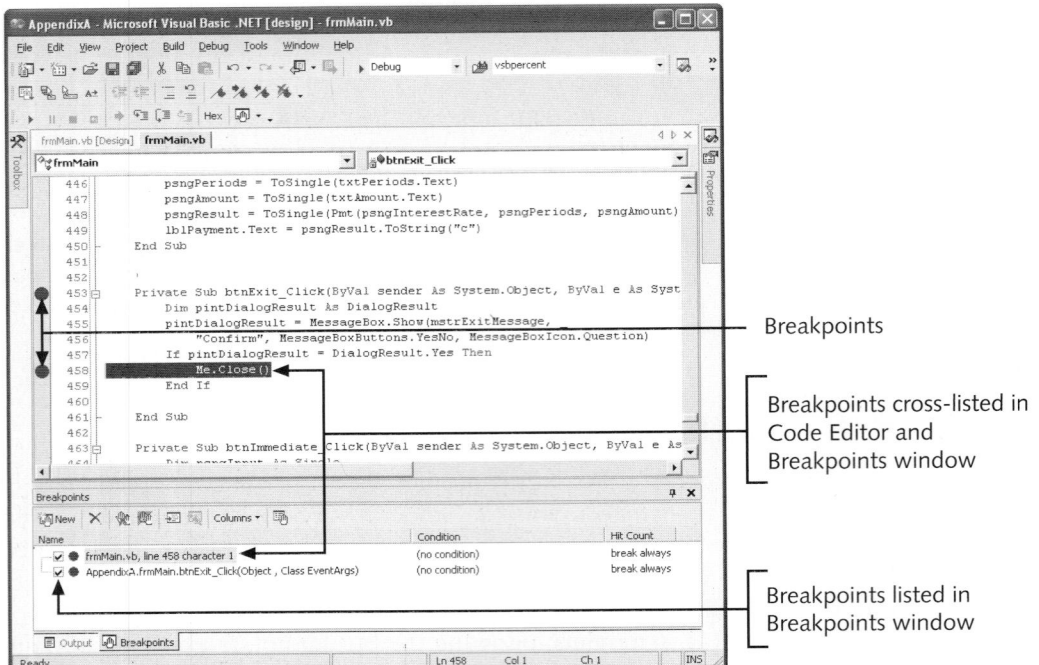

Figure A-3   Code Editor and Breakpoints window

Breakpoints can be enabled or disabled. If a breakpoint is enabled, then Visual Studio .NET will suspend execution just before executing the statement containing the breakpoint. A disabled breakpoint exists but will not suspend execution. A disabled breakpoint appears with an unfilled circle in the left margin of the Code Editor instead of a filled circle. To disable a breakpoint, right-click the line containing the breakpoint in the Code Editor, and select Disable Breakpoint from the context menu.

As you debug an application, you may create any number of breakpoints. Furthermore, you may add and remove breakpoints as you see fit, and enable and disable them. Note that breakpoints are consistent from one invocation of Visual Studio .NET to the next. That is, if breakpoints are set in the current project, and then you exit Visual Studio .NET, the breakpoints will appear the next time that you load the project.

You can set and remove breakpoints in different ways. In the Code Editor, you can set or remove a breakpoint by clicking in the left margin of the Code Editor next to the executable statement or procedure call for which you want to set the breakpoint. Clicking on the filled circle marking the breakpoint will remove that breakpoint. In addition, you can use the Breakpoints window.

A

To set a breakpoint:

1. Make sure that Visual Studio .NET is in design mode. Activate the Code Editor, if necessary. Locate the **Click** event handler for the button named **btnExit**. Set the breakpoint on the following line by clicking in the left margin to the left of the following statement:

```
Me.Close()
```

A filled circle appears in the left margin of the Code Editor. In addition, the statement containing the breakpoint appears highlighted. Note also that you can set a breakpoint by clicking on a statement, and then pressing Ctrl+B.

2. In the same procedure, try to set a breakpoint on the following statement:

```
Dim pintDialogResult As DialogResult
```

A message appears in the status bar indicating that you cannot set a breakpoint on this statement. You cannot set a breakpoint on any declaration statement. Breakpoints can only be set on executable statements and procedure declarations.

3. Activate the Breakpoints window by clicking **Debug**, pointing to **Windows**, and then clicking **Breakpoints**.

The Breakpoints window appears. Typically the Breakpoints window, along with the other debugging windows, appears docked along the bottom of the Visual Studio .NET IDE.

4. In the Breakpoints window, click **New** to activate the New Breakpoint dialog box shown in Figure A-4. Enter the name **btnExit_Click** as shown in Figure A-4.

5. Click **OK** to add the breakpoint. The breakpoint appears in the Breakpoints window, and a filled circle appears to the left of the line containing the breakpoint in the Code Editor.

6. Run the solution. Click the **Exit** button. The procedure name appears highlighted, indicating that the procedure named btnExit_Click is about to execute. Execution is suspended because you set a breakpoint on the procedure call.

7. Press **F5** to continue running the application.

8. A message box appears. In the message box, click **Yes** to try to end the solution and return to design mode. Visual Studio .NET suspends execution and highlights the statement containing the breakpoint, indicating that this is the next statement that will be executed.

Had you clicked No in the message box, no attempt would have been made to execute the statement between the If and the End If statements. Thus, the breakpoint would have never been hit. Again, tracing execution can be helpful to determine which part of a decision-making statement is executing, or how many times the statements in a loop execute.

9. Click the **Step Out** button to continue execution and exit the program.

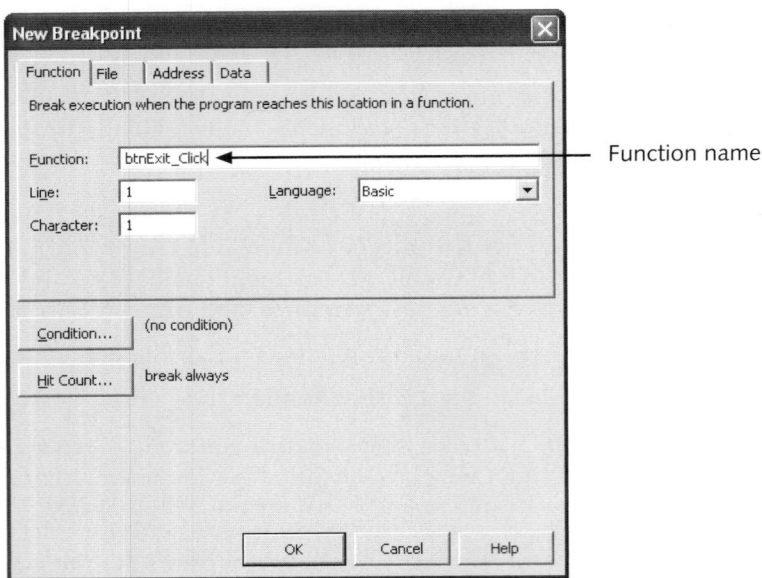

Figure A-4   New Breakpoint window

 When you are finished debugging an application, you can clear all of the breakpoints by clicking Debug, and then clicking Clear All Breakpoints on the Visual Studio .NET menu bar.

In addition to setting a simple breakpoint that suspends execution before a particular statement executes, you can also set hit count breakpoints and conditional breakpoints. A **hit count** breakpoint suspends execution after the breakpoint statement has executed some number of times. A **conditional breakpoint** suspends execution when some condition is met. The condition in a conditional breakpoint looks like the condition in an If statement and must evaluate to a Boolean value.

To set a conditional breakpoint:

1. Clear all of the existing breakpoints by clicking **Debug**, and then clicking **Clear All Breakpoints** .

2. Activate the Code Editor, if necessary, and then locate the **Scroll** event handler for the vertical scroll bar named **vsbPercent**.

3. In the following line of the event hander, click in the left margin to set a breakpoint on the following statement:

```
pintPercent = vsbPercent.Value
```

4. Right-click the line containing the breakpoint, and then click **Breakpoint Properties** from the context menu to activate the Breakpoint Properties dialog

box. Click the **Condition** button to define a condition for the breakpoint. Enter the value **vsbPercent.Value > 100** in the text box, as shown in Figure A-5.

Enter breakpoint condition

Breakpoint will occur when condition is true

Figure A-5   Breakpoint Condition dialog box

Note that the Breakpoint Condition dialog box contains two radio buttons. If the "is true" radio button is selected, the breakpoint will occur when the condition becomes true. If the "has changed" radio button is selected, then the breakpoint will occur whenever the value of the condition changes.

5. Accept the default radio button value of "is true" to suspend execution when the condition becomes true. Click **OK** to close the Breakpoint Condition dialog box, and then click **OK** again to close the Breakpoint Properties dialog box.

6. Run the solution. Click in the scroll region of the scroll bar to change its value by the amount of the LargeChange property. Continue to click the scroll region. As you change the value of the scroll bar, a Label control instance appears below the scroll bar to display the current value. When the value becomes greater than 100, the conditional breakpoint will be activated and Visual Studio .NET will suspend execution, highlighting the line containing the breakpoint.

7. End the solution by clicking the Stop Debugging button, and then clear all breakpoints.

Two points need to be made about the preceding conditional breakpoint. If you used the thumb of the scroll bar to change the value, the breakpoints may have been activated differently. As you drag the scroll bar using the thumb, Windows will likely raise several Scroll events. Thus, the Scroll event handler will fire several times. Each time the Scroll event fires, the value of the scroll bar will be changed.

To illustrate the second point, examine the following assignment statement appearing in the Scroll event handler:

```
pintPercent = vsbPercent.Value
```

Suppose that you had set the following conditional breakpoint on the previous statement:

```
pintPercent > 100
```

While on the surface, the two conditional breakpoints may appear to have the same effect, they do not. When Visual Studio .NET tests the condition for the conditional breakpoint, the assignment statement has not yet executed. PintPercent, a local variable, has a value of 0. The local variable is reinitialized each time the procedure is called, thus the value would always be zero, so the condition would never be met.

 Conditional breakpoints can be very useful in certain situations. For example, when working with arrays, you may receive "subscript out of range" exceptions because of trying to reference an array element outside the bounds of the array. In such a case, set a conditional breakpoint on the variable used as the subscript. Create the condition such that the breakpoint will be hit when the subscript variable is outside of the array bounds.

Hit count breakpoints are useful when debugging loops or working with statements that involve array processing. For example, suppose that you have created a loop that executes its statements thousands of times. You can create a hit count breakpoint to suspend execution periodically through the loop.

To create a hit count breakpoint:

1. Activate the Code Editor, if necessary, and then select the **Click** event hander for the button named **btnWatch**.

2. In the following line of the event handler, click in the left margin to set a breakpoint on the following statement:

```
pintTotal += pintCount
```

3. Right-click on the breakpoint line, and then click **Breakpoint Properties** to activate the Breakpoint Properties dialog box. Click **Hit Count** to activate the Breakpoint Hit Count dialog box.

4. In the list box, select **break when the hit count is a multiple of**. In the text box on the right, enter a value of **100**. Your screen should resemble Figure A-6. These settings will cause Visual Studio .NET to suspend execution when the statements in the loop have executed 100 times.

Figure A-6   Breakpoint Hit Count dialog box

A

5. Click **OK** to close the Breakpoint Hit Count dialog box. Click **OK** to close the Breakpoint Properties dialog box.

6. Test the solution. Click the **Watch** button on the main form. After the loop has executed 100 times, the breakpoint will be activated and displayed in the Code Editor. Point to the variable **pintCount**. The value of the variable appears in a ToolTip. Note that its value is 100. Press **F5** to continue running the solution. After the statements in the loop have executed 100 more times, the breakpoint is hit again.

7. Clear all of the breakpoints, and then end the solution.

Examining the Breakpoint Hit Count dialog box, you can select other hit count options as described in the following list:

- The option **break always** will cause Visual Studio .NET to suspend execution whenever the statement containing the breakpoint is reached.

- The option **break when the hit count is equal to** causes execution to be suspended after the statement has executed some number of times.

- The option **break when the hit count is greater than or equal to** causes execution to be suspended when the hit count is greater than or equal to the hit count value.

USING THE COMMAND WINDOW

The Command window operates in two modes: Command mode and Immediate mode. In Command mode, you send commands to the Visual Studio .NET IDE. These are the same commands as those found on the Visual Studio .NET menu bar. For example, you can use the Command window in Command mode to open or save a solution file. Figure A-7 shows the Command window.

The title bar of the Command window displays the current mode (Command or Immediate). When the Command window is in Command mode, a greater than (>) symbol appears in the first column. When the Command window is in Immediate mode, no character appears in the first column. To toggle the Command window from Command mode to Immediate mode, type "immed" in the Command window, and then press Enter. To toggle the Command window from Immediate mode to Command mode, type ">cmd" in the Command window, and then press Enter.

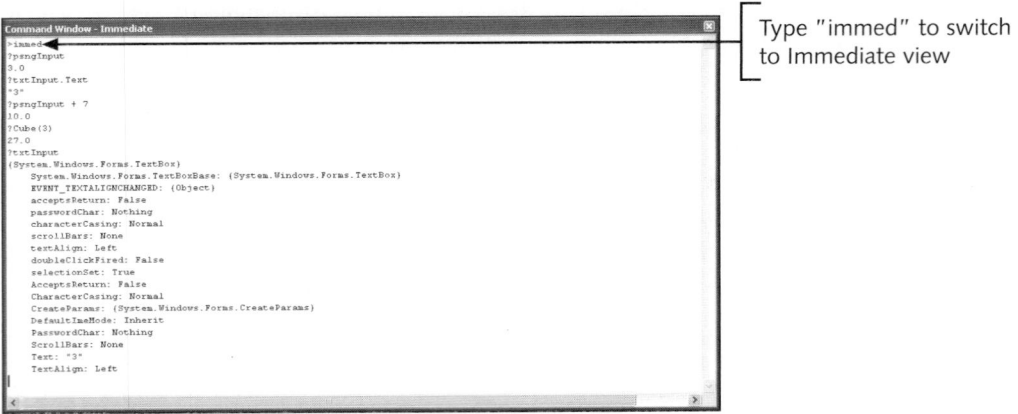

Type "immed" to switch to Immediate view

Figure A-7 Command window

You use the Command window and Immediate mode to examine the values of variables and object properties, and to change those values as follows:

- Typing a question mark (?) followed by an expression, followed by pressing the Enter key, causes Visual Studio .NET to evaluate the expression and display the result of that expression.

- Typing a question mark (?) followed by a procedure name, followed by pressing the Enter key, causes Visual Studio .NET to call the procedure having the corresponding signature.

Typically you use the Command window to examine values of variables or properties as you trace program execution, or after a breakpoint has been hit.

To use the Command window:

1. Activate the Code Editor, if necessary, and then set a breakpoint on the following line in the **Click** event handler for the button named **btnImmediate:**

   ```
   lblSquared.Text = psngSquared.ToString
   ```

2. Run the solution. Enter the number 3 in the text box appearing in the Breakpoints section. Click the **Command Window** button on the form.

3. When the breakpoint fires, activate the Command window, if necessary, by clicking **View**, selecting **Other Windows**, and then clicking **Command Window**.

4. If necessary, change the mode of the Command window to Immediate mode by typing **immed**, and then pressing **Enter**. Note that, by default, the Command window appears docked along the bottom of the Visual Studio .NET IDE.

5. Enter the following expression in the Command window, and then press Enter to evaluate the statement:

`?psngInput`

The statement

`psngInput = ToSingle(txtInput.Text)`

in the event handler has already executed, causing the value 3.0 to be stored in the variable psngInput. Thus, the Command window displays the value of the variable, which is 3.0.

6. In addition to getting the value of a variable, you can examine the properties of objects. Enter the following statement in the Command window to examine the Text property of the TextBox control instance named txtInput:

`?txtInput.Text`

Remember that you entered a value of 3 in the text box. That value is displayed in the Command window.

7. Finally, you can enter expressions containing arithmetic operators. Enter the following statement in the Command window:

`?psngInput + 7`

Visual Studio .NET evaluates the expression and returns the value 10.0. Note that you can evaluate much more complex expressions than the one shown in the preceding statement. Visual Studio .NET can evaluate any expression that can appear on the right side of an assignment statement.

8. Enter the following statement to call a procedure:

`?Cube(3)`

Visual Studio .NET calls the procedure and returns the cube of the number 3, which is 27.0.

If you enter an expression that contains an object, such as a TextBox control instance, Visual Studio .NET will display the properties pertaining to that object.

9. Enter the following expression in the Command window:

`?txtInput`

The Command window displays selected properties of the TextBox control instance.

The Command window is very flexible in the output that it can display. For example, if you enter an expression containing an array, the Command window will display the values for each of the array elements. If you enter an expression that is a structure, then the Command window will display the members of that structure. If you enter an expression that is an object, then the Command window will display the properties of that object.

In addition to examining the values of properties and variables, you can use the Command window in Immediate mode to assign a value to a property or a variable. When you assign values to variables in the Command window, the changes remain in effect only while the solution runs. After the solution ends, the changes are lost. This is logical because all data is initialized when a solution starts running.

To set a property from the Command window:

1. Enter the following statement in the Command window:

   ```
   txtInput.Text = "32"
   ```

2. Press **F5** to continue to run the solution. Note that the value you just entered appears on the main form in the TextBox control instance named txtInput. Note also that you can store a value in a variable using the same syntax.

3. Clear all the breakpoints, and then end the solution by clicking the Stop Debugging button.

 As you debug a program, you may notice that a value is incorrect. Changing the value dynamically allows you to correct it, and then continue debugging, without starting the debugging session over from the beginning. Of course, you will ultimately need to modify the incorrect program statement.

WATCH EXPRESSIONS

Watch expressions provide a useful alternative to entering the same commands repeatedly in the Command window. Each time Visual Studio .NET enters break mode, the values of watch expressions appear in one of four Watch windows. Like breakpoints, watch expressions are persistent from one invocation of Visual Studio .NET to the next.

You can create watch expressions in one of four Watch windows. Each Watch window works exactly the same way. Visual Studio .NET supplies four windows so that you can organize the variables you want to watch into functional or logical groups. The choice of which of the 4 Watch windows you want to use is arbitrary, and is up to you. Figure A-8 shows the first Watch window with four expressions.

As shown in Figure A-8, you can watch a variable or create more complex expressions. Generally speaking, any statement that can appear as the right side of an assignment statement can be used as a watch expression. The Watch window contains three columns. The Name column contains the name of the expression, the Value column displays the current value, and the Type column displays the data type of the watch expression.

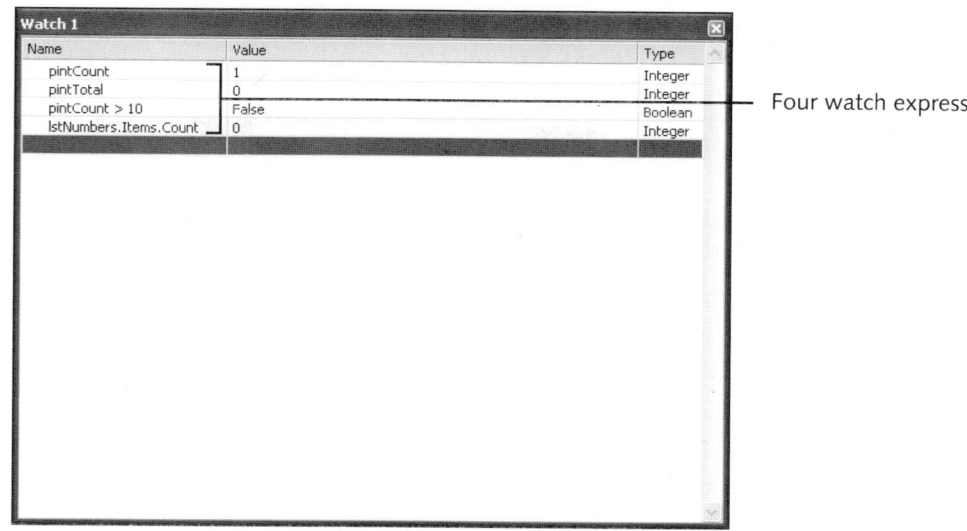

Four watch expressions

Figure A-8 Watch window

To create watch expressions:

1. Activate the Code Editor, if necessary, and then locate the **Click** event handler for the button named **btnWatch**. Set a breakpoint on the following line:

```
lstNumbers.Items.Add(pintCount.ToString)
```

2. Run the solution, and then click the **Watch** button on the form. Visual Studio .NET suspends execution at the breakpoint you just created.

3. Click **Debug**, point to **Windows**, point to **Watch**, and then click **Watch 1**.

4. In the first row of the Name column, enter **pintCount**.

5. In the second row of the Name column, enter **pintTotal**.

6. In the third row of the Name column, enter **pintCount > 10**.

7. Finally, enter **lstNumbers.Items.Count** in the fourth row of the Name column.

8. Press **F11** several times. Each time the value of one of the watched variables changes, the value is updated in the corresponding Watch window.

9. Clear all breakpoints, and then end the solution.

Visual Studio .NET allows you to edit a watch expression while a solution is in break mode. To edit a watch expression, click a watch expression in the desired Watch window, and then click the desired row in the Name column. Finally, change the watch expression, as necessary. You can only delete a watch expression while Visual Studio .NET is in break mode. To delete a watch expression, click the watch expression in the desired Watch window, and then press the Delete key.

THE CALL STACK WINDOW

The Call Stack window allows you to view the procedures called, and the order in which those procedures have been called. Figure A-9 shows the Call Stack window.

Procedure calls appear

Figure A-9 Call Stack window

As shown in Figure A-9, the Call Stack window displays procedures in the order in which they were called—from the most recently called procedure to the least recently called procedure. The lines that appear dimmed contain procedures that Visual Studio .NET executes internally. These internal procedures set up event handlers and allow Visual Studio .NET to call those event handlers along with the procedures you create.

In addition to displaying the procedures that have been called, the Call Stack window can be useful to display events that have fired. In an event-driven language, improper logic can cause events to raise one another indefinitely. This phenomenon is called **cascading events**. Such a problem can arise when a statement fires a TextChanged event for one control instance. That control instance, in turn, fires a TextChanged event in a second control instance, and so on. If a control instance down the line fires a TextChanged event in the first control instance, the execution path becomes circular. That is, the events will continue firing each other indefinitely.

Consider a simple example involving two text boxes. After each text box receives input focus, assume that it sets the focus to the other text box, and the focus shifts back and forth between the two text boxes indefinitely. The solution seems to lock up, and you cannot click any other control instance on the form while the two text boxes continue updating one another.

 When a solution seems to lock due to cascading events, press the Break button on the Debug toolbar, and then examine the Call Stack window to examine the relationship between the event handlers in the solution.

To examine cascading events with the Call Stack window:

1. In the **TextChanged** event handler for the text box named **txtCascade1**, set a breakpoint on the following line:

```
txtCascade2.Text = mintCount1.ToString
```

2. In the **TextChanged** event handler for the text box named **txtCascade2**, set a breakpoint on the following line:

```
txtCascade1.Text = mintCount2.ToString
```

3. Run the solution. In the group box titled Cascading Events, type **5** in the top text box.

4. Press **F11** five times to fire the cascading TextChanged events.

5. On the Visual Studio .NET menu bar, click **Debug**, point to **Windows**, and then click **Call Stack** to view the Call Stack window.

   In the Call Stack window, you will see the event handlers named txtCascade1_ TextChanged and txtCascade2_TextChanged being called several times, indicating cascading event handlers.

6. End the solution. On the menu bar, click **Debug**, and then click **Clear All Breakpoints**.

In addition to locating cascading events, you can use the Call Stack window to examine the order in which Visual Studio .NET has called the procedures you wrote. This capability is useful in situations where you are not sure if a procedure has been called or the order in which several procedures have been called.

1. Set a breakpoint on the following line in the **Click** event handler for the button named **btnCallStack**:

```
Call Print(e)
```

2. Run the solution, and then click the button named **Examine Call Stack**. Visual Studio .NET enters break mode when the statement is reached.

3. Activate the **Call Stack** window.

4. Press **F11** several times to execute the Print, PrintHeadings, and PrintColumn1 procedures. As each procedure is called, Visual Studio .NET updates the Call Stack window. As each procedure completes, it is removed from the Call Stack window.

5. Clear all the breakpoints, and then end the solution.

THE LOCALS WINDOW

The Locals window displays the local variables pertaining to the currently executing event handler or any other executing procedure. As one procedure calls another procedure, Visual Studio .NET updates the Locals window to display the information pertaining to the currently executing procedure. Like the other debugging windows, the Locals window operates only while Visual Studio .NET is in break mode. Figure A-10 shows the Locals window.

Name	Value	Type
⊞ Me	{AppendixA.frmMain}	Appendix
⊞ sender	{System.Windows.Forms.Button}	Object
⊟ e	{System.EventArgs}	System.E
— Object	{System.EventArgs}	Object
⊞ Empty	{System.EventArgs}	System.E
psngAmount	10000.0	Single
psngInterestRate	0.05	Single
psngPeriods	360.0	Single
psngResult	-500.000031	Single

Locals | Watch 1

Figure A-10   Locals window

As shown in Figure A-10, the Me keyword appears. As always, the Me keyword references the current class instance. In this case, the class instance is the form itself. Expanding the Me keyword, you can examine the form's objects and the form level variables. The sender and e variables provide the references to the currently executing event handler's arguments. Finally, the variables psngAmount, psngInterestRate, psngPeriods, and psngResult are the local variables declared in the currently executing event handler.

As shown in Figure A-10, the Locals window has an Explorer-style interface. Clicking the plus sign expands an object, and clicking the minus sign collapses the object. The objects supplied by Me are hierarchical. That is, Me may contain a text box, which will in turn support properties.

To use the Locals window:

1. Set a breakpoint on the following line in the **Click** event handler for the button named **btnTypeMismatch**:

   ```
   lblPayment.Text = psngResult.ToString("c")
   ```

2. Run the solution. In the text boxes inside the Examine Run-Time Errors group box, enter an interest rate of **0.05, 360** for the periods, and **10000** for the amount, and then click the **Type Mismatch** button. Visual Studio .NET will enter break mode when the breakpoint is reached.

3. On the menu bar, click **Debug**, point to **Windows**, and then click **Locals** to view the Locals window. Expand the e argument so you can see the arguments to the event handler.

4. End the solution and clear all of the breakpoints.

THE AUTOS WINDOW

The Autos window is something of a convenience window used to examine the values of objects and variables surrounding the currently executing statement. It contains three columns. The Name column displays the value of objects and variables for the statement surrounding the currently executing statement. The Value column contains the value of the object property or variable. The Type column lists the data type. Figure A-11 shows the Autos window.

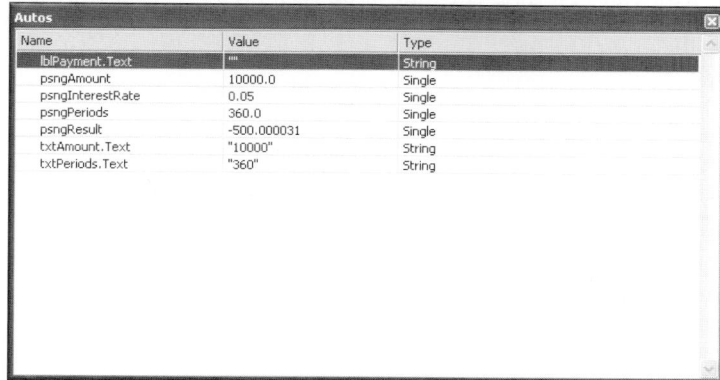

Figure A-11   Autos window

To use the Autos window:

1. Set a breakpoint on the following line in the **Click** event handler for the button named **btnTypeMismatch**:

   ```
   lblPayment.Text = psngResult.ToString("c")
   ```

2. Run the solution. In the text boxes inside the Examine Run–Time Errors group box, enter an interest rate of **0.05**, **360** for the periods, and **10000** for the amount, and then click the **Type Mismatch** button. Visual Studio .NET will enter break mode when the breakpoint is reached.

3. On the menu bar, click **Debug**, point to **Windows**, and then click **Autos** to display the Autos window shown in Figure A-11.

APPENDIX SUMMARY

This appendix presented an overview of the tools you can use to debug solutions. These tools include tracing the execution of a program, setting breakpoints and watch expressions, and using the Command window in Immediate view. You can use these tools as you see fit to locate and fix the programming errors you make.

❑ You can trace the execution of the statements in a program using the Step Into, Step Over, and Step Out buttons.

❑ As you debug a program, you typically set one or more breakpoints. Breakpoints are persistent from one invocation of Visual Studio .NET to the next. To set a simple breakpoint, click in the left margin of the Code Editor to the left of the executable statement for which you want to set a breakpoint. To remove all breakpoints in the program, click Debug, and then click Clear All Breakpoints. Note that you can also set conditional breakpoints.

❑ When Visual Studio .NET temporarily suspends program execution, thereby entering break mode, you can examine the values of variables and object properties using the Command window in Immediate view. To evaluate an expression, type a question mark followed by the expression that you want to evaluate. Visual Studio .NET will display the result of the expression. Call a procedure by entering a question mark followed by the procedure name, followed by any required arguments. Visual Studio .NET will execute the procedure, and then display the result in the Command window. To store a value in a variable or object property, enter the assignment statement but omit the question mark character.

❑ Watch expressions provide an alternative to entering the same expressions again and again in the Command window. Visual Studio .NET supports four Watch windows, which all operate the same way. You use the various windows to organize the variables you want to watch.

❑ The Call Stack window provides the means for you to examine the order in which the procedures in a program have been called.

❑ The Locals and Autos windows allow you to examine the values of local variables and the variables surrounding the currently executing statement, respectively.

Index

Out of Many

COMBINED EDITION

OUT OF MANY

A HISTORY
OF THE
AMERICAN PEOPLE

THIRD EDITION

JOHN MACK FARAGHER
Yale University

MARI JO BUHLE
Brown University

DANIEL CZITROM
Mount Holyoke College

SUSAN H. ARMITAGE
Washington State University

Prentice Hall, Upper Saddle River, New Jersey 07458

Library of Congress Cataloging–in–Publication Data
Out of many: a history of the American people / John Mack Faragher
 . . . [et al.]. — 3rd ed., Combined ed.
  p. cm.
 Includes bibliographical references and index.
 ISBN 0-13-949760-9
 1. United States—History. I. Faragher, John Mack
E178.1.0935 2000   98–34110
973—dc21   CIP

Editorial Director: Charlyce Jones Owen
Executive Editor: Todd R. Armstrong
Development Editor: David Chodoff
Production Editor: Louise Rothman
Creative Director: Leslie Osher
Art Director: Anne Bonanno Nieglos
Editor-in-Chief of Development: Susanna Lesan
Marketing Manager: Sheryl Adams
Interior and Cover Designer: Thomas Nery
Cover Art: William Hahn, *Market Scene, Sansome Street,*
     San Francisco (detail), Crocker Art Museum, Sacramento,
     CA. E.B. Crocker Collection.

AVP, Director of Production and Manufacturing: Barbara Kittle
Manufacturing Manager: Nick Sklitsis
Manufacturing Buyer: Lynn Pearlman
Photo Researcher: Barbara Salz
Photo Editor: Lorinda Morris-Nantz
Copy Editor: Sylvia Moore
Editorial Assistant: Holly Jo Brown
Line Art Coordinator: Guy Ruggiero
Cartographers: Alice and William Thiede/
     CARTO-GRAPHICS
Electronic Page Layout: Scott Garrison and Rosemary Ross

Credits and acknowledgments for materials borrowed from other sources and reproduced,
with permission, in this textbook appear on pages C–1 – C–3.

This book was set in 11/12 Weiss by the HSS in-house formatting
and production services groups and was printed and bound by RR Donnelley & Sons Company.
The cover was printed by Phoenix Color Corp.

Printed in the United States of America
10 9 8 7 6 5 4 3 2 1

ISBN 0-13-949760-9

Prentice-Hall International (UK) Limited, *London*
Prentice-Hall of Australia Pty. Limited, *Sydney*
Prentice-Hall Canada Inc., *Toronto*
Prentice-Hall Hispanoamericana, S.A., *Mexico*
Prentice-Hall of India Private Limited, *New Delhi*
Prentice-Hall of Japan, Inc., *Tokyo*
Pearson Education Asia Pte. Ltd., *Singapore*
Editora Prentice-Hall do Brasil, Ltda., *Rio de Janeiro*

TO OUR STUDENTS,
OUR SISTERS,
AND OUR BROTHERS

BRIEF CONTENTS

CONTENTS

16 The Civil War, 1861–1865 447

MAPS

CHARTS, GRAPHS, AND TABLES

PREFACE

Out of Many, A History of the American People, third edition, offers a distinctive and timely approach to American history, highlighting the experiences of diverse communities of Americans in the unfolding story of our country. These communities offer a way of examining the complex historical forces shaping people's lives at various moments in our past. The debates and conflicts surrounding the most momentous issues in our national life—independence, emerging democracy, slavery, westward settlement, imperial expansion, economic depression, war, technological change—were largely worked out in the context of local communities. Through communities we focus on the persistent tensions between everyday life and those larger decisions and events that continually reshape the circumstances of local life. Each chapter opens with a description of a representative community. Some of these portraits feature American communities struggling with one another: African slaves and English masters on the rice plantations of colonial Georgia, or Tejanos and Americans during the Texas war of independence. Other chapters feature portraits of communities facing social change: the feminists of Seneca Falls, New York, in 1848; the sitdown strikers of Flint, Michigan, in 1934; and the African Americans of Montgomery, Alabama, in 1955. As the story unfolds we find communities growing to include ever larger groups of Americans: The soldiers from every colony who forged the Continental Army into a patriotic national force at Valley Forge during the American Revolution; the movie-goers who dreamed a collective dream of material prosperity and upward mobility during the 1920s; and the Americans linked in ever-growing numbers in the virtual communities of cyberspace as the twenty-first century begins.

Out of Many is also the only American history text with a truly continental perspective. With community vignettes from New England to the South, the Midwest to the far West, we encourage students to appreciate the great expanse of our nation. For example, a vignette of seventeenth-century Santa Fé, New Mexico illustrates the founding of the first European settlements in the New World. We present territorial expansion into the American West from the point of view of the Mandan villagers of the upper Missouri River of North Dakota. We introduce the policies of the Reconstruction era through the experience of African Americans in the Sea Island of South Carolina. This continental perspective drives home to students that American history has never been the preserve of any particular region.

In these ways *Out of Many* breaks new ground, but without compromising its coverage of the traditional turning points that we believe are critically important to an understanding of the American past. Among these watershed events are the Revolution and the struggle over the Constitution, the Civil War and Reconstruction, and the Great Depression and World War II. In *Out of Many*, however, we seek to *integrate* the narrative of national history with the story of the nation's many diverse communities. The Revolutionary and Constitutional period tried the ability of local communities to forge a new unity, and success depended on their ability to build a nation without compromising local identity. The Civil War and Reconstruction formed a second great test of the balance between the national ideas of the revolution and the power of local and sectional communities. The Depression and the New Deal demonstrated the impotence of local communities and the growing power of national institutions during the greatest economic challenge in our history. *Out of Many* also looks back in a new and comprehensive way—from the vantage point of the beginning of a new century and the end of the Cold War—at the salient events of the last fifty years and their impact on American communities. The community focus of *Out of Many* weaves the stories of the people and of the nation into a single compelling narrative.

SPECIAL FEATURES

With each edition of *Out of Many* we have sought to strengthen its unique integration of the best of traditional American history with its innovative community-based focus and strong continental perspective. A wealth of special features and pedagogical aids reinforces our narrative and helps students grasp key issues.

◆ **Community and Diversity.** *Out of Many*, third edition, opens with an introduction, titled "Community and Diversity," that acquaints students with the major themes of the book, providing them with a framework for understanding American history.

◆ **Immigration and Community: The Changing Face of Ethnicity in America.** This feature, new to this edition, highlights the impact of the immigrant experience on the formation of American communities. There are four Immigration and Community features in the book. The first covers the colonial period through 1800, the second covers from 1800 to 1860, the third covers from 1860 to 1930, and the last covers the period since 1930. Each is six pages long and opens with an overview of the character of immigration during the period in question. This overview is followed by a section called "In Their Own Words" that consists of extracts from primary sources written by immigrants themselves and by native-born Americans in response to the new arrivals. Study questions at the end of each Immigration and Community feature ask students to relate issues raised in the overview and documents to broader issues in American history.

◆ **History and the Land.** These features focus on the geographical dimension of historical change to give students an appreciation of the relationship between geography and history. Each elucidates an important historical trend or process with a map and a brief explanatory essay.

◆ **American Communities.** Each chapter opens with an American Communities vignette that relates the experience of a particular community to the broader issues discussed in the chapter.

◆ **Maps.** *Out of Many*, third edition, has more maps than any other American history textbook. Many maps include topographical detail that helps students appreciate the impact of geography on history.

◆ **Overview tables.** Overview tables, also new to this edition, provide students with a summary of complex issues.

◆ **Graphs, charts and tables.** Every chapter includes one or more graphs, charts, or tables that help students understand important events and trends.

◆ **Photos and illustrations.** The abundant illustrations in *Out of Many*, third edition, include many images that have never before been used in an American history text. None of the images is anachronistic—each one dates from the historical period under discussion. Extensive captions treat the

images as visual primary source documents from the American past, describing their source and explaining their significance.

◆ **Chapter-opening outlines and key topics lists.** These pedagogical aids provide students with a succinct preview of the material covered in each chapter.

◆ **Chronologies.** A chronology at the end of each chapter helps students build a framework of key events.

◆ **Review Questions.** Review questions help students review, reinforce, and retain the material in each chapter and encourage them to relate the material to broader issues in American history.

◆ **Recommended Reading and Additional Bibliography.** The works on the short, annotated Recommended Reading list at the end of each chapter have been selected with the interested introductory student in mind. The extensive Additional Bibliography provides a comprehensive overview of current scholarship on the subject of the chapter.

CLASSROOM ASSISTANCE PACKAGE

In classrooms across the country, many instructors encounter students who perceive history as merely a jumble of names, dates, and events. *Out of Many*, third edition, brings our dynamic past alive for these students with a text and accompanying print and multimedia classroom assistance package that combine sound scholarship, engaging narrative, and a rich array of pedagogical tools.

PRINT SUPPLEMENTS

Instructor's Resource Manual

A true time-saver in developing and preparing lecture presentations, the *Instructor's Resource Manual* contains chapter outlines, detailed chapter overviews, lecture topics, discussion questions, readings, and information on audio-visual resources.

Test Item File

Prepared by Gisela Ables, Mike McCormick, and David Aldstadt, Houston Community College

The *Test Item File* offers a menu of more than 1,500 multiple-choice, identification, matching, true-false, and essay test questions and 10–15 questions per chapter on maps found in each chapter. The guide includes a collection of blank maps that can be photo-copied and used for map testing purposes or for other class exercises.

Prentice Hall Custom Test

This commercial-quality computerized test management program, available for Windows, DOS, and Macintosh environments, allows instructors to select items from the Test Item File and design their own exams.

Transparency Pack

Prepared by Robert Tomes, St. John's University

This collection of more than 160 full-color transparency acetates provides instructors with all the maps, charts, and graphs in the text for use in the classroom. Each transparency is accompanied by a page of descriptive material and discussion questions.

Study Guide, Volumes I and II

Prepared by Elizabeth Neumeyer, Kellogg Community College, and S. Ross Doughty, Ursinus College

Each chapter in the *Study Guide* includes a chapter commentary and outline, identification terms, multiple-choice questions, short essay questions, map questions, and questions based on primary source extracts.

Documents Set, Volumes I and II

Prepared by John Mack Faragher, Yale University, and Daniel Czitrom, Mount Holyoke College

The authors have selected and carefully edited more than 300 documents that relate directly to the themes and content of the text and organized them into five general categories: community, social history, government, culture, and politics. Each document is approximately two pages long and includes a brief introduction and study questions intended to encourage students to analyze the document critically and relate it to the content of the text. The Documents Set is available at a substantial discount when packaged with *Out of Many*.

Retrieving the American Past: A Customized U.S. History Reader

Written and developed by leading historians and educators, this reader is an on-demand history database that offers 52 compelling modules on topics in American History, such as: Women on the Frontier, The Salem Witchcraft Scare, The Age of Industrial Violence, and Native American Societies, 1870–1995. Approximately 35 pages in length, each module includes an introduction, several primary documents and secondary sources, follow-up questions, and recommendations for further reading. By deciding which modules to include and the order in which they will appear, instructors can compile the reader they want to use. Instructor-originated material—other readings, exercises—can be included. Contact your local Prentice Hall Representative for more information about this exciting custom publishing option.

Understanding and Answering Essay Questions

Prepared by Mary L. Kelley, San Antonio College

This brief guide suggests helpful study techniques as well as specific analytical tools for understanding different types of essay questions and provides precise guidelines for preparing well-crafted essay answers. The guide is available free to students when packaged with *Out of Many*.

Reading Critically About History

Prepared by Rose Wassman and Lee Rinsky, both of DeAnza College

This brief guide provides students with helpful strategies for reading a history textbook. It is available free when packaged with *Out of Many*.

Themes of the Times

Themes of the Times is a newspaper supplement prepared jointly by Prentice Hall and the premier news publication, *The New York Times*. Issued twice a year, it contains recent articles pertinent to American history. These articles connect the classroom to the world. For information about a reduced-rate subscription to *The New York Times*, call toll-free: (800) 631–1222.

MULTIMEDIA SUPPLEMENTS

History on the Internet

This brief guide introduces students to the origin and innovations behind the Internet and World Wide Web and provides clear strategies for navigating the web to find historical materials. Exercises within and at the end of the chapters allow students to practice searching the wealth of resources available to the student of history. This 48-page supplementary book is free to students when packaged with *Out of Many*.

Out of Many CD-ROM

This innovative electronic supplement takes advantage of the interactive capabilities of multimedia technology to enrich students' understanding of the geographic dimension of history with animated maps, timelines, and related on-screen activities tied to key issues in each chapter of *Out of Many*.

Out of Many Companion Website
Address: http://www.prenhall.com/faragher

With the *Out of Many* Companion Website, students can now take full advantage of the World Wide Web and use it in tandem with the text to enrich their study of American history. The Companion Website ties the text to related material available on the Internet. Its instructional features include chapter objectives, study questions, news updates, and labeling exercises.

The American History CD-ROM
This vast library of more than 2500 images was compiled by Instructional Resources Corporation for instructors for creating slide shows and supplementing lectures. Among its resources are 68 film sequences, 200 works of art, and more than 100 maps. It also includes an overview of historical periods narrated by Charles Kuralt.

ACKNOWLEDGMENTS

In the years it has taken to bring *Out of Many* from idea to reality and to improve it in successive editions, we have often been reminded that although writing history sometimes feels like isolated work, it actually involves a collective effort. We want to thank the dozens of people whose efforts have made the publication of this book possible.

At Prentice Hall, Todd Armstrong, Executive Editor, gave us his full support and oversaw the entire publication process. David Chodoff, Senior Development Editor, greatly helped to strengthen the book's most distinctive features with his careful attention to detail and clarity. Susanna Lesan, now Editor-in-Chief of Development, worked with us on the first edition of the text; without her efforts this book would never have been published. Louise Rothman, Production Editor, oversaw the entire complicated production process in an exemplary fashion. Barbara Salz, our photo researcher, expertly tracked down the many pertinent new images that appear in this edition.

Among our many other friends at Prentice Hall we also want to thank: Phil Miller, President; Charlyce Jones Owen, Editorial Director; Sheryl Adams, Marketing Manager; Leslie Osher, Creative Design Director; Anne Nieglos, Art Director; Patterson Lamb, Copy Editor; and Holly Jo Brown, Editorial Assistant.

Although we share joint responsibility for the entire book, the chapters were individually authored: John Mack Faragher wrote chapters 1–8; Mari Jo Buhle wrote chapters 18–20, 25–26, 29–30; Daniel Czitrom wrote chapters 17, 21–24, 27–28, 31; and Susan Armitage wrote chapters 9–16.

Historians around the country greatly assisted us by reading and commenting on our chapters for this and previous editions. We want to thank each of them for the commitment of their valuable time.

Donald Abbe, Texas Tech University, TX
Richard H. Abbott, Eastern Michigan University, MI
Guy Alchon, University of Delaware, DE
Don Barlow, Prestonsburg Community College, KY
William Barney, University of North Carolina, NC
Alwyn Barr, Texas Tech University, TX
Debra Barth, San Jose City College, CA
Peter V. Bergstrom, Illinois State University, IL
William C. Billingsley, South Plains College, TX
Peter H. Buckingham, Linfield College, OR
Bill Cecil-Fronsman, Washburn University of Topeka, KS
Victor W. Chen, Chabot College, CA
Jonathan M. Chu, University of Massachusetts, MA
P. Scott Corbett, Oxnard College, CA
Matther Coulter, Collin Country Community College, TX
Virginia Crane, University of Wisconsin, Oshkosh, WI
Jim Cullen, Harvard University, MA
Thomas J. Curran, St. John's University, NY
Richard V. Damms, Ohio State University, OH
Elizabeth Dunn, Baylor University, TX
Emmett G. Essin, Eastern Tennessee State Unversity, TN
Mark F. Fernandez, Loyola University, IL
Leon Fink, University of North Carolina, Chapel Hill, NC
Michael James Foret, University of Wisconsin, Stevens Point, WI
Joshua B. Freeman, Columbia University, NY
Glenda E. Gilmore, Yale University, CT
Don C. Glenn, Diablo Valley College, CA
Lawrence Glickman, University of South Carolina, SC
Kenneth Goings, Florida Atlantic University, FL
Mark Goldman, Tallahassee Community College, FL
Gregory L. Goodwin, Bakersfield College, CA
Gretchen Green, University of Missouri, Kansas City, MO
Emily Greenwald, University of Nebraska at Lincoln, NE
Mark W. T. Harvey, North Dakota State University, ND
James A. Hijiya, University of Massachusetts at Dartmouth, MA
Raymond M. Hyser, James Madison University, VA
John Inscoe, University of Georgia, GA

John C. Kesler, Lakeland Community College, OH
Peter N. Kirstein, Saint Xavier University, IL
Frank Lambert, Purdue University, IN
Susan Rimby Leighow, Millersville University, PA
Janice M. Leone, Middle Tennessee University, TN
Glenn Linden, Southern Methodist University, Dallas, TX
George Lipsitz, University of California, San Diego, CA
Judy Barrett Litoff, Bryant College, RI
Jesus Luna, California State University, CA
Larry Madaras, Howard Community College, MD
Lynn Mapes, Grand Valley State University, MI
John F. Marszalek, Mississippi State University, MS
Scott C. Martin, Bowling Green State University, OH
Robert L. Matheny, Eastern New Mexico University, NM
Thomas Matijasic, Prestonsburg Community College, KY
M. Delores McBroome, Humboldt State University, CA
Gerald McFarland, University of Massachusetts, Amherst, MA
Sam McSeveney, Vanderbilt University, TN
Warren Metcalf, Arizona State University, AZ
M. Catherine Miller, Texas State University, TX
Norman H. Murdoch, University of Cincinnati, OH
Gregory H. Nobles, Georgia Institute of Technology, GA
Dale Odom, University of Texas at Denton, TX
Sean O'Neill, Grand Valley State University, MI
Edward Opper, Greenville Technical College, Greenville, SC
Charles K. Piehl, Mankato State University, MN
Carolyn Garrett Pool, University of Central Oklahoma, OK
Christie Farnham Pope, Iowa State University, IA
Susan Porter-Benson, University of Missouri, MO
Russell Posner, City College of San Francisco, CA
John Powell, Penn State University, Erie, PA
Sarah Purcell, Central Michigan University, MI
Joseph P. Reidy, Howard University, DC
Marilyn D. Rhinehart, North Harris College, TX

Leo P. Ribuffo, George Washington University, DC
Judy Ridner, California State University at Northridge, CA
Neal Salisbury, Smith College, MA
Roberto Salmon, University of Texas-Pan American, TX
Steven Schuster, Brookhaven Community College, TX
Megan Seaholm, University of Texas, Austin, TX
Nigel Sellars, University of Oklahoma, Norman, OK
John David Smith, North Carolina State University, NC
Patrick Smith, Broward Community College, FL
Mark W. Summers, University of Kentucky, KY
John D. Tanner, Jr., Palomar College, CA
Robert R. Tomes, St. John's University, NY
Michael Miller Topp, University of Texas at El Paso, TX
John Trickel, Richland Community College, IL
Steve Tripp, Grand Valley State University, MI
Fred R. Van Hartesveldt, Fort Valley State University, GA
Philip H. Vaughan, Rose State College, OK
Robert C. Vitz, Northern Kentucky University, KY
F. Michael Williams, Brevard Community College, FL
Charles Regan Wilson, University of Mississippi, MS
Harold Wilson, Old Dominion University, VA
William Woodward, Seattle Pacific University, WA
Loretta E. Zimmerman, University of Florida, FL

Each of us depended on a great deal of support and assistance with the research and writing that went into this book. We want to thank: Kathryn Abbott, Nan Boyd, Krista Comer, Crista DeLuzio, Keith Edgerton, Carol Frost, Jesse Hoffnung Garskof, Jane Gerhard, Todd Gernes, Melani McAlister, Cristiane Mitchell, J. C. Mutchler, Tricia Rose, Gina Rourke, and Jessica Shubow.

Our families and close friends have been supportive and ever so patient over the many years we have devoted to this project. But we want especially to thank Paul Buhle, Meryl Fingrutd, Bob Greene, and Michele Hoffnung.

ABOUT THE AUTHORS

Chris Freitag

JOHN MACK FARAGHER

John Mack Faragher is Arthur Unobskey Professor of American History at Yale University. Born in Arizona and raised in southern California, he received his B.A. at the University of California, Riverside, and his Ph.D. at Yale University. He is the author of *Women and Men on the Overland Trail* (1979), which won the Frederick Jackson Turner Award of the Organization of American Historians, *Sugar Creek: Life on the Illinois Prairie* (1986), and *Daniel Boone: The Life and Legend of an American Pioneer* (1992). He is also the editor of *The American Heritage Encyclopedia* (1988).

DANIEL CZITROM

Daniel Czitrom is Professor and Chair of History at Mount Holyoke College. He received his B.A. from the State University of New York at Binghamton and his M.A. and Ph.D. from the University of Wisconsin, Madison. He is the author of *Media and the American Mind: From Morse to McLuhan* (1982), which won the First Books Award of the American Historical Association. His scholarly articles and essays have appeared in the *Journal of American History, American Quarterly, The Massachusetts Review,* and *The Atlantic*. He is currently completing *Mysteries of the City: Culture, Politics, and the Underworld in New York, 1870–1920.*

MARI JO BUHLE

Mari Jo Buhle is Professor of American Civilization and History at Brown University, specializing in American women's history. She is the author of *Women and American Socialism, 1870–1920* (1981) and *Feminism and its Discontents: A Century of Struggle with Psychoanalysis* (1998). She is also coeditor of *Encyclopedia of the American Left,* second edition (1998). She currently serves as an editor of a series of books on women and American history for the University of Illinois Press. Professor Buhle held a fellowship (1991–1996) from the John D. and Catherine T. MacArthur Foundation.

SUSAN H. ARMITAGE

Susan H. Armitage is Professor of History at Washington State University. She earned her Ph.D. from the London School of Economics and Political Science. Among her many publications on western women's history are three coedited books, *The Women's West* (1987), *So Much To Be Done: Women on the Mining and Ranching Frontier* (1991), and *Writing the Range: Race, Class, and Culture in the Women's West* (1997). She is the editor of *Frontiers: A Journal of Women's Studies.*

COMMUNITY & DIVERSITY

One of the most characteristic features of our country has always been its astounding variety. The American people include the descendants of native Indians, colonial Europeans, Africans, and migrants from virtually every country and continent. Indeed, as we enter the new century the nation is absorbing a tide of immigrants from Latin America and Asia that rivals the great tide of immigrants from eastern and southern Europe that arrived at the beginning of the twentieth century. Moreover, the United States is one of the world's largest nations, incorporating more than 3.6 million square miles of territory. The struggle to make a nation out of our many communities is what much of American history is all about. That is the story told in this book.

Every human society is made up of communities. A community is a set of relationships that link men, women, and their families into a coherent social whole, more than the sum of its parts. In a community people develop the capacity for unified action. In a community people learn, often through trial and error, how to transform and adapt to their environment. The sentiment that binds the members of a community together is the origin of group identity and ethnic pride. In the making of history, communities are far more important than even the greatest of leaders, for the community is the institution most capable of passing a distinctive historical tradition to future generations.

Communities bind people together in multiple ways. They can be as small as the local neighborhood, in which people maintain face-to-face relations, or as large as the imagined entity of the nation. This book examines American history from the perspective of community life—an ever widening frame that has included larger and larger groups of Americans.

Networks of kinship and friendship, and connections across generations and among families, establish the bonds essential to community life. Shared feelings about values and history establish the basis for common identity. In communities, people find the power to act collectively in their own interest. But American communities frequently took shape as a result of serious conflicts among groups, and within communities there often has been significant fighting among competing groups or classes. Thus the term community,

John L. Krimmel, Election Day in Philadelphia (1815).

John L. Krimmel, Painting, (1786–1821), oil on canvas, H. 16⅞" x W. 25⅝". (AN.59.131) Courtesy, Winterthur Museum, Election Day in Philadelphia (1815).

as we employ it here, includes tension and discord as well as harmony and agreement.

For years there have been persistent laments about the "loss of community" in modern America. But community has not disappeared—it is continually being reinvented. Until the late eighteenth century, community was defined primarily by space and local geography. The closer one gets to the present, the more community is reshaped by new and powerful historical forces such as the nation state, the marketplace, industrialization, the corporation, mass immigration, and electronic media.

The American Communities vignettes that open each chapter of *Out of Many* reflect this shift. Most of the vignettes in the pre–Civil War chapters focus on geographically-defined communities, such as the ancient Indian city at Cahokia, or the experiment in industrial urban planning in early nineteenth-century Lowell, Massachusetts. In the post–Civil War chapters different and more modern kinds of communities make their appearance—the community of Hollywood movie audiences in the 1920s, or the "virtual communities" made possible by new computer technologies. Also, the nearer we get to the present, the more we find Americans struggling to balance their membership in several communities simultaneously. These are defined not simply by local spatial arrangements, but by categories as varied as racial and ethnic groups, occupations, political affiliations, and consumer preferences.

The title for our book was suggested by the Latin phrase selected by John Adams, Benjamin Franklin, and Thomas Jefferson for the Great Seal of the United States: *E Pluribus Unum*—"Out of Many Comes Unity." These men understood that unity could not be imposed by a powerful central authority but had

Ralph Fasanella, Sunday Afternoon—Stickball Game, 1953

to develop out of mutual respect among Americans of different backgrounds. The revolutionary leadership expressed the hope that such respect could grow on the basis of a remarkable proposition: "We hold these truths to be self-evident, that all men are created equal; that they are endowed by their Creator with certain unalienable rights; that among these are life, liberty, and the pursuit of happiness." The national government of the United States would preserve local and state authority but would guarantee individual rights. The nation would be strengthened by guarantees of difference.

Out of Many—that is the promise of America, and the premise of this book. The underlying dialectic of American history, we believe, is that as a people

William Hahn, Market Scene, Sansome Street, San Francisco.

we need to locate our national *unity* in the celebration of the *differences* that exist among us; these differences can be our strength, as long as we affirm the promise of the Declaration. Protecting the "right to be different," in other words, is absolutely fundamental to the continued existence of democracy, and that right is best protected by the existence of strong and vital communities. We are bound together as a nation by the ideal of local and cultural differences protected by our common commitment to the values of our revolution.

Today—with the many social and cultural conflicts that abound in the United States—some Americans have lost faith in that vision. But our history shows that the promise of American unity has always been problematic. Centrifugal forces have been powerful in the American past, and at times the country has seemed about to fracture into its component parts. Our transformation from a collection of groups and regions into a nation has been marked by painful and often violent struggles. Our past is filled with conflicts between Indians and colonists, masters and slaves, Patriots and Loyalists, Northerners and Southerners, Easterners and Westerners, capitalists and workers, and sometimes the government and the people. Americans often appear to be little more than a contentious collection of peoples with conflicting interests, divided by region and background, race and class.

Our most influential leaders also sometimes suffered a crisis of faith in the American project of "liberty and justice for all." Thomas Jefferson not only believed in the inferiority of African Americans, but he feared that immigrants from outside the Anglo-American tradition might "warp and bias" the development of the nation "and render it a heterogeneous, incoherent, distracted mass." We have not always lived up to the American promise, and there is a dark side to our history. It took the bloodiest war in American history to secure the human rights of African Americans, and the struggle for full equality continues nearly a century and a half later. During the great influx of immigrants in the early twentieth century, fears much like Jefferson's led to movements to *Americanize* the foreign born by forcing them, in the words of one leader, "to give up the languages, customs, and methods of life which they have brought with them across the ocean, and adopt instead the language, habits, and customs of this country, and the general standards and ways of American living." Similar thinking motivated Congress at various times to bar the immigration of Asians and other ethnic groups into the country, and to force assimilation on American Indians by denying them the freedom to practice their religion or even to speak their own language. Such calls for restrictive unity resound in our own day.

But other Americans have argued for a more idealistic version of *Americanization*. "What is the American, this new man?" asked the French immigrant Michel Crévecoeur in 1782. "A strange mixture of blood which you will find in no other country," he answered; in America, "individuals of all nations are melted into a new race of men." A century later Crévecoeur was echoed by historian Frederick Jackson Turner, who believed that "in the crucible of the frontier, the immigrants were Americanized, liberated, and fused into a mixed race, English in neither nationality nor characteristics. The process has gone on from the early days to our own."

The process by which diverse communities have come to share a set of common American values is one of the most fundamental aspects of our history. It did not occur, however, because of compulsory *Americanization* programs, but because of free public education, popular participation in democratic politics, and the impact of popular culture. Contemporary America does have a common culture: we laugh at the same television sitcoms and share the same aspirations to own a home and send our children to college—all unique American traits.

To a degree that too few Americans appreciate, this common culture resulted from a complicated process of mutual discovery that took place when different ethnic and regional groups encountered one another. Consider just one small and unique aspect of our culture, the barbecue. Americans have been barbecuing since before the beginning of written history. Early settlers adopted this technique of cooking from the Indians—the word itself comes from a native term for a framework of sticks over a fire on which meat was slowly cooked. Colonists typically barbecued pork, fed on Indian corn. African slaves lent their own touch by introducing the use of hot sauces. Thus the ritual that is a part of nearly every American family's Fourth of July silently celebrates the heritage of diversity that went into making our common culture.

The American educator John Dewey recognized this diversity early in this century. "The genuine American, the typical American is himself a hyphenated character," he declared, "international and interracial in his make-up." The point about our "hyphenated character," Dewey believed, "is to see to it that the hyphen connects instead of separates." We, the authors of *Out of Many*, share Dewey's perspective on American history. "Creation comes from the impact of diversity," wrote the American philosopher Horace Kallen. We also endorse Kallen's vision of the American promise: "A democracy of nationalities, cooperating voluntarily and autonomously through common institutions, . . . a multiplicity in a unity, an orchestration of mankind." And now, let the music begin.

CHAPTER ONE

A CONTINENT OF VILLAGES

TO 1500

AMERICAN COMMUNITIES
Cahokia: Thirteenth-Century Life on the Mississippi

As the sun rose over the rich floodplain, the people of the riverbank city set about their daily tasks. Some went to shops where they manufactured tools, crafted pottery, worked metal, or fashioned ornamental jewelry—goods destined to be exchanged in the far corners of the continent. Others left their densely populated neighborhoods for the outlying countryside, where in the summer heat they worked the seemingly endless fields that fed the city. From almost any point people could see the great temple that rose from the center of their city—the temple where priests in splendid costumes acted out public rituals of death and renewal.

This thirteenth-century city was not in preindustrial Europe but in North America. It flourished long before the first European explorer arrived. Its residents lived and worked on the alluvial soil of the Mississippi River, across from present-day St. Louis, at a place archaeologists have named Cahokia. In its heyday, in the mid-1200s, Cahokia was an urban cluster of perhaps 30,000 people. Its farm fields were abundant with corn, beans, and pumpkins, crops no European had ever seen. The temple, a huge earthwork pyramid, covered fifteen acres at its base and rose as high as a ten-story building. On top were the sacred residences of chiefs and priests, who dressed in elaborate headdresses made from the plumage of American birds.

By the fourteenth century, Cahokia had been abandoned, but its great central temple mound and dozens of smaller ones in the surrounding area, as well as hundreds more throughout the Mississippi Valley, remained to puzzle the European immigrants who resettled the valley in the eighteenth and nineteenth centuries. Treasure seekers plundered the mounds, and most were eventually dynamited and plowed under for farmland. Only a few were saved, inside parks or estates. Cahokia's central mound survived because in the nineteenth century its summit became the site of a monastery, now long gone.

The Europeans who first explored and excavated these mounds were convinced they were the ruins of a vanished civilization, but could not believe they were the work of Native Americans. The first comprehensive study of Cahokia, published in 1848 under the sponsorship of the Smithsonian Institution, noted that "the mound-builders were an agricultural people, considerably advanced in arts, manners, habits, and religion." But because "Indians were hunters averse to labor, and not known to have constructed any works approaching [the] skillfulness of design or [the] magnitude" of Cahokia, surely these wonders must have been constructed by a "lost race."

The Smithsonian scientists were wrong. Thanks to modern archaeology and anthropology we now know that it was the ancestors of contemporary Native Americans who began to construct massive earthworks in the Mississippi Valley as early as 1300 B.C.E. (Before the Common Era) at a place called Poverty Point in Louisiana. The vast urban complex of Cahokia flourished from the tenth to the fourteenth century and at its height stretched six miles along the Mississippi. Its residents were not nomadic hunters but farmers, members of an agricultural society—which archaeologists call the Mississippian—that had developed highly productive techniques of cultivation. Hundreds of acres of crops fed the people of Cahokia, which was the most populated urban community north of the Valley of Mexico. Mississippian farmers constructed ingenious raised plots of land on which they heaped compost in wide ridges for improved drainage and protection from unseasonable frosts. To their square houses of wood and mud they attached pens in which they kept flocks of domesticated turkeys and, perhaps, small herds of young deer that they slaughtered for meat and hides. Cahokia was at the center of a long-distance trading system that linked it to Indian towns over a vast area. Cahokia's specialized artisans were renowned for the manufacture of high-quality flint hoes, exported throughout the Mississippi Valley. Copper came to the city from Lake Superior, mica from the southern Appalachians, conch shells from the Atlantic coast.

The archaeological evidence suggests that Cahokia was emerging as a state supported by tribute and taxation. Like the awe-inspiring public works of early urban societies in other parts of the world—the pyramids of ancient Egypt, the acropolis of Athens—the great temple mound of Cahokia reflected the city's wealth and power. The great mound and other colossal public works at Cahokia were monuments of a society dominated by an elite class of priests and rulers. From their residences and temples atop the mound the city's elite could look down on their awe-struck subjects. There is no indication, however, that the Mississippian peoples had developed a system of writing that would permit us to glimpse their own version of their history.

As the words of the 1848 Smithsonian report on Cahokia make clear, the stereotypical view of Indians that emerged in the nineteenth and twentieth centuries was that they all lived in isolated hunting bands. But the great variety of lifeways Indian peoples developed in their long occupation of North America belies this stereotype. All Native Americans lived in strong vibrant communities that ranged from small hunting bands to large agricultural cities like Cahokia and splendid imperial capitals like that of the Aztecs of Mexico. Before the coming of the Europeans, North America was, as one historian phrases it, "a continent of villages," a land with thousands of local communities. Over many centuries the Indian peoples of North America developed a variety of community types, each with its own system of family and social organization, each integrated with its natural surroundings. The wonders of Cahokia are but one aspect of the little-understood history of the Indians of the Americas.

Cahokia

KEY TOPICS

- The peopling of the Americas by migrants from Asia
- The adaptation of native cultures to the distinctive regions of North America

- The increase in complexity of many native societies following the development of farming
- The nature of Indian cultures in the three major regions of European invasion and settlement

SETTLING THE CONTINENT

"Why do you call us Indians?" a Massachusetts native complained to Puritan missionary John Eliot in 1646. More than a hundred years earlier, Christopher Columbus had mistaken the Arawaks of the Caribbean for the people of the East Indies and called them *Indios*. By the middle of the sixteenth century this Spanish word had passed into English as "Indians" and was widely used to refer to all the native peoples of the Americas. Today anthropologists often use the term "Amerindians," and many people prefer "Native Americans." But most indigenous Americans refer to themselves as "Indian people."

Who Are the Indian People?

At the time of their first contacts with Europeans, near the close of the fifteenth century, the native inhabitants of the Western Hemisphere represented more than 2,000 distinct cultures, spoke hundreds of different languages, and lived and worked in scores of different environments. Just as the term "European" includes such different peoples as the English, French, and Spanish, so "Indian" covers an enormous diversity of peoples. For example, the people of the mid-Atlantic coast called themselves *Lenni Lenape*, meaning "true men"; those of the northern Great Plains were *Lakota*, or "the allies"; and the hunters of the Southwest used the name *Dine* (pronounced "dee-nay"), meaning simply "the people." Interestingly, Europeans came to know these three groups by rather different names: the *Delawares* (from the principal river of the mid-Atlantic region), the *Sioux*, and the *Apaches* (both of which meant "enemy" in the language of a neighboring tribe).

Once Europeans realized that the Americas were in fact a "New World" rather than part of the Asian continent, they began debating how people might have moved there from Europe and Asia, where the Judeo-Christian Bible indicated human life had begun. Over the succeeding centuries writers proposed elaborate theories of transoceanic migrations that linked native Americans variously to ancient Greeks, Carthaginians, Tartars, Chinese, and Welsh; one theory even held they were the survivors of the mythical Atlantis. Common to all these theories was a belief that the Americas had been populated for a few thousand years at most and that native American societies were the degenerate offspring of a far superior Old World culture.

A number of Spanish observers thought more deeply about the question of Indian origins. In 1590 Joseph de Acosta reasoned that because Old World animals were present in the Americas, they must have crossed by a land bridge that could have been used by humans as well. A few years later, Enrico Martín speculated that since no such land passage had been found between the Americas and Europe, it must exist in the unexplored far northwest of the continent, and thus the people using it must have been Asian. In the 1650s Bernabé Cobo, who had lived most of his life in the Caribbean, argued that the great variety of native American languages showed that Indian peoples must have lived on the continent for centuries. But, he continued, their physical similarities suggested that "it was doubtless one nation or family of men which passed to people this land." Here were the principal elements of the migration hypothesis: Indian peoples were descended from a common stock of Asian migrants, they arrived by way of a northwestern land passage, and they had experienced a long and independent history in the Americas.

Certainly no single physical type characterized all the native peoples of the Americas. Although most had straight, black hair and dark, almond-shaped eyes, their skin ranged in color from mahogany to light brown and few fit the "yellow men" or "redskin" descriptions given them by colonists and settlers of the eighteenth and nineteenth centuries. Indeed, it was only when Europeans compared Indian peoples with natives of other continents, such as Africans, that they seemed similar enough to be classified as a group.

Migration from Asia

The theory most widely held today is that the native American peoples moved to this hemisphere from Asia some 25,000 to 30,000 years ago—about the

OVERVIEW

ORIGINS OF SOME INDIAN TRIBAL NAMES	
Cherokee	A corruption of the Choctaw *chiluk-ki,* meaning "cave people," an allusion to the many caves in the Cherokee homeland. The Cherokees called themselves *Ani-Yun-Wiya,* or "real people."
Cheyenne	From the Sioux *Sha-hiyena,* "people of strange speech." The Cheyennes called themselves *Dzi-tsistas,* meaning "our people."
Hopi	A shortening of the Hopis' own name for themselves, *Hópitu,* which means "peaceful ones."
Mohawk	From the Algonquian *Mohawaúuck,* meaning "man-eaters." The Mohawks called themselves *Kaniengehaga,* "people of the place of the flint."
Pawnee	From the Pawnee term *paríki,* which describes a distinctive style of dressing the hair with paint and fat to make it stand erect like a horn. The Pawnees called themselves *Chahik-sichahiks,* "men of men."

time that Japan and the countries of Scandinavia were being settled. Evidence supporting this view includes a common dental pattern found among the most ancient human fossils in the Americas and those in northeastern Asia. The most distinctive marker of modern native American peoples is blood type, for although the vast majority have type O blood and a few have type A, almost none have type B. Because modern Asian populations exhibit all three blood types, scientists have postulated that migrations to the New World took place before the evolution of type B, which they believe occurred about 30,000 years ago. Studies of genetic evolution suggest that it took at least 20,000 years to evolve the variety of physical traits found among native American populations today. And modern linguists, agreeing essentially with Cobo's observation, cited earlier, estimate that it would require about 25,000 years to develop, from a common base, the nearly 500 distinct languages of the Americas.

At the time of the proposed migration from Asia to the Americas, the Northern Hemisphere was experiencing the Ice Age that characterized the geological epoch known as the Pleistocene. Huge glaciers locked up massive volumes of water, and sea levels were as much as 300 feet lower than they are today. Asia and North America were joined by a huge subcontinent of ice-free, treeless grassland, 750 miles wide from north to south. Geologists have named this area Beringia, from the Bering Straits. Summers there were warm, winters were cold, dry, and almost snowfree. This was a perfect environment for large mammals— mammoth and mastodon, bison, horse, reindeer, camel, and saiga (a goatlike antelope).

Beringia also attracted Stone Age hunter-gatherers who lived in small, nomadic bands and subsisted almost entirely on these animals. The animals provided them not only with food but with hides for clothing and shelter, dung for fuel, and bones for tools and weapons. Hunting bands were driven to expand their territories by the powerful force of their own population growth and the pressure it placed on local resources. Today's few remaining hunting-and-gathering peoples have an annual population growth rate of 0.5 percent, which would double their populations only every 140 years. Ancient Asian hunters, with seemingly limitless open country into which they could move, likely had growth rates that were much higher, and their expansion into new territory was correspondingly rapid. Following the big game, and accompanied by a husky-like species of dog, hunting bands gradually penetrated Beringia, moving as far east as the Yukon River basin of northern Canada.

Until recently most scientists dated the first migrations at about 15,000 years ago, but there is growing evidence that people were moving from Asia considerably earlier. Because much of Beringia was later submerged beneath rising seas, definitive archaeological evidence of migration from Asia is difficult to find. No fossil human bones have yet been uncovered there. But in 1966, field excavations in the Yukon basin uncovered what appeared to be fossilized bone tools estimated to be 27,000 years old. Fieldworkers found that these tools fit perfectly into their hands and had worn edges exactly where one would expect them to be. Later digs in the area produced the jawbones of several dogs estimated to be at least 30,000 years old. The most persuasive evidence for an earlier migration,

Migration Routes from Asia to America   *During the Ice Age, Asia and North America were joined where the Bering Straits are today, forming a migration route for hunting peoples. Either by boat along the coast, or through a narrow corridor between the huge northern glaciers, these migrants began making their way to the heartland of the continent as much as 30,000 years ago.*

however, comes from the other end of the hemisphere, in South America. Archaeologists working at separate sites in the Amazon basin and in southern Chile in the early 1990s found striking evidence of human tool-making, house-building, and rock painting that date from at least 12,000 years ago. The ancestors of those peoples must have crossed Beringia many thousands of years before. The consensus today is that the migration from Asia probably began about 30,000 years ago.

Huge glaciers to the south of Beringia blocked passage during most of the last Ice Age, but occasionally a narrow land corridor opened up along the eastern base of the Rocky Mountains. As early as 25,000 years ago, hunting bands following this corridor south could have emerged onto the northern Great Plains—a hunter's paradise teeming with animals of great variety. Migrants probably also moved south in boats, following the Pacific coastline. Rapid population growth would have permitted these groups to populate the entire Western Hemisphere in a few thousand years. Remarkably, the oral traditions of many Indian peoples depict a long journey from a distant place of

origin to a new homeland. Europeans have recorded the Pima people of the Southwest singing this "Emergence Song":

> *This is the White Land; we arrive singing,*
> *Headdresses waving in the breeze.*
> *We have come! We have come!*
> *The land trembles with our dancing and singing.*

Clovis: The First American Technology

The earliest tools found at North American archaeological sites, crude choppers and scrapers made of stone or bone, are similar to artifacts from the same period found in Europe or Asia. About 12,000 years ago, however, a much more sophisticated style of tool-making seems to have developed. Named after the site of its discovery in 1932, near Clovis, New Mexico, the Clovis tradition was a powerful new and more sophisticated technology, unlike anything found in the archaeology of the Old World. In the years since the initial discovery, archaeologists have unearthed Clovis artifacts at sites ranging from Montana to Mexico,

Nova Scotia to Arizona. All these finds date back to within one or two thousand years of one another, suggesting that Clovis spread quickly throughout the continent. This discovery has led, in turn, to speculation that the settlement of North America might then have been entering its final phase, as the continent filled with people. Scientists theorize that it was to feed their expanding populations that communities were driven to find a more efficient way to hunt and developed this greatly improved technology.

The evidence suggests that Clovis users were mobile peoples who traveled in communities numbering perhaps thirty to fifty individuals from several interrelated families. They returned to the same hunting camps year after year, migrating seasonally within territories of several hundred square miles. Near Delbert, Nova Scotia, archaeologists discovered the floors of ten tents arranged in a semicircle, their doors opening south to avoid the prevailing northerly winds. Both this camp and others found throughout the continent were placed so that they overlooked watering places that would attract game. Clovis blades have been excavated amid the remains of mammoth, camel, horse, giant armadillo, and sloth. Hunters apparently drove these animals into shallow bogs, killed them with spears, and butchered them on the spot.

These Clovis points are typical of thousands that archaeologists have found at sites all over the continent, dating from a period about 12,000 years ago. When inserted in a spear shaft, these three- to six-inch fluted points made effective weapons for hunting mammoth and other big game.

THE BEGINNING OF REGIONAL CULTURES

About 15,000 years ago a global warming trend began to alter the North American climate. The giant continental glaciers began to melt, a shift so pronounced by 8000 B.C.E. that it is used to mark the passing of the Pleistocene epoch. As the glaciers retreated, the northern latitudes were colonized by plants, animals, and humans. Meltwater created the lake and river systems of today and raised the level of the surrounding seas, flooding Beringia as well as vast stretches of the Atlantic and Gulf coasts and creating fertile tidal pools and offshore fishing banks. These monumental transformations produced new patterns of wind, rainfall, and temperature, reshaping the ecology of the entire continent and producing the distinct North American regions of today. The great integrating force of a single continental climate faded, and, with its passing, the continental Clovis culture fragmented into many different regional patterns.

Regions have ever since played an important role in American history. Variations in climate and geography combine to form the distinct regions of North America: the Arctic and Subarctic, the Northwest, the Great Plains, the Northeast, California, the Great Basin, the Southwest, the South, the Caribbean, and Mexico. Within these regions, human communities have had to adapt to nature, evolving their own ways of life. Indian peoples were the first in North America to embark on the long journey toward regionally distinct cultures, developing a wide variety of food sources to support their growing populations.

Hunting Traditions of the Plains and Forests

One of the most important effects of this massive climatological shift was the stress it placed on the big-game animals best suited to an Ice Age environment. The archaeological record details the extinction of thirty-two classes of large New World animals, including not only the mammoth and mastodon but the horse and camel, both of which evolved in America and then migrated to Asia across Beringia. It seems likely that lowered reproduction and survival rates of large animals forced hunting bands to intensify their efforts, and the combined effects of warmer climate and increased hunting eventually led to what some archaeologists have called the "Pleistocene Overkill."

As the other large-mammal populations declined, hunters on the Great Plains concentrated on the herds of American bison, more commonly called buffalo. To hunt these animals people needed a weapon they could throw quickly with great accuracy and velocity at fast-moving targets over distances of as much as a hundred yards. The Folsom technology, a refinement of the Clovis tradition, featured points that were more delicate and lighter in weight, but deadlier.

Folsom points were named for the site of their first major excavation, at Folsom, New Mexico, where the tools uncovered were judged to be about 10,000 years old. In one dramatic find, a Folsom point was discovered embedded between the fossilized ribs of an ancient species of bison. Hunters probably hurled the lances to which these points were attached with wooden spear-throwers, achieving far greater velocity than they could with their arms alone. By 7000 B.C.E., Folsom had evolved into a technology that archaeologists call Plano, and the points are often found with grinding tools suitable for processing vegetable foods. This association indicates that peoples of the Great Plains were in the process of developing a varied diet.

Archaeological finds also suggest the growing complexity of early Indian communities. Folsom and Plano hunters frequently stampeded herds of bison or other animals into canyon traps or over cliffs. At one such kill site in southeastern Colorado, estimated to be 8,500 years old, archaeologists uncovered the remains of nearly 200 bison that had been slaughtered and then systematically butchered on a single occasion. This job would have required at least 150 men and women and a sophisticated division of labor, which in turn probably involved the cooperation of a number of communities. Taking food in such quantities indicates a knowledge of basic preservation techniques: these people must have been among the first to make jerky, or dried strips of meat, and pemmican, a mixture of dried meat, animal fat, and berries that can keep into the winter when stored in hide containers. These characteristic products of the Great Plains later became the staple foods of European fur traders in the North American West.

The passing of the Pleistocene epoch and the submergence of Beringia were preceded by a second wave of Beringia migrants—the Athapascans, or Na-Dene people. After entering North America they moved southeast from Alaska, following the melting glacier that had formerly blocked passage. From 7,000 to 4,000 years ago, they settled the forests of the continent's Northwest. Although they eventually adopted a technology for making weapons and tools similar to that of neighboring peoples, the Na-Dene maintained a separate cultural and linguistic identity. The ancestors of the Athapascan-speaking Navajos and Apaches later migrated from this northern country, journeying across the Great Plains to the Southwest.

In a final migration from Asia that took place about 5,000 years ago, the Inupiat—more commonly known as Eskimos—and the Aleuts, other hunting peoples, crossed the flooded Bering Straits by boat.

When in 1927 archaeologists at Folsom, New Mexico, uncovered this dramatic example of a projectile point embedded in the ribs of a long-extinct species of bison it was the first proof that Indians had been in North America for many thousands of years.

The Eskimos colonized the polar coasts of the Arctic, the Aleuts the Aleutian Islands (later named for them) and the southern coast of Alaska.

Desert Culture in Western America

As the glaciers began to retreat, people developed new ways of finding food. During what archaeologists call the Archaic period (which corresponds to the late phases of the Stone Age in Eurasia and Africa), varying modes of subsistence evolved in different regions of North America. Between about 10,000 and 2,500 years ago, desert foraging began in the arid Great Basin, fishing along the Northwest coast of the Pacific, and hunting and gathering in the forests of the humid eastern half of the continent.

In the Great Basin of present-day Utah and Nevada the warming trend associated with the end of the Ice Age created a desert where once there had been enormous inland seas. Here, Indian people developed Desert Culture, a way of life based on the pursuit of small game and intensified foraging for plant foods. Small communities or bands of desert foragers migrated seasonally within a small range. They collected seeds,

PACIFIC OCEAN

Hudson Bay

CASCADES

ROCKY MOUNTAINS

Columbia R.

Snake R.

SIERRA NEVADA

GREAT BASIN

Colorado R.

COLORADO PLATEAU

GREAT

PLAINS

Missouri R.

L. Superior

L. Michigan

L. Huron

L. Erie

L. Ontario

St. Lawrence R.

APPALACHIAN HIGHLANDS

ATLANTIC OCEAN

OZARK HIGHLANDS

Ohio R.

Arkansas R.

Red R.

Tennessee R.

Mississippi R.

ATLANTIC COASTAL PLAIN

Rio Grande

GULF COASTAL PLAIN

GULF OF MEXICO

Frozen polar tundra
Subarctic forests
Humid temperate woodlands
Arid deserts and grasslands
Tropical jungles
Highlands

The Regions of Native North America

Occupying more than a third of the continent, the United States is alone among the world's nations in encompassing all five general classes of global climate: tropical jungles, arid deserts and grasslands, temperate woodlands, subarctic forests, and frozen polar tundra.

The country also contains some of the world's largest lakes, most extensive grasslands, and mightiest rivers.

All peoples must adjust their diet, shelter, and other material aspects of their lives to the physical conditions of the world around them; thus a knowledge of the way in which geography and

fiber, and prickly pear from the yucca one season, then moved to highland mesas to gather grass seed, acorns, juniper berries, and piñon nuts, and next to mountain streams to spear and net fish. This strategy required considerable skill in handicrafts: fiber baskets for collecting, pitch-lined baskets for cooking, nets and traps, and stone grinders for processing seeds and nuts, as well as stone knives, hammers, and mauls.

Archaeologists know that desert foragers lived in caves and rock shelters, for their artifacts are found there today. In addition to stone tools these artifacts include objects of wood, hide, and fiber, wonderfully preserved for thousands of years in the dry climate. The Desert Culture persisted into the nineteenth century among modern Shoshoni and Ute communi-

ties. Although these people were once scornfully labeled "Diggers" because of their practice of gathering edible roots and were ridiculed for their "primitive" life ways, we now appreciate the very sophisticated adjustments they made to a harsh environment.

Descriptions of the culture of the modern Shoshonis suggest that the force of community was strong among the people of the desert. An emphasis on sharing and gift giving, the condemnation of hoarding, and the limitations posed by a nomadic lifestyle on the accumulation of material goods prevented individuals or families from acquiring excessive wealth. Thus, desert communities were characterized by general social equality. Decisions were made by consensus among the adults, and lead-

ARCTIC

SUBARCTIC

NORTHWEST

CALIFORNIA

GREAT
BASIN

GREAT
PLAINS

NORTHEAST

SOUTHWEST

SOUTH

ARCTIC

SUBARCTIC

Elevation	
Feet	Meters
10,000	3,050
5,000	1,525
2,000	610
1,000	305
0	0

climate combine to form regions is a prerequisite to understanding the cultures of the peoples of America. Using the concept of "culture areas," anthropologists divide the continent into several fundamental regions, which have played an important role in the history of the continent for the past 10,000 years.

The Indian peoples of North America were first to develop distinct cultures suited to the regions in which they lived. Just as regions shaped the life-ways and history of Indian peoples, after the coming of the Europeans they nurtured the development of regional American cultures.

ership tended to be informal, based on achievement and reputation. The men of one band generally married women from another, and wives came to live with the people of their husbands, creating important linkages between groups that contributed to the sense of shared ethnic identity.

The innovative practices of the Desert Culture gradually spread from the Great Basin to the Great Plains and the Southwest, where foraging techniques began to supplement intensive hunting. About 6,000 years ago, archaeologists estimate, colonists from the Great Basin carried Desert Culture farther west to California. There, in the natural abundance of the valleys and coasts, Indian peoples developed an econ-omy capable of supporting some of the densest popu-

lations and the first permanently settled communities in North America. Another dynamic center in the West developed along the Northwest Pacific coast, where native American communities developed a way of life based on the exploitation of abundant fish and sea mammals. This Old Cordilleran Culture became the basis for the historic cultures of the Plateau and Northwest, which also included densely populated sedentary communities.

Forest Efficiency

Similar trends were at work east of the Mississippi. Before European settlers destroyed countless acres of forest during the eighteenth and nineteenth centuries, the whole of eastern North America was a vast wood-

9

land. Hardwoods grew in the north, southern pine in the south. The Winnebagos of the Great Lakes region sang of these forests:

> *Pleasant it looked,*
> *this newly created world.*
> *Along the entire length and breadth*
> *of the earth, our grandmother*
> *extended the green reflection*
> *of her covering*
> *and the escaping odors*
> *were pleasant to inhale.*

Archaic forest communities achieved a comfortable and secure life based on what archaeologists call "forest efficiency"—a sophisticated exploitation of their rich and diverse resources. Archaic Indian communities of the forest hunted small game and gathered seeds, nuts, roots, and other wild plant foods. They also developed the practice of burning the woodlands and prairies to stimulate the growth of berries, fruits, and edible roots. The resulting meadows and forest edge produced harvestable foods and attracted grazing animals, which were then hunted for their meat and hides. Another important resource was the abundant fish of the rivers.

Archaeological sites in the East suggest that during the late Archaic period community populations grew and settlements became increasingly permanent, providing convincing evidence of the viability of forest efficiency. The artifacts these people buried with their dead—axes, fishhooks, and animal bones with males, nut-cracking stones, beads, and pestles with females—reflect the different roles of men and women in their society.

THE DEVELOPMENT OF FARMING

The exploitation of a wide variety of food sources during the Archaic period eventually led many Indian people to develop and adopt the practice of farming. The dynamic center of this development in North America was the highlands of Mexico, from which the new technology spread north and east.

Mexico

At the end of the Stone Age, people in four different parts of the world developed farming systems, each based on a different crop: rice in Southeast Asia, wheat in West Asia, maize (or Indian corn) in Mexico, and potatoes in the Andean highlands of South America. In Mexico a great variety of other crops—most importantly beans and squash, but also tomatoes, peppers, avocados, cocoa (chocolate), and vanilla—supplemented maize. Today the two American staples—maize and potatoes—contribute more to the world's

food supply than do wheat and rice. These "miracle crops" fueled the expansion of European human and livestock populations in the three centuries after 1650. Without these and other New World crops such as tobacco, American cotton, and rubber—each the basis of important new industries and markets—the history of the modern world would have been far different.

Archaeological evidence suggests that plant cultivation in the highlands of central Mexico began about 5,000 years ago. Ancient Mexicans developed crops that responded well to human care and produced larger quantities of food in a limited space than did plants occurring naturally. Maize was particularly productive; over time it was adapted to a wide range of American climates, and farming spread throughout the temperate regions of North America.

As farming became increasingly important, it radically reshaped social life. Where a foraging society might require 100 square miles to support 100 people, a farming society required only one square mile. Population growth and the need for people to remain near their fields throughout the year led to the appearance of villages and permanent architecture and eventually to the emergence of large, densely settled communities like Cahokia. Autumn harvests had to be stored during winter months, and the storage and distribution of food had to be managed. The division of labor increased with the appearance of specialists like toolmakers, craftsworkers, administrators, priests, and rulers as well as farmers and food processors. Ultimately, unequal access to wealth and power resulted in the emergence of classes.

By 1000 B.C.E., urban communities governed by permanent bureaucracies had begun to form in Mesoamerica, the region stretching from central Mexico to Central America. By the beginning of the first millenium C.E. (Common Era) highly productive farming was supporting complex urban civilizations in the Valley of Mexico (the location of present-day Mexico City), the Yucatan Peninsula, and other parts of Mesoamerica. Like many of the ancient civilizations of Asia and the Mediterranean, these Mesoamerican civilizations were characterized by the concentration of wealth and power in the hands of an elite class of priests and rulers, the construction of impressive temples and other public structures, and the development of systems of mathematics and astronomy, and several forms of hieroglyphic writing. The civilizations of Mesomerica were also marked by warfare between states and by terrifying public rituals of human sacrifice.

The great city of Teotihuacan in the Valley of Mexico, which emerged about 100 B.C.E., had a population of as many as 200,000 at the height of its power around C.E. 500. Teotihuacan's elite class of religious and political leaders controlled an elaborate state-sponsored trading system that stretched from present-day

Mesoamerican maize cultivation, as illustrated by an Aztec artist for the Florentine Codex, *a book prepared a few years after the Spanish conquest. The peoples of Mesoamerica developed a greater variety of cultivated crops than those of any other region in the world, and their agricultural productivity helped sustain one of the world's great civilizations.*

Arizona south to Central America and may have included coastal shipping connections with the pre-Inca civilizations of Peru. The city had a highly specialized division of labor. Artisans manufactured tools and produced textiles, stoneware, pottery, and obsidian blades; the bureaucratic elite collected taxes and tribute; farmers left the city every day to work the fields that fed its people; and armies of workers constructed such monumental edifices as the Pyramids of the Sun and Moon, which still dominate the city's ruins.

Teotihuacan began to decline in the sixth century, and by the eighth century it was mostly abandoned. A new empire, that of the Toltecs, dominated central Mexico from the tenth to the twelfth century. By the fourteenth century a people known as the Aztecs, migrants from the north, had settled in the Valley of Mexico and begun a dramatic expansion into a formidable imperial power (see Chapter 2).

The Mayan peoples of the Yucatan peninsula developed a group of competing city-states that flourished from about 300 B.C.E. until about C.E. 900. The achievements of the Mayans included Mesoamerica's most advanced writing and calendrical systems and a sophisticated knowledge of mathematics that included the concept of zero.

The Resisted Revolution

Historians once described the development of farming as the "Neolithic Revolution" (*neolithic* means "New, or Later, Stone Age"). They believed that agricultural communities offered such obvious advantages that neighboring peoples must have rushed to adopt this way of life. Societies that remained without a farming tradition must simply have been too "primitive" to achieve this breakthrough; vulnerability to fickle nature was the penalty for their ignorance. This interpretation was based on a scheme of social evolution that viewed human history as the story of technological progress, in which savage hunters gradually developed into civilized farmers.

But there is very little evidence to support the notion that such a "revolution" occurred during a short, critical period. The adoption of farming was a gradual process, one that required hundreds, even thousands of years. Moreover, ignorance of cultivation was never the reason that cultures failed to take up farming, for all hunter-gatherer peoples understand a great deal about plant reproduction. When the Menomini Indians of the northern forests of Wisconsin gathered wild rice, for example, they purposely allowed some of it to fall back into the water to ensure a crop for the next season, and Desert Paiutes of the Great Basin systematically irrigated stands of their favorite wild food sources.

The way today's remaining hunter-gatherers view the farming way of life is instructive. Foragers generally look upon their own method of getting food as vastly superior to any other. The food sources of desert gatherers, for example, are considerably more varied and higher in protein than those of desert farmers, whose diets concentrate almost exclusively on grains. Because foragers took advantage of natural diversity, they were also less vulnerable to climatological stress; although gathering communities frequently experienced periods of scarcity and hunger, unlike farming societies they were rarely devastated by famine. Foragers also point out that farming requires much more work. Why sweat all day in the fields producing tasteless corn, they argue, when in an hour or two one can gather enough sweet prickly pear to last a week? Indeed, rather than freeing men and women from the tyranny of nature, farming tied people to a work discipline unlike anything previously known in human history. Finally, foragers consider their migratory ways far more interesting than village life, which they claim is dull and monotonous, preferred only by those whose possessions are too cumbersome to move.

As the techniques of large-scale agriculture became available, cultures in different regions assessed its advantages and limitations. In California and the Pacific Northwest, acorn gathering or salmon fishing made the cultivation of food crops seem a waste of time. In the Great Basin, several peoples attempted to farm, but without success. Before the invention of modern irrigation systems, which require sophisticated engineering, only the Archaic Desert Culture could prevail in this harsh environment. In the neighboring Southwest, however, farming resolved certain ecological dilemmas and transformed the way of life. Like the development of more sophisticated traditions of tool manufacture, farming represented another stage in the economic intensifications that kept populations and available resources in balance. It seems that where climate favored cultivation, people tended to adopt farming as a way of increasing the production of food, thus continuing the Archaic tradition of squeezing as much productivity as they could from their environment. But in a few areas farming resulted in a truly revolutionary transformation, pushing in the direction of an urban civilization like that of central Mexico or Cahokia on the banks of the Mississippi.

Increasing Social Complexity

Farming created the basis for much greater social complexity within Indian communities. Most important were elaborate systems of kinship. Greater population density prompted families to group themselves into clans responsible for different social, political, or ritual functions. These clans became an important mechanism for binding together the people of several communities into a tribe. A tribe, based on ethnic, linguistic, and territorial unity, was led by a leader or chief from an honored clan, who was often advised by councils of elders, all of whom were also clan leaders. In all likelihood, the city of Cahokia was governed by such a system. The tribal council sometimes arbitrated disputes between individuals or families, but most crimes—theft, adultery, rape, murder—were avenged by the aggrieved kinship group itself.

The primary function of the ruling council was to supervise the economy—to see that the harvest was collected and stored and that the food stores were distributed to the clans. Differences in wealth—small by the standards of modern societies—could develop between the families of a farming tribe, but these inequalities were kept in check by a system of redistribution that followed the principles of sharing characteristic of foraging communities. Nowhere in North America did Indian cultures develop a concept of the private ownership of land. Invariably, land was a common resource of the people and thus worked collectively.

Indian communities practiced a rather strict division of labor by gender that in its details varied greatly from culture to culture. Among foraging peoples, hunting was generally the work of men,

whereas the gathering of food and the maintenance of home-base camps were the responsibility of women. This pattern probably originated during the early years of the Archaic period. But the development of farming disrupted these patterns. In Mexico, where communities became almost totally dependent on crops, both men and women worked in the fields. Where hunting remained important, the older division of labor continued, with women responsible for field work. In general, however, Indian patterns contrasted in important ways with the norms of colonizing Europeans, prompting much misunderstanding. When English colonists saw Indian women working in the cornfields, for example, they thought them greatly oppressed; Indians, on the other hand, thought colonial men who labored in the fields were performing "women's work."

In most North American Indian farming communities, women and men belonged to separate social groupings, each with its own rituals and lore. Membership in these societies was one of the most important elements of a person's identity. Marriage ties, on the other hand, were relatively weak, and in most Indian communities divorce was easy. The couple simply separated, the children almost always remaining with the mother. Indian women were free to determine the timing of reproduction as well as to use herbs to prevent pregnancy, induce abortion, or ease the pain of childbirth. The status and role of Indian women were strikingly different from European patterns, in which the rule of men over women and fathers over households was the norm.

Farming communities were far more complex than foraging communities, but they were also less stable. Growing populations demanded increasingly large surpluses of food, and this need frequently led to social conflict and warfare among farming communities. Moreover, farming systems were especially vulnerable to climatological disruptions such as drought, as well as to ecological crises of their own creation, such as soil depletion or erosion.

The Religions of Foragers and Farmers

The religions of Indian peoples were shaped primarily by the two great traditions of foraging and farming. The first, rooted deep in the Archaic past, is sometimes called the Hunting Tradition. This complex of beliefs centered in the relationship of hunters and prey and celebrated the existence of a "Master of Animals," often portrayed as the sacred bear. Associated with this tradition was the vision quest, a practice in which young men and women sought out personal protective spirits by going alone into the wilderness, exposing themselves to the elements, fasting, and inducing hallucinations and dreams. An individual who developed a special sensitivity to spiritual forces might

Human figures dance on this characteristic piece of red-on-buff pottery of the Hohokams (dated about C.E. 1000). The Hohokams, located on the floodplain of the Gila River near present-day Phoenix, Arizona, were the first irrigation farmers of North America. The Pima and Papago people of Arizona may be descended from them.

The creation of man and woman depicted on a pot (dated about C.E.1000) from the ancient villages of the Mimbres River of southwestern New Mexico, the area of Mogollon culture. Mimbres pottery is renowned for its spirited artistry. Such artifacts were usually intended as grave goods, to honor the dead.

become a shaman—a "medicine" man or woman of the community. The Hunting Tradition was important throughout the continent but was strongest in the northern latitudes, where hunting played a prominent role in the economy.

With the northward spread of maize farming came a second religious complex, known as the Agrarian Tradition, which emphasized and celebrated the notion of fertility in ritual festivals marking the annual change of seasons. At Cahokia, archaeological evidence of posts used to mark the summer and winter solstices suggests that the Agrarian Tradition was honored there. Because this tradition was associated with the greater social complexity of the farming way of life, it was generally characterized by organized cults and priesthoods rather than by individualistic shamans. At its most elaborate, it featured a war-sacrifice-cannibalism ideology that glorified violence and included the ritual consumption of enemy flesh, a tradition whose origins may be related to those of the awe-inspiring sacrificial rituals performed by the priests and leaders of the Mesoamerican city-states.

Although religious beliefs were probably as distinctive as the local communities that held them, some combination of the Hunting and Agrarian traditions characterized most of the Indian cultures of North America. Natural and supernatural forces were thought to be inseparable, a system of belief called *pantheism;* people were thought to share a basic kinship

with animals, plants, inanimate objects, and natural forces. Although many native religions recognized the existence of a paramount spiritual force, they were also generally polytheistic, with numerous gods and spirits.

The Earliest Farmers of the Southwest

Farming communities began to emerge in the arid Southwest during the first millenium B.C.E. Among the first to develop a settled farming way of life were the Mogollon people, who lived along what is today the southern Arizona–New Mexico border from around 250 B.C.E. to around C.E. 1450. Living along mountain ridges and near streams in permanent villages of ingenious pit houses well suited to the region's temperature extremes, these people used digging sticks to cultivate maize, beans, and squash. Some of the Mogollon pit structures may have been what Southwestern peoples today call *kivas,* which are used for community religious rituals.

From about C.E. 300 to 1500 the people of the Hohokam ("those who are gone," in the language of the modern Pimas and Papagos of the area) culture flourished in the region along the floodplain of the Salt and Gila Rivers in southern Arizona. The Hohokams, who lived in agricultural villages, built and maintained the first irrigation system in America north of Mexico, channeling river water many miles to desert fields of maize, beans, squash, tobacco, and cotton. They made jewelry from shells and developed a process for etching shells with animal designs. They shared many traits with Mesoamerican civilization to the south, including platform mounds for religious ceremonies and large courts for ball playing. One thoroughly excavated Hohokam community site is a place the Pimas call Skoaquik, or Snaketown. Located near present-day Phoenix, Snaketown includes the

In Chaco Canyon, in northern New Mexico, lie the ruins of Pueblo Bonito, built in the twelfth century C.E. during the golden age of the Anasazis, an agricultural people who created a complex urban civilization amid the arid landscape of the Colorado Plateau. Until the invention of the modern construction techniques, Pueblo Bonito held the record as the world's largest apartment house.

remains of a hundred pit houses spread over 300 acres. The number and variety of goods from central Mexico uncovered at the site—rubber balls, mirrors of pyrite mosaics, copper bells, and fashionable ear ornaments—suggest that it may have housed a community of merchants who traded Mesoamerican manufactured goods for locally mined turquoise.

The Anasazis

The best-known farming culture of the Southwest is that of the Anasazis ("ancient outsiders," in the Navajo language), which developed around the first century C.E. several hundred miles to the north of the Hohokam communities in the Four Corners area, where today Arizona, New Mexico, Utah, and Colorado meet on the eastern portion of the great plateau of the Colorado River. Around 750, possibly in response to population pressure and an increasingly dry climate, the Anasazis

began a shift from pit-house villages to densely populated, multistoried apartment complexes called *pueblos* ("towns" in Spanish, for they were named by Spanish invaders). These complexes clustered around central plazas with circular underground *kivas*. The Anasazis grew high-yield varieties of maize in terraced fields irrigated by canals flowing from mountain catchment basins. To supplement this vegetable diet they hunted animals for their meat, using the bow and arrow that first appeared in the region about C.E. 500.

Anasazi culture extended over an area larger than California. The sites of more than 25,000 Anasazi communities are known in New Mexico alone. Only a few have been excavated, so there is much that archaeologists do not yet understand. The most prominent of the Anasazi centers was Pueblo Bonito in Chaco canyon. Completed in the twelfth century, this complex of 650 interconnected rooms is a monument to the golden age of the Anasazis. Hundreds of miles of arrow-straight roads and an interpueblo communication system consisting of mountaintop signaling stations connect Chaco Canyon to outlying sites, making it the center of a food distribution, trading, and ceremonial network.

During the thirteenth century, drought conditions in the Southwest worsened. Growing Anasazi populations redoubled their efforts to improve their production methods, building increasingly complex irrigation canals, dams, and terraced fields. Many large fields were mulched with small stones to retain moisture more effectively. But these measures were not sufficient. Scientific analysis of the varying size of the growth rings of ancient tree trunks reveals that between 1276 and 1293 there was a prolonged and devastating drought that must have resulted in repeated crop failures and eventual famine.

The Anasazis were confronted with an additional difficulty—the arrival of bands of Athapascan migrants who for a thousand years or more had been gradually moving south from Subarctic regions. If the Athapascans were anything like their immediate descendants, the Navajos and the Apaches, they must have been fierce fighters. By the fourteenth and fifteenth centuries, the Athapascans were raiding Anasazi farming communities, taking food, goods, and possibly slaves. The dramatic Anasazi cliff dwellings at Mesa Verde, Colorado, constructed about this time, may have been built as a defense against these raiders. Gradually the Anasazis abandoned the Four Corners area altogether. Their movements have not yet been fully traced, but most seem to have resettled in communities along the Rio Grande, joining with local residents to form the Pueblo people of modern times.

Farmers of the Eastern Woodlands

Archaeologists date the beginning of the farming culture of eastern North America, known as Woodland, from the first appearances of pottery in the region about 3,000 years ago. The Woodland culture was based on a sophisticated way of life that combined gathering and hunting with the cultivation of a few crops. People lived most of the year at permanent community sites but left them seasonally to take advantage of resources at different locations. Their crops included sunflowers and other locally domesticated plants. The discovery of clay pipes in archaeological excavations suggests that the early Woodlands people may also have cultivated tobacco, which was first domesticated in the Caribbean region.

Woodlands peoples began cultivating maize during the first millenium C.E., but even before then they had begun to adopt an increasingly settled existence and a more complex social organization in some regions. Between 1700 and 700 B.C.E. the people of the Poverty Point culture in the lower Mississippi Valley erected a remarkable site consisting of a series of concentric semicircular earth mounds covering an area about a mile square. The people of the Adena culture (the name is taken from a site on the upper Ohio River) occupied the Ohio River basin from present-day Indiana to Pennsylvania from before 1000 B.C.E. to about C.E. 250. They lived in permanent or semipermanent villages and built large burial mounds.

Between about 200 B.C.E. and fifth century C.E. the Hopewell people settled in the Mississippi-Ohio Valley. Hopewell communities were devoted to mortuary cults, in which the dead were honored through ceremony, display, and the construction of enormous and elaborate burial mounds. In support of this tradition, Hopewell chiefs mobilized an elaborate trade network that acquired obsidian from the Rocky Mountains, copper from the Great Lakes, mica from the Appalachians, and shells from the Gulf coast. Hopewell artisans converted these materials into distinctive and artistically sophisticated goods that played an important role in Hopewell trade and were buried with the dead in Hopewell graves.

Mississippian Society

The Hopewell culture collapsed in the fifth century, perhaps as a result of shifting climate patterns. Local communities continued to practice their late Archaic subsistence strategies, but abandoned the expensive cultural displays demanded by the Hopewell mortuary cult. Following the collapse of Hopewell, however, several important innovations were introduced in the East. The bow and arrow, developed on the Great Plains, appeared east of the Mississippi about the seventh century, greatly increasing the efficiency of hunting. Also between 450 and 800, maize farming spread widely in the east. Indian farmers had developed a new variety of maize called Northern Flint, with large cobs and plentiful kernels that matured in a short enough time to make it suitable for cultivation in temperate northern latitudes. Also about this time a shift from digging sticks to flint hoes took place, further increasing the productive potential of maize farming.

It was on the basis of these innovations that, in the seventh or eighth century, the powerful new Mississippian culture arose. The Mississippians were master maize farmers who lived in permanent villages along the floodplain of the Mississippi River. Cahokia, the most important of these, was the urban heart of Mississippian America. Cahokia's dense urban center with its monumental temple, its residential neighborhoods, and its surrounding farmlands were mirrored in many other regional centers, each with thousands of residents. There were cities on the Arkansas River near Spiro, Oklahoma; on the Black Warrior River at Moundville, Alabama; at Hiwassee Island on the Tennessee River; and along the Etowah and Ocmulgee Rivers in Georgia. Like Cahokia, these centers of civilization were probably characterized by a sophisticated division of labor that

The Great Serpent Mound in southern Ohio, the shape of an uncoiling snake more than 1,300 feet long, is the largest effigy earthwork in the world. Monumental public works like these suggest the high degree of social organization of the Mississippian people.

Native North American Trade Networks, ca. C.E.1400   *By determining the places of origin of artifacts found at ancient sites, historians have devised a conjectural map of Indian trade networks. Among large regional centers and smaller local ones, trade connected Indian peoples of many different communities and regions.*

Legend:
● Regional centers
• Local centers
→ Customary trading connections

included artisans, priests, and an elite class of rulers. The Great Serpent Mound, the largest effigy earthwork in the world, was constructed by Mississippian peoples in southern Ohio.

Linked by the vast water transportation system of the Mississippi and its many tributaries, these communities became the earliest city-states north of Mexico, hierarchical chiefdoms that extended political control over the farmers of the surrounding countryside. With continued population growth, these cities engaged in vigorous and probably violent competition for the limited space along the rivers. It may have been the need for more orderly ways of allocating territories that stimulated the evolution of political hierarchies. The tasks of preventing local conflict, storing large food surpluses, and redistributing foodstuffs from farmers to artisans and elites required a leadership class with the power to command. Mound-building and the use of tribute labor in the construction of other public works testified to the power the chiefs wielded from their sumptuous quarters atop the commanding mounds. If politics is defined as the orga-

nized contest for power among people and groups, then the Mississippians and the Anasazis were the first truly political societies north of Mexico.

Mississippian culture reached its height between the eleventh and thirteenth centuries C.E., the same period in which the Anasazis were constructing their desert cities. Both groups adapted the technology that was spreading northward from Mexico to their particular environments, both developed impressive artistic traditions, and their feats of engineering reflect the beginnings of science and technology. These were complex societies characterized by urbanism, social stratification, craft specialization, and regional trade. Except for a formal system of writing, they had all the traits of European and Asian civilizations.

The Politics of Warfare and Violence

The late thirteenth century marked the end of several hundred years of climatological conditions that were very favorable to maize farming and the beginning of a century and a half of cool, dry conditions.

Although the changes in climate in the Mississippi Valley were not as severe as those that devastated the Anasazis of the Southwest, over the long term they significantly lowered the potential of farming to support growing urban populations. Some archaeologists have suggested that this extended drought sharpened political conflict in both areas and greatly increased violence and social disorder.

Warfare among Indian peoples certainly predated the colonial era. Organized violence was probably rare among hunting bands, which could seldom muster the manpower for more than a small raid against an enemy. Certain hunting peoples, though, such as the southward-moving Athapascans, undoubtedly engaged in systematic raiding of settled farming communities. Warfare was also common among farming societies fighting to gain additional lands for cultivation. The first Europeans in what is now the South of the United States described highly organized combat among large tribal armies. The bow and arrow was a deadly weapon of war, and the practice of scalping seems to have originated among warring tribes, who believed one could capture a warrior's spirit by taking his hair. (During the period of colonial warfare, the practice of scalping spread widely among both European colonists and the Indian tribes of other regions.) Sculpted images of human sacrifice found at Mississippian sites suggest that these peoples, like the inhabitants of Mexican city-states, not only waged war but practiced human sacrifice and cannibalism.

The archaeological remains of Cahokia reveal that during the thirteenth and fourteenth centuries the people of that great city surrounded its central sections with a heavy log stockade. This defensive structure suggests that there may have been a great deal of violent warfare with other nearby communities. Indeed, the fourteenth century may have been a period of intense conflict and war among competing city-states throughout the valleys of the Mississippi, each based on the domination of farming countrysides by metropolitan centers. Eventually conditions in the upper Mississippi Valley deteriorated so far that Cahokia and many other sites were abandoned altogether, and as the cities collapsed, people relocated in smaller, decentralized communities. Nevertheless, as we will see, among the peoples of the South, Mississippian patterns continued into the period of colonization.

NORTH AMERICA ON THE EVE OF COLONIZATION

The first Europeans to arrive in North America found a continent populated by more than 350 native societies speaking nearly as many distinct languages. Although anthropologists of the early twentieth century estimated that the population of the entire area north of Mexico was little more than a million, historians have now raised this estimate substantially.

The Indian Population of America

In determining the precolonial population of the Americas, today's historical demographers consider a number of factors—the population densities that different technological and economic systems could support, the archaeological evidence, the very earliest European accounts, and the estimated impact of epidemic diseases. (For a discussion of epidemics among Indian peoples, see Chapter 2.) Although estimates vary, most historians now believe that the population of America north of Mexico in the early sixteenth century numbered between 7 and 10 million. Moreover, probably another 25 million were concentrated in the complex societies of the Mexican highlands. Thus at the time of their first contact with European explorers and settlers, the peoples of the Western Hemisphere numbered some 60 to 70 million, about the same as Europe's population.

Population density in North America varied widely according to ways of life. Only scattered bands populated the Great Basin, the Great Plains, and Subarctic regions, but the Northwest and what is today California were densely settled because the foraging peoples of those areas maintained highly productive fishing and gathering economies. The Southwest, South, and Northeast contained the largest populations, and it was in these areas that European explorers, conquerors, and colonists first concentrated their efforts.

The Southwest

The single overwhelming fact of life in the Southwest is aridity. Summer rains average only ten to twenty inches annually, and on much of the dry desert cultivation is impossible. Several rivers, however, flow southward out of pine-covered mountain plateaus to the Gulf of Mexico and the Gulf of California. Narrow bands of green vegetation in parched sands of brown and red, they have made irrigation farming possible.

On the eve of European colonization, Indian farmers in the Southwest had been cultivating fields for nearly 3,000 years. In the floodplain of the Gila and Salt Rivers lived the Pimas and Papagos, descendants of the ancient Hohokams. Working small irrigated fields along the Colorado River and even on the floor of the Grand Canyon were the Yuman peoples. These desert farmers cultivated corn, beans, squash, sunflowers, and cotton, which they traded throughout the Southwest. They lived in dispersed

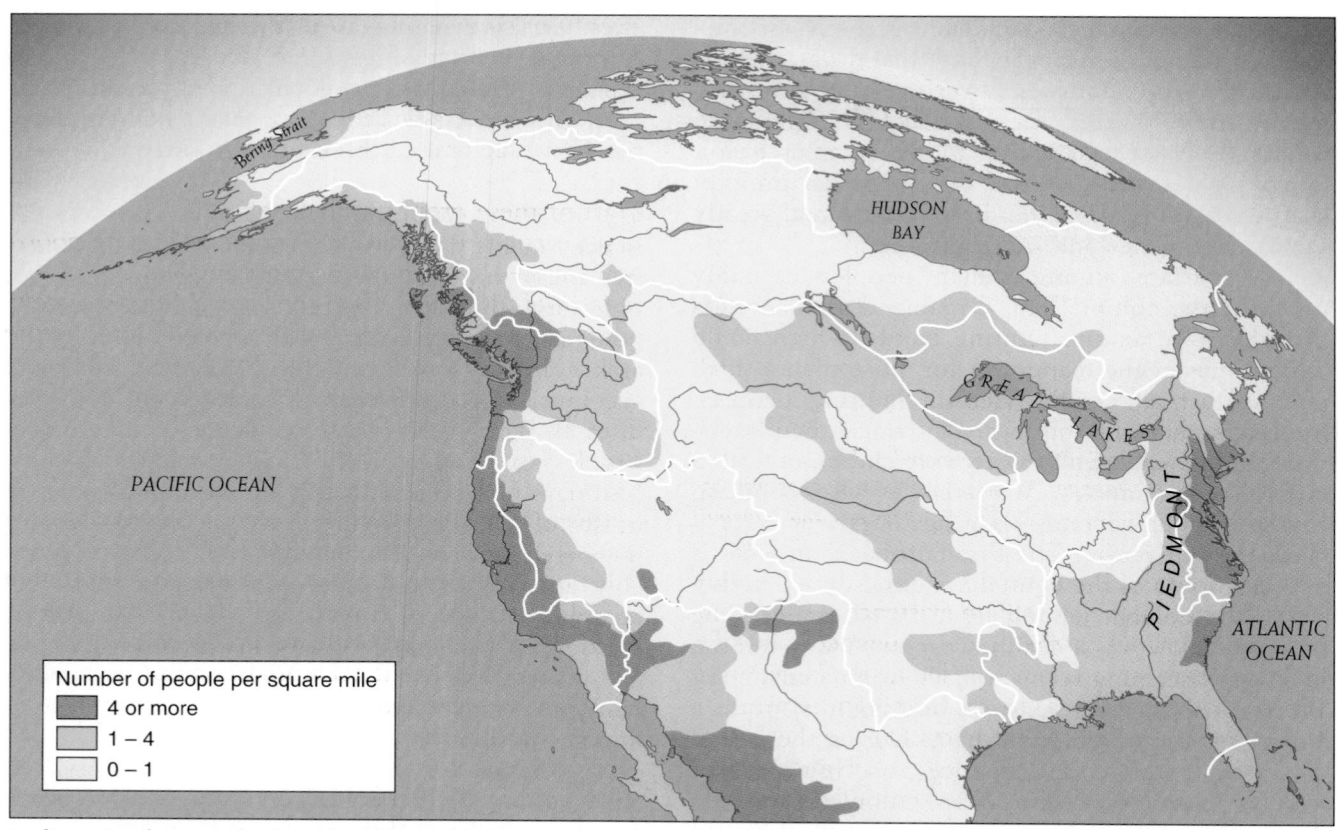

PACIFIC OCEAN

HUDSON BAY

ATLANTIC OCEAN

Number of people per square mile
- 4 or more
- 1 – 4
- 0 – 1

Indian Settlement before European Colonization   *Based on what is called the "carrying capacity" of different subsistence strategies—the population density they could support—historical demographers have mapped the hypothetical population density of Indian societies in the fifteenth century, before the era of European colonization. Populations were most dense in farming societies or in coastal areas with marine resources and least dense in extreme environments like the Great Basin.*

settlements that the Spanish called *rancherias* (meaning "settlements"), which were separated by as much as a mile. That way, say the Pimas, people avoid getting on each other's nerves. Rancherias were governed in general by councils of adult men whose decisions required unanimous consent, although a headman was chosen to manage the irrigation works. Ceremonies focused, appropriately, on rainmaking; one ritual required everyone to drink cactus wine until thoroughly drunk, a state of presumed purification that was thought to bring rain.

East of the Grand Canyon, in their unique dwellings of stacked, interconnected apartments, lived the Pueblo peoples, who inherited this architectural form, as well as their farming techniques and religious practices, from their Anasazi forebears. Although the many Pueblo peoples spoke several languages, as a group they shared a commitment to communal village life that differentiated them from the individualistic desert farmers. A strict communal code of behavior regulating personal conduct was enforced by the Pueblos through a maze of matrilin-

eal clans and secret religious societies; unique combinations of these clans and societies formed the governing systems of different Pueblo villages. Seasonal public ceremonies in the village squares featured colorful impersonations, with singing, chanting, and dancing, of ancestral sacred spirits called *kachinas.* "Clowns" mimicked in slapstick style those who did not conform to the communal ideal, pretending to drink urine or eat dirt, for example, in front of the home of a person who kept an unclean house.

The Pueblos inhabit the oldest continuously occupied towns in the United States. The village of Oraibi, Arizona, dates from the twelfth century, when the Hopis ("peaceful ones") founded it in the isolated central mesas of the Colorado Plateau. Using dry-farming methods and drought-resistant plants, these western Pueblo Indians produced rich harvests of corn and squash amid shifting sand dunes. On a mesa top about fifty miles southwest of present-day Albuquerque, New Mexico, Anasazi immigrants from Mesa Verde built Acoma, the "sky city," in the late thirteenth century. The Pueblo people established approximately

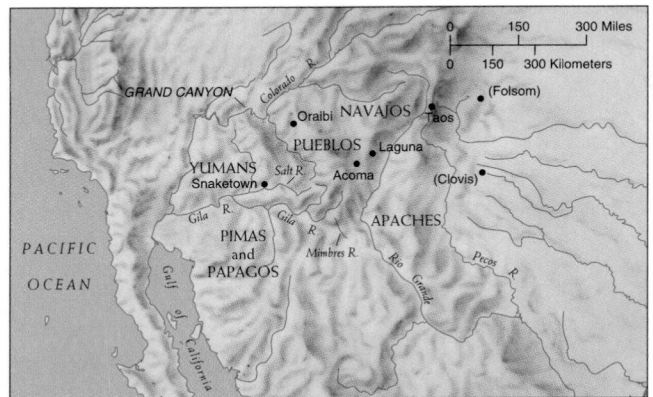

Southwestern Indian Groups on the Eve of Colonization   *The Southwest was populated by desert farmers like the Pimas, Papagos, Yumans, and Pueblos, as well as by nomadic hunters and raiders like the Apaches and Navajos.*

seventy other villages during the next two hundred years; fifty of these were still in existence in the seventeenth century when the Spanish founded Santa Fé, and two dozen survive today, including the large Indian towns of Laguna, Isleta, Santo Domingo, Jémez, San Felipe, and Taos (see the map on p. 52).

In the arid deserts and mountains surrounding these towns were bands of nomadic hunters, some of whom had lived in the region thousands of years. But there were also the Athapascans who, as we have seen, began arriving in the fourteenth and fifteenth centuries and who hunted and foraged, traded meat and medicinal herbs with farmers, and frequently raided and plundered these same villages and rancherias. Gradually, some of the Athapascan people surrounding the Pueblo villages adopted their neighbors' farming and handicraft skills; these people were the Navajos. Others, who came be known as the Apaches, were more heavily influenced by the hunting and gathering traditions of the Great Basin and Great Plains and remained nomadic.

The South

The South enjoys a mild, moist climate with short winters and long summers, ideal for farming. From the Atlantic and Gulf coasts, a broad fertile plain extends inland to the Piedmont, a plateau separating the coastal plains from the Appalachian Mountains. The transition between plateau and coastal plain is marked by the fall line, an area of rapids and waterfalls in the descending rivers. The upper courses of the waterways originating in the Appalachian highlands offered ample rich bottomland for farming, and the extensive forests, mostly of yellow pine, offered abundant animal resources. In the sixteenth century, large populations of Indian peoples farmed this rich land, fishing or hunting to supplement their diets. They lived in communities ranging from villages of

twenty or so dwellings to large towns of a thousand or more inhabitants.

Mississippian cultural patterns continued among the peoples of the South. They were organized into confederacies of farming towns, the most powerful living along the river floodplains. Because most of these groups were quickly decimated in the first years of European colonization, they are poorly documented. We know the most about the Natchez, farmers of the rich lands in the lower Mississippi delta who survived into the eighteenth century before being destroyed in a war with the French. Overseeing the Natchez was a ruler known as the Great Sun, who lived in royal splendor on a ceremonial mound in his village capital. When out among his subjects he was carried on a litter, the path before him swept by his retinue of servants and wives. Natchez society was class based. Noble families were represented on the Great Sun's council of advisers and appointed village peace and war chiefs. The majority of people, however, were a subordinate group known as the "Stinkards." Persistent territorial conflict with other confederacies elevated warfare to an honored status among the Natchez, and public torture and human sacrifice of enemies were commonplace. The Natchez give us our best glimpse at what life may have been like in ancient Cahokia.

The Indians of Florida also lived in sophisticated chiefdoms characterized by class systems, monarchs, and priests. Archaeological evidence implies that central towns dominated farmers in the countryside, demanding from them large quantities of maize, squash, and other cultivated plants grown on fields large enough to support populations numbering in the tens of thousands. As in the Natchez villages and the city of Cahokia, life in these Florida towns centered around the ceremonial mounds where the ruling families resided. Honored clans

Southern Indian Groups on the Eve of Colonization   *On the eve of colonization the Indian societies of the South shared many traits of the complex Mississippian farming culture.*

Neg. No. 324281, photographed by Rota, engraving by de Bry Courtesy Department Library Services, American Museum of Natural History.

The New Queen Being Taken to the King, engraved by Theodor de Bry in the sixteenth century from a drawing by Jacques le Moyne, an early French colonist of Florida. The communities of Florida were hierarchical, with classes and hereditary chiefs, some of whom were women. Here le Moyne depicted a "queen" being carried on an ornamental litter by men of rank.

lived in the plaza below, with ordinary people on the fringes of town and in the countryside.

Eventually, these chiefdoms proved highly vulnerable to conquest, but the looser confederacies of the interior were considerably more resilient. Among the latter the most prominent were the Choctaws of present-day Mississippi and Alabama, the Chickasaws in western Tennessee, and the Creeks of Georgia, each confederacy, including several dozen towns. On the mountain plateaus lived the Cherokees, who made up the single largest confederacy, of more than sixty towns. Farming was somewhat less important in the highlands than along the coast, hunting somewhat more so. There were no ruling classes or kings, and leaders were either women or men. Most peoples reckoned their descent matrilineally (that is, through their mothers, grandmothers, and so on), and at marriage husbands left the homes of their mothers to reside with the families of their wives. Women controlled household and village life and were influential as well in the

matrilineal clans that linked communities together. Councils of elderly men governed the confederacies but were joined by clan matrons for annual meetings at the central council house. These gatherings could last days or even weeks, since all clan members, male and female, were given the opportunity to speak.

All the peoples of the South farmed the same crops, hunted in the same kind of piney woods, and lived in similar villages. They celebrated a common round of agricultural festivals that brought clans together from surrounding communities. At the harvest festival, for example, people thoroughly cleaned their homes and villages. They fasted and purified themselves by consuming the "black drink," a vision-inducing libation made from roasted leaves of the cassina plant. They extinguished old fires, lit new ones, and then celebrated the new crop of sweet corn with dancing and other festivities. During the following days, villages, clans, and groups of men and women competed against each other in the ancient stick-and-ball game that the French named lacrosse; in the evenings men and women played chunkey, a gambling game.

The Northeast

The Northeast, the colder sector of the eastern woodlands, has a varied geography of coastal plains and mountain highlands, great rivers, lakes, and valleys. After C.E. 500, cultivation became the main support of the Indian economy in those places where the growing season was long enough to bring a crop of corn to maturity. In such areas of the Northeast—along the coasts and in the river valleys—Indian populations were large and dense.

The Iroquois of present-day Ontario and upstate New York, who have lived in these areas for at least 4,500 years, were among the first northeastern peoples to adopt cultivation. As they shifted from primary reliance on fishing and hunting to maize farming, they apparently relocated their villages from river floodplains to hilltops. There Iroquois women produced crops of corn, beans, squash, and sunflowers sufficient to support fifty longhouses, each occupied by a large matrilineal, extended family. Some of those houses were truly long; archaeologists have excavated the foundations of 400-foot-long dwellings that may have housed dozens of families. Typically, these villages were surrounded by substantial wooden walls, clear evidence of intergroup conflict and warfare.

Population growth and the resulting intensification of farming in Iroquois country stimulated the development of chiefdoms there as elsewhere. By the fifteenth century several centers of population, each in a separate river system, had coalesced from east to west across upstate New York. These were the five Iroquois chiefdoms or "nations": the Mohawks, Oneidas, Onondagas, Cayugas, and Senecas. Iroquois oral histories collected during the nineteenth century recall this as a period of persistent violence, possibly the consequence of conflicts over territory.

Historians believe that the Iroquois founded a confederacy to control this violence. The confederacy outlawed warfare among the member nations and established regulated forms of gift exchange and payment to replace revenge. According to Iroquois oral history, Chief Deganawida—known as the lawgiver—founded the confederacy. It is said that he "blocked out the sun" as a demonstration of his powers; it may be that these events took place during the full solar eclipse that was visible in the Northeast in 1451. Deganawida's message was proclaimed by his supporter, Hiawatha, a great orator, who convinced all the five Iroquois nations to join. As a model, the confederacy used the powerful metaphor of the longhouse; each nation, it was said, occupied

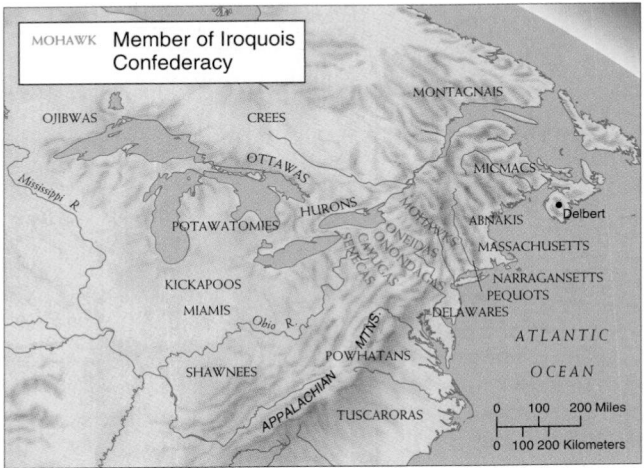

Northeastern Indian Groups on the Eve of Colonization *The Indians of the Northeast were mostly village peoples. In the fifteenth century five Iroquois groups— the Mohawks, Oneidas, Onondagas, Cayugas, and Senecas— joined together to form the Iroquois Five Nation Confederacy.*

a separate hearth but acknowledged descent from a common mother. As in the longhouse, women played important roles in choosing the male leaders who would represent their lineages and chiefdom on the Iroquois council. The confederacy suppressed violence among its members but did not hesitate to encourage war against outside groups such as the neighboring Hurons or the Eries, who constructed defensive confederacies of their own at about the same time. The Iroquois Confederacy would become one of the most powerful contenders in the struggles among competing Indian and European forces during the colonial period.

The Iroquois spoke Iroquoian. The other major language group of the Northeast was Algonquian, whose speakers belonged to at least fifty distinct cultures. In contrast to the Iroquois, most Algonquian peoples were patrilineal. In general, they lived in less extensive dwellings and in smaller villages than the Iroquois, often without palisade fortifications. The Algonquian peoples north of the Great Lakes and in northern New England were hunters and foragers, organized into bands with loose ethnic affiliations. Several of these peoples, including the Micmacs, Crees, Montagnais, and Ojibwas (also known as Chippewas), were the first to become enmeshed in the early fur trade with European newcomers. Among the Algonquians of the Atlantic coast from present-day Massachusetts south to Virginia, as well as among those in the Ohio Valley, farming led to the development of settlements as densely populated as those of the Iroquois, although the abundance of coastal and riverine resources made

CHRONOLOGY

30,000–15,000 B.C.E.	First humans in the Americas	250 B.C.E.	Beginning of Mogollon culture in the Southwest
13,000 B.C.E.	Global warming trend begins	200 B.C.E.–C.E. 400	Hopewell culture flourishes
10,000 B.C.E.	Clovis technology	650	Bow and arrow, flint hoes, and Northern Flint corn in the Northeast
9000 B.C.E.	Extinction of big-game animals		
8000 B.C.E.	Beginning of the Archaic period	775–1150	Hohokam site of Snaketown reaches its greatest extent
7000 B.C.E.	First cultivation of plants in the Mexican highlands	1000	Tobacco in use throughout North America
5000 B.C.E.	Athapascan migrations to America begin	1150	Founding of Hopi village of Oraibi, oldest continuously occupied town in the United States
4000 B.C.E.	First settled communities along the Pacific coast		
3000 B.C.E.	Inupiat and Aleut migrations begin	1200	High point of Mississippian and Anasazi cultures
1500–1000 B.C.E.	Maize and other Mexican crops introduced into the Southwest	1276	Severe drought begins in the Southwest
1000 B.C.E.	Beginning of Adena culture	1300	Arrival of Athapascans in the Southwest
	First urban communities in Mexico	1451	Founding of Iroquois Confederacy

the bow and arrow and the fishing spear as important to these people as the hoe.

Algonquian communities, although relatively autonomous from one another, also began to form confederacies during the fifteenth and sixteenth centuries. Among these groupings were those of the Massachusetts, Narragansets, and Pequots of New England, the Delawares and the peoples of Powhatan's confederacy on the mid-Atlantic coast, and the Shawnees, Miamis, Kickapoos, and Potawatomis of the Ohio Valley.

CONCLUSION

Over the thousands of years that elapsed between the settlement of the North American continent and the invasion of Europeans at the end of the fifteenth century, Indian peoples developed hundreds of distinctive cultures that were fine-tuned to the geographic and climatological possibilities and limitations of their homelands. In the northern forests they hunted game and perfected the art of processing furs and hides. Along the coasts and rivers they harvested the abundant runs of fish and learned to navigate the waters with sleek and graceful boats. In the arid Southwest they mastered irrigation farming and made the deserts bloom, while in the humid Southeast they mastered the large-scale production of crops that could sustain large cities with sophisticated political systems. North America was not a "virgin" continent, as so many of the Europeans believed. Indians had transformed the natural world, making it over into a human landscape.

"Columbus did not discover a new world," writes the historian J. H. Perry. "He established contact between two worlds, both already old." North America had a rich history, one that Europeans did not understand and later generations of Americans have too frequently ignored. The European colonists who came to settle encountered thousands of Indian communities with deep roots and vibrant traditions. In the confrontation that followed, Indian communities viewed the colonists as invaders and called upon their traditions and their gods to help them defend their homelands.

REVIEW QUESTIONS

1. List the evidence for the hypothesis that the Americas were settled by migrants from Asia.
2. Discuss the impact of environmental change and human hunting on the big-game populations of North America.
3. Review the principal regions of the North American continent and the human adaptations that made social life possible in each of them.
4. Define the concept of "forest efficiency." How does it help to illuminate the major development of the Archaic period?
5. Why did the development of farming lead to increasing social complexity? Discuss the reasons why organized political activity began in farming societies.
6. What were the Hunting and Agrarian Traditions? In what ways did the religious beliefs of Indian peoples reflect their environmental adaptations?
7. What factors led to the organization of the Iroquois Confederacy?

RECOMMENDED READING

Tom D. Dillehay and David J. Miltzer, eds., *The First Americans: Search and Research* (1991). A summary of the most recent archaeological findings, suggesting a much earlier migration to the Americas. For the newest discoveries, see recent issues of *National Geographic* and *Scientific American.*

Thomas E. Emerson, *Cahokia and the Archaeology of Power* (1997). The fascinating story of North America's first metropolis.

Brian M. Fagan, *The Great Journey: The Peopling of Ancient America* (1987). An anthropologist's account of the Asian migration to the Americas.

Stuart J. Fiedel, *Prehistory of the Americas* (1987). The best introduction for the nonspecialist, covering the first migrations, the development of technologies, and the spread of farming.

Alvin M. Josephy Jr., ed., *America in 1492* (1992). Important essays by the leading scholars of the North American Indian experience. Includes beautiful illustrations and maps as well as an excellent bibliography.

Alvin M. Josephy Jr., *500 Nations: An Illustrated History of North American Indians* (1995). A magnificent volume that includes historic illustrations as well as fascinating computer re-creations of the pre-European human landscape of America.

Alice B. Kehoe, *North American Indians: A Comprehensive Account* (1992). The best general anthropological survey of the history and culture of the Indians of North America. Organized by culture areas, the new edition covers all the peoples of the continent and includes the most recent scholarship.

Robert Silverberg, *Mound Builders of Ancient America: The Archaeology of a Myth* (1968). A brilliant history of opinion and theory about the mound builders, combined with a review of the best archaeological evidence then available.

William C. Sturtevant, general editor, *Handbook of North American Indians,* 20 vols. proposed (1978–). The most comprehensive collection of the best current scholarship. The completed series will include a volume for each of the culture regions of North America; volumes on origins, Indian-white relations, languages, and art; a biographical dictionary; and a general index.

Russell Thornton, *American Indian Holocaust and Survival: A Population History since 1492* (1987). The best introduction to the historical demography of North America. In a field of great controversy, it provides a judicious review of all the evidence.

ADDITIONAL BIBLIOGRAPHY

Settling the Continent

Larry D. Agenbroad, et al., eds., *Megafauna and Man* (1990)

John Bierhorst, ed., *The Red Swan: Myths and Tales of the American Indians* (1976)

Warwick M. Bray, et al., *The New World: The Making of the Past* (1977)

Mark Nathan Cohen, *The Food Crisis in Prehistory: Overpopulation and the Origins of Agriculture* (1977)

E. James Dixon, *Quest for the Origins of the First Americans* (1993)

Henry F. Dobyns, *Native American Historical Demography: A Critical Bibliography* (1976)

Richard Erdoes and Alfonso Ortiz, eds., *American Indian Myths and Legends* (1984)

Jonathon E. Ericson, et al., eds., *Peopling of the New World* (1982)

Brian M. Fagan, *Ancient North America: The Archaeology of a Continent,* Second Edition (1995)

Jeffrey Goodman, *American Genesis: The American Indian and the Origins of Modern Man* (1981)

Ted Hirschfield, *Middle Mississippians: Encounters with the Prehistoric Amerindians* (1996).

Lee Eldridge Huddleston, *Origins of the American Indians: European Concepts, 1492–1729* (1967)

Jesse D. Jennings, ed., *Ancient North Americans* (1983)

George Kubler, *Esthetic Recognition of Ancient Amerindian Art* (1991)

William S. Laughlin and Albert B. Harper, eds., *The First Americans: Origins, Affinities, and Adaptations* (1979)

James L. Phillips and James A. Brown, eds., *Archaic Hunters and Gatherers in the American Midwest* (1983)

Hanns J. Prem, *The Ancient Americas: A Brief History and Guide to Research* (1997).

Heather Anne Pringle, *In Search of Ancient North America: An Archaeological Journey to Forgotten Cultures* (1996).

Paul Shao, *The Origin of Ancient American Cultures* (1983)

Richard Shutler Jr., ed., *Early Man in the New World* (1983)

Richard F. Townsend, ed., *The Ancient Americas: Art from Sacred Landscapes* (1992)

Waldo R. Wedel, *Prehistoric Man on the Great Plains* (1961)

Gordon R. Willey, *An Introduction to American Archaeology* (1966)

The Beginning of Regional Cultures

Michael A. Adler, ed., *The Prehistoric Pueblo World, A.D. 1150–1350* (1996).

Frances R. Berdan, *The Aztecs of Central Mexico* (1982)

David S. Brose, et al., *Ancient Art of the American Woodland Indians* (1985)

David S. Brose and N'omi Greber, eds., *Hopewell Archaeology* (1979)

Michael D. Coe, *Mexico* (1967)

Linda S. Cordell, *Prehistory of the Southwest* (1984)

Munro Edmondson, ed., *Sixteenth-Century Mexico: The Works of Sahagun* (1974)

Richard I. Ford, ed., *Prehistoric Food Production in North America* (1985)

Melvin L. Fowler, *Perspectives in Cahokia Archeology* (1975)

Emil W. Haury, *The Hohokam* (1976)

William F. Keegan, ed., *Emergent Horticultural Economies of the Eastern Woodlands* (1987)

A. L. Kroeber, *Cultural and Natural Areas of Native North America* (1939)

Barker H. Morrow and V. B. Price, eds., *Anasazi Architecture and American Design* (1997)

Timothy R. Pauketat and Thomas E. Emerson, eds., *Cahokia: Domination and Ideology in the Mississippian World* (1997)

W. H. Wills, *Early Prehistoric Agriculture* (1988)

Eric Wolf, *Sons of the Shaking Earth* (1959)

The Eve of Colonization

James Axtell, ed., *The Indian Peoples of Eastern America: A Documentary History of the Sexes* (1981)

Elizabeth M. Brunfiel and John W. Fox, *Factional Competition and Political Development in the New World* (1993)

Lyle Campbell and Marianne Mithun, eds., *The Languages of Native America* (1979)

Olive P. Dickason, *Canada's First Nations: A History of Founding Peoples* (1992)

Edward P. Dozier, *The Pueblo Indians of North America* (1970)

Harold E. Driver, *Indians of North America* (1961)

James A. Ford, *A Comparison of Formative Cultures in the Americas* (1969)

Charles Hudson, *The Southeastern Indians* (1976)

Mallory McCane O'Connor, *Lost Cities of the Ancient Southeast* (1995)

Alfonso Ortiz, ed., *New Perspectives on the Pueblos* (1972)

Howard S. Russell, *Indian New England before the Mayflower* (1980)

Bruce D. Smith, *The Mississippian Emergence* (1990)

Frank G. Speck, *Penobscot Man* (1940)

Robert F. Spencer and Jesse D. Jennings, et al., *The Native Americans: Ethnology and Backgrounds of the North American Indians* (1977)

John R. Swanton, *The Indians of the Southeastern United States* (1946)

Bruce Trigger, *The Children of Aaeaentsic: A History of the Huron People to 1660* (1976)

Wilcomb E. Washburn, *The Indian in America* (1975)

J. Leitch Wright Jr., *The Only Land They Knew* (1981)

CHAPTER TWO

WHEN WORLDS COLLIDE

1492–1590

The French, under the command of Jean Ribault, discover the River of May (St. Johns River) in Florida on 1 May 1562. Colored engraving, 1591, by Theodor de Bry after a now lost drawing by Jacques Le Moyne de Morgues; the Granger Collection.

F. Maij

2

AMERICAN COMMUNITIES
The English and the Algonquians at Roanoke

It was late August 1590 when English ships sailed through Hatteras Inlet into Pamlico Sound, off the coast of present-day North Carolina, and made their way north through rough seas to Roanoke Island, where Governor John White had left the first English community in North America three years before. Anxiously, White went ashore in search of the sixty-five single men and twenty families including that of his own daughter, son-in-law, and granddaughter Virginia Dare, the first English baby born in America. Finding the houses "taken down" and possessions "spoiled and scattered about," White suddenly noticed some writing on a tree trunk: "in fair capital letters was graven CROATOAN." Because this was the name of a friendly Indian village fifty miles south and because White found no sign of a cross, which he had instructed the colonists to leave if they were in trouble, he felt sure that his people awaited him at Croatoan, and he returned to his ship, anxious to speed to their rescue.

The Roanoke settlement had been sponsored by Walter Raleigh, a wealthy adventurer who sought profit and prestige by organizing an English colony in the New World. When his men returned from a reconnoitering expedition to the area in 1584, they reported that the coastal region was densely populated by a "very handsome and goodly people." These Indians, the most southerly of the Algonquian coastal peoples, enjoyed a prosperous livelihood farming, fishing, and hunting from their small villages of one or two dozen communal houses. At an island the Indians called Roanoke, the English had been "entertained with all love and kindness" by a chief named Wingina. The leader of several surrounding villages, Wingina welcomed the English as potential allies in his struggle to extend his authority over still others. So when Raleigh's adventurers asked the chief's permission to establish a settlement on the island, he readily granted it, even sending two of his men back to England to assist in preparations for the enterprise. Manteo and Wanchese, the Indian emissaries, worked with Thomas Harriot, an Oxford scholar, and John White, a trained artist. The four men learned one another's language, and there seems to have been a good deal of mutual respect among them.

But when an all-male force of Englishmen returned the subsequent year, 1585, to establish the colony of Virginia (christened in honor of England's virgin queen, Elizabeth I), the two Indian ambassadors offered Wingina conflicting reports. Although Manteo, from the village of Croatoan, argued that the English technology and weaponry would make these men powerful allies, Wanchese described the disturbing inequalities of English society and warned of potential brutality. Wanchese was right to suspect English intentions, for Raleigh's plans were based not on respect for the Indians but on the expectation of exploiting them. He had directed the mission's commander to "proceed with extremity" should the Indians prove difficult and "bring them all in subjection to civility," meaning that they should be made serfs to English colonial masters. Raleigh anticipated that his colony would return profits through a lucrative trade in furs, or a flourishing plantation agriculture, or, best of all, mines of gold or silver. In any case, the Indians would supply the labor.

A colony like this—some 100 soldiers and adventurers with plunder foremost in their minds—was incapable of supporting itself. After building a rough fort on the island, the English went to Wingina for supplies of food. With his harvest in the storage pits, with fish running in the streams and game in the woods, Wingina did the hospitable thing. It was, after all, the duty of a chief to distribute presents and thus to create obligations on the part of recipients. But as fall turned to winter and the stores declined, the constant English demands began to tax the Indians' resources. Rather than hunt or fish, the colonists were out exploring for precious metals. They attacked several outlying villages, burning Indian homes and cornfields and kidnapping Indian women. By spring—traditionally the "starving season" for the Indians, before the crops were up or the game fat—Wingina and his people had had enough. But before the Indians could act, the English caught wind of the rising hostility, and in May 1586 they surprised the Roanoke villagers, killing several of the leading men and beheading Wingina. With the plan of using Indian labor now clearly impossible, the colonists returned to England.

John White and Thomas Harriot, who had spent their time exploring the physical and human world of the coast and recording their findings in notes and sketches, were appalled by this turn of events. Back in England Harriot insisted to Raleigh that the attack on the villagers came "upon causes that on our part might easily enough have been borne" and argued that "through discreet dealing" the Indians might "honor, obey, fear and love us." White proposed a new plan for a colony of real settlers, a community of English families who might live in harmony with the Indians. Harriot and White clearly thought English civilization was superior to the civilization of the Indians, but their vision of colonization was considerably different from that of the plunderers.

In 1587 Raleigh arranged for White to return to America as governor of a new family colony. But despite good intentions, the colonists could not overcome the legacy of

violence and hatred left by the former expedition. Within a month one of White's colonists had been shot full of arrows by attackers under the leadership of Wanchese, who after Wingina's death became the most militant opponent of the English among the Roanoke Indians. White retaliated by attacking Wanchese's village, but the Indians fled into the forest with few casualties. Knowing that their entire mission hung in the balance but lacking a vessel large enough to carry them all back to England, the colonists begged White to return home in their only seaworthy ship to press Raleigh for support. Reluctantly, White set sail but arrived in England to find war threatening between England and Spain. Three anxious years elapsed before White was able to return to Roanoke, only to find the settlement destroyed and the colonists gone.

As White and his crew set their sights for Croatoan that August morning in 1590, a great storm blew up. "We drove fast into the shore," White wrote, and all hands feared imminent shipwreck. Several times they dropped anchor, but each time the cable broke. Finally, White and the ship's captain agreed that they would have to leave the sound for deeper waters. It proved to be White's last glimpse of America. Tossed home to England on a stormy sea, he never returned. The English settlers of Roanoke became known as the Lost Colony, their disappearance and ultimate fate one of the enduring mysteries of colonial history.

The Roanoke experience is a reminder of the underlying assumptions of New World colonization. "The English would act just as the Spanish had done in creating their empire," writes the historian and geographer Carl Sauer; they had "naked imperial objectives." It also suggests the wasted opportunity of the Indians' initial welcome. But in an unexpected way, the Roanoke story also emphasizes the importance of community. Many historians believe that the lost colonists lived out the rest of their lives in an Algonquian village. Many years later an English settler reported that a group of coastal North Carolina Indians had told him that "several of their Ancestors were white People," that "the English were forced to cohabit with them for Relief and Conversation, and that in the process of Time, they conformed themselves to the Manners of their Indian Relations." Thus it may be that Virginia Dare and the other children married into Indian families, creating the first mixed community of English and Indians in North America.

Roanoke

KEY TOPICS

- The European background of American colonization

- Creation of the Spanish New World empire and its first extensions to North America

- The large-scale intercontinental exchange of peoples, crops, animals, and diseases

- The French role in the beginnings of the North American fur trade

- England's first overseas colonies in Ireland and America

THE EXPANSION OF EUROPE

There may have been numerous unrecorded contacts between the peoples of America and the Old World before the fifteenth century. Archaeological excavations at L'Anse aux Meadows on the fogbound Newfoundland coast provide evidence for a tenth- or eleventh-century landing in North America by the Norse people from Scandinavian countries. But earthshaking consequences were triggered by the contact with the Americas established in 1492 by Christopher Columbus. Within a generation of Columbus's first voyage, intercontinental exchanges of peoples, crops, animals, and germs had reshaped the Atlantic world. To appreciate these remarkable changes it is important to understand how Europe was transformed during the several centuries that preceded the voyage of Columbus.

European Communities

Western Europe was an agricultural society, the majority of its people peasant farmers. Farming and livestock raising had been practiced in Europe for thousands of years, but great advances in the technology of farming took place during the late Middle Ages. Water mills, iron plows, improved devices for harnessing ox and horse power, and systems of crop rotation greatly increased productivity. Over several centuries farmers more than doubled the quantity of European land in cultivation. The increased supply of food helped the population of western Europe nearly triple between the eleventh and fourteenth centuries.

Rural Europeans lived in family households clustered in farming villages. Men performed the basic field work; women were responsible for child care, livestock, and food preparation. In the European pattern, a daughter usually left the home and village of her family to take up residence among her husband's people. A woman's family gave her a dowry, or a gift of money at the time of marriage, but in general women were excluded from inheritance. Divorce was almost unknown.

This was a world of social contrasts. Europe was dominated by a social system historians have called "feudalism." The land was divided into hundreds of small territories, each ruled by a family of lords monopolizing wealth and power. From the peasants of their districts the noble lords commanded labor service and tribute in the form of crops. Thus the nobility was the main beneficiary of medieval economic expansion, accumulating great estates and building imposing castles. A relatively small class of freehold farmers prospered as well, but the majority of peasants experienced little improvement in their standard of living.

The majority of Europeans were Christians, united under the authority of the Roman Catholic Church, whose complex organization spanned thousands of local communities with a hierarchy that extended from parish priests all the way to the pope in Rome. At the core of Christian belief was a set of communal values: love of God the father, loving behavior toward other people, and the fellowship of all believers. Nevertheless, the Catholic Church itself was one of the most powerful landowners in Europe, devoting a large portion of its considerable resources to awe-inspiring display rather than the amelioration of poverty and suffering. Counseling the poor and downtrodden to place their hopes in heavenly rewards, the Church provided legitimization for the power relationships of Europe.

Europe was also home to numerous communities of Jews, a people who dispersed from their homeland in Palestine after a series of unsuccessful revolts against Roman rule in the first century C.E. Both church and civic authorities subjected the Jews to discriminatory treatment. Restricted to ghettos and forbidden from owing land, many Jews turned adversity to advantage, becoming merchants who specialized in long-distance trade. But Jewish success only seemed to stimulate Christian hostility, culminating in a series of expulsions in the thirteenth and fourteenth

A French peasant labors in the field before a spectacular castle in a page taken from the illuminated manuscript Tres Riches Heures, *made in the fifteenth century for the duc de Berry. In 1580 the essayist Montaigne talked with several American Indians at the French court who "noticed among us some men gorged to the full with things of every sort while their other halves were beggars at their doors, emaciated with hunger and poverty" and "found it strange that these poverty-stricken halves should suffer such injustice, and that they did not take the others by the throat or set fire to their houses."*

centuries: the Jews were forced out of England in 1290, France in 1394, and Spain in 1492. Religious tolerance was unknown in early modern Europe.

For the great majority of Europeans, those were the bad old days. Most rural people survived on bread and porridge, supplemented with seasonal vegetables and an occasional piece of meat or fish. Infectious diseases abounded; perhaps a third of all children died before their fifth birthday, and only half the population reached adulthood. Famines periodically ravaged the countryside. In the fourteenth century a series of crop failures resulted in widespread starvation and death. Malnutrition paved the way for disease. Between 1347 and 1353 the widespread epidemic of bubonic plague known as the Black Death swept in from Asia and wiped out a third of Europe's population. In many places Jews were accused of spreading the plague by poisoning wells, and there were violent attacks on the ghettos.

By 1500, however, Europe's agricultural economy, strengthened by the technological breakthroughs of the Middle Ages, had recovered and its population had nearly returned to its former peak of about 30 million. Europe's social structure was hierarchical and authoritarian, but its agricultural system had the technological capacity for far greater growth than the farming economy of the Americas.

The Merchant Class and the Renaissance

The economic growth of the late Middle Ages was accompanied by the expansion of commerce, especially trade in basic goods such as minerals, salt, timber, fish, cereals, wool, and wine. Commercial expansion stimulated the growth of markets and towns: the heart of this dynamic European commercialism lay in the city-states of Italy.

During the late Middle Ages, the cities of Venice, Genoa, and Pisa launched armed, commercial fleets that seized control of Mediterranean trade. The merchants of these cities became the principal outfitters of the Crusades, a series of great military expeditions promoted by the Catholic Church to recover Palestine from the Muslims. When the Crusaders conquered the Holy Land at the end of the eleventh century they delivered the silk and spice trades of Asia into the hands of the Italian merchants. Tropical spices—cloves, cinnamon, nutmeg, and pepper—were in great demand, for they made the European diet far less monotonous for the lords who could afford them. Asian civilization also supplied a number of technical innovations that further propelled European economic growth. From China alone came the compass, gunpowder, and the art of printing with movable type. These were, according to the seventeenth-century English philosopher Francis Bacon, "the three greatest inventions known to man."

Contact with Muslim civilization provided Western scholars with access to important ancient Greek and Roman texts that had been lost to them during the Middle Ages but that had been preserved in the great Muslim libraries. The revived interest in classical antiquity that resulted triggered during the fourteenth and fifteenth centuries a period of intellectual and artistic flowering known as the Renaissance. The revolution in learning made possible by the printing press, the beginning of regular postal service,

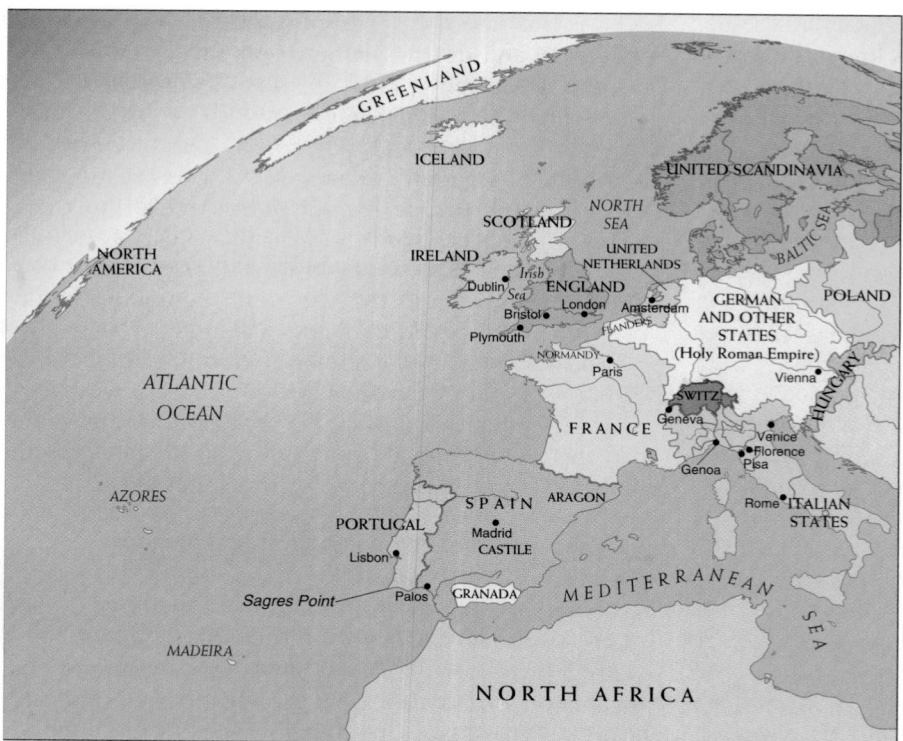

Western Europe in the Fifteenth Century *By the middle of the century, the monarchs of western Europe had unified their realms and begun to build royal bureaucracies and standing armies and navies. These states, all with extensive Atlantic coastlines, sponsored the voyages that inaugurated the era of European colonization.*

and the growth of universities helped spread the Renaissance throughout the elite circles of Europe.

The Renaissance celebrated human possibility. "The nature of all other beings is limited," the Italian intellectual Pico della Mirandola wrote in 1486; "but you, constrained by no limits, in accordance with your own free will, shall ordain for yourself the limits of your nature." This human-centered perspective was evident in architecture. The Gothic style of medieval cathedrals, whose soaring forms were intended to take human thoughts heavenward, gave way to styles borrowed from ancient Greece and Rome, which were thought to encourage rational reflection. In painting and sculpture there was a new focus on the human body. Artists modeled muscles with light and shadow to produce heroic images of men and women. These new artistic trends were aspects of what became known as *humanism*, a revolt against religious authority in which human life on earth took precedence over the afterlife of the soul. This outlook was a critical component of the inquisitive and acquisitive spirit that motivated the exploration of the Americas.

The New Monarchies

The Renaissance flowered amid the ruins that had been wrought by the plague. Famine and disease led to violence, as groups fought for shares of a shrinking economy. In Flanders—a cultural and linguistic region now spread across portions of France, Belgium, and the Netherlands—during the 1320s, peasants rose against both the noble lords and the Church, beginning a series of rebellions that culminated in the great English Peasants' Revolt of 1381. "We are made men in the likeness of Christ," one rebel cried out, "but you treat us like savage beasts!" Meanwhile civil and international warfare among the nobility greatly reduced the power of the landed classes and the Catholic Church was seriously weakened by an internal struggle between French and Italian factions.

During this period of social and political chaos, the monarchs of western Europe began to replace the lords as the new centers of power, building their legitimacy by promising internal order as they unified their realms. They built royal bureaucracies and standing armies and navies. In many cases, these new monarchs found support among the increasingly wealthy merchants, who in return sought lucrative royal contracts and trading monopolies. This alliance between commerce and political power was another of the important developments that prepared the way for European expansion.

Portuguese Explorations

Portugal, a narrow land along the western coast of the Iberian Peninsula with a long tradition of seafaring, became the first of these new kingdoms to explore distant lands. Lisbon, the principal port on the sea route between the Mediterranean and northwestern Europe, was a bustling, cosmopolitan city with large enclaves of Italian merchants. By 1385 local merchants had grown powerful enough to place their own favorite, João I, on the throne, and he laid ambitious plans to establish a Portuguese trading empire.

A central figure in this development was the son of the king, Prince Henry, known to later generations as "the Navigator." In the spirit of Renaissance learning, Henry established an institute of eminent geographers, instrument makers, shipbuilders, and seamen on Sagres Point, the southwestern tip of Portugal. By the mid-fifteenth century, principally as a result of their efforts, all educated Europeans knew the world was "round." (The idea that Europeans believed the world to be flat was invented in the nineteenth century.) The men of Sagres studied the seafaring techniques of Asia and the Muslim world. Incorporating these with European designs, they developed a new ship called the caravel, a faster, more maneuverable, and more seaworthy vessel than any previously known in Europe.

Using this new ship, the Portuguese plied the Atlantic coast of northwestern Africa, where gold mines and a long-established slave trade offered lucrative trading. By the time of Prince Henry's death in 1460, they had colonized the Atlantic islands of the Azores and the Madeiras and had founded bases along the West African Gold Coast. In 1488 the Portuguese captain Bartolomeu Días rounded the southern tip of Africa, known as the Cape of Good Hope, and ten years later Vasco da Gama, with the aid of Arab pilots, followed the same route to reach India. The Portuguese eventually erected strategic trading posts along the coasts of Africa, India, and China. Marrying native women and fitting into indigenous communities rather than trying to dominate them as the Roanoke colonists later would, Portuguese traders created the first and longest-lasting outposts of European world colonization, eventually gaining control of much of the Asian spice trade. Most important for the history of the Americas, however, was their establishment of the slave trade that spanned the Atlantic. (For a full discussion of slavery, see Chapter 4.)

Columbus Reaches the Americas

In 1476, Christopher Columbus, a young Genoan sailor, was shipwrecked off Sagres Point in Portugal. Making his way to Lisbon, he joined his brother, a chart maker in the Italian community there. Over the next ten years Columbus worked as a seafaring merchant seaman, visiting ports from Iceland in the North Atlantic to the Gold Coast in the south. He married and settled on the Portuguese island colony of Madeira in the Atlantic, and it was there that he developed the idea of opening a new route to Asia by sailing west across the

ocean. Such a venture would require royal backing, but when he approached the various monarchs of Europe with his idea, their advisers laughed at his geographic ignorance, pointing out that his calculation of the distance to Asia was much too short. They were right, Columbus was wrong, but it turned out to be an error of monumental good fortune.

Columbus finally sold his idea to the monarchs of Castile and Aragon, Isabella and Ferdinand. This royal couple, who through marriage had joined their kingdoms to form the state of Spain, had just conquered the southern Iberian province of Granada, formerly held by the Moors of North Africa. Their victory completed the *Reconquista* (Reconquest), the centuries-long struggle between Catholics and Muslims for the control of Iberia. Through these many generations of warfare, the Spanish had developed a military tradition that thrived on conquest and plunder. Military service was a popular means by which ordinary men could enrich themselves and rise into the ranks of the noble class. The Catholic monarchs of Spain were eager for new lands to conquer, and observing the successful Portuguese push to the south, they also became interested in opening lucrative trade routes of their own with Asia. Columbus's name for his under-

This ship, thought to be similar to Columbus's Niña, is a caravel, a type of vessel developed by the naval experts at Henry the Navigator's institute at Sagres Point, in Portugal. To the traditional square-rigged Mediterranean ship, they added the "lateen" sail of the Arabs, which permitted much greater maneuverability. Other Asian improvements, such as the stern-post rudder and multiple masting, allowed caravels to travel farther and faster than any earlier ships, and made possible the invasion of America.

taking, "the Enterprise of the Indies," suggested its commercial motive, but his expedition symbolized hopes of both trade and conquest. It did not envision the establishment of a colonial community. Like the adventurers who later peopled the first English colony of Roanoke, the Spanish had material gain in mind.

Columbus's ships left the port of Palos, Spain, in August 1492, pushed west across the Atlantic by the prevailing trade winds. By October flocks of birds and bits of driftwood announced the ships' approach to land, which turned out to be a small, flat island somewhere in the Bahamas. Although scholars disagree on the precise location, many believe it to be a spot now known as Samana Cay. Columbus, however, believed he was somewhere near the Asian mainland. He explored the northern island coasts of Cuba and Hispaniola (now Haiti and the Dominican Republic) before heading home, fortuitously catching the westerly winds that blow from the American coast toward Europe north of the tropics. One of Columbus's most important contributions was the discovery of the clockwise circulation of the Atlantic winds and currents that ultimately carried thousands of ships back and forth between Europe and the Americas.

Leading Columbus's triumphal procession to the royal court were a number of Taino Indians, dressed in bright feathers with ornaments of gold. The natives, Columbus noted, were "of a very acute intelligence" but had "no iron or steel weapons." "Should your majesties command it," Columbus announced to Ferdinand and Isabella, "all the inhabitants could be made slaves." Columbus also reported that "there are many spices and great mines of gold and of other metals." In fact, none of the spices familiar to Europeans grew in the Caribbean, and there were only small quantities of the precious metal in the riverbeds of the islands. But the sight of the little gold ornaments worn by the Indians had infected Columbus with a bad case of gold fever. He had left a small force behind in a rough fort on what is now the isolated northern coast of Haiti with instructions to continue the search for gold—the first European foothold in the Americas.

The Spanish monarchs, enthusiastic about Columbus's report, financed a convoy of 17 ships and 1,500 men that left in late 1493 to begin the colonization of the islands Columbus described as "rich for planting and sowing, for breeding cattle of every kind, for building towns and villages." As later at Roanoke, it was expected that Indians would provide the labor for these enterprises. But on his return to Hispaniola, Columbus found his fort in ruins, his men killed by Indians who, like the Algonquians at Roanoke, lost patience with the demands and brutality of the invading Europeans. Columbus destroyed the nearby native villages, enslaving the Tainos and demanding tribute from them in gold. He took slaves back to Spain, but most soon sickened and died, and the supply of gold quickly ran out. By the time of Columbus's third voyage the Spanish monarchs

This image accompanied Columbus's account of his voyage, which was published in Latin and reissued in many other languages and editions that circulated throughout Europe before 1500. The Spanish King Ferdinand is shown directing the voyage to a tropical island, where the natives flee in terror. Columbus's impression of native Americans as a people vulnerable to conquest shows clearly in this image.

had become so dissatisfied with these results that they ordered the admiral home in leg irons.

Columbus made a fourth and final trip to the Caribbean that was characterized by the same violent slave raiding and obsessive searching for gold. He died in Spain in 1506, still convinced that he had opened the way to Asia, a belief that persisted among many Europeans well into the sixteenth century. But others had already begun to see the discoveries from a different perspective. Amerigo Vespucci of Florence, who voyaged to the Caribbean in 1499, was the first European to describe the lands as *mundus novus*, a New World. When European geographers named these continents in the first decade of the sixteenth century, they called them America, after Vespucci.

THE SPANISH IN THE AMERICAS

A century after Columbus's death, before the English had

The Invasion of America   *In the sixteenth century the Spanish first invaded the Caribbean and used it to stage their successive wars of conquest in North and South America. In the seventeenth century, the French, English, and Dutch invaded the Atlantic coast. The Russians, sailing across the northern Pacific, mounted the last of the colonial invasions in the eighteenth century.*

planted a single New World colony of their own, the Spanish had created a huge and wealthy empire in the Americas. In theory, all law and policy for the empire came from Spain; in practice, the isolation of the settlements permitted a good deal of local autonomy. The Spanish created a caste system, in which a small minority of settlers and their offspring controlled the lives and labor of millions of Indian and African workers. At the same time, theirs was a society in which colonists, Indians, and Africans mixed to form a new people.

The Invasion of America

The first stages of the Spanish invasion of America included frightful violence. Armies led by conquistadors marched across the Caribbean islands, plundering villages, slaughtering men, and capturing women. The Spanish crown created a system known as *encomienda*, in which colonial lords were given the right to the labor of a community of Indians; it was supposed to be a reciprocal relationship, with the lord protecting the Indians as well as exploiting them, but in practice it amounted to simply another

form of slavery. Rather than work, one observer noted, many Indians took poison, "and others hanged themselves." Faced with labor shortages, slavers raided what King Ferdinand labeled the "useless islands" of the Bahamas and soon had entirely depopulated them. The depletion of gold on Hispaniola led to the invasion of the islands of Puerto Rico and Jamaica in 1508, and Cuba in 1511. Meanwhile, rumors of wealthy societies farther west led to scores of probing expeditions. The Spanish invasion of Central America began in 1511, and two years later Vasco Nuñez de Balboa crossed the Isthmus of Panama to what he called the "South Sea," the Pacific Ocean. In 1517 Spaniards landed on the coast of Mexico, and within a year they had made contact with the Aztec empire.

The warlike Aztecs had migrated to the high Valley of Mexico from the harsh deserts of the American Southwest during the thirteenth century in the wake of the collapse of the Toltec Empire (see Chapter 1). They settled the marshy lake district of the valley and built the city of Tenochtitlán. By the early fifteenth century the Aztecs had come to dominate

The Cruelties used by the Spaniards on the Indians, *from a 1599 English edition of* The Destruction of the Indies *by Bartolomé de las Casas. These scenes were copied from a series of engravings produced by Theodore de Bry that accompanied an earlier edition.*

the farming communities of the highlands, in the process building a powerful state. Tribute flowed into Tenochtitlán from all over Mexico and Central America. In public rituals designed to appease their gods, Aztec priests brutally sacrificed captives atop grand pyramids. By 1519, when Hernán Cortés, a veteran of the conquest of Cuba, landed on the Mexican coast, the population of the Aztec capital numbered as much as 300,000, five times the size of the largest city in Spain.

Within two years Cortés and his army had overthrown the Aztec empire, a spectacular military accomplishment that has no parallel in the annals of conquest. The Spanish had superior arms, and they also had horses, which the Indians found terrifying, mistaking mounted men for four-legged monsters. But these were not the principal causes of the Spanish success. Cortés skillfully exploited the resentments of the many native peoples who lived under Aztec domination, forging Spanish-Indian alliances that became a model for the subsequent European colonization of the Americas. Here, as at Roanoke and dozens of other sites of European invasion, colonists found Indians eager for allies to support them in their conflicts with their neighbors. Still, the Aztecs were militarily powerful, successfully driving the Spaniards from Tenochtitlán and putting up a bitter and prolonged defense when they returned to besiege the capital. But in the meantime the Aztecs were hit by a devastating smallpox epidemic that killed thousands and undermined their ability to resist. In the aftermath of conquest, the Spanish

unmercifully plundered Aztec society, providing the Catholic monarchs with wealth beyond their wildest imagining. Later, the discovery of rich silver mines and the exploitation of Mexican labor through the encomienda system turned Spain into the mightiest state in Europe.

The Destruction of the Indies

Like the Aztecs, the other Indian peoples of the Americas resisted Spanish conquest, but most proved a poor match for mounted warriors wielding steel swords and accompanied by vicious bloodhounds. The record of the conquest, however, includes many brave Indian leaders and thousands of martyrs. The Carib people (from whose name "Caribbean" is derived) successfully defended the outermost islands until the end of the sixteenth century, and in the arid lands of northern Mexico the nomadic tribes known collectively as the Chichimecs proved equally difficult to subdue.

Among the Europeans who protested the horrors of the conquest, the most famous may have been Bartolomé de las Casas, a Spanish Catholic priest who had participated in the plunder of Cuba in 1511 but who several years later suffered a crisis of conscience and began to denounce the conquest. The Christian mission in the New World was to convert the Indians, he argued, and "the means to effect this end are not to rob, to scandalize, to capture or destroy them, or to lay waste their lands." Long before the world recognized the concept of universal human rights, Las Casas was proclaiming that "the entire human race is one," a statement that has earned him a reputation as one of the towering moral figures in the early history of the Americas. Las Casas's powerful supporters at court made repeated but unsuccessful attempts to reform the treatment of Indians.

In his brilliant history of the conquest, *The Destruction of the Indies* (1552), Las Casas blamed the Spanish for millions of deaths—in effect, for genocide. Translated into several languages and widely circulated throughout Europe, Las Casas's book was used by other European powers to condemn Spain in an effort to cover up their own dismal colonial records. Later scholars, questioning the accuracy of Las Casas's estimates of huge population losses, condemned his work as contributing to a "Black Legend" of the Spanish conquest. But many of today's historians find Las Casas's figures more believable. Demographic studies suggest that the Tainos of Hispaniola numbered in the hundreds of thousands when Columbus arrived; fifty years later they were reduced to a few hundred, and soon they disappeared from the face of the earth. Over the sixteenth century, the approximately 25 million people thought to have inhabited the highlands of Mexico were reduced to only one million.

Las Casas was incorrect, however, in attributing most of these losses to warfare. To be sure, thousands of lives were lost in battle, but these deaths were but a small proportion of the overall population decline. Thousands more starved because their economies were destroyed or their food stores taken by conquering armies. Even more important, native birth rates fell drastically after the conquest. Indian women were so "worn out with work," one Spaniard wrote, that they avoided conception, induced abortion, and even "killed their children with their own hands so that they [should] not have to endure the same hardships."

But by far the greatest loss of life resulted from the introduction of Old World diseases. The people of the Americas, separated from Asia, Africa, and Europe by the rising oceans following the Ice Age, were isolated from the virulent epidemic diseases that developed along with civilization, diseases such as smallpox, measles, pneumonia, and malaria. Pre-Columbian America was blessed with a remarkably disease-free environment, but the Indian peoples also lacked the antibodies necessary to protect them from European bacteria and viruses. A shipload of colonists carried smallpox to Hispaniola in 1516, causing an epidemic in the Caribbean that by 1520 crossed into Mexico and eventually spread along the trading network through both North and South America. This was the epidemic that provided Cortés with the critical edge in overcoming the Aztecs. Such devastating outbreaks of disease, striking for the first time against a completely unprotected population, are known as "virgin soil epidemics." After the conquest, Mexicans sang of an earlier time:

> There was then no sickness.
> They had then no aching bones.
> They had then no high fever.
> They had then no smallpox.
> They had then no burning chest.
> They had then no abdominal pains.
> They had then no consumption.
> They had then no headache.
> At that time the course of humanity was orderly.
> The foreigners made it otherwise when they arrived here.

This drawing of victims of the smallpox epidemic that struck the Aztec capital of Tenochtitlán in 1520 is taken from the Florentine Codex, *a postconquest history written and illustrated by Aztec scribes. "There came amongst us a great sickness, a general plague," reads the account, "killing vast numbers of people. It covered many all over with sores: on the face, on the head, on the chest, everywhere.... The sores were so terrible that the victims could not lie face down, nor on their backs, nor move from one side to the other. And when they tried to move even a little, they cried out in agony."*

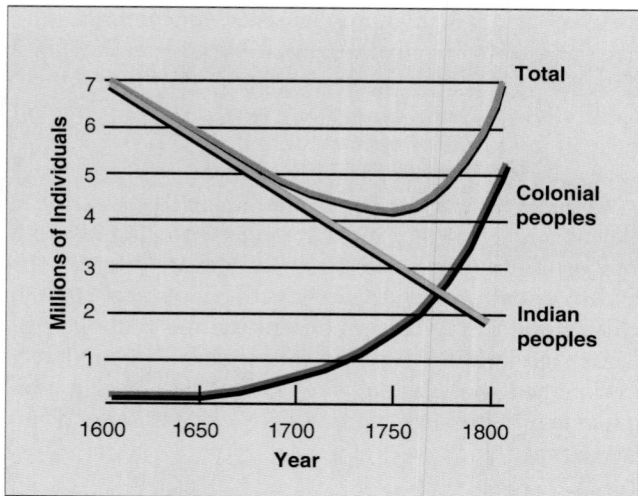

North America's Indian and Colonial Populations in the Seventeenth and Eighteenth Centuries *The primary factor in the decimation of native peoples was epidemic disease, brought to the New World from the Old. In the eighteenth century the colonial population overtook North America's Indian populations.*

Source: *Historical Statistics of the United States* (Washington, D.C.: Government Printing Office, 1976), 8, 1168; Russell Thornton, *American Indian Holocaust and Survival* (Norman: University of Oklahoma Press, 1987), 32.

Warfare, famine, lower birth rates, and epidemic disease knocked the population of Indian America into a downward spiral that did not swing upward until the twentieth century. By that time the native population had fallen by 90 percent. It was the greatest demographic disaster in world history. The outstanding difference between the European colonial experience in the Americas and elsewhere—Africa and Asia, for example—was this radical reduction in the native population.

It is possible that the New World sent one disease back across the Atlantic. On the basis of considerable evidence, archaeologists have concluded that syphilis was present in ancient America but not in the Old World before 1492. The first recorded epidemic of venereal syphilis in Europe took place in Spain in 1493, and many historians think it may have been carried home by the sailors on Columbus's ships. By 1495 the disease was spreading rapidly among Europe's armies, and by the sixteenth century it had found its way to Asia and Africa.

Intercontinental Exchange

The passage of diseases between the Old and New Worlds was just one part of the large-scale intercontinental exchange that marks the beginning of the modern era. The most obvious exchange was the vast influx into Europe of the precious metals plundered

from the Aztec and Incan empires of the New World. "The best thing in the world is gold," wrote Columbus, and Cortés remarked, "We Spaniards suffer from a disease of the heart, the specific remedy for which is gold." Most of the booty was melted down, destroying forever thousands of priceless Indian artifacts. Even more important were the silver mines the Spanish discovered and operated in Mexico and Peru. Between 1500 and 1550 the amount of silver coin circulating in Europe tripled, then tripled again before 1600. The result was runaway inflation, which stimulated commerce and raised profits but lowered the standard of living for most people. During the sixteenth century, for example, rising prices depressed the value of European wages by more than 50 percent.

But of even greater long-term importance were the New World crops brought to Europe. Maize, or corn, from Mexico—the staff of life for most North Americans—became a staple human crop in Mediterranean countries, an important feed crop for livestock elsewhere in Europe, and the primary provision for the slave ships of Africa. Over the next few centuries, potatoes from Peru provided the margin between famine and subsistence for the peasant peoples of northern Europe and Ireland. And, of course, tomatoes transformed the cuisine of Italy. These "miracle crops" provided abundant food sources that went a long way toward ending the persistent problem of famine in Europe.

Although the Spanish failed to locate valuable spices such as black pepper or cloves in the New World, new tropical crops more than compensated. Tobacco, which was first prescribed as an antidote to disease when it appeared in Europe about 1550, soon became widely used as an intoxicant. American vanilla and chocolate both became highly valued commodities, and American cotton proved superior to Asian varieties for the production of cheap textiles. These native crops, together with crops brought from the Old World to the New, like sugar, rice, and coffee, supplied the basis for important new industries and markets that altered the course of world history.

Columbus introduced domesticated animals into Hispaniola and Cuba, and this breeding stock later supplied the conquistadors of Mexico. The movement of Spanish settlement into northern Mexico was greatly aided by an advancing wave of livestock, for not only did these animals supply the colonists with animal power and meat but they disturbed native fields and forests, disrupting Indian societies and preparing the way for conquest. Horses, used by Spanish stockmen to tend their cattle, also spread northward. Eventually they reached the Great

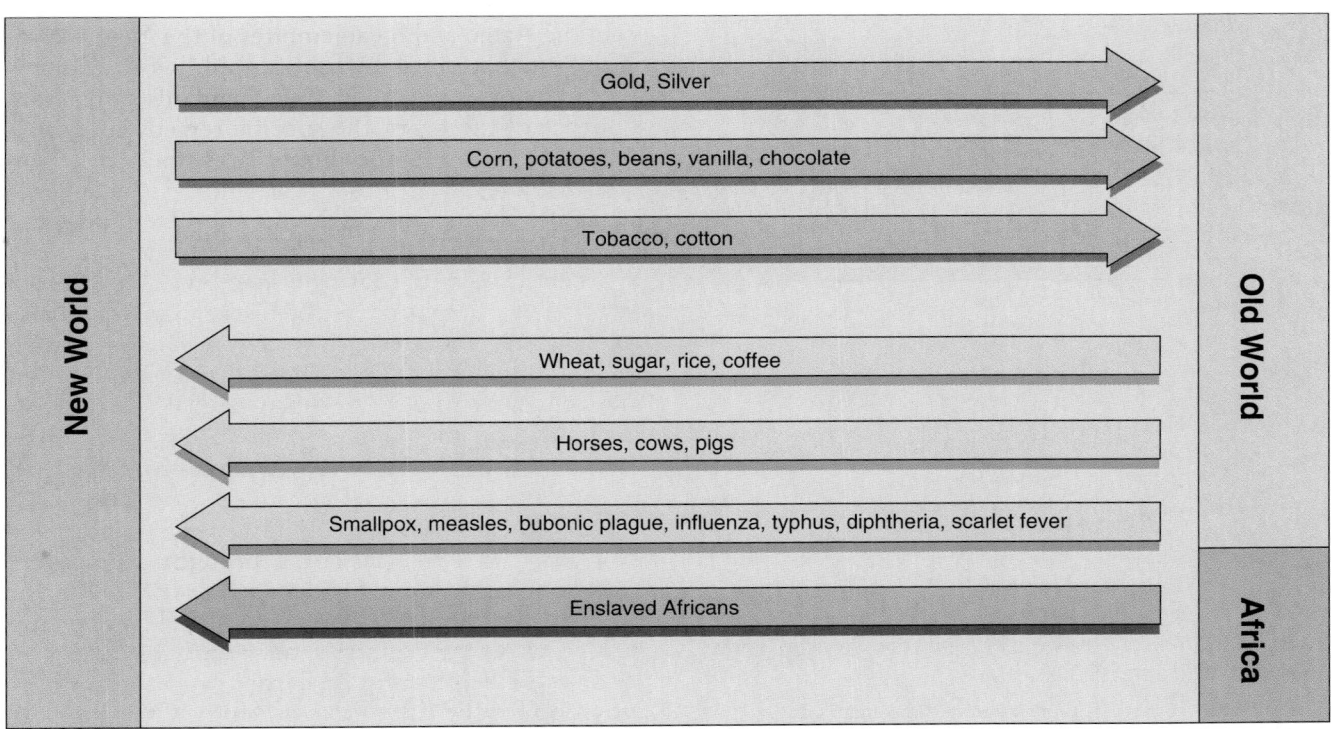

Intercontinental Exchange   *The exchange between continents of crops and animals, microbes and men, marks the beginning of the modern era of world history.*

Plains of North America, where they transformed the lives of the nomadic hunting Indians.

The First Europeans in North America

Juan Ponce de León, governor of Puerto Rico, was the first conquistador to attempt to extend the Spanish conquest to North America. In 1513 he landed on the southern Atlantic coast, which he named Florida in honor of the Easter season, in Spanish called *pascua florida*. Florida is thus the oldest European place-name in the continental United States. Warriors from some of the powerful Indian chiefdoms of the South beat back Ponce de León's attempts to take slaves and finally killed him in battle in 1521. Seven years later another Spanish attempt to colonize Florida, under the command of Pánfilo de Narváez, also ended in disaster. Most of Narváez's men were lost in a shipwreck, but a small group of them survived, living and wandering for several years among the Indian peoples of the Gulf coast and the Southwest until they were finally rescued in 1536 by Spanish slave hunters in northern Mexico. One of these castaways, Alvar Núñez Cabeza de Vaca, published an account of his adventures in which he told of a North American empire known as Cíbola, with golden cities "larger than the city of Mexico."

Cabeza de Vaca's report inspired two Spanish attempts to penetrate the mystery of North America.

Hernán de Soto, a veteran of the conquest of Peru, landed in Florida in 1539 with a Cuban army of more than 700 men and thousands of hogs and cattle. As he pushed hundreds of miles through the heavily populated South, he commandeered food and slaves from the Mississippian Indian towns in his path. De Soto failed, though, to locate another Aztec empire. In present-day Alabama, thousands of warriors of the powerful Alibamu chiefdom besieged his army, and a few months later the ancestors of the modern Chickasaws chewed the Spaniards apart. His army depleted by half, de Soto desperately drove his men westward, crossing the Mississippi and marching deep into present-day Arkansas before returning to the banks of the great river, where he died in 1542. Some 300 of de Soto's dispirited survivors eventually reached Mexico on rafts in 1543. They told of the great farming fields of the Mississippians but also emphasized the ferocity of the warriors. The native peoples of the South had successfully turned back Spanish invasion. If this were the end of the story, de Soto's expedition would be barely remembered, but his army also introduced epidemic diseases to the South that drastically undermined and depopulated the societies there. When Europeans finally returned to colonize the region in the seventeenth century, they found the descendants of the Mississippian chiefdoms living in much simpler tribal confederacies.

European Exploration, 1492–1591 By the mid-sixteenth century Europeans had
explored most of the Atlantic coast of North America and penetrated into the interior in the
disastrous expeditions of de Soto and Coronado.

The year following the beginning of the de Soto expedition, 1540, Spanish officials in Mexico launched a second attempt to find and conquer the cities of Cíbola, this one aimed at the North American Southwest. Francisco Vásquez de Coronado led 300 mounted men and infantry and 800 Indian porters north along well-marked Indian trading paths, passing through the settlements of Piman Indians near the present border of the United States and Mexico and finally reaching the Pueblo villages along the Rio Grande. The initial resistance of the Pueblo people was quickly quashed. But Coronado was deeply disappointed by these towns "of stone and mud, rudely fashioned." He led his army as far north as the Great Plains, where they observed great herds of "shaggy cows" (buffalo) and made contact with nomadic hunting peoples, but returned without gold. When Coronado and his men failed to find the "new Mexico" for which they had been looking, Spain lost all interest in the Southwest for the next fifty years.

The Spanish New World Empire

Despite these setbacks, by the late sixteenth century the Spanish had control of a powerful empire in the Americas. A century after Columbus, some 200,000 Europeans, most of them Spaniards, had settled in the Americas. Another 125,000 Africans had been forcibly resettled on the Spanish plantations of the Caribbean, as well as on the plantations of Brazil, which the Portuguese had colonized under the terms of the Treaty of Tordesillas, a 1494 agreement between Spain and Portugal setting a line of demarcation between their respective colonial domains. Most of the Spanish settlers resided in the more than 200 urban communities founded during the conquest, including cities such as Santo Domingo in Hispaniola; Havana, Cuba; Mexico City, built atop the ruins of Tenochtitlán; Quito, Peru (today in Ecuador), in the north of the conquered empire of the Incas; and Lima, Peru, near the empire's center. The few Spaniards who lived in the countryside supervised Indian or African workers in mining, ranching, or agriculture.

Because European women constituted only about 10 percent of the immigrants, from the beginning male colonists married or simply lived with African or Indian women. The result was the growth of large mixed-ancestry groups. The Spanish communities were characterized by what has been called a "frontier of inclusion," with a great deal of sexual mixing and marriage between male colonists and native women. Hundreds of thousands of Indians died, but Indian genes were passed on to generations of mestizo (European-Indian) and mulatto (European-African) peoples, who became the majority population in the mainland Spanish American empire.

Populated by Indians, Africans, Spanish colonists, and their mixed offspring, the New World colonies of Spain constituted one of the largest empires in the history of the world. In theory, the empire was a highly centralized and bureaucratic system, but in operation there was significant local autonomy. The Council of the Indies, composed of the king's principal advisers, formulated all the laws and regulations of the empire, but the Council was in Spain. In the colonies, halfway around the globe, passive resistance and sometimes outright defiance of central authority were commonplace.

FRENCH AND ENGLISH EXPLORATIONS AND ENCOUNTERS

With the Spanish empire at the height of its power in the sixteenth century, the merchants and monarchs of other important European seafaring states looked across the Atlantic for opportunities of their own. In the early sixteenth century France was first to sponsor intensive expeditions to the New World. At first the French attempted to plant settlements on the coasts of Brazil and Florida, but Spanish opposition ultimately persuaded them to concentrate on the northern regions. It was the second half of the

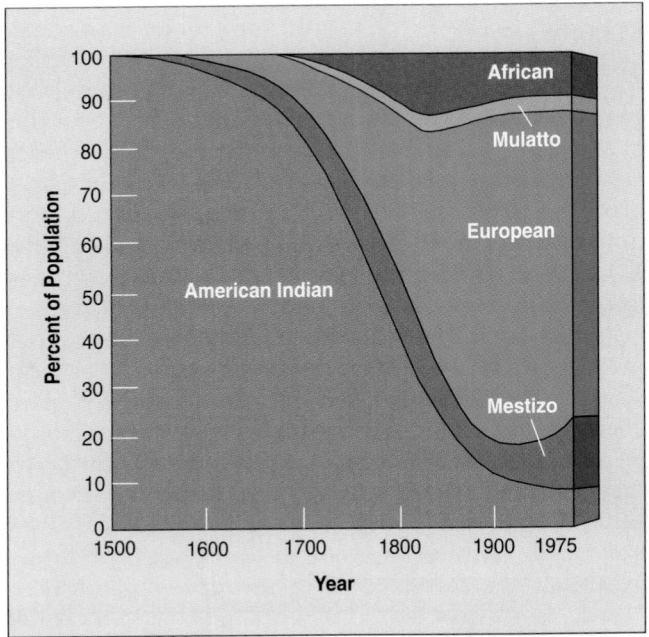

The African, Indian, and European Population of the Americas   *In the 500 years since the European invasion of the Americas, the population has included varying proportions of native, European, and African peoples, as well as large numbers of persons of mixed ancestry.*

Source: Colin McEvedy and Richard Jones, *Atlas of World Population History* (New York: Penguin, 1978), 280.

sixteenth century before England developed plans to colonize North America. With the Spanish in Florida and the French establishing close ties with coastal tribes as far south as present-day Maine, the English focused on the middle latitudes.

The Political Impact of the Reformation

The religious revolt against Catholicism known as the Reformation began in 1517 when the German priest Martin Luther publicized his differences with Rome. Luther declared that eternal salvation was a gift from God, not something earned by good works or service to the Roman Catholic Church. He also emphasized the importance of individual Bible study, underlining the impact of the revolution in printing and literacy and undercutting the authority of priests. As a result of his attacks on the Catholic hierarchy Luther was excommunicated in 1521. But his ideas reflected a growing climate of dissatisfaction throughout Europe with the power and prosperity of the Catholic Church. And when German princes who wished to strengthen their independence from Rome subscribed to Luther's views, the controversy became political, inaugurating a series of bloody religious wars that ravaged Europe for the next century.

Protestantism, as Luther's protest movement came to be called, aroused considerable enthusiasm in France. Catholic persecution of French Protestants in the 1520s, however, caused John Calvin, a prominent reformer even more radical than Luther, to flee to Switzerland. Calvin settled in Geneva, where he organized a model Christian community that by the 1530s was in control of the entire city-state. A former lawyer, Calvin was the most systematic of the early Protestant theologians. His doctrine of predestination proposed that God had chosen a small number of men and women for "election," or salvation, while condemning the vast majority to eternal damnation. Calvinists were encouraged to examine themselves closely for "signs of election," which were usually thought to be prominence and prosperity. The virtues of thrift, industry, sobriety, and personal responsibility, which Calvin argued were essential to the Christian life, likewise promoted material success. This conjunction of spiritual and secular values proved powerful in the growth of the spirit of enterprise that characterized early European capitalism.

Sixteenth-century England also became deeply involved in struggles to reform the Catholic Church. At first King Henry VIII of England (reigned 1509–47) supported the Church against the Protestants. But in England, too, there was great public resentment of the ostentatious display of the Church and the drain of tax money to Rome. When the pope refused to grant Henry an annulment of his marriage to Catherine of Aragon, daughter of Isabella and Ferdinand of Spain, who had not produced a surviving male heir, the king exploited this popular mood. Taking up the cause of reform in 1534, he declared himself head of a separate Church of England. He later confiscated monastic property—the Catholic Church owned about a quarter of the country's land—and used the revenues to begin constructing a powerful English state system, including a standing army and navy. Working through Parliament, Henry carefully enlisted the support of the merchants and landed gentry for his program, parceling out a measure of royal prosperity in the form of titles, offices, lands, and commercial favors. By the mid-sixteenth century he had forged a solid alliance with the wealthy merchant class.

England and France moved in very different directions during the Reformation. Calvin's French followers—known as the Huguenots—were concentrated among merchants and the middle class, but they also included many of the nobility. In 1560 a group of Huguenot nobles tried to seize power, and their defeat initiated nearly forty years of religious struggle, during which France became known as the enemy of the new Protestant faith that was becoming so popular in England. One event that established France's fierce opposition to Protestantism was the St. Bartholomew's Day Massacre of August 24, 1572, in which some 6,000 Huguenots in Paris and thousands more throughout the country were slain at the direction of the French crown. Although in 1589 the Huguenot Henry IV became king of France, he found it impossible to govern until he converted to Catholicism. Henry's Edict of Nantes of 1598 guaranteed freedom of worship and the civil rights of Huguenots, but Henry's conversion, in effect, made Roman Catholicism the official religion of France.

The French Colony in Florida

Efforts by Huguenot leaders to establish a refuge for French Protestants in the New World led to the establishment of a French colony in Florida. In 1562 Jean Ribault and 150 Protestants from Normandy landed on Parris Island, near present-day Beaufort, South Carolina, and began constructing a fort and crude mud huts. Ribault soon returned to France for supplies, where he was caught up in the religious wars. The French colonists nearly starved, finally resorting to cannibalism before being rescued by a passing British ship. In 1564 another French expedition established the Huguenot colony of Fort Caroline on the St. Johns River in Florida, near the present-day city of Jacksonville. When Ribault arrived the next year, he reported that the people of the nearby Timucua villages were friendly and

*This watercolor of Jacques le Moyne, painted in 1564, depicts the friendly relations between
the Timucuas of coastal Florida and the colonists of the short-lived French colony of Fort
Caroline. The Timucuas hoped that the French would help defend them against the Spanish,
who plundered the coast in pursuit of Indian slaves.*

hospitable, welcoming the French colonists into their
homes and honoring them with food and drink. It
seems possible that at Fort Caroline the Huguenots
enjoyed the kinds of relations with the Indians that
John White later hoped for at Roanoke.

The Spanish, however, saw Fort Caroline as a
threat. Uninterested in settlement, the Spanish had
established a foothold along the Atlantic coast of
Florida simply to protect their fleets riding the
offshore Gulf Stream home to Spain. Fort Caroline
was manned not only by Frenchmen but by French
Protestants—deadly enemies of the Catholic
monarchs of Spain. "We are compelled to pass in front
of their port," wrote one official of New Spain, "and
with the greatest ease they can sally out with their
armadas to seek us." In 1565 the Spanish crown sent
Don Pedro Menéndez de Avilés, captain general of
the Indies, to crush the Huguenots. He established
the Spanish fort of St. Augustine on the coast, south
of the French, then marched overland through the
swamps to surprise them with an attack from the rear.
"I put Jean Ribault and all the rest of them to the

knife," Menéndez wrote triumphantly to the king,
"judging it to be necessary to the service of the Lord
Our God and of Your Majesty." More than 500
Frenchmen lay dead on the beaches of Florida; the
French attempt to plant a colony along the South
Atlantic coast had ended in disaster. Today, St. Augus-
tine claims the distinction of being the oldest contin-
uously occupied European city in North America.

Fish and Furs

For the French overseas empire, far more significant
than these efforts at colonization was the entrance of
French fishermen into the waters of the North
Atlantic. It is possible that fishing ships from England,
France, Spain, and Portugal had discovered the great
fishing grounds off North America's northern coast
long before Columbus's voyages. In the Grand Banks,
the waters teemed with "so great multitudes of certain
big fishes," in the words of one early seaman, "that
they sometimes stayed my ships." By 1500, hundreds
of ships and thousands of sailors were regularly fishing the coastal waters of the North Atlantic, many

In his sketch of this "Capitaine" of the Illinois nation (drawn about 1700), the French artist Charles Becard de Granville carefully noted the tattooing of the warrior's face and body, his distinctive costume and feather headdress, his spear and tobacco pipe.

making landfall to take on wood and fuel and to dry their catch. Fishermen were not particularly interested in conquest, and in their contacts with Indian people they established relationships based on the exchange of goods and ideas. Thus the pattern of colonial history in the early Northeast contrasted dramatically with that in the Spanish New World empire—and with later English colonization.

The first official voyages of exploration in the North Atlantic used the talents of experienced European sailors and fishermen. With a crew from Bristol, England, the Genoan navigator John Cabot reached Cape Breton Island or Newfoundland in 1497, and in 1524 the Tuscan captain Giovanni da Verrazano sailed with a crew from France, exploring the North American coast from Cape Fear (in today's North Carolina) to the Penobscot River (in Maine). Anxious to locate a passageway to the spice trade of Asia, the French king next commissioned the experienced captain Jacques Cartier. In 1534 and 1535 Cartier reconnoitered the St. Lawrence River, which led deep into the continental interior, and established France's imperial claim to the lands of Canada.

The northern Indians found the Europeans odd—particularly their beards—but immediately appreciated the usefulness of the textiles, glass, copper, and ironware the Europeans possessed. Seeing Cartier's ship, the Micmacs waved him ashore. "The savages showed marvelous great pleasure in possessing and obtaining iron wares and other commodities," he noted in his report. For his part, Cartier was interested in the fur coats the Indians wore. Europeans, like Indians, used furs for winter clothing. But the growing population of the late Middle Ages had so depleted the wild game of Europe that the price of furs had risen beyond the reach of most people. The North American fur trade thus filled an important demand and produced high profits. Cartier attempted to found a French colony on the St. Lawrence in 1541, but the unremitting winter and the hostility of the Indians forced him to abandon the effort. For the rest of the sixteenth century relations between Europeans and Indians in the Northeast were dominated by commerce, not conquest.

By no means were Indians simply the victims of European traders. Indian traders had a sharp eye for quality, and because of the unbridled competition among the Europeans, they could demand good exchange rates. But the trade also had negative consequences for Indian people. Epidemic European diseases soon began to ravage their communities. Intense rivalry broke out between tribes over hunting territories, resulting in deadly warfare. By the 1580s, disease and violence had turned the St. Lawrence Valley into a virtual no-man's land. Moreover, as European manufactured goods, such as metal knives, kettles, and firearms, became essential to their way of life, the Indians became dependent upon European suppliers. Ultimately, the fur trade was stacked in favor of Europeans.

By the end of the sixteenth century over a thousand ships per year were trading for furs along the northern coast. The trade between Indians and Europeans of many nations grew increasingly important as the century progressed. The village of Tadoussac on the St. Lawrence, where a wide bay offered Europeans safe anchorage, became the customary place for several weeks of trading each summer, a forerunner of the western fur-trade rendezvous of the nineteenth century. Among European traders, the French were probably the most numerous, and later, in the early seventeenth century, they had to move to consolidate their hold by planting colonies along the St. Lawrence.

Social Change in Sixteenth-Century England

Henry VIII of England died in 1547. He was succeeded by his young and sickly son Edward VI, who six years later followed his father to the grave, then by his Catholic daughter Mary, who attempted to reverse her father's Reformation from the top. She added her own chapter to the century's many religious wars, martyring hundreds of English Protestants and gaining the title of "Bloody Mary." But upon Mary's death in 1558, her Protestant half-sister Elizabeth I (reigned 1558–1603) ascended to the throne. Although she outlawed Catholicism, Elizabeth sought to end the religious turmoil by tolerating a variety of views within the English church.

Criticized by radical Protestants for not going far enough and condemned by Catholics for her "pretended title to the kingdom," Elizabeth nevertheless gained popularity among the English people with her moderate approach. The Spanish monarchy, the head of the most powerful empire in the world, declared itself the defender of the Catholic faith and vowed to overthrow her. England and Spain now became the two principal rivals in the Catholic-Protestant confrontation.

In the 1570s several of Elizabeth's closest advisers began to argue that the time had come for England to enter the competition for American colonies. Their analysis linked colonization to social change at home.

Elizabeth I, Armada portrait, c. 1588 (oil on panel) by English School. Private collection/Bridgeman Art Library, London/New York

The Armada Portrait of Elizabeth I, *painted by an unknown artist in 1648. The queen places her hand on the globe, symbolizing the rising seapower of England. Through the open windows we see the battle against the Spanish Armada in 1588 and the destruction of the Spanish ships in a providential storm, interpreted by the queen as an act of divine intervention.*

Algonquian Indian village of Pomeiooc (North Carolina): watercolor, c. 1585, by John White; The Granger Collection.

In July 1585, John White sketched the Algonquian village of Pomeiooc, a palisaded enclosure with an easily guarded entrance. The eighteen longhouses would have made this a rather large community. Note the house with the pyramid-shaped roof. It is thought to have been a ceremonial or religious center.

colonies "upon the mouths of the great navigable rivers" from Florida to the St. Lawrence.

England Turns toward Colonization

Elizabeth's first overseas priority, however, was Ireland, not America. Fearing Spanish subversion on that neighboring Catholic island, she urged enterprising supporters such as Walter Raleigh and his half-brother Humphrey Gilbert to subdue the Irish and settle English families on their land. During the 1560s both those men, and many other colonists as well, did precisely that, invading the island across the Irish Sea and viciously attacking the Irish defenders of their homeland, forcing them to retreat beyond the line of English settlement along the coast.

The English believed the Irish to be "savages," and indeed the Irish fought so ferociously in resisting the English invasions that an image of the "wild Irish" became fixed in the minds of English colonists. Gilbert retaliated with even greater brutality, ordering his soldiers to behead those they captured and line the walk to his quarters with their heads, "so that none should come into his tent for any cause but commonly he must pass through a lane of heads." Their own barbarism did not dissuade the English from considering the Irish an inferior race, and the notion that civilized people could not mix with such "savages" was an assumption that English colonists would carry with them to the Americas.

Like the invasion of Ireland, England's first ventures in the New World were made against the backdrop of its conflict with Spain. The goal of these ventures was to punish the Spanish, particularly to break the Spanish trading monopoly with tropical America. In 1562 John Hawkins inaugurated English participation in the slave trade, violating Spain's prohibition on foreign commerce with its colonies by transporting African slaves to the Caribbean and bringing back valuable tropical goods. In 1567 the Spanish attacked Hawkins, giving English privateers such as Francis Drake an

As New World inflation caused the prices of European goods to rise steeply, English landlords, their rents fixed by custom, sought ways to increase their incomes. Seeking profits in the woolen trade, for example, many fenced off lands traditionally used as common pasture for villagers in order to provide grazing lands for their sheep. The result of this practice, called "enclosure" was the dislocation of farmers; between 1500 and 1650 a third of all the common lands in England were affected. Deprived of their traditional livelihoods, thousands of families left the countryside for the cities, and the roads were crowded with the homeless. In a state paper written for the queen, Richard Hakluyt argued that New World colonies could be populated by these "multitudes of loiterers and idle vagabonds." Such colonies, he said, could provide bases from which to raid the Spanish in the Caribbean, Indian markets for English goods, and plantations for growing tropical products, freeing England from a reliance on the long-distance trade with Asia. He urged Elizabeth to begin the planting of excuse for launching devastating and lucrative raids against Spanish New World ports and fleets. The voyages of these English "Sea Dogs" greatly enriched their investors, including the queen herself. From a voyage that cost several thousand English pounds, Drake was said to have returned with booty valued in the millions. Thus, like the Spanish, the English began their American adventures by slaving and plundering.

It was not until the 1570s that Elizabeth finally authorized and invested in several private attempts at exploration and colonization in North America. In the late 1570s Martin Frobisher conducted three voyages of exploration in the North Atlantic, bringing back an Eskimo man, woman, and child and samples of worthless ores. Fresh from the Irish wars, Raleigh and Gilbert teamed up to plan their first American colonizing venture in 1578, but it failed to get off the ground. In 1583 Gilbert sailed with a flotilla of ships from Plymouth, England, and landed at St. John's Bay, Newfoundland, where he claimed the territory for his queen even though he found fishermen from several other nations there. But Gilbert's ship was lost on the return voyage.

Raleigh followed up Gilbert's efforts with plans to establish a colony to the south, in the more hospitable climate of the mid-Atlantic coast, but, as described in the opening of this chapter, the Roanoke enterprise of 1584–87 eventually failed as well. Nevertheless, it left as a considerable legacy the scientific work of Thomas Harriot and John White, who mapped the area, surveyed its commercial potential, and studied the Indian residents. Harriot's *Briefe and True*

Report of the Newfound Land of Virginia (1588) was addressed mainly to the problem of identifying the "merchantable commodities" that would support settlement, for without products a colonial system was impossible. A later edition of this book included engravings based on White's watercolors of the people and landscape of Virginia. Together Harriot and White provided the most accurate and sensitive description we have of North American Indians at the moment of their contact with Europeans.

King Philip II of Spain was outraged at these English incursions into territory that, in the Treaty of Tordesillas of 1493, the pope had reserved for Spain. Philip had previously authorized the destruction of the French colony in Florida, and England's expanding colonial interests turned the competition between Catholic Spain and Protestant England into war. In 1588 Philip sent the Spanish Armada, a fleet of 130 ships carrying 30,000 men, to invade the British Isles. Countered by men such as Drake and Hawkins, who commanded smaller and more maneuverable ships, and frustrated by an ill-timed storm that the English chose to interpret as an act of divine intervention, the Armada foundered. Half the ships were destroyed, their crews killed or captured. The war continued until 1604, but the Spanish monopoly of the New World was broken in the English Channel.

CONCLUSION

The European colonization of the Americas opened with Columbus's voyage in 1492. For Indian people, assaulted by invasion and disease, the consequences were disastrous. But first in the Caribbean, then most spectacularly in Mexico, the Spanish succeeded in constructing the world's most powerful empire on the backs of Indian and imported African laborers. The New World colonies of Spain were characterized by a great deal of mixing between the mostly male colonists and native women; in this sense they were communities of "inclusion."

Inspired by the Spanish success, in the second half of the sixteenth century both the French and the English attempted to colonize the coast of North America but by the century's end had not succeeded in establishing any lasting communities. Instead, a very different kind of colonial encounter was taking place in Northeast North America, one based on commerce rather than conquest. In the next century the French would turn this development to their advantage in Canada. Along the mid-Atlantic coast in Virginia, however, the English would put their Irish experience to use, pioneering an altogether new kind of American colonialism.

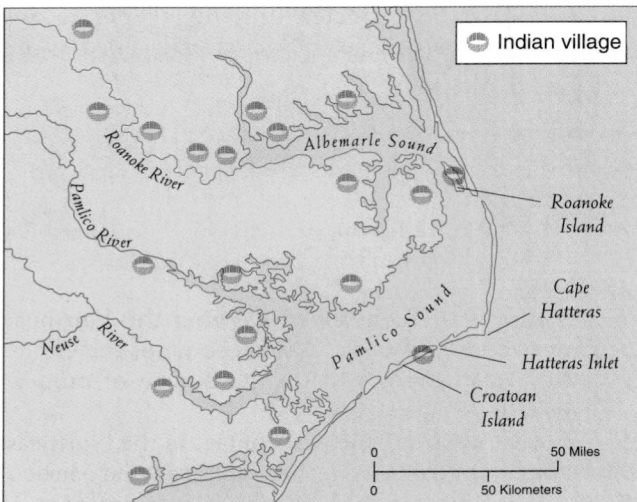

The Roanoke area in 1585 *The surveys of Thomas Harriot and John White revealed that the Roanoke area was densely settled with Indian villages. The information on this map is taken from their report.*

CHRONOLOGY

1000 Norse settlement at L'Anse aux Meadows	**1534** Jacques Cartier first explores the St. Lawrence River
1347–53 Black Death in Europe	**1539–40** Hernán de Soto and Francisco Vásquez de Coronado expeditions
1381 English Peasants' Revolt	
1488 Bartolomeu Días sails around the African continent	**1550** Tobacco introduced to Europe
1492 Christopher Columbus first arrives in the Caribbean	**1552** Bartolomé de Las Casas's *Destruction of the Indies* published
1494 Treaty of Tordesillas	**1558** Elizabeth I of England begins her reign
1497 John Cabot explores Newfoundland	**1562** Huguenot colony planted along the mid-Atlantic coast
1500 High point of the Renaissance	**1565** St. Augustine founded
1508 Spanish invade Puerto Rico	**1572** St. Bartholomew's Day Massacre in France
1513 Juan Ponce de León lands in Florida	
1514 Bartolomé de las Casas begins preaching against the conquest	**1583** Humphrey Gilbert attempts to plant a colony in Newfoundland
1516 Smallpox introduced to the New World	**1584–87** Walter Raleigh's colony on Roanoke Island
1517 Martin Luther breaks with the Roman Catholic Church	**1588** English defeat the Spanish Armada
1519 Hernán Cortés lands in Mexico	**1590** John White returns to find Roanoke colony abandoned

REVIEW QUESTIONS

1. Discuss the roles played by the rising merchant class, the new monarchies, Renaissance humanism, and the Reformation in the development of European colonialism.
2. Define a "frontier of inclusion." In what ways does this description apply to the Spanish empire in the Americas?
3. Make a list of the major exchanges that took place between the Old World and the New World in the centuries following the European invasion of America. Discuss some of the effects these exchanges had on the course of modern history.
4. In what ways did colonial contact in the Northeast differ from contacts in the Caribbean and Mexico?
5. In what ways might the English experience in Ireland have shaped expectations about American colonization?

RECOMMENDED READING

Cyclone Covey, translator and editor, *Cabeza de Vaca's Adventures in the Unknown Interior of America* (1983). The captivity narrative that lured the Spanish into North America. An eye-opening story of the peoples and places of the preconquest Southwest.

Alfred W. Crosby Jr., *The Columbian Exchange: Biological and Cultural Consequences of 1492* (1972). Pathbreaking account of the intersection of the biospheres of the Old and New Worlds.

David Ewing Duncan, *Hernando de Soto: A Savage Quest in the Americas* (1995). A well-written biography of the conquistador and the story of his brutal expedition through the Indian homelands of the Southeast.

Charles Gibson, *Spain in America* (1966). The best introductory history of Spain's American empire.

Lewis Hanke, *The Spanish Struggle for Justice in the Conquest of America* (1949; reprint, 1965). The classic account of Las Casas's attempts to rectify the wrongs committed by the Spanish against the Indians.

Miguel Leon-Portilla, *The Broken Spears: The Aztec Account of the Conquest of Mexico* (1962; expanded ed., 1992). The history of the Spanish conquest as told by the Aztecs, drawn from manuscripts dating as early as 1528, only seven years after the fall of Tenochtitlán.

Samuel Eliot Morison, *The European Discovery of America: The Northern Voyages*, A.D. 500–1600 (1971) and *The Southern Voyages*, A.D. 1492–1616 (1974). The most detailed treatment of all the important European explorations of the Americas.

Anthony Pagden, *Lords of All the Worlds: Ideologies of Empire in Spain, Britain and France c. 1500-c. 1850* (1995). An important comparative history of the European justifications for colonial conquest.

David Beers Quinn, *Set Fair for Roanoke: Voyages and Colonies, 1584–1606* (1985). The story of Roanoke—the Indian village, the English settlement, and the Lost Colony.

Kirkpatrick Sale, *The Conquest of Paradise: Christopher Columbus and the Columbian Legacy* (1990). A harsh view of Columbus, but important information on the world of the Caribbean and the disastrous effects of the encounter with Europeans.

Carl Ortwin Sauer, *Sixteenth Century North America: The Land and the People as Seen by the Europeans* (1971). An excellent source for the explorations of the continent, providing abundant descriptions of the Indians.

David E. Stannard, *American Holocaust: Columbus and the Conquest of the New World* (1992). A provocative argument that the Spanish inaugurated a genocidal policy against the Indians that has continued into the twentieth century.

Hugh Thomas, *Conquest: Montezuma, Cortés, and the Fall of Old Mexico* (1993). A fascinating account, written by a master of historical style, that incorporates the Aztec view as well as the words of the conquerors.

ADDITIONAL BIBLIOGRAPHY

The Expansion of Europe

James M. Blaut, *1492: The Debate on Colonialism, Eurocentrism, and History* (1992)

Fernand Braudel, *The Mediterranean and the Mediterranean World in the Age of Philip II* (1972)

———, *Civilization and Capitalism, 15th–18th Centuries*, 3 vols. (1981)

Carol Cipolla, *Before the Industrial Revolution: European Society and Economy, 1100–1700* (1976)

Patrick Collinson, *The Religion of Protestants: The Church in English Society, 1559–1625* (1982)

Ralph Davis, *The Rise of Atlantic Economies* (1973)

Andre Gunder Frank, *World Accumulation, 1492–1789* (1978)

Douglas North, *The Rise of the Western World: A New Economic History* (1973)

José Casas Pardo, ed., *Economic Effects of the European Expansion, 1492–1824* (1992)

J. H. Parry, *The Age of Reconnaissance* (1963)

———, *Europe and a Wider World: The Establishment of the European Hegemony: Trade and Expansion in the Age of the Renaissance* (1966)

Geoffrey Vaughn Scannell, *The First Imperial Age: European Overseas Expansion c. 1400–1715* (1989)

The Spanish in the Americas

Warner Bowden, *American Indians and Christian Missions: Studies in Cultural Conflict* (1982)

Fredi Chiapelli, ed., *First Images of America: The Impact of the New World on the Old* (1976)

Nobel David Cook and W. George Lovell, *Secret Judgments of God: Old World Disease in Colonial Spanish America* (1991)

Henry F. Dobyns, *Their Number Become Thinned: Native American Population Dynamics in Eastern North America* (1983)

J. H. Elliott, *The Old World and the New, 1492–1650* (1970)

Anthony Grafton, *New Worlds, Ancient Texts: The Power of Tradition and the Shock of Discovery* (1992)

Hugh Honour, *New Golden Land: European Images of America from the Discoveries to the Present Time* (1975)

Charles Hudson, *Knights of Spain, Warriors of the Sun: Hernando De Soto and the South's Ancient Chiefdoms* (1997)

Charles Hudson and Carmen Chaves Tesser, eds., *The Forgotten Centuries: Indians and Europeans in the American South, 1521–1704* (1994)

René Jara and Nicholas Spadaccini, eds., *Amerindian Images and the Legacy of Columbus* (1992)

Elizabeth A. H. John, *Storms Brewed in Other Men's Worlds: The Confrontation of Indians, Spanish, and French in the Southwest, 1540–1795* (1975)

James Lang, *Conquest and Commerce: Spain and England in the Americas* (1975)

James Lockhart and Stuart B. Schwartz, *Early Latin America: A History of Colonial Spanish America and Brazil* (1983)

Peter Mason, *Deconstructing America: Representations of the Other* (1990)

Jerald T. Milanich and Charles Hudson, *Hernando de Soto and the Indians of Florida* (1993)

James Howlett O'Donnell III, *Southeastern Frontiers: Europeans, Africans, and American Indians, 1513–1840: A Critical Bibliography* (1982)

Edmundo O'Gorman, *The Invention of America: An Inquiry into the Historical Nature of the New World and the Meaning of its History* (1961)

David M. Traboulay, *Columbus and Las Casas: The Conquest and Christianization of America, 1492–1566* (1994)

Ronald Wright, *Stolen Continents: The Americas through Indian Eyes since 1492* (1992)

Northern Explorations and Encounters

Alfred Goldsworthy Bailey, *The Conflict of European and Eastern Algonkian Cultures, 1504–1700* (1969)

Carl Bridenbaugh, *Vexed and Troubled Englishmen, 1590–1642* (1968)

Peter Clark and Paul Slack, *English Towns in Transition, 1500–1700* (1976)

Susan Danforth, *Encountering the New World, 1493–1800* (1991)

G. R. Elton, *England under the Tudors* (1974)

C. H. George and Katherine George, *The Protestant Mind of the English Reformation* (1961)

John Guy, *Tudor England* (1988)

Karen Ordahl Kupperman, *Roanoke: The Abandoned Colony* (1984)

Peter Laslett, *The World We Have Lost* (1965)

E. B. Leacock and N. O. Laurie, eds., *North American Indians in Historical Perspective* (1971)

Anthony McFarlane, *The British in the Americas, 1480-1815* (1994).

David B. Quinn, *North America from Earliest Discovery to First Settlements* (1977)

———, *The Roanoke Voyages, 1584–1590*, 2 vols. (1955)

Bernard W. Sheehan, *Savagism and Civility: Indians and Englishmen in Colonial Virginia* (1980)

Russell Thornton, *American Indian Holocaust and Survival* (1987)

Margo Todd, ed., *Reformation to Revolution: Politics and Religion in Early Modern England* (1995)

Marcel Trudel, *The Beginnings of New France, 1524–1663* (1973)

Keith Wrightson, *English Society, 1580–1680* (1982)

Biography

Joe Armstrong, *Champlain* (1987)

Carole Levin, *The Heart and Stomach of a King: Elizabeth I and the Politics of Sex and Power* (1994)

Richard Lee Marks, *Cortés: The Great Adventurer and the Fate of Aztec Mexico* (1993)

Samuel E. Morison, *Admiral of the Ocean Sea: A Life of Christopher Columbus* (1942)

A. L. Rowse, *Eminent Elizabethans* (1983)

John Ure, *Prince Henry the Navigator* (1977)

Henry Raup Wagner, *The Life and Writings of Bartolomé de las Casas* (1967)

CHAPTER THREE

PLANTING COLONIES IN NORTH AMERICA

1588–1701

Navajo painted "Mural" depicting Spanish horsemen, Canyon del Muerto at Canyon de Chelly National Monument, Arizona Jerry Jacka Photography

AMERICAN COMMUNITIES
Communities Struggle with Diversity in Seventeenth-Century Santa Fé

On a hot August day in 1680, frantic messengers rode into the small mission outpost of El Paso with the news that the Pueblo Indians to the north had risen in revolt; corpses of more than 400 colonists lay bleeding in the dust. Two thousand Spanish survivors huddled inside the Palace of Governors in Santa Fé, surrounded by 3,000 angry Indian warriors. The Pueblo leaders had sent two crosses inside the palace—white for surrender, red for death. Which would the Spaniards choose?

Spanish colonists had been in New Mexico for nearly a century. Franciscan priests came first, followed by a military expedition from Mexico in search of precious metals. In 1609, in the picturesque foothills of the Sangre de Cristo Mountains, colonial authorities founded La Villa Real de la Santa Fé de San Francisco—"the royal town of the holy faith of St. Francis"—soon known simply as Santa Fé. Colonization efforts included converting the Pueblo Indians to Christianity, making them subjects of the king of Spain, and forcing them to work for the colonial elite who lived at the edges of the town.

In the face of overwhelming Spanish power—the military might that had retaken Spain from the Moors of North Africa and conquered the great Aztec and Incan civilizations farther south—the Pueblos adopted a flexible attitude. Although 20,000 converted to Christianity, most thought of the new religion as simply an appendage to their already complex culture. The Christian God was but one more of their numerous deities. They incorporated Church holidays into their own religious calendar and celebrated them with native dances and rituals.

Most ethnographers agree that the Pueblos were a sexually spirited people. Many of their public dances included erotic displays, and some ended in public lovemaking. Symbolizing the powerful force that brought the separate worlds of men and women together, sexual intercourse was emblematic of community. Indeed, the celibacy of the Franciscan priests not only astounded the Pueblos but horrified them; they saw the priests as only half-persons.

The Pueblos also found the Franciscan practice of subjecting themselves to prolonged fasts and tortures like self-flagellation completely inexplicable. "You Christians are crazy," one Pueblo chief told a priest. "You go through the streets in groups, flagellating yourselves, and it is not well that the people of this pueblo should be encouraged to commit such madness." The missionaries, for their part, were outraged by what they considered Pueblo sacrileges, and they invaded underground kivas, destroying sacred Indian artifacts, publicly humiliating holy men, and compelling whole villages to perform penance by working in irrigation ditches and fields. When the Spanish governor of New Mexico executed three Pueblo priests and publicly whipped dozens more for secretly practicing their religion, one of these priests, Popé of San Juan Pueblo, vowed to overthrow the Spanish regime and began organizing a conspiracy among more than twenty Indian towns.

Popé's job was not difficult, for there were plenty of local grievances. For example, the Hopis of northern Arizona still tell of a missionary who capped his ever-escalating demands on them with the order that all the young women of the village be brought to live with him. When the revolt of 1680 began throughout the entire colony, the Hopis surrounded the missionary's house. "I have come to kill you," the chief announced. "You can't kill me," the priest cried from behind his locked door. "I will come to life and wipe out your whole tribe." "My gods have more power than you have," the chief shouted back. He and his men broke down the door, hung the missionary from the beams, and lit a fire beneath his feet.

From within Santa Fé's Palace of Governors the Spanish sent back the red cross, signaling that they would fight to the death. But after a siege lasting five days the Pueblos agreed to allow most of them to flee south to El Paso, "the poor women and children on foot and unshod," in the words of one Spaniard's account, and "of such a hue that they looked like dead people." The Indians then ransacked the missions and churches, desecrating the holy furnishings with human excrement and leaving the mutilated bodies of priests lying upon their altars. They transformed the governor's chapel into a traditional kiva, his palace into a communal dwelling. On the elegant inlaid stone floors where the governor had held court, Pueblo women now ground their corn.

Santa Fé became the capital of a Pueblo confederacy led by Popé. Popé first forced Christian Indians to the river to scrub away the taint of baptism and then ordered the general population to destroy everything Spanish. But the latter command met with resistance. The colonists had introduced horses and sheep, fruit trees and wheat, new tools and new crafts—all things that the Indians found useful. In addition, the Pueblos sorely missed the support of the Spanish in their struggle against the Navajos and Apaches, the Pueblos' traditional enemies. Equipped with stolen horses and weapons, these nomadic tribespeople had become considerably more dangerous, and their raids on the unprotected Pueblo villages became much more destructive after the colonists fled. With chaos mounting, Popé was deposed in 1690, and many Indians found themselves thinking the unthinkable: If only the Spanish would come back!

Come back they did, beginning in 1692, and after six years of fighting succeeded in reestablishing Spanish authority. But both sides had learned a lesson, and over the next generation the colonists and the Indians reached an implicit understanding. Pueblos dutifully observed Catholicism in the missionary chapels, while missionaries tolerated the practice of traditional religion in the Indians' underground kivas. Royal officials guaranteed the inviolability of Indian lands, and Pueblos pledged loyalty to the Spanish monarch. Pueblos turned out for service on colonial lands, and colonists abandoned the system of forced labor. Together the Spanish and the Pueblos held off the nomadic tribes for the next 150 years. Colonist and Indian communities remained autonomous, but they were learning to live with one another.

Santa Fé

KEY TOPICS

- A comparison of the European colonies established in North America in the seventeenth century

- The English and Algonquian colonial encounter in the Chesapeake

- The role of religious dissent in the planting of the New England colonies

- The restoration of the Stuart monarchy and the creation of new proprietary colonies

- Indian warfare and internal conflict at the end of the seventeenth century

THE SPANISH AND FRENCH IN NORTH AMERICA

At the end of the sixteenth century the Spanish and the French were the only European powers directly involved in North America. The Spanish had built a series of forts along the Florida coast to protect the Gulf Stream sea lanes used by the convoys carrying wealth from their New World colonies. The French were navigating the St. Lawrence River in pursuit of fur trade. Early in the seventeenth century both were drawn into planting far more substantial colonies—New Mexico and New France—in North America. Because neither France nor Spain was willing or able to transport large numbers of its citizens to populate these colonies, both relied on a policy of converting Indians into subjects, and in New Mexico and New France there was a good deal of cultural and sexual mixing between colonists and natives. These areas became "frontiers of inclusion," where native peoples were part of colonial society, and they contrasted dramatically with the "frontiers of exclusion" established later by the English.

New Mexico

After the 1539 expedition of Francisco Vásquez de Coronado failed to turn up vast Indian empires to conquer in the northern Mexican deserts, the Spanish interest in the Southwest faded. But although the densely settled farming communities of the Pueblos may not have offered wealth to plunder, they did offer a harvest of souls, and by the 1580s Franciscan missionaries had entered the area. Soon, however, rumors drifted back to Mexico City of rich mines along the Rio Grande, and the hopes of Spanish officials that they might find another Aztec empire in what they had called "New Mexico" were rekindled. In 1598 Juan de Oñate, a member of a wealthy mining family, led 130 predominantly Indian and mestizo soldiers and their families, along with some 20 missionaries, north into New Mexico with the intent of mining both gold and souls.

Moving north into the upper Rio Grande Valley, Oñate encountered varying degrees of resistance by the Pueblo Indians. At Acoma, a pueblo set high atop a great outcropping of rock, Oñate met with considerable hostility, and he laid siege to the town. Indian warriors killed dozens of Spaniards with their arrows, and women and even children bombarded the attackers with stones. But in the end, the Spanish succeeded in climbing the rock walls and laying waste the town, killing 800 men,

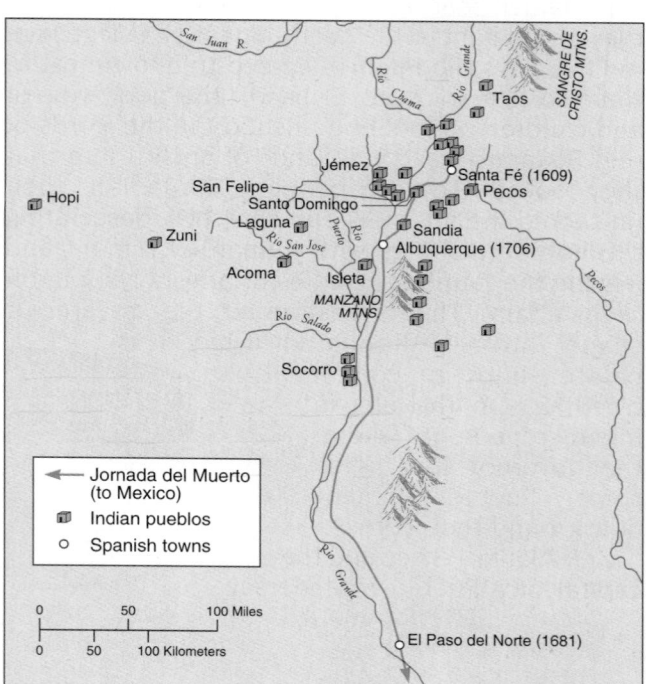

New Mexico in the Seventeenth Century *By the end of the seventeenth century, New Mexico contained 3,000 colonial settlers in several towns, surrounded by an estimated 50,000 Pueblo Indians living in some fifty farming villages. The isolation and sense of danger among the Hispanic settlers are evident in their name for the road linking the colony with New Spain, Jornada del Muerto, "the Road of Death."*

women, and children. The Spanish cut off one foot of each
surviving Indian warrior and
carried off more than 500
persons into slavery. "If you who
are Christians cause so much
harm and violence," a Pueblo
Indian asked one of the priests,
"why should we become Christians?" For their part, the Spanish
authorities in Mexico recalled
Oñate in 1606 for his failure to
locate the fabled gold mines.

The Spanish were about
to abandon the colony, but after
publicizing a surge in Christian
conversions among the Indians,
the Church convinced the
monarchy to subsidize New
Mexico as a special missionary
project. In 1609 the new governor, Don Pedro de Peralta,
founded the capital of Santa Fé,
and from this base the Franciscans penetrated all the surrounding Indian villages.

This illustration, taken from Samuel de Champlain's 1613 account of the founding of New France, depicts him joining the Huron attack on the Iroquois in 1609. The French and their Huron allies controlled access to the great fur grounds of the West. The Iroquois then formed an alliance of their own with the Dutch, who had founded a trading colony on the Hudson River. The palm trees in the background of this drawing suggest that it was not executed by an eyewitness but rather by an illustrator more familiar with South American scenes.

The colonial economy of New Mexico, based
on small-scale agriculture and sheep raising, was never
very prosperous. The Spanish settlers were not inclined
to work—as one Spanish official put it, "One comes to
the Indies not to plow and sow, but only to eat and
loaf"—and forced the Indians to labor for them. After
the initial conquest, few new colonists came up the
dusty road from Mexico. Population growth was almost
entirely the result of natural increase deriving from
unions between colonial men and Indian women. By
the late seventeenth century this northernmost outpost
of the far-flung Spanish American empire contained
some 3,000 mostly mestizo settlers in a few towns
along the Rio Grande, surrounded by an estimated
50,000 Pueblo Indians in some fifty villages.

The First Communities of New France

In the early seventeenth century the French devised a
strategy to monopolize the northern fur trade that had
developed in the sixteenth century. In 1605, Samuel de
Champlain, an agent of the royal Canadian Company,
helped establish the outpost of Port Royal on what is
now Nova Scotia, bordering the Bay of Fundy, and
three years later he founded the town of Quebec at a
site strategically located so that he could intercept the
traffic in furs to the Atlantic. Champlain forged an
alliance with the Huron Indians, who controlled access
to the rich fur territories of the Great Lakes, and joined
them in making war on their traditional enemies, the

Five Nation Iroquois Confederacy. In his diplomacy,
Champlain relied on the tradition of commercial relations that had developed between the French and the
Indians. He sent agents and traders to live among
native peoples, where they learned native languages
and customs and directed the flow of furs to Quebec.

France encouraged families to settle the colony
of Acadia, the tidal shores of the Bay of Fundy, and the
colony of Canada, the narrow belt of fertile land along
the St. Lawrence. It was the second of these that became
the heart of New France. Small clusters of riverbank farmers known as *habitants* lived on the lands of *seigneurs*, or
landlords. The little communities that emerged, with the
manor house of the lord, the Catholic church, and
perhaps a public building or two, resembled the towns of
northern France. Although the growing season was short,
habitants were able to produce subsistence crops by
employing Indian farming techniques, and eventually
they developed a modest export economy.

But the communities of Canada tended to look
west toward the continental interior rather than east
across the Atlantic. It was typical for the sons of *habitants*
to take to the woods in their youth, working as agents for
the fur companies or as independent traders, known as
coureurs de bois, or "runners of the woods." Most eventually
returned to take up farming, but others remained in
Indian villages, where they married Indian women and
raised families. Thus French traders were living on the
Great Lakes as early as the 1620s, and from the late 1660s

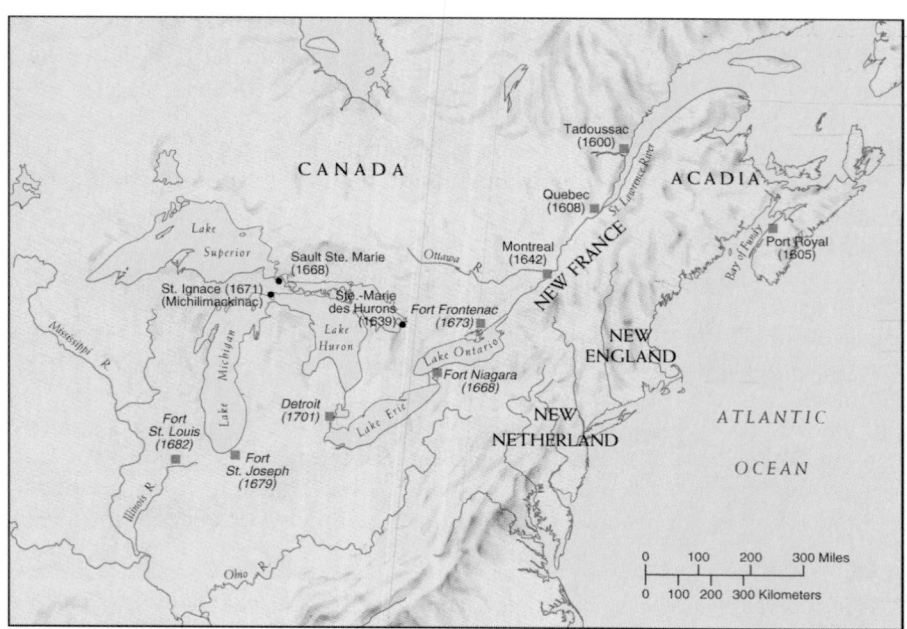

New France in the Seventeenth Century *By the late seventeenth century, French settlements were spread from the town of Port Royal in Acadia to the post and mission at Sault Ste. Marie, on the Great Lakes. But the heart of New France comprised the communities stretching along the St. Lawrence River between the towns of Quebec and Montreal.*

to the 1680s the French established outposts at strategic points on the lakes. By the 1670s French fur traders and missionaries were exploring the reaches of the upper Mississippi River. In 1681–82, fur trade commandant Robert Sieur de La Salle navigated the mighty river to its mouth on the Gulf of Mexico and claimed its entire watershed—a great inland empire—for France.

Thus although both the French and Spanish established societies of inclusion, in which settlers intermarried with native peoples, the early French colonial system differed from that of the Spanish. Whereas the French interest in the Indians was principally commercial, the Spanish organized Indian communities as a labor force for mines, plantations, and ranches. There were also important differences between Spanish and French missionary efforts. The Jesuits, arriving in 1625 and often accompanying French traders—and sometimes leading the way—introduced Christianity as a supplement to the Indian way of life. In contrast, the Franciscans of New Mexico insisted that Indian people accept European cultural norms.

The populations of Acadia and Canada grew throughout the seventeenth century but by 1700 still totaled only 15,000. Quebec City, the colony's administrative capital, was small by Spanish colonial standards, and Montreal, founded in 1642 as a missionary and trading center, remained little more than a frontier outpost. The real strength of New France lay in its extensive fur-trading system.

ENGLAND IN THE CHESAPEAKE

England first attempted to plant colonies in North America during the 1580s, in Newfoundland and on Roanoke Island in present-day North Carolina. Both attempts were failures. England's war with Spain, which lasted from 1588 to 1604, suspended colonization efforts, but at its close the English once again turned to the Americas.

Jamestown and the Powhatan Confederacy

Early in his reign, King James I (reigned 1603–25) issued royal charters for the colonization of the mid-Atlantic region, by then known as Virginia, to English joint-stock companies, which raised capital by selling shares. In 1607 a group of London investors known as the Virginia Company sent ships to the temperate latitudes of Chesapeake Bay, where a hundred men built a fort they named Jamestown, in honor of the king. It was destined to become the first permanent English settlement in North America.

The Chesapeake region was already home to an estimated 20,000 Algonquian people. The English colonists were immediately confronted by Powhatan, the powerful *werowance*, or leader, of a confederacy of Algonquian tribes. Powhatan had mixed feelings about the English. The Spanish had already attempted to plant a base nearby, bringing conflict and disease to his region. But he looked forward to valuable trade with the English as well as to their support for his struggle to extend his confederacy to outlying tribes. As was the case in Mexico and along the St. Lawrence, Indians tried to use Europeans to pursue ends of their own.

The English saw themselves as latter-day conquistadors. Abhorring the idea of physical labor, they survived the first year only with Powhatan's material assistance. Like the first Roanoke colonists (see Chapter 2), they were unable to support themselves. "In our extremity the Indians brought us corn," wrote John Smith, the colony's military leader, "when we rather expected they would destroy us." Jamestown grew so dependent on Algonquian stores that in 1609 Smith and his men began to plunder food from surrounding tribes. In retaliation, Powhatan decided to starve the colonists out. He now realized, as he said to Smith, that the

English had come "not for trade, but to invade my people and possess my country"—the approach not of the French but of the Spanish. During the winter of 1609–10 scores of colonists starved and a number resorted to cannibalism. By spring only 60 remained of the more than 900 colonists sent to Virginia.

Determined to prevail, the Virginia Company sent out a large additional force of men, women, and livestock, committing themselves to a protracted war against the Indians. By 1613 the colonists firmly controlled the territory between the James and York rivers. Worn down by warfare and disease, Powhatan accepted a treaty of peace in 1614. "I am old and ere long must die," he declared; "I know it is better to eat good meat, lie well, and sleep with my women and children, laugh and be merry than to be forced to flee and be hunted." He sent his daughter Pocahontas, fluent in English, on a diplomatic mission to Jamestown. She converted to Christianity and married John Rolfe, a leading settler. But Pocahontas died of disease while visiting England in 1617. Crushed by the news of her death, her father abdicated in favor of his brother Opechancanough and died the following year.

Tobacco, Expansion, and Warfare

Tobacco provided the Virginia colonists with the "merchantable commodity" for which Thomas Harriot, the scientist who accompanied the Roanoke expedition, had searched (see Chapter 2). In 1613 John Rolfe developed a hybrid of hearty North American and mild West Indian varieties, and soon the first commercial shipments of cured Virginia leaf reached England. The revenue from tobacco sales produced the first returns on the investment of the Virginia Company. Its cultivation quickly

The illustration on the left is a detail of John Smith's map of Virginia. It includes the names of many Indian villages, suggesting how densely settled was the Indian population of the coast of Chesapeake Bay. For the inset of Powhatan and his court in the upper left, the engraver borrowed images from John White's drawings of the Indians of the Roanoke area. The illustration on the right, from John Smith's memoirs (1624), was engraved by the artist Robert Vaughn. Seizing Chief Opechancanough, Powhatan's brother, by the scalplock, Smith attempts to obtain needed supplies from the Indians. Opechancanough later succeeded Powhatan and ruled the Chesapeake Algonquian Confederacy for a quarter century.

An eighteenth-century label for Virginia tobacco, featuring an African slave and a native American smoker. Tobacco was introduced to English consumers by Francis Drake in the 1580s, and despite King James's description of the habit as "loathsome to the eye, hateful to the nose, harmful to the brain, dangerous to the lungs," tobacco smoking developed into a craze that created strong consumer demand in the 1610s.

exhausted the soil, however, creating pressures for further expansion into Indian territory.

Because tobacco also required a great deal of hand labor, the company instituted what were called headright grants, or awards of large plantations on the condition that grant recipients transport workers from England at their own cost. Between 1619 and 1624 more than 4,500 English settlers arrived, many with families. But high rates of mortality—probably the result of epidemics of typhoid fever—kept the total population at just over a thousand. In populating their colony with families, the English had chosen a policy quite different from the Spanish practice of sending only male settlers. Moreover, the English emphasis on agriculture and lack of interest in trade with Indian peoples contrasted significantly with the French approach. With no need to incorporate Indians into the population, the English moved in the direction of exclusion, pushing Indian peoples to the periphery rather than incorporating them within colonial communities.

As the English pressed for additional lands, Opechancanough prepared the Chesapeake Algonquians for a final assault on the invaders. He encouraged a cultural revival under the guidance of the shaman Nemattanew, who instructed his followers to reject the English and their ways but to learn the use of firearms. The uprising, which began on Good Friday, March 22, 1622, completely surprised the English. Nearly 350 people, a quarter of the settlers, were killed before Jamestown could mobilize its forces. Yet the colony managed to hang on, and the attack stretched into a ten-year war of attrition. Horrors were committed by both sides, but English officials saw advantages in open warfare. As one wrote, "We may now by right of war, and law of nations, invade the country and destroy them who sought to destroy us, whereby we shall enjoy their cultivated places." Indian territory might now be obtained under the conventions of a "just war."

Long before it ended in 1632, the war bankrupted the Virginia Company. In 1624 the king converted Virginia into a royal colony, with civil authorities appointed by the crown, although the colony's House of Burgesses, created in 1619, continued to include representatives of Virginia's boroughs. Then, despite disease, famine, and warfare, the economy took off, and the English colonial population doubled every five years from 1625 to 1640, by which time it numbered approximately 10,000. Opechancanough emerged from the turmoil as undisputed leader of the still independent Chesapeake Algonquian Confederacy, but other smaller tribes, decimated by casualties and disease, were forced to accept English domination. By 1640 the native population of the Chesapeake had declined to about 40,000.

Numerical strength soon shifted in favor of the English. In 1644, Opechancanough organized a final desperate revolt, in which more than 500 colonists were killed. But the Virginians crushed the Algonquians in 1645, capturing and executing Opechancanough. The colonists then signed a formal treaty with the Indians, who were granted small reserved territories. By the 1670s, when the English population of Virginia numbered more than 40,000, only a dozen tribes and about 2,000 Algonquians remained from the 20,000 who inhabited the area when Jamestown was founded. Today, some 1,500 people who trace their roots to Powhatan's confederacy live in Chesapeake Indian communities near Richmond, Virginia, and Washington, D.C.

Maryland

In 1632, King Charles I (reigned 1625–49) granted 10 million acres at the northern end of Chesapeake Bay to the Calvert family, the Lords Baltimore, important supporters of the monarchy. The Calverts named their colony Maryland, in honor of the king's wife. The first party of colonists founded the settlement of St. Marys

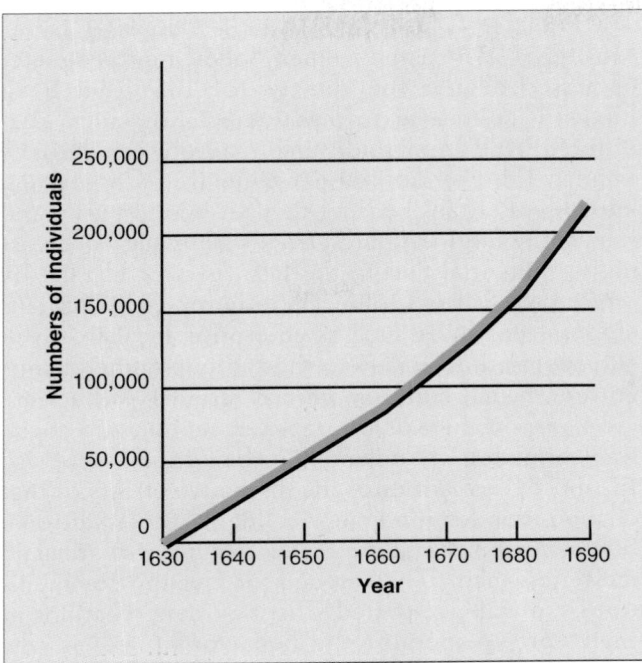

Population Growth of the British Colonies in the Seventeenth Century   *The British colonial population grew steadily through the century, then increased sharply in the closing decade as a result of the new settlements of the Restoration colonies.*

near the mouth of the Potomac River in 1634. Two features distinguished Maryland from Virginia. First, it was a "proprietary" colony. The Calverts were sole owners of all the land, which they planned to carve into feudal manors that would provide them with annual rents, and they appointed all the civil officers. Second, because the proprietors were Catholics, they encouraged settlement by their coreligionists, a persecuted minority in seventeenth-century England. In fact, Maryland became the only English colony in North America with a substantial Catholic minority. Wealthy Catholic landlords were appointed to the governing council, and they came to dominate Maryland's House of Delegates, founded in 1635.

Despite these differences, Maryland quickly assumed the character of neighboring Virginia. Its tobacco plantation economy created pressures for labor and expansion that could not be met under the Calverts' original feudal plans. In 1640 the colony adopted the system of headright grants developed in Virginia, and settlements of independent planters quickly spread out on both sides of the bay. By the 1670s Maryland's English population numbered more than 15,000.

Indentured Servants

At least three-quarters of the English migrants to the Chesapeake came as indentured servants. In exchange for the cost of their transportation to the New World, men and women contracted to labor for a master for a fixed term. Most indentured servants were young, unskilled males, who served for two to seven years, but some were skilled craftsmen, and a few were women and children (the latter were expected to serve until they reached the age of twenty-one). A minority of these laborers were convicts or vagabonds bound into service by English courts for as long as fourteen years.

Masters were obliged to feed, clothe, and house these servants adequately. But work in the tobacco fields was backbreaking, and records include complaints of inadequate care. One Virginia ballad chronicled these complaints:

> *Come all you young fellows wherever you be,*
> *Come listen awhile and I will tell thee,*
> *Concerning the hardships that we undergo,*
> *When we get lagg'd to Virginia*
> *Now in Virginia I lay like a hog,*
> *Our pillow at night is a brick or a log,*
> *We dress and undress like some other sea dog,*
> *How hard is my fate in Virginia.*

Many servants tried to escape, but capture could mean a lengthening of their terms of service. On reaching the end of their service, servants were eligible for "freedom dues": clothing, tools, a gun, a spinning wheel, a little land, or perhaps food—something to help them get started on their own. Most former servants hoped to start farms in the backcountry and thus headed west, even though they thereby risked the danger of Indian attacks.

Reliance on indentured labor was unique to the English colonies. New France had little need for a systematic resort to servitude, for French colonists pretty much did their own labor. The Spanish, on the other hand, in places like Santa Fé, depended on the labor of Indians. African slaves were first introduced to the Chesapeake in 1619, but they were more expensive than servants, and as late as 1680 they made up less than 7 percent of the Chesapeake population. For many servants, however, the distinction between slavery and servitude may have seemed academic. Approximately two of every five servants died during their periods of indenture. In the hard-driving economy of the Chesapeake, many masters treated servants cruelly, and women especially were vulnerable to sexual exploitation. The harsh system of indentured labor prepared the tobacco masters of the Chesapeake for the transition to slavery that occurred during the second half of the seventeenth century. (Chapter 4 discusses the slave system and its implications for the economic and social aspects of American society as well as for slaves and masters themselves.)

Community Life in the Chesapeake

Most migrants were men, and male servants surviving their terms of indenture had a difficult time finding wives. Tobacco masters commonly received offers from men to pay off the indenture of a prospective wife, and free unmarried women often married as soon as they arrived. English men seemed to suffer a higher rate of mortality than English women in the disease-ridden environment of the early Chesapeake. Widows remarried quickly, sometimes within days. Their scarcity provided women with certain advantages. Shrewd widows bargained for remarriage agreements that gave them larger shares of the estate upon the death of their husband. So notable was the concentration of wealth in the hands of these widows that one historian has suggested that early Virginia was a "matriarchy." But because of high mortality rates, family size was smaller and kinship bonds—one of the most important components of community—were weaker than in England.

Visitors from England frequently remarked on the crude conditions of community life. Prosperous planters, investing everything in tobacco production, lived in rough wooden dwellings. Fifty miles inland, on the western edge of the settlements, freed servants lived with their families in shacks, huts, or even caves. Colonists spread across the countryside in search of new tobacco lands, creating dispersed settlements and few towns. Before 1650 there were relatively few community institutions such as schools and churches. The settlements of the Chesapeake, the site of England's premier colony in North America, looked temporary. Meanwhile, the Spanish in the Caribbean and Mexico were building communities that grew into great cities with permanent institutions.

In contrast to the colonists of New France, who were developing a distinctive American identity because of their commercial connections with native Americans, the population of the Chesapeake maintained close emotional ties to England. Colonial politics were shaped less by local developments than by a continuing relationship with the mother country. There was little movement toward a distinctively American point of view in the seventeenth-century Chesapeake.

THE NEW ENGLAND COLONIES

Both in climate and in geography, the northern coast of North America was far different from the Chesapeake. "Merchantable commodities" such as tobacco could not be produced there, and thus the region was far less favored for investment and settlement. Instead, it became a haven for Protestant dissenters from England, who gave the colonies of the North a distinctive character.

The Social and Political Values of Puritanism

Most English men and women, following to a greater or lesser degree the dictates of the Church of England, continued to practice a Christianity that differed little from traditional Catholicism. But the English followers of John Calvin (see Chapter 2), known as Puritans because they wished to purify and reform the English church from within, grew increasingly influential during the last years of Elizabeth's reign. Like Calvin's followers in Europe, the Puritans emphasized values such as enterprise and hard work and appealed especially to those groups—merchants, entrepreneurs, and commercial farmers—who were most responsible for the rapid economic and social transformation of England. But the Puritans were also the most vocal critics of the disruptive effects of that change, condemning the decline of the traditional rural community and the growing number of "idle and masterless men." They argued for reviving communities by placing reformed Christian congregations at their core to monitor the behavior of individuals. Puritanism was thus as much a set of social and political values as religious ones, a way of managing change in troubling times. By the early seventeenth century, Puritans controlled many congregations and had become an influential force at the universities in Oxford and Cambridge, training centers for the future political and religious leaders of England.

King James I, who assumed the throne after Elizabeth's death, abandoned her policy of religious tolerance. His persecution of the Puritans, however, merely stiffened their resolve and turned them toward overt political opposition. An increasingly vocal Puritan minority in Parliament complained that the Church of England was too "Catholic." These Puritans criticized King Charles I, James's son and successor, for supporting High Church policies—which emphasized the authority of the church and its traditional forms of worship—as well as for marrying a Catholic princess. In 1629, determined to rule without these troublesome opponents, Charles dissolved Parliament and launched a campaign of repression against the Puritans. "I am verily persuaded God will bring some heavy affliction upon this land," the Puritan leader John Winthrop despaired. This political turmoil provided the context for the migration of thousands of English Protestants to New England.

Early Contacts in New England

The northern Atlantic coast seemed an unlikely spot for English colonies, for the region was dominated by French and Dutch traders. In the early seventeenth century Samuel de Champlain established trading contacts with coastal Algonquians as far south as Cape Cod. The Dutch, following the explorations of Henry Hudson for the Netherlands, established settlements and a lucrative fur trade on the Hudson River. In 1613 the English, desperate to keep their colonial options open, dispatched a fleet from Jamestown that destroyed the French post at Port Royal on the Bay of Fundy and harassed the Dutch on the Hudson. The following year John Smith explored the northern coastline and christened the region "New England." The land was "so planted with Gardens and Corne fields," he wrote, that "I would rather live here than any where." But Smith's plans for a New England colony were aborted when he was captured and held captive by the French.

Then a twist of fate transformed English fortunes. From 1616 to 1618 a devastating plague ravaged the native peoples of the northern coast. Whole villages disappeared, and the trade system of the French and the Dutch was seriously disrupted. Indians perished so quickly and in such numbers that few remained to bury the dead. Modern estimates confirm the testimony of a surviving Indian that his people were "melted down by this disease, whereof nine-tenths of them have died." The native population of New England as a whole dropped from an estimated 120,000 to less than 70,000. So crippled were the surviving coastal societies that they could not provide effective resistance to the planting of English colonies.

Plymouth Colony and the Mayflower Compact

The first English colony in New England was founded by a group of religious dissenters known to later generations as the Pilgrims. The Pilgrims were English Separatists, people who believed the Anglican establishment so corrupt that they must establish their own independent church. One group of Separatists first moved to Holland in 1609, but, fearful that Dutch society was seducing their children, they soon began exploring the idea of emigrating to North America. Backed by the Virginia Company of London and led by Pilgrim William Bradford, 102 people embarked on the *Mayflower,* sailing from Plymouth, England, in September 1620.

The little group, mostly families but also a substantial number of single men hired by the investors, arrived in Massachusetts Bay at Plymouth, the site of the former Indian village of Patuxet. Soon the hired men began to grumble about Pilgrim authority, and to reassure them Bradford drafted a document known as the Mayflower Compact, in which all the men of the expedition did "covenant and combine [themselves] together into a civil body politic." Signed in November 1620, the Mayflower Compact was the first document of self-government in North America.

Weakened by scurvy and malnutrition, nearly half the Pilgrims perished over the first winter. Like the earlier settlers of Roanoke and Jamestown, however, the Pilgrims were rescued by Indians.

Massasoit, the sachem, or leader, of the local tribe of Wampanoags, offered food and advice in return for an alliance with the newcomers against his enemies, the Narragansets, a powerful neighboring tribe to his immediate west.

The interpreter in these negotiations was an Indian named Squanto who had been kidnapped in 1614 by the captain of one English ship and who had returned to New England five years later as guide on another vessel. Finding that plague had wiped out his village of Patuxet, and knowledgeable in the ways of the Europeans, Squanto became an adviser to Massasoit. With the arrival of the Pilgrims, this last survivor of the Patuxets now resumed his former residence, but as guide and interpreter for the English. Squanto secured seed corn for the colonists and taught them how to sow and cultivate it.

Deeply in debt to its investors, always struggling to meet its payments through the Indian trade, fishing, and lumbering, the Plymouth colony was never a financial success. Most families raised their own crops and kept their own livestock, but produced little for export. Nevertheless, the Pilgrims succeeded in establishing the separate community they wanted. So strong was their communal agreement that the annual meeting of property-owning men reelected William Bradford to thirty consecutive terms as governor. By midcentury, however, the Plymouth population had dispersed into eleven separate communities, and the growth of diverse local interests had begun to disrupt this separatist retreat.

The Massachusetts Bay Colony

In England, the Puritan movement continued its struggle to reform the national church. The political climate of the late 1620s, however, convinced a number of influential Puritans that the only way to protect their congregations was to emigrate. Some went to Ireland, others to the Netherlands or the West Indies, but many decided on New England, where, according to John Winthrop—later the first governor of the colony—they could establish "a city on a hill," a model of reform for England. In 1629 a royal charter was granted to a group of wealthy Puritans who called their enterprise the Massachusetts Bay Company. The company was given exclusive rights to settle and to trade, as well as to "religiously, peaceably and civilly" govern the territory and the native people between the Merrimack and Charles rivers, from the Atlantic "to the south sea on the west part." An advance force of 200 settlers soon left for the fishing settlement of Naumkeag on Massachusetts Bay, which they renamed Salem.

The Puritan emigration to Massachusetts became known as the Great Migration, a phrase that would be repeated many times in American history.

The seal of the Massachusetts Bay Company featured an Indian (dressed more like a native of South America than southern New England) imploring Puritans to "Come over and help us." It was a cynical ploy, for English Puritans were less involved with mission efforts among the Indians than were any of the other colonists in North America.

Between 1629 and 1643 some 20,000 people relocated to New England. Boston, founded in 1630, was their central settlement; within five years it was ringed by towns as far as thirty miles inland. By 1640 settlements had spread seventy-five miles west, into the Connecticut River Valley.

Most colonists arrived in groups from long-established communities in the east of England and were frequently led by men with extensive experience in local English government. Taking advantage of a loophole in their charter, the Puritan leaders transferred company operations to America in 1629, and within a few years they had transformed the company into a civil government. The original charter had established a General Court composed of a governor and his deputy, a board of magistrates (advisers), and the members of the corporation, known as freemen. In 1632 Governor Winthrop and his advisers declared all male heads of household who were also church members to be freemen. Two years later the freemen established their right to select delegates to represent the towns in drafting the laws of the colony. These delegates and the magistrates later separated into two legislative houses. Thus the procedures of a joint-stock company provided the origins for democratic suffrage and the bicameral division of legislative authority in America.

Indians and Puritans

The Algonquian Indians of southern New England found the English considerably different from the French and Dutch traders who had preceded them. The principal concern of the English was not commerce—although the fur trade remained an important part of their economy—but the acquisition of land for their growing settlements. Massasoit attempted to use the colonists to his own advantage. But he soon found that when the English attacked his enemies, their true motive was expansion.

In 1623, on Massasoit's urging, the Pilgrim military commander Miles Standish attacked a group of Massachusetts Indians north of Plymouth. When Standish brought back the sachem's head and placed it on a pike outside the settlement's gates, the meaning of the gesture was not lost on the Wampanoags. If we are allies, one Indian asked, "how cometh it to pass that when we come to Patuxet you stand upon your guard, with the mouths of your pieces [guns] presented to us?" Even the Wampanoags were soon calling their English allies *wotowquenange*, or "cutthroats."

Ravaged by disease, the Wampanoags' northern neighbors, the Massachusetts, were ill prepared for the Puritan settlement that began in 1629. The English believed they had the right to take what they deemed "unused" lands—lands not being used, that is, in the "English way"—and depopulated Massachusetts villages became prime targets. As one colonist wrote: "Their land is spacious and void, and there are few and [they] do but run over the grass, as do also the foxes and wild beasts." Conflicts between settlers over title, however, made it necessary to obtain deeds to the land, and the English used a variety of tactics to pressure the Indians into signing quitclaims, or documents in which the signers relinquish all claim to specified properties. The English allowed their livestock to graze native fields, making them useless for cultivation. They fined Indians for violations of English law, such as working on the Sabbath, and then demanded land as payment. In addition, they made deals with dishonest sachems. For giving up the land that became Charlestown, for example, the "Squaw Sachem" of the Pawtuckets, one of a number of women Algonquian leaders, received twenty-one coats, nineteen fathoms of wampum, and three bushels of corn. Disorganized and demoralized, their populations reduced by disease and warfare, many of the coastal Algonquians surrendered their autonomy and placed themselves under the protection of the English.

Indian peoples to the west, however, remained a formidable presence. They blocked Puritan expansion until they were devastated in 1633–34 by an epidemic of smallpox that spread from the St. Lawrence south to Long Island Sound just as hundreds of English migrants were crowding into coastal towns. "Without this remarkable and terrible stroke of God upon the natives," recorded a town scribe, "we would with much more difficulty have found room, and at far greater charge have obtained and purchased land." In the aftermath of the epidemic, Puritans established many new inland towns.

By the late 1630s the most powerful tribes in the vicinity of the Puritans were the Narragansets of present-day Rhode Island and their traditional enemies the Pequots, principal trading partners of the Dutch. The Pequots lived on Long Island Sound near the mouth of the Connecticut River, where they controlled the production of wampum, woven belts of sea shells used as a medium of exchange in the Indian trade. In 1637 the Narragansets, in alliance with the English, who were looking for an excuse to smash the Dutch, inaugurated the Pequot War. Narraganset warriors and English troops attacked the main Pequot village, killing most of its slumbering residents, including women and children. Unaccustomed to such tactics, the shocked Narragansets cried out to the English: "It is too furious, it slays too many."

New England Communities

Back in England, the standoff between King Charles and the Puritans in Parliament erupted in armed conflict in 1642. The civil war that followed ended in the triumph of the Parliamentarians over royalist forces. The king was executed in 1649, and England proclaimed a "Commonwealth," headed by the Puritan leader Oliver Cromwell. With Cromwell's success, Puritans no longer had the same incentive to leave the country, and in fact many Puritans returned from New England to participate in the war.

New England's economy had depended on the sale of supplies and land to arriving immigrants, but in the 1640s the importance of this "newcomer market" declined with slackening immigration. Lacking a single exportable commodity like tobacco, New Englanders were forced to diversify into farming, fishing, and lumbering. Merchants began construction of what would become, by the end of the century, the largest shipping fleet in the colonies, and became active in the carrying trade between the Caribbean and Chesapeake colonies and Europe. Its diversified economy ultimately provided New England with considerable long-term strength.

The communities of New England were distinct from those of the Chesapeake because the vast majority of the Puritans had come in family groups with relatively few servants. The Puritan ideal was a family governed in the same way that kings ruled over society. "Surely there is in all children a stubbornness, and stoutness of mind arising from natural pride," one Puritan declared, "which must be broken and beaten down." Parents often participated in the choice of mates for their offspring, and children typically married in the order of their births, younger siblings waiting until arrangements had been made for their elders.

Unique among the seventeenth-century colonies in North America, Massachusetts built an impressive system to educate its young. In 1647 the colony required that towns with 50 families or more support a public school; those with 100 families were to establish a "grammar" school that taught Latin, knowledge of which was required for admission to Harvard College, founded in 1636. Connecticut enacted similar requirements. Literacy was higher in New England than elsewhere in the colonies, or even in much of Europe. Far fewer New England women than men could read and write, however, because girls were excluded from

The first map printed in the English colonies, this view of New England was published in Boston in 1677. With north oriented to the right, it looks west from Massachusetts Bay, the two vertical black lines indicating the approximate boundaries of the Commonwealth of Massachusetts. The territory west of Rhode Island is noted as an Indian stronghold, the homelands of the Narraganset, Pequot, and Nipmuck peoples.

The Mason Children, by an unknown Boston artist, c. 1670. These Puritan children—David, Joanna, and Abigail Mason— are dressed in finery, an indication of the wealth and prominence of their family. The cane in young David's hand indicates his position as the male heir, while the rose held by Abigail is a symbol of childhood innocence.

the grammar schools. By 1639 the first printing press in the English colonies was in operation in Boston, and the following year it brought out the first American English publication, *The Bay Psalm Book*.

The Politics of Gender in Massachusetts

The Puritans stressed the importance of well-ordered communities and families. Colonists often emigrated in large kin groups that made up the core of the new towns. The Massachusetts General Court granted townships to proprietors representing the congregation, who then distributed fields, pasture, and woodlands in quantities proportional to the recipient's social status, so that wealthy families received more than humble ones. Settlers clustered their dwellings at the town center, near the meetinghouse that served as both church and civic center. Some towns, particularly those along the coast such as Boston, soon became centers of shipping. These clustered settlements and strong, vital communities made seventeenth-century New England quite different from Chesapeake society.

The family farm economy operated through the combined efforts of husband and wife. Men were generally responsible for field work, women for the work of the household, which included tending the kitchen garden (crops for household use), the dairy, and the henhouse, and securing fuel and water. Women managed an array of tasks, and some housewives independently traded garden products, milk,

and eggs. One New England husband, referring to his wife's domestic management, said, "I meddle not with the geese nor turkeys, for they are hers for she hath been and is a good wife to me." Indeed, women traders helped to create and sustain many of the bonds of New England communities.

It is mistaken to regard the Puritans as "puritanical." Although adultery was a capital crime in New England, Puritans celebrated the sexual expression that took place within marriage. Courting couples were even allowed to lie in bed together, with their lower bodies wrapped in an apron, a custom known as "bundling," free to caress and pet. In the words of an old New England ballad:

> *She is modest, also chaste*
> *While only bare from neck to waist,*
> *And he of boasted freedom sings,*
> *Of all above her apron strings.*

There were certainly many loving Puritan households with contented husbands and wives. Anne Bradstreet, a Massachusetts wife and mother and the first published poet of New England, wrote about her husband and marriage:

> *If ever two are one, then surely we.*
> *If ever man were lov'd by wife, then thee;*
> *If ever wife was happy in a man,*
> *Compare with me ye women if you can.*

Nevertheless, the cultural ideal of the day was the subordination of women to men. "I am but a wife, and therefore it is sufficient for me to follow my husband," wrote Lucy Winthrop Downing, and her brother John Winthrop declared, "A true wife accounts her subjection [to be] her honor and freedom." Married women could neither make contracts nor own property, neither vote nor hold office. The extraordinarily high birth rate of Puritan women was one mark of their "subjection." The average woman, marrying in her early twenties and surviving through her forties, could expect to bear eight children. Aside from abstinence, there was no form of birth control. There was significant cultural suspicion about wives who failed to have children or widows who were economically independent.

These suspicions about women came to the surface most notably in periodic witchcraft scares. During the course of the seventeenth century, according to one historian, 342 New England women were accused by their neighbors of witchcraft. The majority of them were childless or widowed or had reputations among their neighbors for their assertiveness and independence. In the vast majority of cases these accusations were dismissed by authorities. But in Salem,

Massachusetts, in 1692, when a group of girls claimed that they had been bewitched by a number of old men and women, the whole community was thrown into a panic of accusations. Before the colonial governor finally called a halt to the persecutions in 1693, twenty people had been tried, condemned, and executed.

The Salem accusations of witchcraft probably reflected generalized social tensions that found their outlet through an attack on people perceived as outsiders. Salem was a booming port, but although some residents were prospering, others were not. Most of the victims came from the eastern, more commercial section of town, whereas the majority of their accusers lived on the economically stagnant western side. Most of the accused also came from families whose religious sympathies were with sects of Anglicans, Quakers, or Baptists, not Puritans. Finally, a majority of the victims were old women, suspect because they lived alone, without men. The Salem witchcraft trials exposed the dark side of Puritan ideas about women.

Dissent and New Communities

The Puritans emigrated in order to practice their variety of Christianity, but they had little tolerance for other religious points of view. Religious disagreements among them were not accommodated but soon provoked the founding of new colonies. Thomas Hooker, a minister in Cambridge, disagreed with Puritan leaders over the extent of their authority, and believed that suffrage should not be restricted to male church members only. In 1636 he led his followers west to the Connecticut River, where they founded the town of Hartford. Hooker helped write the Fundamental Orders that marked the beginning of the colony of Connecticut.

The second major dissenter was the clergyman Roger Williams, who came to New England in 1631 to take up duties for the congregation in Salem. Williams believed in religious toleration and the separation of church and state. (Chapter 5 discusses these issues at greater length.) He also preached that the colonists had no absolute right to Indian land but must bargain for it in good faith. Because the Puritans believed that theirs was the one true religion, because they believed in the absolute union of church and state, and because they had established their colony on what had been Indian land, they considered Williams's ideas highly dangerous, and in 1636 they banished him from the Bay colony. With a group of followers, Williams emigrated to the Narragansett country, where he purchased land from the Indians and founded the town of Providence.

The next year Boston shook with another religious controversy. Anne Hutchinson, a brilliant woman who had arrived in New England with her merchant husband in 1634, led religious discussion groups that

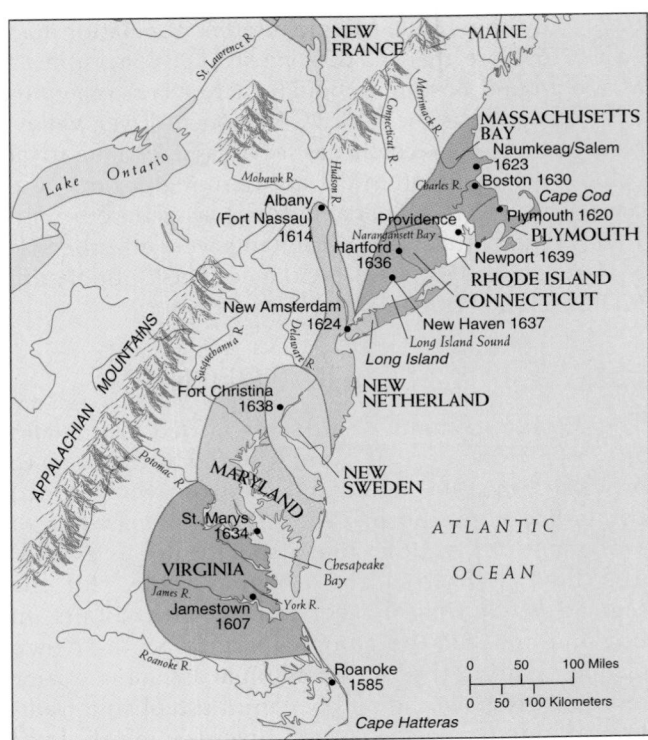

European Colonies of the Atlantic Coast, 1607–1639 *Virginia on Chesapeake Bay was the first English colony in North America, but by the mid-seventeenth century Virginia was joined by settlements of Scandinavians on the Delaware River, and Dutch on the Hudson River, as well as English religious dissenters in New England. The territories indicated here reflect the vague boundaries of the early colonies.*

criticized various Boston ministers for a lack of piety. The concentration of attention on good works, she argued, led people to believe that they could earn their way to heaven, a "popish" or Catholic heresy in the eyes of Calvinists. Hutchinson was called before the General Court, where the Puritan leaders made it clear that they would not tolerate a woman who publicly criticized men. Although she handled herself very skillfully, Hutchinson made the mistake of claiming that she had received a direct "revelation" from God, and so was excommunicated and banished. She and her followers moved to Roger Williams's settlement, where they established their own community in 1638.

A third group of dissenters, Samuel Gorton and his followers, were also banished from the Bay Colony and relocated, like the others, to the Narragansett haven. In 1644, Roger Williams received a charter creating the colony of Rhode Island, named for the principal island in Narragansett Bay, as a protection for these several dissenting communities. A new royal charter of 1663 guaranteed self-government and complete religious liberty and strengthened the colony's territorial claims for its approximately 2,000 English colonial inhabitants.

By the 1670s Massachusetts's population had grown to more than 40,000, most of it concentrated in and around Boston, although there were communities as far west as the lower Connecticut River Valley, New Hampshire—which was set off as a separate royal colony in 1680—and in the northern regions now the state of Maine (not separated from Massachusetts until 1820). Plymouth's 6,000 inhabitants were absorbed by Massachusetts in 1691. Connecticut's population totaled about 17,000.

THE RESTORATION COLONIES

The Puritan Commonwealth established in England after the execution of King Charles attempted to provide a measure of central control over colonial commerce with the passage in 1651 of an Act of Trade and Navigation, aimed specifically at excluding the Dutch from the carrying trade. But the regime was primarily concerned with affairs in England and left the colonies largely to their own devices. During this period colonial assemblies grew increasingly powerful and began to establish a tradition of independence. When Oliver Cromwell, Lord Protector of the Commonwealth, died in 1658, the Puritan new order failed to survive. England was desperate for political stability after decades of civil war and political strife. While retaining for itself certain significant powers of state, in 1660 a new royalist Parliament restored the Stuart monarchy, placing Charles II, son of the beheaded king, on the throne. One of Charles's most important acts was the establishment of several new proprietary colonies in North America, based on the model of the colony of Maryland. As this period in which the monarchy was reestablished was called the Restoration, these became known as the Restoration Colonies.

Early Carolina

In 1663 the king issued the first of the "Restoration" charters, which called for the establishment of the new colony of Carolina stretching from Virginia south to Spanish Florida. Virginians had already begun moving into the northern parts of this territory, and in 1664 the Carolina proprietors appointed a governor for the settlements in the area of Albemarle Sound and created a popularly elected assembly. By 1675, North Carolina, as it became known, was home to 5,000 small farmers and large tobacco planters.

Settlement farther south began in 1670 with the founding of coastal Charles Town (Charleston today). Most South Carolina settlers came from Barbados, a Caribbean colony the English had founded in 1627, which had grown rich from the production and sale of sugar. By the 1670s the island

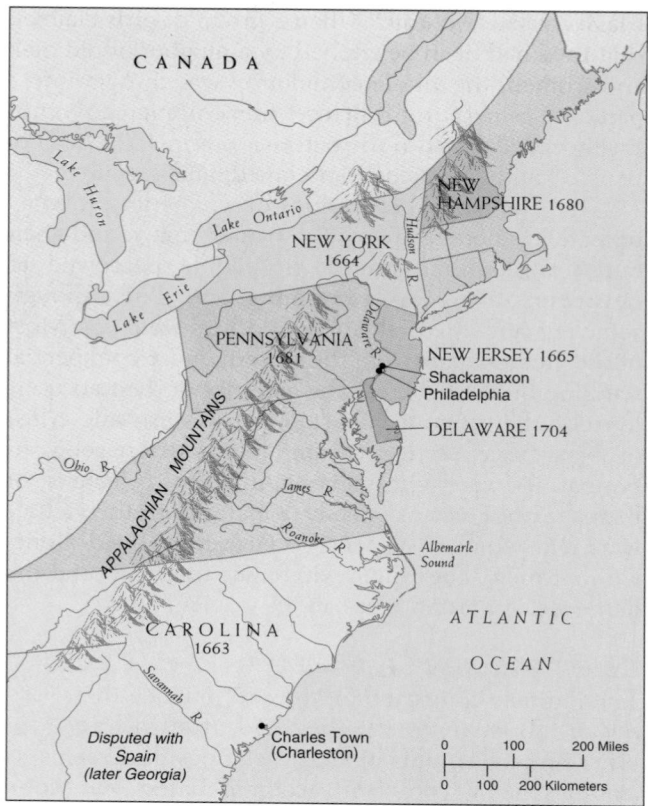

The Restoration Colonies *After the restoration of the Stuart monarchy in 1660, King Charles II of England created the new proprietary colonies of Carolina, New York, Pennsylvania, and New Jersey. New Hampshire was set off as a royal colony in 1680, and in 1704 the lower counties of Pennsylvania became the colony of Delaware.*

had become overpopulated with English settlers and Africans. The latter, imported as slaves to work the plantations, made up a majority of the population. Hundreds of Barbadians, both masters and their African slaves, relocated to South Carolina, lending a distinctly West Indian character to the colony. Adding to the diversity of the community was the arrival of several hundred French Huguenots after the revocation of the Edict of Nantes in 1685. By the end of the seventeenth century South Carolina's nonnative population numbered 6,000, some 2,500 of them enslaved Africans.

From New Netherland to New York

King Charles also coveted the lucrative Dutch colony of New Netherland, which extended from the trading town of Albany down the Hudson to the island city of New Amsterdam. The Netherlands was one of the great maritime trading powers of the seventeenth century, with sugar plantations in Brazil and trading posts in India, Indonesia, and China.

Establishing the colony of New Netherland in the 1620s, the Dutch forged a commercial alliance with the Iroquois Confederacy. The Iroquois, who occupied a strategic position between the coast and the interior, sought to channel the flow of furs through Dutch hands.

Once armed by the Dutch, the Iroquois embarked on a series of military adventures known as the Beaver Wars. They invaded the territories of neighboring peoples, and in the late 1640s they attacked and dispersed the Hurons, who had long controlled the flow of furs from the Great Lakes to the French in Montreal. As a result of these wars, the Dutch trading system was extended deep into the interior of the continent. Meanwhile, persistent conflict between the Iroquois and coastal Algonquians erupted in a series of brutal wars that resulted in the withdrawal of these Indian communities into the interior, opening the way for further Dutch expansion. In 1655 the Dutch succeeded in overwhelming a small colony of Swedes on the lower Delaware River, incorporating that region into their sphere of influence as well.

At that point the English began to challenge the Dutch. The two powers fought an inconclusive naval war in the English Channel during the early 1650s and then, a decade later, clashed along the West African coast. In 1664 Charles decided that the time had come to eliminate Dutch competition in North America. In 1664 an English fleet sailed into Manhattan harbor and forced the surrender of New Amsterdam without firing a shot. The next year, England declared war on the Netherlands, a conflict that lasted until 1667. Only five years of peace transpired before a third and final war broke out. These Anglo-Dutch wars marked the decline of the Dutch and the ascendance of the English in the Atlantic.

Charles granted the newly acquired colony of New Amsterdam to his brother James, the duke of York, renaming it New York in his honor. Otherwise the English government did little to disturb the existing order, preferring simply to reap the benefits of acquiring this profitable and dynamic colony. With settlers of various ethnic backgrounds, speaking many different languages and accommodating a wide range of reli-gious sects, New York became the most heterogeneous colony in North America. In 1674 the colonists were granted the status of English subjects, and in 1683, after persistent appeals, the duke approved the creation of a representative assembly. The communities of the Delaware Valley became the proprietary colony of New Jersey in 1665 but continued to be governed by New York until the 1680s. By the 1670s the combined population of these settlements numbered over 10,000, with more than 1,500 people clustered in the governmental and commercial center of New York City.

The Founding of Pennsylvania

In 1676, proprietary rights to the western portion of New Jersey were sold to a group of English Quakers, among them William Penn, who intended to make the area a religious haven for the Society of Friends, as the Quakers were formally known. A dissenting sect, Quakers were committed to religious toleration and pacifism. Penn himself had been imprisoned four times for publicly expressing these views. But he was the son of the wealthy and influential English admiral Sir William Penn, a close adviser of the king. In 1681, to settle a large debt owed to Sir William, King Charles granted the younger Penn a huge territory west of the Delaware River. The next year Penn supervised the laying out of his capital of Philadelphia, which would become known as "The City of Brotherly Love."

This is the earliest known view of New Amsterdam, printed in 1651. Like the French, the Dutch intended to construct a fur trade network that extended far into the continent, thus the prominent position given to the Indians shown arriving with their goods. They paddle a dugout canoe of distinctive design known to have been produced by the Algonquian peoples in the vicinity of Long Island Sound. Twenty-five years after its founding, the Dutch settlement still occupied only the lower tip of Manhattan Island.

The Delawares presented William Penn with this wampum belt after the Shackamaxon treaty of 1682. In friendship, a Quaker in distinctive hat clasps the hand of an Indian. The diagonal stripes on either side of the figures convey information about the territorial terms of the agreement. Wampum belts like this one, made from strings of white and purple shells, were used to commemorate treaties throughout the colonial period and were the most widely accepted form of money in the northeastern colonies during the seventeenth century.

Penn wanted this colony to be a "holy experiment." In his first Frame of Government, drafted in 1682, he included guarantees of religious freedom, civil liberties, and elected representation. By attempting to deal fairly with the Algonquian Indians, Penn tried to achieve what it took the Spanish and the Pueblo Indians a great deal of bloodshed to accomplish. He refused to permit colonization until settlement rights were negotiated and lands purchased. In 1682 and 1683, he made an agreement with the sachem Tammany of the Delaware tribe at the Indian town of Shackamaxon on the Delaware River. In subsequent years Chief Tammany appeared in many popular stories and myths among the peoples of the mid-Atlantic region. By the time of the Revolution, his name had become emblematic of the American spirit of independence, and later it was adopted by a New York political club. Although Pennsylvania's relations with the Indians later soured, during Penn's lifetime his reputation for fair dealing led a number of Indian groups to take refuge in the Quaker colony.

During the first decade of Pennsylvania's settlement more than 10,000 colonists arrived from England, and agricultural communities were soon spreading from the Delaware into the fertile interior valleys. In 1704 Penn approved the creation of a separate government for the area formerly controlled by the Scandinavians and Dutch, which became the colony of Delaware. In the eighteenth century, Pennsylvania became known as America's breadbasket, and late in the century Philadelphia became the most important colonial port in North America.

CONFLICT AND WAR

Pennsylvania's ability to maintain peaceful relations with the Indians was the great exception of the late seventeenth century. Throughout all the colonial regions of the continent this proved to be a time of

OVERVIEW

CONFLICT AND WAR

King Philip's War	1675–76	The Indian peoples of southern New England and the Puritan colonies fight for the control of land
Bacon's Rebellion	1675–76	Backcountry settlers attack Indians, and colonial authorities try to suppress these attacks
Wars in the South	1670s–1720s	British colonists in the Carolinas incite Creeks, Cherokees, and other Indian tribes to attack and enslave the mission Indians of Spanish Florida
The Glorious Revolution in America	1689	Colonists in Massachusetts, New York, and Maryland rise up against the colonial governments of King James II
King William's War	1689–97	The first of a series of colonial struggles between England and France, these conflicts occur principally on the frontiers of northern New England and New York

persistent warfare between colonists and Indians and of violent conflicts within colonial communities themselves. The revolt of the Pueblo Indians in New Mexico, discussed in the opening of this chapter, was one of the most dramatic examples of such conflict, and the most effective instance of Indian resistance to colonization in the history of North America.

King Philip's War

Another Indian revolt, known as King Philip's War, which erupted in New England in 1675, turned out to be a disaster for Indian people. During the nearly forty years of relative peace that followed the Pequot War of 1637, the Algonquian and English peoples of New England lived in close if tense contact. Several Puritan ministers, including John Eliot and Thomas Mayhew, began to preach to Indian people, and several hundred Algonquian converts eventually relocated in Christian Indian communities called "praying towns." Outside the colonial boundaries, however, there remained a number of independent Indian tribes, including the Wampanoags and Narragansets of Rhode Island and the Abenakis of northern New England. The extraordinary expansion of the Puritan population, coupled with their hunger for land, created pressures for further expansion into those territories.

In 1671 the colonial authorities at Plymouth forced the Wampanoags to concede authority over their homeland territory. This humiliation convinced the Wampanoag sachem Metacomet (called King Philip by his English teachers), son of Massasoit, that his people must break their half-century alliance with Plymouth and take up armed resistance. The New England colonies, meanwhile, prepared for a war of conquest.

In the spring of 1675 Plymouth magistrates arrested three Wampanoag men and executed them for the murder of a Christian Indian. Fearing the moment of confrontation had arrived, Metacomet sent a diplomatic mission to the Narragansetts appealing for a defensive alliance. Arguing that an alliance amounted to an Indian conspiracy, the New England colonies and New York—each hoping for territorial gain—sent armed forces into Narraganset country, attacking and burning a number of villages. What became known as King Philip's War soon engulfed all of New England.

At first things went well for the Indians. They forced the abandonment of English settlements on the Connecticut River and torched several towns less than twenty miles from Boston. But by the beginning of 1676 their campaign was in collapse. A combined colonial army invaded Narraganset country, burning villages, killing women and children, and defeating a large Indian force in a battle known as the Great Swamp Fight. In western New England, Metacomet

Spread of Settlement: British Colonies, 1650–1700
The spread of settlement in the English colonies in the late seventeenth century created the conditions for a number of violent conflicts, including King Philip's War, Bacon's Rebellion, the Southern Indian Wars, and King William's War.

appealed to the Iroquois for supplies and support, but instead they attacked and defeated his forces. Metacomet retreated back to his homeland, where the colonists annihilated his army in August 1676. The victors killed Metacomet and triumphantly marched his head on a pike through their towns. The colonists sold his wife and son, among hundreds of other captives, into West Indian slavery.

In their decisive attack on Metacomet's army, the Iroquois had been motivated by interests of their own. Casting themselves in the role of powerful intermediaries between other tribes and the English colonies, the Iroquois wanted to subjugate all trading rivals. In a series of negotiations conducted at Albany in 1677, the Iroquois Confederacy and the colony of New York created an alliance known as the Covenant Chain, which sought to establish both Iroquois dominance over all other tribes and New York dominance over all other colonies. During the 1680s the Iroquois pressed their claims as far west as the Illinois country, fighting the western Algonquians allied with the French trading system.

King Philip's War, which marked the end of organized Indian resistance in New England, took an enormous toll on human life and property. Approximately 4,000 Algonquians and 2,000 English colonists were dead, and dozens of colonial and native towns

Metacomet, or King Philip, in a mid-eighteenth century engraving by Paul Revere of Boston. Like his father Massasoit, Metacomet tried to cooperate with English colonists but finally had to fight to maintain his authority. For many years after the war, the leaders at Plymouth kept his severed head on display. Because his remains never received an honored burial, say the descendants of the Wampanoags, Metacomet's ghost still rises and walks about his homeland.

lay in smoking ruins. Fearing attack from Indians close at hand, colonists also attacked and destroyed most of the Christian "praying towns." Measured against the size of the population, this was one of the most destructive wars in American history.

Bacon's Rebellion

At the same time as King Philip's War, another English-Indian confrontation took place to the south in the Chesapeake. In the 1670s the Susquehannock people of the upper Potomac River came into conflict with tobacco planters expanding from Virginia. Violent raids in 1675, led by wealthy backcountry settler Nathaniel Bacon, included the indiscriminate murder of Indians. The efforts of Virginia governor

William Berkeley to suppress these unauthorized military expeditions so infuriated Bacon and his followers—many of them former indentured servants—that in the spring of 1676 they turned their fury against the colonial capital of Jamestown itself. Berkeley fled while Bacon pillaged and burned the town. When Bacon suddenly died of dysentery, however, his rebellion collapsed. Two years later, in a replay of these Virginia events, backcountry men in the Albemarle region of North Carolina overthrew the proprietary government in an episode of violence known as Culpeper's Rebellion. The rebels established a government of their own before being suppressed by English authorities.

Little immediate political change resulted from these two rebellions, but they marked an important change of direction for Virginia and North Carolina. During his tenure as "General of Virginia," Bacon had issued a manifesto demanding not only the death or removal of all Indians from the colony but also an end to the rule of aristocratic "grandees" and "parasites." The rebellion thus signaled a developing conflict of interests between the established Tidewater region, where the "Indian problem" had long since been settled, and frontier districts, where settler hunger for land created conflict with natives. Colonial authorities in Virginia and North Carolina, hoping to gain the support of backcountry men by enlarging the stock of available land, soon declared themselves in favor of armed expansion into Indian territory. But at the same time, planters' fears of disorder among former servants encouraged them to accelerate the transition to slave labor.

Wars in the South

There was also massive violence in South Carolina during the 1670s, as colonists there began the operation of a large-scale Indian slave trade. Charleston merchants encouraged Yamasees, Creeks, Cherokees, and Chickasaws to wage war on Indian tribes allied to rival colonial powers and to sell captives into slavery. Among the victims were the mission Indians of Spanish Florida, the Choctaw allies of the French, and the Tuscaroras, trading partners of the Virginians. The Florida mission Indians were hit so hard that by 1710 more than 12,000 of them had been captured and sold, thousands of others had been killed or dispersed, and the Spanish mission system, in operation for more than a century, lay in ruins.

This vicious slave trade extended well into the eighteenth century, resulting in the sale of thousands of southern Indians into captivity. Most of the men were shipped from Charleston to West Indian or northern colonies, but the Indian women remained in South Carolina. Many eventually formed relationships and had children with enslaved African men, forming a racial-ethnic group known as the mustees.

The Glorious Revolution in America

Dynastic change in England was another factor precipitating violence in North America. Upon Charles II's death in 1685, his brother and successor, James II, began a concerted effort to strengthen royal control over the colonies. During the preceding forty years colonial assemblies had grown powerful and independent, and King James was determined to reduce their status. He abolished the New York assembly, which had been particularly troublesome, and placed all power in the hands of the royal governor. Colonial assemblies continued to operate in the other colonies, but many became involved in bitter disputes with their governors.

In his most dramatic action, James abolished altogether the charter governments of the New England, New York, and New Jersey colonies, combining them into what he called the Dominion of New England. Edmund Andros, the royal governor of this dominion, imposed Anglican forms of worship in Puritan areas, violated traditions of local autonomy, and attempted to enforce the Navigation Acts (1651, 1660, 1663), which restricted colonial trade by preventing the colonies from trading directly with any nation other than England.

Within England, the same imperious style on the part of King James II alienated Parliament. In a bloodless transition in 1688, afterward known as the Glorious Revolution, some leaders in Parliament engineered replacing him with his daughter Mary and her Dutch husband, William of Orange. In 1689 the new monarchs agreed to a Bill of Rights, promising to respect traditional civil liberties, to summon and consult with Parliament annually, and to enforce and administer parliamentary legislation. These were significant concessions with profound implications for the future of English politics. England now had a "constitutional monarchy."

These changes unleashed the resentment against King James that had built up in the colonies, and a series of rebellions broke out against the authorities set in place by the king. In the spring of 1689, Governor Andros was attacked by an angry Boston mob, inflamed by rumors that he was a closet Catholic. He was able to escape their wrath but was arrested and deported by the local militia. When news of the Boston revolt arrived in New York, it inspired another uprising there. A group led by German merchant Jacob Leisler, and including many prominent Dutch residents, seized control of the city and called for the formation of a new legislature. In Maryland, rumors of a Catholic plot led to the overthrow of the propri-etary rule of the Calvert family by an insurgent group called the Protestant Association.

The new monarchs carefully measured their response to these uprisings. When Jacob Leisler attempted to prevent the landing of the king's troops in New York, he was arrested, tried, and executed. But the monarchs consented to the dismantling of the Dominion of New England and the end of proprietary rule in Maryland. The outcome of the Glorious Revolution in America was mixed. All the affected English colonies quickly revived their assemblies and returned to their tradition of self-government. But to forestall such disorders in the future, in 1692 the crown decreed that Massachusetts, New York, and Maryland would be royal colonies, with appointed governors, thus extending the control of the monarchy over its troublesome colonists.

King William's War

The year 1689 also marked the beginning of nearly seventy-five years of armed conflict between English and French forces for control of the North American interior. The Iroquois-English Covenant Chain challenged New France to press ever harder in search of commercial opportunities in the interior. In the far North, the English countered French dominance with the establishment of the Hudson's Bay Company, a royal fur-trade monopoly that in 1670 was given exclusive rights to Rupert's Land, the watershed of the great northern Hudson Bay.

Hostilities began with English-Iroquois attacks on Montreal and violence between rival French and English traders on Hudson Bay. These skirmishes were part of a larger conflict between England and France called the War of the League of Augsburg in Europe and King William's War in the North American colonies. In 1690 the French and their Algonquian allies counterattacked, burning frontier settlements in New York, New Hampshire, and Maine and pressing the attack against the towns of the Iroquois. The same year, a Massachusetts fleet briefly captured the strategic French harbor at Port Royal, in Acadia, but a combined English colonial force failed in its attempt to conquer the French settlements along the St. Lawrence. This inconclusive war was ended by the Treaty of Ryswick of 1697, which established an equally inconclusive peace. War between England and France would resume only five years later.

The persistent violence of these years concerned English authorities, who began to fear the loss of their North American possessions either from outside attack or from internal disorder. To shore up central control, in 1701 the English Board of Trade recommended making all charter and proprietary

CHRONOLOGY

1598	Juan de Oñate leads Spanish into New Mexico	1675	King Philip's War
1607	English found Jamestown	1676	Bacon's Rebellion
1608	French found Quebec	1680	Pueblo Revolt
1609	Spanish found Santa Fé	1681–82	Robert Sieur de La Salle explores the Mississippi
1620	Pilgrim emigration		
1622	Indian uprising in Virginia	1688	The Glorious Revolution
1625	Jesuit missionaries arrive in New France	1689	King William's War
1629	Puritans begin settlement of Massachusetts Bay	1698	Spanish reconquest of the Pueblos completed
1637	Pequot War	1701	English impose royal governments on all colonies but Massachusetts, Connecticut, and Pennsylvania
1649	Charles I executed		
1660	Stuart monarchy restored, Charles II becomes king		

governments into royal colonies. After a brief period under royal rule, William Penn regained private control of his domain, but Pennsylvania was the last remaining proprietary colony. Among the charter colonies, only Rhode Island and Connecticut retained their original governments. The result of this quarter-century of violence was the tightening of the imperial reins.

CONCLUSION

At the beginning of the seventeenth century the European presence north of Mexico was extremely limited: a Spanish base in Florida, a few Franciscan missionaries among the Pueblo Indians, and fishermen along the North Atlantic coast. By 1700, however, the human landscape of the Southwest, the South, and the Northeast had been transformed with the establishment of the Spanish colony of New Mexico, the French colonies of New France, and along the Atlantic coast a series of English colonies from New England in the North to the Carolinas in the South. More than a quarter million Europeans and Africans now resided in colonial enclaves. Indian tribal societies had been disrupted, depopulated, and in some cases destroyed. The policies of the various European colonizers differed significantly, and outside the colonial enclaves Indians still constituted the vast majority of the continent's inhabitants, but the profound changes of the seventeenth century had ominous implications for Indian peoples.

During the long civil war in England the English colonies had been left to run their own affairs, but with the Restoration in 1660, and the establishment of the constitutional monarchy in 1689, the English state began to supervise its troublesome colonists more closely, beginning a long struggle over the limits of self-government. The violence and warfare of the last decades of the century suggested that conflict would continue to play a significant role in the future of colonial America.

REVIEW QUESTIONS

1. Using examples drawn from this chapter, discuss the differences between colonizing "frontiers of inclusion" and "exclusion."

2. What factors turned England's Chesapeake colony of Virginia from stark failure to brilliant success?

3. Discuss the role of religious dissent in the founding of the first New England colonies and in stimulating the creation of others.
4. Compare and contrast William Penn's policy with respect to Indian tribes with the policies of other English settlers, in the Chesapeake and New England, and with the policies of the Spanish, the French, and the Dutch.
5. What were the principal causes of colonial violence and warfare of the late seventeenth century?

RECOMMENDED READING

James Axtell, *The European and the Indian: Essays in the Ethnohistory of Colonial America* (1981). A readable introduction to the dynamics of mutual discovery between natives and colonizers.

Carl Bridenbaugh, *Vexed and Troubled Englishmen, 1590–1642* (1968). A social history of the English people on the eve of colonization, emphasizing their religious and economic problems.

W. J. Eccles, *France in America* (1990). The most comprehensive introduction to the history of New France.

Andrew L. Knaut, *The Pueblo Revolt of 1680* (1995). The most complete and sophisticated account of the revolt.

Edmund S. Morgan, *American Slavery, American Freedom* (1975). A classic interpretation of early Virginia.

Morgan argues that early American ideas of freedom for some were based on the reality of slavery for others.

Neal Salisbury, *Manitou and Providence: Indians, Europeans, and the Making of New England* (1982). One of the best examples of the new ethnohistory of Indians; a provocative intercultural approach to the history of the Northeast.

David J. Weber, *The Spanish Frontier in North America* (1992). A powerful overview that includes the history of New Mexico and Florida.

Peter H. Wood, et al., eds., *Powhatan's Mantle: Indians in the Colonial Southeast* (1989). Essays detailing the conflict and consort between colonists and natives in the South.

ADDITIONAL BIBLIOGRAPHY

The Spanish and French in North America

James Axtell, *The Invasion Within: The Contest of Culture in Colonial North America* (1985)

Gilberto Rafael Cruz, *Let There Be Towns: Spanish Municipal Origins in the American Southwest, 1610–1810* (1988)

W. J. Eccles, *The Canadian Frontier, 1534–1760* (1983)

The Chesapeake

Kathleen M. Brown, *Good Wives, Nasty Wenches, and Anxious Patriarchs: Gender, Race, and Power in Colonial Virginia* (1996)

Wesley F. Craven, *White, Red, and Black: The Seventeenth Century Virginian* (1971)

Carville Earle, *The Evolution of a Tidewater Settlement System: All Hallow's Parish, Maryland, 1650–1783* (1975)

Jack P. Greene and J. R. Poole, eds., *Colonial British America: Essays in the New History of the Early Modern Era* (1984)

Karen Ordahl Kupperman, *Settling with the Indians: The Meeting of English and Indian Cultures in America, 1580–1640* (1980)

Gloria L. Main, *Tobacco Colony: Life in Early Maryland, 1650–1720* (1982)

Thad W. Tate and David L. Ammerman, eds., *The Chesapeake in the Seventeenth Century* (1979)

New England

David Grayson Allen, *In English Ways: The Movement of Societies and the Transferal of English Local Law and Custom* (1981)

Bernard Bailyn, *The New England Merchants in the Seventeenth Century* (1955)

Emery Battis, *Saints and Sectaries: Anne Hutchinson and the Antinomian Controversy in the Massachusetts Bay Colony* (1962)

Theodore Dwight Bozeman, *To Live Ancient Lives: The Primitivist Dimension in Puritanism* (1988)

Francis J. Bremer, ed., *Puritanism: Transatlantic Perspectives on a Seventeenth-Century Anglo-American Faith* (1993)

Carl Bridenbaugh, *Fat Mutton and Liberty of Conscience: Society in Rhode Island, 1636–1690* (1974)

David Cressy, *Coming Over: Migration and Communication between England and New England in the Seventeenth Century* (1987)

William Cronon, *Changes in the Land: Indians, Colonists, and the Ecology of New England* (1983)

Bruce Colin Daniels, *Puritans at Play: Leisure and Recreation in Colonial New England* (1995)

John Demos, *A Little Commonwealth: Family Life in Plymouth Colony* (1970)

M. Etienne and E. Leacock, eds., *Women and Colonization* (1980)

Christopher Hill, *The World Turned Upside Down: Radical Ideas during the English Revolution* (1972)

Stephen Innes, *Labor in a New Land* (1983)

Francis Jennings, *The Invasion of America: Indians, Colonialism, and the Cant of Conquest* (1975)

Amy Scrager Lang, *Prophetic Women: Anne Hutchinson and the Problem of Dissent in the Literature of New England* (1987)

Michael Walzer, *The Revolution of the Saints: A Study in the Origins of Radical Politics* (1965)

Restoration Colonies

Wesley F. Craven, *The Southern Colonies in the Seventeenth Century, 1607–1689* (1949)

Melvin B. Endy Jr., *William Penn and Early Quakerism* (1973)

Michael Kammen, *Colonial New York: A History* (1975)

Sung Bok Kim, *Landlord and Tenant in Colonial New York: Manorial Society, 1664–1775* (1978)

H. T. Merrens, *Colonial North Carolina* (1964)

Gary B. Nash, *Quakers and Politics: Pennsylvania, 1681–1726* (1968)

Oliver Rink, *Holland on the Hudson: An Economic and Social History of Dutch New York* (1986)

Robert C. Ritchie, *The Duke's Province: A Study of New York Politics and Society, 1664–1691* (1977)

M. Eugene Sirmans, *Colonial South Carolina: A Political History, 1663–1763* (1966)

Jack M. Sosin, *English America and the Restoration Monarchy of Charles II: Transatlantic Politics, Commerce, and Kinship* (1980)

Conflict and War

Thomas J. Archdeacon, *New York City, 1664–1710* (1976)

Russell Bourne, *The Red King's Rebellion: Racial Politics in New England, 1675–1678* (1990)

Paul Boyer and Stephen Nissenbaum, *Salem Possessed* (1974)

Ramón A. Gutiérrez, *When Jesus Came, the Corn Mothers Went Away: Marriage, Sexuality, and Power in New Mexico, 1500–1846* (1991)

Richard R. Johnson, *Adjustment to Empire: The New England Colonies, 1675–1715* (1981)

D. W. Jordan, *Maryland's Revolution of Government, 1689–1692* (1974)

Carol F. Karlsen, *The Devil in the Shape of a Woman: Witchcraft in Colonial New England* (1987)

Yusuhide Kawashima, *Puritan Justice and the Indian: White Man's Law in Massachusetts, 1630–1763* (1986)

Almon Wheeler Lauber, *Indian Slavery in Colonial Times within the Present Limits of the United States* (1913)

David S. Lovejoy, *The Glorious Revolution in America* (1972)

Michael J. Publisi, *Puritans Besieged: The Legacies of King Philip's War in the Massachusetts Bay Colony* (1991)

Jack M. Sosin, *English America and the Revolution of 1688* (1982)

Wilcomb E. Washburn, *The Governor and the Rebel: A History of Bacon's Rebellion in Virginia* (1957)

Stephen S. Webb, *1676: The End of American Independence* (1980)

Thomas J. Wertenbaker, *Torchbearer of the Revolution: The Story of Bacon's Rebellion and its Leader* (1940)

Biography

Mary M. Dunn, *William Penn, Politics and Conscience* (1967)

J. A. Leo Lemay, *The American Dream of Captain John Smith* (1991)

Edmund S. Morgan, *Puritan Dilemma: The Story of John Winthrop* (1958)

Ann Sanford, *Anne Bradstreet, the Worldly Puritan* (1974)

Marc Simmons, *The Last Conquistador: Juan de Oñate and the Settling of the Far Southwest* (1991)

Robert S. Tilton, *Pocahontas: The Evolution of an American Narrative* (1994)

Alvin Gardner Weeks, *Massasoit of the Wampanoags* (1919)

Selma R. Williams, *Divine Rebel: The Life of Anne Marbury Hutchinson* (1981)

CHAPTER FOUR

SLAVERY AND EMPIRE

1441–1770

AMERICAN COMMUNITIES
African Slaves Build Their Own Community in Coastal Georgia

Africans labored in the steamy heat of the coastal Georgia rice fields, the breeches of the men rolled up over their knees, the sack skirts of the women gathered and tied about their hips, leaving them, in the words of one shocked observer, "two thirds naked." Standing on the banks of canals that channeled water to the fields, African slave drivers, whips at the ready, supervised the work. Upriver, groups cut away cypress and gum trees and cleared the swampland's jungle maze of undergrowth; others constructed levees, preparing to bring more land under cultivation. An English overseer or plantation master could be seen here and there, but overwhelmingly it was a country populated by Africans.

These Georgia plantations were southern extensions of the South Carolina rice belt. Although slavery had been prohibited by Georgia's original colonial charter of 1732, the restriction was lifted when Georgia became a royal colony two decades later. By 1770, 15,000 African Americans lived on several hundred coastal plantations, and the population of the region was 80 percent African. The rice plantations were owned by a small elite, dominated by a tight circle of crown officials and their relatives and associates. Georgia's royal governor and lieutenant governor, for example, owned more than a dozen plantations with over 50,000 acres and 800 slaves. Plantations with names such as Mulberry Grove, New Settlement, and Walnut Hill were among the most recent, and most profitable, additions to the British New World empire.

Rice had become one of the most valuable commodities produced in mainland North America, surpassed in value only by tobacco and wheat. The growth of rice production in the Lower South was matched by an enormous expansion in the Atlantic slave trade. Having no experience in rice cultivation, English colonial planters pressed slave traders to supply them with Africans from rice-growing regions such as the Windward Coast of West Africa. In its workforce, its methods, and even its tools, southern rice culture was patterned on an African model.

Although in the eighteenth century the number of North American blacks who were "country-born" (native to America, and thus born into slavery) grew steadily, the majority on the rice plantations continued to be what were known as "salt-water" Africans. These men and women had endured the shock of enslavement. Ripped from their homeland communities in West Africa by slave raiders, they were brutally marched to coastal forts. There they were imprisoned, subjected to humiliating inspections of their bodies, and branded on the buttocks like animals. Packed into the holds of stinking ships, they endured a nightmarish passage across the Atlantic Ocean. When finally unloaded on a strange continent, they were sold at dockside auctions, then once again marched overland to their destinations on New World plantations. On the rice plantations of isolated coastal Georgia enslaved Africans suffered from overwork and numerous physical ailments caused by poor diet, minimal and inappropriate clothing, and inadequate housing. Mortality rates were exceptionally high, especially for infants. Colonial laws permitted masters to discipline and punish slaves indiscriminately. They were whipped, confined in irons, castrated, or sold to other landowners with little regard for their relations with family or friends.

Africans struggled to make a place for themselves in this inhospitable world. The knowledge of rice cultivation that many slaves brought with them to the rice coast gave them the bargaining power to win acceptance from their masters of the familiar work routines and rhythms of West Africa. Thus, low-country plantations operated according to the task system: once slaves finished their specific jobs, they could use their remaining time to hunt, fish, or cultivate family gardens. Masters frequently complained that "tasking" did not produce the same level of profit as the gang labor system of the sugar plantations, but African rice hands refused to work any other way.

Despite this small degree of control over the form of their servitude, slaves on the Georgia coast ran away, like slaves everywhere in the Americas. Readers of Savannah newspapers were urged to look out for fugitives: Statira, a woman of the "Gold Coast Country" with tribal markings upon her temples, or "a negro fellow named Mingo, about 40 years old, and his wife Quante, a sensible wench about 20 with her child, a boy about 3 years old, all this country born." Some fled in groups, heading for the Creek Indian settlements in northern Florida, or toward St. Augustine, where the Spanish promised them safe haven. Some struck out violently at their masters: in 1759, a group of nine Africans from a Savannah plantation killed their master and stole a boat, planning to head upriver. They were apprehended as they lay in wait to murder their hated overseers as well.

So slaves resisted. But like slaves throughout the New World, the majority of enslaved Africans and African Americans of the Georgia coast remained, and through their strategy and determination, built their own communities within the heartless world of slavery. Plantation slaves throughout the American South married, raised children, and gradually created African American kinship networks. They passed on African names and traditions and created new ones. These links between individuals and families formed the basis for reestablished communities.

African American slave communities combined elements both of African languages and of English to form dialects that allowed newly arrived people from many different African ethnic groups as well as American-born slaves to communicate with one another. Neither individuals nor families alone can make a language; that is something only a community can do. The common African heritage and a common status as slaves supplied the basis for the African American community. Communities provided both newly arrived Africans and the American-born with the opportunity to build relationships. Without African American communities there could have been no African American culture.

Traveling through the Georgia and Carolina low country during the 1740s, an English missionary heard a clamor in the woods along the road. As he peered through the trees he was startled to see a group of slaves "dancing round the fire." The African American community was refitting traditional dance, song, and story to New World circumstances, just as it was reestablishing African arts such as woodworking, iron making, and weaving. Through their culture, the slaves shared a powerful awareness of their common oppression. They told or sang dialect tales of mistreatment, as in this song of Quow, the punished slave:

Was matter Buddy Quow?
I ble Obesha bang you....
Dah Backrow Man go wrong you, Buddy Quow,
Dah Backrow Man go wrong you, Buddy Quow.

[What's the matter Brother Quow?
I believe the overseer's beat you....
The white man's wronged you, Brother Quow,
The white man's wronged you, Brother Quow.]

Just as European settlers planted colonial communities, so Africans, who constituted the largest group of people to come to North America during the colonial era, constructed distinctive communities of their own. The history of African Americans includes the story of the Atlantic slave trade, the plunder of Africa, and the profits of the empire. But it is also a story of achievement under the most difficult of circumstances and of the making of families, kin networks, and communities. They "labor together and converse almost wholly among themselves," a minister wrote of low-country slaves. "They are, as 'twere, a nation within a nation."

Georgia
Sea
Islands

KEY TOPICS

- The development of the slavery system
- The history of the slave trade and the Middle Passage
- Community development among African Americans in the eighteenth century

- The connections between the institution of slavery and the imperial system of the eighteenth century
- The early history of racism in America

THE BEGINNINGS OF AFRICAN SLAVERY

Household slaves had long been a part of the world of Mediterranean Europe. War captives were sold to wealthy families, who put them to work as servants or artisans. In the fifteenth century, Venetian and Genoese merchants led the traffic in captured Slavic peoples—the word "slave" derives from the name Slav—as well as Muslims and Africans. But many Europeans were disturbed by the moral implications of enslaving Christians, which most Slavs were, and in the early fifteenth century the pope excommunicated a number of merchants engaged in selling such captives. The trade in Africans and Muslims, however, continued.

One of the goals of Portuguese expansion in the fifteenth century was access to the lucrative West African trade in slaves that had been dominated by the Moors—today's Algerians, Libyans, and Moroccans—of northern Africa. The first African slaves to arrive in Lisbon were twelve men kidnapped by a Portuguese captain in 1441; three years later another Portuguese crew seized twenty-nine men and women off Cape Blanco and shipped them home. But Portuguese traders found it considerably more efficient to leave the kidnapping to Africans who were willing to sell captives in exchange for European commodities. By the 1450s a small but regular slave trade between Africa and Europe was in place.

Sugar and Slavery

The greatest market for these slaves was the large sugar plantations the Portuguese established on their island colony of Madeira, off the coast of northern Africa. Portuguese masters brutally exploited these Africans, working many of them to death, since profits were high and replacement costs low. Sugar and slaves had gone together since the fourteenth century, when Italian merchants first imported cane sugar from West Asia and set up the first sugar plantations on the islands of the Mediterranean. For the sake of sweetness, Europeans subjected Africans to the suffering of slavery.

One of the first products Columbus introduced to the New World was sugarcane, and soon sugar plantations were operating on the island of Hispaniola. At first the Spanish tried to use native Indian people as a slave labor force, but because disease and warfare had so reduced the indigenous population colonists soon turned to the African slaves who were already working in Spain. The introduction of horse-powered sugar mills around 1510 so increased the demand for labor that in 1518 Spain granted Portuguese slavers an *asiento* (license) to bring slaves to America directly from Africa. Meanwhile, the Portuguese, aided by Dutch financiers, created a center of sugar production in northeast Brazil that became a model of the efficient and brutal exploitation of African labor. By 1600 some 25,000 enslaved Africans labored on the plantations of Hispaniola and Brazil. "As a result of the sugar factories," a colonial Spanish official declared in 1535, "the land seems an…image of Ethiopia itself."

The Dutch, using their experience in Brazil, became responsible for the next extension of slavery in the Americas. In 1630 they seized Brazil and controlled this lucrative colony for the next twenty years. Skilled at finance and commerce, they greatly expanded the European market for sugar, converting it from a luxury item for the rich to a staple for European workers. Along with addictive tropical commodities such as tobacco, coffee, and tea, sugar became what one historian calls a "proletarian hunger-killer," helping to sustain people through increasingly long working days. As the market for sugar expanded, the Dutch expanded their sugar operations throughout the tropics, introducing it, for example, into the small island of Barbados, which soon became the most valuable of England's colonies. Once the profitability of sugar had been demonstrated, the English sought to expand their production by seizing the island of Jamaica from the Spanish in 1655 and making it over in the image of Barbados. Jamaica, much larger than Barbados, soon became the crown jewel of Britain's eighteenth-century empire.

The French repeated the process. They first developed sugar plantations on the small island of

Martinique, then seized the eastern half of Hispaniola from the Spanish and created a sugar colony called St. Domingue (today's Haiti). Caribbean sugar and slaves had become the centerpiece of the European colonial system.

West Africans

The men and women whose labor made these tropical colonies so profitable came from the long-established societies and local communities of West Africa. In the sixteenth century more than a hundred different peoples lived along the coast of West Africa, from Cape Verde south to Angola. In the north were the Wolofs, Mandingos, Hausas, Ashantis, and Yorubas; to the south the Ibos, Sekes, Bakongos, and Mbundus.

In all these societies the most important institution was the local community, which was organized by kinship. Decisions about production, storage, and distribution were generally made by clan leaders and village chiefs; local courts arbitrated disputes. Men frequently took a second or third wife. This marriage system, known as polygyny, produced very large composite families with complex internal relationships. Because of restrictions on sexual relations, however, West African women bore fewer children than the typical European woman, and many enjoyed considerable social and economic independence as tradeswomen.

West African societies were based on sophisticated farming systems many thousands of years old. Farmers cultivated millet, sorghum, and rice on the grassy savannas and fruits, root crops, and other vegetables in the tropical forests that straddled the equator. West Africans had mastered the art of iron making, but because their soils were rather thin and poor, they found no use for iron plows. Rather, like the native farmers of North America, Africans practiced "shifting cultivation": they cleared land by burning, used hoes or digging sticks to work in the ash, rich in nutrients, and when fertility declined after several years, they let their old fields lie fallow and moved on to clear new ones. Men worked at clearing the land, women at cultivation and the sale of surpluses in the lively West African markets.

Farming sustained large populations and thriving networks of commerce, and in some areas kingdoms and states developed. Along the upper Niger River, where the grassland gradually turns to desert, towns such as Timbuktu developed into trading centers. West African metal goods, gold, ivory, and textiles made their way from these towns to the Mediterranean on trans-Saharan caravans organized by Moors and other Muslim traders. The attempt to control the wealth this trade generated led to the rise and fall of a succession of military empires. The most extensive of these was the Mali Empire, whose greatest ruler, Mansa Musa, made Timbuktu a leading intellectual as well as commercial center. When the Portuguese first arrived in the fifteenth century, the most important state in the region was the powerful Muslim kingdom of Songhai (today the African nation of Mali), noted for the cavalry and army with which it controlled the flow of trade. There were also many lesser states and kingdoms along the coast, and it was with these that the Portuguese first bargained for Africans who could be sold as slaves.

Slavery had long been an established institution in Africa. Most enslaved men and women had been captured in war or condemned to servitude as criminal punishment. African slavery was not a permanent condition, however; most slaves were eventually incorporated into the families they served. They were allowed to marry, and their children were born free. "With us they did no more work than other members of the community, even their master," remembered Olaudah Equiano, an Ibo captured and shipped to America as a slave in 1756, when he was a boy of eleven. "Their food, clothing, and lodging were nearly the same as [the others'], except that they were not permitted to eat with those who were born free." When African merchants sold the first slaves to the Portuguese, they must have thought that European slavery would be similar. But as Equiano declared: "How different was their condition from that of the slaves in the West Indies!" Yet it was the West African familiarity with "unfree" labor that made it

This image of Mansa Musa (1312–37), the ruler of the Muslim kingdom of Mali in West Africa, is taken from the Catalan Atlas, *a magnificent map presented to the king of France in 1381 by his cousin, the king of Aragon. In the words of the* Catalan *inscription, Musa was "the richest, the most noble lord in all this region on account of the abundance of gold that is gathered in his land." He holds what was thought to be the world's largest gold nugget. Under Musa's reign, Timbuktu became a capital of world renown.*

The African Slave Trade *The enslaved men, women, and children transported to the Americas came from West Africa, the majority from the lower Niger River (called the Slave Coast) and the region of the Congo and Angola.*

possible for African and European traders to begin the trade in human merchandise.

THE AFRICAN SLAVE TRADE

The movement of Africans across the Atlantic to the Americas was the largest forced migration in world history. Moreover, Africans made up the largest group of people to come to the Americas before the nineteenth century, outnumbering European immigrants by the astounding ratio of six to one. The Atlantic slave trade, which began with the Portuguese in the fifteenth century and did not end in the United States until 1808 (it continued elsewhere in the Americas until the 1870s) is a brutal chapter in the making of America.

The Demography of the Slave Trade
Scholars today estimate that slavers transported 10 to 11 million Africans to the Americas during the four

centuries of the trade. Seventy-six percent arrived from 1701 to 1810—the peak period of colonial demand for labor, when tens of thousands of individuals were shipped from Africa each year. Of this vast multitude, about half were delivered to Dutch, French, or British sugar plantations in the Caribbean, a third to Portuguese Brazil, and 10 percent to Spanish America. A much smaller proportion—about one in twenty, or an estimated 600,000 men, women, and children— were transported from Africa to the British colonies of North America.

Among the Africans brought to the Americas, men generally outnumbered women two to one. Since most Africans were destined for field work, this ratio probably reflected the preferences of plantation owners. The majority of captured and transported Africans were young people, between the ages of fifteen and thirty, and nearly every ethnic group in West Africa was represented among them.

Slavers of All Nations

All the nations of western Europe participated in the slave trade. Dutch slavers began challenging Portuguese control at the end of the sixteenth century, and during the sugar boom of the seventeenth century Holland became the most prominent slave-trading nation. The English also entered the trade in the sixteenth century, beginning with the African voyages of John Hawkins. The Royal African Company, a slave-trading monopoly based in London, was chartered in 1672, but in 1698 England threw open the trade to independent merchants. Soon hundreds of ships from Bristol and Liverpool were competing with those from London. As a result, the number of slaves shipped to North America skyrocketed. The Dutch and Portuguese, however, continued to play important roles, alongside slave traders from France, Sweden, and several German duchies.

For the most part the European presence in Africa was confined to outposts, although the

Slave Colonies of the Seventeenth and Eighteenth Centuries *By the eighteenth century the system of slavery had created societies with large African populations throughout the Caribbean and along the southern coast of North America.*

Portuguese established a colony in Angola. By the early eighteenth century more than two dozen trading forts dotted the 220 miles of the Gold Coast alone. As the slave trade peaked in the middle of the century, however, the forts of trading companies gave way to small coastal clusters of huts where independent traders set up operations with the cooperation of local headmen or chiefs.

This informal manner of trading offered opportunities for small operators, such as the New England slavers who entered the trade in the early eighteenth century. Often bartering rum or salt fish for human beings, these Yankees earned a reputation for crafty dealings. They came by it honestly: "Water your rum as much as possible," one New England merchant instructed his captain, "and sell as much by the short measure as you can." At first, most New England slavers sailed principally from Massachusetts, but after 1750 the center shifted to Rhode Island. Many great New England fortunes were built from profits in the slave trade.

The Shock of Enslavement

The slave trade was a collaboration between European or American and African traders. Dependent on the favor of local rulers, many colonial slave traders lived permanently in coastal forts and married African women, reinforcing their commercial ties with family relations. In many areas a mixed-ancestry group became prominent in the coastal slave trade. Continuing the

Portrait of Olaudah Equiano, *by an unknown English artist, ca. 1780. Captured in Nigeria in 1756 when he was eleven years old, Equiano was transported to America and eventually purchased by an English sea captain. After ten years as a slave, he succeeded in buying his own freedom and dedicated himself to the antislavery cause. His book,* The Interesting Narrative of the Life of Olaudah Equiano *(1789), was published in numerous editions, translated into several languages, and became the prototype for dozens of other slave narratives in the nineteenth century.*

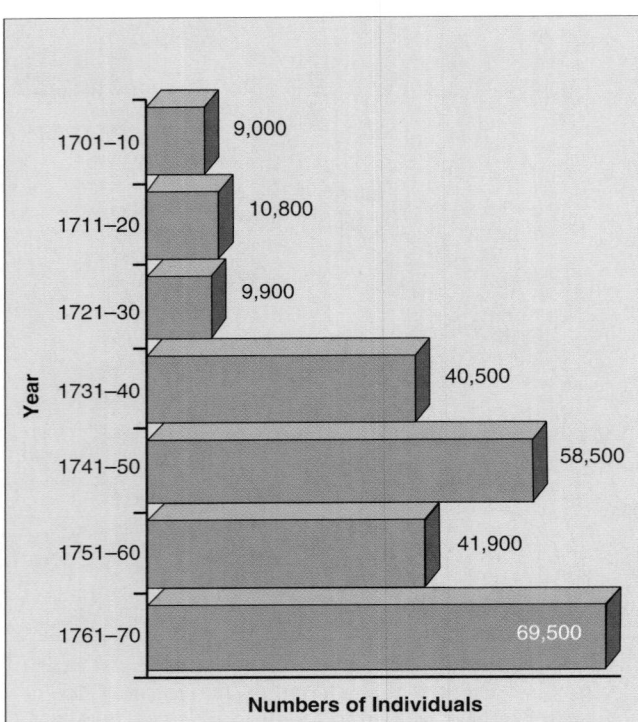

Estimated Number of Africans Imported to British North America, 1701–1775 *These official British statistics include only slaves imported legally and consequently undercount the total number who arrived on American shores. But the trend over time is clear. With the exception of the 1750s, when the British colonies were engulfed by the Seven Years War, the slave trade continued to rise in importance in the decades before the Revolution.*

Source: R. C. Simmons, *The American Colonies: From Settlement to Independence* (London: Longman, 1976), 186.

practice of the Portuguese, the grim business of slave raiding was left to the Africans themselves. Slaves were not at all reticent about condemning the participation of their fellow Africans. "I must own to the shame of my own countrymen," wrote Ottobah Cugoano, who was sold into slavery in the mid-eighteenth century, "that I was first kidnapped and betrayed by [those of] my own complexion."

Most Africans were enslaved through warfare. Sometimes large armies launched massive attacks, burning whole towns and taking hundreds of prisoners. More common were smaller raids in which a group of armed men attacked at nightfall, seized everyone within reach, then escaped with their captives. However, kidnapping, called *panyaring* in the jargon of the slave trade, was also common. One seaman, ashore while his slave ship awaited its cargo, amused himself by peeking at a young African woman bathing. Suddenly two raiders jumped from the bushes and dragged her off. He later saw them carry her on board and sell her to the captain, no questions asked.

As the demand for slaves increased in the eighteenth century with the expansion of the plantation system in the Americas, raids extended deeper and deeper into the African interior. The march to the coast was filled with terrors. One account describes a two-month trip in which many captives died of hunger, thirst, or exhaustion, several attempted suicide, and the whole party was forced to hide to avoid being seized by a rival band of raiders. The captives finally arrived on the coast, where they were sold to an American vessel bound for South Carolina.

Enslavement was an unparalleled shock. Venture Smith, an African born in Guinea in 1729, was eight years old when he was captured. After many years in North American slavery, he still vividly recalled the attack on his village, the torture and murder of his father, and the long march of his people to the coast. "The shocking scene is to this day fresh in my mind," he wrote, "and I have often been overcome while thinking on it." The horror was captured in the song of captives marching to the Slave Coast from the interior kingdom of Bornu, imploring the assistance of one of their gods, a song long remembered by African Americans and published by abolitionists in the nineteenth century:

> *Bornu-land was rich and good,*
> *Wells of water, fields of food;*
> *Bornu-land we see no longer,*
> *Here we thirst, and here we hunger,*
> *Here the Moor man smites in anger;*
> *Where are we going, Rubee?*
> *Where are we going? Where are we going?*
> *Hear us, save us, Rubee!*
> *Moons of marches from our eyes,*
> *Bornu-land behind us lies;*
> *Hot the desert wind is blowing,*
> *Wild the waves of sand are flowing!*
> *Hear us! Tell us, where are we going?*
> *Where are we going, Rubee?*

On the coast, European traders and African raiders assembled their captives. Prisoners waited in dark dungeons or in open pens called barracoons. To lessen the possibility of collective resistance, traders split up families and ethnic groups. Captains carefully inspected each man and woman, and those selected for transport were branded on the back or buttocks with the mark of the buyer. Olaudah Equiano remembered that "those white men with horrible looks, red faces, and long hair, looked and acted…in so savage a manner;…I had never seen among any people such instances of brutal cruelty." Equiano's narrative, written during the 1780s, after he had secured his freedom, is one of the few that

A slave coffle in an eighteenth-century print. As the demand for slaves increased, raids extended deeper and deeper into the African interior. Tied together with forked logs or bark rope, men, women, and children were marched hundreds of miles toward the coast, where their African captors traded them to Europeans.

provide an African account of enslavement. He and his fellow captives became convinced that they "had got into a world of bad spirits" and were about to be eaten by cannibals. A French trader wrote that many prisoners were "positively prepossessed with the opinion that we transport them into our country in order to kill and eat them."

The Middle Passage

In the eighteenth century English sailors christened the voyage of slave ships the Middle Passage, the middle part of a triangle from England to Africa, Africa to America, and America back to England. From coastal forts and barracoons, crews rowed small groups of slaves out to the waiting ships and packed them into shelves below deck only six feet long by two and a half feet high. "Rammed like herring in a barrel," wrote one observer, slaves were "chained to each other hand and foot, and stowed so close, that they were not allowed above a foot and a half for each in breadth." People were forced to sleep "spoon fashion," and the tossing of the ship knocked them about so violently that the skin over their elbows sometimes was worn to the bone from scraping on the planks.

Slavers debated the merits of various packing strategies. One camp argued that additional room lessened mortality and thus increased profits. But the great demand and the price for slaves in the mid-eighteenth century gave the upper hand to the "tight packers," those willing to risk life in order to carry as many men and women as possible. One ship designed to carry 450 slaves regularly crossed the Atlantic with more

than 600. Their holds filled with human cargo, the ships headed toward Cape Verde to catch the trade winds blowing toward America. A favorable voyage from Senegambia to Barbados might be accomplished in as little as three weeks, but a ship from Guinea or Angola becalmed in the doldrums or driven back by storms might take as much as three months.

The voyage was marked by a daily routine. In the morning the crew opened the hatch and brought the captives on deck, attaching their leg irons to a great chain running the length of the bulwarks. After a breakfast of beans came a ritual known as "dancing the slave": while an African thumped an upturned kettle or plucked a banjo, the crew commanded men and women to jump up and down in a bizarre session of exercise. A day spent chained on deck was concluded by a second bland meal and then the stowing away. During the night, according to one seaman, there issued from below "a howling melancholy noise, expressive of extreme anguish." Down in the hold the groans of the dying, the shrieks of women and children, and the suffocating heat and stench combined to create, in the words of Olaudah Equiano, "a scene of horror almost inconceivable."

Among the worst of the horrors was the absence of adequate sanitation. There were "necessary tubs" set below deck, but Africans, "endeavoring to get to them, tumble over their companions," one eighteenth-century ship's surgeon wrote, "and as the necessities of nature are not to be resisted, they ease themselves as they lie." Efficient captains ordered crews to scrape and swab the holds daily, but so sickening was the task that on many ships it was rarely performed and the captive Africans were forced to lie in their own urine and feces. When first taken below deck, the boy Equiano remembered, "I received such a salutation in my nostrils as I had never experienced in my life," and "became so sick and low that I was not able to eat." Atlantic sailors said you could "smell a slaver five miles down wind." Many captives sickened and died in these conditions. Many others contracted dysentery, known as the "flux." Frequent shipboard epidemics of smallpox, measles, and yellow fever added to the misery. Historians estimate that during the Middle Passage of the eighteenth century at least one in every six Africans perished.

Slaves below deck on a Spanish slaver, a sketch made when the vessel was captured by a British warship in the early nineteenth century. Slaves were "stowed so close, that they were not allowed above a foot and a half for each in breadth," wrote one observer. The close quarters and unsanitary conditions created a stench so bad that Atlantic sailors said you could "smell a slaver five miles down wind."

The unwilling voyagers offered plenty of resistance. As long as ships were still within sight of the African coast, hope remained alive and the danger of revolt was great. One historian has found references to fifty-five slave revolts on British and American ships between 1699 and 1845. Once on the open sea, however, captives' resistance took a more desperate form. The sight of the disappearing coast of Africa "left me abandoned to despair," wrote Equiano; "I now saw myself deprived of all chance of returning to my native country, or even the least glimpse of hope of gaining the shore." He witnessed several Africans jump overboard and drown, "and I believe many more would very soon have done the same if they had not been prevented by the ship's crew." Captains took the precaution of spreading netting along the sides of their ships. "Could I have got over the nettings," Equiano declared, "I would have jumped over the side."

Arrival in the New World

As the ship approached its destination, the crew made the human cargo presentable, preparing it for market. All but the most rebellious of Africans were freed from their chains and allowed to wash themselves and move about the deck. One account describes the ship's surgeon plugging captives' rectums with clumps of hemp fiber to prevent potential buyers from seeing the bloody discharge, a symptom of the flux. To impress buyers, slavers sometimes paraded Africans off the ship to the tune of an accordion or the beat of a drum. But the toll taken by the Middle Passage was difficult to disguise. One observer described a disembarking group as "walking skeletons covered over with a piece of tanned leather."

Some cargoes were destined for a single wealthy planter or consigned to a merchant who sold the captives in return for a commission; in other cases the captain himself was responsible. Buyers painstakingly examined the Africans, who once again suffered the indignity of probing eyes and poking fingers. This caused "much dread and trembling among us," wrote Equiano, and "bitter cries." In ports like Charleston sales were generally made either by auction or by a method known as the scramble. In the scramble, standard prices were set in advance for men, women, boys, and girls. Then the Africans were driven into a corral, and at a signal the buyers rushed among them, grabbing their pick of the lot. The noise, clamor, and eagerness of the buyers, Equiano remembered, renewed all the terrible apprehensions of the Africans. "In this manner, without scruple, are relations and friends separated, most of them never to see each other again." Bought by a Virginian, Equiano was taken to an isolated tobacco plantation where he found himself unable to communicate with any of his fellow slaves, who came from other ethnic groups.

Political and Economic Effects on Africa

Africa began the sixteenth century with genuine independence. But as surely as Europe and America grew stronger as a result of the trade and the labor of slaves, so Africa grew weaker by their loss. In the short term, slave-trading kingdoms on the coast increased their power at the expense of interior states. Thus the interior West African state of Songhai gave way to the Gold Coast state of Akwamu. In the Niger delta the slaving states of Nembe, Bonny, and Kalabari arose, and to the south the kingdom of Imbangala drew slaves from central Africa. But these coastal states found that the slave trade was a viper that could easily strike back at them. "Merchants daily seize our own subjects, sons of the land and sons of our noblemen, they grab them and cause them to be sold," King Dom Affonso of the Kongo wrote to the Portuguese monarch in the sixteenth century; "and so great, Sir, is their corruption and licentiousness that our country is being utterly depopulated."

With the loss of millions of men and women over the centuries, the West African economy stagnated. Labor was drawn away from farming and other productive activities, and imported consumer goods such as textiles and metalwares stifled local manufacturing. African traders were expert at driving a hard bargain, and over several centuries they gained an increasing price for slaves—the result of rising demand and increased competition among European slavers. But even when they appeared to get the best of the transaction, the ultimate advantage lay with the Europeans, who in exchange for mere consumer goods got human capital—wealth-producing workers.

For every man or woman taken captive, at least another died in the chronic slave raiding. Many of the new West African states became little more than machines for supplying captives to European traders, and a "gun-slave cycle" pushed neighboring kingdoms into a destructive arms race. The resulting political and cultural demoralization prepared the way for the European conquest of Africa in the nineteenth century. The leaders of West Africa during the centuries of slave trad-

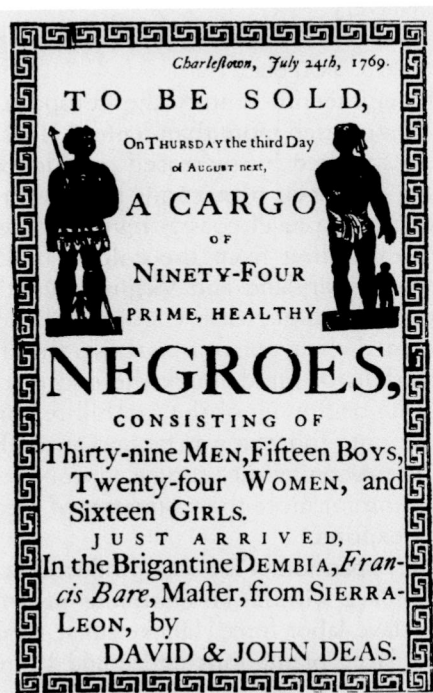

The announcement of the arrival of a consignment of slaves in Charleston, South Carolina, in 1769, where the most common method of sale was by auction. Men and women alike were subjected to intimate inspection before the bidding began. Buyers were quite interested in the ethnic origins of slaves but gave little concern to keeping family members together.

ing, writes the Nigerian poet Chinweizu, "had been too busy organizing our continent for the exploitative advantage of Europe, had been too busy with slaving raids upon one another, too busy decorating themselves with trinkets imported from Europe, too busy impoverishing and disorganizing the land, to take thought and long-range action to protect our sovereignty."

THE DEVELOPMENT OF NORTH AMERICAN SLAVE SOCIETIES

New World slavery was nearly two centuries old before it became an important system of labor in North America. There were slaves in each of the British colonies during the seventeenth century, but in 1700 they constituted only 11 percent of the colonial population. During the eighteenth century slavery greatly expanded, and by 1770 Africans and African Americans in British North America numbered 460,000, or more than 20 percent of the colonial population.

Slavery Comes to North America

The first Africans in Virginia arrived in 1619 when a Dutch slave trader exchanged "20 and odd Negroes" for badly needed provisions. But because slaves generally cost twice as much as indentured servants yet had the same appallingly short life expectancy—because of the frequent epidemics of diseases such as typhoid fever—they offered planters little economic benefit. Consequently, only a relatively small number were brought to Virginia over the next several decades. In fact, there are indications that those Africans who worked in the tobacco fields were not slaves at all, but servants.

An interesting case illustrates the ambiguous status of black Virginians. In 1654 the African John Castor told a local court that "he came unto Virginia for seven or eight years of indenture, yet Anthony Johnson his Master had kept him his servant seven years longer than he should or ought." Johnson claimed that "he had the Negro for his life." The court decided in the master's favor. But strange to say, Johnson himself was an African. He had arrived in 1621 as an indentured servant but achieved his freedom and succeeded in becoming a landowner. Property records reveal that other Africans acquired farms and servants or slaves of their own. Moreover, sexual relations among Africans, Indians, and Europeans produced a sizable group of free people of mixed ancestry known as mulattoes. It was only later that dark skin came to mean slavery, segregation, and lack of rights. Although there surely were slaves among the population in the early years, the first recorded instances of slavery date from around 1640.

In the last quarter of the seventeenth century, however, a number of developments encouraged the expansion of true slavery. As European immigrants discovered opportunities to establish themselves as free farmers in colonies such as Pennsylvania, it became increasingly difficult for southern masters to recruit them as indentured servants. Moreover, after Bacon's Rebellion and the other social conflicts of the 1670s, many colonial leaders began to worry about potential rebellions among former indentured servants in the back country. Because people were living longer, possibly the result of being better fed and more resistant to disease, more servants were surviving their indentures. But these improvements in living conditions also affected Africans, increasing their rates of survival, and planters began to see more advantage in the purchase of slaves. During these same years, the supply of slaves in North America increased when the Royal African Company inaugurated direct shipments from West Africa to the mainland.

Thus the workforce of indentured servants was gradually replaced by a workforce of slaves. By 1700 the number of African slaves had probably surpassed the number of indentured servants. There were some 19,000 Africans in Maryland and Virginia,

about 22 percent of the population. In South Carolina, where indentured servants had never been an important part of the labor force, Africans constituted over 40 percent of the settler population by the end of the seventeenth century.

As the proportions of slaves in the colonial population rose, colonists wrote slavery into law, a process best observed in the case of Virginia. In 1662 colonial officials declared that children inherited the status of their slave mothers; five years later they added that baptism could no longer alter conditions of servitude. Two important avenues to freedom were thus closed. The colony then placed life-threatening violence in the hands of masters, declaring in 1669 that the death of a slave during punishment "shall not be accounted felony." Such regulations accumulated piecemeal until, in 1705, they were gathered together in the comprehensive Virginia Slave Code that became a model for other colonies.

Thus the institution of slavery was strengthened just as the Atlantic slave trade reached flood tide in the eighteenth century. During that century's first decade, more Africans were imported into North America than the total number for the preceding ninety-three years of colonial history. The English colonies were primed for an unprecedented growth of plantation slavery.

The Tobacco Colonies

During the eighteenth century the European demand for tobacco increased more than tenfold. This demand was largely supplied by increased production in the Chesapeake. Tobacco plantations spread through all sections of the sea-level coastal region known as the Tidewater, extending from the colony of Delaware south through Maryland and Virginia into the Albemarle Sound region of North Carolina. Planters eventually extended their operations above the "fall line," where waterfalls or rapids mark the end of the Tidewater and the beginning of the foothill region known as the Piedmont. Tobacco was far and away the single most important commodity produced in North America, accounting for more than a quarter of the value of all colonial exports.

The expansion of tobacco production could not have taken place without an enormous growth in the size of the slave labor force. Unlike sugar, tobacco did not require large plantations and could be produced successfully on relatively small farms. But it was a crop that demanded a great deal of hand labor and close attention, and from the beginnings of Chesapeake colonization its cultivation had been the responsibility of indentured servants and slaves. As tobacco farming grew, slaveholding became widespread. By midcentury slaves were included in a majority of upcountry households

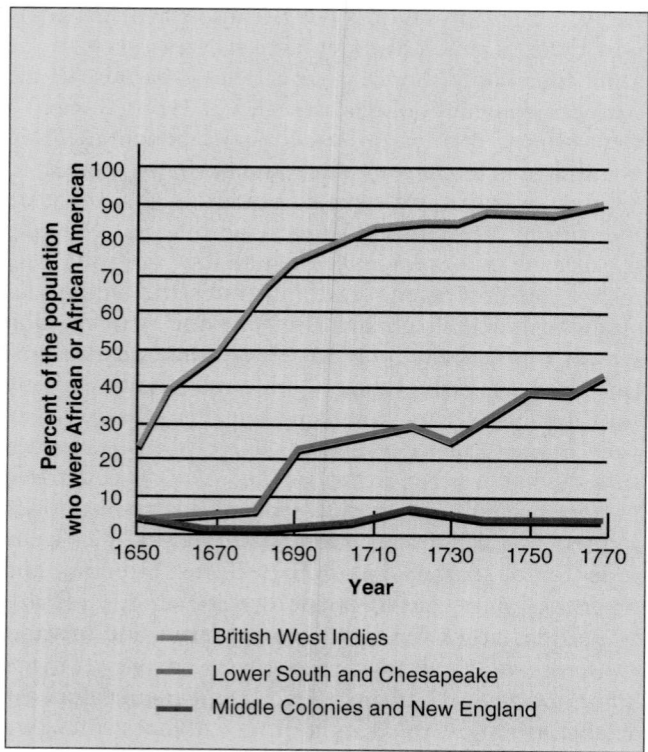

Africans as a Percentage of Total Population of the British Colonies, 1650–1770   *Although the proportion of Africans and African Americans was never as high in the South as in the Caribbean, the ethnic structure of the South diverged radically from that of the North during the eighteenth century.*

Source: Robert W. Fogel and Stanley L. Engerman, *Time on the Cross* (Boston: Little, Brown, 1974), 21.

and as many as three-quarters of the households in the Tidewater. Tobacco farms varied in size, from small establishments where farmers worked side by side with one or two slaves, to large, self-sufficient plantations with dozens of slaves. By 1770 more than a quarter of a million slaves labored in the colonies of the Upper South, and because of the exploding market for tobacco, their numbers were expanding at something like double the rate of the general population.

Shipments from Africa thus accounted for part of the growth of the slave population. From 1700 to 1770 a total of perhaps 80,000 Africans were imported into the Chesapeake colonies, but natural increase in this region was much more important. Indeed, in the 1730s

Benjamin Henry Latrobe, *An Overseer Doing His Duty.* Watercolor on paper. Collection of the Maryland Historical Society, Baltimore.

An Overseer Doing His Duty, *a watercolor sketch made by Benjamin Henry Latrobe during a trip to Virginia in 1798. The majority of masters in the tobacco region owned only one or two slaves and worked with them in the fields. In his portrayal of this overseer, relaxing as he supervises his workers, Latrobe clearly expressed his disgust for slavery.*

the slave population of the Chesapeake was the first in the Western Hemisphere to achieve self-sustained growth. In the Caribbean and Brazil, where the profits from sugar plantations were high, many masters worked their slaves literally to death, replacing them with a constant stream of new arrivals from Africa. These landowners figured that they could make greater profits through extreme exploitation of the labor force than by creating the better living and working conditions that would allow Africans to reproduce at normal rates. In contrast, in Virginia lower rates of profit may have caused tobacco planters to pay more attention to the health of their labor force, establishing work routines that were not so deadly. Food supplies were also more plentiful in North America than in the Caribbean, where nearly every morsel had to be imported, and the better-fed Chesapeake populations of Africans were more resistant to disease. Historians continue to debate these important differences. But whatever the causes, self-sustained population growth among Chesapeake slaves had begun by the 1730s, and by the 1770s the majority of them were "country-born."

The Lower South

For fifty years after the founding of the South Carolina colony in 1670, the area outside the immediate region of Charleston remained a rough and dangerous frontier. English settlers raised cattle, often using slaves with experience in the pastoral economies of West Africa. Others engaged in the deerskin trade, bartering English

goods with the numerous Indian people of the back-country. But in terms of sheer profit, the most valuable part of the early Carolina economy was the Indian slave trade. Practicing a strategy of divide and conquer, in which they encouraged Indian tribes to fight one another, Carolinians enslaved tens of thousands of Indians before the 1730s. Because Indian slaves were dangerous as long as they were near their homelands, most were shipped off to other colonies.

By 1715, as the opening of this chapter illustrates, rice production had become the most dynamic sector of the South Carolina economy, and, like cattle grazing, it depended on the expertise of West Africans. Another important crop was added in the 1740s, when Elizabeth Lucas Pinckney, a young South Carolina woman, successfully adapted West Indian indigo to the low-country climate. It is likely that here as well, the assistance of West Indian slaves skilled in indigo culture was crucial. The indigo plant, native to India, produced

TOBACCO AND RICE EXPORTS TO ENGLAND (IN THOUSANDS OF POUNDS)		
	Tobacco	Rice
1700	37,840	304
1725	21,046	5,367
1750	51,339	16,667
1775	55,968	57,692

Residence and Slave Quarters of Mulberry Plantation, by Thomas Coram, ca. 1770. The slave quarters are on the left in this painting of a rice plantation near Charleston, South Carolina. The steep roofs of the slave cabins, an African architectural feature introduced in America by slave builders, kept living quarters cool by allowing the heat to rise and dissipate in the rafters.

a deep blue dye important in textile manufacture. Rice grew in the lowlands, but indigo could be cultivated on high ground. And because they had different seasonal growing patterns, the two crops harmonized perfectly. Rice and indigo production rose steadily over the next thirty years. By the 1770s they were among the most valuable commodities exported from the mainland colonies of North America.

Like tobacco, the expansion of rice and indigo production depended on the growth of African slavery. Before the importation of slaves to the United States ended in 1808, at least 100,000 Africans had arrived at Charleston. One of every five ancestors of today's African Americans passed through that port on his or her way to the rice and indigo fields.

By the 1740s many of the arriving Africans were being taken to Georgia, a colony created by an act of the English Parliament in 1732. Its leader, James Edward Oglethorpe, hoped to establish a buffer against Spanish invasion from Florida and to create a haven for poor British farmers who could then sell their products in the markets of South Carolina. Under Oglethorpe's influence, Parliament agreed to prohibit slavery in Georgia, but soon the colony's coastal

regions were being settled by South Carolina planters with their slaves. In 1752 Oglethorpe and Georgia's trustees abandoned their experiment, and the colony was opened to slavery under royal authority. The Georgia coast had already become an extension of the Carolina low-country slave system.

By 1770 there were nearly 90,000 African Americans in the Lower South, about 80 percent of the population of coastal South Carolina and Georgia. The slave economy of the Lower South was dominated by large plantations, which had between fifty and seventy-five slaves each. The slaves' work was hard, but the task system, described at the beginning of this chapter, gave them a measure of control over their own lives. The African American communities of the Lower South, like those of the Chesapeake, achieved self-sustained growth by the middle of the eighteenth century.

Slavery in the Spanish Colonies

Slavery was basic to the Spanish colonial labor system, yet doubts about the enslavement of Africans were raised by both the Church and the crown. The papacy many times denounced slavery as a violation of Christian principles, and many priests condemned the institution. The

Catholic Church in Spanish America, however, owned slaves and profited from their labor. The slave system remained intact, and by later in the eighteenth century, when sugar production expanded in Cuba, it had become as brutal there as elsewhere in the Americas.

Still, the character of slavery varied with local conditions. One of the most benign forms operated in Florida, where Spanish colonization was undertaken primarily to create a buffer against the English. In 1699 the Spanish declared Florida a refuge for escaped slaves from the English colonies, offering free land to any fugitives who would help defend the colony and convert to Catholicism. Over the next half-century, refugee Indians and fugitive Africans established many communities in the countryside surrounding St. Augustine. North of the city, Fort Mose was manned by Negro troops commanded by their own officers. Slaves could be found in many Florida settlements, but the conditions of their servitude resembled the household slavery common in Mediterranean and African communities more than the plantation slavery of the British colonies.

In New Mexico, the Spanish depended on the forced labor of Indians. In the sixteenth century the colonial governor sent Indian workers to the mines of Mexico. And the requirement that Pueblo people labor for Spaniards was one of the causes of the Pueblo Revolt (see Chapter 3). During the eighteenth century, the Spanish were much more cautious in their treatment of the Pueblos, who were officially considered Catholics. But they captured and enslaved "infidel Indians" such as the Apaches or nomads from the Great Plains, using them as house servants and field workers.

French Louisiana

Slavery was also important in Louisiana, the colony founded by the French in the lower Mississippi Valley in the early eighteenth century. After Robert Sieur de La Salle's voyage down the Mississippi River in 1681–82, the French planned colonies to anchor their New World empire. In the early eighteenth century French Canadians established bases at Biloxi and Mobile on the Gulf of Mexico, but it was not until 1718 that they laid out the city of New Orleans on the Mississippi delta. Upriver, colonists established an alliance with the powerful Choctaw nation, and with their assistance defeated an opposing confederacy of Chickasaw and Natchez Indians during the 1720s and 1730s.

By 1750 several thousand French colonists, many from New France and the Caribbean, had established farms and plantations on the Gulf coast and in a narrow strip along the Mississippi River. Soon they were exporting rice, indigo, and tobacco, in addition to furs and skins for which they had traded with back-country Indians. Like the Spanish in St. Augustine, however, the French were more interested in defend-

ing their access to the Mississippi against rival colonial threats than in commerce and export. Consequently, African slaves amounted to no more than a third of the colonial population of 10,000. It was not until the end of the eighteenth century that the colony of Louisiana became an important North American slave society.

Slavery in the North

North of the Chesapeake, slavery was much less important. Slaves worked on some farms, but almost never in groups, and they were principally concentrated in port cities. Slaves were first shipped to Philadelphia in the 1680s, and a visitor to the city in 1750 noted that slaves were bought "by almost everyone who could afford [them]." Together with a small group of free blacks, slaves then made up about 9 percent of the city's population.

It was the Quakers, many of whom had themselves kept slaves, who voiced the first antislavery sentiment in the colonies. In *Considerations on the Keeping of Negroes* (1754), John Woolman pointed to the Bible's declaration that all peoples were of one blood. He urged his readers to imagine themselves in the place of the African people:

> Suppose that our ancestors and we had been exposed to constant servitude in the more servile and inferior employments of life; that we had been destitute of the help of reading and good company; that amongst ourselves we had had few wise and pious instructors; that the religious amongst our superiors seldom took notice of us; that while others in ease have plentifully heaped up the fruit of our labour, we had received barely enough to relieve nature, and being wholly at the command of others had generally been treated as a contemptible, ignorant part of mankind. Should we, in that case, be less abject than they now are?

It was not until the Revolution, however, that antislavery sentiment became more widespread.

In New York slavery was somewhat more important. By 1770, New York and New Jersey were home to some 27,000 African Americans, about 10 percent of these colonies' respective populations. Black people were concentrated even more highly in New York City. A British naval officer stationed in the port during the 1750s observed that "the laborious people in general are Guinea negroes." In 1770, 3,000 slaves and 100 free blacks, about 17 percent of the population, lived in the city. The most important center of slavery in the North, however, was Newport, Rhode Island. In 1760 African Americans there made up about 20 percent of the population, a concentration resulting from that port's dominance of the midcentury slave trade. Moreover, the area was unique for the large slave gangs used in cattle and dairy operations in the Narragansett country, some of which were as large as Virginia plantations.

BECOMING AFRICAN AMERICAN

In 1774 a group of enslaved Massachusetts Africans spoke for tens of thousands of others when they petitioned the British authorities for their freedom. "We were unjustly dragged by the cruel hand of power from our dearest friends," they wrote, "and some of us stolen from the bosoms of our tender parents and from a populous, pleasant and plentiful country, and brought hither to be made slaves for life in a Christian land." Men and women from dozens of ethnic groups, representing many different languages, religions, and customs, had been transported across the Atlantic without any of their cultural possessions. In America they were subjected to the control of masters intent on maximizing their work and minimizing their liberty. Yet African Americans carved out lives of their own with a degree of independence. Their African heritage was not erased; it provided them with a fundamental outlook, the basis for a common identity.

The majority of Africans transported to North America arrived during the eighteenth century. They were met by a rapidly growing population of "country-born" slaves, or "creoles" (from the French créole and Spanish criollo, meaning "born" or "raised"), a term first used by slaves in Brazil to distinguish their children, born in the New World, from newly arrived Africans. The perspective of creoles was shaped by their having grown up under slavery, and that perspective helped them to determine which elements of African culture they would incorporate into the emerging culture of the African American community. That community was formed out of the relationship between creoles and Africans, and between slaves and their European masters.

The Daily Life of Slaves

Because slaves made up the overwhelming majority of the labor force that made the plantation colonies so profitable, it is fair to say that Africans built the South. As an agricultural people, Africans—both women and men—were accustomed to the routines of rural labor, and this experience was put to use on the plantations. Most Africans were field hands, and even domestic servants labored in the fields when necessary. As crop production expanded during the eighteenth century, and plantations became larger and more extensive, labor became specialized. On the eighteenth-century Virginia plantation of George Mason, for example, slaves worked as carpenters, coopers, sawyers, blacksmiths, tanners, curriers, shoemakers, spinners, weavers, knitters, and even distillers.

Masters provided their workers with rude clothing, sufficient in the summer but nearly always inadequate in the winter. Increasingly the plantations were supplied by cheap goods from the new industrial looms of England. Stiff shoes were a necessity in the cold months, but they so cramped the feet that everyone looked forward to shedding them in the spring and going barefoot all summer and fall. Hand-me-down clothes from the master's family offered slaves an opportunity to brighten their costumes, and many dressed in a variety of styles and colors. Similarly, they relieved the monotony of their rations of corn and pork with vegetables from their small gardens, game and fish from field and stream, and wild plant foods from the forests. On the whole, their diet must have been sufficient, for they not only survived but rapidly reproduced during the eighteenth century.

The growing African population, and larger plantations on which larger numbers lived and worked together, created the concentration necessary for the emergence of African American communities and African American culture. The typical slave served on a plantation with a workforce of ten or more. On small farms, Africans might work side by side with their owners and, depending on the character of the master, might enjoy living conditions not too different from those of other family members. But plantations offered possibilities for a more autonomous cultural life.

Families and Communities

The family was the most important institution for the development of community and culture. Slave codes did not provide for legal slave marriages, for that would have contradicted the master's freedom to dispose of his property as he saw fit. "The endearing ties of husband and wife are strangers to us," declared the Massachusetts slaves who petitioned for their freedom in 1774, "for we are no longer man and wife than our masters or mistresses think proper." How, they asked, "can a slave perform the duties of a husband to a wife or parent to his child? How can a husband leave master to work and cleave to his wife? How can the [wives] submit themselves to their husbands in all things? How can the [children] obey their parents in all things?" The creation and maintenance of slave family life were essential not only for reproduction but for the physical and psychological well-being of all family members and the development of African American culture.

Despite the barriers, many thousands of Africans in both the Chesapeake and the Lower South had created stable families by the 1730s. On large plantations throughout the southern colonies, travelers found Africans living in nuclear-family households in the slave quarters. But on smaller plantations, men frequently married women from neighboring farms, and with the permission of both owners visited their families in the evenings or on Sundays.

Generally, slave couples married when the woman became pregnant. "Their marriages are generally performed amongst themselves," one visitor to North Carolina wrote of the Africans he observed in the 1730s. "The man makes the woman a present, such as a brass ring or some other toy, which she accepts of, [and] becomes his wife." Common throughout the South was the postnuptial ritual in which the couple jumped over a broomstick together, declaring their relationship to the rest of the community. This custom may have originated in Africa, although versions of it were practiced in medieval Europe as well.

Recent studies of naming practices among eighteenth-century African Americans illustrate their commitment to establishing a system of kinship. Frequently sons were named for their fathers, perhaps a way of strengthening the paternal bonds of men forced to live away from their families. Children of both sexes were named for grandparents and other kin. African names were common; names such as Cudjo (Monday), Quow (Thursday), or Coffee (Friday) continued the African tradition of "weekday" names. Later in the century Anglo names became more general. Margery and Moody, slaves of Francis Jerdone of Louisa County, Virginia, named their six children Sam, Rose, Sukey, Mingo, Maria, and Comba, mixing both African and English traditions. Many Africans carried names known only within their community, and these were often African. In the sea island region of the Lower South, such names were common until the twentieth century.

Emotional ties to particular places, connections between the generations, and relations of kinship and friendship linking neighboring plantations and farms were the foundation stones of African American community life. Kinship was especially important. African American parents encouraged their children to use family terms in addressing unrelated people: "auntie" or "uncle" became a respectful way of addressing older men and women, "brother" and "sister" affectionate terms for age mates. Moreover, during the Middle Passage it was common for adults to address all children as "son" or "daughter." This tradition of "fictive kinship" may have been one of the first devices enslaved Africans used to humanize the world of slavery.

African American Culture

The eighteenth century was the formative period in the development of the African American community, for it was then that the high birth rate and the growing numbers of "country-born" provided the necessary stability for the evolution of culture. During this period, men and women from dozens of African ethnic groups molded themselves into a new people. Distinc-

tive patterns in music and dance, religion, and oral tradition illustrate the resilience of the human spirit under bondage as well as the successful struggle of African Americans to create a spiritually sustaining culture of their own.

Eighteenth-century masters were reluctant to allow their slaves to become Christians, fearing that baptism would open the way to claims of freedom or give Africans dangerous notions of universal brotherhood and equality with masters. One frustrated missionary was told by a planter that a slave was "ten times worse when a Christian than in his state of paganism." Because of this attitude, a Protestant minister wrote from South Carolina in the 1770s, most slaves "are to this day as great strangers to Christianity, and as much under the influence of pagan darkness, idolatry and superstition, as they were at their first arrival from Africa." Thus, the majority of black Southerners before the American Revolution practiced some form of African religion. Many African Americans were not converted to Christianity until the Great Awakening, which swept across the South after the 1760s (see Chapter 5).

One of the most crucial areas of religious practice concerned the rituals of death and burial. In their separate graveyards, African Americans often decorated graves with shells and pottery, an old African custom. African Americans generally believed that the spirits of their dead would return to Africa. "Some destroy themselves [that is, commit suicide] through despair and from a persuasion they fondly entertain, that after death they will return to their beloved friends and native country," wrote one South Carolinian.

The burial ceremony, perhaps the most important of the slave rituals, was often held at night because slave owners objected to the continuation of African traditions. Historical knowledge of these secret proceedings comes from the accounts of a few white observers, from the stories and recollections of slaves, and from the reconstructions of twentieth-century anthropologists. The deceased person was laid out, and around the body men and women would move counterclockwise in a slow dance step while singing ancestral songs. The pace gradually increased, finally reaching a frenzied but joyful conclusion. Dance was a form of worship, a kind of prayer, a means of achieving union with the ancestors and the gods. The circle dance was a widespread custom in West Africa, and in America it became known as the ring shout. As slaves from different backgrounds joined together in the circle, they were beginning the process of cultural unification.

Music and dance may have formed the foundation of African American culture, coming even before a common language. Many eighteenth-century observers commented on the musical and rhythmic gifts of

Abby Aldrich Rockefeller Folk Art Center, Williamsburg, Virginia.

This eighteenth-century painting depicts a celebration in the slave quarters on a South Carolina plantation. The dance—known as "jumping the broomstick"—may have originated in Africa, and the stringed instrument was an African mbanza, *which evolved into the "banjo."*

The Africanization of the South

The African American community often looked to recently arrived Africans for religious leadership. Ancestor worship, divination, and magic were strengthened by constant African infusions through the eighteenth century. Many of these beliefs and practices had much in common with European folklore, especially magic and medicinal lore. In 1729 the governor of Virginia agreed to free one of his elderly slaves, "who has performed many wonderful cures of diseases," after the man revealed the secret formulas of his medical magic. Throughout the South, many whites had as much faith in slave conjurers and herb doctors as the slaves themselves did, one example of the many ways in which white and black Southern-

Africans. Olaudah Equiano remembered his people, the Ibos, as "a nation of dancers, musicians, and poets," and Thomas Jefferson, raised on a Virginia plantation, wrote that blacks "are more generally gifted than the whites, with accurate ears for tune and time." Many Africans were accomplished players of stringed instruments and drums, and their style featured improvisation and rhythmic complexity—elements that would become prominent in African American music. In America, slaves re-created African instruments—the banjo is an example—and mastered the art of the European violin and guitar. Fearing that slaves might communicate by code, authorities frequently outlawed drums. But using bones, spoons, or sticks or simply "patting juba" (slapping their thighs), slaves produced elaborate multirhythmic patterns.

One of the most important developments of the eighteenth century was the invention of African American language. An English traveler during the 1770s complained he could not understand Virginia slaves, who spoke "a mixed dialect between the Guinea and English." But such a language made it possible for "country-born" and "salt-water" Africans to communicate. The two most important dialects were Gullah and Geeche, named after two of the African peoples most prominent in the Carolina and Georgia low country, the Golas and Gizzis of the Windward Coast. These creole languages were a transitional phenomenon, gradually giving way to distinctive forms of so-called black English, although in certain isolated areas like the sea islands of the Carolinas and Georgia they persisted into the twentieth century.

ers came to share a common culture. Acculturation was by no means a one-way street; English men and women in the South were also being Africanized.

Slaves worked in the kitchens of their masters and thus introduced an African style of cooking into colonial diets already transformed by the addition of Indian crops. African American culinary arts are responsible for such southern specialties as barbecue, fried chicken, black-eyed peas, and various greens including collard and mustard. And the liberal African use of red pepper, sesame seeds, and other sharp flavors established the southern preference for highly spiced foods. In Louisiana, a combination of African, French, and Indian elements produced a most distinctive American regional cuisine, exemplified by gumbos (soups) and jambalayas (stews).

Mutual acculturation is also evident in many aspects of material culture. Southern basket weaving used Indian techniques and African designs. Wood-carving often featured African motifs. African architectural designs featuring high, peaked roofs (to drain off the heat) and broad, shady porches gradually became part of a distinctive southern style. The West African ironworking tradition was evident throughout the South, especially in the ornamentation of the homes of Charleston and New Orleans.

Even more important were less tangible aspects of culture. Slave mothers nursed white children as well as their own. As one English observer wrote, "each child has its [black] Momma, whose gestures and accent it will necessarily copy, for children, we all know, are imitative beings." In this way, many Africanisms passed into the English language of the South: "goober" (peanut), "yam," "banjo," "okay," "tote." Some linguists have argued that the Southern "drawl," evident among both black and white speakers, derived from the incorporation of African intonations of words and syllables.

African American music and dance also deeply affected white culture. These art forms offer a good example of mutual acculturation. At eighteenth-century plantation dances, the music was usually provided by Africans playing European instruments and their own, such as the banjo. African American fiddlers were common throughout the South by the time of the Revolution, but the banjo also became the characteristic folk instrument of the white South. Toward the end of the evening, the musicians were often told to play some "Negro jigs," and slaves were asked to demonstrate the African manner of dancing. They sometimes parodied the elegant and rigid dances of their masters, while whites in turn attempted to imitate African rhythmic dance styles. In such a back-and-forth fashion the traditions of both groups were gradually transformed.

Violence and Resistance

Slavery was based on the use of force and violence. Fear underlay the daily life of both masters and slaves. Some owners were humane, but even the kindest could be cruel, and slaves had no guarantees of benevolent treatment. Even the most broad-minded plantation owners of the eighteenth century thought nothing about floggings of fifty or seventy-five lashes. "Der prayer was answered," sang the Africans of South Carolina, "wid de song of a whip." Although the typical planter punished slaves with extra work, public humiliation, or solitary confinement, the threat of the lash was omnipresent. There were also sadistic masters who stabbed, burned, maimed, mutilated, raped, or castrated their slaves.

Yet African Americans demonstrated a resisting spirit. In their day-to-day existence they often refused to cooperate: they malingered, they mistreated tools and animals, they "accidentally" destroyed the master's property.

Flight was also an option, and judging from the advertisements placed by masters in colonial newspapers, even the most trusted Africans ran away. "That this slave should run away and attempt getting his liberty, is very alarming," read the notice of one Maryland master in 1755. "He has always been too kindly used" and was "one in whom his master has put great confidence, and depended on him to overlook the rest of the slaves, and he had no kind of provocation to go off." A South Carolinian noted that his absent slave "may possibly have a ticket that I gave him, mentioning he was in quest of a runaway, [and] as I did not mention when he was to return, he may endeavour to pass by that." An analysis of hundreds of eighteenth-century advertisements for runaways reveals that 80 percent of them were men, most in their twenties, suggesting that flight was an option primarily for young, unattached men.

Runaways were sometimes called *maroons* from the Spanish *cimarrón*, meaning "wild and untamed." The African communities in Spanish Florida were often referred to as maroon colonies. Indeed, as a whole these mixed African and Creek Indian Florida peoples called themselves Seminoles, a name deriving from their pronunciation of *cimarrón*. Maroons also settled in the backcountry of the Lower South. In 1771, Georgia's governor warned that north of Savannah "a great number of fugitive Negroes had committed many robberies and insults," and he sent a detachment of

Fugitive slaves flee through the swamps in Thomas Moran's *Slave Hunt* (1862). *Many slaves ran away from their masters, and colonial newspapers included notices urging readers to be on the lookout for them. Some fled in groups or collected together in isolated communities called "maroon colonies," located in inaccessible swamps and woods.*

Thomas Moran, The Slave Hunt, 1862, oil on canvas, 86.4 x 111.8 cm. The Philbrook Museum of Art, Tulsa, Oklahoma.

militia to destroy their camps. The "black Indian" violence continued, however, and reached catastrophic proportions during the Revolution. Although maroons were less common in the Upper South, a number of fugitive communities existed in the Great Dismal Swamp between Virginia and North Carolina. In the 1730s a group of escaped Africans built a community of grass houses and set up a tribal government there, but they were soon dispersed by the authorities.

The most direct form of resistance was revolt. In the Lower South, where slaves were a majority of the population, there were isolated but violent slave uprisings in 1704, 1720, and 1730. Then in 1738 a series of violent revolts throughout South Carolina and Georgia proved but a prelude to the largest slave rebellion of the colonial period. In September 1739, a group of twenty recently arrived Angolans sacked the armory in Stono, South Carolina. Arming themselves, they began marching toward Florida and freedom. Beating drums to attract other slaves to their cause, they grew to nearly a hundred. Along the way they plundered several planters' homes and killed some thirty colonists. Pausing in a field to celebrate their victory with dance and song, they were overtaken by the militia and destroyed in a pitched battle. That same year there was an uprising in Georgia, probably inspired by the Stono Rebellion, and the next year another took place in South Carolina. Attributing these revolts to the influence of newly arrived Africans, colonial officials shut off the slave trade through Charleston for the next ten years.

The second notable slave uprising of the colonial era occurred in New York City in 1712. Taking an oath of secrecy, twenty-three Africans vowed revenge for what they called the "hard usage" of their masters. They armed themselves with guns, swords, daggers, and hatchets, killed nine colonists, and burned several buildings before being surrounded by the militia. Six of the conspirators committed suicide rather than surrender. Those captured were hanged, burned at the stake, or broken on the wheel. In 1741 New York authorities uncovered what they

thought was another conspiracy. Thirteen black leaders were burned alive, eighteen hanged, and eighty sold and shipped off to the West Indies. A family of colonists and a Catholic priest, accused of providing weapons, were also executed.

Wherever masters held slaves, fears of uprisings persisted. But compared with such slave colonies as Jamaica, Guiana, or Brazil, there were few slave revolts in North America. The conditions favoring revolt—large African majorities, brutal exploitation with correspondingly low survival rates, little acculturation, and geographic isolation—prevailed only in some areas of the Lower South. The very success of African Americans in British North America at establishing families, communities, and a stake in a culture of their own may have made them less likely to risk rebellion.

SLAVERY AND THE STRUCTURE OF EMPIRE

Slavery contributed enormously to the economic growth and development of Europe during the colonial era, and it was an especially important factor in Great Britain's industrial revolution in the eighteenth century. Slavery was the most dynamic force in the Atlantic economy during that century, creating the conditions for industrialization. But because colonists in the South single-mindedly committed their slave resources to the expansion and extension of the plantation system, they derived very little benefit from the economic diversification that characterized industrialization.

Slavery the Mainspring

The slave colonies accounted for 95 percent of exports from the Americas to Great Britain from 1714 to 1773. Most productive were the sugar plantations of the British West Indies (64 percent of total exports), followed by the rice, indigo, and tobacco fields of the mainland South (31 percent). Although approximately half of all Great Britain's American colonists lived in New England and the mid-Atlantic, the colonies in those regions

BRITISH COLONIAL TRADE IN THE AMERICAS, 1714–1773
(IN THOUSANDS OF BRITISH POUNDS STERLING)

	Exports to Britain £	%	Imports from Britain £	%
British West Indies	96,808	64.0	41,653	38.8
Lower South and Chesapeake	47,192	31.2	27,561	25.7
Middle Colonies and New England	7,160	4.7	37,939	35.4
Total	151,160	99.9	107,153	99.9

Source: Eric Williams, *Capitalism and Slavery* (Chapel Hill: University of North Carolina Press, 1944), 225–26.

contributed less than 5 percent of total exports during this period. Moreover, there was the prime economic importance of the slave trade itself, which one economist of the day described as the "foundation" of the British economy, "the mainspring of the machine which sets every wheel in motion." According to another English writer, slavery was "the strength and sinews of this western world." This point is so important it bears repeating: it was the labor of African slaves that made the British empire in the Americas a success.

The profits of individual investors in the slave system varied widely, of course. Slave traders expected a return of 30 percent or more, but many ventures ended in financial disaster. Profits in sugar production during the boom of the seventeenth century easily exceeded 20 percent, but returns fell during the succeeding century. As late as 1776, however, the British economist Adam Smith wrote that "the profits of a sugar plantation in any of our West Indian colonies are generally much greater than those of any other cultivation that is known either in Europe or America." Economic historians estimate that annual profits during the eighteenth century averaged 15 percent of invested capital in the slave trade, 10 percent in plantation agriculture. Some of the first of England's great modern fortunes were made out of slavery's miseries.

Eighteenth-century ships being unloaded of their colonial cargoes on London's Old Custom House Quay. Most of the goods imported into England from the American colonies were produced by slave labor.

The most obvious and direct economic effect of slavery was on the growth of transport: in the eighteenth century better than 10 percent of all English shipping was devoted to the African and American trades. Ships had to be outfitted and provisioned, trade goods had to be manufactured, and the commodities produced on slave plantations had to be processed. The multiplier effects of these activities are best seen in the growth of English ports such as Liverpool and Bristol. There the African and American trades provided employment for an army of ships' crews, dockmen, construction workers, traders, shopkeepers, lawyers, clerks, factory workers, and officials of all ranks down to the humblest employees of the customhouse. It was said of Bristol that "there is not a brick in the city but what is cemented with the blood of a slave."

The profits of the slave trade and slave production resulted in huge accumulations of capital, much of it invested in enterprises in these same cities. One historian estimates that in Great Britain alone during the eighteenth century the slave system generated capital valued at more than 300 million pounds. (Although converting monetary values over several centuries is always imprecise, the eighteenth-century British pound sterling was the equivalent in purchasing power of about $85 in 1990s currency; thus, £300 million would be worth about $25 billion.) This capital funded the first modern banks and insurance companies and eventually found its way into a wide range of economic activities. In the countryside surrounding Liverpool, capital acquired through slavery was invested in the cotton textile industry. Later, the demand for raw cotton to supply cotton textile factories led to the further expansion of American plantation slavery. The connections between slavery and the growth of industry were clear and dramatic.

The Politics of Mercantilism

When imperial officials argued that colonies existed solely for the benefit of the mother country, they had in mind principally the great wealth produced by slavery. To ensure that this wealth benefited their states, European imperial powers created a system of regulations that later became known as mercantilism. The essence of mercantilist policy was the political control of the economy by the state. Just as the new monarchs of western Europe had extended their control over the political affairs of their nations, so they sought to use politics to control the national and colonial economy. In the seventeenth century the French finance minister Jean-Baptiste Colbert formulated the most systematic political approach to mercantilism, and the French empire of Louis XIV became the strongest in the world. But in the eighteenth century mercantilist politics were most successfully applied in Great Britain, where the monarchy and Parliament established a uniform national monetary system, regulated workers and the poor by placing controls on wages and requiring the able-bodied to labor in workhouses, provided subsidies to encourage agriculture and manufacturing, and erected tariff barriers to protect themselves from foreign competition. England also sought to organize and control colonial trade to the maximum advantage of its own shippers, merchants, manufacturers, and bureaucrats. Mercantilists scoffed at the idea that the economy should be left to the free operation of the marketplace.

The mercantilists viewed the world economy as a "zero-sum" game in which total economic gains were equal to total losses. As an English mercantilist put it, "There is but a certain proportion of trade in the world." Profits were thought to result from successful speculation, crafty dealing, or simple plunder—all forms of stealing wealth. The institution of slavery proved the theory, for it was nothing more than a highly developed system by which masters stole the labor of slaves. The essence of the competition between nation-states, the mercantilists argued, was the struggle to acquire and hoard the wealth of the world. The nation that accumulated the largest treasure of gold and silver specie would become the most powerful.

Wars for Empire

The mercantilist era was thus a period of intense and violent competition among European nation-states. Wars usually arose out of Old World issues, spilling over into the New, but they also originated in conflicts over the colonies themselves. In the Anglo-Dutch Wars of the 1650s and 1660s, England replaced Holland as the dominant Atlantic power. Then, beginning with King William's War (1689–97), England and France (generally allied with Spain) opened a long struggle for colonial supremacy in North America that was not concluded until 1763. (For discussion of these conflicts, see Chapter 3.) The fighting took place principally at the peripheries of the empire, on the frontiers separating Spanish Florida from British Georgia and New France from New England.

In the southern region, these wars had everything to do with slavery. The first fighting of the eighteenth century took place during Queen Anne's War (known in Europe as the War of the Spanish Succession), a conflict that pitted Great Britain and its allies against France and Spain. In 1702 troops from South Carolina invaded Florida, plundering and burning St. Augustine in an attempt to destroy the refuge for fugitive slaves there. A combined French and Spanish fleet took revenge in 1706 by bombarding Charleston. But the British finally prevailed over the Spanish, and in 1713, as part of the Peace of Utrecht, Great Britain won the exclusive right to supply slaves to the Spanish colonies in the Americas, a very lucrative business.

The entrance of British slavers into Spanish ports provided an opportunity for illicit trade, and sporadic fighting between the two empires broke out a number of times over the next two decades. Robert Walpole, British prime minister from 1721 to 1748, wished to avoid the outbreak of full-scale war, but a faction in the House of Commons that wanted to bring even more slave colonies into the British orbit looked forward to smashing the Spanish in the Caribbean. In 1739, at the urging of these members of Commons, a one-eared sea captain by the name of Jenkins testified before the House to the indignities suffered by British merchant sailors at the hands of the Spanish. In a dramatic flourish he produced a dried and withered ear, which he claimed they had cut from his head. A public outrage followed, finally forcing Walpole to agree to a war of Caribbean conquest that the British called the War of Jenkins's Ear.

English troops allied with Creek Indians invaded Florida once again, laying waste the last of the old mission stations but failing to capture St. Augustine. In response, Spanish troops, including several companies of African Americans, invaded Georgia. Although the Spanish were defeated

OVERVIEW

THE COLONIAL WARS		
King William's War	1689–97	France and England battle on the northern frontiers of New England and New York.
Queen Anne's War	1702–13	England fights France and Spain in the Caribbean and on the northern frontier of New France. Part of the European conflict known as the War of the Spanish Succession.
War of Jenkins's Ear	1739–43	Great Britain versus Spain in the Caribbean and Georgia. Part of the European War of the Austrian Succession.
King George's War	1744–48	Great Britain and France fight in Acadia and Nova Scotia; the second American round of the War of the Austrian Succession.
French and Indian War	1754–63	Last of the great colonial wars pitting Great Britain against France and Spain. Known in Europe as the Seven Years War.

seventy-five miles south of Savannah, the campaign produced an agreement on the boundary between British Georgia and Spanish Florida that today separates those states. Elsewhere the British were not so lucky: in the Caribbean the imperial fleet suffered disaster at the hands of the Spanish navy.

In the northern region the principal focus of the imperial struggle was control of the Indian trade. In 1704, during Queen Anne's War, the French and their Algonquian Indian allies raided New England frontier towns such as Deerfield, Massachusetts, dragging men, women, and children into captivity in Canada. In turn, the English mounted a series of expeditions against the strategic French fortress of Port Royal, which they captured in 1710. At the war's conclusion in 1713, France was forced to cede Acadia, Newfoundland, and Hudson's Bay to Great Britain in exchange for guarantees of security for the French-speaking residents of those provinces. Thirty years of peace followed, but from 1744 to 1748 England again battled France in King George's War. The French attacked the British in Nova Scotia, Indian and Canadian raids again devastated the border towns of New England and New York, and hundreds of British subjects were killed or captured.

The French, allied with the Spanish and Prussians, were equally successful in Europe. What finally turned the tide of this war was the capture in 1745 of the French fortress of Louisburg on Cape Breton Island by an expedition of Massachusetts troops in conjunction with the royal navy. Deprived of the most strategic of their American ports, and fearful of losing the wealth of their sugar islands, the French

agreed to a negotiated settlement in 1748. But despite the capture of Louisburg, the war had been fought elsewhere to a stalemate, so the treaty restored the prewar status quo, returning Louisburg to France. This disgusted merchants of New England, who wanted to expand their commercial influence in the maritime colonies, and left the North American conflict between France and Britain still simmering. Significantly, however, this was the first time that the concluding battle of a European war had been fought on North American soil, and it was a harbinger of things to come: the next war was destined to start as a conflict between French and British colonists before engulfing Europe (see Chapter 6).

British Colonial Regulation

Mercantilists used means other than war to win the wealth of the world. In the sixteenth century the Spanish monarchy became the first to create a state trading monopoly—the *Casa de Contratación*—to manage the commerce of its empire. This monopoly limited colonial trade to prescribed ports such as Seville or Veracruz, protected traders from attack and plunder, and established a system of great convoys in which merchant ships crossed the oceans under the protection of well-armed galleons. In the seventeenth century other European states followed the Spanish example. The British monarchy, for example, chartered the East India Company, the Hudson's Bay Company, and the Royal African Company as trading monopolies in their respective regions.

English manufacturers complained that the merchant-dominated trading monopolies paid too little attention to the export of their products to colonial markets. Reacting to these charges, between 1651 and 1696 Parliament passed a series of Navigation Acts (see also Chapter 3), which created the legal and institutional structure of Britain's eighteenth-century colonial system. These acts defined the colonies as both suppliers of raw materials and markets for English manufactured goods. Merchants from other nations were expressly forbidden to trade in the colonies, and all trade had to be conducted in ships built either in England or in the British colonies. The regulations specified a list of enumerated goods—colonial products that could be shipped only to England. These included the products of the southern slave colonies (sugar, molasses, rum, tobacco, rice, and indigo), those of the northern Indian trade (furs and skins), as well as the products essential for supplying the shipping industry (masts, tar, pitch, resin, and turpentine). The bulk of these products were not destined for English consumption, however; at great profit English merchants reexported them elsewhere.

England also placed limitations on colonial enterprises that might compete with those at home. A series of enactments—including the Wool Act of 1699, the Hat Act of 1732, and the Iron Act of 1750—forbade the colonial manufacture of those products. Moreover, colonial assemblies were forbidden to impose tariffs on English imports as a way to protect colonial industries. Banking was disallowed, local

coinage prohibited, and the export of coin from England forbidden. Badly in need of a circulating medium, Massachusetts illegally minted copper coin, and several colonies issued paper currency, forcing Parliament to legislate against the practice. The colonists depended mostly on "commodity money" (furs, skins, or hogsheads of tobacco) and the circulation of foreign coin, the most common being the Spanish silver peso and the German silver thaler, which Americans pronounced "dollar." Official rates of exchange between commodity money, colonial paper, foreign currency, and English pounds allowed this chaotic system to operate without too much difficulty.

Certain British interests pressed for even more stringent restrictions. But as the colonies grew more populous, and as the trade in colonial products increased, the British came to agree that it made little sense to tamper with such a prosperous system. Prime Minister Walpole pursued a policy later characterized as one of "salutory neglect": any colonial rules and regulations deemed contrary to good business practice were simply ignored and not enforced. Between 1700 and 1760 the quantity of goods exported from the colonies to the mother country rose 165 percent, while imports from Britain to North America increased by more than 400 percent. In part because of the lax enforcement, but mostly because the system operated to the profit of colonial merchants, colonists

John Greenwood, *Sea Captains Carousing in Surinam*. 1757. Oil on bed ticking, 95.9 × 191.2 cm. The Saint Louis Art Museum, Museum Purchase.

The New England artist John Greenwood painted this amusing view of New England sea captains in Surinam in 1757. By the early eighteenth century New England merchant traders like these had become important participants in the traffic in slaves and sugar to and from the West Indies. Northern ports thus became important pivots in the expanding commercial network linking slave plantations with Atlantic markets.

complained very little about the operation of the mercantilist system before the 1760s.

The Colonial Economy

Despite seemingly harsh mercantilist regulations, then, this economic system benefited planters, merchants, and white colonists in general. Despite being restricted to English markets, southern slave owners made healthy profits on the sale of their commodities. They enjoyed a protected market, in which competing goods from outside the empire were heavily taxed. Moreover, agricultural products more than held their value against the price of manufactures, and planters found themselves with steadily increasing purchasing power.

Pennsylvania, New York, and New England, and increasingly the Chesapeake as well, produced grain and flour, meat and dairy products. None of these was included in the list of enumerated goods, and they could thus be sold freely abroad. They found their most ready market in the British West Indies and the Lower South, where food production was slighted in favor of sugar and rice. Most of this trade was carried in New England ships. Indeed, the New England shipbuilding industry was greatly stimulated by the allowance under the Navigation Acts for ships built and manned in the colonies. So many ships were built for English buyers that by midcentury nearly a third of all British tonnage was American made.

The greatest benefits for the port cities of the North came from their commercial relationship to the slave colonies. New England merchants had become important players in the slave trade by the early eighteenth century, and soon thereafter they began to make inroads as well into the export trade of the West Indian colonies. It was in the Caribbean that New England merchants most blatantly ignored mercantilist regulations. In violation of Spanish, French, and Dutch rules prohibiting foreign trade, New Englanders traded foodstuffs for sugar in foreign colonies. Then, in violation of British regulations prohibiting the importation of sugar from competing colonies, the enterprising Yankees mixed their contraband among legal shipments from the British West Indies. The Molasses Act of 1733, which Parliament enacted under pressure from British West Indian planters, placed a prohibitive duty on sugar products brought from foreign colonies to North America. Had these regulations been strictly applied, they surely would have caused conflict with the colonists, but in fact enforcement was lax. By 1750, more than sixty distilleries in Massachusetts Bay were exporting over 2 million gallons of rum, most of it produced from sugar obtained illegally. Because the restrictive rules and regulations enacted by Britain for its colonies were not enforced, the merchants and manufacturers of the port cities of the North prospered.

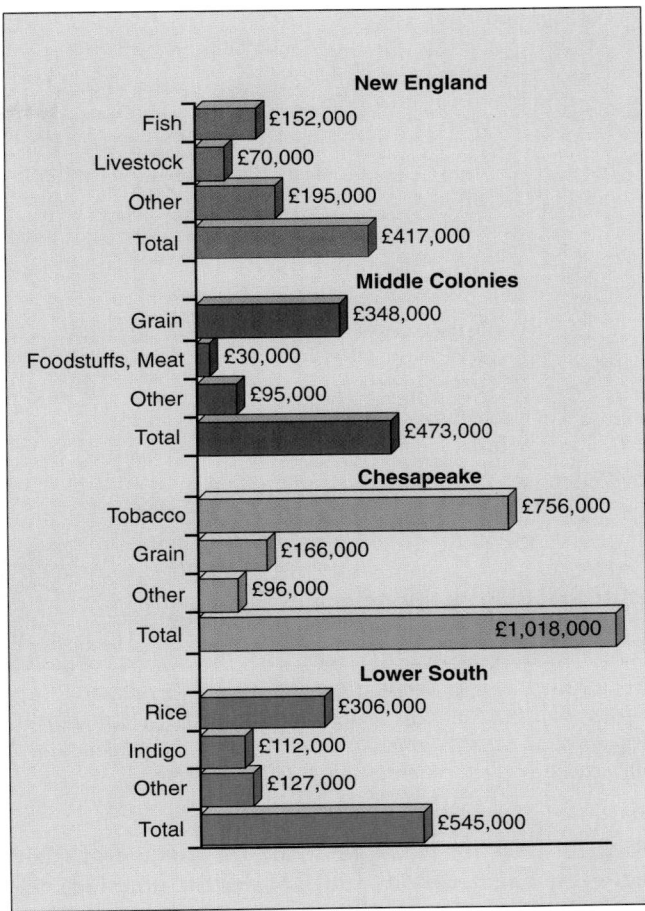

Value of Colonial Exports by Region, Annual Average, 1768–1772 *With tobacco, rice, grain, and indigo, the Chesapeake and Lower South accounted for nearly two-thirds of colonial exports in the late eighteenth century. The Middle Colonies, however, were also becoming major exporters of grain.*

Source: James F. Shepherd and Gary M. Walton, *Shipping, Maritime Trade and the Economic Development of Colonial America* (Cambridge, England: Cambridge University Press, 1972), 211–27.

As early as 1715, the exchange of New England fish, foodstuffs, and lumber for sugar and other tropical products from the West Indies accounted for more than half of the tonnage passing through the port of Boston. The volume of this trade remained steady over the next half-century, but Boston merchants greatly increased their commerce with the slave colonies of the Chesapeake and Lower South, shipping tobacco, rice, and indigo north, then reshipping it to England. A similar pattern is evident in the statistics of other northern ports. This carrying trade in the products of slave labor made it possible for New England and the Middle Colonies to earn the income necessary to purchase British imports despite the relative absence of valuable products from their own regions. Gradually, the commercial economies of the Northeast and the South were becoming integrated. From the 1730s

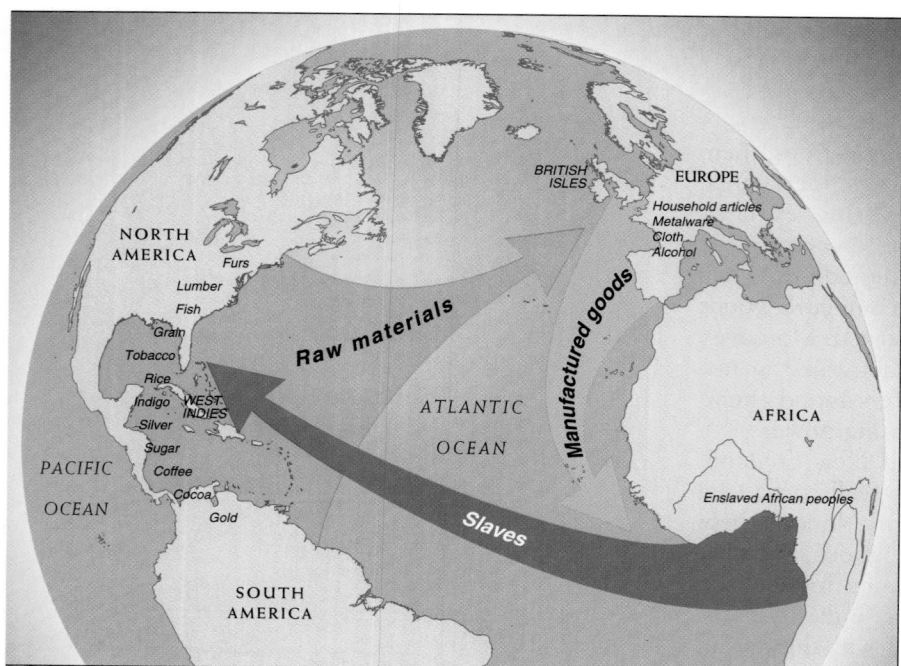

Triangular Trade across the Atlantic   *The pattern of commerce among Europe, Africa, and the Americas became known as the "Triangular Trade." Sailors called the voyage of slave ships from Africa to America the "Middle Passage" because it formed the crucial middle section of this trading triangle.*

to the 1770s, for example, while the volume of trade between Great Britain and Charleston doubled, the trade between Charleston and northern ports grew sevenfold. The same relationship was developing between the Chesapeake and the North. Merchants in Boston, Newport, New York, and Philadelphia increasingly provided southern planters not only with shipping services but with credit and insurance as well. Like London, Liverpool, and Bristol—though on a smaller scale—the port cities of the North became pivots in the expanding trade network linking slave plantations with Atlantic markets. This trade provided northern merchants with the capital that financed commercial growth and development in their cities and the surrounding countryside. Slavery thus contributed to the growth of a score of northern port cities, forming an indirect but essential part of their economies.

SLAVERY AND FREEDOM

The prosperity of the eighteenth-century plantation economy thus improved the living conditions for the residents of northern cities as well as for a large segment of the population of the South, providing them with material opportunities unknown in the preceding century. The price, however, was the oppression and exploitation of millions of Africans and African Americans. Freedom for white men based on the slavery of African Americans

is the most important contradiction in American history.

The Social Structure of the Slave Colonies

At the summit of southern colonial society stood a small elite of wealthy planters, in contrast with the mass of unfree men and women who formed the working population. Slavery had produced a society in which property was concentrated in the hands of a wealthy few. The richest 10 percent of southern colonists owned more than half the cultivated land and over 60 percent of the wealth. Although there was no colonial aristocracy—no nobility or royal appointments—the landed elite of the slave colonies came very close to constituting one.

Among the hundred wealthiest Virginians of the 1770s, for example, more than 80 percent had inherited their wealth from their fathers, and some were third- or fourth-generation colonials. Fewer than 10 percent were "self-made," and most of these men had acquired their fortunes through commerce or the law. The typical wealthy Virginia planter lived in a Tidewater county, owned several thousand acres of prime farmland and more than 100 slaves, resided in a luxurious plantation mansion, built perhaps in the fashionable Georgian style, and had an estate valued at more than 10,000 pounds. Elected to the House of Burgesses, and forming the group from which the magistrates and counselors of the colony were chosen, these "first families of Virginia"—the Carters, Harrisons, Lees, Fitzhughs, Burwells, Randolphs, and others—were a self-perpetuating governing class.

A similar elite ruled the Lower South, although wealthy landowners there spent relatively little time on their plantations. They resided instead in fashionable Charleston, where they constituted a close-knit group who controlled the colonial government. "They live in as high a style here, I believe, as any part of the world," wrote a visitor to Charleston.

A considerable distance separated this slave-owning elite from typical southern landowners. About half the adult white males were small planters and farmers. But although the gap between rich and middling colonists grew larger during the eighteenth century, the prosperity of the plantation economy created generally favorable conditions for this large landed class. Slave ownership, for example, became widespread among this group during the eighteenth century. In Virginia at midcentury, 45 percent of heads of household held one to four slaves, and even poorer farmers kept one or two.

Despite the prosperity that accompanied slavery in the eighteenth century, however, a substantial portion of colonists continued to own no land or slaves at all. Some rented land or worked as tenant farmers, some hired out as overseers or farm workers, and still others were indentured servants. Throughout the plantation region, landless white men constituted about 40 percent of the population. A New England visitor found a "much greater disparity between the rich and poor in Virginia" than at home.

White Skin Privilege

Yet all the white colonists of eighteenth-century North America shared the privileged status of their skin color. In the early seventeenth century there had been more diversity in views about race. For some, black skin was thought to be a sign of God's curse. "The blackness of the Negroes," one Englishman argued, "proceedeth of some natural infection." But not everyone shared those views. "I can't think there is any intrinsic value in one colour more than another," a second Englishman remarked, "nor that white is better than black, only we think it so because we are so." As slavery became increasingly important, however, Virginia officials took considerable care to create legal distinctions between the status of colonists and that of Africans, deliberately encouraging the growth of racism. Beginning in 1670, free Africans were prohibited from owning Christian servants. Ten years later, another law declared that any African, free or slave, who struck a Christian would receive thirty lashes on his bare back. One of the most important measures was designed to suppress intimate interracial contacts between white servants and enslaved Africans. A 1691 act "for prevention of that abominable mixture and spurious issue which hereafter may encrease in this dominion" established severe penalties for interracial sexual relationships. Such penalties were rarely applied to masters, who frequently forced themselves on African women. But some slave women may have willingly established intimate relations with masters to better their condition or the opportunities for their children. The descendants of Sally Hemings, a slave owned by Thomas Jefferson, have long claimed that Jefferson fathered some of her children, and recent scientific tests comparing their DNA with that of descendents of Jefferson's paternal grandfather have confirmed their story. The Hemings children enjoyed a privileged position among Jefferson's slaves and were freed in his will.

Relationships between white masters or indentured servants and African slaves produced a rather large group of mulattoes. Since by law children inherited the bond or free status of their mothers, the children of African mothers became slaves, but a minority, the children of European women and African men, were free. According to a Maryland census of 1755, more than 60 percent of mulattoes were slaves. But mulattoes also made up three-quarters of a small free African American population. This group, about 4,000 in the 1770s, was denied the right to vote, to hold office, or to testify in court—all on the basis of racial

Alexander Spotswood Payne and His Brother, John Robert Dandridge Payne, with Their Nurse, ca. 1790. Oil on canvas, 142.2 x 175.2 cm. Virginia Museum of Fine Arts, Richmond, Gift of Miss Dorothy Payne.

Alexander Spotswood Payne and his brother John Robert Dandridge Payne with their African American nurse, painted by an unknown Virginia artist, ca. 1790. White and black Southerners lived in intimate contact. White children were breast-fed by African nannies, and interracial sex was very much a part of plantation life. But whiteness was the universal badge of freedom, blackness a mark of bondage. Despite their close association, said Thomas Jefferson, the two peoples were divided by "deep rooted prejudices entertained by the whites" and "ten thousand recollections, by the blacks, of the injuries they have sustained."

CHRONOLOGY

1441	African slaves first brought to Portugal	1705	Virginia Slave Code established
1518	Spain grants official license to Portuguese slavers	1706	French and Spanish navies bombard Charleston
1535	Africans constitute a majority on Hispaniola	1710	English capture Port Royal
1619	First Africans brought to Virginia	1712	Slave uprising in New York City
1655	English seize Jamaica	1713	Peace of Utrecht
1662	Virginia law makes slavery hereditary	1721–48	Robert Walpole leads British cabinet
1670	South Carolina founded	1733	Molasses Act
1672	Royal African Company organized	1739	Stono Rebellion / War of Jenkins's Ear
1691	Virginia prohibits interracial sexual contact	1740–48	King George's War
1698	Britain opens the slave trade to all its merchants	1741	Africans executed in New York for conspiracy
1699	Spanish declare Florida a refuge for escaped slaves	1752	Georgia officially opened to slavery
1702	South Carolinians burn St. Augustine	1770s	Peak period of the English colonies' slave trade
		1808	Importation of slaves into the United States ends

background. Denied the status of citizenship enjoyed by even the poorest of white men, free blacks were a pariah group who raised the status of poor white colonials by contrast. Racial distinctions were a constant reminder of the freedom of white colonists and the debasement of all blacks, slave or free.

Racism set up a wall of contempt between colonists and African Americans. Jefferson wrote of "the real distinctions which nature has made" between the races. "In memory they are equal to the whites," he wrote of the slaves, but "in reason much inferior." He gave no consideration to the argument of the freed slave Olaudah Equiano that "slavery debases the mind." Jefferson was on firmer ground when he argued that the two peoples were divided by "deep rooted prejudices entertained by the whites" and "ten thousand recollections, by the blacks, of the injuries they have sustained." Perhaps he knew of these feelings from his long relationship with Sally Hemings. "I tremble for my country when I reflect that God is just," Jefferson concluded in a deservedly famous passage, and remember "that his justice cannot sleep forever."

CONCLUSION

During the eighteenth century nearly half a million Africans were kidnapped from their homes and packed into ships for up to three months before arriving in British North America. They provided the labor that made colonialism pay. Southern planters, northern merchants, and especially British traders and capitalists benefited greatly from the commerce in slave-produced crops, and that prosperity filtered down to affect many of the colonists of British North America. Slavery was "the strength and sinews" of the British empire in North America. The focus of imperial warfare was seizing the slave colonies of other powers and putting them to the service of the mother country. Mercantilism was a system designed to channel the colonial wealth produced by slaves to the nation-state, but as long as profits were high, the British were content to wink at all colonists' violations of mercantilist regulations.

Although African Americans received nothing in return, their labor helped build the greatest accumulation of capital that Europe had ever seen. But despite enormous hardship and suffering, African Americans survived by forming new communities in the colonies, rebuilding families, restructuring language, reforming culture. African American culture added important components of African knowledge and experience to colonial agri-culture, art, music, and cuisine. The African Americans of the British colonies lived better lives than the slaves worked to death on Caribbean sugar plantations, but lives of misery compared to the men they were forced to serve. As the slaves sang on the Georgia coast: "Dah Backrow Man go wrong you, Buddy Quow."

REVIEW QUESTIONS

1. Trace the development of the system of slavery and discuss the way it became entrenched in the Americas.
2. Describe the effects of the slave trade both on enslaved Africans and on the economic and polit-ical life of Africa.
3. Describe the process of acculturation involved in becoming an African American. In what ways did slaves "Africanize" the South?
4. Explain the connection between the institution of slavery and the building of a commercial empire.
5. In what ways did colonial policy encourage the growth of racism?

RECOMMENDED READING

Michael Craton, *Sinews of Empire: A Short History of British Slavery* (1974). An introduction to the British mercantilist system that emphasizes the impor-tance of slavery. Includes a comparison of the mainland colonies with the Caribbean.

Philip D. Curtin, *The African Slave Trade: A Census* (1969). The pioneer work in the quantitative history of the slave trade. All subsequent histories of the slave trade are indebted to Curtin.

Herbert G. Gutman, *The Black Family in Slavery and Freedom, 1750–1925* (1976). A pathbreaking history of the development of the African Amer-ican community in North America. The sections on the eighteenth century provide evidence of the development of multigenerational family and kin networks.

Winthrop D. Jordan, *White over Black: American Attitudes toward the Negro, 1550–1812* (1968). Remains the best and most comprehensive history of racial values and attitudes. A searching examination of British and American literature, folklore, and history.

Peter Kolchin, *American Slavery, 1619–1877* (1993). A survey that features comparisons with slavery in Brazil, the Caribbean, and serfdom in Russia. Includes a comprehensive bibliographic essay.

Walter Rodney, *How Europe Underdeveloped Africa* (1974). A highly influential book that traces the relationship between Europe and Africa from the fifteenth to the twentieth century and demon-strates how Europe's industrialization became Africa's impoverishment.

Mechal Sobel, *The World They Made Together: Black and White Values in Eighteenth-Century Virginia* (1987). Demonstrates the ways in which both Africans and Europeans shaped the formation of American values, perceptions, and identities.

Ian K. Steele, *Warpaths: Invasions of North America* (1994). A new synthesis of the colonial wars from the sixteenth to the eighteenth century that places Indians as well as empires at the center of the action.

Sterling Stuckey, *Slave Culture: Nationalist Theory and the Foundations of Black America* (1987). A study of the African origins of African American culture that concentrates on folklore. Includes important evidence on African American religion in the era before Christianization.

Hugh Thomas, *The Slave Trade: The Story of the Atlantic Slave Trade, 1440–1870* (1997). The horrifying history in brutal detail, told by a master historian.

ADDITIONAL BIBLIOGRAPHY

The African Slave Trade

Jay Coughtry, *The Notorious Triangle: Rhode Island and the African Slave Trade, 1799–1807* (1981)

Philip D. Curtin, *Economic Change in Precolonial Africa: Senegambia in the Era of the Slave Trade* (1975)

Basin Davidson, *The African Slave Trade* (1980)

Elizabeth Donnan, ed., *Documents Illustrative of the History of the Slave Trade to America* 4 vols. (1930–35)

J. E. Inikori, *Forced Migration: The Impact of the Export Slave Trade on African Societies* (1982)

Robert W. July, *A History of the African People* (1992)

Herbert S. Klein, *The Middle Passage: Comparative Studies in the Atlantic Slave Trade* (1978)

Robin Law, *The Slave Coast of West Africa, 1550–1750: The Impact of the Atlantic Slave Trade on an African Society* (1991)

Paul E. Lovejoy, ed., *Africans in Bondage: Studies in Slavery and the Slave Trade* (1986)

Daniel P. Mannix and Malcolm Crowley, *Black Cargoes: A History of the Atlantic Slave Trade* (1962)

David Northrup, ed., *The Atlantic Slave Trade* (1994)

J. A. Rawley, *The Transatlantic Slave Trade* (1981)

Edward Reynolds, *Stand the Storm: A History of the Atlantic Slave Trade* (1985)

A. C. De C. M. Saunders, *A Social History of Black Slaves and Freemen in Portugal, 1441–1555* (1982)

Jon Vogt, *Portuguese Rule on the Gold Coast, 1469–1682* (1979)

The Development of North American Slave Societies

L. R. Bailey, *Indian Slave Trade in the Southwest: A Study of Slave-Taking and the Traffic in Indian Captives* (1966)

T. H. Breen and Stephen Innes, *"Myne Owne Ground": Race and Freedom on Virginia's Eastern Shore* (1980)

Verner W. Crane, *The Southern Frontier, 1670–1732* (1929)

Richard S. Dunn, *Sugar and Slaves: The Rise of the Planter Class in the English West Indies, 1624–1713* (1972)

Laura Foner and Eugene D. Genovese, eds., *Slavery in the New World: A Reader in Comparative History* (1969)

Charles Joyner, *Down by the Riverside: A South Carolina Slave Community* (1984)

Alan Kulikoff, *Tobacco and Slaves: The Development of Southern Cultures in the Chesapeake, 1680–1800* (1986)

Daniel Littlefield, *Rice and Slaves: Ethnicity and the Slave Trade in Colonial South Carolina* (1981)

Paul E. Lovejoy, *Transformations in Slavery: A History of Slavery in Africa* (1983)

Edgar J. McManus, *Black Bondage in the North* (1973)

Gary B. Nash, *Red, White, and Black: The Peoples of Early North America* (1992)

Julia Floyd Smith, *Slavery and Rice Culture in Low Country Georgia, 1750–1860* (1985)

Brenda Stevenson, *Life in Black and White: Family and Community in the Slave South* (1996)

Peter H. Wood, *Black Majority: Negroes in Colonial South Carolina from 1670 through the Stone Rebellion* (1974)

Becoming African American

John B. Boles, *Black Southerners, 1619–1869* (1984)

Joseph E. Harris, ed., *Global Dimensions of the African Diaspora* (1982)

Annette Gordon-Reed, *Thomas Jefferson and Sally Hemings: An American Controversy*, (1997)

Gerald W. Mullin, *Flight and Rebellion: Slave Resistance in Eighteenth-Century Virginia* (1972)

Orlando Patterson, *Slavery and Social Death: A Comparative Study* (1982)

V. B. Thompson, *The Making of the African Diaspora in the Americas, 1441–1900* (1984)

The Structure of Empire

Joyce O. Appleby, *Economic Thought and Ideology in Seventeenth-Century England* (1978)

Eugene Genovese and Elizabeth Fox-Genovese, *Fruits of Merchant Capital: Slavery and Bourgeois Property in the Rise and Expansion of Capitalism* (1983)

E. J. Hobsbawn, *Industry and Empire: The Making of Modern English Society, 1750 to the Present Day* (1968)

Michael Kammen, *Empire and Interest: The American Colonies and the Politics of Mercantilism* (1970)

John J. McCusker and Russell R. Menard, *The Economy of British America, 1607–1787* (1985)

Barbara L. Solow, ed., *Slavery and the Rise of the Atlantic System* (1991)

Eric Williams, *Capitalism and Slavery* (1944)

Slavery and Freedom

David Brion Davis, *The Problem of Slavery in Western Culture* (1966)

Carl N. Degler, *Neither Black nor White: Slavery and Race Relations in Brazil and the United States* (1971)

Edmund S. Morgan, *American Slavery, American Freedom: The Ordeal of Colonial Virginia* (1975)

Joel Williamson, *New People: Miscegenation and Mulattoes in the United States* (1980)

Biography

Philip D. Curtin, ed., *Africa Remembered: Narratives of West Africans from the Era of the Slave Trade* (1967)

Paul Edwards, ed., *The Interesting Narrative of the Life of Olaudah Equiano, or Gustavus Vassa, the African, written by himself* (1987)

James B. Hedges, *The Browns of Providence Plantation* (1952)

Kenneth A. Lockridge, *The Diary and Life of William Byrd II of Virginia, 1674-1744* (1987)

Phinizy Spalding, *Oglethorpe in America* (1977)

Janet Whitman, *John Woolman, American Quaker* (1942)

THE CULTURES OF COLONIAL NORTH AMERICA

1700–1780

Watercolor, fraktur of George and Lady Washington: Abby Aldrich Rockefeller Folk Art Center. Williamsburg. VA

AMERICAN COMMUNITIES
From Deerfield to Kahnawake: Crossing Cultural Boundaries

Two hours before daylight on February 29, 1704, the Reverend John Williams and his wife Eunice of Deerfield, Massachusetts, awoke to "horrid shouting and yelling" and the crash of axes and hatchets breaking open the doors and windows of their house. Leaping out of bed they knew immediately that the town was under attack by Indians and their French allies; this frontier settlement on the northwestern fringe of New England had already been attacked six times in the perennial fighting with New France. Never before, however, had the enemy penetrated the town's stockade. Suddenly the door burst open and "with painted faces and hideous exclamations" Indians began pushing inside. "I reached up my hands for my pistol," Williams remembered, "cocked it, and put it to the breast of the first Indian that came up." It misfired, and as the couple stood trembling in their night clothes, they were bound and dragged into the central hall with their seven children. In horror they were forced to watch the invaders club and kill their resisting six-year-old son, their screaming newborn infant daughter, and the black nursemaid. The family was hustled out into the frigid dawn and, with more than a hundred other captives, marched north through snow and ice toward Canada, leaving the frightful sight of the burning town behind.

The Deerfield raid became one of the most infamous events in the long series of colonial wars. One hundred and forty residents of the town managed to hold off the invasion and survive, but fifty others died in the attack. Among the captives, twenty-one were murdered along the way, in most cases because they were too weak to travel; the murdered included Mrs. Williams, who had not yet recovered from a difficult childbirth just six weeks before. The governor of Massachusetts ordered a day of fasting and prayed that "the Designs of the barbarous Salvages against us be defeated; our exposed Plantations preserved; and the poor Christian Captives in their hands returned." Authorities raised the bounty on Indian scalps from £10 to £100 and organized bloody raids of their own on the French and Indian settlements to the north.

Most of the Deerfield captives were delivered to the French authorities in Montreal. Within two years, fifty-nine of them had been ransomed and returned home to Deerfield, the Reverend Williams and four of his surviving children among them. Williams soon published an account of his captivity, *The Redeemed Captive Returning to Zion*. In colonial America, with its many peoples and cultures, readers were fascinated by the problems and dilemmas of crossing frontiers and boundaries. What was life like for you, people wanted to know, on the other side of the frontier? How were you changed by your experience? Did you remain loyal to your community? Can you still be trusted?

Questions of this sort were vitally important to the colonists, for over the years hundreds of Europeans who had been captured by Indians had chosen to remain with their captors rather than return home. Among the Deerfield captives, thirty-one—including ten-year-old Eunice Williams, her mother's namesake—remained in Canada. Eunice and many of the other Deerfield captives lived at Kahnawake, a community of Catholic Indians near Montreal. Like Deerfield, Kahnawake was a farming town of fifty or sixty homes clustered around a central church and surrounded by a stockade to protect it from enemy raiders. The differences between the two communities, however, were more striking than the similarities.

Founded in the seventeenth century by Jesuit missionaries as a refuge for Iroquois converts, Kahnawake not only became home to a great variety of Native American Catholics but also welcomed people of mixed Indian and European ancestry. The "great mixture of the blood of whites with that of aborigines is observable in the persons of the inhabitants," wrote one visitor, struck by the appearance of people who seemed to be Indians in all respects except their blue eyes. Such mixing was also evident in the community's culture, in the exotic mélange of European and Indian clothing, in the use of both Indian and French names, and in the special ways the community bent Catholic ritual to fit traditional Iroquois practices. Community members crossed boundaries in other ways, too: many residents were smugglers who engaged in the illegal trade of furs and other Indian products across the frontier into New York. According to the frustrated authorities in Montreal, Kahnawake operated as "a sort of republic," insisting on its freedom and independence.

As the historian John Demos writes, Kahnawake was "a unique experiment in bicultural living." Its residents were skilled at offering sympathetic sanctuary to traumatized captive children, and by the time Eunice Williams's father and siblings were ransomed she told the man who had come to fetch her that she was "unwilling to return." Soon she converted to Catholicism. Over the years the father sent several emissaries to retrieve her, but all she would say were two words of Iroquois: *jaghte oghte*, meaning "maybe not." She had apparently forgotten her English tongue, and she refused to acknowledge her English name, having taken another—A'ongonte, which in Iroquois means "she has been planted as a person." In 1713, at the age of sixteen, she married a Kahnawake Mohawk. Father and daughter would meet only once more, the following year, when he went to Kahnawake a final time to beg her to return. But she would "not so much as give me one pleasant look," Williams wrote mournfully. "She is yet obstinatly resolved to live and dye here."

And that is what happened. A'ongonte and her husband remained good Catholics, raising a family and working as traders. John Williams died in 1729, surrounded by his children and grandchildren but longing for his "unredeemed" daughter. It was not until 1739 that A'ongonte found the courage to bring her family south for a visit, for she feared being held in New England against her will. Her brother Stephen wrote in his diary that at long last "we had ye joyfull, Sorrowfull meeting of our poor Sister that we had been Sepratd from fer above 36 years." After that A'ongonte visited only rarely because of the continuing warfare. "We have a great desire of going down to see you," she wrote to her brother through an interpreter near the end of their lives in the 1770s, "but do not know when an oppertunity may offer....I pray the Lord that he may give us grace so to Live in this as to be prepared for a happey meeting in the world to Come." And, perhaps as a sign of reconciliation, she signed the letter, "Loving Sister until death, Eunice Williams."

Deerfield

KEY TOPICS

- The similarities and differences among eighteenth-century Spanish, French, and English colonies

- The impact on British colonial culture of increasing European immigration

- Cultural changes in Indian America brought about by contact with European customs and lifestyles

- Patterns of work and class in eighteenth-century America

- Tensions between Enlightenment thought and the Great Awakening's call to renewed religious devotion

NORTH AMERICAN REGIONS

American colonial history too frequently is written as if only the British colonists along the Atlantic coast really mattered. But as the experience of the Deerfield community and the Williams family suggests, this is a mistake eighteenth-century colonists could not afford to make. In the first place, Indian America was a critically important part of the eighteenth-century world. From the fringes of colonial societies into the native heart of the continent, from the eastern foothills of the Appalachians to the western flank of the Sierra Nevada in California, hundreds of Indian cultures—despite being deeply affected by the spread of colonial culture—remained firmly in control of their homelands. And in addition to the British provinces stretching along the Atlantic coast, there were Hispanic colonists who defended the northern borderlands of the Spanish Caribbean and Mexican empire in isolated communities from Florida to California, and French communities that occupied the valley of the St. Lawrence River and scattered down the Mississippi Valley from the Great Lakes to the Gulf of Mexico. There were impressive similarities among these colonial societies, representing a continuation in the New World of traditional Old World beliefs, customs, and institutions, as well as a general pattern of European adaptation to American conditions.

Indian America

As the native peoples of the Atlantic coastal plain lost their lands to colonists through battles or treaties, and moved into or beyond the Appalachian Mountains, they became active in the European fur trade and dependent on firearms, metal tools, and other manufactured goods to maintain their way of life. Yet through the American Revolution they continued to

assert a proud independence and gained considerable skill at playing colonial powers off against each other. The Iroquois Five Nations battled the French and

A portrait of the Delaware chief Tishcohan by Gustavus Hesselius, painted in 1732. In his purse of chipmunk hide is a clay pipe, a common item of the Indian trade. Tishcohan was one of the Delaware leaders forced by Pennsylvania authorities into signing a fraudulent land deal that reversed that colony's history of fair dealing with Indians over land. He moved west to the Ohio River as settlers poured into his former homeland.

their Indian allies in King William's War, but in 1701 they signed a treaty of neutrality with France that kept them out of harm's way during the next round of conflicts. The Catholic Iroquois of Kahnawake sometimes supported the French, as they did by mounting the Deerfield raid, but they also traded with the English. In the Lower South, the Creeks similarly traded with both the French and the English as a means of maintaining their autonomy.

In general, the French had significantly better relations with native peoples than the English, but inevitably as they pursued their expansionist plans they came into conflict with many Indian groups, and when opposed they could be just as cruel and violent as any other power. In the early eighteenth century the Fox Indians blocked French passage between the Great Lakes and the upper Mississippi, attempting to make themselves into middlemen in the fur trade. After several years of sporadic fighting, the French defeated the tribe in 1716. But Fox warriors rose again in 1726, and only with great violence and not until 1738 could the French force the tribe to sign a treaty. On the lower Mississippi the Natchez and Chickasaw tribes opposed the arrival of the French, engaging them in a series of bloody conflicts during the 1720s that concluded only when the French decimated the Natchez in 1731.

The preeminent concern of the Indians of the eastern half of the continent was the tremendous growth of colonial population in the British Atlantic coastal colonies, especially the movement of settlers westward. In the 1730s and 1740s Pennsylvania perpetrated a series of fraudulent seizures of western lands from the Delawares. Particularly in the light of Pennsylvania's previous history of fair dealing with Indian peoples, these acts offered yet another disturbing sign of things to come. Thus Indian alliances with the French resulted not from any great love and affection on their part toward the French but from their great fear of British expansion.

Growing Use of the Horse by Plains Indians   In the seventeenth and eighteenth centuries, Spanish settlers introduced horses into their New Mexican colony. Through trading and raiding, horses spread northward in streams both west and east of the Rocky Mountains. The horse, whose genetic ancestor had been native to the American continent in pre-Archaic times, offered the Indian peoples of the Great Plains the opportunity to create a distinctive hunting and warrior culture.

Meanwhile, a long-term population decline continued among the Indian peoples of North America. The colonists were relatively immune from dramatic fluctuations in the death rate, but Indian America continued to take a terrific beating from epidemics of European disease. There was no systematic census of North American Indians before the nineteenth century, but historians estimate that from a high of 7 to 10 million native Americans north of Mexico in 1500 the population had probably fallen to around a million by 1800. Thus, during the eighteenth century the colonial population overtook and began to overwhelm the native population of the continent. Population loss did not affect all Indian tribes equally, however. Native peoples with a century or more of colonial contact and interaction had lost 50 percent or more of their numbers, but most Indian societies in the interior had yet to be struck by the horrible epidemics.

Colonization introduced other, less-distressing changes in Indian cultures. By the early eighteenth century, Indians on the southern fringe of the Great Plains were using horses stolen from the Spanish in New Mexico. Horses enabled Indian hunters to exploit the buffalo herds much more efficiently than before, and on the base of this more productive subsistence strategy many groups built a distinctive and elaborate nomadic culture. Great numbers of Indian peoples moved onto the plains during the eighteenth century, pulled by this new way of life, pushed by colonial invasions and disruptions radiating southwest from Canada and north from the Spanish borderlands. By midcentury, the New Mexicans had become regular victims of raids by mounted hunters of the Great Plains. The invention of nomadic Plains Indian culture was another of the dramatic cultural amalgamations and innovations of the eighteenth century. The mounted Plains Indian, so frequently used as a symbol of native America, was actually a product of the colonial era.

The Spanish Borderlands

In the mid-eighteenth century what is today the Sunbelt of the United States formed the periphery of the largest and most prosperous European colony on the North American continent—the viceroyalty of New Spain, which included approximately 1 million Spanish colonists and mestizos and at least 2 million Indians. The administrative capital of Mexico City was the most sophisticated metropolis in the Western Hemisphere, the site of one of the world's great universities, with broad avenues and spectacular baroque architecture. New Spain's northern provinces of Florida, Texas, New Mexico, and California, however, were far removed from this opulence. Officials of the viceroyalty of New Spain, who oversaw these colonies, thought of them as buffer zones, protecting New Spain from the expanding colonial empires of Spain's New World rivals.

In Florida, the oldest of European colonies in North America, fierce fighting among the Spanish, the British, and the Indians had by the early eighteenth century reduced the colonial presence to little more than the forts of St. Augustine on the Atlantic and Pensacola on the Gulf of Mexico, each surrounded by small colonized territories populated with the families of Spanish troops. In their weakened condition, the Spanish had no choice but to establish cooperative relations with the Creek and Seminole Indians who dominated the region,

Region	Population
New France	70,000
New England	400,000
New York	100,000
Pennsylvania	230,000
Chesapeake	390,000
Lower South	100,000
Backcountry	100,000
Northern New Spain	20,000
Indian America	1,500,000

Regions in Eighteenth-Century North America

By the middle of the eighteenth century, European colonists had established a number of distinctive colonial regions in North America. The northern periphery of New Spain, the oldest and most prosperous European colony, stretched from Baja California to eastern Texas, then jumped to the settlements on the northern end of the Florida peninsula; cattle ranching was the dominant way of life in this thinly populated region. New France was like a great crescent, extending from the plantation communities along the Mississippi near New Orleans to the French colonial communities along the St. Lawrence; in between were isolated settlements and forts, connected only by the extensive French trading network.

as well as the hundreds of African American runaways who considered St. Augustine a refuge from the cruel slave regimes in Georgia and Carolina. Like the community of Kahnawake, eighteenth-century Florida included a growing mestizo population as well as a considerable number of free African Americans and Hispanicized Indians from the old missions.

New Mexico, nearly 2,000 miles to the west, was similarly isolated from the mainstream of New Spain. One Spanish observer characterized the province as "little populated and poverty-stricken, although endowed with natural resources." At midcentury New Mexico included some 20,000 Pueblo Indians (their numbers greatly reduced by disease since their first contact with Europeans) and perhaps 10,000 colonists. The prosperity of these colonists, who supported themselves with subsistence agriculture, was severely constrained by a restrictive colonial economic policy that forced them to exchange their wool, pottery, buffalo hides, and buckskin for imported goods at unfavorable rates. Unlike the colonial population of Florida, however, the settlements of New Mexicans were gradually expanding, following the valleys and streams that led

east and north from the original colonial outposts scattered along the upper Rio Grande.

The Spanish also founded new northern outposts during the eighteenth century. Concerned about French colonization of the Mississippi Valley, they established several military posts or *presidios* on the fringes of the colony of Louisiana and in 1716 began the construction of a string of Franciscan missions among the Indian peoples of Texas. By 1750 the settlement of San Antonio had become the center of a developing frontier province. The Spanish also established new colonial outposts west of New Mexico, in what is today southern Arizona. In the 1690s, Jesuit missionaries, led by Father Eusebio Kino, founded missions among the desert Indians of the lower Colorado and Gila River Valleys. Mission San Xavier del Bac near Tucson is acclaimed the most striking example of Spanish colonial architecture in the United States. Cattle ranching, introduced by the Jesuits, and farming as well spread along the lower Rio Grande Valley; in fact, ranching would continue to define the region's economy for the next 200 years.

Midcentury also found the Spanish considering new settlements along the California coast. Juan

The church of San Xavier del Bac, constructed in the late eighteenth century, is located a few miles south of the city of Tucson, where Jesuit Father Eusebio Kino founded a mission among the Pima Indians in 1700. Known as the White Dove of the Desert, it is acclaimed as the most striking example of Spanish colonial architecture in the United States.

Cabrillo, an associate of Hernán Cortés, had first explored the coastal waters in 1542 and was the first European to sail into the fine harbor at San Diego. In 1603 the explorer Sebastián Vizcaíno had come upon Monterey Bay. The Spanish did little to follow up on these finds, but in 1769, acting on rumors of Russian expansion along the northern Pacific coast (for a discussion of Russian America, see Chapter 9), officials in Mexico City ordered Gaspar de Portolá, governor of what is now Baja California, to establish a Spanish presence in the North. With him were Franciscan missionaries led by Junípero Serra, president of the missions in Baja. At the harbor of San Diego, Portolá and Serra founded the first mission and pueblo complex in present-day California. Portolá then proceeded overland, becoming the first European to explore the interior valleys and mountains, and in 1770 he and Serra established their headquarters at Monterey Bay on the central coast. Two years later Juan Bautista de Anza established an overland route across the blistering deserts connecting Arizona and California, and in 1776 he led a colonizing expedition that founded the pueblo of San Francisco. Over the next fifty years the number of California settlements grew to include twenty-one missions and a half-dozen presidios and pueblos, including the town of Los Angeles. Founded in 1781 by a group of mestizo settlers from Sinaloa, Mexico, by the end of the century Los Angeles, with a population of only 300, was California's largest town.

A distinguishing mark of these colonial communities was their close association with the mission system. For the Spanish, conquest demanded conversion, which, according to theory, would lead Indians toward "civilization." Like the efforts of the Jesuits at Kahnawake and elsewhere in New France, the Spanish experiment in cultural transformation was designed to make Indians over into Christians and loyal subjects by educating them and putting them to work raising cattle and crops. The most extensive mission project was in California, where under the direction of priests thousands of Indian laborers produced a flourishing local economy based on irrigation farming as well as horse, cattle, and sheep ranching. Near Los Angeles lay San Gabriel, one of the most prosperous missions, where large vineyards and orchards produced fine wines and brandies. Indian people also constructed the adobe and stone churches, built on Spanish and Moorish patterns, whose ruins symbolize California's colonial society.

But this experiment in culture change was deadly for Indian people. To keep the system functioning, the Franciscan missionaries resorted to cruel and sometimes violent means of controlling their Indian subjects: shackles, solitary confinement, and whipping posts. Indians resisted from the very beginning. In 1775 the villagers around San Diego rose up and killed several priests. The history of many missions was punctuated by revolts, but the arms and organization of Spanish soldiers were usually sufficient to suppress the uprisings. There were also smaller incidents of retaliation, as when at Mission Santa Cruz, on the central coast, a priest who thrashed Indians too often was murdered. Another form of protest was flight: whole villages sometimes fled to the inaccessible mountains.

Foreign observers noted the despondency of California's mission Indians. "I have never seen any of them laugh," one European visitor wrote. "I have never seen a single one look anyone in the face. They have the air of taking no interest in anything." The record of revolt suggests that there may have been more than a little guile in this mask of servility. But overwork, overcrowding, poor nutrition, poor sanitation, and epidemic disease took a terrible toll. The death rate, particularly high for children and women of child-bearing age, exceeded the birth rate, and California's native population fell by at least 25 percent.

As the prominence of mission settlements in California, Texas, and New Mexico suggests, the Catholic Church played a dominant role in the community life of the borderlands. In the eighteenth century, religion was no private affair. It was a deadly serious business dividing nations into warring camps, and the Spanish considered themselves the special protectors of the traditions of Rome. The object of colonization, one colonial promoter wrote in 1584, was "enlarging the glorious gospel of Christ, and leading the infinite multitudes of these simple people that are in error into the right and perfect way of salvation." Although these are the words of the English imperialist Richard Hakluyt, they could as easily have come from the Spanish padres Kino or Serra or the Jesuit missionaries at Kahnawake. There was no tradition of religious dissent. Certain of the truth of their "right and perfect way," the Spanish could see no reason for tolerating the errors of others.

The French Crescent

In France, as in Spain, Church and state were closely interwoven. During the seventeenth century the French prime ministers, Cardinal Richelieu and Cardinal Mazarin, laid out a fundamentally Catholic imperial policy, and under their guidance colonists constructed a second Catholic empire in North America. In 1674 Church and state collaborated in establishing the bishopric of Quebec.

The French Crescent   *The French empire in North America was based on a series of alliances and trade relations with Indian nations linking a great crescent of colonies, settlements, and outposts that extended from the mouth of the St. Lawrence River, through the Great Lakes, and down the Mississippi River to the Gulf of Mexico.*

Under aggressive leadership that office founded local seminaries, oversaw the appointment and review of priests, and laid the foundation of the resolutely Catholic culture of New France. Meanwhile, Jesuit missionaries continued to carry Catholicism deep into the continent.

The number of French colonists rose at an impressive rate from fewer than 15,000 in 1700 to more than 70,000 at midcentury. During the eighteenth century the French used their trade network and alliances with the Indians to establish a great crescent of colonies, military posts, and settlements that extended from the mouth of the St. Lawrence River, southwest through the Great Lakes, then down the Mississippi River to the Gulf of Mexico. The maritime colony of Acadia, populated by fishermen and farmers, anchored the crescent on the northeast; the slave colony of Louisiana held the other end at the mouth of the Mississippi. Over this vast territory the French laid a thin colonial veneer, the beginning of what they planned as a

The persistence of French colonial long lots in the pattern of modern landholding is clear in this enhanced satellite photograph of the Mississippi River near New Orleans. Long lots, the characteristic form of property holding in New France, were designed to offer as many settlers as possible a share of good bottomland as well as a frontage on the waterways, which served as the basic transportation network.

great continental empire that would contain the Protestant British to a narrow strip of Atlantic coastline.

At the heart of the French empire in North America were the farming communities of the colony of Quebec along the banks of the St. Lawrence, including the towns of Montreal and Quebec City. There were also farming communities in the Illinois country, which shipped wheat down the Mississippi to supply the booming sugar plantations of Louisiana. By the mid-eighteenth century, those plantations—extending along the river from Natchez and Baton Rouge to New Orleans—had become the most profitable French enterprise in North America.

One of the most distinctive French stamps on the North American landscape were the "long lots" stretching back from the rivers that provided each settler family a share of good bottomland to farm as well as frontage on the waterways, the "interstate highway system" of the French Crescent. This pattern had first appeared with the seigneurial grants along the St. Lawrence, but French colonists transplanted it throughout their domain; aerial photographs reveal its persistence today. Long lots were laid out along the lower Mississippi in Louisiana and at sites on the upper Mississippi such as Kaskaskia and

Prairie du Chien, as well as at the strategic passages of the Great Lakes, the communities of Mackinac, Sault Ste. Marie, and Detroit. In 1750 Detroit was a stockaded town with a military garrison, a small administrative center, several stores, a Catholic church, and 100 households of *métis* (French for mestizo) families. French and *métis* farmers worked the land along the Detroit River, not far from communities inhabited by more than 6,000 Ottawa, Potawatomi, and Huron Indians.

Communities of this sort that combined both French and Indian elements were in the tradition of the inclusive frontier. Detroit looked like "an old French village," said one observer, except that its houses were "mostly covered with bark," in Indian style. "It is not uncommon to see a Frenchman with Indian shoes and stockings, without breeches, wearing a strip of woolen cloth to cover what decency requires him to conceal," wrote another. "Yet at the same time he wears a fine ruffled shirt and a laced waistcoat, with a fine handkerchief on his head." Detroit had much of the character of the mixed community of Kahnawake on the St. Lawrence.

Family and kinship were also cast in the Indian pattern. Households frequently consisted of several related families, but wives limited their births, having on average only two or three children. There were arranged marriages and occasional polygamy, but women had easy access to divorce and enjoyed property rights. Yet the people focused their activities on commerce and identified themselves overwhelmingly as Catholic. More frequently than not choosing a path of mutual accommodation, the French and Indians established some of the most interesting and distinct of North American communities.

New England

Just as New Spain and New France had their official church, so did the people of New England: local communities in all the New England colonies but Rhode Island were governed by Puritan congregations. Under the plan established in Massachusetts, the local church of a community was free to run its own affairs under the guidance of the General Court (the governor and the representatives selected by the towns). The Puritan colonies allotted each congregation a tract of communal land. Church members divided this land among themselves on the basis of status and seniority, laying out central villages like Deerfield and building churches (called meetinghouses) that were maintained through taxation. Adult male church members constituted the freemen of the town, and thus there was very little distinction between religious and secular authority. At the town meeting the freemen chose their minister, voted on his salary and support, and elected local men to offices ranging from town clerk to fence viewer.

The Puritan tradition, however, was a curious mix of freedom and repression. Although local communities had considerable autonomy, they were tightly bound by the restrictions of the Puritan faith and the General Court. Contrary to the beliefs of many, the Puritans did not come to America to create a society where religion could be freely practiced but to establish their own version of the "right and perfect way," which placed severe restraints on individuals. The General Court, for example, passed a statute threatening that "if any man shall exceed the bounds of moderation, we shall punish him severely." Specifics were left to the imagination. Not only did the Puritans exile dissidents such as Roger Williams and Anne Hutchinson (see Chapter 3), they banned Anglicans and Baptists and jailed, tortured, and even executed members of the Society of Friends, commonly known as the Quakers.

One of the first formal arguments for religious toleration was made by the New Englander Roger Williams, leader of dissenting Rhode Island, in his book *The Bloudy Tenent of Persecution* (1644). "Forced worship," he wrote, "stinks in God's nostrils." This argument gained increasing appeal following the religious excesses of the English civil war. In 1661, lamenting "the sad experience" of the previous generation of religious conflicts, restored King Charles II ordered a stop to religious persecution in Massachusetts. The new climate of opinion was best expressed by the English philosopher John Locke in his *Letter on Tolerance* (1688). Churches were voluntary societies, he argued, and could work only through persuasion. That a religion was sanctioned by the state was no evidence of its truth, because different nations had different official religions. Consequently, the state had no legitimate concern with religious belief. Locke's ideas were embodied in the Toleration Act, passed by Parliament in 1689. New England at first resisted it, but under pressure from English authorities, Massachusetts and Connecticut reluctantly allowed other Protestant denominations to begin worshipping openly in 1700. In both colonies, however, the Puritan, or as it was now called, Congregationalist Church (because of its self-governing congregations) continued to be officially supported through taxation. (It would not be "disestablished" in Massachusetts until 1833.) By the 1730s there were Anglican, Baptist, and Presbyterian congregations in many New England towns.

The system of town and church government was well suited to population growth. As towns grew too large for the available land, groups of residents left together, "hiving off" to form new churches and towns elsewhere. An intricate network of roads and rivers knit the region together. Seventy-five years after the Indians of southern New England suffered their final defeat in King Philip's War (see Chapter 3), Puritan farm communities had taken up most of the available land of Massachusetts, Connecticut, and Rhode Island, leaving only a few communities of Pequots, Narragansets, and Wampanoags on restricted reservations. Northern Algonquians and Catholic Iroquois allied with the French in Quebec, however, maintained a defensive barrier preventing New Englanders from expanding northward into Maine, New Hampshire, and the region later called Vermont. Deerfield represented the far northern limit of safe settlement. By midcentury, then, as the result of growing population, New England was reaching the limit of its land supply.

The Middle Colonies

The colony of New York had one of the most ethnically diverse populations on the continent, in striking contrast to the ethnically homogeneous neighboring New England colonies of Connecticut and Massachusetts. At midcentury society along the lower Hudson River, including the counties in northern New Jersey,

The House of the Seven Gables in Salem, Massachusetts, was constructed in the seventeenth century. In this style of architecture, function prevailed over form as structures grew to accommodate their residents; rooms were added where and when they were needed. In England, wood for building was scarce, but the abundance of forests in North America created the conditions for a golden age of wood construction.

was a veritable mosaic of ethnic communities: the Dutch of Flatbush, the Huguenots of New Rochelle, the Flemish of Bergen County, and the Scots of Perth Amboy were but a few. African Americans, both slave and free, made up more than 15 percent of the lower Hudson population. Congregations of Puritans, Baptists, Quakers, and Catholics worshiped without legal hindrance. New York City also was home to the oldest Jewish community in the country, established in 1654; several hundred Jewish families attended services in North America's first synagogue, built in 1730. Among these communities there was a great deal of intermingling (as there was at places such as Kahnawake), but different ethnic and religious groups would long retain their distinctions, which made New York something of a cultural "salad bowl" if not a "melting pot."

New York City grew by leaps and bounds in the eighteenth century, but the elite who had inherited the rich lands and great manors along the upper Hudson chose to rent to tenants rather than to sell, diminishing the region's attractiveness to immigrants. By contrast, Pennsylvania was what one German immigrant called "heaven for farmers." The colony's Quaker proprietors were willing to sell land to anyone who could pay the relatively modest prices. Thus as the region around New York City filled up, immigrants by the thousand made the decision to land at Philadelphia, Pennsylvania's growing port city on the Delaware River. During the eighteenth century the population of this region and an extended area that encompassed portions of New Jersey, Delaware, and Maryland grew more dramatically than any other in North America. Here, immigration played the dominant role in achieving the astonishing annual growth rate of nearly 4 percent. Boasting some of the best farmland in North America, the region was soon exporting abundant produce through Philadelphia.

The Quakers who had founded Pennsylvania quickly became a minority, but, unlike the Puritans, they were generally comfortable with religious and ethnic pluralism. Many of the founders of the Society of Friends had been imprisoned for their beliefs in pre-Restoration England, and they were determined to prevent a repetition of this injustice in their own province. William Penn himself had been prominent in the struggle for religious toleration. "Force never yet made a good Christian," he argued. Indeed, the Quakers were opposed to all signs of rank, refusing to doff their hats to superiors but greeting all comers, whatever their station, with the extended handshake of brotherhood. To a remarkable extent, these attitudes extended to relations between the sexes as well. English founder George Fox had proclaimed that "in souls there is no sex," and among American Friends, women preached equally with men.

These Quaker attitudes were well suited to the ethnically and religiously diverse population of Penn-

sylvania. Although the Society of Friends remained the affiliation of the governing elite, it never became an established church. Most German immigrants were Lutherans or Calvinists, most North Britons Presbyterians, and there were plenty of Anglicans and Baptists as well. These churches constituted one of the cornerstones of Pennsylvania community life.

The institutions of government were another pillar of community organization. Colonial officials appointed justices of the peace from among the leading local men, and these justices provided judicial authority for the countryside. Property-owning farmers chose their own local officials. Country communities were tied together by kinship bonds and by bartering and trading among neighbors. The substantial stone houses and great barns of the Pennsylvania countryside testified to the social stability and prosperity of this system. The communities of the middle colonies, however, were more loosely bound than those of New England. Rates of mobility were considerably higher, with about half the population moving on in any given decade. Because land was sold in individual lots rather than in communal parcels, farmers tended to disperse themselves at will over the open countryside. Villages gradually developed at crossroads and ferries but with relatively little forethought or planning. It was Pennsylvania, which emphasized individual settlement, that provided the basic model for American expansion.

The Backcountry

By 1750 Pennsylvania's exploding population had pushed beyond the first range of the Appalachian highlands. Settlers occupied the northern reaches of the

This two-story log house, built in Pennsylvania in the early eighteenth century, is one of the oldest surviving examples of the method and style of log construction introduced in America by the Scandinavian colonists on the lower Delaware River. Learning New World farming and woodland hunting techniques from the Indians, these settlers forged a tradition of settlement that proved enormously successful for pioneers.

Great Valley, which extended southwest from Pennsylvania into Virginia. Although they hoped to become commercial farmers, these settlers began more modestly, planting Indian corn and raising hogs, hunting in the woods for meat and furs, and building log cabins. This strategy had originated with the settlers of the New Sweden colony on the lower Delaware River. Scandinavian immigrants brought their hunting traditions and introduced log cabin construction to North America. From the Delaware Indians they incorporated the methods of New World farming and woodland hunting, just as the Indians took from them the use of firearms and metal tools and began to build log structures of their own. These were some of the most successful cross-cultural adaptations of the eighteenth century.

The movement into the Pennsylvania and Virginia backcountry that began during the 1720s was the first of the great pioneer treks that would take Americans into the continental interior. Many, perhaps most, of these pioneers held no legal title to the lands they occupied; they simply hacked out and defended their squatters' claims from Indian tribes and all other comers. Many of these backcountry settlers came from the northern borders of England and Ireland, where there was considerable clan and ethnic violence, and adapted well to the violence of the backcountry. To the Delawares and Shawnees who had been pushed into the interior, or the Cherokees who occupied the Appalachian highlands to the south, however, these pioneers presented a new and deadly threat. Their rising fears and resentments over the expanding colonial population triggered much eighteenth-century warfare.

One of the distinctive characteristics of the backcountry was the settlers' disdain for rank. "The rain don't know broadcloth from bluejeans," they said. But the myth of frontier equality was simply that—myth. Most pioneers owned little or no land, while "big men" held great tracts and dominated local communities with their bombastic style of personal leadership. Here the men were warriors, the women workers. The story was told of one pioneer whose wife began to "jaw at" him. "He pulled off his breeches and threw them down to her, telling her to 'put them on and wear them.'"

The South

The Chesapeake and the Lower South were tri-racial societies, with intermingled communities of white colonists and black slaves, along with substantial Indian communities living on the fringes of colonial settlement. Much of the population growth of the region resulted from the forced migration of enslaved Africans, who by 1750 made up 40 percent of the population. Colonial settlement had filled not only the Tidewater area of the southern Atlantic coast but much of the Piedmont as well. Specializing in rice, tobacco,

Spread of Settlement: Movement into the Backcountry, 1720–1760   *The spread of settlement from 1720 to 1760 shows the movement of population into the backcountry in the midcentury.*

and other commercial crops, these colonies were overwhelmingly rural. Farms and plantations were dispersed across the countryside, and villages or towns were few.

English authorities made the Church of England the state religion in the Chesapeake colonies. Residents paid taxes to support the Church and were required to attend services. No other churches were allowed into Virginia and Maryland, and dissenters were excluded or exiled. Before the 1750s, the Toleration Act was little enforced in the South; at the same time, the Anglican establishment was internally weak. It maintained neither a colonial bishop nor local institutions for training clergy. In Carolina and Georgia, neither Anglicanism nor any other denomination rested on a firm foundation.

Along the rice coast, the dominant institution of social life was the large plantation. Transforming the tangle of woods and swamps along the region's rivers into an ordered pattern of dams, dikes, and flooded fields required a heavy capital investment, which meant that rice cultivation could be undertaken only by men of means. By midcentury, established plantations typically were dominated by a large main house, generally located on a spot of high ground overlooking the fields. Drayton Hall near Charleston, a mansion of the period that still survives, was built of pink brick in classically symmetrical style, with hand-carved interior moldings of imported Caribbean mahogany. Nearby, but a world apart, were the slave quarters, rough wooden cabins lining two sides of a muddy pathway near the outbuildings and barns. In this contrast between "big house" and "quarters" the Lower South was the closest thing in North America to the societies of the Caribbean sugar islands.

Grand plantation houses could be found in the Chesapeake as well. However, because tobacco, unlike rice, could be grown profitably in small plots, the Chesapeake included a greater variety of farmers and a correspondingly diverse landscape. Tobacco quickly drained the soil of its nutrients, and plantings had to be shifted to fresh ground every few years. Former tobacco land could be planted with corn for several years but then required twenty years or more of rest before reuse. The landscape was thus a patchwork of fields, many in various stages of ragged second growth. The poorest farmers lived in wooden cabins little better than the shacks of the slaves. More prosperous farm families lived with two or three slaves in houses that were nevertheless considerably smaller than the substantial homes of New England.

In the Lower South, where the plantations were little worlds unto themselves, there was relatively little community life outside the plantation. But by midcentury the Chesapeake had given rise to well-developed neighborhoods based on kinship networks and economic connections. Encouraging the developing sense of community more than any other institution was the county court, which held both executive and judicial power. On court day, white people of all ranks held a great gathering that included public business, horse racing, and perhaps a barbecue. The gentleman justices of the county, appointed by the governor, included the heads of the leading planter families. These men in turn selected the grand jury, composed of substantial freeholders. One of the most significant bonding forces in this free white population was the growing sense of racial solidarity that developed in response to the increasing proportion of African slaves dispersed throughout the neighborhoods.

Traditional Culture in the New World

In each of these North American colonial societies the family and kinship, the church, and the local community were the most significant factors in everyday life. Throughout the continent, colonists tended to live much as they had in their European homelands at the time their colonies were settled. Thus the residents of New Mexico, Quebec, and New England continued to

be attached to the religious passions of the seventeenth century long after their mother countries had put those religious controversies aside in favor of imperial geopolitics. Nostalgia for Europe helped to fix a conservative colonial attitude toward culture.

These were oral cultures, depending on the transmission of information by the spoken word rather than through print, on the passage of traditions through storytelling and song, music and crafts. North American colonial folk cultures, traditional and suspicious of change, preserved an essentially medieval world view. The rhythms of life were regulated by the hours of sunlight and the seasons of the year. People rose with the sun and went to bed soon after it went down. The demands of the season determined their working routines. They farmed with simple tools and were subject to the whims of nature, for drought, flood, or pestilence might quickly sweep away their efforts. Experience told them that the natural world imposed limitations within which men and women had to learn to live. Even patterns of reproduction conformed to nature's cycle: in nearly every European colonial community of North America the number of births peaked in late winter, then fell to a low point during the summer; for African Americans, by contrast, births peaked in early summer. Historians have not yet

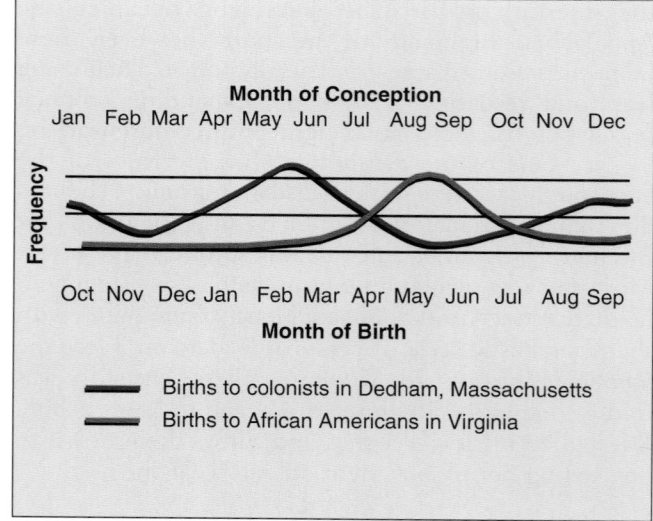

Monthly Frequency of Successful Conceptions
Human reproduction in colonial America corresponded to cycles. But European colonists and African American slaves had different patterns, with white births peaking in March, black births peaking in May and June. Historians do not yet know the cause of this variation, but it is probably tied to old English and African traditions.

Source: James A. Henretta and Gregory H. Nobles, *Evolution and Revolution: American Society, 1600–1820* (Lexington, Mass.: Heath, 1987), 37; Mechal Sobel, *The World They Made Together: Black and White Values in Eighteenth-Century Virginia* (Princeton: Princeton University Press, 1987), 67.

accounted for this intriguing pattern or provided an explanation for the differences between white and black families, but apparently there was some "inner" seasonal clock tied to old European and African patterns. Human sexual activity itself seemed to fluctuate with the rural working demands created by the seasons.

These were also communal cultures. In Quebec villagers worked side by side to repair the roads, in New Mexico they collectively maintained the irrigation canals, in New England they gathered in town meetings to decide the dates when common fields were to be plowed, sowed, and harvested. When in 1620 the Pilgrims and the other Mayflower passengers signed their compact, promising "due submission" to "the general good," they explicitly set down principles with which most North American colonists could agree. Even the artifacts of everyday life reveal this collective emphasis. Houses offered little privacy, with families often sleeping together in the same chamber, sitting together on benches rather than in chairs, and taking their supper from a common bowl or trencher. For most North American colonists of the mid-eighteenth century, the community was more important than the individual.

Throughout North America, most colonists continued the traditional European occupation of working the land. Plantation agriculture was designed to be a commercial system, in which crops were commodities for sale. Commercial farming also developed in some particularly fertile areas, notably southeastern Pennsylvania, which became known as the breadbasket of North America, as well as the country surrounding colonial cities such as New York, Boston, and Quebec. The majority of the farmers of eighteenth-century North America, however, grew crops and raised livestock for their own needs or for local barter, and communities were largely self-sufficient. Most farmers attempted to produce small surpluses as well, which they sold to pay their taxes and buy some manufactured goods. But rather than specializing in the production of one or two crops for sale, they attempted to remain as independent of the market as possible, diversifying their activities. The primary goal was ownership of land and the assurance that children and descendants would be able to settle within the community on lands nearby.

Rural households frequently practiced crafts or trades as a sideline. Farm men were also blacksmiths, coopers, weavers, or carpenters. Some farm women were independent traders in dairy products or eggs. Others became midwives and medicinal experts serving the community. In one Maine community, for example, the midwife Martha Ballard delivered 797 babies over twenty-seven years, and both male and female patients came to her for salves, pills, syrups, ointments, or advice.

In colonial cities, artisans and craftsmen worked at their trades full time. Artisans also followed tradition by organizing themselves according to the European craft system. In the colonial cities of the Atlantic coast, carpenters, iron makers, blacksmiths, shipwrights, and scores of other tradesmen had their own self-governing associations. Young men who wished to pursue a trade served several years as apprentices, working in exchange for learning the skills and secrets of the craft. After completing their apprenticeships they sought employment in a shop. Their search often required them to migrate to some other area, thus becoming "journeymen." Most craftsmen remained at the journeyman level for their whole careers. But by building a good name and carefully saving, journeymen hoped to become master craftsmen, opening shops and employing journeymen and apprentices of their own. As in farming, the ultimate goal was independence, control over one's work.

With the exception of midwifery, there were few opportunities for women outside the household. By law, husbands held managerial rights over family property, but widows received support in the form of a one-third lifetime interest, known as "dower," in a deceased husband's real estate (the rest of the estate being divided among the heirs). And in certain occupations, such as printing (which had a tradition of employing women), widows succeeded their husbands in business. As a result, some colonial women played active roles in eighteenth-century journalism. Ann Smith Franklin, Benjamin Franklin's sister-in-law, took over the operation of her husband's Rhode Island shop after his death. Widow Cornelia Smith Bradford continued to publish her deceased husband's Philadelphia paper and was an important force in publishing throughout the 1750s.

The Frontier Heritage

The colonial societies of eighteenth-century North America also shared perspectives unique to their frontier heritage. European colonists came from Old World societies in which land was scarce and monopolized by property-owning elites. They settled in a continent where, for the most part, land was abundant and cheap. This was probably the most important distinction between North America and Europe. American historians once tied the existence of this "free land" directly to the development of democracy. But although extensive lands were available in all the colonies of North America, the colonial experience encouraged assumptions that were anything but democratic.

One of the most important and widely accepted of these assumptions was that forced labor was legitimate. A woman of eighteenth-century South Carolina once offered advice on how to achieve a good

A carpenter and spinner from The Book of Trades, *an eighteenth-century British survey of the crafts practiced in colonial America. In colonial cities artisans organized themselves into the traditional European craft system, with apprentices, journeymen, and masters. There were few opportunities for the employment of women outside the household, but women sometimes earned income by establishing sidelines as midwives or spinners.*

living. "Get a few slaves," she declared, and "beat them well to make them work hard." In a land where free men and women could work for themselves on their own plot of ground, there was little incentive to work for wages. As a result, labor was in short supply throughout the colonies. Coercion was one of the few ways a landowner could secure an agricultural work force. In the Spanish borderlands, captured Apache children were made lifetime servants, and the Indian slave trade flourished through the eighteenth century. In Quebec one could see African American slaves from the French Caribbean working side by side with enslaved Indians captured by other tribes in the West and sold to French traders. In Philadelphia, according to Benjamin Franklin, wages for free workers were so high that most of the unskilled labor was "performed chiefly by indentured servants." All the colonists came

from European cultures that believed in social hierarchy and subordination, and involuntary servitude was easily incorporated into their world view.

At least half the immigrants to eighteenth-century British America arrived as indentured servants. This system allowed poor immigrants to arrange passage across the Atlantic in exchange for four or five years of service in America. Usually indentured servants were single men, often skilled artisans. Sometimes families without means emigrated as "redemptioners." Under this system, they arranged with the ship's owner to pay their passage on arrival in North America. If no one in the colonies stepped forth to pay, they sold themselves into service for the payment. Thus family members were sometimes separated. In addition, during the eighteenth century the British sent over, mostly to the Chesapeake, some

50,000 convicts sentenced to seven or fourteen years at hard labor. One historian, accounting for the cost of passage and upkeep, estimates that indentured servants earned their masters, on average, about fifty pounds sterling over their terms of service, the equivalent of something like four or five thousand dollars in today's values.

All classes of bound laborers remained on board ship after arrival in America, awaiting inspection by potential buyers, who poked muscles, peered into open mouths, and pinched women. Although servants were not slaves, to the men and women lined up for inspection that may have seemed a distinction without a difference. There were other similarities between indentured servitude and slavery. The ocean crossing was frequently traumatic. One immigrant described a passage across the Atlantic to Philadelphia in which several hundred people were packed like sardines in the ship's hold. "The ship is filled with pitiful signs of distress," he wrote, "smells, fumes, horrors, vomiting, various kinds of sea sickness, fever, dysentery, headaches, heat, constipation, boils, scurvy, cancer, mouth-rot, and similar afflictions. In such misery all the people on board pray and cry pitifully together." In 1750 Pennsylvania was finally compelled to pass a law to prevent the overcrowding of ships filled with indentured passengers. Especially in the Chesapeake, the life of an indentured servant could be filled with harsh and grueling labor, just like a slave's. Running away was common, although it was usually unsuccessful and resulted in extra time to serve: in Pennsylvania a runaway was liable for five times the lost service, in Maryland ten times!

Unlike slaves, however, those servants who endured had a chance of freedom. "Freedom dues" might include a suit of clothes, tools, money, and sometimes land. The social mobility of former servants was limited, however. Of the thousands of men who came to the British colonies under indenture during the seventeenth and early eighteenth centuries, only about 20 percent achieved positions of moderate comfort. The majority died before their terms were completed, returned to England, or continued in miserable poverty. But opportunities for advancement increased somewhat with the overall prosperity of the eighteenth-century British colonies. By midcentury, the chances of moderate success for former servants were probably better than fifty-fifty. The majority of redemptioners, for example, appear to have become small farmers.

The expectation of property ownership was a second important assumption that flowed from the frontier heritage and abundance of land in colonial America. This expectation led to rising popular demands in all regions that more and more land be taken from the Indian inhabitants and opened to white settlement. Some colonists justified the resulting wars of dispossession by arguing, as Puritans did, that Indians deserved to lose their lands because they had failed to use them to their utmost capacity. Others simply maintained that Indians should be dispossessed because they were "savages." But whatever their specific justifications, the majority of colonists—whether British, Spanish, or French—accepted the violence and brutality directed against the Indians as an essential aspect of colonial life. Thus did the Puritan minister Cotton Mather praise Hannah Dustin, a New England woman who escaped her captors during King William's War by killing and scalping nine sleeping Indians, including two women and six children. With this as the model for the behavior of captive women, one can understand why Eunice Williams was hesitant to return to Deerfield after she had married an Indian.

DIVERGING SOCIAL AND POLITICAL PATTERNS

Despite these important similarities among the colonial regions of North America, the eighteenth century also marked a period when the experience of the British colonies began to diverge sharply from that of the French and Spanish. Immigration, economic growth, and provincial political struggles all pushed British colonists in a radically new direction.

Population Growth

All the colonial regions of North America experienced unprecedented growth in the eighteenth century. "Our people must at least be doubled every twenty years," wrote Benjamin Franklin in a remarkable 1751 essay on population, and he was very nearly right. In 1700 there were 290,000 colonists north of Mexico; fifty years later they had grown to approximately 1.3 million, an average annual growth rate of about 3 percent. Typical preindustrial societies grow at rates of less than 1 percent per year, approximately the pace of Europe's expansion in the eighteenth century. But the colonial societies of North America experienced what English economist Thomas Malthus, writing at the end of the eighteenth century, described as "a rapidity of increase probably without parallel in history."

High fertility played an important role in this extraordinary growth. It was common for women in the British colonies to bear seven or more children, and colonial women in the French villages along the St. Lawrence or the towns of New Mexico were equally fertile. In addition, mortality rates were relatively low: in most colonial areas there were fewer than 30 deaths for every 1,000 persons, a rate 15 or 20 percent lower than in Europe. Moreover, levels of infant mortality were low. Blessed with fertile lands and the effective-

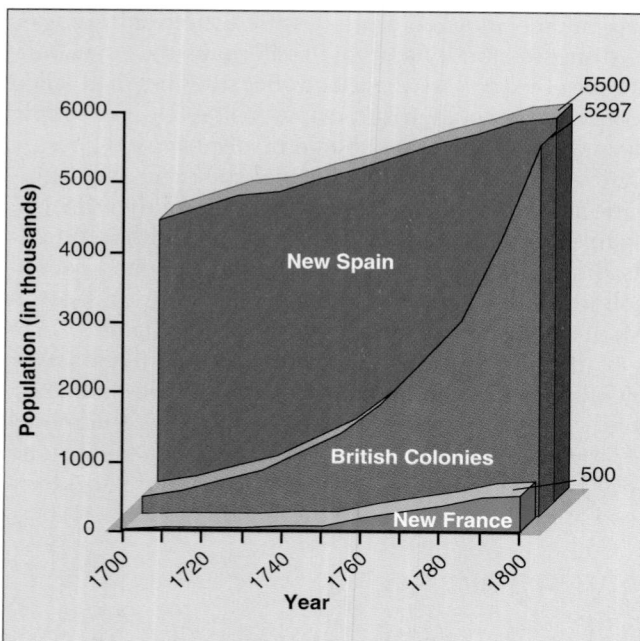

Estimated Total Population of New Spain, New France, and the British North American Colonies, 1700–1780 *Although the populations of all three North American colonial empires grew in the eighteenth century, the explosive growth of the British colonies was unmatched.*

Source: *Historical Statistics of the United States* (Washington, D.C.: Government Printing Office, 1976), 1168.

ness of Indian agricultural techniques, North America had no famines. For the colonists, North America was a remarkably healthy environment.

Yet although all North American colonial societies had high fertility rates, the British colonies grew far more rapidly than those of other nations. The reason for this contrast was the very different colonial policies on immigration. In New France and New Spain restrictive policies curbed the number of European immigrants. By contrast, English authorities allowed a massive immigration of their own subjects to North America in the seventeenth century. A total of 150,000 English men and women had relocated to the colonies by 1700, providing a substantial population base for further growth. In addition, the British were the only colonial power to encourage the immigration of foreign nationals to their colonies. (See "Immigration and Community: The Changing Face of Ethnicity in America, to 1800" on page 222.)

Social Class

Although traditional working roles were transferred to North America, attempts to transplant the European class system by creating monopolies on land were far less successful. In New France the landowning seigneurs claimed privileges similar to those

enjoyed by their aristocratic counterparts at home; the Spanish system of encomienda and the great manors created by the Dutch, and after them the English along the Hudson River, also represented attempts to bring the essence of European feudalism to North America. But in most areas, because settlers had relatively free access to land, these monopolies proved difficult or impossible to maintain. There was, of course, a system of economic rank and an unequal distribution of wealth, prestige, and power. North American society was not aristocratic, but neither was it without social hierarchy.

In New Spain the official criterion for status was racial purity. *Españoles* (Spaniards) or *gente de razón* (literally, "people of reason") occupied the top rung of the social ladder, with mestizos, mulattoes, and others on descending levels; African slaves and Indians were at the bottom. In the isolated northern borderlands, however, these distinctions tended to disappear, with *castas* (persons of mixed background) enjoying considerably more opportunity. Mestizos who acquired land might suddenly be reclassified as españoles. "The only two castes we know of here are the gente de razón and Indians," observed a missionary in California, "and all the former are considered Spaniards." Similarly, census takers in eighteenth-century Texas listed everyone but Indians as españoles, producing curious listings such as "Spaniard from Canada" or "Spaniard from France." Even so, Spanish and French colonial societies were cut in the style of the Old World, with its hereditary ranks and titles. The landlords of New France and the Spanish borderlands may have lacked the means to accumulate real wealth, but they lived lives of elegance compared to the hard toil of the people who owed them labor service or rent.

The upper class of British colonial society— the wealthiest 10 percent of all whites—was made up of large landowners, merchants, and prosperous professionals. In the eighteenth century, property valued at £2,000 marked a family as well-to-do, and £5,000 was real wealth. Leading merchants, with annual incomes in excess of £500, lived in opulence. Despite their lack of titles, the wealthy planters and merchants in the British colonies lived far more extravagantly than the seigneurs of New France or the dons of the Spanish borderlands. What separated the culture of class in the British colonies from that of New France or New Mexico, however, was not so much the material conditions of life as the prevailing attitude toward social rank. In the Catholic cultures, the upper class attempted to obscure its origins, claiming descent from European nobility. But in British North America people celebrated social mobility. The class system was remarkably open, and the entrance

An eighteenth-century Mexican painting of a mixed family, an example of a genre of portraits depicting various racial castas. Here, a Spanish father and Indian mother produce a mestizo child.

of newly successful planters, commercial farmers, and merchants into the upper ranks was not only possible but frequent—although by midcentury most upper-class families had inherited, not earned, their wealth.

To be sure, there was a large lower class in the British colonies. Slaves, bound servants, and poor laboring families made up at least 40 percent of the population. For them the standard of living did not rise above bare subsistence. Most lived from hand to mouth, often suffering through seasons of severe privation. A small proportion of poor whites could expect their condition to improve during their lifetimes, but slaves were a permanently servile population. Enslaved African Americans stood apart from the gains in the standard of living enjoyed by immigrants from Europe. Their lives had been degraded beyond measure from the conditions prevailing in their native lands.

The feature of the class system most frequently commented on by eighteenth-century observers was not the character or composition of the lower ranks but rather the size and strength of the middle class, a rank entirely absent in the colonies of France and Spain. As one Pennsylvanian wrote at midcentury, "The people of this province are generally of the middling sort." More than half the population of the British colonies, and nearly 70 percent of all white settlers, might be so classified. Most were families of landowning farmers of small to moderate means, but the group also included artisans, craftsmen, and small shopkeepers.

At the low end, the colonial middle class included families whose standard of living was barely above subsistence; at the high end were those whose holdings approached real wealth. Households solidly in the center of this broad ranking owned land or other property worth approximately £500 and earned the equivalent of about £100 per year. They enjoyed a standard of living higher than that of the great majority of people in England and Europe. The low mortality of British Americans was important testimony to generally better living conditions. Touring the British Isles at midcentury, Benjamin Franklin was shocked at the squalid conditions of farmers and workers, and he wrote of his renewed appreciation of America, where everyone "lives in a tidy, warm house, has plenty of good food and fuel, with whole cloths from head to foot, the manufacture perhaps of his own family." For the majority of British colonists in North America it was possible to achieve "roast beef and apple pie" comfort.

Economic Growth and Increasing Inequality

One of the most important differences among North American colonial regions in the eighteenth century was the economic stagnation in New France and New Spain compared with the impressive economic growth of the British colonies. Weighed down by royal bureaucracies and overbearing regulations, neither the French Crescent nor New Spain evidenced much prosperity. In British North America, however, per capita production grew at an annual rate of .5 percent. Granted, this was considerably less than the average annual growth rate of 1.5 percent that prevailed during the era of industrialization, from the early nineteenth through the mid-twentieth century. But as economic growth steadily increased the size of the economic pie, most middle- and upper-class British Americans began to enjoy improved living conditions, better than those of any people in Europe. Improving standards of living and relatively open access to land encouraged British colonists to see theirs as a society where hard work and savings could translate into prosperity, thus producing an upward spiral of economic growth.

At the same time, this growth itself produced increasing social inequality. In the commercial cities, for example, prosperity was accompanied by a concentration of assets in the hands of wealthy families. In

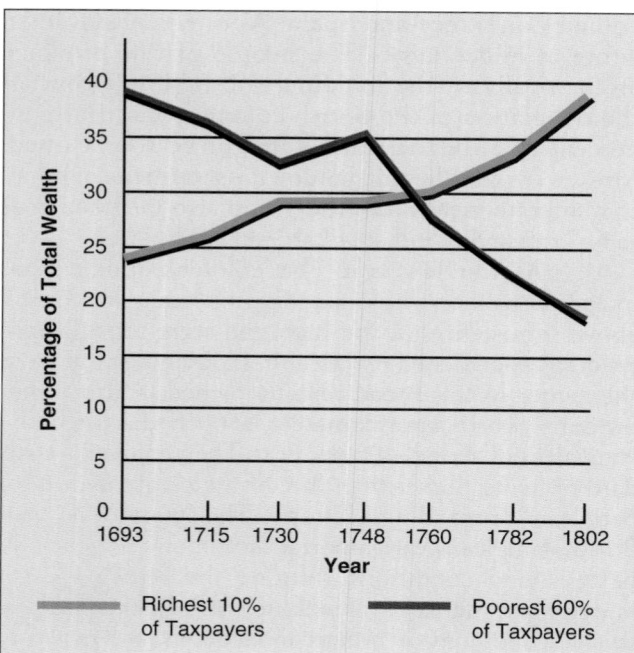

Distribution of Assessed Taxable Wealth in Eighteenth-Century Chester County *This graph charts the concentration of assets in the hands of wealthy families. From 1693 to 1802 the percentage of total wealth held by the richest 10% of taxpayers rose from 24% to 38%, while the percentage held by the poorest 60% of taxpayers fell from 39% to 18%. This pattern was typical for regions dominated by commerce.*

Source: James Lemon and Gary Nash, "The Distribution of Wealth in Eighteenth-Century America," *Journal of Social History* 2 (1968):1–24.

Boston and Philadelphia at the beginning of the century, the wealthiest 10 percent of households owned about half of the taxable property; by about midcentury this small group owned 65 percent or more. In the commercial farming region of Chester County in southeastern Pennsylvania, the holdings of the wealthiest tenth increased more modestly, from 24 to 30 percent during the first half of the century. But at the same time the share of taxable property owned by the poorest third fell from 17 to 6 percent. The general standard of living may have been rising, but the rich were getting richer and the poor poorer. The greatest concentrations of wealth occurred in the cities and in those regions dominated by commercial farming, whether slave or free, while the greatest economic equality continued to be found in areas of self-sufficient farming such as the backcountry.

Another eighteenth-century trend confounded the hope of social mobility in the countryside. As population grew, and as generations succeeded one another in older settlements, all the available land in the towns was taken up. Under the pressure of increased demand, land prices rose almost beyond the reach of families of modest means. As a family's land was divided among the heirs of the second and third generations, parcels became ever smaller and thus more intensively farmed. Eventually the soil was exhausted.

By the eighteenth century, many farm communities did not have sufficient land to provide those of the emerging generation with farms of their own. This problem was particularly acute in New England, where colonists were hemmed in by the French and Indians on the north and the great landed estates of the Hudson Valley on the west. There were notable increases in the number of landless poor in the towns of New England as well as the disturbing appearance of the "strolling poor"—homeless people who traveled from town to town looking for work or a handout. Destitute families crowded into Boston, which by midcentury was expending more than £5,000 annually on relief for the poor, who were required to wear a large red P on their clothing. In other regions, land shortages in the older settlements almost inevitably prompted people to leave in search of cheap or free land.

Young men unable to obtain land in hometowns often moved to the towns and cities of the seaboard, for New England also enjoyed a strong seafaring tradition. Fishing and shipping had first become important during the late seventeenth century, as merchants struggled to find a successful method of earning foreign exchange. The expanding slave market in the South opened new opportunities, prompting the growth of thriving coastal ports such as New Haven, Newport, Salem, and Boston. By midcentury New England had become the most urban of all North America's regions. Boston, the

WEALTH HELD BY RICHEST 10 PERCENT OF THE POPULATION: NORTHERN AND SOUTHERN BRITISH COLONIES COMPARED, 1770		
	North	South
Frontier	33	40
Rural subsistence farming	35	45
Rural commercial farming	45	65
Cities	60	65
Overall	45	55

Source: Jackson Turner Main, *The Social Structure of Revolutionary America* (Princeton: Princeton University Press, 1965), 276n.

largest city in the British colonies, was the metropolis of a region that included not only New England but also the maritime settlements of Nova Scotia and Newfoundland, where New England merchants dominated commerce and recruited seamen for their fishing and shipping fleets.

Contrasts in Colonial Politics

The administration of the Spanish and French colonies was highly centralized. French Canada was ruled by a superior council including the royal governor (in charge of military affairs), the *intendant* (responsible for civil administration), and the bishop of Quebec. New Spain was governed by the Council of the Indies, which sat in Spain, and direct executive authority over all political affairs was exercised by the viceroy in Mexico City. Although local communities enjoyed informal independence, the highly bureaucratized and centralized governments of the French Crescent and the Spanish Borderlands left little room for the development of vigorous traditions of self-government.

The situation in the British colonies was quite different. During the early eighteenth century the British government of Prime Minister Robert Walpole assumed that a decentralized administration would best accomplish the nation's economic goals. Contented colonies, Walpole argued, would present far fewer problems. "One would not strain any point where it can be of no service to our King or country," a British official advised the governor of South Carolina in 1722. "The government should be as easy and mild as possible." Each of the colonies was administered by royally appointed governors, its taxes and finances set by constituent assemblies. Those who owned property could vote for representatives to the assembly. Because many people—mostly white males—owned property, the proportion of adult white men able to vote was 50 percent or higher in all the British colonies. Proportionally, the electorate of the British colonies was the largest in the world.

That did not mean, however, that the British colonies were democratic. The basic principle of order in eighteenth-century British culture was the ideal of deference to natural hierarchies. The well-ordered family—in which children were to be strictly governed by their parents and wives by their husbands—was the common metaphor for civil order. The occupant of each rung on the social ladder was entitled to the respect of those below. Members of subordinate groups, such as women, the non-English, African American slaves, servants, and Indians—who in some colonies constituted nine of every ten adults in the population—could not vote or hold public

office. Moreover, for the most part those men who did vote chose wealthy landowners, planters, or merchants to serve as their leaders. Thus, provincial assemblies were controlled by colonial elites.

The important political developments in eighteenth-century British North America, then, had nothing to do with what we commonly call democracy. To educated British colonists, the word "democracy" implied rule by the mob, the normal order of things turned upside-down. Over the century there was, however, an important trend toward stronger institutions of representative government. By midcentury most colonial assemblies had achieved considerable power over provincial affairs and enjoyed a parity of authority with governors and other imperial officials. They collected local revenues and allocated funds for government programs, asserted the right to audit the accounts of public officers, and in some cases even acquired the power to approve the appointment of provincial officials. Royal governors sometimes balked at such claims of power, but because the assemblies controlled the purse strings, most governors were unable to resist this trend.

The potential power of the assemblies was compromised somewhat by the competition among elite families for patronage and government contracts. The royal governors who were most successful at realizing their agendas were those who became adept at playing off one provincial faction against another. All this conflict had the important effect of schooling the colonial elite in the art of politics. It was not democratic politics, but schooling in the ways of patronage, coalition-building, and behind-the-scenes intrigue had important implications for the development of American institutions.

THE CULTURAL TRANSFORMATION OF BRITISH NORTH AMERICA

Despite broad similarities, therefore, the colonial regions of North America developed along divergent lines during the eighteenth century. The British colonies were marked by increasing ethnic diversity, economic growth, social tensions, and conflictual politics that proved to be training for self-government. The middle decades of the eighteenth century also witnessed significant cultural transformation as new ideas and writings associated with the Enlightenment made their way across the Atlantic on the same ships that transported European goods. In New Spain and New France, by contrast, colonial officials worked diligently to suppress these challenging new ideas. The Catholic Church effectively banned the works of hundreds of authors. In Mexico officials of the Inquisition conducted house-to-house searches in pursuit of prohibited texts that they feared had been smuggled into the country.

The Enlightenment Challenge

Drawing from the discoveries of Galileo, Copernicus, and the seventeenth-century scientists René Descartes and Sir Isaac Newton, Enlightenment thinkers in Britain and on the Continent argued that the universe was governed by natural laws that people could understand and apply to their own advantage. John Locke, for example, articulated a philosophy of reason in proposing that the state existed to provide for the happiness and security of individuals, who were endowed with inalienable rights to life, liberty, and property. Enlightenment writers emphasized rationality, harmony, and order, themes that stood in stark contrast to folk culture's traditional emphasis on the unfathomable mysteries of God and nature and the inevitability of human failure and disorder.

Enlightenment thinking undoubtedly appealed most to those whose ordered lives had improved their lot. The colonial elite had good reason to believe in progress. They sent their sons to college, where the texts of the new thinkers were promoted. Harvard, established in 1636, remained the only institution of higher education in British America until 1693, when Anglicans established the College of William and Mary at Williamsburg, soon to become the new capital of Virginia. Puritans in Connecticut, believing that Harvard was too liberal, founded Yale College in 1701. The curricula of these colleges, modeled on those of Oxford and Cambridge in England, were designed to train ministers, but gradually each institution introduced courses and professors influenced by the Enlightenment. In the 1730s Harvard endowed a chair of mathematics and natural philosophy and to fill it appointed John Winthrop, grandson of the Puritan leader and a disciple of Newton.

A mixture of traditional and Enlightenment views characterized the colonial colleges, as it did the thought of men like Cotton Mather. A conservative defender of the old order, Mather wrote a book supporting the existence of witches. On the other hand, he was also a member of the Royal Society, an early supporter of inoculation against disease, and a defender of the Copernican sun-centered model of the universe. On hearing a scientific lecture of Mather's that could have been construed as raising conflicts with a literal reading of the Bible, one old Boston minister noted in his diary, "I think it inconvenient to assert such problems."

This clergyman's views probably characterized a majority of the reading public. About half the adult men and a quarter

Peter Pelham, *Portrait of Cotton Mather*, c. 1725, oil painting. Courtesy American Antiquarian Society, Worcester, Massachusetts.

The Reverend Cotton Mather (1663–1728), pastor of Boston's Second Congregational Church and author of 450 books on theology, history, government, and science, combined both traditional and Enlightenment views. Although he defended the existence of witches, contributing to the hysteria of the Salem witchcraft trials, he also promoted Copernican science and inoculation against disease.

of the adult women of the British colonies could read, a literacy rate that was comparable to those of England and Scandinavia. In striking contrast, in the French and Spanish colonies reading was a skill confined to a tiny minority of upper-class men. In New England, where the Puritans were committed to Bible reading and had developed a system of public education, literacy rates were 85 percent among men and approximately 50 percent among women—the highest in the entire Atlantic world. But the tastes of ordinary readers ran to traditional rather than Enlightenment fare. Not surprisingly, the best-selling book of the colonial era was the Bible. In second place was that unique American literary form, the captivity narrative. The first publication of that genre was *Sovereignty and Goodness of God* (1682), Mary Rowlandson's story of her captivity among the Indians during King Philip's War, a kind of "pilgrim's progress" through the American wilderness. "It is good for me that I have been afflicted," she wrote, for "I have learned to look beyond present and smaller troubles, and to be quieted under them." Appearing in fifteen editions during the colonial period, Rowlandson's account stimulated the publication of at least 500 other such narratives, including the Reverend John Williams's *Redeemed Captive*, cited in the opening of this chapter, most with a lot less religion and a great deal more gore.

Another popular literary form was the almanac, a combination calendar, astrological guide, and sourcebook of medical advice and farming tips reflecting the concerns of traditional folk culture. The best remembered is Benjamin Franklin's *Poor Richard's Almanac* (1732–57), although it was preceded and outlived by a great many others. But what was so innovative about Franklin's almanac, and what made it so important, was the manner in which the author used this traditional literary form to promote the new Enlightenment emphasis on useful and practical knowledge. Posing as the simple bumpkin "Poor Richard," the highly sophisticated Franklin was one of the first Americans to bring Enlightenment thought to ordinary folk.

The growth of the economy in the British colonies and the development of a colonial upper class stimulated the emergence of a more cosmopolitan "Anglican" culture, particularly in the cities of the Atlantic coast. "The culture of minds by the finer arts and sciences," Franklin wrote in 1749, "was necessarily postponed to times of more wealth and leisure." And now, he added, "these times are come." A rising demand for drama, poetry, essays, novels, and history was met by urban booksellers who imported British publications. In Boston bookshops at midcentury one could buy the works of William Shakespeare and John Milton, the essays of Joseph Addison, Richard Steele, Jonathan Swift, and Samuel Johnson, and editions of the classics. In shops elsewhere around the colonies one might also find editions of novels such as *Moll Flanders* by Daniel Defoe and *Tom Jones* by Henry Fielding—but not in New England, where such works were considered indecent.

A Decline in Religious Devotion

While these new ideas flourished, religion seemed in decline. South of New England, the Anglican Church was weak, its ministers uninspiring, and many families remained "unchurched." A historian of religion has estimated that only one adult in fifteen was a member of a congregation. Although this figure may understate the impact of religion on community life, it helps keep things in perspective.

The Puritan churches of New England also suffered declining membership and falling attendance at services, and many ministers began to warn of Puritanism's "declension," pointing to the "dangerous" trend toward the "evil of toleration." By the second decade of the eighteenth century only one in five New Englanders belonged to an established congregation. When Puritanism had been a sect, membership in the church was voluntary and leaders could demand that followers testify to their religious conversion. But when Puritanism became an established church, attendance was expected of all townspeople, and conflicts inevitably arose over the requirement of a conversion experience. An agreement of 1662, known as the Half-Way Covenant, offered a practical solution: members' children who had not experienced conversion themselves could join as "half-way" members, restricted only from participation in communion. Thus the Puritans chose to manage rather than to resolve the conflicts involved in becoming an established religion. Tensions also developed between congregational autonomy and the central control that traditionally accompanied the establishment of a state church. In 1708 the churches of Connecticut agreed to the Saybrook Platform, which enacted a system of governance by councils of ministers and elders rather than by congregations. This reform also had the effect of weakening the passion and commitment of church members.

In addition, an increasing number of Congregationalists began to question the strict Calvinist theology of predestination—the belief that God had predetermined the few men and women who would be saved in the Second Coming. In the eighteenth century many Puritans turned to the much more comforting idea that God had given people the freedom to choose salvation by developing their faith and good works, a theological principle known as Arminianism (for the sixteenth-century Dutch theologian Jacobus Arminius). This belief was in harmony with the Enlightenment view that men and women were not helpless pawns but rational beings who could actively shape their own destinies. Also implicit in these new views was an image of God as a loving rather than a punishing father. Arminianism became a force at Harvard in the early eighteenth century, and soon a new generation of Arminian ministers began to assume leadership in New England's churches. These "liberal" ideas appealed to groups experiencing economic and social improvement, especially commercial farmers, merchants, and the comfortable middle class with its rising expectations. But among ordinary people, especially those in the countryside where traditional patterns lingered, there was a good deal of opposition to these "unorthodox" new ideas.

The Great Awakening

The first stirrings of a movement challenging this rationalist approach to religion occurred during the 1730s, most notably in the movement sparked by the Reverend Jonathan Edwards in the community of Northampton, in western Massachusetts. As the leaders of the community increasingly devoted their energies to the pursuit of wealth, the enthusiasm had seemed to go out of religion. The congregation adopted rules allowing church membership without evidence of a conversion experience and adopted a seating plan for the church that placed wealthy families in the prominent pews, front and center. But the same economic forces that made the "River Gods"—as the wealthy landowners of the Connecticut Valley were known—impoverished others. Young people from the community's poorer families grew disaffected as they were forced to postpone marriage because of the scarcity and expense of the land needed to set up a farm household. Increasingly they refused to attend church meeting, instead gathering together at night for "frolics" that only seemed to increase their discontent.

The Reverend Edwards made this group of young people his special concern. Believing that they needed to "have their hearts touched," he preached to them in a style that appealed to their emotions. For the first time in a generation, the meetinghouse shook with the fire and passion of Puritan religion. "Before the sermon was done," one Northampton parishioner remembered of one notable occasion, "there was a great moaning and crying through the whole house—What shall I do to be saved?—Oh I am going to Hell!—Oh what shall I do for Christ?" Religious fervor swept through the community, and church membership began to grow. There was more to this than the power of one preacher, for similar revivals were soon breaking out in other New England communities, as well as among German pietists and Scots-Irish Presbyterians in Pennsylvania. Complaining of "spiritual coldness," people abandoned ministers whose sermons read like rational dissertations for those whose preaching was more emotional.

These local revivals became an intercolonial phenomenon thanks to the preaching of George Whitefield, an evangelical Anglican minister from England, who in 1738 made the first of several tours of the colonies. By all accounts, his preaching had a powerful effect. Even Benjamin Franklin, a religious skeptic, wrote of the "extraordinary influence of [Whitefield's] oratory" after attending an outdoor service in Philadelphia where 30,000 people crowded the streets to hear him. Whitefield began as Edwards did, chastising his listeners as "half animals and half devils," but he left them with the hope that God would be responsive to their desire for salvation. "The word was sharper than a two-edged sword," Whitefield wrote after one of his sermons. "The bitter cries and groans were enough to pierce the hardest heart. Some of the people were as pale as death; others were wringing their hands; others lying on the ground; others sinking into the arms of their friends; and most lifting their eyes to heaven and crying to God for mercy. They seemed like persons awakened by the last trumpet, and coming out of their graves to judgement." Whitefield avoided sectarian differences. "God help us to forget party names and become Christians in deed and truth," he declared.

Historians of religion consider this widespread colonial revival of religion, known as the Great Awakening, to be the American version of the second phase of the Protestant Reformation. Religious leaders condemned the laxity, decadence, and officialism of established Protestantism and reinvigorated it with calls for piety and purity. People undergoing the economic and social stresses of the age, unsure about their ability to find land, to marry, to participate in the promise of a growing economy, found relief in religious enthusiasm.

In Pennsylvania, two important leaders of the Awakening were William Tennent and his son Gilbert. An Irish-born Presbyterian, the elder Tennent was an evangelical preacher who established a school in Pennsylvania to train like-minded men for the ministry. Tennent sent many enthusiastic ministers into the field, and his lampooned "Log College" ultimately evolved into the College of New Jersey — later Princeton University—founded in 1746. In the early 1740s, disturbed by what he called the "presumptuous security" of the colonial church, Tennent toured with Whitefield and delivered the famous sermon "The Dangers of an Unconverted Ministry," in which he called upon Protestants to examine the religious

Baptism by full immersion in the Schuylkill River of Pennsylvania, an engraving by Henry Dawkins illustrating events in the history of American Baptists, was published in Philadelphia in 1770. With calls for renewed piety and purity, the Great Awakening reinvigorated American Protestantism. The Baptists preached an egalitarian message, and their congregations in the South often included both white and black Protestants.

convictions of their own ministers. Among Presbyterians, open conflict broke out between the revivalists and the old guard, and in some regions the church hierarchy divided into separate organizations.

In New England similar factions known as the New Lights and the Old Lights accused each other of heresy. The New Lights railed against Arminianism, branding it a rationalist heresy, and called for a revival of Calvinism. The Old Lights condemned emotional enthusiasm as part of the heresy of believing in a personal and direct relationship with God outside the order of the church. Itinerant preachers appeared in the countryside stirring up trouble. The followers of one traveling revivalist burned their wigs, jewelry, and fine clothes in a bonfire, then marched around the conflagration, chanting curses at their opponents, whose religious writings they also consigned to the flames. Many congregations split into feuding factions, and ministers found themselves challenged by their newly awakened parishioners. In one town members of the congregation voted to dismiss their minister, who lacked the emotional fire they wanted in a preacher. When he refused to vacate his pulpit, they pulled him down, roughed him up, and threw him out the church door. Never had there been such turmoil in New England churches.

The Great Awakening was one of the first "national" events in American history. It began somewhat later in the South, developing first in the mid-1740s among Scots-Irish Presbyterians, then achieving its full impact with the organization work of Methodists and particularly Baptists in the 1760s and early 1770s. The revival not only affected white Southerners but introduced many slaves to Christianity for the first time. Local awakenings were frequently a phenomenon shared by both whites and blacks. The Baptist churches of the South in the era of the American Revolution included members of both races and featured spontaneous preaching by slaves as well as masters. In the nineteenth century white and black Christians would go their separate ways, but the joint experience of the eighteenth-century Awakening shaped the religious cultures of both groups.

Many other "unchurched" colonists were brought back to Protestantism by the Great Awakening. But a careful examination of statistics suggests that the proportion of church members in the general population probably did not increase during the middle decades of the century. Although the number of churches more than doubled from 1740 to 1780, the colonial population grew even faster, increasing threefold. The greatest impact was on families already associated with the churches. Before the Awakening, attendance at church had been mostly an adult affair, but throughout the colonies the revival of religion had its

CHRONOLOGY

1636	Harvard College founded	1708	Saybrook Platform in Connecticut
1644	Roger Williams's *Bloudy Tenent of Persecution*	1716	Spanish begin construction of Texas missions
1662	Half-Way Covenant in New England	1730s	French decimate the Natchez and defeat the Fox Indians
1674	Bishopric of Quebec established	1732	Franklin begins publishing *Poor Richard's Almanac*
1680s	William Penn begins recruiting settlers from the European Continent	1738	George Whitefield first tours the colonies
1682	Mary Rowlandson's *Sovereignty and Goodness of God*	1740s	Great Awakening gets under way in the Northeast
1689	Toleration Act passed by Parliament	1740	Parliament passes a naturalization law for the colonies
1690s	Beginnings of Jesuit missions in Arizona	1746	College of New Jersey (Princeton) founded
1693	College of William and Mary is founded	1760s	Great Awakening achieves full impact in the South
1700s	Plains Indians begin adoption of the horse	1769	Spanish colonization of California begins
1701	Yale College founded	1775	Indian revolt at San Diego
	Iroquois sign treaty of neutrality with France	1776	San Francisco founded
1704	Deerfield raid	1781	Los Angeles founded

deepest effects on young people, who flocked to church in greater numbers than ever before. For years the number of people experiencing conversion had been steadily falling, but now full membership surged. Church membership previously had been concentrated among women, leading Cotton Mather, for one, to speculate that perhaps women were indeed more godly. But men were particularly affected by the Great Awakening, and their attendance and membership rose. "God has surprisingly seized and subdued the hardest men, and more males have been added here than the tenderer sex," wrote one Massachusetts minister.

Great Awakening Politics

The Awakening appealed most of all to groups who felt bypassed by the economic and cultural development of the British colonies during the first half of the eighteenth century. Religious factions did not divide neatly into haves and have-nots, but the New Lights tended to draw their greatest strength from small farm-

ers and less prosperous craftsmen. Many members of the upper class and the comfortable "middling sort" were shocked by the excesses of the Great Awakening, viewing them as indications of anarchy, and became even more committed to rational religion.

Some historians have suggested that the Great Awakening had important political implications. In Connecticut, for example, Old Lights politicized the religious dispute by passing a series of laws in the General Assembly designed to suppress the revival. In one town, separatists refused to pay taxes that supported the established church and were jailed. New Light judges were thrown off the bench, and others were denied their elected seats in the assembly. The arrogance of these actions was met with popular outrage, and by the 1760s the Connecticut New Lights had organized themselves politically and, in what amounted to a political rebellion, succeeded in turning the Old Lights out of office. These New Light politicians would provide the leadership for the American Revolution in Connecticut.

Such direct connections between religion and politics were relatively rare. There can be little doubt, however, that for many people the Great Awakening offered the first opportunity to actively participate in public debate and public action that affected the direction of their lives. Choices about religious styles, ministers, and doctrine were thrown open for public discourse, and ordinary people began to believe that their opinions actually counted for something. Underlying the debate over these issues were insecurities about warfare, economic growth, and the development of colonial society. The Great Awakening empowered ordinary people to question their leaders, an experience that would prove critical in the political struggles to come.

CONCLUSION

By the middle of the eighteenth century a number of distinct colonial regions had emerged in North America, all with rising populations pressing for more land to be seized from the Indians. Although colonists lived in traditional and local cultures, they were fascinated with the problems presented by frontiers and boundaries within the increasingly diverse continent. Some colonies attempted to ensure homogeneity, while others embraced diversity. Within the British colonies, New England in particular seemed bound to the past, whereas the Middle Colonies and the backcountry embraced both pluralism and expansion. These developments placed them in direct competition with the expansionist plans of the French and at odds with Indian peoples committed to the defense of their homelands.

The economic development of the British colonies introduced new social and cultural tensions that led to the Great Awakening, a massive revival of religion that was the first transcolonial event in American history. Thousands of people experienced a renewal of religious passions, but rather than resuscitating old traditions, the Awakening pointed people toward a more active role in their own political futures. These transformations added to the differences among the British colonies on the one hand, and those of the Spanish and French on the other.

REVIEW QUESTIONS

1. What were the principal colonial regions of North America? Discuss their similarities and their differences. Contrast the development of their political systems.
2. Why did the Spanish and the French close their colonies to immigration? Why did the British open theirs? How do you explain the ethnic homogeneity of New England and the ethnic pluralism of New York and Pennsylvania?
3. What were the principal trends in the history of Indian America in the eighteenth century?
4. Discuss the development of class differences in the Spanish, French, and British colonies in the eighteenth century.
5. Discuss the effects of the Great Awakening on the subsequent history of the British colonies.

RECOMMENDED READING

Edward Countryman, *Americans: A Collision of Histories* (1996). An important new synthesis that includes the many peoples and cultures of North America.

John Demos, *The Unredeemed Captive: A Family Story from Early America* (1994). A moving history of the Deerfield captives, focusing on the experience of Eunice Williams, the unredeemed captive.

W. J. Eccles, *The Canadian Frontier, 1534–1760* (1983). An introduction to the history of French America by a leading scholar on colonial Canada.

David Hackett Fischer, *Albion's Seed: Four British Folkways in America* (1990). An engaging history with fascinating details on the regions of New England, Pennsylvania, Virginia, and the Backcountry.

Jack P. Greene, *Pursuits of Happiness: The Social Development of Early Modern British Colonies and the Formation of American Culture* (1986). A distillation of a tremendous amount of historical material on community life in British North America.

James A. Henretta and Gregory H. Nobles, *Evolution and Revolution: American Society, 1600–1820* (1987). A useful synthesis of the newest social history of the British colonies. Includes an excellent bibliographic essay.

Jackson Turner Main, *The Social Structure of Revolutionary America* (1965). A detailed treatment of colonial social structure, with statistics, tables, and enlightening interpretations.

Colon McEvedy, *The Penguin Atlas of North American History to 1870* (1988). An unparalleled comparative perspective on the Spanish, French, and British regions of the continent, from precolonial times to the nineteenth century.

D. W. Meinig, *The Shaping of America: Atlantic America, 1492–1800* (1986). A geographer's overview of the

historical development of the North American continent in the era of European colonialism. Provides a survey of the British and French colonies.

David J. Weber, *The Spanish Frontier in North America* (1992). A magnificent treatment of the entire Spanish borderlands, from Florida to California. Includes important chapters on colonial government and social life.

Robert Wells, *The Population of the British Colonies in America before 1776* (1975). The standard source on colonial population growth.

ADDITIONAL BIBLIOGRAPHY

North American Regions

Patricia Albers and Beatrice Medicine, eds., *The Hidden Half: Studies of Plains Indian Women* (1983)

Barbara Allen and Thomas J. Schlereth, eds., *Sense of Place: American Regional Cultures* (1990)

Richard L. Bushman, *From Puritan to Yankee: Character and the Social Order in Connecticut, 1690–1765* (1967)

Edward D. Castillo, ed., *Native American Perspectives on the Hispanic Colonization of Alta California* (1992)

Cornelia Hughes Dayton, *Women before the Bar: Gender, Law, and Society in Connecticut, 1639–1789* (1995)

John C. Ewers, *The Horse in Blackfoot Indian Culture* (1955)

Joseph W. Glass, *The Pennsylvania Culture Region: A View from the Barn* (1986)

Charles E. Hambrick-Stowe, *The Practice of Piety: Puritan Devotional Disciplines in Seventeenth-Century New England* (1982)

Robert F. Heizer, *The Destruction of California Indians* (1974)

Donald A. Hutslar, *The Architecture of Migration: Log Construction in the Ohio Country, 1750–1850* (1986)

Christine Leigh Hyrman, *Commerce and Culture: The Maritime Communities of Colonial Massachusetts* (1984)

Rhys Isaac, *Worlds of Experience: Communities in Colonial Virginia* (1987)

Francis Jennings, *The Ambiguous Iroquois Empire* (1984)

Terry G. Jordan and Matti Kaups, *The American Backwoods Frontier: An Ethnic and Ecological Interpretation* (1988)

Lyle Kohler, *A Search for Power: "The Weaker Sex" in Seventeenth-Century New England, 1650–1750* (1982)

A. C. Land, et al., eds., *Law, Society, and Politics in Early Maryland* (1977)

James T. Lemmon, *The Best Poor Man's Country: A Geographical Study of Early Southeastern Pennsylvania* (1972)

Kenneth Lockridge, *Literacy in Colonial New England* (1974)

James H. Merrell, *The Indians' New World: Catawbas and Their Neighbors from European Contact through the Era of Removal* (1989)

Gary B. Nash, *The Urban Crucible* (1979)

Charles Edwards O'Neill, *Church and State in French Colonial Louisiana: Policy and Politics to 1732* (1966)

Jacqueline Peterson and Jennifer S. H. Brown, eds., *The New Peoples: Being and Becoming Métis in North America* (1985)

Daniel K. Richter, *The Ordeal of the Longhouse: The Peoples of the Iroquois League in the Era of European Colonization* (1992)

Darrett B. Rutman and Anita H. Rutman, *A Place in Time: Middlesex County, Virginia, 1650–1750* (1984)

Marylynn Salmon, *Women and the Law of Property in Early America* (1986)

Sally Schwartz, *A Mixed Multitude: The Struggle for Toleration in Colonial Pennsylvania* (1987)

William S. Simmons, *Spirit of the New England Tribes: Indian History and Folklore, 1620–1984* (1986)

Daniel Blake Smith, *Inside the Great House: Planter Family Life in Eighteenth-Century Chesapeake Society* (1980)

Helen Horbeck Tanner, ed., *Atlas of Great Lakes Indian History* (1987)

Laurel T. Ulrich, *Good Wives: Image and Reality in the Lives of Women in Northern New England, 1650–1750* (1982)

Daniel H. Usner Jr., *Indians, Settlers, and Slaves in a Frontier Exchange Economy: The Lower Mississippi Valley before 1783* (1992)

Diverging Social and Political Patterns

Bernard Bailyn, *The Peopling of British North America: An Introduction* (1986)

Bruce C. Daniels, ed., *Power and Status: Essays on Officeholding in Colonial America* (1986)

Robert J. Dinkin, *Voting in Provincial America: A Study of Elections in the Thirteen Colonies, 1680–1776* (1977)

A. Roger Ekirch, *Bound for America: The Transportation of British Convicts to the Colonies, 1718–1775* (1987)

David W. Galenson, *White Servitude in Colonial America* (1981)

Jack P. Green, *The Quest for Power: The Lower Houses of Assembly in the Southern Royal Colonies, 1689–1776* (1963)

Thomas L. Purvis, *Proprietors, Patronage, and Paper Money: Legislative Politics in New Jersey, 1703–1776* (1986)

Sharon V. Salinger, *"To Serve Well and Faithfully": Labor and Indentured Servants in Pennsylvania, 1682–1800* (1987)

The Cultural Transformation of British North America

Patricia U. Bonomi, *Under the Cope of Heaven: Religion, Society, and Politics in Colonial America* (1986)

Henry Steele Commager, *The Empire of Reason: How Europe Imagined and America Realized the Enlightenment* (1977)

Alan Heimert and Perry Miller, eds., *The Great Awakening* (1967)

Jackson Maine, *The Social Structure of Revolutionary America* (1965)

Barbara B. Oberg and Harry S. Stout, eds., *Benjamin*

Franklin, Jonathan Edwards, and the Representation of American Culture (1993)

Frank Shuffelton, ed., *The American Enlightenment* (1993)

Biography

Milton J. Coalter, *Gilbert Tennent, Son of Thunder* (1986)

Verner W. Crane, *Benjamin Franklin and a Rising People* (1952)

Harry Kelsey, *Juan Rodriguez Cabrillo* (1986)

Martin J. Morgado, *Junípero Serra's Legacy* (1987)

Kenneth Silverman, *The Life and Times of Cotton Mather* (1984)

John Edwin Smith, *Jonathan Edwards: Puritan, Preacher, Philosopher* (1992)

Harry S. Stout, *The Divine Dramatist: George Whitefield and the Rise of Modern Evangelicalism* (1991)

Laurel Ulrich, *A Midwife's Tale: The Life of Martha Ballard, Based on Her Diary, 1785–1812* (1990)

CHAPTER SIX

FROM EMPIRE TO INDEPENDENCE

1750–1776

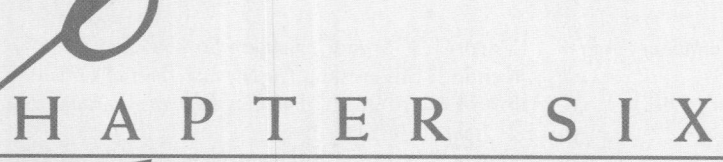

Bostonians protesting the Stamp Act in 1765 by burning the stamps in a bonfire. German colored engraving, 1784. The Granger Collection.

AMERICAN COMMUNITIES
The First Continental Congress Shapes a National Political Community

Although Britain's North American colonies had enjoyed considerable prosperity during the late seventeenth and early eighteenth centuries, beginning with the Stamp Act in 1765 the British government began to put pressures on them, largely in the form of taxes and new trade restrictions, that drew increasing resistance. In convening the first Continental Congress in September 1774, the colonies made clear their displeasure with the government's actions. Fifty-six elected delegates from twelve of the colonies met at Philadelphia to draft a common response to what they called the Intolerable Acts—the closing of the port of Boston, the suspension of Massachusetts government, and several other measures of British repression—that were the latest attempt to force the colonies to accept the power of Parliament to make laws binding them "in all cases whatsoever." This was the first intercolonial meeting since the Stamp Act Congress of 1765 (discussed later in this chapter). If the colonies now failed to act together, they would be "attacked and destroyed by piece-meal," declared Arthur Lee of Virginia. "Every part will in its turn feel the vengeance which it would not unite to repel." Abigail Adams, the politically astute wife of John Adams of Massachusetts, agreed. "You have before you," she wrote to her husband, "the greatest national concerns that ever came before any people."

The opening minutes of the first session of the Continental Congress, on September 5, did not bode well. One delegate moved that they begin with prayer, but another responded that they were "so divided in religious sentiments, some Episcopalians, some Quakers, some Anabaptists, some Presbyterians and some Congregationalists, so that we could not join in the same act of worship." Were the delegates to be stymied from the very beginning by things that separated rather than united them? John Adams's cousin, fellow Massachusetts delegate Samuel Adams, jumped to his feet. He was no bigot, he said, "and could hear a prayer from any gentleman of piety and virtue who was at the same time a friend to his country." The delegates finally agreed to ask a local clergyman, a supporter of the American cause, to officiate. The minister took for his text the Thirty-fifth Psalm: "Plead my cause, O Lord, with them that strive with me; fight against them that fight against me." John Adams was delighted. The minister "prayed with such fervor, such Ardor, such Earnestness and Pathos, and in Language so elegant and sublime," he wrote home, that "it has had an excellent Effect upon every Body here."

This incident highlighted the most important task confronting those attending the Continental Congress: they had to develop trust in one another, for what they were doing was considered treason by the British authorities. And they had to find a way to support the common cause without compromising their local identities. At first it was as if the delegates were "ambassadors from

133

a dozen belligerent powers of Europe," wrote John Adams. The delegates represented different colonies, whose traditions and histories were as distinct as those of separate countries. Moreover, these lawyers, merchants, and planters, who were leaders in their respective colonies, were strangers to one another. Their political opinions ranged from loyalty to the British crown and empire to a belief in the necessity of violent revolution. "Every man," Adams wrote, "is a great man, an orator, a critic, a statesman, and therefore every man, upon every question, must show his oratory, his criticism, and his political abilities." As a result, he continued, "business is drawn and spun out to an immeasurable length. I believe that if it was moved and seconded that we should come to a resolution that three and two make five, we should be entertained with logic and rhetorick, law, history, politicks and mathematics concerning the subject for two whole days."

During seven weeks of deliberations, however, the men of the Continental Congress succeeded in forging an agreement on both the principles and the policies they would have to follow in addressing the most serious crisis in the history of Britain's North American colonies. Equally important, the delegates found ways to work together and harmonize their interests. They immediately resolved that each colony would have one vote, thereby committing themselves to preserving provincial autonomy. They sent their most vexing problems to committees, whose members could sound each other out on the issues without speaking for the public record, and they added to their daily routine a round of dinners, parties, and late-night tippling. The greatest single accomplishment of the Continental Congress was the creation of a community of leadership for the united colonies. "It has taken us much time to get acquainted," John Adams wrote to Abigail, but he left Philadelphia thinking of his fellow representatives as "a collection of the greatest men upon this continent."

The First Continental Congress thus took the initial steps toward the creation of a national political community. The bonds of community can be local, regional, national, or international. In a town or village the feeling of association comes from daily face-to-face contact, but for larger groups these feelings must be created, or "imagined," as the historian Benedict Anderson puts it. The delegates took some of the first steps in this direction. In their final declaration they pledged to "firmly agree and associate, under the sacred ties of virtue, honor and love of our country." They urged their fellow Americans to "encourage frugality, economy, and industry, and promote agriculture, arts and the manufactures of this country," to "discountenance and discourage every species of extravagance and dissipation, especially all horse-racing, and all kinds of gaming, cock fighting, exhibitions of shows, plays, and other expensive diversions and entertainments." In other words, they called upon the common religious and cultural traditions of British Americans. They asked their countrymen to remember "the poorer sort" among them during the coming economic troubles. And in demanding that their fellow Americans "break off all dealings" and treat with contempt anyone violating the compact, the delegates were declaring who was "inside" and who was "outside" their community. Drawing boundaries is the essential first act in the construction of a new community.

Patrick Henry of Virginia, one of the delegates already committed to independence, was exuberant when the Continental Congress adjourned in late October. "The distinctions between Virginians, Pennsylvanians, New Yorkers, and New Englanders, are no more," he declared. "I am not a Virginian, but an American." Although Henry was a little premature in making this remark, he gave expression to an important truth. The Sugar Act, the Stamp Act, and the so-called Intolerable Acts that taxed and restricted colonists in various ways had also aroused a growing resistance among them. Great Britain had forced the colonists to recognize that they shared a community of interest distinct from that of the mother country. The delegates to the Continental Congress would become the core leaders of the national Revolutionary generation. Theirs was a first attempt to overcome local diversity and difference in pursuit of a common national goal. In the months and years to come the strength of local community would sometimes threaten to pull them apart, and the "imagined community" of America would be sorely tested as the colonies cautiously moved toward independence.

Philadelphia

KEY TOPICS

- The final struggle among Great Britain, France, and native American tribes for control of eastern North America

- American nationalism in the aftermath of the French and Indian War

- Great Britain's changing policy toward its North American colonies

- The political assumptions of American republicanism

- The colonies' efforts to achieve unity in their confrontation with Great Britain

THE SEVEN YEARS WAR IN AMERICA

The first attempt at cooperation among the leaders of the British colonies had taken place twenty years earlier, in July 1754, when representatives from New England, New York, Pennsylvania, and Maryland met to consider a joint approach to the French and Indian challenge. Even as the delegates met, fighting between French Canadians and Virginians began on the Ohio River, the first shots in a great global war for empire, known in Europe as the Seven Years War, that pitted Britain (allied with Prussia) against the combined might of France, Austria, Russia, and Spain. In North America, this war—which Americans remembered as the French and Indian War—became the final and most destructive of the armed conflicts between the British and the French before the French Revolution. Ultimately it decided the imperial future of the vast region between the Appalachian Mountains and the Mississippi River, and it laid the groundwork for the conflict between the British and the colonists that led to the American Revolution.

The Albany Conference of 1754

The 1754 meeting, which included an official delegation from the Iroquois Confederacy, took place in the New York town of Albany on the Hudson River. It was convened by officials of the British Board of Trade who wanted the colonies to consider a collective response to the continuing conflict with New France and the Indians of the interior. High on the agenda was the negotiation of a settlement with the leaders of the Iroquois Confederacy, who had grown impatient with colonial land grabbing. "Brother, you are not to expect to hear of me any more," the Iroquois chief Hendrick had declared in disgust to New York officials after a swindle that resulted in the loss of a vast tract. "And brother," he added as he departed, "we desire to hear no more of you." Because the powerful Iroquois Confederacy, and its Covenant

Chain of alliances with other Indian tribes, occupied such a strategic location between New France and the British colonies, the British could ill afford Iroquois disaffection.

The Albany Conference made it clear that the British colonists were not yet ready to unite in common cause. Behind the scenes, while the negotiations took place, real estate agents bribed some minor Iroquois chiefs for their signatures on a "deed" to an enormous tract of land in Pennsylvania, turning the meeting into a vehicle for the very abuses the British were seeking to correct. Angered by these manipulations, the official Iroquois delegation walked out of the conference, refusing all offers to join a British alliance.

The Albany Conference did adopt Benjamin Franklin's Plan of Union, which proposed that Indian affairs, western settlement, and other items of mutual interest to all the colonies be placed under the authority of a grand council composed of representatives elected by the colonial assemblies and led by a royally appointed president. Franklin, who had been appointed by the British government as deputy postmaster general for all of British North America and charged with improving intercolonial communication and commerce, had become extremely sensitive to the need for cooperation among the colonies. Indeed, referring to the Iroquois Confederacy, he declared, "It would be a very strange thing if ignorant savages should be capable of forming a scheme for such a union, and yet a like union should be impracticable for ten or a dozen English colonies." But the colonial assemblies rejected the Albany Plan of Union. As one British official explained, each colony had "a distinct government, wholly independent of the rest, pursuing its own interest and subject to no general command."

Colonial Aims and Indian Interests

The absence of intercolonial cooperation proved to be one of the greatest weaknesses of the British North American empire, for the ensuing war was fought at a

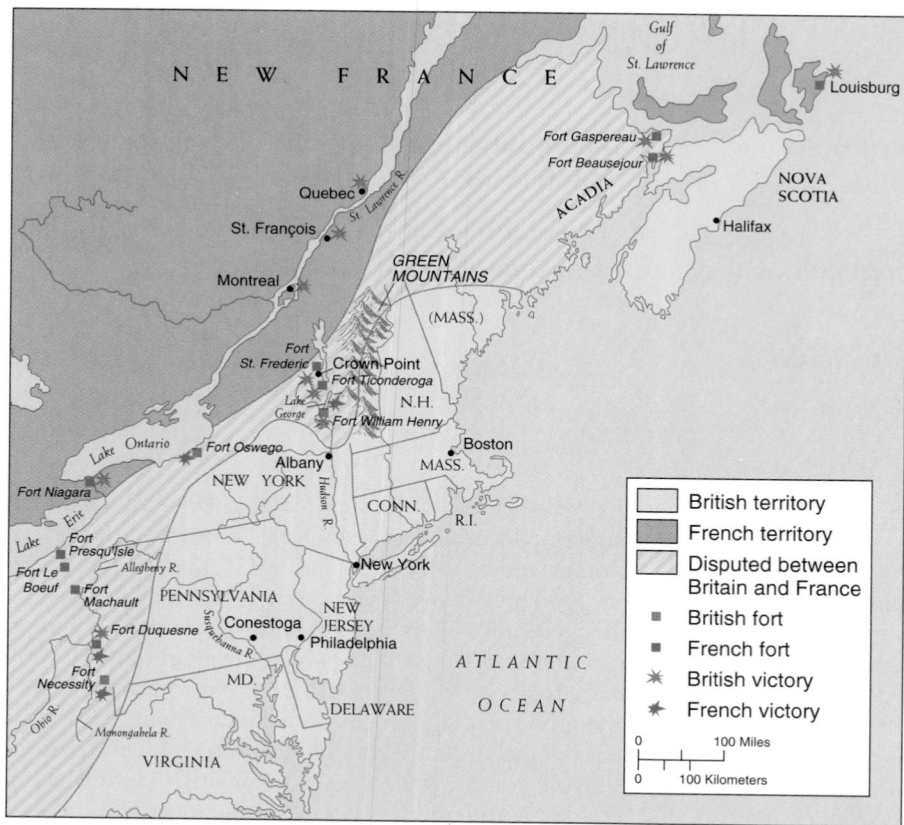

The War for Empire in North America, 1754–1763   *The Seven Years War in America (also known as the French and Indian War) was fought in three principal areas: Nova Scotia and what was then Acadia, the frontier between New France and New York, and the upper Ohio River—gateway to the Great West.*

number of widespread locations. There were three principal flash points of conflict. The first was along the northern Atlantic coast. France had ceded to Britain its colony of Acadia in 1713 (which the British renamed Nova Scotia), but continued to occupy the fortress of Louisburg, from which it guarded its fishing grounds and the St. Lawrence approach to New France. New Englanders had captured this prize in 1745 during King George's War (see Chapter 4), but the French had reclaimed it upon the settlement of that conflict in 1748. They subsequently reinforced Louisburg to such an extent that it became known as the Gibraltar of the New World.

A second zone of conflict was the border region between New France and New York, from Niagara Falls to Lake Champlain, where Canadians and New Yorkers were in furious competition for the Indian trade. Unable to compete effectively against superior English goods, the French resorted to armed might, constructing fortifications on Lake George, south of Lake Champlain, and reinforcing their base at Niagara. This was the homeland of the Iroquois Confederacy, and the loyalty of these tribes would

greatly affect the strategic balance here.

It was the Ohio country—the trans-Appalachian region along the Ohio River—that became the chief focus of British and French attention. This rich land was a prime target of British backcountry settlers and frontier land speculators. The French worried that their isolated settlements at places such as Detroit, Vincennes, and Kaskaskia would be overrun by the expanding British population and that the loss of the Ohio would threaten their entire Mississippi trading empire. To reinforce their claims, in 1749 the French sent a heavily armed force down the Ohio to warn off the British, and in 1752, supported by their northern Indian allies, they expelled a large number of British traders from the region. To prevent the British from returning to the West, in 1753 they began to construct a series of forts running south from Lake Erie to the junction of the Allegheny and Monongahela rivers, a site known as the Forks of the Ohio River.

The French "have stripped us of more than nine parts in ten of North America," one British official cried, "and left us only a skirt of coast along the Atlantic shore." In preparation for a general war, the British established the port of Halifax in Nova Scotia as a counterpart to Louisburg. In northern New York, they strengthened existing forts and constructed new ones. And finally, the British king decided to directly challenge the French claim to the upper Ohio Valley: he conferred an enormous grant of land on the Ohio Company, organized by Virginia and London capitalists, and the company made plans to build a fort at the Forks of the Ohio.

The impending conflict involved more than competing colonial powers, however, for the Indian peoples of the interior had interests of their own. In addition to its native inhabitants, the Ohio country had become a refuge for Indian peoples who had fled the Northeast—Delawares, Shawnees, Hurons, and Iroquois among them. Most of the Ohio Indians opposed the British and were anxious to preserve the Appalachians as a barrier to westward expansion. They were also disturbed by the French movement into their country, although the French outposts, unlike those of the British, did not become centers of expanding agricultural settlements.

The Iroquois Confederacy maintained an official position of neutrality between the rival colonial powers. Iroquois factions allied themselves with either the British or the French, and the confederacy as a whole sought to play off one power against the other, to its own advantage. In the South, the Creeks carved out a similar role for themselves among the British, the French in Louisiana, and the Spanish in Florida; the Cherokees and the Choctaws attempted, less successfully, to do likewise. It was in the interests of these Indian tribes, in other words, to perpetuate the existing colonial stalemate. Their position would be greatly undermined by an overwhelming victory for either side.

Frontier Warfare

At the Albany Congress the delegates received news that Colonel George Washington, a young militia officer from Virginia, had been forced to surrender his troops to a French force near the headwaters of the Monongahela River. The governor of Virginia had sent Washington to expel the French from the region granted to the Ohio Company. Having forced Washington's forces back, the French Canadians now commanded the interior country from their base at Fort Duquesne, which they had built at the Forks of the Ohio and named for the governor of French Canada.

Taking up the challenge, the British government dispatched two Irish regiments under General Edward Braddock across the Atlantic in 1755 to attack and destroy Fort Duquesne. Meanwhile, colonial militias (the equivalent of today's National Guard) commanded by colonial officers were to strike at the New York frontier and the north Atlantic coast. An army of New England militiamen succeeded in capturing two important French forts on the border of Nova Scotia, but the other two prongs of the campaign were complete failures. The offensive in New York was repulsed. And in the worst defeat of a British army during the eighteenth century, Braddock's force was destroyed by a smaller force of French and Indians on the upper Ohio, and Braddock himself was killed.

Braddock's defeat was followed by the outbreak of full-scale warfare between Britain and France in 1756. The fighting of the first two years was a near catastrophe for Great Britain. Canadians captured the British forts in northern New York. Indians pounded backcountry settlements, killed thousands of settlers, and raided deep into the coastal colonies, throwing British colonists into panic. "There is no surer way to sicken the people of the English colonies," a Canadian commander mused, "and to make them desire

the return of peace." The continuing absence of colonial cooperation greatly hampered the British attempt to mount a counterattack. And when British commanders tried to exert direct control over provincial troops, they succeeded only in angering local authorities.

In this climate of defeat, the British enacted a draconian policy of retribution against the French-speaking farmers of Acadia, who had lived peacefully under British rule for over forty years. The Acadians' refusal to swear allegiance to the crown was now used as an excuse for their expulsion. In 1755 New England troops began the forcible removal of approximately 10,000 Acadians, selling their farms at bargain prices to immigrants from New England. Suffering terrible hardship and heartbreak, the Acadians were dispersed throughout the Atlantic world, although a substantial number of them ended up settling in Louisiana, then under Spanish control, where they became known as "Cajuns." The Acadian expulsion is one of the most infamous chapters in the British imperial record in North America.

The Conquest of Canada

In the darkest days of 1757, William Pitt, an enthusiastic advocate of British expansion, assumed the prime ministership of Great Britain. "I know that I can save this country," Pitt declared, "and that no one else can." Deciding that the global war could be won in North America, he subsidized the Prussians to fight in Europe and reserved Britain's own forces and resources for naval and colonial operations. Pitt committed the British to the conquest of Canada and the elimination of all French competition in North America. Such a goal could be achieved only at tremendous cost in men and money. By promising that the war would be fought "at His Majesty's expense," Pitt was able to buy colonial cooperation. A massive infusion of British currency and credit greatly stimulated the North American economy. Pitt dispatched more than 20,000 regular British troops across the Atlantic. Combining them with colonial forces, he massed more than 50,000 armed men against Canada.

The British attracted Indian support for their plans by "redressing the grievances complained of by the Indians, with respect to the lands which have been fraudulently taken from them," in the words of a British official. In 1758 officials promised the Iroquois Confederacy and the Ohio Indians that the crown would "agree upon clear and fixed boundaries between our settlements and their hunting grounds, so that each party may know their own and be a mutual protection to each other of their respective possessions."

Thus did Pitt succeed in reversing the course of the war. Regular and provincial forces captured Louisburg in July 1758, setting the stage for the penetration of the St. Lawrence Valley. A month later a

Benjamin West (1738–1820), *The Death of General Wolfe*, 1770. Oil on canvas, 152.6 x 214.5 cm. Transfer from the Canadian War Memorials, 1921 (Gift of the 2nd Duke of Westminster, Eaton Hall, Cheshire, 1918). National Gallery of Canada, Ottawa, Ontario.

The death of General James Wolfe, at the conclusion of the battle in which the British captured Quebec in 1759, became the subject of American artist Benjamin West's most famous painting, which was exhibited to tremendous acclaim in London in 1770.

force of New Englanders captured the strategic French fort of Oswego on Lake Ontario, thereby preventing the Canadians from resupplying their western posts. Encouraged by British promises, many Indian tribes abandoned the French alliance, and the French were forced to give up Fort Duquesne. A large British force soon took control of the French fort at the Forks of the Ohio, renaming the post Fort Pitt (Pittsburgh today) in honor of the prime minister. "Blessed be God," wrote a Boston editor. "The long looked for day is arrived that has now fixed us on the banks of the Ohio." The last of the French forts on the New York frontier fell in 1759. In the South, regular and provincial British troops invaded the homeland of the Cherokees and crushed them.

British forces now converged on Quebec, the heart of French Canada. In the summer of 1759, following General James Wolfe's order to "burn and lay waste the country," British troops plundered farms and shelled the city of Quebec. Finally, in an epic battle on the Plains of Abraham before the city's walls, the British prevailed over Quebec's defenders. More than 2,000 British, French, American, and Canadian men lost their lives in the battle, including both Wolfe and the French commander, the marquis de Montcalm. Canadian resistance continued for another year, but in 1760 British forces conquered Montreal, completing the destruction of the French Empire in America. "The great day is now come," declared the editor of the *Boston News-Letter*, "the fall of the American Carthage."

In the final two years of the war the British swept French ships from the seas, conquered important French and Spanish colonies in the Caribbean, achieved dominance in India, and even captured the Spanish Philippines. In the Treaty of Paris, signed in 1763, France lost all its possessions on the North American mainland. It ceded its claims east of the Mississippi to Great Britain, with the exception of New Orleans. This city had already been transferred, along with all other French claims to lands west of the Mississippi, to Spain—to keep these territories in the possession of a Catholic monarch. For its part, Spain ceded

Florida to Britain in exchange for the return of all its Caribbean and Pacific colonies. The imperial rivalry in eastern North America that had begun in the sixteenth century now came to an end with total victory for the British empire.

Indians and Europeans Struggle over the West

When the Ohio Indians heard of the French cession of the western country to Britain, they were shocked. "The French had no right to give away [our] country," they told a British trader. "They were never conquered by any nation." A new set of British policies soon shocked them all the more. Both the French and the British had long used gift giving as a way of gaining favor with Indians. The Spanish officials who replaced the French in Louisiana made an effort to continue the old policy. But the British military governor of the western region, General Jeffery Amherst, in one of his first official actions, banned presents to Indian chiefs and tribes, demanding that they learn to live without "charity." Not only were Indians angered by Amherst's reversal of custom, but they were also frustrated by his refusal to supply them with the ammunition they required for hunting. Many were left starving.

In this climate, hundreds of Ohio Indians became disciples of the Indian visionary Neolin (meaning "The Enlightened One," in Algonquian), known to the English as the Delaware Prophet. The core of Neolin's teaching was that Indians had been corrupted by European ways and needed to purify themselves by returning to their traditions and preparing for a holy war. "Drive them out," he declared of the settlers. A confederacy of tribes organized by a group of chiefs who had gained influence by adopting Neolin's ideas laid plans for a coordinated attack against the British in the spring of 1763. The principal figure among them was the Ottawa chief Pontiac, renowned as an orator and political leader. This combination of inspirational religious and political leadership was a pattern in the long history of Indian resistance to colonial expansion in North America. The first instance of this approach on the part of Indian tribes had taken place among the Algonquians of the Chesapeake in the early seventeenth century (see Chapter 3).

In May 1763 the Indian confederacy simultaneously attacked all the British forts in the West. Warriors overran Fort Michilimackinac, at the narrows between Lakes Michigan and Huron, by scrambling

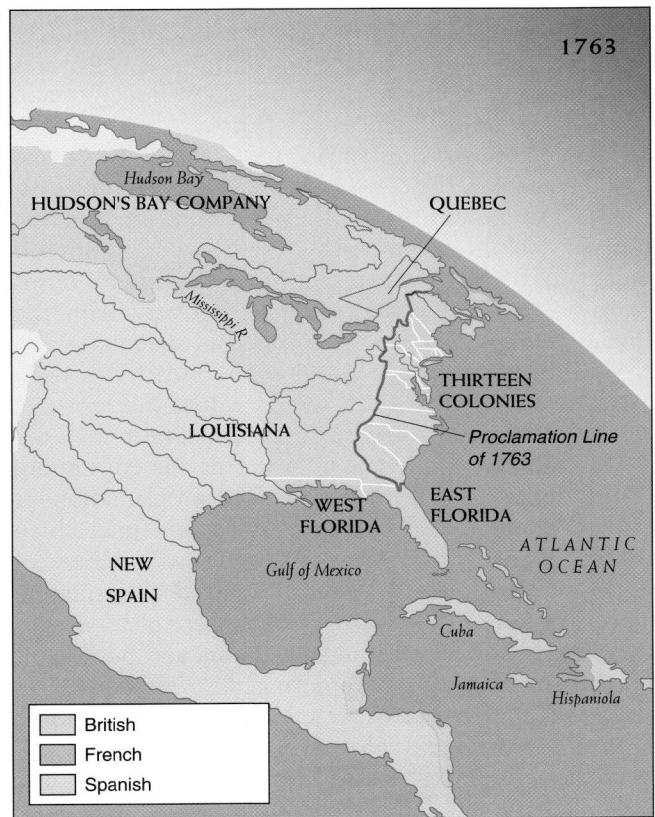

European Claims in North America, 1750 and 1763   *As a result of the British victory in the Seven Years War, the map of colonial claims in North America was fundamentally transformed.*

A treaty between the Delaware, Shawnee, and Mingo (western Iroquois) Indians and Great Britain, July 13, 1765, at the conclusion of the Indian uprising. The Indian chiefs signed with pictographs symbolizing their clans, each notarized with an official wax seal.

through the gates supposedly in pursuit of a lacrosse ball, cheered on by unsuspecting soldiers. In raids throughout the backcountry, Indians killed more than 2,000 settlers. At Fort Pitt, General Amherst proposed that his officers "send the smallpox among the disaffected tribes" by distributing infected blankets from the fort's hospital. This early instance of germ warfare resulted in an epidemic that spread from the Delawares and Shawnees to the southern Creeks, Choctaws, and Chickasaws, killing hundreds of people. Although they sacked and burned eight British posts, the Indians failed to take the key forts of Niagara, Detroit, and Pitt. Pontiac fought on for another year, but most of the Indians sued for peace, fearing the destruction of their villages. For their part, the British came to terms because they knew they could not overwhelm the Indian peoples. The war thus ended in stalemate.

Even before the uprising, the British had been at work on a policy they hoped would help resolve frontier tensions. In the royal Proclamation of 1763, the British government set the terms for continuing British policy toward the Indians. The proclamation set aside the region west of the crest of the Appalachian Mountains as "Indian Country," and any purchase of these protected Indian lands required the specific authorization of the crown. Indians were pleased with the proclamation, but land speculators and backcountry British Americans were outraged.

Colonists had expected that the removal of the French threat would allow them to move unencumbered into the West, regardless of the wishes of the Indian inhabitants. They could not understand why the British would award territory to Indian enemies who had slaughtered more than 4,000 settlers during the previous war. In an act emblematic of the anger back-

country settlers felt about these restrictions, a mob of Pennsylvanians known as the Paxton Boys butchered twenty Indian men, women, and children at the small village of Conestoga on the Susquehanna River in December 1763. When colonial authorities moved to arrest them, 600 frontiersmen marched into Philadelphia in protest. Negotiations led by Benjamin Franklin helped to prevent a bloody confrontation.

In fact, the British proved unable and ultimately unwilling to prevent the westward migration that was a dynamic part of the colonization of British North America. Within a few years of the war, New Englanders by the thousands were moving into the northern Green Mountain district, known as Vermont. In the Middle Colonies, New York settlers pushed ever closer to the homeland of the Iroquois, while others located within the protective radius of Fort Pitt in western Pennsylvania. Hunters, stock herders, and farmers crossed over the first range of the Appalachians in Virginia and North Carolina, planting pioneer communities in what are now West Virginia, western Virginia, and eastern Tennessee.

Moreover, the press of population growth and economic development turned the attention of investors and land speculators to the area west of the Appalachians. George Washington, now a prominent investor in western lands, believed that the Royal Proclamation of 1763 declaring an Appalachian boundary to western expansion was merely "a temporary expedient." In 1768 the Ohio Company sent surveyors to mark out their grant in the upper Ohio Valley. In response to demands by settlers and speculators, British authorities were soon pressing the Iroquois and Cherokees for cessions of land in Indian Country. No longer able to play off rival colonial powers, Indians were reduced to a choice between compliance and resistance. Weakened by the recent war, they chose to sign away lands. In the Treaty of Hard Labor in 1768, the Cherokees ceded a vast tract on the waters of the upper Tennessee River, where British settlers had already planted communities. In the Treaty of Fort Stanwix of the same year, the Iroquois gave up their claim to the Ohio Valley, hoping thereby to deflect English settlement away from their own homeland.

The individual colonies were even more aggressive. Locked in a dispute with Pennsylvania about jurisdiction in the Ohio country, in 1773 the Virginia governor, John Murray, earl of Dunmore, sent a force to occupy Fort Pitt. The next year, in an attempt to gain legitimacy for his dispute with Pennsylvania, Dunmore provoked a frontier war with the Shawnees. After defeating them he forced their cession of the upper Ohio River Valley to Virginia. The Iroquois and Ohio Indians angrily complained about the outcome of what came to be known as Dunmore's

War. The English king, they argued, had guaranteed that the boundary between colonial and Indian land "should forever after be looked upon as a barrier between us." But the Americans "entirely disregard, and despise the settlement agreed upon by their superiors and us." They "are come in vast numbers to the Ohio, and [give] our people to understand that they would settle wherever they pleased. If this is the case we must look upon every engagement you made with us as void and of no effect." This continuing struggle for the West would be an important issue in the coming Revolution.

THE IMPERIAL CRISIS IN BRITISH NORTH AMERICA

No colonial power of the mid-eighteenth century could match Great Britain in projecting empire over the face of the globe. During the years following its victory in the Seven Years War, Britain turned confidently to the reorganization of North America. This new colonial policy plunged British authorities into a new and ultimately destructive conflict with the colonists, who had begun to develop a sense of a separate identity.

The Emergence of American Nationalism

Despite the anger of frontier people over the Proclamation of 1763, the conclusion of the Seven Years War left most colonists proud of their place in the British empire. But during the war many had begun to note important contrasts between themselves and the mother country. The regular soldiers of the British army, for example, shocked Americans with their profane, lewd, and violent behavior. Colonists were equally shocked by the swift and terrible punishment that aristocratic officers used to keep these soldiers in line. David Perry of Massachusetts witnessed the punishment of two soldiers sentenced to 800 lashes apiece. "The flesh appeared to be entirely whipped from their shoulders," he wrote, "and they hung as mute and motionless as though they had long since been deprived of life." A military doctor stood nearby with a vial of smelling salts, periodically reviving the men and taunting them: "Damn you, you can bear it yet!" It was, Perry concluded, "a specimen of British cruelty." Those who had witnessed such scenes later found it easy to believe that the British wished to impose "slavery" on them.

Colonial forces, by contrast, were composed of volunteer companies. Officers tempered their administration of punishment, knowing they had to maintain the enthusiasm of these troops. Discipline thus fell considerably below the standards to which British officers were accustomed. "Riff-raff," one British general said of the colonials, "the lowest dregs

of the people, both officers and men." The British made no secret of their poor opinion of colonial fighting men. "The Americans are in general the dirtiest, most contemptible, cowardly dogs that you can conceive," wrote General Wolfe. For their part, many colonial officers believed that the British ignored the important role the Americans had played in the Seven Years War. Massachusetts, for example, lost between 1,500 and 2,000 fighting men. This mutual suspicion and hostility was often expressed in name calling: British soldiers called New Englanders "Yankees," while colonists heckled the red-coated British with taunts of "Lobster."

If the the Seven Years War left many colonists seeing themselves as distinct from the British, it also strengthened a sense of intercolonial, American identity. Farm boys who never before had ventured outside the communities of their birth fought in distant regions with men like themselves from other colonies. Such experiences reinforced a developing nationalist perspective. From 1735 to 1775, while trade with Britain doubled, commerce among the colonies increased by a factor of four. People and ideas moved along with goods. The first stage lines linking seaboard cities began operation in the 1750s. Spurred by Postmaster Benjamin Franklin, many colonies built or improved post roads for transporting the mails.

One of the most important means of intercolonial communication was the weekly newspaper. Early in the eighteenth century the colonial press functioned as a mouthpiece for the government; editors who criticized public officials could land in jail. In 1735, for example, the New York City editor John Peter Zenger was indicted for seditious libel after printing antigovernment articles. But as it turned out, the Zenger case provided the precedent for greater freedom of the press. "Shall the press be silenced that evil governors may have their way?" Zenger's attorney asked the jury. "The question before the court is not the cause of a poor printer," he declared, but the cause "of every free man that lives under a British government on the main of America." Zenger was acquitted. By 1760, more than twenty highly opinionated weekly newspapers circulated in the British colonies, and according to one estimate, a quarter of all male colonists were regular readers.

The midcentury American press focused increasingly on intercolonial affairs. One study of colonial newspapers indicates that intercolonial coverage increased sixfold over the four decades preceding the Revolution. Editors of local papers increasingly looked at events from what they called a "continental" perspective. This trend accelerated during the Seven Years War, when communities demanded coverage of events

THE New-England Courant.

[Nº 35]

From MONDAY March 26. to MONDAY April 2. 1722.

James Franklin began publishing the New-England Courant *in Boston in 1721. When Franklin criticized the government, he was jailed, and the paper continued under the editorship of his brother Benjamin. The Courant ceased publication in 1726, and the Franklin brothers went on to other papers— James to the* Rhode Island State Gazette, *Benjamin to the* Pennsylvania Gazette *in Philadelphia. Before the Zenger case in 1735, few editors dared to challenge the government.*

in distant colonies where their men might be fighting. During these years the British colonists of North America first began to use the term "American" to denote their common identity. More than any earlier event, the Seven Years War promoted a new spirit of nationalism and a wider notion of community. This was the social base of the political community later forged at the Continental Congress.

Politics, Republicanism, and the Press

The pages of the colonial press reveal the political assumptions held by informed colonists. For decades, royal governors had struggled with colonial assemblies over their respective powers. As commentary on the meaning of these struggles, colonial editors frequently reprinted the writings of the radical Whigs of eighteenth-century England, pamphleteers such as John Trenchard and Thomas Gordon, political theorists such as John Locke, and essayists such as Alexander Pope and Jonathan Swift. These writers warned of the growing threat to liberty posed by the unchecked exercise of power. In their more emotional writings they argued that a conspiracy existed among the powerful—kings, aristocrats, and Catholics—to quash liberty and institute tyranny. Their political principles included extension of the ballot to greater numbers of men, apportionment of legislative representation on the basis of population, and responsiveness by representatives to their constituents. The only effective counterweight to the abuse of power, they argued, was the constant vigilance of the people and their exercise of public virtue— the sacrifice of self-interest for the public good. Outside the mainstream of British political opinion, these ideas came to define the political consensus in the British colonies, a point of view historians call "republicanism."

Republicanism declared that the truly just society provided the greatest possible liberty to individuals. As the power of the state, by its very nature, was antithetical to liberty, it had to be limited. John Locke argued that the authority of a ruler should be conditional rather than absolute and that the people had the inherent right to select their own form of governance and to withdraw their support if the government did not fulfill its trust. The best guarantee of good government, then, was the broad distribution of power to the people, who would not only select their own leaders but vote them out as well. In this view, republican government depended on the virtue of the people, their willingness to make the health and stability of the political community their first priority, and was possible only for an "independent" population that controlled its own affairs. As Thomas Jefferson once wrote, "Dependence begets subservience and venality, suffocates the germ of virtue, and prepares fit tools for the designs of ambition." Individual ownership of property, especially land, he argued, was the foundation of an independent and virtuous people.

This was a political theory that fit the circumstances of American life, with its wide base of property ownership, its tradition of representative assemblies, and its history of struggle with royal authority. Contrast the assumptions of republicans with those of British monarchists, who argued that the good society was one in which a strong state, controlled by a hereditary elite, kept a vicious and unruly people in line.

The Sugar and Stamp Acts

The emerging sense of American political identity was soon tested by British measures designed to raise revenues in the colonies. To quell Indian uprisings and stifle discontent among the French and Spanish populations of Quebec and Florida, 10,000 British regular troops remained stationed in North America at the conclusion of the Seven Years War. The cost of maintaining this force added to the enormous debt Britain had run up during the fighting and created a desperate need for additional revenues. Increased excise taxes at home, however, resulted in disruptive demonstrations in the South of England, and Parliament was flooded by petitions from landlords and merchants protesting any attempt to raise revenues at their expense. In 1764 the Chancellor of the Exchequer, George Grenville, decided to obtain the needed revenue from America and pushed through Parliament a measure known as the Sugar Act.

The Sugar Act placed a prohibitive duty on sugar imported into the colonies and revitalized the customs service, introducing stricter registration procedures for ships and adding more officers. In anticipation of American resistance, the legislation also increased the jurisdiction of the vice-admiralty court at Halifax, where customs cases were heard. Vice-admiralty courts were hated because they stood outside the tradition of the English common law; they made no presumption of innocence and provided the accused with no right to a jury trial. These new regulations promised not only to squeeze the incomes of American merchants but to cut off their lucrative smuggling operations. The merchants had already been hurt by an economic depression that accompanied the decline in public spending at the end of the Seven Years War. Colonial taxes, moreover, which had been raised during the war, remained at an all-time high. In many cities merchants as well as artisans protested loudly. Boston was especially vocal: in response to the sugar tax, the town meeting proposed a boycott of certain English imports. This movement for nonimportation soon spread to other port towns.

James Otis Jr., a Massachusetts lawyer fond of grand oratory, was one of the first Americans to strike a number of themes that would become familiar over the next fifteen years. A man's "right to his life, his liberty, his property" was "written on the heart, and revealed to him by his maker," he argued in language echoing the rhetoric of the Great Awakening. It was "inherent, inalienable, and indefeasible by any laws, pacts, contracts, covenants, or stipulations which man could devise." "An act against the Constitution is void," he declared; there could be "no taxation without representation."

But it was only fair, Grenville countered, that the colonists help pay the costs of the empire, and what better way to do so than by a tax? So in early 1765 Grenville, unswayed by American protests, followed the Sugar Act with a second and considerably more sweeping revenue measure, the Stamp Act. This tax required the purchase of specially embossed paper for all newspapers, legal documents, licenses, insurance policies, ship's papers, and even dice and playing cards.

The Stamp Act Crisis

During the summer and autumn of 1765 the American reaction to the Stamp Act created a crisis of unprecedented proportions. Unlike the Sugar Act, which struck only at merchants, the stamp tax affected lawyers, printers, tavern owners, and other influential colonists. It had to be paid in hard money, and it came during a period of economic stagnation. Many colonists complained, as one did, of being "miserably burdened and oppressed with taxes."

Of more importance for the longer term, however, were the constitutional implications. Although colonial male property-owners elected their own assemblies, they could not vote in British elections. But the British argued that Americans were subject to the acts of Parliament by the fact of "virtual representation." That is, members of Parliament were thought to represent not just their districts but all citizens of the empire. As one British writer put it, the colonists were "represented in Parliament in the same manner as those inhabitants of Britain are who have not voices in elections." But in an influential pamphlet of 1765, *Considerations on the Propriety of Imposing Taxes*, Maryland lawyer Daniel Dulany rejected this theory. Because Americans were members of a separate political community, he insisted, Parliament could impose no tax on them. Instead, he argued for "actual representation," emphasizing the direct relationship that must exist between the people and their political representatives.

It was just such constitutional issues that were emphasized in the Virginia Stamp Act Resolutions, pushed through the Virginia assembly by the passionate young lawyer Patrick Henry in May 1765. Two years before, Henry had established his reputation as a radical by arguing that George III had degenerated "into a tyrant, and forfeits all rights to his subjects' obedience." Now, speaking in favor of these resolutions in the Virginia House of Burgesses, Henry warned the king to heed the fate of earlier tyrants such as Caesar and Charles I, both of whom had lost their lives. To howls of "Treason!" from his conservative colleagues, Henry cried that he spoke in "the interest of his country's dying liberty." Although the Burgesses rejected the most radical of his resolutions, they were all reprinted throughout the colonies. By the end of 1765 the assemblies of eight other colonies had approved similar measures denouncing the Stamp Act and proclaiming their support of "no taxation without representation."

In Massachusetts, the leaders of the opposition to the Stamp Act came from a group of upper- and middle-class men who had long opposed the conservative leaders of the colony. These men had worked for years to establish a political alliance with Boston craftsmen and workers who met at taverns, in volunteer fire companies, or at social clubs. One of these clubs, known as the Loyall Nine, included Samuel Adams (see the opening of this chapter), an associate and friend of James Otis who had made his career in local politics. Using his contacts with professionals, craftsmen, and laboring men as well, Adams helped put together an anti-British alliance that spanned Boston's social classes. "If our trade may be taxed," he reasoned with working men, "why not our lands? Why not the produce of our lands and everything we possess or make use of?" In August 1765, Adams and the Loyall Nine were instru-

mental in organizing a protest of Boston workingmen against the Stamp Act.

The working people of Boston had reasons of their own to be angry. While Boston's elite had prospered during the eighteenth century, the conditions for workers and the poor had worsened. Unemployment, inflation, and high taxes had greatly increased the level of poverty during the depression that followed the Seven Years War, and many were resentful. Concerted action by crowds, as when people took to the streets to demand fair prices for bread, or when posses formed to capture criminals, were commonplace in eighteenth-century communities throughout Europe and the colonies.

It was in this tradition that a large Boston crowd assembled on August 14, 1765, in the shade of a broad "liberty tree" and strung up effigies of several British officials, including Boston's stamp distributor, Andrew Oliver. The restless crowd then proceeded to vandalize Oliver's office and home. At the order of Oliver's brother-in-law, Lieutenant Governor Thomas Hutchinson, leader of the Massachusetts conservatives, the town sheriff tried to break up the crowd, but he was pelted with paving stones and bricks. Soon thereafter, Oliver resigned his commission. The unified action of Boston's social groups had its intended effect.

Twelve days later, however, a similar crowd gathered at the elegant home of Hutchinson himself. As the family fled through the back door, the crowd smashed through the front with axes. Inside they demolished furniture, chopped down the interior walls, consumed the contents of the wine cellar, and looted everything of value, leaving the house a mere shell. As these events demonstrated, it was not always possible to keep popular protests within bounds. During the fall and winter, crowds in commercial towns from Halifax in the North to Savannah in the South forced the resignation of many British tax officials.

In many colonial cities and towns, merchants, lawyers, and respectable craftsmen sought to moderate the resistance movement by seizing control of it. Groups calling themselves the Sons of Liberty encouraged moderate forms of protest. They circulated petitions, published pamphlets, and encouraged crowd actions only as a last resort; always they emphasized limited political goals. Then in October 1765 delegations from nine colonies (New Hampshire and Georgia declined the invitation to attend, and the governors of Virginia and North Carolina prevented their delegates from accepting) met at what has been called the Stamp Act Congress in New York City, where they passed a set of resolutions denying Parliament's right to tax the colonists, since taxation depended on representation. But the delegates also agreed that Parliament

John Singleton Copley (1738–1815), *Samuel Adams*, 1772. Oil on canvas, 127 cm × 102.2 cm. Deposited by the City of Boston. Courtesy, Museum of Fine Arts, Boston.

Samuel Adams, a second cousin of John Adams, was a leader of the Boston radicals and an organizer of the Sons of Liberty. The artist of this portrait, John Singleton Copley, was known for setting his subjects in the midst of everyday objects; here he portrays Adams in a middle-class suit with the charter guaranteeing the liberties of Boston's freemen.

had the authority to pass laws regulating colonial trade. These moderate efforts defused the radicals, and there were few repetitions of mob attacks, but by the end of 1765 almost all the stamp distributors had resigned or fled, making it impossible for Britain to enforce the Stamp Act.

Repeal of the Stamp Act

In the fall of 1765, British merchants, worried about the effects of the growing nonimportation movement among the colonists, began increasingly to petition Parliament to repeal the Stamp Act. About 40 percent of England's exports went to the British colonies in North America. "I rejoice that America has resisted," said William Pitt, who was no longer prime minister but spoke for the merchant interests in Parliament. "It is my opinion that this kingdom has no right to lay a tax upon the colonies." Grenville demanded that the British army be used to enforce the act. "Tell me," he demanded of Pitt, "when the Americans were emancipated." Pitt's response was memorable: "I desire to know when they were made slaves." Parliament heard the testimony of several interested parties, including Benjamin Franklin, who warned that Grenville's proposal to use troops could bring on a rebellion.

It was not, however, until Grenville was replaced by Lord Rockingham, who opposed the Stamp Act, that in March 1766 a bill for repeal passed the House of Commons. This news was greeted with celebrations throughout the American colonies, and the nonimportation associations were disbanded. Overlooked in the mood of optimism was Parliament's assertion in this Declaratory Act of its full authority to make laws binding the colonies "in all cases whatsoever." The notion of absolute parliamentary supremacy over colonial matters was basic to the British theory of empire. Even Pitt, friend of America that he was, asserted "the authority of this kingdom over the colonies to be sovereign and supreme, in every circumstance of government and legislation whatsoever." The Declaratory Act signaled that the conflict had not been resolved, merely postponed.

"SAVE YOUR MONEY AND SAVE YOUR COUNTRY"

Colonial resistance to the Stamp Act was stronger in urban than in rural communities, stronger among merchants, craftsmen, and planters than among farmers and frontiersmen. When Parliament next moved to impose its will on the colonies, as it had claimed the right to do in the Declaratory Act, it placed new duties on imported goods, and the American opposition again adopted the tactic of nonimportation. But this time resistance spread from

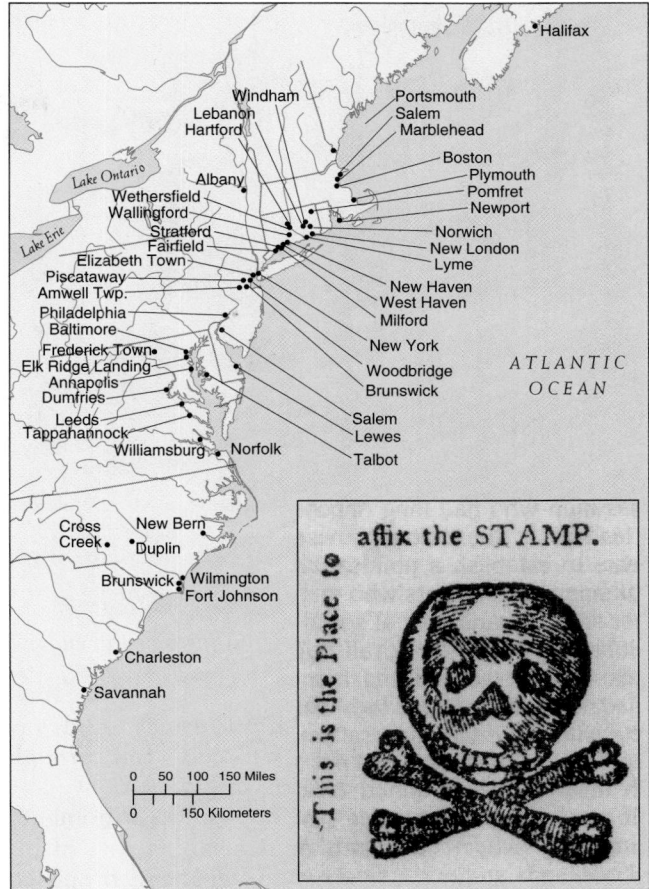

Demonstrations against the Stamp Act, 1765
From Halifax in the North to Savannah in the South, popular demonstrations against the Stamp Act forced the resignation of British tax officials. One newspaper editor cynically proposed that the stamp itself be in the form of a skull and crossbones (inset).

the cities and towns into the countryside. As the editor of the *Boston Gazette* phrased the issue, "Save your money and you save your country." It became the slogan of the movement.

The Townshend Revenue Acts

During the 1760s there was a rapid turnover of government leaders that made it difficult for Britain to form a consistent and even-handed policy toward the colonies. In 1767, after several failed governments, King George III asked William Pitt to again become prime minister. Pitt enjoyed enormous goodwill in America, and a government under his leadership stood a good chance of reclaiming colonial credibility. But, suffering from a prolonged illness, he was soon forced to retire, and his place as head of the cabinet was assumed by Charles Townshend, Chancellor of the Exchequer.

One of the first problems facing Townshend was the national debt. At home there were massive

British politicians bury the Stamp Act in this satirical engraving of 1766.

unemployment, riots over high prices, and tax protests. The large landowners forced a bill through Parliament slashing their taxes by 25 percent. The government feared continued opposition at home far more than opposition in America. So as part of his plan to close the budget gap, Townshend proposed a new measure for the colonies that placed import duties on commodities such as lead, glass, paint, paper, and tea. By means of these new Revenue Acts, enacted in 1767, Townshend hoped to redress colonial grievances against internal taxes like those imposed by the Stamp Act. The new acts provided for the collection of an external tax, that is, a duty imposed on goods at the customhouse, in colonial ports, before they entered colonial markets. In his presentation to the House of Commons, Benjamin Franklin had drawn the distinction between external taxes and internal taxes, and left the impression that colonists would be more accepting of external ones. For most colonial Americans, however, it proved to be a distinction without a difference.

The most influential response to these Revenue Acts came in a series of articles by John Dickinson, *Letters from a Farmer in Pennsylvania*, that were reprinted in nearly every colonial newspaper. In reality a wealthy Philadelphia lawyer, Dickinson posed in these articles as a humble husbandman. Parliament had the right to regulate trade through the use of duties, he conceded. It could place prohibitive tariffs, for example, on foreign products. But it had no constitutional authority to tax goods in order to raise revenues in America. As the preface to the Revenue Acts made

clear, the income they produced would be used to pay the salaries of royal officials in America. Such an arrangement, Dickinson pointed out, would render those in charge of administering colonial affairs independent of elected representatives in the colonial assemblies and thus answerable to no one within the colonies themselves.

Other Americans saw the Revenue Acts as part of a British conspiracy to suppress American liberties. Their fears were confirmed by Townshend's stringent enforcement measures. He created a new and strengthened Board of Commissioners of the Customs and established vice-admiralty courts at Boston, Philadelphia, and Charleston to prosecute violators of the duties—the first time this hated institution had appeared in the most important American port cities. And to demonstrate his power, he also suspended New York's assembly. That body had refused to vote public funds to support the British troops garrisoned in the colony. Until the citizens of New York relented, Townshend declared, they would no longer be represented.

In response to these measures, some men argued for violent resistance. But Dickinson's essays had a great effect on the public debate, not only because of their convincing argument but because of their mild and reasonable tone. "Let us behave like dutiful children," Dickinson urged, "who have received unmerited blows from a beloved parent." As yet, no sentiment for independence existed in America. The colonial response was one of resistance to what were considered unconstitutional measures by the British authorities.

Nonimportation: An Early Political Boycott

Associations of nonimportation and nonconsumption, revived in October 1767 when the Boston town meeting drew up a long list of British products to boycott, became the main weapon of the resistance movement. Over the next few months other port cities, including Providence, Newport, and New York, set up nonimportation associations of their own. Towns such as Philadelphia, however, were unable to overcome conflicts between merchants and artisans. The economy had begun to improve since the earlier boycott, and many merchants saw little advantage in curtailing imports. Craftsmen, on the other hand, supported nonimportation with enthusi-

This British cartoon, A Society of Patriotic Ladies, *ridiculed the efforts of American women to support the Patriot cause by boycotting tea. The moderator of the meeting appears coarse and masculine, while an attractive scribe is swayed by the amorous attention of a gentleman. The activities under the table suggest that these women are neglecting their true duty.*

asm, because it meant that consumers would buy their products rather than foreign ones. Supported by workers, artisans took to the streets in towns and cities throughout the colonies to force merchants to stop importing British goods. The associations published the names of uncooperative importers and retailers. These people then became the object of protesters, who sometimes resorted to violence. Coercion was very much a part of the movement.

Adopting the language of Protestant ethics, nonimportation associations pledged to curtail luxuries and stimulate local industry. These values held great appeal in small towns and rural districts, which previously had been relatively uninvolved in the anti-British struggle. And in 1768 and 1769, colonial newspapers paid a great deal of attention to women's support for the boycott. Groups of women, some styling themselves Daughters of Liberty, organized spinning and weaving bees to produce homespun for local consumption. The actual work performed at these bees was less important than the symbolic message. "The industry and frugality of American

ladies," wrote the editor of the *Boston Evening Post*, "are contributing to bring about the political salvation of a whole continent." Other women renounced silks and satins and pledged to stop serving tea to their husbands. Women sang:

> *Throw aside your topknots of pride,*
> *Wear none but your own country linen.*
> *Of economy boast, let your pride be the most,*
> *To show clothes of your own make and spinning.*

The poet Milcah Martha Moore urged American women to

> *Stand firmly resolv'd, and bid Grenville to see,*
> *That rather than freedom we part with our tea,*
> *And well as we love the dear draught when a-dry,*
> *As American patriots our taste we deny.*

Nonimportation appealed to the traditional values of rural communities—self-sufficiency and independence—and for the first time brought country people into the growing community of resistance.

Nonimportation was greatly strengthened in May 1769 when the Virginia House of Burgesses enacted the first provincial legislation banning the importation of goods enumerated in the Townshend Revenue Acts, and slaves and luxury commodities as well. Over the next few months all the colonies but New Hampshire enacted similar provisions. Because of these efforts, nonimportation was a great success. The value of colonial imports from Britain declined 41 percent the first year. In the largest port cities the decrease was even greater—54 percent in Philadelphia and over 80 percent in New York. The new Townshend duties, meanwhile, collected only about £20,000 in revenue. By 1770 English merchants were again protesting their hardship before Parliament.

The Massachusetts Circular Letter

Boston and Massachusetts were at the center of the agitation over the Townshend Revenue Acts. In February 1768 the Massachusetts House of Representatives approved a letter, drawn up by Samuel Adams, addressed to the speakers of the other provincial assemblies. Designed largely as a propaganda device and having little practical significance, the letter denounced the Townshend Acts, attacked the British plan to make royal officials independent of colonial assemblies, and urged the colonies to find a way to "harmonize with each other." Massachusetts governor Francis Bernard condemned the document for stirring up rebellion and dissolved the legislature. In Britain Lord Hillsborough, secretary of state for the colonies, ordered each royal governor in America to likewise dissolve his colony's assembly if it should endorse the letter. Before this demand reached America, the assemblies of New Hampshire, New Jersey, and Connecticut had commended Massachusetts. Virginia, moreover, had issued a circular letter encouraging a "hearty union" among the colonies and urging common action against the British measures that "have an immediate tendency to enslave us."

Hillsborough now ordered Massachusetts Governor Bernard to force the newly elected House of Representatives to rescind Adams's letter and delete all mention of it from its journal. The radicals could have asked for nothing better; resistance to the Townshend duties had been flagging, but there was great support for the prerogative and independence of the assembly. After protracted debate in June 1768, the representatives voted ninety-two to seventeen to defy Bernard, who immediately shut them down. The "Glorious Ninety-two" became heroes of the hour, and men in taverns throughout the colonies drank "ninety-two toasts" to the brave men of Massachusetts. The "rescinders," meanwhile, were condemned by public and press; in local elections the next year, seven of them lost their seats.

Throughout this crisis there were rumors and threats of mob rule in Boston. "I am no friend to riots, tumult, and unlawful assemblies," Samuel Adams declared, "but when the people are oppressed…they are not to be blamed." Because customs agents pressed on smugglers and honest traders alike, they enraged merchants, seamen, and dockworkers. In June 1768 a crowd assaulted customs officials who had seized John Hancock's sloop *Liberty* for nonpayment of duties. So frightened were the officials that they fled the city. Hancock, reportedly the wealthiest merchant in the colonies and a vocal opponent of the British measures, had become a principal target of the customs officers. In September, the Boston town meeting called on the people to arm themselves, and in the absence of an elected assembly it invited all the other towns to send delegates to a provincial convention. There were threats of armed resistance, but little support for it in the convention, which broke up in chaos. Nevertheless the British, fearing insurrection, occupied Boston with infantry and artillery regiments on October 1, 1768. With this action, they sacrificed a great deal of goodwill and respect and added greatly to the growing tensions.

The Politics of Revolt and the Boston Massacre

The British troops stationed in the colonies were the object of scorn and hostility over the next two years. There were regular conflicts between soldiers and radicals in New York City, often focusing on the Sons of Liberty. These men would erect "liberty poles" festooned with banners and flags proclaiming their cause, and the British troops would promptly destroy them. When the New York assembly finally bowed to Townshend in December 1769 and voted an appropriation to support the troops, the New York City Sons of Liberty organized a demonstration and erected a large liberty pole. The soldiers chopped it down, sawed it into pieces, and left the wood on the steps of a tavern frequented by the Sons. This act led to a riot in which British troops used their bayonets against a few thousand New Yorkers armed with cutlasses and clubs. Several men were wounded.

Confrontations also took place in Boston. In September 1769, James Otis provoked a melee by picking a fight in a tavern catering to British officers. The next month an encounter between a mob and soldiers ended with the troops' firing a volley into the air. The demonstrators were "mutinous desperadoes," wrote General Thomas Gage, guilty of "sedition." Samuel Adams played up reports and rumors of soldiers harassing women, picking fights, or simply taunting residents with versions of "Yankee Doodle." Soldiers were frequently hauled into Boston's courts, and local judges adopted a completely unfriendly attitude toward these members of the occupying army. In February 1770, an eleven-year-old boy was killed when a customs officer opened fire on a rock-throwing crowd. Although no soldiers were involved, this incident heightened the tensions between citizens and troops.

A persistent source of conflict was the competition between troops and townsmen over jobs. Soldiers were permitted to work when off duty, putting them in competition with day laborers. In early March 1770, an off-duty soldier walked into a ropewalk (a long narrow building in which ropes are made) in search of a job. The proprietor told him—using an obscenity—that he could clean the outhouse. The soldier left but returned with his friends, and a small riot ensued. Fighting continued over the next few days in the streets between the wharf and the Common, where the soldiers were encamped. On the evening of March 5, a crowd gathered at the Customs House and began taunting a guard, calling him a "damned rascally scoundrel lobster", and worse. A captain and seven soldiers went to his rescue, only to be pelted with snowballs and stones. Suddenly, without orders, the frightened soldiers began to fire. In what became known as the "Boston Massacre," three of the crowd fell dead immediately, and six more were wounded, two of these dying later. The first blood shed was that of Crispus Attucks, whose mother was Indian and father African American. The soldiers escaped to their barracks, but a mob numbering in the hundreds rampaged through the streets demanding vengeance.

Fearing for the safety of his men and the security of the state, Thomas Hutchinson, now governor of Massachusetts, ordered British troops out of Boston and arrested the soldiers who had fired the shots. The soldiers were tried later that year. Defending them were John Adams and Josiah Quincy Jr., two leaders of the radicals. Adams and Quincy established a reputation for fairness and statesmanship by convincing a jury of Bostonians that the soldiers had fired in fear of their lives. The Boston Massacre became infamous throughout the colonies, in part because of the circulation of an inflammatory print produced by the Boston engraver Paul Revere, which depicted the British as firing on a crowd of unresisting civilians. But for many colonists the incident was a disturbing reminder of the extent to which relations with the mother country had deteriorated. During the next two years, many people found themselves pulling back from the brink. "There seems," one Bostonian wrote, "to be a pause in politics."

The growth of American resistance was slowed as well by the news that Parliament had repealed most of the Townshend Revenue Acts on March 5, 1770—the same day as the Boston Massacre. The nonimportation measures almost immediately collapsed. Over the next three years, the value of British imports rose by 80 percent. The parliamentary retreat on the question of duties, like the earlier repeal of the Stamp Act, was accompanied by a face-saving measure—retention of the tax on tea "as a mark of the supremacy of Parliament," in the words of Frederick Lord North, the new prime minister.

In Paul Revere's version of the Boston Massacre, issued three weeks after the incident, the British fire an organized volley into a defenseless crowd. Revere's print—which he plagiarized from another Boston engraver—may have been inaccurate, but it was enormously effective propaganda. It hung in so many Patriot homes that the judge hearing the murder trial of these British soldiers warned the jury not to be swayed by "the prints exhibited in our houses."

FROM RESISTANCE TO REBELLION

The tax revolt in America was not an isolated incident, but the largest of numerous resistance movements to taxation—in Russa, the Netherlands, Corsica, Ireland, and Great Britain itself. There was a lull in the American controversy during the early 1770s, but the situation turned violent again in 1773, when Parliament infuriated the Americans with an ill-advised tax on tea. The Tea Act propelled the colonists on a swift track from resistance to outright rebellion. The groundwork for these developments, however, was laid during the quiet years that preceded them.

Intercolonial Cooperation

The Townshend Revenue Acts, although repealed, reflected Britain's intention of using customs revenues to pay the salaries of royal officials in the colonies. In June 1772, Governor Hutchinson inaugurated another controversy by announcing that his salary and those of other royally appointed Massachusetts officials would be paid by the crown. In effect, this made the executive and judiciary branches of the colony's government independent of elected representatives. In November, the Boston town meeting appointed a Committee of Correspondence to communicate with other towns regarding this challenge. A few weeks later the meeting issued what became known as the Boston Pamphlet—a series of declarations written by Samuel Adams and other radicals concluding that British encroachments on colonial rights were signs of a plot to enslave Americans.

In March 1773 the Virginia House of Burgesses appointed a standing committee for intercolonial correspondence "to obtain the most early and authentic intelligence" of British actions affecting America, "and to keep up and maintain a correspondence and communication with our sister colonies." The Virginia committee, including Patrick Henry, Richard Henry Lee, and young Thomas Jefferson, served as a model, and within a year all the colonies except Pennsylvania, where conservatives controlled the legislature, had created committees of their own. These committees became the principal channel for sharing information, shaping public opinion, and building intercolonial cooperation before the Continental Congress of 1774.

A British tax man is tarred and feathered and forced to drink tea, while the Boston Tea Party takes place in the background, in this image of 1774.

The information most damaging to British influence came from the radicals in Boston. Governor Hutchinson put himself at the center of controversy by declaring early in 1773 that the colonists were mistaken if they thought they enjoyed all the rights of Englishmen. Furthermore, even though they had removed themselves across the Atlantic, he argued, they were still subordinate to Parliament. "I know of no line that can be drawn," he asserted, "between the supreme authority of Parliament and the total independence of the colonies." This bold declaration outraged colonists, who during the years of agitation against taxes and duties had convinced themselves of the case against parliamentary supremacy.

In June, the Boston committee circulated a set of confidential letters from Hutchinson to the ministry in Britain, obtained in London by Benjamin Franklin from friends within the British government. Because Franklin had pledged to keep the letters to himself, he became the center of a scandal in London, and was dismissed from his position as postmaster

general. But the British cause in the colonies suffered much more than Franklin's reputation. The letters revealed Hutchinson's call for "an abridgement of what are called English liberties" in the colonies. "I wish to see some further restraint of liberty," he had written, "rather than the connection with the parent state should be broken." This statement seemed to be the "smoking gun" of the conspiracy theory, and it created a torrent of anger against the British and their officials in the colonies.

The Boston Tea Party

It was in this context that the colonists received the news that Parliament had passed a Tea Act. Colonists were major consumers of tea, but because of the tax on it that remained from the Townshend duties, the colonial market for tea had collapsed, bringing the East India Company to the brink of bankruptcy. This company was the sole agent of British power in India, and Parliament could not allow it to fail. The British therefore devised a scheme in which they offered tea to Americans at prices that would tempt even the most patriotic back to the beverage. The radicals argued that this was merely a device to make palatable the payment of unconstitutional taxes—further evidence of the British conspiracy to corrupt the colonists.

In October a mass meeting in Philadelphia denounced anyone importing the tea as "an enemy of his country." A group calling itself the Committee for Tarring and Feathering plastered posters all over the city asking if the pilots of ships carrying the tea might like "ten gallons of liquid tar decanted on your pate—with the feathers of a dozen wild geese laid over that to enliven your appearance?" The Philadelphia consignees resigned in terror. Similar protests in New York City forced resignations there as well. The town meeting in Boston passed resolutions patterned on those of Philadelphia, but the tea agents there, among them two of Governor Hutchinson's sons, resisted the call to refuse the shipments.

The first of the tea ships arrived in Boston Harbor late in November. Mass meetings in Old South Church, which included many country people drawn to the scene of the crisis, resolved to keep the tea from being unloaded. Governor Hutchinson was equally firm in refusing to allow the ship to leave the harbor. On December 16, 1773, 8,000 people crowded into and around the church to hear the captain of one tea ship report to Samuel Adams that he could not move his ship. "This meeting can do nothing more to save the country," Adams declared. This was the signal for a disciplined group of fifty or sixty men, including farmers, artisans, merchants, professionals, and even apprentices, to march to the wharf disguised as Indians. There they boarded the ships and dumped into the harbor 45 tons of tea, valued at £18,000, all the while cheered on by Boston's citizens. "Boston Harbor's a tea-pot tonight," the crowd chanted.

Boston's was the first tea party, and other incidents of property destruction followed. When the New York Sons of Liberty learned that a cargo of tea had landed secretly in New York harbor, they, too, dressed themselves as Indians and dumped the tea chests over the sides. At Annapolis a ship loaded with tea was destroyed by fire, and arson also consumed a shipment stored at a warehouse in New Jersey. But it was the action in Boston at which the British railed. The government became convinced that something had to be done about the rebellious colony of Massachusetts. Strong measures were required, King George wrote to Lord North, for "we are now to dispute whether we have, or have not, any authority in that country."

The Intolerable Acts

During the spring of 1774 an angry Parliament passed a series of acts—termed by Americans the Intolerable Acts—that were calculated to punish Massachusetts and strengthen the British hand. The Boston Port Bill prohibited the loading or unloading of ships in any part of Boston harbor until the town fully compensated the East India Company and the customs service for the destroyed tea. The Massachusetts Government Act annulled the colonial charter: delegates to the upper house would no longer be elected by the assembly but henceforth be appointed by the king. Civil officers throughout the province were placed under the authority of the royal governor, and the selection of juries was given over to governor-appointed sheriffs. Town meetings, an important institution of the resistance movement, were prohibited from convening more than once a year except with the approval of the governor, who was to control their agendas. With these acts the

VERVIEW

THE THIRTEEN REPRESSIVE BRITISH MEASURES		
Legislation	**Year**	
Sugar Act	1764	Placed prohibitive duty on imported sugar; provided for greater regulation of American shipping to suppress smuggling
Stamp Act	1765	Required the purchase of specially embossed paper for newspapers, legal documents, licenses, insurance policies, ships' papers, and playing cards; struck at printers, lawyers, tavern owners, and other influential colonists. Repealed in 1766
Declaratory Act	1766	Asserted the authority of Parliament to make laws binding the colonies "in all cases whatsoever"
Townshend Revenue Acts	1767	Placed import duties, collectible before goods entered colonial markets, on many commodities including lead, glass, paper, and tea. Repealed in 1770
Tea Act	1773	Gave the British East India Company a monopoly on all tea imports to America, hitting at American merchants
Intolerable Acts	1774	
Boston Port Bill		Closed Boston harbor
Massachusetts Government Act		Annulled the Massachusetts colonial charter
Administration of Justice Act		Protected British officials from colonial courts by sending them home for trial if arrested
Quartering Act		Legalized the housing of British troops in private homes
Quebec Act		Created a highly centralized government for Canada

The Quebec Act of 1774 *With the Quebec Act, Britain created a centralized colonial government for Canada and extended that colony's administrative control southwest to the Ohio River, invalidating the sea-to-sea boundaries of many colonial charters.*

British terminated the long history of self-rule by communities in the colony of Massachusetts.

Additional measures affected the other colonies and encouraged them to see themselves in league with suffering Massachusetts. The Quartering Act legalized the housing of troops at public expense not only in taverns and abandoned buildings but in occupied dwellings and private homes as well. And the Administration of Justice Act sought to protect British officials from colonial courts, thereby encouraging them to pursue the work of suppression vigorously; those accused of capital crimes committed while putting down riots or collecting revenue, such as the soldiers involved in the Boston Massacre, were now to be sent to England for trial.

Finally, in the Quebec Act, the British authorized a permanent government for the territory taken from France in the late war. Originally, British officials had anticipated creating a popular assembly for Quebec, bringing it in line with the other colonies, but with the continuing American difficulties those plans were shelved. Instead Parliament established an authoritarian, antirepublican administration for

Quebec, with a royal governor and an appointed council. To curry favor with the seigneurial class, the act confirmed the feudal system of land tenure along the St. Lawrence. And the Roman Catholic Church was granted religious toleration and confirmed in its traditional right to collect tithes, thus, in effect, establishing it as the state religion.

To the American colonists the Quebec Act was a frightening preview of what imperial authorities might have in store for them, and it confirmed the prediction of the Committees of Correspondence that there was a British conspiracy to destroy American liberty. The argument was made for them in Parliament by the radical Whig Charles James Fox: "To establish a perfectly despotic government, contrary to the genius and spirit of the British constitution," he warned his colleagues, "carries with it the appearance of a love of despotism, and a settled design to enslave the people of America." Moreover, the act extended Quebec's jurisdiction to the Ohio Valley, thus violating the "sea-to-sea" provisions of many of the colonies' charters. The British appeared to be giving the West back to the very people from whom it had been won.

In May, General Thomas Gage arrived in Boston to replace Hutchinson as governor. The same day, the Boston town meeting called for a revival of nonimportation measures against Britain. In Virginia, the Burgesses declared that Boston was enduring a "hostile invasion" and made provision for a "day of fasting, humiliation, and prayer, devoutly to implore the divine interposition for averting the heavy calamity, which threatens destruction to our civil rights and the evils of civil war." For this expression of sympathy, Governor Dunmore suspended the legislature, but the members adjourned to nearby Raleigh Tavern, where they voted for a Congress of all the colonies. Despite the governor's displeasure, throughout the colony on the first of June, funeral bells tolled, flags flew at half mast, and people flocked to the churches.

The First Continental Congress

It was amid this crisis that town meetings and colonial assemblies alike chose representatives for the Continental Congress described in the opening of this chapter. The delegates who arrived in Philadelphia in September 1774 included the most important leaders of the American cause. Cousins Samuel and John Adams, the radicals from Massachusetts, were joined by Patrick Henry and George Washington from Virginia and Christopher Gadsden of South Carolina. Many of the delegates were conservatives: John Dickinson and Joseph Galloway of Philadelphia, John Jay and James Duane from New York.

With the exception of Gadsden, a hothead who proposed an attack on British forces in Boston, the delegates wished to avoid war and favored a policy of economic coercion.

In one of their first debates, the delegates passed a Declaration and Resolves, in which they asserted that all the colonists sprang from a common tradition and enjoyed rights guaranteed "by the immutable laws of nature, the principles of the English constitution, and the several charters or compacts" of their provinces. Thirteen acts of Parliament, passed since 1763, were declared in violation of these rights. Until these acts were repealed, the delegates pledged, they would impose a set of sanctions against the British. These would include not only the nonimportation and nonconsumption of British goods but a prohibition on the export of colonial commodities to Britain or its other colonies.

To enforce these sanctions, the Continental Congress urged that "a committee be chosen in every county, city, and town, by those who are qualified to vote for representatives in the legislature, whose business it shall be attentively to observe the conduct of all persons." This call for democratically elected local committees in each community had important political ramifications. The following year, these groups, known as Committees of Observation and Safety, took over the functions of local government throughout the colonies. They organized militia companies, convened extralegal courts, and combined to form colony-wide congresses or conventions. By dissolving the colonial legislatures, royal governors unwittingly aided the work of these committees. The committees also scrutinized the activities of fellow citizens, suppressed the expression of Loyalist opinion from pulpit or press, and practiced other forms of coercion. Throughout most of the colonies the committees formed a bridge between the old colonial administrations and the revolutionary governments organized over the next few years. Committees began to link localities together in the cause of a wider American community. It was at this point that people began to refer to the colonies as the American "states."

Lexington and Concord

On September 1, 1774, General Gage sent troops from Boston to seize the stores of cannon and ammunition the Massachusetts militia had stored at armories in Charlestown and Cambridge. In response, the Massachusetts House of Representatives, calling itself the Provincial Congress, created a Committee of Safety empowered to call up the militia. On October 15 the committee authorized the creation of special units, to be known as "minute-

men," who stood ready to be called at a moment's notice. The armed militia of the towns and communities surrounding Boston faced the British army, quartered in the city.

It was no rabble he was up against, Gage wrote to his superiors, but "the freeholders and farmers" of New England who believed they were defending their communities. Worrying that his forces were insufficient to suppress the rebellion, he requested reinforcements. The stalemate continued through the fall and winter. To raise their spirits, the New England militia ridiculed the British army:

> And what have you got now with all your designing,
> But a town without victuals to sit down and dine in;
> And to look on the ground like a parcel of noodles,
> And sing, how the Yankees have beaten the Doodles.
> I'm sure if you're wise you'll make peace for a dinner,
> For fighting and fasting will soon make ye thinner.

But King George was convinced that the time had come for war. "The New England governments are in a state of rebellion," he wrote privately. "Blows must decide whether they are to be subject to this country or independent." In Parliament, Pitt proposed withdrawing troops from Boston, but was overruled by a large margin. Attempting to find a balance between hard-liners and advocates of conciliation, Lord North organized majority support in the House of Commons for a plan in which Parliament would "forbear" to levy taxes for purposes of revenue once the colonies had agreed to tax themselves for the common defense. But simultaneously Parliament passed legislation severely restraining colonial commerce. "A great empire and little minds go ill together," Edmund Burke quipped in March 1775 in a brilliant speech in Parliament opposing this bill. "Let it be once understood that your government may be one thing and their privileges

The First Engagements of the Revolution *The first military engagements of the American Revolution took place in the spring of 1775 in the countryside surrounding Boston.*

another, that these two things may exist without any mutual relation." Then he declared in prophetic words, "The cement is gone, the cohesion is loosened, and everything hastens to decay and dissolution."

In Virginia, at almost the same moment, Patrick Henry predicted that hostilities would soon begin in New England. "Gentlemen may cry peace, peace!—but there is no peace," he thundered in prose later memorized by millions of American schoolchildren. "Is life so dear, or peace so sweet, as to be purchased at the price of chains and slavery? Forbid it, Almighty God! I know not what course others may take, but as for me give me liberty or give me death!" Three weeks later, on April 14, General Gage received instructions to strike at once against the Massachusetts militia. "It will surely be better that the conflict should be brought on upon such ground," argued his superior, "than in a riper state of rebellion."

On the evening of April 18, 1775, Gage ordered 700 men to capture the store of American ammunition at the town of Concord. Learning of the operation, the Boston committee dispatched two men, Paul Revere and William Dawes, to alert the militia of the countryside. By the time the British forces had reached Lexington, midway to their destination, it was dawn. Some seventy armed minutemen had assembled on the green in the center of town,

but they were disorganized and confused. "Lay down your arms, you damned rebels, and disperse!" cried one of the British officers. The Americans began to withdraw in the face of overwhelming opposition, but they took their arms with them. "Damn you, why don't you lay down your arms!" someone shouted from the British lines. "Damn them! We will have them!" No order to fire was given, but shots rang out, killing eight Americans and wounding ten others.

The British marched on to Concord, where they burned a small quantity of supplies and cut down a liberty pole. Meanwhile, news of the skirmish at Lexington had spread through the countryside and the militia companies of communities from miles around converged on the town. Seeing smoke, they mistakenly concluded that the troops were firing homes. "Will you let them burn the town!" one man cried, and the Americans moved to the Concord bridge. There they attacked a British company, killing three soldiers—the first British casualties of the Revolution. The British immediately turned back for Boston, but were attacked by Americans at many points along the way. Reinforcements met them at Lexington, preventing a complete disaster, but by the time they finally marched into Boston 73 were dead and 202 wounded or missing. The British troops were vastly outnumbered by the approximately 4,000 Massachusetts militiamen, who suffered 95 casualties. The engagement forecast what would be a central problem for the British: they would be forced to fight amid an armed population defending their own communities against outsiders.

DECIDING FOR INDEPENDENCE

"We send you momentous intelligence," read the letter received by the Charleston, South Carolina, Committee of Correspondence on May 8, reporting the violence in Massachusetts. Community militia companies mobilized throughout the colonies. At Boston, thousands of militiamen from Massachusetts and the surrounding provinces besieged the city, leaving the British no escape but by sea; the siege would last for nearly a year. Meanwhile, delegates from twelve colonies reconverged on Philadelphia for

Soon after the fighting at Lexington and Concord, the artist Ralph Earl and the engraver Amos Doolittle visited the location and interviewed participants. They produced a series of four engravings of the incident, the first popular prints of the battles of the Revolutionary War. This view shows the British soldiers marching back to Boston through the hail of sniper fire from colonial militiamen.

the second session of the Continental Congress. What would be the political consequences of the armed struggle now under way?

The Second Continental Congress

The members of the Second Continental Congress, which opened on May 10, 1775, represented twelve of the British colonies on the mainland of North America. From New Hampshire to South Carolina, Committees of Observation and Safety had elected colonywide conventions, and these extralegal bodies in turn had chosen delegates. Consequently, few conservatives or Loyalists were among them. Georgia, unrepresented at the first session of the Continental Congress, remained absent at the opening of the second. This newest mainland colony depended heavily on British subsidies, and its leaders were cautious, fearing both slave and Indian uprisings. But in 1775 the political balance in Georgia shifted in favor of the radicals; observing the British attempt to curry favor with Indians elsewhere, Georgia frontier settlers came to believe that the Continental Congress would be more supportive in the matter of encroachments against the Creek Indians. Leaders from the backcountry then joined Whig merchants from Savannah to form a provincial Committee of Safety, and by the end of the summer the colony had delegates in Philadelphia.

The addition of Georgia made thirteen colonies in the revolutionary camp. But what of the other British possessions? The Continental Congress made overtures to a number of them. In one of their first acts, delegates called on "the oppressed inhabitants of Canada" to join in the struggle for "common liberty." After the Seven Years War, the British had treated Quebec as a conquered province, and French Canadians had little sympathy for the British empire. On the other hand, the Americans were traditional enemies, much feared because of their aggressive expansionism. Indeed, when the Canadians failed to respond positively and immediately, the delegates reversed themselves and voted to authorize a military expedition against Quebec to eliminate any possibility of a British invasion from that quarter. They thus killed any chance of the Canadians' joining the anti-British cause and set a course toward the development of separate nations.

Many of the other British colonies, however, harbored significant sympathy for the American struggle against parliamentary authority. For example, the population of Nova Scotia (not then a part of Canada) included many New Englanders who had relocated there after the expulsion of the Acadians. When the British attempted to recruit among them for soldiers to serve in Boston, one community responded that since "[we are] almost all of us born in New England, [we are] divided betwixt natural affection to our nearest relations and good faith and friendship to our king and country." But the British had established a naval stronghold at Halifax, and the province remained secure within the empire. The presence of the British military was decisive in several other locations as well. For example, the British army was able to keep Florida, where there was minimal local government, completely outside the revolutionary struggles. The popular assemblies of Jamaica, Grenada, and Barbados all formally declared themselves in sympathy with the Continental Congress, but the powerful British navy prevented them from sending representatives. Bermuda succeeded in sending a delegation to Philadelphia to plead for support, but so preoccupied were the Americans with more pressing matters that they found themselves unable to assist. Thus it was thirteen colonies against the empire.

Among the delegates at the Continental Congress were many familiar faces and a few new ones. One of the latter was Thomas Jefferson, a plantation owner and lawyer gifted with one of the most imaginative and analytical minds of his time who had served as a junior member of Virginia's Committee of Correspondence. All the delegates carried news of the enthusiasm for war that raged in their home provinces. "A frenzy of revenge seems to have seized all ranks of people," said Jefferson. George Washington attended all the sessions in uniform. "Oh that I was a soldier," an envious John Adams wrote to his wife, Abigail. The delegates agreed that defense was the first issue on their agenda.

On May 15 this Second Continental Congress resolved to put the colonies in a state of defense, but the delegates were divided on how best to do it. They lacked the power and the funds to immediately raise and supply an army. After debate and deliberation, John Adams made the practical proposal that the delegates simply designate as a "Continental Army" the militia forces besieging Boston. On June 14 the Congress resolved to supplement the New England militiamen with six companies of expert riflemen raised in Pennsylvania, Maryland, and Virginia. The delegates agreed that in order to emphasize their national aspirations, they had to select a man from the South to command these New England forces. All eyes turned to George Washington. Although Washington had suffered defeat at the beginning of the Seven Years War, he had subsequently compiled a distinguished record and had been promoted by the British command to brigadier, the highest rank of any native-born American. On June 15, Washington was elected commander in chief of all Continental forces by a unanimous vote. He served without salary. The Continental Congress soon appointed a staff of major generals to support him. On June 22, in a highly significant move, the Congress voted to finance the army with an issue of $2 million in bills of credit, backed by the good faith of the "Confederated Colonies." Thus began the long and complicated process of financing the Revolution.

During its first session in the spring of 1775, the Continental Congress had begun to move cautiously down the path toward independence. Few would admit, even to themselves, however, that this was their goal. John Adams, who was close to advocating independence, wrote that he was "as fond of reconciliation as any man" but found the hope of peaceful resolution unreasonable. "The cancer is too deeply rooted," he thought, "and too far spread to be cured by anything short of cutting it out entire." Still, on July 5, 1775, the delegates passed the so-called Olive Branch Petition, written by John Dickinson of Pennsylvania, in which they professed their attachment to King George and begged him to prevent further hostilities so that there might be an accommodation. The next day they approved a Declaration of the Causes and Necessities of Taking Up Arms, written by Jefferson and Dickinson. Here the delegates adopted a harder tone, resolving "to die freemen rather than to live slaves." Before the Second Continental Congress adjourned at the beginning of August, the delegates appointed commissioners to negotiate with the Indian nations in an attempt to keep them out of the conflict. They also reinstated Benjamin Franklin as postmaster general to keep the mails moving and protect communication among the colonies.

Fighting in the North and South

Both North and South saw fighting in 1775 and early 1776. In May 1775, a small force of armed New Englanders under the command of Ethan Allen of Vermont surprised the British garrison at Fort Ticonderoga on Lake Champlain, demanding—"in the name of Great Jehovah and the Continental Congress"—that

The Connecticut artist John Trumbull painted The Battle of Bunker Hill *in 1785, the first of a series that earned him the informal title of "the Painter of the Revolution." Trumbull was careful to research the details of his paintings but composed them in the grand style of historical romance. In the early nineteenth century he repainted this work, and three other Revolutionary scenes, for the rotunda of the Capitol in Washington, D.C.*

the commander surrender. The Continental Congress, in fact, knew nothing of this campaign, and when news of its arrived, members of the New York delegation were distressed at this New England violation of their territorial sovereignty. With great effort, the Americans transported the fort's cannon overland to be used in the siege of Boston.

At Boston the British hastened to reinforce Gage's forces and by the middle of June 1775 had approximately 6,500 soldiers in the city. By that time the American forces had increased to nearly 10,000. Fearing Gage would occupy the heights south of town, the Americans countered by occupying the Charlestown peninsula to the north. On June 17, British ships in the harbor began to fire on the American positions, and Gage decided on a frontal assault to dislodge them. In bloody fighting that, although it occurred at Breed's Hill, has since been known as the Battle of Bunker Hill, the British finally succeeded in routing the Americans, killing 140 men, but not before suffering over a thousand casualties of their own, including 226 dead. The fierce reaction in England to this enormous loss ended all possibility of any last-minute reconciliation. In August 1775, King George rejected the Olive Branch Petition and issued a royal proclamation declaring the colonists to be in "open and avowed rebellion." "Divers wicked and desperate persons" were the cause of the problem, said the king, and he called on his loyal subjects in America to "bring the traitors to justice."

In June 1775, the Continental Congress had also assembled its expeditionary force against Canada. One thousand Americans moved north up the Hudson River corridor, and in November General Richard Montgomery forced the capitulation of Montreal. Meanwhile, Benedict Arnold set out from Massachusetts with another American army, and after a torturous march through the forests and mountains of Maine, he joined Montgomery outside the walls of Quebec. Unlike the assault of British General Wolfe in 1759, however, the American assault failed to take the city. Montgomery and 100 Americans were killed, and another 300 were taken prisoner. Although Arnold held his position, the American siege was broken the following spring by British reinforcements who had come down the St. Lawrence. By the summer of 1776 the Americans had been forced back from Canada.

Elsewhere there were successes. Washington installed captured British artillery on the heights above Boston, placing both the city and its harbor within cannon range. General William Howe, who had replaced Gage, had little choice but to evacuate. In March, the British sailed out of Boston harbor for the last time, heading north to Halifax with at least 1,000 American Loyalists. In the South, American militia rose against the Loyalist forces of Virginia's Governor Dunmore, who had alienated the planter class by promising freedom to any slave who would fight with the British. After a decisive defeat of his forces, Dunmore retreated to British naval vessels, from which he shelled and destroyed much of the city of Norfolk, Virginia, on January 1, 1776. In North Carolina in February, the rebel militia crushed a Loyalist force at the Battle of Moore's Creek Bridge near Wilmington, ending British plans for an invasion of that province. The British decided to attack Charleston, but at Fort Moultrie in Charleston harbor an American force turned back the assault. It would be more than two years before the British would try again to invade the South.

No Turning Back

Hopes of reconciliation died with the mounting casualties. The Second Continental Congress, which was rapidly assuming the role of a new government for all the provinces, reconvened in September 1775 and received news of the king's proclamation that the colonies were in formal rebellion. Although the delegates disclaimed any intention of denying the sovereignty of the king, they now moved to organize an American navy. They declared British vessels open to capture and authorized privateering. The Congress took further steps toward de facto independence when it authorized contacts with foreign powers through its agents in Europe. In the spring of 1776, after a period of secret negotiations, France and Spain approved the shipping of supplies to the rebellious provinces. The Continental Congress then declared colonial ports open to the trade of all nations but Britain.

The emotional ties to Britain proved difficult to break. But in 1776 help arrived in the form of a pamphlet written by Thomas Paine, a radical Englishman recently arrived in Philadelphia. In *Common Sense,* Paine proposed to offer "simple fact, plain argument, and common sense" on the crisis. For years Americans had defended their actions by wrapping themselves in the mantle of British traditions. But Paine argued that the British system rested on "the base remains of two ancient tyrannies," aristocracy and monarchy, neither of which was appropriate for America. Paine placed the blame for the oppression of the colonists on the shoulders of King George, whom he labeled the "royal Brute." Appealing to the millennial spirit of American Protestant culture, Paine wrote: "We have it in our power to begin the world over again. A situation, similar to the present, hath not happened since the days of Noah until now." *Common Sense* was the single most important piece of writing during the Revolutionary era, selling more than 100,000 copies within a few months of its publication in January 1776. It reshaped popular thinking and put independence squarely on the agenda.

In April the North Carolina convention, which operated as the revolutionary replacement for the old colonial assembly, was first to empower its delegates to vote for a declaration of independence. News that the British were recruiting a force of German mercenaries to use against the Americans provided an additional push toward what now began to seem inevitable. In May the Continental Congress voted to recommend that the individual states move as quickly as possible toward the adoption of constitutions. When John Adams wrote, in the preamble to this statement, that "the exercise of every kind of authority under the said crown should be totally suppressed," he sent a strong signal that the delegates were on the verge of approving a momentous declaration.

The Manner in which the American Colonies Declared themselves INDEPENDENT of the King of ENGLAND, *a 1783 English print. Understanding that the coming struggle would require the steady support of ordinary people, in the Declaration of Independence the upper-class men of the Continental Congress asserted the right of popular revolution and the great principle of human equality.*

The Declaration of Independence

On June 7, 1776, Richard Henry Lee of Virginia offered a motion to the Continental Congress: "That these united colonies are, and of right ought to be, free and independent states, that they are absolved from all allegiance to the British crown, and that all political connection between them and the state of Great Britain is, and ought to be, totally dissolved." After some debate, a vote was postponed until July, but a committee composed of John Adams, Thomas Jefferson, Benjamin Franklin, Roger Sherman of Connecticut, and Robert Livingston of New York was asked to prepare a draft declaration of American independence. The committee assigned the writing to Jefferson.

The intervening month allowed the delegates to sample the public discussion and debate and receive instructions from their state conventions. By the end of the month, all the states but New York had authorized a vote for independence. When the question came up for debate again on July 1, a large majority in the Continental Congress supported independence. The final vote, taken on July 2, was twelve in favor of independence, none against, with New York abstaining. The delegates then turned to the declaration itself and made a number of changes in Jefferson's draft, striking out, for example, a long passage condemning slavery. In this and a number of other ways the final version was somewhat more cautious than the draft, but it was still a stirring document.

Its central section reiterated the "long train of abuses and usurpations" on the part of King George that had led the Americans to their drastic course; there was no mention of Parliament, the principal opponent since 1764. But it was the first section that expressed the highest ideals of the delegates:

> We hold these truths to be self-evident, that all men are created equal, that they are endowed by their creator with certain inalienable rights, that among these are life, liberty, and the pursuit of happiness. That to secure these rights, governments are instituted among men, deriving their just powers from the consent of the governed. That whenever any form of government becomes destructive of these ends, it is the right of the people to alter or to abolish it, and to institute a new government, laying its foundation on such principles, and organizing its powers in such form, as to them shall seem most likely to effect their safety and happiness.

There was very little debate in the Continental Congress about these "truths" and principles. The delegates were mostly men of wealth and position,

CHRONOLOGY

1713	France cedes Acadia to Britain
1745	New Englanders capture Louisburg
1749	French send an expeditionary force down the Ohio River
1753	French begin building forts from Lake Erie to the Ohio
1754	Albany Congress
1755	British General Edward Braddock defeated by a combined force of French and Indians Britain expels Acadians from Nova Scotia
1756	Seven Years War begins in Europe
1757	William Pitt becomes prime minister
1758	Louisburg captured by the British for the second time
1759	British capture Quebec
1763	Treaty of Paris Pontiac's uprising Proclamation of 1763 creates "Indian Country" Paxton Boys massacre
1764	Sugar Act
1765	Stamp Act and Stamp Act Congress
1766	Declaratory Act
1767	Townshend Revenue Acts
1768	Treaties of Hard Labor and Fort Stanwix
1770	Boston Massacre
1772	First Committee of Correspondence organized in Boston
1773	Tea Act Boston Tea Party
1774	Intolerable Acts First Continental Congress Dunmore's War
1775	Fighting begins at Lexington and Concord Second Continental Congress
1776	Americans invade Canada Thomas Paine's *Common Sense* Declaration of Independence

but realizing that the coming struggle for independence would require the steady support of ordinary people they asserted this great principle of equality and the right of revolution without examining the implications or the potential consequences. Surely no statement would reverberate more through American history. The ideal of equality would inspire the poor as well as the wealthy, women as well as men, blacks as well as whites, indeed, people of all races and creeds.

But it was the third and final section that may have contained the most meaning for the delegates: "For the support of this declaration, with a firm reliance on the protection of divine providence, we mutually pledge to each other our lives, our fortunes, and our sacred honor." In voting for independence, the delegates proclaimed their community but they also committed treason against their king. They could be condemned as traitors, hunted as criminals, and might soon stand on the scaffold to be executed for their

sentiments. Yet on July 4, 1776, these men approved the text of the Declaration without dissent.

CONCLUSION

Great Britain emerged from the Seven Years War as the dominant power in North America. Yet despite its attempts at strict regulation and determination of the course of events in its colonies, it faced consistent resistance and often complete failure. Perhaps British leaders assumed that resistance would never be unified. After all, John Adams expressed the same doubts when he likened the delegates at the Continental Congress in 1774 to "ambassadors from a dozen belligerent powers." But the British underestimated the political consensus that existed among the colonists about the importance of "republican" government. They also underestimated the ability of the colonists to inform one another, to work together, to build a sentiment of nationalism that cut across the boundaries of ethnicity, region, and economic status. Through newspapers, pamphlets, Committees of Correspondence, community organizations, and group protest, the colonists discovered the concerns they shared, and in so doing they fostered a new, "American" identity. Without that identity it would have been difficult for them to consent to the treasonous act of declaring independence—especially when the independence they sought was from an international power that dominated much of the globe.

REVIEW QUESTIONS

1. How did overwhelming British success in the Seven Years War lead to an imperial crisis in British North America?
2. Outline the changes in British policy toward the colonies from 1750 to 1776.
3. Trace the developing sense of an American national community over this same period.
4. What were the principal events leading to the beginning of armed conflict at Lexington and Concord?
5. How were the ideals of American republicanism expressed in the Declaration of Independence?

RECOMMENDED READING

Benedict Anderson, *Imagined Communities: Reflections on the Origin and Spread of Nationalism*, revised edition (1991). An argument that the essential first act of national consciousness is the effort to create a community that encompasses more than just local individuals and groups.

Bernard Bailyn, *The Ideological Origins of the American Revolution* (1967). Whereas other accounts stress economic or social causes, this classic argument emphasizes the role of ideas in the advent of the Revolution. Includes an analysis of American views of the imperial crisis.

Eric Foner, *Tom Paine and Revolutionary America* (1976). Combines a biography of Paine with a community study of the Revolution in Philadelphia and Pennsylvania.

Lawrence H. Gipson, *British Empire before the American Revolution*, 8 vols. (1936–49). Although these volumes are heavy going, they offer what is still the best and most comprehensive treatment of the Seven Years War in America.

Robert A. Gross, *The Minute Men and Their World* (1976).

This fascinating and readable history examines the coming of the Revolution from the viewpoint of a New England community.

Francis Jennings, *Empire of Fortune: Crowns, Colonies, and Tribes in the Seven Years War in America* (1988). The French and Indian War examined from the point of view of the Iroquois Confederacy. This is opinionated but exciting history.

Pauline Maier, *American Scripture: Making the Declaration of Independence* (1997). The deep background of this foundation of American democracy.

Richard L. Merritt, *Symbols of American Community, 1735–1775* (1966). A study of colonial newspapers that provides evidence for a rising sense of national community. The French and Indian War emerges as the key period for the growth of nationalist sentiment.

Richard White, *The Middle Ground: Indians, Empires, and Republics in the Great Lakes Region, 1650–1815* (1991). This well-researched history provides a fascinating account of the West from the point of view of imperialists, settlers, and Indians.

ADDITIONAL BIBLIOGRAPHY

The Seven Years War in America

Fred Anderson, *A People's Army: Massachusetts Soldiers and Society in the Seven Years' War* (1984)

Sylvia R. Frey, *The British Soldier in America: A Social History of Military Life in the Colonial Period* (1981)

Dougles E. Leach, *Roots of Conflict: British Armed Forces and Colonial Americans, 1677–1763* (1986)

Richard Middleton, *The Bells of Victory: The Pitt-Newcastle Ministry and the Conduct of the Seven Years' War, 1757–1762* (1985)

Robert C. Newbold, *The Albany Congress and Plan of Union of 1754* (1955)

Howard H. Peckham, *Pontiac and the Indian Uprising* (1947)

William Pencak, *War, Politics, and Revolution in Provincial Massachusetts* (1981)

Alan Rogers, *Empire and Liberty* (1974)

Noel T. St. John Williams, *Red Coats along the Hudson* (1997)

Imperial Crisis in British North America

Thomas C. Barrow, *Trade and Empire: The British Customs Service in Colonial America* (1967)

John Brewer, *Party Ideology and Popular Politics at the Accession of George III* (1976)

Don Cook, *The Long Fuse: How England Lost the American Colonies, 1760–1785* (1995)

Theodore Draper, *A Struggle for Power: The American Revolution* (1996)

Marc Egnal, *A Mighty Empire: The Origins of the American Revolution* (1988)

Alice Hanson Jones, *The Wealth of a Nation to Be* (1980)

John J. McCusker, *Rum and the American Revolution* (1989)

Richard L. Merritt, *Symbols of American Community, 1735–1775* (1966)

J. G. A. Pocock, *The Machiavellian Moment: Florentine Political Thought and the Atlantic Republican Tradition* (1975)

Caroline Robbins, *The Eighteenth-Century Commonwealthman* (1959)

Arthur M. Schlesinger, *The Colonial Merchants and the American Revolution* (1917)

W. A. Speck, *Stability and Strife: England, 1714–1760* (1977)

Peter David Garner Thomas, *Revolution in America: Britain and the Colonies, 1763–1776* (1992)

John W. Tyler, *Smugglers and Patriots: Boston Merchants and the Advent of the American Revolution* (1986)

Carl Ubbelohde, *The Vice-Admiralty Courts and the American Revolution* (1960)

From Resistance to Rebellion

David Ammerman, *In the Common Cause: American Response to the Coercive Acts of 1774* (1974)

T. H. Breen, *Tobacco Culture: The Mentality of the Great Tidewater Planters on the Eve of Revolution* (1985)

Richard D. Brown, *Revolutionary Politics in Massachusetts: The Boston Committee of Correspondence and the Towns, 1772–1774* (1970)

Richard L. Bushman, *King and People in Provincial Massachusetts* (1985)

H. Trevor Colbourn, *The Lamp of Experience: Whig History and the Intellectual Origins of the American Revolution* (1965)

Bernard Donoughue, *British Politics and the American Revolution: The Path to War, 1773–1775* (1964)

Jack P. Greene, *Understanding the American Revolution: Issues and Actors* (1995)

Dirk Hoerder, *Crowd Action in Revolutionary Massachusetts* (1977)

Benjamin W. Labaree, *The Boston Tea Party* (1974)

Pauline Maier, *From Resistance to Rebellion* (1972)

Edmund S. Morgan, *The Birth of the Republic, 1763–1789* (1956)

John Shy, *Toward Lexington: The Role of the British Army in the Coming of the American Revolution* (1965)

Peter David Garner Thomas, *Tea Party to Independence: The Third Phase of the American Revolution, 1773–1776* (1991)

Morton White, *The Philosophy of the American Revolution* (1978)

Gary Wills, *Inventing America* (1978)

Biography

Bernard Bailyn, *The Ordeal of Thomas Hutchinson* (1974)

Della Gray Barthelmas, *The Signers of the Declaration of Independence* (1997)

Richard R. Beeman, *Patrick Henry: A Biography* (1974)

Jeremy Black, *Pitt the Elder* (1992)

John Brooke, *King George III* (1974)

John E. Ferling, *The Loyalist Mind: Joseph Galloway and the American Revolution* (1977)

Milton E. Flower, *John Dickinson: Conservative Revolutionary* (1983)

William M. Fowler, Jr., *The Baron of Beacon Hill: A Biography of John Hancock* (1979)

William M. Fowler, Jr., *Samuel Adams: Radical Puritan* (1997)

David A. McCants, *Patrick Henry, the Orator* (1990)

Peter Shaw, *The Character of John Adams* (1976)

Peter D. G. Thomas, *Lord North* (1974)

CHAPTER SEVEN

THE CREATION
OF THE UNITED STATES

1776–1786

William Ranney, *The Battle of Cowpens.* Oil on canvas. Photo by Sam Holland. Courtesy South Carolina State House.

AMERICAN COMMUNITIES
A National Community
Evolves at Valley Forge

A drum roll ushered in a January morning in 1778, summoning the Continental Army to roll call. Along a two-mile line of log cabins, doors slowly opened and ragged men stepped out onto the frozen ground at Valley Forge. "There comes a soldier," wrote army surgeon Albigense Waldo. "His bare feet are seen through his worn-out shoes, his legs nearly naked from the tattered remains of an only pair of stockings, his breeches not sufficient to cover his nakedness, his shirt hanging in strings, his hair disheveled, his face meagre." The reek of foul straw and unwashed bodies filled the air. "No bread, no soldier!" The chant began as a barely audible murmur, then was picked up by men all along the line. "No bread, no soldier! No bread, no soldier!" At last the chanting grew so loud it could be heard at General Washington's headquarters, a mile away. The 11,000 men of the American army were surviving on little more than "firecake," a mixture of flour and water baked hard before the fire that, according to Waldo, turned "guts to pasteboard." Two thousand men were without shoes, others were without blankets and had to sit up all night about the fires to keep from freezing. Addressing the Continental Congress, Washington wrote, "Three or four days of bad weather would prove our destruction."

Valley Forge was to become a national symbol of endurance. After marching hundreds of weary miles and suffering a series of terrible defeats at the hands of a British force nearly twice their number, the soldiers of the Continental Army had retreated to this winter headquarters only to find themselves at the mercy of indifferent local suppliers. Contractors demanded exorbitant rates for food and clothing, rates the Congress had refused to pay, and as a result local farmers preferred to deal with the British, who paid in pounds sterling, not depreciated Continental currency.

The 11,000 men of the Continental Army, who had not been paid for nearly six months, were divided into sixteen brigades composed of regiments from nine states. An unsympathetic observer described them as "a vagabond army of ragamuffins," and indeed many of the men were drawn from the ranks of the poor and disadvantaged: indentured servants, landless farmers, and nearly a thousand African Americans, both slave and free. Most of the men came from thinly settled farm districts or small towns where precautions regarding sanitation had been unnecessary. Every thaw revealed ground covered with "much filth and nastiness," and officers ordered sentinels to fire on any man "easing himself elsewhere than at ye vaults." Typhoid fever and other infectious diseases spread quickly: along with dysentery, malnutrition, and exposure they claimed as many as 2,500 lives that winter. More than 700 women—wives, lovers, cooks, laundresses, and prostitutes—lived at Valley Forge that winter, and they were kept busy nursing the sick and burying the dead.

"What then is to become of this army?" Washington worried during the depth of the winter. But six months later the force he marched out of Valley Forge was considerably stronger for its experience there. Most important were the strong relationships that formed among the men, twelve of whom bunked together in each cabin, grouped by state regiments and brigade. In these units they fashioned "a band of brotherhood" and "shared with each other their hardships, dangers, and sufferings," wrote common soldier Joseph Plumb Martin, "sympathized with each other in trouble and sickness, assisted in bearing each other's burdens, [and] endeavored to conceal each other's faults." During the coming trials of battle, Washington, who referred to his staff as "family," would rely greatly on the bonds of affection his men had developed during the hard winter. As psychologists know today, it is this sense of community that contributes most to success in warfare.

To some American Patriots—as the supporters of the Revolution called themselves—the European-style Continental Army betrayed the ideals of the citizen-soldier and the autonomy of local communities, central tenets of the Revolution. Washington argued strongly, however, that the Revolution could not be won without a national army insulated from politics and able to withstand the shifting popular mood. Moreover, through the developing sense of community among these men—who came from hundreds of localities and a variety of ethnic backgrounds—the Continental soldiers became living examples of the egalitarian ideals of the Revolution. They were a popular democratic force that counterbalanced the conservatism of the new republic's elite leadership. The national spirit they built at Valley Forge would sustain them through four more years of war and provide momentum for the long process of forging a national political system out of the persistent localism of American politics. "I admire them tremendously!" wrote one European officer serving with Washington. "It is incredible that soldiers composed of men of every age, even children of fifteen, of whites and blacks, almost naked, unpaid, and rather poorly fed, can march so well and withstand fire so steadfastly." Asked to explain why his men served, another officer declared: "Nothing but virtue and that great principle, the love of our country."

Valley Forge

KEY TOPICS

- The major alignments and divisions among Americans during the American Revolution

- Major military campaigns of the Revolution

- The Articles of Confederation and the role of the Confederation Congress during the Revolutionary War

- The states as the setting for significant political change

- The economic crisis in the aftermath of the American Revolution

THE WAR FOR INDEPENDENCE

At the beginning of the Revolution, the British had the world's best-equipped and most disciplined army as well as a navy that was unopposed in American waters. But they greatly underestimated the American capacity to fight. With a native officer corps and considerable experience in the colonial wars of the eighteenth century, the Patriot forces proved formidable. The British also misperceived the sources of the conflict. Seeing the rebellion as the work of a small group of disgruntled conspirators, initially they defined their objective as defeating this Patriot opposition. In the wake of a military victory, they believed, they could easily reassert political control. But the geography of eastern North America offered no single vital center whose conquest would end the war. The Patriots had the advantage of fighting on their own ground and among a population thinly spread over a territory stretching along 1,500 miles of coastline and extending 100 miles or more into the interior. When the British succeeded in defeating the Patriots in one area, resistance would spring up in another. The key factor in the outcome of the war for independence, then, was the popular support for the American cause.

The Patriot Forces

Most American men of fighting age had to face the call to arms. From a population of approximately 350,000 eligible men, more than 200,000 saw action, though no more than 25,000 were engaged at any one time. More than 100,000 served in the Continental Army, under George Washington's command and the authority of the Continental Congress; the others served in Patriot militia companies.

These militias—armed bodies of men drawn from local communities—proved important in the defense of their own areas, where they had homes as well as local reputations to protect. Despite legend, however, the Revolutionary War was not won by these citizen-soldiers who exchanged plows for guns, or back-country riflemen who picked off British soldiers from behind trees. In the exuberant days of 1776, many Patriots did believe that militias alone could win the war against the British. As one observer wrote, "The Rage Militaire, as the French call a passion for arms, has taken possession of the whole Continent." But, serving short terms of enlistment, often with officers of their own choosing, militiamen resisted discipline. Washington's deputy, General Nathanael Greene, declared that they lacked the fortitude "to stand the shocking scenes of war," having never been "steeled by habit or fortified by military pride." Indeed, in the face of battle militia companies demonstrated appalling rates of desertion. During the fierce fighting on Long Island, for example, three-quarters of Connecticut's 8,000 militiamen simply abandoned the field and headed home.

Initially, the Continental Congress refused to invoke a draft of men from all the colonies or to mandate army enlistments exceeding one year. As a result, and because men preferred the militia to the regular army, the states failed to meet their quotas for regiments in the Continental Army. Nevertheless, the final victory in the American Revolution was won essentially by the steady struggle of the Continental Army. And indeed, the Revolution had little in common with modern national liberation movements in which armed populations engage in guerrilla warfare. General Washington and his officers required a force that could directly engage the British, and from the beginning of the war Washington argued with a skeptical Congress that victory could be won only with a full commitment to a truly national army. This view conflicted with popular fears of a standing army: Would they not be defeating their own purpose, many Patriots wondered, by adopting the corrupt institutions of their British enemies?

The failings of the militias in the early battles of the war sobered Congress, however, and it both greatly enlarged state quotas for the army and extended the term of service to three years or the war's duration. To spur enlistment Congress offered bounties, regular wages, and promises of free land after victory. Although the states consistently failed to meet their quotas, by the spring of 1777 Washington's army had grown to nearly 9,000 men.

Discipline was essential in a conflict in which men fired at close range, charged each other with bayonets, and engaged in hand-to-hand combat. One Connecticut man wrote of the effects of cannon on his regiment: "The ball first cut off the head of Smith, a stout heavy man, and dashed it open, then took Taylor across the bowels; it then struck Sergeant Garret of our company on the hip, took off the point of the hip bone." "Oh! What a sight that was," he concluded, "to see within a distance of six rods those men with their legs and arms and guns and packs all in a heap." In New Jersey, a sergeant in the Continental Army witnessed British troops slaughtering Americans lying on the field: "The men that was wounded in the thigh or leg, they dashed out their brains with their muskets and run them through with their bayonets, made them like sieves. This was barbarity to the utmost."

According to the best estimates, a total of 25,674 American men died in the Revolution, approximately 6,000 from wounds suffered in battle, 10,000 from the effects of disease, and the rest as prisoners of war or missing in action. Regiments of the Continental Army experienced the highest casualty rates, sometimes 30 or 40 percent. Indeed, the casualty rate overall was higher than in any other American conflict up to the present day, with the exception of the Civil War. Although in most areas the war was confined to direct engagements between the armies, in the back-country and in the South, where supporters and opponents of independence waged vicious campaigns of violence against each other, there were considerable noncombatant casualties.

Both the Continentals and the militias played important political roles as well. At a time when Americans identified most strongly with their local communities or their states, the Continental Army, through experiences like the Valley Forge winter, evolved into a powerful force for nationalist sentiment. Shortages of food and pay led to many army mutinies, in the most serious of which an officer was killed and two others wounded. But, when the mutineers in this instance set out, in January 1781, for Philadelphia, where they intended to address the Continental Congress, their purpose was not to abandon the American cause but to ask Congress to uphold its commitments to the soldiers who were fighting for the nation. En route to Philadelphia, the soldiers encountered British agents who tried to persuade them to go over to the king. Angry as these Continental soldiers were at the conditions under which their Congress expected them to fight, they were enraged at this attempt at subversion, and they hanged the British agents on the spot. The men from every colony who served in the Continental Army contributed mightily to the unity of purpose—the formation of a national community—that was essential to the process of nation making.

In most communities Patriots seized control of local government during the period of committee organizing in 1774 and 1775 (see Chapter 6), and with war imminent they pressed the obligation to serve in a Patriot militia upon most eligible men. In Farmington, Connecticut, in 1776, eighteen men were imprisoned "on suspicion of their being inimical to America" when they failed to join the muster of the local militia. After individual grilling by the authorities, they petitioned for pardon. "They appeared to be penitent of their former conduct," it was reported, and understood "that there was no such thing" as remaining neutral. Probably the most important role of the Patriot militias was to force even the most apathetic of Americans to think seriously about the Revolution, and to choose sides under the scrutiny of their neighbors.

As men marched off to war, many women assumed the management of family farms and businesses; Abigail Adams, for

Jean Baptiste Antoine de Verger, a French officer serving with the Continental Army, made these watercolors of American soldiers during the Revolution. Some 200,000 men saw action, including at least 5,000 African Americans; more than half of these troops served with the Continental Army.

example, ran the family's farm at Quincy for years. Adams wrote eloquently and often to her husband, John, on issues surrounding the American struggle for independence and, later, on the structure of the new republic. Some women participated even more directly in patriotic politics. The Boston home of Mercy Otis Warren, daughter of James Otis, was a center of Patriot political activity, and this dedicated revolutionary woman published a series of satires supporting the American cause and scorning the Loyalists. When the fighting shifted to their locales, women volunteered as seamstresses, cooks, nurses, and even spies.

When the months of fighting lengthened into years, many women left their homes to join husbands and lovers, fathers and brothers, in army encampments. Some were officially employed, but most took care of their own men, and many fought with them side by side. Best known among the women who stayed by their husbands' sides even in camp were Martha Washington and Catherine Greene, wives of the two most important American generals of the war. But less socially prominent women were remembered as well. Mary Ludwig Hays (later McCauley) earned the name "Molly Pitcher" for her courage in bringing water to the Patriots during the battle of Monmouth, in June 1778. When her husband was overcome by heat, Mary took his place at the cannon. When Margaret Corbin's husband died in battle, she stepped into his position. Other women, such as Deborah Sampson of Massachusetts, disguised themselves as men and enlisted.

The Loyalists

Not all Americans were Patriots. Many sat on the fence, confused by the conflict and waiting for a clear turn in the tide of the struggle before declaring their allegiance. About a fifth of the population, perhaps as many as half a million people, remained loyal to the British crown. They called themselves Loyalists but were known to Patriots as "Tories," the popular name for the conservative party in England, which traditionally supported the authority of the king over Parliament. Loyalism was strongest in the Lower South, weakest in New England. British colonial officials were almost always Loyalists, as were most Anglican clergymen and many lawyers who had worked with colonial administrators. The British cause also attracted ethnic minorities who had been persecuted by the dominant majority, such as the Highland Scots of the Carolinas and western New York, and southern tenant farmers who had Patriot landlords. Many slaves and most Indians identified with the Loyalists, the first because the Patriot leadership in the South was drawn from the ranks of slave owners, the second because they feared aggressive expansion by independent American states. Other

John Singleton Copley's portrait of Mercy Otis Warren captured her at the age of thirty-six, in 1765. During the Revolution her home in Boston was a center of patriotic political activity.

Copley, John Singleton, U.S. 1738–1815 Mrs James Warren (Mercy Otis), ca. 1763. Oil on canvas. 51 1/4 x 41 in. (130.1 x 104.1 cm). Bequest of Winslow Warren. Courtesy. Museum of Fine Art, Boston.

Loyalists were conservatives, fearful of political or social upheaval, or were temperamentally opposed to resistance to established authority.

Patriots passed state treason acts that prohibited speaking or writing against the Revolution. They also punished Loyalists with bills of attainder, by which persons were deprived, without trial, of their civil rights and property (a process later made illegal in the United States Constitution). In some areas, notably New York, South Carolina, Massachusetts, and Pennsylvania, Loyalists faced mob violence. One favorite punishment was the "grand Tory ride," in which a crowd hauled the victim through the streets astride a sharp fence rail. Another was tarring and feathering, in which men were stripped to "buff and breeches" and their naked flesh coated liberally with heated tar and then feathers. One broadside recommended that Patriots "then hold a lighted Candle to the feathers, and try to set it all on fire." The torment rarely went that far, but it was brutally painful nonetheless.

The most infamous American supporter of the British cause was Benedict Arnold, whose name has become synonymous, in the United States, with treason. Arnold was a hero of the early battles of the Revolution. But in 1779, angry and resentful about what he

The TORY'S Day of JUDGMENT.

A Patriot mob torments Loyalists in this print published during the Revolution. One favorite punishment was the "grand Tory ride," in which a crowd hauled the victim through the streets astride a fence rail. In another men were stripped to "buff and breeches" and their naked flesh coated liberally with heated tar and feathers.

perceived to be assignments and rank below his station, he became a paid informer of General Henry Clinton, head of the British army in New York City. In 1780 Patriots uncovered Arnold's plot to betray the strategic post of West Point, which he commanded. After fleeing to the British, who paid him a handsome stipend and pension, he became a brigadier general in the British army. The *bête noire* of the Revolution, Arnold became the most hated man in America. In his hometown of Norwich, Connecticut, a crowd destroyed the gravestones of his family, and in cities and towns throughout America thousands burned his effigy. During the last two years of the war he led British raids against his home state as well as against Virginia, and after the Revolution he lived in England until his death in 1801.

The British strategy for suppressing the Revolution depended on mobilizing the Loyalists, but in most areas this proved impossible. As noted earlier, the Loyalists were not a monolithic group but were divided in their opinions, and many were covertly sympathetic to Patriot arguments. Still, as many as 50,000 Loyalists fought for the king during the Revolution. Many joined Loyalist militias or engaged in irregular warfare, especially in the Lower South. In 1780, when Washington's Continentals numbered about 9,000, there were 8,000 American Loyalists serving in the British army in America.

As many as 80,000 Loyalists fled the country during and after the Revolution, taking up residence in England, the British West Indies, or Canada. Their property was confiscated by the states and sold at public auction. Although the British government compensated many for their losses, most Loyalists were unhappy exiles. "I earnestly wish to spend the remainder of my days in America," wrote William Pepperell, formerly of Maine, from London in 1778. "I love the country, I love the people." Former governor Thomas Hutchinson of Massachusetts wrote that he "had rather die in a little country farm-house in New England than in the best nobleman's seat in old England." Despite their disagreement with the Patriots on essential political questions, they remained Americans, and they mourned the loss of their country.

The Campaign for New York and New Jersey

During the winter of 1775–76 the British developed a strategic plan for the war. From his base at Halifax, Nova Scotia, Sir William Howe was to take his army to New York City, which the British navy would make impregnable. From there Howe was to drive north along the Hudson, while another British army marched south from Canada to Albany. The two armies would converge, cutting New England off from the rest of the colonies, and then turn eastward to reduce the rebellious Yankees into submission. Washington, who had arrived at Boston to take command of the militia forces there in the summer of 1775, anticipated this strategy, and in the spring of 1776 he shifted his forces southward toward New York.

In early July, as Congress was taking its final vote on the Declaration of Independence, the British began their operation at New York City, landing 32,000 men on Staten Island, a third of them Hessian mercenaries (from the German state of Hesse). The Americans, meanwhile, set up fortified positions across the harbor in Brooklyn. Attacking in late August, the British inflicted heavy casualties on the Americans, and the militia forces under Washington's command proved unreliable under fire. The battle of Long Island ended in disaster for the Patriots, and they were forced to withdraw across the East River to Manhattan.

The British now offered Congress an opportunity to negotiate, and on September 6, Benjamin Franklin, John Adams, and Edward Rutledge sat down with General Howe and his brother, Admiral Richard Howe, on Staten Island. But the meeting broke up when the Howes demanded revocation of the Declaration of Independence. The stage was set for another round of violence. Six days later the British invaded Manhattan island, and only an American stand at Harlem Heights prevented the destruction of a large portion of the Patriot army. Enjoying naval control of the harbor, the British quickly outflanked the American positions. In a series of battles over the next few months, they forced Washington back at White Plains and overran the American posts of Fort Washington and Fort Lee, on either side of the Hudson River. By November the Americans were fleeing south across New Jersey in a frantic attempt to avoid the British under General Charles Cornwallis.

With morale desperately low, whole militia companies deserted; others, announcing the end of their terms of enlistment, left for home. American resistance seemed to be collapsing all around Washington. "Our troops will not do their duty," he wrote painfully to Congress as he crossed the Delaware River into Pennsylvania. Upon receiving his message, the delegates in Philadelphia fled to Baltimore. "I think the game is pretty near up," Washington admitted to his brother. But rather than fall back further, which would surely have meant the dissolution of his entire force, he decided to risk a counterattack. On Christmas night Washington led 2,400 troops back across the Delaware, and the next morning defeated the Hessian forces in a surprise attack on their headquarters at Trenton, New Jersey. The Americans inflicted further heavy losses on the British at Princeton, then drove them all the way back to the environs of New York City.

Although these small victories of 1776 and early 1777 had little strategic importance, they salvaged American morale. As Washington settled into winter headquarters at Morristown, he realized he had to pursue a defensive strategy, avoiding direct confrontations with the British while checking their advances and hurting them wherever possible. "We cannot conquer the British force at once," wrote General Greene, "but they cannot conquer us at all." This last sentiment was more of a hope than a conviction, but it defined the essentially defensive American strategy of the Revolution. Most important to that strategy was the survival of the Continental Army.

The Northern Campaigns of 1777

The fighting with the American forces had prevented Howe from moving north up the Hudson, and the British advance southward from Canada had been stalled by American resistance at Lake Champlain. In 1777, however, the British decided to replay their strategy. From Canada they dispatched General John Burgoyne with nearly 8,000 British and German troops. Howe was to move his force from New York, first taking the city of Philadelphia, the seat of the Continental Congress, and then moving north to meet Burgoyne.

Fort Ticonderoga fell to Burgoyne on July 6, but by August the general found himself bogged down and harassed by Patriot militias in the rough country south of Lake George. After several defeats in September at the hands of an American army commanded by General Horatio Gates, Burgoyne retreated to Saratoga. There his army was surrounded by a considerably larger force of Americans, and on October 17, lacking alternatives, he surrendered his nearly 6,000 men. It would be the biggest British defeat until Yorktown, decisive because it forced the nations of Europe to recognize that the Americans had a fighting chance to win their Revolution.

The Americans were less successful against Howe. A force of 15,000 British troops left New York in July, landing a month later at the northern end of Chesapeake Bay. At Brandywine Creek the British outflanked the Americans, inflicting heavy casualties and forcing a retreat. Ten days later the British routed the Americans a second time with a frightful bayonet charge at Paoli that left many Patriots dead. When British troops occupied Philadelphia on September 26, Congress had already fled. Washington attempted a valiant counterattack at Germantown on October 4, but initial success was followed by miscoordination that eventually doomed the operation.

After this campaign the Continentals headed for winter quarters at Valley Forge, about twenty miles from Philadelphia, the bitterness of their defeats muted somewhat by news of the surrender at Saratoga. In taking Philadelphia, the British had gained the most important city in North America, but it proved to have

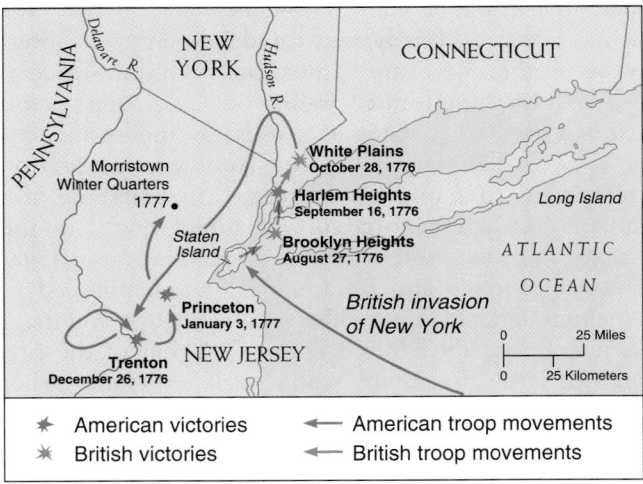

Campaign for New York and New Jersey, 1775–1777

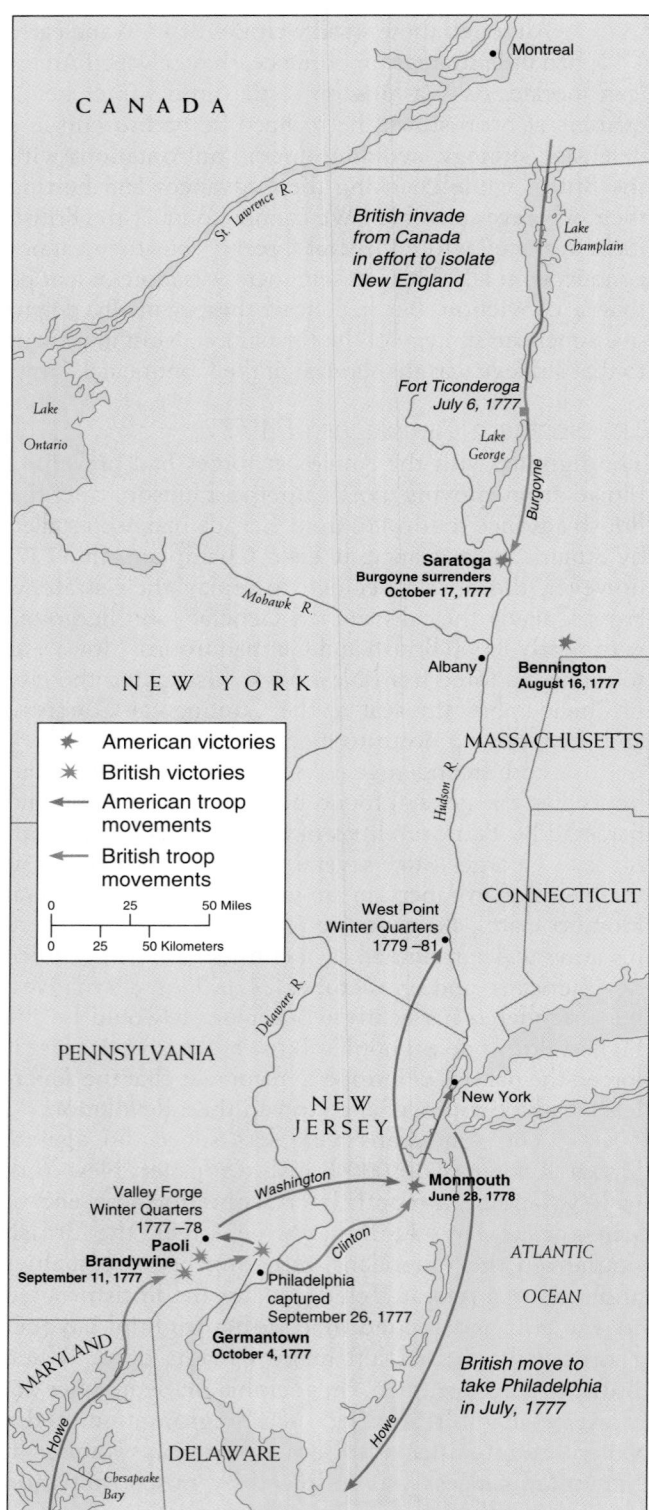

Northern Campaigns, 1777–1778

unified effort suffered little disruption. The British would have done better to move north instead, where they might have saved Burgoyne. At the end of two years of fighting, the British strategy for winning the war had to be judged a failure.

The Politics of the French and Spanish Alliance

During these first two years of fighting, the Americans were sustained by loans from France and Spain, allies in the Bourbon "family compact" of monarchies. Both saw an opportunity to win back North American territories lost to Great Britain in the Seven Years War that concluded in 1763. The Continental Congress maintained a diplomatic delegation in Paris headed by Benjamin Franklin. The urbane and cosmopolitan Franklin, who captured French hearts by dressing in homespun and wearing a "frontiersman" fur cap, maintained excellent relations with the Comte de Vergennes, the French foreign minister. Franklin negotiated with Vergennes for recognition of American independence and a Franco-American alliance against the British in addition to loans to finance the Revolution, but was unable to convince him. France, which wanted to weaken the British empire any way it could, was inclined to support the Americans, but it was reluctant to encourage a republican revolution being fought against monarchy and colonialism.

In England, meanwhile, there was rising opposition to the war among the Tories and the Whigs, their political opponents who took a less authoritarian view of things. "The measures toward America are erroneous," declared Lord Rockingham, "the adherence to them is destruction." William Pitt warned his countrymen to "beware the gathering storm" if and when France decided to support the Americans actively. When British Prime Minister Lord North received the news of Burgoyne's surrender, he dispatched agents to begin peace discussions with Franklin in Paris. The victory at Saratoga, as well as fears of British conciliation with the revolutionaries, finally persuaded Vergennes to intervene on the side of the United States. In mid-December of 1777 he informed Franklin that the king's council had decided to recognize American independence.

In February 1778 the American delegation submitted to Congress a treaty of commerce and alliance it had negotiated with the French. In the treaty, to take effect upon a declaration of war between France and Britain, the French pledged to "maintain effectually the liberty, sovereignty, and independence" of the United States. "Neither of the two parties," the document read, "shall conclude either truce or peace with Great Britain, without the formal consent of the other." The Americans had compelled France to guarantee to the United States all the "northern parts of America" conquered in the war,

little strategic value. The Continental Congress moved to the Pennsylvania backcountry. In any event, central government was virtually nonexistent, and so the ending any thought of a rebirth of New France. But they promised to recognize any French acquisitions of British islands in the West Indies. In June, France declared war, and soon began fighting with Britain.

A year later Spain also entered the war. Spanish officials in New Orleans provided substantial ammunition and provisions for American forts in the West, including herds of cattle, driven to New Orleans by *vaqueros* (cowboys) from Texas. In New Spain the viceroy levied a special tax to pay for these supplies, and borderland colonists contributed their share. Father Junípero Serra, president of the California missions, prescribed a weekly prayer for American victory, and the scene of California Indian converts praying for the freedom of European colonists on the other coast is surely one of the most ironic of the era. But American attempts to establish a formal Spanish alliance met with failure. The Spanish feared the Americans as a danger to their own empire of New Spain but regarded the Revolution as an opportunity to regain Florida from the British and extend their control of the Mississippi Valley. "Its people are active, industrious, and aggressive," one Mexican official wrote of the United States, and "it would be culpable negligence on our part not to thwart their schemes for conquest."

The Spanish zealously pursued their strategy, attacking and taking the Mississippi River towns of Natchez and Baton Rouge in 1779, and the Gulf ports of Mobile in 1780 and Pensacola in 1781; their victory at Pensacola was won with the help of several companies of African Americans. Alarmed by the quick spread of American settlements west of the Appalachians, the Spanish attempted to establish a claim of their own to the British territory north of the Ohio by sending an expedition into the Northwest in 1781, which succeeded in taking the minor British post of St. Joseph, in present-day Michigan.

The first French ambassador to the United States arrived with instructions to do everything he could to prevent the Americans from enlarging their territory at the expense of the Spanish empire in the West. Vergennes also feared the potential power of an independent United States. Several years before, he had warned the British that once the Americans gained their independence they "would immediately set about forming a great marine," and use it in the Caribbean to "conquer both your islands and ours," then sweep south, where it would "not leave a foot of that hemisphere in the possession of any European power." American leaders understood that the treaty with France and the *modus vivendi* with Spain were merely expedients for all sides, and they recognized the dangers that France and Spain posed to the United States. But far more important was the prospect the French treaty offered of victory over Britain.

The entry of France into the war forced the British to rethink their strategy. At first Lord North took a conciliatory approach, sending a peace commission to America with promises to repeal the parliamentary legislation that had provoked the crisis in the first place and pledging never again to impose revenue taxes on the colonies. Three years earlier, such pledges would surely have forestalled the movement toward independence. But the Continental Congress now declared that any person coming to terms with the peace commission was a traitor; the only possible topics of negotiation were the withdrawal of British forces and the recognition of American independence. The peace commission was reduced to attempting to bribe members of Congress and finally to threatening a war of devastation, but to no avail.

Meanwhile the British realized that with France in the war their valuable West Indies colonies were at risk, and they rushed 5,000 men from New York to the Caribbean, where they beat back a French attack. Fearing the arrival of the French fleet along the North American coast, the new British commander in America, General Henry Clinton, evacuated Philadelphia in June 1778. In hot pursuit were Washington's Continentals. At the battle of Monmouth on June 28, the British blunted the American drive and retreated to New York. The Americans, centered at West Point, took up defensive positions surrounding the lower Hudson. Confidence in an impending victory now spread through the Patriot forces. But after a failed campaign with the French against the British forces at Newport, Rhode Island, Washington settled for a defensive strategy. Although the Americans enjoyed several small successes in the Northeast over the next two years, the war there went into a stall.

The war at sea was fought mostly between the British and the French, but Continental, state, and private vessels raided British merchant ships and conducted isolated naval patrols. The foremost American naval hero of the war was John Paul Jones, who, in 1777, raided the coast of Scotland. In 1779, while commanding the French ship *Bonhomme Richard* (named in honor of Franklin's "Poor Richard"), Jones engaged in a celebrated battle with the British warship *Serapis*. When the two ships locked together, the British captain hailed Jones, asking if he were ready to surrender. Jones's reply—"I have not yet begun to fight"—became one of the most quoted lines of the Revolution. Jones won his battle, though it had little military consequence. After the war Congress decommissioned the small American navy and dismissed its officers, including Jones, who went on to serve in the imperial Russian navy.

Gilbert Stuart. *Joseph Brant*, 1786. Oil on canvas, 30" × 25". New York State Historical Association, Cooper-

Joseph Brant, the brilliant chief of the Mohawks who sided with Great Britain during the Revolution, in a 1786 painting by the American artist Gilbert Stuart. After the Treaty of Paris, Brant led a large faction of Iroquois people north into British Canada, where they established a separate Iroquois Confederacy.

Indian Peoples and the Revolution

At the beginning of the conflict both sides solicited the support of the Indians. A committee of the Continental Congress reported that "securing and preserving the friendship of Indian nations appears to be a subject of the utmost moment to these colonies." Most concerned about the stance of the Iroquois Confederacy—long one of the most potent political forces in colonial North America—a delegation from Congress told the Iroquois that the conflict was a "family quarrel" and urged them to avoid it. British agents, on the other hand, pressed the Iroquois to unite against the Americans. Many Indian people were reluctant to get involved: "We are unwilling to join on either side of such a contest," an Oneida chief responded, "for we love you both—old England and new."

But ultimately the British were more persuasive, arguing that a Patriot victory would mean the extension of American settlements into Indian homelands. Native peoples fought in the Revolution for some of the same reasons Patriots did—for political independence, cultural integrity, and the protection of their land and property—but Indian fears of American expansion led them to oppose those who claimed the cause of natural rights and the equality of all men. Almost all the tribes that engaged in the fighting did so on the side of the British.

British officials marshaled the support of Cherokees, Creeks, Choctaws, and Chickasaws in the South, supplying them with arms from the British arsenal at Pensacola. The consequence was a ferocious Indian war in the southern backcountry. In the summer of 1776 a large number of Cherokees, led by the warrior chief Dragging Canoe (Tsiyu-Gunsini), attacked dozens of American settlements. It took hard fighting before Patriot militia companies managed to drive the Cherokees into the mountains, destroying many of their towns. Although the Cherokees eventually made an official peace, sporadic violence between Patriots and Indians continued along the southern frontier.

Among the Iroquois of New York, the Mohawk leader Joseph Brant succeeded in bringing

This American cartoon, published during the Revolution, depicts "the Scalp Buyer," Colonel Henry Hamilton, paying bounties to Indians. In fact, Indian warriors were not simply pawns of the British but fought for the same reasons the Patriots did—for political independence, cultural integrity, and protection of land and property.

Fighting in the West, 1778–1779

most Iroquois warriors into the British camp, although he was opposed by the chiefs of the Oneidas and Tuscaroras, who supported the Patriots. In the summer and fall of 1778, Iroquois and Loyalist forces raided the northern frontiers of Pennsylvania and New York. In retaliation an American army invaded the Iroquois homelands in August 1779, defeating a strong force in the summer and destroying dozens of western villages and thousands of acres of crops during the fall. For the first time since the birth of their confederacy in the fifteenth century, the Iroquois were fighting each other.

Across the mountains the Ohio Indians formed an effective alliance under the British at Detroit in 1777, and during that year and the next American settlements in Kentucky such as Boonesborough were nearly destroyed by Indian attacks. Virginian George Rogers Clark countered by organizing an expedition of militia forces against the French towns in the Illinois country. In July 1778 Clark's men took the British post at Kaskaskia. The following February at Vincennes, Clark captured Colonel Henry Hamilton, British commander in the West, infamous as "the Scalp Buyer" because of the bounty he had placed

on Patriots. But Clark lacked the strength to attack the strategic British garrison at Detroit. Raids back and forth across the Ohio River by Indians and Americans claimed hundreds of lives over the next three years. The war in the West would not end with the conclusion of hostilities in the Revolution; in fact, it would continue for another twenty years.

The War in the South

The hardest and most important fighting of the Revolution took place in the South. There the war had begun with a slave uprising. In late 1775 Lord Dunmore, the last royal governor of Virginia, issued a proclamation calling on slaves to desert their masters and take up arms with the British. More than 800 slaves responded to his call, terrifying Chesapeake planters. When Patriot forces effectively routed Dunmore's army in July 1776, they fought a large number of African American troops wearing sashes emblazoned with the words "Liberty to Slaves." Many of these black soldiers succumbed to smallpox, but at least 300 sailed with Dunmore when he departed.

In December 1778 General Clinton regained the initiative for Britain when he sent a force from New

VIRGINIA

APPALACHIAN MOUNTAINS

Lafayette

Washington and Rochambeau

York R.

Hood and Graves

Yorktown
August 30 – October 19, 1781

Battles of the Virginia Capes
September 5 – 9, 1781

Cornwallis

de Grasse

Guilford Court House
March 15, 1781

Morgan

Cornwallis

Greene

Cornwallis

NORTH
CAROLINA

Cowpens
January 17, 1781

Kings Mountain
October 7, 1780

Camden
August 16, 1780

ATLANTIC
OCEAN

SOUTH   CAROLINA

Cornwallis

Savannah R.

British attempt to push through Carolinas and Virginia

※	British victory
✳	American victory
←	British troop movements
←	American troop movements

0   50   100 Miles
0   50   100 Kilometers

Charleston
May 12, 1780

GEORGIA

Clinton and Cornwallis, March 1780 from New York

Clinton, December 1778 from New York

Savannah
December 29, 1778

Fighting in the South, 1778–1781

York against Georgia, the weakest of the colonies. The British crushed the Patriot militia at Savannah and began to organize the Loyalists in an effort to reclaim the colony. Several American counterattacks failed, including one in which the French fleet bombarded Savannah. Encouraged by their success in Georgia, the British decided to apply the lessons learned there throughout the South. This decision involved a fundamental change from a strategy of military conquest to one of pacification: territory would be retaken step-by-step, then handed over to Loyalists who would reassert colonial authority loyal to the crown. In October 1779 Clinton evacuated Rhode Island, the last British stronghold in New England and, with 8,000 troops, moved south for an attack on Charleston. Outflanking the American defenders, in May Clinton forced the surrender of over 5,000 troops—the most significant American defeat of the war. Horatio Gates, the hero of Saratoga, led a detachment of Continentals southward,

but in August they were defeated by Cornwallis at Camden, South Carolina. Patriot resistance to the British collapsed in the Lower South, and American fortunes were suddenly at their lowest ebb since the beginning of the war.

During the British campaign through the South, thousands of slaves responded to General Clinton's promise of liberty to those who would fight. In response, Maryland, Virginia, and North Carolina grudgingly began to recruit free persons of color and even slaves into their armed forces. Northern states, led by New England, had already solicited African American recruits, and Rhode Island had placed an African American regiment in the field. Some of these men served in the infantry, while many more were commissary workers or teamsters. By war's end at least 5,000 African Americans had served in Patriot militias or the Continental Army, and in the South some slaves won their freedom through military service. In the

Lower South, however, where the numerical superiority of slaves bred fears of rebellion among white people, there was no similar movement.

The southern campaign was marked by vicious violence between partisan militias of Patriots and Loyalists. "The Whigs and Tories persecute each other with little less than savage fury," wrote General Greene, appointed to succeed Gates after the disaster at Camden. "There is nothing but murders and devastations in every quarter." The violence peaked in September 1780 with Cornwallis's invasion of North Carolina, where the Patriots were stronger and better organized. There the British found their southern strategy untenable: plundering towns and farms in order to feed the army in the interior, where it was detached from lines of supply, had the effect of producing angry support for the Patriots. The Patriots won two important battles at Kings Mountain in October 1780 and the Cowpens in January 1781.

Into 1781 the Continentals and militias waged what General Greene called a "fugitive" war of hit and run against the British. "I am quite tired of marching about the country in quest of adventures," Cornwallis wrote; he declared himself "totally in the dark" about what to do next. He won a victory over the Patriots at Guilford Court House in March, but finally deciding that he would not be able to hold the Carolinas so long as Virginia remained a base of support and supply for the Americans, Cornwallis led his army northward in the summer of 1781. After marauding throughout the Virginia countryside he reached the Chesapeake, encamping at Yorktown to await expected reinforcements from New York. This withdrawal from North Carolina allowed Greene to reestablish Patriot control of the Lower South.

Yorktown

While the British raged through the South the stalemate continued in the Northeast. In the summer of 1780, taking advantage of the British evacuation of Rhode Island, the French landed 5,000 troops at Newport under the command of General Comte de Rochambeau. But it was not until the spring of 1781 that the general risked joining his force to Washington's Continentals north of New York. They planned a campaign against the city, but in August Washington learned that the French Caribbean fleet was headed for the Chesapeake. He sensed the possibility of a *coup de grâce* if only he and Rochambeau could move their troops south in coordination with the French naval operation, locking Cornwallis into his camp at Yorktown. Leaving a small force behind as a decoy, Washington and Rochambeau moved quickly down the coast to the Virginia shore.

More than 16,000 American and French troops had converged on the less than 8,000-man British garrison at Yorktown by mid-September. "If you cannot relieve me very soon," Cornwallis wrote to Clinton in New York, "you must expect to hear the worst." French and American heavy artillery hammered the British unmercifully until the middle of October. Cornwallis found it impossible to break the siege, and after the failure of a planned retreat across the York River, he opened negotiations for the surrender of his army. Two days later, on October 19, 1781, between lines of victorious American and French soldiers, the British troops came out from their trenches to surrender, marching to the melancholy tune of "The World Turned Upside Down":

> If buttercups buzzed after the bee,
> If boats were on land, churches on sea,
> If summer were spring and t'other way round,
> Then all the world would be upside down.

It must have seemed that way to Cornwallis, who, pleading illness, sent his second-in-command, General Charles O'Hara, to surrender. Refusing to acknowledge the presence of the Americans, O'Hara first approached General Rochambeau, but the Frenchman waved him toward General Washington. To the British, it was almost incomprehensible that they could be surrendering to former subordinates. Everyone knew this was an event of incalculable importance, but few guessed it was the end of the war, for the British still controlled New York.

In London, at the end of November, Lord North received the news "as he would have taken a ball in the breast," reported the colonial secretary. "Oh God!" he moaned, "it is all over!" British fortunes were at low ebb in India, the West Indies, Florida, and the Mediterranean; the cost of the war was enormous; and there was little support for it among the public and members of Parliament. King George wished to press on, but North submitted his resignation, and in March 1782 the king was forced to accept the ministry of Lord Rockingham, who favored granting Americans their independence.

THE UNITED STATES IN CONGRESS ASSEMBLED

The motion for independence, offered to the Continental Congress by Richard Henry Lee on June 7, 1776, called for a confederation of the states. The Articles of Confederation, the first written constitution of the United States, created a national government of sharply limited powers, an arrangement that reflected the concerns of people fighting to free themselves from a coercive central government. The weak Confederation government found it difficult to forge the unity and assemble the resources necessary to fight the war and win the peace.

The Articles of Confederation

The debate over confederation that took place in the Continental Congress following the Declaration of Independence made it clear that delegates favoring a loose union of autonomous states outnumbered those who wanted a strong national government. Not until the following year did a consensus finally emerge. In November 1777 the Articles of Confederation were formally adopted by the Continental Congress and sent to the states for ratification. The Articles created a national assembly, called the Congress, in which each state had a single vote. Delegates, selected annually in a manner determined by the individual state legislatures, were subjected to term limits, prohibited from serving in more than three years out of any six-year period. Similarly, a president, elected annually by Congress, was eligible to serve no more than one year out of any given three. Votes would be decided by a simple majority of the states, but major questions would require the agreement of nine states.

Congress was granted national authority in the conduct of foreign affairs, matters of war and peace, and maintenance of the armed forces. It could raise loans, issue bills of credit, establish a coinage, and regulate trade with Indian peoples, and it was to be the final authority in jurisdictional disputes between states. It was charged with establishing a national postal system as well as a common standard of weights and measures. Lacking the power to tax citizens directly, however, the national government was to apportion its financial burdens among the states according to the extent of their surveyed land. The Articles explicitly guaranteed the sovereignty of the individual states, reserving to them all powers not expressly delegated to Congress. Ratification or amendment required the agreement of all thirteen states. This constitution thus created a national government of specific, yet sharply circumscribed powers.

The legislatures of twelve states soon voted in favor of the Articles, but final ratification was held up for over three years by the state of Maryland. Representing the interests of states without claims to lands west of the Appalachians, Maryland demanded that states cede to Congress their western claims, the new nation's most valuable resource, for "the good of the whole." Excepted, however, would be the colonial grants made to land companies. The eight states with western claims were reluctant to give them up, and the remaining states included powerful land speculators among their most influential citizens. While the stalemate over western lands continued, Congress remained an extralegal body, but it agreed to work under the terms of the unratified document. It was 1781 before Virginia, the state with the largest western claims, broke the log-jam by promising to cede its lands.

Maryland then agreed to ratification, and in March the Articles of Confederation took effect.

Financing the War

Congress financed the Revolution through grants and loans from friendly foreign powers and by issuing paper currency. The total foreign subsidy by the end of the war approached $9 million, but this was insufficient to back the circulating Continental currency that Congress had authorized, the face value of

The Continental Congress printed currency to finance the Revolution. Because of widespread counterfeiting, engravers attempted to incorporate complex designs, like the unique vein structure in the leaf on this eighteen-pence note. In case that wasn't enough, the engraver of this note also included the warning: "To counterfeit is Death."

which had risen to nearly $200 million by the end of the war. Congress called on the states to raise taxes, payable in Continental dollars, so that this currency could be retired. But most of the states proved unwilling to do this. In fact, the states resorted to printing currency of their own, which totaled another $200 million by the end of the war. The results of this growth in the money supply were rapid depreciation of Continental currency and runaway inflation. People who received fixed incomes for services—Continental soldiers, for example, as well as merchants, landlords, and other creditors—were devastated. When Robert Morris, one of the country's wealthiest merchants, became superintendent of finance in May 1781, Continental currency had ceased to circulate. Things of no value were said to be "not worth a Continental."

Morris persuaded Congress to charter the Bank of North America in Philadelphia, the first private commercial bank in the United States. There he deposited large quantities of gold and silver coin and bills of exchange obtained through loans from Holland and France. He then issued new paper currency backed by this supply. Once confidence in the bank had developed, he was able to begin supplying the army through private contracts. He was also able to meet the interest payments on the debt, which in 1783 he estimated to be about $30 million.

Morris was associated with the nationalists who controlled Congress in the early 1780s. With their support, he proposed amending the Articles of Confederation to empower Congress to levy a 5 percent duty on imports. The Confederation would then have a source of revenue independent of state requisitions. By the fall of 1782, twelve states had approved the "impost amendment," but Rhode Island refused, objecting that state control of import duties was essential to its own revenues. The nationalists continued to press for an independent congressional revenue, but Morris, having failed in his effort, resigned office in 1784.

Negotiating Independence

Peace talks between the United States and Great Britain opened in April 1782, when Benjamin Franklin sat down with the British emissary in Paris. Congress had issued its first set of war aims in 1779. The fundamental demands were recognition of American independence and withdrawal of British forces. Negotiators were to press for as much territory as possible, including Canada, and guarantees of the American right to fish the North Atlantic. As for its French ally, Congress instructed the commissioners to be guided by friendly advice but also by "knowledge of our interests, and by your own discretion, in

which we repose the fullest confidence." But as the British pushed through the South over the next two years and the Americans grew increasingly dependent on French loans and military might, the French ambassador in Philadelphia worked to limit potential American power. In June 1781, partly as a result of French pressure, Congress issued a new set of instructions: the commissioners were to settle merely for a grant of independence and withdrawal of troops, and to be subject to the guidance and control of the French in the negotiations.

Franklin, John Jay, and John Adams, the peace commissioners in Paris, were aware of French attempts to manipulate the outcome of negotiations. In violation of instructions and treaty obligations, and without consulting the French, they signed a preliminary treaty with Britain in November. The British were delighted at the thought of separating the wartime allies. In the treaty, Britain acknowledged the United States as "free, sovereign & independent" and agreed to withdraw its troops from all forts within American territory "with all convenient speed." They guaranteed Americans "the right to take fish" in northern waters. The American commissioners had pressed the British for Canada, but settled for territorial boundaries that extended to the Mississippi. Britain received American promises to erect "no lawful impediments" to the recovery of debts, to cease confiscating Loyalist property, and to try to persuade the states to compensate Loyalist exiles fairly. Finally, the two nations agreed to unencumbered navigation of the Mississippi. The American commissioners had accomplished an astounding coup. The new boundaries, they wrote to Congress, "appear to leave us little to complain of and not much to desire."

France was thus confronted with a *fait accompli*. When Vergennes criticized the commissioners, the Americans responded by hinting that resistance to the treaty provisions could result in a British-American alliance. France thereupon quickly made an agreement of its own with the British.

Spain, the Americans' reluctant ally, was also left out of the negotiations. But as a result of its successful military campaign against the British in the West, Spain now claimed sovereignty over much of the trans-Appalachian territory granted to the United States. The most important issue here was American use of the Mississippi, which depended on access to the Spanish-controlled port of New Orleans. Refusing to deal directly with the Americans, the Spanish arranged their own peace with Great Britain, winning the return of Florida. The final Treaty of Paris—actually a series of separate agreements among the United States, Great Britain, France, and Spain—was signed at Versailles on September 3, 1783.

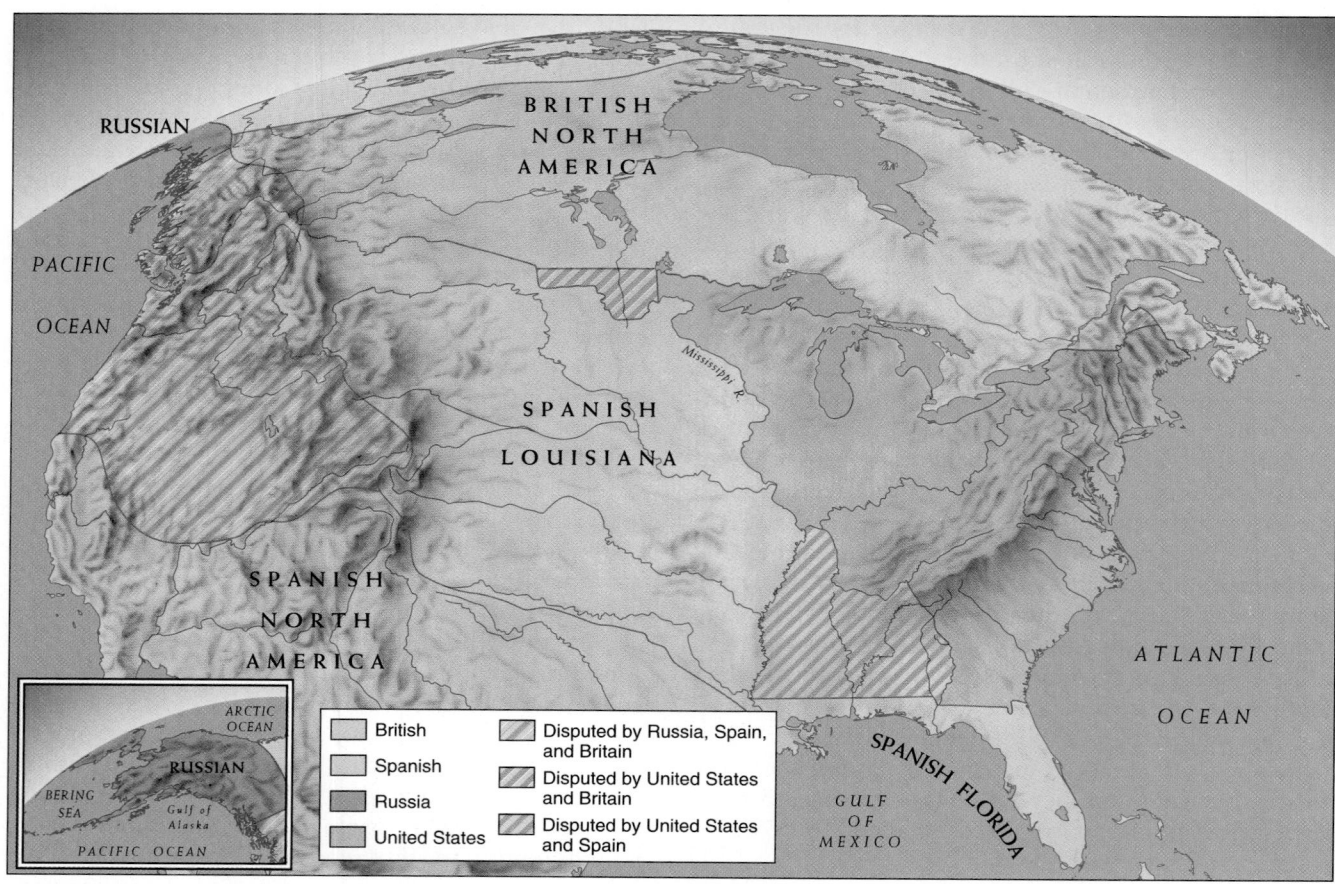

North America after the Treaty of Paris, 1783 *The map of European and American claims to North America was radically altered by the results of the American Revolution.*

The Crisis of Demobilization

During the two years between the surrender at York-town and the signing of the Treaty of Paris, the British continued to occupy New York City, Charleston, and a series of western posts. The Continental Army remained on wartime alert, with some 10,000 men and an estimated 1,000 women encamped at Newburgh, New York, north of West Point. The soldiers had long been awaiting their pay and were concerned about the postwar bounties and land warrants promised them. The most serious problem, however, lay not among the enlisted men but in the officer corps.

Continental officers had extracted a promise from Congress of life pensions at half pay in exchange for enlistment for the duration of the war. By 1783, however, Congress had still not made specific provisions for the pensions. With peace at hand, officers began to fear that the army would be disbanded before the problem was resolved, and they would lose whatever power they had to pressure Congress. In January 1783 a group of prominent senior officers petitioned Congress, demanding that the pensions be converted to a bonus equal to five years of full pay.

"Any further experiments on their patience," they warned, "may have fatal effects." Despite this barely veiled threat of military intervention, Congress rejected their petition.

With the backing of congressional nationalists, a group of army officers associated with General Horatio Gates called an extraordinary meeting of the officer corps at Newburgh. But General Washington, on whom the officers counted for support, condemned the meeting as "disorderly" and called an official meeting of his own. There was enormous tension when the officers assembled on March 15; at stake was nothing less than the possibility of a military coup at the very moment of American victory. Washington strode into the room and mounted the platform. Turning his back in disdain on General Gates, he told the assembly that he wished to read a statement, and then pulled a pair of glasses from his pocket. None of his officers had seen their leader wearing glasses before. "Gentlemen, you must pardon me," said Washington when he noticed their surprise. "I have grown gray in your service and now find myself growing blind." He then went on to denounce any resort to force, but it was his offhand remark about growing gray that made the greatest impact. Who had sacrificed more than their commander in chief? After he left, the officers adopted resolutions rejecting intervention, and a week later, on Washington's urging, Congress decided to convert the pensions to bonuses after all.

Washington's role in this crisis was one of his greatest contributions to the nation. In December 1783 he resigned his commission as general of the army despite calls for him to remain. There is little doubt that he could have assumed the role of American dictator. Instead, by his actions and example, the principle of military subordination to civil authority was firmly established.

As for the common soldiers, they wanted simply to be discharged. "It is not in the power of Congress or their officers to hold them much, if any, longer," Washington wrote Alexander Hamilton in April. The next month, Congress voted the soldiers three months' pay as a bonus and instructed Washington to begin dismissing them. Some troops remained at Newburgh until the British evacuated New York in November, but by the beginning of 1784 the Continental Army had shrunk to no more than a few hundred men.

The Problem of the West

After Yorktown, the British abandoned their Indian allies in the West. When the Indians learned of the armistice, according to one British officer, they were "thunderstruck." Neither the Iroquois nor the Ohio tribes, who had fought with the British, considered themselves defeated, but the United States claimed that its victory over Great Britain was a victory over the Indians as well. A heavily armed American nation now pressed for large grants of territory according to the right of conquest. Even Patriot allies were not exempt. The Oneidas, for example, who had supported the Americans, suffered territorial demands along with the other Iroquois.

Even during the fighting the American migration to the West had continued, and

after the treaty of peace settlers streamed over the mountains and down the Ohio River. The population of Kentucky (still a part of Virginia until admitted as a state in 1792) had grown to more than 30,000 by 1785; in 1790 it numbered 74,000, and the Tennessee area held another 36,000. Thousands of Americans pressed against the Indian country north of the Ohio River, and destructive violence continued along the frontier. British troops continued to occupy posts in the Northwest and encouraged Indian attacks on vulnerable settlements. To the southwest, Spain, refusing to accept the territorial settlement of the Treaty of Paris, closed the Mississippi River to Americans. Westerners who saw that route as their primary access to markets were outraged.

The American leadership saw the West as critical to the continued development of national community sentiment. John Jay, appointed secretary for

State Claims to Western Lands   *The ratification of the Articles of Confederation in 1781 awaited settlement of the western claims of eight states. Vermont, claimed by New Hampshire and New York, was not made a state until 1791, after disputes were settled the previous year. The territory north of the Ohio River was claimed in whole or in part by Virginia, New York, Connecticut, and Massachusetts. All of them had ceded their claims by 1786, except for Connecticut, which had claimed an area just south of Lake Erie, known as the Western Reserve; Connecticut ceded this land in 1800. The territory south of the Ohio was claimed by Virginia, North Carolina, South Carolina, and Georgia; in 1802 the latter became the last state to cede its claims.*

The Northwest Territory and the Land Survey System of the United States

The greatest achievement of the Confederation government was the passing of the Land Ordinance of 1785 and the Northwest Ordinance of 1787. The first act made provision for the federal survey of newly incorporated lands. To avoid the problem of overlapping surveys that could occur under the old system of "metes and bounds" surveying, the authors of the ordinance created an ordered system of survey, dividing the land into townships composed of thirty-six sections of one square mile (640 acres) each. (The differences are clearly evident in the contrast between the patterns of landholding in Ohio, on the left side of the photo, and Pennsylvania, on the right.) The income from section 16 was reserved for the support of local schools, and sections 8, 11, 26, and 29 were held off the market for later sale. First employed in the territory north of the Ohio River, this survey system was used for all the western territory of the United States and has been adopted by many other nations.

With the Northwest Ordinance, Congress established a system of government for the territory north of the Ohio. This legislation established the important principle of eventually bringing new territory

foreign affairs by the Confederation Congress in 1784, attempted to negotiate with the British, but he was told that British troops would not evacuate the Northwest until all outstanding debts from before the war were settled. Jay also attempted to negotiate with the Spanish for guarantees of territorial sovereignty and commercial relations, but he was told that first the United States would have to relinquish free navigation of the Mississippi. Congress would approve no treaty with such terms. Under these frustrating circumstances, some Westerners considered leaving the Confederation. Kentuckians threatened to rejoin the British. The Spanish secretly employed several prominent westerners, including George Rogers Clark and General James Wilkinson, as informants and spies. The people of the West "stand as it were upon a pivot," wrote Washing-

Income from section 16 reserved for school support

16 One section (1 sq. mi.)

THE SURVEY SYSTEM
A township (36 square miles)

Half-section (320 acres)

Quarter-section (160 acres)

Half-quarter-section (80 acres)

Quarter-quarter-sections (40 acres)

into the states on an equal basis with the original thirteen states. The Northwest Territory was eventually divided into the five states that are the focus of this map, and each was admitted to the Union on the date that appears below its name. The Northwest Ordinance also outlawed slavery north of the Ohio River.

Before that process could begin, however, the United States had to establish sovereignty over the country. The British did not abandon the posts that they had continued to occupy after 1783 until June 1, 1796, following the agreement between the United States and Great Britain in Jay's Treaty (1794).

ton in 1784 after a trip down the Ohio. "The touch of a feather would turn them any way." In the West, local community interest continued to override the fragile development of national community sentiment.

In the context of these problems, Congress took up the problem of extending national authority over the West in 1784. Legislation was drafted, principally by Thomas Jefferson, providing for "Government for the Western Territory." The legislation was a remarkable attempt to create a democratic colonial policy. The public domain was to be divided into states, and Congress was to guarantee the settlers in them immediate self-government and republican institutions. Once the population of a territory numbered 20,000, the residents could call a convention and establish a constitution and government of their own choosing. And once the population grew to equal that of the smallest of the original thirteen states, the territory could obtain statehood, provided it agreed to remain forever a member of the Confederation. Fortunately, Congress rejected Jefferson's proposal to provide the future states with names such as Assenisippia and Metropotamia. But it also rejected, by a vote of seven to six, his clause prohibiting slavery.

Passed the following year, the Land Ordinance of 1785 provided for the survey and sale of western lands. To avoid the chaos of overlapping surveys and land claims that had characterized Kentucky, the authors of the ordinance created an ordered system of survey, dividing the land into townships composed of thirty-six sections of one square mile (640 acres) each. This measure would have an enormous impact on the North American landscape, as anyone looking down from an airplane window on the Midwest or West can see. The Land Ordinance also reserved one section in each township for the support of schools; local officials could sell or rent this land to raise money to build schoolhouses or employ teachers. Jefferson argued that all the other land ought to be given away to actual settlers. But Congress, eager to establish a revenue base for the government, provided for the auction of public lands for not less than $1 per acre (the equivalent of $117 in 1990 currency).

In the second Treaty of Fort Stanwix in 1784 and the Treaty of Fort McIntosh in 1785, congressional commissioners forced the Iroquois and some of the Ohio Indians to cede a portion of their territory in what is now eastern Ohio. These treaties were not the result of negotiation; the commissioners dictated the terms by seizing hostages and forcing compliance. Quickly, Congress sent surveyors into the area to divide up the lands. The surveyors did not complete their work and make the lands available for settlers to purchase until the fall of 1788. In the meantime, Congress, desperate for revenue, sold a tract of more than 1.5 million acres to a new land company, the Ohio Company, for $1 million. Jefferson's vision of land for actual settlers seemed to be receding from view.

But thousands of Westerners refused to wait for the official opening of the public land north of the Ohio River. Instead they simply crossed the river and settled illegally. In 1785 Congress raised troops and evicted many of them, but once the soldiers left the squatters returned. The persistence of this problem convinced many congressmen to revise Jefferson's democratic territorial plan. It was necessary, explained Richard Henry Lee of Virginia, "for the security of property among uninformed and perhaps licentious people, as the greater part of those who go there are, that a strong toned government should exist."

In the Northwest Ordinance of 1787, Congress established a system of government for the territory north of the Ohio. Three to five states were to be carved out of the giant Northwest Territory and admitted "on an equal footing with the original states in all respects whatsoever." Slavery was prohibited. But the guarantee of initial self-government in Jefferson's plan was replaced by the rule of a court of judges and a governor appointed by Congress. Once the free white male population of the territory had grown to 5,000, these citizens would be permitted to choose an assembly, but the governor was to have the power of absolute veto on all territorial legislation. National interest would be imposed on the localistic western communities. The Northwest Territory was a huge region that included the future states of Ohio, Indiana, Illinois, Michigan, and Wisconsin. In an early instance of government in the hands of developers, Congress chose Arthur St. Clair, president of the Ohio Company, as the first governor of the Northwest Territory.

The creation of the land system of the United States was the major achievement of the Confederation government. But there were other important accomplishments. Under the Articles of Confederation, Congress led the country through the Revolution and its commissioners negotiated the terms of a comprehensive peace treaty. In organizing the departments of war, foreign affairs, the post office, and finance, the Confederation government created the beginnings of the national bureaucracy.

REVOLUTIONARY POLITICS IN THE STATES

Despite the accomplishments of the Confederation government, most Americans focused not on events in Philadelphia but on those in their own states. Although a strong national community feeling developed during the Revolutionary era, most Americans identified more strongly with their local communities and states than the American nation. People spoke of "these United States," emphasizing the plural, and were relatively unaffected by the national government. The states were the setting for the most important political struggles not only of the Confederation period but for long after.

The Broadened Base of Politics

The political mobilization that took place in 1774 and 1775 greatly broadened political participation. Mass meetings in which ordinary people expressed their opinions, voted, and gained political experience were common, not only in the cities but in small towns and rural communities as well. During these years, a greater proportion of the population began to participate in elections. South Carolina, for example, employed a system of universal white manhood suffrage for the selection of delegates to the Continental Congress, and many other states relaxed property qualifications. Compared with the colonial assemblies, the new state legislatures included more men from rural and western districts—farmers and artisans as well as lawyers, merchants, and large landowners. Many delegates to the Massachusetts provincial congress of 1774 were men from small farming communities who lacked formal education and owned little property.

This transformation was accompanied by a dramatic shift in the political debate. During the colonial period, when only the upper crust of colonial society had been truly engaged by the political process, the principal argument took place between Tory and Whig positions. Tory principles, articulated by royal officials, held that colonial governments were simply convenient instruments of the king's prerogative, serving at his pleasure. The Whig position, on the other hand, was represented by the American colonial elites, who, seeking to preserve and increase their own power, argued for stronger assemblies. They justified their position with arguments about the need for a government balanced with monarchic, aristocratic, and democratic elements, represented by the governor, the upper house, and the assembly, respectively. This debate was ended by the American Revolution. The Tory position lost all legitimacy, indelibly soiled by the taint of Loyalism and treason. There were still plenty of moderate Patriots who took a Whig position on balanced government. But farmers, artisans, and other ordinary people began to argue for a democratic government of the people themselves. For the first time in American history, democracy lost its negative connotations and became a term of approval. One of the most important consequences of the Revolution was a radical shift of the political discourse to the left.

An early post-Revolution debate focused on the appropriate governmental structure for the new states. The new thinking was indicated by the title of a New England pamphlet of 1776, *The People the Best Governors*. Power, the anonymous author argued, should be vested in a single, popularly elected assembly. There should be no property qualifications for either voting or holding office. The governor should simply execute the wishes of the people as voiced by their representatives in the assembly. Judges, too, should be popularly elected, and their decisions reviewed by the assembly. The people, the pamphlet concluded, "best know their wants and necessities, and therefore are best able to govern themselves." The ideal form of government, according to such democrats, was the community or town meeting, in which the people set their own tax rates, created a militia, controlled their own

schools and churches, and regulated the local economy. State government was necessary only for coordination among communities.

Conservative Americans took up the Whig argument on the need for a balanced government. The "unthinking many," wrote another pamphleteer, should be checked by a strong executive and an upper house. Both should be insulated from popular control by property qualifications and long terms in office, designed to draw forth the wisdom and talent of the country's wealthiest and most accomplished men. The greatest danger, according to conservatives, was the possibility of majority tyranny, which might lead to the violation of property rights and to dictatorship. "We must take mankind as they are," one conservative wrote, "and not as we could wish them to be."

The First State Constitutions

Fourteen states—the original thirteen plus Vermont—adopted constitutions between 1776 and 1780. Each of these documents was shaped by debate between radicals and conservatives, democrats and Whigs, and reflected a political balance of power. The constitutions of Pennsylvania, Maryland, and New York typified the political range of the times: Pennsylvania instituted a radical democratic government something like that proposed in *The People the Best Governors*, Maryland created a conservative set of institutions designed to keep citizens and rulers as far apart as possible, and New York adopted a system somewhere in the middle.

In Pennsylvania, a majority of the political conservatives had become Loyalists, allowing the democrats to seize power in 1776. The election of delegates to the constitutional convention was open to every man in the militia, an arrangement that further strengthened the advocates of democracy. The document this convention adopted clearly reflected a democratic agenda. It created a unicameral assembly elected annually by all free male taxpayers. So that delegates would be responsive to their constituents, sessions of the assembly were open to the public and included roll-call votes—the latter somewhat rare in colonial assemblies. There was no governor, but rather an elected executive committee. Judges were removable by the assembly.

By contrast, the Maryland constitution, adopted the same year, was written by conservative planters. It created property requirements for office-holding that left only about 10 percent of Maryland men eligible to serve in the assembly, 7 percent in the senate. A powerful governor, elected by large property owners, controlled a highly centralized government. Judges and other high executive officers served for life. These two states, Maryland and Pennsylvania, represented the political extremes. Georgia, Vermont, and North Carolina followed Pennsylvania's example; South Carolina's constitution was much like Maryland's.

In New York, the constitutional convention of 1777 included a large democratic faction. But conservatives such as John Jay, Gouverneur Morris, and Robert R. Livingston, managing the convention with great skill, helped produce a document that reflected Whiggish principles while still appealing to the people. There would be a bicameral legislature, each house having equal powers. The lower house, or assembly, was democratically elected, but there were stiff property qualifications for election to the upper house, or senate, and senators represented districts apportioned by wealth, not population. The governor, also elected by property owners, had the power of veto, which could be overridden only by a two-thirds vote of both houses. Ultraconservatives wanted a constitution more like Maryland's, but Jay argued that "another turn of the winch would have cracked the cord"; conservatives, in other words, had gotten about as much as they could without alienating the mass of voters. Other states whose constitutions blended democratic and conservative elements were New Hampshire, New Jersey, and Massachusetts.

Declarations of Rights

One of the most important innovations of these constitutions was a guarantee of rights patterned on the Virginia Declaration of Rights of June 1776. Written by George Mason—wealthy planter and brilliant political philosopher—the Virginia declaration set a distinct tone in its very first article: "That all men are by nature equally free and independent, and have certain inherent rights,...namely, the enjoyment of life and liberty, with the means of acquiring and possessing property and pursuing and obtaining happiness and safety." The sixteen articles declared, among other things, that sovereignty resided in the people, that government was the servant of the people, and that the people had the "right to reform, alter, or abolish" that government. There were guarantees of due process and trial by jury in criminal prosecutions, and prohibitions of excessive bail and "cruel and unusual punishments." Freedom of the press was guaranteed as "one of the great bulwarks of liberty," and the people were assured of "the free exercise of religion, according to the dictates of conscience."

Eight state constitutions included a general declaration of rights similar to the first article of the Virginia declaration; others incorporated specific guarantees. A number of states proclaimed the right of the people to engage in free speech and free assembly, to instruct their representatives, and to petition for the redress of grievances—rights either inadvertently or deliberately omitted from Virginia's declaration. These declarations were important precedents for the Bill of Rights, the first ten amendments to the United States Constitution. Indeed, George Mason of Virginia was a leader of those democrats who insisted that the Constitution stipulate such rights.

A Spirit of Reform

The political upheaval of the Revolution raised the possibility of other reforms in American society. The 1776 constitution of New Jersey, by granting the vote to "all free inhabitants" who met the property requirements, enfranchised women as well as men. The number of women voters eventually led to male protests and a new state law explicitly limiting the right to vote to "free white male citizens."

The New Jersey controversy may have been an anomaly, but women's participation in the Revolution wrought subtle but important changes. In 1776 Abigail Adams had written her husband John Adams, away at the Continental Congress: "In the new code of laws which I suppose it will be necessary for you to make I desire you would remember the ladies, and be more generous and favourable to them than your ancestors." In the aftermath of the Revolution, there was evidence of increasing sympathy in the courts for women's property rights and fairer adjudication of women's petitions for divorce. And the postwar years witnessed an increase in opportunities for women seeking an education. From a strictly legal and political point of view, the Revolution may have done little to change women's role in society, but it did seem to help change expectations. Abigail Adams's request to her husband was directed less toward the shape of the new republic than toward the structure of family life. "Do not put such unlimited powers into the hands of husbands," she wrote, "for all men would be tyrants if they could." She had in mind a new, companionate ideal of marriage that contrasted with older notions of patriarchy. Men and women ought to be more like partners, less like master and servant. This new ideal took root in America during the era of the Revolution.

The most steadfast reformer of the day was Thomas Jefferson, who after completing work on the Declaration of Independence returned to Virginia to take a seat in the House of Delegates, convinced that the most important political work lay within his own state. In 1776 he introduced a bill that abolished the law of entails, which had confined inheritance to particular heirs in order that landed property remain undivided. Jefferson believed that entail and primogeniture (inheritance of all the family property by the firstborn son)—legal customs long

By giving the vote to "all free inhabitants," the 1776 constitution of New Jersey enfranchised women as well as men who met the property requirements. The number of women voters eventually led to male protests. Wrote one: "What tho' we read, in days of yore, / The woman's occupation / Was to direct the wheel and loom, / Not to direct the nation." In 1807 a new state law explicitly limited the right of franchise to "free white male citizens."

operating in aristocratic England—had no place in a republican society. The legislation had little practical effect, since relatively few estates were entailed, but the repeal was symbolically important, for it repudiated an aristocratic custom. By 1790, every state but one had followed Virginia's lead (Rhode Island acted in 1798).

Jefferson's other notable success was his Bill for Establishing Religious Freedom. Indeed, he considered this document one of his greatest accomplishments. At the beginning of the Revolution, there were established churches in nine of the thirteen colonies—the Congregationalists in Massachusetts, New Hampshire, and Connecticut, the Anglicans in New York and the South. (See also Chapter 5 for a discussion of colonial religion.) Established religion was increasingly opposed in the eighteenth century, in part because of Enlightenment criticism of the power it had over free and open inquiry but, more important, because of the growing sectarian diversity produced by the religious revival of the Great Awakening. Many Anglican clergymen harbored Loyalist sympathies, and as part of an anti-Loyalist backlash New York, Maryland, the Carolinas, and Georgia had little difficulty passing acts that disestablished the Anglican Church. In Virginia, however, many planters viewed Anglicanism as a bulwark against Baptist and Methodist democratic thinkers, resulting

in bitter and protracted opposition to Jefferson's bill. Patrick Henry, grown conservative, defended state support for the church, and it was not until 1786 that the bill passed.

New England Congregationalists proved even more resistant to change. Although Massachusetts, New Hampshire, and Connecticut allowed dissenters to receive tax support, they maintained the official relationship between church and state well into the nineteenth century. Other states, despite disestablishment, retained religious tests in their legal codes. Georgia, the Carolinas, and New Jersey limited officeholding to Protestants; New York required legislators to renounce allegiance to the pope; and even Pennsylvania, where religious freedom had a long history, required officials to swear to a belief in the divine inspiration of the Old and New Testaments.

Jefferson proposed several more reforms of Virginia law, all of which failed to pass. He would have created a system of public education, revised the penal code to restrict capital punishment to the crimes of murder and treason, and established the gradual emancipation of slaves by law. (This, by the way, marked the third time Jefferson had tried to encourage an end to slavery; the first time in his antislavery clause in the Declaration of Independence, the second with his proposed "Government for the Western Territory" of 1784.) Other states witnessed more progress, but on the whole, the Revolutionary generation, like Jefferson, were more successful in raising these issues than in accomplishing reforms. The problems of penal reform, public education, and slavery remained for later generations of Americans to resolve.

African Americans and the Revolution

For most African Americans, there was little to celebrate in the American victory, because it perpetuated the institution of slavery. Few people were surprised when thousands of black fighters and their families departed with the British at the end of the war, settling in the West Indies, Canada, even Africa. Virginia and South Carolina were said to have lost 30,000 and 25,000 slaves, respectively, as a result of the war.

To many white Americans, as well, there was an obvious contradiction in waging a war for liberty

This portrait of the African American poet Phillis Wheatley was included in the collection of her work published in London in 1773, when she was only twenty. Kidnapped in Africa when a girl, then purchased off the Boston docks, she was more like a daughter than a slave to the Wheatley family, and later married and lived as a free woman of color before her untimely death in 1784.

while continuing to support the institution of slavery. Slavery was first abolished in the state constitution of Vermont in 1777, and in Massachusetts and New Hampshire in 1780 and 1784, respectively. Pennsylvania, Connecticut, and Rhode Island adopted systems of gradual emancipation during these years, freeing the children of slaves at birth. By 1786 every northern state but Delaware had provided for immediate or gradual emancipation of slaves, although as late as 1810, 30,000 African Americans remained enslaved in the North.

In the Upper South, revolutionary idealism, the Christian egalitarianism of Methodists and Baptists, and a shift from tobacco farming to the cultivation of cereal grains such as wheat and corn combined to weaken the commitment of many planters to the slave system. There was a great increase in manumissions—grants of freedom to slaves by individual masters—and a small but important movement encouraged gradual emancipation by convincing masters to free their slaves in their wills. George Washington not only freed several hundred of his slaves on his death but developed an elaborate plan for apprenticeship and tenancy for the able-bodied, lodging and pensions for the aged. Planters in the Lower South, however, heavily dependent on slave labor, resisted the growing calls for an end to slavery. Between 1776 and 1786 all the states but South Carolina and Georgia prohibited or heavily taxed the international slave trade, and this issue became an important point of contention at the Constitutional Convention in 1787 (see Chapter 8).

Perhaps the most important result of these developments was the growth of the free African American population. From a few thousand in 1750, the free African American population grew to more than 200,000 by the end of the century. The increase was most notable in the Upper South. The free black population of Virginia, for example, grew from less than 2,000 in 1780 to approximately 20,000 in 1800. Largely excluded from the institutions of white Americans, the African American community now had sufficient strength to establish schools, churches, and other institutions of its own. Initially this development was opposed. In Williamsburg, Virginia, for instance, the leader of a black congregation was seized and whipped when he attempted to gain recognition from the Baptist Association. But by the 1790s the Williamsburg African Church had more than 500 members, and the association reluctantly recognized it. In Philadelphia the Reverend Absalom Jones established St. Thomas's African Episcopal Church. The incorporation of the term "African" in the names of churches, schools, and mutual benefit societies reflected the pride that African Americans now took in their heritage. New York's African Marine Fund, to take one example, described itself as an organization for assisting "our African brethren and the descendants of our mother country."

A small group of African American writers rose to prominence during the Revolutionary era. Benjamin Banneker, born free in Maryland, where he received an education, was one of the most accomplished mathematicians and astronomers of late-eighteenth-century America. In the 1790s he published a popular almanac that both white and black Americans consulted. Jupiter Hammon, a Long Island slave, took up contemporary issues in his poems and essays, one of the most important of which was his *Address to the Negroes of the State of New York*, published in 1787. The most famous African American writer, however, was Phillis Wheatley, who came to public attention when her *Poems on Various Subjects, Religious and Moral* appeared in London in 1773, while she was still a domestic slave in Boston. Kidnapped as a young girl and converted to Christianity during the Great Awakening, Wheatley wrote poems that combined her piety with a concern for her people. "On Being Brought from Africa to America" is a good example:

> 'Twas mercy brought me from my pagan land,
> Taught my benighted soul to understand
> That there's a God, that there's a Saviour too;
> Once I redemption neither sought nor knew.
> Some view our sable race with scornful eye,
> "Their colour is a diabolic dye."
> Remember, Christians, Negros, black as Cain,
> May be refin'd, and join th'angelic train.

"In every human breast God has implanted a principle, which we call love of freedom; it is impatient of oppression, and pants for deliverance," Wheatley wrote in a letter. "The same principle lives in us."

Economic Problems

During the Revolution, the shortage of goods resulting from the British blockade, the demand for supplies by the army and militias, and the flood of paper currency issued by Congress and the states combined to create the worst inflation that Americans have ever experienced. Continental dollars traded against Spanish dollars at the rate of 3 to 1 in 1777, 40 to 1 in 1779, and 146 to 1 in 1781, by which time Congress had issued more than $190 million in Continentals. Most of this paper ended up in the hands of merchants who paid only a fraction of its face value. There was a popular outcry at the incredible increase in prices, and communities and states in the North responded with laws regulating wages and prices.

The sponsors of wage and price schedules often attributed high prices to hoarding and profiteering. Although it is doubtful that such practices caused the inflation, many merchants did gouge their customers. There were demonstrations and food riots in many communities; men and women demanded fair prices, and when they did not receive them they broke into storehouses and took what they needed. People organized local committees to monitor economic activity and punish wrongdoers. Abigail Adams told of a Boston merchant who refused to sell coffee for the price demanded by the committee. "A number of females, some say a hundred, some say more," she wrote, "seized him by his neck and tossed him into the cart. Upon his finding no quarter he delivered the keys," and the women opened his warehouse and took the coffee. "A large concourse of men stood amazed, silent spectators of the whole transaction."

After the war the primary economic problem was no longer inflation but depression. Political revolution could not alter economic realities: the independent United States continued to be a supplier of raw materials and an importer of manufactured products, and Great Britain remained its most important trading partner. After the Treaty of Paris was signed in 1783, British merchants dumped their unsold goods on the American market, offering easy terms of credit. The production of exportable commodities, however, had been drastically reduced by the fighting.

With few exports to offset all the imports, the trade deficit with Great Britain for the period 1784–86 rose to approximately £5 million in British currency. The deficit acted like a magnet, drawing gold and silver coin from American accounts: according to one estimate, merchants exported £1.3 million in gold and silver coin to Britain during these two years. In turn, these merchants demanded immediate payment from their customers. Short of hard currency, the three commercial banks in the United States—the Bank of North America (Philadelphia), the Bank of New York, and the Bank of Massachusetts (Boston)—insisted on immediate repayment of old loans and refused to issue new ones. The country was left with very little coin in circulation. It all added up to a serious depression, which lasted from 1784 to 1788. At their lowest level, in 1786, prices had fallen 25 percent.

The depression struck while the country was burdened with the huge debt incurred during the Revolution. The total debt owed by the national and state governments amounted to more than $50 million in 1785. (To place this figure in perspective, consider that this debt was approximately sixty-four times greater than the value of American exports for the year 1785; by contrast, the national debt in 1990—considered a crippling burden—was only five times greater than the

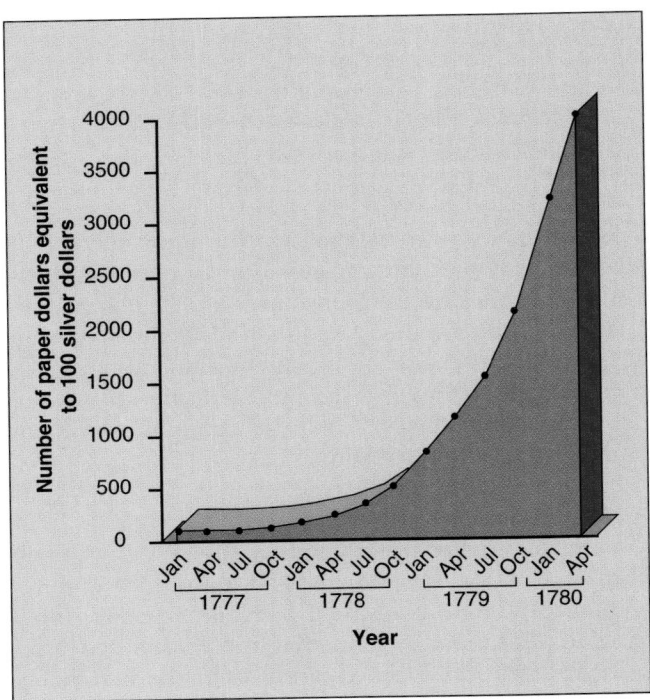

Postwar Inflation, 1777-1780: The Depreciation of Continental Currency (number of paper dollars equal to 100 silver dollars)   *The flood of Continental currency issued by Congress, combined with the shortage of goods resulting from the British blockade, combined to create the worst inflation Americans have ever experienced. Things of no value were said to be "not worth a Continental."*

Source: John McCusker, "How Much Is That in Real Money?" *Proceedings of the American Antiquarian Society,* N.S. 102 (1992): 297–359.

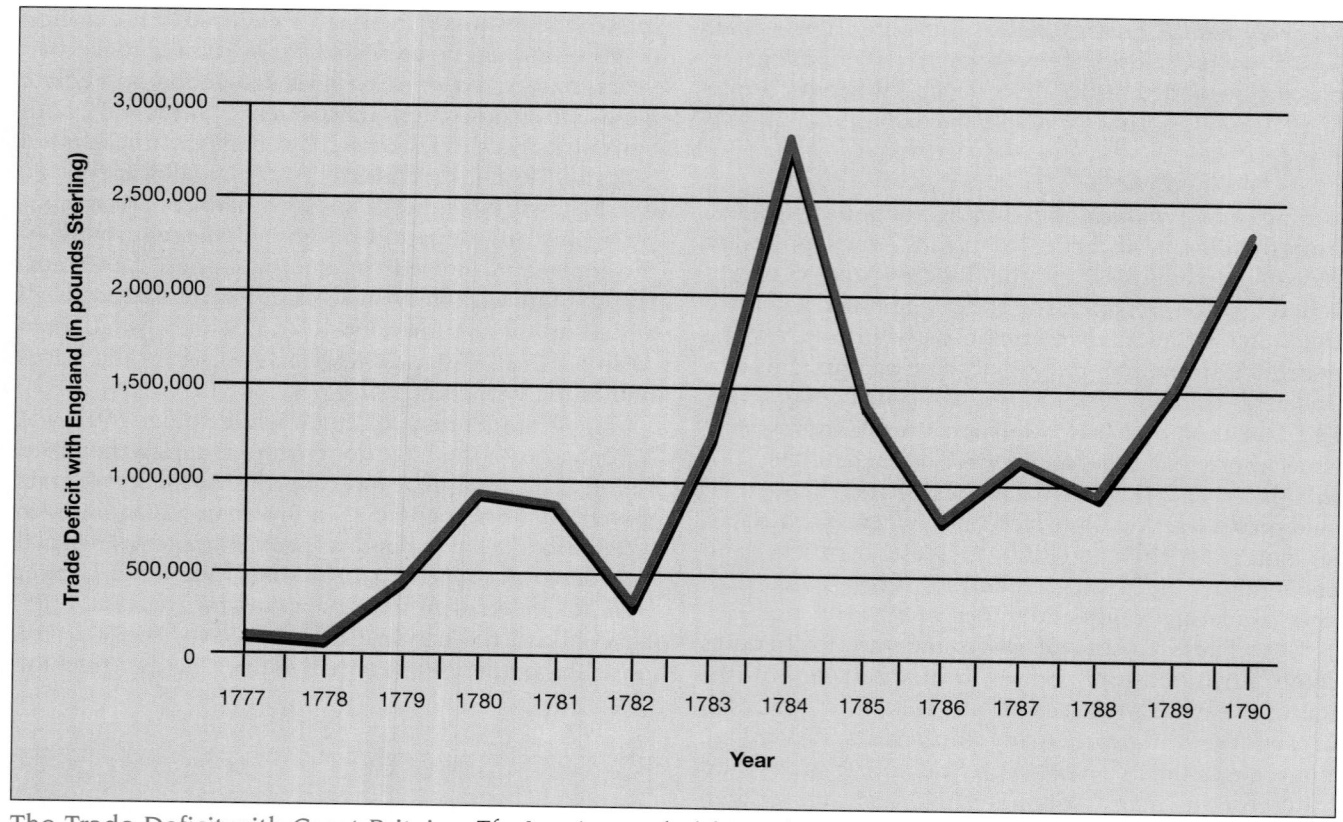

The Trade Deficit with Great Britain *The American trade deficit with Great Britain rose dramatically with the conclusion of the Revolution.*

Source: *Historical Statistics of the United States* (Washington, D.C.:Government Printing Office, 1976), 1176.

value of exports for that year.) Not allowed to raise taxes on its own, the Confederation Congress requisitioned the states for the funds necessary for debt repayment. The states in turn taxed their residents. At a time when there was almost no money in circulation, people rightly feared being crushed by the burden of private debt and public taxes. Thus the economic problem became a political problem.

State Remedies

Where there were manufacturing interests, as in the Northeast, states erected high tariffs to curb imports and protect "infant industries." But shippers could avoid these duties simply by unloading their cargo in nearby seaboard states that lacked tariffs; domestic merchants then distributed the products overland. To be effective, commercial regulation had to be national. Local sentiment had to give way to the unity of a national community. The "means of preserving ourselves," wrote John Adams, [will] "never be secured entirely, until Congress shall be made supreme in foreign commerce, and shall have digested a plan for all the states."

The most controversial economic remedies were those designed to relieve the burden on debtors

and ordinary taxpayers. In some areas, farmers called for laws permitting payment of taxes or debts in goods and commodities, a kind of institutionalized barter. More commonly, farmers and debtors pressed their state governments for "legal tender" laws, laws that would require creditors to accept at specified rates of exchange a state's paper currency—regardless of its worth—for all debts public and private. Understandably, creditors opposed such a plan. But farmers were strong enough to enact currency laws in seven states during the depression. For the most part, these were modest programs that worked rather well, resulted in little depreciation, and did not produce the problems feared by creditors. In most instances, the notes were loaned to farmers, who put up the value of their land as collateral.

It was the radical plan of the state of Rhode Island, however, that received most of the attention. A rural political party campaigning under the slogan "To Relieve the Distressed" captured the legislature in 1786 and enacted a currency law. The supply of paper money issued in relation to the population was much greater under this program than in any other state. The law declared the currency legal tender for all debts. If creditors refused to accept it, people could satisfy their obligations by depositing the money with a county judge, who would then advertise the debt as paid. "In the state of Rogue Island," wrote a shocked merchant, "fraud and injustice" had been "enjoined by solemn law." Conservatives pointed to Rhode Island as an example of the evils that could accompany unchecked democracy. But such programs were perhaps the only alternative without effective national legislation, which required the development of national community sentiment and national political authority.

Shays' Rebellion

In 1786 a rural uprising of communities in Massachusetts shook the nation. Farmers in the western part of the state had been hit particularly hard during the depression, when country merchants pressed them to pay their debts in hard currency they did not possess. About a third of all male heads of household were sued for debt during the 1780s, and the county jails filled with debtors who could not pay. Dozens of towns petitioned the state government for relief, but the legislature, dominated by urban and merchant interests, rejected legal tender and paper currency laws. During the spring and summer of 1786, farmers throughout the rural parts of the state mustered their community militia companies and closed the courts—precisely what they had done during the Revolution. "Whenever any encroachments are made either upon the liberties or properties of the people," declared one rebel, "if redress cannot be had without, it is virtue in them to disturb government."

This uprising quickly became known as Shays' Rebellion, after Daniel Shays, a captain in the Revolution who was one of the leaders of what became known as the Committee of the People. Although the rebellion was most widespread in Massachusetts, similar disorders occurred in every other New England state except Rhode Island, where the farmers had already taken power. There were a number of incidents outside New England as well. A "tumultuary assemblage of the people" closed the court of one Maryland county, and in York, Pennsylvania, 200 armed men stopped a farm auction whose proceeds were marked for debt payment. "Following the example of the insurgents in Massachusetts," a conservative wrote, debtor associations in Virginia prevented auctions and, according to James Madison, officials throughout the state watched "prisons and courthouses and clerks' offices willfully burnt."

The crisis ended when a militia force raised in communities from eastern Massachusetts marched west and crushed the "Shaysites" in January 1787 as they attacked the Springfield armory. Fifteen rebels were subsequently sentenced to death; two were hanged before the remainder were pardoned, and several hundred farmers had to swear an oath of allegiance to the state. In fact, these men had wanted little more than temporary relief from their indebtedness, and rural discontent quickly disappeared once the depression began to lift in 1788.

The most important consequence of Shays' Rebellion was its effect on conservative nationalists unhappy with the distribution of power between the states and national government under the Articles of Confederation. The uprising "wrought prodigious changes in the minds of men respecting the powers of government," wrote the Secretary of War Henry Knox. "Everybody says they must be strengthened and that unless this shall be effected, there is no security for liberty and property." It was time, he declared, "to clip the wings of a mad democracy."

CONCLUSION

The Revolution was a tumultuous era, marked by violent conflict between Patriots and Loyalists, masters and slaves, settlers and Indian peoples. The advocates of independence emerged successful, largely because of their ability to pull together and to begin to define their national community. But fearful of the power of central authority, Americans created a relatively weak national government. People identified strongly with their local and state communities, and these governments became the site for most of the struggles over political direction that characterized the Revolution and its immediate aftermath.

By the mid-1780s, however, many nationalists were paraphrasing Washington's question of 1777: "What then is to become of this nation?" The economic crisis that followed the Revolution sorely tested the

National Portrait Gallery, Smithsonian Institution/Art Resource, NY

A mocking pamphlet of 1787 pictured Daniel Shays and Job Shattuck, two leaders of Shays' Rebellion. The artist gives them uniforms, a flag, and artillery, but the rebels were actually an unorganized group of farmers armed only with clubs and simple muskets. When the rebellion was crushed, Shattuck was wounded and jailed, and Shays along with many others left Massachusetts to settle in a remote region of Vermont.

CHRONOLOGY

1775	Lord Dunmore, royal governor of Virginia, appeals to slaves to support Britain
1776	July: Declaration of Independence
	August: battle of Long Island initiates retreat of Continental Army
	September: British land on Manhattan Island
	December: George Washington counterattacks at Trenton
1777	Slavery abolished in Vermont
	September: British General William Howe captures Philadelphia
	October: British General John Burgoyne surrenders at Saratoga
	November: Continentals settle into winter quarters at Valley Forge
	December: France recognizes American independence
1778	June: France enters the war
	June: battle of Monmouth hastens British retreat to New York
	July: George Rogers Clark captures Kaskaskia
	December: British capture Savannah
1779	Spain enters the war
1780	February: British land at Charleston
	July: French land at Newport
	September: British General Charles Cornwallis invades North Carolina
1781	February: Robert Morris appointed superintendent of finance
	March: Articles of Confederation ratified
	October: Cornwallis surrenders at Yorktown
1782	Peace talks begin
1783	March: Washington mediates issue of officer pensions
	September: Treaty of Paris signed
	November: British evacuate New York
1784	Treaty of Fort Stanwix
	Postwar depression begins
1785	Land Ordinance of 1785
	Treaty of Fort McIntosh
1786	Jefferson's Bill for Establishing Religious Freedom
	Rhode Island currency law
	Shays' Rebellion

resources of local communities, and increasingly people found that local problems were really national problems. Conservative and moderate Patriots, who had been thrown on the defensive by the radical shift of the political debate to the left, saw this as their opportunity to successfully reenter the fray. Led by their Whiggish arguments, increasing numbers of Americans would seek to answer Washington's question by attempting to reform the national government and build a strong new national community.

REVIEW QUESTIONS

1. Assess the relative strengths of the Patriots and the Loyalists in the American Revolution.
2. What roles did Indian peoples and African Americans play in the Revolution?
3. Describe the structure of the Articles of Confederation. What were its strengths and weaknesses?
4. How did the Revolution affect politics within the states?
5. What were the issues in Shays' Rebellion? How do they help to illustrate the political conflict in the nation during the 1780s?

RECOMMENDED READING

Edward Countryman, *The American Revolution* (1985). The best short introduction to the social and political history of the Revolution. Informed by the great outpouring of studies during the twenty years preceding its publication.

Thomas Fleming, *Liberty! The American Revolution* (1997). This well-written account—derived from a public television series—includes wonderful contemporary images.

Merrill Jensen, *The New Nation: A History of the United States during the Confederation, 1781–1789* (1950). Still the standard work on the 1780s.

Charles Patrick Neimeyer, *America Goes to War: A Social History of the Continental Army* (1996). A detailed look at the men who fought and won the Revolution.

Mary Beth Norton, *Liberty's Daughters: The Revolutionary Experience of American Women, 1750–1800* (1980). A provocative and comprehensive history of women in the Revolutionary era. Treats not only legal and institutional change but also the more subtle changes in habits and expectations.

Charles Royster, *A Revolutionary People at War* (1979). A pathbreaking study of the Continental Army and popular attitudes toward it. Emphasizes the important role played by the officer corps and the enlisted men in the formation of the first nationalist constituency.

John Shy, *A People Numerous and Armed* (1976). A series of studies of the local and state militias, demonstrating that their most important contribution was political, not military.

David P. Szatmary, *Shays' Rebellion: The Making of an Agrarian Insurrection* (1980). An excellent study of the famous farmers' rebellion that stimulated conservatives to write the Constitution. Includes a great deal of general background material on the Confederation period, as well as excellent coverage of the specifics of the revolt.

Alfred F. Young, ed., *The American Revolution: Explorations in American Radicalism* (1976). Includes provocative essays on African Americans, Indians, and women.

ADDITIONAL BIBLIOGRAPHY

The War for Independence

Ira Berlin and Ronald Hoffman, eds., *Slavery and Freedom in the Age of the American Revolution* (1983)

Richard Buel Jr., *The Way of Duty: A Woman and Her Family in Revolutionary America* (1984)

Robert M. Calhoon, *The Loyalists in Revolutionary America, 1760–1781* (1973)

Charles E. Claghorn, *Women Patriots of the American Revolution* (1991)

Lawrence D. Cress, *Citizens in Arms: The Army and the Militia in American Society to the War of 1812* (1982)

Paul Finkleman, ed., *Slavery, Revolutionary America, and the New Nation* (1989)

William M. Fowler, *Rebels under Sail: The American Navy during the Revolution* (1976)

Barbara Graymont, *The Iroquois in the American Revolution* (1972)

Ronald Hoffman and Peter J. Albert, eds., *Arms and Independence: The Military Character of the American Revolution* (1984)

Ronald Hoffman and Peter J. Albert, eds., *Women in the Age of the American Revolution* (1989)

Ronald Hoffman and Thad W. Tate, eds., *An Uncivil War: The Southern Backcountry during the American Revolution* (1985)

Mark E. Kann, *A Republic of Men: The American Founders, Gendered Language, and Patriarchial Politics* (1998)

Paul C. Nagel, *The Adams Women: Abigail and Louise Adams, Their Sisters and Daughters* (1987)

Gary B. Nash, *Race and Revolution* (1990)

Mary Beth Norton, *The British Americans: The Loyalist Exiles in England, 1774–1789* (1972)

James O'Donnell, *Southern Indians in the American Revolution* (1973)

Howard W. Peckham, *The Toll of Independence: Engagements and Battle Casualties of the American Revolution* (1974)

Benjamin Quarles, *The Negro in the American Revolution*, rev. ed. (1996)

Jack M. Sosin, *The Revolutionary Frontier, 1763–1783* (1967)

James W. St. G. Walker, *The Black Loyalists* (1976)

Anthony F. C. Wallace, *The Death and Rebirth of the Seneca* (1970)

The United States in Congress Assembled

Robert A. Becker, *Revolution, Reform and the Politics of American Taxation, 1763–1783* (1980)

Richard Beeman, et al., eds., *Beyond Confederation: Origins of the Constitution and American National Identity* (1987)

E. Wayne Carp, *To Starve the Army at Pleasure: Continental Army Administration and American Political Culture, 1774–1783* (1984)

Jack Eblen, *The First and Second United States Empires* (1968)

E. J. Ferguson, *The Power of the Purse: A History of American Public Finance, 1776–1790* (1960)

Calvin C. Jillson, *Congressional Dynamics: Structure, Coordination, and Choice in the First American Congress, 1774–1789* (1994)

Jackson Turner Main, *Political Parties before the Constitution* (1973)

Jack N. Rakove, *The Beginnings of National Politics: An Interpretive History of the Continental Congress* (1979)

Gerald Sourzh, *Benjamin Franklin and American Foreign Policy* (1969)

Gordon S. Wood, *The Creation of the American Republic, 1776–1787* (1969)

Revolutionary Politics in the States

Willi Paul Adams, *The First American Constitutions: Republican Ideology and the Making of the State Constitutions* (1980)

Roger H. Brown, *Redeeming the Republic: Federalists, Taxation, and the Origins of the Constitution* (1993)

Donald S. Lutz, *Popular Consent and Popular Control: Whig Political Theory in the Early State Constitutions* (1980)

Jackson Turner Main, *The Sovereign States, 1775–1789* (1973)

Anne M. Ousterhout, *A State Divided: Opposition in Pennsylvania to the American Revolution* (1987)

Biography

Silvio A. Bedini, *The Life of Benjamin Banneker* (1972)

John Mack Faragher, *Daniel Boone: The Life and Legend of an American Pioneer* (1992)

Douglas Southall Freeman, *George Washington*, 7 vols. (1948–57)

Edith Belle Gelles, *Portia: The World of Abigail Adams* (1992)

Lowell Hayes Harrison, *George Rogers Clark and the War in the West* (1976)

Isabel Thompson Kelsay, *Joseph Brant, 1743–1807: Man of Two Worlds* (1984)

James Kirby Martin, *Benedict Arnold, Revolutionary Hero* (1997)

Willard Sterne Randall, *George Washington: A Life* (1997)

William Henry Robinson, *Phillis Wheatley and Her Writings* (1984)

Rosemarie Zagarri, *A Woman's Dilemma: Mercy Otis Warren and the American Revolution* (1995)

CHAPTER EIGHT

THE UNITED STATES OF NORTH AMERICA

1786–1800

AMERICAN COMMUNITIES
Mingo Creek Settlers Refuse to Pay the Whiskey Tax

On a hot July afternoon in 1794, the federal marshal and the federal tax collector arrived at the backcountry farm of William Miller in Mingo Creek, a community south of Pittsburgh. Like most of his neighbors, Miller had failed to pay the federal excise tax on his homemade whiskey still, and these men had come to serve him with a notice to appear in federal court in Philadelphia. "I felt myself mad with passion," said the farmer, knowing that the fine and the cost of the trip back east would "ruin" him. As the men argued, thirty or forty of Miller's neighbors suddenly appeared, armed with muskets and pitchforks. Members of the Mingo Creek Democratic Society, they had come to fight off this infringement on their liberty. There was an angry confrontation, and someone fired a gun into the air. No one was hit, and after a heated verbal exchange, the two officials rode off. But the farmers were fuming, and they decided to make a "citizen's arrest" of the officials the next day.

At Mingo Creek, poverty was the outstanding fact of life. A third of the farm families owned no land and rented or simply squatted on the acres of others. The tax collector or "exciseman" was one of the great landlords of Mingo Creek, not only controlling most of the local wealth but monopolizing political office as well. Other landlords lived outside the community, the most powerful being President George Washington himself, who owned thousands of acres in the West, much of it in the vicinity of Mingo Creek. The president had evicted so many squatters from his land that local people considered him a grasping speculator. Washington returned the compliment by describing these frontier settlers as "a parcel of barbarians" who were little better than "dogs or cats."

Farm families lived in miserable mud-floored log huts scattered along the creeks of the Monongahela Valley. But despite appearances, the farmers of Mingo Creek were bound together in networks of family and clan, work and barter, religion and politics. The militiamen acted together in what they perceived to be the interests of their community.

Like all the western territories, this was a violent place in a violent time. No-holds-barred fights at local taverns were frequent, and travelers remarked on the presence of one-eyed men, the victims of brutal gougings. Everyone knew of men or women lost in the continuing Indian wars. In 1782 militia companies from the area took their revenge by massacring ninety-six unresisting Christian Indians at Gnadenhutten, north of the Ohio River, hacking their bodies and bringing home their scalps as trophies. The new federal government had committed over 80 percent of its operating budget to defeating the Indians, but the failure of its campaigns left backcountry families resentful.

It was to help pay the costs of these campaigns that Congress had placed the tax on whiskey in 1791. The tax applied to the owners of stills, whether they produced commercially or simply for family and neighbors. Corn was not worth the cost of shipping it east, but whiskey made from corn was another matter, and many a farm family depended on the income from their stills. Farmers throughout America protested that the excise ran counter to Revolutionary principles. "Internal taxes upon consumption," declared the citizens of Mingo Creek, are "most dangerous to the civil rights of freemen, and must in the end destroy the liberties of every country in which they are introduced." Hugh Henry Brackenridge, editor of the *Pittsburgh Gazette*, argued for a tax on the "unsettled lands which all around us have been purchased by speculating men, who keep them up in large bodies and obstruct the population of the country." In other words, Congress should tax land speculators, like President Washington, instead.

Protest followed the course familiar from the Revolution. At first citizens gathered peacefully and petitioned their representatives, but when the tax collectors appeared there was vigilante action. Faces blackened or covered with handkerchiefs, farmers tarred and feathered the tax men. Although the immediate issue was taxation, larger matters were at stake. The Mingo Creek Democratic Society was part of Thomas Jefferson's political movement that supported republicanism and the French Revolution, in opposition to the conservative principles of the Washington administration. The tax protesters made this linkage explicit when they raised banners proclaiming the French slogan of "Liberty, Equality, Fraternity" and adding their own phrase, "and No Excise!" In North Carolina the rebels sang:

Some chaps whom freedom's spirit warms
Are threatening hard to take up arms,
And headstrong in rebellion rise
'Fore they'll submit to that excise:
Their liberty they will maintain,
They fought for't, and they'll
fight again.

But it was only in western Pennsylvania that the protests turned to riot. When the Mingo Creek militia went to arrest the exciseman,

several of their number were killed in the confrontation. The exciseman and his family escaped from their house as it was consumed by a fire set by the farmers. In a community meeting afterward, the farmers resolved to attack and destroy Pittsburgh, where the wealthy and powerful local landlords resided. Terrified residents of the town saved the day by welcoming the rebels with free food and drink. "It cost me four barrels of whiskey that day," declared one man, but "I would rather spare that than a single quart of blood." Destruction was averted, but an angry farmer rode through the street waving a tomahawk and warning: "It is not the excise law only that must go down. A great deal more is to be done. I am but beginning yet."

Declaring the Whiskey Rebellion "the first ripe fruit" of the democratic sentiment sweeping the country, President George Washington organized a federal army of 13,000 men, larger than the one he had commanded during the Revolution, and ordered the occupation of western Pennsylvania. Soldiers dragged half-naked men from their beds and forced them into open pens, where they remained for days in the freezing rain. Authorities arrested twenty people and sent them in irons to Philadelphia, where a judge convicted two of treason and sentenced them to death. The protest gradually died down, and Washington pardoned the felons, sparing their lives.

Federal power had prevailed over the local community. In his Farewell Address to the nation the following year Washington warned of an excessive spirit of localism that "agitates the community with ill-founded jealousies and false alarms; kindles the animosity of one part against another; foments occasionally riot and insurrection." But resistance to the excise remained widespread, and no substantial revenue was ever collected from the tax on whiskey. More important, the whiskey rebels had raised some of the most important issues of the day: the power and authority of the new federal government; the relation of the West to the rest of the nation; the nature of political dissent; and the meaning of the Revolutionary tradition.

Mingo Creek

KEY TOPICS

- The tensions and conflicts between local and national authorities in the decades after the American Revolution

- The struggle to draft the Constitution and to achieve its ratification

- Establishment of the first national government under the Constitution

- The beginning of American political parties

- The first stirrings of an authentic American national culture

FORMING A NEW GOVERNMENT

Eight years before the Whiskey Rebellion a similar rural uprising, Shays' Rebellion (see Chapter 7), had solidified beliefs that the powers of the federal government must be increased lest the budding nation wither. The action at Mingo Creek was the first test of the sovereignty of the newly formed central government, whose strength grew out of the Constitution forged in 1787 by delegates from all the colonies. In putting down the Whiskey Rebellion, federal forces exercised powers that the delegates to the Constitutional Convention agonized over but ultimately granted to the national community they wanted to build.

Nationalist Sentiment

Nationalists had long argued for a strengthened union of the states. Even before ratification of the Articles of Confederation, Alexander Hamilton, a New York lawyer and close associate of George Washington who had served during the Revolution as his aide, was advocating a "solid, coercive union" having "complete sovereignty" over the civil, military, and economic life of the states, along with permanent revenues from taxes and duties. But after emerging victorious from the Revolutionary War, most Americans turned their attention back to the states.

In general, the nationalists were drawn from the elite circles of American life. "Although there are no nobles in America, there is a class of men denominated 'gentlemen,'" the French ambassador to America wrote home in 1786. "They are creditors, and therefore interested in strengthening the government, and watching over the execution of the law. The majority of them being merchants, it is for their interest to establish the credit of the United States in Europe on a solid foundation by the exact payment of debts, and to grant to Congress powers extensive enough to compel the people to contribute for this purpose." In addition to merchants, the ambassador identified others who leaned toward national government: former officers in the Continental Army whose experience with the Continental Congress had made them firm believers in a stronger central government, and conservatives who wanted to restrain what they considered the excessive democracy of the states.

The economic crisis that followed the Revolutionary War (see Chapter 7) provided the nationalists with their most important opportunity to organize. In March 1785 a group of men from Virginia and Maryland, including James Madison, George Mason, and George Washington, drafted an agreement to present to legislatures recommending uniform commercial regulations, duties, and currency laws. Early the next year, at Madison's urging, the Virginia legislature invited all the states to send representatives to a commercial conference to be held at Annapolis.

Only five states sent strong nationalist delegates to the Annapolis Convention in September 1786. Hamilton, who played a leading role at the meeting, drew up a report calling on Congress to endorse a new convention to be held in Philadelphia to discuss all matters necessary "to render the constitution of the federal government adequate to the exigencies of the union." By this time, although there were still serious disagreements between localists and nationalists about the powers of the national government, most Americans agreed that the Articles needed strengthening, especially in regard to commercial regulation and the generation of revenue. Early in 1787, the Confederation Congress cautiously endorsed the plan for a convention "for the sole and express purpose of revising the Articles of Confederation."

The Constitutional Convention

Fifty-five men from twelve states assembled at the Pennsylvania State House in Philadelphia where the convention opened in late May 1787. Rhode Island, where radical localists held power (see Chapter 7), refused to send a delegation. A number of prominent men were missing. Thomas Jefferson and John Adams were serving as ambassadors in Europe, and crusty Patrick Henry declared that he "smelt a rat." Henry had become a localist, and perhaps what bothered him was the predominantly cosmopolitan cast of the meeting. But most of America's best-known leaders were present: George Washington, Benjamin Franklin, Alexander Hamilton, James Madison, George Mason, and Robert Morris. Twenty-nine of them were college educated, thirty-four were lawyers, twenty-four had served in Congress, and twenty-one were veteran officers of the Revolution. At least nineteen owned slaves, and there were also land speculators and merchants. But there were no ordinary farmers or artisans present, and certainly no women, African Americans, or Indians. The Constitution was framed by white men who represented America's social and economic elite.

On their first day of work, the delegates agreed to vote by states, as was the custom in the Confederation Congress. They chose Washington to chair the meeting, and to ensure candid debate they decided to keep their sessions secret. James Madison took voluminous daily minutes, however, providing us with a record of what happened behind the convention's locked doors. Madison, a conservative young Virginian with a profound knowledge of history and political philosophy, had arrived several days before the convention opened, and with his fellow

George Washington presides over a session of the Constitutional Convention, meeting in Philadelphia's State House (now known as Independence Hall), in an engraving of 1799.

Virginians had drafted what became known as the Virginia Plan. Presented by Virginia Governor Edmund Randolph on May 29, it set the convention's agenda.

The authors of the Virginia Plan proposed scrapping the Articles of Confederation in favor of a "consolidated government" having the power to tax and to enforce its laws directly rather than through the states. "A spirit of locality," Madison declared, was destroying "the aggregate interests of the community," by which he meant the great community of the nation. Madison's plan would have reduced the states to little more than administrative districts. Representation in the bicameral national legislature would be based on population: the members of the House of Representatives were to be elected by popular vote, but senators would be

chosen by state legislators so that they might be insulated from democratic pressure. The Senate would lead, controlling foreign affairs and the appointment of officials. An appointed chief executive and a national judiciary would together form a Council of Revision having the power to veto both national and state legislation.

The main opposition to these proposals came from the delegates from small states, which feared being swallowed up by the large ones. After two weeks of debate, William Paterson of New Jersey introduced an alternative, a set of "purely federal" principles known since as the New Jersey Plan. He proposed increasing the powers of the central government but retaining a single-house Congress in which the states were equally represented. After much debate and a series of votes that split the convention down the middle, the delegates finally agreed to what has been called the Great Compromise: proportional representation by population in the House, representation by states in the Senate. The compromise allowed the creation of a strong national government while still providing an important role for the states.

Part of this agreement was a second, fundamental compromise that brought together the delegates from North and South. To boost their power in the new government, the southern delegates wanted to include slaves in the population to be counted for the purpose of determining state representation, but to exclude them when it came to apportioning taxes. Ultimately it was agreed that five slaves would be counted as the equal of three freemen—the "three-fifths rule." Furthermore, the representatives of South Carolina and Georgia demanded protection for the international slave trade, and after bitter debate the delegates included a provision preventing any prohibition of the importation of slaves for twenty years. Another article legitimized the return of fugitive slaves from free states. Although the word "slave" does not appear anywhere in the Constitution (the framers avoided it with such phrases as "other persons" and "persons held to labor," these provisions nonetheless amounted to national guarantees for southern slavery. Many delegates were opposed to slavery and regretted having to give in on this issue, but they agreed with Madison, who wrote that "great as the evil is, a dismemberment of the union would be worse."

There was still much to decide regarding the other branches of government. Madison's Council of Revision was scratched in favor of a strong federal judiciary with the implicit power to declare acts of Congress unconstitutional. Demands for a powerful chief executive raised fears that the office might prove to be, in the words of Edmund Randolph of Virginia, "the fetus of monarchy." But there was considerable support for a president with veto power to check the legislature. In fact, according to James McHenry, a delegate from Maryland, twenty-one delegates favored some form of monarchy, and Alexander Hamilton went on record supporting the creation of a constitutional monarch. To keep the president independent of Congress, the delegates decided he should be elected; but fearing that ordinary voters could never "be sufficiently informed" to select wisely, they insulated the process from popular choice by creating the electoral college. Voters in the states would not actually vote for president. Rather, in a manner to be determined by its legislature, each state would select a slate of "electors" equal in number to the state's total representation in the House and Senate. Following the general election, the electors in each state would meet to cast their ballots and elect the president.

In early September the delegates turned their rough draft of the Constitution over to a Committee of Style that shaped it into an elegant and concise document setting forth the general principles and basic framework of government. But Madison, known to later generations as "the Father of the Constitution," was gloomy, believing that the revisions of his original plan doomed the Union to the kind of inaction that had characterized government under the Articles of Confederation. It was left for Franklin to make the final speech to the convention. "Can a perfect production be expected?" he asked. "I consent, Sir, to this Constitution, because I expect no better, and because I am not sure that it is not the best." The delegates voted their approval on September 17, 1787, and transmitted the document to Congress, agreeing that it would become operative after ratification by nine states. Some congressmen were outraged that the convention had exceeded its charge of simply modifying the Articles of Confederation, but Congress called for a special ratifying convention in each of the states.

Ratifying the New Constitution

The supporters of the new Constitution immediately adopted the name Federalists to describe themselves. Their outraged opponents objected that the existing Confederation already provided for a "federal" government of balanced power between the states and the Union and that the Constitution would replace it with a "national" government. But in this, as in much of the subsequent process of ratification, the Federalists (or nationalists) grabbed the initiative, and their opponents had to content themselves with the label Anti-Federalists. Mercy Otis Warren, a leading critic of the Constitution, commented on the dilemma in which the Anti-Federalists found themselves. "On the one hand," she wrote, "we stand in need of a strong federal government, founded on principles that will support the prosperity and union of the colonies. On the other, we have struggled for liberty and made costly sacrifices at her shrine and there are still many among us who revere her name too much to relinquish, beyond a certain medium, the rights of man for the dignity of government."

The critics of the Constitution were by no means a unified group. Because most of them were localists, they represented a variety of social and regional interests. But most believed the Constitution granted far too much power to the center, weakening the autonomy of communities and states. As local governments "will always possess a better representation of the feelings and interests of the people at large," one critic wrote, "it is obvious that these powers can be deposited with much greater safety with the state than the general government."

All the great political thinkers of the eighteenth century had argued that a republican form of government could work only for small countries. As the French philosopher Montesquieu had observed, "In an extensive republic, the public good is sacrificed to a thousand private views." But in *The Federalist*, a series of brilliant essays in defense of the Constitution written in 1787 and 1788 by Madison, Hamilton, and John Jay, Madison stood Montesquieu's assumption on its head. Rhode Island had demonstrated that the rights of property might not be protected in even the smallest of states. Asserting that "the most common and durable source of factions has been the various and unequal distribution of property," Madison concluded that the best way to control such factions was to "extend the sphere" of government. That way, he continued, "you take in a greater variety of parties and interests; you make it less probable that a majority of the whole will have a common motive to invade the rights of other citizens; or, if such a common motive exists, it will be more difficult for all who feel it to discover their own strength and to act in unison with each other." Rather than a disability, Madison argued, great size is an advantage: interests are so diverse that no single faction is able to gain control of the state, threatening the freedoms of others.

It is doubtful whether Madison's sophisticated argument, or the arguments of the Anti-Federalists for that matter, made much of a difference in the popular voting in the states to select delegates for the state ratification conventions. The alignment of forces generally followed the lines laid down during the fights over economic issues in the years since the Revolution. For example, in Pennsylvania—the first state to convene a ratification convention, in November 1787—48 percent of the Anti-Federalist delegates to the convention were farmers. By contrast, 54 percent of the Federalists were merchants, manufacturers, large landowners, or professionals. What tipped the Pennsylvania convention in favor of the Constitution was the wide support the document enjoyed among artisans and commercial farmers, who saw their interests tied to the growth of a commercial society. As one observer pointed out, "The counties nearest [navigable waters] were in favor of it generally, those more remote, in opposition."

Similar agrarian-localist and commercial-cosmopolitan alignments characterized most of the other states. The most critical convention took place in Massachusetts in early 1788. Five states—Delaware, Pennsylvania, New Jersey, Georgia, and Connecticut—had already voted to ratify, but the states with the strongest Anti-Federalist movements had yet to convene. If the Constitution lost in Massachusetts, its fate would be in great danger. At the convention, Massachusetts opponents of ratification enjoyed a small

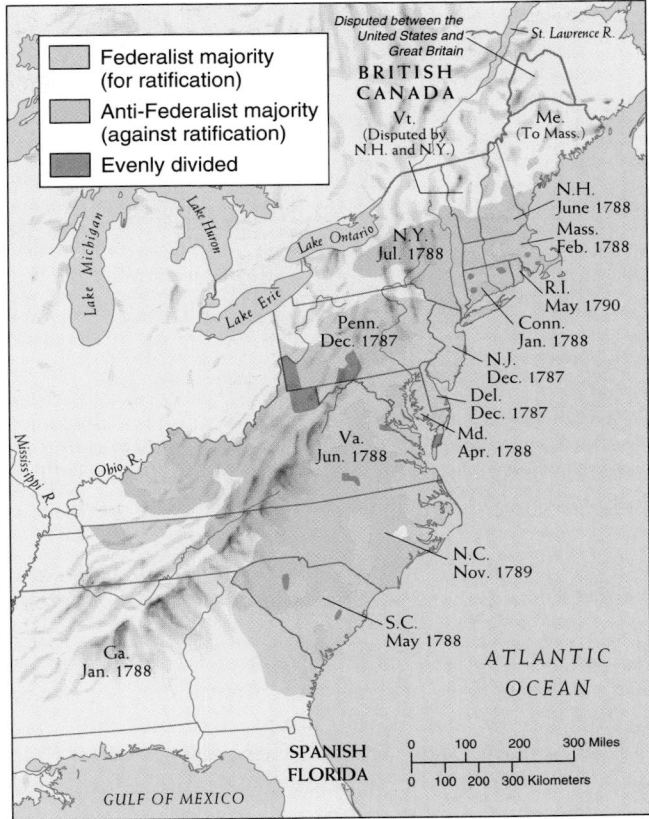

The Ratification of the Constitution, 1787–1790
The distribution of the vote for the ratification of the Constitution demonstrated its wide support in sections of the country linked to the commercial economy and its disapproval in more remote and backcountry sections. (Note that Maine remained a part of Massachusetts until admitted as a separate state in 1820.)

majority. But several important Anti-Federalist leaders, including Samuel Adams, were swayed by the enthusiastic support for the Constitution among Boston's townspeople, and on February 6 the convention voted narrowly in favor of ratification. To no one's surprise, Rhode Island rejected the Constitution in March, but Maryland and South Carolina approved it in April and May. On June 21, New Hampshire became the ninth state to ratify.

Anti-Federalist support was strong in New York, Virginia, and North Carolina. North Carolina voted to reject and did not join the union until the next year; it was followed by a still reluctant Rhode Island in 1790. In New York, the delegates were moved to vote their support by a threat from New York City to secede from the state and join the Union separately if the convention failed to ratify. The Virginia convention was almost evenly divided, but promises to amend the Constitution to protect individual rights persuaded enough delegates to produce a victory for the Consti-

A cartoon published in July 1788 when New York became the eleventh state to ratify the Constitution. After initially voting to reject, North Carolina soon reconsidered, but radical and still reluctant Rhode Island did not join the Union until 1790.

tution. The promise of a Bill of Rights, in fact, was important in the ratification vote of five of the states.

Shaping the Bill of Rights

Although the Bill of Rights—the first ten amendments to the Constitution—was adopted during the first session of the new federal Congress, it was first proposed during the debates over ratification. The Constitutional Convention had considered a Bill of Rights patterned on the declarations of rights in the state constitutions (see Chapter 7) but rejected it as superfluous, agreeing with Madison that the federal government would exercise only those powers expressly delegated to it. However, George Mason, author of Virginia's Declaration of Rights, refused to sign the Constitution because it failed to contain similar provisions. He played an important role in getting the Virginia ratifying convention to endorse a set of constitutional amendments. Campaigning for a seat in the new Congress, Madison was pressed to affirm his willingness to propose and support a set of amendments guaranteeing "essential rights."

The various state ratification conventions had proposed a grab bag of more than 200 potential amendments. Madison set about transforming these into a series that he introduced into the new Congress in June 1789. Congress passed twelve and sent them to the states in September, and ten survived the ratification process to become the Bill of Rights in 1791.

The First Amendment prohibits Congress from establishing an official religion and provides for the freedoms of speech and the press and the right of assembly and petition. The other amendments guarantee the right to bear arms, limit the government's power to quarter troops in private homes, and restrain the government from unreasonable searches or seizures; they assure the people their legal rights under the common law, includ-

ing the prohibition of double jeopardy, the right not to be compelled to testify against oneself, and due process of law before life, liberty, or property can be taken. Finally, the unenumerated rights of the people are protected, and those powers not delegated to the federal government are reserved to the states.

The first ten amendments to the Constitution have been a restraining influence on the growth of government power over American citizens. Their provisions have become an admired aspect of the American political tradition throughout the world. The Bill of Rights is the most important constitutional legacy of the Anti-Federalists.

THE NEW NATION

Ratification of the Constitution was followed by the first federal elections—for the congress and the presidency—and in the spring of 1789 the new federal government assumed power in the temporary capital of New York City. The inauguration of George Washington as the first president of the United States took place on April 30, 1789, on the balcony of Federal Hall, at the corner of Wall and Broad Streets. Reelected without opposition in 1792, Washington would serve until 1797.

The activities of the first federal government were far removed from the everyday lives of most Americans, but as the Whiskey Rebellion demonstrated, there were moments when the two intersected dramatically. Moreover, the first years under the new federal Constitution were especially important for the future, because they shaped the structure of the American state in ways that would be enormously significant for later generations.

The Washington Presidency

During its first month, the Congress debated what to call the president of the United States. Believing that no government could long endure without the awe and veneration of its citizens, Vice President John Adams, sitting as the president of the Senate, proposed "His Highness the President of the United States." But a majority in the House of Representatives saw this title as a dangerous flirtation with "monarchism." When someone proposed that the nation's coinage be stamped with a bust of the president, men of republican persuasion protested that such veneration would be too much like the customs of the British empire. The president himself finally resolved the controversy by declaring the whole topic had been raised "without any privity of knowledge of it on my part," and by custom he came to be addressed simply as "Mr. President." This issue encapsulated an important conflict of these early years—the desire of some nationalists to add to the power of executive authority, versus the faith of localists in a strong Congress.

Although he dressed in plain American broadcloth at his inauguration and claimed to be content with a plain republican title, Washington was counted among the nationalists. He was anything but a man of the people, by nature reserved and solemn, choosing to ride about town in a grand carriage drawn by six horses and escorted by uniformed liverymen. In the tradition of British royalty, he delivered his addresses personally to Congress and received from both houses an official reply. These customs were continued by John Adams, Washington's successor, but ended by Thomas Jefferson, who denounced them as "rags of royalty," and began the practice, continued throughout the nineteenth century, of sending written presidential messages to Congress. On the other hand, Washington worked hard to adhere to the letter of the Constitution, refusing, for example, to use the veto power except where he thought the Congress had acted unconstitutionally, and personally seeking the "advice and consent" of the Senate.

Congress quickly moved to establish departments to run the executive affairs of state, and Wash-

ington soon appointed Thomas Jefferson his secretary of state, Alexander Hamilton to run the Treasury, Henry Knox the War Department, and Edmund Randolph the Justice Department, as attorney general. The president consulted each of these men regularly, and during his first term met with them as a group to discuss matters of policy. By the end of Washington's presidency the secretaries had coalesced in what came to be known as the cabinet, an institution that has survived to the present despite the absence of constitutional authority or enabling legislation giving it formal recognition. Washington was a powerful and commanding personality, but he understood the importance of national unity, and in his style of leadership, his consultations, and his appointments he sought to achieve a balance of conflicting political perspectives and sectional interests. These intentions would be sorely tested during the eight years of his administration.

An Active Federal Judiciary

The most important piece of legislation to emerge from the first session of Congress was the Judiciary Act of 1789, which implemented the judicial clause of the Constitution and set up a system of federal courts.

Daniel Huntington's Republican Court *emphasized the similarities between American republican government and the royal courts of Europe. When Vice President John Adams proposed that the president be addressed as "His Highness," democrats in the Congress argued this was a dangerous flirtation with "monarchism," and Thomas Jefferson urged that the government give up such "rags of royalty."*

Congress provided that the Supreme Court consist of six justices (later increased to nine) and established three circuit and thirteen district courts. Strong nationalists argued for a powerful federal legal system that would provide a uniform code of civil and criminal justice throughout the country. But the localists in Congress fought successfully to retain the various bodies of law that had developed in the states. They wanted to preserve local community autonomy. The act gave federal courts limited original jurisdiction, restricting them mostly to appeals from state courts. But it thereby established the principle of federal judicial review of state legislation, despite the silence of the Constitution on this point.

Under the leadership of Chief Justice John Jay, the Supreme Court heard relatively few cases during its first decade. Still, it managed to raise considerable political controversy. In *Chisholm v. Georgia* (1793) it ruled in favor of two South Carolina residents who had sued the state of Georgia for the recovery of confiscated property. Thus did the Court overthrow the common law principle that a sovereignty could not be sued without its consent, and supported the Constitution's grant of federal jurisdiction over disputes "between a state and citizens of another state." Many localists feared that this nationalist ruling threatened the integrity of the states. In response, they proposed the Eleventh Amendment to the Constitution, ratified in 1798, which declared that no state could be sued by citizens from another state. The Supreme Court nevertheless established itself as the final authority on questions of law when it invalidated a Virginia statute in *Ware v. Hylton* (1796) and upheld the constitutionality of an act of Congress in *Hylton v. U.S.* (1796).

Hamilton's Controversial Fiscal Program

Fiscal and economic affairs pressed upon the new government. Lacking revenues, and faced with the massive national debt contracted during the Revolution, it took power in a condition of virtual bankruptcy. At the urging of James Madison, whose first official position in the United States government was floor leader for the Washington administration in the House of Representatives, Congress passed the Tariff of 1789, a compromise between advocates of protective tariffs (duties so high that they made foreign products prohibitively expensive, thus "protecting" American products) and those who wanted moderate tariffs that produced income. Duties on imported goods, rather than direct taxes on property or incomes, would constitute the bulk of federal revenues until the twentieth century.

After setting this system of duties in place, Congress turned to the problem of the debt. In January 1790, Hamilton submitted a "Report on the Public Credit," in which he recommended that the federal government assume the obligations accumulated by the states during the previous fifteen years and redeem the national debt—owed to both domestic and foreign leaders—by agreeing to a new issue of interest-bearing bonds. To raise the revenue required to retire the debt, Hamilton recommended an excise tax on the manufacture of distilled liquor.

By this means, Hamilton sought to inspire the confidence of domestic and foreign investors in the public credit of the new nation. Congress endorsed his plan to pay off the $11 million owed to foreign creditors but balked at funding the domestic debt of $27 million and assuming the state debts of $25 million. The funding of the domestic debt aroused debate because necessity had forced many individuals to sell off at deep discounts the notes, warrants, and securities the government had issued them during the Revolution. Yet Hamilton now advocated paying these obligations at face value, providing any speculator who held them with fabulous profits. The assumption of state debts aroused even greater debate because some states, mostly those in the South, had already arranged to liquidate their debts, whereas others had left theirs unpaid.

Congress remained deadlocked on these issues for six months, until congressmen from Pennsylvania and Virginia arranged a compromise. Final agreement, however, was stalled by a sectional dispute over the permanent location of the new national capital. Southerners supported Washington's desire to plant it on the Potomac River, but northerners argued for Philadelphia. In return for Madison's pledge to obtain enough southern votes to pass Hamilton's assumption plan—which Madison had earlier opposed as a "radically immoral" windfall for speculators—northern congressmen agreed to a location for the new federal district on the boundary of Virginia and Maryland. In July 1790, Congress passed legislation moving the temporary capital from New York to Philadelphia until the expected completion of the federal city, in 1800, in a "District of Columbia" that would be under the jurisdiction of Congress. Two weeks later it adopted Hamilton's credit program. This was the first of many sectional compromises.

Hamilton now proposed the second component of his fiscal program, the establishment of a Bank of the United States. The bank, a public corporation funded by private capital, would serve as the depository of government funds and the fiscal agent of the Treasury. Congress narrowly approved it, but Madison's opposition raised doubts in the president's mind about the constitutionality of the measure, and Washington solicited the opinion of his cabinet. Here for the first time were articulated the classic interpretations of constitutional authority. Jefferson took a "strict constructionist" position, arguing that the powers of the federal government must be limited to those specifically enumerated in the Constitution. This position came closest to the basic agreement of the men who had drafted the document. Hamilton, on the other hand, reasoned that the Constitution "implied" the power to use whatever means were "necessary and proper" to carry out its enumerated powers—a "loose constructionist" position. Persuaded by Hamilton's opinion, Washington signed the bill, and the bank went into operation in 1791.

Hamilton's "Report on Manufactures," submitted to Congress in December 1791, was the capstone to his comprehensive economic program. It contained an ambitious plan involving the use of government securities as investment capital for "infant industries," federal bounties to encourage innovation, and high protective tariffs. This system, Hamilton hoped, would promote the development of an industrial economy. Congressmen from farming areas, whose previous objections to Hamilton's preference for the "monied interests" had not prevailed, were finally able to frustrate him on this proposal. Hamilton's views, they argued, would limit them to roles exactly like those they had played within the British empire; in effect they would be exchanging British for Boston and New York masters. Of equal importance, the plan failed to inspire American capitalists, who continued to be more interested in investments in shipping or in land speculation than in industrial production.

Many of Hamilton's specific proposals for increased tariff protection became part of a revision of duties that took place in 1792. Moreover, his fiscal program as a whole dramatically restored the financial health of the United States. Foreign investment in government securities increased and along with domestic capital provided the Bank of the United States with enormous reserves. Its bank notes became the most important circulating medium of the North American commercial economy, and their wide acceptance greatly stimulated business enterprise. "Our public credit," Washington declared toward the end of his first term, "stands on that ground which three years ago it would have been considered as a species of madness to have foretold."

The Beginnings of Foreign Policy

The Federalist political coalition, forged during the ratification of the Constitution, was sorely strained by these debates over fiscal policy. By the middle of 1792, Jefferson, representing the southern agrarians, and Hamilton, speaking for northern capitalists, were locked in a full-scale feud within the Washington administration. Hamilton conducted himself more like a prime minister than a cabinet secretary, greatly offending Jefferson, who considered himself the pres-

ident's heir apparent. But the dispute went deeper than a mere conflict of personalities. Hamilton stated the difference clearly when he wrote that "one side appears to believe that there is a serious plot to overturn the State governments, and substitute a monarchy to the present republican system," whereas "the other side firmly believes that there is a serious plot to overturn the general government and elevate the separate powers of the States upon its ruins." The conflict between Hamilton and Jefferson was to grow even more bitter over the issue of American foreign policy.

The commanding event of the Atlantic world during the 1790s was the French Revolution, which had begun in 1789. Most Americans enthusiastically welcomed the fall of the French monarchy. After the people of Paris stormed the Bastille, the new French republic sent Washington the key to the prison's doors as a symbol of the relationship between the two revolutions. But with the beginning in 1793 of the Reign of Terror, whose bloody guillotine claimed the lives of hundreds of aristocrats, American conservatives began to voice their opposition. The execution of King Louis XVI, and especially the onset of war between revolutionary France and monarchical Great Britain in 1793, firmly divided American opinion.

Most at issue was whether the Franco-American alliance of 1778 required the United States to support France in its war with Britain. All of Washington's cabinet agreed on the importance of American neutrality. With France and Britain prowling for each other's vessels on the high seas, the vast colonial trade of Europe was delivered up to neutral powers, the United States prominent among them. Neutrality, in other words, meant windfall profits. Jefferson believed it highly unlikely that the French would call on the Americans to honor the 1778 treaty; the administration should simply wait and see. Hamilton argued, however, that so great was the danger that Washington should immediately declare the treaty "temporarily and provisionally suspended."

These disagreements revealed two contrasting perspectives on the course the United States should chart in international waters. Hamilton believed in the necessity of an accommodation with Great Britain, the most important trading partner of the United States and the world's greatest naval power. Jefferson and Madison, on the other hand, looked for more international independence, pinning their hopes on the future of western expansion. There was room for compromise between these two points of view, but in the debate over the French Revolution positions tended to become polarized.

The debate in the United States grew hotter with the arrival in April 1793 of French ambassador Edmond Genêt. Large crowds of supporters greeted him throughout the nation, and among them he solicited contributions and distributed commissions authorizing American privateering raids against the British. Understandably, a majority of Americans still nursed a hatred of imperial Britain, and many had considerable sympathy for republican France. Like Hamilton, however, conservatives favored a continuation of traditional commercial relations with Britain and feared the anti-aristocratic violence of the French. Washington sympathized with Hamilton's position, but most of all he wished to preserve American independence and neutrality. Knowing he must act before "Citizen" Genêt (as the ambassador was popularly known) compromised American sovereignty and involved the United States in a war with Britain, the president issued a proclamation of neutrality on April 22, 1793. In it he assured the world that the United States intended to pursue "a conduct friendly and impartial towards the belligerent powers," while continuing to do business with all sides.

Hamilton's supporters applauded the president, but Jefferson's were outraged. "The cause of France is the cause of man," declared Hugh Henry Brackenridge of Pittsburgh, "and neutrality is desertion." Throughout the country those sympathetic to France organized Democratic Societies, political clubs modeled after the Sons of Liberty. Society members corresponded with each other, campaigned on behalf of candidates, and lobbied with congressmen. People interpreted the international question in the light of issues of local importance. Thus the members of the Mingo Creek Democratic Society used enthusiasm for the French Revolution as a way of organizing political opposition to the Washington administration. Brackenridge described the society's Mingo Creek chapter as "an engine of election," in other words, a political machine. In a speech to Congress, President Washington denounced what he called these "self-created societies," declaring them "the most diabolical attempt to destroy the best fabric of human government and happiness."

Citizen Genêt miscalculated, however, alienating even his supporters, when he demanded that Washington call Congress into special session to debate neutrality. Jefferson, previously a confidant of the ambassador, now denounced Genêt as "hot-headed" and "indecent towards the President." But these words came too late to save his reputation in the eyes of President Washington, and at the end of 1793 Jefferson left the administration. The continuing upheaval in France soon swept Genêt's party from power, and another minister from France arrived with a warrant for his arrest. Fearing the guillotine, Genêt claimed sanctuary and remained in the United States. The Citizen Genêt affair furthered the division of the Federalist coalition into one faction identifying with Washington, Hamilton, and conservative principles and another faction supporting Jefferson, Madison, democracy, and the French Revolution.

The United States and the Indian Peoples

Among the many problems of the Washington presidency, one of the most pressing concerned the West. The American attempt to treat the western Indian tribes as conquered peoples after the Revolution had resulted only in further violence and warfare. The Northwest Ordinance of 1787 (see Chapter 7) signaled a new approach. "The utmost good faith shall always be observed towards the Indians," it read. "Their lands and property shall never be taken from them without their consent; and in their property, rights, and liberty, they shall never be invaded or disturbed, unless in just and lawful wars authorized by Congress." Although the Constitution was silent regarding Indian policy, Congress endorsed this statutory recognition of the independent character of the Indian tribes when in 1790 it passed the Indian Intercourse Act, the basic law by which the United States would "regulate trade and intercourse with the Indian tribes." To eliminate the abuses of unscrupulous traders, the act created a federal licensing system; subsequent amendments authorized the creation of subsidized trading houses, or "factories," where Indians could obtain goods at reasonable prices. Trade abuses continued unabated for lack of adequate policing power, but

Spread of Settlement: The Backcountry Expands, 1770–1790   *From 1770 to 1790 American settlement moved across the Appalachians for the first time. The Ohio Valley became the focus of bitter warfare between Indians and settlers.*

these provisions indicated the good intentions of the Washington administration.

To clarify the question of Indian sovereignty, the Indian Intercourse Act declared public treaties between the United States and the Indian nations to be the only legal means of obtaining Indian land. Treaty making thus became the procedure for establishing and maintaining relations. Although the federal government frequently applied military pressure to secure the signing of such treaties, the process preserved a semblance of legality. In the twentieth century, a number of Indian tribes have successfully appealed for the return of lands obtained by states or individuals in violation of this provision of the Intercourse Act.

Yet conflict continued to characterize the relationship of Americans and Indian peoples, for one of the American government's highest priorities was the acquisition of Indian land to supply a growing population of farmers. American settlers along the Ohio River, wrote one army officer, "carry on private expeditions against the Indians and kill them whenever they meet them," and there was not a jury in the

Little Turtle, a war chief of the Miami tribe of the Ohio valley, led a large pan-Indian army to victory over the Americans in 1790 and 1791. After his forces were defeated at the Battle of Fallen Timbers in 1794, he became a friend of the United States. This lithograph is a copy of an oil portrait, painted by the artist Gilbert Stuart, which no longer survives.

West, he added, that would dare to punish a man for these crimes. In defense of their homelands, villages of Shawnees, Delawares, and other Indian peoples confederated with the Miamis under their war chief Little Turtle. In the fall of 1790 Little Turtle lured an American expeditionary force led by General Josiah Harmar into the confederacy's stronghold in Ohio and badly mauled them. In November 1791 the confederation inflicted an even more disastrous defeat on a large American force under General Arthur St. Clair, governor of the Northwest Territory. More than 900 Americans were killed or wounded, making this the worst defeat of an army by Indians in North American history.

Spanish and British Hostility

The position of the United States in the West was made even more precarious by the hostility of Spain and Great Britain, which controlled the adjoining terri-

tory. Under the dynamic leadership of King Carlos III and his able ministers, Spain introduced liberal reforms to revitalize the rule-bound economy of its American empire; as a result the economy of New Spain experienced a period of rapid growth in the 1780s. Moreover, Spain had reasserted itself in North America, acquiring the French claims to Louisiana before the end of the Seven Years War, expanding into California, seizing the Gulf coast during the American Revolution, and regaining Florida from Britain in the Treaty of Paris in 1783. The Spanish were deeply suspicious of the Americans. The settlers, the Spanish governor of Florida declared, "were nomadic like Arabs,…distinguished from savages only in their color, language, and the superiority of their depraved cunning and untrustworthiness." Spain claimed for itself most of the territory south of the Ohio River and pursued a policy designed to block the expansion of the new republic.

Spain's anti-American policy in the West had several facets. Controlling both sides of the lower Mississippi, the Spanish closed the river to American shipping, making it impossible for western American farmers to market their crops through the port of New Orleans. The Spanish also sought to create a barrier to American settlement by promoting immigration to Louisiana and Florida. They succeeded in attracting several thousand of the Acadians deported by the British during the Seven Years War, who reassembled their distinctive communities in the bayou country of Louisiana (see Chapter 6). But otherwise the Spanish had little success with immigration and relied mostly on creating a barrier of pro-Spanish Indian nations in the lower Mississippi Valley. In exchange for supplies and Spanish recognition of them as "free and independent nations," the tribes of the South pledged themselves to "the preservation of the Dominion" of Spain in Louisiana and Florida. To consolidate these gains, in the early 1790s the Spanish constructed two new Mississippi River forts at sites that would later become the cities of Vicksburg and Memphis.

North of the Ohio River the situation was much the same. Thousands of Loyalists had fled the United States in the aftermath of the Revolution and settled in the country north of Lakes Ontario and Erie.

They were understandably hostile to the new republic. In 1791 the British Parliament passed the Canada Act, creating the province of Upper Canada (later renamed Ontario) and granting the Loyalists limited self-government. To protect this province British troops remained at a number of posts within American territory at places such as Detroit, where they supplied the Indian nations with arms and ammunition, hoping to create a buffer to American expansion. In early 1794 the governor general of Canada told an assembly of Indian leaders from the Ohio country that war between Britain and the United States was almost certain, and that when it broke out, "a line must then be drawn by the warriors." British soldiers began constructing Fort Miami in the Maumee Valley, west of Lake Erie, well within American territory.

Domestic and International Crises

Washington faced the gravest crisis of his presidency in 1794. In the West, the inability of the federal government to subdue the Indians, to eliminate the British from the northern fur trade, or to arrange with the Spanish for unencumbered use of the Mississippi River stirred frontiersmen to loud protests. There were rumblings of rebellion and secession from western communities. This discontent was strengthened by Hamilton's federal excise tax on whiskey, which hit backcountry farmers hardest, as the opening of this chapter illustrates. "The people of the western counties," wrote an English commentator, find "themselves grievously taxed for the support of the government without enjoying the blessings of it." London and Madrid believed that American settlers in the Northwest and Southwest might quit the Union and join themselves to Canada or Florida, and both English and Spanish secret agents worked to enhance such possibilities with liberal bribes.

In the Atlantic, Great Britain declared a blockade of France, including the seizure of vessels trading with the French West Indies. From 1793 to the beginning of 1794 the British confiscated the cargoes of more than 250 American ships, threatening hundreds of merchants with ruin. The United States was being "kicked, cuffed, and plundered all over the ocean," declared Madi-

In this 1794 painting, President George Washington reviews some 13,000 troops at Fort Cumberland on the Potomac before dispatching them to suppress the Whiskey Rebellion. Washington's mobilization of federal military power dramatically demonstrated the federal commitment to the preservation of the Union and the protection of the western boundary.

son, and in Congress he introduced legislation imposing retaliatory duties on British ships and merchandise.

The Whiskey Rebellion, which broke out in the summer of 1794, thus came at a time when President Washington considered the nation to be under siege. The combination of Indian attack, international intrigue, and domestic insurrection, he believed, created the greatest threat to the nation since the Revolution. In April the president had dispatched Chief Justice John Jay to London to arrange a settlement with the British. At the same time, war seemed increasingly likely, and Washington feared that any sign of federal weakness in the face of western rebellion would invite British or Spanish intervention. With Hamilton's urging he took the decisive course described in the opening of this chapter: he raised a large militia even as he pursued halfhearted negotiations with local authorities and made preparations to occupy the area around Pittsburgh, including Mingo Creek. It is clear now that the president overreacted, for although there was riot and violence in western Pennsylvania, there was no organized insurrection. Nevertheless, his mobilization of federal military power dramatically demonstrated the federal commitment to the preservation of the Union, the protection of the western boundary, and the supremacy of the national over the local community.

This action was reinforced by an impressive American victory against the Indian confederacy. Following the disastrous defeat of St. Clair by Little Turtle, Washington appointed General Anthony Wayne to lead a greatly strengthened American army to subdue the Indian confederacy and secure the Northwest. At the battle of Fallen Timbers, fought in the Maumee country of northern Ohio on August 20, 1794, Wayne crushed the Indians. Retreating, the warriors found the gates of Fort Miami closed and barred, the British inside thinking better of providing the powerful American force with a reason to attack the fort. The victory set the stage for the Treaty of Greenville in 1795, in which the representatives of twelve Indian nations ceded a huge territory encompassing most of present-day Ohio, much of Indiana, and other enclaves in the Northwest, including the town of Detroit and the tiny village of Chicago.

Jay's and Pinckney's Treaties

The strengthened American position in the West encouraged the British to settle their dispute with the United States so that they might concentrate on defeating republican France. In November 1794 Jay and the British signed an agreement providing for British withdrawal from American soil by 1796, limited American trade with the British East and West Indies, and the status of most-favored-nation for both countries (meaning that each would enjoy trade benefits

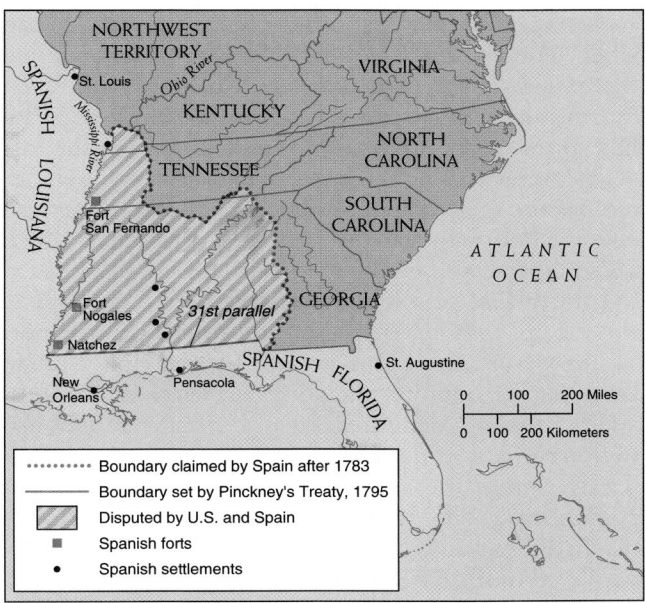

Spanish Claims to American Territory, 1783–1795
Before 1795 the Spanish claimed the American territory of the Old Southwest and barred Americans from access to the port of New Orleans, effectively closing the Mississippi River. This dispute was settled by Pinckney's Treaty in 1795.

equal to those the other accorded any other state). The treaty represented a solid gain for the young republic. With only a small army and no navy to speak of, the United States was in no position to wage war.

As it did on all matters of importance, the Senate debated the treaty in secret session. Details leaked out in a piecemeal fashion that inflamed public debate. The treaty represented a victory for Hamilton's conception of American neutrality. The Jeffersonians might well have opposed any agreement with Great Britain, but they were enraged over this accommodation that virtually unleashed Britain to attack republican France with full force. The absence in the treaty of any mention of compensation for the slaves who had fled to the British side during the Revolution further alienated Southerners. Throughout the country Democratic Societies and Jeffersonian partisans organized protests and demonstrations. Upon his return to the United States, Jay joked, he could find his way across the country by the light of his burning effigies. Despite these protests, the Senate, dominated by supporters of Hamilton, ratified the agreement in June 1795. In the House, a coalition of Southerners, Westerners, and friends of France attempted to stall the treaty by threatening to withhold the appropriations necessary for its implementation and demanding that they be allowed to examine the diplomatic correspondence regarding the whole affair. By refusing this demand, the president established the precedent of executive privilege in matters of state.

The deadlock continued until late in the year, when word arrived that the Spanish had abandoned their claims to the territory south of the Ohio River. Having declared war on revolutionary France, Spain had suffered a humiliating defeat, and fearing the loss of its American empire now found it expedient to mollify the quarrelsome Americans. In 1795 American envoy Thomas Pinckney negotiated a treaty in which Spain agreed to a boundary with the United States at the thirty-first parallel and opened the Mississippi to American shipping, with the right to dock in the port of New Orleans. This treaty fit the Jeffersonian conception of empire, and congressmen from the West and South were delighted with its terms. But administration supporters demanded their acquiescence in Jay's Treaty before the approval of Pinckney's. With this compromise, the long political controversy finally reached a conclusion.

These two important treaties finally established American sovereignty over the land west of the Appalachians and opened to American commerce a vast market extending from Atlantic ports to the Mississippi Valley. From a political standpoint, however, the battle over Jay's Treaty was costly for Washington, for it provided the Jeffersonians an opportunity to claim that in exchange for British gold the administration had sold out American neutrality as well as the republican principles embodied by the French Revolution. Washington's role in the events of 1794 and 1795 brought the president down from his pedestal and subjected him to the rough-and-tumble of political warfare. In the opposition press, he was vilified as "the source of all the misfortunes of our country" and was even accused of having been a traitor during the Revolution. Sick of politics and longing to return to private life, Washington now rejected the offer of a third term.

Washington's Farewell Address

Just two months before the presidential election of 1796, Washington published his Farewell Address to the nation, an appeal for national unity. "With slight shades of difference," Washington said to his countrymen, "you have the same religion, manners, habits, and political principles," and "union ought to be considered as a main prop of your liberty." He warned against sectional loyalty and "the baneful effects of the spirit of party." In the increasingly polarized political debate, however, this appeal fell on deaf ears.

The second part of the address was considerably more influential. "Our detached and distant situation," Washington explained, invited the nation to "defy material injury from external annoyance." He argued not for American isolation, but rather for American disinterest in the affairs of Europe. "The great rule of conduct for us in regard to foreign nations is, in extending our commercial relations to have with them as little political connection as possible." Why, he asked "entangle our peace and prosperity in the toils of European ambition, rivalship, interest, humor, or caprice?" Thomas Jefferson, in his Inaugural Address of 1801, paraphrased this first principle of American foreign policy as "peace, commerce, and honest friendship with all nations, entangling alliances with none." Jefferson's statement underscored the extent to which Washington articulated principles agreed to by all the major political figures of his day.

FEDERALISTS AND REPUBLICANS

The framers of the Constitution envisioned a one-party state in which partisan distinctions would be muted by patriotism and public virtue. "Among the numerous advantages promised by a well constructed Union," Madison had written in *The Federalist*, is "its tendency to break and control the violence of faction." Not only did he fail to anticipate the rise of political parties or factions; he saw them as potentially harmful to the new nation. It is thus ironic that when Madison broke with the Washington administration on questions of fiscal policy, he was the first to take steps toward organizing a political opposition, which would become known as the Democratic Republican Party. At the height of the agitation of the Democratic Societies in 1794, Hamilton cried that "unless soon checked," the "spirit of faction" would "involve the country in all the horrors of anarchy." Yet in acting as Washington's political lieutenant, he did more than anyone else to solidify the "Friends of Order," as his supporters were first known, into a disciplined political party known as the Federalists. Despite the framers' intentions, in the twelve years between the ratification of the Constitution and the federal election of 1800 political parties became a fundamental part of the American system of government.

The Rise of Political Parties

Evident in the debates and votes of Congress from 1789 to 1795 were a series of shifting coalitions that pitted commercial against agrarian interests, representatives from the Atlantic seaboard against those from the frontier, Anglophiles against Francophiles. The greatest potential division, that of Northerners versus Southerners, inspired the greatest fears, and congressmen worked hard to achieve sectional compromise by agreeing to avoid the troublesome issue of slavery. Antislavery petitions submitted to Congress were dismissed by nearly unanimous votes, and a law for the apprehension of fugitive slaves by federal officers anywhere in the Union was approved by a large majority in 1793.

OVERVIEW

THE FIRST AMERICAN PARTY SYSTEM

Federalist Party	Organized by figures in the Washington administration who were in favor of a strong federal government, friendship with the British, and opposition to the French Revolution; its power base was among merchants, property owners, and urban workers tied to the commercial economy. A minority party after 1800, it was regionally strong only in New England.
Democratic Republican Party	Arose as the opposition to the Federalists; its adherents were in favor of limiting federal power, sympathetic to the French Revolution, and hostile to Great Britain; it drew strength from southern planters and northern farmers. The majority party after 1800.

These shifting coalitions first began to polarize into political factions during the debate over Jay's Treaty in 1795, when agrarians, Westerners, Southerners, and supporters of France came together in opposition to the treaty. In the House, Madison acted as a leader of this coalition when it met for the first time and attempted to implement a collective strategy. By the elections of 1796, people had begun to give names to the two factions. The supporters of Hamilton claimed the mantle of Federalism. "I am what the phraseology of politicians has denominated a FEDERALIST," declared one North Carolina candidate for office, "the friend of order, of government, and of the present administration." Forced to find another term, the Jeffersonian opposition used both Democrat (from the Democratic Societies) and Republican, a name carrying the implication that the Federalists were really monarchists at heart. "There are two parties at present in the United States," wrote a New York editor sympathetic to Jefferson, "aristocrats, endeavoring to lay the foundations of monarchical government, and Republicans, the real supports of independence, friends to equal rights, and warm advocates of free elective government." Hamilton insisted on labeling his opponents the Anti-Federalists, while others scorned them as anarchists, Jacobins, or sans-culottes—all labels from the French Revolution. Historians usually call the Jeffersonian coalition the Democratic Republicans.

These two political coalitions played a fitful role in the presidential election of 1796, which pitted John Adams, Washington's vice president, against Thomas Jefferson. Partisan organization was strongest in the Middle States, where there was a real contest of political forces, weakest in New England and the South, where sectional loyalty prevailed and organized

opposition infrequent. When the ballots of the presidential electors, cast in their respective state capitals, were counted in the Senate, Adams was victorious. The authors of the Constitution, not anticipating this level of partisan competition, had provided that the runner-up—Jefferson in this case—would become vice president. Thus the new administration was born divided.

The Adams Presidency

Adams was put in the difficult situation of facing a political opposition led by his own vice president. He nevertheless attempted to conduct his presidency along the lines laid down by Washington, retaining most of the former president's appointees. This arrangement presented Adams with another problem. Although Hamilton had retired the year before, the cabinet remained committed to his advice, actively seeking his opinion and following it. As a result, Adams's authority was further undercut.

On the other hand, Adams benefited from the rising tensions between the United States and France. Angered by Jay's Treaty, the French suspended diplomatic relations at the end of 1796 and inaugurated a tough new policy toward American shipping. During the next two years they seized more than 300 American vessels and confiscated cargoes valued at an estimated $20 million. Hoping to resolve the crisis, Adams sent an American delegation to France. But in dispatches sent back to the United States the American envoys reported that agents of the French foreign ministry had demanded a bribe before any negotiations could be undertaken. Pressed for copies of these dispatches by suspicious Democratic Republicans in Congress, in 1798 Adams released them after substituting the letters X, Y, and Z for the names of the French agents. The documents proved a major liability for the Democratic Republicans, sparking powerful anti-French sentiment throughout the country. To the demand for a bribe, the American delegates had actually answered "Not a sixpence," but in the inflated rhetoric of the day the response became the infinitely more memorable: "Millions for defense, but not one cent for tribute!" The XYZ Affair, as it became known, sent Adams's popularity soaring.

Adams and the Federalists prepared the country for war during the spring of 1798. Congress authorized tripling the size of the army, and Washington came out of retirement to command the force. Fears of a French invasion declined after word arrived of the British naval victory over the French in August 1798 at Aboukir Bay in Egypt, but the "quasi-war" between France and the United States continued.

The Alien and Sedition Acts

In the summer of 1798 the Federalist majority in Congress, with the acquiescence of President Adams, passed four acts severely limiting both freedom of speech and the freedom of the press and threatening the liberty of foreigners in the United States. Embodying the fear that immigrants, in the words of one Massachusetts Federalist, "contaminate the purity and simplicity of the American character" by introducing dangerous democratic and republican ideas, the Naturalization Act extended the period of residence required for citizenship from five to fourteen years. The Alien Act and the Alien Enemies Act authorized the president to order the imprisonment or deportation of suspected aliens during wartime. Finally, the Sedition Act provided heavy fines and imprisonment for anyone convicted of writing, publishing, or speaking anything of "a false, scandalous and malicious" nature against the government or any of its officers.

The Federalists intended these repressive laws as weapons to defeat the Democratic Republicans. Led by Albert Gallatin, a Swiss immigrant and congressman from Pennsylvania (replacing Madison, who had retired from politics to devote his time to his plantation), the Democratic Republicans contested all the Federalist war measures and acted as a genuine opposition party, complete with caucuses, floor leaders, and partisan discipline.

For the first time, the two parties contested the election of Speaker of the House of Representatives, which became a partisan office. The more effective the Democratic Republicans became, the more treasonous they appeared in the eyes of the Federalists. On at least one occasion acrimonious debate in the House gave way to fisticuffs. Matthew Lyon, Democratic Republican of Vermont, spit in the eye of Connecticut Federalist Roger Griswold. Griswold responded by attacking Lyon with a cane, Lyon defended himself with a pair of fire tongs, and the two had to be pulled apart. With the Revolution still fresh in memory, Americans had only a weak understanding of the concept of a loyal opposition. Disagreement with the administration was misconstrued by the Federalists as opposition to the state itself.

The Federalists thus pursued the prosecution of dissent, indicting leading Democratic Republican newspaper editors and writers, fining and imprisoning at least twenty-five of them. The most vilified was Congressman Lyon, scorned by Federalists as "Ragged Matt the Democrat." Lyon was convicted in July 1798 of publishing libelous statements about President Adams and thrown into a Vermont prison. Later that year, however, he conducted a campaign from his cell and was reelected to Congress.

From Virginia, Madison wrote that the Sedition Act "ought to produce universal alarm, because it is levelled against the right of freely examining public characters and measures, and of free commu-

In this contemporary cartoon, Congressional Pugilists, Congress Hall in Philadelphia, February 15, 1798, Roger Griswold, a Connecticut Federalist, uses his cane to attack Matthew Lyon, Vermont Democratic Republican, who retaliates with fire tongs. During the first years of the American republic there was little understanding of the concept of a "loyal opposition," and disagreement with the policy of the Federalist administration was misconstrued as disloyalty.

nication among the people thereon, which has ever been deemed the only effectual guardian of every other right." He and Jefferson anonymously authored resolutions, passed by the Virginia and Kentucky legislatures, that declared the Constitution to be nothing more than a compact between the sovereign states and advocated the power of those states to "nullify" unconstitutional laws. When threatened with overbearing central authority, the Democratic Republicans argued, the states had the right to go their own way. The Virginia and Kentucky Resolves, as they were known, had grave implications for the future of the Union, for they stamped the notion of secession with the approval of two of the founding fathers. The resolutions would later be used to justify the secession of the southern states at the beginning of the Civil War.

The Revolution of 1800

The Alien and Sedition Acts were overthrown by the Democratic Republican victory in the national elections of 1800. As the term of President Adams drew to a close, Federalists found themselves seriously divided. In 1799, by releasing seized American ships and requesting negotiations, the French convinced Adams that they were ready to settle their dispute with the United States. The president also sensed the public mood running toward peace. But the Hamiltonian wing of the party, always scornful of public sentiment, continued to beat the drums of war. When Federalists in Congress tried to block the president's attempt to negotiate, Adams threatened to resign and turn the government over to Vice President Jefferson. In the Convention of 1800, the United States abandoned its demand of compensation for seized cargoes in exchange for French abrogation of its 1778 alliance with the American colonies. "The end of war is peace," Adams declared, "and peace was offered me." Adams considered the settlement of this conflict with France to be one of the greatest accomplishments of his career, but it earned him the scorn of conservative Federalists, including Hamilton.

The Federalists also divided over a domestic controversy. Under their leadership Congress had enacted a direct tax on houses, similar to the earlier tax on whiskey. In eastern Pennsylvania in 1799 several dozen farmers, displaying symbols of the French Revolution, routed the tax collectors and freed from jail a tax resister, one John Fries, who had been involved in the Whiskey Rebellion. Adams sent federal troops to restore order, and for leading Fries's Rebellion, a court issued death sentences for three men, including Fries. The president's cabinet demanded that Adams enforce "exemplary rigor" by

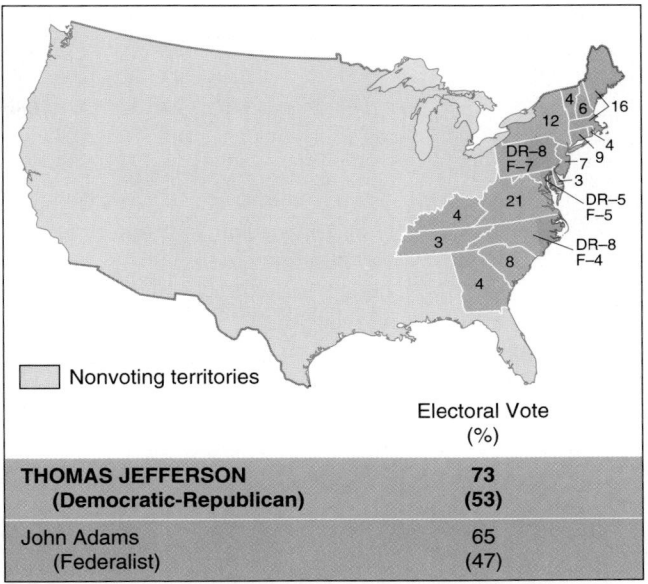

	Electoral Vote (%)
THOMAS JEFFERSON (Democratic-Republican)	**73 (53)**
John Adams (Federalist)	65 (47)

The Election of 1800   *In the presidential election of 1800, Democratic Republican victories in New York and the divided vote in Pennsylvania threw the election to Jefferson. The combination of the South and these crucial Middle States would keep the Democratic Republicans in control of the federal government for the next generation.*

allowing the sentence to be carried out, but in 1800 Adams responded to popular pressure and pardoned the three. To the jeers of conservative Federalists, Adams now dumped the Hamiltonians from his cabinet. During the war scare with France, Washington had insisted that Hamilton be appointed as second in command of the enlarged army. "You crammed him down my throat!" Adams cried. Now he denounced Hamilton as "a bastard, and as much an alien as Gallatin." Hamilton responded by circulating a private letter in which he condemned Adams for his "disgusting egotism," "distempered jealousy," and "vanity without bounds." This letter fell into the hands of Aaron Burr, leader of the New York Democratic Republicans, and he published it, to the consternation of the Federalists.

The Federalists divided at precisely the time when unity was necessary to prevent the Democratic Republicans from consolidating their strengths. The defusing of the crisis with France also helped the Democratic Republicans, who could claim opposition to Federalist warmongering. They captured the state governments of Pennsylvania and New York in 1799, the first important inroads of the party in the North. These states had been taken over, cried a shocked Federalist, by "the most God-provoking Democrats on this side of Hell." From Virginia, Jefferson proclaimed his hope that "with Pennsylvania we can defy the universe!"

The presidential election of 1800 was the first to feature campaign advertising. "T. Jefferson, President of the United States of America," reads the streamer on this election banner, illustrated with an American eagle and a portrait of Jefferson; "John Adams—no more." This was mild rhetoric in a campaign characterized by wild charges. The Republicans labeled Adams a warmonger and a monarchist, while the Federalists denounced Jefferson as an atheist, Jacobin, and sexual libertine.

The presidential campaign of 1800 was the first in which Democratic Republicans and Federalists operated as two national political parties. Caucuses of congressmen nominated respective slates: Adams and Charles Cotesworth Pinckney of South Carolina for the Federalists, Jefferson and Aaron Burr of New York for the Republicans. Both tickets thus represented attempts at sectional balance. The Republicans presented themselves as the party of traditional agrarian purity, of liberty and states' rights, of "government rigorously frugal and simple," in the words of Jefferson. They were optimistic, convinced that they were riding the wave of the future. Divided and embittered, the Federalists waged a defensive struggle for strong central government and public order, and resorted frequently to negative campaigning. They denounced Jefferson as an atheist, a Jacobin, and the father of mulatto children—the first two charges were without foundation, the last apparently true, according to the results of DNA matching tests. One campaign placard put the issue succinctly: "GOD—AND A RELIGIOUS PRESIDENT" or "JEFFERSON—AND NO GOD!"

The balloting for presidential electors took place between October and December 1800. Adams took all the New England states while Jefferson captured the South and West. Jefferson called it "the Revolution of 1800." Party discipline was so effective that one of the provisions of the Constitution was shown to be badly outmoded. By this clause, the candidate receiving a majority of electoral votes became president and the runner-up became vice president. But by casting all their ballots for Jefferson and Burr, Democratic Republican electors unintentionally created a tie and forced the election into the House of Representatives. Because the new Democratic Republican-controlled Congress would not convene until March 1801, the Federalist majority was given a last chance to decide the election. They attempted to make a deal with Burr, who refused but who also would not withdraw his name from consideration. Finally, on the thirty-fifth ballot the Federalists gave up and arranged with their opponents to elect Jefferson without any of them having to cast a single vote in his favor. Congressman Lyon, "Ragged Matt the Democrat," cast the symbolic final vote in a gesture of sweet revenge. The Twelfth Amendment, creating separate ballots for president and vice-president, would be ratified in time for the next presidential election.

With the rise of partisan politics came a transformation in political participation. In 1789 state regulations limited the franchise to a small percentage of the adult population. Women, African Americans, and Indians could not vote, but neither could a third to a half of all free adult males, who were excluded by tax-paying or property-owning requirements. And even among the eligible the turnout was generally low. The traditional manner of voting was by voice: at the polling place in each community individuals announced their selections aloud to the clerk of elections, who wrote them down. Not surprisingly, this system allowed wealthy men, landlords, and employers of the community to pressure poorer voters.

These practices began to change with the increasing competition between Democratic Republicans and Federalists. Popular pressure resulted in the introduction of universal white manhood suffrage in four states by 1800 and the reduction of property requirements in others. These changes inaugurated a movement that would sweep the nation over the next quarter-century, and as a consequence, voter turnout increased in all the states. The growth of popular interest in politics was a transformation as important as the peaceful transition from Federalists to Democratic Republicans in national government.

"THE RISING GLORY OF AMERICA"

In 1771 Philip Freneau and Hugh Henry Brackenridge read an epic poem, "The Rising Glory of America," to their graduating class at Princeton. They admitted that American contributions to learning and the arts had thus far been slim, but they were boundlessly optimistic about the potential of their country. Indeed, judged against the literary and artistic work of individuals in the colonial period, artists and others of the Revolutionary generation accomplished a great deal in their effort to build a national culture.

Art and Architecture

The first American to achieve prominence in the artistic world of Europe was Benjamin West, who painted portraits in his native Pennsylvania before leaving for the Continent and England, where he became popular as a painter of historical scenes. His *Death of General Wolfe* (1770) (see p. 138) was one of the more acclaimed paintings of its day and the first to elevate an American scene to the high status of monumental historical painting. In 1774 West was joined in London by John Singleton Copley, a Boston portraitist who left America because of his loyalist sentiments. Copley's work is renowned for the truth and straightforwardness of his depictions, as in his famous portrait of Samuel Adams (1771) (see p. 144). Both West and Copley remained in England after the Revolution. Their most promising student was Gilbert Stuart, whose work in the fashionable style of the day included a portrait of Mohawk leader Joseph Brant (see p. 172). Stuart returned to

the United States in 1792 to paint what became the most famous portrait of President Washington.

The preeminent painter of the Revolution was Charles Willson Peale, who studied for a time with West in London. He returned to America, however, and during the Revolution turned his talents to producing wartime propaganda. Although the almond eyes and bloated torsos of his figures suggest his technical limitations, Peale's work has a naive charm. His paintings of Washington, for example, seem more revealing of character than Stuart's placid portrait. Inspired by nationalist zeal, Peale planned a public gallery of

In this self-portrait, American artist Charles Willson Peale dramatically lifts the curtain on his Philadelphia Museum. Peale's three sons—whom he named after the artists Raphael, Rembrandt, and Titian—and two of his nieces—Anna and Sarah—also became noted painters, constituting something of a first family of American art in the early years of the new republic.

heroes in Philadelphia that eventually grew into a famous museum of curios, reflecting his interest in natural history, archaeology, and exotic cultures. Federalists joked that its chaotic arrangement of exhibits mirrored Peale's Jeffersonian politics. Part science, part circus, the collection was purchased after Peale's death by the pioneer American entertainer P. T. Barnum.

John Trumbull of Connecticut, who had predicted America's rise to his Yale classmates, served as a soldier during the Revolution, then went to London to study with West. There he painted *The Battle of Bunker's Hill* (1785), the first of a series of Revolutionary scenes (see p. 156), four of which he repainted in the Capitol rotunda in the early nineteenth century. Influenced by the grand style of eighteenth-century historical painting, Trumbull was concerned above all else with documentary detail in his scenes of the birth of America.

Nationalism was also evident in architecture. The greatest architectural project of the day was the new federal capital city, named for President Washington. In 1790, after Congress had agreed on the site, Washington retained Pierre Charles L'Enfant, a French engineer who had served as an officer during the Revolution, to lay out the city. The survey was conducted by Andrew Ellicott, assisted by the African American mathematician Benjamin Banneker. L'Enfant took full advantage of the lay of the land and the Potomac River, placing the Capitol building on a hill "which stands as a pedestal waiting for a monument." He linked public buildings such as the president's house and the Capitol with radial avenues, allowing for what he called "a reciprocity of sight." And he planned a grand mall from the Capitol to the river, along which there would be public museums, academies, and assembly halls. Development during the nineteenth century obscured L'Enfant's original design, but it was revived in 1901. Jefferson recommended "the models of antiquity" for the public buildings of the federal city, a suggestion carried out in William Thornton's original design for the Capitol.

George Town and Federal City, *or City of Washington, a colored aquatint of 1801 by T. Cartwright. When President John Adams first occupied the White House in 1800, Washington was still a small village, its streets merely muddy pathways.*

"Architecture is worth great attention," declared Jefferson, for "as we double our numbers every twenty years, we must double our houses. It is, then, among the most important arts; and it is desirable to introduce taste into an art which shows so much." In New England, architect Asher Benjamin popularized an American variant of the Georgian style, emphasizing economy of decoration and recommending the use of indigenous materials when writing handbooks such as *The Country Builder's Assistant* (1797). A great deal of the urban building undertaken in coastal cities during the shipping boom of the 1790s was characterized by this restrained classicism, which was known as the Federal style.

But the majority of Americans lived in small, bare, even squalid conditions. A nationwide tax on houses produced the first comprehensive survey of the nation's housing in 1798. There was tremendous variation in living conditions. The wealthiest 10 percent lived in dwellings estimated to be worth more than half the total value of all houses. By contrast, the value of housing owned by the wealthiest tenth of Americans today is only 30 percent of the total. Forty percent of American houses in 1798 were valued at $99 or less (the equivalent of about $1,000 today), and were little more than shacks. In the expanding cities, many residents lived along dingy back alleys and in damp basements. In the country, the typical house was a one-story structure of two or three rooms. As the population continued to grow, and Americans continued to move west, many more people would be found in log hovels like those in the community along Mingo Creek.

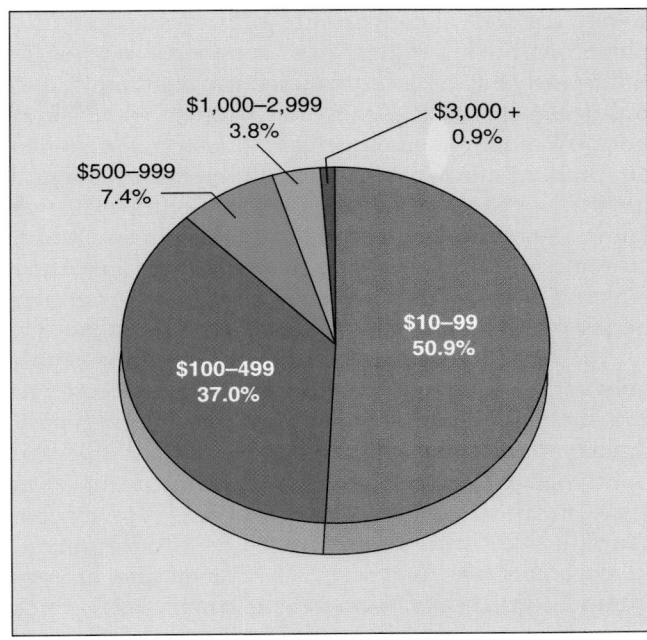

Housing Values, 1798   *In 1798 Congress enacted a direct tax on buildings, resulting in an inventory of American housing that has never been equaled. The data revealed an enormous gap between rich and poor. The majority lived in squalid cabins valued at $99 or less, while the wealthiest 10 percent of Americans lived in dwellings that, taken together, were worth just over half the total value of all the nation's houses.*

Source: Lee Soltow, "Egalitarian America and Its Inegalitarian Housing in the Federal Period," *Social Science History* 9 (1985): 199–213.

The Liberty of the Press

At the beginning of the Revolution in 1775 there were thirty-seven weekly or semiweekly newspapers in the thirteen colonies, only seven of which were Loyalist in sentiment. By 1789 the number of papers in the United States had grown to ninety-two, including eight dailies; three papers were being published west of the Appalachians. Relative to population, there were more newspapers in the United States than in any other country in the world—a reflection of the remarkably high literacy rate of the American people (see Chapter 5). In New England almost 90 percent of the population could read, and even on the frontier, where Brackenridge edited the *Pittsburgh Gazette*, about two-thirds of the males were literate.

During the political controversy of the 1790s, the press became the principal medium of Federalist and Democratic Republican opinion, and papers came to be identified by their politics. In 1789 John Fenno, aided by Alexander Hamilton, began publication of the *Federalist Gazette of the United States*, and in 1791 Jefferson encouraged Philip Freneau to establish the competing *National Gazette*. The columns of these papers broadcast the feud between the two cabinet secretaries.

The prosecutions under the Sedition Act, however, threatened to curb the further development of the media, and in their opposition to these measures Democratic Republicans played an important role in establishing the principle of a free press. In *An Essay on Liberty of the Press* (1799), the Virginia lawyer George Hay, later appointed to the federal bench by President Jefferson, wrote that "a man may say everything which his passions suggest." Were this not true, he argued, the First Amendment would have been "the grossest absurdity that was ever conceived by the human mind." In his first Inaugural Address Jefferson echoed this early champion of the freedom of expression. "Error of opinion may be tolerated," he declared, "where reason is left free to combat it."

The Birth of American Literature

During the post-Revolutionary years there was an enormous outpouring of American publications. In the cities the number of bookstores grew in response to the demand for reading matter. Perhaps even more significant was the appearance in the countryside of numerous book peddlers who supplied farm households with Bibles, gazettes, almanacs, sermons, and political pamphlets. One such peddler was Mason Locke Weems, a man trained as a doctor and ordained an Anglican minister, who gave up these careers in the early 1790s for book selling. Parson Weems, as he was known, wrote that he found his southern backcountry customers "uninformed, their minds bitter, and their manners savage," but that they cried out for "books, books, books!"

The literature of the Revolution understandably reflected the dominating political concerns of the times. Mercy Otis Warren and Hugh Henry Brackenridge wrote propagandistic dramas, and the poet Joel Barlow composed a nationalist epic, *The Vision of Columbus* (1787). *M'Fingal* (1782), a mock epic satirizing the British, was written by John Trumbull (a cousin of the painter), a leader of the literary group known as the Connecticut Wits. It sold copies enough to be considered the best-selling fictional work of the war. But the majority of "best-sellers" during the Revolutionary era were political. The most

important were Thomas Paine's *Common Sense* (1776) and his series of stirring pamphlets, published under the running title *The American Crisis* (1776–83), the first of which began with the memorable phrase, "These are the times that try men's souls."

In the cause of reform, Paine later returned to England and published *The Rights of Man* (1791), a defense of the French Revolution. Banished from Britain for this expression of radical politics, he went to France, jumped into politics, and, in one of the periodic political turns of the revolution, found himself imprisoned for a time. From his jail cell Paine wrote *The Age of Reason* (1795), a powerful attack on organized religion that became one of the most popular American books of its day, loved by Jeffersonians and loathed by Federalists. Book-selling Parson Weems, for example, made a steady profit from the sale of Paine's work, though he offered pious sermons and religious tracts to placate those objecting to Paine's politics.

Some of the most interesting American books of the postwar years examined the developing American character. The French immigrant Michel-Guillaume Jean de Crèvecoeur, in *Letters from an American Farmer* (1782), proposed that the American, a product of many cultures, was a "new man" with ideas new to the world. John Filson, the author of the *Discovery, Settlement, and Present State of Kentucke* (1784), presented the narrative of one such new man, the Kentucky pioneer Daniel Boone. In doing so he took an important step toward the creation of that most American of literary genres, the western. In a satirical novel entitled *Modern Chivalry* (1792), featuring incidents from the Whiskey Rebellion, Pittsburgh editor Brackenridge dipped his pen "in the inkstand of human nature" and produced one of the first dialect portraits of "dat son o'd a whore," the American frontiersman. Brackenridge wrote with an appreciation for his crude characters but expressed frustration that the Revolution had failed to elevate the culture of ordinary people. By shunning simple celebration, however, he was one of the first to take a critical look at the American character.

The single best-selling book of the Revolutionary era

Pages from Noah Webster's famous American Spelling Book, *the largest seller of all American books during the nineteenth century. Believing that "the King's English" reflected aristocratic standards, Webster argued for spelling reform to create "the American language."*

was Noah Webster's *American Spelling Book* (1783), the famous "Blue-Backed Speller," which soon after its publication was selling 200,000 copies annually. It became the largest-selling of all American books, a good indicator of the remarkable literacy of the American people. With it, Webster launched a life-long campaign for a distinctive American form of English, which culminated in his *American Dictionary of the English Language* (1828). In a belief that "the King's English" reflected aristocratic standards, Webster argued for a time that "the American language" must be guided by "republican principles," for example, spelling words as they sounded. "Ther iz no alternativ," he wrote. Eventually he abandoned the most radical of his suggestions, although many of his reforms stuck, dropping the "u" from the English spelling of "colour," for example, in favor of "color." The speller was the first in a graded series of textbooks that included a grammar and a reader designed to "diffuse the principles of virtue and patriotism." These texts included standard selections from not only British but also American writers. Webster compiled a list of important dates beginning with Columbus's voyage and ending with the British surrender at Yorktown—the first attempt at a distinctively American historical chronology.

Other writers produced more formal histories. Not surprisingly, Democratic Republican authors stressed the tradition of resistance to authority, whereas Federalists emphasized the importance, particularly during wartime, of central direction and unity. Fearing criticism by Federalist writers, Democratic Republican Mercy Otis Warren delayed publishing her *History of the Rise, Progress, and Termination of the American Revolution* (1805) until after Jefferson's victory in 1800.

Parson Weems found readers fascinated by the historical heroes of the Revolution, so he drew up plans for a series of "quarter of dollar books on subjects calculated to strike the popular curiosity, printed in very large numbers and properly distributed." When Washington died in December 1799, Weems was already at work on a short biography of the first president. "Washington, you know, is gone!" he wrote to his publisher. "Millions are gaping to read something about him. I am very nearly primed and cocked for 'em." His *Life of Washington* (1800, enlarged edition 1806), became the most popular history of the Revolution and introduced a series of popular and completely fabricated anecdotes, including the story of young Washington and the cherry tree. The book was a pioneering effort in mass culture, and Weems, as one historian puts it, was "the father of the Father of his Country."

Condemned by serious writers and scholars, even at the time of its publication, Weems's biography

In this 1792 cartoon from the Lady's Magazine, the allegorical figure of "Columbia" receives a petition for the "Rights of Woman." In the aftermath of the Revolution, Americans debated the issue of an expanded role for women in the new republic. Many Federalists condemned "women of masculine minds," but there was general agreement among both conservatives and democrats that the time had come for better education for American women.

was loved by ordinary Americans of all political persuasions. In the mid-nineteenth century, Abraham Lincoln recalled that he had read Weems "away back in my childhood, the earliest days of my being able to read," and had been profoundly impressed by "the struggles for the liberties of the country." In praise of Washington, Weems wrote, "all parties join with equal alacrity and earnestness." Although Washington had in fact become a partisan leader of the Federalists during his second term, Weems presented him as a unifying figure for the political culture of the new nation, and this was the way he would be remembered. Jefferson echoed these sentiments in his Inaugural Address in 1801, when as a gesture of conciliation to his opponents he

CHRONOLOGY

1786	Annapolis Convention
1787	Constitutional Convention
1787–88	*The Federalist* published
1788	Constitution ratified
	First federal elections
1789	President George Washington inaugurated in New York City
	Judiciary Act
	French Revolution begins
1790	Agreement on site on the Potomac River for the nation's capital
	Indian Intercourse Act
	Judith Sargent Murray publishes "On the Equality of the Sexes"
1791	Bill of Rights ratified
	Bank of the United States chartered
	Alexander Hamilton's "Report on Manufactures"
	Ohio Indians defeat General Arthur St. Clair's army
1793	England and France at war; America reaps trade windfall
	Citizen Genêt affair
	President Washington proclaims American neutrality in Europe
	British confiscate American vessels
	Supreme Court asserts itself as final authority in *Chisholm v. Georgia*
1794	Whiskey Rebellion
	Battle of Fallen Timbers
	Jay's Treaty with the British concluded
1795	Pinckney's Treaty negotiated with the Spanish
	Treaty of Greenville
	Thomas Paine publishes The Age of Reason
1796	President Washington's Farewell Address
	John Adams elected president
1797–98	French seize American ships
1798	XYZ Affair
	"Quasi-war" with France
	Alien and Sedition Acts
	Kentucky and Virginia Resolves
1799	Fries's Rebellion
1800	Convention of 1800
	Thomas Jefferson elected president
	Mason Locke Weems publishes *Life of Washington*

declared, "We have called by different names brethren of the same principle. We are all Republicans, we are all Federalists."

Women on the Intellectual Scene

One of the most interesting literary trends of the 1790s was the growing demand for books that appealed to women readers. Susanna Haswell Rowson's *Charlotte Temple* (1791), a tale of seduction and abandonment, ran up tremendous sales and remained in print for more than a century. Other romantic works of fiction included *The Power of Sympathy* (1789) by William Hill Brown, sometimes called the first American novel; the gothic novels of Charles Brockden Brown, such as *Arthur Mervyn* (1799); and *The Coquette* (1797) by Hannah Webster Foster. The young republic thus marked the first dramatic appearance of women writers and women readers. Although

women's literacy rates continued to be lower than men's, they rose steadily as girls joined boys in common schools. This increase was one of the most important social legacies of the democratic struggles of the Revolutionary era.

Some writers argued that the new republican order ought to provide new roles for women as well as for men. The first avowed feminist in American history was Judith Sargent Murray, who publicly stated her belief that women "should be taught to depend on their own efforts, for the procurement of an establishment in life." She was greatly influenced by the English feminist Mary Wollstonecraft, but developed her line of thinking independently, as demonstrated by her essay "On the Equality of the Sexes," written in 1779 and finally published in 1790 in a Massachusetts magazine. "I expect to see our young women forming a new era in female history," Murray predicted. Federalists listened to such opinions with horror. "Women of masculine minds," one Boston minister sneered, "have generally masculine manners."

There seemed to be general agreement among all parties, however, that the time had come for better-educated and better-informed women. Republican institutions of self-government were widely thought to depend on the wisdom and self-discipline of the American people. Civic virtue, so indispensable for the republic, must be taught at home. The share that every male citizen had in the government of the country, Benjamin Rush said in 1787, required that women have "suitable education, to concur in instructing their sons in the principles of liberty and government." By placing her learning at the service of her family, the "republican mother" was spared the criticism leveled at independent-minded women such as Murray. "A woman will have more commendation in being the mother of heroes," said a Federalist, "than in setting up, Amazon-like, for a heroine herself." Thus were women provided the opportunity to be not simply "helpmates," but people "learned and wise." But they were also expected to be content with a narrow role, not to wish for fuller participation in American democracy.

CONCLUSION

In 1800, the population of Canada numbered about 500,000. Those of European background in New Mexico and the other Spanish North American colonies numbered approximately 25,000. And the Indian people of the continent numbered anywhere from 500,000 to a million. Overwhelming all these groups was the population of the United States, which stood at 5.3 million and was growing at the astounding annual rate of 3 percent. During the last years of the eighteenth century the United States had adopted a new constitution and established a new national government. It had largely repaid the debt run up during the Revolution and made peace with adversaries abroad and Indian peoples at home. Americans had begun to learn how to channel their disagreements into political struggle. The nation had withstood a first decade of stress, but tensions continued to divide the people. As some of the rebel supporters had promised at the beginning of the Whiskey Rebellion, "their liberty they will maintain, / they fought for't, and they'll fight again." At the beginning of the new century it remained uncertain whether the new nation would find a way to control and channel the energies of an expanding people.

REVIEW QUESTIONS

1. Discuss the conflicting ideals of local and national authority in the debate over the Constitution.
2. What were the major crises faced by the Washington and Adams administrations?
3. Describe the roles of Madison and Hamilton in the formation of the first American political parties.
4. What did Jefferson mean when he talked of "the Revolution of 1800"?
5. Discuss the contributions of the Revolutionary generation to the construction of a national culture.

RECOMMENDED READING

William N. Chambers, *Political Parties in a New Nation: The American Experience, 1776–1809* (1963). An introduction to the formation of the American party system. Though several decades old, it remains essential.

Stanley Elkins and Eric McKitrick, *The Age of Federalism* (1993). A massive and informative account of the politics of the 1790s, from the ratification of the Constitution to the election of Jefferson.

Joseph J. Ellis, *After the Revolution: Profiles of Early American Culture* (1979). A series of portraits of the more important cultural innovators in the young republic.

Reginald Horsman, *The Frontier in the Formative Years, 1783–1815* (1970). A sensitive survey of developments in the West, emphasizing that the "western question" was one of the most important facing the young republic.

Jackson Turner Main, *The Antifederalists: Critics of the Constitution, 1781–1788* (1961). A detailed examination of the localist tradition in early American politics. Includes a discussion of the ratification of the Constitution from the point of view of its opponents.

Willard Sterne Randall, *George Washington: A Life* (1997). The best one-volume biography of "the Father of his Country."

Thomas P. Slaughter, *The Whiskey Rebellion: Frontier Epilogue to the American Revolution* (1986). A detailed history of the rebellion in western Pennsylvania during the 1790s. Includes a thorough examination of the politics and culture of both the backcountry and the federal government at a moment of crisis.

James M. Smith, *Freedom's Fetters: The Alien and Sedition Laws and American Civil Liberties* (1966). Remains the best overview of the Federalist threat to liberty, as well as the Democratic Republican counterattack.

Gerald Stourzh, *Alexander Hamilton and the Idea of Republican Government* (1970). A solid biography of the ultimate Federalist man and his politics.

Gordon Wood, *The Creation of the American Republic, 1776–1787* (1969). This general survey provides the best overview of the Constitutional Convention.

ADDITIONAL BIBLIOGRAPHY

Forming a New Government

Douglass Adair, *Fame and the Founding Fathers*, ed. Trevor Colbourn (1974)

John K. Alexander, *The Selling of the Constitutional Convention: A History of News Coverage* (1990)

Charles A. Beard, *An Economic Interpretation of the Constitution of the United States* (1913)

Max Farrand, ed., *Records of the Federal Convention of 1787*, 4 vols. (1911–37)

Suzette Henberger, *Creatures of the Constitution: The Federalist Constitution and the Shaping of American Politics* (1994)

John P. Kaminski and Gaspare J. Saladino, eds., *The Documentary History of the Ratification of the Constitution* (1982)

Forrest McDonald, *Novus Ordo Seclorum: The Intellectual Origins of the Constitution* (1985)

Richard B. Morris, *Witnesses at the Creation: Hamilton, Madison, Jay and the Constitution* (1985)

Peter Onuf, *Origins of the Federal Republic* (1983)

Josephine F. Pacheco, ed., *Antifederalism: The Legacy of George Mason* (1992)

Herbert J. Storing, ed., *The Complete Anti-Federalist*, 7 vols. (1981)

Garry Wills, *Explaining America: The Federalist* (1981)

The New Nation

Harry Ammon, *The Genêt Mission* (1973)

Steven R. Boyd, ed., *The Whiskey Rebellion: Past and Present Perspectives* (1985)

Collin G. Calloway, *Crown and Calumet: British-Indian Relations, 1783–1815* (1987)

Gerald A. Combs, *The Jay Treaty: Political Battleground of the Founding Fathers* (1970)

Alexander De Conde, *Entangling Alliance: Politics and Diplomacy under George Washington* (1956)

Ralph Ketcham, *Presidents above Party: The First American Presidency, 1789–1829* (1984)

Charles R. Ritcheson, *Aftermath of Revolution: British Policy toward the United States, 1783–1795* (1969)

Wiley Sword, *President Washington's Indian War: The Struggle for the Old Northwest, 1790–1795* (1985)

J. Leitch Wright, *Britain and the American Frontier, 1783–1815* (1975)

Federalists and Republicans

Joyce Appleby, *Capitalism and a New Social Order: The Republican Vision of the 1790s* (1984)

Albert H. Bowman, *The Struggle for Neutrality: Franco-American Diplomacy during the Federalist Era* (1974)

Ralph Adams Brown, *The Presidency of John Adams* (1975)

Richard Buel Jr., *Securing the Revolution: Ideology in American Politics, 1789–1815* (1972)

Nobel E. Cunningham Jr., *The Jeffersonian Republicans: The Formation of Party Organization, 1789–1801* (1957)

Alexander De Conde, *The Quasi-War: Politics and Diplomacy of the Undeclared War with France, 1797–1801* (1966)

Drew McCoy, *The Elusive Republic: Political Economy in Jeffersonian America* (1980)

Andrew W. Robertson, *The Language of Democracy: Political Rhetoric in the United States and Britain, 1790–1900* (1995)

James Roger Sharp, *American Politics in the Early Republic: The New Nation in Crisis* (1993)

Alfred F. Young, *The Democratic Republicans of New York: The Origins, 1763–1797* (1967)

"The Rising Glory of America"

R. A. Burchell, ed., *The End of Anglo-America: Historical Essays in the Study of Cultural Divergence* (1991)

Emory Elliott, *Revolutionary Writers: Literature and Authority in the New Republic* (1982)

Michael Kammen, *A Season of Youth: The American Revolution and the Historical Imagination* (1978)

Linda Kerber, *Women of the Republic: Intellect and Ideology in Revolutionary America* (1980)

Kenneth Silverman, *A Cultural History of the American Revolution* (1976)

Biography

Robert C. Alberts, *Benjamin West: A Biography* (1978)

John R. Alden, *George Washington: A Biography* (1984)

Gay Wilson Allen, *St. John de Crèvecoeur: The Life of an American Farmer* (1987)

Aleine Austin, *Matthew Lyon, "New Man" of the Democratic Revolution, 1749–1822* (1981)

Lance Banning, *The Sacred Fire of Liberty: James Madison and the Founding of the Federal Republic* (1995)

Harvey Lewis Carter, *The Life and Times of Little Turtle: First Sagamore of the Wabash* (1987)

Jacob Ernest Cooke, *Alexander Hamilton* (1982)

Helen A. Cooper, *John Trumbull: The Hand and Spirit of a Painter* (1982)

Herbert Alan Johnson, *John Jay, Colonial Lawyer* (1989)

Dumas Malone, *Jefferson and His Time*, 6 vols. (1948–81)

Jules David Prown, *John Singleton Copley* (1966)

Edgar P. Richardson et al., *Charles Willson Peale and His World* (1983)

K. Alan Synder, *Defining Noah Webster: Mind and Morals in the Early Republic* (1990)

Mason Locke Weems, *The Life of Washington*, ed. Marcus Cunliffe (1962)

Immigration contributed to the growth of the population of the colonies that became the United States of America more than any other factor. Seventeenth-century migration to these colonies was mostly from England, although small but important groups of Dutch, Swedes, and French settled areas of New York, New Jersey, and Maryland.

By 1700 the population of British colonial North America had reached 250,000. The high levels of fertility characteristic of all the colonial societies of North America—British, Spanish, and French—contributed to the growth of population. But only the British encouraged immigration. The French and the Spanish adopted highly restrictive immigration policies. Dedicated to keeping its colonies exclusively Catholic, France turned down the requests of thousands of Protestant Huguenots who desperately sought to emigrate to Canada. The Spanish, fearful of depleting their population at home, severely limited the migration of their own subjects to their colonies and absolutely forbade the immigration of foreigners, with the exception of African slaves.

Yet a veritable flood of immigrants came to British North America during the eighteenth century. Scots, Scots-Irish, Germans, and French joined the English in the trans-Atlantic crossing. Slave traders also brought tens of thousands of Africans to the southern colonies. (For a full discussion of African migration, see Chapter Four.) By 1750 European and African migrants and their descendents outnumbered the Indian population of the continent, and by 1800 had grown to more than 5.3 million, an increase of more than twenty times the population in 1700 over the course of one hundred years.

William Penn was the first British colonial official to encourage the immigration of non-British western Europeans, in the 1680s sending agents to recruit settlers in Holland, France, and the German principalities along the Rhine River. His experiment proved so successful that the leaders of other British colonies soon were employing recruiting agents of their own in Europe. Further encouraging this development, most of the British colonies enacted liberal naturalization laws in the early eighteenth century, allowing immigrants who professed Protestantism and swore allegiance to the British crown to become free "denizens" with all the freedoms and privileges of natural-born subjects. In 1740 Parliament passed a general Naturalization Act that extended these policies to all the colonies. The new legislation continued to prohibit the naturalization of Catholic and Jewish immigrants, however, and these groups remained tiny minorities in the British colonies.

Still, immigration to what would become the United States was characterized by extraordinary ethnic diversity. The two largest migrating groups were the English and the Africans, each totaling, according to good historical estimates, perhaps 400,000 to 500,000 immigrants during the colonial period. There was also substantial emigration from the northern British Isles. Squeezed by economic hardship, an estimated 250,000 Highland Scots and Protestant Irish from the Ulster region (known in America as the "Scots-Irish") emigrated to North America during the eighteenth century. The Germans were another significant group; at least 100,000 of them settled in the British colonies, where they became known as the "Dutch" (from *Deutsch*, the German-language term for German). It should be noted that from half to two-thirds of Europeans came to British North America as indentured servants, or "redemptioners," or else convicts transported to the New World to serve out their sentences laboring on plantations. The Africans were not the only people to come involuntarily to America. A majority of immigrants during the colonial period came in a state of bondage.

The first federal census, conducted in 1790, provides a snapshot of the consequences of eighteenth-century immigration. Forty-nine percent of the population of the thirteen United States was English in origin, and nearly 20 percent was African; 15 percent were Irish or Scots, 7 percent German, 3 percent Dutch, and 2 percent French.

Many of the founders of the American republic worried that the different languages and traditions of these diverse peoples would fracture the nation. In the 1750s, for example, Benjamin Franklin wrote of his fears that German immigrants would not assimilate to English ways. "Why should Pennsylvania," he asked, "founded by English, become a colony of *aliens* who will shortly be so numerous as to Germanize *us* instead of Anglifying them?" Thomas Jefferson worried that immigrants from monarchical countries, untutored in the ways of democracy, would "warp and bias" the direction of American political development. Reflecting such fears, the nation's first Naturalization Act,

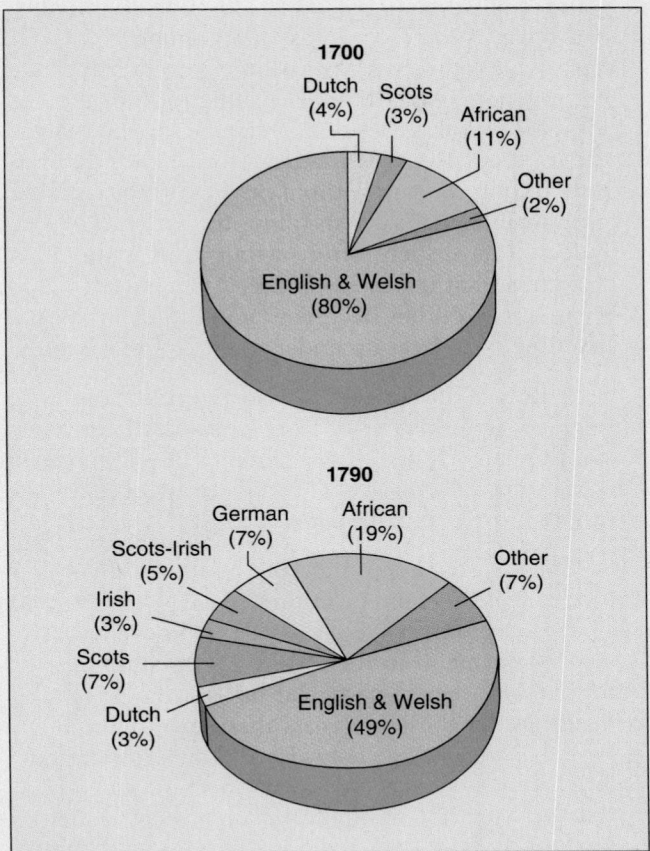

1700

Dutch (4%)
Scots (3%)
African (11%)
Other (2%)
English & Welsh (80%)

1790

German (7%)
African (19%)
Scots-Irish (5%)
Irish (3%)
Scots (7%)
Dutch (3%)
Other (7%)
English & Welsh (49%)

The Ancestry of the British Colonial Population
The legacy of eighteenth-century immigration to the British colonies was a population of unprecedented ethnic diversity.

Source: Thomas L. Purvis, "The European Ancestry of the United States Population," *William and Mary Quarterly* 61 (1984): 85–101.

passed in 1790, required a residency period of five years (a kind of probation period) before immigrants could apply for citizenship, and limited applications to "free white persons." In the nineteenth and early twentieth centuries this clause would be used to bar the naturalization of immigrants from Africa and Asia.

■ IN THEIR OWN WORDS

William Penn was the first colonial leader to actively seek out prospective immigrants for his colony. In 1681 he wrote a promotional account of Pennsylvania that was translated into several European languages and widely circulated.

> The place [Pennsylvania] lies 600 miles nearer the sun than England, for…[it] begins at about the latitude of Naples in Italy, or Montpellier in France. I shall say little in its praise, to excite desires in any, whatever I could truly write as to the soil, air and water. This shall satisfy me, that by the blessing of God, and the honesty and industry of man, it may be a good fruitful land.…
>
> What persons will be fit to go? 1st. Industrious husbandmen and day-labourers, that are hardly able (with extreme labour) to maintain their families and portion [endow] their children.
>
> 2dly. Laborious handicrafts, especially carpenters, masons, smiths, weavers, tailors, tanners, shoemakers, shipwrights, etc., where they may be spared or are low in the world. And as they shall want no encouragement, so their labour is worth more there than here, and their provision cheaper.
>
> 3dly. A plantation [colony] seems a fit place for those ingenious spirits that being low in the world, are much clogged and oppressed about a livelihood, for the means of subsisting being easy there, they may have time and opportunity to gratify their inclinations, and thereby improve science and help nurseries of people.
>
> 4thly. A fourth sort of men for whom a plantation would be proper, takes in those that are younger brothers of small inheritances; yet because they would live in sight of their kindred in some proportion to their quality, and can't do it without a labour that looks like farming, their condition is too straight for them; and if married, their children are often too numerous for the estate, and are frequently bred up to no trades, but are a kind of hangers-on or retainers to the elder brother's table and charity.…
>
> Lastly, there are another sort of persons, not only fit for, but necessary in plantations, and that is men of universal spirits, that have an eye to the good of posterity, and that both understand among a plain and well-intending people. Such persons may find room in colonies for their good counsel and contrivance, who are shut out from being of much use or service to great nations under settled customs. These men deserve much esteem, and would be hearkened to…[1]

Judith Giton (ca. 1665–1711) was twenty years old when she and many other Protestant Huguenots escaped French persecution to settle in South Carolina in 1685. In the following letter to her brother, written from America, she described the harrowing experience of immigration.

> For eight months we had suffered from the contributions and the quartering of the soldiers, on account of religion, enduring many inconveniences. We therefore resolved on quitting France at night, leaving the soldiers in their beds, and abandoning the house with its furniture.…We passed into Holland, in order to go to England.

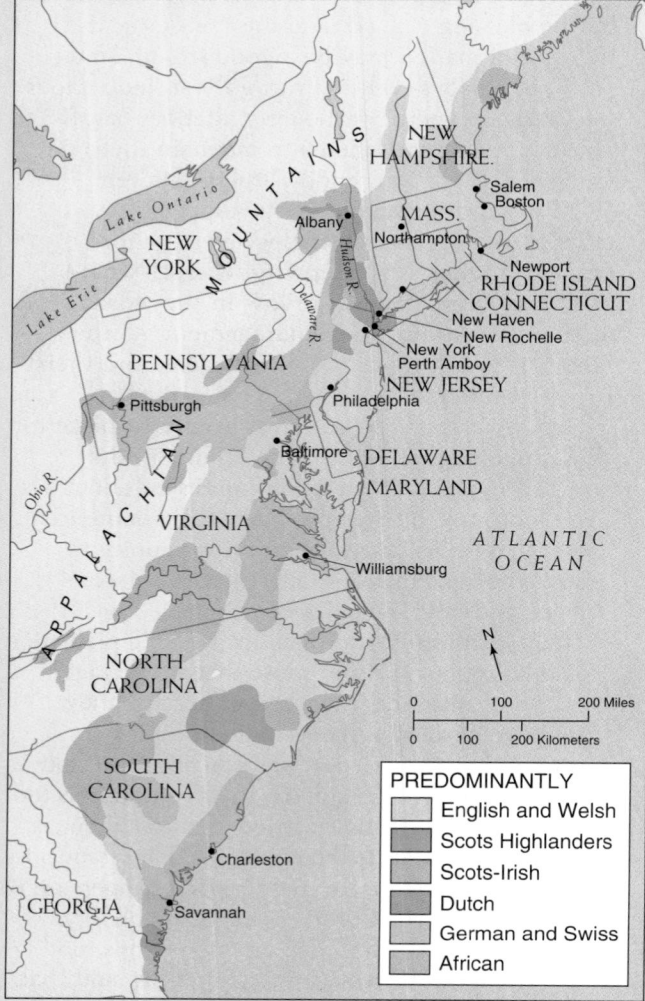

Ethnic Groups in Eighteenth-Century British North America *The first federal census, taken in 1790, revealed remarkable ethnic diversity. New England was filled with people from the British Isles, but the rest of the colonies were a patchwork. Most states had at least three different ethnic groups within their borders, and although the English and Scots-Irish were heavily represented in all colonies, in some they had strong competition from Germans (eastern and southern Pennsylvania) and from African peoples (Virginia and South Carolina).*

We were detained in London for three months, waiting for a vessel ready to sail for Carolina. Once embarked, we were miserably off indeed. The scarlet fever broke out in our ship, and many died, among them our aged mother....Our vessel put in [at Bermuda] for repairs, having been badly injured in a severe storm. Our captain...was thrown into prison, and the ship was seized. It was with the greatest difficulty that we secured our passage in another ship, for our money had all been spent. After our arrival in Carolina, we suffered all sorts of evils. Our eldest brother died of a fever, eighteen months after coming here....We ourselves have been exposed, since leaving France, to all kinds of afflictions, in the forms of sickness, pestilence, famine, poverty, and the roughest labor. I have been for six months at a time in this country without tasting bread, laboring meanwhile like a slave in tilling the ground. Indeed, I have spent three or four years without knowing what it was to eat bread whenever I wanted it. God has been very good to us in enabling us to bear up under trials for every kind.[2]

Robert Parke was a Presbyterian Scot who immigrated with his family from Ireland to Pennsylvania in the early 1720s. Letters home, like this one of Parke's, were an important means of advertising the advantages of American immigration.

Chester Township, the 10th Month 1725
Dear Sister Mary Valentine:
We have not had a day's sickness in the family since we came in to the country, blessed be God for it. My father in particular has not had his health better these ten years than since he came here, his ancient age considered. You write in your letter that there was a talk went back to Ireland that we were not satisfied in coming here, which was utterly false...for there is not one of the family but what likes the country very well and would if we were in Ireland again come here directly it being the best country for working folk and tradesmen of any in the world. But for drunkards and Idlers, they cannot live well anywhere. It is likewise an Extraordinarily healthy country....

Land is of all prices even from ten pounds, to one hundred pounds a hundred, according to the goodness or else the situation thereof, and grows more dear every year by reason of vast quantities of people that come here yearly from several parts of the world, therefore, you and your family or any that I wish well I would desire to make what speed you can to come here the sooner the better....[3]

Gottlieb Mittelberger came to Pennsylvania from Germany in 1750 and served as a schoolmaster and organist in Philadelphia for three years. In this famous account, written after his return to Europe, he paints a horrid picture of the voyage to America, the conditions for indentured servants, and warns his countrymen to remain content at home.

Both in Rotterdam and in Amsterdam the people are packed densely, like herrings so to say, in the large sea vessels. One person receives a place of scarcely 2 feet width and 6 feet length in the bedstead, while many a ship carries four to six hundred souls; not to mention the innumerable implements, tools, provisions, water-barrels and other things which likewise occupy much space.

On account of contrary winds it takes the ships sometimes 2, 3, and 4 weeks to make the trip from Holland to Kaupp [Cowes] in England....When the ships have for the last time weighed their anchors near...Kaupp...., the real misery begins with the long voyage. For from there the ships, unless they have good wind, must often sail 8, 9, 10, to 12 weeks before they reach Philadelphia. But even with the best wind the voyage lasts 7 weeks.

But during the voyage there is on board these ships terrible misery, stanch, fumes, horror, vomiting, many kinds of seasickness, fever, dysentery, headache, heat, constipation, boils, scurvy, cancer, mouth-rot, and the like, all of which come from old and sharply salted food and meat, also from the very bad and foul water, so that many die miserably.

Add to this want of provisions, hunger, thirst, frost, heat, dampness, anxiety, want, afflictions and lamentations, together with other trouble, as *c.v.* the lice abound so frightfully, especially on sick people, that they can be scraped off the body. The misery reaches the climax when a gale rages for 2 or 3 nights and days, so that every one believes that the ship will go to the bottom with all human beings on board. In such a visitation the people cry and pray most piteously....

When the ships have landed at Philadelphia after their long voyage, no one is permitted to leave them except those who pay for their passage or can give good security; the others, who cannot pay, must remain on board the ships till they are purchased, and are released from the ships by their purchasers. The sick always fare the worst, for the healthy are naturally preferred and purchased first; and so the sick and wretched must often remain on board in front of the city for 2 or 3 weeks, and frequently die, whereas many a one, if he could pay his debt and were permitted to leave the ship immediately, might recover and remain alive....

The sale of human beings in the market on board the ship is carried on thus: Every day Englishmen, Dutchmen, and High-German people come from the city of Philadelphia and other places, in part from a great distance, say 20, 30, or 40 hours away, and go on board the newly arrived ship that has brought and offers for sale passengers from Europe, and select among the healthy persons such as they deem suitable for their business, and bargain with them how long they will serve for their passage money, which most of them are still in debt for. When they have come to an agreement, it happens that adult persons bind themselves in writing to serve 3, 4, 5 or 6 years for the amount due by them, according to their age and strength. But very young people, from 10 to 15 years, must serve till they are 21 years old.

One of Philadelphia's many wharves, featured in a hand-colored engraving of 1800. Attracted by the abundant and fertile farmland of the Pennsylvania countryside, more European immigrants passed through Philadelphia than any other North American port of the eighteenth century.

A master potter working with his indentured apprentices, from The Book of Trades, a survey of eighteenth-century American crafts. Of all the Europeans who immigrated to British North America in the eighteenth century, half to two-thirds came as indentured servants

or herself, but also for the deceased. When both parents have died over half-way at sea, their children, especially when they are young and have nothing to pawn or to pay, must stand for their own and their parents' passage, and serve till they are 21 years old. When one has served his or her term, he or she is entitled to a new suit of clothes at parting; and if it has been so stipulated, a man gets in addition a horse, a woman, a cow....

However hard he may be compelled to work in his fatherland, he will surely find it quite as hard, if not harder, in the new country. Besides, there is not only the long and arduous journey lasting half a year, during which he has to suffer, more than with the hardest work; he has also spent about 200 florins which no one will refund to him. If he has so much money, it will slip out of his hands; if he has it not, he must work his debt off as a slave and poor serf. Therefore let every one stay in his own country and support himself and his family honestly. Besides I say that those who suffer themselves to be persuaded and enticed away by the man-thieves, are very foolish if they believe that roasted pigeons will fly into the mouths in America or Pennsylvania without their working for them.[4]

Thomas Jefferson had doubts concerning the effect of mass immigration on American institutions. These comments come from his extended essay, *Notes on the State of Virginia*, published in 1784.

The present desire of America is to produce rapid population by as great importations of foreigners as possible. But is this founded in good policy?...Are there no inconveniences to be thrown into the scale against the advantage expected from a multiplication of numbers by the importation of foreigners? It is for the happiness of those united in society to harmonize as much as possible in matters which they must of necessity transact together. Civil government being the sole object of forming societies, its administration must be conducted by common consent. Every species of government has its specific principles. Ours perhaps are more peculiar than those of any other in the universe. It is a composition of the freest principles of the English constitution, with others derived from natural right and natural reason. To these nothing can be more opposed than the maxims of absolute monarchies. Yet, from such, we are to expect the greatest number of emigrants. They will bring with them the principles of the governments they leave, imbibed in their early youth; or, if able to throw them off, it will be in

Many parents must sell and trade away their children like so many head of cattle; for if their children take the debt upon themselves, the parents can leave the ship free and unrestrained; but as the parents often do not know where and to what people their children are going, it often happens that such parents and children, after leaving the ship, do not see each other again for many years, perhaps no more in all their lives....

It often happens that whole families, husband, wife, and children, are separated by being sold to different purchasers, especially when they have not paid any part of their passage money. When a husband or wife has died at sea, when the ship has made more than half of her trip, the survivor must pay or serve not only for himself exchange for an unbounded licentiousness, passing, as is usual, from one extreme to another. It would be a miracle were they to stop precisely at the point of temperate liberty. These principles, with their language, they will transmit to their children. In proportion to their numbers, they will share with us the legislation. They will infuse into it their spirit, warp and bias its direction, and render it a heterogeneous, incoherent, distracted mass....

Suppose 20 millions of republican Americans thrown all of a sudden into France, what would be the condition of that kingdom? If it would be more turbulent, less happy, less strong, we may believe that the addition of half a million of foreigners to our present numbers would produce a similar effect here. If they come of themselves, they are entitled to all the rights of citizenship: but I doubt the expediency of inviting them by extraordinary encouragements.[5]

In contrast to Jefferson, the French immigrant J. Hector St. Jean de Crèvecoeur celebrated the American cultural blending that resulted from immigration. In his famous *Letters of an American Farmer* (1782), Crèvecoeur was the first to discuss the process by which immigrants were "melted" into a new kind of person, the American.

Whence came all these people? They are a mixture of English, Scotch, Irish, French, Dutch, Germans, and Swedes. From this promiscuous breed, that race, now called Americans, have arisen....

What then is the American, this new man? He is either an European, or the descendant of an European; hence that strange mixture of blood, which you will find in no other country. I could point out to you a man, whose grandfather was an Englishman, whose wife was Dutch, whose son married a French woman, and whose present four sons have now four wives of different nations. *He is an American*, who, leaving behind him all his ancient prejudices and manners, receives new ones from the new mode of life he has embraced, the new government he obeys, and the new rank he holds. He becomes an American by being received in the broad lap of our great Alma Mater.

Here individuals of all nations are melted into a new race of men, whose labours and posterity will one day cause great change in the world. Americans are the western pilgrims, who are carrying along with them that great mass of arts, sciences, vigour, and industry, which began long since in the east; they will finish the great circle. The Americans were once scattered all over Europe; here they are incorporated into one of the finest systems of population which has ever appeared, and which will hereafter become distinct by the power of the different climates they inhabit. The American ought, therefore, to love this country much better than that wherein either he or his forefathers were born. Here the rewards of his industry follow with equal steps the progress of his labour; his labour is founded on the basis of nature, *self-interest*; can it want a stronger allurement? Wives and children, who before in vain demanded of him a morsel of bread, now, fat and frolicsome, gladly help their father to clear those fields whence exuberant crops are to arise to feed and to clothe them all; without any part being claimed either by a despotic prince, a rich abbot, or a mighty lord. Here religion demands but little of him; a small voluntary salary to the minister, and gratitude to God; can he refuse these? The American is a new man, who acts upon new principles; he must therefore entertain new ideas, and form new opinions. From involuntary idleness, servile dependence, penury, and useless labour, he has passed to toils of a very different nature, rewarded by ample subsistence. This is an American.[6]

Questions

1. Identify the major immigrant groups of the colonial period and their proportion in the American population at the end of the eighteenth century.

2. What were the arguments made both in favor of and against immigration to British North America?

3. How would Jefferson respond to Crèvecoeur's argument about "the American, this new man"?

Sources

1. William Penn, "Account of the Province of Pennsilvania," in *Some Account of the Province of Pennsilvania in America* (London: Benjamin Clark, 1681)

2. Ruth Barnes Moynihan, Cynthia Russett, and Laurie Crumpacker, eds., *Second to None: A Documentary History of American Women* (Lincoln: University of Nebraska Press, 1993), 1, 54. Reprinted with permission of the publisher.

3. Robert Parke, "A Letter from Pennsylvania" (1725) from Charles A. Hanna, *The Scotch-Irish in America*, 2 volumes (1902), 2, 64–67

4. Gottlieb Mittelberger, *Journey to Pennsylvania in the Year 1750 and Return to Germany in the Year 1754*, translated by Carl Theo. Eben (Philadelphia: John Jos. McVey, 1898), 19–20, 22, 24–31.

5. Thomas Jefferson, *Notes on the State of Virginia* in *Thomas Jefferson: Writings* (New York, 1984), 210–212

6. J. Hector St. Jean de Crèvecoeur, *Letters from an American Farmer* (London, 1782)

AN AGRARIAN REPUBLIC

1790–1824

Applique quilt, late 18th–early 19th century, by Sarah Furman, with people and village at center. Henry Ford Museum and Greenfield Village.

AMERICAN COMMUNITIES
Expansion Touches Mandan Villages
on the Upper Missouri

In mid-October 1804, news arrived at the Mandan villages, prominently situated on bluffs overlooking the upper Missouri, that an American expedition led by Meriwether Lewis and William Clark was coming up the river. The principal chiefs, hoping for expanded trade and support against their enemies the Sioux, welcomed these first American visitors. As the expedition's three boats and forty-three men approached the village, wrote Clark, "great numbers on both sides flocked down to the bank to view us." That evening the Mandans welcomed the Americans with an enthusiastic dance and gifts of food.

Since the fourteenth century, when they migrated from the East, the Mandans had lived along the Missouri, on the edge of the Great Plains in what is now North Dakota. They believed their homeland was "the very center of the world," and indeed it is in the heart of the North American continent. Mandan men hunted buffalo and Mandan women kept storage pits full with abundant crops of corn, beans, squash, sunflowers, and tobacco grown on the fertile soil of the river bottom. The Mandan villages were also the central marketplace of the northern Plains; at trading time in late summer they filled with Crows, Assiniboins, Cheyennes, Kiowas, and Arapahoes. Well before any of these people, or those of other tribes, had met a European, they were trading in kettles, knives, and guns acquired from the French and English to the east and leatherwork, glassware, and horses acquired form the Spanish in the Southwest.

The eighteenth century was a golden age for the Mandan, who with their closely related Hidatsa neighbors numbered about 3,000 in 1804. In each of their five villages, earth lodges surrounded a central plaza. One large ceremonial lodge was used for community gatherings, and each of the other earth lodges was home to a senior woman, her husband, her sisters (perhaps married to the same man as she, for the Mandans practiced polygamy), their daughters and their unmarried sons, along with numerous grandchildren. Matrilineal clans, the principal institution of the community, distributed food to the sick, adopted orphans, cared for the dependent elderly, and punished wrongdoers. A village council of male clan leaders selected chiefs who led by consensus and lost power when people no longer accepted their opinions.

Lewis and Clark had been sent by President Thomas Jefferson to survey the Louisiana Purchase and to find an overland route to the Pacific Ocean. They were also instructed to inform the Indians that they now owed loyalty—and trade—to the American government, thereby challenging British economic control over the lucrative North American fur trade. Meeting with the village chiefs, the Americans offered the Mandans a military and economic alliance. His people would like nothing better, responded Chief

Black Cat, for the Mandans had fallen on hard times over the past decade. "The smallpox destroyed the greater part of the nation" some twenty years before, the chief said. "All the nations before this malady [were] afraid of them, [but] after they were reduced the Sioux and other Indians waged war, and killed a great many." Black Cat was skeptical that the Americans would deter the Sioux, but Clark reassured him. "We were ready to protect them," Clark reported in his journal, "and kill those who would not listen to our good talk."

The Americans spent the winter with the Mandans, joining in their communal life and establishing firm and friendly relations with them. There were dances and joint hunting parties, frequent visits to the earth lodges, long talks around the fire, and, for many of the men, pleasant nights in the company of Mandan women. Lewis and Clark spent many hours acquiring important geographic information from the Mandans, who drew charts and maps showing the course of the Missouri, the ranges of the Rocky Mountains, and places where one could cross the Continental Divide. The information provided by the Mandans and other Indian peoples to the West was vital to the success of the expedition. Lewis and Clark's "voyage of discovery" depended largely on the willingness of Indian peoples to share their knowledge of the land with the Americans.

In need also of interpreters who could help them communicate with other Indian communities on their way, the Americans hired several multilingual Frenchmen who lived with the Mandans. They also acquired the services of Sacajawea, the fifteen-year-old Shoshoni wife of one of the Frenchmen, who became the only woman to join the westward journey. The presence of Sacajawea and her baby son was a signal, as Clark noted, to "all the Indians as to our friendly intentions"; everyone knew that women and children did not go on war parties.

When the party left the Mandan villages in March, Clark wrote, his men were "generally healthy, except venereal complaints which

is very common amongst the natives and the men catch it from them." After an arduous journey across the Rockies, the party reached the Pacific Ocean at the mouth of the Columbia River, where they spent the winter. Overdue and feared lost, they returned in triumph to St. Louis in September 1806. Before long the Americans had established Fort Clark at the Mandan villages, giving American traders a base for challenging British dominance of the western fur trade. The permanent American presence brought increased contact, and with it much more disease. In 1837 a terrible smallpox epidemic carried away the vast majority of the Mandans, reducing the population to fewer than 150. Four Bears, a Mandan chief who had been a child at the time of the Lewis and Clark visit, spoke these last words to the remnants of his people. "I have loved the whites," he declared. "I have lived with them ever since I was a boy." But in return for the kindness of the Mandans, the Americans had brought this plague. "I do not fear death, my friends," he said, "but to die with my face rotten, that even the wolves will shrink with horror at seeing me, and say to themselves, that is Four Bears, the friend of the whites." "They have deceived me," he pronounced with his last breath. "Them that I always considered as brothers turned out to be my worst enemies."

In sending Lewis and Clark on their "voyage of discovery" to claim the land and the loyalty of the Mandans and other western Indian communities, President Jefferson was motivated by his vision of an expanding American republic of self-sufficient farmers. During his and succeeding presidencies expansion became a key element of national policy and pride. Yet, as the experience of the Mandans showed, what Jefferson viewed as enlargement of "the empire for liberty" had a dark side—the destruction, from disease and coerced displacement, of the communities created by America's first peoples. The effects—economic, political, and social—of continental expansion dominate the history of American communities in the first half of the nineteenth century.

Mandan Villages

KEY TOPICS

- The development of America's economy in a world of warring great powers

- The role of Jefferson's presidency and his agrarian republicanism in forging a national identity

- The ending of colonial dependency by the divisive War of 1812

- Westward expansion becomes a nationalizing force

THE GROWTH OF AMERICAN COMMUNITIES FROM COAST TO COAST

At first glance, the United States of America in 1800 was little different from the scattered colonies of the pre-Revolution era. Two-thirds of the young nation's people still lived in a long thin line of settlement within fifty miles of the Atlantic coast. From New Hampshire to Georgia, most people lived on farms or in small towns, and, because they rarely traveled far from home, their horizons were limited and local.

As famed historian Henry Adams observed, at the beginning of the new century "nature was rather man's master than his servant." Travel in the young republic was slow and difficult, for the roads were poor, and a horse and carriage could go no more than three or four miles an hour. It took two days to travel from New York to Philadelphia, four days to Boston. Nevertheless, the new nation was already transforming itself, not held back by nature but plunging ahead into it. Between 1790 and 1800, according to the first and second federal censuses, the American population grew from 3.9 million to 5.3 million. Growth by migration was greatest in the trans-Appalachian West, a region that was already home to approximately 100,000 Indians. From 1800 to 1850, in an extraordinary burst of territorial expansion, Americans surged westward all the way to the Pacific. At the turn of the century few people would have predicted that within fifty years the nation would encompass the entire continent. In fact, in 1800 several European nations were still mounting significant attempts to settle parts of what is now the United States.

Russian America: Sitka

Russian settlement of what is now Alaska was an extension of its conquest of Siberia, which was driven by the fur trade. In 1741, commissioned by Tsar Peter the Great, the Danish-born naval officer Vitus Bering sailed east from Kamchatka across the sea that now bears his name, explored the Aleutian Islands, and made landfall on the southern coast of Alaska. Although Bering died in a shipwreck on his return voyage, his associates brought back a cargo of sea otter furs, news of the discovery of Alaska, and a navigational report on the Arctic waters of the northern Pacific. In the aftermath of these voyages, Russian and Siberian fur trappers, known as *promyshleniki*, became regular visitors to the Aleutian Islands and the Alaskan coast. By the late 1750s they were shipping a steady supply of furs from Russian America.

The Russians sometimes took furs by force, holding whole villages hostage and brutalizing the native Inuit and Aleut peoples. Within a decade, native resistance had broadened beyond sporadic and local efforts. In 1762, for example, the Aleuts destroyed a fleet of Russian ships from Kamchatka, beginning a series of attacks known as the Aleut Revolt. Finally crushing the Aleuts in 1766, the Russians promised to protect them from abuse, but by the end of the century, the precontact population of 25,000 Aleuts had been greatly reduced. At the same time, sexual relations and intermarriage between fur trappers and Aleut women created a large group of Russian creoles who assumed an increasingly prominent position in the Alaskan fur trade as navigators, explorers, clerks, and traders.

In 1784, the merchant trader Gregory Shelikhov set up a post on Kodiak Island, and over the next several years he established the first permanent Russian settlements in the Gulf of Alaska. In 1799, after his death, Shelikhov's company received a state charter as a quasi-governmental monopoly with rights to the lucrative trade in sea otter pelts. The Russian-American Company set up American headquarters first at Kodiak. When overhunting caused a scarcity of furs, the Russians moved their headquarters south to Sitka, in what is now the southeastern panhandle of Alaska. This was the homeland of the Tlingits, a warrior society, who destroyed the Russians' first fortress in the Tlingit Revolt of 1802. The Russians reestablished

From an engraving by Freidrich H. von Kittlitz, 1827.

This view shows Sitka, the center of Russian activities in Alaska, in 1827. Russian architectural styles and building techniques are apparent in the Church of St. Michael the Archangel in the right background, contrasting with the Asian and Indian origins of most of Sitka's inhabitants.

Sitka by force in 1804, and over the next generation established Russian settlements along the Pacific coast as far south as Fort Ross, which was just north of San Francisco Bay and well within what Spain considered Spanish territory.

Northern New Spain: Los Angeles

Spain had long been concerned about threats to its New World empire from other nations. Fearing incursions by the Russians and British, the Spanish sent naval squadrons north from Mexico to establish their claim to the Pacific coast. By the 1770s, Spain had explored and made claim to the mouth of the Columbia River, Nootka Sound (on Vancouver Island), and the coast of southeastern Alaska. But Spanish attempts to seal off the rich seaborne fur trade from other nations failed. The Russians were a strong presence in Alaska, and the British, already the major power in the land-based fur trade, built a trading post for sea otter furs at Nootka Sound in 1789 in spite of Spanish protests. Americans, who soon dominated the sea otter trade, made their first voyage to the Pacific Northwest in 1787.

In another effort to protect their rich colony of Mexico the Spanish pushed north into Alta (Upper) California, establishing a chain of twenty-one missions that stretched north from San Diego (1769) to Sonoma (1823). The largest of these missions was Los Angeles, which in 1800 had a largely mestizo population of 300. The town, which was the social center for the vast countryside

surrounding it, functioned chiefly as a center of government authority (see Chapter 5). Despite Spain's desire to seal its territory from commerce with other nations, a brisk but illegal trade in otter skins, hides, and tallow developed between the United States and California after the first American ship, the *Lelia Bird*, arrived in 1803.

A French Legacy: New Orleans and St. Louis

For a half-century after its founding by Jean Baptiste le Moyne, Sieur de Bienville, in 1718, New Orleans was controlled by the French. Originally little more than a small port at the mouth of the Mississippi River, its location gave it access to the vast and vaguely defined continental interior that the French called Louisiana. New Orleans came under Spanish rule in 1763 as a result of the Seven Years War, but it continued to be a polyglot, French-dominated society. By 1800 it had a population of about 8,000, half white and half black. Two-thirds of the black population were slaves; the remainder were "free persons of color," who under French law enjoyed legal rights equal to those of white people. The white population was a mixture of French people of European and West Indian origin. Among them were French-speaking exiles from Acadia, who became known in New Orleans as Cajuns (see Chapters 6 and 8). But there were also Spanish, Germans, English, Irish, Americans, and native-born creoles, causing one observer to call the community "a veritable tower of Babel."

All these people were there because New Orleans was becoming a thriving international port. In 1801 it shipped more than $3 million worth of tobacco, sugar, rice, cotton, fruits, and vegetables to Europe. Every year, a greater proportion of the New Orleans trade was supplied by Americans living some distance up the Mississippi River. In 1801 alone, an observer in Natchez counted nearly 600 flatboats on their way to New Orleans from American settlements upriver. Pinckney's 1795 treaty with Spain guaranteed Americans free navigation of the Mississippi River and the right to deposit goods at the port of New Orleans. Nevertheless, Americans were uncomfortably aware that the city's crucial location at the mouth of the Mississippi meant that whatever foreign nation possessed New Orleans had the power to

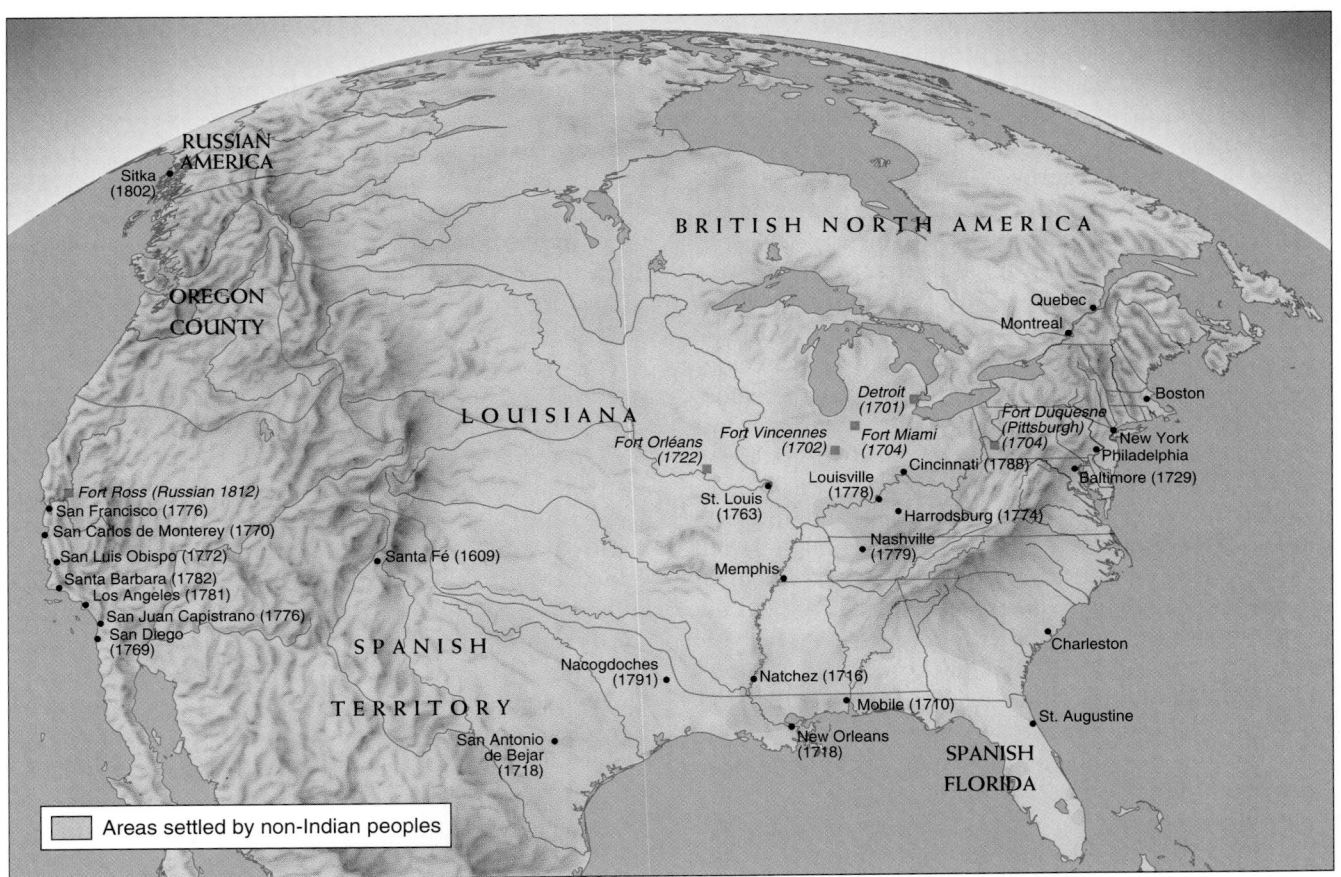

America in 1800   In 1800, the new United States of America was surrounded by territories held by the European powers: British Canada, French Louisiana (secretly ceded that year to France by Spain), Spanish Florida, Spanish Mexico, and Russian Alaska expanding southward along the Pacific coast. Few people could have imagined that by 1850 the United States would span the continent. But the American settlers who had crossed the Appalachians to the Ohio River Valley were already convinced that opportunity lay in the West.

choke off the flourishing trade in the vast Mississippi Valley river system.

More than 600 miles north was the small trading town of St. Louis, founded by the New Orleans trader Pierre Laclède in 1763. By 1800 the town had fewer than a thousand residents, three-quarters of whom were involved in the Indian trade of the Missouri River. Spanish officials tried to supervise that trade from their offices in the town, but real control rested in the hands of the Laclèdes and other French traders. Americans visiting this shabby little place laughed at Pierre Laclède's prediction that St.Louis would become "one of the finest cities in America," but he was right.

Trans-Appalachia: Cincinnati

Within the United States itself, the region of greatest growth was the area west of the Appalachian Mountains. By 1800, 500,000 people (the vast majority from

Virginia and North Carolina) had found rich and fertile land along the splendid rivers of the interior—the Tennessee, the Cumberland, and the Ohio, all draining into the Mississippi River, which marked the western boundary of the United States. Soon there was enough population for statehood. Kentucky (1792) and Tennessee (1796) were the first trans-Appalachian states admitted to the Union.

Migration was a principal feature of American life. Probably 5 to 10 percent of all American households moved each year. In the rural areas of the Atlantic seaboard, a third of the households counted in the 1790 census had moved by 1800; in cities the proportion was closer to half. In the West, meanwhile, rates of migration rose to as high as two-thirds of the community every ten years. Most moves were between neighboring communities or towns, but many families underwent the painful process of long-distance relocation. Migration was generally a family affair, with groups of kin moving together to a new area. One observer wrote of a caravan moving across the mountains, "They had prepared baskets made of fine hickory withe or splints, and fastening two of them together with ropes they put a child in each basket and put it across a pack saddle." Once pioneers had managed to struggle by road over the Appalachians, they gladly took to the rivers, especially the Ohio River, to move farther west.

Cincinnati, strategically situated 450 miles downstream from Pittsburgh, was a particularly dramatic example of the rapid community growth and development that characterized the trans-Appalachian region. Founded in 1788, Cincinnati began life as a military fort defending settlers in the fertile Miami River valley of Ohio from resistance by Shawnee and Miami Indians. Conflict between these Indian peoples and the new settlers was so fierce that the district was grimly referred to as "the slaughterhouse." Trans-Appalachian settlement was not individual but communal: fear of attack led the white settlers to group together for protection. The basic form of settlement in early Kentucky was the "station," or fort; north of the Ohio River, compact settlements on the New England model were favored.

After the battle of Fallen Timbers broke Indian resistance in 1794, Cincinnati became the point of departure for immigrants arriving by the Ohio River on their way to settle the interior of the Old Northwest: Ohio, Indiana, and Illinois. In the boom years of settlement, the number of people passing through was so great that the entire town seemed to consist of hotels and eating places. In 1800, Cincinnati had a population of about 750 people. By 1810, it had tripled in size, confirming its boast to be "the Queen City of the West."

Cincinnati merchants were soon shipping farm goods from the fertile Miami Valley down the Ohio–Mississippi River system to New Orleans, 1,500 miles away. River hazards like snags and sandbars made the downriver trip by barge or keelboat hazardous, and the return trip upriver was slow, more than three months from New Orleans to Cincinnati. Frequently rivermen simply abandoned their flatboats in New Orleans and traveled home overland, on foot or horseback, by the long and dangerous Natchez Trace, an old Indian trail that linked Natchez with Nashville, Tennessee. Nevertheless, river traffic increased yearly, and the control of New Orleans became a key concern of western farmers and merchants. If New Orleans refused to accept American goods, Cincinnati merchants and many thousands of trans-Appalachian farmers would be ruined.

Atlantic Ports: From Charleston to Boston

Although only 3 percent of the nation's population lived in cities, the Atlantic ports continued, as in the colonial era, to dominate the nation economically and politically. Seaports benefited from the advantage of waterborne trade and communication over much slower land travel. Merchants in the seaboard cities found it easier to cross the Atlantic than to venture into their own backcountry in search of trade. In 1800 the nation's most important urban centers were all Atlantic seaports: Charleston (which had a population of 20,000), Baltimore (26,000), Philadelphia (70,000), New York (60,000), and Boston (25,000). Each had a distinctive regional identity.

Charleston, South Carolina, was the South's premier port. In colonial days, Charleston had grown rich on its links with the British West Indies and on trade with England in rice, long-staple cotton, and indigo. The social center for the great low-country plantation owners, Charleston was a multicultural city of white people, African Americans (2,000 of them free), Indian people, and the mixed race offspring of the three groups. One was as likely to hear French, Spanish, or Gullah and Geeche (African-based dialects of low-country slaves) as English. This graceful, elegant city was a center for the slave trade until 1808.

Baltimore was the major port for the tobacco of the Chesapeake Bay region and thus was connected with the slave-owning aristocracy of the Upper South. But proximity to the wheat-growing regions of the Pennsylvania backcountry increasingly inclined the city's merchants to look westward and to consider ways to tap the trade of the burgeoning Ohio country.

Philadelphia, William Penn's "City of Brotherly Love," was distinguished by the commercial and banking skills of Quaker merchants. These merchants had built international trade networks for shipping the farm produce of Pennsylvania's German farmers. Philadelphia served as the nation's capital in the 1790s and was acknowledged as its cultural and intellectual leader as well.

New York, still faintly Dutch in architecture and social customs, was soon to outgrow all the other cities. New York merchants were exceptionally aggressive in their pursuit of trade. Unlike their counterparts in Philadelphia and Boston, New Yorkers accepted the British auction system, which cut out the middleman and offered goods in large lots at wholesale prices at open auctions. Increasingly, British imports entered America through the port of New York. New York's shipping, banking, insurance, and supporting industries boomed, and as early as 1800 a quarter of all American shipping was owned by New York merchants.

Boston, the cockpit of the American Revolution, was also the capital of Massachusetts. The handsome State House, built on Beacon Hill, reflected the origins of Boston's merchant wealth: a carved wooden codfish occupied a place of honor in the new building. By the late eighteenth century, however, Boston's commercial wealth had diversified into shipbuilding and shipping, banking and insurance.

Though small in population, these Atlantic cities led the nation socially, politically, and above all economically. In 1800, the merchants in these seaports still primarily looked across the Atlantic to Europe. In the coming half-century, however, it was the cities that developed the strongest ties with the trans-Appalachian West that were to thrive.

A NATIONAL ECONOMY

In 1800, the United States was a producer of raw materials. The new nation faced the same challenge that developing nations confront today. At the mercy of fluctuating world commodity prices they cannot control, such countries have great difficulty protecting themselves from economic dominance by stronger, more established nations. In 1800, America was in just such a situation.

The Economy of the Young Republic

In 1800 the United States was predominantly rural and agricultural. According to the census of 1800, 94 in 100 Americans lived in communities of fewer than 2,500 people, and 4 in 5 families farmed the land, either for themselves or for others. Farming families followed centuries-old traditions of working with hand tools and draft animals, producing most of their own food and fiber, and most Americans dressed in cloth that had been spun, woven, and tailored by women in their own families. Seaboard farmers of the Middle States and those near urban centers engaged in commercial farming, but for most, crops were grown for home use rather than for sale. Production of a "surplus" to sell was a small sideline. Commodities such as whiskey and hogs (both easy to transport) provided small and irregular cash incomes or items for barter. As late as 1820, only 20 percent of the produce of American farms was consumed outside the local community.

In contrast to this pattern, the plantation agriculture of the South was wholly commercial and international. Slave owners, however, faced a growing dilemma: their heavy capital investment in African American slave labor was not matched by a growth in the demand for tobacco and rice, the traditional export crops. The tobacco trade, which accounted for about a third of the value of all colonial exports, remained at or below pre-Revolutionary levels, and the demand for rice had actually declined.

The demand for a third crop, cotton, was growing rapidly in response to the boom in the indus-

trial production of textiles in England and Europe, but extracting the seeds from the fibers of the variety of cotton that grew best in the southern interior required an enormous investment of labor. The cotton gin, which mechanized this process, was invented in 1793, but not until the nineteenth century did cotton assume a commanding place in the foreign trade of the United States.

In 1790, increasing foreign demand for American goods and services hardly seemed likely. Trade with Britain, still the biggest customer for American raw materials, was considerably less than it had been before the Revolution. As an independent nation, the United States no longer benefited from British mercantilist trade privileges. Britain and France both excluded Americans from their lucrative West Indian trade and taxed American ships with discriminatory duties. It was difficult to be independent in a world dominated by great powers.

Shipping and the Economic Boom

Despite these restrictions on American commerce, the strong shipping trade begun during the colonial era and centered in the Atlantic ports became a major asset in the 1790s, when events in Europe provided America with extraordinary opportunities.

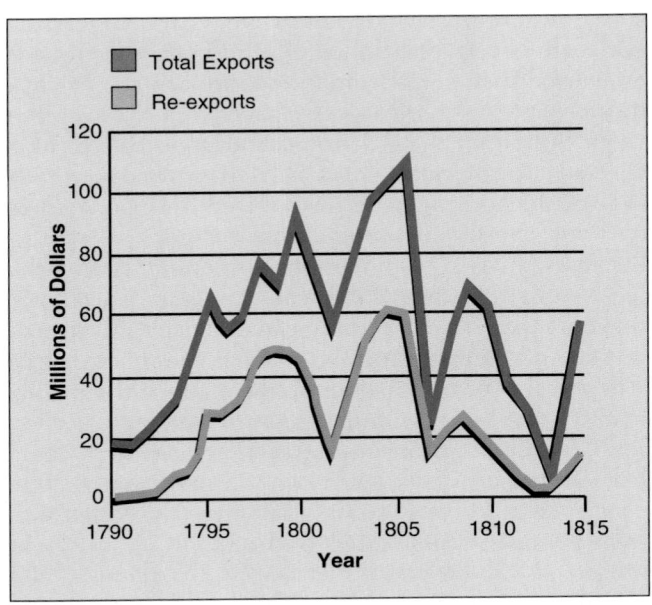

American Export Trade, 1790–1815   *This graph shows how completely the American shipping boom was tied to European events. Exports, half of which were reexports, surged when Britain and France were at war and America could take advantage of its status as neutral. Exports slumped in the brief period of European peace in 1803–1805 and plunged following the Embargo Act of 1807 and the outbreak of the War of 1812.*

Source: Douglass C. North, *The Economic Growth of the United States, 1790–1860* (New York: Norton, 1966), p. 26.

This picture shows the launching of the ship Fame *from Becket's Shipyard in Essex, Massachusetts, in 1802. Shipbuilding was a major New England industry, and a launching was a community event.*

The French Revolution, which began in 1789, soon initiated nearly twenty-five years of warfare between Britain and France. As the European powers converted their ships from international trade to military purposes, American vessels were ready to replace them. All along the Atlantic seaboard, urban centers thrived as American ships carried European goods that could no longer be transported on British ships without danger of French attack (and vice versa). Because America was neutral, its merchants had the legal right to import European goods and promptly reexport them to other European countries. In spite of British and French efforts to prevent the practice (see Chapter 8), reexports amounted to half of the profits in the booming shipping trade.

The vigorous international shipping trade had dramatic effects within the United States. The coastal cities all grew substantially from 1790 to 1820. In 1790, only twelve cities in the United States held more than 5,000 people and only 3 percent of the population was urban; by 1820 city dwellers made up 7 percent of the population and thirty-five cities had a population exceeding 5,000. This rapid urbanization was a sign of vigorous economic growth (rather than a sign that poverty was pushing rural workers off the farms, as occurs in some third world countries today), for it reflected expanding opportunities in the cities. In fact, the rapid growth of cities stimulated farmers to produce the food to feed the new urban dwellers.

The long series of European wars also allowed enterprising Americans to seize such lucrative international opportunities as the China trade. In 1784 the *Empress of China* set sail from New York for Canton with forty tons of ginseng. When it returned in 1785 with a cargo of teas, silks, and chinaware, the sponsors of the voyage, Philadelphia financier Robert Morris and his partners, made a 30 percent profit. Other merchants were quick to follow Morris's example, and to improve on it. In 1787 Robert Gray left Boston in the *Columbia*, sailing south around Cape Horn, then north to Nootka Sound in the Pacific Northwest, where he bought sea otter skins cheaply from the coastal Indians. Then, in 1789, Gray sailed west across the Pacific to China, where he sold the furs at fabulous profits before rounding the Cape of Good Hope and returning to Boston laden with tea. In his second voyage in 1792, Gray discovered the mouth of a major Northwest river, which he named for his ship. (When Lewis and Clark ventured west in 1804, part of their task was to chart the exact path of Gray's "Columbia's River.") Soon New England so dominated the seaborne trade in furs to China that the Pacific Northwest Indians called all Americans "Bostons."

The active American participation in international trade fostered a strong and diversified shipbuilding industry. All the major Atlantic ports boasted expanding shipbuilding enterprises. The average size of full-rigged ships built in one shipyard in Portsmouth, New Hampshire, increased from 361 tons in 1825 to 2,145 tons in 1855. Demands for speed increased as well, resulting in what many people have regarded as the flower of American shipbuilding, the clipper ship. The narrow-hulled, many-sailed clipper ships of the 1840s and 1850s set records for ships of their size. In 1854, *Flying Cloud*, built in the Boston shipyards of Donald McKay, sailed from New York to San Francisco—a 16,000-mile trip that usually took 150 to 200 days—in a mere 89 days. The clipper ships' average of 300 miles a day made them competitive with steamships through the 1850s.

In every seaport, this booming trade stimulated the development of financial services, such as insurance companies, banks, and brokers, geared more to international than to local concerns. By 1820, the United States was well on its way to building a strong and diversified national economy. At the same time, the wealth, confidence, and power of the merchants in the seacoast cities greatly increased.

THE JEFFERSON PRESIDENCY

Thomas Jefferson began his presidency with a symbolic action worthy of a twentieth-century media-wise politician. At noon on March 4, 1801, he walked from his

modest boardinghouse through the swampy streets of the new federal city of Washington to the unfinished Capitol. George Washington and John Adams had ridden in elaborate carriages to their inaugurals. Jefferson, although accepting a military honor guard, demonstrated by his actions that he rejected the elaborate, quasi-monarchical style of the two Federalist presidents, and their (to his mind) autocratic style of government as well.

For all its lack of pretension, Jefferson's inauguration as the third president of the United States was a momentous occasion in American history, for it marked the peaceful transition from one political party, the Federalists, to their hated rivals, the Democratic Republicans. Beginning in an atmosphere of exceptional political bitterness, Jefferson's presidency was to demonstrate that a strongly led party system could shape national policy without leading either to dictatorship or to revolt. It was a great achievement.

Republican Agrarianism

Jefferson brought to the presidency a clearly defined political philosophy. Behind all the events of his administration (1801–09) and those of his successors in what became known as the Virginia Dynasty (James Madison, 1809–17; James Monroe, 1817–25) was a clear set of beliefs that embodied Jefferson's interpretation of the meaning of republicanism for Americans.

Jefferson's years as ambassador to France in the 1780s were particularly important in shaping his political thinking. Recoiling from the extremes of wealth and poverty he saw there, he came to believe that it was impossible for Europe to achieve a just society that could guarantee to most of its members the "life, liberty and...pursuit of happiness" of which he had written in the Declaration of Independence.

Tall, ungainly, and diffident in manner, Thomas Jefferson was nonetheless a man of genius. Jefferson designed and supervised every aspect of the building and furnishing of Monticello, his classical home atop a hill near Charlottesville, Virginia. The process took almost forty years (from 1770 to 1809), for Jefferson constantly changed and refined his design, subjecting both himself and his family to years of uncomfortable living in the partially completed structure. The result, however, was one of the most civilized—and most autobiographical— houses ever built.

The growth of the factory system in England horrified Jefferson, who deplored the squalor of teeming new factory towns such as Manchester in the north of England. He opposed industrialization in America: in the 1790s, when Alexander Hamilton and the Federalists had proposed fostering manufacturing in the United States, Jefferson had responded with outrage (see Chapter 8). He was convinced that the Federalist program would create precisely the same extremes of wealth and the same sort of unjust government that prevailed in Europe.

Jefferson believed that only America provided fertile earth for the true citizenship necessary to a republican form of government. What America had, and Europe lacked, was room to grow. Jefferson envisaged a nation of small family farms clustered together in rural communities—an agrarian republic. He believed that only a nation of roughly equal yeoman farmers, each secure in his own possessions and not dependent on someone else for his livelihood, would exhibit the concern for the community good that was essential in a republic. More romantically, Jefferson also believed that rural contact with the cycles and rhythms of nature was essential to the republican character. Indeed, Jefferson said that "those who labor in the earth are the chosen people of God," and so he viewed himself, though his "farm" was the large slave-owning plantation of Monticello.

Yet another European event influenced Jefferson's thinking. In 1798, the Englishman Thomas Malthus published a deeply pessimistic and widely influential *Essay on the Principle of Population.* Warning of an impending population explosion, Malthus predicted that the British population would soon outstrip the country's food supply. Unless this population growth was checked, misery and poverty would soon be widespread throughout Europe and even, Malthus warned, in America. Malthus's prediction alarmed many Americans, who had taken pride in having one of the fastest rates of population growth in the world, close to 40 percent per decade. Thomas Jefferson was not worried. He used Malthus to underline the opportunity created by America's vast land resources. The Malthusian prediction need not trouble the United States, Jefferson said, as long as the country kept expanding.

Jefferson's vision of an expanding agrarian republic remains to this day one of our most compelling ideas about America's uniqueness and special destiny. But expansionism contained some negative aspects. The lure of the western lands fostered constant mobility and dissatisfaction rather than the stable, settled communities of yeoman farmers that Jefferson envisaged. Expansionism caused environmental damage, in particular soil exhaustion—a consequence of abandoning old lands, rather than conserving them, and moving on to new ones. Finally, expansionism bred a ruthlessness toward Indian peoples, who were pushed out of the way for white settlement or who, like the Mandans, were devastated by the diseases that accompanied European trade and contact. Jefferson's agrarianism thus bred some of the best and some of the worst traits of the developing nation.

Jefferson's Government

Thomas Jefferson came to office determined to reverse the Federalist policies of the 1790s and to ensure an agrarian "republic of virtue." Accordingly, he proposed a program of "simplicity and frugality," promising to cut all internal taxes, reduce the size of the army (from 4,000 to 2,500 men), navy (from twenty-five ships to seven), and government staff, and to eliminate the entire national debt inherited from the Federalists. He kept all of these promises, even the last, although the Louisiana Purchase of 1803 cost the Treasury $15 million. This diminishment of government was a key matter of republican principle to Jefferson. If his ideal yeoman farmer was to be a truly self-governing citizen, the federal government must not, Jefferson believed, be either large or powerful. His cost-cutting measures simply carried out the pledge he had made in his Inaugural Address for "a wise

Ludwig Goettfried von Redeken. *A View of Salem in North Carolina*, 1787. Collection of the Wachovia Historical Society.

Thomas Jefferson based his republican agrarianism on the real lives of prosperous and independent farmers like this one, shown plowing his fields near Salem, North Carolina in 1787.

and frugal government, which shall restrain men from injuring one another, [and] shall leave them otherwise free to regulate their own pursuits."

Perhaps one reason for Jefferson's success was that the federal government he headed was small and unimportant by today's standards. For instance, Jefferson found only 130 federal officials in Washington (a grand total of nine in the State Department, including the secretary of state). The national government's main service to ordinary people was mail delivery, and already in 1800 there were persistent complaints about slowness, unreliability, and expense in the Postal Service! Everything else—law and order, education, welfare, road maintenance, economic control—rested with state or local governments. Power and political loyalty were still local, not national.

This small national government also explains why for years the nation's capital was so unimpressive. The French designer Pierre L'Enfant had laid out a magnificent plan of broad streets and sweeping vistas reminiscent of Paris. Congress planned to pay for the grand buildings with money from land sales in the new city, but few people besides politicians and boardinghouse keepers (a largely female occupation) chose to live in Washington. Construction lagged: the President's House lacked a staircase to the second floor until 1808, and although the House and Senate chambers were soon completed, the central portion of the Capitol was missing. Instead of the imposing dome we know so well today, the early Capitol consisted of two white marble boxes connected by a boardwalk. It is a telling indicator of the true location of national power that a people who had no trouble building new local communities across the continent should have had such difficulty establishing their federal city.

An Independent Judiciary

Although determined to reverse Federalist fiscal policies, Jefferson was much more moderate concerning Federalist officeholders. He resisted demands by other Democratic Republicans that "the board should be swept" and all Federalist officeholders replaced with party loyalists. During his term of office, Jefferson allowed 132 Federalists to remain at their posts, while placing Democratic Republicans in 158 others. This restrained use of patronage did much to attract moderate Federalists to the Democratic Republican party. Jefferson's restraint, however, did not extend to the most notorious Federalist appointees, the so-called midnight judges.

In the last days of the Adams administration, the Federalist-dominated Congress passed a Judiciary Act that created sixteen new judgeships and six new circuit courts. In one of his last acts in office, President Adams appointed Federalists—quickly dubbed the "midnight judges"—to the new positions. This last-minute action angered the Democratic Republicans, who feared that the losing Federalist Party was trying to use the judiciary to increase the power of the federal government over the states. Congress, controlled by the Democratic Republicans, repealed the Judiciary Act, depriving the new judges of their jobs. One of these hapless appointees, William Marbury, sued James Madison, Jefferson's secretary of state, to recover the position he had lost. This action provoked a landmark decision from the Supreme Court, head of the federal judiciary.

At issue was a fundamental constitutional point: Was the federal judiciary an independent and final authority on questions of law, as Supreme Court decisions during the Federalist administrations of the 1790s had asserted, or did the election of a Democratic Republican administration that favored states' rights curtail the powers of federal courts as well? In his celebrated 1803 decision, *Marbury v. Madison*, Chief Justice John Marshall, himself a strong Federalist and an Adams appointee, managed to find a way to please both parties. On the one hand, Marshall proclaimed that the courts had a duty "to say what the law is," thus unequivocally defending the independence of the judiciary and the principle of judicial review. On the other hand, Marshall conceded that the Supreme Court could not force the executive branch to appoint Marbury to a position that no longer existed. At first glance, Jefferson's government appeared to have won the battle over Adams's last-minute appointees. But in the long run, Marshall established the principle that only the federal judiciary could decide what was constitutional. This was a vital step in realizing the three-way balance of power among the branches of the federal government—executive (president), legislative (Congress), judiciary (courts)—envisaged in the Constitution. Equally important, during his long tenure in office (1801–35) Chief Justice Marshall consistently led the Supreme Court in a series of decisions that favored the federal government over state governments. Under Marshall's direction, the Supreme Court became a powerful nationalizing and unifying force.

Opportunity: The Louisiana Purchase

In 1800 the United States was a new and fragile democracy in a world dominated by two contending great powers: Britain and France. This rivalry appeared to threaten both American commerce and national security.

In 1799 the young general Napoleon Bonaparte seized control of France and began a career of military conquests. Four years later, Great Britain went to war against him. Following one year of peace, Britain and France were again at war by 1803, beginning a twelve-year duel that ended only with Napoleon's defeat at the battle of Waterloo in 1815. As had his predecessors, Napoleon looked at North America as a potential battleground on which to fight the British. In 1800, in a secret treaty, France reacquired the Louisiana Territory, the vast western drainage of the Mississippi and Missouri Rivers, from Spain, which had held the region since 1763. From Louisiana, if he chose, Napoleon could launch an attack to regain Canada from the British.

When President Jefferson learned of the secret agreement in 1801, he was alarmed. He feared that French control would threaten the growing American trade on the Mississippi River and force the young nation to take military action. In fact, in 1802 the Spanish commander at New Orleans (the French had not yet taken formal control) closed the port to American shippers, thus disrupting commerce as far away as Cincinnati. As Jefferson feared, Federalists in Congress clamored for military action to reopen the port, and he himself was determined to end this threat to American commerce.

Initially, Jefferson offered to buy New Orleans and the surrounding area for $2 million (or up to $10 million, if necessary). As it happened, Napoleon was eager to sell. A French army of 30,000 men had just withdrawn from the Caribbean island of Santo Domingo (now Haiti), defeated by yellow fever and an army of former slaves led by François Toussaint L'Ouverture. In the wake of the defeat, and in need of money for European military campaigns, Napoleon offered the entire Louisiana Territory, including the crucial port of New Orleans, to the Americans for $15 million. Exceeding his instructions, special American envoy James Monroe seized the opportunity and bought the entire Louisiana Territory from Napoleon in Paris in April 1803.

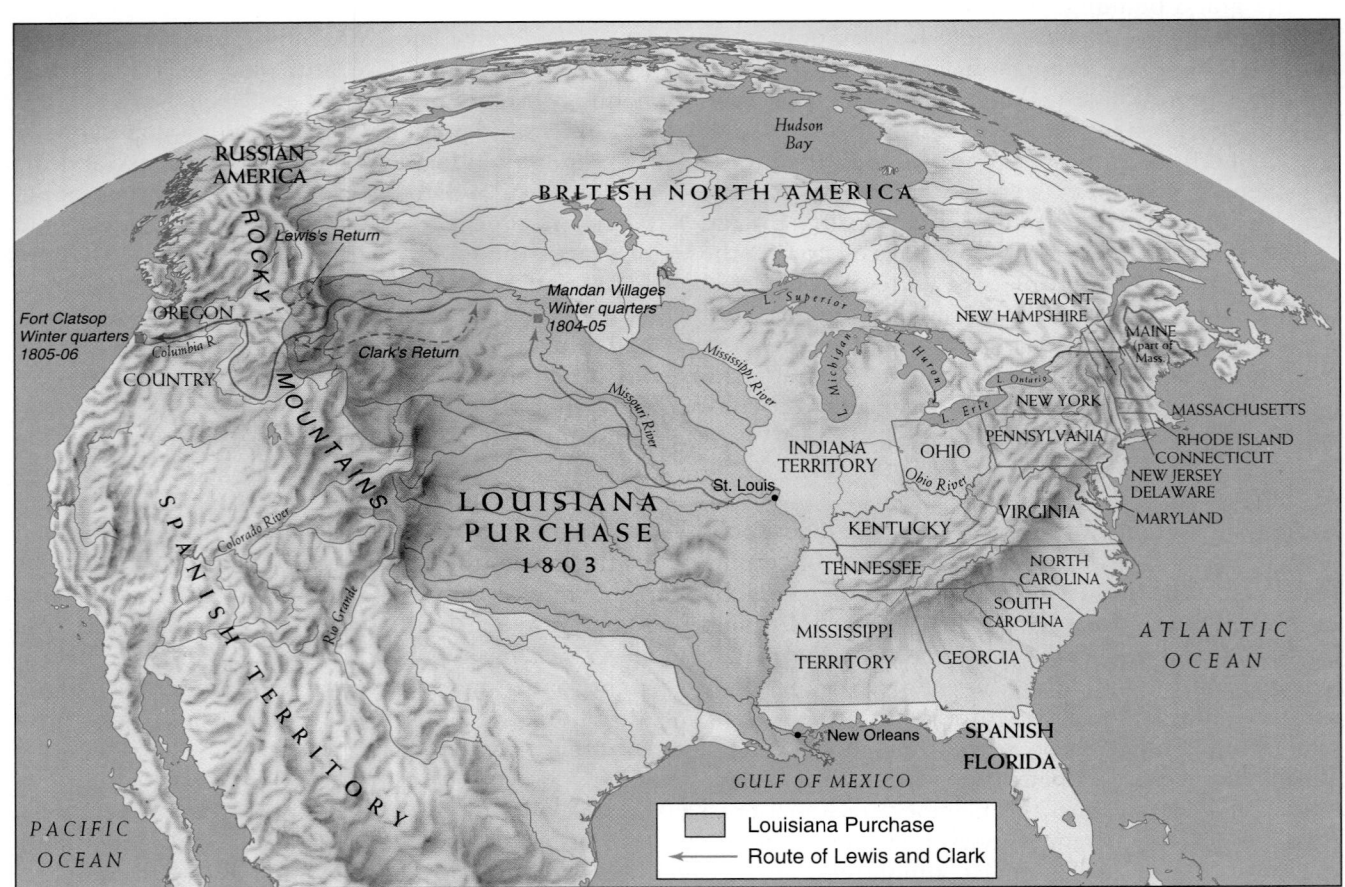

Louisiana Purchase *The Louisiana Purchase of 1803, the largest peaceful acquisition of territory in United States history, more than doubled the size of the nation. The Lewis and Clark expedition (1804–1806) was the first to survey and document the natural and human richness of the area. The American sense of expansiveness and continental destiny owes more to the extra-ordinary opportunity provided by the Louisiana Purchase than to anything else.*

Overnight, the size of the United States more than doubled. It was the largest peaceful acquisition of territory in United States history.

At home, Jefferson suffered brief qualms. The Constitution did not authorize the president to purchase territory, and Jefferson had always rigidly insisted on a limited interpretation of executive rights. But he had also long held a sense of destiny about the West and had planned the Lewis and Clark expedition before the Louisiana Purchase was a reality. In any case, the prize was too rich to pass up. Jefferson now argued that Louisiana was vital to the nation's republican future. "By enlarging the empire of liberty," Jefferson wrote, "we…provide new sources of renovation, should its principles, at any time, degenerate, in those portions of our country which gave them birth." In other words, expansion was essential to liberty.

Congress and the general public joined Jefferson in welcoming the purchase. Of course, the support was not unanimous. Some Federalists disputed Jefferson's claim that expansion would foster liberty and predicted that it would doom the republican form of government. As Federalist Fisher Ames dramatically warned, "By adding an unmeasured world beyond [the Mississippi]…we rush like a comet into infinity."

Incorporating Louisiana

The immediate issue following the Louisiana Purchase was how to treat the French and Spanish inhabitants of the Louisiana Territory. Many people thought that the only way to deal with a population so "foreign" was to wipe out its customs and laws and impose American ones as quickly as possible. But this did not happen. The incorporation of Louisiana into the American federal system was a remarkable story of adaptation between two different communities—American and French.

In 1803, when the region that is now the state of Louisiana became American property, it had a racially and ethnically diverse population of 43,000 people, of whom only 6,000 were American. French and French-speaking people were numerically and culturally dominant, especially in the city of New Orleans. There the French community effectively challenged the initial American plan of rapidly supplanting French culture and institutions with American ones. At a public ball held in New Orleans in January 1804, for example, American and French military officers almost came to blows over whether an English country dance or a French waltz would be played first.

Officials in Washington dismissed the reported conflict as mere frivolity, but the U.S. representative in New Orleans and governor of Lower Louisiana Territory, William Claiborne, did not. Over the next four years Claiborne came to accept the value of French institutions to the region. As a result, with Claiborne's full support, Louisiana adopted a legal code in 1808 that was based on French civil law rather than English common law. This was not a small concession. French law differed from English law in many fundamental respects, such as family property (communal versus male ownership), inheritance (forced heirship versus free disposal), and even contracts, which were much more strictly regulated in the French system. Remnants of the French legal system remain part of Louisiana state law to this day. In 1812, with the required 60,000 free inhabitants, Louisiana was admitted to the Union. New Orleans remained for years a distinctively French city, illustrating the flexibility possible under a federal system.

Texas and the Struggle for Mexican Independence

Spain objected, in vain, to Napoleon's 1803 sale of Louisiana to America. For years Spain had attempted to seal off its rich colony of Mexico from commerce with other nations. Now, American Louisiana shared one vague and disputed boundary with Mexico's northern province of Texas (a parcel of land already coveted by some Americans) and, on the east, a similarly uncertain boundary with Spanish Florida.

Soon Napoleon brought turmoil to all of Mexico. In 1808, he installed his brother Joseph Bonaparte as king of Spain, forcing Spain's king, Charles IV, to renounce his throne. For the next six years, as warfare convulsed Spain, the country's long-prized New World empire slipped away. Mexico, divided between royalists loyal to Spain and populists seeking social and economic justice for mestizos and Indians, edged bloodily toward independence. Two populist revolts—one in 1810 led by Father Miguel Hidalgo and the other in 1813 led by Father José María Morelos—were suppressed by the royalists, who executed both revolutionary leaders. In 1812 a small force, led by Mexican republican Bernardo Gutiérrez but composed mostly of American adventurers, invaded Texas, capturing San Antonio, assassinating the provincial governor Manuel Salcedo, and declaring Texas independent. A year later, however, the Mexican republicans were defeated by a royalist army that then killed suspected collaborators and pillaged the province so thoroughly that the local economy was devastated and the Mexican population declined to fewer than 2,000. Mexico's difficult path toward independence seemed, at least to some Americans, to offer yet another opportunity for expansion.

RENEWED IMPERIAL RIVALRY IN NORTH AMERICA

Fresh from the triumph of the Louisiana Purchase, Jefferson scored a major victory over the Federalist Charles Cotesworth Pinckney in the presidential election of 1804, garnering 162 electoral votes to Pinckney's 14. Jefferson's shrewd wooing of moderate Federalists had been so successful that the remaining Federalists dwindled to a highly principled but sectional group unable to attract voters outside of its home base in New England. Jefferson's Louisiana success was not repeated, however, and few other consequences of the ongoing struggle between Britain and France were so easy to solve. Their rivalry caused problems for America both on the high seas and on the nation's western borders.

Problems with Neutral Rights

In his first Inaugural Address in 1801, Jefferson had announced a foreign policy of "peace, commerce, and honest friendship with all nations, entangling alliances with none." This was a difficult policy to pursue after 1803, when the Napoleonic Wars resumed. By 1805 Napoleon had conquered most of Europe, but Britain, the victor at the great naval battle of Trafalgar, controlled the seas. The United States, trying to profit from trade with both countries, was caught in the middle. The British did not look kindly as their former colonists tried to evade their blockade of the French by claiming neutrality. Beginning in 1805, the British targeted the American reexport trade between the French West Indies and France by seizing American ships bringing French West Indian goods to Europe. Angry Americans viewed these seizures as violations of their neutral rights as shippers.

An even more contentious issue arose from the substantial desertion rate of British sailors. Many deserters promptly signed up on American ships, where they drew better pay and sometimes obtained false naturalization papers as well. The numbers involved were large: as many as a quarter of the 100,000 seamen on American ships were British. Soon the British were stopping American merchant vessels and removing any man they believed to be British, regardless of his papers. The British refusal to recognize genuine naturalization papers (on the principle "once a British subject, always a British subject") was particularly insulting to the new American sense of nationhood.

At least 6,000 innocent American citizens suffered forced impressment into the British navy from 1803 to 1812. In 1807 impressment turned bloody when the British ship *Leopard* stopped the American ship *Chesapeake* in American territorial waters and demanded to search for deserters. When the American captain refused, the *Leopard* opened fire, killing three men, wounding eighteen, and removing four deserters (three with American naturalization papers) from the damaged ship. An indignant public protested British interference and the death of innocent sailors. Had Congress been in session and the country militarily strong, public pressure might very well have forced a declaration of war against Britain then.

The Embargo Act

Fully aware that commerce was essential to the new nation, Jefferson was determined to insist on America's right as a neutral nation to ship goods to Europe. But Britain possessed the world's largest and strongest navy, one the small American navy could not effectively challenge. Jefferson first tried diplomatic protests, then negotiations, and finally threats, all to no avail. In 1806 Congress passed the Non-Importation Act, hoping that a boycott of British goods, which had worked so well during the Revolutionary War, would be effective once again. Presumably, denied their customary American markets British manufacturers would force a change in their government's policy. They did not. The boycott was suspended late in 1806 while the Jefferson administration tried to negotiate with the British; when that effort failed, the boycott was resumed.

Finally, in desperation, Jefferson imposed the Embargo Act in December 1807. This act forbade American ships from sailing to any foreign port, thereby cutting off all exports as well as imports. The act was directed at French as well as British disregard for the neutral rights of American vessels. Its intent was to force both countries to recognize those rights by depriving them of American-shipped raw materials. Jefferson hoped especially for a speedy change of British policy, because Britain's large navy caused much more harm to American shipping than did the smaller French navy.

But the results were a disaster for American trade. The commerce of the new nation, which Jefferson himself had done so much to promote, came to a standstill. Exports fell from $108 million in 1807 to $22 million in 1808, and the nation was driven into a deep depression. There was widespread evasion of the embargo. A remarkable number of ships in the coastal trade found themselves "blown off course" to the West Indies or Canada. Other ships simply left port illegally. Smuggling flourished. Pointing out that the American navy's weakness was due largely to the deep cuts Jefferson had inflicted on it, the Federalists sprang to life with a campaign of outspoken opposition to Jefferson's policy and found a ready audience in New England, the area hardest hit by the embargo.

Madison and the Failure of "Peaceable Coercion"

In this troubled atmosphere, Thomas Jefferson despondently ended his second term, acknowledging the failure of what he called "peaceable coercion." He was followed in office by his friend and colleague, James Madison of Virginia. Although Madison defeated the Federalist candidate—again Charles Cotesworth Pinkney—by 122 electoral votes to 47, Pinckney's share of the votes was three times what it had been in 1804, a reflection of the resentment New Englanders felt to the disproportionate hardships they suffered from the Embargo Act.

Ironically, the Embargo Act had almost no effect on its intended victims. The French used the embargo as a pretext for seizing American ships, claiming they must be British ships in disguise. The British, in the absence of American competition, developed new markets for their goods in South America. And at home, as John Randolph sarcastically remarked, the embargo was attempting "to cure corns by cutting off the toes."

In March 1809 Congress admitted failure, and the Embargo Act was repealed. But the struggle to remain neutral in the confrontation between the European giants continued. The next two years saw passage of several acts—among them the Non-Intercourse Act of 1809 and Macon's Bill Number 2 in 1810—that unsuccessfully attempted to prohibit trade with Britain and France unless they ceased their hostile treatment of U.S. shipping. Frustration with the ineffectiveness of government policy mounted.

A Contradictory Indian Policy

The United States faced other conflicts than those with Britain and France over neutral shipping rights. In the West, the powerful Indian nations of the Ohio Valley were determined to resist the wave of expansion that had carried thousands of white settlers onto their lands. North of the Ohio River lived the Northwest Confederation of the Shawnees, Delawares, Miamis, Potawatomis, and several smaller tribes. To the south of the Ohio were the so-called "Five Civilized Tribes," the Cherokees, Chickasaws, Choctaws, Creeks, and (in Florida) the Seminoles.

According to the Indian Intercourse Act of 1790, the United States could not simply seize Indian land; it could only acquire it when the Indians ceded it by treaty. But this policy conflicted with the harsh reality of westward expansion. Commonly, settlers

This double portrait of two Sac Indians by John Wesley Jarvis, painted in 1833, symbolized the hopes of official American Indian policy. The traditional Indian ways represented by Whirling Thunder's attire would be superseded by the "civilized" attitude represented by his father Black Hawk's European dress.

John Wesley Jarvis, Black Hawk and His Son, Whirling Thunder, 1833. Oil on canvas. 23 x 30 in. (60.3 x 76 cm). Gilcrease Museum, Tulsa, Oklahoma.

pushed ahead of treaty boundaries. When Indian peoples resisted the invasion of their lands, the pioneers fought back and called for military protection. Defeat of an Indian people led to further land cessions. The result for the Indians was a relentless cycle of invasion, resistance, and defeat.

Thomas Jefferson was deeply concerned with the fate of the western Indian peoples. Unlike most of the pioneers, who saw them simply as dangerous obstacles to be removed, Jefferson believed in coexistence and acculturation. His Indian policy was designed to solve the fundamental dilemma of expansion—the conflicting needs of white and Indian peoples. The Indians would cede the lands the pioneers craved, and in return white people would teach them how to farm and live like whites on their new, compressed reservations. Convinced that Indians had to give up hunting in favor of the yeoman-farmer lifestyle he so favored for all Americans, Jefferson directed the governors of the Northwest Territories to "promote energetically" his vision for civilizing the Indians.

Although he himself was notoriously indifferent to organized religion, Jefferson strongly supported efforts to Christianize Indian peoples and educate them in white ways. A number of denominations, among them the Moravians, Quakers, and Baptists, sent missionaries to the western Indians. Others formed special missionary societies, such as the Society for Propagating the Gospel among Indians (1797) and the American Board of Commissioners for Foreign

Ceded before 1784
Ceded 1784 – 1799
Ceded 1800 – 1812
Unceded Indian lands, 1812
Spread of The Prophet's influence
Tecumseh's travel routes

British fort
Spanish fort
American fort
Battle

Missions (1810). The latter was a joint effort of the Congregationalist, Presbyterian, and Dutch Reformed churches. Jefferson's Indian civilization plan was never adequately funded by Congress or supported by territorial governors and settlers. Although missionaries promoted literacy and a knowledge of white ways, they were generally disdainful of Indian culture and created deep divisions within Indian tribes between those who converted to Christianity and those who actively resisted conversion and were unwilling to give up traditional ways, especially hunting. Thus missionary efforts unwittingly weakened tribes already disoriented by the loss of their lands and life ways.

After the Louisiana Purchase, Jefferson offered traditionalist Indian groups new lands west of the Mississippi River, claiming that they would be able to live there undisturbed by white settlers for centuries. But he failed to consider the pace of westward expan-

Tecumseh

Tenskwatawa, The Prophet

Indian Resistance, 1790–1816

American westward expansion put relentless pressure on the Indian nations in the Trans-Appalachian South and West. The Trans-Appalachian region was marked by constant warfare from the time of the earliest settlements in Kentucky in the 1780s to the War of 1812. Tecumseh's Alliance in the Northwest (1809–11) and the Creek Rebellion in the Southwest (1813–14) were the culminating struggles in Indian resistance to the American invasion of the Trans-Appalachian region. Tecumseh, a Shawnee military leader, and his brother Tenskwatawa, a religious leader called The Prophet, led a pan-Indian revitalization and resistance movement that posed a serious threat to American westward

expansion. As the map shows, Tenskwatawa's message had wide appeal in the Northwest. Tecumseh traveled widely, attempting to build a military alliance on his brother's spiritual message. He achieved considerable success in the Northwest, but less in the Southwest, where many Indian peoples put their faith in accommodation. Tecumseh's death at the Battle of the Thames (1813) and British abandonment of their Shawnee allies at the end of the War of 1812 brought an end to organized Indian resistance in the Old Northwest. In the South, Andrew Jackson crushed Creek resisters in the Battle of Horseshoe Bend in 1814, and then demanded the cession of 23 million acres of land from both hostile and friendly Creek peoples.

sion. Less than twenty years later, Missouri, the first trans-Mississippi state, was admitted to the Union. The Indians living in Missouri, some of whom had been removed from the Old Northwest in accord with Jefferson's plan, were forced to move again to lands farther west. Western Indians like the Mandans, who had seemed so remote when Lewis and Clark wintered with them in 1804–05, were now threatened by further westward expansion.

In fact, Jefferson's Indian policy, because it did nothing to slow down the ever-accelerating westward expansion, offered little hope to Indian peoples. The alternatives they faced were stark: acculturation, removal, or extinction. Deprived of hunting lands, decimated by disease, increasingly dependent on the white economy for trade goods and annuity payments in exchange for land cessions, many Indian peoples despaired. Like the Mandans after Lewis and Clark's visit, they came to dread the effects of white contact. Nearly every tribe found itself bitterly split between accommodationists and traditionalists. Some, like groups of Cherokees and associated tribes in the South, advocated adapting their traditional agricultural lifestyles and pursuing a pattern of peaceful accommodation. In the Northwest Territory, however, many Indians chose the path of armed resistance.

Indian Resistance

The Shawnees, a seminomadic hunting and farming tribe (the men hunted, the women farmed) of the Ohio Valley, had resisted white settlement in Kentucky and Ohio since the 1750s. The decisive defeat of the Indian Confederacy led by Little Turtle, a Miami Indian, at Fallen Timbers (1794) and the continuing pressure of American settlement, however, left the Shawnees divided. One group, led by Black Hoof, accepted acculturation. Soon Quaker and Moravian missionaries were converting Black Hoof's band and teaching them farming. The rest of the tribe tried to maintain traditional ways. Most broke into small bands and tried to eke out a living by hunting, but their numbers were reduced by disease and the survivors further demoralized by the alcohol offered them illegally by private traders. One group of traditional Shawnees, however, led by the warrior Tecumseh, sought refuge farther west.

But there was no escape from white encroachment. Between 1801 and 1809, William Henry Harrison, governor of Indiana Territory, concluded fifteen treaties with the Delawares, Potawatomis, Miamis, and other tribes. These treaties opened eastern Michigan, southern Indiana, and most of Illinois to white settlement and forced the Indians into ever-smaller reservations. Many of these treaties were obtained by coercion, bribery, and outright trickery, and most Indians did not accept them.

In 1805 Tecumseh's brother, Tenskwatawa, known as The Prophet, began preaching a message of Indian revitalization: a rejection of all contact with the Americans, including use of American alcohol, clothing, and trade goods, and a return to traditional practices of hunting and farming. He preached an end to quarreling, violence, and sexual promiscuity and to the accumulation of private property. Wealth was valuable only if it was given away, he said. If the Northwest Indians returned to traditional ways, Tenskwatawa promised, "the land will be overturned so that all the white people will be covered and you alone shall inhabit the land."

This was a powerful message, but it was not new. Just six years earlier, Handsome Lake had led the Seneca people of upstate New York in a similar revitalization movement. Tecumseh, however, succeeded in molding his brother's religious following into a powerful pan-Indian military resistance movement. With each new treaty that Harrison concluded, Tecumseh gained new followers among the Northwest Confederation tribes. Significantly, he also had the support of the British, who, after 1807, began sending food and guns to him from Canada.

The pan-Indian strategy was at first primarily defensive, aimed at preventing further westward expansion. But the Treaty of Fort Wayne in 1809, in which the United States gained 3 million acres of Delaware and Potawatomi land in Indiana, led to active resistance. Confronting Harrison directly, Tecumseh argued that the land belonged to the larger community of all the Indian peoples; no one tribe could give away the common property of all. He then warned that any surveyors or settlers who ventured into the 3 million acres would risk their lives.

Tecumseh took his message of common land ownership and military resistance to all the Indian peoples of the Northwest Confederacy. He was not uniformly successful, even among the Shawnees. Black Hoof, for example, refused to join. Tecumseh also recruited, with mixed success, among the tribes south of the Ohio River. In councils with Choctaws, Chickasaws, Creeks, and Cherokees, he promoted active resistance:

> The white race is a wicked race. Since the days when the white race first came in contact with the red men, there has been a continual series of aggressions. The hunting grounds are fast disappearing, and they are driving the red man farther and farther to the west. Such has been the fate of the Shawnees, and surely will be the fate of all tribes if the power of the whites is not forever crushed. The mere presence of the white man is a source of evil to the red men. His whiskey destroys the bravery of our warriors, and his lust corrupts the virtue of our women. The only hope for the red man is a war of extermination against the paleface.

In November 1811, while Tecumseh was still recruiting among the southern tribes, Harrison marched to the pan-Indian village of Tippecanoe with 1,000 soldiers. The 600 to 700 Indian warriors at the town, urged on by Tenskwatawa, attacked Harrison's forces before dawn on November 7, hoping to surprise them. The attack failed, and in the battle that followed the Americans inflicted about 150 Indian casualties, while sustaining about as many themselves. Although Harrison claimed victory, the truth was far different. Dispersed from Tippecanoe, Tecumseh's angry followers fell on American settlements in Indiana and southern Michigan, killing many pioneers and forcing the rest to flee to fortified towns. Tecumseh himself entered into a formal alliance with the British. For western settlers, the Indian threat was greater than ever.

THE WAR OF 1812

Many westerners blamed the British for Tecumseh's attacks on pioneer settlements in the Northwest. British support of western Indians and the long-standing difficulties over neutral shipping rights were the two grievances cited by President Madison when he asked Congress for a declaration of war against Britain on June 1, 1812; Congress obliged him on June 18. But the war had other, more general causes as well.

The War Hawks

A rising young generation of political leaders, first elected to Congress in 1810, strongly resented the continuing influence of Britain, the former mother country, on American affairs. These War Hawks, who included such future leaders as Henry Clay of Kentucky and John C. Calhoun of South Carolina, were young Democratic Republicans from the West and South. They found all aspects of British interference, such as impressment and support for western Indians, intolerable. Eager to assert independence from England once and for all, these young men saw themselves finishing the job begun by the aging revolutionary generation.

The War Hawks were vehemently expansionist, and their dreams of expansion entailed control of peoples of other races—resistant Indians and rebellious African Americans—at the edges of the national boundaries. Southerners wanted to occupy Florida to prevent runaway slaves from seeking refuge with the Seminole Indians. Westerners wanted to invade Canada, hoping thereby to end threats from British-backed Indians in the Northwest such as Tecumseh. As resentments against England and frustrations over border issues merged, the pressure for war—always a strong force for national unity—mounted.

Unaware that the British, seriously hurt by the American trade embargo, were about to adopt a more conciliatory policy, President James Madison yielded to the War Hawks' clamor for action in June 1812, and his declaration of war passed the U.S. Senate by the close vote of 19 to 13, the House by 79 to 49. All the Federalists voted against the war. (The division along party lines continued in the 1812 presidential election, in which Madison garnered 128 electoral votes to 89 for his Federalist opponent, DeWitt Clinton.) The vote was sectional, with New England and the Middle States in opposition and the West and South strongly prowar. Thus the United States entered the War of 1812 more deeply divided along sectional lines than during any other foreign war in American history.

Nor was that the end of the difficulties. As a result of Jefferson's economizing, the American army and navy were small and weak. In contrast, the British,

The War of 1812   On land, the War of 1812 was fought to define the nation's boundaries. In the North, American armies attacked British forts in the Great Lakes region with little success, and the invasion of Canada was a failure. In the South, the battle of New Orleans made a national hero of Andrew Jackson, but it occurred after the peace treaty had been signed. On the sea, with the exception of Oliver Perry's victory in the Great Lakes, Britain's dominance was so complete and its blockade so effective that British troops were able to invade the Chesapeake and burn the capital of the United States.

after almost ten years' entanglement in the Napoleonic Wars, were in fighting trim. As a result, although the War of 1812 brought Americans a few moments of glory, it was on the whole an ignominious struggle that gained them little.

The Campaign against Canada

The American goal of expansion fared badly. Americans envisaged a quick victory over sparsely populated British Canada that would destroy British support for Tecumseh and his Northwest Indian allies, but instead the British-Indian alliance defeated them. In July 1812, a foray into western Canada by General William Hull of Michigan Territory was repulsed by a joint British and Indian force, which went on, in August, to capture Detroit, Fort Dearborn (site of Chicago), and Hull's army of 2,000 men. The American burning of York (now Toronto) in April 1813 achieved little, but in September, at the battle of Put-in-Bay, Captain Oliver H. Perry defeated a British naval squadron on Lake Erie, sending out the famous message, "We have met the enemy and they are ours." Without control of Lake Erie, the British could no longer assure their hold on Detroit. In October, William Henry Harrison retook Detroit and followed its retreating British and Indian defenders. Assisted by naval forces commanded by Perry, Harrison defeated them in the battle of the Thames. Among those slain in the battle was Tecumseh. Later attempts by the United States to invade Canada in the Niagara area failed, but so too did British attempts to invade the United States in the same area.

One reason for the failure of the Canadian invasion, aside from failure to appreciate the strength of the British-Indian forces, was that the New England states actively opposed the war. Massachusetts, Rhode Island, and Connecticut refused to provide militia or supplies, and other New England governors turned a blind eye to the flourishing illegal trade across the U.S.–Canadian border. Another reason was the reaction of Canadians themselves, the majority of whom were former Americans. Ironically, the most decisive effect of the abortive American attacks was the formation of a Canadian sense of national identity and a determination never to be invaded or absorbed by the United States.

War in the South

In the South, warfare similar to that waged against Tecumseh's pan-Indian resistance movement in the Northwest dramatically affected the southern Indian peoples. The first of the southern Indian peoples to battle the Americans were the Creeks, a trading nation with a long history of contacts with the Spanish and the French. When white settlers began to occupy Indian lands in northwestern Georgia and central Alabama early in the century, the Creeks, like the Shawnees in the Northwest, were divided in their response. Although many Creek bands argued for accommodation, a group known as the Red Sticks were determined to fight. During the War of 1812 the Red Sticks, allied with the British and Spanish, fought not only the Americans but other Indian groups.

In August 1813 the Red Sticks attacked Fort Mims on the Alabama River, killing more than 500 Americans and mixed-race Creeks who had gathered there for safety. Led by Andrew Jackson, troops from the Tennessee and Kentucky militias combined with the Creeks' traditional foes—the Cherokees, Choctaws, and Chickasaws—and some opposing bands of Creeks to exact revenge. Jackson's troops matched the Creeks in ferocity, shooting the Red Sticks "like dogs," one soldier reported. At the battle of Horseshoe Bend in March 1814, the Creeks were trapped between American cannon fire and their Indian enemies: more than 800 were killed, more than in any other battle in the history of Indian-white warfare. Jackson then marched on the remaining Red Stick villages, burning and killing as he went. Cornered, one remaining Red Stick leader, Red Eagle, personally confronted Jackson:

> General Jackson, I am not afraid of you. I fear no man, for I am a Creek warrior. I have nothing to request in behalf of myself....But I come to beg you to send for the women and children of the war party, who are now starving in the woods....If I could fight you any longer I would most heartily do so. Send for the women and children. They never did you any harm. But kill me, if the white people want it done.

At the end of the Creek War in 1814 Jackson demanded huge land concessions from the Creeks (including from some Creek bands that had fought on his side): 23 million acres, or more than half the Creek domain. The Treaty of Fort Jackson (1814) confirming these land concessions earned Jackson his Indian name, Sharp Knife.

The war failed to achieve another of its initial goals, that of capturing Florida from Spain. Mobile was captured in 1813, but although Jackson captured Pensacola in 1814, he was unable to hold it. In early 1815 (after the peace treaty had been signed but before news of it arrived in America), Andrew Jackson achieved his best-known victory, an improbable win over veteran British troops in the battle of New Orleans.

The Naval War

At sea the British navy quickly established a strong blockade, harassing coastal shipping along the Atlantic seaboard and attacking coastal settlements at will. In the most humiliating attack, the British burned Washington in the summer of 1814, forcing the president and Congress to flee. Dolley Madison, the president's wife, achieved a permanent footnote in history by saving a portrait of George Washington from the White House as she fled. The indignity of the burning of Washington was somewhat assuaged in September, when Americans beat back a British attack on Baltimore and Fort McHenry. Watching the "rockets' red glare" in the battle, onlooker Francis Scott Key was moved to write the words to the "Star-Spangled Banner." There were a few American naval successes. The American frigate *Constitution* destroyed two British men-of-war, the *Guerrière* and the *Java*, in classic naval battles but failed to lift the British blockade.

The Hartford Convention

America's occasional successes failed to diminish the angry opposition of the New England Federalists to the War of 1812. In late 1814, Federalist representatives from the five New England states met in Hartford, Connecticut, to air their grievances. At first the air was full of talk of secession from the Union, but soon cooler heads prevailed.

The Hartford Convention's final document contained a long list of grievances, but it did not mention secession. It did, however, insist that a state had the right "to interpose its authority" to protect its citizens against unconstitutional federal laws. This nullification doctrine was not new; Madison and Jefferson had proposed it in the Virginia and Kentucky Resolves opposing the Alien and Sedition Acts in 1798 (see Chapter 8). In any event, the nullification threat from Hartford was ignored, for peace with Britain was announced as delegates from the convention made their way to Washington to deliver their message to Congress. There the convention's grievances were treated not as serious business but as an anticlimactic joke.

The Treaty of Ghent

In 1814, as the long Napoleonic Wars in Europe were drawing to a close, the British decided to end their minor war with the Americans. The peace treaty, after months of hard negotiation, was signed at Ghent, Belgium, on Christmas Eve in 1814. Like the war itself, the treaty was inconclusive. The major issues of impressment and neutral rights were not mentioned, but the British did agree to evacuate their western posts, and late in the negotiations they abandoned their insistence on a buffer state for neutral Indian peoples in the Northwest.

For all its international inconsequence, the war did have an important effect on national morale. As one historian has said, Americans had fought "for their chance to grow up." Andrew Jackson's victory at New Orleans allowed Americans to believe that they had defeated the British. It would be more accurate to say that by not losing the war the Americans had ended their own feelings of colonial dependency. Equally important, they convinced the British government to stop thinking of America as its colony. As it turned out, the War of 1812 was the last war the United States and Britain were to fight against each other.

At the same time, the war was a dangerous risk to new and fragile ideas of national unity. It was one of America's most divisive wars, and what made the opposition so serious was its sectional nature. Had the conflict continued, it might have led to the secession of New England.

The only clear losers of the war were the Indian nations in the Northwest and their southern allies. With the death of Tecumseh in 1813 and the defeat of the southern Creeks in 1814, the last hope of a united Indian resistance to white expansion perished forever. Britain's abandonment of its Indian allies in the Treaty of Ghent sealed their fate. By 1815, American settlers were on their way west again.

The burning of Washington by the British was the worst indignity the young American nation suffered in the War of 1812. This contemporary woodcut shows Washington aflame on August 2, 1814.

Spread of Settlement: Westward Surge, 1800–1820
Within a period of twenty years, a quarter of the nation's population had moved west of the Appalachian Mountains. The westward surge was a dynamic source of American optimism.

Map legend:
- Areas settled by 1800
- Areas settled by 1810
- Areas settled by 1820

DEFINING THE BOUNDARIES

With the War of 1812 behind them, Americans turned, more seriously than ever before, to the tasks of expansion and national development. The so-called Era of Good Feelings (1817–23) found politicians largely in agreement on a national agenda, and a string of diplomatic achievements forged by John Quincy Adams gave the nation sharper definition. But the limits to expansion also became clear: the Panic of 1819 showed the dangers in economic growth, and the Missouri Crisis laid bare the sectional split that attended westward expansion.

Another Westward Surge

The end of the War of 1812 was followed by a westward surge to the Mississippi River that populated the Old Northwest (Ohio, Indiana, Illinois, Michigan, and Wisconsin) and the Old Southwest (western Georgia, Alabama, Mississippi, Louisiana). The extent of the population redistribution was dramatic: in 1790, 95 percent of the nation's population had lived in states bordering the Atlantic Ocean; by 1820 fully 25 percent of the population lived west of the Appalachians.

What accounted for the westward surge? There were both push and pull factors. Between 1800 and 1820, the nation's population almost doubled, increasing from 5.3 million to 9.6 million. Although many easterners were attracted to the rapidly growing seacoast cities, 2.5 million, most of them farmers, chose to go westward. Overpopulated farmland in all of the seaboard states pushed farmers off the land, while new land pulled them westward. Defeat and removal of Indians in the War of 1812 was another important pull factor. In the Southwest, the Creeks ceded a huge tract of land amounting to three-fifths of Alabama and one-fifth of Georgia in the Treaty of Fort Jackson (1814); in the Northwest, the threat to settlers posed by Tecumseh's alliance had been removed.

The most important pull factor, however, was the attractive price of western land. The Land Ordinance of 1785 priced western lands too high for all but speculators and the wealthy (see Chapter 7), but since that time realities had slowly forced Congress to

Settlement of the heavily forested Old Northwest and Old Southwest required much heavy labor to clear the land. One common laborsaving method settlers learned from Indians was to "girdle" the trees (cutting the bark all around), thereby killing them. Dead trees could be more easily chopped and burned.

enact land laws more favorable to the small farmer. The most sustained challenge came from "squatters," who repeatedly took up land before it was officially open for sale and then claimed a "preemption" right of purchase at a lower price that reflected the value of improvements made to the land. Congress sought to suppress this illegal settlement and ordered the expulsion of squatters on several occasions, but to no avail. When federal lands were officially opened for sale in Illinois in 1814, for example, there were already 13,000 settlers, forcing Congress to reverse itself and grant them all preemption rights. Finally, in the Land Act of 1820, Congress set the price of land at $1.25 an acre, the minimum purchase at eighty acres (in contrast to the 640-acre minimum in 1785), and a down payment of $100 in cash. This was the most liberal land law yet passed in American history, but the cash requirement still favored speculators, who had more cash than most small farmers.

There were four major migration routes. In upstate New York, the Mohawk and Genesee Turnpike led New England migrants to Lake Erie, where they traveled by boat to northern Ohio. In the Middle States region, the turnpike from Philadelphia to Pittsburgh led to the Ohio River, as did the National Road that began in Baltimore and led to Wheeling. In the South, the Wilderness Road through the Cumberland Gap led to Kentucky, and passes in the mountains of North and South Carolina led to Tennessee. The Federal Road skirted the southern edge of the Appalachians and allowed farmers from South Carolina and eastern Georgia to move directly into Alabama and Mississippi. In this way, geography facilitated lateral westward movement (Northerners tended to migrate to the Old Northwest, Southerners to the Old Southwest). Except in southern Ohio and parts of Kentucky and Tennessee, there was very little contact between regional cultures. New Englanders carried their values and lifestyles

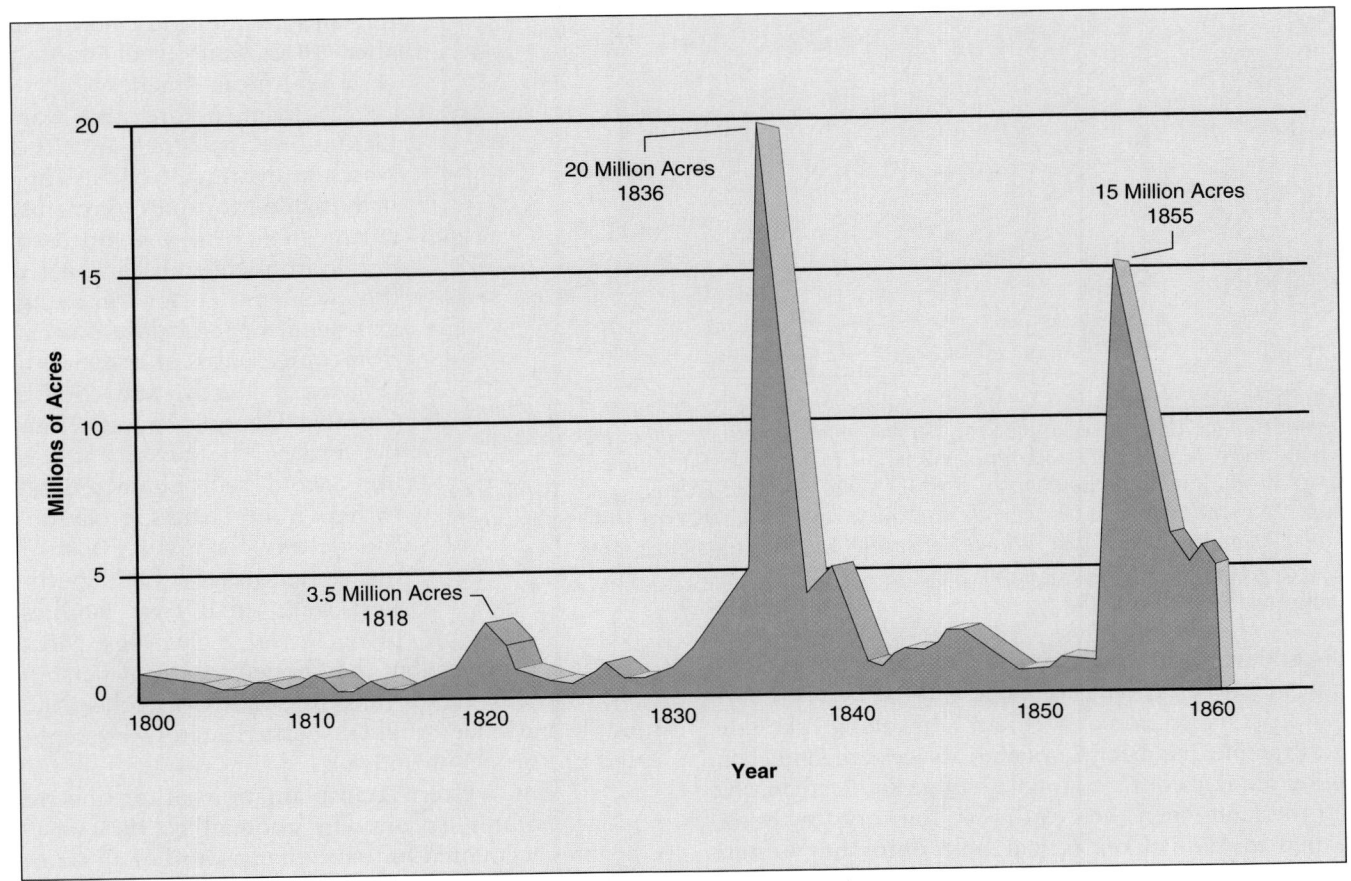

Western Land Sales   *Surges in western land sales reflect surges in westward expansion. Western land sales following the War of 1812 reached an unprecedented 3.5 million acres, but that was small in comparison with what was to come in the 1830s and 1850s. Not all land sales reflected actual settlement, however, and speculation in western lands was rampant. Collapse of the postwar speculative boom contributed to the Panic of 1819, and the abrupt end to the boom of the 1830s led to the Panic of 1837.*

Source: Robert Riegel and Robert Athearn, *America Moves West* (New York: Holt, Rinehart, 1964).

Major Migration Routes, 1800–1820 *The barrier of the Appalachian Mountains permitted only a few routes to the west. Settlers from the northern states took the Genesee Turnpike, Middle States migrants favored the Philadelphia-Pittsburgh Turnpike and the National Road, and Southerners used the Wilderness and Federal Roads. Because most westward movement was lateral, regional mixing among western settlers was rare. New Englanders carried their attitudes West, and Southerners did the same.*

Source: Donald Meinig, *The Shaping of America*, Vol. 2, *Continental America* (New Haven: Yale University Press, 1994).

directly west and settled largely with their own communities; Southerners did the same.

One section of northern Ohio along Lake Erie, for example, had been Connecticut's western land claim since the days of its colonial charter. Rather than give up the land when the Northwest Territory was established in 1787, Connecticut held onto the Western Reserve (as it was known) and encouraged its citizens to move there. Group settlement was common. General Moses Cleaveland of the Revolutionary War led one of the first groups of Yankees, fifty-two in all. In 1795 they settled the community that bears his name (though not his spelling of it). Many other groups followed, naming towns such as Norwalk after those they had left in

Connecticut. These New Englanders brought to the Western Reserve their religion (Congregational), their love of learning (tiny Norwalk soon boasted a three-story academy), and their adamant opposition to slavery.

Western migration in the South was very different. Just as on other frontiers, pioneers hacked wagon roads through the wilderness, encountered resistance from Indian peoples, and cleared the land for settlements and farms. But on this frontier, the hands on the ax handle were likely to be black, the people clearing the land doing it not for themselves but to create plantations for slave owners. More than half of the migrants to the Old Southwest after 1812 were involuntary—enslaved African Americans.

Even before the war, plantation owners in the Natchez district of Mississippi had made fortunes growing cotton, which they shipped to Britain from New Orleans. After the war, as cotton growing expanded, hopeful slave owners from older parts of the South (Virginia, North and South Carolina, Georgia), flooded into the region. The movement was like a gold rush, characterized by high hopes, land speculation, and riches—for a few. Most of the settlers in the Old Southwest were small farm families living in forest clearings. Most did not own slaves, but they hoped to, for ownership of slaves was the means to wealth. Quickly, the lifestyle and values of older southern states were replicated on this new frontier.

This western transplantation of distinctive regional cultures explains why, although by 1820 western states accounted for more than a third of all states (eight out of twenty-three), the West did not form a third, unified political region. Although there were common western issues—in particular, the demand for better roads and other transportation routes—in general, communities in the Old Northwest shared New England political attitudes, whereas those in the Old Southwest shared southern attitudes.

Camp Meeting. Color lithograph by Kennedy and Lucas, after painting by A. Rider, ca. 1835, negative number 26275. Collection of the New York Historical Society, New York City.

The rural and community nature of the Second Great Awakening is captured in this illustration. The preacher exhorts the large audience, which responds with emotion. Many of the most enthusiastic converts were women, who gained a new feeling of moral and social consequence through their religious experience.

The Second Great Awakening on the Frontier

The religious movement known as the Second Great Awakening began quietly in the 1790s in New England, but by 1800 it had spread through the Protestant churches of the entire country. It was most dramatic on the frontier, where church organization was naturally weak. The great institution of western Protestantism became the camp meeting, an outdoor gathering that included many sects and might go on for days. The greatest of the early camp meetings took place at Cane Ridge, Kentucky, in 1801, when an estimated 20,000 people came together for a week of preaching and singing. This was a remarkable assembly considering that the largest town in the West at the time had fewer than 2,000 inhabitants. Preachers shouted from the stand, and in the flickering firelight of evening hundreds of people, overcome with religious enthusiasm, fell to speaking in tongues or jerking uncontrollably. "Many things transpired there," one observer wrote, "that had the same effects as miracles on infidels and unbelievers."

Organized religion became one of the most important institutions within the continuing westward migration. Camp meetings frequently provided the first occasion for the new settlers of an area to come together, and religious meetinghouses were often the first public buildings erected in a community. In the absence of resident ministers, preaching was provided by Methodist circuit riders or perhaps a Baptist farmer who heard "the call" and had himself licensed as a lay preacher. On the frontier as well as in the East, women were often in the majority among church members. They thus played an important role in an institution that was fundamental to the planting of new American communities.

The Election of 1816 and the Era of Good Feelings

In 1816 James Monroe, the last of the Virginia Dynasty, was easily elected president over his Federalist opponent, Rufus King (183 to 34 electoral votes). This was the last election in which Federalists ran a candidate. Monroe had no opponent in 1820 and was reelected nearly unanimously (231 to 1). The triumph of the Democratic Republicans over the Federalists seemed complete. But although the Democratic Republicans kept their name, they had accepted so many Federalist political principles that it was not easy to tell which party had actually triumphed.

Tall, dignified, dressed in the old-fashioned style of knee breeches and white-topped boots that Washington had worn, Monroe looked like a traditional figure. But his politics reflected changing times. Soon after his inauguration, the president made a goodwill tour of the country, the first president since Washington to do so. Reflecting the new geography of the nation, he went the farthest west any president had yet traveled to visit the frontier post of Detroit. When he visited Boston, as recently as 1815 the heart of a secession-minded Federalist region, he received an enthusiastic welcome, prompting the Federalist *Columbian Centinel* to proclaim an "Era of Good Feelings." The phrase has been applied to Monroe's presidency (1817–25) ever since.

Monroe sought a government of national unity, and he chose men from North and South, Democratic Republicans and Federalists, for his cabinet. He selected John Quincy Adams, a former Federalist, as his secretary of state, virtually assuring that Adams, like his father, would become president. To balance Adams, Monroe picked John C. Calhoun of South Carolina, a prominent War Hawk, as secretary of war. And Monroe supported the American System, a program of national economic development that became identified with Westerner Henry Clay, Speaker of the House of Representatives.

In supporting the American System, Monroe was following President Madison, who had proposed the program in his message to Congress of December 1815. Madison and Monroe broke with Jefferson's agrarianism to embrace much of the Federalist program for economic development, including the chartering of a national bank, a tax on imported goods to protect American manufacturers, and a national system of roads and canals. All three of these had first been proposed by Alexander Hamilton in the 1790s (see Chapter 8). At the time they had met with bitter Democratic Republican opposition. The support that Madison and Monroe gave to Hamilton's ideas following the War of 1812 was a crucial sign of the dynamism of the American commercial economy. Many Democratic Republicans now acknowledged that the federal government had a role to play in fostering the economic and commercial conditions in which both yeoman farmer and merchant could succeed. This active support for capitalist development explained why so many former Federalists were willing to join Monroe's party of national unity.

In 1816 Congress chartered the Second Bank of the United States for twenty years. Located in Philadelphia, the bank had a capital of $35 million, of which the government contributed $7 million. The bank was to provide large-scale financing that the smaller state banks could not handle and to create a strong national currency. Because they feared concentrated economic power, Democratic Republicans had allowed the charter of the original Bank of the United States, founded in 1791, to expire in 1811. The Democratic Republican about-face in 1816 was a sign that the strength of commercial interests had grown to rival that of farmers, whose distrust for central banks persisted.

The Tariff of 1816 was the first substantial protective tariff in American history. In 1815, British manufacturers, who had been excluded for eight years (from the Embargo Act of 1807 to the end of the War of 1812), flooded the United States market with their products. American manufacturers complained that the British were dumping goods below cost to prevent the growth of American industries. Congress responded with a tariff on imported woolens and cottons, on iron, leather, hats, paper, and sugar. The measure had southern as well as northern support, although in later years differences over the passage of higher tariffs would become one of the most persistent sources of sectional conflict.

The third item in the American System, funding for roads and canals—internal improvements, as they came to be known—was more controversial. Monroe and Madison both supported genuinely national (that is, interstate) projects such as the National Road from Cumberland, Maryland to Vandalia, Illinois. Congressmen, however, aware of the urgent need to improve transportation in general and scenting the political advantages that could accrue to them from directing funds to their districts, proposed spending federal money on local projects. Both Madison and Monroe vetoed such local proposals, believing them to be unconstitutional. Thus it was that some of the most famous projects of the day, such as the Erie Canal, which lay wholly within New York state, and the early railroads, were financed by state or private money.

The support of Madison and Monroe for measures initially identified with their political opposition was an indicator of their realism. The three aspects of the American System—bank, tariff, roads—were all parts of the basic infrastructure that the American economy needed in order to develop. Briefly, during the Era of Good Feelings, politicians agreed about the need for all three. Later, each would be a source of heated partisan argument.

The Diplomacy of John Quincy Adams

The diplomatic achievements of the Era of Good Feelings were due almost entirely to the efforts of one man, John Quincy Adams, Monroe's secretary of state. Adams set himself the task of tidying up the borders of the United States. Two accords with Britain—the Rush-Bagot Treaty of 1817 and the Convention of 1818—fixed the border between the United States and Canada at the 49th parallel and resolved conflicting U.S. and British claims to Oregon with an agreement to occupy it jointly for ten (eventually twenty) years. The American claim to Oregon (present-day British Columbia, Washington, Oregon, northern Idaho, and parts of Montana) was based on China trader Robert Gray's discovery of the Columbia River in 1792 and on the Lewis and Clark expedition of 1804–06. The British Hudson's Bay Company, however, had land-based fur-trading operations in the region, and established a major base at Fort Vancouver on the Columbia River in 1825.

Adams's major diplomatic accomplishment was the Adams-Onís or Transcontinental Treaty of 1819, in which he skillfully wrested concessions from the faltering Spanish empire. In 1818 General Andrew Jackson led an American force on a mission purportedly to end raids on the Florida border by Seminole Indians against American settlements. Exceeding his orders, Jackson invaded Florida itself, and Spain, preoccupied with revolts throughout its Latin American empire, was unable to repulse him. Jackson's success made it clear that the United States could easily snatch Florida from Spain by force. Adams convinced Spain not only to cede Florida but also to drop all previous claims it had to the Louisiana Territory and Oregon. In return, the United States relinquished claims on Texas and assumed responsibility for the $5 million in claims U.S. citizens had against Spain. Although many Westerners believed Adams should have been able to obtain Texas as well as Florida, the Transcontinental Treaty was hailed at the time as a success. It proved an important spur to American expansionism and highlighted Americans' growing confidence in foreign affairs.

That growing confidence was also apparent in Adams's culminating diplomatic success. In 1821, Mexico achieved its independence from Spain; by 1822, Argentina, Chile, and Colombia were independent as well. Adams picked his way through these remarkable changes in Latin America to the policy that bears his president's name, the Monroe Doctrine. The

United States was the first country outside Latin America to recognize the independence of Spain's former colonies. Many Americans enthusiastically supported the Latin American revolts and were proud to think that they were modeled on the American Revolution, as the Latin American liberator, Simón Bolívar, claimed.

But then the European powers (France, Austria, Russia, and Prussia) began talk of a plan to help Spain recover the lost colonies. What was the United States to do? The British, suspicious of the European powers, proposed a British-American declaration against European intervention in the hemisphere. Others might have been flattered by an approach from the British empire, but Adams would have none of it. Showing the national pride that was so characteristic of the era, Adams insisted on an independent American policy. He therefore drafted for the president the hemispheric policy that the United States has followed ever since.

On December 2, 1823, the president presented the Monroe Doctrine to Congress and the world. He called for the end of colonization of the Western Hemisphere by European nations (this was aimed as much at Russia and its Pacific coast settlements as at other European powers). Intervention by European powers in the affairs of the independent New World nations would be considered by the United States a danger to its own peace and safety. Finally, Monroe pledged that the United States would not interfere in the affairs of European countries or in the affairs of their remaining New World colonies.

All of this was a very large bark from a very small dog. In 1823, the United States lacked the military and economic force to back up its grand statement. In fact, what kept the European powers out of Latin America was British opposition to European intervention, enforced by the Royal Navy. But the Monroe Doctrine was to take on quite another aspect at the end of the century, when the United States did have the power to enforce it. The Monroe Doctrine was more immediately useful in Adams's last diplomatic achievement, the Convention of 1824, in which Russia gave up its claim to the Oregon

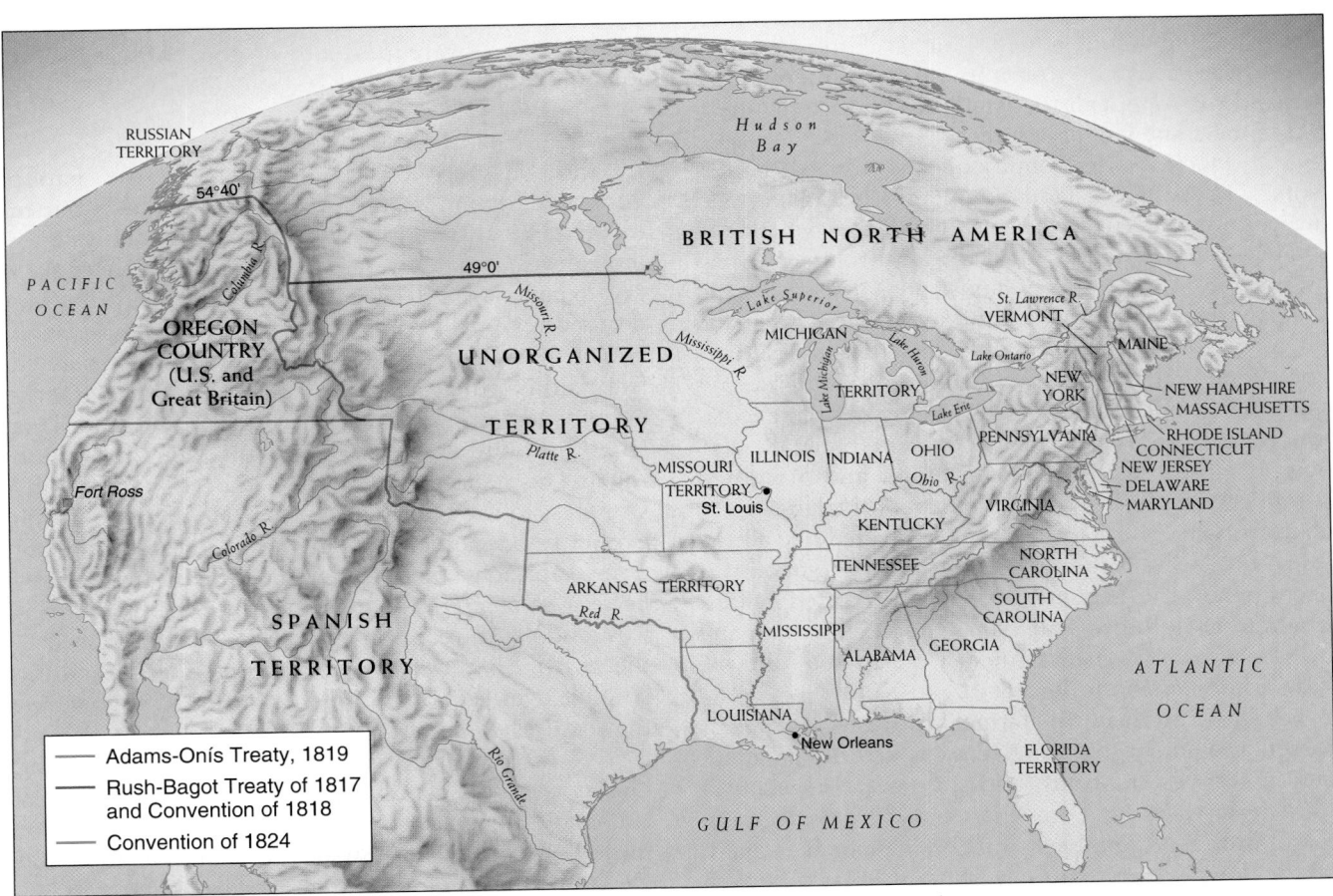

John Quincy Adams's Border Treaties   John Quincy Adams, secretary of state in the Monroe administration (1817–25), solidified the nation's boundaries in several treaties with Britain and Spain. The Rush-Bagot Treaty of 1817 and the Conventions of 1818 and 1824 settled the northern boundary with Canada and the terms of a joint occupancy of Oregon. The Adams-Onís Treaty of 1819 added Florida to the United States and settled the disputed border between the American Louisiana Territory and Spanish possessions in the West.

Territory and accepted 54° 40´ as the southern border of Russian America. Thus Adams contained another possible threat to American continental expansion.

This string of diplomatic achievements—the treaties with Russia, Britain, and Spain and the Monroe Doctrine—represented a great personal triumph for the stubborn, principled John Quincy Adams. A committed nationalist and expansionist, he showed that reason and diplomacy were in some circumstances more effective than force. Adams's diplomatic achievements were a fitting end to the period dominated by the Virginia Dynasty, the trio of enlightened revolutionaries who did so much to shape the new nation.

The Panic of 1819

Across this impressive record of political and economic nation building fell the shadow of the Panic of 1819. A delayed reaction to the end of the War of 1812 and the Napoleonic Wars, the panic forced Americans to come to terms with their economic place in a peaceful world. As British merchant ships resumed trade on routes they had abandoned during the wars, the American shipping boom ended. And as European farm production recovered from the wars, the international demand for American foodstuffs declined and American farmers and shippers suffered.

Domestic economic conditions made matters worse. The western land boom that began in 1815 turned into a speculative frenzy. Land sales, which had totaled 1 million acres in 1815, mushroomed to 3.5 million in 1818. Some lands in Mississippi and Alabama, made valuable by the international demand for cotton, were selling for $100 an acre. Many settlers bought on credit, aided by loans from small and irresponsible "wildcat" state banks. A number of speculators, carried away by the excitement of it all, also bought large tracts of land on credit and promoted them heavily. This was not the first—or the last—speculative boom in western lands. But it ended like all the rest—with a sharp contraction of credit, begun on this occasion by the Second Bank of the United States, which in 1819 forced state banks to foreclose on many bad loans. Many small farmers were ruined, and six years of depression followed.

In response to farmer protests, Congress passed a relief act in 1821 that extended the payment period for western lands, and some state legislatures passed "stay laws" that prevented banks from executing foreclosures. Nonetheless, many small banks failed, taking down their creditors with them. Many western farmers blamed the faraway Bank of the United States for their troubles. In the 1830s Andrew Jackson would build a political movement on their resentment.

Urban workers suffered both from the decline in international trade and from manufacturing failures caused by competition from British imports. As urban workers lobbied for local relief (there was no federal welfare), they found themselves deeply involved in urban politics, where they could express their resentment against the merchants and owners who had laid them off. Thus developed another component of Andrew Jackson's new political coalition.

Another confrontation arose over the tariff. Southern planters, hurt by a decline in the price of cotton, began to actively protest the protective tariff, which kept the price of imported goods high even when cotton prices were low. Manufacturers, hurt by British competition, lobbied for even higher rates, which they achieved in 1824 over southern protests. Southerners then began to express doubts about the fairness of a political system in which they were always outvoted.

The Panic of 1819 was a symbol of this transitional time. It showed how far the country had moved since 1800 from Jefferson's republic of yeoman farmers toward a nation dominated by commerce. And the anger and resentment expressed by the groups harmed by the depression—farmers, urban workers, and southern planters—were portents of the politics of the upcoming Jackson era.

The Missouri Compromise

In the Missouri Crisis of 1819–21, the nation confronted the momentous issue that had been buried in the general enthusiasm for expansion: As America moved west, would the largely southern system of slavery expand as well? Until 1819, this question was decided regionally. As residents of the northern states moved west, the territory into which they expanded (the Old Northwest) was free of slavery. As southerners moved into Alabama, Mississippi, and Louisiana (the Old Southwest), they brought their slaves with them. This regional difference had been mandated by Congress in the Northwest Ordinance of 1787, which explicitly banned slavery in the northern section of trans-Appalachia but made no mention of it elsewhere. Because so much of the expansion into the Old Northwest and Southwest was lateral (Northerners stayed in the north, Southerners in the south), there was little conflict over sectional differences. In 1819, however, the sections collided—in Missouri.

In 1819, Missouri applied for admission to the Union as a slave state. To the slave-owning Kentuckians and Tennesseans who were the territory's major settlers, this extension of slavery seemed natural and inevitable. But Illinois, also an adjacent state, prohibited slavery. The northern states, all of which had abolished slavery by 1819, looked askance at the extension of slavery northward.

In addition to the moral issue of slavery, the Missouri question raised the political issue of sectional balance. Northern politicians did not want to admit another slave state. To do so would tip the balance of power in the Senate, where the 1819 count of slave and free states was eleven apiece. For their part, Southerners believed they needed an advantage in the Senate; because of faster population growth in the North, they were already outnumbered (105 to 81) in the House of Representatives. But above all, Southerners did not believe Congress had the power to limit the expansion of slavery. They were alarmed that Northerners were considering national legislation on the matter. Slavery, in southern eyes, was a question of property and therefore a matter for state rather than federal legislation. Thus, from the very beginning the expansion of slavery raised constitutional issues.

The urgency of these considerations among politicians in 1819 illustrates how delicate matters of sectional balance had already become. Indeed, the aging politician of Monticello, Thomas Jefferson, immediately grasped the seriousness of the question of the expansion of slavery. As he prophetically wrote to a friend, "This momentous question like a fire bell in the night, awakened and filled me with terror. I considered it at once the [death] knell of the Union."

In 1819 Representative James Tallmadge Jr. of New York began more than a year of congressional controversy when he demanded that Missouri agree to the gradual end of slavery as the price of entering the Union. At first, the general public paid little attention, but religious reformers (Quakers prominent among them) organized a number of antislavery rallies in northern cities that made politicians take notice. Former Federalists in the North who had seen their party destroyed by the achievements of Jefferson and his successors in the Virginia Dynasty eagerly seized on the Missouri issue. This was the first time that the growing northern reform impulse

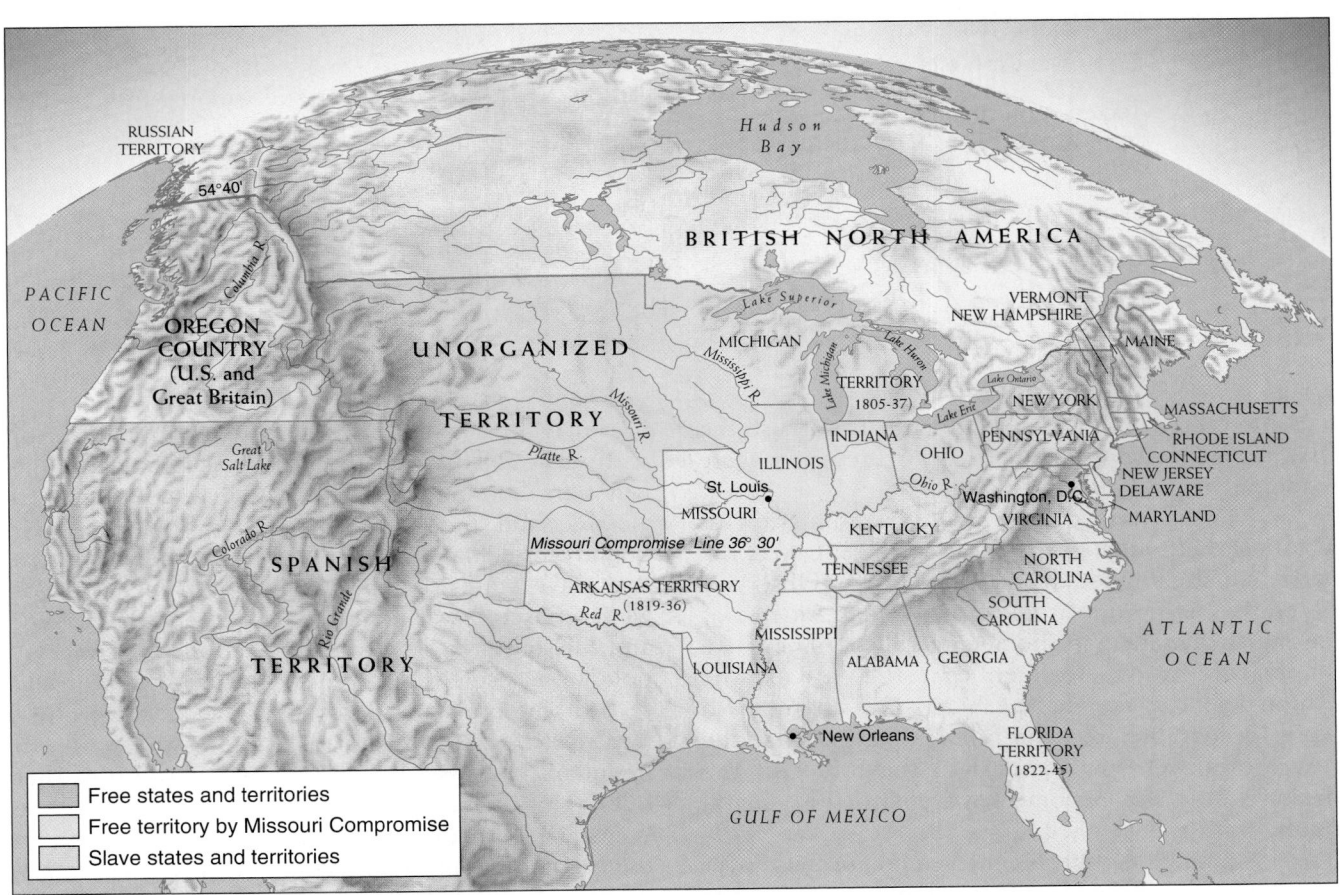

The Missouri Compromise   *Before the Missouri Compromise of 1820, the Ohio River was the dividing line between the free states of the Old Northwest and the slaveholding states of the Old Southwest. The compromise stipulated that Missouri would enter the Union as a slave state (balanced by Maine, a free state), but slavery would be prohibited in the Louisiana Territory north of 36° 30′ (Missouri's southern boundary). This awkward compromise lasted until 1846 when the Mexican-American War reopened the issue of the expansion of slavery.*

CHRONOLOGY

1790s	Second Great Awakening begins			Louisiana admitted to the Union
1800	Thomas Jefferson elected president		**1814**	Hartford Convention Treaty of Ghent
1802	Russian-American Company headquarters established at Sitka, Alaska		**1815**	Battle of New Orleans
1803	Louisiana Purchase *Marbury v. Madison* Ohio admitted to the Union		**1816**	James Monroe elected president Congress charters Second Bank of the United States Indiana admitted to the Union
1804	Lewis and Clark expedition begins Thomas Jefferson reelected president Russians reestablish Sitka following the Tlingit Revolt		**1817**	Mississippi admitted to the Union
			1818	Illinois admitted to the Union Andrew Jackson invades Florida
1807	*Chesapeake-Leopard* incident Embargo Act		**1819**	Panic of 1819 Adams-Onís Treaty Alabama admitted to the Union
1808	James Madison elected president		**1819–20**	Missouri Crisis and Compromise
1809	Tecumseh forms military alliance among Northwest Confederacy peoples		**1820**	James Monroe reelected president Maine admitted to the Union
1811	Battle of Tippecanoe		**1821**	Missouri admitted to the Union as a slave state
1812	War of 1812 begins James Madison reelected president		**1823**	Monroe Doctrine

had intersected with sectional politics. It was also the first time that southern threats of secession were made openly in Congress.

The Senate debate over the admission of Missouri, held in the early months of 1820, was the nation's first extended debate over slavery. Observers noted the high proportion of free African Americans among the listeners in the Senate gallery. They, like Thomas Jefferson, realized that the fate of the Union and the fate of the black race in America were inseparable. But the full realization that the future of slavery was central to the future of the nation would not become apparent to the general public until the 1850s.

In 1820, Congress achieved compromise over the sectional differences. Henry Clay forged the first of the many agreements that were to earn him the title of "the Great Pacificator" (peacemaker). A glance at the map shows the state of Missouri as an awkward intrusion into an otherwise slave-free area, a visual

break in the smooth westward continuation of sectionalism. This visual impression is reflected in the Missouri Compromise itself, which was difficult to arrange and had an awkward air about it. The compromise maintained the balance between free and slave states: Maine (which had been part of Massachusetts) was admitted as a free state in 1820 and Missouri as a slave state in the following year. A policy was also enacted with respect to slavery in the rest of the Louisiana Purchase: slavery was prohibited north of 36° 30′ north latitude—the southern boundary of Missouri—and permitted south of that line. This meant that the vast majority of the Louisiana Territory would be free. In reality, then, the Missouri Compromise could be only a temporary solution, because it left open the question of how the balance between slave and free states would be maintained. The seriousness of the sectional struggle over the Missouri question also directed popular attention to the changing nature of national politics.

CONCLUSION

In complex ways a developing economy, geographical expansion, and even a minor war helped shape American unity. Locally, small, settled, face-to-face communities in both the North and the South began to send their more mobile, expectant members to new occupations in urban centers or west to form new settlements, displacing Indian communities in the process.

The westward movement was the novel element in the American national drama. Europeans believed that large size and a population in motion bred instability

and political disintegration. Thomas Jefferson thought otherwise, and the Louisiana Purchase was the gamble that confirmed his guess. The westward population movement dramatically changed the political landscape and Americans' view of themselves. Few of those changes, though, were fully apparent in 1820.

Expansion would not create the settled communities of yeoman farmers Jefferson had hoped for. Rather, it would breed a nation of restless and acquisitive people and a new kind of national democratic politics that reflected their search for broader definitions of community.

REVIEW QUESTIONS

1. What economic and political problems did the United States face as a new nation in a world dominated by war between Britain and France? How successful were the efforts by the Jefferson, Madison, and Monroe administrations to solve these problems?
2. The anti-European cast of Jefferson's republican agrarianism made it appealing to many Americans who wished to believe in their nation's uniqueness, but how realistic was it?
3. Some Federalists opposed the Louisiana Purchase, warning of the dangers of westward expansion. What are arguments for and against expansion?
4. What contradictions in American Indian policy did the confrontations between Tecumseh's alliance and soldiers and settlers in the Old Northwest reveal? Can you suggest solutions to them?
5. What did the War of 1812 accomplish?
6. What were the issues that made it impossible for the Era of Good Feelings to last?

RECOMMENDED READING

Frank Bergon, ed., *The Journals of Lewis and Clark* (1989). A handy abridgment of the fascinating history of the expedition. (For more intensive study, Gary Moulton's six-volume unabridged edition of the expedition journals is unsurpassed.)

John Boles, *The Great Revival, 1787–1805* (1972). The standard work on the Second Great Awakening.

George Drago, *Jefferson's Louisiana: Politics and the Clash of Legal Traditions* (1975). Provides an illuminating example of the cultural flexibility of the federal system.

R. David Edmunds, *Tecumseh and the Quest for Indian Leadership* (1984). A sympathetic portrait.

Joseph J. Ellis, *American Sphinx: The Character of Thomas Jefferson* (1998). An engaging exploration of Jefferson's many contradictions.

John Mack Faragher, *Sugar Creek* (1987). The fullest examination of the lives of pioneers in the Old Northwest.

Donald Hickey, *The War of 1812: A Forgotten Conflict* (1989). Takes a fresh look at the events and historiography of the war.

Drew McCoy, *The Elusive Republic: Political Economy in Jeffersonian America* (1980). The most useful discussion of the ties between expansion and republican agrarianism.

Glover Moore, *The Missouri Controversy, 1819–1821* (1953). The standard account.

Curtis P. Nettels, *The Emergence of a National Economy, 1775–1815* (1962). A useful overview.

Merrill Peterson, *Thomas Jefferson and the New Nation* (1970). A good one-volume political biography of Jefferson. (The major biography, by Dumas Malone, is a multivolume work.)

James Ronda, *Lewis and Clark among the Indians* (1984). An innovative look at the famous explorers through the eyes of the Indian peoples they encountered.

ADDITIONAL BIBLIOGRAPHY

American Communities from Coast to Coast

James Gibson, *Imperial Russia in Frontier America* (1976)

Marcel Giraud, *A History of French Louisiana, 1698–1715* (1974)

Carey McWilliams, *North from Mexico: The Spanish-Speaking People of the United States* (1948)

Douglas Monroy, *Thrown among Strangers: The Making of Mexican Culture in Frontier California* (1990)

Barbara Sweetland Smith and Redmond Barnett, eds., *Russian America* (1990)

David Weber, *The Spanish Frontier in North America* (1993)

The National Economy

Robert G. Albion, *The Rise of New York Port, 1815–1860* (1939)

W. Eliot Brownlee, *Dynamics of Ascent: A History of the American Economy* (1979)

Stuart Bruchey, *The Roots of American Economic Growth, 1607–1861* (1965)

Samuel Eliot Morison, *Maritime History of Massachusetts: 1783–1860* (1921)

Douglass C. North, *The Economic Growth of the United States, 1790–1860* (1966)

The Jefferson Presidency

Thomas P. Abernathy, *The Burr Conspiracy* (1954)

Henry Adams, *The United States in 1800* (1955)

Noble E. Cunningham, *The Jeffersonian Republicans and Power: Party Operations, 1801–1809* (1963)

Richard E. Ellis, *The Jeffersonian Crisis: Courts and Politics in the Young Republic* (1971)

David Hackett Fischer, *The Revolution of American Conservatism: The Federalist Party in the Era of Jeffersonian Democracy* (1965)

Charles G. Haines, *The Role of the Supreme Court in American Government and Politics, 1789–1835* (1944)

Linda K. Kerber, *Federalists in Dissent: Imagery and Ideology in Jeffersonian America* (1970)

Burton Spivak, *Jefferson's English Crisis: Commerce, Embargo, and the Republican Revolution* (1979)

Robert W. Tucker and David Hendrickson, *Empire of Liberty: The Statecraft of Thomas Jefferson* (1990)

G. Edward White, *The Marshall Court and Cultural Change, 1815–1835*, abridged ed. (1991)

Robert H. Wiebe, *The Opening of American Society: From the Adoption of the Constitution to the Eve of Disunion* (1984)

James S. Young, *The Washington Community: 1800–1828* (1966)

Renewed Imperial Rivalry

Robert F. Berkhofer Jr., *Salvation and Savage: An Analysis of Protestant Missions and American Indian Response, 1787–1862* (1965)

Henry Warner Bowden, *American Indians and Christian Missions: Studies in Cultural Conflict* (1981)

Gregory Evans Dowd, *A Spirited Resistance: The North American Indian Struggle for Unity, 1745–1815*

Reginald Horsman, *Expansion and American Indian Policy, 1783–1812* (1967)

Dorothy Jones, *License for Empire: Colonialism by Treaty in Early America* (1982)

Drew R. McCoy, *The Last of the Fathers: James Madison and the Republican Legacy* (1989)

Francis Paul Prucha, *The Great Father: The United States Government and the American Indians*, 2 vols. (1984)

Bernard Sheehan, *Seeds of Extinction: Jeffersonian Philanthropy and the American Indian* (1973)

The War of 1812

Reginald Horsman, *The Causes of the War of 1812* (1962)

Steven Watts, *The Republic Reborn: War and the Making of Liberal America, 1790–1820* (1987)

Defining the Boundaries

John Boles, *Religion in Antebellum Kentucky* (1976)

Andrew Cayton, *The Frontier Republic: Ideology and Politics in the Ohio Country, 1789–1812* (1986)

———, *Frontier Indiana* (1996)

Paul Conklin, *Cane Ridge: America's Pentecost* (1990)

George Dangerfield, *The Era of Good Feelings* (1952)

Anita Shafer Goodstein, *Nashville, 1780–1860: From Frontier to City* (1989)

Harlan Hatcher, *The Western Reserve: The Story of New Connecticut in Ohio* (1991)

Walter LaFeber, ed., *John Quincy Adams and the American Continental Empire* (1965)

Ernest R. May, *The Making of the Monroe Doctrine* (1975)

Malcolm J. Rohrbough, *The Land Office Business* (1968)

———, *The Trans-Appalachian Frontier: Peoples, Societies, and Institutions, 1775–1850* (1978)

William Ganson Rose, *Cleveland: The Making of a City* (1990)

Richard Slotkin, *Regeneration through Violence: The Mythology of the American Frontier* (1973)

Richard C. Wade, *The Urban Frontier: The Rise of Western Cities, 1790–1850* (1973)

Kenneth J. Winkle, *The Politics of Community: Migration and Politics in Antebellum Ohio* (1988)

Biography

Harry Ammon, *James Monroe: The Quest for National Identity* (1971)

Leonard Baker, *John Marshall: A Life in Law* (1974)

Irving Brant, *James Madison* (1950–61)

Dumas Malone, *Jefferson the President: First Term, 1801–1805* (1970)

———, *Jefferson the President: Second Term, 1805–1809* (1974)

CHAPTER TEN

THE GROWTH OF DEMOCRACY

1824–1840

George Caleb Bingham, *Stump Speaking*, from the Art Collection of NationsBank.

AMERICAN COMMUNITIES
Martin Van Buren Forges a New Kind of Political Community

When Martin Van Buren left Albany for Washington in the fall of 1821 to take up his new position as junior senator from New York, he wrote complacently: "I left the service of the state [of New York] for that of the federal government with my friends in full and almost unquestioned possession of the state government in all its branches, at peace with each other and overflowing with kindly feelings towards myself." Thus did Van Buren sum up more than ten years of intense activity in New York State politics in which he and his allies, nicknamed the Bucktails (for the Indian-inspired insignia, the tail of a buck, that members wore on their hats), created one of the first modern democratic political parties. How could it be, Washington politicians asked, that this short, invariably pleasant but rather nondescript man had triumphed over the renowned DeWitt Clinton?

Tall, handsome, arrogant DeWitt Clinton, governor of New York from 1817 to 1823 (and again from 1825 until his death in 1828), had been swept into office on a tide of enthusiasm for his plan to build a canal the length of the state. Clinton soon gained legislative approval for the project—the Erie Canal—the most ambitious and most successful canal project in an era of canal building. An aristocrat in wealth, connections, and attitude, Clinton represented old style politics. During his first terms as governor he ran the New York Democratic Republican Party as though it were his personal property, dispensing patronage to relatives and friends (many of whom were Federalists) on the basis of their loyalty to him rather than their political principles.

Martin Van Buren was a new kind of politician. Born in the small, Dutch-dominated town of Kinderhook, New York, Van Buren was the son of a tavern keeper, not a member of the wealthy elite. He grew up with an enduring resentment of the aristocratic landowning families such as the Van Schaacks and the Van Rensselaers (and, by extension, the Clintons) who disdained him when he was young. Masking his anger with charming manners, Van Buren took advantage of the growing strength of the Democratic Republican Party in New York State to wrest control of it from Clinton and forge it into a new kind of political organization. Clinton's use of patronage to reward friends at the expense of young party loyalists infuriated Van Buren and other rising politicians. Two years after Clinton became governor, Van Buren wrote bitterly to a friend: "A man to be a sound politician and in any degree useful to his country must be guided by higher and steadier considerations than those of personal sympathy and private regard. . . . In the name of all that is holy, where is the evidence of that towering mind and those superior talents which it has been the business of puffers and toad eaters to attribute to [Clinton]?"

By 1819, Van Buren had gathered together enough other disgruntled Democratic Republicans to form the Bucktail faction and openly challenge Clinton. Two years later, at the state constitutional convention of 1821 (where they made up three fourths of the delegates), the Bucktails sealed their victory. Meeting in Albany to revise the out-of-date constitution of 1777, the convention voted to streamline the organization of state government and sharply curtail the patronage powers of the governor. To cement these changes, delegates enacted nearly total manhood suffrage: all adult male citizens who paid state or local taxes, served in the militia, or worked on state roads—more than four-fifths of the adult male population—were now eligible to vote directly for state legislators, governor, and members of Congress.

This dramatic democratization of politics reflected the state's changing population. Already the bustling port of New York was the nation's largest city, and the state's commercial opportunities were attracting shrewd Yankee traders from New England "whose laws, customs and usages," conservative senator Rufus King complained, "differ from those of New York." The old ruling families, failing to recognize the new commercial and social values of the newcomers, were losing their grip on politics. Rising politicians like Van Buren and other Bucktails, in contrast, found opportunity in these changing conditions. Attuned to popular feeling, they responded to the state's growing and increasingly diverse population by creating a new kind of political community. A political party, they maintained, should be a democratic organization expressing the will of all its members, not an organization dominated by an elite group like Clinton's and bound together only by family ties and political favors. All party members, including leaders, would have to abide by majority rule. Party loyalty, rather than personal opinion or friendship, would be the bond that kept the party together and, rather than aristocratic background, the principal requirement for party leadership. "The first man we see step to the rear," wrote Bucktail Silas Wright Jr., still smarting from the factionalism and favoritism of the Clinton years, "we cut down."

By the time he departed for Washington in the fall of 1821, Van Buren left in Albany a closely knit group of friends and allies who practiced these new political principles. Party decisions, reached by discussion in legislative caucus and publicized by the party newspaper, the *Albany Argus*, were binding on all members and enforced by patronage decisions. The group, dubbed the Albany Regency, ran New York State politics for twenty years. For all those years Martin Van Buren was in Washington, where he was a major architect of the new democratic politics of mass participation that has been called the Second American Party System. This new movement created, for the first time in American history, national communities of political partisans. Van Buren understood how to create these new communities. Organization and discipline were essential not for their own sake but because they allowed the political leader to reach out to public opinion. "Those who have wrought great changes in the world," Van Buren wrote, " never succeeded by gaining over chiefs; but always by exciting the multitude. The first is the resource of intrigue and produces only secondary results, the second is the resort of genius and transforms the face of the universe." The sources and expression of the new politics were linked to wider economic and cultural factors that encouraged national cohesion.

Albany

KEY TOPICS

- The role of Andrew Jackson's presidency in affirming and solidifying the new democratic politics

- The part played by the transportation revolution in unifying the nation

- Establishment of the basic two-party pattern of American political democracy

- The creation of a distinctive American cultural identity by writers and artists

THE NEW DEMOCRATIC POLITICS

The early years of the nineteenth century were a time of extraordinary growth and change for the new republic. The changes pulled the nation in two contradictory directions, toward both sectionalism and nationalism.

The two major sections of the country, the North and the South, had always had different social systems, and from the time of the first Continental Congress they had also always disagreed as to the nature of the political compromises they needed to make. Economic development in the early nineteenth century increased the difference between the sections as the South committed itself to cotton growing and the slave system and the North moved rapidly to a commercial, industrializing economy. Although both North and South were still economically interconnected, the two sections were on very different paths. Had the United States of America still consisted only of the thirteen original states, North-South compromises might well have broken down by the 1820s and split the nation into two parts.

Westward expansion, however, provided a nationalizing force. Because of developments in transportation, in 1840 the larger United States was more closely knit than the original thirteen states had been in 1787. And the nine new states west of the Appalachians that entered the Union between 1800 and 1840—making up one-third of the membership of the U.S. Senate—contributed their own regional perspective to national politics. Although settlement patterns tended to align people in what is now called the Old Northwest (Ohio, Indiana, Illinois, Wisconsin, and Michigan) with New England and those in the Old Southwest (Mississippi and Alabama) and the slave states of the Louisiana Purchase (Louisiana, Arkansas, and Missouri) with the South, Westerners as a whole shared common concerns and attitudes that national politicians from the two older areas could not ignore if they wished to build strong political allegiances in the new region. The political effect of westward expansion in the period 1820–40 was to modify although not to eliminate the basic sectional differences between North and South. But the most dramatic effect of westward expansion was the encouragement it gave to democratic politics.

The Expansion and Limits of Suffrage

Before 1800 most of the original thirteen states limited the vote to property owners or taxpayers, or less than half the white male population. In DeWitt Clinton's New York and other states the wealthy held the levers of political power. In national politics as well, in spite of occasional revolts from below such as the Whiskey Rebellion of 1794 (see Chapter 8), political control remained in the hands of the traditional elite until the end, in 1825, of the Virginia Dynasty of presidents.

Westward expansion changed the nature of American politics. Mobility itself promoted change by undermining the traditional authority structures in the older states. "Old America seems to be breaking up and moving westward," an observer commented in 1817. Rapid westward expansion bolstered the national pride that Americans felt in their successful republican revolution and fostered a spirit of self-reliance. As Andrew Jackson, recruiting troops for the War of 1812, boasted, "We are the free born sons of America; the citizens of the only republic now existing in the world; and the only people on earth who possess rights, liberties, and property which they dare call their own."

The new western states extended the right to vote to all white males over the age of twenty-one. Kentucky entered the Union with universal manhood suffrage in 1792, Tennessee (1796), and Ohio (1803) with low taxpayer qualifications that approached universal suffrage. Soon older states such as New Jersey (1807) and Maryland (1810) dropped their property qualification for voting. By 1820, most of the older states had followed suit. Some states liberalized voting in the hopes of dissuading disgruntled nonvoters from moving west or because it seemed unfair to recruit men to fight in the War of 1812 but not allow them to vote. In most states, however, the driving force behind reform was competition for votes between parties or factions of parties (such as the Bucktails and the Clintonians in New York).

In Connecticut, the Democratic Republicans, appealing to young, democratically minded but propertyless young men, first challenged the state's controlling Federalists in 1802 and finally in 1817 achieved suffrage for all men who paid taxes or served in the militia (that is, nearly everyone). In South Carolina, the rivalry was geographical, pitting the more numerous up-country residents who supported Jefferson's Democratic Republicans against the wealthy Federalist slave-owning political elite of the low country who controlled the state legislature. A compromise agreement of 1808 allocated votes to the lower house by population (favoring the up-country), and to the upper house by wealth (favoring the low country). This redistribution of power led directly to a demand for universal white manhood suffrage, which became law (with a two-year residency requirement) in South Carolina in 1810. There were laggards— Rhode Island, Virginia, and Louisiana did not liberalize their voting qualifications until later— but by 1840, more than 90 percent of adult white males in the nation could vote. And they could vote for more officials: governors and (most important) presidential electors were now elected by direct vote, rather than chosen by small groups of state legislators.

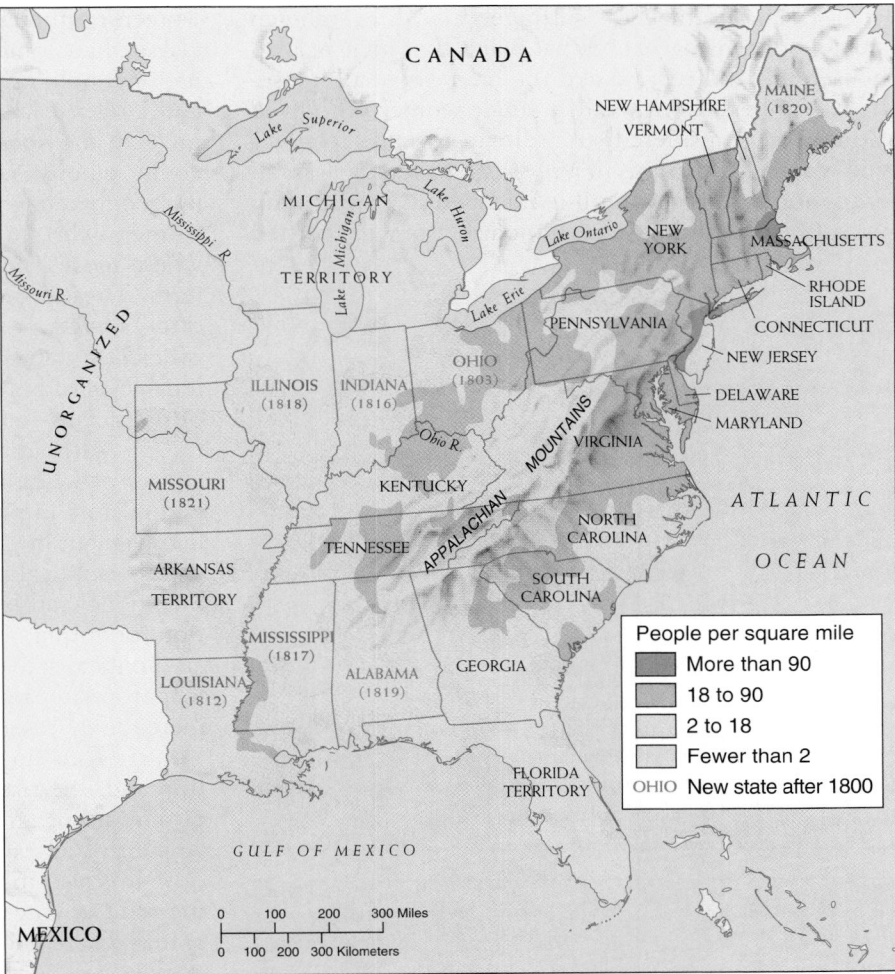

Population Trends: Westward Expansion, 1830   *Westward population movement, a trickle in 1800, had become a flood by 1830. Between 1800 and 1830 the U.S. white and African American population more than doubled (from 5.3 million to 12.9 million), but the trans-Appalachian population grew tenfold (from 370,000 to 3.7 million). By 1830 more than a third of the nation's inhabitants lived west of the original thirteen states.*

Universal white manhood suffrage, of course, was far from true universal suffrage: The right to vote remained barred to most of the nation's 500,000 free African Americans and to women of any race. Only in five New England states (Maine, New Hampshire, Vermont, Massachusetts, and Rhode Island) could free African American men vote before 1865. In most of the other northern states the right of free African American men to vote was limited, first by custom and later by law. In 1821 in New York, for example, the same Bucktail-dominated legislature that voted to extend the franchise to most white men also restricted it among African American men to those with property valued at $250 or more, a very high amount at the time. As a result, only 68 of the nearly 13,000 African Americans in New York City qualified to vote in 1825.

Free African Americans were denied the vote in all southern states—and surprisingly, in the new western states as well. The Ohio constitution of 1802 denied African Americans the rights to vote, to hold public office, and to testify against white men in court cases. Later restrictions barred black men from serving in the state militia and on juries. The constitutions of other western states—Illinois, Indiana, Michigan, Iowa, Wisconsin, and, later, Oregon—attempted to solve the "problem" of free African Americans by simply denying them entry into the state at all.

The denial of suffrage to white women stemmed from the patriarchal belief that men headed households and represented the interests of all household members. Even wealthy single women who lived alone were considered subordinate to male relatives and denied the right to vote. (New Jersey was an exception to this rule until it amended its constitution in 1807 to withdraw the franchise from propertied

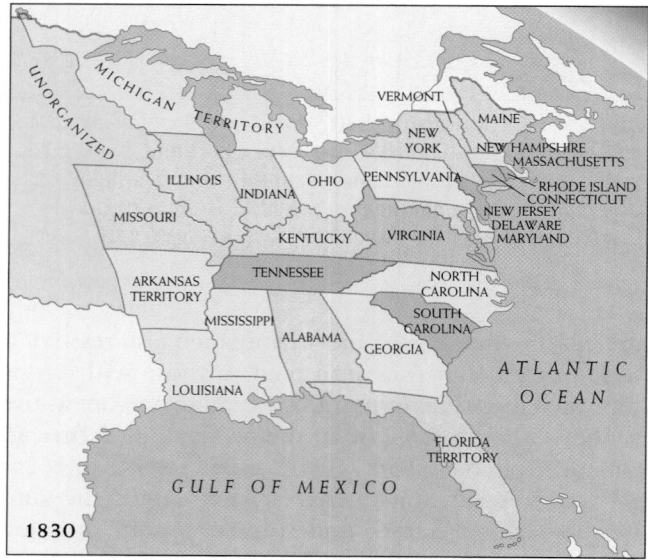

The Growth of Universal White Manhood Suffrage
Kentucky was the first western state to enact white male suffrage without tax or property qualifications. Other western states followed, and by 1820 most of the older states had dropped their suffrage restrictions as well. By 1840, more than 90 percent of the nation's white males could vote. But although voting was democratized for white men, restrictions on free African American male voters grew tighter, and women were excluded completely.

women.) Although unable to vote, women of the upper classes had long played important informal roles in national politics. Presidents' wives like Abigail Adams and Dolley Madison were famous for their ability to provide the social settings in which their husbands could quietly conduct political business. Another unrecognized group of skilled politicians were the women who ran the Washington boardinghouses where most congressmen lived during the legislative term. These women, longtime Washington residents, often served as valuable sources of information and official contacts for their boarders. At the state and local level of politics as well, women—often the wives of politicians—engaged in political activities.

Although the extension of suffrage to all classes of white men seemed to indicate that women had no role in public affairs, in fact women's informal involvement in politics grew along with the increasing pace of political activity. At the same time, however, as "manhood" rather than property became the qualification for voting, men began to ignore women's customary political activity and to regard their participation as inappropriate, an attitude that politically active women increasingly resented.

Thus, in this period famous for democratization and "the rise of the common man" the exclusion of important groups—African American men, and women of all races—marked the limits of liberalization. It is also true that nowhere else in the world was the right to vote so widespread as it was in the United States. The extension of suffrage to the common man marked a major step beyond the republicanism advocated by the Revolutionary generation. Thomas Jefferson had envisaged a republic of property-owning yeoman farmers. Now, however, propertyless farm workers and members of the laboring poor in the nation's cities could vote as well. European observers were curious about the democratization of voting: Could "mob rule" possibly succeed? And how would it affect traditional politics? The election of 1824 provided the first outline of the answer.

The Election of 1824

The 1824 election marked a dramatic end to the political truce that James Monroe had established in 1817. In that "Era of Good Feelings," one big political party, the expanded Democratic Republicans, had absorbed the remaining Federalists. This brief moment of unanimity did not survive the Panic of 1819 and the Missouri Crisis (see Chapter 9). Thus five candidates, all of them members of the Democratic Republican Party, ran for president in the elections of 1824. The candidate chosen by the usual method of congressional caucus was William H. Crawford of Georgia. The traditional stepping stone to the presidency, however, had been the office of secretary of state, giving a strong claim to John Quincy Adams of Massachusetts, who held that position in President Monroe's administration. Adams was nominated by his state legislature, as were two other candidates, Henry Clay of Kentucky and Andrew Jackson of Tennessee. The fifth candidate, John C. Calhoun of South Carolina, Monroe's secretary of war, withdrew before the election to run for vice president. Each candidate was clearly identified with a region: Adams with New England, Crawford and Calhoun with the South, Clay and Jackson with the West. Jackson, a latecomer to the race, was at first not taken seriously because his record as a legislator was lackluster and his political views unknown. His reputation as a military hero, however, enabled him to run as a national candidate despite his regional identification. He won 43 percent of the popular vote and more electoral votes—99—than any other candidate. The runner-up, John Quincy Adams, won 31 percent of the popular vote and 84 electoral votes. But neither had an electoral majority, leaving it up to the House of Representatives, as in the election of 1800, to pick the winner.

After some political dealing, Henry Clay threw his support to Adams and the House elected Adams president. This was customary and proper: the Constitution gave the House the power to decide, and Clay had every right to advise his followers how to vote. But when Adams named Clay his secretary of state, the traditional stepping-stone to the highest office, Jackson's supporters promptly accused them of a "corrupt bargain." Popular opinion, the new element in politics, supported Jackson. John Quincy Adams served four miserable years as president, knowing that Jackson would challenge him, and win, in 1828.

The legislative accomplishments of Adams's presidency were scanty. Adams's ambitious proposals for national development were rebuffed by a hostile Congress, although he did succeed in obtaining funding for an extension of the National Road west from Wheeling—significantly, an issue on which he could count on western votes. Congress stalled Adams's request to send American delegates to a conference in Panama called by the Latin American liberator Simón Bolívar, in part because Southerners feared attendance might lead to recognition of the revolutionary black republic of Haiti. Thus Adams's desire to lead the nation from a position above politics was frustrated by a political opposition that he thought illegitimate but that was in reality an early portent of the emerging two-party system.

Organizing Popular Politics

As the election of 1824 showed, hand-in-hand with the spread of universal manhood suffrage went a change in popular attitudes that spelled the end of personal, elitist politics. The triumph of Van Buren and the Buck-

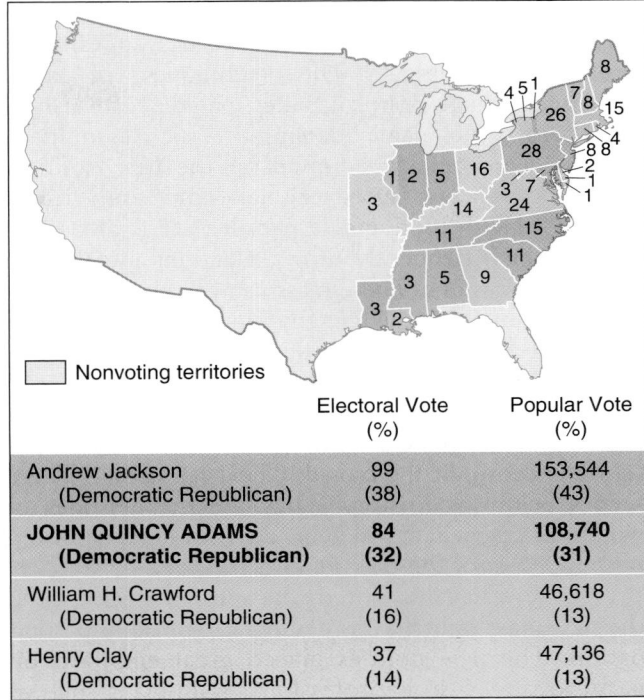

	Electoral Vote (%)	Popular Vote (%)
Andrew Jackson (Democratic Republican)	99 (38)	153,544 (43)
JOHN QUINCY ADAMS (Democratic Republican)	**84 (32)**	**108,740 (31)**
William H. Crawford (Democratic Republican)	41 (16)	46,618 (13)
Henry Clay (Democratic Republican)	37 (14)	47,136 (13)

The Election of 1824 *The presidential vote of 1824 was clearly sectional. John Quincy Adams carried his native New England and little else, Henry Clay carried only his own state of Kentucky and two adjoining states, and Crawford's appeal was limited to Virginia and Georgia. Only Andrew Jackson moved beyond the regional support of the Old Southwest to wider appeal and the greatest number of electoral votes. Because no candidate had a majority, however, the election was thrown into the House of Representatives, which chose Adams.*

tails in New York in 1821 was one example of this sort of change, but politicians in other states shared Van Buren's vision of tightly organized, broad-based political groups. John C. Calhoun of South Carolina was first elected to his state legislature in 1808, the year that the iron political grip of the low-country planters was weakened. Calhoun, himself from the up-country, depended throughout his political career on the up-country voters who achieved universal white manhood suffrage in 1810. In Virginia a group known as the Richmond Junto had control of state politics by 1816, and in Tennessee the Nashville Junto, masterminded by John Overton, held sway by 1822. In New Hampshire, Isaac Hill's Concord Regency was firmly in control by 1825. Each of these organizations, to a greater or lesser extent, aspired to the same discipline and control as the Albany Regency aspired to, and each had wider aspirations. The Nashville Junto led the way by nominating Andrew Jackson for president in 1824.

The crucial element in the success of the new party system, as Van Buren realized, was its mass appeal.

Just as the religion of the day emphasized emotion over reason, so too the new political parties appealed to popular enthusiasms. The techniques of mass campaigns—huge political rallies, parades, and candidates with wide "name recognition" such as military heroes—were quickly adopted by the new political parties. So were less savory techniques such as the distribution of lavish food and (especially) drink at polling places, which frequently turned elections into rowdy, brawling occasions. These mass campaigns were something new. In 1834, the French visitor Michel Chevalier witnessed a mile-long nighttime parade in support of Andrew Jackson. Stunned by the orderly stream of banners lit by torchlight, the portraits of George Washington, Thomas Jefferson, and Jackson, and the enthusiastic cheering of the crowd, Chevalier wrote, "These scenes belong to history. They are the episodes of wondrous epic which will bequeath a lasting memory to posterity, that of the coming of democracy."

As Chevalier noted, the spirit that motivated the new mass politics was democratic pride in participation. The new politics placed great emphasis on party loyalty. Just as professional politicians such as Van Buren were expected to be loyal, so the average voter was encouraged to make a permanent commit-

Politics, abetted by the publication of inexpensive party newspapers, was a great topic of conversation among men in early nineteenth-century America, as Richard Caton Woodville's 1845 painting Politics in an Oyster House *suggests.*

ment to a political party. The party provided some of the same satisfactions that popular sports offer today: excitement, entertainment, and a sense of belonging. In effect, political parties functioned as giant national men's clubs. They made politics an immediate and engrossing topic of conversation and argument for men of all walks of life. In this sense, the political party was the political manifestation of a wider social impulse toward community. But the glue that held political parties together went beyond the appeal of a particular leader or loyalty to one's friends. Political parties were based on genuine differences of political opinion. The task of politicians, as Van Buren recognized, was to emphasize those differences in ways that forged support not just for one election but for permanent, national communities of political interest.

The Election of 1828

The election of 1828 was the first to demonstrate the power and effectiveness of the new party system. With the help of Martin Van Buren, his campaign manager, Andrew Jackson rode the wave of the new democratic politics to the presidency. Jackson's party, the Democratic Republicans (they soon dropped "Republicans" and became simply the Democrats), spoke the language of democracy, and they opposed the special privilege personified for them by President John Quincy Adams and his National Republican (as distinguished from "Democratic Republican") Party. Neither Jackson nor Adams campaigned on his own—that was considered undignified. But the supporters of both candidates campaigned vigorously, freely, and negatively. Jackson's supporters portrayed the campaign as a contest between "the democracy of the country, on the one hand, and a lordly purse-proud aristocracy on the other." In their turn, Adams's supporters depicted Jackson as an illiterate backwoodsman, a murderer (he had killed several men in duels), and an adulterer (apparently unwittingly, he had married Rachel Robards before her divorce was final).

Jackson's running mate for vice president was John C. Calhoun of South Carolina. Although this choice assured Jackson of valuable southern support, it also illustrated the transitional nature of politics, for Calhoun was currently serving as vice president to John Quincy Adams, Jackson's opponent. That Calhoun was able easily to lend his support to a rival faction was a holdover from the old elite and personal politics that would soon be impossible in the new democratic political system.

Jackson won 56 percent of the popular vote (well over 80 percent in much of the South and West) and a decisive electoral majority of 178 votes to Adams's 83. The vote was interpreted as a victory for the common man. But the most important thing about

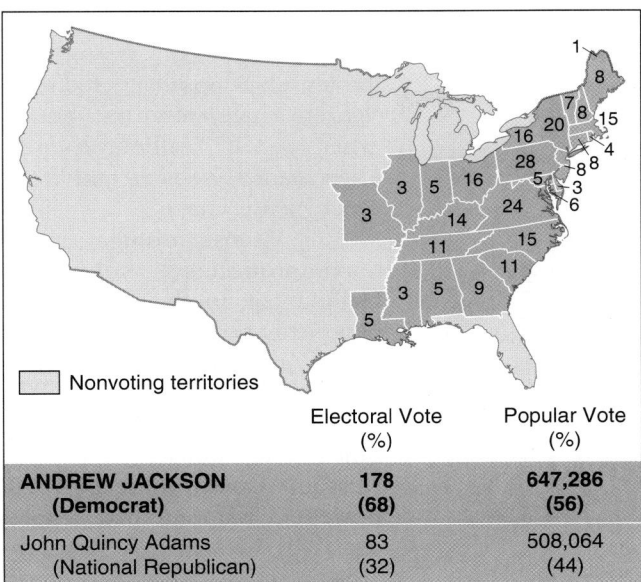

	Electoral Vote (%)	Popular Vote (%)
ANDREW JACKSON (Democrat)	**178 (68)**	**647,286 (56)**
John Quincy Adams (National Republican)	83 (32)	508,064 (44)

The Election of 1828 *Andrew Jackson's victory in 1828 was the first success of the new national party system. The coalition of state parties that elected him was national, not regional. Although his support was strongest in the South and West, his ability to carry Pennsylvania and parts of New York demonstrated his national appeal.*

Jackson's victory was the coalition that achieved it. The new democratically based political organizations—the Richmond and Nashville Juntos, the Albany and Concord Regencies, with help from Calhoun's organization in South Carolina—worked together to elect him. Popular appeal, which Jackson the military hero certainly possessed, was not enough to ensure victory. To be truly national, a party had to create and maintain a coalition of North, South, and West. The Democrats were the first to do this.

THE JACKSON PRESIDENCY

Andrew Jackson's election ushered in a new era in American politics, an era that historians have called "the Age of the Common Man." Jackson himself, however, was no "common man": he was a military hero, a rich slave owner, and an imperious and decidedly undemocratic personality. "Old Hickory," as Jackson was affectionately called, was tough and unbending, just like hickory itself, one of the hardest of woods. Yet he had a mass appeal to ordinary people unmatched—and indeed unsought—by earlier presidents. The secret to Jackson's extraordinary appeal lies in the changing nature of American society. Jackson was the first to respond to the ways in which westward expansion and the extension of the suffrage were changing politics at the national as well as the local and state levels.

A Popular Figure

Jackson was born in 1767 and raised in North Carolina. During the American Revolution he was captured and beaten by the British, an insult he never forgot. As a young man without wealth or family support, he moved west to the frontier "station" of Nashville, Tennessee, in 1788. There he made his career as a lawyer and his considerable wealth as a slave-owning planter. He had a touchy sense of pride and honor that led him into many duels. As he showed in his campaigns against the "Five Civilized Tribes" in the Old Southwest during the War of 1812, he was ruthless toward Indians. He first became a national hero with his underdog win against the British in the battle of New Orleans. In the popular mind, his fierce belligerence came to symbolize pioneer independence. The fact that he had little political experience, which would have made his nomination impossible under the traditional system of politics, was not a hindrance in the new age of popular politics.

On March 4, 1829, Andrew Jackson was inaugurated as president of the United States. Jackson himself was still in mourning for his beloved wife Rachel, whose recent death he attributed to the slanders of the campaign. But everyone else was celebrating. The small community of Washington was crowded with strangers, many of them Westerners and common people who had come especially for Jackson's inauguration. Their celebrating dismayed the city's more respectable citizens. Jackson's brief Inaugural Address was almost drowned out by the cheering of the crowd, and after the ceremony the new president was mobbed by well-wishers. The same unrestrained enthusiasm was evident at a White House reception, where the crowd was large and disorderly. People stood on chairs and sofas to catch glimpses of Jackson and shoved and pushed to reach the food and drink, which was finally carried out to the lawn. In the rush to follow, some people exited through windows rather than the doors. All in all, a disapproving observer noted, this behavior indicated the end of proper government and the beginning of "the reign of King Mob." Indeed, Jackson's administration was different from all those before it.

The Spoils System and the New Politics

Jackson began his term rewarding party loyalists by giving them positions in the national government. Although Jackson himself spoke loftily of democratizing the holding of public office, New York Bucktail William Marcy put the matter more bluntly: there was "nothing wrong in the rule, that to the victor belong the spoils of the enemy." Hence the expression "spoils system" to describe the practice of awarding government appointments to loyalists of the winning party. This attitude toward public office was one of the strongest points of difference between the new politics and the old.

Until 1829, presidential inaugurations had been small, polite, and ceremonial occasions. Andrew Jackson's popularity, however, brought a horde of well-wishers to Washington for his inaugural. Conservative critics, dismayed by the disorderly crowd at Jackson's frontier-style open house at the White House, feared "the reign of King Mob" had begun.

What Jackson did was to transfer a common state practice to the national level and to set a precedent that was followed in national politics until passage of the Pendleton Act of 1883, which began the reform of the civil service system. Jackson opened up all federal positions to party loyalists, and his opponents quickly found examples of corruption and inefficiency among the new officeholders. It is doubtful, though, if any alternative to the spoils system—such as the elite, independent civil service that the British were developing at the time—would have been consistent with the democratic spirit of American politics in the 1820s.

In fact, although the spoils system upset Jackson's opponents more than most of his other controversial actions, the number of officeholders he replaced was rather small—only about 10 percent (of a total of 10,093 offices). As was true in so many other cases, it was not so much the appointments themselves as the manner in which Jackson made them—brooking no argument, not even from supporters—that opponents found so aggravating.

The Nation's Leader vs. Sectional Spokesmen

Despite his western origins, Jackson was a genuinely national figure. He was more interested in asserting strong national leadership than promoting sectional compromise. He believed that the president, who symbolized the popular will of the people, ought to dominate the government. As he put it in his first annual message, "the first principle of our system [is that] the majority is to govern." This was new. Voters were much more accustomed to thinking of politics in

sectional terms. Jackson faced a Congress full of strong and immensely popular sectional figures. Three stood out: Southerner John C. Calhoun, Northerner Daniel Webster, and Westerner Henry Clay.

Intense, dogmatic, and uncompromising, John C. Calhoun of South Carolina had begun his political career as an ardent nationalist and expansionist in his early days as a War Hawk before the War of 1812. Since the debate over the Missouri Compromise in 1820, however, Calhoun had wholeheartedly identified with southern interests, first and foremost among which was the expansion and preservation of slavery. As the South's minority position in Congress became clear over the years, Calhoun's defense of southern economic interests and slavery became more and more rigid. Not for nothing did he earn his nickname "the Cast-Iron Man."

Senator Daniel Webster of Massachusetts was the outstanding orator of the age. Large, dark, and stern, Webster delivered his speeches in a deep, booming voice that, listeners said, "shook the world." He was capable of pathos as well, bringing tears to the eyes of those who heard him say, while defending Dartmouth College before the Supreme Court (in the case of the same name), "It is a small college, sir, but there are those who love it." Webster, a lawyer for business interests, became the main spokesman for the new northern commercial interests, supporting a high protective tariff, a national bank, and a strong federal government. Webster's fondness for comfortable living, and especially brandy, made him less effective as he grew older, but then, as a contemporary of his remarked, "No man could be as great as Daniel Webster looked."

In contrast with the other two, Henry Clay of Kentucky, spokesman of the West, was charming, witty, and always eager to forge political compromises. Clay held the powerful position of Speaker of the House of Representatives from 1811 to 1825 and later served several terms in the Senate. A spellbinding storyteller and well known for his ability to make a deal, Clay worked to incorporate western desires for cheap and good transportation into national politics. It was he who promoted the political agenda known as the American System: a national bank, a protective tariff, and the use of substantial federal funds for internal improvements such as roads, canals, and railroads (see Chapter 9). Clay might well have forged a political alliance between the North and the West if not for the policies of President Jackson, his fellow Westerner and greatest rival. Jackson's preeminence thwarted Clay's own ambition to be president.

The prominence and popularity of these three politicians show that sectional interests remained strong even under a president as determined as Jackson to override them and disrupt "politics as usual" by imposing his own personal style.

A Strong Executive

The mob scene that accompanied Jackson's inauguration was more than a reflection of the popular enthusiasm for Old Hickory. It also signaled a higher level of controversy in national politics. Jackson's personal style quickly stripped national politics of the polite and gentlemanly aura of cooperation it had acquired during the Era of Good Feelings and that Adams had vainly tried to maintain. Jackson had played rough all his life, and he relished controversy. His administration (1829–37) had plenty of it.

Andrew Jackson dominated his administration. Except for Martin Van Buren, whom he appointed secretary of state, he mostly ignored the heads of government departments who made up his official cabinet. Instead he consulted with an informal group, dubbed the "Kitchen Cabinet," made up of Van Buren and old western friends. The Kitchen Cabinet did not include John C. Calhoun, the vice president, or either of the other two great sectional representatives, Henry Clay and Daniel Webster. Jackson never forgave Clay for his role in the "corrupt bargain" of 1825, and he saw Daniel Webster as a representative of his favorite political target, the privileged elite.

Jackson used social distance to separate himself from other politicians. When Jackson's secretary of war, John Henry Eaton, married a beautiful woman of flamboyant reputation, he transgressed the social code of the time. It was rumored that Peggy Eaton had been John's mistress and that there were other men in her past. She was, in nineteenth-century thinking, a fallen woman and unfit for polite society. The respectable ladies of Washington shunned her. But Jackson, aroused by memories of the slanders against his own wife, defended Peggy Eaton and urged his cabinet members to force their wives to call on her. When, to a woman, they refused, Jackson called the husbands henpecked. This episode chilled the social life of cabinet members and their families and drove a wedge between Jackson and Calhoun, whose wife was a leader in the anti-Eaton group. Although Jackson claimed to be motivated only by chivalry, he wanted to keep his distance from Calhoun, and this episode helped him do it. Ironically, it may never have occurred had Jackson not been a widower. His wife Rachel would surely have sided with Mrs. Calhoun in upholding the moral code of the time.

Jackson freely used the tools of his office to strengthen the executive branch of government at the expense of the legislature and judiciary. By using the veto more frequently than all previous presidents combined (twelve vetoes compared with nine by the first six presidents), Jackson forced Congress to constantly consider his opinions. Even more important, Jackson's "negative activism" restricted federal activity, thereby allowing more power to remain in state hands.

In one of his most famous and unexpected actions, the veto of the Maysville Road Bill of 1830, Jackson refused to allow federal funding of a southern spur of the National Road in Kentucky, claiming such funding should be left to the state. Like Presidents James Madison and James Monroe before him, Jackson believed that federal funding for extensive and expensive transportation measures was unconstitutional because it infringed on the "reserved powers" the Constitution left to the states. The veto was unexpected because it disappointed Jackson's strongest supporters, Westerners who wanted better transportation. But by addressing his veto message to a popular audience, not just to Congress, and by dramatically portraying federal funding as a threat to the popular political principle of states' rights (and by making it clear that he was not opposed to federal funding of all internal improvements), Jackson actually gained political support. He also had the satisfaction of defeating a measure central to the American System proposed by his western rival, Henry Clay.

INTERNAL IMPROVEMENTS: BUILDING AN INFRASTRUCTURE

Despite the ongoing constitutional debate over who should fund internal improvements, no one argued that they should not be funded at all. On the contrary, ordinary people and politicians of all persuasions agreed that both federal and state governments had an important role in encouraging economic growth and in fostering the development of a national market. And that role included subsidizing the costs of the basic infrastructure—the canals and railroads—that would tie the national market together.

The Transportation Revolution

Between 1800 and 1840 the United States experienced truly revolutionary improvements in transportation. More than any other development, these improvements encouraged Americans to look beyond their local communities to broader ones and to foster the enterprising commercial spirit for which they became so widely known.

Improved transportation had dramatic effects both on individual mobility and on the economy. By 1840 it was easier for people to move from one locale to another, but even more remarkably people now had easy access in their own cities and towns to commercial goods made in distant centers. Thus even for people who remained in one place, horizons were much broader in 1840 than they had been forty years before. The difference lay in better roads, in improvements in water transport, and in the invention and speedy development of railroads.

In 1800, travel by road was difficult for much of the year. Mud in the spring, dust in the summer, and snow in the winter all made travel by horseback or carriage uncomfortable, slow, and sometimes dangerous. Over the years, localities and states tried to improve local roads or contracted with private turnpike companies to build, maintain, and collect tolls on important stretches of road. In general, however, local roads remained poor.

The federal government demonstrated its commitment to the improvement of interregional transportation by funding the National Road in 1808, at the

time the greatest single federal transportation expense (its eventual cost was $7 million). Built of gravel on a stone foundation, it crossed the Appalachian Mountains at Cumberland, Maryland, thereby opening up the West. Built in stages—to Wheeling, Virginia (now West Virginia), by 1818, to Columbus, Ohio, by 1833, to Vandalia, Illinois, almost at the Mississippi River, by 1850—the National Road tied the East and the West together, providing strong evidence of the nation's commitment to both expansion and cohesion and helping to foster a national community.

Although the federal commitment was great, the states actually spent more than the federal government on internal improvements—canals and railroads as well as roads. In the 1820s, state spending for internal improvements totaled $26 million. Half of this amount was incurred by two states, New York and Pennsylvania, but even smaller states such as South Carolina spent $2 million, largely on canals. In the next decade, state spending for canals, railroads, and turnpikes soared to $108 million. States and towns, especially in newly populated areas of the West, competed against each

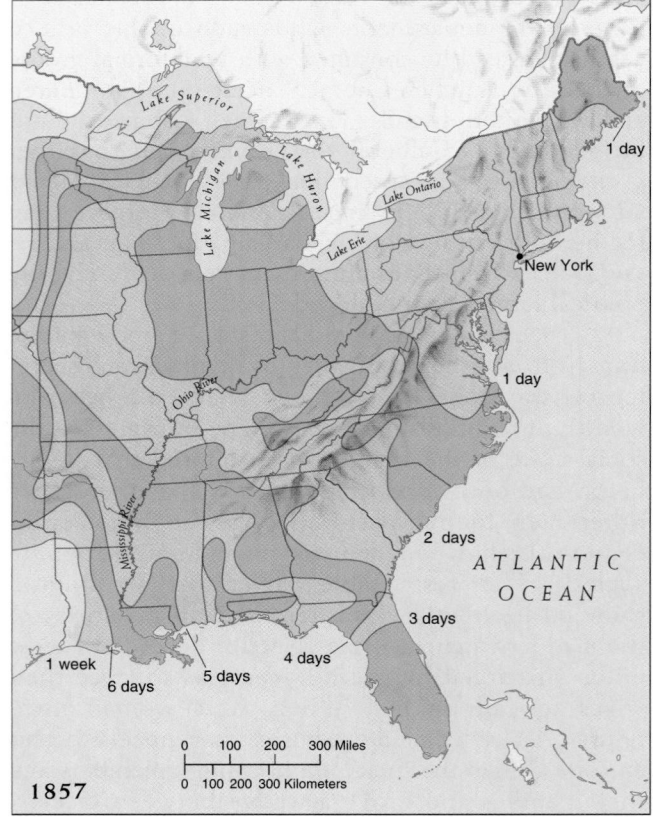

Travel Times, 1800 and 1857   *The transportation revolution dramatically reduced travel times and vastly expanded everyone's horizons. Improved roads, canals, and steamboats and the introduction of railroads made it easier for Americans to move than ever before, and made even those who did not move less isolated. Better transportation linked the developing West to the eastern seaboard and fostered a national identity and pride.*

This 1829 painting of Fairview Inn on the National Road just three miles west of Baltimore illustrates the importance of good transportation. The busy traffic attests to commercial activity and to confidence in westward expansion—the canvas-covered wagons were able to travel as far west as Ohio on the National Road at the time.

other in giving land, subsidies, and other forms of encouragement to road, canal, and railroad companies to provide transportation to their particular localities. Some of these commitments were overly generous and led to financial difficulty: by 1842, nine states (Arkansas, Florida, Illinois, Indiana, Louisiana, Maryland, Michigan, Mississippi, and Pennsylvania) had defaulted on some of their transportation loans, and Ohio and New York were forced to suspend dividends to investors.

Canals and Steamboats

However much they helped the movement of people, the National Road and other roads were unsatisfactory in a commercial sense. Shipment of bulky goods like grain was too slow and expensive by road. Waterborne transportation was much cheaper and still the major commercial link among the Atlantic seaboard states and in the Mississippi-Ohio River system. But before the 1820s most water routes were north-south or coastal (Boston to Charleston, for example); east-west links were urgently needed. Canals turned out to be the answer.

The Erie Canal—the most famous canal of the era—was the brainchild of New York governor DeWitt Clinton, who envisioned a link between New York City and the Great Lakes through the Hudson River and a 364-mile-long canal stretching from Albany to Buffalo. When Clinton proposed the canal in 1817 it was derisively called

"Clinton's Ditch"; the longest then existing American canal was only 27 miles long and had taken nine years to build. Nevertheless, Clinton convinced the New York legislature to approve a bond issue for the canal, and investors (New York and British merchants) subscribed to the tune of $7 million, an immense sum for the day.

Building the canal—40 feet wide, 4 feet deep, 364 miles long, with 83 locks and more than 300 bridges along the way—was a vast engineering and construction challenge. What came to be called Yankee ingenuity showed at every step of the way, from the creation of stump pullers to remove trees from the route, to substitutes for cement (previously imported from England), and to the widespread use of Dupont blasting powder, the forerunner of dynamite (which was not invented for another forty years).

Manpower was another concern. In the early stages nearby farmers worked for $8 a month, but when malaria hit the workforce in the summer of 1819, many went home. They were replaced by 3,000 Irish contract laborers, who were much more expensive—50 cents a day plus room and board—but more reliable (if they survived). Local people regarded the Irish workers as different and frightening, but the importation of foreign contract labor for this job was a portent of the future. Much of the heavy construction work on later canals and railroads was performed by immigrant labor.

DeWitt Clinton had promised, to general disbelief, that the Erie Canal would be completed in less than ten years, and he made good on his promise. The canal was the wonder of the age. On October 26, 1825, Clinton declared it open in Buffalo and sent the first boat, the *Seneca Chief*, on its way to New York at the incredible speed of four miles an hour. (Ironically, the Seneca Indians, for whom the boat was named, had been "removed" from the path of the canal and confined to a small reservation.) The boat reached New York City on November 4, where it was greeted with elaborate ceremonies, including one in which vials of water from the great rivers of the world—the Nile, Ganges, Mississippi, Rhine, and Danube—were emptied into New York harbor to symbolize the opening of commerce between the heart of America and the world.

This grand gesture was appropriate. The Erie Canal provided easy passage to and from the interior, both for people and for goods. It drew settlers like a magnet from the East and, increasingly, from overseas: by 1830, 50,000 people a year were moving west on the canal to the rich farmland of Indiana, Illinois, and territory farther west. Earlier settlers now had a national, indeed an international, market for their produce. Moreover, farm families began purchasing household goods and cloth, formerly made at home. Indeed, one of the most dramatic illustrations of the canal's impact is a rapid decline in the production of homespun cloth. In 1825, the year the Erie Canal opened, New York homesteads produced 16.5 million yards of textiles. By 1835 this figure had shrunk by almost half—8.8 million yards—and by 1855 it had dropped to less than 1 million.

Towns along the canal—Utica, Rochester, Buffalo—became instant cities, each an important commercial center in its own right. Perhaps the greatest beneficiary was the city of New York, which quickly established a commercial and financial supremacy no American city could match. The Erie Canal decisively turned New York's merchants away from Europe and toward America's own heartland, building both interstate commerce and a feeling of community. As the famous song put it,

You'll always know your neighbor,
You'll always know your pal,
If you've ever navigated
On the Erie Canal.

The Impact of the Erie Canal on Household Textile Manufacture   In 1820 the household manufacture of woolen cloth for home use was widespread in New York State, but in 1845, twenty years after the Erie Canal opened, many fewer counties were producing significant quantities of fabric. Because they could now buy cheap manufactured textiles, New York women living near the canal were freed from the time-consuming task of making cloth for their families.

Source: Arthur Harrison Cole, *The American Wool Manufacture* (Cambridge, Mass.: Harvard University Press, 1926), p. 280.

The phenomenal success of the Erie Canal prompted other states to construct similar waterways to tap the rich interior market. Between 1820 and 1840, $200 million was invested in canal building, three-quarters of it provided by state governments. The Blackstone Canal linked Worcester, Massachusetts, with Providence, Rhode Island; the Pennsylvania Main Line Canal ran all the way from Philadelphia to Pittsburgh; and many other canals were built in Maine, Maryland, Ohio, Indiana, and Illinois. None of these waterways achieved the success of the Erie, which collected $8.5 million in tolls in its first nine years. And the port cities they were meant to benefit—Philadelphia and Baltimore, for example—never threatened New York's commercial supremacy. Nevertheless, the spurt of canal building ended the geographical isolation of much of the country. For example, Ohio's canal system opened up the American interior by linking the Ohio River to Lake Erie in the north and to the Pennsylvania canals to the east.

An even more important improvement in water transportation, especially in the American interior, was the steamboat. Robert Fulton first demonstrated the commercial feasibility of steamboats in 1807, and they were soon operating in the East. Redesigned with more efficient engines and shallower, broader hulls, steamboats transformed commerce on the country's great inland river system: the Ohio, the Mississippi, the Missouri, and their tributaries. Steamboats were extremely dangerous, however; boiler explosions, fires, and sinkings were common. Public outrage at these conditions led to one of the first uses of federal regulatory power in the public interest. The first Steamboat Act, passed in 1838 and strengthened in 1852, set standards for the construction, equipment, and operation of steamboat boilers, required measures to prevent fire and collisions, and established an inspection system to make sure the new regulations were carried out. Although steamboats were privately owned and operated, the public that they served insisted on the need for safety standards to promote the wider community welfare.

Dangerous as they were, steamboats greatly stimulated trade in the nation's interior. There had long been downstream trade on flatboats along the Mississippi River system, but it was limited by the return trip overland on the arduous and dangerous Natchez Trace. For a time, steamboats actually increased the down-river flatboat trade, because boatmen could now make more round trips in the same amount of time, traveling home by steamboat in speed and comfort.

The increased river- and canal-borne trade, like the New England shipping boom of a generation earlier, stimulated urban growth and all kinds of commerce. Cities such as Cincinnati, already notable for its rapid growth, experienced a new economic surge. A frontier outpost in 1790, Cincinnati was by the 1830s a center of steamboat manufacture and machine tool production as well as a central shipping point for food for the southern market. Even in sleepy agricultural villages like Mark Twain's hometown of Hannibal, Missouri, the steamboat was a powerful symbol of energy and international

Mary Keys. American (active 1832) *Lockport on the Erie Canal*, 1832. Watercolor on paper 15½ x 20½ inches. Munson–Williams–Proctor Institute Museum of Art, Utica, NY 55.45.

Mary Keys, a local artist, painted this watercolor in 1832 illustrating one of the Erie Canal's engineering triumphs, the famous "combined" locks—two sets of five locks rising side by side for 60 feet—at Lockport. One observer boasted, "Here the great Erie Canal has defied nature."

commerce. As Twain recounts in "Old Times on the Mississippi," the steamboat brought the town to life:

> A negro drayman, famous for his quick eye and prodigious voice, lifts up the cry, "S-t-e-a-m-boat a comin'!"…The town drunkard stirs, the clerks wake up, a furious clatter of drays follows, every house and store pours out a human contribution, and all in a twinkling the dead town is alive and moving. Drays, carts, men, boys, all go hurrying from many quarters to a common center, the wharf….Then such a scramble as there is to get aboard, and to get ashore, and to take in freight and to discharge freight, all at one and the same time; and such a yelling and cursing as the mates facilitate it all with! Ten minutes later the steamer is under way again….After ten more minutes the town is dead again, and the town drunkard asleep by the skids once more.

Railroads

Remarkable as all these transportation changes were, the most remarkable was still to come. Railroads, new in 1830 (when the Baltimore and Ohio Railroad opened with 13 miles of track), grew to an astounding 31,000 miles by 1860. By that date, New England and the Old Northwest had laid a dense network of rails, and several lines had reached west beyond the Mississippi. The South, the least industrialized section of the nation, had fewer railroads. "Railroad mania" surpassed even canal mania as investors—as many as one-quarter of them British—rushed to profit from the new invention.

Early railroads, like the steamboat, had to overcome many technological and supply problems with far-reaching economic effects. For example, locomotives, to generate adequate power, had to be heavy. Heavy locomotives, in turn, required iron rather than wooden rails. The resulting increased demand forced America's iron industry to modernize (at first, railroad iron was imported from England). Heavy engines also required a solid gravel roadbed and strong wooden ties. Arranging steady supplies of both and the labor to lay them was a construction challenge on a new scale. The demand for locomotives and the need to service them fostered the development of a specialized industry, represented by Philadelphia's Baldwin Locomotive Works.

Finally, there were problems of standardization and production quality. Because so many early railroads were short and local, intended simply to connect nearby towns, builders used any gauge (track width) that served their purposes. Thus gauges varied from place to place, forcing long-haul passengers and freight to change trains frequently. For each change, commercial shippers were burdened with the cost of unloading goods from one train and loading them on another. At one time, the trip from Philadelphia to Charleston involved eight gauge changes. Add to this that the early railroads—often hurriedly and poorly built by private companies trying to save money—were prone to frequent breakdowns and accidents, and its not surprising to learn that traveling by ship between Philadelphia and Charleston long remained more pleasant than traveling by rail.

For some years after the introduction of the railroad, canal boats and coastal steamers carried more freight and at lower cost. It was not until the 1850s that consolidation of local railroads into larger systems began in earnest. But already it was clear that this youngest transportation innovation would have far-reaching social consequences.

The Legal Infrastructure

Accompanying the transportation revolution was a series of decisions by federal courts asserting broad federal powers over interstate commerce. The effect of these decisions was to vastly encourage commercial enterprise. By preventing states from interfering with interstate commerce, the government assured entrepreneurs the freedom and security to operate in the risky new national market. Two key decisions were handed down by Chief Justice John Marshall (who had been on the bench since 1801). In *Dartmouth College v. Woodward* (1819) the Supreme Court prevented states from interfering in

contracts, and in *Gibbons v. Ogden* (1824) it enjoined the state of New York from giving a monopoly over a steamboat line to Robert Fulton, inventor of the vessel. Although Fulton's invention was protected by a federal patent, its commercial application was not. Patenting thus encouraged technology, but not at the expense of competition. A decision handed down by Marshall's successor, Roger Taney, *Charles River Bridge v. Warren Bridge* (1837), again supported economic opportunity by denying a monopoly. All three cases involved federal reversal of decisions made at the state level, illustrating how the Supreme Court, under Marshall's leadership, strengthened the power of the federal government and thus fostered national policy rather than localism.

At the state level, another crucial commercial protection was the passage of laws concerning incorporation of businesses that had grown too large for individual proprietorship, family ownership, or limited partnership. Businesses that needed to raise large amounts of capital by attracting many investors found the contractual protections provided by incorporation to be essential. The protection investors wanted most was limited liability—the assurance that they would lose no more than what they had invested in a corporation if it were sued or went bankrupt. Initially transportation companies and banks benefited the most from state charters of incorporation. They were less commonly used by merchants and manufacturers until later in the century. Incorporation increased the powers of government, for it made businesses subject to state regulation. Nevertheless, the net effect of state incorporation laws was to encourage large-scale economic activity and to hasten the commercialization of rural areas.

Commercial Agriculture in the Old Northwest

The impact of the transportation revolution and of technological innovation on rural people (who in spite of the growth of cities still constituted more than two-thirds of the American population) went far beyond the breaking down of rural isolation. Every advance in transportation—better roads, canals, steamboats, railroads—made it easier for farmers to get their produce to market. Improvements in agricultural machinery increased the amount of acreage a farmer could cultivate. These two developments, added to the availability of rich, inexpensive land in the heartland, moved American farmers permanently away from subsistence agriculture and into production for sale.

The impact of the transportation revolution on the Old Northwest was particularly marked. Settlement of the region, ongoing since the 1790s, accelerated. In the 1830s, after the opening of the Erie Canal, migrants from New England streamed into northern Ohio, Illinois, Indiana, southern Wisconsin, and Michigan and began to reach into Iowa.

Government policy strongly encouraged western settlement. The easy terms of federal land sales were an important inducement: terms eased from an initial rate of $2.00 per acre for a minimum of 320 acres in 1800, to $1.25 an acre for 80 acres in 1820. Still, this was too much for most settlers to pay all at once. Some people simply squatted, taking their chances that they could make enough money to buy the land before someone else bought it. Less daring settlers relied on credit, which was extended by banks, storekeepers, speculators, promoters, and, somewhat later, railroads, which received large grants of federal lands.

The very need for cash to purchase land involved western settlers in commercial agriculture from the beginning. Farmers, and the towns and cities that grew up to supply them, needed access to markets for their crops. Canals, steamboats, and railroads ensured that access, immediately tying the individual farm into national and international commercial networks. The long period of subsistence farming that had characterized colonial New England and the early Ohio Valley frontier was superseded by commercial agriculture stimulated by the transportation revolution.

Commercial agriculture in turn encouraged regional specialization. Ohioans shipped corn and hogs first by flatboat and later by steamboat to New Orleans. Cincinnati, the center of the Ohio trade, earned the nickname "Porkopolis" because of the importance of its slaughterhouses. By 1840, the national center of wheat production had moved west of the Appalachians to Ohio. Wheat flowed from the upper Midwest along the Erie Canal to eastern cities and increasingly to Europe. Because in each new western area yields were higher than in earlier ones, farmers in older regions were forced to shift away from wheat to other crops. The constant opening of new farmland encouraged mobility and wasteful soil practices. Many farmers were disinclined to make a permanent commitment to their land, but rather counted on rising land prices and short-term crop profits to improve their financial situation. Prepared to move on when the price was right, they regarded their farmland not as a permanent investment but as a speculation.

At the same time, farmers who grew wheat or any other cash crop found themselves at the mercy of far-off markets, which established crop prices; distant

Cyrus McCormick is shown demonstrating his reaper to skeptical farmers. When they saw that the machine cut four times as much wheat a day as a hand-held scythe, farmers flocked to buy McCormick's invention. Agricultural practices, little changed for centuries, were revolutionized by machines like this.

canal or railroad companies, which set transportation rates; and the state of the national economy, which determined the availability of local credit. This direct dependence on economic forces outside the control of the local community was something new. So, too, was the dependence on technology, embodied in expensive new machines that farmers often bought on credit.

New tools made western farmers unusually productive. John Deere's steel plow (invented in 1837) cut plowing time in half, making cultivation of larger acreages possible. Seed drills were another important advance. But the most remarkable innovation was Cyrus McCormick's reaper, patented in 1834. Earlier, harvesting had depended on manpower alone. A man could cut two or three acres of wheat a day with a cradle scythe, but with the horse-drawn reaper he could cut twelve acres. Impressed by these figures, western farmers rushed to buy the new machines, confident that increased production would rapidly pay for them. In most years, their confidence was justified. But in bad years, farmers found that their new levels of debt could mean failure and foreclosure. They were richer but more economically vulnerable than they had been before.

Effects of the Transportation Revolution

The effects of the transportation revolution were many. The new ease of transportation undergirded economic growth by making distant markets accessible. The startling successes of innovations such as canals and railroads attracted large capital investments, including significant amounts from foreign investors ($500 million between 1790 and 1861) that fueled further

Commercial Links: Rivers, Canals, Roads, 1830, and Rail Lines, 1850   By 1830, the United States was tied together by a network of roads, canals, and rivers. This "transportation revolution" fostered a great burst of commercial activity and economic growth. Transportation improvements accelerated the commercialization of agriculture by getting farmers' products to wider, nonlocal markets. Access to wider markets likewise encouraged new textile and other manufacturers to increase their scale of production. By 1850, another revolutionary mode of transportation, the railroad, had emerged as a vital link to the transportation infrastructure.

growth. In turn, the transportation revolution fostered an optimistic, risk-taking mentality in the United States that stimulated invention and innovation. More than anything, the transportation revolution allowed people to move with unaccustomed ease. Already a restless people compared with Europeans, Americans took advantage of new transport to move even more often—and farther away—than they had before.

There were other, less directly economic effects. Every east-west road, canal, and railroad helped to reorient Americans away from the Atlantic and toward the heartland. This new focus was decisive in the creation of national pride and identity. Transportation improvements such as the Erie Canal and the National Road linked Americans in larger communities of interest beyond the local community in which they lived. Other results were less positive. The technological triumphs of canal building and rail laying fostered a brash spirit of conquest over nature that was to become part of the American myth of the frontier. Furthermore, although every new transportation or communication link broke down local and regional isolation and helped to build a spirit of pride in the nation, it also refocused attention on questions of national politics. The new transportation system caused a subtle political shift, for it strengthened the influence of the North by improving the North's ties with the West more than those of the South. In this way, the new modes of communication and transportation served to heat up the politics of the era.

JACKSON AND HIS OPPONENTS: THE RISE OF THE WHIGS

As transportation improvements, increased commercialization, and the new politics drew the people of the United States out of localism into larger networks, fundamental questions about national unity arose. What was the correct balance between local interests—the rights of the states—and the powers of the central government? The men who wrote the federal Constitution in Philadelphia in 1787 had not been able to reach agreement on this question. Because the Constitution deliberately left the federal structure ambiguous, all subsequent sectional disagreements automatically became constitutional issues that carried a threat to national unity. The great issues of Jackson's presidency expressed this continuing tension between nationalism and sectionalism. Jackson's responses to them created such controversy that a permanent opposition—another political party, known as the Whigs—was born.

The Nullification Crisis
The political issue that came to symbolize the divergent sectional interests of North and South, pitting the rights of individual states against the claims of a federal major-

ity, was the protective tariff. The first substantial protective tariff was enacted in 1816 after northern manufacturing interests clamored for protection from the ruthless British competition that followed the War of 1812 (see Chapter 9). As a group, wealthy southern planters were opposed to tariffs, both because tariffs raised the cost of the luxury goods they imported from Europe and because they believed in the principle of free trade, fearing that American tariffs would cause other countries to retaliate with tariffs against southern cotton. Most southern congressmen, assured that the 1816 tariff was a temporary postwar recovery measure, voted for it. But it was not temporary. As the North industrialized and new industries demanded protection, tariff bills in 1824 and 1828 raised rates still higher and protected more items. Southerners protested, but they were outvoted in Congress by northern and western representatives, who agreed both on the need to protect industry and on the tariff as a way to raise federal revenue.

The 1828 tariff, nicknamed "the Tariff of Abominations," was a special target of southern anger, because Jackson's supporters in Congress had passed it in order to increase northern support for him in the presidential campaign of that year. It imposed especially high tariffs on imported textiles and iron that ranged from a third to half their total value. Southerners in Congress lacked the votes to block the tariff and faced the bleak prospect that their economic interests would always be ignored by the majority. Southern opponents of the tariff insisted that it was not a truly national measure but a sectional one that helped only some groups while harming others. Thus it was unconstitutional because it violated the rights of some of the states.

South Carolina, Calhoun's home state, reacted the most forcefully to the tariff of 1828. Of the older southern states, South Carolina had been the hardest hit by the opening of the new cotton lands in the Southwest, which had drained both population and commerce from the state. One index of South Carolina's changed status was the declining position of Charleston. In 1800 it was still as important a seaport as New York and Boston, but by the 1820s it had been eclipsed by all the major northern ports as well as by Mobile and New Orleans, then the major ports for exporting cotton. To these economic woes were added the first real fears about national attitudes toward slavery. South Carolinians, who had always had close personal ties with slave owners in the Caribbean islands, were shaken by the news that the British Parliament, bowing to popular pressure at home, was planning to emancipate all the slaves in the British West Indies. If Congress had the power to impose tariffs that were harmful to some states, South Carolinians asked, what would prevent it from enacting legislation like Britain's, depriving Southerners of their slaves and, thus, of their livelihood?

The result of these fears was a renewed interest in the doctrine of nullification, a topic that became the subject of widespread discussion in South Carolina in 1828. The doctrine upheld the right of a state to declare a federal law null and void and to refuse to enforce it within the state. This was not a new argument. Thomas Jefferson and James Madison had used it in the Kentucky and Virginia Resolves of 1798, which they wrote in opposing the Alien and Sedition Acts (see Chapter 8). The Hartford Convention of 1814–15, at which Federalists protested grievances related to the War of 1812, had adopted the same position (see Chapter 9). At issue in each case was the power of the state against that of the federal government. Now the same constitutional issue emerged again, this time, linked to the most intractable sectional issue, the South's determination to protect the institution of slavery.

South Carolina had an important supporter of nullification in the person of John C. Calhoun, who wrote a widely circulated defense of the doctrine, the *Exposition and Protest*, in 1828. Because Calhoun was soon to serve as Andrew Jackson's vice president, he wrote the *Exposition* anonymously. He hoped to use his influence with Jackson to gain support for nullification, but he was disappointed.

Where Calhoun saw nullification as a safeguard of the rights of the minority, Jackson saw it as a threat to national unity. As the president said at a famous exchange of toasts at the annual Jefferson Day dinner in 1830, "Our Federal Union, it must be preserved." In response to Jackson, Calhoun offered his own toast: "The Union—next to our liberty most dear. May we always remember that it can only be preserved by distributing equally the benefits and burdens of the Union." The president and the vice president were thus in open disagreement on a matter of crucial national importance. The outcome was inevitable: Calhoun lost all influence with Jackson, and two years later he took the unusual step of resigning the vice presidency. Martin Van Buren was elected to the office for Jackson's second term. Calhoun, his presidential aspirations in ruins, became a senator from South Carolina, and in that capacity participated in the last act of the nullification drama.

In 1832 the nullification controversy became a full-blown crisis. In passing the tariff of 1832, Congress (in spite of Jackson's urging) retained high taxes on woolens, iron, and hemp, although it reduced duties on other items. South Carolina responded with a special convention and an Ordinance of Nullification, in which it rejected the tariff and refused to collect the taxes it required. The state further issued a call for a volunteer militia and threatened to secede from the Union if Jackson used force against it. Jackson responded vehemently, denouncing the nullifiers—"Disunion by armed force is treason"—and obtaining from Congress a Force Bill

authorizing the federal government to collect the tariff in South Carolina at gunpoint if necessary. Intimidated, the other southern states refused to follow South Carolina's lead. More quietly, Jackson also asked Congress to revise the tariff. Henry Clay, the Great Pacificator, swung into action and soon, with Calhoun's support, had crafted the Tariff Act of 1833. This measure appeared to meet southern demands by pledging a return to the tariff rate of 1816 (an average of 20 percent) by 1842 through a series of very small annual decreases for nine years, followed by a large cut in the final year. (In fact, in 1842 Congress quickly voted a return to higher tariff rates.) In 1833 the South Carolina legislature, unwilling to act without the support of other southern states, quickly accepted this face-saving compromise and repealed its nullification of the tariff of 1832. In a final burst of bravado, the legislature nullified the Force Bill, but Jackson defused the crisis by ignoring this second nullification.

The nullification crisis was the most serious threat to national unity that the United States had ever experienced. South Carolinians, by threatening to secede, had forced concessions on a matter they believed of vital economic importance. They—and a number of other Southerners—believed that the resolution of the crisis illustrated the success of their uncompromising tactics. Most of the rest of the nation simply breathed a sigh of relief, echoing Daniel Webster's sentiment, spoken in the heat of the debate over nullification, "Liberty and Union, now and forever, one and inseparable!" Most Americans firmly believed that although every effort should be made to address sectional concerns, national unity and majority rule came first. But another event of the Jackson years, Indian removal, clearly showed how unfair majority rule could be when the minority was not strong enough to force a compromise.

Indian Removal

The official policy of the United States government from the time of Jefferson's administration was to promote the assimilation of Indian peoples by encouraging them to adopt white ways. To Indian groups who resisted "civilization" or who needed more time to adapt, Jefferson offered the alternative of removal from settled areas in the East to the new Indian Territory west of the Mississippi River. Following this logic, at the end of the War of 1812 the federal government signed removal treaties with a number of Indian nations of the Old Northwest, thereby opening up large tracts of land for white settlement (see Chapter 9). In the Southwest, however, the "Five Civilized Tribes"—the Cherokees, Chickasaws, Choctaws, Creeks, and Seminoles—remained. By the 1830s, under constant pressure from settlers, each of the five tribes had ceded most of its lands, but sizable self-governing groups lived in

Georgia, Alabama, Mississippi, and Florida. All of these (except the Seminoles) had moved far in the direction of coexistence with whites, and they resisted suggestions that they should voluntarily remove themselves.

The Cherokees took the most extensive steps to adopt white ways. Their tribal lands in northwestern Georgia boasted prosperous farms, businesses, grain and lumber mills, and even plantations with black slaves. Intermarriage with whites and African Americans had produced an influential group of mixed bloods within the Cherokee nation, some of whom were eager to accept white ways. Schooled by Congregationalist, Presbyterian, and Moravian missionaries, the Cherokees were almost totally literate in English. They took special pride in the alphabet for their own language that was developed by the Cherokee scholar Sequoyah, and in 1828

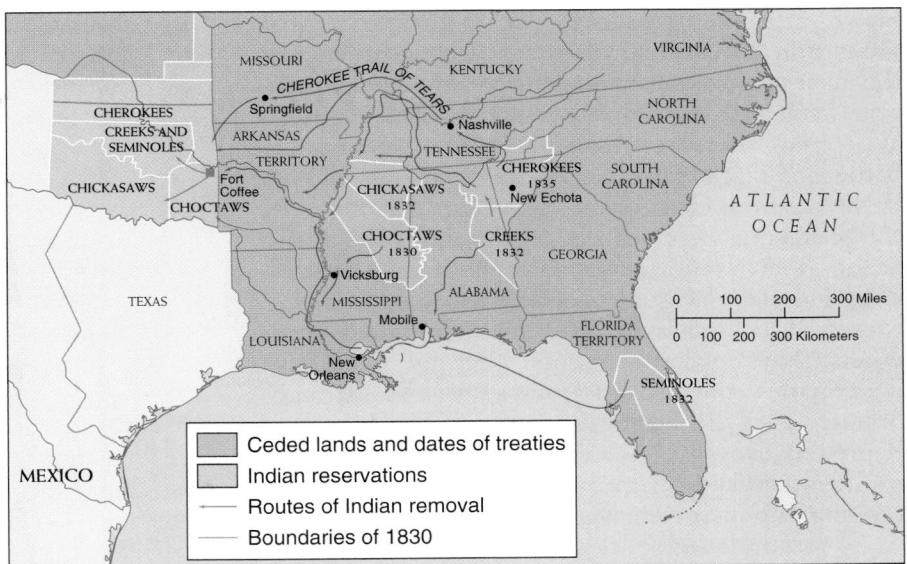

Southern Indian Cessions and Removals, 1830s   *Pressure on the five major southern Indian peoples—the Cherokees, Chickasaws, Choctaws, Creeks, and Seminoles—that began during the War of 1812 culminated with their removal in the 1830s. Some groups from every tribe ceded their southern homelands peacefully and moved to the newly established Indian Territory west of Arkansas and Missouri. Some, like the Seminoles, resisted by force. Others, like the Cherokees, resisted in the courts but finally lost when President Andrew Jackson refused to enforce a Supreme Court decision in their favor. The Cherokees, the last to move, were forcibly removed by the U.S. Army along "the Trail of Tears" in 1838.*

they began publishing a tribal newspaper, the *Cherokee Phoenix*, in both Cherokee and English. A year earlier the tribe abolished its traditional form of government and established a constitutional republic.

Despite the evidence of the Cherokees' successful adaptation to the dominant white culture, in the 1820s the legislatures of Georgia, Alabama, and Mississippi, responding to pressures from land-hungry whites, voted to invalidate federal treaties granting special self-governing status to Indian lands. Because the federal government, not the states, bore responsibility for Indian policy, these state actions constituted a sectional challenge to federal authority. In this instance, however, unlike the Nullification Crisis, the resisting states had presidential support. Living up to his reputation as a ruthless Indian fighter, Jackson determined on a federal policy of wholesale removal of the southern Indian tribes.

In 1830, at President Jackson's urging, the U.S. Congress passed the hotly debated Indian Removal Act, which appropriated funds for relocation, by force if necessary. When Jackson increased the pressure by sending federal officials to negotiate removal treaties with the southern tribes, most reluctantly signed and prepared to move. The Cherokees, however, fought their removal by using the white man's weapon—the law. At first they seemed to have won: in *Cherokee Nation v. Georgia* (1831) and *Worcester v. Georgia* (1832) Chief

Justice John Marshall ruled that the Cherokees, though not a state or a foreign nation, were a "domestic dependent nation" that could not be forced by the state of Georgia to give up its land against its will. However, when President Jackson heard the Supreme Court's decision, he is reputed to have said, "John Marshall has made his decision. Now let him enforce it." Ignoring the decision, Jackson continued his support for removal.

Faced by the Cherokees' de facto defeat, what could the other Indian tribes do? Some Seminoles of Florida chose to fight. Aided by runaway slaves and by their unsurpassed knowledge of their homeland, the Florida Everglades, some Seminole bands fought a guerrilla war that lasted into the 1840s before the U.S. military gave up and allowed them to remain. The majority of Seminoles and members of other tribes were much less fortunate: most of the Choctaws moved west in 1830; the last of the Creeks were forcibly moved by the military in 1836, and the Chickasaws a year later. And in 1838, in the last and most infamous removal, resisting Cherokees were driven west to Oklahoma along what came to be known as "the Trail of Tears." A 7,000-man army escorting them watched thousands (perhaps a quarter of the 16,000 Cherokees) die along the way. Another futile effort to resist removal, the Black Hawk "war," occurred in the Old Northwest. In 1832, Sac and Fox Indians, led by Black

Hawk, attempted to move back to their old tribal grounds in Illinois following removal, but settlers saw the move as an invasion and demanded military protection. Federal troops chased the Black Hawk band to Wisconsin, where more than 300 Indians died in a final battle, and Black Hawk himself was taken prisoner. As in the South, the last of the remaining Indians east of the Mississippi were removed by the end of the 1830s.

Indian removal was a deeply divisive national issue. President Jackson's sweeping policy undoubtedly expressed the opinion of most Southerners and Westerners. But northern opinion, led by Protestant missionaries and reform groups, was so strongly opposed that the Removal Act passed the House of Representatives by only 3 votes (out of 200). Jackson's presidential claim to speak for popular opinion was running into increasing opposition.

The Bank War

The last major event of Jackson's presidency, his refusal to renew the charter of the Second Bank of the United States, had lasting political consequences. Jackson's opponents, already angry about his earlier actions, were so infuriated by the bank episode that they formed the permanent opposition party known as the Whigs. It was from the heat of the Bank War that the now characteristic American two-party system emerged.

The first Bank of the United States had been chartered by Congress in 1791, at Alexander Hamilton's urging. Federalists supported it, Jeffersonians opposed it and allowed its charter to expire in 1811. But after the War of 1812 almost all Democratic Republicans came to appreciate the stability provided by a central bank. Thus in 1816 Congress granted a twenty-year charter to the Second Bank of the United States. Like its predecessor, the Bank played a powerful role in the expanding American economy, encouraging the growth of strong and stable financial interests and curbing less stable and irresponsible ones.

Also, like its predecessor, the Bank was not a government agency but a private institution, the majority of whose directors were appointed by the government. Its stockholders were some of the nation's richest men (New York's John Jacob Astor and Philadelphia's Stephen Girard among them). The bank was directed by the erudite and aristocratic Nicholas Biddle of Philadelphia. Biddle, a friend of Thomas Jefferson and an avid amateur scientist, was the editor of the journals of Lewis and Clark.

The Bank, which with thirty branches was the nation's largest, performed a variety of functions: it held the government's money (about $10 million), sold government bonds, and made commercial loans. But its most important function was the control it exercised over state banks. At the time, America

This figurehead of Andrew Jackson, carved in 1834 for the navy frigate Constitution, captures the unmoveable resolve that made Jackson so popular early in his presidency and so reviled during the Bank War.

Museum of the City of New York (M52.11)

lacked a national currency. The money in circulation was a mixture of paper money (U.S. notes and the notes of state banks) and gold and silver coins (specie, or hard currency), many of them of foreign origin. Because state banks tended to issue more paper money than they could back with hard currency, the Bank always demanded repayment of its loans to them in coin. This policy forced state banks to maintain adequate reserves, curbed inflationary pressures (overprinting of banknotes), and restricted speculative activities such as risky loans. In times of recession, the bank eased the pressure on state banks, demanding only partial payment in coin. Thus the Bank acted as a currency stabilizer by helping to control the money supply. It brought a semblance of order to what we today would consider a chaotic money system—coins of various weights and a multitude of state banknotes, many of which were discounted (not accepted at full face value) in other states.

The concept of a strong national bank was supported by the majority of the nation's merchants and businessmen and was a key element in Henry Clay's American System. Nevertheless, the Bank had many opponents. The objections arose from both sectional and political resentments. A number of state bank directors felt overshadowed by the central bank's size and power. Western land speculators, and many western farmers, chafed at the bank's tight control over the currency reserves of state banks, claiming it was harmful to western development. Both western farmers and urban workers had bitter memories of the Panic of 1819, which the Bank had caused (at least in part) by sharply contracting credit. To some people, the economic power of the Bank was frightening; they feared that monied elites would use it to their own advantage. Although the rapid growth of the national economy made some sort of control necessary, many ordinary people were uneasy not only about the Bank but about banks of all kinds. They believed that a system based on paper currency would be manipulated by bankers in unpredictable and dangerous ways. Among those who held that opinion was Andrew Jackson, who had hated and feared banks ever since the 1790s, when he had lost a great deal of money in a speculative venture.

Early in his administration, Jackson hastened to tell Nicholas Biddle, "I do not dislike your Bank any more than all banks." By 1832, Jackson's opinion had changed and he and Biddle were locked in a personal conflict that harmed not only the national economy but the reputations of both men. Biddle, urged on by Henry Clay and Daniel Webster, precipitated the conflict by making early application for rechartering the Bank. Congress approved the application in July 1832. Clay and Webster, though well aware of Jackson's antibank feelings, believed the president would not risk a veto in an election year. They were wrong. Jackson immediately decided on a stinging veto, announcing to Van Buren, "The bank...is trying to kill me, but I will kill it!"

And kill it he did that same July, with one of the strongest veto messages in American history. Denouncing the Bank as unconstitutional, harmful to states' rights, and "dangerous to the liberties of the people," Jackson presented himself as the spokesman for the majority of ordinary people and the enemy of special privilege. Asserting that the Bank's "exclusive privileges" were benefiting only the rich, Jackson claimed to speak for the "humble members of society—the farmers, mechanics and laborers"—and to oppose injustice and inequality. Nor did Jackson's veto message speak only of the sharp division between social classes. It also aroused sectional and national feelings by its allusions to the many British and eastern bank stockholders who were profiting from the debts of poor Southerners and Westerners. In short, the veto spoke directly to many of the fears and resentments that Americans felt at this time of exceptionally rapid economic and social change. Jackson's message was a campaign document, written to appeal to voters. Most of the financial community was appalled, believing both the veto and the accompanying message to be reckless demagoguery.

Jackson's Reelection in 1832

Nevertheless, Jackson's veto message was a great popular success, and it set the terms for the presidential election of 1832. Henry Clay, the nominee of the anti-Jackson forces, lost the battle for popular opinion. Democrats successfully painted Clay as the defender of the Bank and of privilege. His defeat was decisive: he drew only 49 electoral votes, to Jackson's 219. A handful of votes went to the first third party in American history, the short-lived Anti-Masonic Party. This party played on the resentments of the newly enfranchised "common man" against the traditional political elite, many of whom (including both Jackson and Clay) were members of the Masonic order, a fraternal society with secret rituals and special customs. The Anti-Masonic Party did make one lasting contribution to the political process. It was the first to hold a national nominating convention, an innovation quickly adopted by the other political parties.

Although the election was a triumph for Jackson, the Bank War continued. It was to have serious effects on the economy and on political principle. The Bank charter did not expire until 1836, but Jackson, declaring that "the hydra of corruption is only scotched, not dead," decided to kill the Bank by transferring its $10 million in government deposits to favored state banks ("pet banks," critics called them). Cabinet members objected, but Jackson ignored them. Two secretaries of the treasury refused to carry out Jackson's orders and were abruptly removed. Jackson then found a more pliant man, Roger Taney, for the job. (Jackson later rewarded him with the post of chief justice of the Supreme Court.) Henry Clay led an unprecedented vote of censure in the Senate, but in the House loyal Democrats prevented a censure vote. To all of these protests, Jackson responded that the election had given him a popular mandate to act against the Bank. The president was the direct representative of the people, he claimed, and could act upon the popular will, regardless of the opinion of Congress or even the cabinet. Short of impeachment, there was nothing Congress could do to prevent Jackson from acting on his expansive—and novel—interpretation of presidential powers.

Whigs, Van Buren, and the Election of 1836

But there was someone outside Congress with power to respond: the Bank's director, Nicholas Biddle. "This worthy President thinks that because he has scalped Indians...he is to have his way with the Bank," Biddle commented. "He is mistaken." As the government withdrew its deposits, Biddle abruptly called in the Bank's commercial loans, thereby causing a sharp panic and recession in the winter of 1833–34. Merchants, businessmen, and southern planters were all furious—at Jackson. His opponents, only a loose coalition up to this time, coalesced into a formal opposition party that called itself the Whigs. Evoking the memory of the Patriots who had resisted King George III in the American Revolution, the new party called on everyone to resist tyrannical "King Andrew." Just as Jackson's own calls for popular democracy had appealed to voters in all regions, so his opponents overcame their sectional differences to unite in opposition to his economic policies and arbitrary methods.

The Whigs first tested their strength against Vice President Martin Van Buren, Jackson's designated successor, in the presidential election of 1836. Still not completely free of the methods and attitudes of traditional politics, the Whigs ran four sectional candidates: William Henry Harrison of Ohio, Hugh Lawson White of Tennessee, W. P. Mangum of North Carolina, and Daniel Webster of Massachusetts. The Whigs hoped the combined votes for these regional candidates would deny Van Buren a majority and force the election into the House of Representatives, where they hoped to win. The strategy failed, but not by much: although Van Buren captured 170 electoral votes to the Whigs' 124, the popular vote was much closer, 50.9 percent to 49.1 percent. A shift of only 2,000 votes in Pennsylvania would have thrown the election into the House of Representatives, vindicating the Whig strategy. The Whig defeat drove home the weakness of the traditional sectional politics, but the closeness of the popular vote showed that the basis for a united national opposition did exist. In 1840, the Whigs would prove that they had learned this lesson.

The Panic of 1837

Meanwhile, the consequences of the Bank War continued. The recession of 1833–34 was followed by a wild speculative boom, caused as much by foreign investors as by the expiration of the Bank. Many new state banks were chartered that were eager to give loans, the price of cotton rose rapidly, and speculation in western lands was feverish (in Alabama and Mississippi, the mid-1830s were known as "the Flush Times"). A government surplus of $37 million distributed to the states in 1836 made the inflationary pressures worse. Jackson became alarmed at the widespread use of paper money (which he blamed for the inflation), and in July 1836 he issued the Specie Circular, announcing that the government would accept payment for public lands only in hard currency. At the same time, foreign investors, especially British banks, affected by a world recession, called in their American loans. The sharp contraction of credit led to the Panic of 1837 and a six-year recession, the worst the American economy had yet known. Ironically, Andrew Jackson, whose bad experience with speculation had led him to destroy the Bank of the United States, set in motion the events that caused the boom and bust he so feared. And he left his successor, Martin Van Buren, an impossible political legacy.

In 1837, 800 banks suspended business, refusing to pay out any of their $150 million in deposits. The collapse of the banking system led to business closures and outright failures. Nationwide, the unemployment rate is estimated to have reached more than 10 percent. In the winter of 1837–38 in New York City alone, one-third of all manual laborers were unemployed and an estimated 10,000 were living in abject poverty. New York laborers took to the streets. Four or five thousand protesters carrying signs reading "Bread, Meat, Rent, Fuel!" gathered at City Hall on February 10, 1838, then marched to the warehouse of a leading merchant, Eli Hart. Breaking down the door, they took possession of the thousands of barrels of flour Hart had stored there rather than sell at what the mob considered a fair price. Policemen and state militia who tried to prevent the break-in were beaten by the angry mob.

Nor were the working class and the poor the only victims. Among the many hurt by the panic was Philip Hone, former mayor of New York and once a man of considerable wealth. Hone lost two-thirds of his own fortune and was unable to help his three grown sons when they lost their jobs. "Business of all kinds [is] completely at a stand," Hone noted in 1840, wondering "how the poor man manages to get a dinner for his family." The Panic of 1837 lasted six long years, causing widespread misery. Not until 1843 did the economy show signs of recovery.

In neither 1837 nor 1819 did the federal government take any action to aid victims of economic recession. No banks were bailed out, no bank depositors were saved by federal insurance, no laid-off workers got unemployment payments. Nor did the government undertake any public works projects or pump money into the economy. All of these steps, today seen as essential to prevent economic collapse and to alleviate human suffering, were unheard of in 1819 and 1837. Soup kitchens and charities were mobilized in major cities, but only by private, volunteer groups, not by local or state governments. Panics and depressions were believed to be natural stages in the business cycle, and government intervention was considered unwarranted—although it was perfectly acceptable for government to intervene to promote growth. As a result, workers, farmers, and members of the new business middle class suddenly realized that participation in America's booming economy was very dangerous. The rewards could be great, but so could the penalties.

Martin Van Buren (quickly nicknamed "Van Ruin") spent a dismal four years in the White House presiding over bank failures, bankruptcies, and massive unemployment. Van Buren, who lacked Jackson's compelling personality, could find no remedies to the

This contemporary cartoon bitterly depicts the terrible effects of the Panic of 1837 on ordinary people—bank failures, unemployment, drunkenness, and destitution—which the artist links to the insistence of the rich on payment in specie (as Jackson had required in the Species Circular of 1836). Over the scene waves the American flag, accompanied by the ironic message, "61st Anniversary of our Independence."

depression. His misfortune gave the opposition party, the newly formed Whigs, their opportunity.

THE SECOND AMERICAN PARTY SYSTEM

The First American Party System, the confrontation between the Federalists and the Jeffersonian Democratic Republicans that began in the 1790s, had been widely viewed as an unfortunate factional squabble that threatened the common good of the republic (see Chapter 8). By the 1830s, with the expansion of suffrage, politics and the reality of continuing political disagreements had come to be taken as a fact of life. The political struggles of the Jackson era, coupled with the dramatic social changes caused by expansion and economic growth, created the basic pattern of American politics: two major parties, each with at least some appeal among voters of all social classes and in all sections of the country. That pattern, which we call "the Second American Party System," remains to this day.

Whigs and Democrats

There were genuine differences between the Whigs and the Democrats, but they were not sectional differences. Instead, the two parties reflected just-emerging class and cultural differences. The Democrats, as they themselves were quick to point out, had inherited Thomas Jefferson's belief in the democratic rights of the small, independent yeoman farmer. Because most of the country was rural, it is not surprising that the Democrats had nationwide appeal, especially in the South and West, the most rural regions. As a result of Jackson's presidency, Democrats came to be identified with independence and a distaste for interference, whether from the government or from economic monopolies such as the Bank of the United States. They favored expansion, Indian removal, and the freedom to do as they chose on the frontier. In the politics of the time, these were conservative values. They reflected the opposition of most Democratic voters to the rapid social and economic changes that accompanied the transportation revolution.

OVERVIEW

THE SECOND AMERICAN PARTY SYSTEM

Democrats	First organized to elect Andrew Jackson to the presidency in 1828. The Democratic Party spoke for Jeffersonian democracy, expansion, and the freedom of the "common man" from interference from government or from financial monopolies like the Bank of the United States. It found its power base in the rural South and West and among some northern urban workers. The Democratic Party was the majority party from 1828 to 1860.
Whigs	Organized in opposition to Andrew Jackson in the early 1830s. Heir to Federalism, the Whig Party favored a strong role for the national government in the economy (for example, it promoted Henry Clay's American System) and supported active social reform. Its power base lay in the North and Northwest among voters who benefited from increased commercialization and among some southern planters and urban merchants. The Whigs won the elections of 1840 and 1848.

The Whigs were themselves often the initiators and beneficiaries of economic change and were more receptive to it. Heirs of the Federalist belief in the importance of a strong federal role in the national economy (see Chapter 8), they supported the elements of Henry Clay's American System: a strong central government, the Bank of the United States, a protective tariff, and internal improvements. In fact, when it came to improvements, the Whigs wanted to improve people as well as roads. Religion was an important element in political affiliation, and many Whigs were members of evangelical reforming denominations. Reformers believed that everyone, rich and poor, was capable of the self-discipline that would lead to a good life. Thus Whigs favored government intervention in both economic and social affairs, calling for education and social reforms such as temperance that aimed to improve the ordinary citizen. Many rich men were Whigs, but so were many poorer men who had a democratic faith in the perfectibility of all Americans. The Whigs' greatest strength was in New England and the northern part of the West (the Old Northwest), the areas most affected by commercial agriculture and factory work.

Yet neither party was monolithic. As has continued to be true of American political parties, both the Democrats and the Whigs were a coalition of interests affected by local and regional factors. The job of the party leader, as the Democrats' Martin Van Buren had been among the first to realize, was to forge the divergent local party interests into a winning national majority. Although Jackson's appeal was strongest in the rural South and West, the Democrats also appealed to some workers in northern cities. Reflecting the emerging issues of class and ethnicity, these Democrats, many of them immigrants, voted against the wealthier, native-born Americans, who were mostly Whigs. Urban workers cared little about rural issues, and they were less committed to the slave system than many Southerners, but they shared with Democrats from other regions a dislike of big business. On the other hand, a number of southern planters, who had close ties to merchant and banking interests, and residents of the South's commercial cities were attracted to the Whig policy of a strong federal role in economic development, though they were less active than many northern Whigs in advocating sweeping social reform.

The Campaign of 1840

In 1840, the Whigs set out to beat the Democrats at their own game. Passing over the ever-hopeful Henry Clay, the Whigs nominated a man as much like Andrew Jackson as possible, the aging Indian fighter William Henry Harrison, former governor of the Indiana Territory from 1801 to 1812. In an effort to duplicate Jackson's winning appeal to the South as well as the West, the Whigs balanced the ticket by nominating a Southerner, John Tyler, for vice president. The campaign slogan was "Tippecanoe and Tyler too" (Tippecanoe was the site of Harrison's famous victory over Tecumseh's Indian confederation in 1811). As if this were not enough, Whigs made Harrison out to be a humble man who would be happy to live in a log cabin, although he actually lived in a large and comfortable house. Thus began another long-lived political legend. The Whigs reached out to ordinary people with torchlight parades, barbecues, songs, coonskin caps, bottomless jugs of (hard) cider, and claims that Martin Van Buren, Harrison's hapless opponent, was a man of privilege and aristocratic tastes. Nothing could be further from the truth: Van Buren was the son of a tavern keeper. But Van Buren, a short man who lacked a commanding presence, had always dressed meticulously, and now even his taste in coats and ties was used against him.

The Whig campaign tactics, added to the popular anger at Van Buren because of the continuing depression, gave Harrison a sweeping electoral victory, 234 votes to 60. Even more remarkable, the campaign achieved the greatest voter turnout up to that time (and rarely equaled since), 80 percent.

The Whig Victory Turns to Loss: The Tyler Presidency

Although the Whig victory of 1840 was a milestone in American politics, the triumph of Whig principles was short-lived. William Henry Harrison, who was sixty-eight, died of pneumonia a month after his inauguration. For the first time in American history the vice president stepped up to the presidency. Not for the last time, important differences between the dead president and his successor reshaped the direction of American politics.

John Tyler of Virginia was a former Democrat who had left the party because he disagreed with Jackson's autocratic style. The Whigs had sought him primar-

ily for his sectional appeal and had not inquired too closely into his political opinions, which turned out to be anti-Whig as well as anti-Jackson. President Tyler vetoed a series of bills embodying all the elements of Henry Clay's American System: tariffs, internal improvements, a new Bank of the United States. In exasperation, congressional Whigs read Tyler out of the party, and his entire cabinet of Whigs resigned. To replace them, Tyler appointed former Democrats like himself. Thus the Whig triumph of 1840, one of the clearest victories in American electoral politics, was negated by the stalemate between Tyler and the Whig majority in Congress. The Whigs were to win only one more election, that of 1848.

Although the circumstances that robbed the Whigs of their victory were accidental, the Tyler debacle laid bare the great division that the two-party system was intended to hide: the sectional difference between the North and the South. The Whigs were a short-lived national party because they could not bridge that gap. And by the 1850s not even the Democrats could remain united.

AMERICAN ARTS AND LETTERS

Jackson's presidency was a defining moment in the development of an American identity. His combination of western belligerency and combative individualism was the strongest statement of American distinctiveness since Thomas Jefferson's agrarianism. Did Jackson speak for all of America? The Whigs did not think so. And the definitions of American identity that were beginning to emerge in popular culture and in intellectual circles were more complex than the message coming from the White House. Throughout the nation, however, there was a widespread interest in information and literature of all kinds. The Age of the Common Man would prove to be the period when American writers and painters found the national themes that allowed them to produce the first distinctively American literature and art.

The Spread of the Written Word

The transportation revolution improved communication. The number of newspapers, magazines, and books grew rapidly, helping broaden people's horizons beyond their own community. A print revolution began in 1826 when a reform organization, the American Tract Society, installed the country's first steam-powered press. Three years later the new presses had turned out 300,000 Bibles and 6 million religious tracts, or pamphlets. The greatest growth, however, was in newspapers that reached a mass audience. The number of newspapers soared from 376 newspapers in 1810 to 1,200 in 1835. This rise paralleled the growth of interest in politics, for most newspapers were published by political parties and were

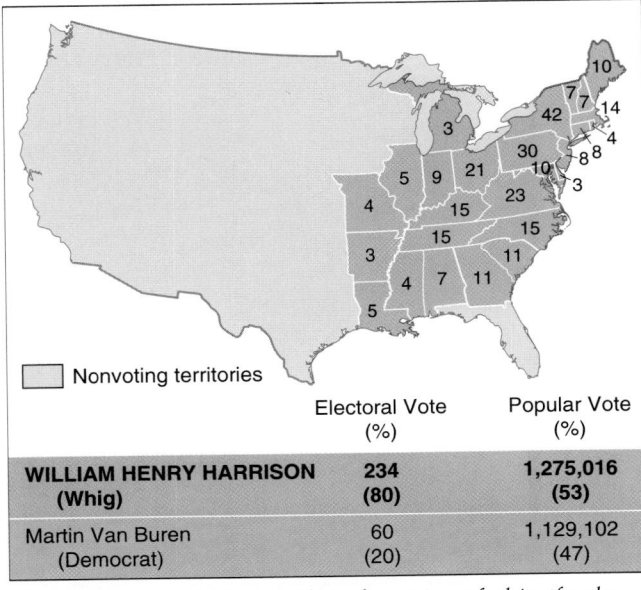

	Electoral Vote (%)	Popular Vote (%)
WILLIAM HENRY HARRISON (Whig)	**234 (80)**	**1,275,016 (53)**
Martin Van Buren (Democrat)	60 (20)	1,129,102 (47)

The Election of 1840 *The Whigs triumphed in the election of 1840 by beating the Democrats at their own game. Whigs could expect to do well in the commercializing areas of New England and the Old Northwest, but their adopted strategy of popular campaigning worked well in the largely rural South and West as well, contributing to Harrison's victory. The Whigs' choice of John Tyler as vice-presidential candidate, another strategy designed to appeal to southern voters, backfired when Harrison died and Tyler, who did not share Whig principles, became America's first vice president to succeed to the presidency.*

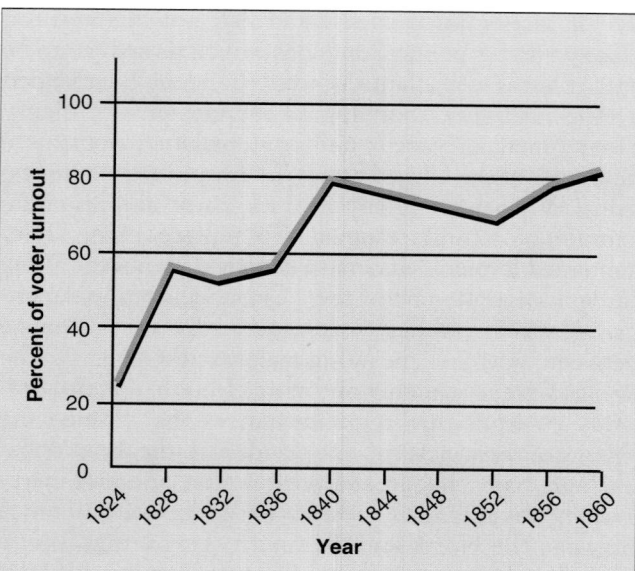

Pre–Civil War Voter Turnout   *The turnout of voters in presidential elections more than doubled from 1824 to 1828, the year Andrew Jackson was first elected. Turnout surged to 80 percent in 1840, the year the Whigs triumphed. The extension of suffrage to all white men and heated competition between two political parties with nationwide membership turned presidential election campaigns into events with great popular appeal.*

openly partisan. Packed with articles that today would be considered libelous and scandalous, newspapers were entertaining and popular reading. For western readers, the popular Crockett almanacs offered a mix of humorous stories and tall tales attributed to Davy Crockett (the boisterous Tennessee "roarer" who died defending the Alamo in 1836) along with meteorological and climate information. Throughout the country, religious literature was still the most widely read, but a small middle-class audience existed for literary magazines and, among women especially, for sentimental magazines and novels.

Accompanying all these changes in print communication was an invention that outsped them all: the telegraph, so innovative that its inventor spent years fruitlesssly seeking private funds to back its application. Finally, with financing from the federal government, Samuel F. B. Morse sent his first message from Washington to Baltimore in 1844. Soon messages in Morse code would be transmitted instantaneously across the continent. The impact of this revolutionary invention, the first to separate the message from the speed at which a human messenger could travel, was immediate. The timeliness of information available to the individual, from important national news to the next train's arrival time, vastly increased. Distant events gained new and exciting immediacy. Everyone's horizon and sense of community was widened.

Creating an American Culture

For all the improvements in communication, the United States was a provincial culture, still looking to Britain for values, standards, and literary offerings, and still mocked by the British. In a famous essay in the *Edinburgh Review* in 1820, Sidney Smith bitingly inquired, "In the four quarters of the globe, who reads an American book? or goes to an American play? or looks at an American picture or statue? What does the world yet owe to American physicians or surgeons? What new substances have their chemists discovered?" The answer was nothing—yet.

In the early years of the nineteenth century, eastern seaboard cities actively built the cultural foundation that would nurture American art and literature. Philadelphia's American Philosophical Society, founded by Benjamin Franklin in 1743, boasted a distinguished roster of scientists, including Thomas Jefferson—concurrently its president and president of the United States—and Nicholas Biddle, Jackson's opponent in the Bank War. Culturally, Boston ran a close second to Philadelphia, founding the Massachusetts General Hospital (1811) and the Boston Athenaeum (1807), a gentleman's library and reading room containing "the works of learning and science in all languages; particularly such rare and expensive publications as are not generally to be obtained in this country." The *North American Review*, published in Boston, emerged as the country's most

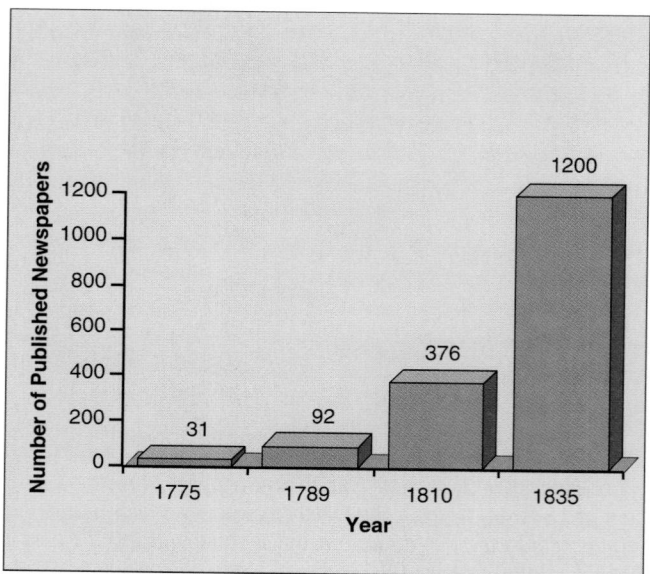

The Burgeoning of Newspapers   *Newspapers have a long history in the United States. Even before the American Revolution the colonies boasted 37 newspapers (see Chapter 6), and within little more than a decade that number had nearly tripled. Toward the end of the century, however, the number of newspapers expanded rapidly, by 1835 numbering more than 30 times that of 1775.*

LIBRARY OF THE ATHENÆUM.

The Boston Athenaeum was one of Boston's leading cultural institutions. The library, shown in this engraving, was probably the finest in the country in the early nineteenth century.

important and long-lasting intellectual magazine. Devoted to keeping its readers in touch with European intellectual developments, the *Review* had a circulation of 3,000 in 1826, about the same as similar British journals. Southern cities were much less successful in supporting culture. Charleston had a Literary and Philosophical Society (founded in 1814), but the widely dispersed residences of the southern elite made urban cultural institutions difficult to sustain. Thus, unwittingly, the South ceded cultural leadership to the North.

The cultural picture was much spottier in the West. A few cities, such as Lexington, Kentucky, and Cincinnati, Ohio, had civic cultural institutions, and some transplanted New Englanders maintained connections with New England culture. A group of pioneers in Ames, Ohio, for example, founded a "coonskin library" composed of books purchased from Boston and paid for in coonskins. But most pioneers were at best uninterested and at worst actively hostile to traditional literary culture. This was neither from lack of literacy nor from failure to read. Newspaper and religious journals both had large readerships in the West: The Methodist *Christian Advo-*

cate, for example, reached 25,000 people yearly (compared with the *North American Review*'s 3,000). The frontier emphasis on the practical was hard to distinguish from anti-intellectualism. As writer Hugh Henry Brackenridge lamented from Pittsburgh, it was not "the want of learning I consider as a defect, but the contempt of it."

Thus in the early part of the nineteenth century, the gap between the intellectual and cultural horizons of a wealthy Bostonian and a frontier farmer in Michigan widened. Part of the unfinished task of building a national society was the creation of a national culture that could fill this gap. For writers and artists, the challenge was to find distinctively American themes.

Of the eastern cities, New York produced the first widely recognized American writers. In 1819, Washington Irving published *The Sketch Book*, thus immortalizing Rip Van Winkle and the Headless Horseman. Within a few years James Fenimore Cooper's Leatherstocking novels (of which *The Last of the Mohicans*, published in 1826, is the best known) achieved wide success in both America and Europe. Cooper's novels featured a heroic frontiersman, Natty Bumppo (modeled on Daniel Boone) who observes favorably the nobility of the Indians even as he participates in their defeat by the forces of civilization. Cooper's novels established the long American experience of westward expansion, of which the conquest of the Indians was a vital part, as a serious and distinctive American literary theme.

It was New England, however, that claimed to be the forge of American cultural independence from Europe. As Ralph Waldo Emerson proclaimed in "The American Scholar," a lecture he delivered in 1837 to the Harvard faculty, "Our day of dependence, our long apprenticeship to the learning of other lands, draws to a close." He went on to encourage American writers to find inspiration in the ordinary details of daily life. The stuff of literature, he declared, were to be found in "the familiar, the low…the milk in the pan; the ballad in the street; the news of the boat." Immensely popular, Emerson was the star of the lyceum circuit, a lecture network that sent speakers on cultural subjects to all parts of the country. He gave more than 1,500 lectures in twenty states between 1833 and 1860. "The American Scholar," his most famous lecture, carried a message of cultural self-sufficiency that Americans were eager to hear.

Artists and Builders

Artists were as successful as novelists in finding American themes. Thomas Cole, who came to America from England in 1818, found great inspiration in the American landscape, painting scenes of New York State's Catskill and Adirondack Mountains that reflect the influence of the British romantic school of landscape painting. With these works, Cole founded the Hudson River school of American painting. The frankly nationalistic style and subject matter of this school are reflected in the comment of New Yorker Philip Hone: "Every American is bound to prove his love of country by admiring Cole."

The western painters—realists such as Karl Bodmer and George Catlin as well as the romantics who followed them, like Albert Bierstadt and Thomas Moran—drew on the dramatic western landscape and its peoples. Their art was an important contribution to the American sense of the land and to the nation's identity. Catlin, driven by a need to document Indian life before it disappeared, spent eight years among the tribes of the upper Missouri River. Then he assembled his collection—more than 500 paintings in all—and toured the country from 1837 to 1851 in an unsuccessful attempt to arouse public indignation about the plight of the western Indian nations. Another unusual western painter, John James Audubon, could at first find no publisher in this country for his striking and sometimes grotesque etchings of American birds. George Caleb Bingham, an accomplished genre painter, produced somewhat tidied-up scenes of real-life American workers, such as flatboatmen on the Missouri River. All these painters found much to

Asher Durand, a member of the Hudson River School of landscape painting, produced this work, Kindred Spirits, *in 1849 as a tribute to Thomas Cole, the school's leader. Cole is one of the figures depicted standing in a romantic wilderness.*

record and to celebrate in American life. Ironically, the inspiration for the most prevalent theme, the American wilderness, was profoundly endangered by the rapid western settlement of which the nation was so proud.

The haste and transiency of American life are nowhere so obvious as in the architectural record of this era, which is sparse. The monumental neoclassical style (complete with columns) that Jefferson had recommended for official buildings in Washington continued to be favored for public buildings elsewhere and by private concerns trying to project an imposing image, such as banks. A few southern planters built impressive mansions, and there were odd experiments such as the prison built in Philadelphia in the 1820s that was designed to look like a medieval castle. The effect of this building on the imagination, one admiring commentator remarked, was "peculiarly impressive, solemn and instructive."

But in general Americans were in too much of a hurry to build for the future, and in balloon-frame construction they found the perfect technique for the present. Balloon-frame structures—which consist of a basic frame of wooden studs fastened with crosspieces top and bottom—could be put up quickly, cheaply, and without the help of a skilled carpenter. Covering the frame with wooden siding was equally simple, and the

CHRONOLOGY

1817	Erie Canal construction begins
1818	National Road completed to Wheeling
1819	*Dartmouth College v. Woodward*
1821	Martin Van Buren's Bucktails defeat DeWitt Clinton in New York
1824	*Gibbons v. Ogden*
	John Quincy Adams elected president by the House of Representatives
1825	Erie Canal opens
1826	First American use of the steam-powered printing press
1828	Congress passes "Tariff of Abominations"
	Andrew Jackson elected president
	John C. Calhoun publishes *Exposition and Protest* anonymously
1830	Jackson vetoes Maysville Road Bill
	Congress passes Indian Removal Act
	Baltimore and Ohio Railroad opens
1832	Nullification Crisis begins
	Jackson vetoes renewal of Bank of the United States charter
	Jackson reelected president
1833	National Road completed to Columbus, Ohio
1834	Cyrus McCormick patents the McCormick reaper
	Whig party organized
1836	Jackson issues Specie Circular
	Martin Van Buren elected president
1837	*Charles River Bridge v. Warren Bridge*
	John Deere invents steel plow
	Ralph Waldo Emerson first presents "The American Scholar"
	Panic of 1837
1838	Cherokee removal along the "Trail of Tears"
1840	Whig William Henry Harrison elected president
1841	John Tyler assumes presidency at the death of President Harrison
1844	Samuel F. B. Morse operates first telegraph

resultant dwelling was as strong, although not as well insulated, as a house of solid timber or logs. Balloon-frame construction was first used in Chicago in the 1830s, where it created the city almost instantly. The four-room balloon-frame house, affordable to many who could not have paid for a traditionally built dwelling, became standard in that decade. This was indeed housing for the common man and his family.

CONCLUSION

Andrew Jackson's presidency witnessed the building of a strong national party system based on nearly universal white manhood suffrage. At the same time that the nation expanded politically (nine new western states were admitted between 1800 and 1840), construction of new roads, canals, and railroads and other improvements in transportation and communication created the infrastructure that united the nation physically. Sectionalism and localism seemed to have been replaced by a more national consciousness that was clearly expressed in the two national political parties, the Whigs and the Democrats. The Second American Party System created new democratic political communities united by common political opinions. Culturally, American writers and artists began to establish a distinctive American identity in the arts. But as the key battles of the Jackson presidency—the Nullification Crisis, Indian removal, the Bank War—attested, the forces of sectionalism resisted the strong nationalizing tendencies of the era. As the next two chapters will show, economic and social forces continued to force the South and the North apart.

REVIEW QUESTIONS

1. What reasons might a person of the 1820s and 1830s give for opposing universal white manhood suffrage? Suffrage for free African American men? For women of all races?
2. Opponents believed that Andrew Jackson was unsuited in both political experience and temperament to be president of the United States, yet his presidency is considered one of the most influential in American history. Explain the changes in political organization and attitude that made his election possible.
3. Both the Nullification Crisis and Indian Removal raised the constitutional issue of the rights of a minority in a nation governed by majority rule. What rights, in your opinion, does a minority have, and what kinds of laws are necessary to defend those rights?
4. Why was the issue of government support for internal improvements so controversial? Who benefited from the transportation revolution? Who lost ground?
5. What were the key differences between Whigs and Democrats? What did each party stand for? Who were their supporters? What were the links between each party's programs and party supporters?
6. What distinctive American themes did the writers, artists, and builders of the 1820s and 1830s express in their works? Are they still considered American themes today?

RECOMMENDED READING

Donald B. Cole, *Martin Van Buren and the American Political System* (1984). An excellent study of Van Buren's key role in the transformation of politics.

Donald B. Cole, *The Presidency of Andrew Jackson* (1993). In this recent work, Jackson is seen as just as influential, but less commanding and more ambiguous in his political attitudes than in earlier studies.

Daniel Feller, *The Jacksonian Promise* (1995). A recent overview of the period 1815–1840 that stresses the optimism and enterprising spirit of the era rather than the anxiety some other historians have discerned.

Ronald P. Formisano, *The Transformation of Political Culture: Massachusetts Parties, 1790s–1840s* (1983). One of many detailed studies that have contributed to our understanding of the development of the second party system.

William W. Freehling, *Prelude to Civil War* (1966). An examination of the Nullification Crisis that stresses the centrality of slavery to the dispute.

Paul W. Gates, *The Farmer's Age: Agriculture, 1815–1860* (1966). The standard source on the growth of commercial agriculture.

Jean V. Matthews, *Toward a New Society: American Thought and Culture, 1800–1830* (1991). A valuable survey of American attitudes toward religion, politics, science, nature, and culture in the early nineteenth century.

Robert Remini, *Andrew Jackson and the Source of American Freedom* (1981). An account of Jackson's White House years by his major biographer.

Carol Sheriff, *The Artificial River: The Erie Canal and the Paradox of Progress, 1817–1862* (1996). Shows how the building of the canal changed personal lives and fostered religious beliefs in human perfectability.

Alan Taylor, *William Cooper's Town: Power and Persuasion on the Frontier of the Early American Republic* (1995). The Pulitzer Prize-winning study of the founding and development of Cooperstown, New York, by the father of novelist James Fenimore Cooper. An engrossing study of the effects of the democratization of politics.

George Rogers Taylor, *The Transportation Revolution, 1815–1860* (1951). The indispensable book on all aspects of the American economy during this period.

Harry L. Watson, *Liberty and Power: The Politics of Jacksonian America* (1990). An excellent recent overview of Jacksonian politics.

ADDITIONAL BIBLIOGRAPHY

The New Democratic Politics and the Jackson Presidency

William L. Anderson, *Cherokee Removal: Before and After* (1991)
Ralph S. Cotterill, *The Southern Indians* (1954)
John Ehle, *Trail of Tears* (1988)
Richard E. Ellis, *The Union at Risk* (1987)
Paul Goodman, *Towards a Christian Republic: Antimasonry and the Great Tradition in New England, 1826–1836* (1988)

Michael D. Green, *The Politics of Indian Removal* (1982)

Lucy Maddox, *Removals: Nineteenth-Century American Literature and the Politics of Indian Affairs* (1991)

Michael Rogin, *Fathers and Children: Andrew Jackson and the Destruction of American Indians* (1975)

Ronald N. Satz, *American Indian Policy in the Jacksonian Era* (1975)

Arthur M. Schlesinger Jr., *The Age of Jackson* (1945)

John Ward, *Andrew Jackson: Symbol for an Age* (1955)

Chilton Williamson, *American Suffrage: From Property to Democracy, 1760–1860* (1960)

Internal Improvements

Allan G. Bogue, *From Prairie to Corn Belt: Farming on the Illinois and Iowa Frontier* (1968)

Clarence Danhof, *Changes in Agriculture: The Northern United States, 1820–1870* (1969)

E. M. Dodd, *American Business Corporations until 1860* (1954)

Albert Fishlow, *American Railroads and the Transformation of the Ante-Bellum Economy* (1965)

Robert W. Fogel, *Railroads and American Economic Growth: Essays in Econometric History* (1964)

Carter Goodrich, *Government Promotion of American Canals and Railroads, 1800–1890* (1960)

John Denis Haeger, *The Investment Frontier: New York Businessmen and the Economic Development of the Old Northwest* (1981)

Oscar Handlin and Mary Handlin, *Commonwealth: A Study of the Role of Government in the American Economy: Massachusetts, 1774–1861* (1947)

Louis Hartz, *Economic Policy and Democratic Thought: Pennsylvania, 1776–1860* (1948)

Erik F. Hiates, James Mak, and Gary M. Walton, *Western River Transportation: The Era of Early Internal Development, 1800–1860* (1975)

Morton J. Horwitz, *The Transformation of American Law, 1780–1860* (1977)

Philip Jordan, *The National Road* (1948)

Karl Raitz, ed., *The National Road* (1995)

Harry N. Scheiber, *The Ohio Canal Era: A Case Study of Government and the Economy, 1820–1861* (1969)

Ronald E. Shaw, *Canals for a Nation: The Canal Era in the United States, 1790–1860* (1990)

Ronald Shaw, *Erie Water West: History of the Erie Canal* (1966)

Peter Temin, *Iron and Steel in Nineteenth-Century America* (1964)

———, *The Jacksonian Economy* (1965)

Peter Way, *Common Labour: Workers and the Digging of North American Canals, 1780–1860* (1993)

The Rise of the Whigs and the Second American Party System

John Ashworth, *Agrarians and Aristocrats: Party Ideology in the United States, 1837–1846* (1983)

R. G. Gunderson, *The Log Cabin Campaign* (1957)

Bray Hammond, *Banks and Politics in America* (1957)

Daniel W. Howe, *The Political Culture of the American Whigs* (1980)

Lawrence F. Kohl, *The Politics of Individualism: Parties and the American Character in the Jacksonian Era* (1989)

Richard P. McCormick, *The Second American Party System: Party Formation in the Jacksonian Era* (1966)

James Roger Sharp, *The Jacksonians versus the Banks: Politics in the United States after the Panic of 1837* (1970)

Joel H. Sibley, *The Partisan Imperative: The Dynamics of American Politics before the Civil War* (1985)

Harry L. Watson, *Jacksonian Politics and Community Conflict: The Emergence of the Second American Party System in Cumberland County, North Carolina* (1981)

American Arts and Letters

John L. Brooke, *Knowledge Is Power: The Diffusion of Information in Early America, 1700–1865* (1989)

Cathy N. Davidson, *Revolution and the Word: The Rise of the Novel in America* (1986)

William J. Gilmore, *Reading Becomes a Necessity of Life: Material and Cultural Life in Rural New England, 1780–1835* (1989)

Neil Harris, *The Artist in American Society: The Formative Years, 1790–1860* (1966)

Nathan O. Hatch, *The Democratization of American Christianity* (1989)

Barbara Novak, *Nature and Culture: American Landscape Painting 1825–1875* (1982)

Albert Von Frank, *The Sacred Game: Provincialism and Frontier Consciousness in American Literature, 1630–1860* (1985)

Gwendolyn Wright, *Building the Dream: A Social History of Housing in America* (1981)

Biography

Irving H. Bartlett, *Daniel Webster* (1978)

Richard Current, *Daniel Webster and the Rise of National Conservatism* (1955)

———, *John C. Calhoun* (1963)

Robert V. Remini, *Henry Clay: Statesman for the Union* (1991)

Leonard L. Richards, *The Life and Times of Congressman John Quincy Adams* (1986)

C. M. Wiltse, *John C. Calhoun: Nullifier, 1829–1839* (1949)

CHAPTER ELEVEN

THE SOUTH AND SLAVERY

1790s–1850s

Taylor. *An American Slave Market.* 1852. Oil on canvas. Chicago Historical Society.

AMERICAN COMMUNITIES
Natchez-under-the-Hill

The wharfmaster had just opened the public auction of confiscated cargoes in the center of Natchez when a great cry was heard. An angry crowd of flatboatmen, Bowie knives in hand, was storming up the bluffs from the Mississippi shouting, as the local newspaper reported, "threats of violence and death upon all who attempted to sell and buy their property." It was November 1837, and the town council had just enacted a restrictive tax of $10 per flatboat, a measure designed to rid the wharf district known as Natchez-under-the-Hill of the most impoverished and disreputable of the riverboatmen. The council had made its first confiscation of cargo after nine captains refused to pay this tax. As the boatmen approached, merchants and onlookers shrank back in fear. But the local authorities had called out the militia, and a company of farmers and planters now came marching into the square with their rifles primed and lowered. "The cold and sullen bayonets of the Guards were too hard meat for the Arkansas tooth-picks," reported the local press, and "there was no fight." The boatmen sullenly turned back down the bluffs. It was the first confrontation in the "Flatboat Wars" that erupted as Mississippi ports tried to bring their troublesome riverfronts under regulation.

The first European to take notice of this "land abundant in subsistence" was a member of Hernando de Soto's expedition in the sixteenth century. The area was "thickly peopled" by the Natchez Indians, he wrote. It was not until the French established the port of Fort Rosalie in the 1720s, however, that Europeans settled in the area. The French destroyed the highly organized society of the Natchez Indians in the 1730s and the port became a major Mississippi River trading center. From Fort Rosalie, the French conducted an extensive frontier trade that brought peoples of different races together, leading to intermarriage and the growth of a mixed-race population. French traders bought deerskins, for which there was a large export market, from Choctaw, Chickasaw, and Creek hunters. During the same period, some Africans who had been imported by the French to work as slaves on plantations found roles in the French-Indian trade as boatmen, hunters, soldiers, and interpreters.

When the Spanish took control of the territory in 1763 they laid out the new town of Natchez high on the bluffs, safe from Mississippi flooding. Fort Rosalie, rechristened Natchez-under-the-Hill, continued to flourish as the produce grown by American farmers in Kentucky and Tennessee moved downriver on flatboats. Thus Americans became the newest additions to the ethnic diversity of this well-established trading center. When Americans took possession of Mississippi in 1798, the district surrounding the port became the most important center of settlement in the Old Southwest. Once again this abundant land of rich, black soil became thickly peopled, but this time with cotton planters and their African American slaves.

Under-the-Hill gained renown as the last stop for boatmen before New Orleans. Minstrel performers sang of their exploits:

Den dance de boatmen dance,
O dance de boatmen dance,
O dance all night till broad daylight,
An go home wid de gals in de morning.

According to one traveler, "They feel the same inclination to dissipation as sailors who have long been out of port." There were often as many as 150 boats drawn up at the wharves. The crowds along the riverfront, noted John James Audubon, who visited in the 1820s, "formed a medley which it is beyond my power to describe." Mingling among American rivermen of all descriptions were trappers and hunters in fur caps, Spanish shopkeepers in bright smocks, French gentlemen from New Orleans in velvet coats, Indians wrapped in their trade blankets, African Americans both free and slave—a pageant of nations and races. Clapboard shacks and flatboats dragged on shore and converted into storefronts served as grog shops, card rooms, dance halls, and hotels. Whorehouses with women of every age and color abounded.

On the bluffs, meanwhile, the town of Natchez had become the winter home to the southwestern planter elite. They built their mansions with commanding views of the river. A visitor attending a ball at one of these homes was dazzled by the display: "Myriads of wax candles burning in wall sconces, sparkling chandeliers, entrancing music, the scent of jasmine, rose and sweet olive, the sparkle of wine mellowed by age, the flow of wit and brilliant repartee, all were there." Sustaining this American aristocracy was the labor of thousands of enslaved men and women, who lived in the squalid quarters behind the great house and worked the endless fields of cotton. It was they who made possible the greatest accumulations of wealth in early-nineteenth-century America.

The Natchez planters, their wealth and confidence growing with cotton's growing dominance of the local economy, found Under-the-Hill an increasing irritant. "A gentleman may game with a gambler by the hour," one resident remembered, "and yet despise him and refuse to recognize him afterward." The Under-the-Hill elite, however—gamblers, saloon keepers, and pimps—disturbed this social boundary when they began staying at hotels and even

building town houses in Natchez town. And in the wake of the slave revolt led by Nat Turner in Virginia in 1831 in which fifty-five white people were killed, the planters began to feel increasingly threatened by the racial mingling of the riverfront.

In the late 1830s the Natchez elite was jolted by rumors that their slaves were conspiring to murder them during Fourth of July celebrations while Under-the-Hill desperadoes looted their mansions. The rumors reinforced the growing conviction among planters that they could no longer tolerate the polyglot community of the riverfront. The measures that ultimately provoked the flatboatmen's threats in November 1837 soon followed.

In response to these threats, the planters issued an extralegal order giving all the gamblers, pimps, and whores of Under-the-Hill twenty-four hours to evacuate the district. As the Mississippi militia sharpened their bayonets, panic swept the wharves, and that night dozens of flatboats loaded with a motley human cargo headed for the more tolerant community of New Orleans. Other river ports issued similar orders of expulsion. "The towns on the river," one resident remembered, "became purified from a moral pestilence which the law could not cure." Three years later a great tornado hit Under-the-Hill, leveling the shacks that had served so long as a rendezvous for the rivermen, and gradually the Mississippi reclaimed the bottom.

These two communities—Natchez, home to the rich slave-owning elite, and Natchez-under-the-Hill, the bustling polyglot trading community—epitomize the paradox of the American South in the early nineteenth century. Enslaved African Americans grew the region's most lucrative crop, cotton. On the resulting profits, aristocratic Southerners built a sumptuous and distinctive lifestyle for themselves. The boatmen and traders of Natchez-under-the-Hill who brought the cotton and other products to market were vital to the planters' prosperity. But the polyglot racial and social mixing of Natchez-under-the-Hill threatened the system of control, built on a rigid distinction between free white people and enslaved black people, by which the planters maintained slavery. Because the slave owners could not control the boatmen, they expelled them. This defensive reaction—to seal off the world of slavery from the wider commercial world—exposed the vulnerability of the slave system at the very moment of its greatest commercial success.

Natchez

KEY TOPICS

- The domination of southern life by the slave system
- The economic implications of "King Cotton"
- The creation of African American communities under slavery
- The social structure of the white South and its increasing defensiveness

KING COTTON AND SOUTHERN EXPANSION

Slavery had long dominated southern life. African American slaves grew the great export crops of the colonial period—tobacco, rice, and indigo—on which slave owners' fortunes were made, and their presence shaped southern society and culture (see Chapter 4). Briefly, in the early days of American independence, the slave system waned, only to be revived by the immense profitability of cotton in a newly industrializing world. Cotton became the dominant crop in a rapidly expanding South that included not only the original states of Maryland, Delaware, Virginia, North and South Carolina, and Georgia, but Kentucky, Tennessee, Missouri, Alabama, Mississippi, Louisiana (the Old Southwest), Arkansas, Florida, and Texas as well. The overwhelming economic success of cotton and of the slave system on which it depended created a distinctive regional culture quite different from that developing in the North.

The Cotton Gin and Expansion into the Old Southwest

Short-staple cotton had long been recognized as a crop ideally suited to southern soils and growing conditions. But it had one major drawback: the seeds were so difficult to remove from the lint that it took an entire day to hand-clean a single pound of cotton. The invention in 1793 that made cotton growing profitable was the result of collaboration between a young Northerner named Eli Whitney, recently graduated from Yale College, and Catherine Greene, a South Carolina plantation owner and widow of Revolu-

tionary War General Nathanael Greene, who hired Whitney to tutor her children. Whitney built a prototype cotton engine, dubbed "gin" for short, a simple device consisting of a hand-cranked cylinder with teeth that tore the lint away from the seeds. At Greene's suggestion, the teeth were made of wire. With the cotton gin it was possible to clean more than fifty pounds of cotton a day. Soon large and small planters in the inland regions of Georgia and South Carolina had begun to grow cotton. By 1811, this area was producing 60 million pounds of cotton a year, and exporting most of it to England.

Other areas of the South quickly followed South Carolina and Georgia into cotton production. New land was wanted because cotton growing rapidly depleted the soil. The profits to be made from cotton growing drew a rush of southern farmers into the so-called black belt—an area stretching through western

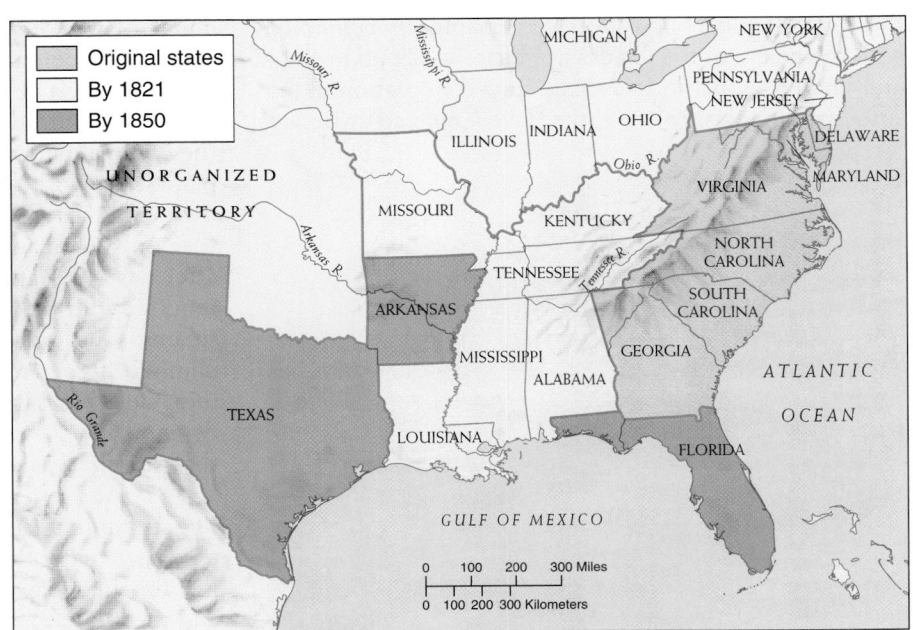

The South Expands, 1790–1850   *This map shows the dramatic effect cotton production had on southern expansion. From the original six states of 1790, westward expansion, fueled by the search for new cotton lands, added another six states by 1821, and three more by 1850.*

Georgia, Alabama, and Mississippi that was blessed with exceptionally fertile soil. Following the War of 1812, southerners were seized by "Alabama fever." In one of the swiftest migrations in American history, white southerners and their slaves flooded into western Georgia and the areas that would become Alabama and Mississippi (the Old Southwest). On this frontier, African American pioneers (albeit involuntary ones) cleared the forests, drained the swamps, broke the ground, built houses and barns, and planted the first crops.

This migration caused the population of Mississippi to double (from 31,306 to 74,448) and that of Alabama to grow sixteenfold (from 9,046 to 144,317) between 1810 and 1820. This and subsequent western land booms dramatically changed the population of the original southern states as well. Nearly half of all white South Carolinians born after 1800 eventually left the state, usually to move west. By 1850 there were more than 50,000 South Carolina natives living in Georgia, almost as many in Alabama, and 26,000 in Mississippi.

Southerners had historically taken the lead in westward expansion. Backcountry residents of Virginia and North Carolina were the first to venture over the Appalachians, and Virginians and Carolinians were the major settlers of the first two trans-Appalachian states, Kentucky (1792) and Tennessee (1796). John C. Calhoun of South Carolina and Henry Clay of Kentucky had been two of the most prominent expansionist War Hawks in Congress before the War of 1812. Like the simultaneous expansion into the Old Northwest, settlement of the Old Southwest took place at the expense of the region's Indian population (see Chapter 9). Beginning with the defeat of the Creeks at Horseshoe Bend in 1814 and ending with the Cherokee forced migration along "the Trail of Tears" in 1838, the "Five Civilized Tribes"—the Cherokees, Chickasaws, Choctaws, Creeks, and Seminoles—were forced to give up their lands and move to Indian Territory (see Chapter 10).

On the southern frontier, as on the northern frontier, the killing, confinement, and removal of Indian peoples was the result of white expansion and settlement motivated by the hunger for land and profit. In the South, however, there was an additional motivation, rooted in slavery, for Indian removal: there was simply no room in the southern social order for anything other than white and black, master and slave. Literate, slave-owning "redskins" confused this simple picture: they were too "civilized" to be like slaves, but the wrong color to be masters. Thus southern Indian removal, like southern expansion, was dictated by the needs of the slave system.

Following "the Alabama Fever" of 1816–20, several later surges of southern expansion (1832–38, and again in the mid–1850s) carried cotton planting over the Mississippi River into Louisiana and deep into Texas. Each surge ignited feverish speculative frenzies, remembered in terms like "the Flush Times" for the heated rush of the 1830s. In the minds of the mobile, enterprising Southerners who sought their fortunes in the West, cotton profits and expansion went hand in hand. But the expansion of cotton meant the expansion of slavery.

The Question of Slavery

Cotton growing was well suited to the southern plantation system of agriculture. That system was characterized by large plantings of a single crop tended by gangs of workers who performed the same operation (planting, hoeing, or picking) under the supervision of an overseer. The southern labor system shifted from white indentured servitude to African slavery during the colonial period because servants would not perform plantation work for others when they could farm their own land (see Chapter 4). White Southerners believed that only African slaves could be forced to work day after day, year after year, at the rapid and brutal pace required in the cotton fields of large plantations in the steamy southern summer. As the production of cotton climbed higher every year in response to a seemingly inexhaustible international demand, so too did the demand for slaves and the conviction of Southerners that slavery was an economic necessity.

At the very moment that the South was committing its future to cotton, however, and assuring the persistence of slavery there, opinion about slavery was changing. Britain outlawed the international slave trade in 1807 and the United States took the same step in 1808. In the preceding quarter century, all the northern states had abolished slavery or passed laws for gradual emancipation (see Chapter 7). Between 1776 and 1786 all the states except South Carolina and Georgia either banned or

Steamboats at New Orleans await loads of cotton, the nation's major export. Just as the giant bales crowd the wharf, so too the culture created by "King Cotton" dominated southern life.

The immense size of the internal slave trade made sights like this commonplace on southern roads. Groups of slaves, chained together in gangs called coffles, were marched from their homes in the Upper South to cities in the Lower South, where they were auctioned to new owners.

heavily taxed the international slave trade, and it was only at the insistence of these two states that the Constitutional Convention prohibited Congress from passing a federal law to outlaw the slave trade for twenty years. All the southern states banned the importation of foreign slaves after the successful slave revolt in Haiti in 1791; Southerners feared that Caribbean revolutionaries might incite their own slaves to rebellion.

Attitudes changed again following the invention of the cotton gin in 1793 and the realization of the riches to be made from cotton. Slave smuggling became so rampant that South Carolina officially reopened the trade in 1804. For the next four years, Charleston boomed as one of the world's largest slaving ports: at least 40,000 Africans were imported. It was clear, however, that national opinion found the international slave trade abhorrent, and on January 1, 1808, the earliest date permitted by the Constitution, a bill to abolish the importation of slaves became law. Although a small number of slaves continued to be smuggled from Africa, the growth of the slave labor force after 1808 depended primarily on natural increase. And the ban on foreign importations vastly increased the importance of the internal slave trade.

The Internal Slave Trade

The cotton boom caused a huge increase in the domestic slave trade. Plantation owners in the Upper South (Delaware, Kentucky, Maryland, Virginia, and Tennessee) sold their slaves to meet the demand for labor in the new and expanding cotton-growing regions of the Old Southwest. In every decade after 1820 at least 150,000 slaves were uprooted either by slave trading or planter migration to the new areas, and in the expansions of the 1830s and the 1850s, the number reached a quarter of a million. Cumulatively, between 1820 and 1860 nearly 50 percent of the slave population of the

Upper South took part against their will in southern expansion.

Purchased by slave traders from owners in the Upper South, slaves were gathered together in notorious "slave pens" like the ones in Richmond and Charleston and then moved south by train or boat. In the interior, they were carried as cargo on steamboats on the Mississippi River, hence the phrase "sold down the river." Often slaves moved on foot, chained together in groups of fifty or more known as "coffles." Coffles were a common sight on southern roads, and one difficult to reconcile with the notion of slavery as a benevolent institution. Arriving at a central market in the Lower South like Natchez, New Orleans, or Mobile, the slaves, after being carefully inspected by potential buyers, were sold at auction to the highest bidder.

Although popular stereotype portrayed slave traders as unscrupulous outsiders who persuaded kind and reluctant masters to sell their slaves, the historical truth is much harsher. Traders, far from being shunned by slave-owning society, were often respected community members. One Charleston trader, Alexander McDonald, served as both an alderman and a bank president and was described as "a man of large means and responsible for all his engagements" who had "the confidence of the public." Similarly, the sheer scale of the slave trade makes it impossible to believe that slave owners only reluctantly parted with their slaves at times of economic distress. Instead, it is clear that many owners sold slaves and separated slave families not out of necessity but to increase their profits. The sheer size and profitability of the internal slave trade made a mockery of Southern claims for the benevolence of the slave system.

The Economics of Slavery

The rapid growth of cotton production was an international phenomenon, prompted by events occurring far from the American South. The insatiable demand for cotton was a result of the technological and social changes that we know today as the industrial revolution. Beginning early in the eighteenth century, a series of inventions resulted in the mechanized spinning and weaving of cloth in the world's first factories in the north of England. The ability of these factories to produce unprecedented amounts of cotton cloth revolutionized the world economy. The invention of the cotton gin came at just the right time. British textile manufacturers were eager to buy all the cotton that the South could produce.

Was the southern plantation system profitable? Clearly, in the years before 1860, southern farmers believed so. The figures for cotton production support this conclusion: from 720,000 bales in 1830, to 2.85 million bales in 1850, to nearly 5 million in 1860. By the time of the Civil War, cotton accounted for almost 60 percent of American exports, representing a total value of nearly $200 million a year.

Cotton's central place in the national economy and its international importance led Senator James Henry Hammond of South Carolina to make a famous boast in 1858:

> Without firing a gun, without drawing a sword, should they make war on us, we could bring the whole world to our feet....What would happen if no cotton was furnished for three years?...England would topple headlong and carry the whole civilized world with her save the south. No, you dare not to make war on cotton. No power on the earth dares to make war upon it. Cotton is King.

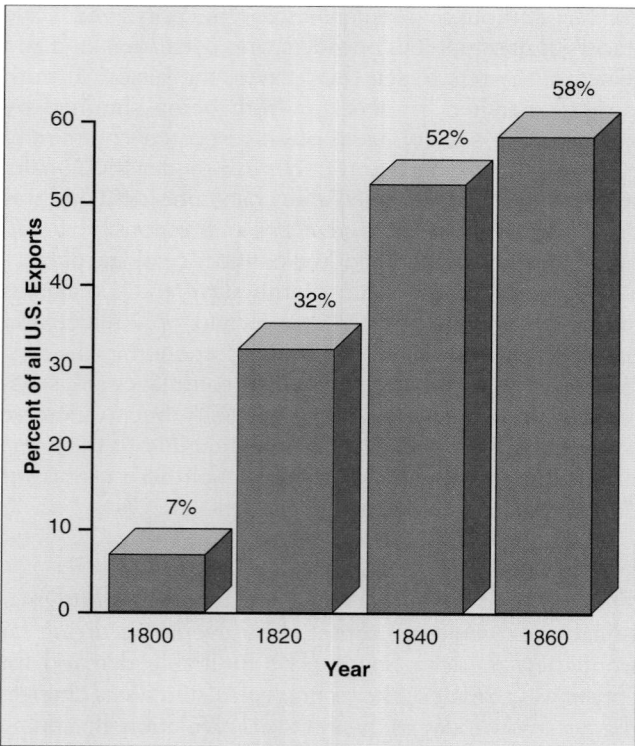

Cotton Exports as a Percentage of All U.S. Exports, 1800–1860 *One consequence of the growth of cotton production was its importance in international trade. The growing share of the export market, and the great value (nearly $200 million in 1860) led southern slave owners to believe that "Cotton Is King." The importance of cotton to the national economy entitled the South to a commanding voice in national policy, many Southerners believed.*

Indeed, the export of cotton from the South was the dynamic force in the developing American economy in the period 1790–1840. Just as the international slave trade had been the dynamic force in the Atlantic economy of the eighteenth century (see Chapter 4), southern slavery financed northern industrial development in the nineteenth century.

The connection between southern slavery and northern industry was very direct. Most mercantile services associated with the cotton trade (insurance, for example) were in northern hands and, significantly, so was shipping. This economic structure was not new. In colonial times, New England ships dominated the African slave trade. Some New England families—like the Browns of Providence who made fortunes in the slave trade—invested some of their profits in the new technology of textile manufacturing in the 1790s. Other merchants—such as the Boston Associates who financed the cotton textile mills at Lowell—made their money from cotton shipping and brokerage. Thus as cotton boomed, it provided capital for the new factories of the North.

Cotton Culture

Northerners, who were caught up in rapid industrialization and urbanization, failed to recognize their economic connection to the South and increasingly regarded it as a backward region. Senator from New York William H. Seward, on his first visit to Virginia, found ample justification for his antislavery convictions:

> It was necessary that I should travel in Virginia to have any idea of a slave state....An exhausted soil, old and decaying towns, wretchedly-neglected roads, and in every respect, an absence of enterprise and improvement, distinguish the region through which we have come, in contrast to that in which we live. Such has been the effect of slavery.

Concentration on plantation agriculture did divert energy and resources from the South's cities. At a time when the North was experiencing the greatest spurt of urban growth in the nation's history, southern cities did not keep pace. Charleston, for example, one of America's five largest cities in 1800, had a population of only 41,000 in 1860, compared with Boston's 177,840 and Baltimore's 212,418. The one exception was New Orleans, the great port at the mouth of the extensive Mississippi River transportation system. In 1860 New Orleans was the nation's fifth largest city, with a population of 169,000. The nine other leading cities were all northern or western. Most of the South remained rural: less than 3 percent of Mississippi's population lived in cities of more than 2,500 residents, and only 10 percent of Virginia's did.

The South also lagged behind the North in industrialization and in canals and railroads. In 1860, only 15 percent of the nation's factories were located in the South. Noteworthy exceptions were the iron industry near Richmond, which in 1860 boasted four rolling mills, fourteen foundries, and various machine shops employing 1,600 mechanics, and William Gregg's cotton textile mills in Graniteville, just east of Augusta, Georgia. Similarly, the South was initially left behind by the transportation revolution. In 1850, only 26 percent of the nation's railroads were in the South, increasing to still only 35 percent in 1860.

The failure of the South to industrialize at the northern rate was not a matter of ignorance but of choice. Southern capital was tied up in land and slaves, and Southerners, buoyed by the world's insatiable demand for cotton, saw no reason to invest in economically risky railroads, canals, and factories. Nor were they eager to introduce the disruptive factor of free wage labor into the tightly controlled slave system. Cotton was safer. Cotton was King.

Thus the cotton boom created a distinctive regional culture. Although cotton was far from being the only crop (the South actually devoted more acreage to corn than to cotton in 1860), its vast profitability affected all aspects of society. In the first half of the nineteenth century, King Cotton reigned supreme over an expanding domain as Southerners increasingly tied their fortunes to the slave system of cotton production. As a British tourist to Mobile wryly noted in the 1850s, the South was a place where "people live in cotton houses and ride in cotton carriages. They buy cotton, sell cotton, think cotton, eat cotton, drink cotton, and dream cotton. They marry cotton wives, and unto them are born cotton children." The South was truly in thrall to King Cotton.

TO BE A SLAVE

The slave population, estimated at 700,000 by 1790, grew to more than 4 million. After 1808 (when official American participation in the international slave trade ceased) the growth occurred because of natural increase—that is, births within the slave population. In spite of the burden of slavery, a distinctive African American community, which had first emerged in the eighteenth century (see Chapter 4), flourished in the years before the Civil War.

The Maturing of the American Slave System

Dependence on King Cotton meant dependence on slave labor. In 1850, 55 percent of all slaves were engaged in cotton growing. Another 20 percent labored to produce other crops: tobacco (10 percent), rice, sugar, and hemp. About 15 percent of all slaves were domestic servants, and the remaining 10 percent worked in mining, lumbering, industry, and construction.

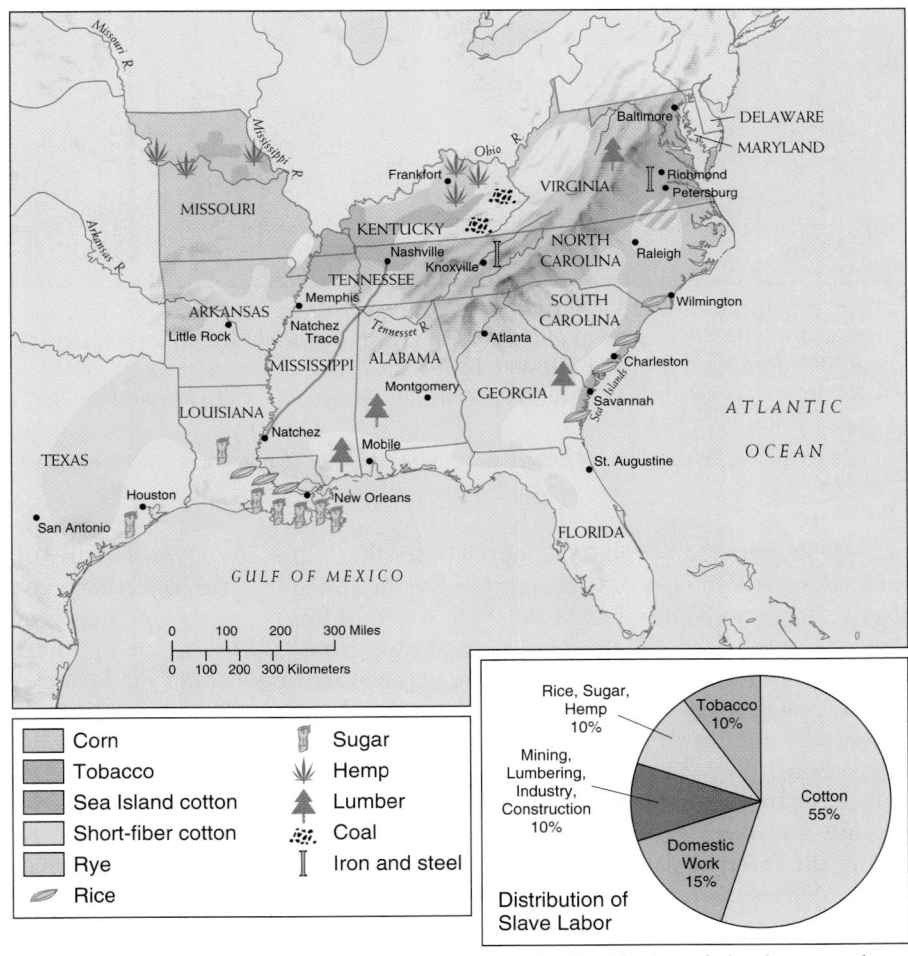

Agriculture, Industry, and Slavery, 1850   *The distribution of the slave population in the South was determined by agricultural and industrial patterns. In 1850, 55 percent of all slaves worked in cotton, 10 percent in tobacco, and another 10 percent in rice, sugar, and hemp. Ten percent worked in mining, lumbering, industry, and construction, and 15 percent worked as domestic servants. Slaves were not generally used to grow corn, the staple crop of the yeoman farmer.*

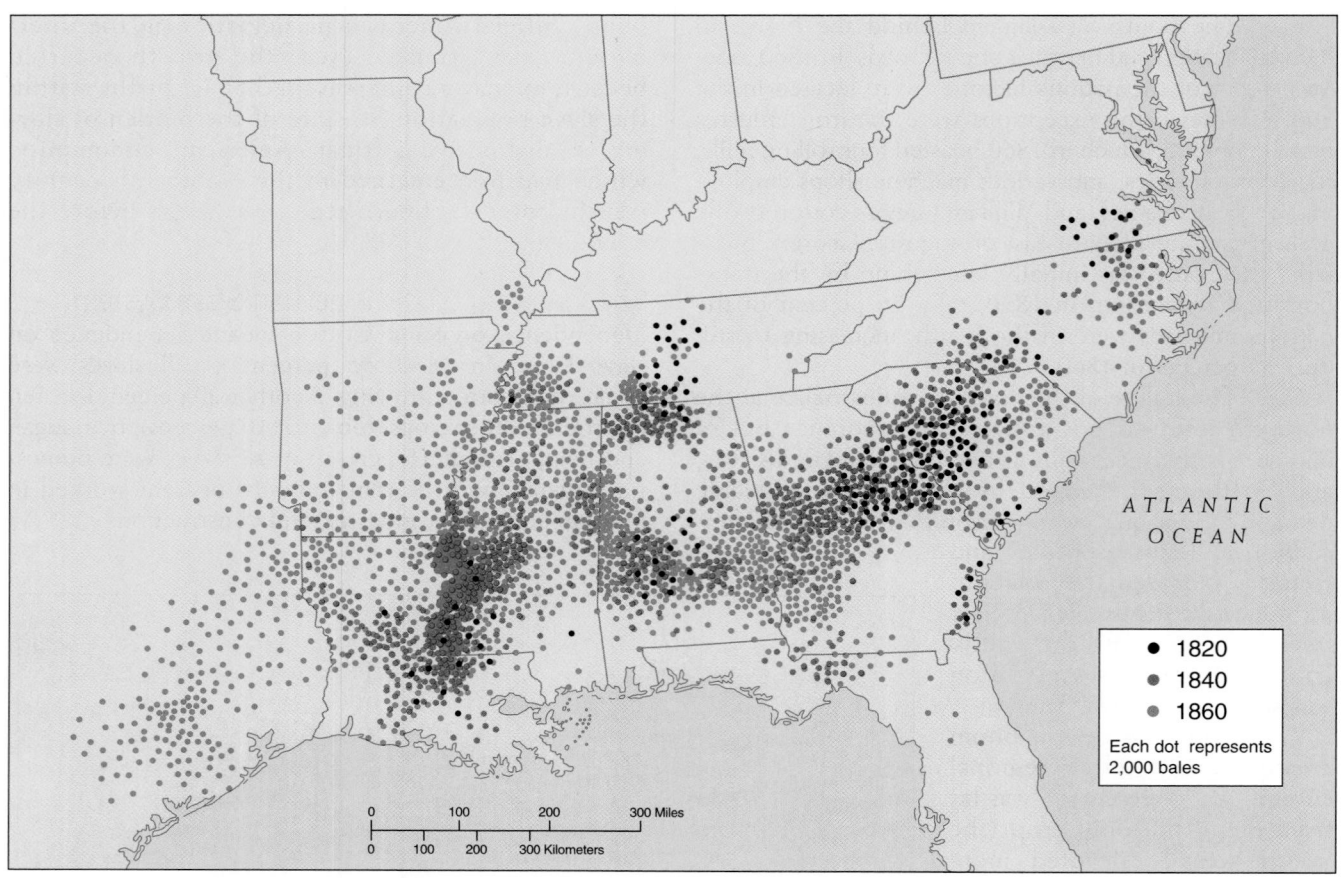

Cotton Production, 1820–1860   *In the forty-year period from 1820 to 1860, cotton production grew dramatically both in quantity and in extent. The westward expansion that cotton
production encouraged in the 1830s and 1850s is reflected in the symbols for 1840 and 1860,
and the growing concentration of cotton production in the black belt (so-called for its rich soils) of
the Lower South is clearly evident.*

Source: Sam Bowers Hilliard, Atlas of Antebellum Southern Agriculture (Baton Rouge: Louisiana State University Press, 1984), pp. 67–71.

Slavery had become distinctively southern: by 1820, as a result of laws passed after the Revolution, all of the northern states had abolished slaveholding. Slaves were increasingly clustered in the Lower South, as Upper South slave owners sold slaves downriver or migrated westward with their entire households. An estimated 1 million slaves migrated involuntarily to the Lower South between 1820 and 1860. Moreover, as expansion to the Southwest accelerated, so did the demand for slaves in the newly settled regions, thus fueling the internal slave trade.

Slaves were not distributed equally among southern slave owners. More than half of all slave owners owned five slaves or fewer, but 75 percent of all slaves lived in groups of ten or more. This disproportionate distribution could have a major impact on a slave's life, for it was a very different matter to be the single slave of a small farmer as opposed to a member of a 100-person black community on a large plantation.

Finally, of all the New World slave societies, the one that existed in the American South was the only one that grew by natural increase rather than the constant importation of captured Africans. This fact alone made the African American community of the South different from the slave societies of Cuba, the Caribbean islands, and Brazil. The first thing to understand, then, are the circumstances of survival.

The Challenge to Survive

The primary challenge facing African Americans was survival. The very young were at risk: mortality rates for slave children under five were twice those for their white counterparts. The reason was clear: pregnant black women were inadequately nourished, worked too hard, or were too frequently pregnant, giving birth to six to eight children at year-and-one-half intervals. When the British actress Fanny Kemble came to live on her husband's Georgia plantation in 1837, what

Slave Population, 1820–1860   *The growth of cotton production caused a redistribution of the enslaved African American population in the South. Although slaves were still used to grow tobacco in Virginia and rice in coastal South Carolina, after 1830 an increasing number were sold "down the river" to work new cotton plantations in the Lower South. Thus although U.S. participation in the international slave trade was outlawed in 1808, the domestic trade in slaves flourished.*

Source: Sam Bowers Hilliard, *Atlas of Antebellum Southern Agriculture* (Baton Rouge: Louisiana State University Press, 1984), pp. 29–34.

shocked her more deeply than any other aspect of the slave system was the treatment of pregnant black women. Sensing her sympathy, pregnant slave women came to Kemble to plead for relief from field work, only to be brusquely ordered back to the fields by the overseer and Kemble's husband.

Health remained a lifelong issue for slaves. Malaria and infectious diseases such as yellow fever and cholera were endemic in the South. White people as well as black died, as the life expectancy figures for 1850 show: 40–43 years for white people and 30–33 years for African Americans. Slaves were more at risk because of the circumstances of slave life: poor housing, poor diet, and constant, usually heavy work. Sickness was chronic: 20 percent or more of the slave labor force on most plantations were sick at any one time. Many owners believed sick slaves were only "malingering." Because of the poor medical knowledge

of the time, they failed to realize that adequate diet, warm housing, and basic sanitation might have prevented the pneumonia and dysentery that killed or weakened many slaves, and that exacted an especially high toll on very young children.

From Cradle to Grave

Slavery was a lifelong labor system, and the constant and inescapable issue between master and slave was how much work the slave would—or could be forced to—do. Southern white slave owners claimed that by housing, feeding, and clothing their slaves from infancy to death they were acting more humanely than northern industrialists who employed people only during their working years. But in spite of occasional instances of manumission—the freeing of a slave—the child born of a slave was destined to remain a slave.

Children lived with their parents (or with their mother if the father was a slave on another farm or plantation) in housing provided by the owner. Slaves owned by small farmers usually had only a bed or mattress to sleep on in the attic or a back room. Larger slave owners housed slaves in one-room cabins with dirt floors and few furnishings (a table, stools, a cooking pot and a few dishes, a bed or corn-shuck mattresses). Fanny Kemble described, with some horror, the one-room slave cabins she found on her husband's plantation:

These cabins consist of one room, about twelve feet by fifteen, with a couple of closets smaller and closer than the state-rooms of a ship, divided off from the main room and each other by rough wooden partitions, in which the inhabitants sleep. They have almost all of them a rude bedstead, with the gray moss of the forests for mattress, and filthy, pestilential-looking blankets for covering. Two families (sometimes eight and ten in number) reside in one of these huts, which are mere wooden frames pinned, as it were, to the earth by a brick chimney outside.

Masters supplied food to their slaves. One common ration for a week was three pounds of meat, a quart of corn meal, and some molasses for each person. Often slaves were encouraged to supplement their diet by keeping their own gardens, and by hunting—though not, of course, with guns. Slaves were also provided with clothes, usually of rough homespun cloth: two shirts, two pairs of pants, and a pair of shoes a year for men, and enough cloth for women to make an equal number of smocks for themselves and their children yearly. This clothing was barely adequate, and in severe winters slaves suffered badly.

From birth to about age seven, slave children played with one another and with white children, observing and learning how to survive. They saw the penalties: black adults, perhaps their own parents, whipped for disobedience; black women, perhaps their own sisters, violated by white men. And they might see one or both parents sold away as punishment or for financial gain. They would also see signs of white benevolence: special treats for children at holidays, appeals to loyalty from the master or mistress, perhaps friendship with a white child. One former slave recalled:

Yessum, when they used to have company in the big house, Miss Ross would bring them to the door to show them us children. And, my blessed, the yard would be black with us children, all string up there next the doorstep looking up in they eyes. Old Missus would say, "Ain't I got a pretty crop of little niggers coming on?"

The children would learn slave ways of getting along: apparent acquiescence in white demands; pilfering; malingering, sabotage, and other methods of slowing the relentless work pace. Fanny Kemble, an accomplished actress, was quick to note the pretense in the "outrageous flattery" she received from her husband's slaves. But many white Southerners genuinely believed that their slaves were both less intelligent and more loyal than they really were. An escaped slave, Jermain Loguen, recalled with some distaste the charade of "servile bows and counterfeit smiles...and other false expressions of gladness" with which he placated his master and mistress. Frederick Douglass, whose fearless leadership of the abolitionist movement made him the most famous African American of his time, wryly noted, "As the master studies to keep the slave ignorant, the slave is cunning enough to make the master think he succeeds."

Most slaves spent their lives as field hands, working in gangs with other slaves under a white overseer, who was usually quick to use his whip to keep up the work pace. But there were other occupations. In the "big house" there were jobs for women as cooks, maids, seamstresses, laundresses, weavers, and nurses. Black men became coachmen, valets, and gardeners, or skilled craftsmen—carpenters, mechanics, and blacksmiths. Some children began learning these occupations at age seven or eight, often in an informal apprentice system. Other children, both boys and girls, were expected to take full care of younger children while the parents were working. Of course black children had no schooling of any kind: in most of the southern states, it was against the law to teach a slave to read, although indulgent owners often rewarded their "pet" slaves by teaching them in spite of the law. At age twelve, slaves were considered full grown and put to work in the fields or in their designated occupation. As Mary Raines, a former slave in South Carolina, recalled, "I was a strong gal, went to de field when I's twelve years old, hoe my acre of cotton, 'long wid de grown ones, and pick my 150 pounds of cotton."

House Servants

At first glance, working in the big house might seem to have been preferable to working in the fields. Physically it was much less demanding, and house slaves were often better fed and clothed. They also had much more access to information, for white people, accustomed to servants and generally confident of their loyalty, often forgot their presence and spoke among themselves about matters of interest to the slaves: local gossip, changes in laws or attitudes, policies toward disobedient or rebellious slaves. As Benjamin Russel, a former slave in South Carolina, recalled:

How did we get the news? Many plantations were strict about this, but the greater the precaution the alerter became the slave, the wider they opened their ears and the more eager they became for outside information. The sources were: girls that waited on the tables, the ladies' maids and the drivers; they would pick up everything they heard and pass it on to the other slaves.

For many white people, one of the worst surprises of the Civil War was the eagerness of their house slaves to flee. Considered by their masters the best treated and the most loyal, these slaves were commonly the first to leave or to organize mass desertions. Even the Confederacy's first family, President Jefferson Davis and his wife Varina, were chagrined by the desertion of their house servants in 1864.

From the point of view of the slave, the most unpleasant thing about being a house servant (or the single slave of a small owner) was the constant presence of white people. There was no escape from white supervision. Many slaves who were personal maids and children's nurses were required to live in the big house and rarely saw their own families. Cooks and other house servants were exposed to the tempers and whims of all members of the white family, including the children, who prepared themselves for lives of mastery by practicing giving orders to slaves many times their own age. And house servants, more than any others, were forced to act grateful and ingratiating. The demeaning images of Uncle Tom and the ever-smiling mammy derive from the roles slaves learned as the price of survival. At the same time, genuine intimacy was possible, especially between black nurses and white children. But these were bonds that the white children were ultimately forced to reject as the price of joining the master class.

Artisans and Skilled Workers

A small number of slaves were skilled workers: weavers, seamstresses, carpenters, blacksmiths, mechanics. More slave men than women achieved skilled status (partly because many jobs considered appropriate for women, like cooking, were not thought of as skilled). Solomon Northup, a northern free African American kidnapped into slavery, explained in his 1853 narrative, *Twelve Years a Slave*, that he had been forced to do a variety of work. He had had three owners and had been hired out repeatedly as a carpenter and as a driver of other slaves in a sugar mill; he had also been hired out to clear land for a new Louisiana plantation and to cut sugar cane. Black people worked as lumberjacks (of the 16,000 lumber workers, almost all were slaves), as miners, as deckhands and stokers on Mississippi riverboats, as stevedores loading cotton on the docks of Charleston, Savannah, and New Orleans, and in the handful of southern factories.

Because slaves were their masters' property, the wages of the slave belonged to the owner, not the slave.

The extent to which slaves made up the laboring class was most apparent in cities. A British visitor to Natchez in 1835 noted slave "mechanics, draymen, hostelers, labourers, hucksters and washwomen and the heterogeneous multitude of every other occupation." In the North, all these jobs were performed by white workers. In part because the South failed to attract as much immigrant labor as the North, southern cities offered both enslaved and free black people opportunities in skilled occupations such as blacksmithing and carpentering that free African Americans in the North were denied.

Field Work

A full 75 percent of all slaves were field workers. Field hands, both men and women, worked from "can see to can't see" (sunup to sundown) summer and winter, and frequently longer at harvest, when eighteen-hour days were common. On most plantations, the bell sounded an hour before sunup, and slaves were expected to be on their way to the fields as soon as it was light. The usual pattern of working in groups of twenty to twenty-five harked back to African communal systems of agricultural work. Many work gangs had black drivers in addition to white overseers. Work continued till noon, and after an hour or so for lunch and rest the slaves worked nearly until dark. In the evening the women prepared dinner at the cabins and everyone snatched a few hours of socializing before bedtime. Work days were shorter in the winter, perhaps only ten hours.

Work was tedious in the hot and humid southern fields, and the overseer's whip was never far away. Cotton growing was hard work: plowing and planting, chopping weeds with a heavy hoe, and picking the ripe cotton from the stiff and scratchy bolls at the rate of 150 pounds a day. In the rice fields, slaves worked knee-deep in water. On sugar plantations, harvesting the cane and getting it ready for boiling was exceptionally heavy work. A strong, hardworking slave—a "prime field hand"—was valuable property, worth at least $1,000 to the master. Slaves justifiably took pride in their strength, as observed by a white Northerner traveling in Mississippi in 1854 who came across a work gang happy to be going home early because of rain:

> First came, led by an old driver carrying a whip, forty of the largest and strongest women I ever saw together...they carried themselves loftily, each having a hoe over the shoulder, and walking with a free, powerful stride. Behind them came the ...[plowhands and their mules], thirty strong, mostly men, but a few of them women....A lean and vigilant white overseer, on a brisk pony, brought up the rear.

That, of course, is only one side of the story. Compare Solomon Northup's memory of cotton picking:

> It was rarely that a day passed by without one or more whippings. The delinquent [who had not picked enough cotton] was taken out, stripped, made to lie upon the ground, face downwards, when he received a punishment proportioned to his offence. It is the literal, unvarnished truth, that the crack of the lash, and the shrieking of the slaves, can be heard from dark till bed time, on [this] plantation, any day almost during the entire period of the cotton-picking season.

Slaves aged fast in this regime. Poor diet and heavy labor undermined health. When they were too old to work, they took on other tasks within the black community, such as caring for young children. Honored by the slave community, the elderly were tolerated by white owners, who continued to feed and clothe them until their deaths. Few actions show the hypocrisy of southern paternalism more clearly than the speed with which white owners evicted their elderly slaves in the 1860s when the end of the slave system was in sight.

THE AFRICAN AMERICAN COMMUNITY

Surely no group in American history has faced a harder job of community building than the black people of the antebellum South. Living in intimate, daily contact with their oppressors, African Americans nevertheless created an enduring culture of their own, a culture that had far-reaching and lasting influence on all of southern society (see Chapter 4). Within their own communities, African American values and attitudes, and especially their own forms of Christianity, played a vital part in shaping a culture of endurance and resistance.

Few African Americans were unfortunate enough to live their lives alone among white people. Over half of all slaves lived on plantations with twenty or more other slaves, and others, on smaller farms, had links with slaves on nearby properties. Urban slaves were able to make and sustain so many secret contacts with other African Americans in cities or towns that slave owners wondered whether slave discipline could be maintained in urban settings. There can be no question that the bonds among African Americans were what sustained them during the years of slavery.

In law, slaves were property, to be bought, sold, rented, worked, and otherwise used (but not abused or killed) as the owner saw fit. But slaves were also human beings, with feelings, needs, and hopes.

Even though most white Southerners believed black people to be members of an inferior, childish race, all but the most brutal masters acknowledged the humanity of their slaves. Furthermore, as a practical matter, white owners had long since learned that unhappy or rebellious slaves were poor workers. White masters learned to live with the two key institutions of African American community life: the family and the African American church.

Slave Families

No southern state recognized slave marriages in law. Most owners, though, not only recognized but encouraged them, sometimes even performing a kind of wedding ceremony for the couple. James Henry Hammond conducted a special ceremony for his slaves, to whom he gave $5.00 for a first marriage and $3.50 for a second marriage. Masters sometimes tried to arrange marriages, but slaves usually found their own mates, sometimes on their own plantation, sometimes elsewhere. Masters encouraged marriage among their slaves, believing it made the men less rebellious, and for economic reasons they were eager for women to have children. Thomas Jefferson, always a clear thinker, put the matter bluntly: "I consider a [slave] woman who [gives birth to] a child every two years as more profitable than the best man on the farm.... What she produces is an addition to the capital." Whatever marriages meant to the masters, to slaves they were a haven of love and intimacy in a cruel world and the basis of the African American community. Husbands and wives had a chance, in their own cabins, to live their own lives among loved ones. The relationship between slave husband and wife was different from that of the white husband and wife. The patriarchal system dictated that the white marriage be unequal, for the man had to be dominant and the woman dependent and submissive. Slave marriages were more equal, for husband and wife were both powerless within the slave system. Both knew that neither could protect the other from abuse at the hands of white people.

Husband and wife cooperated in loving and sheltering their children and teaching them survival skills. Above all, family meant continuity. Parents made great efforts to teach their children the family history. As Alex Haley's *Roots* illustrated, many African American families today maintain strong oral traditions dating back to their African origins. Parents did their best to surround children with a supportive and protective kinship network.

The strength of these ties is shown by the many husbands, wives, children, and parents who searched for each other after the Civil War when slavery came to an end. Observing African Americans' postwar migrations, a Freedmen's Bureau agent commented that "every mother's son among them seemed to be in search of his mother; every mother in search of her children." As the ads in black newspapers indicate, some family searches went on into the 1870s and 1880s, and many ended in failure.

Given the vast size of the internal slave trade, fear of separation was constant—and real. Far from being a rare event prompted only by financial necessity, separations of slave families were common. One in every five slave marriages was broken, and one in every three children sold away from their families. These figures clearly show that slave owners' support for slave marriages was secondary to their desire for profits. The scale of the trade was a strong indication of the economic reality that underlay their protestations of paternalism.

In the face of constant separation, slave communities attempted to act like larger families. Following practices developed early in slavery, children were taught to respect and learn from all the elders, to call all adults of a certain age "aunt" or "uncle," and to call children of their own age "brother" or "sister" (see Chapter 4). Thus, in the absence of their own family, separated children could quickly find a place and a source of comfort in the slave community to which they had been sold.

This emphasis on family and on kinship networks had an even more fundamental purpose. The kinship of the entire community, where old people were respected and young ones cared for, represented a conscious rejection of white paternalism. The slaves' ability, in the most difficult of situations, to structure a community that expressed their values, not those of their masters, was extraordinary. Equally remarkable was the way in which African Americans reshaped Christianity to serve their needs.

African American Religion

Slaves brought religions from Africa but were not allowed to practice them, for white people feared religion would create a bond among slaves that might lead to rebellion. African religions managed to survive in the slave community in forms that white people considered "superstition" or "folk belief," such as the medicinal use of roots by conjurers. Religious ceremonies survived, too, in late-night gatherings deep in the woods where the sound of drumming, singing, and dancing could not reach white ears (see Chapter 4). In the nineteenth century, these African traditions allowed African Americans to reshape white Christianity into their own distinctive faith.

Most masters of the eighteenth century made little effort to Christianize their slaves, afraid they might take the promises of universal brotherhood and

Five generations of one family on a South Carolina plantation are gathered together for this 1862 picture, providing living evidence of the importance of kinship in the building of African American communities.

equality too literally. The Great Awakening, which swept the South after the 1760s, introduced many slaves to Christianity, often in mixed congregations with white people (see Chapter 5). The transformation was completed by the Second Great Awakening, which took root among black and white Southerners in the 1790s. The number of African American converts, preachers, and lay teachers grew rapidly, and a distinctive form of Christianity took shape.

Free African Americans founded their own independent churches and denominations. The first African American Baptist and Methodist churches were founded in Philadelphia in 1794 by the Reverend Absalom Jones and the Reverend Richard Allen. In 1816, the Reverend Allen joined with African American ministers from other cities to form the African Methodist Episcopal (AME) denomination. By the 1830s, free African American ministers like Andrew Marshall of Savannah and many more enslaved black preachers and lay ministers preached, sometimes secretly, to slaves. Their message was one of faith and love, of deliverance, of the coming of the promised land.

African Americans found in Christianity a powerful vehicle to express their longings for freedom and justice. But why did their white masters allow it? Some white people, themselves converted by the revivals, doubtless believed that they should not deny

African cultural patterns persisted in the preference for night funerals and for solemn pageantry and song, depicted in British artist John Antrobus's Plantation Burial, ca. 1860. Like other African American customs, the community care of the dead contained an implied rebuke to the masters' care of the living slaves.

their slaves the same religious experience. But the evangelical religion of the early nineteenth century was also a powerful form of social control. Southern slave owners, seeking to counteract the appeal of African American religion, expected their Christianity to make their slaves obedient and peaceful. Forbidding their slaves to hold their own religious gatherings, owners insisted that their slaves attend white church services. Slaves were quick to realize the owners' purpose. As a former Texas slave recalled: "We went to church on the place and you ought to heard that preachin'. Obey your massa and missy, don't steal chickens and eggs and meat, but nary a word 'bout havin' a soul to save." On many plantations, slaves attended religious services with their masters every Sunday, sitting quietly in the back of the church or in the balcony as the minister preached messages justifying slavery and urging obedience. But at night, away from white eyes, they held their own prayer meetings. Another former Texas slave recalled:

> [We] used to have a prayin' ground down in the hollow and sometimes we come out of the field, between eleven and twelve at night, scorchin' and burnin' up with nothin' to eat, and we wants to ask the good Lawd to have mercy. We put grease in a snuff pan or bottle and make a lamp. We takes a pine torch, too, and goes down to the hollow to pray. Some gits so joyous they starts to holler loud and we has to stop up they mouth [so the whites won't hear].

In churches and in spontaneous religious expressions, the black community made Christianity its own. Fusing Christian texts with African elements of group activity such as the circle dance, the call-and-response pattern, and, above all, group singing, black people created a unique community religion full of emotion, enthusiasm, and protest. Nowhere is this spirit more compelling than in the famous spirituals: "Go Down Moses," with its mournful refrain "Let my people go"; the rousing "Didn't My Lord Deliver Daniel…and why not every man"; the haunting "Steal Away." Some of these spirituals became as well known to white people as to black people, but only African Americans seem to have appreciated the full meaning of their subversive messages.

Nevertheless, this was not a religion of rebellion, for that was unrealistic for most slaves. Black Christianity was an enabling religion: it helped slaves to survive, not as passive victims of white tyranny but as active opponents of an oppressive system that they daily protested in small but meaningful ways. In their faith, African Americans expressed a spiritual freedom that white people could not destroy.

Freedom and Resistance

Whatever their dreams, most slaves knew they would never escape. Freedom was too far away. Almost all successful escapes in the nineteenth century (approximately 1,000 a year) were from the Upper South (Delaware, Maryland, Virginia, Kentucky, Missouri). A slave in the Lower South or the Southwest simply had too far to go to reach freedom. In addition, white Southerners were determined to prevent escapes. Slave patrols were a common sight on southern roads. Any black person without a pass from his or her master was captured (usually roughly) and returned home to certain punishment. But despite almost certain recapture, slaves continued to flee and to help others do so. Escaped slave Harriet Tubman of Maryland, who made nineteen rescue missions freeing 300 slaves in all, had extraordinary determination and skill. As a female runaway, she was unusual, too: most escapees were young men, for women often had small children they were unable to take and unwilling to leave behind.

Much more common was the practice of "running away nearby." Slaves who knew they could not reach freedom still frequently demonstrated their desire for liberty or their discontent over mistreatment by taking unauthorized leave from their plantation. Hidden in nearby forests or swamps, provided with food smuggled by other slaves from the plantation, the runaway might return home after a week or so, often to rather mild punishment. Although in reality most slaves could have little hope of gaining freedom, even failed attempts at rebellion shook the foundations of the slave system and thus temporary flight by any slave was a warning sign of discontent that a wise master did not ignore.

Slave Revolts

The ultimate resistance, however, was the slave revolt. Southern history was dotted with stories of former slave conspiracies and rumors of current plots (see Chapter 4). Every white Southerner knew about the last-minute failure of Gabriel Prosser's insurrection in Richmond in 1800 and the chance discovery of Denmark Vesey's plot in Charleston in 1822. But when in 1831, Nat Turner actually started a rebellion in which a number of white people were killed, southern fears were greatly magnified.

Gabriel Prosser, a literate blacksmith, had gathered more than a thousand slaves for an assault on Richmond. Although the attempt was aborted at the last minute and Prosser and thirty-five others were caught and hanged, white people were especially frightened to learn that Prosser had organized under a banner proclaiming "Death or Liberty" and had hoped for help from the independent black people of Haiti. The notion of an international force of revolutionary slaves demanding their freedom was a fundamental challenge to slave owners' assumptions about their own liberty and power.

Denmark Vesey's conspiracy raised fears among white people concerning African American religion and free black people. Vesey was a well-traveled former seaman who lived in Charleston and worked as a carpenter. Free, well read, and eloquent, he was a lay preacher at Charleston's African Methodist Episcopal Church, where he drew on quotations from the Bible and from the congressional debates during the Missouri Crisis (1819–20) to make a forceful argument against slavery. His co-conspirator, Gullah Jack, was a "conjure-man" who drew on the African religious traditions that flourished among the slaves in the South Carolina low country. Vesey and Gullah Jack drew up a plan to evade the lax city patrol and steal weapons from the Charleston arsenal and horses from livery stables. Then, while mounted and armed slaves beat back white counterattacks in the streets of Charleston, house slaves would capture their owners and murder any who tried to escape. Vesey's aim was to seize Charleston and ultimately to sail to the free black Caribbean nation of Haiti.

Vesey and Gullah Jack recruited at least eighty country and city slaves into the conspiracy, including several trusted house slaves of South Carolina governor Thomas Bennett. Two weeks before the date fixed for the insurrection, the plot was betrayed by a house servant who reported the two slaves who had tried to recruit him into the conspiracy. The accused slaves laughed at the charge and coolly managed to convince the authorities that there was no plot. But two days before the revolt, another house servant confessed, and this time the authorities believed him. In the frantic roundup that followed, thirty-five black people were hanged (Vesey among them) and thirty-seven others sold down the river. But some rebels were not caught because their fellow conspirators died without betraying them. Charlestonians had to live with the knowledge that some of their city's most trusted black servants had conspired to kill their masters—and might still plan to do so.

In the wake of the Vesey conspiracy, Charlestonians turned their fear and anger outward. Planter Robert J. Turnbull wrote bitterly, "By the Missouri question, our slaves thought, there was a charter of liberties granted them by Congress....[The Vesey conspiracy] will long be remembered, as

Harriet Tubman escaped in 1849 from slavery in Maryland, and returned nineteen times to free almost 300 other slaves. Here Tubman (at left), the most famous "conductor" on the Underground Railroad, is shown with some of those she led to freedom.

This drawing shows the moment, almost two months after the failure of his famous and bloody slave revolt, when Nat Turner was accidentally discovered in the woods near his home plantation. Turner's cool murder of his owner and methodical organization of his revolt deeply frightened many white Southerners.

amongst the choicest fruits of that question in Congress." White people attempted to seal off the city from dangerous outside influences. The AME Church (where radical ideas such as the Missouri question had been discussed) was destroyed, and in December 1822 the South Carolina legislature passed a bill requiring that all black seamen be seized and jailed while their ships were in Charleston harbor. Initially most alarmed about free black people from Haiti, Charlestonians soon came to believe that northern free black seamen were spreading antislavery ideas among their slaves.

The most famous slave revolt—Nat Turner's revolt in Southampton County, Virginia—was a partial success. A literate man, Nat Turner was, like Denmark Vesey, a lay preacher, but unlike Vesey he was also a slave. It was Turner's intelligence and strong religious commitment that made him a leader in the slave community and, interestingly, these very same qualities led his master, Joseph Travis, to treat him with kindness even though Turner had once run away for a month after being mistreated by an overseer. Turner began plotting his revolt after a religious vision in which he saw "white spirits and black spirits engaged in battle"; "the sun was darkened—the thunder rolled in the Heavens, and blood flowed in streams." Turner and five other slaves struck on the night of August 20, 1831, first killing Travis, who, Turner said, "was to me a kind master, and placed the greatest confidence in me; in fact, I had no cause to complain of his treatment of me."

Moving from plantation to plantation and killing a total of fifty-five white people, the rebels numbered sixty by the next morning, when they fled from a group of armed white men. More than forty blacks were executed after the revolt, including Turner, who was captured accidentally after he had hidden for two months in the woods. Thomas R. Gray, a white lawyer to whom Turner dictated a lengthy confession before his death, was impressed by Turner's composure. "I looked on him," Gray said, "and my blood curdled in my veins." If intelligent, well-treated slaves such as Turner could plot revolts, how could white Southerners ever feel safe?

Gabriel's Rebellion, the Denmark Vesey plot, and Nat Turner's Revolt were the most prominent examples of organized slave resistance, but they were far from the only ones. Conspiracies and actual or rumored slave resistance began in colonial times (see Chapter 4) and never ceased. These plots exposed the truth white Southerners preferred to ignore: Only force kept Africans and African Americans enslaved, and because no system of control could ever be total, white Southerners could never be completely safe from the possibility of revolt. Nat Turner brought white Southerners' fears to the surface. After 1831, the possibility of slave insurrection was never far from their minds.

Free African Americans

Another source of white disquiet was the growing number of free African Americans. By 1860 nearly 250,000 free black people lived in the South. For most, freedom dated from before 1800, when antislavery feeling among slave owners in the Upper South was widespread and cotton cultivation had yet to boom. In Virginia, for example, the number of manumitted (freed) slaves jumped tenfold in twenty years (see Chapter 7). But a new mood became apparent in 1806 when Virginia tightened its lenient manumission law: now the freed person was required to leave the state within a year or be sold back into slavery. After 1830 manumission was virtually impossible throughout the South.

Most free black people lived in the countryside of the Upper South, where they worked as tenant farmers or farm laborers. Urban African Americans were much more visible. Life was especially difficult for female-headed families because only the most menial work—street peddling and laundry work, for example—was available to free black women. The situation for African American males was somewhat better. Although they were discriminated against in employment and in social life, there were opportunities for skilled black craftsmen in trades such as blacksmithing and carpentering.

Cities such as Charleston, Savannah, and Natchez were home to flourishing free African American communities that formed their own churches and fraternal orders. In Natchez, a free black barber, William Johnson, owned several barber shops, a small farm, and an estate valued at $25,000 in 1851 that included fifteen slaves. Johnson had a white attorney and friends among the city's leading politicians, and he lived in a white neighborhood. Half a dozen other free African Americans in Natchez were similarly prosperous, and they, too, were slave owners. This tiny elite kept a careful social distance from most of Natchez's approximately 1,000 free black people (one-quarter of all free African Americans in Mississippi in 1840), who were miserably poor. This free black elite treated white people with great tact and deference.

Free African Americans had reason to be careful, for their position was increasingly precarious. Throughout the South in the 1830s, state legislatures tightened black codes—laws concerning free black people. Free African Americans could not carry firearms, could not purchase slaves (unless they were members of their own family), and were liable to the criminal penalties meted out to slaves (that is, whippings and summary judgments without a jury trial). They could not testify against whites, hold office, vote, or serve in the militia. In other words, except for the right to own property, free blacks had no civil rights. Following the cleanup of the alarming race mixing in Natchez-under-the-Hill, the Natchez elite focused on free African Americans. In 1841, whites mounted a campaign to deport from the state any free black person who adopted "the practices of the rogue, the incendiary, and the abolitionist." Many poor free African Americans were deported from Natchez that summer and in the following years. William Johnson, whose own security was not threatened, aided some poor black people by quietly helping them obtain attestations of good character from white planters. For

all of his (comparative) wealth, as a black man he could do nothing openly to help his own people.

As this episode shows, white people increasingly feared the influence free black people might have on slaves, for free African Americans were a living challenge to the slave system. Their very existence disproved the basic southern equations of white equals free, and black equals slave. No one believed more fervently in those equations than the South's largest population group, white people who did not own slaves.

YEOMEN AND POOR WHITE PEOPLE

The pervasive influence of the slave system in the South is reflected in the startling contrast of two facts: two-thirds of all Southerners did not own slaves, yet slave owners dominated the social and political life of the region. Who were the two-thirds of white Southerners who did not own slaves, and how did they live? Throughout the south, slave owners occupied the most productive land: tobacco-producing areas in Virginia and Tennessee, coastal areas of South Carolina and Georgia where rice and cotton grew, sugar lands in Louisiana, and large sections of the cotton-producing black belt, which stretched westward from South Carolina to Texas. Small farmers, usually without slaves, occupied the rest of the land. This land ranged from adequate to poor, from depleted, once-rich regions in Virginia to the Carolina hill country and the pine barrens of Mississippi.

Yeomen

The word "yeoman," originally a British term for a farmer who works his own land, is often applied to independent farmers of the South, most of whom lived on family-sized farms. Although yeoman farmers sometimes owned a few slaves, in general they and their families worked their land by themselves. Typical of the yeoman-farmer community was northwestern Georgia, once home to the Creeks and Cherokees, but now populated by communities of small farmers who grew enough vegetables to feed their families, including corn, which they either ate themselves or fed to hogs. In addition, these farmers raised enough cotton every year (usually no more than one or two bales) to bring in a little cash. At least 60 percent owned their own farms, but some were wealthier than others. Isaac Cobb of Carroll County owned 700 acres of land on which he grazed cattle, sheep, and hogs. On 200 of these acres, twelve slaves helped him produce 2,000 bushels of grain and twelve bales of cotton. In contrast, Richard White, of the same county, used only family labor to farm 50 acres devoted to food and grains and the grazing of a few cattle, sheep, and hogs. These two men, and thou-

One of the ways Charleston attempted to control its African American population was to require all slaves to wear badges showing their occupation. After 1848, free black people also had to wear badges, which were decorated, ironically, with a liberty cap.

sands like them, were the yeomen Thomas Jefferson celebrated—economically independent yet intimately tied to a larger but still very local group.

The local community was paramount. Farm men and women depended on their relatives and neighbors for assistance in large farm tasks such as planting, harvesting, and construction. Events requiring lots of hands like logrollings, corn shuckings, and quilting bees were community events. Farmers repaid this help, and obtained needed goods, through complex systems of barter with other members of the community. In their organization, southern farm communities were no different from northern ones, with one major exception—slavery. In the South, one of the key items in the community barter system was the labor of slaves, who were frequently loaned out to neighbors by small slave owners such as Isaac Cobb to fulfill an obligation to another farmer.

Where yeomen and large slave owners lived side by side, as in the Georgia black belt where cotton was the major crop, slavery again provided a link between richer and poorer. Large plantation owners often bought food for their slaves from small local farmers, ground the latter's corn in the plantation mill, ginned their cotton, and transported and marketed it as well. But although planters and much smaller yeomen were part of a larger community network, in the black belt the large slave owners were clearly dominant. Only in their own up-country communities did yeomen feel truly independent.

Poor White People

Not all small farmers were on an equal footing. One-third of the farmers in the Georgia up-country were tenant farmers. Some were farmers' sons, striking out on their own while waiting to inherit their fathers' land. But others were poor whites with little hope of improving their condition. From 30 to 50 percent of all southern white people were landless, a proportion similar to that in the North. But the existence of slavery affected the opportunities for southern poor white people. Slaves made up the permanent, stable work force in agriculture and in many skilled trades. Many poor white people led highly transient lives in search of work, such as farm labor at harvest time, which was only temporary. Others were tenant farmers working under share-tenancy arrangements that kept them in debt to the landowner. Although they farmed poorer land with less equipment than landowning farmers, most tenant farmers grew enough food to sustain their families. Like the yeomen, but with more difficulty, tenant farmers aspired to independence.

Relationships between poor whites and black slaves were complex. White men and women often worked side by side with black slaves in the fields and were socially and sexually intimate with enslaved and free African Americans. White people engaged in clandestine trade to supply slaves with items like liquor that slave owners prohibited, helped slaves to escape, and even (in an 1835 Mississippi case) were executed for their participation in planning a slave revolt. At the same time, the majority of poor white people insisted, sometimes violently, on their racial superiority over blacks. For their part, many African American slaves, better dressed, better nourished, and healthier, dismissed them as "poor white trash." But the fact was that the difficult lives of poor whites, whom one contemporary described as "a third class of white people," served to blur the crucial racial distinction between independent whites and supposedly inferior, dependent black people on which the system of slavery rested. Like the boatmen whom the Natchez slave owners viewed with such alarm, poor white people posed a potential threat to the slave system.

The goal of yeoman farm families was economic independence. Their mixed farming and grazing enterprises, supported by kinship and community ties, afforded them a self-sufficiency epitomized by Carl G. von Iwonski's painting of this rough but comfortable log cabin in New Braunfels, Texas.

Yeoman Values

In 1828 and 1832, southern yeomen and poor white men voted overwhelmingly for Andrew Jackson. They were drawn variously to his outspoken policy of ruthless expansionism, his appeals to the common man, and his rags-to-riches ascent from poor boy to rich slave owner. It was a career many hoped to emulate. The dominance of the large planters was due at least in part to the ambition of many yeomen, especially those with two or three slaves, to expand their holdings and become rich. These farmers, enthusiastic members of the lively democratic politics of the South, supported the leaders they hoped to join.

But for a larger group of yeomen, independence and not wealth was most important. Many southern yeomen lived apart from large slaveholders, in the up-country regions where plantation agriculture was unsuitable. The very high value southern yeomen placed on freedom grew directly from their own experience as self-sufficient property-owning farmers in small, family-based communities. This was a way of life that southern "plain folk" were determined to preserve. It made them resistant to the economic opportunities and challenges that capitalism and industrialization posed for northern farmers, which southern yeomen perceived as encroachments on their freedom.

The irony was that the freedom yeomen so prized rested on slavery. White people could count on slaves to perform the hardest and worst labor, and the degradation of slave life was a daily reminder of the freedom they enjoyed in comparison. Slavery meant that all white people, rich and poor, were equal in the sense that they were all free. This assumption of white skin privilege had formed in the eighteenth century as slavery became the answer to the South's labor problem (see Chapter 4). The democratization of politics in the early nineteenth century and the enactment of nearly universal white manhood suffrage perpetuated the belief in white skin privilege, even though the gap between rich and poor white people was widening.

Southern yeomen did not blindly follow the rich slave owners who were their political leaders. Rather, they supported a freedom they believed they would not have under any other system. But southern unanimity on this point, which looked so strong, was actually very fragile. Anything that appeared to threaten slavery threatened the entire southern social structure, trapping Southerners in ever more rigid and defensive positions.

PLANTERS

Remarkably few slave owners fit the popular stereotype of the rich and leisured plantation owner with hundreds of acres of land and hundreds of slaves. Only

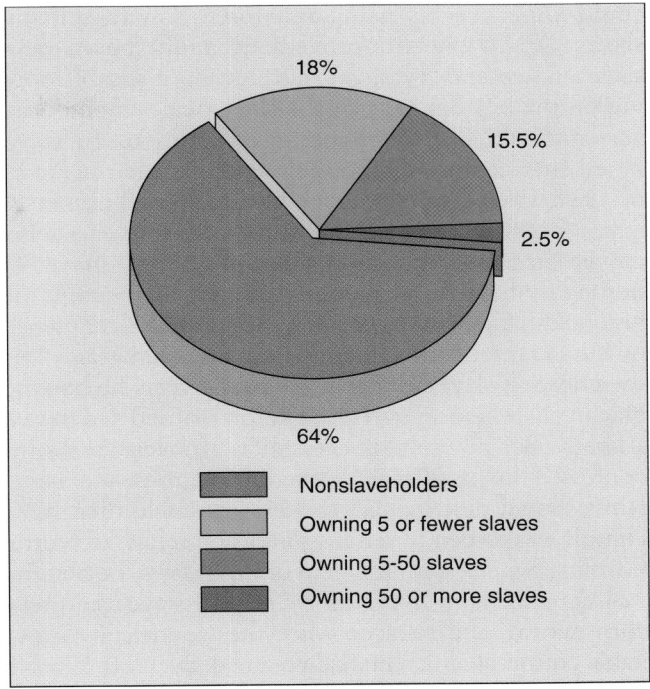

Slaveholding and Class Structure in the South, 1830
The great mass of the southern white population were yeoman farmers. In 1830, slave owners made up only 36 percent of the southern white population; owners of more than fifty slaves constituted a tiny 2.5 percent. Yet they and the others who were middling planters dominated politics, retaining the support of yeomen who prized their freedom as white men above class-based politics.

Source: U.S. Bureau of the Census.

36 percent of southern white people owned slaves in 1830, and only 2.5 percent owned fifty slaves or more. Just as yeomen and poor whites were diverse, so, too, were southern slave owners.

Small Slave Owners

The largest group of slave owners were small yeomen taking the step from subsistence agriculture to commercial production. To do this in the South's agricultural economy, they had to own slaves. But upward mobility was difficult. Owning one or two slaves increased farm production only slightly, and it was hard to accumulate the capital to buy more. One common pattern was for a slave owner to leave one or two slaves to farm while he worked another job (this arrangement usually meant that his wife had unacknowledged responsibility for their supervision). In other cases, small farmers worked side by side with their slaves in the fields. In still other cases, owners hired out their slaves to larger slave owners.

In every case, the owner was economically vulnerable: a poor crop or a downturn in cotton prices could wipe out his gains and force him to sell his slaves. When times improved, he might buy a new slave or two and try again, but getting a secure footing on the bottom rung of the slave owner ladder was very difficult. The roller-coaster economy of the early nineteenth century did not help matters, and the Panic of 1837 was a serious setback to many small farmers.

John Flintoff was an aspiring slave owner who moved from North Carolina to Mississippi in 1841, hoping to make his fortune. Working as an overseer on his uncle's land, Flintoff began his career as a slave owner by buying three slave children (one was seven years old), the cheapest slaves available. Over the years he bought nine in all. While an overseer, Flintoff married and began a family. But he was unsuccessful as an overseer. As he confessed in his diary, "managing negroes and large farms is soul destroying." In 1853 his uncle fired him. Flintoff was forced to sell his slaves and return to North Carolina, where, with the help of his in-laws, he bought 124 acres of land. Assisted by several slaves he grew corn, wheat, and tobacco—not the wonderfully profitable cotton of which he had dreamed. By 1860, Flintoff was modestly successful; wealthy enough to send his son to college and to free his wife from routine farm chores. As he boasted, his wife "has lived a Lady."

For a smaller group of slave owners, the economic struggle was not so hard. Middle-class professional men—lawyers, doctors, and merchants—frequently managed to become large slave owners because they already had capital (the pay from their professions) to invest in land and slaves. Sometimes they received payment for their services not in money but in slaves. These owners were the most likely to own skilled slaves—carpenters, blacksmiths, other artisans—and to rent them out for profit. By steady accumulation, the most successful members of this middle class were able to buy their way into the slave-owning elite and to confirm that position by marrying their sons or daughters into the aristocracy.

Here the career of Andrew Jackson of Tennessee is instructive. Jackson, an orphan, had no family money. He began a profitable career as a prosecutor in Nashville in the 1790s, frequently taking small plots of land as payment for his services. In 1796, the year he was elected Tennessee's delegate to the U.S. House of Representatives, he owned 10 slaves. In 1798 Jackson owned 15 slaves. He widened his economic activities, buying land, partnership in a store, a plantation for himself (the Hermitage), and a racetrack. Then came some bad years—the mercantile business failed, and debts on land came due—and Jackson was soon preoccupied with military matters. But he continued to accumulate slaves: 44 by 1820, 95 by 1828 (the year he was elected president), 150 a few years later, and almost 200 by the time of his death in 1845.

The Old Planter Elite

The slave-owning elite, those 2.5 percent who owned fifty slaves or more, enjoyed the prestige, the political leadership, and the lifestyle to which many white Southerners aspired. Almost all great slave owners inherited their wealth. They were rarely self-made men, although most tried to add to the land and slaves they had inherited. Men of wealth and property had led southern politics since colonial times, but increasingly after 1820 it was men from the middle classes who were most often elected to political office. As the nation moved toward universal manhood suffrage, planters tried to learn how to appeal to the popular vote, but most never acquired "the common touch." It was the smaller slave owners who formed a clear majority in every southern state legislature before 1860.

The eastern seaboard had first given rise to a class of rich planters in the colonial period, as attested by the plantations of William Byrd and Robert "King" Carter of Virginia and the cultured life of the planter elite, centered in Charleston, that had established itself in the South Carolina low country and Sea Islands.

One such planter was Thomas Chaplin, descended from an indentured servant who arrived in 1672 from the British sugar-producing island of Barbados. In 1839 he married Mary McDowell, granddaughter of a rich Charleston merchant, and in 1840 they moved into the old family house on the 376-acre Tombee Plantation on St. Helena Island near Beaufort, South Carolina. Master of sixty to seventy slaves, Chaplin grew sea-island cotton (a long-staple variety), potatoes, and corn and raised beef and mutton. Although St. Helena land was rich and fertile, the climate bred mosquito-borne malaria, epidemic from mid-May until November. Most planters and their families lived in Charleston or the healthier up-country during the "sickly season," and few poorer white people lived on St. Helena at all. As a consequence, by 1845 black people outnumbered white people eight to one on the island (2,000 African Americans to 250 whites). St. Helena and the other Sea Islands of South Carolina were unique in the relative autonomy of their black population and the persistence of African customs and language.

Soon after he took possession of Tombee Plantation, Chaplin was forced to sell off more than half his slaves to settle family debts and lawsuits. Land rich but labor poor, Chaplin fretted in 1850: "So many mouths to feed & so few to work that it is impossible for me to get along." Although completely dependent on his black labor force, Chaplin was indifferent to them as individuals. Unlike many planters, Chaplin refused to attend slave weddings, dismissing them as "tomfoolery," and only grudgingly did he permit his slaves to choose husbands and wives from other plantations. He complained unceasingly about the high rate of infant mortality among slaves, going so far as to accuse mothers of killing their own babies. He failed to realize that overwork and poor nutrition (counteracted only in part by the constant pilfering from his storehouses and barns) were to blame. Unlike most planters, Chaplin never hired an overseer for the work in his fields, but after 1852 he increasingly left the details of management to a black slave driver.

The Natchez "Nabobs"

As Southerners and slave owning spread westward, membership in the elite broadened to include the new wealth of Alabama, Mississippi, Louisiana, and Texas. The rich planters of the Natchez community were popularly called "nabobs" (from a Hindi word for Europeans who had amassed fabulous wealth in India). Frederick Stanton, owner of Stanton Hall in Natchez, was a physician who had immigrated from Northern Ireland. The source of his wealth was not medicine but the cotton commission (brokerage) business. At the time of his death he owned 444 slaves and 15,109 acres of land on six Louisiana and Mississippi plantations that produced more than 3,000 bales of cotton a year. Another great Natchez family, the Surgets, of French origin, traced their wealth further back, to a Spanish land grant of 2,500 acres to Pierre Surget. In the 1850s his grandsons Frank and James Surget controlled some 93,000 acres in Mississippi, Arkansas, and Louisiana (half of it plantation land and half bought on speculation, for resale). Each brother sold 4,000 bales of cotton a year, and between them they owned upwards of 1,000 slaves. Each also owned palatial mansions in Natchez—Cherry Hill and Clifton.

The extraordinary concentration of wealth in Natchez—in 1850 it was the richest county in the nation—fostered a self-consciously elite lifestyle that derived not from long tradition but from suddenly acquired riches. Fastidious Northerners such as Thomas Taylor, a Pennsylvania Quaker who visited Natchez in 1847, noted: "Many of the chivalric gentry whom I have been permitted to see dashing about here on highbred horses, seem to find their greatest enjoyment in recounting their bear hunts, 'great fights,' and occasional exploits with revolvers and Bowie knives—swearing 'terribly' and sucking mint juleps & cherry cobblers with straws."

Plantation Life

The urban life of the Natchez planters was unusual. Many wealthy planters, especially those on new lands in the Old Southwest, lived in isolation on their plantations with their families and slaves. Through family networks, common boarding school experience, political activity, and frequent visiting, the small planter elite consciously worked to create and maintain a distinctive lifestyle that was modeled on that of the English aristocracy, as Southerners understood it. This

William H. Brown, *Hauling the Whole Week's Picking* (detail). 1842. Watercolor. The Historic New Orleans Collection.

This scene is part of a larger mural, created by artist William Henry Brown in 1842, which depicts everyday life at Nitta Yuma, a Mississippi cotton plantation. The elegant white woman, here seen elaborately dressed to go riding, depended for her leisure status on the work of African American slaves, such as this one feeding her horse.

entailed a large estate, a spacious, elegant mansion, and lavish hospitality. For men, the gentlemanly lifestyle meant immersion in masculine activities such as hunting, soldiering, or politics and a touchy concern with "honor" that could lead to duels and other acts of bravado. Women of the slave-owning elite, in contrast, were expected to be gentle, charming, and always welcoming of relatives, friends, and other guests.

But this gracious image was at odds with the economic reality. Large numbers of black slaves had to be forced to work to produce the wealth of the large plantations. Each plantation, like the yeoman farm but on a larger scale, aimed to be self-sufficient, producing not only the cash crop but most of the food and clothing for both slaves and family. There were stables full of horses for plowing, transportation, and show. There were livestock and vegetable gardens to be tended, and carpentering, blacksmithing, weaving, and sewing to be done. A large plantation was an enterprise that required many hands, many skills, and a lot of management. Large plantation owners might have overseers or black drivers to supervise field work, but frequently they themselves had direct financial control of daily operations. Even if they were absentee landlords (like, for example, Thomas Chaplin in South Carolina and the richest of the Natchez elite), planters usually required careful accounts from their overseers and often exercised the right to overrule their decisions.

A paternalistic ideology infused the life of large plantations that permitted the planter elite to rationalize their use of slaves and the submissiveness they demanded of wives. According to this ideology, each plantation was a family composed of both black and white. The master, as head of the plantation, was head of the family, and the mistress was his "help-mate." The master was obligated to provide for all of his family, both black and white, and to treat them with humanity. In return, slaves were to work properly and do as they were told, as children would. Most elite slave owners spoke of their position of privilege as a duty and a burden. (Their wives were even more outspoken about the burdensome aspects of supervising slave labor, which they bore more directly than their husbands.) John C. Calhoun spoke for many slave owners when he described the plantation as "a little community" in which the master directed all operations so that the abilities and needs of every member, black and white, were "perfectly harmonized." Convinced of their own benevolence, slave owners expected not only obedience but gratitude from all members of their great "families."

The Plantation Mistress

Southern paternalism not only laid special burdens on plantation mistresses but put restrictions on their lives and activities not experienced by northern women of the same social rank. For example, although northern women like southern women were barred from public life and taught that their proper role was domestic and family-based, in the North, women came clearly to control the domestic "sphere" and to carry domestic concerns outside the family and into a wide range of activities that addressed various social reforms. Such autonomous behavior was out of the question for plantation mistresses, who were locked by the paternalistic model into positions that bore heavy responsibility but carried no real authority. The difficulties experienced by these in some ways quite privileged women illustrate the way the slave system affected every aspect of the personal life of slave owners.

Plantation mistresses spent most of their lives tending family members—including slaves—in illness and in childbirth, and supervising their slaves' performance of such daily tasks as cooking, housecleaning, weaving, and sewing. In addition, the plantation mistress often had to spend hours, even days, of behind-the-scenes preparation for the crowds of guests she was expected to welcome in her role as elegant and gracious hostess.

Despite the reality of the plantation mistress's daily supervision of an often extensive household, she did not rule it: her husband did. The plantation master was the source of authority to whom wife, children, and slaves were expected to look for both rewards and punishments. A wife who challenged her husband or sought more independence from him

threatened the entire paternalistic system of control. After all, if she were not dependent and obedient, why should slaves be? In addition, although many southern women were deeply affected by evangelical religion and exhortations to care for those in need, their response was personal rather than social. Enlisting in reform movements like their northern counterparts would have been far too threatening to the system of slave control to be tolerated in the South, for it might have led slaves to believe that their lives, too, could be improved.

In addition to their strictly defined family roles, many southern women also suffered deeply from isolation from friends and kin. Sometimes the isolation of life on rural plantations could be overcome by long visits, but women with many small children and extensive responsibilities found it difficult to leave. Plantation masters, on the other hand, often traveled widely for political and business reasons. John C. Calhoun, for example, who spoke so earnestly about the plantation community, spent much less time than his wife on the family plantation, Fort Hill. He spent years in Washington as a politician while Floride Calhoun, who had accompanied him in his early career, remained at Fort Hill after the first five of their ten children were born.

Plantation women in the Old Southwest, many of whom had moved unwillingly and now were far from their families on the eastern seaboard, were particularly lonely. "I seldom see any person aside from our own family, and those employed upon the plantation," Mary Kendall wrote. "For about three weeks I did not have the pleasure of seeing one white female face, there being no white family except our own upon the plantation." The irony is that she was surrounded by women, but the gap between the white mistress and her black slaves was generally unbridgeable.

Although on every plantation black women served as nursemaids to young white children and as lifelong maids to white women, usually accompanying them when they moved as brides into their own homes, there are few historical examples of genuine sympathy and understanding of black women by white women of the slave-owning class. Few of the latter seemed to understand the sadness, frustration, and despair often experienced by their lifelong maids, who were forced to leave their own husbands and children to serve in their mistresses' new homes. A number of southern women did rail against "the curse of slavery," but few meant the inhumanity of the system; most were actually complaining about the extra work entailed by housekeeping with slaves. As one plantation mistress explained, "Slaves are a continual source of more trouble to housekeepers than all other things, vexing them, and causing much sin. We are compelled to keep them in ignorance and much responsibility rests on us." Years later many former slaves remembered their mistresses as being kinder than their masters, but fully a third of such accounts mention cruel whippings and other punishments by white women.

Coercion and Violence

There were generous and benevolent masters, but most large slave owners believed that constant discipline and coercion were necessary to make slaves work hard. Some slave owners used their slaves with great brutality. Owners who killed slaves were occasionally brought to trial (and usually acquitted), but no legal action was taken in the much more frequent cases of excessive punishment, general abuse, and rape.

One of the most common violations of the paternalistic code of behavior (and of southern law) was the sexual abuse of female slaves by their masters. Usually, masters forcibly raped their women slaves at will, and slave women had little hope of defending themselves from these attacks. Sometimes, however, long-term intimate relationships between masters and slaves developed. James Henry Hammond kept two slave mistresses, Sally Johnson and her daughter Louisa, for twenty years and fathered several children by each of them. Hammond's instructions to his (white) son Harry, written in 1856, about the future of his mistresses and slave children tell us much about the boundaries of the slave system: "In the last will I made I left to you…Sally Johnson the mother of Louisa & all the children of both….I cannot free these people & send them North. It would be cruelty to them….Do not let Louisa or any of my children…be the slaves of strangers. Slavery in the family will be their happiest earthly condition."

It was rare for slave owners to publicly acknowledge fathering slave children or to free these children, and black women and their families were helpless to protest their treatment. Equally silenced was the master's wife, who for reasons of modesty as well as her subordinate position was not supposed to notice either her husband's infidelity or his flagrant crossing of the color lines. As Mary Boykin Chesnut, wife of a South Carolina slave owner, vehemently confided to her diary: "God forgive us, but ours is a monstrous system….Like the patriarchs of old, our men live all in one house with their wives and their concubines, and the mulattoes one sees in every family partly resemble the white children. Any lady is ready to tell you who is the father of all the mulatto children in everybody's household but her own. Those, she seems to think, drop from the clouds."

An owner could do what he chose on his plantation, and his sons grew up expecting to do likewise.

This Louisiana slave named Gordon was photographed in 1863 after he had escaped to Union lines during the Civil War. He bears the permanent scars of the violence that lay at the heart of the slave system. Few slaves were so brutally marked, but all lived with the threat of beatings if they failed to obey.

Unchecked power is always dangerous, and it is not surprising that it was sometimes misused. Perhaps the most surprising thing about the southern slave system is how much humanity survived despite the intolerable conditions. For that, most of the credit goes not to white paternalism but to African Americans and the communities they created under slavery.

THE DEFENSE OF SLAVERY

"Slavery informs all our modes of life, all our habits of thought, lies at the basis of our social existence, and of our political faith," announced South Carolina planter William Henry Trescot in 1850, explaining why the South would secede from the Union before giving up slavery. Slavery bound white and black Southerners together in tortuous ways that eventually led, as Trescot had warned, to the Civil War.

Population figures tell much of the story of the complex relationship between whites and blacks: of the

Population Patterns in the South, 1850   *In South Carolina and Mississippi the enslaved African American population outnumbered the white population; in four other Lower South states the percentage was above 40 percent. These ratios frightened many white Southerners. White people also feared the free black population, though only three states in the Upper South and Louisiana had free black populations of over 3 percent. Six states had free black populations that were so small (less than 1 percent) as to be statistically insignificant.*

owners. Once the cotton boom began in the 1790s, this charity was rarely exercised and Jefferson's vision of peaceful emancipation faded. On the contrary, Southerners increasingly sought to justify slavery.

Southern apologists had several conventional lines of defense. They found justifications for slavery in the Bible and in the histories of Greece and Rome, both slave-owning societies. The strongest defense was a legal one: the Constitution allowed slavery. Though never specifically mentioned in the final document, slavery had been a major issue between North and South at the Constitutional Convention in 1787. In the end, the delegates agreed that seats in the House of Representatives would be apportioned by counting all of the white population and three-fifths of the black people (Article I, Section 2, Paragraph 3); they included a clause requiring the return of runaway slaves who had crossed state lines (Article IV, Section 2, Paragraph 3); and they agreed that Congress could not abolish the international slave trade for twenty years (Article I, Section 9, Paragraph 1). There was absolutely no question: the Constitution did recognize slavery.

The Missouri Crisis of 1819–20 alarmed most Southerners, who were shocked by the evidence of widespread antislavery feeling in the North. South Carolinians viewed Denmark Vesey's conspiracy, occurring only two years after the Missouri debate, as an example of the harm that irresponsible northern antislavery talk could cause. After Nat Turner's revolt in 1831, Governor John Floyd of Virginia blamed the uprising on "Yankee peddlers and traders" who supposedly told slaves that "all men were born free and equal." Thus northern antislavery opinion and the fear of slave uprisings were firmly linked in southern minds.

After Nat Turner

In 1831 the South began to close ranks in defense of slavery. Several factors contributed to this regional solidarity. Nat Turner's revolt was important, linked as it was in the minds of many Southerners with antislavery agitation from the North. Militant abolitionist William

12 million people who lived in the South in 1860, 4 million were slaves. Indeed, in the richest agricultural regions, such as the Sea Islands of South Carolina and Georgia and parts of the black belt, black people outnumbered whites. These sheer numbers of African Americans reinforced white people's perpetual fears of black retaliation for the violence exercised by the slave master. Every rumor of slave revolts, real or imagined, kept those fears alive. The basic question was this: What might slaves do if they were not controlled? Thomas Jefferson summed up this dilemma: "We have the wolf by the ears; and we can neither hold him nor safely let him go. Justice is in one scale, and self-preservation in the other."

Developing Proslavery Arguments

In the flush of freedom following the American Revolution, a number of slave owners in the Upper South freed their slaves, and Thomas Jefferson, ever the optimist, claimed that "a total emancipation with the consent of the masters" could not be too far in the future. Nevertheless, southern legislatures were unwilling to write steps toward emancipation into law, preferring to depend on the charity of individual slave

Lloyd Garrison began publishing the *Liberator*, the newspaper that was to become the leading antislavery organ, in 1831. The British gave notice that they would soon abolish slavery on the sugar plantations of the West Indies, an action that seemed to many Southerners much too close to home. Emancipation for West Indian slaves came in 1833. Finally, 1831 was the year before the Nullification Crisis (see Chapter 10) was resolved. Although the other southern states did not support the hotheaded South Carolinians who called for secession, they did sympathize with the argument that the federal government had no right to interfere with a state's special interest (namely, slavery). Following the crisis, other southern states joined with South Carolina in the belief that the only effective way to prevent other federal encroachment was militant and vehement defense of slavery.

In the 1830s, southern states began to barricade themselves against "outside" antislavery propaganda. In 1835, a crowd broke into a Charleston post office, made off with bundles of antislavery literature, and set an enormous bonfire, to fervent state and regional acclaim. By 1835, every southern legislature had tightened its laws concerning control of slaves. For example, they tried to blunt the effect of abolitionist literature by passing laws forbidding slaves to learn how to read. In only three border states—Kentucky, Tennessee, and Maryland—did slave literacy remain legal. By 1860, it is estimated, only 5 percent of all slaves could read. Slaves were forbidden to gather for dances, religious services, or any kind of organized social activity without a white person present. They were forbidden to have whiskey because it might encourage them toward revolt. The penalty for plotting insurrection was death. Other laws made manumission illegal and placed even more restrictions on the lives of free black people (as in Natchez). In many areas slave patrols were augmented and became more vigilant in restricting African American movement and communication between plantations.

In 1836, Southerners introduced a "gag rule" in Washington to prevent congressional consideration of abolitionist petitions. Attempts were made to stifle all open debate about slavery within the South; dissenters were pressured to remain silent or to leave. A few, such as James G. Birney and Sarah and Angelina

Grimké of South Carolina, left for the North to act on their antislavery convictions, but most chose silence. Among those under the greatest pressure to conform were Christian ministers, many of whom professed to believe that preaching obedience to slaves was a vital part of making slavery a humane system.

In addition to fueling fears of slave rebellions, the growing abolitionist sentiment of the 1830s raised the worry that southern opportunities for expansion would be cut off. Southern politicians painted melodramatic pictures of a beleaguered white South hemmed in on all sides by "fanatic" antislavery states, while at home Southerners were forced to contemplate what might happen when they had "to let loose among them, freed from the wholesome restraints of patriarchal authority…an idle, worthless, profligate set of free negroes" whom they feared would "prowl the…streets at night and [haunt] the woods during the day armed with whatever weapons they could lay their hands on."

Finally, southern apologists moved beyond defensiveness to develop proslavery arguments. One of the first to do this was James Henry Hammond, elected a South Carolina congressman in 1834. In 1836 Hammond delivered a major address to Congress in which he denied that slavery was evil. Rather, he claimed, it had produced "the highest toned, the purest, best organization of society that has ever existed on the face of the earth." One wonders what Hammond's slaves, especially Sally and Louisa Johnson, would have thought of this argument.

This 1841 proslavery cartoon contrasts healthy, well-cared-for African American slaves with unemployed British factory workers living in desperate poverty. The comparison between contented southern slaves and miserable northern "wage slaves" was frequently made by proslavery advocates.

CHRONOLOGY

1790s	Second Great Awakening
	Black Baptist and African Methodist Episcopal churches founded
1793	Cotton gin invented
1800	Gabriel Prosser's revolt discovered in Virginia
1806	Virginia tightens law on manumission of slaves
1808	Congress prohibits U.S. participation in the international slave trade
1816–20	"Alabama Fever": migration to the Old Southwest
1819–20	Missouri Crisis
1822	Denmark Vesey's conspiracy in Charleston
1831	Nat Turner's revolt in Virginia
	William Lloyd Garrison begins publishing antislavery newspaper, the *Liberator*
1832	Nullification Crisis
1832–38	"Flush Times": second wave of westward expansion
1832	Virginia legislature debates and defeats a measure for gradual emancipation
1833	Britain frees slaves throughout the empire, including the West Indies
1835	Charleston crowd burns abolitionist literature
	Tightening of black codes completed by southern legislatures
1836	Congress passes "gag rule" to prevent discussion of antislavery petitions
	James Henry Hammond announces to Congress that slavery is not evil
1854	George Fitzhugh publishes *Sociology for the South*, a defense of slavery
1857	Hinton Helper publishes *The Impending Crisis*, an attack on slavery
1858	James Henry Hammond's "King Cotton" speech

In 1854 another southern spokesman, George Fitzhugh, asserted that "the negro slaves of the South are the happiest, and, in some sense, the freest people in the world" because all the responsibility for their care was borne by concerned white masters. Fitzhugh contrasted southern paternalism with the heartless individualism that ruled the lives of northern "wage slaves." Northern employers did not take care of their workers, Fitzhugh claimed, because "selfishness is almost the only motive of human conduct in free society, where every man is taught that it is his first duty to change and better his pecuniary situation." In contrast, Fitzhugh argued, southern masters and their slaves were bound together by a "community of interests."

Changes in the South

In spite of these defensive and repressive proslavery measures, which made the South seem monolithic in northern eyes, there were some surprising indicators of dissent. Most came from up-country nonslaveholders. One protest occurred in the Virginia state legislature in 1832, when nonslaveholding delegates, alarmed by the Nat Turner rebellion, forced a two-week debate on the merits of gradual abolition. In the final vote, abolition was defeated 73 to 58. Although the subject was never raised again, this debate was a startling indicator of frequently unvoiced doubts about slavery that existed in the South.

But slavery was not a static system. From the 1830s on, financial changes increasingly underlined class differences between southern whites. It was harder to become a slaveholder: from 1830 to 1860 slave owners declined from 36 to 25 percent of the population. In 1860 the average slaveholder was ten times as wealthy as the average nonslaveholder. A major reason for the shrinking number of slave owners and their increased wealth was the rapidly increasing price of slaves: a "prime field hand" was worth more than $1,500 in 1855. Such prices caused the internal slave trade to flourish: during the 1850s slave owners from the Upper South sold some 250,000 slaves to the Lower South for handsome profits. Such a difference in the extent of slaveholding between Upper and Lower South threatened regional political unity and provoked concern. One remedy suggested in South Carolina was to reopen the international slave trade!

Economic changes adversely affected poor whites and yeomen as well. Increased commercialization of agriculture (other than cotton) led to higher land prices that made it harder for poor whites to buy or rent land. Extensive railroad building in up-country regions during the boom of the 1850s ended the isolation of many yeomen, exposing them for the first time to the temptations and dangers of the market economy. While slave owners grew increasingly worried about threats from the abolitionist and capitalist North, yeomen worried about local threats to their independence from banks, railroads, and activist state governments. In North Carolina, disputes between slave owners and nonslaveholders erupted in print in 1857, when Hinton Helper published an attack on slavery in a book titled *The Impending Crisis*. His protest was an indicator of the growing tensions between the haves and the have-nots in the South. Equally significant, though, Helper's book was published in New York, where he was forced to move once his views became known.

In spite of these signs of tension and dissent, the main lines of the southern argument were drawn in the 1830s and remained fixed thereafter. The defense of slavery stifled debate within the South, prevented a search for alternative labor systems, and narrowed the possibility of cooperation in national politics. In time, it made compromise impossible.

CONCLUSION

The amazing growth of cotton production after 1793 transformed the South and the nation. Physically, the South expanded explosively westward: in all, seven southern and southwestern states were admitted to the Union between 1800 and 1845. Cotton production fastened the slave system of labor upon the region. Although the international slave trade was abolished in 1808, the internal slave trade flourished, with devastating effects on African American families. Nationally, the profitable cotton trade fueled economic development and provided much of the original capital for the infant factory system of the North. Cotton production was based on the labor of African American slaves, who built strong communities under extremely difficult circumstances. The cohesion of African American families and the powerful faith of African American Christianity were the key community elements that bred a spirit of endurance and resistance. White Southerners, two-thirds of whom did not own slaves, denied their real dependence on slave labor by claiming equality in white skin privilege, while slave owners boasted of their own paternalism. But the extreme fear generated by a handful of slave revolts, the exaggerated reaction to the race mixing of Natchez-under-the Hill, and the growing number of free African Americans in many areas gave the lie to white claims of benevolence. In the 1830s, the South defensively closed ranks against real and perceived threats to the slave system. In this sense, the white South was nearly as trapped as the African American slaves they claimed to control. And in defending the slave system, the South was increasingly different from the dynamic capitalist free labor system that was gaining strength in the North.

REVIEW QUESTIONS

1. How did cotton production after 1793 transform the social and political history of the South? How did the rest of the nation benefit? In what way was it an "international phenomenon"?

2. What were the two key institutions of the African American slave community? How did they function, and what beliefs did they express?

3. The circumstances of three very different groups—poor whites, educated and property-owning American Indians, and free African Americans—put them outside the dominant southern equation of white equals free and black equals slave. Analyze the difficulty each group encountered in the slave-owning South.

4. Who were the yeoman farmers? What was their interest in slavery?

5. Southern slaveholders claimed that their paternalism justified their ownership of slaves, but paternalism implied obligations as well as privileges. How well do you think slaveholders lived up to their paternalistic obligations?

6. How did slaveowners justify slavery? How did their defense change over time?

RECOMMENDED READING

Ira Berlin, *Slaves without Masters* (1974). A full portrait of the lives of free black people in the South before the Civil War.

Charles C. Bolton, *Poor Whites of the Antebellum South: Tenants and Laborers in Central North and Northeast Mississippi* (1994). A careful consideration of a hitherto "invisible" population.

B. A. Botkin, ed., *Lay My Burden Down: A Folk History of Slavery* (1945). One of the first of many volumes drawing on the words of former slaves concerning their memories of slavery.

Orville Vernon Burton, *In My Father's House Are Many Mansions: Family and Community in Edgefield, South Carolina* (1985). A detailed community study that considers the farms, families, and everyday relations of white and black people in the period 1850–80.

Thomas D. Clark and John D. W. Guice, *Frontiers in Conflict: The Old Southwest, 1795–1830* (1989). Considers the Indian nations and their removal, white settlement, and the economic development of the region.

Catherine Clinton, *The Plantation Mistress: Woman's World in the Old South* (1982). Illustrates how slavery shaped the lives of elite white women. The exclusive focus on white women, however, neglects the black women with whom they lived on a daily basis.

Drew Gilpin Faust, *James Henry Hammond and the Old South* (1982). This outstanding biography uses the complex and interesting story of one man's life and ambitions to tell a larger story about southern attitudes and politics.

Lacy K. Ford Jr., *Origins of Southern Radicalism: The South Carolina Upcountry, 1800–1860* (1988). One of a growing number of studies of up-country nonslaveholders and their commitment to liberty and equality.

Eugene Genovese, *Roll, Jordan, Roll: The World the Slaves Made* (1974). The landmark book that redirected the attention of historians from slaves as victims to the slave community as an active participant in the paternalism of the southern slave system.

Steven Hahn, *The Roots of Southern Populism: Yeoman Farmers and the Transformation of the Georgia Upcountry, 1850–1890* (1983). One of the first studies of the changing world of southern yeomen.

Bruce Levine, *Half Slave and Half Free: The Roots of Civil War* (1992). A useful survey of the different lines of development of the northern and southern economies and the political conflicts between the regions.

Stephanie McCurry, *Masters of Small Worlds: Yeoman Households, Gender Relations, and the Political Culture of the Antebellum South Carolina Low Country* (1995). A study of yeomen that links their prized political and economic independence with their strong patriarchal control over their own families.

James Oakes, *The Ruling Race: A History of American Slaveholders* (1982). Oakes disagrees with Genovese's characterization of paternalism and sees slave owners instead as entrepreneurial capitalists. Especially useful for distinguishing the various classes of slave owners.

Peter J. Parish, *Slavery: History and Historians* (1989). A useful survey and synopsis of a large literature.

Brenda Stevenson, *Life in Black and White: Family and Community in the Slave South* (1996). A careful study of families, black and white, in Louden County, Virginia, that illustrates the difficulties both free and enslaved African American families faced.

Michael Tadman, *Speculators and Slaves: Masters, Traders, and Slaves in the Old South* (1989). Examines the extent, organization, and values of the internal slave trade.

ADDITIONAL BIBLIOGRAPHY

King Cotton

Peter A. Coclanis, *The Shadow of a Dream: Economic Life and Death in the South Carolina Low Country, 1670–1920* (1989)

Robert W. Fogel and Stanley Engerman, *Time on the Cross: The Economics of American Negro Slavery* (1974)

Joseph P. Reidy, *From Slavery to Agrarian Capitalism in the Cotton Plantation South: Central Georgia, 1800–1880* (1992)

Harold D. Woodman, *Slavery and the Southern Economy* (1966)

Gavin Wright, *The Political Economy of the Cotton South: Households, Markets, and Wealth in the Nineteenth Century* (1978)

Slavery and African American Communities

John Blassingame, *The Slave Community*, rev. ed. (1979)

Randolph B. Campbell, *An Empire for Slavery: The Peculiar Institution in Texas, 1821–1865* (1989)

Charles T. Davis and Henry Louis Gates Jr., eds., *The Slave's Narrative* (1985)

Carl N. Degler, *Neither White nor Black: Slavery and Race Relations in Brazil and the United States* (1971)

Charles B. Dew, *Bond of Iron: Master and Slave at Buffalo Forge* (1994)

Merton L. Dillon, *Slavery Attacked: Southern Slaves and Their Allies, 1619–1865* (1990)

Douglas Egerton, *Gabriel's Rebellion: The Virginia Slave Conspiracies of 1800 and 1802* (1993)

Paul D. Escott, *Slavery Remembered: A Record of Twentieth-Century Slave Narratives* (1979)

Barbara Field, *Slavery on the Middle Ground: Maryland during the Nineteenth Century* (1985)

Eugene D. Genovese, *From Rebellion to Revolution: Afro-American Slave Revolts in the Making of the Modern World* (1979)

Claudia D. Goldin, *Urban Slavery in the American South, 1820–1860* (1976)

Nathan Huggins, *Black Odyssey: The Afro-American Ordeal in Slavery* (1977)

Michael P. Johnson and James L. Roark, *Black Masters: A Free Family of Color in the Old South* (1984)

————, *No Chariot Down: Charleston's Free People of Color on the Eve of the Civil War* (1984)

Charles Joyner, *Down by the Riverside: A South Carolina Slave Community* (1984)

Peter Kolchin, *American Slavery, 1619–1877* (1993)

Lawrence W. Levine, *Black Culture and Black Consciousness: Afro-American Folk Thought from Slavery to Freedom* (1977)

Ann Patton Malone, *Sweet Chariot: Slave Family and Household Structure in Nineteenth-Century Louisiana* (1992)

Melton McLaurin, *Celia: A Slave* (1991)

Stephen B. Oates, *The Fires of Jubilee: Nat Turner's Fierce Rebellion* (1975)

Albert Raboteau, *Slave Religion: The "Invisible Institution" in the Antebellum South* (1978)

Willie Lee Rose, *A Documentary History of Slavery in North America* (1976)

Kenneth Stampp, *The Peculiar Institution* (1956)

Robert Starobin, *Industrial Slavery in the Old South* (1970)

Sterling Stuckey, *Slave Culture: Nationalist Theory and the Foundation of Black America* (1987)

David E. Swift, *Black Prophets of Justice: Activist Clergy before the Civil War* (1989)

Thomas L. Webber, *Deep Like Rivers: Education in the Slave Quarters, 1831–1865* (1978)

Deborah Gray White, *Arn't I a Woman?* (1985)

Yeomen, Planters, and the Defense of Slavery

David T. Bailey, *Shadow on the Church: Southwestern Evangelical Religion and the Issue of Slavery, 1783–1860* (1985)

Carol Bleser, ed., *In Joy and in Sorrow: Women, Family, and Marriage in the Victorian South, 1830–1900* (1991)

Dickson D. Bruce, *Violence and Culture in the Antebellum South* (1979)

Joan Cashin, *A Family Venture: Men and Women on the Southern Frontier* (1991)

Bill Cecil-Fronsman, *Common White: Class and Culture in Antebellum North Carolina* (1992)

Jane T. Censer, *North Carolina Planters and Their Children, 1800–1860* (1984)

Bruce Collins, *White Society in the Antebellum South* (1985)

William J. Cooper, *The South and the Politics of Slavery, 1829–1856* (1978)

————, *Liberty and Slavery: Southern Politics to 1860* (1983)

Daniel Dupre, *Transforming the Cotton Frontier: Madison County, Alabama, 1800–1840* (1997)

Clement Eaton, *The Freedom of Thought Struggle in the Old South* (1964)

Drew Gilpin Faust, ed. *The Ideology of Slavery: Proslavery Thought in the Antebellum South, 1830–1860* (1981)

Drew Gilpin Faust, *Southern Stories: Slaveholders in Peace and War* (1992)

Elizabeth Fox-Genovese, *Within the Plantation Household* (1988)

John Hope Franklin, *The Militant South 1800–1861* (1956)

George M. Frederickson, *White Supremacy: A Comparative Study in American and South African History* (1981)

————, *The Black Image in the White Mind: The Debate on Afro-American Character and Destiny, 1817–1914* (1971)

Jean Friedman, *The Enclosed Garden: Women and Community in the Evangelical South, 1830–1900* (1985)

J. William Harris, *Plain Folk and Gentry in a Slave Society: White Liberty and Black Slavery in Augusta's Hinterlands* (1985)

Suzanne Lebsock, *The Free Women of Petersburg: Status and Culture in a Southern Town, 1784–1860* (1984)

Donald G. Mathews, *Religion in the Old South* (1977)

John McCardell, *The Idea of a Southern Nation: Southern Nationalists and Southern Nationalism, 1830–1860* (1979)

Christopher Morris, *Becoming Southern: The Evolution of a Way of Life, Warren County and Vicksburg, Mississippi, 1770–1860* (1995)

James Oakes, *Slavery and Freedom: An Interpretation of the Old South* (1990)

Frank Owsley, *Plain Folk in the South* (1949)

Anne F. Scott, *The Southern Lady, from Pedestal to Politics, 1830–1930* (1970)

Steven Stowe, *Intimacy and Power in the Old South: Ritual in the Lives of the Planters* (1987)

Bertram Wyatt-Brown, *Southern Honor: Ethics and Behavior in the Old South* (1982)

CHAPTER TWELVE

INDUSTRY AND THE NORTH
1790s–1840s

Unidentified artist, *Middlesex Company Woolen Mills of Lowell, Mass.* ca. 1848. Oil on canvas. Museum of American Textile History, North Andover, Mass.

AMERICAN COMMUNITIES
Women Factory Workers Form a Community in Lowell, Massachusetts

In the 1820s and 1830s, young farm women from all over New England flocked to Lowell to work a twelve-hour day in one of the first cotton textile factories in America. Living six to eight to a room in nearby boardinghouses, the women of Lowell earned an average of $3 a week. Some also attended inexpensive nighttime lectures or classes. Lowell, considered a model factory town, drew worldwide attention. As one admirer of its educated workers said, Lowell was less a factory than a "philanthropic manufacturing college."

The Boston investors who financed Lowell were businessmen, not philanthropists, but they wanted to keep Lowell free of the dirt, poverty, and social disorder that made English factory towns notorious. Built in 1823, Lowell boasted six neat factory buildings grouped around a central clock tower, the area pleasantly landscaped with flowers, shrubs, and trees. Housing was similarly well ordered: a Georgian mansion for the company agent; trim houses for the overseers; row houses for the mechanics and their families; and boardinghouses, each supervised by a responsible matron, for the workforce that made Lowell famous—young New England farm women.

The choice of young women as factory workers seemed shockingly unconventional. In the 1820s and 1830s, young unmarried women simply did not live alone; they lived and worked with their parents until they married. In these years of growth and westward expansion, however, America was chronically short of labor, and the Lowell manufacturers were shrewd enough to realize that young farm women were an untapped labor force. For farmers' sons, the lure of acquiring their own farms in the West was much stronger than factory wages, but for their sisters, escaping from rural isolation and earning a little money was an appealing way to spend a few years before marriage. To attract respectable young women, Lowell offered supervision both on the job and at home, with strict rules of conduct, compulsory religious services, cultural opportunities such as concerts and lectures, and cash wages.

When they first arrived in Lowell, the young women were often bewildered by the large numbers of townspeople and embarrassed by their own rural clothing and ways of speech. The air of the mill was hot, humid, and full of cotton lint, and the noise of the machinery—"The buzzing and hissing and whizzing of pulleys and rollers and spindles and flyers"—was constant. Very quickly, however, other women workers—often their own sisters or neighbors who had preceded them to the mill—helped them adjust. It was company policy for senior women to train the newcomers. The work itself was simple, consisting largely of knotting broken threads on spinning machines and power looms. Most women enjoyed the work. They were not bothered by the long hours; farm people were accustomed to long days. One woman wrote home: "The work is not disagreeable. It tried my patience sadly at first, but in general I like it very much. It is easy to do, and does not require very violent exertion, as much of our farm work does."

The most novel aspect of textile mills was a rigid work schedule. Power-driven machinery operated at a sustained, uniform pace throughout every mill; human workers had to learn to do the same. Each mill published elaborate schedules and imposed fines and penalties on latecomers. It was this kind of precise work schedule that represented the single largest change from preindustrial work habits; it was the hardest for workers to adjust to. Moreover, each mill positioned one or two overseers on every floor to make sure the pace was maintained. Men held these positions, and they earned more than the women who made up most of the workforce; this arrangement was unquestioned.

Why did young women come to Lowell? Some worked out of need and some to add to their family's income, but most regarded Lowell as opportunity. It was escape from rural isolation and from parental supervision, a chance to buy the latest fashions and learn "city ways," to attend lectures and concerts, to save for a dowry or to pay for an education. As writer Lucy Larcom, one of the most famous workers, said, the young farm women who came to Lowell sought "an opening into freer life." Working side by side and living in company boardinghouses with six to twelve other women, some of whom might be relatives or friends from home, the Lowell women built a close, supportive community for themselves.

The owners of Lowell made large profits. They also drew praise for their carefully managed community with its intelligent and independent workforce. But their success was short-lived. In the 1830s, because of competition and poor economic conditions, the owners imposed wage cuts and work speedups that their model workforce did not take lightly. Although the Lowell women had been brought together under a system of paternalistic control, the close bonds they forged in the boardinghouses gave them the courage and solidarity to "turn out" in spontaneous protests, which were, however, unsuccessful in reversing the wage cuts. By 1850 the "philanthropic manufacturing college" was no more. The original Lowell workforce of New England farm girls had been replaced by poor Irish immigrants of both sexes, who tended more machines for much less pay than their predecessors. Now Lowell was simply another mill town.

The history of Lowell epitomizes the process by which the North (both New England and the Middle Atlantic states) began to change from a society composed largely of self-sufficient farm families (Jefferson's "yeoman farmers") to one of urban wage-workers in an industrial economy. Industrialization did not occur overnight. Large factories were not common until the 1880s, but by that decade most workers had already experienced a fundamental change in their working patterns. Once under way, the market revolution changed the very basis of community: how people worked, how they thought, how they lived. In the early years of the nineteenth century, northern communities led this transformation, fostering attitudes far different from those prevalent in the South.

Lowell

KEY TOPICS

- Preindustrial ways of working and living

- The nature of the market revolution

- The effects of industrialization on workers in early factories

- Ways the market revolution changed the lives of ordinary people

- The emergence of the middle class

PREINDUSTRIAL WAYS OF WORKING

The Lowell mill was a dramatic example of the changes factories imposed on people's accustomed ways of working and interacting with each other. To fully understand the novelty of these changes in long-established patterns of work, it is important to understand traditional ways of working on farms—where 97 percent of all Americans lived in 1800—and in cities.

Rural Life: The Springer Family

The young family of Thomas and Elizabeth Springer began farming near the city of Wilmington in Mill Creek, Delaware, in the 1790s. Although no single family can represent all of the nation's farmers, a close look at the Springers can help to identify traditional patterns and the seeds of commercial change. The Springers, who had two infant daughters, owned 129 acres of farmland, 104 of which Thomas Springer had bought from his father for less than the market price. At twenty-nine, Springer, to whom family wealth had given a substantial advantage, owned four African American slaves: Ace, a young man; Sara and Amelia, young girls; and Will, aged sixty. Ace was in the process of buying his freedom, something he could not have done further south.

Although Delaware remained a slave state until the Civil War, as the case of Ace suggests, it developed differently from states further south. By 1861, only 2 percent of the state's population was still enslaved. In part this decline reflected the strong antislavery feeling that many residents of Delaware shared with people in the neighboring free state of Pennsylvania. But it was primarily because farmers like Thomas Springer found their soil was not suitable for growing cotton, the crop that fastened slavery on the states of the deep south (see Chapter 11).

The Springers had access to a commercial market for their crops. From their herd of thirty or forty sheep and at least fifteen milking cows, the Springers provided Wilmington butchers with some livestock, and they sold wool, milk, and butter in local markets. They also raised oats, hay, and Indian corn to feed the livestock, as well as wheat and vegetables for both family use and commercial sale. They may have sold some of the wheat to Wilmington merchants for transshipment to Philadelphia and then Europe, but in general the Springers, like most preindustrial farm families, planted and produced a diverse range of crops for their own use. Only after their own needs were met did they sell their surplus on the commercial market.

It was Elizabeth Springer who, with the help of the female slaves and perhaps female relatives, was in charge of spinning the wool and collecting the dairy cows' milk that was intended for sale, and she was also responsible for preparing all the farm meals and preserving the vegetables and fruits grown for the family. Both the Springers, who had family living nearby, and all the neighboring farmers who made up the larger community shared their labor with each other in a barter system. They helped each other construct houses and barns, pick apples, thresh wheat, cut firewood, and prune trees. Neighbor women assisted one another in childbirth. Thus the Springers, like their neighbors, produced goods for their own use, for a community network, and for a larger, cash market, in that order. This kind of community network of barter and mutual obligation characterized traditional farming families throughout the nation. But because of the thriving market in nearby Wilmington, the Springers already, in a small way, had begun the transition from traditional to commercial agriculture.

The Family Labor System

In the traditional, preindustrial economy, people like the Springers did most of their work at or near their homes. One kind of traditional work was the labor of caring for the home itself and for its members, including spinning, weaving, and sewing clothes for everyone. These jobs, which fell to the women of the family, were time-consuming, multistage activities that occupied much of the year. Mothers introduced their daughters to the easiest tasks, such as carding wool, at a young age, and taught them the more difficult skills of spinning and weaving as they grew older. This infor-

In the 1840s Edward Hicks painted his childhood home, rendering an idealized image of rural harmony that owes more to faith in republican agrarianism than to the artist's accurate memory. The prosperous preindustrial farm depicted was similar to the Springers' farm described in the text in its mixed yield—sheep, cattle, dairy products, and field crops—and in its employment of an African American farm worker, shown plowing.

goods and services originating in the home were part of the complicated reciprocal arrangements among community residents who knew each other well. The "just price" for an item was set by agreement among neighbors, not by some impersonal market. Another characteristic of traditional rural work was its relatively slow, unscheduled, task-oriented pace. There was no fixed production schedule or specified period of time for task completion. People did their jobs as they needed to be done, along with the daily household routine. "Home" and "work" were not separate locations or activities, but intermixed.

Urban Artisans and Workers

In urban areas, skilled craftsmen had controlled preindustrial production since the early colonial period. Trades were perpetuated through a formal system of apprenticeship in which a boy went to work in the shop of a master, usually at the age of twelve or fourteen. Over the next three to seven years the young apprentice learned all aspects of the craft, gaining increasing responsibility and status as the day approached when he could strike out on his own. During that time, the master not only taught the apprentice his trade but housed, fed, and clothed him. Usually the apprentice lived with the master craftsman and was treated more like a member of the family than an employee. Thus the family-learning model used on farms was formalized in the urban apprenticeship system. At the end of the contract period the apprentice became a journeyman craftsman. Journeymen worked for wages in the shop of a master craftsman until they had enough capital to set up shop for themselves. Generally, they could not afford to marry until they achieved master status.

mal family apprenticeship system was echoed in the barn and field tasks sons learned from their fathers. In this way one generation passed along essential skills to the next generation.

On the rocky farms of New England, where farm surpluses were rare and a home-produced item was cheaper and easier to obtain than an item from Britain or even Boston, many farmers worked off the farm at some other job. Sometimes an entire family developed a skill such as shoemaking that they could practice over the long New England winters. Much of what families crafted was for local and immediate use, not for a distant market. Among New England farmers, the need to find several jobs bred ingenuity and flexibility. As Noah Webster observed in 1785, "Every man is in some measure an artist—he makes a variety of utensils, rough indeed, but such as will answer his purpose—he is a husbandman [farmer] in summer and mechanic in winter."

Two other notable characteristics of rural home production were slated soon to disappear. First, things had no fixed prices, and money rarely exchanged hands. People usually paid for a home-crafted item or a neighbor's help with a particular task in foodstuffs or a piece of clothing or by helping the neighbor with a job he needed to have done. Thus

Like farmers, urban artisans usually kept long hours—sunup to sundown was common—but the pace of work varied enormously with the time of year and the number of orders. And work was frequently interrupted by family activities and neighborliness. Most cities were densely settled, and one bumped into one's neighbors all the time. Sales, business contracts, meals, and other occasions were often accompanied by a friendly drink of rum or other spirits. There was no clear separation between work and leisure.

Although women as well as men did task-oriented skilled work, the formal apprenticeship system was exclusively for men. Because it was assumed that women would marry, most people thought that all girls needed to learn were domestic skills. Women who needed or wanted work, however, found a small niche of respectable occupations as domestic servants, laundresses, or seamstresses, often in the homes of the wealthy, or as cooks in small restaurants or street food vendors. Some owned and managed boardinghouses. Prostitution, another common female occupation (especially in seaport cities) was not respectable.

Patriarchy in Family, Work, and Society

Like the farm family, an entire urban household was commonly organized around one kind of work. Usually the family lived at the shop or store, and all family members worked with the craftsman at his trade. A printer's wife, for example, would be capable of keeping most of the shop's functions going in the printer's absence and of supervising the work of apprentices and

Every small community had artisans such as blacksmiths and wheelwrights who did such essential work as shoeing horses and mending wagons for local farmers. Artist John Neagle's heroic image of the blacksmith Pat Lyon presents him as the very model of honest industry.

her children. Some artisans, like blacksmiths, needed shops separate from their homes but probably relied on their children to fetch and carry and to help with some of the work. Others, like bakers, who generally had to get up in the middle of the night to perform their work, relied on their wives to sell their products during the day.

In both rural and urban settings, working families were organized along strictly patriarchal lines. The man had unquestioned authority to direct the lives and work of family members and apprentices and to decide on occupations for his sons and marriages for his daughters. His wife had many crucial responsibilities—feeding, clothing, child rearing, taking care of apprentices, and all the other domestic affairs of the household—but in all these duties she was subject to the direction of her husband. Men were heads of families and bosses of artisanal shops; although entire families were engaged in the enterprise, the husband and father was the trained craftsman, and assistance by the family was informal and generally unrecognized.

The patriarchal organization of the family was reflected in society as a whole. Legally, men had all the power: neither women nor children had property or legal rights. For example, a married woman's property belonged to her husband, a woman could not testify on her own behalf in court, and in the rare cases of divorce the husband kept the children, for they were considered his property. When a man died, his son or sons inherited his property. It was customary to allow widows the use of one-third of the property, but unfilial sons could deprive their mothers of support if they chose. Some widows successfully continued a family business, and some single daughters received inheritances from rich fathers, but these were exceptions. The basic principle was that the man, as head of the household, represented the common interests of everyone for whom he was responsible—women, children, servants, apprentices. He thus controlled everything of value, and he alone could vote for political office.

The Social Order

In this preindustrial society everyone, from the smallest yeoman farmer to the largest urban merchant, had a fixed place in the social order. The social status of artisans was below that of wealthy merchants but decidedly above that of common laborers. Yeoman farmers, less grand than large landowners, ranked above tenant farmers and farm laborers. Although men of all social ranks mingled in their daily work, they did not mingle as equals, for great importance was placed on rank and status, which were distinguished by dress and manner. Although by the 1790s many artisans who owned property were voters and vocal participants in urban politics, few directly challenged the traditional

Percent	Percent of Wealth Held			
of the Population	1687	1771	1833	1848
Top 1 percent	10%	16%	33%	37%
Top 10 percent	42	65	75	82
Lowest 80 percent	39	29	14	4

WEALTH IN BOSTON, 1687–1848

This table tracing the distribution of wealth in Boston reflects the gains made by merchants during the international shipping boom of 1790–1807 and the way in which intermarriage between wealthy families consolidated these gains.

authority of the rich and powerful to run civic affairs. The rapid spread of universal white manhood suffrage after 1800 democratized politics (see Chapter 10). At the same time, economic changes undermined the preindustrial social order.

Beginning to upset this social order were a few wealthy artisans in seacoast cities like New York. Cabinetmaker Duncan Phyfe, who gave his name to a distinctive style of furniture, is one example. Phyfe, immigrating from Scotland, opened his first shop in 1792. By 1815 he had an elegant salesroom, three workshops employing up to 100 journeymen, and a fortune of $500,000, much of it from real estate investments. Another successful New York artisan, Stephen Allen, began as an apprentice sailmaker. Allen made his fortune when he arranged to bypass the traditional middlemen and buy his materials directly from wholesalers. His sailmaking operation made a profit of $100,000 between 1802 and 1825, and when he retired he was elected mayor of New York, customarily a position reserved for gentlemen. These New York artisans, and others like them in other cities, owed much of their success to the ever-expanding effects of the economic upheaval known as the market revolution.

THE MARKET REVOLUTION

The market revolution, the most fundamental change American communities ever experienced, was the outcome of three interrelated developments: rapid improvements in transportation (see Chapter 10), commercialization, and industrialization. Improved transportation allowed both people and goods to move with new ease and speed. Commercialization involved the replacement of household self-sufficiency and barter with the production of goods for a cash market. And industrialization involved the use of power-driven machinery to produce goods once made by hand. Taken together, these three developments rapidly joined most ordinary Americans into a commercial market that supplied them with abundant quantities of inexpensive manufactured goods.

The Accumulation of Capital

In the northern states, the business community was composed largely of merchants in the seaboard cities: Boston, Providence, New York, Philadelphia, and Baltimore. Many had made substantial profits in the international shipping boom of the period 1790–1807 (as discussed in Chapter 9). During those years, the proportion of American trade carried in American ships jumped from 59 percent to 92 percent, and earnings to American merchants rose from $5.9 million to $42.1 million.

Such extraordinary opportunities attracted enterprising people. Established merchants like Philadelphia's Robert Morris opened up new markets such as the China trade, but there was room for newcomers as well. John Jacob Astor, who had arrived penniless from Germany in 1784, made his first fortune in the Pacific Northwest fur trade with China and eventually dominated the fur trade in the United States through his American Fur Company. Astor made a second fortune in New York real estate, and when he retired in 1834 with $25 million he was reputed to be the wealthiest man in America. Many similar stories of success, though not so fabulous as Astor's, demonstrated that risk-takers might reap rich rewards in international trade.

But the early years of the nineteenth century posed difficulties for international trade. Following the 1807 Embargo Act only the most daring American merchants were willing to risk restrictions and the chance of capture to reap exceptional profits. More cautious men perceived opportunity in the potentially huge domestic American market, deprived of cheap British goods by war in Europe (and later, the War of 1812) and underserved by the traditional family-centered, slow-paced, and localized system of skilled craftsmanship. Mobilizing the capital available within the business community, merchants began to control, transform, and increase American home-based production.

Some of the nation's wealthiest men turned to local investments. In Providence, Rhode Island, Moses Brown and his son-in-law William Almy began to invest some of the profits the Brown family had reaped from a worldwide trade in iron, candles, rum, and African slaves in the new manufacture of cotton textiles. Philadelphia merchant and banker Stephen

Girard, who had made his fortune in the West Indies trade, invested in the Lehigh Valley coalfields and in the canals and railroads that linked the coalfields to Philadelphia. Cincinnati merchants banded together to finance the building of the first steamboats to operate on the Ohio River. And even in rural towns, local merchants and shopkeepers invested in the work of local craftsmen.

Much of the capital for the new investments came from banks, both those in seaport cities that had been established for the international trade and those, like the Lynn, Massachusetts, Mechanics Bank, founded in 1814 by a group of Lynn's Quaker merchants, that served local clients. An astonishing amount of capital, however, was raised through family connections. In the late eighteenth century, members of the business communities in the seaboard cities had begun to consolidate their position and property by intermarriage. In Boston, such a strong community developed that when Francis Cabot Lowell needed $300,000 in 1813 to build the world's first automated cotton mill in Waltham, Massachusetts (the prototype of the Lowell mills), he had only to turn to his family network.

Although much of the original capital for American manufacturing, such as Almy and Brown's collaboration with Samuel Slater, came from the shipping boom of 1790–1807, southern cotton provided the capital for continuing development. Because Northerners built the nation's ships, controlled the shipping trade, and provided the nation's banking, insurance, and financial services, the astounding growth in southern cotton exports enriched northern merchants almost as much as southern planters. In 1825, for example, of the 204,000 bales of cotton shipped from New Orleans, about one-third (69,000) were transshipped through the northern ports of New York, Philadelphia, and Boston. Southerners complained that their combined financial and shipping costs diverted forty cents of every dollar paid for their cotton to northerners. Profits from cotton shipping provided some of the funds the Boston Associates made available to Francis Cabot Lowell. In another example, New York merchant Anson Phelps invested the profits he made from cotton shipping in iron mines in Pennsylvania and metalworks in Connecticut. Although imperfectly understood at the time, the truth is that the development of northern industry was paid for by southern cotton produced by enslaved African American labor.

The Putting-Out System

Initially, the American business community invested not in machinery and factories but in the "putting-out system" of home manufacture, thereby expanding and transforming it. In this significant departure from preindustrial work, people still produced goods at home but under the direction of a merchant, who "put out" the raw materials to them, paid them a certain sum per finished piece, and sold the completed item to a distant market.

A crucial aspect of the new putting-out system was the division of labor. In the preindustrial system, an individual worker or his household made an entire item—a shoe, for example. Now an unskilled worker often made only a part of the finished product in large quantities for low per-piece wages.

The change in the shoe industry in Lynn, Massachusetts, shows how the putting-out system transformed American manufacturing. Long a major center of the shoe industry, Lynn, in 1800, produced 400,000 pairs of shoes—enough for every fifth person in the country. The town's 200 master artisans and their families, including journeymen and apprentices, worked together in hundreds of small home workshops called "ten-footers" (from their size, about ten feet square). The artisans and journeymen cut the leather, the artisans' wives and daughters did the binding of the upper parts of the shoe, the men stitched the shoe together, and children and apprentices helped where needed. In the early days, the artisan commonly bartered his shoes for needed products. For example, in 1773, a Lynn shopkeeper wrote to Providence merchant Nicholas Brown (Moses Brown's brother) offering to trade 100 pairs of shoes for 100 pounds of tea! Sometimes an artisan sold his shoes to a larger retailer in Boston or Salem, and sometimes a sea captain arranged to lend an artisan money for the raw materials and then sold the finished shoes at every port his ship visited. Although production of shoes in Lynn increased yearly from 1780 to 1810 as markets widened, shoes continued to be manufactured in traditional artisanal ways.

The investment of merchant capital in the shoe business changed everything. In Lynn, a small group of Quaker shopkeepers and merchants, connected by family, religious, and business ties, took the lead in reorganizing the trade. Financed by the bank they founded in 1814, Lynn capitalists like Micajah Pratt built large, two-story central workshops to replace the scattered ten-footers. Pratt employed a few skilled craftsmen to cut leather for shoes, but he put out the rest of the shoemaking to less-skilled workers who were no longer connected by family ties. Individual farm women and children sewed the uppers, which, when completed, were soled by farm men and boys. Putting-out workers were paid on a piecework basis; the men and boys earned more than the women and children but much less than a master craftsman or a journeyman. This arrangement allowed the capitalist to employ much more labor for the same investment than with the traditional artisan workshop. Shoe production increased enormously: the largest central shop in 1832 turned out ten times more shoes

Woman at Spinning Wheel, ca. 1850–70. Carved and painted wood and iron. Photographed by Ken Burris. Shelburne Museum, Shelburne, Vermont.

This carved and painted figure, designed as a whirligig and trade sign, shows a woman at a spinning wheel. Until cotton textile mills industrialized this work, spinning was one of the most time-consuming tasks that women and young girls did at home.

than the largest shopkeeper had sold in 1789. Gradually the putting-out system and central workshops replaced artisan's shops. Some artisans became wealthy owners of workshops, but most became wage earners, and the apprenticeship system eventually disappeared.

The putting-out system moved the control of production from the individual artisan households to the merchant capitalists, who could now control labor costs, production goals, and shoe styles to fit certain markets. For example, the Lynn trade quickly monopolized the market for cheap boots for southern slaves and western farmers, leaving workshops in other cities to produce shoes for wealthier customers. This specialization of the national market—indeed, even thinking in terms of a national market—was new. Additionally, and most important from the capitalist's point of view, the owner of the business controlled the workers and could cut back or expand the labor force as economic and marketplace conditions warranted. The unaccustomed severity of economic slumps like the Panics of 1819 and 1837 made this flexibility especially desirable.

While the central workshop system prevailed in Lynn and in urban centers like New York City, the putting-out system also fostered a more dispersed form of home production. By 1810 there were an estimated 2,500 so-called outwork weavers in New England, operating handlooms in their own homes. Other crafts that rapidly became organized according to the putting-out system were flax and wool spinning, straw braiding, glove making, and the knitting of stockings. For example, the palm-leaf hat industry that supplied farm laborers and slaves in the South and West relied completely on women and children, who braided the straw for the hats at home part-time. Absorbed into families' overall domestic routines, the outwork activity seemed small, but the size of the industry itself was surprising: in 1837, 33,000 Massachusetts women braided palm-leaf hats, whereas only 20,000 worked in the state's cotton textile mills. They were producing for a large national market, made possible by the dramatic improvements in transportation that occurred between 1820 and 1840.

Although the putting-out system meant a loss of independence for artisans such as those in Lynn, New England farm families liked it. From their point of view, the work could easily be combined with domestic work, and the pay was a new source of income that they could use to purchase mass-produced goods—among them shoes, boots, hats, buttons, stockings, suspenders, horsewhips, machine-made textiles, and men's work clothes—rather than spend the time required to make these things themselves. It was in this way that farm families moved away from the local barter system and into a larger market economy. The longer-term consequences of industrial capitalism—the destruction of the artisan tradition and the undermining of the patriarchal family—took some years to emerge. For example, apprentices were still taken on in the Lynn shoemaking trade until 1840.

British Technology and American Industrialization

Important as were the transportation revolution and the commercialization made possible by the putting-out system, the third component of the market revolution, industrialization, brought the greatest changes to personal lives. Begun in Britain in the eighteenth century, industrialization was the result of a series of technological changes in the textile trade. Mechanization moved the production of cotton and woolen yarn out of the home to the "manufactory" ("factory" for short), where power-driven machines did the work. In marked contrast to the putting-out system, in which capitalists had dispersed work into many individual households, industrialization required workers to concentrate in factories and pace themselves to the rhythms of power-driven machinery.

Many British people, especially the elite, looked on factories with horror. In England, the first factory workers were orphaned children, women, and poor Irish immigrants. These people flooded into ill-prepared rural factory towns. Horrified at the dirt and squalor of these towns, and by the relentless pace of the machinery, British poet William Blake condemned the entire concept of industrialization, writing ominously of "dark, satanic mills." If this was progress, he wanted no part of it.

Some Americans, most notably Thomas Jefferson, shared these sentiments, basing their dream of American development on the independent yeoman farmer rather than on industrialization. But conditions in New England favored rapid industrialization. New England had swift rivers that could power factory machinery, and it had wealthy merchants looking for new ways to invest their capital. Some of these merchants, whose fortunes derived from shipping southern cotton to textile factories in England, quickly realized that the manufacturing could be done in New England—if Americans could learn the secrets of British industrial technology.

Slater's Mill

The simplest and quickest way for America to industrialize was to copy the British, but the British, well aware of the value of their machinery, enacted laws forbidding its export and even the emigration of skilled workers. Over the years, however, Americans managed to lure a number of British artisans to the United States.

In 1789 Samuel Slater, who had just finished an apprenticeship in the most up-to-date cotton spinning factory in England, disguised himself as a farm laborer and slipped out of England without even telling his mother good-bye. In Providence, Rhode Island, he met Moses Brown and William Almy, who had been trying without success to duplicate British industrial technology. Having carefully committed the designs to memory before leaving England, Slater promptly built copies of the latest British machinery for Brown and Almy. Slater's mill, as it became known, began operation in 1790. It was the most advanced cotton mill in America. Although Slater was a skilled mechanic and improved on the original British machines, it is nonetheless true that American industrialization owed its start to technology that the British had not wished to share.

Following British practice, Slater drew his workforce primarily from among young children (ages seven to twelve) and women, whom he paid much less than the handful of skilled male workers he hired to keep the machines working. The yarn spun at Slater's mill was then put out to local home weavers, who turned it into cloth on handlooms. As a result, home weaving flourished in areas near the mill, giving families a new opportunity to make money at a task with which they were already familiar. In 1790, home weavers had no way of knowing that their profitable occupation would soon be challenged by power looms in factories.

Many others followed Slater's lead, and the rivers of New England were soon dotted with mills wherever waterpower could be tapped. Embargo and war sheltered American factories from British competition from 1807 to 1815, but when the War of 1812 ended, the British cut prices ruthlessly in an effort to drive the newcomers out of business. In 1816 Congress passed the first tariff, aimed largely against British cotton textiles, in response to the clamor by New England manufacturers for protection for their young industry. Interestingly, the issue of tariff protection, usually regarded as a sectional issue between North and South (see "The Nullification Crisis" in Chapter 10) initially aroused controversy in New England, where many seaport merchants opposed it because they saw it as a threat to the international free trade from which they had so richly profited.

This early nineteenth-century watercolor shows Slater's mill, the first cotton textile mill in the United States, which depended on the waterpower of Pawtucket Falls for its energy. New England was rich in swiftly flowing streams that could provide power to spinning machines and power looms.

The Lowell Mills

Another way to deal with British competition was to beat the British at their own game. With the intention of designing better machinery, a young Bostonian, Francis Cabot Lowell, made an apparently casual tour of British textile mills in 1810. Lowell, the founder of the Lowell mills described in the opening of this chapter, made a good impression on his English hosts, who were pleased by his interest and his intelligent questions. They did not know that each night, in his hotel room, Lowell made sketches from memory of the machines he had inspected during the day.

Lowell was more than an industrial spy, however. When he returned to the United States, he went to work with a Boston mechanic, Paul Moody, to improve on the British models. Lowell and Moody not only made the machinery for spinning cotton more efficient, but they also invented a power loom. This was a great advance, for now all aspects of textile manufacture, from the initial cleaning and carding (combing) to the production of finished lengths of cloth, could be gathered together in the same factory. Such a mill required a much larger capital investment than a small spinning mill such as Slater's, but Lowell's family network gave him access to the needed funds. In 1814 he opened the world's first integrated cotton mill in Waltham, near Boston. It was a great success: in 1815, the Boston Associates (Lowell's partners) made profits of 25 percent, and their efficiency allowed them to survive the intense British competition. Many smaller New England mills did not survive, even with the tariff protection voted in 1816. The lesson was clear: size mattered.

Building Types
- ■ Factories
- ▨ Boarding Houses
- ▨ Other company housing
- ▨ Hotels
- ▨ Churches
- ▨ Municipal buildings
- ▨ Other buildings (mostly residences)

Lowell, Massachusetts, 1832 *This town plan of Lowell, Massachusetts, in 1832 illustrates the comprehensive relationship the owners envisaged between the factories and the workforce. The mills are located on the Merrimack River, while nearby are the boardinghouses for the single young female workers, row houses for the male mechanics and their families, and houses for the overseers. Somewhat farther away is the mansion of the company agent.*

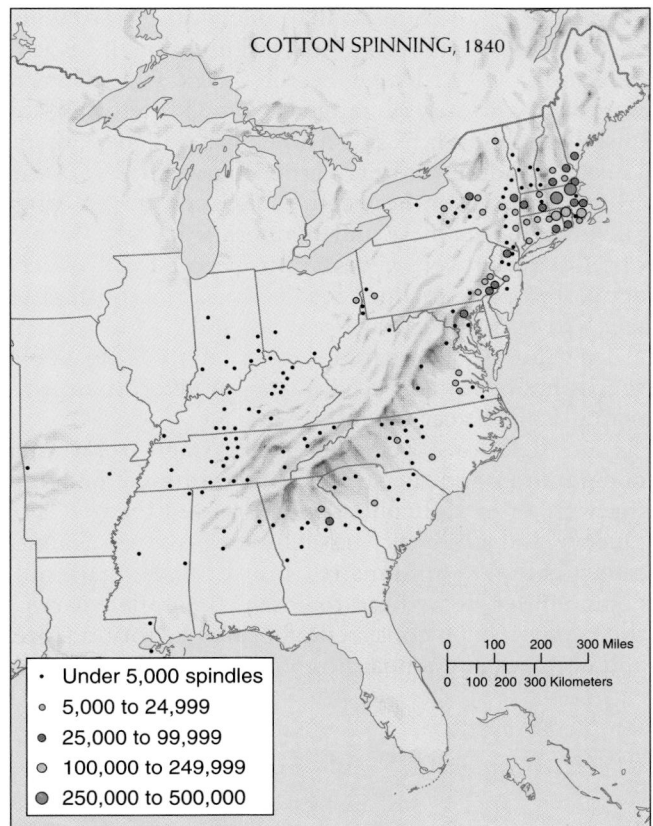

The Growth of Cotton Textile Manufacturing, 1810–1840   *Although cotton textile manufacturing spread to other parts of the country after 1810, New England never lost its early lead. By 1839, the extent of industrialization in New England far outstripped that of other regions. Although much of New England was still rural, more and more residents were drawn into the market economy. Nationally, the proportion of wage laborers rose from 12 percent in 1800 to 40 percent in 1860. The majority of them were New Englanders who had made the transition from artisan to worker.*

Source: *Atlas of the Historical Geography of the United States,* © Carnegie Institute of Washington, Plate 186.

The Boston Associates took the lesson to heart, and when they moved their enterprise to a new location in 1823, they thought big. They built an entire town at the junction of the Concord and Merrimack Rivers where the village of East Chelmsford stood, renaming it Lowell in memory of Francis, who had died, still a young man, in 1817. As the opening of this chapter describes, the new industrial community boasted six mills and company housing for all the workers. In 1826 the town had 2,500 inhabitants; ten years later the population was 17,000.

Family Mills

Lowell was unique. No other textile mill was ever such a showplace. None was as large, integrated so many tasks, or relied on such a homogeneous workforce. Its location in a new town was also unusual. Much more common in the early days of industrialization were small rural spinning mills, on the model of Slater's first

mill, built on swiftly running streams near existing farm communities. Although the economic benefits to local residents were considerable, the presence of the mills and mill workers brought rural communities troubling new issues of authority and diversity.

Because the owners of smaller mills often hired entire families, their operations came to be called family mills. The employment pattern at these mills followed that established by Slater at his first mill in 1790. Children aged eight to twelve, whose customary job was doffing (changing) bobbins on the spinning machines, made up 50 percent of the workforce. Women and men each made up about 25 percent of the workforce, but men had the most skilled and best-paid jobs.

The engagement of an entire family in a particular line of work was hardly new; both farm and artisan families were accustomed to working at a family enterprise. And unless a family member was very highly skilled, more than one worker per family was a necessity. To take one example, in the Rockdale mills, located on Chester Creek in Delaware, wages in the 1840s ranged from $1 a week for unskilled children to $12 a week for skilled workers. Unskilled adult laborers earned between $2.50 and $3.50 a week, or between $110 and $150 a year, allowing for sickness and temporary layoffs. Wages of $300 a year were necessary to keep a family safely above the poverty line. Single workers, who had to pay $70 to $100 a year for room and board, were at a disadvantage compared with a family, who could rent a house for $25 a year and survive on an estimated $200 a year for food.

Relations between these small rural mill communities and the surrounding farming communities were often difficult, as the history of the towns of Dudley and Oxford, Massachusetts, shows. Samuel Slater, now a millionaire, built three small mill communities near these towns in the early years of the century. Each consisted of a small factory, a store, and cottages and a boardinghouse for workers. Slater

In 1816 Connecticut gunsmith Simeon North did what Eli Whitney had only hoped to do. North produced the first gun with interchangeable parts. North's invention, taken up and improved by the national armories at Springfield and Harpers Ferry, formed the basis of the American system of manufactures.

or one of his sons ran the mills personally; they were not absentee owners. Most of Slater's workers came from outside the Dudley-Oxford area. They were a mixed group—single young farm women of the kind Lowell attracted, the poor and destitute, and workers from other factories looking for better conditions. They rarely stayed long: almost 50 percent of the workforce left every year.

Slater's mills provided a substantial amount of work for local people, putting out to them both the initial cleaning of the raw cotton and the much more lucrative weaving of the spun yarn. But in spite of this economic link, relations between Slater and his workers on one side and the farmers and shopkeepers of the Dudley and Oxford communities on the other were stormy. They disagreed over the building of mill dams (essential for the mill power supply, they sometimes flooded local fields), over taxes, over the upkeep of local roads, and over schools. Slater, hoping to save money and exercise more control over his mill workers' time, wanted to set up his own school for factory children. The debates were so constant, and so heated, that in 1831 Slater petitioned the Massachusetts General Court to create a separate town, Webster, that would encompass his three mill communities. For their part, the residents of Dudley and Oxford became increasingly hostile to Slater's authoritarian control, which they regarded as undemocratic. Their dislike carried over to the workers as well. Disdaining the mill workers for their poverty and transiency, people in the rural communities began referring to them as "operatives," making them somehow different in their work roles from themselves. Industrial work thus led to new social distinctions. Even though the people of Dudley and Oxford benefited from the mills, they did not fully accept the social organization on which their new prosperity rested, nor did they feel a sense of community with those who did the work that led to their increased well-being.

"The American System of Manufactures"

Not all American industrial technology was copied from British inventions, for there were many homegrown inventors. Indeed, calling Americans "mechanic[s] by nature," one Frenchman observed that "in Massachusetts and Connecticut there is not a labourer who had not invented a machine or tool." By the 1840s, to take but one example, small towns like St. Johnsbury, Vermont, boasted many small industries based on local inventions such as those by Erastus Fairbanks in scales and plows, Lemuel Hubbard in pumps, and Nicanor Kendall in guns. But perhaps most important was the pioneering American role in the development of standardized parts.

The concept of interchangeable parts, realized first in gun manufacturing, was so unusual that the British soon dubbed it "the American system of manufactures." In this system, a product such as a gun was broken down into its component parts and an exact mold was made for each. All pieces made from the same mold (after being hand filed by inexpensive unskilled laborers) matched a uniform standard. As a result, repairing a gun that malfunctioned required only installing a replacement for the defective part rather than laboriously making a new part or perhaps an entirely new gun.

Eli Whitney, the co-inventor of the cotton gin, was the first to take up the challenge of interchangeable parts, and in 1798 he contracted with the government to make 10,000 rifles in twenty-eight months, an incredibly short period had he been planning to produce each rifle by hand in the traditional way. Whitney's ideas far outran his performance. It took him ten years to fulfill his contract, and even then he had not managed to perfect the production of all the rifle parts. Two other New Englanders, Simeon North and John Hall, created milling machines that could grind parts to the required specifications and brought the concept to fruition, North in 1816 and Hall in 1824. Subsidized by the government to make rifles for the national armory at Harpers Ferry, Virginia, Hall wrote triumphantly to the secretary of war, "I have succeeded in an object which has hitherto baffled...all the endeavors of those who have heretofore attempted it—I have succeeded in establishing methods of fabricating arms exactly alike." When the system of interchangeable machine-made parts was adopted by the other national armory, at Springfield, Massachusetts, the Springfield rifle got its name.

America's early lead in interchangeable parts was a substantial source of national pride. As American gunmaker Samuel Colt boasted, "There is nothing that cannot be made by machine." Standardized production quickly revolutionized the manufacture of items as simple as nails and as complicated as clocks. By 1810 a machine had been developed that could produce 100 nails a minute, cutting the cost of nail making by two-thirds. Finely made wooden and brass clocks, previously made (expensively) by hand, were replaced by mass-produced versions turned out in the Connecticut factories of Eli Terry, Seth Thomas, and Chauncey Jerome and sold nationwide by Yankee peddlers. Now ordinary people could keep precise time rather than estimate time by the sun, and factories could require workers to come to work on time. The need of railroads for precise timekeeping gave further support to the new system of manufacture.

Like the factory system itself, the American system spread slowly. For example, Isaac Singer's sewing machine, first patented in 1851, was not made with fully interchangeable parts until 1873, when the company was already selling 230,000 machines a year. The sewing machine revolutionized the manufacture of clothing, which up to this time had been made by women for their families at home and by hand.

American businesses mass-produced high-quality goods for ordinary people earlier than manufacturers in Britain or any other European country were able to do. The availability of these goods was a practical demonstration of American beliefs in democracy and equality. As historian David Potter has perceptively remarked: "European radical thought is prone to demand that the man of property be stripped of his carriage and his fine clothes. But American radical thought is likely to insist, instead, that the ordinary man is entitled to mass-produced copies, indistinguishable from the originals."

Other Factories

Although cotton textile mills were the first and best known of the early factories, some factories produced other items, among them metal and iron. Like the textile mills, many of these factories were rural because they depended on natural water sources for power or because they needed to be near their raw materials, such as iron ore. And like the early textile mills, these first heavy industries initially coexisted with the traditional artisanal system.

The rapid development of the steamship industry in Cincinnati illustrates both the role of merchant capital and the coexistence of old and new production methods. The first steamboat appeared on the Ohio River in 1811, and Cincinnati's merchants, who had heretofore invested their profits in land and real estate speculation, were quick to see its advantages. Cincinnati's first steamboat, financed by local merchant capital, was commissioned in 1816. It proved so successful that by 1819 one-quarter of all western steamboats were being built in Cincinnati. By 1826, Cincinnati's steamship industry had grown to include four iron foundries employing 54 men, five steam engine and finishing factories employing 126 people, and three boatyards with 200 workers. At the same time, much of the detail work on the steamboat was performed by traditional artisans such as cabinetmakers, upholsterers, tinsmiths, and blacksmiths, who did record-breaking amounts of work in their small, independent shops. In this way, new factory methods and industrial techniques were often coupled with old craft techniques.

The new concepts of specialization and standardization and the increased production they brought about were basic to the system of industrial capitalism. In turn, the system led to vast increases in wealth and in living standards for many—eventually most—of the inhabitants of industrial nations. But for many workers

Steamboats transformed commerce on western rivers and helped to make the fortune of Cincinnati, which became a center of steamboat manufacture. This Currier and Ives print of 1855 shows the Mayflower, one of the most elegant and handsome steamboats on the Mississippi River.

in early-nineteenth-century America, the transition from the old method of production to the new one did not come without a price.

FROM ARTISAN TO WORKER

The changes wrought by the market revolution had major and lasting effects on ordinary Americans. The proportion of wage laborers in the nation's labor force rose from 12 percent in 1800 to 40 percent by 1860. Most of these workers were employed in the North, and almost half were women, performing outwork in their homes. The young farm woman who worked at Lowell for a year or two, then returned home; the master craftsman in Lynn who expanded his shop with the aid of merchant capital; the home weaver who prospered on outwork from Slater's mill—all were participating, often unknowingly, in fundamental personal and social changes.

Personal Relationships

The putting-out system, with its division of each craft into separate tasks, effectively destroyed artisan production and the apprenticeship system. For example, in New York by the mid-1820s, tailors and shoemakers were teaching apprentices only a few simple operations, in effect using them as helpers. Printers undercut the system by hiring partly trained apprentices as journeymen. In almost every trade, apprentices no longer lived with the master's family, and their parents received cash payment for the child's work. Thus in effect the apprenticeship system was replaced by child labor.

Artisans who helped to destroy the older system did so unwillingly, in response to harsh new competition caused by improvements in transportation. For example, in the 1850s Philadelphia's 7,000 shoemakers, shut out of the cheap shoe market by the success of the shoe manufacturers of Lynn, turned to the specialty markets of ladies' shoes and expensive men's shoes and boots. But even in this luxury market, the pressure of cheaper competition forced them to accept the central shop and the putting-out system rather than the individual artisanal shop. To compete, they had to change and adopt the same new labor organization as their rivals.

Although the breakdown of the family work system undoubtedly harmed independent urban artisans, it may have had a liberating effect on the women and children of farm families. About a third of the Lowell women workers did not return to their farm homes, instead remaining in town and marrying urban men or continuing to work. And of the women who did return home, fewer than half married farmers. There is no doubt that working at Lowell provided these women with new options. Women and children who earned wages by doing outwork at home may have found their voices strengthened by this evidence of their power and worth. Patriarchal control over family members was no longer absolute.

The breakdown of the patriarchal relationship between the master craftsman and his workers became an issue in the growing political battle between the North and the South over slavery. Southern defenders of slavery compared their cradle-to-grave responsibility to their slaves with northern employers' "heartless" treatment of their "wage slaves." Certainly the new northern employer assumed less responsibility for individual workers than had the traditional artisan. Although the earliest textile manufacturers, like those at Lowell, provided housing for their workers, workers soon became responsible for their own food and housing. Moreover, northern employers felt no obligation to help or care for old or disabled workers. Southerners were right: this was a heartless system. But Northerners were also right: industrialization was certainly freer than the slave system, freer even than the hierarchical craft system, although it sometimes offered only the freedom to starve.

Mechanization and Women's Work

Industrialization posed a major threat to the status and independence of skilled male workers. In trade after trade, mechanization meant that most tasks could be performed by unskilled labor. For example, the textile mills at Lowell and elsewhere hired a mere handful of skilled mechanics; most of the rest of the workers were unskilled and lower paid. In fact, the work in the textile mills was so simple that children came to form a large part of the workforce. By 1850 in New York City, many formerly skilled trades, including shoemaking, weaving, silversmithing, pottery making, and cabinetmaking, were filled with unskilled, low-paid workers who did one specialized operation or tended machinery. Many former artisans were reduced to performing wage labor for others. Because women were so frequently hired in the putting-out system, male workers began to oppose female participation in the workforce, fearing that it would lower their own wages.

Mechanization changed the nature of women's work in other ways as well. The industrialization of textiles—first in spinning, then in weaving—relieved women of a time-consuming home occupation. To supplement family income, women now had the choice of following textile work into the factory or finding other kinds of home work. At first, these were attractive options, but negative aspects soon developed, especially in the nation's cities.

The 1820s saw the birth of the garment industry. In New York City, employers began hiring women to sew ready-made clothing, at first rough, unfitted clothing for sailors and southern slaves, but later overalls and shirts for Westerners and finer items such as men's shirts. Most women performed this work at low piecework rates in their homes. Although by 1860 Brooks Brothers, the famous men's clothing firm, had 70 "inside" workers in a model central workshop, the firm relied primarily on putting out sewing to 3,000 women who worked at home.

Soon the low pay and seasonal nature of the industry became notorious. Two basic problems were overcrowding of the market and low wages. Women were pushed into the garment trade because they were barred from many occupations considered inappropriate for them, and the oversupply of workers led to wage cutting. To make matters worse, most people believed that "respectable" women did not do factory work (Lowell in its "model" years was the exception that proved the rule), and this disparagement fostered low pay and poor working conditions.

Manufacturers in the garment trade made their profits not from efficient production but by obtaining intensive labor for very low wages. The lower the piece rate, the more each woman, sewing at home, had to produce to earn enough to live. The invention of the sewing machine only made matters worse. Manufacturers dropped their piecework rates still lower, and some women found themselves working fifteen to eighteen hours a day, producing more than they ever had, but earning the same pay.

Time, Work, and Leisure

Preindustrial work had a flexibility that factory work did not, and it took factory workers a while to get accustomed to the constant pace of work. Long hours did not bother them, for they were accustomed to

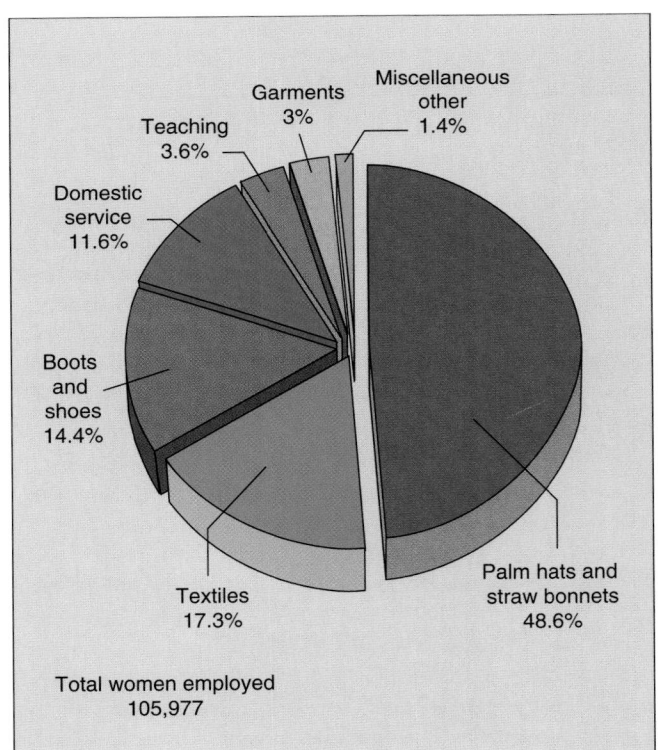

Occupations of Women Wage Earners in Massachusetts, 1837 *This chart shows how important outwork was for women workers. Textile work in factories occupied less than 20 percent of women, while outwork in palm-leaf hats, straw bonnets, and boots and shoes accounted for over half of the total workforce. Teaching was a new occupation for women in 1837. The small percentage of 3.6 would grow in the future.*

Source: Based on Thomas Dublin, *Transforming Women's Work* (Ithaca, N.Y.: Cornell University Press, 1991), table 1.1, p. 20.

twelve-hour workdays and six-day weeks on the farm and in the shop. But in the early days of Slater's mill in Rhode Island, workers sometimes took a few hours off to go berry picking or to attend to other business. And when Slater insisted on a twelve-hour day that required candles for night work, one upset father demanded that his children be sent home at sunset, the traditional end of the workday.

Factory workers gradually adjusted to having their lives regulated by the sound of the factory bell, but they did not necessarily become the docile "hands" the owners wanted. Absenteeism was common, accounting for about 15 percent of working hours, and there was much pilfering. Workers were beginning to think of themselves as a separate community whose interests differed from those of owners, and the tyranny of time over their work was certainly one reason for this.

Another adjustment required by the constant pace was that time now had to be divided into two separate activities—work and leisure. In preindustrial times work and leisure were blended for farmers and artisans.

TIME TABLE OF THE LOWELL MILLS,

To take effect on and after Oct. 21st, 1851.

This timetable from the Lowell Mills illustrates the elaborate time schedules that the cotton textile mills expected their employees to meet. For workers, it was difficult to adjust to the regimentation imposed by clock time, in contrast to approximate times common to preindustrial work.

The place of work—often the home—and the pace made it possible to stop and have a chat or a friendly drink with a visitor. Now, however, the separation of home and workplace and the pace of production not only squeezed the fun out of the long workday but left a smaller proportion of time for leisure activities.

For many workingmen, the favored spot for after-hours and Sunday leisure became the local tavern. Community-wide celebrations and casual sociability, still common in rural areas, began to be replaced in cities by spectator sports—horse racing, boxing, and (beginning in the 1850s) baseball—and by popular entertainments such as plays, operas, minstrel shows, concerts, and circuses. Some of these diversions, such as plays and horse racing, appealed to all social classes, but others, like parades, rowdy dance halls, and tavern games like quoits and ninepins were favored working-class amusements. The effect of these changes was to make working-class amusements more distinct, and visible, than they had been before.

The Cash Economy

Another effect of the market revolution was the transformation of a largely barter system into a cash economy. For example, a farm woman might pay in butter and eggs for a pair of shoes handmade for her by the local shoemaker. A few years later that same woman, now part of the vast New England outwork industry, might buy new footwear with the cash she had earned from braiding straw for hats, making gloves, or sewing shirts at home. Moreover, the shoes would have been commercially manufactured, perhaps in Lynn. In this way, in hundreds of thousands of small transactions, community economic ties were replaced by distant, sometimes national ones.

The rise of the cash economy also changed the relationships among workers and their employers. In some cases the pay envelope was the only direct contact between factory worker and (often absentee) owner. For workers, this change was both unsettling and liberating. On the minus side, workers were no longer part of a settled, orderly, and familiar community. On the plus side, they were now free to labor wherever they could, at whatever wages their skills or their bargaining power could command. That workers took their freedom seriously is evidenced by the very high rate of turnover in the New England textile mills. By the 1830s, at both the small family mills and the model mills at Lowell, almost half the workforce left every year.

But if moving on was a sign of increased freedom of opportunity for some workers, for others it was an unwanted consequence of the market revolution. In New England, for example, many quite prosperous artisans and farmers faced disruptive competition from factory goods and western commercial agriculture. They could remain where they were only if they were willing to become factory workers or commercial farmers. Often the more conservative choice was to move west and try to reestablish one's traditional lifestyle on the frontier.

Free Labor

At the heart of the industrializing economy was the notion of free labor. Originally, "free" referred to individual economic choice—that is, to the right of workers to move to another job rather than be held to a position by customary obligation or the formal contract of apprenticeship or journeyman labor. But "free labor" soon came to encompass as well the range of attitudes—hard work, self-discipline, and a striving for economic independence—that were necessary for success in a competitive, industrializing economy. These were profoundly individualistic attitudes, and owners cited them in opposing labor unions and the use of strikes to achieve wage goals. As the *Cincinnati Gazette* put it in 1857: "We are not speaking of leaving work—that all men have the right to do; but of combining to interrupt and arrest the machinery. The first is a plain, individual right. The last is a conspiracy against the interest, and even the safety of the public." Owners opposed government action, such as proposals for legislation mandating a ten-hour day, on the same grounds: it denied workers wishing to work a twelve-hour day the opportunity to do so!

For their part, many workers were inclined to define freedom more collectively, arguing that their just grievances as free American citizens were not being heard. As a group of New Hampshire female workers rhetorically asked, "Why [is] there...so much want, dependence and misery among us, if forsooth, we are freemen and freewomen?" Or, as the Lowell strikers of 1836 sang as they paraded through the streets:

> Oh! Isn't it a pity, such a pretty girl as I,
> Should be sent to the factory to pine away and die?
> Oh! I cannot be a slave,
> I will not be a slave,
> For I'm so fond of liberty
> That I cannot be a slave.

Early Strikes

Rural women workers led some of the first strikes in American labor history. Because young women formed the majority of the workforce in early textile mills like Lowell, their participation in spontaneous protests is not surprising. What was surprising was that women, whose public role and activities were limited at the time, were the ones who led these protests. In 1824, in one of the first of these actions, women workers at a

Pawtucket, Rhode Island, textile mill led their coworkers, female and male, out on strike to protest wage cuts and longer hours.

More famous were the strikes that the women at the model mill at Lowell led. The first serious trouble came in 1834, when 800 women participated in a spontaneous turnout to protest a wage cut of 25 percent. The owners were shocked and outraged by the strike, considering it both unfeminine and ungrateful. The workers, however, were bound together by a sense of sisterhood and were protesting not just the attack on their economic independence but the blow to their position as "daughters of freemen still." Nevertheless the wage cuts were enforced, as were more cuts in 1836, again in the face of a turnout. Many women simply packed their clothes in disgust and returned home to the family farm.

Like these strikes, most turnouts by factory workers in the 1830s—male or female—were unsuccessful. Owners, claiming that increasing competition made wage cuts inevitable, were always able to find new workers—Irish immigrants, for example—who would work at lower wages. The preindustrial notion of a community of interest between owner and workers had broken down.

Collective labor action by the women workers of Lowell underlined that point. In 1845 they formed the first chapter of the New England Female Labor Reform Association. The chapter soon had over 400 members, and other chapters sprang up in mill towns such as Fall River, Dover, Nashua, and Manchester. The Lowell chapter, led by Sarah Bagley, submitted a petition to the Massachusetts legislature demanding a law limiting the workday to ten hours, which the Lowell owners were unwilling to consider. The ten-hour day, a major labor goal throughout the nation, had first been demanded by skilled male workers in Boston in 1825. When the Massachusetts legislature ignored the Lowell petition on the grounds that many of the signers were nonvoters (because they were women), Bagley broke with customary notions of female propriety and challenged the legislature in a formal address: "For the last half century, it has been deemed a violation of woman's sphere to appear before the public as a speaker: but when our rights are trampled upon and we appeal in vain to our legislator, what are we to do?...Shall not our voice be heard...shall it be [said] to the daughters of New England that they have not political rights?"

The answer seemed at first to be yes. The Massachusetts legislature continued adamantly to ignore the ten-hour-day proposal even when presented with another petition in 1846 that had 10,000 signatures, 4,000 from Lowell women. But in 1847, legislators in New Hampshire, responding to a petition from women workers in Nashua who had refused to work after "lighting up" (after dark), made theirs the first state to enact a ten-hour-day law. Maine followed in 1848 and Pennsylvania in 1849. For the first time, thanks to women's pioneering role in factory protests, a group of workers had obtained state legislation improving their working conditions.

A NEW SOCIAL ORDER

The market revolution reached into every aspect of life, down to the most personal family decisions. It also fundamentally changed the social order, creating a new middle class with distinctive habits and beliefs.

Wealth and Class

There had always been social classes in America. Since the early colonial period planters in the South and merchants in the North had comprised a wealthy elite. Somewhere below the elite but above the mass of people were the "middling sort": a small professional group that included lawyers, ministers, schoolteachers, doctors, public officials, some prosperous farmers, prosperous urban shopkeepers and innkeepers, and a few wealthy artisans such as Boston silversmith Paul Revere. "Mechanics and farmers"—artisans and yeoman farmers—made up another large group, and the laboring poor, consisting of ordinary laborers, servants, and marginal farmers were below them. At the very bottom were the paupers—those dependent on public charity—and the enslaved. This was the "natural" social order that fixed most people in the social rank to which they were born. Although many a male servant in early America aspired to become a small farmer or artisan, he did not usually aspire to become a member of the wealthy elite, nor did serving maids often marry rich men.

The market revolution ended the old social order, creating the dynamic and unstable one we recognize today: upper, middle, and working classes, whose members all share the hope of climbing as far up the social ladder as they can. This social mobility was new, and it fascinated French observer Alexis de Tocqueville: "The first thing that strikes one in the United States is the innumerable crowd of those striving to escape from their original social condition." In the early nineteenth century the upper class remained about the same in size and composition. In the seacoast cities, as the example of Francis Cabot Lowell showed, the elite was a small, intermarried group, so distinctive in its superior cultural style that in Boston its members were nicknamed "Brahmins" (after the highest caste in India). The expanding opportunities of the market revolution enriched this already rich class: by the 1840s, the top 1 percent of the population owned about 40 percent of the nation's wealth. At the other extreme, fully one-third of the population possessed little more than the clothes they wore and some loose change.

The major transformation came in the lives of the "middling sort." As discussed earlier, the market revolution downgraded many independent artisans but elevated others, like Duncan Phyfe and Stephen Allen of New York, who became wealthy businessmen and manufacturers. Other formerly independent artisans or farmers (or more frequently, their children) joined the rapidly growing ranks of managers and white-collar workers such as accountants, bank tellers, clerks, bookkeepers, and insurance agents. Occupational opportunities shifted dramatically in just one generation. In Utica, New York, for example, 16 percent of the city's young men held white-collar jobs in 1855, compared with only 6 percent of their fathers. At the same time, 15 percent fewer younger men filled artisanal occupations than older men.

These new, white-collar workers owed not only their jobs but their lifestyles to the new structure and organization of industry. The new economic order demanded certain habits and attitudes of workers: sobriety, responsibility, steadiness, and hard work. Employers, for their part, were expected to maintain both physical and psychological distance from their workers and to rein in employees' traditional spontaneity and boisterous sociability. Historian Paul Johnson has sketched this change in lifestyle in his study of the city of Rochester: "In 1825 a northern businessman dominated his wife and children, worked irregular hours, consumed enormous amounts of alcohol, and seldom voted or went to church. Ten years later the same man went to church twice a week, treated his family with gentleness and love, drank nothing but water, worked steady hours and forced his employees to do the same." Rochester, a town transformed by the opening of the Erie Canal in 1825, grew from 300 in 1815 to 10,000 in 1830. In this pressure-cooker environment, new middle-class attitudes like that of Johnson's businessman were formed.

WEALTH IN NEW YORK CITY, 1828–1845		
Percent of the Population	Percent of Wealth Held	
	1828	1845
Top 1 percent	40%	50%
Top 4 percent	63	80

The impact of the market revolution on New York City, the nation's largest seaport, is shown by the dramatic increase in wealth of the already wealthy elite in a period of less than 20 years.

The Tea Party *painted by Henry Sargent in 1821 depicts an elegant gathering of what were known as the Boston Brahmins—a small and wealthy group of New England elite. Intermarriage tended to concentrate wealth in this group and to separate them from the "middling sort."*

Religion and Personal Life

Religion, which had undergone dramatic changes since the 1790s, played a key role in the emergence of the new attitudes. The Second Great Awakening (see Chapter 9) had supplanted the orderly and intellectual Puritan religion of early New England. The new evangelistic religious spirit, which stressed the achievement of salvation through personal faith, was more democratic and more enthusiastic than the earlier faith. The old concern with sin survived in dramatic sermons that vividly portrayed hellfire and damnation, but the way to salvation was broader. The concept of original sin, the cornerstone of Puritan belief, was replaced by the optimistic belief that a willingness to be saved was enough to ensure salva-tion. Conversion and repentance were now community experiences, often taking place in huge revival meetings in which an entire congregation focused on the sinners about to be saved. But although continued support from the community was important, the converted bore a heavy personal responsibility to demonstrate their faith in their own daily lives through morally respectable behavior. In this way the new religious feeling fostered individualism and self-discipline.

The Second Great Awakening had its greatest initial success on the western frontier in the 1790s, but by the 1820s evangelical religion was reaching a new audience: the people whose lives were being changed by the market revolution and who needed help in adjusting to the demands made by the new economic conditions. In 1825 in Utica, New York, and other towns along the recently opened Erie Canal, evangelist Charles G. Finney began a series of dramatic revival meetings. His spellbind-ing message reached both rich and poor, converting members of all classes to the new evangelistic religion. In 1830, made famous by these gatherings, Finney was invited by business-men to preach in Rochester. Finney preached every day for six months—three times on Sundays—and his wife, Lydia, made home visits to the unconverted and mobi-lized the women of Rochester for the cause. Under the Finneys' guidance and example, prayer meetings were held in schools and businesses, and impromptu reli-gious services were held in people's homes. As one person recalled, "You could not go upon the streets and hear any conversation, except upon religion."

Evangelism rapidly became the religion of the new middle class. Men soon found that evangelism's stress on self-discipline and individual achievement helped them adjust to new business conditions. More-over, it gave them a basis for demanding the same behavior from their workers. Businessmen now argued that traditional paternalism had no role in the new business world. Because achievement depended on individual character, each worker was responsible for making his own way.

Master artisans, themselves successful businessmen, often took the lead in reforming the habits of younger workers. Stephen Allen, the New York sailmaker who became mayor, attributed his success to long workdays, avoidance of debt, and "employing the utmost economy in all my concerns." Another New York artisan, master baker Thomas Mercein, took advantage of the opening of the Apprentices' Library, founded by the General Society of Mechanics and Tradesmen in 1820, to preach a similar message. "Cherish, I beseech you, a deep-rooted abhorrence of the alluring but fatal paths of vice and dissipation," Mercein told the apprentices. "Industry, ardour, sobriety, and perseverance in your different pursuits will lead to a successful competition in the world."

The New Middle-Class Family

The market revolution and the new evangelism also affected women's family roles. To begin with, the "softer," more emotional aspects of the new religious approach often especially appealed to women, and it was they who made certain that their families joined them in conversion. And as men increasingly concentrated their energies on their careers and occupations, women assumed major new responsibilities for rearing the children and inculcating in them the new attitudes necessary for success in the business world.

As the work roles of middle-class men and women diverged, so did social attitudes about appropriate male and female characteristics and behavior. Men were expected to be steady, industrious, responsible, and painstakingly attentive to their business. They had little choice: in the competitive, uncertain, and rapidly changing business conditions of the early nineteenth century, these qualities were essential for men who hoped to hold their existing positions or to get ahead. In contrast, women were expected to be nurturing, gentle, kind, moral, and selflessly devoted to their families. They were expected to operate within the "woman's sphere"—the home. Neither this division of responsibilities nor the distinction between men's and women's desirable characteristics and behavior was completely new; they were implicit in much earlier thinking about appropriate gender roles. But now clearly defined gender roles became a matter of social importance.

The unsettling demands of the market revolution forced a dramatic change in family life. When the master craftsman became a small manufacturer, or the small subsistence farmer began to manage a large-scale commercial operation, production moved away from both the family home and its members. Husbands and fathers became managers of paid workers—or workers themselves—and although they were still considered the heads of their households, they spent most of the day away from their homes and families. The husband was no longer the undisputed head of a family unit that combined work and personal life. Their wives, on the other hand, remained at home, where they were still responsible for cooking, cleaning, and other domestic tasks but no longer contributed directly to what had previously been the family enterprise. Instead, women took on a new responsibility, that of providing a quiet, well-ordered, and relaxing refuge from the pressures of the industrial world. As Utica author John Mather Austin advised in his manual, *A Voice to the Married*, the husband should regard his home as "an elysium to which he can flee and find rest from the stormy strife of a selfish world."

The invention of photography made possible family portraits that earlier were too expensive for all but the wealthiest. This portrait of the Edward Miner Gallaudet family, photographed by Mathew Brady in the 1860s, exhibits the gender differences expected in the middle-class family: strong, self-reliant men and softer, more clinging women.

Women's magazines like Sarah Josepha Hale's *Ladies' Magazine* gave homemakers some help in creating this refuge for their husbands and families, describing "patterns of virtue, of piety, of intelligence and usefulness in private life." By 1850 this magazine, which Hale merged in 1837 with *Godey's Lady's Book*—a magazine that concentrated on fashion—offered 70,000 readers a popular mixture of advice, recipes, and patterns for everything from simple embroidery to ballgowns to "model cottages," as the new suburban ideal middle-class homes were called.

A sure sign that traditional methods were inadequate for new needs was the appearance of housekeeping guides such as Catharine Beecher's book *Treatise on Domestic Economy*. First published in 1841, this book became the standard guide for a generation of middle-class American women. In it, Beecher combined innovative ideas for household design—she introduced important principles of organization for the kitchen in particular—with medical information, child-rearing advice, recipes, and much discussion of the mother's moral role in the family. Beecher's attempt to help women modernize their traditional housekeeping tasks within the context of their newly defined family role clearly filled a need: her book and the Bible were the only books that many pioneer women carried west.

The maintenance or achievement of a middle-class lifestyle required the joint efforts of husband and wife. More cooperation between them was called for than in the preindustrial, patriarchal family. The nature of the new, companionate marriage that evolved in response to the market revolution was reflected most clearly in decisions concerning children.

Family Limitation

Middle-class couples chose to have fewer children than their predecessors. Children who were being raised to succeed in the middle class placed considerable demands on family resources: they required more care, training, and education than children who could be put to work at traditional tasks at an early age. The dramatic fall in the birth rate during the nineteenth century (from an average of seven children per woman in 1800 to four in 1900) is evidence of conscious decisions about family limitation, first by members of the new middle class and later by working-class families. Few couples used mechanical methods of contraception such as the condom, partly because these were difficult to obtain and partly because most people associated their use with prostitution and the prevention of venereal disease rather than with family planning. Instead, people used birth control methods that relied on mutual consent: coitus interruptus (withdrawal before climax), the rhythm method (intercourse only during the woman's infertile period), and, most often, abstinence or infrequent intercourse. Medical manuals suggested that couples consider ending their sex life after they had reached the desired number of children.

When mutual efforts at birth control failed, married women often sought a surgical abortion, a new technique that was much more reliable than the folk remedies women had always shared among themselves. Surgical abortions were widely advertised after 1830, and widely used, especially by middle-class married women seeking to limit family size. Some historians estimate that one out of every four pregnancies was aborted in the years 1840–60 (about the same rate as in 1990). The rising rate of abortion by married women (in other words, its use as birth control) prompted the first legal bans; by 1860, twenty states had outlawed the practice. Even in the absence of accurate statistics, it is clear that dangerous illegal abortions continued, especially among unmarried women who believed they lacked alternatives.

Accompanying the interest in family limitation was a redefinition of sexuality. Doctors generally recommended that sexual urges be controlled, but they believed that men would have much more difficulty exercising such control than women, partly because, they also believed, women were uninterested in sex. (Women who were visibly interested ran the risk of being considered immoral or "fallen," and thereupon shunned by the middle class.) Medical manuals of the period suggested that it was the task of middle-class women to help their husbands and sons restrain their sexuality by appealing to their higher, moral natures. Although it is always difficult to measure the extent to which the suggestions in advice books were applied in actual practice, it seems that many middle-class women accepted this new and limited definition of their sexuality because of their desire to limit the number of pregnancies.

Many women of the late eighteenth century wanted to be free of the medical risks and physical debility that too-frequent childbearing brought, but they had little chance of achieving that goal until men became equally interested in family limitation. The rapid change in attitudes toward family size that occurred in the early nineteenth century has been repeated around the world as other societies undergo the dramatic experience of industrialization. It is a striking example of the ways economic changes affect our most private and personal decisions.

Motherhood

New responsibilities toward children led to another major redefinition of women's roles. Child rearing had been shared in the preindustrial household, boys learning farming or craft skills from their fathers while girls learned domestic skills from their mothers. The children of the new middle class, however, needed a new kind of upbringing, one that involved a long period of nurturing in the beliefs and personal habits necessary for success. Mothers assumed primary responsibility for this training, in part because fathers were too busy but also because people believed that women's superior qualities of gentleness, morality, and loving watchfulness were essential to the task.

Fathers retained a strong role in major decisions concerning children, but mothers commonly turned to other women for advice on daily matters. Through their churches, women formed maternal associations for help in raising their children to be religious and responsible. In Utica, New York, for example, these extremely popular organizations enabled women to form strong networks sustained by mutual advice and by publications such as *Mother's Magazine*, issued by the Presbyterian Church, and *Mother's Monthly Journal*, put out by the Baptists.

Middle-class status required another sharp break with tradition. As late as 1855, artisanal families expected all children over fifteen to work. Middle-class families, on the other hand, sacrificed to keep their sons in school or in training for their chosen professions, and they often housed and fed their sons until the young men had "established" themselves financially and could marry.

This watercolor, The Happy Home, *illustrates the importance of domesticity for middle class families and the powerful new role for women as they used their moral influence in childrearing.*

Mothers continued to be concerned about their children's character and morality, as women's activities in the great religious revivals of the 1830s showed. They also took the lead in an important informal activity: making sure their children had friends and contacts that would be useful when they were old enough to consider careers and marriage. Matters such as these, rarely considered by earlier generations living in small communities, now became important in the new middle-class communities of America's towns and cities.

Contrary to the growing myth of the self-made man, middle-class success was not a matter of individual achievement. Instead it was usually based on a family strategy in which women's efforts were essential. The reorganization of the family described in this section was successful: from its shelter and support emerged generations of ambitious, responsible, and individualistic middle-class men. But although boys were trained for success, this was not an acceptable goal for their sisters. Women were trained to be the nurturing, silent "support system" that undergirded male success. And women were also expected to ease the tensions of the transition to new middle-class behavior by acting as models and monitors of traditional values.

Sentimentalism

The individualistic competitiveness engendered by the market revolution caused members of the new middle class to place extraordinary emphasis on sincerity and feeling. So-called sentimentalism sprang from nostalgia for the imagined trust and security of the familiar, face-to-face life of the preindustrial village. Sermons, advice manuals, and articles now thundered warnings to young men of the dangers and deceits of urban life, and especially of fraudulent "confidence men and painted ladies" who were not what they seemed. Middle-class women were expected to counteract the impersonality and hypocrisy of the business world by the example of their own morality and sincere feeling.

For guidance in this new role women turned to a new literary form, the sentimental novel. In contrast to older forms like sermons and learned essays, the novel was popular, accessible, and emotionally engrossing. Although denounced by ministers and scholars as frivolous, immoral, and subversive of authority, the novel found a ready audience among American women. Publishers of novels found a lucrative market, one that increased from $2.5 million in 1820 to $12.5 million in 1850. By 1850, *Harper's Magazine* estimated, four-fifths of the reading public were women, and they were reading novels written by women.

To be a "lady novelist" was a new and rather uncomfortably public occupation for women. Several authors, such as Susan Warner, were driven to novel writing when their fathers lost their fortunes in the Panic of 1837. Novel writing could be very profitable: Warner's 1850 novel *The Wide Wide World* went through fourteen editions in two years, and works by other authors such as Lydia Maria Child, Catherine Sedgwick, and E.D.E.N. Southworth sold in the thousands of copies. Sentimental novels concentrated on private life. Religious feeling, antipathy toward the dog-eat-dog world of the commercial economy, and the need to be prepared for unforeseen troubles were common themes. Although the heroines usually married happily at the end of the story, few novels concentrated on romantic love. Most of these domestic novels, as they were known, presented readers with a vision of responsibility and community based on moral and caring family life.

Although sentimentalism originally sprang from genuine fear of the dangers individualism posed to community trust, it rapidly hardened into a rigid code of etiquette for all occasions. Moments of genuine and deep feeling, such as death, were smothered in elaborate rules concerning condolences, expressions of grief, and appropriate clothing. A widow, for example, was expected to wear "deep mourning" for a year—dresses of dull black fabrics and black bonnets covered with long, thick black veils—and in the following year "half mourning"—shiny black silk dresses, perhaps with trim of gray, violet, or white, and hats without veils. Thus sentimentalism rapidly became concerned not with feelings but social codes. Transformed into a set of rules about genteel manners to cover all occasions, sentimentalism itself became a mark of middle-class status. And it became one of the tasks of the middle-class woman to make sure her family conformed to the social code and associated only with other respectable families. In this way, women forged and enforced the distinctive social behavior of the new middle class.

Transcendentalism and Self-Reliance

As the new middle class conformed to the rules of sentimental behavior, it also sought a more general intellectual reassurance. Middle-class men, in particular, needed to feel comfortable about their public assertions of individualism and self-interest. One source of reassurance was the philosophy of transcendentalism and its well-known spokesman, Ralph Waldo Emerson. Originally a Unitarian minister, Emerson quit the pulpit in 1832 and became what one might call a secular minister. Famous as a writer and lecturer, he popularized transcendentalism, a romantic philosophical theory claiming that there was an ideal, intuitive reality transcending ordinary life. The best place to achieve that individual intuition of the Universal Being, Emerson suggested, was not in church or in society but alone in the natural world. As

he wrote in "Nature" (1836), "Standing on the bare ground—my head bathed by the blithe air, and uplifted into infinite space—all mean egotism vanishes. I become a transparent Eyeball; I am nothing; I see all; the currents of the Universal Being circulate through me; I am part and parcel of God." The same assertion of individualism rang through Emerson's stirring polemic "Self-Reliance" (1841). Announcing that "Whoso would be a man, must be a nonconformist," Emerson urged that "Nothing is at last sacred but the integrity of your own mind." Inspirational but down-to-earth, Emerson was just the philosopher to inspire young businessmen of the 1830s and 1840s to achieve success in a responsible manner.

Emerson's younger friend, Henry David Thoreau, pushed the implications of individualism further than the more conventional Emerson. Determined to live the transcendental ideal of association with nature, Thoreau lived in solitude in a primitive cabin for two years at Walden Pond, near Concord, Massachusetts, confronting "the essential facts of life." His experience was the basis for *Walden* (1854), a penetrating criticism of the spiritual cost of the market revolution. Denouncing the materialism that led "the mass of men [to] lead lives of quiet desperation," Thoreau recommended a simple life of subsistence living that left time for spiritual thought. Margaret Fuller, perhaps the most intellectually gifted of the transcendental

Emerson's romantic glorification of nature included the notion of himself as a "transparent eyeball," as he wrote in "Nature" in 1836. A contemporary produced this cartoon.

CHRONOLOGY

1790	Samuel Slater's first mill opens in Rhode Island
1793	Cotton gin invented
1798	Eli Whitney contracts with the federal government for 10,000 rifles, which he undertakes to produce with interchangeable parts
1807	Embargo Act excludes British manufactures
1810	Francis Cabot Lowell tours British textile factories First steamboat on the Ohio River
1812	Micajah Pratt begins his own shoe business in Lynn, Massachusetts
1813	Francis Cabot Lowell raises $300,000 to build his first cotton textile factory at Waltham, Massachusetts
1815	War of 1812 ends; British competition in manufactures resumes
1816	First protective tariff

1820s	Large-scale outwork networks develop in New England
1823	Lowell mills open
1824	John Hall successfully achieves interchangeable parts at Harpers Ferry armory Women lead strike at Pawtucket textile mill
1825	Erie Canal opens
1830	Charles G. Finney's Rochester revivals
1834	First strike at Lowell mills
1836	Ralph Waldo Emerson lecture "Nature" published
1841	Catharine Beecher's *Treatise on Domestic Economy* published
1845	New England Female Labor Reform Association formed
1847	New Hampshire passes first ten-hour-day law

circle, was patronized by Emerson because she was a woman. She expressed her sense of women's wasted potential in her pathbreaking work *Woman in the Nineteenth Century* (1845). Intellectually and emotionally, however, Fuller achieved liberation only when she moved to Europe and participated in the liberal Italian revolution of 1848. The romantic destiny she sought was tragically fulfilled when she, her Italian husband, and their child died in a shipwreck off the New York coast as they returned to America in 1850.

Although Thoreau and Fuller were too radical for many readers, Emerson's version of the romantic philosophy of transcendentalism, seemingly so at odds with the competitive and impersonal spirit of the market revolution, was in fact an essential component of it. Individualism, or, as Emerson called it, self-reliance, was at the heart of the personal transformation required by the market revolution. Sentimentalism, transcendentalism, and evangelical religion all helped the new middle class to forge values and beliefs that were appropriate to their social roles.

CONCLUSION

The market revolution involved three transformations: improvements in transportation, commercialization, and industrialization. Each began at different times. The transportation revolution (discussed in Chapter 10), usually dated from 1825 (the year of the opening of the Erie Canal), accelerated with the building of railroads in the 1830s and 1840s. Commercialization began earlier, around 1805, as a consequence of the reorganization of manufacturing through the putting-out system by northern entrepreneurs. After 1805, the cash purchase of items manufactured elsewhere slowly eroded local barter arrangements. American industrialization began with Samuel Slater's small cotton spinning mill in Rhode Island in 1790, but the most famous early example was the mill town of Lowell, whose factories opened in 1823. These three transformations, taken together, constituted the market revolution that, by changing the ways people worked, changed how they thought.

For most people the changes were gradual. Until midcentury, the lives of rural people were still determined largely by community events, although the spread of democratic politics and the availability of newspapers and other printed material increased their connection to a larger world. Wage earners made up only 40 percent of the working population in 1860, and factory workers made up an even smaller percentage.

The new middle class was most dramatically affected by the market revolution. All aspects of life, including intimate matters of family organization, gender roles, and the number and raising of children, changed. New values—evangelical religion, sentimentalism, and transcendentalism—helped the members of the new middle class in their adjustment. As the next chapter describes, the nation's cities were the first arena where old and new values collided.

REVIEW QUESTIONS

1. What changes in preindustrial life and work were caused by the market revolution?
2. This chapter argues that when people begin doing new kinds of work, their beliefs and attitudes change. Give three examples of such changes described in the chapter. Can you think of other examples?
3. Discuss the opinion offered by historian David Potter that mass production has been an important democratizing force in American politics. Do you agree? Why or why not?
4. Consider the portrait of the nineteenth-century middle-class family offered in this chapter and imagine yourself as a member of such a family. What new aspects of family relations would you welcome? Which would be difficult? Why?

RECOMMENDED READING

Christopher Clark, *The Roots of Rural Capitalism: Western Massachusetts, 1780–1860* (1990). The most thorough examination to date of how the commercial spirit changed rural life.

Alan Dawley, *Class and Community: The Industrial Revolution in Lynn* (1976). A pathbreaking study of the shift from artisanal to wage labor.

Thomas Dublin, *Women at Work: The Transformation of Work and Community in Lowell, Massachusetts, 1826–1860* (1979). A careful look at the female workers of Lowell and their changing conditions.

Thomas Dublin, *Transforming Women's Work: New England Lives in the Industrial Revolution* (1994). A thoughtful study of the effects of women's outwork.

Karen Halttunen, *Confidence Men and Painted Women: A Study of Middle-Class Culture in America* (1982). Explores the development and importance of sentimentalism to the new middle class.

David Houndshell, *From the American System to Mass Production, 1800–1932* (1984). Shows how not only Eli Whitney but an entire network of New England "mechanics" contributed to the invention of interchangeable parts.

Paul Johnson, *A Shopkeeper's Millennium: Society and Revivals in Rochester, New York, 1815–1837* (1978). A study of the changing relationship between masters and workers in Rochester.

Bruce Laurie, *Artisans into Workers: Labor in Nineteenth-Century America* (1989). Using many specific examples, traces the changes in labor described in this chapter.

Jonathan Prude, *The Coming of Industrial Order: Town and Factory Life in Rural Massachusetts, 1810–1860* (1983). A major source of information on family mills.

Steven J. Ross, *Workers on the Edge: Work, Leisure and Politics in Industrializing Cincinnati, 1788–1890* (1985). Studies the growth of wage labor in a major western city.

Mary Ryan, *The Making of the Middle Class* (1981). A study of Utica, New York, that was the first to clearly discern the role of women in the family strategies of the new middle class.

Charles Sellers, *The Market Revolution: Jacksonian America 1815–1846* (1991). A synthesis of the political, religious, and economic change of the period.

Christine Stansell, *City of Women: Sex and Class in New York, 1789–1860* (1983). Exceptionally useful in exploring the range of women's work and the social dynamics of rapidly growing New York City.

ADDITIONAL BIBLIOGRAPHY

The Market Revolution

Thomas C. Cochran, *Frontiers of Change: Early Industrialism in America* (1981)

Robert F. Dalzell Jr., *Enterprising Elite: The Boston Associates and the World They Made* (1987)

L. C. Hunter, *A History of Industrial Power in the United States, 1780–1930*, vol. 1: *Waterpower in the Century of the Steam Engine* (1979)

David J. Jeremy, *Transatlantic Industrial Revolution: The Diffusion of Textile Technology between Britain and America* (1981)

Benjamin W. Labaree, *Patriots and Partisans, The Merchants of Newburyport, 1764–1815* (1962)

Walter Licht, *Industrializing America: The Nineteenth Century* (1995)

Diane Linstrom, *Economic Development in the Philadelphia Region, 1810–1850* (1978)

Merritt R. Smith, *Harpers Ferry Armory and the New Technology* (1977)

Barbara Tucker, *Samuel Slater and the Origins of the American Textile Industry, 1790–1860* (1984)

Caroline F. Ware, *Early New England Cotton Manufacturing* (1931)

From Artisan to Worker

Mary H. Blewett, *Men, Women, and Work: Class, Gender, and Protest in the New England Shoe Industry, 1780–1910* (1988)

John L. Brooke, *The Heart of the Commonwealth: Society and Political Culture in Worcester County, Massachusetts, 1713–1861* (1989)

Robert Doherty, *Society and Power: Five New England Towns, 1800–1860* (1977)

Paul G. Faler, *Mechanics and Manufacturers in the Early Industrial Revolution: Lynn, Massachusetts* (1981)

Michael H. Glickstein, *Concepts of Free Labor in Antebellum America* (1991)

Susan E. Hirsch, *Roots of the American Working Class: The Industrialization of Crafts in Newark, 1800–1860* (1978)

Joan M. Jensen, *Loosening the Bonds: Mid-Atlantic Farm Women, 1750–1850* (1986)

Jack Larkin, *The Reshaping of Everyday Life, 1790–1840* (1988)

Bruce Laurie, *Working People of Philadelphia, 1800–1850* (1980)

Scott C. Martin, *Killing Time: Leisure and Culture in Southwestern Pennsylvania, 1800–1850* (1995)

Howard Rock, *Artisans of the New Republic: Tradesmen of New York City in the Age of Jefferson* (1979)

W. J. Rorabaugh, *The Craft Apprentice: From Franklin to the Machine Age in America* (1986)

Charles G. Steffan, *The Mechanics of Baltimore: Workers and Politics in the Age of Revolution, 1763–1812* (1984)

A New Social Order

Jeanne Boydston, *Home and Work* (1990)

Nancy E. Cott, *The Bonds of Womanhood: "Woman's Sphere" in New England, 1780–1835* (1977)

Betty G. Farrell, *Elite Families: Class and Power in Nineteenth Century Boston* (1993)

Clyde Griffen and Sally Griffen, *Natives and Newcomers: The Ordering of Opportunity in Mid-Nineteenth-Century Poughkeepsie* (1978)

James C. Mohr, *Abortion in America: The Origins and Evolution of National Policy, 1800–1900* (1978)

Edward Pessen, *Riches, Class, and Power before the Civil War* (1973)

James Reed, *From Private Vice to Public Virtue: The Birth Control Movement and American Society since 1830* (1978)

Anthony F. C. Wallace, *Rockdale: The Growth of an American Village in the Early Industrial Revolution* (1977)

Middle-Class Culture

Barbara A. Bardes and Suzanne Gossett, *Declarations of Independence: Women and Political Power in Nineteenth-Century American Fiction* (1990)

Nina Baym, *Woman's Fiction: A Guide to Novels by and about Women in America* (1978)

———, *Feminism and American Literary History* (1992)

Paul F. Boller, *American Transcendentalism, 1830–1860* (1974)

John F. Kasson, *Rudeness and Civility: Manners in Nineteenth-Century America* (1990)

Mary Kelley, *Private Women, Public Stage: Literary Domesticity in Nineteenth-Century America* (1984)

F. O. Matthiessen, *American Renaissance* (1941)

Walter Benn Michaels and Donald E. Pease, eds., *The American Renaissance Reconsidered* (1985)

Leonard Neufeldt, *The Economist: Henry Thoreau and Enterprise* (1989)

Russell Nye, *Society and Culture in America, 1830–1860* (1974)

Lewis Perry, *Intellectual Life in America* (1984)

Ann Rose, *Transcendentalism as a Social Movement* (1981)

Shirley Samuels, ed., *The Culture of Sentiment: Race, Gender, and Sentimentality in Nineteenth-Century America* (1992)

Jane Tompkins, *Sensational Designs: The Cultural World of American Fiction, 1790–1860* (1986)

Joyce W. Warren, *The (Other) American Traditions: Nineteenth-Century Women Writers* (1993)

Biography

Paul Blanchard, *Margaret Fuller: From Transcendentalism to Revolution* (1978)

Walter Harding, *Thoreau: Man of Concord* (1960)

Joel Porte, *Representative Man: Ralph Waldo Emerson in His Time* (1979)

R. D. Richardson Jr., *Henry Thoreau: A Life of the Mind* (1986)

$\mathcal{C}$HAPTER THIRTEEN

COMING TO TERMS
WITH THE NEW AGE

1820s–1850s

The Bootblack, by George Henry Yewell, 1852, oil on canvas, 14 x 12 inches. Collection of the New York Historical Society.

AMERICAN COMMUNITIES
Seneca Falls: Women Reformers Respond to the Market Revolution

In the summer of 1848, a small advertisement appeared in an upstate New York newspaper announcing a "convention to discuss the social, civil, and religious condition and rights of woman," to be held at Seneca Falls on the 19th and 20th of July.

Charlotte Woodward, a nineteen-year-old glove maker who did outwork in her rural home, saw the advertisement and persuaded six friends to join her in the 40-mile journey to the convention. "At first we travelled quite alone," she recalled. "But before we had gone many miles we came on other wagon-loads of women, bound in the same direction. As we reached different crossroads we saw wagons coming from every part of the country, and long before we reached Seneca Falls we were a procession."

To the surprise of the convention organizers, almost 300 people—men as well as women—attended the two-day meeting. The focus of their discussions was the Declaration of Sentiments, a petition for women's rights modeled on the Declaration of Independence. "We hold these truths to be self-evident," it announced: "That all men and women are created equal." As the Declaration of Independence detailed the oppressions King George III had imposed on the colonists, the Declaration of Sentiments detailed, in a series of resolutions, the oppressions men had imposed on women. Men had deprived women of legal rights, of the right to own their own property, of custody of their children in cases of divorce, of the right to higher education (at that time only Oberlin College and Mount Holyoke Female Seminary admitted women), of full participation in religious worship and activity, and of the right to vote. After discussion, the attendees approved all the resolutions, and all but the last of them, which a minority found too radical, unanimously. "Why Lizzie, thee will make us ridiculous!" Quaker Lucretia Mott had exclaimed when Elizabeth Cady Stanton proposed the voting rights measure. Indeed the newspapers reporting on the convention thought the demand for the vote was ridiculously unfeminine. But the group that assembled in Seneca Falls was undeterred. Buoyed by the success of this first women's rights convention, they promptly planned another one three weeks later in New York's largest upstate city, Rochester, to reach new supporters and to develop strategies to implement their resolutions.

The fight for women's rights was only one of many reform movements that emerged in the United States in the wake of the economic and social disruptions of the market revolution. The Seneca Falls region was itself deeply affected by that revolution. A farming frontier in 1800, it had been drawn into national commerce in 1828 when it was reached by an offshoot of the Erie Canal. It was drawn even further into the modern age when the railroad arrived in 1841. A village of 200 in 1824, Seneca Falls had grown to a town of over 4,000 by 1842. It was now a center for flour milling (in 1845, the nine mills in the town produced a total of 2,000 barrels of flour a day) and manufacturing, and a hub of the outwork network of which Charlotte Woodward was a part. Swamped by newcomers (among them a growing number of poor Irish Catholics), the inhabitants of Seneca Falls struggled to maintain a sense of community. They formed volunteer organizations of all kinds—religious, civic, social, educational, recreational. And they became active participants in reform movements seeking to counteract the effects of industrialization, rapid growth, and the influx of newcomers.

Many reformers belonged to liberal religious groups with wide social perspectives. Perhaps a third of those attending the women's rights convention, for example, were members of the Wesleyan Methodist Society of Seneca Falls, which had broken with the national Methodist organization because it would not take a strong stand against slavery. Another quarter were Progressive Quakers of the nearby town of Waterloo, who had broken with their national organization for the same reason. Both groups were outspoken in their belief in the moral equality of all humankind and in their commitment to social activism. The Wesleyans, for example, resolved in 1847 that "we cannot identify our Christian and moral character with societies where women and colored persons are excluded." Seneca Falls had been the site of a "Temperance Reformation" in the early 1840s, and many attendees at the Women's Rights convention were also active in the temperance movement, a more limited but extremely popular reform cause dedicated to promoting abstinence from alcohol.

The idea for the Women's Rights convention emerged during a meeting in early July, 1848, between Lucretia Mott—a Philadelphia Quaker and the nation's best-known woman reformer—and Elizabeth Cady Stanton of Seneca Falls, wife of a well-known antislavery orator and niece of a leading reform philanthropist. Reflecting her many concerns, Mott had just finished a tour of the new penitentiary at Auburn and a nearby Indian reservation and was visiting her sister in Waterloo. Stanton called for tea to renew her acquaintance with Mott, and it was in this context of friendship and shared concern for reform that the two began planning the convention that was held two weeks later.

Stanton and her family had moved from Boston, where, she remembered, they had "near neighbors, a new home with all the modern conveniences, and well-trained

servants." Living in a house on the outskirts of Seneca Falls, her three children suffering from malaria, she had none of those things. "I now fully understood," she mused,

the practical difficulties most women had to contend with....The general discontent I felt with woman's portion as wife, mother, housekeeper, physician and spiritual guide, the chaotic conditions into which everything fell without her constant supervision, and the wearied anxious look of the majority of women impressed me with a strong feeling that some active measures should be taken to remedy the wrongs of society in general, and of women in particular.

As she and Mott spoke of the changes that would be necessary to allow women to care for their families but have energy left over to reform "the wrongs of society," the idea of a women's rights convention was born. The women's rights movement that took shape from this convention proved exceptionally long-lasting. Stanton, soon to form a working partnership with former temperance worker Susan B. Anthony, devoted the rest of her life to women's rights.

But what of Charlotte Woodward, a local farm girl, unaware of the national reform community? Why was she there? In this age of hopefulness and change she wanted a better life for herself. She was motivated, she said, by "all the hours that I sat and sewed gloves for a miserable pittance, which, after it was earned, could never be mine." By law and custom her father, as head of the household, was entitled to her wages. "I wanted to work," she explained, "but I wanted to choose my task and I wanted to collect my wages." The reforming women of Seneca Falls, grouped together on behalf of social improvement, had found in the first women's rights convention a way to speak for the needs of working women such as Charlotte Woodward

All over the North, in communities like Seneca Falls as well as in cities like New York, Americans gathered together in reform organizations to try to solve the problems that the market revolution posed for work, family life, personal and social values, and urban growth. Through these organizations local women and men became participants in wider communities of concern.

Seneca Falls

KEY TOPICS

- The new social problems that accompanied urbanization and immigration
- The responses of reformers

- The origins and political effects of the abolitionist movement
- The involvement of women in reform efforts

URBAN AMERICA

Although the market revolution affected all aspects of American life, nowhere was its impact so noticeable as in the cities. It was within the urban environment, with its stimulating, frightening confusion of rapid physical growth, occupational and ethnic change, and economic competition, that new American political and social forms began to emerge.

The Preindustrial City

The preindustrial cities of eighteenth-century America were small and compact. They were "walking cities," in which people mostly got around on foot. Philadelphia, for example, which had been laid out by William Penn himself in 1682, was an orderly grid of streets bordered by neat row houses in a dense, small-scale housing pattern that fostered neighborliness.

In these cities, rich and poor lived side by side. Merchants lived next door to their businesses, and in the busy streets and public places they daily rubbed elbows with their employees and with artisans and laborers. The wealthy enjoyed unquestioned authority. Merchants sat on the city council, which had broad powers to regulate the public markets, to set prices for basic foodstuffs, to grant licenses to artisans and traders, and to encourage community harmony. The same wealthy men organized charity and relief for the poor in hard times, often walking door to door in their neighborhood to solicit donations. Wealthy men were active in neighborhood volunteer fire departments and in the volunteer watch societies that prevented crime and kept neighborhood order. When larger disturbances such as bread riots broke out, the mayor and other city officials were expected to appear and disperse the mob by force of their own authority.

The Growth of Cities

The market revolution dramatically increased the size of America's cities, with the great seaports leading the way. The proportion of America's population living in cities increased from only 7 percent in 1820 to almost 20 percent in 1860, a rate of growth greater than at any other time in the country's history.

The nation's five largest cities in 1850 were the same as in 1800, with one exception. New York, Philadelphia, Baltimore, and Boston still topped the list, but New Orleans had edged out Charleston (see Chapter 9). The rate of urban growth was extraordinary. All four Atlantic seaports grew at least 25 percent each decade between 1800 and 1860, and often much more. New York, which grew from 60,000 in 1800 to 202,600 in 1830 and to more than 1 million in 1860, emerged as the nation's most populous city, its largest port, and its financial center. Between 1820 and 1830, the decade in which the Erie Canal added commerce with the American interior to the city's long-standing role in international trade, New York's population grew 64 percent.

Philadelphia, which had been the nation's largest city in 1800, was half the size of New York in 1850. Nevertheless, its growth was substantial—from 70,000 in 1800 to 389,000 in 1850 and to 565,529 in 1860. Philadelphia became as much an industrial as a commercial city. Old artisanal industries such as hand-loom weaving, tailoring, and shoe manufacture coexisted with new industries such as the huge Baldwin locomotive works, foundries, and chemical companies.

Baltimore, with 212,418 residents in 1860 was about half the size of Philadelphia. The city's merchants, hoping to counter the threat posed by the Erie Canal to their trade links with the trans-Appalachian West, financed the nation's first important railroad, the Baltimore and Ohio, which began operation in 1830. Although Baltimore remained the east coast center of the tobacco trade with Europe, by 1850 its major partner in foreign trade was Brazil, to which it shipped flour and from which it imported coffee.

Boston, in colonial times, had dominated the triangular trade linking Britain and the West Indies. By 1860, with a population of 177,840, the city had emerged as the center of a new triangular trade: the ships of Boston merchants carried New England cotton cloth, shoes, and other manufactured goods to the South, delivered southern cotton to British and European ports, and returned to Boston with European manufactured goods. Boston still dominated the China trade as well.

New Orleans, fed by the expansion of cotton throughout the South and commercial agriculture in the Mississippi Valley, had a population of 168,675 in 1860. In the 1850s, New Orleans handled about half the nation's cotton exports and by 1860, its exports—$5 million in 1815—had risen to $107 million.

The market revolution oriented the attention of each of these major seaports away from the oceans and toward trade with the nation's interior. Prosperous merchants in these cities now depended on American exports rather than European imports for their profits.

Another result of the market revolution was the appearance of "instant" cities at critical points on the new transportation network. Utica, New York, once a frontier trading post, was transformed by the opening of the Erie Canal into a commercial and manufacturing center. By 1850 the city's population had reached 22,000. Chicago, on the shores of Lake Michigan, was transformed by the coming of the railroad into a major junction for water and rail transport. The city, which emerged as a fur trading center around Fort Dearborn, an army post built in 1803, had become, by the 1850s, a hub of trade boasting grain storage facilities, slaughterhouses, and warehouses of all kinds. Farm implement manufacturers such as Cyrus McCormick built manufacturing plants there to serve the needs of Midwest farmers. By 1860 Chicago had a population of 100,000, making it the nation's eighth largest city (after Cincinnati and St. Louis).

Patterns of Immigration

One of the key aspects of urban growth was a surge in immigration to the United States that began in the 1820s and accelerated dramatically after 1830 (see "Immigration and Community: The Changing Face of Ethnicity in the United States, 1800–1860," on page 380). From an annual figure of about 20,000 in 1831, immigration ballooned to a record 430,000 in 1854 before declining in the years prior to the Civil War. The proportion of immigrants in the population jumped from 1.6 percent in the 1820s to 11.2 percent in 1860. In the nation's cities the proportion was vastly larger: by 1860, nearly half of New York's population (48 percent) was foreign-born.

Most of the immigrants to the United States during this period came from Ireland and Germany. Political unrest and poor economic conditions in Germany and the catastrophic Potato Famine of 1845–1850 in Ireland was responsible for an enormous surge in immigration from those countries between 1845 and 1854. The starving, desperate "Famine Irish" who crowded into eastern seaports were America's first large refugee group. Between them, the Germans and the Irish represented the largest influx of non-English immigrants the country had known (many Americans found the Irish dialect as strange as a foreign language). They were also the poorest: most of the Irish arrived destitute. In addition most of the Irish and half of the Germans were Catholics, an unwelcome novelty to many Protestant Americans.

Many German immigrants made their way to agricultural communities in Ohio, Indiana, Missouri, and Texas, but many others, and most Irish immigrants, settled in America's major cities. Few immigrants found life in the United States pleasant or easy. In addition to the psychological difficulties of leaving a home and familiar ways behind, most immigrants endured harsh living and working conditions. One common immigrant response was to construct ethnic neighborhoods and communities for mutual support. For their inhabitants, these Irish and German neighborhoods were a positive response that eased the difficulties of adaptation to American circumstances. But native-born Americans, unprepared for the "foreignness" and poverty of many new immigrants, reacted with hostility to immigrant clustering, and indeed, to the immigrants themselves. Because the immigrant influx widened the social gap between rich and poor and dramatically altered living patterns, immigration contributed to the social problems that America's urban centers faced—and were unable to solve—in the early nineteenth century.

Class Structure in the Cities

Although per capita income in America is estimated to have doubled between 1800 and 1850, the gap between rich and poor increased and became glaringly apparent in the nation's cities. The benefits of the market revolution were unequally distributed: by the 1840s the top 1 percent of the population owned about 40 percent of the nation's wealth, while, at the other extreme, one-third of the population owned virtually nothing. In the cities, then, there was a very small group of wealthy people worth more than $5,000 (about 3 percent of the population), a very large group of poor people worth $100 or less (nearly 70 percent), and a middle class with incomes in between (25–30 percent).

Differences in income affected every aspect of urban life. Very poor families, including almost all new immigrants, performed unskilled labor in jobs whose future was uncertain at best, lived in cheap rented housing, moved frequently, and depended on more than one income to survive. Artisans and skilled workers with incomes of $500 or more could live adequately, though often in cramped quarters that also served as their shops. A middle-class family with an income of more than $1,000 a year could live comfortably in a house of four to six rooms complete with carpeting, wallpaper, and good furniture. The very rich

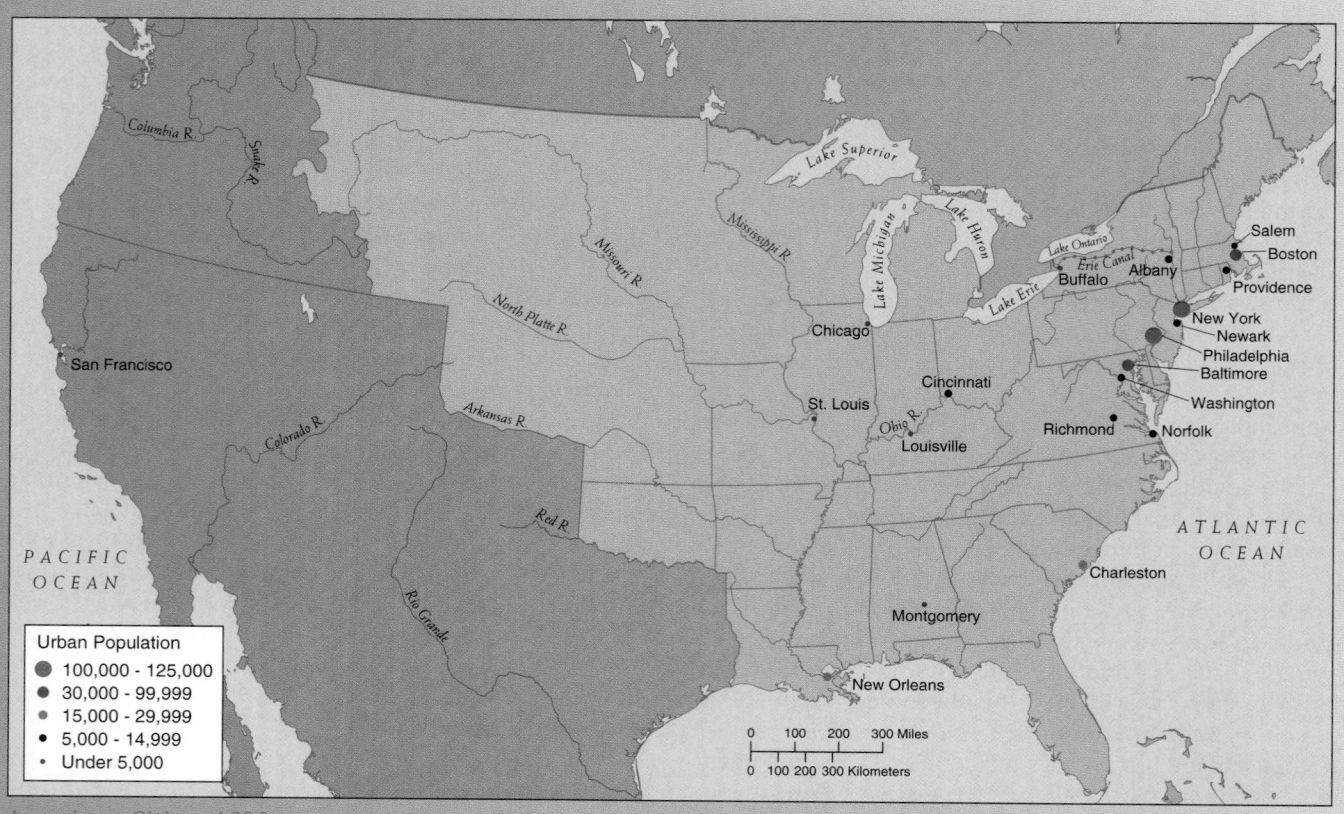

American Cities, 1820

Source: *Statistical Abstract of the United States*

The Growth of Cities, 1820–1860

The cities of North America grew more rapidly between 1820 and 1860 than at any other time in the nation's history. Eastern seaport cities remained the largest, but New York grew to twice the size of the second largest city, Philadelphia. New York's growth, due in large part to the increase in trade following the opening of the Erie Canal, illustrates

built mansions and large town houses and staffed them with many servants. In the summer they left the cities for country estates or homes at seaside resorts such as Newport, Rhode Island, which attracted wealthy families from all over the country.

Sanitation and Living Patterns

Early-nineteenth-century cities lacked municipal water supplies, sewers, and garbage collection. People drank water from wells, used outdoor privies that often contaminated the water supply, and threw garbage and slop out the door to be foraged by roaming herds of pigs. Clearly, this was a recipe for disease, and every American city suffered epidemics of sanitation-related diseases such as yellow fever, cholera, and typhus. Philadelphia's yellow fever epidemic of 1793 caused 4,000 deaths and stopped all business with the outside world for more than a month.

Yet the cities were slow to take action. In response to the yellow fever epidemic Philadelphia completed a city water system in 1801, but users had to pay a fee, and only the richest subscribed in the early days. Neither New York nor Boston had a public water system until the 1840s. Garbage collection remained a private service, and cities charged property owners for the costs of sewers, water mains, and street paving. Poorer areas of the cities could not afford the costs.

Provision of municipal services forced residential segregation. Richer people clustered in neighborhoods that had the new amenities. One of New York's first wealthy areas, Gramercy Park, was developed in 1831 by a speculator who transformed what had been Gramercy Farm into "an ornamental private square or park, with carriageways and footwalks." Only purchasers of the surrounding lots had keys to the park; everyone else was

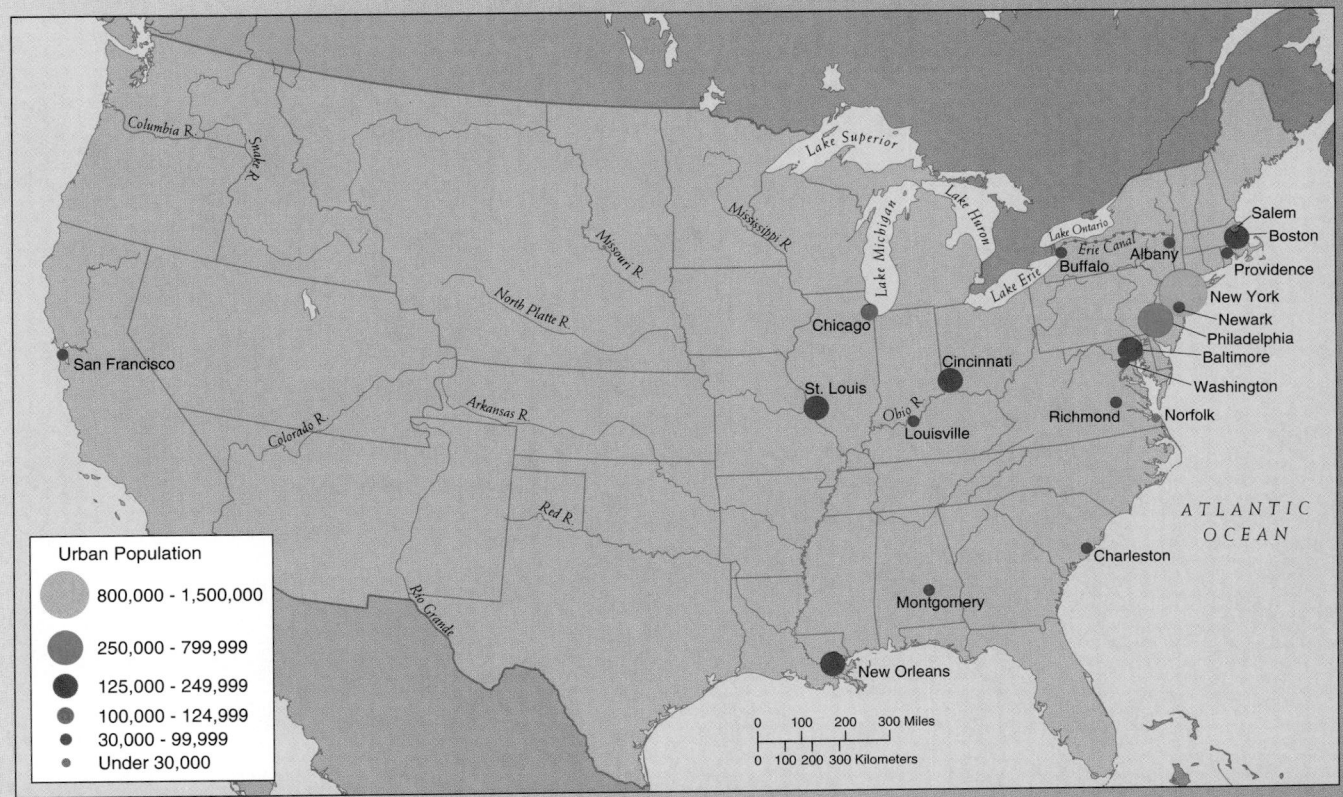

American Cities, 1860

Source: *Statistical Abstract of the United States*

Urban Population

800,000 - 1,500,000
250,000 - 799,999
125,000 - 249,999
100,000 - 124,999
30,000 - 99,999
Under 30,000

the importance of trade between port cities and the nation's interior. Inland river cities like Cincinnati and St. Louis and the great Mississippi seaport of New Orleans grew rapidly. San Francisco, Louisville, and Buffalo—still villages in 1820—grew also, but Chicago, which rapidly emerged as a hub for both water and rail transport, surpassed them all.

excluded. By the 1850s the middle class began to escape cities completely by moving to the new "streetcar suburbs," named for the new mode of urban transportation that connected these nearby areas to the city itself.

As the middle class left the city, the poor clustered in bad neighborhoods that became known as slums. The worst New York slum in the nineteenth century was Five Points, a stone's throw from city hall. There immigrants, free black people, and criminals were crammed into rundown buildings known in the slang of the time as "rookeries." Notorious gangs of thieves and pickpockets with names such as the Plug Uglies and the Shirt Tails dominated the district. Starvation and murder were commonplace.

Five Points was grim even in comparison with the notorious slums of London. As knowledgeable an Englishman as the author Charles Dickens exclaimed on a visit to the district in 1842, "All that is loathsome, drooping and decayed is here…Where dogs would howl to lie, women, and men and boys slink off to sleep, forcing the dislodged rats to move away in quest of better lodgings." With the influx of European immigrants after 1830, middle-class Americans increasingly saw slums as the home of strange and foreign people, who deserved less than American-born citizens. In this way, residential patterns came to embody larger issues of class and citizenship.

Ethnic Neighborhoods

To poverty-stricken Irish immigrants, these same slums represented not only family ties and familiar ways but community support as they learned how to survive in new surroundings. Isolated partly by their own beliefs (for Catholics fully reciprocated the hatred and fear

The Five Points neighborhood in lower Manhattan illustrates the segregated housing patterns that emerged as New York City experienced rapid growth. Immigrants, free African Americans, the poor and criminals were crowded together in New York's most notorious slum, while wealthier people moved to more prosperous neighborhoods.

Protestants showed them), Irish immigrants created their own communities in Boston and New York, their major destinations. They raised the money to erect Catholic churches with Irish priests. They established parochial schools with Irish nuns as teachers and sent their children to them in preference to the openly anti-Catholic public schools. They formed mutual aid societies based on kinship or town of origin in Ireland. Men and women formed religious and social clubs, lodges, and brotherhoods and their female auxiliaries. Irishmen manned fire and militia companies as well. This dense network of associations served the same purpose that social welfare organizations do today: providing help in time of need and offering companionship in a hostile environment.

Germans who settled in urban areas also built their own ethnic enclaves—"Little Germanies"—in which they sought to duplicate the rich cultural life of German cities. In general, German immigrants were skilled workers and not as poor as the Irish. Like the Irish, however, the Germans formed church societies, mutual benefit societies, and fire and militia companies to provide mutual support. Partly because their communities were more prosperous than those of the Irish, the Germans also formed a network of leisure organizations: singing societies, debating and political clubs, concert

halls like New York's Beethoven Hall, theaters, *turnvereins* (gymnastics associations), and beer gardens. They published German-language newspapers as well.

Ethnic clustering, then, allowed new immigrants to hold onto aspects of their culture that they valued and to transplant them to American soil. Many native-born Americans, however, viewed ethnic neighborhoods with deep suspicion. The Boston *American* expressed the sentiments of many in 1837 when it remarked:

> our foreign population are too much in the habit of retaining their own national usages, of *associating too* exclusively *with each other,* and living in groups together. *It would be the part of wisdom, to ABANDON AT ONCE ALL USAGES AND ASSOCIATIONS WHICH MARK THEM AS FOREIGNERS, and to become in feeling and custom, as well as in privileges and rights, citizens of the United States.*

Urban Popular Culture

The size, diversity, and changing working conditions in American cities bred a new urban popular culture with New York, the largest city, leading the way. In the period 1820–60, urban workers experienced the replacement of artisanal labor by wagework, two serious depressions (1837–43 and 1857), and vastly increased competition from immigrant labor. In response to these pressures, working-class amusements became rougher and rowdier. Taverns that served as neighborhood centers of drink and sociability were also frequent centers of brawls and riots. Community groups such as fire engine companies that had once included men of all social classes now attracted rough young laborers who formed their own youth gangs and defended "their" turf against other gangs. Some trades, such as that of butcher, became notorious for starting fights in taverns and grog shops.

Theaters, which had been frequented by men of all social classes, provided another setting for violence. Few women, except for the prostitutes who met their customers in the third tier of the balcony, attended. In the 1820s, a long-standing tradition of small-scale rioting by poorer patrons against unpopular actors began to change into more serious violence. The Astor Place Riot of 1849 began as a theater riot

against a British actor but escalated into a pitched battle between the mob and the militia that left twenty-two dead.

By the 1830s, middle-class and upper-class men withdrew to more respectable theaters to which they could bring their wives and daughters. Workers found new amusements in theaters such as the Lafayette Circus that featured dancing girls and horseback riders as well as theatrical acts. Another popular urban working-class amusement was the blackface minstrel show. White actors (often Irish) blacked their faces and entertained audiences with songs (including the famous "Dixie," written by an Irishman as a blackface song), dances, theatrical skits, and antiblack political jokes. Cruel stereotypes such as Zip Coon, an irresponsible free black man, and Jim Crow, a slow-witted slave, entertained white audiences. Historians have speculated that the popularity of blackface expressed not only white racism but also nostalgia for the freer behavior of preindustrial life that was now impossible for white workers but that

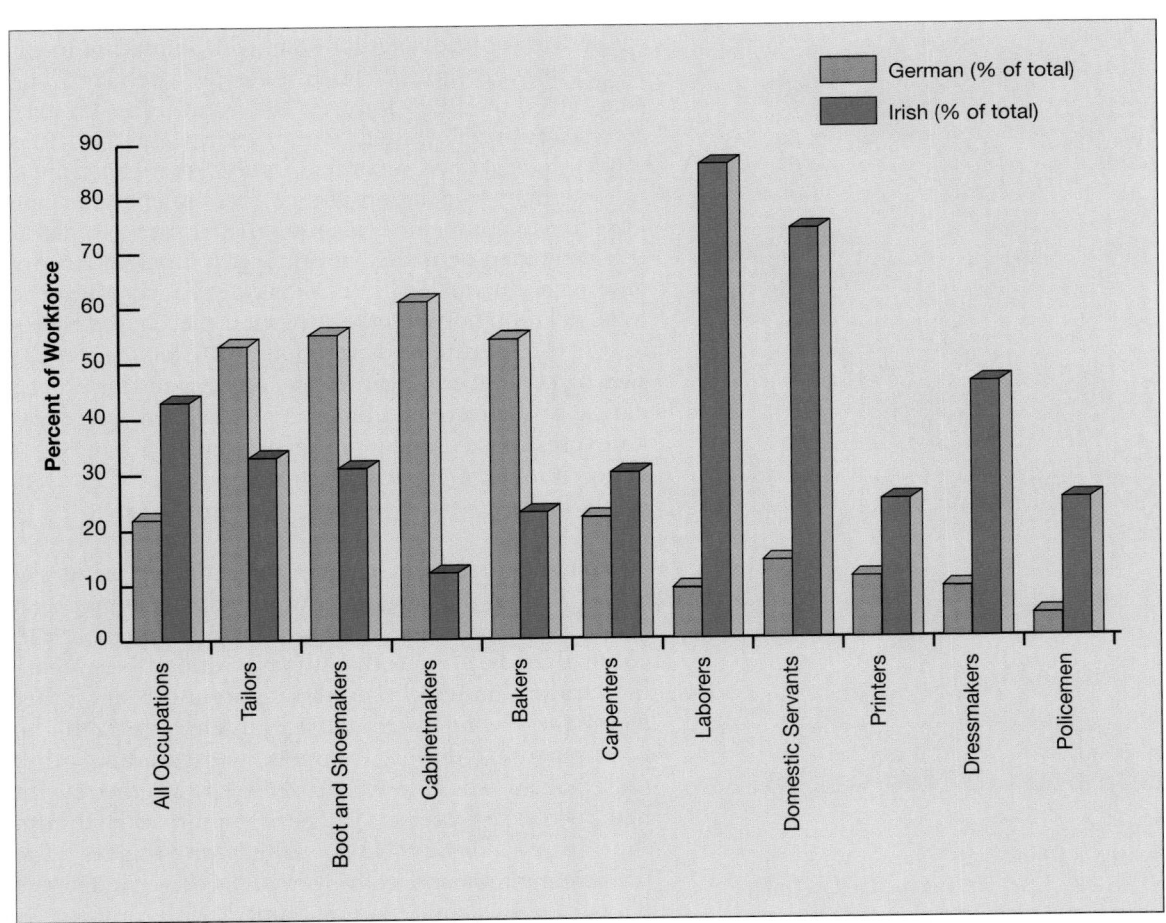

Participation of Irish and German Immigrants in the New York City Workforce for Selected Occuptations, 1855

Source: Robert Ernst, *Immigrant Life in New York City* 1825-1863 (Syracuse: Syracuse University Press, 1994).

they imagined African American slaves continued to enjoy in carefree dependency.

The new working-class culture flourished especially on the Bowery, a New York City street filled with artisanal workshops, small factories, shops with cheap goods, dance halls, theaters, ice cream parlors, and oyster bars. Here working-class youth, the "Bowery b'hoys" (slang pronunciation of "boy") and "gals," found Saturday night amusements and provided it for themselves with outrageous clothing and behavior. The deliberately provocative way they dressed was in effect a way of thumbing their noses at the more respectable classes. The costumes worn by the characters in one long-running series of melodramas staged by the Bowery Theater imitated this style. Mose, the hero of the series, dressed more like a pirate captain

This 1848 playbill promotes A Glance at New York, *which featured two well-known working-class figures, Mose, the Bowery B'hoy, and his gal, Lise. His exaggerated clothing and hairstyle and her flashy colors were deliberate parodies aimed at New York's respectable middle class for the benefit of the rowdy working-class culture that grew up in the Bowery district of the city in the 1830s.*

than a worker, and his gal Lise wore a bright-colored, body-hugging dress that challenged the discreet, sober fashions worn by middle-class women.

Another challenge to middle-class respectability came from the immensely popular "penny papers" (so called from their price), the *New York Morning Post* and the *New York Sun*, which began appearing in 1833. These papers, with lurid headlines such as "Double Suicide," and "Secret Tryst," and "Bloody Murder," fed the same popular appetite for scandal, as did other popular reading such as the *Police Gazette* magazine, pamphlets about murder trials, swindlers, and pirates, and temperance dime novels such as *Franklin Evans; or, The Inebriate* written in 1842 by the struggling young newspaperman, Walter (later Walt) Whitman. Urban journalist, Democratic Party activist, and poet, Whitman distilled his passionate love for the variety and commonness of the American people in *Leaves of Grass*, a book of free-verse poems published in 1855. Regarded at the time as scandalous because of its frank language, Whitman's poetry nevertheless captured the driving energy and democratic spirit of the new urban popular culture. In a rather more sinister way, so did the writings of Edgar Allan Poe, who found the inspiration for his gothic horror stories such as "The Murders in the Rue Morgue" (1841) and "The Mystery of Marie Roget" (1842) not in Europe (as his titles might suggest) but in contemporary American crimes.

This fascination with urban violence led one observer to comment cynically in 1859 that "No narrative of human depravity or crime can shock or horrify an American reader." But Alexis de Tocqueville, the famous French observer who visited the United States in 1831–32 wrote with foreboding, "I look upon the size of certain American cities, and especially on the nature of their population, as a real danger." Here was an expression of a new fear in American urban life—concern about civic order.

Civic Order

Tocqueville's fears for civic order echoed that of the urban middle class, who now found menacing even traditions of lower-class amusement that dated back to colonial times. New York City's tradition of New Year's Eve "frolics," in which laborers, apprentices, and other members of the lower classes paraded through the streets playing drums, trumpets, whistles, and other noisemakers, was an example. By the 1820s the revelry had been taken over by gangs of young workers from the lower classes who called themselves the Callithumpian Band. On New Year's Eve 1828, the band, 4,000 strong and equipped with drums, tin kettles, rattles, horns, and whistles, marched through the city. On their way they overturned carts and broke windows in the commercial district, in some wealthy homes near Battery Park, and in an African American church. They then marched to the City Hotel, where middle-class couples were just leaving a ball, and obstructed traffic. The indignant couples watched helplessly as several hundred watchmen called to disperse the mob cautiously declined to do so. In the following year, the traditional New Year's Eve parade was banned by the city government.

The prosperous classes were frightened by the urban poor and by working-class rowdyism. They resented having to avoid many parts of the city that were unsafe for them, and they disliked even more the disturbances in "their" parts of the city, as this irritable notation in the diary of merchant Philip Hone indicates: "Riot, disorder, and violence increase in our city, every night is marked by some outrage committed by gangs of young ruffians who prowl the streets insulting females, breaking into the houses of unoffending publicans [tavern keepers], making night hideous by yells of disgusting inebriety, and—unchecked by the city authorities—committing every sort of enormity with apparent impunity."

In colonial days, civic disturbances had been handled informally: members of the city watch asked onlookers for such assistance as was necessary to keep the peace. New York City's first response in the 1820s and 1830s to increasing civic disorder was to hire more city watchmen and to augment them with constables and marshals. When riots occurred, the militia were called, and deaths were increasingly common as they forcibly restrained mobs. Finally, in 1845, the city created a permanent police force with a mandate to keep the poor in order. There had been substantial opposition to the idea of this first professional police force in the United States on the grounds that it infringed personal liberty, but as middle-class fear of what became known as "the dangerous classes" grew, police protection came to seem necessary. Here was an indication that the harmonious preindustrial urban community no longer existed.

But even with police forces in place, the pressures of rapid urbanization, immigration, and the market revolution proved to be more than America's cities could contain. The violence was more than just rowdyism and socially disapproved behavior. Beginning in the 1830s, a series of urban riots broke out against the two poorest urban groups: Catholics and free black people. As if their miserable living conditions were not enough, Irish immigrants were met with virulent anti-Catholicism. In 1834 rioters burned an Ursuline convent in Charlestown, Massachusetts; in 1844 a Philadelphia mob attacked priests and nuns and vandalized Catholic churches; in 1854 a mob destroyed an Irish neighborhood in Lawrence, Massachusetts. Often the Irish replied in kind—for example, in the 1806 riot in New York when they counterattacked a mob that disrupted their Christmas Eve mass in a Catholic church on Augustus Street. But the most common targets of urban violence were free African Americans.

Urban Life of Free African Americans

By 1860, there were nearly half a million free African Americans in the United States, constituting about 11 percent of the country's total black population. More than half of all free African Americans lived in the North, mostly in cities, where they competed with immigrants and native-born poor white people for jobs as day laborers and domestic servants. Their relative social position is reflected in statistics on per capita annual income in Boston in the 1850s—$91 for black people and $131 for Irish immigrants compared to $872 for the population at large. Philadelphia and New York had the largest black communities: 22,000 African Americans in Philadelphia and 12,500 in New York (another 4,313 lived just across the East River in Brooklyn). There were much smaller but still significant black communities in the New England cities of Boston, Providence, and New Haven and in Ohio cities like Cincinnati.

Free African Americans in northern cities faced residential segregation (except for the domestic servants who lived in with white families), pervasive job discrimination, segregated public schools, and severe limitations on their civil rights. In addition to these legal restrictions there were matters of custom: African Americans of all economic classes endured daily affronts, such as exclusion from public concerts, lectures, and libraries and segregation or exclusion from public transportation. For example, in Massachusetts—which had the reputation of being more hospitable to black people than any other northern state—the famed African American abolitionist Frederick Douglass was denied admission to a zoo on Boston Common, a public lecture and revival meeting, a restaurant, and a public omnibus, all within the space of a few days.

In common with Irish and German immigrants, African Americans created defenses against the larger hostile society by building their own community structures. They formed associations for aiding the poorest members of the community, for self-improvement, and for socializing. Tired of being insulted by the white press, African American communities supported their own newspapers. The major community organization was the black Baptist or African Methodist Episcopal (AME) church, which served, as one historian put it, as "a place of worship, a social and cultural center, a political meeting place, a hiding place for fugitives, a training ground for potential community leaders, and one of the few places where blacks could express their true feelings."

Free African Americans suffered many forms of discrimination, but as this 1850 daguerreotype of an unknown woman shows, they sought to achieve the same levels of education and economic comfort as other Americans.

Employment prospects for black men deteriorated from 1820 to 1850. Those who had held jobs as skilled artisans were forced from their positions, and their sons denied apprenticeships, by white mechanics and craftsmen who were themselves suffering from the effects of the market revolution. Limited to day labor, African Americans found themselves in direct competition with the new immigrants, especially the Irish, for jobs. On the waterfront, black men lost their jobs as carters and longshoremen to the Irish. One of the few occupations to remain open to them was that of seaman. More than 20 percent of all American sailors in 1850 were black, and over the years their ranks included an increasing number of runaway slaves. The pay was poor and the conditions miserable, but many black men found more equality aboard ship than they did ashore. Mothers, wives, and daughters were left ashore to work as domestic servants (in competition with Irishwomen), washerwomen, and seamstresses.

Free African Americans remained committed to their enslaved brethren in the South. In New York, for example, black communities rioted four times—in 1801, 1819, 1826, and 1832—against slave catchers taking escaped slaves back to slavery. But even more frequently, free African Americans were themselves targets of urban violence. An 1829 riot in Cincinnati sent a thousand black people fleeing to Canada in fear for their lives; a three-day riot in Providence in 1831 destroyed an African American district; and an 1834 New York riot destroyed a church, a school, and a dozen homes. Philadelphia, "the City of Brotherly Love," had the worst record. Home to the largest free African American community in the North, Philadelphia was repeatedly rocked by antiblack riots in the period between 1820 and 1859. A riot in 1834 destroyed two churches and thirty-one homes and left one African American dead and many injured. In 1842, a predominantly Irish mob attacked black marchers celebrating Jamaican Emancipation Day. The marchers counterattacked, wounding three Irish boys and provoking widespread arson, which firemen refused to put out for fear of the mob. The disturbance ended only when the mayor called out seven companies of the militia. Other cities had similar stories. Urban riots of all kinds had cost 125 lives by 1840, by 1860 more than 1,000.

THE LABOR MOVEMENT AND URBAN POLITICS

Universal white manhood suffrage and the development of mass politics (see Chapter 10), coupled with the rapid growth of cities, changed urban politics. The traditional leadership role of the wealthy elite waned, and members of the wealthiest class gradually withdrew from direct participation in urban politics. In New York City, elite political leaders had disappeared by 1845. In their place were professional politicians whose job it was to make party politics work. In New York and in other large cities, this change in politics was spurred by working-class activism.

The Tradition of Artisanal Politics

The nation's urban centers had long been strongholds of craft associations for artisans and skilled workers. These organizations, and their parades and celebrations, were recognized parts of the urban community. Groups of master craftsmen marching in community parades with signs such as "By Hammer and Hand All Arts Do Stand" were visible symbols of the strength and solidarity of workers' organizations.

Also traditional were riots and demonstrations by workers (usually journeymen or apprentices, not the master artisans themselves) over matters as political and far-reaching as the American Revolution or as practical and immediate as the price of bread. In fact, protests by urban workers had been an integral part of the older social order controlled by the wealthy elite. In the eighteenth century, when only men of property could vote, such demonstrations usually indicated widespread discontent or economic difficulty among workers. They served as a warning signal that the political elite rarely ignored.

By the 1830s the status of artisans and independent craftsmen in the nation's cities had changed. As discussed in Chapter 12, the artisanal system was crumbling, undercut by competition between cities (the result of the transportation revolution) and by the growth of the putting-out system. Furthermore, the rapid influx of immigrants changed the character of the labor force. New York provides a particularly dramatic example. The city's rapid growth as a manufacturing center was based on the labor of Irish and German immigrant workers, who made up 65 percent of the workforce by 1855. Germans clustered primarily in the skilled trades, while the Irish performed most of the low-paid labor. Indeed, 86 percent of day laborers were Irishmen, while Irishwomen made up 74 percent of the domestic servants.

This seal of the General Society of Mechanics and Tradesmen illustrates in its motto— "By Hammer and Hand All Arts Do Stand"—the personal and community pride artisans took in their work.

There was no safety net for workers who lost their jobs—no unemployment insurance or welfare—and no public regulation of wages and conditions of work. The first protests against these harsh conditions came from the women workers at the new cotton textile factories in Lowell and elsewhere. The members of urban workers' associations, increasingly angry over their declining status in the economic and social order, also became—tentatively at first, but then with growing conviction—active defenders of working-class interests.

What was new was the open antagonism between workers and employers. The community of interest between masters and workers in preindustrial times broke down. Workers realized they had to depend on other workers, not employers, for support. In turn, employers and members of the middle class began to take urban disorders much more seriously than their grandfathers might have done.

The Union Movement

Urban worker protest against changing conditions quickly took the form of party politics. The Workingmen's Party was founded in Philadelphia in 1827, and chapters quickly formed in New York and Boston as well. Using the language of class warfare—"two distinct classes…those that live by their own labor and they

that live upon the labor of others"—the "Workies" campaigned for the ten-hour day and the preservation of the small artisanal shop. They also called for the end of government-chartered monopolies—banks were high on the list—and for a public school system and cheap land in the West. Although the Workies themselves did not survive as a party, Jacksonian Democrats were quick to pick up on some of their themes. The Democrats attracted many workers' votes in 1832, the year Andrew Jackson campaigned against the "monster" Bank of the United States.

Both major parties competed for the votes of urban workers. In New York City in 1835 a radical antimonopoly branch of the Democratic Party known officially as the Equal Rights Party attracted some worker support. For their part, the Whigs wooed workers by assuring them that Henry Clay's American System, and tariff protection in particular, would be good for the economy and for workers' jobs. Nevertheless, neither major political party really spoke to the primary need of workers—for well-paid, stable jobs that assured them independence and respect. Unsatisfied with the response of political parties, workers turned to labor organization to achieve their goals.

Between 1833 and 1837 a wave of strikes in New York City cut the remaining ties between master craftsmen and the journeymen who worked for them. In 1833, journeymen carpenters struck for higher wages. Workers in fifteen other trades came to their support, and within a month the strike was won. The lesson was obvious: if skilled workers banded together across craft lines, they could improve their conditions. The same year, representatives from nine different craft groups formed the General Trades Union of New York. By 1834 similar groups had sprung up in over a dozen cities—Boston, Louisville, and Cincinnati among them. In New York alone, the GTU helped organize almost forty strikes between 1833 and 1837, and it encouraged the formation of more than fifty unions. In 1834 also, representatives of several local GTUs met in Baltimore and organized the National Trades Union. In its founding statement the NTU criticized the "unjustifiable distribution of the wealth of society in the hands of a few individuals," which had created for working people "a humiliating, servile dependency, incompatible with…natural equality."

Naturally, employers disagreed with the NTU's criticism of the economic system. Convinced that unions were dangerous, New York employers took striking journeymen tailors to court in 1836. Judge Ogden Edwards pronounced the strikers guilty of conspiracy and declared unions un-American. He assured the strikers that "the road of advancement is open to all" and that they would do better to strive to be masters themselves rather than "conspire" with their fellow workers. The GTU responded with a mass rally at which Judge Edwards was burned in effigy. A year later, stunned by the effects of the Panic of 1837, the GTU collapsed. The founding of these general unions, a visible sign of a class-based community of interest among workers, is generally considered to mark the beginning of the American labor movement. However, these early unions included only white men in skilled trades who made up only a small percentage of all workers. The majority of workers—men in unskilled occupations, all free African Americans, and all women—were excluded.

Big-City Machines

Although workers were unable to create strong unions or stable political parties that spoke for their economic interests, they were able to shape urban politics. As America's cities experienced unprecedented growth, the electorate mushroomed. In New York, for example,

By 1855, half the voters in New York City were foreign-born. This 1858 engraving of an Irish bar in the Five Points area appeared in the influential Harper's Weekly. It expressed the dislike of temperance reformers for immigrants and their drinking habits and the dismay of political reformers that immigrant saloons and taverns were such effective organizing centers for urban political machines.

the number of voters grew from 20,000 in 1825 to 88,900 in 1855. Furthermore, by 1855 half of the voters were foreign-born. At the time, America was the only country in the world where propertyless white men had the vote. The job of serving this largely working-class electorate and making the new mass political party work at the urban level fell to a new kind of career politician—the boss—and a new kind of political organization—the machine.

Just as the old system of elite leadership had mirrored the social unity of eighteenth-century cities, so the new system of machine politics reflected the class structure of the rapidly growing nineteenth-century cities. Feelings of community, which had arisen naturally out of the personal contact that characterized neighborhoods in earlier, smaller cities, now were cultivated politically. The existence of distinct ethnic neighborhoods fostered political organization. Because immigrants clustered in neighborhoods, their impact on politics could be concentrated and manipulated. Legally, three years' residence in the United States was required before one could apply for citizenship, but there was clear evidence of swifter naturalization in large cities with effective political organizations. In New York, for example, the Irish-dominated districts quickly became Democratic Party strongholds. Germans, who were less active politically than the Irish, nevertheless voted heavily for the new Republican Party in the 1850s. Between them, these two new blocs of immigrant voters destroyed the Whig Party that had controlled New York politics before the immigrants arrived.

In New York City, the Tammany Society, begun in the 1780s as a fraternal organization of artisans, slowly evolved into the key organization of the new mass politics. (Named after the Delaware chief mentioned in Chapter 3, the society met in a hall called the Wigwam and elected "sachems" as their officers.) Tammany, which was affiliated with the national Democratic Party, reached voters by using many of the techniques of mass appeal made popular earlier by craft organizations—parades, rallies, current songs, and party newspapers.

Along with these new techniques of mass appeal went new methods of organization: a tight system of political control beginning at the neighborhood level with ward committees and topped by a chairman of a citywide general committee. At the citywide level, ward leaders—bosses—bartered the loyalty and votes of their followers for positions on the city payroll for party members and community services for their neighborhood. This was machine politics. Through it workers, although they lacked the political or organizational strength to challenge the harmful effects of the market revolution, could use their

numbers to ameliorate some of its effects at the local level. Machine politics served to mediate increasing class divisions and ethnic diversity as well. The machines themselves offered personal ties and loyalties—community feeling—to recent arrivals in the big cities (increasingly, immigrants from Europe) and help in hard times to workers who cast their votes correctly.

In America's big cities the result was apparent by midcentury: the political "machine" controlled by the "boss"—the politician who represented the interests of his group and delivered their votes in exchange for patronage and favors.

Critics said that big-city machines were corrupt, and indeed they often were. Antagonism between reformers, who were usually members of the upper and middle classes, and machine politicians, who spoke for the working class, was evident by the 1850s. This antagonism was to become chronic in American urban politics. One result of the market revolution was the political expression, in a democratic society, of the conflict of interests between owners and workers.

SOCIAL REFORM MOVEMENTS

The passion for reform that had become such an important part of the new middle-class thinking was focused on the problems of the nation's cities. As the opening of this chapter describes, the earliest response to the dislocations caused by the market revolution was community-based and voluntary. Middle-class people tried to deal with social changes in their communities by joining organizations devoted to reforms such as temperance, education, prisons and asylums, women's rights, abolitionism, and, above all, the spread of evangelical religion. The reform message was vastly amplified by inventions such as the steam printing press, which made it possible to publish reform literature in great volume. Soon there were national networks of reform groups.

Alexis de Tocqueville commented on the vast extent of American voluntary associations and their many purposes. "In no country in the world," he noted, "has the principle of association been more successfully used, or more unsparingly applied to a multitude of different objects, than in America." The widespread reform movements of the era depended on the energy and hope of communities of like-minded people.

Evangelism, Reform, and Social Control
Evangelical religion was fundamental to social reform. Men and women who had been converted to the enthusiastic new faith assumed personal responsibility for making changes in their own lives. Personal reform quickly led to social reform; recall, for example, the northern businessman described in Chapter 12 who

gave up drinking alcohol and insisted that his employees do the same. Religious converts were encouraged in their social activism by such leading revivalists as Charles G. Finney, who preached a doctrine of "perfectionism," claiming it was possible for all Christians to personally understand and live by God's will and thereby become "as perfect as God." Furthermore, Finney predicted, "the complete reformation of the whole world" could be achieved if only enough converts put their efforts into moral reform. This new religious feeling was intensely hopeful: members of evangelistic religions really did expect to convert the world and create the perfect moral and religious community on earth.

Much of America was swept by the fervor of moralistic reform, and it was the new middle class, who applied new notions of morality to the movement, that set the agenda for reform. Reform efforts arose from the recognition that the traditional methods of small-scale local relief were no longer adequate. In colonial times, families (sometimes at the request of local government) had housed and cared for the ill or incapacitated. Small local almshouses and prisons had housed the poor and the criminal. Reformers now realized that large cities had to make large-scale provisions for social misfits and that institutional rather than private efforts were needed. This thinking was especially true of the institutional reform movements that began in the 1830s, such as the push for insane asylums. At this time, of course, the federal government provided no such relief.

A second characteristic of the reform movements was a belief in the basic goodness of human nature. All reformers believed that the condition of the unfortunate—the poor, the insane, the criminal—would improve in a wholesome environment. Thus insane asylums were built in rural areas, away from the noise and stress of the cities, and orphanages had strict rules that were meant to encourage discipline and self-reliance. Prison reform carried this sentiment to the extreme. On the theory that bad social influences were largely responsible for crime, some "model" prisons completely isolated prisoners from one another, making them eat, sleep, work, and do required Bible reading in their own cells. The failure of these prisons to achieve dramatic changes for the better in their inmates (a number of isolated prisoners went mad, and some committed suicide) or to reduce crime was one of the first indications that reform was not a simple task.

A third characteristic of the reform movements was their moralistic dogmatism. Reformers were certain they knew what was right and were determined to see their improvements enacted. It was a short step from developing individual self-discipline to imposing discipline on others. The reforms that

were proposed thus took the form of social controls. Lazy, sinful, intemperate, or unfit members of society were to be reformed for their own good, whether they wanted to be or not. This attitude was bound to cause controversy; by no means did all Americans share the reformers' beliefs, nor did those for whom it was intended always take kindly to being the targets of the reformers' concern.

Indeed, some aspects of the social reform movements were harmful. The evangelical Protestantism of the reformers promoted hostility to Catholic immigrants from Ireland and Germany beginning in the 1830s. The temperance movement, in particular, targeted immigrants for their free drinking habits. Seeking uniformity of behavior rather than tolerance, the reformers thus helped to promote the virulent nativism that infected American politics between 1840 and 1860 (see Chapter 15 and "Immigration and Community: The Changing Face of Ethnicity in America, 1800–1865" on page 380).

Regional and national reform organizations quickly grew from local projects to deal with social problems such as drinking, prostitution, mental illness, and crime. In 1828, for example, Congregationalist minister Lyman Beecher joined other ministers in forming a General Union for Promoting the Observance of the Christian Sabbath; the aim was to prevent business on Sundays. To achieve its goals, the General Union adopted the same methods used by political parties: lobbying, petition drives, fund-raising, and special publications. These and other efforts, Beecher said, were all for the purpose of establishing "the moral government of God."

In effect, the sabbath reformers engaged in political action but remained aloof from direct electoral politics, stressing their religious mission. In any case, their goal was controversial. Workingmen (who usually worked six days a week) were angered when the General Union forced the Sunday closure of their favorite taverns and were quick to vote against the Whigs, the party most sympathetic to reform thinking. Other reforms likewise muddied the distinction between political and social activity. It is not surprising that women, who were barred from electoral politics but not from moral and social activism, were major supporters of reform.

Education and Women Teachers

Women became deeply involved in reform movements through their churches. It was they who did most of the fund-raising for the home missionary societies that were beginning to send the evangelical message worldwide—at first by ministers alone, later by married couples. Nearly every church had a maternal association, where mothers gathered to discuss ways to raise

Catharine Beecher, a member of one of America's leading families of religious reformers, advocated teaching as a suitable employment for young single women because it called for the nurturing skills and moral values she claimed all women possessed.

their children as true Christians. These associations reflected a new and more positive definition of childhood. The Puritans had believed that children were born sinful and that their wills had to be broken before they could become godly. Early schools reflected these beliefs: teaching was by rote, and punishment was harsh and physical. Educational reformers, however, tended to believe that children were born innocent and needed gentle nurturing and encouragement if they were to flourish. At home, mothers began to play the central role in child rearing. Outside the home, women helped spread the new public education pioneered by Horace Mann, secretary of the Massachusetts State Board of Education.

Although literacy had long been valued, especially in New England, schooling since colonial times had been a private enterprise and a personal expense. Town grammar schools, required in Massachusetts since 1647, had been supported primarily by parents' payments, with some help from local property taxes. In 1827, Massachusetts pioneered compulsory education by legislating that public schools be supported by public taxes. Soon schooling for white children between the ages of five and nineteen was common, although, especially in rural schools, the term might be only a month or so long. Uniformity in curriculum

and teacher training, and the grading of classes by ability—measures pioneered by Horace Mann in the 1830s—quickly caught on in other states. In the North and West (the South lagged far behind), more and more children went to school, and more and more teachers, usually young single women, were hired to teach them.

The spread of public education created the first real career opportunity for women. Horace Mann insisted that to learn well, children needed schools with a pleasant and friendly atmosphere. One important way to achieve that atmosphere, Mann recommended, was to group children by ages rather than combining everyone in the traditional ungraded classroom and to pay special attention to the needs of the youngest pupils. Who could better create the friendly atmosphere of the new classroom than women? The great champion of teacher training for women was Catharine Beecher, daughter of Lyman, who clearly saw her efforts as part of the larger work of establishing "the moral government of God." Arguing that women's moral and nurturing nature ideally suited them to be teachers, Beecher campaigned tirelessly on their behalf. Since "the mind is to be guided chiefly by means of the affections," she argued, "is not woman best fitted to accomplish these important objects?"

By 1850 women were dominant in primary school teaching, which had come to be regarded as an acceptable occupation for educated young women during the few years between their own schooling and marriage. For some women, teaching was a great adventure; they enthusiastically volunteered to be "schoolmarms" on the distant western frontiers of Wisconsin and Iowa. Still others thought globally. The young women who attended Mary Lyon's Mount Holyoke Female Seminary in Massachusetts, founded in 1837, hoped to be missionary teachers in distant lands. For others, a few years of teaching was quite enough. Low pay (half of what male schoolteachers earned) and community supervision (women teachers had to board with families in the community) were probably sufficient to make almost any marriage proposal look appealing.

Temperance

Reformers believed not only that children could be molded but that adults could change. The largest reform organization of the period, the American Society for the Promotion of Temperance founded in 1826, boasted more than 200,000 members by the mid-1830s. Dominated by evangelicals, local chapters used revival methods—lurid temperance tracts detailing the evils of alcohol, large prayer and song meetings, and heavy group pressure—to encourage young men to stand up, confess their bad habits, and

Per Capita Consumption of Alcohol, 1800–1860
The underlying cause for the dramatic fall in alcohol consumption during the 1830s was the changing nature of work brought about by the market revolution. Contributing factors were the shock of the Panic of 1837 and the untiring efforts of temperance reformers.

Source: W. J. Rorabaugh, *The Alcoholic Republic: An American Tradition* (New York: Oxford University Press, 1979).

"take the pledge" (not to drink). Here again, women played an important role.

Excessive drinking was a national problem, and it appears to have been mostly a masculine one, for respectable women did not drink in public. (Many did, however, drink alcohol-based patent medicines. Lydia Pinkham's Vegetable Compound, marketed for "female complaints," was 19 percent alcohol.) Men drank hard liquor—whiskey, rum, and hard cider—in abundance. Traditionally, drinking had been a basic part of men's working lives. It concluded occasions as formal as the signing of a contract and accompanied such informal activities as card games. Drink was a staple offering at political speeches, rallies, and elections. In the old artisanal workshops, drinking had been a customary pastime. Much of the drinking was well within the bounds of sociability, but the widespread use (more than seven gallons of hard liquor per capita in 1830—more than twice as much as today's rate) must have encouraged drunkenness.

There were many reasons to support temperance. Heavy-drinking men hurt their families economically by spending their wages on drink. Women had no recourse: the laws of the time gave men complete

financial control of the household, and divorce was difficult as well as socially unacceptable. Excessive drinking also led to violence and crime, both within the family and in the larger society.

But there were other reasons as well. The new middle class, preoccupied with respectability and morality, found the old easygoing drinking ways unacceptable. As work patterns changed, employers banned alcohol at work and increasingly considered drinking men not only unreliable but immoral. Temperance became a social and political issue. Whigs, who embraced the new morality, favored it; Democrats, who in northern cities consisted increasingly of immigrant workers, were opposed. Both German and Irish immigrants valued the social drinking that occurred in beer gardens and saloons and were hostile to temperance reform.

The Panic of 1837 affected the temperance movement. Whereas most temperance crusaders in the 1820s had been members of the middle class, the long depression of 1837–43 prompted artisans and skilled workers to give up or at least cut down substantially on drinking. Forming associations known as Washington Temperance Societies, these workers spread the word that temperance was the workingman's best chance to survive economically and to maintain his independence. Their wives, gathered together in Martha Washington Societies, were frequently even more committed to temperance than their husbands. While the men's temperance groups were often deeply involved in working-class politics, the women's groups stressed the harm that alcoholism could do to homes and families and provided financial help to distressed women and children.

Campaigns against alcohol were frequent and successful. By the mid-1840s alcohol consumption had been more than halved, to less than two gallons per capita, about the level of today. Concern over drinking would remain constant throughout the nineteenth century and into the twentieth.

Moral Reform, Asylums, and Prisons

Alcohol was not the only "social evil" that reform groups attacked. Another was prostitution, which was common in the nation's port cities. The customary approach of evangelical reformers was to "rescue" prostitutes, offering them the salvation of religion, prayer, and temporary shelter. The success rate was not very high. As an alternative to prostitution, reformers usually offered domestic work, a low-paying and restrictive occupation that many women scorned. Nevertheless, campaigns against prostitution, generally organized by women, continued throughout the nineteenth century.

One of the earliest and most effective antiprostitution groups was the Female Moral Reform Society. Founded by evangelical women in New York in 1834 (the first president was Lydia Finney), it boasted 555 affiliates throughout the country by 1840. It was surprising that so many respectable women were willing to acknowledge the existence of something so disreputable as prostitution. Even more surprising was the speed with which the societies realized that prostitution was not so much a moral as an economic issue. The societies rapidly moved to organize charity and work for poor women and orphans. They also took direct action against the patrons of prostitutes by printing their names in local papers, and they successfully lobbied the New York state legislature for criminal penalties against the male clients as well as the women themselves.

Another dramatic example of reform was the asylum movement, spearheaded by a woman evangelist, Dorothea Dix. In 1843, Dix horrified the Massachusetts state legislature with the results of her several years of study into the conditions to which insane women were subjected. She described in graphic detail how the women were incarcerated with ordinary criminals, locked up in "cages, closets, stalls, pens! Chained, naked, beaten with rods, and lashed into obedience!" Dix's efforts led to the establishment of a state asylum for the insane in Massachusetts and to similar institutions in other states. Between 1843 and 1854 Dix traveled more than 30,000 miles to publicize the movement for humane treatment of the insane. By 1860 twenty-eight states had public institutions for the insane.

Other reformers were active in related causes, such as prison reform and the establishment of orphanages, homes of refuge, and hospitals. Model penitentiaries were built in Auburn and Ossining (known as "Sing Sing"), New York, and in Philadelphia and Pittsburgh. Characterized by strict order and discipline, these prisons were supposed to reform rather than simply incarcerate their inmates, but their regimes of silence and isolation caused despair more often than rehabilitation.

Utopianism and Mormonism

Amid all the political activism and reform fervor of the 1830s, a few people chose escape into utopian communities and new religions. The upstate New York area along the Erie Canal was the seedbed for this movement, just as it was for evangelical revivals and reform movements like the Seneca Falls convention. The area was so notable for its reform enthusiasms that it has been termed "the Burned-Over District," a reference to the waves of reform that swept through like forest fires.

Apocalyptic religions tend to spring up in places experiencing rapid social change. The Erie Canal region, which experienced the full impact of the

Temperance tracts, produced in the hundreds of thousands, painted lurid pictures of the perils of alcohol. Both melodramatic stories of ruin and cartoons like this 1826 tract, "The Drunkard's Progress," spread the temperance message in popular, easily understood forms.

Reform Movements in the Burned-Over District
The so-called Burned-Over District, the region of New York State most changed by the opening of the Erie Canal, was a seedbed of religious and reform movements. The Mormon Church originated there and Utopian groups and sects like the Millerites and the Fourierists thrived. Charles G. Finney held some of his most successful evangelical revivals in the district. Antislavery feeling was common in the region, and the women's rights movement began at Seneca Falls.

Source: Whitney Cross, *The Burned-Over District* (1950; reprint, New York: Hippocrene Books, 1981).

market revolution in the early nineteenth century, was such a place. A second catalyst is hard times, and the prolonged depression that began with the Panic of 1837 led some people to embrace a belief in imminent catastrophe. The Millerites (named for their founder, William Miller) believed that the Second Coming of Christ would occur on October 22, 1843. In anticipation, members of the church sold their belongings and bought white robes for their ascension to heaven. When the Day of Judgment did not take place as expected, most of Miller's followers drifted away. But a small group persisted. Revising their expectations, they formed the core of the Seventh-Day Adventist faith, which is still active today.

The Shakers, founded by "Mother" Ann Lee in 1774, were the oldest utopian group. An offshoot of the Quakers, the Shakers espoused a radical social philosophy that called for the abolishment of the traditional family in favor of a family of brothers and sisters joined in equal fellowship. Despite its insistence on celibacy, the Shaker movement grew between 1820 and 1830, eventually reaching twenty settlements in eight states with a total membership of 6,000. The Shaker's simple and highly structured lifestyle, their isolation from the changing world, and their belief in equality drew new followers, especially among women. In contrast, another utopian commu-

nity, the Oneida Community, became notorious for its sexual freedom. Founded by John Humphrey Noyes in 1848, the Oneida community, like the Shaker community, viewed itself as one family. But rather than celibacy, members practiced "complex marriage," a system of highly regulated group sexual activity. Only "spiritually advanced" males (Noyes himself and a few others) could father children, who were raised communally. These practices gave the sect a notorious reputation as a den of "free love" and "socialism," preventing Noyes from increasing its membership beyond 200.

Still other forthrightly socialist communities flourished briefly. New Harmony, Indiana, founded by the famous Scottish industrialist Robert Owen in 1825, was to be a manufacturing community without poverty and unemployment. The community survived only three years. Faring little better were the "phalanxes," huge communal buildings structured on the socialist theories of the French thinker Charles Fourier. Based on his belief that there was a rational way to divide work, Fourier suggested, for example, that children would make the best garbage collectors because they didn't mind dirt! And Louisa May Alcott (who later wrote *Little Women* and many other novels and stories) lived with her family at Fruitlands in Massachusetts, which had begun as a rural community of transcendentalists. The rapid failure of these socialist communities was due largely to inadequate planning and organization. Another reason may have been, as Alcott suggested in her satirical reminiscence, *Transcendental Wild Oats*, that the women were left to do all the work while the men philosophized. Nevertheless, it is striking that at a time when so many voluntary associations successfully organized the activities of their members so few cooperative communities succeeded.

The most successful of the nineteenth-century communitarian movements was also a product of the Burned-Over District. In 1830, a young man named Joseph Smith founded the Church of Jesus Christ of Latter-Day Saints based on the teachings of the *Book of Mormon*, which he claimed to have received from an angel in a vision.

Initially, Mormonism, as the new religion became known, seemed little different from the many other new religious groups and utopian communities of the time. But under the benevolent but absolute authority of its patriarch, Joseph Smith, it rapidly gained distinction for its extraordinary communitarianism. Close cooperation and hard work made the Mormon community successful, attracting both new followers and the animosity of neighbors, who resented Mormon exclusiveness and economic success. The Mormons were harassed in New York and driven west to Ohio and then Missouri. Finally they seemed to find an ideal home in Nauvoo, Illinois, where in 1839 they built a model community, achieving almost complete self-government and isolation from non-Mormon neighbors. But in 1844, dissension within the community over Joseph Smith's new doctrine of polygamy (marriage between one man and more than one woman, simultaneously) gave outsiders a chance to intervene. Smith and his brother were arrested peacefully but were killed by a mob from which their jailers failed to protect them.

The beleaguered Mormon community decided to move beyond reach of harm. Led by Brigham Young, the Mormons migrated in 1846 to the Great Salt Lake in present-day Utah. After several lean years (once, a grasshopper plague was stopped by the providential arrival of sea gulls, who ate the insects), the Mormon method of communal settlement proved successful. Their hopes of isolation were dashed, however, by the California Gold Rush of 1849.

ANTISLAVERY AND ABOLITIONISM

The antislavery feeling that was to play such an important role in the politics of the 1840s and 1850s also had its roots in the religious reform movements that began in the 1820s and 1830s. Three groups—free African Americans, Quakers, and militant white reformers—worked to bring an end to slavery, but each in different ways. Their efforts eventually turned a minor reform movement into the dominant political issue of the day.

Antislavery activity was not new. For free African Americans the freedom of other black people had always been a major goal, but in order to achieve legal change they needed white allies. In 1787 antislavery advocates had secured in the Constitution a clause specifying a date after which American participation in the international slave trade could be made illegal, and Congress outlawed it in 1808. By 1800 slavery had been abolished or gradual emancipation enacted in most northern states. In 1820 the Missouri Compromise prohibited slavery in most of the Louisiana Purchase lands. None of these measures, however, addressed the continuing reality of slavery in the South.

The American Colonization Society

The first attempt to "solve" the problem of slavery was a plan for gradual emancipation of slaves (with compensation to their owners) and their resettlement in Africa. This plan was the work of the American Colonization Society, formed in 1817 by northern religious reformers (Quakers prominent among them) and a number of southern slave owners, most from the Upper South and the border states (Kentuckian Henry Clay was a supporter). Northerners were especially eager to send the North's 250,000 free black people back to Africa, describing them, in the words of the society's 1829 report, as "notoriously ignorant, degraded and miserable, mentally diseased, [and] broken-spirited," a characterization that completely ignored the legal and social discrimination they faced. Some northern members of the society also supported laws disenfranchising and restricting the rights of free African Americans. The American Colonization Society was remarkably ineffective; by 1830, it had managed to send only 1,400 black people to a colony in Liberia, West Africa. Critics pointed out that more slaves were born in a week than the society sent back to Africa in a year.

African Americans' Fight against Slavery

Most free African Americans rejected colonization, insisting instead on a commitment to the immediate end of slavery and the

Hannah Harrison Cohoon, *Tree of Life*, 1845, tempera on paper. From the collection of Hancock Shaker Village, Pittsfield, Mass.

Shaker Hannah Cohoon's 1845 painting of the Tree of Life—*her effort to reproduce a vision she had seen while in a religious trance—communicates the intense spirituality of Shaker life.*

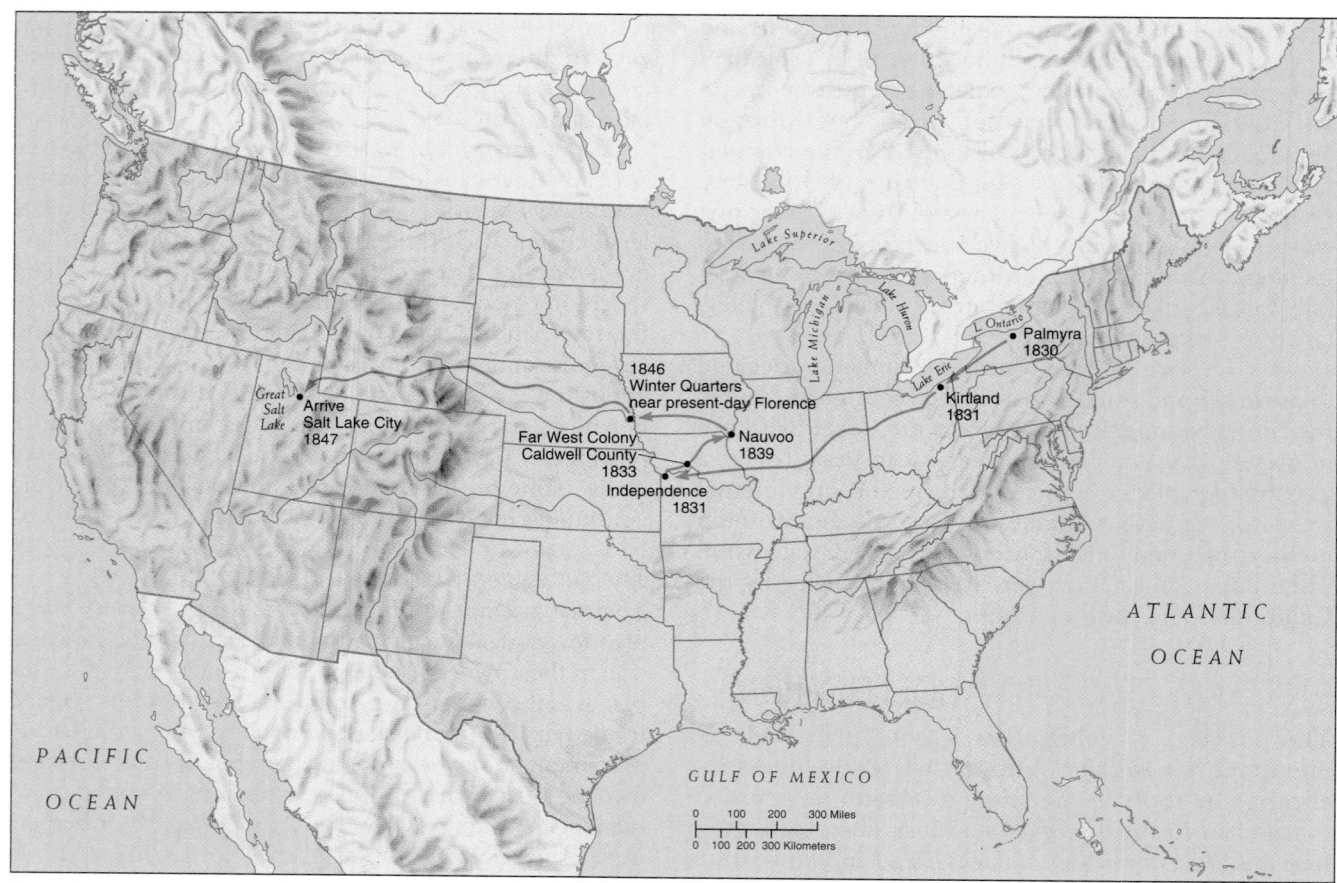

The Mormon Migration, 1830—1847   *The Mormon church and community, founded by Joseph Smith of Palmyra, New York, in 1830, aroused intense opposition. Two early settlements, one in Kirtland, Ohio, and another near Independence, Missouri, were driven out in 1838. The Mormons regrouped and prospered in Nauvoo, Illinois, until the mob murder of Joseph Smith in 1844. Their escape to the west began in 1846, first to Winter Quarters, Nebraska, and finally to the desolate Great Salt Lake region of Utah, where the Mormons hoped to be free of outside interference.*

equal treatment of black people in America. "We are natives of this country," an African American minister in New York pointed out. Then he added bitterly, "We only ask that we be treated as well as foreigners." By 1830 there were at least fifty black abolitionist societies in the North. These organizations held yearly national conventions, where famous African American abolitionists like Frederick Douglass, Harriet Tubman, and Sojourner Truth spoke. The first African American newspaper, founded in 1827 by John Russwurm and Samuel Cornish, announced its antislavery position in its title, *Freedom's Journal.*

In 1829 David Walker, a free African American in Boston, wrote a widely distributed pamphlet, *Appeal to the Colored Citizens of the World*, that encouraged slave rebellion. "We must and shall be free...in spite of you," Walker warned whites. "And woe, woe will be it to you if we have to obtain our freedom by fighting." White Southerners blamed pamphlets such as these and the militant articles of African American journalists for stirring up trouble among southern slaves, and in particular for Nat Turner's revolt in 1831. The vehemence of white southern reaction testifies to the courage of that handful of determined free African Americans who persisted in speaking for their enslaved brothers and sisters long before most white Northerners even noticed.

Abolitionists

The third and best-known group of antislavery reformers was headed by William Lloyd Garrison. In 1831 Garrison broke with the gradualist persuaders of the American Colonization Society and began publishing his own paper, the *Liberator*. In the first issue Garrison declared, "I am in earnest—I will not equivocate—I will not excuse—I will not retreat a single inch—AND I WILL BE HEARD." Garrison, the embodiment of moral indignation, was totally incapable of compromise. His approach was to mount a sweeping crusade condemning slavery as sinful and demanding its immediate abolishment. Garrison's crusade, like evangelical religion, was personal and moral. In reality, Garrison did not expect that all slaves would be freed immediately, but he did want and expect everyone to acknowledge the immorality of slavery. On the other hand, Garrison took the truly radical step of demanding full social equality for African Americans, referring to them individually as "a man and a brother" and "a woman and a sister." Garrison's determination electrified the antislavery movement, but his inability to compromise limited his effectiveness as a leader.

Garrison's moral vehemence radicalized northern antislavery religious groups. Theodore Weld, an evangelical minister, joined Garrison in 1833 in forming the American Anti-Slavery Society. The following year, Weld encouraged a group of students at Lane Theological Seminary in Cincinnati to form an antislavery society. When the seminary's president, Lyman Beecher, sought to suppress it, the students moved en masse to Oberlin College in northern Ohio, where they were joined by revivalist Charles Finney, who became president of the college. Oberlin soon became known as the most liberal college in the country, not only for its antislavery stance but for its acceptance of African American students and of women students as well.

Moral horror over slavery engaged many Northerners deeply in the abolitionist movement. They flocked to hear firsthand accounts of slavery by Frederick Douglass and Sojourner Truth, and by the white sisters from South Carolina, Angelina and Sarah Grimké. Northerners eagerly read slave narratives and books such as Theodore Weld's 1839 *American Slavery As It Is* (based in part on the recollections of Angelina Grimké, whom Weld had married) that provided graphic details of abuse. Lyman Beecher's daughter, Harriet Beecher Stowe, was to draw on the

The different dates on these two widely used antislavery images are important. The title page of Thomas Branagan's 1807 book includes a then already commonly used image of a male slave. The engraving of a chained female slave was made by Patrick Reason, a black artist, in 1835. The accompanying message, "Am I Not a Woman and a Sister?" spoke particularly to white female abolitionists in the North, who were just becoming active in antislavery movements in the 1830s.

The Philadelphia Anti-Slavery Society was one of the largest and best-known local chapters of the American Anti-Slavery Society, founded in 1833. The national society depended on local chapters to collect signatures for petitions, organize local meetings, and raise the money to print and distribute more than a million pieces of antislavery literature. The Philadelphia chapter, founded in 1832, included a number of Quakers, among whom Lucretia Mott (second from right in the front row) was prominent.

Grimké-Weld book for her immensely popular antislavery novel, *Uncle Tom's Cabin*, published in 1852.

The style of abolitionist writings and speeches was similar to the oratorical style of the religious revivalists. Northern abolitionists believed that a full description of the evils of slavery would force southern slave owners to confront their wrongdoing and lead to a true act of repentance—freeing their slaves. They were confrontational, denunciatory, and personal in their message, much like the evangelical preachers. Southerners, however, regarded abolitionist attacks as libelous and abusive.

Abolitionists adopted another tactic of revivalists and temperance workers when, to enhance their powers of persuasion, they began to publish great numbers of antislavery tracts. In 1835 alone they mailed more than a million pieces of antislavery literature to southern states. This tactic also drew a backlash: southern legislatures banned abolitionist literature, encouraged the harassment and abuse of anyone distributing it, and looked the other way when (as in South Carolina) proslavery mobs seized and burned it. The Georgia legislature even offered a $5,000 reward to anyone who would kidnap William Lloyd Garrison and bring him to the South to stand trial for inciting rebellion. Most seriously, most southern states reacted by toughening laws concerning emancipation, freedom of movement, and all aspects of slave behavior. Hoping to prevent the spread of the abolitionist message, most southern states reinforced laws making it a crime to teach a slave how to read. Ironically, then, the immediate impact of abolitionism in the South was to stifle dissent and make the lives of slaves harder (see Chapter 11).

Even in the North, controversy over abolitionism was common. Some places were prone to anti-abolitionist violence. The Ohio Valley, settled largely by Southerners, was one such place, as were northern cities experiencing the strains of rapid growth, such as Philadelphia. Immigrant Irish, who found themselves pitted against free black people for jobs, were often violently antiabolitionist. A tactic that abolitionists borrowed from revivalists—holding large and emotional meetings—opened the door to mob action. Crowds of people often disrupted such meetings, especially those addressed by Theodore Weld, whose oratorical style earned him the title of "the Most Mobbed Man in the United States." William Lloyd Garrison was stoned, dragged through the streets, and on one occasion almost hanged by a Boston mob. In the three-day New York riot of 1834, abolitionist Arthur Tappan's home and store were sacked at the same time that black churches and homes were damaged and free blacks attacked. In 1837, antislavery editor Elijah P. Lovejoy of Alton, Illinois, was killed and his press destroyed. In 1838, a mob threatened a meeting of the Philadelphia Female Anti-Slavery Society one night and, the next night, burned down the hall in which they had met.

Abolitionism and Politics

Abolitionism began as a social movement but soon intersected with sectional interests and became a national political issue. In the 1830s, massive abolitionist petition drives gathered a total of nearly 700,000 petitions requesting the abolition of slavery and the slave trade in the District of Columbia but were rebuffed by Congress. At southern insistence and with President Andrew Jackson's approval, Congress passed a "gag rule" in 1836 that prohibited discussion of antislavery petitions.

Many Northerners viewed the gag rule and censorship of the mails, which Southerners saw as necessary defenses against abolitionist frenzy, as alarming threats to free speech. First among them was Massachusetts representative John Quincy Adams, the only former president ever to serve in Congress after leaving the executive branch. Adams so publicly and persistently denounced the gag rule as a violation of the constitutional right to petition that it was repealed in 1844. Less well-known Northerners like the thousands of women who canvassed their neighborhoods with petitions made personal commitments to abolitionism that they did not intend to abandon.

John Quincy Adams was also a key figure in the abolitionists' one undoubted victory, the fight to free the fifty-three slaves on the Spanish ship *Amistad* and return them to Africa. Although the Africans successfully mutinied against the *Amistad's* crew in 1839, when the ship was found in American waters a legal battle over their "ownership" ensued, during which the Africans themselves were held in jail. Prominent abolitionists, most notably Lewis Tappan, financed the legal fight which went all the way to the Supreme Court, where Adams won the case for the *Amistad* defendants against the American government, which supported the Spanish claim.

Although abolitionist groups raised the nation's emotional temperature, they failed to achieve the moral unity they had hoped for, and they began to splinter. One perhaps inevitable but nonetheless distressing split was between white and black abolitionists. Frederick Douglass and William Lloyd Garrison parted ways when Douglass, refusing to be limited to a simple recital of his life as a slave, began to make specific suggestions for improvements in the lives of free African Americans. When Douglass chose the path of political action, Garrison denounced him as "ungrateful." Douglass and other free African Americans worked under persistent discrimination, even from antislavery whites; some of the latter refused to hire black people or to meet with them as equals. For example, some Philadelphia Quaker meetings, though devoted to the antislavery cause, maintained segregated seating for black people in their churches. While many white reformers eagerly pressed for civil equality for African Americans, they did not accept the idea of social equality. On the other hand, black and white "stations" worked closely in the risky enterprise of passing fugitive slaves north over the famous Underground Railroad, as the various routes by which slaves made their way to freedom were called. Contrary to abolitionist legend, however, it was free African Americans, rather than white people, who played the major part in helping the fugitives.

Among white abolitionists, William Lloyd Garrison remained controversial, especially after 1837, when he espoused a radical program that included women's rights, pacifism, and the abolition of the prisons and asylums that other reformers were working to establish. In 1840 the abolitionist movement formally split. The majority moved toward party politics (which Garrison abhorred), founding the Liberty Party and choosing James G. Birney (whom Theodore Weld had converted to abolitionism) as their presidential candidate. Thus the abolitionist movement, which began as an effort at moral reform, took its first major step into politics, and this step in turn led to the formation of the Republican Party in the 1850s and to the Civil War.

For one particular group of antislavery reformers, the abolitionist movement opened up new possibilities for action. Through their participation in antislavery activity, some women came to a vivid realization of the social constraints on their activism.

THE WOMEN'S RIGHTS MOVEMENT

American women, without the vote or a role in party politics, found a field of activity in social reform movements. There was scarcely a reform movement in which women were not actively involved. Often men

Women's gatherings, like the first women's rights convention in Seneca Falls in 1848 and this meeting of strikers in Lynn in 1860, were indicators of widespread female activism.

were the official leaders of such movements, and some women—especially those in the temperance, moral reform, and abolitionist movements—formed all-female chapters to define and implement their own policies and programs.

The majority of women did not participate in these activities, for they were fully occupied with housekeeping and child rearing (families with five children were the average). A few women—mostly members of the new middle class, who could afford servants—had the time and energy to look beyond their immediate tasks. Touched by the religious revival, these women enthusiastically joined reform movements. Led thereby to challenge social restrictions, some, like the Grimké sisters, found that their commitment carried them beyond the limits of what was considered acceptable activity for women.

The Grimké Sisters

Sarah and Angelina Grimké, members of a prominent South Carolina slaveholding family, rejected slavery out of religious conviction and moved north to join a Quaker community near Philadelphia. In the 1830s, these two sisters found themselves drawn into the growing antislavery agitation in the North. Because they knew about slavery firsthand, they were in great demand as speakers. At first they spoke to "parlor meetings" of women only, as was considered proper. But interested men kept sneaking into the talks, and soon the sisters found themselves

speaking to mixed gatherings. The meetings got larger and larger, and soon the sisters realized that they had become the first female public speakers in America. In 1837 Angelina Grimké became the first woman to address a meeting of the Massachusetts state legislature (Sarah Bagley, the Lowell worker, was the second).

The sisters challenged social norms on two grounds. The antislavery movement was widely disapproved, and many famous male orators were criticized by the press and mobbed at meetings. The Grimké sisters were criticized for speaking because they were women. A letter from a group of ministers cited the Bible in reprimanding the sisters for stepping out of "woman's proper sphere" of silence and subordination. Sarah Grimké answered the ministers in her 1838 *Letters on the Equality of the Sexes and the Condition of Women*, claiming that "men and women were CREATED EQUAL....Whatever is right for a man to do, is right for woman." She followed with this ringing assertion: "I seek no favors for my sex. I surrender not our claim to equality. All I ask of our brethren is, that they will take their feet from off our necks and permit us to stand upright on that ground which God designed us to occupy."

Not all female assertiveness was as dramatic as Sarah Grimké's, but women in the antislavery movement found it a constant struggle to be heard. Some solved the problem of male dominance by forming their own groups, like the Philadelphia Female Anti-Slavery Society. In the antislavery movement and other reform groups as well, men accorded women a secondary role, even when—as was frequently the case—women constituted a majority of the members.

Women's Rights

The Seneca Falls Convention of 1848, the first women's rights convention in American history, was an outgrowth of almost twenty years of female activity in social reform. Every year after 1848 women gathered to hold women's rights conventions and to work for political, legal, and social equality. Over the years, in response to persistent lobbying, states passed property laws more favorable to women and altered divorce laws to allow women to retain custody of

CHRONOLOGY

1817	American Colonization Society founded
1820s	Shaker colonies grow
1825	New Harmony founded, fails three years later
1826	American Society for the Promotion of Temperance founded
1827	Workingmen's Party founded in Philadelphia *Freedom's Journal* begins publication Public school movement begins in Massachusetts
1829	David Walker, *Appeal to the Colored Citizens of the World*, published
1830	Joseph Smith founds Church of Jesus Christ of Latter-Day Saints (Mormon Church) Charles G. Finney's revivals in Rochester
1831	William Lloyd Garrison begins publishing antislavery newspaper, the *Liberator*
1832	Immigration begins to increase
1833	American Anti-Slavery Society founded by Garrison and Theodore Weld
1834	First Female Moral Reform Society founded in New York National Trades Union formed

1836	Congress passes "gag rule" to prevent discussion of antislavery petitions
1837	Antislavery editor Elijah P. Lovejoy killed Angelina Grimké addresses Massachusetts legislature Sarah Grimké, *Letters on the Equality of the Sexes and the Condition of Women* Panic begins seven-year recession
1839	Theodore Weld publishes *American Slavery As It Is*
1840s	New York and Boston complete public water systems
1840	Liberty Party founded
1843	Millerites await the end of the world Dorothea Dix spearheads asylum reform movement
1844	Mormon leader Joseph Smith killed by mob
1845	New York creates city police force Beginning of Irish Potato Famine and heavy Irish immigration
1846	Mormons begin migration to the Great Salt Lake
1848	Women's Rights Convention at Seneca Falls John Noyes founds Oneida Community

children. Teaching positions in higher education opened up to women, as did jobs in some other occupations, and women gained the vote in some states, beginning with Wyoming Territory in 1869. In 1920, seventy-two years after universal woman suffrage was first proposed at Seneca Falls, women's right to vote was at last guaranteed in the Nineteenth Amendment to the Constitution.

Historians have only recently realized how much the reform movements of this "Age of the Common Man" were due to the efforts of the "common woman." Women played a vital role in all the social movements of the day. In doing so they implicitly chal-

lenged the popular notion of separate spheres for men and women—the public world for him, home and family for her. The separate spheres argument, although it heaped praise on women for their allegedly superior moral qualities, was meant to exclude them from political life. The reforms discussed in this chapter show clearly that women reformers believed they had a right and a duty to propose solutions for the moral and social problems of the day. Empowered by their own religious beliefs and activism, the Seneca Falls reformers spoke for all American women when they demanded an end to the unfair restrictions they suffered as women.

CONCLUSION

Beginning in the 1820s, the market revolution changed the size and social order of America's preindustrial cities and towns. Immigration, dramatically rapid population growth, and changes in working life and class structure created a host of new urban problems ranging from sanitation to civic order. These changes occurred so rapidly that they seemed overwhelming. Older, face-to-face methods of social control no longer worked. To fill the gap, new kinds of associations—the political party, the religious crusade, the reform cause, the union movement—sprang up. These associations were new manifestations of the deep human desire for social connection, for continuity, and—especially in the growing cities—for social order. A striking aspect of these associations was the uncompromising nature of the attitudes and beliefs on which they were based. Most groups were formed of like-minded people who wanted to impose their will on others. Such intolerance boded ill for the future. If political parties, religious bodies, and reform groups were to splinter along sectional lines (as happened in the 1850s), political compromise would be very difficult. In the meantime, however, Americans came to terms with the market revolution by engaging in a passion for improvement. As a perceptive foreign observer, Francis Grund, noted, "Americans love their country not as it is but as it will be."

REVIEW QUESTIONS

1. What impact did the new immigration of the 1840s and 1850s have on American cities?
2. Why did urbanization produce so many problems?
3. What motivated the social reformers of the period? Were they benevolent helpers or dictatorial social controllers? Study several reform causes and discuss similarities and differences among them.
4. Abolitionism differed little from other reforms in its tactics, but the effects of antislavery activism were politically explosive. Why was this so?

RECOMMENDED READING

Arthur Bestor, *Backwoods Utopias* (1950). The standard work on utopian communities.

Paul Boyer, *Urban Masses and Moral Order in America, 1820–1920* (1978). Interprets reform as an effort to reestablish the moral order of the preindustrial community.

Amy Bridges, *A City in the Republic: Antebellum New York and the Origins of Machine Politics* (1984). An innovative look at the transition from elite political control to machine politics.

Paul A. Gilje, *The Road to Mobocracy: Popular Disorder in New York City, 1763–1834* (1987). Provides an interesting and entertaining description of the many varieties of civic disorder of the day.

Oscar Handlin, *Boston's Immigrants: A Study in Acculturation* (rev. ed., 1959). A pathbreaking exploration of conflict and adaptation among Boston's Irish community.

Daniel Walker Howe, "The Evangelical Movement and Political Culture in the North during the Second Party System," *Journal of American History*, 78:1 (March 1991). An award-winning article that explores the connections among religion, politics, and reform.

Leon Litwack, *North of Slavery: The Negro in the Free States,* 1790–1860 (1961). The standard source on free black people in the North.

Eric Lott, *Love and Theft: Blackface Minstrelsy and the American Working Class* (1993). Explores the complicated relationships between working-class amusements and racial attitudes.

Steven Mintz, *Moralists and Modernizers: America's Pre-Civil War Reformers* (1995). A brief but inclusive study of reforms and reformers.

David Roediger, *The Wages of Whiteness* (1991). Explores the links between artisanal republicanism, labor organization, and white racism.

David Rothman, *The Discovery of the Asylum: Social Order and Disorder in the New Republic* (1971). Explores institutional reforms.

Kathryn Sklar, *Catharine Beecher: A Study in American Domesticity* (1973). An absorbing "life and times" that explores the possibilities and limits of women's roles in the early nineteenth century.

Sean Wilentz, *Chants Democratic: New York City and the Rise of the American Working Class, 1788–1850* (1983). An important book, rooted in social history, that reveals how workers acted upon their understanding of republicanism in confronting the changes wrought by the market revolution.

ADDITIONAL BIBLIOGRAPHY

Immigration

Kathleen Neils Conzen, *Immigrant Milwaukee, 1836–1860* (1976)
Hasia Diner, *Erin's Daughters in America* (1983)
Jay P. Dolan, *The Immigrant Church: New York's Irish and German Catholics, 1815–1865* (1975)
Oscar Handlin, *The Uprooted* (1951; 2nd ed. 1973)
Noel Ignatiev, *How the Irish Became White* (1995)
Kerby A. Miller, *Emigrants and Exiles: Ireland and the Irish Exodus to North America* (1985)
Stanley Nadel, *Little Germany: Ethnicity, Religion, and Class in New York City, 1845–1880* (1990)
LaVern J. Rippley, *The German-Americans* (1976)
Dennis P. Ryan, *Beyond the Ballot Box: A Social History of the Boston Irish, 1845–1917* (1989)

Urban and Labor

Oliver E. Allen, *The Tiger: The Rise and Fall of Tammany Hall* (1995)
W. Jeffrey Bolster, *Black Jacks: African American Seamen in the Age of Sail* (1997)
Michael Feldberg, *The Philadelphia Riots of 1844: A Study of Ethnic Conflict* (1975)
Herbert G. Gutman, *Work, Culture, and Society in Industrializing America: Essays in American Working-Class History* (1976)
James Oliver Horton, *Free People of Color: Inside the African American Community* (1993)
James Oliver Horton and Lois E. Horton, *Black Bostonians: Family Life and Community Struggle in the Antebellum North* (1979)
David Montgomery, *Citizen Worker: The Experience of Workers in the United States with Democracy and the Free Market during the Nineteenth Century* (1993)
Gary B. Nash, *Forging Freedom: Philadelphia's Black Community, 1720–1840* (1988)
Edward Pessen, *Most Uncommon Jacksonians: The Radical Leaders of the Early Labor Movement* (1967)
Mary Ryan, *Civic Wars: Democracy and Public Life* (1997)
Amy Gilman Srebnick, *The Mysterious Death of Mary Roberts, Sex and Culture in the Nineteenth Century* (1995)
Sam Bass Warner, *The Private City: Philadelphia in Three Periods of Its Growth* (1968)

Religion, Reform, and Utopianism

Lawrence Cremin, *American Education: The National Experience, 1783–1861* (1981)
Whitney R. Cross, *The Burned-Over District: The Social and Intellectual History of Enthusiastic Religion in Western New York, 1800–1850* (1950)
Jed Dannenbaum, *Drink and Disorder: Temperance Reform in Cincinnati from the Washingtonian Revival to the WCTU* (1984)
Barbara Epstein, *The Politics of Domesticity: Women, Evangelism, and Temperance in Nineteenth Century America* (1981)
Michael Fellman, *The Unbounded Frame: Freedom and Community in Nineteenth-Century American Utopianism* (1973)
Lori D. Ginzberg, *Women and the Work of Benevolence: Morality, Politics, and Class in the Nineteenth-Century United States* (1990)
Klaus J. Hansen, *Mormonism and the American Experience* (1981)
Carl F. Kaestle, *Pillars of the Republic: Common Schools and American Society, 1780–1860* (1983)
Louis J. Kern, *An Ordered Love: Sex Roles and Sexuality in Victorian Utopias—The Shakers, the Mormons, and the Oneida Community* (1981)
W. J. Rorabaugh, *The Alcoholic Republic: An American Tradition* (1979)
Ann C. Rose, *Transcendentalism as a Social Movement, 1830–1850* (1981)
Timothy L. Smith, *Revivalism and Social Reform: American Protestantism on the Eve of the Civil War* (1980)

Abolitionism

R.J.M. Blackett, *Building an Antislavery Wall: Black Americans in the Abolitionist Movement, 1830–1860* (1983)
David Brion Davis, *The Problem of Slavery in the Age of Revolution, 1770–1823* (1975)
Louis Gerteis, *Morality and Utility in American Antislavery Reform* (1987)
Howard Jones, *Mutiny on the Amistad* (1987).
Jean Fagan Yellin, *Women and Sisters: The Antislavery Feminists in American Culture* (1989)

Women's Rights

Carl N. Degler, *At Odds: Women and the Family in America from the Revolution to the Present* (1980)
Ellen C. Dubois, *Feminism and Suffrage: The Emergence of an Independent Women's Movement in America, 1848–1869* (1978)
Keith Melder, *Beginnings of Sisterhood: The American Women's Rights Movement, 1800–1850* (1977)
Sandra S. Weber, *Special History Study, Women's Rights National Historical Park, Seneca Falls, New York* (1985)

Biography

Robert H. Abzug, *Passionate Liberator, Theodore Dwight Weld and the Dilemma of Reform* (1980)
Frederick Douglass, *The Narrative of the Life of Frederick Douglass, An American Slave* (1845)
Elisabeth Griffith, *In Her Own Right: The Life of Elizabeth Cady Stanton* (1984)
Nathan I. Huggins, *Slave and Citizen: The Life of Frederick Douglass* (1980)
Gerda Lerner, *The Grimké Sisters from South Carolina: Pioneers for Women's Rights and Abolition* (1967)
John L. Thomas, *The Liberator: William Lloyd Garrison* (1963)

The Changing Face of Ethnicity in America

1800 – 1860

Between 1790 and 1820, the rate of immigration to the United States was low, held in check by the Napoleonic Wars in Europe. It began to pick up in the 1820s, increased sharply in the 1830s, and reached a record 430,000 in 1854. As immigration increased, the ethnic composition of the immigrant stream changed. Most of the new immigrants were Irish, driven from home by the Potato Famine of 1845, and German, driven by economic and political unrest in the German Principalities.

Until the 1880s, the task of receiving immigrants fell completely on cities and states, not the federal government. New York City, by far the largest port of entry, did not even establish an official reception center until 1855, when Castle Garden, at the bottom of Manhattan Island (near present-day Battery Park), was so designated.

The influx of mostly poor, mostly Catholic foreigners provoked nativist hostility among many Protestant, native-born Americans, including many leaders of the major reform movements. It would be a mistake, however, to think that immigration was unwelcome to everyone. Industries needed willing workers, and western states were eager for settlers. In 1852 Wisconsin appointed a commissioner of emigration with responsibility for attracting Europeans to the state. Soon Iowa and Minnesota joined Wisconsin in advertising widely in Europe for settlers.

Immigrant labor fueled the nation's expanding economy and helped turn wilderness into farmland. Many of the changes in industry and transportation that accompanied the market revolution would have been impossible without immigrants. Irish contract workers, for example, were essential to the completion of the Erie Canal in 1825. And Irish women and men kept the mills at Lowell operating when the mill operators, facing increasing competition, sought cheaper labor to replace their original labor force of farm women.

Irish immigration to the United States dated from colonial times. Many of Ireland's young people, with no hope of owning land at home, had long looked to America for better opportunities. But in 1845 Ireland's green fields of potato plants turned black with blight, and for five years a catastrophic famine ravaged the land. The Irish had two choices: starve or leave. One million people died, and another 1.5 million emigrated, most to the United States. The Famine Irish were America's first major refugee group. Starving, suffering from disease (thousands died of typhus during the voyage), and destitute, hundreds of thousands disembarked in the east-coast ports of New York, Philadelphia, Boston, and Baltimore. Lacking the money to go inland, they remained in the cities. Crowded together in miserable housing, desperate for work at any wages, foreign in their religion and pastimes (drinking and fighting, their critics said), tenaciously nationalistic and bitterly anti-British, they created ethnic enclaves of a kind new to American cities.

The largest number of Irish immigrants settled in New York. Fewer settled in Boston, but that city, smaller and more homogeneous than New York, was overwhelmed by the influx. By 1850, a quarter of Boston's population was Irish. The home of Puritanism and the center of American intellectualism, Boston was not welcoming. All over the city in places of business and in homes normally eager for domestic servants the signs went up: "No Irish Need Apply." The Irish were able to get only the worst and poorest-paying jobs and could afford housing only in an area of East Boston that was described by a health committee in 1849 as "a perfect hive of human beings, without comforts and mostly without common necessaries; in many cases, huddled together like brutes, without regard to sex or age or sense of decency."

Despite poverty and local hostility, the Irish created within their neighborhoods an impressive network of Catholic churches and schools, mutual aid societies, and religious and social clubs. And almost from the moment of their arrival, the Irish sent huge sums of money back to Ireland so that relatives could join them in America. For however bad the conditions in the adopted country, they were better than those in Ireland. As one newcomer wrote, "There is a great many ill conveniences here, but no empty bellies."

Irish immigrants changed American urban politics. In Boston, they quickly took over the local Democratic Party, opposing that city's traditional, Whig-dominated power structure. Irish political strength lay at the neighborhood level. Many politicians were saloonkeepers, for the saloon was the secular center of Irish society—much to the horror of temperance reformers. One Irish saloonkeeper, Patrick Joseph Kennedy, founded one of America's most famous political dynasties. Barely a century after Patrick's birth into a poor immigrant family in Boston, his grandson John Fitzgerald Kennedy was elected the first Irish Catholic president of the United States.

The typical German immigrant was a small farmer or artisan dislodged by the same market forces that were at work in America: the industrialization of manufacturing and the commercialization of farming. The first two major ports of embarkation for the Germans were Bremen (in northern Germany) and Le Havre (in northern France), which were also the main ports for the importation of American tobacco and cotton. The tobacco boats bore the Bremen passengers to Baltimore, and the cotton ships took them to New Orleans, a major entry point for European immigrants until the Civil War. From these ports, many Germans made their way up the Mississippi and Ohio valleys, where they settled in Milwaukee, Pittsburgh, Cincinnati, and St. Louis and on farms in Ohio, Indiana, Missouri, and Texas. In Texas the nucleus of a German community began with a Mexican land grant in the 1830s. Few Germans settled in the South.

German agricultural communities took a distinctive form that fostered cultural continuity. Immigrants formed predominantly German towns by clustering, or taking up adjoining land. A small cluster could support German churches, German-language schools, and German customs and thereby attract other Germans, some directly from Europe and some from other parts of the United States. Non-German neighbors often sold out and moved on, but the Germans stayed and passed on

their land to succeeding generations. They used soil conservation practices that were unusual for the time. German cluster communities still endure in Texas, the Midwest, and the Pacific Northwest, and more American farm families are today of German origin than of any other background.

Large German populations settled in "little Germanies" in New Orleans, St. Louis, Cincinnati, and Milwaukee, and in the eastern cities of New York, Philadelphia, and Baltimore. There they developed a flourishing community culture, with German language schools, theater groups, and a German-language press. In the summer, entire families frequented beer gardens, where there was always music, in the semi-rural outskirts of the cities. At first the Germans were greeted with hostility (temperance societies were especially unhappy about the beer gardens), but by 1860, German culture, with its emphasis on music, intellectual interests, and love of nature, had become widely influential. Among its contributions to American life were not only beer (then a new drink to most Americans) but gymnasiums and candle-lit Christmas trees. Germans also had an important impact on American public education, which was then in its formative years. The first kindergarten in America was founded by Margarethe Schurz in Watertown, Wisconsin, where she and her husband, Carl Schurz, settled in 1856. German ideas were also influential in the development of music programs, gymnastics, vocational training, and high schools.

Other areas attracting immigrants in the early nineteenth century were Gold Rush California, which drew, among others, numbers of Chinese, and Utah Territory, where the Mormon Church recruited many former English factory workers to its new Zion. In Texas and Mexico, a high proportion of residents were listed as foreign-born in 1860 who were in fact native-born Mexicans who had become foreigners only by virtue of the conquest of their homeland by the United States in the Mexican-American war.

The Chinese who came to California in the 1850s following the Gold Rush worked in the mines, most as independent prospectors. Other miners disliked their industriousness and their clannishness. One reporter noted groups of twenty or thirty "Chinamen, stools, tables,

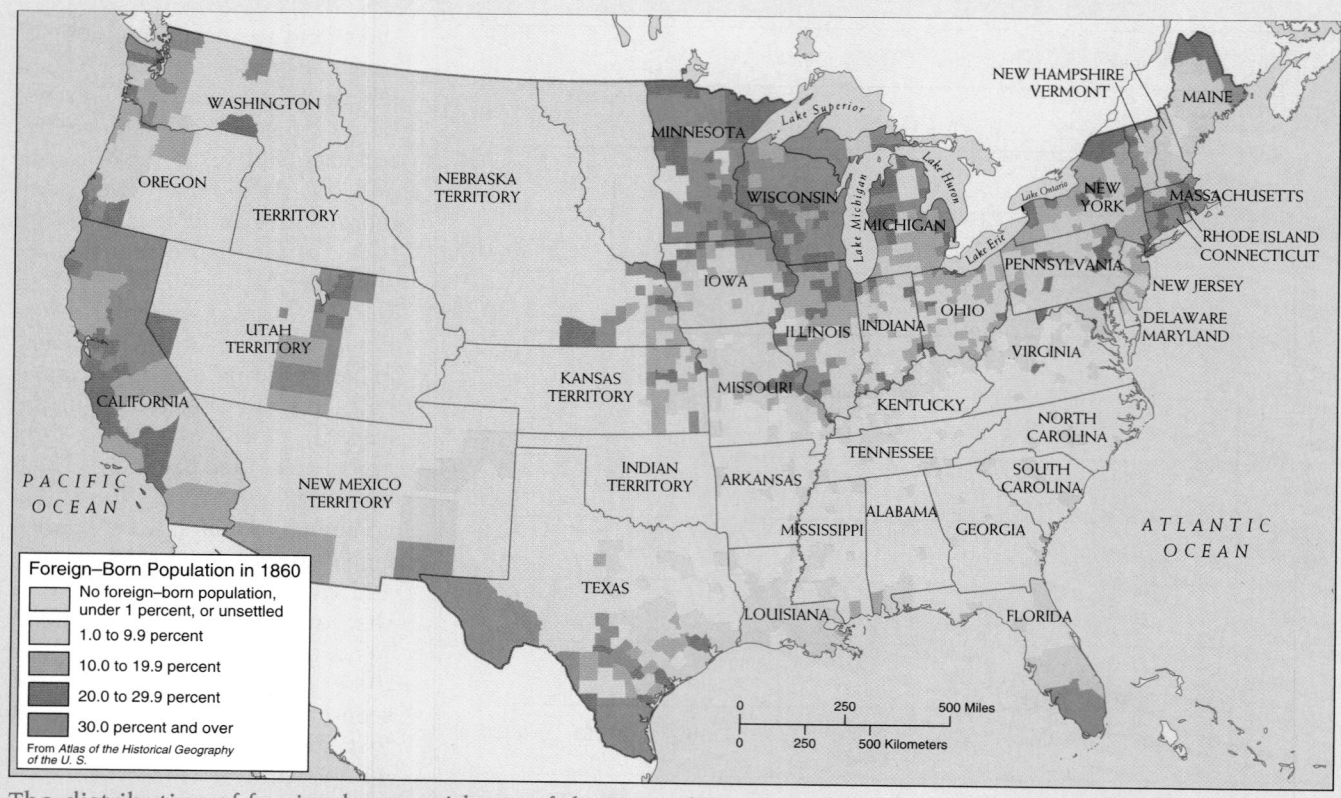

The distribution of foreign-born residents of the United States in 1860.

cooking utensils, bunks, etc., all huddled up together in indiscriminate confusion, and enwreathed with dense smoke, inhabiting close cabins, so small that one would not be of sufficient size to allow a couple of Americans to breathe in it." In 1852 the California legislature enacted a Foreign Miner's Tax aimed at the Chinese. By the time the tax was repealed in 1870, it had cost Chinese miners five million dollars. By the mid-1860s, Chinese workers made up 90 percent of the laborers building the Central Pacific Railroad, replacing more expensive white laborers and sowing the seeds of the long-lasting hostility of American workers toward Chinese. In the meantime, however, San Francisco's Chinatown, the oldest Chinese ethnic enclave in America, became a well established, thriving community. In the years to come, as hostility against the Chinese broke into violence, Chinatowns in San Francisco and elsewhere served a vital function as safe refuges for the Chinese who remained in the United States.

■ IN THEIR OWN WORDS

The unprecedented immigration of the 1840s and 1850s evoked the first organized nativist (antiforeign) movement in American history. As immigration swelled the country's previously small Catholic population, Protestant ministers became alarmed. One of them was Reverend Lyman Beecher, who equated Catholicism with the antidemocratic powers of Europe and suggested that Catholic immigrants followed their bidding. Despite his disclaimer, Beecher viewed immigration as a religious as well as a political threat.

Catholic Europe is throwing swarm on swarm [of immigrants] upon our shores. There is evidently a supervision abroad—and one here—by which they come, and set down together, in city or country, as a Catholic body, and are led or followed quickly by a Catholic priesthood, who maintain over them in the land of strangers and unknown tongues an ascendency as absolute as they are able to exert in Germany itself.

In the beginning this eruption of revolutionary Europe was not anticipated, and we opened our doors wide to the influx and naturalization of foreigners. But it is becoming a terrific inundation; it has increased upon our native population from five to thirty-seven percent, and is every year advancing. It seeks, of course, to settle down upon the unoccupied territory of the West, and may at no distant day equal, and even outnumber the native population.

But what if this emigration, self-moved and slow in the beginning, is now rolling its broad tide at the bidding of the powers of Europe hostile to free institutions, and associated in holy alliance to arrest and put them down? Is this a vain fear? Are not the continental powers alarmed at the march of liberal opinions, and associated to put them down?…A tenth part of the suffrage of the nation,…condensed and wielded by the Catholic powers of Europe, might decide our elections, perplex our policy, inflame and divide the nation, break the bond of our union, and throw down our free institutions.…

I have no fear of the Catholics, considered simply as a religious denomination, and unallied to the church and state establishments of the European governments hostile to republican institutions.

Let the Catholics mingle with us as Americans, and come with their children under the full action of our common schools and republican institutions, and the various powers of assimilation, and we are prepared cheerfully to abide the consequences. If in these circumstances the Protestant religion cannot stand before the Catholic, let it go down, and we will sound no alarm, and ask no aid, and make no complaint. It is no ecclesiastical quarrel to which we would call the attention of the American nation.[1]

Compelled by the Potato Famine to migrate to America, many Irish felt an enduring longing for their homeland, as the following song of lament reflects.

Farewell to thee, Erin mavourneen,
Thy valleys I'll tread nevermore;
This heart that now bleeds for thy sorrows,
Will waste on a far distant shore.
The green sods lie cold on my parents,
A cross marks the place of their rest,—
The wind that moans sadly above them,
Will waft their poor child to the West.[2]

Few personal memoirs from Irish immigrants of this period survive, but the combined effects of the Famine Exodus and the hostile American reception were felt in later generations, as William Alfred's memoir of his great-grandmother, Anna Maria Gavin, attests.

Of Ireland she rarely spoke, save to recall that she was often hungry there and that for her main meal she often ate cress out of the brooks on oaten bread with a bit of lard. Although she always used to say she had no desire to return to Ireland to live, she lived out of a trunk to her dying day, and taught her children to do the same. I myself, till well on in my twenties, felt that Ireland, which I had never seen, was my true country. When, over eighty, she died, it did not seem strange six months afterward to receive a clipping from an Irish newspaper, which read: "Died in Exile: Anna Maria Gavin Egan."

Of her first years here, she never tired of speaking. She and her mother landed at Castle Garden and walked up Broadway to City Hall, with bundles of clothes and pots and featherbeds in their arms. The singing of the then exposed telegraph wires frightened them, as did the bustle of the people in the streets. They lost their fear when they met an Irish policeman who directed them to a rooming house on Baxter Street.

Her training as a "manty-maker" (mantua-maker, in other words, dressmaker) gave her an advantage over other girls of her age. She got a job fast. On her way from work the first year, she nightly passed a house in whose tall, lit first-floor windows sat the most beautiful women she had ever seen, dressed to the nines, their hair as trimly curled, their faces painted fresh as new French china dolls. After weeks of gawking, she built up the courage to hazard a smile. "Come up here…," one of the women called to her, "and we'll wipe that smile off your face."[3]

On the other edge of the continent in California, another new immigrant group, the Chinese, were making their presence felt. By 1852 there were nearly 25,000 Chinese in California, attracted by the Gold Rush. They did not always, at first, encounter hostility, as the following report in a California paper of 1852 suggests.

Quite a large number of the Celestials [Chinese] have arrived among us of late, enticed thither by the golden romance that has filled the world. Scarcely a ship arrives that does not bring an increase to this worthy integer of our population. [Soon] the China boys will vote at the same polls, study at the same schools and bow at the same altar as our own countrymen.[4]

German Beer Halls, like this one pictured on New York's Bowery, offered music and contact with nature as well as beer from the owners' own breweries. Much to the dismay of American temperance reformers, German immigrants viewed beer halls and gardens as gathering places for the entire family.

Samuel Waugh's The Bay and Harbor of New York, *painted in 1855, shows the newly opened Castle Garden, the city's first official reception center for immigrants, receiving a boatload of newcomers from Ireland and perhaps from Germany. Note the anti-Irish caricatures, including the trunk on the right labeled "Pat Murfy for Ameriky." A Chinese junk rides at anchor in the harbor, a reminder that not all immigration in this period was from Europe.*

Another newspaper report described the emerging Chinatown of San Francisco.

The majority of the houses were of Chinese importation and were stores, stocked with hams, tea, dried fish, dried ducks, and other Chinese eatables, besides copper pots and kettles, fans, shawls, chessmen, and all sorts of curiosities. Suspended over the doors were brilliantly-colored boards covered with Chinese writings, and with several yards of red ribbon streaming from them; while the streets thronged with Celestials, chattering vociferously as they rushed about from store to store.[5]

The large German immigrant population was more geographically dispersed than either the Irish or the Chinese. Their experience is also better documented with firsthand accounts, because many more German immigrants than Irish sent letters home to family members and wrote reminiscences. Many German immigrants brought farming skills with them to America and put them to use, often in company with kin and friends, in rural ethnic clusters. Wilhelmina Stille, her brother Wilhelm Stille, and her fiance Wilhelm Krumme settled together along the Ohio River near Wheeling, Virginia (now West Virginia). The following letter, written in October 1838, is from Wilhelmina Stille to her mother.

We got married on August 10th. We've bought 80 acres of land and our brother has too, they are next to one another but his is so much better it cost 400 talers and ours 300 talers, we paid 200 talers of it since we didn't have any more. So we're asking you, dear mother and brothers in the name of the Lord, send me the rest of my money, please don't fail me because we have nowhere else to turn. I also want to tell you that my brother Wilhelm left his boss last fall and went down the river on a boat that was loaded with all kinds of goods, flour, potatoes, string beans, cabbage, onions, apples and two others had a quarter of it each. The city is called Neuoliens [New Orleans] which is 15 hundred miles away it's in South America there they can't grow such things. When he got back he started to work on his land, he's built himself a house and has already cleared 3 acres of farmland. We live 3 hours away from Wilingen [Wheeling] right on the road and are very happy for I have a happy marriage and live in peace.[6]

Another German immigrant, Carl Blümer, settled in Santa Fé before the Mexican-American War. As the following letter of October 31, 1852, suggests, he and his brother August were caught up in some of the dramatic events of America's westward expansion.

My dearest, my eternally beloved mother: Your reproach, my dear mother, is justified; years have passed without my writing to you; I don't want to try to excuse myself, only to the extent that I knew for certain that August [his brother] had sent you all my news until he left for California. Mother! Mother! Brother August is no more! August came here, to Santa Fé, in the spring of 1849; but he only stayed with me for a few months, and went from here to California, thinking and hoping to make a fortune more quickly there. He arrived safely in California; went to the gold mines and wrote his *last* letter to me from the gold mines in Mariposa, in California, in the winter of 1849. Then I didn't hear anything from him for a long time, until I finally received a letter the following year from his brother-in-law, who informed me that he had died in August 1850 in the gold mines on the Yuba River in California. He fell ill with abdominal ailments, and he passed away, calm and composed, after about a month. A German, who worked with him, wrote that he was buried decently. Peace be to his ashes in a foreign land, in an unknown place! His spirit will hover about us in love!...

I myself, my dear mother, have almost always been well, in this country, since 1836; the climate here is one of the nicest, at least the healthiest, on earth. I've been married for about 4 years; my wife is a Mexican, the youngest daughter of a good but poor family; she is named Felisiana Quintana y Alarid. She is pretty about 26 years old. She presented me with a daughter as a first-born child, whom we baptized Carlota, (Charlotte). My second is a boy; named Carlos (Karl or Charles) and is about 15 months old. My business here has almost always been as a merchant; about a year ago I gave up my trading company and am mostly employed in the service of the government. Since the United States of North America took possession of this country, as a result of the war, since the year 1846, I have always had one or other government post; *Treasurer* I have had since 1846 and I still have; my yearly salary is 500 dollars, about 700 Prussian talers. Felisiana sends you, dear mother, her filial love and devotion, and all of you a dear and sisterly kiss.

Farewell!/Forever/ Your true son
and your true brother and uncle, Carl Blümer[7]

Carl Schurz, who emigrated from Germany in 1852 when the nativist political movement was at its height, gained great prominence in the United States, becoming a general in the Union Army, a senator from Missouri, and secretary of the interior in the administration of Rutherford B. Hayes. In this letter to a German friend, he reflects with pride on some of his accomplishments in his adopted country.

Here in America I lived for several years quietly and unobtrusively in an ideally happy family circle until at last in the year '56, when the movement against slavery developed magnificently, I found myself drawn into public life. I knew that I should accomplish something. America is the country for ambitious capability, and the foreigner who studies its conditions thoroughly, and with full appreciation, can procure for himself an even greater field of activity than the native. My success surprised even myself; I found my boldest expectations outdone. I flung myself with all my heart into the Antislavery Movement and thus showed the Americans something new....It is said that I made Lincoln President. That is certainly not true; but the fact that people say it indicates that I did contribute something toward raising the wind which bore Lincoln into the presidential chair and thus shook the slave system to its very foundations.[8]

Study Questions

1. Why did immigrant groups of the 1830s through the 1850s generate more controversy than earlier groups?
2. Many immigrants regarded ethnic neighborhoods as essential to their economic and cultural survival, but many native-born Americans regarded them as hindrances to complete adoption of "American" customs and attitudes. What is your opinion?
3. In what ways did Irish, German, and Chinese immigrants participate in the social, political, economic, and cultural life of the United States?
4. Do you see any validity in the arguments of nativists like Lyman Beecher?

Sources

1. Lyman Beecher, *Plea for the West* (1835)
2. "The Emigrant's Farewell," *Boston Pilot*, August 16, 1862
3. William Alfred, "An Irish Integrity," in Thomas C. Wheeler, ed., *The Immigrant Experience: The Anguish of Becoming American* (1972)
4. *Daily Alta California* (San Francisco), May 12, 1852, quoted in Ronald Takaki, *A Different Mirror: A History of Multicultural America* (1993)
5. Thomas Chinn, H.M. Lai, and Philip Choy, *A History of the Chinese in California* (1969)
6. Walter D. Kamphoefner, Wolfgang Helbich, and Ulrike Summer, eds., *News from the Land of Freedom: German Immigrants Write Home* (1991)
7. *Ibid.*
8. Letter from Carl Schurz to Theodor Petrasch, Bonn, September 24, 1863, quoted in A.E. Zucker, ed. *The Forty-Eighters, Political Refugees of the German Revolution of 1848* (1950)

CHAPTER FOURTEEN

THE TERRITORIAL EXPANSION OF THE UNITED STATES

1830s–1850s

Samuel Chamberlain, *General Wool Crossing the Military Plaza, San Antonio,* c. 1856. San Jacinto Museum of History Association.

AMERICAN COMMUNITIES
Texans and Tejanos
"Remember the Alamo!"

For thirteen days in February and March 1836, a force of 187 Texans held the mission fortress known as the Alamo against a siege by 5,000 Mexican troops under General Antonio López de Santa Anna, president of Mexico. Santa Anna had come north to subdue rebellious Texas, the northernmost part of the Mexican province of Coahuila y Texas, and to place it under central authority. On March 6 he ordered a final assault, and in brutal fighting that claimed over 1,500 Mexican lives, his army took the mission. All the defenders were killed, including Commander William Travis and the well-known frontiersmen Jim Bowie and Davy Crockett. It was a crushing defeat for the Texans, but the cry "Remember the Alamo!" rallied their remaining forces, which, less than two months later, routed the Mexican army and forced Santa Anna to grant Texas independence from Mexico. Today the Alamo, in San Antonio, is one of the most cherished historic shrines in the United States.

But memory is selective: some things tend to be forgotten. Within a generation of the uprising few remembered that many *Tejanos*, Spanish-speaking people born in Texas, had joined with American settlers fighting for Texas independence. The Americans were concentrated in the central and eastern portions of the huge Texas territory, where during the 1820s the Mexican government had authorized several colonies managed by *empresarios* (land agents) like Stephen F. Austin. These settler communities consisted mostly of farmers from the Mississippi Valley, who introduced slavery and cotton growing to the rich lands of coastal and upland Texas.

The Tejano community, descended from eighteenth-century Spanish and Mexican settlers, included wealthy *rancheros* who raised cattle on the shortgrass prairies of south Texas, as well as the cowboys known as *vaqueros* and the *peónes*, or poor tenant farmers. Although there was relatively little contact between the Americans and Tejanos, their leaders interacted in San Antonio, the center of regional government. The Tejano elite welcomed the American immigrants and were enthusiastic about their plans for the economic development of Texas. Many Americans married into elite Tejano families, who hoped that by thus assimilating and sharing power with the Americans they could not only maintain but strengthen their community.

The Mexican state, however, was politically and socially unstable during these first years after its successful revolt against Spain in 1821. Liberals favored a loose federal union, conservatives a strong central state. As a northern frontier province, Texas did not have the benefits of statehood; as a result most Tejanos found themselves taking the liberal side in the struggle, opting for more local control over government activities. When, in 1828, the conservative centralists came to power in Mexico City and decided the Americans had too much influence in Texas, many Tejanos rose up with the Americans in opposition. In 1832 the Tejano elite of San Antonio and many prominent rancheros went on record in favor of provincial autonomy and a strong role for the Americans.

One of the leaders of the San Antonio community was the wealthy ranchero Juan Nepomuceno Seguín. As Santa Anna's army approached from the south, Seguín recruited a company of Tejano volunteers and joined the American force inside the walls of the Alamo. During the siege, Commander Travis sent Seguín and some of his men for reinforcements. Stopped by Mexican troops on his way across the lines, Seguín called out, "¡Somos paisanos!" (We are countrymen), confusing the guards just long enough for Seguín and his men to make their escape despite the hail of gunfire that quickly ensued. Seguín returned from his unsuccessful mission to find the burned bodies of the Alamo defenders, including seven San Antonio Tejanos. "Texas será libre!" Seguín called out as he directed the burial of the Alamo defenders—"Texas shall be free!" In April, Seguín led a regiment of Tejanos in the decisive battle of San Jacinto that won independence for Texas.

At first Tejanos were pleased with independence and played an important political role in the new Republic of Texas. The liberal Lorenzo de Zavala was chosen vice president, and Seguín became the mayor of San Antonio. But soon things began to change, illustrating a recurring pattern in the American occupation of new lands—a striking shift in the relations between different cultures in frontier areas. Most commonly, in the initial stage newcomers blended with native peoples, creating a "frontier of inclusion." The first hunters, trappers, and traders on every American frontier—west of the Appalachians, in the Southwest, and in the Far West—married into the local community and tried to learn native ways. Outnumbered Americans adapted to local societies as a matter of simple survival.

A second, unstable stage occurred when the number of Americans increased and they began occupying more and more land or, as in California, "rushing" in great numbers to mine gold, overrunning native communities. The usual result was warfare and the rapid growth of hostility and racial prejudice—all of which was largely absent in earlier days. A third stage—that of stable settlement—occurred when the native community had been completely "removed" or isolated. In this "frontier of exclusion," racial mixing was rare. Generally, when Europeans pushed American Indians onto reservations they cut themselves off from sources of human history that could have helped them more fully understand the country into which they had moved. And in Texas, American settlers—initially invited in by Mexicans and Tejanos—developed an anti-Mexican passion, regarding all Spanish-speakers as Mexican enemies rather than Tejano allies.

Unscrupulous Americans exploited these prejudices to acquire Tejano property. If the rancheros were "sufficiently scared," one wrote, they would "make an advantageous sale of their lands," and if "two or three hundred of our troops should be stationed here, I have no doubt but a man could make some good speculations." Tejanos were attacked and forced from their homes; some of their villages were burned to the ground. "On the pretext that they were Mexicans," Seguín wrote, Americans treated Tejanos "worse than brutes…My countrymen ran to me for protection against the assaults or exactions of these adventurers." But even in his capacity as mayor Seguín could do little, and in 1842 he and his family, like hundreds of other Tejano families, fled south to Mexico in fear for their lives.

Thus the Tejanos became symbols of a romanticized past rather than full participants in the building of western communities. Spanish-speaking communities in Texas, and later in New Mexico and California, like the communities of Indians throughout the West, became conquered peoples. "White folks and Mexicans were never made to live together," a Texas woman told a traveler a few years after the revolution. "The Mexicans had no business here," she said, and the Americans might "just have to get together and drive them all out of the country." The descendants of the first European settlers of the American Southwest had become foreigners in the land their people had lived in for two centuries.

San Antonio

KEY TOPICS

- Continental expansion and the concept of Manifest Destiny

- The contrasting examples of frontier development in Oregon, Texas, and California

- How the political effects of expansion heightened sectional tensions

EXPLORING THE WEST

There seemed to be no stopping the expansion of the American people. By 1840 they had occupied all of the land east of the Mississippi River and had organized all of it (except for Florida and Wisconsin) into states. Of the ten states admitted to the Union between 1800 and 1840, all but one were west of the Appalachian Mountains. Less than sixty years after the United States gained its independence, the majority of its population lived west of the original thirteen states.

The speed and success of this expansion were a source of deep national pride that whetted appetites for more. Many Americans looked eagerly westward to the vast unsettled reaches of the Louisiana Purchase: to Texas, Santa Fé, and trade with Mexico, and even to the Far West, where New England sea captains had been trading for furs since the 1790s. By 1848 the United States had gained all of these coveted western lands. This chapter examines the way the United States became a continental nation, forming many frontier communities in the process. Exploring the vast continent of North America and gaining an understanding of its geography took several centuries and the efforts of many people.

The Fur Trade

The fur trade, which flourished from the 1670s to the 1840s, was an important spur to exploration on the North American continent. In the 1670s the British Hudson's Bay Company and its French Canadian rival, Montreal's North West Company, began exploring beyond the Great Lakes in the Canadian West in search of beaver pelts. Traders and trappers for both companies depended on the goodwill and cooperation of the native peoples of the region, in particular the Assiniboins, Crees, Gros Ventres, and Blackfeet, all of whom moved freely across what later became the U.S.-Canadian border. From the marriages of European men with native women arose a distinctive mixed-race group, the *métis* (see Chapter 5). In 1821 the Hudson's Bay Company absorbed its Montreal rival and ran the fur trade from trading posts in the far Canadian North

such as Norway House, Cumberland House, and Fort George. British, French Canadian, and métis employees of the Hudson's Bay Company also trapped and explored throughout the Canadian West and in the Oregon Country, then jointly occupied by the British and Americans (see Chapter 9).

Not until the 1820s were American companies able to challenge British dominance of the trans-Mississippi fur trade. In 1824, William Henry Ashley of the Rocky Mountain Fur Company instituted the "rendezvous" system. This was a yearly trade fair, held deep in the Rocky Mountains (Green River and Jackson Hole were favored locations), to which trappers brought their catch of furs. There they traded them for goods transported by the fur companies from St. Louis: traps, guns, ammunition, tobacco, beads and fabrics (for later trade with Indian peoples), and alcohol. These yearly fur rendezvous were modeled on traditional Indian trade gatherings such as the one at the Mandan villages on the upper Missouri and the huge gathering that took place every year at Celilo Falls on the Columbia River during the annual salmon run. Like its Indian model, the fur rendezvous was a boisterous, polyglot, many-day affair at which trappers of many nationalities—Americans and Indian peoples, French Canadians and métis, as well as Mexicans from Santa Fé and Taos—gathered to trade, drink, and gamble.

For the "mountain men" employed by the American fur companies, the rendezvous was their only contact with American society. The rest of the year they spent deep in the mountains trapping beaver and living in some sort of relationship with local Indian peoples. Some lived in a constant state of danger, always alert to the possibility of attack by parties of local people. But most trappers sought accommodation and friendship: nearly half of them contracted long-lasting marriages with Indian women, who not only helped in the trapping and curing of furs but also acted as vital diplomatic links between the white and Indian worlds. Contemporaries often viewed the mountain men—tough, bearded, leather-clad, fluent in Indian tongues—as half-savage, but we should perhaps see them as an example of successful adaptation to frontier life. Indeed, one

The artist Alfred Jacob Miller, a careful observer of the western fur trade, shows us a mountain man and his Indian wife in his 1837 Bourgeois Walker and His Wife. Both Walker and his wife worked together to trap and prepare beaver pelts for market.

Stephen Long's exploration and mapping of the Great Plains in the years 1819–20 was part of a show of force meant to frighten British fur trappers out of the West. Then, in 1843 and 1844, another military explorer, John C. Frémont, mapped the overland trails to Oregon and California. In the 1850s, the Pacific Railroad surveys explored possible transcontinental railroad routes. The tradition of government-sponsored western exploration continued after the Civil War in the famous geological surveys, the best known of which is the 1869 Grand Canyon exploration by Major John Wesley Powell.

Beginning with Long's expedition, the results of these surveys were published by the government, complete with maps, illustrations, and, after the Civil War, photographs. These publications fed a strong popular appetite for pictures of the breathtaking scenery of the Far West and information about its inhabitants. Artists like Karl Bodmer, who accompanied a private expedition by the scientifically inclined German prince Maximilian in the years 1833–34, produced stunning portraits of American Indians. Over the next three decades Thomas Moran, Albert Bierstadt, and other landscape artists traveled west with government expeditions and came home to paint grand (and sometimes fanciful) pictures of Yosemite Valley and Yellowstone (later designated among the first national parks). All these images of the American West made a powerful contribution to the emerging American self-image. American pride in the land—the biggest of this, the longest of that, the most spectacular of something else—was founded on the images brought home by government surveyors and explorers.

In the wake of the pathfinders came hundreds of government geologists and botanists as well as the surveyors who mapped and plotted the West for settlement according to the Land Ordinance of 1785. The basic pattern of land survey and sale established by these measures (see Chapter 7) was followed all the way to the Pacific Ocean. The federal government sold the western public lands at low prices and, to veterans of the War of 1812, gave away land in the Old Northwest. And following policies established in the Old Northwest (see Chapter 9), the federal government also shouldered the expense of Indian removal, paying

legendary trapper became a Crow chief: the African American Jim Beckwourth, who married a Crow woman and was accepted into her tribe.

For all its adventure, the American fur trade was short-lived. By the 1840s, the population of beaver in western streams was virtually destroyed, and the day of the mountain man was over. But with daring journeys like that of Jedediah Smith, the first American to enter California over the Sierra Nevada mountains, the mountain men had helped forge a clear picture of western geography. Soon permanent settlers would follow the trails they had blazed.

Government-Sponsored Exploration

The federal government played a major role in the exploration and development of the West. Thomas Jefferson decisively influenced American westward expansion with the Louisiana Purchase of 1803. When he dispatched the Lewis and Clark expedition the next year it may have been largely to satisfy his own intense scientific and geographic curiosity about the West, but he also instructed Meriwether Lewis and William Clark to draw the western Indians into the American trading network, away from the British.

The exploratory and scientific aspects of the Lewis and Clark expedition set a precedent for many government-financed quasi-military expeditions. In 1806 and 1807, Lieutenant Zebulon Pike led an expedition to the Rocky Mountains in Colorado. Major

Exploration of the Continent, 1804–1830   *Lewis and Clark's "voyage of discovery" of 1804–06 was the first of many government-sponsored western military expeditions. Crossing the Great Plains in 1806, Lieutenant Zebulon Pike was captured by the Spanish in their territory and taken to Mexico but returned in 1807 via Texas. Major Stephen Long, who crossed the Plains in 1819–20, found them "arid and forbidding." Meanwhile fur trappers, among them the much-traveled Jedediah Smith, became well acquainted with the West as they hunted beaver for their pelts.*

the soldiers or the officials who fought or talked Indian peoples into giving up their lands and making long-term commitments to compensate the Indian people themselves. The government also supported the forts and soldiers whose task was to maintain peace between settlers and Indian peoples in newly opened areas.

Expansion and Indian Policy

While American artists were painting the way of life of western Indian peoples, eastern Indian tribes were being removed from their homelands to Indian Territory (present-day Oklahoma, Kansas, and Nebraska), west of Arkansas, Missouri, and Iowa on the eastern edge of the

Great Plains, a region widely regarded as unfarmable and popularly known as the Great American Desert. The justification for this western removal, as Thomas Jefferson had explained early in the century, was the creation of a space where Indian people could live undisturbed by white people while they slowly adjusted to "civilized" ways. But the government officials who negotiated the removals failed to predict the tremendous speed at which white people would settle the West.

As a result, encroachment on Indian Territory was not long in coming. The territory was crossed by the Santa Fé Trail, established in 1821; in the 1840s the northern part was crossed by the heavily traveled

Overland Trails to California, Oregon, and the Mormon community in Utah. In 1854, the government abolished the northern half of Indian Territory, establishing the Kansas and Nebraska Territories in its place and opening them to immediate white settlement. The tribes of the area—the Potawatomis, Wyandots, Kickapoos, Sauks, Foxes, Delawares, Shawnees, Kaskaskias, Peorias, Piankashaws, Weas, Miamis, Omahas, Otos, and Missouris—signed treaties accepting either vastly reduced reservations or allotments. Those who accepted allotments—sections of private land—often sold them, under pressure, to white people. Thus many of the Indian people who had hoped for independence and escape from white pressures in Indian Territory lost both their autonomy and their tribal identity.

The people in the southern part of Indian Territory, in what is now Oklahoma, fared somewhat better. Those members of the southern tribes—the Cherokees, Chickasaws, Choctaws, Creeks, and Seminoles—who had survived the trauma of forcible removal from the Southeast in the 1830s quickly created impressive new communities. The five tribes divided up the territory and established self-governing nations with their own schools and churches. The societies they created were not so different from the American societies from which they had been expelled. The five tribes even carried slavery west with them: an elite economic group established plantations and shipped their cotton to New Orleans like other Southerners. Until after the Civil War, these southern tribes were able to withstand outside pressures and remain the self-governing communities that treaties had assured them they would be.

The removal of the eastern tribes did not solve "the Indian Problem," the term many Americans used to describe their relationship with the first occupants of the land. West of Indian Territory were the nomadic and warlike Indians of the Great Plains: the Sioux, Cheyennes, Arapahoes, Comanches, and Kiowas. Beyond them were the seminomadic tribes of the Rocky Mountains—the Blackfeet, Crows, Utes, Shoshonis, Nez Percé, and Salish peoples—and, in the Southwest, the farming cultures of the Pueblos, Hopis, Acomas, Zunis, Pimas, and Papagos and the migratory Apaches and Navajos. Even farther west were hundreds of small tribes in California and the Pacific Northwest. Clearly, all of these people could not be "removed," for where could they go? The first western pioneers ignored the issue. Beginning in the 1840s, they simply passed through the far western tribal lands on their way to establish new frontiers of settlement in California and Oregon. Later, after the Civil War, the government would undertake a series of Indian wars that ultimately left the remaining Indian peoples penned up on small reservations.

THE POLITICS OF EXPANSION

America's rapid expansion had many consequences, but perhaps the most significant was that it reinforced Americans' sense of themselves as pioneering people. In the 1890s Frederick Jackson Turner, America's most famous historian, observed that the repeated experience of settling new frontiers across the continent had shaped Americans into a uniquely adventurous, optimistic, and democratic people. Other historians have disagreed with Turner, but there is no question that his view of the frontier long ago won the battle for popular opinion. Ever since the time of Daniel Boone, venturing into the wilderness has held a special place in the American imagination, seen almost as an American right.

Manifest Destiny, an Expansionist Ideology

How did Americans justify their restless expansionism? After all, the United States was already a very large country with much undeveloped land. To push beyond existing boundaries was to risk war with Great Britain, which claimed the Pacific Northwest, and with Mexico, which held what is now Texas, New Mexico, Arizona, Utah, Nevada, California, and part of Colorado. If the United States prevailed it would be reducing 75,000 Spanish-speaking people and 150,000 Indian people to subject status. Undertaking such a conquest required a rationale.

In 1845 newspaperman John O'Sullivan provided it. It was, he wrote, "our manifest destiny to overspread the continent allotted by Providence for the free development of our yearly multiplying millions." Sullivan argued that Americans had a God-given right to bring the benefits of American democracy to other, more backward peoples—meaning Mexicans and Indians—by force, if necessary. The notion of manifest destiny summed up the powerful combination of pride in what America had achieved and missionary zeal and racist attitudes toward other peoples that lay behind the thinking of many expansionists. Americans were proud of their rapid development: the surge in population, the remarkable canals and railroads, the grand scale of the American enterprise. Why shouldn't it be even bigger? Almost swaggering, Americans dared other countries—Great Britain in particular—to stop them.

Behind the bravado was concern about the economic future of the United States. After the devastating Panic of 1837 (see Chapter 10), many politicians became convinced that the nation's prosperity depended on vastly expanded trade with Asia. Senator Thomas Hart Benton of Missouri had been advocating trade with India by way of the Missouri and Columbia Rivers since the 1820s (not the easiest of routes, as Lewis and Clark had shown). Soon Benton and others were pointing out

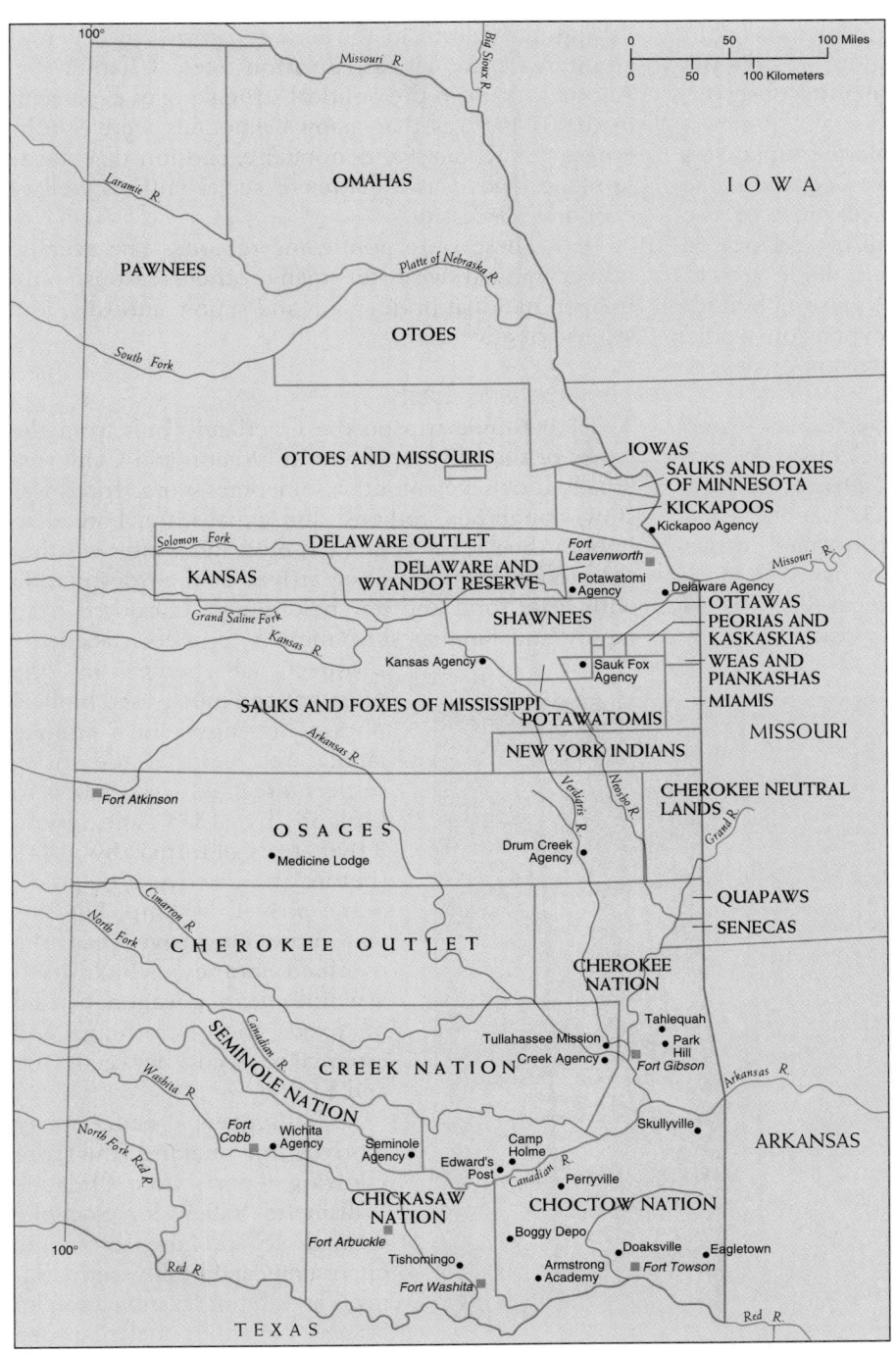

Indian Territory before the Kansas-Nebraska Act of 1854 *Indian Territory lay west of Arkansas, Missouri, and Iowa and east of Spanish Territory. Most of the Indian peoples who lived there in the 1830s and the 1840s had been "removed" from east of the Mississippi River. The southern part (now Oklahoma) was inhabited by peoples from the Old Southwest: the Cherokees, Chickasaws, Choctaws, Creeks, and Seminoles. North of that (in what is now Kansas and Nebraska) lived peoples who had been removed from the Old Northwest. All these Indian peoples had trouble adjusting not only to a new climate and a new way of life but to the close proximity of some Indian tribes who were their traditional enemies.*

how greatly Pacific trade would increase if the United States held the magnificent harbors of the west coast, among them Puget Sound in the Oregon Country held jointly with Britain and the bays of San Francisco and San Diego, both in Mexican-held California.

In one sense, manifest destiny was evangelical religion on a larger scale. The same revivalist fervor that Charles G. Finney had sparked in Rochester in 1830 had a continental echo: missionaries were among the first to travel to the Far West to Christianize Indian people. Just as many of Finney's eastern converts mounted reform movements aimed at changing the lives of workers, so did the western missionaries attempt to "civilize" the Indian peoples. They believed that the only way to do so was to destroy their cultures and to surround them with good American examples.

Expansionism was also tied to national politics. O'Sullivan, whose "manifest destiny" became the expansionist watchword, was not a neutral observer: he was the editor of the *Democratic Review*, a party newspaper. Most Democrats were wholehearted supporters of expansion, whereas many Whigs (especially in the North) opposed it. Whigs welcomed most of the changes wrought by industrialization but advocated strong government policies that would guide growth and development within the country's existing boundaries; they feared (correctly) that expansion would raise the contentious issue of the extension of slavery to new territories.

On the other hand, many Democrats feared the industrialization that the Whigs welcomed. Where the Whigs saw economic progress, Democrats saw economic depression (the Panic of 1837 was the worst the nation had experienced), uncontrolled urban growth, and growing social unrest. For many Democrats, the answer to the nation's social ills was to continue to follow Thomas Jefferson's vision of estab-lishing agriculture in the new territories in order to counterbalance industrialization (see Chapter 9). Another factor in the political struggle over expansion in the 1840s was that many Democrats were Southerners, for whom the continual expansion of cotton-growing lands was a matter of social faith as well as economic necessity.

These were politicians' reasons. The average farmer moved west for many other reasons: land hunger, national pride, plain and simple curiosity, and a sense of adventure.

The Overland Trails

The 2,000-mile trip on the Overland Trails from the banks of the Missouri River to Oregon and California usually took seven months, sometimes more. Travel was slow, dangerous, tedious, and exhausting. Forced to lighten their loads as animals died and winter weather threatened, pioneers often arrived at their destination with little food and few belongings. Uprooted from family and familiar surroundings, pioneers faced the prospect of being, in the poignant and much-used biblical phrase, "strangers in a strange land." Yet despite the risks, settlers streamed west: 5,000 to Oregon by 1845 and about 3,000 to California by 1848 (before the discovery of gold). Some arrived by ship, but this was more expensive than the overland journey, which itself was not cheap: a wagon, a team of oxen, food, clothing, and essential tools cost between $500 and $1,000.

Pioneers had many motives for making the trip. Glowing reports from Oregon's Willamette Valley, for example, seemed to promise economic opportunity and healthy surroundings, an alluring combination to farmers in the malaria-prone Midwest who had been hard hit by the Panic of 1837. But rational motives do not tell the whole story. Many men were motivated by a sense of adventure, by a desire to experience the unknown, or, as they put it, to "see the elephant." Women were more likely to think of the trip as *A Pioneer's Search for an Ideal Home*, the title that Phoebe Judson chose for

The Overland Trails, 1840   *All the great trails west started at the Missouri River. The Oregon, California, and Mormon Trails followed the Platte River into Wyoming, crossed South Pass, and divided in western Wyoming. The much harsher Santa Fé Trail stretched 900 miles southwest across the Great Plains. All of the trails crossed Indian Territory and, to greater or lesser extent, Mexican possessions as well.*

her account of her family's 1852 trip to Oregon.

Few pioneers traveled alone, partly because they feared Indian attack (which was rare) but largely because they needed help fording rivers or crossing mountains with heavy wagons. Most Oregon pioneers traveled with their families but usually also joined a larger group, forming a "train." In the earliest years, when the route was still uncertain, trains hired a "pilot," generally a former fur trapper. Often the men of the wagon train drew up semimilitary constitutions, electing a leader. Democratic as this process appeared, not everyone was willing to obey the leader, and many trains experienced dissension and breakups along the trail. But in essence all pioneers—men, women, and children—were part of a new, westward-moving community in which they had to accept both the advantages and disadvantages of community membership.

J. Goldsborough Bruff, one of thousands who rushed to California for gold in 1849, sketched many events in his Overland Trail journey. Here he depicts several wagons being ferried over the Platte River. The need for individuals to cooperate is obvious. Less obvious in this sketch is the danger: most river crossing points lacked ferries, and both people and livestock often drowned trying to ford them.

Joseph Goldsborough Bruff, Ferriage of the Platte above the Mouth of Deer Creek, July 20, 1849. The Henry E. Huntington Library and Art Gallery, San Marino, Calif.

Wagon trains started westward as soon as the prairies were green (thus ensuring feed for the livestock). The daily routine was soon established. Men took care of the moving equipment and the animals, while the women cooked and kept track of the children. Slowly, at a rate of about fifteen miles a day, the wagon trains moved west along the Platte River, crossing the Continental Divide at South Pass in present-day Wyoming. West of the Rockies the climate was much drier. The long, dusty stretch along the Snake River in present-day southern Idaho finally gave way to Oregon's steep and difficult Blue Mountains and to the dangerous rafting down the Columbia River, in which many drowned and all were drenched by the cold winter rains of the Pacific Northwest. California-bound migrants faced even worse hazards: the complete lack of water in the Humbolt Sink region of northern Nevada and the looming Sierra Nevadas, which had to be crossed before the winter snows came. (Members of the ill-fated Donner party, snowbound on the Nevada side of that range in 1846–47, resorted to cannibalism before they were rescued.)

In addition to the ever-present tedium and exhaustion, wagon trains were beset by such trail hazards as illness and accident. Danger from Indian attack, which all pioneers feared, was actually very small. Before the 1849 California Gold Rush, conflicts between wagon trains and Indians claimed the lives of only thirty-four white people (twenty-four in one wagon train) and twenty-five Indians. In subsequent years, as thousands of gold rushers flocked west, the deaths increased, but, significantly, more Indians than white people died. It appears that unprovoked white attacks on Indians were more common than the reverse.

In contrast, cholera killed at least a thousand people a year in 1849 and the early 1850s when it stalked sections of the trail along the Platte River. Spread by contaminated water, cholera caused vomiting and diarrhea, which in turn led to extreme dehydration and death, often in one night. In the afflicted regions, trailside graves were a frequent and grim sight. Drownings were not uncommon, nor were accidental ax wounds or shootings, and children sometimes fell out of wagons and were run over. The members of the wagon train community did what they could to arrange decent burials, and they provided support for survivors: men helped widows drive their wagons onward, women nursed and tended babies whose mothers were dead, and at least one parentless family, the seven Sager children, were brought to Oregon in safety.

By 1860 almost 300,000 people had traveled the Overland Trails to Oregon or California. Ruts from the wagon wheels can be seen in a number of places along the route even today. In 1869 the completion of the transcontinental railroad marked the end of the wagon train era (although many people made shorter trips to other western locations by wagon). In retrospect, the pioneers remembered their journey as more dangerous and less tedious than it actually was. The stories that came down to their grandchildren told of a heroic adventure. These "pioneers' tales" were not the truth as it had

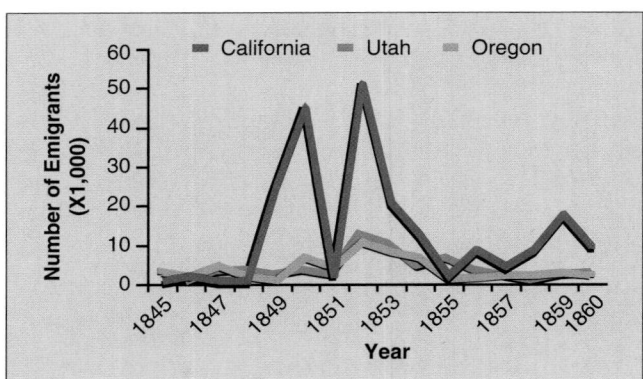

Overland Emigration to Oregon, California, and Utah, 1840–1860 *Before 1849 the westward migration consisted primarily of family groups going to Oregon or Utah. The discovery of gold in California dramatically changed the migration: through 1854 most migrants were single men "rushing" to California, which remained the favored destination up until 1860. Over the twenty-year period from 1840 to 1860 the Overland Trails were transformed from difficult and dangerous routes to well-marked and well-served thoroughfares.*

Source: John Unruh Jr., *The Plains Across* (Champaign-Urbana: University of Illinois Press, 1979), pp. 119–20.

really happened but an effort to find the true heroism in an important episode by making a good story out of it.

Oregon

The American settlement of Oregon provides a capsule example of the stages of frontier development. The first contacts between the region's Indian peoples and Europeans were commercial. Spanish, British, Russian, and American ships traded for sea otter skins from the 1780s to about 1810. Subsequently land-based groups scoured the region for beaver skins as well. In this first "frontier of inclusion" there were frequent, often sexual contacts between Indians and Europeans.

Both Great Britain and the United States claimed the Oregon Country by right of discovery, but in the Convention of 1818 the two nations agreed to occupy it jointly, postponing a final decision on its disposition. In reality, the British clearly dominated the region. In 1824 the Hudson's Bay Company consolidated Britain's position by establishing a major fur trading post at Fort Vancouver, on the banks of the Columbia River. Like all fur-trading ventures, the post exemplified the racial mixing of a "frontier of inclusion." Fort Vancouver housed a polyglot population of eastern Indians (Delawares and Iroquois), local Chinook Indians, French and métis from Canada, British traders, and Hawaiians. Discovered by British Captain James Cook in 1778, Hawaii was visited by the first American ship in 1790. The island kingdom quickly became a favorite stop for American and British traders in sea otter furs destined for China and later for New England whaling

ships. Hawaiian men, famous for their sailing skills, often joined the crews of American and British ships and served, as at Fort Vancouver, as workers in the fur trade. But the effect of the fur trade on native tribes in Oregon was catastrophic; suffering the fate of all Indian peoples after their initial contact with Europeans, they were decimated by European diseases.

The first permanent European settlers in Oregon were retired fur trappers and their Indian wives and families. They favored a spot in the lush and temperate Willamette Valley that became known as French Prairie, although the inhabitants were a mixed group of Americans, British, French Canadians, Indian peoples, and métis. The next to arrive were Protestant and Catholic missionaries, among them Methodist Jason Lee in 1834, Congregationalists Marcus and Narcissa Whitman in 1837, Franciscan priests Frances Blanchet and Modeste Demers in 1838, and Jesuit Pierre-Jean De Smet in 1840. None of these missionaries was very successful. Epidemics had taken the lives of many of the region's peoples, and those who were left were disinclined to give up their nomadic life and settle down as the missionaries wanted them to do.

Finally, in the 1840s, came the Midwest farmers who would make up the majority of Oregon's permanent settlers, carried on the wave of enthusiasm known as "Oregon fever" and lured by free land and patriotism. By 1845 Oregon boasted 5,000 American settlers, most of them living in the Willamette Valley and laying claim to lands to which they had as yet no legal right because neither Britain nor the United States had concluded land treaties with Oregon's Indian peoples. Their arrival signaled Oregon's shift from a "frontier of inclusion" to a "frontier of exclusion."

For these early settlers, life was at first very difficult. Most arrived in late autumn, exhausted from the strenuous overland journey. They could not begin to farm until the spring, and so they depended on the earlier settlers for their survival over the winter. Ironically, in the earliest years American settlers got vital help from the Hudson's Bay Company, even though its director, John McLoughlin, had been ordered by the British government not to encourage American settlement. McLoughlin disregarded his orders, motivated both by sympathy for the plight of the newcomers and by a keen sense of the dangers his enterprise would face if he were outnumbered by angry Americans.

The handful of American settlers in Oregon found themselves in possession of a remote frontier. One of the first things they did was to draw up their own constitution. When the first Oregon settlers (including a number of former mountain men) met in the summer of 1843 to draft a constitution, they prohibited African Americans (both free and enslaved) from settling in the territory. By avoiding the divisive issue of slavery, they hoped to build community feeling between white settlers from the North and the South. In spite of the law, some Southerners did bring their slaves to Oregon with them, but when an early free African American pioneer, George Bush, came to Oregon, he deliberately settled north of the Columbia River, in what later became Washington Territory. Thus Oregon got African American slaves that it did not want and lost a free man who became renowned for his willingness to cooperate with others and his community spirit.

The influx of American settlers and their efforts to establish their own government created strains between the United States and Britain. Campaigning for the presidency in 1844, James K. Polk coined the belligerent slogan "Fifty-four Forty or Fight," suggesting that the United States would go to war if it didn't get control of all the territory south of latitude 54°40´, the border between Russian Alaska and British Canada. In office, however, Polk was willing to compromise. In June, 1846, Britain and the United States concluded a treaty establishing the forty-ninth parallel as the U.S.-Canada border but leaving the island of Vancouver in British hands. The British then quietly wound up their declining fur trade in the region. In 1849 the Hudson's Bay Company closed Fort Vancouver and moved its operations to Victoria, thus ending the Pacific Northwest's largely successful experience with joint occupancy. Oregon's

Donation Land Claim Act of 1850 codified the practice of giving 320 acres to each white male age eighteen or over and 640 acres to each married couple to settle in the territory (African Americans, Hawaiians, and American Indians were excluded).

The white settlers realized that they had to forge strong community bonds if they hoped to survive on their distant frontier. Cooperation and mutual aid were the rule. Until well into the 1850s, residents organized yearly parties that traveled back along the last stretches of the Oregon Trail to help straggling parties making their way to the territory. Kinship networks were strong and vital: many pioneers came to join family who had migrated before them. Although most settlers lived on their own land claims rather than in towns, neighborly cooperation was crucial. Food sharing and mutual labor were essential in the early years, when crop and livestock loss to weather or natural predators was common. Help, even to total strangers, was customary in times of illness or death.

Although this community feeling did not extend to Indian groups as a whole, relations with the small and unthreatening disease-thinned local Indian tribes were generally peaceful until 1847, when Cayuse Indians killed the missionaries Marcus and Narcissa Whitman. Their deaths triggered a series of "wars" against the remaining native people. A "frontier of exclusion" had been achieved. Nonetheless the process by which Oregon became part of the United States (it was admitted as a state in 1859) was relatively peaceful, especially when compared to American expansion into the Spanish provinces of New Mexico and Texas.

The Santa Fé Trade

Santa Fé, first settled by colonists from Mexico in 1609 and the center of the Spanish frontier province of New Mexico, had long attracted American frontiersmen and traders. But Spain had forcefully resisted American penetration. For example, Lieutenant Zebulon Pike's Great Plains and Rocky Mountain exploration of 1806–07 ended ignominiously with his capture by Spanish soldiers.

When Mexico gained its independence from Spain in 1821, this exclusionary policy changed. American traders were now welcome in Santa Fé, but the trip over the legendary Santa Fé Trail from Independence,

James Warre, American Settlement of Oregon City, 1846. Watercolor. Courtesy American Antiquarian Society

This watercolor of tiny Oregon City in 1846 suggests how small the American population of the Oregon Territory was when its status was being decided in America's favor. With just 953 inhabitants in 1850, Oregon City was the largest city in the territory.

Missouri, was a forbidding 900 miles of arid plains, deserts, and mountains. On the Santa Fé trail, unlike the Oregon Trail, there was serious danger of Indian attack, for neither the Comanches nor the Apaches of the southern high plains tolerated trespassers. In 1825, at the urging of Senator Benton and others, Congress voted federal protection for the Santa Fé Trail, even though much of it lay in Mexican territory. The number of people venturing west in the trading caravans increased yearly because the profits were so great (the first American trader to reach Santa Fé, William Becknell, realized a thousand percent profit). By the 1840s a few hundred American trappers and traders (called *extranjeros*, or foreigners) lived permanently in New Mexico. In Santa Fé, some American merchants married daughters of important local families, suggesting the start of the inclusive stage of frontier contact.

Settlements and trading posts soon grew up along the long Santa Fé Trail. One of the most famous was Bent's Fort, on the Arkansas River in what is now eastern Colorado, which did a brisk trade in beaver skins and buffalo robes. Like most trading posts, it had a multiethnic population. In the 1840s the occupants included housekeeper Josefa Tafoya of Taos, whose husband was a carpenter from Pennsylvania; an African American cook; a French tailor from New Orleans; Mexican muleteers; and a number of Indian women, including the two Cheyenne women who were the (successive) wives of William Bent, cofounder of the fort. The three small communities of Pueblo, Hardscrabble, and Greenhorn, spinoffs of Bent's Fort, were populated by men of all nationalities and their Mexican and Indian wives. All three communities lived by trapping, hunting, and a little farming. This racially and economically mixed existence was characteristic of all early trading frontiers, but another western frontier, the American agricultural settlement in Texas, was different from the start.

Mexican Texas

In 1821, when Mexico gained its independence from Spain, there were 2,240 *Tejano* (Spanish-speaking) residents of Texas. Established in 1716 as a buffer against possible French attack on New Spain, the main Texas settlements of Nacogdoches, Goliad, and San Antonio remained small, far-flung frontier outposts (see Chapter 5). As was customary throughout New Spain, communities were organized around three centers: missions and *presidios* (forts), which formed the nucleus of towns, and the large cattle-raising *ranchos* on which rural living depended. As elsewhere in New Spain, society was divided into two classes: the *ricos* (rich), who claimed Spanish descent, and the mixed-blood *pobres* (poor). Tejano town life was traditionally hierarchical, dominated by the ricos who were connected by blood or marriage with the great ranching families. The most colorful figures on the ranchos were mestizo (mixed-blood) vaqueros, renowned for their horsemanship; Americanization of their name made "buckaroos" of the American cowboys to whom they later taught their skills. Most Tejanos were neither ricos nor vaqueros but small farmers or common laborers who led hardscrabble frontier lives. But all Tejanos, rich and poor, faced the constant threat of raids by Comanche Indians.

The Comanches exemplified the revolutionary changes brought about in the lives of Plains Indians by the reintroduction of horses into the American continent (see Chapter 5). "A Comanche on his feet is out of his element...but the moment he lays his hands upon his horse," said artist George Catlin, "I doubt very much whether any people in the world can surpass [him]." Legendary warriors, the Comanches raided the small Texas settlements at will and even struck deep into Mexico itself. Once they raided so far

Alfred Jacob Miller painted the busy life of Fort Laramie, a multiracial trading fort, in 1837. Bent's Fort, another multiracial trading center, would have looked much like this.

south that they saw brightly plumed birds (parrots) and "tiny men with tails" (monkeys); apparently they had reached the tropical Yucatán. The nomadic Comanches followed the immense buffalo herds on which they depended for food and clothing. Their relentless raids on the Texas settlements rose from a determination to hold onto this rich buffalo territory, for the buffalo provided all that they wanted. They had no interest in being converted by mission priests or incorporated into mixed-race trading communities.

Americans in Texas

In 1821, seeking to increase the strength of its buffer zone between the heart of Mexico and the

Painted by George Catlin about 1834, this scene, Comanche Village, *shows how the everyday life of the Comanches was tied to buffalo. The women in the foreground are scraping buffalo hide, and buffalo meat can be seen drying on racks. The men and boys may be planning their next buffalo hunt.*

marauding Comanches, the Mexican government granted Moses Austin of Missouri an area of 18,000 square miles within the territory of Texas. Moses died shortly thereafter, and the grant was taken up by his son Stephen F. Austin, who became the first American *empresario* (land agent). From the beginning the American settlement of Texas differed markedly from that of other frontiers. Elsewhere, Americans frequently settled on land to which Indian peoples still held title, or, as in the case of Oregon, they occupied lands to which other countries also made claim. In contrast, the Texas settlement was fully legal: Austin and other empresarios owned their lands as a result of formal contracts with the Mexican government. In exchange, Austin agreed that he and his colonists would become Mexican citizens and would adopt the Catholic religion. It is difficult to say which of these two provisions was the more remarkable, for most nineteenth-century Americans defined their Americanness in terms of citizenship and the Protestant religion.

Additionally, in startling contrast with the usual frontier free-for-all, Austin's community was populated with handpicked settlers, Austin insisting that "no frontiersman who has no other occupation than that of hunter will be received—no drunkard, no gambler, no profane swearer, no idler." Neither Austin nor later empresarios had any trouble finding Americans to apply, for the simple reason that Mexican land grants were magnificent: a square league (4,605 acres) per family. Soon Americans (including African American slaves, to whose presence the Mexican government turned a blind eye) outnumbered Tejanos by nearly two to one: in 1830 there were an estimated 7,000 Americans and 4,000 Tejanos living in Texas.

The Austin settlement of 1821 was followed by others, twenty-six in all, concentrating in the fertile river bottoms of east Texas (along the Sabine River) and south central Texas (the Brazos and the Colorado). These large settlements were highly organized farming enterprises whose principal crop was cotton, grown by African American slave labor, which was sold in the international market. By the early 1830s, Americans in Texas were exporting an estimated $500,000 worth of goods yearly to New Orleans, two-thirds of it cotton.

Austin's colonists and those who settled later were predominantly Southerners who viewed Texas as a natural extension of settlement in Mississippi and Louisiana. These settlers created enclaves (self-contained communities) that had little contact with Tejanos or Indian peoples. In fact, although they lived in Mexican territory, most Americans never bothered to learn Spanish. Nor, in spite of Austin's promises, did they become Mexican citizens or adopt the Catholic religion. Yet because of the nature of agreements made by the empresarios, the Americans could not set up local American-style governments like the one created by settlers in Oregon. Like the immigrants who flooded into east coast cities (see Chapter 13) the Americans in Texas were immigrants to another country—but one they did not intend to adapt to.

The one exception to American exclusiveness occurred in San Antonio, the provincial government center. There, just as in Santa Fé, a handful of wealthy Americans married into the Tejano elite with ease. One such marriage in San Antonio linked wealthy Louisianan James Bowie, the legendary fighter for whom the Bowie knife is named, and Ursula Veramendi, daughter of the vice governor of Texas. With the marriage, Bowie became a wealthy, honored, and well-connected Mexican citizen. Only after the death of his wife and children in a cholera epidemic in 1833 did Bowie support the cause of Anglo-Texan independence, going on to fight—and die—at the Alamo.

The great ranchos excited the admiration of many Americans, who later made cattle raising a major western industry. In these early days in Texas, Americans watched and learned as Tejanos rounded up range cattle, branded them, and drove more than 20,000 each year to Nacogdoches for the U.S. market. Praise for Tejano horsemanship was unstinting: they are "not surpassed perhaps by any other people in the Globe," enthused one American immigrant. Tejano customs, especially multiday celebrations that mixed religious ceremonies, feasting, horse racing, and elaborate *fandangos* (dances), offered striking evidence of the richly textured community life created by Tejanos of all social classes.

For a brief period Texas was big enough to hold three communities: Comanche, Tejano, and American. The nomadic Comanches rode the high plains of northern and western Texas, raiding settlements primarily for horses. The Tejanos maintained their ranchos and missions mostly in the South, while American farmers occupied the eastern and south central sections. Each group would fight to hold its land: the Comanches, their rich hunting grounds, the Mexicans, their towns and ranchos; and the newcomers, the Americans, their rich land grants.

The Texas Revolt

The balance between the three communities in Texas was broken in 1828, when centrists gained control of the government in Mexico City and, in a dramatic shift of policy, decided to exercise firm control over the northern province. As the Mexican government restricted American immigration, outlawed slavery, levied customs duties and taxes, and planned other measures, Americans seethed and talked of rebellion. Bolstering their cause were as many as 20,000 additional Americans, many of them openly expansionist, who flooded into Texas after 1830. These most recent settlers did not intend to become Mexican citizens. Instead, they planned to take over Texas. What ensued was reminiscent of the American Revolution, at least in the eyes of some Americans. But for all the invocations of the Revolution, the real issue in Texas was conquest.

Whereas many of the older American settlers in Texas found much that was admirable, or at least understandable, in Spanish Mexican culture, many of the post-1830 immigrants were vehemently anti-Mexican. Many had grievances: failure to obtain a land grant, restrictions on trade because of Mexican customs regulations, difficulties in understanding Hispanic law, which differed markedly from the Anglo-American legal tradition. Above all, in the eyes of many Americans, there was the matter of race. Statements of racial superiority were commonplace, and even Stephen Austin wrote in 1836 that he saw the Texas conflict as one of barbarism on the part of "a mongrel Spanish-Indian and negro race, against civilization and the Anglo-American race." Most recent American migrants to Texas had come from the South, and racist statements of this sort made political compromise with the Mexican government, a step favored by many of the older American settlers, impossible.

Between 1830 and 1836, in spite of the mediation efforts of Austin (who was imprisoned for eighteen months by the Mexican government for his pains), the mood on both the Mexican and the American-Texan sides became more belligerent. In the fall of 1835 war finally broke out, and a volunteer American Texan and Tejano army seized Goliad and San Antonio, in the heart of Mexican Texas, from the small Mexican army that was sent to quell them. Believing they had won, the Americans were caught off guard by a major counterattack led by the Mexican general and president Antonio López de Santa Anna. As described in the opening of this chapter, on March 6, 1836, Santa Anna and his forces overwhelmed the 187 men who refused to surrender—or to escape from—the Alamo in San Antonio. At Santa Anna's orders, the women at the Alamo—one American woman and several Tejanas—and an African American slave named Joe were spared so that Texans could hear their eyewitness accounts. From those accounts the legend of the Alamo was born.

From San Antonio, Santa Anna divided his army and led part of it in pursuit of the remaining army of American and Tejano volunteers commanded by General Sam Houston. On April 21, 1836, at the San Jacinto River in eastern Texas, Santa Anna thought he had Houston trapped at last. Confident of victory against the exhausted Texans, Santa Anna's army rested in the afternoon, failing even to post sentries. Although Houston advised against it, Houston's men voted to attack immediately rather than wait till the next morning. Shouting "Remember the Alamo!" for the first time, the Texans completely surprised their opponents and won an overwhelming victory. On May 14, 1836, Santa Anna signed a treaty fixing the southern boundary of the newly independent Republic of Texas at the Rio Grande. The Mexican Congress, however, repudiated the treaty and refused to recognize Texan independence. It also rejected the offer by President Andrew Jackson to solve the matter through purchase.

The Republic of Texas

Despite the military triumph of the Americans who had proclaimed the Republic of Texas, the land between the Rio Grande and the Nueces River remained disputed territory. In the eyes of the Mexicans, the American insistence on the Rio Grande boundary was little more than a blatant effort to stake a claim to New Mexico, an older and completely separate Spanish settlement. An effort by the Republic of Texas in 1841 to capture Santa Fé was easily repulsed.

The Republic of Texas was unexpectedly rebuffed in another quarter as well. The U.S. Congress refused to grant it statehood when, in 1837, Texas applied for admission to the Union. Petitions opposing the admission of a fourteenth slave state (there were then thirteen free states) poured into Congress.

Texas: From Mexican Province to U.S. State   *In the space of twenty years, Texas changed shape three times. Initially part of the Mexican province of Coahuila y Tejas, it became the Republic of Texas in 1836, following the Texas Revolt, and was annexed to the United States in that form in 1845. Finally, in the Compromise of 1850 following the Mexican-American War, it took its present shape.*

Congressman John Quincy Adams of Massachusetts, known as the conscience of New England, led the opposition to the admission of Texas. Adams was (and is still) the only former president to subsequently serve in Congress, and his unprecedented position gave immense authority to his opinions. Congress debated and ultimately dropped the Texas application. Although President Jackson was sympathetic to the Texan cause, he knew that he did not have the power to quell the controversy that the admission of Texas would arouse. But he did manage to extend diplomatic recognition to the Republic of Texas, on March 3, 1837, less than twenty-four hours before he left office. Breaking the good news to Texas agents at the White House, Jackson offered toasts to the Republic of Texas and to its president, his old friend Sam Houston.

Sam Houston must often have wondered whether the presidency of the Republic of Texas was an honor worth having. The unresolved conflict with Mexico put heavy stress on American-Tejano relations. Immediately after the revolt, many Tejano residents fled to Mexico, and American squatters moved in to claim their lands. In some regions, vigilantes forced Tejanos to leave. San Antonio, however, the most important city of Mexican Texas, saw an accommodation between the old elite and the new American authorities. Although they slowly lost political power, members of the Tejano elite were not immediately dispossessed of their property. As before, ambitious Anglos married into the Tejano elite. The intermarriages made it easier for the Tejano elite to adjust to the changes in law and commerce that the Americans quickly enacted. But following a temporary recapture of San Antonio by Mexican forces in 1842, positions hardened. Many more of the Tejano elite fled to Mexico, and Americans discussed banishing or imprisoning all Tejanos until the border issue was settled. This was, of course, impossible. Culturally, San Antonio remained a Mexican city long after the Americans had declared independence. The Americans in the Republic of Texas were struggling to reconcile American ideals of democracy with the reality of subordinating those with a prior claim, the Tejanos, to the status of a conquered people.

Ethnocentric attitudes quickly triumphed. Tejanos and other Mexicans were soon being blamed by Americans for their own subordination. Senator Edward Hannegan of Indiana was one of the most outspoken: "Mexico and the United States are peopled by two distinct and utterly unhomogeneous races," he announced in 1847. "In no reasonable period could we amalgamate." In the same year, the *Democratic Review*, completely ignoring the Spanish discovery and conquest of the Americas, offered the following rationalization: "Had Mexico been settled by a vigorous race of Europeans...that would have

turned its advantages to account, developed its wealth, increased its commerce and multiplied its settlements, she would not now be in danger of losing her lands by emigration from the North."

American control over the other Texas residents, the Indians, was also slow in coming. Although the coastal Indian peoples were soon killed or removed, the Comanches still rode the high plains of northern and western Texas. West of the Rio Grande, equally fierce Apache bands were in control. Both groups soon learned to distrust American promises to stay out of their territory, and they did not hesitate to raid and to kill trespassers. Not until after the Civil War and major campaigns by the U.S. Army were these fierce Indian tribes conquered.

Texas Annexation and the Election of 1844

Martin Van Buren, who succeeded Andrew Jackson as president in 1837, was too cautious to raise the Texas issue during his term of office. But Texans themselves continued to press for annexation to the United States while at the same time seeking recognition and support from Great Britain. The idea of an independent and expansionist republic on its southern border that might gain the support of America's traditional enemy alarmed many Americans. Annexation thus became an urgent matter of national politics. This issue also added to the troubles of a governing Whig Party that was already deeply divided by the policies of John Tyler, who had become president by default when William Harrison died in office (see Chapter 10). Tyler raised the issue of annexation in 1844, hoping thereby to ensure his reelection, but the strategy backfired. Presenting the annexation treaty to Congress, Secretary of State John Calhoun awakened sectional fears by connecting Texas with the urgent need of southern slave owners to extend slavery.

In a storm of antislavery protest, Whigs rejected the treaty proposed by their own president and ejected Tyler himself from the party. In his place they chose Henry Clay, the party's longtime standard-bearer, as their presidential candidate. Clay took a noncommittal stance on Texas, favoring annexation, but only if Mexico approved. Since Mexico's emphatic disapproval was well known, Clay's position was widely interpreted as a politician's effort not to alienate voters on either side of the fence.

In contrast, in the Democratic Party whole-hearted and outspoken expansionists seized control. Sweeping aside their own senior politician, Van Buren, who like Clay tried to remain uncommitted, the Democrats nominated their first "dark horse" candidate, James K. Polk of Tennessee. Southerners and Westerners among the Democrats—including such notables as Robert Walker of Mississippi, Stephen Douglas of Illinois, and Lewis Cass of Michigan—beat the drum of manifest destiny, promising that expansion meant a glorious extension of democracy. They enthusiastically endorsed Polk's platform, which called for "the re-occupation of Oregon and the re-annexation of Texas at the earliest practicable period."

Polk won the 1844 election by the narrow margin of 40,000 popular votes (although he gained 170 electoral votes to Clay's 105). An ominous portent for the Whigs was the showing of James G. Birney of the Liberty Party, who polled 62,000 votes, largely from northern antislavery Whigs. Birney's third-party campaign was the first political sign of the growing strength of antislavery opinion. Nevertheless, the 1844 election was widely interpreted as a mandate for expansion. Thereupon John Tyler, in one of his last actions as president, pushed through Congress a joint resolution (which did not require the two-thirds approval by the Senate necessary for treaties) for the annexation of Texas. Three months later the Texas congress approved annexation, and thus nine years after its founding the Republic of Texas disappeared. Florida had just been approved for statehood as well, and when Texas entered the Union in December 1845 it was the twenty-eighth state and the fifteenth slave state.

THE MEXICAN–AMERICAN WAR

James K. Polk lived up to his campaign promises. In 1846 he peacefully added Oregon south of the forty-ninth parallel to the United States; in 1848, following the Mexican-American War, he acquired Mexico's northern provinces of California and New Mexico as well. Thus, with the annexation of Texas, the United States, in the short space of three years, had added 1.5 million square

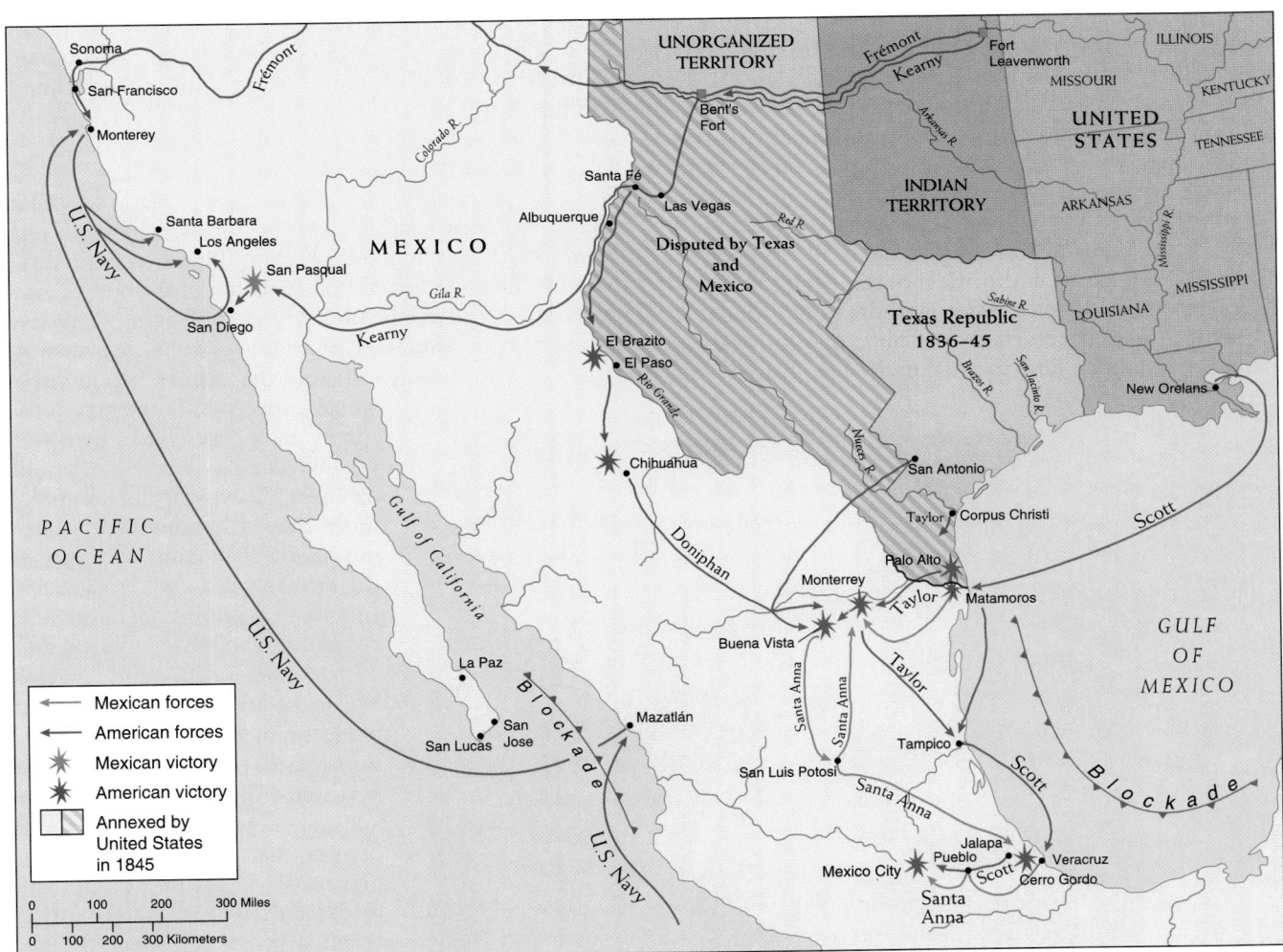

The Mexican-American War, 1846–1848   *The Mexican-American War began with an advance by U.S. forces into the disputed area between the Nueces River and the Rio Grande in Texas. The war's major battles were fought by General Zachary Taylor in northern Mexico and General Winfield Scott in Vera Cruz and Mexico City. Meanwhile Colonel Stephen Kearny secured New Mexico and, with the help of the U.S. Navy and John C. Frémont's troops, California.*

miles of territory, an increase of nearly 70 percent. Polk was indeed "the manifest destiny" president.

Origins of the War

In the spring of 1846, just as the controversy over Oregon was drawing to a peaceful conclusion, tensions with Mexico grew more serious. As soon as Texas was granted statehood in 1845, the Mexican government broke diplomatic relations with the United States. In addition, because the United States accepted the Texas claim of all land north of the Rio Grande, it found itself embroiled in a border dispute with Mexico. In June 1845, Polk sent General Zachary Taylor to Texas, and by October a force of 3,500 Americans were on the Nueces River with orders to defend Texas in the event of a Mexican invasion.

Polk had something bigger than border protection in mind. He coveted the continent clear to the Pacific Ocean. At the same time that he sent Taylor to Texas, Polk secretly instructed the Pacific naval squadron to seize the California ports if Mexico declared war. He also wrote the American consul in Monterey, Thomas Larkin, that a peaceful takeover of California by its residents—Spanish Mexicans and Americans alike—would not be unwelcome. When, in addition, the federally commissioned explorer John C. Frémont and a band of armed men appeared in California in the winter of 1845–46, Mexican authorities became alarmed and ordered him to leave. After withdrawing briefly to Oregon, Frémont returned to California and was on hand in Sonoma in June to assist in the Bear Flag Revolt,

in which a handful of American settlers, declaring that they were playing "the Texas game," announced California's independence from Mexico.

Meanwhile, in November 1845, Polk followed up his warlike gestures by sending a secret envoy, John Slidell, to Mexico with an offer of $30 million or more for the Rio Grande border in Texas and Mexico's provinces of New Mexico and California. When the Mexican government refused even to receive Slidell, an angry Polk ordered General Taylor and his forces south to the Rio Grande, into the territory that Mexicans considered their soil. In April 1846 a brief skirmish between American and Mexican soldiers broke out in the disputed zone. Polk seized on the event, sending a war message to Congress: "Mexico has passed the boundary of the United States, has invaded our territory and shed American blood upon American soil….War exists, and, notwithstanding all our efforts to avoid it, exists by the act of Mexico herself." This last claim of President Polk's was, of course, contrary to fact. On May 13, 1846, Congress declared war on Mexico.

Mr. Polk's War

From the beginning, the Mexican-American War was politically divisive. Whig critics in Congress, among them a gawky young congressman from Illinois named Abraham Lincoln, questioned Polk's account of the border incident. They accused the president of misleading Congress and of maneuvering the country into an unnecessary war. It is with these suspicions that the history of Congressional concern over the way presidents have exercised their war powers begins. The issue would again be prominent, for example, more than a hundred years later during the Vietnam War and in the Reagan years. As the Mexican-American War dragged on and casualties and costs mounted—13,000 Americans and 50,000 Mexicans died and the United States spent $97 million—opposition increased, especially among northern antislavery Whigs. More and more people came to the opinion that the war was nothing more than a plot by Southerners to expand slavery. Many Northerners asked why Polk had been willing to settle for only a part of Oregon but was so eager to pursue a war for slave territory. Thus expansionist dreams served to fuel sectional antagonisms.

General Winfield Scott's amphibious attack on the Mexican coastal city of Vera Cruz in March 1847 was a considerable military feat that was greeted with wide popular acclaim in the United States. Popular interest in the battles of the Mexican-American War was fed by illustrations such as this in newspapers and magazines.

The northern states witnessed both mass and individual protests against the war. In Massachusetts, the legislature passed a resolution condemning Polk's declaration of war as unconstitutional, and philosopher-writer Henry David Thoreau went to jail rather than pay the taxes he believed would support the war effort. Thoreau's dramatic gesture was undercut by his aunt, who paid his fine after he had spent only one night in jail. Thoreau then returned to his cabin on Walden Pond, where he wrote his classic essay "Civil Disobedience," justifying the individual's moral right to oppose an immoral government. In the early twentieth century, the Indian nationalist Mohandas Gandhi used Thoreau's essay to justify his campaign of "passive resistance" against British imperial rule in India. In turn, Martin Luther King and others used Gandhi's model of civil disobedience as a basis for their activities in the civil rights movement of the 1950s and 1960s.

Whigs termed the war with Mexico "Mr. Polk's War," but the charge was not just a Whig jibe. Although he lacked a military background, Polk assumed the overall planning of the war's strategy (a practice that the critical Mr. Lincoln was to follow in the Civil War). By his personal attention to the coordination of civilian political goals and military requirements, Polk gave a new and expanded definition to the role of the president as commander in chief during wartime. In 1846 Polk sent General Taylor south into northeastern Mexico and Colonel Stephen Kearny to New Mexico and California. Taylor captured the northern Mexico cities of Palo Alto in May and Monterrey in September 1846. Meanwhile, Kearny marched his men 900 miles to Santa Fé, which surrendered peacefully. Another march of roughly the same distance brought him by fall to southern California, which he took with the help of naval forces and Frémont's irregular troops.

The northern provinces that Polk had coveted were now secured, but contrary to his expectations, Mexico refused to negotiate. In February 1847, General Santa Anna of Alamo fame attacked American troops led by General Taylor at Buena Vista but was repulsed by Taylor's small force. A month later, in March 1847, General Winfield Scott launched an amphibious attack on the coastal city of Veracruz and rapidly captured it. Americans celebrated these twin victories joyously, but they were to be the last easy victories of the war. It took Scott six months of brutal fighting against stubborn Mexican resistance on the battlefield and harassing guerrilla raids to force his way to Mexico City. American troops reacted bitterly to their high casualty rates, retaliating against Mexican citizens with acts of murder, robbery, and rape. Even General Scott himself admitted that his troops had "committed atrocities to make Heaven weep and

Territory Added, 1845–1853   *James K. Polk was elected president in 1844 on an expansionist platform. He lived up to most of his campaign rhetoric by gaining the Oregon Country (to the forty-ninth parallel) peacefully from the British, Texas by the presidential action of his predecessor John Tyler, and present-day California, Arizona, Nevada, Utah, New Mexico, and part of Colorado by war with Mexico. In the short space of three years, the size of the United States grew by 70 percent. In 1853, the Gadsden Purchase added another 30,000 square miles.*

every American of Christian morals blush for his country." In September, Scott took Mexico City, and Mexican resistance came to an end.

With the American army went a special envoy, Nicholas Trist, who delivered Polk's terms for peace. In the Treaty of Guadalupe Hidalgo, signed February 2, 1848, Mexico ceded its northern provinces of California and New Mexico (which included present-day Arizona, Utah, Nevada, and part of Colorado) and accepted the Rio Grande as the boundary of Texas. The United States agreed to pay Mexico $15 million and assume about $2 million in individual claims against that nation.

When Trist returned to Washington with the treaty, however, Polk was furious. He had actually recalled Trist after Scott's sweeping victory, intending to send a new envoy with greater demands, but Trist had ignored the recall order. "All Mexico!" had become the phrase widely used by those in favor of further expansion, Polk among them. But two very different groups opposed further expansion. The first group, composed of northern Whigs, included such notables as Ralph Waldo Emerson, who grimly warned, "The United States will conquer Mexico, but it will be as the man swallows arsenic, which brings him down in turn. Mexico will poison us." The second group was composed of Southerners who realized that Mexicans could not be kept as conquered people but would have to be offered territorial government as Louisiana had in 1804. Senator John C. Calhoun of South Carolina, leading the opposition, warned against admitting "colored and mixed-breed" Mexicans "on an equality with people of the United States." "We make a great mistake, sir," he argued on the floor of the Senate, "when we suppose that all people are capable of self-government." Bowing to these political protests, Polk reluctantly accepted the treaty. A later addition, the $10 million Gadsden Purchase of parts of present-day New Mexico and Arizona, added another 30,000 square miles to the United States in 1853. This purchase, made to facilitate a southern transcontinental railroad route through arid borderland, was a far cry from the rich heartland of Mexico that Polk had hoped to annex.

The Press and Popular War Enthusiasm

The Mexican-American War was the first war in which regular, on-the-scene reporting by representatives of the press caught the mass of ordinary citizens up in the

Woodville, War News from Mexico, oil on canvas. Manovgian Foundation on loan to the National Gallery of Art, Washington, D.C.

The unprecedented immediacy of the news reporting of the Mexican-American War, transmitted for the first time by telegraph, is captured here by Richard Caton Woodville in War News from Mexico *(1848). By including an African American man and child, the artist is also voicing a political concern about the effect of the war on slavery.*

war's daily events. Thanks to the recently invented telegraph, newspapers could get the latest news from their reporters, who were among the world's first war correspondents. The "penny press," with more than a decade's experience of reporting urban crime and scandals, was quick to realize that the public's appetite for sensational war news was apparently insatiable. For the first time in American history, accounts by journalists, and not the opinions of politicians, became the major shapers of popular attitudes toward a war. From beginning to end, news of the war stirred unprecedented popular excitement.

The reports from the battlefield united Americans in a new way: they became part of a temporary but highly emotional community linked by newsprint and buttressed by public gatherings. In the spring of 1846, news of Zachary Taylor's victory at Palo Alto prompted the largest meeting ever held in the cotton textile town of Lowell, Massachusetts. In May 1847, New York City celebrated the twin victories at Veracruz and Buena Vista with fireworks, illuminations, and a "grand procession" estimated at 400,000 people. Generals Taylor and Scott became overnight heroes, and in time both became presidential candidates. Exciting, sobering, and terrible, war news had a deep hold on the popular imagination. It was a lesson newspaper publishers never forgot.

CALIFORNIA AND THE GOLD RUSH

In the early 1840s California was inhabited by many seminomadic Indian tribes whose people numbered approximately 50,000. There were also some 7,000 Californios, descendants of the Spanish Mexican pioneers who had begun to settle in 1769. The American presence in California at first consisted of a few traders and settlers who often intermarried with Californios. Even American annexation at the end of the Mexican-American War changed little for the handful of Americans on this remote frontier. But then came the Gold Rush of 1849, which changed California permanently.

Russian-Californio Trade

The first outsiders to penetrate the isolation of Spanish California were not Americans but Russians. Because the distance between California and Mexico City was so great, the Spanish had found it difficult to maintain the elaborate system of twenty-one missions first established in the eighteenth century (see Chapter 5). Nevertheless, Spanish officials in Mexico insisted on isolation, forbidding the colonists to trade with other nations. Evading Spanish regulations, Californios conducted a small illegal trade in cattle hides with American merchant ships (for the shoes made in the workshops of Massachusetts), and

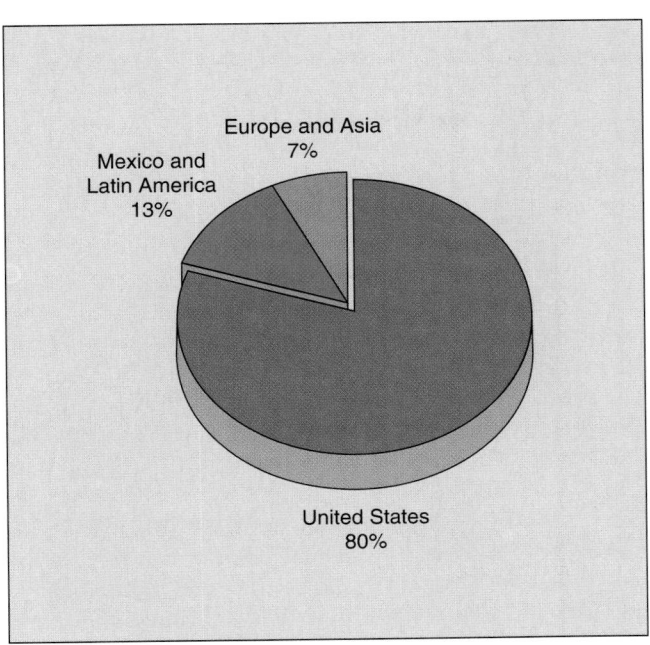

Where the Forty-Niners Came From   *Americans drawn to the California Gold Rush of 1849 encountered a more diverse population than most had previously known. Nearly as novel to them as the 20 percent from foreign countries was the regional variety from within the United States itself.*

a much larger trade with the Russian American Fur Company in Sitka, Alaska. A mutually beneficial barter of California food for iron tools and woven cloth from Russia was established in 1806. This arrangement became even brisker after the Russians settled Fort Ross (near present-day Mendocino) in 1812, and led in time to regular trade with Mission San Rafael and Mission Sonoma. That the Russians in Alaska, so far from their own capital, were better supplied with manufactured goods than the Californios is an index of the latter's isolation.

When Mexico became independent in 1821, the California trade was thrown open to ships of all nations. Nevertheless, Californios continued their special relationship with the Russians, exempting them from the taxes and inspections that they required of Americans. However, agricultural productivity declined after 1832, when the Mexican government ordered the secularization of the California missions, and the Russians regretfully turned to the rich farms of the Hudson's Bay Company in the Pacific Northwest for their food supply. In 1841, they sold Fort Ross, and the Russian-Californio connection came to an end.

Early American Settlement

It was Johann Augustus Sutter, a Swiss who had settled in California in 1839, becoming a Mexican citizen, who served as a focal point for American settlement in

the 1840s. Sutter held a magnificent land grant in the Sacramento Valley. At the center of his holdings was Sutter's Fort, a walled compound that was part living quarters and part supply shop for his vast cattle ranch, which was run largely on forced Indian labor. In the 1840s, Sutter offered valuable support to the handful of American overlanders who chose California over Oregon, the destination preferred by most pioneers. Most of these Americans, keenly aware that they were interlopers in Mexican territory, settled near Sutter in California's Central Valley, away from the Californios clustered along the coast.

The 1840s immigrants made no effort to intermarry with the Californios or to conform to Spanish ways. They were bent on taking over the territory. In June 1846 these Americans banded together at Sonoma in the Bear Flag Revolt (so called

California in the Gold Rush   *This map shows the major gold camps along the Mother Lode in the western foothills of the Sierra Nevada mountains. Gold seekers reached the camps by crossing the Sierra Nevadas near Placerville on the Overland Trail or by sea via San Francisco. The main area of Spanish-Mexican settlement, the coastal region between Monterey and Los Angeles, was remote from the gold fields.*

Source: Warren A. Beck and Ynez D. Haase, *Historical Atlas of California* (Norman: University of Oklahoma Press, 1974), map 50.

This drawing of the bar of a gambling saloon in San Francisco in 1855 shows the effects of the Gold Rush on California. Men from all parts of the world are gathered at this elegant bar in the large cosmopolitan city of San Francisco, which had been only a small trading post before gold was discovered in 1849.

because their flag bore a bear emblem), declaring independence from Mexico. The American takeover of California was not confirmed until the Treaty of Guadalupe Hidalgo in 1848. In the meantime, California was regarded by most Americans merely as a remote, sparsely populated frontier, albeit one with splendid potential. Polk and other expansionists coveted the magnificent harbors in San Diego and San Francisco as the basis for Pacific trade with Asia, but in 1848 this prospect was still only a dream.

Gold!

In January 1848 carpenter James Marshall noticed small flakes of gold in the millrace at Sutter's Mill (present-day Coloma). Soon he and all the rest of John Sutter's employees were panning for gold in California's streams. The news, which they had hoped to keep secret, spread, and before long it seemed that all the men in California were at the mines. When explorer John Frémont returned to San Francisco in June 1848, he found it almost deserted because of the "gold fever."

In the autumn of 1848, the east coast heard the first rumors about the discovery of gold in California. The reports were confirmed in mid-November when an army courier arrived in Washington carrying a tea caddy full of gold dust and nuggets. The spirit of excitement and adventure so recently aroused by the Mexican-American War was now directed toward California, the new El Dorado. Thousands left farms and jobs and headed west, by land and by sea, to make their fortune. Later known as "forty-niners" for the year the gold rush began in earnest, these people came from all parts of the

United States—and indeed, from all over the world. They transformed what had been a quiet ranching paradise into a teeming and tumultuous community in search of wealth in California's rivers and streams.

Eighty percent of the forty-niners were Americans. They came from every state. The Gold Rush was an eye-opening expansion of their horizons for the many who had known only their hometown folks before. The second largest group of migrants were from nearby Mexico and the west coast of Latin America (13 percent). The remainder came from Europe and Asia.

The presence of Chinese miners surprised many Americans. Several hundred Chinese arrived in California in 1849 and 1850, and in 1852 more than 20,000 landed in San Francisco hoping to share in the wealth of Gum Sam (Golden Mountain). Most came, like the Americans, as temporary sojourners, intending to return home as soon as they made some money. Again, like most of the American miners, the majority of Chinese were men who left their wives at home. Dressed in their distinctive blue cotton shirts, baggy pants, and broad-brimmed hats, and with long queues hanging down their backs, hardworking Chinese miners soon became a familiar sight in the gold fields, as did the presence of "Chinatowns." The distinctive appearance of the Chinese, added to the threat of economic competition that they posed, quickly aroused American hostility. A special tax was imposed on foreign miners in 1852, and in the 1870s, Chinese immigration was sharply curtailed.

In 1849, as the gold rush began in earnest, San Francisco, the major entry port and supply point, sprang to life. From a settlement of 1,000 in 1848 it grew to a city of 35,000 in 1850. This surge suggested that the real money to be made in California was not in panning for gold but from feeding, clothing, housing, provisioning, and entertaining the miners. Among the first to learn that lesson was the German Jewish immigrant Levi Strauss, who sold so many tough work pants to miners that his name became synonymous with his product. And Jerusha Marshall, who opened a twenty-room boardinghouse in the city, candidly wrote to her eastern relatives: "Never was there a better field for making money than now presents itself in this place....We are satisfied to dig our gold in San Francisco." From these "instant" beginnings San Francisco stabilized to become a major American city. Meanwhile, the white population of California had jumped from an estimated pre-Gold Rush figure of 11,000 to more than 100,000 by 1852. California was admitted as a state in 1850.

Mining Camps

Most mining camps, like San Francisco, boomed almost instantly to life, but unlike San Francisco, they were empty again within a few years. In spite of the aura of glamour that surrounds the names of the famous camps—Poker Flat, Angels Camp, Whiskey Bar, Placerville, Mariposa—they were generally dirty and dreary places. Most miners lived in tents or hovels, unwilling to take time from mining to build themselves decent quarters. They cooked monotonous meals of beans, bread, and bacon or, if they had money, bought meals at expensive restaurants and boardinghouses (where the table might be no more than a plank over two flour barrels). Many migrants traveled to the mines with relatives or fellow townspeople. But often they split up in California—each man with his own idea of where he could find gold the easiest—and ended up on their own. They led a cheerless, uncomfortable, and unhealthy existence, especially during the long, rainy winter months, with few distractions apart from the saloon, the gambling hall, and the prostitute's crib.

Most miners were young, unmarried, and unsuccessful. Only a small percentage ever struck it rich in California. Gold deposits that were accessible with pick and shovel were soon exhausted, and the deeper deposits required capital and machinery. Some of the workings at the Comstock Lode in Virginia City, Nevada, a later mining center, were half a mile deep. But many men were ashamed to come home until they had "made their pile." Increasingly, as they stayed on in California, they had to give up the status of independent miners and become wage earners for large mining concerns.

As in San Francisco, a more reliable way to earn money in the camps was to supply the miners. Every mining community had its saloonkeepers, gamblers, prostitutes, merchants, and restauranteurs. Like the miners themselves, these people were tran-

sients, always ready to pick up and move at the word of a new gold strike. The majority of women in the early mining camps were prostitutes. Some grew rich or married respectably, but most died young of drugs, venereal disease, or violence. Most of the other women were hardworking wives of miners, and in this predominantly male society they made good money doing domestic work: keeping boardinghouses, cooking, doing laundry. Even the wives of professional men who in the East might have been restrained by propriety succumbed to the monetary opportunities and kept boardinghouses.

Partly because few people put any effort into building communities—they were too busy seeking gold—violence was endemic in mining areas, and much of it was racial. Discrimination, especially against Chinese, Mexicans, and African Americans, was common. Frequently miners' claims were "jumped": thieves would rob them of the gold they had accumulated, kill them, or chase them away, and then file their own claim for the victims' strike. Or unscrupulous miners might use the law to their advantage to secure the claims of others without violence—for example by taking advantage of the prohibitively high mining tax on foreigners.

In the end, most mining camps were at best temporary communities. The gold "played out" and people moved on, leaving ghost towns behind. By the

Chinese first came to California in 1849 attracted by the Gold Rush. Frequently, however, they were forced off their claims by intolerant whites. Rather than enjoy an equal chance in the gold fields they were often forced to work as servants or in other menial occupations.

mid-1850s, the immediate effects of the Gold Rush had passed. California had a booming population, a thriving agriculture, and a corporate mining industry. The Gold Rush also left California with a population that was larger, more affluent, and (in urban San Francisco) more culturally sophisticated than that in other newly settled territories. It was also significantly more multicultural than the rest of the nation, for many of the Chinese and Mexicans, as well as immigrants from many European countries, remained in California after the Gold Rush subsided. But the Gold Rush left some permanent scars, and not just on the foothills landscape: the virtual extermination of the California Indian peoples, the dispossession of many Californios who were legally deprived of their land grants, and the growth of racial animosity toward the Chinese in particular. The major characteristics of the mining frontier, evident first in the California Gold Rush and repeated many times thereafter in similar "rushes" in Colorado, Montana, Idaho, South Dakota, and Arizona, were a lack of stable communities and a worsening of racial tensions.

THE POLITICS OF MANIFEST DESTINY

In three short years, from 1845 to 1848, the territory of the United States grew an incredible 70 percent and became a continental nation. This expansion and the concept of manifest destiny that justified it quickly became the dominant issues in national politics.

The "Young America" Movement

One source of the belief in manifest destiny was national pride—the conviction that American democracy was so superior it would lead inevitably to the expansion of the nation. The swift victory in the Mexican-American War and the "prize" of California gold seemed to confirm that conviction. European events in 1848 also served to foster American pride. In that year a series of democratic revolutions—in Italy, France, Germany, Hungary, and parts of the Austrian Empire—swept the Continent. Expansionists assumed that American democracy and manifest destiny were the models for these liberal revolutions. When Lajos Kossuth, the famed Hungarian revolutionary, visited the United States in 1851, he was given a hero's welcome, and Daniel Webster complacently assured him that "we shall rejoice to see our American model upon the lower Danube."

In an even more confident gesture, President Franklin Pierce dispatched Commodore Matthew Perry across the Pacific to Japan, a nation famous for its insularity and hostility to outsiders. The mission resulted in 1854 in a commercial treaty that opened Japan to American trade. Perry's feat caused a newspaper in tiny Olympia, Washington, to boast, "We shall have the boundless Pacific for a market in manifest destiny. We were born to command it."

But efforts closer to home by the Young America movement, as expansionist Democrats styled themselves, were more controversial. Victory in the Mexican-American War and the evident weakness of the

Details of Perry's ship and military parade from Japanese print, Ukiyo-e school, Landing of Commodore Perry in Japan.

This Japanese painting shows Commodore Matthew Perry landing in Japan in 1854. The commercial treaty Perry signed with the Japanese government, which opened a formerly closed country to American trade, was viewed in the United States as another fruit of manifest destiny.

EXPANSION CAUSES THE FIRST SPLITS IN THE SECOND AMERICAN PARTY SYSTEM

1844	Whigs reject President John Tyler's move to annex Texas and expel him from the Whig Party.
	Southern Democrats choose expansionist James K. Polk as their presidential candidate, passing over Martin Van Buren, who is against expansion.
	Liberty Party runs abolitionist James Birney for president, attracting northern antislavery Whigs.
1846	The Wilmot Proviso, proposing to ban slavery in the territories that might be gained in the Mexican-American War, splits both parties: southern Whigs and Democrats oppose the measure; northern Whigs and Democrats support it.
1848	The new Free-Soil Party runs northern Democrat Martin Van Buren for president, gaining 10 percent of the vote from abolitionists, antislavery Whigs, and some northern Democrats. This strong showing by a third party causes Democrat Lewis Cass to lose the electoral votes of New York and Pennsylvania, allowing the Whig Zachary Taylor to win.

Mexican government whetted the appetite of some southern expansionists for more territory. But most American politicians were cautious about further gains. When in the spring of 1848 Polk recommended American intervention in the civil war in the Mexican province of Yucatán, Congress rebuffed him. Senator John C. Calhoun, harking back to Polk's manipulation of Congress in 1846, cautioned, "I did hope that the experience of the Mexican War—that precipitate and rash measure which has cost the country so dearly in blood and treasure—would have taught the administration moderation and caution." In the winter of 1848, rumors swept Washington that Polk had offered Spain up to $100 million for Cuba (compared with the $15 million paid for Mexico's provinces of California and New Mexico). The nation was spared a raging political battle when Spain spurned all offers.

Thus the Mexican-American War was divisive even after it was won. A small group of expansionists, most from the South, wanted more, in spite of clear evidence that most Americans had had enough. Throughout the 1850s, these expansionists continued to covet Mexico, Central America, and Cuba. Adventures in these directions, all organized by Southerners intent on acquiring new lands for cotton, further inflamed the festering sectional differences of the 1850s that are discussed in Chapter 15.

The Wilmot Proviso

In 1846, almost all the northern members of the Whig Party opposed Democratic president James Polk's belligerent expansionism on antislavery grounds. Northern Whigs correctly feared that expansion would reopen the issue of slavery in the territories. "We appear…to be rushing upon perils headlong, and with our eyes all open," Daniel Webster warned in 1847. His remedy? "We want no extension of territory; we want no accession of new states. The country is already large enough." But the outpouring of enthusiasm for the Mexican-American War drowned Webster's words and convinced most Whig congressmen that they needed to vote military appropriations for the war in spite of their misgivings.

Ironically it was not the Whigs but a freshman Democratic congressman from Pennsylvania, David Wilmot, who opened the door to sectional controversy over expansion. In August 1846, only a few short months after the beginning of the Mexican-American War, Wilmot proposed, in an amendment to a military appropriations bill, that slavery be banned in all the territories acquired from Mexico. He was ready, Wilmot said, to "sustain the institutions of the South as they exist. But sir, the issue now presented is not whether slavery shall exist unmolested where it is now, but whether it shall be carried to new and distant regions, now free, where the footprint of a slave cannot be found." In the debate and voting that followed, something new and ominous occurred: southern Whigs joined southern Democrats to vote against the measure, while Northerners of both parties supported it. Sectional interest had triumphed over party loyalty. Wilmot's Proviso triggered the first breakdown of the national party system and reopened the debate about the place of slavery in the future of the nation.

The Wilmot Proviso was so controversial that it was deleted from the necessary military appropriations bills during the Mexican-American War. But in 1848, following the Treaty of Guadalupe Hidalgo, the question of the expansion of slavery could no longer be avoided or postponed. Antislavery advocates from the North argued with proslavery Southerners in a debate that was much more prolonged and more bitter than the Missouri Crisis of 1819. Civility quickly wore thin: threats were uttered and fistfights broke out on the floor of the House of Representatives. The Wilmot Proviso posed a fundamental challenge to both parties. Neither the Democrats nor the Whigs could take a strong stand on the amendment because neither party could get its northern and southern wings to agree. Decisive action, for or against, was a serious threat to party unity. Webster's fear that expansion would lead to sectional conflict had become a reality.

The Free-Soil Movement

Why did David Wilmot propose this controversial measure? Wilmot, a northern Democrat, was propelled not by ideology but by the pressure of practical politics. The dramatic rise of the Liberty Party, founded in 1840 by abolitionists, threatened to take votes away from both the Whig and the Democratic parties. The Liberty Party won 62,000 votes in the 1844 presidential election, all in the North. This was more than enough to deny victory to the Whig candidate, Henry Clay. Neither party could afford to ignore the strength of this third party.

The Liberty Party took an uncompromising stance against slavery. As articulated by Ohio's Salmon P. Chase, the party platform called for the "divorce of the federal government from slavery." The party proposed to prohibit the admission of slave states to the Union, end slavery in the District of Columbia, and abolish the interstate slave trade that was vital to the expansion of cotton growing into the Old Southwest (see Chapter 11). Liberty Party members also favored denying office to all slaveholders (a proposal that would have robbed all the southern states of their senators) and forbidding the use of slave labor on federal construction projects. In short, the party proposed to quickly strangle slavery. The popularity of this radical program among northern voters in 1844 was an indication of the moral fervor of abolitionism (see Chapter 13).

But Liberty Party doctrine was too uncompromising for the mass of northern voters, who immediately realized that the southern states would leave the Union before accepting it. Still, as the 1844 vote indicated, many Northerners opposed slavery. From this sentiment the Free-Soil Party was born. The free-soil argument was a calculated adjustment of abolitionist principles to practical politics. It shifted the focus from the question of the morality of slavery to the ways in which slavery posed a threat to northern expansion. The free-soil doctrine thus established a direct link between expansion, which most Americans supported, and sectional politics.

Free-soilers were willing to allow slavery to continue in the existing slave states because they supported the Union, not because they approved of slavery. They were unwilling, however, to allow the extension of slavery to new and unorganized territory. If the South were successful in extending slavery, they argued, northern farmers who moved west would find themselves competing at an economic disadvantage with large planters using slave labor. Free-soilers also insisted that the northern values of freedom and individualism would be destroyed if the slave-based southern labor system were allowed to spread. To free-soilers, the South was composed of little more than corrupt aristocrats, degraded slaves, and a large class of poor whites who were deprived of opportunity because they did not understand the value of honest labor.

Finally, many free-soilers really meant "antiblack" when they said "antislavery." They proposed to ban all African American people from the new territories (a step that four states—Indiana, Illinois, Iowa, and Oregon—took but did not always enforce). William Lloyd Garrison promptly denounced the free-soil doctrine as "whitemanism," a racist effort to make the territories white. There was much truth to his charge, but there was no denying that the free-soil doctrine was popular. Although abolitionists were making headway in their claim for moral equality regardless of skin color, most Northerners were unwilling to consider social equality for African Americans, free or slave. Banning all black people from the western territories seemed a simple solution.

Finally, the free-soil movement was a repudiation of the sectional compromise of 1820. If the Missouri Compromise line were carried westward to the Pacific Ocean, as Secretary of State James Buchanan proposed in 1848, much of present-day New Mexico and Arizona and the southern half of California would have been admitted as slave states, and everything to the north would have been free. Free-soilers opposed this arrangement. Their opposition in 1848 to the Missouri Compromise line indicated how influential antislavery feeling was becoming in the North.

The Election of 1848

A swirl of emotions—pride, expansionism, sectionalism, abolitionism, free-soil sentiment—surrounded the election of 1848. The Treaty of Guadalupe Hidalgo had been signed earlier in the year, and the vast northern Mexican provinces of New Mexico and California and the former

Republic of Texas had been incorporated into the United States. But the issues raised by the Wilmot Proviso remained to be resolved, and every candidate had to have an answer to the question of whether slavery should be admitted in the new territories.

Lewis Cass of Michigan, the Democratic nominee for president (Polk, in poor health, declined to run for a second term), proposed to apply the doctrine of popular sovereignty to the crucial slave–free issue. This democratic-sounding notion of leaving the decision to the citizens of each territory was based on the Jeffersonian faith in the common man's ability to vote both his own self-interest and the common good. In fact, however, popular sovereignty was an admission of the nation's failure to resolve sectional differences. It simply shifted decision making on the crucial issue of the expansion of slavery from national politicians to the members of territorial legislatures, who, belonging to different parties, were in as much disagreement as members of Congress and just as unable to resolve it.

In 1848, *the Whigs once again adopted the campaign strategy that had worked so successfully for them in the presidential election of 1840. They nominated a hero of the Mexican-American War, General Zachary Taylor, who ran on his military exploits. In this poster, every letter of Taylor's name is decorated with scenes from the recent war, which had seized the popular imagination in a way no previous conflict had done. Emphasizing Taylor's reputation as a national hero (and therefore above petty politics), the Whigs were able to evade the question of whether or not he favored the extension of slavery into the territories.*

As Cass stated it, the doctrine of popular sovereignty was deliberately vague about when a territory would choose its status. Would it do so during the territorial stage? at the point of applying for statehood? Clearly, this question was crucial, for no slave owner would invest in new land if the territory could later be declared free, and no abolitionist would move to a territory that was destined to become a slave state. Cass hoped his ambiguity on this point would win him votes in both North and South. Even so, sectional differences ran so deep that the Democrats found it necessary to print two campaign biographies of Cass. The biography circulated in the North touted Cass's doctrine of popular sovereignty as the best way to keep slavery out of the territories; the biography in the South implied the opposite.

For their part, the Whigs passed over perennial candidate Henry Clay and turned once again to a war hero, General Zachary Taylor. Taylor, a Louisiana slaveholder, refused to take a position on the Wilmot Proviso, allowing both northern and southern voters to hope that he agreed with them. Privately, Taylor opposed the expansion of slavery. In public, he evaded the issue by running as a war hero and a national leader who was above sectional politics.

The deliberate vagueness of the two major candidates displeased many northern voters. An uneasy mixture of disaffected Democrats (among them David Wilmot) and Whigs joined former Liberty Party voters to support the candidate of the Free-Soil Party, former president Martin Van Buren. Van Buren, angry at the Democratic Party for passing him over in 1844 and displeased with the growing southern dominance of the Democratic Party, ran as a spoiler. He knew he could not win the election, but he could divide the Democrats. In the end, Van Buren garnered 10 percent of the vote (all in the North). The vote for the Free-Soil Party cost Cass the electoral votes of New York and Pennsylvania, and General Taylor won the election with only 47 percent of the popular vote. This was the second election after 1840 that the Whigs had won by running a war hero who could duck hard questions by claiming to be above politics. Uncannily, history was to repeat itself: Taylor, like William Henry Harrison, died before his term was completed, and the chance he offered to maintain national unity—if ever it existed—was lost.

CHRONOLOGY

1609	First Spanish settlement in New Mexico		1833–34	Prince Maximilian and Karl Bodmer visit Plains Indians
1670s	British and French Canadians begin fur trade in western Canada		1834	Jason Lee establishes first mission in Oregon Country
1716	First Spanish settlements in Texas		1835	Texas revolts against Mexico
1769	First Spanish settlement in California		1836	Battles of the Alamo and San Jacinto
				Republic of Texas formed
1780s	New England ships begin sea otter trade in Pacific Northwest		1843–44	John C. Frémont maps trails to Oregon and California
1790	First American ship visits Hawaii		1844	Democrat James K. Polk elected president on an expansionist platform
1803	Louisiana Purchase			
1804–06	Lewis and Clark expedition		1845	Texas annexed to the United States as a slave state
1806	Russian-Californio trade begins			John O'Sullivan coins the phrase "manifest destiny"
1806–07	Zebulon Pike's expedition across the Great Plains to the Rocky Mountains		1846	Oregon question settled peacefully with Britain
				Mexican-American War begins
1819–20	Stephen Long's expedition across the Great Plains			Bear Flag Revolt in California
				Wilmot Proviso
1821	Hudson's Bay Company gains dominance of western fur trade		1847	Cayuse Wars begin in Oregon
	Mexico seizes independence from Spain			Americans win battles of Buena Vista, Veracruz, and Mexico City
	Santa Fé Trail opens, soon protected by U.S. military		1848	Treaty of Guadalupe Hidalgo
	Stephen F. Austin becomes first American empresario in Texas			Free-Soil Party captures 10 percent of the popular vote in the North
1824	First fur rendezvous sponsored by Rocky Mountain Fur Company			General Zachary Taylor, a Whig, elected president
	Hudson's Bay Company establishes Fort Vancouver in Oregon Country			
1830	Indian Removal Act moves eastern Indians to Indian Territory		1849	California Gold Rush

CONCLUSION

In the decade of the 1840s, westward expansion took many forms, from relatively peaceful settlement in Oregon, to war with Mexico over Texas, to the sheer overwhelming numbers of gold rushers who changed California forever. Most of these frontiers—in Oregon, New Mexico, and California—began as frontiers of inclusion in which a small number of Americans were eager for trade, accommodation, and intermarriage with the original inhabitants. Texas, with its agricultural enclaves, was the exception to this pattern. Yet on every frontier, as the number of American settlers increased, so did the sentiment for exclusion, so that by 1850, whatever their origins, the farflung American continental settlements were more similar than different and the success of manifest destiny seemed overwhelming.

The election of 1848, virtually a referendum on manifest destiny, yielded ironic results. James K. Polk, who presided over the unprecedented expansion, did not run for a second term, and thus the Democratic Party gained no electoral victory to match the military one. The electorate that had been so thrilled by the war news voted for a war hero—who led the antiexpansionist Whig Party. The election was decided by Martin Van Buren, the Free-Soil candidate who voiced the sentiments of the abolitionists, a reform group that had been insignificant just a few years before. The amazing expansion achieved by the Mexican-American War—America's manifest destiny—made the United States a continental nation but stirred up the issue that was to tear it apart. Sectional rivalries and fears now dominated every aspect of politics. Expansion, once a force for unity, now divided the nation into Northerners and Southerners, who could not agree on the community they shared—the federal Union.

REVIEW QUESTIONS

1. Define and discuss the concept of manifest destiny.
2. Trace the different ways in which the frontiers in Oregon, Texas, and California moved from frontiers of inclusion to frontiers of exclusion.
3. Take different sides (Whig and Democrat) and debate the issues raised by the Mexican-American War.
4. Referring back to Chapter 13, compare the positions of the Liberty Party and the Free-Soil Party. Examine the factors that made the free-soil doctrine politically acceptable to many, and abolitionism so controversial.

RECOMMENDED READING

Arnoldo De Leon, *The Tejano Community, 1836–1900* (1982). Traces the changing status of Tejanos after Texas came under the control of American Texans.

John Mack Faragher, *Women and Men on the Overland Trail* (1979). One of the first books to consider the experience of women on the journey west.

William Goetzman, *Exploration and Empire: The Explorer and the Scientist in the Winning of the American West* (1966). Considers the many government-sponsored explorations of the West.

Thomas R. Hietala, *Manifest Design: Anxious Aggrandizement in Late Jacksonian America* (1985). An interesting reassessment of manifest destiny from the perspective of party politics.

Julie Roy Jeffrey, *Converting the West: A Biography of Narcissa Whitman* (1991). Makes a clear connection between the missionary Whitman's evangelical upbringing and her failure to understand the culture of Oregon's Cayuse Indians.

Robert W. Johannsen, *To the Halls of the Montezumas: The Mexican War in the American Imagination* (1985). A lively book that explores the impact of the Mexican-American War on public opinion.

Paul D. Lack, *The Texas Revolutionary Experience: A Political and Social History, 1835–1836* (1992). A political and social history that stresses the chaotic and discordant nature of the Texas Revolt.

Janet Lecompte, *Pueblo, Hardscrabble, Greenhorn: The Upper Arkansas, 1832–1856* (1978). A social history that portrays the racial and ethnic diversity of the trading frontier.

Michael Morrison, *Slavery and the American West: The Eclipse of Manifest Destiny and the Coming of the Civil War* (1997). In a study of competing ideas over the future of the West, the author stresses the links between expansion and sectional disagreements.

Malcolm Rohrbough, *Days of Gold: The California Gold Rush and the American Nation* (1997). A lively history that emphasizes the effects of this "great American epic" on the national self-image.

David J. Weber, *The Mexican Frontier, 1821–1846: The American Southwest under Mexico* (1982). A fine study of the history of the Southwest before American conquest. The author is a leading borderlands historian.

Richard White, *"It's Your Misfortune and None of My Own": A History of the American West* (1991). A major reinterpretation that focuses on the history of the region itself rather than on the westward expansion of Americans. Pays much more attention to Spanish Mexicans and Indian peoples than earlier texts.

ADDITIONAL BIBLIOGRAPHY

Exploration, the Fur Trade, and Expansion

Jennifer S. H. Brown, *Strangers in Blood: Fur Trade Company Families in Indian Country* (1980)

William H. Goetzmann, *Army Exploration in the American West, 1803–1863* (1959)

William H. Goetzmann and William N. Goetzmann, *The West of the Imagination* (1986)

Norman A. Graebner, *Empire on the Pacific: A Study in American Continental Expansion* (1955)

LeRoy R. Hafen, ed., *The Mountain Men and the Fur Trade of the Far West*, 10 vols. (1968–72)

Reginald Horsman, *Race and Manifest Destiny* (1981)

Theodore J. Karaminski, *Fur Trade and Exploration: Opening of the Far Northwest, 1821–1852* (1983)

Patricia Nelson Limerick, *The Legacy of Conquest: The Unbroken Past of the Unbroken West* (1987)

Frederick Merk, *Manifest Destiny and Mission in American History: A Reinterpretation* (1963)

———, *History of the Westward Movement* (1978)

Dale Morgan, *Jedediah Smith and the Opening of the West* (1982)

Peter Nabakov, ed., *Native American Testimony: An Anthology of Indian and White Relations* (1978)

James P. Ronda, *Astoria and Empire* (1990)

Henry Nash Smith, *Virgin Land: The American West as Symbol and Myth* (1950)

Edward H. Spicer, *Cycles of Conquest: The Impact of Spain, Mexico, and the United States on the Indians of the Southwest, 1533–1960* (1981)

Robert A. Trennert, *Alternative to Extinction: Federal Indian Policy and the Beginnings of the Reservation System, 1846–1851* (1975)

Sylvia Van Kirk, *"Many Tender Ties": Women in Fur Trade Society in Western Canada, 1670–1870* (1980)

Albert K. Weinberg, *Manifest Destiny: A Study of Nationalist Expansionism in American History* (1957)

Peter Booth Wiley with Korogi Ichiro, *Yankees in the Land of the Gods: Commodore Perry and the Opening of Japan* (1990)

David J. Wishart, *The Fur Trade of the American West, 1807–1840: A Geographic Synthesis* (1979)

California and Oregon

John W. Caughey, *The California Gold Rush* (1975)

Malcolm Clark Jr., *Eden Seekers: The Settlement of Oregon, 1818–1862* (1981)

Douglas H. Daniels, *Pioneer Urbanites: A Social and Cultural History of Black San Francisco* (1980)

James R. Gibson, *Farming the Frontier: The Agricultural Opening of Oregon Country, 1786–1846* (1985)

Albert L. Hurtado, *Indian Survival on the California Frontier* (1988)

Julie Roy Jeffrey, *Frontier Women: Civilizing The West?, 1840–1860* (1998)

David Johnson, *Founding the Far West: California, Oregon, and Nevada, 1840–1890* (1992)

Alvin Josephy, *The Nez Perce and the Opening of the Northwest* (1965)

Rodman W. Paul, *California Gold: The Beginning of Mining in the Far West* (1974)

Leonard Pitt, *The Decline of the Californios: A Social History of the Spanish-Speaking Californians, 1846–1890* (1966)

James J. Rawls, *Indians of California: The Changing Image* (1984)

Kevin Starr, *Americans and the California Dream, 1850–1915* (1973)

John I. Unruh Jr., *The Plains Across: Overland Emigrants and the Trans-Mississippi West, 1840–1860* (1979)

Texas and the Mexican-American War

K. Jack Bauer, *The Mexican War, 1846–1848* (1974)

William C. Binkley, *The Texas Revolution* (1952)

Gene M. Brack, *Mexico Views Manifest Destiny* (1976)

Donald E. Chipman, *Spanish Texas, 1519–1821* (1992)

Seymour Conner and Odie Faulk, *North America Divided: The Mexican War, 1846–1848* (1971)

Arnoldo De Leon, *They Called Them Greasers: Anglo Attitudes toward Mexicans in Texas, 1821–1900* (1983)

John S. D. Eisenhower, *So Far from God: The U.S. War with Mexico 1846–1848* (1989)

Neil Harlow, *California Conquered: War and Peace on the Pacific, 1846–1850* (1982)

Ernest McPherson Lander Jr., *Reluctant Imperialist: Calhoun, South Carolina, and the Mexican War* (1980)

Timothy Matovina, *Tejano Religion and Ethnicity: San Antonio, 1921–1860* (1995)

Frederick Merk, *Slavery and the Annexation of Texas* (1972)

David Montejano, *Anglos and Mexicans in the Making of Texas, 1836–1986* (1987)

Chaplain W. Morrison, *Democratic Politics and Sectionalism: The Wilmot Proviso Controversy* (1967)

Stanley Noyes, *Los Comanches: The Horse People, 1751–1845* (1994)

David Pletcher, *The Diplomacy of Annexation: Texas, Oregon, and the Mexican War* (1973)

Joseph G. Raybeck, *Free Soil: The Election of 1848* (1970)

Andreas V. Reichstein, *Rise of the Lone Star: The Making of Texas* (1989)

John H. Schroeder, *Mr. Polk's War: American Opposition and Dissent, 1846–1848* (1971)

Joel H. Sibley, *The Shrine of Party: Congressional Voting Behavior, 1841–1852* (1967)

Otis A. Singletary, *The Mexican War* (1960)

Jésus F. de la Teja, *San Antonio de Béxar: A Community on New Spain's Northern Frontier* (1995)

Biography

Marquis James, *The Raven: The Story of Sam Houston* (1929)

Charles G. Sellers, *James K. Polk: Jacksonian, 1795–1843* (1957)

———, *James K. Polk: Continentialist, 1843–1846* (1966)

CHAPTER FIFTEEN

THE COMING CRISIS

THE 1850s

AMERICAN COMMUNITIES
Illinois Communities Debate Slavery

On seven occasions through the late summer and autumn of 1858, each at one of seven small Illinois towns—Ottawa, Freeport, Jonesboro, Charleston, Galesburg, Quincy, and Alton—thousands of Illinois farmers and townspeople put aside their daily routines and customary chores; climbed into carriages, farm wagons, carts, and conveyances of all sorts; and converged on the town green. Entertained by brass bands, pageantry, and vast quantities of food and local gossip, they waited impatiently for the main event, the chance to take part in the debate on the most urgent question of the day—slavery. Two Illinois politicians—Democratic senator Stephen A. Douglas and his Republican challenger, Springfield lawyer Abraham Lincoln, the principal figures in the debates—presented their views in three hours of closely reasoned argument. But they did not speak alone. Cheers, boos, groans, and shouted questions from active, engaged listeners punctuated all seven of the now famous confrontations between the two men. Although commonly referred to as the Lincoln-Douglas debates, these were really community events in which Illinois citizens—people who, like Americans everywhere, held varying political beliefs—took part. Some individuals were proslavery, some antislavery, and many were undecided, but all were agreed that democratic politics gave them the means to air their opinions and resolve their differences.

"The prairies are on fire," announced the *New York Evening Post* correspondent who covered the debates. "It is astonishing how deep an interest in politics this people take." The reason was clear: by 1858, the American nation was in deep political crisis. The decade-long effort to solve the problem of the future of slavery had failed. For most of this time Washington politicians trying to build broad national parties with policies acceptable to voters in both the North and the South had done their best not to talk about slavery. Thus, that the Lincoln-Douglas debates were devoted to one issue alone—slavery and the future of the Union—showed how serious matters had become.

Democrat Stephen Douglas was the leading Democratic contender for the 1860 presidential nomination, but before he could mount a campaign for national office he had first to win reelection to the Illinois seat he had held in the U.S. Senate for twelve years. His vote against allowing slavery in Kansas had alienated him from the strong southern wing of his own party and had put him in direct conflict with its top leader, President James Buchanan. Because the crisis of the Union was so severe and Douglas's role so pivotal, his reelection campaign clearly previewed the 1860 presidential election. For the sake of its future, the Republican Party had to field a strong opponent: it found its candidate in Abraham Lincoln.

Lincoln had represented Illinois in the House of Representatives in the 1840s but had lost political support in 1848 because he opposed the Mexican-American War. Developing a prosperous Springfield law practice, he had been an influential member of the Illinois Republican Party since its founding in 1856. Although he had entered political life as a Whig, Lincoln was radicalized by the issue of the extension of slavery. Even though his wife's family were Kentucky slave owners, Lincoln's commitment to freedom and his resistance to the spread of slavery had now become absolute: for him, freedom and Union were inseparable.

Much less well known than Douglas, Lincoln was the underdog in the 1858 Senate race and thus it was he who challenged Douglas to debate. As they squared off in the seven Illinois towns, Douglas and Lincoln were an amusing sight. Douglas was short (5 feet, 4 inches) and his build was very square; his nickname was "the Little Giant." Lincoln, on the other hand, was very tall (6 feet, 4 inches) and very thin. Both were eloquent and powerful speakers—and they had to be. The three-hour debates were held without amplification of any kind. Nevertheless, in every town, audiences of 10,000 to 15,000 listened attentively and responded vocally to each speaker's long and thought-packed arguments.

Douglas had many strengths going into the debates. He spoke for the Union, he claimed, pointing out that the Democratic Party was a national party whereas the Republican Party was only sectional. He repeatedly appealed to the racism of much of his audience with declarations such as, "I would not blot out the great inalienable rights of the white men for all the negroes that ever existed!" He repeatedly called his opponent a "Black Republican," implying that Lincoln and his party favored the social equality of whites and blacks, even race mixing.

Lincoln did *not* believe in the social equality of the races, but he did believe wholeheartedly that slavery was a moral wrong. Pledging the Republican Party to the "ultimate extinction" of slavery, Lincoln continually warned that Douglas's position would lead to the opposite result: the spread of slavery everywhere. Although in this argument Lincoln was addressing the northern fear of an expansionist "slave power," he strove at the same time to present himself as a moderate. He did not favor the breakup of the Union, but he never wavered from his antislavery stance.

The first of the seven debates, held in Ottawa on Saturday, August 21, 1858, showed not only the seriousness but the exuberance of the democratic politics of the time. By early morning the town was jammed with people. The clouds of dust raised by carriages driving to Ottawa, one observer complained, turned the town into "a vast smoke house." By one o'clock the town square was filled to overflowing. At two o'clock, just as the debate was about to begin, the wooden awning over the speakers' platform collapsed under the weight of those sitting on it, delaying the start for half an hour. But then the debate got under way, enthralling an estimated 12,000 people. Ottawa, in northern Illinois, was pro-Republican, and the audience heckled Douglas unmercifully. At the second debate, a week later in Freeport, Douglas's use of the phrase "Black Republicans" drew angry shouts of "White, white" from the crowd. But as the debates moved south in the state, where Democrats predominated, the tables were turned, and Lincoln sometimes had to plead for a chance to be heard.

Although Douglas won the 1858 senatorial election in Illinois, the acclaim that Lincoln gained in the famous debates helped establish the Republicans' claim to be the only party capable of stopping the spread of slavery and made Lincoln himself a strong contender for the Republican presidential nomination in 1860. But the true winners of the Lincoln-Douglas debates were the people of Illinois who gathered peacefully to discuss the most serious issue of their time. The young German immigrant Carl Schurz, who attended the Quincy debate, was deeply impressed by its democratic character. He noted, "There was no end of cheering and shouting and jostling on the streets of Quincy that day. But in spite of the excitement created by the political contest, the crowds remained very good-natured, and the occasional jibes flung from one side to the other were uniformly received with a laugh." The Illinois people who participated in the community debates of 1858 showed the strong faith Americans held in their democratic institutions and the hope—finally shattered in the election of 1860—that a lasting political solution to the problem of slavery could be found.

Illinois

KEY TOPICS

- The failure of efforts by the Whigs and the Democrats to find a lasting political compromise on the issue of slavery

- The end of the Second American Party System and the rise of the Republican Party

- The secession of the southern states following the Republican Party victory in the election of 1860

AMERICA IN 1850

In 1850, after half a century of rapid growth and change, America was a very different nation from the republic of 1800. Geographic expansion, population increase, economic development, and the changes wrought by the market revolution had transformed the struggling new nation. Economically, culturally, and politically Americans had forged a strong sense of national identity.

Expansion and Growth

America was now a much larger nation than it had been in 1800. Through war and diplomacy, the country had grown to continental dimensions, more than tripling in size from 890,000 to 3 million square miles. Its population had increased enormously: from 5.3 million in 1800 to more than 23 million, 4 million of whom were African American slaves and 2 million new immigrants, largely from Germany and Ireland. Comprising just sixteen states in 1800, America in 1850 had thirty-one, and more than half of the population lived west of the Appalachians. America's cities had undergone the most rapid half-century of growth they were ever to experience.

America was also much richer: it is estimated that real per capita income doubled between 1800 and 1850, moving the nation decisively out of the "developing" category. Southern cotton, which had contributed so much to American economic growth, continued to be the nation's principal export, but it was no longer the major influence on the domestic economy. The growth of manufacturing in the Northeast and the rapid opening up of rich farmlands in the Midwest fostered the interdependence of these two regions, which was aided by the rapid growth and consolidation of railway links between them in the 1850s. The future of the United States as a manufacturing nation, second only to Britain, and as a major exporter of agricultural products was assured. Nevertheless, the development of manufacturing in the Northeast and the increased economic importance of the Midwest had serious domestic political implications. As the South's share of responsibility for economic growth waned, so did its political importance—at least in the eyes of many Northerners. Thus the very success of the United States both in geographic expansion and economic development served to undermine the role of the slave South in national politics and to hasten the day of open conflict between it and the free-labor North and Midwest.

Cultural Life and Social Issues

By 1850 the first shock of the far-reaching social changes caused by the market revolution had been absorbed. The conflicting social impulses played out in the politics and reform movements of the Jacksonian period were gradually giving way to new middle-class values, institutions, and ideas. Newspapers, magazines, and communication improvements of all kinds created a national audience for American scholars and writers. Since the turn of the century, American writers had struggled to find distinctive American themes, and these efforts bore fruit in the 1850s in the burst of creative activity termed "the American Renaissance." During this decade, Henry Thoreau, Nathaniel Hawthorne, Walt Whitman, Herman Melville, Emily Dickinson, Frederick Douglass, and others wrote works of fiction and nonfiction that are considered American classics.

During the American Renaissance, American writers pioneered new literary forms. Nathaniel Hawthorne, in stories like "Young Goodman Brown" (1835), raised the short story to a distinctive American literary form. Poets like Walt Whitman and Emily Dickinson experimented with unrhymed and "off-rhyme" verse, Whitman (in *Leaves of Grass*, published in 1855) to celebrate the boisterous pleasures of everyday life in New York City, Dickinson (who lived as a recluse in Amherst, Massachusetts) to catch her every fleeting thought and feeling in scraps of poetry that were not published until after her death. Another recluse, Henry David Thoreau, published *Walden* in 1854. A pastoral celebration of his life at Walden Pond, in Concord, Massachusetts, the essay was also a searching meditation on the cost to the individual of the loss of contact with nature that was a consequence of the market revolution.

Indeed, most of the writers of the American Renaissance were social critics. In *The Scarlet Letter* (1850) and *The House of the Seven Gables* (1851), both set in Puritan New England in the colonial period, Nathaniel Hawthorne brilliantly explored the moral choices faced by individuals as they try to reconcile repressive social expectations with private desires. Hawthorne's friend Herman Melville, in his great work *Moby Dick* (1851), drew on his own personal experience to write about the lives of ordinary sailors on a whaling voyage, but the story had deeper meanings. Melville's novel of Captain Ahab's obsessive search for the white whale is a profound study of the nature of good and evil and a critique of American society in the 1850s. The strongest social critique, however, was Frederick Douglass's starkly simple autobiography, *Narrative of the Life of Frederick Douglass* (1845), which told of his brutal life as a slave.

The most successful American novel of the mid-nineteenth century was about the great issue of the day, slavery. In writing *Uncle Tom's Cabin*, Harriet Beecher Stowe combined the literary style of the then-popular women's domestic novels (discussed in Chapter 12) with vivid details of slavery culled from firsthand accounts by northern abolitionists and escaped slaves. Stowe, the daughter of the reforming clergyman Lyman Beecher,

had married a Congregational minister and was herself a member of the evangelical movement. She had long been active in antislavery work, and a new Fugitive Slave Law passed in 1850 impelled her to write a novel that would persuade everyone of the evils of slavery. She wrote every night at her kitchen table after putting her six children to bed, and, as she said later, the events of the novel came to her "with a vividness that could not be denied," making her feel like "an instrument of God."

Stowe's famous novel told a poignant story of the Christ-like slave Uncle Tom, who patiently endured the cruel treatment of an evil white overseer, Simon Legree. Published in 1851, it was a runaway best seller. More than 300,000 copies were sold in the first year, and within ten years the book had sold more than 2 million copies, becoming the all-time American best-seller in proportion to population. Turned into a play that remained popular throughout the nineteenth century, Uncle Tom's Cabin reached an even wider audience. Scenes from the novel such as that of Eliza carrying her son across the ice-choked Ohio River to freedom, Tom weeping for his children as he was sold south, and the death of little Eva are among the best-known passages in

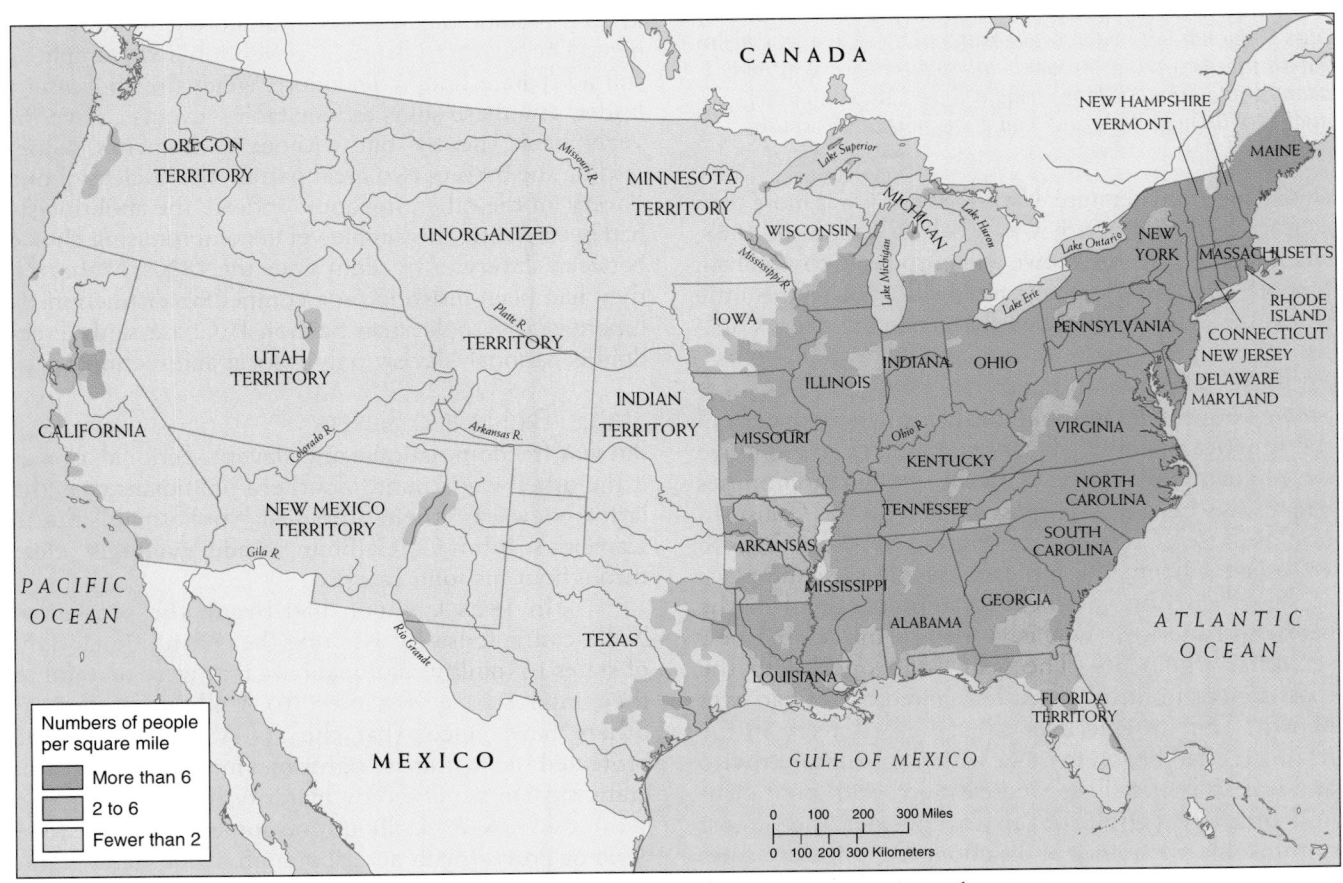

U.S. Population and Settlement, 1850   *By 1850, the United States was a continental nation. Its people, whom Thomas Jefferson had once thought would not reach the Mississippi River for forty generations, had not only passed the river but leapfrogged to the west coast. In comparison to the America of 1800 (see the map on p. 233) the growth was astounding.*

The Webbs, a free African American family, toured northern cities performing dramatic readings from Uncle Tom's Cabin. *An all-time best-seller, the novel outlasted the Civil War and, adapted into dramatic form, remained popular with theater audiences through the second half of the nineteenth century.*

all of American literature. *Uncle Tom's Cabin* was more than a heart-tugging story: it was a call to action. In 1863, when Harriet Beecher Stowe was introduced to Abraham Lincoln, the president remarked, "So you're the little woman who wrote the book that made this great war!"

Political Parties and Slavery

Stowe's novel clearly spoke to the growing concern of the American people. Slavery had long been a divisive issue in national politics. Until the 1840s, compromises had always been found, most notably in the Constitution itself (see Chapter 8) and in the Missouri Crisis of 1820 (see Chapter 9). But the struggle over the place of slavery in the vast new territories gained in the Mexican-American War gave rise to intractable new sectional arguments. The year 1850 opened to the most serious political crisis the United States had ever known. The struggle over the issue of slavery in the territories had begun in 1846 with the Wilmot Proviso and was still unresolved. Increasingly, both politicians and ordinary people began to consider the almost unthinkable possibility of disunion. As politician James Buchanan wrote to a friend early in the year, "The blessed Union of these states is now in greater danger than it has ever been since the adoption of the federal

Constitution." He feared that the two great national parties, the Whigs and the Democrats, would not be able to find a solution to the increasingly sectional division between North and South over slavery.

The Second American Party System forged in the great controversies of Andrew Jackson's presidency (see Chapter 10) was a national party system. In their need to mobilize great masses of recently enfranchised voters to elect a president every four years, politicians created organized party structures that overrode deeply rooted sectional differences. Politicians from all sections of the country cooperated because they knew their party could not succeed without national appeal. At a time when the ordinary person still had very strong sectional loyalties, the mass political party created a national community of like-minded voters. Yet by the election of 1848 sectional interests were eroding the political "glue" in both parties. Although each party still appeared united, sectional fissures already ran deep.

Political splits were preceded by divisions in other social institutions. Disagreements about slavery had already split the country's great religious organizations into northern and southern groups, the Presbyterians in 1837, the Methodists in 1844, and the Baptists in 1845. (Some of these splits turned out to be permanent. The Southern Baptist Convention, for example, is still a separate body.) Theodore Weld, the abolitionist leader, saw these splits as inevitable: "Events...have for years been silently but without a moment's pause, settling the basis of two great parties, the nucleus of one slavery, of the other, freedom." Indeed, the abolitionists had been posing this simple yet uncompromising choice between slavery or freedom since the 1830s. Moreover, they had been insisting on a compelling distinction: as Liberty Party spokesman Salmon P. Chase said, "Freedom is national; slavery only is local and sectional."

States' Rights and Slavery

But was freedom national and slavery sectional, or was it the other way around? Southern politicians took the latter view, as their foremost spokesman, South Carolina's John C. Calhoun, made ringingly clear throughout his long career.

In 1828 Calhoun had begun the protracted Nullification Crisis by asserting the constitutional right of states to "nullify" national laws that were harmful to their interests (see Chapter 10). Calhoun argued, as others have since, that the states' rights doctrine protected the legitimate rights of a minority in a democratic system governed by majority rule.

In 1847, Calhoun responded to the 1846 Wilmot Proviso with an elaboration of the states' rights argument. In spite of the apparent precedents of the Northwest Ordinance of 1787 and the Missouri Compromise, Calhoun argued that Congress did not have a constitutional right to prohibit slavery in the territories. The territories, he said, were the common property of all the states, north and south, and Congress could not discriminate against slave owners as they moved west. On the contrary, Calhoun argued, slave owners had a constitutional right to the protection of their property wherever they moved. Of course, Calhoun's legally correct description of African American slaves as property enraged abolitionists. But on behalf of the South, Calhoun was expressing the belief—and the fear—that his interpretation of the Constitution was the only protection for slave owners, whose right to own slaves (a fundamental right in southern eyes) was being attacked. Calhoun's position on the territories quickly became southern dogma: anything less than full access to the territories was unconstitutional. Slavery, Calhoun and other Southerners insisted, had to be national.

As Congressman Robert Toombs of Georgia put the case in 1850, there was very little room for compromise:

> I stand upon the great principle that the South has the right to an equal participation in the territories of the United States....She will divide with you if you wish it, but the right to enter all or divide I shall never surrender....Deprive us of this right and appropriate the common property to yourselves, it is then your government, not mine. Then I am its enemy....Give us our just rights, and we are ready...to stand by the Union....Refuse [them], and for one, I will strike for independence.

Northern Fears of "The Slave Power"

The words of Southerners like Calhoun and Toombs confirmed for many Northerners the warnings of antislavery leaders that they were endangered by a menacing "slave power." Liberty Party leader James Birney, in a speech in 1844, was the first to add this phrase to the nation's political vocabulary. "The slave power," Birney explained, was a group of aristocratic slave owners who not only dominated the political and social life of the South but conspired to control the federal government as well, posing a danger to free speech and free institutions throughout the nation.

Birney's "slave power" was a caricature of the influence slave owners wielded over southern politics and of the increasingly defensive and monolithic response of southern representatives in national politics after 1830 (see Chapter 11). The proslavery strategy of maintaining supremacy in the Senate by having at least as many slave as free states admitted to the Union (a plan that required slavery expansion) and of maintaining control, or at least veto power, over presidential nominees seemed, in southern eyes, to be nothing less

This strident poster warns that "the Slave Power" aims "to control the government of the nation, and make it subservient to its wicked designs." For good measure, the poster also appeals to nativist fears and to workers.

than ordinary self-defense. But to antislavery advocates, these actions looked like a conspiracy by sectional interests to control national politics. Birney's warnings about "the slave power" seemed in 1844 merely the overheated rhetoric of an extremist group of abolitionists. But the defensive southern political strategies of the 1850s were to convince an increasing number of northern voters that "the slave power" did in fact exist. Thus in northern eyes the South became a demonic monolith that threatened the national government.

Two Communities, Two Perspectives

Ironically, it was a common belief in expansion that made the arguments between Northerners and Southerners so irreconcilable. Southerners had been the strongest supporters of the Mexican-American War, and they still hoped to expand into Cuba, believing that the slave system must grow or wither. On the other hand, although many northern Whigs had opposed the Mexican-American War, most did so for antislavery reasons, not because they opposed expansion. The strong showing of the Free-Soil Party (which evolved out of the Liberty Party) in the election of 1848 (10 percent of the popular vote) was proof of that. Basically, both North and South believed in manifest destiny, but each on its own terms.

Similarly, both North and South used the language of basic rights and liberties in the debate over expansion. But Free-Soilers were speaking of personal liberty, whereas Southerners meant their right to own a particular kind of property (slaves) and to maintain a way of life based on the possession of that property. In defending its own rights, each side had taken measures that infringed on the rights of the other. Southerners pointed out that abolitionists had libeled slave owners as a class and that they had bombarded the South with unwanted literature, abused the right of petition to Congress, incited slaves to rebellion, and actively helped slaves to escape. For their part, Northerners accused slave owners of censorship of the mails; imposition of the "gag rule" (repealed in 1844), which prohibited any petition against slavery from being read to or discussed by Congress; suppression of free speech in the South; and, of course, of committing the moral wrong of enslaving others in the first place.

By 1850, North and South had created different communities. To antislavery Northerners, the South was an economic backwater dominated by a small slave-owning aristocracy that lived off the profits of forced labor and deprived poor whites of their democratic rights and the fruits of honest work. The slave system was not only immoral but a drag on the entire nation, for, in the words of Senator William Seward of New York, it subverted the "intelligence, vigor and energy" that were essential for national growth. In contrast, the dynamic and enterprising commercial North boasted a free labor ideology that offered economic opportunity to the common man and ensured his democratic rights (see Chapter 12).

Things looked very different through southern eyes. Far from being economically backward, the South, through its export of cotton, was, according to Southerners, the great engine of national economic growth from which the North benefited. Slavery was not only a blessing to an inferior race but the cornerstone of democracy, for it ensured the freedom and independence of all white men without entailing the bitter class divisions that marked the North. Slave owners accused northern manufacturers of hypocrisy for practicing "wage slavery" without the paternal benevolence they claimed to bestow on their slaves. The North, James Henry Hammond of South Carolina charged, had eliminated the "name [of slavery], but not the thing," for "your whole hireling class of manual laborers and 'operatives'...are essentially slaves."

By the early 1850s, these vastly different visions of the North and the South—the result of many years of political controversy—had become fixed, and the chances of national reconciliation increasingly slim. Over the course of the decade, many Americans came to believe that the place of slavery in the nation's life had to be permanently settled. And they increasingly wondered whether their two sectional communities—one slave, one free—could continue to be part of a unitary national one.

THE COMPROMISE OF 1850

By 1850 the issue raised by the Wilmot Proviso—whether slavery should be extended to the new territories—could no longer be ignored. Overnight, the California Gold Rush had turned a remote frontier into a territory with a booming population. In 1849 both

In 1850, *the three men who had long represented America's three major regions attempted to resolve the political crisis brought on by the applications of California and Utah for statehood. Henry Clay is speaking; John C. Calhoun stands third from right; and Daniel Webster is seated at the left with his head in his hand. Both Clay and Webster were ill, and Calhoun died before the compromise of 1850 was arranged by a younger group of politicians led by Stephen A. Douglas.*

Missouri Compromise	1820	Admits Missouri to the Union as a slave state and Maine as a free state; prohibits slavery in the rest of the Louisiana Purchase Territory north of 36°30'.
		Territory Covered: The entire territory of the Louisiana Purchase, exclusive of the state of Louisiana, which had been admitted to the Union in 1812.
Compromise of 1850	1850	Admits California to the Union as a free state, settles the borders of Texas (a slave state); sets no conditions concerning slavery for the rest of the territory acquired from Mexico.
		Territory Covered: The territory that had been part of Mexico before the end of the Mexican-American War and the Treaty of Guadalupe Hidalgo (1848): part of Texas, California, Utah Territory (now Utah, Nevada, and part of Colorado), and New Mexico Territory (now New Mexico and Arizona).

California and Utah applied for statehood. Should these territories be admitted as slave or free states? A simmering border war between Texas (a slave state) and New Mexico, which seemed likely to be a free state, had to be settled, as did the issue of the debts Texas had incurred as an independent republic. Closer to home, antislavery forces demanded the end of slavery in the District of Columbia, while slave owners complained that Northerners were refusing to return escaped slaves, as federal law mandated.

Debate and Compromise

The Compromise of 1850 was the final act in the political careers of the three aging men who in the public mind best represented America's sections: Westerner Henry Clay; Southerner John C. Calhoun; and Daniel Webster, spokesman for the North. It was sadly appropriate to the bitter sectional argument of 1850 that the three men contributed great words to the debate but that the compromise itself was enacted by younger men. Calhoun brought an aura of death with him to the Senate as he sat, shrouded in flannels, listening to the speech that he was too ill to read for himself. He died less than a month later, still insisting on the right of the South to secede if necessary to preserve its way of life. Daniel Webster claimed to speak "not as a Massachusetts man, nor as a Northern man, but as an American....I speak today for the preservation of the Union." He rejected southern claims that peaceable secession was possible or desirable and pleaded with abolitionists to compromise

enough to keep the South in the Union. Clay, claiming he had "never before risen to address any assemblage so oppressed, so appalled, and so anxious," argued eloquently for compromise, but left the Senate in ill health before his plea was answered.

On July 9, 1850, in the midst of the debate, President Zachary Taylor died of acute gastroenteritis, caused by a hasty snack of fruit and cold milk at a Fourth of July celebration. A bluff military man, Taylor had been prepared to follow Andrew Jackson's precedent during the Nullification Crisis of 1832 and simply demand that southern dissidents compromise. When Vice President Millard Fillmore assumed the presidency, however, he helped adjust the Compromise of 1850 to southern liking. Fillmore was a moderate northern Whig and more prosouthern than the southern-born Taylor had been. Moreover, although Clay had assembled all the necessary parts of the bargain, it was not he but members of a younger political generation, and in particular the rising young Democrat from Illinois, Stephen Douglas, who drove the Compromise of 1850 through Congress. The final product consisted of five separate bills (it had been impossible to obtain a majority for a comprehensive measure), embodying three separate compromises.

First, California was admitted as a free state, but the status of the remaining former Mexican possessions was left to be decided by popular sovereignty (a vote of the territory's inhabitants) when they applied for statehood. (Utah's application for statehood was not accepted until 1896 because of controversy over the Mormon practice of polygamy.) The result was, for the time being,

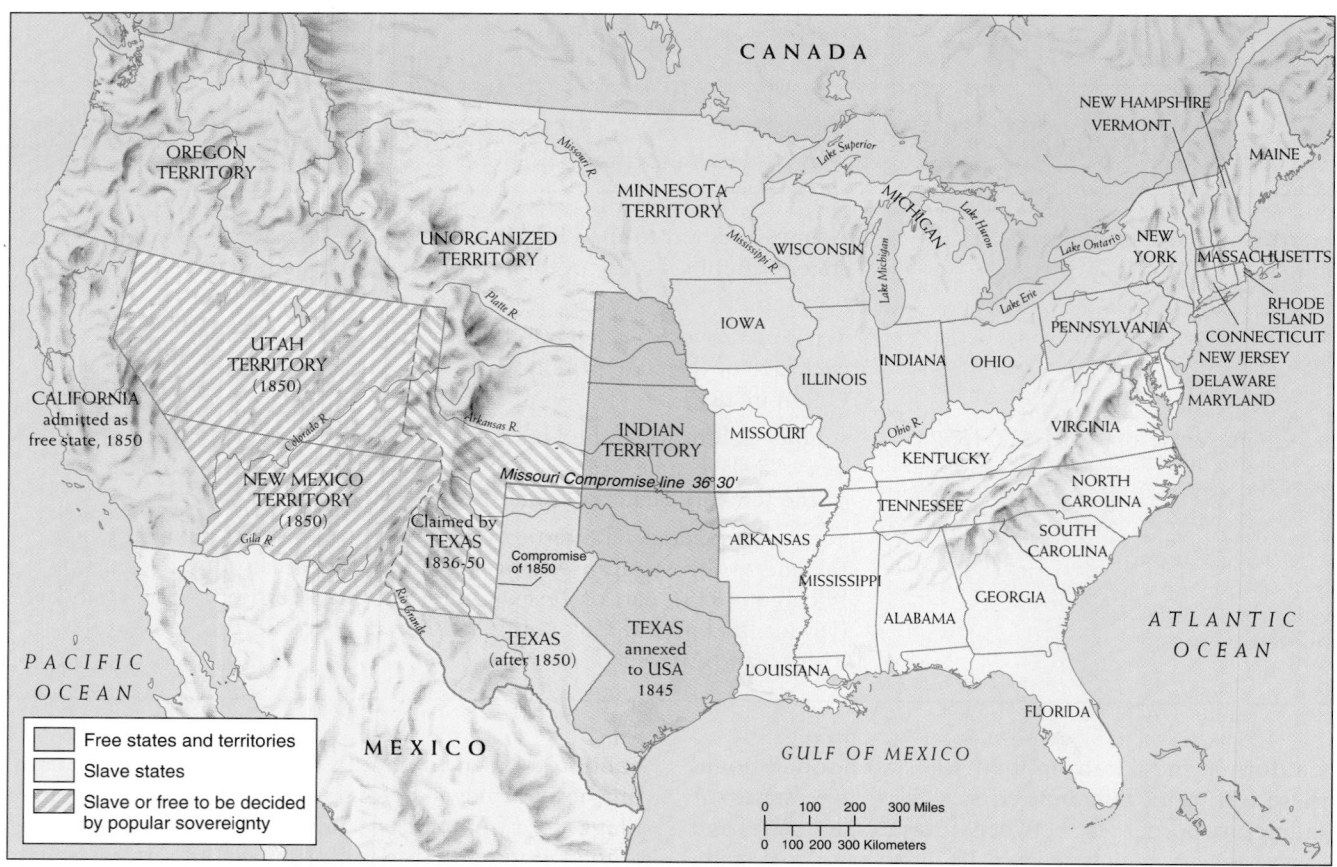

The Compromise of 1850 *The Compromise of 1850 reflected heightened sectional tensions by being even messier and more awkward than the Missouri Compromise of 1820. California was admitted as a free state, the borders of Texas were settled, and the status of the rest of the former Mexican territory was left to be decided later by popular sovereignty. No consistent majority voted for the five separate bills that made up the compromise.*

fifteen slave states and sixteen free states. Second, Texas (a slave state) was required to cede land to New Mexico Territory (free or slave status undecided). In return, the federal government assumed $10 million of debts Texas incurred before it became a state. Finally, the slave trade, but not slavery itself, was ended in the District of Columbia, but a stronger fugitive slave law was enacted.

Jubilation and relief greeted the news that compromise had been achieved. In Washington, where the anxiety and concern had been greatest, drunken crowds serenaded Congress, shouting, "The Union is saved!" That was certainly true for the moment, but analysis of the votes on the five bills that made up the compromise revealed no consistent majority. The sectional splits within each party that had existed before the compromise remained. Antislavery northern Whigs and proslavery southern Democrats, each the larger wing of their party, were the least willing to compromise. Southern Whigs and northern Democrats were the forces for moderation, but each group was dwindling in popular appeal as sectional animosities grew.

In the country as a whole, the feeling was that the problem of slavery in the territories had been solved. The *Philadelphia Pennsylvanian* was confident that "peace and tranquillity" had been ensured, and the *Louisville Journal* said that a weight seemed to have been lifted from the heart of America. But as former Liberty Party spokesman Salmon P. Chase, now a senator from Ohio, soberly noted, "The question of slavery in the territories has been avoided. It has not been settled." The most immediately inflammatory measure of the compromise was the Fugitive Slave Act.

The Fugitive Slave Act

From the early days of their movement, northern abolitionists had urged slaves to escape, promising assistance and support when they reached the North. Some free African Americans had offered far more than verbal support. Among them, Harriet Tubman, an escaped slave from Maryland, was one of the most famous. Tubman made nineteen return trips and brought almost 300 slaves to freedom, among them all the other members of her family. Northerners had long been appalled by professional slave catchers, who zealously seized African Americans in the North and took them south into slavery again. Most abhorrent in northern eyes was that captured black people were at the mercy of slave catchers because they had no legal right to defend themselves. In more than one case, a northern free African American was captured in his own community and helplessly shipped into slavery.

Solomon Northup was one such person. In his widely sold account *Twelve Years a Slave*, published in 1853, he told a harrowing tale of being kidnapped in Washington, the nation's capital, and shipped south. Northup spent twelve years as a slave before he was able to send a message to northern friends to bring the legal proof to free him. As a result of stories like Northup's and the very effective publicity generated by abolitionists, nine northern states passed personal liberty laws between 1842 and 1850, serving notice that they would not cooperate with federal recapture efforts. These northern laws enraged Southerners, who had long been convinced that all Northerners, not just abolitionists, were actively hindering efforts to reclaim their escaped slaves. At issue were two distinct definitions of "rights": Northerners were upset at the denial of legal and personal rights to escaped slaves; Southerners saw illegal infringement of their property rights. Southerners insisted that a strong federal law be part of the Compromise of 1850.

The Fugitive Slave Law, enacted in 1850, dramatically increased the power of slave owners to capture escaped slaves. The full authority of the federal government now supported slave owners, and although fugitives were guaranteed a hearing before a federal commissioner, they were not allowed to testify on their own behalf. Furthermore, the new law imposed federal penalties on citizens who protected or assisted fugitives, or who did not cooperate in their return. In Boston, the center of the abolitionist movement, reaction to the new law was fierce. When an escaped slave named Shadrach Minkins was seized in February 1851, a group of African American men broke into the courtroom, overwhelmed the federal marshals, seized Minkins, and sent him safely to Canada. Although the action had community support—a Massachusetts jury defiantly refused to convict the perpetrators—many people, including Daniel Webster and President Fillmore, condemned it as "mob rule."

The federal government responded with overwhelming force. In April 1851, 300 armed soldiers were mobilized to prevent the rescue of Thomas Sims, who was being shipped back into slavery. In the most famous case in Boston, a biracial group of armed abolitionists led by Unitarian clergyman Thomas Wentworth Higginson stormed the federal courthouse in 1854 in an attempt to save escaped slave Anthony Burns. The rescue effort failed, and a federal deputy marshal was killed. President Pierce sent marines, cavalry, and artillery to Boston to reinforce the guard over Burns and ordered a federal ship to be ready to deliver the fugitive back into slavery. When the effort by defense lawyers to argue for Burns's freedom failed, Bostonians raised money to buy his freedom. But the U.S. attorney, ordered by the president to enforce the Fugitive Slave Law in all circumstances, blocked the purchase. The case was lost, and Burns was marched to the docks through streets lined with sorrowing abolitionists. Buildings were shrouded in black and draped with American flags hanging upside down, while bells tolled as if for a funeral.

The Burns case radicalized many Northerners. Conservative Whig George Hilliard wrote to a friend, "When it was all over, and I was left alone in my office, I put my face in my hands and wept. I could do nothing less." During the 1850s, 322 black fugitives were sent back into slavery; only 11 were declared free. Northern popular sentiment and the Fugitive Slave Law, rigorously enforced by the federal government, were increasingly at odds. The northern abolitionists who used force to rescue captured slaves were breaking the law, but they were winning the battle for public opinion.

In this volatile atmosphere, escaped African Americans wrote and lectured bravely on behalf of freedom. Frederick Douglass, the most famous and eloquent of the fugitive slaves, spoke out fearlessly in support of armed resistance. "The only way to make the Fugitive Slave Law a dead letter," he said in 1853, "is to make a half dozen or more dead kidnappers." Openly active in the underground network that helped slaves reach safety in Canada, Douglass himself had been constantly in danger of capture until his friends bought his freedom in 1847. Harriet Jacobs, who escaped to the North after seven years in hiding in the South, wrote bitterly in her *Incidents in the Life of a Slave Girl* (1861) that the Fugitive Slave Law made her feel that "I was, in fact, a slave in New York, as subject to slave laws as I had been in a slave state....I had been chased during half my life, and it seemed as if the chase were never to end." Threatened by owners who came north for her, Jacobs went into hiding again, until she was informed that friends had arranged her purchase: "A gentleman near me said, 'It's true; I have seen the bill of sale.' 'The bill of sale!' Those words struck me like a blow. So I was sold at last! A human being sold in the free city of New York!"

The Fugitive Slave Law brought home the reality of slavery to residents of the free states. In effect, this law made slavery national and forced northern communities to confront what that meant. Although most people were still unwilling to grant social equality to the free African Americans who lived in the northern states, more and more had come to believe that the institution of slavery was wrong. The strong northern reaction against the Fugitive Slave Law also had consequences in the South. As Democrat Cave Johnson of Tennessee warned, "If the fugitive slave bill is not enforced in the North, the moderate men of the South...will be overwhelmed by the 'fire-eaters,'" the extremists who favored immediate secession. Northern protests against the Fugitive Slave Law bred suspicion in the South and encouraged secessionist thinking. These new currents of public opinion were reflected in the election of 1852.

The Election of 1852

The first sign of the weakening of the national party system in 1852 was the difficulty both parties experienced at their nominating conventions. With long-time party leaders like Henry Clay now dead, William Seward of New York became the unofficial party head, much to the displeasure of southern Whigs. Seward preferred General Winfield Scott (a military hero like the party's previous two candidates) to the prosouthern Fillmore, and after fifty-two ballots, managed to get him nominated. Many southern Whigs were angered and alienated by the choice and either abstained during the voting, like Georgia's Alexander Stephens, or, like Robert Toombs, cast a protest vote for the Democratic candidate. Although southern Whigs were still elected to Congress, their loyalty to the national party was strained to the breaking point. The Whigs never again fielded a presidential candidate.

The Democrats had a wider variety of candidates: Lewis Cass of popular sovereignty fame; Stephen Douglas, architect of the Compromise of 1850; and James Buchanan, described as a "Northern man with Southern principles." Cass, Douglas, and Buchanan competed for forty-nine ballots, each strong enough to block the others but not strong enough to win. Finally the party turned to a handsome, affable nonentity, Franklin Pierce of New Hampshire, who was thought to have southern sympathies. Uniting on a platform pledging "faithful execution" of all parts of the Compromise of 1850, including the Fugitive Slave Law, Democrats polled well in the South and in the North. Most Democrats who had voted for the Free-Soil Party in 1848 voted for Pierce. So, in record numbers, did immigrant Irish and German voters, who were eligible for citizenship after three years' residence. The strong immigrant vote for Pierce was a sign of the strength of the Democratic machines in northern cities (see Chapter 13), and reformers complained, not for the last time, about widespread corruption and "vote buying" by urban ward bosses. Overall, however, "Genl. Apathy is the strongest candidate out here," as one Ohioan reported. Pierce easily won the 1852 election, 254 electoral votes to 42. Voter turnout was below 70 percent, lower than it had been since 1836.

"Young America": The Politics of Expansion

Pierce entered the White House in 1853 on a wave of good feeling. Massachusetts Whig Amos Lawrence reported, "Never since Washington has an administration commenced with the hearty [good]will of so large a portion of the country." This goodwill was soon strained by Pierce's support for the expansionist adventures of the "Young America" movement.

The "Young America" movement was a group within the Democratic Party whose members used manifest destiny to justify their desire for conquest of Central America and Cuba. Young America expansionists had glanced covetously southward since the end of the Mexican-American War. President Polk himself had wanted to buy Cuba and to intervene in Mexican politics but was rebuffed by Congress (see Chapter 14). During the Pierce administration, several private "filibusters" (from the Spanish *filibustero*, meaning an "adventurer" or "pirate") invaded Caribbean and Central American countries, usually with the declared intention of extending slave territory. The best-known of the filibusters, William Walker, was also the most improbable. Short, slight, and soft-spoken, Walker led not one but three invasions of Nicaragua. After the first invasion in 1855, Walker became ruler of the country and encouraged settlement by southern slave owners, but was unseated by a regional revolt in 1857. His subsequent efforts to regain control of the country failed, and on the last he was captured and executed by firing squad in Honduras.

The Pierce administration, not directly involved in the filibustering, was deeply involved in an effort to obtain Cuba. In 1854, Pierce authorized his minister to Spain, Pierre Soulé, to try to force the unwilling Spanish to sell Cuba for $130 million. Soulé met in Ostend, Belgium, with the American ministers to France and England, John Mason and James Buchanan, to compose the offer, which was a mixture of cajolements and threats. At first appealing to Spain to recognize the deep affinities between the Cubans and American Southerners that made them "one people with one destiny," the document went on to threaten to "wrest" Cuba from Spain if necessary. This amazing document, which became known as the Ostend Manifesto, was supposed to be secret but was soon leaked to the press. Deeply embarrassed, the Pierce administration was forced to repudiate it.

The complicity between the Pierce administration and proslavery expansionists was foolhardy and lost it the northern goodwill with which it had begun. The sectional crisis that preceded the Compromise of 1850 had made obvious the danger of reopening the territorial issue. Ironically, it was not the Young America expansionists but the prime mover of the Compromise of 1850 himself, Stephen A. Douglas, who reignited the sectional struggle over slavery expansion.

THE CRISIS OF THE NATIONAL PARTY SYSTEM

In 1854, Douglas introduced the Kansas-Nebraska Act, proposing to open those lands that had been the northern part of Indian Territory to American settlers under the principle of popular sovereignty. He thereby reopened the question of slavery in the territories. Douglas knew he was taking a political risk, but he believed he could satisfy both his expansionist aims and his presidential ambitions. He was wrong. Instead, he pushed the national party system into crisis, first killing the Whigs and then destroying the Democrats.

The Kansas-Nebraska Act

Until 1854, white Americans thought of Kansas only as a passageway to other places farther west. A part of Indian Territory, Kansas was peopled largely by tribes who had been moved from their original homes in the East. In the great Indian removals of the 1830s, these tribes had been promised the Kansas lands "as

long as grass grows and water flows." The promise was broken in 1854, when prior treaties were ignored and the northern part of Indian Territory was thrown open to white settlement.

Stephen Douglas introduced the Kansas-Nebraska Act to further the construction of a transcontinental railroad, which he ardently supported as a way to foster American democracy and commerce. He wanted the rail line to terminate in Chicago, in his own state of Illinois, rather than in the rival St. Louis, but for that to happen, the land west of Iowa and Missouri had to be organized into territories (the first step toward statehood). To get Congress to agree to the organization of the territories, however, Douglas would need the votes of southern Democrats, who would be unwilling to support him unless the territories were open to slavery. Douglas also coveted his party's nomination for the presidency in 1856, and would need the continuing support of southern Democrats to secure it.

Douglas thought he was solving his problem by proposing that the status of slavery in the new

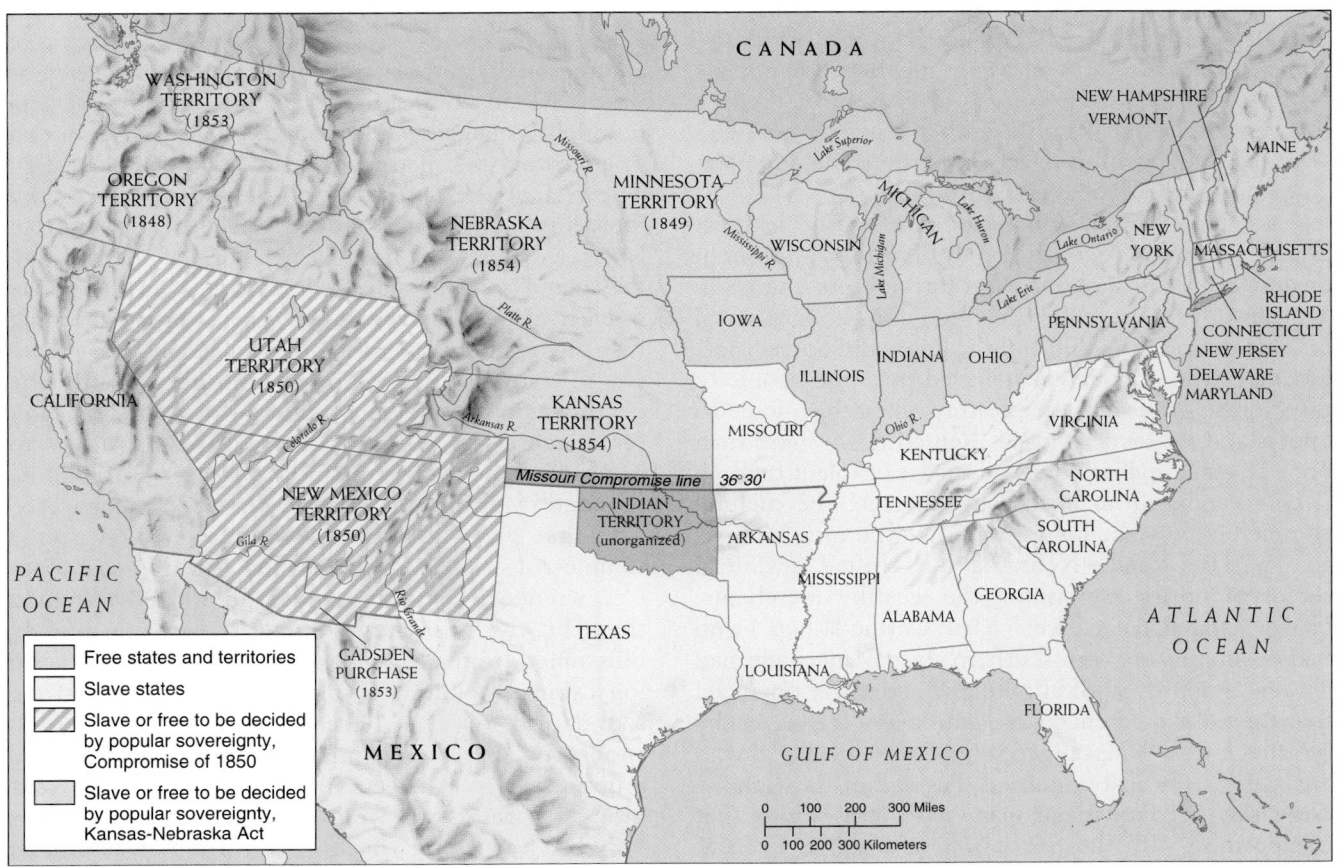

The Kansas-Nebraska Act, 1854   *The Kansas-Nebraska Act, proposed by Steven A. Douglas in 1854, opened the central and northern Great Plains to settlement. The act had two major faults: it robbed Indian peoples of half the territory guaranteed to them by treaty, and, because it repealed the Missouri Compromise Line, it opened up the lands to warring proslavery and antislavery factions.*

territories be governed by the principle of popular sovereignty. Democratic politicians had favored this democratic-sounding slogan, vague enough to appeal to both proslavery and antislavery voters, ever since 1848. Douglas thought Southerners would support his bill because of its popular sovereignty provision, and Northerners because it favored a northern route for the transcontinental railroad. Privately, Douglas believed that the topography of the Kansas-Nebraska region was unsuitable for slave agriculture and that the region's inhabitants would decide to enter the Union as free states. Douglas chose also to downplay the price he had to pay for southern support—by allowing the possibility of slavery in the new territories his bill in effect repealed the Missouri Compromise of 1820, which barred slavery north of latitude 36°30′.

The Kansas-Nebraska bill passed, but it badly strained the major political parties. Southern Whigs voted with southern Democrats in favor of the measure, northern Whigs rejected it absolutely, creating an irreconcilable split that left Whigs unable to field a presidential candidate in 1856. The damage to the Democratic Party was almost as great. In the congressional elections of 1854, northern Democrats lost two-thirds of their seats (a drop from ninety-one to twenty-five), giving the southern Democrats (who were solidly in favor of slavery extension) the dominant voice both in Congress and within the party.

Douglas had committed one of the greatest miscalculations in American political history. A storm of protest arose throughout the North. More than 300 large anti-Nebraska rallies occurred during congressional consideration of the bill, and the anger did not subside. Douglas, who confidently believed that "the people of the North will sustain the measure when they come to understand it," found himself shouted down more than once at public rallies when he tried to explain the bill. "I could travel from Boston to Chicago," he ruefully commented, "by the light of my own [burning] effigy."

The Kansas-Nebraska bill shifted a crucial sector of northern opinion: the wealthy merchants, bankers, and manufacturers (called "Cotton Whigs") who had economic ties with southern slave owners and had always disapproved of abolitionist activity. Convinced that the bill would encourage antislavery feeling in the North, Cotton Whigs urged southern politicians to vote against it, only to be ignored. Passage of the Kansas-Nebraska Act convinced many northern Whigs that compromise with the South was impossible. Even as sober a newspaper as the *New York Times* regarded the act as "part of this great scheme for extending and perpetuating the supremacy of the Slave Power." Joining the antislavery cause were some Cotton Whigs like manufacturer Amos Lawrence of Massachusetts, who had so

warmly welcomed the prospect of sectional peace at the beginning of the Pierce administration. Lawrence provided the financial backing for the first group of antislavery New Englanders who settled Kansas in 1854, and in gratitude they named their town for him.

In Kansas itself in 1854, hasty treaties were concluded with the Indian tribes who owned the land. Some, such as the Kickapoos, Shawnees, Sauks, and Foxes, agreed to relocate to small reservations. Others, like the Delawares, Weas, and Iowas, agreed to sell their lands to whites. Still others, such as the Cheyennes and Sioux, kept the western part of Kansas Territory (now Colorado)—until gold was discovered there in 1859. Once the treaties were signed, both proslavery and antislavery white settlers began to pour in, and the battle was on.

"Bleeding Kansas"

The first to claim land in Kansas were residents of nearby Missouri, itself a slave state. Egged on by Democratic senator David Atchison of Missouri (who took a leave of absence from Congress to lead them), Missourians took up land claims, established proslavery strongholds such as the towns of Leavenworth, Kickapoo, and Atchison, and repeatedly and blatantly swamped Kansas elections with Missouri votes. In 1855, in the second of several notoriously fraudulent elections, 6,307 ballots were cast in a territory that had fewer than 3,000 eligible voters. The rest of the votes—all proslavery—were cast by "border ruffians," as they proudly called themselves, from Missouri. These were frontiersmen, fond of boasting that they could "scream louder, jump higher, shoot closer, get drunker at night and wake up soberer in the morning than any man this side of the Rocky Mountains."

Northerners quickly responded, with the encouragement of sympathetic politicians. Free-Soil (antislavery) New Englanders were recruited to Kansas by the New England Emigrant Aid Society, founded by abolitionist Eli Thayer of Massachusetts. The first party of New Englanders arrived in the summer of 1854 and established the free-soil town of Lawrence. More than a thousand others had joined them by the following summer. Lawrence quickly blossomed from a town of tent homes to one of solid log cabins, a church, a sawmill, stores, and a stone foundation for what became the Free State Hotel, sponsored by the Emigrant Aid Society. These migrants were all free-soilers, and many were religious reformers as well. The contrast of values between them and the border ruffians was almost total. When nondrinking William Phillips stiffly refused a friendly offer of a drink from a Missourian, the border ruffian burst out, "That's just it! This thing of temperance and abolitionism and the Emigrant Aid Society are all the same kind of thing."

Kansas soon became a bloody battleground as the two factions struggled to secure the mandate of "popular sovereignty." Free-Soilers in Lawrence received shipments of heavy crates, innocuously marked "BOOKS" but actually containing Sharps repeating rifles, sent by eastern supporters. For their part, the border ruffians—already heavily armed, with Bowie knives in their boots, revolvers at their waists, rifles slung from their shoulders, and swords at their sides—called for reinforcements. David Atchison exhorted Alabamans: "Let your young men come forth to Missouri and Kansas! Let them come well armed!"

In the summer of 1856 these lethal preparations exploded into open warfare. First, proslavery forces burned and looted the town of Lawrence. The Free State Hotel, among other buildings, was burned to the ground. In retaliation, a grim old man named John Brown led his sons in a raid on the proslavery settlers of Pottawatomie Creek, killing five unarmed people. A wave of violence ensued. Armed bands roamed the countryside, and burnings and killings became commonplace. John Brown and his followers were just one of many bands of marauding murderers who were never arrested, never brought to trial, and never stopped from committing further violence. Peaceful residents of large sections of rural Kansas were repeatedly forced to flee to the safety of military forts when rumors of one or another armed band reached them.

This engraving shows "Border Ruffians" from Missouri lining up to vote for slavery in the Kickapoo, Kansas Territory election of 1855. The widespread practice of illegal voting and of open violence earned Kansas the dreadful nickname of "Bleeding Kansas."

The rest of the nation watched in horror as the residents of Kansas slaughtered each other in the pursuit of sectional goals. Americans' pride in their nation's great achievements was threatened by the endless violence in one small part—but a part that increasingly seemed to represent the divisions of the whole.

The Politics of Nativism

Meanwhile, sectional pressures continued to reshape national politics. The breakup of the Whig Party coincided with one of the strongest bursts of nativism, or anti-immigrant feeling, in American history, a reaction to the Democratic Party's success in capturing the support of the rapidly growing population of mostly Catholic foreign-born voters (see Chapter 13 and "Immigration and Community: The Changing Nature of Ethnicity in America, 1800–1860," p. 380).

Irish immigrants in particular voted Democratic, both in reaction to Whig hostility (as in Boston) and because of their own antiblack prejudices. Frequently in competition with free African Americans for low-paying jobs, Irish immigrants were more likely to share the attitudes of Southerners than those of abolitionists. Violent urban riots in which free African Americans were the scapegoats periodically erupted in northern cities such as Cincinnati (1829), Providence (1831), New York (1834), and Philadelphia (1834 and 1842).

The reformist and individualistic attitudes of many Whigs inclined them toward nativism and toward the new American Party, which formed in 1850 to give political expression to anti-immigrant feeling. Many Whigs disapproved of the new immigrants because they were poor, Catholic, and often disdainful of the temperance movement. The Catholic Church's opposition to the liberal European revolutions of 1848 also fueled anti-Catholic fears. If America's new Catholic immigrants opposed the revolutions in which other Americans took such pride (believing them to be modeled on the American example), how could the future of America's own democracy be ensured? Finally, nativist Whigs held immigration to be solely responsible for the increases in crime and the rising cost of relief for the poor that accompanied the rapid urban growth of the 1830s and 1840s.

Women reformers were as prone to nativism as men. As early as 1838, the influential Lydia Sigourney wrote in alarm in her *Letters to Mothers* about the "influx of untutored foreigners" that had made the United States "a repository for the waste and refuse of other nations." Sigourney urged women to organize an internal missionary movement that would carry the principles of middle-class American domesticity to the unenlightened foreigners.

Nativism drew former Whigs, especially young men in white-collar and skilled blue-collar

Cartoons like this one sought to couple concerns about temperance (suggested by the barrels of Irish whiskey and German lager beer) with nativist claims that immigrant voters were voting illegally (indicated by the struggle in the background).

occupations, to the new American Party. At the core of the party were several secret fraternal societies open only to native-born Protestants who pledged never to vote for a Catholic (on the grounds that all Catholics took their orders straight from the pope in Rome—a fear that was to be voiced again by Southern Baptists in 1960 when John F. Kennedy ran for president). When questioned about their beliefs, party members maintained secrecy by answering, "I know nothing"— Hence the popular name for American Party members, Know-Nothings. Few Know-Nothings were wealthy: most were workers or small farmers whose jobs or ways of life were threatened by the cheap labor and unfamiliar culture of the new immigrants.

Know-Nothings scored startling victories in northern state elections in 1854, winning control of the legislature in Massachusetts and polling 40 percent of the vote in Pennsylvania. No wonder one Pennsylvania Democrat reported, "Nearly everybody seems to have gone altogether deranged on Nativism." Although most of the new immigrants lived in the North, resentment and anger against them was national, and the American Party initially polled well in the South, attracting the votes of many former southern Whigs. But in the 1850s, no party could ignore slavery, and in 1855 the American Party split into northern (antislavery) and southern (proslavery) wings. Soon after this split, many people who had voted for the Know-Nothings shifted their support to another new party, one that combined many characteristics of the Whigs with a westward-looking, expansionist, free-soil policy. This was the Republican Party, founded in 1854.

The Republican Party and the Election of 1856

In 1854 a Massachusetts voter described the elections in his state in terms of "freedom, temperance, and Protestantism against slavery, rum, and Romanism," linking nativism with sectional politics. "Slavery, rum, and Romanism" were supposed to describe the national Democratic Party, whose supporters included southern slave owners and northern immigrant Catholics. "Freedom, temperance, and Protestantism," were meant to characterize the Republican Party. Many constituencies, however, found room in the new party. Its supporters included many former northern Whigs who opposed slavery absolutely, many Free-Soil Party supporters who opposed the expansion of slavery but were willing to tolerate it in the South, and many northern reformers concerned about temperance and Catholicism. The Republicans also attracted the economic core of the old Whig Party—the merchants and industrialists who wanted a strong national government to promote economic growth by supporting a protective tariff, transportation improvements, and cheap land for western farmers. In quieter times it would have taken this party a while to sort out all its differences and become a true political community. But because of the sectional crisis, the fledgling party nearly won its very first presidential election.

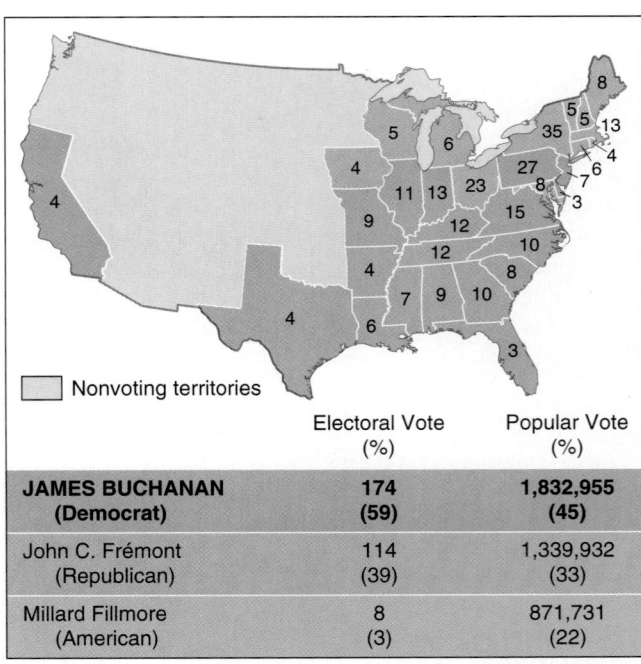

| Nonvoting territories |

	Electoral Vote (%)	Popular Vote (%)
JAMES BUCHANAN (Democrat)	**174 (59)**	**1,832,955 (45)**
John C. Frémont (Republican)	114 (39)	1,339,932 (33)
Millard Fillmore (American)	8 (3)	871,731 (22)

The Election of 1856   *Because three parties contested the 1856 election, Democrat James Buchanan was a minority president. Although Buchanan alone had national support, Republican John Frémont won most of the free states, and Millard Fillmore of the American Party gained 40 percent of the vote in most of the slave states.*

The immediate question facing the nation in 1856 was which new party, the Know-Nothings or the Republicans, would emerge the stronger. But the more important question was whether the Democratic Party could hold together. The two strongest contenders for the Democratic nomination were President Pierce and Stephen A. Douglas. Douglas had proposed the Kansas-Nebraska Act and Pierce had actively supported it. Both men therefore had the support of the southern wing of the party. But it was precisely their support of this act that made Northerners oppose both of them. The Kansas-Nebraska Act's divisive effect on the Democratic Party now became clear: no one who had voted on the bill, either for or against, could satisfy both wings of the party. A compromise candidate was found in James Buchanan of Pennsylvania, the "Northern man with Southern principles." Luckily for him, he had been ambassador to Great Britain at the time of the Kansas-Nebraska Act and thus had not had to commit himself.

The election of 1856 appeared to be a three-way contest that pitted Buchanan against explorer John C. Frémont of the Republican Party and the American (Know-Nothing) Party's candidate, former president Millard Fillmore. In fact, the election was two separate contests, one in the North and one in the South. The southern race was between Buchanan and Fillmore. Frémont's name appeared on the ballot in only four southern states, all in the Upper South, and even there he polled almost no votes. Fillmore received strong support from many former southern Whigs. Although he carried only the state of Maryland, he attracted more than 40 percent of the vote in ten other slave states. Buchanan, though, won the electoral votes in all those states.

Frémont decisively defeated Buchanan in the North, winning eleven of sixteen free states. Nationwide he garnered 1.3 million votes to Buchanan's 1.8 million. Buchanan won the election with only 45

OVERVIEW

POLITICAL PARTIES SPLIT AND REALIGN

Whig Party	Ran its last presidential candidate in 1852. The candidate, General Winfield Scott, alienated many southern Whigs and the party was so split it could not field a candidate in 1856.
Democratic Party	Remained a national party through 1856, but Buchanan's actions as president made southern domination of the party so clear that many northern Democrats were alienated. Stephen Douglas, running as a northern Democrat in 1860, won 29 percent of the popular vote; John Breckinridge, running as a southern Democrat, won 18 percent.
Liberty Party	Antislavery party ran James G. Birney for president in 1844. He won 62,000 votes, largely from northern antislavery Whigs.
Free-Soil	Ran Martin Van Buren, former Democratic president, in 1848. Gained 10 percent of the popular vote, largely from Whigs but also from some northern Democrats.
American (Know-Nothing) Party	Nativist party made striking gains in 1854 congressional elections, attracting both northern and southern Whigs. In 1856, its presidential candidate Millard Fillmore won 21 percent of the popular vote.
Republican Party	Founded in 1854. Attracted many northern Whigs and northern Democrats. Presidential candidate John C. Frémont won 33 percent of the popular vote in 1856; in 1860 Abraham Lincoln won 40 percent and was elected in a four-way race.

percent of the popular vote because he was the only national candidate. His southern support, plus the electoral votes of Pennsylvania, New Jersey, Illinois, Indiana, and California gave him the victory. But the Republicans, after studying the election returns, claimed "victorious defeat," for they realized that in 1860 the addition of just two more northern states to their total would mean victory. Furthermore, the Republican Party had clearly defeated the American Party in the battle to win designation as a major party. These were grounds for great optimism—and for great concern, for the Republican Party was a sectional rather than a national party; it drew almost all its support from the North. Southerners viewed its very existence as an attack on their vital interests. Thus the rapid rise of the Republicans posed a growing threat to national unity.

The election of 1856 attracted one of the highest voter turnouts in American history—79 percent. Ordinary people had come to share the politicians' concern about the growing sectional rift. The combined popular vote for Buchanan and Fillmore (67 percent) showed that most voters, north and south, favored politicians who at least claimed to speak for national rather than sectional interests. The northern returns also showed something else. Northerners had decided that the threat posed by the expansion of slavery was greater than that posed by the new immigrants; although it never disappeared, nativism subsided. The Buchanan administration, however, proved unequal to the task of resolving the free versus slave issue, and the nation began an inexorable slide into civil war.

THE DIFFERENCES DEEPEN

In one dreadful week in 1856 the people of the United States heard, in quick succession, about the looting and burning of Lawrence, Kansas, about John Brown's retaliatory massacre at Pottawatomie, and about unprecedented violence on the Senate floor. In the last of these incidents, Senator Charles Sumner of Massachusetts suffered permanent injury in a vicious attack by Congressman Preston Brooks of South Carolina. Trapped at his desk, Sumner was helpless as Brooks beat him so hard with his cane that it broke. Blood streaming from his head, Sumner escaped only by wrenching loose his desk from the screws that held it to the floor. A few days earlier, Sumner had given an insulting antislavery speech entitled "The Crime against Kansas." Using the abusive, accusatory style favored by abolitionists, he had singled out for ridicule

Senator Andrew Butler of South Carolina, charging him with choosing "the harlot, slavery" as his mistress. Senator Butler was Preston Brooks's uncle; in Brooks's mind, he was simply avenging an intolerable affront to his uncle's honor. So far had the behavioral codes of North and South diverged that each man found his own action perfectly justifiable and the action of the other outrageous. Their attitudes were mirrored in their respective sections.

The *Dred Scott* Decision

Although James Buchanan firmly believed that he alone could hold together the nation so riven by hatred and violence, his self-confidence outran his abilities. When he entered the White House in March 1857 Buchanan was the oldest president (sixty-five) ever elected and a veteran of forty years of politics. Unfortunately, despite his experience, he was indecisive at moments that called for firm leadership. He was also so deeply indebted to the strong southern wing of the Democratic Party that he could not take the impartial actions necessary to heal "Bleeding Kansas." And his support for a momentous prosouthern decision by the Supreme Court further aggravated sectional differences.

In *Dred Scott v. Sandford,* decided on March 6, 1857, two days after James Buchanan was sworn in, a southern-dominated Supreme Court attempted—and failed—to solve the political controversy over slavery. Dred Scott had been a slave all his life. His owner, army surgeon John Emerson, had taken Scott on his military assignments during the 1830s to Illinois (a free state) and Wisconsin Territory (a free territory by the Missouri Compromise line). During that time Scott married another slave, Harriet, and their daughter Eliza was born in free territory. Emerson and the Scotts then returned to Missouri (a slave state) and there, in 1846, Dred Scott sued for his freedom and that of his wife and the daughter born in Wisconsin Territory (who as women had no legal standing of their own) on the grounds that residence in free lands had made them free. It took eleven years for the case to reach the Supreme Court, and by then its importance was obvious to everyone.

Chief Justice Roger B. Taney, of Maryland, seventy-nine years old, hard of hearing and failing of sight, insisted on reading his majority opinion in its entirety, a process that took four excruciating hours. Declaring the Missouri Compromise

SOUTHERN CHIVALRY — ARGUMENT versus CLUB'S.

The beating of Senator Charles Sumner by Congressman Preston Brooks on the Senate floor horrified Northerners but won the approval of Southerners.

unconstitutional, Taney asserted that the federal government had no right to interfere with the free movement of property throughout the territories. Taney was in effect making John C. Calhoun's states' rights position, always considered an extremist southern position, the law of the land. He then dismissed the Dred Scott case on the grounds that only citizens could bring suits before federal courts and that black people—slave or free—were not citizens. With this bold judicial intervention into the most heated issue of the day, Taney intended to settle the controversy over the expansion of slavery once and for all. Instead, he enflamed the conflict.

The five southern members of the Supreme Court concurred in Taney's decision, as did one Northerner, Robert C. Grier. Historians have found that President-elect Buchanan had pressured Grier, a fellow Pennsylvanian, to support the majority. Two of the three other Northerners vigorously dissented, and the last voiced other objections. This was clearly a sectional decision, and the response to it was sectional. Southerners expressed great satisfaction and strong support for the Court. The *Louisville Democrat* said, "The decision is right…but whether or not [it is right], what this tribunal decides the Constitution to be, that it is; and all patriotic men will acquiesce." More bluntly, the *Georgia Constitutionalist* announced, "Southern opinion upon the subject of southern slavery…is now the supreme law of the land…and opposition to southern opinion upon this subject is now opposition to the Constitution, and morally treason against the Government."

Northerners disagreed. Few were quite so contemptuous as the *New York Tribune*, which declared that the decision was "entitled to just as much moral weight as would be the judgment of a majority of those congregated in any Washington bar-room." Still, many were so troubled by the Dred Scott decision that for the first time they found themselves seriously questioning the power of the Supreme Court to establish the "law of the land." Many northern legislatures denounced the decision. New York passed a resolution declaring that the Supreme Court had lost the confidence and respect of the people of that state and another refusing to allow slavery within its borders "in any form or under any pretense, or for any time, however short." New York Republicans also proposed an equal suffrage amendment for free African Americans, who were largely disenfranchised by a stringent property qualification for voting. But this was too liberal for the state's voters, who defeated it. This racist attitude was a bitter blow to free African Americans in the North. Frederick Douglass was so disheartened that he seriously considered emigrating to Haiti.

For the Republican Party, the Dred Scott decision represented a formidable challenge. By invalidating the Missouri Compromise, the decision

These sympathetic portraits of Harriet and Dred Scott and their daughters in 1857 helped to shape the northern reaction to the Supreme Court decision that denied the Scotts' claim for freedom. The infamous Dred Scott decision, which was intended to resolve the issue of slavery expansion, instead heightened angry feelings in both North and South.

swept away the free soil foundation of the party. But to directly challenge a Supreme Court decision was a weighty matter. The most sensational Republican counterattack—made by both Abraham Lincoln and William Seward—was the accusation that President Buchanan had conspired with the southern Supreme Court justices to subvert the American political system by withholding the decision until after the presidential election. Lincoln also raised the frightening possibility that "the next Dred Scott decision" would legalize slavery even in free states that abhorred it. President Buchanan's response to events in Kansas, including the drafting of a proslavery constitution, also stoked political antagonisms.

The Lecompton Constitution

In Kansas, the doctrine of popular sovereignty led to continuing civil strife and the political travesty of two territorial governments. The first election of officers to a territorial government in 1855 produced a lopsided proslavery outcome that was clearly the result of illegal voting by Missouri border ruffians. Free-soilers protested by forming their own government, giving Kansas both a proslavery territorial legislature in Lecompton and a free-soil government in Topeka. Because free-soil voters boycotted a June 1857 election for a convention to write a constitution for the territory once it reached statehood, the convention had a proslavery majority that wrote the proslavery Lecompton constitution and applied to Congress for admission to the Union under its terms. In the meantime, in October free-soil voters had participated in relatively honest elections for the territorial legislature, elections that returned a clear free-soil majority. Nevertheless, Buchanan, in the single most disastrous mistake of his administration, endorsed the proslavery constitution because he feared to lose the support of southern Democrats. It seemed that Kansas would enter the Union as a sixteenth slave state, making the number of slave and free states equal.

Unexpected congressional opposition came from none other than Stephen Douglas, author of the legislation that had begun the Kansas troubles in 1854. Now, in 1857, in what was surely the bravest step of his political career, Douglas opposed the Lecompton constitution on the grounds that it violated the principle of popular sovereignty. He insisted that the Lecompton constitution must be voted upon by Kansas voters in honest elections (as indeed Buchanan had initially promised). Douglas's decision was one of principle, but it was also motivated by the realization that a proslavery vote would never be accepted by the northern wing of the Democratic Party. Defying James Buchanan, his own president, Douglas voted with the majority in Congress in April 1858 to refuse admission to Kansas under the Lecompton constitution. In a new referendum, the people of Kansas also rejected the Lecompton constitution, 11,300 to 1,788. In 1859 Kansas held another constitutional convention, this one dominated by delegates from the new Republican Party. Kansas was finally admitted as a free state in January 1861.

The defeat of the Lecompton constitution did not come easily. There was more bloodshed in Kansas: sporadic ambushes and killings, including a mass shooting of nine free-soilers. And there was more violence in Congress: a free-for-all involving almost thirty congressmen broke out in the House late one night after an exchange of insults between Republicans and southern Democrats. There was conflict on still another level—the Democratic Party was breaking apart. Douglas had intended to preserve the Democrats as a national party, but instead he lost the support of the southern wing. Southerners reviled him, one claiming that Douglas was "stained with the dishonor of treachery without a parallel." Summing up these events, Congressman Alexander

Stephens of Georgia wrote glumly to his brother: "All things here are tending my mind to the conclusion that the Union cannot and will not last long."

The Panic of 1857

Adding to the growing political tensions was the short but sharp depression of 1857 and 1858. Technology played a part. In August 1857, the failure of an Ohio investment house—the kind of event that had formerly taken weeks to be widely known—was the subject of a news story flashed immediately over telegraph wires to Wall Street and other financial markets. A wave of panic selling ensued, leading to business failures and slowdowns that threw thousands out of work. The major cause of the panic was a sharp but temporary downturn in agricultural exports to Britain, and recovery was well under way by early 1859. In the meantime, Republicans and some northern Democrats in Congress proposed to raise tariffs to help industries hurt by the depression but were outvoted by about half of northern Democrats and almost all southern representatives. The South had resisted protective tariffs since the 1820s (see Chapter 10), but now the opposition was regarded, in the bitter

This painting by Charles G. Rosenberg and James H. Cafferty shows a worried crowd exchanging the latest news on Wall Street during the Panic of 1857. This was the first economic depression in which the telegraph played a part by carrying bad financial news in the West to New York much more rapidly than in the past.

words of one Republican, as yet another example of a Congress "shamelessly prostituted, in a base subserviency to the Slave Power."

Because it affected cotton exports less than northern exports, the Panic of 1857 was less harmful to the South than to the North. Southerners took this as proof of the superiority of their economic system to the free-labor system of the North, and some could not resist the chance to gloat. Senator James Henry Hammond of South Carolina drove home the point in his celebrated "King Cotton" speech of March 1858:

> When the abuse of credit had destroyed credit and annihilated confidence; when thousands of the strongest commercial houses in the world were coming down…when you came to a dead lock, and revolutions were threatened, what brought you up?…We have poured in upon you one million six hundred thousand bales of cotton just at the moment to save you from destruction.…We have sold it for $65,000,000, and saved you.

It seemed that all matters of political discussion were being drawn into the sectional dispute. The next step toward disunion was an act of violence perpetrated by the grim abolitionist from Kansas, John Brown.

John Brown's Raid

In the heated political mood of the late 1850s, some improbable people became heroes. None was more improbable than John Brown, the self-appointed avenger who slaughtered unarmed proslavery men in Kansas in 1856. In 1859, Brown proposed a wild scheme to raid the South and start a general slave uprising. He believed, as did most northern abolitionists, that discontent among southern slaves was so great that such an uprising needed only a spark to get going. Significantly, free African Americans—among them Frederick Douglass—did not support Brown, thinking his first planned foray, to raid the federal arsenal at Harpers Ferry, Virginia, was doomed to failure. They were right. On October 16, 1859, Brown led a group of twenty-two white and African American men against the arsenal. However, he had made no provision for escape. Even more incredible, he had not notified the Virginia slaves whose uprising it was supposed to be. In less than a day the raid was over. Eight of Brown's men (including two of his sons) were dead, no slaves had joined the fight, and Brown himself was captured. Moving quickly to prevent a lynching by local mobs, the state of Virginia tried and convicted Brown, while he was still weak from the wounds of battle, of treason, murder, and fomenting insurrection.

Ludicrous in life, possibly insane, Brown was nevertheless a noble martyr. In his closing speech prior

JOHN BROWN AT HARPER'S FERRY.

In a contemporary engraving, John Brown and his followers are shown trapped inside the armory at Harper's Ferry in October 1859. Captured, tried, and executed, Brown was regarded as a martyr in the North and a terrorist in the South.

to sentencing, Brown was magnificently eloquent: "Now, if it is deemed necessary that I should forfeit my life for the furtherance of the end of justice, and mingle my blood further with the blood of my children and with the blood of millions in this slave country whose rights are disregarded by wicked, cruel, and unjust enactments, I say, let it be done."

Brown's death by hanging on December 2, 1859, was marked throughout northern communities with public rites of mourning not seen since the death of George Washington. Church bells tolled, buildings were draped in black, ministers preached sermons, prayer meetings were held, abolitionists issued eulogies. Ralph Waldo Emerson said that Brown would "make the gallows as glorious as the cross," and Henry David Thoreau called him "an angel of light." In a more militant frame of mind, abolitionist Wendell Phillips announced, "The lesson of the hour is insurrection." Naturally, not all Northerners supported Brown's action. Northern Democrats and conservative opinion generally repudiated him. In New York, for example, 20,000 merchants signed a petition for a public meeting designed to reassure the South of northern good intentions. But many people, while rejecting Brown's raid, did support the antislavery cause that he represented.

Brown's raid shocked the South because it aroused the greatest fear, that of slave rebellion. Southerners believed that northern abolitionists were provoking slave revolts, a suspicion apparently confirmed when documents captured at Harpers Ferry revealed that Brown had the financial support of half a dozen members of the northern elite. These "Secret Six"— Gerrit Smith, George Stearns, Franklin Sanborn, Thomas Wentworth Higginson, Theodore Parker, and Samuel Gridley Howe—had been willing to finance armed attacks on the slave system.

Even more shocking to Southerners than the raid itself was the extent of northern mourning for Brown's death. Although the Republican Party disavowed Brown's actions, Southerners simply did not believe the party's statements. Southerners wondered how they could stay in the Union in the face of "Northern insolence." The *Richmond Enquirer* reported, "The Harpers Ferry invasion has advanced the cause of disunion more than any other event that has happened since the formation of [the] government." The alarm in up-country South Carolina was so great that vigilance committees were formed in every district. Throughout the next year, these committees remained armed and ready to deal with strangers (they might be abolitionists) and any hint of slave revolt. This extreme defensiveness was not a good portent for the election year of 1860. Looking to the presidential race, Senator Robert Toombs of Georgia warned that the South would "never permit this Federal government to pass into the traitorous hands of the Black Republican party."

Talk of secession as the only possible response to the northern "insults" of the 1850s—the armed protests against the Fugitive Slave Law, the rejection of the Lecompton constitution, and now the support for John Brown's raid—was common throughout the South. Although the majority of Southerners probably rejected secession, the political passions of the election year fostered secessionist thinking.

THE SOUTH SECEDES

By 1860, sectional differences had caused one national party, the Whigs, to collapse. The second national party, the Democrats, stood on the brink of dissolution. Not only the politicians but ordinary people in both the North and the South were coming to believe there was no way to avoid what in 1858 William Seward (once a Whig, now a Republican) had called an "irrepressible conflict."

The Election of 1860

The split of the Democratic Party into northern and southern wings that had occurred during President Buchanan's tenure became official at the Democratic nominating conventions in 1860. The party convened first in Charleston, South Carolina, the center of seces-

sionist agitation. It was the worst possible location in which to attempt to reach unity. Although Stephen Douglas had the support of the plurality of delegates, he did not have the two-thirds majority necessary for nomination. As the price of their support, Southerners insisted that Douglas support a federal slave code—a guarantee that slavery would be protected in the territories. Douglas could not agree without violating his own belief in popular sovereignty and losing his northern support. After ten days, fifty-nine ballots, and two southern walkouts, the convention ended where it had begun: deadlocked. Northern supporters of Douglas were angry and bitter: "I never heard Abolitionists talk more uncharitably and rancorously of the people of the South than the Douglas men," one reporter wrote. "They say they do not care...where the South goes."

In June, the Democrats met again in Baltimore. The Douglasites, recognizing the need for a united party, were eager to compromise wherever they could, but most southern Democrats were not. More than a third of the delegates bolted. Later, holding a convention of their own, they nominated Buchanan's vice president John C. Breckinridge of Kentucky. The remaining two-thirds of the Democrats nominated Douglas, but everyone knew that a Republican victory was inevitable. To make matters worse, some southern Whigs joined with some border-state nativists to form the Constitutional Union Party, which nominated John Bell of Tennessee.

Republican strategy was built on the lessons of the 1856 "victorious defeat." The Republicans planned to carry all the states Frémont had won, plus Pennsylvania, Illinois, and Indiana. The two leading Republican contenders were Senator William H. Seward of New York and Abraham Lincoln of Illinois. Seward, the party's best-known figure, had enemies among party moderates, who thought he was too radical, and among nativists with whom he had clashed in the New York Whig Party. Lincoln, on the other hand, appeared new, impressive, more moderate than Seward, and certain to carry Illinois. Lincoln won the nomination on the third ballot.

The election of 1860 presented voters with one of the clearest choices in American history. On the key issue of slavery, Breckinridge supported its extension to the territories; Lincoln stood firmly for its exclusion. Douglas attempted to hold the middle ground with his principle of popular sovereignty; Bell vaguely favored compromise as well. The Republicans offered other platform planks designed to appeal to northern voters: a homestead act (free western lands), support for a transcontinental railroad, other internal improvements, and a higher tariff. Although they spoke clearly against the extension of slavery, Republicans sought to dispel their radical abolitionist image. The Republican platform condemned John Brown's raid as "the gravest of crimes," repeatedly denied that Republicans favored the social

THE IRREPRESSIBLE CONFLICT

Declaration of Independence	1776	Thomas Jefferson's denunciation of slavery deleted from the final version.
Northwest Ordinance	1787	Slavery prohibited in the Northwest Territory (north of the Ohio River).
Constitution	1787	Slavery unmentioned but acknowledged in Article I, section 2, counting three-fifths of all African Americans, slave and free, in a state's population, and in Article I, section 9, which barred Congress from prohibiting the international slave trade for twenty years.
Louisiana Purchase	1803	Louisiana admitted as a slave state in 1812; no decision about the rest of Louisiana Purchase.
Missouri Compromise	1820	Missouri admitted as a slave state, but slavery prohibited in Louisiana Purchase north of 36°30'.
Wilmot Proviso	1846	Proposal to prohibit slavery in territory that might be gained in Mexican-American War causes splits in national parties.
Compromise of 1850	1850	California admitted as free state; Texas (already admitted, 1845) is a slave state, the rest of Mexican Cession to be decided by popular sovereignty. Ends the slave trade in the District of Columbia but a stronger Fugitive Slave Law, leading to a number of violent recaptures, arouses northern antislavery opinion.
Kansas-Nebraska Act	1854	At the urging of Stephen A. Douglas, Congress opens Kansas and Nebraska Territories for settlement under popular sovereignty. Open warfare between proslavery and antislavery factions breaks out in Kansas.
Lecompton Constitution	1857	President James Buchanan's decision to admit Kansas to the Union with a proslavery constitution is defeated in Congress.
Dred Scott Decision	1857	The Supreme Court's denial of Dred Scott's case for freedom is welcomed in the South, condemned in the North.
John Brown's Raid and Execution	1859	Northern support for John Brown shocks the South.
Democratic Party Nominating Conventions	1860	The Democrats are unable to agree on a candidate; two candidates, one northern (Stephen A. Douglas) and one southern (John C. Breckinridge) split the party and the vote, thus allowing Republican Abraham Lincoln to win.

equality of black people, and strenuously affirmed that they sought to preserve the Union. In reality, Republicans simply did not believe the South would secede if Lincoln won. In this the Republicans were not alone; few Northerners believed southern threats—Southerners had threatened too many times before.

Breckinridge insisted that he and his supporters were loyal to the Union—as long as their needs

concerning slavery were met. The only candidate who spoke urgently and openly about the impending threat of secession was Douglas. Breaking with convention, Douglas campaigned personally, in both the North and, bravely, in the hostile South, warning of the danger of dissolution and presenting himself as the only truly national candidate. Realizing his own chances for election were slight, he told his private

This Republican Party poster for the election of 1860 combines the party's major themes: free land, free soil, opposition to "the Slave Power" (the slogan "Free Speech"), and higher tariffs. But above all was the message, "THE UNION MUST AND SHALL BE PRESERVED."

secretary, "Mr. Lincoln is the next President. We must try to save the Union. I will go South."

In accordance with tradition, Lincoln did not campaign for himself, but many other Republicans spoke for him. In an estimated 50,000 campaign speeches they built the image of "Honest Abe," the candidate who really had been born in a log cabin. The Republicans made a special effort, headed by Carl Schurz, to attract the German immigrant vote. They were successful with German Protestants but less so with Catholics, who were put off by the Republicans' lingering reputation for nativism. The general mood among the northern electorate was one of excitement and optimism. The Republicans were almost certain to win and to bring, because of their uncompromising opposition to the expansion of slavery, an end to the long sectional crisis. "I will vote the Republican ticket next Tuesday," wrote New York businessman and former Whig George Templeton Strong. "The only alternative is everlasting submission to the South." The Republicans did not campaign in the South; Breckinridge did not campaign in the North. Each side was therefore free to believe the worst about the other. All parties, North and South, campaigned with oratory, parades and rallies, free food and drink. Even in the face of looming crisis, this presidential campaign was the best entertainment of the day.

In spite of Breckinridge's protestations of loyalty to the Union, the mood in the Deep South was close to mass hysteria. Rumors of slave revolts—in Texas,

Alabama, and South Carolina— swept the region, and vigilance committees sprang up to counter the supposed threat. Responding to the rumors, Alabaman Sarah R. Espy wrote in her diary, "The country is getting in a deplorable state owing to the depredations committed by the Abolitionist[s] especially in Texas; and the safety of the country depend[s] on who is elected to the presidency." Apparently, southern voters talked of little else, as another Alabaman, Benjamin F. Riley, recalled: "Little else was done this year, than discuss politics. Vast crowds would daily assemble at the places of popular resort, to canvass the questions at issue. Stump speaking was a daily occurrence. Men were swayed more by passion than by calm judgment."

In the South Carolina up-country, the question of secession dominated races for the state legislature. Candidates such as A. S. Wallace of York, who advocated "patriotic forbearance" if Lincoln won, were soundly defeated. The very passion and excitement of the election campaign moved Southerners toward extremism. Even the weather—the worst drought and heat wave the South had known for years—contributed to the tension.

The election of 1860 produced the second highest voter turnout in U.S. history (81.2 percent, topped only by 81.8 percent in 1876). The election turned out to be two regional contests: Breckinridge versus Bell in the South, Lincoln versus Douglas in the North. Breckinridge carried eleven slave states with 18 percent of the popular vote; Bell carried Virginia, Tennessee, and Kentucky with 13 percent of the popular vote. Lincoln won all eighteen of the free states (he split New Jersey with Douglas) and almost 40 percent of the popular vote. Douglas carried only Missouri, but gained nearly 30 percent of the popular vote. Lincoln's electoral vote total was overwhelming: 180 to a combined 123 for the other three candidates. But although Lincoln had won 54 percent of the vote in the northern states, his name had not even appeared on the ballot in ten southern states. The true winner of the 1860 election was sectionalism.

The South Leaves the Union

Charles Francis Adams, son and grandson of presidents, wrote in his diary on the day Lincoln was elected, "The great revolution has actually taken

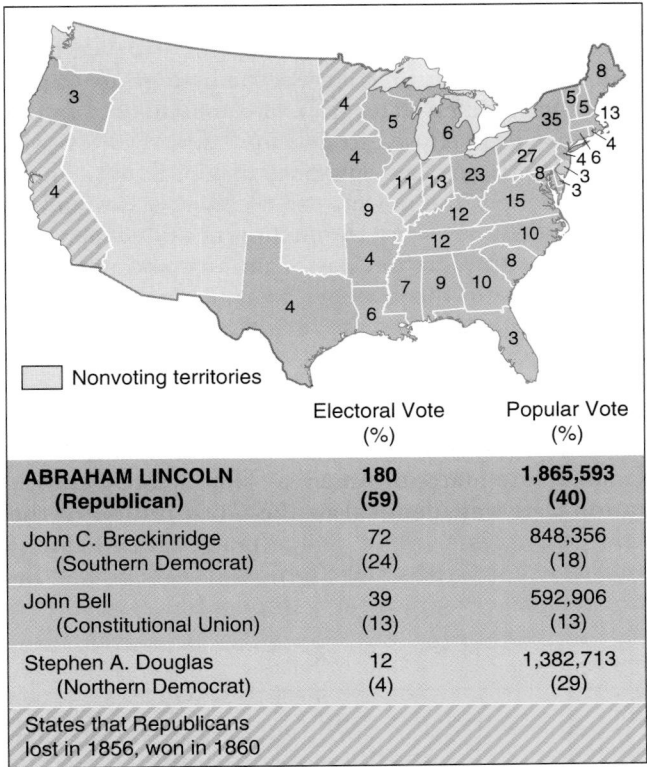

	Electoral Vote (%)	Popular Vote (%)
ABRAHAM LINCOLN (Republican)	**180 (59)**	**1,865,593 (40)**
John C. Breckinridge (Southern Democrat)	72 (24)	848,356 (18)
John Bell (Constitutional Union)	39 (13)	592,906 (13)
Stephen A. Douglas (Northern Democrat)	12 (4)	1,382,713 (29)

☐ Nonvoting territories

▨ States that Republicans lost in 1856, won in 1860

The Election of 1860 *The election of 1860 was a sectional election. Lincoln won no votes in the South, Breckinridge none in the North. The contest in the North was between Lincoln and Douglas, and although Lincoln swept the electoral vote, Douglas's popular vote was uncomfortably close. The large number of northern Democratic voters opposed to Lincoln was a source of political trouble for him during the Civil War.*

place....The country has once and for all thrown off the domination of the Slaveholders." That was precisely what the South feared.

The results of the election shocked Southerners. They were humiliated and frightened by the prospect of becoming a permanent minority in a political system dominated by a party pledged to the elimination of slavery. In southern eyes the Republican triumph meant they would become unequal partners in the federal enterprise, their way of life (the slave system) existing on borrowed time. As a Georgia newspaper said ten days after Lincoln's election, "African slavery, though panoplied by the Federal Constitution, is doomed to a war of extermination. All the powers of a Government which has so long sheltered it will be turned to its destruction. The only hope for its preservation, therefore, is out of the Union." And Mary Boykin Chesnut, member of a well-connected South Carolina family, confided to her diary, "The die is cast—no more vain regrets—sad forebodings are useless. The stake is life or death."

The governors of South Carolina, Alabama, and Mississippi, each of whom had committed his state to

secession if Lincoln were elected, immediately issued calls for special state conventions. At the same time, calls went out to southern communities to form vigilance committees and volunteer militia companies. A visiting Northerner, Sereno Watson, wrote to his brother in amazement: "This people is apparently gone crazy. I do not know how to account for it & have no idea what might be the end of it. Union men, Douglas men, Breckinridge men are alike in their loud denunciation of submission to Lincoln's administration. There are of course those who think differently but they scarcely dare or are suffered to open their mouths." In the face of this frenzy, cooperationists (the term used for those opposed to immediate secession) were either intimidated into silence or simply left behind by the speed of events.

On December 20, 1860, a state convention in South Carolina, accompanied by all the hoopla and excitement of bands, fireworks displays, and huge rallies, voted unanimously to secede from the Union. James Buchanan, the lame-duck president (Lincoln would not be inaugurated until March), did nothing. In the weeks that followed, conventions in six other southern states (Mississippi, Florida, Alabama, Georgia, Louisiana, and Texas) followed suit, with the support, on average, of 80 percent of their delegates. Although there was genuine division of opinion in the South (especially in Georgia and Alabama, along customary up-country—low-country lines) none of the Deep South states held anywhere near the number of Unionists that Republicans had hoped. Throughout the South, secession occurred because Southerners no longer believed they had a choice. "Secession is a desperate remedy," acknowledged South Carolina's David Harris, "but of the two evils I do think it is the lesser."

In every state that seceded, the joyous scenes of South Carolina were repeated as the decisiveness of action replaced the long years of anxiety and tension. People danced in the streets, most believing the North had no choice but to accept secession peacefully. They ignored the fact that eight other slave states (Delaware, Maryland, Kentucky, Missouri, Virginia, North Carolina, Tennessee, and Arkansas) had not acted—though the latter four states would secede after war broke out. Just as Republicans had miscalculated in thinking southern threats a mere bluff, so secessionists now miscalculated in believing they would be able to leave the Union in peace.

The North's Political Options

What should the North do? Buchanan continued to do nothing. The decision thus rested with Abraham Lincoln, even before he officially became president. One possibility was compromise, and many proposals were suggested, ranging from full adoption of the Breckinridge campaign platform to reinstatement of the Missouri Compromise line. Lincoln cautiously refused them all, making it clear that he would not compromise on the extension of slavery, which was the South's key demand. He hoped, by appearing firm but moderate, to discourage additional southern states from seceding while giving pro-Union Southerners time to organize. He succeeded in his first aim, but not in the second. Lincoln and most of the Republican Party had seriously overestimated the strength of pro-Union sentiment in the South.

A second possibility, suggested by Horace Greeley of the *New York Tribune*, was to let the seven seceding states "go in peace." This is what many secessionists expected, but too many Northerners—including Lincoln himself—believed in the Union for this to happen. As Lincoln said, what was at stake was "the necessity of proving that popular government is not an absurdity. We must settle this question now, whether in a free government the minority have the right to break up the government whenever they choose." At stake was all the accumulated American pride in the federal government as a model for democracies the world over.

The third possibility was force, and this was the crux of the dilemma. Although he believed their action was wrong, Lincoln was loath to go to war to force the seceding states back into the Union. On the other hand, he refused to give up federal powers over military forts and customs posts in the South. These were precisely the powers the seceding states had to command if they were to function as an independent nation. A confrontation was bound to come. Abraham Lincoln, not for the last time, was prepared to wait for the other side to strike the first blow.

Establishment of the Confederacy

In February, delegates from the seven seceding states met in Montgomery, Alabama, and created the Confederate States of America. They wrote a constitution that was identical to the Constitution of the United States, with a few crucial exceptions: it strongly supported states' rights and made the abolition of slavery practically impossible. These two

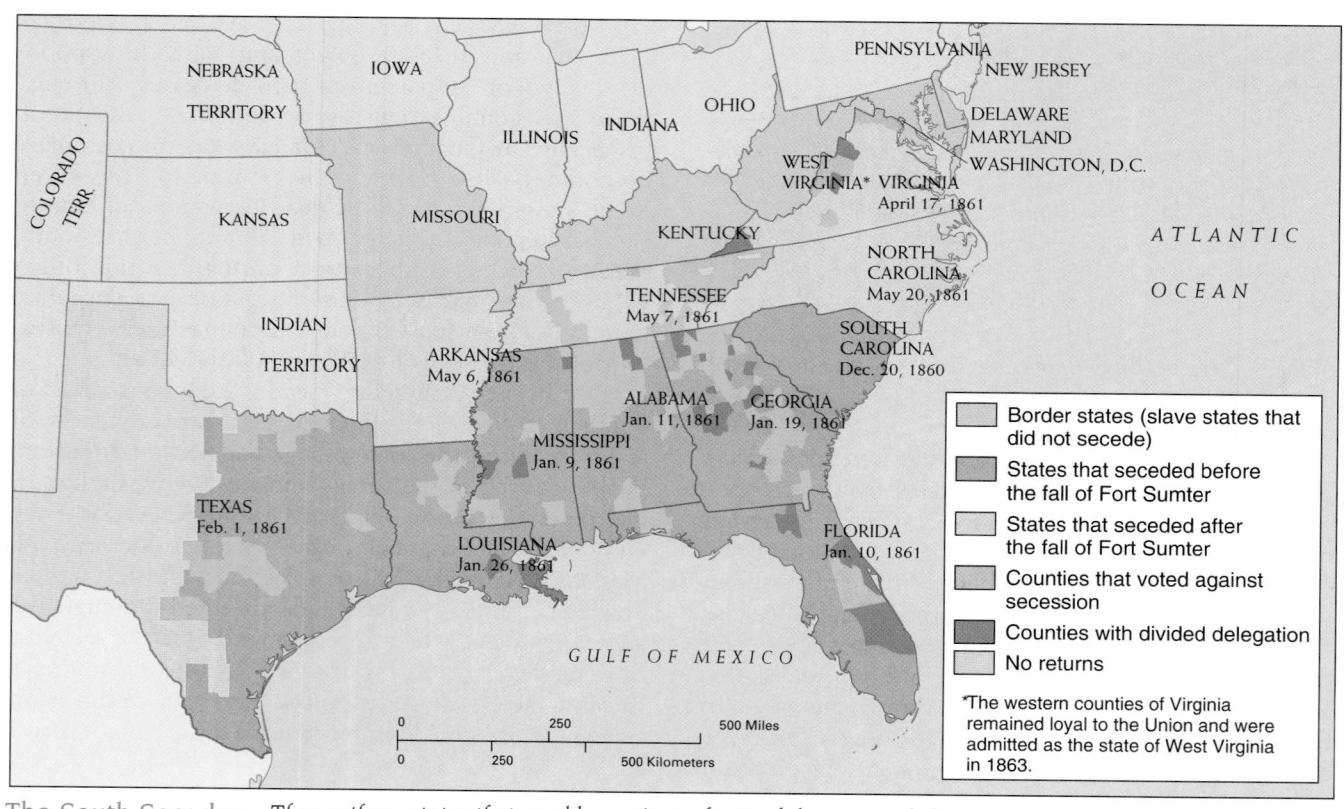

The South Secedes   *The southern states that would constitute the Confederacy seceded in two stages. The states of the Lower South seceded before Lincoln took office. Arkansas and three states of the Upper South—Virginia, North Carolina, and Tennessee—waited until after the South fired on Fort Sumter. And four border slave states—Delaware, Maryland, Kentucky and Missouri—chose not to secede. Every southern state (except South Carolina) was divided on the issue of secession, generally along up-country—low-country lines. In Virginia, this division was so extreme that West Virginia split off to become a separate nonslave state and was admitted to the Union in 1863.*

clauses did much to define the Confederate enterprise. It was difficult to avoid the conclusion that the structure of the new Confederacy had been decided by the southern dependence on slave labor. L. W. Spratt of South Carolina confessed as much in 1859: "We stand committed to the South, but we stand more vitally committed to the cause of slavery. It is, indeed, to be doubted whether the South [has] any cause apart from the institution which affects her." The South's entire defense of slavery was built on a commitment to individualism and decentralization: the rights of the slave owner over his slaves; the right of freedom claimed by all white men; and the rights of individual states versus the federal government. The military defense of the South, however, would require a strong central government. This was to be the South's basic dilemma throughout the Civil War.

The Montgomery convention passed over the fire-eaters—the men who had been the first to urge secession—and chose Jefferson Davis of Mississippi as president and Alexander Stephens of Georgia as vice president of the new nation. Both men were known as moderates. Davis, a slave owner who had been a general in the Mexican-American War and secretary of war in the Pierce administration, who was currently a senator from Mississippi, had expressed his own uncertainties by retaining his Senate seat for two weeks after Mississippi seceded. Stephens, a former leader in the Whig party, had been a cooperationist delegate to Georgia's convention, where he urged that secession not be undertaken hastily.

The choice of moderates was deliberate, for the strategy of the new Confederate state was to argue that secession was a normal, responsible, and expectable course of action, and nothing for the North to get upset about. This was the theme that President Jefferson Davis of the Confederate States of America struck in his Inaugural Address, delivered to a crowd of 10,000 from the steps of the State Capitol at Montgomery, Alabama on February 18, 1861. "We have changed the constituent parts," Davis said, "but not the system of our Government." Secession was a legal and peaceful step that, Davis said, quoting from the Declaration of Independence, "illustrates the American idea that governments rest on the consent of the governed...and that it is the right of the people to alter or abolish them at will whenever they become destructive of the ends for which they were established." After insisting that "a just perception of mutual interest [should] permit us peaceably to pursue our separate political [course]," Davis concluded, "Obstacles may retard, but they cannot long prevent, the progress of a movement sanctified by its justice and sustained by a virtuous

Abraham Lincoln's inauguration on March 4, 1861, shown here in Leslie's Illustrated Newspaper, *symbolized the state of the nation. As he took the oath to become president of a divided country, Lincoln stood before a Capitol building with a half-finished dome and was guarded by soldiers who feared a Confederate attack. Politicians had long been concerned about the dangers of sectionalism in American life. But most ordinary people had taken for granted the federal Union of states—and the ability of slave and nonslave states to coexist.*

people." This impressive inaugural prompted a deeply moved correspondent for the *New York Herald* to report, "God does not permit evil to be done with such earnest solemnity, such all-pervading trust in His Providence, as was exhibited by the whole people on that day."

Lincoln's Inauguration

The country as a whole waited to see what Abraham Lincoln would do, which at first appeared to be very little. In Springfield, Lincoln refused to issue public statements before his inaugural (although he sent many private messages to Congress and to key military officers), for fear of making a delicate situation worse. Similarly, during a twelve-day whistle-stopping rail-

CHRONOLOGY

1820	Missouri Compromise
1828–32	Nullification Crisis
1846	Wilmot Proviso
1848	Treaty of Guadalupe Hidalgo ends Mexican-American War Zachary Taylor elected president Free-Soil Party formed
1849	California and Utah seek admission to the Union as free states
1850	Compromise of 1850 California admitted as a free state American (Know-Nothing) Party formed Zachary Taylor dies, Millard Fillmore becomes president
1851	North reacts to Fugitive Slave Law Harriet Beecher Stowe's *Uncle Tom's Cabin* published
1852	Franklin Pierce elected president
1854	Ostend Manifesto Kansas-Nebraska Act Treaties with Indians in northern part of Indian Territory renegotiated Republican Party formed as Whig Party dissolves
1855	William Walker leads first filibustering expedition to Nicaragua
1856	Burning and looting of Lawrence, Kansas John Brown leads Pottawatomie massacre Attack on Senator Charles Sumner James Buchanan elected president
1857	Dred Scott decision President Buchanan accepts proslavery Lecompton constitution in Kansas Panic of 1857
1858	Congress rejects Lecompton constitution Lincoln-Douglas debates
1859	John Brown's raid on Harpers Ferry
1860	Four parties run presidential candidates Abraham Lincoln elected president South Carolina secedes from Union
1861	Six other Deep South states secede Confederate States of America formed Lincoln takes office

road trip east from Springfield, he was careful to say nothing controversial. Eastern intellectuals, already suspicious of a mere "prairie lawyer," were not impressed. Finally, hard evidence of an assassination plot forced Lincoln to abandon his whistle-stops at Harrisburg and, protected by Pinkerton detectives, to travel incognito into Washington "like a thief in the night," as he complained. These signs of moderation and caution did not appeal to an American public with a penchant for electing military heroes. Americans wanted leadership and action.

Lincoln continued, however, to offer nonbelligerent firmness and moderation. And at the end of his Inaugural Address on March 4, 1861, as he stood ringed by federal troops called out in case of a Confederate attack, the new president offered unexpected eloquence:

I am loath to close. We are not enemies, but friends. We must not be enemies. Though passion may have strained, it must not break our bonds of affection. The mystic chords of memory, stretching from every battlefield, and patriot grave, to every living heart and hearthstone, all over this broad land, will yet swell the chorus of the Union, when again touched, as surely they will be, by the better angels of our nature.

CONCLUSION

Americans had much to boast about in 1850. Their nation was vastly larger, richer, and more powerful than it had been in 1800. But the issue of slavery was slowly dividing the North and the South, two communities with similar origins and many common bonds. The following decade was marked by frantic efforts at political compromise, beginning with the Compromise of 1850, continuing with the Kansas-Nebraska Act of 1854, and culminating in the Supreme Court's 1859 decision in the Dred Scott case. Increasingly, the ordinary people of the two regions demanded resolution of the crisis. The two great parties of the Second American Party System, the Democrats and the Whigs, unable to find a solution, were destroyed. Two new sectional parties—the Republican Party and a southern party devoted to the defense of slavery—fought the 1860 election, but Southerners refused to accept the national verdict. Politics had failed: the issue of slavery was irreconcilable. The only remaining recourse was war. But although Americans were divided, they were still one people. That made the war, when it came, all the more terrible.

REVIEW QUESTIONS

1. What aspects of the remarkable economic development of the United States in the first half of the nineteenth century contributed to the sectional crisis of the 1850s?

2. How might the violent efforts by abolitionists to free escaped slaves who had been recaptured and the federal armed enforcement of the Fugitive Slave Act have been viewed differently by merchants (the so-called Cotton Whigs), Irish immigrants, and abolitionists?

3. Consider the course of events in "Bloody Kansas" from Douglas's Kansas-Nebraska Act to the Congressional rejection of the Lecompton constitution. Were these events the inevitable result of the political impasse in Washington, or could other decisions have been taken that would have changed the outcome?

4. The nativism of the 1850s that surfaced so strongly in the Know-Nothing Party was eclipsed by the crisis over slavery. But nativist sentiment has been a recurring theme in American politics. Discuss why it was strong in the 1850s and why it might have emerged periodically since then.

5. Evaluate the character and actions of John Brown. Was he the hero proclaimed by northern supporters or the terrorist condemned by the South?

6. Imagine that you lived in Illinois, home state to both Douglas and Lincoln, in 1860. How would you have voted in the presidential election, and why?

RECOMMENDED READING

William L. Barney, *The Secessionist Impulse: Alabama and Mississippi in 1860* (1974). Covers the election of 1860 and the subsequent conventions that led to secession.

Don E. Fehrenbacher, *The Dred Scott Case: Its Significance in American Law and Politics* (1978). A major study by the leading historian on this controversial decision.

Eric Foner, *Free Soil, Free Labor, Free Men: The Ideology of the Republican Party before the Civil War* (1970). A landmark effort that was among the first studies to focus on free labor ideology of the North and its importance in the political disputes of the 1850s.

Lacey K. Ford Jr., *Origins of Southern Radicalism: The South Carolina Upcountry, 1800–1860* (1988). One of a number of recent studies of the attitudes of upcountry farmers, who in South Carolina supported secession wholeheartedly.

Homan Hamilton, *Prologue to Conflict: The Crisis and Compromise of 1850* (1964). The standard source on the Compromise of 1850.

Bruce Levine, *Half Slave and Half Free: The Roots of the Civil War* (1992). Good survey of the contrasting attitudes of North and South.

Alice Nichols, *Bleeding Kansas* (1954). The standard source on the battles over Kansas.

David M. Potter, *The Impending Crisis, 1848-1861* (1976). A comprehensive account of the politics leading up to the Civil War.

Anne C. Rose, *Voices of the Marketplace: American Thought and Culture, 1830–1860* (1995). A new study that considers the effects of the concepts of Christianity, democracy, and capitalism on American cultural life.

Kenneth M. Stampp, *America in 1857: A Nation on the Brink* (1990). A study of the "crucial" year by a leading southern historian.

Albert J. Von Frank, *The Trials of Anthony Burns: Freedom and Slavery in Emerson's Boston* (1998). An eloquent study of the trial and the links between transcendentalist and abolitionist opinion.

ADDITIONAL BIBLIOGRAPHY

The Controversy over Slavery

Richard H. Abbott, *Cotton and Capital: Boston Businessmen and Antislavery Reform, 1854–1868* (1991)

Eugene Berwanger, *The Frontier against Slavery: Western Anti-Negro Prejudice and the Slavery Extension Controversy* (1967)

Stanley W. Campbell, *The Slave Catchers* (1970)

David B. Davis, *The Slave Power Conspiracy and the Paranoid Style* (1969)

W. Ehrlich, *They Have No Rights: Dred Scott's Struggle for Freedom* (1979)

P. Finkelman, *An Imperfect Union: Slavery, Freedom, and Comity* (1981)

C. C. Goen, *Broken Churches, Broken Nation* (1985)

Thomas F. Grossett, *Uncle Tom's Cabin and American Culture* (1985)

Joseph Herring, *The Enduring Indians of Kansas: A Century and a Half of Acculturation* (1990)

J. R. McKivigan, *The War against Proslavery Religion* (1984)

William Lee Miller, *Arguing About Slavery: The Great Battle in the United States Congress* (1996)

H. Craig Miner and William E. Unrau, *The End of Indian Kansas* (1978)

Thomas D. Morris, *Free Men All: The Personal Liberty Laws of the North, 1780–1861* (1974)

Allan Nevins, *The Ordeal of the Union*, vols. 1–2 (1947)

Roy Nichols, *The Disruption of American Democracy* (1948)

Joseph G. Rayback, *Free Soil: The Election of 1848* (1970)

J. Rossbach, *Ambivalent Conspirators: John Brown, the Secret Six and a Theory of Black Political Violence* (1982)

Thomas P. Slaughter, *Bloody Dawn: The Christiana Riots and Racial Violence in the Antebellum North* (1991)

Kenneth M. Stampp, *The Causes of the Civil War*, rev. ed. (1974)

Joanna L. Stratton, *Pioneer Women: Voices from the Kansas Frontier* (1981)

Gerald W. Wolff, *The Kansas-Nebraska Bill: Party, Section, and the Coming of the Civil War* (1977)

Bertram Wyatt-Brown, *Yankee Saints and Southern Sinners* (1985)

The Crisis of the National Party System

Thomas B. Alexander, *Sectional Stress and Party Strength* (1967)

Tyler Anbinder, *Nativism and Slavery: The Northern Know-Nothings and the Politics of the 1850s* (1992)

J. H. Baker, *Affairs of Party: The Political Culture of Northern Democrats in the Mid-Nineteenth Century* (1983)

F. J. Blue, *The Free Soilers: Third Party Politics* (1973)

G. B. Forgie, *Patricide in the House Divided* (1981)

Ronald Formisano, *The Birth of Mass Political Parties: Michigan, 1827–1861* (1971)

William E. Gienapp, *The Origins of the Republican Party, 1852–1856* (1987)

Michael Holt, *Forging a Majority: The Formation of the Republican Party in Pittsburgh, 1848–1860* (1969)

———, *The Political Crisis of the 1850's* (1978)

Thelma Jennings, *The Nashville Convention* (1980)

Robert W. Johannsen, *The Lincoln-Douglas Debates* (1965)

Paul Kleppner, *The Third Electoral System, 1853–1892: Parties, Voters, and Political Cultures* (1979)

John Mayfield, *Rehearsal for Republicanism: Free Soil and the Politics of Antislavery* (1980)

Richard Sewell, *Ballots for Freedom: Antislavery Politics in the United States, 1837–1865* (1976)

The South Secedes

William. L. Barney, *The Road to Secession* (1972)

Charles H. Brown, *Agents of Manifest Destiny: The Lives and Times of the Filibusters* (1980)

Steven A. Channing, *Crisis of Fear: Secession in South Carolina* (1970)

William J. Cooper, *The South and the Politics of Slavery* (1978)

Avery O. Craven, *The Growth of Southern Nationalism 1848–1861* (1953)

John Hope Franklin, *A Southern Odyssey: Travelers in the Antebellum North* (1976)

———, *The Militant South 1800–1861* (1956)

William W. Freehling, *The Road to Disunion*, vol. I: *Secessionists at Bay, 1776–1854* (1991)

William H. Goetzmann, *When the Eagle Screamed: The Romantic Horizon in American Diplomacy, 1800–1860* (1966)

Michael P. Johnson, *Toward a Patriarchal Republic: The Secession of Georgia* (1977)

———, *Secession and Conservatism in the Lower South: The Social and Ideological Bases of Secession in Georgia, 1860–1861* (1983)

Michael P. Johnson and James L. Roark, eds., *No Chariot Let Down: Charleston's Free People of Color on the Eve of the Civil War* (1984)

Robert E. May, *The Southern Dream of a Caribbean Empire, 1854–1861* (1973)

John McCardell, *The Idea of a Southern Nation: Southern Nationalists and Southern Nationalism, 1830–1861* (1979)

Rollin G. Osterweis, *Romanticism and Nationalism in the Old South* (1949)

David M. Potter, *The South and the Sectional Conflict* (1968)

Basil Rauch, *American Interest in Cuba* (1948)

William O. Scroggs, *Filibusters and Financiers: The Story of William Walker and His Associates* (1960)

K. M. Stampp, *And the War Came: The North and the Secession Crisis 1860–1861* (1950)

Joe A. Stout, *The Liberators: Filibustering Expeditions into Mexico, 1848–1862, and the Last Thrust of Manifest Destiny* (1973)

Ronald L. Takaki, *A Proslavery Crusade: The Agitation to Reopen the African Slave Trade* (1971)

J. Mills Thornton, *Politics and Power in a Slavery Society* (1978)

Eric H. Walter, *The Fire-Eaters* (1992)

C. Vann Woodward, *American Counterpoint: Slavery and Racism in the North–South Dialogue* (1971)

R. A. Wooster, *The Secession Conventions of the South* (1962)

Biography

K. J. Bauer, *Zachary Taylor: Soldier, Planter, Statesman of the Old Southwest* (1985)

D. H. Donald, *Charles Sumner and the Coming of the Civil War* (1960)

Donald E. Fehrenbacher, *Prelude to Greatness: Lincoln in the 1850's* (1962)

Joan Hedrick, *Harriet Beecher Stowe: A Life* (1994)

Robert W. Johannsen, *Stephen A. Douglas* (1973)

Stephen Oates, *To Purge This Land with Blood: A Biography of John Brown* (1970)

———, *With Malice toward None: A Life of Abraham Lincoln* (1977)

CHAPTER SIXTEEN

THE CIVIL WAR

1861–1865

AMERICAN COMMUNITIES
Mother Bickerdyke Connects Northern Communities to Their Boys at War

In May 1861 the Reverend Edward Beecher interrupted his customary Sunday service at Brick Congregational Church in Galesburg, Illinois, to read a disturbing letter to the congregation. Two months earlier, Galesburg had proudly sent 500 of its young men off to join the Union army. They had not yet been in battle. Yet, the letter reported, an alarming number were dying of diseases caused by inadequate food, medical care, and sanitation at the crowded military camp in Cairo, Illinois. Most army doctors were surgeons, trained to operate and amputate on the battlefield. They were not prepared to treat soldiers sick with dysentery, pneumonia, typhoid, measles—all serious, frequently fatal diseases that could often be cured with careful nursing. The letter writer, appalled by the squalor and misery he saw around him, complained of abuses by the army. The Union army, however, was overwhelmed with the task of readying recruits for battle and had made few provisions for their health when not in combat.

The shocked and grieving members of Beecher's congregation quickly decided to send not only supplies but one of their number to inspect the conditions at the Cairo camp and to take action. In spite of warnings from a veteran of the War of 1812 that army regulations excluded women from encampments, the congregation voted to send their most qualified member, Mary Ann Bickerdyke, a middle-aged widow who made her living as a "botanic physician." This simple gesture of community concern launched the remarkable Civil War career of "the Cyclone in Calico," who defied medical officers and generals alike in her unceasing efforts on behalf of ill, wounded, and convalescent Union soldiers.

"Mother" Bickerdyke, as she was called, let nothing stand in the way of helping her "boys." When she arrived in Cairo, she immediately set to work cleaning the hospital tents and the soldiers themselves and finding and cooking nourishing food for them. Ordered to leave by the hospital director, who resented her interference, she blandly continued her work. When he reported her to the commanding officer, General Benjamin Prentiss, she quickly convinced the general to let her stay. "I talked sense to him," she later said.

From a peacetime point of view, what Mother Bickerdyke was doing was not unusual. Every civilian hospital had a matron who made sure patients were supplied with clean bed linen and bandages and were fed the proper convalescent diet. But in the context of the war—the sheer number of soldiers, the constant need to set up new field hospitals and commandeer scarce food for an army on the move—it was unusual indeed and required an unusual person. A plain spoken, hardworking woman, totally unfazed by rank or tender masculine egos, Mother Bickerdyke single-mindedly devoted herself to what she called "the Lord's work." The ordinary soldiers loved her; wise generals supported her. Once, when an indignant officer's wife complained about Bickerdyke's rudeness, General William Tecumseh Sherman joked, "You've picked the one person around here who outranks me. If you want to lodge a complaint against her, you'll have to take it to President Lincoln."

By their actions, Mother Bickerdyke and others like her exposed the War Department's inability to meet the needs of the nation's first mass army. And like the Galesburg congregation, other communities all over the North rallied to make up for the department's shortcomings with supplies and assistance. The efforts of women on the local level—for example, to make clothing for men from their communities who had gone off to the war—quickly took on national dimensions. The Women's Central Association of Relief (WCAR), whose organizers were mostly reformers experienced in the abolitionist, temperance, and education movements, eventually had 7,000 chapters throughout the North. Its volunteers raised funds, made and collected a variety of items—food, clothes, medicine, bandages, and more than 250,000 quilts and comforters—and sent them to army camps and hospitals. Volunteers also provided meals, housing, and transportation to soldiers on furlough. All told, association chapters supplied an estimated $15 million worth of goods to the Union troops.

In June 1861, responding to requests by officials of the WCAR for formal recognition of the organization, President Abraham Lincoln created the United States Sanitary Commission and gave it the power to investigate and advise the Medical Bureau. Henry Bellows, a Unitarian clergyman, became president of the organization, and Frederick Law Olmsted, the author of influential books about the slaveholding South and later the designer of New York's Central Park, was named its executive secretary. The commission's more than 500 "sanitary inspectors" (usually men) instructed soldiers in such matters as water supply, placement of latrines, and safe cooking.

Although at first she worked independently and remained suspicious of all organizations (and even of many other relief workers), in 1862 Mother Bickerdyke was persuaded to become an official agent of "the Sanitary," as it was known. The advantage to her was access to the commission's warehouses and the ability to order from them precisely what she needed. The advantage to the Sanitary was that Mother Bickerdyke was an unequaled fundraiser. In speaking tours throughout Illinois, she touched her female listeners with moving stories of wounded boys whom she had cared for as if they were her own sons. Her words to men were more forceful. It was a man's business to fight, she said. If he was too old or ill to fight with a gun, he should fight with his dollars. With the help of Bickerdyke's blunt appeals, the Sanitary raised $50 million for the Union war effort.

As the Civil War continued, Mother Bickerdyke became a key figure in the medical support for General Ulysses S. Grant's campaigns along the Mississippi River. She was with the army at Shiloh, and as Grant slowly fought his way to Vicksburg she set up convalescent hospitals in Memphis. Grant authorized her to commandeer any army wagons she needed to transport supplies. Between fifty and seventy "contrabands" (escaped former slaves) worked on her laundry crew. On the civilian side, the Sanitary Commission authorized her to draw on its supply depots in Memphis, Cairo, Chicago, and elsewhere. She was thus in a practical sense a vital "middlewoman" between the home front and the battlefield—and in a symbolic and emotional sense too, as a stand-in for all mothers who had sent their sons to war.

The Civil War was a community tragedy, ripping apart the nation's political fabric and producing more casualties than any other war in the nation's history. Yet in another sense, it was a community triumph. Local communities directly supported and sustained their soldiers on a massive scale in unprecedented ways. As national unity failed, the strength of local communities, symbolized by Mother Bickerdyke, endured.

Memphis

KEY TOPICS

- **The social and political changes created by the unprecedented nature and scale of the Civil War**

- **The major military campaigns of the war**

- **The central importance of the end of slavery to the war efforts of North and South**

COMMUNITIES MOBILIZE FOR WAR

A neutral observer in March 1861 might have seen ominous similarities. Two nations—the United States of America (shorn of seven states in the Deep South) and the Confederate States of America—each blamed the other for the breakup of the Union. Two new presidents—Abraham Lincoln and Jefferson Davis—each faced the challenging task of building and maintaining national unity. Two regions—North and South—scorned each other and boasted of their own superiority. But the most basic similarity was not yet apparent: both sides were unprepared for the ordeal that lay ahead.

Fort Sumter: The War Begins

In their Inaugural Addresses, both Abraham Lincoln and Jefferson Davis prayed for peace but positioned themselves for war. Careful listeners to both addresses realized that the two men were on a collision course. Jefferson Davis claimed that the Confederacy would be forced to "appeal to arms...if...the integrity of our territory and jurisdiction [is] assailed." Lincoln said, "The power confided to me will be used to hold, occupy, and possess the property and places belonging to the government." One of those places, Fort Sumter, in South Carolina, was claimed by both sides.

Fort Sumter, a major federal military installation, sat on a granite island at the entrance to Charleston harbor. So long as it remained in Union hands, Charleston, the center of secessionist sentiment, would be immobilized. Realizing its military and symbolic importance, South Carolinians had begun demanding that the fort be turned over to them even before they seceded. Thus it was hardly surprising that Fort Sumter would provide President Lincoln with his first crisis.

With the fort dangerously low on supplies, Lincoln had to decide whether to abandon it or risk the fight that might ensue if he ordered it resupplied. In a process he would follow on many other occasions, Lincoln first hesitated, canvassed opinions of all kinds, and then took cautious and careful action (even as some of his cabinet urged more decisive steps). On April 6, Lincoln notified the governor of South Carolina that he was sending a relief force to the fort carrying only food and no military supplies. Now the decision rested with Jefferson Davis. Like Lincoln, Davis faced a divided cabinet; unlike Lincoln, however, he opted for decisive action. On April 10 he ordered General P. G. T. Beauregard to demand the surrender of Fort Sumter and to attack it if the garrison did not comply. On April 12, as Lincoln's relief force neared Charleston harbor, Beauregard opened fire. Two days later, the defenders surrendered and the Confederate Stars and Bars rose over Fort Sumter. The people of Charleston celebrated wildly. "I did not know," wrote Mary Boykin Chesnut in her diary, "that one could live such days of excitement."

The Call to Arms

Even before the attack on Fort Sumter, the Confederate Congress had authorized a volunteer army of 100,000 men to serve for twelve months. There was no difficulty finding volunteers. Men flocked to enlist, and their communities sent them off in ceremonies featuring bands, bonfires, and belligerent oratory. Most of that oratory, like Jefferson Davis's Inaugural Address (see Chapter 15), evoked the Revolutionary War and the right of free people to resist tyranny. In many places, the response to the hostilities at Fort Sumter was even more visceral. The first war circular, printed in Hickman County, Tennessee, trumpeted, "To Arms! Our Southern soil must be defended. We must not stop to ask who brought about war, who is at fault, but let us go and do battle...and then settle the question of who is to blame." Exhilarated by their own rapid mobilization, most Southerners believed that Unionists were cowards who would not be able to face up to southern bravery. "Just throw three or four shells among those blue-bellied Yankees," one North Carolinian boasted, "and they'll scatter like sheep." The cry of "On to Washington!" was raised throughout the South, and orators confidently predicted that the city would be captured and the war concluded within sixty days. For the early recruits, war was a patriotic adventure.

The "thunderclap of Sumter" startled the North into an angry response. The apathy and uncertainty that had prevailed since Lincoln's election disappeared, to be replaced by strong feelings of patriotism. On April 15, Lincoln issued a proclamation calling for 75,000 state militiamen to serve in the federal army for ninety days. Enlistment offices were swamped with so many enthusiastic volunteers that many men were sent home. Free African Americans, among the most eager to serve, were turned away: this was not yet a war for or by black people.

Public outpourings of patriotism were common. New Yorker George Templeton Strong recorded one example on April 18: "Went to the [City] Hall. The [Sixth] Massachusetts Regiment, which arrived here last night, was marching down on its way to Washington. Immense crowd; immense cheering. My eyes filled with tears, and I was half choked in sympathy with the contagious excitement. God be praised for the unity of feeling here! It is beyond, very far beyond, anything I hoped for."

The mobilization in Chester, Pennsylvania, was typical of the northern response to the outbreak of war. A patriotic rally was held at which a company of volunteers (the first of many from the region) calling themselves the "Union Blues" were mustered into the Ninth Regiment of Pennsylvania Volunteers amid cheers and band music. As they marched off to Washington (the gathering place for the Union army), companies of home guards were organized by the men who remained behind. Within a month, the women of Chester had organized a countywide system of war relief that sent a stream of clothing, blankets, bandages, and other supplies to the local troops and provided assistance to their families at home. Such relief organizations, some formally organized, some informal, emerged in every community, North and South, that sent soldiers off to the Civil War. These organizations not only played a vital role in supplying the troops but maintained the human, local link on which so many soldiers depended. In this sense, every American community accompanied its young men to war. And every American community stood to suffer terrible losses when its young men went into battle.

This patriotic painting shows the departure of New York's Seventh Regiment for Washington in mid-April of 1861. Stirring scenes like this occurred across the nation following "the thunderclap of Sumter" as communities mobilized for war.

George Hayward (1834–1872). *Departure of the Seventh Regiment*, N.Y.S.M. April 19, 1861. Pencil, watercolor, and gouache. M. and M. Karolik Collection. Courtesy, Museum of Fine Arts, Boston.

The Border States

The first secession, between December 20, 1860, and February 1, 1861, had taken seven Deep South states out of the Union. Now, in April, the firing on Fort Sumter and Lincoln's call for state militias forced the other southern states to take sides. Courted—and pressured—by both North and South, four states of the Upper South (Virginia, Arkansas, Tennessee, and North Carolina) joined the original seven in April and May 1861. Virginia's secession tipped the other three toward the Confederacy. The capital of the Confederacy was now moved to Richmond. This meant that the two capitals—Richmond and Washington—were less than 100 miles apart.

Still undecided was the loyalty of the northernmost tier of slave-owning states: Missouri, Kentucky, Maryland, and Delaware. Each controlled vital strategic assets. Missouri not only bordered the Mississippi River but controlled the routes to the west. Kentucky controlled the Ohio River. The main railroad link with the West ran through Maryland and the hill region of western Virginia (which split from Virginia to become the free state of West Virginia in 1863). Delaware controlled access to Philadelphia. Finally, were Maryland to secede, the nation's capital would be completely surrounded by Confederate territory.

Delaware was loyal to the Union (less than 2 percent of its population were slaves), but Maryland's loyalty was divided, as an ugly incident on April 19 showed. When the Sixth Massachusetts Regiment (the one Strong had cheered in New York) marched through Baltimore, a hostile crowd of 10,000 Southern sympathizers, carrying Confederate flags, pelted the troops with bricks, paving stones, and bullets. Finally, in desperation the troops fired on the crowd, killing twelve people and wounding others. In retaliation, Southern sympathizers burned the railroad bridges to the North and destroyed the telegraph line to Washington, cutting off communication between the capital and the rest of the Union for six days.

Lincoln's response was swift and stern. He stationed Union troops along Maryland's crucial railroads, declared martial law in Baltimore, and arrested the suspected ringleaders of the pro-Confederate mob and held them without trial. In July, he ordered the detention of thirty-two secessionist legislators and many sympathizers. Thus was Maryland's loyalty to the Union ensured.

In detaining the Baltimore agitators, Lincoln suspended the writ of habeas corpus, the constitutional requirement that authorities explain to a court their reasons for arresting someone. Chief Justice Roger B. Taney of the Supreme court ruled that the president had no right to do this, but Lincoln at first ignored him. Later Lincoln argued that the suspension of certain civil rights might be necessary to suppress rebellion. The arrests in Maryland were the first of a number of violations of basic civil rights during the war, all of which the president justified on the basis of national security.

Like Maryland, the loyalties of the other border states were also divided. Missouri was plagued by guerrilla battles (reminiscent of the prewar "Bleeding Kansas") throughout the war. In Kentucky, division took the form of a huge illegal trade with the Confederacy through neighboring Tennessee, to which Lincoln, determined to keep Kentucky in the Union, turned a blind eye. The conflicting loyalties of the border states were often mirrored within families. Kentucky senator John J. Crittenden had two sons who were major generals, one in the Union army and the other in the Confederate army. Such family divisions reached all the way to the White House: three brothers of Kentucky-born Mary Todd Lincoln, the president's wife, died fighting for the Confederacy.

That Delaware, Maryland, Missouri, and Kentucky chose to stay in the Union was a severe blow to the Confederacy. Among them, the four states could have added 45 percent to the white population and military manpower of the Confederacy and 80 percent to its manufacturing capacity. Almost as damaging, the decision of four slave states to stay in the Union punched a huge hole in the Confederate argument that the southern states were forced to secede to protect the right to own slaves.

The Battle of Bull Run

Once sides had been chosen and the initial flush of enthusiasm had passed, the nature of the war, and the mistaken notions about it, soon became clear. The event that shattered the illusions was the first battle of Bull Run, at Manassas Creek in Virginia in July 1861. Confident of a quick victory, a Union army of 35,000 men marched south, crying "On to Richmond!" So lighthearted and unprepared was the Washington community that the troops were accompanied not only by journalists but by a crowd of politicians and sightseers. At first the Union troops held their ground against the 25,000 Confederate troops commanded by General P. G. T. Beauregard (of Fort Sumter fame). But when 2,300 fresh Confederate troops arrived as reinforcements, the untrained northern troops broke ranks in an uncontrolled retreat that swept up the frightened sightseers as well. Soldiers and civilians alike retreated in disarray to Washington. Confederate Mary Boykin Chesnut recorded in her diary, "We might have walked into Washington any day for a week after Manassas, such was the consternation and confusion there." But the Confederates lacked the organization and the strength to follow the retreating Union troops and capture the capital.

Bull Run was sobering—and prophetic. The Civil War was the most lethal military conflict in American history, leaving a legacy of devastation on the battlefield and desolation at home. It claimed the lives of nearly 620,000 soldiers, more than the the First and Second World Wars combined. One out of every four soldiers who fought in the war never returned home.

The Relative Strengths of North and South

Overall, in terms of both population and productive capacity, the Union seemed to have a commanding edge over the Confederacy. The North had two and a half times the South's population (22 million to 9 million, of whom 3.5 million were slaves) and enjoyed an even greater advantage in industrial capacity (nine times that of the South). The North produced almost all of the nation's firearms (97 percent), had 71 percent of its railroad mileage, and produced 94 percent of its cloth and 90 percent of its footwear. The North seemed able to feed, clothe, arm, and transport all the soldiers it chose. These assets were ultimately to prove decisive: by the end of the war the Union had managed to field more than 2 million soldiers to the Confederacy's 800,000.

But in the short term the South had important assets to counter them.

The first was the nature of the struggle. For the South, this was a defensive war in which, as the early volunteers showed, the most basic principle of the defense of home and community united almost all white citizens, regardless of their views about slavery. The North would have to invade the South and then control it against guerrilla opposition to win. The parallels with the Revolutionary War were unmistakable. Most white Southerners were confident that the North, like Great Britain in its attempt to subdue the rebellious colonies, would turn out to be a lumbering giant against whom they could secure their independence.

Second, the military disparity was less extreme than it appeared. Although the North had manpower, its troops were mostly untrained. The professional federal army numbered only 16,000, and most of its experience had been gained in small Indian wars. Moreover, the South, because of its tradition of honor and belligerence (see Chapter 11), appeared to have an advantage in military leadership. More than a quarter of

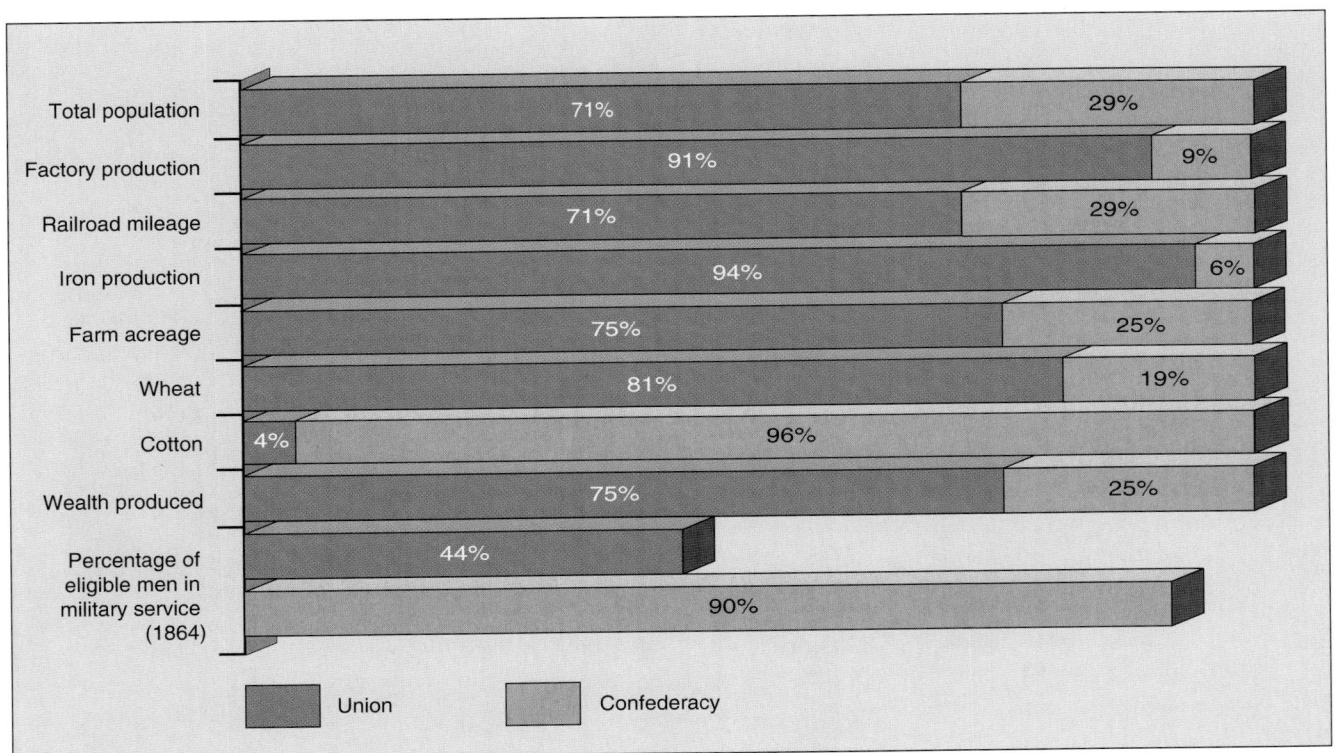

Comparative Resources, North and South, 1861   *By 1865, the North's overwhelming advantage in population, industrial strength, railroad mileage, agricultural productivity, and wealth had proved decisive in assuring victory. But initially these strengths made little difference in a struggle that began as a traditional war of maneuver in which the South held the defensive advantage. Only slowly did the Civil War become a modern war in which all of the resources of society, including the property and lives of civilians, were mobilized for battle.*

Source: *The Times Atlas of World History* (Maplewood, New Jersey: Hammond, 1978).

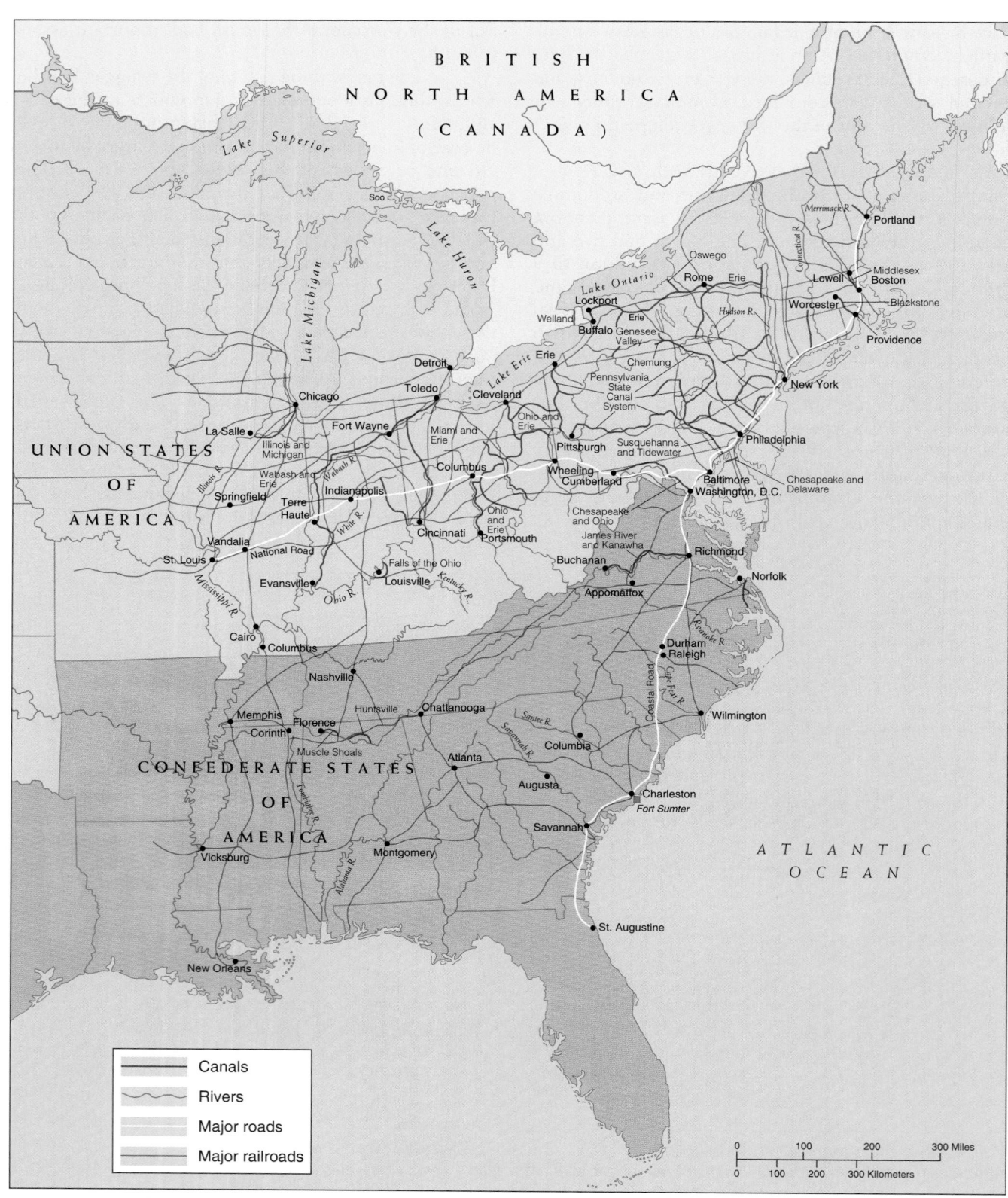

Comparative Transportation Systems, 1860 *Transportation systems were an important index of comparative strength: the North had almost three times the railroad mileage of the South. The relative lack of transportation hurt the Confederacy by hindering its ability to move troops and to distribute military and medical supplies.*

all the regular army officers chose to side with the South. The most notable was Robert E. Lee. Offered command of the Union army by President Lincoln, Lee hesitated but finally decided to follow his native state, Virginia, into the Confederacy, saying, "I have been unable to make up my mind to raise my hand against my native state, my relatives, my children, and my home."

Finally, the North's economic advantages, which were eventually decisive, initially seemed unimportant. The South could feed itself, and many soldiers brought their own weapons, uniforms, horses, and sometimes slaves when they enlisted. It was widely believed that slavery would work to the South's advantage, for slaves could continue to do the vital plantation work while their masters went off to war. But above all, the South had the weapon of cotton. "Cotton is King," James Henry Hammond had announced in 1858, at the height of the cotton boom that made the 1850s the most profitable decade in southern history. Because of the crucial role of southern cotton in industrialization, Hammond had declared, "The slaveholding South is now the controlling power of the world." Southerners were confident that the British and French need for southern cotton would soon bring those countries to recognize the Confederacy as a separate nation.

This aerial view of Washington shows the nation's capital during the Civil War as it underwent an abrupt transition from a small slave-owning community to the busy hub of the Union's war effort. Throughout the Civil War, the unfinished dome of the Capitol Building loomed over the city, its incompleteness symbolizing the divided state of the nation.

THE LINCOLN PRESIDENCY

The Civil War forced the federal government to assume powers unimaginable just a few years before. Abraham Lincoln took as his primary task to lead and unify the nation in his responsibility as commander in chief. He found the challenge almost insurmountable. Fortunately, the nation had found in Lincoln a man with the moral courage and the political skill to chart a course through the many conflicting currents of northern public opinion.

Lincoln as Party Leader and War President

Lincoln's first task as president was to assert control over his own cabinet. Because he had few national contacts outside the Republican Party, Lincoln chose to staff his cabinet with other Republicans, including, most unusually, several who had been his rivals for the presidential nomination. Secretary of State William

Seward, widely regarded as the leader of the Republican Party, at first expected to "manage" Lincoln as he had Zachary Taylor in 1848, but he soon became the president's willing partner. On the other hand, Treasury Secretary Salmon P. Chase, a staunch abolitionist, adamantly opposed concessions to the South and considered Lincoln too conciliatory. Chase, a key member of a group known as the Radical Republicans, remained a vocal and dangerous critic. That the Republican Party was a not-quite-jelled mix of former Whigs, abolitionists, moderate Free-Soilers, and even some prowar Democrats made Lincoln's task as party leader much more difficult than it might otherwise have been.

After the fall of Fort Sumter, military necessity prompted Lincoln to call up the state militias, order a naval blockade of the South, and vastly expand the military budget. Breaking with precedent, he took these actions without congressional sanction because Congress was not in session. Military necessity—the need to hold the border states—likewise prompted other early actions, such as the suspension of habeas corpus and the acceptance of Kentucky's ambiguous neutrality. Over howls of protest from abolitionists, the president also repudiated an unauthorized declaration issued by General John C. Frémont, military commander in Missouri, in August 1861 that would have freed Missouri's slaves, because he feared it would lead to the secession of Kentucky and Maryland.

Although James K. Polk had assumed responsibility for overall American military strategy during the

President Abraham Lincoln visits General George McClellan in 1862 after Antietam. Although as a young congressman Lincoln had objected to President James K. Polk's active participation in Mexican-American War strategy, he found himself taking a major role as commander in chief during the Civil War. His relationship with McClellan was especially difficult, for he could never convince the general to overcome his habitual caution.

Mexican-American War (see Chapter 14), Lincoln was the first president to act as commander in chief in both a practical and a symbolic way. He actively directed military policy, although he sometimes wondered whether he would ever find generals capable of carrying out his orders. Lincoln's involvement in military strategy sprang from his realization that a civil war presented problems different from those of a foreign war of conquest. Lincoln wanted above all to persuade the South to rejoin the Union, and his every military move was dictated by the hope of eventual reconciliation—hence his cautiousness, and his acute sense of the role of public opinion. Today we recognize Lincoln's exceptional abilities and eloquent language, but in his own time some of his most moving statements fell on deaf ears.

The War Department

The greatest expansion in government power during the war was in the War Department, which by early 1862 was faced with the unprecedented challenge of feeding, clothing, and arming 700,000 Union soldiers. Initially the government relied on the individual states to equip and supply their vastly expanded militias. States often contracted directly with textile mills and shoe factories to clothe their troops. In many northern cities volunteer groups sprang up to recruit regiments, buy them weapons, and send them to Washington. Other such community groups, like the one in Chester, Pennsylvania, focused on clothing and providing medical care to soldiers. By January 1862 the War Department, under the able direction of Edwin M.

Stanton, a former Democrat from Ohio, was able to perform many basic functions of procurement and supply without too much delay or corruption. But the size of the Union army and the complexity of fully supplying it demanded constant efforts at all levels—government, state, and community—throughout the war. Thus, in the matter of procurement and supply, as in mobilization, the battlefront was related to the home front on a scale that Americans had not previously experienced.

Taxes and the Greenback Dollar

Although Lincoln was an active commander in chief, he did not believe it was the job of the president to direct economic policy. This, he believed, was the task of Congress. In this important respect, the Civil War was fundamentally different from American wars of the twentieth century, during which executive control over economic policy was deemed essential. Yet the need for money for the vast war effort was pressing. Treasury Secretary Chase worked closely with Congress to develop ways to finance the war. They naturally turned to the nation's economic experts—private bankers, merchants, and managers of large businesses. With the help of Philadelphia financier Jay Cooke, the Treasury used patriotic appeals to sell war bonds to ordinary people in amounts as small as $50. Cooke sold $400 million in bonds, taking for himself what he considered a "fair commission." By the war's end, the United States had borrowed $2.6 billion for the war effort, the first example in American history of the mass financing of war. Additional sources of revenue were sales taxes and the first federal income tax (of 3 percent). Imposed in August 1861, the income tax affected only the affluent: anyone with an annual income under $800 was exempt.

Most radical of all was Chase's decision—which was authorized only after a bitter congressional fight—to print and distribute Treasury notes (paper money). Until then, the money in circulation had been a mixture of coins and state bank notes issued by 1,500 different state banks. The Legal Tender Act of February 1862 created a national currency, which, because of its color, was popularly known as the greenback. In 1863 Congress passed the National Bank Act, which prohibited state banks from issuing their own notes and forced them to apply for federal charters. Thus was the first uniform national currency created, at the expense of the independence that many state banks had prized. "These are extraordinary times, and extraordinary measures must be resorted to in order to save our Government and preserve our nationality," pleaded Congressman Elbridge G. Spaulding, sponsor of the legislation. Only through this appeal to wartime necessity were Spaulding and his allies able to overcome the opposition, for the switch to a national currency was widely recognized as a major step toward centralization of economic power in the hands of the federal government. Such a measure would have been unthinkable if southern Democrats had still been part of the national government. The absence of southern Democrats also made possible passage of a number of Republican economic measures not directly related to the war.

Politics and Economics: The Republican Platform

Although the debate over slavery had overshadowed everything else, in 1860 the Republican Party had campaigned on a comprehensive program of economic development. Once in office, Republicans quickly passed the Morrill Tariff Act (1861); by 1864, this and subsequent measures had raised tariffs to more than double their prewar rate. In 1862 and 1864, Congress created two federally chartered corporations to build a transcontinental railroad—the Union Pacific Railroad Company, to lay track westward from Omaha, and the Central Pacific, to lay track eastward from California—thus fulfilling the dreams of the many expansionists who believed America's economic future lay in trade with Asia across the Pacific Ocean. Two other measures, both passed in 1862, had long been sought by Westerners. The Homestead Act gave 160 acres of public land to any citizen who agreed to live on it for five years, improve it by building a house and cultivating some of the land, and pay a small fee. The Morrill Land Grant Act gave states public land that would allow them to finance land-grant colleges offering education to ordinary citizens in practical skills such as agriculture, engineering, and military science. Coupled with this act, the establishment of a federal Department of Agriculture in 1862 gave American farmers a big push toward modern commercial agriculture.

This package revealed the Whig origins of many Republicans, for in essence the measures amounted to an updated version of Henry Clay's American System of national economic development (see Chapter 9). They were to have a powerful nationalizing effect, connecting ordinary people to the federal government in new ways. As much as the extraordinary war measures, the enactment of the Republican program increased the role of the federal government in national life. Although many of the executive war powers lapsed when the battles ended, the accumulation of strength by the federal government, which southern Democrats would have opposed had they been in Congress, was never reversed.

Diplomatic Objectives

To Secretary of State William Seward fell the job of making sure that Britain and France did not extend diplomatic recognition to the Confederacy. Although Southerners had been certain that King Cotton would gain them European support, they were wrong. British public opinion, which had strongly supported the abolition of slavery within the British Empire in the 1830s, would not now countenance the recognition of a new nation based on slavery. British cotton manufacturers found economic alternatives, first using up their backlog of southern cotton and then turning to Egypt and India for new supplies. In spite of Union protests, however, both Britain and France did allow Confederate vessels to use their ports, and British shipyards sold six ships to the Confederacy. But in 1863, when the Confederacy commissioned Britain's Laird shipyard to build two ironclad ships with pointed prows for ramming, the Union threatened war and the British government made sure that the Laird rams were never delivered. Seward had wanted to threaten Britain with war earlier, in 1861, when the prospect of diplomatic recognition for the Confederacy seemed most likely, but Lincoln had overruled him, cautioning, "One war at a time."

Nonbelligerence was also the Union response in 1863, when France took advantage of the Civil War to invade Mexico and install the Austrian archduke Maximilian as emperor. This was a serious violation of the Monroe Doctrine that could have led to war, but fearing that France might recognize the Confederacy or invade Texas, Seward had to content himself with refusing to recognize the new Mexican government. In the meantime he directed Union troops to gain a stronghold in Texas as soon as possible. In November, five months after the French marched into Mexico City, Union troops seized Brownsville, a town on the Texas-Mexico border, sending a clear signal to the French to go no further. In 1866, after the Civil War, strong diplomatic pressure from Seward convinced the French to withdraw from Mexico. The following year, the hapless Maximilian was captured and shot during a revolt led by a future Mexican president, Benito Juárez.

Although the goal of Seward's diplomacy—preventing recognition of the Confederacy by the European powers—was always clear, its achievement was uncertain for more than two years. Northern fears and southern hopes seesawed with the fortunes of battle. Not until the victories at Vicksburg and Gettysburg in July 1863 could Seward be reasonably confident of success.

Confederate President Jefferson Davis (in the largest chair) and his cabinet are shown meeting with Confederate general Robert E. Lee in this 1866 lithograph. Davis carefully selected his cabinet to represent the South's major states. Shown here, left to right, are Stephen R. Mallory, Judah P. Benjamin, Leroy P. Walker, Davis, Lee, John Reagan, Christopher Memminger, Alexander Stephens, and Robert Toombs.

THE CONFEDERACY

Lincoln faced a major challenge in keeping the North unified enough to win the war, but Jefferson Davis's challenge was even greater. He had to create a Confederate nation. The Confederate States of America was a loose grouping of eleven states, each believing strongly in states' rights. Yet in the Confederacy, as in the Union, the conduct of the war required central direction.

Jefferson Davis as President

Although Jefferson Davis had held national cabinet rank (as secretary of war under president Franklin Pierce), had experience as an administrator, and was a former military man (none of which was true of Abraham Lincoln), he was unable to hold the Confederacy together. Perhaps no one could have. Born, like Lincoln, in Kentucky, Davis ultimately settled in Mississippi, where he became a rich planter. Davis was thus a "cotton nabob" (one of the newly rich class of slave owners), and as such was as scorned by some members of the old southern aristocracy as was Abraham Lincoln by some members of the northern elite. Davis's problems, however, were as much structural as they were personal.

Davis's first cabinet of six men, appointed in February 1861, included a representative from each of the states of the first secession except Mississippi, which was represented by Davis himself. This careful attention to the equality of the states pointed to the fundamental problem that Davis was unable to overcome. For all of its drama, secession was a conservative strategy for preserving the slavery-based social and political structure that existed in every southern state. A shared belief in states' rights—that is, in their own autonomy—was a poor basis on which to build a unified nation. Davis, who would have preferred to be a general rather than a president, lacked Lincoln's persuasive skills and political astuteness. Although he saw the need for unity, he was unable to impose it. Soon his autonomous style of leadership—he wanted to decide every detail himself—angered his generals, alienated cabinet members, and gave southern governors reason to resist his orders. By the second year of the war, when rich slave owners were refusing to give up their privileges for the war effort, Davis no longer had the public confidence and support he needed to coerce them. After the first flush of patriotism had passed, the Confederacy never lived up to its hope of becoming a unified nation.

Diplomatic Hopes

The failure of "cotton diplomacy" was a crushing blow. White Southerners were stunned that Britain and France would not recognize their claim to independence. Well into 1863, the South hoped that a decisive battlefield victory would change the minds of cautious Europeans. In the meantime, plantations continued to grow cotton, but the Confederacy withheld it from market, hoping that lack of raw material for their textile mills would lead the British and French to recognize the Confederacy. The British reacted indignantly, claiming that the withholding of cotton was economic blackmail and that to yield "would be ignominious beyond measure," as Lord Russell put it. Because British textile manufacturers found new sources of cotton, when the Confederacy ended the embargo in 1862 and began to ship its great surplus, the world price of cotton plunged. Then too, the Union naval blockade, weak at first, began to take effect. Cotton turned out to be not so powerful a diplomatic weapon after all.

The Sinews of War

Perhaps the greatest southern failure was in the area of finances. At first the Confederate government tried to raise money from the states, but governors refused to impose new taxes. By the time uniform taxes were levied in 1863, it was too late. Heavy borrowing and the printing of great sums of paper money produced runaway inflation (a ruinous rate of 9,000 percent by 1865, compared with 80 percent in the North). Inflation, in turn, caused incalculable damage to morale and prospects for unity.

After the initial surge of volunteers, enlistment in the military fell off, as it did in the North also. In April 1862, the Confederate Congress passed the first draft law in American history, and the Union Congress followed suit in March 1863. The southern law declared that all able-bodied men between eighteen and thirty-five were eligible for three years of military service. Purchase of substitutes was allowed, as in the North, but in the South the price was uncontrolled, rising eventually to $10,000 in Confederate money. The most disliked part of the draft law was a provision exempting one white man on each plantation with twenty or more slaves. This provision not only seemed to disprove the earlier claim that slavery freed white men to fight, but it aroused class resentments. A bitter phrase of the time complained, "It's a rich man's war but a poor man's fight."

Contradictions of Southern Nationalism

In the early days of the war, Jefferson Davis successfully mobilized feelings of regional identity and patriotism.

Many Southerners felt part of a beleaguered region that had been forced to resist northern tyranny. But most Southerners felt loyalty to their own state and local communities, not to a Confederate nation. The strong belief in states' rights and aristocratic privilege undermined the Confederate cause. Some Southern governors resisted potentially unifying actions such as moving militias outside their home states. Broader measures, such as general taxation, were widely evaded by rich and poor alike. The inequitable draft was only one of many things that convinced the ordinary people of the South that this was a war for privileged slave owners, not for them. With its leaders and citizens fearing (perhaps correctly) that centralization would destroy what was distinctively southern, the Confederacy was unable to mobilize the resources—financial, human, and otherwise—that might have prevented its destruction by northern armies.

THE FIGHTING THROUGH 1862

Just as political decisions were often driven by military necessity, the basic northern and southern military strategies were affected by political considerations as much as by military ones. The initial policy of limited war, thought to be the best route to ultimate reconcil-

Cook Collection. Valentine Museum, Richmond, Virginia.

The contrast between the hope and valor of these young southern volunteer soldiers, photographed shortly before the first battle of Bull Run, and the later advertisements for substitutes is marked. Southern exemptions for slave owners and lavish payment for substitutes increasingly bred resentment among the ordinary people of the South.

SUBSTITUTE NOTICES.

WANTED—A SUBSTITUTE for a conscript, to serve during the war. Any good man over the age of 35 years, not a resident of Virginia, or a foreigner, may hear of a good situation by calling at Mr. GEORGE BAGBY'S office, Shockoe Slip, to-day, between the hours of 9 and 11 A. M. [jy 9—1t*] A COUNTRYMAN.

WANTED—Two SUBSTITUTES—one for artillery, the other for infantry or cavalry service. Also, to sell, a trained, thoroughbred cavalry HORSE. Apply to DR. BROOCKS, Corner Main and 12th streets, or to
jy 9—3t* T. T. BROOCKS, Petersburg, Va.

WANTED—Immediately, a SUBSTITUTE. A man over 35 years old, or under 18, can get a good price by making immediate application to Room No. 50, Monument Hotel, or by addressing "J. W.," through Richmond P. O. jy 9—1t*

WANTED—A SUBSTITUTE, to go into the 24th North Carolina State troops, for which a liberal price will be paid. Apply to me at Dispatch office this evening at 4 o'clock P. M.
jy 9---1t* R. R. MOORE.

WANTED—A SUBSTITUTE, to go in a first-rate Georgia company of infantry, under the heroic Jackson. A gentleman whose health is impaired, will give a fair price for a substitute. Apply immediately at ROOM, No. 13, Post-Office Department, third story, between the hours of 10 and 3 o'clock. jy 9—6t*

WANTED—Two SUBSTITUTES for the war. A good bonus will be given. None need apply except those exempt from Conscript. Apply to-day at GEORGE I. HERRING'S,
jy 9—1t* Grocery store, No. 56 Main st.

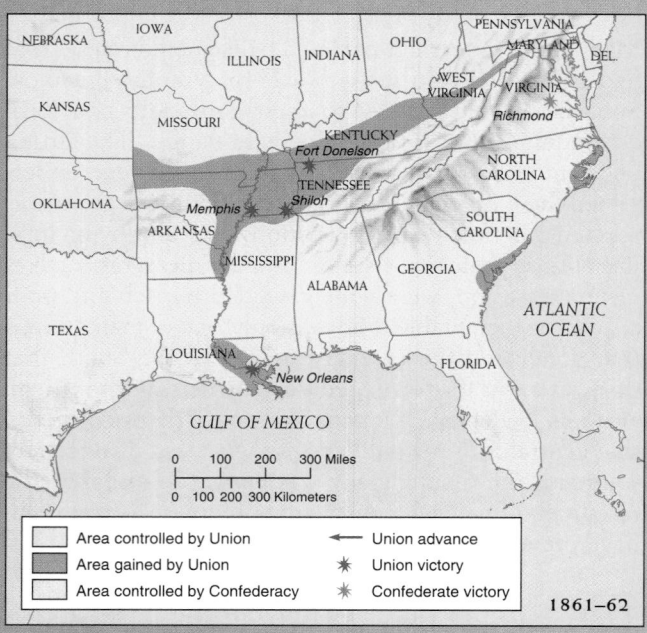

Legend:
- Area controlled by Union
- Area gained by Union
- Area controlled by Confederacy
- Union advance
- ✳ Union victory
- ✳ Confederate victory

1861–62

1863

1864–65

Overall Strategy of the Civil War

In 1861 General Winfield Scott, then the Union's general in chief, proposed the so-called Anaconda plan for subduing the South, which involved strangling it by a blockade at sea and control of the Mississippi rather than directly assaulting its territory. Important aspects of this plan—the blockade of the Confederate coast and the attempt to divide the Confederacy by controlling the Mississippi—became part of the Union's overall war strategy. Union leaders realized, however, that they could not win the war without conquering Confederate territory. The South's strategy was defensive. If its armies could hold out long enough for the North to tire of fighting, its independence would be secured.

By the end of 1862, the Union had captured the sea islands of South Carolina and Georgia and areas of North Carolina, Ulysses S. Grant had won important victories in Tennessee, and Admiral David Farragut had taken New Orleans and advanced up the Mississippi. But in the East, Union armies were consistently stymied by Robert E. Lee's Army of Northern Virginia.

The turning point of the war came in 1863 with General George Gordon Meade's defeat of Lee at Gettysburg (July 1–3) and Grant's capture of Vicksburg (July 4). These two great victories turned the tide in favor of the Union. The Confederates never again mounted a major offensive, and total Union control of the Mississippi exposed the Lower South to Union advance.

In 1864–65, Grant (now in command of all the Union armies) and General William Tecumseh Sherman brought the war home to the South. Sherman's destructive "March to the Sea" divided the South's heartland, and Grant's hammering tactics kept Lee under constant pressure in northern Virginia. Finally, on April 9, 1865, Lee surrendered to Grant at Appomattox, thus ending the bloodiest war in the nation's history.

iation, ran into difficulties because of the public's impatience for victories. But victories, as the mounting slaughter made clear, were not easy to achieve.

The War in Northern Virginia

The initial northern strategy, dubbed by critics the Anaconda Plan (after the constricting snake), envisaged slowly squeezing the South with a blockade at sea and on the Mississippi River. Proposed by the general in chief, Winfield Scott, a native of Virginia, it avoided invasion and conquest in the hope that a strained South would recognize the inevitability of defeat and thus surrender. Lincoln accepted the basics of the plan, but public clamor for a fight pushed him to agree to the disastrous battle of Bull Run and then to a major buildup of Union troops in northern Virginia under General George B. McClellan.

Dashing in appearance, McClellan was extremely cautious in battle. In March 1862, after almost a year spent drilling the raw Union recruits and after repeated exhortations by an impatient Lincoln, McClellan committed 120,000 troops to what became known as the Peninsular campaign. The objective was to capture Richmond, the Confederate capital. McClellan had his troops and their supplies ferried from Washington to Fortress Monroe, near the mouth of the James River, in 400 ships, an effort that took three weeks. Inching up the James Peninsula toward Richmond, he tried to avoid battle, hoping his overwhelming numbers would convince the South to surrender. By June, McClellan's troops were close enough to Richmond to hear the church bells ringing—but not close enough for victory. In a series of battles known as the Seven Days, Robert E. Lee (who had just assumed command of the Confederacy's Army of Northern Virginia) boldly counterattacked, repeatedly catching McClellan off guard. Taking heavy losses as well as inflicting them, Lee drove McClellan back. In August, Lee routed another Union army, commanded by General John Pope, at the second battle of Bull Run (Second Manassas). Lincoln, alarmed at the threat to Washington and disappointed by McClellan's inaction, ordered him to abandon the Peninsular campaign and return to the capital.

Jefferson Davis, like Abraham Lincoln, was an active commander in chief. And like Lincoln, he responded to a public that clamored for more action than a strictly defensive war entailed. After the Seven Days victories, Davis supported a Confederate attack on Maryland. At the same time, he issued a proclamation urging the people of Maryland to make a separate peace. But in the brutal battle of Antietam on September 17, 1862, which claimed more than 5,000 dead and 19,000 wounded, McClellan's army checked Lee's advance. Lee retreated to Virginia, inflicting terrible losses on northern troops at Fredricksburg when they

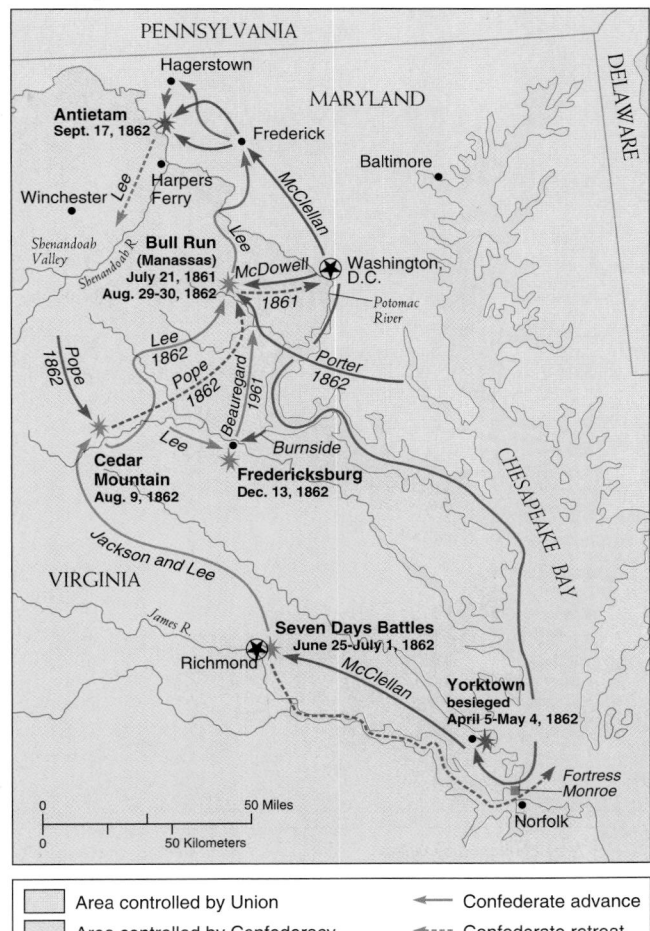

Area controlled by Union	Confederate advance
Area controlled by Confederacy	Confederate retreat
Union advance	Union victory
Union retreat	Confederate victory

Major Battles in the East, 1861–1862 *Northern Virginia was the most crucial and the most constant theater of battle. The prizes were the two opposing capitals, Washington and Richmond, only 70 miles apart. By the summer of 1862, George B. McClellan, famously cautious, had achieved only stalemate in the Peninsular campaign. He did, however, turn back Robert E. Lee at Antietam in September.*

again made a thrust toward Richmond in December, 1862. The war in northern Virginia was stalemated: neither side was strong enough to win, but each was too strong to be defeated.

Shiloh and the War for the Mississippi

Although most public attention was focused on the fighting in Virginia, battles in Tennessee and along the Mississippi River proved to be the key to eventual Union victory. The rising military figure in the West was Ulysses S. Grant, who had once resigned from the service because of a drinking problem. Reenlisting as a colonel after the capture of Fort Sumter, Grant was promoted to brigadier general within two months. In February 1862

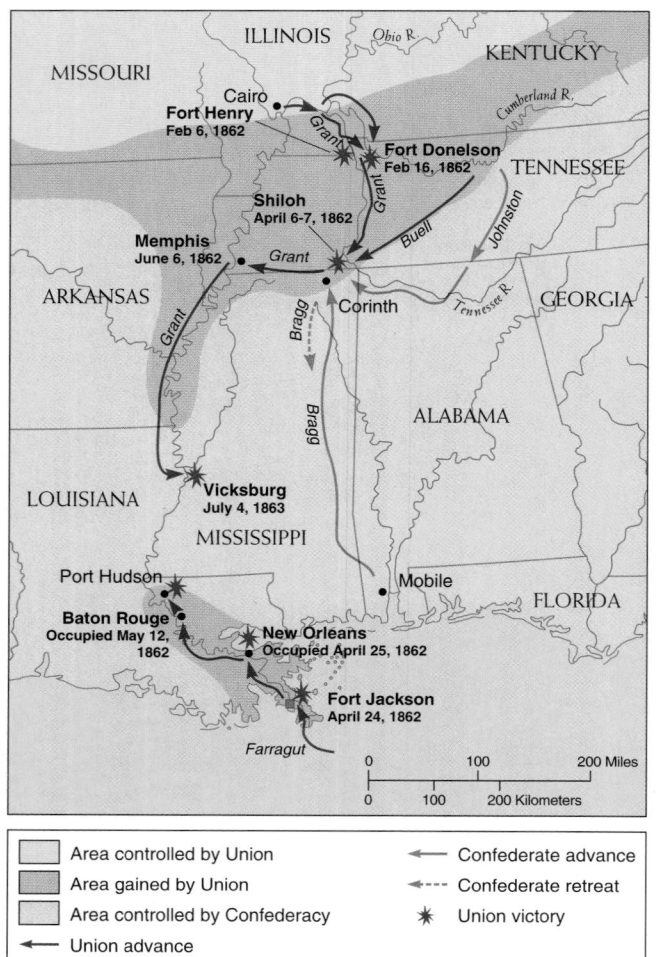

Major Battles in the West, 1862–1863   *Ulysses S. Grant waged a mobile war, winning at Fort Henry and Fort Donelson in Tennessee in February 1862 and at Shiloh in April, and capturing Memphis in June. He then laid siege to Vicksburg, as Admiral David Farragut captured New Orleans and began to advance up the Mississippi River.*

Grant captured Fort Henry and Fort Donelson, on the Tennessee and Cumberland Rivers, establishing Union control of much of Tennessee and forcing Confederate troops to retreat into northern Mississippi.

Moving south with 28,000 men, Grant met a 40,000-man Confederate force commanded by General Albert Sidney Johnston at Shiloh Church in April. Seriously outnumbered on the first day, Grant's forces were reinforced by the arrival of 35,000 troops under the command of General Don Carlos Buell. After two days of bitter and bloody fighting in the rain, the Confederates withdrew. The losses on both sides were enormous: the North lost 13,000 men, the South 11,000, including General Johnston, who bled to death. McClellan's Peninsular campaign was already under way when Grant won at Shiloh, and Jefferson Davis,

concerned about the defense of Richmond, refused to reinforce the generals who were trying to stop Grant. Consequently, Union forces kept moving, capturing Memphis in June and beginning a campaign to eventually capture Vicksburg, "the Gibraltar of the Mississippi." Grant and other Union generals faced strong Confederate resistance, and progress was slow. Earlier that year, naval forces under Admiral David Farragut had captured New Orleans and then continued up the Mississippi River. By the end of 1862 it was clearly only a matter of time before the entire river would be in Union hands. Arkansas, Louisiana, and Texas would then be cut off from the rest of the Confederacy.

The War in the Trans-Mississippi West

Although only one western state, Texas, seceded from the Union, the Civil War was fought in small ways in many parts of the West. Southern hopes for the extension of slavery into the Southwest were reignited by the war. Texans mounted an attack on New Mexico, which they had long coveted, and kept their eyes on the larger prizes of Arizona and California. A Confederate force led by General Henry H. Sibley occupied Santa Fe and Albuquerque early in 1862 without resistance, thus posing a serious Confederate threat to the entire Southwest. Confederate hopes were dashed, however, by a ragtag group of 950 miners and adventurers organized into the first Colorado Volunteer Infantry Regiment. After an epic march of 400 miles from Denver, which was completed in thirteen days despite snow and high winds, the Colorado militia stopped the unsuspecting Confederate troops in the battle of Glorieta Pass on March 26–28, 1862. This dashing action, coupled with the efforts of California militias to safeguard Arizona and Utah from seizure by Confederate sympathizers, secured the Far West for the Union.

Other military action in the West was less decisive. The chronic fighting along the Kansas-Missouri border set a record for brutality when Confederate William Quantrill's Raiders made a predawn attack on Lawrence, Kansas, in August 1863, massacring 150 inhabitants and burning the town. Another civil war took place in Indian Territory, south of Kansas. The southern Indian tribes who had been removed there from the Old Southwest in the 1830s included many who were still bitter over the horrors of removal by federal troops and sympathized with the Confederacy. Furthermore, the Confederacy actively sought Indian support by offering Indian people representation in the Confederate Congress. Consequently, many Indians fought for the South, among them Stand Watie, who became a Confederate military officer. Union victories at Pea Ridge (in northwestern Arkansas) in 1862 and near Fort Gibson (in Indian Territory) in 1863 secured the area for the Union but did little to stop dissension among the Indian groups themselves. After the Civil War the victorious federal government used the tribes' wartime support for the Confederacy as a justification for demanding further land cessions.

Elsewhere in the West, other groups of Indians found themselves caught up in the wider war. An uprising by the Santee Sioux in Minnesota occurred in August 1862, just as McClellan conceded defeat in the Peninsular campaign in Virginia. Alarmed whites, certain that the uprising was a Confederate plot, ignored legitimate Sioux grievances and responded in kind to Sioux ferocity. In little more than a month, 500–800 white settlers and an even greater number of Sioux were killed. Thirty-eight Indians were hanged in a mass execution in Mankato on December 26, 1862, and subsequently all Sioux were expelled from Minnesota. In 1863, U.S. Army Colonel Kit Carson invaded Navajo country in Arizona in retaliation for Indian raids on U.S. troops. Eight thousand Navajos were forced on the brutal "Long Walk" to Bosque Redondo on the Pecos River in New Mexico, where they were held prisoner until a treaty between the United States and the Navajos was signed in 1868.

The hostilities in the West showed that no part of the country, and none of its inhabitants, could remain untouched by the Civil War.

The Naval War

The Union's naval blockade of the South, intended to cut off commerce between the Confederacy and the rest of the world, was initially unsuccessful. The U.S. Navy had only thirty-three ships with which to blockade 189 ports along 3,500 miles of coastline. Southern blockade runners evaded Union ships with ease: only an estimated one-eighth of all Confederate shipping was stopped in 1862. Moreover, the Confederacy licensed British-made privateers to strike at northern shipping. In a two-year period one such Confederate raider, the *Alabama*, destroyed sixty-nine Union

ships with cargoes valued at $6 million. Beginning in 1863, however, as the Union navy became larger, the blockade began to take effect. In 1864 a third of the blockade runners were captured, and in 1865 half of them. As a result, fewer and fewer supplies reached the South.

North and South also engaged in a brief duel featuring the revolutionary new technology of ironcladding. The Confederacy refitted a scuttled Union vessel, the *Merrimac*, with iron plating and renamed it the *Virginia*. On March 8, 1862, as McClellan began his Peninsular campaign, the *Virginia* steamed out of Norfolk harbor to challenge the Union blockade. The iron plating protected the *Virginia* from the fire of the Union ships, which found themselves defenseless against its ram and

The War in the Trans-Mississippi West   *Far removed from the major theaters of battle, the Far West was nevertheless a rich prize in the Civil War. Battles in remote places like Glorieta Pass, New Mexico, were decisive in holding the Far West for the Union. The battles in Kansas and Indian Territory, however, arose primarily from prewar antagonisms and settled little.*

Source: Warren Beck and Ynez Haase, *Historical Atlas of the American West* (Norman: University of Oklahoma Press, 1989).

its powerful guns. Two Union ships went down, and the blockade seemed about to be broken. But the North had an experimental ironclad of its own, the *Monitor*, which was waiting for the *Merrimac* when it emerged from port on March 9. The *Monitor*, which looked like "an immense shingle floating on the water, with a gigantic cheese box rising from its center," was the ship of the future, for the "cheese box" was a revolving turret, a basic component of battleships to come. The historic duel between these first two ironclads was inconclusive, and primitive technology together with limited resources made them of little consequence for the rest of the war. But this brief duel prefigured the naval and land battles of the world wars of the twentieth century as much as did the massing of huge armies on the battlefield.

For the Union, the most successful naval operation in the first two years of the war was not the blockade but the seizing of exposed coastal areas. The Sea Islands of South Carolina were taken, as were some of the North Carolina islands and Fort Pulaski, which commanded the harbor of Savannah, Georgia. Most damaging to the South was the capture of New Orleans.

The Black Response

The capture of Port Royal in the South Carolina Sea Islands in 1861 was important for another reason. Whites fled at the Union advance, but 10,000 slaves greeted the troops with jubilation and shouts of gratitude. Union troops had unwittingly freed these slaves in advance of any official Union policy on the status of slaves in captured territory.

Early in the war, an irate Southerner who saw three of his slaves disappear behind Union lines at Fortress Monroe, Virginia, demanded the return of his property, citing the Fugitive Slave Law. The Union commander, Benjamin Butler, replied that the Fugitive Slave Law no longer applied and that the escaped slaves were "contraband of war." News of Butler's decision spread rapidly among the slaves in the region of Fortress Monroe. Two days later, eight runaway slaves appeared; the next day, fifty-nine black men and women arrived at the fort. Union commanders had found an effective way to rob the South of its basic workforce. The "contrabands," as they were known, were put to work building fortifications and doing other useful work in northern camps. Washington, D.C., became a refuge for contrabands, who crowded into the capital to join the free black people who lived there (at 9,000, they were one of the largest urban black populations outside the Confederacy). Many destitute contrabands received help from the Contraband Relief Association. Modeled on the Sanitary Commission, the association was founded by former slave Elizabeth Keckley, seamstress to Mary Todd Lincoln, the president's wife.

As Union troops drove deeper into the South, the black response grew. When Union General William Tecumseh Sherman marched his army through Georgia in 1864, 18,000 slaves—entire families, people of all ages—flocked to the Union lines. By the war's end, nearly a million black people, fully a quarter of all the slaves in the South, had "voted with their feet" for the Union.

THE DEATH OF SLAVERY

The overwhelming response of black slaves to the Union advance changed the nature of the war. As increasing numbers of slaves flocked to Union lines, the conclusion was unmistakable: the southern war to defend the slave system did not have the support of slaves themselves. Any northern policy that ignored the issue of slavery and the wishes of the slaves was unrealistic.

The Politics of Emancipation

Abraham Lincoln had always said that this was a war for the Union, not a war about slavery. In his Inaugural Address, he had promised to leave slavery untouched in the South. Although Lincoln personally abhorred slavery, his official policy was based on a realistic assessment of several factors. At first, he hoped to give pro-Union forces in the South a chance to consolidate and to prevent the outbreak of war. After the war began, he was impelled by the military necessity of holding the border states (Delaware, Maryland, Kentucky, and Missouri), where slavery was legal.

Finally, Lincoln was worried about unity in the North. Even within the Republican Party, before the war only a small group of abolitionists had favored freeing the slaves. Most Republicans were more concerned about the expansion of slavery than they were about the lives of slaves themselves. They did not favor the social equality of black people, whom they considered inferior. The free-soil movement, for example, was as often antiblack as it was antislave. For their part, most northern Democrats were openly antiblack. Irish workers in northern cities had rioted against free African Americans, with whom they often competed for jobs. There was also the question of what would become of slaves who were freed. Even the most fervent abolitionists had refused to face up to this issue. Finally, northern Democrats effectively played on racial fears in the 1862 congressional elections, warning that freed slaves would pour into northern cities and take jobs from white laborers.

Nevertheless, the necessities of war edged Lincoln toward a new position. In March 1862 he proposed that every state undertake gradual, compensated emancipation, after which former slaves would be resettled in Haiti and Panama (neither of which was under U.S. control). This unrealistic colonization scheme, as well as the reluctance of politicians in the border states to consider emancipation, doomed the proposal.

Radical Republicans chafed at Lincoln's conservative stance. In August 1862 Horace Greeley, editor of the *New York Tribune*, pressed the point in an open letter to the president: "On the face of this wide earth, Mr. President, there is not one disinterested, determined, intelligent champion of the Union cause who does not feel that all attempts to put down the Rebellion and at the same time uphold its inciting cause are preposterous and futile." Greeley's statement was incorrect, for many Northerners did not care what happened to the slaves but did care what happened to the Union. Lincoln's famous answer implicitly acknowledged the many shades of public opinion and cast his decision in terms of military necessity: "If I could save the Union without freeing any slave, I would do it; and if I could save it by freeing all the slaves, I would do it; and if I could do it by freeing some and leaving others alone, I would also do that. What I do about Slavery and the colored race, I do because I believe it helps to save this Union."

In fact, Lincoln had already made up his mind to issue an Emancipation Proclamation, and was simply waiting for the right moment. Following the Union victory at Antietam in September 1862, Lincoln issued a preliminary decree: unless the rebellious states returned to the Union by January 1, 1863, he would declare their slaves "forever free." Although Lincoln did not expect the Confederate states to surrender because of his proclamation, the decree increased the pressure on the South by directly linking the slave system to the war effort. Thus the freedom of black people became part of the struggle. Frederick Douglass, the voice of black America, wrote, "We shout for joy that we live to record this righteous decree."

On January 1, 1863, Lincoln duly issued the final Emancipation Proclamation, which turned out to be just as tortuous as his response to Greeley in August. The proclamation freed the slaves in the areas of rebellion—the areas the Union did not control—but specifically exempted slaves in the border states and in former Confederate areas conquered by the Union. Lincoln's purpose was to meet the abolitionist demand for a war against slavery while not losing the support of conservatives, especially in the border states. But the proclamation was so equivocal that Lincoln's own secretary of state, William Seward, remarked sarcastically, "We show our sympathy with slavery by emancipating slaves where we cannot reach them and holding them in bondage where we can set them free." And in Britain, where Lincoln had hoped to make a favorable impression on the public, government officials were more puzzled than impressed by the proclamation.

One group greeted the Emancipation Proclamation with open celebration. On New Year's Day, hundreds of African Americans gathered outside the White House and cheered the president. They called to him, as pastor Henry M. Turner recalled, that "if he would come out of that palace, they would hug him to death." Realizing the symbolic importance of the proclamation, free African Americans predicted that the news would encourage southern slaves either to flee to Union lines or refuse to work for their masters. Both of these things were already happening as African Americans seized on wartime changes to reshape white-black relations in the South. In one sense, then, the Emancipation Proclamation simply gave a name to a process already in motion.

Abolitionists set about moving Lincoln beyond his careful stance in the Emancipation Proclamation. Reformers such as Elizabeth Cady Stanton and Susan B. Anthony lobbied and petitioned for a constitutional amendment outlawing slavery. Lincoln agreed with them, and encouraged the Republican Party to support such an amendment in its 1864 election platform. Congress, at Lincoln's urging, approved and sent to the states a statement banning slavery throughout the United States. Quickly ratified by the Union states in 1865, the statement became the Thirteenth Amendment to the Constitution. (The southern states, being in a state of rebellion, could not vote.) Lincoln's firm support for this amendment is a good indicator of his true feelings about slavery when he was free of the kinds of military and political considerations taken into account in the Emancipation Proclamation.

Black Fighting Men

As part of the Emancipation Proclamation, Lincoln gave his support for the first time to the recruitment of black soldiers. Early in the war, eager black volunteers had been bitterly disappointed at being turned away. Many, like Robert Fitzgerald, a free African American from Pennsylvania, found other ways to serve the Union cause. Fitzgerald first drove a wagon and mule for the Quartermaster Corps, and later, in spite of persistent seasickness, he served in the Union navy. After the Emancipation Proclamation, however, Fitzgerald was able to do what he had wanted to do all along: be a soldier. He enlisted in the Fifth Massachusetts Cavalry, a regiment that, like all the units in which black soldiers served, was 100 percent African American but commanded by white officers. The most famous black regiment, the Fifty-fourth Massachusetts Colored Infantry, was commanded by abolitionist Robert Gould Shaw of Boston, who was killed in action along with half of his troops in a fruitless attack on Fort Wagner, South Carolina, in 1863. Thomas Wentworth Higginson, the Unitarian minister who had supported John Brown, led another of the first black regiments, the First South Carolina Volunteers.

In Fitzgerald's company of eighty-three men, half came from slave states and had run away to enlist; the other half came mostly from the North but also from Canada, the West Indies, and France. Other regiments had volunteers from Africa. The proportion of volunteers from the loyal border states (where slavery was still legal) was upwards of 25 percent—a lethal blow to the slave system in those states.

After a scant two months of training, Fitzgerald's company was sent on to Washington and thence to battle in northern Virginia. Uncertain of the reception they would receive in northern cities with their history of antiblack riots, Fitzgerald and his comrades were pleasantly surprised. "We are cheered in every town we pass through," he wrote in his diary. "I was surprised to see a great many white people weeping as the train moved South." White people had reason to cheer: black volunteers, eager and willing to fight, made up 10 percent of the Union army. Nearly 200,000 African Americans (one out of every five black males in the nation) served in the Union army or navy.

A fifth of them—37,000—died defending their own freedom and the Union.

Military service was something no black man could take lightly. He faced prejudice of several kinds. In the North, most white people believed that black people were inferior both in intelligence and in courage. Most army officers shared these opinions— but usually not those who had volunteered to lead black troops. Thus African American soldiers had to prove themselves in battle. The performance of black soldiers at Fort Wagner and in battles near Vicksburg, Mississippi, in 1863 helped to change the minds of the Union army command. In the battle of Milliken's Bend, untrained and poorly armed former slaves fought desperately—and successfully. "The bravery of the blacks...completely revolutionized the sentiment of the army with regard to the employment of negro troops," wrote Charles Dana, assistant secretary of war. "I heard prominent officers who formerly in private had sneered at the idea of negroes fighting express themselves after that as heartily in favor of it."

Among the Confederates, however, the feeling was very different. They hated and feared African American troops and threatened to treat any captured black soldier as an escaped slave subject to execution. On at least one occasion, the threats were carried out. In 1864 Confederate soldiers massacred 262 black soldiers at Fort Pillow, Tennessee, after they had surrendered. Although large-scale episodes such as this were rare (especially after President Lincoln threatened retaliation), smaller ones were not. On duty near Petersburg, Virginia, Robert Fitzgerald's company lost a picket to Confederate hatred: wounded in the leg, he was unable to escape from Confederate soldiers, who smashed his skull with their musket butts. Fitzgerald wrote in his diary, "Can such men eventually triumph? God forbid!"

Another extraordinary part of the story of the African American soldiers was their reception by black people in the South, who were overjoyed at the sight of armed black men, many of them former slaves themselves, wearing the uniform of the Union army. As his regiment entered Wilming-

When the family of Robert and Cornelia Fitzgerald posed for a group picture in the 1890s, Robert Fitzgerald proudly dressed in the Union Army uniform he had worn during the Civil War. Fitzgerald's pride in his war service, doubtless shared by many African American veterans, was an important family memory of the fight against slavery.

ton, North Carolina, one soldier wrote, "Men and women, old and young, were running throughout the streets, shouting and praising God. We could then truly see what we have been fighting for."

Robert Fitzgerald's own army career was brief. Just five months after he enlisted, he caught typhoid fever. Hearing of his illness, Fitzgerald's mother traveled from Pennsylvania and nursed him, probably saving his life. Eventually, 117 members of his regiment died of disease—and only 7 in battle. Eight months after he had enlisted, Fitzgerald was discharged for poor eyesight. His short military career nevertheless gave him, in the words of a granddaughter, the distinguished lawyer Pauli Murray, "a pride which would be felt throughout his family for the next century."

African American soldiers were not treated equally by the Union army. They were segregated in camp, given the worst jobs, and paid less than white soldiers ($10 a month rather than $13). Although they might not be able to do much about the other kinds of discrimination, the men of the Fifty-fourth Massachusetts found an unusual way to protest their unequal pay: they refused to accept it, preferring to serve the army for free until it decided to treat them as free men. The protest was effective; in June 1864 the War Department equalized the wages of black and white soldiers.

In other ways the army service of black men made a dent in northern white racism. Massachusetts, the state where abolitionist feeling was the strongest, went the furthest by enacting the first law forbidding discrimination against African Americans in public facilities. Some major cities, among them San Francisco, Cincinnati, Cleveland, and New York, desegregated their streetcars. Several states—Ohio, California, Illinois—repealed statutes that had barred black people from testifying in court or serving on juries. But above all, as Frederick Douglass acutely saw, military service permanently changed the status of African Americans. "Once let the black man get upon his person the brass letters, U.S., let him get an eagle on his button and a musket on his shoulder and bullets in his pocket," Douglass said, and "there is no power on earth that can deny that he has earned the right to citizenship."

THE FRONT LINES AND THE HOME FRONT

Civil War soldiers wrote millions of letters home, more proportionately than in any American war. Their letters and the ones they received in return were links between the front lines and the home front, between the soldiers and their home communities. They are a testament to the patriotism of both Union and Confederate troops, for the story they tell is frequently one of slaughter and horror.

The Toll of War

In spite of early hopes for what one might call a "brotherly" war, one that avoided excessive brutality, Civil War battles were appallingly deadly. One reason was technology: improved weapons, particularly modern rifles, had much greater range and accuracy than the muskets they replaced. The Mexican-American War had been fought with smooth-bore muskets, which were slow to reload and accurate only at short distances. As Ulysses Grant said, "At a distance of a few hundred yards, a man could fire at you all day [with a musket] without your finding out." The new Springfield and Enfield rifles were accurate for a quarter of a mile or more.

Civil War generals, however, were slow to adjust to this new reality. Almost all Union and Confederate generals remained committed to the conventional military doctrine of massed infantry offensives—the Jomini doctrine—that they had learned in their military classes at West Point. Part of this strategy had been to "soften up" a defensive line before an infantry assault, but now the range of the new rifles made artillery itself vulnerable to attack. As a result, generals relied less on "softening up" than on immense numbers of infantrymen, hoping that enough of them would survive the withering rifle fire to overwhelm the enemy line. Enormous casualties were a consequence of this basic strategy.

Medical ignorance was another factor in the casualty rate. Because the use of antiseptic procedures was in its infancy, men often died because minor wounds became infected. Gangrene was a common cause of death. Disease was an even more frequent killer, taking twice as many men as were lost in battle. The overcrowded and unsanitary conditions of many camps were breeding grounds for smallpox, dysentery, typhoid, pneumonia, and, in the summer, malaria. The devastating effect of disease was apparent, for example, in McClellan's Peninsular campaign. Among his 130,000 men, nearly a quarter of the unwounded were ill in July 1862. The knowledge that this situation could only deteriorate during August and September—the most disease-ridden months—was one of the reasons Lincoln decided to recall McClellan and his army.

Both North and South were completely unprepared to handle the supply and health needs of their large armies. Twenty-four hours after the battle of Shiloh, most of the wounded still lay on the field in the rain. Many died of exposure; some, unable to help themselves, drowned. Nor were the combatants prepared to deal with masses of war prisoners, as the shocking example of the Confederate prison camp of Andersonville in northern Georgia demonstrated. Andersonville was an open stockade with no shade or shelter erected early in 1864 to hold 10,000 northern prisoners, but by midsummer it held 33,000. During the worst weeks of that summer, 100 prisoners died of disease, exposure, or malnutrition each day.

Army Nurses

Many medical supplies that the armies were unable to provide were donated by the United States Sanitary Commission in the North, as described in the opening of this chapter, and by women's volunteer groups in the South. But in addition to supplies, there was also an urgent need for skilled nurses to care for wounded and convalescent soldiers. Nursing within a family context was widely considered to be women's work. Caring for sick family members was a key domestic responsibility for women, and most had considerable experience with it. But taking care of strange men in hospitals was another thing. There were strong objections that such work was "unseemly" for respectable women.

Under the pressure of wartime necessity, and over the objections of most army doctors—who resented the challenge to their authority from people no different than their daughters or wives—women became army nurses. Hospital nursing, previously considered a job only disreputable women would undertake, now became a suitable vocation for middle-class women. Under the leadership of veteran reformer Dorothea Dix of the asylum movement (see Chapter 13), and in cooperation with the Sanitary Commission (and with the vocal support of Mother Bickerdyke), by the war's end more than 3,000 northern women had worked as paid army nurses and many more as volunteers.

One of the volunteers was Ellen Ruggles Strong of New York, who, over her husband's objections, insisted on nursing in the Peninsular campaign of 1862. "The little woman has come out amazingly strong during these two months," George Templeton Strong wrote in his diary with a mixture of pride and condescension. "Have never given her credit for a tithe of the enterprise, pluck, discretion, and force of character that she has shown. God bless her." Other women organized other volunteer efforts outside the Sanitary Commission umbrella. Perhaps the best known was Clara Barton, who had been a government clerk before the war and consequently knew a number of influential members of Congress. Barton organized nursing and the distribution of medical supplies; she also used her congressional contacts to force reforms in army medical practice, of which she was very critical.

Southern women were also active in nursing and otherwise aiding soldiers, though the South never boasted a single large-scale organization like the Sanitary Commission. The women of Richmond volunteered when they found the war on their doorstep in the summer of 1862. During the Seven Days Battles, thousands of wounded poured into Richmond; many died in the streets because there was no room for them in hospitals. Richmond women first established informal "roadside hospitals" to meet the need, and their activities expanded from there. As in the North, middle-class women at first faced strong resistance from army doctors and even their own families, who believed that a field hospital was "no place for a refined lady." Kate Cumming of Mobile, who nursed in Corinth, Mississippi, after the Battle of Shiloh, faced down such reproofs, though she confided to her diary that nursing wounded men was very difficult: "Nothing that I had ever heard or read had given me the faintest idea of the horrors witnessed here." She and her companion nurses persisted and became an important part of the Confederate medical services. For southern women, who had been much less active in the public life of their communities than their northern reforming sisters, this Civil War activity marked an important break with prewar tradition.

Although women had made important advances, most army nurses and medical support staff were men. One volunteer nurse was the poet Walt Whitman, who visited wounded soldiers in the hospital in Washington, D.C. Horrified at the suffering he saw, Whitman also formed a deep admiration for the "incredible

Nurse Ann Bell shown preparing medicine for a wounded soldier. Prompted by the medical crisis of the war, women such as Bell and "Mother" Bickerdyke actively participated in the war effort as nurses.

dauntlessness" of the common soldier in the face of slaughter and privation. While never denying the senselessness of the slaughter, Whitman nevertheless found hope in the determined spirit of the common man and woman.

The Life of the Common Soldier

The conditions experienced by the eager young volunteers of the Union and Confederate armies included massive, terrifying, and bloody battles, apparently unending, with no sign of victory in sight. Soldiers suffered from the uncertainty of supply, which left troops, especially in the South, without uniforms, tents, and sometimes even food. They endured long marches over muddy, rutted roads while carrying packs weighing fifty or sixty pounds. Disease was rampant in

The Metropolitan Museum of Art, Gift of Mrs. Frank B. Porter.

This painting helped to establish the reputation of the young artist Winslow Homer, for in it he broke with the tradition of heroic battle scenes and focused instead on the psychology of defeat. In a landscape devastated by battle, three disarmed Confederate prisoners of war await the decision of a Union general on their future. The prisoners, although bedraggled, appear psychologically undefeated, evoking an expression of sympathy from their captor.

their dirty, verminous, and unsanitary camps, and hospitals were so dreadful that more men left them dead than alive. Many soldiers had entered military service with unrealistic, even romantic ideas about warfare. The Mexican-American War had been short and glorious (or at least far enough away to seem so), and the Revolutionary War was even more shrouded in myth. Reality was thus a rude shock, and not all soldiers reacted as nobly as those glorified by Walt Whitman. Desertion was common: an estimated one of every nine Confederate soldiers and one of every seven Union soldiers deserted. Unauthorized absence was another problem. At Antietam, Robert E. Lee estimated that unauthorized absence reduced his strength by a third to a half.

Another widespread phenomenon was fraternization between the two sides. A southern private, for example, wrote about how he celebrated the Fourth of July after the Seven Days Battles in 1862: "There are blackberries in the fields so our boys and the Yanks made a bargain not to fire at each other, and went out in the field, leaving one man on each post with the arms, and gathered berries together and talked over the fight, and traded tobacco and coffee and newspapers as peacefully and kindly as if they had not been engaged for…seven days in butchering one another." In October 1861 a Louisiana man wrote to his brother-in-law: "You spoke as if you had some notion of volunteering. I advise you to stay at home." Once the initial patriotic fervor had waned, attitudes such as his were increasingly common, both on the battlefield and at home.

Wartime Politics

In the earliest days of the war, Northerners had joined together in support of the war effort. Democrat Stephen A. Douglas, Lincoln's defeated rival, paid a visit to the White House to offer Lincoln his support, then traveled home to Illinois, where he addressed a huge rally of Democrats in Chicago: "There can be no neutrals in this war, only patriots— or traitors!" Within a month, Douglas was dead at age forty-eight. The Democrats had lost the leadership of a broad-minded man who might have done much on behalf of northern unity. By 1862 Democrats had split into two factions: the War Democrats and the Peace Democrats, or Copperheads (from the poisonous snake).

Despite the split in the party in 1860 and the secession of the South, the Democratic Party remained a powerful force in northern politics. It had received 44 percent of the popular vote in the North in the 1860 election and its united opposition to the emancipation of slaves explains much of Lincoln's equivocal action on this issue. But the Peace Democrats went far beyond opposition to emancipation, denouncing the draft, martial law, and the high-handed actions of "King Abraham." Echoing old complaints against the Whigs, Peace Democrats appealed to the sympathies of western farmers by warning that agriculture was being hurt by the Republican Party's tariff and industrial policies. At the same time, they appealed to urban workers and immigrants with racist warnings that Republican policies would bring a flood of black workers into northern cities.

The leader of the Copperheads, Clement Vallandigham, a former Ohio congressman, advocated an armistice and a negotiated peace that would "look only to the welfare, peace and safety of the white race, without reference to the effect that settlement may have on the African." Western Democrats, he threatened, might form their own union with the South, excluding New England with its radical abolitionists and high-tariff industrialists.

At the time, long before Grant captured Vicksburg and gained control of the Mississippi River, Lincoln could not afford to take Vallandigham's threats lightly. Besides, he was convinced that some Peace Democrats were members of secret societies—the Knights of the Golden Circle and the Sons of Liberty—that had been conspiring with the Confederacy. In 1862, Lincoln proclaimed that all people who discouraged enlistments in the army or otherwise engaged in disloyal practices would be subject to martial law. In all, 13,000 people were arrested and imprisoned, including Vallandigham, who was exiled to the Confederacy. Lincoln rejected all protests, claiming that his arbitrary actions were necessary for national security.

Lincoln also faced challenges from the radical faction of his own party. As the war continued, the Radicals gained strength: it was they who pushed for emancipation in the early days of the war and for harsh treatment of the defeated South after it ended. The most troublesome Radical was Salmon P. Chase, who in December 1862 caused a cabinet crisis when he encouraged Senate Republicans to complain that Secretary of State William Seward was "lukewarm" in his support for emancipation. This Radical challenge was a portent of the party's difficulties after the war, which Lincoln did not live to see—or prevent.

Economic and Social Strains on the North

Wartime needs caused a surge in northern economic growth, but the gains were unequally distributed. Early in the war, some industries suffered: textile manufacturers could not get cotton, and shoe factories that had made cheap shoes for slaves were without a market. But other industries boomed—bootmaking, shipbuilding, and the manufacture of woolen goods such as blankets and uniforms, to give just three examples. Coal mining expanded, as did ironmaking, especially the manufacture of iron rails for railroads. Agricultural goods were in great demand, promoting further mechanization of farming. The McCormick brothers grew rich from sales of their reapers. Once scorned as a "metal grasshopper," the ungainly-looking McCormick reaper made hand harvesting of grain a thing of the past and led to great savings in manpower. Women, left to tend the family farm while the men went to war, found that with mechanized equipment they could manage the demanding task of harvesting.

Meeting wartime needs enriched some people honestly, but speculators and profiteers also flourished, as they have in every war. By the end of the war, government contracts had exceeded $1 billion. Not all of this business was free from corruption. New wealth was evident in every northern city. *Harper's Monthly* reported that "the suddenly enriched contractors, speculators, and stock-jobbers...are spending money with a profusion never before witnessed in our country." Some people were appalled at the spectacle of wealth in the midst of wartime suffering. Still, some of the new wealth went to good causes. Of the more than $3 million raised by the female volunteers of the United States Sanitary Commission, some came from gala Sanitary Fairs designed to attract those with money to spend.

For most people, however, the war brought the day-to-day hardship of inflation. During the four years of the war, the North suffered an inflation rate of 80 percent, or nearly 15 percent a year. This annual rate, three times what is generally considered tolerable, did much to inflame social tensions. Wages rose only half as much as prices, and workers responded by joining unions and striking. Thirteen occupational groups, among them tailors, coal miners, and railroad engineers, formed unions during the Civil War. Manufacturers, bitterly opposed to unions, freely hired strikebreakers (many of whom were African Americans, women, or immigrants) and formed organizations of their own to prevent further unionization and to blacklist union organizers. Thus both capital and labor moved far beyond the small, localized confrontations of the early industrial period. The formation of large-scale organizations, fostered by wartime demand, laid the groundwork for the national battle between workers and manufacturers that would dominate the last part of the nineteenth century.

Another major source of social tension was conscription. The Union draft, introduced in March 1863, was based on the theory that the very threat of coercion would stimulate reenlistments and encourage volunteering. It soon became clear, however, that coercion, backed by federal marshals, was necessary to fill the ranks. Especially unpopular was a provision in the draft law that allowed the hiring of substitutes or the payment of a commutation fee of $300. The most likely source of substitutes was recent immigrants who had not yet filed for citizenship and were thus not yet eligible to be drafted. It is estimated that immigrants (some of whom were citizens) made up 20 percent of the Union army. Substitution had been accepted in all previous European and American wars. It was so common that President Lincoln, though overage, tried to set an example by paying for a substitute himself. The Democratic Party, however, made substitution an inflammatory issue.

Pointing out that $300 was almost a year's wages for an unskilled laborer, they denounced the draft law (88 percent of Democratic congressmen had voted against it). They appealed to popular resentment by calling it "aristocratic legislation" and to fear by running headlines such as "Three Hundred Dollars or Your Life."

As practiced in the local communities, conscription was indeed often marred by favoritism and prejudice. Local officials called up many more poor than rich men and selected a higher proportion of immigrants than nonimmigrants. In reality, however, only 7 percent of all men called to serve actually did so. About 25 percent hired a substitute, another 45 percent were exempted for "cause" (usually health reasons), and another 20–25 percent simply failed to report to the community draft office. Nevertheless, by 1863 many northern urban workers believed that the slogan "a rich man's war but a poor man's fight," though coined in the South, applied to them as well.

A *black man is lynched during the New York City Draft Riots in July 1863. Free black people and their institutions were major victims of the worst rioting in American history until then. The riots were less a protest against the draft than an outburst of frustration over urban problems that had been festering for decades.*

The New York City Draft Riots

In the spring of 1863 there were protests against the draft throughout the North. Riots and disturbances broke out in many cities, and several federal enrollment officers were killed. The greatest trouble occurred in New York City between July 13 and July 16, 1863, where a wave of working-class looting, fighting, and lynching claimed the lives of 105 people, many of them African American. The rioting, the worst up to that time in American history, was quelled only when five units of the U.S. Army were rushed from the battlefield at Gettysburg, where they had been fighting Confederates the week before.

The riots had several causes. Anger at the draft and racial prejudice were what most contemporaries saw. George Templeton Strong, a staunch Republican, believed that the "brutal, cowardly ruffianism and plunder" was instigated by Confederate agents stirring up "the rabble" of "the lowest Irish day laborers." From a historical perspective, however, the riots had less to do with the war than with the urban growth and tensions described in Chapter 13. The Civil War made urban problems worse and heightened the visible contrast between the lives of the rich and those of the poor.

These tensions exploded, but were not solved, during those hot days in the summer of 1863.

Ironically, African American men, a favorite target of the rioters' anger, were a major force in easing the national crisis over the draft. Though they had been barred from service until 1863, African American volunteers ultimately composed one-tenth of the Union army. Nearly 200,000 black soldiers filled the manpower gap that the controversial draft was meant to address.

The Failure of Southern Nationalism

The war brought even greater changes to the South. As in the North, war needs led to expansion and centralization of government control over the economy. In many cases, Jefferson Davis himself initiated government control (over railroads, shipping, and war production, for example), often in the face of protest or inaction by governors who favored states' rights. The expansion of government brought sudden urbanization, a new experience for the predominantly rural South. The population of Richmond, the Confederate capital, almost tripled, in large part because the Confederate bureaucracy grew to 70,000 people. Because of the need for military manpower, a good part of the Confederate bureaucracy consisted of women, who were referred to as "government girls." All of this—government control, urban growth, women in the paid workforce—was new to Southerners, and not all of it was welcomed.

Even more than in the North, the voracious need for soldiers fostered class antagonisms. When small yeoman farmers went off to war, their wives and families struggled to farm on their own, without the help of mechanization, which they could not afford, and without the help of slaves, which they had never owned. But wealthy men could be exempted from the draft if they had more than twenty slaves. Furthermore, many upper-class Southerners—at least 50,000—avoided military service by paying liberally ($5,000 and more) for substitutes. In the face of these inequities, desertions from the Confederate army soared. One Mississippi soldier spoke for many when he said that "he did not propose to fight for the rich men while they were at home having a good time." But the rich men, the South's traditional ruling class, paid little attention to such complaints.

Worst of all was the starvation. The North's blockade and the breakdown of the South's transportation system restricted the availability of food in the South, and these problems were vastly magnified by runaway inflation. Prices in the South rose by an unbelievable 9,000 percent. Speculation and hoarding by the rich made matters even worse. Women and children were left destitute, and a government-sponsored civilian relief program was soon diverted to meet the pressing needs of the military. Ordinary people suffered. "It is folly for a poor mother to call on the rich people about here," one woman wrote bitterly. "Their hearts are of steel; they would sooner throw what they have to spare to the dogs than give it to a starving child."

In the spring of 1863 food riots broke out in four Georgia cities (Atlanta among them) and in North Carolina. In Richmond, more than a thousand people, mostly women, broke into bakeries and snatched loaves of bread, crying "Bread! Bread! Our children are starving while the rich roll in wealth!" When the bread riot threatened to turn into general looting, Jefferson Davis himself appealed to the crowd to disperse—but found he had to threaten the rioters with gunfire before they would leave. A year later, Richmond stores sold eggs for $6 a dozen and butter for $25 a pound. One woman wept, "My God! How can I pay such prices? I have seven children; what shall I do?"

Increasingly, the ordinary people of the South, preoccupied with staying alive, refused to pay taxes, to provide food, or to serve in the army. Soldiers were drawn home by the desperation of their families as well as the discouraging course of the war. By January 1865 the desertion rate had climbed to 8 percent a month.

At the same time, the life of the southern ruling class was irrevocably altered by the changing nature of slavery. By the end of the war, one-quarter of all slaves had fled to the Union lines, and those who remained often stood in a different relationship to their owners. As white masters and overseers left to join the army, white women were left behind on the plantation to cope with shortages, grow crops, and manage the labor of slaves. Lacking the patriarchal authority of their husbands, white women found that white-black relationships shifted, sometimes drastically (as when slaves fled) and sometimes more subtly. Slaves increasingly made their own decisions about when and how they would work, and they refused to accept the punishments that would have accompanied this insubordination in prewar years. One black woman, implored by her mistress not to reveal the location of a trunk of money and silver plate when the invading Yankees arrived, looked her in the eye and said, "Mistress, I can't lie over that; you bought that silver plate when you sold my three children."

Peace movements in the South were motivated by a confused mixture of realism, war weariness, and the animosity of those who supported states' rights and opposed Jefferson Davis. The anti-Davis faction was led by his own vice president, Alexander Stephens, who early in 1864 suggested a negotiated peace. Peace sentiment was especially strong in North Carolina, where more than a hundred public meetings in support of negotiations were held in the summer of 1863. Davis would have none of it, and he commanded enough votes in the Confederate Congress to enforce his will and to suggest that peace sentiment was traitorous. The Confederacy, which lacked a two-party system, had no official way to consider alternatives. Thus the peace sentiment, which grew throughout 1864, flourished outside the political system in secret societies such as the Heroes of America and the Red Strings. As hopes of Confederate victory slipped away, conflict expanded beyond the battlefield to include the political struggles that southern civilians were fighting among themselves.

THE TIDE TURNS

As Lincoln's timing of the Emancipation Proclamation showed, by 1863 the nature of the war was changing. The proclamation freeing the slaves struck directly at the southern home front and the civilian workforce. That same year, the nature of the battlefield war changed as well. McClellan's notion of a limited war with modest battlefield casualties was gone forever. The Civil War became the first total war.

The Turning Point of 1863

In the summer of 1863 the moment finally arrived when the North could begin to hope for victory. But for the Union army the year opened with stalemate in the East and slow and costly progress in the West. For the South, 1863 represented its highest hopes for military success and for diplomatic recognition by Britain or France.

Attempting to break the stalemate in northern Virginia, General Joseph "Fighting Joe" Hooker and a

Union army of 130,000 men attacked a Confederate army half that size at Chancellorsville in May. In response, Robert E. Lee daringly divided his forces, sending General Thomas "Stonewall" Jackson and 30,000 men on a day-long flanking movement that caught the Union troops by surprise. Although Jackson was killed (shot by his own men by mistake), Chancellorsville was a great Confederate victory. However, Confederate losses were also great: 13,000 men, representing more than 20 percent of Lee's army (versus 17,000 Union men).

Though weakened, Lee moved to the attack. In June, in his second and most dangerous single thrust into Union territory, he moved north into Maryland and Pennsylvania. His purpose was as much political as military: he hoped that a great Confederate victory would lead Britain and France to intervene in the war and demand a negotiated peace. The ensuing battle of Gettysburg, July 1–3, 1863, was another horrible slaughter. On the last day, Lee sent 15,000 men, commanded by George Pickett, to attack the heavily defended Union center. The charge was suicidal. When the Union forces opened fire at 700 yards, one southern officer reported, "Pickett's division just seemed to melt away....Nothing but stragglers came back." The next day a Union officer reported, "I tried to ride over the field but could not, for dead and wounded lay too thick to guide a horse through them."

Pickett's Charge, one historian has written, was the perfect symbol of the entire Confederate war effort: "matchless valor, apparent initial success, and ultimate disaster." Lee retreated from the field, leaving more than one-third of his army behind—28,000 men killed, wounded, or missing. Union general George Meade elected not to pursue with his battered Union army (23,000 casualties). "We had them in our grasp," Lincoln said in bitter frustration. "We had only to stretch forth our arms and they were ours. And nothing I could say or do could make the Army move." Nevertheless, Lee's great gamble had failed; he never again mounted a major offensive.

The next day, July 4, 1863, Ulysses S. Grant took Vicksburg, Mississippi, after a costly siege. The combined news of Gettysburg and Vicksburg dissuaded Britain and France from recognizing the Confederacy and checked the northern peace movement. It also tightened the North's grip on the South, for the Union now controlled the entire Mississippi River. In November, Generals Grant and Sherman broke the Confederate hold on Chattanooga, Tennessee, thereby opening the way to Atlanta.

Grant and Sherman

In March 1864, President Lincoln called Grant east and appointed him general in chief of all the Union

Area controlled by Union	Confederate retreat
Area controlled by Confederacy	Union victory
Union advance	Confederate victory
Confederate advance	

The Turning Point: 1863   *In June, Lee boldly struck north into Maryland and Pennsylvania, hoping for a victory that would cause Britain and France to demand a negotiated peace on Confederate terms. Instead, he lost the hard-fought battle of Gettysburg, July 1–3. The very next day, Grant's long siege of Vicksburg succeeded. These two great Fourth of July victories turned the tide in favor of the Union. The Confederates never again mounted a major offensive. Total Union control of the Mississippi now exposed the Lower South to attack.*

forces. Lincoln's critics were appalled. Grant was an uncouth Westerner (like the president) and (unlike the president) was rumored to have a drinking problem. Lincoln replied that if he knew the general's brand of whiskey he would send a barrel of it to every commander in the Union army.

Grant devised a plan of strangulation and annihilation. While he took on Lee in northern Virginia, he sent General William Tecumseh Sherman to defeat Confederate general Joe Johnston's Army of Tennessee, which was defending the approach to Atlanta. Both Grant and Sherman exemplified the new kind of warfare. They aimed to inflict maximum damage on the fabric of southern life,

Sherman's Campaign in Georgia, 1864   Ulysses S. Grant and William Tecumseh Sherman, two like-minded generals, commanded the Union's armies in the final push to victory. While Grant hammered away at Lee in northern Virginia, Sherman captured Atlanta in September (a victory that may have been vital to Lincoln's reelection) and began his March to the Sea in November 1864.

The Final Battles in Virginia, 1864–1865   In the war's final phase early in 1865, Sherman closed one arm of a pincers by marching north from Savannah while Grant attacked Lee's last defensive positions in Petersburg and Richmond. Lee retreated from them on April 2 and surrendered at Appomattox Court House on April 9, 1865.

hoping that the South would choose to surrender rather than face total destruction. This decision to broaden the war so that it directly affected civilians was new in American military history and prefigured the total wars of the twentieth century.

In northern Virginia, Grant pursued a policy of destroying civilian supplies. He said he "regarded it as humane to both sides to protect the persons of those found at their homes, but to consume everything that could be used to support or supply armies." One of those supports was slaves. Grant welcomed fleeing slaves to Union lines and encouraged army efforts to put them to work or enlist them as soldiers. He also cooperated with the efforts of groups like the New England Freedmen's Aid Society, which sent northern volunteers (many of them women) into Union-occupied parts of the South to educate former slaves. (The Freedmen's Bureau, authorized by Congress in March 1865, continued this work into Reconstruction. One of the northern teachers who

went south in 1866 to work for the bureau was Robert Fitzgerald, the former soldier.) But the most famous example of the new strategy of total war was General Sherman's 1864 march through Georgia.

Sherman captured Atlanta on September 2, 1864, after outmaneuvering and outfighting Johnson and his successor, John Bell Hood. Atlanta lay in ruins as Sherman and his troops entered the city. With the rest of Georgia now vulnerable, gloom enveloped the South. "Since Atlanta I have felt as if all were dead within me, forever," Mary Boykin Chesnut wrote in her diary. "We are going to be wiped off the earth."

In November, Sherman set out to march the 285 miles to the coastal city of Savannah, living off the land and destroying everything in his path. His military purpose was to tighten the noose around Robert E. Lee's army in northern Virginia by cutting off Mississippi, Alabama, and Georgia from the rest of the Confederacy. But his second purpose, openly stated, was to "make war so terrible" to the people of the South, to "make them so sick of war that generations would pass away before they would again appeal to it." Accordingly, he told his men to seize, burn, or destroy everything in their path (but, significantly, not to harm civilians).

One Union soldier wrote to his father, "You can form no idea of the amount of property destroyed by us on this raid....A tornado 60 miles in width from Chattanooga to this place 290 miles away could not have done half the damage we did." A southern woman supplied the details: "The fields were trampled down and the road was lined with carcasses of horses, hogs and cattle that the invaders, unable either to consume or to carry with them, had wantonly shot down to starve our people and prevent them from making their crops. The stench in some places was unbearable." It was estimated that Sherman's army did $100 million worth of damage. "They say no living thing is found in Sherman's track," Mary Boykin Chesnut wrote, "only chimneys, like telegraph poles, to carry the news of [his] attack backwards."

Terrifying to white southern civilians, Sherman was initially hostile to black Southerners as well. In the interests of speed and efficiency, his army turned away many of the 18,000 slaves who flocked to it in Georgia, causing a number to be recaptured and reenslaved. This callous action caused such a scandal in Washington that Secretary of War Edwin Stanton arranged a special meeting in Georgia with Sherman and twenty African American ministers who spoke for the freed slaves. This meeting in itself was extraordinary: no one had ever asked slaves what they wanted. Equally extraordinary was Sherman's response in Special Field Order 15, issued in January 1865: he set aside more than 400,000 acres of Confederate land to be given to the freed slaves in forty-acre parcels. This was war of a kind that white Southerners had never imagined.

The 1864 Election

The war complicated the 1864 presidential election, aggravating the usual political factionalism. Public opinion about Lincoln and the conduct of the war had been on a roller coaster, soaring to great heights with news of Union victories and plunging during long periods of stalemate. Just as in the Mexican-American War, the "instant news" provided by the telegraph and special correspondents pulled people out of their daily lives and fixed their attention on the war. But the Civil War was much larger and much nearer. Almost everyone had a son or a father or a brother at the front, or knew someone in their community who did. The war news was personal.

Lincoln was renominated during a low period. Opposed by the Radicals, who thought he was too conciliatory toward the South, and by Republican conservatives, who disapproved of the Emancipation Proclamation, Lincoln had little support within his own party. Secretary of the Treasury Salmon P. Chase, a man of immense ego, went so far as to encourage his supporters to propose him, rather than Lincoln, as the party's nominee.

The Democrats had an appealing candidate: General George McClellan, a war hero (always a favorite with American voters) who was known to be sympathetic to the South, although he was unwilling to endorse the plank of the Democratic Party platform that proclaimed the war a failure and proposed an armistice to end it. Other Democrats played shamelessly on the racist fears of the urban

This striking photograph by Thomas C. Roche shows a dead Confederate soldier, killed at Petersburg on April 3, 1865, only six days before the surrender at Appomattox. The new medium of photography conveyed the horror of the war with a gruesome reality to the American public.

working class, accusing Republicans of being "negro-lovers" and warning that racial mixing lay ahead.

A deeply depressed Lincoln fully expected to lose the election. "I am going to be beaten," he told an army officer in August 1864, "and unless some great change takes place badly beaten." A great change did take place: Sherman captured Atlanta on September 2. Jubilation swept the North: some cities celebrated with 100-gun salutes. Lincoln won the election with 55 percent of the popular vote. Seventy-eight percent of the soldiers voted for him rather than for their former commander. The vote probably saved the Republican Party from extinction. Furthermore, the election was important evidence of northern support for Lincoln's policy of uncondi-tional surrender for the South. There would be no negotiated peace; the war would continue.

In many ways, Lincoln's reelection was extraor-dinary. Ordinary people and war-weary soldiers had voted to continue a difficult and divisive conflict. This was the first time in American history that the people had been able to vote on whether they were willing to continue wartime hardships, and that 45 percent of the electorate voted against Lincoln suggests how severe those hardships were.

Nearing the End

As Sherman devastated the lower South, Grant was locked in struggle with Lee in northern Virginia.

Abraham Lincoln toured Richmond, the Confederate capital, just hours after Jefferson Davis had fled. This photograph, taken April 4, 1865, shows Yankee cavalry horses in the foreground and the smoldering city in the background. It gives a sense of the devastation suffered by the South and the immense task of rebuilding and reconciliation that Lincoln would not live to accomplish.

Grant did not favor subtle strategies. He bluntly said, "The art of war is simple enough. Find out where your enemy is. Get at him as soon as you can. Strike at him as hard as you can, and keep moving on." Following this plan, Grant eventually hammered Lee into submission, but at enormous cost. Lee had learned the art of defensive warfare (his troops called him "the King of Spades" because he made them dig trenches so often), and he inflicted heavy losses on the Union army in a succession of bloody encounters in the spring and summer of 1864: almost 18,000 at the battle of the Wilderness, more than 8,000 at Spotsylvania, and 12,000 at Cold Harbor. At Cold Harbor, Union troops wrote their names and addresses on scraps of paper and pinned them to their backs, so certain were they of being killed or wounded in battle. Grim and terrible as Grant's strat-egy was, it proved effective. Rather than pulling back after his failed assaults, he kept moving South, finally settling in for a prolonged siege of Lee's forces at Petersburg. The North's great advantage in popula-tion finally began to tell. There were more Union soldiers to replace those lost in battle, but there were no more white Confederates.

In desperation, the South turned to what had hitherto been unthinkable: arming slaves to serve as soldiers in the Confederate army. As Jefferson Davis said in February 1865, "We are reduced to choosing whether the negroes shall fight for or against us." But—and this was the bitter irony—the African American soldiers and their families would have to be promised freedom or they would desert to the Union at the first chance they had. Even though Davis's proposal had the support of General Robert E. Lee, the Confederate Congress balked at first. As one member said, the idea was "revolting to Southern sentiment, Southern pride, and Southern honor." Another candidly admitted, "If slaves make good soldiers our whole theory of slavery is wrong." Finally, on March 13, the Confederate Congress authorized a draft of black soldiers—without mentioning freedom. Although two regi-ments of African American soldiers were immediately orga-nized in Richmond, it was too late. The South never had to publicly acknowledge the paradox of having to offer slaves freedom so that they would fight to defend slavery.

By the spring of 1865, public support for the war simply disintegrated in the South. Starvation, inflation, dissension, and the prospect of military defeat were too much. In February, Jefferson Davis sent his vice president, Alexander Stephens, to negotiate terms at a peace conference at Hampton Roads. Lincoln would not countenance anything less than full surrender, although he did offer gradual emancipation with compensation for slave owners. Davis, however, insisted on southern independence at all costs. Consequently, the Hampton Roads conference failed and southern resistance faded away. In March 1865, Mary Boykin Chesnut recorded in her diary: "I am sure our army is silently dispersing. Men are going the wrong way all the time. They slip by now with no songs nor shouts. They have given the thing up."

Lincoln's assassination, just days after Lee's surrender at Appomattox, was a stunning blow. This lithograph shows the elaborate funeral cortege in New York City on April 25, 1865, just one of the many ceremonies that marked Lincoln's final trip to Springfield, Illinois, his burying place.

Appomattox

Grant's hammering tactics worked—slowly. In the spring of 1865 Lee and his remaining troops, outnumbered two to one, still held Petersburg and Richmond. Starving, short of ammunition, and losing men in battle or to desertion every day, Lee retreated from Petersburg on April 2. The Confederate government fled Richmond, stripping and burning the city. Seven days later, Lee and his 25,000 troops surrendered to Grant at Appomattox Court House. Grant treated Lee with great respect and set a historic precedent by giving the Confederate troops parole. This meant they could not subsequently be prosecuted for treason. Grant then sent the starving army on its way with three days' rations for every man. Jefferson Davis, who had hoped to set up a new government in Texas, was captured in Georgia on May 10. The war was finally over.

Death of a President

Sensing that the war was near its end, Abraham Lincoln visited Grant's troops when Lee withdrew from Petersburg on April 2. Thus it was that Lincoln came to visit Richmond, and to sit briefly in Jefferson Davis's presidential office, soon after Davis had left it. As Lincoln walked the streets of the burned and pillaged city, black people poured out to see him and surround him, shouting "Glory to God! Glory! Glory! Glory!" Lincoln in turn said to Admiral David Porter: "Thank God I have lived to see this. It seems to me that I have been dreaming a horrid dream for four years, and now the nightmare is gone." Lincoln had only the briefest time to savor the victory. On the night of April 14, President and Mrs. Lincoln went to Ford's Theater in Washington. There Lincoln was shot at point-blank range by John Wilkes Booth, a Confederate sympathizer. He died the next day. For the people of the Union, the joy of victory was muted by mourning for their great leader. After a week of observances in Washington, Lincoln's coffin was loaded on a funeral train that slowly carried him back to Springfield. All along the railroad route, day and night, in small towns and large, people gathered to see the train pass and to pay their last respects. At that moment, the Washington community and the larger Union community were one and the same.

The nation as a whole was left with Lincoln's vision for the coming peace, expressed in the unforgettable words of his Second Inaugural Address:

> With malice toward none, with charity for all, with firmness in the right as God gives us to see the right, let us strive on to finish the work we are in, to bind up the nation's wounds, to care for him who shall have borne the battle and for his widow and his orphan, to do all which may achieve and cherish a just and lasting peace among ourselves and with all nations.

CHRONOLOGY

1861	March: Morrill Tariff Act
	April: Fort Sumter falls; war begins
	April: Mobilization begins
	April–May: Virginia, Arkansas, Tennessee, and North Carolina secede
	June: United States Sanitary Commission established
	July: First Battle of Bull Run
1862	February: Legal Tender Act
	February: Battles of Fort Henry and Fort Donelson
	March: Battle of Pea Ridge
	March: Battle of the *Monitor* and the *Merrimack*
	March–August: George B. McClellan's Peninsular campaign
	March: Battle of Glorieta Pass
	April: Battle of Shiloh
	April: Confederate Conscription Act
	April: David Farragut captures New Orleans
	May: Homestead Act
	June–July: Seven Days Battles
	July: Pacific Railway Act
	July: Morrill Land Grant Act
	August: Santee Sioux Uprising, Minnesota
	September: Battle of Antietam
	December: Battle of Fredericksburg
1863	January: Emancipation Proclamation
	February: National Bank Act
	March: Draft introduced in the North
	March: Colonel Kit Carson sends 8,000 Navajos on the "Long Walk" to Bosque Redondo, New Mexico Territory
	April: Richmond bread riot
	May: Battle of Chancellorsville
	June: French occupy Mexico City
	July: Battle of Gettysburg
	July: Surrender of Vicksburg
	July: New York City Draft Riots
	November: Battle of Chattanooga
	November: Union troops capture Brownsville, Texas
1864	March: Ulysses S. Grant becomes general in chief of Union forces
	April: Fort Pillow massacre
	May: Battle of the Wilderness
	May: Battle of Spotsylvania
	June: Battle of Cold Harbor
	September: Atlanta falls
	November: Abraham Lincoln reelected president
	November–December: William Tecumseh Sherman's March to the Sea
1865	April: Richmond falls
	April: Robert E. Lee surrenders at Appomattox
	April: Lincoln assassinated
	December: Thirteenth Amendment to the Constitution becomes law

CONCLUSION

In 1865, a divided people had been forcibly reunited by battle. Their nation, the United States of America, had been permanently changed by civil war. Devastating losses among the young men of the country—the greatest such losses the nation was ever to suffer—would affect not only their families but all of postwar society. Politically, the deepest irony of the Civil War was that only by fighting it had America become completely a nation. For it was the war that broke down local isolation. Ordinary citizens in local communities, North and South, developed a national perspective as they sent their sons and brothers to be soldiers, their daughters to be nurses and teachers. Then, too, the federal government, vastly strengthened by wartime necessity, reached the lives of ordinary citizens more than ever before. The question now was whether this strengthened but divided national community, forged in battle, could create a just peace.

REVIEW QUESTIONS

1. At the outset of the Civil War, what were the relative advantages of the North and the South, and how did they affect the final outcome?

2. In the absence of the southern Democrats, in the early 1860s the new Republican Congress was able to pass a number of party measures with little opposition. What do these measures tell you about the historical roots of the Republican Party? More generally, how do you think we should view legislation passed in the absence of the customary opposition, debate, and compromise?

3. The greatest problem facing Jefferson Davis and the Confederacy was the need to develop a true feeling of nationalism. Can the failure of this effort be blamed on Davis's weakness as a leader alone, or are there other causes?

4. In what ways can it be said that the actions of African Americans, both slave and free, came to determine the course of the Civil War?

5. Wars always have unexpected consequences. List some of these consequences both for soldiers and for civilians in the North and in the South.

6. Today, Abraham Lincoln is considered one of our greatest presidents, but he did not enjoy such approval at the time. List some of the contemporary criticisms of Lincoln, and evaluate them.

RECOMMENDED READING

Nina Brown Baker, *Cyclone in Calico: The Story of Mary Ann Bickerdyke* (1952). Mother Bickerdyke's wartime career is told in homely detail.

Iver Bernstein, *The New York City Draft Riots* (1990). A social history that places the famous riots in the context of the nineteenth century's extraordinary urbanization.

Paul Escott, *After Secession: Jefferson Davis and the Failure of Confederate Nationalism* (1978). A thoughtful study of Davis's record as president of the Confederacy.

Drew Gilpin Faust, *Mothers of Invention: Women of the Slaveholding South in the American Civil War* (1996). A major study that considers the importance of gender at the white South's "moment of truth."

Alvin Josephy, *The Civil War in the West* (1992). A long-needed study, by a noted western historian, of the course of the war in the Trans-Mississippi West.

William Quentin Maxwell, *Lincoln's Fifth Wheel: The Political History of the United States Sanitary Commission* (1956). A useful study of the major northern volunteer organization.

James M. McPherson, *The Negro's Civil War: How American Negroes Felt and Acted during the War for the Union* (1965). One of the earliest documentary collections on African American activity in wartime.

———, *Battle Cry of Freedom: The Civil War Era* (1988). An acclaimed, highly readable synthesis of much scholarship on the war.

———, *The Atlas of the Civil War* (1994). Detailed battle diagrams with clear descriptions.

Pauli Murray, *Proud Shoes: The Story of an American Family* (1956). Murray tells the proud story of her African American family and her grandfather, Robert Fitzgerald.

Phillip Shaw Paludan, *"A People's Contest": The Union at War, 1861–1865* (1988). A largely successful social history of the North during the war.

ADDITIONAL BIBLIOGRAPHY

The Lincoln Presidency and the Northern Home Front

Richard Franklin Bensel, *Yankee Leviathan: The Origins of Central State Authority in America, 1859–1877* (1991)

David Donald, *Liberty and Union* (1978)

Eric Foner, *Politics and Ideology in the Age of the Civil War* (1980)

George M. Frederickson, *The Inner Civil War: Northern Intellectuals and the Crisis of the Union* (1965)

J. Matthew Gallman, *The North Fights the Civil War: The Home Front* (1994)

Ernest A. McKay, *The Civil War and New York City* (1990)

James M. McPhersen, *Abraham Lincoln and the Second American Revolution* (1990)

Mark E. Neely, *The Fate of Liberty: Abraham Lincoln and Civil Liberties* (1991)

Phillip Shaw Paludan, *The Presidency of Abraham Lincoln* (1994)

William E. Parrish, *Turbulent Partnership: Missouri and the Union, 1861–1865* (1963)

James Rawley, *The Politics of Union: Northern Politics during the Civil War* (1974)

Heather Cox Richardson, *The Greatest Nation of the Earth: Republican Economic Policies during the Civil War* (1997)

Anne C. Rose, *Victorian America and the Civil War* (1992)

Joel Sibley, *A Respectable Minority: The Democratic Party in the Civil War Era, 1860–1868* (1977)

Lewis P. Simpson, *Mind and the American Civil War* (1989)

John L. Thomas, ed., *Abraham Lincoln and the American Political Tradition* (1986)

Hans L. Trefousse, *The Radical Republicans* (1968)

Thomas H. O'Connor, *Civil War Boston: Homefront and Battlefield* (1997)

Bell I. Wiley, *The Life of Johnny Reb* (1943)

————, *The Life of Billy Yank* (1952)

Maris A. Vinovskis, ed., *Toward a Social History of the American Civil War: Exploratory Essays* (1990)

T. Harry Williams, *Lincoln and His Generals* (1952)

Gary Wills, *Lincoln at Gettysburg: Words that Remade America* (1992)

The Death of Slavery

Herman Belz, *A New Birth of Freedom: The Republican Party and Freedmen's Rights, 1861–1866* (1976)

Ira Berlin, et al., *Slaves No More: Three Essays on Emancipation and the Civil War* (1992)

Ira Berlin, et al., eds., *Freedom, A Documentary History of Emancipation, 1861–1867*, Series 1, Volume I: *The Destruction of Slavery* (1985)

————, et al., eds. *Freedom, A Documentary History of Emancipation, 1861–1867*, Series 1, Volume II: *The Wartime Genesis of Free Labor: The Upper South* (1993)

————, et al., eds. *Freedom, A Documentary History of Emancipation, 1861–1867*, Series 1, Volume III: *The Wartime Genesis of Free Labor: The Lower South* (1990)

————, et al., eds. *Freedom, A Documentary History of Emancipation, 1861–1867*, Series 2: *The Black Military Experience* (1988)

John Hope Franklin, *The Emancipation Proclamation* (1963)

Benjamin Quarles, *The Negro in the Civil War* (1953)

Willie Lee Rose, *Rehearsal for Reconstruction: The Port Royal Experiment* (1964)

The Confederacy and the Southern Home Front

Steven V. Ash, *When the Yankees Came: Conflict and Chaos in the Occupied South 1861–1865* (1995)

Daniel W. Crofts, *Reluctant Confederates: Upper South Unionists in the Secession Crisis* (1989)

William C. Davis, *"A Government of Our Own": The Making of the Confederacy* (1994)

Wayne K. Durrill, *War of Another Kind: A Southern Community in the Great Rebellion* (1990)

Clement Eaton, *A History of the Southern Confederacy* (1954)

Drew Gilpin Faust, *The Creation of Confederate Nationalism* (1988)

Robert M. Myers, ed., *The Children of Pride: A True Story of Georgia and the Civil War* (1972)

Phillip S. Paludan, *Victims: A True History of the Civil War* (1981)

George C. Rable, *Civil Wars: Women and the Crisis of Southern Nationalism* (1989)

————, *The Confederate Republic: A Revolution against Politics* (1994)

Charles W. Ramsdell, *Behind the Lines in the Southern Confederacy* (1944)

James L. Roark, *Masters without Slaves: Southern Planters in the Civil War and Reconstruction* (1978)

Daniel E. Sutherland, *Seasons of War: The Ordeal of a Confederate Community 1861–1865* (1995)

Emory M. Thomas, *The Confederate Nation, 1861–1865* (1979)

LeeAnn Whites, *The Civil War as a Crisis in Gender: Augusta, Georgia, 1860–1890* (1995)

Bell I. Wiley, *The Plain People of the Confederacy* (1943)

The Fighting

Michael Barton, *Good Men: The Character of Civil War Soldiers* (1981)

Ken Burns, *The Civil War* (1990)

Bruce Catton, *A Stillness at Appomattox* (1953)

Shelby Foote, *The Civil War: A Narrative*, 3 vols. (1958–1974)

Joseph T. Glatthaar, *Forged in Battle: The Civil War Alliance of Black Soldiers and White Officers* (1990)

————, *The March to the Sea and Beyond: Sherman's Troops in the Savannah and Carolinas Campaign* (1985)

Mark Grimsley, *The Hard Hand of War: Union Policy toward Southern Civilians, 1861–1865* (1995)

Edward Hagerman, *The American Civil War and the Origins of Modern Warfare* (1988)

Gerald F. Linderman, *Embattled Courage: The Experience of Combat in the American Civil War* (1987)

Reid Mitchell, *The Vacant Chair: The Northern Soldier Leaves Home* (1993)

Allan Nevins, *The War for the Union*, 4 vols. (1959–71)

Edwin S. Redkey, ed., *A Grand Army of Black Men: Letters from African-American Soldiers in the Union Army, 1861–1865* (1992)

Charles Royster, *The Destructive War: William Tecumseh Sherman, Stonewall Jackson, and the Americans* (1991)

Biography

William C. Davis, *Jefferson Davis: The Man and His Hour* (1991)

William S. Feeley, *Grant: A Biography* (1980)

Thomas E. Schott, *Alexander H. Stephens of Georgia: A Biography* (1988)

Stephen W. Sears, *George B. McClellan: The Young Napoleon* (1988)

Emory M. Thomas, *Robert E. Lee: A Biography* (1995)

RECONSTRUCTION

1863–1877

Theodor Kaufmann, *On to Liberty*, 1867, oil on canvas, 36"×56". The Metropolitan Museum of Art, Gift of Erving and Joyce Wolf, 1982. (1982.443.3). Photograph © 1982 The Metropolitan Museum of Art.

AMERICAN COMMUNITIES
Hale County, Alabama: From Slavery to Freedom in a Black Belt Community

On a bright Saturday morning in May 1867, 4,000 former slaves eagerly streamed into the town of Greensboro, bustling seat of Hale County in west-central Alabama. They came to hear speeches from two delegates to a recent freedmen's convention in Mobile and to find out about the political status of black people under the Reconstruction Act just passed by Congress. Tensions mounted in the days following this unprecedented gathering as military authorities began supervising voter registration for elections to the upcoming constitutional convention that would rewrite the laws of Alabama. On June 13, John Orrick, a local white, confronted Alex Webb, a politically active freedman, on the streets of Greensboro. Webb had recently been appointed a voter registrar for the district. Orrick swore he would never be registered by a black man, and shot Webb dead. Hundreds of armed and angry freedmen formed a posse to search for Orrick, but failed to find him. Galvanized by Webb's murder, 500 local freedmen formed a chapter of the Union League, the Republican Party's organizational arm in the South. The chapter functioned as both a militia company and a forum to agitate for political rights.

Violent political encounters between black people and white people were common in southern communities in the wake of the Civil War. The war had destroyed slavery and the Confederacy, but left the political and economic status of newly emancipated African Americans unresolved. Communities throughout the south struggled over the meaning of freedom in ways that reflected their particular circumstances. The 4 million freed people constituted roughly one-third of the total southern population, but the black–white ratio in individual communities varied enormously. In some places the Union army had been a strong presence during the war, hastening the collapse of the slave system and encouraging experiments in free labor. Other areas remained relatively untouched by the fighting. In some areas small farms prevailed; in others, including Hale County, large plantations dominated economic and political life.

West-central Alabama had emerged as a fertile center of cotton production just two decades before the Civil War. There African Americans, as throughout the South's black belt, constituted more than three-quarters of the population. The region was virtually untouched by fighting until the very end of the Civil War. But with the arrival of federal troops in the spring of 1865, African Americans in Hale County, like their counterparts elsewhere, began to challenge the traditional organization of plantation labor.

One owner, Henry Watson, found that his entire workforce had deserted him at the end of 1865. "I am in the midst of a large and fertile cotton growing country," Watson wrote to a partner.

"Many plantations are entirely without labor, many plantations have insufficient labor, and upon none are the laborers doing their former accustomed work." Black women refused to work in the fields, preferring to stay home with their children and tend garden plots. Nor would male field hands do any work, such as caring for hogs, that did not directly increase their share of the cotton crop.

Above all, freed people wanted more autonomy. Overseers and owners thus grudgingly allowed them to work the land "in families," letting them choose their own supervisors and find their own provisions. The result was a shift from the gang labor characteristic of the antebellum period, in which large groups of slaves worked under the harsh and constant supervision of white overseers, to the sharecropping system, in which African American families worked small plots of land in exchange for a small share of the crop. This shift represented less of a victory for newly freed African Americans than a defeat for plantation owners, who resented even the limited economic independence it forced them to concede to their black workforce.

Only a small fraction—perhaps 15 percent—of African American families were fortunate enough to be able to buy land. The majority settled for some version of sharecropping, while others managed to rent land from owners, becoming tenant farmers. Still, planters throughout Hale County had to change the old routines of plantation labor. Local African Americans also organized politically. In 1866 Congress had passed the Civil Rights Act and sent the Fourteenth Amendment to the Constitution to the states for ratification; both promised full citizenship rights to former slaves. Hale County freedmen joined the Republican Party and local Union League chapters. They used their new political power to press for better labor contracts, demand greater autonomy for the black workforce, and agitate for the more radical goal of land confiscation and redistribution. "The colored people are very anxious to get land of their own to live upon independently; and they want money to buy stock to make crops," reported one black Union League organizer. "The only way to get these necessaries is to give our votes to the [Republican] party . . . making every effort possible to bring these blessings about by reconstructing the State." Two Hale County former slaves, Brister Reese and James K. Green, won election to the Alabama state legislature in 1869.

It was not long before these economic and political gains prompted a white counterattack. In the spring of 1868, the Ku Klux Klan—a secret organization devoted to terrorizing and intimidating African Americans and their white Republican allies—came to Hale County. Disguised in white sheets, armed with guns and whips, and making nighttime raids on horseback, Klansmen flogged, beat, and murdered freed people. They intimidated voters and silenced political activists. Planters used Klan terror to dissuade former slaves from leaving plantations or organizing for higher wages.

With the passage of the Ku Klux Klan Act in 1871, the federal government cracked down on the Klan, breaking its power temporarily in parts of the former Confederacy. But no serious effort was made to stop Klan terror in the west Alabama black belt, and planters there succeeded in reestablishing much of their social and political control.

The events in Hale County illustrate the struggles that beset communities throughout the South during the Reconstruction era after the Civil War. The destruction of slavery and the Confederacy forced African Americans and white people to renegotiate their old economic and political roles. These community battles both shaped and were shaped by the victorious and newly expansive federal government in Washington. In the end, Reconstruction was only partially successful. Not until the "Second Reconstruction" of the twentieth-century civil rights movement would the descendants of Hale County's African Americans begin to enjoy the full fruits of freedom—and even then not without challenge.

Greensboro

KEY TOPICS

- Competing political plans for reconstructing the defeated Confederacy

- Difficult transition from slavery to freedom for African Americans

- The political and social legacy of Reconstruction in the southern states

- Post–Civil War transformations in the economic and political life of the North

THE POLITICS OF RECONSTRUCTION

When General Robert E. Lee's men stacked their guns at Appomattox, the bloodiest war in American history ended. More than 600,000 soldiers had died during the four years of fighting, 360,000 Union and 260,000 Confederate. Another 275,000 Union and 190,000 Confederate troops had been wounded. Although President Abraham Lincoln insisted early on that the purpose of the war was to preserve the Union, by 1863 it had evolved as well into a struggle for African American liberation. Indeed the political, economic, and moral issues posed by slavery were the root cause of the Civil War, and the war ultimately destroyed slavery, although not racism, once and for all.

The Civil War also settled the Constitutional crisis provoked by the secession of the Confederacy and its justification in appeals to states' rights . The name "United States" would from now on be understood as a singular rather than a plural noun, signaling an important change in the meaning of American nationality. The old notion of the United States as a voluntary union of sovereign states gave way to the new reality of a single nation in which the federal government took precedence over the individual states. The key historical developments of the Reconstruction era revolved around precisely how the newly strengthened national government would define its relationship with the defeated Confederate states and the 4 million newly freed slaves.

The Defeated South

The white South paid an extremely high price for secession, war, and defeat. In addition to the battlefield casualties, the Confederate states sustained deep material and psychological wounds. Much of the best agricultural land lay waste, including the rich fields of northern Virginia, the Shenandoah Valley, and large sections of Tennessee, Mississippi, Georgia, and South Carolina. Many towns and cities—including Richmond, Atlanta, and Columbia, South Carolina—were in ruins. By 1865, the South's most precious commodities, cotton and African American slaves, no longer were measures of wealth and prestige. Retreating

Confederates destroyed most of the South's cotton to prevent its capture by federal troops. What remained was confiscated by Union agents as contraband of war. The former slaves, many of whom had fled to Union lines during the latter stages of the war, were determined to chart their own course in the reconstructed South as free men and women.

It would take the South's economy a generation to overcome the severe blows dealt by the war. In 1860 the South held roughly 25 percent of the nation's wealth; a decade later it controlled only 12 percent. Many white Southerners resented their conquered status, and white notions of race, class, and "honor" died hard. A white North Carolinian, for example, who had lost almost everything dear to him in the war—his sons, home, and slaves—recalled in 1865 that in spite of all his tragedy he still retained one thing. "They've left me one inestimable privilege—to hate 'em. I git up at half-past four in the morning, and sit up till twelve at night, to hate 'em." As late as 1870 the Reverend Robert Lewis Dabney of Virginia wrote: "I do not forgive. I try not to forgive. What! forgive those people, who have invaded our country, burned our cities, destroyed our homes, slain our young men, and spread desolation and ruin over our land! No, I do not forgive them."

Emancipation proved the bitterest pill for white Southerners to swallow, especially the planter elite. Conquered and degraded, and in their view robbed of their slave property, white people responded by regarding African Americans more than ever as inferior to themselves. In the antebellum South white skin had defined a social bond that transcended economic class. It gave even the lowliest poor white a badge of superiority over even the most skilled slave or prosperous free African American. Emancipation, however, forced white people to redefine their world. Many believed that without white direction, the freed people would languish, become wards of the state, or die off. Most white people believed that African Americans were too lazy to take care of themselves and survive. At the very least, whites reasoned, the South's agricultural economy would suffer at the hands of allegedly undisciplined and inefficient African Americans. The specter of political power and social equality for African Americans made

Charleston, South Carolina, in 1865, after Union troops had burned the city. In the aftermath of the Civil War, scenes like this were common throughout the South. The destruction of large portions of so many southern cities and towns contributed to the postwar economic hardships faced by the region.

racial order the consuming passion of most white Southerners during the Reconstruction years. In fact, racism can be seen as one of the major forces driving Reconstruction and, ultimately, undermining it.

Abraham Lincoln's Plan

By late 1863, Union military victories had convinced President Lincoln of the need to fashion a plan for the reconstruction of the South (see Chapter 16). Lincoln based his reconstruction program on bringing the seceded states back into the Union as quickly as possible. He was determined to respect private property (except in the case of slave property), and he opposed imposing harsh punishments for rebellion. His Proclamation of Amnesty and Reconstruction of December 1863 offered "full pardon" and the restoration of property, not including slaves, to white Southerners willing to swear an oath of allegiance to the United States and its laws, including the Emancipation Proclamation. Prominent Confederate military and civil leaders were excluded from Lincoln's offer, though he indicated that he would freely pardon them.

The president also proposed that when the number of any Confederate state's voters who took the oath of allegiance reached 10 percent of the number who had voted in the election of 1860, this group could establish a state government that Lincoln would recognize as legitimate. Fundamental to this Ten Percent Plan was acceptance by the reconstructed governments of the abolition of slavery. Lincoln's plan was designed less as a blueprint for Reconstruction than as a way to shorten

the war and gain white people's support for emancipation. It angered those Republicans—known as Radical Republicans—who advocated not only equal rights for the freedmen but a tougher stance toward the white South. As a result, when Arkansas and Louisiana met the president's requirements for reentry into the Union, Congress refused to seat their representatives.

In July 1864, Senator Benjamin F. Wade of Ohio and Congressman Henry W. Davis of Maryland, both Radicals, proposed a harsher alternative to the Ten Percent Plan. The Wade-Davis bill required 50 percent of a seceding state's white male citizens to take a loyalty oath before elections could be held for a convention to rewrite the state's constitution. The bill also guaranteed equality before the law (although not suffrage) for former slaves. Unlike the president, the Radicals saw Reconstruction as a chance to effect a fundamental transformation of southern society. They thus wanted to delay the process until war's end and to limit participation to a small number of southern Unionists. Lincoln viewed Reconstruction as part of the larger effort to win the war and abolish slavery. He wanted to weaken the Confederacy by creating new state governments that could win broad support from southern white people. The Wade-Davis bill threatened his efforts to build political consensus within the southern states, and Lincoln therefore pocket-vetoed it, by refusing to sign it within ten days of the adjournment of Congress.

Redistribution of southern land among former slaves posed another thorny issue for Lincoln, Congress, and federal military officers. As Union armies occupied parts of the South, commanders had improvised a variety of arrangements involving confiscated plantations and the African American labor force. For example, in 1862 General Benjamin F. Butler began a policy of transforming slaves on Louisiana sugar plantations into wage laborers under the close supervision of occupying federal troops. Butler's policy required slaves to remain on the estates of loyal planters, where they would receive wages according to a fixed schedule, as well as food and medical care for the aged and sick. Abandoned plantations would be leased to northern investors. Butler's successor, General Nathaniel P. Banks, extended this system throughout occupied Louisiana. By 1864 some 50,000 African American laborers on nearly 1,500 Louisiana estates worked either directly for the government or for individual planters under contracts supervised by the army.

In January 1865, General William T. Sherman issued Special Field Order 15, setting aside the Sea Islands off the Georgia coast and a portion of the South Carolina low-country rice fields for the exclusive settlement of freed people. Each family would receive forty acres of land and the loan of mules from the army—the origin, perhaps, of the famous call for "forty acres and a

FREEDOM TO SLAVES!

Whereas, the President of the United States did, on the first day of the present month, issue his *Proclamation* declaring "that *all persons held as Slaves in certain designated States, and parts of States, are, and henceforward shall be free*," and that the Executive Government of the United States, including the Military and Naval authorities thereof, would recognize and maintain the freedom of said persons. *And Whereas*, the county of *Frederick* is included in the territory designated by the Proclamation of the President, in which the *Slaves should become free*, I therefore hereby notify the citizens of the city of Winchester, and of said County, of said Proclamation, and of my intention to maintain and enforce the same.

I expect all citizens to yield a ready compliance with the Proclamation of the Chief Executive, and I admonish all persons disposed to resist its peaceful enforcement, that upon manifesting such disposition by acts, they will be regarded as rebels in arms against the lawful authority of the Federal Government and dealt with accordingly.

All persons liberated by said Proclamation are admonished to abstain from all violence, and immediately betake themselves to useful occupations.

The officers of this command are admonished and ordered to act in accordance with said proclamation and to yield their ready co-operation in its enforcement.

R. H. Milroy,
Brig. Gen'l Commanding.

Winchester Va.
Jan. 5th, 1863.

A Union commander notifies the citizens of Winchester, Virginia, of President Abraham Lincoln's Emancipation Proclamation. Union officers throughout the South had to improvise arrangements for dealing with African Americans who streamed into Union army camps. For many newly freed slaves, the call for taking up "useful occupations" meant serving the Union forces in their neighborhoods as laborers, cooks, spies, and soldiers.

mule" that would soon capture the imagination of African Americans throughout the South. Sherman's intent was not to revolutionize southern society but to relieve the demands placed on his army by the thousands of impoverished African Americans who followed his march to the sea. By the summer of 1865 some 40,000 freed people, eager to take advantage of the general's order, had been settled on 400,000 acres of "Sherman land."

Conflicts within the Republican Party prevented the development of a systematic land distribution program. Still, Lincoln and the Republican Congress supported other measures to aid the emancipated slaves. In March 1865 Congress established the Freedmen's Bureau. Along with providing food, clothing, and fuel to destitute former slaves, the bureau was charged with supervising and managing "all the abandoned lands in the South and the control of all subjects relating to refugees and freedmen." The act that established the bureau also stated that forty acres of abandoned or confiscated land could be leased to freed slaves or white Unionists, who would have an option to purchase after three years and "such title thereto as the United States can convey." To guarantee the end of slavery once the war ended, Republicans drafted the Thirteenth Amendment, declaring that "neither slavery nor involuntary servitude, except as a punishment for crime . . . , shall

exist within the United States." This amendment passed both houses of Congress by January 1865 and was ratified by the necessary three-fourths of the states on December 18, 1865—eight months after Lee's surrender.

At the time of Lincoln's assassination, his Reconstruction policy remained unsettled and incomplete. In its broad outlines the president's plans had seemed to favor a speedy restoration of the southern states to the Union and a minimum of federal intervention in their affairs. But with his death the specifics of postwar Reconstruction had to be hammered out by a new president, Andrew Johnson of Tennessee, a man whose personality, political background, and racist leanings put him at odds with the Republican-controlled Congress.

Andrew Johnson and Presidential Reconstruction

Andrew Johnson, a Democrat and former slaveholder, was a most unlikely successor to the martyred Lincoln. By trade a tailor, educated by his wife, Johnson overcame his impoverished background and served as state legislator, governor, and U.S. senator. Throughout his career Johnson had championed yeoman farmers and viewed the South's plantation aristocrats with contempt. He was the only southern member of the U.S. Senate to remain loyal to the Union, and he held the planter elite responsible for secession and defeat. In 1862 Lincoln appointed Johnson to the difficult post of military governor of Tennessee. There he successfully began wartime Reconstruction and cultivated Unionist support in the mountainous eastern districts of that state.

In 1864 the Republicans, in an appeal to northern and border state "War Democrats," nominated Johnson for vice president. But despite Johnson's success in Tennessee and in the 1864 campaign, many Radical Republicans distrusted him, and the hardscrabble Tennessean remained a political outsider in Republican circles. In the immediate aftermath of Lincoln's murder, however, Johnson appeared to side with those Radical Republicans who sought to treat the South as a conquered province. "Treason is a crime and must be made odious," Johnson declared. "Traitors must be impoverished. . . . They must not only be punished, but their social power must be destroyed." The new president also hinted at indicting prominent Confederate officials for treason, disfranchising them, and confiscating their property.

Such tough talk appealed to Republicans. But support for Johnson quickly faded as the new president's policies unfolded. Johnson defined Reconstruction as the province of the executive, not the legislative branch, and he planned to restore the Union as quickly as possible. He blamed individual Southerners—the planter elite—rather than entire states for leading the South down the disastrous road to secession. In line with this philosophy, Johnson outlined mild terms for reentry to the Union.

In the spring of 1865 Johnson granted amnesty and pardon, including restoration of property rights except slaves, to all Confederates who pledged loyalty to the Union and support for emancipation. Fourteen classes of Southerners, mostly major Confederate officials and wealthy landowners, were excluded. But these men could apply individually for presidential pardons. The power to pardon his former enemies—the Old South's planter elite—gratified Johnson and reinforced his class bias. It also helped win southern support for his lenient policies, for Johnson pardoned former Confederates liberally. In September 1865 Johnson granted an average of a hundred pardons a day, and during his tenure he pardoned roughly 90 percent of those who applied. Significantly, Johnson instituted this plan while Congress was not in session.

Johnson also appointed provisional governors for seven of the former Confederate states, requiring them to hold elections for state constitutional conventions. Participation in this political process was limited to white people who had been pardoned or who had taken a loyalty oath. Johnson also called on state conventions to repudiate secession, acknowledge the abolition of slavery, and void state debts incurred during the war. By the fall of 1865 ten of the eleven Confederate states claimed to have met Johnson's requirements to reenter the Union. On December 6, 1865, in his first annual message to Congress, the president declared the "restoration" of the Union virtually complete. But a serious division within the federal government was taking shape, for the Congress was not about to allow the president free rein in determining the conditions of southern readmission.

Andrew Johnson used the term "restoration" rather than "reconstruction." A lifelong Democrat with ambitions to be elected president on his own in 1868, Johnson hoped to build a new political coalition composed of northern Democrats, conservative Republicans, and southern Unionists. Firmly committed to white supremacy, he opposed political rights for the freedmen. In 1866, after Frederick Douglass and other black leaders had met with him to discuss black suffrage, Johnson told an aide: "Those damned sons of bitches thought they had me in a trap! I know that damned Douglass; he's just like any nigger, and he would sooner cut a white man's throat than not." Johnson's open sympathy for his fellow white Southerners, his antiblack bias, and his determination to control the course of Reconstruction placed him on a collision course with the powerful Radical wing of the Republican Party.

The Radical Republican Vision

Most Radicals were men whose careers had been shaped by the slavery controversy. At the core of their thinking lay a deep belief in equal political rights and equal economic opportunity, both guaranteed by a powerful national government. They argued that once free labor, universal education, and equal rights were implanted in the South, that region would be able to share in the North's material wealth, progress, and fluid social mobility. Representative George W. Julian of Indiana typified the Radical vision for the South. He called for elimination of the region's "large estates, widely scattered settlements, wasteful agriculture, popular ignorance, social degradation, the decline of manufactures, contempt for honest labor, and a pampered oligarchy." This process would allow Republicans to develop "small farms, thrifty tillage, free schools, social independence, flourishing manufactures and the arts, respect for honest labor, and equality of political rights."

In the Radicals' view, the power of the federal government would be central to the remaking of southern society, especially in guaranteeing civil rights and suffrage for freedmen. In the most far-reaching proposal, Representative Thaddeus Stevens of Pennsylvania called for the confiscation of 400 million acres belonging to the wealthiest 10 percent of Southerners, to be redistributed to black and white yeomen and northern land buyers. "The whole fabric of southern society must be changed," Stevens told Pennsylvania Republicans in September 1865, "and never can it be done if this opportunity is lost. How can republican institutions, free schools, free churches, free social intercourse exist in a mingled community of nabobs and serfs? If the South is ever to be made a safe republic let her lands be cultivated by the toil of the owners."

Northern Republicans were especially outraged by the stringent "black codes" passed by South Carolina, Mississippi, Louisiana, and other states. These were designed to restrict the freedom of the black labor force and keep freed people as close to slave status as possible. Laborers who left their jobs before contracts expired would forfeit wages already earned and be subject to arrest by any white citizen. Vagrancy, very broadly defined, was punishable by fines and involuntary plantation labor. Apprenticeship clauses obliged black children to work without pay for employers. Some states attempted to bar African Americans from land ownership. Other laws specifically denied African Americans equality with white people in civil rights, excluding them from juries and prohibiting interracial marriages.

The black codes underscored the unwillingness of white Southerners to accept the full meaning of freedom for African Americans. Mississippi's version contained a catchall section levying fines and possible imprisonment for any former slaves "committing riots, routs, affrays, trespasses, malicious mischief, cruel treatment to animals, seditious speeches, insulting gestures, language, or acts, or assaults on any person, disturbance of the peace, exercising the function of a minister of

This wood engraving appeared in Frank Leslie's Illustrated Newspaper, May 5, 1864. It depicted "vagrant" African Americans in New Orleans being rounded up by the Provost Guard, in compliance with Louisiana's restrictive "Black Code." These types of images helped raise concerns in the North about the treatment of recently freed slaves.

the Gospel without a license . . . vending spiritous or intoxicating liquors, or committing any other misdemeanor, the punishment of which is not specifically provided for by law."

The Radicals, although not a majority of their party, were joined by moderate Republicans as growing numbers of Northerners grew suspicious of white southern intransigence and the denial of political rights to freedmen. When the Thirty-ninth Congress convened in December 1865, the large Republican majority prevented the seating of the white Southerners elected to Congress under President Johnson's provisional state governments. Republicans also established the Joint Committee on Reconstruction. After hearing extensive testimony from a broad range of witnesses, it concluded that not only were old Confederates back in power in the South but that black codes and racial violence required increased protection for African Americans.

As a result, in the spring of 1866 Congress passed two important bills designed to aid African Americans. The landmark Civil Rights bill, which bestowed full citizenship on African Americans, overturned the 1857 Dred Scott decision and the black codes. It defined all persons born in the United States (except Indian peoples) as national citizens, and it enumerated various rights, including the rights to make and enforce contracts, to sue, to give evidence, and to buy and sell property. Under this bill, African Americans acquired "full and equal benefit of all laws and proceedings for the security of person and property as is enjoyed by white citizens."

Congress also voted to enlarge the scope of the Freedmen's Bureau, empowering it to build schools and pay teachers, and also to establish courts to prosecute those charged with depriving African Americans of their civil rights. The bureau achieved important, if limited, success in aiding African Americans. Bureau-run schools helped lay the foundation for southern public education. The bureau's network of courts allowed freed people to bring suits against white people in disputes involving violence, nonpayment of wages, or unfair division of crops. The very existence of courts hearing public testimony by African Americans provided an important psychological challenge to traditional notions of white racial domination.

An angry President Johnson vetoed both of these bills. In opposing the Civil Rights bill, Johnson denounced the assertion of national power to protect African American civil rights, claiming it was a "stride toward centralization, and the concentration of all legislative powers in the national Government." In the case of the Freedmen's Bureau, Johnson argued that Congress lacked jurisdiction over the eleven unrepresented southern states. But Johnson's intemperate attacks on the Radicals—he damned them as traitors unwilling to restore the Union—united moderate and Radical Republicans and they succeeded in overriding the vetoes. Congressional Republicans, led by the Radical faction, were now unified in challenging the president's power to direct Reconstruction and in using national authority to define and protect the rights of citizens.

In June 1866, fearful that the Civil Rights Act might be declared unconstitutional and eager to settle the basis for the seating of southern representatives, Congress passed the Fourteenth Amendment. The amendment defined national citizenship to include former slaves ("all persons born or naturalized in the United States") and prohibited the states from violating the privileges of citizens without due process of law. It also empowered Congress to reduce the representation of any state that denied the suffrage to males over twenty-one. Republicans adopted the Fourteenth Amendment as their platform for the 1866 congressional elections and suggested that southern states would have to ratify it as a condition of readmission. President Johnson, meanwhile, took to the stump in August to support conservative Democratic and Republican candidates. His unrestrained speeches often degenerated into harangues, alienating many voters and aiding the Republican cause.

For their part, the Republicans skillfully portrayed Johnson and northern Democrats as disloyal and white Southerners as unregenerate. Republicans began an effective campaign tradition known as "waving the bloody shirt"—reminding northern voters of the hundreds of thousands of Yankee soldiers left dead or maimed by the war. In the November 1866 elections, the Republicans increased their majority in both the House and the Senate and gained control of all the northern states. The stage was now set for a battle between the president and Congress. Was it to be Johnson's "restoration" or Congressional Reconstruction?

Congressional Reconstruction and the Impeachment Crisis

United against Johnson, Radical and moderate Republicans took control of Reconstruction early in 1867. In March Congress passed the First Reconstruction Act over Johnson's veto. This act divided the South into five military districts subject to martial law. To achieve restoration, southern states were first required to call new constitutional conventions, elected by universal manhood suffrage. Once these states had drafted new constitutions, guaranteed African American voting rights, and ratified the Fourteenth Amendment, they were eligible for readmission to the Union. Supplementary legislation, also passed over the president's veto, invalidated the provisional governments established by Johnson, empowered the military to administer voter registration, and required an oath of loyalty to the United States.

Congress also passed several laws aimed at limiting Johnson's power. One of these, the Tenure of Office Act, stipulated that any officeholder appointed by the president with the Senate's advice and consent could not be removed until the Senate had approved a successor. In this way, congressional leaders could protect Republi-

Reconstruction of the South, 1866–1877   *Dates for the readmission of former Confederate states to the Union and the return of Democrats to power varied according to the specific political situations in those states.*

cans, such as Secretary of War Edwin M. Stanton, entrusted with implementing Congressional Reconstruction. In August 1867, with Congress adjourned, Johnson suspended Stanton and appointed General Ulysses S. Grant interim secretary of war. This move enabled the president to remove generals in the field that he judged to be too radical and replace them with men who were sympathetic to his own views. It also served as a challenge to the Tenure of Office Act. In January 1868, when the Senate overruled Stanton's suspension, Grant broke openly with Johnson and vacated the office. Stanton resumed his position and barricaded himself in his office when Johnson attempted to remove him once again.

Outraged by Johnson's relentless obstructionism, and seizing upon his violation of the Tenure of Office Act as a pretext, Radical and moderate Republicans in the House of Representatives again joined forces and voted to impeach the president by a vote of 126 to 47 on February 24, 1868, charging him with eleven counts of high crimes and misdemeanors. To ensure the support of moderate Republicans, the articles of impeachment focused on violations of the Tenure of Office Act. The case against Johnson would have to be made on the basis of willful violation of the law. Left unstated were the Republicans' real reasons for wanting the president removed: Johnson's political views and his opposition to the Reconstruction Acts.

An influential group of moderate Senate Republicans feared the damage a conviction might do to the constitutional separation of powers. They also worried about the political and economic policies that might be pursued by Benjamin Wade, the president pro tem of the Senate and a leader of the Radical Republicans, who, because there was no vice president, would succeed to the presidency if Johnson were removed from office. Behind the scenes during his Senate trial, Johnson agreed to abide by the Reconstruction Acts. In May, the Senate voted 35 for conviction, 19 for acquittal—one vote shy of the two-thirds necessary for removal from office. Johnson's narrow acquittal established the precedent that only criminal actions by a president—not political disagreements—warranted removal from office.

The Election of 1868

By the summer of 1868, seven former Confederate states (Alabama, Arkansas, Florida, Louisiana, North Carolina, South Carolina, and Tennessee) had ratified the revised constitutions, elected Republican governments, and ratified the Fourteenth Amendment. They had thereby earned readmission to the Union. Though Georgia, Mississippi, Texas, and Virginia still awaited readmission, the presidential election of 1868 offered some hope that the Civil War's legacy of sectional hate and racial tension might finally ease.

Republicans nominated Ulysses S. Grant, the North's foremost military hero. An Ohio native, Grant had graduated from West Point in 1843, served in the Mexican War, and resigned from the army in 1854. Unhappy in civilian life, Grant received a second chance during the Civil War. He rose quickly to become commander in the western theater, and he later destroyed Lee's army in Virginia. Although his armies suffered terrible losses, Grant enjoyed tremendous popularity after the war, especially when he broke with Johnson. Totally lacking in political experience, Grant admitted after receiving the nomination that he had been forced into it in spite of himself: "I could not back down without leaving the contest for power for the next four years between mere trading politicians, the elevation of whom, no matter which party won, would lose to us, largely, the results of the costly war which we have gone through."

Significantly, at the very moment that the South was being forced to enfranchise former slaves as a prerequisite for readmission to the Union, the Republicans rejected a campaign plank endorsing black suffrage in the North. Their platform left "the question of suffrage in all the loyal States . . . to the people of those States." State referendums calling for black suffrage failed in eight northern states between 1865 and 1868, succeeding only in Iowa and Minnesota. The Democrats, determined to reverse Congressional Reconstruction, nominated Horatio Seymour, former governor of New York and a long-

time foe of emancipation and supporter of states' rights. Democrats North and South exploited the race question to garner votes. Their platform blasted the Republicans for subjecting the nation "in time of profound peace, to military despotism and negro supremacy." The party sought "the abolition of the Freedmen's Bureau; and all political instrumentalities designed to secure negro supremacy."

Throughout the South, violence marked the electoral process. The Ku Klux Klan, founded as a Tennessee social club in 1866, emerged as a potent instrument of terror (see the opening of this chapter). In Louisiana, Arkansas, Georgia, and South Carolina the Klan threatened, whipped, and murdered black and white Republicans to prevent them from voting. This terrorism enabled the Democrats to carry Georgia and Louisiana, but it ultimately cost the Democrats votes in the North. In the final tally, Grant carried twenty-six of the thirty-four states for an electoral college victory of 214 to 80. But he received a popular majority of less than 53 percent, beating Seymour by only 306,000 votes. Significantly, more than 500,000 African American voters cast their ballots for Grant, demonstrating their overwhelming support for the Republican Party. The Republicans also retained large majorities in both houses of Congress.

In February 1869, Congress passed the Fifteenth Amendment, providing that "the right of citizens of the United States to vote shall not be denied or abridged . . . on account of race, color, or previous condition of servitude." Noticeably absent was language prohibiting the states from imposing educational, residential, or other qualifications for voting. Moderate Republicans feared that filling these discriminatory loopholes might make it difficult to obtain ratification for the amendment by the required three-quarters of the states. To enhance the chances of ratification, Congress required the three remaining unreconstructed states—Mississippi, Texas, and Virginia—to ratify both the Fourteenth and Fifteenth Amendments before readmission. They did so and rejoined the Union in early 1870. The Fifteenth Amendment was ratified in February 1870. In the narrow sense of simply readmitting the former Confederate states to the Union, Reconstruction was complete.

Woman Suffrage and Reconstruction

The battles over the political status of African Americans proved an important turning point for women as well. The Fourteenth and Fifteenth Amendments, which granted citizenship and the vote to freedmen, both inspired and frustrated women's rights activists. Many of these women had long been active in the abolitionist movement. During the war, they had actively supported the union cause through their work

OVERVIEW

RECONSTRUCTION AMENDMENTS TO THE CONSTITUTION, 1865–1870		
Amendment and Date Passed by Congress	Main Provisions	Ratification Process (¾ of all states including ex-Confederate states required)
13 (January 1865)	Prohibited slavery in the United States	December 1865 (27 states, including 8 southern states)
14 (June 1866)	• Conferred national citizenship on all persons born or naturalized in the United States • Reduced state representation in Congress proportionally for any state disfranchising male citizens • Denied former Confederates the right to hold state or national office • Repudiated Confederate debt.	July 1868 (after Congress makes ratification a prerequisite for readmission of ex-Confederate states to the Union)
15 (February 1869)	Prohibited denial of suffrage because of race, color, or previous condition of servitude	March 1870 (ratification required for readmission of Virginia, Texas, Mississippi, and Georgia)

in the National Woman's Loyal League and the United States Sanitary Commission. Elizabeth Cady Stanton and Susan B. Anthony, two leaders with long involvement in both the antislavery and feminist movements, objected to the inclusion of the word "male" in the Fourteenth Amendment. "If that word 'male' be inserted," Stanton predicted in 1866, "it will take us a century at least to get it out."

Insisting that the causes of the African American vote and the women's vote were linked, Stanton, Anthony, and Lucy Stone founded the American Equal Rights Association in 1866. The group launched a series of lobbying and petition campaigns to remove racial and sexual restrictions on voting from state constitutions. In Kansas, for example, an old antislavery battlefield, the association vigorously supported two 1867 referendums that would have removed the words "male" and "white" from the state's constitution. But Kansas voters rejected both woman suffrage and black suffrage. Throughout the nation, the old abolitionist organizations and the Republican Party emphasized passage of the Fourteenth and Fifteenth Amendments and withdrew funds and support from the cause of woman suffrage. Disagreements over these amendments divided suffragists for decades.

The radical wing, led by Stanton and Anthony, opposed the Fifteenth Amendment, arguing that ratification would establish an "aristocracy of sex," enfranchising all men while leaving women without political privileges. In arguing for a Sixteenth Amendment that would secure the vote for women, they used racist and elitist appeals. They urged "American women of wealth, education, virtue, and refinement" to support the vote for women and oppose the Fifteenth Amendment "if you do not wish the lower orders of Chinese, Africans, Germans, and Irish, with their low ideas of womanhood to make laws for you and your daughters." Other women's rights activists, including Lucy Stone and Frederick Douglass, asserted that "this hour belongs to the Negro." They feared a debate over woman suffrage at the national level would jeopardize passage of the two amendments.

By 1869 woman suffragists had split into two competing organizations. The moderate American Woman Suffrage Association (AWSA), led by Lucy Stone, Julia Ward Howe, and Henry Blackwell, focused on achieving woman suffrage at the state level. It maintained close ties with the Republican Party and the old abolitionist networks, worked for the Fifteenth Amendment, and actively sought the support of men. The more radical wing founded the all-female National Woman

Susan B. Anthony (1820–1906) and Elizabeth Cady Stanton (1815–1902), the two most influential leaders of the woman suffrage movement, ca. 1892. Anthony and Stanton broke with their longtime abolitionist allies after the Civil War when they opposed the Fifteenth Amendment. They argued that the doctrine of universal manhood suffrage it embodied would give constitutional authority to the claim that men were the social and political superiors of women. As founders of the militant National Woman Suffrage Association, Stanton and Anthony established an independent woman suffrage movement with a broader spectrum of goals for women's rights and drew millions of women into public life during the late nineteenth century.

Suffrage Association (NWSA). For the NWSA, the vote represented only one part of a broad spectrum of goals inherited from the Declaration of Sentiments manifesto adopted at the first women's rights convention held in 1848 at Seneca Falls, New York (see Chapter 13).

Although women did not win the vote in this period, they did establish an independent suffrage movement that eventually drew millions of women into political life. The NWSA in particular demonstrated that self-government and democratic participation in the public sphere were crucial for women's emancipation. Stanton and Anthony toured the country, speaking to women's

audiences and inspiring the formation of suffrage societies. The NWSA's weekly magazine, *Revolution*, became a forum for feminist ideas on divorce laws, unequal pay, women's property rights, and marriage. The failure of woman suffrage after the Civil War was less a result of factional fighting than of the larger defeat of Radical Reconstruction and the ideal of expanded citizenship.

THE MEANING OF FREEDOM

For 4 million slaves, freedom arrived in various ways in different parts of the South. In many areas, slavery had collapsed long before Lee's surrender at Appomattox. In regions far removed from the presence of federal troops, African Americans did not learn of slavery's end until the spring of 1865. There were thousands of sharply contrasting stories, many of which revealed the need for freed slaves to confront their owners. One Virginia slave, hired out to another family during the war, had been working in the fields when a friend told her she was now free. "Is dat so?" she exclaimed. Dropping her hoe, she ran the seven miles to her old place, confronted her former mistress, and shouted, "I'se free! Yes, I'se free! Ain't got to work fo' you no mo'. You can't put me in yo' pocket now!" Her mistress burst into tears and ran into the house. That was all the former slave needed to see. But regardless of specific regional circumstances, the meaning of "freedom" would be contested for years to come.

The deep desire for independence from white control formed the underlying aspiration of newly freed slaves. For their part, most southern white people sought to restrict the boundaries of that independence. As individuals and as members of communities transformed by emancipation, former slaves struggled to establish economic, political, and cultural autonomy. They built on the twin pillars of slave culture—the family and the church—to consolidate and expand African American institutions and thereby laid the foundation for the modern African American community.

Emancipation greatly expanded the choices available to African Americans. It helped build confidence in their ability to effect change without deferring to white people. Freedom also meant greater uncertainty and risk. But the vast majority of African Americans were more than willing to take their chances. Many years later, one former Texas slave pondered the question "What I likes bes, to be slave or free?" She answered: "Well, it's dis way. In slavery I owns nothin' and never owns nothin'. In freedom I's own de home and raise de family. All dat cause me worryment and in slavery I has no worryment, but I takes de freedom."

Moving About

The first impulse of many emancipated slaves was to test their freedom. The simplest, most obvious way to do this involved leaving home. By walking off a plantation, coming and going without restraint or fear of punishment, African Americans could savor freedom. Throughout the summer and fall of 1865, observers in the South noted enormous numbers of freed people on the move. One former slave squatting in an abandoned tent outside Selma, Alabama, explained his feeling to a northern journalist: "I's want to be free man, cum when I please, and nobody say nuffin to me, nor order me roun'." When urged to stay on with the South Carolina family she had served for years as a cook, a slave woman replied firmly: "No, Miss, I must go. If I stay here I'll never know I am free."

Yet many who left their old neighborhoods returned soon afterward to seek work in the general vicinity, or even on the plantation they had left. Many wanted to separate themselves from former owners, but not from familial ties and friendships. Others moved away altogether, seeking jobs in nearby towns and cities. Many former slaves left predominantly white counties, where they felt more vulnerable and isolated, for new lives in the relative comfort of predominantly black communities. In most southern states, there was a significant population shift toward black belt plantation counties and towns after the war. Many African Americans, attracted by schools, churches, and fraternal societies as well as the army, preferred the city. Between 1865 and 1870, the African American population of the South's ten largest cities doubled, while the white population increased by only 10 percent.

Disgruntled planters had difficulty accepting African American independence. During slavery, they had expected obedience, submission, and loyalty from African Americans. Now many could not understand why so many former slaves wanted to leave despite urgent pleas to continue working at the old place. The deference and humility white people expected from African Americans could no longer be taken for granted. Indeed, many freed people went out of their way to reject the old subservience. Moving about freely was one way of doing this, as was refusing to tip one's hat to white people, ignoring former masters or mistresses in the streets, and refusing to step aside on sidewalks. After encountering an African American who would not step aside, Eliza Andrews, a Georgia plantation mistress, complained, "It is the first time in my life that I have ever had to give up the sidewalk to a man, much less to negroes!" When freed people staged parades, dances, and picnics to celebrate their new freedom, as they did, for example, when commemorating the Emancipation Proclamation, white people invariably condemned them angrily for "insolence," "outrageous spectacles," or "putting on airs."

The African American Family

Emancipation allowed freed people to strengthen family ties. For many former slaves, freedom meant the opportunity to reunite with long-lost family members. To track down relatives, freed people trekked to faraway places, put ads in newspapers, sought the help of Freedmen's Bureau agents, and questioned anyone who might have information about loved ones. Many thousands of family reunions, each with its own story, took place after the war. To William Curtis of Georgia, whose father had been sold to a Virginia planter, "that was the best thing about the war setting us free, he could come back to us." One North Carolina slave, who had seen his parents separated by sale, recalled many years later what for him had been the most significant aspect of freedom. "I has got thirteen great-gran' chilluns an' I know whar dey ever'one am. In slavery times dey'd have been on de block long time ago."

Thousands of African American couples who had lived together under slavery streamed to military and civilian authorities and demanded to be legally married. By 1870, the two-parent household was the norm for a large majority of African Americans. "In their eyes," a Freedmen's Bureau agent reported, "the work of emancipation was incomplete until the families which had been dispersed by slavery were reunited." For many freed people the attempt to find lost relatives dragged on for years. Searches often proved frustrating, exhausting, and ultimately disappointing. Some "reunions" ended painfully with the discovery that spouses had found new partners and started new families.

Emancipation brought changes to gender roles within the African American family as well. By serving in the Union army, African American men played a more direct role than women in the fight for freedom. In the political sphere, black men could now serve on juries, vote, and hold office; black women, like their white counterparts, could not. Freedmen's Bureau agents designated the husband as household head and established lower wage scales for women laborers. African American editors, preachers, and politicians regularly quoted the biblical injunction that wives submit to their husbands. African American men asserted their male authority, denied under slavery, by insisting their wives work at home instead of in the fields.

For years after 1865, southern planters complained about the scarcity of women and children available for field work. African American women generally wanted to devote more time than they had under slavery to caring for their children and to performing such domestic chores as cooking, sewing, gardening, and laundering. Yet African American women continued to work outside the home, engaging in seasonal field labor for wages or working a family's rented plot. Most rural black families barely eked out a living, and thus the labor of every family member was essential to survival. The key difference from slave times was that African American families themselves, not white masters and overseers, decided when and where women and children worked.

African American Churches and Schools

The creation of separate African American churches proved the most lasting and important element of the energetic institution building that went on in post-emancipation years. Before the Civil War, southern Protestant churches had relegated slaves and free African Americans to second-class membership. Black worshipers were required to sit in the back during services, they were denied any role in church governance, and they were excluded from Sunday schools. Even in larger cities, where all-black congregations sometimes built their own churches, the law required white pastors. In rural areas, slaves preferred their own preachers to the sermons of local white ministers who quoted Scripture to justify slavery and white supremacy. "That old white preachin' wasn't nothin'," former slave Nancy Williams recalled. "Old white preachers used to talk with their tongues without sayin' nothin', but Jesus told us slaves to talk with our hearts."

In communities around the South, African Americans now pooled their resources to buy land and build their own churches. Before these structures were completed, they might hold services in a railroad boxcar, where Atlanta's First Baptist Church began, or in an outdoor arbor, the original site of the First Baptist Church of Memphis. By late 1866 Charleston's African American community could boast of eleven churches in the city—five Methodist, two Presbyterian, two Episcopalian, one Baptist, and one Congregational. In rural areas, different denominations frequently shared the same church building. Churches became the center not only for religious life but for many other activities that defined the African American community: schools, picnics, festivals, and political meetings. They also helped spawn a host of organizations devoted to benevolence and mutual aid, such as burial societies, Masonic lodges, temperance clubs, and trade associations.

The church became the first social institution fully controlled by African Americans. In nearly every community ministers, respected for their speaking and organizational skills, were among the most influential leaders. By 1877 the great majority of black Southerners had withdrawn from white-dominated churches. In South Carolina, for example, only a few hundred black Methodists attended biracial churches, down from over 40,000 in 1865. The various Protestant denominations competed for the allegiance of African American worshipers. Among Methodists, the African Methodist

Episcopal Church, originally founded in 1816, gained ascendancy over white-dominated rivals. Black Baptist churches, with their decentralized and democratic structure and more emotional services, attracted the greatest number of freed people. By the end of Reconstruction the vast majority of African American Christians belonged to black Baptist or Methodist churches.

The rapid spread of schools reflected African Americans' thirst for self-improvement. Southern states had prohibited education for slaves. But many free black people managed to attend school, and a few slaves had been able to educate themselves. Still, over 90 percent of the South's adult African American population was illiterate in 1860. Access to education thus became a central part of the meaning of freedom. Freedmen's Bureau agents repeatedly expressed amazement at the number of makeshift classrooms organized by African Americans in rural areas. A bureau officer described these "wayside schools": "A negro riding on a loaded wagon, or sitting on a hack waiting for a train, or by the cabin door, is often seen, book in hand delving after the rudiments of knowledge. A group on the platform of a depot, after carefully conning an old spelling book, resolves itself into a class."

African American communities received important educational aid from outside organizations. By 1869 the Freedmen's Bureau was supervising nearly 3,000 schools serving over 150,000 students throughout the South. Over half the roughly 3,300 teachers in these schools were African Americans, many of whom had been free before the Civil War. Other teachers included dedicated northern white women, volunteers sponsored by the American Missionary Association (AMA). The bureau and the AMA also assisted in the founding of several black colleges, including Tougaloo, Hampton, and Fisk, designed to train black teachers. Black self-help proved crucial to the education effort. Throughout the South in 1865 and 1866, African Americans raised money to build schoolhouses, buy supplies, and pay teachers. Black artisans donated labor for construction, and black families offered room and board to teachers.

Land and Labor after Slavery

Most newly emancipated African Americans aspired to quit the plantations and to make new lives for themselves. Leaving the plantation was not as simple as walking off. Some freed people did find jobs in railroad building, mining, ranching, or construction work. Others raised subsistence crops and tended vegetable gardens as squatters. However, white planters tried to retain African Americans as permanent agricultural laborers. Restricting the employment of former slaves was an important goal of the black codes. For example, South Carolina legislation in 1865 provided that "no person of color shall pursue or practice the art, trade, or business of an artisan, mechanic, or shopkeeper, or any other trade employment, or business, besides that of husbandry, or that of a servant under contract for service or labor" without a special and costly permit.

The majority of African Americans hoped to become self-sufficient farmers. As *DeBow's Review* observed in 1869, the freedman showed "great anxiety to have his little home, with his horse, cow, and hogs, separate and apart from others." Many former slaves believed they were entitled to the land they had worked throughout their lives. General Oliver O. Howard, chief commissioner of the Freedmen's Bureau, observed that many "supposed that the Government [would] divide among them the lands of the conquered owners, and furnish them with all that might be necessary to begin life as an independent farmer." This perception was not merely a wishful fantasy. The Freedmen's Bureau Act of 1865 specifically required that abandoned land be leased for three years in forty-acre lots, with an option to buy. Frequent reference in the Congress and the press to the question of land distribution made the idea of "forty acres and a mule" not just a pipe dream but a matter of serious public debate.

Above all, African Americans sought economic autonomy, and ownership of land promised the most independence. "Give us our own land and we take care of ourselves," was how one former slave saw it. "But widout land, de ole massas can hire us or starve us, as dey please." At a Colored Convention in Montgomery, Alabama, in May 1867, delegates argued that the prop-

erty now owned by planters had been "nearly all earned by the sweat of our brows, not theirs. It has been forfeited to the government by the treason of its owners, and is liable to be confiscated whenever the Republican Party demands it."

But by 1866 the federal government had already pulled back from the various wartime experiments involving the breaking up of large plantations and the leasing of small plots to individual families. President Johnson directed General Howard of the Freedmen's Bureau to evict tens of thousands of freed people settled on confiscated and abandoned land in southeastern Virginia, southern Louisiana, and the Georgia and South Carolina low country. These evictions created a deep sense of betrayal among African Americans. A former Mississippi slave, Merrimon Howard, bitterly noted that African Americans had been left with "no land, no house, not so much as a place to lay our head. . . . We were friends on the march, brothers on the battlefield, but in the peaceful pursuits of life it seems that we are strangers."

A variety of labor arrangements could be found in southern agriculture in the immediate postwar years. Each featured both advantages and disadvantages for planters and freed people. Writing in 1866, white planter Percy Roberts identified three distinct "systems of hire" for working the land: money wages, share wages, and sharecropping. Under both the money wage and share wage systems, planters contracted former slaves to work in large gangs, paying them either in

Leaving for Kansas, Harper's Weekly, May 17, 1879. *This drawing depicts a group of southern freedpeople on their way to Kansas. Black disillusionment following the end of Reconstruction led thousands of African Americans to migrate to Kansas, where they hoped to find the political rights, economic opportunities, and freedom from violence denied them in the South. Most of these "Exodusters" (after the biblical story of the Israelite Exodus from Egypt) lacked the capital or experience to establish themselves as independent farmers on the Great Plains. Yet few chose to go back to the South, where their former masters had returned to political and economic power.*

cash (money wage) or with a share of the crop that the workers divided among themselves (share wage). Freedmen's Bureau agents, who generally advocated the money wage arrangement, would often help freedmen negotiate labor contracts with planters. Planters tended to prefer the money wage system because it clearly defined laborers as hirelings and gave planters more direct control over the labor force—for example, by enabling them to discharge the hands they thought

inefficient. Yet most planters were forced to adopt share wages at the insistence of black laborers who were adamantly opposed to serving as mere hirelings.

But both the money wage and share wage systems were unsatisfactory from the perspective of freed people. Both systems relied on the gang labor approach so reminiscent of slavery. And both systems often left African Americans at the mercy of unscrupulous planters who cheated them of their wages or fair

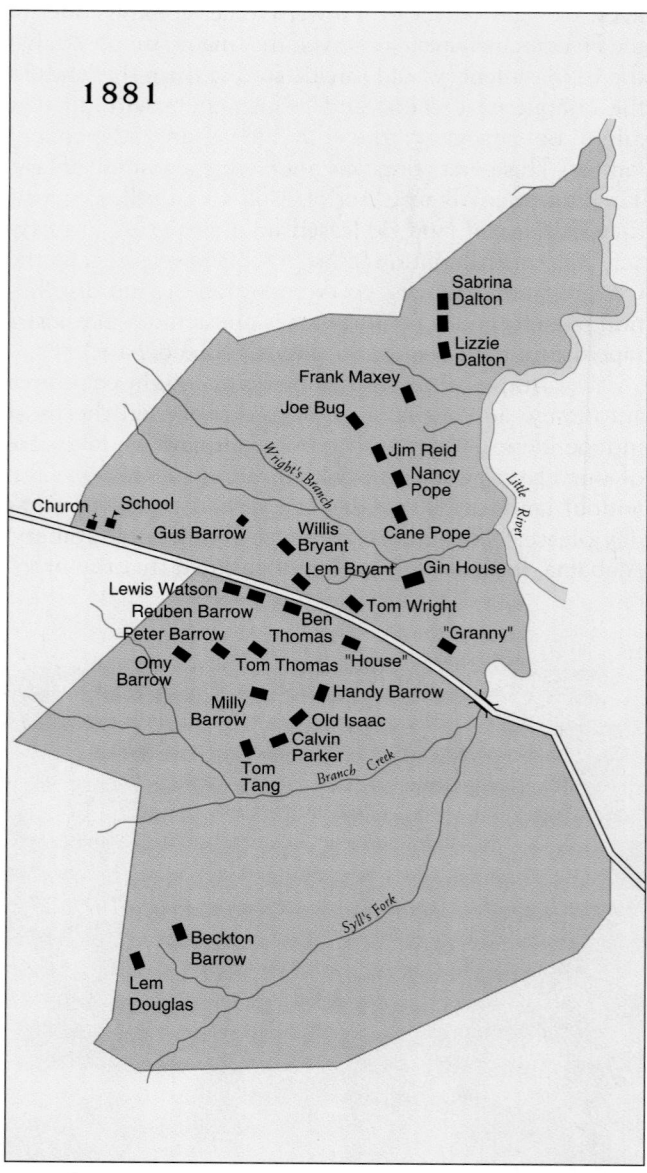

The Barrow Plantation, Oglethorpe County, Georgia, 1860 and 1881 (approx. 2,000 acres)   These two maps, based on drawings from Scribner's Monthly, April 1881, show some of the changes brought by emancipation. In 1860 the plantation's entire black population lived in the communal slave quarters, right next to the white master's house. In 1881 black sharecropper and tenant families lived on individual plots, spread out across the land. The former slaves had also built their own school and church.

shares. Above all, the deep desire for economic improvement and greater autonomy led many African Americans to press for an alternative. By the late 1860s, black people's resistance to working in gangs and their desire to establish independent homesteads forced planters into a compromise system, sharecropping, that emerged as the dominant form of working the land.

Under sharecropping arrangements, individual families contracted with landowners to be responsible for a specific plot. Large plantations were thus broken into family-sized farms. Generally, sharecropper families received one-third of the year's crop if the owner furnished implements, seed, and draft animals, or one-half if they provided their own supplies. African Americans preferred sharecropping to gang labor, as it allowed families to set their own hours and tasks and offered freedom from white supervision and control. For planters, the system stabilized the work force by requiring sharecroppers to remain until the harvest and to employ all family members. It also offered a way around the chronic shortage of cash and credit that plagued the postwar South. But as the *Southern Argus* of Selma, Alabama, editorialized, sharecropping was "an unwilling concession to the freedmen's desire to become a proprietor. . . . It is not a voluntary association from similarity of aims and interests." Freed people did not aspire to sharecropping. Owning land outright or tenant farming (renting land) were both more desirable. But though black sharecroppers clearly enjoyed more autonomy than in the past, the vast majority never achieved economic independence or land ownership. They remained a largely subordinate agricultural labor force.

Sharecropping came to dominate the southern agricultural economy and African American life in particular. By 1880 about 80 percent of the land in the black belt states—Mississippi, Alabama, and Georgia—had been divided into family-sized farms. Nearly three-quarters of black Southerners were sharecroppers. Through much of the black belt, family and community were one. Often several families worked adjoining parcels of land in common, pooling their labor in order to get by. Men usually oversaw crop production. Women went to the fields seasonally during planting or harvesting, but they mainly tended to household chores and child care. In addition, women frequently held jobs that might bring in cash, such as raising chickens or taking in laundry. The cotton harvest engaged all members of the community, from the oldest to the youngest. Cotton picking remained a difficult, labor-intensive task that took priority over all other work.

The Origins of African American Politics

Although the desire for autonomy had led African Americans to pursue their economic and religious goals largely apart from white people, inclusion rather than separation was the objective of early African American political activity. The greatest political activity by African Americans occurred in areas occupied by Union forces during the war. In 1865 and 1866, African Americans throughout the South organized scores of mass meetings, parades, and petitions that demanded civil equality and the right to vote. In the cities, the growing web of churches and fraternal societies helped bolster early efforts at political organization.

Hundreds of African American delegates, selected by local meetings or churches, attended statewide political conventions held throughout the South in 1865 and 1866. Previously free African Americans, as well as black ministers, artisans, and veterans of the Union army, tended to dominate these proceedings, setting a pattern that would hold throughout Reconstruction. Convention debates sometimes reflected the tensions within African American communities, such as friction between poorer former slaves and better-off free black people, or between lighter- and darker-skinned African Americans. But most of these state gatherings concentrated on passing resolutions on issues that united all African Americans. The central concerns were suffrage and equality before the law. Black Southerners firmly proclaimed their identification with the nation's history and republican traditions. The 1865 North Carolina freedmen's convention was typical in describing universal manhood suffrage as "an essential and inseparable element of self-government." It also praised the Declaration of Independence as "the broadest, the deepest, the most comprehensive and truthful definition of human freedom that was ever given to the world."

The passage of the First Reconstruction Act in 1867 encouraged even more political activity among African Americans. The military started registering the South's electorate, ultimately enrolling approximately 735,000 black and 635,000 white voters in the ten unreconstructed states. Five states—Alabama, Florida, Louisiana, Mississippi, and South Carolina—had black electoral majorities. Fewer than half the registered white voters participated in the elections for state constitutional conventions in 1867 and 1868. In contrast, four-fifths of the registered black voters cast ballots in these elections. Much of this new African American political activism was channeled through local Union League chapters throughout the South. However, as the fate of Alex Webb in Hale County, Alabama, again makes clear, few whites welcomed this activism.

Begun during the war as a northern, largely white middle-class patriotic club, the Union League now became the political voice of the former slaves. Union League chapters brought together local African Americans, soldiers, and Freedmen's Bureau agents to demand the vote and an end to legal discrimination

Electioneering at the South, Harper's Weekly, July 25, 1868. *Throughout the Reconstruction-era South, newly freed slaves took a keen interest in both local and national political affairs. The presence of women and children at these campaign gatherings illustrates the importance of contemporary political issues to the entire African American community.*

against African Americans. It brought out African American voters, instructed freedmen in the rights and duties of citizenship, and promoted Republican candidates. Not surprisingly, newly enfranchised freedmen voted Republican and formed the core of the Republican Party in the South.

In 1867 and 1868, the promise of Radical Reconstruction enlarged the scope of African American political participation and brought new leaders to the fore. Many were teachers, preachers, or others with useful skills, such as literacy. For most ordinary African Americans, politics was inseparable from economic issues, especially the land question. Grassroots political organizations frequently intervened in local disputes with planters over the terms of labor contracts. African American political groups closely followed the congressional debates over Reconstruction policy and agitated for land confiscation and distribution. Perhaps most important, politics was the only arena where black and white Southerners might engage each other on an equal basis. As the delegates to an Alabama convention asserted in 1867: "We claim exactly the same rights, privileges and immunities as are enjoyed by white men—we ask nothing more and will be content with nothing less. . . . The law no longer knows white nor black, but simply men, and consequently we are entitled to ride in public conveyances, hold office, sit on juries and do everything else which we have in the past been prevented from doing solely on the ground of color."

SOUTHERN POLITICS AND SOCIETY

By the summer of 1868, when the South had returned to the Union, the majority of Republicans believed the task of Reconstruction to be finished. Ultimately, they put their faith in a political solution to the problems facing the vanquished South. That meant nurturing a viable two-party system in the southern states, where no Republican Party had ever existed. If that could be accomplished, Republicans and Democrats would compete for votes, offices, and influence, just as they did in northern states. Most Republican congressmen were moderates, conceiving Reconstruction in limited terms. They rejected radical calls for confiscation and redistribution of land, as well as permanent military rule of the South. The Reconstruction Acts of 1867 and 1868 laid out the requirements for the readmission of southern states, along with the procedures for forming and electing new governments.

Yet over the next decade the political structure created in the southern states proved too restricted and fragile to sustain itself. Republicans had to employ radical means to protect their essentially conservative goals. To most southern whites the active participation of African Americans in politics seemed extremely dangerous. Federal troops were needed to protect Republican governments and their supporters from violent opposition. Congressional action to monitor southern elections and protect black voting rights became routine. Despite initial successes, southern Republicanism proved an unstable coalition of often conflicting elements, unable to sustain effective power for very long. By 1877, Democrats had regained political control of all the former Confederate states.

Southern Republicans

Three major groups composed the fledgling Republican coalition in the postwar South. African American voters made up a large majority of southern Republicans throughout the Reconstruction era. Yet African Americans outnumbered whites in only three southern states—South Carolina, Mississippi, and Louisiana. They made up roughly one-quarter of the population in Texas, Tennessee, and Arkansas, and between 40 and 50 percent in Virginia, North Carolina, Alabama, Florida, and Georgia. Thus, Republicans would have to attract white support to win elections and sustain power.

A second group consisted of white Northerners, derisively called "carpetbaggers" by native white Southerners. One Democratic congressman in 1871 said the term "applied to the office seeker from the North who came here seeking office by the negroes, by arraying their political passions and prejudices against the white people of the community." In fact, most carpet-baggers combined a desire for personal gain with a commitment to reform the "unprogressive" South by developing its material resources and introducing Yankee institutions such as free labor and free public schools. Most were veterans of the Union army who stayed in the South after the war. Others included Freedmen's Bureau agents and businessmen who had invested capital in cotton plantations and other enterprises.

Carpetbaggers tended to be well educated and from the middle class. Albert Morgan, for example, was an army veteran from Ohio who settled in Mississippi after the war. When he and his brother failed at running a cotton plantation and sawmill, Morgan became active in Republican politics as a way to earn a living. He won election to the state constitutional convention, became a power in the state legislature, and risked his life to keep the Republican organization alive in the Mississippi delta region. Although they made up a tiny percentage of the population, carpetbaggers played a disproportionately large role in southern politics. They won a large share of Reconstruction offices, particularly in Florida, South Carolina, and Louisiana and in areas with large African American constituencies.

The third major group of southern Republicans were the native whites pejoratively termed "scalawags." They had even more diverse backgrounds and motives than the northern-born Republicans. Some were prominent prewar Whigs who saw the Republican Party as their best chance to regain political influence. Others viewed the party as an agent of modernization and economic expansion. "Yankees and Yankee notions are just what we want in this country," argued Thomas Settle of North Carolina. "We want their capital to build factories and workshops. We want their intelligence, their energy and enterprise." Their greatest influence lay in the up-country strongholds of southern Unionism, such as eastern Tennessee, western North Carolina, and northern Alabama. Loyalists during the war, traditional enemies of the planter elite (most were small farmers), these white Southerners looked to the Republican Party for help in settling old scores and relief from debt and wartime devastation.

Deep contradictions strained the alliance of these three groups. Southern Republicans touted themselves as the "party of progress and civilization" and promised a new era of material progress for the region. Republican state conventions in 1867 and 1868 voiced support for internal improvements, public schools, debt relief, and railroad building. Yet few white Southerners identified with the political and economic aspirations of African Americans. Nearly every party convention split between "confiscation radicals" (generally African Americans) and moderate elements committed to white

control of the party and to economic development that offered more to outside investors than to impoverished African Americans and poor whites.

Reconstructing the States: A Mixed Record

With the old Confederate leaders barred from political participation, and with carpetbaggers and newly enfranchised African Americans representing many of the plantation districts, Republicans managed to dominate the ten southern constitutional conventions of 1867–69. Well-educated carpetbaggers usually chaired the important committees and drafted key provisions of the new constitutions. Most of the delegates were southern white Republicans. African Americans formed a majority of the conventions in Louisiana and South Carolina, but they were generally underrepresented. In all, there were 258 African Americans among the 1,027 convention delegates at the ten conventions.

This poster, ca. 1880, honored seven prominent ex-slaves, including U.S. Senators Hiram R. Revels and Blanche K. Bruce, both representing Mississippi. In the center is Frederick Douglass. This poster was typical of many other Reconstruction-era prints celebrating the entry of African Americans into state and national legislatures.

Most of the conventions produced constitutions that expanded democracy and the public role of the state. The new documents guaranteed the political and civil rights of African Americans, and they abolished property qualifications for officeholding and jury service, as well as imprisonment for debt. They created the first state-funded systems of education in the South, to be administered by state commissioners. The new constitutions also mandated establishment of orphanages, penitentiaries, and homes for the insane. The changes wrought in the South's political landscape seemed quite radical to many. In 1868, only three years after the end of the war, Republicans came to power in most of the southern states. By 1869 new constitutions had been ratified in all the old Confederate states. "These constitutions and governments," one South Carolina Democratic newspaper vowed bitterly, "will last just as long as the bayonets which ushered them into being, shall keep them in existence, and not one day longer."

Republican governments in the South faced a continual crisis of legitimacy that limited their ability to legislate change. They had to balance reform against the need to gain acceptance, especially by white Southerners. Their achievements were thus mixed. In the realm of race relations there was a clear thrust toward equal rights and against discrimination. Republican legislatures followed up the federal Civil Rights Act of 1866 with various antidiscrimination clauses in new constitutions and laws prescribing harsh penalties for civil rights violations. While most African Americans supported autonomous African American churches, fraternal societies, and schools, they insisted that the state be color-blind. African Americans could now be employed in police forces and fire departments, serve on juries, school boards, and city councils, and hold public office at all levels of government.

Segregation, though, became the norm in public school systems. African American leaders often accepted segregation because they feared that insistence on integrated education would jeopardize funding for the new school systems. They generally agreed with Frederick Douglass that separate schools were "infinitely superior" to no schools at all. So while they opposed constitutional language requiring racial segregation in schools, most African Americans were less interested in the abstract ideal of integrated education than in ensuring educational opportunities for their children and employment for African American teachers. Many, in fact, believed all-black schools offered a better chance of securing these goals.

Patterns of discrimination persisted. Demands by African Americans to prohibit segregation in railroad cars, steamboats, theaters, and other public spaces revealed and heightened the divisions within the Republican Party. Moderate white Republicans feared such laws would only further alienate potential white supporters. But by the early 1870s, as black influence and assertiveness grew, laws guaranteeing equal access to transportation and public accommodation were passed in many states. By and large, though, such civil rights laws were difficult to enforce in local communities.

In economic matters, Republican governments failed to fulfill African Americans' hopes of obtaining land. Few former slaves possessed the cash to buy land in the open market, and they looked to the state for help. Republicans tried to weaken the plantation system and promote black ownership by raising taxes on land. Yet even when state governments seized land for nonpayment of taxes, the property was never used to help create black homesteads. In Mississippi, for example, 6 million acres, or about 20 percent of the land, had been forfeited by 1875. Yet virtually all of it found its way back to the original owners after they paid minimal penalties.

Republican leaders emphasized the "gospel of prosperity" as the key to improving the economic fortunes of all Southerners, black and white. Essentially, they envisioned promoting northern-style capitalist development—factories, large towns, and diversified agriculture—through state aid. Much Republican state lawmaking was devoted to encouraging railroad construction. Between 1868 and 1873 state legislatures passed hundreds of bills promoting railroads. Most of the government aid consisted not of direct cash subsidies but of official endorsements of a company's bonds. This government backing gave railroad companies credibility and helped them raise capital. In exchange, states received liens on railroads as security against defaults on payments to bondholders.

Between 1868 and 1872 the southern railroad system was rebuilt and over 3,000 new miles of track added, an increase of almost 40 percent. But in spite of all the new laws, it proved impossible to attract significant amounts of northern and European investment capital. The obsession with railroads drew resources from education and other programs. As in the North, it also opened the doors to widespread corruption and bribery of public officials. Finally, the frenzy of railroad promotion soon led to an overextension of credit and to many bankruptcies, saddling Republican governments with enormous debts. Railroad failures eroded public confidence in the Republicans' ability to govern. The "gospel of prosperity" ultimately failed to modernize the economy or solidify the Republican Party in the South.

White Resistance and "Redemption"

The emergence of a Republican Party in the reconstructed South brought two parties but not a two-party system to the region. The opponents of Reconstruction, the Democrats, refused to acknowledge Republi-

The Ku Klux Klan emerged as a potent political and social force during Reconstruction, terrorizing freedpeople and their white allies. An 1868 Klan warning threatens Louisiana governor Henry C. Warmoth with death. Warmoth, an Illinois-born "carpetbagger," was the state's first Republican governor. Two Alabama Klansmen, photographed in 1868, wear white hoods to protect their identities.

cans' right to participate in southern political life. In their view, the Republican Party, supported primarily by the votes of former slaves, was the partisan instrument of the northern Congress. Since Republicans controlled state governments, this denial of legitimacy meant, in effect, a rejection of state authority itself. In each state, Republicans were split between those who urged conciliation in an effort to gain white acceptance and those who emphasized consolidating the party under the protection of the military.

From 1870 to 1872 the Ku Klux Klan fought an ongoing terrorist campaign against Reconstruction governments and local leaders. Although not centrally organized, the Klan was a powerful presence in nearly every southern state. It acted as a kind of guerrilla military force in the service of the Democratic Party, the planter class, and all those who sought the restoration of white supremacy. Klansmen employed violence to intimidate African Americans and white Republicans, murdering innocent people, driving them from their homes, and destroying their property. Planters sometimes employed Klansmen to enforce labor discipline

by driving African Americans off plantations to deprive them of their harvest share.

In October 1870, after Republicans carried Laurens County in South Carolina, bands of white people drove 150 African Americans from their homes and murdered 13 black and white Republican activists. In March 1871, three African Americans were arrested in Meridian, Mississippi, for giving "incendiary" speeches. At their court hearing, Klansmen killed two of the defendants and the Republican judge, and thirty more African Americans were murdered in a day of rioting. The single bloodiest episode of Reconstruction era violence took place in Colfax, Louisiana, on Easter Sunday 1873. Nearly 100 African Americans were murdered after they failed to hold a besieged courthouse during a contested election. One former Confederate officer observed that the Klan's goal was "to defy the reconstructed State Governments, to treat them with contempt, and show that they have no real existence."

Southern Republicans looked to Washington for help. In 1870 and 1871 Congress passed three Enforcement Acts designed to counter racial terrorism.

These declared interference with voting a federal offense, provided for federal supervision of voting, and authorized the president to send the army and suspend the writ of habeas corpus in districts declared to be in a state of insurrection. The most sweeping measure was the Ku Klux Klan Act of April 1871, which made the violent infringement of civil and political rights a federal crime punishable by the national government. Attorney General Amos T. Akerman prosecuted hundreds of Klansmen in North Carolina and Mississippi. In October 1871 President Grant sent federal troops to occupy nine South Carolina counties and round up thousands of Klan members. By the election of 1872 the federal government's intervention had helped break the Klan and restore a semblance of law and order .

The Civil Rights Act of 1875 outlawed racial discrimination in theaters, hotels, railroads, and other public places. But the law proved more an assertion of principle than a direct federal intervention in southern affairs. Enforcement required African Americans to take their cases to the federal courts, a costly and time-consuming procedure.

As wartime idealism faded, northern Republicans became less inclined toward direct intervention in southern affairs. They had enough trouble retaining political control in the North. In 1874 the Democrats gained a majority in the House of Representatives for the first time since 1856. Key northern states also began to fall to the Democrats. Northern Republicans slowly abandoned the freedmen and their white allies in the South. Southern Democrats were also able to exploit a deepening fiscal crisis by blaming Republicans for excessive extension of public credit and the sharp increase in tax rates. Republican governments had indeed spent public money for new state school systems, orphanages, roads, and other internal improvements.

Gradually, conservative Democrats "redeemed" one state after another. Virginia and Tennessee led the way in 1869, North Carolina in 1870, Georgia in 1871, Texas in 1873, and Alabama and Arkansas in 1874. In Mississippi, white conservatives employed violence and intimidation to wrest control in 1875 and "redeemed" the state the following year. Republican infighting in Louisiana in 1873 and 1874 led to a series of contested election results, including bloody clashes between black militia and armed whites, and finally to "redemption" by the Democrats in 1877. Once these states returned to Democratic rule, African Americans faced obstacles to voting, more stringent controls on plantation labor, and deep cuts in social services.

Several Supreme Court rulings involving the Fourteenth and Fifteenth Amendments effectively constrained federal protection of African American civil rights. In the so-called Slaughterhouse cases of 1873, the Court issued its first ruling on the Fourteenth Amendment. The cases involved a Louisiana charter that gave a New Orleans meat-packing company a monopoly over the city's butchering business on the grounds of protecting public health. A rival group of butchers had sued, claiming the law violated the Fourteenth Amendment, which prohibited states from depriving any person of life, liberty, or property without due process of law. The Court held that the Fourteenth Amendment protected only the former slaves, not butchers, and that it protected only national citizenship rights, not the regulatory powers of states. The ruling in effect denied the original intent of the Fourteenth Amendment—to protect against state infringement of national citizenship rights as spelled out in the Bill of Rights.

Three other decisions curtailed federal protection of black civil rights. In *U.S. v. Reese* (1876) and *U.S. v. Cruikshank* (1876) the Court restricted congressional power to enforce the Ku Klux Klan Act. Future prosecution would depend on the states rather than on federal authorities. In these rulings the Court held that the Fourteenth Amendment extended the federal power to protect civil rights only in cases involving discrimination by states; discrimination by individuals or groups was not covered. The Court also ruled that the Fifteenth Amendment did not guarantee a citizen's right to vote; it only barred certain specific grounds for denying suffrage—"race, color, or previous condition of servitude." This interpretation opened the door for southern states to disfranchise African Americans for allegedly nonracial reasons. States back under Democratic control began to limit African American voting by passing laws restricting voter eligibility through poll taxes and property requirements.

Finally, in the 1883 Civil Rights Cases decision, the Court declared the Civil Rights Act of 1875 unconstitutional, holding that the Fourteenth Amendment gave Congress the power to outlaw discrimination by states, but not by private individuals. The majority opinion held that black people must no longer "be the special favorite of the laws." Together, these Supreme Court decisions marked the end of federal attempts to protect African American rights until well into the next century.

"King Cotton" and the Crop Lien System

The Republicans' vision of a "New South" remade along the lines of the northern economy failed to materialize. Instead, the South declined into the country's poorest agricultural region. Unlike midwestern and western farm towns burgeoning from trade in wheat, corn, and livestock, southern communities found themselves

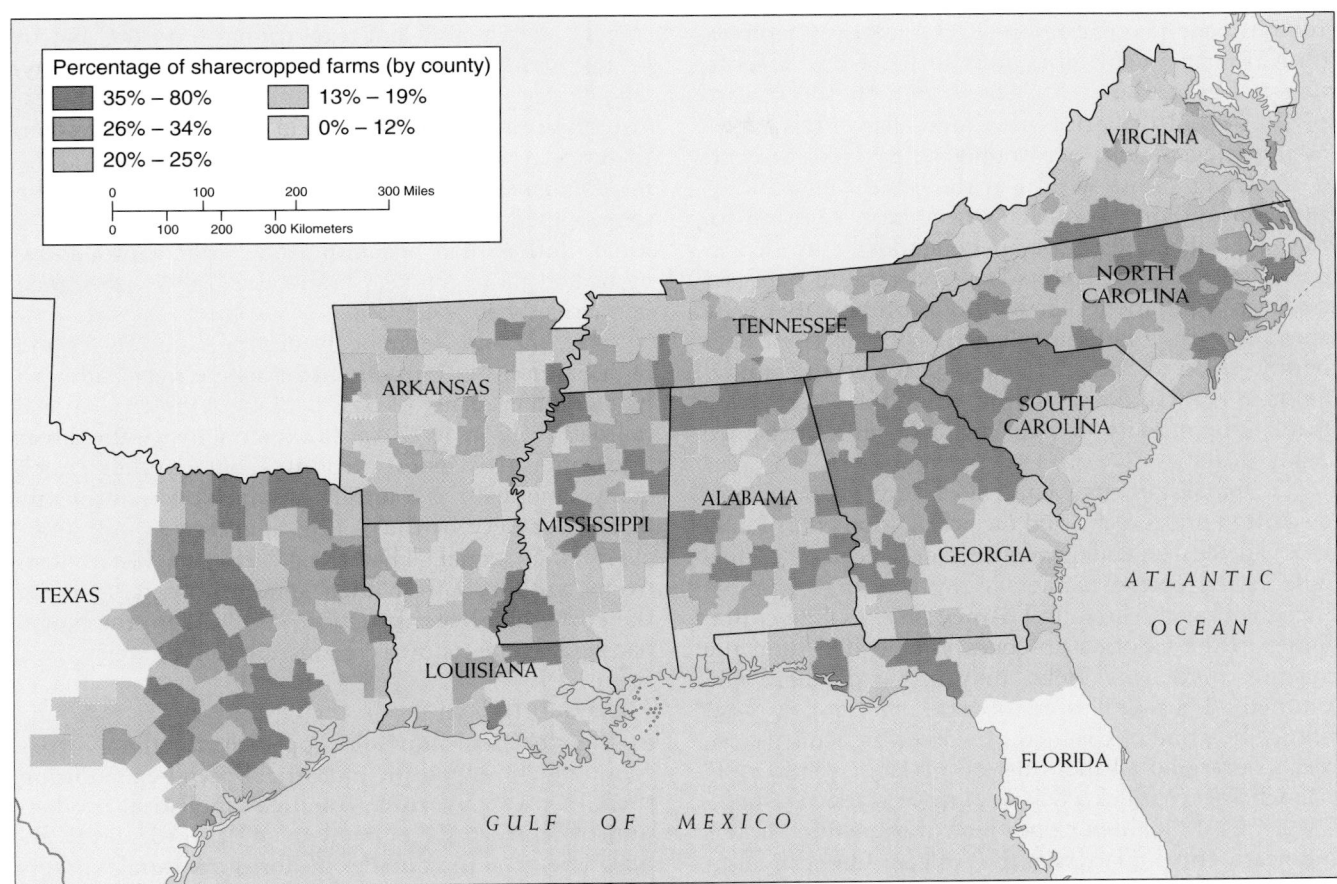

Southern Sharecropping and the Cotton Belt, 1880 *The economic depression of the 1870s forced increasing numbers of southern farmers, both white and black, into sharecropping arrangements. Sharecropping was most pervasive in the cotton belt regions of South Carolina, Georgia, Alabama, Mississippi, and east Texas.*

almost entirely dependent on the price of one commodity. Cotton growing had defined the economic life of large plantations in the coastal regions and black belt communities of the antebellum South. In the post–Civil War years "King Cotton" expanded its realm, as greater numbers of small white farmers found themselves forced to switch from subsistence crops to growing cotton for the market. The transition to cotton dependency developed unevenly, at different speeds in different parts of the South. Penetration by railroads, the availability of commercial fertilizers, and the opening up of new lands to cultivation were key factors in transforming communities from diversified, locally oriented farming to the market-oriented production of cotton.

The spread of the crop lien system as the South's main form of agricultural credit forced more and more farmers, both white and black, into cotton growing. This system developed because a chronic

shortage of capital and banking institutions made local merchants and planters the sole source of credit. They advanced loans to small owners, sharecroppers, and tenant farmers only in exchange for a lien, or claim, on the year's cotton crop. Merchants and planters frequently charged exorbitant interest rates on advances, as well as marking up the prices of the goods they sold in their stores. Taking advantage of the high illiteracy rates among poor Southerners, landlords and merchants easily altered their books to inflate the figures. At the end of the year, sharecroppers and tenants found themselves deep in debt to stores (many owned by Northerners) for seed, supplies, and clothing. Despite hard work and even bountiful harvests, few small farmers could escape from heavy debt.

As more and more white and black farmers turned to cotton growing as the only way to obtain credit, expanding production depressed prices. Competition from new cotton centers in the world market, such as Egypt and India, accelerated the downward spiral. As cotton prices declined alarmingly, from roughly eleven cents per pound in 1875 to five cents in 1894, per capita wealth in the South fell steadily, equaling only one-third that of the East, Midwest, or West by the 1890s. Cotton dependency had other repercussions. The planters lacked capital to purchase the farm equipment needed to profitably cultivate wheat or corn, and their reliance on cheap labor kept them wedded to cotton. Planters persisted in employing hand labor and mule power. As soil depletion took its toll, crop outputs, or yields per acre, either remained steady or fell.

Small farmers caught up in a vicious cycle of low cotton prices, debt, and dwindling food crops found their old ideal of independence sacrificed to the cruel logic of the cotton market. Many must have sympathized with men like John F. Armstrong, a white cotton farmer in the Georgia up-country, who fled from the crushing burdens of debt, only to be captured and returned. "I just got tired of working for the other fellow," he grimly explained. "I worked and toiled from year to year and all the fruits of my labor went to the man who never struck a lick. . . . I never made anything."

By 1880, about one-third of the white farmers and nearly three-quarters of the African American farmers in the cotton states were sharecroppers or tenants. Of the roughly 1.1 million farms in the nine large cotton-planting states that year, sharecroppers worked 301,000 of them. Many former slaves and poor white people had tried subsistence farming in the undeveloped backcountry. Yet to obtain precious credit, most found themselves forced to produce cotton for market and thus became enmeshed in the debt-ridden crop lien system. In traditional cotton producing areas, especially the black belt, landless farmers growing cotton had replaced slaves growing cotton. In the up-country and newer areas of cultivation, cotton-dominated commercial agriculture, with landless tenants and sharecroppers as the main workforce, had replaced the more diversified subsistence economy of the antebellum era.

RECONSTRUCTING THE NORTH

Abraham Lincoln liked to cite his own rise as proof of the superiority of the northern system of "free labor" over slavery. "There is no permanent class of hired laborers amongst us," Lincoln asserted. "Twenty-five years ago, I was a hired laborer. The hired laborer of yesterday, labors on his own account today; and will hire others to labor for him tomorrow. Advancement—improvement in condition—is the order of things in a society of equals." But the triumph of the North brought with it fundamental changes in the economy, labor relations, and politics that brought Lincoln's ideal vision into question. The spread of the factory system, the growth of large and powerful corporations, and the rapid expansion of capitalist enterprise all hastened the development of a large unskilled and routinized work force. Rather than becoming independent producers, more and more workers found themselves consigned permanently to wage labor.

The old Republican ideal of a society bound by a harmony of interests had become overshadowed by a grimmer reality of class conflict. A violent national railroad strike in 1877 was broken only with the direct intervention of federal troops. That conflict struck many Americans as a turning point. Northern society, like the society of the South, appeared more hierarchical than equal. That same year, the last federal troops withdrew from their southern posts, marking the end of the Reconstruction era. By then, the North had undergone its own "reconstruction" as well.

The Age of Capital

In the decade following Appomattox, the North's economy continued the industrial boom begun during the Civil War. By 1873, America's industrial production had grown 75 percent over the 1865 level. By that time, too, the number of nonagricultural workers in the North had surpassed the number of farmers. Between 1860 and 1880 the number of wage earners in manufacturing and construction more than doubled, from 2 million to over 4 million. Only Great Britain boasted a larger manufacturing economy than the United States. During the same period, nearly 3 million immigrants arrived in America, almost all of whom settled in the North and West.

The railroad business both symbolized and advanced the new industrial order. Shortly before the Civil War, enthusiasm mounted for a transcontinental line. Private companies took on the huge and expensive job of construction, but the federal government funded the project, providing the largest subsidy in American history. The Pacific Railway Act of 1862 granted the Union Pacific and the Central Pacific rights to a broad swath of land extending from Omaha, Nebraska, to Sacramento, California. An 1864 act bestowed a subsidy of $15,000 per mile of track laid over smooth plains country and varying larger amounts up to $48,000 per mile in the foothills and mountains of the Far West. The Union Pacific employed gangs of Irish American and African American workers to lay track heading west from Omaha, while the Central Pacific brought in more than 10,000 men from China to handle the difficult work in the Sierra Nevada mountain region.

Completion of the transcontinental railroad, May 10, 1869, as building crews for the Union Pacific and Central Pacific meet at Promontory Point, Utah. The two locomotive engineers salute each other, while the chief engineers for the two railroads shake hands. Construction had begun simultaneously from Omaha and Sacramento in 1863, with the help of generous subsidies from Congress. Work crews, consisting of thousands of ex-soldiers, Irish immigrants, and imported Chinese laborers, laid nearly 1,800 miles of new track.

On May 10, 1869, Leland Stanford, the former governor of California and president of the Central Pacific Railroad, traveled to Promontory Point in Utah Territory to hammer a ceremonial golden spike, marking the finish of the first transcontinental line. Other railroads went up with less fanfare. The Southern Pacific, chartered by the state of California, stretched from San Francisco to Los Angeles, and on through Arizona and New Mexico to connections with New Orleans. The Atchison, Topeka, and Santa Fe reached the Pacific in 1887 by way of a southerly route across the Rocky Mountains. The Great Northern, one of the few lines financed by private capital, extended west from St. Paul, Minnesota, to Washington's Puget Sound.

Railroads paved the way for the rapid settlement of the West, and both rural and urban areas grew dramatically over the next several decades. The combined population of Minnesota, the Dakotas, Nebraska, and Kansas, for example, jumped from 300,000 in 1860 to over 2 million in 1880. In the fifty years after 1870, the nation's railroad system expanded to more than a quarter million miles—more than all the rest of the world's railroad track combined.

Railroad corporations became America's first big businesses. Railroads required huge outlays of investment capital, and their growth increased the economic power of banks and investment houses centered in Wall Street. Bankers often gained seats on boards of directors, and their access to capital some-

times gave them the real control of lines. By the early 1870s the Pennsylvania Railroad stood as the nation's largest single company, with more than 20,000 employees. A new breed of aggressive entrepreneur sought to ease cutthroat competition by absorbing smaller companies and forming "pools" that set rates and divided the market. A small group of railroad executives, including Cornelius Vanderbilt, Jay Gould, Collis P. Huntington, and James J. Hill, amassed unheard-of fortunes. When he died in 1877, Vanderbilt left his son $100 million. By comparison, a decent annual wage for working a six-day week was around $350.

A growing number of Republican politicians maintained close connections with railroad interests. Railroad promoters, lawyers, and lobbyists became ubiquitous figures in Washington and state capitals, wielding enormous influence among lawmakers. "The galleries and lobbies of every legislature," one Republican leader noted, "are thronged with men seeking . . . an advantage." Railroads benefited enormously from government subsidies. Between 1862 and 1872 Congress alone awarded more than 100 million acres of public lands to railroad companies and provided them over $64 million in loans and tax incentives.

Some of the nation's most prominent politicians routinely accepted railroad largesse. Republican senator William M. Stewart of Nevada, a member of the Committee on Pacific Railroads, received a gift of 50,000 acres of land from the Central Pacific for his services. Senator Lyman Trumbull of Illinois took an annual retainer from the Illinois Central. The worst scandal of the Grant administration grew out of corruption involving railroad promotion. As a way of diverting funds for the building of the Union Pacific Railroad, an inner circle of Union Pacific stockholders created the dummy Crédit Mobilier construction company. In return for political favors, a group of prominent Republicans received stock in the company. When the scandal broke in 1872, it ruined Vice President Schuyler Colfax politically and led to the censure of two congressmen.

Other industries also boomed in this period, especially those engaged in extracting minerals and processing natural resources. Railroad growth stimulated expansion in the production of coal, iron, stone, and lumber, and these also received significant government aid. For example, under the National Mineral Act of 1866, mining companies received millions of acres of free public land. Oil refining enjoyed a huge expansion in the 1860s and 1870s. As with railroads, an early period of fierce competition soon gave way to concentration. By the late 1870s John D. Rockefeller's Standard Oil Company controlled almost 90 percent of the nation's oil-refining capacity. The production of pig iron tripled from 1 million tons in 1865 to 3 million tons in 1873. Between 1869 and 1879 both the capital investment and the number of workers in iron nearly doubled. Coal production shot up from 17 million tons in 1861 to 72 million tons in 1880. The size of individual ironworks and coal mines—measured by the number of employees and capital invested—also grew in these years, reflecting the expanding scale of industrial enterprise as a whole.

Liberal Republicans and the Election of 1872

With the rapid growth of large-scale, capital-intensive enterprises, Republicans increasingly identified with the interests of business rather than the rights of freedmen or the antebellum ideology of "free labor." The old Civil War–era Radicals had declined in influence. State Republican parties now organized themselves around the spoils of federal patronage rather than grand causes such as preserving the Union or ending slavery. Despite the Crédit Mobilier affair, Republicans had no monopoly on political scandal. In 1871 New York City newspapers reported the shocking story of how Democratic Party boss William M. Tweed and his friends had systematically stolen tens of millions from the city treasury. The "Tweed Ring" had received enormous bribes and kickbacks from city contractors and businessmen. Grotesquely caricatured by Thomas Nast's cartoons in *Harper's Weekly*, Tweed emerged as the preeminent national symbol of an increasingly degraded and dishonest urban politics. But to many, the scandal represented only the most extreme case of the routine corruption that now plagued American political life.

By the end of President Grant's first term, a large number of disaffected Republicans sought an alternative. They were led by a small but influential number of intellectuals, professionals, businessmen, and reformers who articulated an ideology that helped reshape late-nineteenth-century politics. The Liberal Republicans, as they called themselves, shared several core values. First, they emphasized the doctrines of classical economics, stressing the law of supply and demand, free trade, defense of property rights, and individualism. They called for a return to limited government, arguing that bribery, scandal, and high taxes all flowed from excessive state interference in the economy.

Liberal Republicans were also suspicious of expanding democracy. "Universal suffrage," Charles Francis Adams Jr. wrote in 1869, "can only mean in plain English the government of ignorance and vice— it means a European, and especially Celtic, proletariat on the Atlantic coast, an African proletariat on the shores of the Gulf, and a Chinese proletariat on the Pacific." Liberal Republicans believed that politics ought to be the province of "the best men"—educated and well-to-do men like themselves, devoted to the "science of government." They proposed civil service reform as the best way to break the hold of party machines on patronage. Competitive examinations, they argued, were the best way to choose employees for government posts. At a time when only a very small fraction of Americans attended college, this requirement would severely restrict the pool of government workers.

Although most Liberal Republicans had enthusiastically supported abolition, the Union cause, and equal rights for freedmen, they now opposed continued federal intervention in the South. The national government had done all it could for the former slaves; they must now take care of themselves. "Root, Hog, or Die" was the harsh advice offered by Horace Greeley, editor of the *New York Tribune*. In the spring of 1872 a diverse collection of Liberal Republicans nominated Greeley to run for president. A longtime foe of the Democratic Party, Greeley nonetheless won that party's presidential nomination as well. He made a new policy for the South the center of his campaign against Grant. The "best men" of both sections, he argued, should support a more generous Reconstruction policy based on "universal amnesty and impartial suffrage." All Americans, Greeley urged, must put the Civil War behind them and "clasp hands across the bloody chasm."

Grant easily defeated Greeley, carrying every state in the North and winning 56 percent of the popular vote. Most Republicans were not willing to abandon the regular party organization, and "waving the bloody shirt" was still a potent vote-getter. But the 1872 election accelerated the trend toward federal abandonment of African American citizenship rights. The Liberal Republicans quickly faded as an organized political force. But their ideas helped define a growing conservative consciousness among the northern public. For the rest of the century, their political and economic views attracted a growing number of middle-class professionals and businessmen. This agenda included retreat from the ideal of racial justice, hostility toward trade unions, suspicion of working-class and immigrant political power, celebration of competitive individualism, and opposition to government intervention in economic affairs.

The Depression of 1873

In the fall of 1873 the postwar boom came to an abrupt halt as a severe financial panic triggered a deep economic depression. The collapse resulted from commercial overexpansion, especially speculative investing in the nation's railroad system. The investment banking house of Jay Cooke and Company failed in September 1873 when it found itself unable to market millions of dollars in Northern Pacific Railroad bonds. Soon other banks and brokerage houses, especially those dealing in railroad securities, caved in as well, and the New York Stock Exchange suspended operations. By 1876 half the nation's railroads had defaulted on their bonds. Over the next two years more than 100 banks folded and 18,000 businesses shut their doors. The depression that began in 1873 lasted sixty-five months—the longest economic contraction in the nation's history until then.

The human toll of the depression was enormous. As factories began to close across the nation, the unemployment rate soared to about 15 percent. In many cities the jobless rate was much higher; roughly one-quarter of New York City workers were unemployed in 1874. Many thousands of men took to the road in search of work, and the "tramp" emerged as a new and menacing figure on the social landscape. The

The Tramp, Harper's Weekly, *September 2, 1876. The depression that began in 1873 forced many thousands of unemployed workers to go "on the tramp" in search of jobs. Men wandered from town to town, walking or riding railroad cars, desperate for a chance to work for wages or simply for room and board. The "tramp" became a powerful symbol of the misery caused by industrial depression and, as in this drawing, an image that evoked fear and nervousness among the nation's middle class.*

Pennsylvania Bureau of Labor Statistics noted that never before had "so many of the working classes, skilled and unskilled . . . been moving from place to place seeking employment that was not to be had." Farmers were also hard hit by the depression. Agricultural output continued to grow, but prices and land values fell sharply. As prices for their crops fell, farmers had a more difficult time repaying their fixed loan obligations; many sank deeper into debt.

During the winter of 1873, New York labor leaders demanded to know what measures would be taken "to relieve the necessities of the 10,000 homeless and hungry men and women of our city whose urgent appeals have apparently been disregarded by our public servants." Mass meetings of workers in New York and other cities issued calls to government officials to create jobs through public works. But these appeals were rejected. Indeed, many business leaders and political figures denounced even meager efforts at charity. E. L. Godkin wrote in the Christmas 1875 issue of the *Nation* that "free soup must be prohibited, and all classes must learn that soup of any kind, beef or turtle, can be had only by being paid for." Men such as Godkin saw the depression as a natural, if painful, part of the business cycle, one that would allow only the strongest enterprises (and workers) to survive. They dismissed any attempts at government interference, in the form of either job creation or poor relief.

Increased tensions, sometimes violent, between labor and capital reinforced the feeling of many Americans that the nation was no longer immune from European-style class conflict. The depression of the 1870s prompted workers and farmers to question the old free-labor ideology that celebrated a harmony of interests in northern society. More people voiced anger at and distrust of large corporations that exercised great economic power from outside their communities. Businessmen and merchants, meanwhile, especially in large cities, became more conscious of their own class interests. New political organizations such as Chicago's Citizens' Association united businessmen in campaigns for fiscal conservatism and defense of property rights. In national politics, the persistent depression made the Republican Party, North and South, more vulnerable than ever.

The Electoral Crisis of 1876

With the economy mired in depression, Democrats looked forward to capturing the White House in 1876. New scandals plaguing the Grant administration also weakened the Republican Party. In 1875, a conspiracy surfaced between distillers and U.S. revenue agents to cheat the government out of millions in tax revenues. The government secured indictments against more than 200 members of this "Whiskey Ring," including Orville E. Babcock, Grant's private secretary. Though acquitted, thanks to Grant's intervention, Babcock resigned in disgrace. In 1876, Secretary of War William W. Belknap was impeached for receiving bribes for the sale of trading posts in Indian Territory, and he resigned to avoid conviction.

Though Grant himself was never implicated in any wrongdoing, Democrats hammered away at his administration's low standard of honesty in government. For president they nominated Governor Samuel J. Tilden of New York, who brought impeccable reform credentials to his candidacy. In 1871 he had helped expose and prosecute the "Tweed Ring" in New York City. As governor he had toppled the "Canal Ring," a graft-ridden scheme involving inflated contracts for repairs on the Erie Canal. In their platform, the Democrats linked the issue of corruption to an attack on Reconstruction policies. They blamed the Republicans for instituting "a corrupt centralism" that subjected southern states to "the rapacity of carpetbag tyrannies," riddled the national government "with incapacity, waste, and fraud," and "locked fast the prosperity of an industrious people in the paralysis of hard times."

Republican nominee Rutherford B. Hayes, governor of Ohio, also sought the high ground. As a lawyer in Cincinnati he had defended runaway slaves. Later he had distinguished himself as a general in the Union army. Republicans charged Tilden with disloyalty during the war, income tax evasion, and close relations with powerful railroad interests. Hayes promised, if elected, to support an efficient civil service system, to vigorously prosecute officials who betrayed the public trust, and to introduce a system of free universal education.

On an election day marred by widespread vote fraud and violent intimidation, Tilden received 250,000 more popular votes than Hayes. But Republicans refused to concede victory, challenging the vote totals in the electoral college. Tilden garnered 184 uncontested electoral votes, one shy of the majority required to win, while Hayes received 165. The problem centered in 20 disputed votes from Florida, Louisiana, South Carolina, and Oregon. In each of the three southern states two sets of electoral votes were returned. In Oregon, which Hayes had unquestionably carried, the Democratic governor replaced a disputed Republican elector with a Democrat.

The crisis was unprecedented. In January 1877 Congress moved to settle the deadlock, estab-

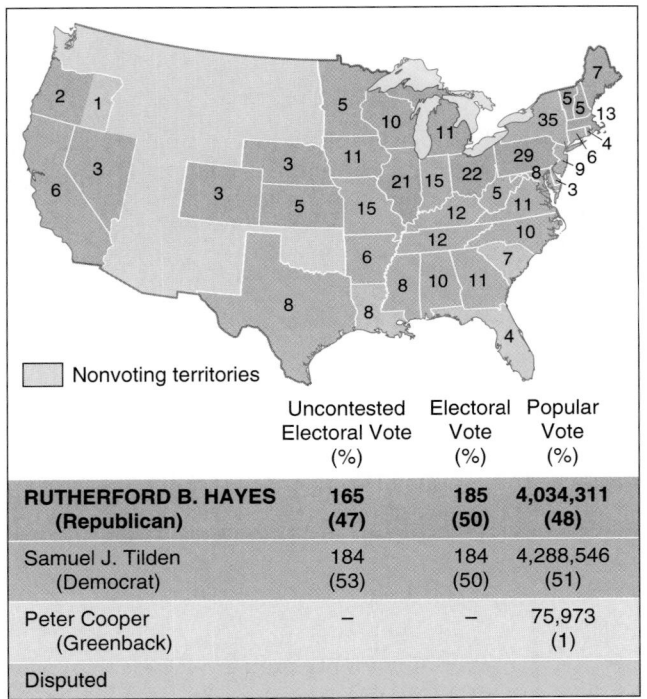

Nonvoting territories

	Uncontested Electoral Vote (%)	Electoral Vote (%)	Popular Vote (%)
RUTHERFORD B. HAYES (Republican)	**165 (47)**	**185 (50)**	**4,034,311 (48)**
Samuel J. Tilden (Democrat)	184 (53)	184 (50)	4,288,546 (51)
Peter Cooper (Greenback)	–	–	75,973 (1)
Disputed			

The Election of 1876   *The presidential election of 1876 left the nation without a clear-cut winner.*

lishing an Electoral Commission composed of five senators, five representatives, and five Supreme Court justices; eight were Republicans and seven were Democrats. The commission voted along strict partisan lines to award all the contested electoral votes to Hayes. Outraged by this decision, Democratic congressmen threatened a filibuster to block Hayes's inauguration. Violence and stalemate were avoided when Democrats and Republicans struck a compromise in February. In return for Hayes's ascendance to the presidency, the Republicans promised to appropriate more money for Southern internal improvements, to appoint a Southerner to Hayes's cabinet, and to pursue a policy of noninterference ("home rule") in southern affairs.

Shortly after assuming office, Hayes ordered removal of the remaining federal troops in Louisiana and South Carolina. Without this military presence to sustain them, the Republican governors of those two states quickly lost power to Democrats. "Home rule" meant Republican abandonment of freed people, Radicals, carpetbaggers, and scalawags. It also effectively nullified the Fourteenth and Fifteenth Amendments and the Civil Rights Act of 1866. The "Compromise of 1877" completed repudiation of the idea, born during the Civil War and pursued during Congressional

Reconstruction, of a powerful federal government protecting the rights of all American citizens. As one black Louisianan lamented, "The whole South—every state in the South—had got into the hands of the very men that held us slaves." Other voices hailed this turning point in policy. "The negro," declared the *Nation,* "will disappear from the field of national politics. Henceforth, the nation, as a nation, will have nothing more to do with him."

CONCLUSION

Reconstruction succeeded in the limited political sense of reuniting a nation torn apart by civil war. The Radical Republican vision, emphasizing racial justice, equal civil and political rights guaranteed by the Fourteenth and Fifteenth Amendments, and a new southern economy organized around independent small farmers, never enjoyed the support of the majority of its party or the northern public. By 1877 the political force of these ideals was spent and the national retreat from them nearly complete.

The end of Reconstruction left the way open for the return of white domination in the South. The freed people's political and civil equality proved only temporary. It would take a "Second Reconstruction," the civil rights movement of the next century, to establish full black citizenship rights once and for all. The federal government's failure to pursue land reform left former slaves without the economic independence needed for full emancipation. Yet the newly autonomous black family, along with black-controlled churches, schools, and other social institutions, provided the foundations for the modern African American community. If the federal government was not yet fully committed to protecting equal rights in local communities, the Reconstruction era at least pointed to how that goal might be achieved.

Even as the federal government retreated from the defense of equal rights for black people, it took a more aggressive stance as the protector of business interests. The Hayes administration responded decisively to one of the worst outbreaks of class violence in American history by dispatching federal troops to several northern cities to break the Great Railroad Strike of 1877. In the aftermath of Reconstruction, the struggle between capital and labor had clearly replaced "the southern question" as the number one political issue of the day. "The overwhelming labor question has dwarfed all other questions into nothing," wrote an Ohio Republican. "We have home questions enough to occupy attention now."

CHRONOLOGY

1865	Freedmen's Bureau established
	Abraham Lincoln assassinated
	Andrew Johnson begins Presidential Reconstruction
	Black codes begin to be enacted in southern states
	Thirteenth Amendment ratified
1866	Civil Rights Act passed
	Congress approves Fourteenth Amendment
	Ku Klux Klan founded
1867	Reconstruction Acts, passed over President Johnson's veto, begin Congressional Reconstruction
	Tenure of Office Act
	Southern states call constitutional conventions
1868	President Johnson impeached by the House, but acquitted in Senate trial
	Fourteenth Amendment ratified
	Most southern states readmitted to Union
	Ulysses S. Grant elected president
1869	Congress approves Fifteenth Amendment
	Union Pacific and Central Pacific tracks meet at Promontory Point in Utah Territory
	Suffragists split into National Woman Suffrage Association and American Woman Suffrage Association
1870	Fifteenth Amendment ratified
1871	Ku Klux Klan Act passed
	"Tweed Ring" in New York City exposed
1872	Liberal Republicans break with Grant and Radicals, nominate Horace Greeley for president
	Crédit Mobilier scandal
	Grant reelected president
1873	Financial panic and beginning of economic depression
	Slaughterhouse cases
1874	Democrats gain control of House for first time since 1856
1875	Civil Rights Act
1876	Disputed election between Samuel Tilden and Rutherford B. Hayes
1877	Electoral Commission elects Hayes president
	President Hayes dispatches federal troops to break Great Railroad Strike and withdraws last remaining federal troops from the South

REVIEW QUESTIONS

1. How did various visions of a "reconstructed" South differ? How did these visions reflect the old political and social divisions that had led to the civil war?
2. What key changes did emancipation make in the political and economic status of African Americans? Discuss the expansion of citizenship rights in the post–Civil War years. To what extent did women share in the gains made by African Americans?
3. What role did such institutions as the family, the church, schools, and political parties play in the African American transition to freedom?
4. How did white Southerners attempt to limit the freedom of former slaves? How did these efforts succeed, and how did they fail?
5. Evaluate the achievements and failures of Reconstruction governments in the southern states.
6. What were the crucial economic changes occurring in the North and South during the Reconstruction era?

RECOMMENDED READING

Michael Les Benedict, *The Impeachment and Trial of Andrew Johnson* (1973). The best history of the impeachment crisis.

Laura F. Edwards, *Gendered Strife & Confusion: The Political Culture of Reconstruction* (1997). An ambitious analysis of how gender ideologies played a key role in shaping the party politics and social relations of the Reconstruction-era South.

Michael W. Fitzgerald, *The Union League Movement in the Deep South* (1989). Uses the Union League as a lens through which to examine race relations and the close connections between politics and economic change in the post–Civil War South.

Eric Foner, *Reconstruction: America's Unfinished Revolution, 1863–1877* (1988). The most comprehensive and thoroughly researched overview of the Reconstruction era.

William Gillette, *Retreat from Reconstruction: A Political History, 1867–1878* (1979). Covers the national political scene, with special attention to the abandonment of the ideal of racial equality.

Jacqueline Jones, *Labor of Love, Labor of Sorrow* (1985). Includes excellent material on the work and family lives of African American women in slavery and freedom.

Leon Litwack, *Been in the Storm So Long: The Aftermath of Slavery* (1979). A richly detailed analysis of the transition from slavery to freedom; excellent use of African American sources.

Michael Perman, *Emancipation and Reconstruction, 1862–1879* (1987). A short but very useful overview of Reconstruction, emphasizing racial issues and the end of slavery.

Edward Royce, *The Origins of Southern Sharecropping* (1993). A sophisticated, tightly argued work of historical sociology that explains how sharecropping emerged as the dominant form of agricultural labor in the post–Civil War South.

Mark W. Summers, *Railroads, Reconstruction, and the Gospel of Prosperity* (1984). The best study of the economic and political importance of railroad building in this era.

Allen W. Trelease, *White Terror: The Ku Klux Klan Conspiracy and Southern Reconstruction* (1971). The most complete account of Klan activity and the efforts to suppress it.

ADDITIONAL BIBLIOGRAPHY

The Politics of Reconstruction

Richard H. Abbott, *The Republican Party and the South, 1855–1877* (1986)

Herman Belz, *Emancipation and Equal Rights* (1978)

Michael Les Benedict, *A Compromise of Principle: Congressional Republicans and Reconstruction* (1974)

Michael Kent Curtis, *No State Shall Abridge: The Fourteenth Amendment and the Bill of Rights* (1990)

Ellen Carol DuBois, *Feminism and Suffrage* (1978)

Eric Foner, *Politics and Ideology in the Age of the Civil War* (1980)

William C. Harris, *With Charity for All: Lincoln and the Restoration of the Union* (1997)

Robert Kaczorowski, *The Politics of Judicial Interpretation: The Federal Courts, Department of Justice, and Civil Rights, 1866–1876* (1985)

James McPherson, *Ordeal by Fire: The Civil War and Reconstruction* (1982)

Kenneth M. Stampp, *The Era of Reconstruction, 1865–1877* (1965)

The Meaning of Freedom

Ira Berlin et al., eds., *Freedom: A Documentary History*, 3 vols. (1985–91)

W. E. B. Du Bois, *Black Reconstruction* (1935)

Barbara J. Fields, *Slavery and Freedom on the Middle Ground* (1985)

Eric Foner, *Freedom's Lawmakers: A Directory of Black Officeholders during Reconstruction* (1996)

Herbert G. Gutman, *The Black Family in Slavery and Freedom* (1976)

Thomas Holt, *Black over White: Negro Political Leadership in South Carolina during Reconstruction* (1977)

Lynda J. Morgan, *Emancipation in Virginia's Tobacco Belt* (1992)

Nell Irvin Painter, *Exodusters* (1977)

Howard N. Rabinowitz, *Race Relations in the Urban South, 1865–1890* (1978)

Roger L. Ransom and Richard Sutch, *One Kind of Freedom: The Economic Consequences of Emancipation* (1977)

Southern Politics and Society

Dan T. Carter, *When the War Was Over: The Failure of Self Reconstruction in the South, 1865–1877* (1985)

Richard N. Current, *Those Terrible Carpetbaggers* (1988)

Stephen Hahn, *The Roots of Southern Populism* (1983)

William C. Harris, *The Day of the Carpetbagger: Republican Reconstruction in Mississippi* (1979)

Michael S. Perman, *Reunion without Compromise: The South and Reconstruction, 1865–1868* (1973)

———, *The Road to Redemption: Southern Politics, 1868–1979* (1984)

Howard N. Rabinowitz, *The First New South, 1865–1920* (1991)

James Roark, *Masters without Slaves* (1977)

Jonathan M. Wiener, *Social Origins of the New South* (1978)

Reconstructing the North

Stephen Buechler, *The Transformation of the Woman Suffrage Movement* (1986)

Morton Keller, *Affairs of State* (1977)

James C. Mohr, ed., *Radical Republicans in the North* (1976)

David Montgomery, *Beyond Equality: Labor and the Radical Republicans, 1862–1872* (1967)

Keith I. Polakoff, *The Politics of Inertia: The Election of 1876 and the End of Reconstruction* (1973)

Mark W. Summers, *The Era of Good Stealings* (1993)

Margaret S. Thompson, *The "Spider Web": Congress and Lobbying in the Age of Grant* (1985)

C. Vann Woodward, *Reunion and Reaction: The Compromise of 1877 and the End of Reconstruction* (1956)

Biography

Fawn M. Brodie, *Thaddeus Stevens* (1959)

David Donald, *Charles Sumner and the Rights of Man* (1970)

Russell Duncan, *Freedom's Shore: Tunis Campbell and the Georgia Freedmen* (1986)

William S. McFeely, *Frederick Douglass* (1989)

———, *Grant: A Biography* (1981)

———, *Yankee Stepfather: General O. O. Howard and the Freedmen* (1968)

Hans L. Trefousse, *Andrew Johnson* (1989)

CHAPTER EIGHTEEN

CONQUEST AND SURVIVAL
THE TRANS-MISSISSIPPI WEST, 1860–1900

John Gast, *American Progress.*

AMERICAN COMMUNITIES
The Oklahoma Land Rush

Decades after the event, cowboy Evan G. Barnard vividly recalled the preparations made by settlers when Oklahoma territorial officials announced the opening of No Man's Land to the biggest "land rush" in American history. "Thousands of people gathered along the border. . . . As the day for the race drew near the settlers practiced running their horses and driving carts." Finally the morning of April 22, 1889, arrived. "At ten o'clock people lined up . . . ready for the great race of their lives." Like many others, Barnard displayed his guns prominently on his hips, determined to discourage competitors from claiming the 160 acres of prime land that he intended to grab for himself.

Evan Barnard's story was one strand in the larger tale of the destruction and creation of communities in the trans-Mississippi West. In the 1830s, the federal government designated what was to become the state of Oklahoma as Indian Territory, reserved for the Five Civilized Tribes (Cherokees, Chickasaws, Choctaws, Creeks, and Seminoles) that had been forcibly removed from their eastern lands. All five tribes had reestablished themselves as sovereign republics in Indian Territory. The Cherokees and Chocktaws became prosperous cotton growers. The Creeks managed large herds of hogs and cattle, and the Chickasaws grazed not only cattle but sheep and goats on their open fields. The Five Tribes also ran sawmills, gristmills, and cotton gins. Indian merchants were soon dealing with other tribespeople as well as licensed white traders and even contracting with the federal government.

The Civil War, however, took a heavy toll on their success. Some tribes, slaveholders themselves, sided with the Confederacy; others with the Union. When the war ended, more than 10,000 people—nearly one-fifth of the population of Indian Territory—had died. To make matters worse, new treaties required the Five Tribes to cede the entire western half of the territory for the resettlement of tribes from other regions, including the former northern Indian territory of Nebraska and Kansas.

Western Oklahoma thereby became home to thousands of newly displaced peoples, including the Pawnees, Peorias, Ottawas, Wyandots, and Miamis. Many small tribes readily took to farming and rebuilt their communities. But the nomadic, buffalo-hunting Kiowas, Cheyennes, Comanches, and Arapahoes did not settle so peacefully. They continued to traverse the plains until the U.S. Army finally forced them onto reservations. Eventually, more than 80,000 tribespeople were living on twenty-one separate reservations in western Oklahoma, all governed by agents appointed by the federal government.

The opening of the unassigned far western district of Oklahoma known as No Man's Land to non-Indian homesteading, however, signaled the impending end of Indian sovereignty. Many non-Indians saw this almost 2 million acre strip as a Promised

Oklahoma Territory

Oklahoma Territory *Land openings to settlers came at different times, making new land available through various means.*

Map labels:

NO MAN'S LAND
Added to Oklahoma Territory
by Organic Act May 2, 1890

1. Opened by Run, September 22, 1891
2. Tonkawa Lands by Allotment, 1891
3. Pawnee Lands by Allotment, 1892
4. Opened by Run, May 23, 1895
5. Ponca and Oto-Missouri Lands by Allotment, 1904
6. Kaw Lands by Allotment, 1906

0   50   100 Miles
0   50   100 Kilometers

CHEROKEE OUTLET
Opened by Run
September 16, 1893

CHEYENNES AND ARAPAHOS
Opened by Lottery
July 9 to August 6 1901

KAWS
OSAGE RESERVATION
Lands by Allotment 1906
CHEROKEE NATION

PAWNEES
UNASSIGNED LANDS
Opened by Run April 22, 1889
IOWAS
KICKAPOOS
SACS AND FOXES
CREEK NATION
SEMINOLE NATION

WICHITAS AND CADDOS

GREER COUNTY
Attached to Oklahoma following decision of United States Supreme Court March 16, 1896

COMANCHES, KIOWAS, AND APACHES

BIG PASTURE
Opened by Sealed Bids December 1906

POTAWATOMIS AND SHAWNEES

CHICKASAW NATION

CHOCTAW NATION

Land, perfect for dividing into thousands of small farms. African Americans, many of whom were former slaves of Indian planters, appealed to the federal government for the right to stake claims there. Another group of would-be homesteaders, known as "Boomers," quickly tired of petitioning and invaded the district in 1880, only to be booted out by the Tenth Cavalry. Meanwhile, the railroads, seeing the potential for lucrative commerce, put constant pressure on the federal government to open No Man's Land for settlement. In 1889 the U.S. Congress finally gave in.

Cowboy Barnard was just one of thousands to pour into No Man's Land on April 22, 1889. Many homesteaders simply crossed the border from Kansas. Southerners, dispossessed by warfare and economic ruin in their own region, were also well represented. Market-minded settlers claimed the land nearest the railroads, and by nightfall of April 22 had set up tent cities along the tracks. In a little over two months, after 6,000 homestead claims had been filed, the first sod houses appeared, sheltering growing communities of non-Indian farmers, ranchers, and other entrepreneurs.

Dramatic as it was, the land rush of 1889 was only

Indian Territory (Oklahoma)

one in a series of events that soon dispossessed Oklahoma's Indians of their remaining lands. First the federal government broke up the estates held collectively by various tribes in western Oklahoma, assigning to individuals the standard 160-acre allotment and allowing non-Indian homesteaders to claim the rest. In 1898, Congress passed the Curtis Act, formally dissolving Indian Territory and dispossessing the Five Tribes. Members of the former Indian nations were directed to dismantle their governments, abandon their estates, and join the ranks of other homesteaders. They nevertheless retained many of their tribal customs and managed to regain sovereign status in 1977.

Later generations of Oklahomans often celebrated their historic ties to the Indian nations. At formal ceremonies marking statehood, just before the newly elected governor took the oath of office, a mock wedding ceremony united a tough and virile cowboy with a demure and submissive Indian maiden. By this time, in 1907, tribespeople were outnumbered in Oklahoma by ten to one.

By this time also, nearly one-quarter of the entire population of the United States lived west of the Mississippi River. Hundreds of new communities, supported primarily by cattle ranching, agriculture, mining, or other industries, had not only grown with the emerging national economy but helped to shape it in the process. The newcomers displaced communities that had formed centuries earlier. They also drastically transformed the physical landscape.

Through their activities and the support of Easterners, the United States realized an ambition that John L. O'Sullivan had described in 1845 as the nation's "manifest destiny to overspread the continent" and remake it in a new image.

515
515

KEY TOPICS

- The impact of western expansion on Indian societies

- The West as an "internal empire" and the development of new technologies and new industries

- The creation of new communities and the displacement of old communities

- The West as myth and legend

INDIAN PEOPLES UNDER SIEGE

The tribespeople living west of the Mississippi River keenly felt the pressure of the gradual incorporation of the West into the nation. The Oregon Trail opened the Northwest to large numbers of non-Indian settlers, and by 1845 nearly 5,000 people had braved the six- to eight-month journey by wagon to reach present-day Oregon and Washington. The following year, the United States reached an agreement with Great Britain for the division of the Oregon Country. Then came the addition of the vast territories taken from Mexico following the Mexican-American War. California quickly became a state in 1850, Oregon in 1859. Congress consolidated the national domain in the next decades by granting territorial status to Utah, New Mexico, Washington, Dakota, Colorado, Nevada, Arizona, Idaho, Montana, and Wyoming. The purchase of Alaska in 1867 added an area twice the size of Texas and extended the nation beyond its contiguous borders so that it reached almost to Russia and the North Pole. The federal government made itself the custodian of all these thinly settled regions, permitting limited self-rule, with appointed governors supervising the transition from territorial status to statehood.

Tribespeople struggled to preserve their ways of life under these changing conditions, but their prospects dimmed considerably following the discovery of gold in California in 1848 and the completion of the transcontinental railroad in 1869. White settlers, hoping to build a new life for themselves, rushed into these new territories and repeatedly invaded Indian lands west of the Mississippi. Violent outbreaks between white emigrants and Indian peoples became increasingly commonplace. Since the Jefferson administration, federal officials had promoted the assimilation of Indian peoples; they now became even more determined to break up their tribal councils and to bring them into the American mainstream.

On the Eve of Conquest

Before the European colonists reached the New World, tribespeople of the Great Plains, Southwest, and Far West had occupied the lands for more than twenty thousand years. Hundreds of tribes totaling perhaps a million members had adapted to such extreme climates as the desert aridity of present-day Utah and Nevada, the bitter cold of the northern plains, and the seasonally heavy rain of the Pacific Northwest. Many cultivated maize (corn), foraged for wild plants, fished, or hunted game. Several tribes built cities with several thousand inhabitants and traded across thousands of miles of western territory.

Invasion by the English, Spanish, and other Europeans brought disease, religious conversion, and new patterns of commerce. But geographic isolation still gave many tribes a margin of survival unknown in the East. At the close of the Civil War, approximately 360,000 Indian people still lived in the trans-Mississippi West, the majority of them in the Great Plains.

The surviving tribes adapted to changing conditions. The Plains Indians learned to ride the horses and shoot the guns introduced by Spanish and British traders. The Pawnees migrated farther westward to evade encroaching non-Indian settlers, while the Sioux and the Comanches fought neighboring tribes to gain control of large stretches of the Great Plains. The southwestern Hopis and Zunis, conquered earlier by the Spanish, continued to trade extensively with the Mexicans who lived near them. Some tribes took dramatic steps toward accommodation with white ways. Even before they were uprooted and moved across the Mississippi River, the Cherokees had become literate in English, converted to Christianity, established a constitutional republic, and become a nation of farmers.

Legally, the federal government had long regarded Indian tribes as autonomous nations residing within American boundaries and had negotiated numerous treaties with them over land rights and commerce. But pressured by land-hungry whites, several states had violated these federal treaties so often that the U.S. Congress passed the Indian Removal Act of 1830 (Chapter 10), which provided funds to relocate all eastern tribes by force if necessary. The Cherokees challenged this legislation, and

Major Indian Battles and Indian Reservations, 1860–1900   *As commercial routes and white populations passed through and occupied Indian lands, warfare inevitably erupted. The displacement of Indians to reservations opened access by farmers, ranchers, and investors to natural resources and to markets.*

the Supreme Court ruled in their favor in *Cherokee Nation v. Georgia* (1831). Ignoring the court's decision, President Andrew Jackson, known as a hardened Indian fighter, forced many tribes to cede their land and remove to Indian Territory. There, it was believed, they might live undisturbed by whites and gradually adjust to "civilized" ways. But soon, the onslaught of white settlers, railroad entrepreneurs, and prospectors rushing for gold pressured tribes to cede millions of their acres to the United States. In 1854, to open the Kansas and Nebraska Territories for white settlement, the federal government simply abolished the northern half of Indian Territory. As demand for resources and land accelerated, the entire plan for a permanent Indian Territory fell apart.

Reservations and the Slaughter of the Buffalo

As early as the 1840s, highly placed officials had outlined a plan to subdue the intensifying rivalry over natural resources and land. Under the terms of their proposal, individual tribes would agree to live within clearly defined zones—reservations—and, in exchange, the Bureau of Indian Affairs would provide guidance while U.S. military forces ensured protection. This reservation policy also reflected the vision of many "Friends of the Indian," educators and Protestant missionaries who aspired to "civilize the savages." By the end of the 1850s eight western reservations had been established where Indian peoples were induced to speak English, take up farming, and convert to Christianity. The U.S. commissioner of Indian affairs

Luke Lea predicted that reservations would speed the "ultimate incorporation" of the Indians "into the great body of our citizen population."

Several tribes did sign treaties, although often under duress. High-handed officials, such as governor Isaac Stevens of Washington Territory, made no attempt at legitimate negotiations, choosing instead to intimidate or deceive Indian peoples into signing away their lands. Most of the tribes in Washington responded by remaining in their old villages. But Stevens finally had his way. State officials moved the Indians onto three reservations after their leaders signed away 45,000 square miles of tribal land. The Suquamish leader Seattle admitted defeat but warned the governor: "Your time of decay may be distant, but it will surely come."

Those tribes that moved to reservations often found federal policies inadequate to their needs. The federal government repeatedly reduced the size of land allotments, forcing tribes to compete with each other for increasingly scarce resources and making subsistence farming on the reservation virtually impossible. The Medicine Lodge Treaty of 1867 assigned reservations in existing Indian Territory to Comanches, Plains (Kiowa) Apaches, Kiowas, Cheyennes, and Arapahoes, bringing these tribes together with Sioux, Shoshones, Bannocks, and Navajos. All told, more than 100,000 people found themselves competing intensely for survival. Over the next decade, a group of Quakers appointed by President Ulysses S. Grant attempted to mediate differences among the tribes and to supply the starving peoples with food and seed. At the same time, white prospectors and miners continued to flood the Dakota Territory. "They crowded in," Iron Teeth recalled bitterly, "so we had to move out." Moreover, corrupt officials of the Bureau of Indian Affairs routinely diverted funds for their own use and reduced food supplies, a policy promoting malnutrition, demoralization, and desperation.

The nomadic tribes that traditionally hunted and gathered over large territories saw their freedom sharply curtailed. The Lakotas, or Western Sioux, a loose confederation of bands scattered across the northern Great Plains, were one of the largest and most adaptive of all Indian nations. Seizing buffalo-hunting territory from their rivals, the Pawnees and the Crows, the Sioux had learned to follow the herds on horseback. Buffalo meat and hides fed and clothed the Sioux and satisfied many of their other needs as well. Images of buffalo appeared in their religious symbols and ceremonial dress. The Sioux were also vision seekers. Young men and women pursued dreams that would provide them guidance for a lifetime; elders themselves followed dreams that might guide the destiny of the entire tribe or nation.

The mass slaughter of the buffalo by whites brought the crisis provoked by the increasing restriction of the Plains peoples to a peak. In earlier eras, vast herds of buffalo had literally darkened the western horizon. Buffalo grazed over distances of several hundred miles, searching for water and wallowing in mud to fend off insects. As gunpowder and the railroad came to the range, the number of buffalo fell rapidly. Non-Indian traders avidly sought buffalo fur for coats, hide for leather, and heads for trophies. New rifles, like the .50 caliber Sharps, could kill at 600 feet; one sharpshooter bragged of killing 3,000 buffalo. Army commanders encouraged the slaughter, accurately predicting that starvation would break tribal resistance to the reservation system. Their food sources practically destroyed and their way of life undermined, many Great Plains tribes, including many Sioux, concluded that they could only fight or die.

The Indian Wars

Under these pressures, a handful of tribes organized themselves and their allies to resist both federal poli-

Chief Red Cloud in an 1868 photograph. The Oglala Sioux spiritual leader is seen with Red Dog, Little Wound, interpreter John Bridgeman (on his right), American Horse, and Red Shirt (on his left). He ventured to Washington with his delegation to discuss with President Ulysses S. Grant the various provisions of the peace treaty, just signed, to end the violent conflict over the Bozeman Trail.

cies and the growing wave of white settlers. The over-whelming majority of tribespeople did not take up arms. But settlers, thousands of them Civil War veterans with weapons close at hand, responded to real or imaginary threats with their own brands of violence.

Large-scale war erupted in 1864. Having decided to terminate all treaties with tribes in eastern Colorado, territorial governor John Evans encouraged a group of white civilians, the Colorado Volunteers, to stage repeated raids through Cheyenne campgrounds. Seeking protection, chief Black Kettle brought a band of 800 Cheyennes to a U.S. fort and received orders to set up camp at Sand Creek. Feeling secure in this arrangement, Black Kettle sent out most of his men to hunt. The next morning, on November 29, 1864, the Colorado Volunteers attacked. While Black Kettle held up a U.S. flag and a white truce banner, the disorderly group of 700 men, many of them drunk, slaughtered 105 Cheyenne women and children and 28 men. They mutilated the corpses and took scalps back to Denver to exhibit as trophies. Iron Teeth, a Cheyenne woman who survived, remembered seeing a woman "crawling along on the ground, shot, scalped, crazy, but not yet dead." Months after the Sand Creek Massacre, bands of Cheyennes, Sioux, and Arapahoes were still retaliating, burning civilian outposts and sometimes killing whole families.

The Sioux played the most dramatic roles in the Indian Wars. In 1851, believing the U.S. government would recognize their own rights of conquest over other Indian tribes, the Sioux relinquished large tracts of land as a demonstration of good faith. But within a decade, a mass invasion of miners and the construction of military forts along the Bozeman Trail in Wyoming, the Sioux's principal buffalo range, threw the tribe's future into doubt. During the Great Sioux War of 1865–67, the Oglala Sioux warrior Red Cloud fought the U.S. Army to a stalemate and forced the government to abandon its forts, which the Sioux then burned to the ground. The Treaty of Fort Laramie, signed in 1868, created the Great Sioux Reservation, which included the present state of South Dakota west of the Missouri River, but restored only a temporary peace to the region.

The Treaty of Fort Laramie granted the Sioux the right to occupy the Black Hills, or Paha Sapa, their sacred land, "as long as the grass shall grow," but the discovery of gold soon undermined this guarantee. White prospectors hurriedly invaded the territory. Directed to quash rumors of fabulous deposits of the precious metal, Lieutenant Colonel George Armstrong Custer led a surveying expedition to the Black Hills during the summer of 1874, but, contrary to plan, the Civil War hero described rich veins of ore that could be cheaply extracted. The U.S. Congress then pushed

Preparing for a War Expedition, *ca. 1887. This sketch on paper was made by an Indian artist, Silverhorn, who had himself taken part in the final revolt of the Kiowas in 1874. He later became a medicine man, and then served as a private in the U.S. Cavalry at Fort Sill, Oklahoma Territory.*

to acquire the territory for Americans. To protect their land, Sioux, Cheyenne, and Arapaho warriors, ranging between two thousand and nine thousand in number, moved into war camps during the summer of 1876 and prepared for battle.

The most flamboyant of army commanders (and in the eyes of many of his own troops, the most irresponsible), Custer developed an ambitious plan to subdue the rebellious tribes. He even invited newspaper reporters to come along as he set off to establish a fort in the Black Hills. After several skirmishes, he decided to rush ahead of other army regiments to a site that was known to white soldiers as Little Bighorn and to Lakotas as Greasy Grass. This foolhardy move offered the allied Cheyenne and Sioux warriors a perfect opportunity to cut off Custer's logistical and military support. On June 25, 1876, Custer and his troops were wiped out by one of the largest Indian contingents ever assembled, an estimated 2,000 to 4,000 warriors.

"Custer's Last Stand" gave Indian-haters the emotional ammunition to whip up public excitement. After Custer's defeat, spiritual leader Sitting Bull reportedly said, "Now they will never let us rest." The U.S. Army tracked down the disbanded Indian contingents one by one and forced them to surrender. In February, 1877, the U.S. government formally took possession of the Black Hills. After the defiant warrior Crazy Horse was fatally stabbed while under arrest at a U.S. army camp, Sioux leadership in the Indian Wars came to an end.

Among the last to hold out against the reservation system were the Apaches in the Southwest. Most Apache bands had abided the Medicine Lodge Treaty of 1867, and in 1872 Cochise, one of the ablest

Apache chiefs, agreed to live with his people on a reservation on a portion of the tribe's ancestral land. Cochise died two years later, and some of the Apache bands, unable to tolerate the harsh conditions on the reservation, returned to their old ways of seizing territory and stealing cattle. For the next ten years, Cochise's successor Geronimo led intermittent raids against white outposts in the rough Arizona terrain.

Pursued by the U.S. Army, the Apaches earned a reputation as intrepid warriors. Their brilliant strategists and horse-riding braves became legendary for lightning-swift raids followed by quick disappearances. The Kiowas and the Comanches, both powerful tribes, joined the Apaches in one of the bloodiest conflicts, the Red River War of 1874–75. The U.S. Army ultimately prevailed less by military might than by denying Indians access to food. Even after the Red River War, small-scale warfare sputtered on. Not until September 1886, his band reduced to only thirty people, did Geronimo finally surrender, ending the Indian Wars.

The Nez Percé

In crushing the Plains tribes, the U.S. government had conquered those peoples who had most actively resisted the advance of non-Indians into the West. But even tribes that had long tried to cooperate found themselves embattled. The Nez Percé (pierced nose), given their name by French Canadian trappers who thought they had seen members of the tribe wearing shells in their septums, for generations regarded themselves as good friends to white traders and settlers. Living in the plateau where Idaho, Washington, and Oregon now meet, they saved the Lewis and Clark expedition from starvation. The Nez Percé occasionally assisted U.S. armies against hostile tribes, and many of them were converts to Christianity.

The discovery of gold on Nez Percé territory in 1860 changed their relations with whites for the worse. Pressed by prospectors and mining companies, government commissioners, in the treaty of 1863, demanded the Nez Percé cede 6 million acres, nine-tenths of their land, at less than ten cents per acre. Some the Nez Percé leaders agreed to the terms of the treaty, which had been fraudulently signed on behalf of the entire tribe, but others refused. Old Chief Tukekas, one of the first to convert to Christianity, threw away his Bible and returned to his old religion. His son and successor, Chief Joseph, swore to protect the peoples of the Wallowa Valley in present-day Oregon. At first federal officials listened to Nez Percé complaints against the treaty and decided to allow them to remain on their land. Responding to pressure from settlers and politicians, however, they almost immediately reversed their decision, ordering the Nez Percé, including Chief

Joseph and his followers, to sell their land and to move onto the reservation.

Intending to comply, Chief Joseph's band set out from the Wallowa Valley with their livestock and all the possessions they could carry. When U.S. troops fired on a Nez Percé truce team, however, the Nez Percé fought back, repulsing the attackers and killing one-third of them. Chief Joseph and his people then undertook a monumental journey in search of sanctuary in Canada. Brilliantly outmaneuvering vengeful U.S. troops sent to intercept them, the 750 Nez Percé—including women, children, and the elderly—retreated for some 1,400 miles into Montana and Wyoming through mountains and prairies, and across the Bitterroot range. Along the way they unintentionally terrified tourists at the newly created Yellowstone National Park. Over the three and a half months of their journey, Nez Percé braves fought 2,000 regular U.S. troops and eighteen Indian auxiliary detachments in eighteen separate engagements and two major battles. U.S. troops finally trapped the Nez Percé in the Bear Paw Mountains of northern Montana, just 30 miles from the Canadian border. Suffering from hunger and cold, they surrendered.

General Sherman remarked admiringly at the Nez Percé's ingenious tactics, courage, and avoidance of cruelty. Newspapers described Chief Joseph as a "Red Napoleon" defying overwhelming odds. (Actually, Joseph did not plan military strategy but mainly attended to the needs of dependent tribal members.)

Promised they would be returned to Oregon, the Nez Percé were sent instead to disease-ridden bottomland near Fort Leavenworth in Kansas, and then to Oklahoma. Arguing for the right of his people to return to their Oregon reservation, Joseph spoke eloquently, through an interpreter, to Congress in 1879. "Treat all men alike. Give them all the same law. Give them all an even chance to live and grow. All men were made by the same Great Spirit Chief," Joseph pleaded. Government officials appeared willing to allow him and his people to return to their homeland until white settlers in Idaho objected. The last remnant of Joseph's band were deported under guard to a non-Nez Percé reservation in Washington, where Chief Joseph died in 1904 "of a broken heart" and where his descendants continue to live in exile to this day.

THE INTERNAL EMPIRE

Since the time of Christopher Columbus, the Americas had inspired in Europeans visions of a land of incredible wealth, free for the taking. In the nineteenth century, the North American continent, stretching across scarcely populated territories toward the Pacific Ocean, revived this fantasy, espe-

Railroad Routes, Cattle Trails, Gold and Silver Rushes, 1860–1900   *By the end of the nineteenth century, the vast region of the West was crosscut by hundreds of lines of transportation and communication. The trade in precious metals and in cattle helped build a population almost constantly on the move, following the rushes for gold or the herds of cattle.*

Source: Encyclopedia of American Social History.

cially as early reports conjured dreams of mountains of gold and silver. Determined to make their fortunes, be it from copper in Arizona, wheat in Montana, or oranges in California, numerous adventurers traveled west. As a group they carried out the largest migration and greatest commercial expansion in American history.

But the settlers themselves also became the subjects of a huge "internal empire" whose financial, political, and industrial centers of power remained in

the East. A vast system of international markets also shaped the development of mines, farms, and new communities even as Americans romantically imagined the West to be the last frontier of individual freedom and wide-open spaces. Only a small number of settlers actually struck it rich. Meanwhile, older populations—Indian peoples, Hispanic peoples, and more recently settled communities like the Mormons—struggled to create places for themselves in this new order.

Mining Communities

The discovery of gold in California in 1848 roused fortune seekers from across the United States, Europe, and as far away as China and Chile. Within a year, prospecting parties overran the western territories, setting a pattern for intermittent rushes for gold, silver, and copper that extended from the Colorado mountains to the Arizona deserts to California, Oregon, Washington, and Alaska to the Black Hills of South Dakota. Mining camps and boomtowns soon dotted what had once been thinly settled regions. The population of California alone jumped from 14,000 in 1848 to 223,856 just four years later. More than any other industry or commercial enterprise, mining fostered western expansion.

The first miners required little preparation to stake their claims. The miner needs nothing, the military governor of California announced, "but his pick

A *"hard rock"* miner demonstrates the tiring and often dangerous task of hammering a drill into a rock to prepare a blasting hole. New technologies, such as diamond-headed drills, quickly revolutionized the extractive process, but potentially lethal hazards, including cave-ins and poisonous gases, remained great.

Artist unknown, [Miners Underground], 1897, glass plate negative, Mazzulla Collection—Mining, © Amon Carter Museum, Fort Worth, Texas. Mazzulla Collection.

and shovel and tin pan with which to dig and wash the gravel." A handful of individual prospectors did strike it rich. Many more found themselves employees of the so-called bonanza kings, the owners or operators of the most lucrative enterprises. Only in 1896–97, with news of "gold on the Klondike" in Alaska, did prospectors again hit on a vein worth millions of dollars.

The mining industry quickly grew from its treasure-hunt origins into a grand corporate enterprise. The Comstock Lode of silver, discovered by Henry Comstock along the Carson River in Nevada in 1858, sent about 10,000 miners across the Sierra Nevada from California, but few individuals came out wealthy. Comstock himself eventually sold his claims for a mere $11,000 and two mules. Those reaping the huge profits were the entrepreneurs who could afford to invest in the heavy—and expensive—equipment necessary to drill more than 3,000 feet deep and to hire engineers with the technical knowledge to manage the operations. Having secured a capital investment of nearly $900,000, the owners of the Gould and Curry mill, built on the Comstock Lode, did very well.

The most successful mineowners bought out the smaller claims and built an entire industry around their stakes. They found investors to finance their expansion and used the borrowed capital to purchase the latest in extractive technology, such as new explosives, compressed-air or diamond-headed rotary drills, and wire cable. They gained access to timber to fortify their underground structures and water to feed the hydraulic pumps that washed down mountains. They built smelters to refine the crude ore into ingots and often financed railroads to transport the product to distant markets. By the end of the century, the Anaconda Copper Mining Company had expanded into hydroelectricity to become one of the most powerful corporations in the nation.

The mining corporations laid the basis for a new economy as well as an interim government and established many of the region's first white settlements. Before the advent of railroads, ore had to be brought out of and supplies brought into mining areas by boats, wagons, and mules traveling hundreds of miles over rough territory. The railroad made transportation of supplies and products easier and faster. The shipping trade meanwhile grew into an important industry of its own, employing thousands of merchants, peddlers, and sailors. Dance halls, saloons, theaters, hospitals, and newspapers followed. Gold Hill and nearby Virginia City, Nevada, began as a cluster of small mining camps and by the early 1860s became a thriving urban community of nearly 6,000 people. A decade later, the population had quadrupled, but it subsequently fell sharply as the mines gave out. Occasionally, ore veins lasted long enough—as in Butte, Montana, center of the copper-mining district—to create permanent cities.

Many short-lived boomtowns were known as "Helldorados." Men outnumbered women by as much as ten to one, and very few lived with families or stayed very long. They often bunked with male kin and worked alongside friends or acquaintances from their hometown. Some lived unusually well, feasting on oysters trucked in at great expense. Amateur sporting events, public lectures, and large numbers of magazines and books filled many of their leisure hours. But the town center was usually the saloon, where, as one observer complained, men "without the restraint of law, indifferent to public opinion, and unburdened by families, drink whenever they feel like it, whenever they have the money to pay for it, and whenever there is nothing else to do."

The western labor movement began in these camps, partly as a response to dangerous working conditions. In the hardrock mines of the 1870s, one of every thirty workers was disabled, one of eighty killed. Balladeers back in Ireland sang of Butte as the town "where the streets were paved with Irish bones," and departing emigrants promised their mothers that they would never go underground in Montana. Miners began to organize in the 1860s, demanding good pay for dangerous and life-shortening work. By the end of the century they had established the strongest unions in the West.

Violence on both sides characterized western labor relations. When mineowners' private armies "arrested" strikers or fought their unions with rifle fire, miners burned down the campsites, seized trains loaded with ore, and sabotaged company property. The miners' unions also helped to secure legislation mandating a maximum eight-hour day for certain jobs and workmen's compensation for injuries. Such laws were enacted in Idaho, Arizona, and New Mexico by the 1910s, long before similar laws in most eastern states.

The unions fought hard, but they did so exclusively for the benefit of white workers. The native-born and the Irish and Cornish immigrants (from Cornwall, England) far outnumbered other groups before the turn of the century, when Italians, Slavs, and Greeks began to replace them. Labor unions eventually admitted these new immigrants, but refused Chinese, Mexican, and Indian workers. In 1869 white miners at the Comstock Lode rioted to protest the employment of Chinese miners. In Arizona, Mexican Americans had secured jobs in the copper and silver mines, but they usually received less pay and worked under worse conditions than white workers.

When prices and ore production fell sharply, not even unions could stop the owners from shutting down the mines and leaving ghost towns in their wake.

Often they also left behind an environmental disaster. Hydraulic mining, which used water cannons to blast hillsides and expose gold deposits, drove tons of rock and earth into the rivers and canyons. By the late 1860s southern California's rivers were clogged, producing floods that wiped out towns and farms. In 1893 Congress finally passed the Caminetti Act, giving the state the power to regulate the mines. (The act also created the Sacramento River Commission, which began to replace free-flowing rivers with canals and dams). Underground mining continued unregulated, using up whole forests for timbers and filling the air with dangerous, sulfurous smoke.

Mormon Settlements

While western expansion fostered the growth of new commercial cities such as the numerous if unstable mining towns, it simultaneously placed new restrictions on established communities. The Mormons (members of the Church of Jesus Christ of Latter-Day Saints) had fled western New York in the 1830s for Illinois and Missouri, only to face greater persecution in the Midwest. When their founder, Joseph Smith, was lynched after proclaiming the doctrine of polygamy (plural wives), the community sought refuge in the West. Led by their new prophet, Brigham Young, the Mormons migrated in 1846–47 to the Great Basin in present-day Utah and formed an independent theocratic state, called Deseret. However, their dream was cut short in 1850 when Congress set up Utah Territory. In 1857 President James Buchanan declared the Mormons to be in "a state of substantial rebellion" (for being an independent state in U.S. territory) and sent the U.S. Army to occupy the territory.

Although federal troops remained until the outbreak of the Civil War in 1861, the Mormon population continued to grow. By 1860 more than 40,000 Mormons lived in Utah Territory. Contrary to federal law, church officials forbade the selling of land. Mormons instead held property in common. They created sizable settlements complemented by satellite villages joined to communal farmlands and a common pasture. Relying on agricultural techniques learned from local Indian tribes, the Mormons built dams for irrigation and harvested a variety of crops from desert soil. Eventually nearly 500 Mormon communities spread from Oregon to Idaho to Arizona.

But as territorial rule tightened, the Mormons saw their unique way of life once again threatened. The newspapers and the courts repeatedly assailed the Mormons for the supposed sexual excesses of their system of "plural marriage," condemning them as heathens and savages. "There is an irrepressible conflict," one journalist wrote, "between the Mormon power and the principles upon which our free institu-

Mormon Cultural Diffusion, ca. 1883 *Mormon settlements permeated many sparsely populated sections of Idaho, Nevada, Arizona, Wyoming, Colorado, and New Mexico. Built with Church backing and the strong commitment of community members, they survived and even prospered in adverse climates.*

tions are established, and one or the other must succumb." Preceded by prohibitory federal laws enacted in 1862 and 1874, the Supreme Court finally ruled against polygamy in the 1879 case of *United States v. Reynolds*, which granted the freedom of belief but not the freedom of practice. In 1882 Congress passed the Edmunds Act, which effectively disfranchised those who believed in or practiced polygamy and threatened them with fines and imprisonment. Equally devastating was the Edmunds-Tucker Act, passed five years later, which destroyed the temporal power of the Mormon Church by confiscating all assets over $50,000 and establishing a federal commission to over-

see all elections in the territory. By the early 1890s Mormon leaders officially renounced plural marriage.

Polygamy had actually been practiced by no more than 15 percent to 20 percent of Mormon families, but it had been important to their sense of messianic mission. Forced to abandon the practice, they gave up most other aspects of their distinctive communal life, including the common ownership of land. By the time Utah became a state in 1896, Mormon communities resembled in some ways the society that the original settlers had sought to escape. They nevertheless combined their religious cohesion with leadership in the expanding regional economy to become a major political force in the West.

The Southwest

American expansionism transformed deserts and grasslands that had been contested for centuries among world powers. In 1845, Texas was annexed as a state, and the following year President James K. Polk whipped up a border dispute with Mexico into a war. The one-sided conflict ended in 1848 with the United States taking fully half of all Mexican territory—the future states of Arizona, California, Nevada, and Utah and parts of New Mexico, Wyoming, and Colorado. The Gadsden Purchase of 1853 rounded off this prize, giving the United States possession of all the land north of the Rio Grande.

The Treaty of Guadalupe Hidalgo, which ended the Mexican-American War, allowed the Hispanic people north of the Rio Grande to choose between immigrating to Mexico or staying in what was now the United States. But the new Mexican-American border, one of the longest unguarded boundaries in the world, could not successfully sever communities that had been connected for centuries. Despite the change in sovereignty, elites and common folk alike continued to travel back and forth between the two nations, and the majority of people who became U.S. citizens retained their identity as Mexicans. Even those who migrated farther north, a process that accelerated after the discovery of gold in California and the silver strikes in Nevada, kept their ties with friends and family in Mexico. What gradually emerged was an economically and socially interdependent zone, the Anglo-Hispanic borderlands linking the United States and Mexico.

Equality, however, did not provide the basis for relationships between the two nations and their peoples. Although under the treaty all Hispanics were formally guaranteed citizenship and the "free enjoyment of their liberty and property," local Anglos (as the Mexicans called white Americans) often violated these provisions and, through fraud or coercion, took control of the land. The Sante Fe Ring, a group of lawyers, politicians, and land speculators, stole millions of acres from the public

Thomas Allen, *Market Plaza*, 1878–1879. Oil on canvas, 26 x 39½ in. Witte Museum, San Antonio, Texas.

Mexican Americans in San Antonio continued to conduct their traditional market bazaar well after the incorporation of this region into the United States. Forced off the land and excluded from the better-paying jobs in the emerging regional economy, many Mexicanos and especially women sought to sell the products of their own handiwork for cash or for bartered food and clothing.

prominent merchants became territorial delegates to Congress.

The majority of Mexicans who had lived in the mountains and deserts of the Southwest for well over two centuries were less prepared for these changes. Most had worked outside the commercial economy, farming and herding sheep for their own subsistence. Before 1848 they had few contacts with the outside world. With the Anglos came land closures as well as commercial expansion prompted by railroad, mining, and timber industries. Many poor families found themselves crowded onto plots too small for subsistence farming. Many turned to seasonal labor on the new Anglo-owned commercial farms, where they became the first of many generations of poorly paid migratory workers. Other Mexicanos adapted by taking jobs on the railroad or in the mines. Meanwhile their wives and daughters moved to the new towns and cities in such numbers that by the end of the century Mexicanos had become a predominantly urban population, dependent on wages for survival.

Women were quickly drawn into the expanding network of market and wage relations. They tried to make ends meet by selling produce from their back-yard gardens; more often they worked as seamstresses or laundresses. Formerly at the center of a communal society, Mexicanas found themselves with fewer options in the cash economy. What wages they could now earn fell below even the low sums paid to their husbands, and women lost status within both the family and community.

domain and grabbed over 80 percent of the Mexicano landholdings in New Mexico alone. More often, Anglos used new federal laws to their own benefit.

For a time, Arizona and New Mexico seemed to hold out hope for a mutually beneficial interaction between Mexicanos and Anglos. A prosperous class of Hispanic landowners, with long-standing ties to Anglos through marriage, had established itself in cities like Albuquerque and Tucson, old Spanish towns that had been founded in the seventeenth and eighteenth centuries. Estevan Ochoa, merchant, philanthropist, and the only Mexican to serve as mayor of Tucson following the Gadsden Purchase, managed to build one of the largest business empires in the West. In Las Cruces, New Mexico, an exceptional family such as the wealthy Amadors could shop by mail from Bloomingdales, travel to the World's Fair in Chicago, and send their children to English-language Catholic schools. Even the small and struggling Mexicano middle class could afford such modern conveniences as kitchen stoves and sewing machines. These Mexican elites, well integrated into the emerging national economy, continued to wield political power as ranchers, landlords, and real estate developers until the end of the century. They secured passage of bills for education in their regions and often served as superintendents of local schools. Several

Occasionally, Mexicanos organized to reverse these trends or at least to limit the damage done to their communities. In South Texas in 1859, Juan Cortina and sixty of his followers pillaged white-owned stores and killed four Anglos who had gone unpunished for murdering several Mexicans. "Cortina's War" marked the first of several sporadic rebellions. As late as the 1880s, Las Corras Blancas, a band of agrarian rebels in New Mexico, were destroying railroad ties and posting demands for justice on fences of the new Anglo farms and ranches. Other Mexicanos organized more peacefully. *El Alianzo Hispano-Americano* (the Hispanic-American Alliance) was formed "to protect and fight for the rights of Spanish Americans" through political action. *Mutualistes* (mutual aid societies) provided sickness and death benefits to Mexican families.

Despite many pressures, Mexicanos preserved much of their cultural heritage. Many persisted in older ways because they had few choices and because their family and religion reinforced tradition. The Roman Catholic Church retained its influence in the community, and most Mexicans continued to turn to the church to baptize infants, to celebrate the feast day of their patron saints, to marry, and to bury the dead. Special saints like the Virgin of Guadalupe and distinctive holy days like the Day of the Dead survived along with fiestas celebrating the change of seasons. Many communities continued to commemorate Mexican national holidays, such as *Cinco de Mayo* (the fifth of May), marking the Mexican victory over French invaders in the battle of Puebla in 1862. Spanish language and Spanish place names continued to distinguish the Southwest.

But for the encroaching Anglo majority, large regions in the West had been "won" from the populations who had previously settled the region. Americans had brought in commercial capitalism, their political and legal systems, as well as many of their social and cultural institutions. Ironically, though, even after statehood, white settlers would still be only distant representatives of an empire whose financial, political, and industrial centers remained in the Northeast. In return for raw produce or ore drawn out of soil or rock, they received washtubs, clothes, and whiskey; model legal statutes; and doctors, lawyers, and teachers. But they were often frustrated by their continued isolation and enraged at the federal regulations that governed them and at the eastern investors and lawyers who seemed poised on all sides to rob them of the fruits of their labor. Embittered Westerners, along with Southerners, would form the core of a nationwide discontent that would soon threaten to uproot the American political system.

THE CATTLE INDUSTRY

The slaughter of the buffalo made way for the cattle industry, one of the most profitable businesses in the West. Texas longhorns, introduced by the Spanish, numbered over 5 million at the close of the Civil War and represented a potentially plentiful supply of beef for eastern consumers. In the spring of 1866, entrepreneurs such as Joseph G. McCoy began to build a spectacular cattle market in the western part of Kansas, where the Kansas Pacific Railroad provided crucial transportation links to slaughtering and packing houses and commercial distributors in Kansas City, St. Louis, and Chicago.

In 1867 only 35,000 head of cattle reached McCoy's new stockyards in Abilene, but 1868 proved the first of many banner years. Drovers pushed herd after herd north from Texas through Oklahoma on the trail marked out by part-Cherokee trader Jesse Chisholm. Great profits were made on Texas steers bought for $7–$9 a head and sold in Kansas for upward of $30. In 1880 nearly 2 million cattle were slaughtered in Chicago alone. For two decades, cattle represented the West's bonanza industry.

Cowboys

The great cattle drives depended on the cowboy, a seasonal or migrant worker. After the Civil War, cowboys—one for every 300–500 head on the trail—rounded up herds of Texas cattle and drove them as much as 1,500 miles north to grazing ranches or to the stockyards where they were readied for shipping by rail to eastern markets. The boss supplied the horses, the cowboy his own bedroll, saddle, and spurs. The workday lasted from sunup to sundown, with short night shifts for guarding the cattle. Scurvy, a widespread ailment, could be traced to the basic chuckwagon menu of sowbelly, beans, and coffee, a diet bereft of fruits and vegetables. The cowboy worked without protection from rain or hail, and severe dust storms could cause temporary blindness. As late as 1920, veterans of the range complained that no company would sell life insurance to a cowboy.

In return for his labor, the cowboy received at the best of times about $30 per month. Wages were usually paid in one lump sum at the end of a drive, a policy that encouraged cowboys to spend their money quickly and recklessly in the booming cattle towns of Dodge City, Kansas, or Cheyenne, Wyoming. In the 1880s, when wages began to fall along with the price of beef, cowboys fought back by stealing cattle or by forming unions. In 1883 many Texas cowboys struck for higher wages; nearly all Wyoming cowboys struck in 1886. Aided by the legendary camaraderie fostered in the otherwise desolate conditions of the long drive, cowboys, along with miners, were among the first western workers to organize against employers.

Like other parts of the West, the cattle range was ethnically diverse. Between one-fifth and one-third of all workers were Indian, Mexican, or African American. Indian cowboys worked mainly on the northern plains and in Indian Territory; the vaqueros, who had previously worked on the Mexican cattle haciendas, or huge estates, predominated in South Texas and California. After the Civil War, hundreds of African Americans took the trail north from Texas.

Like the vaqueros, African American cowboys were highly skilled managers of cattle. Some were sons of former slaves who had been captured from the African territory of Gambia, where cattle-raising was an age-old art. Unlike Mexicans, they earned wages comparable to those paid to Anglos and especially during the early years worked in integrated drover parties. By the 1880s, as the center of the cattle industry shifted to the more settled regions around the northern ranches, African Americans were forced out and turned to other kinds of work. Although the majority of Anglo cowboys also came from the South and shared with former slaves the hope of escaping the postwar economic devastation of their region, they usually remained loyal to the racial hierarchy of the Confederacy.

Cowgirls and Prostitutes

Sally Redus, wife of an early Texas cattleman, once accompanied her husband on the long drive from Texas to Kansas. Carrying her baby on her lap, she most likely rode the enormous distance "sidesaddle," with both legs on one side of the horse. Although few women worked as trail hands, they did find jobs on the ranches, usually in the kitchen or laundry. Occasionally a husband and wife worked as partners, sharing even the labor of wrangling cattle, and following her husband's death, a woman might take over altogether. The majority of women attended to domestic chores, caring for children and maintaining the household. Their daughters, however, enjoyed better prospects. By the end of the century, women reared on ranches were riding astride, "clothespin style," roping calves, branding cattle or cutting their ears to mark

them, and castrating bulls. But not until 1901 did a woman dare to enter an official rodeo contest.

In cattle towns, many women worked as prostitutes. During the first cattle drive to Abilene in 1867, a few women were so engaged; but by the following spring, McCoy's assistant recalled, "they came in swarms, & as the weather was warm 4 or 5 girls could huddle together in a tent very comfortably." Although some women worked in trailside "hoghouses," the best-paid prostitutes congregated in "brothel districts" or "tenderloins." Most cattle towns boasted at least one dance hall where prostitutes plied their trade. Dodge city had two: one with white prostitutes for white patrons; another with black prostitutes for both white and black men. Although prostitution was illegal in most towns, the laws were rarely enforced until the end of the century, when reformers led campaigns to shut down the red-light districts.

Perhaps 50,000 women engaged in prostitution west of the Mississippi during the second half of the nineteenth century. Like most cowboys, most prostitutes were unmarried and in their teens or twenties. Often fed up with underpaid jobs in dressmaking or domestic service, they found few alternatives to prostitution in the cattle towns, where the cost of food and lodging was notoriously high. Still, earnings in prostitution were slim, except during the cattle-shipping season when young men outnumbered women by as much as three to one.

In the best of times, a fully employed Wichita prostitute might earn $30 per week, nearly two-thirds of which would go for room and board. Injury or even death from violent clients, addiction to narcotics such as cocaine or morphine, and venereal disease were workaday dangers.

Community and Conflict on the Range

The combination of prostitution, gambling, and drinking discouraged the formation of stable communities. According to a Kansas proverb, "There's no Sunday west of Junction City and no god west of Salina." Personal violence was notoriously commonplace on the streets and in the barrooms of cattle towns and mining camps populated mainly by young, single men. Many western towns such as Wichita outlawed the carrying of handguns, but

Curly Wolves Howled on Saturday Night, *a commercial woodcut from the 1870s. The artist, recording this scene at a tavern near Billings, Montana, captured what he called a "Dude and a Waitress" dancing the "Bull Calves' Medley on the Grand Piano." Illustrations depicting a wild and lively West appeared prominently in magazines like* Harper's Weekly, *which circulated mainly among readers east of the Mississippi.*

enforcement usually lagged. Local specialty shops and mail-order catalogues continued to sell weapons with little regulation. But contrary to popular belief, gunfights were relatively rare. Local police officers, such as Wyatt Earp and "Wild Bill" Hickok, worked mainly to keep order among drunken cowboys.

After the Civil War, violent crime, assault, and robbery rose sharply throughout the United States. In the West, the most prevalent crimes were horse theft and cattle rustling, which peaked during the height of the open range period and then fell back by the 1890s. Death by legal hanging or illegal lynching—at "necktie parties" in which the victims were "jerked to Jesus"— was the usual sentence. In the last half of the century, vigilantes acting outside the law mobilized more than 200 times, claiming altogether more than 500 victims.

The "range wars" of the 1870s produced violent conflicts. By this time, both farmers and sheep herders were encroaching on the fields where cattle had once grazed freely. Sheep chew grass down to its roots, making it practically impossible to raise cattle on land they have grazed. Farmers meanwhile set about building fences to protect their domestic livestock and property. Great cattle barons fought back against farmers by ordering cowboys to cut the new barbed-wire fences. Rivalry among the owners of livestock was even more vicious, particularly in the Southwest and Pacific Northwest. In these areas, Mexicano shepherds and Anglo cattlemen often fought each other for land. In Lincoln County, New Mexico, the feuds grew so intense in 1878 that one faction hired gunman Billy the Kid to protect its interests. President Rutherford B. Hayes finally sent troops to halt the bloodshed.

The cattle barons helped to bring about their own demise, but they did not go down quietly. Ranchers eager for greater profits, and often backed by foreign capital, overstocked their herds, and eventually the cattle began to deplete the limited supply of grass. Finally, in 1885–87, a combination of summer drought and winter blizzards killed 90 percent of the cattle in the West. Prices also declined sharply. Many big ranchers fell into bankruptcy. Along the way, they often took out their grievances against the former cowboys who had gathered small herds for themselves. They charged these small ranchers with cattle rustling, taking them to court or, in some cases, rounding up lynching parties. As one historian has written, violence was "not a mere sideshow" but "an intrinsic part of western society."

Statehood and Ethnic Settlement

The process for admitting new states to the Union was established by Congress in the Northwest Ordinance of 1787, before the ratification of the Constitution. Although the pace at which this process operated and the way it was controlled varied from region to region and over time, its formal rules changed little. Each new state was admitted when its free population reached 60,000 and its constitution was approved by Congress, entitling those citizens eligible to vote to become full participants in the political system.

Each of the western states that entered the Union in the late nineteenth and early twentieth centuries had its own distinctive ethnic and racial composition. North Dakota, which became a state in 1889, had long had a large Native American population. An influx of newcomers, many of them European immigrants, boosted its population quickly by 1900. As the map at the right indicates, ethnic groups of European background tended to settle in clusters, mainly where they had purchased large blocs of fertile land from promoters. Nonwhites sought (or were confined to) remote locations. Much of the state remained practically uninhabited.

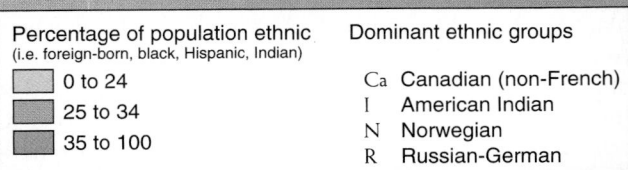

Percentage of population ethnic (i.e. foreign-born, black, Hispanic, Indian)	Dominant ethnic groups
☐ 0 to 24	Ca Canadian (non-French)
☐ 25 to 34	I American Indian
☐ 35 to 100	N Norwegian
	R Russian-German

Source: James R. Shortridge, *The Great Plains.* Cayton, Gorn, Williams, *Encyclopedia of American History,* II.

FARMING COMMUNITIES ON THE PLAINS

The vision of a huge fertile garden extending from the Appalachians to the Pacific Ocean had inspired Americans since the early days of the republic. But the first explorers who actually traveled through the Great Plains quashed this dream. "The Great Desert" was the name they gave to the region stretching west from Kansas and Nebraska, north to Montana and the Dakotas, and south again to Oklahoma and Texas. Few trees fended off the blazing sun of summer or promised a supply of lumber for homes and fences. The occasional river or stream flowed with "muddy gruel" rather than pure, sweet water. Economically, the entire region appeared as hopelessly barren as it was vast. It took massive improvements in both transportation and farm technology—as well as unrelenting advertising and promotional campaigns—to open the Great Plains to widescale agriculture.

The Homestead Act

The Homestead Act of 1862 offered the first incentive to prospective white farmers. This act granted a quarter section (160 acres) of the public domain free to any settler who lived on the land and improved it for at least five years; or a settler could buy the land for $1.25 per acre after only six months' residence. Approximately 605 million acres of public domain became available for settlement.

Homesteaders achieved their greatest success in the central and upper Midwest where the soil was rich and weather relatively moderate. But those settlers lured to the Great Plains by descriptions of land "carpeted with soft grass—a sylvan paradise" found themselves locked in a fierce struggle with the harsh climate and arid soil. The average holding could rarely furnish a livelihood, even with hard work.

Rather than filing a homestead claim with the federal government, most settlers acquired their land outright. State governments and land companies usually held the most valuable land near transportation and markets, and the majority of farmers were willing to pay a hefty price for these benefits. A few women speculators did very well, particularly in the Dakotas, where they acquired acreage under the generous terms of the Homestead Act, not to farm but to sell when prices for land increased. Before the turn of the century, farm acreage west of the Mississippi had tripled, but perhaps only 10 percent of all farmers got their start under homestead provisions. The big-time land speculators gained the most, plucking choice locations at bargain prices.

The dream of a homestead nevertheless died hard. Five years after the passage of the Homestead Act, *New York Tribune* editor Horace Greeley still advised his readers to strike off "into the broad, free West" and "make yourself a farm from Uncle Sam's generous domain, you will crowd nobody, starve nobody, and . . . neither you nor your children need evermore beg for Something to Do." He was wrong. Although the Homestead Act did spark the largest migration in American history, it did not lay the foundation for a nation of prosperous family farms.

Populating the Plains

The rapid settlement of the West could not have taken place without the railroad. Although the Homestead Act offered prospective farmers free land, it was the railroad that promoted settlement, brought people to their new homes, and carried crops and cattle to eastern markets. The railroads therefore wielded tremendous economic and political power throughout the West. Their agents—reputed to know every cow in the district—made major decisions regarding territorial welfare. In designing routes and locating depots, railroad companies put whole communities "on the map," or left them behind.

Along with providing transportation links between the East and West and potential markets as distant as China, the western railroads directly encouraged settlement. Unlike the railroads built before the Civil War, which followed the path of villages and towns, the western lines preceded settlement. Bringing people west became their top priority, and the railroad companies conducted aggressive promotional and marketing campaigns. Agents enticed Easterners and Europeans alike with long-term loans and free transportation by rail to distant points in the West. The railroads also sponsored land companies to sell parcels of their own huge allotments from the federal government. The National Land Company, founded in Chicago in 1869, alone organized sixteen colonies of mainly European immigrants in parts of Kansas and Colorado. The Santa Fe Railroad sent agent C. B. Schmidt to Germany, where he managed to entice nearly 60,000 Germans to settle along the rail line.

More than 2 million Europeans, many recruited by professional promoters, settled the Great Plains between 1870 and 1900. Some districts in Minnesota seemed to be virtual colonies of Sweden; others housed the largest number of Finns in the New World. In sparsely settled North Dakota, Scandinavians constituted 30 percent of the population, with Norwegians the largest group. Nebraska, whose population as early as 1870 was 25 percent foreign-born, concen-

trated Germans, Swedes, Danes, and Czechs. A smaller portion of European immigrants reached Kansas, still fewer the territories to the south where Indian and Hispanic peoples and African Americans remained the major ethnic populations. But Germans outnumbered all other immigrants by far.

Many immigrants found life on the Great Plains difficult but endurable. "Living in Nebraska," the locals joked, "is a lot like being hanged; the initial shock is a bit abrupt, but once you hang there for awhile you sort of get used to it." The German Russians who settled the Dakotas discovered soil similar to that of their homeland but weather that was even more severe. Having earlier fled religious persecution in Germany for Russia, they brought with them heavy coats and the technique of using sun-dried bricks to build houses in areas where lumber was scarce. These immigrants often provided examples for other settlers less familiar with such harsh terrain.

Having traveled the huge distance with kin or members of their Old World villages, immigrants tended to form tight-knit communities on the Great Plains. Often they advised others still at home to join them and gradually enlarged their distinctive settlements. Many married only within their own group. For example, only 3 percent of Norwegian men married women of a different ethnic background. Like many Mexicanos in the Southwest, several immigrant groups retained their languages well into the twentieth century, usually by sponsoring parochial school systems and publishing their own newspapers. A few groups closed their communities to outsiders. The Poles who migrated to central Nebraska in the 1880s, for example, formed an exclusive settlement; and the German Hutterites, who disavowed private property, lived as much as possible in seclusion in the Bon Homme colony of South Dakota, established in 1874.

Among the native-born settlers of the Great Plains, the largest number had migrated from states bordering the Mississippi River, all of which lost population in the decade after the enactment of the Homestead Act. Settling as individual families rather than as whole communities, they faced an exceptionally solitary life on the Great Plains. The usual rectangular homestead of 160 acres placed farm families at least a half-mile and often much farther from each other. To stave off isolation, homesteaders sometimes built their homes on the adjoining corners of their plots. Still, the prospect of doing better, which brought most homesteaders to the Great Plains in the first place, caused many families to keep seeking greener pastures. Mobility was so high that between one-third and one-half of all households pulled up stakes within a decade.

Communities eventually flourished in prosperous towns like Grand Island, Nebraska; Coffeyville, Kansas; and Fargo, North Dakota, that served the larger agricultural region. Built alongside the railroad, they grew into commercial centers, home to banking, medical, legal, and retail services. Town life fostered a special intimacy; even in the county graveyard, it was said, a town resident remained among neighbors. But closeness did not necessarily promote social equality or even friendship. A social hierarchy based on education (for the handful of doctors and lawyers) and, more important, investment property (held mainly by railroad agents and bankers) governed relationships between individuals and families. Religion also played a large part in defining these differences. Upwards of 70 percent of town residents were church-affiliated, the largest group comprising Roman Catholics, followed by Methodists, Lutherans, Baptists, and Presbyterians. Reinforced by family ties and ethnic affiliation, religious allegiances just as often provided a basis for conflict as for community.

Work, Dawn to Dusk

By the 1870s the Great Plains, once the home of buffalo and Indian hunters, was becoming a vast farming region populated mainly by immigrants from Europe and white Americans from east of the Mississippi. In place of the first one-room shanties, sod houses, and log cabins stood substantial frame farmhouses, along with a variety of other buildings like barns, smokehouses, and stables. But the built environment took nothing away from the predominating vista—the expansive fields of grain. "You have no idea, Beulah," wrote a Dakota farmer to his wife, "of what [the wheat farms] are like until you see them. For mile after mile there is not a sign of a tree or stone and just as level as the floor of your house. . . . Wheat never looked better and it is nothing but wheat, wheat, wheat."

Most farm families survived, and prospered if they could, through hard work, often from dawn to dusk. Men's activities in the fields tended to be seasonal, with heavy work during planting and harvest; at other times, their labor centered on construction or repair of buildings and on taking care of livestock. Women's activities were usually far more routine, week in and week out: cooking and canning of seasonal fruit and vegetables, washing, ironing, churning cream for butter, and keeping chickens for their eggs. Women might occasionally take in boarders, usually young men working temporarily in railroad construction, and they tended to the young children. Many women complained about the ceaseless drudgery, especially when they watched their husbands invest in farm equipment rather than domestic appliances. Others, however, relished the challenge. An Iowa woman, for example, liked "to have whole control of my house; can say I am monarch of all I survey and none to dispute my right."

Children also joined in the family's labors. Milking the cows, hauling water, and running errands to neighboring farms could be done by the children, once they had reached the age of nine or so. The "one-room school," where all grades learned together, taught the basics of literacy and arithmetic that a future farmer or commercial employee would require. Sons might be expected to work for ten to twenty years on the family farm, generally for their subsistence alone. Older sons and daughters alike might move to the nearest town to find wagework and contribute their earnings to the family coffer.

The harsh climate and unyielding soil nevertheless

These homesteaders in Nebraska, 1886, confronted the typically harsh conditions of treeless plains by erecting sod huts. They often brought with them an assortment of seeds and seedlings for spring plantings and a small number of livestock. A good fall harvest would provide the cash for building more substantial frame houses and outbuildings and encourage other homesteaders to settle near them. Communities eventually grew from these crude beginnings.

forced all but the most reclusive families to seek out friends and neighbors. Many hands were needed to clear the land for cultivation or for road beds, to raise houses and barns, or to bring in a harvest before a threatening storm. Neighbors might agree to work together haying, harvesting, and threshing grain. They also traded their labor, calculated by the hour, for use of equipment or for special assistance. A well-to-do farmer might "rent" his threshing machine in exchange for a small cash fee and, for instance, three days' labor. His wife might barter her garden produce for her neighbor's bread and milk or for help during childbirth or disability. Women often combined work and leisure in quilting bees and sewing circles, where they made friends while sharing scraps of material and technical information. Whole communities turned out for special events, such as the seasonal husking bees and apple bees, which were organized mainly by women.

Much of this informal barter, however, resulted from lack of cash rather than a lasting desire to cooperate. When annual harvests were bountiful, even the farm woman's practice of bartering goods with neighbors and local merchants—butter and eggs in return for yard goods or seed—diminished sharply, replaced by cash transactions. Still, wheat production proved unsteady in the last half of the nineteenth century, and few farm families could remain reliant wholly on themselves.

For many farmers, the soil simply would not yield a livelihood, and they often owed more money than they took in. Start-up costs, including the purchase of land and equipment, put many farmers deep in debt to local creditors. Some lost their land altogether. By 1880, when the Bureau of the Census began to compile statistics on tenant-operated farms, nearly 18 percent of the farms in Nebraska were worked by tenants; a decade later the portion had risen to nearly one-quarter. By the turn of the century, more than one-third of all farmers in the United States were tenants on someone else's land.

The Garden of Eden was not to be found on the prairies or on the plains, no matter how hard the average farm family worked. Again and again foreclosures wiped out the small landowner through dips in commodity prices, bad decisions, natural disasters, or illness. In one especially bad year, 1881, a group of farmers in western Iowa chose to burn off rather than harvest their wheat because the yield promised to be so small. Many farmers stood only a step away from financial disaster, wondering if they had chosen the best life for themselves and their families. The swift growth of rural population soon ended. Although writers and orators alike continued to celebrate the family farm as the source of virtue and economic well-being, the hard reality of big money and political power told a far different story.

THE WORLD'S BREADBASKET

During the second half of the nineteenth century western farms employed the most intensive and extensive methods of agricultural production in the world. Hard-working farmers brought huge numbers of acres under cultivation, while new technologies allowed them to achieve unprecedented levels of efficiency in the planting and harvesting of crops. As a result, western agriculture became increasingly tied to international trade, and modern capitalism soon ruled western agriculture, as it did the mining and cattle industries.

New Production Technologies

Only after the trees had been cleared and grasslands cut free of roots could the soil be prepared for planting. But as farmers on the Great Plains knew so well, the sod west of the Mississippi did not yield readily to cultivation and often broke the cast-iron plows typically used by eastern farmers. Farther west, some farmers resorted to drills to plant seeds for crops such as wheat and oats. Even in the best locations, where loamy, fertile ground had built up over centuries into eight or more inches of decayed vegetation, the preliminary breaking, or "busting," of the sod required hard labor. One man would guide a team of five or six oxen pulling a plow through the soil, while another regulated the depth of the cut, or furrow. But, as a North Dakota settler wrote to his wife back in Michigan, after the first crop the soil became as "soft as can be, any team [of men and animals] can work it."

Agricultural productivity depended as much on new technology as on the farmers' hard labor. In 1837 John Deere had designed his famous "singing plow" that easily turned prairie grasses under and turned up even highly compacted soils. Around the same time, Cyrus McCormick's reaper began to be used for cutting

This "thirty-three horse team harvester" was photographed at the turn of the century in Walla Walla, Washington. Binding the grain into sheaves before it could hit the ground, the "harvester" cut, threshed, and sacked wheat in one single motion.

HAND VS. MACHINE LABOR ON THE FARM, CA. 1880

Crop	Time Worked		Labor Cost	
	Hand	Machine	Hand	Machine
Wheat	61 hours	3 hours	$3.55	$0.66
Corn	39 hours	15 hours	3.62	1.51
Oats	66 hours	7 hours	3.73	1.07
Loose Hay	21 hours	4 hours	1.75	0.42
Baled Hay	35 hours	12 hours	3.06	1.29

grain; by the 1850s his factories were turning out reapers in mass quantities. McCormick's design featured ridges of triangular knives, like sharks' teeth, that mechanically sliced through the stalks as the reaper moved forward under horse-power or, later, machine-power. The harvester, invented in the 1870s, drew the cut stalks upward to a platform where two men could bind them into sheaves; by the 1880s an automatic knotter tied them together. Drastically reducing the number of people traditionally required for this work, the harvester increased the pace many times over.

Improvements were not limited to the reaper and harvester, although these machines underwent continuous redesign and were enhanced first by steam and eventually gas power. From the 1840s on, the U.S. Patent Office recorded an astonishing number of agricultural inventions. The introduction of mechanized corn planters and mowing or raking machines for hay all but completed the technological arsenal.

In the 1890s, the U.S. commissioner of labor measured the impact of technology on farm productivity. Before the introduction of the wire binder in 1875, he reported, a farmer could not plant more than 8 acres of wheat if he were to harvest it successfully without help; by 1890 the same farmer could rely on his new machine to handle 135 acres with relative ease and without risk of spoilage. The improvements in the last half of the century allowed an average farmer to produce up to ten times more than was possible with the old implements.

Scientific study of soil, grain, and climatic conditions was another factor in the record output. Heretofore, farmers had to rely on tradition or to experiment with whatever the grain merchants had to offer. Beginning in the mid-nineteenth century, federal and state governments added inducements to the growing body of expertise, scientific information, and hands-on advice. Through the Morrill Act of 1862, "land-grant" colleges acquired space for campuses in return for promising to institute agricultural programs. The Department of Agriculture, which attained cabinet status in

1889, and the Weather Bureau (transferred from the War Department in 1891) also made considerable contributions to farmers' knowledge. The federal Hatch Act of 1887, which created a series of experimental agricultural stations, passed along new information, especially in the areas of soil minerals and plant growth. Many states added their own agricultural stations, usually connected with state colleges and universities.

Nature nevertheless often reigned over technological innovation and seemed in places to take revenge against these early successes. West of the 98th meridian—a north–south line extending through western Oklahoma, central Kansas and Nebraska, and eastern Dakota—perennial dryness due to an annual rainfall of less than 28 inches constantly threatened to turn soil into dust and to break plows on the hardened ground. Summer heat burned out crops and ignited grass fires. Mountains of winter snows turned rivers into spring torrents that flooded fields; heavy fall rains washed crops away. Even good weather invited worms and flying insects to infest the crops. During the 1870s grasshoppers in clouds a mile long ate everything organic, including tree bark and clothes. Mormons erected a statue to the gulls who made a surprise appearance in Utah to eat the "hoppers"; however, most farmers were not as lucky as the Mormons.

Producing for the Market

From the Midwest to the far reaches of the Great Plains, farming changed in important ways during the last third of the nineteenth century. Although the family remained the primary source of labor, farmers tended to put more emphasis on production for exchange rather than for home use. They continued to plant vegetable gardens and often kept fowl or livestock for the family's consumption, but farmers raised crops mainly for the market and measured their own success or failure in terms of cash products.

Most large-scale farmers specialized in one or two crops, such as corn, rye, or barley, and sent their goods by railroad to eastern distributors and thence to national and international markets. Wheat farmers in particular prospered. With the world population increasing at a rapid rate, the international demand for wheat was enormous, and American farmers made huge profits from the sale of this crop. Wheat production ultimately served as a barometer of the agricultural economy in the West. Farmers in all corners of the region, from Nebraska to California, expanded or contracted their holdings and planned their crops according to the price of wheat.

The new machines and expanding market did not necessarily guarantee success. Land, draft animals, and equipment remained very expensive, and start-up costs could keep a family in debt for decades. A year of good returns often preceded a year of financial disaster. Weather conditions, international markets, and railroad and steamship shipping prices all proved equally unpredictable and heartless.

Farmers who settled on good lands in the 1860s and 1870s were more fortunate than those to follow. These pioneers, who began with only a little capital and worked twenty or thirty years to build up livestock and crops, frequently reached old age knowing that they could leave productive farmland to their sons or daughters. Latecomers found most of the good land already locked up in production or too expensive to acquire.

The new technology and scientific expertise favored the large, well-capitalized farmer over the small one. Such is the story of the large-scale wheat operations in the great Red River Valley of North Dakota. Here a shrewd worker such as Oliver Dalrymple could take advantage of a spectacular bonanza. When Dalrymple started out in 1875, he managed a farm owned by two officials of the Northern Pacific Railroad. He cleared their land, planted wheat, and yielded a sizable harvest the first year. He did much better the second year and began to invest in his own farm. A decade later his operations included 32,000 acres in wheat and 2,000 in oats. Dalrymple now had the financial resources to use the latest technology to harvest these crops and to employ up to one thousand seasonal laborers at a time. The majority of farmers with fewer resources expanded at more modest rates. Between 1880 and 1900 average farm size in the seven leading grain-growing states increased from 64.4 acres to more than 100 acres.

California

The trend toward big farms reached an apex in California, where farming as a business quickly superseded farming as a way of life. The conclusion of the Mexican-American War in 1848 coincided with the beginning of the Gold Rush, and the Anglos flooding the new territory wanted the land that had been occupied for centuries by the Spanish-speaking peoples, the Californios. The U.S. Congress created the Lands Claims Commission in 1851 to examine the great land-grant system that had been introduced by the Spaniards. Although many Californios ultimately saw their holdings validated by the Supreme Court, the cost of litigation had forced many into debt. Then, after a period of frenzied land speculation, capitalists mainly from San Francisco and Sacramento took ownership of many farms in northern California. Many of these haciendas held some of the best farming land in the state and were replete with dams, canals, and other expensive earthworks demanded by the arid soil. The new owners introduced new technologies and invested huge amounts of capital, setting the pattern for the state's prosperous agribusiness. Farms of nearly 500 acres dominated the California landscape in 1870; by the turn of the century, two-thirds of the state's arable land was in 1,000-acre farms. As land reformer and social commentator Henry George noted, California was "not a country of farms but a country of plantations and estates."

This scale of production made California the national leader in wheat production by the mid-1880s. But it also succeeded dramatically with fruit and vegetables. Large- and medium-sized growers, shrewdly combined in cooperative marketing associations during the 1870s–80s, used the new refrigerator cars to ship their produce in large quantities to the East and even to Europe. By 1890, cherries, apricots, and oranges, packed with mountains of ice, made their way into homes across the United States.

California growers learned quickly that they could satisfy consumer appetites and even create new ones. Orange producers packed their products individually in tissue paper, a technique designed to convince eastern consumers that they were about to eat a luxury fruit. By the turn of the century, advertisers for the California Citrus Growers' Association described oranges as a necessity for good health, inventing the trademark "Sunkist" to be stamped on each orange. Meanwhile California's grape growing grew into a big business, led by promoter and winemaker Paul Masson. Long considered inferior to French wines, California wines found a ready market at lower prices. Other grape growers made their fortunes in raisins. By the early twentieth century, one association trademarked its raisins as "Sun Maid" and packaged them for schoolchildren in the famous nickel box.

By 1900, California had become the model for American agribusiness, not the home of self-sufficient homesteaders but the showcase of heavily capitalized farm factories. Machines soon displaced animals and even many people. Many Californios tried to hold onto their traditional forms of labor if not their land, only to become the backbone of the state's migrant work force. Intense battles in the state legislature over land and irrigation rights underscored the message that powerful forces had gathered in California to promote large-scale agricultural production.

The Toll on the Land

The delicate ecologies of the West perished more quickly under human pressure than those prevailing anywhere else on the continent. Viewing the land as a resource to command, the new inhabitants often looked past the existing flora and fauna toward a landscape remade strictly for commercial purposes. The changes they produced in some areas were nearly as cataclysmic as those that occurred during the Ice Age.

Banishing many existing species, farmers "improved" the land by introducing exotic plants and animals—that is, biological colonies indigenous to other regions and continents. Some of the new plants and animals flourished in alien surroundings; many did not. Farmers also unintentionally introduced new varieties of weeds, insect pests, and rats. Surviving portions of older grasslands and meadows eventually could be found only alongside railroad tracks, in graveyards, or inside national parks.

Numerous species disappeared altogether or suffered drastic reduction. The grizzly bear, for example, an animal exclusive to the West, could once be found in large numbers from the Great Plains to California and throughout much of Alaska; by the early decades of the twentieth century, one nature writer estimated that only 800 survived, mostly in Yellowstone National Park. At the same time the number of wolves declined from perhaps as many as 2 million to just 200,000. "If you count the buffalo for hides and the antelope for backstraps and the passenger pigeons for target practice and the Indian ponies (killed by whites, to keep the Indian poor)," one scholar estimates, "it is conceivable that 500 million creatures died" on the Plains alone. By the mid-1880s, no more than 5,000 buffalo survived in the entire United States, and little remained of the once vast herds but great heaps of bones sold for $7.50 per ton.

The slaughter of the buffalo had a dramatic impact, not only on the fate of the species but also on the grasslands of the Great Plains. Overall, the biological diversity of the region had been drastically reduced. Unlike the grizzly and wolf, buffalo had not been exclusively Western animals. Before European colonization they had grazed over an area of 3 million square miles, nearly to the east coast; as the herds moved on, the grasslands were replenished. Having killed off the giant herds, ranchers and farmers quickly shifted to cattle and sheep production. Unlike the roaming buffalo, these livestock did not range widely

and soon devoured the native grasses down to their roots. With the ground cover destroyed, the soil eroded and became barren. By the end of the century, huge dust storms formed across the windswept plains.

New forests, many settlers hoped, would improve the weather, restore the soil, and also provide a source for fencing and fuel. In 1873 the U.S. Congress passed the Timber Culture Act, which allotted homesteaders an additional 160 acres of land in return for planting and cultivating forty acres of trees. Because residence was not required, and because tree planting could not be assessed for at least thirteen years, speculators filed for several claims at once, then turned around and sold the land without having planted a single tree. Although some forests were restored, neither the weather nor the soil improved.

Large-scale commercial agriculture also took a heavy toll on inland waters. Before white settlement, rainfall had drained naturally into lakes and underground aquifers, and watering spots were abundant throughout the Plains. Farmers mechanically rerouted and dammed water to irrigate their crops, causing many bodies of water to disappear and the water table to drop significantly. Successful farmers pressed for ever greater supplies of water. In 1887 the state of California formed irrigation districts, securing bond issues for construction of canals, and other western states followed. But by the 1890s, irrigation had seemed to reach its limit without federal support. The Newlands or National Reclamation Act of 1902 added 1 million acres of irrigated land, and state irrigation districts added more than 10 million acres. Expensive to taxpayers, and ultimately benefiting corporate farmers rather than small landowners, these projects further diverted water and totally transformed the landscape.

Although western state politicians and federal officials debated water rights for decades, they rarely considered the impact of water policies on the environment. Lake Tulare in California's Central Valley, for example, had occupied up to 760 square miles. After farmers began to irrigate their land by tapping the rivers that fed Tulare, the lake shrank dramatically, covering a mere 36 square miles by the early twentieth century. Finally the lake, which had supported rich aquatic and avian life for thousands of years, disappeared entirely. The land left behind, now wholly dependent on irrigation, grew so alkaline in spots that it could no longer be used for agricultural purposes.

The need to maintain the water supply indirectly led to the creation of national forests and the Forest Service. Western farmers supported the General Land Revision Act of 1891, which gave the president the power to establish forest reserves to protect watersheds against the threats posed by lumbering, overgrazing, and forest fires. In the years that followed,

The Establishment of National Parks and Forests *The setting aside of land for national parks saved large districts of the West from early commercial development and industrial degradation, setting a precedent for the later establishment of additional parks in economically marginal but scenic territory. The West, home to the vast majority of park space, became a principal site of tourism by the end of the nineteenth century.*

President Benjamin Harrison established 15 forest reserves exceeding 16 million acres, and President Grover Cleveland added more than 21 million acres. But only in 1897 did the secretary of the interior finally gain the authority to regulate the use of these reserves.

The Forest Management Act of 1897 and the National Reclamation Act of 1902 set the federal government on the path of large-scale regulatory activities. The Forest Service was established in 1905, and in 1907 forest reserves were transferred from the Department of the Interior to the Department of Agriculture. The federal government would now play an even larger role in economic development of the West, dealing mainly with corporate farmers and ranchers eager for improvements.

THE WESTERN LANDSCAPE

Throughout the nineteenth century, many Americans viewed western expansion as the nation's "manifest destiny," and just as many marveled at the region's natural and cultural wonders. Their fascination grew with the proliferation of printed literature, "Wild West" entertainments, sideshows, and traveling exhibits featuring western themes. The public east of the Mississippi craved stories about the West and visual images of its sweeping vistas. Artists and photographers built their reputations in what they saw and imagined. Scholars, from geologists and botanists to historians and anthropologists, toured the trans-Mississippi West in pursuit of new data. The region and its peoples came to represent what was both unique and magnificent about the American landscape.

Nature's Majesty

Alexis de Tocqueville, the famed commentator on American society, found little beauty in the land west of the Mississippi. Writing in the 1830s, he described the landscape as "more and more uneven and sterile," the soil "punctured in a thousand places by primitive rocks sticking out here and there like the bones of a skeleton when sinews of flesh have perished." By the end of the century, scores of writers had provided an entirely different image of the American West. They described spectacular, breathtaking natural sites like the

Grand Tetons and High Sierras, vast meadows of waving grasses and beautiful flowers, expansive canyons and rushing white rivers, and exquisite deserts covered with sagebrush or dotted with flowering cactus and enticing precisely for their stark qualities. A traveler through Yellowstone country recalled "the varied scenery" of the West and its "stupendous & remarkable manifestations of nature's forces," an impression destined to stay with him "as long as memory lasts."

Moved by such reveries, the federal government began to set aside huge tracts of land as nature reserves. In 1864 Congress passed the Yosemite Act, which placed the spectacular cliffs and giant sequoias under the management of the state of California. Meanwhile, explorers returned to the East awestruck by the varied terrain of the Rocky Mountains, the largest mountain chain in North America. These early visitors described huge sky-high lakes, boiling mud, and spectacular waterfalls. Finally, in 1871, the federal government funded a major undertaking by a team of researchers from the Geological and Geographical Survey of the Territories, which included the early landscape photographer William H. Jackson and the painter Thomas Moran. These researchers brought back to Congress visual proof of the monumental scenery of the West, including the Grand Canyon. In 1872 Congress named Yellowstone the first national park. Yosemite and Sequoia in California, Crater Lake in Oregon, Mount Ranier in Washington, and Glacier in Montana all became national parks between 1890 and 1910.

Landscape painters, particularly the group that became known as the Rocky Mountain School, also piqued the public's interest in western scenery. Exhibited in galleries and museums and reproduced in popular magazines, their sketches and paintings circulated western imagery throughout the country and through much of Europe. In the 1860s German-born Albert Bierstadt, equipped with a camera, traveled the Oregon Trail. Using his photographs as inspiration, Bierstadt painted mountains so wondrous that they seemed nearly surreal, projecting a divine aura behind the majesty of nature. His "earthscapes"— huge canvases with exacting details of animals and plants— thrilled viewers and sold for tens of thousands of dollars.

The Legendary Wild West

Legends of the Wild West grew into a staple of popular culture just as the actual work of cowboys became more routine. By the end of the century, many Americans, rich and poor alike, imagined the West as a land of promise and opportunity and, above all, of excitement and adventure. Future president Theodore Roosevelt helped to promote this view. Soon after his election to the New York state assembly in 1882, Roosevelt was horrified to see himself lampooned in the newspapers as a dandy and weakling. A year later, after buying a ranch in South Dakota, he began to reconstruct his public image. He wrote three books recounting his adventures in the West, claiming that they had not only instilled in him personal bravery and "hardihood" but self-reliance. In 1886 he was back in New York, running for mayor as the "Cowboy of the Dakotas." In April 1899, he addressed the members of Chicago's elite Hamilton Club, inviting them to join him in "the strenuous life" as exemplified by their Indian-fighter ancestors. Indeed, by this time many Americans had joined Roosevelt in imagining the West as a source of rejuvenation and virility. Young men at Harvard and Yale universities, for example, had named their hunting clubs after Daniel Boone and Davy Crockett. The West, as Roosevelt insisted, meant "vigorous manhood."

The first "westerns," the "dime novels" that sold in the 1860s in editions of 50,000 or more, reflected

Albert Bierstadt, Merced River, Yosemite Valley, 1866. Oil on canvas, 36 x 50 in. The Metropolitan Museum of Art, Gift of the sons of William Paton, 1909.

Albert Bierstadt became one of the first artists to capture on enormous canvases the vastness and rugged terrain of mountains and western wilderness. Many other artists joined Bierstadt to form the Rocky Mountain School. In time, the camera largely replaced the paintbrush, and most Americans formed an image of these majestic peaks from postcards and magazine illustrations.

these myths. Competing against stories about pirates, wars, crime, and sea adventures, westerns outsold the others. Edward Zane Carroll Judson's *Buffalo Bill, the King of the Border Men*, first published in 1869, spawned hundreds of other novels, thousands of stories, and an entire magazine devoted to Buffalo Bill. Even before farmers had successfully halted the free-grazing of cattle, writers made tough cowboys and high-spirited women into legends of the Wild West. Real-life African American cowboy Nat Love lived on in the imaginations of many generations as Edward L. Wheeler's dime novel hero "Deadwood Dick," who rode the range as a white cowboy in black clothes in over thirty stories. His girlfriend "Calamity Jane"—"the most reckless bucharia in ther Hills"—also took on mythic qualities.

Buffalo Bill's "Wild West Show" poster from 1899. William Cody's theatrical company toured the United States and Europe for decades, reenacting various battles and occasionally switching to football (cowboys versus Indians). Cody's style set the pace for both rodeos and Western silent films.

Railroad promoters and herd owners actively promoted these romantic and heroic images. Cowman Joseph McCoy staged Wild West shows in St. Louis and Chicago, where Texas cowboys entertained prospective buyers by roping calves and breaking horses. Many cowboys played up this imaginary role, dressing and talking to match the stories told about them. "The drovers of the seventies were a wild and reckless bunch," recalled cowboy Teddy Blue. Typically, they had worn a "wide brimmed beaver hat, black or brown with a low crown, fancy shirts, high heeled boots, and sometimes a vest." In the 1880s cowboys adopted the high-crowned Stetson hat, ornately detailed shirts with pockets, and striped or checked pants. The first professional photographers often made their living touring the West, setting up studios where cowboys and prostitutes posed in elaborate costumes.

For thirty years, Wild West shows toured the United States and Europe. The former Pony Express rider, army scout, and famed buffalo hunter William F. Cody hit upon the idea of an extravaganza that would bring the legendary West to those who could never experience it in person. "Buffalo Bill" Cody made sharpshooter Annie Oakley a star performer. Entrancing crowds with her stunning accuracy with pistol or rifle, Oakley shot dimes in midair and cigarettes from her husband's mouth. Cody also hired Sioux Indians and hundreds of cowboys to perform in mock stagecoach robberies and battles. Shows like Custer's Last Stand thrilled crowds, including Britain's Queen Victoria. Revamped as the rodeo, the Wild West show long outlasted Buffalo Bill, who died in 1917.

With far less fanfare, many veteran cowboys enlisted themselves on "dude ranches" for tourists or performed as rope twirlers or yodeling singers in theaters across the United States. In 1902 Owen Wister's novel *The Virginian* fixed in the popular imagination the scene of the cowboy facing down the villain and saying, "When you call me that, smile."

The "American Primitive"

New technologies of graphic reproduction encouraged painters and photographers to provide new images of the West, authentic as well as fabricated. A young German American artist, Charles Schreyvogel, saw Buffalo Bill's tent show in Buffalo and decided to make the West his life's work. His canvases depicted Indian warriors and U.S. cavalry fighting furiously but without blood and gore. Charles Russell, a genuine cowboy, painted the life he knew, but also indulged in imaginary scenarios, producing paintings of buffalo hunts and first encounters between Indian peoples and white explorers.

Frederic Remington, the most famous of all the western artists, left Yale Art School to visit Montana in 1881, became a Kansas sheep herder and tavern owner, and then returned to painting. Inspired by newspaper stories of the army's campaign against the Apaches, he made himself into a war correspondent and captured vivid scenes of battle in his sketches. Painstakingly accurate in physical details, especially of horses, his paintings celebrated the "winning of the West" from the Indian peoples. By the turn of the century, Remington was the chief magazine illustrator of western history.

Remington joined hundreds of other painters and engravers in reproducing the most popular historic event: Custer's Last Stand. Totally fictionalized by white artists to show a heroic General Custer personally holding off advancing Indian warriors, these renditions dramatized the romance and tragedy of conquest. Indian artists recorded Custer's defeat in far less noble fashion.

Photographers often produced highly nuanced portraits of Indian peoples. Dozens of early photographers from the Bureau of American Ethnology captured the gaze of noble tribespeople or showed them hard at work digging clams or grinding corn. President Theodore Roosevelt praised Edward Sheriff Curtis for vividly conveying tribal virtue. Generations later, in the 1960s and 1970s, Curtis's photographs again captured the imagination of western enthusiasts, who were unaware or unconcerned that this sympathetic artist had often posed his subjects or retouched his photos to blur out any artifacts of white society.

Painters and photographers led the way for scholarly research on the various Indian societies. The early ethnographer and pioneer of fieldwork in anthropology, Lewis Henry Morgan, devoted his life to the study of Indian family or kinship patterns, mostly of eastern tribes such as the Iroquois, who adopted him into their Hawk Clan. In 1851 he published *League of the Ho-de-no-sau-nee, or Iroquois*, considered the first scientific account of an Indian tribe. A decade later Morgan ventured into Cheyenne country to examine the naming patterns of this tribe. In his major work, *Ancient Society*, published in 1877, he posited a universal process of social evolution leading from savagery to barbarism to civilization.

One of the most influential interpreters of the cultures of living tribespeople was the pioneering ethnographer Alice Cunningham Fletcher. In 1879, Fletcher met Suzette (Bright Eyes) La Flesche of the Omaha tribe, who was on a speaking tour to gain support for her people, primarily to prevent their removal from tribal lands. Fletcher, then forty-two years old, accompanied La Flesche to Nebraska, telling the Omahas that she had come "to learn, if you will let me, something about your tribal organization, social customs, tribal rites, traditions and songs. Also to see if I can help you in any way." After transcribing hundreds of songs, Fletcher became well known as an expert on Omaha music. She also supported the Omahas' campaign to gain individual title to tribal lands, eventually drafting legislation that was enacted

by Congress as the Omaha Act of 1882. In 1885 Fletcher produced for the U.S. Senate a report titled *Indian Education and Civilization*, one of the first general statements on the status of Indian peoples. As a founder of the American Anthropological Society and president of the American Folk-Lore Society, she encouraged further study of Indian societies.

While white settlers and the federal government continued to threaten the survival of tribal life, Indian lore became a major pursuit of scholars and amateurs alike. Adults and children delighted in turning up arrowheads. Fraternal organizations such as the Elks and Eagles borrowed tribal terminology. The Boy Scouts and Girl Scouts, the nation's premier youth organizations, used tribal lore to instill strength of character. And the U.S. Treasury stamped images of tribal chiefs and of buffalo on the nation's most frequently used coins.

THE TRANSFORMATION OF INDIAN SOCIETIES

In 1871, the U.S. government formally ended the treaty system, eclipsing without completely abolishing the sovereignty of Indian nations. Still, the tribes persisted. Using a mixture of survival strategies from farming and trade to the leasing of reservation lands, they both adapted to changing conditions and maintained old traditions.

Reform Policy and Politics

By 1880, many Indian tribes had been forcibly resettled on reservations, but very few had adapted to white ways. For decades, reformers, mainly from the Protestant churches, had lobbied Congress for a program of salvation through assimilation, and they looked to the Board of Indian Commissioners, created in 1869, to carry out this mission. The board often succeeded in mediating conflicts among the various tribes crowded onto reservations but made far less headway in converting them to Christianity or transforming them into prosperous farming communities. The majority of Indian peoples lived in poverty and misery, deprived of their traditional means of survival and more often than not subjected to fraud by corrupt government officials and private suppliers. Reformers who observed these conditions firsthand nevertheless remained unshaken in their belief that tribespeople must be raised out of the darkness of ignorance into the light of civilization. Many conceded, however, that the reservation system might not be the best means to this end.

Unlike most Americans, who saw the conquest of the West as a means to national glory, some reformers were genuinely outraged by the government's continuous violation of treaty obligations and the military enforcement of the reservation policy. One of the most influential was Helen Hunt Jackson, a noted poet and author of children's stories. In 1879 Jackson had attended a lecture in Hartford, Connecticut, by a chief of the Ponca tribe whose destitute people had been forced from their Dakota homeland. Heartstruck, Jackson lobbied former abolitionists such as Wendell Phillips to work for Indians' rights and herself began to write against government policy. Her book-length exposé, *A Century of Dishonor*, published in 1881, detailed the mistreatment of Indian peoples.

Jackson threw herself into the Indian Rights Association, an offshoot of the Women's National Indian Association (WNIA), which had been formed in 1874 to rally public support for a program of assimilation. The two organizations helped to place Protestant missionaries in the West to work to eradicate tribal customs as well as to convert Indian peoples to Christianity. According to the reformers' plans, men would now farm as well as hunt, while women would leave the fields to take care of home and children. Likewise, all communal practices would be abandoned in favor of individually owned homesteads, where families could develop in the "American" manner and even celebrate proper holidays such as the Fourth of July. Children, hair trimmed short, would be placed in boarding schools where, removed

from their parents' influence, they would shed traditional values and cultural practices. By 1882 the WNIA had gathered 100,000 signatures on petitions urging Congress to phase out the reservation system, establish universal education for Indian children, and award title to 160 acres to any individual willing to work the land.

The Dawes Severalty Act, passed by Congress in 1887, incorporated many of these measures and established federal Indian policy for decades to come. The act allowed the president to distribute land not to tribes but to individuals legally "severed" from their tribes. The commissioner of Indian affairs rendered the popular interpretation that "tribal relations should be broken up, socialism destroyed and the family and autonomy of the individual substituted. The allotment of land in severalty, the establishment of local courts and police, the development of a personal sense of independence and the universal adoption of the English language are means to this end."

Those individuals who accepted the land allotment of 160 acres and agreed to allow the government to sell unallotted tribal lands (with some funds set aside for education) could petition to become citizens of the United States. A little over a decade after its enactment, many reformers believed that the Dawes Act had resolved the basis of the "Indian problem." Hollow Horn Bear, a Sioux chief, offered a

OVERVIEW

MAJOR INDIAN TREATIES AND LEGISLATION OF THE LATE NINETEENTH CENTURY		
1863	Nez Percé Treaty	Signed illegally on behalf of the entire tribe in which the Nez Percé abandoned 6 million acres of land in return for a small reservation in northeastern Oregon. Led to Nez Percé wars, which ended in 1877 with surrender of Chief Joseph.
1867	Medicine Lodge Treaty	Assigned reservations in existing Indian Territory to Comanches, Plains (Kiowa), Appaches, Kiowas, Cheyennes, and Arapahoes, bringing these tribes together with Sioux, Shoshones, Bannocks, and Navajos.
1868	Treaty of Fort Laramie	Successfully ended Red Cloud's war by evacuating federal troops from Sioux Territory along the Bozeman Trail; additionally granted Sioux ownership of the western half of South Dakota and rights to use Powder River county in Wyoming and Montana.
1871		Congress declares end to treaty system.
1887	Dawes Severalty Act	Divided communal tribal land, granting the right to petition for citizenship to those Indians who accepted the individual land allotment of 160 acres. Successfully undermined sovereignty.

Students at Toledo Indian School, Iowa, August 1899. Young women of various tribes boarded at this school, which offered them lessons in several subjects and training for adult life among white Americans. Their teachers hoped to prepare them for a future Christian marriage and motherhood.

different opinion, judging the Dawes Act to be "only another trick of the whites."

The Dawes Act successfully undermined tribal sovereignty but offered little compensation. Indian religions and sacred ceremonies were banned, the telling of legends and myths forbidden, and shaman and medicine men imprisoned or exiled for continuing their traditional practices. "Indian schools" forbade Indian languages, clothing styles, and even hair fashions in order to "kill the Indian . . . and save the man," as one schoolmaster put it.

These and other measures did little to integrate Indians into white society. Treated as savages, Indian children fled most white schools. Nor did adults receive much encouragement to become property holders. Government agencies allotted them inferior farmland, inadequate tools, and little training for agricultural self-sufficiency. Seeing scant advantage in assimilating, only a minority of adults dropped their tribal religion for Christianity or their communal ways for the accumulation of private property. Within the next forty years, the Indian peoples lost 60 percent of the reservation land remaining in 1887 and 66 percent of the land allotted to them as homesteaders. The tenets of the Dawes Act were not reversed until 1934. In that year, Congress passed the Indian Reorganization Act, which affirmed the integrity of Indian cultural institutions and returned some land to tribal ownership (see Chapter 24).

The Ghost Dance

After the passage of the Dawes Severalty Act, one more cycle of rebellion remained for the Sioux. In 1888, the Paiute prophet Wovoka, ill with scarlet fever, had a vision during a total eclipse of the sun. In his vision, the Creator told him that if the Indian peoples learned to love each other, they would be granted a special place in the afterlife. The Creator also gave him the Ghost Dance, which the prophet performed for others and soon spread throughout the tribe. The Sioux came to believe that when the day of judgment came, all Indian peoples who had ever lived would return to their lost world and white peoples would vanish from the earth. The chant sounded:

> *The whole world is coming.*
> *A nation is coming, a nation is coming.*
> *The Eagle has brought the message to the tribe.*
> *The father says so, the father says so.*
> *Over the whole earth they are coming.*
> *The buffalo are coming, the buffalo are coming.*
> *The Crow has brought the message to the tribe,*
> *The Father says so, the Father says so.*

Many white settlers and federal officials feared the Ghost Dancers, even though belief in a sudden divine judgment was common among Christians and Jews. Before the Civil War, Protestant groups such as the Millerites had renounced personal property and prepared themselves for the millennium. But after decades of Indian warfare, white Americans took the Ghost Dance as a warning of tribal retribution rather than a religious ceremony. As thousands of Sioux danced to exhaustion, local whites demanded the practice be stopped. A group of the Sioux led by Big Foot, now fearing mass murder, moved into hiding in the Bad Lands of South Dakota.

The U.S. Seventh Cavalry, led in part by survivors of the battle of Little Bighorn, pursued them. The three hundred undernourished Sioux, freezing and without horses, agreed to accompany the troops to Wounded Knee Creek on the Pine Ridge Reservation. There, on December 29, 1890, while the peace-seeking Big Foot, who had personally raised a white flag of surrender, lay dying of pneumonia, they were surrounded by soldiers armed with automatic guns. The U.S. troops expected the Sioux to surrender their few remaining weapons, but an accidental gunshot from one deaf brave who misunderstood the command caused panic on both sides.

Within minutes, 200 Sioux had been cut down and dozens of soldiers wounded, mostly by their own cross fire. For two hours soldiers continued to shoot at anything that moved—mostly women and children straggling away. Many of the injured froze to

This 1916 photograph of Chief American Horse shows the Oglala Sioux leader accepting his tribe's allotment from government agents at Pine Ridge, South Dakota. A veteran of the "Fetterman Massacre" during Red Cloud's war for the Bozeman Trail during the 1860s, American Horse had seen his people's territory reduced in size from more than 2.5 million acres to less than 150,000.

symbolism into their religion, learned to speak English, and even fought with the U.S. cavalry against the Apaches. Still, the Pimas saw their lands stolen, their precious waterways diverted, and their families impoverished.

The similarly peaceful Yana tribes of California, hunters and gatherers rather than farmers, were even less fortunate. Suffering enslavement, prostitution, and multiple new diseases from white settlers, they faced near extinction within a generation. One Yana tribe, the Yahi, chose simply to disappear. For more than a decade, they lived in caves and avoided all contact with white settlers.

Many tribes found it difficult to survive in the proximity of white settlers. The Flatheads, for example, seemed to Indian commissioners in the Bitterroot region of Montana to be destined for quick assimilation. They had refused to join the Ghost Dance and had agreed to

death in the snow; others were transported in open wagons and finally laid out on beds of hay under Christmas decorations at the Pine Ridge Episcopal church. The massacre, which took place almost exactly four hundred years after Columbus "discovered" the New World for Christian civilization, seemed to mark the final conquest of the continent's indigenous peoples.

Black Elk later recalled, "I can see that something else died there in the bloody mud, and was buried in the blizzard. A people's dream died there. It was a beautiful dream. . . . The nation's hoop is broken and scattered. There is no center any longer, and the sacred tree is dead."

Endurance and Rejuvenation

The most tenacious tribes were those occupying land rejected by white settlers or distant from their new communities. Still, not even an insular, peaceful agricultural existence on semi-arid, treeless terrain necessarily provided protection. Nor did a total willingness to accept white offers peacefully prevent attack.

The Pimas of Arizona, for instance, had a well-developed agricultural system adapted to a scarce supply of water, and they rarely warred with other tribes. After the arrival of white settlers, they integrated Christian

sell their rich tribal land and move to a new reservation. But while waiting to be moved, the dispossessed Flatheads nearly starved. When they finally reached the new reservation in October 1891, the remaining 250 Flatheads put on their finest war paint and whooped and galloped their horses, firing guns in the air in celebration. But disappointment and tragedy lay ahead. The federal government drastically reduced the size of the reservation, using a large part of it to provide a national reserve for buffalo. Only handfuls of Flatheads, mostly elderly, continued to live together in pockets of rural poverty.

A majority of tribes, especially smaller ones, sooner or later reached numbers too low to maintain their collective existence. Intermarriage, although widely condemned by the white community, drew many young people outside their Indian communities. Some tribal leaders also deliberately chose a path toward assimilation. The Quapaws, for example, formally disbanded in the aftermath of the Dawes Severalty Act. The minority that managed to prosper in white society as tradespeople or farmers abandoned their language, religious customs, and traditional ways of life. Later generations petitioned the federal government and regained tribal status, established ceremonial grounds and cultural centers (or bingo halls), and built up one of the most durable powwows in the state. Even so, much of the tribal lore that had underpinned distinct identity had simply vanished.

A small minority of tribes, grown skillful in adapting to dramatically changing circumstances, managed to persist and even grow. Never numbering more than a few thousand people, during the late eighteenth century the Cheyennes had found themselves caught geographically between aggressive tribes in the Great Lakes region and had migrated into the Missouri area, where they split into small village-sized communities. By the mid-nineteenth century they had become expert horse traders on the Great Plains, well prepared to meet the massive influx of white settlers by shifting their location frequently. They avoided the worst of the pestilence that spread from the diseases white people carried, and likewise survived widespread intermarriage with the Sioux in the 1860s and 1870s. Instructed to settle, many Cheyenne took up elements of the Christian religion and became farmers, also without losing their tribal identity. Punished by revenge-hungry soldiers after the battle of Little Bighorn, their lands repeatedly taken away, they still held on. The Cheyennes were survivors.

The Navajos experienced an extraordinary renewal, largely because they built a life in territory considered worthless by whites. Having migrated to the Southwest from the northwestern part of the continent perhaps 700 years earlier, the *Diné* ("the People") as they called themselves had already survived earlier invasions by the Spanish. In 1863 they had been conquered again through the cooperation of hostile tribes led by the famous Colonel Kit Carson. Their crops burned, their fruit trees destroyed, 8,000 Navajo were forced in the 300-mile "Long Walk" to the desolate Bosque Redondo reservation, where they nearly starved. Four years later, the Indian Bureau allowed the severely reduced tribe to return to a fraction of its former lands.

CHRONOLOGY

1848	Treaty of Guadalupe Hidalgo
1849–1860s	California Gold Rush
1853	Gadsden Purchase
1858	Comstock Lode discovered
1859	Cortina's War in South Texas
1862	Homestead Act makes free land available
	Morrill Act authorizes "land-grant" colleges
1865–1867	Great Sioux War
1866	Texas cattle drives begin
	Medicine Lodge Treaty established reservation system
	Alaska purchased
1869	Board of Indian Commissioners created
	Buffalo Bill, the King of the Border Men, sets off "Wild West" publishing craze
1870s	Grasshopper attacks on the Great Plains
1872	Yellowstone National Park created
1873	Timber Culture Act
	Red River War
1874–1875	Sioux battles in Black Hills of Dakotas
1876	Custer's Last Stand
1877	Defeat of the Nez Percé
1881	Helen Hunt Jackson, *A Century of Dishonor*
1882	Edmunds Act outlaws polygamy
1885–87	Droughts and severe winters cause the collapse of the cattle boom
1887	Dawes Severalty Act
1890	Sioux Ghost Dance movement
	Massacre of Lakota Sioux at Wounded Knee
	Census Bureau announces the end of the frontier line
1887	Forest Management Act gives the federal government authority over forest reserves

By 1880 the Navajos' population had returned to nearly what it had been before their conquest by white Americans. Quickly depleting the deer and antelope on their hemmed-in reservation, they had to rely on sheep alone as a food reserve for years of bad crops. With their wool rugs and blankets much in demand in the East, the Navajos increasingly turned to crafts, including eventually silver jewelry as well as weaving, to survive. Although living on the economic margin, they persevered to become the largest Indian nation in the United States.

The nearby Hopis, like the Navajos, survived by stubbornly clinging to lands unwanted by white settlers and by adapting to drastically changing conditions. A famous tribe of "desert people," the Hopis had lived for centuries in their cliff cities. Their highly developed theological beliefs, peaceful social system, sand paintings, and kachina dolls interested many educated and influential whites. The resulting publicity helped them gather the public supporters and financial resources to fend off further threats to their reservations.

Fortunate northwestern tribes remained relatively isolated from white settlers until the early twentieth century, although they had begun trading with white visitors centuries earlier. Northwestern peoples relied largely on salmon and other resources of the region's rivers and bays. In potlatch ceremonies, leaders redistributed tribal wealth and maintained their personal status and the status of their tribe by giving lavish gifts to invited guests. Northwest peoples also made intricate wood carvings, including commemorative "totem" poles, that recorded their history and identified their regional status. Northwestern peoples maintained their cultural integrity in part through connections with kin in Canada, as did southern tribes with kin in Mexico.

In Canada and Mexico, native populations suffered less pressure from new populations and retained more tribal authority than in the United States.

Indian nations approached their nadir as the nineteenth century came to a close. The descendants of the great pre-Columbian civilizations had been conquered by foreigners, their population reduced to fewer than 250,000. Under the pressure of assimilation, the remaining tribespeople became known to non-Indians as "the vanishing Americans." It would take several generations before Indian sovereignty experienced a resurgence.

CONCLUSION

The transformation of the trans-Mississippi West pointed up the larger meaning of expansion. Almost overnight, mines opened, cities grew, and farms and cattle ranches spread out across the vast countryside. New communities formed rapidly and often displaced old ones. In 1890 the director of the U.S. Census announced that the nation's "unsettled area has been so broken into by isolated bodies of settlement that there can hardly be said to be a frontier line."

The development of the West met the nation's demand for mineral resources for its expanding industries and agricultural products for the people of the growing cities. Envisioning the West as a cornucopia whose boundless treasures would offer themselves to the willing pioneer, most of the new residents failed to calculate the odds against their making a prosperous livelihood as miners, farmers, or petty merchants. Nor could they appreciate the long-term consequences of the violence they brought with them from the battlefields of the Civil War to the far reaches of the West.

REVIEW QUESTIONS

1. Discuss the role of federal legislation in accelerating and shaping the course of westward expansion.
2. How did the incorporation of western territories into the United States affect Indian nations such as the Sioux or the Nez Percé? Discuss the causes and consequences of the Indian Wars. Discuss the significance of reservation policy and the Dawes Severalty Act for tribal life.
3. What were some of the major technological advances in mining and in agriculture that promoted the development of the western economy?
4. Describe the unique features of Mexicano communities in the Southwest before and after the mass

immigration of Anglos. How did changes in the economy affect the patterns of labor and the status of women in these communities?
5. What role did the Homestead Act play in western expansion? How did farm families on the Great Plains divide chores among their members? What factors determined the likelihood of economic success or failure?
6. Describe the responses of artists, naturalists, and conservationists to the western landscape. How did their photographs, paintings, and stories shape perceptions of the West in the East?

RECOMMENDED READING

Alfred L. Bush and Lee Clark Mitchell, *The Photograph and the American Indian* (1994). A comprehensive study of photos of Indians by various American photographers from 1840 to the present.

William Cronon, George Miles, and Jay Gitlin, eds., *Under an Open Sky: Rethinking America's Western Past* (1992). A useful collection of essays. Reinterpreting older evidence and adding new data, these essays stress the bitter conflicts over territory, the racial and gender barriers against democratic community models, and the tragic elements of western history.

Jon Gjerde, *The Minds of the West: Ethnocultural Evolution in the Rural Middle West, 1830–1914* (1997). A combination cultural and economic history that weighs the importance of ethnicity in the shaping of American identities in the farming regions of the Middle West. Gjerde pays close attention to the religious institutions and systems of belief of European immigrants as the basis of community formation.

Lisbeth Haas, *Conquests and Historical Identities in California, 1769–1936* (1995). A multiethnic history, centered in San Juan Capistrano, that examines the political intersection of geography and community formation. The author studies the processes of Americanization among the Spanish and Indian populations who settled this land.

John C. Hudson, *Making the Corn Belt: A Geographical History of Middle-Western Agriculture* (1994). An ecologically oriented study of corn growing that traces its development from Indians to Southerners moving westward.

Elizabeth Jameson and Susan Armitage, eds., *Writing the Range* (1997). A collection of essays on women in the U.S. West that presents an inclusive historical narrative based on the experiences of women of differing backgrounds, races, and ethnic groups.

Patricia Nelson Limerick, *The Legacy of Conquest: The Unbroken Past of the American West* (1987). A controversial and popular revisionist history of the West. Focused on conflict, Limerick's study shows the frontier most of all as a site of racial antagonism.

John G. Neihardt, *Black Elk Speaks: Being the Life Story of a Holy Man of the Oglala Sioux* (1961). A classic "as-told-to" autobiographical account published originally in 1932. Black Elk recalls the tragedy of his tribe's destruction with the events around George Armstrong Custer and the battle of Little Bighorn.

Glenda Riley, *Building and Breaking Families in the American West* (1996). Essays covering the variety of cultures in the American West and organized topically to highlight courtship, marriage and intermarriage, and separation and divorce.

Thomas E. Sheridan, *Los Tucsonenses: The Mexican Community in Tucson, 1854–1941* (1986). A highly readable account of Mexican-American communities in the Southwest. Sheridan shows how a mid-century accommodation of Anglos and Mexicanos faded with the absorption of the region into the national economy and with the steady displacement of Mexicano community from its agricultural landholdings.

Robert M. Utley, *The Lance and the Shield: The Life and Times of Sitting Bull* (1993). A careful reinterpretation of a spiritual leader's attempt to secure religious freedom for Indian peoples.

Richard White, *"It's Your Misfortune and None of My Own": A History of the American West* (1991). A wide-ranging history of the West with emphasis on cultural contact and the environment. White shows that conflicting cultures with little understanding of each other clashed tragically, with great losses to the environment and the hopes of a democratic American community.

ADDITIONAL BIBLIOGRAPHY

Indian Peoples and Indian-White Relations

Patricia Albers and Beatrice Medicine Albers, *The Hidden Half: Studies of Plains Indian Women* (1983)

Morris W. Foster, *Being Comanche: A Social History of an American Indian Community* (1991)

E. Richard Hart, ed., *Zuni and the Courts: A Struggle for Sovereign Land Rights* (1995)

Frederick E. Hoxie, *A Final Promise: The Campaign to Assimilate the Indians, 1880–1920* (1984)

Douglas R. Hurt, *Indian Agriculture in America* (1987)

Albert L. Hurtado, *Indian Survival on the California Frontier* (1988)

Douglas C. McChristian, *The U.S. Army in the West, 1870–1880: Uniforms, Weapons and Equipment* (1995)

Catherine Price, *The Oglala People, 1841–1879* (1996)

Glenda Riley, *Women and Indians on the Frontier, 1825–1915* (1984)

Richard White, *The Roots of Dependency: Subsistence, Environment, and Social Change among the Choctaws, Pawnees, and Navajos* (1983)

Robert Wooster, *The Military and United States Indian Policy, 1865–1902* (1988)

Internal Empire

Susan Armitage and Elizabeth Jameson, eds., *The Women's West* (1987)

Susan Armitage, Ruth B. Moynihan, and Christiane Fischer Dichamp, eds., *So Much to Be Done: Women Settlers on the Mining and Ranching Frontier* (1990)

Sarah Deutsch, *No Separate Refuge: Culture, Class and Gender on an Anglo-Hispanic Frontier in the American Southwest, 1880–1940* (1987)

David M. Emmons, *The Butte Irish: Class and Ethnicity in an American Mining Town, 1875–1925* (1989)

Mario R. Garcia, *Desert Immigrants: The Mexicans of El Paso, 1880–1920* (1981)

Marion S. Goldman, *Gold Diggers and Silver Miners: Prostitution and Social Life on the Comstock* (1981)

Richard Griswold del Castillo, *The Los Angeles Barrio, 1850–1890* (1979)

B. Carmon Hardy, *Solemn Covenant: The Mormon Polygamous Passage* (1992)

Douglas Monroy, *Thrown among Strangers: The Making of Mexican Culture in Frontier California* (1993)

David Montejano, *Anglos and Mexicans in the Making of Texas, 1836–1986* (1987)

Robert J. Rosenbaum, *Mexicano Resistance in the Southwest* (1981)

Jonathan D. Rosenblum, *Copper Crucible: How the Arizona Miners' Strike of 1893 Recast Labor-Management Relations in America* (1996)

Lucy E. Salyer, *Laws Harsh as Tigers: Chinese Immigrants and the Shaping of Modern Immigration Law* (1996)

Ranching and Farming

Leonard J. Arrington and Davis Bitton, *The Mormon Experience*, 2d ed. (1992)

Allan G. Bogue, *From Prairie to Corn Belt: Farming on the Illinois and Iowa Prairies in the Nineteenth Century* (1963)

Anne M. Butler, *Daughters of Joy, Sisters of Misery: Prostitutes in the American West, 1865–1890* (1985).

Harry Sinclair Drago, *The Great Range Wars* (1985)

Philip Durham and Everett L. Jones, *The Negro Cowboys* (1965)

C. Mark Hamilton, *Nineteenth-Century Mormon Architecture and City Planning* (1995)

Robert C. Haywood, *Victorian West: Class and Culture in Kansas Cattle Towns* (1991)

Stan Hoig, *The Oklahoma Land Rush of 1889* (1984)

Lawrence Jelinek, *Harvest Empire: A History of California Agriculture*, 2d ed. (1982)

Frederick C. Luebke, ed., *Ethnicity on the Great Plains* (1980).

D. Aidan McQuillan, *Prevailing over Time: Ethnic Adjustment on the Kansas Prairies, 1875–1925* (1990)

Donald J. Pisani, *From Family Farm to Agribusiness* (1984)

Sonya Salamon, *Prairie Patrimony: Family, Farming, and Community in the Midwest* (1992)

Paul I. Wellman, *The Trampling Herd: The Story of the Cattle Range in America* (1988)

Jack Weston, *The Real American Cowboy* (1985)

Ellen Jane Marris Wheeler, ed., *Cherokee Outlet Cowboy: Recollections of Laban S. Records* (1996)

The West, the Land, and the Imagination

Robert F. Berkhoffer Jr., *The White Man's Indian: Images of the American Indian from Columbus to the Present* (1978)

Christine Bold, *Selling the West: Popular Western Fiction, 1860–1960* (1987)

William H. Goetzmann and William N. Goetzmann, *The West of the Imagination* (1986)

L.G. Moses, *Wild West Shows and the Images of American Indians, 1883–1933* (1996)

Alexander Nemertov, *Frederic Remington & Turn-of-the-Century America* (1995)

Richard Orsi, Alfred Runte, and Marlene Smith-Barazini, eds., *Yosemite and Sequoia: A Century of California National Parks* (1993)

Donald J. Pisani, *To Reclaim a Divided West: Water, Law, and Public Policy, 1848–1901* (1993)

Joseph G. Rosa, *Wild Bill Hickok: The Man and His Myth* (1996)

Richard Slotkin, *Gunfighter Nation: The Myth of the Frontier in 20th-Century America* (1992)

Raymond William Steadman, *Shadows of the Indian: Stereotypes in American Culture* (1982)

Richard White and Patricia Nelson Limerick, *The Frontier in American Culture* (1994)

Donald Worcester, *Rivers of Empire: Water, Aridity, and the Growth of the American West* (1985)

Biography

Matthew Baigell, *Albert Bierstadt* (1981)

Louise Barnett, *Touched by Fire: The Life, Death, and Mythic Afterlife of George Armstrong Custer* (1996)

Angie Debo, *Geronimo* (1976)

Joan T. Mark, *A Stranger in Her Native Land: Alice Fletcher and the American Indians* (1988)

Valerie Mathes, *Helen Hunt Jackson and Her Indian Reform Legacy* (1990)

Glenda Riley, *Life and Legacy of Annie Oakley* (1994)

Mari Sandoz, *Crazy Horse, the Strange Man of the Oglalas* (1961)

Elinore Pruitt Stewart, *Letters of a Woman Homesteader* (1914; 1989)

Edwin R. Sweeny, *Cochise, Chiricahua Apache Chief* (1991)

John Tusha, *Billy the Kid, His Life and Legend* (1994)

CHAPTER NINETEEN

THE INCORPORATION OF AMERICA

1865–1900

Looking north on State Street, Chicago, in 1899, oil over a photograph. The Granger Collection.

AMERICAN COMMUNITIES
Packingtown, Chicago, Illinois

A pproaching Packingtown, the neighborhood adjoining the Union Stockyards, the center of Chicago's great meat-packing industry, one noticed first the pungent odor, a mixture of smoke, fertilizer, and putrid flesh, blood, and hair from the slaughtered animals. A little closer, the stench of the uncovered garbage dump blended in. Finally one crossed "Bubbly Creek," a lifeless offshoot of the Chicago River aptly named for the effect of the carbolic acid gas that formed from the decaying refuse poured in by the meat-packing plants. Railroads crisscrossed the entire area, bringing in thousands of animals each day and carrying out meat for sale in markets across the country.

Packingtown occupied about one square mile of land bounded by stockyards, packing plants, and freight yards. With a population of 30,000–40,000 at the end of the nineteenth century, it was a rapidly growing community of old and new immigrants who depended on the meat-packing industry for their livelihood. An average household included six or seven people—parents, two or three children, and two or three boarders. They lived typically in wooden houses divided into four or more flats. Although Irish, Germans, Bohemians, Poles, Lithuanians, and Slovaks were squeezed together in this solidly working-class neighborhood, strong ethnic identities persisted. Few households included residents of more than one nationality, and interethnic marriages were rare. Nearly everyone professed the Roman Catholic faith, yet each ethnic group maintained its own church and often its own parochial school, where children were taught in their parents' language. Political organizations, fraternal societies, and even gymnastic clubs and drama groups reflected these ethnic divisions.

The one local institution that bridged the different groups was the saloon. Located on virtually every street corner, saloons offered important services to the community, hosting weddings and dances, providing meeting places for trade unions and fraternal societies, and cashing paychecks. During the frequent seasons of unemployment, Packingtown workers spent a lot of time in saloons. Here they often made friends across ethnic divisions, an extension of their common work experience in the nearby stockyard and packinghouses.

Most of the meat-packing industry's first "knife men"—the skilled workers in the "killing gangs" that managed the actual slaughtering and cutting operations—were German and Irish. Many had learned their butcher's craft in the Old Country. Below them were the common laborers, mainly recent immigrants from eastern Europe. Having no previous experience in meat packing, these workers found themselves in the lowest paid jobs, such as the by-product manufacturing of glue and oleo. A sizable portion had never before earned wages. They soon discovered, as one Lithuanian laborer put it, that "money was everything and a man without money must die." But the money available—a daily wage of $2 (or less)—was often not enough. The death rate from tuberculosis in Packingtown was thought to be the highest in Chicago and among the highest in the nation.

The Packingtown community was bound into an elaborate economic network that reached distant parts of the United States, transforming the way farmers raised livestock and grains, railroads operated, and consumers ate their meals. These workers helped make Chicago a gateway city, a destination point for raw materials coming in from the West as well as a point of export for products of all kinds.

Chicago meat packers, led by the "big five" of Armour, Cudahy, Morris, Schwarzschild and Sulzberger, and Swift, expanded more than 900 percent between 1870 and 1890, dominating the national market for meat and establishing a standard for monopoly capitalism in the late nineteenth century. In the process, they also became the city's largest manufacturing employer. They built huge, specialized factories during the 1860s and 1870s that speeded the killing process and— thanks to mountains of ice brought by rail from ponds and lakes—operated year round. The introduction of

an efficiently refrigerated railroad car in the 1880s made it possible to ship meat nationwide. Consumers had long believed that only meat butchered locally was safe to eat, but now cheap Chicago-packed beef and pork began to appear on every meat-eater's table. Local packinghouses throughout the Midwest succumbed to the ruthless competition from Chicago.

Chicago's control of the mass market for meat affected all aspects of the industry. Midwestern farmers practically abandoned raising calves on open pastures. Instead, they bought two-year-old steers from the West and fattened them on homegrown corn in feedlots, making sure that bulk went into edible parts rather than muscle and bone. The feedlot—a kind of rural factory—replaced pasture just as pasture had earlier supplanted prairie grasslands.

Few of the workers in Chicago's stockyards had seen a farm since they left their homelands. But as the working hands of what poet Carl Sandburg would later call the "City of the Big Shoulders," "Hog Butcher for the World," they played their part, along with the farmer, the grain dealer, the ironworker, the teamster, and many others in bringing together the neighboring countryside, distant regions, and the city in a common endeavor.

Chicago

KEY TOPICS

- The rise of big business and the formation of the national labor movement
- The growth of cities
- The transformation of southern society

- The Gilded Age
- Changes in education
- Commercial amusements and organized sports

THE RISE OF INDUSTRY, THE TRIUMPH OF BUSINESS

At the time of the Civil War, the typical American business firm was a small enterprise, owned and managed by a single family, and producing goods for a local or regional market. By the turn of the century, businesses depending on large-scale investments had organized as corporations and grown to unforeseen size. These mammoth firms could afford to mass-produce goods for national and even international markets. At the helm stood unimaginably wealthy men such as Andrew Carnegie, Philip Danforth Armour, Jay Gould, and John D. Rockefeller, all powerful leaders of a new national business community.

A Revolution in Technology

In the decades after the Civil War, American industry transformed itself into a new wonder of the world. The Centennial Exposition of 1876, held in Philadelphia, celebrated not so much the American Revolution 100 years earlier as the industrial and technological promise of the century to come. Its central theme was power. In the main building—at the time the largest on earth—the visiting emperor of Brazil marked the opening day by throwing a switch on a giant steam engine. Examining the telephone, which he had never before seen in operation, he gasped, "My God, it talks!" Patented that year by Alexander Graham Bell, the telephone signaled the rise of the United States to world leadership in industrial technology.

The year 1876 also marked the opening of Thomas Alva Edison's laboratory in Menlo Park, New Jersey, one of the first devoted to industrial research. Not yet thirty years old, Edison could already claim credit for the mimeograph, the multiplex telegraph, and the stock ticker. In October 1879 his research team hit upon its most marketable invention, an incandescent lamp that burned for more than thirteen hours. On December 31 Edison brought 3,000 people by a special train to witness the sight of hundreds of electric lights illuminating his shop and neighborhood streets. By 1882 the Edison Electric Light Company had launched its service in New York City's financial district. A wondrous source of light and power, electricity revolutionized both industry and urban life.

By this time American inventors, who had filed nearly half a million patents since the close of the Civil War, were previewing the marvels of the next century. Henry Ford, working as an electrical engineer for the Detroit Edison Company, was already experimenting with the gasoline-burning internal combustion engine and designing his own automobile. By 1900 American companies had produced more than 4,000 automobiles. The prospect of commercial aviation emerged in 1903 when Wilbur and Orville Wright staged the first airplane flight near Kitty Hawk, North Carolina.

A major force behind economic growth in the decades after the Civil War was the completion of the transcontinental railroad in 1869. The addition of three more major lines (Southern Pacific, Northern Pacific, and the Atchison, Topeka, and Santa Fe) in the early 1880s and the Great Northern a decade later completed the most extensive transportation network in the world. The nation's first big business, railroads linked cities in every state and serviced a nationwide market for goods. Freight trains carried the bountiful natural resources, such as iron, coal, and minerals that supplied the raw materials for industry, as well as food for the growing urban populations.

Advances in transportation and communication promoted the progressively westward relocation of industry. The geographic center of manufacturing (as computed by the gross value of products) was near the middle of Pennsylvania in 1850, in western Pennsylvania by 1880, and near Mansfield, Ohio, in 1900. Flour milling moved from the east coast to Rochester, New York, then to Ohio, and finally to Minneapolis and Kansas City. The manufacture of agricultural equipment relocated from central New York to Illinois and Wisconsin, while the production of wire moved from Massachusetts to Illinois.

Industry grew at an unprecedented and previously unimaginable pace. The output of capital goods rose at more than 7 percent per year (compared to less than 5 percent annually before the Civil War). In 1865

A whimsical rendition of Thomas Edison's laboratories in Menlo Park, New Jersey, ca. 1880. The commercial artist imagined a giant electric light illuminating the entire region. Six weeks after Edison announced the invention of the electric light in 1879, the stock market turned jittery and gas company shares fell sharply: investors feared his "magic."

the annual production of goods was estimated at $2 billion; by 1900 it stood at $13 billion, transforming the United States from fourth to first in the world in terms of productivity. By the early twentieth century, American industry manufactured one-third of the world's goods.

Mechanization Takes Command

This second industrial revolution depended on many factors, but none was more important than the application of new technologies to increase the productivity of labor and the volume of goods. Machines, factory managers, and workers together created a system of continuous production by which more could be made, and faster, than anywhere else on earth. Higher productivity depended not only on machinery and technology but on economies of scale and speed, reorganization of factory labor and business management, and the unparalleled growth of a market for goods of all kinds.

All these changes depended in turn on a new source of fuel, anthracite coal, which was widely used after 1850. By the late 1880s many factories had begun to replace waterpower with steam, generated by huge boilers fired by coal or coke. These reliable and relatively inexpensive sources of energy made possible dramatic changes in the industrial uses of light, heat, and motion. Equally important, coal fueled the great open-hearth furnaces and mills of the iron and steel industry. By the end of the century, the United States steel industry was the world's largest, churning out rails to carry trains and frames and parts to speed production by machines. Not only machines for manufacturing goods but machines for making more machines were at the heart of mass production.

In addition to new machinery, new systems of mass production replaced wasteful and often chaotic practices and speeded up the delivery of finished goods. In the 1860s meat packers set up one of the earliest production lines. The process of converting livestock into meat began with a live animal. A chain around the hind leg whirled the body to an overhead rail, which carried it to slaughter—all in barely half a minute's time. Then hair and bristles were removed by a scraping machine, the carcass shifted to a conveyer belt where the chest was split and the organs removed, and the body placed in a cooler. This "disassembly line" displaced patterns of hand labor that were centuries old. Although opponents of meat eating looked with horror upon the mechanization of animal slaughter, comparing the process to modern warfare, the production line became standard in most areas of manufacturing.

Sometimes the invention of a single machine could instantly transform production, mechanizing every stage from processing the raw material to packaging the product. The cigarette-making machine, patented in 1881, shaped the tobacco, encased it in an endless paper tube, and snipped off the tube at cigarette-length intervals. This machine could produce more than 7,000 cigarettes per hour, replacing the worker who at best made 3,000 per day. After a few more improvements, fifteen machines could meet the total demand for American cigarettes. Diamond brand matches were soon produced in the same fashion and came to dominate the world market. Within a generation, continuous production also revolutionized the making of furniture, cloth, grain products, soap, and canned goods; the refining, distilling, and processing of animal and vegetable fats; and eventually the manufacture of automobiles.

The Expanding Market for Goods

To distribute the growing volume of goods, businesses demanded new techniques of marketing and merchandising. For generations, legions of sellers, or "drummers," had worked their routes, pushing goods, especially hardware and patent medicines, to individual buyers and retail stores. The appearance of mail-order houses after the Civil War accompanied the consolidation of the railroad lines and the expansion of the postal system. Rates were lowered for freight and

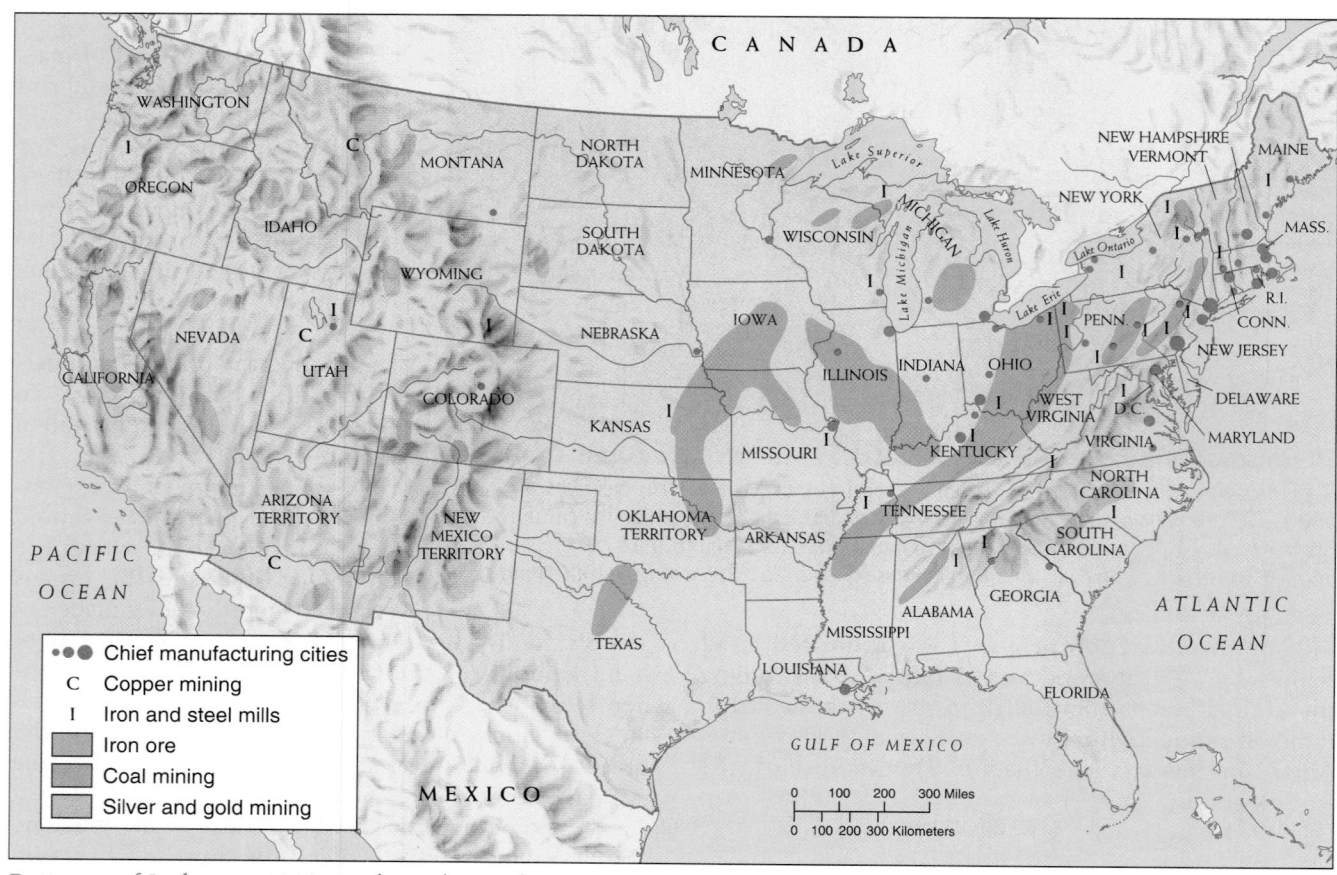

Patterns of Industry, 1900   *Industrial manufacturing concentrated in the Northeast and Midwest, while the raw materials for production came mostly from other parts of the nation.*

postage alike, and railroad stations opened post offices and sold money orders. By 1896 rural free delivery had reached distant communities.

Growing directly out of these services, the successful Chicago-based mail-order houses drew rural and urban consumers into a common marketplace. Sears, Roebuck and Company (which began by selling watches by mail) and Montgomery Ward (which started out with a mail-order catalogue of merchandise) offered an enormous variety of goods, from shoes to buggies to gasoline stoves and cream separators. The Montgomery Ward catalogue provided "a real link between us and civilization," a Nebraska farmwoman wrote. The mail-order catalogue also returned to rural folks the fruits of their own labor, now processed and packaged for easy use. The Sears catalogue offered Armour's summer sausage as well as Aunt Jemima's Pancake Flour and Queen Mary Scotch Oatmeal, both made of grains that came from the agricultural heartland. In turn, the purchases made by farm families through the Sears catalogue sent cash flowing into Chicago.

The chain store achieved similar economies of scale. By 1900, a half-dozen grocery chains had sprung up. The largest was A&P, originally named the Great Atlantic and Pacific Tea Company to celebrate the completion of the transcontinental railroad. Frank and Charles Woolworth offered inexpensive variety goods in five-and-ten-cent stores, of which more than 1,000 were established in the United States and Great Britain by 1919. Other chains selling drugs, costume jewelry, shoes, cigars, and furniture soon appeared, offering a greater selection of goods and lower prices than the small, independent stores. Hurt financially by this competition, community-based retailers headed the lobby for antichain legislation.

The department stores reigned over the urban market. These palaces of merchandise, with their attractive displays and convenient arrangements of goods, enticed buyers and browsers alike. Opening shortly after the Civil War, department stores began to take up much of the business formerly enjoyed by specialty shops, offering a spectrum of services that included restaurants, rest rooms, ticket agencies, nurseries, reading rooms, and post offices. Elegantly appointed with imported carpets, sweeping marble staircases, and crystal chandeliers, the department store

Montgomery Ward & Company, *Chicago, ca. 1870s. This "sectional view" imaginatively strips away exterior walls to show the activity of each department of the great mail-order firm. The artist suggests that all who work at the Ward Company must be overwhelmingly busy simply to meet customer demand.*

raised retailing to new heights. By the close of the century, the names of Marshall Field of Chicago, Filene's of Boston, The Emporium of San Francisco, Wanamaker's of Philadelphia, and Macy's of New York had come to represent the splendors of those great cities as well as the apex of mass retailing.

Advertising lured customers to the department stores, the chains, and the independent neighborhood shops. The advertising revolution began in 1869, when Francis Wayland Ayer founded the earliest advertising agency, but the firm did not hire its first full-time copy writers until 1891. Ayer's handled the accounts of such companies as Montgomery Ward, Procter & Gamble, and the National Biscuit Company. With the help of this new sales tool, gross revenues of retailers raced upward from $8 million in 1860 to $102 million in 1900.

Integration, Combination, and Merger

Business leaders moved purposefully to exercise greater control of the American economy and to enlarge their own commercial empires. In every aspect of their business, from procurement of raw materials to the organization of production, from the conditions of labor to

the climate of public opinion, they acted shrewdly. The contracts and high protective tariffs of the Civil War era had given American businesses an enormous boost. The business cycle, alternating between rapid growth and sharp decline, also promoted the rise of big business. Major economic setbacks in 1873 and 1893 wiped out weaker competitors, allowing the strongest firms to rebound swiftly and to expand their sales and scale of operation during the recovery period. Purchasing more efficient machines and speeding up production, American corporations commanded the heights of the national and even world markets in the last half of the century.

Businesses grew in two distinct if overlapping ways. Through vertical integration a firm aspired to control production at every step of the way—from raw materials through processing to transport and merchandising of the finished items. Agricultural processing firms such as Gustavus Swift in meat and James Buchanan Duke's American Tobacco Company often integrated "forward" in this fashion. In 1899 the United Fruit Company began to build a network of wholesale houses, and within two years it had opened distribution centers in twenty-one major cities. Eventually United Fruit directed an elaborate system of Central American plantations and temperature-controlled shipping and storage facilities for its highly perishable bananas. The firm became one of the nation's largest corporations, its "empire in bananas" dominating the economic and political life of whole nations in Central America.

The second means of growth, horizontal combination, entailed gaining control of the market for a single product. The most famous case was the Standard Oil Company, founded by John D. Rockefeller in 1870. Operating out of Cleveland in a highly competitive but lucrative field, Rockefeller recognized the urgency of bringing "some order out of what has rapidly become a state of chaos." He first secured preferential rates from railroads to transport Standard's oil. He then convinced or coerced other local oil operators to sell their stock to him; by 1880 he controlled over 90 percent of the nation's oil-refining industry.

The Standard Oil Trust, established in 1882, "was the first in the field," wrote journalist Ida Tarbell, "and it has furnished the methods, the charter, and the traditions for its followers." Rockefeller himself recognized the larger implications. "This movement," he wrote proudly, "was the origin of the whole system of modern economic administration. It has revolutionized the way of doing business all over the world. . . . The day of combination is here to stay."

Horizontal combinations, which secured unprecedented control over output and prices, produced a highly concentrated business economy over which a few very large firms prevailed. To protect trade and commerce and restore competition by encouraging small business, Congress in 1890 passed the Sherman Antitrust Act, which outlawed "every . . . combination . . . in restraint of trade." Ironically, the courts interpreted the law in ways that inhibited the organization of trade unions (on the ground that they restricted the free flow of labor) while supporting the consolidation of business. Between 1898 and 1902, more than 2,600 firms vanished, 1,200 in 1899 alone. By 1910 the industrial giants that would dominate the American economy until the last half of the twentieth century—U.S. Rubber, Goodyear, American Smelting and Refining, Anaconda Copper, General Electric, Westinghouse, Nabisco, Swift and Company, Armour, International Harvester, Eastman-Kodak, and American Can—had already been created.

The Gospel of Wealth

The preeminent financiers and corporation magnates not only took pride in the collective triumph of the business community but felt spiritually fulfilled by the accumulation of wealth. Ninety percent of the nation's business leaders were Protestant, and the majority attended church services regularly. They attributed their personal achievement to hard work and perseverance and made these the principal tenets of a new faith that imbued the pursuit of wealth with old-time religious zeal. "God gave me my money," declared John D. Rockefeller, and Baptist minister Russell Conwell's pamphlet *Acres of Diamonds*, which sold more than 1 million copies, argued that to build a fortune was a profound Christian duty. "To make money honestly," he preached, "is to preach the gospel."

One version of this "gospel of wealth" justified the ruthless behavior of entrepreneurs who accumulated unprecedented wealth and power through shady deals and conspiracies. Speculator Jay Gould, known in the popular press as "the Worst Man in the World," wrung his fortune, it was widely believed, from the labor of others. Through a series of financial maneuvers (one of which allegedly drove a partner to suicide) and such high-handed measures as sending armed employees to seize a factory, he rose quickly from his modest origins in western New York state. After abandoning his tanning business for stock trading, Gould gained notoriety on Wall Street for bribing, threatening, and conspiring against his competitors.

Speculation in railroads proved to be Gould's forte. He took over the Erie Railroad, paying off New York legislators to get the state to finance its expansion. Now a major player, Gould acquired the U.S. Express Company by pressuring and tricking its stockholders. Threatened with arrest, he sold off his shares for $9 million and moved on to the Union Pacific, where he cut wages, precipitated strikes, and manipulated elections in the western and Plains states. When caricatured in the press as a great swindler, Gould bought

the leading newspapers and kept reporters in line by giving them valuable tips on stocks. At his death, the New York World called Jay Gould "an incarnation of cupidity and sordidness" whose life symbolized "idolatrous homage [to] the golden calf."

Andrew Carnegie—"the Richest Man in the World"—offered a strikingly different model of success. He represented the "captain of industry" who had risen from the ranks through diligence and who refused to worship wealth for its own sake. A poor immigrant boy from Scotland, Carnegie had studied bookkeeping at night while working days in a textile mill. At age thirteen he had become a messenger for Western Union, and by age seventeen he was the fastest telegraph key operator in Pittsburgh. In 1852 the superintendent of the Penn-

The Two Philanthropists *by Joseph Keppler, from* Puck Magazine, *February 23, 1888. This famous artist of the late nineteenth century drew caricatures of magnates Jay Gould and Cornelius Vanderbilt, stressing not their "good works" but their less than beneficent control of the nation's railroads and telegraph systems. Illustrated magazines, such as* Puck, *reproduced such drawings in quantity, due in part to technological advances in the lithographic process.*

sylvania Railroad's western division hired the young man as his secretary and personal telegrapher. Well placed to learn the principles of the business, Carnegie stepped into the superintendent's job seven years later. He improved passenger train service while investing brilliantly to build up funds for his next venture, steel. By exploiting his talents for management and self-promotion, Carnegie was soon able to place the new industry on the same powerful financial footing as the railroads.

A genius at vertical integration, Carnegie built an empire in steel. He consistently undercut his strongest competitors by using the latest technology, following his own system of cost analysis, and selling steel as cheaply as possible. By 1900 Carnegie managed the most efficient steel mills in the world and accounted for one-third of American output. When he sold out to J. P. Morgan's new United States Steel Corporation for $480 million in 1901, his personal share came to $225 million.

By 1890 Carnegie, only five feet three inches tall, was an industrial giant with a personality to match. From one point of view, he was still a factory despot who underpaid his employees and ruthlessly managed their work lives. But to the patrons of the public libraries, art museums, concert halls, colleges, and universities he funded, he was the greatest philanthropist of the age. At the time of his death, he had given away his massive personal fortune. In his book *The Gospel of Wealth* (1900) Carnegie insisted that "there is no genuine, praiseworthy success in life if you are not honest, truthful, and fair-dealing."

Whether following the rough road of Gould or the smooth path of Carnegie, the business community effected sweeping changes in the larger society. One such change took place in the way most Americans perceived greatness. Even as they schemed to control market forces, the captains of industry praised the system of free enterprise. They endorsed the principles of social Darwinism, or survival of the fittest—the timely doctrine devised from the famed naturalist Charles Darwin's scientific theories of evolution that purportedly explained, and justified, why some Americans grew rich while others remained poor. Meanwhile, Horatio Alger published more than 100 rags-to-riches novels celebrating the outrageous good fortune of self-made men. Some Americans nevertheless feared that the cost of progress achieved by such principles might be more than the nation could afford.

LABOR IN THE AGE OF BIG BUSINESS

It was a common item of faith among most working people that, as labor reformer George E. McNeill put it in 1877, "labor produces all the wealth of the

world. . . . [The laborer] makes civilization possible." Like the gospel of wealth, the "gospel of work" affirmed the dignity of hard work, the virtue of thrift, and the importance of individual initiative. Both doctrines elaborated the simple phrase adorning many needlework samplers, "Work Is Prayer." But unlike business leaders, the philosophers of American working people did not believe in riches as the proof of work well done, or in the lust for power as the driving force of progress. On the contrary, they contended that honesty and competence should become the cornerstones of a society "so improved that labor shall become a blessing instead of a curse," recognized by all as the badge of the morally responsible citizen.

This faith inspired a slender minority, less than 3 percent of the work force, to form unions in various trades and industries. Despite its small size, the labor movement represented the most significant and lasting response of workers to the rise of big business and the consolidation of corporate power.

The Changing Status of Labor
The momentous growth of manufacturing in the last half of the nineteenth century required a parallel expansion of the workforce. Self-employment became less common, and the United States became a nation of wage workers or employees. The 1870 census revealed that wage workers already totaled almost 5 million (3.5 million in industry) of the nearly 13 million gainfully employed persons. Farmers still accounted for 3 million or so, agricultural laborers for nearly 4 million. By the end of the century, two-thirds of all Americans worked for wages.

The new system required a vast number of people. Many young men and women fled the family farm for the promise of a paying job in industry. A smaller number escaped the peonage system of agricultural labor in the South. By far the largest proportion came from Europe or Asia. Between 1860 and 1890, 10 million people immigrated to the United States. Although the lure of jobs brought many to American shores, political or economic crisis in their homelands also proved a major incentive. The Irish were forced off the land in their native country, while in Germany and Great Britain many factory workers fled industrial depressions. A 1910 report on twenty-one industries estimated that nearly 53 percent of all wage workers were foreign-born, with two-thirds coming from southern and eastern Europe. In many occupations—meat processing, clothing and textile manufacturing, cigar making, and mining, for example—immigrants predominated.

The accelerating growth of industry, especially the steady mechanization of production, shaped this expanding pool of wage workers in two major ways: it

Between 1852 and the Chinese Exclusion Act of 1882, approximately 322,000 Chinese immigrated to the United States. Many helped to built the Central Pacific Railroad and, after fulfilling their labor contracts, moved on to work as cooks or laundry workers in mining and timber camps. Nearly 90 percent of all American Chinese settled in the West. This family, celebrating a wedding, posed for a photographer in Idaho City, Idaho, their new hometown.

dramatically changed employer-employee relations; and it created wholly new categories of workers. Both, in turn, fostered competition among workers and created often hazardous work conditions.

For most craft workers, the new system destroyed long-standing practices and chipped away at their customary autonomy. As the pioneer of scientific management, Frederick Winslow Taylor, explained, the company must "take all the important decisions . . . out of the hands of workmen." Although only a few companies adopted Taylor's specific policies before the turn of the century, workers in major industries lost control over production processes. Teams of iron-workers, for example, had previously set the rules of production as well as their wages while the company supplied equipment and raw materials. Once steel replaced iron, most companies gradually introduced a new managerial structure. Workers now faced constant supervision, higher production quotas, and new, faster machinery. Highly skilled cabinetmakers, who for generations had brought their own tools to the factory, were largely replaced with "green hands"—immigrants, including many women, who could operate new woodworking machines with minimal training and close supervision.

Not all trades conformed to this pattern. The garment industry, for example, grew at a very fast pace in New York, Boston, Chicago, Philadelphia, Cleveland, and St. Louis but retained older systems of labor along with the new. On the one hand were highly mechanized factories that employed hundreds of thou-

sands of young immigrant women. On the other was the outwork system, established well before the Civil War, which employed ever-larger numbers of families working at home on sewing machines or by hand. Companies fostered extreme competition between these two groups of workers, continually speeding up the pace by increasing daily production quotas. Paid by the piece—a seam stitched, a collar turned, a button attached—workers labored faster and longer at home or in the factory to forestall a dip in wages. Meanwhile, in older trades such as machine tooling and textiles, the surviving craft jobs continued to pass from fathers to sons, nephews, or family friends.

Wholly new trades or expanding occupational fields brought an unprecedented number of women into the wage system. In the trades least affected by technological advances, such as domestic service, African American and immigrant women in particular found employment in cities such as Atlanta, Boston, New York, and Chicago. Meanwhile, English-speaking white women moved into clerical positions in the rapidly expanding business sector. After the typewriter and telephone came into widespread use in the 1890s, the number of women employed in office work rose even faster. In retailing there was a legion of nearly 60,000 saleswomen ruled over by male superintendents, floorwalkers, and buyers. Overall, at the turn of the century, 8.6 million women worked outside their homes—nearly triple the number in 1870.

By contrast, African American men found themselves excluded from many fields. In Cleveland, for example, the number of black carpenters declined after 1870, just as the volume of construction increased rapidly. African American men were also driven from restaurant service and barred from newer trades like boilermaking, plumbing, electrical work, and paperhanging, which European immigrants secured for themselves.

The impact of discriminatory or exclusionary practices fell hardest on workers who had been recruited from China in earlier decades. Driven by severe famine and political turmoil in their homeland and drawn by news of jobs in the California Gold Rush, 322,000 Chinese—mostly young men between the ages of sixteen and twenty-four—came to the United States between 1850 and 1882. Many signed up as contract laborers, agreeing to work for four or five years in railroad construction without wages in return for ocean transport. Once their contracts expired and they sought other jobs, they were viewed as potential competitors by white workers and proprietors of small businesses. In 1877 rioters calling for deportation measures destroyed Chinese neighborhoods. In 1882 Congress passed the Chinese Exclusion Act, which suspended Chinese immigra-

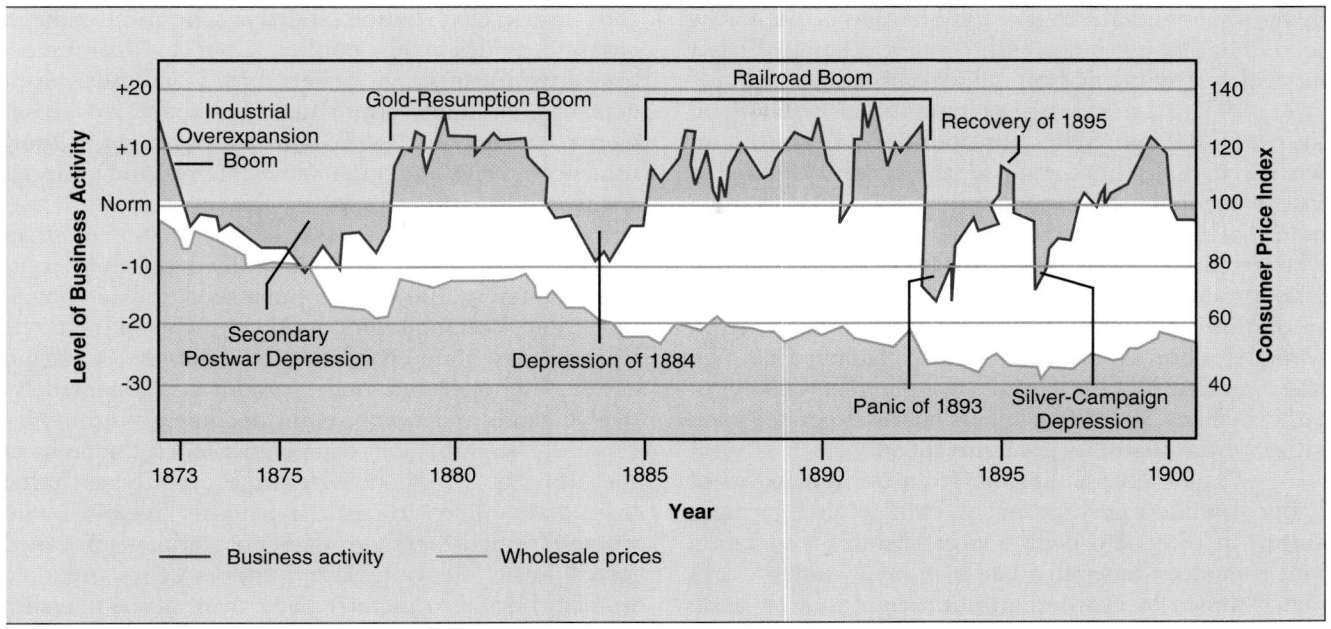

U.S. Economy, 1873–1900   *The economy of the late nineteenth century was a series of sharp ups and downs. Each "boom" was swiftly followed by a "bust," often of greater duration. Although wholesale prices fell, most consumers lacked sufficient income to enjoy fully the bounty of cheaper goods.*

Source: Bernard Bailyn et al., *The Great Republic*, 3d ed. (Lexington, Mass.: D. C. Heath, 1985), p. 552.

tion, limited the civil rights of resident Chinese, and forbade their naturalization.

For even the best-placed wage earners, the new workplace could be unhealthy, even dangerous. Meat packing produced its own hazards—the dampness of the pickling room, the sharp blade of the slaughtering knife, and the noxious odors of the fertilizer department. Factory owners often locked fire doors from the outside, failed to mark high-voltage wires, and took little or no action to limit the emission of toxic fumes. Extractive workers, such as coal and copper miners, endured the worst conditions of all. Mineshaft air could suddenly turn poisonous; sudden cave-ins could make escape all but impossible. Moreover, machines ran faster in American factories than anywhere else in the world, and workers who could not keep up or suffered serious injury found themselves without a job.

Even under less hazardous conditions, workers complained about the tedium of performing repetitive tasks for many hours each day. Although federal employees had been granted the eight-hour day in 1868, most workers still toiled upward of ten or twelve hours. "Life in a factory," one textile operative grumbled, "is perhaps, with the exception of prison life, the most monotonous life a human being can live." Nor could glamour be found in the work of saleswomen in the elegant department stores. Clerks could not sit down, despite workdays as long as sixteen hours in the busy season, or hold "unnec-

essary conversations" with customers or other clerks. Despite these disadvantages, most women preferred sales and manufacturing jobs to domestic service. Household workers, especially live-in servants, were on call seven days a week, enjoying at best an occasional afternoon off. Most workers tolerated unsafe conditions or tedious jobs as the price of steady employment.

The boom-and-bust business cycle made periods of unemployment routine in the lives of most workers. Between 1866 and 1897, fourteen years of prosperity stood against seventeen of hard times. The major depressions of 1873–79 and 1893–97 were the worst in the nation's history up to that time. Three "minor" recessions (1866–67, 1883–85, and 1890–91) did not seem insignificant to the millions who lost their jobs during those periods. "At one time they drive us like slaves," a labor official complained in 1883, "and at other times we have to beg for work." During that year, 40 percent of all industrial workers lived below the poverty line ($500 per year). Whereas a highly skilled worker might earn between $800 and $1,000 per year, a common laborer received only $1.50 for a day's work.

Mobilization against the Wage System

Many workers who abhorred the wage system experimented with worker-owned factories. Others dismissed such an alternative as far-fetched and concentrated instead on improving conditions in their trades by stabilizing wages and above all by shortening hours. In the second half of the nineteenth century, a national labor movement embracing both views took shape.

The National Labor Union (NLU) was formed in 1866. William Sylvis, its founder and president, wished to halt the spread of the wage system. He insisted that through "cooperation we will become a nation of employers—the employers of our own labor. The wealth of the land will pass into the hands of those who produce it." Annual NLU conventions passed resolutions advocating banking reforms to permit workers to borrow enough money to launch their own factories. The NLU achieved a maximum enrollment of approximately 300,000 members but disintegrated soon after Sylvis's death, its goal unrealized.

The Noble and Holy Order of the Knights of Labor, founded by a group of Philadelphia garment cutters in 1869, became the largest labor organization in the nineteenth century. Led by Grand Master Workman Terence V. Powderly, the order sought to bring together all wage earners regardless of skill in a "great brotherhood." Only by organizing widely, one member insisted, would workers be able to achieve their "emancipation" from "the thraldom and loss of wage slavery." Growing slowly at first, the Knights enrolled 110,000 members by 1885.

The Knights endorsed a variety of reform measures—more land set aside for homesteading, the abolition of contract and child labor, monetary reform, and a graduated income tax—to offset the power of the manufacturers. Above all they advocated a system of producers' cooperatives. Local assemblies launched thousands of small co-ops, such as the Our Girls Cooperative Manufacturing Company established by Chicago seamstresses. These worker-run factories generated great enthusiasm among the participants, who shared all profits and made collective decisions on prices and wages. The Knights also sponsored consumer cooperatives for members, often operating small grocery stores from their own assembly buildings. Other co-ops, such as cigar shops, sold items to the broader working-class community. Local banks and other businesses, however, viewed co-ops as competitors, and many refused to extend them credit or sell them goods at wholesale prices. Ultimately, the co-ops could not compete against heavily capitalized enterprises such as chain or department stores.

The Knights reached their peak during the great campaign for a shorter workday. At the close of the Civil War, eight-hour leagues had formed to advocate a "natural" rhythm of eight hours for work, eight hours for sleep, and eight hours for leisure. After staging petition campaigns, marches, and a massive strike in New York City, the movement collapsed during the economic recession of the 1870s. But it was revived early in the next decade, and this time the campaign aroused widespread public support. Consumers boycotted those brands of beer, bread, and other products made in longer-hour shops. Newspaper advertisements announced "eight-hour" shoes, "eight-hour" romance novels, and "eight-hour" picnics and concerts sponsored by groups eager for the reform.

During the first weeks of May 1886, more than a third of a million workers walked off their jobs. Approximately 200,000 of them won shorter hours, including Packingtown's workers, who joined the Knights of Labor en masse. To celebrate, Chicago cattle butchers led a huge parade, accompanied by twelve bands and twenty-eight decorated wagons.

The eight-hour campaign swelled the ranks of the Knights of Labor. Workers ordinarily excluded from craft unions joined the Knights. Nearly 3,000 women formed their own "ladies assemblies" or joined mixed locals. Leonora Barry, appointed to organize women, helped to increase their share of membership to 10 percent, or nearly 50,000 workers from the textile, garment, shoe, and carpet industries. African Americans—20,000 to 30,000 of them nationally—also joined the Knights, forming separate assemblies within the organization. Like the NLU, however, the Knights supported the Chinese Exclusion Act and advocated further restrictions on immigration.

A tragedy in Chicago's Haymarket Square on May 4, 1886, however, undercut the Knights' gains. A protest rally on that day against police violence following a series of confrontations between strikers and police was unfolding quietly when an unidentified person threw a bomb. One police officer was killed outright and seven others were fatally wounded. The police then fired wildly into the dispersing crowd, killing several people. During the next weeks, newspaper editorials warned of imminent, bloody revolution in the nation's streets. In several cities, club-wielding police broke up rallies, raided the offices of labor assemblies and ethnic fraternal clubs, and threatened immigrant unionists with deportation. Chicago authorities arrested anarchist leaders and in a sensational trial sentenced them to death, although no evidence linked them to the actual bombing. Four of the anarchists were hanged, another committed suicide, and three others remained jailed until Illinois governor John Peter Altgeld pardoned them in 1893.

The Knights of Labor suffered irreparable setbacks during the rest of 1886 and 1887. Employers' associations successfully pooled funds to rid their factories of troublesome organizers and announced that companies would no longer bargain with unions. In Packingtown, the Big Five firms drew up a blacklist to get rid of labor organizers and quickly reinstituted the ten-hour day. The Knights' leadership, shaken by these events, desperately sought to regain respectability by denouncing the "Haymarket martyrs." Most remaining members simply dropped out. The wage system had triumphed.

The American Federation of Labor

The events of 1886 also signaled the rise of a very different kind of organization, the American Federation of Labor (AFL). Unlike the NLU or the Knights, the AFL accepted the wage system. Following a strategy of "pure and simple unionism," the AFL sought to gain recognition of its union status to bargain with employers for better working conditions, higher wages, and shorter hours. In return it offered compliant firms the benefit of amenable day-to-day relations with the most highly skilled wage earners. Only if companies refused to bargain in good faith would union members strike.

The AFL originated in the craft unions revived from earlier times or founded in the decade after the Civil War. National organizations for individual crafts, such as machinists and typographers, set their own agendas. At the same time, combined assemblies of skilled workers appeared in most major cities outside the South. During the business upswing of the early 1880s, delegates from eight national unions formed the Federation of Organized Trades and Labor Unions of the United States and Canada. In 1886 this organization became the American Federation of Labor.

The new federation, with twelve national unions and 140,000 affiliated members, declared war on the Knights of Labor. In the wake of the Haymarket tragedy and collapse of the eight-hour movement, the AFL pushed ahead of its rival by organizing craft workers. AFL president Samuel Gompers refused to include unskilled workers, including African Americans, women, and most new immigrants. As Gompers put it, such a "heterogeneous stew of divergent and discordant customs, languages and institutions" was "impossible to organize" and even unworthy of equal status. By successfully limiting the job market and policing unskilled workers for employers, the AFL unionist became the "aristocrat of labor," the best-paid worker in the world.

By the end of the century, the AFL had enrolled only 10 percent of the nation's workers. It could not slow the steady advance of mechanization, which diminished the craft worker's autonomy and eliminated some of the most desirable jobs. But the AFL had achieved a degree of respectability that the Knights of Labor had commanded only briefly. Local politicians courted AFL members' votes, and Labor Day, first celebrated in the 1880s, became a national holiday in 1894.

THE INDUSTRIAL CITY

Before the Civil War, manufacturing had centered in the countryside, in burgeoning factory towns such as Lowell, Massachusetts, and Troy, New York. The expanding rail system promoted new growth in the older commercial cities of Boston, Philadelphia, and New York and created urban outposts like Minneapolis, Kansas City, and Denver. By the end of the nineteenth century, 90 percent of all manufacturing took place in cities. The metropolis stood at the center of the growing industrial economy, a magnet drawing raw material, capital, and labor and the key distribution point for manufactured goods.

The industrial city inspired both great hope and great trepidation. Civic leaders often bragged about its size and rate of growth; immigrants wrote to their countryfolk of its pace, both exciting and exhausting. Philosopher Josiah Strong described the city as the nation's "storm center." "Here luxuries are gathered—everything that dazzles the eye, or tempts the appetite" as well as, he pointedly added, "the desperation of starvation." Whatever the assessment, the city dominated the nation's economic, social, and cultural life.

Populating the City

The United States was on its way to becoming an urban nation. The population of cities grew at double the rate of the nation's population as a whole. In 1860 only sixteen cities had more than 50,000 residents. By 1890 one-third of all Americans were city dwellers. Eleven cities claimed more than 250,000 people. Both Chicago and Philadelphia had 1 million inhabitants. By 1900 New York City was home to almost 3.5 million people.

The major cities—New York, Chicago, Philadelphia, St. Louis, Boston, and Baltimore—achieved international fame for the size and diversity of their populations. Many of their new residents had migrated from rural communities within the United States. Between 1870 and 1910, an average of nearly 7,000 African Americans moved north each year, hoping to escape the poverty and oppression prevailing in the South and to find better-paying jobs. By the end of the century, nearly 80 percent of African Americans in the North lived in urban areas. Among those aged sixteen to thirty-five in all native-born groups, urban women outnumbered men. Whereas young white men in particular aspired to inherit the family farm or seek a fortune in the West, their sisters sought jobs in urban manufacturing, commercial trades, and housekeeping.

Immigrants and their children were the major source of urban population growth in the late nineteenth century. Most of those in the first wave of immi-

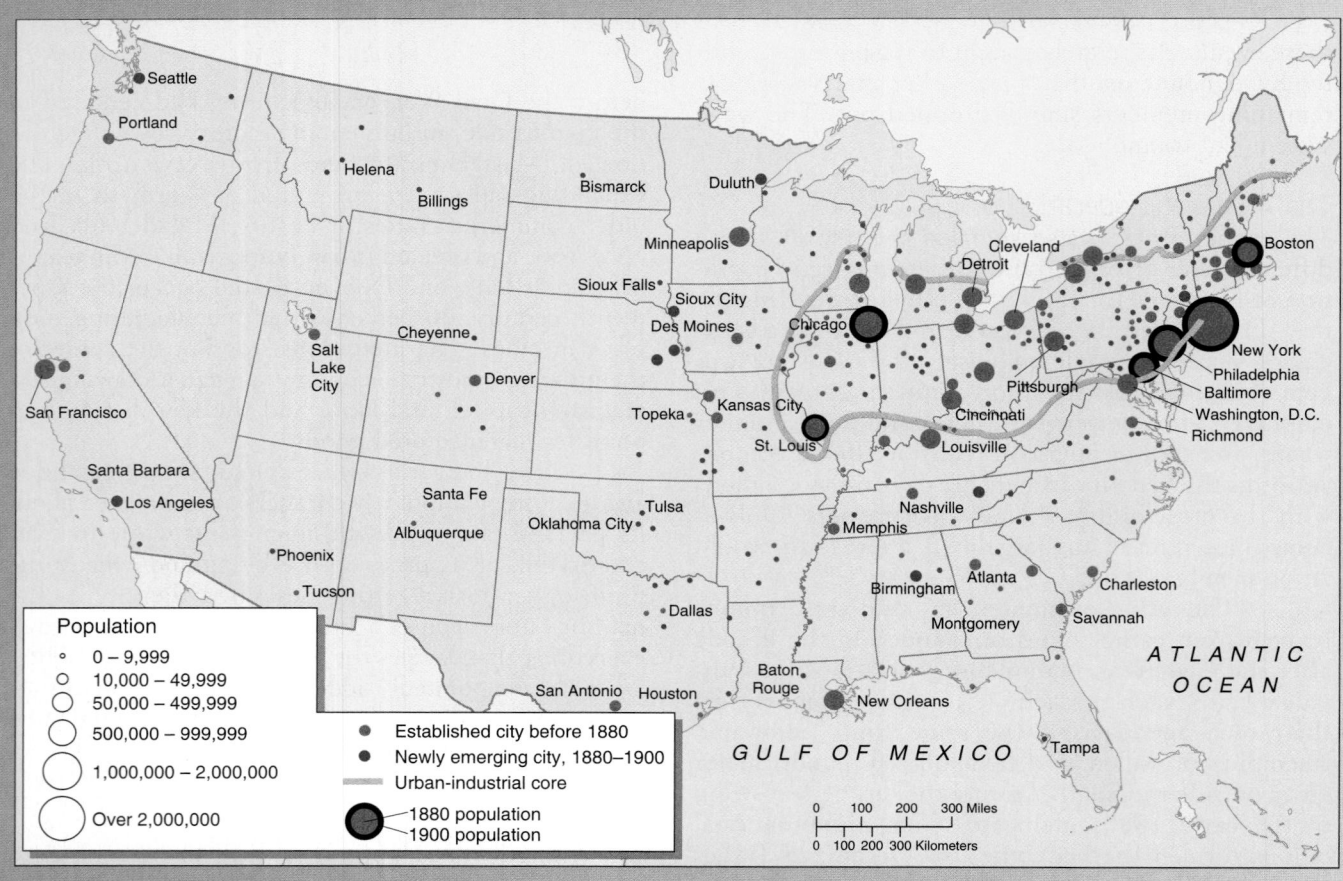

Patterns in Urban Growth in Turn-of-the-Century America

By the turn of the century, the ten largest cities in the United States were located in the Northeast and the Midwest. The rapid growth of these cities reflected the rise of industry and commerce in the nation's urban-industrial core and the demand for labor that accompanied it. New York City, Chicago, Philadelphia, St. Louis, and Boston, for example, attracted new immigrants who found jobs in the these cities' huge ready-to-wear clothing industries and other light manufacturing shops. Chicago, Pittsburgh, Detroit,

and Buffalo became the home of working-class families who looked for their livelihood to these cities' giant steel mills and packinghouse plants.

The growth of cities in the western and southern states reflected the expansion of the nation's railroads in those regions and the efficient transportation of goods and people that expansion made possible. The growth of Atlanta, for example, was tied to the expansion of the southern rail system. Like Chicago in the Midwest and Los Angeles in the West, Atlanta became a hub and distribution center for regionally produced goods.

gration, before the Civil War, had settled in the countryside. In contrast, after the war it was the industrial city that drew the so-called "new" immigrants, who came primarily from eastern and southern Europe. At the turn of the century Chicago had more Germans than all but a few German cities and more Poles than most Polish cities; New York had more Italians than a handful of the largest Italian cities, and Boston had nearly as many Irish as Dublin. In almost every group except the Irish, men outnumbered women.

Like rural migrants, immigrants came to the American city to take advantage of the expanding opportunities for employment. While many hoped to build a new home in the land of plenty, many others intended to work hard, save money, and return to their families in the Old Country. In the 1880s, for example, nearly half of all Italian, Greek, and Serbian men returned to their native lands. Others could not return to their homelands or did not wish to. Jews, for instance, had emigrated to escape persecution in Russia

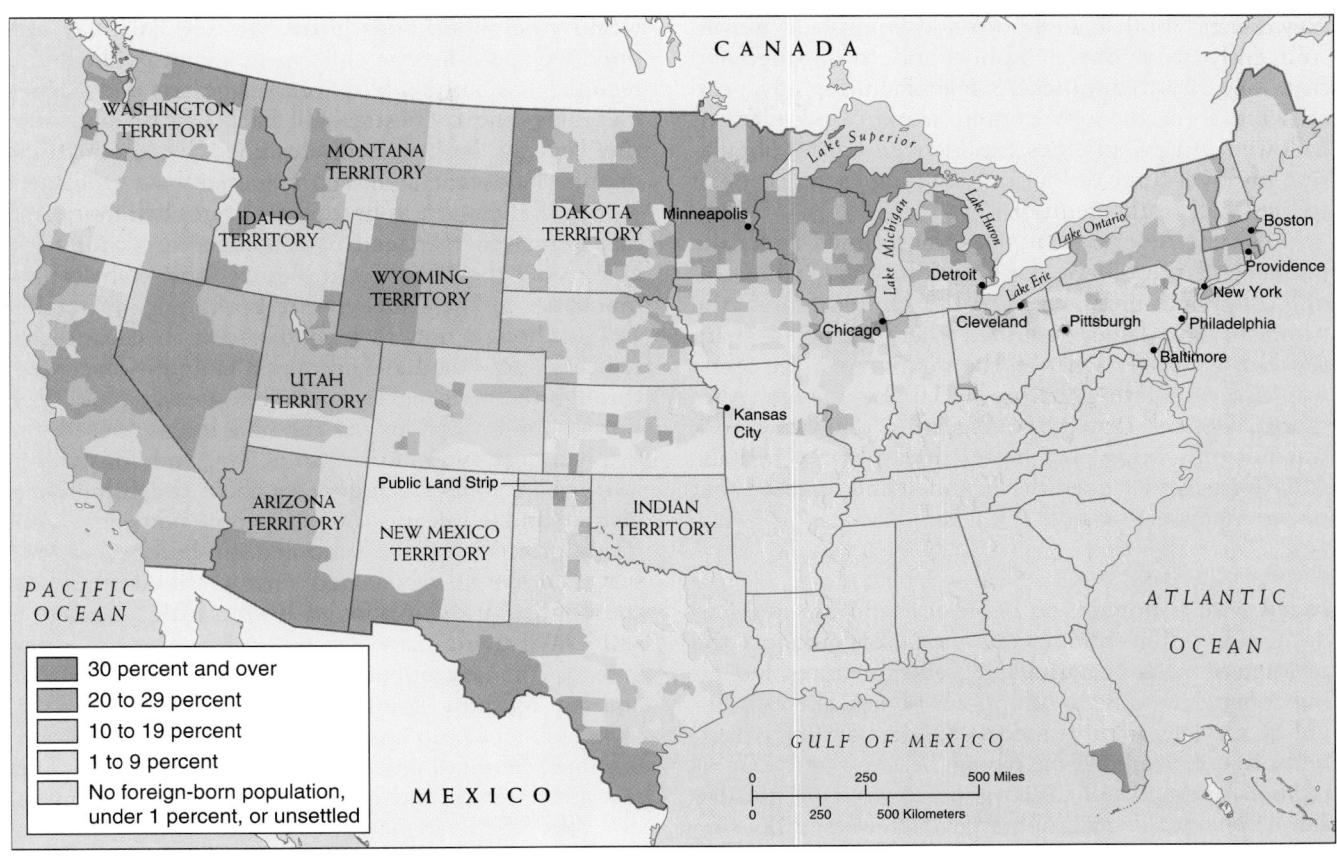

Population of Foreign Birth by Region, 1880   *European immigrants after the Civil War settled primarily in the industrial districts of the northern Midwest and parts of the Northeast. French Canadians continued to settle in Maine, Cubans in Florida, and Mexicans in the Southwest, where earlier immigrants had established thriving communities.*

Source: Clifford L. Lord and Elizabeth H. Lord, *Lord & Lord Historical Atlas of the United States* (New York: Holt, 1953).

and Russian-dominated Polish and Romanian lands. A Yiddish writer later called this generation the "Jews without Jewish memories. . . . They shook them off in the boat when they came across the seas. They emptied out their memories."

Of all groups, Jews had the most experience with urban life. Forbidden to own land in most parts of Europe and boxed into shtetls (villages), Jews had also formed thriving urban communities in Vilna, Berlin, London, and Vienna. Many had worked in garment manufacturing in, for example, London's East End, and followed a path to American cities like New York, Rochester, Philadelphia, or Chicago where the needle trades flourished.

Other groups, the majority coming from rural parts of Europe, sought out their kinfolk in American cities, where they could most easily find housing and employment. Bohemians settled largely in Chicago, Pittsburgh, and Cleveland. They often lived and worked near German immigrants, although in poorer

housing and in less skilled jobs as lumberyard workers, cigar rollers, and garment workers. French Canadians, a relatively small group of a few hundred thousand, emigrated from Quebec and settled almost exclusively in New England and upper New York State. Finding work mainly in textile mills, they transformed smaller industrial cities like Woonsocket, Rhode Island, into French-speaking communities. Cubans, themselves often first- or second-generation immigrants from Spain, moved to Ybor City, a section of Tampa, Florida, to work in cigar factories. Still other groups tended toward cities dominated by fishing, shoemaking, or even glassblowing, a craft carried directly from the Old Country. Italians, the most numerous among the new immigrants, settled mainly in northeastern cities. With few skills and little education, they often became laborers, laying railroad track, excavating subways, and erecting buildings.

Resettlement in an American city did not necessarily mark the end of the immigrants' travels.

Newcomers, both native-born and immigrant, moved frequently from one neighborhood to another and from one city to another. As manufacturing advanced outward from the city center, working populations followed. American cities experienced a total population turnover three or four times during each decade of the last half of the century.

The American city was transformed under the pressure of these various groups. In 1882, when 1.2 million people immigrated to the United States, the novelist Henry James described what he called a "sharp sense of dispossession." To the immigrants, the scene was also disquieting. Before he left his village, Allesandro DeLuca remembered hearing that New York was not only bigger but better than any city in Italy. After he arrived, he felt disillusioned and doubted that he would ever "find here my idea."

The Urban Landscape

Faced with a population explosion and an unprecedented building boom, the cities encouraged the creation of many beautiful and useful structures, including commercial offices, sumptuous homes, and efficient public services—but at a cost. Builders and city planners often disregarded the natural beauty and the architectural landmarks of earlier generations. Laid out in a simple geometric gridiron pattern, streets and housing ran over the sites of hills that had been leveled, ponds that had been filled, farmlands and farm houses that had been eradicated. Factories often occupied the best sites, near waterways where goods could be easily transported and wastes dumped.

The majority of the population, who worked in dingy factories, lived in crowded tenements designed to maximize the use of space by impoverished families. Built by the thousands after the Civil War, the typical "dumbbell" model in New York City sat on a lot 25 feet by 100 feet and rose to five stories. Each floor was subdivided into four family units of no more than three rooms each. One room served as a combined cooking and living room, the remaining two as bedrooms. By 1890 New York's Lower East Side packed more than 700 people per acre into back-to-back buildings, producing one of the highest population densities in the world.

At the other end of the urban social scale, New York's Fifth Avenue, St. Paul's Summit Avenue, Chicago's Michigan Avenue, and San Francisco's Nob Hill fairly gleamed with new mansions and town houses. Commonwealth Avenue marked Boston's fashionable Back Bay district, built on a filled-in 450-acre tidal flat. State engineers planned this community, with its magnificent boulevard, uniform five-story brownstones, and back alleys designed for deliveries. Like

wealthy neighborhoods in other cities, Back Bay also provided space for the city's magnificent public architecture, its stately public library, fine arts and science museums, and orchestra hall. Back Bay opened onto the Fenway Park system designed by the nation's premier landscape architect, Frederick Law Olmsted.

Cities such as Boston, Chicago, Baltimore, and San Francisco managed to rebuild after major fires, employing the latest technological and architectural innovations. The Chicago Fire broke out in October 1871—though not, as legend had it, because "Mrs. O'Leary's cow" had kicked over a lantern—and swept through the ramshackle wooden houses that had been thrown up for workers. By the time it was doused, the fire had destroyed more than 60,000 buildings within four square miles, including much of the commercial district, and left nearly 100,000 people homeless. Louis H. Sullivan, recently schooled in Europe, eagerly surveyed the newly cleared sites in the aftermath of the conflagration. Although he did little to improve residential living, he came up with a plan for a new type of commercial building, the skyscraper, a "proud and soaring thing, rising in [such] sheer exultation that from bottom to top it is a unit without a single dissenting line." Emphasizing vertical grandeur rising as high as twenty stories, and using iron, steel, and masonry to deter fires, Sullivan made the skyscraper the symbol of the modern city.

Architects played a key role in what is sometimes called the American Renaissance or City Beautiful movement. Grand concrete boulevards were constructed at enormous public cost. New sports amphitheaters dazzled the public and evoked pride in the city's accomplishments. New schools, courthouses, capitols, hospitals, museums, and department stores arose. Influenced by the Parisian Beaux-Arts style, architects regularly replaced the simple Greek Revival buildings constructed earlier in the century with domed palaces. These massive, often highly ornate structures expressed the city's pride in its commercial success. The city center also became more congested and noisy, making it a more desirable place to visit than to live.

The city inspired other architectural marvels. Opened in 1883, the Brooklyn Bridge won wide acclaim from engineers, journalists, and poets as the most original American construction. Designed by John Roebling, who died from an accident early in its construction, and by his son Washington Roebling, who became an invalid during its construction, the bridge was considered an aesthetic and practical wonder. Its soaring piers, elegant arches, and intricate steel cables convey an image of strength and elasticity, inspiring a belief among artists and writers in the potential of technology to unite function and beauty. The Brooklyn

Bridge also helped to speed the transformation of rural townships into suburban communities.

The emergence of inexpensive, rapid mass transportation systems also altered the spatial design of cities. Like the railroad but on a smaller scale, streetcars and elevated railroads changed business dramatically because they moved traffic of many different kinds—information, people, and goods—faster and farther than before. Although San Francisco introduced the first mechanically driven cable car in 1873, within a decade Chicago would claim the most extensive cable car system in the world. By 1895 more than 800 communities operated systems of electrically powered cars or trolleys on track reaching 10,000 miles. Two years later Boston rerouted a mile and a half of track underground, establishing the nation's first subway trolley. In 1902 New York opened its subway system, which would grow to become the largest in the nation.

In his watercolor The Bowery at Night, *painted in 1895, W. Louis Sonntag Jr. shows a New York City scene transformed by electric light. Electricity transformed the city in other ways as well, as seen in the electric streetcars and elevated railroad.*

By making it possible for a great number of workers to live in communities distant from their place of employment, mass transportation also allowed cities to grow dramatically. In 1880 New York City's surface transit system alone accommodated more than 150 million riders annually, a large proportion traveling into Manhattan from Queens and Brooklyn. Suburbs like Dorchester and Brookline sprang up outside Boston, offering many professional workers quiet residential retreats from the city's busy downtown. New retail and service businesses followed as the dynamism of the great city radiated outward while the bulk of industry and pollution remained behind.

The City and the Environment

Electric trolleys eliminated the tons of waste from horsecars that had for decades fouled city streets. But the new rail systems also increased congestion and created new safety hazards for pedestrians. During the 1890s, 600 people were killed each year by Chicago's trains. To relieve congestion, Chicago as well as New York and Boston elevated portions of their rapid transit systems and in the process placed entire communities under the shadow of noisy and rickety wooden platforms. Despite many technologi-

cal advances, the quality of life in the nation's cities did not necessarily improve.

In the half-century after the Civil War, efforts to improve sanitary conditions absorbed many urban tax dollars. Modern water and sewer systems constituted a hidden city of pipes and wires mirroring the growth of the visible city above ground. Although cast iron pipes and steam pumps had delivered water into cities since the early part of the century, the filtration systems introduced in the 1890s greatly improved water quality and, by providing cleaner water, played an important role in reducing the incidence of typhoid. By the 1880s, bathrooms with showers and flush toilets had become standard features in hospitals and in many middle-class homes.

These advances did not in themselves eradicate serious environmental problems. Most cities continued to dump sewage in nearby bodies of water. Moreover, rather than outlawing upriver dumping by factories, municipal governments usually moved to establish separate clean-water systems through the use of reservoirs. Meanwhile the filthy rivers, such as the Providence and Woonasquatucket Rivers in Providence, Rhode Island, were paved over as they passed through downtown. The Chicago River was reversed through an engineering feat so as to transport sewage away from Lake Michigan, the city's source of drinking water. Chicago's residents enjoyed cleaner tap water, but downriver communities began to complain about the unendurable stench from the diverted flow.

The unrestricted burning of coal to fuel the railroads and to heat factories and homes after 1880 greatly intensified urban air pollution. Noise levels continued to rise in the most compacted living and industrial areas. Overcrowded conditions and inadequate sanitary facilities bred tuberculosis, smallpox, and scarlet fever, among other contagious diseases. Children's diseases like whooping cough and measles spread rapidly through poor neighborhoods such as Packingtown. A major yellow fever epidemic in 1878 prompted the creation of the National Board of Health, which in turn began to advise state and city officials and provide emergency assistance. But only after the turn of the century, amid an intensive campaign against municipal corruption, did laws and administrative practices address the serious problems of public health (see Chapter 21).

Meanwhile the distance between the city and the countryside narrowed. Naturalists had hoped for large open spaces—a buffer zone—to preserve farmland and wild areas, protect future water supplies, and diminish regional air pollution. But soon the industrial landscape invaded the countryside. Nearby rural lands not destined for private housing or commercial development became sites for water treatment and sewage plants, garbage dumps, and graveyards—services essential to the city's growing population.

THE NEW SOUTH

"Fifteen years have gone over" since the Civil War, journalist Whitelaw Reid complained, yet the South "still sits crushed, wretched, busy displaying and bemoaning her wounds." Physically and financially devastated by the war, the South had little investment capital and relatively few banks to manage it. The area was economically stagnant, its per capita wealth only 27 percent of that of the northeastern states. The South's remote countryside receded into greater isolation, while its few urban regions moved very slowly into the era of modern industry and technology. As late as 1880 mining and manufacturing employed only 5 percent of Alabama's workforce. At the turn of the century southern industries lagged far behind enterprises in other regions of the country. Their progress was held back by dependence on northern finance capital, continued reliance on cotton production, and the legacy of slavery.

Industrialization

In the 1870s a vocal and powerful new group of Southerners headed by Henry Woodfin Grady, editor of the *Atlanta Constitution*, insisted that the region enjoyed a great potential in its abundant natural resources of coal, iron, turpentine, tobacco, and lumber. Grady and his peers envisioned a "New South" where modern textile mills operated efficiently and profitably close to the sources of raw goods, the expansive fields of cotton, and a plentiful and cheap supply of labor, unrestricted by unions or by legal limitations on the employment of children. Arguing against those planters who aspired to rejuvenate the agricultural economy based on the cultivation of a few staple crops, this group forcefully promoted industrial development and welcomed northern investors.

Northern investors secured huge concessions from state legislatures, including land, forest, and mineral rights and large tax exemptions. Exploiting the incentives, railroad companies laid over 22,000 miles of new track, connecting the region to national markets and creating new cities. By 1890 a score of large railroad companies, mainly centered in New York, held more than half of all the track in the South. Northern-owned lumber companies meanwhile stripped southern forests.

Northerners also employed various means to protect their investments from southern competition. By the late 1870s southern merchants, with help from foreign investors, had begun to run iron factories around Birmingham, Alabama. Southern iron production was soon encroaching on the northeastern market. Andrew Carnegie toured the city's iron mills and then declared, "The South is Pennsylvania's most formidable industrial enemy." Carnegie first attempted to stave off competition by ordering the railroads to charge higher freight fees to Birmingham's iron producers. By the turn of the century, his successor corporation, U.S. Steel, implemented a simpler solution: buying several Birmingham plants and taking over production.

The production of cotton textiles followed a similar course. Powerful merchants and large landowners, realizing that they could make high profits by controlling the cotton crop from field to factory, promoted the vertical integration of the cotton industry. The Mississippi Valley Cotton Planters' Association, for example, advised planters to "set up spindles in the cotton fields"—that is, to build mills on their land. Meanwhile, New South promoters in Atlanta hosted the International Cotton Exposition of 1881 in a bold public relations campaign to attract investors.

The number of mills in the South grew from 161 in 1880 to 400 in 1900. The latest machines ran the new mills, and the South boasted the first factory fully equipped with electricity. Production in the four leading cotton-manufacturing states—North Carolina, South Carolina, Georgia, and Alabama—skyrocketed, far outpacing the New England mills.

Yet this achievement did not necessarily represent an absolute gain for the South. Northern manufacturers, including many New England mill owners, responded creatively to the report of the 1900 census on manufacturing that "the return upon investment in southern cotton mills has greatly exceeded that upon factories in the North." Recognizing the potential for great profit in new factories and cheap labor, they shifted their investments to the South. By the 1920s, northern investors held much of the South's wealth, including the major textile mills, but returned through employment or social services only a small share of the profits to the region's people.

Beyond iron or steel and textiles, southern industry remained largely extractive and, like the South itself, rural. Turpentine and lumbering businesses pushed ever farther into diminishing pine forests, the sawmills and distilleries moving with them. Toward the end of the century, fruit canning and sugar refining flourished. For the most part, southern enterprises mainly produced raw materials for consumption or use in the North, thereby perpetuating the economic imbalance between the sections.

The governing role of capital investments from outside the region reinforced long-standing relationships. Even rapid industrialization—in iron, railroad, and textiles—did not match the level achieved in the North. The rise of the New South reinforced, rather than refuted, the region's status as a dependent economy: the South relied on the North for capital and administration while deriving few long-term benefits from the relationship.

Southern Labor

Reconstruction and its demise (see Chapter 17) profoundly affected working conditions in the region. For instance, Captain Ellison Alger Smyth, who organized a group of white Southerners, the Red Shirts, to curtail the political influence of African Americans, established a whites-only policy for the workforce of his Pelzer Mill, which he founded in 1881 in Greenville, South Carolina. Textile barons such as Smyth, who became known as the "dean of southern Cotton manufacturers," helped to pass legislation and to devise informal rules that spread racial segregation throughout southern society.

The advance of southern industry did little to improve the working lives of most African Americans, although large numbers moved to the new manufacturing centers and growing cities in search of better-paying jobs. African American men did find work with the railroads; in booming cities like Atlanta they even gained skilled positions in the construction trades and worked as bricklayers, carpenters, and painters. For the most part, however, African Americans were limited to unskilled, low-paying jobs. In the textile mills and cigarette factories, which employed both black and white workers, the work force was rigidly

African American women working as sweepers, Belton, South Carolina, in 1899. Despite the rise of industry in the New South, African Americans found few new avenues for employment. The majority continued to work in agricultural labor or domestic service.

segregated. African Americans were assigned mainly to janitorial jobs and rarely worked alongside the white workers who tended the machines. Nearly all African American women who earned wages did so as household workers. Girls as young as ten years worked as domestics or as child-nurses, while the vast majority of older women did laundry. By 1880 Atlanta's washerwomen outnumbered the African American men who worked as common laborers.

In general, white workers fiercely protected their relatively privileged positions. Locals of the all-white carpenters' union maintained a segregation policy so absolute that if too few members were available for a job, the union would send for out-of-town white workers rather than employ local members of the black carpenters' union. In Atlanta in 1897, 1,400 white women mill operatives went on strike when the company proposed to hire two black spinners.

Only at rare moments did southern workers unite across racial lines. In the 1880s, the Knights of Labor briefly organized both black and white workers. At its high point, the Knights' local union, District Assembly 92, enrolled two-thirds of Richmond's 5,000 tobacco operatives and made significant inroads among quarry workers, coopers, typographers, iron molders, and builders. But when white politicians and local newspapers began to raise the specter of black domination, the Knights were forced to retreat. Across the region their organization collapsed. The few successful unions remained for generations the exclusive claim of white skilled workers.

Wages throughout the South were low for both black and white workers. In Richmond, white skilled workers in the iron trades, including plumbers, carpenters, and gas fitters, made 10 percent to 30 percent less in 1890 than comparable workers elsewhere in the United States. Southern textile workers' wages were barely half those of New Englanders. In the 1880s, when investors enjoyed profits ranging from 30 percent to 75 percent, southern mill workers earned as little as twelve cents per hour. Black men earned at or below the poverty line of $300 per year, while black women rarely earned more than $120 and white women about $220 annually. The poorest paid workers were children.

As industry expanded throughout the nation, so too did the number of children earning wages, especially in the South. In 1896 only one in twenty Massachusetts mill operatives was younger than sixteen, but one in four North Carolina cotton mill workers was. Traditions rooted in the agricultural economy reinforced the practice of using the labor of all family members, even the very young. The same principle operated among Polish immigrant families in the South: even five-year-olds joined their parents to work in oyster-canning factories. Seasonal labor, such as picking crops or grinding sugarcane, put families on the move, making community life and formal education all but impossible. Not until well into the twentieth century did compulsory school attendance laws effectively restrict child labor in the South.

A system of convict labor also thrived in the South. Public work projects of all kinds, especially in remote areas, employed disciplinary methods and created living and working conditions reminiscent of slavery. With African Americans constituting up to 90 percent of the convict work force, public officials felt little need to justify the occasional practice of capturing unsuspecting black strangers and placing them alongside criminals in labor gangs. Transported and housed like animals—chained together by day and confined in portable cages at night—these workers suffered high mortality rates. Southern leaders took pride in what they called the "good roads movement"—the chief use of convict labor—as proof of regional progress.

The Transformation of Piedmont Communities

The impact of the New South was nowhere greater than in the Piedmont. The region, where the tidewater ends and water power can be used for mills, extends from southern Virginia and the central Carolinas into northern Alabama and Georgia. After 1870, long-established farms and plantations gave way to railroad tracks, textile factories, numerous mill villages, and a few sizable cities. By the turn of the century, five Piedmont towns had populations over 10,000. Even more dramatic was the swelling number of small towns with populations between 1,000 and 5,000—from fourteen in 1870 to fifty-two in 1900. Once the South's backcountry, the Piedmont now surpassed New England to stand first in the world in the production of yarn and cloth.

Rural poverty, even more than persuasive arguments by labor recruiters, encouraged many farm families to strike out for a new life in the mill town. As prices of cotton or tobacco fell and farmers' debts to the merchants rose, many families turned to tenant farming and its life of hopeless indebtedness. Those with the least access to land and credit—mainly widows and their children and single women—were the first to go into the mills. Then families sent their children. Some families worked in the mills on a seasonal basis, between planting and harvesting. But as the agricultural crisis deepened, more and more people abandoned the countryside entirely for what they called "public work." In the mill, workers hoped, they could do better.

The majority of these families found themselves residents of a company town, owned "lock, stock and barrel" by the manufacturers who employed them. A mill community typically comprised rows of single-family houses, a small school, several churches, a company-owned store, and the home of the superintendent who governed everyone's affairs. The manager of the King Cotton Mill in Burlington, North Carolina, not only kept the company's accounts in order, purchased raw material, and sold the finished yarn, but even bought Christmas presents for the workers' children. It was not unknown for a superintendent to prowl the neighborhood to see which families burned their lanterns past nine o'clock at night and, finding a violator, to knock on the door and tell the offenders to go to bed. Millworkers frequently complained that they had no private life at all. A federal report published shortly after the turn of the century concluded that "all the affairs of the village and the conditions of living of all the people are regulated entirely by the mill company. Practically speaking, the company owns everything and controls everything, and to a large extent controls everybody in the mill village."

Mill superintendents also relied on schoolteachers and clergy to set the tone of community life. They hired and paid the salaries of Baptist and Methodist ministers to preach a faith encouraging workers to be thrifty, orderly, temperate, and hardworking. Ministers conducted evening prayer services, brought men and women into the choir, and sponsored Bible classes and missionary societies. The schools, similarly subsidized by the company, reinforced the lesson of moral and social discipline required of industrial life and encouraged students to follow their parents into the mill. But it was mainly young children between six and eight years old who attended school. When more hands were needed in the mill, superintendents plucked out these youngsters and sent them to join their older brothers and sisters who were already at work.

Piedmont mill villages like Greenville, South Carolina, and Burlington, Charlotte, and Franklinville, North Carolina, nevertheless developed a cohesive character typical of isolated rural communities. The new residents maintained many aspects of their agricultural pasts, tilling small gardens and keeping chickens, pigs, and cows in their yards. Factory owners rarely paved roads or sidewalks or provided adequate sanitation. Mud, flies, and diseases such as typhoid fever flourished. Millworkers endured poverty and health hazards by strengthening community ties through intermarriage. Within a few generations, most of the village residents had, according to one study, "some connection to each other, however distant, by marriage," blood, or both. Even the men and women without families boarded in households where privacy was scarce and collective meals created a familylike atmosphere. Historians have called this complex of intimate economic, family, and community ties the customs of incorporation.

CULTURE AND SOCIETY IN THE GILDED AGE

The growth of industry and spread of cities had a profound impact on all regions of the United States. During the final third of the century the standard of living climbed, although unevenly and erratically. Real wages (pay in relation to the cost of living) rose, fostering improvements in nutrition, clothing, and housing. More and cheaper products were within the reach of all but the very poor. Food from the farms became more abundant and varied—grains for bread or beer; poultry, pork, and beef; fresh fruits and vegetables from California. Although many Americans continued to acknowledge the moral value of hard work, thrift, and self-sacrifice, the explosion of consumer goods and services promoted sweeping changes in behavior and beliefs. Nearly everyone felt the impact of the nation's wealth, although in vastly different ways.

"Conspicuous Consumption"

Labeled the "Gilded Age" by humorist and social critic Mark Twain, the era following the Civil War favored the growth of a new class united in its pursuit of money and leisure. The well-to-do enjoyed great status throughout the nineteenth century, but only after the war did upper-class Americans form national networks to consolidate their power. Business leaders built diverse stock portfolios and often served simultaneously on the boards of several corporations. Similarly, they intertwined their interests by joining the same religious, charitable, athletic, and professional societies. They sent their sons to private boarding schools such as St. Paul's, then on to Harvard, Yale, or Princeton. Their wives and children vacationed together in the sumptuous new seashore and mountain resorts, while they themselves made deals at their leisure in new downtown social clubs and on the golf links of suburban country clubs. Just as Dun and Bradstreet ranked the leading corporations, the Social Register identified the 500 families that controlled most of the nation's wealth.

According to economist and social critic Thorstein Veblen, the rich had created a new style of "conspicuous consumption." The Chicago mansion of real estate tycoon Potter Palmer, for example, was constructed in 1885 without exterior doorknobs. Not only could no one enter uninvited, but a visitor's calling card supposedly passed through the hands of twenty-seven servants before admittance was allowed. At the nearby McCormick mansion, dinner guests chose from a menu printed in French. A vice president of the Chicago & Northwestern Railroad, Perry H. Smith, built his marble palace in the style of the Greek Renaissance. Its ebony staircase was trimmed in gold, its butler's pantry equipped with faucets not only for hot and cold water but for iced champagne. The women who oversaw these elaborate households themselves served as measures of their husbands' status, according to Veblen, by adorning themselves in jewels, furs, and dresses of the latest Paris design.

"Conspicuous consumption" reached toward new heights of extravagance. In New York, wealthy families hosted dinner parties for their dogs or pet monkeys, dressing the animals in fancy outfits for the occasion. Railroad magnate "Diamond Jim" Brady commonly enjoyed after-theater snacks at the city's "lobster palaces," where he consumed vast quantities of food—oysters for an appetizer, two soups, fish, a main dinner of beef and vegetables, punches and sherbet on the side, dessert, and coffee and quarts of orange juice.

Perhaps no display of wealth matched the ostentation of the "cottages" of Newport, Rhode Island, where the rich created a summer community centering on consumption. Architect H. H. Richardson and his protégés built manor houses more magnificent than the English homes they mimicked. Here wealthy young men and women engaged in new amateur sports such as polo, rowing, and lawn tennis. Young and old alike joined in yachting and golf tournaments.

Toward the end of the century, the wealthy added a dramatic public dimension to the "high life."

New York's Waldorf-Astoria hotel, which opened in 1897, incorporated the grandeur of European royalty but with an important difference. Because rich Americans wanted to be watched, the elegantly appointed corridors and restaurants were visible to the public through huge windows, and floor-to-ceiling mirrors allowed diners to observe one another. The New York rich also established a unique custom to welcome the New Year: they opened wide the curtains of their Fifth Avenue mansions so that passersby could marvel at the elegant decor.

The wealthy also became the leading patrons of the arts as well as the chief importers of art treasures from Europe and Asia. They provided the bulk of funds for the new symphonies, operas, and ballet companies, which soon rivaled those of Continental Europe. Nearly all major museums and art galleries, including the Boston Museum of Fine Arts, the Philadelphia Museum of Art, the Art Institute of Chicago, and the Metropolitan Museum of Art in New York, were founded during the last decades of the nineteenth century. Many were the gifts of individual donors, such as the libraries, museums, and galleries in Pittsburgh that all bore the name "Carnegie."

Gentility and the Middle Class

A new middle class, very different from its predecessor, formed during the last half of the century. The older middle class comprised the owners or superintendents of small businesses, doctors, lawyers, teachers, and ministers and their families. The new middle class included these professionals but also the growing number of salaried employees—the managers, technicians, clerks, and engineers who worked in the complex web of corporations and government. Long hours of labor earned their families a modest status and sufficient income to live securely in style and comfort.

Most middle-class American families valued their home not simply as a sign of their social station but as a haven from the tumultuous society outside. For as little as $10 a month, a family could finance the construction of a suburban retreat from the noise, filth, and dangers of the city. This peaceful domestic setting, with its manicured lawns and well-placed shrubs, afforded family members both privacy and rejuvenation. But to accomplish this goal, middle-class families had to separate business activities from leisure, and the breadwinner from his family for most of the day. Assisted by modern transportation systems, men often traveled one to two hours each day, five or six days a week, to their city offices and back again. Women and children stayed behind.

The interior design of middle-class homes reflected a desire for refinement. A rush of new magazines and volumes on homemaking, like Harriet Spof-

ford's *Art Decoration* (1879), set the standards, including elaborate front entryways, wallpapers stenciled by housewives themselves, stained-glass windows, and solid furniture. Reserved for visitors, the parlor featured upholstered furniture, inexpensive prints of famous paintings, and framed photographs of family members. Outside, the fenced-in yard served as a safe playground for small children and their pets.

Middle-class women found themselves devoting a large part of their day to housework. They frequently employed one or two servants but relied increasingly on the many new household appliances to get their work done. Improvements in the kitchen stove, such as the conversion from wood fuel to gas, saved a lot of time. Yet, simultaneously, with the widespread circulation of cookbooks and recipes in newspapers and magazines, as well as the availability of new foods, the preparation of meals became more complex and time-consuming. New devices such as the eggbeater speeded some familiar tasks, but the era's

Franklin Park, Boston *by Maurice Prendergast, ca. 1897, reflects the "impressionist" influence on changing artistic sensibility. Influenced by current European techniques, many contemporary American painters abandoned realist or photographic-like representational styles for a subjective artistic view of nature or society. One of their favorite subjects was the emerging middle class at play.*

Maurice Brazil Prendergast (American, 1858–1924), *Franklin Park, Boston*, 1895–97, watercolor and graphite on paper, 17½ x 13⅛ inches, Daniel J. Terra Collection, Terra Museum of American Art. Photograph © 1996, Terra Museum of American Art, Chicago.

fancy culinary practices offset any gains. Similarly, the new carpet sweepers surpassed the broom in efficiency, but the fashionable high-napped carpeting demanded more care. The foot-powered treadle sewing machine, a staple of the middle-class home, encouraged the fashion-conscious housewife to produce fancier clothing for herself and her family. Thus, rather than diminishing with technological innovation, household work expanded to fill the time available.

Almost exclusively white, Anglo-Saxon, and Protestant, the new middle class embraced "culture" not for purposes of "conspicuous consumption" but as a means of self-improvement and moral uplift. Whole families visited the new museums and art galleries. One of the most cherished institutions, the annual week of lectures at the Chautauqua campgrounds in upstate New York, brought thousands of families together in pursuit of knowledge of literature and the fine arts. The middle class also provided the bulk of patrons for the new public libraries.

Middle-class families applied the same standards to their leisure activities. What one sporting-goods entrepreneur rightly called the "gospel of EXERCISE" involved men and women in calisthenics and outdoor activities, not so much for pleasure as for physical and mental discipline. Hiking was a favorite among both men and women and required entirely new outfits: for women, loose upper garments and skirts short enough to prevent dragging; for men, rugged outer wear and jaunty hats. Soon men and women began camping out, with almost enough amenities to re-create a middle-class home in the woods. Roller skating and ice skating, which became crazes shortly after the Civil War, took place in specially designed rinks in almost every major town. By the 1890s, the "safety" bicycle had also been marketed. It replaced the large-wheel variety, which was difficult to keep upright. A good-quality "bike" cost $100 and, like the piano, was a symbol of middle-class status.

Leisure became the special province of middle-class childhood. Removed from factories and shops and freed from many domestic chores, children enjoyed creative play and physical activity. Summer camps, offering several weeks of sports and handicrafts, attracted many children to New England during this period. The toy market boomed, and lower printing prices helped children's literature flourish. *The Brownie Book* (1898), about imaginary elflike beings, was tremendously popular. Children's magazines such as *St. Nicholas* and *Youth's Companion* were filled with stories, poems, and pictures. Slightly older children read Westerns, sports novels of many kinds, and such perennial and uplifting classics as *Little Women* and *Black Beauty*.

Life in the Streets

Immigrants often weighed the material abundance they found in the United States against their memories of the Old Country. One could "live better" here, but only by working much harder. In letters home, immigrants described the riches of the new country but warned friends and relatives not to send weaklings, who would surely die of stress and strain. Even if their bodies thrived, their spirits might sink amid the alien and intense commercialism of American society. In many immigrant communities, alcoholism and suicide rates did soar above contemporary European standards. Germans in Chicago, it was said half jokingly, drank more beer and whiskey than all the Germans in Germany. Each group had its own phrase to express its feelings of disenchantment. Embittered German immigrants called their new land Malhuerica, "misfortune"; Jews called it Ama Reka, Hebrew for "without soul"; and Slavs referred to it as Dollerica.

To alleviate the stress of adjustment to life in an unfamiliar city, newcomers often established close-knit ethnic communities. European immigrants usually preferred to live together with people from their own country of origin, if possible from their home district. The poorest of new immigrants, like the Italians of Providence, Rhode Island, or the Slavs of Homestead, Pennsylvania, made special sacrifices to resettle with people who would be familiar to them. Aunts and uncles became almost as dear as parents, cousins as close as brothers and sisters. Young adults married within their communities, often setting up households within a few blocks of their parents and not infrequently within the same "triple-decker" or tenement.

Many newcomers, having little choice about their place of residence, concentrated in districts marked off by racial or ethnic lines. In San Francisco, city ordinances prevented Chinese from operating laundries in most of the city's neighborhoods, effectively confining the population to Chinatown. In Los Angeles and San Antonio, Mexicans lived in distinctive barrios. In most cities, African American families were similarly compelled to remain in the dingiest, most crime-ridden, and dangerous sections of town.

Young people who had left their families behind, whether in Europe or in the American countryside, usually took rooms in small residential hotels or boardinghouses. The Young Men's Christian Association, established in the 1850s, and the Young Women's Christian Association, organized a decade later, provided temporary residences mainly to native-born, white, self-supporting men and women. The most successful "women adrift," such as clerical workers and retail clerks, lived in the new furnished-room districts bordering the city's business center. The least prosperous landed on skid row, where homeless people spent time in the rough taverns, eating free lunches in return for purchased beer, waiting for casual labor, and sometimes trading sexual favors for money.

The working-class home did not necessarily ensure privacy or offer protection from the dangers of the outside world. In the tenements, families often shared their rooms with other families or paying boarders. During the summer heat, adults, children, and boarders alike competed for a sleeping place on the fire escape or roof, and all year round noise resounded through paper-thin walls. But so complex and varied were income levels and social customs that no single pattern emerged. Packingtown's Slovaks, Lithuanians, and Poles, for example, frequently took in boarders, yet Bohemians rarely did. Neither did the skilled iron rollers who worked at the Carnegie Steel Company in Homestead, Pennsylvania. These well-paid craft workers often owned their own homes, boasting parlors and even imported Belgian carpets. At the other extreme, Italian immigrants, who considered themselves fortunate to get work with a shovel, usually lived in overcrowded rented apartments, just a paycheck away from eviction.

Whether it was a small cottage or a tenement flat, the working-class home involved women and children in routines of household labor without the aid of the new mechanical devices. In addition to cooking and cleaning, women used their cramped domestic space for work that provided a small income. They gathered their children—and their husbands after a hard day's labor—to sew garments, wrap cigars, string beads, or paint vases for a contractor who paid them by the piece. And they cooked and cleaned for the boarders whose rent supplemented the family income. In short, the home was a second workplace, usually involving the entire family.

Despite working people's slim resources, their combined buying power created new and important markets for consumer goods. Often they bought shoddy replicas of products sold to the middle class: cheaper canned goods, inferior cuts of meat, and partially spoiled fruit. Several leading clothing manufacturers specialized in inexpensive ready-to-wear items, usually copied from patterns designed for wealthier consumers but constructed hastily from flimsy materials. Patent medicines for ailments caused by working long periods in cramped conditions sold well in working-class communities, where money for doctors was scarce. These nostrums failed to restore health, except perhaps through the power of suggestion. On the other hand, their high alcohol content might lift people's spirits, if only temporarily.

The close quarters of the urban neighborhood allowed immigrants to preserve many Old World

The intersection of Orchard and Hester Streets on New York's Lower East Side, photographed ca. 1905. Unlike the middle classes, who worked and played hidden away in offices and private homes, the Jewish lower-class immigrants who lived and worked in this neighborhood spent the greater parts of their lives on the streets. Here children and adults mingle, partaking in both business and conversation.

customs. In immigrant communities such as Chicago's Packingtown, Pittsburgh's Poletown, New York's Lower East Side, or San Francisco's Chinatown, people usually spoke their native language while visiting their friends and relatives. The men might play cards while women and children gathered in the stairwell or on the front stoop to trade stories. In good weather they walked and talked, an inexpensive pastime common in European cities. No organization was as important as the fraternal society, which sponsored social clubs and provided insurance benefits. Immigrants also re-created Old World religious institutions such as the church or synagogue, or secular institutions such as German family-style taverns or Russian Jewish tearooms. They replicated their native cuisine (as much as available foods allowed), sang their own songs accompanied by polka, mazurka, or tamburitza music according to tradition, and married, baptized children, and buried the dead according to Old World customs.

In the cosmopolitan cities, immigrants, by being innovative entrepreneurs as well as best customers, helped to shape the emerging popular culture. German immigrants, for example, created Tin Pan Alley, the center of the popular music industry, and wrote such well-liked ballads as "Down by the Old Mill Stream." They also became the first promoters of ragtime, which found its way north from Storyville, the red-light district of New Orleans. Created by African American and creole bands, ragtime captivated those teenage offspring of immigrants who rushed to the new dance halls. Disdaining their parents' sentimental favorites, such as "Beautiful Dreamer," the youngsters seemed to associate the new syncopated sounds with the pulse of urban life. They also gave ragtime musicians paying work and budding musical entrepreneurs the idea that music with African American roots could become the biggest commercial entertainment of all.

In the same years, the first great amusement parks began to enthrall masses of immigrants and other city dwellers. The most spectacular was Coney Island, at the southern edge of Brooklyn, New York, which grew out of a series of fancy hotels and gambling (and prostitution) parlors. When developers realized that "wholesome fun" for the masses could pay better than upper-class leisure or lower-class vice, they decided to transform Coney Island into a magnificent seaside park filled with ingenious amusements such as water slides, mechanized horse races, roller coasters, and fun houses. It opened in 1895. On the rides or at the nearby beach, young men and women could easily meet apart from their parents, cast off their inhibitions, and enjoy a hug or kiss. Or they could simply stroll through the grounds, looking at exotic performers, enjoying make-believe trips to the Far East or even the moon, entranced by fantastic towers, columns, minarets, and lagoons lit up at night to resemble dreams rather than reality. Here millions of working-class people enjoyed cheap thrills that offset the hardships of their working lives.

CULTURES IN CONFLICT, CULTURE IN COMMON

The new commercial entertainments gave Americans from various backgrounds more in common than they would otherwise have had. On New York's Lower East Side, for instance, theater blossomed with dramas that Broadway would adopt years later, while children dreamed of going "uptown" where the popular songs they heard on the streets were transcribed onto sheet music and sold in stores throughout the city. Even so, nothing could smooth the tensions caused by conflicting claims to the same resources, such as public schools and urban parks.

Education

As industries grew and cities expanded, so did the nation's public school system. Business and civic leaders realized that the welfare of society now depended on an educated population, one possessing the skills and knowledge required to keep both industry and government running. In the last three decades of the nineteenth century, the idea of universal free schooling, at least for white children, took hold. Kindergartens in particular flourished. St. Louis, Missouri, opened the first public school kindergarten in 1873, and by the turn of the century more than 4,000 similar programs throughout the country enrolled children between the ages of three and seven.

The number of public high schools also increased, from 160 in 1870 to 6,000 by the end of the century. In Chicago alone, average daily attendance increased sixfold. Despite this spectacular growth, which was concentrated in urban industrial areas, as late as 1890 only 4 percent of children between the ages of fourteen and seventeen were enrolled in school, the majority of them girls planning to become teachers or office workers. Most high schools continued to serve mainly the middle class. In 1893 the National Education Association reaffirmed the major purpose of the nation's high schools as preparation for college, rather than for work in trades or industry, and endorsed a curriculum of rigorous training in the classics, such as Latin, Greek, and ancient history. The expected benefits of this kind of education rarely outweighed the immediate needs of families who depended on their children's wages.

Higher education also expanded along several lines. Agricultural colleges formed earlier in the century developed into institutes of technology and took their places alongside the prestigious liberal arts colleges. To extend learning to the "industrial classes," Representative Justin Morrill of Vermont sponsored the Morrill Federal Land Grant Act of 1862, which funded a system of state colleges and universities for teaching agriculture and mechanics "without excluding other scientific and classic studies." Meanwhile, established private institutions like Harvard, Yale, Princeton, and Columbia grew, with the help of huge endowments from business leaders such as Rockefeller and Carnegie. By 1900, sixty-three Catholic colleges were serving mainly the children of immigrants from Ireland and eastern and southern Europe. Still, as the overall number of colleges and universities grew from 563 in 1870 to nearly 1,000 by 1910, only 3 percent of the college-age population took advantage of these new opportunities.

One of the most important developments occurred in the area of professional training. Although medical and law schools dated from the mid-eighteenth century, their numbers grew rapidly after the Civil War. Younger professions, such as engineering, pharmacy, and journalism, also established specialized training institutions. In 1876 the Johns Hopkins University pioneered a program of research and graduate studies, and by the end of the century several American universities, including Stanford University and the University of Chicago, offered advanced degrees in the arts and sciences.

This expansion benefited women, who previously had had little access to higher education. After the Civil War, a number of women's colleges were founded, beginning in 1865 with Vassar, which set the academic standard for the remainder of the century. Smith and Wellesley followed in 1875, Bryn Mawr in 1885. By the end of the century 125 women's colleges offered a first-rate education comparable to that given to men at Harvard, Yale, or Princeton. Meanwhile, coeducation grew at an even faster rate; by 1890, 47 percent of the nation's colleges and universities admitted women. The proportion of women college students changed dramatically. Women constituted 21 percent of undergraduate enrollments in 1870, 32 percent in 1880, and 40 percent in 1910. Despite these gains, many professions remained closed to women.

An even greater number of women enrolled in vocational courses. Normal schools, which offered one- or two-year programs for women who planned to become elementary school teachers, developed a collegiate character after the Civil War and had become accredited state teachers' colleges by the end of the century. Normal schools enrolled many women from rural areas, particularly from poor families. Upon graduation, these women filled the personnel ranks of the rapidly expanding system of public education. Other institutions, many founded by middle-class philanthropists, also prepared women for vocations. For example, the first training school for nurses opened in Boston in 1873, followed in 1879 by a diet kitchen that taught women to become cooks in the city's hospitals. Founded in 1877, the Women's Educational and Industrial Union offered a multitude of classes to Boston's wage-earning women, ranging from elementary French and German to drawing, watercolors, oil and china painting, to dressmaking, millinery, stenography, typing, as well as crafts less familiar to women, such as upholstering, cabinetmaking, and carpentry. In the early 1890s, when the entering class at a large women's college like Vassar still averaged under 100, the Boston Women's Educational and Industrial Union reported that its staff of 83 served an estimated 1,500 clients per day. By that time, one of its most well-funded programs was a training school for domestic servants.

The leaders of the business community had also begun to promote manual training for working-class and immigrant boys. One leading San Francisco merchant described the philosophy behind this movement as a desire to train boys "to earn a living with little study and plenty of work." Craft unionists in several cities actively opposed this development, preferring their own methods of apprenticeship to training programs they could not control. But local associations of merchants and manufacturers lobbied hard for "industrial education" and raised funds to supplement the public school budget. In 1884 the Chicago Manual Training School opened teaching "shop work" along with a few academic subjects, and by 1895 all elementary and high schools in the city offered courses that trained working-class boys for future jobs in industry and business.

The expansion of education did not benefit all Americans or benefit them all in the same way. Because African Americans were prohibited from enrolling in colleges attended by white students, special colleges were founded in the southern states shortly after the Civil War. All-black Atlanta and Fisk both soon offered a rigorous curriculum in the liberal arts. Other institutions, such as Hampton, founded in 1868, specialized in vocational training, mainly in manual trades. Educator Booker T. Washington encouraged African Americans to resist "the craze for Greek and Latin learning" and to strive for practical instruction. In 1881 he founded the Tuskegee Institute in Alabama to provide industrial education and moral uplift. By the turn of the century, Tuskegee enrolled 1,400 men and women in more than thirty different vocational courses, including special cooking classes for homemakers and domestic servants. Black colleges, including Tuskegee, trained so many teachers that by the century's end the majority of black schools were staffed by African Americans.

The nation's educational system was becoming more inclusive and yet more differentiated. The majority of children attended school for several years or more. At the same time, students were tracked—by race, gender, and class—to fill particular roles in an industrial society.

Leisure and Public Space

Most large cities set aside open land for leisure-time use by residents. New York's Central Park opened for ice skating in 1858, providing a model for urban park systems across the United States. These parks were rolling expanses, cut across by streams and pathways and footbridges and set off by groves of trees, ornamental shrubs, and neat flower gardens. According to the designers' vision, the urban middle class might find here a respite from the stresses of modern life. To ensure this possibility, posted regulations forbade many activities, ranging from walking on the grass to gambling, picnicking or ball playing without permission, and speeding in carriages.

The working classes had their own ideas about the use of parks and open land. Trapped in overcrowded tenements, they wanted space for sports, picnics, and lovers' trysts. Young people openly defied ordinances that prohibited play on the grassy knolls, while their elders routinely voted against municipal bonds that did not include funds for more recreational space in their communities. Immigrant ward representatives on the Pittsburgh city council, for instance, argued that band shells for classical music meant little to their constituents, while spaces suitable for sports meant much.

Eventually, most park administrators set aside some sections for playgrounds and athletic fields and others for public gardens and band shells. Yet intermittent conflicts erupted. The Worcester, Massachusetts, park system, for example, allowed sports leagues to schedule events but prohibited pickup games. This policy gave city officials more control over the use of the park for outdoor recreation but at the same time forced many ball-playing boys into the streets. When working-class parents protested, city officials responded by instituting programs of supervised play, to the further dismay of the children.

Public drinking of alcoholic beverages, especially on Sunday, provoked similar disputes. Pittsburgh's "blue laws," forbidding businesses to open on Sunday, were rigidly enforced when it came to neighborhood taverns, while large firms like the railroads enjoyed exemptions. Although the Carnegie Institute hoped to discourage Sunday drinking by sponsoring alternative events, such as free organ recitals and other concerts, many working people, especially beer-loving German immigrants, continued to treat Sunday as their one day of relaxation and gathered for picnics in the city's parks.

Toward the end of the century, many park administrators relaxed the rules and expanded the range of permitted activities. By this time, large numbers of the middle class had become sports enthusiasts and pressured municipal governments to turn meadowlands into tennis courts and golfing greens. In the 1890s bicycling brought many women into the parks. Still, not all city residents enjoyed these facilities. Officials in St. Louis, for example, barred African Americans from the city's grand Forest Park and set aside the smaller Tandy Park for their use. After challenging this policy in court, African Americans won a few concessions, such as the right to picnic at any time in Forest Park and to use the golf course on Monday mornings.

One of the finest American painters of the period, known for realistic depictions of physical exertion in amateur athletics, Thomas Eakins here turned his attention to the commercial baseball park. The batter and catcher appear as well-poised athletes, dignified in their dress and manner—everything that the baseball player of the late nineteenth century was not very likely to be.

Thomas Eakins. *Baseball Players.* 1875. Watercolor. The Rhode Island School of Design Museum of Art

National Pastimes

Toward the end of the century, the younger members of the urban middle class had begun to find common ground in lower-class pastimes, especially ragtime music. Introduced to many Northerners by the African American composer Scott Joplin at the Chicago World's Fair of 1893, "rag" quickly became the staple of entertainment in the new cabarets and nightclubs. Middle-class urban dwellers began to seek out ragtime bands and congregated in nightclubs and even on rooftops of posh hotels to listen and dance and even to drink.

Vaudeville, the most popular form of commercial entertainment since the 1880s, also bridged middle- and working-class tastes. Drawing on a variety-show tradition of singers, dancers, comedians, jugglers, and acrobats who had entertained Americans since colonial days, "vaude" became a big business that made ethnic and racial stereotypes and the daily frustrations of city life into major topics of amusement. Vaudeville palaces—ten in New York, six in Philadelphia, five in Chicago, and at least one in every other large city—attracted huge, "respectable" crowds that sampled between twenty and thirty dramatic, musical, and comedy acts averaging fifteen minutes each. One study estimated that before vaudeville gave way to movie theaters in the 1920s, between 14 and 16 percent of all city dwellers attended shows at least once a week. Sunday matinees were especially popular with women and children.

Sports, however, outdistanced all other commercial entertainments in appealing to all kinds of fans and managing to create a sense of national identity. No doubt the most popular parks in the United States were the expanses of green surrounded by grandstands and marked by their unique diamond shape—the baseball field. During the last quarter of the nineteenth century the amateur sport of gentlemen and Union soldiers suddenly became the "national pastime." Both American and English children had for years been playing a form of baseball, known mainly as "rounders," when a group of young men in Manhattan formed the Knickerbocker Base Ball Club in 1845 and proceeded to set down the game's rules in writing. Baseball clubs soon formed in many cities, and shortly after the Civil War traveling teams with regular schedules made baseball a professional sport. The formation of the National League in 1876 encouraged other spectator sports, but for generations baseball remained the most popular.

Rowdy behavior gave the game a working-class ambience. Well-loved players known for their saloon brawls occasionally disappeared for a few days on "benders." Team owners, themselves often proprietors of local breweries, counted heavily on beer sales

in the parks. Having to contend with hundreds of drunken fans, officials maintained order only with great difficulty. Outfielders occasionally leaped into the grandstand to punch spectators who had heckled them. To attract more subdued middle-class fans, the National League raised admission prices, banned the sale of alcohol, and observed Sunday blue laws. Catering to a working-class audience, the American Association kept the price of admission low, sold liquor, and played ball on Sunday.

Baseball, like many other sports, soon became tied to the larger business economy. Entrepreneur Albert Spalding, manager and then president of the Chicago White Stockings, quickly came to see baseball as a source of multiple profits. He procured the exclusive rights to manufacture the official ball and the rule book, while producing large varieties of other sporting equipment. Meanwhile, he built impressive baseball parks in Chicago with seating for 10,000 and special private boxes above the grandstands for the wealthy. He easily became the foremost figure in the National League.

Spalding also succeeded in tightening the rules of participation in the sport. In 1879 he dictated

CHRONOLOGY

1862	Morrill Act authorizes "land-grant" colleges		Chinese Exclusion Act passed
			Standard Oil Trust founded
1866	National Labor Union founded	1886	Campaigns for eight-hour workday peak
1869	Knights of Labor founded		Haymarket riot and massacre discredit the Knights of Labor
1870	Standard Oil founded		American Federation of Labor founded
1871	Chicago Fire		
1873	Financial panic brings severe depression	1890	Sherman Antitrust Act passed
1876	Baseball's National League founded	1893	Stock market panic precipitates severe depression
	Alexander Graham Bell patents the telephone	1895	Coney Island opens
1879	Thomas Edison invents the incandescent bulb	1896	Rural free delivery begins
	Depression ends	1900	Andrew Carnegie's *Gospel of Wealth* recommends honesty and fair dealing
1881	Tuskegee Institute founded	1901	U.S. Steel Corporation formed
1882	Peak of immigration to the United States (1.2 million) in the nineteenth century		

the "reserve clause" that prevented players from negotiating a better deal and leaving the team that originally signed them. He encouraged his player-manager "Cap" Anson to forbid the White Stockings to play against any team with an African American member, thereby setting the standard for professional baseball. The firing of Moses "Fleet" Walker from the Cincinnati team in 1884 marked the first time the color line had been drawn in a major professional sport. Effectively excluded, African Americans organized their own traveling teams. In the 1920s they formed the Negro Leagues, which produced some of the nation's finest ballplayers.

Players occasionally organized to regain control over their sport. They frequently complained about low wages and arbitrary rules, and like factory workers in the 1880s they formed their own league, the Brotherhood of Professional Base Ball Players, with profits divided between participants and investors. This effort failed, partly because fans would not desert the established leagues, but mostly because successful baseball franchises demanded large quantities of capital. American sports had become big business.

As attendance continued to grow, the enthusiasm for baseball straddled major social divisions, bringing together Americans of many backgrounds, if only on a limited basis. By the end of the century, no section of the daily newspaper drew more readers than the sports pages. Although it interested relatively few women, sports news riveted the attention of men from all social classes. Loyalty to the "home team" helped to create an urban identity, while individual players became national heroes.

CONCLUSION

By the end of the nineteenth century, industry and the growing cities had opened a new world for Americans. Fresh from Europe or from the native countryside, ordinary urban dwellers struggled to form communities of fellow newcomers through work and leisure, in the factory, the neighborhood, the ballpark, and the public school. Their "betters," the wealthy and the new middle class, meanwhile made and executed the decisions of industry and marketing, established the era's grand civic institutions, and set the tone for high fashion and art.

Rich and poor alike shared many aspects of the new order. Yet inequality persisted and increased, as much a part of the new order as the Brooklyn Bridge or advertising. During the mostly prosperous 1880s, optimists believed that unfair treatment based on region, on class, and perhaps even on race and gender might ease in time. By the depressed 1890s, however, these hopes had worn thin, and the lure of overseas empire appeared as one of the few goals that held together a suffering and divided nation.

REVIEW QUESTIONS

1. Discuss the sources of economic growth in the decades after the Civil War. Historians often refer to this period as the era of the "second industrial revolution." Do you agree with this description?

2. Describe the impact of new technologies and new forms of production on the routines of industrial workers. How did these changes affect African American and women workers in particular? What role did trade unions play in this process?

3. Choose one major city, such as Boston, New York, Chicago, Birmingham, or San Francisco, and discuss changes in its economy, population, and urban space in the decades after the Civil War.

4. Discuss the role of northern capital in the development of the New South. How did the rise of industry affect the lives of rural Southerners? Analyze these changes from the point of view of African Americans.

5. How did urban life change during the Gilded Age? How did economic development affect residential patterns? How did the middle class aspire to live during the Gilded Age? How did their lifestyles compare with those of working-class urbanites?

6. How did the American educational system change to prepare children for their adult roles in the new industrial economy?

7. How did the rise of organized sports and commercial amusements reflect and shape social divisions at the end of the century? Which groups were affected most (or least) by new leisure activities?

RECOMMENDED READING

James R. Barrett, *Work and Community in the Jungle* (1987). A very close study of the Packingtown district of Chicago, Illinois, at the turn of the century. Barrett describes the transformation of animals to meat in great stockyards and processing plants. He also provides rich documentation of neighborhood life.

Alfred D. Chandler Jr., *The Visible Hand: The Managerial Revolution in American Business* (1977). A highly acclaimed study of corporate management. Chandler shows how the rapid growth in the scale of business, as well as its influence in public life, brought about a new type of executive with skills for national decision making and close links with others of his kind.

William Cronon, *Nature's Metropolis* (1991). Analyzes the changing economic and political relationship between the city of Chicago and the surrounding countryside. Cronon demonstrates through a variety of evidence the tight interdependence of urban and rural regions.

Herbert G. Gutman, *Work, Culture and Society in Industrializing America: Essays in American Working-Class and Social History* (1977). Influential essays on the formation of working-class communities in the nineteenth century. Gutman focuses on the role of immigrants in transforming the values and belief systems of working-class Americans in the throes of industrialization.

John F. Kasson, *Amusing the Millions: Coney Island at the Turn of the Century* (1978). A heavily illustrated account of America's favorite amusement park. Kasson sees Coney Island as the meeting point for shrewd entrepreneurs and pleasure-seeking immigrants, its amusements and architectural styles emblematic of a special era in American history.

Alice Kessler-Harris, *Out to Work: A History of Wage-Earning Women in the United States* (1982). A comprehensive survey of women's increasing participation in the labor force. Kessler-Harris documents women's role in trade unions but also the impact on family patterns and ideas about women's role in American society.

Kenneth L. Kusmer, *A Ghetto Takes Shape, Black Cleveland, 1870–1930* (1976). A keen analysis of a long-standing African American community. Kusmer shows how blacks suffered downward mobility and increased segregation as their skilled jobs and small-business opportunities were given to European immigrants.

Lawrence H. Larsen, *The Rise of the Urban South* (1985). Studies of the changing South. In Larson's view, the true New South was the city, for relatively few had lived there before the late nineteenth century, but rural values remained vital, especially in religious life and voting patterns.

David F. Noble, *America by Design: Science, Technology and the Rise of Corporate Capitalism* (1977). A view of scientific advancement and its connections with the expanding economy. Noble shows how scientific breakthroughs were often created for, but especially adapted to, corporate purposes.

Dave Roediger and Franklin Rosemont, eds., *Haymarket Scrapbook* (1986). A large, beautifully illustrated book about the events and consequences of the Haymarket tragedy.

Roy Rosenzweig, *Eight Hours for What We Will: Workers and Leisure in an Industrial City, 1870–1920* (1983). Analyzes class and cultural conflicts over recreational space. This valuable book treats the city park as the arena for conflict over whether public community life should be uplifting (devoted to nature walks and concerts) or entertaining (for drinking, courting, and amusement).

Alan Trachtenberg, *The Incorporation of America: Culture and Society in the Gilded Age* (1982). One of the best and most readable overviews of the post–Civil War era. Trachtenberg devotes great care to describing the rise of the corporation to the defining institution of national life, and the reorientation of culture to reflect the new middle classes employed by the corporation.

ADDITIONAL BIBLIOGRAPHY

Science, Technology, and Industry

David A. Hounshell, *From the American System to Mass Production, 1800–1932* (1984)

David Landes, *The Unbound Prometheus: Technological Change and Industrial Development* (1969)

Walter Licht, *Industrializing America: The Nineteenth Century* (1995)

A. J. Millard, *Edison and the Business of Innovation* (1990)

Leonard S. Reich, *The Making of American Industrial Research: Science and Business at G.E. and Bell, 1876–1926* (1985)

Howard Segal, *Technological Utopianism in American Culture* (1985)

Business and the Economy

Wendy Gambler, *The Female Economy: The Millinery and Dressmaking Trades, 1860–1930* (1997)

Robert Higgs, *Competition and the Economy: Blacks in the American Economy, 1865–1914* (1977)

Howard Horwitz, *By the Law of Nature: Form and Value in Nineteenth Century America* (1990)

John Ingham, *Iron Barons: A Social Analysis of an Urban Elite* (1978)

Naomi R. Lamoreaux, *The Great Merger Movement in American Business, 1895–1904* (1985)

Daniel Nelson, *Managers and Workers: Origins of the Factory System in the United States, 1880–1920* (1975)

Sarah Lyons Watts, *Order against Chaos: Business Culture and Labor Ideology in America, 1800–1915* (1991)

Olivier Zunz, *Making America Corporate, 1870–1920* (1990)

Working Class and Labor

Eric Arnesen, *Waterfront Workers of New Orleans: Race, Class, and Politics, 1863–1923* (1991)

John Bodnar, *Immigration and Industrialization: Ethnicity in an American Mill Town* (1977)

Lisa M. Fine, *The Souls of the Skyscraper: Female Clerical Workers in Chicago, 1870–1930* (1990)

Leon Fink, *Workingmen's Democracy: The Knights of Labor and American Politics* (1983)

Victoria C. Hattam, *Labor Visions and State Power* (1993)

David M. Katzman, *Seven Days a Week: Women and Domestic Service in Industrializing America* (1978)

David Montgomery, *The Fall of the House of Labor: The Workplace, the State, and American Labor Activism, 1865–1925* (1987)

Dominic A. Pacyga, *Polish Immigrants and Industrial Chicago* (1991)

Daniel T. Rodgers, *The Work Ethic in Industrial America, 1850–1920* (1978)

The Industrial City

Lewis F. Fried, *Makers of the City* (1990)

John S. Garner, ed., *The Midwest in American Architecture* (1991)

James Gilbert, *Perfect Cities: Chicago's Utopias of 1893* (1991)

Dolores Hayden, *The Grand Domestic Revolution: A History of Feminist Designs for American Homes, Neighborhoods, and Cities* (1981)

Scott Molloy, *Trolley Wars: Streetcar Workers on the Line* (1996)

Roy Rosenzweig and Elizabeth Blackmar, *The Park and the People: A History of Central Park* (1993)

John R. Stilgoe, *Borderland: Origins of the American Suburb, 1820–1939* (1988)

The New South

Edward L. Ayers, *The Promise of the New South* (1992)

Don Doyle, *New Men, New Cities, New South* (1990)

Jacquelyn D. Hall, et al., *Like a Family: The Making of a Southern Cotton Mill World* (1987)

Gerald D. Jaynes, *Branches without Roots: Genesis of the Black Working Class in the American South, 1862–1882* (1986)

Cathy McHugh, *Mill Family: The Labor System in the Southern Textile Industry, 1880–1915* (1988)

Allen Tullos, *Habits of Industry: White Culture and the Transformation of the Carolina Piedmont* (1989)

Society and Culture

Elaine S. Abelson, *When Ladies Go A-Thieving* (1989)

Stuart Blumin, *The Emergence of the Middle Class* (1989)

Perry Duis, *The Saloon: Public Drinking in Chicago and Boston, 1880–1920* (1983)

John F. Kasson, *Rudeness and Civility: Manners in Nineteenth-Century Urban America* (1992)

Lawrence W. Levine, *Black Culture and Black Consciousness* (1977)

Patricia Marks, *Bicycles, Bangs, and Bloomers: The New Woman in the Popular Press* (1990)

Steven A. Riess, *City Games: The Evolution of American Urban Society and the Rise of Sports* (1989)

Barbara M. Solomon, *In the Company of Educated Women: A History of Women and Higher Education in America* (1985)

Louise L. Stevenson, *The Victorian Homefront: American Thought and Culture, 1860–1880* (1991)

Biography

Robert V. Bruce, *Alexander Graham Bell and the Conquest of Solitude* (1973)

Helen Lefkowitz Horowitz, *The Power and Passion of M. Carey Thomas* (1994)

Stuart B. Kaufman, *Samuel Gompers and the Rise of the American Federation of Labor, 1884–1896* (1973)

Murray Klein, *The Life and Legend of Jay Gould* (1986)

Emily Toth, *Kate Chopin: The Life of the Author of* The Awakening (1990)

Robert C. Twombly, *Louis Sullivan* (1986)

COMMONWEALTH AND EMPIRE

1870–1900

R. F. Zogbaum, *Dewey at Manila*, 1899. Oil on canvas, 60 x 48 inches, Vermont State House, Montpelier, Vermont.

CHAPTER OUTLINE

AMERICAN COMMUNITIES
The Cooperative Commonwealth

Edward Bellamy's *Looking Backward* (1888), the century's best-selling novel after Harriet Beecher Stowe's *Uncle Tom's Cabin*, tells the story of a young man who awakens in the year 2000 after a sleep lasting more than 100 years. He is surprised to learn that Americans had solved their major problems. Poverty, crime, war, taxes, air pollution—even housework—no longer exist. Nor are there politicians, capitalists, bankers, or lawyers. Most amazing, gone is the great social division between the powerful rich and the suffering poor. In the year 2000 everyone lives in material comfort, happily and harmoniously. No wonder Bellamy's hero shudders at the thought of returning to the late nineteenth century, a time of "worldwide bloodshed, greed and tyranny."

Community and cooperation are the key concepts in Bellamy's utopian tale. The nation's businesses, including farms and factories, have been given over to the collective ownership of the people. Elected officials now plan the production and distribution of goods for the common well-being. With great efficiency, they even manage huge department stores and warehouses full of marvelous manufactured goods and oversee majestic apartment complexes with modern facilities for cooking, dining, and laundering. To get the necessary work done, an industrial army enlists all adult men and women, but automated machinery has eliminated most menial tasks. The workday is only four hours; vacations extend to six months of each year. At forty-five everyone retires to pursue hobbies, sports, and culture.

Bellamy envisioned his technological utopia promoting the "highest possible physical, as well as mental, development for everyone." There was nothing fantastic in this plan, the author insisted. It simply required Americans to share equally the abundant resources of their land. If the nation's citizens actually lived up to their democratic ideals, Bellamy declared, the United States would become a "cooperative commonwealth," that is, a nation governed by the people for their common welfare.

Bellamy, a journalist and writer of historical fiction from Chicopee Falls, Massachusetts, moved thousands of his readers to action. His most ardent fans endorsed his program for a "new nation" and formed the Nationalist movement, which by the early 1890s reached an apex of 165 clubs. Terence V. Powderly of the Knights of Labor declared himself a Nationalist. Many leaders of the woman suffrage movement also threw in their support. They endorsed *Looking Backward*'s depiction of marriage as a union of "perfect equals" and admired Bellamy's sequel, *Equality* (1897), which showed how women might become "absolutely free agents" by ending their financial dependence on men.

During the 1890s Bellamy's disciples actually attempted to create new communities along the lines set forth in *Looking Backward*. The best known and longest lasting of these settlements was

579

established in Point Loma, California, in 1897. Situated on 330 acres, with avenues winding through gardens and orchards newly planted with groves of eucalyptus trees, Point Loma was known for its physical beauty. Many young married couples chose to live in small bungalows, which were scattered throughout the colony's grounds; others opted for private rooms in a large communal building. Either way, they all met twice daily to share meals and usually spent their leisure hours together. On the ocean's edge the residents constructed an outdoor amphitheater and staged plays and concerts.

The colony's founder, Katherine Tingley, described Point Loma as "a practical illustration of the possibility of developing a higher type of humanity." No one earned wages, but all 500 residents lived comfortably. They dressed simply in clothes manufactured by the community's women. The majority of the men worked in agriculture. They conducted horticultural experiments that yielded new types of avocados and tropical fruits and eventually produced over half of the community's food supply. Children, who slept in a special dormitory from the time they reached school age, enjoyed an outstanding education. They excelled in the fine arts, including music and drama, and often demonstrated their talents to audiences in nearby San Diego.

The Point Loma community never met all its expenses, but with the help of donations from admirers across the country it remained solvent for decades. Baseball entrepreneur Albert Spalding, who lived there during his retirement, helped make up the financial deficit. As late as the 1950s the community still had some seventy-five members living on about 100 acres of land.

Even relatively successful cooperative communities such as Point Loma, however, could not bring about the changes that Bellamy hoped to see, and he knew it. Only a mobilization of citizens nationwide could overturn the existing hierarchies and usher in the egalitarian order depicted in *Looking Backward*. Without such a rigorous challenge, the economic and political leadership that had been emerging since the Civil War would continue to consolidate its power and become even further removed from popular control.

The last quarter of the nineteenth century saw just such a challenge, producing what one historian calls "a moment of democratic promise." Ordinary citizens sought to renew the older values of community through farm and labor organizations as well as philanthropic and charitable societies. They could not clearly see, however, that the fate of the nation depended increasingly on events beyond its territorial boundaries. Business leaders and politicians had proposed their own vision of the future: an American empire extending to far distant lands.

Point Loma

KEY TOPICS

- The growth of federal and state governments and the consolidation of the modern two-party system

- The development of mass protest movements

- Economic and political crisis in the 1890s

- The United States as a world power

- The Spanish-American War

TOWARD A NATIONAL GOVERNING CLASS

The basic structure of government changed dramatically in the last quarter of the nineteenth century. Mirroring the fast-growing economy, public administration expanded at all levels—municipal, county, state, and federal—and took on greater responsibility for regulating society, especially market and property relations. Whereas most political theorists continued to advise that the best government is the one that governs least, governments began to do much more than simply maintain order.

This expansion offered ample opportunities for politicians who were eager to compete against one another for control of the new mechanisms of power. Political campaigns, especially those staged for the presidential elections, became mass spectacles, and votes became precious commodities. The most farsighted politicians attempted to rein in the growing corruption and to promote both efficiency and professionalism in the expanding structures of government.

The Growth of Government

Before the Civil War, local governments attended mainly to the promotion and regulation of trade and relied on private enterprise to supply vital services such as fire protection and water supply. As cities became more responsible for their residents' well-being, they introduced professional police and firefighting forces and began to finance school systems, public libraries, and parks. Municipal ownership and administration of basic services became so common that by the end of the century only nine of the nation's fifty largest cities still depended on private corporations for their water supplies.

This expansion demanded huge increases in local taxation. Boston, for example, spent five times more per resident in 1875 than it did just thirty years earlier, and its municipal debt rose from $784,000 to more than $27 million. The city now paid the salaries of many civil servants, including a growing class of sanitary engineers. By 1880 one of every eight New York voters appeared on a government payroll.

At the national level, mobilization for the Civil War and Reconstruction had demanded an unprecedented degree of coordination, and the federal government continued to expand under the weight of new tasks and responsibilities. Federal revenues also skyrocketed, from $257 million in 1878 to $567 million in 1900. The administrative bureaucracy also grew dramatically, from 50,000 employees in 1871 to 100,000 only a decade later.

The modern apparatus of departments, bureaus, and cabinets took shape amid this upswing. The Department of Agriculture was established in 1862 to provide information to farmers and to consumers of farm products. The Department of the Interior, which had been created in 1849, grew into the largest and most important federal department after the Post Office. It came to comprise more than twenty agencies, including the Bureau of Indian Affairs, the U.S. Geological Survey, and the Bureau of Territorial and International Affairs. The Department of the Treasury, responsible for collecting federal taxes and customs as well as printing money and stamps, grew from 4,000 employees in 1873 to nearly 25,000 in 1900. The Pension Act of 1890 made virtually

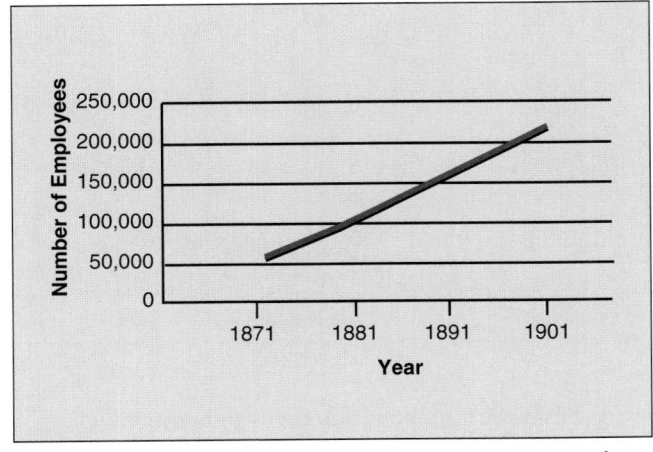

Federal Employment by Decade, 1871–1901 *The expansion of government created a bureaucracy of employees and great opportunities for political patronage.*

Source: David Nachmias and David H. Rosenbloom, *Bureaucratic Government USA* (New York: St. Martin's Press, 1980), p. 39.

OVERVIEW

PRESIDENTIAL POLITICS, 1868–1900

Presidential election year	Winning candidate (party)	Popular vote margin	Major issues
1868	Ulysses S. Grant (Republican)	5.4 percent	• Reconstruction • Suffrage for African American men • Monetary reform
1872	Ulysses S. Grant (Republican)	11.9 percent	• Civil Service reform • Government regulation • Reconstruction
1876	Rutherford B. Hayes (Republican)	-3 percent (election decided in House)	• Reconstruction • Corruption
1880	James A. Garfield (Republican)	.4 percent	• Monetary reform • Civil Service reform • Pensions for veterans • Chinese exclusion • Tariff
1884	Grover Cleveland (Democratic)	.3 percent	• Corruption • Civil Service reform • Tariff • Monetary reform
1888	Benjamin Harrison (Republican)	-.7 percent (Harrison won with a majority of electoral votes)	• Tariff • Veteran pension
1892	Grover Cleveland (Democratic)	3.1 percent	• Tariff • Government ownership of railroads • Monetary reform
1896	William McKinley (Republican)	3.4 percent	• Tariff • Monetary reform • Regulation of railroads
1900	William McKinley (Republican)	6.2 percent	• Imperialism • Monetary reform • Tariff

every Union army veteran and his dependents eligible for benefits; within a decade the Veterans Bureau became known as "the largest executive bureau in the world," employing nearly 60,000 men and women.

The nation's first independent regulatory agency, the Interstate Commerce Commission (ICC), was created in 1887 to bring order to the growing patchwork of state laws concerning railroads. The five-member commission appointed by the president approved freight and passenger rates set by the railroads. The ICC could take public testimony on possible violations, examine company records, and generally oversee enforcement of the law. This set a precedent for future regulation of trade as well as for positive government—that is, for the intervention of the government into the affairs of private enterprise. The establishment of the ICC also marked a shift in the balance of power from the states to the federal government.

The Machinery of Politics

Only gradually did Republicans and Democrats adapt to the demands of governmental expansion. The Republican Party continued to run on its Civil War record, pointing to its achievements in reuniting the nation and in passing new reform legislation. Democrats, by contrast, sought to reduce the influence of the federal government, slash expenditures, repeal legislation, and protect states' rights. While Republicans held on to their long-time constituencies, Democrats gathered support from southern white voters and immigrants newly naturalized in the North. But neither party commanded a clear majority of votes until the century drew to a close.

Presidents in the last quarter of the century—Rutherford B. Hayes (1877–81), James A. Garfield (1881), Chester A. Arthur (1881–85), Grover Cleveland (1885–89), Benjamin Harrison (1889–93), and Cleveland again (1893–97)—did not espouse a clear philosophy of government. They willingly yielded power to Congress and the state legislatures. Only 1 percent of the popular vote separated the presidential candidates in three of five elections between 1876 and 1892. Congressional races were equally tight, less than 2 percentage points separating total votes for Democratic and Republican candidates in all but one election in the decade before 1888. Democrats usually held a majority in the House and Republicans a majority in the Senate, but neither party had sufficient strength to govern effectively. One result was that Congress passed little legislation before 1890.

One major political issue of the late nineteenth century was the tariff. First instituted in 1789 to raise revenue for the young republic, the tariff imposed a fee on imported goods, especially manufactured commodities. Soon its major purpose became the protection of the nation's "infant industries" from foreign competition. Manufacturing regions, especially the Northeast, favored a protective policy, while agricultural regions like the South opposed high tariffs as unfair to farmers who had to pay the steep fees on imported necessities. Democrats, with a stronghold among southern voters, argued for sharp reductions in the tariff as a way to save the rural economy and to give a boost to workers. Republicans, who represented mainly business interests, raised tariffs to new levels on a wide array of goods during the Civil War and retained high tariffs as long as they held power.

Although their platforms encompassed broad national issues, none more important than the tariff, both political parties operated essentially as state or

This wooden noisemaker was designed for Grover Cleveland's presidential campaign in 1892. Pursuing the voters, political campaigners devised ingenious signs, buttons, and other miscellaneous novelties for supporters to display, especially at public demonstrations. When shaken vigorously, noisemakers literally demanded the attention of bystanders.

local organizations. Successful politicians responded primarily to the particular concerns of their constituents. To please local voters, Democrats and Republicans repeatedly crosscut each other by taking identical positions on controversial issues.

Candidates of both parties urged their "regulars" to turn out and pursued swing voters furiously. "We work through one campaign," quipped one candidate, "take a bath and start in on the next." Election paraphernalia—leaflets or pamphlets, banners, hats, flags, buttons, inscribed playing cards, or clay pipes featuring a likeness of a candidate's face or the party symbol—became a major expense for both parties. Partisans embraced the Democratic donkey or the Republican elephant as symbols of party fidelity. And voters did turn out. During the last quarter of the century, participation in presidential elections peaked at nearly 80 percent of those eligible to vote. Thousands, in fact, voted several times on any given election day; voters who had died, or had never lived, also miraculously cast ballots.

The rising costs of maintaining local organizations and orchestrating mammoth campaigns drove party leaders to seek ever-larger sources of revenue. Winners often seized and added to the "spoils" of office through an elaborate system of payoffs. Legislators who supported government subsidies for railroad corporations, for instance, commonly received stock in return and sometimes cash bribes. At the time, few politicians or business leaders regarded these practices as unethical.

At the local level, powerful bosses and political machines dominated both parties. Democrats William Marcy Tweed of New York's powerful political organization, Tammany Hall, and Michael "Hinky Dink" Kenna of Chicago specialized in giving municipal jobs to loyal voters and holiday food baskets to their families. Tweed's machine wooed working-class voters by expanding city services in their neighborhoods and even by staging major sporting events or entertainments for the Irish Americans and German Americans who made up over half of New York City's population. Hundreds of smaller political machines ruled cities and rural courthouses through a combination of "boodle" (bribe money) and personal favors.

Many federal jobs, meanwhile, changed hands each time the presidency passed from one party to another. More than 50 percent of all federal jobs were patronage positions—nearly 56,000 in 1881—jobs that could be awarded to loyal supporters as part of the "spoils" of the winner. Observers estimated that decisions about congressional patronage filled one-third of all legislators' time.

Noted critic John Jay Chapman, looking back at the history of candidates and elections, suggested that "the change of motive power behind the party organizations—from principles to money—was silently effected during the thirty years which followed the [Civil] war." No wonder Bellamy's utopian community operated without politicians and political parties.

One Politician's Story

A typical politician of the age was James Garfield, the nation's twentieth president. Born in a frontier Ohio log cabin in 1831, Garfield briefly worked as a canal boat driver, an experience he later exploited as proof of his humble origins. A Civil War hero—he fought at Shiloh, was honored for gallantry at Chickamauga, and was a major general when he took a seat in Congress in 1863—the Ohio legislator carefully prepared his move into the national political arena.

While serving in Congress, Garfield seemed at first committed to social reform. He introduced a bill to create a Department of Education, arguing that public education would prove the best stepping-stone to equality. He denounced his own Republican Party for allowing corruption to flourish during Ulysses S. Grant's administration. The nation's "next great fight," he insisted, would pit the people against the corporations.

With the failure of Reconstruction, Garfield shifted his stance and began to espouse more conservative views. Nearly defeated in a Democratic congressional landslide in 1874, he concluded that "the intelligence of the average American citizen" fell short of the demands of the democratic system. As a result, he came out against universal suffrage. Garfield now looked to the probusiness faction of the Republican Party as a vehicle for realizing his personal ambition. After six years of shrewd maneuvering, trading votes and favors to build his reputation, Garfield became the party's candidate for the 1880 presidential election. In a mediocre race with no outstanding issues, Garfield won by less than 40,000 popular votes out of 9 million cast.

Garfield the idealist had grown into Garfield the machine politician and lackluster president. He had already shown himself indecisive and even indifferent to governing when a frustrated patronage seeker shot him just 200 days after his inauguration. Like other presidents of his era, Garfield assumed that the nation's chief executive served as his party's titular leader and played mainly a ceremonial role in office.

The Spoils System and Civil Service Reform

For decades, critics in both parties had been calling without success for legislation to improve the quality of government. As early as 1865, Republican representative Thomas A. Jenckes of Rhode Island proposed a bill for civil service reform. Congress, however, feared that such a measure would hamper candidates in their relentless pursuit of votes. President Hayes took up the cause, introducing a few reforms in the New York Customhouse and federal post offices, but Congress again refused to join in a major reform effort. Finally, a group consisting of mainly professors, newspaper editors, lawyers, and ministers organized the Civil Service Reform Association and enlisted Democratic senator George H. Pendleton to sponsor reform legislation in Congress.

In January 1883, a bipartisan congressional majority passed the Pendleton Civil Service Reform Act. This measure allowed the president to create, with Senate approval, a three-person commission to draw up a set of guidelines for executive and legislative appointments. The commission established a system of standards for various federal jobs and instituted "open, competitive examinations for testing the fitness of applicants for public service." The Pendleton Act also barred political candidates from soliciting campaign contributions from government workers. Patronage did not disappear, but public service did improve.

Many departments of the federal government took on a professional character similar to that which doctors, lawyers, and scholars were imposing on their fields through regulatory societies such as the American Medical Association and the American Historical Association. At the same time, the federal judiciary began to act more aggressively to establish the parameters of government. With the Circuit Courts of Appeals Act of 1891, Congress granted the U.S. Supreme Court the right to review any case—state or federal—at will.

The move to transform government into a professional enterprise involved people from many walks of life, but no group more than lawyers. Lawyers began to organize citywide and statewide societies and in 1878 formed the American Bar Association (ABA). In 1894 New York introduced an examining board to control admission to legal practice, and many states followed its example. By the turn of the century, more than 40 percent of the members of Congress were lawyers, and lawyers dominated in the Senate.

Despite reforms like the Pendleton Act and the increasing dominance of legal professionals in government, many observers, Edward Bellamy among them, remained convinced that "insiders" controlled government, pulling the levers of party machinery or spending money to influence important decisions. Bellamy, concluding that the growing legion of politicians and civil servants failed to address the needs of ordinary citizens, advised Americans to organize their communities for the specific purpose of wresting control of government from the hands of politicians.

FARMERS AND WORKERS ORGANIZE THEIR COMMUNITIES

In the late 1860s farmers and workers began to organize. Within two decades, they built powerful national organizations to oppose, as a Nebraska newspaper put it, "the wealthy and powerful classes who want the control of government to plunder the people." Though short on financial resources, farmers and workers raised the most significant challenge to the two-party system since the Civil War—the populist movement.

The Grange

In 1867 farmers on the Great Plains formed the Patrons of Husbandry for their own "social, intellectual, and moral improvement." Led by Oliver H. Kelley, an employee of the Department of Agriculture, this fraternal society resembled the secretive Masonic order. Whole families staffed a complex array of offices engaged in mysterious rituals involving passwords, flags, songs, and costumes. In many farming communities, the headquarters of the local chapter, known as the Grange (a word for "farm"), became the center of social activity, the site of summer dinners and winter dances.

As a result of economic hardship among farmers, the Grange movement spread rapidly. The price of

Kingfisher Reformer, May 3, 1894

The symbols chosen by Grange artists represented their faith that all social value could be traced to honest labor and most of all to the work of the entire farm family. The hardworking American required only the enlightenment offered by the Grange to build a better community.

wheat and corn had boomed in the immediate aftermath of the Civil War, but following the Panic of 1873, farm families saw their hopes for prosperity wither. Blizzards, drought, and grasshopper infestations in the early 1870s left farmers on the Great Plains barely surviving. Competition from producers in Canada, Australia, Argentina, Russia, and India, meanwhile, contributed to steadily falling prices for grains and cotton, hurting farmers throughout the trans-Mississippi West and the South. Most farmers found themselves operating at a loss; many slid to the verge of bankruptcy. In the hope of improving their condition through collective action, many farmers joined their local Grange. The Patrons of Husbandry soon swelled to more than 1.5 million members.

Grangers blamed hard times on the exorbitant fees of big businesses, especially railroads and banks, which they reviled as a band of "thieves in the night." They fumed at American farm equipment manufacturers, such as Cyrus McCormick, for selling their wares more cheaply in Europe than in the United States. To purchase equipment and raw materials, farmers borrowed money, accruing debts averaging twice that of Americans not engaged in business. Eastern land companies, Grangers charged, not only imposed usurious interest rates but granted mortgages on terms too short to allow farmers to turn their fortunes around.

Grangers mounted their most concerted assault on the railroad corporations. With bribes, the railroads had secured the support of state legislators for a highly discriminatory rate policy. Farmers commonly paid more to ship their crops short distances than over long hauls. In 1874 several midwestern states responded to Granger pressure and passed a series of so-called Granger laws establishing maximum shipping rates.

Grangers also complained to their lawmakers about the price-fixing policies of grain wholesalers, warehousers, and operators of grain elevators. In 1873 the Illinois legislature passed a Warehouse Act establishing maximum rates for storing grains. Chicago firms challenged the legality of this measure, but in *Munn v. Illinois* (1877) the Supreme Court upheld the law, ruling that states had the power to regulate private property in the public interest.

Determined to "buy less and produce more," Grangers created a vast array of cooperative enterprises for both the purchase of supplies and the marketing of crops. They established local grain elevators, set up retail stores, and even manufactured some of their own farm machinery. As early as 1872 the Iowa Grange claimed to control one-third of the grain elevators and warehouses in the state. In other states Grangers ran banks as well as fraternal life and fire insurance companies.

The deepening depression of the late 1870s came at the worst possible moment for the Patrons of Husbandry, wiping out most of their cooperative programs. By 1880 Grange membership had fallen to 100,000. Meanwhile, the Supreme Court overturned most of the key legislation regulating railroads. The Patrons of Husbandry had nonetheless promoted a model of cooperation that would remain at the heart of agrarian protest movements until the end of the century.

The Farmers' Alliance

Agrarian unrest did not end with the decline of the Grange but instead moved south. In the 1880s farmers organized in communities where both poverty and the crop-lien system prevailed (see Chapter 17). Conservative newspaper writers and politicians advised farmers to trim expenditures and to diversify out of cotton into other crops. But with household budgets that had already fallen from $50 to as low as $10 a year, southern farmers had no leeway to cut expenses. And the cost of shipping perishable crops made diversification untenable despite the low price of cotton. In response to these conditions, Texas farmers—proclaiming "Equal Rights to All, Special Privileges to None"—began to organize.

In 1889, under the leadership of Charles W. Macune and William Lamb, several regional organizations joined forces to create the National Farmers' Alliance and Industrial Union. The next year the combined movement claimed 3 million white members. African American farmers joined the separate Colored Farmers' Alliance and Cooperative Union, which emerged in Texas and Arkansas and quickly spread across the South, ultimately claiming more than a million members of its own. The development of these parallel organizations reflected both practical necessity in a region of increasing racial segregation and the racism of white farmers.

The Farmers' Alliance claimed that power concentrated in the hand of a new governing class had resulted in "the impoverishment and bondage of so many." Members pledged themselves to restore democracy through "agitation, education, and cooperation."

Southern farmers readily translated their anger over falling cotton prices into intense loyalty to the one organization pledged to the improvement of their lot. With more than 500 chapters in Texas alone, and cooperative stores complemented by cooperative merchandising of crops, the Southern Farmers' Alliance became a viable alternative to the capitalist marketplace—if only temporarily. The alliance-run Texas Cotton Exchange failed in 1889, mainly because banks refused to accept as legal tender the vouchers its members used among themselves.

Large farmers' organizations in Minnesota, Nebraska, Iowa, Kansas, and the Dakota territory joined forces in the Northern Farmers' Alliance on the Plains states. During 1886 and 1887, summer drought followed winter blizzards and ice storms, reducing wheat harvests by one-third on the Plains. Locusts and cinch bugs ate much of the rest. As if this were not enough, prices on the world market fell sharply for what little remained. Many farmers left the land; western Kansas lost nearly half its population by the early 1890s. Skilled agitators played upon these hardships—especially the overpowering influence of railroads over the farmers' lives— boosting the alliance movement. By 1890 the Kansas Alliance alone claimed 130,000 members.

Grangers had pushed legislation that would limit the salaries of public officials, provide public school students with books at little or no cost, establish a program of teacher certification, and widen the admissions policies of the new state colleges. But only rarely did they put up candidates for office. In comparison, the Farmers' Alliance had few reservations about taking political stands or entering electoral races. At the end of the 1880s regional alliances drafted campaign platforms demanding state ownership of the railroads, a graduated income tax, lower tariffs, restriction of land ownership to citizens, and easier access to money through "the free and unlimited coinage of silver." In several states, alliance candidates for local and state office won local elections. By 1890 the alliances had gained control of the Nebraska legislature and held the balance of power in Minnesota and South Dakota.

Workers Search for Power

Like farmers, urban workers organized protest movements during the 1870s. The depression following the Panic of 1873, which produced 25 percent unemployment in many cities, served as a catalyst for organization. In New York City, a group marched to City Hall to present a petition on behalf of 10,000 workers who were without jobs or homes. Turned back repeatedly by the police, the organizers decided to stage a rally to advertise their demand for a steady job at a living wage. City officials refused to grant a permit. When 7,000 working-class men and women showed up on January 13, 1874, a battalion of 1,600 police—nearly two-thirds of the city's force—rushed into the crowd and began striking out indiscriminately with their clubs. This incident, known as the Tompkins Square Riot, inaugurated an era of unprecedented labor conflict and violence.

The railroad industry became the focus of protests by workers and farmers alike. Within the few months after the Panic of 1873, workers struck so many times that the New York Railroad Gazette complained, "Strikes are . . . as much a disease of the body politic as the measles or indigestion are of our physical organization." Although most of these strikes ended in failure, they revealed the readiness of workers to spell out their grievances in a direct and dramatic manner. They also suggested how strongly many townspeople, including merchants who depended on workers' wages, would support local strikes.

Despite these warnings, the railroad corporations were unprepared for the Great Uprising of 1877, the first nationwide strike. The strike began in Martinsburg, West Virginia, where workers protesting a 10 percent wage cut uncoupled all engines. No trains would run, they promised, until wages were restored. Within a few days, the strike had spread along the railroad routes to New York, Buffalo, Pittsburgh, Chicago, Kansas City, and San Francisco. In all these cities, workers in various industries and masses of the unemployed formed angry crowds, defying armed militia ordered to disperse them by any means. Meanwhile, strikers halted train traffic. They seized carloads of food for hungry families, and in St. Louis workers even took over the city's administration.

The rioting persisted for nearly a week, spurring business leaders to call for the deportation, arrest, or execution of strike leaders. Law and Order Leagues swept through working-class neighborhoods and broke up union meetings. Fearing a "national insurrection," President Hayes set a precedent by calling in the U.S. Army to suppress the strike. In Pittsburgh, federal troops equipped with semi-automatic machine guns fired into a

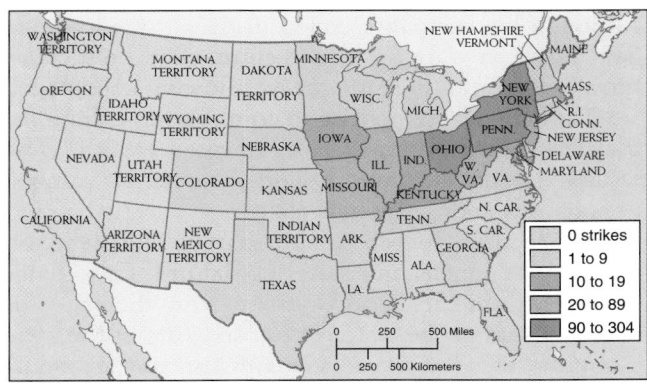

Strikes by State, 1880   *Most strikes after the Uprising of 1877 could be traced to organized trades, concentrated in the manufacturing districts of the Northeast and Midwest.*

Source: Carville Earle, *Geographical Inquiry and American Historical Problems* (Stanford, Calif.: Stanford University Press, 1992).

crowd and killed more than 20 people. By the time the strike finally ended, more than 100 people were dead.

Memories of the Uprising of 1877 haunted business and government officials for decades, prompting the creation of the National Guard and the construction of armories in working-class neighborhoods. Workers also drew lessons from the events. Before the end of the century, more than 6 million workers would strike in industries ranging from New England textiles to southern tobacco factories to western mines. The labor movement also expanded its sphere of influence to the halls of city government. While the Farmers' Alliance put up candidates in the South and Plains states, workers launched labor parties in dozens of industrial towns and cities.

In New York City, popular economist and land reformer Henry George, with the ardent support of the city's Central Labor Council and the Knights of Labor, put himself forward in 1886 as candidate for mayor on the United Labor Party ticket. His best-selling book, *Progress and Poverty* (1879), advocated a sweeping tax on all property to generate enough revenue to allow all Americans to live in comfort. Especially popular among Irish Americans, who had seen their homeland swallowed up by British landlords, George's ideas also appealed to German Americans, who, with the Irish, made up the heart of the city's labor movement. George called upon "all honest citizens" to join in independent political action as "the only hope of exposing and breaking up the extortion and speculation by which a standing army of professional politicians corrupt the people whom they plunder."

Tammany Hall delivered many thousands of the ballots cast for George straight into the Hudson River. Nevertheless, George managed to finish a respectable second with 31 percent of the vote, running ahead of young patrician Theodore Roosevelt.

Although his campaign ended in defeat, George had issued a stern warning to the entrenched politicians. Equally important, his impressive showing encouraged labor groups in other cities to form parties calling for the defeat of the "power of aggregated wealth." The results, in local elections around the country, stunned Republicans and Democrats alike.

In the late 1880s labor parties won seats on many city councils and state legislatures. Candidates of the Milwaukee People's Party won the race for mayor, a seat in the state senate, six seats in the state assembly, and one seat in Congress. In smaller industrial towns where workers outnumbered the middle classes, labor parties did especially well. In Rochester, New Hampshire, with a population of only 7,000, the Knights of Labor encouraged workers in shoe factories to put up their own candidates for office. From 1889 through 1891 Rochester workers elected a majority slate, from city council to mayor.

Women Build Alliances

Women helped build both the labor and agrarian protest movements while campaigning for their own rights as citizens. Like woman suffrage leader Elizabeth Cady Stanton, they believed that "government based on caste and class privilege cannot stand." In its place, as Bellamy predicted in *Equality*, would arise a new cooperative order in which women would be "absolutely free agents in the disposition of themselves."

Women in the Knights of Labor endorsed the order's political planks while putting forth their own set of demands. In 1886 sixteen women attending the

Sixteen women were among the 660 delegates attending the 1886 convention of the Knights of Labor in Richmond, Virginia. Elizabeth Rodgers, who holds her two-week-old daughter, joined the organization as a housewife. The mother of twelve children, she was also the first woman elected to head a district assembly. The majority of women delegates worked in shoe factories or textile mills.

national convention lobbied for the creation of a special department "to investigate the abuses of which our sex is subjected by unscrupulous employers, to agitate the principles which our Order teaches of equal pay for equal work and the abolition of child labor." The delegates accepted the plan with little dissent and appointed knit-goods worker Leonora M. Barry general investigator. With perhaps 65,000 women members at its peak, the Knights ran day-care centers for the children of wage-earning mothers and occasionally even set up bakery cooperatives to reduce the drudgery of cooking.

Women made a similar mark on farmers' organizations. The Patrons of Husbandry issued a charter to a local chapter only when women were well represented on its rolls, and in the 1870s delegates to its conventions routinely gave speeches endorsing woman suffrage and even dress reform. The Farmers' Alliance continued this policy, enjoining women to assist their fathers, husbands, or sons in agitation efforts. Whole families shared in social programs, such as songfests on Sunday afternoons, lecture series, and contests featuring antimonopoly games. In both the Northern and Southern Alliances, women made up perhaps one-quarter of the membership, and several advanced through the ranks to become leading speakers and organizers. Mary E. Lease, who achieved lasting fame for advising farmers to raise less corn and more hell, vividly expressed their sense of purpose. "Ours is a grand, a holy mission," she proclaimed, "to drive from our land and forever abolish the triune monopoly of land, money, and transportation."

Women in both the Knights of Labor and the Farmers' Alliance found their greatest leader in Frances E. Willard, the most famous woman of the nineteenth century. Willard assumed that the women who guarded their families' physical and spiritual welfare would, if granted the right to vote, extend their influence throughout the whole society. From 1878 until her death in 1897, Willard presided over the Woman's Christian Temperance Union (WCTU), at the time the largest organization of women in the world, and encouraged her numerous followers to "do everything." She mobilized nearly 1 million women to, in her words, "make the whole world HOMELIKE." WCTU members preached total abstinence from the consumption of alcohol, but they also worked to reform the prison system, eradicate prostitution, and eliminate the wage system. Willard went so far as to draw up plans for a new system of government whereby all offices, right up to the presidency, would be shared jointly by men and women. She also became a member of the Knights of Labor and endorsed the platform of the Farmers' Alliance.

Under Willard's leadership, the WCTU grew into the major force behind the campaign for woman suffrage, far surpassing the American Woman Suffrage Association and the National Woman Suffrage Association. By 1890, when the two rival suffrage associations merged to form the National American Woman Suffrage Association, the WCTU had already pushed the heart of the suffrage campaign into the Plains states and the West. In Iowa, Nebraska, Colorado, and especially Kansas, agitation for the right to vote provided a political bridge among women organized in the WCTU, Farmers' Alliance, Knights of Labor, and various local suffrage societies.

In 1891 representatives from various women's organizations formed the National Women's Alliance. The founding convention called for "full equality of the sexes," "harmony and unity of action among the Sisterhood" of the nation, "prevention of war," and the rejection of alcohol, tobacco, and narcotics as injurious to health. The organization's newspaper, the *Farmer's Wife*, spelled out basic principles in epigrams like "Give our women encouragement and victory is yours" and "Put 1000 women lecturers in the field and the revolution is here."

Although women lecturers such as Kansas's Annie Diggs were outstanding crowd pleasers, women in the Knights of Labor and the Farmers' Alliance failed to gain equality within the protest movements. Most political parties endorsed by these organizations included planks calling for equal wages for equal work but refused to endorse woman suffrage. Only in Colorado did local third-party candidates support the 1893 campaign that secured women's right to vote in that state. In the Southern Alliance, women themselves opposed women's enfranchisement. It was, however, an increasing emphasis on electoral politics that effectively placed voteless women on the sidelines.

Farmer-Labor Unity

In December 1890 the Farmers' Alliance called a meeting at Ocala, Florida, to press for a national third-party movement. This was a risky proposition because local chapters, like the Grangers before them, often allied themselves with Democrats or Republicans. The Southern Alliance hoped to capture control of the Democratic Party, while many farmers in the Plains states voted Republican. In some areas, though, the Farmers' Alliance established its own parties, put up full slates of candidates for local elections, won majorities in state legislatures, and even sent a representative to Congress. Reviewing these successes, delegates at Ocala decided to push ahead and form a national party, and they appealed to other farm, labor, and reform organizations to join them. Edward Bellamy advised his followers to take advantage of "the largest opportunity yet presented in the history of our movement" and support the third-party effort.

The time had come, the Alliance announced, "to establish the moral solidarity of the farmer and toiler societies." In February 1892, representatives from the Farmers' Alliance, the Knights of Labor, and the National Colored Farmers' Alliance, among others, met in St. Louis under a broad banner that read: "We do not ask for sympathy or pity. We ask for justice." After much deliberation, the 1,300 delegates adopted a platform for the new People's Party. It called for government ownership of railroads, banks, and telegraph lines, prohibition of large landholding companies, a graduated income tax, an eight-hour workday, and restriction of immigration. Its preamble, written by Minnesota's Ignatius Donnelly, declared: "We seek to restore the government of the Republic to the hands of 'the plain people' with which class it originated." The People's Party convened again in Omaha in July 1892 and nominated James Baird Weaver of Iowa for president and, to please the South, the Confederate veteran James Field from Virginia for vice president.

The Populists, as supporters of the People's Party styled themselves, quickly became a major factor in American politics. In some southern states, Populists cooperated with local Republicans in sponsoring "pepper and salt" state and local tickets that put black and white candidates on a single slate. To hold their voters, some Democrats adopted the Populist platform wholesale; others resorted to massive voter fraud and intimidation. In the West, Democrats threw their weight behind the Populist ticket mainly to defeat the ruling Republicans.

Democrat Grover Cleveland regained the presidency in 1892 (he had previously served from 1885 to 1889), but Populists scored a string of local victories. They ran strongest in Idaho, Nevada, Colorado, Kansas, and North Dakota, winning 50 percent or more of the vote. Nationwide, they elected three governors, ten representatives to Congress, and five senators. The national ticket received more than 1 million votes (8.5 percent of the total) and 22 electoral college votes—the only time since the Civil War that a third party had received any electoral votes. Despite poor showings among urban workers east of the Mississippi, Populists looked forward to the next round of state elections in 1894. But the great test would come with the presidential election in 1896.

THE CRISIS OF THE 1890s

Populist Ignatius Donnelly wrote in the preface to his pessimistic novel *Caesar's Column* (1891) that industrial society appears to be a "wretched failure" to "the great mass of mankind." On the road to disaster rather than to the egalitarian community that Bellamy had envisioned, "the rich, as a rule, hate the poor; and the poor are coming to hate the rich . . . society divides itself into two hostile camps. . . . They wait only for the drum beat and the trumpet to summon them to armed conflict."

A series of events in the 1890s shook the confidence of many citizens in the reigning political system. But nothing was more unsettling than the severe economic depression that consumed the nation. Many feared—while others hoped—that the entire political system would topple.

Financial Collapse and Depression

Railroads were at the center of the economic growth of the late nineteenth century. By the early 1890s they represented capital totaling $2.5 billion. As a result, when the nation's major rail lines went bankrupt in 1893, the business boom of nearly two decades ended and the entire economy ground to a halt. The depression that followed made the hard times of the 1870s appear a mere rehearsal for worse misery to come.

Jacob Coxey's "Commonwealth of Christ Army," 1894. Attracting the sympathetic attention of working people and the hostility of most of the wealthier classes, "Industrial Armies" marched through U.S. cities en route to the nation's capital.

The collapse of the Philadelphia and Reading Railroad in March 1893, followed by the downfall of the National Cordage Company, precipitated a crisis in the stock market and sent waves of panic splashing over banks across the country. In a few months, more than 150 banks went into receivership and hundreds more closed; nearly 200 railroads and more than 15,000 businesses also slipped into bankruptcy. In the steel industry alone thirty companies collapsed within six months of the panic. Agricultural prices meanwhile plummeted to new lows. Subsequent bank failures and stock market declines held back recovery until 1897, when the economy slowly began to pick up again. The new century arrived before prosperity returned.

The depression brought untold hardships. In many cities, unemployment rates reached 25 percent; Samuel Gompers, head of the American Federation of Labor (AFL), estimated nationwide unemployment at 3 million. "I have seen more misery in this last week than I ever saw in my life before," wrote a young reporter from Chicago. Few people starved, but millions suffered. Inadequate diets prompted a rise in communicable diseases, such as tuberculosis and pellagra.

Men and women begged for food or turned to charities for free bread and clothing. Tens of thousands "rode the rails" or went "on the tramp" to look for work, hoping that their luck might change in a new city or town. Some panhandled for the nickel that could buy a mug of beer and a free lunch at a saloon. By night they slept in parks or, in the colder months, flocked to the "bum tanks" of the city jail or to fleabag hotels. In New York City alone, with more than 20,000 homeless people, thousands ended up in jail. Newspapers warned against this "menace" and blamed the growing crime rates on the "dangerous classes."

Another Populist, Jacob Sechler Coxey, decided to gather the masses of unemployed into a huge army and then to march to Washington, D.C., to demand from Congress a public works program. On Easter Sunday, 1894, Coxey left Massillon, Ohio, with several hundred followers. Meanwhile, brigades from Boston, Los Angeles, San Francisco, Tacoma, Denver, Salt Lake City, Reno, Butte, and Omaha joined his "petition in boots." Communities across the country welcomed the marchers, but U.S. attorney general Richard C. Olney, a former lawyer for the railroad companies, conspired with state and local officials to halt them. Only 600 men and women reached the nation's capital, where the police first clubbed and then arrested the leaders for trespassing on the grass. Coxey's Army quickly disbanded, but not before voicing the public's growing impatience with government apathy toward the unemployed.

Strikes and Labor Solidarity

Meanwhile, in several locations the conflict between labor and capital had escalated to the brink of civil war.

In 1892, general strikes shut down industries in New Orleans and Buffalo and spread throughout the mining territories of east Tennessee.

Wage cuts in the silver and lead mines of northern Idaho led to one of the bitterest conflicts of the decade. To put a brake on organized labor, mineowners had formed a "protective association," and in March 1892 they announced a lower wage scale throughout the Coeur d'Alene district. After the miners' union refused to accept the cut, the owners locked out all union members and brought in strikebreakers. After three months of stalemate, union members loaded a railcar with explosives and blew up a mine. Strikebreakers fled while mineowners appealed to the Idaho governor for assistance. A force of 1,500 state and federal troops occupied the district. Strikebreakers were brought back in, and more than 300 union members were herded into bullpens, where they were kept under unsanitary conditions for several weeks before their trial. Ore production meanwhile resumed, and by November, when troops were withdrawn, the mineowners declared a victory. But the miners' union survived, and most members eventually regained their jobs. "We have made a fight that we are proud of and propose to continue it to the end," one striker declared. The following spring, Coeur d'Alene miners sent delegates to Butte, Montana, where they helped form the Western Federation of Miners, which soon became one of the strongest labor organizations in the nation.

Coeur d'Alene strikers had been buoyed by the news that steelworkers at Homestead, Pennsylvania, had likewise taken guns in hand to defend their union. Members of the Amalgamated Iron, Steel and Tin Workers, the most powerful union of the AFL, had carved out an admirable position for themselves in the Carnegie Steel Company. Well paid, proud of their skills, the unionists customarily directed their unskilled helpers without undue influence of company supervisors. Determined to gain control over every stage of production, Carnegie and his chairman, Henry C. Frick, decided not only to lower wages but to break the union.

In 1892, when the Amalgamated's contract expired, Frick announced a drastic wage cut. He also ordered a wooden stockade built around the factory, with grooves for rifles and barbed wire on top. The workers went on strike in late June. When Homestead's city government refused to assign police to disperse them, Frick sent in a heavily armed private army to do the job. After a day-long gun battle between strikers and the hired army, the governor sent the Pennsylvania National Guard to restore order. Carnegie's factory reopened, with strikebreakers doing the work.

After four months, the union was forced to concede a crushing defeat, not only for itself but in effect for all steelworkers. The Carnegie company reduced its work force by 25 percent, lengthened the workday, and cut wages 25 percent for those who remained on the job. If the Amalgamated Iron, Steel and Tin Workers, known throughout the industry as the "aristocrats of labor," could be brought down, less-skilled workers could expect little from the corporate giants. Within a decade, every major steel company operated without union interference.

But the spirit of labor solidarity did not die. Just two years after the strikes at Coeur d'Alene and Homestead, the greatest railway strike since 1877 again dramatized the extent of collusion between the government and corporations to crush the labor movement.

Like Lowell, Massachusetts, sixty years earlier, the town of Pullman, Illinois, just south of Chicago, had been regarded as a model industrial community. Its creator and proprietor, George Pullman, had manufactured luxurious "sleeping cars" for railroads since 1881. He built his company as a self-contained community, with the factory at the center, surrounded by modern cottages, a library, churches, an independent water supply, and even its own cemetery. The Pullman Palace Car Company deducted rent, library fees, and grocery bills from each worker's weekly wages. In good times workers enjoyed a decent livelihood, although many resented Pullman's autocratic control of their daily affairs.

When times grew hard, the company cut wages by as much as one-half, in some cases down to less than $1 a day. Charges for food and rent remained unchanged. Furthermore, factory supervisors sought to make up for declining profits by driving workers to produce more. In May 1894, after Pullman fired members of a committee that had drawn up a list of grievances, workers voted to strike.

Pullman workers found their champion in Eugene V. Debs, who had recently formed the American Railway Union (ARU) to bring all railroad workers into one organization. Just one month before the Pullman workers voted to strike, Debs and the ARU had scored a victory over the Great Northern rail line. Debs now advised caution, but delegates to an ARU convention voted to support a nationwide boycott of all Pullman cars. This action soon turned into a sympathy strike by railroad workers across the country. Support for the strike was especially strong in the western states.

Compared to the Uprising of 1877, the orderly Pullman strike at first produced little violence. ARU officials urged strikers to ignore all police provocations and hold their ground peacefully. But Attorney General Olney, claiming that the ARU was disrupting mail shipments (actually Debs had banned such interference), issued a blanket injunction against the strike. On July 4, President Cleveland sent federal troops to Chicago, over Illinois governor John Peter Altgeld's objections. After a bitter confrontation that left thirteen people dead and more than fifty wounded, the army dispersed the strikers. For the next week, railroad workers in twenty-six other states resisted federal troops, and a dozen more people were killed. On July 17, the strike finally ended when federal marshals arrested Debs and other leaders. Debs was sentenced to six months in jail.

"The Debs of fable," wrote the editor of a Unitarian weekly, "lighted a fire in the car yards of Chicago. The Debs of fact lighted an idea in the dangerous shadows of the Republic." Assailing the arrogance of class privilege that encouraged the government to use brute force against its citizens, Debs concluded that the labor movement could not regain its dignity under the present system. An avid fan of Bellamy's *Looking Backward*, he came out of jail a committed socialist. A few years later he tried to create a utopian colony that would prove the viability of cooperation in both working and living arrangements. This attempt failed to get off the ground, and in 1898 Debs moved on to help form a socialist political party.

Across the industrial belt and in the West and Southwest, in railroad towns, factory villages, and farms, tens of thousands of people supported Debs. Debs ran for president as a Socialist in 1900 and in four subsequent elections. But as prosperity returned after the depression of the 1890s, the odds against him grew. Debs, however, made his point on moral grounds. His friend James Whitcomb Riley, the nation's most admired sentimental poet, wrote in rural dialect that Debs had "the kindest heart that ever beat/betwixt here and the jedgment [judgment] seat."

The Social Gospel

Like Edward Bellamy, a growing number of Protestant and Catholic clergy and lay theologians noted a discrepancy between the ideals of Christianity and prevailing attitudes toward the poor. Like Bellamy, they could no longer sanction an economic system that allowed so many to toil long hours under unhealthy conditions and for subsistence wages. Moved by the human suffering accompanying the major depressions of the 1870s and 1890s, leading clergy envisioned a new cooperative order based on the principles of Christ's gospels and demanded that the church lead the way. In 1889 Episcopalian clergyman W. D. P. Bliss, a charter member of Boston's Bellamy Nationalist club, began to publish a monthly magazine, the *Dawn*, whose motto was "He works for God who works for man."

Coinciding with an upswing in religious revivals in the nation's cities, some liberal congregations broke away from established churches to side with the working class and the immigrant poor. Ministers called for civil service reform and the end of child labor. Supporting labor's right to organize and, if necessary, to strike, they petitioned government officials to regulate corporations and place a limit on profits. Washington Gladden, a Congregationalist minister, warned that if

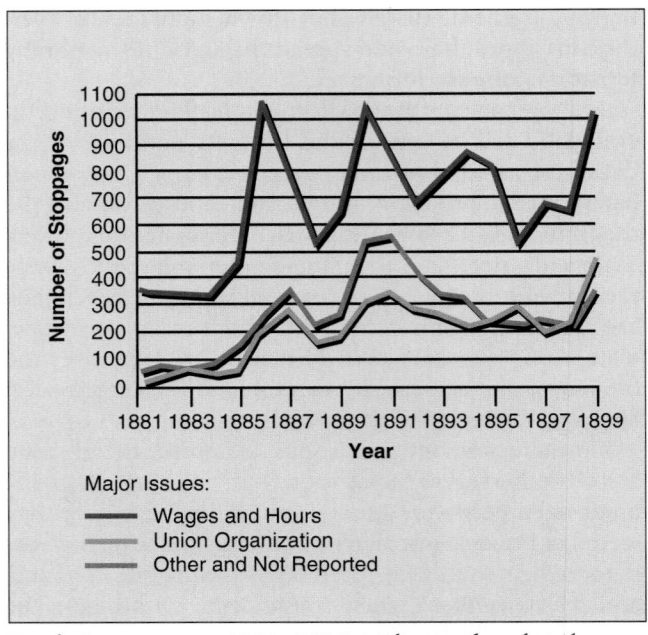

Work Stoppages, 1881–1899 *The number of strikes over wages and hours peaked in the years of 1886, 1890, and 1899, as workers in various trades and industries acted to protect or better their situations. By contrast, strikes for union recognition by employees—waged mostly by skilled workers—rose slowly but steadily until the economic depression of the 1890s. As the depression eased, strikes again increased.*

Source: United States Bureau of the Census, *Historical Statistics of the United States, Colonial Times to 1957* (Washington, D.C.: Bureau of the Census, 1960), p. 99.

churches continued to ignore pressing social problems they would devolve into institutions whose sole purpose was to preserve obscure rituals and superstitions. In the wake of the great railroad strikes of 1877, he had called upon his congregation in Columbus, Ohio, to take an active part in the fight against social injustice. Gladden's *Applied Christianity* (1886) appealed to the nation's business leaders to return to Christ's teachings.

Less famous but more numerous, local Protestant ministers and community leaders likewise sought to restore what they considered the true spirit of Christianity. As labor reformer George McNeill wrote in 1890, some ministers might be the servants of wealth, but in the long run "the influence of the teachings of the Carpenter's Son" will "counteract the influence of Mammon," the biblical embodiment of greed. McNeill looked forward to the day when "every man shall have according to his needs." Although the social gospel spread most rapidly through the northern industrial cities, southern African Americans espoused their own version. They reinterpreted the Gospel as Jesus' promise to emancipate their race from satanic white power brokers. The biblical republic of "Beulahland" became their model of redemption.

The depression of the 1890s produced an outpouring of social gospel treatises. The very popular *If Christ Came to Chicago* (1894), by British journalist W. T. Stead, forced readers to confront the "ugly sight" of a city with 200 millionaires and 200,000 unemployed men. It inspired Edward Everett Hale's *If Jesus Came to Boston* (1894), which similarly questioned social inequalities. The most famous tract, *In His Steps* (1896), by Methodist minister Charles M. Sheldon of Topeka, Kansas, urged readers to rethink their actions in the light of the simple question "What would Jesus do?" By 1933 Sheldon's book had sold more than 23 million copies.

Catholics, doctrinally more inclined than Protestants to accept poverty as a natural condition, joined the social gospel movement in smaller numbers. In the early 1880s Polish Americans broke away from the Roman Catholic Church to form the Polish National Church, which was committed to the concerns of working people. Irish Americans, especially prominent in the Knights of Labor, encouraged priests to ally themselves with the labor movement. Pope Leo XIII's encyclical *Rerum Novarum* (1891) endorsed the right of workers to form trade unions.

Women guided the social gospel movement in their communities. In nearly every city, groups of women affiliated with various evangelical Protestant sects raised money to establish small, inexpensive residential hotels for working women, whose low wages rarely covered the price of safe, comfortable shelter. Many of these groups joined to form the Young Women's Christian Association (YWCA), which by 1900 had more than 600 local chapters. The "Y" sponsored a range of services for needy Christian women, ranging from homes for the elderly and for unmarried mothers to elaborate programs of vocational instruction and physical fitness. The Girls Friendly Societies, an organization of young women affiliated with Episcopal churches, sponsored similar programs. Meanwhile Catholic lay women and nuns served the poor women of their faith, operating numerous schools, hospitals, and orphanages.

Although centered in the cities, the social gospel rallied many small-town and rural women, especially ardent admirers of Frances Willard. "The time will come," Willard insisted, "when the human heart will be so much alive that no one could sleep in any given community; if any of that group of human beings were cold, hungry, or miserable."

POLITICS OF REFORM, POLITICS OF ORDER

The severe hardships of the 1890s, following decades of popular unrest and economic uncertainty, led to a crisis in the two-party system, making the presidential election of 1896 a turning point in American politics. Republicans and Democrats continued to enjoy long-standing voter loyalties among specific groups or regions. Particularly in the South, the Democrats could generally depend on the masses of white voters to unite against any movement threatening to compromise the "color line." But Populists showed surprising ingenuity and courage in breaking down barriers against political insurgents.

The Free Silver Issue

Grover Cleveland owed his victory in 1892 over Republican incumbent Benjamin Harrison to the predictable votes of the Democratic "solid South" and to the unanticipated support of such northern states as Illinois and Wisconsin, whose German-born voters turned against the increasingly nativist Republicans. But when the economy collapsed the following year, Cleveland and the Democrats who controlled Congress faced a public eager for action. Convinced that the economic crisis was "largely the result of financial policy . . . embodied in unwise laws," the president called a special session of Congress to reform the nation's currency.

For generations, reformers had advocated "soft" currency—that is, an increase in the money supply that would loosen credit, accelerate economic development, and allow farmers to repay bank loans with "cheaper" money than they had borrowed. "Hard money" conservatives insisted that such a measure would throw the economy into chaos. Nevertheless, during the Civil War the federal government took decisive action, replacing state bank notes with a national paper currency popularly called "greenbacks" (from the color of the bills). In 1873 President Grant signed a Coinage Act that added silver to gold as the precious metal base of currency, presumably lowering the value of specie by adding to its supply. This measure had little real impact on the economy but opened the door to yet more tinkering.

In hard times especially, the currency question simmered. In 1876 philanthropist Peter Cooper ran an independent presidential campaign on a soft money platform and won 50,000 votes. Four years later, Civil War General James Baird Weaver ran on a similar platform for the Greenback-Labor Party and gathered an impressive 300,000 votes. Meanwhile, the gold-standard advocates, concentrated mostly in the business community, argued that the economy had already been damaged by the Coinage Act of 1873, which they called the "Crime of '73." The compromise Sherman Silver Purchase Act of 1890 directed the Treasury to increase the amount of currency coined from silver mined in the West and also permitted the U.S. government to print paper currency backed by the silver. Eastern members of Congress supported this measure when Westerners agreed, in turn, to support the McKinley tariff of 1890, which established the highest import duties yet on foreign goods.

With the economy in ruins, a desperate President Cleveland now demanded the repeal of the Sherman Act, insisting that only the gold standard could pull the nation out of depression. By exerting intense pressure on congressional Democrats, Cleveland got his way in October 1893, but not without ruining his chances for renomination. The midterm elections in 1894 brought the largest shift in congressional power in American history: the Republicans gained 117 seats, while the Democrats lost 113. The "Silver Democrats" of Cleveland's own party vowed revenge and began to look to the Populists, mainly Westerners and farmers who favored "free silver"—that is, the unlimited coinage of silver. Republicans confidently began to prepare for the presidential election of 1896, known as the "battle of the standards."

Populism's Last Campaigns

Populists had been buoyed by the 1894 election, which delivered to their candidates nearly 1.5 million votes, a gain of 42 percent over their 1892 totals. They made impressive inroads into several southern states. West of the Mississippi, political excitement steadily increased. David Waite, the Populist governor of Colorado, talked of a coming revolution and declared, "It is better, infinitely better, that blood should flow [up] to the horses' bridles rather than our national liberties should be destroyed." Still, even in the Midwest where Populists doubled their vote, they managed to win less than 7 percent of the total.

As Populists prepared for the 1896 election, they found themselves at a crossroad: What were they to do with the growing popularity of Democrat William Jennings Bryan? Son of an Illinois judge who had run for Congress unsuccessfully on the Greenback ticket, Bryan had relocated to Nebraska, where he practiced law. A spellbinding orator, he won a congressional seat in 1890. After seizing the Populist slogan "Equal Rights to All, Special Privilege to None," Bryan became a major contender for president of the United States.

Noting the surging interest in free silver, Bryan became its champion. "I don't know anything about free silver," he once admitted, but "the people of Nebraska are for free silver and I am for free silver. I will look up the arguments later." For two years before the 1896 election, Bryan wooed potential voters in a speaking tour that took him to every state in the nation. Pouring new life into his divided party, Bryan pushed Silver Democrats to the forefront.

At the 1896 party convention, the thirty-six-year-old orator thrilled delegates with his evocation of agrarian ideals. "Burn down your cities and leave our farms," Bryan preached, "and your cities will spring up again as if by magic; but destroy our farms and the grass will grow in the streets of every city in the country." What became one of the most famous speeches in Amer-

This Republican campaign poster of 1896 depicts William McKinley standing on sound money and promising a revival of prosperity. The depression of the 1890s shifted the electorate into the Republican column.

ican political history closed on a yet more dramatic note. Spreading his arms to suggest the crucified Christ figure, Bryan pledged to answer all demands for a gold standard by saying, "You shall not press down upon the brow of labor this crown of thorns, you shall not crucify mankind upon a cross of gold." The next day, Bryan won the Democratic presidential nomination.

The Populists knew that the Democrats, in nominating Bryan, had stolen their thunder. Although many feared that the growing emphasis on currency would overshadow their more important planks calling for government ownership of the nation's railroads and communications systems, few Populists had expected either major party to come out for free silver. As the date of their own convention approached, delegates divided over strategy: they could endorse Bryan and give up their independent status; or they could run an independent campaign and risk splitting the silver vote. Neither choice was good. "If we fuse," one Populist explained, "we are sunk; if we don't fuse, all the silver men we have will leave us for the more powerful Democrats."

In the end, the Populists nominated Bryan for president and chose one of their own ranks, the popular Georgian Tom Watson, for the vice-presidential candidate. Most of the state Democratic Party organizations, however, refused to put the "fusion" ticket on the ballot, and Bryan and his Democratic running mate, Arthur Sewall, simply ignored the Populist campaign.

The Republican Triumph

After Cleveland's blunders, Republicans anticipated an easy victory in 1896, but Bryan's nomination, as party stalwart Mark Hanna warned, "changed everything." Luckily, they had their own handsome, knowledgeable, courteous, and ruthless candidate, Civil War veteran William McKinley. Equally important, the Republicans enjoyed an efficient and well-financed machine. Hanna guided a campaign strategy that raised up to $7 million and outspent Bryan more than ten to one. The sheer expense and skill of coordination outdid all previous campaigns and established a precedent for future presidential elections. Using innumerable pamphlets, placards, hats, and parades, Republicans advertised their promise to "re-build out of the ruins of the last four years the stately mansions of national happiness, prosperity and self-respect." In the campaign's final two weeks, organizers dispatched 1,400 speakers to spread the word. Fearful of divisions in their own ranks, Republicans played down the silver issue while emphasizing the tariff and consistently cast adversary Bryan as a dangerous naysayer willing to risk the nation's well-being and cost voters their jobs or worse.

McKinley triumphed in the most important presidential election since Reconstruction. Bryan won 46 percent of the popular vote but failed to carry the Midwest, West Coast, or Upper South. The free silver campaign alienated traditionally Democratic urban voters, who feared soft money would bring higher prices. Many Catholics, uncomfortable with Bryan's Protestant moral piety, also deserted the Democrats, while German American Lutherans voted in especially large numbers for McKinley and for a Republican Congress. Finally, neither the reform-minded middle classes nor impoverished blue-collar workers were convinced that Bryan's grand reform vision really included them. The Populist following, disappointed and disillusioned, dwindled away.

For sixteen years after the 1896 election, Democrats dominated no region but the South. With Republican victories seemingly inevitable, apathy set in, and voter participation began to spiral downward.

Once in office, McKinley promoted a mixture of probusiness and expansionist measures. He supported the Dingley tariff of 1897, which raised

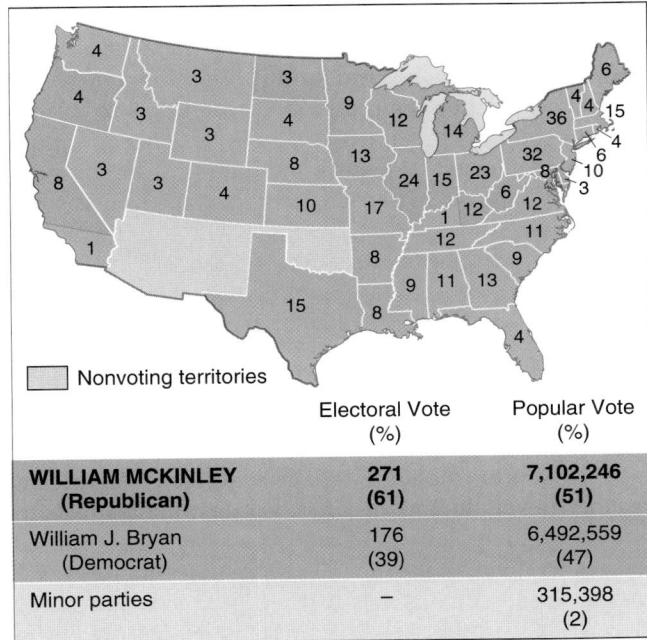

	Electoral Vote (%)	Popular Vote (%)
WILLIAM MCKINLEY (Republican)	**271 (61)**	**7,102,246 (51)**
William J. Bryan (Democrat)	176 (39)	6,492,559 (47)
Minor parties	–	315,398 (2)

Election of 1896, by States   *Democratic candidate William Jennings Bryan carried most of rural America but could not overcome Republican William McKinley's stronghold in the populous industrial states.*

import duties to an all-time high and favored the passage of the Gold Standard Act of 1900. In 1897 McKinley also encouraged Congress to create the United States Industrial Commission, which would plan business regulation; in 1898 he promoted a bankruptcy act that eased the financial situation of small businesses; and in the same year he proposed the Erdman Act, which established a system of arbitration to avoid rail strikes. The Supreme Court ruled in concert with the president, finding eighteen railways in violation of antitrust laws and granting states the right to regulate hours of labor under certain circumstances.

McKinley's triumph ended the popular challenge to the nation's governing system. With prosperity returning by 1898 and nationalism rising swiftly, McKinley encouraged Americans to go for "a full dinner pail," the winning Republican slogan of the 1900 presidential election.

The Limits of Democracy

Campaign rhetoric aside, McKinley and Bryan differed only slightly on the major problems facing the nation in 1896. Neither Bryan the reformer nor McKinley the prophet of prosperity addressed the escalation of racism and nativism (anti-immigrant feeling) throughout the nation. After the election, McKinley made white supremacy a major tenet of his foreign policy; Bryan, twice more a presidential contender, championed white rule in the South.

Toward the end of the century, many political observers noted, the nation's patriotic fervor took on a strongly nationalistic and antiforeign tone. Striking workers and their employers alike tended to blame "foreigners" for the hard times. AFL leader Samuel Gompers, himself a Jewish immigrant from Europe, lobbied Congress to restrict immigration from eastern and southern Europe, and even the sons and daughters of earlier immigrants attacked the newcomers as unfit for democracy. Imagining a Catholic conspiracy directed by the pope, semisecret organizations such as the American Protective Association sprang up to defend American institutions. Fourth of July orators continued to celebrate freedom and liberty but more often boasted about the might and power of their nation.

White violence against African Americans reached levels unknown since Reconstruction. Meanwhile, southern local and state governments codified racist ideology by passing discriminatory and segregationist legislation, which became known as Jim Crow laws. Wealthy planters, merchants, and farmers organized to disfranchise black voters and to extend the practice of

Billboard produced for the Mississippi constitutional convention of 1890. Rallying under the banner of "white supremacy," the delegates successfully disfranchised African Americans.

segregation to cover facilities such as restaurants, public transportation, and even drinking fountains. The United States Supreme Court upheld the new discriminatory legislation. Its decisions in the *Civil Rights Cases* (1883) overturned the Civil Rights Act of 1875, and in *Plessy v. Ferguson* (1896) the Court upheld a Louisiana state law formally segregating railroad cars on the basis of the "separate but equal" doctrine. In *Cumming v. Richmond County Board of Education* (1899), the Court allowed separate schools for blacks and whites, even where facilities for African American children did not exist.

The new restrictions struck especially hard at the voting rights of African Americans. Southern states enacted new literacy tests and property qualifications for voting, demanding proof of $300 to $500 in property and the ability to read and write. Loopholes permitted poor whites to vote even under these conditions, except where they threatened the Democratic Party's rule. "Grandfather clauses," invented in Louisiana, exempted from all restrictions those who had been entitled to vote on January 1, 1867, together with their sons and grandsons, a measure that effectively enfranchised whites while barring African Americans. In 1898 the Supreme Court ruled that poll taxes and literacy requirements enacted in order to prevent blacks (and some poor whites) from voting were a proper means of restricting the ballot to "qualified" voters. By this time, only 5 percent of the southern black electorate voted, and African Americans were barred from public office and jury service. Supreme Court Justice John Marshall Harlan, the lone dissenter in *Plessy v. Ferguson*, lamented that the Court's majority rulings gave power to the states "to place in a condition of legal inferiority a large body of American citizens." Depriving African Americans of equal rights and protection under the law, Jim Crow legislation encouraged states outside the South to pass similar measures.

Racial violence in turn escalated. Not only race riots but thousands of lynchings took place. Between 1882 and the turn of the century, the number of lynchings usually exceeded 100 each year; 1892 produced a record 230 deaths (161 black, 69 white). Mobs often burned or dismembered victims in order to drag out their agony and entertain the crowd of onlookers. Announced in local newspapers, lynchings became public spectacles for entire white families, and railroads sometimes offered special excursion rates for travel to these events.

Antilynching became the one-woman crusade of Ida B. Wells, young editor of a black newspaper in Memphis. After three local black businessmen were lynched in 1892, Wells vigorously denounced the outrage, blaming white business competitors of the victims. Her stand fanned the tempers of local whites, who destroyed her press and forced the outspoken editor to leave the city.

Wells set out to investigate lynching in a systematic fashion. She paid special attention to the common defense of lynching—that it was a necessary response to attempts by black men to rape white women. Her 1895 pamphlet *A Red Record* showed that the vast majority of black lynching victims had not even been accused of rape. In fact, Wells showed, lynching was primarily a brutal device to eliminate African Americans who had become too prosperous or competed with white businesses.

Wells launched an international movement against lynching, lecturing across the country and in Europe, demanding an end to the silence about this barbaric crime. Her work also inspired the growth of a black women's club movement. The National Association of Colored Women, founded in 1896, provided a home for black women activists who had been excluded from white women's clubs. United by a growing sense of racial pride, black women's clubs took up the antilynching cause and also fought to protect black women from exploitation by white men and from charges of sexual depravity.

Tom Watson

Few white reformers rallied to defend African Americans. At its 1899 convention, the National American Woman Suffrage Association appeased new southern white members by voting down a resolution condemning racial segregation in public facilities. A far greater tragedy was a racist turn in the Populist movement, whose leaders even in the South had at times challenged white supremacy. The story of Thomas E. Watson, briefly a champion of interracial unity, illustrates the rise and fall of hopes for an egalitarian South.

Son of a prosperous cotton farmer who had been driven into bankruptcy during the depression of the 1870s, Tom Watson had once campaigned to restore the civil rights of southern African Americans. "Why is not the colored tenant [farmer] open to the conviction that he is in the same boat as the white tenant; the colored laborer with the white laborer?" he asked. Watson planned to overturn Democratic rule by capturing and building up the black vote for the People's Party.

Watson's followers in Georgia were jailed, shot at, denied the protection of the courts, and driven from their churches. Yet tens of thousands regarded him as a savior. Flowers decorated the bridges along his speaking routes, crowds standing in pouring rain begged him to continue speaking, and wagons of loyalists carried Winchester rifles to defend him from armed attack. Preaching government ownership of railroads and banks and political equality for both races, Watson stirred the only truly grass-roots interracial movement the South had yet seen.

By early 1896, however, Watson perceived that the increasing ardor for free silver and the move toward cooperation with Democrats would doom the Populist movement. He nevertheless accepted the nomination for vice president on the "fusion" ticket and campaigned in several states. After McKinley's triumph, Watson withdrew from politics, returning to his Georgia farm to write popular histories of the United States and to plot his future.

Watson returned to public life after the turn of the century but with a totally different approach to race relations. He still bitterly attacked the wealthy classes but now blamed black citizens for conspiring against poor whites. Political salvation now hinged, he concluded, on accommodation to white supremacy. Watson expressed a southern variation of the new national creed that prepared Americans to view the luckless inhabitants of distant lands as ripe for colonization by the United States.

"IMPERIALISM OF RIGHTEOUSNESS"

Many Americans attributed the crisis of 1893–97 not simply to the collapse of the railroads and the stock market but to basic structural problems: an overbuilt economy and an insufficient market for goods. Profits from total sales of manufactured and agricultural products had grown substantially over the level achieved in the 1880s, but output increased even more rapidly. While the number of millionaires shot up from 500 in 1860 to more than 4,000 in 1892, the majority of working people lacked enough income to buy back a significant portion of what they produced. As Republican Senator Albert J. Beveridge of Indiana put it, "We are raising more than we can consume . . . making more than we can use. Therefore, we must find new markets for our produce, new occupation for our capital, new work for our labor."

In 1893 Frederick Jackson Turner reminded Americans that the continent had now been settled. Having passed "from the task of filling up the vacant spaces of the continent," the nation is now "thrown back upon itself," the young historian concluded. Obviously, Americans required a new "frontier" if democracy were to survive.

The White Man's Burden

Turner read his famous essay, "The Significance of the Frontier in American History," at the meeting of the American Historical Association, which was held in Chicago at the time of the World's Fair, less than two months after the nation's economy collapsed. On May Day 1893 crowds flocked to the fair—"a little ideal world, a realization of Utopia . . . [foreshadowing] some far away time when the earth should be as pure, as beautiful, and as joyous as the White City itself." A complex of more than 400 buildings, newly constructed in beaux arts design, commemorated the four hundredth anniversary of Columbus's landing. Such expositions, President McKinley explained, served as "timekeepers of progress."

The captains of Chicago's industry—Armour, Swift, McCormick, Field, and Pullman—had campaigned hard to bring the fair to Chicago and delighted in its triumphant display of American business ingenuity. Agriculture Hall showcased the production of corn, wheat, and other crops and featured a gigantic globe encircled by samples of American-manufactured farm machinery. The symbolism was evident: all eyes were on worldwide markets for American products. Another building housed a model of a canal cut across Nicaragua, suggesting the ease with which American traders might reach Asian markets if transport ships could travel directly from the Caribbean to the Pacific. One of the most popular exhibits, attracting 20,000 people a day, featured a mock ocean liner built to scale by the International Navigation Company, where fair-goers could imagine themselves as "tourists," sailing in luxury to distant parts of the world.

The World's Fair also "displayed" representatives of the people who populated foreign lands. The Midway Plaisance, a strip nearly a mile long and more than 600 feet wide, was an enormous sideshow of re-created Turkish bazaars and South Sea island huts. There were Javanese carpenters, Dahomean drummers, Egyptian swordsmen, and Hungarian Gypsies as well as Eskimos, Syrians, Samoans, and Chinese. Very popular was the World Congress of Beauty, parading "40 Ladies from 40 Nations" dressed in native costume. Another favorite attraction was "Little Egypt," who performed at the Persian Palace of Eros; her *danse du ventre* became better known as the hootchy-kootchy. According to the guidebook, these peoples had come "from the nightsome North and the splendid South, from the wasty West and the effete East, bringing their manners, customs, dress, religions, legends, amusements, that we might know them better." One of the exposition's directors, Frederick Ward Putnam, head of Harvard's Peabody Museum of American Archeology and Ethnology, explained more fully that the gathering gave fair-goers "a grand opportunity to see . . . the material advantages which civilization brings to mankind."

By celebrating the brilliance of American industry and simultaneously presenting the rest of the world's people as a source of exotic entertainment, the planners of the fair delivered a powerful message. Former abolitionist Frederick Douglass, who attended the fair on "Colored People's Day," recognized it immediately. He noted that the physical layout of the fair, by carefully grouping exhibits, sharply divided the United States and Europe from the rest of the world, namely from the nations of Africa, Asia, and the Middle East. Douglass objected to the stark contrast setting off Anglo-Saxons from people of color, an opposition between "civilization" and "savagery." Douglass and Ida

B. Wells jointly wrote a pamphlet that referred to the famed exposition as "a whited sepulcher." Wells advised African Americans to boycott the fair, but Douglass chose to attend. He used the occasion to deliver a speech upbraiding those white Americans who labeled the African American "a moral monster."

The Chicago World's Fair gave material shape to prevalent ideas about the superiority of American civilization and its racial order. At the same time, by showcasing American industries, it made a strong case for commercial expansion abroad. Social gospeler Josiah Strong, a Congregational minister who had begun his career trying to convert Indians to Christianity, provided a timely synthesis. He argued that the United States, as the most economically advanced and most Christian nation in the world, commanded a providential role. Thus linking economic and spiritual expansion, Strong advocated an "imperialism of righteousness." The rest of the world "is to be Christianized and civilized," Strong insisted, by the white Americans, who were best suited to this greatest task of all time. "Pure spiritual Christianity" and a "genius for colonizing" compelled Americans to move beyond their own national interests to consider the needs of the people of Africa and the Pacific and beyond. It was the white American, Strong argued, who had been "divinely commissioned to be, in a peculiar sense, his brother's keeper."

Senator Beveridge faithfully carried this message to Congress, insisting that God "has made us [white, English-speaking people] adept in government that we may administer governments among savages and senile peoples. . . . He has marked the American people as His chosen nation to finally lead in the regeneration of the world." According to many newspaper reporters and editorialists, it would be morally wrong for Americans to shirk what the British poet Rudyard Kipling called the "White Man's Burden."

Foreign Missions

The push for overseas expansion coincided with a major wave of religious evangelism and foreign missions. Early in the nineteenth century, Protestant missionaries, hoping to fulfill what they believed to be a divine command to carry God's message to all peoples and to win converts for their church, had focused on North America. Many disciples, like Strong himself, headed west and stationed themselves on Indian reservations. Others worked among the immigrant populations of the nation's growing cities. As early as the 1820s, however, a few missionaries had traveled to the Sandwich Islands (Hawai'i) in an effort to supplant the indigenous religion with Christianity. After the Civil War, following the formation of the Women's Union Missionary Society of Americans for Heathen Lands, the major evangelical Protestant denominations all sponsored missions directed at foreign lands.

Funded by wealthy men and the vigorous campaigns of female church members, these societies soon attracted a large membership. By the 1890s college campuses blazed with missionary excitement, and the intercollegiate Student Volunteers for Foreign Missions spread rapidly under the slogan "The Evangelicization of the World in This Generation." Magazines bristled with essays such as "The Anglo-Saxon and the World's Redemption." Young Protestant women rushed to join foreign missionary societies. In 1863 there had been only 94 Methodist women missionaries in China; by 1902 the number had jumped to 783. In all, some twenty-three American Protestant churches had established missions in China by the turn of the century, the majority staffed by women. By 1915, more than 3 million women had enrolled in forty denominational missionary societies, surpassing in size all other women's organizations in the United States. Their foreign missions ranged from India and Africa to Syria, the Pacific Islands, and nearby Latin America.

With so many agents in the field, missionaries scored numerous successes. They recruited many "natives," including the "rice-Christians" who feigned conversion in order to be fed by the missions. By 1898 Protestants claimed to have made Christians of more than 80,000 Chinese, a tiny portion of the population but a significant stronghold for American interests in their nation. The missionaries did more than spread the gospel. They taught school, provided rudimentary medical care, offered vocational training programs, and sometimes encouraged young men and women to pursue a college education in preparation for careers in their homelands. Such work depended on, and in turn inspired, enthusiastic church members in the United States.

Outside the churches proper, the YMCA and YWCA, which had set up nondenominational missions for the working poor in many American cities, also embarked on a worldwide crusade to reach non-Christians. By the turn of the century, the YWCA had foreign branches in Ceylon (present-day Sri Lanka) and China. After foreign branches multiplied in the next decade, a close observer ironically suggested that the United States had three great occupying forces: the army, the navy, and the "Y." He was not far wrong.

Missionaries played an important role both in generating public interest in foreign lands and in preparing the way for American economic expansion. As Josiah Strong aptly put it, "Commerce follows the missionary."

An Overseas Empire

Not only missionaries but business and political leaders had set their sights on distant lands. In the 1860s secretary of state William Henry Seward, under Abraham Lincoln and then under Andrew Johnson, encouraged Americans to defer to "a political law—and when I say political law, I mean higher law, a law of Providence—that empire has [had], for the last three thousand years." Seward correctly predicted that foreign trade would play an increasingly important part in the American economy. Between 1870 and 1900 exports more than tripled, from about $400 million to over $1.5 billion. But as European markets for American goods began to contract, business and political leaders of necessity looked more eagerly to Asia as well as to lands closer by.

Since the American Revolution, many Americans had regarded all nearby nations as falling naturally within their own territorial realm, destined to be acquired when opportunity allowed. Seward advanced these imperialist principles in 1867 by negotiating the purchase of Alaska (known at the time as Seward's Icebox) from Russia for 7.2 million dollars, and hoped someday to see the American flag flying over Canada and Mexico. Meanwhile, with European nations launched on their own imperialist missions in Asia and Africa, the United States increasingly viewed the Caribbean as an "American lake" and all of Latin America as a vast potential market for U.S. goods. The crisis of the 1890s transformed this long-standing desire into a perceived economic necessity. Large-scale conquest, however, appeared to American leaders more expensive and less appealing than economic domination and selective colonization. Unlike European imperialists, powerful Americans dreamed of empire without large-scale permanent military occupation and costly colonial administration.

Americans focused their expansionist plans on the Western Hemisphere, determined to dislodge the dominant power, Great Britain. In 1867, when Canada became a self-governing dominion, American diplomats hoped to annex their northern neighbor, believing that Great Britain would gladly accede in order to concentrate its imperial interests in Asia. But Great Britain refused to give up Canada, and the United States backed away. Central and South America proved more accommodating to American designs.

Republican stalwart James G. Blaine, secretary of state under presidents Garfield and Harrison, determined to work out a Good Neighbor policy (a phrase coined by Henry Clay in 1820). "What we want," he explained, "are the markets of these neighbors of ours that lie to the south of us. We want the $400,000,000 annually which to-day go to England, France, Germany and other countries. With these markets secured new life would be given to our manufactures, the product of the Western farmer would be in demand, the reasons for and inducements to strikers, with all their attendant evils, would cease." Bilateral treaties with Mexico, Colombia, the British West Indies, El Salvador, and the Dominican Republic allowed American business to dominate local economies, importing their raw materials at low prices

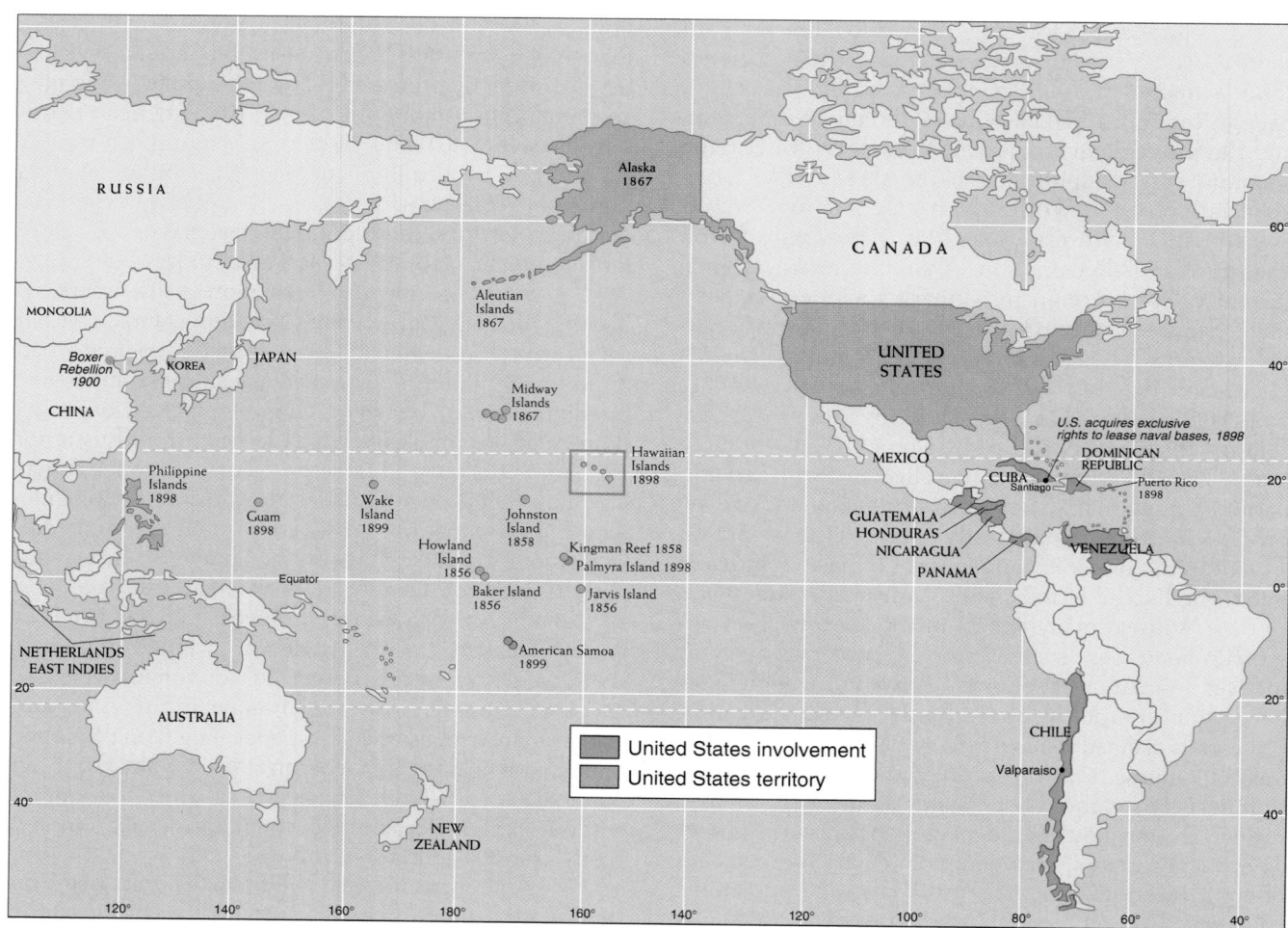

The American Domain, ca. 1900 *The United States claimed numerous islands in the South Pacific and intervened repeatedly in Latin America to secure its economic interests.*

and flooding their local markets with goods manufactured in the United States. Often American investors simply took over the principal industries of these small nations, undercutting national business classes. The first Pan-American Conference, held in 1889–90, marked a turning point in hemispheric relations.

The Good Neighbor policy depended, Blaine knew, on peace and order in the Latin American states. As early as 1875, when revolt shook Venezuela, the Department of State warned European powers not to meddle. If popular uprisings proved too much for local officials, the U.S. Navy would intervene and return American allies to power.

In 1883, wishing to enforce treaties and protect overseas investments, Congress appropriated funds to build up American seapower. Beginning with ninety small ships, over one-third of them wooden, the navy grew quickly to become known as the Great White Fleet. One of the most popular exhibits at the Chicago World's Fair featured full-sized models of the new armor-plated steel battleships. Congress also established

the Naval War College in Newport, Rhode Island, in 1884 to train the officer corps. One of its first presidents, Captain Alfred Thayer Mahan, prescribed an imperialist strategy based on command of the seas. His book, *The Influence of Sea Power upon American History, 1660–1873* (1890), helped to define American foreign policy at the time. Mahan insisted that international strength rested not only on open markets but on the control of colonies. He advocated the annexation of bases in the Caribbean and the Pacific to enhance the navy's ability to threaten or wage warfare.

The annexation of Hawai'i on July 7, 1898, followed nearly a century of economic penetration and diplomatic maneuver. American missionaries, who had arrived in the 1820s to convert Hawai'ians to Christianity, began to buy up huge parcels of land and to subvert the existing feudal system of landholding. They also encouraged American businesses to buy into sugar plantations, and by 1875 U.S. corporations dominated the sugar trade. They tripled the number of plantations by 1880 and sent Hawai'ian sugar duty-free to the

Brought to power with the assistance of American businessmen, Queen Liliuokalani nevertheless sought to limit the outsiders' influence. American marines, Christian missionaries, and sugar planters joined in 1893 to drive her from her throne. A century later, the U.S. government apologized to Hawai'ians for this illegal act.

United States. By this time Hawai'i appeared, in Blaine's opinion, to be "an outlying district of the state of California," and he began to push for annexation. In 1887 a new treaty allowed the United States to build a naval base at Pearl Harbor on the island of Oahu.

The next year, American planters took a step further, arranging the overthrow of a weak king, Kalakaua, and securing a new government allied to their economic interests. In 1891, the new ruler, Queen Liliuokalani, struck back by issuing a constitution granting her more discretionary power. The U.S. minister, prompted by the pineapple magnate Sanford B. Dole, responded by calling for military assistance. On January 16, 1893, U.S. sailors landed on Hawai'i to protect American property. Liliuokalani was deposed, a new provisional government was installed, and Hawai'i was proclaimed an American protectorate (a territory protected and partly controlled by the United States). The American diplomat John L. Stevens, stationed in Hawai'i, eagerly wired Washington that the "Hawai'ian

pear is now fully ripe, and this is the golden hour for the United States to pluck it." President Cleveland refused to consider annexation, but five years later McKinley affirmed a joint congressional resolution under which Hawai'i would become an American territory in 1900. The residents of Hawai'i were not consulted about this momentous change in their national identity.

Hawai'i was often viewed as a stepping-stone to the vast Asian markets. A U.S. admiral envisioned the happy future: "The Pacific is the ocean bride of America—China, Japan and Korea—and their innumerable islands, hanging like necklaces about them, are the bridesmaids. . . . Let us as Americans . . . determine while yet in our power, that no commercial rival or hostile flag can float with impunity over the long swell of the Pacific sea."

To accelerate railroad investment and trade, a consortium of New York bankers created the American China Development Company in 1896. They feared, however, that the tottering Manchu dynasty would fall to European, Russian, and Japanese colonial powers, which would then prohibit trade with the United States. Secretary of State John Hay responded in 1899 by proclaiming the Open Door policy. According to this doctrine, outlined in notes to six major powers, the United States enjoyed the right to advance its commercial interests anywhere in the world, at least on terms equal to those of the other imperialist nations. The Chinese marketplace was too important to lose.

Nationalist rebellion, however, threatened to overwhelm all the outsiders' plans for China. An antiforeign secret society known as the Harmonious Righteous Fists (dubbed "Boxers" by the Western press) rioted repeatedly in 1898 and 1899, actually occupying the capital city of Beijing and surrounding the foreign embassies. Shocked by the deaths of thousands, including many Chinese converts to Christianity, and determined to maintain American economic interests, President McKinley, not bothering to request congressional approval, contributed five thousand U.S. troops to an international army that put down the uprising. The Boxer Rebellion dramatized the Manchu regime's inability to control its own subjects and strengthened John Hay's determination to preserve the economic status quo. A second series of Open Door notes by the secretary of state restated the intention of the United States to trade in China and laid the basis for twentieth-century foreign policy.

THE SPANISH-AMERICAN WAR

During his 1896 campaign, William McKinley firmly committed himself to the principle of economic expansion. It was for him the proper alternative to Edward Bellamy's program for a cooperative commonwealth. Indeed, he once described his "greatest ambition" as achieving American supremacy in world markets. As president, McKinley not only reached out for markets but took his nation into war.

A "Splendid Little War" in Cuba

Cuba had long tempted American investors. As early as the 1840s, advocates of expansion described the nearby Caribbean island, still owned by Spain, as a fruit ripe for picking. Before the Civil War, Southerners hoped to acquire Cuba as a new region for cotton production and the expansion of slavery. After the Civil War Americans invested heavily in sugar mills, tobacco plantations, and mines, and by the early 1890s they held nearly $50 million worth of property on Cuba. In 1894, however, the Wilson-Gorman tariff placed stiff restrictions on Cuban imports to the United States, cutting the volume of trade by as much as 50 percent. The Cuban economy, along with American investments, went into a deep recession, setting the stage for revolution.

As unemployment and unrest spread, nationalist leader José Martí declared that "Cuba must be free from Spain and the United States." Cubans rallied under his leadership until Spanish troops ambushed and killed Martí in May 1895. Martí's martyrdom fueled the flames of rebellion.

Many Americans, invoking the legacy of their own war for independence, supported the movement for *Cuba Libre*. Grisly stories of Spain's treatment of captured insurrectionists circulated in American newspapers and aroused popular sympathy for the Cuban cause. President Cleveland refused to back the Cuban revolutionaries but urged Spain to grant the island a limited autonomy. Even when Congress passed a resolution in 1896 welcoming the future independence of Cuba, Cleveland and his advisers demurred, determined to avoid war with Spain.

When McKinley took over the presidency, he immediately perceived that the insurrection harmed U.S. investments and might destroy the entire Cuban economy. He nevertheless drew back. In his Inaugural Address he declared, "We want no wars of conquest; we must avoid the temptation of territorial aggression." The tide turned, however, when Spain appeared unable to maintain order. In early 1898 American newspapers published a private letter written by a Spanish diplomat in Washington characterizing the president as weak and opportunistic. Public indignation, whipped up by tabloid press head-

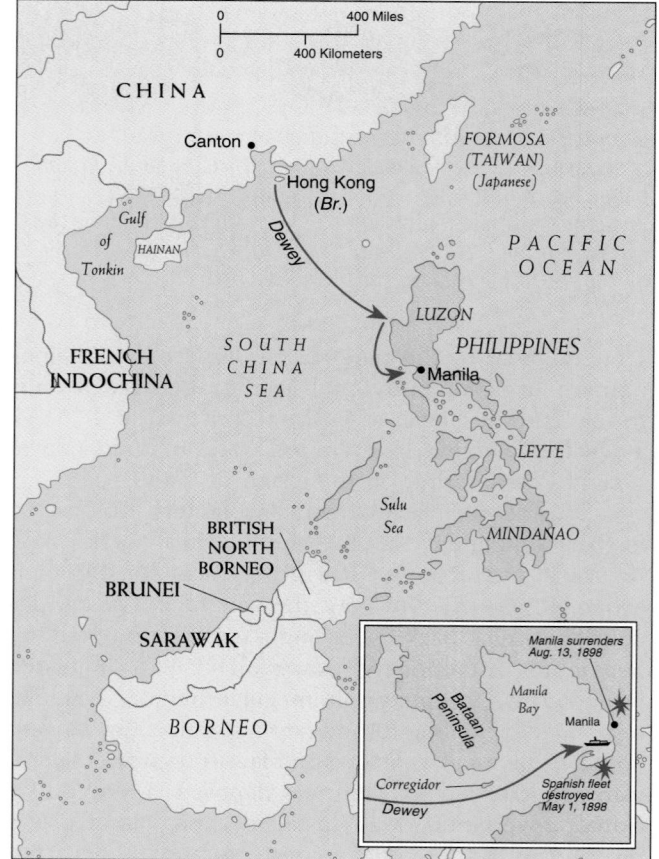

The Spanish-American War   *In two theaters of action, the United States used its naval power adeptly against a weak foe.*

lines and sensational stories, turned into frenzy five days later, on February 15, when an explosion ripped through the battleship USS Maine, stationed in Havana harbor ostensibly to rescue American citizens living in Cuba.

McKinley, suspecting war was close, had already begun to prepare for intervention. While newspapers ran banner headlines charging a Spanish conspiracy, the president established a commission to investigate the explosion, which proved to be an accident rather than an act of Spanish aggression. The impatient public meanwhile demanded revenge for the death of 266 American sailors. Soon a new slogan appeared: "Remember the Maine and to Hell with Spain!"

Finally, on April 11, McKinley asked Congress for a declaration of war against Spain. Yet the Senate barely passed the war resolution by a vote of 42 to 35, and only with the inclusion of an amendment by Republican senator Henry Teller of Colorado that disclaimed "any disposition or intention to exercise sovereignty, jurisdiction or control over said island, except for the pacification thereof." McKinley, who opposed any plan to annex Cuba, signed the declaration of war on April 29, 1898.

An outpouring of patriotic joy inspired massive parades, topical songs, and an overpowering enthusiasm. "Populists, Democrats, and Republicans are we," went one jingle, "But we are all Americans to make Cuba free."

Ten weeks later the war was all but over. On land, Lieutenant Colonel Theodore Roosevelt—who boasted of killing Spaniards "like jackrabbits"—led his Rough Riders to victory. On July 3, the main Spanish fleet near Santiago Bay was destroyed; two weeks later Santiago itself surrendered, and the war drew to a close. Although fewer than 400 Americans died in battle, disease and the inept treatment of the wounded claimed more than 5,000 lives. Roosevelt nevertheless felt invigorated by the conflict, agreeing with John Hay that it had been a "splendid little war."

On August 12, at a small ceremony in McKinley's office marking Spain's surrender, the United States secured Cuba's independence but nevertheless denied the island an official role in the proceedings. American businesses tightened their hold on Cuban sugar plantations, while U.S. military forces oversaw the formation of a constitutional convention that made Cuba a protectorate of the United States. Under the Platt Amendment, sponsored by Republican senator Orville H. Platt of Connecticut in 1901, Cuba promised to provide land for American bases; to devote national revenues to paying back debts to the United States; to sign no treaty that would be detrimental to American interests; and to acknowledge the right of the United States to intervene at any time to protect its interests in Cuba. After American troops withdrew from Cuba, the amendment was incorporated into the Cuban-

American Treaty of 1903. This treaty, which remained in place until 1934, paved the way for American domination of the island's sugar industry and contributed to anti-American sentiment among Cuban nationalists.

The United States further advanced its interests in the Caribbean to include Puerto Rico, ceded by Spain, and eventually the Virgin Islands of St. Thomas and St. John, purchased from Denmark in 1917. The acquisition of Pacific territories, including Guam, marked the emergence of the United States as a global colonial power.

War in the Philippines

The Philippines, another of Spain's colonies, seemed an especially attractive prospect, its 7,000 islands a natural way station to the markets of mainland Asia. In 1897 Assistant Secretary of the Navy Theodore Roosevelt and President McKinley had discussed the merits of taking the Pacific colony in the event of war with Spain. At the first opportunity, McKinley acted to bring these islands into the U.S. strategic orbit. Shortly after Congress declared war on Spain, on May 4, the president dispatched 5,000 troops to occupy the Philippines. George Dewey, a Civil War veteran who commanded the American Asiatic Squadron, was ordered to "start offensive action." During the first week

Rebel Cubans, 1898, painted by Herbert Orth. Badly supplied Cuban insurrectos had practiced guerrilla warfare against the Spanish colonizers since the mid-1890s, but after the explosion on the USS Maine, American forces took over the war and abandoned the cause of Cuban self-determination. This picture, by the young U.S. volunteer, was one of a series of sketches later transformed into watercolor and oil paintings.

Courtesy of Mrs. Charles Johnson Post and Miss Phyllis B. Post.

of the conflict, he demolished the Spanish fleet in Manila Bay through seven hours of unimpeded target practice. Once the war ended, McKinley refused to sign the armistice unless Spain relinquished all claims to its Pacific islands. When Spain conceded, McKinley quickly drew up plans for colonial administration. He pledged "to educate the Filipinos, and to uplift and civilize and Christianize them." But after centuries of Spanish rule, the majority of islanders—already Christians—were eager to create their own nation.

The Filipino rebels, like the Cubans, at first welcomed American troops and fought with them against Spain. But when the war ended and they perceived that American troops were not preparing to leave, the rebels, led by Emilio Aguinaldo, turned against their former allies and attacked the American base of operations in Manila in February 1899. Predicting a brief skirmish, American commanders seriously underestimated the population's capacity to endure great suffering for the sake of independence.

U.S. troops had provoked this conflict in various ways. Military leaders, the majority veterans of the Indian wars, commonly described the natives as "gu-gus," and reported themselves, as one said, as "just itching to get at the niggers." While awaiting action, American soldiers repeatedly insulted or physically abused civilians, raped Filipino women, and otherwise whipped up resentment.

The resulting conflict took the form of modern guerrilla warfare, with brutalities on both sides. Instructed to regard every male Filipino over ten years of age as a potential enemy who could be shot without provocation, U.S. troops attacked civilians and destroyed their food, housing, and water supplies. Many American soldiers appeared indifferent to the sight of bloodshed. A. A. Barnes of the Third Regiment, describing the slaughter of 1,000 men, women, and children, wrote home, "I am probably growing hard-hearted, for I am in my glory when I can sight my gun on some dark-skin and pull the trigger." Ordered to take no prisoners, American soldiers forced Filipino civilians to dig their own graves and bragged about killing the wounded. By the time the fighting slowed down in 1902, 4,300 American lives had been lost, and one of every five Filipinos had died in battle or from starvation or disease. On some of the Philippine islands, intermittent fighting lasted until 1935.

The United States nevertheless refused to pull out. In 1901 William Howard Taft headed a commission that established a government controlled by Americans; after 1905, the president appointed a Filipino governor general to maintain the provincial government. Meanwhile, Americans bought up the best land and invested heavily in the island's sugar economy.

The conquest of the Philippines, which remained a U.S. territory until 1946, evoked for its defenders the vision of empire.

"Uncle Sam Teaches the Art of Self-Government," editorial cartoon, 1898. Expressing a popular sentiment of the time, a newspaper cartoonist shows the rebels as raucous children who constantly fight among themselves and need to be brought into line by Uncle Sam. The Filipino leader, Emilio Aguinaldo, appears as a dunce for failing to learn properly from the teacher. The two major islands where no uprising took place, Puerto Rico and Hawai'i, appear as passive but exotically dressed women, ready to learn their lessons.

Once again, Josiah Strong proclaimed judgment over an era. His famous treatise *Expansion* (1900) roundly defended American overseas involvements by carefully distinguishing between freedom and independence. People could achieve freedom, he argued, only under the rule of law. And because white Americans had proven themselves superior in the realm of government, they could best bring "freedom" to nonwhite peoples by setting aside the ideal of national independence for a period of enforced guidance. Many began to wonder, however, whether the United States could become an empire without sacrificing its democratic spirit, and to ask whether the subjugated people were so fortunate under the rule of the United States.

Critics of Empire

No mass movement formed to forestall U.S. expansion, but distinguished figures like Mark Twain, Andrew Carnegie, William Jennings Bryan, and Harvard philosopher William James voiced their opposition strongly. Dissent followed two broad lines of argument. In 1870, when President Grant urged the annexation of Santo Domingo, the nation-state occupying half of the island of Hispaniola (Haiti occupy-

CHRONOLOGY

1867	Grange founded		**1892**	Coeur d'Alene miners' strike
	Secretary of State Seward negotiates the purchase of Alaska			Homestead strike
				Ida B. Wells begins crusade against lynching
1874	Tompkins Square Riot		**1893**	Western Federation of Miners formed
	Granger laws begin to regulate railroad shipping rates			Financial panic and depression
				World's Columbian Exhibition opens in Chicago
1877	Rutherford B. Hayes elected president		**1894**	"Coxey's Army" marches on Washington, D. C.
	Great Uprising of 1877			Pullman strike
1879	Henry George publishes *Progress and Poverty*		**1896**	*Plessy v. Ferguson* upholds segregation
1881	President James A. Garfield assassinated; Chester A. Arthur becomes president			William McKinley defeats William Jennings Bryan for president
1883	Pendleton Act passed		**1897**	Dingley tariff again raises import duties to an all-time high
1884	Grover Cleveland elected president		**1898**	Eugene V. Debs helps found Social Democratic Party
1887	Interstate Commerce Act creates the Interstate Commerce Commission			Hawai'i is annexed
				Spanish-American War begins
				Anti-Imperialist League formed
1888	Edward Bellamy publishes *Looking Backward*		**1899**	*Cumming v. Richmond County Board of Education* sanctions segregated education
	National Colored Farmers' Alliance and Cooperative Union formed			Secretary of State John Hay announces Open Door policy
	Benjamin Harrison elected president			Guerrilla war begins in the Philippines
1889	National Farmers' Alliance and Industrial Union formed		**1900**	Gold Standard Act
1890	Sherman Silver Purchase Act			Josiah Strong publishes *Expansion*
	McKinley tariff enacted			
	National American Woman Suffrage Association formed			
1891	National Women's Alliance formed			
	Populist (People's) Party formed			

ing the other half), opponents countered by insisting that the United States stood unequivocally for the right of national self-determination and the consent of the governed. Others opposed annexation on the ground that dark-skinned and "ignorant" Santo Domingans were unworthy of American citizenship. These two contrary arguments, democratic and racist, were sounded repeatedly as the United States joined other nations in the armed struggle for empire.

Organized protest to military action, especially against the widely reported atrocities in the Philippines, owed much to the Anti-Imperialist League, which was founded by a small group of prominent Bostonians. In historic Faneuil Hall, which had witnessed the birth of both the American Revolution and the antislavery movement, a mass meeting was convened in June 1898 to protest the "insane and wicked ambition which is driving the nation to ruin." Within a few months, the league reported 25,000 members. Most supported American economic expansion but advocated free trade rather than political domination as the means to reach this goal. All strongly opposed the annexation of new territories. The league drew followers from every walk of life, including such famous writers as Charles Francis Adams and Mark Twain, *Nation* editor E. L. Godkin, African American scholar W.E.B. Du Bois, and Civil War veteran Thomas Wentworth Higginson.

The Anti-Imperialist League brought together like-minded societies from across the country, encouraged mass meetings, and published pamphlets, poems, and broadsides. *The National Labor Standard* expressed the common hope that all those "who believe in the Republic against Empire should join." By 1899, the league claimed a half-million members. A few outspoken anti-imperialists, such as former Illinois governor John Peter Altgeld, openly toasted Filipino rebels as heroes. Morrison Swift, leader of the Coxey's Army contingent from Massachusetts, formed a Filipino Liberation Society and sent antiwar materials to American troops. Others, such as Samuel Gompers, a league vice president, felt no sympathy for conquered peoples, describing Filipinos as "perhaps nearer the condition of savages and barbarians than any island possessed by any other civilized nation on earth." Gompers simply wanted to prevent colonized nonwhites from immigrating to the United States and "inundating" American labor.

Military leaders and staunch imperialists did not distinguish between racist and nonracist anti-imperialists. They called all dissenters "unhung traitors" and demanded their arrest. Newspaper editors accused universities of harboring antiwar professors, although college students as a group were enthusiastic supporters of the war.

Within the press, which overwhelmingly supported the Spanish-American War, the voices of opposition appeared primarily in African American and labor papers. The *Indianapolis Recorder* asked rhetorically in 1899, "Are the tender-hearted expansionists in the United States Congress really actuated by the desire to save the Filipinos from self-destruction or is it the worldly greed for gain?" The *Railroad Telegrapher* similarly commented, "The wonder of it all is that the working people are willing to lose blood and treasure in fighting another man's battle."

Most Americans put aside their doubts and welcomed the new era of aggressive nationalism. Untouched by the private tragedies of dead or wounded American soldiers and the mass destruction of civilian society in the Philippines, the vast majority could approve Theodore Roosevelt's defense of armed conflict: "No triumph of peace is quite so great as the supreme triumphs of war."

CONCLUSION

The conflicts marking the last quarter of the nineteenth century that pitted farmers, workers, and the proprietors of small businesses against powerful outside interests had offered Americans an important moment of democratic promise. By the end of the century, however, the rural and working-class campaigns to retain a large degree of self-government in their communities had been defeated, their organizations destroyed, their autonomy eroded. The rise of a national governing class and its counterpart, the large bureaucratic state, established new rules of behavior, new sources of prestige, and new rewards for the most successful citizens.

But the nation would pay a steep price, in the next era, for the failure of democratic reform. Regional antagonisms, nativist movements against the foreign-born, and above all deepening racial tensions blighted American society. As the new century opened, progressive reformers moved to correct flaws in government while accepting the framework of a corporate society and its overseas empire. But they found the widening divisions in American society difficult—if not impossible—to overcome.

REVIEW QUESTIONS

1. Discuss some of the problems accompanying the expansion of government during the late nineteenth century. What role did political parties play in this process? Explain how a prominent reformer such as James Garfield might become a leading "machine" politician?

2. What were the major causes and consequences of the populist movement of the 1880s and 1890s? Why did the election of 1896 prove so important to the future of American politics?

3. Discuss the role of women in both the Grange and the People's Party. What were their specific goals?

4. Discuss the causes and consequences of the financial crisis of the 1890s. How did various reformers and politicians respond to the event? What kinds of programs did they offer to restore the economy or reduce poverty?

5. How did the exclusion of African Americans affect the outcome of populism? Explain the rise of Jim Crow legislation in the South, and discuss its impact on the status of African Americans.

6. Describe American foreign policy during the 1890s. Why did the United States intervene in Cuba and the Philippines? What were some of the leading arguments for and against overseas expansion?

RECOMMENDED READING

Ruth Bordin, *Woman and Temperance: The Quest for Power and Liberty, 1873–1900* (1981). Relates the history of the WCTU to other campaigns for women's emancipation in the late nineteenth century and highlights the leadership of Frances E. Willard. Bordin demonstrates the central position temperance occupied in the political struggles of the era.

John G. Cawelti, *Apostles of the Self-Made Man* (1965). Examines the popular cultural obsession with the idea of success. Cawelti analyzes both the myths behind the notion of equal opportunity for all and the methods of popularizing success in the various media of the time.

Lawrence Goodwyn, *Democratic Promise: The Populist Moment in America* (1976). The most detailed study of populism, this book focuses on the economic cooperation and visionary schemes that preceded the populist electoral actions of the 1890s. Goodwin shows that populism was above all a movement aimed to turn back the monopolistic trend in the market economy and return power to the nation's citizens.

Lewis L. Gould, *The Presidency of William McKinley* (1980). A biography and political study of the president who represented a new kind of national leader in several key ways. Gould presents McKinley as product of "machine" politics but also an enlightened and modern administrator.

Michael Kazin, *The Populist Persuasion: An American History* (1995). A fresh interpretation of populist-style movements through the nineteenth and twentieth century that suggests such movements can be either "right" or "left" depending upon circumstances.

Walter LaFeber, *The New Empire: An Interpretation of American Expansion, 1860–1898* (1963). The best overview of U.S. imperial involvement in the late nineteenth century. LaFeber shows how overseas commitments grew out of the economic expansionist assumptions of American leaders and expanded continuously, if often chaotically, with the opportunities presented by the crises experienced by the older imperial powers.

Nell Irvin Painter, *Standing at Armageddon: The United States, 1877–1919* (1987). Presents a broad overview of racial and industrial conflicts and the political movements that formed in their wake. Painter attempts to show how this period proved decisive to the future history of the United States.

Thomas C. Reeves, *Gentleman Boss: The Life of Chester Alan Arthur* (1975). A detailed treatment of President Arthur as a product of a particular stage in the American political system. Reeves analyzes the conflicts within the Republican Party and the chaos of the Democratic Party, which made Arthur's rise possible.

Emily S. Rosenberg, *Spreading the American Dream: American Economic and Cultural Expansion, 1890–1945* (1982). Insightfully examines the significance of expansionist ideology. Rosenberg studies the cultural and social roots of American foreign policy.

William Appleman Williams, *Empire as a Way of Life: An Essay on the Causes and Character of America's Present Predicament* (1982). A lucid general exploration of American views of empire. Williams shows that Americans allowed the idea of empire and, more generally, economic expansion, to dominate their concept of democracy, especially in the last half of the nineteenth century.

C. Vann Woodward, *The Strange Career of Jim Crow*, 3d rev. ed. (1974). The classic study of southern segregation. Woodward shows how racist laws and customs tightened in the South and in many parts of the North in the last decades of the nineteenth century and how the ideologies of southern society encouraged the rise of Jim Crow legislation.

ADDITIONAL BIBLIOGRAPHY

The Nation and Politics

Cindy Sondik Aron, *Ladies and Gentlemen of the Civil Service* (1987)

Paula C. Baker, *The Moral Frameworks of Public Life: Gender, Politics and the State in Rural New York, 1870–1930* (1991)

Michael Lewis Goldberg, *An Army of Women: Gender and Politics in Gilded Age Kansas* (1997)

Charles Hoffman, *The Depression of the Nineties* (1970)

Morton Keller, *Affairs of the State: Public Life in Late Nineteenth*

Century America (1977)

J. Morgan Kousser, *The Shaping of Southern Politics: Suffrage Restriction and the Establishment of a One Party South* (1974)

Gwendolyn Mink, *Old Labor and New Immigrants in American Political Development* (1986)

Homer E. Socolofsky and Allan B. Spetter, *The Presidency of Benjamin Harrison* (1987)

Tom E. Terrell, *The Tariff, Politics and American Foreign Policy, 1874–1901* (1973)

Richard E. Welch Jr., *The Presidencies of Grover Cleveland* (1988)

Populism

Steven Hahn, *The Roots of Southern Populism* (1983)

Robert C. McMath, *American Populism: A Social History* (1993)

Scott G. McNall, *The Road to Rebellion: Class Formation and Kansas Populism 1865–1900* (1988)

Theodore R. Mitchell, *Political Education in the Southern Farmers' Alliance, 1887–1900* (1987)

Norman Pollack, *The Human Economy: Populism, Capitalism and Democracy* (1990)

Protest and Reform Movements

Beverly Beeton, *Women Vote in the West: The Suffrage Movement, 1869–1896* (1986)

Paul Buhle, *From the Knights of Labor to the New World Order: Labor and Culture in America* (1996)

Susan Curtis, *A Consuming Faith: The Social Gospel and Modern American Culture* (1991)

Barbara Leslie Epstein, *The Politics of Domesticity: Women, Evangelism, and Temperance in Nineteenth-Century America* (1981)

Philip S. Foner, *The Great Labor Uprisings of 1877* (1977)

Paul Krause, *The Battle for Homestead, 1880–1892* (1992)

Ralph E. Luker, *The Social Gospel in Black and White* (1991)

Nina Mjagkij and Margaret Spratt, eds., *Men and Women Adrift: The YMCA and the YWCA in the City* (1997)

Carlos A. Schwantes, *Coxey's Army* (1985)

Sheldon Stromquist, *A Generation of Boomers: The Patterns of Railroad Labor Conflict in Nineteenth Century America* (1987)

Mary Martha Thomas, *The New Woman in Alabama: Social Reform and Suffrage, 1890–1920* (1992)

Imperialism and Empire

Robert L. Beisner, *Twelve against Empire: The Anti-Imperialists, 1898–1900* (1968)

Nupur Chauduri and Margaret Strobel, eds., *Western Women and Imperialism* (1992)

Willard B. Gatewood Jr., *Black Americans and the White Man's Burden* (1975)

David Healy, *Drive to Hegemony: The United States in the Caribbean, 1888–1917* (1988)

Patricia Hill, *The World Their Household: The American Women's Foreign Mission Movement and Cultural Transformation, 1870–1920* (1985)

Amy Kaplan and Donald E. Pease, eds., *Cultures of United States Imperialism* (1993)

Martin Ridge, ed., *History, Frontier and Section: Three Essays by Frederick Jackson Turner* (1993)

Robert W. Rydell, *All the World's a Fair: Vision of Empire at the American International Expositions, 1876–1916* (1984)

Anders Stephanson, *Manifest Destiny: American Expansion and the Empire of Right* (1995)

Rubin F. Weston, *Racism in American Imperialism* (1972)

Spanish-American War and the Philippines

H. W. Brands, *Bound to Empire: The United States and the Philippines* (1992)

Kenton Clymer, *Protestant Missionaries in the Philippines, 1898–1916* (1986)

Graham A. Cosmos, *An Army for Empire* (1971)

Glenn Anthony May, *Battle for Batangas: A Philippine Province at War* (1991)

———, *Social Engineering in the Philippines: The Aims, Execution, and Impact of American Colonial Policy, 1900–1913* (1980)

Stuart Creighton Miller, *"Benevolent Assimilation": The American Conquest of the Philippines, 1899–1903* (1982)

William J. Pomeroy, *Philippines: Colonialism, Collaboration, Resistance* (1992)

Winfred Lee Thompson, *The Introduction of American Law in the Philippines and Puerto Rico, 1889–1905* (1989)

David F. Trask, *The War with Spain in 1898* (1981)

Richard E. Welch, *Response to Imperialism: The United States and the Philippine-American War* (1979)

Biography

Ruth Bordin, *Frances Willard: A Biography* (1986)

Mari Jo Buhle, Paul Buhle, and Harvey J. Kaye, eds., *The American Radical* (1995)

Jane Taylor Nelson, *A Prairie Populist: The Memoirs of Luna Kellie* (1992)

Allan Peskin, *Garfield: A Biography* (1978)

Martin Ridge, *Ignatius Donnelly* (1962)

Nick Salvatore, *Eugene V. Debs* (1982)

Mildred Thompson, *Ida B. Wells-Barnett: An Exploratory Study of an American Black Woman* (1990)

C. Van Woodward, *Tom Watson* (1963)

CHAPTER TWENTY-ONE

URBAN AMERICA AND
THE PROGRESSIVE ERA

1900–1917

AMERICAN COMMUNITIES
The Henry Street Settlement House:
Women Settlement House Workers
Create a Community of Reform

A shy and frightened young girl appeared in the doorway of a weekly home-nursing class for women on Manhattan's Lower East Side. The teacher beckoned her to come forward. Tugging on the teacher's skirt, the girl pleaded in broken English for the teacher to come home with her. "Mother," "baby," "blood," she kept repeating. The teacher gathered up the sheets that were part of the interrupted lesson in bed making. The two hurried through narrow, garbage-strewn, foul-smelling streets, then groped their way up a pitch-dark, rickety staircase. They reached a cramped, two-room apartment, home to an immigrant family of seven and several boarders. There, in a vermin-infested bed, encrusted with dried blood, lay a mother and her newborn baby. The mother had been abandoned by a doctor because she could not afford his fee.

The teacher, Lillian Wald, was a twenty-five-year-old nurse at New York Hospital. Years later she recalled this scene as her baptism by fire and the turning point in her life. Born in 1867, Wald enjoyed a comfortable upbringing in a middle-class German Jewish family in Rochester. Despite her parents' objections, she moved to New York City to become a professional nurse. Resentful of the disdainful treatment nurses received from doctors and horrified by the inhumane conditions at a juvenile asylum she worked in, Wald determined to find a way of caring for the sick in their neighborhoods and homes. With nursing school classmate Mary Brewster, Wald rented a fifth-floor walk-up apartment on the Lower East Side and established a visiting nurse service. The two provided professional care in the home to hundreds of families for a nominal fee of ten to twenty-five cents. They also offered each family they visited information on basic health care, sanitation, and disease prevention. In 1895, philanthropist Jacob Schiff generously donated a red brick Georgian house on Henry Street as a new base of operation.

The Henry Street Settlement stood in the center of perhaps the most overcrowded neighborhood in the world, New York's Lower East Side. Roughly 500,000 people were packed into an area only as large as a midsized Kansas farm. Population density was about 500 per acre, roughly four times the figure for the rest of New York City and far more concentrated than even the worst slums of London or Calcutta. A single city block might have as many as 3,000 residents. Home for most Lower East Siders was a small tenement apartment that might include paying boarders squeezed in alongside the immediate family. Residents were mostly recent immigrants from southern and eastern Europe: Jews, Italians, Germans, Greeks, Hungarians, Slavs. Men, women, and children toiled in the garment shops, small factories, retail stores, breweries, and warehouses to be found on nearly every street. An Irish-dominated machine controlled local political affairs.

The Henry Street Settlement became a model for a new kind of reform community composed essentially of college-educated women who encouraged and supported one another in a wide variety of humanitarian, civic, political, and cultural activities. Settlement house living arrangements closely resembled those in the dormitories of such new women's colleges as Smith, Wellesley, and Vassar. Like these colleges, the settlement house was an "experiment," but one designed, in settlement house pioneer Jane Addams's words, "to aid in the solution of the social and industrial problems which are engendered by the modern conditions of urban life." Unlike earlier moral reformers who tried to impose their ideas from outside, settlement house residents lived in poor communities and worked for immediate improvements in the health and welfare of those communities. Yet as Addams and others repeatedly stressed, the college-educated women were beneficiaries as well. The settlement house allowed them to preserve a collegial spirit, satisfy the desire for service, and apply their academic training.

With its combined moral and social appeal, the settlement house movement attracted many educated young women and grew rapidly. There were six settlement houses in the United States in 1891, 74 in 1897, more than 200 by 1900, and more than 400 by 1910. Few women made settlement work a career. The average stay was less than five years. Roughly half of those who worked in the movement eventually married. Those who did make a career of settlement house work, however, typically chose not to marry, and most lived together with female companions. As the movement flourished, settlement house residents called attention to the plight of the poor and fostered respect for different cultural heritages in countless articles and lectures. Leaders of the movement, including Jane Addams, Lillian Wald, and Florence Kelley, emerged as influential political figures during the progressive era.

Wald attracted a dedicated group of nurses, educators, and reformers to live at the Henry Street Settlement. By 1909 Henry Street had more than forty residents, supported by the donations of well-to-do New Yorkers. Wald and her allies convinced the New York Board of Health to assign a nurse to every public school in the city. They lobbied the Board of Education to create the first school lunch programs. They persuaded the city to set up municipal milk stations to ensure the purity of milk. Henry Street also pioneered tuberculosis treatment and prevention. Its leaders became powerful advocates for playground construction, improved street cleaning, and tougher housing inspection. The settlement's Neighborhood Playhouse became an internationally acclaimed center for innovative theater, music, and dance.

As settlement house workers expanded their influence from local neighborhoods to larger political and social circles, they became, in the phrase of one historian, spearheads for reform. Lillian Wald became a national figure—an outspoken advocate of child labor legislation and woman suffrage and a vigorous opponent of American involvement in World War I. She offered Henry Street as a meeting place to the National Negro Conference in 1909, out of which emerged the National Association for the Advancement of Colored People. It was no cliché for Wald to say, as she did on many occasions, "The whole world is my neighborhood."

New York City

KEY TOPICS

- The political, social, and intellectual roots of progressive reform
- Tensions between social justice and social control

- The urban scene and the impact of new immigration
- Political activism by the working class, women, and African Americans
- Progressivism in national politics

THE CURRENTS OF PROGRESSIVISM

Between the 1890s and World War I, a large and diverse number of Americans claimed the political label "progressive." Progressives could be found in all classes, regions, and races. They shared a fundamental ethos, or belief, that America needed a new social consciousness to cope with the problems brought on by the enormous rush of economic and social change in the post–Civil War decades. Yet progressivism was no unified movement with a single set of principles. It is best understood as a varied collection of reform communities, often fleeting, uniting citizens in a host of political, professional, and religious organizations, some of which were national in scope.

Progressivism drew from deep roots in hundreds of local American communities. At the state level it flowered in the soil of several key issues: ending political corruption, bringing more businesslike methods to governing, and offering a more compassionate legislative response to the excesses of industrialism. As a national movement, progressivism reached its peak in 1912, when the four major presidential candidates all ran on some version of a progressive platform. This last development was an important measure of the extent to which local reform movements like the Henry Street Settlement and new intellectual currents had captured the political imagination of the nation.

The many contradictions and disagreements surrounding the meaning of progressivism have led some historians to dismiss the term as hopelessly vague. Some progressives focused on expanding state and federal regulation of private interests for the public welfare. Others viewed the rapid influx of new immigrants and the explosive growth of large cities as requiring more stringent social controls. Another variant emphasized eliminating corruption in the political system as the key to righting society's wrongs. In the South, progressivism was for white people only. Progressives could be forward looking in their vision or nostalgic for a nineteenth-century world rapidly disap-

pearing. Self-styled progressives often found themselves facing each other from opposite sides of an issue.

Yet at the local, state, and finally national levels, reform rhetoric and energy shaped most of the political and cultural debates of the era. Understanding progressivism in all its complexity thus requires examining what key reform groups, thinkers, and political figures actually did and said under its ambiguous banner.

Unifying Themes

Three basic attitudes underlay the various crusades and movements that emerged in response to the fears gnawing at large segments of the population. The first was anger over the excesses of industrial capitalism and urban growth. At the same time, progressives shared an essential optimism about the ability of citizens to improve social and economic conditions. They were reformers, not revolutionaries. Second, progressives emphasized social cohesion and common bonds as a way of understanding how modern society and economics actually worked. They largely rejected the ideal of individualism that had informed nineteenth-century economic and political theory. For progressives, poverty and success hinged on more than simply individual character; the economy was more than merely a sum of individual calculations. Progressives thus opposed social Darwinism, with its claim that any effort to improve social conditions would prove fruitless because society is like a jungle in which only the "fittest" survive. Third, progressives believed in the need for citizens to intervene actively, both politically and morally, to improve social conditions. They pushed for a stronger government role in regulating the economy and solving the nation's social problems.

Progressive rhetoric and methods drew on two distinct sources of inspiration. One was evangelical Protestantism, particularly the late-nineteenth-century social gospel movement. Social gospelers rejected the idea of original sin as the cause of human suffering. They emphasized both the capacity and the duty of Christians to purge the world of poverty, inequality, and economic greed. A second strain of progressive

OVERVIEW

CURRENTS OF PROGRESSIVISM

	Key Figures	Issues	Institutions/Achievements
Local Communities	Jane Addams, Lillian Wald, Florence Kelley, Frederic C. Howe, Samuel Jones	• Improving health, education, welfare in urban immigrant neighborhoods • Child labor, eight-hour day • Celebrating immigrant cultures • Reforming urban politics • Municipal ownership/regulation of utilities	• Hull House Settlement • Henry Street Settlement • National Consumers League • New York Child Labor Committee • Bureau of Municipal Research
State	Robert M. LaFollette, Hiram Johnson, Al Smith	• Limiting power of railroads, other corporations • Improving civil service • Direct democracy • Applying academic scholarship to human needs	• "Wisconsin Idea" • State Workmen's Compensation • Unemployment Insurance • Public utility regulation
	James K. Vardaman, Hoke Smith	• Disfranchisement of African Americans	• Legalized segregation
National	Theodore Roosevelt	• Trustbusting • Conservation and Western development • National regulation of corporate and financial excesses	• Reclamation Bureau (1902) • U.S. Forest Service (1905) • Food and Drug Administration (1906) • Meat Inspection Act (1906) • Hepburn Act–ICC (1906)
	Woodrow Wilson	• National regulation of corporate and financial excesses • Reform of national banking	• Graduated Income Tax (1913) • Federal Reserve Act (1913) • Clayton Antitrust Act (1914) • Federal Trade Commission (1914)
Intellectual/ Cultural	Jacob Riis	• Muckraking	• *How the Other Half Lives* (1890)
	Lincoln Steffens, Ida Tarbell, Upton Sinclair, S.S. McClure		• *Shame of the Cities* (1902) • *History of Standard Oil* (1904) • *The Jungle* (1906) • *McClure's Magazine*
	John Dewey	• Education reform	• *Democracy and Education* (1916)
	Louis Brandeis	• Sociological jurisprudence	• *Muller v. Oregon* (1908)
	Edwin A. Ross	• Empowering "ethical elite"	• *Social Control* (1901)

Lewis Hine took this photo of a young girl working on a thread spinning frame in a North Carolina cotton mill. Between 1908 and 1918 Hine worked for the National Child Labor Committee, documenting the widespread abuse of child labor in the nation's mills, factories, mines, and canneries. "These pictures," Hine wrote, "speak for themselves and prove that the law is being violated."

thought looked to natural and social scientists to develop rational measures for improving the human condition, believing that experts trained in statistical analysis and engineering could make government and industry more efficient. Progressivism thus offered an uneasy combination of social justice and social control, a tension that would characterize American reform for the rest of the twentieth century.

Women Spearhead Reform

In the 1890s the settlement house movement had begun to provide an alternative to traditional concepts of private charity and humanitarian reform. Settlement workers found they could not transform their neighborhoods without confronting a host of broad social questions: chronic poverty, overcrowded tenement houses, child labor, industrial accidents, public health. As on Henry Street, college-educated, middle-class women constituted a key vanguard in the crusade for social justice. As reform communities, settlement houses soon

discovered the need to engage the political and cultural life of the larger communities that surrounded them.

Jane Addams founded one of the first settlement houses, Hull House, in Chicago in 1889 after years of struggling to find work and a social identity equal to her talents. A member of one of the first generation of American women to attend college, Addams was a graduate of Rockford College. Many educated women were dissatisfied with the life choices conventionally available to them: early marriage or the traditional female professions of teaching, nursing, and library work. Settlement work provided these women with an attractive alternative. Hull House was located in a run-down slum area of Chicago. It had a day nursery, a dispensary for medicines and medical advice, a boardinghouse, an art gallery, and a music school. Addams often spoke of the "subjective necessity" of settlement houses. By this she meant that they gave young, educated women a way to satisfy their powerful desire to connect with the real world. "There is nothing after disease, indigence and guilt," she wrote, "so fatal to life itself as the want of a proper outlet for active faculties."

Social reformer Florence Kelley helped direct the support of the settlement house movement behind groundbreaking state and federal labor legislation. Arriving at Hull House in 1891, Kelley found what she described as a "colony of efficient and intelligent women." In 1893, she wrote a report detailing the dismal conditions in sweatshops and the effects of long hours on the women and children who worked in them. This report became the basis for landmark legislation in Illinois that limited women to an eight-hour workday, barred children under fourteen from working, and abolished tenement labor. Illinois governor John Peter Altgeld appointed Kelley as chief inspector for the new law. In 1895 Kelley published *Hull House Maps and Papers*, the first scientific study of urban poverty in America. Moving to Henry Street Settlement in 1898, Kelley served as general secretary of the new National Consumers' League. With Lillian Wald she established the New York Child Labor Committee and pushed for the creation of the U.S. Children's Bureau, established in 1912.

Kelley, Addams, Wald, and their circle consciously used their power as women to reshape politics in the progressive era. Electoral politics and the state were historically male preserves, but female social progressives turned their gender into an advantage. They built upon the tradition of female moral reform, where women had long operated outside male-dominated political institutions to agitate and organize. Activists like Kelley used their influence in civil society to create new state powers in the service of social justice. They left a legacy that simultaneously expanded the social welfare function of the state and increased women's public authority and influence.

The Urban Machine

Women had to work outside existing political institutions not just because they could not vote, but also because city politics had become a closed and often corrupt system. By the turn of the century Democratic Party machines, usually dominated by first- and second-generation Irish, controlled the political life of most large American cities. The keys to machine strength were disciplined organization and the delivery of essential services to both immigrant communities and business elites. The successful machine politician viewed his work as a business, and he accumulated his capital by serving people who needed assistance. For most urban dwellers, the city was a place of economic and social insecurity. Recent immigrants in particular faced frequent unemployment, sickness, and discrimination. In exchange for votes, machine politicians offered their constituents a variety of services. These included munic-

ipal jobs in the police and fire departments, work at city construction sites, intervention with legal problems, and food and coal during hard times.

For those who did business with the city—construction companies, road builders, realtors—staying on the machine's good side was simply another business expense. In exchange for valuable franchises and city contracts, businessmen routinely bribed machine politicians and contributed liberally to their campaign funds. George Washington Plunkitt, a stalwart of New York's Tammany Hall machine, good-naturedly defended what he called "honest graft": making money from inside information on public improvements. "It's just like lookin' ahead in Wall Street or in the coffee or cotton market. . . . I seen my opportunities and I took 'em."

The machines usually had close ties to a city's vice economy and commercial entertainments. Organized prostitution and gambling, patronized largely by visitors to the city, could flourish only when "protected" by politicians who shared in the profits. Many machine figures began as saloonkeepers, and liquor dealers and beer brewers provided important financial support for "the organization." Vaudeville and burlesque theaters, boxing, horse racing, and professional baseball were other urban enterprises with economic and political links to machines. Entertainment and spectacle made up a central element in the machine political style as well. Constituents looked forward to the colorful torchlight parades, free summer picnics, and riverboat excursions regularly sponsored by the machines.

On New York City's Lower East Side, where the Henry Street Settlement was located, Timothy D. "Big Tim" Sullivan embodied the popular machine style. Big Tim, who had risen from desperate poverty, remained enormously popular with his constituents until his death in 1913. "I believe in liberality," he declared. "I am a thorough New Yorker and have no narrow prejudices. I never ask a hungry man about his past; I feed him, not because he is good, but because he needs food. Help your neighbor but

This publicity photograph of neighborhood children taking an art class at the Henry Street Settlement, New York City, around 1910, suggested that cultural pursuits and learning could flourish in slum neighborhoods with the help of a settlement house.

keep your nose out of his affairs." Critics charged that Sullivan controlled the city's gambling and made money from prostitution. But his real fortune came through his investments in vaudeville and the early movie business. Sullivan, whose district included the largest number of immigrants and transients in the city, provided shoe giveaways and free Christmas dinners to thousands every winter. To help pay for these and other charitable activities, he informally taxed the saloons, theaters, and restaurants in the district.

Progressive critics of machine politics routinely exaggerated the machine's power and influence. State legislatures, controlled by Republican rural and small-town elements, proved a formidable check on what city-based machines could accomplish. Reform campaigns that publicized excessive graft and corruption sometimes led voters to throw machine-backed mayors and aldermen out of office. And there were never enough patronage jobs for all the people clamoring for appointments. In the early twentieth century, to expand their base of support, political machines in the Northeast began concentrating more on passing welfare legislation beneficial to working-class and immigrant constituencies. In this way machine politicians often allied themselves with progressive reformers in state legislatures. In New York, for example, Tammany Hall figures such as Robert Wagner, Al Smith, and Big Tim Sullivan worked with middle-class progressive groups to pass child labor laws, factory safety regulations, worker compensation plans, and other efforts to make government more responsive to social needs. As Jewish and Catholic immigrants expanded in number and proportion in the city population, urban machines also began to champion cultural pluralism, opposing prohibition and immigration restrictions and defending the contributions made by new ethnic groups in the cities.

Political Progressives and Urban Reform

Political progressivism originated in the cities. It was both a challenge to the power of machine politics and a response to deteriorating urban conditions. City governments, especially in the Northeast and industrial Midwest, seemed hardly capable of providing the basic services needed to sustain large populations. For example, an impure water supply left Pittsburgh with one of the world's highest rates of death from typhoid, dysentery, and cholera. Most New York City neighborhoods rarely enjoyed street cleaning, and playgrounds were nonexistent. "The challenge of the city," Cleveland progressive Frederic C. Howe said in 1906, "has become one of decent human existence."

Reformers placed much of the blame for urban ills on the machines and looked for ways to restructure city government. The "good government" movement, led by the National Municipal League, fought to make city management a nonpartisan, even nonpolitical, process by bringing the administrative techniques of large corporations to cities. Reformers revised city charters in favor of stronger mayoral power and expanded use of appointed administrators and career civil servants. The New York Bureau of Municipal Research, founded in 1906, became a prototype for similar bureaus around the country. It drew up blueprints for model charters, ordinances, and zoning plans designed by experts trained in public administration.

Business and professional elites became the biggest boosters of structural reforms in urban government. In the summer of 1900 a hurricane in the Gulf of Mexico unleashed a tidal wave on Galveston, Texas. To cope with this disaster, leading businessmen convinced the state legislature to replace the mayor-council government with a small board of commissioners. Each commissioner was elected at large, and each was responsible for a different city department. Under this plan voters could more easily identify and hold accountable those responsible for city services. The city commission, enjoying both policy-making and administrative powers, proved very effective in rebuilding Galveston. By 1917 nearly 500 cities, including Houston, Oakland, Kansas City, Denver, and Buffalo, had adopted the commission form of government. Another approach, the city manager plan, gained popularity in small and midsized cities. In this system, a city council appointed a professional, nonpartisan city manager to handle the day-to-day operations of the community.

Progressive politicians who focused on the human problems of the industrial city championed a different kind of reform, one based on changing policies rather than the political structure. In Toledo, Samuel "Golden Rule" Jones served as mayor from 1897 to 1904. A capitalist who had made a fortune manufacturing oil well machinery, Jones created a strong base of working-class and ethnic voters around his reform program. He advocated municipal ownership of utilities, built new parks and schools, and established an eight-hour day and a minimum wage for city employees. In Cleveland, wealthy businessman Thomas L. Johnson served as mayor from 1901 to 1909. He emphasized both efficiency and social welfare. His popular program included lower streetcar fares, public baths, milk and meat inspection, and an expanded park and playground system.

Progressivism in the Statehouse

Their motives and achievements were mixed, but progressive politicians became a powerful force in many state capitals. In Wisconsin, Republican dissident Robert M. La Follette forged a coalition of angry farmers, small businessmen, and workers with his fiery attacks on railroads and other large corporations. Leader of the progressive faction of the state Republicans, "Fighting Bob" won three terms as governor (1900–1906), then served as a U.S. senator until his death in 1925. As governor he pushed through tougher corporate tax rates, a direct primary, an improved civil service code, and a railroad commission designed to regulate freight charges. La Follette used faculty experts at the University of Wisconsin to help research and write his bills. Other states began copying the "Wisconsin Idea"—the application of academic scholarship and theory to the needs of the people.

La Follette railed against "the interests" and invoked the power of the ordinary citizen. In practice, however, his railroad commission accomplished far less than progressive rhetoric claimed. It essentially represented special interests—commercial farmers and businessmen seeking reduced shipping rates. Ordinary consumers did not see lower passenger fares or reduced food prices. And as commissioners began to realize, the national reach of the railroads limited the effectiveness of state regulation. Although La Follette championed a more open political system, he also enrolled state employees in a tight political machine of his own. The La Follette family would dominate Wisconsin politics for forty years.

Western progressives displayed the greatest enthusiasm for institutional political reform. In the early 1900s, Oregon voters approved a series of constitutional amendments designed to strengthen direct democracy. The two most important were the initiative, which allowed a direct vote on specific measures put on the state ballot by petition, and the referendum, which allowed voters to decide on bills referred to them by the legislature. Other reforms included the direct primary, which allowed voters to cross party lines, and the recall, which gave voters the right to remove elected officials by popular vote. Widely copied throughout the West, all these measures intentionally weakened political parties.

Western progressives also targeted railroads, mining and timber companies, and public utilities for reform. Large corporations such as Pacific Gas and Electric and the Southern Pacific Railroad had amassed enormous wealth and political influence. They were able to corrupt state legislatures and charge consumers exorbitant rates. An alliance between middle-class progressives and working-class voters reflected growing disillusionment with the ideology of individualism that had helped pave the way for the rise of the big corporation. In California, attorney Hiram Johnson won a 1910 progressive campaign for governor on the slogan "Kick the Southern Pacific Railroad Out of Politics." In addition to winning political reforms, Johnson also put through laws regulating utilities and child labor, mandating an eight-hour day for working women, and providing a state worker compensation plan.

In the South, reform governors, such as James Vardaman of Mississippi and Hoke Smith of Georgia, often drew on the agrarian program and flamboyant oratory of populism. But southern progressives were typically city professionals or businessmen rather than farmers. Like their northern and western counterparts, they focused their attention on strengthening state regulation of railroads and public utilities, improving educational facilities, reforming city governments, and reining in the power of large corporations.

While southern populism had been based in part on a biracial politics of protest, southern progressivism was for white people only. A strident racism accompanied most reform campaigns against entrenched conservative Democratic machines, reinforcing racial discrimination and segregation. Southern progressives supported black disfranchisement as an electoral reform. With African Americans removed from political life, they argued, the direct primary system of nominating candidates would give white voters more influence. Between 1890 and 1910 southern states passed a welter of statutes specifying poll taxes, literacy tests, and property qualifications with the explicit goal of preventing voting by blacks. This systematic disfranchisement of African American voters stripped black communities of any political power. To prevent the disfranchisement of poor white voters under these laws, states established so-called understanding and grandfather clauses. Election officials had discretionary power to decide whether an illiterate person could understand and reasonably interpret the Constitution when read to him. Unqualified white men were also registered if they could show that their grandfathers had voted.

Southern progressives also supported the push toward a fully segregated public sphere. Between 1900 and 1910 southern states strengthened laws requiring separation of races in restaurants, streetcars, beaches, and theaters. Schools were separate but hardly equal. A 1916 Bureau of Education study found that per capita expenditures for education in southern states averaged $10.32 a year for white children and $2.89 for black children. And African American teachers received far lower salaries than their white counterparts. The legacy of southern progressivism was thus closely linked to the strengthening of the legal and institutional guarantees of white supremacy.

New Journalism: Muckraking

Changes in journalism helped fuel a new reform consciousness by drawing the attention of millions to urban poverty, political corruption, the plight of industrial workers, and immoral business practices. As early as 1890, journalist Jacob Riis had shocked the nation with his landmark book *How the Other Half Lives,* a portrait of New York City's poor. A Danish immigrant who arrived in New York City in 1871, Riis became a newspaper reporter, covering the police beat and learning about the city's desperate underside. Riis's book included a remarkable series of photographs he had taken in tenements, lodging houses, sweatshops, and saloons. These striking pictures, combined with Riis's analysis of slum housing patterns, had a powerful impact on a whole generation of urban reformers.

Within a few years, magazine journalists had turned to uncovering the seamier side of American life. The key innovator was S. S. McClure, a young Midwestern editor who in 1893 started America's first large-circulation magazine, *McClure's.* Charging only a dime for his monthly, McClure effectively combined popular fiction with articles on science, technology, travel, and recent history. He attracted a new readership among the urban middle class through aggressive subscription and promotional campaigns, as well as newsstand sales. By the turn of the century *McClure's* and several imitators—*Munsey's, Cosmopolitan, Collier's, Everybody's,* and the *Saturday Evening Post*—had circulations in the hundreds of thousands. Making extensive use of photographs and illustrations, these cheap upstarts soon far surpassed older, more staid and expensive magazines such as the *Atlantic Monthly* and *Harper's* in circulation.

In 1902 McClure began hiring talented reporters to write detailed accounts of the nation's social problems. Lincoln Steffens's series *The Shame of the Cities* (1902) revealed the widespread graft at the center of American urban politics. He showed how big-city bosses routinely worked hand in glove with businessmen seeking lucrative municipal contracts for gas, water, electricity, and mass transit. Ida Tarbell, in her *History of the Standard Oil Company* (1904), thoroughly documented how John D. Rockefeller ruthlessly squeezed out competitors with unfair business practices. Ray Stannard Baker wrote detailed portraits of life and labor in Pennsylvania coal towns.

McClure's and other magazines discovered that "exposure journalism" paid off handsomely in terms of increased circulation. The middle-class public responded to this new combination of factual reporting and moral exhortation. A series such as Steffens's fueled reform campaigns that swept individual communities. Between 1902 and 1908, magazines were full of articles exposing insurance scandals, patent medicine frauds, and stock market swindles. Upton Sinclair's 1906 novel *The Jungle,* a socialist tract set among Chicago packinghouse workers, exposed the filthy sanitation and abysmal working conditions in the stockyards and the meatpacking industry. In an effort to boost sales, Sinclair's publisher devoted an entire issue of a monthly magazine it owned, *World's Work,* to articles and photographs that substantiated Sinclair's devastating portrait.

In 1906, David Graham Phillips, in a series for *Cosmopolitan* called "The Treason of the Senate," argued that many conservative U.S. senators were no more than mouthpieces for big business. President Theodore Roosevelt, upset by Phillips's attack on several of his friends and supporters, coined a new term when he angrily denounced Phillips and his colleagues as "muckrakers" who "raked the mud of society and never looked up." Partly due to Roosevelt's outburst, the muckraking vogue began to wane. By 1907, S. S. McClure's original team of reporters had broken up.

In his landmark book, How the Other Half Lives (1890), *Jacob Riis made innovative use of photographs and statistics to argue for housing reform. This photograph depicts an Italian immigrant family of seven living in a one-room apartment. Overcrowded and dilapidated tenements threatened the entire city "because they are the hot-beds of the epidemics that carry death to the rich and poor alike; the nurseries of pauperism and crime that fill our jails and police courts."*

But muckraking had demonstrated the powerful potential for mobilizing public opinion on a national scale. Reform campaigns need not be limited to the local community. Ultimately, they could engage a national community of informed citizens.

Intellectual Trends Promoting Reform

On a deeper level than muckraking, a host of early-twentieth-century thinkers challenged several of the core ideas in American intellectual life. Their new theories of education, law, economics, and society provided effective tools for reformers. The emergent fields of the social sciences—sociology, psychology, anthropology, and economics—emphasized empirical observation of how people actually lived and behaved in their communities. Progressive reformers linked the systematic analysis of society and the individual characteristic of these new fields of inquiry to the project of improving the material conditions of American society. In doing so they called on the academy for something it had never before been asked to provide—practical help in facing the unprecedented challenges of rapid industrialization and urbanization.

Sociologist Lester Frank Ward, in his pioneering work *Dynamic Sociology* (1883), offered an important critique of social Darwinism, the then orthodox theory that attributed social inequality to natural selection and the "survival of the fittest." Ward argued that the conservative social theorists responsible for social Darwinism, such as Herbert Spencer and William Graham Sumner, had wrongly applied evolutionary theory to human affairs. They had confused organic evolution with social evolution. Nature's method was genetic: unplanned, involuntary, automatic, and mechanical. An octopus had to lay 50,000 eggs to maintain itself; a codfish hatched a million young fish a year in order that two might survive. By contrast, civilization had been built on successful human intervention in the natural processes of organic evolution. The human method was telic: planned, voluntary, rational, dynamic. "Every implement or utensil," Ward argued, "every mechanical device, every object of design, skill, and labor, every artificial thing that serves a human purpose, is a triumph of mind over the physical forces of nature in ceaseless and aimless competition."

Philosopher John Dewey criticized the excessively rigid and formal approach to education found in most American schools. In books such as *The School and Society* (1899) and *Democracy and Education* (1916), Dewey advocated developing what he called "creative intelligence" in students, which could then be put to use in improving society. Schools ought to be "embryonic communities," miniatures of society, where children were encouraged to participate actively in different types of experiences. By cultivating imagination and openness to new experiences, schools could develop creativity and the habits required for systematic inquiry. Dewey placed excessive faith in the power of schools to promote community spirit and democratic values. But his belief that education was the "fundamental method of social progress and reform" inspired generations of progressive educators.

At the University of Wisconsin, John R. Commons founded the new field of industrial relations and organized a state industrial commission that became a model for other states. Working closely with Governor Robert M. La Follette, Commons and his students helped draft pioneering laws in worker compensation and public utility regulation. Another Wisconsin faculty member, economist Richard Ely, argued that the state was "an educational and ethical agency whose positive aim is an indispensable condition of human progress." Ely believed the state must directly intervene to help solve public problems. He rejected the doctrine of laissez faire as merely "a tool in the hands of the greedy." Like Commons, Ely worked with Wisconsin lawmakers, applying his expertise in economics to reforming the state's labor laws.

Progressive legal theorists began challenging the conservative view of constitutional law that had dominated American courts. Since the 1870s the Supreme Court had interpreted the Fourteenth Amendment (1868) as a guarantee of broad rights for corporations. That amendment, which prevented states from depriving "any person of life, liberty, or property, without due process of law," had been designed to protect the civil rights of African Americans against violations by the states. But the Court, led by Justice Stephen J. Field, used the due process clause to strike down state laws regulating business and labor conditions. The Supreme Court and state courts had thus made the Fourteenth Amendment a bulwark for big business and a foe of social welfare measures.

The most important dissenter from this view was Oliver Wendell Holmes Jr. A scholar and Massachusetts judge, Holmes believed the law had to take into account changing social conditions. And courts should take care not to invalidate social legislation enacted democratically. After his appointment to the Supreme Court in 1902, Holmes authored a number of notable dissents to conservative court decisions overturning progressive legislation. Criticizing the majority opinion in *Lochner v. New York* (1905), in which the Court struck down a state law setting a ten-hour day for bakers, Holmes insisted that the Constitution "is not intended to embody a particular theory."

Holmes's pragmatic views of the law seldom convinced a majority of the Supreme Court before the late 1930s. But his views influenced a generation of lawyers who began practicing what came to be called sociological jurisprudence. In *Muller v. Oregon* (1908), the Court upheld an Oregon law limiting the maximum hours for working women. Noting that "woman's physical structure and the performance of maternal functions place her at a disadvantage," the Court found that "the physical well-being of woman becomes an object of public interest and care." Louis Brandeis, the state's attorney, amassed statistical, sociological, and economic data, rather than traditional legal arguments, to support his arguments. The "Brandeis Brief" became a common strategy for lawyers defending the constitutionality of progressive legislation.

The new field of American sociology concentrated on the rapidly changing nature of community. German social theorist Ferdinand Tönnies developed an extremely influential model for describing the recent evolution of western society from *Gemeinschaft* to *Gesellschaft*: from a static, close-knit, morally unified community to a dynamic, impersonal, morally fragmented society. If the new urban-industrial order had weakened traditional sources of morality and values—the family, the church, the small community—then where would the mass of people now learn these values?

This question provided the focus for Edward A. Ross's landmark work *Social Control* (1901), a book whose title became a key phrase in progressive thought. Ross argued that society needed an "ethical elite" of citizens "who have at heart the general welfare and know what kinds of conduct will promote this welfare." The "surplus moral energy" of this elite—ministers, educators, professionals—would have to guide the new mechanisms of social control needed in America's *Gesellschaft* communities.

SOCIAL CONTROL AND ITS LIMITS

Many middle- and upper-class Protestant progressives feared that immigrants and large cities threatened the stability of American democracy. They worried that alien cultural practices were disrupting what they viewed as traditional American morality. Viewing themselves as part of what sociologist Edward Ross called the "ethical elite," progressives often believed they had a mission to frame laws and regulations for the social control of immigrants, industrial workers, and African Americans. This was the moralistic and frequently xenophobic side of progressivism, and it provided a powerful source of support for the regulation of drinking, prostitution, leisure activities, and schooling. Organizations devoted to social control constituted other versions of reform communities. But these attempts at moral reform met with mixed success amid the extraordinary cultural and ethnic diversity of America's cities.

The more extreme proponents of these views also embraced the new pseudo-science of eugenics, based on the biological theories of the English scientist Francis Galton. Eugenicists stressed the primacy of inherited traits over environmental conditions for understanding human abilities and deficiencies. They argued that human society could be bettered only by breeding from the best stock and limiting the offspring of the worst. By the 1920s, these theories had gained enough influence to contribute to the drastic curtailing of immigration to America (see Chapter 23).

The Prohibition Movement
During the last two decades of the nineteenth century, the Woman's Christian Temperance Union had grown into a powerful mass organization. The WCTU appealed especially to women angered by men who used alcohol and then abused their wives and children. It directed most of its work toward ending the production, sale, and consumption of alcohol. But local WCTU chapters put their energy into nontemperance activities as well, including homeless shelters, Sunday schools, prison reform, child nurseries, and woman suffrage. The WCTU thus provided women with a political forum in which they could fuse their traditional moral posture as guardians of the home with broader public concerns. By 1911 the WCTU, with a quarter million members, was the largest women's organization in American history.

Other temperance groups had a narrower focus. The Anti-Saloon League, founded in 1893, began by organizing local-option campaigns in which rural counties and small towns banned liquor within their geographical limits. It drew much of its financial support from local businessmen, who saw a link between closing a community's saloons and increasing the productivity of workers. The league was a one-issue pressure group that played effectively on anti-urban and anti-immigrant prejudice. League lobbyists targeted state legislatures, where big cities were usually underrepresented. They hammered away at the close connections among saloon culture, liquor dealers, brewers, and big-city political machines.

The prohibition movement found its core strength among Protestant, native-born, small-town, and rural Americans. But prohibition found support as well in the cities, where the battle to ban alcohol revealed deep ethnic and cultural divides within America's urban communities. Opponents of alcohol were generally "pietists" who viewed the world from a position of moral absolutism. These included native-born, middle-class Protestants associated with evangelical churches along with some old-stock Protestant immigrant denominations. Opponents of prohibition were generally "ritualists" with less arbitrary notions of personal morality. These were largely new-stock, working-class Catholic and Jewish immigrants, along with some Protestants, such as German Lutherans.

The Social Evil

Many of the same reformers who battled the saloon and drinking also engaged in efforts to eradicate prostitution. Crusades against "the social evil" had appeared at intervals throughout the nineteenth century. But they reached a new level of intensity between 1895 and 1920. In part, this new sense of urgency stemmed from the sheer growth of cities and the greater visibility of prostitution in red-light districts and neighborhoods. Antiprostitution campaigns epitomized the diverse makeup and mixed motives of so much progressive reform. Male business and civic leaders joined forces with feminists, social workers, and clergy to eradicate "commercialized vice."

Between 1908 and 1914 exposés of the "white slave traffic" became a national sensation. Dozens of books, articles, and motion pictures alleged an international conspiracy to seduce and sell girls into prostitution. Most of these materials exaggerated the practices they attacked. They also made foreigners, especially Jews and southern Europeans, scapegoats for the sexual anxieties of native-born whites. In 1910 Congress passed legislation that permitted the deportation of foreign-born prostitutes or any foreigner convicted of procuring or employing them. That same year, the Mann Act made it a federal offense to transport women across state lines for "immoral purposes."

But most antiprostitution activity took place at the local level. Between 1910 and 1915, thirty-five cities and states conducted thorough investigations of prostitution. The progressive bent for defining social problems through statistics was nowhere more evident than in these reports. Vice commission investigators combed red-light districts, tenement houses, hotels, and dance halls, drawing up detailed lists of places where prostitution took place. They interviewed prostitutes, pimps, and customers. These reports agreed that commercialized sex was a business run by and for the profit and pleasure of men. They also documented the dangers of venereal disease to the larger community. The highly publicized vice reports were effective in forcing police crackdowns in urban red-light districts.

Reformers had trouble believing that any woman would freely choose to be a prostitute; such a choice was antithetical to conventional notions of female purity and sexuality. But for wage-earning women, prostitution was a rational choice in a world of limited opportunities. Maimie Pinzer, a prostitute, summed up her feelings in a letter to a wealthy female reformer: "I don't propose to get up at 6:30 to be at

work at 8 and work in a close, stuffy room with people I despise, until dark, for $6 or $7 a week! When I could, just by phoning, spend an afternoon with some congenial person and in the end have more than a week's work could pay me." The antivice crusades succeeded in closing down many urban red-light districts and larger brothels, but these were replaced by the streetwalker and call girl, who were more vulnerable to harassment and control by policemen and pimps. Rather than eliminating prostitution, reform efforts transformed the organization of the sex trade.

The Redemption of Leisure

Progressives faced a thorny issue in the growing popularity of commercial entertainment. For large numbers of working-class adults and children, leisure meant time and money spent at vaudeville and burlesque theaters, amusement parks, dance halls, and motion picture houses. These competed with municipal parks, libraries, museums, YMCAs, and school recreation centers. For many cultural traditionalists, the flood of new urban commercial amusements posed a grave threat. As with prostitution, urban progressives sponsored a host of recreation and amusement surveys detailing the situation in their individual cities. "Commercialized leisure," warned Frederic C. Howe in 1914, "must be controlled by the community, if it is to become an agency of civilization rather than the reverse."

By 1908 movies had become the most popular form of cheap entertainment in America. One survey estimated that 11,500 movie theaters attracted 5 million patrons each day. For five or ten cents "nickelodeon" theaters offered programs that might include a slapstick comedy, a Western, a travelogue, and a melodrama. Early movies were most popular in the tenement and immigrant districts of big cities, and with children. As the films themselves became more sophisticated and as "movie palaces" began to replace cheap storefront theaters, the new medium attracted a large middle-class clientele as well.

Progressive reformers seized the chance to help regulate the new medium as a way of improving the commercial recreation of the urban poor. Movies held out the promise of an alternative to the older entertainment traditions, such as concert saloons and burlesque theater, that had been closely allied with machine politics and the vice economy. In 1909, New York City movie producers and exhibitors joined with the reform-minded People's Institute to establish the voluntary National Board of Censorship (NBC). Movie entrepreneurs, most of whom were themselves immigrants, sought to shed the stigma of the slums, attract more middle-class patronage, and increase profits. A revolving group of civic activists reviewed new movies, passing them, suggesting changes, or condemning

Movies, *by John Sloan, 1913, the most talented artist among the so-called Ashcan realist school of painting. Active in socialist and bohemian circles, Sloan served as art editor for* The Masses *magazine for several years. His work celebrated the vitality and diversity of urban working-class life and leisure, including the new commercial culture represented by the motion picture.*

them. Local censoring committees all over the nation subscribed to the board's weekly bulletin. They aimed at achieving what John Collier of the NBC called "the redemption of leisure." By 1914 the NBC was reviewing 95 percent of the nation's film output.

Standardizing Education

Along with reading, writing, and mathematics, schools inculcated patriotism, piety, and respect for authority. Progressive educators looked to the public school primarily as an agent of "Americanization." Elwood Cubberley, a leading educational reformer, expressed the view that schools could be the vehicle by which immigrant children could break free of the parochial ethnic neighborhood. "Our task," he argued in *Changing Conceptions of Education* (1909), "is to break up these groups or settlements, to assimilate and amalgamate these people as a part of our American race, and to implant in their children, so far as can be done, the Anglo-Saxon conception of righteousness, law and order, and popular government."

The most important educational trends in these years were the expansion and bureaucratization of the nation's public school systems. In most cities centralization served to consolidate the power of older urban elites who felt threatened by the large influx of immigrants. Children began school earlier and stayed there longer. Kindergartens spread rapidly in large cities.

They presented, as one writer put it in 1903, "the earliest opportunity to catch the little Russian, the little Italian, the little German, Pole, Syrian, and the rest and begin to make good American citizens of them." By 1918 every state had some form of compulsory school attendance. High schools also multiplied, extending the school's influence beyond the traditional grammar school curriculum. In 1890 only 4 percent of the nation's youth between fourteen and seventeen were enrolled in school; by 1930 the figure was 47 percent.

High schools reflected a growing belief that schools be comprehensive, multifunctional institutions. In 1918 the National Education Association offered a report defining Cardinal Principles of Secondary Education. These included instruction in health, family life, citizenship, and ethical character. Academic programs prepared a small number of students for college. Vocational programs trained boys and girls for a niche in the new industrial order. Boys took shop courses in metal trades, carpentry, and machine tools. Girls learned typing, bookkeeping, sewing, cooking, and home economics. The Smith-Hughes Act of 1917 provided federal grants to support these programs and set up a Federal Board for Vocational Education.

Educational reformers also established national testing organizations such as the College Entrance Examination Board (founded in 1900) and helped standardize agencies for curriculum development and teacher training. In 1903 E. L. Thorndike published *Educational Psychology*, which laid the groundwork for education research based on experimental and statistical investigations. Progressives led in the development of specialized fields such as educational psychology, guidance counseling, and educational administration.

WORKING-CLASS COMMUNITIES AND PROTEST

The industrial revolution, which had begun transforming American life and labor in the nineteenth century, reached maturity in the early twentieth. In 1900, out of a total labor force of 28.5 million, 16 million people worked at industrial occupations and 11 million on farms. By 1920, in a labor force of nearly 42 million, almost 29 million were in industry, but farm labor had declined to 10.4 million. The world of the industrial worker included large manufacturing towns in New England; barren mining settlements in the West; primitive lumber and turpentine camps in the South; steelmaking and coal-mining cities in Pennsylvania and Ohio; and densely packed immigrant ghettos from New York to San Francisco, where workers toiled in garment trade sweatshops.

All these industrial workers shared the need to sell their labor for wages in order to survive. At the same time, differences in skill, ethnicity, and race proved powerful barriers to efforts at organizing trade unions that could bargain for improved wages and working conditions. So, too, did the economic and political power of the large corporations that dominated much of American industry. Yet there were also small, closely knit groups of skilled workers, such as printers and brewers, who exercised real control over their lives and labors. And these years saw many labor struggles that created effective trade unions or laid the groundwork for others. Industrial workers also became a force in local and national politics, adding a chorus of insistent voices to the calls for social justice.

The New Immigrants

On the eve of World War I, close to 60 percent of the industrial labor force was foreign-born. Most of these workers were among the roughly 9 million new immigrants from southern and eastern Europe who arrived in the United States between 1900 and 1914. In the nineteenth century, much of the overseas migration had come from the industrial districts of northern and western Europe. English, Welsh, and German artisans had brought with them skills critical for emerging industries such as steelmaking and coal mining. Unlike their predecessors, the new Italian, Polish, Hungarian, Jewish, and Greek immigrants nearly all lacked indus-

IMMIGRATION TO THE UNITED STATES (1901–1920)

Total: 14,532,000		% of Total
Italy	3,157,000	22%
Austria-Hungary	3,047,000	21
Russia and Poland	2,524,000	17
Canada	922,000	6
Great Britain	867,000	6
Scandinavia	709,000	5
Ireland	487,000	3
Germany	486,000	3
France and Low Countries (Belgium, Netherlands, Switz.)	361,000	2
Mexico	268,000	2
West Indies	231,000	2
Japan	213,000	2
China	41,000	*
Australia and New Zealand	23,000	*

*Less than 1% of total

Source: U.S. Bureau of the Census, *Historical Statistics of the United States from Colonial Times to* 1970, Washington, D.C., 1975.

trial skills. They thus entered the bottom ranks of factories, mines, mills, and sweatshops.

These new immigrants had been driven from their European farms and towns by several forces, including the undermining of subsistence farming by commercial agriculture; a falling death rate that brought a shortage of land; and religious and political persecution. American corporations also sent agents to recruit cheap labor. Except for Jewish immigrants, a majority of whom fled virulent anti-Semitism in Russia and Russian Poland, most newcomers planned on earning a stake and then returning home. Hard times in America forced many back to Europe. In the depression year of 1908, for example, more Austro-Hungarians and Italians left than entered the United States.

The decision to migrate usually occurred through social networks—people linked by kinship, personal acquaintance, and work experience. These "chains," extending from places of origin to specific destinations in the United States, helped migrants cope with the considerable risks entailed by the long and difficult journey. A study conducted by the U.S. Immigration Commission in 1909 found that about 60 percent of the new immigrants had their passage arranged by immigrants already in America. An Italian who joined his grandfather and cousins in Buffalo in 1906 recalled, "In western New York most of the first immigrants from Sicily went to Buffalo, so that from 1900 on, the thousands who followed them to this part of the state also landed in Buffalo."

Immigrant communities used ethnicity as a collective resource for gaining employment in factories, mills, and mines. One Polish steelworker recalled how the process operated in the Pittsburgh mills: "Now if a Russian got his job in a shear department, he's looking for a buddy, a Russian buddy. He's not going to look for a Croatian buddy. And if he sees the boss looking for a man he says, 'Look, I have a good man,' and he's picking out his friends. A Ukrainian department, a Russian department, a Polish department. And it was a beautiful thing in a way." Such specialization of work by ethnic origin was quite common throughout America's industrial communities.

In 1892 *the federal government opened the immigration station on Ellis Island, located in New York City's harbor, where about 80 percent of the immigrants to the United States landed. As many as 5,000 passengers per day reported to federal immigration officers for questions about their background and for physical examinations, such as this eye exam. Only about 1 percent were quarantined or turned away for health problems.*

The low-paid, backbreaking work in basic industry became nearly the exclusive preserve of the new immigrants. In 1907, of the 14,359 common laborers employed at Pittsburgh's U.S. Steel mills, 11,694 were eastern Europeans. For twelve-hour days and seven-day weeks, two-thirds of these workers made less than $12.50 a week, one-third less than $10.00. This was far less than the $15.00 that the Pittsburgh Associated Charities had estimated as the minimum for providing necessities for a family of five. Small wonder that the new immigration was disproportionately male. One-third of the immigrant steelworkers were single, and among married men who had been in the country less than five years, about two-thirds reported that their wives were still in Europe. Workers with families generally supplemented their incomes by taking in single men as boarders.

Not all the new immigrants came from Europe. Between 1898 and 1907 more than 80,000 Japanese entered the United States. The vast majority were young men working as contract laborers in the West, mainly in California. American law prevented Japanese immigrants (the Issei) from obtaining American citizenship, because they were not white. This legal discrimination, along with informal exclusion from many occupations, forced the Japanese to create niches for themselves within local economies. Most Japanese settled near Los Angeles, where they established small communities centered around fishing, truck farming, and the flower and nursery business. In 1920 Japanese farmers produced 10 percent of the dollar volume of California agriculture on 1 percent of the farm acreage. By 1930 over 35,000 Issei and their children (the Nisei) lived in Los Angeles.

Mexican immigration also grew in these years, providing a critical source of labor for the West's farms, railroads, and mines. Between 1900 and 1914, the number of people of Mexican descent living and working in the United States tripled, from roughly 100,000 to 300,000. Economic and political crises spurred tens of thousands of Mexico's rural and urban poor to emigrate north. Large numbers of seasonal agricultural workers regularly came up from Mexico to work in the expanding sugar beet industry and then returned. But a number of substantial resident Mexican communities also emerged in the early twentieth century.

Throughout Texas, California, New Mexico, Arizona, and Colorado, western cities developed barrios, distinct communities of Mexicans. Mexican immigrants attracted by jobs in the smelting industry made El Paso the most thoroughly Mexican city in the United States. In San Antonio, Mexicans worked at shelling pecans, becoming perhaps the most underpaid and exploited group of workers in the country. By 1910, San Antonio contained the largest number of Mexican immigrants of any city. In southern California, labor agents for railroads recruited Mexicans to work on building new interurban lines around Los Angeles. Overcrowding, poor sanitation, and deficient public services made many of these enclaves unhealthy places to live. Mexican barrios suffered much higher rates of disease and infant mortality than surrounding Anglo communities.

Urban Ghettos

In large cities, new immigrant communities took the form of densely packed ghettos. By 1920, immigrants and their children constituted almost 60 percent of the population of cities over 100,000. They were an even larger percentage in major industrial centers such as Chicago, Pittsburgh, Philadelphia, and New York. The sheer size and dynamism of these cities made the immigrant experience more complex than in smaller cities and more isolated communities. Workers in the urban garment trades toiled for low wages and suffered layoffs, unemployment, and poor health. But conditions in the small, labor-intensive shops of the clothing industry differed significantly from those in the large-scale, capital-intensive industries like steel.

New York City had become the center of both Jewish immigration and America's huge ready-to-wear clothing industry. The city's Jewish population was 1.4 million in 1915, almost 30 percent of its inhabitants. New York produced 70 percent of all women's clothing and 40 percent of all men's clothing made in the country. In small factories, lofts, and tenement apartments some 200,000 people, most of them Jews, some of them Italians, worked in the clothing trades. Most of the industry operated on the grueling piece-rate, or task, system, in which manufacturers and subcontractors paid individuals or teams of workers to complete a certain quota of labor within a specific time.

The garment industry was highly seasonal. A typical work week was sixty hours, with seventy common during busy season. But there were long stretches of unemployment in slack times. Even skilled cutters, all men, earned an average of only $16 per week. Unskilled workers, nearly all of them young single women, made only $6 or $7 a week. Perhaps a quarter of the work force, classified as "learners," earned only $3 to $6 a week. Often forced to work in cramped, dirty, and badly lit rooms, garment workers strained under a system in which time equaled money. Morris Rosenfeld, a presser of men's clothing who wrote Yiddish poetry, captured the feeling:

> The tick of the clock is the boss in his anger
> The face of the clock has the eye of a foe
> The clock—I shudder—Dost hear how it draws me?
> It calls me "Machine" and it cries to me "Sew!"

In November 1909 two New York garment manufacturers responded to strikes by unskilled women workers by hiring thugs and prostitutes to beat up pickets. The strikers won the support of the Women's Trade Union League, a group of sympathetic female reformers that included Lillian Wald, Mary Dreier, and prominent society figures. At a dramatic mass meeting in Cooper Union Hall, Clara Lemlich, a teenage working girl speaking in Yiddish, made an emotional plea for a general strike. She called for everyone in the crowd to take an old Jewish oath: "If I turn traitor to the cause I now pledge, may this hand wither from the arm I now raise." The Uprising of the 20,000, as it became known, swept through the city's garment district.

The strikers demanded union recognition, better wages, and safer and more sanitary conditions. They drew support from thousands of suffragists, trade unionists, and sympathetic middle-class women as well. Hundreds of strikers were arrested, and many were beaten by police. After three cold months on the picket line, the strikers returned to work without union recognition. But the International Ladies Garment Workers Union (ILGWU), founded in 1900, did gain strength and negotiated contracts with some of the city's shirt-

New York City Police set up this makeshift morgue to help identify victims of the disastrous Triangle Shirtwaist Company fire, March 25, 1911. Unable to open the locked doors of the sweatshop and desperate to escape from smoke and flames, many of the 146 who died had leaped eight stories to their death.

waist makers. The strike was an important breakthrough in the drive to organize unskilled workers into industrial unions. It opened the doors to women's involvement in the labor movement and created new leaders, such as Lemlich, Pauline Newman, and Rose Schneiderman.

On March 25, 1911, the issues raised by the strike took on new urgency when a fire raced through three floors of the Triangle Shirtwaist Company. As the flames spread, workers found themselves trapped by exit doors locked from the outside. Fire escapes were nonexistent. Within half an hour, 146 people, mostly young Jewish women, had been killed by smoke or had leaped to their death. In the bitter aftermath, women progressives led by Florence Kelley and Frances Perkins of the National Consumers' League joined with Tammany Hall leaders Al Smith, Robert Wagner, and Big Tim Sullivan to create a New York State Factory Investigation Commission. Under Perkins's vigorous leadership, the commission conducted an unprecedented round of public hearings and on-site inspections, leading to a series of state laws that dramatically improved safety conditions and limited the hours for working women and children.

Company Towns

Immigrant industrial workers and their families often established their communities in a company town, where a single large corporation was dominant. Cities such as Lawrence, Massachusetts; Gary, Indiana; and Butte, Montana, revolved around the industrial enter-

prises of Pacific Woolen, U.S. Steel, and Anaconda Copper. Workers had little or no influence over the economic and political institutions of these cities. In the more isolated company towns, residents often had no alternative but to buy their food, clothing, and supplies at company stores, usually for exorbitantly high prices. But they did maintain some community control in other ways. Family and kin networks, ethnic lodges, saloons, benefit societies, churches and synagogues, and musical groups affirmed traditional forms of community in a setting governed by individualism and private capital.

On the job, modern machinery and industrial discipline meant high rates of injury and death. In Gary, immigrant steelworkers suffered twice the accident rate of English-speaking employees, who could better understand safety instructions and warnings. A 1910 study of work accidents revealed that nearly a fourth of all new steelworkers were killed or injured each year. As one Polish worker described the immigrant's lot to his wife: "If he comes home sick then it is trouble, because everybody is looking only for money to get some of it, and during the sickness most will be spent." Mutual aid associations, organized around ethnic groups, offered some protection through cheap insurance and death benefits.

In steel and coal towns, women not only maintained the household and raised the children, they also boosted the family income by taking in boarders, sewing, and laundry. Many women also tended gardens and raised chickens, rabbits, and goats. Their produce and income helped reduce dependence on the company store. Working-class women felt the burdens of housework more heavily than their middle-class sisters. Pump water, indoor plumbing, and sewage disposal were often available only on a pay-as-you-go basis. The daily drudgery endured by working-class women far outlasted the "man-killing" shift worked by the husband. Many women struggled with the effects of their husbands' excessive drinking and faced early widowhood.

The adjustment for immigrant workers was not so much a process of assimilation as adaptation and resistance. Efficiency experts, such as Frederick Taylor (see Chapter 19), carefully observed and analyzed the time and energy needed for each job, then set standard methods for each worker. In theory, these standards would increase efficiency and give managers more control over their workers. But work habits and Old World cultural traditions did not always mesh with factory discipline or Taylor's "scientific management." A Polish wedding celebration might last three or four days. A drinking bout following a Sunday funeral might cause workers to celebrate "St. Monday" and not show up for work. Employers made much of the few Slavs allowed to work their way up into the ranks of skilled workers and foremen. But most immigrants were far more concerned with job security than with upward mobility. The newcomers learned from more skilled and experienced British and American workers that "slowing down" or "soldiering" spread out the work. As new immigrants became less transient and more permanently settled in company towns, they increased their involvement in local politics and union activity.

The power of large corporations in the life of company towns was most evident among the mining communities of the West, as was violent labor conflict. The Colorado Fuel and Iron Company (CFI) employed roughly half of the 8,000 coal miners who labored in that state's mines. In mining towns such as Ludlow and Trinidad, the CFI thoroughly dominated the lives of miners and their families. "The miner," one union official observed, "is in this land owned by the corporation that owns the homes, that owns the boarding houses, that owns every single thing there is there . . . not only the mines, but all the grounds, all the buildings, all the places of recreation, as well as the school and church buildings." By the early twentieth century, new immigrants, such as Italians, Greeks, Slavs, and Mexicans, composed a majority of the population in these western mining communities. About one-fifth of CFI miners spoke no English.

In September 1913, the United Mine Workers led a strike in the Colorado coalfields, calling for improved safety, higher wages, and recognition of the union. Thousands of miners' families moved out of company housing and into makeshift tent colonies provided by the union. In October, Governor Elias Ammons ordered the Colorado National Guard into the tense strike region to keep order. The troops, supposedly neutral, proceeded to ally themselves with the mine operators. By spring the strike had bankrupted the state, forcing the governor to remove most of the troops. The coal companies then brought in large numbers of private mine guards who were extremely hostile toward the strikers. On April 20, 1914, a combination of guardsmen and private guards surrounded the largest of the tent colonies at Ludlow, where more than a thousand mine families lived. A shot rang out (each side accused the other of firing), and a pitched battle ensued that lasted until the poorly armed miners ran out of ammunition. At dusk, the troops burned the tent village to the ground, routing the families and killing fourteen, eleven of them children. Enraged strikers attacked mines throughout southern Colorado in an armed rebellion that lasted ten days, until President Woodrow Wilson ordered the U.S. Army into the region. News of the Ludlow Massacre shocked millions and aroused widespread protests and demonstrations against the policies of Colorado Fuel and Iron and its owner, John D. Rockefeller Jr.

The AFL: "Unions, Pure and Simple"

Following the depression of the 1890s, the American Federation of Labor emerged as the strongest and most stable organization of workers. Samuel Gompers's strategy of recruiting skilled labor into unions organized by craft had paid off. Union membership climbed from under 500,000 in 1897 to 1.7 million by 1904. Most of this growth took place in AFL affiliates in coal mining, the building trades, transportation, and machine shops. The national unions—the United Mine Workers of America, the Brotherhood of Carpenters and Joiners, the International Association of Machinists—represented workers of specific occupations in collective bargaining. Trade autonomy and exclusive jurisdiction were the ruling principles within the AFL.

But the strength of craft organization also gave rise to weakness. In 1905 Gompers told a union gathering in Minneapolis that "caucasians" would not "let their standard of living be destroyed by negroes, Chinamen, Japs, or any others." Those "others" included the new immigrants from eastern and southern Europe, men and women, who labored in the steel mills and garment trades. Each trade looked mainly to the welfare of its own. Many explicitly barred women and African Americans from membership. There were some important exceptions. The United Mine Workers of America followed a more inclusive policy, recruiting both skilled underground pitmen and the unskilled aboveground workers. The UMWA even tried to recruit strikebreakers brought in by coal operators. With 260,000 members in 1904, the UMWA became the largest AFL affiliate.

AFL unions had a difficult time holding on to their gains. Economic slumps, technological changes, and aggressive counterattacks by employer organizations could be devastating. Trade associations using management-controlled efficiency drives fought union efforts to regulate output and shop practices. The National Association of Manufacturers, a group of smaller industrialists founded in 1903, launched an "open shop" campaign to eradicate unions altogether. "Open shop" was simply a new name for a workplace where unions were not allowed. The NAM supplied strikebreakers, private guards, and labor spies to employers. It also formed antiboycott associations to prevent unions in one trade from supporting walkouts in another.

Unfriendly judicial decisions also hurt organizing efforts. In 1906 a federal judge issued a permanent injunction against an iron molders strike at the Allis Chalmers Company of Milwaukee. In the so-called Danbury Hatters' Case (*Loewe v. Lawler*, 1908), a federal court ruled that secondary boycotts, aimed by strikers at other companies doing business with their employer, such as suppliers of materials, were illegal under the Sherman Antitrust Act. Long an effective labor tactic, secondary boycotts were now declared a conspiracy in restraint of trade. Not until the 1930s would unions be able to count on legal support for collective bargaining and the right to strike.

The IWW: "One Big Union"

Some workers developed more radical visions of labor organizing. In the harsh and isolated company towns of Idaho, Montana, and Colorado, miners suffered from low wages, poor food, and primitive sanitation, as well as injuries and death from frequent cave-ins and explosions. The Western Federation of Miners (WFM) had gained strength in the metal mining regions of the West by leading several strikes marred by violence. In 1899, during a strike in the silver mining district of Coeur d'Alene, Idaho, the Bunker Hill and Sullivan Mining Company had enraged the miners by hiring armed detectives and firing all union members. Desperate miners retaliated by destroying a company mill with dynamite. Idaho's governor declared martial law and obtained federal troops to enforce it. In a pattern that would become familiar in western labor relations, the soldiers served as strikebreakers, rounding up hundreds of miners and imprisoning them for months in makeshift bullpens.

In response to the brutal realities of labor organizing in the West, most WFM leaders embraced socialism and industrial unionism. In 1905, leaders of the WFM, the Socialist Party, and various radical groups gathered in Chicago to found the Industrial Workers of the World (IWW). The IWW charter proclaimed bluntly, "The working class and the employing class have nothing in common. . . . Between these two classes a struggle must go on until the workers of the world unite as a class, take possession of the earth and the machinery of production, and abolish the wage system."

William D. "Big Bill" Haywood, an imposing, one-eyed, hard-rock miner, emerged as the most influential and flamboyant spokesman for the IWW, or Wobblies, as they were called. Haywood, a charismatic speaker and effective organizer, regularly denounced the AFL for its conservative emphasis on organizing skilled workers by trade. He insisted that the IWW would exclude no one from its ranks. The Wobblies concentrated their efforts on miners, lumberjacks, sailors, "harvest stiffs," and other casual laborers. They glorified transient and unskilled workers in speeches and songs, aiming to counter their hopelessness and degradation. Openly contemptuous of bourgeois respectability, the IWW stressed the power of collective direct action on the job—strikes and, occasionally, sabotage.

The IWW briefly became a force among eastern industrial workers, tapping the rage and growing militance of the immigrants and unskilled. In 1909, an IWW-led steel strike at McKees Rocks, Pennsylvania,

challenged the power of U.S. Steel. In the 1912 "Bread and Roses" strike in Lawrence, Massachusetts, IWW organizers turned a spontaneous walkout of textile workers into a successful struggle for union recognition. Wobbly leaders such as Haywood, Elizabeth Gurley Flynn, and Joseph Ettor used class-conscious rhetoric and multilingual appeals to forge unity among the ethnically diverse Lawrence work force of 25,000.

These battles gained the IWW a great deal of sympathy from radical intellectuals, along with public scorn from the AFL and employers' groups. The IWW failed to establish permanent organizations in the eastern cities, but it remained a force in the lumber camps, mines, and wheat fields of the West. In spite of its militant rhetoric, the IWW concerned itself with practical gains. "The final aim is revolution," said one Wobbly organizer, "but for the present let's see if we can get a bed to sleep in, water enough to take a bath in and decent food to eat."

The occasional use of violence by union organizers sometimes backfired against the labor movement. On October 1, 1910, two explosions destroyed the printing plant of the *Los Angeles Times*, killing twenty-one workmen. When John and James McNamara, two brothers active in the ironworkers' union, were charged with the bombing and indicted for murder, unionists of all political persuasions rallied to their defense. Leaders of the AFL, IWW, and Socialist Party joined in a massive campaign that stressed the labor-versus-capital aspects of the case. The *Los Angeles Times* and its influential owner Harrison Gray Otis, they noted, were strongly antiunion and had helped keep Los Angeles a largely nonunion city. Some even suggested that Otis himself, looking to give labor a black eye, was responsible for the bombs. On Labor Day 1911, as the trial approached, huge crowds in America's largest cities gathered to proclaim the McNamara brothers innocent. But they were guilty. In the middle of the trial, the McNamaras confessed to the dynamiting, shocking their many supporters. A Socialist candidate for mayor of Los Angeles, favored to win the election, was decisively defeated, and the city remained a nonunion stronghold.

Rebels in Bohemia

During the 1910s, a small but influential community of painters, journalists, poets, social workers, lawyers, and political activists coalesced in the New York City neighborhood of Greenwich Village. These cultural radicals, nearly all of middle-class background and hailing from provincial American towns, shared a deep sympathy toward the struggles of labor, a passion for modern art, and an openness to socialism and anarchism. "Village bohemians," especially the women among them, challenged the double standard of Victorian sexual morality, rejected traditional marriage and sex roles, advocated birth control, and experimented with homosexual relations. They became a powerful national symbol for rebellion and the merger of political and cultural radicalism.

The term "bohemian" referred to anyone who had artistic or intellectual aspirations and who lived with disregard for conventional rules of behavior. Other American cities, notably Chicago at the turn of the century, had supported bohemian communities. But the Village scene was unique, if fleeting. The neighborhood offered cheap rents, studio space, and good ethnic restaurants, and it was close to the exciting political and labor activism of Manhattan's Lower East Side. The world view of the Village's bohemian community found expression in *The Masses*, a monthly magazine founded in 1911 by socialist critic Max Eastman, who was also its editor. "The broad purpose of *The Masses*," wrote John Reed, one of its leading writers, "is a social one—to everlastingly attack old systems, old morals, old prejudices—the whole weight of outworn thought that dead men have saddled upon us." Regular contributors included radical labor journalist Mary Heaton Vorse, artists John Sloan and George Bellows, and writers Floyd Dell and Sherwood Anderson.

At private parties and public events, the Village brought together a wide variety of men and women looking to combine politics, art, and support for the labor movement. Birth control activist Margaret Sanger found a sympathetic audience, as did IWW leader Big Bill Haywood. Journalist Walter Lippmann lectured on the new psychological theory of Sigmund Freud. Anarchist and feminist Emma Goldman wooed financial supporters for her magazine *Mother Earth*. Photographer Alfred Stieglitz welcomed artists to his gallery-studio "291."

For some, Greenwich Village offered a chance to experiment with sexual relationships or work arrangements. For others, it was an escape from small-town conformity or a haven for like-minded artists and activists. Yet the Village bohemians were united in their search for a new sense of community. Mary Heaton Vorse expressed their deeply pessimistic conviction that modern American society could no longer satisfy the elemental needs of community. "This is our weakness," she wrote. "Our strength does not multiply in our daily lives. There is a creative force in people doing things together." Intellectuals and artists, as well as workers, feeling alienated from the rest of society, sought shelter in the collective life and close-knit social relations of the Village community.

The Paterson, New Jersey, silk workers' strike of 1913 provided the most memorable fusion of bohemian sensibility and radical activism. After hearing Haywood speak about the strike at Mabel Dodge's apartment, John Reed offered to organize a pageant on

the strikers' behalf at Madison Square Garden. The idea was to publicize the strike to the world and also raise money. The Villagers helped write a script, designed sets and scenery, and took care of publicity. A huge crowd watched more than a thousand workers reenact the silk workers' strike, complete with picket line songs, a funeral, and speeches by IWW organizers.

The spectacular production was an artistic triumph. One critic described the pageant as "a new art form, a form in which the workers would present their own story without artifice or theatricality, and therefore with a new kind of dramatic power." But the pageant was also a financial disaster. The Village bohemia lasted only a few years, a flame snuffed out by the chill political winds accompanying America's entry into World War I. Yet for decades Greenwich Village remained a mecca for young men and women searching for alternatives to conventional ways of living.

Publicity poster for the 1913 pageant, organized by John Reed and other Greenwich Village radicals, supporting the cause of striking silk workers in Paterson, New Jersey. This poster drew on aesthetic styles associated with the Industrial Workers of the World, typically including a heroic, larger than life image of a factory laborer.

WOMEN'S MOVEMENTS AND BLACK AWAKENING

Progressive era women were at the forefront of several reform campaigns, such as the settlement house movement, prohibition, suffrage, and birth control. Millions of others took an active role in new women's associations that combined self-help and social mission. These organizations gave women a place in public life, increased their influence in civic affairs, and nurtured a new generation of female leaders.

In fighting racial discrimination, African Americans had a more difficult task. As racism gained ground in the political and cultural spheres, black progressives fought defensively to prevent the rights they had secured during Reconstruction from being further undermined. Still, they managed to produce leaders, ideas, and organizations that would have a long-range impact on American race relations.

The New Woman

The settlement house movement discussed in the opening of this chapter was just one of the new avenues of opportunity that opened to progressive era women. A steady proliferation of women's organizations attracted growing numbers of educated, middle-class women in the early twentieth century. With more men working in offices, more children attending school, and family size declining, the middle-class home was emptier. At the same time, more middle-class women were graduating from high school and college. In 1900, only 7 percent of Americans went to high school, but 60 percent of those who graduated were women. Moreover, in 1870, only 1 percent of college-age Americans had attended college, about 20 percent of them women; by 1910 about 5 percent of college-age Americans attended college, but the proportion of women among them had doubled to 40 percent.

Single-sex clubs brought middle-class women into the public sphere by celebrating the distinctive strengths associated with women's culture: cooperation, uplift, service. The formation of the General Federation of Women's Clubs in 1890 brought together 200 local clubs representing 20,000 women. By 1900 the federation boasted 150,000 members, and by World War I it claimed to represent over a million women. The women's club movement combined an earlier focus on self-improvement and intellectual pursuits with newer benevolent efforts on behalf of working women and children. The Buffalo Union, for example, sponsored art lectures for housewives and classes in typing, stenography, and bookkeeping for young working women. It also maintained a library, set up a "noon rest" downtown where women could eat lunch, and ran a school for training domestics. In Chicago the Women's

Club became a powerful ally for reformers, and club member Louise Bowen, a Hull House trustee, gave the settlement three-quarters of a million dollars.

For many middle-class women the club movement provided a new kind of female-centered community. As one member put it: "What college life is to the young woman, club life is to the woman of riper years, who amidst the responsibilities and cares of home life still wishes to keep abreast of the time, still longs for the companionship of those who, like herself, do not wish to cease to be students because they have left school." Club activity often led members to participate in other civic ventures, particularly "child-saving" reforms, such as child labor laws and mothers' pensions. Some took up the cause of working-class women, fighting for protective legislation and offering aid to trade unions. As wives and daughters of influential and well-off men in their communities, clubwomen had access to funds and could generate support for projects they undertook.

Other women's associations made even more explicit efforts to bridge class lines between middle-class homemakers and working-class women. The National Consumers' League (NCL), started in 1898 by Maud Nathan and Josephine Lowell, sponsored a "white label" campaign in which manufacturers who met safety and sanitary standards could put NCL labels on their food and clothing. Under the dynamic leadership of Florence Kelley, the NCL took an even more aggressive stance by publicizing labor abuses in department stores and lobbying for maximum-hour and minimum-wage laws in state legislatures. In its efforts to protect home and housewife, worker and consumer, the NCL embodied the ideal of "social housekeeping." "The home does not stop at the street door," said Marion Talbot, dean of women at the University of Chicago in 1911. "It is as wide as the world into which the individual steps forth."

Birth Control

The phrase "birth control," coined by Margaret Sanger around 1913, described her campaign to provide contraceptive information and devices for women. Sanger had seen her own mother die at age forty-nine after bearing eleven children. In 1910, Sanger was a thirty-year-old nurse and housewife living with her husband and three children in a New York City suburb. Excited by a socialist lecture she had attended, she convinced her husband to move to the city, where she threw herself into the bohemian milieu. She became an organizer for the IWW, and in 1912 she wrote a series of articles on female sexuality for a socialist newspaper.

When postal officials confiscated the paper for violating obscenity laws, Sanger left for Europe to learn more about contraception. She returned to New York determined to challenge the obscenity statutes with her own magazine, the *Woman Rebel*. Sanger's journal

Margaret Sanger (second from left) is shown outside the first birth control clinic, which she founded in Brooklyn, New York, in 1916. Sanger campaigned tirelessly to educate working-class women about contraception: she wrote and distributed pamphlets, lectured around the country, and invited arrest by publicly breaking obscenity laws. "Women cannot be on an equal footing with men," she wrote, "until they have full and complete control over their reproductive function."

celebrated female autonomy, including the right to sexual expression and control over one's body. When she distributed her pamphlet *Family Limitation*, postal inspectors confiscated copies and she found herself facing forty-five years in prison. In October 1914 she fled to Europe again. In her absence, anarchist agitator Emma Goldman and many women in the Socialist Party took up the cause.

An older generation of feminists had advocated "voluntary motherhood," or the right to say no to a husband's sexual demands. The new birth control advocates embraced contraception as a way of advancing sexual freedom for middle-class women as well as responding to the misery of those working-class women who bore numerous children while living in poverty. Sanger returned to the United States in October 1915. After the government dropped the obscenity charges, she embarked on a national speaking tour. In 1916 she again defied the law by opening a birth control clinic in a working-class neighborhood in Brooklyn and offering birth control information without a physician present. Arrested and jailed, she gained more publicity for her crusade. Within a few years, birth control leagues and clinics could be found in every major city and most large towns in the country.

Racism and Accommodation

At the turn of the century, four-fifths of the nation's 10 million African Americans still lived in the South, where most eked out a living working in agriculture. In the cities, most blacks were relegated to menial jobs, but a small African American middle class of entrepreneurs and professionals gained a foothold by selling services and products to the black community. They all confronted a racism that was growing in both intensity and influence in American politics and culture. White racism came in many variants and had evolved significantly since slavery days. The more virulent strains, influenced by Darwin's evolutionary theory, held that blacks were a "degenerate" race, genetically predisposed to vice, crime, and disease and destined to lose the struggle for existence with whites. By portraying blacks as incapable of improvement, racial Darwinism justified a policy of repression and neglect toward African Americans.

Southern progressives articulated a more moderate racial philosophy. They also assumed the innate inferiority of blacks, but they believed that black progress was necessary to achieve the economic and political progress associated with a vision of the New South. Their solution to the "race problem" stressed paternalist uplift. Edgar Gardner Murphy, an Episcopal clergyman and leading Alabama progressive, held that African Americans need not be terrorized. The black man, Murphy asserted, "will accept in the white man's country the place assigned him by the white man, will do his work, not by stress of rivalry, but by genial cooperation with the white man's interests."

African Americans also endured a deeply racist popular culture that made hateful stereotypes of black people a normal feature of political debate and everyday life. Benjamin Tillman, a U.S. senator from South Carolina, denounced the African American as "a fiend, a wild beast, seeking whom he may devour." Thomas Dixon's popular novel *The Clansman* (1905) described the typical African American as "half child, half animal, the sport of impulse, whim, and conceit . . . a being who, left to his will, roams at night and sleeps in the day, whose speech knows no word of love, whose passions, once aroused, are as the fury of a tiger." In northern cities "coon songs," based on gross caricatures of black life, were extremely popular in theaters and as sheet music. As in the antebellum minstrel shows, these songs reduced African Americans to creatures of pure appetite—for food, sex, alcohol, and violence. The minstrel tradition of white entertainers "blacking up"—using burnt cork makeup to pretend they were black—was still a widely accepted convention in American show business.

Amid this political and cultural climate, Booker T. Washington won recognition as the most influential black leader of the day. Born a slave in 1856, Washington was educated at Hampton Institute in Virginia, one of the first freedmen's schools devoted to industrial education. In 1881 he founded Tuskegee Institute, a black school in Alabama devoted to industrial and moral education. He became the leading spokesman for racial accommodation, urging blacks to focus on economic improvement and self-reliance, as opposed to political and civil rights. In an 1895 speech delivered at the Cotton States Exposition in Atlanta, Washington outlined the key themes of accommodationist philosophy. "Cast down your buckets where you are," Washington told black people, meaning they should focus on improving their vocational skills as industrial workers and farmers. "In all things that are purely social," he told attentive whites, "we can be as separate as the fingers, yet one as the hand in all things essential to mutual progress."

Washington's message won him the financial backing of leading white philanthropists and the respect of progressive whites. His widely read autobiography, *Up from Slavery* (1901), stands as a classic narrative of an American self-made man. Written with a shrewd eye toward cementing his support among white Americans, it stressed the importance of learning values such as frugality, cleanliness, and personal morality. But Washington also gained a large following among African Americans, especially those who aspired to business success. With the help of Andrew Carnegie he founded the National Negro Business League to preach the virtue of black business development in black communities.

Presidents Theodore Roosevelt and William Howard Taft consulted Washington on the few political patronage appointments given to African Americans. Washington also had a decisive influence on the flow of private funds to black schools in the South. Publicly he insisted that "agitation of questions of social equality is the extremest folly." But privately Washington also spent money and worked behind the scenes trying to halt disfranchisement and segregation. He offered secret financial support, for example, for court cases that challenged Louisiana's grandfather clause, the exclusion of blacks from Alabama juries, and railroad segregation in Tennessee and Georgia.

Racial Justice and the NAACP

Washington's focus on economic self-help remained deeply influential in African American communities long after his death in 1915. But alternative black voices challenged his racial philosophy while he lived. In the

In July 1905, a group of African American leaders met in Niagara Falls, Ontario, to protest legal segregation and the denial of civil rights to the nation's black population. This portrait was taken against a studio backdrop of the falls. In 1909, the leader of the Niagara movement, W.E.B. Du Bois (second from right, middle row) founded and edited the Crisis, the influential monthly journal of the National Association for the Advancement of Colored People.

early 1900s, scholar and activist W. E. B. Du Bois created a significant alternative to Washington's leadership. A product of the black middle class, Du Bois had been educated at Fisk University and Harvard, where in 1895 he became the first African American to receive a Ph.D. His book *The Philadelphia Negro* (1899) was a pioneering work of social science that refuted racist stereotypes by, for example, discussing black contributions to that city's political life and describing the wide range of black business activity. In *The Souls of Black Folk* (1903), Du Bois declared prophetically that "the problem of the twentieth century is the problem of the color line." Through essays on black history, culture, education, and politics, Du Bois explored the concept of "double consciousness." Black people, he argued, would always feel the tension between an African heritage and their desire to assimilate as Americans.

Unlike Booker T. Washington, Du Bois did not fully accept the values of the dominant white society. He worried that "our material wants had developed much faster than our social and moral standards." *Souls* represented the first effort to embrace African American culture as a source of collective black strength and something worth preserving. Spiritual striving, rooted in black folklore, religion, music, and history, were just as important as industrial education.

Du Bois criticized Booker T. Washington's philosophy for its acceptance of "the alleged inferiority of the Negro." The black community, he argued, must fight for the right to vote, for civic equality, and for higher education for the "talented tenth" of their youth. In 1905 Du Bois and editor William Monroe Trotter brought together a group of educated black men to oppose Washington's conciliatory views. Discrimination they encountered in Buffalo, New York, prompted the men to move their meeting to Niagara Falls, Ontario. "Any discrimination based simply on race or color is barbarous," they declared. "Persistent manly agitation is the way to liberty." The Niagara movement protested legal segregation, the exclusion of blacks from labor unions, and the curtailment of voting and other civil rights.

The Niagara movement failed to generate much change. But in 1909 many of its members, led by Du Bois, attended a National Negro Conference held at the Henry Street Settlement in New York. The group included a number of white progressives sympathetic to the idea of challenging Washington's philosophy. A new, interracial organization emerged from this conference, the National Association for the Advancement of Colored People. Du Bois, the only black officer of the original NAACP, founded and edited the *Crisis*, the influential NAACP monthly journal. For the next several decades the NAACP would lead struggles to overturn legal and economic barriers to equal opportunity.

NATIONAL PROGRESSIVISM

The progressive impulse had begun at local levels and percolated up. Progressive forces in both major political parties pushed older, entrenched elements to take a more aggressive stance on the reform issues of the day. Both Republican Theodore Roosevelt and Democrat Woodrow Wilson laid claim to the progressive mantle during their presidencies—a good example of how on the national level progressivism animated many perspectives. In their pursuit of reform agendas, both significantly reshaped the office of the president. As progressivism moved to Washington, nationally organized interest groups and public opinion began to rival the influence of the old political parties in shaping the political landscape.

Theodore Roosevelt and Presidential Activism

The assassination of William McKinley in 1901 made forty-two-year-old Theodore Roosevelt the youngest

man to hold the office of president before or since. Born to a wealthy New York family in 1858, Roosevelt overcame a sickly childhood through strenuous physical exercise and rugged outdoor living. After graduating from Harvard he immediately threw himself into a career in the rough and tumble of New York politics. He won election to the state assembly, ran an unsuccessful campaign for mayor of New York, served as president of the New York City Board of Police Commissioners, and went to Washington as assistant secretary of the navy. During the Spanish-American War, he won national fame as leader of the Rough Rider regiment in Cuba. Upon his return, he was elected governor of New York and then in 1900 vice president. Roosevelt viewed the presidency as a "bully pulpit"—a platform from which he could exhort Americans to reform their society—and he aimed to make the most of it.

Roosevelt was a uniquely colorful figure, a shrewd publicist, and a creative politician. His three-year stint as a rancher in the Dakota Territory; his fondness for hunting and nature study; his passion for scholarship, which resulted in ten books before he became president—all these set "T.R." apart from most of his upper-class peers. Roosevelt preached the virtues of "the strenuous life," and he believed that educated and wealthy Americans had a special responsibility to serve, guide, and inspire those less fortunate.

In style, Roosevelt made key contributions to national progressivism. He knew how to inspire and guide public opinion. He stimulated discussion and aroused curiosity like no one before him. In 1902 Roosevelt demonstrated his unique style of activism when he personally intervened in a bitter strike by anthracite coal miners. Using public calls for conciliation, a series of White House bargaining sessions, and private pressure on the mineowners, Roosevelt secured a settlement that won better pay and working conditions for the miners, but without recognition of their union. Roosevelt also pushed for efficient government as the solution to social problems. Unlike most nineteenth-century Republicans, who had largely ignored economic and social inequalities, Roosevelt frankly acknowledged them. Administrative agencies run by experts, he believed, could find rational solutions that could satisfy everyone.

Trustbusting and Regulation

One of the first issues Roosevelt faced was growing public concern with the rapid business consolidations taking place in the American economy. In 1902 he directed the Justice Department to begin a series of prosecutions under the Sherman Antitrust Act. The first target was the Northern Securities Company, a huge merger of transcontinental railroads brought about by financier J. P. Morgan. The deal would have created a giant holding company controlling nearly all the long-distance rail lines from Chicago to California. The Justice Department fought the case all the way through a hearing before the Supreme Court. In *Northern Securities v. U.S.* (1904), the Court held that the stock transactions constituted an illegal combination in restraint of interstate commerce.

This case established Roosevelt's reputation as a "trustbuster." During his two terms, the Justice Department filed forty-three cases under the Sherman Antitrust Act to restrain or dissolve business monopolies. These included actions against the so-called tobacco and beef trusts and the Standard Oil Company. Roosevelt viewed these suits as necessary to publicize the issue and assert the federal government's ultimate authority over big business. But he did not really believe in the need to break up large corporations. Unlike many progressives, who were nostalgic for smaller companies and freer competition, Roosevelt accepted centralization as a fact of modern economic life.

Roosevelt considered government regulation the best way to deal with big business. After easily defeating Democrat Alton B. Parker in the 1904 election, Roosevelt felt more secure in pushing for regulatory legislation. In 1906 Roosevelt responded to public pressure for greater government intervention and, overcoming objections from a conservative Congress, signed three important measures into law. The Hepburn Act strengthened the Interstate Commerce Commission (ICC), established in 1887 as the first independent regulatory agency, by authorizing it to set maximum railroad rates and inspect financial records.

Two other laws passed in 1906 also expanded the regulatory power of the federal government. The battles surrounding these reforms demonstrate how progressive measures often attracted supporters with competing motives. The Pure Food and Drug Act established the Food and Drug Administration (FDA), which tested and approved drugs before they went on the market. The Meat Inspection Act empowered the Department of Agriculture to inspect and label meat products. In both cases, supporters hailed the new laws as providing consumer protection against adulterated or fraudulently labeled food and drugs. Sensational exposés by muckrakers, documenting the greed, corruption, and unhealthy practices in the meatpacking and patent medicine industries, contributed to public support for the measures. Upton Sinclair's best-selling novel *The Jungle*, depicting the horrible conditions in Chicago's packinghouses, was the most sensational and influential of these.

But regulatory legislation found advocates among American big business as well. Large meat packers such as Swift and Armour strongly supported stricter federal regulation as a way to drive out smaller compa-

nies that could not meet tougher standards. The new laws also helped American packers compete more profitably in the European export market by giving their meat the official seal of federal inspectors. Large pharmaceutical manufacturers similarly supported new regulations that would eliminate competitors and patent medicine suppliers. Thus these reforms won support from large corporate interests that viewed stronger federal regulation as a strategy for consolidating their economic power. Progressive era expansion of the nation-state had its champions among—and benefits for—big business as well as American consumers.

Conservation, Preservation, and the Environment

As a naturalist and outdoorsman, Theodore Roosevelt also believed in the need for government regulation of the natural environment. He worried about the destruction of forests, prairies, streams, and the wilderness. The conservation of forest and water resources, he argued, was a national problem of vital import. In 1905 he created the U.S. Forest Service and named conservationist Gifford Pinchot to head it. Pinchot recruited a force of forest rangers to manage the reserves. By 1909 total timber and forest reserves had increased from 45 to 195 million acres, and more than 80 million acres of mineral lands had been withdrawn from public sale. Roosevelt also sponsored a National Conservation Commission, which produced the first comprehensive study of the nation's mineral, water, forest, and soil resources.

On the broad issue of managing America's natural resources, the Roosevelt administration took the middle ground between preservation and unrestricted commercial development. Pinchot established the basic pattern of federal regulation based on a philosophy of what he called the "wise use" of forest reserves. "Wilderness is waste," Pinchot was fond of saying, reflecting an essentially utilitarian vision that balanced the demands of business with wilderness conservation. But other voices championed a more radical vision of conservation, emphasizing the preservation of wilderness lands against the encroachment of commercial exploitation.

The most influential and committed of these was John Muir, an essayist and founder of the modern environmentalist movement. Muir made a passionate and spiritual defense of the inherent value of the American wilderness. Wild country, he argued, had a mystical power to inspire and refresh. "Climb the mountains and get their good tidings," he advised. "Nature's peace will flow into you as the sunshine into the trees. The winds will blow their freshness into you, and the storms their energy, while cares will drop off like autumn leaves."

Muir had been a driving force behind the Yosemite Act of 1890. Yosemite Park, located in a

William Hahn (1829–1887), Yosemite Valley from Glacier Point, 1874. 27¼ x 46¼ inches. California Historical Society, gift of Albert M. Bender.

William Hahn, Yosemite Valley from Glacier Point (1874). *Congress established Yosemite as a national park in 1890. Paintings like this one, along with contemporary photographs, helped convince Congress of the uniqueness of Yosemite's natural beauty.*

valley amid California's majestic Sierra Nevada range, became the nation's first preserve consciously designed to protect wilderness. Muir served as first president of the Sierra Club, founded in 1892 to preserve and protect the mountain regions of the west coast as well as Yellowstone National Park in Wyoming, Montana, and Idaho. Muir was a tireless publicist, and his writings won wide popularity among Americans, who were increasingly drawn to explore and enjoy the outdoors. By the turn of the century, misgivings about the effects of "overcivilization" and the association of untamed lands with the nation's frontier and pioneer past had attracted many to his thinking.

A bitter, drawn-out struggle over new water sources for San Francisco revealed the deep conflicts between conservationists, represented by Pinchot, and preservationists, represented by Muir. After a devastating earthquake in 1906, San Francisco sought federal approval to dam and flood the spectacular Hetch Hetchy Valley, located 150 miles from the city in Yosemite National Park. The project promised to ease the city's chronic freshwater shortage and to generate hydroelectric power. Conservationists and their urban progressive allies argued that developing Hetch Hetchy would be a victory for the public good over greedy private developers, since the plan called for municipal control of the water supply. To John Muir

and the Sierra Club, Hetch Hetchy was a "temple" threatened with destruction by the "devotees of ravaging commercialism."

Both sides lobbied furiously in Congress and wrote scores of articles in newspapers and magazines. Congress finally approved the reservoir plan in 1913; utility and public development triumphed over the preservation of nature. Although they lost the battle for Hetch Hetchy, the preservationists gained much ground in the larger campaign of alerting the nation to the dangers of a vanishing wilderness. A disappointed John Muir took some consolation from the fact that "the conscience of the whole country has been aroused from sleep." Defenders of national parks now realized that they could not make their case simply on scenic merit alone. They began to use their own utilitarian rationales, arguing that national parks would encourage economic growth through tourism and provide Americans with a healthy escape from urban and industrial areas. In 1916 the preservationists obtained their own bureaucracy in Washington with the creation of the National Park Service.

The Newlands Reclamation Act of 1902 represented another important victory for the conservation strategy of Roosevelt and Pinchot. With the goal of turning arid land into productive family farms through irrigation, the act established the Reclamation Bureau within the Department of the Interior and provided federal funding for dam and canal projects. But in practice, the bureau did more to encourage the growth of large-scale agribusiness and western cities than small farming. The Roosevelt Dam on Arizona's Salt River, along with the forty-mile Arizona Canal, helped develop the Phoenix area. The Imperial Dam on the Colorado River diverted water to California's Imperial and Coachella Valleys. The bureau soon became a key player in western life and politics, with large federally funded water projects providing flood control and the generation of electricity, as well as water for irrigation. The Newlands Act thus established a growing federal presence in managing water resources, the critical issue in twentieth-century western development.

Republican Split

When he won reelection in 1904, Roosevelt proclaimed his support for a "Square Deal" for all people. He was still essentially a conservative who supported progressive reform as the best way to head off the potential of class war. By the end of his second term, Roosevelt had moved beyond the idea of regulation to push for the most far-reaching federal economic and social programs ever proposed. He saw the central problem as "how to exercise . . . responsible control over the business use of vast wealth." To that end, he proposed restrictions on the use of court injunctions against labor strikes, as well as an eight-hour day for federal employees, a worker compensation law, and federal income and inheritance taxes.

In 1908, Roosevelt kept his promise to retire after a second term. He chose Secretary of War William Howard Taft as his successor. Taft easily defeated Democrat William Jennings Bryan in the 1908 election. During Taft's presidency, the gulf between "insurgent" progressives and the "stand pat" wing split the Republican Party wide open. To some degree, the battles were as much over style as substance. Compared with Roosevelt, the reflective and judicious Taft brought a much more restrained concept of the presidency to the White House. He supported some progressive measures, including the constitutional amendment legalizing a graduated income tax (ratified in 1913), safety codes for mines and railroads, and the creation of a federal Children's Bureau (1912). But in a series of bitter political fights involving tariff, antitrust, and conservation policies, Taft alienated Roosevelt and many other progressives.

After returning from an African safari and a triumphant European tour in 1910, Roosevelt threw himself back into national politics. He directly challenged Taft for the Republican Party leadership. In a dozen bitter state presidential primaries (the first ever held), Taft and Roosevelt fought for the nomination.

Although Roosevelt won most of these contests, the old guard still controlled the national convention and renominated Taft in June 1912. Roosevelt's supporters stormed out, and in August the new Progressive Party nominated Roosevelt and Hiram Johnson of California as its presidential ticket. Roosevelt's "New Nationalism" presented a vision of a strong federal government, led by an activist president, regulating and protecting the various interests in American society. The platform called for woman suffrage, the eight-hour day, prohibition of child labor, minimum-wage standards for working women, and stricter regulation of large corporations.

The Election of 1912: A Four-Way Race

With the Republicans so badly divided, the Democrats sensed a chance for their first presidential victory in twenty years. They chose Governor Woodrow Wilson of New Jersey as their candidate. Although not nearly as well known nationally as Taft and Roosevelt, Wilson had

This political cartoon, drawn by Charles Jay Budd, appeared on the cover of Harper's Weekly, September 28, 1912. It employed the imagery of autumn county fairs to depict voters as unhappy with their three choices for president. Note that the artist did not include the fourth candidate, Socialist Eugene Debs, who was often ignored by more conservative publications such as Harper's.

built a strong reputation as a reformer. The son of a Virginia Presbyterian minister, Wilson spent most of his early career in academia. He studied law at the University of Virginia and then earned a Ph.D. in political science from Johns Hopkins. After teaching history and political science at several schools, he became president of Princeton University in 1902. In 1910, he won election as New Jersey's governor, running against the state Democratic machine. He won the Democratic nomination for president with the support of many of the party's progressives, including William Jennings Bryan.

Wilson declared himself and the Democratic Party to be the true progressives. Viewing Roosevelt rather than Taft as his main rival, Wilson contrasted his New Freedom campaign with Roosevelt's New Nationalism. Crafted largely by progressive lawyer Louis Brandeis, Wilson's platform was far more ambiguous than Roosevelt's. The New Freedom emphasized restoring conditions of free competition and equality of economic opportunity. Wilson did favor a variety of progressive reforms for workers, farmers, and consumers. But in sounding older, nineteenth-century Democratic themes of states' rights and small government, Wilson argued against allowing the federal government to become as large and paternalistic as Roosevelt advocated. "What this country needs above everything else," Wilson argued, "is a body of laws which will look after the men who are on the make rather than the men who are already made."

Socialist party nominee Eugene V. Debs offered the fourth and most radical choice to voters. The Socialists had more than doubled their membership since 1908, to more than 100,000. On election days Socialist strength was far greater than that, as the party's candidates attracted increasing numbers of voters. By 1912 more than a thousand Socialists held elective office in thirty-three states and 160 cities. Geographically, Socialist strength had shifted to the trans-Mississippi South and West.

Debs had been a national figure in American politics since the 1890s, and he had already run for president three times. An inspiring orator who drew large and sympathetic crowds wherever he spoke, Debs proved especially popular in areas with strong labor movements and populist traditions. He wrapped his socialist message in an apocalyptic vision. Socialists would "abolish this monstrous system and the misery and crime which flow from it." His movement would "tear up all privilege by the roots, and consecrate the earth and all its fullness to the joy and service of all humanity." Debs and the Socialists also took credit for pushing both Roosevelt and Wilson further toward the left. Both the Democratic and Progressive Party platforms contained proposals considered extremely radical only ten years earlier.

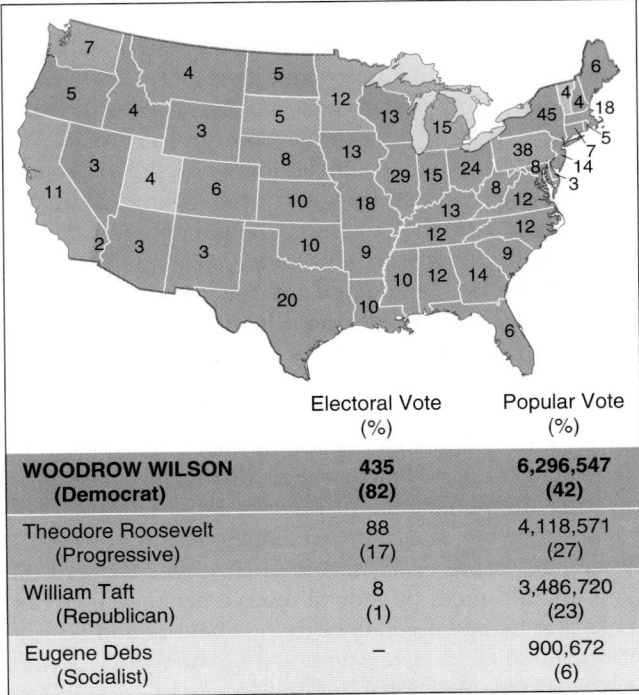

	Electoral Vote (%)	Popular Vote (%)
WOODROW WILSON (Democrat)	**435 (82)**	**6,296,547 (42)**
Theodore Roosevelt (Progressive)	88 (17)	4,118,571 (27)
William Taft (Republican)	8 (1)	3,486,720 (23)
Eugene Debs (Socialist)	—	900,672 (6)

The Election of 1912   *The split within the Republican Party allowed Woodrow Wilson to become only the second Democrat since the Civil War to be elected president. Eugene Debs's vote was the highest ever polled by a Socialist candidate.*

In the end, the divisions in the Republican Party gave the election to Wilson. He won easily, polling 6.3 million votes to Roosevelt's 4.1 million. Taft came in third with 3.5 million. Eugene Debs won 900,000 votes, 6 percent of the total, for the strongest Socialist showing in American history. Even though he won with only 42 percent of the popular vote, Wilson swept the electoral college with 435 votes to Roosevelt's 88 and Taft's 8, giving him the largest electoral majority ever to that time. In several respects, the election of 1912 was the first "modern" presidential race. It featured the first direct primaries, challenges to traditional party loyalties, an issue-oriented campaign, and a high degree of interest group activity.

Woodrow Wilson's First Term

As president, Wilson followed Roosevelt's lead in expanding the activist dimensions of the office. He became more responsive to pressure for a greater federal role in regulating business and the economy. This increase in direct lobbying—from hundreds of local and national reform groups, Washington-based organizations, and the new Progressive Party—was itself a new and defining feature of the era's political life. With the help of a Democratic-controlled Congress, Wilson pushed through a significant battery of reform proposals. By 1916 his reform program looked more like the New Nationalism that

Theodore Roosevelt had run on in 1912 than Wilson's own New Freedom platform. Four legislative achievements in Wilson's first term stand out.

The Underwood-Simmons Act of 1913 substantially reduced tariff duties on a variety of raw materials and manufactured goods, including wool, sugar, agricultural machinery, shoes, iron, and steel. Taking advantage of the newly ratified Sixteenth Amendment, which gave Congress the power to levy taxes on income, it also imposed the first graduated tax (up to 6 percent) on personal incomes. The Federal Reserve Act that same year restructured the nation's banking and currency system. It created twelve Federal Reserve Banks, regulated by a central board in Washington. Member banks were required to keep a portion of their cash reserves in the Federal Reserve Bank of their district. By raising or lowering the percentage of reserves required, "the Fed" could either discourage or encourage credit expansion by member banks. Varying the interest rate charged on loans and advances by federal reserve banks to member banks also helped regulate both the quantity and cost of money circulating in the national economy. By giving central direction to banking and monetary policy, the Federal Reserve Board diminished the power of large private banks.

Wilson also supported the Clayton Antitrust Act of 1914, which replaced the old Sherman Act of 1890 as the nation's basic antitrust law. Clayton reflected the growing political clout of the American Federation of Labor. It exempted unions from being construed as illegal combinations in restraint of trade, and it forbade federal courts to issue injunctions against strikers. But Wilson adopted the view that permanent federal regulation was necessary for checking the abuses of big business. The Federal Trade Commission (FTC), established in 1914, sought to give the federal government the same sort of regulatory control over corporations that the ICC had over railroads. Wilson believed a permanent federal body like the FTC would provide a method for corporate oversight superior to the erratic and time-consuming process of legal trustbusting. Wilson's hope that the FTC would usher in an era of harmony between government and business recalled the aims of Roosevelt and his big business backers in 1912.

On social issues, Wilson proved more cautious in his first two years. His initial failure to support federal child labor legislation and rural credits to farmers angered many progressives. A Southerner, Wilson also sanctioned the spread of racial segregation in federal offices. "I would say," he explained in 1913, "that I do approve of the segregation that is being attempted in several of the departments." As the reelection campaign of 1916 approached, Wilson worried about defections from the labor and social justice wings of his party. He proceeded to support a rural credits act providing

government capital to federal farm banks, as well as federal aid to agricultural extension programs in schools. He also came out in favor of child labor reform and a worker compensation bill for federal employees. But by 1916 the dark cloud of war in Europe had already begun to cast its long shadow over progressive reform.

CONCLUSION

The American political and social landscape was significantly altered by progressivism, but these shifts reflected the tensions and ambiguities of progressivism itself. A review of changes in election laws offers a good perspective on the inconsistencies that characterized progressivism. Nearly every new election law had the effect of excluding some people from voting while including others. For African Americans, progressivism largely meant disfranchisement from voting altogether. Direct primary laws eliminated some of the most blatant abuses of big-city machines, but in cities and states dominated by one party, the majority party's primary effectively decided the general election. Stricter election laws made it more difficult for third parties to get on the ballot, another instance in which progressive reform had the effect of reducing political options available to voters. Voting itself steadily declined in these years.

Overall, party voting became a less important form of political participation. Interest group activity, congressional and statehouse lobbying, and direct appeals to public opinion gained currency as ways of influencing government. Business groups such as the National Association of Manufacturers and individual trade associations were among the most active groups pressing their demands on government. Political action often shifted from legislatures to the new administrative agencies and commissions created to deal with social and economic problems. Popular magazines and journals grew significantly in both number and circulation, becoming more influential in shaping and appealing to national public opinion.

Social progressives and their allies could point to significant improvements in the everyday lives of ordinary Americans. On the state level, real advances had been made through a range of social legislation covering working conditions, child labor, minimum wages, and worker compensation. Social progressives, too, had discovered the power of organizing into extra-party lobbying groups such as the National Consumers' League and the National American Woman Suffrage Association. Yet the tensions between fighting for social justice and the urge toward social control remained unresolved. The emphasis on efficiency, uplift, and rational administration often collided with humane impulses to aid the poor, the immigrant, the slum dweller. The large majority of African Americans, blue-collar workers, and urban poor remained untouched by federal assistance programs.

Progressives had tried to confront the new realities of urban and industrial society. What had begun as a discrete collection of local and state struggles had by 1912 come to reshape state and national

politics. Politics itself had been transformed by the calls for social justice. Federal and state power would now play a more decisive role than ever in shaping work, play, and social life in local communities. That there was so much contention over the "true meaning" of progressivism is but one measure of its defining role in shaping early-twentieth-century America.

CHRONOLOGY

1889	Jane Addams founds Hull House in Chicago
1890	Jacob Riis publishes *How the Other Half Lives*
1895	Booker T. Washington addresses Cotton States Exposition in Atlanta, emphasizing an accommodationist philosophy
	Lillian Wald establishes Henry Street Settlement in New York
1898	Florence Kelley becomes general secretary of the new National Consumers' League
1900	Robert M. La Follette elected governor of Wisconsin
1901	Theodore Roosevelt succeeds the assassinated William McKinley as president
1904	Lincoln Steffens publishes *The Shame of the Cities*
1905	President Roosevelt creates U.S. Forest Service and names Gifford Pinchot head
	Industrial Workers of the World is founded in Chicago
1906	Upton Sinclair's *The Jungle* exposes conditions in the meatpacking industry
	Congress passes Pure Food and Drug Act and Meat Inspection Act and establishes Food and Drug Administration
1908	In *Muller v. Oregon* the Supreme Court upholds a state law

	limiting maximum hours for working women
1909	Uprising of the 20,000 in New York City's garment industries helps organize unskilled workers into unions
	National Association for the Advancement of Colored People (NAACP) is founded
1911	Triangle Shirtwaist Company fire kills 146 garment workers in New York City
	Socialist critic Max Eastman begins publishing *The Masses*
1912	Democrat Woodrow Wilson wins presidency, defeating Republican William H. Taft, Progressive Theodore Roosevelt, and Socialist Eugene V. Debs
	Bread and Roses strike involves 25,000 textile workers in Lawrence, Massachusetts
	Margaret Sanger begins writing and speaking in support of birth control for women
1913	Sixteenth Amendment, legalizing a graduated income tax, is ratified
1914	Clayton Antitrust Act exempts unions from being construed as illegal combinations in restraint of trade
	Federal Trade Commission is established
	Ludlow Massacre occurs
1916	National Park Service is established

REVIEW QUESTIONS

1. Discuss the tensions within progressivism between the ideals of social justice and the urge for social control. What concrete achievements are associated with each wing of the movement? What were the driving forces behind them?

2. Describe the different manifestations of progressivism at the local, state, and national levels. To what extent did progressives redefine the role of the state in American politics?

3. What gains were made by working-class communities in the progressive era? What barriers did they face?

4. How did the era's new immigration reshape America's cities and workplaces? What connections can you draw between the new immigrant experience and progressive era politics?

5. Analyze the progressive era from the perspective of African Americans. What political and social developments were most crucial, and what legacies did they leave?

6. Evaluate the lasting impact of progressive reform. How do the goals, methods, and language of progressives still find voice in contemporary America?

RECOMMENDED READING

John D. Buenker, *Urban Liberalism and Progressive Reform* (1973). Explores the contributions of urban ethnic voters and machine-based politicians to the progressive movement.

Robert M. Crunden, *Ministers of Reform: The Progressives' Achievement in American Civilization, 1889–1920* (1982). Emphasizes the moral and religious traditions of middle-class Protestants as the core of the progressive ethos.

Alan Dawley, *Struggles for Justice: Social Responsibility and the Liberal State* (1991). Offers an important interpretation of progressivism that focuses on how the working class and women pushed the state toward a more activist role in confronting social problems.

Susan A. Glenn, *Daughters of the Shtetl: Life and Labor in the Immigrant Generation* (1990). A sensitive analysis of the experiences of immigrant Jewish women in the garment trades.

Dewey Grantham, *Southern Progressivism: The Reconciliation of Progress and Tradition* (1982). Examines the contradictions within the southern progressive tradition.

James R. Green, *The World of the Worker: Labor in Twentieth Century America* (1980). Includes a fine overview of life and work in company towns and urban ghettos in the early twentieth century.

Morton Keller, *Regulating a New Society: Public Policy and Social Change in America, 1900–1930* (1994). A comprehensive study of public policy making on local and national levels in early twentieth-century America.

Arthur Link and Richard L. McCormick, *Progressivism* (1983). The best recent overview of progressivism and electoral politics.

Kathryn Kish Sklar, *Florence Kelley and the Nation's Work* (1995). The first installment in a two-volume biography, this book brilliantly brings Florence Kelley alive within the rich context of late-nineteenth-century women's political culture.

Robert Wiebe, *The Search for Order, 1877–1920* (1967). A pathbreaking study of how the professional middle classes responded to the upheavals of industrialism and urbanization.

ADDITIONAL BIBLIOGRAPHY

The Currents of Progressivism

Walter M. Brasch, *Forerunners of Revolution: Muckrakers and the American Social Conscience* (1990)

John D. Buenker, John C. Burnham, and Robert M. Crunden, *Progressivism* (1977)

Mina Carson, *Settlement Folk: Social Thought and the American Settlement Movement, 1885–1930* (1990)

Allen F. Davis, *Spearheads for Reform: The Social Settlements and the Progressive Movement, 1890–1914* (1967)

Leon Fink, *Progressive Intellectuals and the Dilemmas of Democratic Commitment* (1997)

Richard Hofstadter, *The Age of Reform: From Bryan to FDR* (1955)

James T. Kloppenberg, *Uncertain Victory: Social Democracy and Progressivism in European and American Thought, 1870–1920* (1986)

William A. Link, *The Paradox of Southern Progressivism, 1880–1930* (1992)

Richard McCormick, *The Party Period and Public Policy* (1986)

Nell Irvin Painter, *Standing at Armageddon: The United States, 1877–1919* (1987)

Martin J. Schiesl, *The Politics of Efficiency: Municipal Administration and Reform in America* (1977)

Social Control and Its Limits

Paul M. Boyer, *Urban Masses and Moral Order in America, 1820–1920* (1978)

Mark T. Connelly, *The Response to Prostitution in the Progressive Era* (1980)

Eldon J. Eisenach, *The Lost Promise of Progressivism* (1994)

Alan M. Kraut, *Silent Travelers: Germs, Genes, and the "Immigrant Menace"* (1994)

W. J. Rorabaugh, *The Alcoholic Republic* (1979)

Ruth Rosen, *The Lost Sisterhood: Prostitutes in America, 1900–1918* (1982)

David Tyack and Elizabeth Hansot, *Managers of Virtue: Public School Leadership in America, 1820–1980* (1982)

Working-Class Communities and Protest

John Bodnar, *The Transplanted* (1985)

Melvyn Dubofsky, *We Shall Be All: A History of the Industrial Workers of the World* (1969)

Leslie Fishbein, *Rebels in Bohemia* (1982)

Alice Kessler-Harris, *Out to Work: A History of Wage Earning Women in the United States* (1969)

J. Anthony Lukas, *Big Trouble* (1997)

David Montgomery, *The Fall of the House of Labor* (1987)

Kathy Peiss, *Cheap Amusements: Working Women and Leisure in Turn of the Century New York* (1986)

Roy Rosenzweig, *Eight Hours for What We Will* (1983)

Ronald Takaki, *Strangers from a Different Shore: A History of Asian Americans* (1989)

Women's Movements and Black Awakening

Paula Baker, *The Moral Frameworks of Public Life* (1991)

Mari Jo Buhle, *Women and American Socialism* (1983)

Ellen Fitzpatrick, *Endless Crusade: Women Social Scientists and Progressive Reform* (1990)

Linda Gordon, *Woman's Body, Woman's Right: A Social History of Birth Control* (1976)

Louis R. Harlan, *Booker T. Washington: Wizard of Tuskegee, 1901–1915* (1983)

Charles F. Kellogg, *NAACP* (1967)

J. Morgan Kousser, *The Shaping of Southern Politics* (1974)

Molly Ladd-Taylor, *Mother Work: Women, Child Welfare, and the State, 1890–1930* (1994)

David Levering Lewis, *W.E.B. Du Bois: Biography of a Race, 1868–1919* (1993)

Elaine Tyler May, *Great Expectations: Marriage and Divorce in Post Victorian America* (1980)

National Progressivism

Kendrick A. Clements, *The Presidency of Woodrow Wilson* (1992)

John M. Cooper Jr., *The Warrior and the Priest: Theodore Roosevelt and Woodrow Wilson* (1983)

Stephen R. Fox, *The American Conservation Movement: John Muir and His Legacy* (1981)

Lewis L. Gould, *The Presidency of Theodore Roosevelt* (1991)

Thomas K. McCraw, *Prophets of Regulation* (1984)

Michael McGerr, *The Decline of Popular Politics* (1986)

Roderick Nash, *Wilderness and the American Mind* (1967)

Melvin I. Urofsky, *Louis D. Brandeis and the Progressive Tradition* (1981)

Biography

Ellen Chesler, *Woman of Valor: Margaret Sanger and the Birth Control Movement in America* (1992)

Allen F. Davis, *American Heroine: The Life and Legend of Jane Addams* (1973)

Helen L. Horowitz, *The Power and Passion of M. Carey Thomas* (1994)

J. Joseph Huthmacher, *Senator Robert F. Wagner and the Rise of Urban Liberalism* (1971)

Justin Kaplan, *Lincoln Steffens* (1974)

W. Manning Marable, *W.E.B. Du Bois* (1986)

Nick Salvatore, *Eugene V. Debs: Citizen and Socialist* (1982)

David P. Thelen, *Robert M. La Follette and the Insurgent Spirit* (1976)

Bernard A. Weisberger, *The LaFollettes of Wisconsin* (1994)

Robert Westbrook, *John Dewey and American Democracy* (1991)

CHAPTER TWENTY-TWO

WORLD WAR I

1914–1920

AMERICAN COMMUNITIES
Vigilante Justice in Bisbee, Arizona

Early in the morning of July 12, 1917, two thousand armed vigilantes swept through Bisbee, Arizona, acting on behalf of the Phelps-Dodge mining company and Bisbee's leading businessmen to break a bitter strike that had crippled Bisbee's booming copper industry. The vigilantes seized miners in their homes, on the street, and in restaurants and stores. Any miner who wasn't working or willing to work was herded into Bisbee's downtown plaza, where two machine guns commanded the scene. From the Plaza more than 2,000 were marched to the local baseball park. There, mine managers gave them a last chance to return to work. Hundreds accepted and were released. The remaining 1,400 were forced at gunpoint onto a freight train, which took them 173 miles east to Columbus, New Mexico, where they were dumped in the desert.

The Bisbee deportation occurred against a complex backdrop. America had just entered World War I, corporations were seeking higher profits, and labor militancy was on the rise. Bisbee was only one of many American communities to suffer vigilantism during the war. Any number of offenses—not displaying a flag, failing to buy war bonds, criticizing the draft, alleged spying, any apparently "disloyal" behavior—could trigger vigilante action. In western communities like Bisbee, vigilantes used the superpatriotic mood to settle scores with labor organizers and radicals.

Arizona was the leading producer of copper in the United States. With a population of 8,000, Bisbee lay in the heart of the state's richest mining district. The giant Phelps-Dodge Company dominated Bisbee's political and social life. It owned the town's hospital, department store, newspaper, library, and largest hotel. With the introduction of new technology and open pit mining after 1900, unskilled laborers—most of them Slavic, Italian, Czech, and Mexican immigrants—had increasingly replaced skilled American and English-born miners in Bisbee's workforce.

America's entry into the war pushed the price of copper to an all-time high, prompting Phelps-Dodge to increase production. Miners viewed the increased demand for labor as an opportunity to flex their own muscle and improve wages and working conditions. Two rival union locals, one affiliated with the American Federation of Labor (AFL), the other with the more radical Industrial Workers of the World (IWW), or "Wobblies," sought to organize Bisbee's workers. On June 26, 1917, Bisbee's Wobblies went on strike. They demanded better mine safety, an end to discrimination against union workers, and a substantial pay increase. The IWW, making special efforts to attract lower-paid foreign-born workers to their cause, even hired two Mexican organizers. Although the IWW had only 300 or 400 members in Bisbee, more than half the town's 4,700 miners supported the strike.

The walkout was peaceful, but Walter Douglas, district manager for Phelps-Dodge, was unmoved. "There will be no compromise," he declared, "because you cannot compromise with a rattlesnake." Douglas, Cochise County Sheriff Harry Wheeler, and Bisbee's leading businessmen met secretly to plan the July 12 deportation. The approximately 2,000 men they deputized to carry it out were members of Bisbee's Citizens' Protective League and the Workers Loyalty League. These vigilantes included company officials, small businessmen, professionals, and anti-union workers. Local telephone and telegraph offices agreed to isolate Bisbee by censoring outgoing messages. The El Paso and Southwestern Railroad, a subsidiary of Phelps-Dodge, provided the waiting boxcars.

The participants in this illegal conspiracy defended themselves by exaggerating the threat of organized labor. They also appealed to patriotism and played on racial fears. The IWW opposed American involvement in the war, making it vulnerable to charges of disloyalty. A proclamation, posted in Bisbee the day of the deportation, claimed, "There is no labor trouble—we are sure of that—but a direct attempt to embarrass and injure the government of the United States." Sheriff Wheeler told a visiting journalist he worried that Mexicans "would take advantage of the disturbed conditions of the strike and start an uprising, destroying the mines and murdering American women and children."

An army census of the deportees, who had found temporary refuge at an army camp in Columbus, New Mexico, offered quite a different picture. Of the 1,400 men, 520 owned property in Bisbee. Nearly 500 had already registered for the draft, and more than 200 had purchased Liberty Bonds. More than 400 were married with children; only 400 were members of the IWW. Eighty percent were immigrants, including nearly 400 Mexicans. A presidential mediation committee concluded that "conditions in Bisbee were in fact peaceful and free from manifestations of disorder or violence." The deported miners nonetheless found it difficult to shake the accusations that their strike was anti-American and foreign inspired.

At their camp, the miners organized their own police force and elected an executive committee to seek relief. In a letter to President Wilson, they claimed "Common American

citizens here are now convinced that they have no constitutional rights." They promised to return to digging copper if the federal government operated the nation's mines and smelters. IWW leader William D. "Big Bill" Haywood threatened a general strike of metal miners and harvest workers if the government did not return the deportees to their homes. The presidential mediation committee criticized the mine companies and declared the deportation illegal. But it also denied the federal government had any jurisdiction in the matter. Arizona's attorney general refused to offer protection for a return to Bisbee.

In September, the men began gradually to drift away from Columbus. Only a few ever returned to Bisbee. The events convinced President Wilson that the IWW was a subversive organization and a threat to national security. The Justice Department began planning an all-out legal assault that would soon cripple the Wobblies. But Wilson could not ignore protests against the Bisbee outrage from such prominent and patriotic Americans as Samuel Gompers, head of the American Federation of Labor. To demonstrate his administration's commitment to harmonious industrial relations, the president appointed a special commission to investigate and mediate wartime labor conflicts. But Arizona's mines would remain union free until the New Deal era of the 1930s.

America's entry into the war created a national sense of purpose and an unprecedented mobilization of resources. Unifying the country and winning the war now took precedence over progressive reforms. The war also aroused powerful political emotions and provided an excuse for some citizens to try to cleanse their communities of anyone who did not conform. In a 1918 speech, Arizona State Senator Fred Sutter hailed the benefits of vigilante justice. "And what are the results in Bisbee since the deportation?" he asked. "They are, sir, a practically 100 percent American camp; a foreigner to get a job there today had to give a pretty good account of himself. The mines are today producing more copper than ever before and we are a quiet, peaceful, law-abiding community and will continue so, so long as the IWWs or other enemies of the government let us alone."

Bisbee

KEY TOPICS

- America's expanding international role
- From neutrality to participation in the Great War

- Mobilizing the society and the economy for war
- Dissent and its repression
- Woodrow Wilson's failure to win the peace

BECOMING A WORLD POWER

In the first years of the new century the United States pursued a more vigorous and aggressive foreign policy than it had in the past. Presidents Theodore Roosevelt, William Howard Taft, and Woodrow Wilson all contributed to "progressive diplomacy," in which commercial expansion was backed by a growing military presence in the Caribbean, Asia, and Mexico. This policy reflected a view of world affairs that stressed moralism, order, and a special, even God-given, role for the United States. By 1917, when the United States entered the Great War, this policy had already secured the country a place as a new world power.

Roosevelt: The Big Stick

Theodore Roosevelt left a strong imprint on the nation's foreign policy. Like many of his class and background, "T.R." took for granted the superiority of Protestant Anglo-American culture and the goal of spreading its values and influence. He believed that to maintain and increase its economic and political stature, America must be militarily strong. In 1900 Roosevelt summarized his activist views, declaring, "I have always been fond of the West African proverb, 'Speak softly and carry a big stick, you will go far.' "

Roosevelt brought the "big stick" approach to several disputes in the Caribbean region. Since the 1880s, several British, French, and American companies had pursued various plans for building a canal across the Isthmus of Panama, thereby connecting the Atlantic and Pacific Oceans. The canal was a top priority for Roosevelt, and he tried to negotiate a leasing agreement with Colombia, of which Panama was a province. But when the Colombian Senate rejected a final American offer in the fall of 1903, Roosevelt invented a new strategy. A combination of native forces and foreign promoters associated with the canal project plotted a revolt against Colombia. Roosevelt kept in touch with at least one leader of the revolt, Philippe Bunau-Varilla, an engineer and agent for the New Panama Canal Company, and the president let him know that U.S. warships were steaming toward Panama.

On November 3, 1903, just as the USS Nashville arrived in Colón harbor, the province of Panama declared itself independent of Colombia. The United States immediately recognized the new Republic of Panama. Less than two weeks later, Bunau-Varilla, serving as a minister from Panama, signed a treaty granting the United States full sovereignty in perpetuity over a ten-mile-wide canal zone. America guaranteed Panama's independence and agreed to pay it $10 million initially and an additional $250,000 a year for the canal zone. Years after the canal was completed, the U.S. Senate voted another $25 million to Colombia as compensation.

The Panama Canal was a triumph of modern engineering and gave the United States a tremendous strategic and commercial advantage in the Western Hemisphere. It took eight years to build and cost hundreds of poorly paid manual workers their lives. Several earlier attempts to build a canal in the region had failed. But with better equipment and a vigorous campaign against disease, the United States succeeded. In 1914, after $720 million in construction costs, the first merchant ships sailed through the canal.

"The inevitable effect of our building the Canal," wrote Secretary of State Elihu Root in 1905, "must be to require us to police the surrounding premises." Roosevelt agreed. He was especially concerned that European powers might step in if America did not. In 1903 Great Britain, Germany, and Italy had imposed a blockade on Venezuela in a dispute over debt payments owed to private investors. To prevent armed intervention by the Europeans, Roosevelt in 1904 proclaimed what became known as the Roosevelt Corollary to the Monroe Doctrine. "Chronic wrongdoing, or an impotence which results in a general loosening of the ties of civilized society," the statement read, justified "the exercise of an international police power" anywhere in the hemisphere. Roosevelt invoked the corollary to justify U.S. intervention in the region, beginning with the Dominican Republic in 1905. To counter the protests of European creditors (and the implied threat of armed intervention), Washington assumed management of the Dominican debt and customs services. Roosevelt and later presidents cited

This 1905 *cartoon portraying President Theodore Roosevelt,* The World's Constable, *appeared in* Judge *magazine. In depicting the president as a strong but benevolent policeman bringing order in a contentious world, the artist Louis Dalrymple drew on familiar imagery from Roosevelt's earlier days as a New York City police commissioner.*

the corollary to justify armed intervention in the internal affairs of Cuba, Haiti, Nicaragua, and Mexico.

American diplomacy in Asia reflected the Open Door policy formulated by Secretary of State John Hay in 1899. Japan and the western European powers had carved key areas of China into spheres of influence, in which individual nations enjoyed economic dominance. The United States was a relative latecomer to the potentially lucrative China market, and Hay sought guarantees of equal opportunity for its commercial interests there. In a series of diplomatic notes Hay won approval for the so-called Open Door approach, giving all nations equal access to trading and development rights in China. The outbreak of war between Japan and Russia in 1905 threatened this policy. Roosevelt worried that a total victory by Russia or Japan could upset the balance of power in East Asia and threaten American business enterprises. He became especially concerned after the Japanese scored a series of military victories over Russia and began to loom as a dominant power in East Asia.

Roosevelt mediated a settlement of the Russo-Japanese War at Portsmouth, New Hampshire, in 1905 (for which he was awarded the 1906 Nobel Peace Prize). In this settlement, Japan won recognition of its dominant position in Korea and consolidated its economic control over Manchuria. Yet repeated incidents of anti-Japanese racism in California kept American-Japanese relations strained. In 1906, for example, the San Francisco school board, responding to nativist fears of a "yellow peril,"

ordered the segregation of Japanese, Chinese, and Korean students. Japan angrily protested. In 1907, in the so-called gentlemen's agreement, Japan agreed not to issue passports to Japanese male laborers looking to emigrate to the United States and Roosevelt promised to fight anti-Japanese discrimination. He then persuaded the San Francisco school board to exempt Japanese students from the segregation ordinance.

But Roosevelt did not want these conciliatory moves to be interpreted as weakness. He thus built up American naval strength in the Pacific, and in 1908 he sent battleships to visit Japan in a muscle-flexing display of sea power. In that same year, the two burgeoning Pacific powers reached a reconciliation. The Root-Takahira Agreement affirmed the "existing status quo" in Asia, mutual respect for territorial possessions in the Pacific, and the Open Door trade policy in China. From the Japanese perspective, the agreement recognized Japan's colonial dominance in Korea and southern Manchuria.

Taft: Dollar Diplomacy

Roosevelt's successor, William Howard Taft, believed he could replace the militarism of the big stick with the more subtle and effective weapon of business investment. Taft and his secretary of state, corporate lawyer Philander C. Knox, followed a strategy (called "dollar diplomacy" by critics) in which they assumed that political influence would follow increased U.S. trade and investment. As Taft explained in 1910, he advocated "active intervention to secure for our merchandise and our capitalists opportunity for profitable investment." He hoped to substitute "dollars for bullets," but he was to discover limits to this approach in both the Caribbean and Asia.

Overall American investment in Central America grew rapidly, from $41 million in 1908 to $93 million by 1914. Most of this money went into railroad construction, mining, and plantations. The United Fruit Company alone owned about 160,000 acres of land in the Caribbean by 1913. But dollar diplomacy ended up requiring military support. The Taft administration sent the navy and the marines to intervene in political disputes in Honduras and Nicaragua, propping up factions pledged to protect American business interests. A contingent of U.S. Marines remained in Nicaragua until 1933. The economic and political structures of Honduras and Nicaragua were controlled by both the dollar and the bullet.

In China, Taft and Knox pressed for a greater share of the pie for U.S. investors. They gained a place for U.S. bankers in the European consortium building the massive new Hu-kuang Railways in southern and central China. But Knox blundered by attempting to "neutralize" the existing railroads in China. He tried to secure a huge international loan for the Chinese government that would allow it to buy up all the foreign railways and develop new ones. Both Russia and Japan, which had fought wars over their railroad interests in Manchuria, resisted this plan as a threat to the arrangements hammered out at Portsmouth with the help of Theodore Roosevelt. Knox's "neutralization" scheme, combined with U.S. support for the Chinese Nationalists in their 1911 revolt against the ruling Manchu dynasty, prompted Japan to sign a new friendship treaty with Russia. The Open Door to China was now effectively closed, and American relations with Japan began a slow deterioration that ended in war thirty years later.

The United States in the Caribbean, 1865–1933 *An overview of U.S. economic and military involvement in the Caribbean during the late nineteenth and early twentieth centuries. Victory in the Spanish-American War, the Panama Canal project, and rapid economic investment in Mexico and Cuba all contributed to a permanent and growing U.S. military presence in the region.*

Wilson: Moralism and Realism

Right after he took office in 1913, President Woodrow Wilson observed that "it would be the irony of fate if my administration had to deal chiefly with foreign affairs." His political life up to then had centered on achieving progressive reforms in the domestic arena. As it turned out, Wilson had to face international crises from his first day in office. These were of a scope and complexity unprecedented in U.S. history. Wilson had no experience in diplomacy, but he brought to foreign affairs a set of fundamental principles that combined a moralist's faith in American democracy with a realist's understanding of the power of international commerce. He believed that American economic expansion, accompanied by democratic principles and Christianity, was a civilizing force in the world. "Our industries," he told the Democratic National Convention in 1912, "have expanded to such a point that they will burst their jackets if they cannot find a free outlet to the markets of the world. . . . Our domestic markets no longer suffice. We need foreign markets."

Wilson, like most corporate and political leaders of the day, emphasized foreign investments and industrial exports as the keys to the nation's prosperity. He believed that the United States, with its superior industrial efficiency, could achieve supremacy in world commerce if artificial barriers to free trade were removed. He championed and extended the Open Door principles of John Hay, advocating strong diplomatic and military measures "for making ourselves supreme in the world from an economic point of view." Wilson often couched his vision of a dynamic, expansive American capitalism in terms of a moral crusade. As he put it in a speech to a congress of salesmen, "[Since] you are Americans and are meant to carry liberty and justice and the principles of humanity wherever you go, go out and sell goods that will make the world more comfortable and more happy, and convert them to the principles of America." Yet he quickly found that the complex realities of power politics could interfere with moral vision.

Wilson's policies toward Mexico, which foreshadowed the problems he would encounter in World War I, best illustrate his difficulties. The 1911 Mexican Revolution had overthrown the brutally corrupt dictatorship of Porfirio Díaz, and popular leader Francisco Madero had won wide support by promising democracy and economic reform for millions of landless peasants. U.S. businessmen, however, were nervous about the future of their investments, which totaled over $1 billion, an amount greater than Mexico's own investment and more than all other foreign investment in that country combined. Wilson at first gave his blessing to the revolutionary movement, expressed regret over the Mexican-American War of 1846–48, and

disavowed any interest in another war. "I have constantly to remind myself," he told a friend, "that I am not the servant of those who wish to enhance the value of their Mexican investments."

But right before he took office, Wilson was stunned by the ousting and murder of Madero by his chief lieutenant, General Victoriano Huerta. Other nations, including Great Britain and Japan, recognized the Huerta regime, but Wilson refused. He announced that the United States would support only governments that rested on the rule of law. An armed faction opposed to Huerta known as the Constitutionalists and led by Venustiano Carranza emerged in northern Mexico. Both sides rejected an effort by Wilson to broker a compromise between them. Carranza, an ardent nationalist, pressed for the right to buy U.S. arms, which he won in 1914. Wilson also isolated Huerta diplomatically by persuading the British to withdraw their support in exchange for American guarantees of English property interests in Mexico.

But Huerta stubbornly remained in power. In April 1914 Wilson used a minor insult to U.S. sailors in Tampico as an excuse to invade. American naval forces bombarded and then occupied Veracruz, the main port through which Huerta received arms shipments. Nineteen Americans and 126 Mexicans died in the battle, which brought the United States and Mexico close to war and provoked anti-American demonstrations in Mexico and throughout Latin America. Wilson accepted the offer of the ABC Powers—Argentina, Brazil, and Chile—to mediate the dispute. Huerta rejected a plan for him to step aside in favor of a provisional government. But then in August Carranza managed to overthrow Huerta. Playing to nationalist sentiment, Carranza too denounced Wilson for his intervention.

As war loomed in Europe, Mexico's revolutionary politics continued to frustrate Wilson. For a brief period Wilson threw his support behind Francisco "Pancho" Villa, Carranza's former ally who now led a rebel army of his own in the North. But Carranza's forces dealt Villa a major setback in April, 1915, and in October, its attention focused on the war in Europe, the Wilson administration recognized Carranza as Mexico's *de facto* president. Meanwhile Pancho Villa, feeling betrayed, turned on the United States and tried to provoke a crisis that might draw Washington into war with Mexico. Villa led several raids in Mexico and across the border in early 1916 that killed a few dozen Americans. The man once viewed by Wilson as a fighter for democracy was now dismissed as a dangerous bandit.

In March 1916, enraged by Villa's defiance, Wilson dispatched General John J. Pershing and an army that eventually numbered 15,000 to capture him. For a year, Pershing's troops chased Villa in vain, penetrating 300 miles into Mexico. The invasion made Villa a

Mexican revolutionary leaders and sometime allies Francisco "Pancho" Villa (center) and Emiliano Zapata (right) are shown at the National Palace in Mexico City, ca. 1916. Zapata's army operated out of a base in the southern agricultural state of Morelos, while Villa's army controlled large portions of Mexico's North. In 1914 Villa captured the imagination of American reformers, journalists, and moviemakers with his military exploits against the oppressive Huerta regime. But in 1916, after several border clashes between his forces and U.S. military units, President Wilson dispatched a punitive expedition in pursuit of Villa.

before the United States entered World War I, Wilson officially recognized the Carranza regime.

Wilson's attempt to guide the course of Mexico's revolution and protect U.S. interests left a bitter legacy of suspicion and distrust in Mexico. It also suggested the limits of a foreign policy tied to a moral vision rooted in the idea of American exceptionalism. Militarism and imperialism, Wilson had believed, were hallmarks of the old European way. American liberal values—rooted in capitalist development, democracy, and free trade—were the wave of the future. Wilson believed the United States could lead the world in establishing a new international system based on peaceful commerce and political stability. In both the 1914 invasion and the 1916 punitive expedition, Wilson declared that he had no desire to interfere with Mexican sovereignty. But in both cases that is exactly what he did. The United States, he argued,

symbol of national resistance in Mexico, and his army grew from 500 men to 10,000 by the end of 1916. Villa's effective hit-and-run guerrilla tactics kept the U.S. forces at bay. A frustrated General Pershing complained that he felt "just a little bit like a man looking for a needle in a haystack." He urged the U.S. government to occupy the northern Mexican state of Chihuahua and later called for the occupation of the entire country.

Pershing's invasion angered the Carranza government and the Mexican public. Skirmishes between American forces and Carranza's army brought the two nations to the brink of war again in June 1916. Wilson prepared a message to Congress asking permission for American troops to occupy all of northern Mexico. But he never delivered it. There was fierce opposition to war with Mexico throughout the country. Perhaps more important, mounting tensions with Germany caused Wilson to hesitate. He told an aide that "Germany is anxious to have us at war with Mexico, so that our minds and our energies will be taken off the great war across the sea." Wilson thus accepted negotiations by a face-saving international commission. In early 1917, with America moving toward direct involvement in the European war, Wilson began withdrawing American troops. Just a month

must actively use its enormous moral and material power to create the new order. That principle would soon engage America in Europe's bloodiest war and its most momentous revolution.

THE GREAT WAR

World War I, or the Great War, as it was originally called, took an enormous human toll on an entire generation of Europeans. The unprecedented slaughter on the battlefields of Verdun, Ypres, Gallipoli, and scores of other places appalled the combatant nations. At the war's start in August 1914, both sides had confidently predicted a quick victory. Instead, the killing dragged on for more than four years and in the end transformed the old power relations and political map of Europe. The United States entered the war reluctantly, and American forces played a supportive rather than a central role in the military outcome. Yet the wartime experience left a sharp imprint on the nation's economy, politics, and cultural life, one that would last into the next decades.

The Guns of August

In August 1914 a relatively minor incident plunged the European continent into the most destructive war in its history until then. The last decades of the nineteenth century had seen the major European nations, especially Germany, enjoy a great rush of industrial development. During the same period, these nations acquired extensive colonial empires in Africa, Asia, and the Middle East. Only a complex and fragile system of alliances had kept the European powers at peace with each other since 1871. Two great competing camps had evolved by 1907: the Triple Alliance (also known as the Central Powers), which included Germany, Austria-Hungary, and Italy; and the Triple Entente (also known as the Allies), which included Great Britain, France, and Russia. At the heart of this division was the competition between Great Britain, long the world's dominant colonial and commercial power, and Germany, which had powerful aspirations for an empire of its own.

The alliance system managed to keep small conflicts from escalating into larger ones for most of the late nineteenth and early twentieth centuries. But its inclusiveness was also its weakness: the alliance system threatened to entangle many nations in any war that did erupt. On June 28, 1914, Archduke Franz Ferdinand, heir to the throne of the unstable Austro-Hungarian Empire, was assassinated in Sarajevo, Bosnia. The archduke's killer was a Serbian nationalist who believed the Austro-Hungarian province of Bosnia ought to be annexed to neighboring Serbia. Germany pushed Austria-Hungary to retaliate against Serbia, and the Serbians in turn asked Russia for help.

By early August both sides had exchanged declarations of war and begun mobilizing their forces. Germany invaded Belgium and prepared to move across the French border. But after the German armies were stopped at the River Marne in September, the war settled into a long, bloody stalemate. New and grimly efficient weapons, such as the machine gun and the tank, and the horrors of trench warfare meant unprecedented casualties for all involved. Centered in northern France, the fighting killed 5 million people over the next two and a half years.

American Neutrality

The outbreak of war in Europe shocked Americans. President Wilson issued a formal proclamation of neutrality and urged citizens to be "impartial in thought as well as in action." Most of the country shared the editorial view expressed that August in the New York Sun: "There is nothing reasonable in such a war, and it would be folly for the country to sacrifice itself to the frenzy of dynastic policies and the clash of ancient hatreds which is urging the Old World to destruction."

In practice, powerful cultural, political, and economic factors made the impartiality advocated by Wilson impossible. The U.S. population included many ethnic groups with close emotional ties to the Old

World. Out of a total population of 92 million in 1914, about one-third were "hyphenated" Americans, either foreign-born or having one or both parents who were immigrants. Strong support for the Central Powers could be found among the 8 million German Americans, as well as the 4 million Irish Americans, who shared their ancestral homeland's historical hatred of English rule. On the other side, many Americans were at least mildly pro-Allies due to cultural and language bonds with Great Britain and the tradition of Franco-American friendship.

Both sides bombarded the United States with vigorous propaganda campaigns. The British effectively exploited their bonds of language and heritage with Americans. Reports of looting, raping, and the killing of innocent civilians by German troops circulated widely in the press. Many of these atrocity stories were exaggerated, but verified German actions—the invasion of neutral Belgium, submarine attacks on merchant ships, and the razing of towns—lent them credibility. German propagandists blamed the war on Russian expansionism and France's desire to avenge its defeat by Germany in 1870–71. It is difficult to measure the impact of war propaganda on American public opinion. As a whole, though, it highlighted the terrible human costs of the war and thus strengthened the conviction that America should stay out of it.

Economic ties between the United States and the Allies were perhaps the greatest barrier to true neutrality. Early in the war Britain imposed a blockade on all shipping to Germany. The United States, as a neutral country, might have insisted on the right of nonbelligerents to trade with both sides, as required by international law. But in practice, although Wilson protested the blockade, he wanted to avoid antagonizing Britain and disrupting trade between the United States and the Allies. Trade with Germany all but ended while trade with the Allies increased dramatically. As war orders poured in from Britain and France, the value of American trade with the Allies shot up from $824 million in 1914 to $3.2 billion in 1916. By 1917 loans to the Allies exceeded $2.5 billion compared to loans to the Central Powers of only $27 million. Increased trade with the Allies helped produce a great economic boom at home—transforming the economy in places like Bisbee, Arizona—and the United States became neutral in name only.

Preparedness and Peace

In February 1915, Germany declared the waters around the British Isles to be a war zone, a policy that it would enforce with unrestricted submarine warfare. All enemy shipping, despite the requirements of international law to the contrary, would be subject to surprise submarine attack. Neutral powers were warned that the problems of identification at sea put their ships at risk. The United States issued a sharp protest to this policy, calling it "an indefensible violation of neutral rights," and threatened to hold Germany accountable.

On May 7, 1915, a German U-boat sank the British liner Lusitania off the coast of Ireland. Among the 1,198 people who died were 128 American citizens. The Lusitania was in fact secretly carrying war materials, and passengers had been warned about a possible attack. Wilson nevertheless denounced the sinking as illegal and inhuman, and the American press loudly condemned the act as barbaric. An angry exchange of diplomatic notes led Secretary of State William Jennings Bryan to resign in protest against a policy he thought too warlike.

Tensions heated up again in March 1916 when a German U-boat torpedoed the Sussex, an unarmed French passenger ship, injuring four Americans. President Wilson threatened to break off diplomatic relations with Germany unless it abandoned its methods of submarine warfare. He won a temporary diplomatic victory when Germany promised that all vessels would be visited prior to attack. But the crisis also prompted Wilson to begin preparing for war. The National Security League, active in large eastern cities and bankrolled by conservative banking and commercial interests, helped push for a bigger army and navy and, most important, a system of universal military training. In June 1916 Congress passed the National Defense Act, which more than doubled the size of the regular army to 220,000 and integrated the state National Guards under federal control. In August, Congress passed a bill that dramatically increased spending for new battleships, cruisers, and destroyers.

Not all Americans supported these preparations for battle, and opposition to military buildup found expression in scores of American communities. As early as August 29, 1914, 1,500 women clad in black had marched down New York's Fifth Avenue in the Woman's Peace Parade. Out of this gathering evolved the American Union against Militarism, which lobbied against the preparedness campaign and against intervention in Mexico. Antiwar feeling was especially strong in the South and Midwest. Except for its vitally important cotton exports, the South generally had weaker economic ties to the Allies than other parts of the nation, as well as a historical suspicion of military power concentrated in Washington. The Midwest included communities with large German and socialist influences, both of which opposed U.S. aid to the Allies.

A group of thirty to fifty House Democrats, led by majority leader Claude Kitchin of North Carolina, stubbornly opposed Wilson's buildup. Jane Addams, Lillian D. Wald, and many other prominent progressive reformers spoke out for peace. A large

Jane Addams (right), shown here in the late 1920s, remained active in the women's world peace movement until her death in 1935. In 1915 she had cofounded the Women's Peace Party, whose pacifist platform representing the views of the "mother half of humanity" attracted 25,000 members. But the American entry into World War I led to the Party's rapid demise.

reservoir of popular antiwar sentiment flowed through the culture in various ways. Movie director Thomas Ince won a huge audience for his 1916 film *Civilization*, which depicted Christ returning to reveal the horrors of war to world leaders. Two of the most popular songs of 1915 were "Don't Take My Darling Boy Away" and "I Didn't Raise My Boy to Be a Soldier."

To win reelection in 1916, Wilson had to acknowledge the active opposition to involvement in the war. In the presidential campaign, Democrats adopted the winning slogan "He Kept Us Out of War." Wilson made a strong showing in the West, where antiwar sentiment was vigorous, and he managed to draw hundreds of thousands of votes away from the antiwar Socialist Party as well. Wilson made a point of appealing to progressives of all kinds, stressing his support for the eight-hour day and his administration's efforts on behalf of farmers. The war-induced prosperity no doubt helped him to defeat conservative Republican Charles Evans Hughes in a very close election. But Wilson knew that the peace was as fragile as his victory.

Safe for Democracy

By the end of January 1917, Germany's leaders had decided against a negotiated peace settlement, placing their hopes instead in a final decisive offensive against the Allies. On February 1, 1917, Germany resumed its policy of unrestricted submarine warfare, with no warnings, against all neutral and belligerent shipping. (These attacks had been temporarily restrained in 1916, following U.S. protests.) This decision was made with full knowledge that it might bring America into the conflict. In effect, German leaders were gambling that they could destroy the ability of the Allies to fight before the United States would be able to effectively mobilize manpower and resources.

Halt the Hun. *This 1918* Liberty Loan *poster used anti-German sentiment to encourage the purchase of war bonds. Its depiction of an American soldier as the protector of an innocent mother and child implied that the Germans were guilty of unspeakable war crimes.*

Howard Chandler Christy, *Fight or Buy Bonds*, poster, 1917. Museum of the City of New York, gift of John Campbell.

Wilson was indignant and disappointed. He still hoped for peace, but Germany had made it impossible for him to preserve his twin goals of U.S. neutrality and freedom of the seas. Reluctantly, Wilson broke off diplomatic relations with Germany and called on Congress to approve the arming of U.S. merchant ships. On March 1, the White House shocked the country when it made public a recently intercepted coded message, sent by German foreign secretary Arthur Zimmermann to the German ambassador in Mexico. The Zimmermann note proposed that an alliance be made between Germany and Mexico if the United States entered the war. Zimmermann suggested that Mexico take up arms against the United States and receive in return the "lost territory in New Mexico, Texas, and Arizona." The note caused a sensation and became a very effective propaganda tool for those who favored U.S. entry into the war. "As soon as I saw it," wrote Republican senator Henry Cabot Lodge of Massachusetts, an interventionist, "I knew it would arouse the country more than any other event." The specter of a German-Mexican alliance helped turn the tide of public opinion in the Southwest, where opposition to U.S. involvement in the war had been strong.

Revelation of the Zimmermann note stiffened Wilson's resolve. He issued an executive order in mid-March authorizing the arming of all merchant ships and allowing them to shoot at submarines. In that month, German U-boats sank seven U.S. merchant ships, leaving a heavy death toll. Anti-German feeling increased, and thousands took part in prowar demonstrations in New York, Boston, Philadelphia, and other cities. Wilson finally called a special session of Congress to ask for a declaration of war.

On April 2, on a rainy night before a packed and very quiet assembly, Wilson made his case. He reviewed the escalation of submarine warfare, which he called "warfare against mankind," and said that neutrality was no longer feasible or desirable. But the conflict was not merely about U.S. shipping rights, Wilson argued:

> The world must be made safe for democracy. Its peace must be planted upon the tested foundations of political liberty. We have no selfish ends to serve. . . . We shall fight for the things which we have always carried nearest our hearts,—for democracy, for the right of those who submit to authority to have a voice in their own Governments, for the rights and liberties of small nations.

This was a bold bid to give the United States a new role in international affairs. It asserted not just the right to protect U.S. interests but called also for change in basic international structures. Wilson's eloquent speech won over the Congress, most of the press, and even his bitterest political critics, such as

Theodore Roosevelt. The Senate adopted the war resolution 82 to 6, the House 373 to 50. On April 6, President Wilson signed the declaration of war. All that remained was to win over the American public.

AMERICAN MOBILIZATION

The overall public response to Wilson's war message was enthusiastic. Most newspapers, religious leaders, state legislatures, and prominent public figures endorsed the call to arms. But the Wilson administration was less certain about the feelings of ordinary Americans and their willingness to fight in Europe. It therefore took immediate steps to win over public support for the war effort, place a legal muzzle on antiwar dissenters, and establish a universal military draft. War mobilization was above all a campaign to unify the country.

Selling the War

Just a week after signing the war declaration, Wilson created the Committee on Public Information (CPI) to organize public opinion. It was dominated by its civilian chairman, the journalist and reformer George Creel. He had become a personal friend of Wilson's while handling publicity for the 1916 Democratic campaign. Creel quickly transformed the CPI from its original function as coordinator of government news into a sophisticated and aggressive agency for promoting the war. Creel remarked that his aim was to mold Americans into "one white-hot mass . . . with fraternity, devotion, courage, and deathless determination."

To sell the war, Creel raised the art of public relations to new heights. He enlisted more than 150,000 people to work on a score of CPI committees. They produced more than 100 million pieces of literature—pamphlets, articles, books—that explained the causes and meaning of the war. The CPI also created posters, slides, newspaper advertising, and films to promote the war. It called upon movie stars such as Charlie Chaplin, Mary Pickford, and Douglas Fairbanks to help sell war bonds at huge rallies. Famous journalists like the muckraker Ida Tarbell and well-known artists like Charles Dana Gibson were recruited. Across the nation, a volunteer army of 75,000 "Four Minute Men" gave brief patriotic speeches before stage and movie shows.

Three major themes dominated the materials disseminated by the CPI: America as a unified moral community; the war as an idealistic crusade for peace and freedom; and the image of a despicable enemy. The last of these featured an aggressively negative campaign against all things German. Posters and advertisements depicted the Germans as Huns, bestial monsters outside the civilized world. The CPI supported films such as *The Kaiser: The Beast of Berlin* and *The Prussian Cur.* German music and literature, indeed

Founded by Clara Barton after the Civil War, the American Red Cross grew in both size and importance during World War I. Female volunteers, responding to humanitarian and patriotic appeals combined in posters like this one, provided most of the health and sanitary services to military and civilian casualties of the war.

the German language itself, were suspect, and were banished from the concert halls, schools, and libraries of many communities. The CPI also urged ethnic Americans to abandon their Old World ties, to become "unhyphenated Americans." The CPI's push for conformity would soon encourage thousands of local, sometimes violent, campaigns of harassment against German Americans, radicals, and peace activists.

Fading Opposition to War

By defining the call to war as a great moral crusade, President Wilson was able to win over many Americans who had been reluctant to go to war. In particular, many liberals and progressives were attracted to the possibilities of war as a positive force for social change. Many progressives identified with President Wilson's definition of the war as an idealistic crusade to defend democracy, spread liberal principles, and redeem European decadence and militarism. John Dewey, the influential philosopher, believed the war offered great "social possibilities" for developing the public good through science and greater efficiency.

Social welfare advocates, suffragists, tax reformers, even many socialists, now viewed war as a unique opportunity. War would require greater direct and coordinated involvement by the government in nearly every phase of American life. A group of prominent progressives quickly issued a statement of support for Wilson's war policy. They argued that "out of the sacrifice of war we may achieve broader democracy in Government, more equitable distribution of wealth, and greater national efficiency in raising the level of the general welfare."

The writer and cultural critic Randolph Bourne was an important, if lonely, voice of dissent among intellectuals. A former student of Dewey's at Columbia University, Bourne wrote a series of antiwar essays warning of the disastrous consequences for reform movements of all kinds. He was particularly critical of "war intellectuals" such as Dewey who were so eager to shift their energies to serving the war effort. "War is essentially the health of the State," Bourne wrote, and he accurately predicted sharp infringements on political and intellectual freedoms.

The Woman's Peace Party, founded in 1915 by feminists opposed to the preparedness campaign, dissolved. Most of its leading lights—Florence Kelley, Lillian D. Wald, and Carrie Chapman Catt—threw themselves into volunteer war work. Catt, leader of the huge National American Woman Suffrage Association (NAWSA), believed that supporting the war might help women win the right to vote. She joined the Women's Committee of the Council of National Defense and encouraged suffragists to mobilize women for war service of various kinds. A few lonely feminist voices, such as Jane Addams, continued steadfastly to oppose the war effort. But war work proved very popular among activist middle-class women. It gave them a leading role in their communities—selling bonds, coordinating food conservation drives, and working for hospitals and the Red Cross.

"You're in the Army Now"

The central military issue facing the administration was how to raise and deploy U.S. armed forces. When war was declared, there were only about 200,000 men in the army. Traditionally, the United States had relied on volunteer forces organized at the state level. But volunteer rates after April 6 were less than they had been for the Civil War or the Spanish-American War, reflecting the softness of prowar sentiment. The administration thus introduced the Selective Service Act, which provided for the registration and classification for military service of all men between ages twenty-one and thirty-five. Secretary of War Newton D. Baker was anxious to prevent the widespread, even violent, opposition to the draft that had occurred during the Civil War. Much of the anger over the Civil War draft stemmed from the unpopular provision that allowed draftees to buy their way out by paying $300 for a substitute. The new draft made no such allowances. Baker stressed the democratic procedures for registration and the active role of local draft boards in administering the process.

On June 5, 1917, nearly 10 million men registered for the draft. There was scattered organized resistance, but overall, registration records offered evidence of national support. A supplemental registration in August 1918 extended the age limits to eighteen and forty-five. By the end of the war some 24 million men had registered. Of the 2.8 million men eventually called up for service, about 340,000, or 12 percent, failed to show up. Another 2 million Americans volunteered for the various armed services.

U.S. *soldiers leaving training camp, on their way to the European front, 1918. In just over a year national mobilization expanded the armed forces twentyfold, to nearly 5 million men and women. By November 1918, when the fighting ended, more than 2 million American troops were in Europe.*

The vast, polyglot army posed unprecedented challenges of organization and control. But progressive elements within the administration also saw opportunities for pressing reform measures involving education, alcohol, and sex. Army psychologists gave the new Stanford-Binet intelligence test to all recruits and were shocked to find illiteracy rates as high as 25 percent. The low test scores among recent immigrants and rural African Americans undoubtedly reflected the cultural biases embedded in the tests and, for many test takers, their lack of proficiency in English. Most psychologists at the time, however, interpreted low scores in terms of racial theories of innate differences in intelligence. After the war, intelligence testing became a standard feature of America's educational system.

Ideally, the army provided a field for social reform and education, especially for the one-fifth of U.S. soldiers born in another country. "The military tent where they all sleep side by side," Theodore Roosevelt predicted, "will rank next to the public schools among the great agents of democratization." The recruits themselves took a more lighthearted view, while singing the army's praises:

> *Oh, the army, the army, the democratic army,*
> *They clothe you and feed you because the army needs you*
> *Hash for breakfast, beans for dinner, stew for suppertime,*
> *Thirty dollars every month, deducting twenty-nine.*
> *Oh, the army, the army, the democratic army,*
> *The Jews, the Wops, and the Dutch and Irish Cops,*
> *They're all in the army now!*

Racism in the Military

But African Americans who served found severe limitations in the U.S. military. They were organized into totally segregated units, barred entirely from the marines and the Coast Guard, and largely relegated to working as cooks, laundrymen, stevedores, and the like in the army and navy. Thousands of black soldiers endured humiliating, sometimes violent treatment, particularly from southern white officers. African American servicemen faced hostility from white civilians as well, North and South, often being denied service in restaurants and admission to theaters near training camps. The ugliest incident occurred in Houston, Texas, in August 1917. Black infantrymen, incensed over continual insults and harassment by local whites, seized weapons from an armory and killed seventeen civilians. The army executed thirty black soldiers and imprisoned forty-one others for life, denying any of them a chance for appeal.

More than 200,000 African Americans eventually served in France, but only about one in five saw combat, as opposed to two out of three white soldiers. Black combat units served with distinction in various

The military reinforced old patterns of racism in American life by segregating African American troops and assigning most of them to menial and support tasks. Yet African Americans generally supported the war effort. The leading black newspaper of the day, the Chicago Defender, predicted optimistically: "The colored soldier who fights side by side with the white American will hardly be begrudged a fair chance when the victorious armies return."

divisions of the French army. The all-black 369th U.S. Infantry, for example, saw the first and longest service of any American regiment deployed in a foreign army, serving in the trenches for 191 days. The French government awarded the *Croix de Guerre* to the entire regiment, and 171 officers and enlisted men were cited individually for exceptional bravery in action. African American soldiers by and large enjoyed a friendly reception from French civilians as well. The contrast with their treatment at home would remain a sore point with these troops upon their return to the United States.

Americans in Battle

Naively, many Americans had assumed that the nation's participation in the war could be limited to supplying economic aid and military hardware. At first, the main contribution came on the sea. German U-boats were sinking Allied ships at a rate of 900,000 tons each month; one of four British ships never returned to port. The United States began sending warships and destroyers to protect large convoys of merchant ships and to aid the British navy in assaulting U-boats. Within a year, shipping tonnage lost each month to submarine warfare had been reduced to 200,000; the flow of weapons, supplies, and troops continued. No American soldiers were lost on the way to Europe.

The Western Front, 1918   *American units saw their first substantial action in late May, helping to stop the German offensive at the battle of Cantigny. By September, more than 1 million American troops were fighting in a counteroffensive campaign at St. Mihiel, the largest single American engagement of the war.*

President Wilson appointed General John J. Pershing, recently returned from pursuing Pancho Villa in Mexico, as commander of the American Expeditionary Force (AEF). Pershing insisted that the AEF maintain its own identity, distinct from that of the French and British armies. He was also reluctant to send American troops into battle before they had received at least six months' training. The AEF's combat role would be brief but intense: not until early 1918 did AEF units reach the front in large numbers; eight months later the war was over.

Like Ulysses S. Grant, Pershing believed the object of war to be total destruction of the enemy's military power. He expressed contempt for the essentially defensive tactics of trench warfare pursued by both sides. But the brutal power of modern military technology had made trench warfare inevitable from 1914 to 1917. The awesome firepower of the machine gun and long-range artillery made the massed frontal confrontations of the Civil War era obsolete. The grim reality of life in the trenches—cold, wet, lice-ridden, with long periods of boredom and sleeplessness—also made a mockery of older notions about the glory of combat.

In the early spring of 1918 the Germans launched a major offensive that brought them within fifty miles of Paris. In early June about 70,000 AEF soldiers helped the French stop the Germans in the battles of Château-Thierry and Belleau Wood. In July, Allied forces led by Marshal Ferdinand Foch of France, began a counteroffensive designed to defeat Germany once and for all. American reinforcements began flooding the ports of Liverpool in England and Brest and Saint-Nazaire in France. The "doughboys" (a nickname for soldiers dating back to Civil War-era recruits who joined the army for the money) streamed in at a rate of over 250,000 a month. By September, General Pershing had more than a million Americans in his army.

In late September 1918, the AEF took over the southern part of a 200-mile front in the Meuse-Argonne offensive. In seven weeks of fighting, most through terrible mud and rain, U.S. soldiers used more ammunition than the entire Union army had in the four years of the Civil War. The Germans, exhausted and badly outnumbered, began to fall back and look for a cease-fire. On November 11, 1918, the war ended with the signing of an armistice.

The massive influx of American troops and supplies no doubt hastened the end of the war. About two-thirds of the U.S. soldiers saw at least some fighting, but even they managed to avoid the horrors of the sustained trench warfare that had marked the earlier years of the war. For most Americans at the front, the war experience was a mixture of fear, exhaustion, and fatigue. Their time in France would remain a decisive moment in their lives. In all, more than 52,000 Americans died in battle. Another 60,000 died from influenza and pneumonia, half of these while still in training camp. More than 200,000 Americans were wounded in the war. These figures, awful as they were, paled against the estimated casualties (killed and wounded) suffered by the European nations: 9 million for Russia, more than 6 million for Germany, nearly 5 million for France, and over 2 million each for Great Britain and Italy.

OVER HERE

In one sense, World War I can be understood as the ultimate progressive crusade, a reform movement of its own. Nearly all the reform energy of the previous two decades was turned toward the central goal of winning the war. The federal government would play a larger role than ever in managing and regulating the wartime economy. Planning, efficiency, scientific analysis, and cooperation were key principles for government agencies and large volunteer organizations. Although much of the regulatory spirit was temporary, the war experience started some important and lasting organizational trends in American life.

Organizing the Economy

In the summer of 1917 President Wilson established the War Industries Board (WIB) as a clearinghouse for industrial mobilization to support the war effort. Led by the successful Wall Street speculator Bernard M. Baruch, the WIB proved a major innovation in expanding the regulatory power of the federal government. It was given broad authority over the conversion of industrial plants to wartime needs, the manufacture of war materials, and the purchase of supplies for the United States and the Allies. The WIB had to balance price controls against war profits. Only by ensuring a fair rate of return on investment could it encourage stepped-up production.

The WIB eventually handled 3,000 contracts worth $14.5 billion with various businesses. Standardization of goods brought large savings and streamlined production. Baruch continually negotiated with business leaders, describing the system as "voluntary cooperation with the big stick in the cupboard." At first Elbert Gary of U.S. Steel refused to accept the government's price for steel and Henry Ford balked at limiting private car production. But when Baruch warned that he would instruct the military to take over their plants, both industrialists backed down.

In August 1917, Congress passed the Food and Fuel Act, authorizing the president to regulate the production and distribution of the food and fuel necessary for the war effort. To lead the Food Administration (FA), Wilson appointed Herbert Hoover, a millionaire engineer who had already won fame for directing a program of war relief for Belgium. He became one of the best-known figures of the war administration. Hoover imposed price controls on certain agricultural commodities, such as sugar, pork, and wheat. These were purchased by the government and then sold to the public through licensed dealers. The FA also raised the purchase price of grain so that farmers would increase production. But Hoover stopped short of imposing mandatory food rationing, preferring to rely on persuasion, high prices, and voluntary controls.

Hoover's success, like George Creel's at the CPI, depended on motivating hundreds of thousands of volunteers in thousands of American communities. The FA coordinated the work of local committees that distributed posters and leaflets urging people to save food, recycle scraps, and substitute for scarce produce. The FA directed patriotic appeals for "Wheatless Mondays, Meatless Tuesdays, and Porkless Thursdays." Hoover exhorted Americans to "go back to simple food, simple clothes, simple pleasures." He urged them to grow their own vegetables. These efforts resulted in a sharp cutback in the consumption of sugar and wheat as well as a boost in the supply of livestock. The resultant increase in food exports helped sustain the Allied war effort.

The enormous cost of fighting the war, about $33 billion, required unprecedentedly large expenditures for the federal government. The tax structure shifted dramatically as a result. Taxes on incomes and profits replaced excise and customs levies as the major source of revenue. The minimum income subject to the graduated federal income tax, in effect only since 1913, was lowered to $1,000 from $3,000, increasing the number of Americans who paid income tax from 437,000 in 1916 to 4,425,000 in 1918. Tax rates were as steep as 70 percent in the highest brackets.

The bulk of war financing came from government borrowing, especially in the form of the popular Liberty Bonds sold to the American public. Bond drives became highly organized patriotic campaigns that ultimately raised a total of $23 billion for the war effort. The administration also used the new Federal Reserve Banks to expand the money supply, making borrowing easier. The federal debt jumped from $1 billion in 1915 to $20 billion in 1920.

The Business of War

Overall, the war meant expansion and high profits for American business. Between 1916 and 1918, Ford Motor Company increased its workforce from 32,000 to 48,000, General Motors from 10,000 to 50,000. Total capital expenditure in U.S. manufacturing jumped from $600 million in 1915 to $2.5 billion in 1918. Corporate profits as a whole nearly tripled between 1914 and 1919, and many large businesses did much better than that. Annual prewar profits for United States Steel had averaged $76 million; in 1917 they were $478 million. The Bethlehem Shipbuilding Company increased its annual profits from $6 million in peacetime to $49 million in wartime. Du Pont quadrupled its assets. The demand for foodstuffs led to a boom in agriculture as well. The total value of farm produce rose from $9.8 billion in 1914 to $21.3 billion by 1918. Expanded farm acreage and increased investment in farm machinery led to a jump of 20–30 percent in overall farm production.

The most important and long-lasting economic legacy of the war was the organizational shift toward corporatism in American business. The wartime need for efficient management, manufacturing, and distribution could be met only by a greater reliance on the productive and marketing power of large corporations. Never before had business and the federal government cooperated so closely. Under war administrators like Baruch and Hoover, entire industries (such as radio manufacturing) and economic sectors (such as agriculture and energy) were organized, regulated, and subsidized. War agencies used both public and private power—legal authority and voluntarism—to hammer out and enforce agreements. Here was the genesis of the modern bureaucratic state.

Some Americans worried about the wartime trend toward a greater federal presence in their lives. As the *Saturday Evening Post* noted, "All this government activity will be called to account and re-examined in due time." Although many aspects of the government–business partnership proved temporary, some institutions and practices grew stronger in the postwar years. Among these were the Federal Reserve Board, the income tax system, the Chamber of Commerce, the Farm Bureau, and the growing horde of lobbying groups that pressed Washington for special interest legislation.

One key example of the long-range impact of the government–business partnership was the infant radio industry. Wireless communication technology found many uses among naval and ground forces in wartime. As in most industries, the Justice Department guaranteed radio manufacturers protection against patent infringement and antitrust suits. These guarantees helped stimulate research and the mass production of radios for airplanes, ships, and infantry. In 1919 the government helped create the Radio Corporation of America (RCA), which bought out a British company that had dominated America's wireless system. As part of the deal, the U.S. military was allowed a permanent representative on the RCA board of directors. The creation of RCA, jointly owned by General Electric, American Telephone and Telegraph, and Westinghouse, assured the United States a powerful position in the new age of global communications. It also set the stage for the new radio broadcasting industry of the 1920s.

Labor and the War

Organized labor's power and prestige, though by no means equal to those of business or government, clearly grew during the war. The expansion of the economy, combined with army mobilization and a decline in immigration from Europe, caused a growing wartime labor shortage. As the demand for workers intensified, the federal government was forced to recognize that labor, like any other resource or commodity, would have to be more carefully tended to than in peacetime. For the war's duration, working people generally enjoyed higher wages and a better standard of living. Trade unions, especially those affiliated with the American Federation of Labor (AFL), experienced a sharp rise in membership. In effect, the government took in labor as a junior partner in the mobilization of the economy.

Samuel Gompers, president of the AFL, emerged as the leading spokesman for the nation's trade union movement. An English immigrant and cigar maker by trade, Gompers had rejected the socialism of his youth for a philosophy of "business unionism." By stressing the concrete gains that workers could win through collective bargaining with employers, the AFL had reached a total membership of about 2 million in 1914. Virtually all its members were skilled white males, organized in highly selective crafts in the building trades, railroads, and coal mines.

Gompers pledged the AFL's patriotic support for the war effort, and in April 1918 President Wilson appointed him to the National War Labor Board (NWLB). During 1917 the nation had seen thousands of strikes involving more than a million workers. Wages were usually at issue, reflecting workers' concerns with spiraling inflation and higher prices. The NWLB, co-chaired by labor attorney Frank Walsh and former president William H. Taft, acted as a kind of supreme court for labor, arbitrating disputes and working to prevent disruptions in production. The great majority of these interventions resulted in improved wages and reduced hours of work.

Most important, the NWLB supported the right of workers to organize unions and furthered the acceptance of the eight-hour day for war workers—central aims of the labor movement. It also backed time-and-a-half pay for overtime, as well as the principle of equal pay for women workers. AFL unions gained more than a million new members during the war, and overall union membership rose from 2.7 million in 1914 to more than 5 million by 1920. The NWLB established important precedents for government intervention on behalf of labor.

Wartime conditions often meant severe disruptions and discomfort for America's workers. Overcrowding, rapid workforce turnover, and high inflation rates were typical in war-boom communities. In Bridgeport, Connecticut, a center for small-arms manufacturing, the population grew by 50,000 in less than a year. In 1917 the number of families grew by 12,000, but available housing stock increased by only 6,000 units. Chronic congestion became common in many cities; Philadelphia reported the worst housing shortage in its history.

In the Southwest, the demand for wartime labor temporarily eased restrictions against the movement of Mexicans into the United States. The Immigration Act of 1917, requiring a literacy test and an $8 head tax, had cut Mexican immigration nearly in half, down to about 25,000 per year. But employers complained of severe shortages of workers. Farmers in Arizona's Salt River Valley and southern California needed hands to harvest grain, alfalfa, cotton, and fruit. El Paso's mining and smelting industries, Texas's border ranches, and southern Arizona's railroads and copper mines insisted they depended on unskilled Mexican labor as well.

Responding to these protests, in June 1917 the Department of Labor suspended the immigration law for the duration of the war and negotiated an agreement with the Mexican government permitting some 35,000 Mexican contract laborers to enter the United States. Mexicans let in through this program had to demonstrate they had a job waiting before they could cross the border. They received identification cards and transportation to their place of work from American labor contractors. Pressure from southwestern employers kept the exemptions in force until 1921, well after the end of the war, demonstrating the growing importance of cheap Mexican labor to the region's economy.

If the war boosted the fortunes of the AFL, it also spelled the end for more radical elements of the U.S. labor movement. The Industrial Workers of the World (IWW) had followed a different path from the "pure and simple" trade unionism of Gompers. Unlike the AFL, the IWW concentrated on organizing unskilled workers into all-inclusive industrial unions. The Wobblies denounced capitalism as an unreformable system based on exploitation and they opposed U.S. entry into the war. IWW leaders advised their members to refuse induction for "the capitalists' war."

With vigorous organizing, especially in the West, the IWW had grown in 1916 and 1917. It gained strength among workers in several areas crucial to the

For Every Fighter a Woman Worker, 1917, *by Ernest Hamlin Baker. This poster, part of the United War Work Campaign of the Young Women's Christian Association, depicted America's women as a civilian army, ready and able to take the place of male workers gone off to fight.*

war effort: copper mining, lumbering, and wheat harvesting. In September 1917, just after the vigilante attack in Bisbee and the IWW's efforts to expose it, the Wilson administration responded to appeals from western business leaders for a crackdown on the Wobblies. Justice Department agents, acting under the broad authority of the recently passed Espionage Act, swooped down on IWW offices in more than sixty towns and cities, arresting more than 300 people and confiscating files. The mass trials and convictions that followed broke the back of America's radical labor movement and marked the beginning of a powerful wave of political repression.

Women at Work

For many of the 8 million women already in the labor force, the war meant a chance to switch from low-paying jobs, such as domestic service, to higher-paying industrial fields. About a million women workers joined the labor force for the first time. Of the estimated 9.4 million workers directly engaged in war work, some 2.25 million were women. Of these, 1.25 million worked in manufacturing. Female munitions plant workers, train engineers, drill press operators, streetcar conductors, and mail carriers became a common sight around the country.

In response to the widened range of female employment, the Labor Department created the Women in Industry Service (WIS). Directed by Mary Van Kleeck, the service advised employers on using female labor and formulated general standards for the treatment of women workers. The WIS represented the first attempt by the federal government to take a practical stand on improving working conditions for women. Its standards included the eight-hour day, equal pay for equal work, a minimum wage, the prohibition of night work, and the provision of rest periods, meal breaks, and restroom facilities. These standards had no legal force, however, and WIS inspectors found that employers often flouted them. They were accepted nonetheless as goals by nearly every group concerned with improving the conditions of working women.

Many women resented the restrictiveness of the WIS guidelines. Myrtle Altenburg, a Wisconsin widow, complained of being prevented from working on a local railroad. "It is my belief," she wrote the state railway commission, "that a woman can do everything that a man can do that is within her strength. Hundreds and hundreds of women might work and release men for war or war work, could they, the women, be employed on the railroads." Even when hired, women suffered discrimination over pay. Government surveys found that women's average earnings were roughly half of men's in the same industries.

At war's end, women lost nearly all their defense-related jobs. Wartime women railroad workers, for example, were replaced by returning servicemen through the application of laws meant to protect women from hazardous conditions. But the war accelerated female employment in fields already dominated by women. By 1920, more women who worked outside the home did so in white-collar occupations—as telephone operators, secretaries, and clerks, for example—than in manufacturing or domestic service. The new awareness of women's work led Congress to create the Women's Bureau in the Labor Department, which continued the WIS wartime program of education and investigation through the postwar years.

Woman Suffrage

The presence of so many new women wageworkers, combined with the highly visible volunteer work of millions of middle-class women, helped finally to secure the vote for women. Volunteer war work—selling bonds, saving food, organizing benefits—was very popular among housewives and clubwomen. These women played a key role in the success of the Food Administration, and the Women's Committee of the Council of National Defense included a variety of women's organizations.

Until World War I, the fight for woman suffrage had been waged largely within individual states. Western states and territories had led the way. Various forms of woman suffrage had become law in Wyoming in 1869, followed by Utah (1870), Colorado (1893), Idaho (1896), Washington (1910), California (1911), Arizona and Oregon (1912), and Montana and Nevada (1914). The reasons for this regional pattern had less to do with dramatically different notions of gender roles in the West than with the distinctiveness of western politics and society. Rocky Mountain and Pacific coast states did not have the sharp ethnocultural divisions between Catholics and Protestants that hindered suffrage efforts in the East. The close identification in the East between the suffrage and prohibition movements led many Catholic immigrants and German Lutherans to oppose the vote for women because they feared it would lead to prohibition. Mormons in Utah supported woman suffrage as a way to preserve polygamy and defend their distinctive social order from attack.

The U.S. entry into the war provided a unique opportunity for suffrage groups to shift their strategy to a national campaign for a constitutional amendment granting the vote to women. The most important of these groups was the National American Woman Suffrage Association. Before 1917, most American suffragists had opposed the war. Under the leadership of Carrie Chapman Catt, NAWSA threw its support behind the war effort and doubled its membership to 2 million. Catt gambled that a strong show of patriotism would help clinch the century-old fight to win the vote for women. NAWSA pursued a moderate policy of lobbying Congress for a constitutional amendment and calling for state referendums on woman suffrage.

At the same time, more militant suffragists led by a young Quaker activist, Alice Paul, injected new energy and more radical tactics into the movement. Paul had spent several years in England working with militant suffragists there, and in 1913 she returned to the United States to form the Congressional Union within the NAWSA to lobby for a federal amendment. Dissatisfied with the NAWSA's conservative strategy of quiet lobbying and orderly demonstrations, Paul left the organization in 1916. She joined forces with western women voters to form the National Woman's Party. Borrowing from English suffragists, this party pursued a more aggressive and dramatic strategy of agitation. Paul and her supporters picketed the White House, publicly burned President Wilson's speeches, and condemned the president and the Democrats for failing to produce an amendment. In one demonstration they chained themselves to the White House fence and after their

Members of the National Woman's Party picketed President Wilson at the White House in 1917. Their militant action in the midst of the war crisis aroused both anger and sympathy. The NWP campaign helped push the president and the Congress to accept woman suffrage as a "war measure."

arrest went on a hunger strike in jail. The militants generated a great deal of publicity and sympathy.

Although some in the NAWSA objected to these tactics, Paul's radical approach helped make the NAWSA position more acceptable to Wilson. Carrie Chapman Catt used the president's war rhetoric as an argument for granting the vote to women. The fight for democracy, she argued, must begin at home, and she urged passage of the woman suffrage amendment as a "war measure." She won Wilson's support, and in 1917 the president urged Congress to pass a woman suffrage amendment as "vital to the winning of the war." The House did so in January 1918 and a more reluctant Senate approved it in June 1919. Another year of hard work was spent convincing the state legislatures. In August 1920, Tennessee gave the final vote needed to ratify the Nineteenth Amendment to the Constitution, finally making woman's vote legal nationwide.

Prohibition

Significantly, another reform effort closely associated with women's groups triumphed at the same time. The movement to eliminate alcohol from American life had attracted many Americans, especially women, since before the Civil War. Temperance advocates saw drinking as the source of many of the worst problems faced by the working class, including family violence, unemployment, and poverty. By the early twentieth century

the Woman's Christian Temperance Union, with a quarter-million members, had become the single largest women's organization in American history.

The moral fervor that accompanied America's entry into the war provided a crucial boost to the cause. With so many breweries bearing German names, the movement benefited as well from the strong anti-German feeling of the war years. Outlawing beer and whiskey would also help to conserve precious grain, prohibitionists argued.

In 1917, a coalition of progressives and rural fundamentalists in Congress pushed through a constitutional amendment providing for a national ban on alcoholic drinks. The Eighteenth Amendment was ratified by the states in January 1919 and became the law of the land one year later. Although Prohibition would create a host of problems in the postwar years, especially as a stimulus for the growth of organized crime, many Americans, particularly native Protestants, considered it a worthy moral reform.

Public Health

Wartime mobilization brought deeper government involvement with public health issues, especially in the realm of sex hygiene, child welfare, and disease prevention. The rate of venereal disease among draftees was as high as 6 percent in some states, presenting a potential manpower problem for the army. In April 1917 the War Department mounted a vigorous campaign against venereal disease, which attracted the energies of progressive era sex reformers—social hygienists and antivice crusaders. Under the direction of Raymond Fosdick and the Commission on Training Camp Activities, the military educated troops on the dangers of contracting syphilis and gonorrhea and distributed condoms to soldiers. "A Soldier who gets a dose," warned a typical poster, "is a Traitor." More than a hundred red-light districts near military bases were closed down, and the army established five-mile "pure zones" to keep prostitutes away from the camps. Yet the sexual double standard still operated. Female activists angrily protested when military authorities, while refusing to arrest soldiers for patronizing prostitutes, arrested women en masse and held them in detention centers.

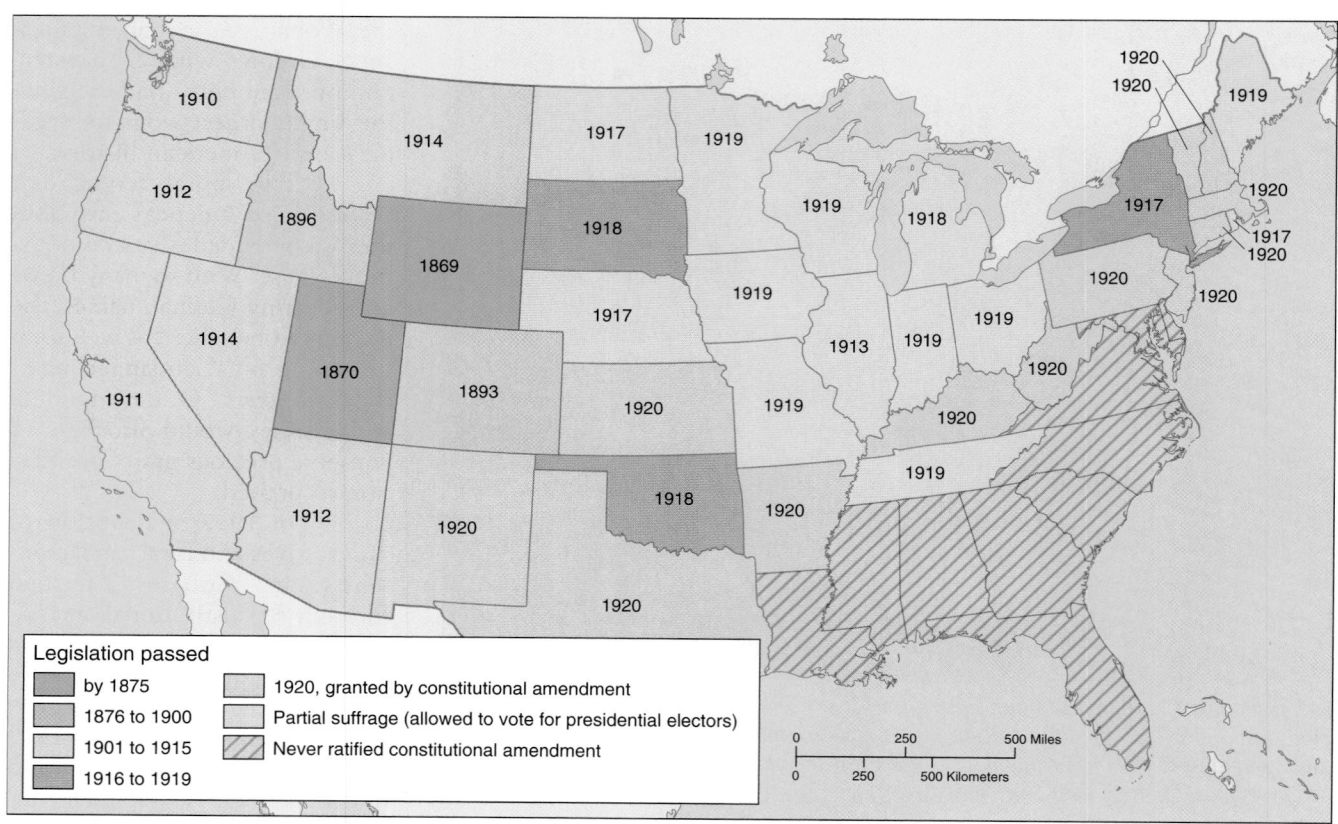

Woman Suffrage by State, 1869–1919 *Dates for the enactment of woman suffrage in the individual states. Years before ratification of the Nineteenth Amendment in 1920, a number of western states had legislated full or partial voting rights for women. In 1917 Montana suffragist Jeannette Rankin became the first woman elected to Congress.*

Source: Barbara G. Shortridge, *Atlas of American Women* (New York: Macmillan, 1987).

The scientific discussions of sex to which recruits were subjected in lectures, pamphlets, and films were surely a first for the vast majority of them. Venereal disease rates for soldiers declined by more than 300 percent during the war. The Division of Venereal Diseases, created in the summer of 1918 as a branch of the U.S. Public Health Service, established clinics offering free medical treatment to infected persons. It also coordinated an aggressive educational campaign through state departments of health.

The wartime boost to government health work continued into the postwar years. The Children's Bureau, created in 1912 as a part of the Labor Department, undertook a series of reports on special problems growing out of the war: the increase in employment of married women, finding day care for children of working mothers, and the growth of both child labor and delinquency. In 1918 Julia C. Lathrop, chief of the bureau, organized a "Children's Year" campaign designed to promote public protection of expectant mothers and infants and to enforce child labor laws. Millions of health education pamphlets were distrib-

uted nationwide, and mothers were encouraged to have their infants and children weighed and measured. Thousands of community-based committees enrolled some 11 million women in the drive.

In 1917, Lathrop, who had come to the Children's Bureau from the settlement house movement, proposed a plan to institutionalize federal aid to the states for protection of mothers and children. Congress finally passed the Maternity and Infancy Act in 1921, appropriating over $1 million a year to be administered to the states by the Children's Bureau. In the postwar years, clinics for prenatal and obstetrical care grew out of these efforts and greatly reduced the rate of infant and maternal mortality and disease.

The disastrous influenza epidemic of 1918–19 offered the most serious challenge to national public health during the war years. Part of a worldwide pandemic that claimed as many as 20 million lives, few Americans paid attention to the disease until it swept through military camps and eastern cities in September 1918. A lethal combination of the "flu" and respiratory complications (mainly pneumonia) killed roughly

550,000 Americans in ten months. Most victims were young adults between ages twenty and forty. Professional groups such as the American Medical Association called for massive government appropriations to search for a cure. Congress did appropriate a million dollars to the Public Health Service to combat and suppress the epidemic, but it offered no money for research.

The Public Health Service found itself overwhelmed by calls for doctors, nurses, and treatment facilities. Much of the care for the sick and dying came from Red Cross nurses and volunteers working in local communities across the nation. With a war on, and the nation focused on reports from the battlefront, even a public health crisis of this magnitude went relatively unnoticed. Although funding for the Public Health Service continued to grow in the 1920s, public and private expenditures on medical research were barely one-fiftieth of what they would become after World War II.

REPRESSION AND REACTION

World War I exposed and intensified many of the deepest social tensions in American life. On the local level, as exemplified by the Bisbee deportations, vigilantes increasingly took the law into their own hands to punish those suspected of disloyalty. The push for national unity led the federal government to crack down on a wide spectrum of dissenters from its war policies. The war inflamed racial hatred, and the worst race riots in the nation's history exploded in several cities. At war's end, a newly militant labor movement briefly asserted itself in mass strikes around the nation. Over all these developments loomed the 1917 Bolshevik Revolution in Russia. Radicals around the world had drawn inspiration from what looked like the first successful revolution against a capitalist state. Many conservatives worried that similar revolutions were imminent. From 1918 through 1920 the federal government directed a repressive antiradical campaign that had crucial implications for the nation's future.

Muzzling Dissent:
The Espionage and Sedition Acts

The Espionage Act of June 1917 became the government's key tool for the suppression of antiwar sentiment. It set severe penalties (up to twenty years' imprisonment and a $10,000 fine) for anyone found guilty of aiding the enemy, obstructing recruitment, or causing insubordination in the armed forces. The act also empowered the postmaster general to exclude from the mails any newspapers or magazines he thought treasonous. Within a year the mailing rights of forty-five newspapers had been revoked. These included several anti-British and pro-Irish publications, as well as such

leading journals of American socialism as the Kansas-based *Appeal to Reason*, which had enjoyed a prewar circulation of half a million, and *The Masses*.

To enforce the Espionage Act, the government had to increase its overall police and surveillance machinery. Civilian intelligence was coordinated by the newly created Bureau of Investigation in the Justice Department. This agency was reorganized after the war as the Federal Bureau of Investigation (FBI). In May 1918 the Sedition Act, an amendment to the Espionage Act, outlawed "any disloyal, profane, scurrilous, or abusive language intended to cause contempt, scorn, contumely, or disrepute" to the government, Constitution, or flag.

In all, more than 2,100 cases were brought to trial under these acts. They became a convenient vehicle for striking out at socialists, pacifists, radical labor activists, and others who resisted the patriotic tide. The most celebrated prosecution came in June 1918 when federal agents arrested Eugene Debs in Canton, Ohio, after he gave a speech defending antiwar protesters. Sentenced to ten years in prison, Debs defiantly told the court: "I have been accused of having obstructed the war. I admit it. Gentlemen, I abhor war. I would oppose the war if I stood alone." Debs served thirty-two months in federal prison before being pardoned by President Warren G. Harding on Christmas Day 1921.

The Supreme Court upheld the constitutionality of the acts in several 1919 decisions. In *Schenck v. United States* the Court unanimously agreed with Justice Oliver Wendell Holmes's claim that Congress could restrict speech if the words "are used in such circumstances and are of such a nature as to create a clear and present danger." The decision upheld the conviction of Charles Schenck for having mailed pamphlets urging potential army inductees to resist conscription. In *Debs v. United States*, the Court affirmed the guilt of Eugene Debs for his antiwar speech in Canton, even though he had not explicitly urged violation of the draft laws. Finally, in *Abrams v. United States*, the Court upheld Sedition Act convictions of four Russian immigrants who had printed pamphlets denouncing American military intervention in the Russian Revolution. The nation's highest court thus endorsed the severe wartime restrictions on free speech.

The deportation of striking miners in Bisbee offered an extreme case of vigilante activity. Thousands of other instances took place as government repression and local vigilantes reinforced each other. The American Protective League, founded with the blessing of the Justice Department, mobilized 250,000 self-appointed "operatives" in more than 600 towns and cities. Members of the league, mostly businessmen, bankers, and former policemen, spied on their neighbors and staged a series of well-publicized "slacker" raids on antiwar protesters and draft evaders. Many communities, inspired by Committee on Public Information campaigns, sought to

OVERVIEW

THE GREAT MIGRATION: BLACK POPULATION GROWTH IN SELECTED NORTHERN CITIES, 1910–1920

City	1910 No.	1910 Percent	1920 No.	1920 Percent	Percent Increase
New York	91,709	1.9%	152,467	2.7%	66.3%
Chicago	44,103	2.0	109,458	4.1	148.2
Philadelphia	84,459	5.5	134,229	7.4	58.9
Detroit	5,741	1.2	40,838	4.1	611.3
St. Louis	43,960	6.4	69,854	9.0	58.9
Cleveland	8,448	1.5	34,451	4.3	307.8
Pittsburgh	25,623	4.8	37,725	6.4	47.2
Cincinnati	19,739	5.4	30,079	7.5	53.2
Indianapolis	21,816	9.3	34,678	11.0	59.0
Newark	9,475	2.7	16,977	4.1	79.2
Kansas City	23,566	9.5	30,719	9.5	30.4
Columbus	12,739	7.0	22,181	9.4	74.1
Gary	383	2.3	5,299	9.6	1,283.6
Youngstown	1,936	2.4	6,662	5.0	244.1
Buffalo	1,773	0.4	4,511	0.9	154.4
Toledo	1,877	1.1	5,691	2.3	203.2
Akron	657	1.0	5,580	2.7	749.3

Source: U.S. Department of Commerce.

ban the teaching of the German language in their schools or the performance of German music in concert halls.

The Great Migration and Racial Tensions

Economic opportunity brought on by war prosperity triggered a massive migration of rural black Southerners to northern cities. From 1914 to 1920, somewhere between 300,000 and 500,000 African Americans left the rural South for the North. Chicago's black population increased by 65,000, or 150 percent; Detroit's by 35,000, or 600 percent. Acute labor shortages led northern factory managers to recruit black migrants to the expanding industrial centers. The Pennsylvania Railroad alone drew 10,000 black workers from Florida and south Georgia. Black workers eagerly left low-paying jobs as field hands and domestic servants for the chance at relatively high-paying work in meat-packing plants, shipyards, and steel mills.

Kinship and community networks were crucial in shaping what came to be called the Great Migration. They spread news about job openings, urban residential districts, and boardinghouses in northern cities. Black clubs, churches, and fraternal lodges in southern communities frequently sponsored the migration of their members, as well as return trips to the South. Single African American women often made the trip first because they could more easily obtain steady work as maids, cooks, and laundresses. One recalled that "if [white employers] liked the way the women would work in their homes or did ironing, they might throw some work to your husband or son." Relatively few African American men actually secured high-paying skilled jobs in industry or manufacturing. Most had to settle for work as construction laborers, teamsters, janitors, porters, or other low-paid jobs.

The persistence of lynching and other racial violence in the South no doubt contributed to the Great Migration. But racial violence was not limited to the South. Two of the worst race riots in American history occurred as a result of tensions brought on by wartime migration. On July 2, 1917, in East St. Louis, Illinois, a ferocious mob of whites attacked African Americans, killing at least 200. Before this riot, some of the city's manufacturers had been steadily recruiting black labor as a way to keep local union demands down. Unions had refused to allow black workers as members, and politicians had cynically exploited white racism in appealing for votes. In Chicago, on July 27,

1919, antiblack rioting broke out on a Lake Michigan beach. For two weeks white gangs hunted African Americans in the streets and burned hundreds out of their homes. Twenty-three African Americans and 15 whites died, and more than 500 were injured.

In both East St. Louis and Chicago, local authorities held African Americans responsible for the violence. President Wilson refused requests for federal intervention or investigation. A young black veteran who had been chased by a mob in the Chicago riot asked: "Had the ten months I spent in France been all in vain? Were all those white crosses over dead bodies of those dark skinned boys lying in Flanders field for naught? Was democracy a hollow sentiment?"

In terms of service in the armed forces, compliance with the draft, and involvement in volunteer work, African Americans had supported the war effort as faithfully as any group. In 1917, despite a segregated army and discrimination in defense industries, most African Americans thought the war might improve their lot. "If we again demonstrate our loyalty and devotion to our country," advised the *Chicago Defender*, "those injustices will disappear and the grounds for complaint will no longer exist." By the fall of 1919, writing in the *Crisis*, the journal of the National Association for the Advancement of Colored People (NAACP), black author James Weldon Johnson gloomily concluded that "an increased hatred of race was an integral part of wartime intolerance."

This southern African American family is shown arriving in Chicago around 1915. Black migrants to northern cities often faced overcrowding, inferior housing, and a high death rate from disease. But the chance to earn daily wages of $6 to $8 (the equivalent of a week's wages in much of the South), as well as the desire to escape persistent racial violence, kept the migrants coming.

Black disillusionment about the war grew quickly. So did a newly militant spirit. A heightened sense of race consciousness and activism was evident among black veterans and the growing black communities of northern cities. Taking the lead in the fight against bigotry and injustice, the NAACP held a national conference in 1919 on lynching. It pledged to defend persecuted African Americans, publicize the horrors of lynch law, and seek federal legislation against "Judge Lynch." By 1919 membership in the NAACP had reached 60,000 and the circulation of its journal exceeded half a million.

Labor Strife

The relative labor peace of 1917 and 1918 dissolved after the armistice. More than 4 million American workers were involved in some 3,600 strikes in 1919 alone. This unprecedented strike wave had several causes. Most of the modest wartime wage gains were wiped out by spiraling inflation and high prices for food, fuel, and housing. With the end of government controls on industry, many employers withdrew their recognition of unions. Difficult working conditions, such as the twelve-hour day in steel mills, were still routine in some industries. The quick return of demobilized servicemen to the labor force meant layoffs and new concerns about job security.

Several of the postwar strikes received widespread national attention. They seemed to be more than simple economic conflicts, and they provoked deep fears about the larger social order. In February 1919 a strike in the shipyards of Seattle, Washington, over wages escalated into a general citywide strike involving 60,000 workers. A strike committee coordinated the city's essential services for a week in a disciplined, nonviolent fashion. But the local press and Mayor Ole Hanson denounced the strikers as revolutionaries. Hanson effectively ended the strike by requesting federal troops to occupy the city.

In September, Boston policemen went out on strike when the police commissioner rejected a citizens' commission study that recommended a pay raise. Massachusetts governor Calvin Coolidge called in the National Guard to restore order and won a national reputation by crushing the strike. The entire police force was fired. Coolidge declared, "There is no right to strike against the public safety by anybody, anywhere, any time."

The biggest strike took place in the steel industry, involving some 350,000 steelworkers. Centered in several midwestern cities, this epic struggle lasted from September 1919 to January 1920. The AFL had hoped to build on wartime gains in an industry that had successfully resisted unionization before the war. The major demands were union recognition, the eight-hour day, and wage increases. The steel companies used black strike-

The General Strike Committee of Seattle distributed groceries to union families in February 1919. The Seattle general strike had been triggered when shipyard workers walked off the job after failing to gain wage hikes to offset spiraling postwar inflation. The conservative Los Angeles Times *saw the strike as evidence that Bolshevism was a right here and now American menace.*

breakers and armed guards to keep the mills running. Elbert Gary, president of U.S. Steel, directed a sophisticated propaganda campaign that branded the strikers as revolutionaries. Public opinion turned against the strike and condoned the use of state and federal troops to break it. A riot in Gary, Indiana, left eighteen strikers dead. The failed steel strike proved to be the era's most bitter and devastating defeat for organized labor.

AN UNEASY PEACE

The armistice of November 1918 ended the fighting on the battlefield, but the war continued at the peace conference. In the old royal palace of Versailles near Paris, delegates from twenty-seven countries spent five months hammering out a settlement. Yet neither Germany nor Russia was represented. The proceedings were dominated by leaders of the "Big Four": David Lloyd George (Great Britain), Georges Clemenceau (France), Vittorio Orlando (Italy), and Woodrow Wilson (United States). President Wilson saw the peace conference as a historic opportunity to project his domestic liberalism onto the world stage. But the stubborn realities of power politics would frustrate Wilson at Versailles and lead to his most crushing defeat at home.

The Fourteen Points
Wilson arrived in Paris with the United States delegation in January 1919. He brought with him a plan for peace that he had outlined a year earlier in a speech to Congress on U.S. war aims. The Fourteen Points, as they were called, had originally served wartime

purposes: to appeal to war opponents in Austria-Hungary and Germany, to convince Russia to stay in the war, and to help sustain Allied morale. As a blueprint for peace, they contained three main elements. First, Wilson offered a series of specific proposals for setting postwar boundaries in Europe and creating new countries out of the collapsed Austro-Hungarian and Ottoman empires. The key idea here was the right of all peoples to "national self-determination." Second, Wilson listed general principles for governing international conduct, including freedom of the seas, free trade, open covenants instead of secret treaties, reduced armaments, and mediation for competing colonial claims. Third, and most important, Wilson called for a League of Nations to help implement these principles and resolve future disputes.

The Fourteen Points offered a plan for world order deeply rooted in the liberal progressivism long associated with Wilson. The plan reflected a faith in efficient government and the rule of law as means for solving international problems. It looked to free trade and commercial development as the key to spreading prosperity. It advocated a dynamic democratic capitalism as a middle ground between Old World autocracy and revolutionary socialism. Wilson's vision was a profoundly moral one, and he was certain it was the only road to a lasting and humane peace.

The most controversial element, both at home and abroad, would prove to be the league. The heart of the league covenant, Article X, called for collective security as the ultimate method of keeping the peace: "The members of the League undertake to respect and preserve as against external aggression the territorial integrity and existing political independence of all Members." In the United States, Wilson's critics would focus on this provision as an unacceptable surrender of the nation's sovereignty and independence in foreign affairs. They also raised constitutional objections, arguing that the American system vested the power to declare war with the Congress. Would membership in the league violate this basic principle of the Constitution?

Wilson in Paris
The president was pleased when the conference at first accepted his plan as the basis for discussions. He also enjoyed wildly enthusiastic receptions from the public

in Paris and several other European capitals he visited. France's Clemenceau was less enamored. He sarcastically observed, "God gave us the Ten Commandments, and we broke them. Wilson gave us the Fourteen Points. We shall see." Wilson's plan could not survive the hostile atmosphere at Versailles.

Much of the negotiating at Versailles was in fact done in secret among the Big Four. The ideal of self-determination found limited expression. The independent states of Austria, Hungary, Poland, Yugoslavia, and Czechoslovakia were carved out of the homelands of the beaten Central Powers. But the Allies resisted Wilson's call for independence for the colonies of the defeated nations. A compromise mandate system of protectorates gave the French and British control of parts of the old German and Turkish empires in Africa and West Asia. Japan won control of former German colonies in China. Among those trying, but failing, to influence the treaty negotiations were the sixty-odd delegates to the first Pan African Congress, held in Paris at the same time as the peace talks. The group included Americans W.E.B. Du Bois and William Monroe Trotter as well as representatives from Africa and the West Indies. All were disappointed with the failure of the peace conference to grant self-determination to thousands of Africans living in former German colonies.

Another disappointment for Wilson came with the issue of war guilt. He had strongly opposed the extraction of harsh economic reparations from the Central Powers. But the French and British, with their awful war losses fresh in mind, insisted on making Germany pay. The final treaty contained a clause attributing the war to "the aggression of Germany," and a commission later set German war reparations at $33 billion. Bitter resentment in Germany over the punitive treaty helped sow the seeds for the Nazi rise to power in the 1930s.

The final treaty was signed on June 28, 1919, in the Hall of Mirrors at the Versailles palace. The Germans had no choice but to accept its harsh terms. President Wilson had been disappointed by the secret deals and the endless compromising of his ideals, no doubt underestimating the stubborn reality of power politics in the wake of Europe's most devastating war. He had nonetheless won a commitment to the League of Nations, the centerpiece of his plan, and he was confident that the American people would accept the treaty. The tougher fight would be with the Senate, where a two-thirds vote was needed for ratification.

The Treaty Fight

Preoccupied with peace conference politics in Paris, Wilson had neglected politics at home. His troubles had actually started earlier. Republicans had captured both the House and the Senate in the 1918 elections.

Woodrow Wilson, Georges Clemenceau, and David Lloyd George are among the central figures depicted in John Christen Johansen's Signing of the Treaty of Versailles. But all the gathered statesmen appear dwarfed by their surroundings.

Wilson had then made a tactical error by including no prominent Republicans in the U.S. peace delegation. He therefore faced a variety of tough opponents to the treaty he brought home.

Wilson's most extreme enemies in the Senate were a group of about sixteen "irreconcilables," opposed to a treaty in any form. Some were isolationist progressives, such as Republicans Robert M. La Follette of Wisconsin and William Borah of Idaho, who opposed the League of Nations as steadfastly as they opposed American entry into the war. Others were racist xenophobes like Democrat James Reed of Missouri. He objected, he said, to submitting questions to a tribunal "on which a nigger from Liberia, a nigger from Honduras, a nigger from India, and an unlettered gentleman from Siam, each have votes equal to the great United States of America."

The less dogmatic but more influential opponents were led by Republican Henry Cabot Lodge of Massachusetts, powerful majority leader of the Senate. They had strong reservations about the League of Nations, especially the provisions for collective security in the event of a member nation's being attacked. Lodge argued that this provision impinged on congressional authority to declare war and placed unacceptable restraints on the nation's ability to pursue an independent foreign policy. Lodge proposed a series of amendments that would have weakened the league. But Wilson refused to compromise, motivated in part by the long-standing hatred he and Lodge felt toward each other. The president decided instead to take his case directly to the American people.

In September, Wilson set out on a speaking tour across the country to drum up support for the league and the treaty. His train traveled 8,000 miles— through the Midwest, to the Pacific, and then back East. The crowds were large and responsive, but they did not change any votes in the Senate. The strain took its toll. On September 25, after speaking in Pueblo, Colorado, the sixty-three-year-old Wilson collapsed from exhaustion. His doctor canceled the rest of the trip. A week later, back in Washington, the president suffered a stroke that left him partially paralyzed. In November, Lodge brought the treaty out of committee for a vote, having appended to it fourteen reservations—that is, recommended changes. A bedridden Wilson stubbornly refused to compromise and instructed Democrats to vote against the Lodge version of the treaty. On November 19, Democrats joined with the "irreconcilables" to defeat the amended treaty, 39 to 55.

Wilson refused to budge. In January, he urged Democrats to either stand by the original treaty or vote it down. The 1920 election, he warned, would be "a great and solemn referendum" on the whole issue. In the final vote, on March 19, 1920, twenty-one Democrats broke with the president and voted for the Lodge version, giving it a majority of 49 to 35. But this was seven votes short of the two-thirds needed for ratification. As a result, the United States never signed the Versailles Treaty, nor did it join the League of Nations. The absence of the United States weakened the League and made it more difficult for the organization to realize Wilson's dream of a peaceful community of nations.

The Russian Revolution and America's Response

Since early 1917, the turmoil of the Russian Revolution had changed the climate of both foreign affairs and domestic politics. The repressive and corrupt regime of Czar Nicholas II had been overthrown in March 1917 by a coalition of forces demanding change. The new provisional government, headed by Alexander Kerensky, vowed to keep Russia in the fight against Germany. But the war had taken a terrible toll on Russian soldiers and civilians, and had become very unpopular. The radical Bolsheviks, led by V. I. Lenin, gained a large following by promising "peace, land, and bread," and they began plotting to seize power. The Bolsheviks followed the teachings of German revolutionary Karl Marx, emphasizing the inevitability of class struggle and the replacement of capitalism by communism.

In November 1917 the Bolsheviks took control of the Russian government. In March 1918, to the dismay of the Allies, the new Bolshevik government negotiated a separate peace with Germany, the Treaty of Brest-Litovsk. Russia was now lost as a military ally, and her defection made possible a massive shift of German troops to the Western Front. As civil war raged within Russia, British and French leaders wanted to help counterrevolutionary forces overthrow the new Bolshevik regime, as well as reclaim military supplies originally sent for use against the Germans.

Although sympathetic to the March revolution overthrowing the czar, President Wilson refused to recognize the authority of the Bolshevik regime. Bolshevism represented a threat to the liberal-capitalist values that Wilson believed to be the foundation of America's moral and material power and that provided the basis for the Fourteen Points. At the same time, however, Wilson at first resisted British and French pressure to intervene in Russia, citing his commitment to national self-determination and noninterference in other countries' internal affairs. "I believe in letting them work out their own salvation, even though they wallow in anarchy for a while," he wrote to one Allied diplomat.

By August 1918, as the Russian political and military situation became increasingly chaotic, Wilson agreed to British and French plans for sending troops to Siberia and northern Russia. Meanwhile, Japan poured troops into Siberia and northern Manchuria in a bid to control the commercially important Chinese Eastern and Trans-Siberian Railways. After the Wilson administration negotiated an agreement that placed these strategic railways under international control, the restoration and protection of the railways became the primary concern of American military forces in Russia. Wilson justified the intervention on trade and commercial grounds, telling Congress, "It is essential that we maintain the policy of the Open Door." But however reluctantly, the United States had in fact become an active, anti-Bolshevik participant in the Russian civil war.

Wilson's idealistic support for self-determination had succumbed to the demands of international power politics. Eventually, some 15,000 American troops served in northern and eastern Russia, with some remaining until 1920. They stayed for two reasons: to counter Japanese influence, and because Wilson did not want to risk alienating the British and French, who opposed withdrawal. The Allied armed intervention widened the gulf between Russia and the West. In March 1919, Russian Communists established the Third International, or Comintern. Their call for a worldwide revolution deepened Allied mistrust, and the Paris Peace Conference essentially ignored the new political reality posed by the Russian Revolution.

The Red Scare

In the United States, strikes, antiwar agitation, even racial disturbances were increasingly blamed on foreign radicals and alien ideologies. Pro-German sentiment, socialism, the IWW, and trade unionism in general, all were conveniently lumped together. The accusation of Bolshevism became a powerful weapon for turning public opinion against strikers and political dissenters of all kinds. In the 1919 Seattle general strike, for example, Mayor Ole Hanson claimed against all evidence that the strikers "want to take possession of our American Government and try to duplicate the anarchy of Russia." Months later the Seattle *Post-Intelligencer*, referring to the IWW, said: "We must smash every un-American and anti-American organization in the land. We must put to death the leaders of this gigantic conspiracy of murder, pillage, and revolution."

In truth, by 1919 the American radicals were already weakened and badly split. The Socialist Party had around 40,000 members. Two small Communist Parties, made up largely of immigrants, had a total of perhaps 70,000. In the spring of 1919, a few extremists mailed bombs to prominent business and political leaders. That June, simultaneous bombings in eight cities killed two people and damaged the residence of Attorney General A. Mitchell Palmer. With public alarm growing, state and federal officials began a coordinated campaign to root out subversives and their alleged Russian connections.

Palmer used the broad authority of the 1918 Alien Act, which enabled the government to deport any immigrant found to be a member of a revolutionary organization prior to or after coming to the United States. In a series of raids in late 1919, Justice Department agents in eleven cities arrested and roughed up several hundred members of the IWW and the Union of Russian Workers. Little evidence of revolutionary intent was found, but 249 people were deported, including prominent anarchists Emma Goldman and Alexander Berkman. In early 1920 some 6,000 people in thirty-three cities, including many U.S. citizens and noncommunists, were arrested and herded into prisons and bullpens. Again, no evidence of a grand plot was found, but another 600 aliens were deported. The Palmer raids had a ripple effect around the nation, encouraging other repressive measures against radicals. In New York, the state assembly refused to seat five duly elected Socialist Party members.

A report prepared by a group of distinguished lawyers questioned the legality of the attorney general's tactics. Palmer's popularity had waned by the spring of 1920, when it became clear that his predictions of revolutionary uprisings were wildly exaggerated. But the Red Scare left an ugly legacy: wholesale violations of constitutional rights, deportations of hundreds of innocent people, fuel for the fires of nativism and intolerance. Business groups, such as the National Association of Manufacturers, found "Red-baiting" to be an effective tool in postwar efforts to keep unions out of their factories. Indeed, the government-sanctioned Red Scare reemerged later in the century as a powerful political force.

The Red Scare took its toll on the women's movement as well. Before the war, many suffragists and feminists had maintained ties and shared platforms with socialist and labor groups. The suffrage movement in particular had brought together women from very different class backgrounds and political perspectives. But the calls for "100 percent Americanism" during and after the war destroyed the fragile alliances that had made a group such as the National American Woman Suffrage Association so powerful. After the war, many women's organizations that had been divided over American involvement in the war reunited under the umbrella of the National Council for Prevention of War. But when military spokesmen in the early 1920s attacked the group for advocating communism, two of its largest affiliates—the General Federation of Women's Clubs and the Parent-Teacher Association—withdrew in fear. Hostility to radicalism marked the political climate of the 1920s, and this atmosphere narrowed the political spectrum for women activists.

The Election of 1920

The presidential contest of 1920 suggested that Americans wanted to retreat from the internationalism, reform fervor, and social tensions associated with the war. Woodrow Wilson had wanted the 1920 election to be a "solemn referendum" on the League of Nations and his conduct of the war. Ill and exhausted, Wilson did not run for reelection. A badly divided Democratic Party compromised on Governor James M. Cox of Ohio as its candidate. A proven vote-getter, Cox distanced himself from Wilson's policies, which had come under withering attack from many quarters.

The Republicans nominated Senator Warren G. Harding of Ohio. A political hack, the handsome and genial Harding had virtually no qualifications to be president, except that he looked like one. Harding's campaign was vague and ambiguous about the Versailles Treaty and almost everything else. He struck a chord with the electorate in calling for a retreat from Wilsonian idealism. "America's present need," he said, "is not heroics but healing; not nostrums but normalcy; not revolution but restoration."

The notion of a "return to normalcy" proved very attractive to voters exhausted by the war, inflation, big government, and social dislocation. Harding won the greatest landslide in history to that date, carrying every state outside the South and taking the popular vote by 16 million to 9 million. Republicans retained their majorities in the House and Senate as well. Socialist Eugene

Debs, still a powerful symbol of the dream of radical social change, managed to poll 900,000 votes from jail. But the overall vote repudiated Wilson and the progressive movement. Americans seemed eager to pull back from moralism in public and international controversies. Yet many of the economic, social, and cultural changes wrought by the war would accelerate during the 1920s. In truth, there could never be a "return to normalcy."

CHRONOLOGY

1903	U.S. obtains Panama canal rights
1904	Roosevelt Corollary justifies U.S. intervention in the Americas
1905	President Theodore Roosevelt mediates peace treaty between Japan and Russia at Portsmouth Conference
1908	Root-Takahira Agreement with Japan affirms status quo in Asia and Open Door policy in China
1911	Mexican Revolution begins
1914	U.S. forces invade Mexico
	Panama Canal opens
	First World War begins in Europe
	President Woodrow Wilson issues proclamation of neutrality
1915	Germany declares war zone around Great Britain
	German U-boat sinks *Lusitania*
1916	Pancho Villa raids New Mexico, is pursued by General Pershing
	Wilson is reelected
	National Defense Act establishes preparedness program
1917	February: Germany resumes unrestricted submarine warfare
	March: Zimmermann note, suggesting a German-Mexican alliance, shocks Americans
	April: U.S. declares war on the Central Powers
	Committee on Public Information is established
	May: Selective Service Act is passed
	June: Espionage Act is passed
	July: Race riot occurs in East St. Louis

	War Industries Board is established
	August: Food Administration and Fuel Administration are established
	November: Bolshevik Revolution begins in Russia
1918	January: Wilson unveils Fourteen Points
	April: National War Labor Board is established
	May: Sedition Act is passed
	June: Eugene Debs is arrested for defending antiwar protesters
	U.S. troops begin to see action in France
	U.S. troops serve in Russia
	November: Armistice ends war
1919	January: Eighteenth Amendment (Prohibition) is ratified
	Wilson serves as Chief U.S. negotiator at Paris Peace Conference
	June: Versailles Treaty is signed in Paris
	July: Race riot breaks out in Chicago
	Steel strike begins in several midwestern cities
	September: Wilson suffers stroke while touring country in support of Versailles Treaty
	November: Henry Cabot Lodge's version of the Versailles Treaty is rejected by the Senate
	Palmer raids begin
1920	March: Senate finally votes down Versailles Treaty and League of Nations
	August: Nineteenth Amendment (woman suffrage) is ratified
	November: Warren G. Harding is elected president

CONCLUSION

Compared to the casualties and social upheavals endured by the European powers, the Great War's impact on American life might appear slight. Yet the war created economic, social, and political dislocations that helped reshape American life long after Armistice Day. Republican administrations invoked the wartime partnership between government and industry to justify an aggressive peacetime policy fostering cooperation between the state and business. Wartime production needs contributed to what economists later called "the second industrial revolution." Patriotic fervor and the exaggerated specter of

Bolshevism were used to repress radicalism, organized labor, feminism, and the entire legacy of progressive reform.

The wartime measure of national prohibition evolved into perhaps the most contentious social issue of peacetime. Sophisticated use of sales techniques, psychology, and propaganda during the war helped define the newly powerful advertising and public relations industries of the 1920s. The growing visibility of immigrants and African Americans, especially in the nation's cities, provoked a xenophobic and racist backlash in the politics of the 1920s. More than anything else, the desire for "normalcy" reflected the deep anxieties evoked by America's wartime experience.

REVIEW QUESTIONS

1. What central issues drew the United States deeper into international politics in the early years of the century? How did American presidents justify a more expansive role? What diplomatic and military policies did they exploit for these ends?

2. Compare the arguments for and against American participation in the Great War. Which Americans were most likely to support entry? Which were more likely to oppose it?

3. How did mobilizing for war change the economy and its relationship to government? Which of these changes, if any, spilled over to the postwar years?

4. How did the war affect political life in the United States? What techniques were used to stifle dissent? What was the war's political legacy?

5. To what extent was the war an extension of progressivism?

6. Analyze the impact of the war on American workers. How did the conflict affect the lives of African Americans and women?

7. What principles guided Woodrow Wilson's Fourteen Points? How would you explain the United States' failure to ratify the Treaty of Versailles?

RECOMMENDED READING

Robert H. Ferrell, *Woodrow Wilson and World War I* (1985). A close analysis of Wilson's handling of wartime diplomacy and domestic politics.

Martin Gilbert, *The First World War: A Complete History* (1994). An ambitious overview of the Great War from a global perspective.

Maureen Greenwald, *Women, War, and Work* (1980). The best account of the impact of the war on working women.

David M. Kennedy, *Over Here* (1980). The best, most comprehensive one-volume history of the political and economic impact of the war on the domestic front.

Thomas J. Knock, *To End All Wars: Woodrow Wilson and the Quest for a New World Order* (1992). A fine analysis of Wilson's internationalism, its links to his domestic policies, and his design for the League of Nations.

Walter LaFeber, *The American Age* (1989). A fine survey of the history of U.S. foreign policy that includes an analysis of the pre–World War I era.

Paul L. Murphy, *World War I and the Origin of Civil Liberties* (1979). A good overview of the various civil liberties issues raised by the war and government efforts to suppress dissent.

Ronald Schaffer, *America in the Great War: The Rise of the War Welfare State* (1991). Excellent material on how the war transformed the relationship between business and government and spurred improved conditions for industrial workers.

Joe William Trotter Jr., ed., *The Great Migration in Historical Perspective* (1991). An excellent collection of essays examining the Great Migration, with special attention to issues of class and gender within the African American community.

Neil A. Wynn, *From Progressivism to Prosperity: World War I and American Society* (1986). An illuminating account of the social impact of the war on Amer-ican life. Effectively connects the war experience with both progressive era trends and postwar developments in the 1920s.

ADDITIONAL BIBLIOGRAPHY

Becoming a World Power

Richard H. Collin, *Theodore Roosevelt's Caribbean* (1990)

John Dobson, *America's Ascent: The United States Becomes a Great Power, 1880–1914* (1978)

Akira Iriye, *Pacific Estrangement* (1972)

Friedrich Katz, *The Secret War in Mexico* (1981)

Burton I. Kaufman, *Efficiency and Expansion* (1974)

Walter LaFeber, *The Panama Canal* (1978)

Lester E. Langley, *The Banana Wars: An Inner History of American Empire, 1900–1934* (1983)

Emily S. Rosenberg, *Spreading the American Dream* (1982)

The Great War

Lloyd E. Ambrosius, *Woodrow Wilson and the American Diplo-matic Tradition* (1987)

Paul Fussell, *The Great War and Modern Memory* (1973)

James Joll, *The Origins of the First World War* (1984)

C. Roland Marchand, *The American Peace Movement and Social Reform, 1898–1918* (1973)

American Mobilization

A. E. Barbeau and Florette Henri, *The Unknown Soldiers: Black American Troops in World War I* (1974)

John W. Chambers, *To Raise an Army: The Draft in Modern America* (1987)

J. Garry Clifford, *Citizen Soldiers* (1972)

Edward M. Coffman, *The War to End All Wars* (1968)

Charles Gilbert, *American Financing of World War I* (1970)

Stephen Vaughn, *Holding Fast the Inner Lines: Democracy, Nationalism, and the Committee on Public Information* (1980)

Russell Weigley, *The American Way of War* (1973)

Over Here

Daniel R. Beaver, *Newton D. Baker and the American War Effort, 1917–1919* (1966)

Allen J. Brandt, *No Magic Bullet: A Social History of Venereal Disease in the United States since 1880* (1985)

Valerie J. Conner, *The National War Labor Board* (1983)

Frank L. Grubbs Jr., *Samuel Gompers and the Great War* (1982)

Ellis W. Hawley, *The Great War and the Search for Modern Order*, 2d ed. (1992)

Jeffrey Haydu, *Making American Industries Safe for Democracy* (1997)

John F. McClymer, *War and Welfare: Social Engineering in Amer-ica, 1890–1925* (1980)

David Montgomery, *The Fall of the House of Labor* (1987)

Barbara Steinson, *American Women's Activism in World War I* (1982)

Repression and Reaction

David Brody, *Labor in Crisis: The Steel Strike of 1919* (1965)

James P. Grossman, *Land of Hope: Chicago, Black Southerners, and the Great Migration* (1989)

Florette Henri, *Black Migration: Movement Northward, 1900–1920* (1975)

Frederick C. Luebke, *Bonds of Loyalty: German Americans and World War I* (1974)

Harold C. Peterson and Gilbert Fite, *Opponents of War, 1917–1918* (1968)

William Preston Jr., *Aliens and Dissenters: Federal Suppression of Radicals, 1903–1933* (1966)

William M. Tuttle Jr., *Race Riot: Chicago in the Red Summer of 1919* (1970)

An Uneasy Peace

Dana Frank, *Purchasing Power: Consumer Organizing, Gender, and the Seattle Labor Movement, 1919–1929* (1994)

Lloyd Gardner, *Safe for Democracy: The Anglo-American Response to Revolution, 1913–1923* (1984)

Robert D. Johnson, *The Peace Progressives and American Foreign Relations* (1995)

N. Gordon Levin Jr., *Woodrow Wilson and World Politics* (1968)

Robert K. Murray, *Red Scare: A Study in National Hysteria, 1919–1920* (1955)

Richard Polenberg, *Fighting Faiths: The Abrams Case, the Supreme Court, and Free Speech* (1987)

Stuart Rochester, *American Liberal Disillusionment in the Wake of World War I* (1977)

Ralph Stone, *The Irreconcilables: The Fight against the League of Nations* (1970)

Biography

Bruce Clayton, *Forgotten Prophet: The Life of Randolph Bourne* (1984)

Kendrick Clements, *Woodrow Wilson: World Statesman* (1987)

Stanley Coben, *A. Mitchell Palmer* (1963)

Arthur S. Link, *Woodrow Wilson: War, Revolution, and Peace* (1979)

Jordan Schwarz, *The Speculator: Bernard M. Baruch in Washing-ton, 1917–1965* (1981)

Frank E. Vandiver, *Black Jack: The Life and Times of John J. Pershing* (1977)

Jacqueline van Voris, *Carrie Chapman Catt* (1987)

CHAPTER TWENTY-THREE

THE TWENTIES

1920–1929

Thomas Hart Benton. *City Activities with Dance Hall* from *America Today*. 1930. Distemper and egg tempera with oil glaze on gessoed linen, 92 x 134 ½ in. Collection, The Equitable Life Assurance Society of the United States. Photo 1988 by Dorothy Zeidman.

AMERICAN COMMUNITIES
The Movie Audience and Hollywood: Mass Culture Creates a New National Community

Inside midtown Manhattan's magnificent new Roxy Theater, a sellout crowd eagerly settled in for opening night. Outside, thousands of fans cheered wildly at the arrival of movie stars such as Charlie Chaplin, Gloria Swanson, and Harold Lloyd. A squadron of smartly uniformed ushers guided patrons under a five-story-tall rotunda to some 6,200 velvet-covered seats. The audience marveled at the huge gold and rose-colored murals, classical statuary, plush carpeting, and Gothic-style windows. It was easy to believe newspaper reports that the theater had cost $10 million to build. Suddenly, light flooded the orchestra pit and 110 musicians began playing "The Star Spangled Banner." A troupe of 100 performers took the stage, dancing ballet numbers and singing old southern melodies such as "My Old Kentucky Home" and "Swanee River." Congratulatory telegrams from President Calvin Coolidge and other dignitaries flashed on the screen. Finally, the evening's feature presentation, *The Love of Sunya*, starring Gloria Swanson, began. Samuel L. "Roxy" Rothapfel, the theater's designer, had realized his grand dream—to build "the cathedral of the motion picture."

When Roxy's opened in March 1927, nearly 60 million Americans "worshiped" each week at movie theaters across the nation. The "movie palaces" of the 1920s were designed to transport patrons to exotic places and different times. As film pioneer Marcus Loew put it, "We sell tickets to theaters, not movies." Every large community boasted at least one opulent movie theater. Houston's Majestic was built to represent an ancient Italian garden; it had a ceiling made to look like an open sky, complete with stars and cloud formations. The Tivoli in Chicago featured opulent French Renaissance decor; Grauman's Egyptian in Los Angeles re-created the look of a pharaoh's tomb; and Albuquerque's Kimo drew inspiration from Navajo art and religion.

The remarkable popularity of motion pictures, and later radio, forged a new kind of community. A huge national audience regularly went to the movies, and the same entertainment could be enjoyed virtually anywhere in the country by just about everyone. Movies emerged as the most popular form in the new mass culture, with an appeal that extended far beyond the films themselves, or even the theaters. Americans embraced the cult of celebrity, voraciously consuming fan magazines, gossip columns, and news of the stars. By the 1920s, the production center for this dream world was Hollywood, California, a suburb of Los Angeles that had barely existed in 1890.

Motion picture companies found Hollywood an alluring alternative to the east coast cities where they had been born. Its reliably sunny and dry climate was ideal for year-round filming. Its unique surroundings offered a perfect variety of scenic locations—mountains, desert, ocean—and downtown Los Angeles was only an hour away. Land was cheap and plentiful. And because Los Angeles was the leading nonunion, open-shop city in the country, so was labor. By the early 1920s Hollywood produced more than 80 percent of the nation's motion pictures and was assuming mythical status. The isolation of the town, its great distance from the eastern cities, its lack of traditional sources of culture and learning—all contributed to movie folk looking at life in a self-consciously "Hollywood" way.

With its feel of a modern frontier boom-town, Hollywood was a new kind of American community. It lured the young and cosmopolitan with the promise of upward mobility and a new way of life. Most of the top studio executives were Jewish immigrants from eastern and central Europe. In contrast to most Americans, who hailed from rural areas or small towns, more than half of Holly-wood's writers, directors, editors, and actors were born in cities of over 100,000. Two-thirds of its performers were under thirty-five, and three-fourths of its actresses were under twenty-five. More than 90 percent of its writers (women made up one-third to one-half of this key group) had attended college or worked in journalism. The movies this untypical community created evoked the pleasures of leisure, consumption, and personal freedom, redefining the nation's cultural values in the 1920s.

Movie stars dominated Hollywood. Charlie Chaplin, Mary Pickford, Rudolph Valentino, Gloria Swanson, and Douglas Fairbanks became popular idols as much for their highly publicized private lives as for their roles on screen.

Hollywood

Many accumulated great wealth, becoming the nation's experts on how to live well. Movie folk built luxurious mansions in a variety of architectural styles and outfitted them with swimming pools, tennis courts, golf courses, and lavish gardens.

Visitors often noted that Hollywood had no museums, art galleries, live theater, or other traditional institutions of high culture. How would the town's wealthy movie elite spend their time and money? By 1916 Charlie Chaplin, a working-class immigrant from the London slums, was earning $10,000 a week for the comedies that made his the most famous face in the world. He recalled trying to figure out what to do with his new wealth. "The money I earned was legendary, a symbol in figures, for I had never actually seen it. I therefore had to do something to prove I had it. So I procured a secretary, a valet, a car, a chauffeur."

Ordinary Americans found it easy to identify with movie stars despite their wealth and status. Unlike industrialists or politicians, stars had no social authority over large groups of employees or voters. They, too, had to answer to a boss, and most had risen from humble beginnings. But above all, Hollywood, like the movies it churned out, represented for millions of Americans new possibilities: freedom, material success, upward mobility, and the chance to remake one's very identity. By the end of the decade the Hollywood "dream factory" had helped forge a national community whose collective aspirations and desires were increasingly defined by those possibilities, even if relatively few Americans realized them during the 1920s.

KEY TOPICS

- A second industrial revolution that transforms the economy

- The promise and limits of prosperity in the 1920s

- New mass media and the culture of consumption

- Republican Party dominance

- Political and cultural opposition to modern trends

POSTWAR PROSPERITY AND ITS PRICE

Republican Warren G. Harding won the presidency in 1920, largely thanks to his nostalgic call for a "return to normalcy." But in the decade following the end of World War I, the American economy underwent profound structural changes that guaranteed life would never be "normal" again. The 1920s saw an enormous increase in the efficiency of production, a steady climb in real wages, a decline in the length of the average employee's work week, and a boom in consumer goods industries. Americans shared unevenly in the postwar prosperity, and by the end of the decade certain basic weaknesses in the economy helped to bring on the worst depression in American history. Yet overall, the nation experienced crucial transformations in how it organized its business, earned its living, and enjoyed its leisure time.

The Second Industrial Revolution

The prosperity of the 1920s rested on what historians have called the "second industrial revolution" in American manufacturing, in which technological innovations made it possible to increase industrial output without expanding the labor force. Electricity replaced steam as the main power source for industry in these years, making possible the replacement of older machinery with more efficient and flexible electric machinery. In 1914 only 30 percent of the nation's factories were electrified; by 1929, 70 percent relied on the electric motor rather than the steam engine.

Much of the newer, automatic machinery could be operated by unskilled and semiskilled workers, and it boosted the overall efficiency of American industry. Thus in 1929 the average worker in manufacturing produced roughly three-quarters more per hour than he or she had in 1919. The machine industry itself, particularly the manufacture of electrical machinery, led in productivity gains, enjoying one of the fastest rates of expansion. It employed more workers than any other manufacturing sector—some 1.1 million in 1929—supplying not only a growing home market but 35 percent of the world market as well.

During the late nineteenth century heavy industries such as machine tools, railroads, iron, and steel had pioneered mass-production techniques. These industries manufactured what economists call producer-durable goods. In the 1920s, modern mass-production techniques were increasingly applied as well to newer consumer-durable goods—automobiles, radios, washing machines, and telephones—permitting firms to make large profits while keeping prices affordable. Other consumer-based industries, such as canning, chemicals, synthetics, and plastics, began to change the everyday lives of millions of Americans. With more efficient management, greater mechanization, intensive product research, and ingenious sales and advertising methods, the consumer-based industries helped to nearly double industrial production in the 1920s.

America experienced a building boom during the 1920s, and its construction industry played a large role in the new prosperity. Expenditures for residential housing, nonresidential building, and public construction projects all showed steady growth after 1921. The demand for new housing was unprecedented, particularly with the backlog created during World War I, when little new construction took place. The growth in automobile ownership, as well as improvements in public mass transit, made suburban living more attractive to families and suburban construction more profitable for developers. Commercial banks, savings and loan associations, and insurance companies provided greatly expanded credit for home buying. America's residential mortgage debt jumped from about $8 billion in 1919 to $27 billion in 1929.

The Modern Corporation

The organization and techniques of American business underwent crucial changes during the postwar decade. In the late nineteenth century, individual entrepreneurs such as John D. Rockefeller in oil and Andrew Carnegie in steel had provided a model for

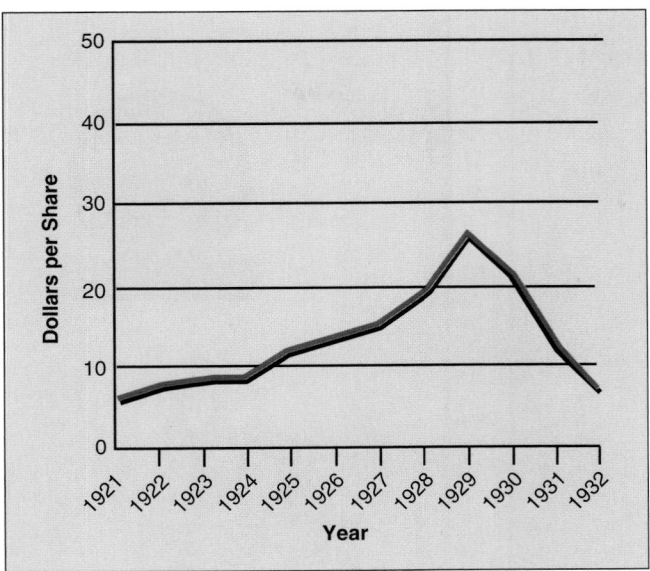

Stock Market Prices, 1921–1932 *Common stock prices rose steeply during the 1920s. Although only about 4 million Americans owned stocks during the period, "stock watching" became something of a national sport.*

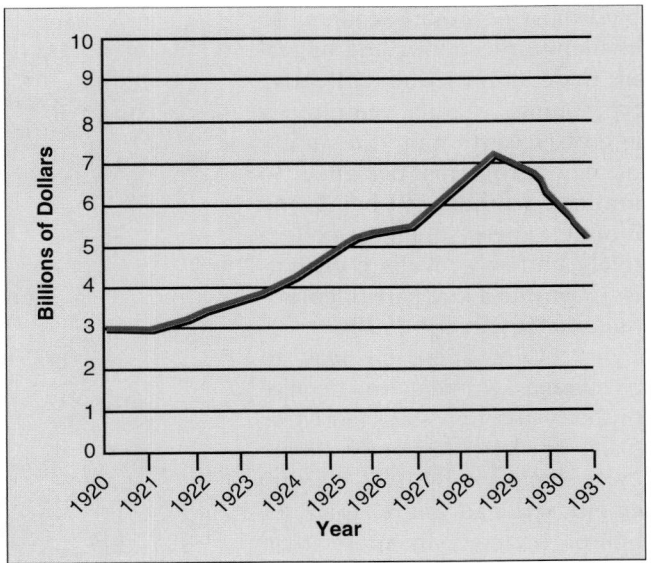

Consumer Debt, 1920–1931 *The expansion of consumer borrowing was a key component of the era's prosperity. These figures do not include mortgages or money borrowed to purchase stocks. They reveal the great increase in "installment buying" for such consumer durable goods as automobiles and household appliances.*

success. They maintained both corporate control (ownership) and business leadership (management) in their enterprises. In the 1920s, a managerial revolution increasingly divorced ownership of corporate stock from the everyday control of businesses. The new corporate ideal was to be found in men such as Alfred P. Sloan of General Motors and Owen D. Young of the Radio Corporation of America. A growing class of salaried executives, plant managers, and engineers formed a new elite who made corporate policy without themselves having a controlling interest in the companies they worked for. They stressed scientific management and the latest theories of behavioral psychology in their effort to make their workplaces more productive, stable, and profitable.

During the 1920s, the most successful corporations were those that led in three key areas: the integration of production and distribution; product diversification; and the expansion of industrial research. Until the end of World War I, for example, the chemical manufacturer Du Pont had specialized in explosives such as gunpowder. After the war Du Pont moved aggressively into the consumer market with a diverse array of products. The company created separate but integrated divisions that produced and distributed new fabrics (such as rayon), paints, dyes, and celluloid products (such as artificial sponges). The great electrical manufacturers—General Electric and Westinghouse—similarly transformed themselves after the war. Previously

concentrating on lighting and power equipment, they now diversified into household appliances like radios, washing machines, and refrigerators. The chemical and electrical industries also led the way in industrial research, hiring personnel to develop new products and test their commercial viability.

By 1929 the 200 largest corporations owned nearly half the nation's corporate wealth—that is, physical plant, stock, and property. Half the total industrial income—revenue from sales of goods—was concentrated in 100 corporations. Oligopoly—the control of a market by a few large producers—became the norm. Four companies packed almost three-quarters of all American meat. Another four rolled nine out of every ten cigarettes. National chain grocery stores, clothing shops, and pharmacies began squeezing out local neighborhood businesses. One grocery chain alone, the Great Atlantic and Pacific Tea Company (A&P), accounted for 10 percent of all retail food sales in America. Its 15,000 stores sold a greater volume of goods than Ford Motor Company at its peak. These changes meant that Americans were increasingly members of national consumer communities, buying the same brands all over the country, as opposed to locally produced goods.

Welfare Capitalism

The wartime gains made by organized labor and the active sympathy shown to trade unions by government agencies such as the National War Labor Board troubled most corporate leaders. To challenge the power and appeal of trade unions and collective bargaining, large employers aggressively promoted a variety of new programs designed to improve worker well-being and morale. These schemes, collectively known as welfare capitalism, became a key part of corporate strategy in the 1920s.

One approach was to encourage workers to acquire property through stock-purchase plans or, less frequently, home ownership plans. By 1927, 800,000 employees had more than $1 billion invested in more than 300 companies. Other programs offered workers insurance policies covering accidents, illness, old age, and death. By 1928 some 6 million workers had group insurance coverage valued at $7.5 billion. Many plant managers and personnel departments consciously worked to improve safety conditions, provide medical services, and establish sports and recreation programs for workers. Employers hoped such measures would

The A&P grocery chain expanded from 400 stores in 1912 to more than 15,000 by the end of the 1920s, making it a familiar sight in communities across America. A&P advertisements, like this one from 1927, emphasized cleanliness, order, and the availability of name brand goods at discount prices.

encourage workers to identify personally with the company and discourage complaints on the job. To some extent they succeeded. But welfare capitalism could not solve the most chronic problems faced by industrial workers: seasonal unemployment, low wages, long hours, and unhealthy factory conditions.

Large corporations also mounted an effective anti-union campaign in the early 1920s called "the American plan," a name meant to associate unionism with foreign and un-American ideas. Backed by powerful business lobbies such as the National Association of Manufacturers and the Chamber of Commerce, campaign leaders called for the open shop, in which no employee would be compelled to join a union. If a union existed, nonmembers would still get whatever wages and rights the union had won—a policy that put organizers at a disadvantage in signing up new members.

The open shop undercut the gains won in a union shop, where new employees had to join an existing union, or a closed shop, where employers agreed to hire only union members. As alternatives, large employers such as U.S. Steel and International Harvester began setting up company unions. Their intent was to substitute largely symbolic employee

representation in management conferences for the more confrontational process of collective bargaining. Company unions were often established simultaneously with anti-union campaigns in specific industries or communities.

These management strategies contributed to a sharp decline in the ranks of organized labor. Total union membership dropped from about 5 million in 1920 to 3.5 million in 1926. A large proportion of the remaining union members were concentrated in the skilled crafts of the building and printing trades. A conservative and timid union leadership was also responsible for the trend. William Green, who became president of the American Federation of Labor after the death of Samuel Gompers in 1924, showed no real interest in getting unorganized workers like those in the growing mass-production industries of automobiles, steel, and electrical goods into unions. The federal government, which had provided limited wartime support for unions, now reverted to a more probusiness posture. The Supreme Court in particular was unsympathetic toward unions, consistently upholding the use of injunctions to prevent strikes, picketing, and other union activities.

The Auto Age

In their classic community study *Middletown* (1929), sociologists Robert and Helen Lynd noted the dramatic impact of the car on the social life of Muncie, Indiana. "Why on earth do you need to study what's changing this country?" asked one life-long Muncie resident in 1924. "I can tell you what's happening in just four letters: A-U-T-O!" This remark hardly seems much of an exaggeration today. No other single development could match the impact of the postwar automobile explosion on the way Americans worked, lived, and played. The auto industry offered the clearest example of the rise to prominence of consumer durables. During the 1920s, America made approximately 85 percent of all the world's passenger cars. By 1929 the motor vehicle industry was the most productive in the United States in terms of value. In that year the industry added 4.8 million new cars to the more than 26 million—roughly one for every five people—already on American roads.

This extraordinary new industry had mushroomed in less than a generation. Its great pioneer, Henry Ford, had shown how the use of a continuous assembly line could drastically reduce the number of worker hours required to produce a single vehicle. Ford revolutionized the factory shop floor with new, custom-built machinery, such as the engine-boring drill press and the pneumatic wrench, and a more efficient layout. "Every piece of work in the shop moves," Ford boasted. "It may move on hooks or overhead chains, going to assembly in the exact order in which the parts are required; it may travel on a moving platform, or it may go by gravity, but the point is that there is no lifting or trucking of anything other than materials." In 1913 it took thirteen hours to produce one automobile. In 1914, at his sprawling new Highland Park assembly plant just outside Detroit, Ford's system finished one car every ninety minutes. By 1925, cars were rolling off his assembly line at the rate of one every ten seconds.

In 1914 Ford startled American industry by inaugurating a new wage scale: $5 for an eight-hour day. This was roughly double the going pay rate for industrial labor, and a shorter workday as well. But in defying the conventional economic wisdom of the day, Ford acted less out of benevolence than out of shrewdness. He understood that workers were consumers as well as producers, and the new wage scale helped boost sales of Ford cars. It also reduced the high turnover rate in his labor force and increased worker efficiency. Roughly two-thirds of the labor force at Ford consisted of immigrants from southern and eastern Europe. By the early 1920s Ford also employed about 5,000 African Americans, more

Finished automobiles roll off the moving assembly line at the Ford Motor Company, Highland Park, Michigan, ca.1920. During the 1920s Henry Ford achieved the status of folk hero, as his name became synonymous with the techniques of mass production. Ford cultivated a public image of himself as the heroic genius of the auto industry, greatly exaggerating his personal achievements.

than any other large American corporation. Ford's mass-production system and economies of scale permitted him to progressively reduce the price of his cars, bringing them within the reach of millions of Americans. The famous Model T, thoroughly standardized and available only in black, cost just under $300 in 1924—about three months' wages for the best-paid factory workers.

By 1927 Ford had produced 15 million Model Ts. But by then the company faced stiff competition from General Motors, which had developed an effective new marketing strategy. Under the guidance of Alfred P. Sloan, GM organized into separate divisions, each of which appealed to a different market segment. Cadillac, for example, produced GM's most expensive car, which was targeted at the wealthy buyer; Chevrolet produced its least expensive model, which was targeted at working-class and lower-middle-class buyers. The GM business structure, along with its attempts to match production with demand through sophisticated market research and sales forecasting, became a widely copied model for other large American corporations.

The auto industry provided a large market for makers of steel, rubber, glass, and petroleum products. It stimulated public spending for good roads and extended the housing boom to new suburbs. Showrooms, repair shops, and gas stations appeared in thousands of communities. New small enterprises, from motels to billboard advertising to roadside diners, sprang up as motorists took to the highway. The rapid development of Florida and California, in particular, was partly a response to the growing influence of the automobile and the new possibilities it presented for seeing far-off places.

Automobiles widened the experience of millions of Americans. They made the exploration of the world outside the local community easier and more attractive. For some the car merely reinforced old social patterns, making it easier for them to get to church on Sunday, for example, or visit neighbors. Others used their cars to go to new places, shop in nearby cities, or take vacations. The automobile made leisure, in the sense of getting away from the routines of work and school, a more regular part of everyday life. It undoubtedly also changed the courtship practices of America's youth. Young people took advantage of the car to gain privacy and distance from their parents. "What on earth do you want me to do?" complained one Middletown high school girl to her anxious father. "Just sit around home all evening?" Many had their first sexual experiences in a car.

Cities and Suburbs

Cars also promoted urban and suburban growth. The federal census for 1920 was the first in American history in which the proportion of the population that lived in urban places (those with 2,500 or more people) exceeded the proportion of the population living in rural areas. More revealing of urban growth was the steady increase in the number of big cities. In 1910 there were sixty cities with more than 100,000 inhabitants; in 1920 there were sixty-eight; and by 1930 there were ninety-two. During the 1920s New York grew by 20 percent to nearly 7 million, whereas Detroit, home of the auto industry, doubled its population, to nearly 2 million.

Cities promised business opportunity, good jobs, cultural richness, and personal freedom. They attracted millions of Americans, white and black, from small towns and farms, as well as immigrants from abroad. Immigrants were drawn to cities by the presence there of family and people of like background in already established ethnic communities. In a continuation of the Great Migration that began during World War I, roughly 1.5 million African Americans from the rural south migrated to cities in search of economic opportunities during the 1920s, doubling the black populations of New York, Chicago, Detroit, and Houston.

Until 1924 Henry Ford had disdained national advertising for his cars. But as General Motors gained a competitive edge by making yearly changes in style and technology, Ford was forced to pay more attention to advertising. This ad was directed at "Mrs. Consumer," combining appeals to both female independence and motherly duties.

Cities grew both vertically and horizontally in these years. Skylines around the country were remade as architects took advantage of steel-skeleton construction technology to build skyscrapers. By 1930, American cities boasted nearly 400 buildings more than 20 stories tall. New York's Empire State Building, completed in 1931, was the tallest building in the world, rising 1,250 feet into the sky. It had room for 25,000 commercial and residential tenants in its 102 stories.

Houston offers a good example of how the automobile shaped an urban community. In 1910 it was a sleepy railroad town with a population of about 75,000 that served the Texas Gulf coast and interior. The enormous demand for gasoline and other petroleum products helped transform the city into a busy center for oil refining. Its population soared to 300,000 by the end of the 1920s. Abundant cheap land and the absence of zoning ordinances, combined with the availability of the automobile, pushed Houston to expand horizontally rather than vertically. It became the archetypal decentralized, low-density city, sprawling miles in each direction from downtown, and thoroughly dependent upon automobiles and roads for its sense of community. Other

Sunbelt cities, such as Los Angeles, Miami, and San Diego, experienced similar land use patterns and sharp population growth during the decade.

Suburban communities grew at twice the rate of their core cities, also thanks largely to the automobile boom. Undeveloped land on the fringes of cities became valuable real estate. Grosse Pointe, near Detroit, and Elmwood Park, near Chicago, grew more than 700 percent in ten years. Long Island's Nassau County, just east of New York City, tripled in population. All the new "automobile suburbs" differed in important ways from earlier suburbs built along mass transit lines. The car allowed for a larger average lot size, and in turn lower residential density. It also became essential for commuting to work and encouraged the movement of workplaces out of the central city. The suburbs would increasingly become not only places to live but centers for working and shopping as well.

Exceptions: Agriculture, Ailing Industries

Amid prosperity and progress, there were large pockets of the country that lagged behind. Advances in real income and improvements in the standard of living for workers and farmers were uneven at best. During the 1920s one-quarter of all American workers were employed in agriculture, yet the farm sector failed to share in the general prosperity. The years 1914–19 had been a kind of golden age for the nation's farmers. Increased wartime demand, along with the devastation of much of European agriculture, had led to record-high prices for many crops. In addition, the wartime Food Administration had encouraged a great increase in agricultural production. But with the war's end, American farmers began to suffer from a chronic worldwide surplus of such farm staples as cotton, hogs, and corn.

Prices began to drop sharply in 1920. Cotton, which sold at thirty-seven cents a pound in mid-1920, fell to fourteen cents by year's end. Hog and cattle prices declined nearly 50 percent. By 1921 net farm income was down more than half from the year before. Land values also dropped, wiping out billions in capital investment. Behind these aggregate statistics were hundreds of thousands of individual human tragedies on the nation's 6 million farms. A 1928 song, "Eleven Cent Cotton," expressed the farmer's lament:

'Leven cent cotton, forty cent meat,
How in the world can a poor man eat?
Pray for the sunshine, 'cause it will rain,
Things gettin' worse, drivin' us insane.

During the war many farmers had gone heavily into debt to buy land and expand operations with new machinery. Farm mortgages doubled between 1910 and 1920, from $3.3 billion to $6.7 billion, and another $2.7 billion was added to the total by 1925. These debts saddled farmers with fixed expenses that grew crushingly burdensome as prices spiraled downward. American farm products, moreover, faced stiffer competition abroad from reviving European agriculture and the expanding output from Canada, Argentina, and Australia. Efforts to ease the farmer's plight through governmental reform were largely unsuccessful. Individual farmers, traditionally independent, could not influence the price of commodities they sold or bought. It was extremely difficult for farmers to act collectively.

To be sure, some farmers thrived. Wheat production jumped more than 300 percent during the 1920s. Across the plains of Kansas, Nebraska, Colorado, Oklahoma, and Texas, wheat farmers brought the methods of industrial capitalism to the land. They hitched disc plows and combined harvester-threshers to gasoline-powered tractors, tearing up millions of acres of grassland to create a vast wheat factory. With prices averaging above $1 per bushel over the decade, mechanized farming created a new class of large-scale wheat entrepreneurs on the plains. Ida Watkins, "the Wheat Queen" of Haskell County, Kansas, made a profit of $75,000 from her 2,000 acres in 1926. Hickman Price needed twenty-five combines to harvest the wheat on his Plainview, Texas, farm—34,500 acres stretching over fifty-four square miles. When the disastrous dust storms of the 1930s rolled across the grassless plains, the long-range ecological impact of destroying so much native vegetation became evident.

Improved transportation and chain supermarkets allowed for a wider and more regular distribution of such foods as oranges, lemons, and fresh green vegetables. Citrus, dairy, and truck farmers in particular profited from the growing importance of national markets. But per capita farm income remained well below what it had been in 1919, and the gap between farm and nonfarm income widened. By 1929 the average income per person on farms was $223, compared with $870 for nonfarm workers. By the end of the decade, hundreds of thousands had quit farming altogether for jobs in mills and factories. And fewer farmers owned their land. In 1930, 42 percent of all farmers were tenants, compared with 37 percent in 1919.

The most important initiatives for federal farm relief were the McNary-Haugen bills, a series of complicated measures designed to prop up and stabilize farm prices. The basic idea, borrowed from the old populist proposals of the 1890s, was for the government to purchase farm surpluses and either store them until prices rose or sell them on the world market. The result was supposed to be higher domestic prices for farm products. But President Calvin Coolidge viewed these measures as unwarranted federal interference in the economy and vetoed the McNary-Haugen Farm Relief bill of 1927 when it finally passed Congress. Hard-pressed farmers would not benefit from government relief until the New Deal programs implemented in response to the Great Depression in the 1930s.

Other large sectors of American industry also failed to share in the decade's general prosperity. As oil and natural gas gained in importance, America's coal mines became a less important source of energy. A combination of shrinking demand, new mining technology, and a series of losing strikes reduced the coal labor force by one-quarter. The United Mine Workers, perhaps the strongest AFL union in 1920 with 500,000 members, had shrunk to 75,000 by 1928. Economic hardship was widespread in many mining communities dependent on coal, particularly in Appalachia and the southern Midwest. And those miners who did work earned lower hourly wages.

The number of miles of railroad track actually decreased after 1920 as automobiles and trucks began to displace trains. In textiles, shrinking demand and overcapacity (too many factories) were chronic problems. The women's fashions of the 1920s generally required less material than had earlier fashions, and competition from synthetic fibers such as rayon depressed demand for cotton textiles. To improve profit margins, textile manufacturers in New England and other parts of the Northeast began a long-range shift of operations to the South, where nonunion shops and substandard wages became the rule. Between 1923 and 1933, 40 percent of New England's textile factories closed and nearly 100,000 of the 190,000 workers employed there lost their jobs. Older New England manufacturing centers such as Lawrence, Lowell, Nashua, Manchester, and Fall River were hard hit by this shift.

The center of the American textile industry shifted permanently to the Piedmont region of North and South Carolina. Southern mills increased their work force from 220,000 to 257,000 between 1923 and 1933. By 1933 they employed nearly 70 percent of the workers in the industry. One of the biggest new textile communities was Gastonia, North Carolina, which proudly called itself "the South's City of Spindles." As the dominant employers and overall economic powers in southern textile communities, manufacturers aggressively tried to improve productivity and cut costs. Southern mills generally operated night and day, used the newest labor-saving machinery, and cut back on the wage gains of the World War I years. Southern mill hands paid the

price for what they called "stretch-out"—a catchall term describing the changes that had them tending more and more machines, receiving lower wages, working nights, and losing nearly all control over the pace and method of production.

THE NEW MASS CULTURE

New communications media reshaped American culture in the 1920s. The nickname "Roaring Twenties" captures the explosion of image- and sound-making machinery that came to dominate so much of American life. Movies, radio, new kinds of journalism, the recording industry, and a more sophisticated advertising industry were deeply connected with the new culture of consumption. They also encouraged the parallel emergence of celebrity as a defining element in modern life. As technologies of mass impression, the media established national standards and norms for much of our culture—habit, dress, language, sounds, social behavior. For millions of Americans, the new media radically altered the rhythms of everyday life and redefined what it meant to be "normal." To be sure, most working-class families had only limited access to the world of mass consumption—and many had only limited interest in it. But the new mass culture helped redefine the ideal of "the good life" and made the images, if not the substance, of it available to a national community.

Movie-Made America

The early movie industry, centered in New York and a few other big cities, had made moviegoing a regular habit for millions of Americans, especially immigrants and the working class. They flocked to cheap, storefront theaters, called nickelodeons, to watch short Westerns, slapstick comedies, melodramas, and travelogues. By 1914 there were about 18,000 "movie houses" showing motion pictures, more than 7 million daily admissions, and $300 million in annual receipts. With the shift of the industry westward to Hollywood, movies entered a new phase of business expansion.

Large studios such as Paramount, Fox, Metro-Goldwyn-Mayer (M-G-M), Universal, and Warner Brothers dominated the business with longer and more expensively produced movies—feature films. These companies were founded and controlled by immigrants from Europe, all of whom had a talent for discovering and exploiting changes in popular tastes. Adolph Zukor, the Hungarian-born head of Paramount, had been a furrier in New York City. Warsaw-born Samuel Goldwyn, a founder of M-G-M, had been a glove salesman. William Fox, of Fox Pictures, began as a garment cutter in Brooklyn. Most of the immigrant moguls had started in the business by

Mary Pickford, one of the most popular movie stars of the 1910s and 1920s, shown here reading a feminist newspaper in a publicity photo ca.1917. Pickford frequently portrayed young women struggling for economic freedom from men. She wrote weekly columns for women in which she backed suffrage and urged her female readers to be more self-sufficient. Pickford embodied the new, mass media-based "celebrity" of the 1920s.

buying or managing small movie theaters before beginning to produce films.

The studio system, which came to dominate moviemaking, was based on industrial principles. Each studio combined the three functions of production, distribution, and exhibition, and each controlled hundreds of movie theaters around the country. The era of silent films ended when Warner Brothers scored a huge hit in 1927 with *The Jazz Singer*, starring Al Jolson, which successfully introduced sound. New genres—musicals, gangster films, and screwball comedies—soon became popular. The higher costs associated with "talkies" also increased the studios' reliance on Wall Street investors and banks for working capital.

At the heart of Hollywood's success was the star system and the accompanying cult of celebrity. Stars became vital to the fantasy lives of millions of fans. For many in the audience, there was only a vague line separating the on-screen and off-screen adventures of the stars. Studio publicity, fan magazines, and gossip columns reinforced this ambiguity. Film idols, with their mansions, cars, parties, and private escapades, became the national experts on leisure and consumption. Their movies generally emphasized sexual themes and celebrated youth, athleticism, and the liberating power of consumer goods. Young Americans in particular looked to

movies to learn how to dress, wear their hair, talk, or kiss. One researcher looking into the impact of moviegoing on young people asked several to keep "motion picture diaries." "Upon going to my first dance I asked the hairdresser to fix my hair like Greta Garbo's," wrote one eighteen-year-old college student. "In speaking on graduation day I did my best to finish with the swaying-like curtsy which Pola Negri taught me from the screen."

Moviemakers attracted new fans by producing more spectacular movies and by building elegant "movie palaces," like the Roxy Theater described in the opening of this chapter, in which to watch them. But many Americans, particularly in rural areas and small towns, worried about Hollywood's impact on traditional sexual morality. They attacked the permissiveness associated with Hollywood life, and many states created censorship boards to screen movies before allowing them to be shown in theaters. In 1921, the popular comedian Roscoe "Fatty" Arbuckle became embroiled in a highly publicized sex scandal when he was accused of raping and murdering actress Virginia Rappe. Although Arbuckle was acquitted, the sensational atmosphere surrounding the case badly frightened studio heads. They resolved to improve their public image.

To counter growing calls for government censorship, Hollywood's studios came up with a plan to censor themselves. In 1922 they hired Will Hays to head the Motion Picture Producers and Distributors of America. Hays was just what the immigrant moguls needed. An Indiana Republican, elder in the Presbyterian Church, and former postmaster general under President Harding, he personified midwestern Protestant respectability. As the movie industry's czar, Hays lobbied against censorship laws, wrote pamphlets defending the movie business, and began setting guidelines for what could and could not be depicted on the screen. He insisted that movies be treated like any other industrial enterprise, for he understood the relationship between Hollywood's success and the growth of the nation's consumer culture. "More and more," Hays argued in 1926, "is the motion picture being recognized as a stimulant to trade. No longer does the girl in Sullivan, Indiana, guess what the styles are going to be in three months. She knows because she sees them on the screen."

Radio Broadcasting

In the fall of 1920, Westinghouse executive Harry P. Davis noticed that amateur broadcasts from the garage of an employee had attracted attention in the local Pittsburgh press. A department store advertised radio sets capable of picking up these "wireless concerts." Davis converted this amateur station to a stronger one at the Westinghouse main plant. Beginning with the presidential election returns that November, station KDKA offered regular nightly broadcasts that were probably heard by only a few hundred people. Radio broadcasting, begun as a service for selling cheap radio sets left over from World War I, would soon sweep the nation.

Before KDKA, wireless technology had been of interest only to the military, the telephone industry, and a few thousand "ham" (amateur) operators who enjoyed communicating with each other. The "radio mania" of the early 1920s was a response to the new possibilities offered by broadcasting. By 1923 nearly 600 stations had been licensed by the Department of Commerce, and about 600,000 Americans had bought radios. Early programs included live popular music, the playing of phonograph records, talks by college professors, church services, and news and weather reports. For millions of Americans, especially in rural areas and small towns, radio provided a new and exciting link to the larger national community of consumption.

Who would pay for radio programs? In the early 1920s, owners and operators of radio stations included radio equipment manufacturers, newspapers, department stores, state universities, cities, ethnic societies, labor unions, and churches. But by the end of the decade commercial (or "toll") broadcasting emerged as the answer. The dominant corporations in the industry—General Electric, Westinghouse, Radio Corporation of America (RCA), and American Telephone and Telegraph (AT&T)—settled on the idea that advertisers would foot the bill for radio. Millions of listeners might be the consumers of radio shows, but sponsors were to be the customers. Only the sponsors and their advertising agencies enjoyed a direct relationship with broadcasters. Sponsors advertised directly or indirectly to the mass audience through such shows as the *Eveready Hour*, the *Ipana Troubadors*, and the *Taystee Loafers*. AT&T leased its nationwide system of telephone wires to allow the linking of many stations into powerful radio networks, such as the National Broadcasting Company (1926) and the Columbia Broadcasting System (1928).

Radio broadcasting created a national community of listeners, just as motion pictures created one of viewers. NBC and CBS led the way in creating popular radio programs that relied heavily on older cultural forms. The variety show, hosted by vaudeville comedians, became network radio's first important format. Radio's first truly national hit, *The Amos 'n' Andy Show* (1928), was a direct descendant of nineteenth-century "blackface" minstrel entertainment. Radio did more than any previous medium to publicize and commer-

cialize previously isolated forms of American music such as country-and-western, blues, and jazz. Broadcasts of baseball and college football games proved especially popular. In 1930, some 600 stations were broadcasting to more than 12 million homes with radios, or roughly 40 percent of American families. By that time all the elements that characterize the present American system of broadcasting—regular daily programming paid for and produced by commercial advertisers, national networks carrying shows across the nation, and mass ownership of receiver sets in American homes—were in place.

New Forms of Journalism

A new kind of newspaper, the tabloid, became popular in the postwar years. The *New York Daily News*, founded in 1919 by Joseph M. Patterson, was the first to develop the tabloid style. Its folded-in-half page size made it convenient to read on buses or subways. The *Daily News* devoted much of its space to photographs and other illustrations. With a terse, lively reporting style that emphasized sex, scandal, and sports, *Daily News* circulation reached 400,000 in 1922 and 1.3 million by 1929.

This success spawned a host of imitators in New York and elsewhere. New papers like the *Chicago Times* and the *Los Angeles Daily News* brought the tabloid style to cities across America, while some older papers, such as the *Denver Rocky Mountain News*, adopted the new format. The circulation of existing dailies was little affected. Tabloids had instead discovered an audience of millions who had never read newspapers before. Most of these new readers were poorly educated working-class city dwellers, many of whom were immigrants or children of immigrants.

The tabloid's most popular new feature was the gossip column, invented by Walter Winchell, an obscure former vaudevillian who began writing his column "Your Broadway and Mine" for the *New York Daily Graphic* in 1924. Winchell described the secret lives of public figures with a distinctive, rapid-fire, slangy style that made the reader feel like an insider. He chronicled the connections among high society, show business stars, powerful politicians, and the underworld. By the end of the decade, scores of newspapers "syndicated" Winchell's column, making him the most widely read—and imitated—journalist in America.

Many critics dismissed the tabloids for being, as one put it, "synonomous with bad taste, vulgarity, and a degenerate sensationalism." But the popularity of the tabloids forced advertising agencies to expand their definition of the consumer market to include working-class and immigrant readers. And advertisers borrowed freely from tabloid techniques—"true confession" stories, racy headlines, shocking photos, sexually charged images—to reach that market.

Journalism followed the larger economic trend toward consolidation and merger. Newspaper chains like Hearst, Gannett, and Scripps-Howard flourished during the 1920s. There was a sizable increase in the number of these chains and in the percentage of total daily circulation that was chain-owned. By the early 1930s, the Hearst organization alone controlled twenty-six dailies in eighteen cities, accounting for 14 percent of the nation's newspaper circulation. One of every four Sunday papers sold in America was owned by the Hearst group. One journalist lamented this standardization in 1930: "When one travels through the country on a Sunday on a fast train and buys Sunday papers, one finds the same 'comics,' the same Sunday magazines, the same special 'features' in almost all of them and, of course, in most of them precisely the same Associated Press news." New forms of journalism, like radio and the movies, contributed to the growth of a national consumer community.

Advertising Modernity

A thriving advertising industry both reflected and encouraged the growing importance of consumer goods in American life. Previously, advertising had been confined mostly to staid newspapers and magazines and offered little more than basic product information. The most creative advertising was usually for dubious products, such as patent medicines. The successful efforts of the government's Committee on Public Information, set up to "sell" World War I to Americans, suggested that new techniques using modern communication media could convince people to buy a wide range of goods and services. As a profession, advertising reached a higher level of respectability, sophistication, and economic power in American life during the 1920s. Total advertising volume in all media—newspapers, magazines, radio, billboards—jumped from $1.4 billion in 1919 to $3 billion in 1929.

The larger ad agencies moved toward a more scientific approach by sponsoring market research and welcoming the language of psychology to their profession. Advertisers began focusing on the needs, desires, and anxieties of the consumer rather than on the qualities of the product. "There are certain things that most people believe," noted one ad agency executive in 1927. "The moment your copy is linked to one of those beliefs, more than half your battle is won." Ad agencies and their clients invested extraordinary amounts of time, energy, and money trying to discover and, to some extent, shape those beliefs. Leading agencies such as Lord and Thomas in Chicago and J. Walter Thompson in New York combined knowledge gained from market research and consumer surveys with carefully prepared ad copy and graphics to sell their clients' wares.

High-powered ad campaigns made new products like Fleischmann's Yeast and Kleenex household words across the country. One of the more spectacular examples of advertising effectiveness involved an old product, Listerine, which had been marketed as a general antiseptic for years by Lambert Pharmaceutical Company. A new ad campaign touting Listerine as a cure for halitosis—a scientific-sounding term for bad breath—boosted Lambert's profits from $100,000 in 1922 to more than $4 million in 1927.

Above all, advertising celebrated consumption itself as a positive good. In this sense the new advertising ethic was a therapeutic one, promising that products would contribute to the buyer's physical, psychic, or emotional well-being. Certain strategies, such as appeals to nature, medical authority, or personal freedom, were used with great success. Many of these themes and techniques are still famil-

Cigarette smoking increased enormously in the 1920s among both men and women, and tobacco companies were among the largest national advertisers. This ad linked smoking to male sexual prowess.

iar today. Well-financed ad campaigns were especially crucial for marketing newer consumer goods such as cars, electrical appliances, and personal hygiene products.

The Phonograph and the Recording Industry

Like radio and movies, the phonograph came into its own in the 1920s as a popular entertainment medium. Originally marketed in the 1890s, early phonographs used wax cylinders that could both record and replay. But the sound quality was poor, and the cylinders were difficult to handle. The convenient permanently grooved disc recordings introduced around World War I were eagerly snapped up by the public, even though discs could not be used to make recordings at home. The success of records transformed the popular music business, displacing both cylinders and sheet music as the major source of music in the home.

Dance crazes such as the fox trot, tango, and grizzly bear, done to complex ragtime and Latin rhythms, boosted the record business tremendously. Dixieland jazz, which recorded well, also captured the public's fancy in the early 1920s, and records provided the music for new popular dances like the Charleston and the black bottom. In 1921 more than 200 companies produced some 2 million records and annual record sales exceeded 100 million.

Record sales declined toward the end of the decade due to competition from radio. But in a broader cultural sense, records continued to transform American popular culture. Record companies discovered lucrative regional and ethnic markets for country music, which appealed primarily to white Southerners, and blues and jazz, which appealed primarily to African Americans. Country musicians like the Carter Family and Jimmie Rodgers and blues singers like Blind Lemon Jefferson and Ma Rainey had their performances put on records for the first time. Their records sold mainly in specialized "hillbilly" and "race" markets. Yet they were also played over the radio, and millions of Americans began to hear musical styles and performers who had previously been isolated. Blues great Bessie Smith sold hundreds of thousands of records and single-handedly kept the fledgling Columbia Record Company profitable. The combination of records and radio started an extraordinary cross-fertilization of American musical styles that continues to this day.

Sports and Celebrity

During the 1920s, spectator sports enjoyed an unprecedented growth in popularity and profitability. As radio, newspapers, magazines, and newsreels exhaustively documented their exploits, athletes took their place alongside movie stars in defining a new culture of celebrity. Big-time sports, like the movies, entered a new corporate phase. Yet it was the athletes themselves, performing extraordinary feats on the field and transcending their often humble origins, who attracted millions of new fans. The image of the modern athlete—rich, famous, glamorous, and often a rebel against social convention—came into its own during the decade.

Major league baseball had more fans than any other sport, and its greatest star, George Herman "Babe" Ruth, embodied the new celebrity athlete. In 1920 the game had suffered a serious public relations disaster with the unfolding of the "Black Sox" scandal. The previous year, eight members of the poorly paid Chicago White Sox had become involved in a scheme to "throw" the World Series in exchange for large sums of money from gamblers. Although they were acquitted in the courts, baseball commissioner Judge Kenesaw Mountain Landis, looking to remove any taint of gambling from the sport, banned the accused players for life. Landis's actions won universal acclaim, but doubts about the integrity of "the national pastime" lingered.

Ruth did more than anyone to repair the damage and make baseball more popular than ever. Born in 1895, he was a product of Baltimore's rough waterfront district. After spending most of his youth in an orphanage for delinquent boys, he broke into baseball as a pitcher for the Boston Red Sox. Traded to the New York Yankees in 1920, he switched to the outfield and began attracting enormous attention with the length and frequency of his home runs. He hit fifty-four in his first year in New York, eclipsing the old record by twenty-nine. The next year he hit fifty-nine. "The Sultan of Swat," as one sportswriter dubbed him, transformed the game. Before Ruth, the "homer" was an infrequent event in a game built around pitching, defense, and speed. Fans now flocked to games in record numbers to see the new, more offensive-oriented baseball.

Ruth was a larger-than-life character off the field as well as on. In New York, media capital of the nation, newspapers and magazines chronicled his enormous appetites—for food, whiskey, expensive cars, and big-city nightlife. He hobnobbed with politicians, movie stars, and gangsters, and he regularly visited sick children in hospitals. Ruth became the first athlete avidly sought after by manufacturers for celebrity endorsement of their products. As one of the most photographed individuals of the era, Ruth's round, beaming face became a familiar image around the world. In 1930, at the onset of the Great Depression, when a reporter told him that his $80,000 salary was more than President Herbert Hoover's, the Babe replied good naturedly, "Well, I had a better year than he did."

Baseball attendance exploded during the twenties, reaching a one-year total of 10 million in 1929. The attendance boom prompted urban newspapers to increase their baseball coverage, and the larger dailies featured separate sports sections. The best sportswriters, such as Grantland Rice, Heywood Broun, and Ring Lardner, brought a poetic sensibility to descriptions of the games and their stars. William K. Wrigley, owner of the Chicago Cubs, discovered that by letting local radio stations broadcast his team's games, the club could win new fans, especially among housewives.

Baseball owners solidified their monopolistic control of the game in 1922 when the Supreme Court, ruling in an antitrust suit, declared that baseball, while obviously a business, was not "trade or commerce in the commonly accepted use of those words." By exempting baseball from antitrust prosecution, the Court gave the game a uniquely favored legal status and also ensured the absolute control of owners over their players. Among those excluded from major league baseball were African Americans, who had been banned from the game by an 1890s' "gentleman's agreement" among owners.

During the 1920s black baseball players and entrepreneurs developed a world of their own, with several professional and semiprofessional leagues catering to expanding African American communities in cities. The largest of these was the Negro National League, organized in 1920 by Andrew "Rube" Foster. Black ball clubs also played exhibitions against, and frequently defeated, teams of white major leaguers. African Americans had their own baseball heroes, such as Josh Gibson and Satchel Paige, who no doubt would have been stars in the major leagues if not for racial exclusion.

The new media configuration of the 1920s created heroes in other sports as well. Radio broadcasts and increased journalistic coverage made college football a big-time sport, as millions followed the exploits of star players such as Illinois's Harold E. "Red" Grange and Stanford's Ernie Nevers. Teams like Notre Dame, located in sleepy South Bend, Indiana, but coached by the colorful Knute Rockne, could gain a wide national following. Sportswriter Grantland Rice contributed to the school's mystique when he dubbed its backfield "the Four Horsemen of Notre Dame." The earnings potential of big-time athletics was not lost on college administrators, and it blurred the old lines separating amateur and professional sports. The center of college football shifted from the old elite schools of the Ivy League to the big universities of the Midwest and Pacific coast, where most of the players were now second-generation Irish, Italians, and Slavs. Athletes like boxers Jack Dempsey and Gene Tunney, tennis players Bill Tilden and Helen Wills, and swimmers Gertrude Ederle and Johnny Weissmuller became household names who brought legions of new fans to their sports.

A New Morality?

Movie stars, radio personalities, sports heroes, and popular musicians became the elite figures in a new culture of celebrity defined by the mass media. They were the model for achievement in the new age. Great events and abstract issues were made real through movie close-ups, radio interviews, and tabloid photos. The new media relentlessly created and disseminated images that are still familiar today: Babe Ruth trotting around the bases after hitting a home run; the wild celebrations that greeted Charles Lindbergh after he completed the first solo transatlantic airplane flight in 1927; the smiling gangster Al Capone, bantering with reporters who transformed his criminal exploits into important news events.

But images do not tell the whole story. Consider one of the most enduring images of "the Roaring Twenties," the flapper. She was usually portrayed on screen, in novels, and in the press as a young, sexually aggressive woman with bobbed hair, rouged cheeks, and short skirt. She loved to dance to jazz music, enjoyed smoking cigarettes, and drank bootleg liquor in cabarets and dance halls. She could also be competitive, assertive, and a good pal. As writer Zelda Fitzgerald put it in 1924: "I think a woman gets more happiness out of being gay, light hearted, unconventional, mistress of her own fate. . . . I want [my daughter] to be a flapper, because flappers are brave and gay and beautiful."

Was the flapper a genuine representative of the 1920s? Did she embody the "new morality" that was so widely discussed and chronicled in the media of the day? The flapper certainly did exist, but she was neither as new nor as widespread a phenomenon as the image would suggest. The delight in sensuality, personal pleasure, and rhythmically complex dance and music had long been key elements of subcultures on the fringes of middle-class society: bohemian enclaves, communities of political radicals, African American ghettos, working-class dance halls. In the 1920s, these activities became normative for a growing number of white middle-class Americans, including women. Jazz, sexual experimentation, heavy makeup, and cigarette smoking spread to college campuses.

Several sources, most of them rooted in earlier years, can be found for the increased sexual openness of the 1920s. Troops in the armed forces during World War I had been exposed to government-sponsored sex education. New psychological and social theories like those of Havelock Ellis, Ellen

Key, and Sigmund Freud stressed the central role of sexuality in human experience, maintaining that sex is a positive, healthy impulse that, if repressed, could damage mental and emotional health. The pioneering efforts of Margaret Sanger in educating women about birth control had begun before World War I (see Chapter 21). In the 1920s, Sanger campaigned vigorously—through her journal *Birth Control Review,* in books, on speaking tours—to make contraception freely available to all women.

Advertisers routinely used sex appeal to sell products. Tabloid newspapers exploited sex with "cheesecake" photos, but they also provided features giving advice on sex hygiene and venereal disease. And movies, of course, featured powerful sex symbols such as Rudolph Valentino, Gloria Swanson, John Gilbert, and Clara Bow. Movies also taught young people an etiquette of sex. One typical eighteen-year-old college student wrote in the motion picture diary she kept for a sociological study: "These passionate pictures stir such longings, desires, and urges as I never expected any person to possess. Just the way the passionate lover held his sweetheart suggests so many beautiful and intimate relations, which even my reenacting a scene does not satisfy any more."

Sociological surveys also suggested that genuine changes in sexual behavior began in the prewar years among both married and single women. Katherine Bement Davis's pioneering study of 2,200 middle-class women, carried out in 1918 and published in 1929, revealed that most used contraceptives and described sexual relations in positive terms. A 1938 survey of 777 middle-class females found that among those born between 1890 and 1900, 74 percent were virgins before marriage; for those born after 1910 the figure dropped to 32 percent. Women born after the turn of the century were twice as likely to have had premarital sex as those born before 1900. The critical change took place in the generation that came of age in the late teens and early twenties. By the 1920s, male and female "morals" were becoming more alike.

THE STATE, THE ECONOMY, AND BUSINESS

Throughout the 1920s, a confident Republican Party dominated national politics, certain that it had ushered in a "new era" in American life. A new and closer relationship between the federal government and American business became the hallmark of Republican policy in both domestic and foreign affairs during the administrations of three successive Republican presidents: Warren Harding (1921–1923), Calvin Coolidge (1923–1929), and Herbert Hoover (1929–1933). And Republicans never tired of claiming that the business-government partnership their policies promoted was responsible for the nation's economic prosperity.

Harding and Coolidge

Handsome, genial, and well-spoken, Warren Harding may have looked the part of a president—but acting like one was

This 1925 *Judge* cartoon, Sheik with Sheba, *drawn by John Held, Jr., offered one view of contemporary culture. The flashy new automobile, the hip flask with illegal liquor, the cigarettes, and the stylish "new woman" were all part of the "Roaring Twenties" image.*

another matter. Harding was a product of small-town Marion, Ohio, and the machine politics in his native state. Republican Party officials had made a point of keeping Senator Harding, a compromise choice, as removed from the public eye as possible in the 1920 election. They correctly saw that active campaigning could only hurt their candidate by exposing his shallowness and intellectual weakness. Harding understood his own limitations. He sadly told one visitor to the White House shortly after taking office, "I knew that this job would be too much for me."

Harding surrounded himself with a close circle of friends, "the Ohio gang," delegating to them a great deal of administrative power. The president often conducted business as if he were in the relaxed, convivial, and masculine confines of a small-town saloon. Alice Roosevelt Longworth, Theodore Roosevelt's daughter, described the scene she encountered in Harding's crony-filled study when she tagged along with her husband, Congressman Nicholas Longworth, to a card game: "The air heavy with tobacco smoke, trays with bottles containing every imaginable brand of whiskey [standing] about, cards and poker chips ready at hand—a general atmosphere of waistcoat unbuttoned, feet on the desk, and spitoons alongside." In the summer of 1923 Harding began to get wind of the scandals for which his administration is best remembered. He wearily told his friend Kansas journalist William Allen White: "This is a hell of a job! I have no trouble with my enemies. . . . But my damned friends, . . . White, they're the ones that keep me walking the floor nights."

A series of congressional investigations soon revealed a deep pattern of corruption. Attorney General Harry M. Daugherty had received bribes from violators of the Prohibition statutes. He had also failed to investigate graft in the Veterans Bureau, where Charles R. Forbes had pocketed a large chunk of the $250 million spent on hospitals and supplies. The worst affair was the Teapot Dome scandal involving Interior Secretary Albert Fall. Fall received hundreds of thousands of dollars in payoffs when he secretly leased navy oil reserves in Teapot Dome, Wyoming, and Elk Hills, California, to two private oil developers. He eventually became the first cabinet officer ever to go to jail.

But the Harding administration's legacy was not all scandal. Andrew Mellon, an influential Pittsburgh banker, served as secretary of the treasury under all three Republican presidents of the 1920s. One of the richest men in America, and a leading investor in the Aluminum Corporation of America and Gulf Oil, Mellon believed government ought to be run on the same conservative principles as a corpo-

ration. He was a leading voice for trimming the federal budget and cutting taxes on incomes, corporate profits, and inheritances. These cuts, he argued, would free up capital for new investment and thus promote general economic growth. Mellon's program sharply cut taxes for both higher-income brackets and for businesses. By 1926, a person with an income of a million a year paid less than a third of the income tax he or she paid in 1921. Overall, Mellon's policies succeeded in rolling back much of the progressive taxation associated with Woodrow Wilson.

When Harding died in office of a heart attack in August 1923, Calvin Coolidge succeeded to the presidency. Coolidge seemed to most people the temperamental opposite of Harding. Born and raised in rural Vermont, elected governor of Massachusetts, and coming to national prominence only through the 1919 Boston police strike (see Chapter 22), "Silent Cal" was the quintessential New England Yankee. Taciturn, genteel, and completely honest, Coolidge believed in the least amount of government possible. He spent only four hours a day at the office. His famous aphorism, "The business of America is business," perfectly captured the core philosophy of the Republican new era. He was in awe of wealthy

Calvin Coolidge combined a spare, laconic political style with a flair for publicity. He frequently posed in the dress of a cowboy, farmer, or Indian chief.

men such as Andrew Mellon, and he thought them best suited to make society's key decisions.

Coolidge easily won election on his own in 1924. He benefited from the general prosperity and the contrast he provided with the disgraced Harding. Coolidge defeated little-known Democrat John W. Davis, the compromise choice of a party badly divided between its rural and urban wings. Also running was Progressive Party candidate Robert M. La Follette of Wisconsin, who mounted a reform campaign that attacked economic monopolies and called for government ownership of utilities.

In his full term, Coolidge showed most interest in reducing federal spending, lowering taxes, and blocking congressional initiatives. He saw his primary function as clearing the way for American businessmen. They, after all, were the agents of the era's unprecedented prosperity.

Herbert Hoover and the "Associative State"

The most influential figure of the Republican new era was Herbert Hoover, who as secretary of commerce dominated the cabinets of Harding and Coolidge before becoming president himself in 1929. A successful engineer, administrator, and politician, Hoover effectively embodied the belief that enlightened business, encouraged and informed by the government, would act in the public interest. In the modern industrial age, Hoover believed, the government needed only to advise private citizens' groups about what national or international polices to pursue. "Reactionaries and radicals," he wrote in *American Individualism* (1922), "would assume that all reform and human advance must come through government. They have forgotten that progress must come from the steady lift of the individual and that the measure of national idealism and progress is the quality of idealism in the individual."

Hoover thus fused a faith in old-fashioned individualism with a strong commitment to the progressive possibilities offered by efficiency and rationality. Unlike an earlier generation of Republicans, Hoover wanted not just to create a favorable climate for business but to actively assist the business community. He spoke of creating an "associative state," in which the government would encourage voluntary cooperation among corporations, consumers, workers, farmers, and small businessmen. This became the central occupation of the Department of Commerce under Hoover's leadership. Under Hoover, the Bureau of Standards became one of the nation's leading research centers, setting engineering standards for key American industries such as machine tools and automobiles. The bureau also helped standardize the styles, sizes, and designs of many consumer products such as canned goods and refrigerators.

Hoover actively encouraged the creation and expansion of national trade associations. By 1929 there were about 2,000 of them. At industrial conferences called by the Commerce Department, government officials explained the advantages of mutual cooperation in figuring prices and costs and then publishing the information. The idea was to improve efficiency by reducing competition. To some this practice violated the spirit of antitrust laws, but in the 1920s the Justice Department's Antitrust Division took a very lax view of its responsibility. In addition, the Supreme Court consistently upheld the legality of trade associations. Hoover also had a strong influence on presidential appointments to regulatory commissions; most of these went to men who had worked for the very firms the commissions had been designed to supervise. Regulatory commissions thus benefited from the technical expertise brought by industry leaders, but they in turn tended to remain uncritical of the industries they oversaw.

The government thus provided an ideal climate for the concentration of corporate wealth and power. The trend toward large corporate trusts and holding companies had been well under way since the late nineteenth century, but it accelerated in the 1920s. By 1929, the 200 largest American corporations owned almost half the total corporate wealth and about a fifth of the total national wealth. Concentration was particularly strong in manufacturing, retailing, mining, banking, and utilities. The number of vertical combinations—large, integrated firms that controlled the raw materials, manufacturing processes, and distribution networks for their products—also increased. Vertical inegration became common not only in older industries but in the automobile, electrical, radio, motion picture, and other new industries as well.

War Debts, Reparations, Keeping the Peace

The United States emerged from World War I the strongest economic power in the world. The war transformed it from the world's leading debtor nation to its most important creditor. European governments owed the U.S. government about $10 billion in 1919. In the private sector, the war ushered in an era of expanding American investment abroad. As late as 1914 foreign investments in the United States were about $3 billion more than the total of American capital invested abroad. By 1919 that situation was reversed: America had $3 billion more invested abroad than foreigners had invested in the United States. By 1929 the surplus was $8 billion. New York replaced London as the center of international finance and capital markets.

During the 1920s, war debts and reparations were the single most divisive issue in international economics. In France and Great Britain, which both owed the United States large amounts in war loans, many concluded that the Uncle Sam who had offered assistance during wartime was really a loan shark in disguise. In turn, many Americans viewed Europeans as ungrateful debtors. As President Coolidge acidly remarked, "They hired the money, didn't they?" In 1922 the U.S. Foreign Debt Commission negotiated an agreement with the debtor nations that called for them to repay $11.5 billion over a sixty-two-year period. But by the late 1920s, the European financial situation had become so desperate that the United States agreed to cancel a large part of these debts. Continued insistence by the United States that the Europeans pay at least a portion of the debt fed anti-American feeling in Europe and isolationism at home.

The Germans believed that war reparations, set at $33 billion by the Treaty of Versailles, not only unfairly punished the losers of the conflict but, by saddling their civilian economies with such massive debt, also deprived them of the very means to repay. In 1924 Herbert Hoover and Chicago banker Charles Dawes worked out a plan to aid the recovery of the German economy. The Dawes Plan reduced Germany's debt, stretched out the repayment period, and arranged for American bankers to lend funds to Germany. These measures helped stabilize Germany's currency and allowed it to make reparations payments to France and Great Britain. The Allies, in turn, were better able to pay their war debts to the United States.

The horrors of the Great War led millions of citizens, as well as government officials, to advocate curbs on the world's armed forces. In 1921 Secretary of State Charles Evans Hughes took the initiative on arms limitations by inviting representatives from Great Britain, Japan, Italy, France, and China to meet in Washington to discuss reductions in military budgets. Hughes offered to scrap thirty major American ships and asked for comparable actions by the British and Japanese. He asked for a ten-year moratorium on the construction of new battleships and cruisers and proposed limiting naval tonnage. The following year the Five-Power Treaty agreed to this scaling down of navies and also pledged to respect the territorial integrity of China. But the Italians and Japanese soon complained about the treaty's restraints, and ultimately the limits placed on navy construction were abandoned.

The United States never joined the League of Nations, but it maintained an active, if selective, involvement in world affairs. In addition to the Dawes Plan and the American role in naval disarmament, the United States joined the league-sponsored World Court in 1926 and was represented at numerous league conferences. In 1928, with great fanfare, the United States and sixty-two other nations signed the Pact of Paris (better known as the Kellogg-Briand Pact for the U.S. secretary of state Frank B. Kellogg and French foreign minister Aristide Briand who initiated it), which grandly and naively renounced war in principle. Peace groups, such as the Woman's Peace Party and the Quaker-based Fellowship of Reconciliation, hailed the pact for formally outlawing war. But critics charged that the Kellogg-Briand Pact was essentially meaningless since it lacked powers of enforcement and relied solely on the moral force of world opinion. Within weeks of its ratification, the U.S. Congress had appropriated $250 million for new battleships.

Commerce and Foreign Policy

Secretary of State Charles Evans Hughes, a former governor of New York and the Republican candidate for president in 1916, played a leading role in shaping America's postwar foreign policy. Hughes argued that the United States must seek "to establish a *Pax Americana* maintained not by arms but by mutual respect and good will and the tranquilizing processes of reason." Hughes's push for the arms reduction agreements of 1921 went hand in hand with his deep belief that America's economic wealth—not military or political power—could help create a new and prosperous international system free of the rivalries that had led to the disastrous Great War.

Throughout the 1920s, Hughes and other Republican leaders pursued policies designed to expand American economic activity abroad. They understood that capitalist economies must be dynamic; they must expand their markets if they were to thrive. The focus must be on friendly nations and investments that would help foreign citizens to buy American goods. Toward this end, Republican leaders urged close cooperation between bankers and the government as a strategy for expanding American investment and economic influence abroad. They insisted that investment capital not be spent on U.S. enemies, such as the new Soviet Union, or on nonproductive enterprises such as munitions and weapons. Throughout the 1920s, investment bankers routinely submitted loan projects to Hughes and Secretary of Commerce Hoover for informal approval, thus reinforcing the close ties between business investment and foreign policy.

Foreign policy makers were not shy about brandishing America's postwar economic power to gain advantage. In 1926, the British tried to drive up the world price of rubber, a crucial product for the burgeoning automobile industry. Hoover retaliated by threatening a less friendly U.S. attitude toward British loans and war debts and by encouraging American investors to enlarge their rubber plantations in Southeast Asia and Liberia. Within three months, Hoover had succeeded in driving down the price of rubber from $1.21 a pound to 40 cents. For Hoover and other policy makers, American business abroad was simply rugged individualism at work around the globe.

American oil, autos, farm machinery, and electrical equipment supplied a growing world market. Much of this expansion took place through the establishment of branch plants overseas by American companies. America's overall direct investment abroad increased from $3.8 billion in 1919 to $7.5 billion in 1929. Leading the American domination of the world market were General Electric, Ford, and Monsanto Chemical. American oil companies, with the support of the State Department, also challenged Great Britain's dominance in the oil fields of the Middle East and Latin America, forming powerful cartels with English firms.

The strategy of maximum freedom for private enterprise, backed by limited government advice and assistance, significantly boosted the power and profits of American overseas investors. But in Central and Latin America, in particular, aggressive U.S. investment also fostered chronically underdeveloped economies, dependent on a few staple crops (sugar, coffee, cocoa, bananas) grown for export. American investments in Latin America more than doubled between 1924 and 1929, from $1.5 billion to over $3.5 billion. A large part of this money went to taking over vital mineral resources, such as Chile's copper and Venezuela's oil. The growing wealth and power of U.S. companies made it more difficult for these nations to grow their own food or diversify their economies. U.S. economic dominance in the hemisphere also hampered the growth of democratic politics by favoring autocratic, military regimes that could be counted on to protect U.S. investments.

During the 1920s, U.S. negotiators peacefully resolved long-simmering disputes with Mexico over oil and mineral holdings of American companies. The United States withdrew its marines from the Dominican Republic in 1924, after many years of direct military intervention. But in Nicaragua, American troops continued to prop up the conservative government of Adolfo Díaz, who had worked closely with the State Department since the first U.S. intervention in 1911. When a popular revolt led by General Augustino Sandino broke out in 1927, American marines landed and wound up supervising Nicaraguan elections over the next five years. They were not finally withdrawn until 1933, leaving a bitter legacy that would lead to crisis once again in the 1980s.

RESISTANCE TO MODERNITY

One measure of the profound cultural changes of the 1920s was the hostility and opposition expressed toward them by large sectors of the American public. Deep and persistent tensions, with ethnic, racial, and geographical overtones, characterized much of the decade's politics. The postwar Red Scare had given strength to the forces of antiradicalism in politics and traditionalism in culture. Resentments over the growing power of urban culture were very strong in rural and small-town America. The big city, in this view, stood for all that was alien, corrupt, and immoral in the country's life. Several trends and mass movements reflected this anger and the longing for a less complicated past.

Prohibition

The Eighteenth Amendment, banning the manufacture, sale, and transportation of alcoholic beverages, took effect in January 1920. Prohibition was the culmination of a long campaign that associated drinking with the degradation of working-class family life and the worst evils of urban politics. Supporters, a coalition of women's temperance groups, middle-class progressives, and rural Protestants, hailed the new law as "a noble experiment." But it became clear rather quickly that enforcing the new law would be extremely difficult. The Volstead Act of 1919 established a federal Prohibition Bureau to enforce the Eighteenth Amendment. Yet the bureau was severely understaffed, with only about 1,500 agents to police the entire country.

The public demand for alcohol, especially in the big cities, led to widespread lawbreaking. Drinking was such a routine part of life for so many Americans that bootlegging quickly became a big business. Illegal stills and breweries, as well as liquor smuggled in from Canada, supplied the needs of those Americans who continued to drink. Nearly every town and city had at least one "speakeasy," where people could drink and enjoy music and other entertainment. Local law enforcement personnel, especially in the cities, were easily bribed to overlook these illegal establishments. By the early 1920s many eastern states no longer made even a token effort at enforcing the law.

But because liquor continued to be illegal, prohibition gave an enormous boost to violent organized crime. The profits to be made in the illegal liquor trade dwarfed the traditional sources of criminal income—gambling, prostitution, and robbery. The pattern of organized crime in the 1920s closely resembled the larger trends in American business: smaller operations gave way to larger and more complex combinations. Successful organized crime figures, like Chicago's Al "Scarface" Capone, became celebrities in their own right and received heavy coverage in the mass media. Capone himself shrewdly used the rhetoric of the Republican new era to defend himself: "Everybody calls me a racketeer. I call myself a businessman. When I sell liquor it's bootlegging. When my patrons serve it on a silver tray on Lake Shore Drive, it's hospitality."

Organized crime, based on its huge profits from liquor, also made significant inroads into legitimate businesses, labor unions, and city government. By the time Congress and the states ratified the Twenty-first Amendment in 1933, repealing Prohibition, organized crime was a permanent feature of American life. Politically, Prohibition continued to be a controversial issue in national politics, as "wets" and "drys" debated the merits of the law. Prohibition did, in fact, significantly reduce per capita consumption of alcohol. In 1910, annual per capita consumption stood at 2.6 gallons; in 1934 the figure was less than a gallon. Many drinkers—especially wage earners—probably consumed less because of the higher price of bootleg beer and spirits. Yet among young people, especially college students, the excitement associated with speakeasies and lawbreaking contributed to increased drinking during Prohibition.

Immigration Restriction

Sentiment for restricting immigration, growing since the late nineteenth century, reached its peak immediately after World War I. Anti-immigrant feeling reflected the growing preponderance after 1890 of "new immigrants"—those from southern and eastern Europe—over the immigrants from northern and western Europe who had predominated before 1890. Between 1891 and 1920, roughly 10.5 million immigrants arrived from southern and eastern Europe. This was nearly twice as many as arrived in the same years from northern and western Europe.

The "new immigrants" were mostly Catholic and Jewish, and they were darker-skinned than the "old immigrants." To many Americans they seemed more exotic, more foreign, and less willing and able to assimilate the nation's political and cultural values. They were also relatively poorer, more physically isolated in the nation's cities, and less politically strong than earlier immigrants. In the 1890s, the anti-Catholic American Protective Association called for a curb on immigration, and by exploiting the economic depression of that decade it reached a membership of 2.5 million. In 1894 a group of prominent Harvard graduates, including Henry Cabot Lodge and John Fiske, founded the Immigration Restriction League, providing an influential forum for the fears of the nation's elite. The league used newer scientific arguments, based on a flawed application of Darwinian evolutionary theory and genetics, to support its call for immigration restriction.

Theories of scientific racism, which had become more popular in the early 1900s, reinforced anti-immigrant bias. The most influential statement of racial hierarchy was Madison Grant's *The Passing of the Great Race* (1916), which distorted genetic theory to argue that America was committing "race suicide." According to Grant, inferior Alpine, Mediterranean, and Jewish stock threatened to extinguish the superior Nordic race that had made America great. Eugenicists, who enjoyed considerable vogue in these years, held that heredity determined almost all of a person's capacities and that genetic inferiority predisposed people to crime and poverty. Such pseudoscientific thinking sought to explain historical and social development solely as a function of "racial" differences.

Against this background, the war and its aftermath provided the final push for immigration restriction. The "100 percent American" fervor of the

Population Composition of Selected Cities, 1920 By 1920 the demographic impact of several decades of heavy immigration was especially evident in the nation's cities. The combined population of the foreign-born and those born of foreign parents frequently surpassed that of the native-born of native parents.

war years fueled nativist passions. So did the Red Scare of 1919–20, which linked foreigners with Bolshevism and radicalism of all kinds in the popular mind. The postwar depression coincided with the resumption of massive immigration, bringing much hostile comment on the relationship between rising unemployment and the new influx of foreigners. The American Federation of Labor proposed stopping all immigration for two years. Sensational press coverage of organized crime figures, many of them Italian or Jewish, also played a part.

In 1921 Congress passed the Immigration Act, setting a maximum of 357,000 new immigrants each year. Quotas limited annual immigration from any European country to 3 percent of the number of its natives counted in the 1910 U.S. census. But restrictionists complained that the new law still allowed too many southern and eastern Europeans in, especially since the northern and western Europeans did not fill their quotas. The Johnson-Reed Immigration Act of 1924 revised the quotas to 2 percent of the number of foreign-born counted for each nationality in the census for 1890, when far fewer southern or eastern Europeans were present in the United States. The maximum total allowed each year was also cut, to 164,000. The quota laws did not apply to Canada, Mexico, or any other nation in the western hemisphere.

The immigration restriction laws reversed earlier practices and became a permanent feature of national policy. Republican congressman Albert Johnson of Washington, co-author of the 1924 act, defended it by claiming that "our capacity to maintain our cherished institutions stands diluted by a stream of alien blood, with all its inherited misconceptions respecting the relationships of the governing power to the governed. . . . The day of unalloyed welcome to all peoples, the day of indiscriminate acceptance of all races, has definitely ended." In effect, Congress had accepted the racial assumptions of such popular, pseudoscientific writers as Madison Grant, basing immigration restriction on a presumed hierarchy of superior and inferior "races."

The Ku Klux Klan

If immigration restriction was resurgent nativism's most significant legislative expression, a revived Ku Klux Klan was its most effective mass movement. The original Klan had been formed in the Reconstruction South as an instrument of white racial terror against newly freed slaves (see Chapter 17). It had died out in the 1870s. The new Klan, born in Stone Mountain, Georgia, in 1915, was inspired by D. W. Griffith's racist spectacle *The Birth of a Nation*, a film released in that year depicting the original KKK as a heroic organization. The new

Klan patterned itself on the secret rituals and antiblack hostility of its predecessor, and until 1920 it was limited to a few local chapters in Georgia and Alabama.

When Hiram W. Evans, a dentist from Dallas, became imperial wizard of the Klan in 1922, he transformed the organization. Evans hired professional fund-raisers and publicists and directed an effective recruiting scheme that paid a commission to sponsors of new members. The Klan advocated "100 per cent Americanism" and "the faithful maintenance of White Supremacy." The Klan also staunchly supported the enforcement of Prohibition, and it attacked birth control and Darwinism. The new Klan made a special target of the Roman Catholic Church, labeling it a hostile and dangerous alien power. In a 1926 magazine piece titled "The Klan's Fight for Americanism," Evans alleged that the Church's "theocratic autocracy and its claim to full authority in temporal as well as spiritual matters, all make it impossible for it as a church, or for its members if they obey it, to cooperate in a free democracy in which Church and State have been separated."

The new Klan presented itself as the righteous defender of the embattled traditional values of small-town Protestant America. But ironically, to build its membership rolls, it relied heavily on the publicity, public relations, and business techniques associated with modern urban culture. By 1924 the new Klan counted more than 3 million members across the country. President Harding had joined in a special White House ceremony. Its slogan, "Native, White, Protestant Supremacy," proved especially attractive in the Midwest and South, including many cities. Klansmen boycotted businesses, threatened families, and sometimes resorted to violence—public whippings, arson, and lynching—against their chosen enemies. The Klan's targets sometimes included white Protestants accused of sexual promiscuity, blasphemy, or drunkenness, but most were African Americans, Catholics, and Jews. Support for Prohibition enforcement probably united Klansmen more than any single issue.

On another level, the Klan was a popular social movement. Many members were more attracted by the Klan's spectacular social events and its efforts to reinvigorate community life than by its attacks on those considered outsiders. Perhaps a half million women joined the Women of the Ku Klux Klan, and women constituted nearly half of the Klan membership in some states. Klanswomen drew on family and community traditions, such as church suppers, kin reunions, and gossip campaigns, to defend themselves and their families against what they saw as corruption and immorality. One northern Indiana Klanswoman recalled, "Store owners,

Women members of the Ku Klux Klan in New Castle, Indiana, August 1, 1923. The revived Klan was a powerful presence in scores of American communities during the early 1920s, especially among native-born white Protestants who feared cultural and political change. In addition to preaching "100 percent Americanism," local Klan chapters also served a social function for members and their families.

teachers, farmers . . . the good people, all belonged to the Klan. They were going to clean up the government, and they were going to improve the school books that were loaded with Catholicism." The Klan's power was strong in many communities precisely because it fit so comfortably into the everyday life of white Protestants.

Studies of Klan units suggest that the appeal and activities of the organization varied greatly from community to community. Local conditions and circumstances often attracted followers more than the extremist and nativist appeals of the national office. In Anaheim, California, for example, most Klansmen were migrants from midwestern states who attended mainstream Protestant churches. They focused their anger on the local economic elite, whom they held responsible for failure to enforce Prohibition, a rising crime rate, and runaway economic growth. In Colorado, Prohibition and vice law violations appeared to be the main concern. Vigilante attacks on Catholic priests and Jewish synagogues were more prevalent in cities like Denver and Pueblo, which had small but visible nonwhite Protestant communities.

At its height, the Klan also became a powerful force in Democratic Party politics in Texas, Okla-

homa, Indiana, Colorado, Oregon, and other states. It had a strong presence among delegates to the 1924 Democratic National Convention. The Klan began to fade in 1925 when its Indiana leader, Grand Dragon David C. Stephenson, became involved in a sordid personal affair. Stephenson had picked up a young secretary at a party, got her drunk on bootleg liquor, and then assaulted her on a train. After the woman took poison and died, Stephenson was convicted of manslaughter. With one of its most famous leaders disgraced and in jail, the new Klan began to lose members and influence. The success of immigration restriction, the receding concern over Bolshevism, wrangling among Klan leaders, and the general economic prosperity also contributed to the movement's rapid decline by the late 1920s.

Religious Fundamentalism

Paralleling political nativism in the 1920s was the growth of religious fundamentalism. In large numbers of Protestant churches, congregations focused less on religious practice and worship than on social and reform activities in the larger community. By the early 1920s, a fundamentalist revival had developed in reaction to these tendencies. The fundamentalists

Clarence Darrow (left) and William Jennings Bryan at the Scopes Trial in Dayton, Tennessee, in 1925. Their courtroom battle embodied the larger cultural conflict between religious fundamentalism and secular values. In the trial's most dramatic moment, Darrow called Bryan to the witness stand to testify as an expert on the Bible.

Darrow, the most famous trial lawyer in America. The prosecution was led by William Jennings Bryan, the old Democratic standard-bearer who had thrown himself into the fundamentalist and anti-evolutionist cause. Held in a circus atmosphere in sweltering heat, the trial attracted thousands of reporters and partisans to Dayton and was broadcast across the nation by the radio.

The Scopes "monkey trial"—so called because fundamentalists trivialized Darwin's theory into a claim that humans were descended from monkeys—became one of the most publicized and definitive moments of the decade. The real drama was the confrontation between Darrow and Bryan. Darrow, denied the right to call scientists to testify for the defense, put "the Great Commoner," Bryan, himself on the stand as an expert witness on the Bible. Bryan delighted his supporters with a staunch defense of biblical literalism. But he also drew scorn from many of the assembled journalists, including cosmopolitan types such as H. L. Mencken of the Baltimore Sun, who ridiculed Bryan's simplistic faith. Scopes's guilt was never in question. The jury convicted him quickly, although the verdict was later thrown out on a technicality. Bryan died a week after the trial; his epitaph read simply, "He kept the Faith." The struggle over the teaching of evolution continued in an uneasy stalemate; state statutes were not repealed, but prosecutions for teaching evolution ceased. Fundamentalism, a religious creed and a cultural defense against the uncertainties of modern life, continued to have a strong appeal for millions of Americans.

emphasized a literal reading of the Bible, and they rejected the tenets of modern science as inconsistent with the revealed word of God. Fundamentalist publications and Bible colleges flourished, particularly among Southern Baptists.

One special target of the fundamentalists was the theory of evolution, first set forth by Charles Darwin in his landmark work *The Origin of Species* (1859). Using fossil evidence, evolutionary theory suggested that over time many species had become extinct and that new ones had emerged through the process of natural selection. These ideas directly contradicted the account of one, fixed creation in the Book of Genesis. Although most Protestant clergymen had long since found ways of blending the scientific theory with their theology, fundamentalists launched an attack on the teaching of Darwinism in schools and universities. By 1925 five southern state legislatures had passed laws restricting the teaching of evolution.

A young biology teacher, John T. Scopes, deliberately broke the Tennessee law in 1925 in order to challenge it in court. The resulting trial that summer in Dayton, a small town near Chattanooga, drew international attention to the controversy. Scopes's defense team included attorneys from the American Civil Liberties Union and Clarence

PROMISES POSTPONED

The prosperity of the twenties was unevenly distributed and enjoyed across America. Older, progressive reform movements that had pointed out inequities faltered in the conservative political climate. But the Republican new era did inspire a range of critics deeply troubled by unfulfilled promises in American life. Feminists sought to redefine their movement in the wake of the suffrage victory. Mexican immigration to the United States shot up, and in the burgeoning Mexican American communities of the Southwest and Midwest, economic and social conditions were very difficult. African Americans, bitterly disappointed by their treatment during and after the war, turned to new political and cultural strategies. Many American intellectuals found themselves deeply alienated from the temper and direction of modern American society.

Feminism in Transition

The achievement of the suffrage removed the central issue that had given cohesion to the disparate forces of female reform activism. In addition, female activists of all persuasions found themselves swimming against a national tide of hostility to political idealism. During the 1920s, the women's movement split into two main wings over a fundamental disagreement about female identity. Should activists stress women's differences from men—their vulnerability and the double burden of work and family—and continue to press for protective legislation, such as laws that limited the length of the work week for women? Or should they emphasize the ways that women were like men—sharing similar aspirations—and push for full legal and civil equality?

In 1920, the National American Woman Suffrage Association reorganized itself as the League of Women Voters. The league represented the historical mainstream of the suffrage movement, those who believed that the vote for women would bring a nurturing sensibility and a reform vision to American politics. This view was rooted in politicized domesticity, the notion that women had a special role to play in bettering society: improving conditions for working women, abolishing child labor, humanizing prisons and mental hospitals, and serving the urban poor. Most league members continued working in a variety of reform organizations, and the league itself concentrated on educating the new female electorate, encouraging women to run for office, and supporting laws for the protection of women and children.

A newer, smaller, and more militant group was the National Woman's Party (NWP), founded in 1916 by militant suffragist Alice Paul. The NWP downplayed the significance of suffrage and argued that women were still subordinate to men in every facet of life. The NWP opposed protective legislation for women, claiming that such laws reinforced sex stereotyping and prevented women from competing with men in many fields. Largely representing the interests of professional and business women, the NWP focused on passage of a brief Equal Rights Amendment (ERA) to the Constitution, introduced in Congress in 1923: "Men and women shall have

equal rights throughout the United States and every place subject to its jurisdiction."

Since the ERA would wipe out sex as a legal category, its opponents worried about the loss of hard-won protective legislation that benefited poor and working-class women. Many of the older generation of women reformers opposed the ERA as elitist, arguing that far more women benefited from protective laws than were injured by them. "So long as men cannot be mothers," Florence Kelley declared, "so long legislation adequate for them can never be adequate for wage-earning women; and the cry Equality, Equality, where nature has created inequality, is as stupid and as deadly as the cry of Peace, Peace, where there is no Peace." Mary Anderson, director of the Women's Bureau in the Department of Labor, argued that "women who are wage earners, with one job in the factory and another in the home, have little time and energy left to carry on the fight to better their economic status. They need the help of other women and they need labor laws."

ERA supporters countered that maximum hours laws or laws prohibiting women from night work prevented women from getting many lucrative jobs. According to Harriot Stanton Blatch, daughter of feminist pioneer Elizabeth Cady Stanton, "In many highly paid trades women have been pushed into the lower grades of work, limited in earning capacity, if not shut out of the trade entirely by these so-called protective laws." M. Carey Thomas, president of Bryn Mawr College, defended the ERA with language reminiscent of laissez faire: "How much better by one blow to do away with discriminating against women in work, salaries, promotion and opportunities to compete with men in a fair field with no favour on either side!"

But most women's groups did not think there was a "fair field." Positions solidified. The League of Women Voters, the National Consumers' League, and the Women's Trade Union League opposed the ERA. ERA supporters generally stressed individualism, competition, and the abstract language of "equality" and "rights." ERA opponents emphasized the grim reality of industrial exploitation and the concentration of women workers in low-paying jobs in which they did not compete directly with men. ERA advocates dreamed of a labor market that might be, one in which women might have the widest opportunity. Anti-ERA forces looked at the labor market as it was, insisting it was more important to protect women from existing exploitation. The NWP campaign failed to get the ERA passed by Congress, but the debates it sparked would be echoed during the feminist movement of the 1970s, when the ERA became a central political goal of a resurgent feminism.

A small number of professional women made real gains in the fields of real estate, banking, and journalism. The press regularly announced new "firsts" for women, such as Amelia Earhart's 1928 airplane flight across the Atlantic. Anne O'Hare McCormick won recognition as the "first lady of American journalism" for her reporting and editorial columns in the *New York Times*. As business expanded, a greater percentage of working women were employed in white-collar positions, as opposed to manufacturing and domestic service. In 1900 less than 18 percent of employed women worked in clerical, managerial, sales, and professional areas. By 1930 the number was 44 percent. But studies showed that most of these women were clustered in the low-paying areas of typing, stenography, bookkeeping, cashiering, and sales clerking. Men still dominated in the higher-paid and managerial white-collar occupations.

The most significant, if limited, victory for feminist reformers was the 1921 Sheppard-Towner Act, which established the first federally funded health care program, providing matching funds for states to set up prenatal and child health care centers. These centers also provided public health nurses for house calls. Although hailed as a genuine reform breakthrough, especially for women in rural and isolated communities, the act aroused much opposition. The NWP disliked it for its assumption that all women were mothers. Birth control advocates such as Margaret Sanger complained that contraception was not part of the program. The American Medical Association (AMA) objected to government-sponsored health care and to nurses who functioned outside the supervision of physicians. By 1929, largely as a result of intense AMA lobbying, Congress cut off funds for the program.

Mexican Immigration

While immigration restriction sharply cut the flow of new arrivals from Europe, the 1920s also brought a dramatic influx of Mexicans to the United States. Mexican immigration, which was not included in the immigration laws of 1921 and 1924, had picked up substantially after the outbreak of the Mexican Revolution in 1911, when political instability and economic hardships provided incentives to cross the border to *El Norte*. According to the U.S. Immigration Service, an estimated 459,000 Mexicans entered the United States between 1921 and 1930, more than double the number for the previous decade. The official count no doubt underrepresented the true numbers of immigrants from Mexico. Many Mexicans shunned the main border crossings at El Paso, Texas; Nogales, Arizona; and Calexico, California, and thus avoided paying the $8 head tax and $10 visa fee.

The primary pull was the tremendous agricultural expansion occurring in the American Southwest. Irrigation and large-scale agribusiness had begun transforming California's Imperial and San Joaquin Valleys from arid desert into lucrative fruit and vegetable fields. Cotton pickers were needed in the vast plantations of Lower Rio Grande Valley in Texas and the Salt River Valley in Arizona. The sugar beet fields of Michigan, Minnesota, and Colorado also attracted many Mexican farm workers. American industry had also begun recruiting Mexican workers, first to fill wartime needs and later to fill the gap left by the decline in European immigration.

The new Mexican immigration appeared more permanent than previous waves—that is, more and more newcomers stayed—and, like other immigrants, settled in cities. By 1930 San Antonio's Mexican community accounted for roughly 70,000 people out of a total population of a quarter million. Around 100,000 Mexicans lived in Los Angeles, including 55,000 who attended city schools. Substantial Mexican communities also flourished in midwestern cities such as Chicago, Detroit, Kansas City, and Gary. Many of the immigrants alternated between agricultural and factory jobs, depending on seasonal availability of work. Mexican women often worked in the fields alongside their husbands. They also had jobs as

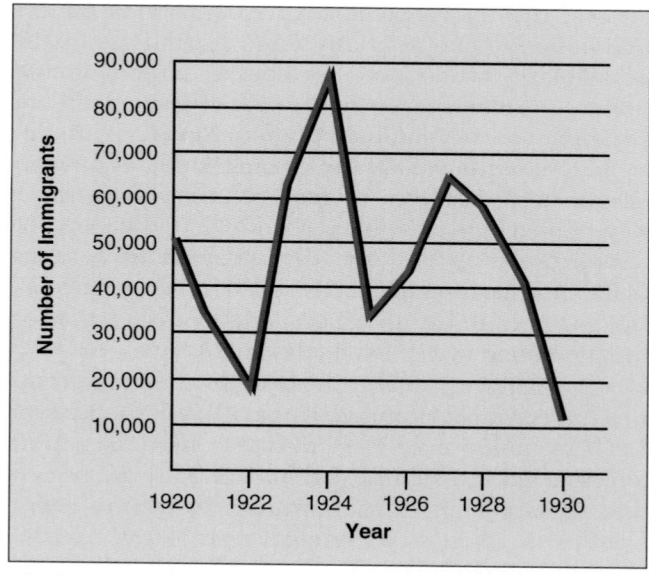

Mexican Immigration to the United States in the 1920s *Many Mexican migrants avoided official border crossing stations so they would not have to pay visa fees. Thus these official figures probably underestimated the true size of the decade's Mexican migration. As the economy contracted with the onset of the Great Depression, immigration from Mexico dropped off sharply.*

Mexican American farm workers are shown pitting apricots near Canoga Park, Los Angeles County, 1924. Most of the more than half million Mexicans who migrated to the United States during the 1920s worked as farm laborers. Migrant families usually traveled and worked together, following the crop harvests.

domestics and seamstresses or took in laundry and boarders.

Racism and local patterns of residential segregation confined most Mexicans to barrios. Housing conditions were generally poor, particularly for recent arrivals, who were forced to live in rude shacks without running water or electricity. Disease and infant mortality rates were much higher than average, and most Mexicans worked at low-paying, unskilled jobs and received inadequate health care. Legal restrictions passed by states and cities made it difficult for Mexicans to enter teaching, legal, and other professions. Mexicans were routinely banned from local public works projects as well. Many felt a deep ambivalence about applying for American citizenship. Loyalty to the Old Country was strong, and many cherished dreams of returning to live out their days in Mexico.

Ugly racist campaigns against Mexicans were common in the 1920s, especially when "cheap Mexican labor" was blamed for local unemployment or hard times. Stereotypes of Mexicans as "greasers" or "wetbacks" were prevalent in newspapers and movies of the day. Nativist efforts to limit Mexican immigration were thwarted by the lobbying of powerful agribusiness interests. The Los Angeles Chamber of Commerce typically employed racist stereotyping in arguing to keep the borders open. Mexicans, it claimed, were naturally suited for agriculture, "due to their crouching and bending habits . . . , while the white is physically unable to adapt himself to them."

Mutual aid societies—*mutualistas*—became key social and political institutions in the Mexican communities of the Southwest and Midwest. They provided death benefits and widows' pensions for members and also served as centers of resistance to

Black Population, 1920   *Although the Great Migration had drawn hundreds of thousands of African Americans to the urban north, the southern states of the former Confederacy still remained the center of the African American population in 1920.*

civil rights violations and discrimination. In 1928, the Federation of Mexican Workers Unions formed in response to a large farm labor strike in the Imperial Valley of California. A group of middle-class Mexican professionals in Texas organized the League of United Latin American Citizens (LULAC) in 1929. The founding of these organizations marked only the beginnings of a long struggle to bring economic, social, and racial equality to Mexican Americans.

The "New Negro"

The Great Migration spurred by World War I showed no signs of letting up during the 1920s, and African American communities in northern cities grew rapidly. By far the largest and most influential of these communities was New York City's Harlem, the demographic and cultural capital of black America. Previously a residential suburb, Harlem began attracting middle-class African Americans in the prewar years. After the war, heavy black migration from the South and the Caribbean encouraged real estate speculators and landlords to remake Harlem as an exclusively black neighborhood. Between 1920 and 1930 nearly

90,000 new arrivals settled in Harlem, giving it a black population of nearly 200,000.

The demand for housing in this restricted geographical area led to skyrocketing rents, but most Harlemites held low-wage jobs. This combination produced extremely overcrowded apartments, unsanitary conditions, and the rapid deterioration of housing stock. Disease and death rates were abnormally high. Harlem was well on its way to becoming a slum. Yet Harlem also boasted a large middle-class population and supported a wide array of churches, theaters, newspapers and journals, and black-owned businesses. It became a magnet for African American intellectuals, artists, musicians, and writers from all over the world. Poet Langston Hughes expressed the excitement of arriving in the community in 1921: "I can never put on paper the thrill of the underground ride to Harlem. I went up the steps and out into the bright September sunlight. Harlem! I stood there, dropped my bags, took a deep breath and felt happy again."

Harlem became the political and intellectual center for what writer Alain Locke called the "New Negro." Locke was referring to a new spirit in the work of black writers and intellectuals, an optimistic faith that encouraged African Americans to develop and celebrate their distinctive culture, firmly rooted in the history, folk culture, and experiences of African American people. This faith was the common denominator uniting the disparate figures associated with the Harlem Renaissance. The assertion of cultural independence resonated in the poetry of Langston Hughes and Claude McKay, the novels of Zora Neale Hurston and Jessie Fauset, the essays of Countee Cullen and James Weldon Johnson, the acting of Paul Robeson, and the blues singing of Bessie Smith. Most would agree with Johnson when he wrote in 1927 that "nothing can go farther to destroy race prejudice than the recognition of the Negro as a creator and contributor to American civilization."

There was a political side to the "New Negro" as well. The newly militant spirit that black veterans had brought home from World War I matured and found a variety of expressions in the Harlem of the 1920s. New leaders and movements began to appear alongside established organizations like the National Association for the Advancement of Colored People. A. Philip Randolph began a long career as a labor leader, socialist, and civil rights activist in these years, editing the *Messenger* and organizing the Brotherhood of Sleeping Car Porters. Harlem was also headquarters to Marcus Garvey's Universal Negro Improvement Association. An ambitious Jamaican immigrant who had moved to Harlem in 1916, Garvey created a mass movement that stressed black economic self-determination and unity among the black communities of the United States, the Caribbean, and Africa. His newspaper, *Negro World*, spoke to black communities around the world, urging black businesses to trade among themselves. With colorful parades and rallies and a central message affirming pride in black identity, Garvey attracted as many as a million members worldwide.

Garvey's best-publicized project was the Black Star Line, a black-owned and -operated fleet of ships that would link people of African descent around the world. But insufficient capital and serious financial mismanagement resulted in the spectacular failure of the enterprise. In 1923, Garvey was found guilty of mail fraud in his fund-raising efforts; he later went to jail and was subsequently deported to England. Despite the disgrace, Harlem's largest newspaper, the *Amsterdam News*, explained Garvey's continuing appeal to African Americans: "In a world where black is despised, he taught them that black is beautiful. He taught them to admire and praise black things and black people."

Harlem in the 1920s also became a popular tourist attraction for "slumming" whites. Nightclubs like the Cotton Club were often controlled by white

A 1925 *pensive portrait of Langston Hughes, one of the leading literary voices of the Harlem Renaissance. Winold Reiss's work suggested Hughes's determination to create poetry out of the everyday life experiences of Harlem's burgeoning African American population.*

organized crime figures. They featured bootleg liquor, floor shows, and the best jazz bands of the day, led by Duke Ellington, Fletcher Henderson, Cab Calloway, and Louis Armstrong. Yet these clubs were rigidly segregated. Black dancers, singers, and musicians provided the entertainment, but no African Americans were allowed in the audience. Chronicled in novels and newspapers, Harlem became a potent symbol to white America of the ultimate good time. Yet the average Harlemite never saw the inside of a nightclub. For the vast majority of Harlem residents, working menial jobs for low wages and forced to pay high rents, the day-to-day reality was depressingly different.

Intellectuals and Alienation

War, Prohibition, growing corporate power, and the deep currents of cultural intolerance troubled many intellectuals in the 1920s. Some felt so alienated from the United States that they left to live abroad. In the early 1920s Gertrude Stein, an American expatriate writer living in Paris, told the young novelist Ernest Hemingway: "All of you young people who served in the war, you are a lost generation." The phrase "a lost generation" was widely adopted as a label for American writers, artists, and intellectuals of the postwar era. Yet it is difficult to generalize about so diverse a community. For one thing, living abroad attracted only a handful of American writers. Alienation and disillusion with American life were prominent subjects in the literature and thought of the 1920s, but artists and thinkers developed these themes in very different ways.

The mass slaughter of World War I provoked revulsion and a deep cynicism about the heroic and moralistic portrayal of war so popular in the nineteenth century. Novelists Hemingway and John Dos Passos, who both served at the front as ambulance drivers, depicted the war and its

Clifford K. Berryman's 1928 political cartoon interpreted that year's presidential contest along sectional lines. It depicted the two major presidential contenders as each setting off to campaign in the regions where their support was weakest. For Democrat Al Smith, that meant the West, and for Republican Herbert Hoover, the East.

aftermath in world-weary and unsentimental tones. The search for personal moral codes that would allow one to endure life with dignity and authenticity was at the center of Hemingway's fiction. In the taut, spare language of *The Sun Also Rises* (1926) and *A Farewell to Arms* (1929), he questioned idealism, abstractions, and large meanings. As Jake Barnes, the wounded war hero of *The Sun Also Rises* explained, "I did not care what it was all about. All I wanted to know was how to live it."

Hemingway and F. Scott Fitzgerald were the most influential novelists of the era. Fitzgerald joined the army during World War I but did not serve overseas. His work celebrated the youthful vitality of "the Jazz Age" (a phrase he coined) but was also deeply distrustful of the promises of American prosperity and politics. His first novel, *This Side of Paradise* (1920), won a wide readership around the country with its exuberant portrait of "a new generation," "dedicated more than the last to the fear of poverty and the worship of success; grown up to find all Gods dead, all wars fought, all faiths in man shaken." Fitzgerald's finest work, *The Great Gatsby* (1925), written in the south of France, depicted the glamorous parties of the wealthy while evoking the tragic limits of material success.

At home, many American writers engaged in sharp attacks on small-town America and what they viewed as its provincial values. Essayist H. L. Mencken, caustic editor of the *American Mercury*, heaped scorn on fundamentalists, Prohibition, and nativists, while ridiculing what he called the "American booboisie." Mencken understood the power of the small town and despaired of reforming politics. "Our laws," he wrote, "are invented, in the main, by frauds and fanatics, and put upon the statute books by poltroons and scoundrels." Fiction writers also skewered small-town America, achieving commercial and critical success in the process. Sherwood Anderson's *Winesburg, Ohio* (1919) offered a spare, laconic, pessimistic yet compassionate view of middle America. He had a lasting influence on younger novelists of the 1920s.

The most popular and acclaimed writer of the time was novelist Sinclair Lewis. In a series of novels satirizing small-town life, such as *Main Street* (1920) and especially *Babbitt* (1922), Lewis affectionately mocked his characters. His treatment of the central character in *Babbitt*—George Babbitt of Zenith—also had a strong element of self-mockery, for Lewis could offer no alternative set of values to Babbitt's crass self-promotion, hunger for success, and craving for social acceptance.

In 1930 Lewis became the first American author to win the Nobel Prize for literature.

The playwright Eugene O'Neill revolutionized the American stage with his naturalistic and brooding dramas. O'Neill's depictions of the darker side of family life and his exploration of race relations helped push American theater past the melodramatic conventions of the late nineteenth century. Among his influential early plays were *Beyond the Horizon* (1920), *The Emperor Jones* (1921), and *The Great God Brown* (1926). Two expatriate poets, T. S. Eliot and Ezra Pound, were breaking Victorian conventions by pushing American verse in revolutionary new directions. Eliot's *The Waste Land* (1922), perhaps the most influential poem of the century, used the metaphor of impotence to comment on the postwar world.

Another side of intellectual alienation was expressed by writers critical of industrial progress and the new mass culture. The most important of these were a group of poets and scholars centered in Vanderbilt University in Nashville, Tennessee, collectively known as the Fugitives. They included Allen Tate, John Crowe Ransom, Donald Davidson, and Robert Penn Warren, all of whom invoked traditional authority, respect for the past, and older agrarian ways as ideals to live by. The Fugitives attacked industrialism and materialism as modern-day ills. Self-conscious Southerners, they looked to the antebellum plantation-based society as a model for a community based on benevolence toward dependents (such as black people and women) and respect for the land. Their book of essays, *I'll Take My Stand* (1930), was a collective manifesto of their ideas.

Not all intellectuals, of course, were critics of modern trends. Some, like the philosopher John Dewey, retained much of the prewar optimism and belief in progress. But many others, such as Walter Lippmann and Joseph Wood Krutch, articulated a profound uneasiness with the limits of material growth. In his 1929 book *A Preface to Morals*, the urbane and sophisticated Lippmann expressed doubts about the moral health of the nation. Modern science and technological advances could not address more cosmic questions of belief. The erosion of old religious faiths and moral standards, along with the triumph of the new mass culture, had left many people with nothing to believe in. Lippmann called for a new "religion of the spirit" to offer a guide for living an ethical life. He was unclear as to just what the "religion of the spirit" might be. But he was certain that the moralist would have to persuade rather than command people to live the good life. His job would be "not to exhort men to be good but to elucidate what the good is."

The Election of 1928

The presidential election of 1928 served as a kind of national referendum on the Republican new era. It also revealed just how important ethnic and cultural differences had become in defining American politics. The contest reflected many of the deepest tensions and conflicts in American society in the 1920s: native-born versus immigrant; Protestant versus Catholic; Prohibition versus legal drinking; small-town life versus the cosmopolitan city; fundamentalism versus modernism; traditional sources of culture versus the new mass media.

The 1928 campaign featured two politicians who represented profoundly different sides of American life. Al Smith, the Democratic nominee for president, was a pure product of New York City's Lower East Side. Smith came from a background that included Irish, German, and Italian ancestry, and he was raised as a Roman Catholic. After attending parochial school and working in the Fulton Fish Market, he rose through the political ranks of New York's Tammany Hall machine. A personable man with a deep sympathy for poor and working-class people, Smith won a reputation as an effective state legislator in Albany. He served four terms as governor of New York, pushing through an array of laws reforming factory conditions, housing, and welfare programs. Two of his closest advisers were the progressives Frances Perkins and Belle Moskowitz. Smith thus fused older-style machine politics with the newer reform emphasis on state intervention to solve social problems.

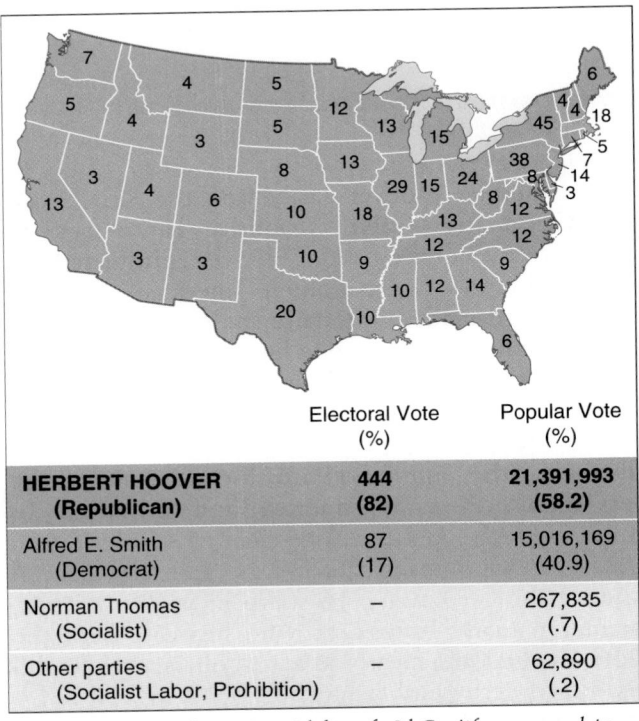

	Electoral Vote (%)	Popular Vote (%)
HERBERT HOOVER (Republican)	**444** **(82)**	**21,391,993** **(58.2)**
Alfred E. Smith (Democrat)	87 (17)	15,016,169 (40.9)
Norman Thomas (Socialist)	–	267,835 (.7)
Other parties (Socialist Labor, Prohibition)	–	62,890 (.2)

The Election of 1928   *Although Al Smith managed to carry the nation's twelve largest cities, Herbert Hoover's victory in 1928 was one of the largest popular and electoral landslides in the nation's history.*

CHRONOLOGY

1920	Prohibition takes effect
	Warren G. Harding is elected president
	Station KDKA in Pittsburgh goes on the air
	Census reports that urban population is greater than rural population for the first time
1921	First immigration quotas are established by Congress
	Sheppard-Towner Act establishes first federally funded health care program
1922	Washington conference produces Five-Power Treaty scaling down navies
1923	Equal Rights Amendment is first introduced in Congress
	Harding dies in office; Calvin Coolidge becomes president
1924	Ku Klux Klan is at height of its influence
	Dawes Plan for war reparations stabilizes European economies

	Johnson-Reed Immigration Act tightens quotas established in 1921
1925	Scopes trial pits religious fundamentalism against modernity
	F. Scott Fitzgerald publishes *The Great Gatsby*
1926	National Broadcasting Company establishes first national radio network
1927	McNary-Haugen Farm Relief bill finally passed by Congress but is vetoed by President Coolidge as unwarranted federal interference in the economy
	Warner Brothers produces *The Jazz Singer,* the first feature-length motion picture with sound
	Charles Lindbergh makes first solo flight across the Atlantic Ocean
1928	Kellogg-Briand Pact renounces war
	Herbert Hoover defeats Al Smith for the presidency
1929	Robert and Helen Lynd publish their classic community study, *Middletown*

Herbert Hoover easily won the Republican nomination after Calvin Coolidge announced he would not run for reelection. Hoover epitomized the successful and forward-looking American. An engineer and self-made millionaire, he offered a unique combination of experience in humanitarian war relief, administrative efficiency, and probusiness policies. Above all, Hoover stood for a commitment to voluntarism and individualism as the best method for advancing the public welfare. He was one of the best-known men in America and promised to continue the Republican control of national politics.

Smith himself quickly became the central issue of the campaign. His sharp New York accent, jarring to many Americans who heard it over the radio, marked him clearly as a man of the city. So did his brown derby and fashionable suits, as well as his promise to work for the repeal of Prohibition. As the first Roman Catholic nominee of a major party, Smith also drew a torrent of anti-Catholic bigotry, especially in the South and Midwest. Nativists and Ku Klux

Klanners shamelessly exploited old anti-Catholic prejudices and intimidated participants in Democratic election rallies. But Smith was also attacked from more respectable quarters. Bishop James Cannon, head of the Southern Methodist Episcopal Church, insisted that "no subject of the Pope" should be permitted to occupy the White House. William Allen White, the old and influential progressive editor from Kansas, denounced Smith as the candidate of gambling, prostitution, and liquor interests.

For his part, Smith ran a largely conservative race. He appointed John Raskob, a Republican vice president of General Motors, to manage his campaign, and tried to outdo Hoover in his praise for business. He avoided economic issues such as the unevenness of the prosperity, the plight of farmers, or the growing unemployment. Democrats remained regionally divided over Prohibition, Smith's religion, and the widening split between rural and urban values. Hoover did not have to do much, other than take credit for the continued prosperity.

In retrospect, probably no Democrat could have won in 1928. The incumbent majority party would not lose during prosperous times. Hoover polled 21 million votes to Smith's 15 million, and swept the electoral college 444 to 87, including New York State. Even the Solid South, reliably Democratic since the Civil War, gave five states to Hoover—a clear reflection of the ethnocultural split in the party. Yet the election offered important clues to the future of the Democrats. Smith ran better in the big cities of the North and East than any Democrat in modern times. He outpolled Hoover in the aggregate vote of the nation's twelve largest cities and carried six of them, thus pointing the way to the Democrats' future control of the urban vote.

CONCLUSION

America's big cities, if not dominant politically, now defined the nation's cultural and economic life as never before. The mass media of motion pictures, broadcasting, and chain newspapers brought cosmopolitan entertainments and values to the remotest small communities. The culture of celebrity knew no geographic boundaries. New consumer durable goods associated with mass-production techniques— automobiles, radios, telephones, household appliances—were manufactured largely in cities. The advertising and public relations companies that sang their praises were also distinctly urban enterprises. Even with the curtailing of European immigration, big cities attracted a kaleidoscopic variety of migrants: white people from small towns and farms, African Americans from the rural South, Mexicans from across the border, intellectuals and professionals looking to make their mark.

Many Americans, of course, remained deeply suspicious of postwar cultural and economic trends. Yet the partisans of Prohibition, members of the Ku Klux Klan, and religious fundamentalists usually found themselves on the defensive against what they viewed as alien cultural and economic forces centered in the metropolis. Large sectors of the population did not share in the era's prosperity. But the large numbers who did—or at least had a taste of good times—ensured Republican political dominance throughout the decade. Thus America in the 1920s balanced dizzying change in the cultural and economic realms with conservative politics. The reform crusades that attracted millions during the progressive era were a distant memory. Political activism was no match for the new pleasures promised by technology and prosperity.

REVIEW QUESTIONS

1. Describe the impact of the "second industrial revolution" on American business, workers, and consumers. Which technological and economic changes had the biggest impact on American society?
2. Analyze the uneven distribution of the decade's economic prosperity. Which Americans gained the most, and which were largely left out?
3. How did an expanding mass culture change the contours of everyday life in the decade following World War I? What role did new technologies of mass communication play in shaping these changes? What connections can you draw between the "culture of consumption," then and today?
4. What were the key policies and goals articulated by Republican political leaders of the 1920s? How did they apply these to both domestic and foreign affairs?
5. How did some Americans resist the rapid changes taking place in the post–World War I world? What cultural and political strategies did they employ?
6. Discuss the 1928 election as a mirror of the divisions in American society.

RECOMMENDED READING

John Braemer et al., eds., *Change and Continuity in Twentieth Century America: The 1920s* (1968). A wide-ranging collection of essays on the period, with especially good studies of the resistance to modernity.

Nancy F. Cott, *The Grounding of American Feminism* (1987). Includes a sophisticated analysis of the debates among and between feminists during the 1920s.

Lynn Dumenil, *The Modern Temper: America in the 1920s* (1995). An excellent synthesis of recent scholarship which emphasizes the ambivalence that many Americans felt toward the emergence of modern society.

James J. Flink, *The Car Culture* (1975). The best single volume on the history of the automobile and how it changed American life.

Ellis W. Hawley, *The Great War and the Search for Modern Order* (1979). An influential study of the relations between the state and business and the growth of mass consumer society.

Nancy Maclean, *Behind the Mask of Chivalry: The Making of the Second Ku Klux Klan* (1994). A fine case study of the KKK in Athens, Georgia, with important insights on the Klan's relationship to issues involving gender and class difference.

Roland Marchand, *Advertising the American Dream: Making Way for Modernity, 1920–1940* (1985). A superb, beautifully illustrated account of the rise of the modern advertising industry.

Geoffrey Perrett, *America in the Twenties* (1982). A useful overview of the decade, with very good anecdotal material.

Emily S. Rosenberg, *Spreading the American Dream* (1982). A fine study of American economic and cultural expansion around the world from 1890 to 1945.

Susan Smulyan, *Selling Radio: The Commercialization of American Broadcasting, 1920–1934* (1994). The best analysis of the rise of commercial radio broadcasting in the 1920s.

ADDITIONAL BIBLIOGRAPHY

Postwar Prosperity and Its Price

Irving Bernstein, *The Lean Years: A History of the American Worker, 1919–1933* (1960)

David Brody, *Workers in Industrial America* (1980)

Gilbert C. Fite, *American Farmers: The New Minority* (1981)

Kenneth T. Jackson, *Crabgrass Frontier* (1985)

William Leuchtenberg, *The Perils of Prosperity, 1914–1932* (1958)

Clay McShane, *Down the Asphalt Path* (1994)

Gwendolyn Wright, *Building the American Dream* (1981)

Gerald Zahavi, *Workers, Managers, and Welfare Capitalism* (1988)

The New Mass Culture

Beth A. Bailey, *From Front Porch to Back Seat: Courtship in Twentieth Century America* (1988)

Daniel J. Czitrom, *Media and the American Mind* (1982)

John D'Emilio and Estelle B. Freedman, *Intimate Matters: A History of Sexuality in America* (1988)

Stewart Ewen, *Captains of Consciousness* (1976)

Roland Gelatt, *The Fabulous Phonograph*, rev. ed. (1977)

Jackson Lears, *Fables of Abundance: A Cultural History of Advertising in America* (1994)

Robert Lynd and Helen Lynd, *Middletown* (1929)

Lary May, *Screening Out the Past: The Birth of Mass Culture and the Motion Picture Industry* (1980)

Robert Sklar, *Movie Made America*, rev. ed. (1995)

The State, the Economy, and Business

Guy Alchon, *The Invisible Hand of Planning* (1985)

Warren I. Cohen, *Empire without Tears* (1987)

Louis Galambos and Joseph Pratt, *The Rise of the Corporate Commonwealth* (1988)

Ellis W. Hawley, ed., *Herbert Hoover as Secretary of Commerce* (1974)

John D. Hicks, *Republican Ascendancy, 1921–1933* (1960)

Charles L. Mee, *The Ohio Gang: The World of Warren G. Harding* (1981)

Robert K. Murray, *The Politics of Normalcy* (1973)

Mira Wilkins, *The Maturing of Multinational Enterprise* (1974)

Joan Hoff Wilson, *American Business and Foreign Policy* (1971)

Resistance to Modernity

Katherine M. Blee, *Women and the Klan: Racism and Gender in the 1920s* (1991)

Norman H. Clark, *Deliver Us from Evil: An Interpretation of American Prohibition* (1976)

Lyle W. Dorsett, *Billy Sunday and the Redemption of Urban America* (1991)

John Higham, *Strangers in the Land: Patterns of American Nativism, 1860–1925* (1955)

Henry B. Leonard, *The Open Gates: The Protest against the Movement to Restrict Immigration, 1896–1924* (1980)

George M. Marsden, *Fundamentalism and American Culture* (1980)

Promises Postponed

Stanley Coben, *Rebellion against Victorianism* (1991)

Ruth Schwartz Cowan, *More Work for Mother* (1982)

Ann Douglas, *Terrible Honesty: Mongrel Manhattan in the 1920s* (1995)

Sara M. Evans, *Born for Liberty: A History of Women in America* (1989)

Nathan I. Huggins, *Harlem Renaissance* (1971)

Allan J. Lichtman, *Prejudice and the Old Politics: The Presidential Election of 1928* (1979)

Cary D. Mintz, *Black Culture and the Harlem Renaissance* (1988)

Kathy H. Ogren, *The Jazz Revolution: Twenties America and the Meaning of Jazz* (1989)

Gilbert Osofsky, *Harlem: The Making of a Ghetto* (1965)

Mark Reisler, *By the Sweat of Their Brow: Mexican Immigrant Labor in the United States, 1900–1940* (1976)

George J. Sanchez, *Becoming Mexican American* (1993)

Judith Stein, *The World of Marcus Garvey* (1985)

Biography

Edith L. Blumhofer, *Aimee Semple McPherson* (1993)

David Burner, *Herbert Hoover: The Public Life* (1979)

Robert Creamer, *Babe: The Legend Comes to Life* (1975)

Paula Elder, *Governor Alfred E. Smith: The Politician as Reformer* (1983)

Neal Gabler, *Winchell: Gossip, Power, and the Culture of Celebrity* (1994)

Fred Hobson, *Mencken: A Life* (1994)

Arnold Rampersad, *The Life of Langston Hughes*, 2 vols. (1986–88)

Randy Roberts, *Jack Dempsey* (1979)

David Robinson, *Chaplin* (1985)

Joan Hoff Wilson, *Herbert Hoover: Forgotten Progressive* (1975)

IMMIGRATION & COMMUNITY

The Changing Face of Ethnicity in America
1860-1930

Annual immigration to the United States, which had declined during the late 1850s from a peak of more than 400,000 in 1854, dropped sharply at the onset of the Civil War. But even before the war ended, the pace of immigration revived. From the late nineteenth century until World War I, as America's unprecedented industrial expansion created an unprecedented demand for labor, the rate of immigration increased dramatically, surpassing 1,000,000 in 1905. At the same time, the ethnic background of the immigrants changed, creating a corresponding change in the nation's ethnic landscape.

Before the Civil War most immigrants came from Ireland and Germany. After the war immigrants from Germany and northwestern Europe continued at first to predominate, but by 1896 they had been overtaken by the so-called "New Immigrants" from the countries of southern and eastern Europe. Immigration from Latin America and many Asian countries, although far lower than that from Europe, also increased. Immigration from China, however, slowed considerably after the passage of the Chinese Exclusion Act of 1882.

Overall, between 1860 and 1920 about 28.2 million people immigrated to the United States, and by 1920 these immigrants and their children represented more than one-third of the nation's population. The vast majority of New Immigrants sought better lives for themselves and their families. Driven by economic dislocation, political turmoil, and overpopulation at home, millions of people left their villages for opportunity in distant lands, including Canada, Argentina, Brazil, Australia, and New Zealand as well as the United States. Italians were the largest group among the New Immigrants: between 1880 and 1930 nearly five million came to the United States. Of them, 80 percent were peasants from southern Italy left landless by an agricultural depression.

Religious and ethnic persecution combined with economic hardship to drive the Jews of Russia, Poland, and other eastern European countries to emigrate. Laws in Russia dictated where Jews could live and restricted their opportunities for employment and education. Beginning in 1881, the Russian government encouraged violent attacks known as *pogroms* on Jewish communities. These hardships made the United States appear a beacon of salvation. As a result, the Jewish population of the United States grew from 250,000 in 1877 to more than 4 million in 1927.

Most New Immigrants settled in the nation's urban manufacturing centers, not on farms. Generally poorly educated and lacking industrial skills, they entered the bottom ranks in factories, mines, mills, slaughterhouses, and garment shops. Employers benefited from their numbers to reorganize the workplace and reduce their reliance on highly paid skilled workers. Jews, however, were an exception to this pattern. Many had come from cities and were skilled in craft work and business. Nearly 77 percent of immigrant Jewish men qualified for skilled work in such specialized trades as cigar manufacturing, printing, carpentry, and garment manufacturing. Japanese immigrants—more than 111,000 by 1920—likewise fared well. They had a literacy rate of 99 percent and were able to translate the agricultural experience they brought from Japan to establish themselves as successful farmers of market garden crops in California, where the majority settled.

Most New Immigrants were unmarried young men, and many did not intend to settle permanently in the United States. They hoped instead to earn enough money to return home and buy land or set up a small business. Italian immigrants, nearly 80 percent of them male, and Greek immigrants, more than 90 percent male, had the highest rate of remigration—almost 50 percent. Jews, facing persecution at home, were the least likely to return home. Only 5 percent remigrated. Instead, they saved their wages to bring other family members to the United States. As a result, Jews were the most evenly distributed by sex of the New Immigrants. Only among the Irish did women form the majority of newcomers.

Whether they planned to remigrate or stay, the New Immigrants quickly established distinctive communities, mainly in the nation's large cities or along the West Coast. In 1920 three-quarters of the foreign-born lived in cities. The vast majority of Italians, for example, entered through the port of New York, and nearly one-quarter of them settled nearby. By 1920, 400,000 Italian immigrants were living in sizable communities in Manhattan, Brooklyn, the Bronx, Queens, and Staten Island. In Chicago, one-third of all Italians lived in a single neighborhood on the city's West Side. Across the continent in California, where Italians represented the single largest immigrant group, they gave North Beach in San Francisco a special ethnic flavor.

In many cities the New Immigrants became the numerical majority and dominated political and

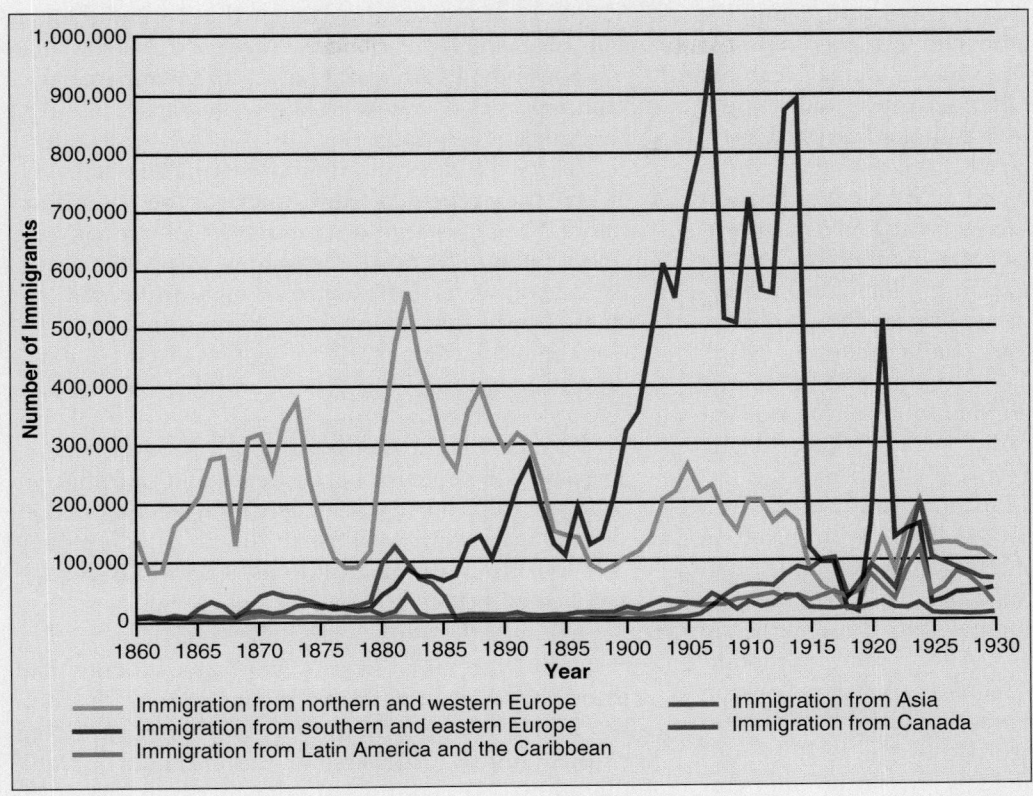

Annual Immigration to the United States, 1860–1930

social institutions. By 1910 in Passaic, New Jersey, for example, 52 percent of the population was foreign-born, most from Russia, Austria-Hungary, or Italy; 32 percent was second-generation (the children of foreign-born); and only 14 percent native-born whites. The immigrant population reshaped Passaic's political landscape, eventually forcing a sweeping reorganization of city government.

Although all New Immigrants tended to concentrate in neighborhoods near the factories or the steel mills where they worked, Italians were the most likely to cluster in so-called ethnic ghettos. Here, in "Little Italy," they spoke their native language, ate familiar foods, and helped their compatriots find jobs and housing. As immigrant communities grew, they sought to recreate Old World cultural patterns through schools, businesses, mutual-aid societies, and fraternal orders. Religious institutions—church and temple—provided the most important link to cultural traditions. Foreign-language newspapers—Germans and Jews produced the largest number—likewise helped forge community solidarity.

Although most old-stock Americans welcomed immigrant labor, many feared the "alien" cultural values and mores of the immigrants themselves. Before the Civil War, nativist, or anti-immigrant, sentiment was directed primarily against Catholics; shortly after the war, its focus was the Chinese. As the new immigration gathered steam in the 1880s, nativist sentiment increasingly turned against *all* immigrants. The nativist reaction to the new immigration found justification in certain intellectual currents of the late nineteenth century. So-called "scientific racism" purported to demonstrate that some racial groups were inherently superior to others, with western Europeans, especially Anglo-Saxons, inevitably ranked at the top, Africans at the bottom, and southern and eastern Europeans not much above them. Social Darwinism similarly claimed to justify social ranking with evolutionary theory.

Until the late nineteenth century, the federal government did little to regulate immigration and instead allowed state governments to set their own policies. But a turning point was reached with the Immigration Act of 1882, which gave the federal government the right to regulate immigration in cooperation with the states. The act laid the foundation for the kind of selective immigration based on race or ethnicity that the Chinese Exclusion Act, also passed in 1882, put into practice. The Immigration Act of 1891 gave the federal government the exclusive power to regulate immigration. The following year, in 1892, the newly centralized immigration reception center opened on Ellis Island.

In 1896, in the midst of a severe economic depression, a bipartisan majority in Congress passed a law requiring all immigrants to pass a literacy test, but it was vetoed by President McKinley. Subsequent efforts to enact such a law met a similar fate until 1917, when fear that the nation would face a wave of immigrants fleeing Europe at the end of World War I generated enough support for Congress to override President Wilson's veto and enact the Immigration Act of 1917. This landmark legislation implemented a literacy test and created an "Asiatic Barred Zone" to deny admission to people from India, Burma, Siam, Afghanistan, Arabia, the Malay Islands, and Polynesia. Foreshadowing the Red Scare that followed World War I, it also tightened restrictions on radicals to exclude members of anarchist and revolutionary organizations.

The era of open-door immigration came to a decisive end in the 1920s. Bills were introduced in Congress to suspend immigration altogether, but legislators compromised on a quota plan based on national origins, which was incorporated into the emergency restriction law passed in 1921. After a series of modifications and heated debates, Congress enacted a law on May 26, 1924, limiting immigration of specific groups to 2 percent of the number recorded by the 1890 census. The consequences were dramatic. European immigration dropped from more than 800,000 in 1921 to less than 150,000 by 1929. In that year, Congress passed the National Origins Act that put the quota system in place on a permanent basis, which, along with the Great Depression, reduced immigration to the United States in the 1930s to the lowest level since 1820.

■ IN THEIR OWN WORDS

Most immigrants came to the United States hoping to provide a better life for themselves and their families. Walter Lindstrom, who emigrated from Sweden in 1914, began to prepare for this journey when he was only fourteen. After he settled in Chicago, he worked for a time as a hospital orderly, then as a fireman for the railroad, and finally as a cement contractor. At age eighty-three Lindstrom recalled his expectations of a new beginning in America during his childhood on a farm in Sweden.

My family [in Sweden] had about fifteen acres of poor soil, which did not yield much in the way of crops....I was the oldest child in the family, and also a boy, so I had many chores to do. I had to chop wood, split kindling, carry hay, carry water, and take care of the farm animals....Then in the summer the fields had to be plowed, potatoes planted, harvest to be gathered in the fall, barley to be threshed....Work, work, all the time. No end. No compensation. Only an existence.

I kept on pressing my father that I wanted to go. Somewhere, someplace. Anyplace. Maybe on a ship. Maybe to America. I always remembered the alluring tales of the Wild West—Indians, buffaloes, everything.

And what tales the immigrants had to tell when they returned from America, the promised land! Nuggets of gold hanging on Christmas trees, diamonds on the waysides, sparkling pearls in crystal water begging to be held in human hands. And how good those homecomers looked—fur coats, cuffs on well-creased trousers, and money! Sure, big American bills. Not small like Swedish bills....

I remember the day I left home. Mother had prepared some home-baked beans and salt pork. She was very quiet when I left. Maybe she cried later. Father went with me to the railroad station. He looked pretty sad and I saw tears in his eyes as he wished me well.[1]

By the turn of the century, Italians had created the largest immigrant community in Philadelphia. Many came to the city as laborers contracted by the highly successful entrepreneur, Frank DiBaradino. An immigrant himself from the rural region of Abruzzo, DiBaradino advertised for workers throughout Italy, and, as the proprietor of a steamship ticket agency, he offered them interest-free loans to pay for the Atlantic crossing. By 1940 approximately 37,000 immigrants had taken advantage of his services, which often extended to matchmaking. He not only found jobs on the railroads and in the mines but often personally introduced these men to the women who would become their wives. DiBaradino eventually became the largest labor contractor in Philadelphia. His son later described his father's effective recruiting techniques:

Agents travelled through the countryside of Abruzzo encouraging and channelizing emigration to Philadelphia with promises of immediate employment. They came as couriers of good fortune. Villagers and country dwellers alike passed on the good tidings that in Philadelphia, some place in America, there were "paesans" who not only had good jobs to give, but who also lent emigrants assistance in obtaining passage across the ocean and in becoming settled among other "paesans" and friends in a strange country. The branch office of the Philadelphia contractors, located in strategic places throughout Abruzzo, became the direct link between the hintermost hamlet in Abruzzo and adjacent regions and the Italian colony in Philadelphia.[2]

Italian immigrants, ca. 1900, on Ellis Island, the main receiving station for nearly three-fourths of all the immigrants from its opening in 1892 until its closing in 1954. Italians were the largest group among the new immigrants.

we had congee in a large serving bowl with some cookies. Then at night we had rice with a main dish. You picked at some of it…and that was that. We ate in a huge dining hall.…They allowed us to go outside to the yard or even out to the dock, where there were grass and trees, tall and fan-like. The women were allowed to wander around, jump around, and stick our hands or feet into the water to fish out seaweed. Otherwise, the day would have been hard to pass.…

I was interrogated one day for several hours. They asked me so much, I broke out in a sweat. Sometimes they would try to trip you: "Your husband said such-and-such and now you say this?" But the answer was out already and it was too late to take it back, so I couldn't do anything about it. If they said you were wrong, then it was up to them whether to land you or not. Later, upon landing, I noticed a white man kept coming around to my husband's laundry and looking at me through the glass window. That was how they checked you out to make sure you didn't go elsewhere.[3]

It was common for men from Eastern Europe to precede other family members. As soon as they earned enough money to pay for the trip and found housing, they usually sent for their wives and children. Such was the case for Abraham Blum, who was born in Romania in 1855 and moved several times in his homeland before deciding to immigrate to the United States. He settled in Philadelphia among his "landsmen," other Jewish immigrants from Romania, and sent for his family. His son, Samuel, later recounted the family's journey to Philadelphia and described the city's checkerboard of ethnic enclaves.

My father was the first to leave Romania.…As far as could be verified, he travelled overland, boarded ship at Antwerp and landed in Philadelphia on March 23, 1900.…The second contingent was made up of [his children] Ben, Rose, Gitel and Gitel's fiancé, Moyshe. They traveled a similar route and landed, also in Philadelphia, several months later.

They apparently lost little time in setting up living quarters. Gitel did the house-keeping and the others found work; Rose and Ben in the needle industry and Moyshe at tailoring. My father, I believe, found work as a shoe cutter.…

My mother was in charge of bringing the rest of her brood; Kate, myself and Ester, aged ten, six and three respectively. Across Europe to Antwerp and across four thousand miles of ocean, fourteen days of ocean travel, to our destination in Philadelphia. As I finish the foregoing sentence I hesitate, to

In 1910 the U.S. Immigration Commission opened the Angel Island detention center, off the coast of San Francisco, for the few Chinese who were allowed to enter the United States following a loosening of the Exclusion Act of 1882. Modeled after Ellis island, the point of entry for most European immigrants, Angel Island housed new arrivals until U.S. immigration inspectors determined whether they were eligible to settle in the United States. The experience made a lasting, often unpleasant impression on the nearly 175,000 Chinese who were detained there before 1940, when the center shut down. In the following passage, a woman immigrant recalls her detention at Angel Island in 1913 when she was nineteen years old.

There was not much for us to do on the island. In the morning we got up and washed our faces. Afterwards, we had breakfast. After we ate, we napped or washed our own clothes. At lunch time marvel at the fortitude and daring of the undertaking, and I well up anew with admiration.

The area in which we settled was at the time a sort of concentrated repository for Jewish immigrants from Russia, Poland and Romania....From Catherine Street south, the Italian element predominated but they were left behind in a sort of "Little Italy" as the Jewish community by-passed them and began again at about Federal Street, continuing to spread further south. From Second Street east, the Slavic and Polish immigrants were apparently more comfortable, and north of Lombard and west of Sixth was the domain of the earlier arrivals already established and "Americanized"; there were few, if any, black people living in the area at that time.

I recollect that in our immediate area there were Romanian restaurants, Romanian "Chainas" (Tea Houses), their signs showing a large teapot with a smaller teapot superimposed on the same, and there was the "Romanish shiel" (Romanian synagogue), still there on Lombard Street.[4]

Rose Schneiderman (1882–1972), who became a prominent trade union organizer, emigrated from Russia with her family. In this account, published in a popular magazine, *The Independent*, in 1905, she recounts with pride the ups and downs of her family's fortunes and her response to the burdens that fell upon her.

My name is Rose Schneiderman, and I was born in some small city of Russian Poland. I don't know the name of the city, and have no memory of that part of my childhood. When I was about five years of age my parents brought me to this country and we settled in New York.

So my earliest recollections are of living in a crowded street among the East Side Jews, for we also are Jews.

My father got work as a tailor, and we lived in two rooms on Eldridge Street, and did very well, though not so well as in Russia, because mother and father both earned money, and here father alone earned the money, while mother attended to the house. There were then two other children besides me, a boy of three and one of five.

I went to school until I was nine years old, enjoying it thoroughly and making great progress, but then my father died of brain fever and mother was left with three children and another one coming. So I had to stay at home to help her and she went out to look for work....

I was the house worker, preparing the meals and looking after the other children—the baby, a little girl of six years, and a boy of nine. I managed very well, tho the meals were not very elaborate. I could cook simple things like porridge, coffee and eggs, and mother used to prepare the meat before she went away in the morning, so that all I had to do was to put it in the pan at night....

I was finally released by my little sister being taken by an aunt, and the two boys going to the Hebrew Orphan Asylum, which is a splendid institution, and turns out good men. One of these brothers is now a student in the City College, and the other is a page in the Stock Exchange.

When the other children were sent away mother was able to send me back to school, and I stayed in this school (Houston Street Grammar) till I had reached the Sixth Grammar Grade.

Then I had to leave in order to help support the family. I got a place in Hearn's as a cash girl, and after working there three weeks changed to Ridley's, where I remained for two and a half years. I finally left because the pay was so very poor and there did not seem to be any chance of advancement, and a friend told me that I could do better making caps.[5]

After Texas gained its independence from Mexico in 1836 and became a state in 1845, conflict between Anglo Texans and Mexicans persisted, becoming especially acute in the late nineteenth century when political turmoil and economic decline in their homeland prompted many Mexicans to travel northward in search of jobs or education. José Vasconcelos (1882–1959), who became a prominent educator and politician in Mexico, experienced a clash of cultures first-hand after his parents crossed the border to secure better schooling for their children. In his autobiography, *Ulises criollo*, published in 1945, Vasconcelos recalls the ethnic and national rivalries that surfaced in the classroom and on the playground. In the passage below he alludes to the divergent views of Mexicans and Anglos over the legacy of the Battle of the Alamo, a key event in the revolt against Mexico that secured Texas independence.

Piedras Negras [Mexico, opposite Eagle Pass, Texas] was a prosperous town, but it lacked a good school. On the other side of the border, the Yankees matched their concern with material progress with careful attention to education. Because of that my family moved to Eagle Pass when I was about ten years old....

We discussed issues in a democratic manner; the teacher confined herself to directing the debates. Texas independence and the war of 1847 divided the class into rival camps. We constantly talked about the Alamo, the cruel executions carried on

New York City's Lower East Side, photographed by Jacob Riis (1849–1914), ca. 1900. A large number of immigrants established small businesses and lived and worked in this district.

by Santa Anna, and the [treatment of] prisoners of war. There were only a few Mexicans in the class, but we were determined [to defend Mexico]. When I refer to Mexicans I include many who, despite their residence in Texas and their parents' U.S. citizenship, sided with me because of ethnic affinity. Had they done otherwise, they would have still been considered Mexicans because Anglos labeled them as such. Full-fledged Mexicans rarely went to the school. For years I was the only one.

I never felt obligated to make excuses [about Mexican history or Mexican society]. But when it was affirmed in class that one hundred Yankees could chase off one thousand Mexicans, I would rise and say, "That isn't true." I would get even more angry when someone would assert, "Mexicans are a semicivilized people." At home I always heard the opposite, that it was the Yankees who were the newcomers to culture. I would intervene, remarking [to the other students], "But look at Joe [José Vasconcelos]. He is a Mexican. Isn't he civilized? Isn't he a gentleman?" For the moment, that just observation would reestablish cordiality. But that would last only until the next lesson, until we would again read in our textbook phrases and judgments that drove me to ask for permission to refute them. Passions would rise anew. We would make challenging signs to each other. At first I would only have to remain alert in class and be ready to launch my verbal defenses. The other Mexicans would support me and take care of my rivals; during school holidays they would fight them.[6]

Questions

1. Identify the major groups known as the "New Immigrants."
2. Why did the New Immigrants leave their homelands, and why did they choose to settle in particular regions of the United States?
3. What were the major changes in immigration law during 1860–1930 period?
4. How did old-stock Americans greet the New Immigrants?

Sources

1. Joan Morrison and Charlotte Fox Zabusky, *American Mosaic: The Immigrant Experience in the Words of Those Who Lived It* (Pittsburgh: University of Pittsburgh Press, 1993)
2. Jerre Mangione and Ben Morreale, *La Storia: Five Centuries of the Italian American Experience* (New York: HarperCollins, 1992), 50
3. Him Mark Lai, Genny Lim, and Judy Yung, eds., *Island: Poetry and History of Chinese Immigrants on Angel Island, 1910–1940* (Seattle: University of Washington Press, 1980), 72, 117
4. Samuel Blum, unpublished memoir. Copyright Selma Chodoff, 1977.
5. Rose Schneiderman, "A Cap Maker's Story," *The Independent,* 58 (April 27, 1905), pp. 935–936
6. José Vasconcelos, *Ulises criolo,* 2 vols. (Mexico City: Ediciones Botas, 1945), 1:22, 24–27, 29–33, trans. Oscar J. Martinez; reprinted in Oscar J. Martinez, ed., *U.S.–Mexico Borderlands: Historical and Contemporary Perspectives* (Wilmington, Del.: Scholarly Resources, Inc, 1996), 103–106

CHAPTER TWENTY-FOUR

THE GREAT DEPRESSION AND THE NEW DEAL

1929–1940

Domenica del Corriere, Demonstration in New York. Unemployed, depression.

AMERICAN COMMUNITIES
Sit-Down Strike at Flint: Automobile Workers Organize a New Union

In the gloomy evening of February 11, 1937, 400 tired, unshaven, but very happy strikers marched out of the sprawling automobile factory known as Fisher Body Number 1. Most carried American flags and small bundles of clothing. A makeshift banner on top of the plant announced "Victory Is Ours." A wildly cheering parade line of a thousand supporters greeted the strikers at the gates. Shouting with joy, honking horns, and singing songs, the celebrants marched to two other factories to greet other emerging strikers. After forty-four days, the great Flint sit-down strike was over.

Flint, Michigan, was the heart of production for General Motors, the largest corporation in the world. In 1936 GM's net profits had reached $285 million, and its total assets were $1.5 billion. Originally a center for lumbering and then carriage making, Flint had boomed with the auto industry during the 1920s. Thousands of migrants streamed into the city, attracted by assembly line jobs averaging about $30 a week. By 1930 Flint's population had grown to about 150,000 people, 80 percent of whom depended on work at General Motors. A severe housing shortage made living conditions difficult. Tar-paper shacks, tents, even railroad cars were the only shelter available for many. Parts of the city resembled a mining camp.

The Great Depression hit Flint very hard. Employment at GM fell from a 1929 high of 56,000 to fewer than 17,000 in 1932. As late as 1938 close to half the city's families were receiving some kind of emergency relief. By that time, as in thousands of other American communities, Flint's private and county relief agencies had been overwhelmed by the needs of the unemployed and their families. Two new national agencies based in Washington, D.C., the Federal Emergency Relief Administration and the Works Progress Administration, had replaced local sources of aid during the economic crisis.

The United Automobile Workers (UAW) came to Flint in 1936 seeking to organize GM workers into one industrial union. The previous year, Congress had passed the National Labor Relations Act (also known as the Wagner Act), which made union organizing easier by guaranteeing the right of workers to join unions and bargain collectively. The act established the National Labor Relations Board to oversee union elections and prohibit illegal anti-union activities by employers. But the obstacles to labor organizing were still enormous. Unemployment was high, and GM had maintained a vigorous anti-union policy for years. By the fall of 1936, the UAW had signed up only a thousand members. The key moment came with the seizure of two Flint GM plants by a few hundred auto workers on December 30, 1936. The idea was to stay in the factories until strikers could achieve a collective bargaining agreement with General Motors. "We don't aim to keep the plants or try to run them," explained one sit-downer to a reporter, "but we want to see that nobody takes our jobs. We don't think we're breaking the law, or at least we don't think we're doing anything really bad."

The sit-down strike was a new and daring tactic that gained popularity among American industrial workers during the 1930s. In 1936 there were 48 sit-downs involving nearly 90,000 workers, and in 1937 some 400,000 workers participated in 477 sit-down strikes. Sit-downs expressed the militant exuberance of the rank and file. As one union song of the day put it:

> *When they tie the can to a union man,*
> *Sit down! Sit down!*
> *When they give him the sack they'll take him back,*
> *Sit down! Sit down!*
> *When the speed up comes, just twiddle your thumbs,*
> *Sit down! Sit down!*
> *When the boss won't talk don't take a walk,*
> *Sit down! Sit down!*

The Flint strikers carefully organized themselves into what one historian called "the sit down community." Each plant elected a strike committee and appointed its own police chief and sanitary engineer. Strikers were divided into "families" of fifteen, each with a captain. No alcohol was allowed, and strikers were careful not to destroy company property. Committees were organized for every conceivable purpose: food, recreation, sanitation, education, and contact with the outside. Sit-downers formed glee clubs and small orchestras to entertain themselves. Using loudspeakers, they broadcast concerts and speeches to their supporters outside the gates. A Women's Emergency Brigade—the strikers' wives, mothers, and daughters—provided crucial support preparing food and maintaining militant picket lines.

As the sit-down strike continued through January, support in Flint and around the nation grew. Overall production in the GM empire dropped from 53,000 vehicles per week to 1,500. Reporters and union supporters flocked to the plants. On January 11, in the so-called Battle of Running Bulls, strikers and their supporters clashed violently with Flint police and private GM guards. Michigan governor Frank Murphy, sympathetic to the strikers, brought in the National Guard to protect them. He refused to enforce an injunction obtained by GM to evict the strikers.

In the face of determined unity by the sit-downers, GM gave in and recognized the UAW as the exclusive bargaining agent in all sixty of its factories. The strike was perhaps the most important in American labor history, sparking a huge growth in union membership in the automobile and other mass-production industries. Rose Pesotta, a textile union organizer, described the wild victory celebration in Flint's overflowing Pengelly Building: "People sang and joked and laughed and cried, deliriously joyful. Victory meant a freedom they had never known before. No longer would they be afraid to join unions."

Out of the tight-knit, temporary community of the sit-down strike emerged a looser yet more permanent kind of community: a powerful, nation-wide trade union of automobile workers. The UAW struggled successfully to win recognition and collective bargaining rights from other carmakers, such as Chrysler and Ford. The national UAW, like other new unions in the mass-production industries, was composed of locals around the country. The permanent community of unionized auto workers won significant improvements in wages, working conditions, and benefits. Locals also became influential in the political and social lives of their larger communities—industrial cities such as Flint, Detroit, and Toledo. Nationally, organized labor became a crucial component of the New Deal political coalition and a key power broker in the Democratic Party. The new reality of a national community of organized labor would alter the national political and economic landscape for decades to come.

Flint

KEY TOPICS

- Causes and consequences of the Great Depression

- The politics of hard times

- Franklin D. Roosevelt and the two New Deals

- The expanding federal sphere in the West

- American cultural life during the 1930s

- Legacies and limits of New Deal reform

HARD TIMES

No event of the twentieth century had a more profound impact on American life than the Great Depression of the 1930s. Statistics can document a slumping economy, mass unemployment, and swelling relief rolls—but these numbers tell only part of the story. The emotional and psychological toll of these years, what one writer called "the invisible scar," must also be considered in understanding the worst economic crisis in American history. Even today, depression-era experiences retain a central, even mythical, place in the lives and memories of millions of American families.

The Bull Market

Stock trading in the late 1920s captured the imagination of the broad American public. The stock market resembled a sporting arena, millions following stock prices as they did the exploits of Babe Ruth or Jack Dempsey. Many business leaders and economists as much as told Americans that it was their duty to buy stocks. John J. Raskob, chairman of the board of General Motors, wrote an article for the *Ladies' Home Journal* titled "Everybody Ought to Be Rich." A person who saved $15 each month and invested it in good common stocks would, he claimed, have $80,000 within twenty years. The *Saturday Evening Post* printed a poem that captured the fever:

> *Oh, hush thee, my babe, granny's bought some more shares*
> *Daddy's gone out to play with the bulls and the bears,*
> *Mother's buying on tips and she simply can't lose,*
> *And baby shall have some expensive new shoes!*

During the bull market of the 1920s, stock prices increased at roughly twice the rate of industrial production. Paper value far outran real value. By the end of the decade, stocks that had been bought mainly on the basis of their earning power, which was passed on to stockholders in the form of dividends, now came to be purchased only for the resale value after their prices rose. Anyone reading the financial pages of a newspaper would be amazed at the upward climb. In

1928 alone, for example, the price of Radio Corporation of America stock shot up from 85 points to 420; Chrysler stock more than doubled, from 63 to 132.

Yet only about 4 million Americans owned any stocks at all, out of a total population of 120 million. Many of these stock buyers had been lured into the market through easy-credit, margin accounts. Margin accounts allowed investors to purchase stocks by making a small down payment (as low as 10 percent), borrowing the rest from a broker, and using the shares as collateral, or security, on the loan. Just as installment plans had stimulated the automobile and other industries, "buying on the margin" brought new customers to the stock market. Investment trusts, similar to today's mutual funds, attracted many new investors with promises of high returns based on their managers' expert knowledge of the market. Corporations with excess capital found that lending money to stockbrokers was more profitable than plowing it back into their own plants to develop new technologies. All these new approaches to buying stock contributed to an expansive and optimistic atmosphere on Wall Street.

The Crash

Although often portrayed as a one- or two-day catastrophe, the Wall Street crash of 1929 was in reality a steep downward slide. The bull market peaked in early September, and prices drifted downward. On October 23 the Dow Jones industrials lost 21 points in one hour, and many large investors concluded the boom was over. The boom itself rested on expectations of continually rising prices; once those expectations began to melt, the market had to decline. On Monday, October 28, the Dow lost 38 points, or 13 percent of its value. On October 29, "Black Tuesday," the bottom seemed to fall out. Over 16 million shares, more than double the previous record, were traded as panic selling took hold. For many, stocks no buyers were available at any price.

The situation worsened. The market's fragile foundation of credit, based on the margin debt, quickly crumbled. Many investors with margin accounts had no choice but to sell when stock values fell. Since the shares themselves represented the security for their

Stockbrokers, their customers, and employees of the New York Stock Exchange gather nervously on Wall Street during the stock market crash of 1929. October 29 was the worst single day in the 112-year history of the exchange, as panic selling caused many stocks to lose half their value.

loans, more money had to be put up to cover the loans when prices declined. By mid-November about $30 billion in the market price of stocks had been wiped out. Half the value of the stocks listed in the *New York Times* index was lost in ten weeks.

The nation's political and economic leaders downplayed the impact of Wall Street's woes. "The fundamental business of the country," President Herbert Hoover told Americans in late October, "is on a sound and prosperous basis." Secretary of the Treasury Andrew Mellon spoke for many in the financial world when he described the benefits of the slump: "It will purge the rottenness out of the system. High costs of living and high living will come down. People will work harder, live a more moral life. Values will be adjusted, and enterprising people will pick up the wrecks from less competent people." At the end of

1929 hardly anyone was predicting that a depression would follow the stock market crash.

Underlying Weaknesses

It would be oversimple to say that the stock market crash "caused" the Great Depression. But like a person who catches a chill, the economy after the crash became less resistant to existing sources of infection. The resulting sickness revealed underlying economic weaknesses left over from the previous decade. First, workers and consumers by and large received too small a share of the enormous increases in labor productivity. Better machinery and more efficient industrial organization had increased labor productivity enormously. But wages and salaries had not risen nearly as much.

In effect, the automobile of American capitalism had one foot pressed to the accelerator of produc-

DISTRIBUTION OF TOTAL FAMILY INCOME AMONG VARIOUS SEGMENTS OF THE POPULATION, 1929–1944 (IN PERCENTAGES)

Year	Poorest Fifth	Second Poorest Fifth	Middle Fifth	Second Wealthiest Fifth	Wealthiest Fifth	Wealthiest 5 Percent
1929		12.5	13.8	19.3	54.4	30.0
1935–1936	4.1	9.2	14.1	20.9	51.7	26.5
1941	4.1	9.5	15.3	22.3	48.8	24.0
1944	4.9	10.9	16.2	22.2	45.8	20.7

Source: Adapted from U.S. Bureau of the Census, *Historical Statistics of the United States, Colonial Times to 1970,* Bicentennial Edition (Washington, D.C.: U.S. Government Printing Office, 1975), p. 301.

tion and another on the brake of consumption. Between 1923 and 1929 manufacturing output per worker-hour increased by 32 percent. But wages during the same period rose only 8 percent, or one-quarter the rise in productivity. Moreover, the rise in productivity itself had encouraged overproduction in many industries. The farm sector had never been able to regain its prosperity of the World War I years. Farmers suffered under a triple burden of declining prices for their crops, a drop in exports, and large debts incurred by wartime expansion (see Chapter 23).

The most important weakness in the economy was the extremely unequal distribution of income and wealth. In 1929, the top 0.1 percent of American families (24,000 families) had an aggregate income equal to that of the bottom 42 percent (11.5 million families). The top 5 percent of American families received 30 percent of the nation's income; the bottom 60 percent got only 26 percent. About 71 percent of American families had annual incomes below $2,500. Nearly 80 percent of the nation's families (21.5 million households) had no savings; the top 0.1 percent held 34 percent of all savings. The top 0.5 percent of Americans owned 32.4 percent of the net wealth of the entire population—the greatest such concentration of wealth in the nation's history.

The stock market crash undermined the confidence, investment, and spending of businesses and the well-to-do. Manufacturers decreased their production and began laying off workers, and layoffs brought further declines in consumer spending and another round of production cutbacks. A spurt of consumer spending might have checked this downward spiral, but consumers had less to spend as industries laid off workers and reduced work hours. With a shrinking market for products, businesses were hesitant to expand. A large proportion of the nation's banking funds were tied to the speculative bubble of Wall Street stock buying. Many banks began to fail

as anxious depositors withdrew their funds, which were uninsured. Thousands of families lost their savings to these failures. An 86 percent plunge in agricultural prices between 1929 and 1933, compared to a decline in agricultural production of only 6 percent, brought suffering to America's farmers.

Mass Unemployment

At a time when unemployment insurance did not exist and public relief was completely inadequate, the loss of a job could mean economic catastrophe for workers

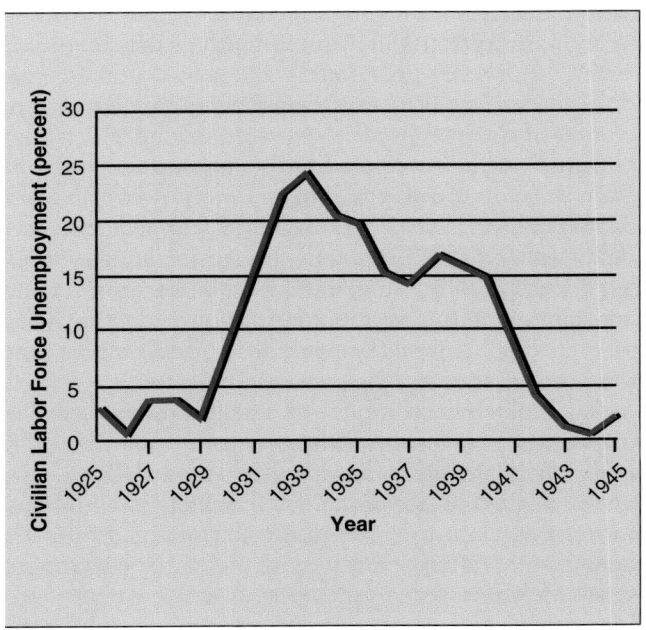

Unemployment, 1929–1945   In 1939, *despite six years of New Deal programs, unemployment still hovered around 18 percent of the workforce. Only the onset of World War II ended the unemployment crisis.*

Source: U.S. Bureau of the Census, *Historical Statistics of the United States, Colonial Times to 1970,* Bicentennial Edition (Washington, D.C.: U.S. Government Printing Office, 1975), p. 135.

and their families. Massive unemployment across America became the most powerful sign of a deepening depression. In 1930 the Department of Labor estimated that 4.2 million workers, or roughly 9 percent of the labor force, were out of work. These figures nearly doubled in 1931, and by 1933, 12.6 million workers—over one-quarter of the labor force—were without jobs. Other sources put the figure that year above 16 million, or nearly one out of every three workers. None of these statistics tells us how long people were unemployed or how many Americans found only part-time work.

What did it mean to be unemployed and without hope in the early 1930s? Figures give us only an outline of the grim reality. Many Americans, raised believing that they were responsible for their own fate, blamed themselves for their failure to find work. Contemporary journalists and social workers noted the common feelings of shame and guilt expressed by the unemployed. Even those who did not blame themselves struggled with feelings of inadequacy, uselessness, and despair. One unemployed Houston woman told a relief caseworker, "I'm just no good, I guess. I've given up ever amounting to anything. It's no use." "Drives a man crazy, or drives him to drink, hangin' around," said an out-of-work Connecticut knife maker. For many, nighttime was the worst. "What is going to become of us?" wondered an Arizona man. "I've lost twelve and a half pounds this month, just thinking. You can't sleep, you know. You wake up about 2 A.M., and you lie and think." A West Virginia man wrote his senator to complain, "My children have not got no shoes and clothing to go to school with, and we haven't got enough bed clothes to keep us warm." For the most desperate, contemplating suicide was not unusual. "Can you be so kind as to advise me as to which would be the most human way to dispose of my self and family, as this is about the only thing that I see left to do," one despondent Pennsylvania man inquired of a state relief agency.

Joblessness proved especially difficult for men between the ages of thirty-five and fifty-five, the period in their lives when family responsibilities were heaviest. Nathan Ackerman, a psychiatrist who went to Pennsylvania to observe the impact of prolonged unemployment on coal miners, found an enormous sense of "internal distress":

> They hung around street corners and in groups. They gave each other solace. They were loath to go home because they were indicted, as if it were their fault for being unemployed. A jobless man was a lazy good-for-nothing. The women punished the men for not bringing home the

Dorothea Lange captured the lonely despair of unemployment in White Angel Bread Line, San Francisco, 1933. *During the 1920s Lange had specialized in taking portraits of wealthy families, but by 1932 she could no longer stand the contradiction between her portrait business and "what was going on in the street." She said of this photograph: "There are moments such as these when time stands still and all you can do is hold your breath and hope it will wait for you."*

bacon, by withholding themselves sexually. . . . These men suffered from depression. They felt despised, they were ashamed of themselves. They cringed, they comforted one another. They avoided home.

Unemployment upset the psychological balance in many families by undermining the traditional authority of the male breadwinner. Women, because their labor was cheaper than men's, found it easier to hold onto jobs. Female clerks, secretaries, maids, and waitresses earned much less than male factory workers, but their jobs were more likely to survive hard times. Men responded in a variety of ways to unemployment. Some withdrew emotionally; others became angry or took to drinking. A few committed suicide. One Chicago social worker, writing about unemployment in 1934, summed up the strains she found in families: "Fathers feel they have lost their prestige in the home; there is much nagging, mothers nag at the fathers, parents nag at the children. Children of working age who earn meager salaries find it hard to turn over all their earnings and deny themselves even the greatest necessities and as a result leave home."

Pressures on those lucky enough to have a job increased as well. Anna Novak, a Chicago meat packer, recalled the degrading harassment at the hands of foremen: "You could get along swell if you let the boss slap you on the behind and feel you up. God, I hate that stuff, you don't know!" Fear of unemployment and a deep desire for security marked the depression generation. "I mean there's a conditioning here by the Depression," a sanitation worker told an interviewer many years later. "I'm what I call a security cat. I don't dare switch [jobs]. 'Cause I got too much whiskers on it, seniority."

Hoover's Failure

The enormity of the Great Depression overwhelmed traditional—and meager—sources of relief. In most communities across America these sources were a patchwork of private agencies and local government units, such as towns, cities, or counties. They simply lacked the money, resources, and staff to deal with the worsening situation. In large urban centers like Detroit and Chicago, unemployment approached 50 percent by 1932. Smaller communities could not cope either. One West Virginia coal-mining county with 1,500 unemployed miners had only $9,000 to meet relief needs for that year. Unemployed transients, attracted by warm weather, posed a special problem for communities in California and Florida. By the end of 1931 Los Angeles had 70,000 nonresident jobless and homeless men; new arrivals numbered about 1,200 a day.

There was great irony, even tragedy, in President Hoover's failure to respond to human suffering. He had administered large-scale humanitarian efforts during World War I with great efficiency. Yet he seemed to most people a man with little personal warmth. Hoover made his reputation as an engineer and as one who believed in the importance of objective studies of social and economic problems, yet he failed to face the facts of the depression. He ignored

Isaac Soyer's Employment Agency, *a 1937 oil painting, offered one of the decade's most sensitive efforts at depicting the anxiety and sense of isolation felt by millions of depression-era job hunters.*

Isaac Soyer, Employment Agency, 1937. Oil on canvas 34¼ x 45 inches, (87 x 114.3). Whitney Museum of Art, New York.

all the mounting evidence to the contrary when he claimed in his 1931 State of the Union Address, "Our people are providing against distress from unemployment in true American fashion by magnificent response to public appeal and by action of the local governments."

Hoover resisted the growing calls from Congress and local communities for a greater federal role in relief efforts or public works projects. He worried, as he told Congress after vetoing one measure, about injuring "the initiative and enterprise of the American people." The President's Emergency Committee for Unemployment, established in 1930, and its successor, the President's Organization for Unemployment Relief (POUR), created in 1931, did little more than encourage local groups to raise money to help the unemployed. Walter S. Gifford, chairman of POUR and president of AT&T, insisted that local relief groups could handle the needs of Americans in distress. "My sober and considered judgement," he told Congress in early 1932, "is that at this stage Federal aid would be a disservice to the unemployed."

Hoover's plan for recovery centered on restoring business confidence. His administration's most important institutional response to the depression was the Reconstruction Finance Corporation (RFC), established in early 1932 and based on the War Finance Corporation of the World War I years. The RFC was designed to make government credit available to ailing banks, railroads, insurance companies, and other businesses, thereby stimulating economic activity. The key assumption here was that the credit problem was one of supply (for businesses) rather than demand (from consumers). But given the public's low purchasing power, most businesses were not interested in obtaining loans for expansion.

The RFC managed to save numerous banks and other businesses from going under, but its approach did not hasten recovery. And Hoover was loath to use the RFC to make direct grants to states, cities, or individuals. In July 1932, congressional Democrats pushed through the Emergency Relief Act, which authorized the RFC to lend $300 million to states that had exhausted their own relief funds. Hoover grudgingly signed the bill, but less than $30 million had actually been given out by the end of 1933. Although Congress authorized the RFC to spend money on public works, only a small fraction of its $2 billion budget went to such programs.

Protest and the Election of 1932

By 1932, the desperate mood of many Americans was finding expression in direct, sometimes violent protests that were widely covered in the press. On March 7, communist organizers led a march of several thousand Detroit auto workers and unemployed to the Ford River Rouge factory in nearby Dearborn. When the demonstrators refused orders to turn back, Ford-controlled police fired tear gas and bullets, killing four and seriously wounding fifty others. Some 40,000 people attended a tense funeral service a few days later. Desperate farmers in Iowa organized the Farmers' Holiday Association, aimed at raising prices by refusing to sell produce. In August, some 1,500 farmers turned back cargo trucks outside Sioux City, Iowa, and made a point by dumping milk and other perishables into ditches.

The spring of 1932 also saw the "Bonus Army" begin descending on Washington, D.C. This protest took its name from a 1924 act of Congress that had promised a $1,000 bonus—in the form of a bond that would not mature until 1945—to every veteran of World War I. The veterans who were gathering in Washington demanded immediate payment of the bonus in cash. By summer they and their families numbered around 20,000 and were camped out all over the capital city. Their lobbying convinced the House to pass a bill for immediate payment, but the Senate rejected the bill and most of the veterans left. At the end of July U.S. Army troops led by Chief of Staff General Douglas MacArthur forcibly evicted the remaining 2,000 veterans from their encampment. MacArthur exaggerated the menace of the peaceful demonstrators, insisting they were driven by "the essence of revolution." The spec-

tacle of these unarmed and unemployed men, the heroes of 1918, driven off by bayonets and bullets provided the most disturbing evidence yet of the failure of Hoover's administration.

The congressional elections of 1930 had already revealed a growing dissatisfaction with Hoover's approach. Democrats had won control of the House of Representatives for the first time since 1916 and gained eight seats in the Senate. In 1932, Democrats nominated Franklin D. Roosevelt, governor of New York, as their candidate. Roosevelt's acceptance speech stressed the need for reconstructing the nation's economy. "I pledge you, I pledge myself," he said, "to a new deal for the American people."

Roosevelt's plans for recovery were vague at best. He frequently attacked Hoover for reckless and extravagant spending and accused him of trying to center too much power in Washington. He also spoke of the need for government to meet "the problem of underconsumption" and to help in "distributing wealth and products more equitably." Hoover bitterly condemned Roosevelt's ideas as a "radical departure" from the American way of life. But with the depression growing worse every day, probably any Democrat would have defeated Hoover. The Democratic victory was overwhelming. Roosevelt carried forty-two states, taking the electoral college 472 to 59 and the popular vote by about 23 million to 16 million. Democrats won big majorities in both the House and the Senate. The stage was set for FDR's "new deal."

FDR AND THE FIRST NEW DEAL

No president of this century had a greater impact on American life and politics than Franklin Delano Roosevelt. To a large degree, the New Deal was a product of his astute political skills and the sheer force of his personality. The only president ever elected to four terms, FDR would loom as the dominant personality in American political life through depression and war. Roosevelt's leadership also inaugurated a forty-year-long period during which the Democrats would be the nation's majority party.

FDR the Man

Franklin Delano Roosevelt was born in 1882 in Dutchess County, New York, where he grew up an only child, secure and confident, on his family's vast estate. Franklin's father, James, had made a fortune through railroad investments, but he was already in his fifties when Franklin was born, and it was his mother, Sara Delano, who was the dominant figure in his childhood. Roosevelt's education at Groton, Harvard, and Columbia Law School reinforced the aristocratic values of his family: a strong sense of civic duty, the impor-

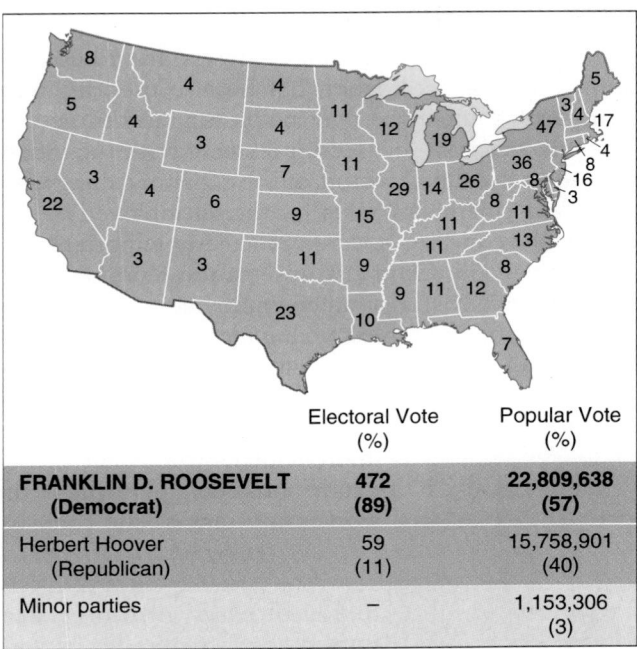

	Electoral Vote (%)	Popular Vote (%)
FRANKLIN D. ROOSEVELT (Democrat)	**472 (89)**	**22,809,638 (57)**
Herbert Hoover (Republican)	59 (11)	15,758,901 (40)
Minor parties	–	1,153,306 (3)

The Election of 1932   *Democrats owed their overwhelming victory in 1932 to the popular identification of the depression with the Hoover administration. Roosevelt's popular vote was about the same as Hoover's in 1928, and FDR's electoral college margin was even greater.*

tance of competitive athletics, and a commitment to public service.

In 1905 Franklin married his distant cousin, Anna Eleanor Roosevelt, niece of President Theodore Roosevelt. Eleanor would later emerge as an influential adviser and political force on her own. Franklin turned to politics as a career early on. He was elected as a Democrat to the New York State Senate in 1910, served as assistant navy secretary from 1913 to 1920, and was nominated for vice president by the Democrats in the losing 1920 campaign.

In the summer of 1921 Roosevelt was stricken with polio at his summer home. He was never to walk again without support. The disease strengthened his relationship with Eleanor, who encouraged him not only to fight his handicap but to continue his political career. The disease and FDR's response to it proved a turning point. His patience and determination in fighting the illness transformed him. The wealthy aristocrat, for whom everything had come relatively easy, now personally understood the meaning of struggle and hardship. "Once I spent two years lying in bed trying to move my big toe," he recalled. "After that anything else seems easy."

Elected governor of New York in 1928, Roosevelt served two terms and won a national reputation for reform. As governor, his achievements included instituting unemployment insurance, strength-

ening child labor laws, providing tax relief for farmers, and providing pensions for the old. As the depression hit the state, he slowly increased public works and set up a Temporary Emergency Relief Administration. With his eye on the White House, he began assembling a group of key advisers, the "brains trust," who would follow him to Washington. The central figures were Columbia Law School professor and progressive Raymond Moley; two economists, Rexford G. Tugwell and Adolf A. Berle; and attorneys Samuel Rosenman, Basil O'Connor, and Felix Frankfurter. The "brain trusters" shared a faith in the power of experts to set the economy right and a basic belief in government-business cooperation. They rejected the old progressive dream of re-creating an ideal society of small producers. Structural economic reform, they argued, must accept the modern reality of large corporate enterprise based on mass-production and distribution.

Restoring Confidence

In the first days of his administration Roosevelt conveyed a sense of optimism and activism that helped restore the badly shaken confidence of the nation. "First of all," he told Americans in his Inaugural Address on March 4, 1933, "let me assert my firm belief that the only thing we have to fear is fear itself." The very next day he issued an executive order calling for a four-day "bank holiday" to shore up the country's ailing financial system. More than 1,300 banks failed in 1930, more than 2,000 in 1931. Contemporary investigations had revealed a disquieting pattern of stock manipulation, illegal loans to bank officials, and tax evasion that helped erode public confidence in the banking system. Between election day and the inauguration, the banking system had come alarmingly close to shutting down altogether due to widespread bank failures and the hoarding of currency.

Roosevelt therefore called for a special session of Congress to deal with the banking crisis as well as with unemployment aid and farm relief. On March 12 he broadcast his first "fireside chat" to explain the steps he had taken to meet the financial emergency. These radio broadcasts became a standard part of Roosevelt's political technique, and they proved enormously successful. They gave courage to ordinary Americans and communicated a genuine sense of compassion from the White House.

Congress immediately passed the Emergency Banking Act, which gave the president broad discretionary powers over all banking transactions and foreign exchange. It authorized healthy banks to reopen only under licenses from the Treasury Department and provided for greater federal authority in managing the affairs of failed banks. By the middle of March about half the country's banks, holding about

90 percent of the nation's deposits, were open for business again. Banks began to attract new deposits from people who had been holding back their money. The bank crisis had passed.

The Hundred Days

From March to June of 1933—"the Hundred Days"—FDR pushed through Congress an extraordinary number of acts designed to combat various aspects of the depression. What came to be called the New Deal was no unified program to end the depression but rather an improvised series of reform and relief measures, some

This 1933 Vanity Fair *cartoon depicting the inauguration of Franklin D. Roosevelt captures the contrasting moods of the ebullient, victorious FDR and the glum, defeated Herbert Hoover.*

of which seemed to contradict each other. Roosevelt responded to pressures from Congress, from business, and from organized labor, but he also used his own considerable influence over public opinion to get his way. His program focused on reviving both the industrial and agricultural sectors of the economy along with providing emergency relief for the unemployed.

Five measures were particularly important and innovative. The Civilian Conservation Corps (CCC), established in March as an unemployment relief effort, provided work for jobless young men in protecting and conserving the nation's natural resources. Road construction, reforestation, flood control, and national park improvements were some of the major projects performed in work camps across the country. CCC workers received room and board and $30 each month, up to $25 of which had to be sent home to dependents. By the time the program was phased out in 1942, more than 2.5 million youths had worked in some 1,500 CCC camps.

In May, Congress authorized $500 million for the Federal Emergency Relief Administration (FERA). Half the money went as direct relief to the states; the rest was distributed on the basis of a dollar of federal aid for every three dollars of state and local funds spent for relief. This system of outright federal grants differed significantly from Hoover's approach, which provided only for loans. Establishment of work relief projects, however, was left to state and local governments. To direct the FERA Roosevelt turned to Harry Hopkins, an experienced reformer from the world of New York social work. A brilliant administrator with a special commitment to ending racial discrimination in relief work, Hopkins became the New Deal's most influential figure in relief policies and one of Roosevelt's most trusted advisers.

The Agricultural Adjustment Administration (AAA) was set up to provide immediate

KEY LEGISLATION OF THE FIRST NEW DEAL ("HUNDRED DAYS," MARCH 9–JUNE 16, 1933)

Legislation	Purpose
Emergency Banking Relief Act	Enlarged federal authority over private banks Government loans to private banks
Civilian Conservation Corps	Unemployment relief Conservation of natural resources
Federal Emergency Relief Administration	Direct federal money for relief, funneled through state and local governments
Agricultural Adjustment Administration	Federal farm aid based on parity pricing and subsidy
Tennessee Valley Authority	Economic development and cheap electricity for Tennessee Valley
National Industrial Recovery Act	Self-regulating industrial codes to revive economic activity
Public Works Administration	Federal public works projects to increase employment and consumer spending

relief to the nation's farmers. The AAA established a new federal role in agricultural planning and price setting. It established parity prices for basic farm commodities, including corn, wheat, hogs, cotton, rice, and dairy products. The concept of parity pricing was based on the purchasing power that farmers had enjoyed during the prosperous years of 1909 to 1914. That period now became the benchmark for setting the prices of farm commodities. The AAA also incorporated the principle of subsidy, whereby farmers received benefit payments in return for reducing acreage or otherwise cutting production where surpluses existed. The funds for these payments were to be raised from new taxes on food processing.

The AAA raised total farm income and was especially successful in pushing up the prices of wheat, cotton, and corn. But it had some troubling side effects as well. Landlords often failed to share their AAA payments with tenant farmers, and they frequently used benefits to buy tractors and other equipment that displaced sharecroppers. Many Americans were disturbed, too, by the sight of surplus crops, livestock, and milk being destroyed while millions went hungry. The Southern Tenant Farmers Union (STFU), founded in 1934, emerged as an important voice of protest

against AAA policies. Active in six states and composed of about thirty thousand tenant farmers (over half of whom were black), the STFU protested evictions, called strikes to raise farm labor wages, and challenged landlords to give tenants their fair share of subsidy payments. The STFU succeeded in drawing national attention to the plight of sharecroppers and tenant farmers, but it failed to influence national farm policy. The 1937 Bankhead-Jones Tenancy Act offered a very limited program of loans to tenant farmers, and the AAA remained a boon to large landlords.

The Tennessee Valley Authority (TVA) proved to be one of the most unique and controversial projects of the New Deal era. It had its origins in the federal government's effort during World War I to build a large hydroelectric power complex and munitions plant on the Tennessee River at Muscle Shoals, Alabama. During the 1920s, Republican senator George W. Norris of Nebraska had led an unsuccessful fight to provide for permanent government operation of the Muscle Shoals facilities on behalf of the area's population. The TVA, an independent public corporation, built dams and power plants, produced cheap fertilizer for farmers, and, most significantly, brought cheap electricity for the first time to thousands of people in six southern states. Denounced by some as a dangerous step toward socialism, the TVA stood for decades as a model of how careful government planning could dramatically improve the social and economic welfare of an underdeveloped region.

On the very last of the Hundred Days, Congress passed the National Industrial Recovery Act, the closest attempt yet at a systematic plan for economic recovery. It had two main parts. The National Recovery Administration (NRA) sought to stimulate production and competition in business by means of industrial codes regulating prices, output, and trade practices. In theory, each industry would be self-governed by a code hammered out by representatives of business, labor, and the consuming public. Once approved by the NRA in Washington, led by General Hugh Johnson and symbolized by the distinctive Blue Eagle stamp, the codes would have the force of law. In practice, almost all the NRA codes were written by the largest firms in any given industry; labor and consumers got short shrift. The sheer administrative complexities involved with code writing and compliance made a great many people unhappy with the NRA's operation. Overall, the NRA looked to business and industry leaders to find a way to recovery.

The second component, the Public Works Administration (PWA), led by Secretary of the Interior Harold Ickes, authorized $3.3 billion for the construction of roads, public buildings, and other projects. The idea was to provide jobs and thus stimulate the economy through increased consumer spending. A favorite image for this kind of spending was "priming the pump." Just as a farmer had to prime a pump with water before it could draw more water from the well, the government had to prime the economy with jobs for the unemployed. Eventually the PWA spent over $4.2 billion building roads, schools, post offices, bridges, courthouses, and other public buildings around the country. In thousands of communities today, these structures remain the most tangible reminders of the New Deal era.

LEFT TURN AND THE SECOND NEW DEAL

The Hundred Days legislative package tried to offer something for everybody. Certainly the active, can-do spirit in Washington brought reassurance that the nation was back on track. Yet the depression remained a stark reality for many millions. From the beginning, the New Deal had loud and powerful critics who complained bitterly that FDR had overstepped the traditional boundaries of government action. Others were angry that Roosevelt had not done nearly enough. These varied voices of protest helped shape the political debates of FDR's first term. Ultimately, they would push the New Deal in more radical directions.

Roosevelt's Critics

Criticism of the New Deal came from the right and the left. On the right, pro-Republican newspapers and the American Liberty League, a group of conservative businessmen organized in 1934, denounced Roosevelt and his advisers. They held the administration responsible for what they considered an attack on property rights, the growing welfare state, and the decline of personal liberty. Dominated by wealthy executives of Du Pont and General Motors, the league attracted support from a group of conservative Democrats, including Al Smith, the former presidential candidate, who declared the New Deal's laws "socialistic." The league supported anti-New Dealers for Congress, but in the 1934 election Democrats built up their majorities from 310 to 319 in the House and from 60 to 69 in the Senate—an unusually strong showing for the incumbent party in a midterm election.

Some of Roosevelt's staunchest early supporters turned critical. Father Charles E. Coughlin, a Catholic priest in suburban Detroit, attracted a huge national radio audience of 40 million listeners with passionate sermons attacking Wall Street, international bankers, and "plutocratic capitalism." Coughlin at first supported Roosevelt and the New Deal, and he tried to build a close personal relationship with the president. But by 1934 the ambitious Coughlin, frustrated by his limited influence on the administration, began attacking FDR. Roosevelt was a tool of special interests, he charged, who wanted dictatorial powers. New Deal policies were part of a communist conspiracy, threatening community autonomy with centralized federal power. Coughlin finally broke with FDR and founded the National Union for Social Justice. In 1936 the Coughlin-dominated Union Party nominated William Lemke, an obscure North Dakota congressman, to run for president. Lemke polled only 900,000 votes, but Coughlin continued his biting attacks on Roosevelt through 1940.

More troublesome for Roosevelt and his allies were the vocal and popular movements on the left. These found the New Deal too timid in its measures. In California, well-known novelist and socialist Upton Sinclair entered the 1934 Democratic primary for governor by running on a program he called EPIC, for End Poverty in California. He proposed a $50 a month pension for all poor people over age sixty. His campaign also emphasized a government-run system of "production for use" (rather than profit) workshops for the unemployed. Sinclair shocked local and national Democrats by winning the primary easily. He lost a close general election only because the Republican candidate received heavy financial and tactical support from wealthy Hollywood studio executives and frightened regular Democrats.

of which had never been seen before. The dust storms were largely the consequence of years of stripping the landscape of its natural vegetation. During World War I, wheat fetched record-high prices on the world market, and for the next twenty years Great Plains farmers turned the region into a vast wheat factory.

The wide flatlands of the Great Plains were especially suited to mechanized farming, and gasoline-powered tractors, disc plows, and harvester-thresher combines increased productivity enormously. Back in 1830 it had taken some fifty-eight hours of labor to bring an acre of wheat to the granary; in much of the Great Plains a hundred years later it required less than three hours. As wheat prices fell in the 1920s, farmers broke still more land to make up the difference with increased production. Great Plains farmers had created an ecological time bomb that exploded when drought returned in the early 1930s. With native grasses destroyed for the sake of wheat growing, there was nothing left to prevent soil erosion. Dust storms blew away tens of millions of acres of rich topsoil, and thousands of farm families left the region. Those who stayed suffered deep economic and psychological losses from the calamity. The hardest-hit regions were western Kansas, eastern Colorado, western Oklahoma, the Texas Panhandle, and eastern New Mexico. It was the calamity in this southern part of the Plains that prompted a Denver journalist to coin the phrase "Dust Bowl."

Black blizzards of dust a mile and a half high rolled across the landscape, darkening the sky and whipping the earth into great drifts that settled over hundreds of miles. Dust storms made it difficult for humans and livestock to breathe and destroyed crops and trees over vast areas. Dust storms turned day into night, terrifying those caught in them. "Dust pneumonia" and other respiratory infections afflicted thousands, and many travelers found themselves stranded in automobiles and trains unable to move. The worst storms occurred in the early spring of 1935. A Garden City, Kansas, woman gave an account of her experience for the *Kansas City Times*:

> All we could do about it was just sit in our dusty chairs, gaze at each other through the fog that filled the room and watch that fog settle slowly and silently, covering everything—including ourselves—in a thick, brownish gray blanket. When we opened the door swirling whirlwinds of soil beat against us unmercifully. The door and windows were all shut tightly, yet those tiny particles seemed to seep through the very walls. It got into cupboards and clothes closets; our faces were as dirty as if we had rolled in the dirt; our hair was gray and stiff and we ground dirt between our teeth.

Several federal agencies intervened directly to relieve the distress. Many thousands of Great Plains farm families were given direct emergency relief by the Resettlement Administration. Other federal assistance included crop and seed loans, moratoriums on loan payments, and temporary jobs with the Works Progress Administration. In most Great Plains counties, from one-fifth to one-third of the families applied for relief; in the hardest-hit communities, as many as 90 percent of the families received direct government aid. The Agricultural Adjustment Administration paid wheat farmers millions of dollars not to grow what they could not sell and encouraged the diversion of acreage from soil-depleting crops like wheat to soil-enriching crops such as sorghum.

To reduce the pressure from grazing cattle on the remaining grasslands, the Drought Relief Service of the Department of Agriculture purchased more than 8 million head of cattle in 1934 and 1935. For a brief time, the federal government was the largest cattle owner in the world. This agency also lent ranchers money to feed their remaining cattle. The Taylor Grazing Act of 1934 brought stock grazing on 8 million acres of public domain lands under federal management.

The federal government also pursued longer-range policies designed to alter land-use patterns, reverse soil erosion, and nourish the return of grass-

The Dust Bowl, 1935–1940   *This map shows the extent of the Dust Bowl in the southern Great Plains. Federal programs designed to improve soil conservation, water management, and farming practices could not prevent a mass exodus of hundreds of thousands out of the Great Plains.*

YEARS OF DUST

RESETTLEMENT ADMINISTRATION
Rescues Victims
Restores Land to Proper Use

Years of Dust. This 1936 poster by the artist and photographer Ben Shahn served to publicize the work of the Resettlement Administration, which offered aid to destitute farm families hit hard by the Dust Bowl. Shahn's stark imagery here was typical of the documentary aesthetic associated with Depression-era art and photography.

lands. The Department of Agriculture, under Secretary Henry A. Wallace, sought to change farming practices. The spearhead for this effort was the Soil Conservation Service (SCS), which conducted research into controlling wind and water erosion, set up demonstration projects, and offered technical assistance, supplies, and equipment to farmers engaged in conservation work on farms and ranches. The SCS pumped additional federal funds into the Great Plains and created a new rural organization, the soil conservation district, which administered conservation regulations locally.

By 1940 the acreage subject to blowing in the Dust Bowl area of the southern plains had been reduced from roughly 50 million acres to less than 4 million acres. In the face of the Dust Bowl disaster, New Deal farm policies had restricted market forces

in agriculture. But the return of regular rainfall and the outbreak of World War II led many farmers to abandon the techniques that the SCS had taught them to accept. Wheat farming expanded and farms grew as farmers once again pursued commercial agriculture with little concern for its long-term effects on the land.

While large landowners and ranchers reaped sizable benefits from AAA subsidies and other New Deal programs in the southern plains, tenant farmers and sharecroppers received very little. In the cotton lands of Texas, Oklahoma, Missouri, and Arkansas, thousands of tenant and sharecropper families were forced off the land. They became part of a stream of roughly 300,000 people, disparagingly called "Okies," who migrated to California in the 1930s. California migrants included victims of the Dust Bowl, but the majority were blue-collar workers and small businessmen looking to improve their economic lot. California suffered from the depression along with the rest of the nation, but it still offered more jobs, higher wages, and higher relief payments than the states of the southern plains. Most Okies could find work only as poorly paid agricultural laborers in the fertile San Joaquin and Imperial Valley districts. There they faced discrimination and scorn as "poor white trash" while they struggled to create communities amid the squalor of migrant labor camps. Only with the outbreak of World War II and the pressing demand for labor were migrants able to significantly improve their situation.

Mexican farm laborers faced stiff competition from Dust Bowl refugees. By the mid-1930s they no longer dominated California's agricultural workforce. In 1936 an estimated 85 to 90 percent of the state's migratory workers were white Americans, as compared to less than 20 percent before the depression. Mexican farm worker families who managed to stay employed in California, Texas, and Colorado saw their wages plummet.

Southwestern communities, responding to racial hostility from unemployed whites and looking for ways to reduce their welfare burden, campaigned to deport Mexicans and Mexican Americans. Employers, private charities, and the Immigration and Naturalization Service joined in this effort. Authorities made little effort to distinguish citizens from aliens; most of the children they deported had been born in the United States and were citizens. Los Angeles County had the most aggressive campaign, using boxcars to ship out more than 13,000 Mexicans between 1931 and 1934. The hostile climate convinced thousands more to leave voluntarily. Approximately one-third of Los Angeles's 150,000 Mexican and Mexican American residents left the city in the early 1930s. Overall, nearly one-half million left the United States during the decade. Some

Mexican deportees crossed the border with a melancholy song on their lips:

> And so I take my leave,
> may you be happy.
> Here the song ends,
> but the depression goes on forever.

Water Policy

The New Deal ushered in the era of large-scale water projects designed to provide irrigation and cheap power and to prevent floods. The long-range impact of these undertakings on western life was enormous. The key government agency in this realm was the Bureau of Reclamation of the Department of the Interior, established under the National Reclamation Act of 1902. The bureau's original responsibility had been to construct dams and irrigation works and thereby encourage the growth of small farms throughout the arid regions of the West. Until the late 1920s the bureau's efforts had been of little consequence, providing irrigation for only a very small portion of land. But its fortunes changed when its focus shifted to building huge multipurpose dams designed to control entire river systems.

The first of these projects was the Boulder Dam (later renamed the Hoover Dam). The dam, actually begun during the Hoover administration, was designed to harness the Colorado River, wildest and most isolated of the major western rivers. Its planned benefits included flood prevention, the irrigation of California's Imperial Valley, the supplying of domestic water for southern California, and the generation of cheap electricity for Los Angeles and southern Arizona. Hoover, however, had opposed the public power aspect of the project, arguing that the government ought not to compete with private utility companies. This position was contrary to that of most Westerners, who believed cheap public power was critical for development. Roosevelt's support for government-sponsored power projects was a significant factor in his winning the political backing of the West in 1932 and subsequent election years.

Boulder Dam was completed in 1935 with the help of funds from the Public Works Administration. Its total cost was $114 million, which was to be offset by the sale of the hydroelectric power it generated. Los Angeles and neighboring cities built a 259-mile aqueduct, costing $220 million, to channel water to their growing populations. Lake Mead, created by construction of the dam, became the world's largest artificial lake, extending 115 miles up the canyon and providing a popular new recreation area. The dam's irrigation water helped make the Imperial Valley, covering over 500,000 acres, one of the most productive agricultural districts in the world.

The success of Boulder Dam transformed the Bureau of Reclamation into a major federal agency with huge resources at its disposal. In 1938 it completed the All-American Canal—an 80-mile channel connecting the Colorado River to the Imperial Valley, with a 130-mile branch to the Coachella Valley. The canal cost $24 million to build and carried a flow of water equal to that of the Potomac River. More than a million acres of desert land were opened up to the cultivation of citrus fruits, melons, vegetables, and cotton. Irrigation districts receiving water promised to repay, without interest, the cost of the canal over a forty-year period. This interest-free loan was in effect a huge government subsidy to the private growers who benefited from the canal.

In 1935 the bureau began the giant Central Valley Project (CVP). The Central Valley, stretching through the California interior, is a 500-mile oblong watershed with an average width of 125 miles. The idea was to bring water from the Sacramento River in the North down to the arid lands of the larger San Joaquin Valley in the South. Completed in 1947, the project eventually cost $2.3 billion. The CVP stored water and transferred it to the drier southern regions of the state. It also provided electricity, flood control, and municipal water. The federal government, local municipalities, and buyers of electric power paid most of the cost, and the project proved a boon to large-scale farmers in the Sacramento and San Joaquin River Valleys.

The largest power and irrigation project of all was the Grand Coulee Dam, northwest of Spokane, Washington. Completed in 1941, it was designed to convert the power of the Columbia River into cheap electricity and to irrigate previously uncultivated land, thereby stimulating the economic development of the Pacific Northwest. The construction of Grand Coulee employed tens of thousands of workers and pumped millions of dollars into the region's badly depressed economy. Between 1933 and 1940 Washington State ranked first in per capita federal expenditures. In the longer run, Grand Coulee provided the cheapest electricity in the United States and helped attract new manufacturing to a region previously dependent on the export of raw materials, such as lumber and metals.

These technological marvels and the new economic development they stimulated were not without an environmental and human cost. The Grand Coulee and smaller dams nearby reduced the Columbia River, long a potent symbol of the western wilderness, to a string of lakes. Spawning salmon could no longer run the river above the dam. In California, the federal guarantee of river water made a relative handful of large farmers fabulously wealthy. But tens of thousands of farm workers, mostly of Mexican descent, labored in the newly fertile fields for very low wages, and their health suffered from contact with pesticides.

The New Deal and Water   *This map illustrates U. S. drainage areas and the major large-scale water projects begun or completed by federal agencies in them during the New Deal. By providing irrigation, cheap power, flood control, and recreation areas, these public works had a historically unprecedented impact on America's western communities.*

The Colorado River, no longer emptying into the Pacific, began to build up salt deposits, making its water increasingly unfit for drinking or irrigation. Water pollution in the form of high salinity continues to plague the 2,000 mile river to this day.

A New Deal for Indians

The New Deal brought important changes and some limited improvements to the lives of Indians. In 1933 some 320,000 Indian people, belonging to about 200 tribes, lived on reservations. Most were in Oklahoma, Arizona, New Mexico, and South Dakota. Indian people suffered from the worst poverty of any group in the nation and an infant mortality rate twice that of the white population. The incidence of alcoholism and other diseases such as tuberculosis and measles was much higher on the reservation than off. Half of all those on reservations were landless, forced to rent or live with relatives. The Bureau of Indian Affairs (BIA), oldest of the federal bureaucracies in the West, had a long history of corruption and mismanagement. The

BIA had for years tried to assimilate Indians through education and had routinely interfered with Indian religious affairs and tribal customs. In 1928 the Merriam Report, prepared by the Institute for Government Research, had offered a scathing and widely publicized critique of BIA mismanagement. But the Hoover administration made no effort to reform the agency.

In 1933 President Roosevelt appointed John Collier to bring change to the BIA. Collier had deep roots in progressive-era social work and community organizing in eastern big-city slums. During the 1920s he had become passionately interested in Indian affairs after spending time in Taos, New Mexico. He became involved with the struggle of the Pueblo Indians to hold onto their tribal lands, and he had served as executive secretary of the American Indian Defense Association. As the new BIA head, Collier pledged to "stop wronging the Indians and to rewrite the cruel and stupid laws that rob them and crush their family lives." Collier brought a reformer's zeal to his new job, and he quickly demonstrated his bureaucratic skills. He halted the sale of Indian lands, obtained emergency conservation work for 77,000 Indians under the CCC program, and secured millions of dollars in PWA funds to finance Indian day schools on the reservations. He also fired incompetent and corrupt BIA officials and insisted that those who remained respect tribal customs.

Most important, Collier became the driving force behind the Indian Reorganization Act (IRA) of 1934. The IRA reversed the allotment provisions of the Dawes Severalty Act of 1887, which had weakened tribal sovereignty by shifting the distribution of land from tribes to individuals (see Ch.18). The new legislation permitted the restoration of surplus reservation lands to tribal ownership and allocated funds for the purchase of additional lands and for economic development. At its heart, the IRA sought to restore tribal structures by making the tribes instruments of the federal government. Any tribe that ratified the IRA could then elect a tribal council that would enjoy federal recognition as the legal tribal government. In this way, Collier argued, tribes would be "surrounded by the protective guardianship of the federal government and clothed with the authority of the federal government." He fought first to get the legislation through a reluctant Congress, which, uneasy with reversing the long-standing policy of Indian assimilation, insisted on many changes to Collier's original plan.

The more difficult battle involved winning approval by Indian peoples. Collier's efforts to win acceptance of the IRA met with mixed results on the reservations. Linguistic barriers made it nearly impossible for some tribes to fully assess the plan. The Papagos of southern Arizona, for example, had no words for "budget" and "representative." Their language made no distinction among the terms "law," "rule," "charter," and "constitution," and they used the same word for "president," "reservation agent," "king," and "Indian commissioner." In all, 181 tribes organized governments under the IRA, while 77 tribes rejected it.

The Navajos, the nation's largest tribe with over 40,000 members, rejected the IRA, illustrating some of the contradictions embedded in federal policy. The Navajo refusal came as a protest against the BIA's forced reduction of their livestock, part of a soil conservation program. The government blamed Navajo sheep for the gullying and erosion that threatened to fill in Lake Mead and make Boulder Dam inoperable. But the hundreds of thousands of sheep in the Navajos' herds were central to their economy and society. They used sheep for barter, to pay religious leaders, and as their primary source of meat.

The Navajos believed the erosion stemmed not from overgrazing but from lack of sufficient water and inadequate acreage on the reservation. Howard Gorman, a Navajo political leader, angrily responded to Collier's last-minute personal appearance before the

tribal council: "This thing, the thing you said that will make us strong, what do you mean by it? We have been told that not once but many times this same thing, and all it is is a bunch of lies. . . . You're wasting your time coming here and talking to us." Facing loss of half their sheep, Navajos took their anger out on Collier, rejecting the reorganization plan.

Under Collier's tenure, the BIA became much more sensitive to Indian cultural and religious freedom. The number of Indian people employed by the BIA itself increased from a few hundred in 1933 to more than 4,600 in 1940. Collier trumpeted the principle of Indian political autonomy, a radical idea for the day. But in practice, both the BIA and Congress regularly interfered with reservation governments, especially in money matters. Collier often dictated economic programs for tribes, which Congress usually underfunded. For the long run, Collier's most important legacy was the reassertion of the status of Indian tribes as semisovereign nations. In 1934 a Department of the Interior lawyer, Nathan Margold, wrote a legal opinion that tribal governments retained all their original powers—their "internal sovereignty"—except when these were specifically limited by acts of Congress. In later years U.S. courts would uphold the Margold Opinion, leading to a significant restoration of tribal rights and land to Indian peoples of the West.

DEPRESSION-ERA CULTURE

American culture in the 1930s, like all other aspects of national life, was profoundly shaped by the Great Depression. The themes and images in various cultural forms frequently reflected depression-related problems. Yet contradictory messages coexisted, sometimes within the same novel or movie. With American capitalism facing its worst crisis, radical expressions of protest and revolution were more common than ever. But there were also strong celebrations of individualism, nostalgia for a simpler, rural past, and searches for core American virtues. The 1930s also saw important shifts in the organization and production of culture. For a brief but significant moment, the federal government offered substantial and unprecedented support to artists and writers. In the realm of popular culture, Hollywood movies, network radio broadcasting, and big-band jazz achieved a central place in the everyday lives of Americans.

A New Deal for the Arts

The depression hit America's writers, artists, and teachers just as hard as blue-collar workers. In 1935, the WPA allocated $300 million for the unemployed in these fields. Over the next four years, Federal Project No. 1, an umbrella agency covering writing, theater, music, and the visual arts, proved to be one of the most

NEW YORK PUBLIC LIBRARY

A *Works Progress Administration* (WPA) *poster from 1938. The primary goal of federal relief projects, WPA officials stressed, was to rebuild the individual worker's confidence and self-respect. Typically, this poster uses only male laborers in its illustrations, reflecting a gender bias common in New Deal relief efforts.*

innovative and successful New Deal programs. "Federal One," as it was called, offered work to desperate artists and intellectuals, enriched the cultural lives of millions, and left a substantial legacy of artistic and cultural production. Nearly all these works were informed by the spirit of the documentary impulse, a deep desire to record and communicate the experiences of ordinary Americans. Photographer Lewis Hine defined the documentary attitude simply and clearly: "I wanted to show the things that had to be corrected. I wanted to show the things that had to be appreciated."

At its height, the Federal Writers Project employed 5,000 writers on a variety of programs. Most notably, it produced a popular series of state and city guidebooks, each combining history, folklore, and tourism. The 150-volume "Life in America" series included valuable oral histories of former slaves, studies of ethnic and Indian cultures, and pioneering collections of American songs and folk tales. Work on the Writers Project helped many American writers to survive, hone their craft, and go on to great achievement and prominence. These included Ralph Ellison, Richard Wright, Margaret Walker, John Cheever, Saul Bellow, and Zora Neale Hurston. Novelist Anzia Yezierska recalled a strong spirit of camaraderie among the writers: "Each morning I walked to the Project as light hearted as if I

were going to a party." For poet Muriel Rukeyser, the FWP embodied an essential part of the era: "The key to the 30s was the joy to awake and see life entire and tell the stories of real people."

The Federal Theater Project (FTP), under the direction of the dynamic Hallie Flanagan of Vassar College, reached as many as 30 million Americans with its productions. The FTP sought to expand the audience for theater beyond the regular patrons of the commercial stage. Tickets for its productions were cheap, and it made variety of dramatic forms available. Among its most successful productions were the "Living Newspaper" plays based on contemporary controversies and current events. *Power* concerned the public ownership of utilities; *Triple A Plowed Under* dealt with farm problems; *Injunction Granted* documented unionizing struggles. Other FTP productions brought classics as well as new plays to communities. Among the most successful productions were T. S. Eliot's *Murder in the Cathedral*, Maxwell Anderson's *Valley Forge*, and Orson Welles's version of *Macbeth*, set in Haiti with an all-black cast.

The FTP often came under attack from congressional critics who found it too radical. But Flanagan defended her vision of a theater that confronted political issues. If the plays were mixed with politics, she wrote, "it was because life in our country was mixed with politics. These Arts projects were coming up, through, and out of the people." The FTP supported scores of community-based theatrical units around the country, giving work and experience to actors, playwrights, directors, and set designers. It brought vital and exciting theater to millions who had never attended before.

Two smaller but similar programs were the Federal Music Project (FMP) and the Federal Art Project (FAP). The FMP, under Nikolai Sokoloff of the Cleveland Symphony Orchestra, employed 15,000 musicians and financed hundreds of thousands of low-priced public concerts by touring orchestras. The Composers' Forum Laboratory supported new works by American composers such as Aaron Copland and William Schuman.

Among the painters who received government assistance through the FAP were Willem de Kooning, Jackson Pollock, and Louise Nevelson. The FAP also employed painters and sculptors to teach studio skills and art history in schools, churches, and settlement houses. The *Index of American Design* was a comprehensive compilation of American folk art from colonial times. The FAP also commissioned artists to paint hundreds of murals on the walls of post offices, meeting halls, courthouses, and other government buildings. Many of these, done in the style of the revolutionary Mexican muralists Diego Rivera and José Clemente Orozco, emphasized political and social themes. All these projects, declared Holger Cahill, director of the FAP, were aimed at "raising a generation sensitive to their visual environment and capable of helping to improve it."

The Documentary Impulse

"You can right a lot of wrongs with 'pitiless publicity,'" Franklin Roosevelt once declared. Social change, he argued, "is a difficult thing in our civilization unless you have sentiment." During the 1930s an enormous number of artists, novelists, journalists, photographers, and filmmakers tried to document the devastation wrought by the depression in American communities. They also depicted people's struggles to cope with and reverse hard times. Some of these efforts were consciously linked to promoting political action, often as part of a radical commitment to overthrowing capitalism. Others were interested less in fomenting social change than in recording vanishing ways of life. Mainstream mass media, such as the photo essays found in *Life* magazine or "March of Time" newsreels, also adapted this stance.

Regardless of political agendas or the medium employed, what one historian calls "the documentary impulse" became a prominent style in 1930s cultural expression. At its core, the documentary impulse directly influenced its audience's intellect and feelings through documentary "evidence" of social problems and human suffering. The most direct and influential expression of the documentary style was the photograph. In 1935 Roy Stryker, chief of the Historical Section of the Resettlement Administration (later part of the Farm Security Administration), gathered a remarkable group of photographers to help document the work of the agency. Stryker encouraged them to photograph whatever caught their interest, even if the pictures had no direct connection with RA projects. These photographers, including Dorothea Lange, Walker Evans, Arthur Rothstein, Russell Lee, Ben Shahn, and Marion Post Wolcott, left us the single most significant visual record of the Great Depression.

The photographers traveled through rural areas, small towns, and migrant labor camps, often not stopping even long enough to learn the names of their subjects. They produced powerful images of despair and resignation as well as hope and resilience. These photographs were reproduced in newspapers and magazines across America. Individual images could be interpreted in different ways, depending on context and captions. Stryker believed that the faces of the subjects were most memorable. "You could look at the people," he wrote, "and see fear and sadness and desperation. But you saw something else, too. A determination that not even the depression could kill. The photographers saw it—documented it."

That double vision, combining a frank portrayal of pain and suffering with a faith in the possibility of overcoming disaster, could be found in many other cultural works of the period. John Steinbeck's *Grapes of Wrath* (1939) sympathetically portrayed the hardships of Oklahoma Dust Bowl migrants on their way to California. "We ain't gonna die out," Ma Joad asserts near the end of the book. "People is goin' on—changing' a little, maybe, but goin' right on." A similar, if more personal, ending could be found in Margaret Mitchell's 1936 bestseller *Gone with the Wind*. Although this romantic novel was set in the Civil War–era South, many Americans identified with Scarlett O'Hara's determination to overcome the disaster of war and the loss of Rhett Butler. "With the spirit of her people who would not know defeat, even when it stared them in the face, she raised her chin. She could get Rhett back. She knew she could."

Many writers interrupted their work to travel around the country and discover the thoughts and feelings of ordinary people. "With real events looming larger than any imagined happenings," novelist Elizabeth Noble wrote, "documentary films and still photographs, reportage and the like have taken the place once held by the grand invention." Writers increasingly used documentary techniques to communicate the sense of upheaval around the nation. In *Puzzled America* (1935), Sherwood Anderson wrote of the psychological toll taken by unemployment. American men, especially, he wrote, were losing "that sense of being some part of the moving world of activity, so essential to an American man's sense of his manhood—the loss of this essential something in the joblessness can never be measured in dollars." Yet writers also found a remarkable absence of bitterness and a great deal of faith. James Rorty, in *Where Life Is Better* (1936), was actually encouraged by his cross-country trip. "I had rediscovered for myself a most beautiful land, and a most vital, creative, and spiritually unsubdued people."

Waiting for Lefty

For some, the capitalist system itself, with its enormous disparities of private wealth amid desperate poverty, was the culprit responsible for the Great Depression. Relatively few Americans became communists or socialists in the 1930s (at its height, the Communist

Sharecropper Family, *by Walker Evans, 1939. This photograph of the Bud and Ivy Woods family was first published in the 1941 book* Let Us Now Praise Famous Men, *with text by James Agee. Unlike some documentary photographers of the era, Evans's spare, direct pictures revealed his subjects to be not merely victims but strong and complex individuals as well. Largely ignored in the 1930s, Evans's work enjoyed a critical revival during the 1960s.*

Party of the United States had perhaps 100,000 members), and many of these remained active for only a brief time. Yet Marxist analysis, with its emphasis on class conflict and the failures of capitalism, had a wide influence on the era's thought and writing.

Some writers joined the Communist Party believing it to be the best hope for political revolution. They saw in the Soviet Union an alternative to an American system that appeared mired in exploitation, racial inequality, and human misery. Communist writers, like the novelist Michael Gold and the poet Meridel LeSueur, sought to radicalize art and literature, and they celebrated collective struggle over individual achievement. Gold's *Jews without Money* (1930) was one of the more successful attempts at a proletarian novel. It dramatized the sense of being locked into a system that could deliver only despair rather than prosperity. Granville Hicks, an editor of the communist magazine the *New Masses*, flatly declared: "If there is any other working interpretation of the apparent chaos than that which presents itself in terms of the class struggle, it has not been revealed."

A more common pattern for intellectuals, especially when they were young, was brief flirtation with communism. Many African American writers, attracted by the Communist Party's militant opposition to lynching, job discrimination, and segregation, briefly joined the party or found their first supportive audiences there. These included Richard Wright, Ralph Ellison, and Langston Hughes. Many playwrights and actors associated with New York's influential Group Theater were part of the Communist Party orbit in those years. One production of the group, Clifford Odets's *Waiting for Lefty* (1935), depicted a union organizing drive among taxi drivers. At the play's climax, the audience was invited to join the actors in shouting "Strike!" A commercial and political success, it offered perhaps the most celebrated example of radical, politically engaged art.

Left-wing influence reached its height after 1935 during the "Popular Front" period. Alarmed by the rise of fascism in Europe, communists around the world followed the Soviet line of uniting with liberals and all other antifascists. The American Communist Party adopted the slogan "Communism is Twentieth-Century Americanism." Communists became strong supporters of Roosevelt's New Deal, and their influence was especially strong within the various WPA arts projects. Some 3,200 Americans volunteered for the Communist Party–organized Abraham Lincoln Brigade, which fought in the Spanish civil war on the republican side against the fascists led by Francisco Franco. The Lincolns' sense of commitment and sacrifice appealed to millions of Americans sympathetic to the republican cause. Communists and other radicals, known for their dedication and effectiveness, also played a leading role in the difficult CIO unionizing drives in the auto, steel, and electrical industries. The successful sit-down strike at General Motors in Flint benefited from the organizing efforts of Communist Party activists who lent their expertise and helped keep the strikers and their families focused and supplied with food.

Hollywood in the 1930s

Commercial popular culture also boomed in the depression years. The coming of "talking pictures" toward the end of the 1920s helped make movies the most popular entertainment form of the day. More than 60 percent of Americans attended one of the nation's 20,000 movie houses each week. Through fan maga-

Reginald Marsh, Twenty Cent Movie, *1936. Marsh documented the urban landscape of the 1930s with great empathy, capturing the city's contradictory mix of commercialism, optimism, energy, and degradation. The popularity of Hollywood films and their stars reached new heights during the Great Depression.*

Reginald Marsh, *Twenty Cent Movie*, 1936. Egg tempera on composition board. 40 x 40 in. Whitney Museum of American Art, New York.

zines and gossip columns they followed the lives and careers of movie stars more avidly than ever. With so many movies being churned out by Hollywood studios for so many fans, it is difficult to generalize about the cultural impact of individual films. Moviegoing itself, usually enjoyed with friends, family, or a date, was perhaps the most significant development of all.

It is too easy to dismiss movies as mere escapism. The more interesting question is, What were people escaping to? Several film genres proved enormously popular during the 1930s. Gangster films did very well in the early depression years. *Little Caesar* (1930), starring Edward G. Robinson, and *Public Enemy* (1931), with James Cagney, set the standard. They all depicted violent criminals brought to justice by society—but along the way they gave audiences a vicarious exposure to the pleasures of wealth, power, and lawbreaking. Social disorder could also be treated comically, as in such Marx Brothers films as *Duck Soup* (1933) and *A Night at the Opera* (1935). Mae

West's popular comedies, such as *She Done Him Wrong* (1933) and *I'm No Angel* (1933), made people laugh by subverting expectations about sex roles. West was an independent woman, not afraid of pleasure. When Cary Grant asked her, "Haven't you ever met a man who could make you happy?" she replied, "Sure, lots of times."

Movie musicals offered audiences extravagant song-and-dance spectacles, as in Busby Berkeley's *Gold Diggers of 1933* and *42nd Street* (1933). "Screwball comedies" featured sophisticated, fast-paced humor and usually paired popular male and female stars: Clark Gable and Claudette Colbert in *It Happened One Night* (1934), Katharine Hepburn and Cary Grant in *Bringing Up Baby* (1938). A few movies, notably from the Warner Brothers studio, tried to offer a more "socially conscious" view of depression-era life. These included *I Am a Fugitive from a Chain Gang* (1932), *Wild Boys of the Road* (1933), and *Black Legion* (1936). By and large, however, Hollywood avoided confronting controversial social or political issues.

Some 1930s filmmakers expressed highly personal visions of core American values. Two who succeeded in capturing both popular and critical acclaim were Walt Disney and Frank Capra. By the mid-1930s, Disney's animated cartoons had become moral tales that stressed keeping order and following the rules. The Mickey Mouse cartoons and the full-length features, such as *Snow White and the Seven Dwarfs* (1937), pulled back from the fantastic stretching of time and space in earlier cartoons. Capra's comedies, such as *Mr. Deeds Goes to Town* (1936) and *You Can't Take It with You* (1938), idealized a small-town America with close families and comfortable homes. Although Capra's films dealt with contemporary problems more than most—unemployment, government corruption, economic monopoly—he made no critique of the social and economic system. Rather, he seemed to suggest that most of the country's ills could be solved if only its leaders learned the old-fashioned values of "common people"—kindness, loyalty, charity.

The Golden Age of Radio

Radio broadcasting emerged as the most powerful medium of communication in the home, profoundly changing the rhythms and routines of everyday life. In 1930 roughly 12 million American homes, 40 percent of the total, had a radio set. By the end of the decade radios could be found in 90 percent of the nation's homes. Advertisers dominated the structure and content of American radio, forming a powerful alliance with the two large networks, the National Broadcasting Company (NBC) and the Columbia Broadcasting System (CBS). The Federal Communications Commission, established in 1934, continued long-standing policies that favored commercial broadcasting over other arrangements, such as municipal or university programming. By 1937 NBC and CBS controlled about 90 percent of the wattage in the American broadcasting industry. Nearly all network shows were produced by advertising agencies.

The depression actually helped radio expand. An influx of talent arrived from the weakened worlds of vaudeville, ethnic theater, and the recording industry. The well-financed networks offered an attractive outlet to advertisers seeking a national audience. Radio programming achieved a regularity and professionalism absent in the 1920s, making it much easier for a listener to identify a show with its sponsor. Companies with national distribution paid thousands of dollars an hour to networks; by 1939 annual radio advertising revenues totaled $171 million.

Much of network radio was based on older cultural forms. The variety show, hosted by comedians and singers and based on the old vaudeville format, was the first important style. It featured stars like Eddie Cantor, Ed Wynn, Kate Smith, and Al Jolson, who constantly plugged the sponsor's product. The use of a studio audience re-created the human interaction so necessary in vaudeville. The popular comedy show *Amos 'n' Andy* adapted the minstrel "blackface" tradition to the new medium. White comedians Freeman Gosden and Charles Correll used only their two voices to invent a world of stereotyped African Americans for their millions of listeners.

The spectacular growth of the daytime serial, or soap opera, dominated radio drama. Aimed mainly at women working in the home, these serials alone constituted 60 percent of all daytime shows by 1940. Soaps such as *Ma Perkins, Helen Trent,* and *Clara Lou and Em* revolved around strong, warm female characters who provided advice and strength to weak, indecisive friends and relatives. Action counted very little; the development of character and relationships was all-important. Contemporary studies found that the average soap opera fan regularly tuned in to six or more different series. Evening radio dramas included thrillers such as *Inner Sanctum* and *The Shadow,* which emphasized crime and suspense. These shows made great use of music and sound effects to sharpen their impact.

In the later 1930s serious drama bloomed briefly, independent of commercial sponsorship, over CBS's Columbia Workshop. Archibald MacLeish's *Fall of the City,* a parable about fascism, and Orson Welles's *War of the Worlds,* a superrealistic adaptation of the H. G. Wells classic, proved the persuasive power of radio. Welles's show convinced many who tuned in that a Martian invasion was actually underway. Radio became a key factor in politics as well, as President Roosevelt showed early on with his popular fireside chats.

Finally, radio news arrived in the 1930s, showing the medium's potential for direct and immediate coverage of events. Network news and commentary shows multiplied rapidly over the decade. Complex political and economic issues and the impending European crisis fueled a news hunger among Americans. A 1939 survey found that 70 percent of Americans relied on the radio as their prime source of news. Yet commercial broadcasting, dominated by big sponsors and large radio manufacturers, failed to cover politically controversial events, such as labor struggles. The most powerful station in the country, WLW in Cincinnati, refused to even mention strikes on the air. NBC routinely canceled programs it feared might undermine "public confidence and faith."

The Swing Era

One measure of radio's cultural impact was its role in popularizing jazz. Before the 1930s, jazz was heard largely among African Americans and a small coterie of white fans and musicians. Regular broadcasts of live performances began to expose a broader public to the music. So did radio disc jockeys who played jazz records on their shows. Bands led by black artists such as Duke Ellington, Count Basie, and Benny Moten began to enjoy reputations outside of traditional jazz centers like Chicago, Kansas City, and New York.

Benny Goodman became the key figure in the "swing era," largely through radio exposure. Goodman, a white, classically trained clarinetist, had been inspired by African American bandleaders Fletcher Henderson and Don Redman. These men created arrangements for big bands that combined harmonic call-and-response patterns with breaks for improvised solos. Goodman purchased a series of arrangements from Henderson, smoothing out the sound but keeping the strong dance beat. His band's late-Saturday-night broadcasts began to attract attention.

The Benny Goodman band at the Meadowbrook Lounge, Cedar Grove, New Jersey, 1941. After his breakthrough into national prominence in 1935, Goodman became one of the first white bandleaders to hire and feature African American musicians. Although most in the audience were undoubtedly dancing to "the King of Swing," note the crowd of serious listeners gathered around the bandstand.

In 1935, at the Palomar Ballroom in Los Angeles, Goodman made the breakthrough that established his enormous popularity. When the band started playing the Henderson arrangements, the young crowd, primed by the radio broadcasts, roared its approval and began to dance wildly. Goodman's music was perfect for doing the jitterbug or lindy hop, dances borrowed from African American culture. As "the King of Swing," Goodman helped make big-band jazz a hit with millions of teenagers and young adults from all backgrounds. In the late 1930s, big-band music by the likes of Goodman, Basie, Jimmie Lunceford, and Artie Shaw accounted for the majority of million-selling records.

Despite the depression, the mass culture industry expanded enormously during the 1930s. Millions of Americans no doubt used mass culture as a temporary escape from their problems, but the various meanings they drew from movies, radio, and popular music were by no means monolithic. In most communities, Americans, especially young people, identified more closely than ever with the national communities forged by modern media. If mass culture offered little in the way of direct responses to the economic and social problems of the day, it nonetheless played a more integral role than ever in shaping the rhythms and desires of the nation's everyday life.

THE LIMITS OF REFORM

In his second Inaugural Address Roosevelt emphasized that much remained to be done to remedy the effects of the depression. Tens of millions of Americans were still denied the necessities for a decent life. "I see one third of a nation ill-housed, ill-clad, ill-nourished," the president said. With his stunning electoral victory, the future for further social reform seemed bright. Yet by 1937 the New Deal was in retreat. A rapid political turnaround over the next two years put continuing social reform efforts on the defensive.

Court Packing

FDR and his advisers were frustrated by several Supreme Court rulings declaring important New Deal legislation unconstitutional. In May 1935, in *Schecter v. United States*, the Court found the National Recovery Administration unconstitutional in its entirety. The grounds included excessive delegation of legislative power to the executive and the regulation of business that was intrastate, as opposed to national, in character. In early 1936, ruling in *Butler v. United States*, the Court invalidated the Agricultural Adjustment Administration, declaring it an unconstitutional attempt at regulating agriculture. The Court was composed mostly of Republican appointees, six of whom were over seventy. Roosevelt looked for a way to get more friendly judges on the high court.

In February 1937 FDR asked Congress for legislation that would expand the Supreme Court from nine to a maximum of fifteen justices. The president would be empowered to make a new appointment whenever an incumbent judge failed to retire upon reaching age seventy. Roosevelt argued that age prevented justices from keeping up with their workload, but few people believed this logic. Newspapers almost unanimously denounced FDR's "court-packing bill."

Even more damaging was the determined opposition from a coalition of conservatives and outraged New Dealers in the Congress, such as Democratic senator Burton K. Wheeler of Montana. The president gamely fought on, maintaining that his purpose was simply to restore the balance of power among the three branches of the federal government. As the battle dragged on through the spring and summer, FDR's claims weakened. Conservative justice Willis Van Devanter announced plans to retire, giving Roosevelt the chance to make his first Court appointment.

More important, the Court upheld the constitutionality of some key laws from the second New Deal, including the Social Security Act and the National Labor Relations Act. At the end of August, FDR backed off from his plan and accepted a compromise bill that reformed lower court procedures but left the Supreme Court untouched. FDR lost the battle for his judiciary proposal, but he may have won the war for a more responsive Court. Still, the political price was very high. The Court fight badly weakened Roosevelt's relations with Congress. Many more conservative Democrats now felt free to oppose further New Deal measures.

The Women's Network

The Great Depression and the New Deal brought some significant changes for women in American economics and politics. Most women continued to perform unpaid domestic labor within their homes, work that was not covered by the Social Security Act. A growing minority, however, also worked for wages and salaries outside the home. Women represented 24.3 percent of all workers in 1930; by 1940, 25.1 percent of the workforce was female. There was also an increase in married working women as a result of hard times. Between 1930 and 1940 the proportion of married women among the female workforce jumped from 28.8 percent to 35 percent. Jobs in which men predominated, such as construction and heavy industry, were hardest hit by the depression. In contrast, secretarial, sales, and other areas long associated with women's labor were less affected. But sexual stereotyping still routinely forced women into low-paying and low-status jobs.

The New Deal brought a measurable, if temporary, increase in women's political influence. For those women associated with social reform, the New Deal opened up possibilities to effect change. A "women's network," linked by personal friendships and professional connections, made its presence felt in national politics and government. Most of the women in this network had long been active in movements promoting suffrage, labor law reform, and welfare programs.

Eleanor Roosevelt became a powerful political figure in her own right, actively using her prominence as First Lady to fight for the liberal causes she believed in. She revolutionized the role of the political wife by taking a position involving no institutional duties and turning it into a base for independent action. Privately, she enjoyed great influence with her husband, and her support for a cause could give it instant credibility. She worked behind the scenes with a wide network of women professionals and reformers whom she had come to know in the 1920s. She was a strong supporter of protective labor legislation for women, and her overall outlook owed much to the social reform tradition of the women's movement. "When all is said and done," she wrote in *It's Up to the Women* (1933), "women are different from men. They are equal in many ways, but they cannot refuse to acknowledge their differences. . . . Their physical functions in life are different and perhaps in the same way the contributions which they are to bring to the spiritual side of life are different."

One of Eleanor Roosevelt's first public acts as First Lady was to convene a White House Conference on the Emergency Needs of Women, in November 1933. She helped Ellen Woodward, head of women's projects in the Federal Emergency Relief Administration, find jobs for 100,000 women, ranging from nursery school teaching to sewing. Roosevelt worked vigorously for anti-lynching legislation, compulsory health insurance, and child labor reform and fought racial discrimination in New Deal relief programs. She saw herself as the guardian of "human values" within the administration, a buffer between depression victims and government bureaucracy. She frequently testified before legislative committees, lobbied her husband privately and the Congress publicly, and wrote a widely syndicated newspaper column.

Eleanor Roosevelt's closest political ally was Molly Dewson. A long-time social worker and suffragist, Dewson wielded a good deal of political clout as director of the Women's Division of the national Democratic Party. Under her leadership women for the first time played a central role in shaping the party platform and running election campaigns. Dewson proved a tireless organizer, traveling to cities and towns around the country and educating women about Democratic policies and candidates. Her success impressed the president, and he relied on her judgment in recommending political appointments. Dewson placed more than a hundred women in New Deal positions.

Perhaps Dewson's most important success came in persuading FDR to appoint Frances Perkins secretary of labor—the first woman cabinet member in U.S. history. A graduate of Mount Holyoke College and a veteran activist for social welfare and reform, Perkins had served as FDR's industrial commissioner in New York before coming to Washington. As labor secretary, Perkins embodied the gains made by women in appointive offices. Her department was responsible for creating the Social Security Act and the Fair Labor Standards Act of 1938, both of which incorporated protective measures long advocated by women reformers. Perkins defined feminism as "the movement of women to participate in service to society." Yet despite the best efforts of the "women's network," women never constituted more than 19 percent of those employed by work relief programs, even though they made up 37 percent of the unemployed.

Eleanor Roosevelt on a campaign tour with her husband in Nebraska, 1935. Long active in women's organizations and Democratic Party circles, she used political activity both to maintain her independence and make herself a valuable ally to FDR. "The attitude of women toward change in society," she argued, "is going to determine to a great extent our future in this country."

New Deal agencies opened up spaces for scores of women in the federal bureaucracy. These women were concentrated in Perkins's Labor Department, the FERA and WPA, and the Social Security Board. In addition, the social work profession, which remained roughly two-thirds female in the 1930s, grew enormously in response to the massive relief and welfare programs. In sum, although the 1930s saw no radical challenges to existing male and female roles, working-class women and professional women held their own and managed to make some gains.

A New Deal for Minorities?

"The Negro was born in Depression," recalled Clifford Burke. "It only became official when it hit the white man." Long near the bottom of the American economic ladder, African Americans suffered disproportionately through the difficult days of the 1930s . The old saying among black workers that they were "last hired, first fired" was never more true than during times of high unemployment. With jobs made scarce by the depression, even traditional "Negro occupations"—domestic service, cook-

ing, janitorial work, elevator operating—were coveted. One white clerk in Florida expressed a widely held view among white Southerners when he defended a lynch mob attack on a store with black employees: "A nigger hasn't got no right to have a job when there are white men who can do the work and are out of work."

Overall, the Roosevelt administration made little overt effort to combat the racism and segregation entrenched in American life. FDR was especially worried about offending the powerful southern Democratic congressmen who were a key element in his political coalition. And local administration of many federal programs meant that most early New Deal programs routinely accepted discrimination. The CCC established separate camps for African Americans. The NRA labor codes tolerated lower wages for black workers doing the same jobs as white workers. African Americans could not get jobs with the TVA. In Atlanta, relief payments for black clients averaged $19.29 per month, compared with $32.66 for white clients. When local AAA committees in the South reduced acreage and production to boost prices, thousands of black sharecroppers and farm laborers were forced off the land. Racism was also embedded in the entitlement provisions of the Social Security Act. The act excluded domestics and casual laborers—workers whose ranks were disproportionately African Americans—from old-age insurance.

Yet some limited gains were made. President Roosevelt issued an executive order in 1935 banning discrimination in WPA projects. In the cities the WPA, paying minimum wages of $12 a week, enabled thousands of African Americans to survive. Between 15 and 20 percent of all WPA employees were black people, although African Americans made up less than 10 percent of the nation's population. The Public Works Administration, under Harold Ickes, constructed a number of integrated housing complexes and employed more than its fair share of black workers in construction.

FDR appointed several African Americans to second-level positions in his administration. This group became known as "the Black Cabinet." Mary McLeod Bethune, an educator who rose from a sharecropping background to found Bethune-Cookman College, proved a superb leader of the Office of Minority Affairs in the National Youth Administration. Her most successful programs substantially reduced black illiteracy. Harvard-trained Robert Weaver advised the president on economic affairs and in 1966 became the first black cabinet member when he was appointed secretary of housing and urban development. Yet Roosevelt himself was diffident about advancing civil rights. Typically, he spoke out against lynching in the South, but unlike his wife, he refused to support legislation making it a federal crime. Nor would he risk alienating white Southerners by working for long-denied voting rights for African Americans in the South.

Hard times were especially trying for Mexican Americans as well. As the Great Depression drastically reduced the demand for their labor, they faced massive layoffs, deepening poverty, even starvation. In Houston, a settlement association survey made in 1935 reported that "no group are greater sufferers from the present economic situation than members of the Mexican colony." As with African Americans, New Deal programs did little to help Mexicans and Mexican Americans. The AAA benefited large growers, not stoop laborers. Neither the National Labor Relations Act nor the Social Security Act made any provisions for farm laborers. The Federal Emergency Relief Administration and the Works Progress Administration did, at first, provide relief and jobs to the needy irrespective of citizenship status. But after 1937 the WPA eliminated aliens from eligibility, causing great hardship for thousands of Mexican families. In San Antonio, for example, the WPA allocated 1,800 jobs for needy pecan shellers, but only 700 Mexicans could qualify due to citizenship requirements.

The New Deal record for minorities was mixed at best. African Americans, especially in the cities, benefited from New Deal relief and work programs, though this assistance was not color-blind. Black industrial workers made inroads into labor unions affiliated with the CIO. The New Deal made no explicit attempt to attack the deeply rooted patterns of racism and discrimination in American life. The deteriorating economic and political conditions faced by Mexicans and Mexican Americans resulted in a mass reverse exodus. Yet by 1936, for the first time ever, a majority of black voters had switched their political allegiance to the Democrats—concrete evidence that they supported the directions taken by FDR's New Deal.

The Roosevelt Recession

The nation's economy had improved significantly by 1937. Unemployment had declined to "only" 14 percent (9 million people), farm prices had improved to 1930 levels, and industrial production was slightly higher than the 1929 mark. Economic traditionalists, led by Secretary of the Treasury Henry Morgenthau, called for reducing the federal deficit, which had grown to more than $4 billion in fiscal year 1936. Roosevelt, always uneasy about the growing national debt, called for large reductions in federal spending, particularly in WPA and farm programs. Federal Reserve System officials, worried about inflation, tightened credit policies.

Rather than stimulating business, the retrenchment brought about a steep recession. The stock market collapsed in August 1937, and industrial output and farm prices plummeted. Most alarming was the big increase in unemployment. By March 1938 the jobless rate hovered around 20 percent, with more than 13 million people looking for work. As conditions worsened, Roosevelt began to blame the "new depression" on a "strike of capital," claiming businessmen had refused to invest because they wanted to hurt his prestige. In truth, the administration's own severe spending cutbacks were more responsible for the decline.

The blunt reality was that even after five years the New Deal had not brought about economic recovery. Throughout 1937 and 1938 the administration drifted. Roosevelt received conflicting advice on the economy. Some advisers, suspicious of the reluctance of business to make new investments, urged a massive antitrust campaign against monopolies. Others urged a return to the Keynesian strategy of "priming the economic pump" with more federal spending. Emergency spending bills in the spring of 1938 pumped new life into the WPA and the PWA. But Republican gains in the 1938 congressional elections (eighty seats in the House, seven in the Senate) made it harder than ever to get new reform measures through.

There were a couple of important exceptions. The 1938 Fair Labor Standards Act established the first federal minimum wage (twenty-five cents an hour) and set a maximum work week of forty-four hours for all employees engaged in interstate commerce. The National Housing Act of 1937, also known as the Wagner-Steagall Act, funded public housing construction and slum clearance and provided rent subsidies for low-income families. But by and large, by 1938 the reform whirlwind of the New Deal was over.

CONCLUSION

Although American capitalism and democracy survived the cataclysm of the Great Depression, the New Deal failed in its central mission. It was never able to bring full economic recovery or end the scourge of mass unemployment. Only the economic boom that accompanied World War II would do that. Far from being the radical program its conservative critics charged, the New Deal did little to alter fundamental property relations or the distribution of wealth. Indeed, most of its programs largely failed to help the most powerless groups in

America—migrant workers, tenant farmers and share-croppers, African Americans, and other minorities.

But the New Deal profoundly changed many areas of American life. Overall, it radically increased the role of the federal government in American lives and communities. Western and southern communities in particular were transformed through federal intervention in water, power, and agricultural policies. Relief programs and the Social Security system established at least the framework for a welfare state. For the first time in American history, the national government took responsibility for assisting its needy citizens. And also for the first time, the federal government guaranteed the rights of workers to join trade unions, and it set standards for minimum wages and maximum hours. In politics, the New Deal established the Democrats as the majority party. Some version of the Roosevelt New Deal coalition would dominate the nation's political life for another three decades.

The New Deal's efforts to end racial and gender discrimination were modest at best. Some of the more ambitious programs, such as subsidizing the arts or building model communities, enjoyed only brief success. Other reform proposals, such as national

---

CHRONOLOGY

1929	Stock market crash
1930	Democrats regain control of the House of Representatives
1932	Reconstruction Finance Corporation established to make government credit available
	Bonus Army marches on Washington
	Franklin D. Roosevelt elected president
1933	Roughly 13 million workers unemployed
	The "hundred days" legislation of the First New Deal
	Twenty-first Amendment repeals Prohibition (Eighteenth Amendment)
1934	Indian Reorganization Act repeals Dawes Severalty Act and reasserts the status of Indian tribes as semisovereign nations
	Growing popularity of Father Charles E. Coughlin and Huey Long, critics of Roosevelt
1935	Second New Deal
	Committee for Industrial Organization (CIO) established
	Dust storms turn the southern Great Plains into the Dust Bowl
	Boulder Dam completed
1936	Roosevelt defeats Alfred M. Landon in reelection landslide
	Sit-down strike begins at General Motors plants in Flint, Michigan
1937	General Motors recognizes United Automobile Workers
	Roosevelt's "Court-packing" plan causes controversy
	Memorial Day Massacre in Chicago demonstrates the perils of union organizing
	"Roosevelt recession" begins
1938	CIO unions withdraw from the American Federation of Labor to form the Congress of Industrial Organizations
	Fair Labor Standards Act establishes the first federal minimum wage

health insurance, never got off the ground. Conservative counterpressures, especially after 1937, limited what could be changed.

Still, the New Deal did more than strengthen the presence of the national government in people's lives. It also fed expectations that the federal presence would intensify. Washington became a much greater center of economic regulation and political power, and the federal bureaucracy grew in size and influence. With the coming of World War II, the direct role of national government in shaping American communities would expand beyond the dreams of even the most ardent New Dealer.

REVIEW QUESTIONS

1. What were the underlying causes of the Great Depression? What consequences did it have for ordinary Americans, and how did the Hoover administration attempt to deal with the crisis?

2. Analyze the key elements of Franklin D. Roosevelt's first New Deal program. To what degree did these succeed in getting the economy back on track and in providing relief to suffering Americans?

3. How did the so-called Second New Deal differ from the first? What political pressures did Roosevelt face that contributed to the new policies?

4. How did the New Deal reshape western communities and politics? What specific programs had the greatest impact in the region? How are these changes still visible today?

5. Evaluate the impact of the labor movement and radicalism on the 1930s. How did they influence American political and cultural life?

6. To what extent were the grim realities of depression reflected in popular culture? To what degree were they absent?

7. Discuss the long- and short-range effects of the New Deal on American political and economic life. What were its key successes and failures? What legacies of New Deal-era policies and political struggles can you find in contemporary America?

RECOMMENDED READING

Anthony J. Badger, *The New Deal: The Depression Years, 1933–1940* (1989). Recent and very useful overview that emphasizes the limited nature of New Deal reforms.

John Braeman et al., eds., *The New Deal: The State and Local Levels* (1975). Good collection of essays analyzing the workings of the New Deal in local communities throughout the nation.

Alan Brinkley, *The End of Reform: New Deal Liberalism in Recession and War* (1995). A sophisticated analysis of the political and economic limits faced by New Deal reformers from 1937 through World War II.

Lizabeth Cohen, *Making a New Deal: Industrial Workers in Chicago, 1919–1939* (1990). A brilliant study that demonstrates the transformation of immigrant and African American workers into key actors in the creation of the CIO and in New Deal politics and illuminates the complex relationship between ethnic cultures and mass culture.

Michael Demming, *The Cultural Front: The Laboring of American Culture in the Twentieth Century* (1997). A provocative reinterpretation of 1930s culture, emphasizing the impact of the Popular Front and its lasting influence on American modernism and mass culture.

Richard Lowitt, *The New Deal and the West* (1984). A comprehensive study of the New Deal's impact in the West, with special attention to water policy and agriculture.

Robert S. McElvaine, *The Great Depression: America, 1929–1941* (1984). The best one-volume overview of the Great Depression. It is especially strong on the origins and early years of the worst economic calamity in American history.

Lois Scharf, *To Work and to Wed* (1980). Examines female employment and feminism during the Great Depression.

Harvard Sitkoff, *A New Deal for Blacks* (1978). Focuses on the narrow gains made by African Americans from New Deal measures, as well as the racism that pervaded most government programs.

William Stott, *Documentary Expression and Thirties America* (1973). A very thoughtful account of the documentary impulse and its relationship to the political and social upheavals of the era.

Studs Terkel, *Hard Times* (1970). The best oral history of the Great Depression. It includes a very wide range of voices recalling life in the depression era.

ADDITIONAL BIBLIOGRAPHY

Hard Times

Michael A. Bernstein, *The Great Depression* (1987)
David Burner, *Herbert Hoover* (1978)
Roger Daniels, *The Bonus March* (1971)
John A. Garraty, *The Great Depression* (1986)
Susan E. Kennedy, *The Banking Crisis of 1933* (1973)
Robert S. McElvaine, ed., *Down and Out in the Great Depression* (1983)
Janet Poppendieck, *Breadlines Knee-Deep in Wheat* (1986)
Elmos Wicker, *The Banking Panics of the Great Depression* (1996)

FDR and the First New Deal

Paul K. Conkin, *The New Deal*, 2d ed. (1975)
Steve Fraser and Gary Gerstle, eds., *The Rise and Fall of the New Deal Order* (1988)
Ellis Hawley, *The New Deal and the Problem of Monopoly* (1966)
William Leuchtenberg, *The FDR Years* (1995)
Percy M. Merill, *Roosevelt's Forest Army* (1981)
James S. Olson, *Saving Capitalism* (1988)
Albert U. Romasco, *The Politics of Recovery: Roosevelt's New Deal* (1983)
Theodore M. Saloutos, *The American Farmer and the New Deal* (1982)

Left Turn and the Second New Deal

Kristi Andersen, *The Creation of a Democratic Majority, 1928–1936* (1979)
Irving Bernstein, *The Turbulent Years: A History of the American Worker, 1933–1941* (1970)
Alan Brinkley, *Voices of Protest: Huey Long, Father Coughlin, and the New Deal* (1982)
Peter Friedlander, *The Emergence of a UAW Local* (1975)
Gary Gerstle, *Working Class Americanism* (1989)
Robin D. G. Kelley, *Hammer and Hoe: Alabama Communists during the Great Depression* (1990)
Joseph P. Lash, *Dealers and Dreamers* (1988)
Roy Lubove, *The Struggle for Social Security* (1968)
Robert H. Zieger, *The CIO, 1935–1955* (1995)

The New Deal and the West

James M. Gregory, *American Exodus: The Dust Bowl Migration and Okie Culture in California* (1989)
Norris Hundley Jr., *The Great Thirst: California and Water, 1770s–1990s* (1992)
Laurence Kelly, *The Assault on Assimilation: John Collier and the Origins of Indian Policy Reform, 1920–1954* (1983)
Vicki Ruiz, *Cannery Women/Cannery Lives: Mexican Women, Unionization, and the California Food Processing Industry, 1930–1950* (1987)
Charles J. Shindo, *Dust Bowl Migrants in the American Imagination* (1997)
Graham D. Taylor, *The New Deal and American Indian Tribalism* (1980)
Donald Worster, *Dust Bowl* (1979)

Depression-Era Culture

Vivian Gornick, *The Romance of American Communism* (1976)
Harvey Kleher, *The Heyday of American Communism* (1984)
J. Fred MacDonald, *Don't Touch That Dial* (1979)
Richard McKinzie, *The New Deal for Artists* (1973)
Barbara Melosh, *Engendering Culture: Manhood and Womanhood in New Deal Public Art and Theater* (1991)
David P. Peeler, *Hope among Us Yet* (1987)
Richard H. Pells, *Radical Visions and American Dreams: Culture and Social Thought in the Depression Years* (1973)
Thomas Schatz, *The Genius of the System: Hollywood Filmmaking in the Studio Era* (1988)
Richard Schickel, *The Disney Version* (1968)
Martin Williams, *Jazz in Its Own Time* (1989)

The Limits of Reform

Francisco E. Balderrama, *Decade of Betrayal: Mexican Repatriation in the 1930's* (1995)
Mark Naison, *Communists in Harlem during the Depression* (1983)
James T. Patterson, *Congressional Conservatism and the New Deal* (1967)
Winifred Wandersee, *Women's Work and Family Values: 1920–1940* (1981)
Susan Ware, *Beyond Suffrage: Women in the New Deal* (1981)
_____, *Partner and I: Molly Dewson, Feminism, and New Deal Politics* (1987)
Nancy J. Weiss, *Farewell to the Party of Lincoln: Black Politics in the Age of FDR* (1983)
Robert L. Zangrando, *The NAACP Crusade against Lynching* (1980)

Biography

Blanche W. Cook, *Eleanor Roosevelt*, vol. 1 (1992)
Kenneth S. Davis, *FDR*, 4 vols. (1972, 1975, 1986, 1992)
Steven Fraser, *Labor Will Rule: Sidney Hillman and the Rise of American Labor* (1991)
Dorothy Healey and Maurice Isserman, *California Red: A Life in the American Communist Party* (1990)
J. Joseph Huthmacher, *Robert F. Wagner and the Rise of Urban Liberalism* (1968)
Nelson Lichtenstein, *The Most Dangerous Man in Detroit: Walter Reutter and the Fate of American Labor* (1995)
George Martin, *Madame Secretary: Frances Perkins* (1976)
George McJimsey, *Harry Hopkins* (1987)
Karen Becker Ohrn, *Dorothea Lange and the Documentary Tradition* (1980)
Lois Scharf, *Eleanor Roosevelt* (1987)
Robert Zieger, *John L. Lewis* (1988)

CHAPTER TWENTY-FIVE

WORLD WAR II

1941–1945

AMERICAN COMMUNITIES
Los Alamos, New Mexico

On Monday, July 16, 1945, at 5:29:45 A.M., Mountain War Time, the first atomic bomb exploded in a brilliant flash visible in three states. Within just seven minutes, a huge, multicolored, bell-shaped cloud soared 38,000 feet into the atmosphere and threw back a blanket of smoke and soot to the earth below. The heat generated by the blast was four times the temperature at the center of the sun, and the light produced rivaled that of nearly twenty suns. Even ten miles away people felt a strong surge of heat. The giant fireball ripped a crater a half-mile wide in the ground, fusing the desert sand into glass. The shock wave blew out windows in houses more than 200 miles away. The blast killed every living creature—squirrels, rabbits, snakes, plants, and insects—within a mile and the smells of death lingered for nearly a month.

Very early that morning, Ruby Wilkening had driven to a nearby mountain ridge, where she joined several other women waiting for the blast. Wilkening worried about her husband, a physicist, who was already at the test site. No one knew exactly what to expect, not even the scientists who developed the bomb.

The Wilkenings were part of a unique community of scientists who had been marshaled for war. President Franklin D. Roosevelt, convinced by Albert Einstein and other physicists that the Nazis might successfully develop an atomic bomb, had inaugurated a small nuclear research program in 1939. Soon after the United States entered World War II, Roosevelt, convinced by scientists that they could produce an atomic weapon in time to affect the outcome of the war, increased the resources available to what was now known as the Manhattan Project and placed it under the direction of the Army Corps of Engineers. By December 1942 a team headed by Italian-born Nobel Prize-winner Enrico Fermi had produced the first chain reaction in uranium under the University of Chicago's football stadium. Now the mission was to build a new, formidable weapon of war, the atomic bomb.

The government moved the key researchers and their families to Los Alamos in the remote and sparsely populated Sangre de Cristo Mountains of New Mexico, a region of soaring peaks, ancient Indian ruins, modern Pueblos, and villages occupied by the descendents of the earliest Spanish settlers. The scientists and their families arrived in March 1943. They occupied a former boys' preparatory school until new houses could be built. Some families doubled up in rugged log cabins or nearby ranches. Telephone service to the outside world was poor, and the mountain roads were so rough that changing flat tires became a tiresome but familiar routine. Construction of new quarters proceeded slowly, causing nasty disputes between the "long-hairs" (scientists) and the "plumbers" (army engineers) in charge of the grounds. Despite the chaos, outstanding American and European scientists eagerly signed up. Most were young, with an average age of twenty-seven, and quite a few were recently married. Many couples began their families at Los Alamos, producing a total of nearly a thousand babies between 1943 and 1949.

The scientists and their families formed an exceptionally close-knit community, united by the need for secrecy and their shared antagonism toward their army guardians. The military atmosphere was oppressive. Homes and laboratories were cordoned off by barbed wire and guarded by military police. Everything, from linens to food packages, was stamped "Government Issue." Security personnel followed the scientists whenever they left Los Alamos. The scientists' homes were wired for sound, and several scientists were reprimanded for discussing their work with their wives. All outgoing mail was censored. Well-known scientists commonly worked under aliases—Fermi became "Eugene Farmer"—and code names were used for such terms as atom, bomb, and uranium fission. The birth certificates of babies born at Los Alamos listed their place of birth simply as rural Sandoval County, and children registered without surnames at nearby public schools. Even automobile accidents went unreported, and newspapers carried no wedding announcements or obituaries. Only a group thoroughly committed to the war effort could accept such restrictions on personal liberty.

A profound urgency motivated the research team, which included refugees from Nazi Germany and Fascist Italy and a large proportion of Jews. The director of the project, California physicist J. Robert Oppenheimer, promoted a scientific élan that offset the military style of commanding general Leslie Groves. Just thirty-eight, slightly built, and deeply emotional, "Oppie" personified the idealism that helped the community of scientists overcome whatever moral reservations they held about placing such a potentially ominous weapon in the hands of the government.

Los Alamos

In the Technical Area of Los Alamos, Oppenheimer directed research from an office with a desk, long tables, and blackboard along the walls in a typical two-story army building. At seven o'clock each workday morning, the siren dubbed "Oppie's Whistle" called the other scientists to their laboratories to wrestle with the theoretical and practical problems of building an atomic device. Once a week Oppenheimer called together the heads of the various technical divisions to discuss their work in round-table conferences. From May to November 1944, after the bomb had been designed, the key issue was testing it. Many scientists feared a test might fail, scattering the precious plutonium at the bomb's core and discrediting the entire project. Finally, with plutonium production increasing, the Los Alamos team agreed to test "the gadget" at a site 160 miles away.

The unprecedented scientific mobilization at Los Alamos mirrored changes occurring throughout American society as the nation rallied behind the war effort. Sixteen million men and women left home for military service and nearly as many moved to take advantage of wartime jobs. Several states in the South and Southwest experienced huge surges in population. California alone grew by 2 million people, a large proportion from Mexico. Many broad social changes with roots in earlier times—the economic expansion of the West, the erosion of farm tenancy among black people in the South and white people in Appalachia, and the increasing employment of married women—accelerated during the war. The United States, initially reluctant to enter the war, emerged from it the world's leading superpower and free from the weight of the Great Depression. The events of the war eroded old communities, created new ones like Los Alamos, and transformed nearly all aspects of American society.

KEY TOPICS

- The events leading to Pearl Harbor and declaration of war

- The marshaling of national resources for war

- American society during wartime

- The mobilization of Americans into the armed forces

- The war in Europe and Asia

- Diplomacy and the atomic bomb

THE COMING OF WORLD WAR II

The Great Depression was not confined to the United States. It was a worldwide economic decline that further undermined a political order that had been shaky since World War I. Production declined by nearly 40 percent, international trade dropped by as much as two-thirds, and unemployment rose. While rivalries for markets and access to raw materials intensified, political unrest spread across Europe and Asia. Demagogues played upon nationalist hatreds, fueled by old resentments and current despair, and offered solutions in the form of territorial expansion by military conquest.

Preoccupied with restoring the domestic economy, President Franklin D. Roosevelt had no specific plan to deal with growing conflict elsewhere in the world. Moreover, the majority of Americans strongly opposed foreign entanglements. But as debate over diplomatic policy heated up, terrifying events overseas pulled the nation steadily toward war.

The Shadows of War

War spread first across Asia. Militarist-imperialist leaders in Japan, which suffered economically from loss of trade during the 1930s, determined to make their nation the richest in the world. The Japanese army seized control of Manchuria in 1931 and in 1932 installed a puppet government there. When reprimanded by the League of Nations, Japan simply withdrew from the organization. In 1937 Japan provoked full-scale war with an invasion of northern China. When it seized control of the capital city of Nanking, Japan's army murdered as many as 300,000 Chinese men, women, and children and destroyed much of the city. Within the year Japan controlled all but China's western interior and threatened all Asia and the Pacific.

Meanwhile, the rise of authoritarian nationalism in Italy and Germany cast a dark shadow over Europe. The economic hardships brought on by the Great Depression—and in Germany resentment over the harsh terms of the Versailles Treaty that ended World War I—fueled the rise of demagogic mass movements. Glorifying war as a test of national viril-

ity, the Italian Fascist dictator Benito Mussolini, who had seized power in 1922, declared, "We have buried the putrid corpse of liberty." In Germany, the National Socialists (Nazis), led by Adolf Hitler, combined militaristic rhetoric with a racialist doctrine of Aryan (Nordic) supremacy that claimed biological superiority for the blond-haired and blue-eyed peoples of northern Europe and classified nonwhites, including Jews, as "degenerate races."

Hitler, who had the backing of major industrialists such as the weapons manufacturer Krupp and the support of about a third of the German electorate, was appointed Chancellor of Germany in 1933. With his brown-shirted storm troopers ruling the streets, he quickly seized absolute authority, destroying opposition parties and effectively making himself dictator of the strongest nation in central Europe. Renouncing the disarmament provisions of the Versailles treaty, he began, with no effective protest from France and Britain, to rebuild Germany's armed forces. Intending to make Germany the center of a new civilization, the Nazi leader built up a vast industrial infrastructure for an army of a half-million men poised to conquer Europe. In 1936 Italy allied with Germany to form the Rome-Berlin Axis. In November 1937 Hitler announced plans to obtain *Lebensraum*—living space and farmland for Germany's growing population—through territorial expansion. The prospect of war grew as both Mussolini and Hitler began to act on their imperial visions. In 1935 Italy sent troops to Ethiopia and formally claimed the impoverished African kingdom as a colony. Both Germany and Italy supported the fascist insurrection of General Francisco Franco in the Spanish Civil War that broke out in 1936. In 1936 also, Hitler sent troops to occupy the Rhineland, a region demilitarized by the Versailles Treaty, and prepared to advance on central Europe. In 1938 he sent troops into his native Austria, annexing it to Germany.

Hitler next turned his attention to Czechoslovakia, a country which both Britain and France were pledged by treaty to assist. War seemed imminent. But Britain and France surprised Hitler by agreeing, at a conference in Munich the last week of September 1938, to allow Germany to annex the Sudetenland, a part of Czechoslovakia bordering Germany. In return, Hitler pledged to stop his territorial advance. Less than six months later, in March 1939, Hitler seized the rest of Czechoslovakia.

By the fall of 1938, the world was becoming increasingly aware of the shocking character of Hitler's regime, especially its virulent racial doctrines. After 1935, when Hitler published the notorious Nuremberg Laws denying civil rights to Jews, the campaign against them became steadily more vicious. On the night of November 9, 1938, Nazi storm troopers rounded up Jews, beating them mercilessly and murdering an untold number. They smashed windows in Jewish shops, hospitals, and orphanages and burned synagogues to the ground. This attack came to be known as *Kristallnacht*, "the Night of Broken Glass." The Nazi government soon expropriated Jewish property and excluded Jews from all but the most menial forms of employment. Pressured by Hitler, Hungary and Italy also enacted laws against Jews.

Isolationism

Americans responded cautiously to these events. World War I had left a legacy of strong isolationist sentiment. Popular films such as *All Quiet on the Western Front* (1930) vividly depicted the horrors of war, including atrocities against civilians. Senseless slaughter might be a centuries-old way of life in Europe, many reasoned, but not for the United States, which should stay clear of foreign wars. As late as 1937, nearly 70 percent of Americans responding to a Gallup poll stated that U.S. involvement in World War I had been a mistake.

This sentiment won strong support in Congress. In 1934, a special committee headed by Republican senator Gerald P. Nye of North Dakota had charged weapons manufacturers with driving the United States into World War I in the hopes of windfall profits, which, in fact, many realized. To deter future entanglements, Congress passed three Neutrality Acts in 1935, 1936, and 1937 authorizing the president to deny American firms the right to sell or ship munitions to belligerent nations.

College students, seeing themselves as future cannon fodder, strongly opposed foreign entanglements. In 1933, 39 percent of those polled stated that they would refuse to fight in any war; 33 percent would fight only if the United States were attacked. Three years later, 500,000 boycotted classes in a nationwide "student strike" to demonstrate their opposition to any preparation for war.

Isolationism spanned the political spectrum. In 1938 socialist Norman Thomas gathered leading liberals and trade unionists into the Keep America Out of War Congress; the communist-influenced American League against War and Fascism claimed more than 1

million members. Meanwhile, Republican senator Robert A. Taft of Ohio, son of former president William Howard Taft, argued that a new war would harm American democracy by enlarging the federal government and tightening its grip on the citizenry.

In 1940 the arch-conservative America First Committee was formed to oppose U.S. intervention. The group was particularly strong in the Midwest. Some America Firsters championed the Nazis while others simply advocated American neutrality. Chaired by top Sears executive Robert E. Wood, the America First Committee quickly gained attention because its members included such well-known personalities as movie stars Robert Young and Lillian Gish, automobile manufacturer Henry Ford, and Charles A. Lindbergh, famous for his 1927 solo flight across the Atlantic. Within a year, America First had launched more than 450 chapters.

Roosevelt Readies for War

While Americans looked on anxiously, the twists and turns of world events prompted President Franklin D. Roosevelt to ready the nation for war. In October 1937 he had called for international cooperation to "quarantine the aggressors." "Let no one imagine that America will escape, that America may expect mercy, that this Western Hemisphere will not be attacked." But a poll of Congress revealed that a two-thirds majority opposed economic sanctions, calling any such plan a "back door to war." Forced to draw back, Roosevelt nevertheless won from Congress $1 billion in appropriations to enlarge the navy. But as late as January 1939, in his annual address to Congress, Roosevelt insisted that the United States must use all means "short of war" to deter aggression.

Everything changed on September 1, 1939, when Hitler invaded Poland. Committed by treaty to defend Poland against unprovoked attack, Great Britain and France issued a joint declaration of war against Germany two days later. After the fall of Warsaw at the end of the month, the fighting slowed to a near halt. Even along their border, French and German troops did not exchange fire. From the east, however, the invasion continued. Just two weeks before Hitler overran Poland, the Soviet Union had stunned the world by signing a nonaggression pact with its former enemy. The Red Army now entered Poland, and the two great powers proceeded to split the hapless nation between them. Soviet forces then headed north, invading Finland on November 30. The European war had begun.

Calculating that the United States would stay out of the war, Hitler began a crushing offensive against western Europe in April 1940. Using the technique of *Blitzkrieg* (lightning war)—massed, fast-moving columns of tanks supported by air power—that had overwhelmed Poland, Nazi troops moved first against

OCTOBER 2, 1938
EUROPEAN WAR

If England and France go to war against Germany do you think the United States can stay out?

Yes	57%
No	43

By Region

	Yes	No
New England	46%	54%
Middle Atlantic	61	39
East Central	60	40
West Central	57	43
South	60	40
West	51	49

Interviewing Date 9/15–20/1938, Survey #132, Question #4

FEBRUARY 21, 1940
EUROPEAN WAR

If it appears that Germany is defeating England and France, should the United States declare war on Germany and send our army and navy to Europe to fight?

Yes	23%
No	77

7 percent expressed no opinion.

Interviewing Date 2/2–7/1940, Survey #183-K, Question #6

DECEMBER 16, 1940
EUROPEAN WAR

Do you think it was a mistake for the United States to enter the last World War?

Yes	39%
No	42
No opinion	19

By Political Affiliation
Democrats

Yes	33%
No	46
No opinion	21

Republicans

Yes	46%
No	38
No opinion	16

Interviewing Date 11/21–30/1940, Survey #244-K, Question #6

Gallup Polls: European War and World War I, 1938–1940   *These three polls conducted by the American Institute of Public Opinion indicate the persistence of isolationist sentiment and popular criticism of U.S. involvement in World War I. Many respondents believed the United States, despite its commitments to European allies, should stay out of war. After 1940, in the aftermath of Nazi military victories in Europe, many Americans reconsidered their opposition, fearing a threat to democracy in their own nation.*

Germany's northern neighbors. After taking Denmark and Norway, the Nazi armored divisions swept over Holland, Belgium, and Luxembourg and sent more than 338,000 British troops into retreat across the English Channel from Dunkirk. Hitler's army, joined by the Italians, easily conquered France in June 1940. Hitler now turned toward England. In the battle of Britain, Nazi bombers pounded population and industrial centers while U-boats cut off incoming supplies.

Even with Great Britain under attack, opinion polls indicated Americans' determination to stay out of the war. But most Americans, like Roosevelt himself, believed that the security of the United States depended on both a strong defense and the defeat of Germany. Invoking the Neutrality Act of 1939, which permitted the sale of arms to Britain, France, and China, the president clarified his position: "all aid to the Allies short of war." In May 1940 he began to transfer surplus U.S. planes and equipment to the Allies. In September the president secured the first peacetime military draft in American history, the Selective Service Act of 1940, which sent 1.4 million men to army training camps by July 1941. Yet even when he secured huge congressional appropriations for the production of airplanes and battleships, Roosevelt did so in the name of "hemispheric defense," not intervention.

President Roosevelt could not yet admit the inevitability of U.S. involvement—especially during an election year. His popularity had dropped with the "Roosevelt recession" that began in 1937, raising doubts that he could win what would be an unprecedented third term. Waiting until July 1940, the eve of the Democratic Party convention, Roosevelt announced that world events compelled him to accept a party "draft" for renomination. In his campaign he promised voters not to "send your boys to any foreign wars." Roosevelt and his vice-presidential candidate Henry Wallace won by a margin of 5 million popular votes over the Republican dark-horse candidate, Wendell L. Willkie of Indiana.

Roosevelt now moved more aggressively to aid the Allies in their struggle with the Axis powers. In his annual message to Congress, he proposed a bill that would allow the president to sell, exchange, or lease arms to any country whose defense appeared vital to

Japanese attack planes devastated the U.S. fleet stationed on the Hawaiian island of Oahu. Before December 7, 1941, few Americans had heard of Pearl Harbor, but the "sneak" attack became a symbol of Japanese treachery and the necessity for revenge.

U.S. security. Passed by Congress in March, 1941, the Lend-Lease Act made Great Britain the first beneficiary of massive aid. Roosevelt also extended the U.S. "security zone" nearly halfway across the Atlantic Ocean and ordered the Coast Guard to seize any German-controlled or German ships that entered an American port. He directed Germany and Italy to close their U.S. consulates and ordered U.S. ships to shoot any Nazi vessel in U.S. "defensive waters" on sight. After Congress authorized the merchant marine to sail fully armed while conveying lend-lease supplies directly to Britain, a formal declaration of war was only a matter of time.

In August 1941 Roosevelt met secretly at sea off Newfoundland with British prime minister Winston Churchill to map military strategy and declare "common principles." Known as the Atlantic Charter, their proclamation specified the right of all peoples to live in freedom from fear, want, and tyranny. The Atlantic Charter also called for free trade among all nations, an end to territorial seizures, and disarmament. Eventually endorsed by the Soviet Union and fourteen other nations, the Atlantic Charter pledged to all nations—vanquished as well as victors—the right to self-determination.

By this time the European war had moved to a new stage. Hitler had conquered the Balkans and then set aside the expedient Nazi-Soviet Pact to resume his quest for the entire European continent. In June 1941

Hitler launched an invasion of the Soviet Union, promising its rich agricultural land to German farmers. Observing this dramatic escalation, the United States moved closer to intervention.

Pearl Harbor

Throughout 1940 and much of 1941 the United States focused on events in Europe, but the war in Asia went on. Roosevelt, anticipating danger to American interests in the Pacific, had directed the transfer of the Pacific Fleet from bases in California to Pearl Harbor, on the island of Oahu, Hawai'i, in May 1940. On September 27 Japan formally joined Germany and Italy as the Asian partner of the Axis alliance. Under the terms of the expanded alliance, Germany would support Japan's seizure of Dutch, British, and French colonial possessions as part of its attempt to create a regional bloc under its rule.

The United States and Japan each played for time. Roosevelt wanted to save his resources to fight against Germany, while Japan's leaders gambled that America's preoccupation with Europe might allow them to conquer all of Southeast Asia, including the French colonies in Indochina (Vietnam, Cambodia, and Laos) and the British possessions of Burma and India. When Japan occupied Indochina in July, 1941, however, Roosevelt responded by freezing Japanese assets in the United States and cutting off its oil supplies.

Confrontation with Japan now looked likely. U.S. intelligence had broken the Japanese diplomatic code, and the president knew that Japan was preparing for war against the western powers. Roosevelt's advisers expected an attack in the southern Pacific or British Malaya sometime after November. General Douglas MacArthur alerted his command in the Philippines.

Japan, however, intended to knock the United States out of the Pacific in a single blow. Early Sunday morning, December 7, 1941, Japanese carriers launched an attack on Pearl Harbor that caught American forces completely off guard. Sailors on the decks of American ships looked up to see Japanese dive-bombers in the sky above them. Loudspeakers warned: "Japs are coming! Japs attacking us! Go to your battle stations!" Within two hours, Japanese pilots had destroyed nearly 200 American planes and badly damaged the fleet; more than 2,400 Americans were killed and nearly 1,200 wounded. On the same day, Japan struck U.S. bases on the Philippines, Guam, and Wake Island.

On December 8, declaring the attack on Pearl Harbor a date that "will live in infamy," Roosevelt asked Congress for a declaration of war against Japan. With only one dissenting vote—by pacifist Jeannette Rankin of Montana, who had voted against U.S. entry into World War I in 1917—Congress acceded. The United States had not yet declared war on Japan's European allies, but Hitler made that unnecessary when he asked the Reichstag on December 11 to support war against the "half Judaized and the other half Negrified" American nation. Mussolini joined him in the declaration, and the United States on the same day recognized that a state of war existed with Germany and Italy. World War II now began for Americans.

President Franklin D. Roosevelt signs the declaration of war against Japan, December 8, 1941, a day after the attack on Pearl Harbor. Congressional leaders, many of whom had earlier hoped to keep the United States out of war, here unite around the president and his policies.

ARSENAL OF DEMOCRACY

Late in 1940 President Roosevelt called upon all Americans to make the nation "an arsenal of democracy." During the next three years, the economic machinery that had failed during the 1930s was swiftly retooled for military purposes, with dramatic results. The Great Depression suddenly ended. Never before had the federal government poured so much energy and money into production or assigned such a great army of experts to manage it. This marshaling of resources involved a concentration of power in the federal government that exceeded anything planned by the New Deal.

Mobilizing for War

A few days after the United States declared war on Germany, Congress passed the War Powers Act, which established a precedent for executive authority that would endure long after the war's end. The president gained the power to reorganize the federal government and create new agencies; to establish programs censoring all news and information and abridging civil liberties; to seize property owned by foreigners; and even to award government contracts without competitive bidding.

Roosevelt promptly created special wartime agencies. At the top of his agenda was a massive reorientation and management of the economy, and an alphabet soup of new agencies arose to fill any gaps in production. The Supply Priorities and Allocation Board (SPAB) oversaw the use of scarce materials and resources vital to the war, adjusting domestic consumption (even ending it for some products such as automobiles) to military needs. The Office of Price Administration (OPA) checked the threat of inflation from the government's sudden massive spending by imposing price controls. The National War Labor Board (NWLB) mediated disputes between labor and management, halting strikes and also controlling inflation by limiting wage increases. The War Manpower Commission (WMC) directed the mobilization of military and civilian services. And the Office of War Mobilization (OWM), headed by James F. Byrnes, coordinated operations among all these agencies.

Several new agencies focused on domestic propaganda. The attack on Pearl Harbor evoked an outpouring of rage against Japan and effectively quashed much opposition to U.S. intervention. Still, for most Americans, World War II would remain a foreign war, and the government stepped in to fan the fires of patriotism and to shape public opinion. In June 1942 the president created the Office of War Information (OWI) to coordinate information from the multiplying federal agencies and to engage the press, radio, and film industry in an informational campaign—in short, to sell the war to the American people.

The OWI gathered data and controlled the release of news, emphasizing the need to make reports on the war both dramatic and encouraging. Like the Committee on Public Information during World War I, during the first twenty-one months of the war the new agency banned the publication of advertisements, photographs, and newsreels showing American dead, fearing that such images would demoralize the public. In 1943, worrying that Americans had become overconfident, officials changed their policy. A May issue of *Newsweek* featured graphic photographs of Americans wounded in battle, explaining that "to harden home-front morale, the military services have adopted a new policy of letting civilians see photographically what warfare does to men who fight." To spare families unnecessary grief, throughout the war the OWI prohibited the publication of any photograph revealing the identity of the American dead. The OWI also published leaflets and booklets for the armed services and flooded enemy ranks with subversive propaganda.

Propaganda also fueled the selling of war bonds. Secretary of the Treasury Henry Morgenthau Jr. not only encouraged Americans to buy government bonds to finance the war but planned a campaign "to use bonds to sell the war, rather than vice versa." Bonds, the ads for them claimed, were a good investment that gave everyone an opportunity "to have a financial stake in American democracy." Buying them would "mean bullets in the bellies of Hitler's hordes!" Discovering through research that Americans felt more antagonism to Japan than Germany, Morgenthau directed his staff to use more negative stereotypes of the Japanese in their advertising copy. Polls showed, however, that most depression-stung Americans bought war bonds mainly to invest safely, to counter inflation, and to save for postwar purchases.

The federal government also sponsored various measures to prevent subversion of the war effort. Concerned about enemy propaganda, the Office of Facts and Figures hired political scientist Harold Lasswell of Yale University to devise a means to measure the patriotic content of magazines and newspapers. The Federal Bureau of Investigation (FBI) was kept busy, its appropriation rising from $6 million to $16 million in just two years. The attorney general authorized wiretapping in cases of espionage or sabotage, but the FBI used it extensively—and illegally—in domestic surveillance. The Joint Chiefs of Staff created the Office of Strategic Services (OSS) to assess the enemy's military strength, to gather intelligence information, and to oversee espionage activities. Its head, Colonel William Donovan, envisioned the OSS as an "adjunct to military strategy" and engaged leading social scientists to plot psychological warfare against the enemy.

Effects of War Spending, 1940–1945   *Wartime spending had a multiplier effect on the U.S. economy. Government contracts with industry rapidly increased the gross national product, and the sharp upswing in production utilized all available workers and sharply reduced unemployment.*

Source: Robert L. Heilbroner, *The Economic Transformation of America* (New York: Harcourt, Brace, 1977), p. 205.

One important outcome of these activities was to increase the size of the government many times over its New Deal level, which conservatives already considered far too large. It cost about $250 million a day to fight the war. As a result, the federal government spent twice as much during the war as it had during the nation's entire history up to then. The federal budget grew to ten times its peacetime amount during the New Deal. Defense spending rose from $9 million to $98 million, and the number of federal employees nearly quadrupled, from a little over 1 million in 1940 to nearly 4 million by the war's end.

Despite this pattern of expansion, however, the New Deal itself fell victim to the war. As President Roosevelt announced in 1942, "Dr. New Deal" had been replaced by "Dr. Win the War." No longer carrying the heavy responsibility of bringing the nation out of the Great Depression, his administration directed all its resources toward securing the planes, ships, guns, and food required for victory. Moreover, the 1942 elections weakened the New Deal coalition by unseating many liberal Democrats. The Republicans gained forty-six new members in the House of Representatives, nine in the Senate. Republicans now had greater opportunity to quash proposals to extend the social programs instituted during the 1930s.

One by one, New Deal agencies vanished. One of the most popular programs, the Civilian Conservation Corps, secured funds from Congress, but only to cover its liquidation. In December 1942 the Works Progress Administration, which handled various forms of work relief, was given, in Roosevelt's words, a "wartime furlough"; a few months later Congress granted the agency an "honorable discharge." Major New Deal agencies, including the National Youth Administration and the Federal Writers Project, were dismantled by 1943.

Economic Conversion

The decisive factor for victory, even more than military prowess and superior strategy, would be, many observers agreed, the ability of the United States to outproduce its enemies. The country enjoyed many advantages to meet this challenge: a large industrial base, abundant natural resources (largely free from interference by the war), and a civilian population large enough to permit it to increase both its labor force and its armed forces. The war would lift the United States out of the Great Depression and create the biggest economic boom in the history of any nation. But first the entire civilian economy had to be both expanded and transformed for the production of arms and other military supplies.

Economic conversion resulted from a combination of government spending and foreign orders for military supplies. The American public firmly opposed rearmament until 1938, when expenditures for military purposes amounted to only 1.5 percent of the federal budget. The revision of neutrality legislation in 1939 eased previous restrictions on the sale of war materials to France and Great Britain, creating a huge market and boosting production significantly. By the summer of 1941 the federal government was pouring vast amounts into defense production. Six months after the attack on Pearl Harbor its allocations topped $100 billion for equipment and supplies that exceeded what American firms had produced in any previous war. Facing war orders too large to fill, American industries were now primed for all-out production.

Before the Japanese attack on Pearl Harbor, President Roosevelt counted on American businesses to manage their own war-related industries. After announcing a goal of 60,000 planes, 45,000 tanks, and 8 million tons of ships for 1942, Roosevelt formed the War Production Board in January of that year. He directed the new agency to "exercise general responsibility" for the economy. By June, nearly half of everything produced in the United States was war material.

Every economic indicator pointed upward. The gross national product (accounting for inflation) rose from $88.6 billion in 1939 to $198.7 billion in five years. Investment in new plants and equipment, including the manufacture of newly discovered synthetic rubber and fabrics, made possible an increase of 50 percent in the nation's productive capacity and the creation of 17 million jobs. Factories operated around-the-clock, seven days a week. With better equipment and more motivation, American workers proved twice as productive as the Germans, five times as productive as the Japanese. No wonder the actual volume of industrial output expanded at the fastest rate in American history. Military production alone grew from 2 percent of the 1939 total gross national product to 40 percent of the 1943 total. "Something is happening," announced Time magazine, "that Adolf Hitler does not understand . . . it is the miracle of production."

Businesses scored huge profits from military contracts. The government provided low-interest loans and even direct subsidies for the expansion of construction of facilities, with generous tax write-offs for retooling. The 100 largest corporations, which manufactured 30 percent of all goods in 1940, garnered 70 percent of all war and civilian contracts and the bulk of the war profits. On the other hand, many small businesses closed, a half-million between 1941 and 1943 alone.

Defense production transformed entire regions. The impact was strongest in the West—the major staging area for the war in the Pacific—where the federal government spent nearly $40 billion for military and industrial expansion. California secured 10 percent of all federal funds, and by 1944 Los Angeles had become the nation's second largest manufacturing center, only slightly behind Detroit. The South also benefited from 60 of the army's 100 new camps. Its textile factories hummed: the army alone required nearly 520 million pairs of socks and 230 million pairs of pants. The southern branch of the Manhattan Project, the Oak Ridge, Tennessee, facility for the production of uranium, employed more than 80,000 workers during 1945, its peak year. The economic boom lifted entire populations out of sharecropping and tenancy into well-paid industrial jobs in the cities and pumped unprecedented profits into southern business. Across the country the rural population decreased by almost 20 percent.

Despite a "Food for Freedom" program, American farmers could not keep up with the rising international demand or even the domestic market for milk, potatoes, fruits, and sugar. The Department of Agriculture reached its goals only in areas such as livestock production, thanks to skyrocketing wholesale prices for meat. The war also speeded the development of large-scale, mechanized production of crops, including the first widespread use of chemical fertilizers and pesticides. By 1945 farm income had doubled, but thousands of small farms had disappeared, never to return.

New Workers

The wartime economy brought an unprecedented number of new workers into the labor force. The *bracero* program, negotiated by United States and Mexico in 1942, opened to Mexicans short-term employment in trades previously closed to them, such as shipbuilding on the Pacific coast. More than 200,000 Mexicans entered the United States legally to help harvest crops. In 1944 a survey published by the Bureau of Indian Affairs reported that more than 46,000 Indian peoples were working in either agriculture or industry. The Sioux and Navajos, for example, were hired in large numbers to help build military depots and military training centers. African Americans found new opportunities in industry, and the number of black workers rose from 2,900,000 to 3,800,000.

The war most dramatically altered the wage-earning patterns of women. The female labor force grew by over 50 percent, reaching 19.5 million in 1945. The rate of growth proved especially high for white women over the age of thirty-five, and for the first time married women became the majority of female wage earners. The employment rate changed comparatively little for African American women; fully 90 percent had been in the labor force in 1940. However, many black women left domestic service for higher-paying jobs in manufacturing.

Despite this jump in employment rates, neither government nor industry rushed to recruit women. Well into the summer of 1942 the Department of War advised

Facing a shortage of workers and increased production demands, the War Manpower Commission and the Office of War Information conducted a campaign to recruit women into the labor force. Women were encouraged to "take a job for your husband/son/brother" and to "keep the world safe for your children." Higher wages also enticed many women to take jobs in factories producing aircraft, ships, and ordnance. This photograph shows women working on the assembly line at Douglas Aircraft's plant in Long Beach, California, in 1944.

cut and welded sheet metal, and operated forklifts and drill presses. On the Pacific coast, more than one-third of all workers in aircraft and shipbuilding were women. One female African American ship welder recalled: "There is nothing in the training to prepare you for the excruciating noise you get down in the ship. Any who were not heart-and-soul determined to stick it out would fade out right away. . . . And it isn't only your muscles that must harden. It's your nerve, too."

Compared to the Great Depression, when married women were barred from many jobs, World War II opened up new fields. The number of women automobile workers, for example, jumped from 29,000 to 200,000, that of women electrical workers from 100,000 to 374,000. Polled near the end of the war, the overwhelming majority—75 percent—of women workers expressed a desire to keep working, preferably at the same jobs. One woman spoke for many in describing her wartime work as "thrilling" and "exciting," adding that it was also "something women have never been allowed to do before." Many also candidly admitted that they most of all liked earning good money. One woman reported that her assembly-line job in the aircraft industry paid $1.15 per hour, a huge increase over the hourly wage she formerly earned as a waitress: 20 cents, with no tips allowed.

Although wartime employment changed the lives and raised the expectations of many new workers, the major advances proved short-lived. As early as 1943 some industries began planning to lay off women as war production wound down. With jobs reserved for returning veterans, women in industry saw their numbers diminish rapidly; as many as 4 million lost their jobs between 1944 and 1946. Although skyrocketing inflation propelled many married women back into the labor force by the end of the decade, they did not pick up lucrative jobs in heavy industry.

Wartime Strikes

Although 17 million new jobs were created during the war, the economic gains were unevenly distributed. Wages increased by as much as 50 percent but never as fast as profits or prices. This widely reported dispar-

businesses to hold back from hiring women "until all available male labor in the area had first been employed." Likewise, neither government nor industry expected women to stay in their jobs when the war ended. Recruitment campaigns targeted "Mrs. Stay-at-Home" yet underscored the temporary aspect of her wartime service. "Rosie the Riveter" appeared in posters and advertisements as the model female citizen, but only "for the duration." In Washington, D.C., women bus drivers were given badges to wear on their uniforms that read: "I am taking the place of a man who went to war."

For the most part, advertisers used conventional gender stereotypes to make wartime jobs appealing to women. Recruitment posters and informational films depicted women's new industrial jobs as simple variations of domestic tasks. Where once housewives sewed curtains for their kitchens, they now produced silk parachutes. Their skill with a vacuum cleaner easily translated into riveting on huge ships. "Instead of cutting a cake," one newsreel explained, "this woman [factory worker] cuts the pattern of aircraft parts. Instead of baking a cake, this woman is cooking gears to reduce the tension in the gears after use."

In practice, however, many stereotypes broke down. Women mined coal, repaired aircraft engines,

	STRIKES AND LOCKOUTS IN THE UNITED STATES, 1940–1945			
Year	Number of Strikes	Number of Workers Involved	Number of Man-Days Idle	Percent of Total Employed
1940	2,508	576,988	6,700,872	2.3
1941	4,288	2,362,620	23,047,556	8.4
1942	2,968	839,961	4,182,557	2.8
1943	3,752	1,981,279	13,500,529	6.9
1944	4,956	2,115,637	8,721,079	7.0
1945	4,750	3,467,000	38,025,000	12.2

Despite "no-strike" pledges, workers staged wildcat strikes in the war years. Union leaders negotiated shorter hours, higher wages, and seniority rules and helped to build union membership to a new height. When the war ended, nearly 30 percent of all nonagricultural workers were union members.

Source: "Work Stoppages Caused by Labor-Management Disputes in 1945," *Monthly Labor Review,* May 1946, p. 720; and Martin Glaberman, *War Time Strikes* (Detroit: Bewick, 1980), p. 36.

ity produced one of the most turbulent periods in American labor history.

Labor strife began even before U.S. involvement in World War II. Only two weeks after the 1940 election, workers struck at the Vultee aircraft plant in Los Angeles. After the attorney general denounced the strikers as unpatriotic and the FBI began to harass participants, workers throughout the city walked off their jobs in sympathy with the aircraft workers. In April 1941 the president himself intervened in a large strike at Allis Chalmers near Milwaukee, threatening seizure of the plant and forcing a settlement after 75 days of work stoppage. Later that year Roosevelt ordered troops to break the North American Aviation strike at Inglewood, California.

More workers went on strike in 1941, before the United States entered the war, than in any previous year except 1919. Rising production orders and tightening labor markets made strikes feasible: jobs were plentiful, and business leaders, anticipating hefty profits, had reason to settle quickly. This climate prompted a militant union drive at Ford Motor Company's enormous River Rouge plant, and the United Auto Workers (UAW) emerged as one of the most powerful labor organizations in the world.

Once the United States entered the war, the major unions agreed to no-strike pledges for its duration. The National War Labor Board, with representatives from business and labor, encouraged employers to allow unions in their plants, and unions secured contracts that included automatic dues checkoff, high wages, and new fringe benefits such as pension plans. Total union membership increased from 10.5 million to 14.7 million, with women's share alone rising from 11 to 23 percent.

Unions also enrolled 1,250,000 African Americans, twice the prewar number. But many white workers resisted this change. "Hate strikes" broke out in plants across the country when African Americans were hired or promoted to jobs customarily held by white workers. For example, at a U.S. Rubber Company factory in Detroit, more than half the workers walked out in 1943 when African American women began to operate the machinery. Such strikes usually ended quickly because black workers refused to back down.

Rank-and-file union members staged other illegal "wildcat" strikes. The most dramatic, a walkout of more than a half-million coal miners in 1943 led by the rambunctious John L. Lewis, withstood the attacks of the government and the press. Roosevelt repeatedly ordered the mines seized, only to find, as Lewis retorted, that coal could not be mined with bayonets. The Democratic majority in Congress passed the first federal antistrike bill, giving the president power to penalize strikers, even to draft them. And yet the strikes grew in size and number, reaching a level greater than in any other four-year period in American history.

THE HOME FRONT

Most Americans thoroughly appreciated the burst of prosperity brought on by wartime production. But they also experienced dramatic and unanticipated changes in the ways they worked and lived. Food rationing, long workdays, and separation from loved ones were just a few of the new conditions of daily life. Americans in communities across the country endured four intense years of adjustment.

Most Americans were happy and proud to make whatever sacrifices they could to help bring about the Allied victory. But alongside national unity ran deep conflicts on the home front. Racial and ethnic hostilities flared repeatedly and on several occasions erupted in violence.

Families in Wartime

Despite the uncertainties of wartime, or perhaps because of them, men and women rushed into marriage. The surge in personal income caused by the wartime economic boom meant that many young couples could afford to set up their own households—something their counterparts in the 1930s had not been able to do. As one social scientist remarked at the time, "Economic conditions were ripe for a rush to the altar." For other couples, the prospect of separation provided the incentive. The U.S. Census Bureau estimated that between 1940 and 1943 at least a million more people married than would have been expected had there been no war. The marriage rate skyrocketed, peaking in 1946. The median age for first marriage for women dropped to an unprecedented low of 20.3 years. But by 1946 the number of divorces also set records.

Housing shortages were acute, and rents were high. So scarce were apartments that taxi drivers became, for an extra fee, up-to-the-minute guides to vacancies. Able to set their own terms, landlords frequently discriminated against families with children and even more so against racial minorities. To ease these pressures, the National Housing Agency kicked off the "Share Your Home" campaign, which ultimately encouraged 1.5 million families to open their homes to friends, relatives, or strangers. The federal government also financed the construction of low-cost housing projects, which furnished approximately 2 million new residential units.

Supplying a household was scarcely less difficult. Although retailers extended their store hours into the evenings and weekends, shopping had to be squeezed in between long hours on the job. Extra planning was necessary for purchasing government-rationed staples such as meat, cheese, sugar, milk, coffee, gasoline, and even shoes. Many women found it nearly impossible to manage both a demanding job and a household; this dual responsibility contributed to high turnover and absentee rates in factories. A 1943 survey reported that 40 percent of all women who left war plants did so for marital or household reasons rather than because of unsatisfactory wages or working conditions.

The care of small children became a major problem. Wartime employment or military service often separated husbands and wives, leaving children

Students at Officers' Training School at Northwestern University, who were not allowed to marry until they were commissioned as ensigns, apply for marriage licenses in Chicago, August 20, 1943, shortly before graduation. These young couples helped the marriage rate skyrocket during World War II.

in the hands of only one parent. But even when families stayed together, both adults often worked long hours, sometimes on different shifts. Although the War Manpower Commission estimated that as many as 2 million children needed some form of child care, federally funded day-care centers served less than 10 percent of defense workers' children. Polls indicated that the majority of mothers would in any case refuse to send their youngsters to a public child-care center. In some communities, industries and municipal governments established limited facilities that could not keep up with the rapid increase in the number of "latchkey" children.

Juvenile delinquency rose during the war. With employers often relaxing minimum age requirements for employment, many teenagers quit school for the high wages of factory jobs. Between 1941 and 1944 high school enrollments decreased by 1.2 million. Runaways drifted from city to city, finding temporary work at wartime plants or at military installations. Gangs formed in major urban areas, leading to brawling, prostitution, or automobile thefts for joy rides. Overall, however, with so many young men either employed or serving in the armed forces, crime by juvenile as well as adult males declined. In contrast, complaints against girls, mainly for sexual offenses or for running away from home, increased significantly. In response, local officials created various youth agencies and charged them with developing more recreational and welfare programs.

In 1944 the U.S. Office of Education and the Children's Bureau inaugurated a back-to-school campaign. Local school boards appealed to employers to hire only older workers, and toward the end of the war the student dropout rate began to decline. The public schools, meanwhile, expanded their curriculums to include nutrition, hygiene, first aid, and the political context of the war itself. Although many teachers had quit to take better-paying jobs in industry, those who remained often organized scrap and salvage missions, war bond drives, Victory gardens, and letter-writing campaigns. In many localities, the school stood at the center of community war efforts.

Public health improved greatly during the war. Forced to cut back on expenditures for medical care during the Great Depression, many Americans now spent large portions of their wartime paychecks on doctors, dentists, and prescription drugs. But even more important were the benefits provided to the more than 16 million men inducted into the armed forces and their dependents. The majority of young, well-trained physicians and dentists worked in uniform, providing their services at government expense. The number of doctors and dentists also increased dramatically: the graduating classes of 1944 were twice as large as those of any prewar year. Nationally, incidences of such communicable diseases as typhoid fever, tuberculosis, and diphtheria dropped considerably, the infant death rate fell by more than a third, and life expectancy increased by three years. The death rate in 1942, excluding battle deaths, was the lowest in the nation's history. In the South and Southwest, however, racism and widespread poverty combined to halt or even reverse these trends. These regions continued to have the highest infant and maternal mortality rates in the nation.

The Internment of Japanese Americans

After the attack on Pearl Harbor, many Americans feared an invasion of the mainland and suspected Japanese Americans of secret loyalty to an enemy government. On December 8, 1941, the federal government froze the financial assets of those born in Japan, known as Issei, who had been barred from U.S. citizenship. Politicians, patriotic organizations, and military officials, meanwhile, called for the removal of all Americans of Japanese descent from Pacific coastal areas. Although a State Department intelligence report certified their loyalty, Japanese Americans—two-thirds of whom were American-born citizens—became the only ethnic group singled out for legal sanctions.

Charges of sedition masked long-standing racial prejudices. The press began to use the word "Jap" in headlines, while political cartoonists employed blatant racial stereotypes. Popular songs appeared with titles like "You're a Sap, Mister Jap, to Make a Yankee Cranky." The head of the Western Defense Command, General John L. DeWitt, called the Japanese "an enemy race," bound by "racial affinities" to their homeland no matter how many generations removed. "The very fact that no sabotage has taken place to date," an army report suggested, with twisted logic, "is a disturbing and confirming indication that action will be taken."

On February 19, 1942, President Roosevelt signed Executive Order 9066, suspending the civil rights of Japanese Americans and authorizing the exclusion of approximately 110,000 men, women, and children from (mainly) California, Oregon, Washington, and southern Arizona. While the government confiscated most of their personal property, the army began to round up and remove them from the communities where they lived and worked.

During the spring of 1942, Japanese American families received one week's notice to close up their businesses and homes before being transported to one of the ten internment camps managed by the War Relocation Authority. The guarded camps were located as far away as Arkansas, although the majority had been set up in isolated districts of Utah, Colorado, Idaho, Arizona, Wyoming, and California. Karl G. Yoneda described his quarters at Manzanar, California:

There were no lights, stoves, or window panes. My two cousins and I, together with seven others, were crowded into a 25 x 30 foot room. We slept on army cots with our clothes on. The next morning we discovered that there were no toilets or washrooms. . . . We saw GIs manning machine guns in the watchtowers. The barbed wire fence which surrounded the camp was visible against the background of the snow-covered Sierra mountain range. "So this is the American-style concentration camp," someone remarked.

By August, virtually every West Coast resident who had at least one Japanese grandparent had been interned.

The Japanese American Citizens League charged that "racial animosity" rather than military necessity had dictated the internment policy. Despite the protest of the American Civil Liberties Union and several church groups against the abridgment of the civil rights of Japanese Americans, the Supreme Court in *Korematsu v. U.S.* (1944) upheld the constitutionality of relocation on grounds of national security. By this time a program of gradual release was in place, although the last center, at Tule Lake, California, did not close until March 1946. In protest, nearly 6,000 Japanese Americans renounced their U.S. citizenship. Japanese Americans had lost homes and businesses valued at $500 million in what many historians judge the worst violation of American civil liberties during the war. Not until 1988 did the U.S. Congress vote reparations of $20,000 and a public apology to each of the 60,000 surviving victims.

Civil Rights and Race Riots

Throughout the war, African American activists conducted a "Double V" campaign, mobilizing not only for Allied victory but for their own rights as citizens. "The army is about to take me to fight for democracy," one Detroit resident said, "but I would as leave fight for democracy right here." Black militants demanded, at a minimum, fair housing and equal employment opportunities. President Roosevelt responded in a lukewarm fashion, supporting advances in civil rights that would not, in his opinion, disrupt the war effort.

Before the United States entered the war, A. Philip Randolph, president of both the Brotherhood of Sleeping Car Porters and the National Negro Congress, had organized the March on Washington Movement. At a planning meeting in Chicago a black woman had proposed sending African Americans to Washington, D.C., "from all over the country, in jalopies, in trains, and any way they can get there until we get some action from the White House." Local rallies were held across the country in preparation for the "great rally" of no less than 100,000 people at the Lincoln Memorial on the Fourth of July.

Eager to stop the movement, President Roosevelt met with Randolph, who proposed an executive order "making it mandatory that Negroes be permitted to work." Randolph reviewed several drafts before approving the text that became, on June 25, 1941, Executive Order 8802 banning discrimination in defense industries and government. The president later appointed a Fair Employment Practices Committee to hear complaints and to take "appropriate steps to redress grievances." Randolph called off the march but did not disband his all-black March on Washington organization. He remained determined to "shake up white America."

Byron Takashi Tsuzuki, Forced Removal, Act II, 1944. This Japanese American artist illustrates the forced relocation of Japanese Americans from their homes to one of ten inland camps in 1942. About 110,000 Japanese Americans were interned during World War II, some for up to four years. Beginning in January 1945, they were allowed to return to the Pacific coast.

Other civil rights organizations formed during wartime to fight both discrimination and Jim Crow practices, including segregation in the U.S. armed forces. The interracial Congress of Racial Equality (CORE), formed by pacifists in 1942, staged sit-ins at Chicago, Detroit, and Denver restaurants that refused to serve African Americans. In several cities, CORE used nonviolent means to challenge racial segregation in public facilities. Meanwhile, membership in the National Association for the Advancement of Colored People (NAACP), which took a strong stand against discrimination in the military, grew from 50,000 in 1940 to 450,000 in 1946.

The struggle for equality took shape within local communities. Approximately 1.2 million African Americans left the rural South to take jobs in wartime industries. They faced not only serious housing shortages but whites who were determined to keep them out of the best jobs and neighborhoods. In February 1942, when twenty black families attempted to move into new federally funded apartments adja-

cent to a Polish American community in Detroit, a mob of 700 white protesters halted the moving vans and burned a cross on the project's grounds. The police overlooked the white rioters but arrested black youths. Finally, two months later, 1,000 state troopers supervised the move of these families into the Sojourner Truth Homes, named after the famous abolitionist and former slave.

Racial violence reached its wartime peak during the summer of 1943, when 274 conflicts broke out in nearly fifty cities. In Detroit, twenty-five blacks and nine whites were killed and more than 700 were injured. After the riot, one writer reported: "I thought that I had witnessed an experience peculiar to the Deep South. On the streets of Detroit I saw again the same horrible exhibition of uninhibited hate as they fought and killed one another—white against black—in a frenzy of homicidal mania, without rhyme or reason." The poet Langston Hughes, who supported U.S. involvement in the war, wrote:

> *Looky here, America*
> *What you done done—*
> *Let things drift*
> *Until the riots come*
>
> *Yet you say we're fighting*
> *For democracy.*
> *Then why don't democracy*
> *Include me?*
>
> *I ask you this question*
> *Cause I want to know*
> *How long I got to fight*
> *BOTH HITLER—AND JIM CROW.*

The poet and educator Pauli Murray summed up the situation in a letter sent to President Roosevelt: "It is my conviction . . . that the problem of race, intensified by economic conflict and war nerves . . . will eventually . . . occupy a dominant position as a national domestic problem." Her words proved prescient.

Zoot-suit Riots

On the night of June 4, 1943, sailors poured into nearly 200 cars and taxis to drive through the streets of East Los Angeles in search of Mexican Americans dressed in zoot suits. The sailors assaulted their victims at random, even chasing one youth into a movie theater and stripping him of his clothes while the audience cheered. Riots broke out and continued for five days.

Two communities had collided, with tragic results. The sailors had only recently been uprooted from their hometowns and regrouped under the strict discipline of boot camp. Now stationed in southern California while awaiting departure overseas, they came face-to-face with

This painting is by Horace Pippin, a self-taught African American artist who began painting as therapy for an injury suffered while serving with the U.S. Army's 369th Colored Infantry Regiment during World War I. It is one of a series drawn during World War II illustrating the contradiction between the principles of libery and justice, for which Americans were fighting abroad, and the reality of race prejudice at home.

Mexican American teenagers wearing long-draped coats, pegged pants, pocket watches with oversized chains, and big floppy hats. To the sailors, the zoot suit was not just a flamboyant fashion. Unlike the uniform the young sailors wore, the zoot suit signaled a lack of patriotism.

The zoot-suiters, however, represented less than 10 percent of their community's youth. More than 300,000 Mexican Americans were serving in the armed forces, in numbers greater than their proportion of the draft-age population and in the most hazardous branches, the paratrooper and marine corps. Many others were employed in war industries in Los Angeles, which had become home to the largest community of Mexican Americans in the nation. For the first time Mexican Americans were finding well-paying jobs, and, like African Americans, they expected their government to protect them from discrimination.

There were several advances during the war. The Fair Employment Practices Committee fostered a limited expansion of civil rights. The Spanish-Speaking People's Division in the Office of Inter-American Affairs established centers in Denver, Salt Lake City, and Los Angeles to bring together community, business, and educational leaders in programs on Latin American culture. The office also developed programs to instill cultural pride and self-esteem among Mexican American children. School districts in California and throughout the Southwest introduced lessons on the Mexican heritage and encouraged bilingual education. Many schools also added vocational training classes to channel graduates into wartime industry.

But these new programs did little to ease the bitter racial and cultural conflict that on occasion became vicious. In Los Angeles, military and civilian authorities eventually contained the zoot-suit riots by ruling several sections of the city off limits to military personnel. The Los Angeles City Council passed legislation making the wearing of a zoot suit in public a criminal offense. Later, the Joint Finding Committee on Un-American Activities in California conducted hearings to determine whether foreign enemy agents had plotted the unrest. Nevertheless, many Mexican Americans expressed concern about their personal safety; some feared that, after the government rounded up the Japanese, they would be the next group sent to internment camps.

Popular Culture and "The Good War"

Global events shaped the lives of American civilians but appeared to touch them only indirectly in their everyday activities. Food shortages, long hours in the factories, and even fears for loved ones abroad did not take away all the pleasures of full employment and prosperity. With money in their pockets, Americans spent freely at vacation resorts, country clubs, race-tracks, nightclubs, dance halls, and movie theaters. Sales of books skyrocketed, and spectator sports attracted huge audiences.

This Mexican American zoot-suiter wears the typical thigh-length, broad-lapel jacket with padded shoulders, baggy trousers pegged at the cuff, and a broad-brimmed felt hat. A dramatic contrast to the military uniforms of the day, the zoot suit symbolized cultural rebellion.

Popular culture, especially music, seemed to bridge the growing racial divisions of the neighborhood and the workplace. Transplanted southern musicians, black and white, brought their regional styles to northern cities and adapted them quickly to the electric amplification of nightclubs and recording studios. "They'd made them steel guitars cry and whine," Ray Charles later remembered. Played on jukeboxes in bars, bus stations, and cafes, "country" and "rhythm & blues" not only won over new audiences but also inspired musicians themselves to crisscross old boundaries. The International Sweethearts of Rhythm, a group of black and white women singers, started in the Mississippi Delta but soon pleased audiences throughout the United States.

Many songs featured war themes. Personal sentiment meshed with government directive to depict a "good war," justifying massive sacrifice and dedicated to a worthy and even noble cause. The plaintive "A Rainbow at Midnight" by country singer Ernest Tubb expressed the hope of a common "dogface" soldier looking beyond the misery and horror to the promise of a brighter tomorrow. "Till Then," recorded by the harmonious black quartet, the Mills Brothers, offered the prospect of a romantic reunion when "the world will be free." The era's best-known tune, Irving Berlin's "White Christmas," evoked a lyrical nostalgia of past celebrations with family and friends close by. On the lighter side, novelty artist Spike Jones made his name with the "razz" or "Bronx cheer," in "We're Going to Ffft in the Fuehrer's Face."

Hollywood artists meanwhile threw themselves into a perpetual round of fund-raising and morale-boosting public events. Movie stars called on fans to buy war bonds and to support the troops. Combat films such as *Action in the North Atlantic* made heroes of ordinary Americans under fire, depicting GIs of different races and ethnicities discovering their common humanity. Movies with antifascist themes, such as *Tender Comrade,* promoted friendship among Russians and Americans, while films like *Since You Went Away* portrayed the loyalty and resilience of families with servicemen stationed overseas.

The wartime spirit also infected the juvenile world of comics. The climbing sales of nickel "books" spawned a proliferation of patriotic superheroes such as Flash, Hawkman, the Green Lantern, Captain Marvel, and the more comical Plastic Man. Captain America, created by the famed comic artist Jack Kirby, was a frail soldier who, when injected with a wonder drug, began delivering punches at Adolf Hitler even before the United States entered the war. Kirby went on to create "boy Commandos," intensifying juvenile identification with battlefield action. Even Bugs Bunny put on a uniform and fought sinister-looking enemies.

Fashion designers did their part. Padded shoulders and straight lines became popular for both men and women; BVD, a leading manufacturer of underwear, designed civilian clothing to resemble military attire. Patriotic Americans, such as civil defense volunteers and Red Cross workers, fancied uniforms, and women employed in defense plants wore pants, often for the first time. Restrictions on materials also influenced fashion. Production of nylon stockings was halted because the material was needed for parachutes. To save material, women's skirts were shortened, while the War Production Board encouraged cuffless "Victory Suits" for men. Executive Order M-217 restricted the colors of shoes manufactured during the war to "black, white, navy blue, and three shades of brown."

Never to see a single battle, safeguarded by two oceans, many Americans nevertheless experienced the war years as the most intense of their entire lives. Popular music, Hollywood movies, radio programs, and advertisements—all screened by the Office of War Information—encouraged a sense of personal involvement in a collective effort to preserve democracy at home and to save the world from fascism. No one was excluded, no action considered insignificant. Even casual conversation came under the purview of the government, which warned that "Loose Lips Sink Ships."

MEN AND WOMEN IN UNIFORM

During World War I, American soldiers served for a relatively brief period and in small numbers. A quarter-century later, World War II mobilized 16.4 million Americans into the armed forces. Although only 34 percent of men who served in the army saw combat—the majority during the final year of the war—the experience had a powerful impact on nearly everyone. Whether working in the steno pool at Great Lakes Naval Training Center in northern Illinois or slogging through mud with rifle in hand in the Philippines, many men and women saw their lives reshaped in unpredictable ways. Uprooted from their communities, they suddenly found themselves among strangers, in an unfamiliar geographical setting, and under a severe military regimen.

Creating the Armed Forces

Before the European war broke out in 1939, the majority of the 200,000 men in the U.S. armed forces were employed as military police, engaging in such tasks as patrolling the Mexican border or occupying colonial possessions, such as the Philippines. Neither the army nor the navy was prepared for the scale of combat World War II entailed. Only the Marine Corps, which had been planning since the 1920s to wrest control of the western Pacific from Japan, was poised to fight. Once mobilized for war, however, the United States became a first-rank military power.

On October 16, 1940, National Registration Day, all men between the ages of twenty-one and thirty-six were legally obligated to register for military service. Just two weeks later more than 5,000 local draft boards began to draw the first numbers to send men off to camps for one year of training. After the United States entered the war, the draft age was lowered to eighteen, and local boards were instructed to choose first from the youngest.

One-third of the men examined by the Selective Service were rejected. Surprising numbers were refused induction because they were physically unfit for military service, and nearly 1 million were rejected because of "neuropsychiatric disorders or emotional problems." At a time when only one American in four graduated from high school, induction centers turned away many conscripts because they were functionally illiterate.

But those who passed the screening tests joined the best-educated army in history: nearly half of white draftees had graduated from high school and 10 percent had attended college. Once inducted, soldiers spent the first month learning basic military skills such as shooting a rifle, pitching a tent, digging a foxhole, and saluting an officer.

The officer corps, whose top-ranking members were from the Command and General Staff School at Fort Leavenworth, tended to be highly professional, politically conservative, and personally autocratic. General Douglas MacArthur, supreme commander in the Pacific theater, was said to admire the discipline of the German army and to disparage political democracy. General Dwight D. Eisenhower, however, supreme commander of the Allied forces in Europe, projected a new and contrasting spirit. Distrusted by MacArthur and many of the older brass, Eisenhower appeared to his troops a model of fair play, encouraging young men to follow him into the officer corps for idealistic rather than career reasons.

The democratic rhetoric of the war and the sudden massive expansion of the armed forces contributed to this transformation of the officer corps. A shortage of officers during World War I had prompted a huge expansion of the Reserve Officer Training Corps, but its drilling and discipline alone

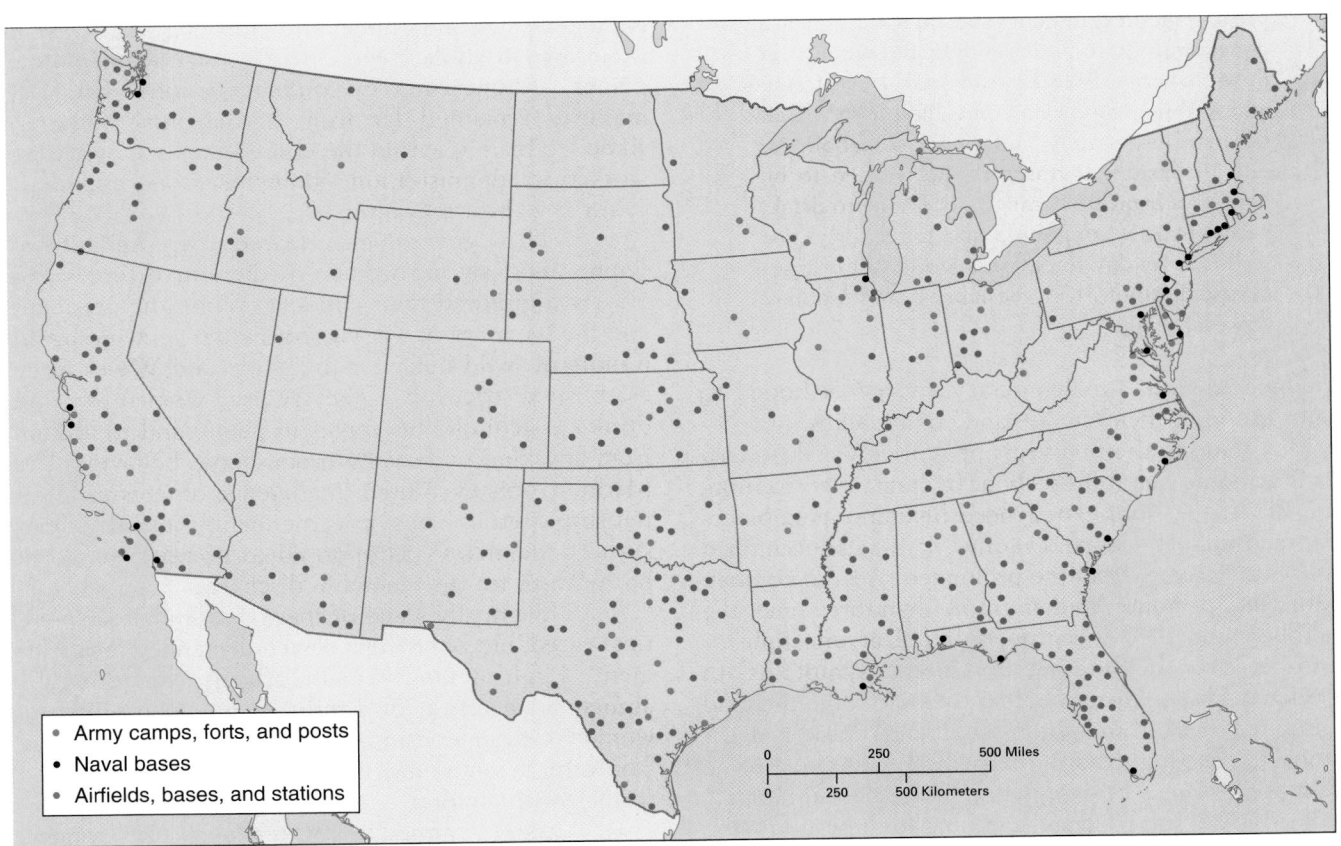

- Army camps, forts, and posts
- Naval bases
- Airfields, bases, and stations

Wartime Army Camps, Naval Bases, and Airfields   *Their locations chosen for political as well as defense reasons, military facilities were rapidly constructed in every state. The many facilities located in the South and West helped open these areas to economic development and an influx of new migrants.*

Source: Clifford L. Lord and Elizabeth H. Lord, *Lord & Lord Historical Atlas of the United States*, rev. ed. (New York: Holt, 1953), p. 309.

could not create good officers, and it was still insufficient to meet the demand for trained officers. Racing to make up for the deficiency, Army Chief of Staff George Marshall opened schools for officer candidates. In 1942, in seventeen-week training periods, these schools produced more than 54,000 platoon leaders. Closer in sensibility to the civilian population, these new officers were the kinds of leaders Eisenhower sought.

Most GIs (short for "government issue"), who were the vast majority of draftees, had limited contact with officers at the higher levels and instead forged bonds with their company commanders and men within their own combat units. "Everyone wants someone to look up to when he's scared," one GI explained. Most of all, soldiers depended on the solidarity of the group and the loyalty of their buddies to pull through the war.

The majority of GIs endured military discipline "to get the task done," as revealed in numerous polls. They longed foremost for peace. "In the magazines," wrote the popular war correspondent Ernie Pyle,

> war seemed romantic and exciting, full of heroics and vitality. . . . Certainly there were great tragedies, unbelievable heroism, even a constant undertone of comedy. But when I sat down to write, I saw instead men . . . suffering and wishing they were somewhere else . . . all of them desperately hungry for somebody to talk to besides themselves, no women to be heroes in front of, damned little wine to drink, precious little song, cold and fairly dirty, just toiling from day to day in a world full of insecurity, discomfort, homesickness and a dulled sense of danger.

Pledged to fight for democracy, most GIs hoped to return soon to their families and communities.

During the first years of World War II, Americans at home heard little about its human devastation, but GIs at the front experienced firsthand its unprecedented brutality, fear, and agony. Many GIs succumbed to "battle fatigue" from the prolonged stress of combat. More than 1 million soldiers, more than three times the number who died in battle, suffered at one time or another from debilitating psychiatric symptoms. In France, where soldiers spent up to 200 days in the field without a break from fighting, thousands cracked, occasionally inflicting wounds on themselves in order to be sent home. One who simply fled the battlefront, Private Eddie Slovik, was tried and executed for desertion—the first such execution since the Civil War. Slovik had been singled out as an example. Most deserters were sentenced to hard labor in military stockades. Only in 1944 did the army devise a rotation system to relieve exhausted soldiers.

Women Enter the Military

Before World War II women served in the armed forces mainly as nurses and clerical workers. The Army Nurse Corps, created in 1901, and the Navy Nurse Corps, formed in 1908, were scarcely military organizations. Recruits earned neither military pay nor rank and received scant public recognition for their services.

With the approach of World War II, Massachusetts Republican congresswoman Edith Nourse Rogers proposed legislation for the formation of a women's corps. The army instead drafted its own bill, which Rogers sponsored, creating in May 1942 the Women's Army Auxiliary Corps (WAAC), later changed to Women's Army Corps (WAC). In 1942–43 other bills established a women's division of the navy (WAVES), the Women's Airforce Service Pilots, and the Marine Corps Women's Reserve. Overall, more than 350,000 women served in World War II, two-thirds of them in the WACS and WAVES. As a group, they were better educated and more skilled than the average soldier.

Although barred from combat, women were not necessarily protected from danger. Nurses accompanied the troops into combat in Africa, Italy, and France, treated men under fire, and dug and lived in their own foxholes. More than 1,000 women flew planes, although not in combat missions. The vast majority remained far from battlefronts, however, stationed mainly within the United States, where they worked in administration, communications, and clerical or health-care facilities.

The government feared the spread of "immorality" among women in the armed forces and closely monitored their conduct. While the president and the secretary of war vigorously denied widespread rumors of "wild behavior" by Wacs and Waves, they established strict rules. They advised women to avoid drinking alcoholic beverages in public and to abstain from any kind of sexually promiscuous behavior. The Marine Corps even used intelligence officers to ferret out suspected lesbians or women who showed "homosexual tendencies" (as opposed to homosexual acts), both causes for dishonorable discharge.

Eventually some of these discriminatory practices eased, but only after women demanded fair treatment. High-ranking female officers, for example, argued for a repeal of a military policy prohibiting women from supervising male workers, even in offices. The armed forces did not, however, lift its ban on women with children.

Like the armed forces in general, the women's services were marked by racial segregation, despite government declarations of egalitarianism. Black women and white women ate in separate mess halls and slept in separate barracks. At the beginning of the war, black nurses were admitted to serve only black

New recruits to the Women's Army Corps (WAC) pick up their clothing "issue" (allotment). These volunteers served in many capacities, from nursing men in combat to performing clerical and communications duties "stateside" (within the United States). Approximately 140,000 women served in the WACS during World War II.

soldiers, and the WAVES refused all black women on the ground that the navy had no black airmen to attend. Only in 1944 did Roosevelt order the navy to incorporate black Waves, and fewer than 100 served.

Old Practices and New Horizons

The draft brought hundreds of thousands of young African American men into the army, where they would join all-black regiments commanded by white officers. Secretary of War Henry Stimson refused to challenge this policy, saying that the army could not operate effectively as "a sociological laboratory." African Americans nevertheless enlisted at a rate 60 percent above their proportion of the general population.

By 1944 black soldiers represented 10 percent of the army's troops, and overall approximately 1 million African Americans served in the armed forces during World War II. The majority served in the Signal, Engineer, and Quartermaster Corps, mainly in construction or stevedore work. Only a small minority were permitted to rise to fighting status and lower officer ranks, and only toward the end of the war when the shortage of infantry neared a crisis. An all-black tank squadron earned distinction in Germany. And despite the very small number of African Americans admitted to the Air Force, the 99th Pursuit Squadron gained high marks in action against the feared German air force, the Luftwaffe. Even the Marine Corps and the Coast Guard agreed to end their historic exclusion of African Americans, although they recruited and promoted only a small number.

The ordinary black soldier, sailor, or marine, saw no benefit from the late-in-the-war gains of a few. Throughout 1941 race riots initiated by whites against blacks broke out at training bases, especially in the South. Serving in segregated, low-prestige units, African Americans encountered discrimination everywhere, from the army canteen to the religious chapels. Even the blood banks kept blood segregated by race (although a black physician, Dr. Charles Drew, had process for storing plasma). Toward the ne war, segregation began to break down, if y in post stores and recreational facilities.

The army also grouped Japanese Americans into segregated units, sending most to fight far from the Pacific theater. Better educated than the average soldier, many Nisei soldiers who knew Japanese served state-side as interpreters and translators. When the army decided to create a Nisei regiment, more than 10,000 volunteers stepped forward, only one in five of whom was accepted. The Nisei 442d fought heroically in Italy and France and became the most decorated regiment in the war.

Despite segregation, the armed forces ultimately pulled Americans of all varieties out of their communities. Many Jews and other second-generation European immigrants, for example, described their stint in the military as an "Americanizing" experience. Many Indian peoples left reservations for the first time, approximately 25,000 serving in the armed forces. For many African Americans, military service provided a bridge to postwar civil rights agitation. Amzie Moore, who later helped to organize the Mississippi Freedom Democratic Party, traced his understanding that "people are just people" to his experiences in the armed forces during World War II.

Many homosexuals also discovered a wider world. Despite a policy barring them from military service, most slipped through mass screening at induction centers. Moreover, the emotional pressures of wartime, especially the fear of death, encouraged close friendships, and homosexuals in the military often found more room than in civilian life to express their sexual orientation openly. In army canteens, for example, men often danced with one another, whereas in civilian settings they would have been subject to ridicule or even arrest for such activity. "The war is a tragedy to my mind and soul," one gay soldier confided, "but to my physical being, it's a memorable experience." Lesbian Wacs and Waves had similar tales.

Most soldiers looked back at the war, with all its dangers and discomforts, as the greatest experience they would ever know. As the *New Republic* predicted in 1943, they met fellow Americans from every part of the country and recognized for the first time in their lives "the bigness and wholeness of the United States." "Hughie was a Georgia cracker, so he knew something about moonshine," remembered one soldier. Another fondly recalled "this fellow from Wisconsin we called 'Moose.'" The army itself promoted these expectations of new experience. *Twenty-Seven Soldiers* (1944), a government-produced film for the troops, showed Allied soldiers of several nationalities all working together in harmony.

Overseas Occupation

As a liberating or occupying force, Americans stationed overseas had a mixed record. Children especially welcomed the GIs, who brought candy and chewing gum. But civilians in areas not controlled by Axis powers often resented the presence of American troops, whose demands for entertainment could turn their communities into red-light zones for drinking and prostitution.

Few Britishers welcomed the nearly 3 million GIs who were stationed in their country between 1942 and 1945. "It is difficult to go anywhere in London without having the feeling that Britain is now Occupied Territory," complained novelist George Orwell in 1943. The privileges of American troops also irked the British. American soldiers enjoyed a standard of living that surpassed that of both the military and civilian populations of Europe. A GI earned three times as much pay as his British counterpart, and consumed an average of four pounds of rations daily. Even their uniforms outshone those of the British, who mocked: "They're overfed, overpaid, overdressed, oversexed—and over here."

The relationship between GIs and civilians was worse on the Continent. At first, the French welcomed the American troops as soldiers of liberation. But the Americans arrived in 1944, when several million Europeans were without homes and nearly everyone was living on the brink of starvation. The GIs themselves were war-weary or war-crazed, and not a few committed petty robberies or rapes in towns and villages en route to Paris. "Intoxication," one study found, "was the largest contributing factor to crime in the European Theater of Operations."

In Belgium and southern Holland, however, where Nazi rule had been harsh, American soldiers were greeted as heroes. City restaurants were renamed "Cafe Texas" or "Cafe Alaska." Civilians cheered the Americans and eagerly shared—or traded sexual favors for—their supply of chewing gum, cash, and cigarettes. Despite government-sponsored precautions, the rate of venereal disease ran at 42 per 1,000 soldiers.

Prisoners of War

Approximately 120,000 Americans became prisoners of war (POWs). Those captured by the Germans were taken back to camps—*Olfags* for officers or *Stalags* for enlisted men—where they sat out the remainder of the war, mainly fighting boredom. Registered by the Swiss Red Cross, they could receive packages of supplies and occasionally join work brigades. By contrast, Russian POWs were starved and occasionally murdered in German camps.

Conditions for POWs in the Pacific were, however, worse than abysmal. Of the 20,000 Americans captured in the Philippines early in the war, only 40 percent survived to return home in 1945. At least 6,000 American and Filipino prisoners, beaten and denied food and water, died on the notorious eighty-

A *painting by Sidney Simon of American POWs freed from Japanese captors at Bilibid prison, in Manila, 1945, after the U.S. reconquest of the Philippines. The battle of the Philippine Sea and the battle of Leyte Gulf during the previous year had nearly broken Japanese resistance in the area, but the cleanup process revealed the awful price that Americans and their Filipino allies had paid. As prisoners of war, they had suffered terribly from malnutrition and improperly attended wounds and from an unsparing and inhumane Japanese military code of behavior.*

Sidney Simon, *P.O.W.s at Bilibid Prison*, 1945. Oil on canvas, 25 x 30 inches. Center of Military History, U.S. Army.

mile "Death March" through the jungles on the Bataan Peninsula in 1942. After the survivors reached the former U.S. air base Camp O'Donnell, hundreds died weekly in a cesspool of disease and squalor.

The Japanese army felt only contempt for POWs; its own soldiers evaded capture by killing themselves. The Imperial Army assigned its most brutal troops to guard prisoners and imposed strict and brutal discipline in the camps. In a postwar survey, 90 percent of former POWs from the Pacific reported that they had been beaten. A desire for retribution, as well as racist attitudes, prompted GIs to treat Japanese prisoners far more brutally than enemy soldiers captured in Europe or Africa.

THE WORLD AT WAR

During the first year of declared war, the Allies remained on the defensive. Hitler's forces held the European Continent and pounded England with aerial bombardments while driving deep into Russia and across northern Africa to take the Suez Canal. The situation in the Pacific was scarcely better. Just two hours after the attack on Pearl Harbor, Japanese planes struck the main U.S. base in the Philippines and demolished half the air force commanded by General Douglas MacArthur. Within a short time, MacArthur was forced to withdraw his troops to the Bataan Peninsula, admitting that Japan had practically seized the Pacific.

The War in Europe

Roosevelt called the news "all bad," and his military advisers predicted a long fight to victory.

But the Allies enjoyed several important advantages: vast natural resources and a skilled workforce with sufficient reserves to accelerate the production of weapons and ammunitions; the determination of millions of antifascists throughout Europe and Asia; and the capacity of the Soviet Union to endure immense losses. Slowly at first, but then with quickening speed, these advantages made themselves felt.

Soviets Halt Nazi Drive

The weapons and tactics of World War II were radically different from those of World War I. Unlike World War I, which was fought by immobile armies kept behind trenches by bursts of machine-gun fire, World War II

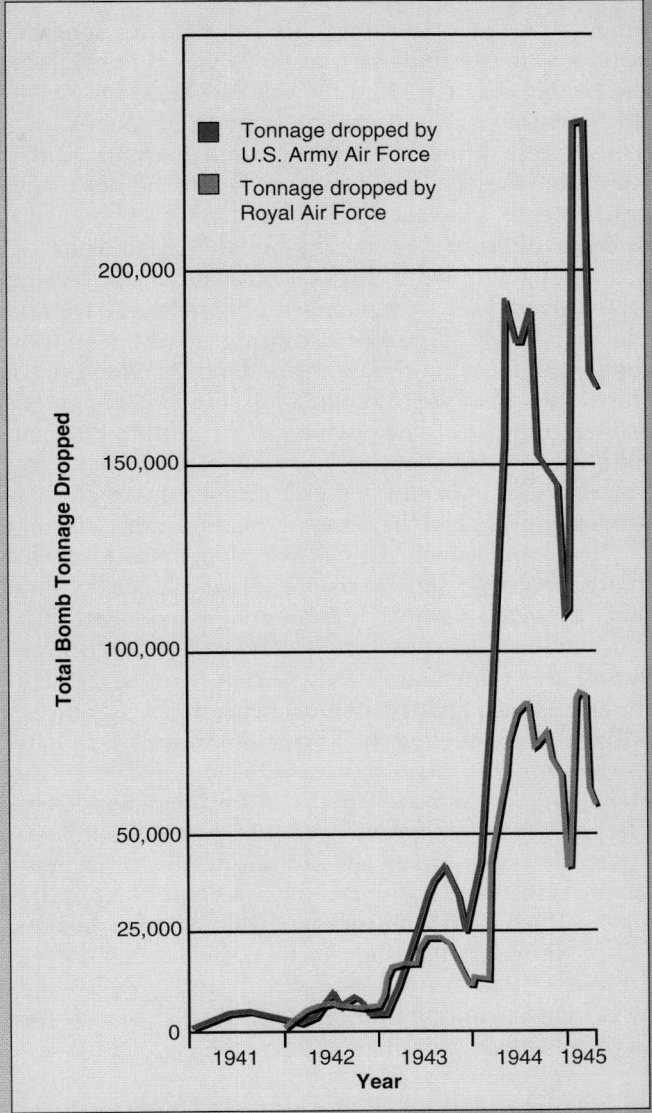

World War II: *Personnel and Bombs*

The offensive phase of the Allied campaign against the Axis unfolded late in the war. Major defeats in the Soviet Union and Africa deprived Germany of the resources needed to expand the war. The British and Americans, with an almost endless supply of materials and personnel, proceeded to overpower Germany and its European allies. Germans had ruled the skies early in the war. By 1943, Allied planes destroyed the German and Italian systems of transportation and supply, making cities almost unlivable. As British and Americans troops continued to pour into Europe, Allied victory became inevitable.

was a war of offensive maneuvers punctuated by surprise attacks. Its chief weapons were tanks and airplanes, combining mobility and concentrated firepower. Also of major importance were artillery and explosives, which according to some estimates accounted for over 30 percent of the casualties. Major improvements in communication systems, mainly two-way radio transmission and radiotelephony permitting commanders to stay in contact with division leaders, also played a decisive role from the beginning of the war.

Early on, Hitler had used these methods to seize the advantage, purposefully creating terror among the stricken populations of western Europe as he routed their armies. The Royal Air Force, however, fought the Luftwaffe to a standstill in the Battle of Britain, frustrating Hitler's hopes of invading England. In the summer of 1941, he turned his attention to the east, hoping to invade and conquer the Soviet Union before the United States entered the war. But he had to delay the invasion to come to the support of Mussolini, whose weak army had been pushed back in North Africa and Greece. The attack on Russia did not come until June 22, six weeks later than planned and too late to achieve its goals before the brutal Russian winter.

The burden of the war now fell on the Soviet Union. From June to September, Hitler's forces overran the Red Army, killing or capturing nearly 3 million soldiers and leaving thousands to die from exposure or starvation. But Nazi commanders did not count on civilian resistance. The Soviets rallied, cutting German supply lines and sending every available resource to Soviet troops concentrated just outside Moscow. After furious fighting and the onset of severe winter weather, the Red Army launched a massive counterattack, catching the freezing German troops off guard. For the first time, the Nazi war machine suffered a major setback.

Turning strategically away from Moscow, during the summer of 1942 German troops headed toward Crimea and the rich oil fields of the Caucasus. Still set on conquering the Soviet Union and turning its vast resources to his own use, Hitler decided to attack Stalingrad, a major industrial city on the Volga River. The Soviets suffered more casualties during the following battles than Americans did during the entire war. But intense house-to-house and street fighting and a massive Soviet counteroffensive took an even greater toll on the Nazi fighting machine. By February 1943 the German Sixth Army had met defeat, overpowered by Soviet war troops and weapons. More than 100,000 German soldiers surrendered.

Already in retreat but plotting one last desperate attempt to halt the Red Army, the Germans threw most of their remaining armored vehicles into action at Kursk, in the Ukraine, in July 1943. The clash quickly developed into the greatest land battle in history. More than 2 million troops and 6,000 tanks went into action. After another stunning defeat, the Germans had decisively lost the initiative. Their only option was to delay the advance of the Red Army against their homeland.

Meanwhile, the Soviet Union had begun to recover from its early losses, even as tens of millions of its own people remained homeless and near starvation. Assisted by the U.S. Lend-Lease program, by 1942 the Soviets were outproducing Germany in many types of weapons and other supplies. Nazi officers and German civilians alike began to doubt that Hitler could win the war. The Soviet victories had turned the tide of the war.

The Allied Offensive

In the spring of 1942, Germany, Italy, and Japan commanded a territory extending from France to the Pacific Ocean. They controlled central Europe and a large section of the Soviet Union as well as considerable parts of China and the southwestern Pacific. But their momentum was flagging. American shipbuilding outpaced the punishment Nazi submarines inflicted on allied shipping, and sub-sinking destroyers greatly reduced the submarines' threat. The United States far outstripped Germany in the production of landing craft and amphibious vehicles, two of the most important innovations of the war. Also outnumbered by the Allies, the German air force was limited to defensive action. On land, the United States and Great Britain had the trucks and jeeps to field fully mobile armies, while German troops marched in and out of Russia with packhorses.

Still, German forces represented a mighty opponent on the European Continent. Fighting the Nazis there almost by themselves, the Soviets repeatedly appealed for the creation of a Second Front, an Allied offensive against Germany from the West. The Allies focused instead on securing North Africa and then on an invasion of Italy, hoping to move from there into Central Europe.

On the night of October 23–24, 1942, near El Alamein in the deserts of western Egypt, the British Eighth Army halted a major offensive by the German Afrika Korps, headed by General Edwin Rommel, the famed "Desert Fox." Although suffering heavy losses— approximately 13,000 men and more than 500 tanks— their forces destroyed the Italian North African Army and much of Germany's Afrika Korps. Americans entered the war in Europe as part of Operation Torch, the landing of British and American troops on the coast of Morocco and Algeria in November 1942 that was the largest amphibious military landing to that date. The Allies then fought their way along the coast, entering Tunis in triumph six months later. With the surrender of a quarter-million Germans and Italians in Tunisia in May 1943, the Allies controlled North Africa and had a secure position in the Mediterranean.

During the North African campaign, the Allies announced that they would accept nothing less than the unconditional surrender of their enemies. In January 1943, Roosevelt and Churchill had met in Casablanca in Morocco and ruled out any possibility of negotiation with the Axis powers. Roosevelt's supporters hailed the policy as a clear statement of goals, a promise to the world that the scourge of fascism would be completely banished. Stalin, who did not attend the meeting, criticized the policy, fearing that it would only increase the enemy's determination to fight to the end. Other critics similarly charged that the demand for total capitulation would serve to prolong the war and lengthen the casualty list.

Allied aerial bombing further increased pressure on Germany. Many U.S. leaders believed that in the B-17 Flying Fortress, the air force possessed the ultimate weapon, "the mightiest bomber ever built."

The U.S. Army Air Corps described this bomber as a "humane" weapon, capable of hitting specific military targets and sparing the lives of civilians. But when weather or darkness required pilots to depend on radar for sightings, they couldn't distinguish clearly between factories and schools or between military barracks and private homes, and bombs might fall within a range of nearly two miles from the intended target. American pilots preferred to bomb during daylight hours, while the British bombed during the night. Bombing missions over the Rhineland and the Ruhr successfully took out many German factories. But the Germans responded by relocating their plants, often dispersing light industry to the countryside.

Determined to break German resistance, the Royal Air Force redirected its main attack away from military sites to cities, including fuel dumps and public transportation. Hamburg was practically leveled. Between 60,000 and 100,000 people were killed, and 300,000 buildings were destroyed. Sixty other cities were hit hard, leaving 20 percent of Germany's total residential area in ruins. The very worst raid of the war—650,000 incendiary bombs dropped on the city of Dresden, destroying 8 square miles and killing 135,000 civilians—had no military value.

The Allied strategic air offensive weakened the German economy and undermined civilian morale. Moreover, in trying to defend German cities and factories, the *Luftwaffe* sacrificed many of its fighter planes. When the Allies finally invaded western Europe in the summer and fall of 1944, they would enjoy superiority in the air.

The Allied Invasion of Europe

During the summer of 1943, the Allies began to advance on southern Italy. On July 10 British and American troops stormed Sicily from two directions and conquered the island in mid-August. King Vittorio Emmanuel dismissed Mussolini, calling him "the most despised man in Italy," and Italians, by now disgusted with the Fascist government, celebrated in the streets. Italy surrendered to the Allies on September 8, and Allied troops landed on the southern Italian peninsula. But Hitler sent new divisions into Italy, occupied the northern peninsula, and effectively stalled the Allied campaign. When the European war ended, the German and Allied armies were still battling on Italy's rugged terrain.

Elsewhere in occupied Europe, armed uprisings against the Nazis spread. The brutalized inhabitants of Warsaw's Jewish ghetto repeatedly rose up against their tormentors during the winter and spring of 1943. Realizing that they could not hope to defeat superior forces, they finally sealed off their quarter, executed collaborators, and fought invaders, street by street and house by house. Scattered revolts followed in the Nazi labor camps, where military prisoners of war and civilians were being worked to death on starvation rations.

Partisans were active in many sections of Europe, from Norway to Greece and from Poland to France. Untrained and unarmed by any military standard, organized groups of men, women, and children risked their lives to distribute antifascist propaganda, taking action against rich and powerful Nazi collaborators. They smuggled food and weapons to clandestine resistance groups and prepared the way for Allied offensives. As Axis forces grew weaker and partially withdrew, the partisans worked more and more openly, arming citizens to fight for their own freedom.

Meanwhile, Stalin continued to push for a second front. Stalled in Italy, the Allies prepared in early 1944 for Operation Overlord, a campaign to retake the continent with a decisive counterattack through France. American and British forces began by filling the southern half of England with military camps. All leaves were canceled. New weapons, such as amphibious armored vehicles, were carefully camouflaged. Fortunately, Hitler had few planes or ships left, so the Germans could defend the coast only with fixed bunkers whose location the Allies ascertained. Operation Overlord began with a preinvasion air assault that dropped 76,000 tons of bombs on Nazi targets.

The Allied invasion finally began on "D-Day," June 6, 1944. Under steady German fire the Allied fleet brought to the shores of Normandy more than 175,000 troops and more than 20,000 vehicles—an accomplishment unimaginable in any previous war. Although the Germans had responded slowly, anticipating an Allied strike at Calais instead, at Omaha Beach they had prepared their defense almost perfectly. Wave after wave of Allied landings met machine gun and mortar fire, and the tides filled with corpses and those pretending to be dead. Some 2,500 troops died, many before they could fire a shot. In the next six weeks, nearly 1 million more Allied soldiers came ashore, broke out of Normandy, and prepared to march inland.

As the fighting continued, all eyes turned to Paris, the premier city of Europe. Allied bombers pounded factories producing German munitions on the outskirts of the French capital. As dispirited German soldiers retreated, many now hoping only to survive, the French Resistance unfurled the French flag at impromptu demonstrations on Bastille Day, July 14. On August 10, railway workers staged one of the first successful strikes against Nazi occupiers, and three days later the Paris police defected to the Resistance, which proclaimed in leaflets that "the hour of liberation has come." General Charles de Gaulle, accompanied by

D-Day landing, June 6, 1944, marked the greatest amphibious maneuver in military history. Troop ships ferried Allied soldiers from England to Normandy beaches. Within a month, nearly 1 million men had assembled in France, ready to retake western and central Europe from German forces.

Allied troops, arrived in Paris on August 25 to become president of the reestablished French Republic.

One occupied European nation after another now swiftly fell. But the Allied troops had only reached a resting place between bloody battles.

The High Cost of European Victory

In September 1944 Allied commanders searched for a strategy to end the war quickly. Missing a spectacular chance to move through largely undefended territory and on to Berlin, they turned north instead, intending to open the Netherlands for Allied armies on their way to Germany's industrial heartland. Faulty intelligence reports overlooked a well-armed German division at Arnhem, Holland, waiting to cut Allied paratroopers to pieces. By the end of the battle, the Germans had captured 6,000 Americans.

In a final, desperate effort to reverse the Allied momentum, Hitler directed his last reserves, a quarter-million men, at Allied lines in the Belgian forest of the Ardennes. In what is known as the Battle of the Bulge, the Germans took the Allies by surprise, driving them back 50 miles before they were stopped. This last effort—the bloodiest single campaign Americans had been involved in since the battle of Gettysburg—exhausted the German capacity for counterattack. After Christmas day 1944, the Germans fell back, retreating toward their own territory.

The end was now in sight. In March 1945 the Allies rolled across the Rhine and took the Ruhr valley with its precious industrial resources. The defense of Germany, now hopeless, had fallen into the hands of young teenagers and elderly men. By the time of the German surrender, May 8, Hitler had committed suicide in a Berlin bunker and high Nazi officials were planning their escape routes. The casualties of the Allied European campaign had been enormous, if still small compared to those of the Eastern Front: more than 200,000 killed and almost 800,000 wounded, missing, or dead in nonbattle accidents and unrelated illness.

The War in Asia and the Pacific

The war that had begun with Pearl Harbor rapidly escalated into scattered fighting across a region of the world far larger than all of Europe, stretching from Southeast Asia to the Aleutian Islands. Japan followed up its early advantage by cutting the supply routes between Burma and China, crushing the British navy, and seizing the Philippines, Hong Kong, Wake Island, British Malaya, and Thailand. Although China offically joined the Allies on December 9, 1941, and General Stillwell arrived in March as commander of the China-Burma-India theater, the military mission there remained on the defensive. Meanwhile, after tenacious fighting at the Bataan Peninsula and on the island of Corregidor, the U.S. troops not captured or killed retreated to Australia.

At first, nationalist and anticolonial sentiment played into Japanese hands. Japan succeeded with only 200,000 men because so few inhabitants of the imperial colonies of Britain and France would fight to defend them. Japan installed puppet "independent" governments in Burma and the Philippines. But the new Japanese empire proved terrifyingly cruel. A panicky exodus of refugees precipitated a famine in Bengal, India, which took nearly 3,500,000 lives in 1943. Nationalists from Indochina to the Philippines turned against the Japanese, establishing guerrilla armies that cut Japanese supply lines and prepared the way for Allied victory.

Six months after the disaster at Pearl Harbor, the United States began to regain naval superiority in the central Pacific and halt Japanese expansion. In a carrier duel with spectacular aerial battles at the Battle of the Coral Sea on May 7 and 8, the United States blocked a Japanese threat to Australia. A month later, the Japanese fleet converged on Midway Island, which was strategically vital to American communications and the defense of Hawai'i. American strategists, however, thanks to specialists who had broken Japanese codes, knew when and where the Japanese planned to attack. The two carrier fleets, separated by hundreds of miles, clashed at the Battle of Midway on June 4. American planes sank four of Japan's vital aircraft carriers and destroyed hundreds of planes, ending Japan's offensive threat to Hawai'i and the west coast of the United States.

But the war for the Pacific was far from over. By pulling back their offensive perimeter, the Japanese concentrated their remaining forces. Their commanders calculated that bitter fighting, with high casualties on both sides, would wear down the American troops. The U.S. command, divided between General Douglas MacArthur in the southwest Pacific

and Admiral Chester Nimitz in the central Pacific, needed to develop a counterstrategy to strangle the Japanese import-based economy and to retake strategic islands closer to the homeland.

The Allies launched their counteroffensive campaign on the Solomon Islands and Papua, near New Guinea. American and Australian ground forces fought together through the jungles of Papua, while the marines prepared to attack the Japanese stronghold of Guadalcanal. American forces ran low on food and ammunition during the fierce six-month struggle on Guadalcanal, while the Japanese were reduced to eating roots and berries. American logistics were not always well planned: a week before Christmas in the subtropical climate, a shipment of winter coats arrived! But with strong supply lines secured in a series of costly naval battles, the Amer-

War in the Pacific   *Across an ocean battlefield utterly unlike the European theater, Allies battled Japanese troops near their homeland.*

icans were finally victorious in February 1943 when the Japanese abandoned Guadalcanal.

For the next two years, the U.S. navy and marine corps, in a strategy known as "island hopping," pushed to capture a series of important atolls from their well-armed Japanese defenders and open a path to Japan. The first of these assaults, which cost more than 1,000 Marines their lives, was on Tarawa, in November 1943, in the Gilbert Islands. In subsequent battles in 1944, American forces occupied Guam, Saipan, and Tinian in the Marianas Islands, within air range of the Japanese home islands. In another decisive naval engagement, the Battle of the Philippine Sea, fought in June 1944, the Japanese fleet suffered a crippling loss.

In October 1944 General MacArthur led a force of 250,000 to retake the Philippines. In a bid to defend the islands, practically all that remained of the Japanese navy threw itself at American invaders in the Battle of Leyte Gulf, the largest naval battle in history. The Japanese lost eighteen ships, leaving the United States in control of the Pacific. While MacArthur continued to advance toward Luzon, the marines waged a successful battle on the small but important island of Iwo Jima. The ground fighting in the Philippines, meanwhile, cost 100,000 Filipinos their lives and left Manila devastated.

The struggle for the island of Okinawa, 800 miles southwest of Tokyo, proved even more bloody. The invasion of the island, which began on Easter Sunday, April 1, 1945, was the largest amphibious operation mounted by Americans in the Pacific war. It was met by waves of Japanese airborne *kamikaze* (or "divine wind") pilots flying suicide missions in planes with a 500-pound bomb and only enough fuel for a one-way flight. On the ground, U.S. troops used flame-throwers, each with three hundred gallons of napalm, against the dug-in Japanese. More Americans died or were wounded here than at Normandy. In all, the fighting killed more than 200,000 people.

Air and sea attacks on mainland Japan had begun to take their toll. U.S. submarines had drastically reduced the ability of ships to reach Japan with supplies. Since the taking of Guam, American bombers had been able to reach Tokyo and other Japanese cities, with devastating results. Massive fire bombings burned thousands of civilians alive in their mostly wood or bamboo homes and apartments and left hundreds of thousands homeless.

Japan could not hold out forever. Without a navy or air force, the government could not transport the oil, tin, rubber, and grain needed to maintain its soldiers. Great Britain and particularly the United States, however, pressed for quick unconditional surrender. They had special reasons to hurry. Earlier seeking a commitment from the Soviet Union to invade Japan, they now looked beyond the war, determined to prevent the Red Army from taking any territories held

by the Japanese. These calculations and the anticipation that an invasion would be extremely bloody set the stage for the use of a secret weapon that American scientists had been preparing: the atomic bomb.

THE LAST STAGES OF WAR

From the attack on Pearl Harbor until mid-1943, President Roosevelt and his advisers focused on military strategy rather than on plans for peace. But once the defeat of Nazi Germany appeared in sight, high government officials began to reconsider their diplomatic objectives. Roosevelt wanted both to crush the Axis powers and to establish a system of collective security to prevent another world war. He knew he could not succeed without the cooperation of the other key leaders, Stalin and Churchill.

During 1944 and 1945, the "Big Three" met to hammer out the shape of the postwar world. Although none of these nations expected to reach a final agreement, neither did they anticipate how quickly they would be confronted with momentous global events. It soon became clear that the only thing holding the Allies together was the mission of destroying the Axis.

The Holocaust

Not until the last stages of the war did Americans learn the extent of Hitler's atrocities. As part of his "final solution to the Jewish question," Hitler had ordered the systematic extermination of not only Jews but Gypsies, homosexuals, and others of "inferior" races. Beginning in 1933, and accelerating after 1941, the Nazis murdered millions of people from Germany and the European nations they conquered.

During the war the U.S. government released little information on what came to be known as the Holocaust. Although liberal magazines such as the *Nation* and small committees of intellectuals tried to call attention to what was happening in German concentration camps, major news media like the *New York Times* and *Time* magazine treated reports of the camps and killings as minor news items. The experience of World War I, during which the press had published stories of German atrocities that proved in most cases to have been fabricated by the British, had bred a skeptical attitude in the American public. As late as 1943, only 43 percent of Americans polled believed that Hitler was systematically murdering European Jews.

Roosevelt and his advisers maintained that the liberation of European Jews depended primarily on a speedy and total Allied victory. When American Jews pleaded for a military strike against the rail lines leading to the notorious extermination camp in Auschwitz,

Leslie Cole, *Belsen Camp: The Compound for Women.* Imperial War Museum. London.

Belsen Camp: The Compound for Women, *painted by American artist Leslie Cole, depicts Belsen as the Allied troops found it when they invaded Germany in 1945.*

Poland, the War Department replied that Allied armed forces would not be employed "for the purpose of rescuing victims of enemy oppression unless such rescues are the direct result of military operations conducted with the objective of defeating the armed forces of the enemy." In short, the government viewed civilian rescue as a diversion of precious resources.

Allied troops discovered the death camps when they invaded Germany and liberated Poland. When Eisenhower and General George S. Patton visited the Ohrdruf concentration camp in April 1945, they found barracks crowded with corpses and crematories still reeking of burned flesh. "I want every American unit not actually in the front lines to see this place," Eisenhower declared. "We are told that the American soldier does not know what he is fighting for. Now, at least, he will know what he is fighting against." At Buchenwald in the first three months of 1944, more than 14,000 prisoners were murdered. In all, the Holocaust claimed the lives of as many as 6 million Jews, 250,000 Gypsies, and 60,000 homosexuals, among others.

The Yalta Conference

In preparing for the end of the war, Allied leaders began to reassess their goals. The Atlantic Charter, drawn up before the United States had entered the war, stated noble objectives for the world after the defeat of fascism: national self-determination, no territorial aggrandizement, equal access of all peoples to raw materials and collaboration for the improvement of economic opportunities, freedom of the seas, disarmament, and "freedom from fear and want." Now, four years later, Roosevelt—ill and exhausted—realized that neither Great Britain nor the Soviet Union intended to abide by any code of conduct that compromised its national security or conflicted with its economic interests in other nations or in colonial territories. Stalin and Churchill soon reached a new agreement, one that projected their respective "spheres of influence" over the future of central Europe.

In February 1945 Roosevelt held his last meeting with Churchill and Stalin at Yalta, a Crimean resort on the Black Sea. Seeking their cooperation, the president recognized that prospects for postwar peace also depended on compromise. Although diplomats avoided the touchy phrase "spheres of influence"—the principle according to which the great powers of the nineteenth century had described their claims to dominance over other nations—it was clear that this principle guided all negotiations. Neither the United States nor Great Britain did more than object to the Soviet Union's plan to retain the Baltic states and part of Poland as a buffer zone to protect it against any future German aggression. In return, Britain planned to reclaim its empire in Asia, and the United States hoped to hold several Pacific islands in order to monitor any military resurgence in Japan. Stalin also affirmed his pledge to enter the war against Japan and approved plans for a future world organization, which Roosevelt championed.

Roosevelt announced to Congress that the Yalta meeting had been a "great success," proof that the wartime alliance remained intact. Privately, however, the president concluded that the outcome of the conference revealed that the Atlantic Charter had been nothing more than "a beautiful idea."

The death of Franklin Roosevelt of a stroke on April 12, 1945 cast a dark shadow over all hopes for long-term, peaceful solutions to global problems. Stung by a Republican congressional comeback in 1942, Roosevelt had rebounded in 1944 to win an unprecedented fourth term as president. In an overwhelming electoral college victory (432 to 99), he had defeated Republican New York governor Thomas E. Dewey. Loyal Democrats continued to link their

On August 6, 1945, a U.S. B-29 *bomber dropped "Little Boy," an atomic bomb, on Hiroshima, killing nearly 80,000 Japanese civilians and injuring another 70,000. Three days later, "Fat Man" destroyed Nagasaki, killing 40,000 and injuring 60,000 more. On August 14, the government of Japan surrendered, bringing an end to the war.*

hopes for peace to Roosevelt's leadership, but the president did not live to witness the surrender of Germany on May 8, 1945. And now, as new and still greater challenges were appearing, the nation's great pragmatic idealist was gone.

The Atomic Bomb

Roosevelt's death made cooperation among the Allied nations much more difficult. His successor, Harry S. Truman, who had been a Kansas City machine politician, a Missouri judge, and a U.S. senator, lacked diplomatic experience as well as Roosevelt's personal finesse. The new president had no intention of making concessions to the war-devastated Soviets.

Shortly after taking office, Truman announced to his secretary of state, "We must stand up to the Russians at this point and not be easy with them."

As a result, negotiations at the Potsdam Conference, held just outside Berlin from July 17 to August 2, 1945, lacked the spirited cooperation characteristic of the wartime meetings of Allied leaders that Roosevelt had attended. The American, British, and Soviet delegations had a huge agenda, including reparations, the future of Germany, and the status of other Axis powers such as Italy. They agreed to demand Japan's unconditional surrender and to try Nazi leaders as war criminals. But they were sharply divided over most other issues.

It was during the Potsdam meetings that Truman first learned about the successful testing of an atomic bomb in New Mexico. Until this time, the United States had been pushing the Soviet Union to enter the Pacific war as a means to avoid a costly U.S. land invasion. But after Secretary of State Stimson received a cable reading "Babies satisfactorily born," U.S. diplomats concluded that they no longer needed assistance from the Soviet Union to bring the war to an end.

American diplomats knew that the emperor of Japan was prepared to end the fighting if the Allies would set aside the stipulation of unconditional surrender. At first, Truman considered accepting a slight modification, such as allowing the emperor to continue to head the Japanese nation. But the president also went forward with the plan to deploy the atomic bomb. As Truman later stated, he had no moral reservations about making this decision. He understood that the three bombs on hand had been developed specifically for this purpose. He therefore endorsed the principal outcome of the Potsdam Conference, a warning to Japan to surrender immediately or face "complete and utter destruction."

On August 3, 1945, Japan wired its refusal to surrender. Three days later, the Army Air Force B-29 bomber Enola Gay dropped the bomb that destroyed the Japanese city of Hiroshima. Approximately 80,000 people died on August 6; in the following weeks thousands more died from radiation poisoning or burns; by 1950 the death toll reached 200,000. "I was greatly moved," Truman reported when he heard the news.

An editorialist wrote in the Japanese *Nippon Times*, "This is not war, this is not even murder; this is pure nihilism . . . a crime against God which strikes at the very basis of moral existence." In the United States, several leading religious publications echoed this view. The *Christian Century* interpreted the use of the bomb as a "moral earthquake" that made the long-denounced use of poison gas by Germany in World War I utterly insignificant by comparison.

CHRONOLOGY

1931	September: Japan occupies Manchuria
1933	March: Adolf Hitler seizes power
	May: Japan quits League of Nations
1935	October: Italy invades Ethiopia
1935–1937	Neutrality Acts authorize the president to block the sale of munitions to belligerent nations
1937	August: Japan invades China
	October: Franklin D. Roosevelt calls for international cooperation against aggression
1938	March: Germany annexes Austria
	September: Munich Agreement lets Germany annex Sudeten Czechoslovakia
	November: Kristallnacht, Nazis attack Jews and destroy Jewish property
1939	March: Germany annexes remainder of Czechoslovakia
	August: Germany and the Soviet Union sign nonaggression pact
	September: Germany invades Poland; World War II begins
	November: Soviet Union invades Finland
1940	April–June: Germany's *Bliztkrieg* sweeps over Western Europe
	September: Germany, Italy, and Japan—the Axis powers— conclude a military alliance
	First peacetime military draft in American history
	November: Roosevelt is elected to an unprecedented third term
1941	March: Lend-Lease Act extends aid to Great Britain
	May: German troops secure the Balkans
	A. Philip Randolph plans March on Washington movement for July
	June: Germany invades Soviet Union

	Fair Employment Practices Committee formed
	August: The United States and Great Britain agree to the Atlantic Charter
	December: Japanese attack Pearl Harbor; United States enters the war
1942	January: War mobilization begins
	February: Executive order mandates internment of Japanese Americans
	May–June: Battles of Coral Sea and Midway give the United States naval superiority in the Pacific
	August: Manhattan Project begins
	November: United States stages amphibious landing in North Africa; Operation Torch begins
1943	January: Casablanca conference announces unconditional surrender policy
	February: Soviet victory over Germans at Stalingrad
	April–May: Coal miners strike
	May: German Afrika Korps troops surrender in Tunis
	July: Allied invasion of Italy
	Summer: Race riots break out in nearly fifty cities
1944	June–August: Operation Overlord and liberation of Paris
	November: Roosevelt elected to fourth term
1945	February: Yalta Conference renews American-Soviet alliance
	February–June: United States captures Iwo Jima and Okinawa in Pacific
	April: Roosevelt dies in office; Harry Truman becomes president
	May: Germany surrenders
	July–August: Potsdam Conference
	August: United States drops atomic bombs on Hiroshima and Nagasaki; Japan surrenders

Most Americans learned about the atomic bomb for the first time on August 7, when the news media reported the destruction and death it had wrought in Hiroshima. But concerns about the implications of this new weapon were soon overwhelmed by an outpouring of relief when Japan surrendered on August 14 after a second bomb destroyed Nagasaki. In Los Alamos, New Mexico, horns and sirens blared in exultation. Proud of his scientific accomplishment, Oppenheimer nevertheless reported that he was a "little scared of what I have made."

The decision to use the atomic bomb against Japan remains one of the most controversial aspects of the war. Although Truman stated in his memoirs, written much later, that he gave the order with the expectation of saving "a half a million American lives" in ground combat, no such official estimate exists. An intelligence document of April 30, 1946, states, "The dropping of the bomb was the pretext seized upon by all leaders as the reason for ending the war, but . . . [even if the bomb had not been used] the Japanese would have capitulated upon the entry of Russia into the war." There is no question, however, that the use of nuclear force did strengthen the U.S. diplomatic mission. It certainly intimidated the Soviet Union, which would soon regain its status as a major enemy of the United States. Truman and his advisers in the State Department knew that their atomic monopoly could not last, but they hoped that in the meantime the United States could play the leading role in building the new world order.

CONCLUSION

The new tactics and weapons of the Second World War, such as massive air raids and the atomic bomb, made warfare incomparably more deadly than before to both military and civilian populations. Between 40 and 50 million people died in World War II—four times the number in World War I—and half the casualties were women and children. More than 405,000 Americans died and more than 670,000 were wounded. Although slight compared to the casualties suffered by other Allied nations—more than 20 million Soviets died during the war—the human cost of World War II for Americans was second only to that of the Civil War.

Coming at the end of two decades of resolutions to avoid military entanglements, the war pushed the nation's leaders to the center of global politics and into risky military and political alliances that would not outlive the war. The United States emerged the strongest nation in the world, but in a world where the prospects for lasting peace appeared increasingly remote.

If World War II raised the nation's international commitments to a new height, its impact on ordinary Americans was not so easy to gauge. Many new communities formed as Americans migrated in mass numbers to new regions that were booming as a result of the wartime economy. Enjoying a rare moment of full employment, many workers new to well-paying industrial jobs anticipated further advances against discrimination. Exuberant at the Allies' victory over fascism and the return of the troops, the majority were optimistic as they looked ahead.

REVIEW QUESTIONS

1. Describe the response of Americans to the rise of nationalism in Japan, Italy, and Germany during the 1930s. How did President Franklin D. Roosevelt ready the nation for war?
2. What role did the federal government play in gearing up the economy for wartime production?
3. How did the war affect the lives of American women?
4. Discuss the causes and consequences of the Japan-ese American internment program.
5. Describe the role of popular culture in promoting the war effort at home.
6. How did military service affect the lives of those who served in World War II?
7. What were the main points of Allied military strategy in both Europe and Asia?
8. How successful were diplomatic efforts in ending the war and in establishing the terms of peace?

RECOMMENDED READING

Stephen E. Ambrose, *D-Day, June 6, 1944: The Climactic Battle of World War II* (1994). A vivid and extremely readable, moment-by-moment reconstruction of the preparation and battle, relying heavily upon the oral histories of American veterans.

Allan Berube, *Coming Out under Fire: The History of Gay Men and Women in World War Two* (1991). A study of government policy toward homosexuals during the war and the formation of a gay community. Berube offers many insights into the new opportunities offered homosexuals through travel and varied companionship and of the effects of sanctions against them.

John Morton Blum, *V Was for Victory: Politics and American Culture during World War II* (1976). A colorful narration of American society and culture during wartime. Blum seeks to recreate the patriotic spirit that quelled potential conflict among diverse groups during wartime.

Paul Boyer, *By the Bomb's Early Light: American Thought and Culture at the Dawn of the Atomic Age* (1985). An analysis of the intellectual and cultural assumptions in relation to atomic weaponry. Boyer examines the development of a political logic, on the part of President Harry Truman and others, that made use of atomic weapons against the Japanese inevitable.

Wayne S. Cole, *Roosevelt and the Isolationists, 1932–45* (1983). Shows the president and his critics sparring over foreign policy issues. Cole analyzes the complexities of liberal-conservative divisions over war and offers insights into the logic of conservatives who feared the growth of a permanent bureaucratic, militarized state.

Richard M. Dalfiume, *Desegregation of the U.S. Armed Forces: Fighting on Two Fronts, 1939–1953* (1969). Analyzes wartime race relations in the military. By examining the official mechanisms to end discrimination and the remaining patterns of racism in the armed forces, Dalfiume reveals how changing attitudes from the top ran up against old assumptions among enlisted men and women.

Roger Daniels, *Concentration Camps USA: Japanese Americans and World War II* (1981). Perhaps the best account of Japanese American internment. Daniels details the government programs, the experiences of detention and camp life, and the many long-term consequences of lost liberty.

Sherna Berger Gluck, *Rosie the Riveter Revisited: Women, the War, and Social Change* (1987). An oral history-based study of women workers during World War II. Gluck's interviewees reveal the diversity of experiences and attitudes of women workers as well as their common feelings of accomplishment.

Gerald F. Linderman, *The World within War: America's Combat Experience in World War II* (1997). Emphasizes the less glamorous aspects of war, mainly the strains placed on the combat soldiers on the front lines. Linderman examines in especially close detail the grim experiences of Army infantrymen and the Marine riflemen who fought in the Pacific campaign.

Katrina R. Mason, *Children of Los Alamos: An Oral History of the Town Where the Atomic Age Began* (1995). Recollections of those who spent their childhood in Los Alamos. They describe their affection for the geographical setting as well as sense of safety growing up in a community so well protected. They also comment on the ethnic diversity of those who populated the town and on the pride they took in their parents' contribution to building the bomb and ending the war.

Neil R. McMillan, ed., *Remaking Dixie: The Impact of World War II on the American South* (1997). A collection of essays on the impact of World War II on the South that pay special attention to the experiences of African Americans and women. Several authors question the degree to which southern society was transformed by wartime mobilization.

Robert J. Moskin, *Mr. Truman's War: The Final Victories of World War II and the Birth of the Postwar World* (1996). A lively history of the final stages of World War II, including the surrender of Germany and the emergence of postwar foreign policy. Moskin provides an assessment of the impact of the war on social and economic conditions in the United States.

William M. Tuttle Jr., *"Daddy's Gone to War": The Second World War in the Lives of America's Children* (1993). Draws from 2,500 letters that the author solicited from men and women in their fifties and sixties about their wartime childhood memories.

David S. Wyman, *The Abandonment of the Jews: America and the Holocaust, 1941–1945* (1984). A detailed examination of U.S. immigration policy and response to Hitler's program of genocide. Wyman shows both the indifference of the Roosevelt administration to appeals for Allied protection of Jews and the inclinations of leading American Jewish organizations to stress the formation of a future Jewish state above the protection of European Jewry.

ADDITIONAL BIBLIOGRAPHY

Coming of World War II

Cynthia Ellet, *Conscientious Objectors and the Second World War* (1991)

Sheldon H. Harris, *Factories of Death: Japanese Biological Warfare, 1932–1945, and the American Cover Up* (1994)

Akira Iriye, *The Origins of the Second World War in Asia and the Pacific* (1988)

Deborah Lipstadt, *Beyond Belief: The American Press and the Coming of the Holocaust, 1933–1945* (1992)

Ernest Mandel, *The Meaning of the Second World War* (1986)

Frank P. Mintz, *Revisionism and the Origins of Pearl Harbor* (1985)

Geoffrey S. Smith, *To Save a Nation* (1992)

Arsenal of Democracy and the Home Front

Karen Anderson, *Wartime Women* (1981)

Beth Bailey and David Farber, *The First Strange Place: The Alchemy of Race and Sex in World War II Hawaii* (1993)

Alison R. Bernstein, *American Indians and World War II* (1991)

Dominic J. Capeci and Martha Wilkerson, *Layered Violence: The Detroit Rioters of 1943* (1991)

Paul D. Casdorph, *Let the Good Times Roll: Life at Home in America during World War II* (1989)

Thomas Doherty, *Hollywood, American Culture and World War II* (1993)

Lewis A. Erenberg and Susan E. Hirsch, eds., *The War in American Culture: Society and Consciousness during World War II* (1996)

George Q. Flynn, *The Mess in Washington: Manpower Mobilization in World War II* (1979)

Evelyn Nakano Glenn, *Issei, Nisei, War Bride* (1986)

Maurice Isserman, *Which Side Were You On? The American Communist Party during World War II* (1982)

John W. Jeffries, *Wartime America* (1996)

Amy Kesselman, *Fleeting Opportunities: Women Shipyard Workers in Portland and Vancouver during World War II* (1990)

Nelson Lichtenstein, *Labor's War at Home: The CIO in World War II* (1982)

Gary Y. Okihiro, *Whispered Silences: Japanese Americans and World War II* (1996)

Richard Polenberg, *War and Society: The United States, 1941–1945* (1972).

George H. Roeder, *The Censored War: American Visual Experience during World War II* (1993)

Ronald Schaffer, *America in the Great War: The Rise of the War Welfare State* (1991)

Bartholomew H. Sparrow, *From the Outside In: World War II and the American State* (1996)

Harold Vatter, *The U.S. Economy in World War II* (1985)

World at War

Russell A. Buchanan, *Black Americans in World War II* (1977)

Jean H. Cole, *Women Pilots of World War II* (1992)

Conrad C. Crane, *Bombs, Cities, and Civilians* (1993)

John W. Dower, *War without Mercy* (1986)

Paul Fussell, *Wartime: Understanding Behavior in the Second World War* (1989)

Akira Iriye, *Power and Culture: The Japanese-American War, 1941–1945* (1981)

Peter Maslowski, *Armed with Cameras: The American Military Photographers of World War II* (1996)

Nathan Miller, *War at Sea: A Naval History of World War II* (1995)

Brenda L. Moore, *To Serve My Country: The Story of the Only African American WACS Stationed Overseas During World War II* (1996)

David Reynolds, *Rich Relations: The American Occupation of Britain, 1942–1945* (1995)

Ronald H. Spector, *Eagle against the Sun: The American War with Japan* (1985)

Mark A. Stoler, *The Politics of the Second Front* (1977)

Russell P. Weigley, *Eisenhower's Lieutenants: The Campaign for France and Germany, 1944–1945* (1981)

Last Stages of War

Lloyd C. Gardner, *Architects of Illusion* (1970).

____, *Spheres of Influence: The Great Powers Partition Europe, from Munich to Yalta* (1993)

Gabriel Kolko, *Politics of War* (1968, 1990)

Charles E. Neu, *The Troubled Encounter: The United States and Japan* (1975, 1979)

Keith Sainsbury, *The Turning Point: Roosevelt, Stalin, Churchill, and Chiang-Kai-Shek, 1943* (1985)

Kenneth E. Shewmaker, *Americans and Chinese Communists, 1927–1945* (1971)

Paul Varg, *The Closing of the Door: Sino-American Relations, 1936–1946* (1973)

Atomic Bomb

Gar Alperovitz, *The Decision to Use the Atomic Bomb and the Architecture of an American Myth* (1995)

Barton J. Bernstein, ed., *The Atomic Bomb* (1976)

Michael S. Sherry, *The Rise of American Air Power* (1987)

Martin J. Sherwin, *A World Destroyed: The Atomic Bomb and the Grand Alliance* (1975)

Michael B. Stoff and Jonathan F. Fanton, eds., *The Manhattan Project* (1991)

Biography

Stephen E. Ambrose, *Supreme Commander: War Years of General Dwight D. Eisenhower* (1970)

Robert Dallek, *Franklin D. Roosevelt and American Foreign Policy* (1979)

Carlo D'Este, *Patton: A Genius for War* (1995)

Thomas Hughes, *Over Lord: General Pete Quesada and the Triumph of Tactical Air Power in World War II* (1995)

Steve Neal, *Dark Horse: A Biography of Wendell Willkie* (1984)

Paula F. Pfeffer, *A. Philip Randolph* (1990)

John Hubbard Preston, *Apocalypse Undone: My Survival of Japanese Imprisonment during World War II* (1990)

CHAPTER TWENTY-SIX

THE COLD WAR

1945–1952

Poster from 1947: *Is This Tomorrow—America under Communism!* Michael Barson/Archive Photos.

AMERICAN COMMUNITIES
University of Washington, Seattle: Students and Faculty Face the Cold War

In May 1948, a philosophy professor at the University of Washington in Seattle answered a knock on his office door. Two state legislators, members of the state's Committee on Un-American Activities, entered. "Our information," they charged, "puts you in the center of a communist conspiracy."

The accused professor, Melvin Rader, had never been a communist. A self-described liberal, Rader drew fire because he had joined several organizations supported by communists. During the 1930s, in response to the rise of Nazism and fascism, Rader had become a prominent political activist in his community. At one point he served as president of the University of Washington Teacher's Union, which had formed during the upsurge of labor organizing during the New Deal. When invited to join the Communist Party, Rader bluntly refused. "The experience of teaching social philosophy had clarified my concepts of freedom and democracy," he later explained. "I was an American in search of a way—but it was not the communist way."

Despite this disavowal, Rader was caught up in a Red Scare that curtailed free speech and political activity on campuses throughout the United States. At some universities, such as Yale, the Federal Bureau of Investigation (FBI) set up camp with the consent of the college administration, spying on students and faculty, screening the credentials of job or scholarship applicants, and seeking to entice students to report on their friends or roommates. The University of Washington administration turned down the recommendation of the Physics Department to hire J. Robert Oppenheimer because the famed atomic scientist had become a vocal opponent of the arms race and the proliferation of nuclear weapons.

Although one state legislator claimed that "not less than 150 members" of the University of Washington faculty were subversives, the state's Committee on Un-American Activities turned up just six members of the Communist Party. These six were brought up before the university's Faculty Committee on Tenure and Academic Freedom, charged with violations ranging from neglect of duty to failing to inform the university administration of their party membership. Three were ultimately dismissed, while the other three were placed on probation.

What had provoked this paranoia? Instead of peace in the wake of World War II, a pattern of cold war—icy relations—prevailed between the United States and the Soviet Union. Uneasy allies during World War II, the two superpowers now viewed each other as archenemies, and nearly all other nations lined up with one or the other of them. Within the United States, the cold war demanded pledges of absolute loyalty from citizens in every institution, from the university to trade unions and from the mass media to government itself.

If not for the outbreak of the cold war, this era would have marked one of the most fruitful in the history of higher education. The Servicemen's Readjustment Act, popularly known as the GI Bill of Rights, passed by Congress in 1944, offered stipends covering tuition and living expenses to veterans attending vocational schools or college. By the 1947–48 academic year, the federal government was subsidizing nearly half of all male college students. Between 1945 and 1950, 2.3 million students benefited from the GI Bill, at a cost of more than $10 billion.

At the University of Washington the student population in 1946 had grown by 50 percent over its prewar peak of 10,000, and veterans represented fully two-thirds of the student body. A quickly expanded faculty taught into the evening to use classroom space efficiently. Meanwhile, the state legislature pumped in funds for the construction of new buildings, including dormitories and prefabricated units for married students.

According to many observers, a feeling of community flourished among these war-weary undergraduates. Often the first in their families to attend college, they joined fellow students in campaigns to improve the campus. Married, often fathers of young children, they expected university administrators to treat them as adults. They wanted less supervision of undergraduate social life, more affordable housing, and better cultural opportunities than had previously been the case. On some campuses, film societies and student-run cooperatives vied with fraternities and sororities as centers of undergraduate social activity.

The cold war put a damper on these community-building efforts. FBI director J. Edgar Hoover testified that the college campuses were centers of "red propaganda," full of teachers "tearing down respect for agencies of government, belittling tradition and moral custom and . . . creating doubts in the validity of the American way of life." Due to communistic teachers and "communist-line textbooks," a senator lamented, thousands of parents sent "their sons and daughters to college as good Americans," only to see them return home "four years later as wild-eyed radicals."

These extravagant charges were never substantiated, but conservatives who had long regarded campuses as centers of homosexuality and atheism leaped at the opportunity presented by the cold war to take revenge on them. Several states, including Washington, enacted or revived "loyalty acts," obligating all state employees to swear in writing their loyalty to the United States and to disclaim membership in any subversive organization. Nationwide, approximately 200 faculty members were dismissed outright and many others were denied tenure. Thousands of students simply left school, dropped out of organizations, or changed friends after "visits" from FBI agents or interviews with administrators. The main effect on campus was the restraint of free speech generally and fear of criticizing U.S. racial, military, or diplomatic policies in particular.

This gloomy mood reversed the wave of optimism that had swept through America only a few years earlier. V-J Day, marking Victory over Japan, had erupted into a two-day national holiday of wild celebrations, complete with ticker-tape parades, spontaneous dancing, and kisses for returned GIs. Americans, living in the richest and most powerful nation in the world, finally seemed to have gained the peace they had fought and sacrificed to win. But peace proved fragile and elusive.

Seattle

KEY TOPICS

- Prospects for world peace at end of World War II
- Diplomatic policy during the cold war
- The Truman presidency

- Anticommunism and McCarthyism
- Cold war culture and society
- The Korean War

GLOBAL INSECURITIES AT WAR'S END

The war that had engulfed the world from 1939 to 1945 created an international interdependence that no country could ignore. The legendary African American folk singer Leadbelly (Huddie Ledbetter) added a fresh lyric to an old spiritual melody: "We're in the same boat, brother. . . . And if you shake one end you're going to rock the other." Never before, not even at the end of World War I, had hopes been so strong for a genuine "community of nations." But most Americans also recognized, a 1945 opinion poll revealed, that prospects for a durable peace rested on harmony among the Allies, especially between the Soviet Union and the United States.

Diplomatic conflict between these two competitors for world leadership had been the rule since the Russian Revolution of 1917. The threat of fascism had merely placed this rivalry on hold. Following World War II, opposing national interests and combative leaders made a continued U.S.-Soviet alliance impossible. Only the prospect of mutual destruction prevented the United States and the Soviet Union, the world's two most powerful nations, from precipitating another world war.

"The American Century"

In 1941 Henry Luce, publisher of *Time, Life,* and *Fortune* magazines, had forecast the dawn of "the American Century." Americans must, he wrote, "accept whole-heartedly our duty and our opportunity as the most powerful and vital nation in the world and in consequence to assert upon the world the full impact of our influence, for such means as we see fit." This bold pronouncement reflected the prevailing faith that, with the rest of the world in ruins, the United States should establish the principles of world order.

Americans had good reason to be confident about their prospects for setting the terms of peace. Compared with Great Britain and France, reduced to second-rate powers too weak to hold their once vast empires, the United States had not only escaped the ravages of the war but had actually prospered from it.

Between 1940 and 1944 industrial production rose by 90 percent, agricultural output by 20 percent. By June 1945 the capital assets of manufacturing had increased 65 percent over prewar levels, largely because of government subsidies, and were equal in value to approximately half the entire world's goods and services.

And yet the foundation of this vigorous economy appeared fragile. Above all, Americans feared the return of widespread unemployment. Memories of the Great Depression were still fresh, and many older Americans could recall the steep economic downturn that had followed World War I. Economists understood that it was the massive government spending associated with wartime industry, rather than New Deal programs, that had ended the nightmare of the 1930s. A great question loomed: What would happen when wartime production slowed and millions of troops returned home?

"We need markets—big markets—in which to buy and sell," answered Assistant Secretary of State for Economic Affairs Will Clayton. Just to maintain the current level of growth, the United States needed an estimated $14 billion in exports—an unprecedented amount. Many business leaders looked to the Soviet Union as a potential trading partner. The president of the U.S. Chamber of Commerce testified that the Soviet Union, desperate to rebuild its war-torn society, could become, "if not our biggest, at least our most eager consumer." But as diplomatic relations became increasingly strained, this prospect vanished. With eastern European markets threatened and large chunks of former colonial territories closed off, U.S. business and government leaders became yet more determined to secure Europe for American trade and investment.

During the final stages of the war, President Franklin D. Roosevelt's advisers laid plans to secure U.S. primacy in the postwar global economy. In July 1944 representatives from forty-four Allied nations met at Bretton Woods, New Hampshire, and established the International Bank for Reconstruction and Development (World Bank) and the International Monetary Fund (IMF) to help rebuild war-torn Europe and to assist the nations of Asia, Latin America, and Africa. By stabilizing exchange rates to permit the expansion of international trade, the IMF would deter currency conflicts and trade wars—two maladies of the 1930s that were largely responsible for the political instability and national rivalries leading to World War II. The IMF was also seen as a means for blocking any rivals to U.S. economic leadership.

As the principal supplier of funds for the IMF and the World Bank—more than $7 billion to each—the United States could unilaterally shape the world economy by determining the allocation of loans. Its representatives could withhold funds from those nations that threatened to nationalize industry, for instance, while generously rewarding those that opened themselves to American investments. Foreign currencies were pegged to the U.S. dollar, a monetary policy that further enhanced the power of American bankers.

The Soviet Union interpreted "the American Century," and especially its aggressive economic programs, as a return to the policy that had guided international affairs since the Russian Revolution: a strategy to destroy communism. For this reason, the Soviet Union simply refused to join either the World Bank or the IMF, regarding them as part of a concerted endeavor by the United States to remake the world in its own capitalist image. By spurning these financial institutions, the Soviet Union cut off the possibility of aid to its own people as well as to its eastern European client states. Equally important, the Soviet Union isolated itself economically.

The United Nations and Hopes for Collective Security

A thin hope remained amid the gloom of disunity between the two superpowers. A month after the conference at Bretton Woods, Allied leaders met to lay

Appointed to the UN delegation by President Harry Truman in 1946, Eleanor Roosevelt (1884–1962) pressured the organization to adopt the Declaration of Human Rights in 1948. In this photograph, taken in 1946, the former First Lady is exchanging ideas with Warren Austin, also a delegate to the United Nations.

plans for a system of collective security, the United Nations (UN). The dream of international cooperation had been seeded earlier by President Roosevelt. Had Americans agreed to join the League of Nations—as President Woodrow Wilson had pleaded in 1919—then perhaps, Roosevelt suggested, the second world war might have been averted. In late summer and fall 1944 at the Dumbarton Oaks estate in Washington, D.C., and again in April 1945 in San Francisco, the Allies worked to shape the United Nations as an international agency that would arbitrate disputes among members as well as impede aggressors, by military force if necessary. Opinion polls showed that nearly 80 percent of Americans favored U.S. membership in the UN.

From its inception the UN had only limited ability to carry out its mission. The organization represented all member nations through its General Assembly, which met for the purpose of debate but not for adjudication. The "primary responsibility for the maintenance of international peace and security" lay exclusively with the Security Council, which had five permanent members (the United States, Great Britain, the Soviet Union, France, and Nationalist China) and six temporary members elected for two-year terms. Because each permanent member enjoyed absolute veto power, the Security Council could censure an act of aggression by any of its members only if that nation abstained from the vote. Without this provision, the United States would not have joined the United Nations, but because of it, the UN could not assume the role of world peacekeeper that its architects had envisioned.

During its first decade, the UN operated strictly along lines dictated by the cold war. The Western nations held the balance of power and rigorously maintained their position by controlling the admission of new member nations. They successfully excluded Communist China, for example, thus ensuring that the UN would bolster their own political interests. The polarization between East and West made negotiated settlements virtually impossible.

The UN achieved its greatest success with its humanitarian programs for the victims of world war. Its relief agency provided the war-torn countries of Europe and Asia with billions of dollars for medical supplies, food, and clothing. The UN also dedicated itself to protecting human rights; its high standards for human dignity were due significantly to the lobbying of Eleanor Roosevelt, the president's widow and one of the first U.S. delegates to the world organization. In December 1948 the UN adopted the Universal Doctrine of Human Rights that affirmed the inalienable rights of all people to religious and civil liberty.

The trial of top Nazi officials by the International Court of Justice in 1945 and 1946 proved to be a high point of post-war international cooperation. At these proceedings, known as the Nuremberg trials, twenty-one of the twenty-four defendants were found guilty of "war crimes and atrocities." The testimony revealed the ghastly details of the organized cruelty of the Nazi regime, including the attempt to exterminate Jews, Gypsies, homosexuals, and others in the "final solution." Responding to the attempt by the accused to defend themselves with the claim that they had only followed orders, the panel of judges propounded the Nuremberg Principle: No soldier or civilian could be required, or should obey, an order—whatever its source—that conflicted with basic humanitarian tenets. Put forward by Robert Jackson, associate justice of the U.S. Supreme Court and chief U.S. prosecutor at the trials, this ruling was later affirmed by the United Nations. In the long run, however, the UN lacked the power and authority to enforce these principles any more than the ideals of human rights.

The Division of Europe

The Atlantic Charter of 1941 committed the Allies to recognize the right of all nations to self-determination and renounce all claims to new territories as the spoils of war. Following a limited period of occupation, the Allies pledged to hold free, democratic elections in those areas taken from the Axis powers and then to relinquish control to the new governments. As polls revealed, however, most Americans were skeptical of this plan. The Allied leaders themselves, moreover, violated the charter's main points before the war had ended, dividing occupied Europe into spheres of influence (see Chapter 25).

So long as Franklin Roosevelt remained alive, this strategy had seemed reconcilable with world peace. Convinced of his ability to maneuver Josef Stalin and the Soviets person to person and situation by situation, the president had balanced his own international idealism with his belief that the United States was entitled to extraordinary influence in Latin America and the Philippines and that other great powers might have similar privileges or responsibilities elsewhere. "We shall have to take the responsibility for world collaboration," he said in an address to Congress, "or we shall have to bear the responsibility for another world conflict."

Roosevelt also recognized the diplomatic consequences of the brutal European ground war that had been fought largely on Soviet territory: the Soviet Union's unnegotiable demand for territorial security along its European border. The nation lay in ruins, with 20 million dead, more than 70,000 villages destroyed, and nearly 25 million people homeless; its steel and agricultural production was down to half of prewar levels. Roosevelt believed that by offering economic assistance he might ease Stalin's fears and loosen the Soviet grip on conquered nations. But by the time of

the Potsdam Conference in July 1945, the Soviet Union had already consolidated its influence over most of eastern Europe and the little Baltic states. Only the Yugoslavians and Albanians, who had turned back fascist forces without the Red Army's assistance, could claim nominal independence.

Hopes for cooperation between the Soviet Union and the United States further unraveled in central Europe. France, Great Britain, the Soviet Union, and the United States had divided Germany temporarily into four occupation zones, each governed by one of them. But the Allies could not agree on long-term plans. Having borne the brunt of German aggression, France and the Soviet Union both opposed reunification of Germany. The Soviet Union also demanded heavy reparations along with a limit on postwar reindustrialization. Roosevelt appeared to agree with the Soviets. "We have got to be tough with Germany, and I mean the German people not just the Nazis," he concluded. "We . . . have got to treat them in such a manner so they can't just go on reproducing people who want to continue the way they have in the past." But American business leaders, envisioning a new center for U.S. commerce, shared Winston Churchill's hope of rebuilding Germany into a powerful counterforce against the Soviet Union and a strong market for U.S. and British goods.

The division of Germany forecast the shape of the new world order. West Germany became more and more "American" as the United States directed the reconstruction of its capitalist economy and canceled voters' mandates for government ownership of coal mines and major industries. While guiding liberal politicians into top government positions, U.S. advisers began a program of amnesty for a former Nazi elite, which controlled large sectors of business and the civil service, in order to stabilize the government against a resurgence of a once-strong German socialist movement. Meanwhile, the Soviets dragged industrial equipment out of impoverished East Germany for their own domestic needs and imposed a harsh discipline on the inhabitants. Despite promising to deliver the economy over to German workers, the Soviets took no steps toward democracy in East Germany.

"The main prize of the victory" over the Axis powers was, a State Department document had noted in November 1945, a "limited and temporary power to establish the kind of world we want to live in." But this prediction failed to account for the dissolution of the alliance between the western powers and the Soviet Union. Winston Churchill, swearing to preserve the British colonial empire, had himself parleyed with Stalin to establish spheres of influence. Yet he refused to accept Soviet demands for control over eastern Europe as a buffer against future invasions from the West. The more forcefully Stalin resisted plans for Western-style governments and Western influence right up to the Soviet borders, the more Western leaders cried foul. In a speech delivered in Fulton, Missouri, in March 1946, Churchill declared that "an iron curtain has descended across the [European] Continent." The dream of a community of nations had dissolved, but perhaps it had never been more than a fantasy contrived to maintain a fragile alliance amid the urgency of World War II.

THE POLICY OF CONTAINMENT

Many Americans believed that Franklin D. Roosevelt, had he lived, would have been able to stem the tide of tensions between the Soviet Union and the United States. Harry S. Truman, who became president when FDR died in April 1945, sorely lacked FDR's talent for diplomacy. More comfortable with southern or conservative Democrats than with polished New Dealers, the new president liked to talk tough and act defiantly. He did not hesitate to flaunt the U.S. monopoly of the atomic bomb. Just ten days after he took office, Truman complained that U.S.-Soviet negotiations had been a "one-way street." He vowed to "baby" the Soviets no longer, adding that if they did not like it they could "go to hell."

Truman replaced Roosevelt's diplomatic advisers with a hard-line team of new advisers. Drawing on their advice, he aimed to establish U.S. leadership in the world through a race for power that would exhaust communist resources. In the short run, Truman determined to maintain U.S. military superiority and prevent communism from spreading outside the Soviet Union. Containment, a doctrine uniting military, economic, and diplomatic strategies to turn back communism and to secure for the United States the leading role in world affairs, now became the linchpin of U.S. foreign policy.

The Truman Doctrine

Truman showed his cards early in 1947 when a crisis erupted in the Mediterranean, a region considered a British sphere. When civil war broke out in Greece and Great Britain announced its plan to withdraw all economic and military aid, U.S. diplomatic leaders began to fear a move into this territory by the Soviet Union. They knew that Stalin was not directly involved in the crisis, but they also recognized that the Soviet Union would derive enormous benefits from a communist victory in nearby Greece. To forestall this possibility, Truman decided to take over Britain's historic role as the dominant power in this area. The president made his case by insisting that without U.S. intervention all of the oil-rich Middle East would fall under Soviet control.

Such a commitment demanded something many Americans feared: an expenditure of hundreds of millions of dollars and the responsibility for controlling a region far outside the Western Hemisphere and the Pacific. If he hoped to sway public opinion as well as the fiscally conservative Republican Congress, advised Republican senator Arthur H. Vandenberg of Michigan, chair of the Foreign Relations Committee, the president would have to "scare hell out of the country."

In early March 1947 Truman swung into action. Speaking at Baylor University, he linked the survival of the American system of free enterprise to Western victory in Greece. A week later, on March 12, appearing before Congress, the president argued: "At the present moment in world history, nearly every nation must choose between alternative ways of life. . . . One way of life is based upon the will of the majority, and is distinguished by free institutions . . . and freedom from political oppression. The second way of life is based upon the will of a minority forcibly imposed on the majority . . . and the suppression of personal freedoms." Never mentioning the Soviet Union by name, the president appealed for all-out resistance to a "certain ideology," wherever it appeared in the world. The preservation of peace and the freedom of all Americans depended, Truman insisted, on containing communism.

Truman won the day. Congress approved his request to appropriate $400 million in aid for Greece and Turkey, and this assistance helped the Greek monarchy crush the rebel movement. Truman's victory took the sting out of Republican criticisms and buoyed his popularity for the upcoming 1948 election. It also helped to turn Americans against their former ally and to generate popular support for a campaign against communism, both at home and abroad. Moreover, by exaggerating the immediacy of the Soviet threat, Truman was able to wield his executive power to control the legislative agenda, much as a president would do in time of war.

The significance of what became known as the Truman Doctrine far outlasted the events in the Mediterranean: the United States had declared its right to intervene to save other nations from communist subversion. As early as February 1946, foreign-policy adviser George Kennan had sent an 8,000-word "long telegram" to the State Department insisting that Soviet fanaticism could be quelled only by ongoing military and diplomatic pressure. In July 1947 he reaffirmed his belief. Writing under the pseudonym "X" in *Foreign Affairs*, Kennan explained that the future of democracy depended on two possibilities: "either the break-up [of communism] or the gradual mellowing of Soviet power." Despite complaints from critics such as Walter Lippmann, who described this position as a "strategic monstrosity," requiring an

OVERVIEW

MAJOR COLD WAR POLICIES

Policy	Date	Provisions
Truman Doctrine	1947	Pledged the United States to the containment of communism in Europe and elsewhere. The doctrine was the foundation of Truman's foreign policy. It impelled the United States to support any nation whose stability was threatened by communism or the Soviet Union.
Federal Employees Loyalty and Security Program	1947	Established by Executive Order 9835, this program barred communists and fascists from federal employment and outlined procedures for investigating current and prospective federal employees.
Marshall Plan	1947	U.S. program to aid war-torn Europe, also known as the European Recovery Program. The Marshall Plan was a cornerstone in the U.S. use of economic policy to contain communism.
National Security Act	1947	Established Department of Defense (to coordinate the three armed services), the National Security Council (to advise the president on security issues), and the Central Intelligence Agency (to gather and evaluate intelligence data).
North Atlantic Treaty Organization (NATO)	1948	A military alliance of twelve nations formed to deter possible aggression of the Soviet Union against Western Europe.
NSC-68	1950	National Security Council Paper calling for an expanded and aggressive U.S. defense policy, including greater military spending and higher taxes.
Internal Security Act (also known as the McCarran Act and the Subversive Activities Control Act)	1950	Legislation providing for the registration of all communist and totalitarian groups and authorizing the arrest of suspect persons during a national emergency.
Immigration and Nationality Act (also known as McCarran-Walter Immigration Act)	1952	Reaffirmed the national origins quota system but tightened immigration controls, barring homosexuals and people considered subversive from entering the United States.

endless diffusion of American resources for military operations around the world, containment served as the cornerstone of U.S. foreign policy for the next several decades.

The Marshall Plan

The Truman Doctrine directly inspired the European Recovery Program, commonly known as the Marshall Plan. Introduced in a commencement speech at

Harvard University on June 5, 1947, by secretary of state and former army chief of staff George C. Marshall, the plan aimed to reduce "hunger, poverty, desperation, and chaos" and to restore "the confidence of the European people in the economic future of their own countries and of Europe as a whole." In this region, the Truman administration did not fear a Soviet invasion as much as the political consequences of total disintegration of the region's economy. Indirectly, the Marshall Plan aimed to turn back both socialist and communist bids for power in northern and western Europe.

The Marshall Plan in effect brought recipients of aid into a bilateral agreement with the United States. The western European nations, seventeen in all, received nearly $13 billion between 1948 and 1951; more than half went to West Germany, France, and Great Britain. The seventeen nations also ratified the General Agreement on Tariffs and Trade (GATT), which reduced commercial barriers among member nations and opened all to U.S. trade.

Considered by many historians the most successful postwar U.S. diplomatic venture, the Marshall Plan created the climate for a viable capitalist economy in western Europe. Industrial production in that region rose by 200 percent between 1947 and 1952. Deflationary programs cut wages and increased unemployment, but profits soared and the standard of living improved. Under U.S. leadership, the nations of western Europe rallied to become a major center of American trade and investment.

The Marshall Plan drove a further wedge between the United States and the Soviet Union. Stalin denounced the plan as an American scheme to rebuild Germany and to incorporate it into an anti-Soviet bloc. The architects of the Marshall Plan, however, had never expected the Soviet Union to participate. As one planner noted, if the recovery program included funds to help the communist nations, "the whole project would probably be unworkable." As

Located deep within communist East Germany, West Berlin was suddenly cut off from the West when Josef Stalin blockaded all surface traffic in an attempt to take over the war-torn city. Between June 1948 and May 1949, British and U.S. pilots made 272,000 flights, dropping food and fuel to civilians. The Berlin Airlift successfully foiled the blockade, and the Soviet Union reopened access on May 12.

the president readily acknowledged, the Truman Doctrine and the Marshall Plan were "two halves of the same walnut."

The Berlin Crisis and the Formation of NATO

Once the Marshall Plan was in place, the strategy of containment began to take clear shape in Germany. In June 1948 the Western allies decided to incorporate the American, French, and British occupation zones into a single nation, the Federal Republic of West Germany. Already alarmed by their plan to rebuild German industry, Stalin perceived this new move as yet another threat to Soviet security. On June 24, 1948, he responded by stopping all traffic to West Berlin, formally controlled by the Western allies but located hundreds of miles within Soviet-occupied East Germany.

Divided Europe   *During the cold war, Europe was divided into opposing military alliances, the North American Treaty Organization (NATO) and the Warsaw Pact (communist bloc).*

The Soviet retaliation created for Truman both a crisis and an opportunity for confrontation. The president believed that Stalin intended to take over Berlin, thus putting not only the future of Germany but the governing role of the Western powers in jeopardy. Although his advisers were reluctant to risk war by challenging Stalin militarily, the president refused to show any sign of weakness. He threatened to use atomic weapons against the Soviets, and he even sent two squadrons of B-29s to the U.S. military base in Great Britain. But this plan was quickly abandoned, and the United States began, with help from the Royal Air Force, an airlift of historic proportions—Operation Vittles, which delivered nearly 2 million tons of supplies to West Berliners. Finally, in May 1949, the Soviet Union conceded defeat and lifted the blockade.

Within a few weeks, East Germany and West Germany were established as separate states.

The Berlin crisis made a U.S.-led military alliance against the Soviets attractive to western European nations. In April 1949 ten European nations, Canada, and the United States formed the North Atlantic Treaty Organization (NATO), a mutual defense pact in which "an armed attack against one or more of them . . . shall be considered an attack against them all." NATO complemented the Marshall Plan, strengthening economic ties among the member nations by, according to one analyst, keeping "the Russians out, the Americans in, and the Germans down." It also deepened divisions between eastern and western Europe, making a permanent military mobilization on both sides almost inevitable.

By mid-1949 Truman and his advisers were basking in the glow of their victories. The U.S. Senate had ratified the first formal military treaty with a European nation since the Revolutionary War era—a giant step away from isolationism. Congress also approved $1.3 billion in military aid, which involved the creation of U.S. Army bases and the deployment of American troops abroad. Critics such as isolationist senator Robert A. Taft warned that the United States could not afford to police all of Europe without sidetracking domestic policies and undercutting the UN. But opinion polls revealed strong support for Truman's tough line against the Soviets.

Between 1947 and 1949, the Truman administration had defined the policies that would shape the cold war for decades to come. The Truman Doctrine explained the ideological basis of containment; the Marshall Plan put into place its economic underpinnings in western Europe; and NATO created the mechanisms for military enforcement. When NATO extended membership to a rearmed West Germany in May 1955, the Soviet Union responded by creating a counterpart, the Warsaw Pact, including East Germany. The division of East and West was complete.

The Cold War in Asia

Triumphant in western Europe, Truman managed only a mixed record in Asia. In some areas, he proved that the United States could contain communism without massive displays of military strength. Elsewhere, the Truman Doctrine did not work, and the results were disastrous for the president.

The United States achieved its greatest success in occupied Japan. General Douglas MacArthur directed an interim government in a modest reconstruction program that included land reform, the creation of independent trade unions, abolition of contract marriages and granting of woman suffrage, sweeping demilitarization, and, eventually, a constitutional democracy that barred communists from all posts. Increasingly more wary of the Soviet Union than of a resurgent Japan, American leaders planned to rebuild the Japanese economy and integrate Japan, like West Germany, into an anti-Soviet bloc. In return for its sovereignty, granted in 1952, Japan agreed to house huge U.S. military bases, thus placing U.S. troops and weapons strategically close to the Soviet Union's Asian rim. U.S. advisers, meanwhile, prepared a new group of business leaders who were eager to build a capitalist economy in Japan and willing to quash anti-American dissent with a powerful national police. Economically, the United States took control, forbidding Japan to trade with the Soviet Union and, later, the People's Republic of China.

Truman scored smaller but significant victories in both Indonesia and the Philippines. When a nationalist revolution in the Dutch East Indies began to threaten U.S. interests, the State Department forced Holland to grant independence to its colony, and the sovereign state of Indonesia was created in 1949. The United States had granted formal independence to the Philippines in 1946 but retained major naval bases there as well as influence over Filipino foreign and domestic affairs. In response to a major uprising of peasants hungry for land, the United States directed massive amounts of aid to nationalist leader Ramón Magsaysay, who crushed the rebellion. General MacArthur adamantly defended the role of the United States, describing the Philippines to Congress in 1950 as a "mighty bulwark of Christianity in the Far East."

The situation in China could not be handled so easily. Unwilling to take strong diplomatic or economic measures against the escalating Japanese invasion during the 1930s, American officials nevertheless felt compelled to prop up the corrupt and sagging Jiang Jieshi (Chiang Kai-shek) regime after China officially joined the Allies in 1941. Under General Joseph Stilwell, however, the U.S. military mission of the China-Burma-India theater remained largely defensive. The Communist Red Army, led by Mao Zedong, assumed more and more of the fighting as the war drew to a close.

American diplomats on the scene, observing the shift of forces closely, warned Jiang that without major reforms—especially the breaking up of large landholdings and the feeding of starving people—his forces were bound to lose the loyalty of ordinary Chinese. Increasingly desperate for a solution, the Americans tried to convince Jiang to turn over the reins of government to a less corrupt group of moderates. Some urged reconciliation of the U.S. government with the rising military and political hero, Mao, either alone or in coalition with Jiang.

All these plans failed when Jiang insisted on fighting the communists after Japan had been defeated. Sorely misjudging his resources and launching an all-out offensive against his communist adversaries, Jiang precipitated the collapse of his government. When the victory of Mao's forces became inevitable, U.S. diplomats broke off relations with Jiang, and Secretary of State Dean Acheson issued a 1,054-page "White Paper" explaining that the situation was "beyond the control of the government of the United States." By mid-1949, the majority of Jiang's troops surrendered, and his Nationalist government retreated to the island of Formosa (Taiwan). Enjoying wide support among the rural 85 percent of China's population, Mao took control of the mainland.

The news of China's "fall" to communism created an uproar in the United States. The Asia First wing of the Republican Party, which envisioned the Far East rather than Europe as the prime site of future U.S. overseas economic expansion, blamed the Truman administration for "losing" China. Although China was never America's possession to lose, the bipartisan anti-communist sentiment fueled by Truman's actions placed him in the delicate position of holding the "Iron Curtain" in place across the world. Republicans described Truman's explanation for communist victory as a "white-wash of a wishful, do-nothing policy," and the Democrats as a "party of treason" to national security.

The president had repeatedly insisted that communism was a "conspiracy" of depraved power-mongers with no basis of popular support. The "China Lobby," which represented economic interests but also had roots in Christian missionary ties to Asia, continued to use Truman's own rhetoric against him. *Time* magazine, the voice of publisher and China Lobby enthusiast Henry Luce, was especially vitriolic. Boxed in, Truman seemed once more as he had to many during his early months in office, a small-time politician power-less and incompetent to shape American affairs.

After Stalin signed a formal alliance with Mao in February 1950, the rhetoric of the cold war became yet more pronounced. The perceived threat of "international communism" came to dominate American foreign policy for the next twenty years.

Atomic Diplomacy

The policy of containment depended on the ability of the United States to back up its commitments through military means, and Truman relied on the U.S. monopoly of atomic weapons to pressure the Soviets to cooperate. On August 9, 1945, the day U.S. planes bombed Nagasaki, the president told Americans, "We must constitute ourselves trustees of this new force—to prevent its misuse, and to turn it into the channels of service to mankind." In a survey conducted one month later, 85 percent of the respondents wanted the United States to retain sole possession of the bomb for as long as possible. Many scientists nevertheless warned that once the bomb had been exploded, the "secret" could no longer be guarded.

After the war, many Americans favored control of atomic power by the United Nations. But a plan drafted by American financier Bernard M. Baruch failed to win approval by the Soviet Union. When negotiations stalled, the United States quickly put aside all plans for international cooperation. In 1946 Congress passed the Atomic Energy Act, which granted the newly established Atomic Energy Commission control of all research and development under the strictest standards of national security.

The United States began to stockpile atomic weapons and conduct additional tests on the Bikini Islands in the Pacific. By 1949, the number of bombs had grown from thirteen to fifty. By 1950, as a scientific adviser subsequently observed, the United States "had a stockpile capable of somewhat more than reproducing World War II in a single day."

Despite warnings to the contrary by leading scientists, U.S. military analysts continued to downplay Soviet nuclear capability. The Military Intelligence Division of the War Department estimated it would take the Soviet Union three to ten years to produce an atomic bomb. In August 1949, the Soviet Union proved them wrong by testing its own atomic bomb. "There is only one thing worse than one nation having the atomic bomb," Nobel Prize-winning scientist Harold C. Urey said, "that's two nations having it."

Within a few years, both the United States and the Soviet Union had tested hydrogen bombs a thousand times more powerful than the primitive weapons dropped on Hiroshima and Nagasaki in 1945. Both proceeded to stockpile bombs and to put nuclear warheads on missiles, inaugurating the fateful nuclear arms race that scientists had feared since 1945. The two superpowers were now firmly locked into the cold war. The nuclear arms race imperiled their futures, diverted their economies, and fostered fears of impending doom. When he heard of the Soviet detonation of the bomb, Senator Vandenberg remarked presciently, "This is now a different world." Prospects for global peace had faded, and despite the Allied victory in World War II, the world had again divided into hostile camps.

THE TRUMAN PRESIDENCY

Truman's aggressive, gutsy personality suited the confrontational mood of the cold war. He linked the Soviet threat in Europe to the need for a strong presidency. Meanwhile, he reached out to voters alarmed at Republican intent on dismantling the New Deal. Pressed to establish his own political identity, "Give 'em Hell" Harry successfully portrayed himself as a fierce fighter against all challengers, yet loyal to Roosevelt's legacy.

"To Err Is Truman"

In marked contrast with his illustrious predecessor, Harry Truman was a virtual unknown to most Americans. Within a year of assuming office, he rated lower in public approval than any twentieth-century president except Roosevelt's own predecessor, Herbert Hoover, who had been blamed for the Great Depression. The twin responsibilities of reestablishing peacetime conditions—demobilizing the troops and reconverting the economy—seemed to overwhelm the new president's administration. Repeatedly lashing out at his detractors and withdrawing unpopular proposals after public outcries, he also had trouble convincing Americans of his sincerity. "To err is Truman," critics jeered.

As commander in chief, Truman angered servicemen and -women eager to return home. Quite a few combat veterans were surprised to find themselves shipped off to the Philippines to put down labor and agrarian unrest. Members of Congress received bundles of protest letters, "Bring Daddy Home" clubs formed throughout the country, and in January 1946 demonstrations broke out in Manila. Spreading across the Pacific, the "Bring the Boys Home" movement so alarmed Truman that he reversed course and, in a dramatic radio address, promised a rapid demobilization. Under his orders the War Department gave in, but the president had already damaged his record.

At home, Truman did no better. In handling the enormous task of reconverting the economy to peacetime production, he appeared both inept and mean-spirited. The president faced millions of restless would-be consumers tired of rationing and eager to spend their wartime savings. The demand for consumer items rapidly outran supply, fueling inflation and creating a huge black market; business profits skyrocketed along with retail prices. When Congress proposed to extend wartime controls over prices, Truman vetoed the bill.

In 1945 and 1946, the country appeared ready to explode. While homemakers protested rising prices by boycotting neighborhood stores, industrial workers struck in unprecedented numbers. Employers, fearing a rapid decline to depression-level profits, determined to slash wages or at least hold them steady; workers wanted a bigger cut of the huge war profits they had

heard about. As police and strikers clashed, citywide general strikes spread from transit workers to other laborers. In Oakland, Pittsburgh, and Rochester, the strikes halted all commerce for days. Alarmed by the spectacle of nearly 4.6 million workers on picket lines, the new president proposed to seize the mines and to induct striking railroad workers into the army. The Senate, however, killed this plan by a 70 to 13 vote.

Congress defeated most of Truman's proposals for reconversion. One week after Japan's surrender, the president introduced a twenty-one-point program that included greater unemployment compensation, higher minimum wages, and housing assistance. Later he added proposals for national health insurance and atomic energy legislation. Congress turned back the bulk of these bills, passing the Employment Act of 1946 only after substantial modification. The act created a new executive body, the Council of Economic Advisers, which would confer with the president and formulate policies for maintaining employment, production, and purchasing power. But the measure failed to grant the fiscal means to guarantee full employment, thus undermining Truman's chief effort to advance beyond the New Deal.

By 1946 Truman's popularity had dipped to 32 percent. One joke began with a reflection on what

Police and strikers confront each other in Los Angeles during one of many postwar strikes in 1946. Employers wanted to cut wages, and workers refused to give up the higher living standard achieved during the war.

Roosevelt would do if still alive, only to end by asking "What would Truman do if he were alive?" Republicans, sensing victory in the upcoming off-year elections, asked the voters, "Had enough?" Apparently the voters had. They censored Truman and the Democrats, giving Republicans majorities in both houses of Congress and in the state capitols. In office, the Republicans set out to turn back the New Deal. And in a symbolic repudiation of Roosevelt they passed an amendment establishing a two-term limit for the presidency.

The Republicans, dominant in Congress for the first time since 1931, prepared a full counteroffensive against the constituency most hated by business: organized labor. Unions had by this time reached a peak in size and power, with membership topping 15 million and encompassing nearly 40 percent of all wage earners. To halt this movement, the Republican-dominated Eightieth Congress passed the Taft-Hartley Act in 1947.

The Labor-Management Relations Act, as Taft-Hartley was officially known, outlawed many practices approved by the Wagner Act of 1935 (see Chapter 24), such as the closed shop, the secondary boycott, and the use of union dues for political activities. It also mandated an eighty-day cooling-off period in the case of strikes affecting national safety or health. Called the "slave labor bill" by union activists, Taft-Hartley furthermore required all union officials to swear under oath that they were not communists—a cold war mandate that abridged freedoms ordinarily guaranteed by the First Amendment. Those unions that refused to cooperate were denied the services of the National Labor Relations Board, which arbitrated strikes and issued credentials to unions. In short, the Taft-Hartley Act made it more difficult for workers to establish unions in their industry or trade.

Truman regained some support from organized labor when he vetoed the Taft-Hartley Act, saying it would "conflict with important principles of our democratic society." Congress, however, overrode his veto, and Truman himself went on to invoke the act against strikers. Members of the president's own party now proposed that he resign or sought to persuade General Dwight Eisenhower to accept the Democratic nomination for president in the upcoming national election.

The 1948 Election

Although lacking a strong candidate, Democrats gingerly approached the 1948 election—the first presidential contest since the inauguration of the cold war—as an opportunity to campaign for their own post-New Deal agenda. In preparation, a group headed by Eleanor Roosevelt, labor leaders Philip Murray and Walter Reuther, and theologian Reinhold Niebuhr, among others, met in January 1947 to form Americans for Democratic Action (ADA). This body became the most important liberal lobby of the postwar era. Deter-

mined to defeat the Republicans, ADA moved to reorient the Democratic Party itself, which appeared to be breaking up on the shoals of cold war politics.

"As long as Franklin Roosevelt was President," wrote a journalist in the British *New Statesman* in 1948, "life was politically simple. . . . There was a place for [liberals] on the New Deal bandwagon, and until the driver died, some of them were permitted to sit on the front seat." The new president, however, had already divided the liberal community. Truman frankly considered some of Roosevelt's closest advisers to be "crackpots and the lunatic fringe." By late 1946 he had forced out the remaining social planners who had staffed the Washington bureaus for over a decade, including one of the best-loved New Dealers, Secretary of the Interior Harold Ickes.

Truman had also fired his secretary of commerce, Henry A. Wallace, for advocating a more conciliatory policy toward the Soviet Union. Wallace, however, would not retreat and made plans to run for president as candidate of the newly formed Progressive Party. Having served as Roosevelt's vice president and secretary of agriculture, Wallace was well known as a long-time champion of New Deal liberalism. He vowed to expand New Deal programs, to move swiftly and boldly toward full employment, racial equality, and stronger trade unions, and to work in harmony with the Soviet Union. As the election neared, Wallace remarked after a speech before 32,000 enthusiastic supporters, "We're on the march. We're really rolling now."

The deepening cold war soon quashed Wallace's chances. Rallying around the president, ADA denounced the Progressive Party for lining up "with the force of Soviet totalitarianism." Truman himself, as well as many conservatives, accused Wallace of being a tool of communists. These timely Red-baiting attacks took a toll on the poorly organized and underfunded Wallace campaign, driving many liberals from its ranks, including future Democratic presidential candidate George McGovern. Moreover, Wallace, who never subscribed to communism, refused to fend off these charges, considering them a dangerous by-product of anticommunist hysteria.

Meanwhile, Truman, in an unusually shrewd strategic move, repositioned himself to discredit congressional Republicans. He proposed programs calling for federal funds for education and new housing and a national program of medical insurance that he knew the Republicans would kill, and he called Congress back for a fruitless special session in 1948. He then hammered away at the Republican controlled "do-nothing Congress" to good effect in his reelection campaign, warning voters that if Republicans won the White House, the United States would become "an economic colony of Wall Street."

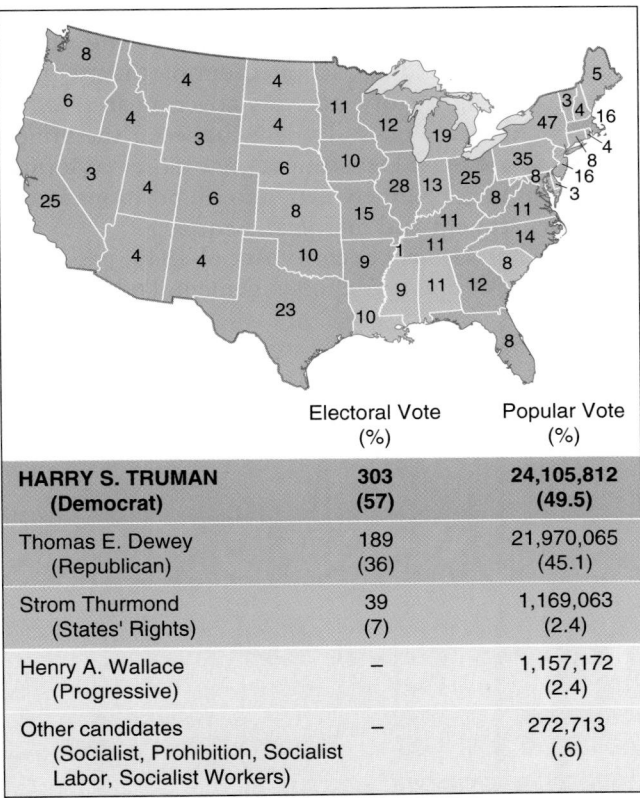

	Electoral Vote (%)	Popular Vote (%)
HARRY S. TRUMAN (Democrat)	**303 (57)**	**24,105,812 (49.5)**
Thomas E. Dewey (Republican)	189 (36)	21,970,065 (45.1)
Strom Thurmond (States' Rights)	39 (7)	1,169,063 (2.4)
Henry A. Wallace (Progressive)	–	1,157,172 (2.4)
Other candidates (Socialist, Prohibition, Socialist Labor, Socialist Workers)	–	272,713 (.6)

The Election of 1948   *Harry Truman holds up a copy of the* Chicago Tribune *with headlines confidently and mistakenly predicting the victory of his opponent, Thomas E. Dewey. An initially unpopular candidate, Truman made a whistle-stop tour of the country by train to win 49.5 percent of the popular vote to Dewey's 45.1 percent.*

A second tactic seemed to backfire. Pressed by ADA leaders to cut Wallace's lead on civil rights, Truman issued executive orders in July 1948 desegregating the armed forces and banning discrimination in the federal civil service. He also endorsed a plank on racial equality that he personally considered too

strongly worded. In response, some 300 southern delegates bolted from the Democratic National Convention and formed a States' Rights ("Dixiecrat") ticket headed by Governor J. Strom Thurmond of South Carolina, known for his segregationist views. With the South as good as lost, and popular New York governor Thomas E. Dewey heading the Republican ticket, Truman appeared hopelessly far from victory.

Yet as the election neared, Truman managed to restore essential components of the New Deal coalition. Fear of the Republicans won back the bulk of organized labor, while the recognition of the new State of Israel in May 1948 helped prevent the defection of many liberal Jewish voters from Democratic ranks. The success of the Berlin airlift also buoyed Truman's popularity. By election time, Truman had deprived Henry Wallace of nearly all his liberal support. Meanwhile, Dewey, who had run a hard-hitting campaign against Roosevelt in 1944, expected to coast to victory. By campaigning vigorously, Truman won back Democrats except in the South, where Thurmond took four states. The president carried most of the states and trounced Dewey 303 to 189 in the electoral college. Congressional Democrats again had majorities in both houses. Truman's campaign had retained the loyalty of those Americans who feared a reversal of the New Deal. "Harry Truman won the election," concluded the *New Republic*, "because Franklin Roosevelt had worked so well."

The Fair Deal

President Truman laid out his domestic agenda in January 1949. "Every segment of our population and every individual has a right to expect from our Government a fair deal," he affirmed. The return of Democratic majorities in the House and Senate, he hoped, would enable him to translate campaign promises into concrete legislative achievements. But a powerful bloc of conservative southern Democrats and midwestern Republicans defeated most of the president's plans.

Truman could claim only a few victories. Congress passed a National Housing Act in 1949, promoting federally funded construction of low-income housing. It also raised the minimum wage from forty to seventy-five cents per hour and expanded the Social Security program to cover an additional 10 million people. Otherwise, Truman made little headway. He and congressional liberals introduced a variety of bills to weaken southern segregationism: making lynching a federal crime; outlawing the poll tax; prohibiting discrimination in interstate transportation. These measures were all defeated by southern-led filibusters. Proposals to create a national health insurance plan, provide federal aid for education, and repeal or modify Taft-Hartley remained bottled up in committees. Truman himself appeared to lose interest in the liberal agenda as his cold war foreign policy increasingly took priority over domestic issues.

Truman managed best to lay out the basic principles of cold war liberalism. Toning down the rhetoric of economic equality espoused by the visionary wing of the Roosevelt coalition, his Fair Deal exalted economic growth—not the reapportionment of wealth or political power—as the proper mechanism for ensuring social harmony and national welfare. His administration insisted, therefore, on an ambitious program of expanded foreign trade while relying on the federal government to encourage high levels of productivity at home. Although dropping at the end of World War II, federal expenditures remained at least seven times greater than during their New Deal peak in the 1930s.

The Truman administration effectively used the threat of military confrontation with the Soviet Union to increase the size of the defense budget. By the end of Truman's second term, defense allocations accounted for 10 percent of the gross national product, directly or indirectly employed hundreds of thousands of well-paid workers, and subsidized some of the nation's most profitable corporations. This vast financial outlay, guided through Congress by legislators seeking economic benefits for their constituents, created the rationale for permanent, large-scale military spending as a basic stimulus to economic growth. A vigorous anticommunist crusade at home strengthened the underpinnings of this ambitious cold war program.

THE COLD WAR AT HOME

In June 1946, Attorney General Tom C. Clark announced that the United States had become the target of "a sinister and deep-seated plot on the part of Communists, ideologists, and small groups of radicals" to capture unions, cause strikes, and prevent lawful authorities from maintaining order. FBI director J. Edgar Hoover estimated that there were at least 100,000 communists in the nation. Four years later, Republican senator Joseph R. McCarthy announced that he held lists of communists serving secretly in government agencies. This information, he declared, showed that the United States had already fallen prey to subversive influences. The specter of a prolonged cold war with the Soviet Union had encouraged many Americans, including the nation's leaders, to become obsessed with problems of national security, real or imagined, and to resort to extreme measures to solve them.

The National Security State

The cold war served as the rationale for a massive reordering of governmental power. Only a powerful leader in charge of a vast bureaucracy, it was argued, could hope to curtail the international communist

conspiracy. Invoking national security, the president now claimed executive authority normally reserved for wartime. Within a decade after the end of World War II, a huge federal bureaucracy, dependent on military spending and increasingly devoted to surveillance at home and abroad, had greatly changed the relationship of the federal government to everyday affairs.

National defense took up increasingly large portions of the nation's resources. Shortly before the war, the federal workforce totaled about 900,000 civilians, with about 10 percent engaged in security work; by war's end, the government employed nearly 4 million people, of whom 75 percent worked in national security agencies. The Pentagon, which had opened in 1943 as the largest office building in the world, housed the Joint Chiefs of Staff and 35,000 military personnel. Similarly, when the State Department consolidated its various divisions in 1961, it abandoned the nearly thirty separate buildings acquired during the 1950s to take over an eight-story structure covering an area the size of four city blocks. The ties between the armed forces and the State Department grew closer, as former military officers routinely began to fill positions in the State Department and diplomatic corps.

The National Security Act of 1947, passed by Congress with Truman's encouragement, laid the foun-

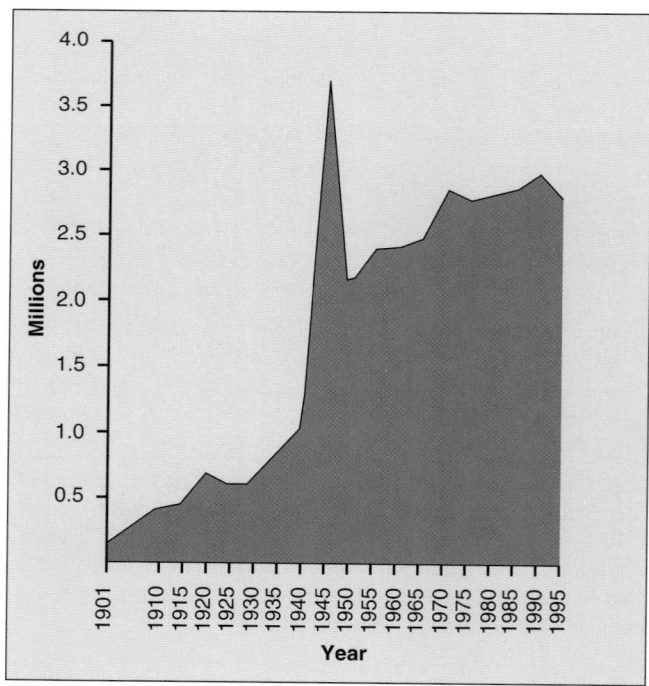

Number of Employees in the Executive Branch, *1901–1995   The federal bureaucracy, which reached a peak of nearly four million people during World War II, remained at unprecedentedly high levels during the cold war.*

Source: U.S. Bureau of the Census, *Historical Statistics of the United States, Colonial Times through* 1970; *Statistical Abstract of the United States,* 1997 dation for this expansion. The act established the Department of Defense and the National Security Council (NSC) to administer and coordinate defense policies and to advise the president. The Central Intelligence Agency (CIA), with roots in the wartime Office of Strategic Services, was established to obtain political, military, and economic information from around the world. Although information about the CIA was classified—that is, secret from both Congress and the public—historians have estimated that the agency soon dwarfed the State Department in number of employees and size of budget. By late 1947, as Harrison Baldwin of the *New York Times* noted, there was an ominous trend toward "militarization of [the] government and of the American state of mind."

In March 1947, Truman signed Executive Order 9835, establishing the Federal Employees Loyalty and Security Program. The program barred members of the Communist Party—as well as fascists and anyone guilty of "sympathetic association" with either—from federal employment. It also outlined procedures for investigating current and prospective federal employees. An employee could be dismissed merely on "reasonable grounds for belief that the person is disloyal." Later amendments added "homosexuals" as potential security risks on the grounds that they might succumb to blackmail by enemy agents.

Many state and municipal governments enacted loyalty programs and required public employees, including teachers at all levels, to sign loyalty oaths. In Detroit, the loyalty review board included city officials, FBI agents, and executives from the auto industry. Positions involving security clearances were closed off to many scientists and engineers, including several who had worked on the Manhattan Project. In all, some 6.6 million people underwent loyalty and security checks. Although no spies or saboteurs turned up, nearly 500 government workers were fired and nearly 6,000 more chose to resign.

Attorney General Clark aided this effort by publishing a list of hundreds of potentially subversive organizations selected by criteria so vague that any views "hostile or inimical to the American form of government" (as Clark's assistants noted in a memo) could make an organization liable for investigation and prosecution. There was, moreover, no right of appeal.

Although designed primarily to screen federal employees, the attorney general's list effectively outlawed many political and social organizations, indirectly stigmatizing hundreds of thousands of individuals who had done nothing illegal. Church associations, civil rights organizations, musical groups, and even summer camps appeared on the list. Some, like the Civil Rights Congress, played important roles in defending imprisoned African Americans. Others, like the Jewish Music

Alliance and Camp Kinderland, mainly served the cultural interests of Jewish Americans.

Membership in a listed group provided the rationale for dismissal at nearly every level of government. Fraternal and social institutions, especially popular among aging European immigrants of various nationalities, were among the largest organizations destroyed. The state of New York, for example, legally dismantled the International Workers' Order, which had provided insurance to nearly 200,000 immigrants and their families. Only a handful of organizations had the funds to challenge the listing legally; most simply closed their doors. Even past membership in a listed group—during the desperate 1930s many liberals had been briefly active in communist or communist-related movements—quickly became grounds for suspicion and likely dismissal. As a result, millions faced investigation and potential ruin.

In 1950 Congress overrode the president's veto to pass a bill that Truman called "the greatest danger to freedom of press, speech, and assembly since the Sedition Act of 1798." The Internal Security (McCarran) Act required communist organizations to register with the Subversive Activities Control Board and authorized the arrest of suspect persons during a national emergency. The Immigration and Nationality Act, sponsored by Republican senator Pat McCarran of Nevada and adopted in 1952, again over Truman's veto, barred people deemed "subversive" or "homosexual" from becoming citizens or even from visiting the United States. It also empowered the attorney general to deport immigrants who were members of communist organizations, even if they had become citizens. Challenged repeatedly on constitutional grounds, the Subversive Activities Control Board remained in place until 1973, when it was terminated.

The Red Scare in Hollywood

Anticommunist Democratic representative Martin Dies of Texas, who had chaired a congressional committee on "un-American activities" since 1938, told reporters at a press conference in Hollywood in 1944:

> Hollywood is the greatest source of revenue in this nation for the Communists and other subversive groups. . . . Two elements stand out in . . . the making of pictures which extoll foreign ideology—propaganda for a cause which seeks to spread its ideas to our people[,] and the "leftist" or radical screenwriters. . . . In my opinion, [motion picture executives] will do well to halt the propaganda pictures and eliminate every writer who has un-American ideas.

A few years later, Dies's successor, J. Parnell Thomas of New Jersey (later convicted and imprisoned for bribery), directed the committee to investigate supposed communist infiltration of the movie industry.

Renamed and made a permanent standing committee in 1945, the House Un-American Activities Committee (HUAC) conducted an investigation of the entertainment industry that was one of the most spectacular and troubling domestic antisubversive campaigns of the cold war. HUAC had the power to subpoena witnesses and to compel them to answer all questions or face contempt of Congress charges. The results were sometimes absurd. In well-publicized hearings held in Hollywood in October 1947, HUAC heard the mother of actress Ginger Rogers explain that her daughter, duped into appearing in the pro-Soviet wartime film *Tender Comrade* (1943), "had been forced" to read the subversive line "Share and share alike, that's democracy." Conservative novelist Ayn Rand added that *The Song of Russia* (1944) had intentionally deceived the American public by showing Russians smiling! The committee found ample evidence of leftist sympathies but none of the subversive activity it alleged. Meanwhile, the studios announced that no writer, technician, or actor who refused to denounce communism would be employed again.

HUAC encouraged testimony by "friendly witnesses" such as Ronald Reagan and Gary Cooper. Barbara Stanwyck testified that her husband, Robert Taylor, another friendly witness, could not have been influenced by communist ideas because he never read books; he even prepared gourmet meals solely "from the pictures" in cookbooks. The committee intimidated many witnesses into naming suspect friends and coworkers in order to be cleared for future work in Hollywood. Only a few former communists, such as television superstar Lucille Ball, were too popular to be damaged by the bad publicity.

A small but prominent minority refused to cooperate with HUAC. By claiming the freedoms of speech and association guaranteed by the First and Sixth Amendments to the Constitution, they became known as "unfriendly witnesses." Many had worked in Hollywood films celebrating America's working people, a popular depression-era theme but now considered indicative of subversive intentions. During World War II, many of these same screenwriters and actors had teamed up on films attacking fascism. Among the most prominent "unfriendly witnesses" were actors Orson Welles, Zero Mostel, and Charlie Chaplin, and Oscar-winning screenwriter Ring Lardner Jr. Humphrey Bogart led a stars' delegation to "Defend the First Amendment" before Congress, but generated only headlines. A handful of dissenters served prison sentences for contempt of Congress. Meanwhile, the privately published *Red Channels: The Report of Communist Influence in Radio and Television* (1950) persuaded advertisers to cancel their accounts

with many programs considered friendly to the Soviet Union, the United Nations, or liberal causes. Hollywood studios refused to employ any writer, director, or actor who refused to cooperate with HUAC. The resulting blacklist, which remained in effect until the 1960s, limited the production of films dealing directly with social or political issues.

Hollywood studios themselves played into the mounting fears, releasing by 1954 more than forty films with titles such as *I Married a Communist* (1950) and *The Red Menace* (1949) that sensationalized the communist threat. The television industry sponsored the dramatic series *The Hunter*, featuring the adventures of an American businessman fighting communist agents throughout the Free World. Few of these films or programs were popular, however.

Spy Cases

In August 1948, HUAC opened public hearings with a star witness: Whittaker Chambers, *Time* magazine editor and former communist, who confessed to spying for the Soviet Union during the 1930s. Chambers named as a fellow communist Alger Hiss, a veteran of Roosevelt's State Department, Roosevelt's adviser at Yalta, and at the time of the hearings president of the prestigious Carnegie Endowment for International Peace. After Hiss denied any affiliation with the Communist Party and proceeded to sue his accuser for slander, Chambers revealed a cache of microfilms of secret documents—hidden in a pumpkin patch on his farm in Maryland—he claimed Hiss had passed to him.

Republican representative Richard Nixon of California described this evidence as proof of "the most serious series of treasonable activities . . . in the history of America" but refused to allow anyone to examine the mysterious documents. (Many years later, the notorious "Pumpkin Papers" were revealed to be Bureau of Standards data, available in most public libraries.) Because a statute of limitations for espionage precluded a charge of treason, a federal grand jury in January 1950 convicted Hiss of perjury only (for denying he knew Chambers), and he received a five-year prison term.

Many Democrats, including Truman himself, at first dismissed the allegations against Hiss—conveniently publicized at the start of the 1948 election campaign—as a red herring, a Republican maneuver to convince the public that Democrats had allowed communists to infiltrate the federal government. Indeed, Nixon himself circulated a pamphlet entitled *The Hiss Case* to promote his candidacy for vice president. Two years later, Hiss was released from prison, still claiming his innocence.

The most dramatic spy case of the era involved Julius Rosenberg, former government engineer, and his wife, Ethel, who were accused of stealing and plotting

I Married a Communist, *movie poster, 1950. In this Hollywood movie, an evil subversive blackmails a shipping executive with a shady past, while fellow communists fool longshoremen into striking. This sensationalistic treatment of the "communist threat" merges the familiar image of the gangster with the malevolent Soviet Union. Like most anticommunist films,* I Married a Communist *was commercially unsuccessful.*

citizens' committees and their convictions protested in large-scale demonstrations. Scientist Albert Einstein, the pope, and the president of France, among many prominent figures, all pleaded for clemency. The Rosenbergs maintained their innocence to the end, insisting they were being persecuted as Jews and for holding leftist political beliefs. They died in the electric chair on June 19, 1953.

McCarthyism

In a sensational Lincoln Day speech to the Republican Women's Club of Wheeling, West Virginia, on February 9, 1950, Republican senator Joseph R. McCarthy of Wisconsin announced that the United States had been sold out by the "traitorous actions of those who have been treated so well by the nation." These "bright young men who have been born with silver spoons in their mouths"—such as Secretary of State Dean Acheson, whom McCarthy called a "pompous diplomat in striped pants, with a phony English accent"—were part of a conspiracy, he charged, of more than 200 communists working in the State Department.

A few days later, after a drinking bout, McCarthy, pressed by reporters to name some of these alleged communists, said "I'm not going to tell you anything. I just want you to know I've got a pailful [of dirt] . . . and I'm going to use it where it does the most good." Actually, he had no names, and later investigations uncovered not a single communist in the State Department. But for several years, McCarthy issued wild accusations and led a flamboyant offensive against not only New Deal Democrats but the entire Truman administration for failing to defend the nation's security. Democrats were "soft on communism," he charged; they had "lost" China. His name has provided the label for the entire campaign to silence critics of the cold war: McCarthyism.

to convey atomic secrets to Soviet agents during World War II. The government's case against the Rosenbergs rested on the testimony of their supposed accomplices, some of them secretly coached by the FBI. In March 1951 a jury found them guilty of conspiring to commit espionage. The American press showed them no sympathy, but around the world the Rosenbergs were defended by

Behind the blitz of publicity—McCarthy's staff assistant, lawyer Roy Cohn, called it "show-biz"—the previously obscure junior senator from Wisconsin had struck a chord. Communism seemed to many Americans to be much more than a military threat—indeed, nothing less than a demonic force capable of undermining basic values. It compelled patriots to proclaim themselves ready for atomic warfare: "Better Dead Than Red." McCarthy also had help from the American Legion and the Chamber of Commerce, prominent religious leaders such as the Catholic Francis Cardinal Spellman, and union leaders wishing to consolidate their power by eliminating dissenters. Many of his fellow campaigners shared his deep resentment toward the east coast diplomatic elite who had come to power with the New Deal. McCarthyism, as a historian wrote at the time, was at least partly "the revenge of the noses that for 20 years of fancy parties were pressed against the outside window pane."

Ironically, however, the targets of McCarthyism were not members of the elite but groups with little political clout, such as African Americans, Jews, the foreign-born, and homosexuals. They were carefully chosen not so much for their political sympathies but because they would be too weak or fearful to strike back at their accusers. Civil rights organizations faced the severest persecution since the 1920s. The Civil Rights Congress and the Negro Youth Council, for instance, were destroyed after frequent charges of communist influence. W. E. B. Du Bois, the renowned African American historian, and famed concert singer (and former All-American football hero) Paul Robeson had public appearances canceled and their right to travel abroad abridged.

In attacks on women's organizations and homosexual groups, meanwhile, anticommunist rhetoric cloaked deep fears about changing sexual mores. HUAC published a pamphlet quoting a Columbia professor as saying that "girls' schools and women's colleges contain some of the most loyal disciples of Russia . . . often frustrated females." Republican Party chair Guy Gabrielson warned that "sexual perverts" who were possibly "as dangerous as actual Communists" had infiltrated the government. Aided by FBI reports, the federal government fired up to sixty homosexuals per month in the early 1950s. Dishonorable discharges from the U.S. armed forces for homosexuality, an administrative procedure without appeal, also increased dramatically, to 2,000 per year. Noted historian Arthur Schlesinger Jr., bitterly opposed to the former vice president Henry Wallace's crusade against the cold war, accused Wallace's supporters of wanting "something secret, sweaty and furtive," acting like "homosexuals in a boys' school." Critics of cold war policies, Schlesinger Jr. suggested, were not "real" men or, perhaps, "real" women either.

Hank Walker, Life-Time Magazine

The tables turned on Senator Joseph McCarthy (1908–57) after he instigated an investigation of the U.S. Army for harboring communists. A congressional committee then investigated McCarthy for attempting to make the Army grant special privileges to his staff aide, Private David Schine. During the televised hearings, Senator McCarthy—shown here with his staff assistant Roy Cohn—discredited himself. In December 1954, the Senate voted to censure him.

But much of this rhetoric was merely divisive opportunism, a ruthless attempt to gain power and fame by exploiting cold war fears. Although McCarthy's own chief aide, Roy Cohn, was himself a secret homosexual, and FBI director J. Edgar Hoover a secret transvestite, both used their influence to heighten anxieties about such "abnormal" or "perverted" orientations.

McCarthy succeeded in his campaign of intimidation partly because he brilliantly used the media to his own advantage. He also perfected the inquisitorial technique, asking directly, "Are you now, or have you ever been, a Communist?" By showing the press a blatantly doctored photo of Democratic senator Millard E. Tydings of Maryland talking with Soviet leaders, he helped defeat Tydings for reelection in 1950. When the distinguished liberal Republican Margaret Chase Smith of Maine appealed to fellow senators for support in a "Declaration of Conscience" against McCarthy's smear tactics, she secured only nine votes.

McCarthyism took hold so effectively because the way had been paved for it by the inflammatory rhetoric of the Truman Doctrine. Conservatives and liberals alike routinely compared communists to Satan or invasive bacteria, thereby promoting not only paranoia but hysteria. Attorney General J. Howard McGrath sounded a typical alarm in 1949: "Communists . . . are everywhere—in factories, offices, butcher shops, on street corners, in private businesses. . . . At this very moment [they are] busy at work—undermining your government, plotting to destroy the liberties of every citizen, and feverishly trying in whatever way they can, to aid the Soviet Union."

Joseph McCarthy and his fellow Red-hunters eventually burned themselves out. During televised congressional hearings in 1954, not only did McCarthy fail to prove wild charges of communist infiltration of the army but in the glare of the television cameras he appeared deranged. Cowed for years, the Senate finally condemned him for "conduct unbecoming a member." Although its energy was spent, McCarthyism left great damage in its wake. Many repressive state and federal laws remained in effect and basic freedoms of speech and assembly had been eroded. Dissent had become dangerous.

AGE OF ANXIETY

At the end of World War II, while much of the world lay in rubble, the United States began the longest, steadiest period of economic growth and prosperity in its history. "We have about 50 percent of the world's wealth," George Kennan noted in 1948, "but only 3.6 percent of its population." Very large pockets of poverty remained, and not all Americans benefited from the postwar abundance. Nonetheless, millions of Americans achieved middle-class status, often through programs subsidized by the federal government.

Prosperity did not dispel an anxious mood, fueled in part by the reality and the rhetoric of the cold war and nuclear proliferation. Many Americans also feared an economic backslide. If war production had ended the hardships of the Great Depression, how would the economy fare in peacetime? No one could say. Above all, peace itself seemed precarious. President Truman himself suggested that World War III appeared inevitable, and his secretary of state, Dean Acheson, warned the nation to keep "on permanent alert." McCarthyism raised the spectre of internal as well as distant enemies. To ease their apprehensions, many Americans turned their attention inward, focusing on a personal life they could understand and influence instead of the uncertainties of foreign affairs.

Even the ultimate symbol of postwar prosperity, the new home in the suburbs, reflected more than simple self-confidence. In 1950 the *New York Times* ran advertisements that captured a chilling quality of the boom in real estate: country properties for the Atomic Age located at least fifty miles outside major cities—the most likely targets, it was believed, of a Soviet nuclear attack. To protect their families in light of this possibility, not a few suburbanites built bomb shelters adjoining their homes. These underground structures reinforced with concrete and steel and outfitted with sufficient provisions to maintain a family for several weeks after an atomic explosion signaled a widespread anxiety about life in postwar American communities.

The Two-Income Family

The postwar prosperity propelling the suburban boom helped to strengthen the domestic ideal of the nuclear family. But many Americans also interpreted their rush toward marriage and parenthood, as one writer put it, as

| | | Second | | Second | | |
| | Poorest | Poorest | Middle | Wealthiest | Wealthiest | Wealthiest |
Year	Fifth	Fifth	Fifth	Fifth	Fifth	5 Percent
1947	3.5	10.6	16.7	23.6	45.6	18.7
1950	3.1	10.5	17.3	24.1	45.0	18.2
1960	3.2	10.6	17.6	24.7	44.0	17.0
1970	3.6	10.3	17.2	24.7	44.1	16.9

DISTRIBUTION OF TOTAL PERSONAL INCOME AMONG VARIOUS SEGMENTS OF THE POPULATION, 1947–1970 (IN PERCENTAGES)*

Despite the general prosperity of the postwar era, the distribution of income remained essentially unchanged.

*Monetary income only.

Source: Adapted from U.S. Bureau of the Census, Historical Statistics of the United States, Colonial Times to 1970, Bicentennial ed. (Washington, D.C.: U.S. Government Printing Office, 1975), p. 292.

a "defense—an impregnable bulwark" against the anxieties of the era. Financial well-being could not in itself offset the insecurities provoked by the cold war.

Young couples were marrying younger and producing more children than at any time in the past century. The national fertility rate had reached an all-time low during the Great Depression, bottoming out in 1933 at 75 per 1,000 women. A decade later, after wartime production had revived the economy, the birth rate climbed to nearly 109 per 1,000 women. The U.S. Census Bureau predicted that this spurt would be temporary. To everyone's surprise, the birth rate continued to grow at a record pace, peaking at over 118 per 1,000 women in 1957. The "baby boom" lasted well into the 1960s.

This model is displaying the ideal kitchen of the 1950s. The "American way of life," defined as a high standard of living, was one of the tangible fruits of U.S. victory in World War II.

Postwar prosperity also sparked a spending spree of trailblazing proportions. "The year 1946," Life magazine proclaimed, "finds the U.S. on the threshold of marvels, ranging from runless stockings and shineless serge suits to jet-propelled airplanes that will flash across the country in just a little less than the speed of sound." The conversion from wartime to peacetime production took longer than many eager shoppers had hoped, but by 1950 the majority of Americans could own consumer durables, such as automatic washers, and small appliances, from do-it-yourself power tools to cameras. By the time Harry Truman left office two-thirds of all American households claimed at least one television set.

These two trends—the baby boom and high rates of consumer spending—encouraged a major change in the middle-class family. Having worked during World War II, often in occupations traditionally closed to them, many women wished to continue in full-time employment. Reconversion to peacetime production forced the majority from their factory positions, but most women quickly returned, taking jobs at a faster rate than men and providing half the total growth of the labor force. By 1952, 2 million more wives worked than during the war. Gone, however, were the high-paying unionized jobs in manufacturing. Instead, most women found minimum-wage jobs in the expanding service sector: clerical work, health care and education, and restaurant, hotel, and retail services. Mothers of young children

were the most likely to be employed. "If it weren't for the children," one wife explained,

I'd be tempted to try to get along on one salary, even if it meant skimping. But we need two incomes to enable us to have a house with a yard that the children can play in; to live in a neighborhood where I don't have to worry about their playmates; to provide a guitar for the musical one and dancing lessons for the one who needs to improve her muscular co-ordination—not to mention teeth-straightening and medical insurance and the bonds we are stowing away for their education.

Older women whose children were grown might work because they had come to value a job for its own sake. Younger women often worked for reasons of "economic necessity"—that is, to maintain a middle-class standard of living that now required more than one income.

Even though most women sought employment primarily to support their families, they ran up against popular opinion and expert advice urging them to return to their homes. Public opinion registered resounding disapproval—by 86 percent of those surveyed—of a married woman's working if jobs were scarce and her husband could support her. Commentators even appealed for a return to an imaginary "traditional" family, where men alone were breadwinners and women stayed happily at home, as a bulwark against communism. Noting that most Soviet women worked in industry, nervous writers insisted that American men and women must stop the spread of communism by playing complementary but utterly different roles. Just as the Truman Doctrine and the Marshall Plan responded to pitfalls abroad, the American family might limit, or "contain," dangers at home—if "restored" to its "traditional" form and function in the democratic nation.

This campaign began on a shrill note. Ferdinand Lundberg and Marynia Farnham, in their best-selling *Modern Woman: The Lost Sex* (1947), attributed the "super-jittery age in which we live" to women's abandonment of the home to pursue careers. To counter this trend, they proposed federally funded psychotherapy to readjust women to their housewifely roles and cash subsidies to encourage them to bear more children.

Articles in popular magazines, television shows, and high-profile experts chimed in with similar messages. Talcott Parsons, the distinguished Harvard sociologist, delineated the parameters of the "democratic" family: husbands served as breadwinners while wives—"the emotional hub of the family"—stayed home to care for their families. In the first edition of *Baby and Child Care* (1946), the child-rearing advice manual that soon outsold the Bible, Benjamin Spock similarly advised women to devote themselves full time, if financially possible, to their maternal responsibilities. "Women have many careers," another expert explained, "but only one vocation—motherhood."

Patterns of women's higher education reflected this conservative trend. Having made slight gains during World War II when college-age men

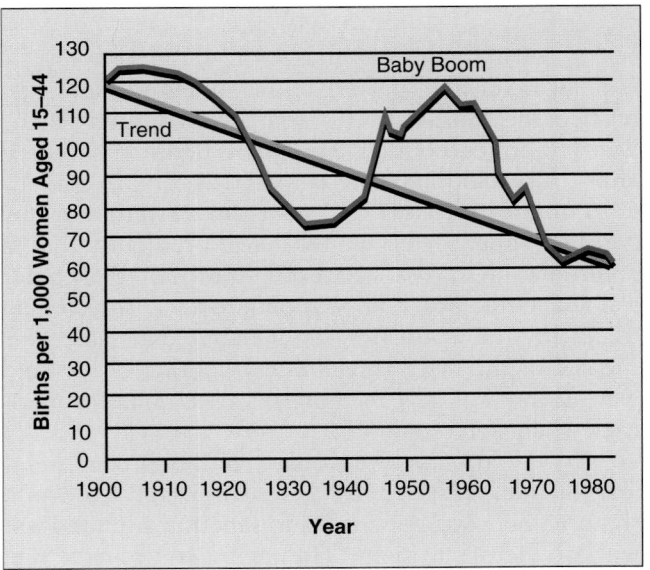

U.S. Birth Rate, 1930–1980   *The bulge of the "baby boom," a leading demographic factor in the postwar economy, stands out for this fifty-year period.*

were serving in the armed forces or working in war industries, women lost ground after the GI Bill created a huge upsurge in male enrollment. Women represented 40 percent of all college graduates in 1940 but only 25 percent a decade later. College administrators, disturbed by the trend toward women's employment, called for a new curriculum that would prepare women instead for marriage and motherhood. James Madison Wood, president of Stephens College in Columbia, Missouri, prescribed home economics as the foundation of women's higher education, with such curriculum highlights as child care and interior decoration. "The college years," he argued, "must be rehearsal periods for the major performance"—that is, for their roles as wives and mothers—of women's lives.

These policies and prescriptions ran counter to the trend that was bringing ever more middle-class women into the workforce to help support their families. As early as 1947 *Life* magazine reflected an awareness of this conflict in a thirteen-page feature, "American Woman's Dilemma." How could women comfortably take part in a world beyond the home, the article asked, and at the same time heed the advice of FBI director J. Edgar Hoover, who exhorted the nation's women to fight "the twin enemies of freedom—crime and communism" by fulfilling their singular role as "homemakers and mothers"?

Religion and Education

Cold war fears helped to make Baptist Billy Graham one of the most popular evangelical ministers of the era and star of the first major televised "crusades" for religious revival. Born in Charlotte, North Carolina, in 1918, Graham had grown up believing that all doubts about the literal truth of the Bible were traps set by Satan. He gave a spiritual twist to cold war anxieties, warning against the decline of "God-centered homes" and the increased number of wives who tried to "wear the trousers" of the family. Moral contagion, juvenile delinquency, and communism could be halted only by what Graham called an "immediate decision for Christ." Politically, Graham aligned himself with the Republican Party and supported a large military budget to protect the United States, which he saw as the last hope of Christianity.

The message of anticommunism also permeated public education. In an era of higher education reshaped by the GI Bill, and of primary education expanding to meet the postwar baby boom, the nation invested more than funds in its school system. According to guidelines set down by the Truman administration, teachers were to "strengthen national security through education," specifically redesigning their lesson plans to illustrate the superiority of the American democratic system over

Soviet communism. In 1947 the federal Office of Education launched the "Zeal for Democracy" program for implementation by school boards nationwide. Meanwhile, schoolchildren were also taught to prepare themselves for a surprise Soviet attack by ducking under their desks and closing their eyes against the blinding light of a nuclear bomb.

Leading historians, such as Samuel Eliot Morison, insisted that fellow scholars shape their interpretations of the nation's past to highlight traditional values, especially the sanctity of private property. Richard Hofstadter's prize-winning *American Political Tradition* (1948) described in detail the uniquely American faith in "the economic virtues of capitalist culture as necessary qualities of man." Historians like Hofstadter portrayed earlier critics of this consensus, such as the populists, as mentally unbalanced and dangerous to American democracy.

Many teachers and students spurned these new educational programs and interpretations of American history. A fearless minority of scholars protested infringements on their academic freedom by refusing to sign loyalty oaths and by writing books pointing out the potential dangers of U.S. foreign and domestic policies of the cold war. But the chilling atmosphere, such as the political climate pervading the campus of the University of Washington, made many individuals more reluctant to express contrary opinions or ideas.

The Cultural Noir

Anxieties intensified by the cold war surfaced as major themes in popular culture. One of the most acclaimed Hollywood films of the era, the winner of nine Academy Awards, *The Best Years of Our Lives* (1946), followed the stories of three returning veterans as they tried to readjust to civilian life. The former soldiers found that the dreams of reunion with family and loved ones that had sustained them through years of fighting now seemed hollow. In some cases, their wives and children had become so self-reliant that the men had no clear function to perform in the household; in other cases, the prospect for employment appeared dim. The feeling of community shared with wartime buddies dissipated, leaving only a profound sense of loneliness.

The genre of film *noir* (French for "black") deepened this mood into an aesthetic. Movies like *Out of the Past, Detour,* and *They Live by Night* featured stories of ruthless fate and betrayal. Their protagonists were usually strangers or loners falsely accused of crimes or trapped into committing them. The high-contrast lighting of these black and white films accentuated the difficulty of distinguishing friend from foe. Feelings of frustration and loss of control came alive in tough, cynical characters played by actors such as Robert Mitchum and Robert Ryan. The Hollywood blacklist,

however, soon barred many of the most talented directors and writers of *noir* films from further production.

Plays and novels also described alienation and anxiety in vivid terms. Playwright Arthur Miller, in *Death of a Salesman* (1949), sketched an exacting portrait of self-destructive individualism. Willy Loman, the play's hero, is obsessively devoted to his career in sales but nevertheless a miserable failure. Worse, he has trained his sons to excel in personal presentation and style—the very methods prescribed by standard American success manuals—making them both shallow and materialistic. J. D. Salinger's widely praised novel *Catcher in the Rye* (1951) explored the mental anguish of a teenage boy estranged from the crass materialism of his parents.

Cold war anxiety manifested itself in a flurry of unidentified flying object (UFO) sightings. Thousands of Americans imagined that a communistlike invasion from outer space was already under way, or they hoped that superior creatures might arrive to show the way to world peace. The U.S. Air Force discounted the sightings of flying saucers, but dozens of private researchers and faddists claimed to have been contacted by aliens. Hollywood films fed these beliefs. The popular movie *The Day the Earth Stood Still* (1951) delivered a message of world peace in which a godlike being implores earthlings to abandon their weaponry before they destroy the planet. Other popular science fiction films carried a different message. In *The Invasion of the Body Snatchers* (1956), for example, a small town is captured by aliens who take over the minds of its inhabitants when they fall asleep, a subtle warning against apathy toward the threat of communist "subversion."

END OF THE DEMOCRATIC ERA

Cold war tensions festered first in Europe and had pushed the United States and Soviet Union to the brink of armed conflict during the Berlin crisis. Well after the resolution of the Berlin crisis, Truman's advisers continued to watch events in eastern Europe. Neither superpower would have predicted that a confrontation in Asia would soon transform their political and ideological competition into a war threatening to destroy the world. Yet, in June 1950, Korea became the site of the first major military conflict of the cold war. Within a few years more than 1.8 million Americans would serve in Korea.

For Truman, the Korean conflict proved political suicide. Trapped by his own tough cold war rhetoric, he asked Americans to sanction a limited war with no victory in sight. The raging controversy that followed Truman's actions in Korea ended the twenty-year Democratic lock on the presidency and the greatest era of reform in U.S. history.

American soldiers fought in Korea under the command of General Douglas MacArthur until President Truman named General Matthew Ridgway as his replacement in April 1951. Nearly 1.8 million Americans served in Korea.

The Korean War

On June 25, 1950, President Truman was called back to Washington, D.C., from his home in Independence, Missouri. The State Department had just received a cablegram reporting a military attack on South Korea by communist-controlled North Korea. Secretary of State Acheson immediately set up an emergency meeting of the UN Security Council to request action. Determined to carve a niche in history by "being tough" on communists, Truman now had to live up to his promise.

Korea, a colony of Japan since 1910, had been divided along its 38th parallel between U.S. and Soviet forces following the Axis defeat in 1945, making its two halves into zones of occupation cold war-style. By mid-1949, the two superpowers had withdrawn from the small peninsula, leaving their respective dependent governments in charge. In the South (the Republic of Korea) the United States backed the unpopular dictatorship of Syngman Rhee, while the Soviet Union sponsored a communist government in North Korea (the Democratic People's Republic of Korea) under Kim Il Sung.

Some experienced diplomats such as George Kennan regarded the conflict between the two Koreas as a civil war. Truman, however, treated the invasion as a major Soviet test of the U.S. policy of containment, an act of aggression that had to be met with force. "Korea is the Greece of the Far East," the president announced. "If we are tough enough now, if we stand up to them like we did in Greece three years ago, they won't take any next steps," he explained. The Soviets, on the other hand, regarded the invasion as the consequence of former anti-Japanese military leader Kim Il Sung's plan to overthrow a government of past collaborators with the Japanese and unite the two Koreas. While supplying military equipment, Moscow insisted that it had neither ordered nor directed the attack. Having recently been accused of "selling out" eastern Europe and "losing" China, Truman felt compelled to act.

Three days after the invasion, the president sought approval from the UN Security Council to send in troops. Due to a boycott of the Council by the Soviet delegate, who could have vetoed the decision, the Security Council agreed. Two-thirds of Americans polled approved the president's decision to send troops under the command of General Douglas MacArthur.

Military events seemed at first to justify the president's decision. Seoul, the capital of South Korea, had fallen to North Korean troops within weeks of the invasion, and communist forces continued to push south until they had taken most of the peninsula. The situation appeared grim until Truman authorized MacArthur to carry out an amphibious landing at Inchon, which he did on September 15, 1950. With tactical brilliance and good fortune, the general orchestrated a military campaign that halted the communist drive. By October, UN troops had retaken South Korea.

Basking in victory, the Truman administration could not resist the temptation to expand its war aims. Hoping to prove that Democrats were not soft on communism, the president and his advisers decided to roll back the communists beyond the 38th parallel to

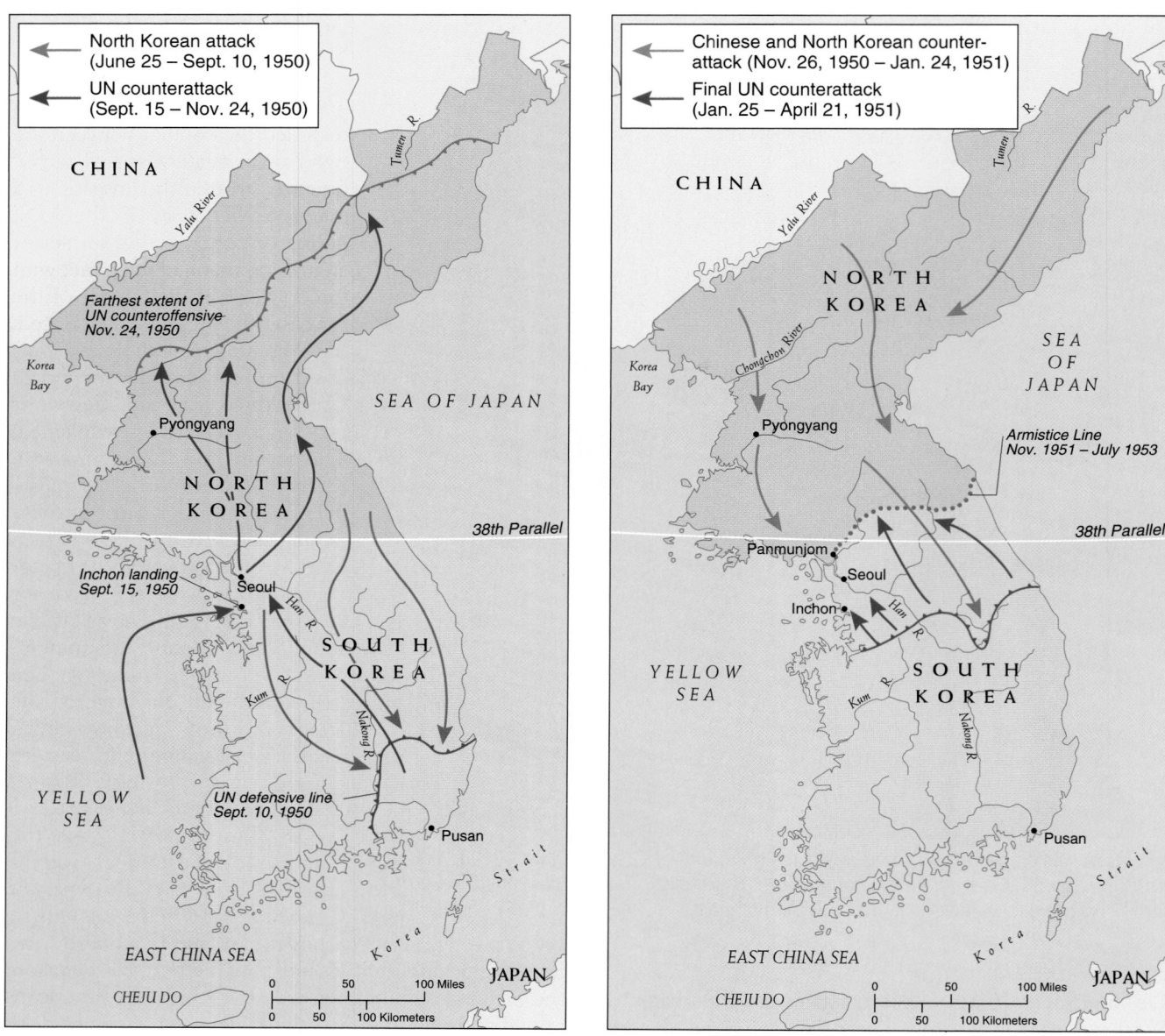

The Korean War   *The intensity of battles underscored the strategic importance of Korea in the cold war.*

the Chinese border and thereby reunite Korea as a showcase for democracy. Until this point, China had not been actively involved in the war. But it now warned that any attempt to cross the dividing line would be interpreted as a threat to its national security. Truman flew to Wake Island in the Pacific on October 15 for a conference with MacArthur, who assured the president of a speedy victory, promising to have the UN troops "home by Christmas."

Overconfident, MacArthur had sorely miscalculated. Chinese premier Zhou Enlai ordered Chinese troops to mass at the Yalu River. Suddenly, and without any air support, the Chinese attacked on November 26. MacArthur's force was all but crushed. European allies

warned against escalation, and White House officials debated using the atomic bomb. The Chinese drove the UN troops back into South Korea, where they regrouped and in March began pushing back to the 38th parallel. By summer 1951, a stalemate had been reached very near the old border. Negotiations for a settlement went on for the next eighteen months amid heavy fighting.

"There is no substitute for victory," MacArthur insisted as he tried without success to convince Truman to prepare for a new invasion of communist territory. Encouraged by strong support at home, he continued to provoke the president by speaking out against official policy, calling for bombing of supply lines in China and a naval blockade of the Chinese coast—actions certain to lead to a Chinese-American war. Finally, on April 10, 1951, Truman dismissed MacArthur for insubordination and other unauthorized activities. As General Omar N. Bradley later remarked, MacArthur had proposed "the wrong war, at the wrong place and at the wrong time, and with the wrong enemy." He had also placed himself above the civilian commander in chief of the armed forces.

The Legacy of "The Sour Little War"

The Korean War had profound implications for the use of executive power. By instituting a peacetime draft in 1948 and then ordering American troops into Korea, Truman had bypassed congressional authority. Senator Robert Taft called the president's actions "a complete usurpation" of democratic checks and balances. Truman sidestepped such criticisms and their constitutional implications by carefully referring to the military deployment not as a U.S. war but as a UN-sanctioned "police action."

The president derived his authority from NSC-68, a paper adopted by the National Security Council in April 1950 that reinterpreted the basic policy of containment as well as decision making at the highest levels of government. Describing communism as "a new fanatic faith" that "seeks to impose its absolute authority over the rest of the world," NSC-68 pledged the United States not only to drive back communist influence wherever it appeared but also to "foster the seeds of destruction within the Soviet Union." As Dean Acheson observed later, NSC-68 was the new "fundamental" paper of U.S. foreign policy. Its use demonstrated, one historian observed, a "centralization of power" in which the entire government "had literally been compressed or consolidated into the President and his like-minded appointees."

The Korean War, which permitted Truman to activate NSC-68, also provided the president the public rationale for a rapid and permanent military buildup, including the allocation of at least 20 percent of the gross national product to national defense. Between 1950 and 1953, when the conflict subsided, military spending rose from $13 billion to more than $50 billion annually. By 1952 the U.S. Army had grown to 3.6 million, or six times its size at the beginning of the conflict. At the same time, the federal government accelerated the development of nuclear bombs and weapons, including the first hydrogen, or H, bomb, which was tested in November 1952. By the time it ended, the war had cost the United States approximately $100 billion.

The outcome of the Korean War did nothing to improve Truman's case for rolling back communism. Negotiations and fighting proceeded in tandem until the summer of 1953, when a settlement was reached in which both North Korea and South Korea occupied almost the same territory as when the war began. Approximately 54,000 Americans died in Korea; the North Koreans and Chinese lost well over 2 million people. The UN troops had employed both "carpet bombing" (intense, destructive attack on a given area) and napalm (jellied gasoline bombs), destroying most of the housing and food supplies in both Koreas. True to the pattern of modern warfare, which emerged during World War II, the majority of civilians killed were women and children. Nearly 1 million Koreans were left homeless.

For the United States, the Korean War extended the principle of containment far beyond Europe and enlarged the geographical range of the cold war to include East Asia. The war also lined up the People's Republic of China and the United States as unwavering enemies for the next twenty years and heightened the U.S. commitment to Southeast Asia. Now, as one historian commented, the "frontiers on every continent were going to remain frontiers in the traditional American meaning of a frontier—a region to penetrate and control and police and civilize."

The Korean War, moreover, did much to establish an ominous tradition of "unwinnable" conflicts that left many Americans skeptical of official policy. Truman had initially rallied popular support for U.S. intervention by contrasting the communist North with the "democratic" South, thus casting the conflict in the ideological terms of the cold war. MacArthur's early victories had promised the liberation of North Korea and even the eventual disintegration of the Soviet and Chinese regimes. But with the tactical stalemate came mass disillusionment.

In retrospect many Americans recognized that Truman, in fighting communism in Korea, had pledged the United States to defend a corrupt government and a brutal dictator. Decades later the Korean War inspired the dark comedy *M*A*S*H*, adapted for television from the film written by Hollywood screenwriter Ring Lardner Jr., an "unfriendly witness" before HUAC who was jailed during the Korean War for contempt of Congress. As late as 1990, members of Congress were still debating the terms of a Korean War memorial. "It ended on a sad note for Americans," one historian has concluded, "and the war and its memories drifted off into a void."

Truman's Downfall

There was only one burning issue during the election campaign of 1952: the Korean War. Opinion polls indicated widespread frustration with Truman's conduct of the war. Although respondents did not know what they wanted instead—an invasion of China, as MacArthur had planned, or an immediate withdrawal of U.S.

troops—they were clearly angry at the leader who had created the bloody deadlock.

Truman's popularity had wavered continually since he took office in 1945, but it sank to an all-time low in the early 1950s shortly after he dismissed MacArthur as commander of the UN troops in Korea. The White House received thousands of letters and telegrams calling for Truman's impeachment. If Congress did not get rid of the Truman-Acheson team, McCarthy roared, "Asia, the Pacific and Europe may be lost to Communism" and "Red waters may lap at all of our shores." MacArthur, meanwhile, returned home a hero, welcomed by more than 7 million fans in New York City alone.

A furious but short-lived MacArthur-for-president campaign began. On April 19, 1951, MacArthur gave an

Richard Nixon used the new medium of television to convince American voters that he had not established an illegal slush fund in his campaign for the vice presidency in 1952. Viewers responded enthusiastically to his melodramatic delivery and swamped the Republican campaign headquarters with telegrams endorsing his candidacy.

impassioned address to a joint session of the Congress. Legislators, many with tears in their eyes, gave him a standing ovation. But over the next two months, as the Senate Armed Services and Foreign Relations Committees conducted joint hearings about MacArthur's dismissal, the general's popularity rapidly fell. George Marshall, Omar Bradley, and the Joint Chiefs all testified that they had never subscribed to MacArthur's strategy for the war. Moreover, in light of General MacArthur's challenge to presidential authority, they believed that there had been "no other course but to relieve him" of his duties in Korea.

While discrediting MacArthur, the hearings also revealed the extent of popular dissatisfaction with Truman. Newspapers reported that officials in his administration had been dealing in kickbacks for government contracts, just the kind of corruption that critics had predicted when Truman replaced veteran New Dealers with his political cronies. Business and organized labor complained about the price and wage freezes imposed during the Korean War. A late-1951 Gallup poll showed the president's approval rating at 23 percent. In early 1952, Truman announced he would not run for reelection, a decision rare for a president eligible for another term.

Truman left the Democratic Party in disarray. The Democrats' best hope for victory now lay in convincing Dwight Eisenhower to run on the Demo-

cratic ticket, although his reputation as a moderate conservative suggested no continuity with party traditions. When Eisenhower politely refused their offers, Democratic leaders turned to the popular but uncharismatic governor of Illinois, Adlai E. Stevenson Jr.

Admired for his honesty and intelligence, Stevenson offered no solutions to the conflict in Korea, the accelerating arms race, or the cold war generally. Accepting the Democratic nomination, Stevenson candidly admitted that "the ordeal of the twentieth century is far from over," a prospect displeasing to voters aching for peace.

The Republicans made the most of the Democrats' dilemma. Without proposing any sweeping answers of their own, they pointed to all the obvious shortcomings of their opponents. The Korean stasis dovetailed with the "K_1C_2"—Korea, communism, and corruption—line of attack on the Democratic administration. Traditional Republican conservatives wanted to nominate Robert Taft, shrewd critic of Truman's "imperial" presidency and author of the anti-labor Taft-Hartley Act. But when opinion polls showed that Dwight Eisenhower possessed an "unprecedented" 64 percent approval rating, and when "Ike" allowed himself to be "drafted" for the Republican nomination, his candidacy was certain.

Eisenhower styled himself the moderate. He wisely avoided the negative impressions made by the unsuccessful 1948 Republican candidate, Thomas

CHRONOLOGY

1941 Henry Luce forecasts the dawn of "the American Century"

1944 GI Bill of Rights benefits World War II veterans

International Monetary Fund and World Bank founded

1945 Franklin D. Roosevelt dies in office; Harry S. Truman becomes president

United Nations charter signed

World War II ends

Strike wave begins

Truman proposes program of economic reforms

1946 Employment Act creates Council of Economic Advisers

Churchill's Iron Curtain speech

Atomic Energy Act establishes Atomic Energy Commission

Republicans win control of Congress

Benjamin Spock publishes *Baby and Child Care*

1947 Americans for Democratic Action founded

Truman Doctrine announced; Congress appropriates $400 million in aid for Greece and Turkey

Federal Employees Loyalty and Security Program established and attorney general's list of subversive organizations authorized

Marshall Plan announced

Taft-Hartley Act restricts union activities

National Security Act establishes Department of Defense, the National Security Council, and the Central Intelligence Agency

House Un-American Activities Committee hearings in Hollywood

1948 Ferdinand Lundberg and Marynia Farnham publish *Modern Woman: The Lost Sex*

State of Israel founded

Berlin blockade begins

Henry Wallace nominated for president on Progressive Party ticket

Truman announces peacetime draft and desegregates U.S. armed forces and civil service

Truman wins election; Democrats sweep both houses of Congress

1949 Truman announces Fair Deal

North Atlantic Treaty Organization (NATO) created

Communists led by Mao Zedong take power in China

Berlin blockade ends

Soviet Union explodes atomic bomb

1950 Alger Hiss convicted of perjury

Senator Joseph McCarthy begins anticommunist crusade

Soviet Union and the People's Republic of China sign an alliance

Adoption of NSC-68 consolidates presidential war powers

Korean War begins

Internal Security (McCarran) Act requires registration of communist organizations and arrest of communists during national emergencies

1951 Truman dismisses General Douglas MacArthur

Armistice talks begin in Korea

1952 Immigration and Nationality Act retains quota system, lifts ban on immigration of Asian and Pacific peoples, but bans "subversives" and homosexuals

United States explodes first hydrogen bomb

Dwight D. Eisenhower wins presidency; Richard Nixon becomes vice president

1953 Julius and Ethel Rosenberg executed for atomic espionage

Armistice ends fighting in Korea

1954 Army-McCarthy hearings end

1955 Warsaw Pact created

Dewey, who had seemed as aggressive as Truman on foreign policy and simultaneously eager to overturn the New Deal domestic legislation. Eisenhower knew better: voters wanted peace and government-assisted prosperity. He neither threatened to widen the war nor supported the stalemate created by Truman. Eisenhower promised instead "an early and honorable" peace and avoided questions of finance or the economy. His advisers warned him: "The chief reason that people want to vote for you is because they think you have more ability to keep us out of another war."

Meanwhile, Eisenhower's vice-presidential candidate, Richard Nixon, waged a relentless and defamatory attack on Stevenson, calling him "Adlai the Appeaser" and the "Ph.D. graduate of Dean Acheson's cowardly College of Communist Containment." Senator Joseph McCarthy chimed in, proclaiming that with club in hand he might be able to make "a good American" of Stevenson. A month before the election, McCarthy went on network television with his requisite "exhibits" and "documents," this time purportedly showing that the Democratic presidential candidate had promoted communism at home and abroad. These outrageous charges kept the Stevenson campaign off balance.

The Republican campaign was itself not entirely free of scandal: the vice-presidential candidate had been caught accepting personal gifts from wealthy benefactors. Nixon chose to plead his case on national television. Describing his wife Pat's "good Republican cloth coat" and their modest style of living, he contritely admitted that he had indeed accepted one gift, a puppy named Checkers that his daughters loved and that he refused to give back. "The Poor Richard Show," as critics called the event, defused the scandal without answering the most important charges.

Eisenhower, meanwhile, continued to enchant the voters as a peace candidate. Ten days before the election he dramatically announced, "I shall go to Korea" to settle the war. Eisenhower received 55 percent of the vote and carried thirty-nine states, in part because he brought out an unusually large number of voters in normally Democratic areas. He won the popular vote in much of the South and in the northern cities of New York, Chicago, Boston, and Cleveland. The New Deal coalition of ethnic and black voters, labor, northern liberals, and southern conservatives no longer commanded a majority. But the victory was most clearly a sign of Eisenhower's own popularity. Riding his coattails, the Republicans regained control of Congress, but their margin in the Senate was only one seat.

CONCLUSION

Dwight Eisenhower's election diminished the intensity of the cold war mood without actually halting the conflict. "The Eisenhower Movement," wrote Walter Lippmann, was a "mission in American politics" to restore a sense of community among the American people. In a larger sense, many of the issues of the immediate post–World War II years seemed to have been settled, or put off for a distant future. The international boundaries of communism were frozen with the Chinese Revolution, the Berlin blockade, and now the Korean War. Meanwhile, at home cold war defense spending had become a permanent part of the national budget, an undeniable drain on tax revenues but an important element in the government contribution to economic prosperity. If the nuclear arms race remained a cause for anxiety, joined by more personal worries about the changing patterns of family life, a sense of relative security nevertheless spread. Prospects for world peace had dimmed, but the worst nightmares of the 1940s had eased as well.

REVIEW QUESTIONS

1. Discuss the origins of the cold war and the sources of growing tensions between the United States and the Soviet Union at the close of World War II.
2. Describe the basic elements of President Harry Truman's policy of containment. How did the threat of atomic warfare affect this policy?
3. Compare the presidencies of Franklin D. Roosevelt and Harry S. Truman, both Democrats.
4. Describe the impact of McCarthyism on American political life. How did the anticommunist campaigns affect the media? What were the sources of Senator Joseph McCarthy's popularity? What brought about his downfall?
5. How did the cold war affect American culture?
6. Discuss the role of the United States in Korea in the decade after World War II. How did the Korean War affect the 1952 presidential election?
7. Why did Dwight D. Eisenhower win the 1952 presidential election?

RECOMMENDED READING

Warren I. Cohen, *America in the Age of Soviet Power, 1945–1991* (1993). A volume in the "Cambridge History of American Foreign Relations" series, this study examines the origins of the cold war in policies ending World War II, including the breakup of the colonial empires, and concludes with the collapse of communism in the Soviet Union.

Martin Bauml Duberman, *Paul Robeson* (1988). A biography of the renowned African American singer and actor who was driven from the stage for political reasons. Duberman shows Robeson as a great artist but also a self-conscious representative of black rights who felt compelled to oppose U.S. foreign policy and suddenly lost his public career as a result.

Townsend Hoopes and Douglas Brinkley, *FDR and the Creation of the U.N.* (1997). A concise account of the founding the United Nations, from Franklin D. Roosevelt—whose "initiative and determination" laid the groundwork for the world organization—to Harry Truman.

Joyce Kolko and Gabriel Kolko, *The Limits of Power: The World and United States Foreign Policy, 1945–1954* (1972). A detailed commentary arguing that U.S. efforts to control the post-war world were thwarted by the complexities of international politics, especially the efforts of colonized nations to gain independence.

George Lipsitz, *A Rainbow at Midnight: Labor and Culture in the 1940s* (1994). A vivid account of economic and cultural hopes, uneasiness, and disappointments after World War II. Lipsitz shows how struggles for economic democracy were defeated and how popular culture—for example, country-and-western music and rock 'n' roll, as well as stock car racing and roller derby—arose in blue-collar communities.

Elaine Tyler May, *Homeward Bound: American Families in the Cold War Era* (1988). A lively account of the effects on family life and women's roles of the national mood of "containment." May argues that government policy became part of a popular culture that solidified the cold war era's "feminine mystique."

David G. McCullough, *Truman* (1992). An uncritical rendition of Truman's personal life and political career. Through personal correspondence and other documents, McCullough details Truman's view of himself and the generally favorable view of him held by supporters of cold war liberalism.

Patrick McGilligan and Paul Buhle, *Tender Comrades: A Backstory of the Hollywood Blacklist* (1997). A collection of interviews with thirty-five victims of the Hollywood Blacklist, including some of the most important writers, directors, and film stars. The collection is especially valuable for its detailing of film production during the years of World War II and afterward, including the creation of *film noir*.

Joanne Meyerowitz, ed., *Not June Cleaver: Women and Gender in Postwar America, 1945–1960* (1994). A collection of essays that refute the common stereotype of women as homebound during the postwar era.

Victor S. Navasky, *Naming Names* (1980). A fascinating account of government informants, McCarthyism, and the blacklist. Navasky presents especially interesting treatments of academic life, where blacklisting had only a slight impact, and Hollywood, where McCarthyism changed American popular culture.

David M. Oshinsky, *A Conspiracy So Immense: The World of Joe McCarthy* (1983). A study of McCarthyism that presents a keen view of McCarthy as a product of his background and the political conditions of the time, as well as a clever politician who found widespread support in the Republican Party.

Daniel Yergin, *Shattered Peace: The Origins of the Cold War and the National Security State* (1977). A lucid analysis of the motives of the Americans and the Soviets that led to a full-scale arms race. Yergin argues that each side misinterpreted the motives of the other and thereby lost the opportunity to attain world peace.

ADDITIONAL BIBLIOGRAPHY

Global Insecurities and the Policy of Containment

H. W. Brands Jr., *The Devil We Knew: Americans and the Cold War* (1993)

Robert Frazier, *Anglo-American Relations with Greece: The Coming of the Cold War, 1942–47* (1991)

James L. Gormly, *The Collapse of the Grand Alliance, 1945–1948* (1987)

Burton Hersh, *The Old Boys: The American Elite and the Origins of the CIA* (1992)

Michael J. Hogan, *The Marshall Plan* (1987)

Timothy P. Ireland, *Creating the Entangling Alliance: The Origins of NATO* (1981)

Bruce R. Kuniholm, *The Origins of the Cold War in the Near East* (1980)

Walter LeFeber, *America, Russia, and the Cold War, 1945–1980*, 7th ed. (1993)

Robert L. Messer, *The End of an Alliance: James F. Byrnes, Roosevelt, Truman, and the Origins of the Cold War* (1982)

Thomas G. Paterson, *Meeting the Communist Threat* (1988)

Michael Schaller, *American Occupation of Japan: The Origins of the Cold War in Asia* (1985)

Telford Taylor, *The Anatomy of the Nuremberg Trials: A Personal Memoir* (1992)

Imanuel Wexler, *The Marshall Plan Revisited* (1983)

The Truman Presidency

Jack Ballard, *Shock of Peace* (1983)

Andrew J. Dunar, *The Truman Scandals and the Politics of Morality* (1984)

Melvyn P. Leffler, *A Preponderance of Power: National Security, the Truman Administration, and the Cold War* (1992)

Donald McCoy, *The Presidency of Harry S. Truman* (1984)

Gary W. Reichard, *Politics as Usual* (1988)

The Cold War at Home

Michael R. Belknap, *Cold War Political Justice: The Smith Act, the Communist Party, and American Civil Liberties* (1977)

David Callahan, *Dangerous Capabilities: Paul Nitze and the Cold War* (1990)

Larry Ceplair and Steven Englund, *The Inquisition in Hollywood: Politics in the Film Community, 1930–1960* (1980)

Sigmund Diamond, *Compromised Campus: The Collaboration of Universities with the Intelligence Communities, 1945–1995* (1992)

Richard M. Freeland, *The Truman Doctrine and the Origins of McCarthyism* (1972, 1985)

Richard M. Fried, *Nightmare in Red* (1990)

Robert Griffith, *The Politics of Fear: Joseph R. McCarthy and the Senate*, 2d ed. (1987)

Mike Nielson and Gene Mailes, *Hollywood's Other Blacklist: Union Struggles in the Studio System* (1996)

Kenneth O'Reilly, *Hoover and the Un-Americans: The FBI, HUAC, and the Red Menace* (1983)

Ellen W. Schrecker, *No Ivory Tower: McCarthyism in the Universities* (1988)

Age of Anxiety

Michael Barson, *"Better Dead Than Red!" A Nostalgic Look at the Golden Years of Russiaphobia, Red-Baiting, and Other Commie Madness* (1992)

Paul Boyer, *By the Bomb's Early Light: American Thought and Culture at the Dawn of the Atomic Age* (1985)

Ann Fagan Ginger and David Christian, eds., *The Cold War against Labor: An Anthology* (1987)

Fred Inglis, *The Cruel Peace: Everyday Life in the Cold War* (1991)

Stuart W. Leslie, *The Cold War and American Science* (1993)

J. Fred MacDonald, *Television and the Red Menace* (1985)

Lary May, ed., *Recasting America: Culture and Politics in the Age of the Cold War* (1989)

Richard G. Powers, *G-Men: Hoover's FBI in American Popular Culture* (1983)

Andrews Ross, *No Respect: Intellectuals and Popular Culture* (1989)

Leila Rupp and Verta Taylor, *Survival in the Doldrums: The American Women's Rights Movement, 1945 to the 1960s* (1987)

Nora Sayre, *Running Time: Films of the Cold War* (1982)

Arlene Skolnick, *Embattled Paradise: The American Family in an Age of Uncertainty* (1991)

Korean War

Albert Cowdrey, *The Medics' War* (1987)

Bruce Cumings, *The Origins of the Korean War* (1981)

Rosemary Foot, *The Wrong War* (1985)

Jon Halliday and Bruce Cumings, *Korea* (1988)

D. Clayton James, *Refighting the Last War: Command and Crisis in Korea, 1950–1953* (1992)

John Toland, *In Mortal Combat: Korea, 1950–1953* (1992)

Biography

Curt Gentry, *J. Edgar Hoover: The Man and the Secrets* (1991)

Wilson D. Miscamble, *George F. Kennan and the Making of American Foreign Policy, 1947–1950* (1992)

Robert P. Newman, *Owen Lattimore and the "Loss" of China* (1992)

Michael Schaller, *Douglas MacArthur* (1989)

Athan G. Theoharis and John Stuart Cox, *The Boss: J. Edgar Hoover and the Great American Inquisition* (1988)

CHAPTER TWENTY-SEVEN

AMERICA AT MIDCENTURY

1952–1963

Andy Warhol, *Campbell's Soup Can*. Saatchi Collection, London/A.K.G., Berlin/Superstock.

AMERICAN COMMUNITIES
Popular Music in Memphis

The nineteen-year-old singer was peering nervously out over the large crowd. He knew that people had come to Overton Park's outdoor amphitheater that hot, sticky July day in 1954 to hear the headliner, country music star Slim Whitman. Sun Records, a local Memphis label, had just released the teenager's first record, and it had begun to receive some airplay on local radio. But the singer and his two bandmates had never played in a setting even remotely as large as this one. And their music defied categories: it wasn't black and it wasn't white; it wasn't pop and it wasn't country. But when the singer launched into his version of a black blues song called "That's All Right," the crowd went wild. "I came offstage," the singer later recalled, "and my manager told me that they was hollering because I was wiggling my legs. I went back out for an encore, and I did a little more, and the more I did, the wilder they went." Elvis Presley had arrived.

Elvis combined a hard-driving, rhythmic approach to blues and country music with a riveting performance style, inventing the new music known as rock 'n' roll. An unprecedented cultural phenomenon, rock 'n' roll was a music made largely for and by teenagers. In communities all over America, rock 'n' roll brought teens together around jukeboxes, at sock hops, in cars, and at private parties. It demonstrated the enormous consumer power of American teens. Rock 'n' roll also embodied a postwar trend accelerating the integration of white and black music. This cultural integration prefigured the social and political integration won by the civil rights movement.

Located halfway between St. Louis and New Orleans on the Mississippi River, Memphis had become a thriving commercial city by the 1850s, with an economy centered on the lucrative cotton trade of the surrounding delta region. It grew rapidly in the post–Civil War years, attracting a polyglot population of white businessmen and planters, poor rural whites and blacks, and German and Irish immigrants. By the early twentieth century Memphis also boasted a remarkable diversity of popular theater and music, including a large opera house, numerous brass bands, vaudeville and burlesque, minstrel shows, jug bands, and blues clubs.

Like most American cities, Memphis enjoyed healthy growth during World War II, with lumber mills, furniture factories, and chemical manufacturing supplementing the cotton market as sources of jobs and prosperity. And like the rest of the South, Memphis was a legally segregated city; whites and blacks lived, went to school, and worked apart. Class differences among whites were important as well. Like thousands of other poor rural whites in these years, Elvis Presley had moved from Mississippi to Memphis in 1949, where his father found work in a munitions plant. The Presleys were poor enough to qualify for an apartment in Lauderdale Courts, a Memphis public housing project. To James Conaway, who grew up in an all-white, middle-class East Memphis neighborhood, people like the

Presleys were "white trash." Negroes, he recalled, were "not necessarily below the rank of a country boy like Elvis, but of another universe, and yet there was more affection for them than for some whites."

Gloria Wade-Gayles, who lived in the all-black Foote Homes housing project, vividly remembered that her family and neighbors "had no illusion about their lack of power, but they believed in their strength." For them, strength grew from total immersion in a black community that included ministers, teachers, insurance men, morticians, barbers, and entertainers. "Surviving meant being black, and being black meant believing in our humanity, and retaining it, in a world that denied we had it in the first place."

Yet in the cultural realm, class and racial barriers could be challenged. Elvis Presley grew up a dreamy, shy boy, who turned to music for emotional release and spiritual expression. He soaked up the wide range of music styles available in Memphis. The Assembly of God Church his family attended featured a renowned hundred-voice choir. Elvis and his friends went to marathon all-night "gospel singings" at Ellis Auditorium, where they enjoyed the tight harmonies and emotional style of white gospel quartets.

Elvis also drew from the sounds he heard on Beale Street, the main black thoroughfare of Memphis and one of the nation's most influential centers of African American music. In the postwar years, local black rhythm and blues artists like B. B. King, Junior Parker, and Muddy Waters attracted legions of black and white fans with their emotional power and exciting showmanship. At the Handy Theater on Beale Street, the teenaged Elvis Presley, like thousands of other white young people, heard black performers at the "Midnight Rambles"—late shows for white people only. Elvis himself performed along with black contestants in amateur shows at Beale Street's Palace Theater. Nat D. Williams, a prominent black Memphis disc jockey and music promoter, recalled how black audiences responded to Elvis's unique style. "He had a way of singing the blues that was distinctive. He could sing 'em not necessarily like a Negro, but he didn't sing 'em altogether like a typical white musician. . . . Always he

had that certain humanness about him that Negroes like to put in their songs."

The expansion of the broadcasting and recording industries in the postwar years also contributed to the weakening of racial barriers in the musical realm. Two Memphis radio stations featured the hard-driving rhythm and blues music that was beginning to attract a strong following among young white listeners. These Memphis stations also featured spirituals by African American artists such as Mahalia Jackson and Clara Ward.

Elvis himself understood his debt to black music and black performers. "The colored folks," he told an interviewer in 1956, "been singing and playing it just like I'm doing now, man, for more years than I know. They played it like that in the shanties and in their juke joints and nobody paid it no mind until I goosed it up. I got it from them."

Dissatisfied with the cloying pop music of the day, white teenagers across the nation were increasingly turning to the rhythmic drive and emotional intensity of black rhythm and blues. They quickly adopted rock 'n' roll (the term had long been an African American slang expression for dancing and sexual intercourse) as their music. But it was more than just music: it was also an attitude, a celebration of being young, and a sense of having something that adult authority could not understand or control.

When Sun Records sold Presley's contract to RCA Records in 1956, Elvis became an international star. Records like "Heartbreak Hotel," "Don't Be Cruel," and "Jailhouse Rock" shot to the top of the charts and blurred the old boundaries between pop, country, and rhythm and blues. By helping to accustom white teenagers to the style and sound of black artists, Elvis helped establish rock 'n' roll as an interracial phenomenon. Institutional racism would continue to plague the music business—many black artists were routinely cheated out of royalties and severely underpaid—but the music of postwar Memphis at least pointed the way toward the exciting cultural possibilities that could emerge from breaking down the barriers of race. It also gave postwar American teenagers a newfound sense of community.

Memphis

KEY TOPICS

- Post–World War II prosperity

- Suburban life: ideal and reality

- The emergence of youth culture

- Television, mass culture, and their critics

- Foreign policy in the Eisenhower years

- John F. Kennedy and the promise of a New Frontier

AMERICAN SOCIETY AT MIDCENTURY

With the title of his influential work, *The Affluent Society* (1958), economist John Kenneth Galbraith gave a label to postwar America. Galbraith observed that American capitalism had worked "quite brilliantly" in the years since World War II. But Americans, he argued, needed to spend less on personal consumption and devote more public funds to schools, medical care, cultural activities, and social services. For most Americans, however, strong economic growth was the defining fact of the postwar period. A fierce desire for consumer goods and the "good life" imbued American culture, and the deeply held popular belief in a continuously expanding economy and a steadily increasing standard of living—together with the tensions of the cold war—shaped American social and political life.

The Eisenhower Presidency

Dwight D. Eisenhower's landslide election victory in 1952 set the stage for the first full two-term Republican presidency since that of Ulysses S. Grant. At the core of Eisenhower's political philosophy lay a conservative vision of community. He saw America as a corporate commonwealth, similar to the "associative state" envisioned by Herbert Hoover a generation earlier (see Chapter 23). Eisenhower believed the industrial strife, high inflation, and fierce partisan politics of the Truman years could be corrected only through cooperation, self-restraint, and disinterested public service. As president, Eisenhower emphasized limiting the New Deal trends that had expanded federal power, and he encouraged a voluntary, as opposed to regulatory, relationship between government and business. Social harmony and "the good life" at home were closely linked, in his view, to maintaining a stable and American-led international order abroad.

Eisenhower viewed his leadership style as crucial for achieving the goal of a harmonious, corporate-led society. That style owed something to his roots in turn-of-the-century Kansas and his socialization in the military. In the army he had risen through the command structure by playing it safe, keeping his own counsel, and allowing his subordinates to apprise him of his options. He once described his views on leadership to a critic: "It's persuasion—and conciliation—and patience. It's long, slow, tough work. That's the only kind of leadership I know or believe in—or will practice."

Consciously, Eisenhower adopted an evasive style in public, and he was fond of the phrase "middle of the road." He told a news conference, "I feel pretty good when I'm attacked from both sides. It makes me more certain I'm on the right track." Intellectuals and liberals found it easy to satirize Eisenhower for his blandness, his frequent verbal gaffes, his vagueness, and his often contradictory pronouncements. The majority of the American public, however, evidently agreed with Eisenhower's easygoing approach to his office. He kept the conservative and liberal wings of his party united and appealed to many Democrats and independents.

Eisenhower wanted to run government in a businesslike manner while letting the states and corporate interests guide domestic policy and the economy. He appointed nine businessmen to his first cabinet, including three with ties to General Motors. Former GM chief Charles Wilson served as secretary of defense and epitomized the administration's economic views with his famous aphorism "What's good for General Motors business is good for America." In his appointments to the Federal Trade Commission, the Federal Communications Commission, and the Federal Power Commission, Eisenhower favored men congenial to the corporate interests they were charged with regulating. Eisenhower also secured passage of the Submerged Lands Act in 1953, which transferred $40 billion worth of disputed offshore oil lands from the federal government to the Gulf states. This transfer ensured a greater role for the states and private companies in the oil business—and cost the Treasury billions in lost revenues.

In the long run, the Eisenhower administration's lax approach to government regulation accelerated a trend toward the destruction of the natural environment. Oil exploration in Louisiana's bayous, for example, began the massive degradation of America's largest wetlands. Water diversion policies in Florida seriously damaged the biggest tropical forest in the United States. The increased use of toxic chemicals, begun during World War II and largely unregulated by law, placed warehouses of poisons in hundreds of sites, many abutting military installations. Virtually unregulated use and disposal of the pesticide DDT poisoned birds and other animals and left permanent toxic scars in the environment.

At the same time, Eisenhower accepted the New Deal legacy of greater federal responsibility for social welfare. He rejected calls from conservative Republicans, for example, to dismantle the Social Security system. His administration

This photo, which appeared in a 1950 issue of Life Magazine, *posed a family of pioneer suburbanites in front of their Levittown, New York, home. The prefabricated house was built in 1948.*

agreed to a modest expansion of Social Security and unemployment insurance and small increases in the minimum wage. Ike also created the Department of Health, Education and Welfare, appointing Oveta Culp Hobby as its secretary, making her the second woman to hold a cabinet post. In agriculture, Eisenhower continued the policy of parity payments designed to sustain farm prices. Between 1952 and 1960, federal spending on agriculture jumped from about $1 billion to $7 billion.

Eisenhower proved hesitant to use fiscal policy to pump up the economy, which went into recession after the Korean War ended in 1953 and again in 1958, when the unemployment rate reached 7.5 percent. The administration refused to cut taxes or increase spending to stimulate growth. Eisenhower feared starting an inflationary spiral more than he worried about unemployment or poverty. By the time he left office, he could proudly point out that real wages for an average family had risen 20 percent during his term. With low inflation and steady, if modest, growth, the Eisenhower years brought greater prosperity to most Americans. Long after he retired from public life, Ike liked to remember his major achievement as having created "an atmosphere of greater serenity and mutual confidence."

Subsidizing Prosperity

During the Eisenhower years the federal government played a crucial role in subsidizing programs that helped millions of Americans achieve middle-class status. Federal aid helped people to buy homes, attend college and technical schools, and live in newly built suburbs. Much of this assistance expanded on programs begun during the New Deal and World War II. The Federal Housing Administration (FHA), established in 1934, extended the government's role in subsidizing the housing industry. The FHA insured long-term mortgage loans made by private lenders for home building. By putting the full faith and credit of the federal government behind residential mortgages, the FHA attracted new private capital into home building and revolutionized the industry. A typical FHA mortgage required less than 10 percent for a down payment and spread low-interest monthly payments over thirty years.

Yet FHA policies also had long-range drawbacks. FHA insurance went overwhelmingly to new residential developments, usually on the fringes of urban areas, hastening the decline of older, inner-city neighborhoods. A bias toward suburban, middle-class communities manifested itself in several ways: it was FHA policy to favor the construction of single-family projects while discouraging multi-unit housing, to refuse loans for the repair of older structures and rental units, and to require for any loan guarantee an "unbiased professional estimate" rating the property, the prospective borrower, and the neighborhood. In practice, these estimates resulted in blatant discrimination against communities that were racially mixed. The FHA's Underwriting Manual bluntly warned: "If a neighborhood is to retain stability, it is necessary that properties shall continue to be occupied by the same social and racial classes." FHA policies in effect inscribed the racial and income segregation of suburbia in public policy.

Wife and children of the typical white, middle-class family greet the breadwinning father arriving home from work. Such images, which appeared frequently in popular magazines, idealized the home as the safe haven from the tensions of the office and enshrined the family as the source of happiness and security.

The majority of suburbs were built as planned communities. One of the first was Levittown, which opened in Hempstead, Long Island, in 1947, on 1,500 acres of former potato fields. Developer William Levitt, who described his firm as "the General Motors of the housing industry," was the first entrepreneur to bring mass-production techniques to home building. All building materials were precut and prefabricated at a central factory, then assembled on-site into houses by largely unskilled, nonunion labor. In this way Levitt put up hundreds of identical houses each week. Eventually, Levittown encompassed more than 17,000 houses and 82,000 people. Yet in 1960 not one of Levittown's residents was African American.

The revolution in American life wrought by the 1944 Servicemen's Readjustment Act, known as the GI Bill of Rights, extended beyond its impact on higher education (see Chapter 26). In addition to educational grants, the act provided returning veterans with low-interest mortgages and business loans, thus subsidizing the growth of the suburbs as well as the postwar expansion of higher education. Through 1956, nearly 10 million veterans received tuition and training benefits under the act. VA-insured loans totaled more than $50 billion by 1962, providing assistance to millions of former GIs who started businesses.

The Federal Highway Act of 1956 gave another key boost to postwar growth, especially in the suburbs. It originally authorized $32 billion for the construction of a national interstate highway system. Financing was to come from new taxes on gasoline, as well as on oil, tires, buses, and trucks. Key to this ambitious program's success was that these revenues were held separately from general taxes in a Highway Trust Fund. By 1972 the program had become the single largest public works program in American history; 41,000 miles of highway were built at a cost of $76 billion. Federal subsidy of the interstate highway system stimulated both the automobile industry and suburb building. But it also accelerated the decline of American mass transit and older cities. By 1970, the nation possessed the world's best roads and one of its worst public transportation systems.

The shadow of the cold war prompted the federal government to take new initiatives in aid for education. After the Soviet Union launched its first Sputnik satellite in the fall of 1957, American officials worried that the country might be lagging behind the

Soviets in training scientists and engineers. The Eisenhower administration, with the bipartisan support of Congress, pledged to strengthen support for educating American students in mathematics, science, and technology. The National Defense Education Act (NDEA) of 1958 allocated $280 million in grants—tied to matching grants from the states—for state universities to upgrade their science facilities. The NDEA also created $300 million in low-interest loans for college students, who had to repay only half the amount if they went on to teach in elementary or secondary school after graduation. In addition, the NDEA provided fellowship support for graduate students planning to go into college and university teaching. The NDEA represented a new consensus on the importance of high-quality education to the national interest.

Suburban Life

The suburban boom strengthened the domestic ideal of the nuclear family as the model for American life. In particular, the picture of the perfect suburban wife—efficient, patient, always charming—became a dominant image in television, movies, and magazines. Suburban domesticity was usually presented as women's only path to happiness and fulfillment. This cultural image often masked a stifling existence defined by housework, child care, and boredom. In the late 1950s Betty Friedan, a wife, mother, and journalist, began a systematic survey of her Smith College classmates. She found "a strange discrepancy between the reality of our lives as women and the image to which we were trying to conform." Friedan expanded her research and in 1963 published *The Feminine Mystique*, a landmark book that articulated the frustrations of suburban women and helped to launch a revived feminist movement.

The postwar rebirth of religious life was strongly associated with suburban living. In 1940 less than half the American population belonged to institutionalized churches; by the mid-1950s nearly three-quarters identified themselves as church members. A church-building boom was centered in the expanding suburbs. Best-selling religious authors such as Norman Vincent Peale and Bishop Fulton J. Sheen offered a shallow blend of reassurance and "the power of positive thinking." They stressed individual solutions to problems, opposing social or political activism. Their emphasis on the importance of belonging, of fitting in, meshed well with suburban social life and the ideal of family-centered domesticity.

California came to embody postwar suburban life. At the center of this lifestyle was the automobile. Cars were a necessity for commuting to work. California also led the nation in the development of drive-in facilities: motels, movies, shopping malls, fast-food restaurants, and banks. More than 500 miles of highways would be constructed around Los Angeles alone. In Orange County,

southeast of Los Angeles, the "centerless city" emerged as the dominant form of community. The experience of one woman resident was typical: "I live in Garden Grove, work in Irvine, shop in Santa Ana, go to the dentist in Anaheim, my husband works in Long Beach, and I used to be the president of the League of Women Voters in Fullerton."

Contemporary journalists, novelists, and social scientists contributed to the popular image of suburban life as essentially dull, conformist, and peopled exclusively by the educated middle class. John Cheever, for example, won the National Book Award for *The Wapshot Chronicle* (1957), a novel set in fictional Remsen Park, "a community of four thousand identical homes." Psychiatrist Richard Gordon's *Split Level Trap* (1960) focused on the emotional problems he observed among the suburban families of Bergen County, New Jersey. Yet these writers tended to obscure the real class and ethnic differences found among and between suburban communities. Many new suburbs had a distinctively blue-collar cast. Milpitas, California, for example, grew up around a Ford auto plant about fifty miles outside San Jose. Its residents were blue-collar assembly line workers and their families rather than salaried, college-educated, white-

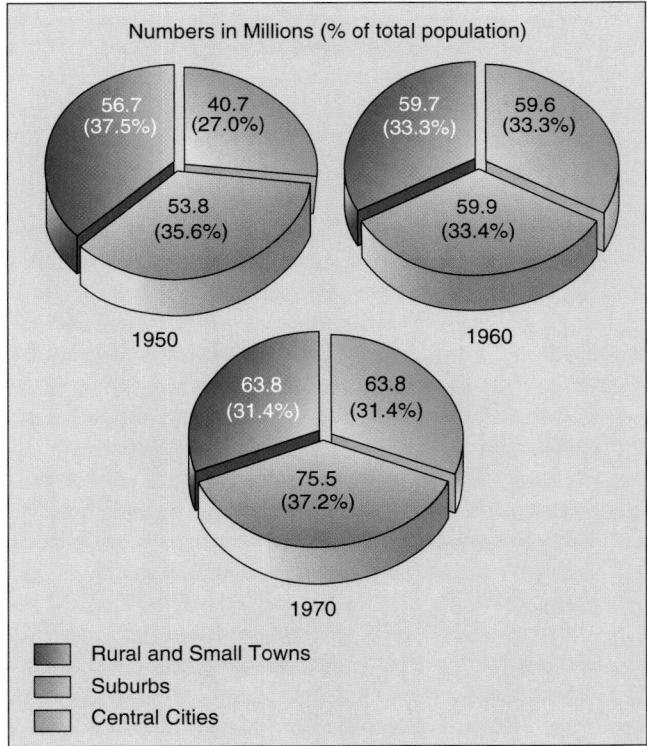

The Growth of the Suburbs, 1950–1970   *Suburban growth, at the expense of older inner cities, was one of the key social trends in the twenty-five years following World War II. By 1970, more Americans lived in suburbs than in either inner cities or rural areas.*

Source: Adapted from U.S. Bureau of the Census, *Current Censuses,* 1930–1970 (Washington, D.C.: U.S. Government Printing Office, 1975).

Los Angeles in the 1950s

- Industrial district
- Urbanized area
- Freeway
- Freeway under construction
- Federal or state highway

Ethnic Groups by Census Tract, 1950
- Asian (30 percent or more)
- Black (40 percent or more)
- Hispanic (40 percent or more)

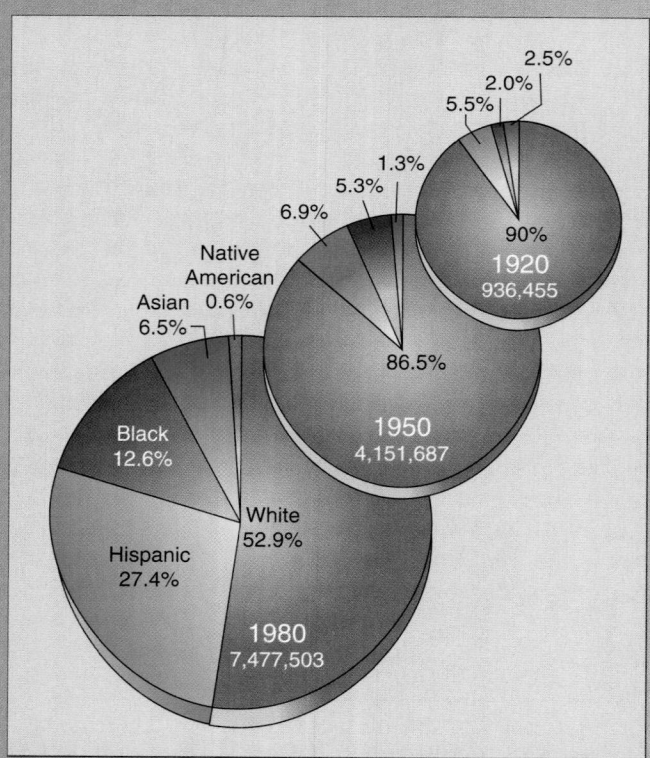

L. A. County Population

1920 — 936,455
- 90%
- 5.5%
- 2.0%
- 2.5%

1950 — 4,151,687
- 86.5%
- 6.9%
- 5.3%
- 1.3%

1980 — 7,477,503
- White 52.9%
- Hispanic 27.4%
- Black 12.6%
- Asian 6.5%
- Native American 0.6%

The Changing Face of Postwar Los Angeles

Los Angeles epitomized two postwar American trends: the rapid growth of western cities and the rapid expansion of the suburbs. Spurred by government funding, it boasted the highest per capita ownership of both private homes and automobiles of any American city. Federal tax policies subsidized home ownership, and loan guarantees through the Federal Housing Administration and the Veterans Administration made home mortgages available to millions. The state's Collier-Burns Act of 1947 committed gasoline taxes and auto registration fees to building a high-speed freeway system in metropolitan Los Angeles. The Federal Highway Act of 1956 supplemented these funds by incorporating some of the freeways into the national highway system. By 1960 Los Angeles had 250 miles of freeways. By the 1970s, about two-thirds of downtown Los Angeles was devoted to the automobile.

Postwar Los Angeles also evolved into one of the most ethnically diverse cities in the nation. What had been an overwhelmingly white Protestant population began to change during World War II with the influx of African American, Mexican, and Indian factory workers. By the 1970s Korean, Filipino, Vietnamese, and other Asian immigrants, along with newcomers from Mexico and Central America, had radically altered the city's ethnic character. But Los Angeles neighborhoods and suburbs remained largely segregated by race and ethnicity.

collar employees. Self-segregation and zoning ordinances gave some new suburbs as distinctively Italian, Jewish, or Irish ethnic identities as older urban neighborhoods. For millions of new suburbanites, architectural and psychological conformity was an acceptable price to pay for the comforts of home ownership, a small plot of land, and a sense of security and status.

Lonely Crowds and Organization Men

Perhaps the most ambitious and controversial critique of postwar suburban America was sociologist David Riesman's *The Lonely Crowd* (1950). Riesman argued that modern America had given birth to a new kind of character type, the "other-directed" man. Previously the nation had cultivated "inner-directed" people—self-reliant individualists who early on in life had internalized self-discipline and moral standards. By contrast, the "other-directed" person typical of the modern era was peer-oriented. Morality and ideals came from the overarching desire to conform. Americans, Riesman thought, were now less likely to take risks or act independently. Their thinking and habits had come to be determined by cues they received from the mass media.

Similarly, William H. Whyte's *Organization Man* (1956), a study of the Chicago suburb of Park Forest, offered a picture of people obsessed with fitting into their communities and jobs. In place of the old Protestant ethic of hard work, thrift, and competitive struggle, Whyte believed, middle-class suburbanites now strived mainly for a comfortable, secure niche in the system. They held to a new social ethic, he argued: "a belief in the group as the source of creativity; a belief in 'belongingness' as the ultimate need of the individual." Sloan Wilson's *Man in the Grey Flannel Suit*, a 1955 best-seller, featured a hero who rejects the top position at his firm. His boss sympathizes with this reluctance to sacrifice, telling him, "There are plenty of good positions where it's not necessary for a man to put in an unusual amount of work."

The most radical critic of postwar society, and the one with the most enduring influence, was Texas-reared sociologist C. Wright Mills. In *White Collar* (1951), Mills analyzed the job culture that typified life for middle-class salaried employees, office workers, and bureaucrats. "When white collar people get jobs," he wrote, "they sell not only their time and energy, but their personalities as well. They sell by the week or month their smiles and their kindly gestures, and they must practice the prompt repression of resentment and aggression." In *The Power Elite* (1956), Mills argued that a small, interconnected group of corporate executives, military men, and political leaders had come to dominate American society. The arms race in particular, carried out in the name of cold war policies, had given an unprecedented degree of power to the military-industrial complex.

The Expansion of Higher Education

American higher education experienced rapid growth after the war. This expansion both reflected and reinforced other trends in postwar society. The number of students enrolled in colleges and universities climbed from 2.6 million in 1950 to 3.2 million in 1960. It then more than doubled—to 7.5 million—by 1970, as the baby boom generation came of age. Most of these new students attended greatly enlarged state university systems. Main campuses at state universities in Michigan, Wisconsin, California, and other states grew bigger than ever, enrolling as many as 40,000 students. Technical colleges and "normal schools" (designed originally for the training of teachers) were upgraded and expanded into full-fledged universities, as in the branches of the State University of New York, founded in 1948.

Several factors contributed to this explosion. A variety of new federal programs, including the GI Bill and the National Defense Education Act, helped subsidize college education for millions of new students. Government spending on research and development in universities, especially for defense-related projects, pumped further resources into higher education. Much of this money supported programs in graduate work, reflecting an important postwar shift in the priorities of American universities. Graduate education and faculty research now challenged traditional undergraduate teaching as the main locus of university activity and power.

Colleges and universities by and large accepted the values of postwar corporate culture. By the mid-1950s, 20 percent of all college graduates majored in business or other commercial fields. The college degree was a gateway to the middle class. It became a requirement for a whole range of expanding white-collar occupations in banking, insurance, real estate, advertising and marketing, and other corporate enterprises. As much as educating young people, colleges trained them for careers in technical, professional, and management positions. Most administrators accommodated large business interests, which were well represented on university boards of trustees. Universities themselves were increasingly run like businesses, with administrators adopting the language of input-output, cost effectiveness, and quality control.

Researchers found college students in the 1950s generally absorbed the conventions and attitudes associated with working in a corporate environment. A typical Iowa State student told one writer, "You have to be very careful not to associate with the wrong clan of people, an introvert that isn't socially acceptable, guys who dress in the fashion of ten years ago. These people are just not accepted—and, if you associate with them, you're not accepted either."

Health and Medicine

Dramatic improvements in medical care allowed many Americans to enjoy longer and healthier lives. During the war the federal government had poured unprecedented amounts of money into medical research and the diffusion of new techniques. The armed forces had immunized and treated millions of servicemen and women for diseases ranging from syphilis to tuberculosis. New antibiotics such as penicillin were manufactured and distributed on a mass basis, and after the war they became widely available to the general population. Federal support for research continued after the war with the reorganization of the National Institutes of Health in 1948. Federal agencies, led by the National Institute of Mental Health, founded in 1949, also expanded research on and treatment of mental illness.

By 1960 many dreaded epidemic diseases, such as tuberculosis, diphtheria, whooping cough, and measles, had virtually disappeared from American life. Perhaps the most celebrated achievement of postwar medicine was the victory over poliomyelitis. Between 1947 and 1951 this disease, which usually crippled those it did not kill, struck an annual average of 39,000 Americans. In 1952, 58,000 cases, most of them children, were reported. Frightened parents warned children to stay away from crowded swimming pools and other gathering places. In 1955 Jonas Salk pioneered the first effective vaccine against the disease, using a preparation of killed virus. A nationwide program of polio vaccination, later supplemented by the oral Sabin vaccine, virtually eliminated polio by the 1960s.

Yet the benefits of "wonder drugs" and advanced medical techniques were not shared equally by all Americans. More sophisticated treatments and expensive new hospital facilities sharply increased the costs of health care. The very poor and many elderly Americans found themselves unable to afford modern medicine. Thousands of communities, especially in rural areas and small towns, lacked doctors or decent hospital facilities. Critics of the medical establishment charged that the proliferation of medical specialists and large hospital complexes had increased the number of unnecessary surgical operations, especially for women and children. The decline of the general practitioner— the family doctor—meant fewer physicians made house calls; more and more people went to hospital emergency rooms or outpatient clinics for treatment. Unreasonable faith in sophisticated medical technologies also contributed to the proliferation of iatrogenic ailments— sickness brought on by treatment for some other illness.

The American Medical Association (AMA), which certified medical schools, did nothing to increase the flow of new doctors. The number of physicians per 100,000 people actually declined between 1950 and 1960; the shortage was made up by doctors trained in other countries. The AMA also lobbied hard against efforts to expand government responsibility for the public's health. President Harry Truman had advanced a plan for national health insurance, to be run along the lines of Social Security. President Dwight Eisenhower had proposed a program that would offer government assistance to private health insurance companies. The AMA denounced both proposals as "socialized medicine." It helped block direct federal involvement in health care until the creation of Medicare (for the elderly) and Medicaid (for the poor) in 1965.

YOUTH CULTURE

The term "teenager," describing someone between thirteen and nineteen, entered standard usage only at the end of World War II. According to the *Dictionary of American Slang*, the United States is the only country with a word for this age group and the only country to consider it "a separate entity whose influence, fads, and fashions are worthy of discussion apart from the adult world." The fifteen years following World War II saw unprecedented attention to America's adolescents. Deep fears were expressed about everything from teenage sexuality and juvenile delinquency to young people's driving habits, hairstyles, and choice of clothing. At the same time, advertisers and businesses pursued the disposable income of America's affluent youth with a vengeance. Teenagers often found themselves caught between their desire to carve out their own separate sphere and the pressure to become an adult as quickly as possible.

Dr. Jonas E. Salk and nurse administered polio vaccine to Pauline Antloger, a student at Sunnyside School in Pittsburgh, 1955. Dr. Salk's scientific breakthrough of a killed-virus polio vaccine led to an array of viral vaccines to cure other diseases, such as hepatitis.

The Youth Market

Birth rates had accelerated gradually during the late 1930s and more rapidly during the war years. The children born in those years had by the late 1950s grown into the original teenagers, the older siblings of the celebrated baby boom of 1946–64. They came of age in a society that, compared with that of their parents and the rest of the world, was uniquely affluent. Together, the demographic growth of teens and the postwar economic expansion created a burgeoning youth market. Manufacturers and advertisers rushed to cash in on the special needs and desires of young consumers: cosmetics, clothing, radios and phonographs, and cars.

Before Elvis Presley became the ultimate teen idol, his life in Memphis mirrored the experiences of millions of American teenagers. In high school he was an average student at best, and he took part-time jobs to help out the family; after graduation he worked as a truck driver and as an electrician's helper. He enjoyed making the rounds of movies, roller rinks, and burger joints with his friends, and he dreamed of owning his own Cadillac. Like many teens, Elvis obsessed over the latest stylish clothing—which he could not afford. He could often be found haunting the shop windows at the Lansky Brothers clothing store on Beale Street in Memphis.

In 1959, *Life* summarized the new power of the youth market. "Counting only what is spent to satisfy their special teenage demands," the magazine reported, "the youngsters and their parents will shell out about $10 billion this year, a billion more than the total sales of GM." In addition, advertisers and market researchers found that teenagers often played a critical, if hard-to-measure, role as "secret persuaders" in a family's large purchases. Specialized market research organizations, such as Eugene Gilbert & Company and Teen-Age Survey Incorporated, sprang up to serve business clients eager to attract teen consumers and instill brand loyalty. Through the 1950s and into the 1960s, teenagers had a major, sometimes dominant, voice in determining America's cultural fads.

To many parents, the emerging youth culture was a dangerous threat to their authority. One mother summarized this fear in a revealing, if slightly hysterical, letter to *Modern Teen:*

> Don't you realize what you are doing? You are encouraging teenagers to write to each other, which keeps them from doing their school work and other chores. You are encouraging them to kiss and have physical contact before they're even engaged, which is morally wrong and you know it. You are encouraging them to have faith in the depraved individuals who

make rock and roll records when it's common knowledge that ninety per cent of these rock and roll singers are people with no morals or sense of values.

The increasing uniformity of public school education also contributed to the public recognition of the special status of teenagers. In 1900, about one of every eight teenagers was in school; by the 1950s, the figure was six out of eight. Psychologists wrote guidebooks for parents, two prominent examples being Dorothy Baruch's *How to Live with Your Teenager* (1953) and Paul Landis's *Understanding Teenagers* (1955). Social scientists stressed the importance of peer pressure for understanding teen behavior. "The teenage group," Landis observed in *Understanding Teenagers*, "is self sufficient now as in no previous generation." The larger point here is that traditional sources of adult authority and socialization—the marketplace, schools, childrearing manuals, the mass media—all reinforced the notion of teenagers as a special community, united by age, rank, and status.

"Hail! Hail! Rock 'n' Roll!"

The demands of the new teen market, combined with structural changes in the postwar American mass media, reshaped the nation's popular music. As television broadcasting rapidly replaced radio as the center of family entertainment, people began using radios in new ways. The production of portable transistor radios and car radios grew rapidly in the 1950s as listeners increasingly tuned them in for diversion from or an accompaniment to other activities. Locally produced radio shows, featuring music, news, and disc jockeys, replaced the old star-studded network programs. By 1956, 2,700 AM radio stations were on the air across the United States, with about 70 percent of their broadcast time given to record shows. Most of these concentrated on popular music for the traditional white adult market: pop ballads, novelty songs, and show tunes.

In the recording industry, meanwhile, a change was in the air. Small independent record labels led the way in aggressively recording African American rhythm and blues artists. Atlantic, in New York, developed the most influential galaxy of artists, including Ray Charles, Ruth Brown, the Drifters, Joe Turner, LaVerne Baker, and the Clovers. Chess, in Chicago, had the blues-based singer-songwriter-guitarists Chuck Berry and Bo Diddley and the "doo-wop" group the Moonglows. In New Orleans, Imperial had the veteran pianist-singer Fats Domino, while Specialty unleashed the outrageous Little Richard on the world. On radio, over jukeboxes, and in record stores, all of these African American artists "crossed over," adding millions of white teenagers to their solid base of black fans.

The older, more established record companies, such as RCA, Decca, M-G-M, and Capitol, had largely ignored black music. Their response to the new trend was to offer slick, toned-down "cover" versions by white pop singers of rhythm and blues originals. Cover versions were invariably pallid imitations, artistically inferior to the originals. One has only to compare, say, Pat Boone's covers of Fats Domino's "Ain't That a Shame" or Little Richard's "Tutti Frutti" to hear how much was lost. While African American artists began to enjoy newfound mass acceptance, there were limits to how closely white kids could identify with black performers. Racism, especially in so sexually charged an arena as musical performance, was still a powerful force in American life. Because of the superior promotional power of the major companies and the institutional racism in the music business, white cover versions almost always outsold the black originals.

This photo of Elvis Presley singing at a 1956 state fair in Memphis captured his dramatic stage presence. Performing with only a trio, his sound was spare but hard driving. Both the music and Presley's stage moves owed a great deal to African American rhythm and blues artists.

Alan Freed, a popular white Cleveland disc jockey, refused to play cover versions on his "Moondog Matinee" program. He played only original rhythm and blues music, and he popularized the term "rock 'n' roll" to describe it. Freed promoted concerts around the Midwest featuring black rhythm and blues artists, and these attracted enthusiastic audiences of both black and white young people. In 1954 the music trade magazine *Billboard* noted this trend among white teenagers: "The present generation has not known the rhythmically exciting dance bands of the swing era. It therefore satisfies its hunger for 'music with a beat' in modern r&b (rhythm and blues) groups." The stage was thus set for the arrival of white rock 'n' roll artists who could exploit the new sounds and styles.

As a rock 'n' roll performer and recording artist, Elvis Presley reinvented American popular music. His success challenged the old lines separating black music from white, and pop from rhythm and blues or country. As a symbol of rebellious youth and as the embodiment of youthful sexuality, Elvis revitalized American popular culture. In his wake came a host of white rock 'n' rollers, many of them white Southerners like Elvis: Jerry Lee Lewis, Buddy Holly, the Everly Brothers, Roy Orbison. But the greatest songwriter and the most influential guitarist to emerge from this first "golden age of rock 'n' roll" was Chuck Berry, an African Amer-

ican from St. Louis who worked part-time as a beautician and house painter. Berry proved especially adept at capturing the teen spirit with humor, irony, and passion. He composed hits around the trials and tribulations of school ("School Days"), young love ("Memphis"), cars ("Maybellene"), and making it as a rock 'n' roller ("Johnny B. Goode"). As much as anyone, Berry created music that defined what it meant to be young in postwar America.

Almost Grown

At least some of the sense of difference, of uniqueness, associated with adolescence came from teens themselves. Teenage consumers remade the landscape of popular music into their own turf. The dollar value of annual record sales nearly tripled between 1954 and 1959, from $213 million to $603 million. New magazines aimed exclusively at teens flourished in the postwar years. *Modern Teen, Teen Digest,* and *Dig* were just a few. Most teen magazines, like rock 'n' roll music, focused on the rituals, pleasures, and sorrows surrounding teenage courtship. Paradoxically, behavior patterns among white middle-class teenagers in the 1950s and early 1960s exhibited a new kind of youth orientation and at the same time a more pronounced identification with adults.

While many parents worried about the separate world inhabited by their teenage children, many teens seemed determined to become adults as quickly as possible. Postwar affluence multiplied the number of two-car families, making it easier for sixteen-year-olds to win driving privileges formerly reserved for eighteen-year-olds. Girls began dating, wearing brassieres and nylon stockings, and using cosmetics at an earlier age than before—twelve or thirteen rather than fifteen or sixteen. Several factors contributed to this trend, including a continuing decline in the age of menarche (first menstruation), the sharp drop in the age of marriage after World War II, and the precocious social climate of junior high schools (institutions that became widespread only after 1945). The practice of going steady, derived from the college custom of fraternity and sorority pinning, became commonplace among high schoolers. By the late 1950s, eighteen had become the most common age at which American females married.

Teenagers often felt torn between their identification with youth culture and pressures to assume adult responsibilities. Many young people juggled part-time jobs with school and very active social lives. Teen-oriented magazines, music, and movies routinely dispensed advice and sympathy regarding this dilemma. Rock 'n' roll songs offered the most sympathetic treatments of the conflicts teens experienced over work ("Summertime Blues"), parental authority ("Yakety Yak"), and the desire to look adult ("Sweet Little Sixteen"). By 1960 sociologist James S. Coleman reflected a growing consensus when he noted that postwar society had given adolescents "many of the instruments which can make them a functioning community: cars, freedom in dating, continual contact with the opposite sex, money, and entertainment, like popular music and movies, designed especially for them."

Deviance and Delinquency

Many adults held rock 'n' roll responsible for the apparent decline in parental control over teens. A psychiatrist writing in the *New York Times* described rock as "a cannibalistic and tribalistic kind of music" and "a communicable disease." Many clergymen and church leaders declared it "the devil's music." Much of the opposition to rock 'n' roll, particularly in the South, played on long-standing racist fears that white females might be attracted to black music and black performers. The undercurrent beneath all this opposition was a deep anxiety over the more open expression of sexual feelings by both performers and audiences.

Paralleling the rise of rock 'n' roll was a growing concern with an alleged increase in juvenile delinquency. An endless stream of magazine articles, books, and newspaper stories asserted that criminal behavior among the nation's young was chronic. Gang fights, drug and alcohol abuse, car theft, and sexual offenses received the most attention. The U.S. Senate established a special subcommittee on juvenile delinquency. Highly publicized hearings in 1955 and 1956 convinced much of the public that youthful criminals were terror-

izing the country. Although crime statistics do suggest an increase in juvenile crime during the 1950s, particularly in the suburbs, the public perception of the severity of the problem was surely exaggerated.

In retrospect, the juvenile delinquency controversy tells us more about anxieties over family life and the erosion of adult authority than about crime patterns. Teenagers seemed more defined by and loyal to their peer culture than to their parents. A great deal of their music, speech, dress, and style was alien and threatening. The growing importance of the mass media in defining youth culture brought efforts to regulate or censor media forms believed to cause juvenile delinquency. For example, psychologist Fredric Wertham led a crusade that forced the comic book industry to adopt a code strictly limiting the portrayal of violence and crime.

As reactions to two of the most influential "problem youth" movies of the postwar era indicate, teens and their parents frequently interpreted depictions of youthful deviance in the mass media in very different ways. In *The Wild One* (1954), Marlon Brando played the crude, moody leader of a vicious motorcycle gang. Most adults thought of the film as a critique of mindless gang violence, but many teenagers identified with the Brando character, who, when asked, "What are you rebelling against?" coolly replied, "Whattaya got?" In *Rebel without a Cause* (1955), James Dean, Natalie Wood, and Sal Mineo played emotionally troubled youths in an affluent California suburb. The movie suggests that parents can cause delinquency when they fail to conform to conventional roles—Dean's father wears an apron and his mother is domineering. But on another level, the film suggests that young people can form their own families, without parents.

Brando and Dean, along with Elvis, were probably the most popular and widely imitated teen idols of the era. For most parents, they were vaguely threatening figures whose sexual energy and lack of discipline placed them outside the bounds of middle-class respectability. For teens, however, they offered an irresistible combination of rough exterior and sensitive core. They embodied, as well, the contradiction of individual rebellion versus the attractions of a community defined by youth.

MASS CULTURE AND ITS DISCONTENTS

No mass medium ever achieved such power and popularity as rapidly as television. The basic technology for broadcasting visual images with sound had been developed by the late 1930s, and television demonstrations were among the most popular exhibits at the 1939 New York World's Fair. But World War II and corporate competition postponed television's introduction to the public until 1946. By 1960, nearly nine in ten American families owned at least one set, which was turned on an average of more than five hours a day. Television reshaped leisure time and political life. It also helped create a new kind of national community defined by the buying and selling of consumer goods.

Important voices challenged the economic trends and cultural conformity of the postwar years. Academics, journalists, novelists, and poets offered a variety of works criticizing the overall direction of American life. These critics of what was dubbed "mass society" were troubled by the premium American culture put on conformity, status, and material consumption. Although a distinct minority, these critics were persistent. Many of their ideas and prescriptions would reverberate through the political and cultural upheavals of the 1960s and 1970s.

Television: Tube of Plenty

Television constituted a radical change from radio, and its development as a mass medium was quicker and less chaotic. The three main television networks—NBC, CBS, ABC—grew directly from radio organizations. A short-lived fourth network, Dumont, grew from a television manufacturing business. The Federal Communications Commission oversaw the licensing of stations and set technical standards. The networks led the industry from the start, rather than following individual stations, as radio had done. Nearly all TV stations were affiliated with one or more of the networks; only a handful of independent stations could be found around the country.

Television not only depended on advertising, it also transformed the advertising industry. The television business, like radio, was based on the selling of time to advertisers who wanted to reach the mass audiences tuning into shows. Radio had offered entire shows produced by and for single sponsors, usually advertisers who wanted a close identification between their product and a star. But the higher costs of television production forced key changes. Sponsors left production of programs to the networks, independent producers, and Hollywood studios.

Sponsors now bought scattered time slots for spot advertisements rather than bankrolling an entire show. Ad agencies switched their creative energy to producing slick thirty-second commercials rather than entertainment programs. A shift from broadcasting live shows to filming them opened up lucrative opportunities for reruns and foreign export. The total net revenue of the TV networks and their affil-

iated stations in 1947 was about $2 million; by 1957 it was nearly $1 billion. Advertisers spent $58 million on TV shows in 1949; ten years later the figure was almost $1.5 billion.

The staple of network radio, the comedy-variety show, was now produced with pictures. The first great national TV hit, *The Milton Berle Show*, followed this format when it premiered in 1948. Radio stars such as Jack Benny, Edgar Bergen, George Burns and Gracie Allen, and Eddie Cantor switched successfully to television. Boxing, wrestling, the roller derby, and other sporting events were also quite popular. For a brief time, original live drama flourished on writer-oriented shows such as *Goodyear Television Playhouse* and *Studio One*. In addition, early television featured an array of situation comedies with deep roots in radio and vaudeville.

Set largely among urban ethnic families, early shows like *I Remember Mama, The Goldbergs, The Life of Riley, Life with Luigi,* and *The Honeymooners* often featured working-class families struggling with the dilemmas posed by consumer society. Most plots turned around comic tensions created and resolved by consumption: contemplating home ownership,

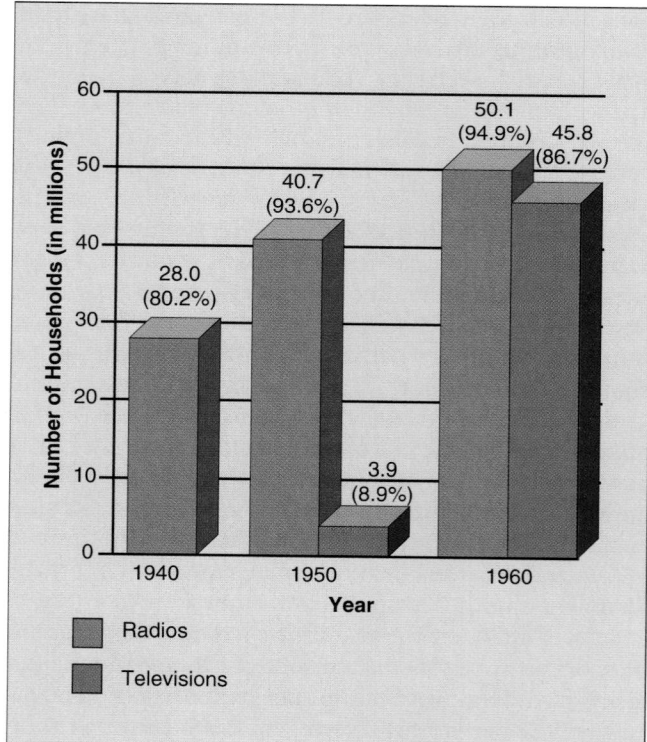

Radio and Television Ownership, 1940–1960
By 1960 *nearly 90 percent of American households owned at least one television set, as TV replaced radio as the nation's dominant mass medium of entertainment. Radio ownership rose as well, but Americans increasingly listened to radio as an accompaniment to other activities, such as driving.*

A *Motorola television advertisement from* Woman's Home Companion, 1951. *Manufacturers designed* TV *sets as living room furniture and emphasized their role in fostering family togetherness.*

going out on the town, moving to the suburbs, buying on credit, purchasing a new car. Generational discord and the loss of ethnic identity were also common themes. To some degree, these early shows mirrored and spoke to the real dilemmas facing families that had survived the Great Depression and the Second World War and were now finding their place in a prosperous consumer culture.

By the late 1950s all the urban ethnic comedy shows were off the air. A new breed of situation comedies presented non-ethnic white, affluent, and insular suburban middle-class families. Shows like *Father Knows Best, Leave It to Beaver, The Adventures of Ozzie and Harriet,* and *The Donna Reed Show* epitomized the ideal suburban American family of the day. Their plots focused on genial crises, usually brought on by children's mischief and resolved by kindly fathers. In retrospect, what is most striking about these shows is what is absent—politics, social issues, cities, white ethnic groups, African Americans, and Latinos were virtually unrepresented.

Television cut deeply into the filmgoing habits of Americans. The audience for movies began a steep decline from the high point of 1948. Hollywood tried desperately to compete with its new rival by pushing spectacular new techniques such as Cinerama, CinemaScope, and 3-D. By the mid-1950s, studios had begun to sell off their valuable backlog of films to the networks; old movies thus became a staple of television programming. Many TV shows were produced on the same Hollywood back lots that had churned out "B" pictures in the 1930s and 1940s. Two of the most popular genres of television in these years were old movie standbys:

Westerns (*Gunsmoke, Cheyenne, The Rifleman*) and crime dramas (*Dragnet, Highway Patrol, The Untouchables*).

Television also demonstrated a unique ability to create overnight fads and crazes across the nation. Elvis Presley's 1956 appearances on several network television variety shows, including those hosted by Milton Berle and Ed Sullivan, catapulted him from regional success to international stardom. Successful television advertising campaigns made household names out of previously obscure products. A memorable example of TV's influence came in 1955 when Walt Disney produced a series of three one-hour shows on the life of frontier legend Davy Crockett. The tremendous success of the series instantly created a $300 million industry of Davy Crockett shirts, dolls, toys, and coonskin caps.

Television and Politics

Prime-time entertainment shows carefully avoided any references to the political issues of the day. Network executives bowed to the conformist climate created by the domestic cold war. Any hint of political controversy could scare off sponsors, who were extremely sensitive to public protest. Anticommunist crusaders set themselves up as private watchdogs, warning of alleged subversive influence in the broadcasting industry. In 1950 one such group published *Red Channels* (see Chapter 26), a book branding 151 of the most well-known writers, directors, and actors in radio and television as communists or communist dupes. Television executives responded by effectively blacklisting many talented individuals.

As in Hollywood, the cold war chill severely restricted the range of political discussion on television. Any honest treatment of the conflicts in American society threatened the consensus mentality at the heart of the television business. Even public affairs and documentary programs were largely devoid of substantial political debate. An important exception was Edward R. Murrow's *See It Now* on CBS—but that show was off the air by 1955. Television news did not come into its own until 1963, with the beginning of half-hour nightly network newscasts. Only then did television's extraordinary power to rivet the nation's attention during a crisis become clear.

Still, some of the ways that TV would alter the nation's political life emerged in the 1950s. Television made Democratic senator Estes Kefauver of Tennessee a national political figure through live coverage of his 1951 Senate investigation into organized crime. It also contributed to the political downfall of Senator Joseph McCarthy in 1954 by showing his cruel bullying tactics during Senate hearings into alleged subversive influence in the army. In 1952, Republican vice-presidential candidate Richard M. Nixon effectively used an emotional, direct television appeal to voters—the "Checkers" speech—to counter charges of corruption (see Chapter 26).

The 1952 election also brought the first use of TV political advertising for presidential candidates. The Republican Party hired a high-powered ad agency, Batten, Barton, Durstine & Osborn, to create a series of short, sophisticated advertisements touting Dwight D. Eisenhower. The Democrats were content to buy a few half-hour blocks of TV time for long speeches by their nominee, Adlai Stevenson. The BBD&O campaign saturated TV with twenty-second Eisenhower spots for two weeks before election day. Ever since then, television image making has been the single most important element in American electoral politics.

Culture Critics

From both the left and the right, an assortment of writers expressed anger, fear, and plain disgust with the power of American mass culture. It would, they feared, overwhelm traditional standards of beauty, truth, and quality. Indeed, the urge to denounce the mass media for degrading the quality of American life tended to unite radical and conservative critics. Thus Marxist writer Dwight Macdonald sounded an old conservative warning when he described mass culture as "a parasite, a cancerous growth on High Culture." Society's most urgent problem, Macdonald claimed, was a "a tepid, flaccid Middlebrow Culture that threatens to engulf everything in its spreading ooze."

Critics of mass culture argued that the audiences for the mass media were atomized, anonymous, and detached. The media themselves had become omnipotent, capable of manipulating the attitudes and behavior of the isolated individuals in the mass. These critics undoubtedly overestimated the power of the media. They ignored the preponderance of research suggesting that most people watched and responded to mass media in family, peer group, and other social settings. The critics also missed the genuine vitality and creative brilliance to be found within mass culture: African American music; the films of Nicholas Ray, Elia Kazan, and Howard Hawks; the experimental television of Ernie Kovacs; the satire of *Mad* magazine.

Many of these critics achieved great popularity themselves, suggesting that the public was deeply ambivalent about mass culture. One of the best-selling authors of the day was Vance Packard, whose 1957 exposé *The Hidden Persuaders* showed how advertisers exploited motivational research into the irrational side of human behavior. Paul Goodman won a wide audience for his *Growing Up Absurd* (1960), which charged that America made it difficult for young

Jack Kerouac, founding voice of the Beat literary movement, in front of a neon lit bar, ca. 1950. Kerouac's public readings, often to the accompaniment of live jazz music, created a performance atmosphere underlining the connections between his writing style and the rhythms and sensibility of contemporary jazz musicians.

people to find meaningful work, sexual fulfillment, or a true sense of community. Goodman was only one of the thinkers at the end of the decade whose work pointed toward the coming youth rebellion in culture and politics.

The Beats

Some of the sharpest dissents from the cultural conformity of the day came from a group of writers known collectively as the Beats. Led by the novelist Jack Kerouac and the poet Allen Ginsberg, the Beats shared a distrust of the American virtues of progress, power, and material gain. Kerouac, born and raised in a working-class French Canadian family in Lowell, Massachusetts, coined the term "beat" in 1948. It meant for him a "weariness with all the forms of the modern industrial state"—conformity, militarism, blind faith in technological progress. The Beat sensibility celebrated spontaneity, friendship, jazz, open sexuality, drug use, and the outcasts of American society. Like Elvis Presley and other white rock 'n' rollers, the Beats also identified with black music and black culture. But for the Beats, it was the music, language, and dress of jazz musicians that caught their attention rather than the rhythm and blues that had attracted so many white teenagers.

Kerouac championed what he called the "spontaneous prose" style of writing—"first thought, best thought"—and he filled scores of notebooks with his observations, poems, and accounts of his friends' lives. These notebooks provided the basis for his published works. His novel *On the Road* became the Beat manifesto. Originally written in 1951, the novel was not published until 1957. It chronicled the tumultuous adventures of Kerouac's circle of friends as they traveled by car back and forth across America. The main character, Dean Moriarty, became a potent symbol of freedom and rebellion, "mad to live, mad to talk, mad to be saved, desirous of everything at the same time." Many readers mistook Dean for Kerouac, a sensitive and complex artist. The instant celebrity brought by the book exacerbated the alcoholism that drove Kerouac to an early death at age forty-seven in 1969.

Allen Ginsberg had grown up in New Jersey in an immigrant Jewish family. His father was a poet and teacher, and his mother had a history of mental problems. After being expelled from Columbia University, Ginsberg grew close to Kerouac and another writer, William Burroughs. At a 1955 poetry reading in San Francisco, Ginsberg introduced his epic poem *Howl* to a wildly enthusiastic audience:

> I saw the best minds of my generation destroyed
> by madness, starving hysterical naked,
> dragging themselves through the negro streets at dawn
> looking for an angry fix,
> angelheaded hipsters burning for the ancient heavenly
>   connection
> to the starry dynamo in the machinery of night.

Howl was published in 1956 and was quickly confiscated by police as "obscene and indecent." A highly publicized trial led to a landmark legal decision that the poem was literature, not pornography. *Howl* became one of the best-selling poetry books in the history of publishing, and it established Ginsberg as an important new voice in American literature.

Beat writers received a largely antagonistic, even virulent reception from the literary establishment. But millions of young Americans read their work and became intrigued by their alternative visions. The mass media soon managed to trivialize the Beats. A San Francisco journalist coined the term "beatnik," and by the late 1950s it had become associated with affected men and women dressed in black, wearing sunglasses and berets, and acting rebellious and alienated. *Life* did a highly negative photo portrayal of beatniks, hiring models for the spread. On television, *The Many Loves of Dobie Gillis* even featured a comic beatnik character, Maynard G. Krebs. But Beat writers like Kerouac, Ginsberg, Burroughs, Diane DiPrima, Gary Snyder, LeRoi Jones, and others continued to produce serious work that challenged America's official culture. They foreshadowed the mass youth rebellion and counterculture to come in the 1960s.

THE COLD WAR CONTINUED

Eisenhower's experience in foreign affairs had been one of his most attractive assets as a presidential candidate. His success as supreme commander of the Allied forces in World War II owed as much to diplomatic skill as to military prowess. As president, Eisenhower sustained the anticommunist rhetoric of cold war diplomacy, and his administration persuaded Americans to accept the cold war stalemate as a more or less permanent fact. Eisenhower developed new strategies for containment and for the support of United States power abroad, including a greater reliance on nuclear weapons and the aggressive use of the Central Intelligence Agency (CIA) for covert action. Yet Eisenhower also resolved to do everything he could to forestall an all-out nuclear conflict. He recognized the limits of raw military power. He accepted a less than victorious end to the Korean War, and he avoided a full military involvement in Indochina. Ironically, Eisenhower's promotion of high-tech strategic weaponry fostered development of a military-industrial complex. By the time he left office in 1961, he felt compelled to warn the nation of the growing dangers posed by burgeoning military spending.

The "New Look" in Foreign Affairs

Although Eisenhower recognized that the United States was engaged in a long-term struggle with the Soviet Union, he feared that permanent mobilization for the cold war might overburden the American economy and result in a "garrison state." He therefore pursued a high-tech, capital intensive defense policy that emphasized America's qualitative advantage in strategic weaponry. The "new look" in foreign affairs promised to reduce the military budget by exploiting America's atomic and air superiority.

The emphasis on massive retaliation, the administration claimed, would also make possible cuts in the military budget. As Secretary of Defense Charles Wilson said, the goal was to "get more bang for the buck." Eisenhower largely succeeded in stabilizing the defense budget. Between 1954 and 1961 absolute spending rose only $800 million, from $46.6 billion to $47.4 billion. Military spending as an overall percentage of the federal budget fell from 66 percent to 49 percent during his two terms. Much of this saving was gained through the increased reliance on nuclear weapons and long-range delivery systems, which were relatively less expensive than conventional forces.

Secretary of State John Foster Dulles emerged as a key architect of American policy, giving shape to Eisenhower's views. Raised a devout Presbyterian and trained as a lawyer, Dulles had been involved in diplomatic affairs since World War I. He brought a strong sense of righteousness to his job, an almost missionary belief in America's responsibility to preserve the "free world" from godless, immoral communism. Dulles articulated a more assertive policy toward the communist threat by calling not simply for containment but for a "rollback." The key would be

President Dwight D. Eisenhower (left), meeting with John Foster Dulles, who served as secretary of state until his death in 1959.

greater reliance on America's nuclear superiority. This policy appealed to Republicans, who had been frustrated by the restriction of United Nations forces to conventional arms during the Korean War.

The "new look" conflicted, however, with Eisenhower's own sense of caution, especially during moments of crisis in eastern Europe and potential military confrontation with the Soviet Union. The limits of a policy based on nuclear strategy became painfully clear when American leaders faced tense situations that offered no clear way to intervene without provoking full-scale war.

When East Berliners rebelled against the Soviets in 1953, cold war hard-liners thought they saw the long awaited opportunity for rollback. But precisely how could the United States respond? Public bitterness over the Korean conflict merged with Eisenhower's sense of restraint and in the end, apart from angry denunciations, the United States did nothing to prevent the Soviets from crushing the rebellion. U.S. leaders faced the same dilemma on a grander scale when Hungarians revolted against their Soviet-dominated communist rulers in 1956, staging a general strike and taking over the streets and facto-

ries in Budapest and other cities. The United States opened its gates to thousands of Hungarian refugees, but despite urgent requests, it refused to intervene when Soviet tanks and troops crushed the revolt. Eisenhower recognized that the Soviets would defend their own borders, and all of eastern Europe as well, by all-out military force if necessary.

The death of Josef Stalin in 1953 and the worldwide condemnation of his crimes, revealed by his successor, Nikita Khrushchev, in 1956, gave Eisenhower fresh hope for a new spirit of peaceful coexistence between the two superpowers. Khrushchev, in a gesture of goodwill, withdrew Soviet troops from Austria. The first real rollback had been achieved by negotiations and a spirit of common hope, not threats or force. In 1958 Khrushchev, probing American intentions and hoping to redirect the Soviet economy toward the production of more consumer goods, unilaterally suspended nuclear testing. Tensions rose again that year when the Soviet leader, threatened by a revived West Germany, demanded that the Western Allies leave Berlin within six months. But after Khrushchev made a twelve-day trip to America in 1959, he suspended the deadline and relations warmed. Khrushchev visited an Iowa farm, went sightseeing in Hollywood, and spent time with Eisenhower at Camp David, the presidential retreat in Maryland.

The two leaders achieved nothing concrete, but with summit diplomacy seeming to offer at least a psychological thaw in the cold war, the press began referring to "the spirit of Camp David." In early 1960 Khrushchev called for another summit in Paris, to discuss German reunification and nuclear disarmament. Eisenhower, meanwhile, planned his own friendship tour of the Soviet Union. But in May 1960 the Soviets shot down an American U-2 spy plane gathering intelligence on Soviet military installations. A deeply embarrassed Eisenhower at first denied the existence of U-2 flights, but the Soviets produced the pilot, Francis Gary Powers, who readily confessed. The summit collapsed when Eisenhower refused Khrushchev's demands for an apology and an end to the spy flights.

The U-2 incident demonstrated the limits of personal diplomacy in resolving the deep structural rivalry between the superpowers. Although Eisenhower knew from earlier U-2 flights that the Soviet Union had undertaken no major military buildup, he had agreed with Congress to a hike of $2.5 billion in military spending in 1957. The launching of the first space-orbiting satellite by the Soviets in October of that year provided a new incentive. Sputnik demonstrated Soviet technological prowess and upset Americans' precarious sense of security. Urged to sponsor the building of "fallout shelters" for the entire population in case of nuclear attack, Eisenhower rejected what he called "the negative stuff." He supported instead a program of more federal funds for science education, as provided in the National Defense Education Act of 1958. Yet, in Congress a bipartisan majority voted to increase the military budget by another $8 billion in 1958, thereby accelerating the arms race and expanding the defense sector of the economy.

Covert Action

Eisenhower combined the overt threat of massive retaliation in his "new look" approach to foreign affairs with a heavy reliance on covert interventions by the Central Intelligence Agency (CIA). He had been an enthusiastic supporter of covert operations during World War II, and during his presidency CIA-sponsored covert paramilitary operations became a key facet of American foreign policy. With the American public wary of direct U.S. military interventions, the CIA promised a cheap, quick, and quiet way to depose hostile or unstable regimes. Eisenhower increasingly relied on the CIA to destabilize emerging third world governments deemed too radical or

too friendly with the Soviets. Covert actions also proved vital for propping up more conservative regimes under siege by indigenous revolutionaries. These actions were particularly effective in the former colonial areas of Asia, Africa, and the Caribbean.

For CIA director, Eisenhower named Allen Dulles, brother of the secretary of state and a former leader in the CIA's World War II precursor, the Office of Strategic Services. The CIA's mandate was to collect and analyze information, but it did much more under Dulles's command. Thousands of covert agents stationed all over the world carried out a wide range of political activities. Some agents arranged large, secret financial payments to friendly political parties, such as the conservative Christian Democrats in Italy and Latin America or foreign trade unions opposed to socialist policies. Other agents secretly funded and guided intellectuals in, for instance, the Congress of Cultural Freedom, a prestigious group of liberal writers in Europe and the United States.

While the United States moderated its stance toward the Soviet Union and its eastern European satellites, it hardened its policies in the third world. The need for anticommunist tactics short of all-out military conflict pushed the Eisenhower administration to develop new means of fighting the cold war. The premise rested on encouraging confusion or rivalry within the communist sphere and on destabilizing or destroying anticapitalist movements around the world.

The Soviet Union tried to win influence in Africa, Asia, and Latin America by appealing to a shared "anti-imperialism" and by offering modest amounts of foreign aid. In most cases, communists played only small roles in third world independence movements. But the issue of race and the popular desire to recover national resources from foreign investors inflamed already widespread anti-European and anti-American feelings. When new nations or familiar allies threatened to interfere with U.S. regional security arrangements, or to expropriate the property of American businesses, the Eisenhower administration turned to covert action and military intervention.

Intervening around the World

The Central Intelligence Agency produced a swift, major victory in Iran in 1953. The country's popular prime minister, Mohammed Mossadegh, had nationalized Britain's Anglo-Iranian Oil Company, and the State Department worried that this might set a precedent throughout the oil-rich Middle East. Kermit Roosevelt, CIA chief in Iran, organized and financed an opposition to Mossadegh within the Iranian army and on the streets of Teheran. This CIA-led move-

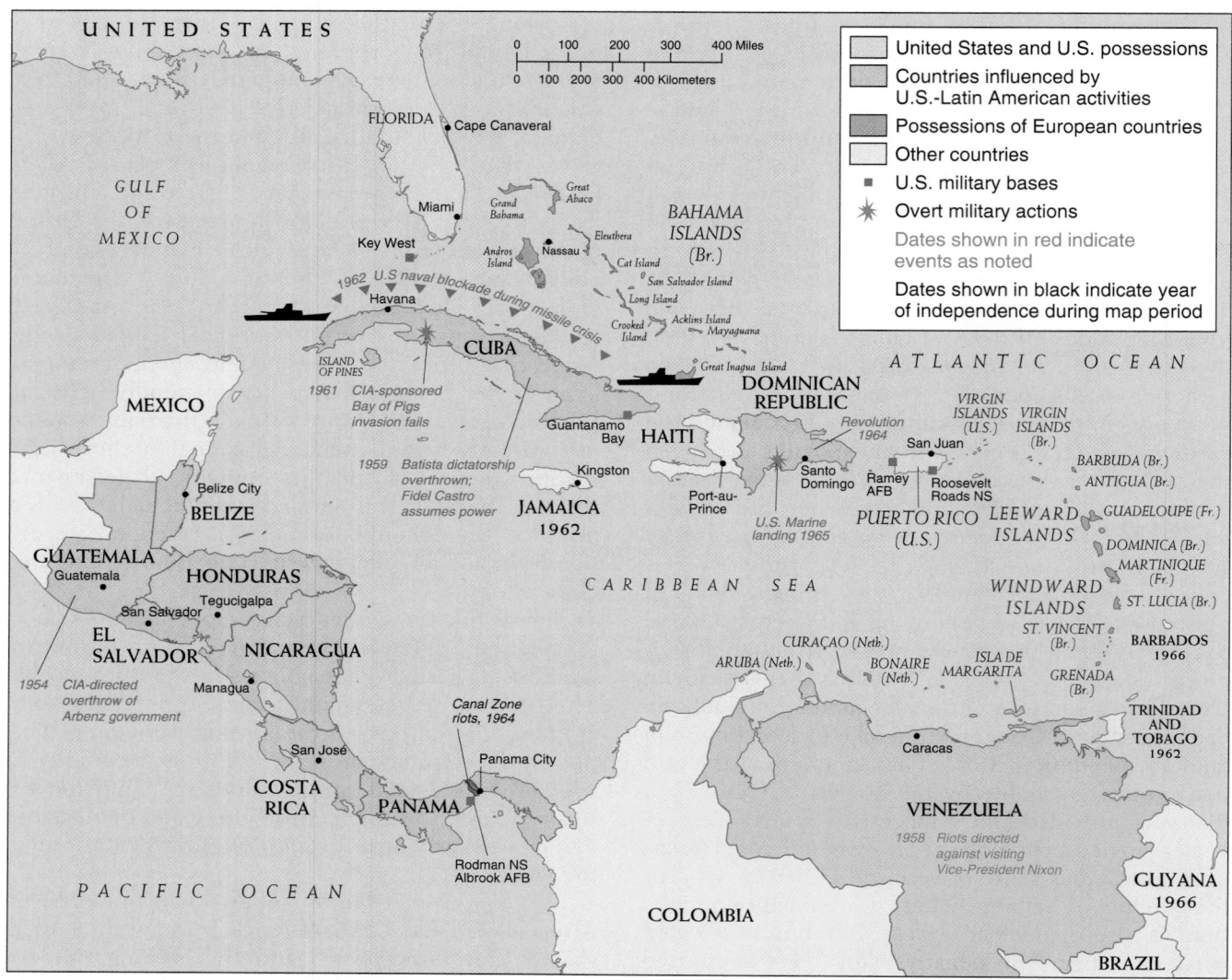

The U.S. in the Caribbean, 1948–1966   *U.S. military intervention and economic presence grew steadily in the Caribbean following World War II. After 1960, opposition to the Cuban Revolution dominated U.S. Caribbean policies.*

ment forced Mossadegh out of office and replaced him with Riza Shah Pahlavi. The shah proved his loyalty to his American sponsors by renegotiating oil contracts so as to assure American companies 40 percent of Iran's oil concessions.

The rivalry between Israel and its Arab neighbors complicated U.S. policy in the rest of the Middle East. The Arab countries launched an all-out attack on Israel in 1948 immediately after the United States and the Soviet Union had recognized its independence. Israel repulsed the attack, drove thousands of Palestinians from their homes, occupied territory that hundreds of thousands of others had fearfully fled, and seized lands far in excess of the terms of a United Nations-sponsored armistice of 1949. The Arab states refused to recognize Israel's right to exist

and subjected it to a damaging economic boycott. Meanwhile, hundreds of thousands of Palestinians languished in refugee camps. Eisenhower believed that Truman had perhaps been too hasty in encouraging the Israelis. Yet most Americans supported the new Jewish state as a refuge for a people who had suffered so much persecution.

Israel stood as a reliable U.S. ally in an unstable region. Arab nationalism continued to vex American policy makers, culminating in the Suez crisis of 1956. Egyptian president Gamal Abdel Nasser, a leading voice of Arab nationalism, looked for American and British economic aid. He had long dreamed of building the Aswan High Dam on the Nile to create more arable land and provide cheap electric power. When negotiations broke down, Nasser announced he would nationalize the strategically sensitive Suez Canal, and he turned to the Soviet Union for aid. Eisenhower refused European appeals for U.S. help in seizing the Suez Canal and returning it to the British. When British, French, and Israeli forces attacked Egypt in October 1956, the United States sponsored a UN resolution calling for a cease-fire and a withdrawal of foreign forces. Yielding to this pressure and to Soviet threats of intervention, the British and French withdrew, and eventually so did the Israelis. Eisenhower had won a major diplomatic battle through patience and pressure, but he did not succeed in bringing lasting peace to the troubled region.

The most publicized CIA intervention of the Eisenhower years took place in Guatemala, where a fragile democracy had taken root in 1944. President Jácobo Arbenz Guzmán, elected in 1950, aggressively pursued land reform and encouraged the formation of trade unions. At the time, 2 percent of the Guatemalan population owned 72 percent of all farmland. Arbenz also challenged the long-standing dominance of the American-based United Fruit Company by threatening to expropriate hundreds of thousands of acres that United Fruit was not cultivating. The company had powerful friends in the administration (CIA director Dulles had sat on its board of trustees), and it began intensive lobbying for U.S. intervention. United Fruit linked the land reform program to the evils of international communism, and the CIA spent $7 million training antigovernment dissidents based in Honduras.

The American navy stopped ships bound for Guatemala and seized their cargo, and on June 14, 1954, a U.S.-sponsored military invasion began. Guatemalan citizens resisted by seizing United Fruit buildings, but U.S. Air Force bombing saved the invasion effort. Guatemalans appealed in vain to the United Nations for help. Meanwhile, President Eisenhower publicly denied any knowledge of CIA activities. The newly appointed military leader, Carlos Castillo Armas, flew to the Guatemalan capital in a U.S. embassy plane. Widespread terror followed, unions were outlawed, and thousands arrested. United Fruit circulated photos of Guatemalans murdered by the invaders, labeling them "victims of communism." In 1957 Castillo Armas was assassinated, and a decades-long civil war ensued between military factions and peasant guerrillas.

American intervention in Guatemala increased suspicion of and resentment against American foreign policy throughout Central and Latin America. Vice President Nixon declared that the new Guatemalan government had earned "the overwhelming support of the Guatemalan people." But in 1958, while making a "goodwill" tour of Latin America, Nixon was stoned by angry mobs in Caracas, Venezuela, suggesting that U.S. actions in the region had triggered an anti-American backlash.

In Indochina, the United States provided France with massive military aid and CIA cooperation in its desperate struggle to maintain its colonial empire. From 1950 to 1954 the United States poured $2.6 billion (about three-quarters of the total French costs) into the fight against the nationalist Vietminh movement, led by communist Ho Chi Minh. When Vietminh forces surrounded 25,000 French troops at Dien Bien Phu in March 1954, France pleaded with the United States to intervene directly. Secretary of State Dulles and Vice President Nixon, among others, recommended the use of tactical nuclear weapons and a commitment of ground troops. But Eisenhower, recalling the difficulties of the Korean conflict, rejected this call. "I can conceive of no greater tragedy," he said, "than for the United States to become engaged in all-out war in Indochina."

At the same time, Eisenhower feared that the loss of one country to communism would inevitably lead to the loss of others. As he put it, "You have a row of dominoes set up, and you knock over the first one and what will happen to the last one is the certainty that it will go over quickly." According to this so-called domino theory, the "loss" of Vietnam would threaten other Southeast Asian nations, such as Laos, Thailand, the Philippines, and perhaps even India and Australia. After the French surrender at Dien Ben Phu, a conference in Geneva established a cease-fire and a temporary division of Vietnam along the 17th parallel into northern and southern sectors. The Geneva accord called for reunification and national elections in 1956. But the United States, although it had attended the conference along with the Soviet Union and China, refused to sign the accord. In response to the Vietnam situation the Eisenhower administration created the Southeast Asia Treaty Organization (SEATO) in 1954. This NATO-like security pact included the United States, Great Britain, France, Australia, New Zealand, Thailand, the Philippines, and Pakistan, and was dominated by the United States.

South Vietnamese leader Ngo Dinh Diem, a former Japanese collaborator and a Catholic in a country that was 90 percent Buddhist, quickly alienated many peasants with his corruption and repressive policies. American economic and military aid, along with continuing covert CIA activity, was crucial in keeping the increasingly isolated Diem in power. Both Diem and Eisenhower refused to permit the 1956 elections stipulated in Geneva, because they knew popular hero Ho Chi Minh would easily win. By 1959 Diem's harsh and unpopular government in

Venezuelan soldiers (right) tried to disperse rioters who attacked Vice President Richard M. Nixon's car in Caracas during his 1958 "goodwill tour." Demonstrations such as these revealed a reservoir of resentment in Latin America against the interventionist policies of the United States in the region.

Saigon faced a civil war; thousands of peasants had joined guerrilla forces determined to drive him out. Eisenhower's commitment of military advisers and economic aid to South Vietnam, based on cold war assumptions, laid the foundation for the Vietnam War of the 1960s.

Ike's Warning: The Military-Industrial Complex

Throughout the 1950s small numbers of peace advocates in the United States had pointed to the ultimate illogic of the "new look" in foreign policy. The increasing reliance on nuclear weapons, they argued, did not strengthen national security but rather threatened the entire planet with extinction. They demonstrated at military camps, atomic test sites, and missile-launching ranges, often getting arrested to make their point. Reports of radioactive fallout around the world rallied a larger group of scientists and prominent intellectuals against further nuclear testing. In Europe, a Ban the Bomb movement gained a wide following; an American counterpart, the National Committee for a Sane Nuclear Policy (SANE), claimed 25,000 members by 1958. The

Women's International League for Peace and Freedom collected petitions calling for a test ban. The Student Peace Union, founded in 1959, established units on many campuses. Small but well-publicized actions against civil defense drills took place in several big cities: protesters marched on the streets rather than entering bomb shelters.

As he neared retirement, President Eisenhower came to share some of the protesters' anxiety and doubts about the arms race. Ironically, Eisenhower found it difficult to restrain the system he helped create. He chose to devote his Farewell Address, delivered in January 1961, to warning the nation about the dangers of what he termed "the military-industrial complex." Its total influence, he cautioned, "economic, political, even spiritual—is felt in every city, every statehouse, every office of the federal government." The conjunction of a large military establishment and a large arms industry, Eisenhower noted, was new in American history. "The potential for the disastrous rise of misplaced power exists and will persist. We must never let the weight of this combination endanger our liberties or democratic processes."

The old soldier understood perhaps better than most the dangers of raw military force. Eisenhower's public posture of restraint and caution in foreign affairs accompanied an enormous expansion of American economic, diplomatic, and military strength. Yet the Eisenhower years also demonstrated the limits of power and intervention in a world that did not always conform to the simple dualistic assumptions of cold war ideology.

JOHN F. KENNEDY AND THE NEW FRONTIER

No one could have resembled Dwight Eisenhower less in personality, temperament, and public image than John Fitzgerald Kennedy. The handsome son of a prominent, wealthy Irish American diplomat, husband of a fashionable, trend-setting heiress, forty-two-year-old JFK embodied youth, excitement, and sophistication. As only the second Catholic candidate for president—the first was Al Smith in 1928—Kennedy ran under the banner of the New Frontier. His liberalism inspired idealism and hope in millions of young people at home and abroad. In foreign affairs, Kennedy generally followed, and in some respects deepened, the cold war precepts that dominated postwar policy making. But by the time of his assassination in 1963, he may have been veering away from the hard-line anticommunist ideology he had earlier embraced. What a second term might have brought remains debatable, but his death ended a unique moment in American public life.

The Election of 1960

John F. Kennedy's political career began in Massachusetts, which elected him to the House in 1946 and then the Senate in 1952. Kennedy won the Democratic nomination after a bruising series of primaries in which he defeated party stalwarts Hubert Humphrey of Minnesota and Lyndon B. Johnson of Texas. Unlike Humphrey and Johnson, Kennedy had not been part of the powerful group of insiders who dominated the Senate. But he drew strength and financial support from a loyal coterie of friends and family, including his father, Joseph P. Kennedy, and his younger brother Robert. Vice

President Richard M. Nixon, the Republican nominee, had faithfully served the Eisenhower administration for eight years, and was far better known than his younger opponent. The Kennedy campaign stressed its candidate's youth and his image as a war hero. During his World War II tour of duty in the Pacific, Kennedy had bravely rescued one of his crew after their PT boat had been sunk. Kennedy's supporters also pointed to his intellectual ability. JFK had won the Pulitzer Prize in 1957 for his book *Profiles in Courage,* which in fact had been written largely by aides.

The election featured the first televised presidential debates. Political analysts have long argued over the impact of these four encounters, but agree that they moved television to the center of presidential politics, making image and appearance more critical than ever. Nixon appeared nervous and the camera made him look unshaven. Kennedy, in contrast, benefited from a confident manner and telegenic good looks. Both candidates emphasized foreign policy. Nixon defended the Republican record and stressed his own maturity and experience. Kennedy hammered away at the alleged "missile gap" with the Soviet Union and promised more vigorous executive leadership. He also countered the anti-Catholic prejudice of evangelical Protestants with a promise to keep church and state separate.

Kennedy squeaked to victory in the closest election since 1884. He won by a little more than 100,000 votes out of nearly 69 million cast. He ran

Studio television set for one of the four Kennedy-Nixon presidential debates, October 1960. Howard K. Smith of CBS News was the moderator. Eighty-five million viewers watched at least one of the debates, which both reflected and increased the power of television in the electoral process.

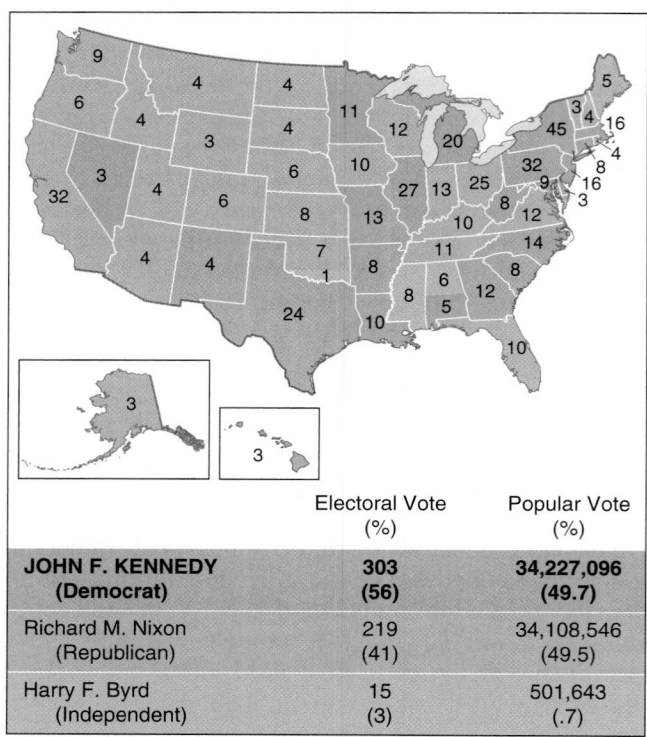

	Electoral Vote (%)	Popular Vote (%)
JOHN F. KENNEDY (Democrat)	**303 (56)**	**34,227,096 (49.7)**
Richard M. Nixon (Republican)	219 (41)	34,108,546 (49.5)
Harry F. Byrd (Independent)	15 (3)	501,643 (.7)

The Election of 1960   *Kennedy's popular vote margin over Nixon was only a little over 100,000, making this one of the closest elections in American history.*

poorly in the South, but won the Catholic vote so overwhelmingly that he carried most of the Northeast and Midwest. Though the margin of victory was tiny, Kennedy was a glorious winner. Surrounding himself with prestigious Ivy League academics, Hollywood movie stars, and talented artists and writers, he imbued the presidency with an aura of celebrity. The inauguration brought out a bevy of poets, musicians, and fashionably dressed politicians from around the world. The new administration promised to be exciting and stylish, a modern-day Camelot peopled by heroic young men and beautiful women. The new president's ringing inaugural address ("Ask not what your country can do for you—ask what you can do for your country") had special resonance for a whole generation of young Americans.

New Frontier Liberalism

Kennedy promised to revive the long-stalled liberal domestic agenda. His New Frontier advocated such liberal programs as a higher minimum wage, greater federal aid for education, increased Social Security benefits, medical care for the elderly, support for public housing, and various antipoverty measures. Yet the thin margin of his victory and the stubborn opposition of conservative southern Democrats in Congress made it difficult to achieve these goals. Congress refused, for

example, to enact the administration's attempt to extend Social Security and unemployment benefits to millions of uncovered workers. Congress also failed to enact administration proposals for aid to public schools, mass-transit subsidies, and medical insurance for retired workers over sixty-five.

There were a few New Frontier victories. Congress did approve a modest increase in the minimum wage (to $1.25 per hour), agreed to a less ambitious improvement in Social Security, and appropriated $5 billion for public housing. It also passed the Manpower Retraining Act, appropriating $435 million to train the unemployed. The Area Redevelopment Act provided federal funds for rural, depressed Appalachia. The Higher Education Act of 1963 offered aid to colleges for constructing buildings and upgrading libraries. One of the best-publicized New Frontier programs was the Peace Corps, in which thousands of mostly young men and women traveled overseas for two-year stints in underdeveloped countries. There they provided technical and educational assistance in setting up health care programs and improving agricultural efficiency. As a force for change, the Peace Corps produced modest results, but it epitomized Kennedy's promise to provide opportunities for service for a new generation of idealistic young people.

Kennedy helped revive the issue of women's rights with his Presidential Commission on the Status of Women, led by Eleanor Roosevelt. The commission's 1963 report was the most comprehensive study of women's lives ever produced by the federal government. It documented the ongoing discrimination faced by American women in the workplace and in the legal system, as well as the inadequacy of social services such as day care. It called for federally supported day-care programs, continuing education programs for women, and an end to sex bias in Social Security and unemployment benefits. The commission also insisted that more women be appointed to policy-making positions in government. One concrete legislative result, the Equal Pay Act of 1963, made it illegal for employers to pay men and women different wages for the same job. The law did not do much to improve women's economic status, since most working women were employed in job categories, such as secretary or clerk, that included no men. But the issue of economic inequality had at least been put on the public agenda. President Kennedy also directed executive agencies to prohibit sex discrimination in hiring and promotion. The work of the commission contributed to a new generation of women's rights activism.

Taking a more aggressive stance on stimulating economic growth and creating new jobs than had Eisenhower, Kennedy relied heavily on Walter Heller, chair of the Council of Economic Advisers (CEA).

Heller emphasized the goal of full employment, which he believed could be attained through deficit spending, encouragement of economic growth, and targeted tax cuts. The administration thus pushed lower business taxes through Congress, even at the cost of a higher federal deficit. The Revenue Act of 1962 encouraged new investment and plant renovation by easing tax depreciation schedules for business. Kennedy also gained approval for lower U.S. tariffs as a way to increase foreign trade. To help keep inflation down, he intervened in the steel industry in 1961 and 1962, pressuring labor to keep its wage demands low and management to curb price increases.

Kennedy also increased the federal commitment to a wholly new realm of government spending: the space program. The National Aeronautics and Space Administration (NASA) had been established under Eisenhower in response to the Soviet success with Sputnik. In 1961, driven by the cold war motivation of beating the Soviets to the moon and avoiding "another Sputnik," Kennedy won approval for a greatly expanded space program. He announced the goal of landing an American on the moon by the end of the decade. NASA eventually spent $33 billion before reaching this objective in 1969. This program of manned space flight—the Apollo missions—appealed to the public, acquiring a science fiction aura. In space, if not on earth, the New Frontier might actually be reached.

Overall, Kennedy's most long-lasting achievement as president may have been his strengthening of the executive branch itself. He insisted on direct presidential control of details that Eisenhower had left to advisers and appointees. Moreover, under Kennedy the White House staff assumed many of the decision-making and advisory functions previously held by cabinet members. This arrangement increased Kennedy's authority, since these appointees, unlike cabinet secretaries, escaped congressional oversight and confirmation proceedings. White House aides also lacked an independent constituency; their power and authority derived solely from their ties to the president. Kennedy's aides, "the best and the brightest," as he called them, dominated policy making. With men such as McGeorge Bundy directing foreign affairs and Theodore Sorensen coordinating domestic issues, Kennedy began a pattern whereby American presidents increasingly operated through small groups of fiercely loyal aides, often acting in secret.

Kennedy and the Cold War

During Kennedy's three years in office his approach to foreign policy shifted from aggressive containment to efforts at easing U.S.-Soviet tensions. Certainly when he first entered office, Kennedy and his chief aides considered it their main task to confront the communist threat. In his first State of the Union Address, in January 1961, Kennedy told Congress that America must seize the initiative in the cold war. The nation must "move outside the home fortress, and . . . challenge the enemy in fields of our own choosing." To head the State Department Kennedy chose Dean Rusk, a conservative former assistant to Truman's secretary of state, Dean Acheson. Secretary of Defense Robert McNamara, a Republican and Ford Motor Company executive, was determined to streamline military procedures and weapons buying. McNamara typified the technical, cost-efficient, superrational approach to policy making. Allen Dulles, Eisenhower's CIA director, remained at his post. These and other officials believed with Kennedy that Eisenhower had timidly accepted stalemate when the cold war could have been won.

Kennedy built up American nuclear and conventional weapons systems. Between 1960 and 1962 defense appropriations increased by nearly a third, from $43 billion to $56 billion. JFK expanded Eisenhower's policy of covert operations, deploying the Army's elite Special Forces as a supplement to CIA covert operations in counterinsurgency battles against third world guerrillas. These soldiers, fighting under the direct orders of the president, could provide "rapid response" to "brush-fire" conflicts where Soviet influence threatened American interests. The Special Forces, authorized by Kennedy to wear the green berets that gave them their unofficial name, reflected the president's desire as president to acquire greater flexibility, secrecy, and independence in the conduct of foreign policy.

The limits on the ability of covert action and the Green Berets to further American interests became

Astronaut John H. Glenn as he prepared for the first American manned space orbit of the earth. The space program of the early 1960s emphasized the technical training and courage of astronauts, consciously creating a set of public heroes as a way to ensure popular support and congressional funding.

apparent in Southeast Asia. In Laos, where the United States had ignored the 1954 Geneva agreement and installed a friendly military regime, the CIA-backed government could not defeat Soviet-backed Pathet Lao guerrillas. The president had to arrange with the Soviets to neutralize Laos. In neighboring Vietnam, the situation proved more difficult. When Communist Vietcong guerrillas launched a civil war in South Vietnam against the U.S.-supported government in Saigon, Kennedy began sending hundreds of Green Berets and other military advisers to support the rule of Ngo Dinh Diem. In May 1961, in response to North Vietnamese aid to the Vietcong, Kennedy ordered a covert action against Ho Chi Minh's government that included sabotage and intelligence gathering.

Kennedy's approach to Vietnam reflected an analysis of the situation in that country by two aides, General Maxwell Taylor and Walt Rostow, who saw it through purely cold war eyes. "The Communists are pursuing a clear and systematic strategy in Southeast Asia," Taylor and Rostow concluded, ignoring the inefficiency, corruption, and unpopularity of the Diem government. By 1963, with Diem's army unable to contain the Vietcong rebellion, Kennedy had sent nearly 16,000 support and combat troops to South Vietnam. By then, a wide spectrum of South Vietnamese society had joined the revolt against the hated Diem, including highly respected Buddhist monks and their students. Americans watched in horror as television news reports showed footage of Buddhists burning themselves to death on the streets of Saigon—the ultimate protest against Diem's repressive rule. American press and television also reported the mounting casualty lists of U.S. forces in Vietnam. The South Vietnamese army, bloated by U.S. aid and weakened by corruption, continued to disintegrate. In the fall of 1963, American military officers and CIA operatives stood aside with approval as a group of Vietnamese generals removed President Diem, killing him and his top advisers. It was the first of many coups that racked the South Vietnamese government over the next few years.

In Latin America, Kennedy looked for ways to forestall various revolutionary movements that were gaining ground. The erosion of peasant landholdings had accelerated rapidly after 1950. Huge expanses of fertile land long devoted to subsistence farming were converted to business-dominated agriculture that grew staple crops for export (bananas, coffee, sugar). Millions of impoverished peasants were forced to relocate to already overcrowded cities. In 1961 Kennedy unveiled the Alliance for Progress, a ten-year, $100 billion plan to spur economic development in Latin America. The United States committed $20 billion to the project, with the Latin nations responsible for the rest. The main goals included greater industrial growth and agricultural productivity, more equitable distribution of income, and improved health and housing.

Kennedy intended the program as a kind of Marshall Plan that would benefit the poor and middle classes of the continent. The alliance did help raise growth rates in Latin American economies. But the expansion in export crops and in consumption by the tiny upper class did little to aid the poor or encourage democracy. The United States hesitated to challenge the power of dictators and extreme conservatives who were staunch anticommunist allies. Thus the alliance soon degenerated into just another foreign aid program, incapable of generating genuine social change.

The Cuban Revolution and the Bay of Pigs

The direct impetus for the Alliance for Progress was the Cuban Revolution of 1959, which loomed over Latin America. The U.S. economic domination of Cuba that began with the Spanish American War (see Chapter 20) had continued through the 1950s. American-owned business controlled all of Cuba's oil production, 90 percent of its mines, and roughly half of its railroads and sugar and cattle industries. Havana, the island's capital, was an attractive tourist center for Americans, and U.S. crime syndicates shared control of the island's lucrative gambling, prostitution, and drug trade with dictator Fulgencio Batista. In the early 1950s a peasant-based revolutionary movement, led by Fidel Castro, began gaining strength in the rural districts and mountains outside Havana.

On New Year's Day 1959, after years of guerilla war, the rebels entered Havana and seized power amid great public rejoicing. For a brief time, Castro seemed a hero to many North Americans as well. The *New York Times* had conducted sympathetic interviews with Castro in 1958, while he was still fighting in Cuba's mountains. Many young people visited the island and returned with enthusiastic reports. Famous writers such as James Baldwin and Ernest Hemingway embraced Castro. The CIA and President Eisenhower, however, shared none of this exuberance. Castro's land reform program, involving the seizure of acreage from the tiny minority that controlled much of the fertile land, threatened to set an example for other Latin American countries. Although Castro had not joined the Cuban Communist Party, he turned to the Soviet Union after the United States withdrew economic aid. He began to sell sugar to the Soviets and soon nationalized American-owned oil companies and other enterprises. Eisenhower established an economic boycott of Cuba in 1960, then severed diplomatic relations.

Kennedy inherited from Eisenhower plans for a U.S. invasion of Cuba, including the secret arming and training of Cuban exiles. The CIA drafted the invasion plan, which was based on the assumption that a U.S.-led invasion would trigger a popular uprising of the Cuban people and bring down Castro. Kennedy went along with the plan, but at the last moment decided not to supply an Air Force cover for the operation. On April 17, 1961, a ragtag army of 1,400 counterrevolutionaries led by CIA operatives landed at the Bay of Pigs, on Cuba's south coast. Castro's efficient and loyal army easily subdued them. At the United Nations, Ambassador Adlai Stevenson, deceived by presidential aides, flatly denied any U.S. involvement, only to learn the truth later.

The debacle revealed that the CIA, blinded by cold war assumptions, had failed to understand the Cuban Revolution. There was no popular uprising against Castro. Instead, the invasion strengthened Castro's standing among the urban poor and peasants, already attracted by his programs of universal literacy and medical care. As Castro stifled internal opposition, many Cuban intellectuals and professionals fled to the United States. An embarrassed Kennedy reluctantly took the blame for the abortive invasion, and his administration was censured time and again by third world delegates to the United Nations. American liberals criticized Kennedy for plotting Castro's overthrow, while conservatives blamed him for not supporting the invasion. Despite the failure, Kennedy remained committed to getting rid of Castro and keeping up the economic boycott. The CIA continued to support anti-Castro operations and launched at least eight attempts to assassinate the Cuban leader.

The Missile Crisis

The aftermath of the Bay of Pigs led to the most serious confrontation of the cold war: the Cuban missile crisis of October 1962. Frightened by U.S. belligerency, Castro asked Soviet premier Khrushchev for military help. Khrushchev responded in the summer of 1962 by shipping to Cuba a large amount of sophisticated weaponry, including intermediate-range nuclear missiles. In early October U.S. reconnaissance planes found camouflaged missile silos dotting the island. Several Kennedy aides demanded an immediate bombing of Cuban bases, arguing that the missiles had decisively changed the strategic global advantage the United States had previously enjoyed. Other aides rejected this analysis, pointing out that American cities had been vulnerable to Soviet intercontinental ballistic missiles (ICBMs) since 1957.

A tense meeting of President John F. Kennedy (bending over table at right) and his Cabinet, October 29, 1962, in the midst of the Cuban missile crisis. The White House released a carefully selected series of such photos to convey the seriousness of the choices faced by the president and his advisers.

The president and his advisers pondered their options in a series of tense meetings. Secretary of Defense McNamara was probably closest to the truth when he asserted, "I don't believe it's primarily a military problem. It's primarily a domestic political problem." Kennedy's aggressive attempts to exploit Cuba in the 1960 election now came back to haunt him, as he worried that his critics would accuse him of weakness in failing to stand up to the Soviets. The disastrous Bay of Pigs affair still rankled. Even some prominent Democrats, including Senator J. William Fulbright, chair of the Senate Foreign Relations Committee, called for an invasion of Cuba.

Kennedy went on national television on October 22. He announced the discovery of the missile sites, demanded the removal of all missiles, and ordered a strict naval blockade of all offensive military equipment

Vice President Lyndon B. Johnson took the oath of office as president aboard Air Force One after the assassination of John F. Kennedy, November 22, 1963. Onlookers included the grief-stricken Jacqueline Kennedy (right) and Lady Bird Johnson (left). This haunting photo captured both the shock of Kennedy's assassination and the orderly succession of power that followed.

shipped to Cuba. He also requested an emergency meeting of the UN Security Council and promised that any missiles launched from Cuba would bring "a full retaliatory response upon the Soviet Union." For a tense week, the American public wondered if nuclear Armageddon was imminent. Eyeball to eyeball, the two superpowers waited for each other to blink. On October 26 and 27 Khrushchev yielded, ordering twenty-five Soviet ships off their course to Cuba, thus avoiding a challenge to the American blockade.

Khrushchev offered to remove all the missiles in return for a pledge from the United States not to invade Cuba. Khrushchev later added a demand for removal of American weapons from Turkey, as close to the Soviet Union as Cuba is to the United States. Kennedy secretly assured Khrushchev that the United States would dismantle the obsolete Jupiter missiles in Turkey. On November 20, after weeks of delicate negotiations, Kennedy publicly announced the withdrawal of Soviet missiles and bombers from Cuba, pledged to respect Cuban sovereignty, and promised that U.S. forces would not invade the island.

The crisis had passed. The Soviets, determined not to be intimidated again, began the largest weapons buildup in their history. For his part Kennedy, perhaps chastened by this flirtation with nuclear disaster, made important gestures toward peaceful coexistence with the Soviets. In a June 1963 address at American University, Kennedy called for a rethinking of cold war diplomacy. Both sides, he said, had been "caught up in a vicious and dangerous cycle in which suspicion on one side breeds suspicion on the other, and new weapons beget counterweapons." It was important "not to see only a distorted and desperate view of the other side. . . . No government or social system is so evil that its people must be considered as lacking in virtue."

Shortly after, Washington and Moscow set up a "hot line"—a direct phone connection to permit instant communication during times of crisis. More substantial was the Limited Nuclear Test-Ban Treaty, signed in August by the United States, the Soviet Union, and Great Britain. The treaty prohibited aboveground, outer space, and underwater nuclear weapons tests. It eased international anxieties over radioactive fallout. But underground testing continued to accelerate for years. The limited test ban was perhaps more symbolic than substantive, a psychological breakthrough in East-West relations after a particularly tense three years.

The Assassination of President Kennedy

The assassination of John F. Kennedy in Dallas on November 22, 1963, sent the entire nation into shock and mourning. Just forty-six years old and president

CHRONOLOGY

1950	David Riesman publishes *The Lonely Crowd*
1952	Dwight D. Eisenhower is elected president
1953	CIA installs Riza Shah Pahlavi as leader of Iran
1954	Vietminh force French surrender at Dien Bien Phu
	CIA overthrows government of Jácobo Arbenz Guzmán in Guatemala
	United States explodes first hydrogen bomb
1955	Jonas Salk pioneers vaccine for polio
	James Dean stars in the movie *Rebel without a Cause*
1956	Federal Highway Act authorizes Interstate Highway System
	Elvis Presley signs with RCA
	Eisenhower is reelected
	Allen Ginsberg publishes *Howl*
1957	Soviet Union launches Sputnik, first space-orbiting satellite
	Jack Kerouac publishes *On the Road*
1958	National Defense Education Act authorizes grants and loans to college students
1959	Nikita Khrushchev visits the United States
1960	Soviets shoot down U-2 spy plane
	John F. Kennedy is elected president
	Almost 90 percent of American homes have television
1961	President Kennedy creates "Green Berets"
	Bay of Pigs invasion of Cuba fails
1962	Cuban missile crisis brings the world to the brink of a superpower confrontation
1963	Report by the Presidential Commission on the Status of Women documents ongoing discrimination
	Limited Nuclear Test-Ban Treaty is signed
	President Kennedy is assassinated
	Betty Friedan publishes *The Feminine Mystique*

for only three years, Kennedy quickly ascended to martyrdom in the nation's consciousness. Millions had identified his strengths—intelligence, optimism, wit, charm, coolness under fire—as those of American society. In life, Kennedy had helped place television at the center of American political life. Now in the aftermath of his death, television riveted a badly shocked nation. One day after the assassination, the president's accused killer, an obscure political misfit named Lee Harvey Oswald, was himself gunned down before television cameras covering his arraignment in Dallas. Two days later tens of millions watched the televised spectacle of Kennedy's funeral, trying to make sense of the brutal murder. Although a special commission headed by Chief Justice Earl Warren found the killing to be the work of Oswald acting alone, many Americans doubted this conclusion. Kennedy's death gave rise to a host of conspiracy theories, none of which seems provable. In 1979 a House committee concluded that more than one gunman had fired on the presidential motorcade; but FBI scientists disputed this finding.

As Adlai Stevenson, one of Kennedy's longtime political rivals in the Democratic Party, noted in his eulogy to the president, "No one will ever know what this blazing political talent might have accomplished had he been permitted to live and labor long in the cause of freedom." We will never know, of course, what Kennedy might have achieved in a second term. But in his 1,000 days as president, he demonstrated a capacity to change and grow in office. Having gone to the brink during the missile crisis, he managed to launch new initiatives toward peaceful coexistence. At the time of his death, relations between the United States and the Soviet Union were more amicable than at any time since the end of World War II. Much of the domestic liberal agenda of the New Frontier would be finally implemented by Kennedy's successor, Lyndon B. Johnson, who dreamed of creating a Great Society.

CONCLUSION

America in 1963 still enjoyed the full flush of its post-war economic boom. To be sure, millions of Americans, particularly African Americans and Latinos, did not share in the good times. But millions of others had managed to achieve middle-class status since the early 1950s. An expanding economy, cheap energy, government subsidies, and a dominant position in the world marketplace had made the hallmarks of "the good life" available to more Americans than ever. The postwar "American dream" promised home ownership, college education, secure employment at decent wages, affordable appliances, and the ability to travel—for one's children if not for one's self. The nation's public culture—its schools, mass media, politics, advertising—presented a powerful consensus based on the idea that the American dream was available to all who would work for it.

The presidential transition from the grandfatherly Dwight Eisenhower to the charismatic John F. Kennedy symbolized for many a generational shift as well. By 1963 young people had more influence than ever before in shaping the nation's political life, its media images, and its burgeoning consumer culture. Kennedy himself inspired millions of young Americans to pursue public service and to express their political idealism. But even by the time of Kennedy's death, the postwar consensus and the conditions that nurtured it were beginning to unravel.

REVIEW QUESTIONS

1. How did postwar economic prosperity change the lives of ordinary Americans? Which groups benefited most and which were largely excluded from "the affluent society"?

2. What role did federal programs play in expanding economic opportunities?

3. Analyze the origins of postwar youth culture. How was teenage life different in these years from previous eras? How did popular culture both reflect and distort the lives of American youth?

4. How did mass culture become even more central to American everyday life in the two decades following World War II? What problems did various cultural critics identify with this trend?

5. How did cold war politics and assumptions shape American foreign policy in these years? What were the key interventions the United States made in Europe and the third world?

6. Evaluate the domestic and international policies associated with John F. Kennedy and the New Frontier. What continuities with Eisenhower-era politics do you find in the Kennedy administration? How did JFK break with past practices?

RECOMMENDED READING

Erik Barnouw, *Tube of Plenty* (1982). The best one-volume history of television, with excellent material on the new medium's impact upon cultural and political life.

James B. Gilbert, *A Cycle of Outrage* (1986). An insightful analysis of juvenile delinquency and its treatment by social scientists and the mass media during the 1950s.

Peter Guralnick, *Last Train to Memphis: The Rise of Elvis Presley* (1994). The best biography of Presley and a stunning portrait of the milieu that produced him.

Kenneth T. Jackson, *Crabgrass Frontier* (1985). The most comprehensive overview of the history of American suburbs. Jackson provides a broad historical context for understanding postwar suburbanization, and offers an excellent analysis of the impact of government agencies such as the Federal Housing Administration.

George Lipsitz, *Time Passages* (1990). An illuminating set of essays charting developments in American popular culture, especially strong analysis of music and early television.

Elaine Tyler May, *Homeward Bound: American Families in the Cold War* (1988). A thoughtful social history linking family life of the 1950s with the political shadow of the cold war.

Gerald Nicosia, *Memory Babe: A Critical Biography of Jack Kerouac* (1983). Both the best biography of this key Beat writer and the best analysis of the Beat generation.

Chester Pach Jr. and Elmo Richardson, *The Presidency of Dwight D. Eisenhower*, rev. ed. (1991). A good recent overview of the Eisenhower administration.

Herbert Parmet, *JFK* (1983). A solid, balanced examination of the Kennedy presidency.

James T. Patterson, *Grand Expectations: Postwar America, 1945–1974* (1996). A comprehensive overview of postwar life that centers on the "grand expectations" evoked by unprecedented prosperity.

ADDITIONAL BIBLIOGRAPHY

American Society at Mid-Century

Charles C. Alexander, *Holding the Line: The Eisenhower Era, 1952–1961* (1975)
David Calleo, *The Imperious Economy* (1982)
Barbara B. Clowse, *Brainpower for the Cold War* (1981)
Stephanie Coontz, *The Way We Never Were* (1992)
John P. Diggins, *The Proud Decades: America in War and Peace, 1941–1960* (1988)
Scott Donaldson, *The Suburban Myth* (1969)
Benita Eisler, *Private Lives: Men and Women of the Fifties* (1986)
Herbert Gans, *The Levittowners* (1967)
Delores Hayden, *Redesigning the American Dream* (1984)
Kenneth W. Olson, *The GI Bill, the Veterans, and the Colleges* (1974)

Youth Culture

Wini Breines, *Young, White, and Miserable: Growing Up Female in the Fifties* (1992)
Thomas Doherty, *Teen Pics* (1994)
Nelson George, *The Death of Rhythm and Blues* (1988)
Charlie Gillett, *The Sound of the City*, rev. ed. (1983)
William Graebner, *Coming of Age in Buffalo* (1990)
John A. Jackson, *Big Beat Heat: Alan Freed and the Early Years of Rock 'n' Roll* (1991)
Douglas T. Miller and Marion Novak, *The Fifties: The Way We Really Were* (1977)
David P. Szatmary, *Rockin' in Time: A Social History of Rock and Roll* (1991)
Ed Ward et al., *Rock of Ages* (1987)

Mass Culture and Its Discontents

James L. Baughman, *The Republic of Mass Culture* (1992)
George Lipsitz, *Class and Culture in Cold War America* (1981)
J. Fred MacDonald, *Television and the Red Menace* (1985)
David Marc, *Demographic Vistas: Television and American Culture* (1984)
Karal Ann Merling, *As Seen On TV: The Visual Culture of Everyday Life in the 1950's* (1995)
Richard H. Pells, *The Liberal Mind in a Conservative Age* (1984)
Lynn Spigel, *Make Room for TV* (1992)
Ella Taylor, *Prime Time Families* (1989)
Stephen J. Whitfield, *The Culture of the Cold War* (1991)

The Cold War Continued

Stephen Ambrose, *Ike's Spies* (1981)
David L. Anderson, *Trapped by Success: The Eisenhower Administration and Vietnam, 1953–1961* (1991)
Richard J. Barnet, *Intervention and Revolution* (1972)
Robert Divine, *Eisenhower and the Cold War* (1981)
Richard Immerman, *The CIA in Guatemala* (1982)
Gabriel Kolko, *Confronting the Third World* (1988)
Richard A. Melanson and David A. Mayers, eds., *Reevaluating Eisenhower* (1986)
Peter Wyden, *Bay of Pigs* (1980)

John F. Kennedy and the New Frontier

Michael Beschloss, *The Crisis Years* (1991)
Thomas Brown, *JFK: The History of an Image* (1988)
Noam Chomsky, *Rethinking Camelot* (1993)
James N. Giglio, *The Presidency of John F. Kennedy* (1991)
Trumbull Higgins, *The Perfect Failure: Kennedy, Eisenhower and the CIA at the Bay of Pigs* (1988)
Walter LaFeber, *Inevitable Revolutions* (1983)
Richard Mahoney, *JFK: Ordeal in Africa* (1983)
Thomas G. Paterson, ed., *Kennedy's Quest for Victory* (1989)
Richard E. Welch Jr., *Response to Revolution: The United States and Cuba, 1959–1961* (1985)
Garry Wills, *The Kennedy Imprisonment* (1983)

Biography

Stephen Ambrose, *Eisenhower*, 2 vols. (1983, 1984)
Chuck Berry, *The Autobiography* (1987)
David Burner, *John F. Kennedy and a New Generation* (1988)
Carol George, *God's Salesman: Norman Vincent Peale and the Power of Positive Thinking* (1993)
Townsend Hoopes, *The Devil and John Foster Dulles* (1973)
Daniel Horowitz, *Vance Packard and American Social Criticism* (1994)
Irving L. Horowitz, *C. Wright Mills: American Utopian* (1983)
Barry Miles, *Allen Ginsberg* (1989)
Thomas C. Reeves, *A Question of Character: A Life of John F. Kennedy* (1991)

CHAPTER TWENTY-EIGHT

THE CIVIL RIGHTS MOVEMENT

1945–1966

Romare Bearden, *Watching the Trains Go By*, 1964. Collection of Philip J. and Suzanne Schiller, American Social Commentary Art, 1930–1970. Photo by Sharon Goodman. © Romare Bearden Foundation/Licensed by VAGA, New York, NY.

AMERICAN COMMUNITIES
The Montgomery Bus Boycott: An African American Community Challenges Segregation

A steady stream of cars and pedestrians jammed the streets around the Holt Street Baptist Church in Montgomery, Alabama. By early evening a patient, orderly, and determined crowd of more than 5,000 African Americans had packed the church and spilled over onto the sidewalks. Loudspeakers had to be set up for the thousands who could not squeeze inside. After a brief prayer and a reading from Scripture, all attention focused on the twenty-six-year-old minister who was to address the gathering. "We are here this evening," he began slowly, "for serious business. We are here in a general sense because first and foremost we are American citizens, and we are determined to apply our citizenship to the fullness of its means."

Sensing the expectant mood of the crowd, the minister got down to specifics. Rosa Parks, a seamstress and well-known activist in Montgomery's African American community, had been taken from a bus, arrested, and put in jail for refusing to give up her seat to a white passenger on December 1, 1955. Composing roughly half the city's 100,000 people, Montgomery's black community had long endured the humiliation of a strictly segregated bus system. Drivers could order a whole row of black passengers to vacate their seats for one white person. And black people had to pay their fares at the front of the bus and then step back outside and reenter through the rear door. The day of the mass meeting, more than 30,000 African Americans had answered a hastily organized call to boycott the city's buses in protest of Mrs. Parks's arrest. As the minister quickened his cadence and drew shouts of encouragement, he seemed to gather strength and confidence from the crowd. "You know, my friends, there comes a time when people get tired of being trampled over by the iron feet of oppression. There comes a time, my friends, when people get tired of being flung across the abyss of humiliation, when they experience the bleakness of nagging despair."

Even before he concluded his speech, it was clear to all present that the bus boycott would continue for more than just a day. The minister laid out the key principles that would guide the boycott—nonviolence, Christian love, unity. In his brief but stirring address the minister created a powerful sense of communion. "If we are wrong, justice is a lie," he told the clapping and shouting throng. "And we are determined here in Montgomery to work and fight until justice runs down like water and righteousness like a mighty stream." Historians would look back at Montgomery, he noted, and have to say: " 'There lived a race of people, black people, fleecy locks and black complexion, of people who had the moral courage to stand up for their rights.' And thereby they injected a new meaning into the veins of history and of civilization."

The Reverend Dr. Martin Luther King Jr. made his way out of the church amid waves of applause and rows of hands reaching out to touch him. His prophetic speech catapulted him into leadership of the Montgomery bus boycott—but he had not started the movement. When Rosa Parks was arrested, local activists with deep roots in the black protest tradition galvanized the community with the idea of a boycott. Mrs. Parks herself had served for twelve years as secretary of the local NAACP chapter. She was a committed opponent of segregation and was thoroughly respected in the city's African American community. E. D. Nixon, president of the Alabama NAACP and head of the local Brotherhood of Sleeping Car Porters union, saw Mrs. Parks's arrest as the right case on which to make a stand. It was Nixon who brought Montgomery's black ministers together on December 5 to coordinate an extended boycott of city buses. They formed the Montgomery Improvement Association (MIA) and chose Dr. King as their leader.

While Nixon organized black ministers, Jo Ann Robinson, an English teacher at Alabama State College, spread the word to the larger black community. Robinson led the Women's Political Council (WPC), an organization of black professional women founded in 1949. With her WPC allies, Robinson wrote, mimeographed, and distributed 50,000 copies of a leaflet telling the story of Mrs. Parks's arrest and urging all African Americans to stay off city buses on December 5. They did. Now the MIA faced the more difficult task of keeping the boycott going. Success depended on providing alternate transportation for the 30,000 to 40,000 maids, cooks, janitors, and other black working people who needed to get to work.

The MIA coordinated an elaborate system of car pools, using hundreds of private cars and volunteer drivers to provide as many as 20,000 rides each day. Many people walked. Local authorities, although shocked by the discipline and sense of purpose shown by Montgomery's African American community, refused to engage in serious negotiations. With the aid of the NAACP, the MIA brought suit in federal court against bus segregation in Montgomery. Police harassed boycotters with traffic tickets and arrests. White racists exploded bombs in the homes of Dr. King and E. D. Nixon. The days turned into weeks, then months, but still the boycott continued. All along, mass meetings in Montgomery's African American churches helped boost morale with singing, praying, and stories of individual sacrifice. One elderly woman, refusing all suggestions that she drop out of the boycott on account of her age, made a spontaneous remark that became a classic refrain of the movement: "My feets is tired, but my soul is rested."

The boycott reduced the bus company's revenues by two-thirds. In February 1956 city officials obtained indictments against King, Nixon, and 113 other boycotters under an old law forbidding hindrance to business without "just cause or legal excuse." A month later King went on trial. A growing contingent of newspaper reporters and TV crews from around the country watched as the judge found King guilty, fined him $1,000, and released him on bond pending appeal. But on June 4, a panel of three federal judges struck down Montgomery's bus segregation ordinances as unconstitutional. On November 13 the Supreme Court affirmed the district court ruling. After eleven hard months and against all odds, the boycotters had won.

The struggle to end legal segregation took root in scores of southern cities and towns. African American communities led these fights, developing a variety of tactics, leaders, and ideologies. With white allies, they engaged in direct-action protests such as boycotts, sit-ins, and mass civil disobedience as well as strategic legal battles in state and federal courts. The movement was not without its inner conflicts. Tensions between local movements and national civil rights organizations flared up regularly. Within African American communities, long-simmering distrust between the working classes and rural folk on the one hand and middle-class ministers, teachers, and business people on the other sometimes threatened to destroy political unity. There were generational conflicts between African American student activists and their elders. But overall, the civil rights movement created new social identities for African Americans and profoundly changed American society.

Montgomery

KEY TOPICS

- Legal and political origins of the African American civil rights struggle
- Martin Luther King's rise to leadership
- Student protesters and direct action in the South
- Civil rights and national politics
- Civil Rights Act of 1964 and Voting Rights Act of 1965
- America's other minorities

ORIGINS OF THE MOVEMENT

The experiences of African Americans during World War II and immediately after laid the foundation for the civil rights struggle of the 1950s and 1960s. Nearly 1 million black men and women had served in the armed forces. The discrepancy between fighting totalitarianism abroad while enduring segregation and other racist practices in the military embittered many combat veterans and their families. Between 1939 and 1945 nearly 2 million African Americans found work in defense plants and another 200,000 entered the federal civil service. Black union membership doubled, reaching more than 1.2 million. But the wartime stress on national unity and consensus largely muted political protests. With the war's end, African Americans and their white allies determined to push ahead for full political and social equality.

Civil Rights after World War II

The boom in wartime production spurred a mass migration of nearly a million black Southerners to northern cities. Forty-three northern and western cities saw their black population double during the 1940s. Although racial discrimination in housing and employment was by no means absent in northern cities, greater economic opportunities and political freedom continued to attract rural African Americans after the war. With the growth of African American communities in northern cities, black people gained significant influence in local political machines in such cities as New York, Chicago, and Detroit. Within industrial unions such as the United Automobile Workers and the United Steel Workers, white and black workers learned the power of biracial unity in fighting for better wages and working conditions. Harlem congressman Adam Clayton Powell Jr. captured the new mood of 1945 when he wrote that black people were eager "to make the dream of America become flesh and blood, bread and butter, freedom and equality."

After the war, civil rights issues returned to the national political stage for the first time since Reconstruction. Black voters had already begun to switch their allegiance from the Republicans to the Democrats during the New Deal. A series of symbolic and substantial acts by the Truman administration solidified that shift. In 1946 Truman created a President's Committee on Civil Rights. Its report, *To Secure These Rights* (1947), set out an ambitious program to end racial inequality. Recommendations included a permanent civil rights division in the Justice Department, voting rights protection, antilynching legislation, and a legal attack on segregated housing. Yet, although he publicly endorsed nearly all the proposals of the new committee, Truman introduced no legislation to make them law.

Truman and his advisers walked a political tightrope on civil rights. They understood that black voters in several key northern states would be pivotal in the 1948 election. At the same time, they worried about the loyalty of white southern Democrats adamantly opposed to changing the racial status quo. In July 1948 the president made his boldest move on behalf of civil rights, issuing an executive order barring segregation in the armed forces. When liberals forced the Democratic National Convention to adopt a strong civil rights plank that summer, a group of outraged Southerners walked out and nominated Governor Strom Thurmond of South Carolina for president on a States' Rights ticket. Thurmond carried four southern states in the election. But with the help of over 70 percent of the northern black vote, Truman barely managed to defeat Republican Thomas E. Dewey in November. The deep split over race issues would continue to rack the national Democratic Party for a generation.

Electoral politics was not the only arena for civil rights work. During the war, membership in the National Association for the Advancement of Colored People had mushroomed from 50,000 to 500,000. Working- and middle-class urban black people provided the backbone of this new membership. The NAACP conducted voter registration drives and lobbied against discrimination in housing and employment. Its Legal Defense and Education Fund, vigorously led by special counsel Thurgood Marshall, mounted several significant legal challenges to segregation laws. In *Morgan v. Virginia* (1946), the Supreme

Court declared that segregation on interstate buses was an undue burden on interstate commerce. Other Supreme Court decisions struck down all-white election primaries, racially restrictive housing covenants, and the exclusion of blacks from law and graduate schools.

The NAACP's legal work demonstrated the potential for using federal courts in attacking segregation. Courts were one place where black people, using the constitutional language of rights, could make forceful arguments that could not be voiced in Congress or at political conventions. But federal enforcement of court decisions was often lacking. In 1947 a group of black and white activists tested compliance with the Morgan decision by traveling on a bus through the Upper South. This "Freedom Ride" was cosponsored by the Christian pacifist Fellowship of Reconciliation (FOR) and its recent offshoot, the Congress of Racial Equality (CORE), which was devoted to interracial, nonviolent direct action. In North Carolina, several riders were arrested and sentenced to thirty days on a chain gang for refusing to leave the bus.

Two symbolic "firsts" raised black expectations and inspired pride. In 1947 Jackie Robinson broke the color barrier in major league baseball, winning rookie-of-the-year honors with the Brooklyn Dodgers. Robinson's courage in the face of racial epithets from fans and players paved the way for the black ballplayers who soon followed him to the big leagues. In 1950 United Nations diplomat Ralph Bunche won the Nobel Peace Prize for arranging the 1948 Arab-Israeli truce. However, Bunche later declined an appointment as undersecretary of state because he did not want to subject his family to the humiliating segregation laws of Washington, D.C.

Cultural change could have political implications as well. In the 1940s, African American musicians created a new form of jazz that revolutionized American music and asserted a militant black consciousness. Although black musicians had pioneered the development of swing and, earlier, jazz, white bandleaders and musicians had reaped most of the recognition and money from the public. Artists such as Charlie Parker, Dizzy Gillespie, Thelonius Monk, Bud Powell, and Miles Davis revolted against the standard big-band format of swing, preferring small groups and competitive jam sessions to express their musical visions. The new music, dubbed "bebop" by critics and fans, demanded a much more sophisticated knowledge of harmony and melody and featured more complex rhythms and extended improvisation than previous jazz styles.

In urban black communities the "boppers" consciously created a music that, unlike swing, white popularizers found difficult to copy or sweeten. These black artists insisted on independence from the white-defined norms of show business. Serious about both their music and the way it was presented, they refused

to cater to white expectations of grinning, easygoing black performers. Although most boppers had roots in the South, they preferred the relative freedom they found in northern urban black communities. Many northern black (and white) youths identified with the distinctive music, language, and dress of the boppers. In both their music and their public image, these musicians presented a rebellious alternative to the traditional image of the African American entertainer.

The Segregated South

In the postwar South, still home to over half the nation's 15 million African Americans, the racial situation had changed little since the Supreme Court had sanctioned "separate but equal" segregation in *Plessy v. Ferguson* (discussed in Chapter 20). In practice, segregation meant separate but unequal. A tight web of state and local ordinances enforced strict separation of the races in schools, restaurants, hotels, movie theaters, libraries, restrooms, hospitals, even cemeteries, and the facilities for black people were consistently inferior to those for whites. There were no black policemen in the Deep South and only a handful of black lawyers. "A white man," one scholar observed, "can steal from or maltreat a Negro in almost any way without fear of reprisal, because the Negro cannot claim the protection of the police or courts."

Charlie Parker (alto sax) and Miles Davis (trumpet) with their group in 1947, at the Three Deuces Club in New York City. Parker and Davis were two creative leaders of the "bebop" movement of the 1940s. Working in northern cities, boppers reshaped jazz music and created a distinct language and style that was widely imitated by young people. They challenged older stereotypes of African American musicians by insisting that they be treated as serious artists.

*Signs designating "White" and "Colored" rest rooms, waiting rooms, entrances, benches, and
even water fountains were a common sight in the segregated South. They were a constant
reminder that legal separation of the races in public spaces was the law of the land.*

In the late 1940s only about 10 percent of eligible southern black people voted, most of these in urban areas. A combination of legal and extralegal measures kept all but the most determined black people disfranchised. Poll taxes, all-white primaries, and discriminatory registration procedures reinforced the belief that voting was "the white man's business." African Americans who insisted on exercising their right to vote, especially in remote rural areas, faced physical violence—beatings, shootings, lynchings. A former president of the Alabama Bar Association expressed a commonly held view when he declared, "No Negro is good enough and no Negro will ever be good enough to participate in making the law under which the white people of Alabama have to live."

Outsiders often noted that despite Jim Crow laws (see Chapter 20) contact between blacks and whites was ironically close. The mass of black Southerners worked on white-owned plantations and in white households. One black preacher neatly summarized the nation's regional differences this way: "In the South, they don't care how close you get as long as you don't get too big; in the North, they don't care how big you get as long as you don't get too close." The South's racial code forced African Americans to accept, at least outwardly, social conventions that reinforced their low standing with whites. A black person did not shake hands with a white person, or enter a white home through the front door, or address a white person except formally.

In these circumstances, survival and self-respect depended to a great degree on patience and stoicism. Black people learned to endure humiliation by keeping their thoughts and feelings hidden from white people. Paul Laurence Dunbar, an African American poet, captured this bitter truth in his turn-of-the-century poem "We Wear the Mask."

> *We wear the mask that grins and lies,*
> *It hides our cheeks and shades our eyes,*
> *This debt we pay to human guile;*
> *With torn and bleeding hearts we smile,*
> *And mouth with myriad subtleties.*
> *Why should the world be over-wise,*
> *In counting all our tears and sighs?*
> *Nay, let them only see us, while*
> *We wear the mask.*

Brown v. Board of Education

Since the late 1930s, the NAACP had chipped away at the legal foundations of segregation. Rather than making a frontal assault on the *Plessy* separate-but-equal rule, civil rights attorneys launched a series of suits seeking complete equality in segregated facilities. The aim of this strategy was to make segregation so prohibitively expensive that the South would be forced to dismantle it. In the 1939 case *Missouri v. ex.rel. Gaines*, the Supreme Court ruled that the University of Missouri law school must either admit African Americans or build another, fully equal law school for them. NAACP lawyers pushed their arguments further, asserting that equality could not be measured simply by money or physical plant. In *McLaurin v. Oklahoma State Regents* (1950), the Court agreed with Thurgood Marshall's argument that regulations forcing a black law student to sit, eat, and study in areas apart from white students inevitably created a "badge of inferiority."

By 1951, Marshall had begun coordinating the NAACP's legal resources for a direct attack on the separate-but-equal doctrine. The goal was to overturn *Plessy* and the constitutionality of segregation itself. For a test case, Marshall combined five lawsuits challenging segregation in public schools. One of these suits argued the case of Oliver Brown of Topeka, Kansas, who sought to overturn a state law permitting cities to maintain segregated schools. The law forced Brown's eight-year-old daughter Linda to travel by bus to a black school even though she lived only three blocks from an all-white elementary school. The Supreme Court heard initial arguments on the cases, grouped together as *Brown v. Board of Education*, in December 1952.

In his argument before the Court, Thurgood Marshall tried to establish that separate facilities, by definition, denied black people their full rights as American citizens. Marshall used sociological and psychological evidence that went beyond standard legal arguments. For example, he cited the research of African American psychologist Kenneth B. Clark, who had studied the self-esteem of black children in New York City and in segregated schools in the South. Using black and white dolls and asking the children which they preferred, Clark illustrated how black children educated in segregated schools developed a negative self-image. When Chief Justice Fred Vinson died suddenly in 1953, President Dwight Eisenhower appointed California Governor Earl Warren to fill the post. After hearing further arguments, the Court remained divided on the issue of overturning *Plessy*. Warren, eager for a unanimous decision, patiently worked at convincing two holdouts. Using his political skills to persuade and achieve compromise, Warren urged his colleagues to affirm a simple principle as the basis for the decision.

On May 17, 1954, Warren read the Court's unanimous decision aloud. "Does segregation of children in public schools solely on the basis of race . . . deprive the children of the minority group of equal educational opportunities?" The chief justice paused. "We believe that it does." Warren made a point of citing several of the psychological studies of segregation's effects. He ended by directly addressing the constitutional issue. Segregation deprived the plaintiffs of the equal protection of the laws guaranteed by the Fourteenth Amendment. "We conclude that in the field of public education the doctrine of 'separate but equal' has no place. Separate educational facilities are inherently unequal." "Any language in *Plessy v. Ferguson* contrary to this finding is rejected."

African Americans and their liberal allies around the country hailed the decision and the legal genius of Thurgood Marshall. Marshall himself predicted that all segregated schools would be abolished within five years. Black newspapers were full of stories on the imminent dismantling of segregation. The *Chicago Defender* called the decision "a second emancipation proclamation." But the issue of enforcement soon dampened this enthusiasm. To gain a unanimous decision, Warren had had to agree to let the Court delay for one year its ruling on how to implement desegregation. This second *Brown* ruling, handed down in May 1955, assigned responsibility for desegregation plans to local school boards. The Court left it to federal district judges to monitor compliance, requiring only that desegregation proceed "with all deliberate speed." Thus, although the Court had made a momentous and clear constitutional ruling, the need for compromise dictated gradual enforcement by unspecified means.

Crisis in Little Rock

Resistance to *Brown* took many forms. Most affected states passed laws transferring authority for pupil assignment to local school boards. This prevented the NAACP from bringing statewide suits against segregated school systems. Counties and towns created layers of administrative delays designed to stop implementation of *Brown*. Some school boards transferred public school property to new, all-white private "academies." State legislatures in Virginia, Alabama, Mississippi, and Georgia, resurrecting pre–Civil War doctrines, passed resolutions declaring their right to "interpose" themselves between the people and the federal government and to "nullify" federal laws. In 1956, 101 congressmen from the former Confederate states signed the Southern Manifesto, urging their states to refuse compliance with desegregation. President Dwight Eisenhower declined to publicly endorse *Brown*, contributing to the spirit of southern resistance. "I don't believe you can change the hearts of men with laws or decisions," he said. Privately, the pres-

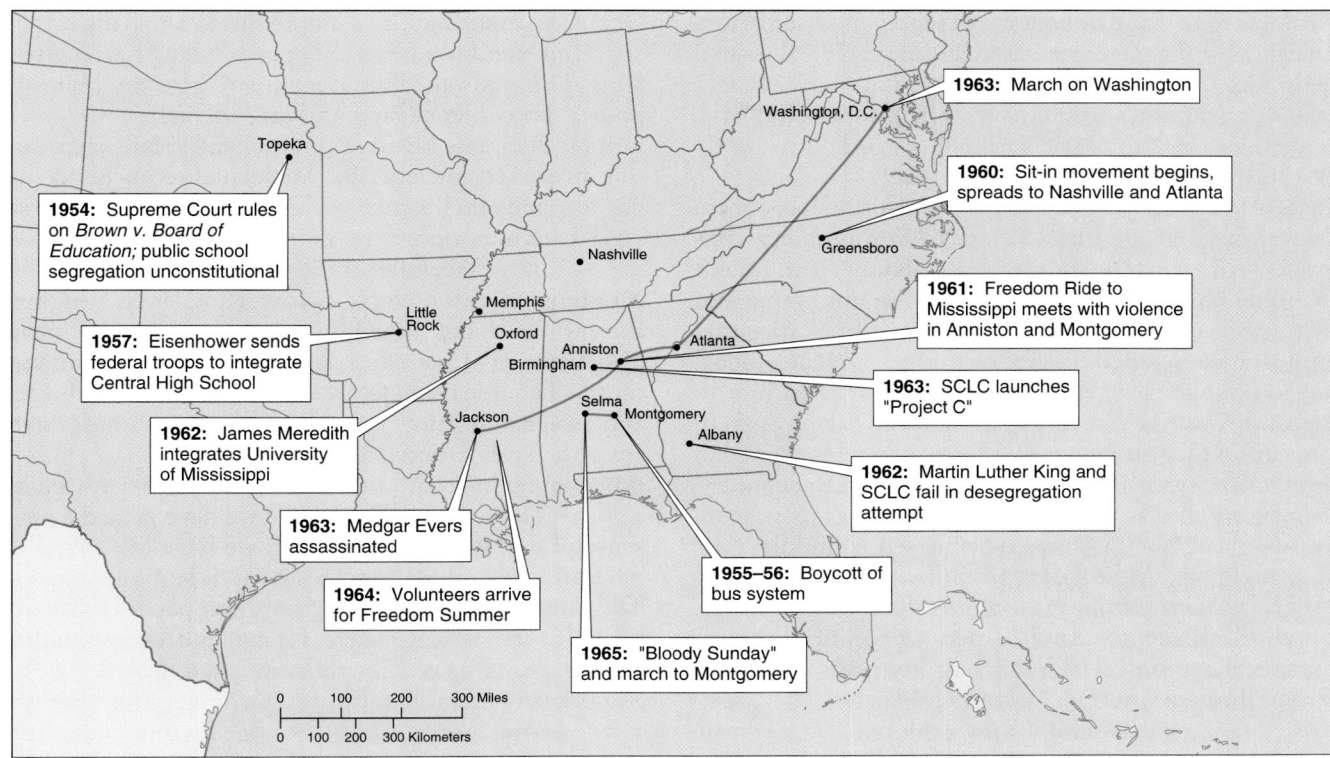

1963: March on Washington

Washington, D.C.

Topeka

1954: Supreme Court rules on *Brown v. Board of Education;* public school segregation unconstitutional

Nashville

1960: Sit-in movement begins, spreads to Nashville and Atlanta

Greensboro

Memphis

Little Rock

1957: Eisenhower sends federal troops to integrate Central High School

Oxford

Anniston

Atlanta

1961: Freedom Ride to Mississippi meets with violence in Anniston and Montgomery

Birmingham

1962: James Meredith integrates University of Mississippi

1963: SCLC launches "Project C"

Jackson

Selma

Montgomery

Albany

1962: Martin Luther King and SCLC fail in desegregation attempt

1963: Medgar Evers assassinated

1955–56: Boycott of bus system

1964: Volunteers arrive for Freedom Summer

1965: "Bloody Sunday" and march to Montgomery

0   100   200   300 Miles

0   100   200   300 Kilometers

Map of the Civil Rights Movement   *Key battlegrounds in the struggle for racial justice in communities across the South.*

ident opposed the *Brown* decision, and he later called his appointment of Earl Warren as chief justice "the biggest damn fool mistake I ever made."

In Little Rock, Arkansas, the tense controversy over school integration became a test case of state versus federal power. A federal court ordered public schools to begin desegregation in September 1957, and the local school board made plans to comply. But Governor Orval Faubus, facing a tough reelection fight, decided to make a campaign issue out of defying the court order. He dispatched Arkansas National Guard troops to Central High School to prevent nine black students from entering. For three weeks, armed troops stood guard at the school. Screaming crowds, encouraged by Faubus, menaced the black students, beat up two black reporters, and chanted "Two, four, six, eight, we ain't going to integrate."

At first, President Eisenhower tried to intervene quietly, gaining Faubus's assurance that he would protect the nine black children. But when Faubus suddenly withdrew his troops, leaving the black students at the mercy of the white mob, Eisenhower had to move. On September 24 he placed the Arkansas National Guard under federal control and ordered a thousand paratroopers of the 101st Airborne Division to Little Rock. The nine black students arrived in a U.S. Army car. With fixed bayonets, the soldiers protected the students

as they finally integrated Little Rock High School. Eisenhower, the veteran military commander, justified his actions on the basis of upholding federal authority and enforcing the law. He made no endorsement of desegregation. But as the first president since Reconstruction to use armed federal troops in support of black rights, Eisenhower demonstrated that the federal government could, indeed, protect civil rights. Unfazed, Governor Faubus kept Little Rock high schools closed during the 1958–59 academic year to prevent what he called "violence and disorder."

NO EASY ROAD TO FREEDOM, 1957–62

The legal breakthrough represented by the *Brown* decision heartened opponents of segregation everywhere. Most important, *Brown* demonstrated the potential for using the federal court system as a weapon against discrimination and as a means of protecting the full rights of citizenship. Yet the widespread opposition to *Brown* and its implications showed the limits of a strictly legal strategy. In Little Rock, the ugly face of white racism received wide coverage in the mass media and quickly sobered the more optimistic champions of integration. However welcome Eisenhower's intervention, his reluctance to endorse desegregation suggested that civil rights activists could still not rely on federal help. As the Montgomery bus boycott had proved, black communities would have to help themselves first.

Martin Luther King and the SCLC

When it ended with the Supreme Court decision in November 1956, the 381-day Montgomery bus boycott had made Martin Luther King a prominent national figure. In January 1957 *Time* magazine put King on its cover. The *New York Times Magazine* published a detailed history of the bus boycott, focusing on King's role. NBC's *Meet the Press* invited him to become only the second African American ever to appear on that program. Speaking invitations poured in from universities and organizations around the country. King himself was an extraordinary and complex man. Born in 1929 in Atlanta, he enjoyed a middle-class upbringing as the son of a prominent Baptist minister. After graduating from prestigious Morehouse College, an all-black school, King earned a divinity degree at Crozer Theological Seminary in Pennsylvania and a Ph.D. in theology from Boston University.

In graduate school King explored a very diverse range of philosophers and political thinkers—the ancient Greeks, French Enlightenment thinkers, the German idealists, and Karl Marx. He was drawn to the social Christianity of American theologian Walter Rauschenbusch, who insisted on connecting religious faith with struggles for social justice. Above all King admired Mohandas Gandhi, a lawyer turned ascetic who had led a successful nonviolent resistance movement against British colonial rule in India. Gandhi taught his followers to confront authorities with a readiness to suffer, in order to expose injustice and force those in power to end it. This tactic of nonviolent civil disobedience required discipline and sacrifice from its followers, who were sometimes called upon to lay their lives on the line against armed police and military forces.

Like Gandhi and many of the Christian saints he had studied, King grappled with inner doubts about his faith and true mission. Since childhood he had suffered from extreme mood swings. He was charming and popular, but also self-restrained and dignified. Even after becoming pastor of Montgomery's

Dexter Avenue Baptist Church in 1954, King often agonized over his inner emotions, including his religious faith. The rigorous discipline required by the philosophy of nonviolence helped King to master his inner turmoil. A unique blend of traditional African American folk preacher and erudite intellectual, King used his passion and intelligence to help transform a community's pain into a powerful moral force for change.

In a December 1956 address celebrating the Montgomery bus boycott victory, King laid out six key lessons from the year-long struggle. "(1) We have discovered that we can stick together for a common cause; (2) our leaders do not have to sell out; (3) threats and violence do not necessarily intimidate those who are sufficiently aroused and non-violent; (4) our church is becoming militant, stressing a social gospel as well as a gospel of personal salvation; (5) we have gained a new sense of dignity and destiny; (6) we have discovered a new and powerful weapon—non-violent resistance." The influence of two visiting northern pacifists, Bayard Rustin of the War Resisters' League and Glenn Smiley of the Fellowship of Reconciliation, had helped deepen King's own commitment to the Gandhian philosophy.

King recognized the need to exploit the momentum of the Montgomery movement. In early 1957, with the help of Rustin and other aides, he brought together nearly 100 black ministers to found the Southern Christian Leadership Conference (SCLC). The clergymen elected King president and his close friend, the Reverend Ralph Abernathy, trea-

After eleven months of nonviolent struggle, the Reverend Dr. Martin Luther King, Jr., leader of the Montgomery Bus Boycott, and the Reverend Glenn Smiley, of the Fellowship of Reconciliation, were among the group enjoying the first integrated bus ride in Montgomery. They were pictured here sitting at the front of the bus.

The second day of the sit-in at the Greensboro, North Carolina, Woolworth's lunch counter, February 2, 1960. From left: Joseph McNeil, Franklin McCain, Billy Smith, and Clarence Henderson. The Greensboro protest sparked a wave of sit-ins across the South, mostly by college students, demanding an end to segregation in restaurants and other public places.

surer. The SCLC called upon black people "to understand that nonviolence is not a symbol of weakness or cowardice, but as Jesus demonstrated, nonviolent resistance transforms weakness into strength and breeds courage in the face of danger."

Previously, the struggle for racial equality had been dominated by a northern elite focusing on legal action. The SCLC now envisioned the southern black church, preaching massive nonviolent protest, as leading the fight. The SCLC gained support among black ministers, and King vigorously spread his message in speeches and writings. But the organization failed to spark the kind of mass, direct-action movement that had made history in Montgomery. Instead, the next great spark to light the fire of protest came from what seemed at the time a most unlikely source: black college students.

Sit-Ins: Greensboro, Nashville, Atlanta

On Monday, February 1, 1960, four black freshmen from North Carolina Agricultural and Technical College in Greensboro sat down at the whites-only lunch counter in Woolworth's. They politely ordered coffee and doughnuts. As the students had anticipated while planning the action in their dorm rooms, they were refused service. Although they could buy pencils or toothpaste, black people were not allowed to eat in Woolworth's. But the four students stayed at the counter until closing time. Word of their actions spread quickly, and the next day they returned with over two dozen supporters. On the third day, students occupied sixty-three of the sixty-six lunch counter seats. By Thursday they had been joined by three white students from the Women's College of the University of North Carolina in Greensboro. Scores of sympathizers overflowed Woolworth's and started a sit-in down the street in S. H. Kress. On Friday hundreds of black students and a few whites jammed the lunch counters.

The week's events made Greensboro national news. City officials, looking to end the protest, offered to negotiate in exchange for an end to demonstrations. But white business leaders and politicians proved unwilling to change the racial status quo, and the sit-ins resumed on April 1. In response to the April 21 arrest of forty-five students for trespassing, an outraged African American community organized an economic boycott of targeted stores. With the boycott cutting deeply into merchants' profits, Greensboro's leaders reluctantly gave in. On July 25, 1960, the first African American ate a meal at Woolworth's.

The Greensboro sit-in sent a shock wave throughout the South. During the next eighteen months 70,000 people—most of them black students, a few of them white allies—participated in sit-ins against segregation in dozens of communities. More than 3,000 were arrested. African Americans had discovered a new form of direct-action protest, dignified and powerful, which white people could not ignore. The sit-in movement also transformed participants' self-image, empowering them psychologically and emotionally. Franklin McCain, one of the original four Greensboro students, later recalled a great feeling of soul cleansing: "I probably felt better on that day than I've ever felt in my life. Seems like a lot of feelings of guilt or what-have-you suddenly left me, and I felt as though I had gained my manhood, so to speak, and not only gained it, but had developed quite a lot of respect for it."

In Nashville, Reverend James Lawson, a northern-born black minister, had led workshops in nonviolent resistance since 1958. Lawson had served a jail term as a conscientious objector during the Korean War and had become active in the Fellowship of Reconciliation. He had also spent three years as a missionary in India, where he learned close-up the Gandhian methods of promoting social change. Lawson gathered around him a group of deeply committed black students from Fisk, Vanderbilt, and other Nashville colleges. Young activists there talked not only of ending segregation but also of creating a "Beloved Community" based on Christian idealism and Gandhian principles.

In the spring of 1960 more than 150 Nashville students were arrested in disciplined sit-ins aimed at desegregating downtown lunch counters. Lawson, who preached the need for sacrifice in the cause of justice, found himself expelled from the divinity school at Vanderbilt. Lawson and other veterans of the Nashville sit-ins, such as John Lewis, Diane Nash, and Marion Barry, would go on to play influential roles in the national civil rights movement. The Nashville group developed rules of conduct that became a model for protesters elsewhere: "Don't strike back or curse if abused. . . . Show yourself courteous and friendly at all times. . . . Report all serious incidents to your leader in a polite manner. Remember love and nonviolence."

The most ambitious sit-in campaign developed in Atlanta, the South's largest and richest city, home to the region's most powerful and prestigious black community. Students from Morehouse, Spelman, and the other all-black schools that made up Atlanta University took the lead. On March 15, 1960, 200 young black people staged a well-coordinated sit-in at restaurants in City Hall, the State Capitol, and other government offices. Police arrested and jailed seventy-six demonstrators that day, but the experience only strengthened the activists' resolve. Led by Julian Bond and Lonnie King, two Morehouse undergraduates, the students formed the Committee on an Appeal for Human Rights. In full-page advertisements in Atlanta newspapers the students demanded an end to segregation and also demanded jobs, equal housing and education, and better health services for the city's black people. We will "use every legal and non-violent means at our disposal to secure full citizenship rights as members of this great democracy of ours," the students promised. Over the summer they planned a fall campaign of large-scale sit-ins at major Atlanta department stores and a boycott of downtown merchants. Their slogan became "Close out your charge account with segregation, open up your account with freedom." In October 1960 Martin Luther King and thirty-six students were arrested when they sat down in the all-white Magnolia Room restaurant in Rich's Department Store. As in Greensboro and Montgomery, the larger African American community in Atlanta supported the continuing sit-ins, picketing, and boycotts. The campaign stretched on for months, and hundreds of protesters went to jail. The city's business leaders finally relented in September 1961, and desegregation came to Atlanta.

SNCC and the "Beloved Community"

The sit-in movement pumped new energy into the civil rights cause, creating a new generation of activists and leaders. Mass arrests, beatings, and vilification in the southern white press only strengthened the resolve of those in the movement. Students also had to deal with the fears of their families, many of whom had made great sacrifices to send them off to college. John Lewis, a seminary student in Nashville, remembered his mother in rural Alabama pleading with him to "get out of that mess, before you get hurt." Lewis wrote to his parents that he acted out of his Christian conscience: "My soul will not be satisfied until freedom, justice, and fair play become a reality for all people."

The new student militancy also caused discord within black communities. The authority of local African American elites had traditionally depended on their influence and cooperation with the white establishment. Black lawyers, schoolteachers, principals, and businessmen had to maintain regular and cordial relations with white judges, school boards, and politicians. Student calls for freedom disturbed many community leaders worried about upsetting traditional patronage networks. Some black college presidents, pressured by trustees and state legislators, sought to moderate or stop the movement altogether. The president of Southern University in Baton Rouge, the largest black college in the nation, suspended eighteen sit-in leaders in 1960 and forced the entire student body of 5,000 to reapply to the college so that agitators could be screened out.

An April 1960 conference of 120 black student activists in Raleigh, North Carolina, underlined the generational and radical aspects of the new movement. The meeting had been called by Ella Baker, executive director of the SCLC, to help the students assess their experiences and plan future actions. Fifty-five at the time, Baker had for years played an important behind-the-scenes role in the civil rights cause, serving as a community organizer and field secretary for the NAACP before heading the staff of the SCLC. She understood the psychological importance of the students' remaining independent of adult control. She counseled them to resist affiliating with any of the national civil rights organizations. Baker also encouraged the trend toward group-centered leadership among the students. She later commented that social movements needed "the development of people who are interested not in being leaders as much as in developing leadership among other people."

With Baker's encouragement, the conference voted to establish a new group, the Student Nonviolent Coordinating Committee (SNCC). The strong influence of the Nashville students, led by James Lawson, could be found in the SNCC statement of purpose:

> We affirm the philosophical or religious ideal of nonviolence as the foundation of our purpose, the presupposition of our faith, and the manner of our action. Nonviolence as it grows from Judaic-Christian tradition seeks a social order of justice permeated by love. Integration of human endeavor represents the crucial first step towards such a society.
>
> By appealing to conscience and standing on the moral nature of human existence, nonviolence nurtures the atmosphere in which reconciliation and justice become actual possibilities.

In the fall of 1960 SNCC established an organizational structure, a set of principles, and a new style of civil rights protest. The emphasis was on fighting segregation through direct confrontation, mass action, and civil disobedience. SNCC fieldworkers initiated and supported local, community-based activity. Three-quarters of the first fieldworkers were less than twenty-two years old. Leadership was vested in a nonhierarchical Coordinating Committee, but local groups were free to determine their own direction. SNCC people distrusted bureaucracy and structure; they stressed spontaneity and improvisation. Bob Moses, a former Harvard graduate student and New York City schoolteacher, best expressed the freewheeling SNCC attitude: "Go where the spirit say go and do what the spirit say do." Over the next few years SNCC was at the forefront of nearly every major civil rights battle.

The Election of 1960 and Civil Rights

The issue of race relations was kept from center stage during the very close presidential campaign of 1960. As vice president, Richard Nixon had been a leading Republican voice for stronger civil rights legislation. In contrast, Democratic nominee Senator John F. Kennedy had played virtually no role in the congressional battles over civil rights during the 1950s. But during the campaign, their roles reversed. Kennedy praised the sit-in movement as part of a revival of national reform spirit. He declared, "It is in the American tradition to stand up for one's rights—even if the new way is to sit down." While the Republican platform contained a strong civil rights plank, Nixon, eager to court white southern voters, minimized his own identification with the movement. In October, when Martin Luther King was jailed after leading a demonstration in Atlanta, Kennedy telephoned Coretta Scott King to reassure her and express his personal support. Kennedy's brother Robert telephoned the judge in the case and angrily warned him that he had violated King's civil rights and endangered the national Democratic ticket. The judge released King soon afterward.

News of this intervention did not gain wide attention in the white South, much to the relief of the Kennedys. The race was tight, and they knew they could not afford to alienate traditional white southern Democrats. But the campaign effectively played up the story among black voters all over the country. Kennedy won 70 percent of the black vote, which helped put him over the top in such critical states as Illinois, Texas, Michigan, and Pennsylvania and secure his narrow victory over Nixon. Many civil rights activists optimistically looked forward to a new president who would have to acknowledge his political debt to the black vote.

But the very closeness of his victory constrained Kennedy on the race question. Democrats had lost ground in the House and Senate, and Kennedy had to worry about alienating conservative southern Democrats who chaired key congressional committees. Passage of major civil rights legislation would be virtually impossible. The new president told leaders such as Roy Wilkins of the NAACP that a strategy of "minimum legislation, maximum executive action" offered the best road to change. The president did appoint some forty African Americans to high federal positions, including Thurgood Marshall to the federal appellate court. He established a Committee on Equal Employment Opportunity, chaired by Vice President Lyndon B. Johnson, to fight discrimination in the federal civil service and in corporations that received government contracts.

Most significantly, the Kennedy administration sought to invigorate the Civil Rights Division of the Justice Department. That division had been created by the Civil Rights Act of 1957, which authorized the attorney general to seek court injunctions to protect people denied their right to vote. But the Eisenhower administration had made little use of this new power. Robert Kennedy, the new attorney general, began assembling a staff of brilliant and

A *Freedom Riders' bus burns after being firebombed in Anniston, Alabama, May 14, 1961. After setting the bus afire, whites attacked the passengers fleeing the smoke and flames. Violent scenes like this one received extensive publicity in the mass media and helped compel the Justice Department to enforce court rulings banning segregation on interstate bus lines.*

committed attorneys, headed by Washington lawyer Burke Marshall. Kennedy encouraged them to get out of Washington and get into the field wherever racial troubles arose. In early 1961, when Louisiana school officials balked at a school desegregation order, Robert Kennedy warned them that he would ask the federal court to hold them in contempt. When Burke Marshall started court proceedings, the state officials gave in. But the new, more aggressive mood at Justice could not solve the central political dilemma: how to move forward on civil rights without alienating southern Democrats. Pressure from the newly energized southern civil rights movement soon revealed the true difficulty of that problem. The movement would also provoke murderous outrage from white extremists determined to maintain the racial status quo.

Freedom Rides

In the spring of 1961 James Farmer, national director of CORE, announced plans for an interracial Freedom Ride through the South. The goal was to test compliance with court orders banning segregation in interstate travel and terminal accommodations. CORE had just recently made Farmer its leader in an effort to revitalize the organization. One of the founders of CORE in 1942, Farmer had worked for various pacifist and socialist groups and served as program director for the NAACP. He designed the Freedom Ride to induce a crisis, in the spirit of the sit-ins. "Our intention," Farmer declared, "was to provoke

the southern authorities into arresting us and thereby prod the Justice Department into enforcing the law of the land." CORE received financial and tactical support from the SCLC and several NAACP branches. It also informed the Justice Department and the Federal Bureau of Investigation of its plans, but received no reply.

On May 4 seven blacks and six whites split into two interracial groups and left Washington on public buses bound for Alabama and Mississippi. At first the two buses encountered only isolated harassment and violence as they headed south. But when one bus entered Anniston, Alabama, on May 14 an angry mob surrounded it, smashing windows and slashing tires. Six miles out of town, the tires went flat. A firebomb tossed through a window forced the passengers out. The mob then beat the Freedom Riders with blackjacks, iron bars, and clubs, and the bus burst into flames. A caravan of cars organized by the Birmingham office of the SCLC rescued the wounded. Another mob attacked the second bus in Anniston, leaving one Freedom Rider close to death and permanently brain-damaged.

The violence escalated. In Birmingham, a mob of forty whites waited on the loading platform and attacked the bus that managed to get out of Anniston. Although police had been warned to expect trouble, they did nothing to stop the mob from beating the Freedom Riders with pipes and fists, nor did they make any arrests. FBI agents observed and took notes but did nothing. The remaining Freedom Riders decided to travel as a single group on the next lap, from Birmingham to Montgomery, but no bus would take them. Stranded and frightened, they reluctantly boarded a special flight to New Orleans arranged by the Justice Department. On May 17 the CORE-sponsored Freedom Ride disbanded.

But that was not the end of the Freedom Rides. SNCC leaders in Atlanta and Nashville assembled a fresh group of volunteers to continue the trip. On May 20 twenty-one Freedom Riders left Birmingham for Montgomery. The bus station in the Alabama capital was eerily quiet and deserted as they pulled in. But when the passengers left the bus a mob of several hundred whites rushed them, yelling "Get those niggers!" and clubbing people to the ground. James Zwerg, a white Freedom Rider from the University of Wisconsin, had his spinal cord severed. John Lewis, veteran of the Nashville sit-in movement, suffered a brain concussion. As he lay in a pool of blood, a policeman handed him a state court injunction forbidding interracial travel in Alabama. The mob indiscriminately beat journalists and clubbed John Siegenthaler, a Justice Department attorney sent to observe the scene. It took police more than an hour to halt the rioting. Montgomery's police commissioner later said, "We have no intention of standing guard for a bunch of troublemakers coming into our city."

The mob violence and the indifference of Alabama officials made the Freedom Ride page-one news around the country and throughout the world. Newspapers in Europe, Africa, and Asia denounced the hypocrisy of the federal government. The Kennedy administration, preparing for the president's first summit meeting with Soviet premier Nikita Khrushchev, saw the situation as a threat to its international prestige. On May 21, an angry mob threatened to invade a support rally at Montgomery's First Baptist Church. A hastily assembled group of 400 U.S. marshals, sent by Robert Kennedy, barely managed to keep the peace. The attorney general called for a cooling-off period, but Martin Luther King, James Farmer, and the SNCC leaders announced that the Freedom Ride would continue. When Robert Kennedy warned that the racial turmoil would embarrass the president in his meeting with Khrushchev, Ralph Abernathy of the SCLC replied, "Doesn't the Attorney General know that we've been embarrassed all our lives?"

A bandaged but spirited group of twenty-seven Freedom Riders prepared to leave Montgomery for Jackson, Mississippi, on May 24. To avoid further violence Robert Kennedy arranged a compromise through Mississippi senator James Eastland. In exchange for a guarantee of safe passage through Mississippi, the federal government promised not to interfere with the arrest of the Freedom Riders in Jackson. This Freedom Ride and several that followed thus escaped violence. But more than 300 people were arrested that summer in Jackson on charges of traveling "for the avowed purpose of inflaming public opinion." Sticking to a policy of "jail, no bail," Freedom Riders clogged the prison, where they endured beatings and intimidation by prison guards that went largely unreported in the press. Their jail experiences turned most of them into committed core leaders of the student movement.

The Justice Department eventually petitioned the Interstate Commerce Commission to issue clear rules prohibiting segregation on interstate carriers. At the end of 1962 CORE proclaimed victory in the battle against Jim Crow interstate travel. By creating a crisis, the Freedom Rides had forced the Kennedy administration to act. But they also revealed the unwillingness of the federal government to fully enforce the law of the land. The Freedom Rides exposed the ugly face of southern racism to the world. At the same time, they reinforced white resistance to desegregation. The jailings and brutality experienced by Freedom Riders made clear to the civil rights community the limits of moral suasion alone for effecting change.

The Albany Movement: The Limits of Protest

Where the federal government chose not to enforce the constitutional rights of black people, segregationist forces tenaciously held their ground, especially in the more remote areas of the Deep South. In Albany, a small city in southwest Georgia, activists from SNCC, the NAACP, and other local groups formed a coalition known as the Albany movement. Starting in October 1961 and continuing for more than a year, thousands of Albany's black citizens marched, sat in, and boycotted as part of a citywide campaign to integrate public facilities and win voting rights. More than a thousand people spent time in jail. In December, the arrival of Martin Luther King and the SCLC transformed Albany into a national symbol of the struggle.

But the gains at Albany proved minimal. Infighting among the various civil rights organizations hurt the cause. Local SNCC workers opposed the more cautious approach of NAACP officials, even though the more established organization paid many of the campaign's expenses. The arrival of King guaranteed national news coverage, but local activists worried that his presence might undermine the community focus and their own influence. Most important, Albany police chief Laurie Pritchett shrewdly deprived the movement of the kind of national sympathy won by the Freedom Riders. Pritchett filled the jails with black demonstrators, kept their mistreatment to a minimum, and prevented white mobs from running wild. "We met 'nonviolence' with 'nonviolence,' " he boasted.

King himself was twice arrested in the summer of 1962, but Albany officials quickly freed him to avoid negative publicity. The Kennedy administration kept clear of the developments in Albany, hoping to help the gubernatorial campaign of "moderate" Democrat Carl Sanders. By late 1962 the Albany movement had collapsed, and Pritchett proudly declared the city "as segregated as ever." One activist summed up the losing campaign: "We were naive enough to think we could fill up the jails. Pritchett was hep to the fact that we couldn't. We ran out of people before he ran out of jails." Albany showed that mass protest without violent white reaction and direct federal intervention could not end Jim Crow.

The successful battle to integrate the University of Mississippi in 1962 contrasted with the failure at Albany and reinforced the importance of federal intervention for guaranteeing civil rights to African Americans. In the fall of 1962 James Meredith, an Air Force veteran and a student at all-black Jackson State College, tried to register as the first black student at the university. Governor Ross Barnett defied a federal court order and personally blocked Meredith's path at the admissions office. When Barnett refused to assure Robert Kennedy that Meredith would be protected, the attorney general dispatched 500 federal marshals to the campus. Over the radio, Barnett encouraged resistance to the "oppressive power of the United States," and an angry mob of several thousand whites, many of them armed, laid siege to the campus on September 30. A night of violence left 2 people dead and 160 marshals wounded, 28 from gunfire. President Kennedy ordered 5,000 army troops onto the campus to stop the riot. A federal guard remained to protect Meredith, who graduated the following summer.

THE MOVEMENT AT HIGH TIDE, 1963–65

The tumultuous events of 1960–62 convinced civil rights strategists that segregation could not be dismantled merely through orderly protest and moral persuasion. Only comprehensive civil rights legislation, backed by the power of the federal government, could guarantee full citizenship rights for African Americans. To build the national consensus needed for new laws, civil rights activists looked for ways to gain broader support for their cause. By 1963, their sense of urgency had led them to plan dramatic confrontations that would expose the violence and terror routinely faced by southern blacks. With the whole country—indeed, the whole world—watching, the movement reached the peak of its political and moral power.

Birmingham

At the end of 1962, Martin Luther King and his SCLC allies decided to launch a new campaign against segregation in Birmingham, Alabama. After the failure in Albany, King and his aides looked for a way to shore up his leadership and inject new momentum into the freedom struggle. They needed a major victory. Birmingham was the most segregated big city in America, and it had a deep history of racial violence. African Americans endured total segregation in schools, restaurants, city parks, and department store dressing rooms. Although black people constituted more than 40 percent of the city's population, fewer than 10,000 of Birmingham's 80,000 registered voters were black. The city's prosperous steel industry relegated black workers to menial jobs.

Working closely with local civil rights groups led by the longtime Birmingham activist Reverend Fred Shuttlesworth, the SCLC carefully planned its campaign. The strategy was to fill the city jails with protesters, boycott downtown department stores, and enrage Public Safety Commissioner Eugene "Bull" Connor. In April, King arrived with a manifesto demanding an end to racist hiring practices and segregated public accommodations and the creation of a biracial committee to oversee desegregation. "Here in Birmingham," King told reporters, "we have reached the point of no return." Connor's police began jailing hundreds of demonstrators, including King himself, who defied a state court injunction against further protests.

Held in solitary confinement for several days, King managed to write a response to a group of Birmingham clergy who had deplored the protests. King's *Letter from Birmingham Jail* was soon widely reprinted and circulated as a pamphlet. It set out the key moral issues at stake, and scoffed at those who claimed the campaign was illegal and ill timed. King wrote:

> We know through painful experience that freedom is never voluntarily given by the oppressor; it must be demanded by the oppressed. Frankly, I have never yet engaged in a direct action campaign that was "well timed" in the view of those who have not suffered unduly from the disease of segregation. For years now I have heard the word "Wait!" It rings in the ear of every Negro with a piercing familiarity. This "Wait" has almost always meant "Never." We must come to see, with one of our distinguished jurists, that "justice too long delayed is justice denied."

After King's release on bail, the campaign intensified. The SCLC kept up the pressure by recruiting thousands of Birmingham's young students for a "children's crusade." In early May, Bull Connor's forces

Police dogs attacked a seventeen-year-old civil rights demonstrator for defying an anti-parade ordinance in Birmingham, Alabama, May 3, 1963. He was part of the "children's crusade" organized by SCLC in its campaign to fill the city jails with protesters. More than 900 Birmingham schoolchildren went to jail that day.

began using high-powered water cannons, billy clubs, and snarling police dogs to break up demonstrations. Millions of Americans reacted with horror to the violent scenes from Birmingham shown on national television. Many younger black people, especially from the city's poor and working-class districts, began to fight back, hurling bottles and bricks at police. On May 10, mediators from the Justice Department negotiated an uneasy truce. The SCLC agreed to an immediate end to the protests. In exchange, businesses would desegregate and begin hiring African Americans over the next three months, and a biracial city committee would oversee desegregation of public facilities.

King claimed "the most magnificent victory for justice we've ever seen in the Deep South." But whites such as Bull Connor and Governor George Wallace denounced the agreement. A few days after the announcement, more than a thousand robed Ku Klux Klansmen burned a cross in a park on the outskirts of Birmingham. When bombs rocked SCLC headquarters and the home of King's brother, a Birmingham minister, enraged blacks took to the streets and pelted police and fire fighters with stones and bottles. President Kennedy ordered 3,000 army troops into the city and prepared to nationalize the Alabama Guard. The violence receded, and white city business people and politicians began to carry out the agreed-upon pact. But in September a bomb killed four black girls in a Birmingham Baptist church, reminding the city and the world that racial harmony was still a long way off.

The Birmingham campaign and the other protests it sparked over the next seven months engaged more than 100,000 people and led to nearly 15,000 arrests. The civil rights community now drew support from millions of Americans, black and white, who were inspired by the protesters and repelled by the face of southern bigotry. At the same time, Birmingham changed the nature of black protest. The black unemployed and working poor who joined in the struggle brought a different perspective from that of the students, professionals, and members of the religious middle class who had dominated the movement before Birmingham. They cared less about the philosophy of nonviolence and more about immediate gains in employment and housing and an end to police brutality. The urgent cries for "Freedom now!" were more than simply a demand to end legal segregation, and they were a measure as well of how far the movement had traveled in the seven years since the end of the Montgomery bus boycott.

JFK and the March on Washington

The growth of black activism and white support convinced President Kennedy the moment had come to press for sweeping civil rights legislation. Continuing white resistance in the South also made clearer than ever the need for federal action. In June 1963, Alabama governor George Wallace threatened to personally block the admission of two black students to the state university. Only the deployment of National Guard troops, placed under federal control by the president, ensured the students' safety and their peaceful admission into the University of Alabama.

It was a defining moment for Kennedy. On June 11 the president went on national television and offered his personal endorsement of the civil rights activism. Reviewing the racial situation, Kennedy told his audience that America would not be fully free until all its citizens were free. "We face . . . a moral crisis as a country and a people. It cannot be met by repressive police action. It cannot be left to increased demonstrations in the streets. It cannot be quieted by token moves or talk. It is a time to act in the Congress, in your state and local legislative body, and, above all, in all our daily lives." The next week Kennedy asked Congress for a broad law that would ensure voting rights, outlaw segregation in public facilities, and bolster federal authority to deny funds for discriminatory programs. Knowing they would face a stiff fight from congressional conservatives, administration officials began an intense lobbying effort in support of the law. After three years of fence sitting, Kennedy finally committed his office and his political future to the civil rights cause.

Movement leaders lauded the president's initiative. Yet they understood that racial hatred still haunted the nation. Only a few hours after Kennedy's television speech, a gunman murdered Medgar Evers, leader of the Mississippi NAACP, outside his home in Jackson. To pressure Congress and demonstrate the

Reverend Dr. Martin Luther King, Jr., acknowledging the huge throng at the historic March on Washington for "jobs and freedom," August 28, 1963. The size of the crowd, the stirring oratory and song, and the live network television coverage produced one of the most memorable political events in the nation's history.

urgency of their cause, a broad coalition of civil rights groups planned a massive, nonviolent March on Washington. The idea had deep roots in black protest. A. Philip Randolph, head of the Brotherhood of Sleeping Car Porters, had originally proposed such a march in 1941 to protest discrimination against blacks in the wartime defense industries. Now, more than twenty years later, Randolph, along with his aide Bayard Rustin, revived the concept and convinced leaders of the major civil rights groups to support it.

The Kennedy administration originally opposed the march, fearing it would jeopardize support for the president's civil rights bill in Congress. But as plans for the rally solidified, Kennedy reluctantly gave his approval. Leaders from the SCLC, the NAACP, SNCC, the Urban League, and CORE—the leading organizations in the civil rights community—put aside their tactical differences to forge a broad consensus for the event. John Lewis, the young head of SNCC who had endured numerous brutal assaults, planned a speech that denounced the Kennedys as hypocrites. Lewis's speech enraged Walter Reuther, the white liberal leader of the United Auto Workers union, which had helped finance the march. Reuther threatened to turn off the loudspeakers he was paying for, believing Lewis's speech would embarrass the Kennedys. Randolph, the acknowledged elder statesman of the movement, convinced Lewis at the last moment to tone down his remarks. "We've come this far," he implored. "For the sake of unity, change it."

On August 28, 1963, more than a quarter of a million people, including 50,000 whites, gathered at the Lincoln Memorial to rally for "jobs and freedom." Union members, students, teachers, clergy, professionals, musicians, actors—Americans from all walks of life joined the largest political assembly in the nation's history until then. The sight of all those people holding hands and singing "We Shall Overcome," led by the white folk singer Joan Baez, would not be easily forgotten. At the end of a long, exhilarating day of speeches and freedom songs, Martin Luther King provided an emotional climax. Combining the democratic promise of the Declaration of Independence with the religious fervor of his Baptist heritage, King stirred the crowd with his dream for America:

> I have a dream today that one day this nation will rise up and live out the true meaning of its creed: "We hold these truths to be self-evident—that all men are created equal." . . . When we allow freedom to ring, when we let it ring from every village and every hamlet, from every state and every city, we will be able to speed up that day when all of God's children—black men and white men, Jews and Gentiles, Protestants and Catholics—will be able to join hands and sing in the words of the old Negro spiritual, "Free at last! Free at last! Thank God almighty, we are free at last!"

LBJ and the Civil Rights Act of 1964

An extraordinary demonstration of interracial unity, the March on Washington stood as the high-water mark in the struggle for civil rights. It buoyed the spirits of movement leaders as well as the liberals pushing the new civil rights bill through Congress. But the assassination of John F. Kennedy on November 22, 1963, in Dallas threw an ominous cloud over the whole nation and the civil rights movement in particular. In the Deep South, many ardent segregationists welcomed the president's death because of his support for civil rights. Most African Americans probably shared the feelings of Coretta Scott King, who recalled her family's vigil: "We felt that President Kennedy had been a friend of the

Cause and that with him as President we could continue to move forward. We watched and prayed for him."

Lyndon Baines Johnson, Kennedy's successor, had never been much of a friend to civil rights. As a senator from Texas (1948–60, including six years as majority leader), Johnson had been one of the shrewdest and most powerful Democrats in Congress. Throughout the 1950s he had worked to obstruct the passage and enforcement of civil rights laws—though as vice president he had ably chaired Kennedy's working group on equal employment. Johnson reassured a grieving nation that "the ideas and the ideals which [Kennedy] so nobly represented must and will be translated into effective action." Even so, civil rights activists looked upon Johnson warily as he took over the Oval Office.

As president, Johnson realized that he faced a new political reality, one created by the civil rights movement. Eager to unite the Democratic Party and prove himself as a national leader, he seized on civil rights as a golden political opportunity. "I knew that if I didn't get out in front on this issue," he later recalled, "they [the liberals] would get me. They'd throw up my background against me, they'd use it to prove that I was incapable of bringing unity to the land I loved so much. . . . I had to produce a civil rights bill that was even stronger than the one they'd have gotten if Kennedy had lived." Throughout the early months of 1964, the new president let it be known publicly and privately that he would brook no compromise on civil rights.

Johnson exploited all his skills as a political insider. He cajoled, flattered, and threatened key members of the House and Senate. Working with the president, the fifteen-year-old Leadership Conference on Civil Rights coordinated a sophisticated lobbying effort in Congress. Groups such as the NAACP, the AFL-CIO, the National Council of Churches, and the American Jewish Congress made the case for a strong civil rights bill. The House passed the bill in February by a 290–130 vote. The more difficult fight would be in the Senate, where a southern filibuster promised to block the bill or weaken it. But by June, Johnson's persistence had paid off and the southern filibuster had collapsed.

On July 2, 1964, Johnson signed the Civil Rights Act of 1964. Every major provision had survived intact. This landmark law represented the most significant civil rights legislation since Reconstruction. It prohibited discrimination in most places of public accommodation; outlawed discrimination in employment on the basis of race, color, religion, sex, or national origin; outlawed bias in federally assisted programs; authorized the Justice Department to institute suits to desegregate public schools and other facilities; created the Equal Employment Opportunity Commission; and provided technical and financial aid to communities desegregating their schools.

OVERVIEW

LANDMARK CIVIL RIGHTS LEGISLATION, SUPREME COURT DECISIONS, AND EXECUTIVE ORDERS

Year	Decision, law, or executive order	Significance
1939	*Missouri v. ex.rel.Gaines*	Required University of Missouri Law School either to admit African Americans or build another, fully equal law school
1941	Executive Order 8802 (by President Roosevelt)	Banned racial discrimination in defense industry and government offices; established Fair Employment Practices Committee to investigate violations
1946	*Morgan v. Virginia*	Ruled that segregation on interstate buses violated federal law and created an "undue burden" on interstate commerce
1948	Executive Order 9981 (by President Truman)	Desegregated the U.S. armed forces
1950	*McLaurin v. Oklahoma State Regents*	Ruled that forcing an African American student to sit, eat, and study in segregated facilities was unconstitutional because it inevitably created a "badge of inferiority"
1950	*Sweatt v. Painter*	Ruled that an inferior law school created by the University of Texas to serve African-Americans violated their right to equal protection and ordered Herman Sweatt to be admitted to University of Texas Law School
1954	*Brown v. Board of Education of Topeka I*	Declared "separate educational facilities are inherently unequal," thus overturning *Plessy v. Ferguson* (1896) and the "separate but equal" doctrine as it applied to public schools
1955	*Brown v. Board of Education of Topeka II*	Ordered school desegregation to begin with "all deliberate speed," but offered no timetable
1957	Civil Rights Act	Created Civil Rights Division within the Justice Department
1964	Civil Rights Act	Prohibited discrimination in employment and most places of public accommodation on basis of race, color, religion, sex, or national origin; outlawed bias in federally assisted programs; created Equal Employment Opportunity Commission
1965	Voting Rights Act	Authorized federal supervision of voter registration in states and counties where fewer than half of voting age residents were registered; outlawed literacy and other discriminatory tests in voter registration

Mississippi Freedom Summer

While President Johnson and his liberal allies won the congressional battle for the new civil rights bill, activists in Mississippi mounted a far more radical and dangerous campaign than any yet attempted in the South. In the spring of 1964 a coalition of workers led by SNCC launched the Freedom Summer project, an ambitious effort to register black voters and directly challenge the iron rule of segregation. Mississippi stood as the toughest test for the civil rights movement, racially and economically. It was the poorest, most backward state in the nation, and had remained largely untouched by the freedom struggle. African Americans constituted 42 percent of the state's population, but fewer than

After they were barred from the floor of the August 1964 National Democratic convention, members of the Mississippi Freedom Democratic Party were led by Fanny Lou Hamer in a song-filled protest outside the hotel.

5 percent could register to vote. Median black family income was under $1,500 a year, roughly one-third that of white families. A small white planter elite controlled most of the state's wealth, and a long tradition of terror against black people had maintained the racial caste system.

Bob Moses of SNCC and Dave Dennis of CORE planned Freedom Summer as a way of opening up this closed society to the glare of national publicity. The project recruited over 900 volunteers, mostly white college students, to aid in voter registration, teach in "freedom schools," and help build a "freedom party" as an alternative to Mississippi's all-white Democratic Party. Organizers expected violence, which was precisely why they wanted white volunteers. Dave Dennis later explained their reasoning: "The death of a white college student would bring on more attention to what was going on than for a black college student getting it. That's cold, but that was also in another sense speaking the language of this country." Mississippi authorities prepared for the civil rights workers as if expecting a foreign army, beefing up state highway patrols and local police forces.

On June 21, while most project volunteers were still undergoing training in Ohio, three activists disappeared in Neshoba County, Mississippi, when they went to investigate the burning of a black church that was supposed to serve as a freedom school. Six weeks later, after a massive search belatedly ordered by President Johnson, FBI agents discovered the bodies of the three—white activists Michael Schwerner and Andrew Goodman, and a local black activist, James

Chaney—buried in an earthen dam. Goodman and Schwerner had been shot once; Chaney had been severely beaten before being shot three times. Over the summer, at least three other civil rights workers died violently. Project workers suffered 1,000 arrests, 80 beatings, 35 shooting incidents, and 30 bombings in homes, churches, and schools.

Within the project, simmering problems tested the ideal of the Beloved Community. Black veterans of SNCC resented the affluent white volunteers, many of whom had not come to terms with their own racial prejudices. White volunteers, staying only a short time in the state, often found it difficult to communicate in the southern communities with local African Americans, who were wary of breaking old codes of deference. Sexual tensions between black male and white female volunteers also strained relations. A number of both black and white women, led by Ruby Doris Robinson, Mary King, and Casey Hayden, began to raise the issue of women's equality as a companion goal to racial equality. The day-to-day reality of violent reprisals, police harassment, and constant fear took a hard toll on everyone.

The project did manage to rivet national attention on Mississippi racism, and it won enormous sympathy from northern liberals. Among their concrete accomplishments, the volunteers could point with pride to more than forty freedom schools that brought classes in reading, arithmetic, politics, and African American history to thousands of black children. Some 60,000 black voters signed up to join the Mississippi Freedom Democratic Party (MFDP). In August 1964 the MFDP sent a slate of delegates to the Democratic

National Convention looking to challenge the credentials of the all-white regular state delegation.

In Atlantic City, the idealism of Freedom Summer ran into the more cynical needs of the national Democratic Party. Lyndon Johnson opposed the seating of the MFDP because he wanted to avoid a divisive floor fight. He was already concerned that Republicans might carry a number of southern states in November. But MFDP leaders and sympathizers gave dramatic testimony before the convention, detailing the racism and brutality in Mississippi politics. "Is this America," asked Fannie Lou Hamer, "the land of the free and the home of the brave, where we are threatened daily because we want to live as decent human beings?" Led by vice-presidential nominee Senator Hubert Humphrey, Johnson's forces offered a compromise that would have given the MFDP a token two seats on the floor. Bitter over what they saw as a betrayal, the MFDP delegates turned the offer down. Within SNCC, the defeat of the MFDP intensified African American disillusionment with the Democratic Party and the liberal establishment.

Malcolm X and Black Consciousness

Frustrated with the limits of nonviolent protest and electoral politics, younger activists within SNCC found themselves increasingly drawn to the militant rhetoric and vision of Malcolm X, who since 1950 had been the preeminent spokesman for the black nationalist religious sect, the Nation of Islam (NOI). Founded in depression-era Detroit by Elijah Muhammad, the NOI, like the followers of black nationalist leader Marcus Garvey in the 1920s (see Chapter 23) aspired to create a self-reliant, highly disciplined, and proud community—a separate "nation" for black people. Elijah Muhammad preached a message of racial solidarity and self-help, criticized crime and drug use, and castigated whites as "blue-eyed devils" responsible for the world's evil. During the 1950s the NOI (also called Black Muslims) successfully organized in northern black communities, appealing especially to criminals, drug addicts, and others living on the margins of urban life. It operated restaurants, retail stores, and schools as models for black economic self-sufficiency.

The man known as Malcolm X had been born Malcolm Little in 1925 and raised in Lansing, Michigan. His father, a preacher and a follower of Marcus Garvey, was killed in a racist attack by local whites. In his youth, Malcolm led a life of petty crime, eventually serving a seven-year prison term for burglary. While in jail he educated himself and converted to the Nation of Islam. He took the surname "X" to symbolize his original African family name, lost through slavery. Emerging from jail in 1952, he became a dynamic organizer, editor, and speaker for the Nation of Islam. He spoke frequently on college campuses as well on the street corners of black neighborhoods like New York's Harlem. He

Born Malcolm Little, Malcolm X (1925–65) took the name "X" as a symbol of the stolen identity of African slaves. He emerged in the early 1960s as the foremost advocate of racial unity and black nationalism. The Black Power movement, initiated in 1966 by SNCC members, was strongly influenced by Malcolm X.

encouraged his audiences to take pride in their African heritage and to consider armed self-defense rather than relying solely on nonviolence—in short, to break free of white domination "by any means necessary."

Malcolm ridiculed the integrationist goals of the civil rights movement. Black Muslims, he told audiences, do not want "to integrate into this corrupt society, but to separate from it, to a land of our own, where we can reform ourselves, lift up our moral standards, and try to be godly." In his best-selling *Autobiography of Malcolm X* (1965), he admitted that his position was extremist. "The black race here in North America is in extremely bad condition. You show me a black man who isn't an extremist," he argued, "and I'll show you one who needs psychiatric attention."

In 1964, troubled by Elijah Muhammad's personal scandals (he faced paternity suits brought by two young female employees) and eager to find a more politically effective approach to improving conditions for blacks, Malcolm X broke with the Nation of Islam. He made a pilgrimage to Mecca, the Muslim holy city, where he met Islamic peoples of all colors and underwent a "radical alteration in my whole outlook about 'white' men." He returned to the United States as El-Hajj Malik El-Shabazz, abandoned his black separatist views, and founded the Organization of Afro-American Unity. Malcolm now looked for common ground with the civil rights movement, addressing a Mississippi Freedom Democrats rally in Harlem and meeting with SNCC activists. He stressed the international links between the civil rights struggle in America and the problems facing emerging African nations. On February 21, 1965, Malcolm X was assassinated during a speech at Harlem's Audubon Ballroom. His assailants were members of a New Jersey branch of the NOI, possibly infiltrated by the FBI.

"More than any other person," remarked black author Julius Lester, "Malcolm X was responsible for the new militancy that entered The Movement in 1965." SNCC leader John Lewis thought Malcolm had been the most effective voice "to articulate the aspirations, bitterness, and frustrations of the Negro people," forming "a living link between Africa and the civil rights movement in this country." In his death he became a martyr for the idea that soon became known as Black Power. As much as anyone, Malcolm X pointed the way to a new black consciousness that celebrated black history, black culture, the African heritage, and black self-sufficiency.

Selma and the Voting Rights Act of 1965

Lyndon Johnson won reelection in 1964 by a landslide, capturing 61 percent of the popular vote. Of the 6 million black people who voted in the election, 2 million more than in 1960, an overwhelming 94 percent cast their ballots for Johnson. Republican candidate Senator Barry Goldwater managed to carry only his home state of Arizona and five Deep South states, where fewer than 45 percent of eligible black people could vote. With Democrats in firm control of both the Senate and the House, civil rights leaders believed the time was ripe for further legislative gains. Johnson and his staff began drafting a tough voting rights bill in late 1964, partly with an eye toward countering Republican gains in the Deep South with newly registered black and Democratic voters. Martin Luther King and the SCLC shared this goal of passing a strong voting rights law that would provide southern black people with direct federal protection of their right to vote.

Once again, movement leaders plotted to create a crisis that would arouse national indignation, pressure Congress, and force federal action. King and his aides chose Selma, Alabama, as the target of their campaign. Selma, a city of 27,000 some fifty miles west of Montgomery, had a notorious record of preventing black voting. Of the 15,000 eligible black voters in Selma's Dallas County, registered voters numbered only in the hundreds. In 1963, local activists Amelia Boynton and Reverend Fred Reese had invited SNCC workers to aid voter registration efforts in the community. But they had met a violent reception from county sheriff Jim Clark. Sensing that Clark might be another Bull Connor, King arrived in Selma in January 1965, just after accepting the Nobel Peace Prize in Oslo. "We are not asking, we are demanding the ballot," he declared. King, the SCLC staff, and SNCC workers led daily marches on the Dallas County Courthouse, where hundreds of black citizens tried to get their names added to voter lists. By early February, Clark had imprisoned more than 3,000 protesters.

Despite the brutal beating of Reverend James Bevel, a key SCLC strategist, and the killing of Jimmy

Voting rights demonstrators rallied in front of the state capitol in Montgomery, Alabama, March 25, 1965, after a four day, fifty-four mile trek from Selma. The original 3,000 marchers were joined by over 30,000 supporters by the end of their journey.

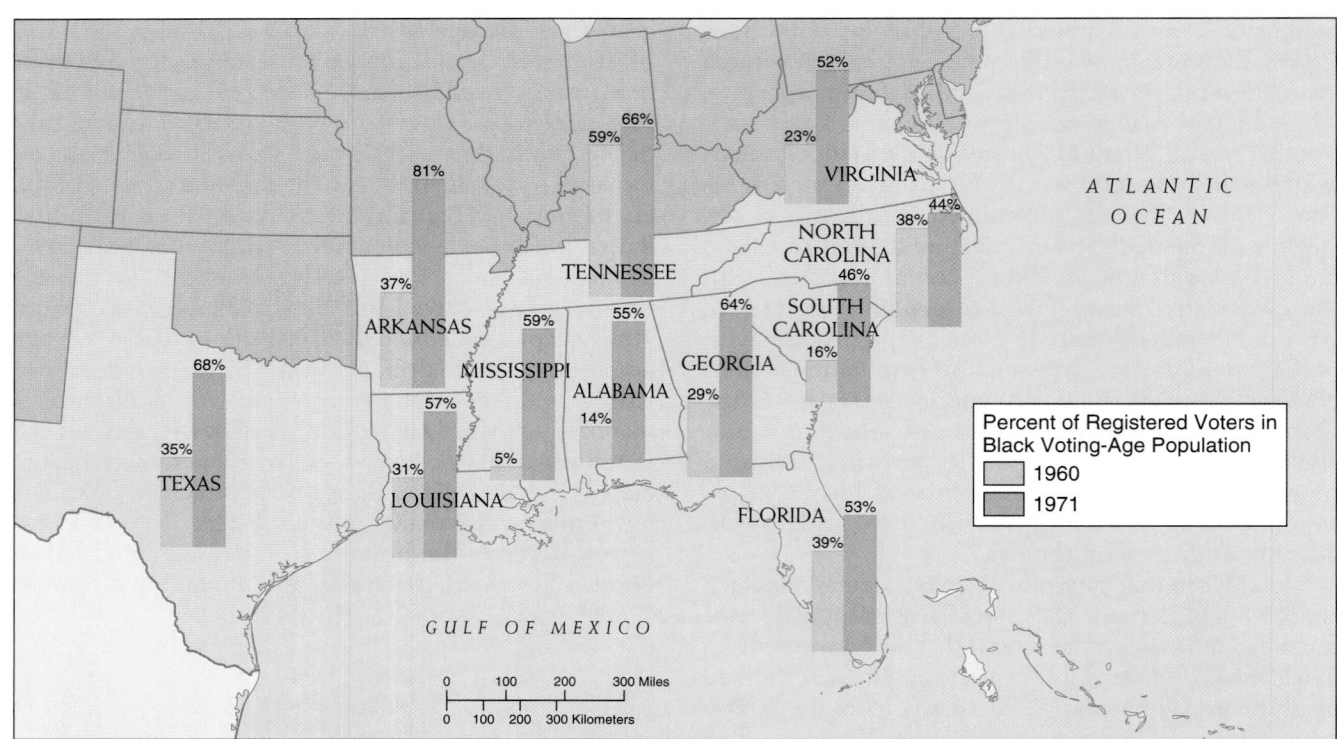

Impact of the Voting Rights Act of 1965   *Voter registration among African Americans in the South increased significantly between 1960 and 1971.*

Lee Jackson, a young black demonstrator in nearby Marion, the SCLC failed to arouse the level of national indignation it sought. Consequently, in early March SCLC staffers called on black activists to march from Selma to Montgomery, where they planned to deliver a list of grievances to Governor Wallace. On Sunday, March 7, while King preached to his church in Atlanta, a group of 600 marchers crossed the Pettus Bridge on the Alabama River, on their way to Montgomery. A group of mounted, heavily armed county and state lawmen blocked their path and ordered them to turn back. When the marchers did not move, the lawmen attacked with billy clubs and tear gas, driving the protesters back over the bridge in a bloody rout. More than fifty marchers had to be treated in local hospitals.

The dramatic "Bloody Sunday" attack received extensive coverage on network television, prompting a national uproar. Demands for federal intervention poured into the White House from all over the country. King issued a public call for civil rights supporters to come to Selma for a second march on Montgomery. But a federal court temporarily enjoined the SCLC from proceeding with the march. King found himself trapped. He reluctantly accepted a face-saving compromise: in return for a promise from Alabama authorities not to harm marchers, King would lead his followers across the Pettus Bridge, stop, pray briefly,

and then turn back. This plan outraged the more militant SNCC activists and sharpened their distrust of King and the SCLC.

But just when it seemed the Selma movement might die, white racist violence revived it. A gang of white toughs attacked four white Unitarian ministers who had come to Selma to participate in the march. One of them, Reverend James J. Reeb of Boston, died of multiple skull fractures. His death brought new calls for federal action. On March 15, President Johnson delivered a televised address to a joint session of Congress to request passage of a voting rights bill. In a stirring speech, the president fused the political power of his office with the moral power of the movement. "Their cause must be our cause, too. Because it is not just Negroes, but really all of us who must overcome the crippling legacy of bigotry and injustice. And," he concluded firmly, invoking the movement's slogan, "we shall overcome." Johnson also prevailed upon federal judge Frank Johnson to issue a ruling allowing the march to proceed, and he warned Governor Wallace not to interfere.

On March 21 Martin Luther King led a group of more than 3,000 black and white marchers out of Selma on the road to Montgomery, where the bus boycott that marked the beginning of his involvement had occurred nine years before. Four days later they arrived at the Alabama statehouse. Their ranks had been swelled by more than 30,000 supporters, including hundreds of prominent politicians, entertainers, and black leaders. "I know some of you are asking today," King told the crowd, " 'How long will it take?' " He went on in a rousing, rhythmic cadence:

> I come to say to you this afternoon, however difficult the moment, however frustrating the hour, it will not be long because truth pressed to earth will rise again. How long? Not long, because no lie can live forever. How long? Not long, because you will reap what you sow. How long? Not long, because the arc of the moral universe is long but it bends toward justice. How long? Not long, because mine eyes have seen the glory of the coming of the Lord!

In August 1965 President Johnson signed the Voting Rights Act into law. It authorized federal supervision of registration in states and counties where fewer than half of voting-age residents were registered. It also outlawed literacy and other discriminatory tests that had been used to prevent blacks from registering to vote. Between 1964 and 1968, black registrants in Mississippi leaped from 7 percent to 59 percent of the statewide black population; in Alabama, from 24 percent to 57 percent. In those years the number of southern black voters grew from 1 million to 3.1 million. For the first time in their lives, black Southerners in hundreds of small towns and rural communities could enjoy full participation in American politics. Ten years after the Montgomery bus boycott, the civil rights movement had reached a peak of national influence and interracial unity.

FORGOTTEN MINORITIES, 1945–65

The civil rights movement revolved around the aspirations and community strength of African Americans. The historic injustices of slavery, racism, and segregation gave a moral and political urgency to the black struggle for full citizenship rights. Yet other minorities as well had long been denied their civil rights. After World War II, Latinos, Indian peoples, and Asian Americans began making their own halting efforts to improve their political, legal, and economic status. They faced strong opposition from institutional racism and various economic interests that benefited from keeping these groups in a subordinate position. By the late 1960s, the success of the black civil rights movement had inspired these minority groups to adopt more militant strategies of their own.

Mexican Americans

The Mexican American community in the West and Southwest included both longtime U.S. citizens—who found white authorities nonetheless unwilling to recognize their rights—and non-citizen immigrants from Mexico. After World War II, several Mexican American political organizations sought to secure equal rights and equal opportunity for their community by stressing its American identity. The most important of these groups were the League of United Latin American Citizens (LULAC), founded in Texas in 1928, and the GI Forum, founded in Texas in 1948 by Mexican American veterans of World War II. Both emphasized the learning of English, assimilation into American society, improved education, and the promotion of political power through voting. LULAC successfully pursued two important legal cases that anticipated *Brown v. Board of Education.* In *Mendez v. Westminster,* a 1947 California case, and in the 1948 *Delgado* case in Texas, the Supreme Court upheld lower-court rulings that declared segregation of Mexican Americans unconstitutional. Like *Brown,* these two decisions did not immediately end segregation, but they offered pathbreaking legal and psychological victories to Mexican American activists. LULAC won another significant legal battle in the 1954 *Hernandez* decision, in which the Supreme Court ended the exclusion of Mexican Americans from Texas jury lists.

Mexican migration to the United States increased dramatically during and after World War II. The *bracero* program, a cooperative effort between the U.S. and Mexican governments, brought some 300,000 Mexicans to the United States during the war as temporary agricultural and railroad workers. American agribusiness came to depend on Mexicans as a key source of cheap farm labor, and the program continued after the war. Most *braceros* endured harsh work, poor food, and substandard housing in the camps in which they lived. Some migrated into the newly emerging barrio neighborhoods in cities such as San Antonio, Los Angeles, El Paso, and Denver. Many *braceros* and their children became American citizens, but most returned to Mexico. Another group of postwar Mexican immigrants were the *mojados,* or "wetbacks," so called because many swam across the Rio Grande River to enter the United States illegally.

In 1954, in an effort to curb the flow of undocumented immigrants from Mexico, the Eisenhower administration launched the massive "Operation Wetback." Over the next three years Immigration Service agents rounded up some 3.7 million allegedly illegal migrants and sent them back over the border. Immigration agents made little effort to distinguish the so-called illegals from *braceros* and Mexican American citizens. Many families were broken up, and thousands who had lived in the United States for a decade or more found

Delegates to the 1948 National Convention of the League of United Latin American Citizens met in Kingsville, Texas. After World War II, LULAC grew to about 15,000 members active in two hundred local councils, mostly in Texas and California.

themselves deported. Many deportees were denied basic civil liberties, such as due process, and suffered physical abuse and intimidation. Most Mexican Americans had ambivalent feelings about *mojados* and Operation Wetback. The deportations tended to improve job opportunities and wages for those who remained. Yet the so-called illegals were considered members of *la raza,* the larger Mexican American community, and family ties between these groups were common. LULAC and the *Asociación Nacional Mexico-Americana,* founded in 1950, tried in vain to curb abuses against aliens and Mexican Americans. Among Mexican Americans, Operation Wetback left a bitter legacy of deep mistrust and estrangement from Anglo culture and politics.

Puerto Ricans

The United States took possession of the island of Puerto Rico in 1898, during the final stages of the Spanish-American War. The Jones Act of 1917 made the island an unincorporated territory of the United States and granted U.S. citizenship to all Puerto Ricans. Over the next several decades, Puerto Rico's economic base shifted from a diversified, subsistence-oriented agriculture to a single export crop—sugar. U.S. absentee owners dominated the sugar industry, claiming most of the island's arable land, previously tilled by small farmers growing crops for local consumption. Puerto Rico's sugar industry grew enormously profitable, but few island residents benefited from this expansion. By the

1930s, unemployment and poverty were widespread and the island was forced to import its foodstuffs.

Small communities of Puerto Rican migrants had begun to form in New York City during the 1920s. The largest was on the Upper East Side of Manhattan—*el barrio* in East Harlem. During World War II, labor shortages led the federal government to sponsor the recruitment of Puerto Rican workers for industrial jobs in New Jersey, Philadelphia, and Chicago. But the "great migration" took place from 1945 to 1964. During these two decades the number of Puerto Ricans living on the mainland jumped from less than 100,000 to roughly 1 million. Economic opportunity was the chief impetus for this migration, for the island suffered from high unemployment rates and low wages.

The advent of direct air service between Puerto Rico and New York in 1945 made the city easily accessible. The Puerto Rican community in East (or Spanish) Harlem mushroomed, and new communities in the South Bronx and Brooklyn began to emerge. By 1970 there were about 800,000 Puerto Ricans in New York—more than 10 percent of the city's population. New Puerto Rican communities also took root in Connecticut, Massachusetts, New Jersey, and the Midwest. Puerto Ricans frequently circulated between the island and the mainland, often returning home when economic conditions on the mainland were less favorable.

The experience of Puerto Rican migrants both resembled and differed from that of other immigrant groups in significant ways. Like Mexican immigrants, Puerto Ricans were foreign in language, culture, and experience, yet unlike them they entered the United States as citizens. Many Puerto Ricans were also African Americans. Racial and ethnic discrimination came as a double shock, since Puerto Ricans, as citizens, entered the United States with a sense of entitlement. In New York, Puerto Ricans found themselves barred from most craft unions, excluded from certain neighborhoods, and forced to take jobs largely in the low-paying garment industry and service trades. Puerto Rican children were not well served by a public school system insensitive to language differences and too willing to track Spanish-speaking students into obsolete vocational programs.

By the early 1970s, Puerto Rican families were substantially poorer on average than the total population of the country, and they had the lowest median income of any Latino groups. The steep decline in manufacturing jobs and in the garment industry in New York during the 1960s and 1970s hit the Puerto Rican community especially hard. So did the city's fiscal crisis, which brought sharp cuts in funding for schools, health care, libraries, government jobs, and other public services traditionally available to immigrant groups. The structural shift in the U.S. economy away from manufacturing and toward service and high-technology jobs reinforced the Puerto Rican community's goal of improving educational opportunities for its members. The struggle to establish and improve bilingual education in schools became an important part of this effort. Most Puerto Ricans, especially those who had succeeded in school and achieved middle-class status, continued to identify strongly with their Puerto Rican heritage and the Spanish language.

Indian Peoples

The postwar years also brought significant changes in the status and lives of Indian peoples. Congress reversed the policies pursued under the New Deal, which had stressed Indian sovereignty and cultural independence. Responding to a variety of pressure groups, including mining and other economic interests wishing to exploit the resources on Indian reservations, Congress adopted a policy known as "termination," designed to cancel Indian treaties and terminate sovereignty rights. In 1953 it passed House Concurrent Resolution 108, which allowed Congress to terminate a tribe as a political entity by passing legislation specific to that tribe. The leader of the termination forces, Senator Arthur Watkins of Utah, declared the new law meant that "the concept that the Indian people exist within the United States as independent nations has been rejected." Supporters of termination had varied motives, but the policy added up to the return of enforced assimilation for solving the "Indian problem."

George Gillette (left foreground), chairman of the Fort Berthold Indian Council, wept as Secretary of Interior J. A. Krug signed a contract buying 155,000 acres of the tribe's best land in North Dakota for a reservoir project, May 20, 1948. "The members of the tribal council sign this contract with heavy hearts," Gillette said.

Between 1954 and 1962, Congress passed twelve termination bills covering more than sixty tribes, nearly all in the West. Even when tribes consented to their own termination, they discovered that dissolution brought unforeseen problems. For example, members of the Klamaths of Oregon and the Paiutes of Utah received large cash payments from the division of tribal assets. But after these one-time payments were spent, members had to take poorly paid, unskilled jobs to survive. Many Indian peoples became dependent on state social services and slipped into poverty and alcoholism.

Along with termination, the federal government gave greater emphasis to a relocation program aimed at speeding up assimilation. The Bureau of Indian Affairs encouraged reservation Indians to relocate to cities, where they were provided housing and jobs. For some, relocation meant assimilation, intermarriage with whites, and the loss of tribal identity. Others, homesick and unable to adjust to an alien culture and place, either returned to reservations or wound up on the margins of city life. Still others regularly traveled back and forth. In some respects, this urban migration paralleled the larger postwar shift of rural peoples to cities and suburbs.

Indians increasingly came to see termination as a policy geared mainly to exploiting resources on Indian lands. By the early 1960s a new movement was emerging to defend Indian sovereignty. The National Congress of American Indians (NCAI) condemned termination, calling for a review of federal policies and a return to self-determination. The NCAI led a political and educational campaign that challenged the goal of assimilation and created a new awareness among white people that Indians had the right to remain Indians. When the termination policy ended in the early 1960s, it had affected only about 3 percent of federally recognized Indian peoples.

Taking their cue from the civil rights movement, Indian activists used the court system to reassert sovereign rights. Indian and white liberal lawyers, many with experience in civil rights cases, worked through the Native American Rights Fund, which became a powerful force in western politics. A series of Supreme Court decisions, culminating in *U.S. v. Wheeler* (1978), reasserted the principle of "unique and limited" sovereignty. The Court recognized tribal independence except where limited by treaty or Congress.

The Indian population had been growing since the early years of the century, but most reservations had trouble making room for a new generation. Indians suffered increased rates of poverty, chronic unemployment, alcoholism, and poor health. The average Indian family in the early 1960s earned only one-third of the average family income in the United States. Those who remained in the cities usually became "ethnic Indians," identifying themselves more as Indians than as members of specific tribes. By the late 1960s ethnic Indians had begun emphasizing civil rights over tribal rights, making common cause with African Americans and other minorities. The National Indian Youth Council (NIYC), founded in 1960, tried to unite the two causes of equality for individual Indians and special status for tribes. But the organization faced difficult contradictions between a common Indian identity, emphasizing Indians as a single ethnic group, and tribal identity, stressing the citizenship of Indians in separate nations.

Asian Americans

The harsh relocation program of World War II devastated the Japanese American community on the west coast (see Chapter 25). But the war against Nazism also helped weaken older notions of white superiority and racism. During the war the state of California had aggressively enforced an alien land law by confiscating property declared illegally held by Japanese. In November 1946 a proposition supporting the law appeared on the state ballot. But, thanks in part to a campaign by the Japanese American Citizens League (JACL) reminding voters of the wartime contributions of Nisei (second-generation) soldiers, voters overwhelmingly rejected the referendum. One JACL leader hailed the vote as proof that "the people of California will not approve discriminatory and prejudiced treatment of persons of Japanese ancestry." Two years later the Supreme Court declared

the law unconstitutional, calling it "nothing more than outright racial discrimination."

The 1952 Immigration and Nationality Act (see Chapter 26) removed the old ban against Japanese immigration, and also made Issei (first-generation Japanese Americans) eligible for naturalized citizenship. Japanese Americans, who lobbied hard for the new law, greeted it with elation. "It gave the Japanese equality with all other immigrants," said JACL leader Harry Takagi, "and that was the principle we had been struggling for from the very beginning." By 1965 some 46,000 immigrant Japanese, most of them elderly Issei, had taken their citizenship oaths. One of these wrote a poem to celebrate the achievement:

> *Going steadily to study English,*
> *Even through the rain at night,*
> *I thus attain,*
> *Late in life,*
> *American citizenship.*

The Immigration and Nationality Act allowed immigration from the "Asian-Pacific Triangle." It was nonetheless racially discriminatory, in that each country in Asia was permitted only 100 immigrants a year. In addition, the act continued the national-origins quotas of 1924 for European countries. The civil rights struggle helped spur a movement to reform immigration policies. "Everywhere else in our national life, we have eliminated discrimination based on national origins," Attorney General Robert Kennedy told Congress in 1964. "Yet, this system is still the foundation of our immigration law."

In 1965 Congress passed a new Immigration and Nationality Act, abolishing the national-origins quotas and providing for the admission each year of 170,000 immigrants from the Eastern Hemisphere and 120,000 from the Western Hemisphere. The new law set a limit of 20,000 per country from the Eastern Hemisphere—these immigrants to be admitted on a first-come, first-served basis—and established preference categories for professional and highly skilled immigrants.

The 1965 act would have a profound effect on Asian American communities, opening the way for a new wave of immigration. In the twenty years following the act the number of Asian Americans soared from 1 million to 5 million. Four times as many Asians settled in the United States in this period as in the entire previous history of the nation. This new wave also brought a strikingly different group of Asian immigrants. In 1960 the Asian American population was 52 percent Japanese, 27 percent Chinese, and 20 percent Filipino. In 1985, the composition was 21 percent Chinese, 21 percent Filipino, 15 percent

CHRONOLOGY

1941	Executive Order 8802 forbids racial discrimination in defense industries and government
1946	In *Morgan v. Virginia*, U.S. Supreme Court rules that segregation on interstate buses is unconstitutional
	President Harry Truman creates the Committee on Civil Rights
1947	Jackie Robinson becomes the first African American on a major league baseball team
1948	President Truman issues executive order desegregating the armed forces
1954	In *Brown v. Board of Education*, Supreme Court rules segregated schools inherently unequal
1955	Supreme Court rules that school desegregation must proceed "with all deliberate speed"
	Montgomery bus boycott begins
1956	Montgomery bus boycott ends in victory as the Supreme Court affirms a district court ruling that segregation on buses is unconstitutional
1957	Southern Christian Leadership Conference (SCLC) is founded
	President Dwight Eisenhower sends in federal troops to protect African American students integrating Little Rock, Arkansas, high school
1960	Sit-in movement begins as four college students sit at a lunch counter in Greensboro, North Carolina, and ask to be served
	Student Nonviolent Coordinating Committee (SNCC) founded

1960	Board of Indian Commissioners is created
	Buffalo Bill, the King of the Border Men, sets off "Wild West" publishing craze
1961	Freedom Rides begin
1962	James Meredith integrates the University of Mississippi
	The Albany movement fails to end segregation in Albany, Georgia
1963	SCLC initiates campaign to desegregate Birmingham, Alabama
	Medgar Evers, leader of the Mississippi NAACP, is assassinated
	March on Washington; Martin Luther King Jr. delivers his historic "I Have a Dream" speech
1964	Mississippi Freedom Summer project brings students to Mississippi to teach and register voters
	President Johnson signs the Civil Rights Act of 1964
	Civil rights workers Michael Schwerner, James Chaney, and Andrew Goodman are found buried in Philadelphia, Mississippi
	Mississippi Freedom Democratic Party (MFDP) is denied seats at the 1964 Democratic Presidential Convention
1965	SCLC and SNCC begin voter registration campaign in Selma, Alabama
	Malcolm X is assassinated
	Civil rights marchers walk from Selma to Montgomery
	Voting Rights Act of 1965 is signed into law

Japanese, 12 percent Vietnamese, 11 percent Korean, 10 percent Asian Indian, 4 percent Laotian, and 3 percent Cambodian. These newcomers included significant numbers of highly educated professionals and city dwellers, a sharp contrast with the farmers and rural peoples of the past.

CONCLUSION

The mass movement for civil rights was arguably the most important domestic event of the twentieth century. The struggle that began in Montgomery in December 1955 ultimately transformed race relations in thousands of American communities. By the early 1960s this community-based movement had placed civil rights at the very center of national political life. It achieved its greatest successes by invoking the law of the land to destroy legal segregation and win individual freedom for African Americans. The Civil Rights Act of 1964 and the Voting Rights Act of 1965 testified to the power of an African American and white liberal coalition. Yet the persistence of racism, poverty, and ghetto slums challenged a central assumption of liberalism: that equal protection of constitutional rights would give all Americans equal opportunities in life. By the mid-1960s, many black people had begun to question the core values of liberalism, the benefits of alliance with whites, and the philosophy of nonvio-

lence. At the same time, a conservative white backlash against the gains made by African Americans further weakened the liberal political consensus.

In challenging the persistence of widespread poverty and institutional racism, the civil rights movement called for deep structural changes in American life. By 1967, Martin Luther King was articulating a broad and radical vision linking the struggle against racial injustice to other defects in American society. "The black revolution," he argued, "is much more than a struggle for the rights of Negroes. It is forcing America to face all its interrelated flaws—racism, poverty, militarism, and materialism. It is exposing evils that are deeply rooted in the whole structure of our society." Curing these ills would prove far more difficult than ending legal segregation.

REVIEW QUESTIONS

1. What were the key legal and political antecedents to the civil rights struggle in the 1940s and early 1950s? What organizations played the most central role? Which tactics continued to be used, and which were abandoned?

2. How did African American communities challenge legal segregation in the South? Compare the strategies of key organizations, such as the NAACP, SNCC, SCLC, and CORE.

3. Discuss the varieties of white resistance to the civil rights movement. Which were most effective in slowing the drive for equality?

4. Analyze the civil rights movement's complex relationship with the national Democratic Party between 1948 and 1964. How was the party transformed by its association with the movement? What political gains and losses did that association entail?

5. What legal and institutional impact did the movement have on American life? How did it change American culture and politics? Where did it fail?

6. What relationship did the African American struggle for civil rights have with other American minorities? How—if at all—did these minorities benefit? Did they build their own versions of the movement?

RECOMMENDED READING

Taylor Branch, *Parting the Waters: America in the King Years, 1954–1963* (1988); *Pillar of Fire: America in the King Years, 1963–1965* (1998). A deeply researched and monumental narrative history of the southern civil rights movement organized around the life and influence of Reverend Martin Luther King Jr.

Clayborne Carson, *In Struggle: SNCC and the Black Awakening of the 1960s* (1981). The most comprehensive history of the Student Nonviolent Coordinating Committee, arguably the most important civil rights organization. Carson stresses the evolution of SNCC's radicalism during the course of the decade.

William Chafe, *Civilities and Civil Rights: Greensboro, North Carolina, and the Black Struggle for Equality* (1980).

Examines the community of Greensboro from 1945 to 1975. Chafe focuses on the "etiquette of civility" and its complex relationship with the promise of racial justice, along with black protest movements and relations between the city's blacks and whites.

David Chappell, *Inside Agitators: White Southerners in the Civil Rights Movement* (1994). The best recent analysis of white involvement in the movement.

Sara Evans, *Personal Politics: The Roots of Women's Liberation in the Civil Rights Movement and the New Left* (1979). A pathbreaking study showing the important connections between the struggle for black rights and the rebirth of feminism.

Aldon D. Morris, *The Origins of the Civil Rights Movement: Black Communities Organizing for Change* (1984). An important study combining history and social theory. Morris emphasizes the key role of ordinary black people, acting through their churches and other community organizations before 1960.

Howell Raines, *My Soul Is Rested: Movement Days in the Deep South Remembered* (1977). The best oral history of the civil rights movement, drawing from a wide range of participants and points of view. It is brilliantly edited by Raines, who covered the events as a journalist.

Jo Ann Gibson Robinson, *The Montgomery Bus Boycott and the Women Who Started It*, ed. David J. Garrow (1987). An important memoir by one of the key behind-the-scenes players in the Montgomery bus boycott. Robinson stresses the role of middle- and working-class black women in the struggle.

Mark Tushnet, *Making Civil Rights Law: Thurgood Marshall and the Supreme Court, 1936–1961* (1994). An in-depth examination of Marshall's critical role in leading the legal fight against segregation.

Robert Weisbrot, *Freedom Bound: A History of America's Civil Rights Movement* (1990). One of the best single-volume syntheses of the movement. Weisbrot is especially strong on the often turbulent relations between black activists and white liberals and the relationship between civil rights and broader currents of American reform.

ADDITIONAL BIBLIOGRAPHY

Origins of the Movements

Michael R. Belknap, *Federal Law and Southern Order* (1987)

William C. Berman, *The Politics of Civil Rights in the Truman Administration* (1970)

A. Russell Buchanan, *Black Americans in World War II* (1977)

Richard M. Dalfiume, *Desegregation of the U.S. Armed Forces* (1969)

Scott DeVeaux, *The Birth of BeBop* (1998)

Elizabeth Huckaby, *Crisis at Central High* (1980)

Martin Luther King Jr., *Stride toward Freedom* (1958)

Richard Kluger, *Simple Justice* (1977)

Bernard Schwartz, *Inside the Warren Court* (1987)

___, *The NAACP's Legal Strategy against Segregated Education* (1987)

Jules Tygiel, *Baseball's Great Experiment: Jackie Robinson and His Legacy* (1983)

Stephen J. Whitfield, *A Death in the Delta: The Story of Emmett Till* (1989)

C. Vann Woodward, *The Strange Career of Jim Crow*, 3d ed. (1974)

No Easy Road to Freedom, 1957–62

Jack Bloom, *Class, Race, and the Civil Rights Movement* (1987)

James Farmer, *Lay Bare the Heart* (1985)

James Forman, *The Making of Black Revolutionaries* (1985)

David J. Garrow, *The FBI and Martin Luther King Jr.* (1983)

Ann Moody, *Coming of Age in Mississippi* (1970)

Cleveland Sellers with Robert Terrell, *The River of No Return* (1973)

Harris Wofford, *Of Kennedys and Kings* (1980)

Miles Wolff, *Lunch at the 5&10* (1990)

Howard Zinn, *SNCC: The New Abolitionists* (1965)

The Movement at High Tide, 1963–65

Seth Cagin and Philip Dray, *We Are Not Afraid* (1988)

David J. Garrow, *Protest at Selma* (1978)

Hugh Davis Graham, *The Civil Rights Era* (1990)

Henry Hampton and Steve Fayer, *Voices of Freedom: An Oral History of the Civil Rights Movement* (1990)

Stephen Lawson, *Black Ballots* (1976)

Doug McAdam, *Freedom Summer* (1988)

Harvard Sitkoff, *The Struggle for Black Equality, 1954–1992* (1993)

Mark Stern, *Calculating Visions: Kennedy, Johnson, and Civil Rights* (1992)

Sheyann Webb and Rachel West Nelson, *Selma, Lord, Selma* (1980)

Charles Whalen and Barbara Whalen, *The Longest Debate: A Legislative History of the 1964 Civil Rights Act* (1985)

Forgotten Minorities, 1945–65

Rodolfo Acuna, *Occupied America*, 3d ed. (1981)

Manuel Alers-Montalvo, *The Puerto Rican Migrants of New York* (1985)

Frank T. Bean and Marta Tienda, *The Hispanic Population of the United States* (1988)

Larry Burt, *Tribalism in Crisis: Federal Indian Policy, 1953–1961* (1982)

Donald Fixico, *Termination and Relocation: Federal Indian Policy, 1945–1960* (1986)

Mario T. Garcia, *Mexican Americans* (1989)

Virginia Sanchez Korrol, *From Colonia to Community* (1983)

Benjamin Marquez, *LULAC* (1993)

Ronald Takaki, *Strangers from a Different Shore: A History of Asian Americans* (1989)

Biography

Paul K. Conkin, *Big Daddy from the Pedernales: Lyndon Baines Johnson* (1986)

David J. Garrow, *Bearing the Cross: Martin Luther King, Jr., and the Southern Christian Leadership Conference* (1986)

David Levering Lewis, *King: A Biography*, 2d ed. (1978)

Malcolm X, with Alex Haley, *The Autobiography of Malcolm X* (1965)

Kay Mills, *This Little Light of Mine: The Life of Fannie Lou Hamer* (1993)

Bruce Perry, *Malcolm: The Life of a Man Who Changed Black America* (1991)

Paula F. Pfeffer, *A. Philip Randolph* (1990)

$\mathcal{C}$HAPTER TWENTY-NINE

WAR ABROAD, WAR AT HOME

1965–1974

Bernard Perlin, *Mayor Richard Daley*, 1968. Collection of Philip J. and Suzanne Schiller, American Social Commentary Art, 1930–70.

AMERICAN COMMUNITIES
Uptown, Chicago, Illinois

During Freedom Summer of 1964, while teams of northern college students traveled south to join voter registration campaigns among African Americans, a small group moved to Chicago to help the city's poor people take control of their communities and to demand better city services. They targeted a neighborhood known as Uptown, a one-mile-square section five miles north of the Loop, the city center. The residents, many only recently transplanted from the poverty of the Appalachian South, lived in crowded tenements or in once-elegant mansions now subdivided into tiny, run-down apartments. Four thousand people lived on just one street running four blocks, 20 percent of them on welfare. Chicago civic authorities had also selected this neighborhood for improvement. Designating it a Conservation Area under the terms of the Urban Renewal Act, they applied for federal funds in order to upgrade the housing for middle-income families and, in effect, to clear out the current residents. In contrast, the student organizers intended to mobilize the community "so as to demand an end to poverty and the construction of a decent social order."

With the assistance of the Packinghouse Workers union, the students formed Jobs or Income Now (JOIN), opened a storefront office, and invited local residents to work with them to halt the city's plans. They spent hours and hours listening to people, drawing out their ideas and helping them develop scores of additional programs. Confronting the bureaucracy of the welfare and unemployment compensation offices stood high on their list. They also campaigned against Mayor Richard Daley's policy of "police omnipresence" that had a fleet of squad cars and paddy wagons continually patrolling the neighborhood. To curb police harassment, they demanded the creation of civilian review boards. They also helped establish new social clubs, a food-buying cooperative, a community theater, and a health clinic. Within a few years, Uptown street kids had formed the Young Patriots organization, put out a community newspaper, *Rising Up Angry*, and staffed free breakfast programs.

Chicago JOIN was one of ten similar projects sponsored by Students for a Democratic Society (SDS). Impatient with the nation's chronic poverty and cold war politics, twenty-nine students from nine universities had met in June 1960 to form a new kind of campus-based political organization. SDS soon caught the attention of liberal students, encouraging them, as part of the nation's largest college population to date, to make their voices heard. By its peak in 1968, SDS had 350 chapters and between 60,000 and 100,000 members. Its principle of participatory democracy—with its promise to give people control over the decisions affecting their lives—appealed to a wider following of more than a million students.

In June 1962 in Port Huron, Michigan, the founding members of SDS issued a declaration of principles, drafted mainly by graduate student Tom Hayden. "We are people . . . bred in at least modest comfort, housed now in universities," *The Port Huron Statement* opened, "looking uncomfortably to the world we inherit." The dire effects of poverty and social injustice, it continued, were not the only dismaying things about American society. A deeper ailment plagued American politics. Everyone, including middle-class students with few material wants, suffered from a sense of "loneliness, estrangement, and alienation." *The Port Huron Statement* defined SDS as a new kind of political movement that would bring people "out of isolation and into community." Through participatory democracy, not just the poor but all Americans could overcome their feelings of "powerlessness [and hence] resignation before the enormity of events." As one organizer explained, programs like JOIN were attempts to create a poor people's movement as well as a means for students themselves to live an "authentic life" outside the constraints of middle-class society.

SDS began with a campaign to reform the university, especially to disentangle the financial ties between campus-based research programs and the military-industrial complex. Later it expanded to the nation's cities, sending small groups of students to live and organize in the poor communities of Boston, Louisville, Cleveland, and Newark as well as Chicago.

Ultimately, few of these projects succeeded in mobilizing the poor to political action. Protests against local government did little to combat unemployment, and campaigns for better garbage collection or more playgrounds rarely evolved into lasting movements. Nevertheless, organizers did succeed in bringing many neighborhood residents "out of isolation and into community." By late 1967 SDS prepared to leave JOIN in the hands of the people it had organized, which was its goal from the beginning.

Initially, even Lyndon Baines Johnson promoted the ideal of civic participation. The Great Society, as the president called his domestic program, promised more than the abolition of poverty and racial inequality. In May 1964 at the University of Michigan the president described his goal as a society "where every child can find knowledge to enrich his mind and to enlarge his talents," where "the city of man serves not only the needs of the body and the demands of commerce but the desire for beauty and the hunger for community."

By 1967 the Vietnam War had upset the domestic agendas of both SDS and the Johnson administration. If SDSers had once believed they could work with liberal Democrats to reduce poverty in the United States, they now interpreted social injustice at home as the inevitable consequence of dangerous and destructive foreign policies pursued by liberals and conservatives alike. SDS threw its energies into the movement against the war in Vietnam. President Johnson, meanwhile, pursued a foreign policy that would swallow up the funding for his own plans for a war on poverty and precipitate a very different war at home, Americans against Americans. As hawks and doves lined up on opposite sides, the Vietnam War created a huge and enduring rift. SDS member Richard Flacks had warned that the nation had to "choose between devoting its resources and energies to maintaining military superiority and international hegemony or rechanneling those resources and energies to meeting the desperate needs of its people." Ultimately, even President Johnson himself understood that the "bitch of a war" in Asia ruined "the woman I really loved—the Great Society." The dream of community did not vanish, but consensus appeared increasingly remote as the United States fought—and eventually lost—the longest war in its history.

Chicago

KEY TOPICS

- Widening U.S. involvement in the war in Vietnam

- "The sixties generation" and the antiwar movement

- Poverty and urban crisis

- The election of 1968

- The rise of "liberation" movements

- The Nixon presidency and the Watergate conspiracy

VIETNAM: AMERICA'S LONGEST WAR

The Vietnam War had its roots in the Truman Doctrine and its goal of containing communism (see Chapter 26). After the defeat of the French by the communist forces of Ho Chi Minh in 1954, Vietnam emerged as a major zone of cold war contention. President John Kennedy called it "the cornerstone of the Free World in Southeast Asia, the keystone in the arch, the finger in the dike," a barrier to the spread of communism throughout the region and perhaps the world. President Lyndon Johnson sounded the same note at the beginning of his presidency. He told the public that North Vietnam was intent on conquering South Vietnam, defeating the United States, and extending "the Asiatic dominion of communism." With American security at stake, he concluded, Americans had little choice but to fight for "the principle for which our ancestors fought in the valleys of Pennsylvania."

Vietnam was not Valley Forge, however, and the United States ultimately paid a huge price for its determination to turn back communism in Indochina. More than 50,000 Americans died in an unwinnable overseas war that only deepened divisions at home.

Johnson's War

Although President Kennedy had greatly increased the number of military advisors in South Vietnam (see Chapter 27), it was his successor, Lyndon B. Johnson, who made the decision to engage the United States in a major war there. At first, Johnson simply hoped to stay the course in Vietnam. Facing a presidential election in November 1964, he knew that a major military setback would cripple his election campaign. But he was equally determined to avoid the fate of President Truman, who had bogged down politically after "losing" China to communism and producing a stalemate in Korea. Within days of taking office, the new president said he intended to do his utmost to help South Vietnam win its "contest against the externally directed and supported Communist conspiracy."

Throughout the winter and spring of 1964, as conditions grew steadily worse in South Vietnam, Johnson and his advisors quietly laid the groundwork for a sustained bombing campaign against North Vietnam. In early August, they found a pretext to set this plan in motion. After two U.S. destroyers in the Gulf of Tonkin, off the coast of North Vietnam, reported attacks by North Vietnamese patrol boats, Johnson retaliated by ordering air strikes against bases in North Vietnam.

Johnson now appealed to Congress to pass a resolution giving him the authority "to take all necessary measures" and "all necessary steps" to defend U.S. armed forces and to protect Southeast Asia "against aggression or subversion." This Tonkin Gulf resolution, secretly drafted six weeks before the incident for which it was named, passed the Senate on August 7 with only two dissenting votes and moved unanimously through the House. It served, in Undersecretary of State Nicholas Katzenbach's words, as the "functional equivalent" of a declaration of war.

Ironically, Johnson campaigned for the presidency with a call for restraint in Vietnam. He assured voters that "we are not about to send American boys nine or ten thousand miles away from home to do what Asian boys ought to be doing for themselves." This strategy helped him win a landslide victory over conservative Republican Barry Goldwater of Arizona, who had proposed the deployment of nuclear weapons in Vietnam.

With the election behind him, Johnson now faced a hard decision. The limited bombing raids against North Vietnam had failed to slow the movement of the communist Vietcong forces across the border into the South. Meanwhile, the government in Saigon, the capital city of South Vietnam, appeared near collapse. Faced with the prospect of a communist victory, the president chose to escalate U.S. involvement in Vietnam massively.

Deeper into the Quagmire

In early February 1965, Johnson found a rationale to justify massive bombing of the North. The Vietcong had fired at the barracks of the U.S. Marine base at Pleiku in the central highlands of Vietnam, killing 8 and wounding more than 100 Americans. Waving the list of casualties, the president rushed into an emergency meeting of the National Security Council to announce that the time had passed for keeping "our guns over the mantel and our shells in the cupboard." He ordered immediate reprisal bombing of North Vietnam and one week later, on February 13, authorized Operation Rolling Thunder, a campaign of gradually intensifying air attacks.

Johnson and his advisers hoped that the air strikes against North Vietnam would demonstrate U.S. resolve "both to Hanoi and to the world" and make the deployment of ground forces unnecessary. Intelligence reports, however, suggested that the bombing had little impact and noted, moreover, that North Vietnam was now sending troops into South Vietnam. With retreat his only alternative, Johnson decided to introduce ground troops for offensive operations.

Once Rolling Thunder had begun, President Johnson found it increasingly difficult to speak frankly with the American public about his policies. Initially, he announced that only two battalions of marines were being assigned to Danang to defend the airfields where bombing runs began. But six week later 50,000 U.S. troops were in Vietnam. By November 1965 the total topped 165,000, and more troops were on the way. But even after Johnson authorized a buildup to 431,000 troops in mid-1966, victory was still nowhere in sight.

The strategy pursued by the Johnson administration and implemented by General William Westmoreland—a war of attrition—was based on the premise that continued bombing would eventually exhaust North Vietnam's resources. Meanwhile, U.S. ground forces would defeat the Vietcong in South Vietnam, forcing its soldiers to defect and supporters to scatter, thereby restoring political stability to South Vietnam's pro-western government. As Johnson once boasted, the strongest military power in the world surely could crush a communist rebellion in a "pissant" country of peasants.

In practice, the United States wreaked havoc in South Vietnam, tearing apart its society and bringing ecological devastation to its land. Intending to locate and eradicate the support network of the Vietcong, U.S. ground troops conducted search-and-destroy missions throughout the countryside. They attacked villagers and their homes. Seeking to ferret out Vietcong sympathizers, U.S. troops turned at any one time as many as 4 million people—approximately one quarter of the population of South Vietnam—into refugees. By late 1968, the United States had dropped more than 3 million tons of bombs on Vietnam, and eventually delivered more than three times the tonnage dropped by the Allies on all fronts during World War II. The United States also conducted the most destructive chemical warfare in history. To deprive the Vietcong of camouflage, American troops used herbicides to defoliate forests. During Operation Ranch Hand, which ran between 1965 and 1971, 17.6 million gallons of Agent Orange were sprayed over approximately 3.6 million acres of South Vietnam.

Several advisers urged the president to inform the American people about his decisions on Vietnam, even to declare a state of national emergency. But Johnson feared he would lose momentum on domestic reform, including his antipoverty programs, if he drew attention to foreign policy. Seeking to avoid "undue excitement in the Congress and in domestic public opinion," he held to a course of intentional deceit.

The Credibility Gap

Johnson's popularity had surged at the time of the Tonkin Gulf resolution, skyrocketing in one day from 42 to 72 percent, according to a Louis Harris poll. But afterward it waned rapidly. The war dragged on. Every night network television news publicized the latest American body count. No president had worked so hard to control the news media, but by 1967 Johnson found himself badgered at press conferences by reporters who accused the president of creating a credibility gap.

Scenes of human suffering and devastation recorded by television cameras increasingly undermined the administration's moral justification of the war with claims that it was a necessary defense of freedom and democracy in South Vietnam. During the early 1960s network news had either ignored Vietnam or had been patriotically supportive of U.S. policy. Beginning with a report on a ground operation against the South Vietnamese village of Cam Ne by Morley Safer for CBS News in August 1965, however, the tenor of news reporting changed. Although government officials described the operation as a strategic destruction of "fortified Vietcong bunkers," the CBS *Evening News* showed pictures of Marines setting fire to the thatched homes of civilians. After CBS aired Safer's report, President Johnson complained bitterly to the news director. But more critical commentary soon followed. By 1967, according to a noted media observer, "every subject tended to become Vietnam." Televised news reports now told of new varieties of American cluster bombs, which released up to 180,000 fiberglass shards, and showed the nightmarish effects of the defoliants used on forests in South Vietnam to uncover enemy strongholds.

Coverage of the war in the print media also became more skeptical of Johnson's policies. By 1967 independent news teams were probing the government's official claims. Harrison Salisbury, Pulitzer Prize-winning *New York Times* reporter, questioned the administration's claims that its bombing of the North precisely targeted military objectives, charging that U.S. planes had bombed the population center of Hanoi, capital of North Vietnam, and intentionally ravaged villages in the South. As American military deaths climbed at the rate of more than 800 per month during the first half of 1967, newspaper coverage of the war focused yet more intently on such disturbing events.

The most vocal congressional critic of Johnson's war policy was Democratic senator J. William Fulbright of Arkansas, who chaired the Senate Foreign Relations Committee and who had personally speeded the passage of the Tonkin Gulf resolution. A strong supporter of the cold war, Fulbright had decided that the war in Vietnam was unwinnable and destructive to domestic reform. In *Arrogance of Power,* a book published in 1966 that became a national best-seller, he proposed a negotiated withdrawal from a neutralized Southeast Asia. At first Fulbright stood nearly alone: in October 1966 only 15 percent of Congress favored a negotiated

Refugees, Binh Dinh Province, 1967. The massive bombing and ground combat broke apart the farming communities of South Vietnam, creating huge numbers of civilian casualties and driving millions into quickly constructed refugee camps or already overcrowded cities. Approximately 25 percent of the South Vietnamese population fled their native villages, many never to return.

settlement. But he soon persuaded prominent Democrats in Congress, such as Frank Church, Mike Mansfield, and George McGovern, to put aside their personal loyalty to Johnson and oppose his conduct of the war. In 1967 the Congress passed a nonbinding resolution appealing to the United Nations to help negotiate an end to hostilities. Meanwhile, some of the nation's most trusted European allies called for restraint in Vietnam.

The impact of the war, which cost Americans $21 billion per year, was also felt at home. Johnson convinced Congress to levy a 10 percent surcharge on individual and corporate taxes. Later adjustments in the national budget tapped the Social Security fund, heretofore safe from interference. Inflation raced upward, fed by spending on the war. Johnson replaced advisers who questioned his policy, but as casualties multiplied, more and more Americans began to question his handling of the war.

A GENERATION IN CONFLICT

As the war in Vietnam escalated, Americans from all walks of life demanded an end to U.S. involvement. Debates raged everywhere, from families to informal community meetings to the halls of Congress. Eventually the antiwar movement won over a majority. But between 1965 and 1971, its years of peak activity, it had a distinctly generational character. At the forefront were the baby boomers who were just coming of age.

This so-called sixties generation, the largest generation in American history, was also the best educated so far. By the late 1960s, nearly half of all young adults between the ages of 18 and 21 were enrolled in college. In 1965 there were 5 million college students; in 1973 the number had doubled to 10 million. Public universities made the largest gains; by 1970 eight had more than 30,000 students apiece. Many of these young people combined protest against the war in Vietnam with a broader, penetrating critique of American society. Through music, dress, and even hairstyle, many expressed a deep estrangement from the values and aspirations of their parents' generation. As early as 1967, when opposition to the war had begun to swell, "flower children" were putting daisies in the rifle barrels of troops stationed to quash campus protests, providing a seemingly innocent counterpoint to the grim news of slaughter abroad.

These young people believed they heralded a "culture of life" against the "culture of death" symbolized by the war. Campus organizations such as SDS, which had begun in the early 1960s in an attempt to build community, now turned against the government. SDS encouraged many college students to take a militant stand against the war, calling for an immediate and unconditional withdrawal of U.S. troops from Vietnam.

"The Times They Are A-Changin'"

The first sign of a new kind of protest was the free speech movement at the University of California at Berkeley in 1964. That fall, civil rights activists returned to the campus from Freedom Summer in Mississippi. They soon began to picket Bay Area stores that practiced discrimination in hiring and to recruit other students to join them. When the university administration moved to prevent them from setting up information booths on campus, eighteen groups protested, including the arch-conservative Students for Goldwater, claiming that their right to free speech had been abridged. The administration responded by sending police to break up the protest rally and arrest participants. University president Clark Kerr met with students, agreed not to press charges, and seemed set to grant them a small space on campus for political activity. Then, under pressure from conservative regents, Kerr reversed himself and announced in November that the university planned to press new charges against the free speech movement's leaders. On December 2 a crowd of 7,000 gathered to protest this decision. Joining folk singer Joan Baez in singing "We Shall Overcome," a group of students marched toward the university's administration building where they planned to stage a sit-in until Kerr rescinded his order. The police arrested nearly 800 students in the largest mass arrest in California history.

Mario Savio, a Freedom Summer volunteer and philosophy student, explained that the free speech movement wanted more than just the right to conduct political activity on campus. He spoke for many students when he complained that the university had become a faceless bureaucratic machine rather than a community of learning. Regulating the activities of students while preparing them for colorless lives as corporation clerks, the university made them "so sick at heart" that they had decided to put their "bodies upon the gears" to make it stop.

The free speech movement's social critique resonated among college students. Across the country they began to demand a say in the structuring of their education. Brown University students, for example, demanded a revamp of the curriculum that would eliminate all required courses and make grades optional. Students also protested campus rules that treated students as children instead of as adults. After a string of campus protests, most large universities, including the University of California, relinquished *in loco parentis* (in the place of parents) policies and allowed students to live off-campus and to set their own hours.

Across the bay in San Francisco, other young adults staked out a new form of community —a counterculture. In 1967, "the Summer of Love," the population of the Haight-Ashbury district swelled by 75,000 as youthful adventurers gathered for the most celebrated "be-in" of the era. Although the *San Francisco Chronicle* featured a headline reading "Mayor Warns Hippies to Stay Out of Town," masses of long-haired young men and women dressed in bell-bottoms and tie-dyed T-shirts were undeterred. They congregated in "the Haight" to listen to music, take drugs, and "be" with each other. "If you're going to San Francisco," a popular rock group sang, "be sure to wear some flowers in your hair . . . you're going to meet some gentle people there." In the fall, the majority returned to their own communities, often bringing with them a new lifestyle. *Time* magazine announced the appearance of new "hippie enclaves . . . in every major U.S. city from Boston to Seattle, from Detroit to New Orleans."

The generational rebellion took many forms, including a revolution in sexual behavior that triggered countless quarrels between parents and their maturing sons and daughters. During the 1960s more teenagers experienced premarital sex—by the decade's end three-quarters of all college seniors had engaged in sexual intercourse—and far more talked about it openly than in previous eras. With birth control widely available, including the newly developed "pill," many young women, who were no longer deterred from sex by fear of pregnancy, rejected premarital abstinence. "We've

Young women, dressed in hippie garb, flash the peace sign in protest against the war in Vietnam.

discarded the idea that the loss of virginity is related to degeneracy," one college student explained. "Premarital sex doesn't mean the downfall of society, at least not the kind of society that we're going to build." Many heterosexual couples chose to live together outside marriage, a practice few parents condoned. A much smaller but significant number formed communes—approximately 4,000 by 1970—where members could share housekeeping and child care as well as sexual partners.

Psychedelic and other hallucinogenic drugs played a large part in this counterculture. Harvard professor Timothy Leary urged young people to "turn on, tune in, drop out" and also advocated the mass production and distribution of LSD (lysergic acid diethylamide), which was not criminalized until 1968. Marijuana, illegal yet readily available,

An antiwar demonstrator places a flower, a symbol of peace, in the rifle barrel of troops during the March on the Pentagon in October 1967. Nearly 100,000 opponents of the Vietnam War gathered in Washington, D.C., and hundreds were arrested as they attempted to storm the entrance to the Pentagon.

was often paired with rock music in a collective ritual of love and laughter. Singer Bob Dylan taunted adults with the lyrics of his hit single, "Everybody must get stoned."

Music played a large part in defining the counterculture. With the emergence of rock 'n' roll in the 1950s, popular music had begun to express a deliberate generational identity (see Chapter 27), a trend that gained momentum with the emergence of the British rock group, the Beatles, in 1964. Folk music, which had gained popularity on campuses in the early 1960s with the successful recordings of Peter, Paul, and Mary, Phil Ochs, Judy Collins, as well as Joan Baez, continued to serve the voice of protest. Shortly after Freedom Summer, folk singer Bob Dylan issued a warning to parents:

> Your sons and your daughters
> are beyond your command
> Your old road is
> rapidly agin'.
> Please get out of the new one
> If you can't lend your hand
> For the times they are a-changin'.

By 1965 Dylan himself had turned to the electric guitar and rock, which triumphed as the musical emblem of a generation.

At a farm near Woodstock, New York, more than 400,000 people gathered in August 1969 for a three-day rock concert and to give witness to the ideals of the counterculture. Thousands took drugs while security officials and local police stood by, some stripped off their clothes to dance or swim, and a few even made love in the grass. "We were exhilarated," one reveler recalled. "We felt as though we were in liberated territory."

The Woodstock Nation, as the counterculture was renamed by the media, did not actually represent the sentiments of most young Americans. But its attitudes and styles, especially its efforts to create a new community, did speak for the large minority seeking a peaceful alternative to the intensifying climate of war. "We used to think of ourselves as little clumps of weirdos," rock star Janis Joplin explained. "But now we're a whole new minority group." Another interpreter, Charles Reich, whose The Greening of America (1970) became a best-seller, defined the counterculture as a generation's attempt to create "a form of community in which love, respect, and a mutual search for wisdom replace the competition and separation of the past." The slogan "Make Love, Not War" linked generational rebellion and opposition to the U.S. invasion of Vietnam.

From Campus Protest to Mass Mobilization

Three weeks after the announcement of Operation Rolling Thunder in 1965, peace activists called for a day-long boycott of classes so that students and faculty might meet to discuss the war. At the University of

Antiwar Protests on College and University Campuses, 1967–1969   *Campus-based protests against the war in Vietnam, at first centered on the east coast and in California, spread to nearly every region of the country and around the world by the decade's end.*

Michigan in Ann Arbor, more than 3,000 students turned out for sessions held through the night because administrators bowed to pressure of state legislators and refused to cancel classes. During the following weeks, "teach-ins" spread across the United States and as far away as Europe and Japan.

Students also began to protest against war-related research on their campuses. The expansion of higher education in the 1960s had depended largely on federally funded programs, including military research on counterinsurgency tactics and new chemical weapons. Student protesters demanded an end to these programs and, receiving no response from university administrators, turned to civil disobedience. In October 1967, the Dow Chemical Company, manufacturers of napalm, a form of jellied gasoline often used against civilians, sent job recruiters to the University of Wisconsin at Madison despite warnings that a group of students would try to prevent them from conducting interviews. A few hundred students staged a sit-in at the

building where the recruitment interviews were scheduled, and 2,000 onlookers gathered outside. Ordered by university administrators to disperse the crowd, the city's police broke glass doors, dragged students through the debris, and clubbed those who refused to move. Suddenly the campus erupted. Students chanted *Sieg Heil* at the police, who attempted to disperse them with tear gas and Mace. Undergraduate students and their teaching assistants boycotted classes for a week. During the next three years, hundreds of similar strikes took place on campuses in every region of the country.

Many student strikes merged opposition to the war with other campus and community issues. At Columbia University, students struck in 1968 against the administration's plans to build a new gymnasium in a city park used by residents of neighboring Harlem. In the Southwest, Mexican American students demonstrated against the use of funds for military projects that might otherwise be allocated to antipoverty and educational programs.

By the late 1960s the peace movement had spread well beyond the campus and commanded a diverse following. While some protesters marched, others held prayer vigils, staged art fairs, distributed leaflets door to door, or simply engaged friends and neighbors in conversation about Vietnam. In April 1967 a day-long antiwar rally at the Sheep Meadow in Manhattan's Central Park drew more than 300,000 people—more than had taken part in the civil rights movement's 1965 March on Washington. Meanwhile, 60,000 protesters turned out in San Francisco. By summer, Vietnam Veterans against the War began to organize returning soldiers and sailors, encouraging them to cast off the medals and ribbons they had won in battle.

The steadily increasing size of antiwar demonstrations provoked conservatives and prowar Democrats to take a stronger stand in support of the war. On the weekend following the huge turn-out in Central Park, the Veterans of Foreign Wars staged a "Loyalty Day" parade in New York City under the banner "One Country, One Flag, Love It or Leave It." Although only 7,500 people participated, the event signaled a hardening of opposition to the peace movement. Several newspaper and magazine editorialists called for the arrest of antiwar leaders on charges of treason. Secretary of State Dean Rusk, appearing on NBC's *Meet the Press*, expressed his concern that "authorities in Hanoi" might conclude, incorrectly, that the majority of Americans did not back their president and that "the net effect of these demonstrations will be to prolong the war, not to shorten it."

Many demonstrators themselves concluded that mass mobilizations alone had little impact on U.S. policy. Some sought to serve as moral witnesses. Despite a congressional act of 1965 providing for a five-year jail term and a $10,000 fine for destroying a draft card, nearly 200 young men destroyed their draft cards at the April Sheep Meadow demonstration and encouraged approximately a half-million more to resist the draft or refuse induction. Two Jesuit priests, Daniel and Philip Berrigan, raided the offices of the draft board in Catonsville, Maryland, in May 1968 and poured homemade napalm over records. A few protesters even doused their clothes with gasoline and set fire to themselves, as Buddhist monks protesting the war had done in Vietnam. Other activists determined to "bring the war home." An estimated 40,000 bombing incidents or bomb threats took place from January 1969 to April 1970; more than $21 million of property was damaged, and forty-three people were killed. Most of the perpetrators were never identified.

Observers at the time noted a similarity between the violence in Vietnam and the violence in the United States. Parallel wars were now being fought, one between two systems of government in Vietnam, another between the American government and masses of its citizens. Those Americans sent to Vietnam were caught in between.

Teenage Soldiers

The Vietnam War era witnessed not only a generation gap but a fissure within the generation of young adults. Whereas the average age of the World War II soldier was twenty-six, the age of those who fought in Vietnam hovered around nineteen. Until late 1969 the Selective Service System—the draft—gave deferments to college students and to workers in selected occupations while recruiting hard in poor communities, advertising the armed forces as a provider of vocational training and social mobility. Working-class young men, disproportionately African American and Latino, signed up in large numbers under these inducements. They also bore the brunt of combat. Whereas college graduates constituted only 12 percent of all soldiers and 9 percent of those who were killed in combat, high school dropouts were the most likely to serve in Vietnam and by far the most likely to die there. This disparity created a rupture that would last well past the end of the war.

Yet the soldiers were not entirely isolated from the changes affecting their generation. GIs in significant numbers smoked marijuana, listed to rock music, and participated in the sexual revolution. In 1968 more than 200 soldiers from Fort Hood, Texas, attended a be-in. But most condemned antiwar protest as the expressions of their privileged peers who did not have to fight.

As the war dragged on, however, some soldiers began to show their frustration. By 1971 many GIs were putting peace symbols on their combat helmets, joining antiwar demonstrations, and staging their own events such as "Armed Farces Day." Sometimes entire companies refused to carry out duty assignments or even to enter battle. A smaller number took revenge by "fragging" their commanding officers with grenades meant for the enemy. Meanwhile African American soldiers closed ranks and often flaunted their racial solidarity by weaving their bootlaces into "slave bracelets" and carrying Black Power canes, which were ebony-colored and topped with a clenched fist. Some openly complained about being asked to fight "a white man's war" and emblazoned their helmets with slogans like "No Gook Ever Called Me Nigger." By 1971, at least fourteen organizations claimed affiliation with RITA, an acronym for "Resistance in the Army." The largest was the American Servicemen's Union, which claimed more than 10,000 members and published its own newspaper, *The Bond*.

The nature of the war fed feelings of disaffection in the armed forces. U.S. troops entering South Vietnam expected a warm welcome from the people whose homeland they had been sent to defend.

Instead, they encountered anti-American demonstrations and placards with slogans like "End Foreign Dominance of Our Country." Hostile Vietnamese civilians viewed the Americans as invaders. The enemy avoided open engagements in which the Americans could benefit from their superior arms and air power. Soldiers found themselves instead stumbling into booby traps as they chased an elusive guerrilla foe through deep, leech-infested swamps and dense jungles swarming with fire ants. They could never be sure who was friend and who was foe. Patently false U.S. government press releases that heralded glorious victories and extolled the gratitude of Vietnamese civilians deepened bitterness on the front lines.

Approximately 8.6 million men and women served in the armed forces, and many returned to civilian life quietly and without fanfare, denied the glory earned by the combat veterans of previous wars. They reentered a society divided over the cause for which they had risked their lives. Tens of thousands suffered debilitating physical injuries. As many as 40 percent of them came back with drug dependencies or symptoms of post-traumatic stress disorder, haunted and depressed by troubling memories of atrocities. Moreover, finding and keeping a job proved to be particularly hard in the shrinking economy of the 1970s. The situation was especially bleak for African American veterans who returned to communities with unemployment rates at least triple the national average. Many veterans felt betrayed either by their own generation or by their government.

WARS ON POVERTY

During the early 1960s, the civil rights movement spurred a new awareness of and concern with poverty. As poor African Americans from both the rural South and the urban North got involved in political protests, they added the issues of unemployment, low wages, and slum housing to the demands for desegregation and voting rights. The civil rights movement also revealed the close link between racial discrimination and economic inequalities. What good was winning the right to sit at a lunch counter if one could not afford to buy a hamburger?

One of the most influential books of the times, Michael Harrington's *The Other America* (1962), added fuel to this fire. Harrington argued that one-fifth of the nation—as many as 40 to 50 million people—suffered from bad housing, malnutrition, poor medical care, and other deprivations of poverty. He documented the miseries of what he called the "invisible land of the other Americans," the rejects of society who simply did not exist for affluent suburbanites or the mass media. The other America, Harrington wrote, "is populated

President Lyndon B. Johnson talks to James Truesville of Raleigh, North Carolina, at Camp Catoctin, Maryland, where young men from fourteen states were receiving training in basic job skills. One of the most highly touted programs of the War on Poverty, the Job Corps suffered from underfunding and a tendency to teach young trainees obsolete technical skills.

by failures, by those driven from the land and bewildered by the city, by old people suddenly confronted with the torments of loneliness and poverty, and by minorities facing a wall of prejudice."

These arguments motivated President Johnson to expand the antipoverty program that he had inherited from the Kennedy administration. "That's my kind of program," he told his advisers. "It will help people. I want you to move full speed ahead on it." Ironically, it was another kind of war that ultimately undercut his aspiration to wage "an unconditional war on poverty."

The Great Society

In his State of the Union message in 1964, Johnson announced his plans to build a Great Society. Over the next two years, he used the political momentum of the civil rights movement and the overwhelming Democratic majorities in the House and Senate to push through the most ambitious reform program since the New Deal. In August 1964 the Economic Opportunity Act launched the War on Poverty. It established an Office of Economic Opportunity (OEO), which coordinated a network of federal programs designed to increase opportunities in employment and education.

The programs had mixed results. The Job Corps provided vocational training mostly for urban black youth considered unemployable. Housed in dreary barrackslike camps far from home, trainees often found themselves learning factory skills that were already obsolete. The dropout rate was very high. The Neighborhood Youth Corps managed to provide work for about 2 million young people aged sixteen to twenty-one. But nearly all of these were low-paying, make-work jobs. Educational programs proved more successful. VISTA (Volunteers in Service to America) was a kind of domestic Peace Corps that brought several thousand idealistic teachers into poor school districts.

The most innovative and controversial element of the OEO was the Community Action Program (CAP). The program invited local communities to establish community action agencies (CAAs), to be funded through the OEO. The Economic Opportunity Act included language requiring these agencies to be "developed, conducted, and administered with the maximum feasible participation of residents of the areas and members of the groups served." In theory, as the SDS organizers had also believed, community action would empower the poor by giving them a direct say in mobilizing resources to attack poverty.

By 1966 the OEO was funding more than 1,000 CAAs, mostly in black neighborhoods of big cities. The traditional powers in cities—mayors, business elites, and

political machines—generally resisted the CAP's promotion of institutional change. They looked at CAAs as merely another way to dispense services and patronage, with the federal government picking up the tab. A continual tug-of-war over who should control funding and decision making plagued the CAP in most cities, sparking intense power struggles that helped to cripple the antipoverty effort. Such was the case in Chicago, where Mayor Richard Daley demanded absolute control over the allocation of federal funds. After being challenged by OEO activists, Daley denounced the program for "fostering class struggle."

The most successful and popular offshoots of the CAP were the so-called national-emphasis programs, designed in Washington and administered according to federal guidelines. The Legal Services Program, staffed by attorneys, helped millions of poor people in legal battles with housing authorities, welfare departments, police, and slumlords. Head Start and Follow Through reached more than 2 million poor children and significantly improved the long-range educational achievement of participants. Comprehensive Community Health Centers—one-stop clinics—provided basic medical services to poor patients who could not afford to see doctors. Upward Bound helped low-income teenagers develop the skills and confidence needed for college. Birth control programs dispensed contraceptive supplies and information to hundreds of thousands of poor women.

But the root cause of poverty lay in unequal income distribution. The Johnson administration never committed itself to the redistribution of income or wealth. Spending on social welfare jumped from 7.7 percent of the gross national product in 1960 to 16 percent in 1974. But roughly three-quarters of social welfare payments went to the nonpoor. The largest sums went to Medicare, established by Congress in 1965 to provide basic health care for the aged, and to expanded Social Security payments and unemployment compensation. The major surge in federal spending on poor people resulted from the explosive growth of Aid to Families with Dependent Children (AFDC), a program begun during the New Deal. But the total cost of AFDC in the mid-1970s was only about $5 billion per year, compared with $65 billion annually for the roughly 30 million Americans receiving Social Security payments.

The War on Poverty, like the Great Society itself, became a forgotten dream. "More than five years after the passage of the Economic Opportunity Act," a 1970 study concluded, "the war on poverty has barely scratched the surface. Most poor people have had no contact with it, except perhaps to hear the promises of a better life to come." The OEO finally expired in 1974. Having made the largest commitment to federal spending on social welfare since the New Deal, Johnson could take pride in the gains scored in the War on Poverty. At

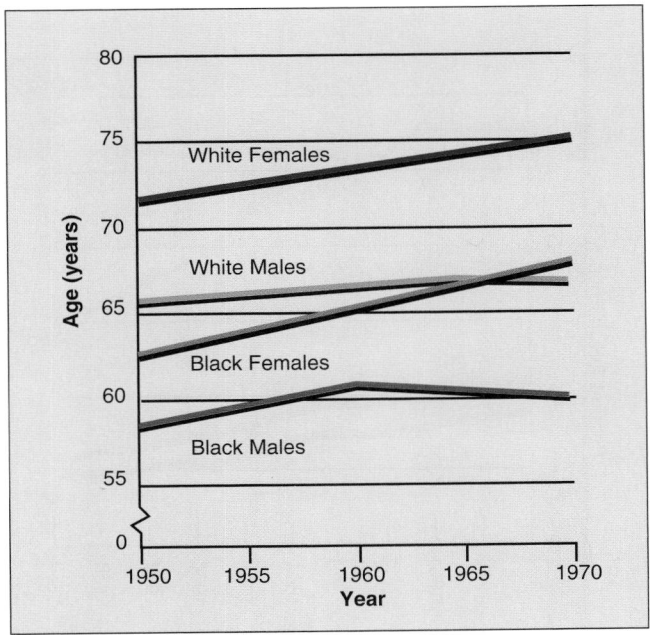

Comparative Figures on Life Expectancy at Birth by Race and Sex, 1950–1970 *Shifting mortality statistics suggested that the increased longevity of females increasingly cut across race lines, but did not diminish the difference between white people and black people as a whole.*

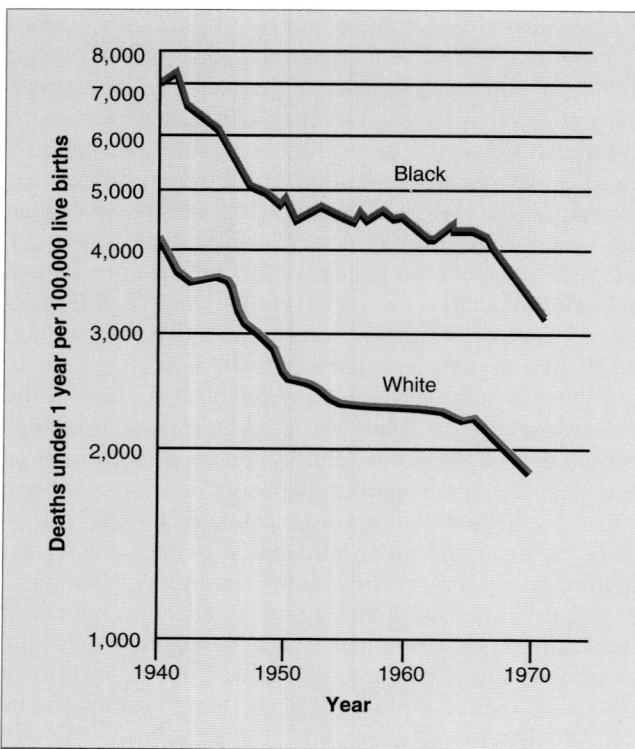

Comparative Figures on Infant Mortality by Race, 1940–1970 *The causes of infant mortality such as inadequate maternal diets, prenatal care, and medical services were all rooted in poverty, both rural and urban. Despite generally falling rates of infant mortality, nonwhite people continued to suffer the effects more than white people.*

ing loans to support the building of new homes in suburban areas (see Chapter 27). The federal government also encouraged "redlining," which left people in poor neighborhoods without access to building loans. In these areas, the supply of adequate housing declined sharply. Slumlords took advantage of this situation, collecting high rents while allowing their properties to deteriorate. City officials meanwhile appealed for federal funds under Title I of the 1949 Housing Act to upgrade housing. Designed as a program of civic revitalization, these urban renewal projects more often than not sliced apart poor neighborhoods with new highways, demolished them in favor of new office complexes, or, as in Chicago's Uptown, favored new developments for the middle class rather than the poor. In 1968 a federal survey showed that 80 percent of those residents who had been displaced under this program were nonwhite, a finding that prompted civil rights leaders to call urban renewal programs "Negro removal." As a result, the inner city became not only increasingly crowded in the 1960s but more segregated.

Urban employment opportunities declined with the urban housing stock. The industries and corporations that had lured working men and women to the cities a century earlier either automated their plants, thus scaling back their workforces, or relocated to the suburbs or other regions, such as the South and Southwest, that promised lower corporate taxes and nonunion labor. Nationwide, military spending prompted by the escalation of the Vietnam War brought the unemployment rate down from 6 percent,

the same time, he had raised expectations higher than could be reached without a more drastic redistribution of economic and political power. Even in the short run, the president could not sustain the welfare programs and simultaneously fight a lengthy and expensive war abroad.

Crisis in the Cities

As Harrington's *The Other America* pointed out, some of the nation's poorest communities were located in the Appalachian mountains and in the Deep South. But since World War II, urban areas had suffered disproportionally from a steady process of decay. "White flight"—the exodus of white people to the suburbs—had reduced the tax base for public services of all kinds, especially schools and recreational facilities. Johnson's War on Poverty scarcely addressed the problems plaguing the nation's metropolitan areas (defined by the U.S. Census as those with populations of 250,000 people or more). On the contrary, urban conditions grew worse.

With funds for new construction limited during the Great Depression and World War II, and the postwar boom taking place in the suburbs, the housing stock in the cities diminished and deteriorated. The Federal Housing Administration had encouraged this trend by insur-

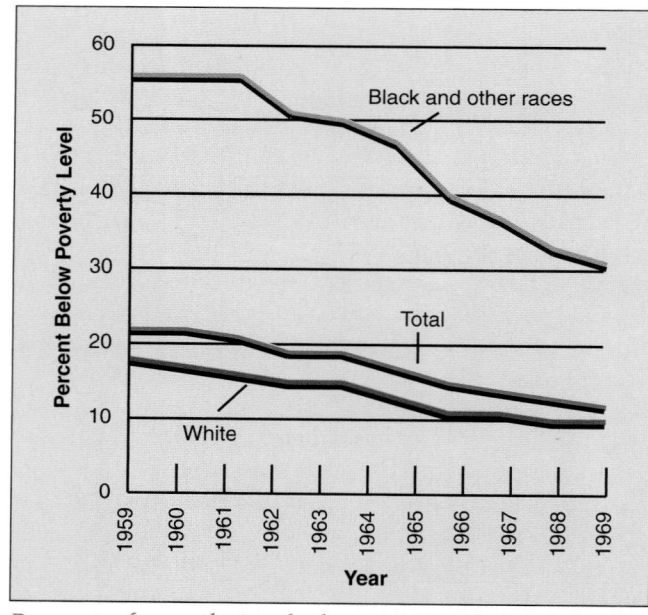

Percent of population below poverty level, by race, 1959–1969

Note: The poverty threshold for a nonfarm family of four was $3,743 in 1969 and $2,973 in 1959.

Source: *Congressional Quarterly, Civil Rights: A Progress Report,* 1971, p. 46.

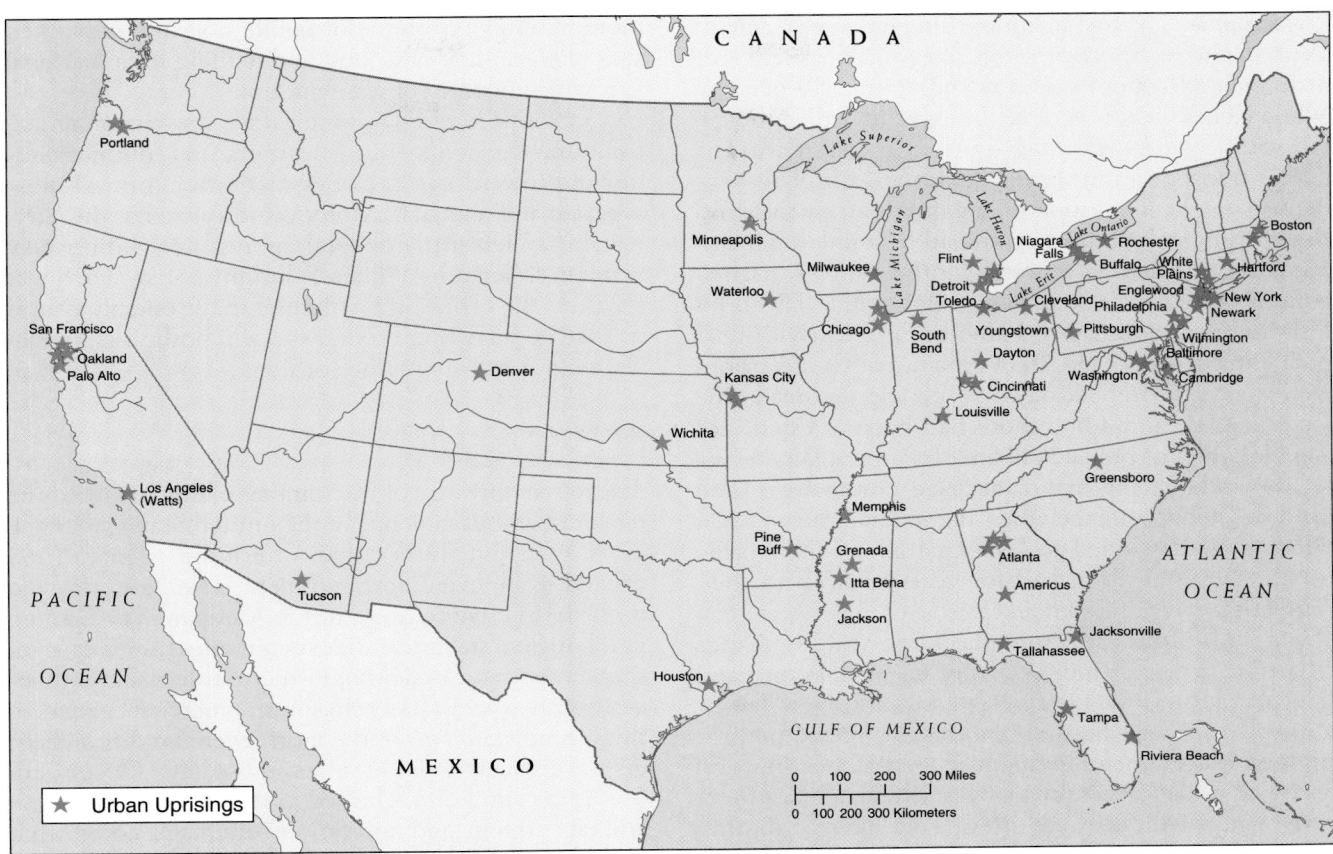

Urban Uprisings, 1965–1968   *After World War II urban uprisings precipitated by racial conflict increased in African American communities. In Watts in 1965 and in Detroit and Newark in 1967 rioters struck out at symbols of white control of their communities, such as white-owned businesses and residential properties.*

where it was in 1960, to 4 percent in 1966, where it remained until the end of the decade. Black unemployment, however, was nearly twice that of white unemployment. New jobs were concentrated in the defense-related industries in the South and Southwest. In northern cities, the proportion of the workforce employed in the higher-paying manufacturing jobs declined precipitously while the proportion working in minimum-wage service industries rose at a fast rate. In short, African Americans were losing good jobs and steadily falling further behind whites.

Pollution, which had long plagued traffic-congested cities like Los Angeles and industrial cities like steel-producing Pittsburgh, became an increasingly pervasive urban problem. Cities like Phoenix that once had clean air began to issue smog alerts. Pointing to high levels of lead in the blood of urban children, scientists warned of the long-term threat of pollution to public health.

Despite deteriorating conditions, millions of Americans continued to move to the cities, mainly African Americans from the Deep South, white people from the Appalachian mountains, and Latinos from Puerto Rico. By the mid-1960s African Americans had become near majorities in the nation's decaying inner cities. Since World War II nearly 3 million African Americans had left the South for northern cities. In that time, New York's black population had more than doubled, and Detroit's had tripled. The vast majority of these African Americans fled rural poverty only to find themselves earning minimum wages at best and living in miserable, racially segregated neighborhoods.

Urban Uprisings

These deteriorating conditions brought urban pressures to the boiling point in the mid-1960s. In the "long, hot summers" of 1964 to 1968 the nation was rocked by more than 100 urban uprisings. As poet Imamu Amiri Baraka (formerly LeRoi Jones) noted, these incidents were spontaneous rebellions against authority. Unlike the race riots of the 1920s and 1940s, when angry whites assaulted blacks, masses of African Americans now took revenge for the white domination of their communities and specifically for police abuse.

In 1964, waves of turbulence rippled through the black neighborhoods of Harlem, Rochester, and

Philadelphia. The first major uprising erupted in August 1965 in the Watts section of Los Angeles. Here, the male unemployment rate hovered around 30 percent. Watts lacked health care facilities—the nearest hospital was twelve miles away—and in a city with little public transportation, fewer than one-fifth of its residents owned cars. It took only a minor arrest to set off the uprising, which quickly spread fifty miles. Throwing rocks and bottles through store windows, participants reportedly shouted, "This is for Selma! This is for Birmingham!" and "Burn, baby, burn!" Nearly 50,000 people turned out, and 20,000 National Guard troops were sent in. After six days, 34 people lay dead, 900 were injured, and 4,000 more had been arrested. Los Angeles chief of police William H. Parker blamed civil rights workers, the mayor accused communists, and both feigned ignorance when the media reported that white police assigned to "charcoal alley," their name for the Watts district, had for years referred to their nightsticks as "nigger knockers."

The following summer, large-scale uprisings occurred in San Francisco, Milwaukee, Dayton, and Cleveland. On July 13, 1967, in Newark, New Jersey, a city with severe housing shortages and the nation's highest black unemployment rate, the beating and arrest of a black taxi driver by a white police officer provoked a widespread protest. Five days of looting and burning of white-owned buildings ended with twenty-five people killed by the bullets of police and the National Guard. One week later the Detroit "Great Rebellion" began. This time a vice squad of the Detroit police had raided a bar and arrested the after-hours patrons. One spectator called out, "Don't let them take our people away.... Let's get the bricks and bottles going." *Time* magazine later reported, "Detroit became the scene of the bloodiest uprising in a half century and the costliest in terms of property damage in U.S. history." Army tanks and paratroopers were brought in to quell the massive disturbance, which lasted a week and left 34 people dead and 7,000 under arrest.

The uprisings seemed at first to prompt badly needed reforms. After Watts, President Johnson set up a task force headed by Deputy Attorney General Ramsey Clark and allocated funds for a range of antipoverty programs. Several years later the Kerner Commission, headed by Governor Otto Kerner of Illinois, studied the riots and found that the participants in the uprisings were not the poorest or least-educated members of their communities. They suffered instead from heightened expectations sparked by the civil rights movement and Johnson's promise of a Great Society, expectations that were not to be realized. The Kerner Commission concluded its report by indicting "white racism" for creating an "explosive mixture" of poverty and police brutality and recommending a yet more extensive program of public housing, integrated schools, 2 million new jobs, and funding for a "national system of income supplementation."

But Congress ignored both the recommendations and the commission's warning that "our nation is moving toward two societies, one black, one white— separate and unequal." Moreover, the costs of the Vietnam War left little federal money for antipoverty programs. Senator William Fulbright noted, "Each war feeds on the other, and, although the President assures us that we have the resources to win both wars, in fact we are not winning either of them."

1968

The urban uprisings of the summer of 1967 marked the most drawn-out violence in the United States since the Civil War. But, rather than offering a respite, 1968 proved to be even more turbulent. The bloodiest and most destructive fighting of the Vietnam War resulted in a hopeless stalemate that soured most Americans on the conflict and undermined their faith in U.S. invincibility in world affairs. Disillusionment deepened in the spring when two of the most revered political leaders were struck down by assassins' bullets. Once again protesters and police clashed on the nation's campuses and city streets, and millions of Americans asked what was wrong with their country. Why was it so violent? A former graduate student at Columbia University, Mike Wallace, spoke for many when he later recalled, "1968 just cracked the universe open for me."

The Tet Offensive

On January 30, 1968, the North Vietnamese and their Vietcong allies launched the Tet Offensive (named for the Vietnamese lunar new year holiday), stunning the U.S. military command in South Vietnam. The Vietcong managed to push into the major cities and provincial capitals of the South, as far as the courtyard of the U.S. embassy in Saigon. U.S. troops ultimately halted the offensive, suffering comparatively modest casualties of 1,600 dead and 8,000 wounded. The North Vietnamese and Vietcong suffered more than 40,000 deaths, about one-fifth of the total forces. Civilian casualties ran to the hundreds of thousands. As many as 1 million South Vietnamese became refugees, their villages totally ruined.

The Tet Offensive, despite U.S. success in stopping it, shattered the credibility of American officials who had repeatedly claimed the enemy to be virtually beaten. Television and press coverage—including scenes of U.S. personnel shooting from the embassy windows in Saigon—dismayed the public. Americans saw the beautiful, ancient city of Hue devastated almost beyond recognition and heard a U.S. officer casually remark about a village in the Mekong delta, "We had to destroy home. For the first time, polls showed strong opposition to the war, 49 percent concluding that the entire operation in Vietnam was a mistake. The majority believed that the stalemate was hopeless. Meanwhile, in Rome, Berlin, Paris, and London, students and others turned out in huge demonstrations to protest U.S. involvement in Vietnam. At home, sectors of the antiwar movement began to shift from resistance to open rebellion.

The Tet Offensive also opened a year of political drama at home. Congress resoundingly turned down a request for a general increase in troops issued by General Westmoreland. President Johnson, facing the 1968 election campaign, knew the odds were now against him. He watched as opinion polls showed his popularity plummet to an all-time low. After he squeaked to a narrow victory in the New Hampshire primary, Johnson decided to step down. On March 31 he announced he would not seek the Democratic Party's nomination. He also declared a bombing halt over North Vietnam and called Hanoi to peace talks, which began in Paris in May. Like Truman almost thirty years earlier, and despite his determination not to repeat that bit of history, Johnson had lost his presidency in Asia.

King, the War, and the Assassination

By 1968 the civil rights leadership stood firmly in opposition to the war, and Martin Luther King Jr. had reached a turning point in his life. The Federal Bureau of Investigation had been harassing King, tapping his telephones and spreading malicious rumors about him. Despite the threat from the FBI (Bureau chief J. Edgar Hoover had sworn to "destroy the burrhead"), King abandoned his customary caution in criticizing U.S. policy in Vietnam. In the fall of 1965 he began to connect domestic unrest

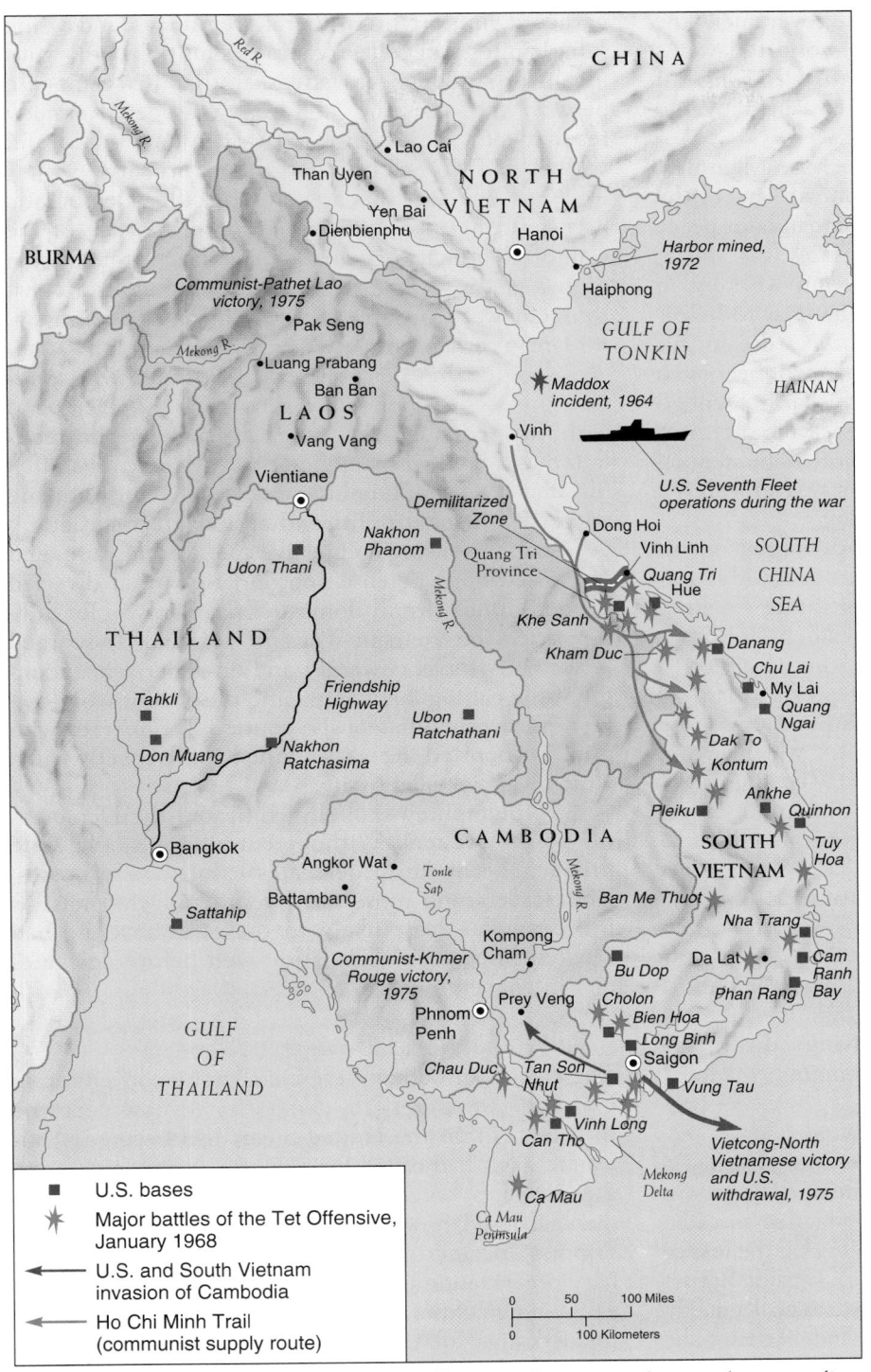

The Southeast Asian War *The Indo-Chinese subcontinent, home to long-standing regional conflict, became the center of a prolonged war with the United States.*

it, in order to save it." Television newscasters began to warn parents: "The following scenes might not be suitable viewing for children."

The United States had chalked up a major military victory during the Tet Offensive but lost the war at with the war abroad, calling the U.S. government the "greatest purveyor of violence in the world today." As he became more militant in opposing the war, King lost the support of liberal Democrats who remained loyal to Johnson. King refused to compromise.

In the spring of 1968 King chose Memphis, Tennessee, home of striking sanitation workers, as the place to inaugurate a Poor People's Campaign for peace and justice. Noting that the United States was "much, much sicker" than when he had begun working in 1955, he nonetheless delivered, in what was to be his final speech, a message of hope. "I have a dream this afternoon that the brotherhood of man will become a reality," King told the crowd. "With this faith, I will go out and carve a tunnel of hope from a mountain of despair." The next evening, April 4, 1968, as he stepped out on the balcony of his motel, King was shot in the head by a lone assassin, James Earl Ray.

Throughout the world crowds turned out to mourn King's death. The *New York Times* declared King's murder "a national disaster." Cheers, however, rang through the regional FBI office. President Johnson, who had ordered the investigation of King, declined to attend the funeral, sending the vice president in his place. Student Nonviolent Coordinating Committee leader Stokely Carmichael stormed, "When white America killed Dr. King, she declared war on us."

Riots broke out in more than 100 cities. Chicago Mayor Richard Daley ordered his police to shoot to kill. In Washington, D.C., U.S. Army units set up machine guns outside the Capitol and the White House. By week's end, nearly 27,000 African Americans had been jailed. The physical scars of these riots remained for years, as banks redlined black neighborhoods and refused funds for rebuilding. The psychic scars survived even longer. With King's death, his vision of humanity as a "Beloved Community" faded.

The Democratic Campaign

The dramatic events of the first part of the year had a direct impact on the presidential campaign. For those liberals dissatisfied with Johnson's conduct of the war, and especially for African Americans suffering the loss of their greatest national leader, New York senator Robert F. Kennedy emerged as the candidate of choice. Kennedy enjoyed a strong record on civil rights, and, like King, he had begun to interpret the war as a mirror of injustice at home. Kennedy insisted during the Tet Offensive that "our nation must be told the truth about this war, in all its terrible reality." On this promise he began to build a campaign for the Democratic nomination.

Ironically, Kennedy faced an opponent who agreed with him, Minnesota senator Eugene McCarthy. The race for the Democratic nomination positioned McCarthy, the witty philosopher, against Kennedy, the charismatic campaigner. McCarthy garnered support from liberal Democrats and white suburbanites. On college campuses his popularity with idealistic students was so great that his campaign became known as the "children's crusade." Kennedy reached out successfully to African Americans and Latinos and won all but the Oregon primary.

Kennedy appeared to be the Democratic Party's strongest candidate as June 4, the day of the California primary, dawned. But as the final tabulation of his victory came in just past midnight, Robert Kennedy was struck down by the bullet of an assassin, Jordanian Sirhan Sirhan.

Vice President Hubert H. Humphrey, a long-time presidential hopeful, was now the sole Democrat with the credentials to succeed Johnson. But his reputation as a cold war Democrat had become a liability. In the 1950s Humphrey had delivered stirring addresses for civil rights and antipoverty legislation; yet he also sponsored repressive cold war measures and supported huge defense appropriations that diverted needed funds from domestic programs. He fully supported the Vietnam War and had publicly scorned peace activists as cowardly and un-American. Incongruously calling his campaign "the Politics of Joy," Humphrey simultaneously courted Democrats who grimly supported the war and the King-Kennedy wing, which was sickened by it.

Humphrey skillfully cultivated the Democratic power brokers. Without entering a single state primary, he lined up delegates loyal to city bosses, labor leaders, and conservative southern Democrats. As the candidate least likely to rock the boat, he had secured his party's nomination well before delegates met in convention.

"The Whole World Is Watching!"

The events surrounding the Democratic convention in Chicago, August 21–26, demonstrated how deep the divisions within the United States had become. Antiwar activists had called for a massive demonstration at the delegates' hotel and at the convention center. The media focused, however, on the plans announced by the "Yippies," or Youth International Party, a largely imaginary organization of politicized hippies led by jokester and counterculture guru Abbie Hoffman. Yippies called for a Festival of Life, including a "nude-in" on Lake Michigan beaches and the release of a greased pig—Pigasus, the Yippie candidate for president. Still reeling from the riots following King's assassination, Chicago's Mayor Richard Daley refused to issue parade permits. According to later accounts, he sent hundreds of undercover police into the crowds to encourage rock throwing and generally incite violence so that retaliation would appear necessary and reasonable.

Daley's strategy boomeranged when his officers staged what a presidential commission later termed a

The "police riot" in Chicago, August 1968, during the Democratic National Convention capped a spring and summer of violence. Mayor Richard Daley had prepared his city for the anticipated protest against the war by assembling more than 20,000 law enforcement officials, including police, National Guard, and U.S. Army troops carrying flame throwers and bazookas. Television cameras and photographers recorded the massive clubbing and teargassing of demonstrators as well as bystanders and news reporters.

Realistic, Demand the Impossible!" Similar protests against authority occurred in eastern Europe. In Prague, Czechoslovakia, students wearing blue jeans and singing Beatles songs threw rocks at Soviet tanks. Meanwhile, demonstrations in Japan, Italy, Ireland, Germany, and England all brought young people into the streets to demand democratic reforms in their own countries and an end to the war in Vietnam.

THE POLITICS OF IDENTITY

The tragic events of 1968 brought whole sectors of the counterculture into political activism. But, remember, hippie Tuli Kupferberg warned them, "the first revolution (but not of course the last) is in yr own head." Many young Americans seemed to hear his message,

"police riot," randomly assaulting demonstrators, casual passersby, and television crews filming the events. For one of the few times in American history, the media appeared to join a protest against civil authorities. Angered by the embarrassing publicity, Daley sent his agents to raid McCarthy's campaign headquarters, where Democrats opposed to the war had gathered.

Inside the convention hall, a raging debate over a peace resolution underscored the depth of the division within the party over the war. Representative Wayne Hays of Ohio lashed out at those who substituted "beards for brains . . . [and] pot [for] patriotism." When the resolution failed, McCarthy delegates put on black armbands and followed folk singer Theodore Bikel in singing "We Shall Overcome." Later, as tear gas used against the demonstrators outside turned the amphitheater air acrid, delegates heard the beaming Humphrey praise Mayor Daley and Johnson's conduct of the Vietnam War. When Senator Abraham Ribicoff of Connecticut addressed the convention and protested the "Gestapo tactics" of the police, television cameras focused on Mayor Daley saying, "You Jew son of a bitch . . ., go home!" The crowd outside chanted, "The whole world is watching! The whole world is watching!" Indeed, through satellite transmission, it was.

Protest and social strain spread worldwide. Across the United States the antiwar movement picked up steam. In Paris, students took over campuses and workers occupied factories. Young people scrawled on the walls such humorous and half-serious slogans as "Be

intensifying their protest against the war while at the same time expressing their own political grievances and promoting their own sense of collective identity. United in their opposition to "the Establishment"—that is, the politicians and business leaders who maintained the status quo—these baby boomers sought also to empower themselves and their communities in myriad smaller but vital movements.

With great media fanfare, gay liberation and women's liberation movements emerged in the late 1960s. By the early 1970s young Latinos, Asian Americans, and Indian peoples had pressed their own claims. In different ways, these groups drew their own lessons from the nationalist movement that formed in the wake of Malcolm X's death—Black Power. Soon, "Brown Power," "Yellow Power," and "Red Power" became the slogans of movements constituted distinctly as new communities of protest.

Black Power

In African American communities, when the Great Society programs failed to lessen poverty and black men began to die in disproportionate numbers in Vietnam, faith in the old ways lapsed. Impatient with the strategies of social change based on voting rights and integration, many younger activists spurned the tactics of civil disobedience of King's generation for direct action and militant self-defense. In 1966 Stokely Carmichael, who had helped turn SNCC into an all-black organization, began to advocate Black

OVERVIEW

Year	Organization/ Movement	Description
1962	Students for a Democratic Society (SDS)	Organization of college students that became the largest national organization of left-wing white students. Calling for "participatory democracy," SDS involved students in community-based campaigns against poverty and for citizens' control of neighborhoods. SDS played a prominent role in the campaign to end the war in Vietnam.
1964	Free Speech Movement	Formed at the University of California at Berkeley to protest the banning of on-campus political fund-raising. Decried the bureaucratic character of the "multiuniversity" and advocated an expansion of student rights.
1965	Anti-Vietnam War Movement	Advocated grass-roots opposition to U.S. involvement in Southeast Asia. By 1970 a national mobilization committee organized a demonstration of a half-million protesters in Washington, D.C.
1965	*La raza*	A movement of Chicano youth to advance the cultural and political self-determination of Mexican Americans. *La raza* included the Brown Berets, which addressed community issues, and regional civil rights groups such as the Crusade for Social Justice, formed in 1965.
1966	Black Power	Militant movement that emerged from the civil rights campaigns to advocate independent institutions for African Americans and pride in black culture and African heritage. The idea of Black Power, a term coined by Stokely Carmichael, inspired the formation of the paramilitary Black Panthers.
1968	American Indian Movement (AIM)	Organization formed to advance the self-determination of Indian peoples and challenge the authority of the Bureau of Indian Affairs. Its most effective tactic was occupation. In February, 1973, AIM insurgents protesting land and treaty violations occupied Wounded Knee, South Dakota, the location of an 1890 massacre, until the FBI and BIA agents drove them out.
1968	Women's Liberation	Movement of mainly young women that took shape following a protest at the Miss America Beauty Pageant. Impatient with the legislative reforms promoted by the National Organization for Women, founded in 1966, activists developed their own agenda shaped by the slogan "The Personal Is Political." Activities included the formation of "consciousness-raising" groups and the establishment of women's studies programs.
1968	Asian American Political Alliance (AAPA)	Formed at the University of California at Berkeley, the AAPA was one of the first pan-Asian political organizations to struggle against racial oppression. The AAPA encouraged Asian Americans to claim their own cultural identity and to protest the war against Asian peoples in Vietnam.
1969	Gay Liberation	Movement to protest discrimination against homosexuals and lesbians that emerged after the Stonewall Riots in New York City. Unlike earlier organizations such as the Mattachine Society, which focused on civil rights, Gay Liberationists sought to radically change American society and government, which they believed were corrupt.

Power as a means for African Americans to take control of their own communities.

Derived from a century-long tradition of black nationalism, the key tenets of Black Power were self-determination and self-sufficiency. National conferences of activists, held annually beginning in 1966, adopted separatist resolutions, including a plan to partition the United States into black and white nations. Black Power also promoted self-esteem by affirming the unique history and heritage of African peoples.

The movement's boldest expression was the Black Panther Party for Self-Defense, founded in Oakland, California, in 1966 by Huey P. Newton and Bobby Seale. "We want freedom," Newton demanded. "We want power. . . . We want full employment. . . . We want all black men to be exempt from military service. We want . . . an end to POLICE BRUTALITY. . . . We want land, bread, housing, education, clothing, and justice." Armed self-defense was the Panthers' strategy, and they adopted a paramilitary style—black leather jackets, shoes, black berets, and firearms—that infuriated local authorities. Monitoring local police, a practice Panthers termed "patrolling the pigs," was their major activity. In several communities, Panthers also ran free breakfast programs for schoolchildren, established medical clinics, and conducted educational classes. For a time the Panthers became folk heroes in the black community. Persecuted by local police and the FBI—there were more than thirty raids on Panther offices in eleven states during 1968 and 1969—the Panthers were arrested, prosecuted, and sentenced to long terms in jail that effectively destroyed the organization.

Black Power nevertheless continued to grow during the late 1960s and became a multifaceted movement. The Reverend Jesse Jackson, for example, rallied African Americans in Chicago to boycott the A&P supermarket chain until the firm hired 700 black workers. A dynamic speaker and skillful organizer, Jackson encouraged African Americans to support their own businesses and services. "We are going to see to it," he explained in 1969, "that the resources of the ghetto are not siphoned off by outside groups. . . . If a building goes up in the black community, we're going to build it." His program, Operation Breadbasket, strengthened community control. By 1970 it had spread beyond Chicago to fifteen other cities.

Cultural nationalism became the most enduring component of Black Power. In their popular book *Black Power* (1967), Stokely Carmichael and Charles V. Hamilton urged African Americans "to assert their own definitions, to reclaim their history, their culture; to create their own sense of community and togetherness." Thousands of college students responded by calling for more scholarships and for more classes on African American history and culture. At San Francisco

The war in Vietnam contributed to the growing racial militancy in the United States. African Americans served on the front lines in Vietnam in disproportionate numbers, and many came to view the conflict as a "white man's war."

State University, students formed the Black Student Union and, with help from the Black Panthers, demanded the creation of a black studies department. After a series of failed negotiations with the administration, the black students called for a campuswide strike and in December 1968 shut down the university. In the end, 134 school days later, the administration agreed to fund a black studies department but also fired about 25 faculty members and refused to drop charges against 700 arrested campus activists. Strikes for "third world studies" soon broke out on other campuses, including the Newark campus of Rutgers University, the San Diego and Berkeley campuses of the University of California, and the University of Wisconsin at Madison, where the national guard was brought in to quell the protest.

Meanwhile, trend setters put aside Western dress for African-style dashikis and hairdos, and black parents gave their children African names. Many well-known African Americans such as Imamu Amiri Baraka (formerly LeRoi Jones), Muhammad Ali (formerly Cassius Clay), and Kwame Touré (formerly Stokely Carmichael) rejected their "slave names." The African

American holiday Kwanzaa began to replace Christmas as a seasonal family celebration. This deepening sense of racial pride and solidarity was summed up in the popular slogan "Black Is Beautiful."

Sisterhood Is Powerful

Betty Friedan's best-selling *Feminine Mystique* (1963) had swelled feelings of discontent among many middle-class white women who had come of age in the 1950s (see Chapter 27) and sparked the formation of the National Organization for Women (NOW) in 1966. NOW pledged itself "to take action to bring women into full participation in the mainstream of American society now." Members spearheaded campaigns for the enforcement of laws banning sex discrimination in work and in education, for maternity leaves for working mothers, and for government funding of day-care centers. NOW also came out for the Equal Rights Amendment, first introduced in Congress in 1923, and demanded the repeal of legislation that prohibited abortion or restricted birth control.

The second half of the decade produced a different kind of movement: women's liberation. Like Black Power, the women's liberation movement attracted especially women who had been active in civil rights, SDS, and campus antiwar movements. These women resented the sexist attitudes and behaviors of their fellow male activists. Women must come to understand, one angry woman wrote, that "they are not inferior—nor chicks, nor bunnies, nor quail, nor cows, nor bitches, nor ass, nor meat," but agents of their own destiny. Like Black Power, the women's liberation movement issued its own separatist plan.

In 1967 small groups of women broke off from male-led protest movements. They formed myriad all-women organizations such as Radical Women and Redstockings in New York, the Women's Liberation Union in Chicago, Berkeley, and Dayton, and Bread and Roses and Cell 16 in Boston. Impatient with the legislative reforms promoted by NOW, and angered by the sexism of SNCC and SDS, these women proclaimed "Sisterhood Is Powerful." "Women are an oppressed class. Our oppression is total, affecting every facet of our lives," read the Redstocking Manifesto of 1969. "We are exploited as sex objects, breeders, domestic servants, and cheap labor."

The women's liberation movement developed a scathing critique of patriarchy—that is, the power of men to dominate all institutions, from the family to business to the military to protest movements themselves. Patriarchy, they argued, was the prime cause of exploitation, racism, and war. Outraged and sometimes outrageous, radical feminists, as they called themselves, conducted "street theater" at the 1968 Miss America Beauty Pageant in Atlantic City, crowning a live sheep queen and "throwing implements of female torture" (bras, girdles, curlers, and copies of the *Ladies' Home Journal*) into a "freedom trash can." A few months later, the Women's International Terrorist Conspiracy from Hell (WITCH) struck in Lower Manhattan, putting a hex on the male-dominated New York Stock Exchange.

The media focused on the audacious acts and brazen pronouncements of radical feminists, but the majority involved in the women's liberation movement were less flamboyant women who were simply trying to rise above the limitations imposed on them because of their sex. Most of their activism took place outside the limelight in consciousness-raising (CR) groups. CR groups, which multiplied by the thousands in the late 1960s and early 1970s, brought women together to discuss the relationship between public events and private lives, particularly between politics and sexuality. Here women shared their most intimate feelings toward men or other women and established the constituency for the movement's most important belief, expressed in the aphorism "The personal is political." Believing that no aspect of life lacked a political dimension, women in these groups explored the power dynamics of the institutions of family and marriage as well as the workforce and government. "The small group has served as a place where thousands of us have learned to support each other," one participant reported, "where we have gained new feelings of self-respect and learned to speak about what we are thinking and to respect other women."

Participants in the women's liberation movement engaged in a wide range of activities. Some staged sit-ins at *Newsweek* to protest demeaning media depictions of women. Others established health clinics, day-care centers, rape crisis centers, and shelters for women fleeing abusive husbands or lovers. The women's liberation movement also had a significant educational impact. Feminist bookstores and publishing companies, such as the Feminist Press, reached out to eager readers. Scholarly books such as Kate Millett's *Sexual Politics* (1970) found a wide popular audience. By the early 1970s campus activists were demanding women's studies programs and women's centers. Like black studies, women's studies programs included traditional academic goals, such as the generation of new scholarship, but also encouraged personal change and self-esteem. Between 1970 and 1975, as many as 150 women's studies programs had been established. The movement continued to grow; by 1980 nearly 30,000 women's studies courses were offered at colleges and universities throughout the United States.

The women's liberation movement remained, however, a bastion of white middle-class women. The appeal to sisterhood did not unite women across race or class or even sexual orientation. Lesbians, who charged the early leaders of NOW with homophobia, found large pockets of "heterosexism" in the women's liberation movement and broke off to form their own organizations. Although some African American women were outraged at the posturing of Black Power leaders like Stokely Carmichael, who joked that "the only position for women in SNCC is prone," the majority remained wary of white women's appeals to sisterhood. African American women formed their own "womanist" movement to address their distinct cultural and political concerns. Similarly, by 1970 a Latina feminist movement had begun to address issues uniquely relevant to women of color in an Anglo-dominated society.

Although the women's liberation movement could not dispel ethnic or racial differences, it fostered a sense of community among many women. By August 1970 hundreds of thousands of women responded to NOW's call for a Women's Strike for Equality, a mass demonstration marking the fiftieth anniversary of the woman suffrage amendment and the largest turnout for women's rights in U.S. history.

Gay Liberation

The gay community had been generations in the making but gained visibility during World War II (see Chapter 25). By the mid-1950s two pioneering homophile organizations, the Mattachine Society and the Daughters of Bilitis, were campaigning to reduce discrimination against homosexuals in employment, the armed forces, and all areas of social and cultural life. Other groups, such as the Society for Individual Rights, rooted themselves in New York's Greenwich Village, San Francisco's North Beach, and other centers of gay night life. But it was during the tumultuous 1960s that gay and lesbian movements encouraged many men and women to proclaim publicly their sexual identity: "Say It Loud, Gay Is Proud."

The major event prompting gays to organize grew out of repeated police raids of gay bars and harassment of their patrons. In February 1966 New York City's popular liberal mayor John Lindsay announced a crackdown against "promenading perverts" and assigned police to patrol the bars between Times Square and Washington Square. The American Civil Liberties Union responded by pointing out that the mayor was "confusing deviant social behavior with criminal activity." Lindsay's police commissioner soon announced the end of the entrapment policy by which undercover police had been luring homosexuals into breaking the law, but various forms of individual harassment continued. Finally, on Friday, June 27, 1969, New York police raided the Stonewall Inn, a well-known gay bar in Greenwich Village, and provoked an uprising of angry homosexuals that lasted the entire night. The next day, "Gay Power" graffiti appeared on buildings and sidewalks throughout the neighborhood.

The Stonewall Riot, as it was called, sparked a new sense of collective identity among many gays and lesbians and touched off a new movement for both civil rights and liberation. Gay men and women in New York City formed the Gay Liberation Front (GLF), announcing themselves as "a revolutionary homosexual group of men and women formed with the realization that complete sexual liberation for all people cannot come about unless existing social institutions are abolished. We reject society's attempt to impose sexual roles and definitions of our nature. We are stepping outside these roles and simplistic myths. We are going to be who we are." The GLF also took a stand against the war in Vietnam and supported the Black Panthers. It quickly adopted the forms of public protest, such as street demonstrations and sit-ins, developed by the civil rights movement and given new direction by antiwar protesters.

Changes in public opinion and policies followed. As early as 1967 a group of Episcopal priests had urged church leaders to avoid taking a moral position against same-sex relationships. The San Francisco-based Council on Religion and Homosexuality established a network for clergy sympathetic to gay and lesbian parishioners. In 1973 the American Psychiatric Association, which since World War II had viewed homosexuality as a treatable mental illness, reclassified it as a normal sexual orientation. Meanwhile, there began a slow process of decriminalization of homosexual acts between consenting adults. In 1975 the U.S. Civil Service Commission ended its ban on the employment of homosexuals.

The founders of gay liberation encouraged not only legal changes and the establishment of supporting institutions but self-pride. "Gay Is Good" (like "Black Is Beautiful" and "Sisterhood Is Powerful") expressed the aspiration of a large hidden minority (estimated at 10 million or more people) to "come out" and demand public acceptance of their sexual identity. The Gay Activist Alliance, founded in 1970, demanded "freedom of expression of our dignity and value as human beings." By the mid-1970s Gay Pride marches held simultaneously in several cities were drawing nearly 500,000 participants.

The Chicano Rebellion

By the mid-1960s young Mexican Americans had created, according to one historian, a moral community founded on collectivist principles and a determination to resist Anglo domination. Mainly high school and college students, they adopted the slang term *Chicano*, in preference to Mexican American, to express a militant

Major Indian Reservations, 1976   *Although sizable areas, designated Indian reservations represented only a small portion of territory occupied in earlier times.*

ethnic nationalism. Chicano militants demanded not only equality with white people but cultural and political self-determination. Tracing their roots to the heroic Aztecs, they identified *la raza* (the race or people) as the source of a common language, religion, and heritage.

Between 1965 and 1969 the Chicano movement reached its peak. Students staged "blowouts" or strikes in East Los Angeles high schools to demand educational reform and a curricular emphasis on the history, literature, art, and language of Mexican Americans. In 1968 President Johnson had signed the Bilingual Education Act, which reversed state laws that prohibited the teaching of classes in any language but English. Nevertheless, as Sal Castro, an East Los Angeles teacher, complained, "If a kid speaks in Spanish, he is criticized. If a kid has a Mexican accent, he is ridiculed. If a kid talks back, in any language, he is arrested. . . . We have a gun-point education. The school is a prison." Castro encouraged 15,000 students from five Los Angeles schools to strike against poor educational facilities. The police conducted a mass arrest of protesters, and within a short time students in San Antonio and Denver were conducting their own blowouts, holding placards

reading "Teachers, Sí, Bigots, No!" By 1969, on September 16, Mexican Independence Day, high school students throughout the Southwest skipped classes in the First National Chicano Boycott. Meanwhile, students organized to demand Mexican American studies on their campuses. In 1969, a group staged a sit-in at the administrative offices of the University of California–Berkeley, which one commentator called "the first important public appearance of something called Brown Power."

In 1967 David Sanchez of East Los Angeles formed the Brown Berets, modeled on the Black Panthers, to address such community issues as housing and employment and generally to encourage teenagers to express *Chicanismo*, or pride in their Mexican American identity and heritage. By 1972, when the organization disbanded, the Brown Berets had organized twenty chapters, published a newspaper, *La Causa*, and run a successful health clinic. From college campuses spread a wider cultural movement that spawned literary journals in "Spanglish" (a mixture of English and Spanish), theatrical companies and music groups, and murals illustrating ethnic themes on buildings in Los Angeles and elsewhere.

Chicano nationalism inspired a variety of regional political movements in the late 1960s. Several organizations, such as Corky Gonzales's Crusade for Justice, formed in 1965 to protest the failure of the Great Society's antipoverty programs. A former boxer and popular poet, Gonzales was especially well liked by barrio youth and college students. He led important campaigns for greater job opportunities and land reform throughout the Southwest well into the 1970s. In Colorado and New Mexico, the *Alianza Federal de Mercedes*, formed in 1963 by Reies López Tijerina, fought to reclaim land fraudulently appropriated by white settlers. The Texas-based *La Raza Unida* Party (LRUP), meanwhile, increased Mexican American representation in local government and established social and cultural programs. The student-led Mexican American Youth Organization (MAYO) worked closely with the LRUP to help Mexican Americans take political power in Crystal City, Texas. The two organizations registered voters, ran candidates for office, and staged a massive boycott of Anglo-owned businesses.

Mexican American activists, even those who won local office, soon discovered that economic power remained out of community hands. Stifled by poverty, ordinary Mexican Americans had less confidence in the political process, and many fell back into apathy after early hopes of great, sudden change. Despite these setbacks, a sense of collective identity had been forged among many young people. A member of the Brown Berets summed up: "We're not in the melting pot sort of thing. Chicanos don't melt."

Red Power

Having battled government programs to terminate their tribal status (see Chapter 28), Indian peoples entered the 1960s determined to reassert themselves. The Civil Rights Act passed in 1968 restored the legitimacy of tribal laws on the reservations, and Lyndon Johnson personally promised a "new goal" that "erases old attitudes of paternalism." Although economic and social reforms were limited by a shortage of antipoverty and educational funds, a movement to build a sense of Indian identity spread widely among young people. In the 1970 census, many of the 800,000 respondents who identified themselves as Indians did so for the first time.

The American Indian Movement (AIM) was founded in 1968 by Chippewas George Mitchell and Dennis Banks. Like the Black Panthers and Brown Berets, AIM was organized for self-defense, to protect Indians in Minneapolis from police harassment and brutality. The group's activities soon expanded to include a direct challenge of the Bureau of Indian Affairs' guidance over tribal life. Affirming Indian dignity while calling for greater economic opportunities and an end to police

harassment, AIM quickly inspired a plethora of new publications and local organizations. In 1969 the new militancy created national headlines when a group of young Indians occupied the deserted federal prison on Alcatraz Island in San Francisco Bay and demanded government funds for a cultural center and university. The federal government did not respond, however, and the Indians eventually pulled out.

The most dramatic series of events of the Red Power movement began in November 1972, when tribal members occupied the headquarters of the Bureau of Indian affairs for nearly a week. Soon AIM insurgents took over the site of the 1890 massacres at Wounded Knee, South Dakota, swearing to hold their position by force if necessary. Occupiers asked only that the federal government honor treaty rights. Instead, dozens of FBI agents invaded under shoot-to-kill orders, leaving two Indians dead and one federal marshal wounded. AIM

Members of the American Indian Movement (AIM) guard the door to the Bureau of Indian Affairs in Washington, D.C., during a week-long occupation in November 1972 meant to dramatize their grievances. Formed in 1968 to work for equal rights and better living conditions, AIM had led a march of Indian peoples along the "Trail of Broken Treaties" before occupying the BIA offices.

902 War Abroad, War at Home, 1965–1974

gained widespread support for its actions but alienated the more conservative leaders of various tribes.

Several tribes won in court, by legislation or by administrative fiat, small parts of what had earlier been taken from them. The sacred Blue Lake was returned to Pueblo Indians in Taos, New Mexico, and Alaskan natives were granted legal title to 40 million acres (and compensation of almost $1 billion). The Native American Rights Fund (NARF), established in 1971, gained additional thousands of acres in Atlantic coast states. Despite these victories, tribal lands continued to suffer from industrial and government dumping and other commercial uses. On reservations and in urban areas with heavy Indian concentrations, alcohol abuse and ill health remained serious problems.

The 1960s also marked the beginning of an "Indian Renaissance." New books like Vine Deloria Jr.'s *Custer Died for Your Sins* (1969), Dee Brown's *Bury My Heart at Wounded Knee* (1971), and the classic *Black Elk Speaks* (1961), reprinted from the 1930s, reached millions of readers inside and outside Indian communities. A wide variety of Indian novelists, historians, and essayists, such as Pulitzer Prize–winning N. Scott Momaday and Leslie Silko, followed up these successes, and fiction and nonfiction works about Indian life and lore continued to attract a large audience.

The Asian American Movement

Inspired by the Black Power movement, college students of Asian ancestry sought to unite fellow Asian Americans in a struggle against racial oppression "through the power of a consolidated yellow people." In 1968 students at the University of California at Berkeley founded the Asian American Political Alliance (AAPA), one of the first pan-Asian political organizations bringing together Chinese, Japanese, and Filipino American activists. Similar organizations soon appeared on campuses throughout California and spread quickly to the east coast and Midwest.

These groups took a strong stand against the war in Vietnam, condemning it as a violation of the national sovereignty of the small Asian country. They also protested the racism directed against the peoples of Southeast Asia, particularly the practice common among American soldiers of referring to the enemy as "Gooks." This racist epithet, first used to denigrate Filipinos during the Spanish-American War, implied that Asians were something less than human and therefore proper targets for slaughter. In response, Asian American activists rallied behind the people of Vietnam and proclaimed racial solidarity with their "Asian brothers and sisters."

The antiwar movement brought many young Asian Americans into political organizations such as the AAPA that encouraged them to claim their own cultural identity. In 1968 and 1969 students at San Francisco State College and the University of California at Berkeley, for example, rallied behind the slogan "Shut It Down!" and waged prolonged campus strikes to demand the establishment of ethnic studies programs. These students sought alternatives to the goal of assimilation into mainstream society, promoting instead a unique sense of ethnic identity, a pan-Asian counterculture. Berkeley students, for example, sponsored the "Asian American Experience in America—Yellow Power" conference, inviting their peers to learn about "Asian American history and destiny, and the need to express Asian American solidarity in a predominantly white society."

Between 1968 and 1973, major universities across the country introduced courses on Asian American studies, and a few, such as the City College of New York, set up interdisciplinary departments. Meanwhile, artists, writers, documentary filmmakers, oral historians, and anthropologists worked to recover the Asian American past. Writer Frank Chin, who advocated a language that "coheres the people into a community by organizing and codifying the symbols of the people's common experience," wrote the first Asian American drama, *The Year of the Dragon*, to be produced on national television. It was, however, Maxine Hong Kingston's *Woman Warrior: A Memoir of a Girlhood among Ghosts* (1976) that became the major best-seller.

Looking to the example of the Black Panthers, young Asian Americans also took their struggle into the community. In 1968, activists presented the San Francisco municipal government with a list of grievances about conditions in Chinatown, particularly the poor housing and medical facilities, and organized a protest march down the neighborhood's main street. They led a communitywide struggle to save San Francisco's International Hotel, a low-income residential facility for mainly Filipino and Chinese men, which was ultimately leveled for a new parking lot.

Community activists ranging from college students to neighborhood artists worked in a variety of campaigns to heighten public awareness. The Redress and Reparations Movement, initiated by Sansei (third-generation Japanese Americans), for example, encouraged students to ask their parents about their wartime experiences and prompted older civil rights organizations, such as the Japanese American Citizens League, to bring forward the issue of internment. At the same time, trade union organizers renewed labor organizing among new Asian workers, mainly in service industries such as hotel and restaurant work, and in clothing manufacturing. Other campaigns reflected the growing diversity of the Asian population. Filipinos, the fastest growing group, organized to protest the destructive role of

U.S.-backed Philippine dictator Ferdinand Marcos. Students from South Korea similarly denounced the repressive government in their homeland. Samoans sought to publicize the damage caused by nuclear testing in the Pacific Islands. Ultimately, however, in blurring intergroup differences, the Asian American movement failed to reach the growing populations of new immigrants, especially the numerous Southeast Asians fleeing their devastated homeland.

Despite its shortcomings, the politics of identity would continue to grow through the next two decades of mainly conservative rule, broadening the content of literature, film, television, popular music, and even the curriculum of the nation's schools. Collectively, the various movements for social change pushed issues of race, gender, and sexual orientation to the forefront of American politics and simultaneously spotlighted the nation's cultural diversity as a major resource.

THE NIXON PRESIDENCY

The sharp divisions among Americans in 1968, due to a large degree to President Johnson's policies in Vietnam, paved the way for the election of Richard Milhous Nixon. The new Republican president inherited not only an increasingly unpopular war but a nation riven by internal discord. Without specifying his plans, he promised a just and honorable peace in Southeast Asia and the restoration of law and order at home. Yet, once in office, Nixon puzzled both friends and foes. He ordered unprecedented illegal government action against private citizens while agreeing with Congress to enhance several welfare programs and improve environmental protection. He widened and intensified the war in Vietnam, yet made stunning moves toward détente with the People's Republic of China. An architect of the cold war in the 1950s, Nixon became the first president to foresee its end. Nixon worked hard in the White House, centralizing authority and reigning defiantly as an Imperial President—until he brought himself down.

The Southern Strategy

In 1968, Republican presidential contender Richard Nixon deftly built on voter hostility toward youthful protesters and the counterculture. He represented, he said, the "silent majority"—those Americans who worked, paid taxes, and did not demonstrate, picket, or protest loudly, "people who are not haters, people who love their country." Recovering from defeats in runs for the presidency in 1960 and the governorship of California in 1962, Nixon declared himself the one candidate who could restore law and order to the nation.

After signing the landmark Civil Rights Act of 1964, President Johnson said privately, "I think we just

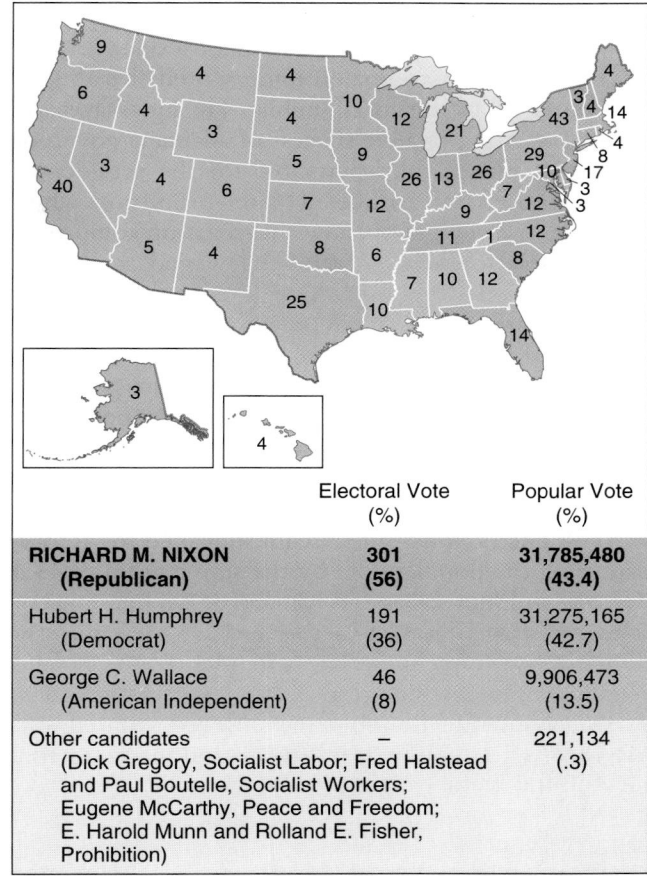

	Electoral Vote (%)	Popular Vote (%)
RICHARD M. NIXON (Republican)	**301 (56)**	**31,785,480 (43.4)**
Hubert H. Humphrey (Democrat)	191 (36)	31,275,165 (42.7)
George C. Wallace (American Independent)	46 (8)	9,906,473 (13.5)
Other candidates (Dick Gregory, Socialist Labor; Fred Halstead and Paul Boutelle, Socialist Workers; Eugene McCarthy, Peace and Freedom; E. Harold Munn and Rolland E. Fisher, Prohibition)	–	221,134 (.3)

The Election of 1968 *Although the Republican Nixon-Agnew team won the popular vote by only a small margin, the Democrats lost in most of the northern states that had voted Democratic since the days of FDR. Segregationist Governor George Wallace of Alabama polled more than 9 million votes.*

delivered the South to the Republicans for a long time to come." Republican strategists moved quickly to make this prediction come true. They also recognized the growing electoral importance of the Sunbelt, where populations grew with the rise of high-tech industries and retirement communities. A powerful conservatism dominated this region, home to many military bases, defense plants, and an increasingly influential Protestant evangelism. Nixon appealed directly to these voters by promising to appoint to federal courts judges who would undercut liberal interpretations of civil rights and be tough on crime. Nixon also promised to roll back the Great Society. "I say it's time," he announced, "to quit pouring billions of dollars into programs that have failed."

Nixon selected as his running mate Maryland governor Spiro T. Agnew, known for his vitriolic oratory. Agnew treated dissent as near treason. He courted the silent majority by attacking all critics of the war as "an effete corps of impudent snobs" and blasted liberal newscasters as "nattering nabobs of negativism."

Democratic nominee Hubert Humphrey chose as his running mate Maine senator Edmund Muskie.

The 1968 campaign underscored the antiliberal sentiment of the voting public. The most dramatic example was the relative success of Alabama governor George Wallace's third-party bid for the presidency. Wallace took state office in 1963 promising white Alabamans "Segregation now! Segregation tomorrow! Segregation forever!" In 1968 he waged a national campaign around a conservative hate list that included school busing, antiwar demonstrations, and urban uprisings. His running mate in the American Independent Party, retired air force general Curtis LeMay, proposed the use of nuclear weapons to "bomb the North Vietnamese back to the Stone Age." Winning only five southern states, Wallace nevertheless captured 13.5 percent of the popular vote.

The Nixon-Agnew team squeaked to victory, capturing the popular vote by the slim margin of 43.4 percent to Humphrey and Muskie's 42.7 percent but taking nearly all the West's electoral votes. Bitterly divided by the campaign, the Democrats would remain out of presidential contention for decades, except when the Republicans suffered scandal and disgrace. The Republicans in 1968 had inaugurated a new political era.

Nixon's War

Nixon promised to bring "peace with honor." Yet, despite this pledge, the Vietnam War raged for four more years before a peace settlement was reached.

Much of the responsibility for the prolonged conflict rested with Henry A. Kissinger. A dominating personality on the National Security Council, Kissinger insisted that the United States could not retain its global leadership by appearing weak to either allies or enemies. "However we got into Vietnam," he wrote in 1969, the United States "cannot accept a military defeat, or a change in the political structure of South Vietnam brought about by external military forces." Brilliant and ruthless, Kissinger helped Nixon centralize foreign policy making in the White House. Together, they overpowered those members of the State Department who had concluded that the majority of Americans no longer supported the war.

In public Nixon followed a policy of "Vietnamization." On May 14, 1969, he announced that the time was approaching "when the South Vietnamese . . . will be able to take over some of the fighting." During the next several months, he ordered the withdrawal of 60,000 U.S. troops. Hoping to placate public opinion, Nixon also intended to "demonstrate to Hanoi that we were serious in seeking a diplomatic settlement." In private, with Kissinger's guidance,

---

In view of the developments since we entered the fighting in Vietnam, do you think the United States made a mistake sending troops to fight in Vietnam?	
Yes	52%
No	39
No opinion	9

Interviewing Date 1/22–28/1969, Survey #774-K, Question #6/Index #45

Public Opinion on the War in Vietnam *By 1969 Americans were sharply divided in their assessments of the progress of the war and peace negotiations. The American Institute of Public Opinion, founded in 1935 by George Gallup, charted a growing dissatisfaction with the war in Vietnam.*

Source: *The Gallup Poll: Public Opinion, 1935–1974* (New York: Random House, 1974), p. 2189.

Nixon mulled over the option of a "knockout blow" to the North Vietnamese.

On April 30, 1970, Nixon made one of the most controversial decisions of his presidency. Without seeking congressional approval, Nixon added Cambodia (through which North Vietnam had been ferrying troops and supplies south) to the war zone. Although Nixon had authorized secret bombing raids of Cambodia in 1969, he now ordered U.S. troops to invade the tiny nation. Nixon had hoped in this way to end North Vietnamese infiltration into the South, but he had also decided to live up to what he privately called his "wild man" or "mad bomber" reputation. The enemy would be unable to anticipate the location or severity of the next U.S. strike, Nixon reasoned, and would thus feel compelled to negotiate.

Nixon could not have predicted the outpouring of protest that followed the invasion of Cambodia. The largest series of demonstrations and police-student confrontations in the nation's history took place on campuses and in city streets. At Kent State University in Ohio, twenty-eight National Guardsmen apparently panicked. Shooting into an unarmed crowd of about 200 students, they killed four and wounded nine. Ten days later, on May 14, at Jackson State University, a black school in Mississippi, state troopers entered a campus dormitory and began shooting wildly, killing two students and wounding twelve others. Demonstrations broke out on 50 campuses.

The nation was shocked. Thirty-seven college and university presidents signed a letter calling on the president to end the war. A few weeks later the Senate adopted a bipartisan resolution outlawing the use of funds for U.S. military operations in Cambodia, starting July 1, 1970. Although the House rejected the resolution, Nixon saw the writing on the wall. He had planned to negotiate a simultaneous withdrawal of North Vietnamese and U.S. troops, but he could no longer afford to hold out for this condition.

The president, still goaded by Kissinger, did not accept defeat easily. In February 1971 Nixon directed the South Vietnamese army to invade Laos and cut supply lines, but the demoralized invading force suffered a quick and humiliating defeat. Faced with enemy occupation of more and more territory during a major offensive in April 1972, Nixon ordered the mining of North Vietnamese harbors and directed B-52s on massively destructive bombing missions in Cambodia and North Vietnam.

Nixon also sent Kissinger to Paris for secret negotiations with delegates from North Vietnam. They agreed to a cease-fire specifying the withdrawal of all U.S. troops and the return of all U.S. prisoners of war. Knowing these terms ensured defeat, South Vietnam's president refused to sign the agreement. On Christmas Day 1972, hoping for a better negotiating position, Nixon ordered one final wave of bomb attacks on North Vietnam's cities. To secure a halt to the bombing, the North Vietnamese offered to resume negotiations. But the terms of the Paris Peace Agreement, signed by North Vietnam and the United States in January 1973, differed little from the settlement Nixon could have procured in 1969, hundreds of thousands of deaths earlier. Beginning in March 1973, the withdrawal of U.S. troops left the outcome of the war a foregone conclusion. By December of that year only 50 American military personnel remained, and the government of South Vietnam had no future.

In April 1975 North Vietnamese troops took over Saigon, and the communist-led Democratic Republic of Vietnam soon united the small nation. The war was finally over. It had cost the United States 58,000 lives and $150 billion. The country had not only failed to achieve its stated war goal but had lost an important post in Southeast Asia. Equally important, the policy of containment introduced by Truman had proved impossible to sustain.

While Nixon was maneuvering to bring about "peace with honor," the chilling crimes of war had already begun to haunt Americans. In 1971 the army court-martialed a young lieutenant, William L. Calley Jr., for the murder of "at least" twenty-two Vietnamese civilians during a 1968 search-and-destroy mission subsequently known as the My Lai Massacre. Calley's platoon had destroyed a village and slaughtered more than 350 unarmed South Vietnamese, raping and beating many of the women before killing them. "My Lai was not an isolated incident," one veteran attested, but "only a minor step beyond the standard official United States policy in Indochina." Commander of the platoon at My Lai,

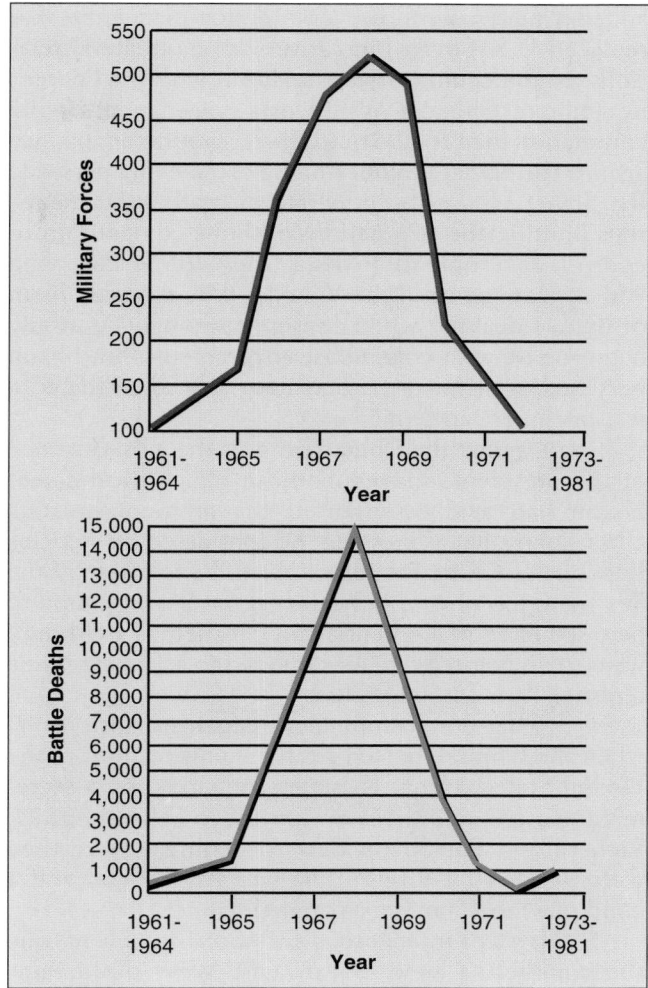

U.S. Military Forces in Vietnam and Casualties, 1961–1981   *The United States government estimated battle deaths between 1969 and 1973 for South Vietnamese troops at 107,504 and North Vietnamese and Vietcong at more than a half-million. Although the United States suffered fewer deaths, the cost was enormous.*

Source: U.S. Department of Defense, *Selected Manpower Statistics,* annual, and unpublished data; beginning 1981, National Archives and Records Service, "Combat Area Casualty File" (3-330-80-3).

Calley was first sentenced to life imprisonment before being given a reduced term of ten years. The secretary of the army paroled Calley after he served three years under house arrest in his apartment.

"The China Card"

Apart from Vietnam, Nixon's foreign policy defied the expectations of liberals and conservatives alike. Actually, he followed traditions of previous Republican moderates such as Herbert Hoover and Dwight Eisenhower, who had so effectively "proved" their anticommunism that they could conciliate international foes without undermining their popularity at home. Nixon added a new page, however, a policy of détente that replaced U.S.-Soviet bipolarity with multilateral relations. Nixon could cultivate relations with the People's Republic of China, a rising world power more rigidly communist than the Soviet Union, to form an alliance against the Soviet Union. And he could easily persuade the Soviet Union to cooperate on trade agreements, thus limiting the two nations' ruthless competition to control governments in Asia, the Middle East, and Africa. Opponents of the Vietnam War accused Nixon of double dealing, while conservatives howled at any compromise with communist governments. But Nixon persisted in his plans, anticipating an end to the cold war on American terms.

Playing "the China card" was the most dramatic of the president's moves. Early in his political career Nixon had avidly supported the arch-conservative China lobby. But as president he considered the People's Republic of China too important to be isolated by the West and too obviously hostile to the Soviet Union to be discounted as a potential ally. "If there is anything I want to do before I die," he confided to a *Time* magazine reporter, "it is to go to China."

"Ping-pong diplomacy" began in April 1971, when the Chinese hosted a table tennis team from the United States. Henry Kissinger embarked on a secret mission a few months later. Finally, in February 1972, Richard and Pat Nixon flew to Beijing, where they were greeted by foreign minister Zhou Enlai and a band playing "The Star-Spangled Banner."

It was a momentous and surprising event, one that marked a new era in East-West diplomacy. Nixon claimed that he had succeeded in bridging "16,000 miles and twenty-two years of hostility." The president's move successfully increased diplomatic pressure on the Soviet Union but simultaneously weakened the Nationalist Chinese government in Taiwan, which now slipped into virtual diplomatic obscurity.

Next the president went to Moscow to negotiate with Soviet leader Leonid Brezhnev, who was anxious about U.S. involvement with China and eager for economic assistance. Declaring, "There must be room in this world for two great nations with different systems to live together and work together," Nixon offered to sell $1 billion of grain to the Soviets. Winning the favor of American wheat farmers, this deal simultaneously relieved U.S. trade deficits and crop surpluses. Afterward, the Soviet leader became visibly more cautious about supporting revolutions in the third world. Nixon also completed negotiations of the Strategic Arms Limitation Treaty (SALT, known later as SALT I). A limited measure, SALT I represented the first success at strategic arms control since the opening

of the cold war and a major public relations victory for the leaders of the two superpowers.

Nixon's last major diplomatic foray proved far less effective. The president sent Kissinger on a two-year mission of "shuttle diplomacy" to mediate Israeli-Arab disputes, to ensure the continued flow of oil, and to increase lucrative U.S. arms sales to Arab countries. The Egyptians and Israelis agreed to a cease-fire in their October 1973 Yom Kippur War, but little progress toward peace in the area was achieved.

Domestic Policy

Nixon deeply desired to restore order in American society. "We live in a deeply troubled and profoundly unsettled time," he noted. "Drugs, crime, campus revolts, racial discord, draft resistance—on every hand we find old standards violated, old values discarded." Despite his hostility to liberalism, however, Nixon had some surprises for conservatives. Determined to win reelection in 1972, he supported new Social Security benefits and subsidized housing for the poor and oversaw the creation of the Environmental Protection Agency and the Occupational Safety and Health Administration. Most notable was his support, under the guidance of Democratic adviser Daniel P. Moynihan, for the Family Assistance Plan, which proposed a minimal income for the poor in place of welfare benefits. Conservatives judged the plan too generous while liberals found it inadequate. Moreover, the plan was expensive. Bipartisan opposition ultimately killed the bill.

Nixon also embraced a policy of fiscal liberalism. Early in 1971 he accepted the idea of deficit spending. Later that year he ordered a first: he took the nation off the gold standard. Subsequently, the dollar's value would float on the world market rather than being tied to the value of gold. His ninety-day freeze on wages, rents, and prices, designed to halt the inflation caused by massive spending on the Vietnam War, also closely resembled Democratic policies. Finally, Nixon's support of "black capitalism"—adjustments or quotas favoring minority contractors in construction projects—created an explosive precedent for set-aside programs later blamed on liberals.

Nixon lined up with conservatives, however, on most civil rights issues and thus enlarged southern Republican constituencies. He accepted the principle of school integration but rejected the busing programs required to implement racial balance. His nominees to the Supreme Court were far more conservative than those appointed by Eisenhower. Warren E. Burger, who replaced Chief Justice Earl Warren, steered the Court away from the liberal direction it had taken since the 1950s.

One of the most newsworthy events of Nixon's administration was a distant result of President Kennedy's determination to outshine the Soviets in outer space (see Chapter 27). On July 21, 1969, the lunar module of Apollo 11 descended to the moon's Sea of Tranquility. As millions watched on television, astronauts Neil Armstrong and Buzz Aldrin stepped out to plant an American flag and to bear the message, "We came in peace for all mankind."

WATERGATE

At times Richard Nixon expressed his yearning for approval in strange ways. A few days after the bombing of Cambodia in May 1970, he wandered out of the White House alone at 5:00 in the morning to talk to antiwar demonstrators. He tried to engage them in small talk about football and pleaded, "I know that probably most of you think I'm an SOB, but I want you to know I understand just how you feel." According to H. R. Haldeman, one of Nixon's closest advisers, the killings at Kent State deeply troubled the president.

Yet only a few months later Nixon ordered illegal wiretaps of news professionals. He also reaffirmed his support of Central Intelligence Agency (CIA) surveillance of U.S. citizens and organizations—a policy specifically forbidden by the CIA charter—and encouraged members of his administration to spy on Democrats planning for the 1972 election campaign. When news of these illegal activities surfaced, one of the most canny politicians in American history found himself the first president since Andrew Johnson to face the likelihood of impeachment proceedings.

Foreign Policy as Conspiracy

Nixon's conduct of foreign policy offered early clues into his political character. Although he had welcomed the publicity surrounding his historic moves toward détente with the Soviet Union and normalized relations with China, Nixon generally handled the nation's foreign affairs in surreptitious fashion. But as opposition to the Vietnam War mounted in Congress, he began to face hard questions about this practice. As early as 1970 Republicans as well as Democrats had condemned covert operations in foreign countries. In response, the president, the Department of State, and the CIA developed plans to tighten security even further. Nixon issued a tough mandate against all leaks of information by government personnel, news specialists, or politicians.

At the time, apart from the highly publicized tour to China, Nixon revealed little about his policy for other parts of the globe. Unknown to most Americans, he accelerated the delivery of arms supplies to foreign dictators, including the shah of Iran, Ferdinand Marcos of the Philippines, and the regime of Pieter William Botha in South Africa. His CIA assistants trained and aided SAVAK, the Iranian secret police force notorious for torturing political dissidents. They also stood behind the South African government in its effort to curtail the activities of the antiapartheid African National Congress. In Latin America, Nixon provided financial assistance and military aid to repressive regimes such as that of Anastasio Somoza of Nicaragua, notorious for its blatant corruption and repeated violations of human rights.

Still more controversial was Nixon's plan to overthrow the legally elected socialist government of Salvador Allende in Chile. With the assistance of nongovernment agencies, such as the AFL-CIO's American Institute for Free Labor Development, the CIA destabilized the regime by funding right-wing parties, launching demonstrations, and preparing the Chilean army for a coup. In September 1973, a military junta killed President Allende and captured, tortured, or murdered thousands of his supporters. Nixon and Kissinger warmly welcomed the new ruler, Augusto Pinochet, granting him financial assistance to restabilize the country.

Toward the end of Nixon's term, members of Congress who had been briefed on these policies began to break silence, and reports of clandestine operations flooded the media. Several former CIA agents issued anguished confessions of their activities in other countries. More troubling to Nixon, in spite of all his efforts the United States continued to lose ground as a superpower.

The Age of Dirty Tricks

As Nixon approached the 1972 reelection campaign, he tightened his inner circle of White House staff who assisted him in withholding information from the public, discrediting critics, and engaging in assorted "dirty tricks." Circle members solicited illegal contributions for the campaign and laundered the money through Mexican bank accounts. They also formed a secret squad, "the plumbers," to halt the troublesome leaks of information. This team, headed by former CIA agent E. Howard Hunt and former FBI agent G. Gordon Liddy, assisted in conspiracy at the highest levels of government.

The first person on the squad's "hit list" was Daniel Ellsberg, a former researcher with the Department of Defense, who in 1971 had turned over to the press secret documents outlining the military history of American involvement in Vietnam. The so-called Pentagon Papers exposed the role of presidents and military leaders in deceiving the public and Congress about the

Richard Nixon bid a final farewell to his White House staff as he left Washington, D.C., in August 1974. The first president to resign from office, Nixon had become so entangled in the Watergate scandal that his impeachment appeared certain. He was succeeded by Vice President Gerald Ford, who appears next to the helicopter on the right.

conduct of the United States in Southeast Asia. Nixon sought to bar publication by the *New York Times*, but the Supreme Court ruled in favor of the newspaper on the basis of the First Amendment. Within weeks, a complete version of the Pentagon Papers became a best-selling book, and in 1972 the *New York Times* won a Pulitzer Prize for the series of articles. Frustrated in his attempt to suppress the report, Nixon directed the Department of Justice to prosecute Ellsberg on charges of conspiracy, espionage, and theft. Meanwhile, Hunt and Liddy, seeking to discredit Ellsberg, broke into the office of his former psychiatrist. They found nothing that would make their target less heroic in the eyes of an increasingly skeptical public, and by 1973 the charges against Ellsberg were dropped after the Nixon administration itself stood guilty of misconduct.

At the same time, Nixon ran a skillful negative campaign charging George McGovern, the liberal Democrat who had won his party's nomination on the first ballot, with supporting "abortion, acid [LSD], and amnesty" for those who had resisted the draft or deserted the armed forces. The Republicans also informed the news media that McGovern's running

mate, Senator Thomas Eagleton, had once undergone electric shock therapy for depression, thus forcing his resignation from the Democratic team. Voter turnout fell to an all-time low, and McGovern lost every state but Massachusetts. (Later, when Nixon faced disgrace, bumper stickers appeared reading, "Don't Blame Me, I'm from Massachusetts.")

The Committee to Re-Elect the President (CREEP) enjoyed a huge war chest and spent a good portion on dirty tricks designed to divide the Democrats and discredit them in the eyes of the voting public. The most ambitious plan—wiretapping the Democratic National Committee headquarters—backfired.

On June 17, 1972, a security team had tripped up a group of intruders hired by CREEP to install listening devices in the Washington, D.C., Watergate apartment and office complex where the Democrats were headquartered. The police arrested five men, who were later found guilty of conspiracy and burglary. Although Nixon disclaimed any knowledge of the plan, two *Washington Post* reporters, Bob Woodward and Carl Bernstein, followed a trail of evidence back to the nation's highest office.

CHRONOLOGY

1964	President Lyndon Johnson calls for "an unconditional war on poverty" in his state of the union address
	Tonkin Gulf resolution
	The Economic Opportunity Act establishes the Office of Economic Opportunity
	Free speech movement gets under way at University of California at Berkeley
	Johnson defeats conservative Barry Goldwater for president
1965	President Johnson authorizes Operation Rolling Thunder, the bombing of North Vietnam
	Teach-ins begin on college campuses
	First major march on Washington for peace is organized
	Watts uprising begins a wave of rebellions in black communities
1966	J. William Fulbright publishes *The Arrogance of Power*
	Black Panther Party is formed
	National Organization for Women (NOW) is formed
1967	Antiwar rally in New York City draws 300,000
	Vietnam Veterans against the War is formed
	Uprisings in Newark, Detroit, and other cities
	Hippie "Summer of Love"
1968	U.S. ground troops levels in Vietnam number 500,000
	Tet Offensive in Vietnam, followed by international protests against U.S. policies
	Martin Luther King Jr. is assassinated; riots break out in more than 100 cities
	Vietnam peace talks begin in Paris
	Robert Kennedy is assassinated
	Democratic National Convention, held in Chicago, nominates Hubert Humphrey; "police riot" against protesters

	Richard Nixon elected president
	American Indian Movement (AIM) founded
1969	Woodstock music festival marks the high tide of the counterculture
	Stonewall Riot in Greenwich Village sparks the gay liberation movement
	Apollo 11 lands on the moon
1970	U.S. incursion into Cambodia sparks campus demonstrations; students killed at Kent State and Jackson State Universities
	Women's Strike for Equality marks the fiftieth anniversary of the woman suffrage amendment
1971	Lieutenant William Calley Jr. court-martialed for My Lai Massacre
	New York Times starts publishing the Pentagon Papers
1972	Nixon visits China and Soviet Union
	SALT I limits offensive intercontinental ballistic missiles
	Intruders attempting to "bug" Democratic headquarters in the Watergate complex are arrested
	Nixon is reelected in a landslide
	Nixon orders Christmas Day bombing of North Vietnam
1973	Paris Peace Agreement ends war in Vietnam
	FBI seizes Indian occupants of Wounded Knee, South Dakota
	Watergate burglars tried; congressional hearings on Watergate
	CIA destabilizes elected Chilean government, which is overthrown
	Vice President Spiro T. Agnew resigns
1974	House Judiciary Committee adopts articles of impeachment against Nixon
	Nixon resigns the presidency

Televised Senate hearings opened to public view more than a pattern of presidential wrongdoing: they showed an attempt to impede investigations of the Watergate case. Testifying before the committee, a former Nixon aide revealed the existence of secret tape recordings of conversations held in the Oval Office. After special prosecutor Archibald Cox refused to allow Nixon to claim executive privilege and withhold the tapes, the president ordered Cox fired. This "Saturday Night Massacre," as it came to be called, further tarnished Nixon's reputation and swelled curiosity about the tapes. On June 24, 1974, the Supreme Court voted unanimously that Nixon had to release the tapes to a new special prosecutor, Leon Jaworski.

The Fall of the Executive

The case against the president gained strength. Although incomplete, the Watergate tapes proved damning. They documented Nixon's ravings against his enemies, including anti-Semitic slurs, and his conniving efforts to harass private citizens through federal agencies. The tapes also proved that Nixon had not only known about plans to cover up the Watergate break-in but had ordered it. The news media enjoyed a field day with the revelations. In July 1974, the House Judiciary Committee adopted three articles of impeachment, charging Nixon with obstructing justice.

Charges of executive criminality had clouded the Nixon administration since his vice president had resigned in disgrace. In 1972 Spiro Agnew had admitted accepting large kickbacks while governor of Maryland. Pleading no contest to this and to charges of federal income tax evasion, Agnew resigned from office in October 1973. Gerald Ford, a moderate Republican representative from Michigan, had replaced him and now stood in the wings while the president's drama unfolded.

Facing certain impeachment by the House of Representatives, Richard Nixon became, on August 9, 1974, the first U.S. president to resign from office.

CONCLUSION

The resignations of Richard Nixon and Spiro Agnew brought little to relieve the feeling of national exhaustion that attended the Vietnam War. U.S. troops had pulled out of Vietnam in 1973 and the war officially ended in 1975, but bitterness lingered over the unprecedented—and, for many, humiliating—defeat. Morover, confidence in the government's highest office was severely shaken. The passage of the War Powers Act in 1973, written to compel any future president to seek congressional approval for armed intervention abroad, dramatized both the widespread suspicion of presidential intentions and a yearning for peace. But the positive dream of community that had inspired Johnson, King, and a generaton of student activists could not be revived. No other vision took its place.

In 1968 seven prominent antiwar protesters had been brought to trial for allegedly conspiring to disrupt the Democratic National Convention in Chicago. Just a few years later, the majority of Americans had concluded that presidents Johnson and Nixon had conspired to do far worse. They had intentionally deceived the public about the nature and fortunes of the war. This moral failure signaled a collapse at the center of the American political system. Since Dwight Eisenhower left office warning of the potential danger embedded in "the military-industrial complex," no president had survived the presidency with his honor intact. Watergate, then, appeared to cap the politics of the cold war, its revelations only reinforcing futility and cynicism. The United States was left psychologically at war with itself.

REVIEW QUESTIONS

1. Discuss the events that led up to and contributed to U.S. involvement in Vietnam. How did U.S. involvement in the war affect domestic programs?

2. Discuss the reasons the protest movement against the Vietnam War started on college campuses. Describe how these movements were organized and how the opponents of the war differed from the supporters.

3. Discuss the programs sponsored by Johnson's plan for a Great Society. What was their impact on urban poverty in the late 1960s?

4. What was the impact of the assassinations of Martin Luther King Jr. and Robert Kennedy on the election of 1968? How were various communities affected?

5. How were the "politics of identity" movements different from earlier civil rights organizations? In what ways did the various movements resemble one another?

6. Why did Richard Nixon enjoy such a huge electoral victory in 1972? Discuss his foreign and domestic policies. What led to his sudden downfall?

RECOMMENDED READING

Terry H. Anderson, *The Movement and the Sixties* (1995). A richly detailed and highly readable account of the political and cultural movements of the 1960s, beginning with an overview of the significance of the cold war and ending with an assessment of the impact of the various movements, including the counterculture.

Loren Baritz, *Backfire: A History of How American Culture Led Us into Vietnam and Made Us Fight the Way We Did* (1985). A keen study of U.S. military policies and dissent within the military during the Vietnam War. Baritz shows how decisions for aggressive military policies in Vietnam divided poorer young men from middle- and upper-class men by sending to war those who did not or could not manage deferments. He analyzes the increasing bitterness toward the government and the military by the men who fought the war.

Alexander Bloom and Wini Breines, eds., *Takin' It to the Streets: A Sixties Reader* (1996). A useful and popular anthology of documents from the time that emphasizes the connections of political and cultural developments.

Mary C. Brennan, *Turning Right in the Sixties: The Conservative Capture of the GOP* (1995). Challenges the conventional depiction of the 1960s as a time when liberals and radicals flourished. Brennan discusses the rise of conservatives within the Republican party and their emergence as the dominant force in American politics by 1980. She focuses on grassroots organizations and their ability to appeal to discontented but generally apolitical Americans.

Susan J. Douglas, *Where the Girls Are: Growing Up Female with the Mass Media* (1994). A witty and perceptive interpretation of the images created for young women in the 1960s and the ways in which they responded.

Michael H. Hunt, *Lyndon Johnson's War: America's Cold War Crusade in Vietnam, 1945–1968* (1996). Tracks Johnson's decisions to wage all-out war in Vietnam. Hunt interprets Johnson's actions as consistent with the Cold War foreign policy that had prevailed since the Truman Administration and its pledge to "contain" communism.

Neil Sheehan, *A Bright Shining Lie: John Paul Vann and America in Vietnam* (1988). A study of U.S. government deception of the public, conducted with greater and greater intensity as losses in Vietnam increased. Sheehan especially emphasizes the ways in which prowar messages played on false images of a noble and committed South Vietnamese government and a military program always on the verge of defeating an unpopular enemy.

Fred Turner, *Echoes of Combat: The Vietnam War in American Memory* (1996). Examines the paradox of a war that many Americans hope to forget and the rise of a "memory industry" devoted to its preservation. Turner asks two main questions: What are Americans remembering? What are they trying to forget?

William L. Van Deburg, *New Day in Babylon: The Black Power Movement and American Culture, 1965–1975* (1992). A well-researched and lively study of the transformation of racial consciousness among African Americans.

Bob Woodward and Carl Bernstein, *The Final Days* (1976). Journalistic accounts of the Watergate cover-up by the news team that broke the first stories. The authors trace the series of events that led to the resignation of President Nixon.

Marilyn B. Young, *The Vietnam Wars, 1945–1990* (1991). An excellent overview of the involvement of the French and the American military and diplomatic forces in Vietnam from the 1910s to 1975, and of the various movements against them. Young presents a thematic continuity that highlights the nationalism of the Vietnamese as ultimately more powerful than the troops and weaponry of their opponents.

ADDITIONAL BIBLIOGRAPHY

Vietnam: America's Longest War

David L. Anderson, *Shadow on the White House: Presidents and the Vietnam War, 1945–1975* (1993)

Christian G. Appy, *Working-Class War: American Combat Soldiers in Vietnam* (1993)

Larry Berman, *Lyndon Johnson's War* (1989)

Robert Buzzanco, *Masters of War: Military Dissent and Politics in the Vietnam War Era* (1996)

David L. DiLeo, *George Ball, Vietnam, and the Rethinking of Containment* (1991)

Virginia Elwood-Akers, *Women War Correspondents in the Vietnam War, 1961–1975* (1988)

George C. Herring, *America's Longest War: The United States and Vietnam, 1950–1975*, 2d ed. (1986)

———, *LBJ and Vietnam: A Different Kind of War* (1994)

———, ed., *The Pentagon Papers*, abridged ed. (1993)

Martha Hess, *Then the Americans Came: Voices from Vietnam* (1993)

Arnold R. Isaacs, *Without Honor* (1983)

Richard Moser, *The New Winter Soldiers: GI and Veteran Dissent during the Vietnam Era* (1996)

Robert D. Schulzinger, *A Time for War: The United States and Vietnam, 1941–1975* (1997)

Randy Shilts, *Conduct Unbecoming: Lesbians and Gays in the U.S. Military, Vietnam to the Persian Gulf* (1993)

Dennis E. Showalter and John G. Albert, eds., *An American Dilemma: Vietnam, 1964–1973* (1993)

James E. Westheider, *Fighting on Two Fronts: African Americans and the Vietnam War* (1997)

James R. Wilson, *Landing Zones: Southern Veterans Remember Vietnam* (1990)

Clarence R. Wyatt, *Paper Soldiers: The American Press and the Vietnam War* (1993)

A Generation in Conflict

John Morton Blum, *Years of Discord* (1991)

Wini Breines, *Community and Organization in the New Left* (1982)

David Chalmers, *And the Crooked Places Made Straight: The Struggle for Social Change in the 1960s* (1991)

Charles DeBeneditti, *An American Ordeal: The Antiwar Movement of the Vietnam Era* (1990)

David Farber, *The Age of Great Dreams: America in the 1960s* (1994)

———, ed., *The Sixties: From Memory to History* (1994)

Ronald Fraser, et al., *1968: A Student Generation in Revolt* (1988)

Sherry Gottlieb, *Hell No, We Won't Go* (1991)

Kenneth Heineman, *Campus Wars: The Peace Movement at American State Universities in the Vietnam Era* (1993)

Paul Lyons, *New Left, New Right, and the Legacy of the Sixties* (1996)

Jim Miller, *"Democracy Is in the Streets"* (1987)

Timothy Miller, *The Hippies and American Values* (1991)

Edward P. Morgan, *The 60s Experience* (1991)

W. J. Rorabaugh, *Berkeley at War: The 1960s* (1989)

Sohnya Sayres, et al., ed., *The 60s without Apology* (1984)

David Steigerwald, *The Sixties and the End of Modern America* (1995)

Barbara L. Tischler, ed., *Sights on the Sixties* (1992)

Tom Wells, *The War Within: America's Battle over Vietnam* (1994)

The Politics of Identity

Barry D. Adam, *The Rise of a Gay and Lesbian Movement* (1987)

Elaine Brown, *A Taste of Power* (1993)

James Button, *Black Violence: Political Impact of the 1960s Riots* (1978)

Jack Campisi, *The Mashpee Indians* (1991)

Margaret Cruikshank, *The Gay and Lesbian Liberation Movement* (1992)

John D'Emilio, *Making Trouble: Essays on Gay History, Politics, and the University* (1992)

Martin Duberman, *Stonewall* (1993)

Gerald Horne, *Fire This Time: The Watts Uprising and the 1960s* (1996)

Blance Linden-Ward, *American Women in the 1960s* (1992)

Manning Marable, *Race, Reform, and Rebellion* (1984)

Eric Marcus, *Making History: The Struggle for Gay and Lesbian Equal Rights, 1945–1990: An Oral History* (1992)

Marguerite V. Marin, *Social Protest in an Urban Barrio: A Study of the Chicano Movement, 1966–1972* (1991)

Peter Matthiessen, *In the Spirit of Crazy Horse* (1991)

Armando Navarro, *Mexican American Youth Organization: Avant-Garde of the Chicano Movement in Texas* (1995)

M. Rivka Polatnick, *Strategies for Women's Liberation: A Study of a Black and White Group of the 1960s* (1987)

The Nixon Presidency and Watergate

Carl Bernstein and Bob Woodward, *All the President's Men* (1974)

John Ehrlichman, *Witness to Power* (1982)

Lewis L. Gould, *1968: The Election That Changed America* (1993)

Jim Hougan, *Secret Agenda: Watergate, Deep Throat, and the CIA* (1984)

Diane Kunz, ed., *The Diplomacy of the Crucial Decade* (1994)

Michael Schudson, *Watergate in American History* (1992)

Biography

Stephen E. Ambrose, *Nixon*, 3 vols. (1987–91)

LeRoy Ashby and Rod Gramer, *Fighting the Odds: The Life of Senator Frank Church* (1994)

Elaine Brown, *A Taste of Power: A Black Woman's Story* (1992)

Paul Buhle and Edward Rice-Maximin, *William Appleman Williams: The Tragedy of Empire* (1995)

Jody Carlson, *George C. Wallace and the Politics of Powerlessness* (1981)

David T. Dellinger, *From Yale to Jail: A Memoir* (1993)

Brian Dooley, *Robert Kennedy: The Final Years* (1996)

Robert Alan Goldberg, *Barry Goldwater* (1995)

Elliot Gorn, ed., *Muhammed Ali: The People's Champ* (1996)

David Hilliard and Lewis Cole, *This Side of Glory: The Autobiography of David Hilliard and the Story of the Black Panther Party* (1993)

Joan Hoff, *Nixon Reconsidered* (1994)

Walter Isaacson, *Kissinger* (1992)

Jonah Raskin, *For the Hell of It: The Life and Times of Abbie Hoffman* (1996)

Herb Schandler, *The Unmaking of a President: Lyndon Johnson and Vietnam* (1977)

Arthur M. Schlesinger Jr., *Robert Kennedy and His Times* (1974)

Tom Wicker, *One of Us: Richard Nixon and the American Dream* (1991)

Randall Bennett Woods, *Fulbright: A Biography* (1995)

CHAPTER THIRTY

THE OVEREXTENDED SOCIETY

1974–1980

AMERICAN COMMUNITIES
Three Mile Island, Pennsylvania

On Wednesday, March 28, 1979, a series of mechanical problems and judgment errors at the nuclear generating facility at Three Mile Island (TMI), near Harrisburg, Pennsylvania, led to the loss of a reactor's protective blanket of water. As much as two-thirds of the nuclear core was uncovered, causing the formation of a dangerously explosive hydrogen bubble and a massive release of radioactive gas into the atmosphere and posing the danger of a catastrophic core meltdown. The plant director declared a site emergency and reported a "slight problem" to the governor at 7:40 A.M. By 9:00 A.M. President Jimmy Carter had been notified. The Associated Press issued a national news bulletin announcing a general emergency but stating (mistakenly) that no radiation had been released. Metropolitan Edison, which ran the TMI facility, denied the existence of any danger.

At 8:00 A.M. on Friday, when a higher-than-anticipated radiation level above a vent was recorded, staff at the Nuclear Regulatory Commission suggested an evacuation of people living near the plant. Fearing panic, the governor urged residents within ten miles of TMI to stay indoors with their windows shut. Only pregnant women and preschool children within five miles of the facility were advised to leave the area. Federal officials ordered the shipment to Pennsylvania of massive doses of potassium iodide, which, taken orally, saturates the thyroid gland and inhibits absorption of radiation. The mayor of nearby Middletown later recalled:

> Friday was the day. . . . A lot of the kids thought about dying and wrote their last wills and testaments. Fifth and sixth grade kids! People were concerned. You could tell they were afraid because a lot of people who left town left their doors wide open, unlocked. They just put anything in the car and took off. . . . I had a bus set up in front of City Hall for pregnant women. But heck, most of the people who were in that condition left themselves.

While nearly 150,000 residents fled their homes, President and Rosalynn Carter tried to reassure the stricken community by visiting the site.

Ten days later, on Monday, April 9, Pennsylvania governor Richard Thornburgh announced that the danger of a meltdown had passed. The Nuclear Regulatory Commission, equally eager to end the crisis, reported that the size of the hydrogen bubble had decreased. The situation was now stable, the officials agreed. There was no longer any danger of explosion.

What had seemed an isolated event in one community grew quickly into a regional phenomenon with international repercussions. The world waited, as one newscaster put it, while "the danger faced by man for tampering with natural forces, a theme familiar from the myth of Prometheus to the story of

Frankenstein, moved closer to fact from fantasy." During the crisis, millions of people living in eastern states downwind of TMI stayed glued to their televisions or radios. Ten days after the near meltdown, elevated levels of radioactivity were found in milk supplies several hundred miles away. People throughout the mid-Atlantic area worried for months about consuming contaminated dairy products, meat, vegetables, and even jams or jellies coming from the agricultural region of central Pennsylvania. Massive demonstrations against nuclear power followed the accident, concluding in a rally of more than 200,000 people in New York City.

Closer to TMI, more than 1,000 people eventually became involved in legal claims of mental or physical harm. Protests and lawsuits against the plant's reopening continued for years, and its owner, General Public Utilities, teetered toward bankruptcy. Although steadfast proponents of nuclear energy argued that the events at TMI demonstrated that safety had prevailed even at the moment of the greatest potential danger, the scales had been tipped toward opponents of nuclear power plants.

The events at Three Mile Island capped a wave of community-based mobilizations against nuclear power. In 1975, a less serious accident at Brown's Ferry, Alabama, heightened public concern about safety. Broad coalitions, with members ranging from conservatives to liberals, from rural landowners to urban renters, formed to keep their communities safe from danger. Community groups defeated referendums to fund new nuclear facilities or rallied around candidates who promised to shut down existing ones. If few communities wanted nuclear

Three Mile Island

power plants, fewer still were eager to accept the radioactive wastes they generated.

The economy itself helped slow the development of new plants. At the time of the TMI crisis, more than seventy generating plants had been built, producing altogether about 13 percent of the nation's electrical energy. Of the ninety-six still under construction and the thirty more planned, only a handful would ever be completed. The courts and regional authorities blocked the completed Shoreham plant on Long Island, New York, from going into operation. News of faulty construction and building-cost overruns sometimes topping 1,000 percent and amounting to hundreds of millions of dollars made local governments hesitant to back new projects.

The promoters of nuclear energy in the 1950s had billed it as a source of energy so cheap that utility companies would be able to "turn off the meter." Communities would bask in prosperity, enjoying the fruits of dramatic advances equal to those that followed the introduction of electricity itself seventy-five years earlier. As late as 1974 President Richard Nixon predicted that by 1980 nuclear power would free the United States of its dependence on foreign energy sources.

The end of the dream of unlimited, inexpensive, and safe nuclear energy was one of many disappointments in the 1970s that shattered the expectations of experts and ordinary citizens alike for a time of unsurpassed abundance. Faced with diminishing financial resources, environmental disasters, discredited political leaders, and international defeats, many Americans lowered their expectations. The cold war finally began to wind down, but international affairs remained turbulent. The Middle East, a major source of oil, was becoming the new battleground.

KEY TOPICS

- The economics and politics of "stagflation"
- The Carter presidency
- Crisis in the cities and in the environment

- Community politics and the rise of the New Right
- The Iran hostage crisis
- The Republican presidential victory in 1980

STAGFLATION

In the 1970s Americans faced an unfamiliar combination of skyrocketing prices, rising unemployment, and low economic growth. Economists termed this novel condition "stagflation." The annual rate of economic growth slowed by almost one-quarter from its robust 3.2 percent average of the 1950s. By 1975 the unemployment rate had reached nearly 9 percent, its highest level since the Great Depression, and it remained close to 7 percent for most of the rest of the decade. Inflation, meanwhile, reached double-digit numbers.

The United States had reached a turning point in its economic history. Emerging from World War II as the most prosperous nation in the world and retaining this status through the 1960s, the country suddenly found itself falling behind western Europe and Japan. The standard of living in the United States dropped to fifth place, below that of Denmark, West Germany, Sweden, and Switzerland. Polls conducted at the end of the 1970s revealed that a majority of Americans believed that conditions would worsen. Faith in progress and prosperity, the hallmark of "the American Century," wore thin.

The Oil Crisis

In October 1973 American motorists received a big surprise at the gas pumps. Gasoline prices nearly doubled, in some regions jumping from forty to nearly seventy cents per gallon. Worse, many dealers suddenly ran out of supplies. In New Jersey, gas lines were up to four miles long. Fistfights broke out among frustrated motorists. Gas tank locks enjoyed brisk sales after thieves began to siphon fuel out of parked cars. Several states introduced rationing programs.

Although the oil crisis began suddenly, it had been in the making for decades. The United States, which used about 70 percent of all oil produced in the world, had been able to meet its demand from domestic supplies until the late 1950s. At that point, rising demand outstripped the capacity of national reserves and oil imports began to rise. By 1973 the nation was importing one-third of its total crude oil, mainly from the Middle East.

Although oil prices remained stable through most of the 1960s, rising political and military tensions in the Middle East threatened that stability. After Israel overwhelmed its Arab neighbors in the Six-Day War of 1967, the Arab nations became increasingly bitter toward the United States and other Western supporters of Israel. Then came the Yom Kippur War of 1973, so named because it began with an Arab attack on Israel on that Jewish holy day, which fell on October 6 that year.

On October 17, the Organization of Petroleum Exporting Countries (OPEC), a cartel of mainly Arab oil producers, announced an embargo on oil shipments to Israel's allies, including the United States, Japan, and other Western nations. American experts thought at first that the embargo would be short-lived. But although a cease-fire ended the Yom Kippur War on most fronts on October 25, the oil embargo continued until March 18, 1974, sending a shock wave through the United States. A few weeks after the embargo began, President Nixon, in a dramatic televised speech, announced "a very stark fact: We are heading toward the most acute shortage of energy since World War II." A newspaper headline pessimistically declared, "Things Will Get Worse before They Get Worse."

As oil prices continued to skyrocket through the 1970s, angry motorists usually blamed the Arabs, but some also looked suspiciously at U.S. oil companies. By 1978 almost 50 percent of those polled believed that they were "just being told" that there was a shortage as a pretext for raising prices. Skepticism grew as a congressional committee reported that American-owned Texaco Oil was withholding natural gas from the market and that Gulf Oil had overstated its crude oil costs and charged customers wildly inflated prices. Whatever the cause, whoever the scapegoat, the oil crisis played a major role in the economic downturn of 1974 and 1975, the worst since the Great Depression.

The Bill Comes Due

President Nixon quickly responded to the embargo. He appointed William E. Simon to the new position of "energy czar," paving the way for the creation of the Department of Energy in 1977. Nixon also imposed

Following the oil crisis of 1973, the supply of gasoline for automobiles remained tight. This photograph, taken in 1978, captured a scene that had become familiar to many motorists: cars lined up, bumper to bumper, outside a local filling station.

emergency energy conservation measures. He ordered a 10 percent reduction in air travel and appealed to Congress to lower speed limits on interstate highways to fifty-five miles per hour and to extend daylight saving time into the winter months. Many state governments introduced their own programs, turning down the thermostats in public buildings to sixty-eight degrees, reducing nonessential lighting, and restricting hours of service. Colleges and universities canceled midwinter sessions, and some factories voluntarily shortened their workday.

These conservation measures produced one unintended, positive result: a 23 percent reduction in highway deaths between 1973 and 1974 due to the lower speed limit. Meanwhile, however, children went to school in the dark, workers shivered in their offices, and the poor and elderly succumbed to hypothermia in cold apartments.

Virtually all energy prices rose following the Arab oil embargo, reversing a century-old trend. And with the rising costs of gasoline, home-heating fuel, and electricity, other prices jumped as well, from apartment rents to telephone bills to restaurant checks. In 1974 inflation was at 11 percent and polls showed it to have assumed first place among issues Americans were worried about. By 1980 inflation had reached 13.5 percent. The middle-class lifestyle that schoolteachers, secretaries, factory workers, and others had managed to create for themselves and their families on relatively modest incomes became harder to maintain; for young families it was often impossible to achieve. A San Francisco homemaker told a reporter, "I used to keep a budget, but it got so discouraging. I gave it up. The whole economic picture scares me. It's so unreal."

Falling Productivity

Many Americans had experienced the recessions of the 1950s, millions even remembered the Great Depression, but few were prepared to witness the death of entire sectors of basic industry. The problem, according to many experts, was not simply a result of dependence on foreign oil reserves. It had deeper roots in the failure of the United States to keep up with the rising industrial efficiency of western Europe and Japan. As long as American manufacturers faced scant competition from abroad, they had little incentive to update their machinery or to establish management techniques that took full advantage of the skills of younger, more educated employees. American companies could meet large production quotas, but they could not fabricate quality goods at low cost.

Asian, Latin American, and European manufacturers offered consumers cheaper and better alternatives. As a result, whereas the United States produced 60 percent of the world's steel in 1947, by 1975 it produced only 16 percent. Similar trends developed in related industries. Sales of foreign automobiles in the United States, negligible in 1960, topped 15 percent by the early 1970s and continued to grow. Meanwhile, sales of American-made autos dropped by 11 million in 1973 and another 8 million in 1974. In 1977 more American cars were recalled for defects than were produced in the same year. By the end of the decade foreign manufacturers had also shattered the near monopoly the United States once enjoyed in the production of precision machine tools. In high-tech electronics, the United States scarcely competed against Japanese-made televisions, radios, tape players, cameras, and computers.

Major American corporations began to devise their own strategies to combat falling profits. While General Motors lowered production costs by opening a new, highly automated plant in Lordstown, Ohio, other automakers turned to Mexico, Taiwan, South Korea, and the Philippines for cheaper labor. Many

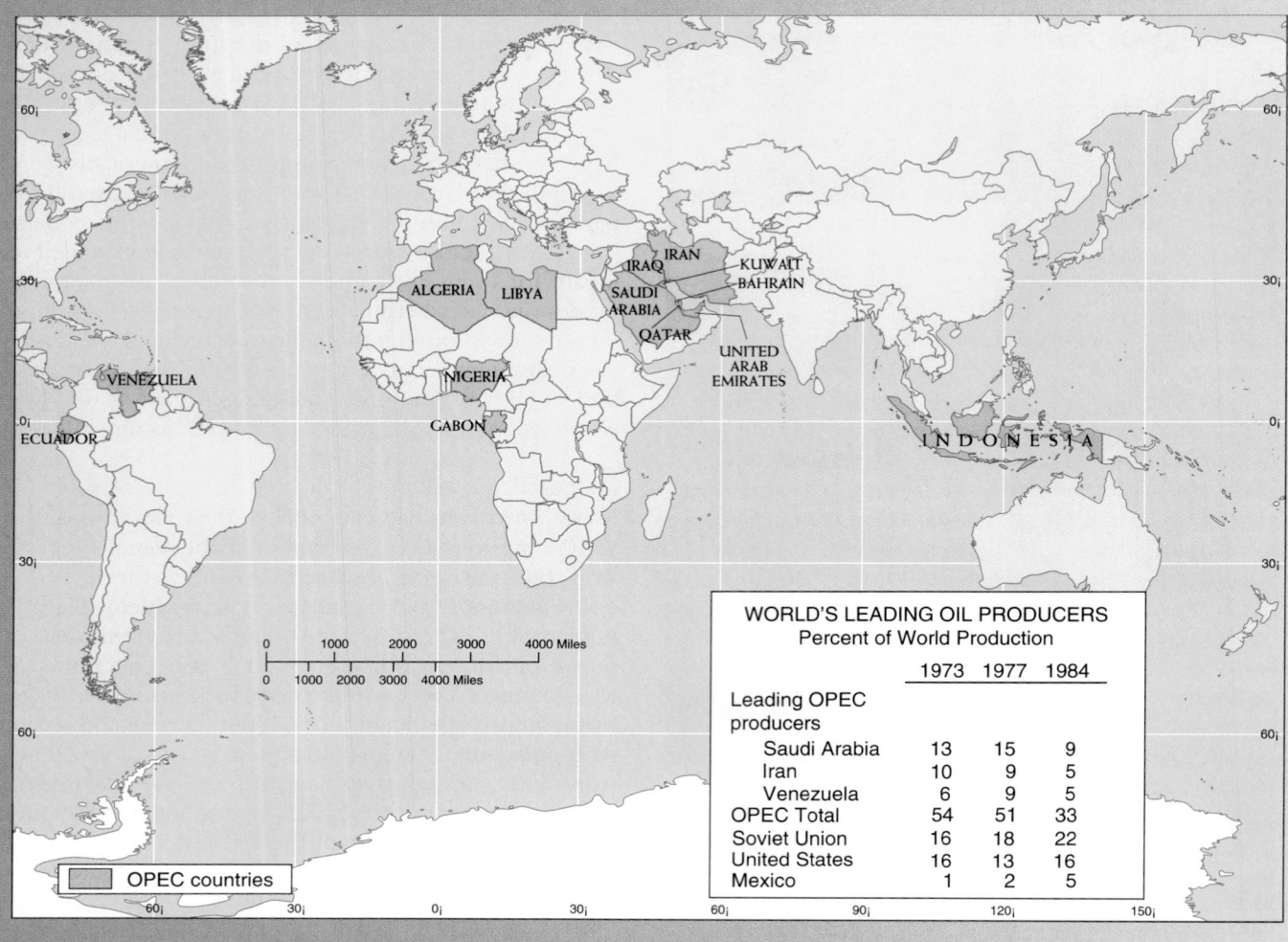

WORLD'S LEADING OIL PRODUCERS Percent of World Production			
	1973	1977	1984
Leading OPEC producers			
Saudi Arabia	13	15	9
Iran	10	9	5
Venezuela	6	9	5
OPEC Total	54	51	33
Soviet Union	16	18	22
United States	16	13	16
Mexico	1	2	5

OPEC countries

parts of American automobiles were "outsourced"—that is, produced abroad and imported into the United States as semifinished materials (which were subject to a lower tariff than finished goods).

A few American corporations tried to improve their production capacities by adopting the model of labor-management relations developed by their foremost competitors. In many Japanese firms a system of benefits and rewards gave employees a sense of security and offered them incentives for helping to improve the quality and speed of production. However, in the United States "quality circles"—American versions of Japanese factory teams—were far less successful than their Japanese counterparts. Older workers feared the new management techniques would undermine their unions, and most new workers doubted the new techniques would bring them significant material benefits.

American industrial productivity continued to lag, increasing 1.4 percent between 1971 and 1975 and only 0.2 percent in the second half of the decade. The balance of trade tipped sharply toward the countries that manufactured and exported better and cheaper products than U.S. firms. An AFL-CIO leader complained that the United States was becoming "a nation of hamburger stands . . . a country stripped of industrial capacity and meaningful work . . . a service economy . . . a nation of citizens busily buying and selling cheeseburgers and root beer floats."

In agriculture the situation was equally grim. Ironically, a shortage of grain in the Soviet Union, Egypt, and the third world during the 1970s hiked up agricultural prices and encouraged American farmers to produce a bounty of crops for export. But the huge increase in oil prices translated into higher gasoline

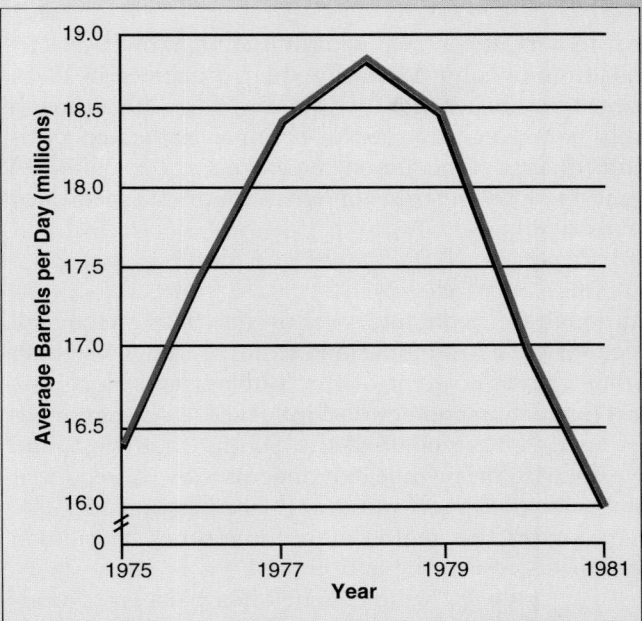

Decline of U.S. Oil Consumption, 1975–1981

Source: Department of Energy, *Monthly Energy Review*, June 1982.

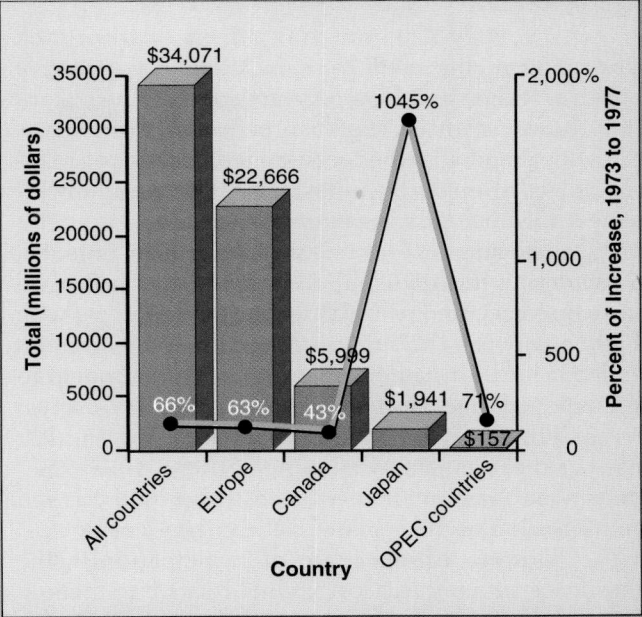

Foreign Direct Investment in the United States, 1977

Source: *Morgan Guaranty Survey*, September 1978.

1970s: *Oil Consumption*

OPEC (the Organization of Petroleum Exporting Countries), which is dominated by large Arab producers in the Middle East, began to use its control of much of the world's oil as a diplomatic lever and successfully increased the world price of crude oil during the 1970s. As a result, all energy prices rose sharply in the United States, leading to a previously unknown combination of inflation and recession that was dubbed "stagflation."

These developments had two dramatic and unanticipated consequences. One was a sharp decline in U.S. oil consumption after 1978. High prices and shortages induced Americans to drive fewer miles and to conserve energy. In some cases the energy squeeze forced factories and businesses to close. A second consequence was increased foreign investment in the United States and with it, increased foreign ownership of U.S. businesses. Despite the role of the oil crisis in triggering this shift, only a small percentage of outside investment came from OPEC entrepreneurs. Most of it came from Europe, Canada, and Japan. Japanese investment in the United States increased more than tenfold between 1973 and 1977.

and fertilizer costs, forcing farmers to borrow heavily from banks. Soon, the high interest rates on borrowed money put many farmers in a state of permanent indebtedness.

When overseas grain sales declined at the end of the 1970s, tens of thousands of farmers defaulted on loans and lost their farms to banks and credit companies. These failures often ended a way of life that was generations old. The remaining farmers often supplemented their income through part-time jobs in town. Many considered themselves fortunate if they could retire on the price offered by land developers who turned their farms into suburban housing. Continuing soil erosion, high costs, and unstable prices offered a gloomy prospect for all but the leaders in corporate-style agribusiness, the 12 percent of farmers who made 90 percent of all farm income.

Blue-collar Blues

In past decades, labor unions had typically responded to inflation by negotiating new contracts or, if necessary, striking for higher pay. When successful, these actions elevated living standards for millions of additional workers because nonunion employers often felt compelled to raise wages as well. But by the 1970s new legislation and legal decisions had changed labor-management relations. The National Labor Relations Board, created during the 1930s to ensure fair elections for union representation, now more frequently ruled in favor of management, making it increasingly difficult to form new union locals. Between 1970 and 1982 the AFL-CIO lost nearly 30 percent of its membership, and its political influence dipped accordingly. Labor-backed measures now routinely failed in Congress.

The only real growth in organized labor took place among public employees, including teachers, civil service workers, and health professionals. Their gains were, however, often less than expected. During the 1970s local and state budgets sagged because of inflation, lower revenues from business, and voters' unwillingness to shoulder a bigger tax burden.

The number of wage-earning women continued to rise during the 1970s. By 1980 more than half of all married women and nearly 60 percent of mothers with children between the ages of six and seventeen were in the labor force. It had become the norm for women to be employed, and most households depended on two wages. The two economic recessions during the last years of the Vietnam War—1969–70 and 1973–75—encouraged many married women to find jobs, as did the high inflation that followed the energy crisis.

Despite a higher rate of participation in the labor force, women had lost ground relative to men. In 1955 women earned 64 percent of the average wages paid to men; in 1980 they earned only 59 percent. The reason for this dip lay in the increasing concentration of women in a few, mostly nonunion occupations. More than 80 percent of employed women worked in only 20 of the 420 occupations listed by the U.S. Census Bureau. In 1973 less than 15 percent of all employed women were in professional occupations. The great majority were clustered in the clerical and service trades, where the lowest wages prevailed.

African American women made some gains. Through Title VII of the Civil Rights Act, which outlawed workplace discrimination by sex or race, and the establishment of the Equal Employment Opportunity Commission to enforce it, they managed to climb the lower levels of the job ladder. By 1980 black women's median earnings in the North were about 95 percent of white women's earnings. Proportionately, slightly more black women than white women were gainfully employed in technical, sales, and administrative jobs.

In contrast, Hispanic women, whose labor force participation leaped by 80 percent during the decade, were restricted to a very few, poorly paid occupations. Puerto Ricans found jobs in the garment industry of the Northeast; Mexican Americans more typically worked as domestics or agricultural laborers in the Southwest. Neither group earned much more than the minimum wage.

Several local organizations were formed in the 1970s to push for equality in the workplace. The most successful of these addressed office workers. In 1973 Boston's Nine to Five drew up an Office Workers' Bill of Rights calling for equal pay for equal work, maternity benefits, and promotion opportunities. California's WAGE (Women Act to Gain Equality) and Chicago's WU (Women United) pressured government agencies for stricter enforcement of antidiscrimination laws. The Coalition of Labor Union Women, organized in 1974, fought for greater rights within the AFL-CIO, although only two women served in national leadership positions in the organization. The leaders of the AFL-CIO continued to regard women as poor prospects for unionization.

Sunbelt/Snowbelt

Although the economic woes of the 1970s affected all sections of the country, some regions fared worse than others. The Snowbelt of the Midwest and Northeast lost population and political influence as its economies slumped. The Sunbelt of the South, Southwest, and West Coast, meanwhile, continued a growth trend that had begun during World War II (see Chapter 25). The economy of this region grew three times faster than that of the rest of the nation.

By the 1970s the Sunbelt boasted a gross product greater than that of many nations and more cars, television sets, houses, and even miles of paved roads than the rest of the United States. Large influxes of immigrants from Latin America, the Caribbean, and Asia combined with the shift of people from the depressed Northeast to boost the region's population. From 56 million people in 1940, the Sunbelt's population more than doubled to 118 million by 1980, just forty years later.

The Sunbelt states had gained enormously from cold war defense spending as well as the expenditure of Social Security and pension income by retirees. The number of residents over the age of sixty-five increased by 30 percent during the 1970s, reaching 26 million by 1980. Armed with retirement packages won decades earlier, "golden agers" created new communities in Florida, Arizona, and southern California, pumping $8 billion a year into the Florida economy alone.

The South witnessed extraordinary changes in its economy and population. High-profit agribusiness emerged to meet the growing demand for poultry, beef, and frozen foods. Giant processing plants like Perdue, Inc., of Salisbury, Maryland, marketed up to 2 million broiler chickens each week through a high-technology mix of computerized feedings, growth hormones, conveyor-belt packaging, and aggressive advertising. The South also gained in manufacturing, in older industries such as textiles, coal, and steel, but also in petrochemicals and automobile parts. As commerce flourished, southern cities began to reverse the century-long trend of African American out-migration. Of the "ten best cities for blacks" listed by *Ebony* magazine in 1978, five—Atlanta, Dallas, Houston, Baltimore, and Washington—were southern cities that had all been rigidly segregated only a few decades earlier. For the first time, African Americans returned south in large numbers.

The Southwest and West changed even more dramatically. With the help of air conditioning, public improvements, large-scale development, and its recreational attractions, California became the nation's most populous state; Texas moved to third, behind New York. Almost overnight farms and deserts were turned into huge suburban developments clogged with automobile traffic. The population of Phoenix grew from 664,000 in 1960 to 1,509,000 in 1980, that of Las Vegas from 127,000 to 463,000. Meanwhile, agribusiness giants turned entire California valleys to the production of a single crop, such as strawberries, lima beans, or artichokes.

The rapidly growing computer industry created California's Silicon Valley (named for the production of silicon chips) south of San Francisco, adding more than a half-million jobs and billions of dollars of profit during the 1970s in Santa Clara County alone. Even when the number of lucrative defense contracts dropped after the Vietnam War, military outlays in high technology increased, with spin-offs in research and development centered in the Los Angeles area.

On the downside, much of the surge in the Sunbelt's wealth tended to be temporary, producing a boom-and-bust economy. Corporate office buildings in cities like Houston emptied almost as fast as they filled. Likewise, textile and similarly labor-intensive industries that had earlier moved to the South for lower wages now relocated to Mexico, the Caribbean, or Asia. Even microchip processing, considered virtually a native Californian industry, gradually moved to Pacific islands and East Asia.

The Sunbelt's economic assets were also very unevenly distributed. Older Hispanic populations made only modest gains, while recent Mexican immigrants and Indian peoples survived on low incomes. Whereas eastern and midwestern states, traditionally dependent on urban political machines and liberal voters, spent significantly on public housing, education, and mass transit, the conservative Sunbelt states concentrated their tax and federal dollars on strengthening police

These newly built houses in Phoenix, Arizona, a popular retirement community as well as the state capital, helped accommodate a 55 percent rise in the city's population between 1970 and 1980. Like other burgeoning cities of the Mountain West, Phoenix experienced many urban tensions during this decade, including racial conflict, antagonism between affluent suburbs and the decaying downtown, air pollution, traffic congestion, and strained water supplies.

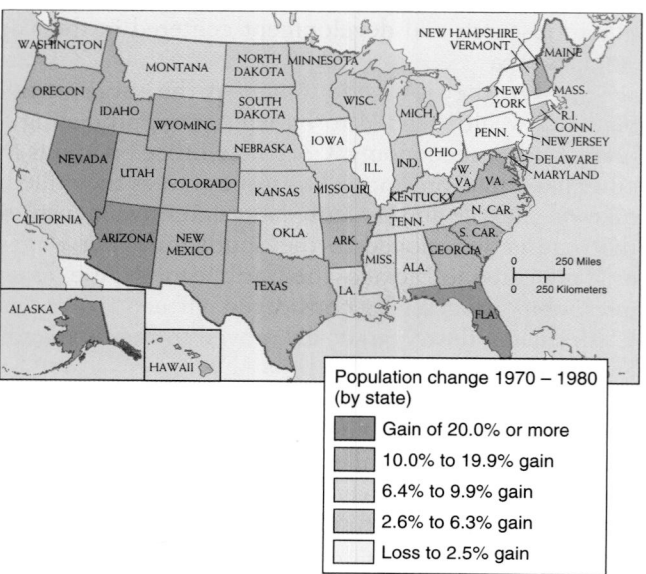

Population change 1970 – 1980 (by state)

- Gain of 20.0% or more
- 10.0% to 19.9% gain
- 6.4% to 9.9% gain
- 2.6% to 6.3% gain
- Loss to 2.5% gain

Population Shifts, 1970–1980   *Industrial decline in the Northeast coincided with an economic boom in the Sunbelt, encouraging millions of Americans to head for warmer climes and better jobs.*

forces, improving roads or sanitation systems for expanding suburbs, and creating budget surpluses.

Meanwhile, the Snowbelt (or "Rustbelt"), as the Northeast and upper Midwest came to be called, suffered population losses following a sharp decline in industry. Of the nineteen metropolitan areas that lost population during the 1970s, all were old manufacturing centers—topped by New York, Cleveland, Pittsburgh, Boston, Philadelphia, and Buffalo. Reduced federal outlays to city governments compounded municipal budget crises, accentuating a feeling of defeat that prevailed in these areas.

Philadelphia, once the nation's most important manufacturing center, was a case in point. From 1969 to 1981, the city lost 14 percent of its residents and 20 percent of its jobs, including 42 percent of its factory jobs. Only service employment grew, but in relatively small numbers (35,000 jobs gained versus more than 130,000 lost in all areas). Restored downtown neighborhoods with cobblestone streets dating to the eighteenth century bordered decayed neighborhoods and vacant commercial and industrial structures. Crime in the City of Brotherly Love increased by 200 percent, the municipal debt ballooned to $167 million, and the only city-owned hospital closed. Ranked fifty-seventh in terms of prosperity and service in a survey of sixty-five American cities, Philadelphia had nearly hit bottom.

New York City offered a still more spectacular example. A fiscal crisis in 1975 forced liberal mayor Abraham Beame to choose between wage freezes for public employees and devastating cuts and layoffs. Eventually, with the municipal government teetering on the brink of bankruptcy, he chose both. In response to cutbacks in mass transit and the deterioration of the city's public health system as well as municipal services generally, a large sector of the middle class left the city. At the same time, the proportion of poor people in the city's population rose from 15 percent in 1969 to nearly 25 percent fourteen years later.

"LEAN YEARS" PRESIDENTS

Gerald R. Ford and Jimmy Carter presided over a depressed economy and a nation of disillusioned citizens. Neither came up with a viable program to stimulate the economy. Carter contributed to voter apathy by admitting that he doubted that the government could solve the country's economic problems. After the 1968 election, voter participation began a two-decade decline, with only a little over half of eligible voters turning out for presidential elections. By the time Carter left office, a majority of those polled agreed that the "people running the country don't really care what happens to you."

"I'm a Ford, not a Lincoln"

When Gerald Ford replaced Nixon as president in August 1974 and Nelson Rockefeller became vice president, an overwhelming majority of Americans reported that they supported the new administration. But only a month after reassuring the public that "our long national nightmare is over," Ford turned around and pardoned Nixon for all the federal crimes he may have committed as president. Amid allegations that a deal had been struck, Ford irrevocably lost the nation's trust.

As president, Ford lacked a clear program and offered few initiatives to put the economy on the road to recovery. At best, he hoped to stimulate slow but steady growth by keeping interest rates stable, raising taxes to reduce federal deficits, and above all restraining federal spending. His voluntary anti-inflation program, Whip Inflation Now, publicized by big red-and-white lapel buttons emblazoned "WIN," failed to restore public confidence.

With inflation and unemployment soaring, the Democrats gained fifty-two seats in the House and four in the Senate in the 1974 midterm elections, eroding the Republican president's congressional support. Ford vetoed more major bills than any other president in the twentieth century, but Congress overrode him on most of them. Ford nevertheless swore to hold fast even against popular measures such as emergency job bills and education, health, and child nutrition programs. When New York City faced bankruptcy, Ford promised "to veto any bill that had as its purpose a federal bail-out." The *New York*

Daily News appeared the next day with the memorable headline "Ford to City: Drop Dead." When Congress united against him, the president relented.

Lyndon Johnson had once quipped: "The trouble with Jerry Ford is that he used to play football without a helmet." And indeed, the image Ford conveyed was that of a pleasant person of modest ability. The press often caught him stumbling or mixing up his ideas. He once claimed that "things are more like they are now than they have ever been."

First Lady Betty Ford, on the other hand, won the admiration of many Americans. Soon after she moved into the White House, she showed her personal courage by candidly discussing her mastectomy for breast cancer. "Lying in the hospital, thinking of all those women going for cancer checkups because of me," she later reported, "I'd come to recognize more clearly the power of the woman in the White House. Not my power, but the power of the position, a power which could be used to help." She soon broke ranks with other Republicans to champion the Equal Rights Amendment (ERA). She once told a television reporter that she supported abortion rights, would not scold her adult daughter for having premarital sex, and probably would have tried marijuana herself if it had been in vogue when she was growing up. Her popularity skyrocketed, and in 1975 *Newsweek* magazine chose her as Woman of the Year. Even after leaving the White House, Betty Ford remained in the spotlight when she openly discussed her dependency on drugs and alcohol.

The 1976 Election

Despite his flagging popularity, Gerald Ford banked on his incumbency and put himself forward in 1976 as the Republican candidate for president. His chief Republican opponent was Ronald Reagan, a film and television actor and a former governor of California who was widely known for his conservative views. Most Republicans feared, however, that a Reagan candidacy would push the party too far to the right and result in a landslide victory for the Democrats. Cautious in the aftermath of Watergate, the Republicans unenthusiastically nominated Ford, who named Senator Robert Dole of Kansas as his running mate.

On the Democratic side, the public's mistrust of government was the most important factor in the selection of a presidential candidate. Jimmy Carter, a former one-term governor of Georgia, depicted himself as an outsider, independent of the Washington establishment. (When Carter told his mother he was running for president, she reportedly asked, "President of what?") Trust and integrity were the chief planks of Carter's campaign for the nation's highest office. Promising to apply the "Golden Rule . . . in all public matters," he further pledged, "I will never lie to you."

A moderate Democrat, Carter appealed to conservative and southern voters by playing up his credentials as a born-again Christian. At the same time he made fairly liberal statements on domestic policy, including civil rights, and favored a strong national defense. Carter also capitalized on the Nixon pardon. His pointed references to the "Nixon-Ford administration," as well as the sagging economy, encouraged voters to try their luck with a Democrat. He entered the campaign with a 30 percent lead over Ford.

Carter and his running mate, Senator Walter Mondale of Minnesota, won the election with just over 50 percent of the popular vote and secured a 297-to-240 margin in the electoral college. Carter won more than 90 percent of the black vote, which provided his margin of victory in Pennsylvania, Ohio, and seven southern states. Apathy proved to be the most important factor, however. A record 46.7 percent of eligible voters, mainly the nation's poor, did not even bother to cast ballots.

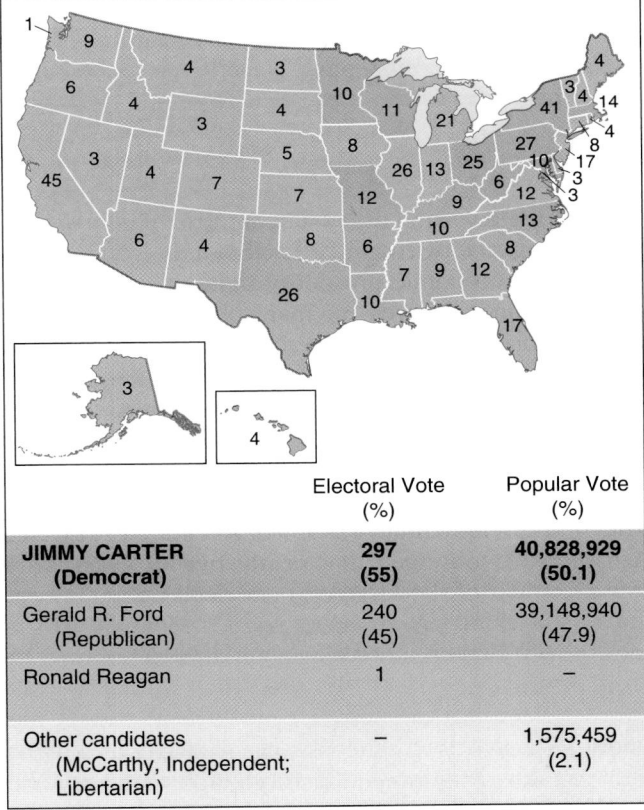

	Electoral Vote (%)	Popular Vote (%)
JIMMY CARTER (Democrat)	**297 (55)**	**40,828,929 (50.1)**
Gerald R. Ford (Republican)	240 (45)	39,148,940 (47.9)
Ronald Reagan	1	–
Other candidates (McCarthy, Independent; Libertarian)	–	1,575,459 (2.1)

The Election of 1976   *Incumbent Gerald Ford could not prevail over the disgrace brought to the Republican Party by Richard Nixon. The lingering pall of the Watergate scandal, especially Ford's pardon of Nixon, worked to the advantage of Jimmy Carter, who campaigned as an outsider to national politics. Although Carter and his running mate Walter Mondale won by only a narrow margin, the Democrats gained control of both the White House and Congress.*

The Carter Presidency

James Earl (Jimmy) Carter, the first president to come of age after World War II, was an enigma to most political analysts. As a professed outsider, he never gained the confidence of congressional Democrats, let alone Republicans, and could never command their votes. Uncertain and hesitant, he reflected the uneasiness that spread across the country in the late 1970s. Lacking an overarching political vision, Carter gradually shifted to the right, so much so that critics called him "a Democrat who often talks and thinks like a Republican."

The stalled economy resisted his best efforts, but Carter made his own mistakes. When he took office, he admitted that the nation's problems might require truly novel solutions but offered only a lackluster legislative program. His tax reform measure of 1977 did little to help the middle classes; his energy bill, enacted in 1978, appeared to benefit the oil companies as much as consumers; and the health reform measures promised during his campaign were never enacted.

Carter's style reflected his managerial outlook as well as his lack of experience as a politician. He generally abstained from the customary bargaining with legislators. Lacking leadership ability, he tended to seek technical solutions to the country's enormous social problems. On occasion he got caught up in trivial details, such as planning a players' schedule for the White House tennis courts. Overall, Carter relied on a small circle of advisers, mainly close friends from Georgia, and kept an unusually low profile for the nation's chief executive.

Carter's decisions nevertheless reflected his sense of political reality. Although he appointed a higher percentage of women, African Americans, and Latinos to full-time federal appointments than any previous president and created a "superfund" to clean up abandoned toxic waste sites, he broke ranks with liberal Democrats on important issues. Like many Southerners, Carter sought to reduce the scale of federal government as well as to lessen its control over the marketplace. He backed legislation that deregulated airlines, bringing fares down for millions of business and vacation travelers. He also backed the easing of congressional regulation of banks, a policy change that inadvertently encouraged fraud, the granting of questionable loans, and eventually a round of disastrous bank failures.

Carter made no effort to renew the social welfare initiatives of his Democratic predecessor, Lyndon B. Johnson. Under Carter's administration, inner-city schools and health and social services declined. The federal funds that might have gone to poverty programs instead bolstered military spending. The press, aided by whistle blowers working inside defense factories, found military spending loaded with fraud and abuse. Exposés of wasteful purchases—such

as $50 screwdrivers—made Carter appear unable or unwilling to challenge dishonesty in government, despite his campaign promises.

Inflation proved to be his worst enemy. As older Americans could recognize, half of all the inflation since 1940 had occurred in just ten years. Interest rates rose, driving mortgages out of reach for many would-be home buyers. Rents in many locations doubled, sales of automobiles and other consumer products slumped, and many small businesses went under. Tuition costs skyrocketed along with unemployment, and many young men and women who could neither afford to go to college nor find a job moved back home. Carter could not deliver on his promise to turn the economy around.

Like Betty Ford, First Lady Rosalynn Carter played a prominent role in her husband's administration, which she described as a family affair. She promoted reforms in mental health care and policies for the elderly, and she served as a goodwill ambassador to South America. She also took a strong stand in support of the ERA. She never achieved Betty Ford's popularity, however. Many Americans believed Rosalynn Carter overstepped her role when she began to attend cabinet meetings.

THE NEW POVERTY

Despite the diversion of federal funds to military spending during the Vietnam War, the nation enjoyed a continuing economic prosperity during the 1960s that raised living standards for many. Income differences between black and white Americans—and between men and women—declined; segregation in schools, housing, and public facilities declined as well. By the mid-1970s, however, it had become clear that many of these gains were short-lived, reversed by a contracting economy and persistent racism. Michael Harrington, author of the highly influential *The Other America* (1962) (see Chapter 29), observed that nearly twenty years "after the President of the United States declared an 'unconditional' war on poverty, . . . we must deal . . . with a new poverty much more tenacious than the old."

A Two-tiered Society

During the 1970s Americans were healthier and living longer than at any time in history. Life expectancy had risen from sixty years in 1930 to seventy-three years, and gains were even greater for those who survived past the age of seventy-five. The majority of Americans also enjoyed greater wealth. Real personal income had doubled since the late 1930s, and by 1977 median family income had reached $15,000.

The gap between rich and poor, however, was starting to grow wider. By 1980 the wealthiest 20 percent

When Jimmy Carter took the oath of office in January 1977, he inherited an office dishonored by the Nixon-Ford administration. Hoping to dispel the political cynicism that had settled over the nation, he smiled broadly as he left the inaugural platform, bypassed his armored limousine, and walked hand-in-hand with Rosalynn Carter. Spectators cheered along the Pennsylvania Avenue parade route, greeting the new president's gesture as the symbolic end of an unhappy era.

black college graduates, and many African Americans found places in the ranks of professional, clerical, managerial, and technical workers. By the late 1970s one-third of all black workers had found white-collar employment.

But although 35 to 45 percent of African American families achieved middle-class status, others fell into poverty in nearly the same proportion. The sociologist William Julius Wilson confirmed "a deepening economic schism . . . in the black community." While middle-class black people were joining white people in the professional workplace and integrated suburbs, the poor stayed behind in increasingly segregated urban neighborhoods and in jobs that did not pay a living wage.

This trend affected the black community in dramatic ways. Until the 1970s the majority of African Americans had shared residential neighborhoods, institutions such as churches, and political outlooks. The growing income and residential disparity, which widened faster among black people than among white people, eventually produced sharp differences among African Americans on social, economic, and political issues as well.

Toward the end of the decade, opportunities for advancement into the middle class dwindled. By 1980 fewer black students attended integrated schools than in 1954, except in the South, where about half the black students did. The turnabout resulted in part from increasing opposition by white parents to court-ordered school busing, which had served since *Brown v. Board of Education* as the principal means of achieving racial balance in urban school systems where residential neighborhoods remained segregated by choice. In 1975 residents of a white neighborhood clashed with black children who had been sent to their school under a court-ordered busing plan. By the end of the decade the busing controversy had nearly disappeared, in part because federal judges hesitated to mandate such programs. But more important was the change in the racial composition of American cities. As a consequence of "white flight" to the suburbs, by 1980 big-city school systems served mainly African American and Latino children, making the issue of integration moot. By this time, the dropout rate of black teenagers had reached 50 percent in inner-city schools.

of American families received about 40 percent of all income, whereas the poorest 20 percent received only about 5 percent. Nearly 26 million Americans—about 12 percent of the population—lived in poverty. Another 12 percent squeaked over the poverty line of $6,000 per family of four only because of welfare assistance. More than 11 million families were receiving welfare assistance from Aid to Families with Dependent Children (AFDC).

The widening gap between rich and poor was sharply defined by race. Although poor white people outnumbered poor black people by two to one, a disproportionate number of African Americans lived below the poverty line. Whereas 8.7 percent of white people lived in poverty in 1978, 30.6 percent of black and 21.6 percent of Hispanic people did (the rate was especially high among Puerto Ricans, low among Cuban Americans). The gains achieved by the civil rights movement and Great Society programs steadily eroded over the 1970s. Black family income, for example rose from 53 percent of white family income in 1954—the year of the *Brown v. Board of Education* decision—to 60 percent in 1969, peaked at 62 percent in 1975, then fell back to 57 percent in 1975. In most cities, residential segregation continued to increase.

Differences among African Americans also became more pronounced during the 1970s. The proportion of the African American population attending college peaked in 1976 at 9.3 percent, a 500 percent increase from 1960. Implementing federal affirmative action mandates, major corporations began to recruit

New legal rulings closed off important routes to employment in the professions. A 1978 U.S. Supreme Court decision dealt a sharp blow to affirmative action. To ensure acceptance of a minimum number of minority students, the University of California–Davis Medical School had established a quota system. In 1973 and 1974 the school denied admission to Allan Bakke, a white student. Bakke sued the university for "reverse discrimination," claiming his academic record was better than that of the sixteen minority students who were admitted. The California Supreme Court ruled in his favor in 1976, and, in a 5 to 4 decision, the Supreme Court upheld the California court's ruling, stating that the use of an "explicit racial classification" in situations where no earlier discrimination had been demonstrated violated the Equal Protection Clause of the Fourteenth Amendment. The Court ordered the University of California to admit Bakke to its medical school. Affirmative action programs could now operate only when "a legacy of unequal treatment" could be proved.

The Feminization of Poverty

Women as a group lost economic ground during the 1970s. The proportion of women in the labor force continued to grow, but most employed women earned less than a living wage. A rising divorce rate also left women—including employed women—at an economic disadvantage. Throughout the 1950s, the divorce rate averaged fifteen per thousand married women between the ages of fourteen and forty-four; by the time President Carter took office, the rate had more than doubled, reaching a new high of thirty-seven per thousand. At the same time, changes in divorce laws worked to men's financial advantage. For example, new no-fault divorce laws reduced or eliminated alimony payments to women. Most men, moreover, defaulted on child-support payments within one year after separation. Whereas divorced men enjoyed an average 42 percent increase in their standard of living, divorced women suffered a 73 percent decline.

During the 1970s the number of poor families headed by women increased nearly 70 percent. Divorce was the most important factor in this trend; more than 50 percent of female-headed families had divorced women as heads of the household, while 31 percent were headed by women separated from their husbands. Another factor was a sharp rise in pregnancy among unwed teenagers, although less than 20 percent of female-headed households were headed by an unwed mother. Unlike those of earlier generations, teenagers of the 1970s tended to keep their babies rather than put them up for adoption. Many dropped out of high school. Too young to have gained either the education or skills to secure more than minimum-wage jobs, unmarried mothers could rarely support themselves and their children.

Separated and divorced women and their children drifted downward into poverty, often from the relative security of the middle class. Even with AFDC payments and food stamps, it was nearly impossible for any single mother to keep her family's income above the poverty line. And with inflation, the real incomes of welfare recipients dropped in many states to a little over half their 1970 levels. In 1982 the National Advisory Council on Economic Opportunity issued a report predicting that, if these trends continued, by the turn of the century female heads of households and their children would account for just about all the poor people in the United States.

By the mid-1970s, the major organization promoting the rights of poor women had itself filed for bankruptcy. Between 1967 and 1975, the National Welfare Rights Organization (NWRO) had coordinated the work of various local welfare rights groups. Led mainly by African American women, the NWRO raised funds from churches and government poverty programs to enable welfare recipients to have a voice in policy decisions. They demanded adequate day-care facilities and job-training programs and insisted on the legitimacy of female-headed households. NWRO activists occasionally staged sit-ins at welfare agencies to secure benefits for their members. More often, they informed poor women of their existing rights and encouraged them to apply for benefits. By 1975, however, NWRO had exhausted itself fighting cutbacks in the federal welfare system.

"The Underclass"

"Behind the [ghetto's] crumbling walls," *Time* magazine announced in 1977, "lives a large group of people who are more intractable, more socially alien and more hostile than almost anyone had imagined. They are the unreachables: the American underclass. . . ." Although the majority of poor Americans lived in rural areas and small towns, with Missouri, South Dakota, and Texas accounting for the nation's largest pockets of poverty, *Time* and other news media spotlighted the inner cities. "The underclass," in their discussions, became a metaphor for the deteriorating conditions of urban America.

Most commentators focused on African Americans, the six out of ten who lived in central cities with rising unemployment rates. The economic boom during the Vietnam War and the expansion of public programs under Johnson's Great Society had built huge municipal payrolls, permitting many African Americans to secure jobs in the public sector. With the drastic cutbacks of the 1970s, many municipal workers were laid off. Jobs became scarcer than they had been at any time since the Great Depression. One unemployed worker in

Kansas City commented that despite the advances brought about by the civil rights movement, conditions appeared no better than they had been during the 1930s: "The truth is that black people ain't no closer to catching up with white than they were before."

The bleak prospects took an especially heavy toll on young African Americans. A black child was twice as likely as a white child to die before reaching his or her first birthday and four times more likely to be killed between the ages of one and four. Among black teenagers, the unemployment rate topped 40 percent; the few jobs available to them were among the lowest-paid in the economy. Despite the paucity of jobs for teenagers, the high school dropout rate skyrocketed during the 1970s. Among dropouts, illiteracy, frequent arrests, alcohol and drug abuse, and long-term reliance on public welfare were endemic.

The growth of teenage poverty also correlated positively with a rise in crime. Rates of violent crimes, such as aggravated assault, robbery, rape, and murder increased dramatically in poor communities throughout the country. The number of serious crimes, such as burglary, car theft, and murder, perpetrated by children between the ages of ten and seventeen increased at an alarming rate.

Although some policy experts attributed the emergence of an "underclass" to declining economic opportunities, the news media revived the "tangle of pathology" argument, which had been at the heart of Daniel Patrick Moynihan's *Negro Family: The Case for National Action* (1965). This report identified the major cause of disorder within the African American community as the prevalence of female-headed households, or what Moynihan called "the black matriarchy." At the time, many civil rights leaders and feminists objected to Moynihan's assessment, claiming that it shifted blame from the causes of poverty to its victims. Over a decade later, this argument still found favor in the news media and with many legislators who linked the emergence of "the underclass" to the increase of single mothers and welfare dependence.

Indian peoples remained the poorest and most disadvantaged of all racial or ethnic groups. They suffered from a high death rate—six times the national average from tuberculosis, and twenty-two times the national average from alcohol-related causes. Tribes continued to struggle for autonomy during the 1970s—that is, to gain authority over their reservations, including mineral and water resources—but often encountered resistance and competing claims from white neighbors. In 1978 the Supreme Court ruled in *United States v. Wheeler* that tribal sovereignty existed "only at the sufferance of Congress." Another case in the same year, *Oliphant v. Suquamish Indian Tribe*, added that tribes had no authority to arrest or punish trespassers who violated their laws. Meanwhile the federal government did little to help integrate Indian peoples who lived off the reservations—slightly less than half of the total Indian population—into mainstream society.

COMMUNITIES AND GRASS-ROOTS POLITICS

The mass demonstrations of the 1960s gave way in the 1970s to a style of political mobilization centered squarely in communities. Unlike national elections, which registered increasing voter apathy, local campaigns brought a great many people to the voting booth and into voluntary associations. "I didn't care so much about my neighborhood until I had children," one city dweller told a sociologist. "I wasn't aware of the various facets of the community. Then came a lot of other things that I began to do as the parent of a child in this neighborhood. We became committed to this area."

The New Urban Politics

In many cities, new groups came into political power. In several college towns, such as Berkeley, California, and Eugene, Oregon, both of which had been centers of antiwar activism during the 1960s, student coalitions were formed to secure seats for their candidates on city councils. In 1973 labor unions, college students, and community groups in Madison, Wisconsin, elected a former student activist to the first of three terms as mayor.

African American candidates scored impressive victories during the 1970s. The newly elected African American mayor of Atlanta, Maynard Johnson, concluded that "politics is the civil rights movement of the 1970s." By 1978, 2,733 African Americans held elected offices in the South, ten times the number a decade earlier. Mississippi, a state where the civil rights movement had encountered violent opposition, had more African American elected officials by 1980 than any other state in the union. Most of these elected officials served on city councils, county commissions, school boards, and law enforcement agencies. But voters also elected African American mayors in the South's premier cities, New Orleans and Atlanta. In other parts of the country, black mayors, such as Coleman Young in Detroit, Richard Hatcher in Gary, and Tom Bradley in Los Angeles, held power along with many minor black officials. Cities with black mayors spent more than other municipalities of similar size on education and social services. They worked hardest at improving community health services and to ensure equity in government employment.

Other racial or ethnic groups advanced more slowly, rarely in proportion to their actual numbers in the population. Mexican Americans had already won offices in Crystal City, Texas, and in 1978 took control

Geronimo, 1981, *by Victor Orozco Ochoa. During the 1970s public murals appeared in many cities, often giving distinctive expression to a community's racial or ethnic identity. The murals painted in the mid-1970s on the outside of the Centro Cultural de la Raza, in San Diego, were among the most striking. After vandals ruined one section, Ochoa, whose grandmother was Yaqui, replaced it with this enormous representation of Geronimo, surrounded by figures of contemporary Chicano cultural life.*

of a major city council, in San Antonio, for the first time. They also scored electoral victories in other parts of Texas and in New Mexico and developed strong neighborhood or ward organizations in southern California. Puerto Ricans elected a handful of local officials in New York, mostly in the Bronx. Asian Americans advanced in similar fashion in parts of Hawai'i.

The fiscal crises of the 1970s undercut these efforts to reform municipal government. Most of these new officials found themselves unable to make the sweeping changes they had promised during their campaigns. In tackling the problem of youth unemployment, they discovered that temporary job programs could not counteract the effects of factory shutdowns and the disappearance of industrial jobs. Moreover, affirmative action programs aroused cries of "reverse discrimination" from angered whites who felt that the progress of others was being made at their expense. But although support for them frequently dissipated when the cycle of poverty and violence could not be slowed, community-based mobilizations remained the political touchstone of the decade.

The City and the Neighborhood

The nation's cities inspired a range of responses from residents who chose to resist the pull of the suburbs

and from those who simply could not afford to leave. For city dwellers, the city's hospitals, public libraries, symphony orchestras, museums, and art galleries became anchoring institutions requiring public support. Changes in federal policies also encouraged local initiative. The Community Development Act of 1974, signed by President Ford, combined federal grant programs for cities into a single program and put mayors and city managers directly in charge of spending. With grants totaling $8.4 billion over three years, city governments could allocate funds as they saw fit to public works, law enforcement, residential redevelopment, or even to salaries for public employees. These community development block grants encouraged citizens to take part in local planning. Communities Organized for Public Service (COPS) in San Antonio, Texas, and the Association of Community Organizations for Reform Now (ACORN) in Little Rock, Arkansas, were formed to advise public officials. In other cities, Save the City campaigns engaged residents in defining problems important to the community, such as traffic, sewerage, or stray dogs.

Groups of preservationists organized to save historic buildings and public spaces and formed land trusts to take over and refurbish old houses or to turn vacant lots into neighborhood parks. In Rhode Island, the Providence Preservation Society worked with city planners and individual donors to restore hundreds of houses, organized festival tours of neighborhoods to lure prospective buyers, and spurred the formation of similar societies in nearby towns.

Local and national foundations joined federal agencies in funding Community Development Corporations (CDCs) through a series of antipoverty agencies. By the end of the 1970s some 700 community-based economic development groups had been formed to infuse capital into neighborhood businesses and housing. These community groups promoted "development banks" that would facilitate "sweat equity"—that is, the granting of low-interest mortgage loans to buyers who were willing to rebuild or refurbish dilapidated housing. They also acted to prevent local banks from closing when a neighborhood became mainly black.

Those who guided the neighborhood campaigns often became known as "local heroes." They usually insisted that tensions between old and new neighborhood residents, problems of housing and schools, and the like could be solved face to face and cooperatively with the resources available to them. In San Francisco during the early 1970s, a law professor, Ray Schonholtz, launched "community boards," neighborhood arbitration centers that he described as "a new justice model . . . a neighborhood stabilization program . . . a volunteer service delivery system" with a "new philosophy about conflict, viewing it positively instead of negatively." Federal assistance proved crucial in maintaining most community-based programs, however, especially in the late 1970s when cities faced major fiscal crises.

In 1979 President Carter's National Commission on Neighborhoods compiled 200 specific recommendations to broaden and speed the development of local institutions. The long-range goal of such efforts, the commission suggested, should be "to reorganize our society . . . to a new democratic system of grassroots involvement." But local advocacy groups often found themselves enmeshed in projects that foundations and federal agencies, not the local groups, thought best for a neighborhood. As a leader of a Bronx advocacy group concluded, he and his fellow activists were "diverted from organizing" and "seen—rightly—as part of the establishment" when they found themselves administering large-scale, well-funded projects that they had not originally intended to create. And even when local preservationists succeeded in restoring entire urban districts to an earlier splendor, "gentrification" often followed, with poor residents displaced by middle-class professionals who craved the increasingly fashionable old homes.

The Endangered Environment

As at Three Mile Island, threats to the environment rallied whole communities. For example, the discovery of high rates of cancer and birth defects among the residents of Love Canal, a neighborhood of Niagara Falls, New York, offered compelling evidence of a growing danger to many American communities. Love Canal had been built over a site used by the Hooker Chemical Laboratory as a dump for toxic wastes, which began oozing into basements and backyards in the late 1970s. Homemaker Lois Gibbs organized a vigorous publicity campaign to draw attention to the grim situation. Residents demanded to be evacuated from the site and compensated for damages. Hooker and the city of Niagara Falls eventually paid a group of former homeowners more than $20,000,000. Many residents of southern Florida, meanwhile, were outraged to learn that modifications of water flow into the Everglades for sugar production and housing developments, undertaken decades earlier by the Army Corps of Engineers, had degraded thousands of acres of wilderness, eliminating natural filtration systems and killing millions of birds and other species. These and similar problems alerted communities nationwide to the perils of industrial and economic development unchecked by concern for their environmental consequences.

The roots of the modern environmental movement can be traced to the works of scientist Rachel Carson, especially *Silent Spring* (1962), which detailed the devastating effects of the then commonly used DDT and other pesticides. By the spring of 1970, opinion polls showed that the public was more concerned about the environment than any other domestic issue. Senator Gaylord Nelson of Wisconsin and Representative Paul "Pete" McCloskey of California invited Americans to devote an entire day—April 22, Earth Day—to discuss the environment. The response was overwhelming; nearly 20 million Americans gathered in local parks, high schools, and colleges and at the nation's capital. Many wore green peace symbols and sang "All we are saying is give earth a chance."

The residents of many communities began to reassess their priorities and even to make changes in the way they lived. Municipal governments introduced recycling programs, encouraging residents to save glass, plastic bottles, and newspapers for reuse. Many families changed their diets to reduce or eliminate beef, which was far more costly to produce than the grains fed to cattle. Backyard vegetable gardens became popular, as did grocers who stocked organic foods, which were grown without pesticides or chemical fertilizers. Nutritionist Frances Moore Lappe's popular *Diet for a Small Planet* (1971) sought to counter the logic of excess that had made Americans consumers of one third of the world's energy resources. Barry Commoner's *Closing*

Circle (1971) helped make the term "ecology" (the name of the branch of biology that deals with the relationship between organisms and their environment) into a synonym for environmental balance ("eco" means "home" in Greek).

The environmentalist movement grew stronger on college campuses and in a handful of long-standing organizations, such as the Audubon Society and the Wilderness Society. The Sierra Club, formed in 1892 as a small society of western mountain hikers, grew to 100,000 members in 1970 and a half-million over the next decade. New groups sprang up in response to the energy crisis, often devoted to developing renewable energy sources such as solar power. Some, like Greenpeace, sponsored direct action campaigns to halt practices that caused harm to the environment.

Environmentalism cut across social and geographic boundaries. The dangers of toxic wastes, the destruction of wetlands, the ruin of fishing industries, and other problems aroused concern even in such traditionally conservative areas as the Deep South (where bumper stickers read "Don't Dump It in Dixie!"). Sometimes campaigns succeeded in blocking massive construction projects, such as nuclear energy plants; more often they halted small-scale destruction—of a particular natural habitat or historic urban district, for example. Most important, all these campaigns made the public more aware of the consequences of private and government decisions about the environment. Responding to organized pressure groups, Congress passed scores of bills designed to protect endangered species, reduce pollution caused by automobile emissions, limit and ban the use of some pesticides, and control strip mining. The Environmental Protection Agency (EPA), established in 1970, grew to become the federal government's largest regulatory agency, employing more than 10,000 people by the end of the decade.

Environmentalists had only limited success, however, in effecting large-scale policy changes. Congress passed clean air mandates to reduce air pollution, but cities often avoided the mandates with petitions for lengthy extensions of the deadlines for meeting them. Despite the introduction of lead-free gasoline, the air in major metropolitan areas grew worse because of a rapid increase in automobile traffic. Environmentalists lost an important campaign when Nixon's secretary of the interior, former Alaska governor Walter Hickel, chose Earth Day to announce the approval of the Alaska pipeline, 800 miles of pipe connecting oil fields with refining facilities. Despite predictions of environmental destruction from leaks and other catastrophes, pipeline construction began in 1973. As White House adviser John Ehrlichman explained, "Conservation is not in the Republican ethic."

Small-town America

A host of unresolved problems, ranging from air pollution to rising crime rates to higher taxes, encouraged a massive exodus from the nation's cities. Between 1970 and 1975, for every 100 people relocating to metropolitan areas, 138 moved out. Newer residential communities in small towns and in semirural or formerly rural areas grew at a fast pace, attracting retirees and others seeking solace or security.

Government programs such as mortgage guarantees and low-interest financing on individual homes promoted these large "low-density" developments of single-family houses. In many regions, the countryside gradually disappeared into "exurbia," a trend that population experts Peter A. Morison and Judith P. Wheeler attributed to the American "wish to love one's neighbor but keep him at arm's length." Opinion poles suggested that many Americans wanted to live in a small town that was not a suburb but was still no more than thirty miles from a major city.

Soon even small towns developed their own suburbs, usually moderate-income tracts of ranch houses squeezed between older wood-frame colonial or Victorian farmhouses. Federal subsidies for the construction of sewage and water lines, originally intended to aid rural communities, now became springboards for further development. Ironically, shopping malls on former farmland drained commercial activity from the small-town centers, channeling the benefits of development to chain stores rather than to local merchants.

Some communities organized to oppose these trends. Following the publication of E. F. Schumacher's *Small Is Beautiful* (1973), groups of people began to question the advantages of "bigness." Seeking to rebuild communities on a smaller, more environmentally sound scale, they opposed new development, new highways, the construction of nuclear power plants, and the dumping of toxic waste. In Vermont, liberal "hippies" and "back-to-the-landers" joined traditionally conservative landowners to defeat a 1974 gubernatorial plan to attract developers. In other locales, such as the Berkshire Mountains, community land trusts were organized to encourage common ownership of the land. "From coast to coast," the *New York Times* reported, "environmental, economic and social pressures have impelled hundreds of cities and towns to adopt limitations on the size and character of their populations." To encourage public discussion of land-use issues, such as the use of open space or farms for commercial development, President Carter created the Small Community and Rural Development Policy group.

Some small towns, especially those without mild climates or nearby cities, did not prosper during

Archie (Carroll O'Connor) and Edith Bunker (Jean Stapleton) endowed television with a social and political complexity that previous situation comedies had scrupulously avoided. First broadcast in 1971, All in the Family featured a working-class family living in Queens, New York, trying to sort out their differences with Archie, the highly bigoted but lovable center of the household. Producer Norman Lear explained that the show "holds a mirror up to our prejudices. . . . We laugh now, swallowing just the littlest bit of truth about ourselves, and it sits there for the unconscious to toss about later."

the 1970s. In parts of Kansas, Iowa, and the Dakotas, where family farms failed at a high rate, other businesses also closed. A "snowball effect" resulted in rundown schools, inadequate medical care, and abandoned movie theaters and grocery stores. Only nursing homes and funeral parlors continued to thrive.

THE NEW CONSERVATISM

While many Americans concentrated their political energies in their communities, others organized to turn back the liberal Great Society programs. Many taxpayers resented having to pay for government programs that benefited minorities or provided expanded social services for the poor. In 1978 California voters staged a "taxpayers' revolt" and approved Proposition 13, which cut property taxes and government revenues for social programs and education. In other, mainly economically hard-pressed urban areas, white voters who resented the gains made by African Americans and Latinos formed a powerful backlash movement. Poles in Chicago, Irish in Boston, and Italians and Jews in Brooklyn, for example, organized to consolidate their political influence. By the end of the decade, the only substantial increase in voter participation was among conservatives.

The New Right

The political surge rightward in the 1970s united many traditionally probusiness conservatives with a new constituency of alienated lower-class white voters. This alliance gained strength from widespread bitterness about both the United States defeat in Vietnam and the growing regulatory powers of the federal government. It gained intellectual respectability from neoconservatives, former liberals who blamed the social movements of the 1960s for the demoralization of the nation. The American Enterprise Institute and the Heritage Foundation, richly funded by major corporations, established major research centers for conservative scholars. These and other foundations also funded campus publications attacking welfare programs, affirmative action, and environmentalism. Leaders of the New Right, as the movement was called, identified themselves with the defense of "family values" and sought to gain political power by influencing legislation and public policy, and most of all by winning elections.

The most sensational element of the New Right was its paramilitary wing, which was concentrated in rural districts of the upper Midwest and Southwest. Inspired by white supremicist author William Pierce's *Turner Diaries* (1978), a novel that predicted the revolt by white "Aryans" against people of color and the federal government, thousands of enthusiasts bolstered their apocalyptic vision by arming themselves with assault weapons and training surreptitiously for combat.

The largest New Right constituency, however, united behind major conservative religious and political leaders to preserve and promote what they viewed as traditional moral values. By decade's end more than 50 million Americans had joined the ranks of evangelical Christians, and Southern Baptists had become the nation's largest Protestant denomination. One year after Billy Graham published his fast-selling *How to Be Born Again* (1977), 40 percent of all Americans, including the nation's president, reported that they were indeed "born again." These evangelical Christians became the backbone of key organizations such as the National Conservative Political Action Committee and, most especially, Moral Majority. Together they raised the funds to wage well-publicized campaigns against abortion, the ERA, gay rights, and the busing of schoolchildren.

The New Right used sophisticated marketing techniques to build its constituency. Conservative political groups were among the first to use direct mail campaigns to mobilize followers and raise funds. In the 1970s approximately 100 conservative organizations each created lists of potential donors, traded or sold these lists, and kept in circulation millions of personally addressed letters requesting financial contributions in return for monthly newsletters, insignia buttons, bumper stickers, or even embossed Bibles.

Phyllis Schlafly led the campaign to defeat ratification of the Equal Rights Amendment. She wrote widely and delivered speeches throughout the country denouncing women's liberation as a threat to the family. The Alton, Illinois, homemaker appears here on the steps of the Illinois State Capitol in 1978.

"Televangelists" enjoyed even greater success in attracting a following. Evangelical programming emerged on the local level in the early days of television. By the late 1960s, several shows had achieved national syndication. Televangelists such as Pat Robertson and Jim Bakker frequently mixed conservative political messages with appeals to prayer. The *Old Time Gospel Hour,* featuring the Reverend Jerry Falwell, was broadcast on more than 200 television stations and 300 radio stations each week. Falwell told his listeners that Christians were morally compelled to support issues and candidates that punish "the enemies of God," including communists, supporters of abortion rights, and the "secular humanist" opponents of prayer in public schools. Christian broadcasters generally endorsed Falwell's faith that "the free-enterprise system is clearly outlined in the Book of Proverbs of the Bible." By the end of the 1970s more than 1,400 radio stations and 30 TV stations specialized in religious broadcasts that reached an audience of perhaps 20 million weekly.

Urging Americans to repent their sins and acknowledge God's authority or suffer terrible wrath, Falwell formed Moral Majority, Inc., as a political lobbying group to urge the rightful "place for biblical moral law in public policy." Moral Majority advocated tough laws against homosexuality and pornography, a reduction of government services, especially welfare payments to poor families, and increased spending for a stronger national defense. It promised campaign funds and votes for, as Falwell put it, "the

mighty man . . . that man of war, that judge, that prophet, that preacher who is willing to call sin by its right name."

Jesse Helms was the first major politician to appeal directly to the New Right and to build his own impressive fund-raising empire with its help. A North Carolina journalist who had fought the integration of public schools and affirmative action programs and defended the Ku Klux Klan, Helms had often attacked Martin Luther King Jr. as a communist-influenced demagogue. Helms entered national politics as a Goldwater supporter in 1964 and ran for the Senate in 1972. Carried to victory with Richard Nixon's success in North Carolina, Helms immediately promoted a host of conservative bills. He introduced legislation to allow automobile owners or dealers to disconnect mandatory antipollution devices. He also defended the Watergate break-ins as necessary to offset the "traitorous conduct" of antiwar activists. By 1978 he had raised $8.1 million, the largest amount ever, for his successful reelection campaign. Helms won few victories in the Senate but built a powerful, loyal, and wealthy following.

Anti-ERA, Antiabortion

The New Right sponsored several important campaigns during the 1970s. Conservatives sought, without success, to pass a Balanced Budget Amendment to the Constitution and to return prayer to the public schools. They endorsed the Supreme Court's decision permitting the resumption of the death penalty in 1977. And in one of the New Right's best-funded campaigns, they sought to

Asked of those who said they had heard
of or read about the Equal Rights
Amendment: Do you favor or oppose this
amendment?

Favor	58%
Oppose	24%
No opinion	18%

By Sex

Male

Favor	63%
Oppose	22%
No opinion	15%

Female

Favor	54%
Oppose	25%
No opinion	21%

Interviewing Date 3/7–10/1975, Survey #925-K

Gallup Poll on the Equal Rights Amendment, 1975
By 1973 thirty of the thirty-eight states required to ratify the ERA had done so. Although the amendment ultimately failed to achieve ratification and died in June 1982, public support was strong. In the 1976 presidential campaign, the platforms of both Democrats and Republicans included planks favoring its passage.

Source: *The Gallup Poll: Public Opinion, 1935–1974* (New York: Random House, 1974).

restore the "traditional family values" that, in their minds, the women's liberation movement had destroyed.

The defeat of the Equal Rights Amendment (ERA) stood at the top of the New Right agenda. Approved by Congress in March 1972, nearly fifty years after its introduction (see Chapter 22), the ERA stated: "Equality of rights under the law shall not be denied or abridged by the United States or by any State on account of sex." Endorsed by both the Democratic and Republican Parties, the amendment appeared likely to be ratified by the individual states. Nearly all mainstream women's organizations, including the Girl Scouts of America, endorsed the ERA. Even the AFL-CIO retracted its long-standing opposition and endorsed the amendment.

Responding to this groundswell of support in favor of the ERA, the New Right swung into action. Phyllis Schlafly, a self-described suburban housewife who had been active in Republican Party politics since the 1950s, headed the STOP ERA campaign. Schlafly described the amendment's supporters as "a bunch of bitter women seeking a constitutional cure for their personal problems." She warned that the ERA would

deprive women of their true rights "such as the right of a wife to be supported by her husband" and that it would lead to unisex public toilets and homosexual marriages. As one woman wrote her senator, "Forced busing, forced mixing, forced housing. Now forced women. No thank you!" Hostile to "Big Government," antiratificationists believed that the ERA would allow the state to intrude further into the private domain of family by requiring massive changes in laws concerning marriage, divorce, and child custody.

The New Right mounted large, expensive campaigns in each swing state, overwhelming pro-ERA resources. By 1979, although thirty-five states had ratified the ERA, the amendment remained three votes short of passage. Despite a three-year extension, the ERA died in 1982.

As part of its counterattack against the women's liberation movement, the New Right also waged a steady campaign against abortion, which the women's movement had defined as a woman's right rather than a mere medical issue. In 1973 the Supreme Court had ruled in *Roe v. Wade* that state laws outlaw-

Would you favor or oppose a law that
would permit a woman to go to a doctor to
end pregnancy at any time during the first
three months?

Favor	40%
Oppose	50%
No opinion	10%

Interviewing Date 11/12–17/1969, Survey #793-K, Question #4, Index #54

The United States Supreme Court has
ruled that a woman may go to a doctor to
end pregnancy at any time during the first
three months of pregnancy. Do you favor
or oppose this ruling?

Favor	47%
Oppose	44%
No opinion	9%

Interviewing Date 3/8–11; 3/15–18/1974, Survey #894-K; 895-K

Gallup Polls on Abortion: 1969, 1974 *During the 1960s, numerous American women began to demand control over their own reproductive processes and the repeal of legislation in place in all fifty states rendering abortion illegal. The American Institute of Public Opinion surveyed Americans in 1969, when abortion was still illegal, and again in 1974, one year after* Roe v. Wade, *the Supreme Court ruling that struck down state laws prohibiting abortion during the first three months of pregnancy.*

Source: *The Gallup Poll: Public Opinion, 1935–1974* (New York: Random House, 1974).

ing abortion during the first two trimesters of pregnancy were unconstitutional because they violated a woman's right to privacy. The decision in effect legalized abortion on demand. Opponents of *Roe* sought a constitutional amendment that would define conception as the beginning of life and outlaw abortion. They argued that the "rights of the unborn" supersede a woman's right to control her own body. The Roman Catholic Church organized the first antiabortion demonstrations after the Supreme Court's decision and sponsored the formation of the National Right to Life Committee, which claimed 11 million members by 1980. Many more groups organized, such as Concerned for Life, Life and Equality, Right to Life, and the American Life Lobby, all framing the issue in terms of a fundamental and sacred "right to life."

Abortion foes rallied behind the conservative representative from Illinois, Henry Hyde, who sponsored a legislative bill that severely restricted the use of Medicaid funds for abortions. Upheld by the Supreme Court in 1980, the Hyde Amendment affected mainly poor women. Antiabortion groups also picketed Planned Parenthood counseling centers and abortion clinics, humiliating and intimidating potential clients. They rallied against government-subsidized day-care centers and against sex education programs in public schools. A small minority turned to more extreme actions, including violence.

"The Me Decade"

During the 1970s many Americans disengaged themselves from politics altogether. In 1976 novelist Tom Wolfe coined the phrase "the Me Decade" to describe an era obsessed with personal well-being, happiness, and emotional security. Health foods and diet crazes, a mania for physical fitness, and a quest for happiness through therapy involved millions of middle-class Americans. The historian Christopher Lasch provided his own label for this enterprise in the title of his best-selling book *The Culture of Narcissism: American Life in an Age of Diminishing Expectations* (1978). "After the political turmoil of the sixties," he explained, "Americans have returned to purely personal preoccupations."

The rise of the "human potential movement" provided a vivid example of this trend. Its most successful manifestation was Erhard Seminars Training (EST), a self-help program that blended insights from psychology and mysticism. Founded by Werner Erhard (a former door-to-door seller of encyclopedias), the institute taught individuals to form images of themselves as successful and satisfied. Through sixty hours of intensive training involving playacting and humiliation, participants learned one major lesson: "You are the one and only source of your experience. You created it." In addition to emphasizing

self-esteem, the seminars taught the value of "power relationships"—that is, the importance of selecting friends or business colleagues who are compatible with one's own goals and ambitions. Priced at $400 for a series of two weekend sessions, EST peaked at 6,000 participants per month, grossing $25 million in revenue in 1980. In the San Francisco Bay Area, where Erhard had established his headquarters, one of every nine college graduates enrolled in EST. Typically white, single, middle class, and between the ages of twenty and forty-five, EST participants appeared to find in therapy what previous generations and other contemporaries found in religion.

Other popular therapies encouraged clients to "live in the present" and to "get in touch with" their body signals rather than make abstract plans for the future. The record-breaking best-seller *Open Marriage: A New Life Style for Couples* (1972), by Nena O'Neill and George O'Neill, for example, urged husbands and wives to stress "personal growth" and to search for "the true ME." Transcendental meditation (TM) promised a shortcut to mental tranquility and found numerous advocates among Wall Street brokers, Pentagon officials, and star athletes. Techniques of TM were taught in more than 200 special centers and practiced by a reputed 350,000 devotees.

Religious cults also formed in relatively large numbers during the 1970s. The Unification Church, founded by the Korean Reverend Sun Myung Moon, extracted intense personal loyalty from its youthful disciples. The parents of many of these disciples, however, were horrified by church practices, which included mass marriage ceremonies of couples selected for pairing by church leaders. Some desperate parents hired private detectives to "kidnap" their own children from the "Moonies." According to a 1977 Gallup survey, the Reverend Moon "elicited one of the most overwhelmingly negative responses ever reported by a major national poll." Moon's financial empire, which included hundreds of retail businesses and the *Washington Times*, a conservative daily newspaper, nevertheless proved very lucrative and kept his church solvent despite numerous lawsuits. By contrast, Jim Jones's People's Temple, a liberal interracial movement organized in the California Bay Area, ended in a mass murder and suicide when Jones induced more than 900 of his followers to drink cyanide-laced Kool-Aid in Guyana in 1978.

Popular music expressed and reinforced the self-absorption of the 1970s. The songs of community and hope that had been common in the late 1960s gave way to songs of despair or nihilism. Bruce Springsteen, whose lyrics lamented the disappearance of the white working class, became the decade's most popular new rock artist. At the same time, heavy metal bands such as Kiss, as well as "punk" and "new wave" artists underscored themes of decadence and drew crowds of mainly young white men to their concerts. At the other end of the popular music scale, country and western music hit its peak with mainstream sales or "crossover" hits, charismatic stars, and numerous new all-country and western radio stations. The songs of Willie Nelson, who was invited to perform at the White House by President Carter, evoked a sense of loneliness and nostalgia that appealed to older, white, working-class Americans.

ADJUSTING TO A NEW WORLD

In April 1975 the North Vietnamese struck Saigon and easily captured the city as the South Vietnamese army fell apart without U.S. assistance. All fighting stopped within a few weeks, and Saigon was renamed Ho Chi Minh City. The Vietnamese had finally triumphed over the French and Americans, and the nation was reunited under a government dominated by communists. For many Americans, this outcome underscored the futility of U.S. involvement.

By the mid-1970s a new realism prevailed in U.S. diplomacy. Presidents Ford and Carter, as well as their chief advisers, acknowledged that the cost of fighting the Vietnam War had been high, speeding the decline of the United States as the world's reigning superpower. The "realists" shared with dissatisfied nationalists a single goal: "No More Vietnams."

A Thaw in the Cold War

The military defeat in Vietnam forced the makers of U.S. foreign policy to reassess priorities. The United States must continue to defend its "vital interests," declared Ford's secretary of state Henry Kissinger, but must also recognize that "Soviet-American relations are not designed for tests of manhood." Both nations had experienced a relative decline of power in world affairs. And both were suffering from the already enormous and relentlessly escalating costs of sustaining a prolonged cold war.

At the close of World War II, the United States could afford to allocate huge portions of its ample economic resources to maintaining and enlarging its global interests. Soon, however, military and defense expenses began to grow at a much faster rate than the economy itself. Whereas the Korean War cost around $69.5 billion, the Vietnam War cost $172.2 billion. But the expenses of military conflicts accounted for only one portion of the defense budget. Clandestine operations, alliance building, spending for the United Nations and NATO, and weapons production accounted for trillions of dollars more. The Voice of America's network of radio stations, which broadcast

anticommunist propaganda abroad, cost $640 million in the 1970s alone.

Military spending at this level eventually took its toll on the American economy, especially as the federal government increasingly relied on deficit spending to cover the bill. The federal debt, which stood at $257 billion in 1950, had jumped to $908 billion by 1980, and an increasingly large part of the federal budget was devoted just to paying the interest on this debt. At the same time, military spending diverted funds from programs that could have strengthened the economy. The results were disastrous. While the United States endured falling productivity levels and rates of personal savings, rising high school dropout rates and a disappearing skilled workforce, other nations rushed ahead. In the 1970s, when Japan and West Germany had emerged as potent economic competitors, *Business Week* noted that the American "colossus" was "clearly facing a crisis of the decay of power."

Western European nations acted to nudge U.S. foreign policy away from its cold war premises.

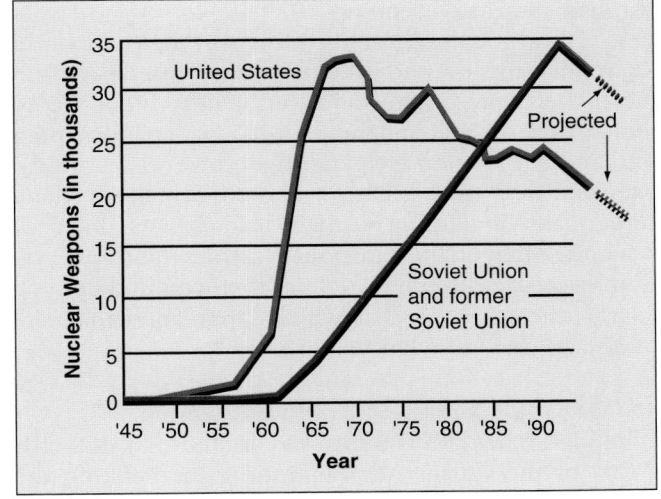

Nuclear Arsenals, the United States and the Soviet Union   *During the cold war, both superpowers built up huge stockpiles of nuclear weapons, including sea and land missiles. President Lyndon Johnson began negotiations with the Soviet Union in an attempt to slow down the perilous nuclear arms race. In 1972, the Strategic Arms Limitation Treaty (SALT) set limits on offensive intercontinental ballistic missiles. SALT II, negotiated by President Carter in 1979, called for further reductions but failed to win approval in the U.S. Senate. Negotiations resumed under President Reagan and culminated in 1991 in the Strategic Arms Reduction Treaty (START), which included plans for the destruction of the stockpile of nuclear weapons.*

Source: James Sterngold, "Milestones of the Nuclear Era," New York Times, December 1, 1992, p. C10. Copyright © The New York Times Company; Illustrations by Rebecca Perry and Martha Hernandez; and the Bulletin of the Atomic Scientists.

In 1975, in Helsinki, Finland, representatives of thirty-five nations approved the national boundaries drawn in eastern and western Europe after World War II, and in return the Soviet Union agreed to enact a more liberal human rights policy, including the loosening of restrictions on the emigration of Soviet Jews. Recognizing that the Soviet Union no longer posed a military threat to their national sovereignty—if indeed it ever had—Western leaders also sought to strengthen economic relations between the two major blocs.

The Soviet Union, whose economy suffered even greater setbacks from defense spending, joined the United States in moving toward détente. The signing of SALT I, the first Strategic Arms Limitation Treaty, during Nixon's administration, followed by the U.S. withdrawal from Vietnam, encouraged new efforts to negotiate on strategic arms control. In November 1974 Ford and Soviet leader Leonid Brezhnev met in Vladivostok to set the terms of SALT II, and Carter secured the final agreement in 1979. The treaty failed to win confirmation from the Senate, however, when the Soviet Union invaded Afghanistan in December, 1979.

Although repeated conflicts in the third world continued to slow the pace toward détente, leaders in both the United States and the Soviet Union recognized that their economic well-being depended on a reduction in defense spending. However haltingly, steps toward reconciliation had to be taken. Many Americans, including business leaders, welcomed or accepted this change in policy as inevitable. "If you think you can run the world and then you find out you can't," the aged journalist Walter Lippmann explained, "you withdraw to what you can run."

Foreign Policy and "Moral Principles"

The historian Gaddis Smith has argued that "the four years of the Carter Administration were among the most significant in the history of American foreign policy in the twentieth century" because each of Carter's major decisions confronted long-entrenched diplomatic policy. In fresh approaches to Latin America and the Middle East in particular, Carter emphasized regional solutions and human rights over "gunboat diplomacy" and competition with the Soviet Union. By the end of the Carter years, however, the familiar U.S. strategies had returned with a vengeance.

In 1977, when Carter took office, he happily admitted his lack of experience in foreign affairs and viewed it as an asset. "We've seen a loss of morality," he noted, "and we're ashamed." His policy would demonstrate "the decency and generosity and common sense of our own people," its "soul" an "absolute" commitment to human rights. Carter condemned policies that had allowed the United States to support "right-wing monarchs and military dictators" in the name of anticommunism. In 1976 a powerful human rights lobby had pressured Congress to pass a bill that required the secretary of state to report annually on the status of human rights in all countries receiving aid from the United States and to cut off assistance to any country with a record of "gross violations." Carter's secretary of state, Cyrus R. Vance, and the assistant secretary for human rights and humanitarian affairs, Pat Derrian, worked to punish or at least to censure repressive military regimes in Brazil, Argentina, and Chile. For the first time, leading U.S. diplomats spoke out against the South African white supremacist "Apartheid" regime rather than commending or quietly supporting that government's avid anticommunism.

But when it came to troubled nations considered vital to U.S. interests, such as South Korea, the Philippines, and several countries in Central America, Carter put aside human rights principles to support brutally antidemocratic governments. Likewise, in restoring diplomatic relations with the People's Republic of China in January 1979, Carter overlooked that nation's imprisonment of dissidents. "The real problem," a U.S. diplomat observed, was that human rights was "not a policy but an attitude." Carter hoped to persuade others without paying any real price for his administration's efforts. The Soviet Union dismissed his initiative as mere propaganda, and many world leaders treated it as typical American political rhetoric.

Carter did attempt, however, to institute reforms at the Central Intelligence Agency (CIA), especially to halt the blatant intervention in the affairs of foreign governments that many Americans found embarrassing after the Vietnam misadventure. Carter appointed Admiral Stansfield Turner, a Rhodes scholar, as the agency's new director and ordered a purge of the "rogue elephants" who had pursued massive covert operations in Southeast Asia. "The CIA must operate within the law," Carter insisted, and restrict its activities mostly to the process of intelligence gathering. Neither Congress nor the president had the determination to press these reforms, however. Limited in their effect, they would be reversed in later years.

Carter scored his biggest moral victory in foreign affairs by paving the way for Panama to assume the ownership, operation, and defense of the Panama Canal Zone. Negotiations with Panama had begun during Lyndon Johnson's administration, following riots by Panamanians against U.S. territorial rule of their country. Carter pressured the Senate to ratify new treaties in 1978 (by a vote of 68 to 32) that would give the Canal over to Panamanian control by the year 2000.

President Carter signs the Middle East Peace Treaty with Egyptian President Anwar Sadat and Israeli Prime Minister Menachem Begin, in Washington, D.C., March 1979. President Carter had invited both leaders to Camp David, the presidential retreat in Maryland, where for two weeks he mediated between them on territorial rights to the West Bank and Gaza Strip. Considered Carter's greatest achievement in foreign policy, the negotiations, known as the Camp David Peace Accords, resulted in not only the historic peace treaty but the Nobel Peace Prize for Begin and Sadat.

The Camp David Accords

Carter nearly triumphed in the Middle East, where U.S. policies had historically balanced military and diplomatic support of Israel with the quest for Arab oil. Following the Israeli victory in the Yom Kippur War of 1973, Henry Kissinger devoted two years to "shuttle diplomacy" between various regimes but could not resolve regional problems. Carter himself had little knowledge of the Middle East before taking over the presidency, although as a born-again Christian he had strong feelings about the "Holy Land." Early in his administration, Carter met privately with Israeli prime minister Menachem Begin to encourage conciliation with Egypt. When negotiations between the two countries stalled in 1978, Carter brought Begin together with Egyptian president Anwar el-Sadat for a planned three-day retreat at Camp David, Maryland, which lasted thirteen days and resulted in unprecedented agreements.

The Camp David Accords, signed in September 1978, set the formal terms for peace in the region. Egypt became the earliest Arab country to recognize Israel's right to exist, the two nations establishing mutual diplomatic relations for the first time since the founding of Israel in 1948. In return, Egypt regained control of the Sinai Peninsula, including important oil fields and airfields. Israel, however, was the biggest winner: it secured a virtual permanent guarantee of greatly enhanced U.S. military support, including three new air force bases that cost several billion dollars. Later in 1979, Begin and Sadat shared the Nobel Prize for Peace.

But disappointment lay ahead. Carter staked his hopes for regional peace on the final achievement of statehood, or at least political autonomy, for Palestinians in a portion of their former lands now occupied by the Israelis. As specified in the new Israeli-Egyptian treaty, Israel would return eventually to its approximate borders of 1967. Begin, who had said "My right eye will fall out, my right hand will fall off, before I ever agree to the dismantling of a single Jewish settlement," did dismantle Israeli settlements in the Sinai—but otherwise refused to budge.

Carter nevertheless continued to believe that the Camp David Accords had set the peace process in motion. He repeatedly pressed Begin to issue promises of Palestinian autonomy within the "Occupied Territories" of the West Bank and Gaza. Begin, however, announced more and more government-sponsored Jewish settlements expropriating Palestinian holdings. The final status of the Palestinians remained in limbo, and so did that of Jerusalem, which many Christians and Muslims felt should be an autonomous holy city, free of any direct government control. Sadat, frustrated and unable to halt Begin, grew increasingly isolated within the Arab world. In 1981, he was assassinated by Islamic fundamentalists. Meanwhile, a new regional war threatened in Lebanon where tens of thousands of Palestinian refugees had relocated.

Carter was only the second American standing president ever to visit the Middle East. But his focus on the region exaggerated his foreign policy failures, and his expressed sympathy for the Palestinian plight weakened his support among some traditionally Democratic Jewish constituencies in his bid for reelection.

CARTER'S "CRISIS OF CONFIDENCE"

Carter's modest victories in Middle East negotiations, as it turned out, marked the final high point of his presidency. By 1979 it was clear that his domestic program for economic recovery had failed. To reassess his priorities, Carter withdrew with his staff to Camp David in July and emerged ten days later with a series of new energy proposals that Congress later rejected. But in his first public speech after the retreat, the president struck a nerve. The nation was experiencing a "crisis of confidence," he complained, and a feeling of "paralysis and stagnation and drift" hung like a dark cloud over the land. He called upon the people to change their attitude, to stop wallowing in personal problems, and to show more faith in their leaders.

Carter's "malaise speech," as it was called, backfired. His public approval rating hardly rose again from its low point of 26 percent. Many Americans resented the president for heaping blame on the public instead of taking responsibility for his own failures. News analysts attacked Carter with zeal, breaking stories of minor scandals in his administration and ridiculing the president in various ways. Far from pleasing the public, Carter lost its respect. His prospects for reelection therefore appeared to rest on his conduct of international affairs. If he could only put his human rights policy on a firm ground, move toward lasting peace in the Middle East, or strike a bargain with the Soviets on arms limitation, he might restore voter confidence. If not, his presidency would end after a single term.

(Mis)Handling the Unexpected

As Carter's first term came to a close, several crises erupted in foreign affairs, and long-standing divisions within the State Department drew the president first one way and then the other in response to them. Secretary of State Cyrus Vance recommended well-planned negotiations to soothe Soviet-U.S. relations and resolve disagreements with third world nations. National Security Adviser Zbigniew Brzezinski, a bitterly anticommunist Polish exile, adhered to a cold war view and interpreted events in even remote sections of Africa or South America as plays in a zero-sum game: wherever the United States lost influence, the Soviet Union gained, and vice versa. Mired in problems inherited from his predecessors, the president found himself disoriented by contradictory advice.

In 1979 the brutal Nicaraguan dictatorship of Anastasio Somoza, a long-time ally of the United States, was overthrown by the revolutionary Sandinista Liberation Front (which took its name from Augustino Sandino, a popular leader who had led the resistance against U.S. occupation forces in the 1920s and 1930s, see Chapter 23). The Sandinistas were not the kind of moderate successor to Somoza that Carter would have preferred. Nonetheless, when they asked for financial help, the president requested $75 million in aid for Nicaragua, but Congress turned him down. The Sandinistas aligned Nicaragua with Cuba and the Soviet Union and began to assist a revolutionary movement in El Salvador against a repressive anticommunist regime supported by the United States. Carter continued to back the Salvadoran government despite atrocities attributed to its ultraright partisans, including the assassination of Catholic archbishop Oscar Romero, who supported the revolutionaries. Following the rape and murder of four U.S. Catholic church women, apparently by members of the ultraright Salvadoran armed forces, who had been trained in the United States, peace activists and other Americans pleaded with Carter to withhold further military aid. Conservatives meanwhile demanded yet more funds to bolster the regime.

Africa posed similarly perplexing problems. Emerging from colonial rule, African nations vacillated between allying with the United States and courting the Soviet Union. In this tricky political territory, UN ambassador (and former civil rights leader) Andrew Young, the first major African American diplomat assigned to Africa, scored an important victory when he persuaded oil-rich Nigeria to resume economic relations with the United States. But Young could not persuade Carter to recognize the antiapartheid

Iranians demonstrate against the United States, burning an American flag and waving signs declaring "The U.S. Is Our Enemy." The Iran hostage crisis, which began November 4, 1979, when a mob of Iranians seized the U.S. embassy in Tehran, contributed to Carter's defeat at the polls the following year. Fifty-two embassy employees were held hostage for 444 days.

government of Angola, which had invited 20,000 Cuban troops to help in its fight against South Africa. Nor did Carter's and Young's verbal criticisms of the South African regime, unaccompanied by economic sanctions, satisfy black Africans. Then, suddenly, Young was forced from office because he had met privately with officials of the Palestine Liberation Organization (PLO). The PLO, although an opponent of apartheid, was also an enemy of Israel, and the meeting exposed Carter to bitter congressional criticism. Without Young, Carter proved even less effective in negotiating with antiapartheid leaders.

Carter had once advised Americans to put their "inordinate fear of Communism" behind them in order to focus more clearly on the pressing problems of the third world. By 1979, however, events in Central America and Africa gave the fear of communism a new twist and caused relations between the United States and the Soviet Union, which supported these revolutionary movements, to slide backward.

The Soviet invasion of neighboring Afghanistan produced a major stalemate. Two Afghan military coups during the 1970s had troubled the Soviets, who feared

that the United States might forge an alliance with a new right-wing government and create yet another border fortified with U.S. missiles. After widespread rioting broke out, 30,000 Soviet troops invaded Afghanistan in December 1979 to prop up a communist government. The invasion precipitated a civil war between Islamic fundamentalist guerillas and the Soviet-backed government that was quickly labeled the "Russian Vietnam" by the American press. Despite their high-technology weapons, the Soviets were stymied by the guerillas, who were intimately familiar with their territory and armed by the United States. As the war bogged down, stories of disillusionment and drug use reminiscent of Vietnam emerged, but this time involving Soviet soldiers. The United States called for an immediate withdrawal of Soviet troops.

President Carter responded to these events with his own corollary to the Monroe Doctrine. The so-called Carter Doctrine asserted U.S. determination to protect its interests in yet another area of the world, the Persian Gulf. Carter acted on the advice of Brzezinski, who believed that the Soviet Union would soon try to secure for itself a warm-water port on the gulf, an area rich in oil and now vital to U.S. interests. The president backed up his policy by halting exports of grain and high technology to the Soviet Union, asking American athletes to boycott the 1980 Olympic Games in Moscow, reinstituting registration for the military draft in the United States, and beginning what would become a massive U.S. arms buildup during the 1980s.

By the end of Carter's term, the cold war had once again heated up. In his State of the Union Address in January 1980, Carter pledged that "the United States will remain the strongest of all nations." With the economy still hurting from the effects of cold war spending, Carter called for yet another increase in the military budget. He also signed Presidential Directive 59, which guaranteed the production of weapons necessary to win a prolonged nuclear war. The prospect of peace and détente dried up.

The Iran Hostage Crisis

On November 4, 1979, Iranian fundamentalists seized the U.S. embassy in Tehran; for the next 444 days they held fifty-two embassy employees hostage. This event made President Carter's previous problems seem small by comparison. "I-R-A-N," Rosalynn Carter later wrote. "Those four letters had become a curse to me."

For decades, U.S. foreign policy in the Middle East had depended on a friendly government in Iran. After the CIA had helped to overthrow the reformist, constitutional government of Prime Minister Mohammed Mossadegh and restored Shah Mohammed Reza Pahlavi to the throne in 1953, millions of U.S. dollars poured into the Iranian economy and the shah's armed forces. By the late 1970s, Iran had become the most Westernized society in the Middle East. President Carter toasted the shah for his "great leadership" and overlooked the rampant corruption in the Iranian government and a well-organized opposition led by the Islamic fundamentalist Ayatollah Ruholla Khomeini. Revolutionary unrest erupted in 1978, and in January 1979, the shah was forced to flee the country.

After Carter allowed the deposed shah to enter the United States to be treated for cancer in November, a group of Khomeini's followers retaliated by storming the U.S. embassy and taking the staff as hostages. Islamic fundamentalists paraded in the streets of Tehran waving placards with anti-American and anti-Carter slogans and calling the United States "the Great Satan."

Cyrus Vance assured Carter that only negotiations could free the Americans while Brzezinski lobbied for decisive action. Carter, beginning his reelection campaign, ordered a nighttime helicopter rescue mission, but decided to abort it when it encountered mechanical problems and a sandstorm. One helicopter crashed, leaving eight Americans dead; their burned corpses were displayed in television broadcasts by the enraged Iranians. Short of an all-out attack, which surely would have resulted in the hostages' death, the United States had used up its options.

The political and economic fallout was heavy. Cyrus Vance resigned, the first secretary of state in sixty-five years to leave office over a political difference with the president. By supporting the shah, whose secret police were notorious for their brutality, Carter had violated his own human rights policy, which was to have been his distinctive mark on U.S. foreign affairs. He had also failed in the one area he had pronounced to be central to the future of the United States—energy. During the hostage crisis, as the price of oil rose by 60 percent, inflation once again soared.

The 1980 Election

Jimmy Carter began his campaign for renomination and reelection in what seemed to be the worst possible light. The *Wall Street Journal* commented in August 1980 that "one continues to look in vain for anything beyond his own reflection that he wants to accomplish with the power of his office, for any consistent purpose or vision." Carter had no significant accomplishments to stand on, not even a program for the future. His Democratic rival from 1976, Washington Senator Henry Jackson, described him as "washed up."

One more surprise dogged Carter. During May, Fidel Castro invited thousands of Cubans, including political prisoners and petty criminals, to leave the island. Dubbed the *Marielitos,"* (because they left the Cuban port of Mariel), these Cuban refugees landed in Florida and demanded asylum. Unable to convince them to leave and unwilling to deport them, Carter established camps that were, according to the inmates, inhumane. Many Americans meanwhile demanded the return of "the boat people" to Cuba. Unconvincingly, Carter answered, "We ought to be thankful we have a country that people want to come to."

Carter's bid for renomination depended more on his incumbency than on his popularity. Delegates at the Democratic National Convention unenthusiastically endorsed Carter along with his running mate Walter Mondale, a similarly uninspiring campaigner. The Republicans nominated former California governor Ronald Reagan, who had come close to displacing Gerald Ford in 1976. Former CIA director and Texas oil executive George Bush, more moderate than Reagan, became the Republican candidate for vice president. Moral Majority placed itself squarely in Reagan's camp, promising a "conservative revolu-

CHRONOLOGY

1973	*Roe v. Wade* legalizes abortion
	Arab embargo sparks oil crisis in the United States
	Construction of Alaska oil pipeline begins
1974	Richard Nixon resigns presidency; Gerald Ford takes office
	President Ford pardons Nixon and introduces anti-inflation program
	Community Development Act funds programs for urban improvement
	Coalition of Labor Union Women is formed
1975	Unemployment rate reaches nearly 9 percent
	South Vietnamese government falls to communists
	Antibusing protests break out in Boston
	New York City government declares itself bankrupt
1976	Percentage of African Americans attending college peaks at 9.3 percent and begins a decline
	Hyde Amendment restricts use of Medicaid funds for abortions
	Tom Wolfe declares "the Me Decade"
	James Earl Carter is elected president
1977	President Carter announces human rights as major tenet in foreign policy

Department of Energy is established

1978 *Bakke v. University of California* decision places new limits on affirmative action programs

Senator Edward Kennedy calls attention to "a permanent under-class"

Panama Canal Treaties arrange for turning the canal over to Panama by 2000

Camp David meeting sets terms for Middle East Peace

California passes Proposition 13, cutting taxes and government social programs

1979 Three Mile Island nuclear accident threatens a meltdown

Moral Majority is formed

SALT II treaty is signed in Vienna but later stalls in the Senate

Nicaraguan Revolution overthrows Anastasio Somoza

Iranian fundamentalists seize the U.S. embassy in Tehran and hold hostages 444 days

Soviets invade Afghanistan

Equal Rights Amendment, three states short of ratification, gets a three-year extension but eventually dies anyway

1980 United States boycotts Olympic Games in Moscow

Inflation reaches 13.5 percent

Ronald Reagan is elected president

---

tion" to end legal abortion, reinstate school prayer, and bear down on communism. Senator Jesse Helms's Congressional Club contributed $4.6 million to the Reagan campaign and funded strident campaigns targeting senatorial liberals.

The Republican campaign made the most of Carter's mismanagement of both domestic and foreign affairs. Reagan repeatedly asked voters, "Are you better off now than you were four years ago?" Although critics questioned Reagan's competence, the attractive, soft-spoken actor shrugged off criticisms while spotlighting the many problems besetting the country.

The Republican ticket cruised to victory. Carter won only 41.2 percent of the popular vote to Reagan's 50.9 percent, 49 votes in the electoral college to Reagan's 489. Liberal Republican John Anderson, running as an independent, won nearly 6 million votes, or 6.6 percent of the popular vote. The Republicans won control of the Senate for the first time since 1952 and with the largest majority since 1928. Still, most Americans remained apathetic toward the electoral process. Barely half of the eligible voters turned out in the 1980 election, bringing Ronald Reagan into office with a thin mandate of 25 percent.

CONCLUSION

Gerald Ford's failure to set a new course either domestically or internationally had completed the Republican debacle of Richard Nixon's administration. Democrat Jimmy Carter, elected to office on a promise to restore public confidence in government, suffered repeated embarrassments and political defeats. Hopeful signs appeared mainly in local communities in the form of campaigns for better schools, neighborhoods, and protection from toxic wastes. Grass-roots activism cut across political lines. At the national level, an unprecedented number of voters disengaged from the process and seemed to suffer from a deep malaise about the machinations of government.

As Carter's tenure in office came to a close, the economic problems that concerned most Americans were exacerbated still further by military spending and dependence on foreign oil. The focus of U.S. foreign policy had begun to shift from the Soviet Union to the Middle East, where diplomatic maneuvers brought neither national security nor a fresh supply of low-cost crude oil. The erosion of America's industrial base meanwhile mirrored the nation's decline from unquestioned superpower status. Like the Soviet Union, the United States had paid too much for the cold war.

REVIEW QUESTIONS

1. Discuss the impact of the accident at the Three Mile Island nuclear plant on communities in the eastern states. How did fears generated by the near meltdown combine with anxieties provoked by the oil crisis?

2. Evaluate the significance of the major population shifts in the United States from the 1940s through the 1970s. How do these shifts relate to changes in the American economy? What was their impact on local and national politics?

3. Discuss the character of the "new poverty" of the 1970s. Why did the poor comprise mainly women and children?

4. Discuss the connections between the energy crisis and the rise of the environmental movement during the 1970s.

5. Why was the 1970s dubbed "the Me Decade"? Interpret the decline of liberalism and the rise of conservative political groups. How did these changes affect Carter's role as president and his chances for reelection?

6. Was the Iran hostage crisis a turning point in American politics or only a thorn in Carter's reelection campaign?

RECOMMENDED READING

Peter N. Carroll, *It Seemed Like Nothing Happened* (1983). A broad overview of the 1970s, including its political and cultural aspects. Carroll captures the everyday lives of Americans, especially their frustrations over their failure to achieve according to their expectations, and finds a bitter comedy in the blunders of the era's mediocre political leaders.

Susan M. Hartmann, *From Margin to Mainstream: American Women and Politics since 1960* (1989). An interpretation of women's growing role in American politics. Hartmann analyzes the important developments of the 1970s, most pointedly women's influence on the Democratic Party, and looks at the forces that pushed the Equal Rights Amendment through Congress but failed to see it ratified in the states.

Jerome L. Himmelstein, *To the Right: The Transformation of American Conservatism* (1990). The story of the decline of "Old Right" fiscal conservatives, isolationists, and Republican "centrists" during the 1970s and the rise of the "New Right" based in evangelical Protestantism. Himmelstein analyzes the New Right's ability to rally support for cold war foreign policy and the rollback of social welfare programs at both federal and state levels of government.

Michael B. Katz, *Improving Poor People: The Welfare State, the "Underclass," and Urban Schools as History* (1995). Provides a broad overview of the history of urban poverty, welfare policy, and public education. Katz examines the "underclass" debates of the 1970s as a function of the interaction between politics and economics within the postindustrial inner city.

William B. Quandt, *Camp David: Peacemaking and Politics* (1986). An insider's story of Jimmy Carter's greatest triumph. Quandt analyzes the Middle Eastern diplomacy as the centerpiece of Carter's otherwise unsuccessful program of world peace through negotiations and better understanding.

Edwin Schur, *The Awareness Trap: Self Absorption Instead of Social Change* (1977). A description of the various contemporary "awareness" movements. Schur includes detailed examples of how programs of self-improvement and religious mysticism appealed to people disoriented by social change and willing to pay money to find "meaning" in their lives.

James L. Sundquist, *The Decline and Resurgence of Congress* (1981). A close political study of changing relations between the two key branches of government. Sundquist underlines the revival of congressional strength after President Johnson's successful broadening of executive powers and the bipartisan tug of war that took place between Congress and its 1970s counterparts: the often haughty Nixon, the congressional-style "weak" president Gerald Ford, and the distant Jimmy Carter.

Andrew Szasz, *EcoPopulism: Toxic Waste and the Movement for Environmental Justice* (1994). A careful analysis of

a turning point in federal regulation of toxic waste. Szasz shows how the prevention of pollution, previously considered a local issue, through strengthened state and federal regulations became a national issue and a springboard for the environmental movement.

Cyrus R. Vance, *Hard Choices: Critical Years of America's Foreign Policy* (1983). A former secretary of state's day-to-day recollections of his time in office during the Carter years. Vance, a career diplomat, reviews the crucial policy decisions concerning Afghanistan and the Middle East as well as the factors that caused him to resign from the Carter administration.

Winifred D. Wandersee, *On the Move: American Women in the 1970s* (1988). A highly readable overview of the changes that brought American women into political life but also kept them at the margins of power. This study includes a close description of the National Organization for Women as well as media personalities, such as Jane Fonda, who gave feminism a public face.

ADDITIONAL BIBLIOGRAPHY

Stagflation and the Oil Crisis

Michael A. Bernstein and David E. Adler, eds., *Understanding American Economic Decline* (1994)

Gordon L. Clark, *Unions and Communities under Siege* (1989)

Sara M. Evans and Barbara J. Nelson, *Wage Justice: Comparable Worth and the Paradox of Technocratic Reform* (1989)

Daniel F. Ford, *Three Mile Island: 30 Minutes to Meltdown* (1982)

Claudia Goldin, *Understanding the Gender Gap: An Economic History of American Women* (1990)

Burton I. Kaufman, *The Arab Middle East and the United States: Inter-Arab Rivalry and Superpower Diplomacy* (1996)

Robert Leppzer, *Voices from Three Mile Island* (1980)

Emma Rothschild, *Paradise Lost: The Decline of the Auto-Industrial Age* (1973)

Bruce J. Schulman, *From Cotton Belt to Sun Belt* (1990)

Richard Sherrill, *The Oil Follies of 1970–1980* (1983)

Jeffrey K. Stine, *Mixing the Waters: Environmental Politics and the Building of the Tennessee-Tombigbee Waterway* (1993)

Jon Teaford, *Cities of the Heartland: The Rise and Fall of the Industrial Midwest* (1993)

"Lean Year" Presidents

Richard J. Barnet, *The Lean Years* (1980)

George C. Edwards III, *At the Margins: Presidential Leadership of Congress* (1989)

Charles O. Jones, *The Trusteeship Presidency: Jimmy Carter and the United States Congress* (1988)

Burton I. Kaufman, *The Presidency of James Earl Carter, Jr.* (1993)

Alexander P. Lamis, *The Two-Party South*, 2d ed. (1990)

Gary Sick, *October Surprise* (1991)

Alan Ware, *The Breakdown of the Democratic Party Organization, 1940–1980* (1985)

The New Poverty

Chicago Tribune, *The American Millstone: An Examination of the Nation's Permanent Underclass* (1986)

James D. Cockcroft, *Outlaws in the Promised Land: Mexican Immigrant Workers and America's Future* (1986)

Barbara Ehrenreich, *Fear of Falling: The Inner Life of the Middle Class* (1989)

Jacqueline Jones, *The Dispossessed: America's Underclasses from the Civil War to the Present* (1992)

Michael B. Katz, ed., *The "Underclass" Debate* (1993)

Ruth Sidel, *The Plight of Poor Women in Affluent America* (1986)

Lenore J. Weitzman, *The Divorce Revolution: The Unexpected Social and Economic Consequences for Women and Children in America* (1985)

William Julius Wilson, *The Declining Significance of Race: Blacks and Changing American Institutions*, rev. ed. (1980)

Grass-roots Politics and the New Conservatism

Carl Abbott, *The New Urban America: Growth and Politics in the Sunbelt Cities* (1987)

Henry F. Bedford, *Seabrook Station: Citizen Politics and Nuclear Power* (1990)

Steve Bruce, *The Rise and Fall of the New Christian Right* (1988)

Pamela Johnston Conover and Virginia Gray, *Feminism and the New Right: Conflict over the American Family* (1983)

Craig Cox, *Storefront Revolution: Food Co-ops and the Counterculture* (1994)

Robert M. Entman, *Democracy without Citizens: Media and the Decay of American Politics* (1989)

Marian Faux, *Roe v. Wade* (1988)

Suzanne Garment, *Scandal: The Crisis of Mistrust in American Politics* (1991)

Joan Hoff-Wilson, ed., *Rights of Passage: The Past and Future of the ERA* (1986)

Rebecca Klatch, *Women of the New Right* (1987)

Michael C. D. MacDonald, *America's Cities: A Report on the Myth of the Urban Renaissance* (1984)

Nicol C. Rae, *The Decline and Fall of the Liberal Republicans* (1989)

Suzanne Staggenborg, *The Pro-Choice Movement: Organization and Activism in the Abortion Conflict* (1991)

Steven M. Tipton, *Getting Saved from the Sixties* (1982)

William Clyde Wilcox, *God's Warriors: The Christian Right in Twentieth-Century America* (1992)

Robert Wuthnow, *The Restructuring of American Religion* (1988)

Foreign Policy

Warren Christopher, et al., *American Hostages in Iran* (1985)

Walter LaFeber, *The Panama Canal* (1978, 1989)

Morris Morley, *Washington, Somoza and the Sandinistas: State and Regime in U.S. Policy toward Nicaragua, 1969–1981* (1994)

A. Glenn Mower Jr., *Human Rights and American Foreign Policy* (1987)

Nancy Peabody Newell and Richard S. Newell, *The Struggle for Afghanistan* (1981)

Robert A. Pastor, *Condemned to Repetition* (1987)

Lars Schoultz, *Human Rights and U.S. Policy toward Latin America* (1981)

Sandy Vogelgesang, *American Dream, Global Nightmare* (1980)

Biography

Peter Carroll, *Famous in America: Jane Fonda, George Wallace, and Phyllis Schlafly* (1986)

Jimmy Carter, *Keeping Faith: Memoirs of a President/Jimmy Carter* (1982, 1995)

Rosalynn Carter, *First Lady from Plains* (1984)

Betty Ford, with Chris Chase, *Betty, a Glad Awakening* (1987)

Ernest B. Furgurson, *The Hard Right: The Rise of Jesse Helms* (1986)

Carolyn G. Heilbrun, *The Education of a Woman: A Life of Gloria Steinem* (1995)

John C. Jeffries, *Justice Lewis F. Powell, Jr.* (1994)

David S. McLellan, *Cyrus Vance* (1985)

Kenneth E. Morris, *Jimmy Carter: American Moralist* (1996)

Richard Reeves, *A Ford and not a Lincoln* (1975)

Kenneth S. Stern, *Loud Hawk: The United States versus the American Indian Movement* (1994)

$\mathcal{C}$HAPTER THIRTY-ONE

THE CONSERVATIVE ASCENDANCY

SINCE 1980

Computerizing Liberty and Sunset Liberty

AMERICAN COMMUNITIES
Virtual Communities
on the Electronic Frontier

When the moving van carrying lawyer Mike Godwin's possessions across the country from Cambridge, Massachusetts, to Washington state caught fire, most of his belongings were destroyed. In a new city, with a new job, Godwin felt uprooted and alone. "I didn't know my new neighbors in Washington," he recalled, "but I knew who my cyberspace neighbors were." Godwin turned to his neighbors on the Whole Earth 'Lectronic Link (WELL), an electronic community of 8,000 based in Sausalito, California. Using his personal computer, Godwin posted news of his misfortune, including a list of books he had lost, books he had been collecting since his youth "And for the next six months," he reported, "not a day went by that I didn't get a book, or a box of books, in the mail."

Cyberspace is the conceptual region occupied by people linked through computers and communications networks. It began with ARPANET, the first computer network, which was created by the Department of Defense in the early 1970s. Computer enthusiasts known as "hackers" created unexpected grass-roots spin-offs from ARPANET, including electronic mail, computer conferencing, and computer bulletin board systems.

In the mid-1980s the boom in cheap personal computers capable of linking to the worldwide telecommunications network began a population explosion in cyberspace. By then tens of thousands of researchers and scholars at universities and in private industry were linked to the Internet—the U.S. government-sponsored successor to ARPANET—through their institutions' computer centers. "Virtual communities" emerged from the Internet (or Net) whenever a group of users with a common interest reached a critical mass.

By 1998 there were more than 40 million cybercitizens in a variety of thriving virtual communities that suggested both the democratic and exploitative possibilities of cyberspace. WELL, for example, began in 1985 as a spin-off of the Whole Earth Review, a magazine with deep roots in the counterculture and ecology movements of the 1960s. Among its original goals were to make it easier for people in the San Francisco Bay area to communicate with each other, to provide sophisticated computer conferencing services, and to provide users who wanted it with electronic mail. Users were charged a small monthly fee plus an hourly rate for the time they spent "online." WELL initially attracted adventurous Bay area computer professionals and journalists, many of whom were given free accounts in exchange for "hosting" conversations. Passionate fans of the rock group the Grateful Dead—known as "Deadheads"—provided another early base of users.

WELL's subscriber list soon grew to the thousands. "What it is is up to us," became the motto of this virtual community. In scores of "public conferences" members of the WELL exchanged information on a wide range of topics under headings such as arts and letters, recreation, parenting, social responsibility and politics, body-mind-health, computers, and, of course, the Grateful Dead. Admission to "private conferences," which covered an equally broad range of subjects, was restricted to those invited by conference hosts. WELL was unusual among virtual communities in that it had a strong geographic locus, the Bay Area, making it easy for members to meet "I.T.R.W."— in the real world—if they chose. "We rent a nice site under the Golden Gate Bridge once a month and sort of see what happens," said Gail Williams, WELL's conferencing manager. As many as 500 people showed up for these gatherings.

Anger, feuds, and "flaming" with abusive interchanges were not unknown among WELL subscribers. But the sense of communal support was strong. For many the virtual community replaced more traditional centers of community like neighborhood, church, and family. Those who faced illness or loss were consoled by "beams" from electronic well-wishers. Howard Rheingold, one WELL pioneer, attributed its appeal to "the hunger for community that grows in the breasts of people around the world as more and more informal public spaces disappear from our real lives." WELL also posed a challenge to corporate-dominated communications media, and it offered a model for revitalizing citizen-based democracy.

Other services, such as Prodigy, Compuserve, and America Online, provided powerful alternatives to the utopian WELL. These nationwide services evolved not from the grass roots but from corporate efforts to commercialize cyberspace. By the mid-1990s each counted between 500,000 and 2 million subscribers. Unlike WELL, they emphasized consumer services over interactive communication. Prodigy, a joint venture of IBM and Sears, cost nearly $1 billion to launch. For a flat monthly fee Prodigy users could play games, make airplane reservations, send electronic mail, and discuss issues in public forums. They also received a steady stream of advertising and had to agree to give Prodigy the right to edit public messages.

By blurring the lines between the public and private spheres, virtual communities created a whole new set of legal, political, and ethical issues that have yet to be fully resolved. In 1995 Congress passed the Communications Decency Act, which imposed jail terms and fines on those who created or solicited online material deemed "obscene, lewd, lascivious, filthy, or indecent."

But in 1997 a unanimous Supreme Court found the act unconstitutional because it abridged the freedom of speech protected by the First Amendment. Noting that "the growth of the Internet has been and continues to be phenomenal," Justice John Paul Stevens' opinion argued that "we presume that governmental regulation of the content of speech is more likely to interfere with the free exchange of ideas than to encourage it." Those who worried about protecting children from "cyberporn" looked to new "gateway" technologies, which would allow parents to block out offensive material from their computers. But free speech advocates and the Internet industry continued to argue that no law can effectively monitor and regulate content on the global web without compromising fundamental freedoms.

Perhaps more ominous than the threat of legal restrictions on the internet is the Orwellian flip side of the utopian dream of virtual community. The same technology that permits citizens to communicate in new ways also opens them to government and corporate surveillance. As more and more intimate and private data about individuals moves into cyberspace, the potential for abuse of that information increases.

Virtual communities are still in their infancy. They will continue to evolve as more Americans join them, but the forms they take and the solutions to the problems they pose resist easy prediction. Can the democratic promise of cyberspace be fulfilled, for example, if poverty or lack of education bar a substantial part of the American population from access to computer technology? Even WELL experienced discontent and grumbling as growth created crowded, impersonal conferences and overloaded the system's technical infrastructure. In 1994 the nonprofit organization that founded WELL sold it to California businessman Bruce Katz, who had made a fortune manufacturing Rockport shoes. The relentless commercialization of cyberspace accelerated in the late 1990s as millions of businesses explored the profit potential of selling goods and services over the Internet. By 1998 there were some 320 million Web sites in the United States, representing everything from large corporations to fringe political groups to personal "home pages." At the close of the twentieth century, more and more Americans were finding—and inventing—versions of community on the electronic frontier of cyberspace.

KEY TOPICS

- Domestic policies under the Reagan administration

- Reagan era foreign policy: Soviet Union, Central America, Middle East

- Structural shifts in the economy and culture of the 1980s

- The growth of inequality

- The new immigration

- Contradictions and difficulties attending America's role in world affairs

- The Clinton presidency and the resurgent right

THE REAGAN REVOLUTION

No other twentieth-century president except Franklin D. Roosevelt left as deep a personal imprint on American politics as Ronald Reagan. Ironically, Reagan himself began his political life as an ardent New Deal Democrat. Even after his transformation into a conservative Republican, Reagan regularly invoked the words and deeds of FDR. Reagan admired Roosevelt as an inspirational leader who had led the nation through depression and war. But by the time he entered the White House in 1981, Reagan had rejected the activist welfare state legacy of the New Deal era. Following his overwhelming electoral victories in 1980 and 1984, Reagan and his conservative allies tried to radically reshape the political and social landscape of the nation.

The Great Communicator

Ronald Reagan was born in 1911 and raised in the small town of Dixon, Illinois. His father, a salesman, was an alcoholic who had a tough time holding a job. His strong-willed mother was a fundamentalist Christian who kept the family together despite frequent moves. During the Great Depression his father obtained a Works Progress Administration (WPA) job that helped the family survive hard times. As a child, Reagan learned to disconnect himself from the difficult scenes at home, withdrawing into himself. He took refuge in his own world of imaginary stories and plays. He identified with real-life sports heroes like Babe Ruth and Jack Dempsey as well as with fictional figures, heroes of the Wild West. Encouraged by his mother, Reagan began acting in church plays and in productions at Eureka College, from which he graduated in 1932.

In 1937 Reagan made a successful screen test with the Warner Brothers studio in Hollywood, beginning an acting career that lasted for a quarter-century. He was never a big star, appearing in scores of mostly

"B" movies, but he became a skilled actor. On screen, he was tall, handsome, and affable, and his characters usually projected an optimistic and sunny personality. In later years, Reagan cheerfully credited his political

Ronald and Nancy Reagan at the Inaugural Ball, January 20, 1981. The Reagans, supported by a circle of wealthy conservative friends from the business world and Hollywood, brought a lavish style to the White House that helped define the culture of the 1980s.

success to his acting experience. He told one interviewer: "An actor knows two important things—to be honest in what he's doing and to be in touch with the audience. That's not bad advice for a politician either. My actor's instincts simply told me to speak the truth as I saw it and felt it."

In Hollywood, Reagan became active in union affairs. While serving as president of the Screen Actors Guild from 1947 to 1952, he became a leader of the anticommunist forces in Hollywood and began to distance himself from New Deal liberalism. In 1954 Reagan became the host of a new national television program, *General Electric Theater,* and began a long stint as a national spokesman for GE. He toured GE plants and surrounding communities across the country, publicizing the TV show and making speeches on behalf of the company. These talks celebrated the achievements of corporate America and emphasized the dangers of big government, excessive liberalism, and radical trade unions.

Reagan's GE experience made him a significant public figure and allowed him to perfect a political style and a conservative message. He switched his party affiliation to the Republicans and became a popular fund-raiser and speaker for the California GOP. Reagan took a leading role in conservative Republican Barry Goldwater's 1964 presidential campaign. A televised address on Goldwater's behalf thrust Reagan himself to national prominence. By this time, Reagan had formulated a standard speech that hammered home his conservative message: antitax, anticommunism, antigovernment. The attack on big government was at the core of the Reagan message. He lashed out at the growing government bureaucracy and celebrated the achievements of entrepreneurs unfettered by governmental regulation or aid. He invoked the nation's founders, who, he claimed, knew "that outside of its legitimate functions, government does nothing as well or as economically as the private sector of the economy."

A group of wealthy, conservative southern Californians encouraged Reagan to run for office himself. These backers, most of whom had made fortunes in California real estate and the oil business, saw themselves as self-made men and shared a basic distrust of government intervention in the economy. With their financial and political support, Reagan defeated Democratic governor Edmund G. Brown in 1966 and won reelection in 1970. As governor, Reagan cut the state welfare rolls, placed limits on the number of state employees, and funneled a large share of state tax revenues back to local governments. He vigorously attacked student protesters and black militants, thereby tapping into the conservative backlash against the activism of the 1960s.

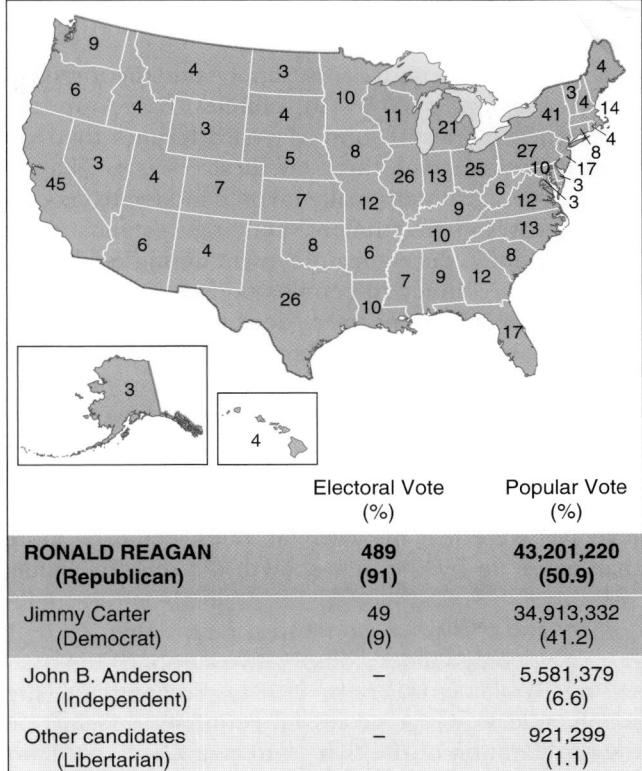

	Electoral Vote (%)	Popular Vote (%)
RONALD REAGAN (Republican)	**489 (91)**	**43,201,220 (50.9)**
Jimmy Carter (Democrat)	49 (9)	34,913,332 (41.2)
John B. Anderson (Independent)	–	5,581,379 (6.6)
Other candidates (Libertarian)	–	921,299 (1.1)

The Election of 1980   *Ronald Reagan won a landslide victory over incumbent Jimmy Carter, who managed to carry only six states and the District of Columbia. Reagan attracted millions of traditionally Democratic voters to the Republican camp.*

As governor, Reagan also perfected a laid-back style of governing that left most of the actual work to his aides and allowed him to concentrate on speech making and fund-raising. In 1980 he became the Republican candidate for president after failing to win the nomination in 1968 and 1976. Exploiting his strengths as an actor and salesman, he was an extremely likable and effective campaigner. The conservatism that had been forced to the backwaters of American politics in 1964 now reemerged as the mainstream. Jimmy Carter's political weakness also helped the Republicans to carry the Senate for the first time since 1952. When Reagan entered the White House in January 1981, his supporters confidently predicted that the "Reagan revolution" would usher in a new age in American political life.

Reaganomics

In the 1980 election Republicans successfully exploited popular discontent over the stagflation of the Carter years—an unprecedented combination of recession, high inflation, and the highest interest rates in American history. During the Reagan presidency, supply-side economic theory, dubbed "Reaganomics," dominated the administration's thinking and helped redirect American economic policy.

Since the mid-1970s, supply-side theorists had urged a sharp break with policies based on the economic theories of John Maynard Keynes that had been dominant since the New Deal era (see Chapter 24). Keynesians traditionally favored moderate tax cuts and increases in government spending to stimulate the economy and reduce unemployment during recessions. Putting more money in people's pockets, they argued, would increase consumer demand and stimulate economic expansion. By contrast, supply-siders called for simultaneous tax cuts and reductions in public spending. This combination, they claimed, would give private entrepreneurs and investors greater incentives to start businesses, take risks, invest capital—and thereby create new wealth and jobs. Whatever revenues were lost in lower tax rates would be more than made up by the new growth. At the same time, spending cuts would keep the federal deficit under control and thereby keep interest rates down.

George Gilder, conservative author of the best-selling *Wealth and Poverty* (1981), summarized the supply-side view: "A successful economy depends on the proliferation of the rich." Perceiving entrepreneurs as the heroes of the American economy, Gilder concluded, "To help the poor and middle classes, one must cut the taxes of the rich." On the political level, supply-siders looked to reward the most loyal Republican constituencies: the affluent and the business community. At the same time, they hoped to reduce the flow of federal dollars received by two core Democratic constituencies: the recipients and professional providers of health and welfare programs.

Reagan quickly won approval for two key pieces of legislation based on these ideas. The Economic Recovery Tax Act of 1981, passed by a very willing Congress, cut income and corporate taxes by $747 billion over five years. For individuals, the act cut taxes across the board by 5 percent in 1981, 10 percent in 1982, and another 10 percent in 1983. It also reduced the maximum tax on all income from 70 percent to 50 percent, lowered the maximum capital gains tax—the tax paid on profitable investments—from 28 percent to 20 percent, and eliminated the distinction between earned and unearned income. This last measure proved a boon to the small and richest fraction of the population, which derives most of its income from rent, dividends, and interest instead of from wages.

With the help of conservative southern and western Democrats in the House, the administration also pushed through a comprehensive program of spending cuts awkwardly known as the Omnibus Reconciliation Act of 1981. This bill mandated cuts of $136 billion in federal spending for the period 1982–84, affecting more than 200 social and cultural programs. The hardest-hit areas included federal appropriations for education, the environment, health, housing, urban aid, food stamps, research on synthetic fuels, and the arts. The conservative coalition in the House allowed only one vote on the entire package of spending cuts, a strategy that allowed conservatives to slash appropriations for a wide variety of domestic programs in one fell swoop. One leading House liberal, Democrat Leon Panetta of California, lamented: "We are dealing with over 250 programs with no committee consideration, no committee hearings, no debate and no opportunity to offer amendments."

The Reagan administration quickly created a chilly atmosphere for organized labor. In the summer of 1981 some 13,000 members of the Professional Air Traffic Controllers Organization (PATCO) went on strike. As federal employees, PATCO members had been bargaining with the government. The president retaliated against the strikers by firing them, and the Federal Aviation Administration started a crash program to replace them. Conservative appointees to the National Labor Relations Board and the federal courts set an anti-union tone throughout the government. The militantly antilabor mood in Washington, combined with the decline of the nation's manufacturing infrastructure, kept trade unions on the defensive. By 1990 fewer than 15 percent of American workers belonged to a labor union, the lowest proportion since before World War II.

Reagan appointed conservatives to head the Environmental Protection Agency, the Occupational Safety and Health Administration, and the Consumer Product Safety Commission. These individuals abolished or weakened hundreds of rules governing environmental protection, workplace safety, and consumer protection, all in the interest of increasing the efficiency and productivity of business. The deregulatory fever dominated cabinet departments as well. Secretary of the Interior James Watt typified the administration's desire to privatize the federal government, opening up formerly protected wilderness areas and wetlands to private developers. Secretary of Transportation Andrew L. "Drew" Lewis Jr. eliminated regulations passed in the 1970s aimed at reducing air pollution and improving fuel efficiency in cars and trucks.

The Reagan administration aggressively curbed the federal government's regulatory authority in the business sphere as well. Following the tenets of supply-side economics, Reagan weakened the Antitrust Division of the Justice Department, the Securities and Exchange Commission, and the Federal Home Loan Bank Board. Large corporations,

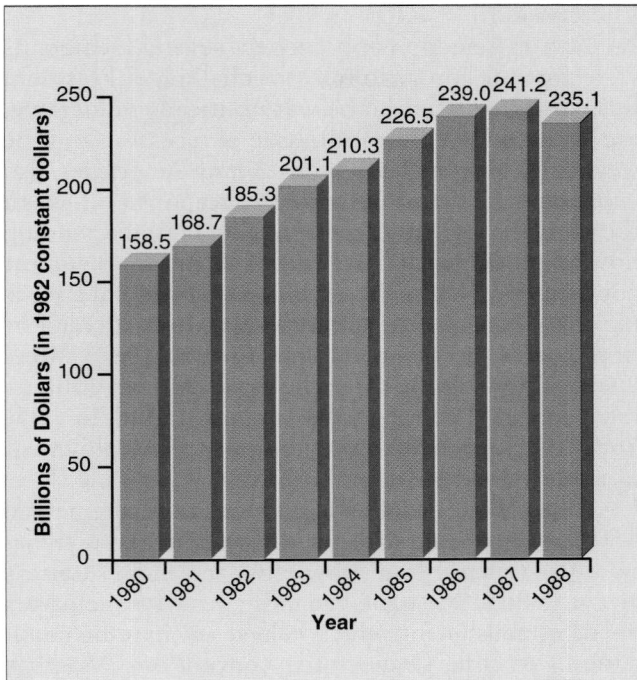

U.S. Military Spending, 1980–1988   *Measured in constant dollars, American military spending grew nearly 50 percent between 1981 and 1987.*

Source: Robert Griffith, ed., *Major Problems in American History since 1945* (Lexington, MA: D.C. Heath, 1992), p. 694. Statistics compiled by David Murphy.

Wall Street stock brokerages, investment banking houses, and the savings and loan industry were all allowed to operate with a much freer hand than ever before. By the late 1980s, the unfortunate consequences of this freedom would become apparent in a series of unprecedented scandals in the nation's financial markets and banking industry.

Military Buildup

During the 1980 election campaign, Reagan argued that American military capability had been seriously weakened since the Vietnam War. His calls to "restore America's defenses" helped reinforce the public perception that President Jimmy Carter had dealt ineffectively with the Iran hostage crisis. For Reagan, there was no contradiction between his campaign vows to cut the cost of government and his intention to increase defense spending. Reduced government spending and a strengthened military posture were both ideological linchpins of Reagan's world view. Military strength symbolized the power of the nation rather than the authority of government.

The Reagan administration greatly accelerated a sharp increase in defense spending that began during the last two years of the Carter presidency. The Pentagon's annual budget expanded from $169

billion in 1981 to $239 billion in 1986. Secretary of Defense Caspar Weinberger and Secretary of State Alexander Haig persistently lobbied Congress for a more potent nuclear arsenal, including the MX missile, based mostly in western states, and the deployment of Cruise and Pershing missiles in western Europe. In 1983, President Reagan proclaimed his Strategic Defense Initiative (SDI), an expensive space-based missile defense system popularly called "Star Wars." Overall, the Reagan budgets for military spending totaled $1.6 trillion over five years.

Defense contracts meant the difference between prosperity and recession for blue- and white-collar workers, merchants, developers, and bankers in scores of communities. The Pacific, Atlantic, and Gulf coast states were the chief beneficiaries. In 1983, California led all states with more than $26 billion in military contracts, followed by New York ($9.6 billion), Texas ($8.2 billion), and Virginia ($7.1 billion). The military buildup of the 1980s reflected a significant shift in federal budget priorities. In 1980, 28 percent of federal spending went to what the Office of Management and Budget calls "human resources" (excluding Social Security and Medicare): housing, education, and urban and social services. By 1987, federal outlays for human resources had declined to only 22 percent of the total. In the same period, defense spending rose from 23 percent to 28 percent of the federal budget.

Recession, Recovery, Fiscal Crisis

The Reagan administration's economic policies had mixed results. In 1982 a severe recession, the worst since the 1930s, gripped the nation. By the end of that year the official unemployment rate reached nearly 11 percent, or more than 11.5 million people. Another 3 million had been out of work so long they no longer actively looked for jobs and therefore were not counted in official statistics. Many communities, particularly in the industrial Midwest and Northeast, experienced depressionlike conditions. In January 1983, 20,000 people lined up for hours in subfreezing weather to apply for 200 jobs at a Milwaukee auto-frame factory. American steel plants operated at only about one-third of capacity.

By the middle of 1983 the economy had begun to recover. During that year unemployment dropped to about 8 percent, and inflation fell below 5 percent. The economy as a whole grew 3.6 percent, the biggest increase since the mid-1970s. Unemployment remained relatively low, and the stock market boomed, pushing the Dow Jones industrial average from 776 in August 1982 to an all-time high of 2,722 in August 1987. Inflation averaged just over 3 percent from 1982 to 1986. The administration took credit for the turnaround, hailing the supply-side fiscal policies that had drastically cut taxes and domestic spending. But critics pointed to other factors: the Federal Reserve Board's tight-money policies, an energy glut and consequent sharp drop in energy prices, and the billions of dollars pumped into the economy for defense spending.

The economic recovery affected the nation's regions, industries, and social classes unequally. It produced over 13 million new jobs between 1981 and 1986, but half of these paid less than $11,661, the federally defined poverty level for a family of four. Real family income rose nearly 11 percent from 1982 to 1986, but with average hourly earnings stagnant, most of this gain came from families adding a second paycheck. While certain industries—computers, electronics, real estate, financial services—boomed, others experienced painful shrinkage—automobiles, steel, rubber, machine tools, and textiles—and the communities they supported thrived or suffered accordingly.

The supply-side formula also intensified an ominous fiscal crisis. Although President Reagan had promised to balance the federal budget, his policies had the opposite effect. The 1981 tax cuts, which shrank the government's revenue base, along with the massive increase in military spending, produced chronic annual budget deficits and a mushrooming federal debt. Before the 1980s, the largest single-year budget deficit in U.S. history had been $66 billion; in 1986 the deficit reached $221 billion. The national debt grew from $907 billion in 1980 to over $2 trillion in 1986, more than the federal government had accumulated in its entire previous history. Expenditures for paying just the interest on the national debt reached 14 percent of the annual budget in 1988, double the percentage set aside for that purpose in 1974.

Deficit spending and a large national debt predated the 1980s, but in the Reagan years they took on proportions that threatened to become a structural problem with newly disturbing and perhaps permanent implications for the American economy. Interest rates rose as the government borrowed the money it needed to pay its own bills. Foreign investors, attracted by high interest rates on government securities, pushed up the value of the dollar in relation to foreign currencies. The overvalued dollar made American products expensive abroad and foreign products cheaper for American consumers. Basic American industries—steel, autos, textiles—thus found it difficult to compete abroad and at home. In 1980, the United States still enjoyed a trade surplus of $166 billion. By 1987 the nation owed foreigners $340 billion. The nation that had been the world's leading creditor since World War I had become, by the mid-1980s, its biggest debtor.

The Election of 1984

As the 1984 election approached, several Democrats vied for the opportunity to challenge President Reagan. They believed he was politically vulnerable, especially on the economic issue of recession and the weakening of social programs. Many Americans also expressed fears over the nuclear weapons buildup of the early 1980s, concerned that such arms spending not only fueled deficits but also made a nuclear confrontation more likely. Polls showed that more than 70 percent of Americans favored a nuclear freeze with the Soviet Union. In June 1982, three-quarters of a million people—the largest political rally in American history—demonstrated in New York City for a halt to spending on and deployment of nuclear weapons.

By early 1984, Walter Mondale had emerged as the leading candidate for the Democratic nomination. As a senator from Minnesota and Jimmy Carter's vice president, Mondale had close ties with the party's liberal establishment, which helped win him the nomination. At the Democratic convention, Mondale named Representative Geraldine Ferraro of New York as his running mate, a first for women in American politics. Charismatic speakers such as the Reverend Jesse Jackson, a dynamic disciple of Martin Luther King Jr., and Governor Mario Cuomo of New York stirred the delegates and many television viewers with their appeals to compassion, fairness, and brotherhood. Opinion polls showed Mondale running even with Reagan. But the president's enormous personal popularity, bolstered by the now-booming economy, overwhelmed the Democratic ticket. While Mondale emphasized the growing deficit and called attention to Americans who were left out of prosperity, Reagan cruised above it all. It was "morning again in America," his campaign ads claimed. The nation was strong, united, and prosperous, a far cry from the dark years of the Carter administration.

As *Newsweek* put it, Reagan embodied "America as it imagined itself to be—the bearer of the traditional Main Street values of family and neighborhood, of thrift, industry, and charity instead of government intervention where self-reliance failed." Reagan, despite his close association with the rich and powerful, remained what one journalist called a "cultural democrat," the affable, friendly, neighborly citizen he had portrayed as a movie actor. Mondale's effort to revive the New Deal coalition failed. In one of the biggest landslides in American history, Reagan won 59 percent of the popular vote and carried every state but Minnesota and the District of Columbia. A quarter of registered Democrats, more than 60 percent of independents, and a majority of blue-collar voters cast their ballots for the president, as

The Reverend Jesse Jackson won wide support from black voters and poor people in the 1984 and 1988 Democratic presidential primaries. His Rainbow Coalition registered thousands of new voters in the South and the inner cities. Jackson's inspiring oratory emphasized the "common ground" shared by Americans of all races and classes.

did 54 percent of women, despite Ferraro's presence on the Democratic ticket. No wonder Republicans believed they now had a chance to replace the Democrats as the nation's majority party.

REAGAN'S FOREIGN POLICY

Against the stark imagery of the Iran hostage crisis, Ronald Reagan campaigned to restore American leadership in world affairs. As president, he revived cold war patriotism and championed American interventionism in the third world, especially the Caribbean. The unprecedented military buildup during the Reagan years would have enormous consequences for the domestic economy as well as for America's international stance. Yet along with its hard-line exhortations against the Soviet Union and international terrorism, the Reagan administration also pursued a less ideological, more pragmatic approach in key foreign policy decisions. Most important, sweeping and unanticipated internal changes within the Soviet Union made the entire cold war framework of American foreign policy largely irrelevant by the late 1980s.

The Evil Empire

Part of Reagan's success in the 1980 campaign lay in appeals to restoring America's will to assert itself in the post–Vietnam era. In the early 1980s the Reagan administration made vigorous anticommunist rhetoric the centerpiece of its foreign policy. In sharp contrast

to President Carter's focus on human rights and President Nixon's pursuit of détente, Reagan brought a return to the cold war mode of the 1950s and early 1960s. In a March 1983 speech to the National Association of Evangelicals, Reagan described the Soviet Union as "an evil empire . . . the focus of evil in the modern world." The president denounced the growing movement for a nuclear freeze, arguing that "we must find peace through strength."

Administration officials asserted that the nation's military strength had fallen dangerously behind that of the Soviet Union during the 1970s. Critics disputed this assertion, pointing out that the Soviet advantage in intercontinental ballistic missiles (ICBMs) was offset by American superiority in submarine-based forces and strategic aircraft. When asked at a congressional hearing whether he would exchange forces with his Soviet counterpart, General John Vessey, chairman of the Joint Chiefs of Staff, replied, "Not on your life." Nonetheless, the administration proceeded with plans designed to enlarge America's nuclear strike force. These included placing multiple-warhead MX missiles in fixed silos in the American West; deploying Cruise and Pershing II missiles in western Europe, a short distance from the Soviet Union; and pressing for 100 new B-1 long-range bombers.

Reagan's call for the Strategic Defense Initiative (SDI) introduced an unsettling new element into relations between the superpowers. The president claimed, though few scientists agreed, that satellites and lasers could create an impregnable shield against nuclear attack. The project eventually grew into a $17 billion research and development program. From the Soviet perspective, SDI looked like a potentially offensive weapon that would enhance U.S. first-strike capability. Not only the Soviets but millions of Europeans and Americans worried about the administration's routine acceptance of the possibility of nuclear war. A National Security Council directive outlined how the United States might "prevail" in a "protracted" nuclear conflict. The Federal Emergency Management Agency published detailed plans for the evacuation of major cities in the event of such a war.

Attempts at meaningful arms control stalled in this atmosphere, and U.S.-Soviet relations deteriorated.

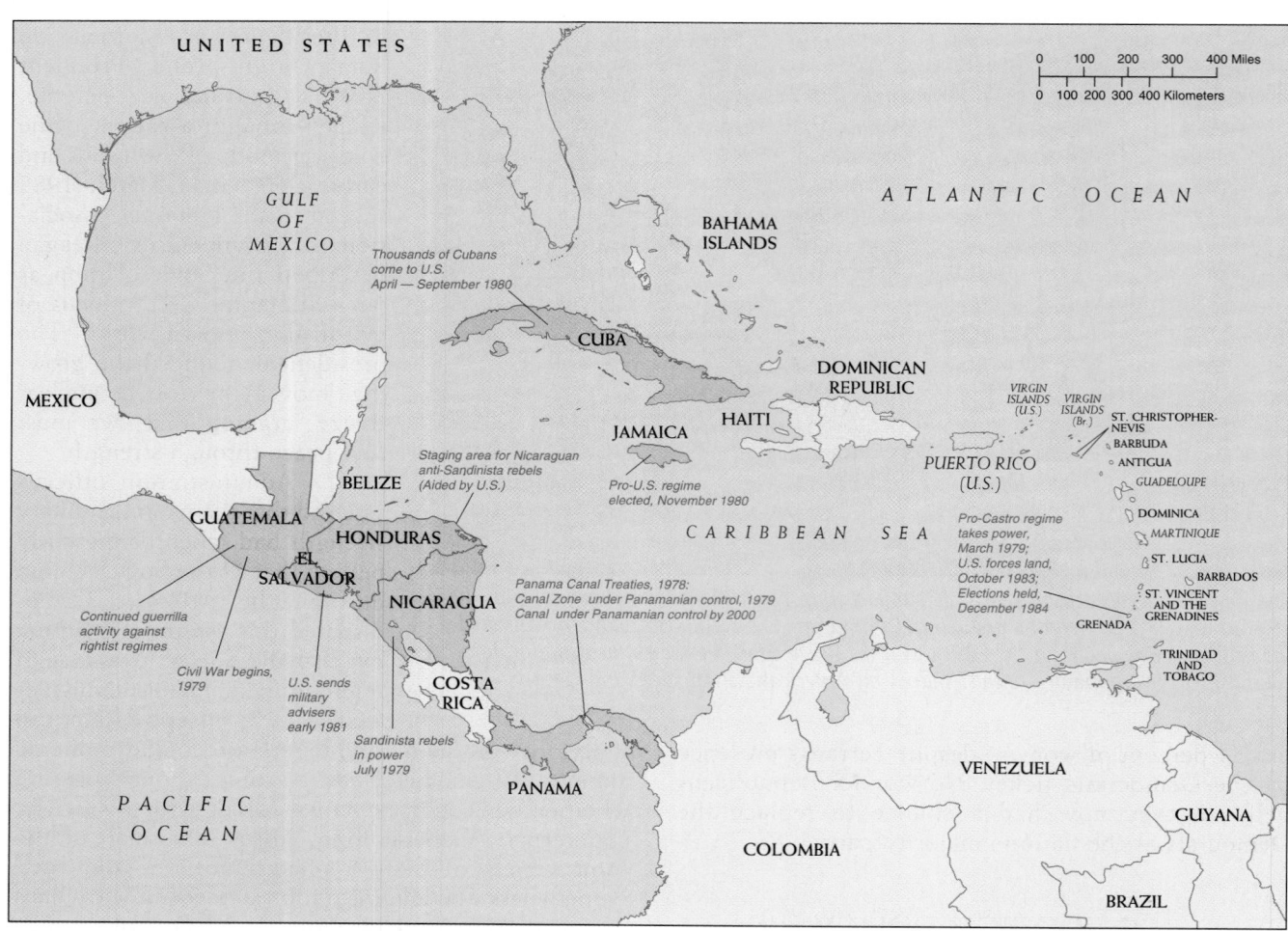

The United States in Central America, 1978–1990 *U.S. intervention in Central America reached a new level of intensity with the so-called Reagan Doctrine. The bulk of U.S. aid came in the form of military support for the government of El Salvador and the Contra rebels in Nicaragua.*

In the fall of 1983, the Soviets shot down a Korean airliner that had strayed over Soviet airspace, killing 269 people. Soviet military officials, believing the plane to be on a spy mission, acted at best in a confused and incompetent manner. President Reagan immediately denounced the act as a deliberate "crime against humanity," and a wave of anti-Soviet sentiment swept the country. The Soviet Union and its eastern European allies boycotted the 1984 Olympic Games in Los Angeles, partly in response to the American boycott of the 1980 Moscow games. While Reagan transformed images of enthusiastic Americans chanting "USA! USA!" and "We're number one!" into an effective backdrop for his reelection campaign, the American-Soviet relationship seemed to have fallen to a new low.

Central America

Declaring the "Vietnam syndrome" over, the president confidently reasserted America's right to inter-

vene anywhere in the world to fight communist insurgency. The Reagan Doctrine, as this declaration was later called, offered a corollary to the notion of the "evil empire." It assumed that social revolution anywhere in the world was directed and controlled by the Soviet Union and its allies. The Reagan Doctrine found its most important expression in Central America, where the United States hoped to reestablish its historical control over the Caribbean basin. In early 1981 the U.S. ambassador to the United Nations, Jean Kirkpatrick, declared, "Central America is the most important place in the world for the United States today."

On the economic front, the Caribbean Basin Initiative (CBI) promised to revitalize friendly nations through $350 million in U.S. aid and what Reagan called "the magic of the marketplace." The idea was to stimulate the Caribbean economy by encouraging the growth of corporations and a freer flow of capital. Yet Congress refused to play by the rules of free trade, placing stiff tariffs and quotas on imports of shoes, leather goods, and sugar that might compete with U.S. products. Many Latin American business people opposed key parts of CBI, such as generous tax breaks for foreign investors. They feared that once large multinational corporations entered their markets, CBI would strengthen the kind of chronic economic dependency that had shaped so much of the region's past.

The administration's policy toward Central America, however, was little influenced by any understanding of the region's history, its internal political struggles, or the grinding poverty of most of its inhabitants. The administration believed, as National Security Adviser Richard Allen argued, that Central America's problems stemmed from "Fidel Castro's Soviet directed, armed, and financed marauders," and required an essentially military solution. Between 1980 and 1983 the United States poured more military aid into Central America than it had during the previous thirty years. In October 1983, American marines landed on the tiny island of Grenada, population 110,000, and quickly ousted its anti-American Marxist regime. The administration claimed that Grenada had become a base for the Cuban military and therefore posed a dangerous threat to the hemisphere. The easy triumph proved popular with most Grenadans and Americans. But in the larger and more complicated nations of El Salvador and Nicaragua, this sort of unilateral military action proved politically and strategically more difficult to carry out.

Unencumbered by the concern for human rights that President Carter had sought, however inconsistently, to incorporate in foreign policy, the Reagan administration stepped up U.S. support for El Salvador's repressive regime in its struggle against a coalition of rebel groups. Salvadoran soldiers received special training in North American camps and from U.S. advisers sent to El Salvador. U.S. military aid to El Salvador jumped from $6 million in 1980 to $82 million in 1982, and economic aid exceeded that to any other Latin American country. Right-wing death squads, backed by representatives of the military in the regime, operated with increasing impunity. In 1980 they had murdered Roman Catholic archbishop Oscar Romero; by 1983, they had tortured and assassinated thousands more opposition leaders. The election in 1984 of centrist president José Napoleón Duarte failed to end the bloody civil war. Some 53,000 Salvadorans, more than one out of every hundred, lost their lives in the conflict. As many as 300,000 Salvadoran refugees entered the United States illegally between 1979 and 1985.

In Nicaragua, the Reagan administration claimed that the revolutionary Sandinista govern-

ment—which had come to power in 1979 after overthrowing the dictatorial regime of the Somoza family—posed "an unusual and extraordinary threat to the national security." U.S. officials accused the Sandinistas of shipping arms to antigovernment rebels in El Salvador. In December 1981 Reagan approved a Central Intelligence Agency (CIA) plan to spend $19 million arming and organizing the Contras—anti-Sandinista Nicaraguan exiles—to fight against the Sandinista government. Reagan described the Contras, made up mostly of former members of the overthrown Somoza regime's National Guard, as "freedom fighters" and "the moral equivalent of the Founding Fathers." As Reagan escalated this undeclared war, the aim became not merely the cutting of Nicaraguan aid to Salvadoran rebels but the overthrow of Nicaragua's Sandinista regime itself.

Toward this end the CIA used neighboring Honduras as a sanctuary and training base for the Contras. In 1984 the CIA secretly mined Nicaraguan harbors. When Nicaragua won a judgment against the United States in the World Court over this violation of its sovereignty, the Reagan administration refused to recognize the court's jurisdiction in the case and ignored the verdict. Predictably, the U.S. covert war pushed the Sandinistas closer to Cuba and the Soviet bloc. Meanwhile, in the United States, grass-roots opposition to Contra aid grew more vocal and widespread. A number of American communities set up sister city projects offering humanitarian and technical assistance to Nicaraguan communities. Scores of U.S. churches offered sanctuary to political refugees from Central America.

In 1984 Congress reined in the covert war by passing the Boland Amendment, forbidding government agencies from supporting "directly or indirectly military or paramilitary operations" in Nicaragua. Denied funding by Congress, President Reagan turned to the National Security Council to find a way to keep the Contra war going. Between 1984 and 1986 the NSC staff secretly ran the Contra assistance effort, raising $37 million in aid from foreign countries and private contributors. In 1987, the revelation of this unconstitutional scheme exploded before the public as part of the Iran-Contra affair. This led to the most damaging political scandal of the Reagan years.

Glasnost and Arms Control

Meanwhile, momentous political changes within the Soviet Union set in motion a reduction in East-West tensions and ultimately the end of the cold war. Soviet premier Leonid Brezhnev, in power since 1964, died toward the end of 1982. His successors, Yuri Andropov and Konstantin Chernenko, both died after brief terms in office. But in 1985 a new, reform-minded leader, Mikhail Gorbachev, won election as general secretary of the Soviet Communist Party. A lifelong communist and a pure product of Soviet education and politics, Gorbachev represented a new generation of disenchanted party members. He initiated a radical new program of economic and political reform under the rubrics of *glasnost* (openness) and *perestroika* (restructuring). Gorbachev's "new thinking" focused on modernizing the rigid Soviet economy, democratizing its politics, and transforming its relations with the rest of the world.

Gorbachev and his advisers opened up political discussion and encouraged internal critiques of the Soviet economy and political culture. There was much to criticize. Inefficiency and chronic shortages plagued Soviet production of such staples as meat, grain, clothing, and housing. Even when consumer goods were available, high prices often put them beyond the means of the average Soviet family. The government released long-time dissidents like Andrei Sakharov from prison and took the first halting steps toward profit-based, private initiatives in the economy. The "new thinking" inspired an unprecedented wave of diverse, often critical perspectives in Soviet art, literature, journalism, and scholarship.

In Gorbachev's view, improving the economic performance of the Soviet system depended first on halting the arms race. A large slice of the Soviet gross national product went to defense spending, while the majority of its citizens still struggled to find even the most basic consumer items in shops. Gorbachev thus took the lead in negotiating a halt to the arms race with the United States. The historical ironies were stunning. Reagan had made militant anticommunism the centerpiece of his political life. He staunchly resisted arms control initiatives and presided over the greatest military buildup in American history. But between 1985 and 1988 Reagan had four separate summit meetings with the new Soviet leader. In October 1986 Reagan and Gorbachev met in Reykjavík, Iceland. Gorbachev proposed a startling 50 percent cut in all strategic nuclear weapons. He also suggested a policy known as "zero option" for intermediate-range nuclear forces (INF), with the Soviets giving up their predominance in missiles in the European theater in exchange for the removal by the United States of its Pershing missiles. But the Iceland summit bogged down over the issue of SDI. Reagan refused to abandon his plan for a space-based defensive umbrella. Gorbachev insisted that the plan violated the 1972 Strategic Arms Limitation Treaty (SALT I) and that SDI might eventually allow the United States to make an all-out attack.

After another year of tough negotiating, the two sides agreed to a modest INF Treaty providing for the elimination of a total of 2,611 medium- and short-range nuclear missiles. This was a small dent in the combined arsenals of the two superpowers, covering less than 4 percent of total nuclear warheads. However, the INF Treaty also called for comprehensive, mutual, on-site inspections, and it provided an important psychological breakthrough. Reagan himself visited Moscow in 1988, a remarkable reversal from the days when he had thundered against the "evil empire." At one of the summits a Soviet leader humorously announced, "We are going to do something terrible to you Americans—we are going to deprive you of an enemy."

The Iran-Contra Scandal

With Gorbachev clearing the way for scaling back the cold war, the Soviet Union no longer presented itself as the overarching foe that had shaped American foreign policy for more than four decades. Yet the gift of glasnost did not eliminate cold war thinking entirely, especially in the continuing covert war in Central America. Nor could it resolve long-standing and complex international disputes in regions like the Middle East. In 1987 the revelations of the Iran-Contra affair laid bare the continuing contradictions and difficulties attending America's role in world affairs. The affair also demonstrated how overzealous and secretive government officials subverted the Constitution and compromised presidential authority under the guise of patriotism.

The Middle East presented the Reagan administration with its most frustrating foreign policy dilemmas. In Afghanistan, the administration expanded military aid, begun under President Carter, to the forces resisting the Soviet-backed regime. In June 1982 Israel invaded Lebanon in an attempt to destroy the Palestine Liberation Organization (PLO). Hoping to shore up a weak Lebanese government threatened by a brutal civil war, President Reagan dispatched marines to Beirut. In October 1983, however, a terrorist bombing in the marine barracks killed 241 American servicemen, and the administration pulled the marines out of Lebanon, shying away from a long-term commitment of U.S. forces in the Middle East.

Terrorist acts, including the seizing of Western hostages and the bombing of commercial airplanes and cruise ships, redefined the politics of the region. These were desperate attempts by small, essentially powerless sects, many of them splinter groups associated with the Palestinian cause or Islamic fundamentalism. In trying to force the Western world to pay attention to their grievances, they succeeded mostly in provoking outrage and anger. The Reagan administration insisted that behind international terrorism lay the sinister influence and money of the Soviet bloc, the

Ayatollah Khomeini of Iran, and Libyan leader Muammar Qaddafi. In the spring of 1986 the president, eager to demonstrate his antiterrorist resolve, ordered the bombing of Tripoli in a failed effort to kill Qaddafi.

Although administration officials railed against "state-sponsored terrorism," they had little luck in capturing terrorists or gaining the release of Western hostages. During the fierce and prolonged war between Iran and Iraq (1980–1988), the administration tilted publicly toward Iraq to please the Arab states around the Persian Gulf. But in 1986 the administration began secret negotiations with the revolutionary Iranian government. In exchange for help in securing the release of Americans held hostage by radical Islamic groups in Lebanon, the United States offered to supply Iran with sophisticated weapons for use against Iraq. A Lebanese magazine broke the story of the arms-for-hostages deal in November 1986, igniting a firestorm of criticism in Congress and the press. The president, it appeared, had broken his oft repeated promise that he would "never negotiate with terrorists."

Subsequent disclosures elevated the story into a major scandal. Some of the money from the arms deal had been secretly diverted into covert aid for the Nicaraguan Contras. The American public soon learned the sordid details from investigative journalists and through televised congressional hearings held during the summer of 1987. In order to escape congressional oversight of the CIA, Reagan and CIA director William Casey had essentially turned the National Security Council, previously a policy-coordinating body, into an operational agency. Under the direction of National Security Advisers Robert McFarlane and later Admiral John Poindexter, the NSC sold TOW and HAWK missiles to the Iranians, using Israel as a go-between. Millions of dollars from these sales were then given to the Contras in blatant and illegal disregard of the Boland Amendment.

In the hearings, NSC staffer and marine lieutenant colonel Oliver North emerged as the figure running what he euphemistically referred to as "the Enterprise." North defiantly defended his actions in the name of patriotism. Some Americans saw the

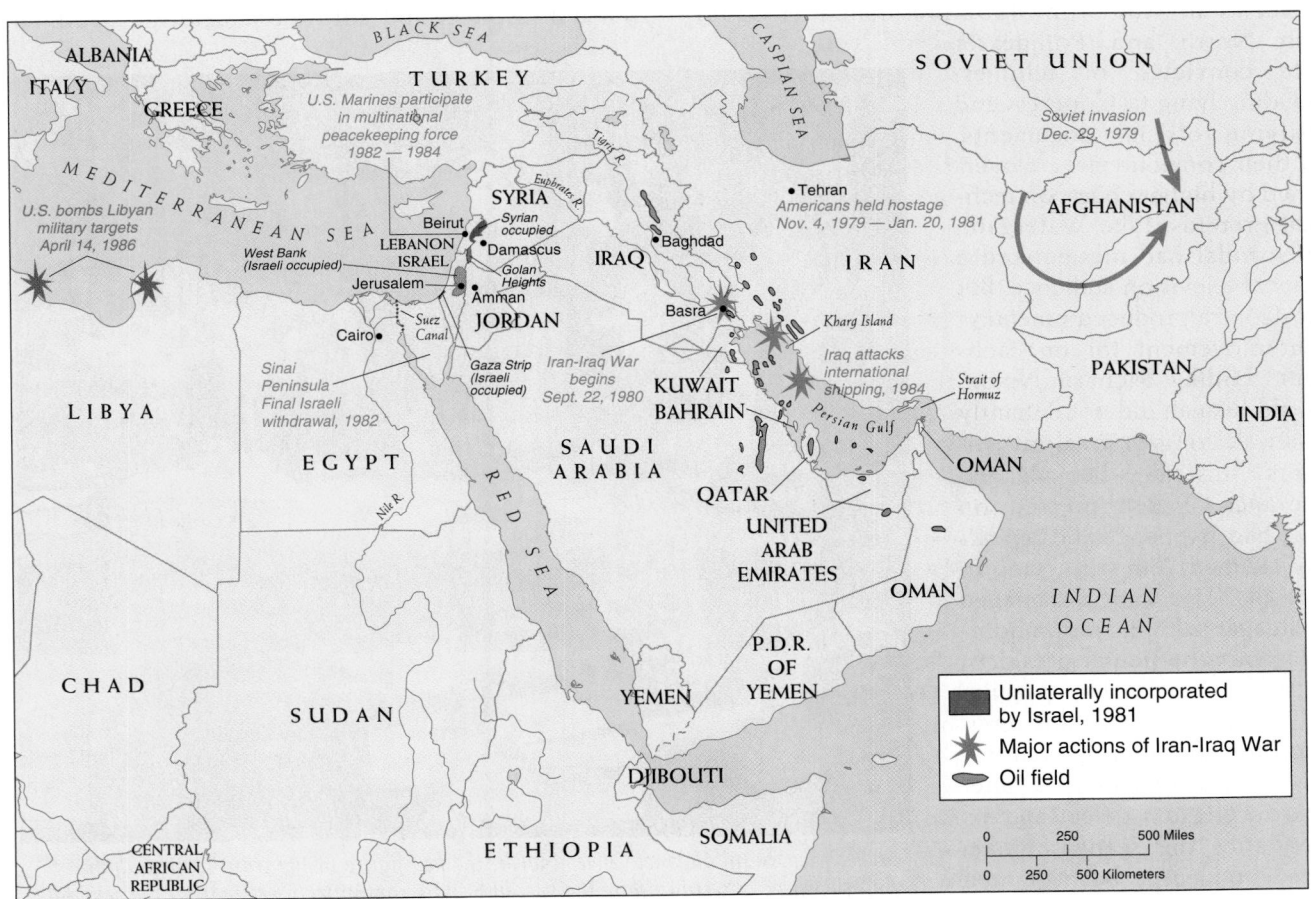

The United States in the Middle East in the 1980s   *The volatile combination of ancient religious and ethnic rivalries, oil, and emerging Islamic fundamentalism made peace and stability elusive in the Middle East.*

handsome and dashing North as a hero, but most were appalled by his and Poindexter's blithe admissions that they had lied to Congress, shredded evidence, and refused to inform the president of details in order to guarantee his "plausible deniability." A blue-ribbon commission led by former senator John Tower concluded that Reagan himself "did not seem to be aware" of the policy or its consequences. But the Tower report offered a stunning portrait of a president who was at best confused and far removed from critical policy-making responsibilities. The joint congressional committee investigating the "profoundly sad" story concluded: "The common ingredients of the Iran and Contra policies were secrecy, deception, and disdain for the law. A small group of senior officials believed that they alone knew what was right."

Ultimately, the Iran-Contra investigation raised more questions than it answered. The full role of CIA director Casey, who died in 1987—particularly his relationships with North and the president—remained murky. The role of Vice President George Bush remained mysterious as well, and it would surface as an issue in the 1992 presidential election. Both North and Poindexter were convicted of felonies, including lying to Congress and falsifying official documents, but their convictions were overturned by higher courts on technical grounds. Like Watergate, the scandal had mesmerized a national television audience. But Iran-Contra produced no equivalent movement for impeachment. Unlike Richard Nixon, Ronald Reagan did not defiantly stonewall congressional investigators. Instead, he pleaded ignorance. When pressed on what had happened, he repeatedly claimed, "I'm still trying to find out." The scandal damaged the Reagan administration politically, but the genial president remained personally popular and was protected by his reputation for not being in charge.

In December 1992, after his own election defeat and six years after the scandal broke, President George Bush granted pardons to six key players in the Iran-Contra affair. Among those pardoned was former secretary of defense Caspar Weinberger, who was scheduled to be tried on four felony counts, including perjury. Bush asserted that the officials had been motivated by "patriotism," and he attacked Special Prosecutor Lawrence Walsh for the "criminalization of policy differences." Yet critics argued that the Bush pardons suggested that government officials might violate the law as long as they believed their actions were good for the country. The Bush pardons made it unlikely that the full truth about the arms-for-hostages affair would ever be known.

BEST OF TIMES, WORST OF TIMES

During the 1980s, American communities experienced economic and social change in profoundly diverse ways. However they judged the economic policies of the Reagan era, all observers agreed that the reality of recession and recovery varied enormously across the nation's regions, cities, and industries. On a deeper structural level, the decade witnessed the rapid expansion of relatively new industries such as microelectronics, biotechnology, robotics, and computers. Simultaneously, old standbys such as steel and auto manufacturing declined

Marine Lieutenant Colonel Oliver North, the key figure in the Iran-Contra affair, being sworn in to testify before the special Senate committee investigating the scandal, July 7, 1987. A joint congressional investigation later found that when North and his compatriots were threatened with exposure, "they destroyed official documents and lied to Cabinet officials, to the public, and to elected representatives in Congress."

A silicon microchip, with imprinted circuit, on a finger. These tiny chips provided the basic building blocks for the rapid development of the computer industry. An aerial view of Santa Clara and Sunnyvale showed semiconductor plants and other microelectronic facilities in the heart of "Silicon Valley."

more quickly than many could have imagined. Communities that had long depended on industry and manufacturing for their livelihood now struggled to create alternative job bases around newer service- and information-based enterprises.

Silicon Valley

In the early 1980s, a thirty-by-ten-mile strip of Santa Clara County, California, emerged as both the real and symbolic capital of the most important new industry in America. Silicon Valley achieved a special place in the American economy and imagination as the center of the microelectronics industry. As recently as the 1950s, the valley was largely uninhabited range land and fruit orchards. Now two dozen cities, each with about 100,000 people, formed a continuous suburban sprawl between San Francisco and San Jose. None of the cities had real centers, unless shopping malls could be considered the heart of a community. Silicon Valley was a suburb of nowhere.

The name "Silicon Valley" referred to the semiconductor chips, made of silicon, that provided the foundation for local high-technology firms. Semiconductors containing complex integrated circuits formed the brains of computers and the basic building blocks of modern electronics. The nucleus for Silicon Valley was formed in the 1950s in Stanford Research Park, a development on previously unused land in Palo Alto that Stanford University started leasing to electronics firms as a way to earn money. Firms such as Hewlett-Packard and Fairchild Semiconductor wanted the advantages of being close to a major research university. Military contracts played a crucial role in the business during the 1950s

and 1960s, but in the 1970s a consumer electronics revolution fueled an explosive new wave of growth. Silicon Valley firms gave birth to pocket calculators, video games, home computers, cordless telephones, digital watches, and almost every other new development in electronics.

Silicon Valley flourished thanks to its unique combination of research facilities, investment capital, attractive environment, and a large pool of highly educated people. By 1980 it was home to some 1,700 high-tech firms that engaged in gathering, processing, or distributing information or in manufacturing information technology. Companies like Atari, Apple, and Intel achieved enormous international success and became household names. Silicon Valley boasted the greatest concentration of new wealth in the United States, and it attracted widespread coverage in trade magazines, business periodicals, and the popular press, which documented the amazing success stories of young entrepreneurs such as Steve Jobs of Apple and Nolan Bushnell of Atari. These tales reinforced the powerful popular image of Silicon Valley as a place where technological breakthroughs and great fortunes emerged from a unique culture of youth, inventiveness, and entrepreneurship.

Silicon Valley became increasingly divided along geographic and class lines. The affluent managers and engineers, nearly all of whom were white males, tended to live in North County communities such as Palo Alto, Mountain View, and Sunnyvale. Manual workers on assembly lines and in low-paying service jobs clustered in San Jose and Gilroy. Most of these were Latino, black, Vietnamese, Chinese, and Filipino men and women. The majority of Silicon Valley workers did not see or enjoy the affluent lifestyle publicized in the mass media; they constituted a cheap, nonunionized labor pool with an extremely high turnover rate. Public services in South County—schools, welfare, police and fire protection—were poor; among Latino public school students in Santa Clara County, the dropout rate reached 50 percent in the mid-1980s.

By the early 1990s the Silicon Valley economy had matured; its rate of growth slowed, as did the infusion of new venture capital. Stiff competition from computer companies in Japan, Korea, and Malaysia made it much more difficult for young entrepreneurs to start successful new companies. And the leap from small, start-up company to large corporation was becoming more and more difficult. The computer industry had diffused around the whole Pacific Rim, of which Silicon Valley was only one part. The crowds, traffic jams, and inflated cost of living led many companies and individuals to move out of the area. The mature Silicon Valley was so well developed and dense that it still had a critical mass of technological and business talent, but the boom-town atmosphere of the early years had faded.

Monongahela Valley

Across the continent, in western Pennsylvania, a different kind of economic transformation reshaped the industrial cities along the Monongahela River Valley. Since the late nineteenth century, the "Mon Valley" had proudly stood as the steelmaking center of the nation and much of the world. The very way of life in cities like Pittsburgh, Homestead, and Clairton revolved around manufacturing jobs at companies like U.S. Steel, Bethlehem, and smaller firms in the area. In the 1980s, however, the American steel industry declined. Part of the problem was the overvalued dollar, which raised the price of American goods relative to imports. As a result, steel companies lost sales, both directly to cheaper imported steel and indirectly as their domestic customers in steel-intensive industries (automobiles, machine tools) also lost sales to imports.

But much of the problem stemmed from the long-term failure of big steel companies to invest in modernizing their operations. Instead they used their profits to diversify into other industries, buying chemical firms, shopping malls, and oil companies. In 1984, U.S. Steel's sales from steel accounted for just 34 percent of its total revenues and only 9 percent of its total operating income. It paid $6 billion to acquire Marathon Oil of Ohio. At the same time, U.S. Steel increased its investments in overseas mining and mineral processing companies, some of which worked closely with foreign steelmakers. This policy of disinvestment had a devastating impact on the people and

Demolished blast furnaces at Pittsburgh's Jones and Laughlin Steel Company testified to the decline of the American steel industry. The permanent loss of high-paying jobs in the manufacturing sector devastated scores of American communities in the 1980s.

communities who had helped build the nation's basic production industries.

Overall employment in the American steel industry dropped from 400,000 in 1980 to 167,000 in 1987. In Mon Valley, U.S. Steel employed 26,500 people in 1979, but just 4,000 by 1990. The company's steelmaking capacity plunged from 8.5 million tons to 2.3 million tons a year in that period. Its Homestead Steel Works, where 15,000 people once made the steel for the Empire State Building, the Golden Gate Bridge, and the Sears Tower, closed for good in 1986. During the 1980s the valley lost 30,000 people, or 10 percent of its population. Those who stayed behind were often middle-aged steelworkers unable to find jobs or sell their homes. A survey of nearly 30,000 laid-off workers found that a majority of those over forty remained either unemployed or underemployed in part-time, low-paying jobs. Many were haunted by mental and physical problems and an overall sense of resignation.

The community of Clairton epitomized these conditions. Situated on a hill about fifteen miles south of Pittsburgh, Clairton was once a bustling small city, with active Slavic, Italian, and Irish communities. At the end of World War II its coke works were the largest in the world, and its by-products division made components for thousands of different products, including fertilizer, resin, and dyes. By the mid-1980s, however, Clairton was suffering a permanent unemployment rate of about 35 percent, and it was bankrupt. The taxes once paid to the city by U.S. Steel dropped from $805,000 in 1980 to $331,000 in 1985. The entire thirteen-member police force had to be laid off. A state-appointed trustee handled Clairton's financial affairs. Several thousand residents have moved out since 1980; others remain trapped and dependent on charity and food banks.

Some Mon Valley communities have made strides toward rebuilding around "postindustrial" enterprises. One plan called for demolishing steel mills to make way for the area's first interstate highway. Another project would turn the valley's steelmaking past into a tourist attraction, transforming the remnants of the Homestead Works into a museum run by the National Park Service. In Pittsburgh, on the former site of Jones and Laughlin Steel, state government, business, and local universities pooled resources to create a high-tech industrial park. Commercial tenants include new ventures born of university research into biotechnology, robotics, and computer software. UPARC (University of Pittsburgh Applied Research Center) has also attracted industrial and academic tenants. Pittsburgh's assets now include the world's largest robotics institute and the biggest research program on industrial uses of artificial intelligence. This modest boom may point the way toward a future in which the old steelmaking center becomes a knowledge-based community.

Indian Country

During the 1970s and 1980s Indians won a series of legal and political victories that cumulatively bolstered the principle of what the Supreme Court in *United States v. Wheeler* (1978) called "unique and limited" sovereignty. The federal government recognized tribal sovereignty except where limited by treaty or Congress. A series of court decisions defined precisely what those limits were. Tribes, for example, could tax corporations located on reservations, were exempted from paying state income taxes, and won greater powers for their own courts. In *United States v. John* (1978), the Court ruled that Indian tribes are essentially self-defined and can only be dissolved by their members, thus negating the policy of termination (see Chapter 28). The 1983 Tribal Government Tax Status Act authorized tribes to be treated like states for certain purposes.

But this strengthening of the principle of self-determination had only a limited impact on the lives of most Indians. The postwar trends toward urbanization and assimilation continued. By the 1980s more than half of the nation's Indian population lived in urban areas, with the largest communities in Los Angeles, Tulsa, Oklahoma City, and Phoenix. More than 50 percent of all Americans identifying themselves as Indians were married to non-Indians. On reservations, most tribes lacked the independence or authority of state governments since they continued to rely on federal funding.

This continued dependence on Washington was underscored in 1981 when the Reagan administration cut appropriations for Indians by a third. As Indians experienced the greatest per capita cut in federal programs of any American citizens, reservations saw a dramatic increase in unemployment and poverty. By the mid-1980s, for example, Navajo per capita income was $1,700, compared to $9,000 for the United States as a whole. In Arizona, a state with a large reservation population, more than a third of reservation Indians lived below the poverty line. On the Pine Ridge Reservation in South Dakota, some 18,000 Oglala Sioux lived amid corrosive poverty and an unemployment rate that averaged well above 50 percent. On Wyoming's Wind River Reservation about 8,000 Northern Arapaho and Eastern Shoshone Indians lived on land without any functioning economy except a few trading posts that brought in tourist dollars.

By the late 1980s a new source of income and economic power emerged for Indian tribes—gambling. An outgrowth of the drive for sovereignty rights, the Indian Gaming Regulatory Act of 1988 allowed tribes to operate any sort of gambling establishment that is legal in their state. Thus, if a church or social club can hold a "Las Vegas night," a tribe can run a casino. Within a few years, at least seventy-five tribes in eighteen states had signed agreements with states to open reservation casinos.

For some tribes, the results proved spectacular. In Ledyard, Connecticut, the Mashantucket

Gamblers crowded around card games and dice tables at the Foxwoods High Stakes Bingo and Casino, on the Ledyard, Connecticut, reservation of the Mashantucket Pequots, 1993. The success of Foxwoods made it one of the biggest employers in southeast Connecticut. It also spurred a host of Indian nations and municipalities across the nation, all eager to rake in profits and create new jobs, to propose plans for more gambling casinos.

Pequots built Foxwoods, a full-scale gambling casino and hotel complex that not only brought riches to the tribe but also reshaped the economic landscape of surrounding communities. To build Foxwoods, the Mashantuckets borrowed $55 million from a Malaysian company that operated hotels and casinos in Asia. Under an agreement between Connecticut and the tribe, state agencies regulated the casino. All profits remained with the tribe after it reimbursed the state for money spent on regulation. The Mashantuckets paid no taxes to the state or federal governments.

Some people in the adjacent community of Ledyard, a traditional New England village of 15,000, worried about traffic congestion, pollution, and crime. Others expressed concern over the human tragedies caused by compulsive gambling. But the potential for Foxwoods to reverse southeastern Connecticut's disastrous economic decline dominated all discussion. A 1990 state study estimated that New London County stood to lose anywhere from 13,000 to 27,000 jobs over the next five years as a result of cutbacks in military spending. Out of 110,000 jobs in the county, 66,000 depended directly on the Pentagon. General Dynamics' Electric Boat Division alone employed 23,000 people

building Seawolf submarines, a program scheduled for cancellation. Forty percent of all households in Ledyard had at least one person in a military-related job. No wonder, then, that more than 25,000 people applied for the 2,300 job openings at Foxwoods. At $3.75 an hour plus tips, dealers and cocktail waitresses would earn as much as $30,000 a year.

By 1998 Foxwoods was the single most profitable gambling casino in the United States. An average of fifty thousand visitors each day brought an estimated annual profit of more than $200 million on gross revenues of more than $400 million. Since 1993, in exchange for permission to install slot machines and a promise from the state not to legalize gambling off the reservation, the Pequots have contributed $100 million a year to Connecticut's treasury. The tribe could now guarantee college tuition for all its children, world travel for its elders, and new homes for its 250 members. It hired its own archaeologist to help recover evidence of lost tribal history. Steady expansion resulted in 1200 hotel rooms, 300,000 square feet of casino space, and a new $135 million Mashantucket Pequot Museum and Research Center.

Foxwoods's success inspired other Indian peoples across the nation. In California the once impoverished Cabayan Mission Indians, who had built the first reservation casino in the early 1980s, constructed a 950-unit housing development and a new power plant and guaranteed universal employment, health care, and education for tribal members. In New Mexico, $16 million in annual gambling profits helped the 600-year-old Sandia tribe reinvigorate its culture and helped revive the economy in Albuquerque.

Not all these ventures were bonanzas. The Wisconsin Winnebago tribe almost went bankrupt when its casinos were mismanaged by a corrupt businessman who had bribed tribal officials to win a lucrative contract to run them. Some Indians opposed casino gambling on philosophical and spiritual grounds, leading to intratribal conflicts. But most shared the view of Reid A. Walker, an executive with the National Indian Gaming Association, who argued that reservation gambling had "brought us new hope. It's a renaissance for Indian country, giving us power to start our own programs in health care, infrastructure, education and more."

An Electronic Culture

Important technological developments helped reconfigure American cultural life during the 1980s. Revolutions in computers and telecommunications merged telephones, televisions, computers, cable, and satellites into a single differentiated system. The new information technologies of the 1980s changed the way people worked and played. They made the nation's cultural life more homogeneous, and they played a greater role than ever in shaping politics. The new world of "compunications" (referring to the merging of computer and communications technologies) speeded the growth of what many analysts call postindustrial society. In this view, the creation, processing, and sale of information and services have replaced the manufacturing and distribution of material goods as society's most important and dynamic wealth-producing activities.

The twin arrivals of cable and the videocassette recorder (VCR) expanded and redefined the power of television. By the end of the 1980s pay cable services and VCRs had penetrated roughly two-

thirds of American homes. Cable offered television viewers scores of new programming choices, especially sports events and movies. For the first time ever, the mass audience for traditional network programming declined as "narrowcasting"—the targeting of specialized audiences—competed with broadcasting. The VCR revolutionized the way people used their sets, allowing them to organize program watching around their own schedules. People also used their televisions to play video games. Hollywood studios began releasing movies on videotape and the rental and sale of movies for home viewing quickly outstripped ticket sales at theaters as the main profit source for filmmakers. The VCR thus radically changed the economics of the entertainment business.

The intensification of television's power could be measured in many ways. In 1981, a new cable channel called MTV (for Music Television) began airing videos of popular music stars performing their work. The intent was to boost sales of the stars' audio recordings, but the music video soon became a new art form in itself. MTV redefined popular music by placing as much emphasis on image as on sound, and it revived dance as a popular performance art as well. Artists who best exploited music video, such as Madonna and Michael Jackson, achieved international superstar status. MTV also transformed smaller, cult musical forms, such as rap and heavy metal, into giant mass-market phenomena. MTV pioneered an imaginative visual style, featuring rapid cutting, animation, and the sophisticated

Pioneer female rappers Salt 'N' Pepa, shown here at the 1995 American Music Awards in Los Angeles. Among the most popular rap groups of the 1980s and '90s, their music and videos celebrated individuality, sexual freedom, and self-confidence for young women.

fusion of sound and image. Television producers, filmmakers, advertisers, and political consultants quickly adapted MTV techniques to just about every kind of image making.

More than ever, television drove the key strategies and tactics defining American political life. Politicians and their advisers focused on shaping a candidate's television image, producing slick campaign commercials, and raising the enormous amounts of money needed to get them on TV. Issues, positions, and debate all paled alongside the key question: How did it look on television? Even Ronald Reagan's harshest critics conceded that the former actor had mastered the art of television-based politics. Fewer citizens voted or took an active role in campaigns, and most relied on television coverage to make their choices. Thus creating an effective television "character" emerged as perhaps the most crucial form of political discourse. Evangelical preachers also discovered that they could use televised appeals to religious faith to make money and gain political power. "Televangelists" like Pat Robertson, Jimmy Swaggart, and Jim and Tammy Bakker attracted large audiences and built lucrative empires by preaching versions of fundamentalist Protestantism over cable networks.

The dominant themes in popular culture were money, status, and power—the values embraced by the Reagan administration. The newly elected president himself set the tone when he responded to a reporter's question asking him what was best about America. "What I want to see above all," Reagan replied, "is that this remains a country where someone can always get rich." Certainly there were many thousands of Americans who made fortunes in the expansive and lucrative sectors of the economy: stock trading, real estate, business services, defense contracting, and high-tech industries. A step below the new rich were the "yuppies" (young upwardly mobile professionals). The term, coined in 1984, gained influence as a tool for the advertising and marketing worlds, a shorthand description of those people most likely to define themselves by their upscale consumer behavior. Yuppies ate gourmet foods, wore designer clothes, drove expensive automobiles, and lived in "gentrified" neighborhoods. They were not necessarily rich, but they patterned their lifestyle after that of the wealthy.

Popular culture reflected and reinforced an obsession with getting rich and living well. Novelist Tom Wolfe called this phenomenon "plutography"—"graphic depictions of the acts of the rich." Hit TV series like *Dallas* and *Dynasty* (and their imitators) focused on the family wars and business intrigues of

oil tycoons and fashion queens. Shows such as *Lifestyles of the Rich and Famous* and *Entertainment Tonight* offered vicarious pleasures by taking viewers into the homes and on the shopping sprees of wealthy celebrities. Movies like *Risky Business* (1983), *Ghostbusters* (1984), and *Working Girl* (1988) that reveled in moneymaking and the entrepreneurial spirit attracted huge audiences. So, too, did films that combined spectacular special effects and science fiction with the comforting verities of so-called traditional family values: *ET: The Extraterrestrial* (1982), *Return of the Jedi* (1983), and *Back to the Future* (1985).

The marketing of marketing drove American culture, as exposure through the mass media became more crucial than ever for business success. Tie-ins proliferated among films, television shows, advertising, newspapers and magazines, popular music, and politicians. A growing concentration of ownership among television networks, movie studios, publishers, and cable companies accelerated this trend. New media forms—the newspaper *USA Today*, the news channel Cable News Network (CNN), the weekly magazine *People*—intensified the national culture of celebrity. On a deeper level, demographic analysis created the most important "communities" in American life—communities of consumer choice. Polls, graphs, and charts increasingly located and divided Americans by race, gender, ethnicity, education, income, and religion so that advertisers, manufacturers, book publishers, moviemakers, television producers, and political candidates—anyone looking to sell a product or provide a service—could define and target the right demographic community.

Epidemics: Drugs, AIDS, Homelessness

The scourge of drug addiction and drug trafficking took on frightening new dimensions in the early 1980s. The arrival of crack, a cheap, smokable, and highly addictive form of cocaine, made that drug affordable to the urban poor. As crack addiction spread, the drug trade assumed alarming new proportions both domestically and internationally. Crack ruined hundreds of thousands of lives and led to a dramatic increase in crime rates. Studies showed that over half the men arrested in the nation's largest cities tested positive for cocaine. The crack trade spawned a new generation of young drug dealers who were willing to risk jail and death for enormous profits. In city after city, drug wars over turf took the lives of dealers and innocents, both caught in the escalating violence. Many ghetto youths looked at the drug trade as the only real business enterprise open to them.

Well-financed and carefully organized groups like the Medellín cartel in Colombia linked coca plant farmers in Bolivia, money laun-derers in Panama, and smugglers in Mexico and the United States. Drug money corrupted many public officials in all of these countries. By the end of the 1980s, opinion polls revealed that Americans identified drugs as the nation's number one problem. The Reagan administration declared a highly publicized "war on drugs" to bring the traffic under control. This multibillion-dollar campaign focused on stopping the flow of illegal drugs into the United States, destroying cocaine-producing labs in Bolivia, and stiff-ening the penalties for those convicted of violating federal drug statutes. Critics charged that the war on drugs needed to focus less on the supply of drugs from abroad and more closely on the demand for them at home. They urged more federal money for drug education, treatment, and rehabilitation. Drug addiction and drug use, they argued, were primarily health problems, not law enforcement issues.

In 1981 doctors in Los Angeles, San Francisco, and New York began encountering a puzzling new medical phenome-non. Young homosexual men were dying suddenly from rare types of pneumonia and cancer. The underlying cause was found to be a mysterious new viral disease that destroyed the body's natural defenses against illness, making its victims susceptible to a host of opportunistic infec-tions. Researchers at the U.S. Public Health Service's Centers for Disease Control (CDC) in Atlanta called the new disease acquired immune deficiency syndrome (AIDS). The virus that causes AIDS (the human immunodeficiency virus, or HIV) is transmitted primarily in semen and blood, but it can be years before a person exposed to HIV develops full-blown AIDS. Thus one could infect others without knowing one had the disease. Although tests emerged to determine whether one carried HIV,

The AIDS Quilt in Washington, D.C., October 1992. The quilt project united thousands of individual memorials to AIDS victims into one powerful statement expressing the national sense of loss from the disease. Mourners were thus able to transcend their personal grief and connect with the larger movement to fight AIDS.

there was no effective treatment for AIDS in these early years. Because the preponderance of early AIDS victims were homosexual men who had been infected through sexual contact, many Americans perceived AIDS as a disease of homosexuals.

As more and more gay men fell victim to the disease, AIDS aroused fear, anguish, and anger. It also brought an upsurge of organization and political involvement. The Gay Men's Health Crisis, formed in New York in 1981, drew thousands of volunteers to care for the sick, raised millions of dollars for education and research, and lobbied vigorously for federal funding of research toward finding a cure. In city after city, gay communities responded to the AIDS crisis with energy and determination. Most gay men changed their sexual habits, practicing "safe sex" to reduce the chances of infection. The Reagan administration, playing to antihomosexual prejudices, largely ignored the epidemic. One important exception was Surgeon General C. Everett Koop, who urged a comprehensive sex education program in the nation's schools, including information about condoms. Individual American communities became bitterly divided over whether school boards and other local agencies ought to take on these responsibilities.

By the 1990s the AIDS epidemic had spread far beyond gay men. The fastest-growing group of AIDS victims were intravenous drug users, their sex partners (including many heterosexuals), and their babies. The AIDS epidemic spread rapidly among African Americans and Latinos as well. Revelations that well-known public figures such as actor Rock Hudson and athletes Magic Johnson and Arthur Ashe were infected helped remove some of the stigma and increased AIDS awareness in the public. More important were the continuing political and educational efforts mounted by groups like the AIDS Coalition to Unleash Power (ACT-UP), Women's Health Action Mobilization (WHAM), and the AIDS Quilt Project, which stitched together a moving tribute to victims out of thousands of individual memorial quilts. In 1994 Congress passed the Comprehensive AIDS Revenue Emergency Act, which pumped hundreds of millions of federal dollars into AIDS research and prevention programs.

By 1997, some 612,000 Americans had contracted AIDS, of whom 379,000 had died. About 900,000 Americans (1 in 300) was infected with the HIV virus. But although the HIV infection rate remained steady, the death rate from AIDS began to drop by 1995. A variety of new drug treatments, such as AZT and protease inhibitors, proved effective in slowing the disease's progress and in relieving some symptoms. For those patients with access to the new drugs, AIDS became a long-term chronic condition rather than an automatic death sentence. But these treatments were enormously expensive and required difficult regimens for patients, thus limiting their effectiveness against the epidemic.

Another chronic social problem plagued America during the 1980s. In cities throughout the country, citizens could not help noticing the disturbing presence of homeless people. Often disoriented, shoeless, and forlorn, growing numbers of "street people" slept over heating grates, on subways, and in parks. Homeless people wandered city sidewalks panhandling and struggling to find scraps of food. Winters proved especially difficult. In the early 1980s, the Department of Housing and Urban Development placed the number of the nation's homeless at between 250,000 and 350,000. But advocates for the homeless estimated that the number was as high as 3 million.

Who were the homeless? Analysts agreed that at least a third were mental patients who had been discharged from hospitals during the 1970s as the result of a large-scale policy of deinstitutionalization. That policy was in part a response to charges that institutionalization violated patients' right. But without adequate community mental health centers to ease their transition, deinstitutionalization proved a disaster for many thousands of the mentally ill. Alcoholics and drug addicts unable to hold jobs also contributed to the growing homeless problem, but the ranks of the homeless also included female-headed families, battered women, Vietnam veterans, AIDS victims, and elderly people with no place to go. Some critics pointed to the decline in decent housing for poor people and the deterioration of the nation's health-care system as a cause of homelessness. Some communities made strong efforts to place their homeless residents in city-run shelters, but violence and theft in the shelters scared away many people. No matter how large and what its components, the permanent class of American homeless reflected the desperate situation of America's poor.

Economic Woes

The government had only mixed success in trying to curb the excesses of economic development in the 1980s. Congress sought to check burgeoning deficits, which had topped $200 billion in the annual budget for 1984. In late 1985, amid great fanfare, Congress enacted the Balanced Budget and Emergency Deficit Reduction Act, more popularly known as Gramm-Rudman after its principal authors, Senators Phil Gramm and Warren Rudman. It mandated automatic spending cuts if the government failed to meet fixed deficit reduction goals. Under the plan, congressional and presidential budget officials would forecast whether target reductions would be met. If not, the General Accounting Office would compile a list of across-the-board reductions, evenly divided between domestic and military programs. Although Gramm-Rudman targeted a deficit of $172 billion for 1986, with further reductions leading to a balanced budget by 1991, the deficit for 1986 reached $238 billion, some $66 billion over the target. In fact, the actual deficit was $283 billion. Congress and the president masked the true size of the deficit by taking the $45 billion surplus from Social Security and other trust funds and spending it on government programs. This tactic of diverting trust funds to reduce the deficit became standard during the 1980s. Congress revised the Gramm-Rudman targets in 1987, but once again the numbers did not add up. The 1989 deficit wound up at $153 billion instead of the promised $136 billion. The 1991 deficit set a record at $269 billion; if the Social Security surplus was subtracted from government spending books, the real deficit totaled $321 billion.

On Wall Street, the bull market of the 1980s ended abruptly in the fall of 1987. The Dow-Jones average of thirty leading industrial stocks had reached an all-time high of 2,722 at the end of August. There followed a gradual slide over the next few weeks and then a resounding crash. On October 19, the Dow lost an incredible 508 points in one day, almost 23 percent of its value. Analysts blamed the decline on computerized program trading, which automatically instructed money managers to sell stock-index futures when prices on the New York Stock Exchange fell below certain levels. The panic on the trading floors recalled the pandemonium set off by the stock market crash of 1929. Millions of Americans now feared that the 1987 crash would signal the onset of a great recession or even a depression.

In late 1986, the Securities and Exchange Commission (SEC) uncovered the biggest stock scandal in history, in the process revealing the inner workings of high finance in the 1980s. Ivan Boesky, one of the nation's leading stock speculators, admitted to using confidential information about upcoming corporate takeovers to trade stocks illegally. Just two years earlier the dapper Boesky had made more than $100 million on two deals. "Greed is all right," he told a cheering University of California Business School audience in 1985. "Everybody should be a little bit greedy. . . . You shouldn't feel guilty."

Now Boesky agreed to pay the U.S. government $100 million to settle civil charges, and he cooperated with SEC investigators. The biggest fish caught in their net was Michael Milken, a Boesky ally and the most successful businessman of the era. An investment banker for Drexel Burnham Lambert, Milken perfected the art of corporate raiding through creative manipulation of debt. He showed how enormous profits could be earned from weak firms that offered tempting targets for takeovers and mergers. Their debt could be used as tax write-offs; less efficient units could be sold off piecemeal; and more profitable units could be retained, merged, or sold again to form new entities. Instead of borrowing from banks, Milken financed his deals by underwriting high-yield, risky "junk bonds"

for companies rated below investment grade. Investors in turn reaped huge profits by selling these junk bonds to hostile-takeover dealers.

Milken and other corporate raiders reshaped the financial world, setting off the greatest wave of buying and selling in American business history. During the 1980s corporate America undertook 25,000 mergers, takeovers, and restructuring deals, cumulatively valued at more than $2 trillion. Between 1984 and 1987, there were twenty-one such deals involving over a billion dollars each. Milken himself made a staggering $550 million in one year alone. Just before filing for bankruptcy in 1990, Drexel Burnham Lambert paid its executives $350 million in bonuses—almost as much as it owed its creditors. Milken was eventually convicted of insider trading and stock fraud and sent to prison. Critics both within and outside the Wall Street world questioned the economic benefits of this "paper entrepreneurialism." Many American businesses enjoyed rising profits and cash flow, but these depended as much on debt manipulation and corporate restructuring as on investment in research and development or the creation of new products.

Growing Inequality

The celebration of wealth, moneymaking, and entrepreneurship dominated much of popular culture, politics, and intellectual life in the 1980s. But grimmer realities lay under the surface. A variety of measures strongly suggested that the nation had moved toward greater inequality, that the middle class was shrinking, and that poverty was on the rise. Analysts disagreed over the causes of these trends. No doubt some reflected structural changes in the American economy and a rapidly changing global marketplace. After eight years of tax cuts, defense buildup, growing budget deficits, and record trade imbalances, the economic future looked uncertain at best. Two of the most cherished basic assumptions about America— that life would improve for most people and their children, and that a comfortable middle-class existence was available to all who worked for it—looked shaky by the early 1990s.

The very wealthy did extremely well during the 1980s. In 1989 the richest 1 percent of American households accounted for 37 percent of the nation's private wealth—up from 31 percent in 1983, a jump of almost 20 percent. This top 1 percent, consisting of 834,000 households with about $5.7 trillion of net worth, owned more than the bottom 90 percent of Americans, the remaining 84 million households, whose total net worth was about $4.8 trillion. The top 1 percent owned a disproportionate share of many types of assets: 78 percent of bonds and trusts, 62

PERCENTAGE SHARE OF AGGREGATE FAMILY INCOME, 1980–1992

	1980	1992
Top 5 Percent	15.3%	17.6%
Highest Fifth	41.6	44.6
Fourth Fifth	24.3	24.0
Third Fifth	17.5	16.5
Second Fifth	11.6	10.5
Lowest Fifth	5.1	4.4

Source: U.S. Bureau of the Census, Current Population Reports: Consumer Incomes, Series P-60, Nos. 167 and 184, 1990, 1993. U.S. federal data compiled by Ed Royce, Rollins College.

SHARE OF TOTAL NET WORTH OF AMERICAN FAMILIES

	1983	1989
Richest 1 percent of families	31%	37%
Next richest 9 percent	35	31
Remaining 90 percent	33	32

Source: *New York Times*, April 21, 1992, from Federal Reserve Survey of Consumer Finances.

percent of business assets, 49 percent of publicly held stock, and 45 percent of nonresidential real estate. The average wealth of the Fortune 500 (the wealthiest individuals in America) jumped from $230 million in 1982 to $682 million in 1990. The total net worth of this group rose from $92 billion to $273 billion over the same period, and the number of billionaires jumped from thirteen to sixty-six.

The most affluent Americans made the biggest gains in family income as well. In 1980 the top 5 percent of families earned 15.3 percent of the nation's total income. By 1992 their share had grown to 17.6 percent, an increase of 15 percent; their average income was $156,000 a year. In 1980 the top 20 percent of families earned 41.6 percent of the nation's total. By 1992 their share had grown to 44.6 percent, an increase of about 7 percent, with an average income of $99,000 a year. In contrast, the bottom 40 percent of families had 16.7 percent of aggregate income in 1980. By 1992 their share had declined to 14.9 percent, a drop of nearly 11 percent, with an average income of about $16,500 a year.

The average weekly earnings of American workers declined from $373 in 1980 to $339 in 1992, and average hourly wages dropped from $10.59 to $9.87 (in 1990 dollars). Both these figures reflected that most of the new jobs created during the 1980s were in low-paying service and manufacturing sectors. Of the roughly 12 million (net) new jobs created between 1979 and 1987, 50.4 percent paid less than the $11,611 poverty-level income for a family of four. Only 12 percent were high-wage jobs paying over $46,445. Millions of families now needed two wage earners to maintain middle-class status where formerly one would have sufficed.

The number and percentage of Americans in poverty grew alarmingly during the decade. In 1979 the government classified about 26.1 million people as poor, 11.7 percent of the total population. By 1992 the number of poor had reached 36.9 million, or 14.5 percent of the population. This represented an increase of more than 23 percent in the nation's poverty rate. In 1992 nearly 22 percent of all American children under eighteen lived in poverty, including 47 percent of all black children and 40 percent of all Hispanic children. Thirty-three percent of all African Americans lived in poverty, as did 29 percent of Hispanics. Female-headed

MEASURES OF AVERAGE EARNINGS, 1980–1992 (IN 1990 DOLLARS)

Year	Average Weekly Earnings	Average Hourly Earnings
1980	$373.81	$10.59
1985	363.30	10.41
1992	339.37	9.87

Source: U.S. House of Representatives, Committee on Ways and Means, *Overview of Entitlement Programs* (Washington, D.C.: GPO, 1993), table 35, p. 557. U.S. federal data compiled by Ed Royce, Rollins College.

NUMBER OF POOR, RATE OF POVERTY, AND POVERTY LINE, 1979–1992

	1979	1992
Millions of poor	26.1	36.9
Rate of poverty	11.7%	14.5%
Poverty line (family of four)	$7,412	$14,335

Source: U.S. Bureau of the Census, Current Population Reports: Consumer Income, Series P-60, Nos. 161 and 185, 1988, 1993. U.S. federal data compiled by Ed Royce, Rollins College.

NET NEW JOB CREATION BY WAGE LEVEL, 1979–1987

	Number of Net New Jobs Created	Percentage of Net New Jobs Created
Low-wage Jobs (less than $11,611)	5,955,000	50.4%
Middle-wage Jobs ($11,612 to $46,444)	4,448,000	31.7%
High-wage Jobs ($46,445 and above)	1,405,000	11.9%

Source: U.S. Senate, Committee on the Budget, *Wages of American Workers in the 1980s* (Washington, D.C.: GPO, 1988). U.S. federal data compiled by Ed Royce, Rollins College.

MEDIAN FAMILY INCOME AND RATIO TO WHITE, BY RACE AND HISPANIC ORIGIN, 1980–1992 (IN 1992 DOLLARS)

Year	All Races	White	Black	Hispanic
1980	$35,839	$37,341	$21,606 (58%)	$25,087 (67%)
1985	36,164	38,011	21,887 (58%)	25,596 (67%)
1992	36,812	38,909	21,161 (54%)	23,901 (61%)

Source: U.S. Bureau of the Census, Current Population Reports, Series P-60, No. 184, 1993. U.S. federal data compiled by Ed Royce, Rollins College.

households, comprising 13.7 million people, accounted for 37 percent of the poor.

END OF AN ERA?

As Americans approached the end of the twentieth century, they faced dramatic changes around the world and at home. The fall of world communism promised to reshape the fundamental premises of the nation's foreign policy. Economic competition with the nations of the Pacific Rim and Europe would replace the ideological rivalry between Marxism-Leninism and capitalism. But capitalism was hardly triumphant. Global economic struggles forced a reassessment of the core beliefs in growth and abundance that had dominated the nation's political and cultural life since World War II. The limits of military power to solve complex political and economic disputes became clear in the aftermath of victory in the Persian Gulf War. Economic inequality and racial divisions continued to plague many American communities. In 1992 Democrats recaptured the White House for the first time since 1976, riding a wave of desire for change. But in 1994 a resurgent and more right-wing Republican Party won control of both houses of Congress for the first time in forty years.

The Election of 1988

For the 1988 campaign, the Republicans nominated Vice President George Bush. Bush embodied the eastern establishment, with a few twists. The son of an investment banker and senator from Connecticut, educated at Yale, he had moved to Texas after serving in World War II as a fighter pilot. Bush made money in the oil business and entered Texas Republican politics. His detractors dismissed him as a "wimp" and "the resume candidate." He had held a string of appointive offices under three presidents—head of the National Republican Committee, UN ambassador, envoy to China, director of the CIA—before being elected vice president. In his campaign for the presidency, Bush promised to continue the policies of his patron, Ronald Reagan.

The Democratic nominee, Governor Michael Dukakis of Massachusetts, stressed competence over ideology and took credit for his state's economic boom. With Reagan retiring, the Democrats believed they had a good chance to recapture the White House in 1988. At first Dukakis led Bush in the polls. But Republican strategists, led by Lee Atwater and Roger Ailes, created and ran a cynical and effective negative campaign that painted Dukakis as outside the mainstream of "American values." They attacked

Dukakis for vetoing a law requiring students to pledge allegiance to the flag; for opposing the death penalty and mandatory school prayer; and for being a "card-carrying member" of the American Civil Liberties Union. Most damaging was an ad campaign accusing Dukakis of being soft on crime by authorizing weekend furloughs for some Massachusetts prison inmates. One TV spot focused on Willie Horton, a black man serving time for rape and assault, who had escaped during a furlough and committed another rape. The gut-level appeal to racist stereotypes was shocking and potent. "If I can make Willie Horton a household name," said Lee Atwater, "we'll win the election."

The Bush campaign succeeded in creating a negative image of Dukakis, especially among undecided voters. While Bush excoriated liberalism, wrapped himself in the flag, and made thinly veiled racist and nativist appeals, Dukakis distanced himself from the campaign and the Democratic Party's liberal tradition. The 1988 election intensified the importance of image over substance in the nation's politics. The creation of daily "sound bites" for the evening news, along with carefully calculated "spin control" by campaign aides, seemed far more crucial than debate over issues. Even during televised debates, the candidates appeared unwilling and incapable of discussing such pressing concerns as the political upheaval in the Soviet Union, the environmental crisis, and the globalization of the world economy. Bush and his running mate, Dan Quayle, won the popular vote by 54 to 46 percent and carried the electoral votes of forty out of fifty states. Above all, the election of 1988 signaled that more sophisticated levels of media manipulation and image making were the keys to success in presidential politics.

The New Immigration

Figures from the 1990 census confirmed what many Americans had observed over the previous decade in their communities and workplaces. The face of the nation was perceptibly changing. The Census Bureau estimated that 6 million legal and 2 million undocumented immigrants entered the country during the 1980s, second only to the 8.8 million foreign immigrants who had arrived between 1900 and 1910. More than a third of the nation's population growth over the decade—from 227 million to 248 million—came from immigration, a greater proportion than in any decade since 1910–1920, when immigration accounted for 40 percent of population growth. Seven states, headed by California, New York, Texas, and Florida, received 75 percent of the newcomers.

Hispanics and Asians led the accelerated trend toward cultural diversity. The Hispanic population

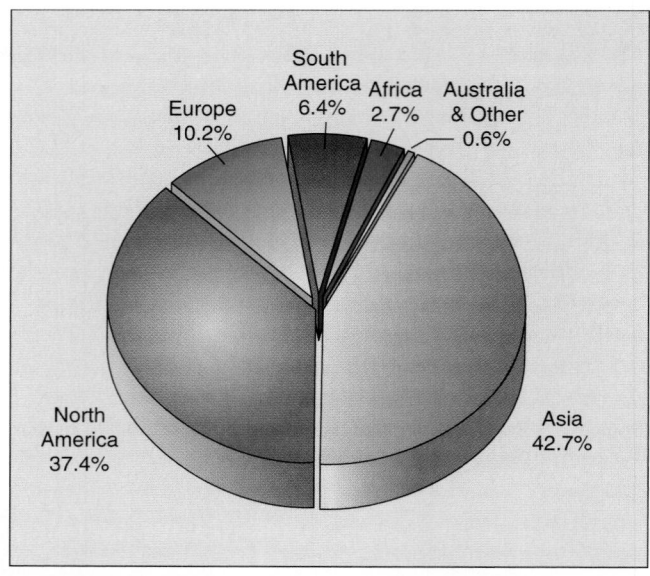

Continent of Birth for Immigrants, 1981–1989

increased by more than 50 percent, from 14.6 million to 22.4 million. One out of every five immigrants living in the United States was Mexican-born, and Mexican Americans accounted for more than 60 percent of the Hispanic population identified in the 1990 census. Hispanics formed over a third of the population of New Mexico, a quarter of the population of Texas, and over 10 percent of the populations of California, Arizona, and Colorado. Nearly a million Mexican Americans lived in Los Angeles alone. Large Hispanic communities, including Cuban, Puerto Rican, Dominican, and Salvadoran Americans, also grew in New York City, Miami, and Chicago. Demographers predicted that by the middle of the next century Hispanics would replace African Americans as the largest minority group in the nation.

The decline of oil prices had a devastating impact on the Mexican economy, worsening poverty and unemployment and spurring more people to seek a better life in North America. Most Mexican Americans struggled in low-paying jobs and fought to hold on to their distinctive cultural heritage. They worked on farms, in garment sweatshops and high-tech assembly plants, and as gardeners and domestics. Through education and business success, many joined the middle class. But almost 20 percent of Mexican Americans lived below the poverty line.

The number of Asian Americans more than doubled, from 3.5 million to 7.3 million. Nearly two out of every five Asian Americans lived in California. The population of Koreatown in Los Angeles approached 300,000. Like earlier immigrant groups, new Americans from Korea, Vietnam, and the Philippines tended to cluster in their own communities and maintain a durable group identity. As a whole, Asian

Americans made mobility through education a priority, along with pooling family capital and labor to support small businesses. Newcomers selected communities with job opportunities or where family members and friends had settled previously. This "chain migration" is illustrated by the large numbers of Hmongs, a tribal group from Laos, living in Minneapolis and St. Paul. The stream of Hmongs began with church-sponsored refugee programs, then gained momentum as more and more family members followed. Minnesota's total Asian population tripled, increasing during the 1980s from 26,000 to 78,000.

The Immigration and Nationality Act of 1965 had eliminated quotas based on national origin. It also gave preferential treatment to highly educated foreigners seeking professional opportunities. The 1965 act set limits of 120,000 immigrants per year from the Western Hemisphere and 170,000 from countries outside the Western Hemisphere. However, many more immigrants entered the nation illegally. By the mid-1980s, growing concern over "illegal aliens" had become a hotly debated political issue, particularly in the Southwest. The Immigration Reform and Control Act of 1986 addressed the concerns of Anglos worried about "illegals" and the increasingly influential Mexican American community. It required employers to vouch for the legal status of their employees. At the same time, it offered an amnesty to all undocumented workers who had entered the country before 1982. The law, critics charged, led to discrimination in hiring. And no matter what Congress did, the desperate economic realities in Mexico and Central America continued to enlarge the flow of illegal immigrants.

Anti-immigrant sentiment re-emerged as a potent political force during the 1990s. Proposition 187, a referendum on California's ballot in 1994, proved a lightning rod for anti-immigrant sentiment. The proposition called for making all undocumented aliens ineligible for any welfare services, schooling, and non-emergency medical care, and it required teachers and clinic doctors to report illegals to the police. Proponents, such as Republican Governor Pete Wilson, argued that illegals created a crushing burden on state and local welfare agencies and school systems. They also hoped the measure would force federal action to stem the flow of illegals. A spokesman for Americans Against Illegal Immigration, a pro-187 Southern California group, asserted, "Enough is enough. We're going broke in this state. . . . It's insanity, it doesn't make sense and the average guy in this country is not going to buy into it anymore." A deep and lingering economic recession during the early 1990s no doubt contributed to the state's increasingly anti-immigrant political mood.

Proposition 187 passed by a 3–2 margin, but it was immediately challenged in the streets and in the courts. In Los Angeles more than 70,000 people marched to protest its passage and the City Council voted not to enforce it. In 1998, after several years of legal wrangling, a Los Angeles federal district court judge ruled that Proposition 187 unconstitutionally usurped federal authority over immigration policy. But the national debate over immigration policy, in which economic issues and racial fears were deeply entangled, continued unabated. As one Stanford law professor who had worked to overturn Proposition 187 put it: "Some people genuinely worry about the problem of too many immigrants in a stagnant economy. But for most, economics is a diversion. Underneath it is race."

The Collapse of Communism

At the end of the 1980s, Americans watched with amazement as the political structures that had defined postwar eastern Europe disintegrated. In the Soviet Union, the political reforms initiated by Mikhail Gorbachev in the mid-1980s ultimately led to the dissolution of the Soviet state. By calling for a greater openness and a new spirit of democracy, Gorbachev had boldly challenged the Communist Party establishment that had dominated Soviet life for three-quarters of a century. He had also inspired open opposition to communist rule throughout eastern Europe. The outright revolt against communist rule gathered strength first in eastern European nations, then hit home in Moscow with stunning swiftness.

In June 1989 Poland held its first free elections since the communists took power after World War II, bringing an overwhelming victory for the Solidarity movement. Solidarity leader Tadeusz Mazowiecki became prime minister, forming a government that shared power with, but was no longer dominated by, communists. In Hungary, the Communist Party changed its name and called for a multiparty system, which in 1990 resulted in the election of a center-right government. In the fall of 1989 angry prodemocracy demonstrations forced out long-time Communist Party leaders in Czechoslovakia, Bulgaria, and Romania.

Most dramatic of all were the events in East Germany. First Hungary opened its border with Austria, allowing the exit of East Germans gathered at the West German Embassy in Budapest. Then huge protests broke out during official celebrations of East Germany's fortieth anniversary, and thousands of refugees flooded routes to the West. The Berlin Wall had suddenly been rendered irrelevant. The wall, which for thirty years had loomed as the ultimate symbol of cold war division, was torn down by gleeful protesters. Revelations of corruption forced East Germany's Communist Party leaders out of power and paved the way for German reunification the next year.

In the Soviet Union political change had progressed more slowly. In 1987, on the seventieth anniversary of the Russian Revolution, Gorbachev had denounced Josef Stalin, helping to legitimize growing criticism of censorship and organs of political repression, including the secret police, or KGB. In March 1989, the Soviet Union held its first free elections since 1917 as a new Congress of People's Deputies replaced the old Communist Party–dominated Supreme Soviet. Hundreds of party officials went down to defeat. In early 1990, over the fierce objections of hard-liners, the Central Committee agreed to Gorbachev's plan to end the Communist Party's constitutional monopoly of power. In elections held in March 1990, prodemocracy groups in Russia, Ukraine, and Byelorussia achieved major gains, and the Communist Party lost control of the local governments in Moscow, Leningrad, and other cities. By the middle of 1991, most of the fifteen republics that constituted the Soviet Union had announced plans to break away from Moscow's control.

German demonstrators defiantly tearing down the Berlin Wall, November 1989. For three decades the wall dividing East and West Berlin had embodied the political divisions of the cold war. Images such as these underscored the passing of an era.

The party's hard-liners made one final attempt to prevent the dissolution of the Soviet Union. In August 1991, they attempted a coup by placing Gorbachev under house arrest at his vacation home in the Crimea, reasserting control of the press, and banning street demonstrations. Boris Yeltsin, president of the Russian Republic, denounced Gorbachev's removal and urged thousands of Muscovites gathered outside the Parliament building to resist. The coup failed when Soviet army troops refused orders to attack the Russian parliament building. Upon his return from the Crimea, Gorbachev resigned as head of the Communist Party and then banned it. As leader of Russia, the largest of the republics, Yeltsin now emerged as the most powerful political leader. At the end of 1991 Russia proclaimed its independence and, along with Ukraine and Byelorussia (now Belarus), formed the Commonwealth of Independent States. Eight more republics quickly joined the new commonwealth, and on Christmas Day 1991 a weary and bitter Gorbachev resigned as president of the Soviet Union and recognized the Commonwealth of Independent States.

In the end, Gorbachev's zeal to reform politics had outrun his ability to reform the economy. As one sympathetic editorial in *Pravda* put it: "Gorbachev was unable to change the living standards of the people, but he changed the people." Attempts to move toward a more open free-market economy had been stymied by resistance of the entrenched and privileged Communist Party apparatchiks. A severe shortage of capital had also hampered plans to shift the economy toward greater production of consumer goods. Promises of economic investment and technical aid from the United States and the European Economic Community ran far behind the actual delivery of assistance. Violent ethnic conflict and a weak economy threatened the future of the new commonwealth. The sticky question of who controlled the enormous nuclear and military might of the former Soviet Union remained unresolved. Gorbachev and the movement he had inspired had wrought revolutionary changes. But the 280 million people of the former Soviet Union faced a very uncertain future.

The Persian Gulf War

Like most Americans, President George Bush greeted the momentous changes in the Soviet Union and eastern Europe with a sense of hope. A consensus emerged among the nation's citizens and elected officials that the cold war was over. The collapse of the Soviet Union meant the end of the great superpower rivalry that had shaped American foreign policy and domestic politics since World War II. What, if anything, would take its place? Bush spoke optimistically of an emerging "new world order" for the post–cold war era, "freer from the threat of terror, stronger in the pursuit of justice, and more secure in the quest for peace, an era in which the nations of the world, East and West, North and South, can prosper and live in harmony." But the first great post–cold war international crisis demonstrated how new kinds of conflicts might now define global politics. Economic competition, ethnic hatreds, and regional struggles for power seemed to replace the old ideological divide between the United States and the Soviet Union as the fulcrum of international conflict.

On August 2, 1990, 120,000 Iraqi troops backed by 850 tanks swept into neighboring Kuwait and quickly seized control of that tiny country. The motives of Saddam Hussein, Iraq's military dictator, were mixed. Like most Iraqis, Saddam believed that oil-rich Kuwait was actually an ancient province of Iraq that had been illegally carved away by British imperial agents in the 1920s as part of the dismemberment of the Ottoman Empire. Control of Kuwait would give Saddam control of its huge oil reserves, as well as Persian Gulf ports for his landlocked country. Rivalry within the Organization of Petroleum Exporting Countries (OPEC) was a factor as well. Iraq, just emerging from an exhausting and inconclusive eight-year war with Iran, bitterly resented Kuwait's production of oil beyond OPEC quotas, which had helped send the world price of oil plummeting from the highs of the 1970s and early 1980s.

The United States responded swiftly to news of the invasion. Its first concern was that Saddam also might attack Saudi Arabia, which the United States had defined as vital to its interests as far back as 1943. On August 15, President Bush ordered U.S. forces to Saudi Arabia and the Persian Gulf, calling the action Operation Desert Shield. The president stressed the importance of oil supplies. "Our jobs, our way of life, our own freedom, and the freedom of friendly countries around the world will suffer if control of the world's great oil reserves fall in the hands of that one man, Saddam Hussein." The United States also led a broad coalition in the United Nations that condemned the Iraqi invasion of Kuwait and declared strict economic sanctions against Iraq if it did not withdraw. By the middle of October, some 230,000 American troops had been sent to the Persian Gulf.

In early November, President Bush announced a change in policy to what he called "an offensive military option," and the U.S. troop deployment quickly doubled to more than 400,000, reaching 580,000 by January 1991. The president also shifted to the moral high ground in justifying the biggest U.S. troop buildup since the Vietnam War. "The fight

U.S. Marines swept into Kuwait City, March 1991. After six weeks of intensive bombing and less than five days after the start of a massive ground offensive, U.S. and allied forces overwhelmed the Iraqi army and ended Saddam Hussein's occupation of Kuwait.

isn't about oil," he insisted. "The fight is about naked aggression that will not stand." Bush administration officials now demonized Saddam as another Adolf Hitler and warned that he controlled a formidable fighting machine of over a million men. The UN sanctions failed to budge Saddam from Kuwait, and the drift to war now looked inevitable. In January 1991, the Senate and House of Representatives vigorously debated a joint resolution authorizing the president to use military force. Opponents urged the president to give the economic sanctions more time to force Iraq out of Kuwait, and they warned of the bloody cost of a drawn-out ground war against Saddam. They also pointed out that only recently the United States had supported Saddam in his war with Iran by providing economic aid, wheat exports, and arms sales. Supporters argued that if war came, it would be both morally just and in the nation's strategic economic interest. The resolution passed narrowly in the Senate (52 to 47) and more comfortably in the House (250 to 183).

A last-minute UN peace mission failed to break the deadlock. On January 16, 1991, President Bush announced the start of Operation Desert Storm. U.S. and Allied air forces began forty-two days of massive bombing of Iraqi positions in Kuwait, as well as Baghdad and other Iraqi cities. They dropped 142,000 tons of bombs on Iraq and Kuwait, roughly

Looters struggled to make off with their booty during the Los Angeles riots of April 1992. Most of the 12,000 people arrested during the riots were from the most economically marginal elements of the L.A. population, including a large number of recent immigrants from Central America and Mexico.

six times the equivalent of the atomic bomb dropped on Nagasaki in World War II. The ground war began on February 24, taking only 100 hours to force Saddam out of Kuwait. Iraqi troops, most of whom were poor conscripts reluctant to fight, surrendered in droves. Saddam's vaunted military machine turned out to be far weaker than advertised. U.S. forces lost only 184 dead, compared with nearly 100,000 Iraqi deaths, mostly from bombing.

At home, the vast majority of Americans supported Operation Desert Storm; the scattered anti-war protests around the nation received scant media coverage. Almost every community in the country had sent men and women to the Gulf either as part of regular armed forces units or as National Guard support personnel. Millions placed yellow ribbons outside their doors as a show of support for American forces. Unlike what occurred during the Vietnam War, television coverage showed virtually no blood or death. The Pentagon required "military escorts" to accompany all reporters, giving army commanders unprecedented control over the press. The Pentagon carefully regulated the release of silent film footage documenting precision bombing runs. On television

these looked more like video games than bombing attacks. American military officials insisted that the bombing had been limited to Iraqi military targets. But subsequent investigations revealed the devastation of Iraq's electrical and communications systems, waterways, bridges, factories, and highways—in short, the nation's entire infrastructure.

Politically, the Persian Gulf War marked the high point of President Bush's popularity. Along with General Norman Schwarzkopf and General Colin Powell, chairman of the Joint Chiefs of Staff, Bush enjoyed enormous acclaim in the afterglow of the swift victory. To most Americans, the war seemed a welcome reassertion of the nation's military prowess and world leadership. Bush received a hero's welcome from a joint session of Congress in March. His approval rating with the public reached nearly 90 percent, higher than President Franklin Roosevelt's during World War II.

Yet nagging questions remained. Saddam himself survived, and the United States abandoned Iraqi opposition forces and the Kurds of northern Iraq after encouraging them to rebel. The United States had succeeded in restoring the government of

Kuwait to power, but that government was itself an undemocratic feudal monarchy. The ecological damage in the Gulf region, mainly due to the torching of Kuwaiti oil wells by Iraqi troops, was extensive. The massive bombing of Iraq led to a severe public health crisis and destroyed the country's economy. Human rights groups reported an appalling toll among civilians. Congressman Jim McDermott (D-Washington), who visited Iraq during the summer after the war, testified before a House committee on the misery he saw and the ethical dilemma posed by American policy. "The Iraqi people did not vote for Saddam Hussein, yet hundreds of thousands of Iraqis, most of them children, are hungry, sick, and dying because of Saddam's intransigence and our commitment to oust Hussein at all cost." The war brought an intense spirit of triumph to the people of the United States. But for the 18 million people of Iraq, heavily bombed and left with Saddam in power, it produced the worst possible outcome.

Multicultural Riot in Los Angeles

In the spring of 1992 a devastating riot in Los Angeles offered the starkest evidence of how racial tensions and desperate poverty continued to plague many American communities. The spark that ignited the worst riot of the century was black outrage over police brutality. Rodney King, a black motorist, had been severely beaten by four white police officers after being stopped and pulled from his vehicle in 1991. An amateur videotape of the incident made by an onlooker was aired widely on television news shows, and it seemed to confirm long-standing charges by minority groups that many Los Angeles police officers were racist.

The four white officers were charged with eleven counts of assault, but they were tried in the white middle-class suburb of Simi Valley. When the jury acquitted them of all but one charge, minority communities erupted in outrage. For three days, rioters swept through South Central Los Angeles and nearby Koreatown, looting and burning businesses. Fifty-one people were killed, more than $750 million in damage was reported, and about 500 buildings were destroyed before L.A. police and National Guard troops managed to restore order. More than 12,000 people were arrested for looting, arson, and violations of curfew. Journalists were quick to make comparisons with the Watts riot of 1965, in which thirty-four people died. But the 1992 riot was different. Not only was it more deadly and more destructive, it was also more complex. The riot was not simply a black-versus-white affair. It was a multicultural riot that involved the large Korean and Latino populations of Los Angeles as well.

A Sheriff's Department analysis of riot-related arrests revealed that 45 percent of those arrested were Latino, 41 percent African American, and 12 percent Anglo. Sixty percent lacked prior criminal records. They included a large number of poor, non-English-speaking recent immigrants from Mexico, El Salvador, and Nicaragua, many of whom were undocumented. These rioters represented the most desperate and marginal people in Los Angeles. They were generally confined to minimum wage jobs as laborers, busboys, domestics, and factory workers, and their unemployment rate had tripled during two years of economic recession. Thousands lived in homeless colonies near the MacArthur Park neighborhood and in the concrete bed of the Los Angeles River. Those who engaged in looting appeared more interested in clothing and food than in televisions or other consumer durables.

The city's large Korean community suffered enormous economic and psychological damage in the riot. Almost 2,000 Korean businesses, mostly liquor stores, groceries, and discount "swap meets," were destroyed. Koreans angrily accused the police of making no effort to defend their stores, and many hired armed guards to patrol their property. Animosity between Korean store owners and African American customers ran deep. Black people had been outraged by the recent acquittal of a Korean grocer who had shot and killed an African American girl she thought was stealing a bottle of orange juice. Black people also complained about the large number of Korean-owned liquor stores in South Central. They resented the success of Korean businesses in black neighborhoods, where very few Koreans lived. The Korean community, generally ambitious and hardworking, questioned why it had been singled out for attack and wondered if the American dream was dead.

For most African Americans, the situation in Los Angeles seemed more desperate than ever, reflecting many of the larger trends in American society over the previous decade. The poverty rate in South Los Angeles was 30.3 percent, over twice the national average. The unemployment rate for adult black males hovered around 40 percent, and a quarter of the population was on welfare. Los Angeles had lost 100,000 manufacturing jobs in the three years before the riot. In 1978, the passage of the statewide Proposition 13 tax cut had led to a sharp reduction in public investment in the inner-city educational system. Drug dealing and gang warfare had escalated, reflecting the sense of despair among young people. The riot exposed the festering ethnic and racial divisions within Los Angeles. "We are all quite isolated in our own communities," a resident of Westwood, a mostly white middle-class neighborhood, explained. "We don't know and don't care about the problems in the inner cities. Driving to work every day most of us don't even know where South Central is—except many of us saw the fires from that direction when we were stuck in traffic."

The Election of 1992

As President Bush's popularity soared after the Persian Gulf War, most political analysts believed that he would win reelection easily. But the glow of military victory faded, and so did Bush's political fortunes. A harsh and lingering recession in 1991 and 1992 dominated the presidential election campaign. The recession was different from other post–World War II slumps in several ways. Although interest rates were low and theoretically should have encouraged investment, business continued to shrink rather than expand. The nation's manufacturers faced stiffer competition than ever, especially from Japan, Korea, and the industrialized nations of Europe. As unemployment climbed above 8 percent, consumer confi-

dence and retail sales plummeted. The effect of previous recessions had been hardest on blue-collar workers, but this one hit white-collar workers severely as well, leaving many in the declining real estate, financial, and computer industries unemployed.

The paradoxes of the Reagan-Bush years became apparent. Conservatives took credit for forcing the fall of communism and reviving America's military strength. Yet the fundamental international problem facing the country seemed to be the erosion of American economic competitiveness and the decline in real wages. In communities devastated by the loss of key industries, millions wondered whether the structural changes transforming the world economy meant an irreversible decline in the American standard of living. Conservatives had made cutting government spending a central premise of their appeal. But after twelve years of Republican rule the national debt stood at an astronomical $4 trillion and threatened to undermine the

Republican President George Bush, Democrat Bill Clinton, and independent H. Ross Perot debated the issues on television three times during the 1992 presidential campaign. Bush emphasized the "character" issue by hammering away at Clinton's failure to serve during the Vietnam War. Clinton focused on the plight of the "forgotten middle class," many of whom had deserted the Democratic Party. Perot made the national debt the centerpiece of his campaign, and he appealed to voter frustration with the two major parties.

nation's economic future. Perhaps the clearest success for Reagan and Bush came in remaking the courts; by 1992, 65 percent of all federal judges and a majority of Supreme Court justices were their appointees. Conservative courts rewrote criminal procedure and allowed states to limit women's access to abortion.

During the primary elections President Bush faced a challenge from the right with the insurgent candidacy of conservative commentator Patrick Buchanan. A former aide to Presidents Nixon and Reagan, Buchanan espoused a conserve ideology that emphasized "traditional values": opposition to abortion and gay rights; celebration of the nuclear family above all others; attacks on government social programs, welfare recipients, and the poor; and a tough stance on crime. Buchanan failed to win any primaries, but his campaign forced the president to shore up his conservative flank. At the Republican National Convention Buchanan and the Reverend Pat Robertson, a conservative fundamentalist, tried to frame the upcoming election as a "cultural war," and in the process they alienated many moderate voters.

After a vigorous primary season the Democrats nominated Governor Bill Clinton of Arkansas. Clinton had begun his political life as a liberal, anti-Vietnam War Democrat. But after suffering defeat in his quest for a second term as governor of Arkansas, he had remade himself politically as a centrist. Clinton's campaign for the nomination effectively adopted many of the conservative themes that had proved so popular for Republicans over the past twelve years. He called for "responsibility" on the part of recipients of social programs, spoke of the importance of stable families, promised to be tough on crime and bureaucracy, and stressed the need for encouraging private investment to create new jobs. Clinton also promised to reform the nation's ailing health care system.

A wild-card element in the 1992 election was the independent campaign of Texas billionaire H. Ross Perot. Perot had made a fortune with a data-processing company that had computerized Social Security and Medicare records in the 1960s and 1970s. He promoted his candidacy through appearances on television talk shows, hoping to bypass traditional media outlets and reach voters directly. With his folksy, East Texas twang, Perot appealed to the deep distrust and anger that millions of people felt toward the two major parties. He made the national debt his central issue, and he argued that a successful businessman like him was better qualified to solve the nation's economic woes than Washington insiders. Perot spent millions of dollars of his own money funding "volunteer" organizations in the fifty states. In July, with polls showing him running nearly even with Bush and Clinton, he abruptly announced

that he was quitting the race. His reasoning was unclear. Two months later, in an effort to restore his damaged reputation, he reentered the race.

All the candidates' campaigns featured sophisticated new media strategies. Clinton, Bush, and Perot appeared frequently on call-in television and radio talk shows in an effort to circumvent the power of professional journalists and connect more directly with voters. Perot spent millions of dollars on half-hour "infomercials" broadcast over the major networks. Clinton made a special effort to reach younger voters by appearing on MTV and youth-oriented programs. As the first baby-boomer candidate, the forty-six-year-old Clinton stressed the theme of generational change.

On election day, the Democrats recaptured the White House after twelve years of Republican control. Clinton won big, beating Bush 43 percent to 38 percent in the popular vote and 370 to 168 in the electoral vote. Although he carried no states, Perot garnered 19 percent of the popular vote, the strongest showing by a third-party candidate since Theodore Roosevelt in 1912. Clinton ran especially strong in the Northeast, the industrial Midwest, and the West, where he became the first Democratic presidential candidate to capture California since Lyndon Johnson in 1964. Clinton won back many of the Reagan Democrats, and his campaign also broke the long Republican grip on the states of the trans-Mississippi West.

"The Era of Big Government Is Over"

With a solidly Democratic House and Senate, President Clinton called for an "American renewal" as he began his first term. A self-styled "new Democrat," he tempered his commitment to activist government with a strategy sensitive to widespread cynicism about Washington politics and "big government" in general. Although his party also controlled Congress, Clinton sought to distance himself from its liberal core. On several key domestic and foreign policy issues Clinton thus found himself fighting with Democrats nearly as much as with Republicans.

As part of a campaign strategy that promised a new government attentiveness to the "forgotten middle class," Clinton pledged a sweeping reform of the nation's health-care system. Nearly 40 million Americans had no health insurance at all. Many simply could not afford it, and others were denied coverage by private insurers because of preexisting conditions such as AIDS and heart disease. Sudden illness or long-term hospital care could wipe out the savings of the uninsured and underinsured. For millions of others, health insurance was tied to the workplace; and a loss or change of jobs threatened

U. S. Secretary of State Madeleine Albright and United Nations Secretary General Kofi Annan begin a session of the Security Council on Africa at UN headquarters, September 25, 1997. Albright, the first woman Secretary of State in American history, embodied President Bill Clinton's commitment to appointing more women to high offices in his administration.

greater reliance on "market forces" and criticized the "big government" approach. Many of these members of Congress had received large campaign donations from political action committees associated with the pharmaceutical industry, insurance companies, and the American Medical Association. One of the most powerful of these special interest groups, the Health Insurance Association of America, spent millions of dollars on a series of television advertisements designed to spread doubts about the administration's plan. After a year of congressional wrangling, no plan was approved and the president was forced to abandon his reform effort.

In foreign affairs Clinton focused on improving America's international trade position as the key to national economic growth. He pushed two important trade agreements through Congress, both of which built on efforts by the Reagan and Bush administrations to expand markets and encourage "free trade." Approved in late 1993, the North American Free Trade Agreement (NAFTA) eased the international flow of goods, services, and investments among the United States, Mexico, and Canada by eliminating tariffs and other trade barriers. Supplemental agreements called for cooperation on environmental and labor concerns. The broad goal of NAFTA was to improve productivity and living standards through a freer flow of commerce in North America. It created the largest free trade zone in the world, comprising 360 million people and an annual gross national product of $6 trillion. In 1994 Congress also approved the General Agreement on Tariffs and Trade (GATT), which slashed tariffs on thousands of goods throughout the world and phased out import quotas imposed by the United States and other industrialized nations. It also established the World Trade Organization to mediate commercial disputes among 117 nations. GATT supporters argued that the agreement would encourage global competition, thereby boosting American export industries and creating new high-wage jobs for American workers.

But NAFTA and GATT barely won approval after bruising congressional fights, and both found their strongest champions among Republicans. Many Democrats in Congress, especially those from traditionally liberal

their coverage. National spending on health care had skyrocketed from roughly $200 billion in 1980 to more than $800 billion in 1992, constituting about one-seventh of the entire domestic economy.

Once in office Clinton appointed his wife, Hillary Rodham Clinton, to head a task force charged with preparing a sweeping legislative overhaul of health care. The task force sought a political middle ground between conservative approaches, which stressed fine tuning the system by making private insurance available to all, and more liberal approaches, which would have the federal government guarantee health care as a right. Indeed, nearly 100 House Democrats supported a "single payer plan" modeled on the Canadian system of government-run, universal health care.

The complex plan that emerged from the task force in the fall of 1993 was difficult to understand and impossible to sell politically. Under this "managed competition" proposal, most Americans would obtain coverage through large purchasing groups called health-care alliances. Employers would be mandated to pay at least 80 percent of their employees' insurance premiums. Private insurance companies would remain at the center of the system.

Powerful forces attacked the Clinton administration's health-care plan immediately. The Chamber of Commerce and National Association of Manufacturers opposed the employer mandate provision. Republicans and conservative Democrats called for districts in the Northeast and Midwest, bitterly opposed the agreements, creating a strain within the party. Critics of GATT questioned the rosy predictions of a net gain in high-wage jobs. Increases in imports, they pointed out, would threaten hundreds of thousands of high-paying jobs in American industries such as automobiles and textiles. Opponents of NAFTA feared that the free trade agreements would mean an exodus of millions of jobs to Mexico because industries would be attracted there by its low wages and lax enforcement of workers' rights. They worried, too, that the environmental sections of the agreement were too weak to prevent Mexico from becoming a haven for corporate polluters.

In the first few years after the passage of NAFTA and GATT many of these fears seemed confirmed. Free trade with the United States was supposed to bring prosperity to Mexico, but instead the peso collapsed and the Mexican economy slipped into a serious depression. From 1994 to 1997 the wages of the average Mexican worker fell from $1.45 per hour to only 78 cents. Trade did boom between the two countries, but a 1997 study conducted by the Department of Labor estimated that some 142,000 U.S. and Canadian jobs had been lost as a direct result of NAFTA. Moreover, the report admitted, many American employers were using the threat of moving plants or facilities to Mexico as a weapon in wage negotiations with workers. There was also increasing evidence that environmental conditions along the U.S.-Mexico border were growing worse, not better, and there were several episodes in which tainted Mexican fruit and vegetables caused local epidemics in American communities.

The failure of health-care reform and the debate over NAFTA revealed a Democratic Party deeply divided against itself. President Clinton's political position was also weakened by publicity attending his personal life. Paula Jones, a former Arkansas state employee, filed a sexual harassment suit against him. Nagging questions arose about real estate deals in which Clinton and his wife were involved while he was still governor of Arkansas—a scandal that became known as Whitewater. Responding to Republican charges that a former business partner of Clinton's had received favorable insider treatment in connection with a failed savings and loan company, the Attorney General eventually appointed an independent counsel, former judge Kenneth Starr.

Reacting to doubts about Clinton's character and leadership, voters in the 1994 congressional elections rewarded Republicans with control of both the House and Senate for the first time in forty years—a disaster of historic proportions for Clinton and the Democratic Party. Congress was now dominated by a new breed of younger, ideologically more conservative

Republicans. Their leader was the new House Speaker, Newt Gingrich of Georgia. First elected to Congress in 1978, Gingrich had quickly won a reputation as a formidable polemicist for the Republican Party's far right. A brilliant organizer and fund raiser, he had moved from the margins to the center of his party's power structure. With his scathing denunciations of big government, attacks on the counterculture of the 1960s, and celebration of entrepreneurship, Gingrich captured the heart of the Republican Party and emerged as potentially the most influential House Speaker in this century.

The Republicans exploited prevailing social conditions. As more and more working-class and middle-class voters expressed fear for their jobs and economic security in the new global economy, race and immigration loomed as effective "hot button" issues for political candidates. With attacks on welfare, affirmative action, and federal initiatives to aid education and the inner cities, conservatives exploited a continuing white backlash against the limited economic and political gains African Americans had achieved in the previous decades. No candidates addressed the deepening poverty and economic inequality that put one of every seven Americans, and one of every five children, below the poverty line.

The Republican victory at the polls allowed Gingrich to challenge Clinton as the key figure setting the nation's political agenda. His priorities were expressed in a set of proposals labeled the "Contract with America." Invoking the "hundred days" of Franklin D. Roosevelt's New Deal in 1933 (Chapter 24), Gingrich promised to bring all these proposals to a vote in the House within 100 days. The House did indeed pass much of the Contract, including a large tax cut, an increase in military spending, cutbacks in federal regulatory power in the environment and at the workplace, a tough anticrime bill, and a sharp reduction in federal welfare programs. Differences with the Senate, however, and the threat of presidential veto thwarted Gingrich's plans and created conditions that allowed President Clinton to make a political comeback.

In December of 1995 the Republican-controlled Congress forced a shutdown of the federal government rather than accede to President Clinton's demand for changes in their proposed budget. The result was a public relations disaster for the Republicans. Gingrich's reputation plummeted, and after little more than a year as Speaker he had become one of the most unpopular figures in American politics.

The Election of 1996 and Clinton's Second Term
Meanwhile, Clinton undercut the Republicans by adapting many of their positions to his own. He endorsed the goal of a balanced federal budget and

The era of divided government at century's end meant that Democrats controlled the White House while Republicans dominated the Congress. Here President Bill Clinton talked to Senate Majority Leader Trent Lott (R-MS), as House Speaker Newt Gingrich (R-GA) looked on, during a White House meeting to discuss combating terrorism, July 29, 1996.

was at home in the halls of Congress but extremely uncomfortable on the campaign trail. Seventy-three years old and a poor public speaker, he proved a pale contrast to Clinton—young, vigorous, and surely one of the most adroit politicians of the century. Sensing Dole's weakness, Ross Perot once again threw his hat into the ring as the candidate of his own Reform Party, siphoning off many potential Dole supporters.

Pursuing a strategy his advisers called "triangulation," the president successfully positioned himself above and between the interests of warring Democrats and Republicans. Welfare reform provided a prominent example of this strategy in action. Despite his attacks on the Republicans as radicals, Clinton opposed his own party's efforts to block a Republican plan to dismantle the federal welfare system in place since the New Deal. The new legislation—the Welfare Reform Act—abolished the sixty-year-old Aid to Families with Dependent Children program (AFDC). Poor mothers with dependent children would now have access to aid for only a limited period and only if they were preparing for or seeking work. When Congress passed the act in August of 1996, Clinton held a public signing ceremony and declared "an end to welfare as we know it."

declared, in his January 1996 State of the Union message, that "the era of big government is over." With such deft maneuvers, the president set the theme for his 1996 reelection campaign, portraying himself as a reasonable conservative and the Republicans in Congress as conservative radicals. In a blitz of effective television ads, Democrats portrayed Republicans as reckless extremists bent on destroying the safety net of Social Security and Medicare and inattentive to the educational needs of children.

Leading Republicans, meanwhile, attacked each other as they fought to win their party's presidential nomination. In the state primaries leading up to the national convention, Robert Dole of Kansas, Majority Leader of the Senate, was forced to move to his right to counter more conservative opponents such as commentator Patrick Buchanan and wealthy publisher Steve Forbes, who advocated replacing the income tax with a so-called "flat tax." Dole had the nomination locked up by June, but the bruising primary battles cost him the support of many voters who worried that Dole's positions were cut from the same cloth as Gingrich's "Contract with America."

Dole waged an inept campaign for president, Clinton a brilliant one. A veteran of the Senate, Dole

Clinton's greatest strength was a resurgent American economy. The recession that had plagued George Bush's presidency bottomed out in 1994, followed over the next two years by strong economic growth, a dramatic rise in the stock market, and a sharp decline in unemployment. Some economists began to talk of a "third industrial revolution," led by high-technology companies, that would produce an extended boom. Others went so far as to suggest that the new, technology-driven global economy might end the historic business cycle of boom and bust. Such claims easily could be dismissed as wildly optimistic speculation—but the political credit for the newly robust economy went largely to President Clinton.

Confounding the predictions of political pundits, who had pronounced his political death after the Republican congressional sweep of 1994, President Bill Clinton won a resounding reelection victory in

November of 1996. But it was a victory without coat-tails; the Republicans retained control of both houses of Congress. The era of big government may have ended, as Clinton had proclaimed, but the era of divided government would continue.

The 1996 campaign had been the most expensive in history. The Democrats spent $250 million, the Republicans $400 million, a total that was more than twice the amount spent in 1992. Both parties created fund-raising machines of enormous ingenuity and dubious legality. In 1997 Republicans organized congressional hearings that exposed Democratic campaign finance abuses, such as soliciting funds in the White House. But with Congress unable to agree on campaign finance reform, the revelations served only to deepen popular cynicism about the electoral process.

The conflict between the Democratic president and the Republican Congress reached historic proportions in 1998. Although the sexual harassment lawsuit brought by Paula Jones was thrown out of court that year, it indirectly led to the deepest crisis of the Clinton presidency. In the summer of 1998, independent counsel Kenneth Starr delivered an explosive report of his investigation to the House Judiciary Committee. The Starr report focused entirely on an extramarital affair the president had conducted with a young White House intern, Monica Lewinsky. Starr claimed his office had discovered evidence of the affair while reviewing depositions from the Paula Jones lawsuit. The report outlined several potentially impeachable offenses, allegedly committed by the president in the course of trying to keep his affair with Lewinsky secret. These included lying under oath, witness tampering, and obstruction of justice.

After agreeing to testify before a grand jury empanelled by Starr—a first for an American president—Clinton made an extraordinary television address to the nation in which he defended his legal position and attacked the Starr inquiry as politically motivated. The Congress and the American people at large fiercely debated the nature of the charges against the president: Were they truly impeachable—"high crimes and misdemeanors" as the Constitution put it—or merely part of a partisan political effort to overturn the election of 1996? In October 1998, the House of Representatives voted along largely partisan lines to begin a full-scale, open-ended inquiry into possible grounds for the impeachment of President Clinton. It was only the third time in American history that the House had taken such action.

Republicans expected the Lewinsky scandal and the impeachment inquiry to bolster their fortunes in the election of 1998, augmenting the gains the party out of power in the White House can traditionally expect in a midterm election. Indeed all summer and fall, virtually every professional pollster and media commentator predicted big Republican gains in the House and Senate.

Instead, for the first time since 1934, the President's party added seats in a midterm election. The Democrats gained five seats in the House, cutting the Republican majority from 228–206 in the 105th Congress to 223–211 in the 106th. In the Senate, Republicans were unable to increase their 55–45 majority.

Voters no doubt had more on their minds than President Clinton's sex life. Democratic candidates benefited from continued strength in the economy, and they made effective appeals on a range of issues, from preserving Social Security and Medicare to protecting a woman's right to choose an abortion. Higher than expected turnout from such core constituencies as union members and African Americans (especially in the South) also contributed to the unexpectedly strong Democratic showing. The election also brought a shakeup in the Republican leadership. Newt Gingrich, under pressure from Republican colleagues angry about a campaign strategy that had narrowly focused on Clinton's impeachment problem, announced his resignation as Speaker of the House and from his seat in Congress. Ironically Gingrich, who had led the Republican resurgence in the 1990s, now appeared to be the first political victim of the Lewinsky scandal.

In the aftermath of the 1998 election, most politicians and analysts, and indeed most Americans, believed the impeachment inquiry to be at a dead end. But the House Judiciary Committee, after raucous televised debate, voted to bring four articles of impeachment—charging President Clinton with perjury, obstruction of justice, witness tampering, and abuse of power—to the full House. But unlike the bipartisan case the Judiciary Committee brought against Richard Nixon in 1974 (see Chapter 29), this time the votes were all along strictly party lines. Neither the 1998 election results, nor polls showing a large majority of Americans opposed to removing the President, curbed the Republican determination to push impeachment through the House. On December 19, 1998, for only the second time in American history, the full House voted to impeach a sitting president, passing articles charging Clinton with perjury and obstruction of justice along party lines and sending them to the Senate for trial. The impeachment drive could be understood as the culmination of divided government and the bitterly partisan turn American politics had taken since 1980.

Changing American Communities

The 1990 census showed that for the first time in U.S. history a majority of Americans lived within large metropolitan areas. The census defined a metropolitan area as "one or more counties including a large population nucleus and nearby communities that have a high degree of interaction." The census divided these areas into two groups: those with populations above 1 million and those with smaller populations. It revealed that nearly 125 million people out of a total population of 249 million lived within the thirty-nine large (over 1 million) metropolitan centers. Greater New York City, with more than 18 million people, was the largest of these areas, followed by Greater Los Angeles, with 14.5 million residents. The nation's fastest-growing large metropolitan areas were all in the West and South. These included Orlando, which grew by 53 percent in the 1980s, Phoenix (40 percent), Sacramento (34 percent), San Diego (34 percent), Dallas-Fort Worth (32 percent), Atlanta (32 percent), and Los Angeles (26 percent).

This historic statistical shift stemmed directly from the expansion of the economy's service sector. The nation's postindustrial economy relied heavily on the growth of management, research and development, marketing, and distribution activities. These required the critical mass of educated people and services that could be found only in metropolitan areas. The proportion of the population with at least a college degree grew disproportionately in those areas, to 22.5 percent, compared with 13 percent in nonmetropolitan areas.

An enormous range of differences could be found both between and within metropolitan area communities. Recent immigrants brought a striking new multiculturalism to many coastal and Sunbelt "port of entry" communities, while smaller communities in the Midwest remained relatively unchanged. In Greater Los Angeles, for example, half the population was Hispanic, black, or Asian, and 27 percent of the residents were foreign-born. But the community that many demographers called typical was Indianapolis, where less than 15 percent of the population was Hispanic, black, or Asian and less than 2 percent of the residents were foreign-born. A larger percentage of people lived in expanding metropolitan areas, but a larger proportion of metropolitan people lived in the suburbs. Metropolitan expansion created huge semiurban sprawls, which erased the old boundaries between many towns. Population and job growth were concentrated at the geographic edges of metropolitan areas.

The suburban city of Plano, Texas, offered a harbinger of the future for many American communities. Part of the Dallas-Fort Worth metropolitan area, Plano's population jumped from 72,000 to 128,000 during the 1980s, an increase of 78 percent. Plano was one of five suburban cities with populations of more than 100,000 in the Dallas-Fort Worth area. The others included Arlington, Garland, Irving, and Mesquite. Altogether, these five suburban cities grew almost twice as much as Dallas and Fort Worth during the 1980s. Whereas the traditional American city was built around a central business district, newer suburban cities grew up around a principal business or economic activity: a collection of computer companies, a large regional medical center, or a sports complex. Plano's economic life revolved around Legacy Park, a huge office development housing one of the world's largest data-processing centers, along with the headquarters of five major corporations. Two large fiber optic communications stations kept Legacy Park plugged into the global economy. A nearby complex of telecommunications manufacturing plants provided another new source of jobs.

Every rush hour, traffic moved in both directions as commuters drove to and from Plano for jobs in office buildings, factories, warehouses, and shopping malls. During the 1980s, Plano began to display many attributes associated with large urban centers. Thai, Chinese, and other ethnic restaurants opened up. A quaint downtown featured antique and crafts shops in storefronts where cotton farmers used to buy supplies. The city boasted its own small chamber music ensemble. Yet the rapid growth of suburban cities like Plano also exposed and reinforced the deepening economic and racial divisions in American society. Plano had a very small immigrant and minority population, and nearly 90 percent of its public school students were white. In Dallas, by contrast, the 1990 census showed that for the first time a majority of the city's population was African American or Latino.

Suburban cities have become even more economically specialized than the industrial centers of the nineteenth century. Yet their gains often meant losses for older cities. As core cities like Fort Worth lost jobs and part of their tax base to suburban cities like Plano, it became more difficult for them to pay the costs of maintaining infrastructure and caring for the elderly, poor, and sick. While suburban cities like Plano often suffered from labor shortages, unemployment increased in the core cities, especially among African Americans and Latinos. Lack of adequate transportation and low-cost housing made it difficult for central-city residents to take advantage of new job opportunities in the suburban city.

CONCLUSION

In the late 1980s and early 1990s, as the nation faced competition from a tougher, more dynamic global economy, citizens, politicians, and business leaders had to rethink some of their most basic assumptions about the American way of life. American society became more stratified along lines of race and income. New immigrant groups, especially from Asia and Latin America, changed the face of the nation's neighborhoods, schools, and workplaces. New epidemics and spreading poverty threatened the public health of whole communities. New media technologies made cultural life more homogenized and caused the manipulation of image to become more crucial than ever in both politics and entertainment.

During these decades the very notion of community itself, once defined entirely in terms of

CHRONOLOGY

1980	Ronald Reagan is elected president
1981	Reagan administration initiates major cuts in taxes and domestic spending
	Military buildup accelerates
	AIDS is recognized and named
	MTV and CNN start broadcasting as cable channels
1982	Economic recession grips the nation
	Nuclear freeze rally attracts 750,000 in New York City
1983	Reagan announces the Strategic Defense Initiative, labeled "Star Wars" by critics
	241 marines are killed in Beirut terrorist bombing
	Marines land on Grenada and oust anti-American Marxist regime
1984	Reagan is reelected overwhelmingly
1985	Mikhail Gorbachev initiates reforms—*glasnost* and *perestroika*—in the Soviet Union
1986	Immigration Reform and Control Act addresses concerns about illegal aliens
	Democrats regain control of the Senate
1987	Iran-Contra hearings before Congress reveal arms-for-hostages deal and funds secretly, and illegally, diverted to Nicaraguan rebels
	Stock market crashes

	Reagan and Gorbachev sign INF Treaty
1988	George Bush is elected president
1989	Communist authority collapses in eastern Europe
1990	August: Iraqi invasion of Kuwait leads to massive U.S. military presence in the Persian Gulf
1991	January–February: Operation Desert Storm forces Iraq out of Kuwait
	Soviet Union dissolves into Commonwealth of Independent States
1992	Rodney King verdict sparks rioting in Los Angeles
	Bill Clinton is elected president
1993	Clinton administration introduces comprehensive health-care reform, but it fails to win passage in Congress
	Congress approves the North American Free Trade Agreement
1994	Republicans win control of Senate and House for first time in forty years
	Congress approves the General Agreement on Tariffs and Trade
	Congress passes the Comprehensive AIDS Revenue Emergency Act
1996	Congress passes Welfare Reform Act
	President Bill Clinton is reelected

space, increasingly became a function of demographics. The proliferation of computer-based communication technologies made it easier to create communities based on the demographic categories of income, profession, education level, and consumption preferences. The mass media, advertisers, and political professionals all intensified their reliance on sophisticated marketing and polling techniques. Thus American culture defined and addressed its citizens less as whole human beings and more as the sums of statistical characteristics. At the same time, new technologies created "virtual communities" with the potential for new kinds of human relationships not defined by corporate values or even by physical familiarity. As American communities continue to evolve in response to a more global, service-oriented, and high-tech economy, they will no doubt be forced to seek both regional and international solutions to the problems posed by the twenty-first century.

REVIEW QUESTIONS

1. Describe the central philosophical assumptions behind "Reaganomics." What were the key policies by which it was implemented? To what extent were these policies a break with previous economic approaches?

2. Evaluate Reagan-Bush era foreign policy. What successes and failures stand out? Which problems from those years remain central and/or unsolved for today's policy makers?

3. Analyze the key structural factors underlying recent changes in American economic and cultural life. Do you see any political solutions for the growth of poverty and inequality?

4. Assess the growing political appeal of conservatism in American life. How would you explain its successes? What future do you see for the liberal and radical traditions?

5. Is the United States entering a "new era" at the turn of the twenty-first century? What effects have the globalized economy and the fall of the Soviet Union had on American life?

RECOMMENDED READING

Donald Barlett and James B. Steele, *America: What Went Wrong* (1992). An expansion of the authors' series in the *Philadelphia Inquirer*. This book offers a mass of interesting data documenting the declining fortunes of the American middle class in the 1980s.

Sidney Blumenthal and Thomas B. Edsall, eds., *The Reagan Legacy* (1988). A collection of critical essays assessing the impact of Reagan's presidency on American society and culture.

Colin Campbell and Bert A. Rockman, eds., *The Clinton Presidency: First Appraisals* (1996). A wide-ranging collection of essays assessing the political and historical significance of the Clinton administration.

Haynes Johnson, *Sleepwalking through History* (1991). A readable, journalistic narrative of the Reagan presidency.

Michael T. Klare and Peter Kornbluh, eds., *Low Intensity Warfare* (1988). A valuable set of essays offering case studies of counterinsurgency and antiterrorist tactics during the 1980s.

Robert Lekachman, *Visions and Nightmares* (1987). An economist's view of Reagan's legacy, emphasizing the long-range impact of military spending, tax cuts, and the shrinking of social programs.

Nicolaus Mills, *Culture in an Age of Money* (1990). An acerbic account of the impact of corporate power and big money on the cultural life of the nation during the 1980s.

New York Times, The Downsizing of America (1996). A well-researched account detailing the devastating impact of corporate "downsizing" on American communities and families.

Kevin Phillips, *The Politics of Rich and Poor* (1990). A fascinating, superbly documented, and often brilliant analysis of the growth in economic inequality that characterized the 1980s. Phillips, a prominent Republican strategist, makes historical comparisons with the 1920s and the late nineteenth century to bolster his argument.

Howard Rheingold, *The Virtual Community* (1994). Very thoughtful examination of the promises and problems posed by the new computer-based technologies associated with "virtual communities."

Micah L. Sifry and Christopher Cerf, eds., *The Gulf War Reader* (1991). An excellent collection of historical essays, government documents, and political addresses that provides a comprehensive overview of the Persian Gulf War.

James B. Stewart, *Den of Thieves* (1991). A well-documented inside look at the people and events at the center of Wall Street's insider trader scandal. Stewart offers a detailed account of the shady financial practices of the 1980s.

ADDITIONAL BIBLIOGRAPHY

The Reagan Revolution

Ryan Barilleaux, *The Post-Modern Presidency* (1988)

Lou Cannon, *President Reagan: The Role of a Lifetime* (1991)

Rowland Evans and Robert Novak, *The Reagan Revolution* (1991)

Dilys Hill et al., *The Reagan Presidency* (1990)

Michael Schaller, *Reckoning with Reagan* (1992)

C. Brant Short, *Ronald Reagan and the Public Lands* (1989)

David Stockman, *The Triumph of Politics* (1986)

Susan Tolchin and Martin Tolchin, *Dismantling America: The Rush to Deregulate* (1983)

Garry Wills, *Reagan's America* (1987)

Reagan's Foreign Policy

Raymond Bonner, *Weakness and Deceit: U.S. Policy and El Salvador* (1984)

William J. Broad, *Teller's War: The Top-Secret Story behind the Star Wars Deception* (1992)

William E. Brock and Robert D. Hormats, eds., *The Global Economy* (1990)

Thomas Crothers, *In the Name of Democracy: U.S. Foreign Policy toward Latin America in the Reagan Years* (1991)

Theodore Draper, *A Very Thin Line: The Iran-Contra Affairs* (1991)

John L. Gaddis, *The United States and the End of the Cold War* (1992)

Stephen R. Graubard, *Mr. Bush's War* (1992)

Roy Gutman, *Banana Diplomacy* (1988)

Jonathan Kwitny, *Endless Enemies* (1984)

David E. Kyvig, ed., *Reagan and the World* (1990)

Walter LaFeber, *Inevitable Revolutions*, 2d ed. (1984)

Michael Mandelbaum, *Reagan and Gorbachev* (1987)

Bob Woodward, *Veil: The Secret Wars of the CIA* (1987)

Best of Times, Worst of Times

Michael A. Bernstein and David A. Adler, eds., *Understanding American Economic Decline* (1994)

Barbara Ehrenreich, *Fear of Falling: The Inner Life of the Middle Class* (1989)

Elizabeth Fee and Daniel M. Fox, eds., *AIDS: The Making of a Chronic Disease* (1992)

Bennet Harrison and Barry Bluestone, *The Great U Turn: Corporate Restructuring and the Polarizing of America* (1988)

James D. Hunter, *Culture Wars: The Struggle to Define America* (1991)

Daniel Ichbiah, *The Making of Microsoft* (1991)

Martin Lowy, *High Rollers: Inside the Savings and Loan Debacle* (1991)

Everett M. Rogers and Judith K. Larsen, *Silicon Valley Fever* (1984)

William Serrin, *Homestead* (1991)

Randy Shilts, *And the Band Played On* (1986)

Richard White, *Rude Awakenings: What the Homeless Crisis Tells Us* (1992)

William Julius Wilson, *The Truly Disadvantaged: The Inner City, the Underclass, and Public Policy* (1987)

Edward N. Wolff, *Top Heavy* (1995)

End of an Era?

Michael R. Beschloss and Strobe Talbott, *At the Highest Levels: The Inside Story of the End of the Cold War* (1994)

Mike Davis, *City of Quartz: Excavating the Future in Los Angeles* (1990)

Michael Duffy, *Marching in Place: The Status Quo Presidency of George Bush* (1992)

Susan Faludi, *Backlash: The Undeclared War against American Women* (1991)

Andrew Hacker, *Two Nations: Black and White, Separate, Hostile, and Unequal* (1992)

Richard Hallion, *Storm over Iraq* (1992)

Denis Lynn Daly Heyck, ed., *Barrios and Borderlands: Cultures of Latinos and Latinas in the United States* (1993)

Bill Ong Hing, *Making and Remaking Asian America through Immigration Policy, 1850–1990* (1993)

Juliet B. Schor, *The Overworked American* (1991)

James B. Stewart, *Blood Sport: The President and His Adversaries* (1996)

Reed Ueda, *Postwar Immigrant America* (1994)

Bob Woodward, *The Agenda: Inside the Clinton White House* (1994)

Biography

Charles F. Allen, *The Comeback Kid: The Life and Career of Bill Clinton* (1992)

Ken Gross, *Ross Perot: The Man behind the Myth* (1992)

Harry Hurt, *The Lost Tycoon: The Many Lives of Donald J. Trump* (1993)

Kitty Kelley, *Nancy Reagan* (1991)

Nicholas King, *George Bush* (1980)

David Maraniss, *First in His Class: A Biography of Bill Clinton* (1995)

Roger Morris, *Partners in Power: The Clintons and Their America* (1996)

Michael Rogin, *Ronald Reagan* (1987)

IMMIGRATION & COMMUNITY

The Changing Face of Ethnicity in America
SINCE 1930

During the last three quarters of the twentieth century, the character and sources of immigration to the United States changed radically. With America's growing power and prominence in the international arena, the laws governing immigration became increasingly tools of foreign policy. The social devastation of World War II and the ideological battles of the Cold War created whole new categories of immigrant, such as that of political refugee. Recent immigration has also reflected the dynamic transformations in the economies of the United States and of the rest of the world. The national quotas established in the 1920s severely limited the flow of immigrants from Europe. But lawmakers, responding to the labor needs of industry and agriculture, had placed no barriers to newcomers from the Western Hemisphere. Thus, Canadians and Mexicans grew into the two largest national immigrant groups. Circular migration shaped the experience of these peoples; they were *transborder peoples*, going frequently back and forth between their homelands and the United States. Dividing their political and cultural loyalties between the United States and their homelands, Mexicans and Canadians developed an ambiguous identity. As a result, they were slower to adopt U.S. citizenship than were other immigrants.

Some 1.4 million Canadians arrived in the United States between 1920 and 1960, with three quarters from British Canada (Ontario, Nova Scotia, New Brunswick) and one quarter from French Canada (Quebec). They settled close to the border, primarily in New England cities, such as Boston, Lowell, Nashua, and Holyoke, as well as in the Great Lakes region. During the same period, more than 840,000 Mexicans arrived as permanent settlers and 4.7 million more as temporary guest workers. They headed mainly for the rich agricultural areas of southern California and the lower Rio Grande Valley of Texas. Many, however, looking for factory work, settled in big Midwestern industrial centers such as Chicago, Detroit, and Kansas City. In the Southwest, Mexicans tended to cluster in isolated *barrios*. In the midwest, in contrast, following the pattern of older European immigrant communities in big cities, they tended to assimilate more.

Perhaps more than any other group, Mexican immigrants were subject to the vagaries of the U.S. economy. The Great Depression drastically reduced the need for their labor and spurred a mass reverse migration. As many as half a million Mexicans were repatriated during the 1930s, often at the urging of local American officials who did not want Mexican aliens on public relief rolls. The onset of World War II brought a new demand for Mexican labor in agriculture and transportation. In 1942 the U.S. and Mexican governments revived the guest worker program of World War I. The *bracero* ("farmhand") program admitted agricultural workers on short-term contracts; they were classified as foreign laborers, not immigrants. By 1947, some 200,000 *braceros* worked in twenty-one states, including 100,000 in California. Congress renewed the program after the war ended. By 1960 Mexicans made up more than one quarter of the nation's farm labor force.

Puerto Ricans, the third largest group of immigrants to the U.S. mainland from the Western Hemisphere, were a special case because, as U.S. citizens since 1917, they could come and go without restriction. Like Canadians and Mexicans, they helped fill the labor demand caused by the restriction of European immigration. Between 1945 and 1965 the Puerto Rican-born population jumped from 100,000 to roughly 1 million. The majority headed for New York City and surrounding communities.

Another growing class of immigrants consisted of refugees uprooted by World War II and the emergence of Communist regimes in Eastern Europe. A series of laws combined the historical notion of America as a haven for the world's oppressed with the new reality of Cold War power politics. The Displaced Persons Act of 1948 was the first law in American history to set refugee policy as opposed to immigration policy. It provided 202,000 visas over a two-year period, allowing permanent settlement in the United States for refugees from fascist and Communist regimes. A 1950 amendment upped the number of visas to 341,000 annually. The Refugee Relief Act of 1953 authorized admission of 205,000 "nonquota" refugees, but limited these to people fleeing persecution from Communist regimes. In practice, this policy gave priority to refugees from the Baltic states and Eastern European Communist nations; only a minority admitted under the act were Jews or other victims of Hitler. Indeed, hundreds of former Nazis, including many scientists, were allowed in under the act in the interest of "national security."

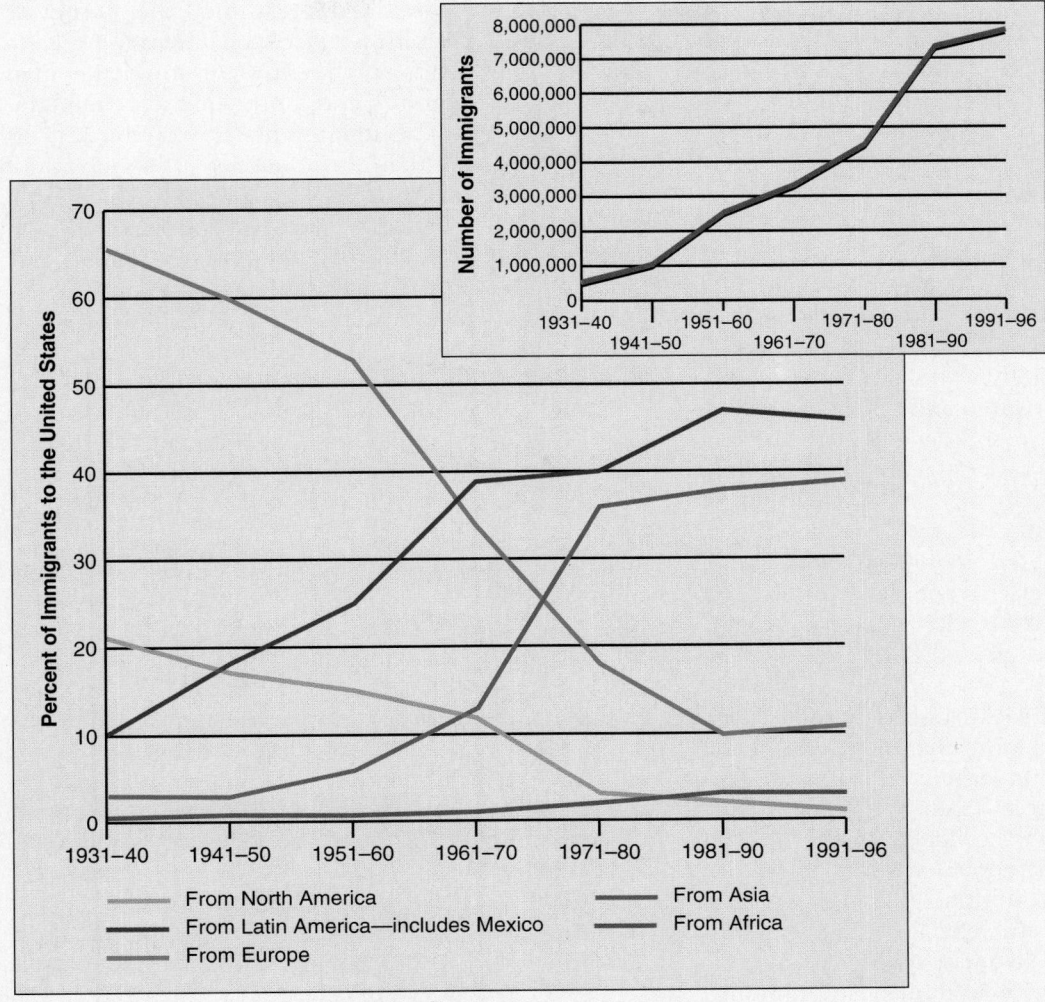

Immigration to the United States, by Decade, 1930–1996

In 1952, as a conservative counterpoint to the growth of refugee legislation, Congress passed the McCarran-Walter Act. Reaffirming the 1920s principle of discriminatory quotas based on national origin, the act specified that 85 percent of those admitted annually were to come from Northern and Western European countries. Yet McCarran-Walter also contained some important liberal innovations. It revoked the denial of admission based on race, and it allowed for small, token quotas for immigrants from China and Japan, ending the long-standing policy of Asian exclusion.

The Immigration Act of 1965, passed almost unnoticed in the context of the egalitarian political climate created by the Civil Rights movement, had revolutionary consequences, some of them unintended. The act abolished the discriminatory national origins quotas that had been in place since the 1920s. But it also limited immigration from the Western Hemisphere for the first time, allowing 120,000 annual visas from

that region, compared to 170,000 from the Eastern Hemisphere. It continued the policy of selective admissions, but with important exceptions. Exempted from numerical quotas were immigrants seeking family reunification with American citizens or resident aliens. In addition, preferences to those with specialized job skills and training were extended to people from the nations of the Eastern Hemisphere.

The high priority given family reunification greatly increased the *chain migration* of people seeking to join relatives already in the United States. After 1965, Asian immigrants made up the fastest growing ethnic groups, with more than 1.5 million arriving during the 1970s, as opposed to roughly 800,000 from Europe. The new Asian migration included many professionals and well-educated technical workers. For example, immigrants from the Philippines and India included a high number of health care professionals, and many Chinese and Korean immigrants found work in professional and managerial occupations. At the same time, low-skilled and impoverished Asians poured into the "Chinatowns" and "Koreatowns" of cities like New York and Los Angeles, seeking work in restaurants, hotels, and garment manufacturing. The end of the Indochina War brought new refugees from Cambodia, Laos, and Vietnam. The 1965 act also created conditions that increased undocumented immigration from Latin America. The new limits on Western Hemisphere migration, along with simultaneous ending of the *bracero* program, tempted many thousands to enter the United States illegally. The Immigration and Naturalization Service arrested and deported 500,000 illegal aliens each year in the decade following the act, most of them from Mexico, Central America, and the Caribbean.

During the 1980s the rate of immigration accelerated. The estimated 6 million legal and 2 million undocumented immigrants who entered the United States during that decade was second only to the 8.8 million who had arrived between 1900 and 1910. By 1990, one out of every five immigrants living in the United States was Mexican-born, and Mexican Americans accounted for more than 60 percent of all Hispanics. Demographers predicted that by 2050 Hispanics would replace African Americans as the largest minority group in the nation. The number of Asian Americans more than doubled during the 1980s, from 3.5 million to 7.3 million. Nearly two out of every five Asian Americans lived in California, with 300,000 in Los Angeles' "Koreatown." Among recent immigrant groups, Asians—Vietnamese, Filipinos, Koreans, and Chinese—gained naturalization (citizenship) at the fastest rate. Asians totaled nearly 50 percent of all people naturalized in the 1980s. Unlike early-twentieth-century Asian migrants, the post-1965 newcomers were mostly intent on settling here permanently, and they migrated in family units. The new Asian immigrants also remade the small ethnic enclaves from earlier migrations, reinvigorating them with new energy, new capital, and a more explicit ethnic consciousness.

By the mid-1980s, growing concern over "illegal aliens" had become a hotly debated political issue, particularly in the Southwest. The Immigration Reform and Control Act of 1986 marked a break with past attempts to address this problem. Instead of mass deportation programs, the law offered an amnesty to all undocumented workers who had entered the country since 1982. Although opening the "front door" of admissions wider, the law also tried to shut the "back door" by imposing sanctions on employers who knowingly hired or recruited undocumented aliens.

Yet no matter what Congress did, the desperate economic realities in Mexico and Central America continued to enlarge the flow of undocumented aliens. At the century's end, both American immigration policy and the immigrants now arriving look radically different than they did 75 years ago. Nativist sentiment and calls for greater immigration restriction are still powerful voices on the political scene, especially during economic downturns and within those states absorbing the bulk of new immigrants. Thus, in 1994, California voters, by a 3–2 margin, approved Proposition 187, which declared all undocumented immigrants ineligible for any welfare services, public schooling, and nonemergency medical care. But in 1998 a federal court ruled that Proposition 187 unconstitutionally usurped federal authority over immigration policy. Nativist appeals and campaigns will likely remain part of the American political landscape—but they have been defeated by the fundamental idea that immigration has ultimately strengthened America's economy, culture, and society. At the dawn of the new millennium, a glance at almost any American city, school, or workplace reinforces that point clearly.

■ IN THEIR OWN WORDS

Born in a small Estonian town in 1939, Anton Tamsarre and his family lived in camps for displaced persons after World War II. They were allowed entry into the United States under the Displaced Persons Act. Private agencies were responsible for placement, and the Tamsaares were sent by a Norwegian Lutheran Church agency to Fargo, North Dakota, in February of 1949.

We came by boat. I remember it sailing into New York. [Laughs.] My father woke me up and showed me the Statue of Liberty. It was kind of nice! And then we took a train across the country. We were met in Fargo by some people from the Lutheran agency. We were taken to a little place with a population of one hundred or so—Arthur, North Dakota—where they had an old-folks home. My father's job was to be a caretaker there, and that's where we ended up for a while....

I had a relatively conventional kind of midwestern American upbringing insofar as school life was concerned. At home, it was still quite foreign. We spoke Estonian, still do when I go home, but it's not a place noted for any immigrant culture. There are no ghettos. People kind of forget that you've come recently. You live just like everyone else....

No one ever made fun of me for being different. I suppose that was helped a little bit because I was a very good student. There was another interesting factor. My parents were very eager for me to succeed. This is not uncommon, I'm sure, with immigrant families, but there was an understanding that I was supposed to be number one in what I chose to do. I did manage to succeed there. I was valedictorian of the high school and of the college and straight A's all the way through. I took a great deal of pleasure in this. This was the way I made my identity.

Let me say just a couple of other things which occur to me as being important. One is this dislocation that occurred, which is so strong with my parents. Going from being upper middle class to lower middle class, this hurt them a great deal. They've dealt with this now. But this is an absolutely overpowering sort of theme. This change of status and then an attempt to gain respectability and wealth in some limited way. That is why they were very careful and very eager to have me do as well as I possibly could, and I'm sure it's also been in the back of my mind.[1]

Duong Van Minh came to the United States in 1975 at age twenty-five. A Catholic, he was raised in Saigon, earned a graduate degree in economics, and worked for the South Vietnamese government. He was one of the 130,000 Vietnamese refugees allowed to enter the United States at the end of the Indochina War.

I had a very wonderful sponsor in El Paso, Texas. The Ashbury United Methodist Church sponsor my family with three persons. They provide everything—house, transportation, food, health, clothing. The minister of the church asked the people to help the Vietnamese. The church was ready to sponsor a family with eight people, but nobody like to come to El Paso. They want to live in a big city with Americans, not to live in El Paso, with about 70 percent Mexican. And they want better weather and sometimes it's 110 degrees there. I'm a person who doesn't mind about that point....I just want people who will help me and show me how to rent an apartment, to get a job.

We go to El Paso. Church prepare everything for us. They have a house belong to church. They repaint that, bring in some furniture and clothing for us. Some people take care of painting, some take care of furniture like committees. One committee for transportation, one for food, one for health and one for education....They give us some money and also show me how to get a high school equivalency diploma. I have a Master Degree in Economics, but I try to forget about that. I get an equivalency diploma and start college. I go for two semesters to University of Texas and work part-time in the library....

I save my money and I send to my parents in Vietnam through France. They get the money and contact some people and they plan to get a ship. They give the money, but still the Communists come and take the ship and we lose the money.

After we settle in El Paso we try to be in touch with friends and relatives from Vietnam. We know some people left but we do not know where they are. So I write note in the newspaper....My sister had a friend from Vietnam and we know he is in the Western United States but not where exactly. She wrote a letter in the paper and he answered from Albuquerque, New Mexico....

Soon my sister's friend came from Albuquerque every week to see her. First he has a low pay job because of English barrier. But he works hard. I see he is a good worker, try very hard to make success and he will take good care of my sister. About ten months after we come to El Paso they want to get married. My parents not here so I think about it and give my permission. Now they both work and he gets steady upgrade. Very good.[2]

In 1984 Rosa Maria Urbina, a thirty-one-year-old widow from Juarez, Mexico, crossed the Rio Grande River looking for work as a housecleaner in El Paso. She had hoped to earn enough money to take her three children out of an orphanage. José Luis, a Juarez farm worker, moved to El Paso permanently in 1981 at the age of twenty-two. The two married and made their life among El Paso's fifty thousand illegal immigrants, known in Mexican slang as "mojados," or "wets," the river people.

West Indian-American Day Parade, Brooklyn New York, 1991

José: The majority of the people in our apartment building have the same problem as my family. All of us are in El Paso without legal papers. I have been living here since 1981.

Rosa: I came in 1984, to find work. After José and I were married and we found a place to live, I brought my children from my previous marriage. We lived across the river in Juárez. But I was born further south, in Zacatecas.

José: My hometown is Juárez. Since I was nine years old, I've been coming to El Paso to work. At first I did gardening in people's yards, but I have stayed in El Paso constantly since 1981, going out to the fields to do farm work. I used to go to Juárez to visit my relatives at least one day each month. But in the last year, I haven't gone, because of the immigration law. To visit Juarez I have to swim across the river. I can't cross the bridge or the *"migra"* [Border Patrol officers] can catch me right there....

Rosa: When I was a teenager, I worked as a hairdresser in a beauty salon, cutting hair. My first husband was a mechanic, fixing cars. We made a good living. But my husband spent the money he made drinking in the *cantinas.* And after a while, he wouldn't let me work, because I had young children to take care of. When he died in 1984, he left me with nothing at all....My children were nine, seven, and three years old. I had to find a way to pay rent and feed them.

At that time, the economy in Mexico had become horrible. Inflation was going crazy. The peso jumped to 500 per dollar. Today it is still climbing at 1,000 per dollar. I found a job working on an assembly line at a factory. We produced rubber gloves for hospitals and medical supplies like caps for syringes. I would go into work at 4:30 in the afternoon and stay until 2:00 A.M. I was paid only 7,000 pesos [$14] each week. That was not enough to feed my kids. And I didn't have any relatives or friends to watch the kids while I worked. So I had no other choice but to put them in a special institution, like an orphanage, for children without parents. This upset me very much. But with my husband dead, and no other form of support, there was nothing I could do.

My only hope was to cross the river to the United States. If I could find a job that paid enough money, my children could join me. I wanted them to have an education and a proper life...to be someone....

Before I met José, I crossed back and forth across the river five days each week to my housekeeping jobs in El Paso. On weekends, I took my children out of the orphanage. Then I had to reluctantly return them to the orphanage on Sunday evenings and prepare to go back across the river.

For a while I traveled alone, which can be dangerous. But after I met José Luis, we crossed together. There are men who carry people across the river on their shoulders. The water is kind of rough, but that's what these men do to make a living. They charge passengers, 1,500 to 2,000 pesos [$1.50 to $2.50]. The water is up to their chests, but they manage to hold us up on their shoulders so we can get to work dry....

José: Farm-labor jobs are not very steady. We just grab whatever is open at the moment. I accept anything, any time, as long as it is work. But suppose I take a job that only pays me $12 a day. It would only be enough to cover my transportation and meals in the field. I must find jobs that pay enough to feed my family.

In order to make $25, I must pick seventy-two buckets of chili peppers. That could take me four or five hours; it depends on how fast my hands are. The total amount of buckets we pick depends upon the amount contracted by the big companies in California. For a big contract, we work as long as necessary to complete the order. But the most I can earn in a day is $35....

Rosa: We would like an ordinary life, but our problems with the *migra* are nothing new. If they catch me again and send me back to Juarez, I will just come back across the river.[3]

Wing Ng, a Cantonese woman born into a poor family, emigrated to California in 1975 at the age of twenty-three. She came alone, but had the sponsorship of her sister's friend in Los Angeles, as well as financial help from the YMCA for the airfare from Hong Kong. She soon relocated to New York's Chinatown.

The reason I wanted to come to the United States is that I heard it is really freedom. That's the first thing. And the second was the education. It's hard to get an education in China. Only the United States can support you to get a good education and a good life. My childhood was not happy. Too many children. Poor. I don't want that again. I graduated from high school but nothing can get you into college. Even though you have good grades and a good record you can never get into college in China. I don't know how it is now but in my experience, when I was young, during the Cultural Revolution, there were no colleges to get into. Every student

Chinese parents reading with their children.

Questions

1. To what extent were different immigrant experiences shaped by post-World War II changes in United States immigration laws?

2. How do the immigrants' narratives reflect their encounters with new gender roles and possibilities in American life?

3. Discuss the importance of educational opportunities for immigrants. Why were these critical for some and not for others?

4. For many immigrants, the trip to the United States was only one of several migrations. What other kinds of migrations shaped their lives before they arrived here?

5. What do the immigrants' stories reveal about the role of economic instability in their decision to emigrate?

Sources

1. June Namias, *First Generation: In the Words of Twentieth Century American Immigrants* (Boston: Beacon Press, 1978), 142–144. Copyright © 1978 by June Namias. Reprinted with the permission of Beacon Press, Boston.

2. Thomas Kessner and Betty Boyd Caroli, *Today's Immigrants/Their Stories: A New Look at the Newest Americans* (New York: Oxford University Press, 1981), 49–51. Copyright © 1981 by Thomas Kessner and Betty Boyd Caroli. Reprinted with the permission of Oxford University Press, Inc.

3. Al Santoli, *New Americans: An Oral History* (New York: Viking/Penguin, 1988), 306–308. Copyright © 1988 by Al Santoli. Reprinted with the permission of Viking Penguin, a division of Penguin Putnam, Inc.

4. Thomas Kessner and Betty Boyd Caroli, *Today's Immigrants/Their Stories: A New Look at the Newest Americans* (New York: Oxford University Press, 1981), 252–254. © 1981 by Thomas Kessner and Betty Boyd Caroli. Reprinted with the permission of Oxford University Press, Inc.

who graduated from high school in 1968, 1970, around that time, was sent to work in the countryside, to become a farmer....

I came first to California. Los Angeles. Then I came here to New York. I had some friends. They told me there were more opportunities to find a good job in New York. To learn English. In Los Angeles everything is far away. You have to drive in a car for hours to get anywhere. There's not that much chance to get an education, to go to school, because of the distance between places. I stayed there just two weeks and then I came to New York.

When I got here I worked as a babysitter. I had a green card and I could have gotten another kind of job but I wanted to learn English. Even though you go to school, you are just listening a lot of the time, and I wanted a job where I could talk English. So I found a job with an American family. They talked to me and corrected me. Told me how to do things. I took care of their little boy. He was seven years old and very easy to take care of. I took him to the park on his bicycle or to the museum. For me it was very interesting....

In February 1978, I started at City University, New York City Community College. There are many Chinese people there, many different races. Many, many. I have helped about twenty people go there myself. Told them it was a very good college, especially for data processing. I promised myself I will go on to a four-year college when I graduate but I do not know how long it will take. First I will get a job and then ask the boss to help me with my education....That first year back in college was very difficult for me. I had to take any kind of job, just to get money. Type. Work in a restaurant. Whatever I could find.[4]

APPENDIX

THE DECLARATION OF INDEPENDENCE

When in the course of human events it becomes necessary for one people to dissolve the political bands which have connected them with another and to assume, among the powers of the earth, the separate and equal station to which the laws of nature and of nature's God entitle them, a decent respect to the opinions of mankind requires that they should declare the causes which impel them to the separation.

We hold these truths to be self-evident, that all men are created equal; that they are endowed by their Creator with certain unalienable rights; that among these are life, liberty, and the pursuit of happiness. That, to secure these rights, governments are instituted among men, deriving their just powers from the consent of the governed; that, whenever any form of government becomes destructive of these ends, it is the right of the people to alter or to abolish it, and to institute a new government, laying its foundation on such principles, and organizing its powers in such form, as to them shall seem most likely to effect their safety and happiness. Prudence, indeed, will dictate that governments long established should not be changed for light and transient causes; and, accordingly, all experience hath shown that mankind are more disposed to suffer, while evils are sufferable, than to right themselves by abolishing the forms to which they are accustomed. But when a long train of abuses and usurpations, pursuing invariably the same object, evinces a design to reduce them under absolute despotism, it is their right, it is their duty, to throw off such government and to provide new guards for their future security. Such has been the patient sufferance of these colonies, and such is now the necessity which constrains them to alter their former systems of government. The history of the present King of Great Britain is a history of repeated injuries and usurpations, all having, in direct object, the establishment of an absolute tyranny over these States. To prove this, let facts be submitted to a candid world:

He has refused his assent to laws the most wholesome and necessary for the public good.

He has forbidden his governors to pass laws of immediate and pressing importance, unless suspended in their operation till his assent should be obtained; and, when so suspended, he has utterly neglected to attend to them.

He has refused to pass other laws for the accommodation of large districts of people, unless those people would relinquish the right of representation in the legislature, a right inestimable to them and formidable to tyrants only.

He has called together legislative bodies at places unusual, uncomfortable, and distant from the depository of their public records, for the sole purpose of fatiguing them into compliance with his measures.

He has dissolved representative houses, repeatedly, for opposing, with manly firmness, his invasions on the rights of the people.

He has refused, for a long time after such dissolutions, to cause others to be elected; whereby the legislative powers, incapable of annihilation, have returned to the people at large for their exercise; the state remaining, in the meantime, exposed to all the danger of invasion from without and convulsions within.

He has endeavored to prevent the population of these States; for that purpose, obstructing the laws for naturalization of foreigners, refusing to pass others to encourage their migration hither, and raising the conditions of new appropriations of lands.

He has obstructed the administration of justice by refusing his assent to laws for establishing judiciary powers.

He has made judges dependent on his will alone for the tenure of their offices and the amount and payment of their salaries.

He has erected a multitude of new offices and sent hither swarms of officers to harass our people and eat out their substance.

He has kept among us, in time of peace, standing armies, without the consent of our legislatures.

He has affected to render the military independent of, and superior to, the civil power.

He has combined with others to subject us to a jurisdiction foreign to our Constitution and unacknowledged by our laws, giving his assent to their acts of pretended legislation—

For quartering large bodies of armed troops among us;

For protecting them, by mock trial, from punishment for any murders which they should commit on the inhabitants of these States;

For cutting off our trade with all parts of the world;

For imposing taxes on us without our consent;

For depriving us, in many cases, of the benefit of trial by jury;

For transporting us beyond seas to be tried for pretended offences;

For abolishing the free system of English laws in a neighboring province, establishing therein an arbitrary government, and enlarging its boundaries, so as to render it at once an example and fit instrument for introducing the same absolute rule into these colonies;

For taking away our charters, abolishing our most valuable laws, and altering, fundamentally, the powers of our governments.

For suspending our own legislatures and declaring themselves invested with power to legislate for us in all cases whatsoever.

He has abdicated government here by declaring us out of his protection and waging war against us.

He has plundered our seas, ravaged our coasts, burnt our towns, and destroyed the lives of our people.

He is, at this time, transporting large armies of foreign mercenaries to complete the works of death, desolation, and tyranny already begun with circumstances of cruelty and perfidy scarcely paralleled in the most barbarous ages, and totally unworthy the head of a civilized nation.

He has constrained our fellow citizens, taken captive on the high seas, to bear arms against their country, to become the executioners of their friends and brethren, or to fall themselves by their hands.

He has excited domestic insurrections amongst us and has endeavored to bring on the inhabitants of our frontiers, the merciless Indian savages, whose known rule of warfare is an undistinguished destruction of all ages, sexes, and conditions.

In every stage of these oppressions, we have petitioned for redress in the most humble terms; our repeated petitions have been answered only by repeated injury. A prince whose character is thus marked by every act which may define a tyrant is unfit to be the ruler of a free people.

Nor have we been wanting in attention to our British brethren. We have warned them, from time to time, of attempts made by their legislature to extend an unwarrantable jurisdiction over us. We have reminded them of the circumstances of our emigration and settlement here. We have appealed to their native justice and magnanimity, and we have conjured them, by the ties of our common kindred, to disavow these usurpations, which would inevitably interrupt our connections and correspondence. They, too, have been deaf to the voice of justice and consanguinity. We must, therefore, acquiesce in the necessity which denounces our separation, and hold them, as we hold the rest of mankind, enemies in war, in peace, friends.

We, therefore, the representatives of the United States of America, in general Congress assembled, appealing to the Supreme Judge of the world for the rectitude of our intentions, do, in the name and by the authority of the good people of these colonies, solemnly publish and declare, that these united colonies are, and of right ought to be, free and independent states: that they are absolved from all allegiance to the British Crown, and that all political connection between them and the state of Great Britain is, and ought to be, totally dissolved; and that, as free and independent states, they have full power to levy war, conclude peace, contract alliances, establish commerce, and to do all other acts and things which independent states may of right do. And, for the support of this declaration, with a firm reliance on the protection of Divine Providence, we mutually pledge to each other our lives, our fortunes, and our sacred honor.

THE CONSTITUTION OF THE UNITED STATES OF AMERICA

We the people of the United States, in order to form a more perfect union, establish justice, insure domestic tranquillity, provide for the common defense, promote the general welfare, and secure the blessings of liberty to ourselves and our posterity, do ordain and establish this Constitution for the United States of America.

Article I

Section 1. All legislative powers herein granted shall be vested in a Congress of the United States, which shall consist of a Senate and House of Representatives.

Section 2. 1. The House of Representatives shall be composed of members chosen every second year by the people of the several States, and the electors in each State shall have the qualifications requisite for electors of the most numerous branch of the State legislature.

2. No person shall be a representative who shall not have attained to the age of twenty-five years, and been seven years a citizen of the United States, and who shall not, when elected, be an inhabitant of that State in which he shall be chosen.

3. Representatives and direct taxes[1] shall be apportioned among the several States which may be included within this Union, according to their respective numbers, which shall be determined by adding to the whole number of free persons, including those bound to service for a term of years, and excluding Indians not taxed, three fifths of all other persons.[2] The actual enumeration shall be made within three years after the first meeting of the Congress of the United States, and within every subsequent term of ten years, in such manner as they shall by law direct. The number of representatives shall not exceed one for every thirty thousand, but each State shall have at least one representative; and until such enumeration shall be made, the State of New Hampshire shall be entitled to choose three, Massachusetts eight, Rhode Island and Providence Plantations one, Connecticut five, New York six, New Jersey four, Pennsylvania eight, Delaware one, Maryland six, Virginia ten, North Carolina five, South Carolina five, and Georgia three.

4. When vacancies happen in the representation from any State, the executive authority thereof shall issue writs of election to fill such vacancies.

5. The House of Representatives shall choose their speaker and other officers; and shall have the sole power of impeachment.

Section 3. 1. The Senate of the United States shall be composed of two senators from each State, chosen by the legislature thereof,[3] for six years; and each senator shall have one vote.

2. Immediately after they shall be assembled in consequence of the first election, they shall be divided as equally as may be into three classes. The seats of the senators of the first class shall be vacated at the expiration of the second year, of the second class at the expiration of the fourth year, and of the third class at the expiration of the sixth year, so that one third may be chosen every second year; and if vacancies happen by resignation, or otherwise, during the recess of the legislature of any State, the executive thereof may make temporary appointments until the next meeting of the legislature, which shall then fill such vacancies.[4]

3. No person shall be a senator who shall not have attained to the age of thirty years, and been nine years a citizen of the United States, and who shall not, when elected, be an inhabitant of that State for which he shall be chosen.

4. The Vice President of the United States shall be President of the Senate, but shall have no vote, unless they be equally divided.

5. The Senate shall choose their other officers, and also a president pro tempore, in the absence of the Vice President, or when he shall exercise the office of the President of the United States.

6. The Senate shall have the sole power to try all impeachments. When sitting for that purpose, they shall be on oath or affirmation. When the President of the United States is tried, the chief justice shall preside: and no person shall be convicted without the concurrence of two thirds of the members present.

7. Judgment in cases of impeachment shall not extend further than to removal from office, and disqualification to hold and enjoy any office of honor, trust or profit under the United States: but the party convicted shall nevertheless be liable and subject to indictment, trial, judgment and punishment, according to law.

Section 4. 1. The times, places, and manner of holding elections for senators and representatives, shall be prescribed in each State by the legislature thereof; but the Congress may at any time by law make or alter such regulations, except as to the places of choosing senators.

2. The Congress shall assemble at least once in every year, and such meeting shall be on the first Monday in December, unless they shall by law appoint a different day.

Section 5. 1. Each House shall be the judge of the elections, returns and qualifications of its own members, and a majority of each shall constitute a quorum to do business; but a smaller number may adjourn from day to day, and may be authorized to compel the attendance of absent members, in such manner, and under such penalties as each House may provide.

2. Each House may determine the rules of its proceedings, punish its members for disorderly behavior, and, with the concurrence of two thirds, expel a member.

3. Each House shall keep a journal of its proceedings, and from time to time publish the same, excepting such parts as may in their judgment require secrecy; and the yeas and nays of the members of either House on any ques-

---

[1]See the Sixteenth Amendment.
[2]See the Fourteenth Amendment.
[3]See the Seventeenth Amendment.

[4]See the Seventeenth Amendment.

tion shall, at the desire of one fifth of those present, be entered on the journal.

4. Neither House, during the session of Congress, shall, without the consent of the other, adjourn for more than three days, nor to any other place than that in which the two Houses shall be sitting.

Section 6. 1. The senators and representatives shall receive a compensation for their services, to be ascertained by law, and paid out of the Treasury of the United States. They shall in all cases, except treason, felony, and breach of the peace, be privileged from arrest during their attendance at the session of their respective Houses, and in going to and returning from the same; and for any speech or debate in either House, they shall not be questioned in any other place.

2. No senator or representative shall, during the time for which he was elected, be appointed to any civil office under the authority of the United States, which shall have been created, or the emoluments whereof shall have been increased, during such time; and no person holding any office under the United States shall be a member of either House during his continuance in office.

Section 7. 1. All bills for raising revenue shall originate in the House of Representatives; but the Senate may propose or concur with amendments as on other bills.

2. Every bill which shall have passed the House of Representatives and the Senate, shall, before it become a law, be presented to the President of the United States; If he approves he shall sign it, but if not he shall return it, with his objections, to that House in which it shall have originated, who shall enter the objections at large on their journal, and proceed to reconsider it. If after such reconsideration two thirds of that House shall agree to pass the bill, it shall be sent, together with the objections, to the other House, by which it shall likewise be reconsidered, and if approved by two thirds of that House, it shall become a law. But in all such cases the votes of both Houses shall be determined by yeas and nays, and the names of the persons voting for and against the bill shall be entered on the journal of each House respectively. If any bill shall not be returned by the President within ten days (Sundays excepted) after it shall have been presented to him, the same shall be a law, in like manner as if he had signed it, unless the Congress by their adjournment prevent its return, in which case it shall not be a law.

3. Every order, resolution, or vote to which the concurrence of the Senate and the House of Representatives may be necessary (except on a question of adjournment) shall be presented to the President of the United States; and before the same shall take effect, shall be approved by him, or being disapproved by him, shall be repassed by two thirds of the Senate and House of Representatives, according to the rules and limitations prescribed in the case of a bill.

Section 8. The Congress shall have the power

1. To lay and collect taxes, duties, imposts, and excises, to pay the debts and provide for the common defense and general welfare of the United States; but all duties, imposts, and excises shall be uniform throughout the United States.

2. To borrow money on the credit of the United States;

3. To regulate commerce with foreign nations, and among the several States, and with the Indian tribes;

4. To establish a uniform rule of naturalization, and uniform laws on the subject of bankruptcies throughout the United States;

5. To coin money, regulate the value thereof, and of foreign coin, and fix the standard of weights and measures;

6. To provide for the punishment of counterfeiting the securities and current coin of the United States;

7. To establish post offices and post roads;

8. To promote the progress of science and useful arts, by securing for limited times to authors and inventors the exclusive right to their respective writings and discoveries;

9. To constitute tribunals inferior to the Supreme Court;

10. To define and punish piracies and felonies committed on the high seas, and offenses against the law of nations;

11. To declare war, grant letters of marque and reprisal, and make rules concerning captures on land and water;

12. To raise and support armies, but no appropriation of money to that use shall be for a longer term than two years;

13. To provide and maintain a navy;

14. To make rules for the government and regulation of the land and naval forces;

15. To provide for calling forth the militia to execute the laws of the Union, suppress insurrections and repel invasions;

16. To provide for organizing, arming, and disciplining the militia, and for governing such part of them as may be employed in the service of the United States, reserving to the States respectively, the appointment of the officers, and the authority of training the militia according to the discipline prescribed by Congress;

17. To exercise exclusive legislation in all cases whatsoever, over such district (not exceeding ten miles square) as may, by cession of particular States, and the acceptance of Congress, become the seat of the government of the United States, and to exercise like authority over all places purchased by the consent of the legislature of the State in which the same shall be, for the erection of forts, magazines, arsenals, dockyards, and other needful buildings; and

18. To make all laws which shall be necessary and proper for carrying into execution the foregoing powers, and all other powers vested by this Constitution in the government of the United States, or any department or officer thereof.

Section 9. 1. The migration or importation of such persons as any of the States now existing shall think proper to admit, shall not be prohibited by the Congress prior to the year one thousand eight hundred and eight, but a tax or duty may be imposed on such importation, not exceeding ten dollars for each person.

2. The privilege of the writ of habeas corpus shall not be suspended, unless when in cases of rebellion or invasion the public safety may require it.

3. No bill of attainder or ex post facto law shall be passed.

4. No capitation, or other direct, tax shall be laid, unless in proportion to the census or enumeration hereinbefore directed to be taken.[5]

5. No tax or duty shall be laid on articles exported from any State.

6. No preference shall be given by any regulation of commerce or revenue to the ports of one State over those of another: nor shall vessels bound to, or from, one State be obliged to enter, clear, or pay duties in another.

7. No money shall be drawn from the treasury, but in consequence of appropriations made by law; and a regular statement and account of the receipts and expenditures of all public money shall be published from time to time.

8. No title of nobility shall be granted by the United States: and no person holding any office of profit or trust under them, shall, without the consent of the Congress, accept of any present, emolument, office, or title, of any kind whatever, from any king, price, or foreign State.

Section 10. 1. No State shall enter into any treaty, alliance, or confederation; grant letters of marque and reprisal; coin money; emit bills of credit; make any thing but gold and silver coin a tender in payment of debts; pass any bill of attainder, ex post facto law, or law impairing the obligation of contracts, or grant, any title of nobility.

2. No State shall, without the consent of the Congress, lay any imposts or duties on imports or exports, except what may be absolutely necessary for executing its inspection laws: and the net produce of all duties and imposts laid by any State on imports or exports, shall be for the use of the treasury of the United States; and all such laws shall be subject to the revision and control of the Congress.

3. No State shall, without the consent of the Congress, lay any duty of tonnage, keep troops, or ships of war in time of peace, enter into any agreement or compact with another State, or with a foreign power, or engage in war, unless actually invaded, or in such imminent danger as will not admit of delay.

Article II

Section 1. 1. The executive power shall be vested in a President of the United States of America. He shall hold his office during the term of four years, and, together with the Vice President, chosen for the same term, be elected, as follows:

2. Each State shall appoint, in such manner as the legislature thereof may direct, a number of electors, equal to the whole number of senators and representatives to which the State may be entitled in the Congress: but no senator or representative, or person holding any office of trust or profit under the United States, shall be appointed an elector.

The electors shall meet in their respective States, and vote by ballot for two persons, of whom one at least shall not be an inhabitant of the same State with themselves. And they shall make a list of all the persons voted for, and of the number of votes for each; which list they shall sign and certify, and transmit sealed to the seat of the government of the United States, directed to the president of the Senate. The president of the Senate shall, in the presence of the Senate and House of Representatives, open all the certificates, and the votes shall then be counted. The person having the greatest number of votes shall be the President, if such number be a majority of the whole number of electors appointed; and if there be more than one who have such majority, and have an equal number of votes, then the House of Representatives shall immediately choose by ballot one of them for President; and if no person have a majority, then from the five highest on the list the said House shall in like manner choose the President. But in choosing the President, the votes shall be taken by States, the representation from each State having one vote; a quorum for this purpose shall consist of a member or members from two thirds of the States, and a majority of all the States shall be necessary to a choice. In every case after the choice of the President, the person having the greatest number of votes of the electors shall be the Vice President. But if there should remain two or more who have equal votes, the Senate shall choose from them by ballot the Vice President.[6]

3. The Congress may determine the time of choosing the electors, and the day on which they shall give their votes; which day shall be the same throughout the United States.

4. No person except a natural born citizen, or a citizen of the United States, at the time of the adoption of this Constitution, shall be eligible to the office of President; neither shall any person be eligible to the office who shall not have attained to the age of thirty-five years, and been fourteen years a resident within the United States.

5. In case of the removal of the President from office, or of his death, resignation, or inability to discharge the powers and duties of the said office, the same shall devolve on the Vice President, and the congress may by law provide for the case of removal, death, resignation or inability, both of the President and Vice President, declaring what officer shall then act as President, and such officer shall act accordingly until the disability be removed, or a President shall be elected.

6. The President shall, at stated times, receive for his services a compensation which shall neither be increased nor diminished during the period for which he shall have been elected, and he shall not receive within that period any other emolument from the United States, or any of them.

7. Before he enter on the execution of his office, he shall take the following oath or affirmation:—"I do

---

[5]See the Sixteenth Amendment.

[6]Superseded by the Twelfth Amendment.

solemnly swear (or affirm) that I will faithfully execute the office of President of the United States, and will to the best of my ability, preserve, protect and defend the Constitution of the United States."

Section 2. 1. The President shall be commander in chief of the army and navy of the United States, and of the militia of the several States, when called into the actual service of the United States; he may require the opinion in writing, of the principal officer in each of the executive departments, upon any subject relating to the duties of their respective offices, and he shall have power to grant reprieves and pardons for offenses against the United States, except in cases of impeachment.

2. He shall have power, by and with the advice and consent of the Senate, to make treaties, provided two thirds of the senators present concur; and he shall nominate, and by and with the advice and consent of the Senate, shall appoint ambassadors, other public ministers and consuls, judges of the Supreme Court, and all other officers of the United States, whose appointments are not herein otherwise provided for, and which shall be established by law; but the Congress may by law vest the appointment of such inferior officers, as they think proper, in the President alone, in the courts of laws, or in the heads of departments.

3. The President shall have power to fill up all vacancies that may happen during the recess of the Senate, by granting commissions which shall expire at the end of their next session.

Section 3. He shall from time to time give to the Congress information of the state of the Union, and recommend to their consideration such measures as he shall judge necessary and expedient; he may, on extraordinary occasions, convene both Houses, or either of them, and in case of disagreement between them with respect to the time of adjournment, he may adjourn them to such time as he shall think proper; he shall receive ambassadors and other public ministers; he shall take care that the laws be faithfully executed, and shall commission all the officers of the United States.

Section 4. The President, Vice President, and all civil officers of the United States, shall be removed from office on impeachment for, and conviction of, treason, bribery, or other high crimes and misdemeanors.

Article III

Section 1. The judicial power of the United States shall be vested in one Supreme Court, and in such inferior courts as the Congress may from time to time ordain and establish. The judges, both of the Supreme and inferior courts, shall hold their offices during good behavior, and shall, at stated times, receive for their services, a compensation, which shall not be diminished during their continuance in office.

Section 2. 1. The judicial power shall extend to all cases, in law and equity, arising under this Constitution, the laws of the United States, and treaties made, or which shall be made, under their authority;—to all cases of admiralty and maritime jurisdiction;—to controversies to which the

United States shall be a party;[7]—to controversies between two or more States;—between a State and citizens of another State;—between citizens of different States;— between citizens of the same State claiming lands under grants of different States, and between a State, or the citizens thereof, and foreign States, citizens or subjects.

2. In all cases affecting ambassadors, other public ministers and consuls, and those in which a State shall be party, the Supreme Court shall have original jurisdiction. In all the other cases before mentioned, the Supreme Court shall have appellate jurisdiction, both as to law and fact, with such exceptions, and under such regulations as the Congress shall make.

3. The trial of all crimes, except in cases of impeachment, shall be by jury; and such trial shall be held in the State where the said crimes shall have been committed; but when not committed within any State, the trial shall be such place or places as the congress may by law have directed.

Section 3. 1. Treason against the United States shall consist only in levying war against them, or in adhering to their enemies, giving them aid and comfort. No person shall be convicted of treason unless on the testimony of two witnesses to the same overt act, or on confession in open court.

2. The Congress shall have power to declare the punishment of treason, but no attainder of treason shall work corruption of blood, or forfeiture except during the life of the person attained.

Article IV

Section 1. Full faith and credit shall be given in each State to the public acts, records, and judicial proceedings of every other State. And the Congress may by general laws prescribe the manner in which such acts, records and proceedings shall be proved, and the effect thereof.

Section 2. 1. The citizens of each State shall be entitled to all privileges and immunities of citizens in the several States.[8]

2. A person charged in any State with treason, felony, or other crime, who shall flee from justice, and be found in another State, shall on demand of the executive authority of the State from which he fled, be delivered up to be removed to the State having jurisdiction of the crime.

3. No person held to service or labor in one State under the laws thereof, escaping into another, shall, in consequence of any law or regulation therein, be discharged from such service or labor, but shall be delivered up on claim of the party to whom such service or labor may be due.[9]

Section 3. 1. New States may be admitted by the Congress into this Union; but no new State shall be formed or erected within the jurisdiction of any other State, nor any State be formed by the junction of two or more States, or parts of States, without the consent of the legislatures of the States concerned as well as of the Congress.

---

[7]See the Eleventh Amendment.
[8]See the Fourteenth Amendment, Sec. 1.
[9]See the Thirteenth Amendment.

2. The Congress shall have power to dispose of and make all needful rules and regulations respecting the territory or other property belonging to the United States; and nothing in this Constitution shall be so construed as to prejudice any claims of the United States, or of any particular State.

Section 4. The United States shall guarantee to every State in this Union a republican form of government, and shall protect each of them against invasion; and on application of the legislature, or of the executive (when the legislature cannot be convened) against domestic violence.

Article V

The Congress, whenever two thirds of both Houses shall deem it necessary, shall propose amendments to this Constitution, or, on the application of the legislatures of two thirds of the several States, shall call a convention for proposing amendments, which in either case shall be valid to all intents and purposes, as part of this Constitution, when ratified by the legislatures of three fourths of the several States, or by conventions in three fourths thereof, as the one or the other mode of ratification may be proposed by the Congress; Provided that no amendment which may be made prior to the year one thousand eight hundred and eight shall in any manner affect the first and fourth clauses in the ninth section of the first article; and that no State, without its consent, shall be deprived of its equal suffrage in the Senate.

Article VI

1. All debts contracted and engagements entered into, before the adoption of this Constitution, shall be as valid against the United States under this Constitution, as under the Confederation.[10]

2. This Constitution, and the laws of the United States which shall be made in pursuance thereof; and all treaties made, or which shall be made, under the authority of the United States, shall be the supreme law of the land; and the judges in every State shall be bound thereby, any thing in the Constitution or laws of any State to the contrary notwithstanding.

3. The senators and representatives before mentioned, and the members of the several State legislatures, and all executive and judicial officers, both of the United States and of the several States, shall be bound by oath or affirmation to support this Constitution; but no religious test shall ever be required as a qualification to any office or public trust under the United States.

Article VII

The ratification of the conventions of nine States shall be sufficient for the establishment of this Constitution between the States so ratifying the same.

Done in Convention by the unanimous consent of the States present the seventeenth day of September in the year of our Lord one thousand seven hundred and eighty-

seven, and of the independence of the United States of America the twelfth. In witness whereof we have hereunto subscribed our names.

[Names omitted]

* * *

Articles in addition to, and amendment of, the Constitution of the United States of America, proposed by Congress, and ratified by the legislatures of the several States, pursuant to the fifth article of the original Constitution.

Amendment I [First ten amendments ratified December 15, 1791]

Congress shall make no law respecting an establishment of religion, or prohibiting the free exercise thereof; or abridging the freedom of speech, or of the press; or the right of the people peaceably to assemble, and to petition the government for a redress of grievances.

Amendment II

A well regulated militia, being necessary to the security of a free State, the right of the people to keep and bear arms, shall not be infringed.

Amendment III

No soldier shall, in time of peace be quartered in any house, without the consent of the owner, nor in time of war, but in a manner to be prescribed by law.

Amendment IV

The right of the people to be secure in their persons, houses, papers, and effects, against unreasonable searches and seizures, shall not be violated, and no warrants shall issue, but upon probable cause, supported by oath or affirmation, and particularly describing the place to be searched, and the persons or things to be seized.

Amendment V

No person shall be held to answer for a capital or otherwise infamous crime, unless on a presentment or indictment of a grand jury, except in cases arising in the land or naval forces, or in the militia, when in actual service in time of war or public danger; nor shall any person be subject for the same offense to be twice put in jeopardy of life or limb; nor shall be compelled in any criminal case to be a witness against himself, nor be deprived of life, liberty, or property, without due process of law; nor shall private property be taken for public use, without just compensation.

Amendment VI

In all criminal prosecutions, the accused shall enjoy the right to a speedy and public trial, by an impartial jury of the State and district wherein the crime shall have been committed, which district shall have been previously ascertained by law, and to be informed of the nature and cause of the accusation; to be confronted with the witnesses against him; to have compulsory process for obtaining witnesses in his favor, and to have the assistance of counsel for his defense.

[10]See the Fourteenth Amendment, Sec. 4.

Amendment VII

In suits at common law, where the value in controversy shall exceed twenty dollars, the right of trial by jury shall be preserved, and no fact tried by a jury shall be otherwise reexamined in any court of the United States, than according to the rules of the common law.

Amendment VIII

Excessive bail shall not be required, nor excessive fines imposed, nor cruel and unusual punishments inflicted.

Amendment IX

The enumeration in the Constitution of certain rights shall not be construed to deny or disparage others retained by the people.

Amendment X

The powers not delegated to the United States by the Constitution, nor prohibited by it to the States, are reserved to the States respectively, or to the people.

Amendment XI [January 8, 1798]

The judicial power of the United States shall not be construed to extend to any suit in law or equity, commended or prosecuted against one of the United States by citizens of another State, or by citizens or subjects of any foreign State.

Amendment XII [September 25, 1804]

The electors shall meet in their respective States, and vote by ballot for President and Vice President, one of whom, at least, shall not be an inhabitant of the same State with themselves; they shall name in their ballots the person voted for as President, and in distinct ballots, the person voted for as Vice President, and they shall make distinct lists of all persons voted for as President and of all persons voted for as Vice President, and of the number of votes for each, which lists they shall sign and certify, and transmit sealed to the seat of the government of the United States, directed to the President of the Senate;—The President of the Senate shall, in the presence of the Senate and House of Representatives, open all the certificates and the votes shall then be counted;—The person having the greatest number of votes for President, shall be the President, if such number be a majority of the whole number of electors appointed; and if no person have such majority, then from the persons having the highest numbers not exceeding three on the list of those voted for as President, the House of Representatives shall choose immediately, by ballot, the President. But in choosing the President, the votes shall be taken by States, the representation from each State having one vote; a quorum for this purpose shall consist of a member or members from two thirds of the States, and a majority of all the States shall be necessary to a choice. And if the House of Representatives shall not choose a President whenever the right of choice shall devolve upon them, before the fourth day of March next following, then the Vice President shall act as President, as in the case of the death or other constitutional disability of the President.

The person having the greatest number of votes as Vice President shall be the Vice President, if such number be a majority of the whole number of electors appointed, and if no person have a majority, then from the two highest numbers on the list, the Senate shall choose the Vice President; a quorum for the purpose shall consist of two thirds of the whole number of Senators, and a majority of the whole number shall be necessary to a choice. But no person constitutionally ineligible to the office of President shall be eligible to that of Vice President of the United States.

Amendment XIII [December 18, 1865]

Section 1. Neither slavery nor involuntary servitude, except as a punishment for crime whereof the party shall have been duly convicted, shall exist within the United States, or any place subject to their jurisdiction.

Section 2. Congress shall have power to enforce this article by appropriate legislation.

Amendment XIV [July 28, 1868]

Section 1. All persons born or naturalized in the United States, and subject to the jurisdiction thereof, are citizens of the United States and of the State wherein they reside. No State shall make or enforce any law which shall abridge the privileges or immunities of citizens of the United States; nor shall any State deprive any person of life, liberty, or property, without due process of law; nor deny to any person within its jurisdiction the equal protection of the laws.

Section 2. Representatives shall be apportioned among the several States according to their respective numbers, counting the whole number of persons in each State, excluding Indians not taxed. But when the right to vote at any election for the choice of electors for President and Vice President of the United States, representatives in Congress, the executive and judicial officers of a State, or the members of the legislature thereof, is denied to any of the male inhabitants of such State, being twenty-one years of age, and citizens of the United States, or in any way abridged, except for participating in rebellion, or other crime, the basis of representation there shall be reduced in the proportion which the number of such male citizens shall bear to the whole number of male citizens twenty-one years of age in such State.

Section 3. No person shall be a senator or representative in Congress, or elector of President and Vice President, or hold any office, civil or military, under the United States, or under any State, who having previously taken an oath, as a member of Congress, or as an officer of the United States, or as a member of any State legislature, or as an executive or judicial officer of any State, to support the Constitution of the United States, shall have engaged in insurrection or rebellion against the same, or given aid or comfort to the enemies thereof. But Congress may by a vote of two thirds of each House, remove such disability.

Section 4. The validity of the public debt of the United States, authorized by law, including debts incurred for payment of pensions and bounties for services in suppressing insurrection or rebellion; shall not be questioned.

But neither the United States nor any State shall assume or pay any debt or obligation incurred in aid of insurrection or rebellion against the United States, or any claim for the loss or emancipation of any slave; but all such debts, obligations, and claims shall be held illegal and void.

Section 5. The Congress shall have the power to enforce, by appropriate legislation, the provisions of this article.

Amendment XV [March 30, 1870]

Section 1. The right of citizens of the United States to vote shall not be denied or abridged by the United States or by any State on account of race, color, or previous condition of servitude.

Section 2. The Congress shall have power to enforce this article by appropriate legislation.

Amendment XVI [February 25, 1913]

The Congress shall have power to lay and collect taxes on incomes, from whatever source derived, without apportionment among the several States, and without regard to any census or enumeration.

Amendment XVII [May 31, 1913]

The Senate of the United States shall be composed of two senators from each State, elected by the people thereof, for six years; and each senator shall have one vote. The electors in each State shall have the qualifications requisite for electors of the most numerous branch of the State legislature.

When vacancies happen in the representation of any State in the Senate, the executive authority of such State shall issue writs of election to fill such vacancies: *Provided,* That the legislature of any State may empower the executive thereof to make temporary appointments until the people fill the vacancies by election as the legislature may direct.

This amendment shall not be so construed as to affect the election or term of any senator chosen before it becomes valid as part of the Constitution.

Amendment XVIII[1] [January 29, 1919]

After one year from the ratification of this article, the manufacture, sale, or transportation of intoxicating liquors within, the importation thereof into, or the exportation thereof from the United States and all territory subject to the jurisdiction thereof for beverage purposes is thereby prohibited.

The Congress and the several States shall have concurrent power to enforce this article by appropriate legislation.

This article shall be inoperative unless it shall have been ratified as an amendment to the Constitution by the legislatures of the several States, as provided in the constitution, within seven years from the date of the submission hereof to the States by Congress.

[1]Repealed by the Twenty-first Amendment.

Amendment XIX [August 26, 1920]

The right of citizens of the United States to vote shall not be denied or abridged by the United States or by any State on account of sex.

Congress shall have the power to enforce this article by appropriate legislation.

Amendment XX [January 23, 1933]

Section 1. The terms of the President and Vice President shall end at noon on the 20th day of January and the terms of Senators and Representatives at noon on the 3d day of January, of the years in which such terms would have ended if this article had not been ratified; and the terms of their successors shall then begin.

Section 2. The Congress shall assemble at least once in every year, and such meeting shall begin at noon on the 3d day of January, unless they shall by law appoint a different day.

Section 3. If, at the time fixed for the beginning of the term of President, the President-elect shall have died, the Vice President-elect shall become President. If a President shall not have been chosen before the time fixed for the beginning of his term, or if the President-elect shall have failed to qualify, then the Vice President-elect shall act as President until a President shall have qualified; and the Congress may by law provide for the case wherein neither a President-elect nor a Vice President-elect shall have qualified, declaring who shall then act as President, or the manner in which one who is to act shall be selected, and such person shall act accordingly until a President or Vice President shall have qualified.

Section 4. The Congress may by law provide for the case of the death of any of the persons from whom, the House of Representatives may choose a President whenever the right of choice shall have devolved upon them, and for the case of the death of any of the persons from whom the Senate may choose a Vice President whenever the right of choice shall have devolved upon them.

Section 5. Sections 1 and 2 shall take effect on the 15th day of October following the ratification of this article.

Section 6. This article shall be inoperative unless it shall have been ratified as an amendment to the Constitution by the legislatures of three-fourths of the several States within seven years from the date of its submission.

Amendment XXI [December 5, 1933]

Section 1. The Eighteenth Article of amendment to the Constitution of the United States is hereby repealed.

Section 2. The transportation or importation into any State, Territory, or possession of the United States for delivery or use therein of intoxicating liquors in violation of the laws thereof, is hereby prohibited.

Section 3. This article shall be inoperative unless it shall have been ratified as an amendment to the Constitution by conventions in the several States, as provided in the Constitution, within seven years from the date of the submission thereof to the States by the Congress.

Amendment XXII [March 1, 1951]

No person shall be elected to the office of the President more than twice, and no person who has held the office of President, or acted as President, for more than two years of a term to which some other person was elected President shall be elected to the office of the President more than once.

But this article shall not apply to any person holding the office of President when this article was proposed by the Congress, and shall not prevent any person who may be holding the office of President, or acting as President, during the term within which this article becomes operative from holding the office of President or acting as President during the remainder of such term.

This article shall be inoperative unless it shall have been ratified as an amendment to the Constitution by the legislatures of three-fourths of the several States within seven years from the date of its submission to the States by the Congress.

Amendment XXIII [March 29, 1961]

Section 1. The District constituting the seat of Government of the United States shall appoint in such manner as the Congress may direct.

A number of electors of President and Vice President equal to the whole number of Senators and Representatives in Congress to which the District would be entitled if it were a State, but in no event more than the least populous State; they shall be in addition to those appointed by the States, but they shall be considered, for the purposes of the election of President and Vice President, to be electors appointed by a State; and they shall meet in the District and perform such duties as provided by the twelfth article of amendment.

Section 2. The Congress shall have power to enforce this article by appropriate legislation.

Amendment XXIV [January 23, 1964]

Section 1. The right of citizens of the United States to vote in any primary or other election for President or Vice President, for electors for President or Vice President, or for Senator or Representative in Congress, shall not be denied or abridged by the United States or any State by reason of failure to pay any poll tax or other tax.

Section 2. The Congress shall have power to enforce this article by appropriate legislation.

Amendment XXV [February 10, 1967]

Section 1. In case of the removal of the President from office or of his death or resignation, the Vice President shall become President.

Section 2. Whenever there is a vacancy in the office of the Vice President, the President shall nominate a Vice President who shall take office upon confirmation by a majority of both Houses of Congress.

Section 3. Whenever the President transmits to the President pro tempore of the Senate and the Speaker of the House of Representatives his written declaration that he is unable to discharge the powers and duties of his office, and until he transmits to them a written declaration to the contrary, such powers and duties shall be discharged by the Vice President as Acting President.

Section 4. Whenever the Vice president and a majority of either the principal officers of the executive departments or of such other body as Congress may by law provide, transmit to the President pro tempore of the Senate and the Speaker of the House of Representatives their written declaration that the President is unable to discharge the powers and duties of his office, the Vice President shall immediately assume the powers and duties of the office as Acting President.

Thereafter, when the President transmits to the President pro tempore of the Senate and the Speaker of the House of Representatives his written declaration that no inability exists, he shall resume the powers and duties of his office unless the Vice President and a majority of either the principal officers of the executive departments or of such other body as Congress may by law provide, transmit within four days to the President pro tempore of the Senate and the Speaker of the House of Representatives their written declaration that the President is unable to discharge the powers and duties of his office. Thereupon Congress shall decide the issue, assembling within forty-eight hours for that purpose if not in session. If the Congress, within twenty-one days after receipt of the latter written declaration, or, if Congress is not in session, within twenty-one days after Congress is required to assemble, determines by two-thirds vote of both Houses that the President is unable to discharge the powers and duties of his office, the Vice President shall continue to discharge the same as Acting President; otherwise, the President shall resume the powers and duties of his office.

Amendment XXVI [June 30, 1971]

Section 1. The right of citizens of the United States who are eighteen years of age or older to vote shall not be denied or abridged by the United States or by any State on account of age.

Section 2. The Congress shall have power to enforce this article by appropriate legislation.

Amendment XXVII[12] [May 7, 1992]

No law, varying the compensation for services of the Senators and Representatives, shall take effect until an election of Representatives shall have intervened.

---

[12]James Madison proposed this amendment in 1789 together with the ten amendments that were adopted as the Bill of Rights, but it failed to win ratification at the time. Congress, however, had set no deadline for its ratification, and over the years—particularly in the 1980s and 1990s—many states voted to add it to the Constitution. With the ratification of Michigan in 1992 it passed the threshold of 3/4ths of the states required for adoption, but because the process took more than 200 years, its validity remains in doubt.

PRESIDENTS AND VICE PRESIDENTS

1. George Washington (1789)
   John Adams (1789)

2. John Adams (1797)
   Thomas Jefferson (1797)

3. Thomas Jefferson (1801)
   Aaron Burr (1801)
   George Clinton (1805)

4. James Madison (1809)
   George Clinton (1809)
   Elbridge Gerry (1813)

5. James Monroe (1817)
   Daniel D. Thompkins (1817)

6. John Quincy Adams (1825)
   John C. Calhoun (1825)

7. Andrew Jackson (1829)
   John C. Calhoun (1829)
   Martin Van Buren (1833)

8. Martin Van Buren (1837)
   Richard M. Johnson (1837)

9. William H. Harrison (1841)
   John Tyler (1841)

10. John Tyler (1841)

11. James K. Polk (1845)
    George M. Dallas (1845)

12. Zachary Taylor (1849)
    Millard Fillmore (1849)

13. Millard Fillmore (1850)

14. Franklin Pierce (1853)
    William R. King (1853)

15. James Buchanan (1857)
    John C. Breckinridge (1857)

16. Abraham Lincoln (1861)
    Hannibal Hamlin (1861)
    Andrew Johnson (1865)

17. Andrew Johnson (1865)

18. Ulysses S. Grant (1869)
    Schuyler Colfax (1869)
    Henry Wilson (1873)

19. Rutherford B. Hayes (1877)
    William A. Wheeler (1877)

20. James A. Garfield (1881)
    Chester A. Arthur (1881)

21. Chester A. Arthur (1881)

22. Grover Cleveland (1885)
    T. A. Hendricks (1885)

23. Benjamin Harrison (1889)
    Levi P. Morgan (1889)

24. Grover Cleveland (1893)
    Adlai E. Stevenson (1893)

25. William McKinley (1897)
    Garret A. Hobart (1897)
    Theodore Roosevelt (1901)

26. Theodore Roosevelt (1901)
    Charles Fairbanks (1905)

27. William H. Taft (1909)
    James S. Sherman (1909)

28. Woodrow Wilson (1913)
    Thomas R. Marshall (1913)

29. Warren G. Harding (1921)
    Calvin Coolidge (1921)

30. Calvin Coolidge (1923)
    Charles G. Dawes (1925)

31. Herbert C. Hoover (1929)
    Charles Curtis (1929)

32. Franklin D. Roosevelt (1933)
    John Nance Garner (1933)
    Henry A. Wallace (1941)
    Harry S. Truman (1945)

33. Harry S. Truman (1945)
    Alben W. Barkley (1949)

34. Dwight D. Eisenhower (1953)
    Richard M. Nixon (1953)

35. John F. Kennedy (1961)
    Lyndon B. Johnson (1961)

36. Lyndon B. Johnson (1963)
    Hubert H. Humphrey (1965)

37. Richard M. Nixon (1969)
    Spiro T. Agnew (1969)
    Gerald R. Ford (1973)

38. Gerald R. Ford (1974)
    Nelson A. Rockefeller (1974)

39. James E. Carter Jr. (1977)
    Walter F. Mondale (1977)

40. Ronald W. Reagan (1981)
    George H. Bush (1981)

41. George H. Bush (1989)
    James D. Quayle III (1989)

42. William J. Clinton (1993)
    Albert Gore (1993)

PRESIDENTIAL ELECTIONS

Year	Number of States	Candidates	Party	Popular Vote*	Electoral Vote†	Percentage of Popular Vote
1789	11	GEORGE WASHINGTON	No party designations		69	
		John Adams			34	
		Other Candidates			35	
1792	15	GEORGE WASHINGTON	No party designations		132	
		John Adams			77	
		George Clinton			50	
		Other Candidates			5	
1796	16	JOHN ADAMS	Federalist		71	
		Thomas Jefferson	Democratic-Republican		68	
		Thomas Pinckney	Federalist		59	
		Aaron Burr	Democratic-Republican		30	
		Other Candidates			48	
1800	16	THOMAS JEFFERSON	Democratic-Republican		73	
		Aaron Burr	Democratic-Republican		73	
		John Adams	Federalist		65	
		Charles C. Pinckney	Federalist		64	
		John Jay	Federalist		1	
1804	17	THOMAS JEFFERSON	Democratic-Republican		162	
		Charles C. Pinckney	Federalist		14	
1808	17	JAMES MADISON	Democratic-Republican		122	
		Charles C. Pinckney	Federalist		47	
		George Clinton	Democratic-Republican		6	
1812	18	JAMES MADISON	Democratic-Republican		128	
		DeWitt Clinton	Federalist		89	
1816	19	JAMES MONROE	Democratic-Republican		183	
		Rufus King	Federalist		34	
1820	24	JAMES MONROE	Democratic-Republican		231	
		John Quincy Adams	Democratic-Republican		1	
1824	24	JOHN QUINCY ADAMS	Democratic-Republican	108,740	84	30.5
		Andrew Jackson	Democratic-Republican	153,544	99	43.1
		William H. Crawford	Democratic-Republican	46,618	41	13.1
		Henry Clay	Democratic-Republican	47,136	37	13.2
1828	24	ANDREW JACKSON	Democrat	647,286	178	56.0
		John Quincy Adams	National-Republican	508,064	83	44.0
1832	24	ANDREW JACKSON	Democrat	687,502	219	55.0
		Henry Clay	National-Republican	530,189	49	42.4
		William Wirt	Anti-Masonic	} 33,108	7	} 2.6
		John Floyd	National-Republican		11	

*Percentage of popular vote given for any election year may not total 100 percent because candidates receiving less than 1 percent of the popular vote have been omitted.

†Prior to the passage of the Twelfth Amendment in 1904, the electoral college voted for two presidential candidates; the runner-up became Vice-President. Data from *Historical Statistics of the United States, Colonial Times to 1957* (1961), pp. 682–683, and *The World Almanac*.

PRESIDENTIAL ELECTIONS
(continued)

Year	Number of States	Candidates	Party	Popular Vote	Electoral Vote	Percentage of Popular Vote
1836	26	MARTIN VAN BUREN	Democrat	765,483	170	50.9
		William H. Harrison	Whig		73	
		Hugh L. White	Whig		26	
		Daniel Webster	Whig	739,795	14	49.1
		W. P. Mangum	Whig		11	
1840	26	WILLIAM H. HARRISON	Whig	1,274,624	234	53.1
		Martin Van Buren	Democrat	1,127,781	60	46.9
1844	26	JAMES K. POLK	Democrat	1,338,464	170	49.6
		Henry Clay	Whig	1,300,097	105	48.1
		James G. Birney	Liberty	62,300		2.3
1848	30	ZACHARY TAYLOR	Whig	1,360,967	163	47.4
		Lewis Cass	Democrat	1,222,342	127	42.5
		Martin Van Buren	Free-Soil	291,263		10.1
1852	31	FRANKLIN PIERCE	Democrat	1,601,117	254	50.9
		Winfield Scott	Whig	1,385,453	42	44.1
		John P. Hale	Free-Soil	155,825		5.0
1856	31	JAMES BUCHANAN	Democrat	1,832,955	174	45.3
		John C. Frémont	Republican	1,339,932	114	33.1
		Millard Fillmore	American ("Know Nothing")	871,731	8	21.6
1860	33	ABRAHAM LINCOLN	Republican	1,865,593	180	39.8
		Stephen A. Douglas	Democrat	1,382,713	12	29.5
		John C. Breckinridge	Democrat	848,356	72	18.1
		John Bell	Constitutional Union	592,906	39	12.6
1864	36	ABRAHAM LINCOLN	Republican	2,206,938	212	55.0
		George B. McClellan	Democrat	1,803,787	21	45.0
1868	37	ULYSSES S. GRANT	Republican	3,013,421	214	52.7
		Horatio Seymour	Democrat	2,706,829	80	47.3
1872	37	ULYSSES S. GRANT	Republican	3,596,745	286	55.6
		Horace Greeley	Democrat	2,843,446	*	43.9
1876	38	RUTHERFORD B. HAYES	Republican	4,036,572	185	48.0
		Samuel J. Tilden	Democrat	4,284,020	184	51.0
1880	38	JAMES A. GARFIELD	Republican	4,453,295	214	48.5
		Winfield S. Hancock	Democrat	4,414,082	155	48.1
		James B. Weaver	Greenback-Labor	308,578		3.4
1884	38	GROVER CLEVELAND	Democrat	4,879,507	219	48.5
		James G. Blaine	Republican	4,850,293	182	48.2
		Benjamin F. Butler	Greenback-Labor	175,370		1.8
		John P. St. John	Prohibition	150,369		1.5
1888	38	BENJAMIN HARRISON	Republican	5,447,129	233	47.9
		Grover Cleveland	Democrat	5,537,857	168	48.6
		Clinton B. Fisk	Prohibition	249,506		2.2
		Anson J. Streeter	Union Labor	146,935		1.3

*Because of the death of Greeley, Democratic electors scattered their votes.

PRESIDENTIAL ELECTIONS
(continued)

Year	Number of States	Candidates	Party	Popular Vote	Electoral Vote	Percentage of Popular Vote
1892	44	GROVER CLEVELAND	Democrat	5,555,426	277	46.1
		Benjamin Harrison	Republican	5,182,690	145	43.0
		James B. Weaver	People's	1,029,846	22	8.5
		John Bidwell	Prohibition	264,133		2.2
1896	45	WILLIAM MCKINLEY	Republican	7,102,246	271	51.1
		William J. Bryan	Democrat	6,492,559	176	47.7
1900	45	WILLIAM MCKINLEY	Republican	7,218,491	292	51.7
		William J. Bryan	Democrat; Populist	6,356,734	155	45.5
		John C. Woolley	Prohibition	208,914		1.5
1904	45	THEODORE ROOSEVELT	Republican	7,628,461	336	57.4
		Alton B. Parker	Democrat	5,084,223	140	37.6
		Eugene V. Debs	Socialist	402,283		3.0
		Silas C. Swallow	Prohibition	258,536		1.9
1908	46	WILLIAM H. TAFT	Republican	7,675,320	321	51.6
		William J. Bryan	Democrat	6,412,294	162	43.1
		Eugene V. Debs	Socialist	420,793		2.8
		Eugene W. Chafin	Prohibition	253,840		1.7
1912	48	WOODROW WILSON	Democrat	6,296,547	435	41.9
		Theodore Roosevelt	Progressive	4,118,571	88	27.4
		William H. Taft	Republican	3,486,720	8	23.2
		Eugene V. Debs	Socialist	900,672		6.0
		Eugene W. Chafin	Prohibition	206,275		1.4
1916	48	WOODROW WILSON	Democrat	9,127,695	277	49.4
		Charles E. Hughes	Republican	8,533,507	254	46.2
		A. L. Benson	Socialist	585,113		3.2
		J. Frank Hanly	Prohibition	220,506		1.2
1920	48	WARREN G. HARDING	Republican	16,143,407	404	60.4
		James M. Cox	Democrat	9,130,328	127	34.2
		Eugene V. Debs	Socialist	919,799		3.4
		P. P. Christensen	Farmer-Labor	265,411		1.0
1924	48	CALVIN COOLIDGE	Republican	15,718,211	382	54.0
		John W. Davis	Democrat	8,385,283	136	28.8
		Robert M. La Follette	Progressive	4,831,289	13	16.6
1928	48	HERBERT C. HOOVER	Republican	21,391,993	444	58.2
		Alfred E. Smith	Democrat	15,016,169	87	40.9
1932	48	FRANKLIN D. ROOSEVELT	Democrat	22,809,638	472	57.4
		Herbert C. Hoover	Republican	15,758,901	59	39.7
		Norman Thomas	Socialist	881,951		2.2
1936	48	FRANKLIN D. ROOSEVELT	Democrat	27,752,869	523	60.8
		Alfred M. Landon	Republican	16,674,665	8	36.5
		William Lemke	Union	882,479		1.9
1940	48	FRANKLIN D. ROOSEVELT	Democrat	27,307,819	449	54.8
		Wendell L. Willkie	Republican	22,321,018	82	44.8
1944	48	FRANKLIN D. ROOSEVELT	Democrat	25,606,585	432	53.5
		Thomas E. Dewey	Republican	22,014,745	99	46.0

PRESIDENTIAL ELECTIONS
(continued)

Year	Number of States	Candidates	Party	Popular Vote	Electoral Vote	Percentage of Popular Vote
1948	48	HARRY S. TRUMAN	Democrat	24,105,812	303	49.5
		Thomas E. Dewey	Republican	21,970,065	189	45.1
		J. Strom Thurmond	States' Rights	1,169,063	39	2.4
		Henry A. Wallace	Progressive	1,157,172		2.4
1952	48	DWIGHT D. EISENHOWER	Republican	33,936,234	442	55.1
		Adlai E. Stevenson	Democrat	27,314,992	89	44.4
1956	48	DWIGHT D. EISENHOWER	Republican	35,590,472	457*	57.6
		Adlai E. Stevenson	Democrat	26,022,752	73	42.1
1960	50	JOHN F. KENNEDY	Democrat	34,227,096	303†	49.9
		Richard M. Nixon	Republican	34,108,546	219	49.6
1964	50	LYNDON B. JOHNSON	Democrat	42,676,220	486	61.3
		Barry M. Goldwater	Republican	26,860,314	52	38.5
1968	50	RICHARD M. NIXON	Republican	31,785,480	301	43.4
		Hubert H. Humphrey	Democrat	31,275,165	191	42.7
		George C. Wallace	American Independent	9,906,473	46	13.5
1972	50	RICHARD M. NIXON‡	Republican	47,165,234	520	60.6
		George S. McGovern	Democrat	29,168,110	17	37.5
1976	50	JIMMY CARTER	Democrat	40,828,929	297	50.1
		Gerald R. Ford	Republican	39,148,940	240	47.9
		Eugene McCarthy	Independent	739,256		
1980	50	RONALD REAGAN	Republican	43,201,220	489	50.9
		Jimmy Carter	Democrat	34,913,332	49	41.2
		John B. Anderson	Independent	5,581,379		
1984	50	RONALD REAGAN	Republican	53,428,357	525	59.0
		Walter F. Mondale	Democrat	36,930,923	13	41.0
1988	50	GEORGE BUSH	Republican	48,901,046	426	53.4
		Michael Dukakis	Democrat	41,809,030	111	45.6
1992	50	BILL CLINTON	Democrat	43,728,275	370	43.2
		George Bush	Republican	38,167,416	168	37.7
		H. Ross Perot	United We Stand, America	19,237,247		19.0
1996	50	BILL CLINTON	Democrat	45,590,703	379	49.0
		Robert Dole	Republican	37,816,307	159	41.0
		H. Ross Perot	Reform	7,874,283		8.0

*Walter B. Jones received 1 electoral vote.

†Harry F. Byrd received 15 electoral votes.

‡Resigned August 9, 1974: Vice President Gerald R. Ford became President.

ADMISSION OF STATES INTO THE UNION

State	Date of Admission	State	Date of Admission
1. Delaware	December 7, 1787	26. Michigan	January 26, 1837
2. Pennsylvania	December 12, 1787	27. Florida	March 3, 1845
3. New Jersey	December 18, 1787	28. Texas	December 29, 1845
4. Georgia	January 2, 1788	29. Iowa	December 28, 1846
5. Connecticut	January 9, 1788	30. Wisconsin	May 29, 1848
6. Massachusetts	February 6, 1788	31. California	September 9, 1850
7. Maryland	April 28, 1788	32. Minnesota	May 11, 1858
8. South Carolina	May 23, 1788	33. Oregon	February 14, 1859
9. New Hampshire	June 21, 1788	34. Kansas	January 29, 1861
10. Virginia	June 25, 1788	35. West Virginia	June 20, 1863
11. New York	July 26, 1788	36. Nevada	October 31, 1864
12. North Carolina	November 21, 1789	37. Nebraska	March 1, 1867
13. Rhode Island	May 29, 1790	38. Colorado	August 1, 1876
14. Vermont	March 4, 1791	39. North Dakota	November 2, 1889
15. Kentucky	June 1, 1792	40. South Dakota	November 2, 1889
16. Tennessee	June 1, 1796	41. Montana	November 8, 1889
17. Ohio	March 1, 1803	42. Washington	November 11, 1889
18. Louisiana	April 30, 1812	43. Idaho	July 3, 1890
19. Indiana	December 11, 1816	44. Wyoming	July 10, 1890
20. Mississippi	December 10, 1817	45. Utah	January 4, 1896
21. Illinois	December 3, 1818	46. Oklahoma	November 16, 1907
22. Alabama	December 14, 1819	47. New Mexico	January 6, 1912
23. Maine	March 15, 1820	48. Arizona	February 14, 1912
24. Missouri	August 10, 1821	49. Alaska	January 3, 1959
25. Arkansas	June 15, 1836	50. Hawaii	August 21, 1959

DEMOGRAPHICS OF THE UNITED STATES

POPULATION GROWTH

Year	Population	Percent Increase
1630	4,600	
1640	26,600	478.3
1650	50,400	90.8
1660	75,100	49.0
1670	111,900	49.0
1680	151,500	35.4
1690	210,400	38.9
1700	250,900	19.2
1710	331,700	32.2
1720	466,200	40.5
1730	629,400	35.0
1740	905,600	43.9
1750	1,170,800	29.3
1760	1,593,600	36.1
1770	2,148,100	34.8
1780	2,780,400	29.4
1790	3,929,214	41.3
1800	5,308,483	35.1
1810	7,239,881	36.4
1820	9,638,453	33.1
1830	12,866,020	33.5
1840	17,069,453	32.7
1850	23,191,876	35.9
1860	31,443,321	35.6
1870	39,818,449	26.6
1880	50,155,783	26.0
1890	62,947,714	25.5
1900	75,994,575	20.7
1910	91,972,266	21.0
1920	105,710,620	14.9
1930	122,775,046	16.1
1940	131,669,275	7.2
1950	150,697,361	14.5
1960	179,323,175	19.0
1970	203,235,298	13.3
1980	226,545,805	11.5
1990	248,709,873	9.8
1996	265,557,000	6.8

Source: *Historical Statistics of the United States* (1975); *Statistical Abstract by the United States* (1991, 1997).
Note: Figures for 1630–1780 include British colonies within limits of present United States only; Native American population included only in 1930 and thereafter.

WORKFORCE

Year	Total Number Workers (1000s)	Farmers as % of Total	Women as % of Total	% Workers in Unions
1810	2,330	84	(NA)	(NA)
1840	5,660	75	(NA)	(NA)
1860	11,110	53	(NA)	(NA)
1870	12,506	53	15	(NA)
1880	17,392	52	15	(NA)
1890	23,318	43	17	(NA)
1900	29,073	40	18	3
1910	38,167	31	21	6
1920	41,614	26	21	12
1930	48,830	22	22	7
1940	53,011	17	24	27
1950	59,643	12	28	25
1960	69,877	8	32	26
1970	82,049	4	37	25
1980	108,544	3	42	23
1990	117,914	3	45	16
1995	124,900	3	46	15

Source: *Historical Statistics of the United States* (1975); *Statistical Abstract of the United States* (1991, 1996).

VITAL STATISTICS
(per thousands)

Year	Births	Deaths	Marriages	Divorces
1800	55	(NA)	(NA)	(NA)
1810	54.3	(NA)	(NA)	(NA)
1820	55.2	(NA)	(NA)	(NA)
1830	51.4	(NA)	(NA)	(NA)
1840	51.8	(NA)	(NA)	(NA)
1850	43.3	(NA)	(NA)	(NA)
1860	44.3	(NA)	(NA)	(NA)
1870	38.3	(NA)	9.6 (1867)	0.3 (1867)
1880	39.8	(NA)	9.1 (1875)	0.3 (1875)
1890	31.5	(NA)	9.0	0.5
1900	32.3	17.2	9.3	0.7
1910	30.1	14.7	10.3	0.9
1920	27.7	13.0	12.0	1.6
1930	21.3	11.3	9.2	1.6
1940	19.4	10.8	12.1	2.0
1950	24.1	9.6	11.1	2.6
1960	23.7	9.5	8.5	2.2
1970	18.4	9.5	10.6	3.5
1980	15.9	8.8	10.6	5.2
1990	16.7	8.6	9.8	4.7
1994	15.0	8.8	9.1	4.6

Source: *Historical Statistics of the United States* (1975); *Statistical Abstract of the United States* (1991, 1997).

RACIAL COMPOSITION OF THE POPULATION
(in thousands)

Year	White	Black	Indian	Hispanic	Asian
1790	3,172	757	(NA)	(NA)	(NA)
1800	4,306	1,002	(NA)	(NA)	(NA)
1820	7,867	1,772	(NA)	(NA)	(NA)
1840	14,196	2,874	(NA)	(NA)	(NA)
1860	26,923	4,442	(NA)	(NA)	(NA)
1880	43,403	6,581	(NA)	(NA)	(NA)
1900	66,809	8,834	(NA)	(NA)	(NA)
1910	81,732	9,828	(NA)	(NA)	(NA)
1920	94,821	10,463	(NA)	(NA)	(NA)
1930	110,287	11,891	(NA)	(NA)	(NA)
1940	118,215	12,866	(NA)	(NA)	(NA)
1950	134,942	15,042	(NA)	(NA)	(NA)
1960	158,832	18,872	(NA)	(NA)	(NA)
1970	178,098	22,581	(NA)	(NA)	(NA)
1980	194,713	26,683	1,420	14,609	3,729
1990	205,710	30,486	2,065	22,354	7,458
1996	219,749	30,503	2,288	28,269	9,743

Source: U.S. Bureau of the Census, *U.S. Census of Population: 1940*, vol. II, part 1, and vol. IV, part 1; *1950*, vol. II, part 1; *1960*, vol. I, part 1; *1970*, vol. I, part B; and *Current Population Reports*, P25-1095 and P25-1104; *Statistical Abstract of the United States* (1997); and unpublished data.

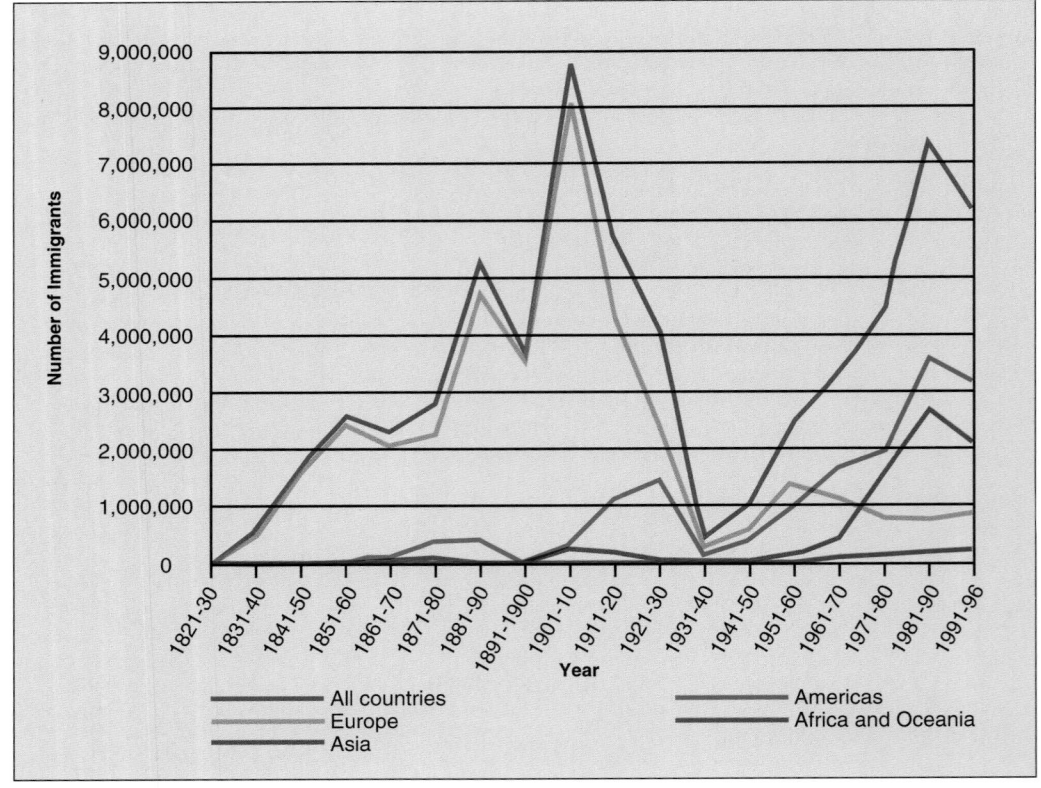

Immigration to the United States since 1820

Source: *Statistical Yearbook of the Immigration and Naturalization Service*, 1996.

PHOTO AND TEXT CREDITS

Boston Athenaeum," 289; New York Public Library, 290 Text: "The Impact of the Erie Canal on Household Textile Manufacture" from Arthur Harrison Cole, The American Wool Manufacture. Copyright 1926 by the President and Fellows of Harvard College. Reprinted with the permission of Harvard University Press, 274

Chapter 11: Photos: Chicago Historical Society, 294; Library of Congress, 298; Wilson S. Armistead, University of Michigan Press, 299; Library of Congress, 307; The Historic New Orleans Collection, 308; Sophia Smith Collection, Smith College, 309; Library of Congress, 310; American Numismatic Society of New York, (left and right), 311; Daughters of the Republic of Texas, Yanaguana Society Collection, 312; The Historic New Orleans Collection, 315; National Archives, 317; Library of Congress, 319

Chapter 12: Photos: American Textile History Museum, 324; Abby Aldrich Rockefeller Folk Art Center, Williamsburg, VA, 328; Museum of Fine Arts, Boston, 329; Library of Congress, 332; Rhode Island Historical Society, 333; James L. Amos, National Geographic Society, (top & bottom) 336; High-Pressure Steamboat Mayflower, 1855, color lithograph by N. Currier. The Bettmann Archive. Corbis-Bettmann, 338; Baker Library, Graduate School of Business Administration, Harvard University, 340; Musuem of Fine Arts, Boston, 343; Mathew Brady/Brown Brothers, 344; The New York Historical Society, 346; Library of Congress, 347

Chapter 13: Photos: The New York Historical Society, 351; The Granger Collection, 358; Library of Congress, 360; Zelsa P. Mackay Collection, Courtesy George Eastman House, 362; "Seabury Champlin's June 3, 1791 Certificate of Membership in NY Mechanic Society," Abraham Godwin, print. Courtesy Winterthur Museum, 363; Frank and Marie-Therese Wood Print Collections, The Picture Bank, 364; The Schlesinger Library, Radcliffe College, 367; Library of Congress, 369; Hannah Harrison, Hancock Shaker Village, 371; Library of Congress (left & right), 373; Sophia Smith Collection, Smith College, 374; Lynn Historical Society, 376

Immigration & Community, 1800–1860: Photos: Dover Publications, Inc., 383; Museum of the City of New York, 384

Chapter 14: Photos: San Jacinto Museum of History Association, 386; Walters Art Gallery, 390; Henry E. Huntington Library and Art Gallery, 395; American Antiquarian Society, 397; The Walters Art Gallery, Baltimore, 398; Art Resource, NY, 399; Brown University Library, 404; National Gallery of Art, 406; The New York Historical Society, 408; California State Library, 409; Bigelow Collection, Museum of Fine Arts, Boston, 410; Steven Laschever/Museum of American Political Life/University of Hartford, 413 Text: "Overland Emigration to Oregon, California, and Utah, 1840-1860" from John Unruh, Jr., The Plains Across: The Overland Emigrants and the Trans-Mississippi West, 1840-60. Copyright © 1979 by the Board of Trustees of the University of Illinois. Reprinted with the permission of the University of Illinois Press., 396; "California in the Gold Rush," from Warren A. Beck and Ynez D. Haase, Historical Atlas of California. Copyright © 1974 by the University of Oklahoma Press. Reprinted with the permission of the publishers., 407

Chapter 15: Photos: The Granger Collection, 417; Harriet Beecher Stowe Center, Hartford, CT, Stowe-Day Foundation, 422; Courtesy American Antiquarian Society, 423; Library of Congress, 424; The Granger Collection, 431; Corbis-Bettmann, 432; New York Public Library, 434; Library of Congress, 435; Museum of the City of New York, 436; The Granger Collection, 437; Library of Congress, 440; United States Senate, 443

Chapter 16: Photos: Armen Shamalian Photographers, Art Resource, NY, 447; Courtesy Museum of Fine Arts, Boston, 451; The Picture Bank, 455; Alexander Gardner, National Archives, 456; Library of Congress, 458; Valentine Museum Library, (left) 459; Library of Congress, 459; Reproduced from Pauli Murray, Proud Shoes: The Story of an American Family,

HarperCollins Publishers, Inc., 1987, 466; Center of Military History, U.S. Army, 468; The Metropolitan Museum of Art, 469; Culvery Pictures, Inc., 471; Thomas C. Roche, Library of Congress, 475; Army Military History Institute, 476; Library of Congress, 477

Chapter 17: Photos: The Metropolitan Museum of Art, 481; National Archives, 485; Chicago Historical Society, 486; The Granger Collection, 488; The Susan B. Anthony House, Rochester, NY, 492; The Picture Bank/Harper's Weekly, 495; Library of Congress, 498; Library of Congress, 499; The University of North Carolina, (left) 501; Rutherford B. Hayes Presidential Center, 501; The Granger Collection, New York, 505; The Picture Bank, Frank and Marie-Therese Wood Print Collection, 507

Chapter 18: Photos: Christie's Images, 513; National Anthropological Archives, 518; Marion Koogler McNay Art Museum, 519; Timothy O'Sullivan, Amon Carter Museum, 522; Witte Museum, 525; Harper's Weekly, 527; Nebraska State Historical Society, Solomon D. Butcher Collection, 531; Library of Congress, 532; The Metropolitan Museum of Art, 537; Library of Congress, 538; Photo courtesy of State Historical Society of Iowa, Iowa City, 541; Edward Truman/The Denver Public Library, Western History Collection, 542 Text: "Oklahoma Territory" from John W. Morrois, Charles R. Goins, and Edwin C. McReynolds, Historical Atlas of Oklahoma, Third Edition. Copyright © 1965, 1976, 1986 by the University of Oklahoma Press. Reprinted with the permission of the publishers., 515; History and the Land feature and "Ethnic Composition of North Dakota, 1900," from John R. Shortridge, "The Great Plains" in Mary Kupiec Cayton, Elliott J. Gorn, and Peter W. Williams, Encyclopedia of American Social History II. Copyright © 1993 by Charles Scribner's Sons. Reprinted with the permission of Scribner's, an imprint of Simon & Schuster Macmillan. 528–529

Chapter 19: Photos: The Granger Collection, 547; U.S. Department of the Interior, National Park Service, Edison National Historic Site, 551 Chicago Historical Society, 553; Color engraving by J. Keppler from Puck, February 23, 1881, Collection of The New York Historical Society, New York City, 554; The Denver Public Library, Western History Collection, 556; Museum of the City of New York, 563; National Archives, 565; Terra Museum of American Art, 568; The Granger Collection, 570; Rhode Island School of Design, 573 Text: "U.S. Economy, 1873-1900" from Bernard Bailyn et al., The Great Republic, Third Edition. Copyright © 1985 by D.D. Heath and Company. Reprinted with the permission of Houghton Mifflin Company., 557

Chapter 20: Photos: Vermont State House, 578; Sally Anderson-Bruce/Museum of American Political Life, 583; Library of Congress, 585; Library of Congress, 588; Library of Congress, 590; The Granger Collection, New York, 594; National Archives, 596; Library of Congress, 601; Library of Congress, 603; Library of Congress, 604

Chapter 21: Photos: San Diego Museum of Art, 609; Lewis W. Hine/George Eastman House, 614; Henry Street Settlement, 615; Museum of the City of New York, 618; The Toledo Museum of Art, 622; Brown Brothers, 624; UPI/Corbis-Bettmann, 626; Collection of The American Labor Museum, Botto House National Landmark, 629; Planned Parenthood ® Federation of America, Inc. At, 810 Seventh Avenue, New York, NY, 10019., 631; Schomburg Center for Research in Black Culture, 632; California Historical Society, 635; Theodore Roosevelt Collection, Harvard College Library/The Houghton Library, Harvard University, 636

Chapter 22: Photos: Corbis-Bettmann, 642; The Granger Collection, 646; Culver Pictures, Inc., 649; Wallace Kirkland Papers, Jane Addams Memorial Collection, Special Collections, The University Library, University of Illinois at Chicago, 651; The Granger Collection, 652; Library of Congress, 653; National Archives, 654; National Archives, 655; Virginia War Museum/War Memorial Museum of Virginia, 659; Library of Congress, 661; Stock Montage Inc./ Historial Pictures Collection, 665;

INDEX

Forest Management Act (1897), 536
Forests, national, 535–36
Fort Gibson, battle at (1863), 462
Fort Jackson, Treaty of (1814), 248, 250
Fort Laramie, Treaty of (1868), 519, 540
Fort McIntosh, Treaty of (1785), 182
Fort Pillow, Tennessee, massacre at (1863), 466
Fortress Monroe, Virginia, 464
Fort Stanwix, Treaty of (1768), 140
Fort Stanwix, Treaty of (1784), 182
Fort Wayne, Treaty of (1809), 246
"Forty–niners," 407, 408
Fosdick, Raymond, 661
Fossils, early American, 4
Foster, Andrew "Rube," 687
Foster, Hannah Webster, 218
Four Bears, Chief, 230
Four Corners, 14
Fourier, Charles, 370
Fourteen Points, 666
Fourteenth Amendment, 483, 489, 502, 509, 619, 854
Fox, Charles James, 152
Fox, George, 114
Fox, William, 682
Fox Indians, 107, 281–82
Foxwoods Casino, Connecticut, 962
France: *See also* New France; World War I; World War
    II; American Revolution and, 170–71, 177;
    British blockade of (1793–1794), 206–7; colo-
    nization by, 39–42; cotton diplomacy in Civil
    War and, 457; Franco-American alliance of
    1778, 203; in French and Indian War, 135–41;
    French Resistance in World War II, 775–76;
    fur trade, 41–42, 53–54; immigration from,
    222, 223–24; in Indochina, 837; Louisiana
    Purchase and, 239–41; Napoleonic Wars, 242,
    248, 249; Reign of Terror, 203; revolution in,
    203–4, 216, 236; sugar plantations, 76–77;
    XYZ affair, 209–10
Franciscan missionaries, 50, 52–53, 109, 110, 396
Franco, Francisco, 738, 751
Frankfurter, Felix, 723
Franklin, Ann Smith, 117
Franklin, Benjamin, 117, 118, 119, 121, 222; American
    culture and, 288; in American Revolution, 169,
    170, 177; colonial newspapers and, 142;
    Constitutional Convention and, 197, 198;
    Declaration of Independence and, 158; on Great
    Awakening, 126; in House of Commons, 146;
    Hutchinson and, 150; Paxton Boys and, 140;
    Plan of Union, 135; *Poor Richard's Almanac*, 125;
    as Postmaster, 141, 156
Franklin, James, 142
Franklin Evans, or the Inebriate (Whitman), 360
Franz Ferdinand, Archduke, 650
Fraternal societies, 570
Fredricksburg, battle of (1862), 461
Freed, Alan, 828
Freedmen, 482–83, 487, 497
Freedmen's Bureau, 474, 486, 488, 494, 495
Freedmen's Bureau Act (1865), 495
Freedom Rides, 860–61
Freedom's Journal, 372
Freedom Summer (Mississippi, 1964), 867–68
Free labor, notion of, 341
Free silver issue, 593–94
Free-Soil Party, 412, 413, 423–24, 430–31, 433
Free speech, wartime restrictions on, 663
Free speech movement, 884
Frémont, John C., 390, 403, 404, 433, 455
French and Indian War, 135–41
French Canadian immigrants, 561
French crescent, 106, 111–12
French Revolution (1789), 203–4, 216, 236
Freneau, Philip, 213, 216
Freud, Sigmund, 688
Frick, Henry C., 591
Friedan, Betty, 823, 898

Friends of Oder, 208
Fries, John, 211
Frobisher, Martin, 45
Frontier heritage, 117–19
Frontiers, 137, 396, 520–28, 530–31; *See also*
    Westward expansion
Fruitlands, Massachusetts, 370
Fugitive Slave Act (1850), 426–28, 464
Fugitive slaves, 75, 91–92, 109, 308–9
Fugitives (scholarly group), 703
Fulbright, J. William, 844, 883
Fuller, Margaret, 347–48
Fulton, Robert, 275, 276
Fundamental Orders, 63
Fur trade, 41–42, 53–54, 106, 107, 231, 236,
    389–90, 397

G

Gabrielson, Guy, 804
Gadsden, Christopher, 152, 153
Gadsden Purchase (1853), 406, 524
Gage, Thomas, 148, 152, 153, 155, 157
Gag rule, 319, 375
Galileo, 124
Gallatin, Albert, 210, 211
Gallaudet, Edward Miner, 344
Galloway, Joseph, 152
Galton, Francis, 620
Gambling, Indian tribes and, 961–63
Gandhi, Mohandas, 405, 856, 858
Gang labor system, 75
Gangster films, 739
Garfield, James A., 583, 584
Garment industry, 339, 556, 626
Garrison, William Lloyd, 318–19, 372–76, 412
Garvey, Marcus, 701, 868
Gary, Elbert, 657, 666
Gates, Horatio, 169, 174, 175, 178
Gavin, Anna Maria, 383
Gay Activist Alliance, 899
Gay Liberation Front (GLF), 899
Gay liberation movement, 899
Gay Men's Health Crisis, 966
Gay Pride marches, 899
Geeche dialect, 90
Gemeinschaft and *Gesellschaft*, 620
General Agreement on Tariffs and Trade (GATT),
    793, 978–79
General Court of Massachusetts Bay Colony, 60, 62,
    63, 112, 113
General Federation of Women's Clubs, 630, 669
General Land Revision Act (1891), 535
General Motors, 658, 677, 679, 715
General Society of Mechanics and Tradesmen, 344
General Trades Union of New York, 365
General Union for Promoting the Observance of the
    Christian Sabbath, 366
Generational conflict, 883–88
Genêt, Edmond, 203–4
Genocide of Spanish conquest, 35
Gente de razón, 120
Gentility, middle class and, 568–69
Geological surveys of West, 390, 537
George, David Lloyd, 666
George, Henry, 534, 587–88
George III of England, King, 143, 145, 151, 153,
    156, 157, 175
Georgia: civil rights movement in, 858, 859; in Civil
    War, 474, 476; colony of, 74–75, 86, 155; slav-
    ery in, 74–75
Georgia Constitutionalist, 435
German immigrants, 224–26, 355, 358, 359, 363,
    365, 380, 381, 384–85; culture of, 381
Germany: Berlin crisis (1948), 793–94; Nazis in, 751,
    775–76; post-World War II division of, 790;
    reparations, 667, 690–91; reunification of, 972;
    World War I and, 650–52, 656–57; World War
    II and, 771–78

Geronimo, 520
Gettysburg, battle of (1863), 460, 473
Ghent, Treaty of (1814), 249
Ghettos, 625–26, 709
Ghost Dance, 541–42
Ghost towns, 523
Gibbons v. Ogden, 276
GI Bill of Rights (1944), 787, 807, 822, 825
Gibson, Charles Dana, 653
Gibson, Josh, 687
Gifford, Walter S., 721
GI Forum, 871
Gilbert, Humphrey, 44, 45
Gilded Age, 567–75
Gilder, George, 950
Gillespie, Dizzy, 852
Gillette, George, 873
Gingrich, Newt, 979–80
Ginsberg, Allen, 832–33
Girard, Stephen, 282, 330–31
Girls Friendly Societies, 593
Gish, Lillian, 752
Giton, Judith, 223–24
Gladden, Washington, 592
Glasnost, 955–56
Global warming trend, 6
Glorieta Pass, battle of (1862), 462
"Glorious Ninety-two," 148
Glorious Revolution, 66, 69
Gnadenhutten, massacre at (1782), 194
Godey's Lady's Book, 345
Godkin, E.L., 508, 606
Gold: in Black Hills, 519; California Gold Rush, 381,
    382, 383–84, 395, 407, 408–10, 516, 522;
    search for in New World, 32–33, 36
Gold, Michael, 738
Goldman, Emma, 629, 631, 669
Gold Standard Act (1900), 595
Goldwater, Barry, 869, 949
Goldwyn, Samuel, 682
Gompers, Samuel, 559, 590, 596, 606, 627, 644, 658,
    678
Gone with the Wind (Mitchell), 737
Gonzales, Corky, 901
Goodman, Andrew, 867
Goodman, Benny, 741
Goodman, Paul, 832
Good Neighbor Policy, 599–600
Gorbachev, Mikhail, 956–57, 971
Gordon, Richard, 823
Gordon, Thomas, 142
Gorman, Howard, 735
Gorton, Samuel, 63
Gospel of Wealth, The (Carnegie), 555
Gospel of work, 555
Gossip column, 684
Gould, Jay, 505, 550, 554
Government: *See also* Politics; balance of power in,
    239; civil service reform, 506, 584–85, 799;
    colonial, 123; commission form of, 616; era of
    divided, 979–81; exploration of West spon-
    sored by, 390; under Jefferson, 238–39;
    machinery of politics, 583–84; post–Civil War
    growth of, 581–83; post-revolutionary, forma-
    tion of, 196–200; spoils system, 269–70,
    584–85; in the twenties, 688–92; urban, struc-
    tural reforms in, 616
Government-business partnership, 658
Graduated income tax, 636
Graduate studies, 571–72; *See also* Colleges and uni-
    versities
Grady, Henry Woodfin, 564
Graham, Billy, 807, 931
Gramercy Park, New York City, 356–57
Gramm-Rudmann Act (1985), 966–67
Grand Banks, fish in, 41–42
Grand Coulee Dam, 733
Grandfather clauses, 596

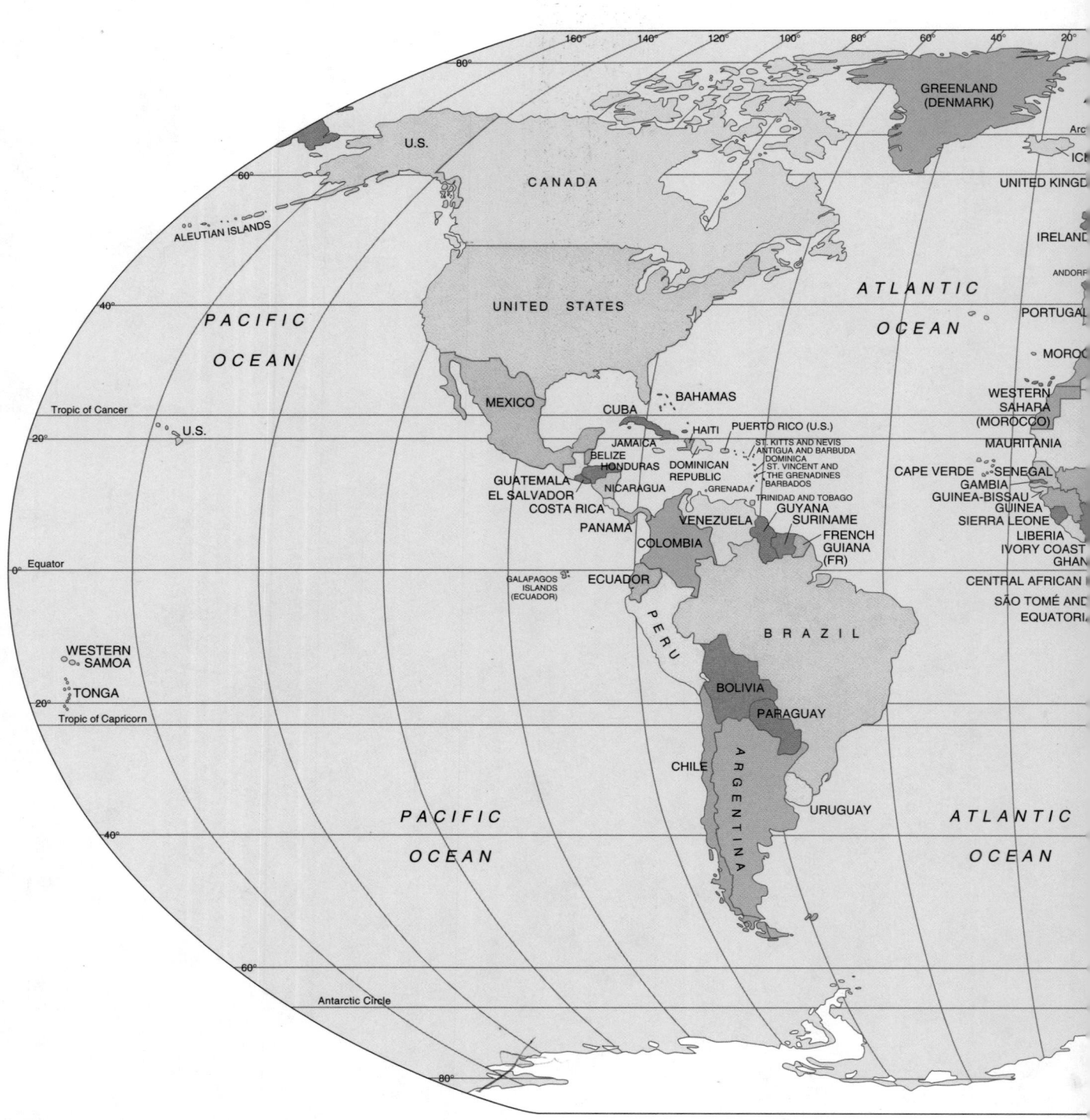